TUKI ENGLISH-SWAHILI DICTIONARY

Kamusi ya Kiingereza-Kiswahili

15,000/-

TUKI ENGLISH-SWAHILI DICTIONARY

Kamusi ya Kiingereza-Kiswahili

INSTITUTE OF KISWAHILI RESEARCH
UNIVERSITY OF DAR ES SALAAM
1996

Institute of Kiswahili Research
University of Dar es Salaam
P.O. Box 35110
Dar es Salaam

First Edition 1996

ISBN 9976 911 29 7

FOREWORD

The long awaited **TUKI English-Swahili Dictionary** is at last in print and ready for its users. Having taken sixty years of waiting, fourteen years of preparation, the heavy and difficult task has now exposed the brains and energy of lexicographers, academic members and the administrative staff of the Institute of Kiswahili Research who consistently and continuously devoted themselves to its accomplishment. However, it would have been far from being complete had it not been for the assistance of others outside the Institute. This dictionary, which is not only new but also the biggest ever among Kiswahili dictionaries is a result of serious and doughty teams of the Institute who spent their precious time on the over 50,000 entries in order to introduce language learners and dictionary users into current language usage. A dictionary of this kind and size needs concerted efforts of many people especially when it is taken into account that the whole work, from compilation to printing, was done in house. The teams that accomplished this work included Lexicographers, Editors, Secretaries, Proofreaders and members of the printing section.

LEXICOGRAPHERS

The first panel took place on 30/7/82 and was chaired by Prof. G. Mhina, who was assisted by Mr. C.W. Temu. This beginning of the great task included the following lexicographers:- Z.N. Tumbo-Masabo, A.R. Chuwa, P. Mbughuni, R. Ohly, H.J.M. Mwansoko, A. MacWilliam, H. Akida, Y. Mganga, J.S. Mdee, C.M.T. Bwenge and M.M.R. Alidina. Unfortunately most of these could not continue with the project to its logical conclusion. To them, we wish to express the Institute's sincere thanks for all their input. We believe that using this dictionary will mean and remind them a lot of things. This team, at different times and stages got support from other members of Institute. We need to specifically mention the team of Lexicographers which really deserve to be congratulated for their patience and tolerance beginning to end. This team is that of the following members:-

Dr. J.S. Mdee - **Team Leader**
Dr. Z.N. Tumbo-Masabo
Prof. H.J.M. Mwansoko
Dr. A.R. Chuwa.
Dr. J.G. Kiango
Prof. A.M. Khamisi
Sister A. MacWilliam

EDITORS

In October 1990 the compilation of the **TUKI English-Swahili Dictionary** was over and the next difficult work was to begin. A team of seven editors was formed (with only four going to the end of the work). The number came down after the real extent of the work ahead was known to them all. Those who opted out might have realized what lay ahead of them. The team of four Editors spent a lot of time in bringing this project to shape. Our sincere gratitudes go to this team below:-

Prof. D.P.B. Massamba - **Team Leader**
Prof. A.M. Khamisi
Prof. S.A.K. Mlacha
Mr. R. Mabala

TECHNICAL EDITORS

The manuscript was submitted to Technical Editors in order to accomplish the task of giving the dictionary a consistent format, taking into account technical aspects of dictionary making. Our thanks go to the following members of the team:

Prof. A.M. Khamisi (**Chief Editor**)
Prof. S.A.K. Mlacha

Some help was received from Prof. D.P.B. Massamba and Mr. M.M.R. Alidina. We wish to express our appreciation for that.

PROOFREADERS

A special team of three was formed to deal with proofreading. For several months each of them looked at each and every letter of this dictionary for more than two times. It is true that, despite their great efforts, such a big work cannot be error free. We highly appreciate what they did and congratulate them for doing this within very limited time. It is here that we should give allowance to human errors, since it was a work done with great care. These thanks go to the following:-

Prof. S.A.K. Mlacha **Team Leader**
Prof. H.J.M. Mwansoko
Dr. A.R. Chuwa

At this stage we also wish to acknowledge the observations and opinions of Dr. Z. Tumbo-Masabo, Dr. J.G. Kiango and Dr. J.S. Mdee who also proofread the manuscript at least once. It was a great contribution.

SECRETARIAL TEAM

Indeed, this whole work would not have been done by the above mentioned teams within reasonable time if it was not for dedicated members of the Institute's secretarial services. The history of the **TUKI English-Swahili Dictionary** passed through manual and electric typewriters to computers. These members were actively involved and moved with those historical and technological developments. This needed understanding, love, care, commitment and great dexterity. The typing and typesetting of this dictionary was mainly the work of this team to whom our devoted thanks go.

Miss Judith Stephen - **Team Leader**
Miss Salome Mlingi
Miss Mbuyagi Mmarika

Miss Apronia Stephen
Mr. Iddi Mkriti
Mr. Aminieli Muwanga.
Miss Joyce Mwakimi
Miss Rukia Mwabba

Special thanks should go to Miss Judith Stephen who, frankly, relives the history of this dictionary. Tirelessly, from the first panel to the last proofs, she has been actively involved. The many hours and energy she lost on this dictionary will always be remembered.

PRINTING TEAM

Printing of this dictionary has been done at the Institute using the manpower of committed members at all the stages. To them it has been an experience while the Institute will never forget their innovative minds and fast thinking. It is a team that managed to make possible what was initially seen as impossible. This team included:-

Mr. I. Omari - **Team Leader**

Mr. E. Semzaba	Mr. M. Mrisho
Mr. M. Rangi	Mr. H. Denis
Miss J. Mwakimi	Mr. I. Mkriti
Miss A. Stephen	Mr. J. Mlacha
Miss S. Mlingi	Mr. M. Dhahabu
Miss J. Stephen	Mr. M. Kisimikwe
Mr. H. Selemani	Mr. D. Mwenda

This team will also join us in appreciating the great help we got from Mr. H. Mrehy and A. Muwanga who over and above their normal duties played a great role in preparing the manuscript for printing. Special thanks go to Mr. I. Omari and J. Mlacha who played a significant role in handling the machines.

DIRECTORS

As it will have been observed, this dictionary would not have been in its present state if at any one stage of its history it would have fallen under the hands of uncaring leadership. It is a dictionary that was supervised by four Directors from 1982 as seen below:-

Mr. C.W. Temu (1982 - 1985)
Prof. D.P.B. Massamba (1985 - 1991)
Dr. T.S.Y. Sengo (1991 - 1994)
Prof. S.A.K. Mlacha (1994 - 1997)

It is through their leadership and concern that, at long last, this new and great dictionary is now in use. Special thanks should be directed to them all. We also wish to express our thanks to other former Directors. It is impossible to expunge their names from our records since they encouraged the idea of having this dictionary prepared. These are Prof. G.A. Mhina and Prof. A.M. Khamisi.

Our sincere thanks go to the University administration which gave us all the necessary support we wanted to accomplish this task. This could not have been easy if it was not for the University Council's keen interest in seeing that the work is carried out successfully to its final stage. We wish to express our gratitudes to:-
The Councillors (1982 - 1996)
The Senators (1982 - 1996)
Mr. N.A. Kuhanga, Former Vice-Chancellor (UDSM)
Prof. G.V. Mmari, Former Vice-Chancellor (UDSM)
Prof. M.L. Luhanga, Vice-Chancellor (UDSM).
The different types of support we received from them cannot be easily enumerated. At long last, we have managed to deliver what they were all waiting for and that their support was worthwhile. I am especially indebted to Prof. M.L. Luhanga for his continuous support and encouragement. Taking this project as part of his projects was more than what any Institution would expect from a Vice-Chancellor. His great concern and close monitoring on the progress of the work gave us the energy to have it completed this year.

EXTERNAL SUPPORT

It has now been clear that single - handedly this dictionary would not have come out. We wish to express our deeply felt gratitudes to Canadian Organization for Development in Education (**CODE) Eastern Africa** for the great support they gave us in terms of printing materials. This immeasurable support can not be expressed in words. It remains in our minds and hearts. Personally, I wish to thank Mr. Scott Walter, who was then the Director of **CODE Eastern Africa**. As the then Institute's Coordinator of Publications I approached him with our request and since then he has left me with memories of a non lexicographer very much committed to the world of dictionary making. His understanding and pursuit of our problem has resulted into this treasure while making **CODE** and Scott Walter sound synonymous in the ears of members of the Institute. The support of a computer and printer we received from Norwegian Council of Universities (**NUFU**) has resulted into the prints we now read. Our many thanks to **NUFU**. While to **CODE** (Canada) and **NUFU** (Norway) this is history, we have these fresh memories of close relationships with the two organizations representing the two countries. To us then, this was support to the whole English-Swahili world.

To all those above and those others who directly or indirectly supported us to this end, we express our sincere thanks. We have great hopes for continued relationship since the final touches of the ***TUKI English-Swahili Dictionary*** have marked the beginning of the ***TUKI Swahili-English Dictionary***.

Institute of Kiswahili Research
University of Dar es Salaam
5th December 1996.

Prof. S.A.K. Mlacha
DIRECTOR

PREFACE

TUKI English - Swahili Dictionary is the most up to date dictionary of current English. It is published after more than a century since Madan published the first English - Swahili Dictionary in 1894, and half a century since Johnson (1939) was published. Johnson (1939) *English - Swahili Dictionary*, hitherto the most elaborate and authoritative dictionary, was compiled with the objective of helping the user to comprehend English texts. With the changing needs of a dictionary user, a new dictionary was necessary for two reasons : (1) to record new words and new meanings of words which the language acquired during the last 55 years, and (2) to provide some lexicographical information that current dictionary users need.

TUKI English-Swahili Dictionary was written with this background. It's vocabulary covers a wide range of lexicon that includes both the general language and specialized language. It has more than 50,000 entries, some of which are technical words. It should however be emphasized that technical words which have been entered in this dictionary are only those which appear in the general language although they still belong to the specialized fields.

English as a world language is not always used the same way throughout the English world. It has some variations in form and meaning of words which are specific to one region or country. The language has also some words that suggest a particular style, attitude or level of formality. It has words which have been borrowed from other languages in recent years. This dictionary provides adequate information about these aspects so as to alert the user on when and where a word can or cannot be used and the connotation it may have to the audience.

This dictionary is both a decoding and an encoding dictionary. Efforts have been made to give every English word an equivalent word in Swahili and where no equivalent one word is found a phrase is provided. A headword which acquires meaning only when it is in a context, is put in a context first and then defined. For example:

> **con**[1] *adv. pro and con* pande zote
> (hasi na chanya)

As an encoding dictionary, it provides some hints on word formation and syntax. Derivatives and compounds of a headword have been explicitly shown in the entry so that the user can see how words which share a common root are formed and the morphological changes that take place during the derivation process. Words which appear with the headword have been illustrated in an example phrase or sentence, or by showing the obligatory and optional elements which the headword takes, e.g. prepositional phrase.

Pronunciation is an important aspect in language learning especially the spoken language. English is not always pronounced as it is written. Moreover it has variations of pronunciation for the same words even for the standard pronunciation.

Pronunciation is thus a very important information in an English dictionary. Inspite of this fact, pronunciation has been omitted in this edition for technical reasons. We hope the readers will bear with us and tolerate the unavoidable omission.

Important Information in a Dictionary Entry

headword → **use** *n* i matumizi, kutumia. *in* ~ inayotumika (tena). *come in* ~ anza kuṭumika. **~ed** *adj* liotumika. **usable** *adj* -a (kuweza) kutumika. **~er** *n* matumiaji. ← entry

homographs
→ **ball**[1] *n* 1 mpira, *throw the* ~ tupa mpira. 2 bonge, donge.
→ **ball**[2] *n* dansi rasmi. ~ **dress** *n* gauni rasmi la dansi.

word class
→ **abattoir** *n* machinjoni
→ **a/an** *indef art.* -o ote, fulani, moja.

alternative spelling of a headword
→ **aneurism, aneurysm** *n (med)* prema: ugonjwa wa kuvimba. tezi
→ **anesthesia** *see* **anaesthesia**

cross-reference
→ **amp** *n* *see* **ampere**
→ **carotene** *also* **carotid** *n* karotini

gloss → **dream** *n* (of things, experiences)

definition → sio dhahiri, sio ya kweli

subject label → **carcinogen** *n* *(med)* kisababisha kansa

usage label → **duck** *n* *(sl)* kipenzi, muhibu

regional label →
mugwump *n* (US) mshaufu
pecker *n* **(GB)** *(sl)* pua

senses separated by numbers →
bastard *n* 1 mtoto wa nje ya ndoa. 2 mkatili, mshenzi 3 asiye na bahati 4 kitu bandia

illustrative examples →
option *n* 1 uchaguzi, hiari, haki ya kutenda. *the ~ is yours* uchaguzi ni wako *there is no ~* hakuna budi *I have no ~ but to go* ni lazima niende.

compounds →
fish *n* 3 (compounds) **~ ball/ ~ cake** andazi la samaki na viazi vya kupondwa **~ bone** mwiba wa samaki **~ knife** kisu cha kulia samaki **~ monger** mchuuzi/mwuza samaki

argue *vi,vt* 1 to hoja (sababu....). shindana kwa maneno, hojiana..... 3 jadili.

derivatives

- **argument** *n* 1 hoja 2 mabishano...
- **argumentative** *adj* -bishi
- **arguable** *adj* -a kujadilika....
- **argumentation** *n* kubishana, kutoa hoja, kuhojiana.

fit *adj* 1 ~ **(for)** -a kufaa, laiki, -enye kustahili the meal is ~ **to eat** chakula kinafaa kuliwa. The proposed time is **~ for us all** muda uliopendekezwa unatufaa sote 2 sawa, -a haki it is not **~ that you should abuse** **your teacher so** si haki kumtukana mwalimu wako 3 - wa tayari feel **~ to do sth** -wa tayari kufanya jambo fulani.

adjectival complementation

live *vt,vi* 1 ishi, -wa na uzima: 2 endelea kuishi, dumu **~ on** jikongoja, endelea kuishi **~ to be live** .... ishi hadi.... **~ as man and wife** kaa kinyumba. 3 pata riziki ~ **by ones wits**. ishi kwa ujanja/mbinu: **~ off the land** tegemea riziki kwa kilimo. **~ on your salary** ishi kwa kutegemea mshahara wako. 6 nenda **~ up to sth** fuata, fikia mataraji fulani. **~ sth down** sahaulisha yaliyopita. **~ with sth** vumilia. 7 **~ sth up** ishi maisha ya anasa.

verb complementation

How to use the dictionary

The following information is given in order to help the reader to use the dictionary efficiently when looking up a word or some information. But before we do that we shall define three important words: dictionary, entry and headword.

1.0.0 The Dictionary, entry and headword

A *dictionary* is a book of words with their semantic and grammatical meaning . It is made up of units called entries.

An *entry* is a block consisting of a headword and the information describing it.

A *headword* is the word listed in the dictionary in alphabetical order and printed in bold letters so that it can catch the eye of the reader easily when he/she looks it up. A headword in this dictionary has been entered two letters off the margin of the text of an entry as follows:

international *adj* - a mataifa; - a kimataifa. **~ money order** hawala ya fedha ya kimataifa. **~ism** n umataifa, nadharia inayotetea masilahi ya kimataifa. **~ist** *n* mtu anayetetea/unga mkono umataifa. **~ize** *vt* fanya -a kimataifa, fanya mali ya mataifa. **~ization** *n.* **~ly** *adv* **~e** *n.* The **internationale** wimbo wa kimapinduzi wa kijamaa.

An entry may have a headword and, sub-headwords and undefined words which are also printed in bold letters but are within the entry and could be either compounds or derivatives. In the entry above, *international* is the headword, and sub-headwords are ~ *money order*, *~ism*, *~ist* and *~ize*. The undefined words are *~ization*, *~ly* and *~e*.

2.0.0 How to find a word in the dictionary

A headword in this dictionary is either a simple word like **use** or **eat**, a derivative like **user** or **usage** and a compound like *cross country* or *cross check*. Before you look up a word in the dictionary you should know first whether it is a simple word, a derived word or a compound word.

2.1.0 Simple words

A simple word is the smallest word without affixes which has a meaning of its own. For example, book, pen, use, house, boy, girl, eat, little, drive, run, small, very, educate, quick, etc., are simple words. All simple words have been entered as headwords.

2.2.0 Derivatives

A derivative is a word formed by adding affixes to a simple word (root). For example: *educate education, educator, educational. etc. use* > *usage, useful, useless, used, useful* etc. Derivatives are usually entered as run ons (sub-headwords) to the headword (which is the simple word). However sometimes a derivative may be entered as a headword if it has high occurrence in the language and a dictionary user would need to look it up often. A derivative entered as a run on to the simple word, may be written as a whole word if its form has slightly changed from the basic form (simple words) as a result of the derivation process. For example: use

> usage. If the derived form is made by adding a suffix to the basic form or sub-headword, the suffix is indicated after a tilde (~) representing the basic word:

intensify *vt,vi* ongeza, zidisha (nguvu n.k.), ongeza, zidi. intensification *n* intensifier *n*. **intensity** *n* mkazo **intent** *adj* - enye dhamira, -enye shauku, makini. **~ion** n nia, kusudi, dhamira.... ~ **ioned** -enye nia; ...~ **ional** *adj* -a makusudi.- ~ **ionally** *adv*.

2.3.0 **Compounds**

A compound word is made up of two or more words written as one word or separate words. Compounds have been entered as headwords or as run ons to a headword which is the word that makes the first part of the compound. A run on compound is usually not written in full. The first part is represented by a tilde (~) and then followed by the second part. For example:

plastic *adj* 1 (of material) -a plastiki, kinamo, -a kunyumbuka. **~explosive/bomb** bomu la plastiki; 2 -a kuumba/kutengeneza **~surgery** utengenezaji upya wa viungo.

A dictionary reader looking up a derivative or a compound has to check first whether it is entered as a headword. If it is not, he/she should look up the simple word for a derivative or the first word of the compound and then look down the entry and he/she will find the word.

2.4.0 **Homographs**

Homographs are different words with different meanings but happen to have the same spelling. Words which are used in more than one grammatical category are treated as homographs which in this dictionary have been entered in separate entries and numbered.

flag[1] *n* bendera, baramu
flag[2] *n* (also ~stone) jiwe bapa linalotumiwa kusakafia
flag[3] *n* (bot) kangaga
fix[1] *vt,vi* 1 kaza, kongomea, imarisha.........
fix[2] *n* 1 matatizo, matata, mkwamo
accord[1] *n* 1 makubaliano, maafikiano - 2 mapatano
accord[2] vi 1 (with) patana (na), lingana (na)......

It is important therefore to know the word class of the word which one is looking up so that he/she does not waste time looking at a different word class. The user should know the context of the word he/she is looking up so that he/she can go through quickly the homographs and identify the relevant one. For example the contexts of **flag**[1] and **flag**[2] or **flag**[3] are different hence one can correctly guess the appropriate one.

2.5.0 **Affixes**

An affix is a part of a word used to form new words. Productive affixes are usually entered as headwords. These precede the root and together form a new word. Affixes which precede the root are called prefixes and those attached after the root are suffixes. For example:

bond - *pref.* -a utumwa **~age** *n* utumwa
ultra- *pref.* -a kupita kiasi -a kuzidi mno
un- pref. (before adj. adv.) 1 sio, hapana ~ **certain** si yakini,
2 (before v) tenda kinyume, **~tie** fungua,
3 (before n) huonyesha kutokuwa na, **~consciousness** kutokuwa na fahamu.

3.0.0 Parts of speech

Every word in this dictionary has been marked with its word class (part of speech) or grammatical category. The traditional parts of speech are: adjective (adj), adverb (adv), conjunction (conj), interjection (interj), noun (n), preposition (prep), pronoun (pron) and verb (v). Other word classes used are: indefinite article (indef art), attributive (attrib), predicative (pred), prefix (pref), verb intransitive (vi) and verb transitive (vt). A headword which functions in more than one word class but has only one meaning for each category or their definitions are related, it is labelled all the word classes simultaneously.

4.0.0 Variants

Words which have alternative spellings, have been entered either in one entry or in different entries, and one is cross-referred to the alternative spelling considered to be more accepted.

fridge *n see* **refrigerator**
dissociate (also disassociate) vt, vi from, tenga, jitenga, kata, weka mbali.

5.0.0 Cross-reference

Words which are related have been cross-referred to one another in order to show the user that they are either the same or related. Words which have been cross-referred to one another are:

1. Words with alternative spellings
   artefact see **artifact**
   armour **(US armor)**
   raze *also* **rase**
2. Verbs of different tenses su past tense (pt) or past participle (pp) are cross-referred to the present tense form.
   arose *see* **arise**
3. Words and their synonyms.
   anal *see* **anus**
   arrange 3 *(music) see* **adaptation**

6.0.0 Usage labels

Labels are used in this dictionary to draw the attention of the user to the limitation the labelled word can be used. Labels have been used to indicate the status of a word, subject field where a word belongs, geographical region or country in which a particular word is often used, a particular period of time when it has been used, or language of origin of a word. Usage labels are printed in italic letters.

6.1.0 Status of words

Many words are used almost everywhere, but some words are restricted to specific situations and audience.

6.1.1 **Formal** This label denotes words which are used in official context or public occasions such as public speeches, government writing, etc.

6.1.2 **Informal** This label marks words or senses that are often used in conversation or writing between friends.

6.1.3 **Slang** This label is for words or meanings which are used very informally by groups of people of the same social status e.g. students, soldiers or criminals.

6.1.4 **Derogative** This label applies to words used to show disapproval of a certain behaviour or to scorn the person or thing referred to.

6.1.5 **Euphemism** This is used for words chosen to refer to something unpleasant in a pleasant way.

6.1.6 **Vulgar** It applies to words and meanings thought to be indecent and offensive when used before groups of people who could be offended by them.

6.1.7 **Jocular**. This label is used for words or phrases intended to be funny.

6.1.8 **Colloquial**. It shows that a word or sense is used mostly in conversation and informal writing.

6.2.0 **Subject labels**

Words which are used mostly in specific fields of study such as biology, zoology, legal, history, grammar. etc. are marked to indicate the subject in which they are used.

battery *n* (mil) kikosi cha askari wa mizinga....

bail[1] *n* (leg) dhamana

polyphony *n* (music) sauti nyingi

6.3.0 **Regional labels**

English is used in many countries besides Great Britain: Australia, New Zealand, Canada, United States, etc. Within Britain there are also some variations hence Scottish English. In each region some new words or spelling of the same words or even meaning of words have developed and used in one region alone. Words and meaning specific to American English, Australian, British or Scottish English, have been marked (US), (Ausl), (GB) and (Scot) respectively.

6.4. .0 **Time labels**

There are words which are used for a particular period of time and then fall out of use or they are used only in special context.

6.4.1 **Archaic**. This label means that a word or meaning which was at one time in common use, is no longer used except in special contexts e.g. in poetry to reflect the past.

6.4.2 **Dated**. This label indicates that the word is no longer in use.

6.5.0 **Labels of language of origin**

Some words have been borrowed from other languages in recent years. The language of origin has been marked.

plaza *n* (Italy) uwanja, soko, gulio

piece *n* (Fr) ~ de resistance chakula kikuu.

raison de'etre *n* (Fr) sababu (za kuwepo kwa kitu)

7.0.0 Syntax of the verb

In the entry of a verb information is provided to show whether a verb takes an object (vt) or does not take one (vi). For example:

interchange vt 1 (of two persons, etc.) badilishana (mashauri n.k.) **we ~ed books**

lumber[2] *vi* 1 enda kwa kishindo, -wa zito the army tanks ~ed past vifaru vya kijeshi vilipita kwa kishindo.

8.0.0 Complementation

In a language there are words which always appear together. These are either fixed or optional. Many adjectives, nouns and verbs take a prepositional phrase or a non-finite construction. These fixed elements are called complementation of adjectives, nouns or verbs. In this dictionary the complementations are indicated in the entry after the word class label. The optional ones are put in parenthesis. The dictionary user can thus choose the correct complementation for the word he/she uses:

resolve *vt* **~ to do sth**
~ that
~ on doing sth
~ sth (into sth)

respect *n* **~ (for)**
have ~ for sb
pay ~ to
with ~ to
in this ~
in all ~
without ~ to

rife *adj* (pred only) be ~, ~ with

9.0.0 Explanation of meaning

The meaning of a headword is usually a Swahili equivalent which is either one word or a phrase:

much *adj* -ingi
mudfish *n* kambare
nainsook *n* nguo laini ya pamba.

9.1.0 Sense discrimination

A word which has more than one meaning, its senses are provided and separated by numbers:

bastard *n* 1 mtoto wa nje ya ndoa 2 mkatili, mshenzi, 3 asiye na bahati. 4 kitu bandia.

Senses which are closely related but slightly different are separated by letters:

ball[1] *n* 3 pl (sl) (a) mapumbu, makende (b) (int) mavi, upuzi mtupu.

9.2.0 Sense elaboration

A gloss is an explanatory comment added to a definition or example sentence in order to make the definition clearer. Sometimes a Swahili equivalent may not be clear enough to give the reader the sense in the English word. In such cases glosses have been used to limit the scope of the definition hence elaborate the sense.

haggard *adj* (of a person, his face)
-liotambarajika, -liosawajika.

drastic *adj* (of action, methods or medicines) kali, -enye athari kubwa, -enye matokeo ya haraka.

10.0.0 **Illustrative examples**

Examples of usage help to elaborate the definition of a headword and thus make it clearer to the reader. Examples of usage also show the words which always appear with the headword in a sentence and guide the user to make sentences of his own by analogy.

option *n* 1 uchaguzi, hiari, haki ya kutenda *the ~ is yours* uchaguzi ni wako. *there is no ~* hakuna budi. *I have no ~ but to go* ni lazima niende.

bad *adj* 1 -baya, *he has a ~character* ana tabia mbaya *from ~ to worse* zidi kuwa mbaya.

11.0.0 **Collocation**

Some words of a language always appear together with other words. A headword and its collocate make a collocation. For example: *be on guard, change guard, keep guard, mount guard, stand guard*

ABBREVIATIONS

abb - abbreviation
adj - adjective
adv - adverb
Am - America
anat - anatomy
arch - archaic
archit - architecture
astron - astronomy
attrib - attributive
Ausl - Australia
aux - auxilliary
bio - biology
bot - botany
chem - chemistry
colloq - colloquial
comm - commerce
conj - conjunction
derog - derogative
elect - electricity
euph - euphemism
fig - figurative
fin . - finance
Fr - France
GB - Great Britain
geol - geology
geom - geometry
gram - grammar
hist - history
imper - imperative
indef art - indefine article
int - intonation
interj - interjection
irreg - irregular
joc - jocular
Lat - Latin
leg - legal
lit - literature
maths - mathematics
mech - mechanic
med - medicine
mil - military
mus - music
myth - mythology
n - noun
naut - nautical
path - pathology
philos - philosophy
phon - phonology
photog - photography
phr - phrases
phys - physics
pl - plural
poet - poetry
pred - predicative
pref - prefix
prep - preposition
pron - pronoun
prov - proverb
RC - Roman Catholic
rel - religion
Scot - Scottish
sl - slang
Sp - Spanish
tech - technical
US - United States
usu - usually
vi - verb intransitive
vt - verb transitive
vul - vulgar
zoo - zoology

A

A,a 1 herufi ya kwanza ya alfabeti ya Kiingereza. 2 barabara; tangu mwanzo hadi mwisho, *he knows the subject from A to Z* analijua hilo somo barabara. *adj* 1 *(naut)* -a daraja la kwanza. 2 *(colloq)* zuri sana, *I am feeling A ~* 1 najisikia vizuri sana. 3 -a daraja la juu *this essay is ~ material* insha hii ni ya daraja la juu.

a/an 1 *indef art* -o ote, fulani, moja k.m. *buy a book* nunua kitabu, (chochote). 2 *(a certain one)* mmoja, yeyote mmojawapo *there is a man to see you* kuna mtu anataka kuonana nawe, *a Mr. Juma* Bwana mmoja aitwaye Juma (*'an'* hutumika badala ya *'a'* kwa majina yanayoanza na irabu k.m. *an egg* yai moja, *twenty miles an hour* maili ishirini kwa saa).

aback *adv* 1 *(arch)* nyuma, kinyume. 2 *be taken ~* shtuka, staajabu, shangaa, duwaa.

abacus *n* abakusi, abaki: kibao maalum chenye shanga kinachotumika kusaidia kuhesabu.

abaft *adv prep (naut)* katika tezi, kuelekea tezi, karibu na tezi, nyuma ya chombo.

abandon *vt* 1 *(desert)* tupa, toka katika gea, telekeza, jitenga na *~ wife and children,* acha, tupa, telekeza mke na watoto. 2 *(Give up)* acha: *~ rights/a property* acha haki/mali. 3 *(phr) ~* **hope** kata tamaa. 4 *(phr) ~* **oneself to sth** jiachia kabisa k.m. huzuni, furaha, dhambi, tamaa. *n* hali ya kutojizuia, kujisahau, kujiachia *they danced with ~* walicheza wakajisahau. **~ed** *adj* 1 *(deserted)* -lioachwa, -liotupwa, -liotelekezwa, -kiwa, *an ~ ed village* kijiji kilichotelekezwa, mahame, tongo. 2 *(profligate)* -ovu, -potovu, fisadi, -asherati. **~ ed ment** *n* 1 tendo/hali ya kutupa/ kutupwa, kuacha kuachwa; tendo/hali ya ufisadi. 2 *(carelessness)* ulegevu, uzembe. 3 *(complete surrender)*. *see* **abandon**.

abase *vt* tusha, fedhehesha, dhalilisha, vunjia heshima/hadhi, shushia hadhi. *~oneself* jitahayarisha, jifedhehesha, jiaibisha. **~ment** *n* 1 utwezo, unyonge, udhalili, udhilifu. 2 unyenyekeo, unyenyekevu (kupita kiasi).

abash *vt* ona haya, aibishwa, fedheheshwa, *to be ~ed* tahayarishwa. **~ ment** *n* fadhaa, haya, tahayuri, fedheha.

abate *vt, vi* 1 punguza, pungua, punguka. 2 komesha. **~ ed ment** *n* 1 kupunguza, kupungua, kupunguka. 2 kukomesha.

abattoir *n* machinjioni.

abb *n (lit)* mtiririko wa vitendo *see* **plot**.

abbess *n (rel)* mama mkuu, bi mkuu (katika nyumba ya watawa wa kike).

abbey *n (rel)* 1 makao ya watawa. 2 jumuiya ya watawa.

abbot *n (rel)* mkuu wa watawa katika nyumba ya watawa wa kiume.

abbreviate *vt* fupisha (hadithi, hotuba, neno n.k.); punguza, kusuru. **abbreviation** *n* ufupisho,kifupi, kifupisho, ufupishaji, k.m. mt. badala ya methali, TZ badala ya Tanzania.

ABC, abc *n* 1 alfabeti. 2 maarifa ya msingi *the ~ of driving* maarifa ya msingi ya udereva.

abdicate *vi* acha/ng'atuka kwenye cheo kikubwa k.v. ufalme . **abdication** *n* kukimbia majukumu.

abdomen *n* fumbatio, tumbo. **abdominal** *adj* -a fumbatio, -a tumbo *~ pain* maumivu ya tumbo; *~ operation* operesheni ya tumbo.

abduct *vt* teka nyara (watu). **~ion** *n* kuteka nyara, kutorosha mtu. **~or** *n* mtekaji nyara, mtoroshaji.

abeam *adv (naut)* kwenye mstari wa pembemraba na chombo, kwa kukingama na chombo.

abed *adj (lit or arch)* kitandani.

abberrant *adj* -potovu, -liokengeuka; -enye kasoro. **aberration** *n* mkengeuko, kupotoka (kwa njia, tabia au akili); kasoro.

abet *vt* saidia, shawishi, shirikiana na (kutenda maovu). **aid and ~** saidia kutenda jinai. **~ment** *n* msaada, ushirika, mshawasha. **~ter, ~tor** *n* mshiriki, mshawishi (hasa kwa mabaya), mbuya; msaidizi jinai.

abeyance *n* kutokutumika kwa muda

this rule is in ~ sheria hii haitumiki n kwa wakati huu.

abhor *vt* chukia sana, chukizwa sana ~ *cruelty to animals* chukia ukatili kwa wanyama. **~rence** *n* chuki kubwa, karaha. **~rent** *adj*

abide *vt* 1 ngoja, ngojea. 2 stahimili, vumilia *he can't ~ him* hawezi kumvumilia, *vi* 1 *(arch)* kaa mahali, tulia mahali, shinda mahali *and they abode there three days* wakakaa huko siku tatu. 2 *(phr)* ~ **by** tii, shikilia, fuata, zingatia (ahadi, kusudi, amri, n.k.) ~ *by an agreement* fuata mapatano. **abiding** *adj* 1 -a kudumu, -a milele. 2 *(leg)* tiifu *law ~ing person,* mtii sheria, mwenye kufuata sheria.

ability *n* 1 uwezo (kimwili, kiakili) *to the best of my* ~ kwa kadri ya uwezo wangu, *a man of great* ~ mtu mwenye uwezo mkubwa. 2 werevu. 3 kipaji *a boy of abilities* mvulana mwenye vipaji vingi. **able** *adj* -enye uwezo, hodari (kimwili, kiakili) *to be ~ to do sth* kuweza kumudu kufanya jambo. *drinkable* -a kunyweka. **ably** *adv* kwa ustadi, kwa akili. *(suf to form adjectives)*

ab initio *adj (leg)* toka mwanzo. **void** ~ batili toka mwanzo.

abject *adj* 1 duni, -nyonge kabisa, fakiri ~ *poverty* ufukara, umaskini kabisa. 2 (of persons) -a kudharauliwa ~ *behaviour*, matendo duni, tabia ya kujidhalilisha mno; *an ~ apology* kitendo cha kuomba msamaha kwa kujidhalilisha mno. **~ly** *adv* ~ **ion** *n* **~ness** *n.*

abjure *vt* acha, kana (kwa kiapo). **abjuration** *n.*

ablate *vt* ondoa kwa kuyeyusha/kukata/kumomonyoa/kukausha. **ablation** *n.*

ablaut *n* ablauti: kubadilishwa irabu ya mzizi wa neno ili kuonyesha nyakati k.m.: *sing, sang, sung, song.*

ablaze *adj,adv* 1 -a kuwaka *the house is* ~ nyumba inawaka moto. 2 -a kung'aa; -a kumeremeta *(fig) the face of the bride was ~with happiness* uso wa bibi harusi ulimeremeta kwa furaha.

ablution *n* 1 kuosha, kuoga; kunawa. 2 (ceremonial) kutawadha, kutia tohara, kuosha maiti, kujitakasa *perform one's ~s* jiosha.

abnegate *vt* 1 kana. 2 jihini, jinyima. **abnegation** *n.*

abnormal *adj* 1 -siyo ya kawaida (hasa enye kuleta hisia hasi). **~ity** *n.*

aboard *adv* chomboni, katika ndege, melini *go ~* panda chomboni; *welcome* ~ karibu(ni) chomboni.

abode *n (arch or lit)* makao, makazi, maskani, mastakimu.

abolish *vt* komesha, futa, ondoa kabisa ~ *tax*, futa kodi; ~ *a law* tangua sheria. **abolition** *n* (of slavery) ukomeshaji wa utumwa.

A-bomb *n* atomiki bomu.

abominate *vt* chukia mno, kirihi. **abominable** *adj* -a kuchukiza mno, makuruhi. **abomination** *n*

aboriginal *adj* (of living creatures) -a asili, -a kwanza, -a awali. **aborigine** *n* mwananchi wa asili. **A ~s** wananchi wa asili ya Australia.

abort *vi* avya, haribu (mimba) *vt.* 1 toa mimba. 2 komesha kitu kisitokee. **~ed** *adj.* **~ion** *n* 1 kutoa mimba. 2 kuharibika mimba. 3 mimba iliyoharibika; *(fig)* (jambo, mradi au mpango) usiofanikiwa. **~ionist** *n* 1 mtoaji mimba. 2 mtetezi wa haki ya kutoa mimba. **~ive** *adj* -sio fanikiwa, viza ~ *coup* maasi yasiyofanikiwa; *prove* ~ kuwa bila mafanikio, via.

abound *vi* 1 ~ **(in/with)** sheheni. 2 jaa tele *the river ~ in fish,* mto umejaa samaki tele.

about[1] *adv* kadiri ya kama ~ *as high as that tree* urefu wa kama mti ule.

about[2] *adv part* potepote, huku na huko, mahali pote *the children were rushing~* watoto walikimbia huku na huko. 2 elekea nyuma. ~ **face** geuka nyuma.

about[3] *prep* 1 hapa na pale *he walked ~ the town* alitembea hapa na pale mjini. 2 kuhusu, juu ya *he wrote* *a story ~ a lion* aliandika hadithi juu ya simba *he is careless~ his personal appearance* hajijali. 3 karibia ~ *to die* karibia kufa, taka kufa *he is ~ to leave* anakaribia kuondoka.

above[1] *adv* 1 juu *from ~* kutoka juu. 2 awali, juu *as was stated ~* kama ilivyosemwa hapo awali. 3 mbinguni. ~ **board** *adv* wazi wazi *The discussion was ~* majadiliano yalikuwa bayana.

above[2] *prep* 1 juu ya *we flew ~ the clouds* tuliruka juu ya mawingu. 2 zidi wastani *the temperature has been ~ average* halijoto imezidi wastani. 3 zaidi ya, kuliko *to value humanity ~ wealth* kuthamini utu zaidi kuliko mali. ~ **all** zaidi ya yote. **over and ~** zaidi ya hayo. 4 safi, sio kifani, zuri mno *she is ~ criticism* hana doa.

abrade *vt* sugua, chubua, kwaruza, chuna (k.m. ngozi). **abrasion** *n (of the skin),* mchubuko wa ngozi. **abrasive** *n (tech)* kichubuo, kikwaruzo, msasa. *adj* -a kuchubua -a kukwaruza; *(fig)* -a kuchukiza ~ *voice* sauti ya madende, ya kuchukiza.

abreast *adv* sambamba, chanjari;*(fig)* **be/keep ~ (of/with)** *the times* jua mambo yanayotokea wakati huo.

abridge *vt* fupisha (hasa maandishi), punguza *an ~ed edition* toleo lililofupishwa. **~ment** *n* ufupishaji.

abroad *adv* 1 ughaibuni, ng'ambo, ugenini *be or travel ~* kuwa/safiri ng'ambo. 2 kila mahali *there is a rumour ~ that* uvumi umeenea kwamba. 3 nje ya nyumba *you are ~ early this morning* umetoka nje mapema sana asubuhi hii.

abrogate *vt (leg)* tangua, batilisha. **abrogation** *n.*

abrupt *adj* 1 -a ghafula, -siotazamiwa. 2 *(of speech, writing or behaviour)* bila nadhari, -a mkato. 3 *(of a slope)* -kali, -kubwa.

abscess *n* usaha.

abscise *vi* pogoka, kongoka. **abscission** *n.*

abscond *vi* toroka, jificha, kimbia kwa ujificha. **~er** *n.*

absence *n* 1 kutokuwako *in my~* wakati sipo. **leave of ~** ruhusa ya kutokuwako. ~ **of mind** usahaulifu. 2 kutokuwapo kimawazo. **absent minded** *adj he is ~* yu msahaulifu. **absent mindedly** *adv.* **absent mindedness** *n.* 3 (lack) ukosefu, ukosekano *there is an ~ of heat* hakuna joto, **absent** *adj* 1 kutokuwepo. *vt* ~ **oneself (from)** acha kuja **~ee** *n* **~ism** *n.*

absolute *adj* 1 kamili ~ *trust* imani kamili. 2 (despotic) -enye amri zote peke yake, -a kidikteta. 3 (infinite) huru, isiyo na masharti wala mipaka. 4 halisi, bila shaka ~ *proof* ushahidi thabiti. **~ly** *adv.* **absolutism** *n* udikteta; nadhari ya siasa ya mtu mmoja kuhodhi madaraka yote.

absolution *n* 1 *(rel)* ghofira, msamaha. **absolve** *vt* 1 samehe, achilia, epusha; ~ *from blame* ondoa hatiani. 2 ghofiri, ondoka dhambi.

absorb *vt* 1 -fyonza, nyonya; sharabu ~ *ink* fyonza wino. 2 shughulisha *his work ~ed him* kazi yake ilimshughulisha sana. **~ent** *adj* -enye kufyonza. **~er** *n* kisharabu. **~ing** *adj: an ~ing novel* riwaya inayoteka. **absorption** *n* 1 ufyonzaji. 2 *(engrossment)* utekwaji (katika fikra au shughuli). **absorptive** *adj.*

abstain *vi* 1 jinyima, jihini, acha kufanya kutumia kitu. *he ~ed from smoking* aliacha kuvuta sigara. **~er** n (mtu) ajinyimaye, *total ~er:* asiyekunywa mvinyo kabisa. **abstemious** *adj* -a kujihini (chakula kinywaji n.k.). **~ness** *n.*

abstention *n* 1 kutokupiga kura. 2 mzio. **abstinence** *n* ~ **(from)** uzuiaji. **abstinent** *adj.*

abstract[1] *adj* 1 dhahania, -a kuwazika tu. 2 -soweza kushikika. ~ **noun** nomino dhahania. **in the ~** kinadharia.

abstract[2] *vt* 1 toa katika, chomoa. **~ed.** **~edly** *adv, adj (engrossed)* 1 -lio tekwa kimawazo. 2 -lio fupishwa

(k.m. kitabu au hotuba).
abstraction *n* 1 usahaulifu; hali ya kushughulika na kuacha kuzingatia mengine. 2 utoaji/ung'oaji wa kitu k.m. ung'oaji jino. 3 dhana au wazo.
abstruse *adj* -gumu kueleweka/ kufahamika, tata, -enye kutatiza. **~ly** *adv*. **~ness** *n* utatanishi.
absurd *adj* -a upuuzi, -a kipumbavu, -a kuchekesha. **~ity** *n*. **~ly** *adv*.
abundant *adj* - ingi, tele. *we have ~ food* tuna vyakula vingi sana. **~ly** *adv* **abundance** *n*.
abuse *vt* 1 tumia vibaya. 2 tukana, tusi. 3 dhulumu, onea. *n* **abusive** *adj ~ language* lugha chafu. **~ly** *adv*. **~ness** *n*.
abut *vi* pakana na, -wa jirani na, egemea. **~ment** *n* mhimili (wa daraja au tao).
abyss *n* lindi kuu; *(fig) the ~ of despair* kukata tamaa kabisa; **abysmal** *adj ~ ignorance* ujuha kabisa. **abysmally** *adv*.
Abyssinia *n* Uhabeshi. **~n** *n* Mhabeshi. *adj* -a kihabeshi.
academic *adj* 1 -a kitaaluma. 2 (discussion) -a kinadharia mno. *n* ulama, mhadhiri. **~lly** *adv*. **~al** *adj* **academicals** *n* mavazi (joho na kofia) wakati wa mahafali au sherehe rasmi za chuo.
academy *n* 1 chuo (cha elimu ya juu). **Military ~** Chuo cha Jeshi, 2 akademia (chama cha maulama). **academician** *n* mwanachama wa chama cha maulama; mwanataaluma.
accede *vi* 1 kubali, ridhia. 2 pata au rithi cheo *when did he ~ to the throne?* alirithi lini kiti cha ufalme?
accelerando *n, adv* (music) mchapuko; kwa mchapuko. *adj* -enye mchapuko.
accelerate 1 *vt; vi* chapuka, chapuza, zidisha mwendo; harakisha. **acceleration** *n* mchapuko. **accelerator** *n* kichapuzi.
accent *n (gram)* 1 kiinitoni. 2 lafudhi. 3 *(colloq)* msisitizo *this year the ~ is on youth*: mwaka huu msisitizo ni wa maendeleo ya vijana. *vt* tamka kwa lafudhi **~ed** *adj*. *vt* ~ **accentuate** tia mkazo. **accentuation** *n*
accept *vt* 1 pokea *~ a bribe* pokea rushwa. 2 kubali, kiri *~ a fact* kubali ukweli. **~able** *adj*. **~ability** *n* ukubalifu. **~ance** *n* kukubali, ridhaa.
access *n* 1 *(means of)* njia ya kufikia. **~ road** barabara ya kuingilia. 2 *(liberty)* fursa ya (kukaribia, kutumia, kuingia) *easy of ~* rahisi sana kuingia. 3 *(sudden burst)* kupandwa ghafla (na hisia, homa) *an ~ of anger* kupandwa hamaki/hasira. **~ible** *adj* -a kuingilika, -a kufikika, -a kupatikana. **~ibility** *n* ufikikaji,upatikanaji.
accessary *n* msaidizi, mshiriki, hasa katika jinai. **accession** *n* 1 kupata au kupanda cheo. 2 (increase) nyongeza *recent ~ to the library* nyongeza za karibuni za vitabu vya maktaba. **accessory** *n* 1 see **accessary** 2 *n* kifuasi, kitu cha ziada *accessoriesof a bicycle* vifuasi vya baiskeli k.m. taa, kengele, pampu.
accidence *n* mbadiliko umbo.
accident *n* 1 ajali *highway ~* ajali barabarani. *(prov)* **~s will happen** ajali haina kinga. 2 bahati *I met him by ~* nimekutana naye kwa bahati. **~al** *adj* -a bahati. **~ally** *adv*. kwa bahati.
acclaim *vt* 1 karibisha/pokea kwa shangwe, tangaza kwa shangwe, (k.m. rais/mfalme) *n* himidi, shangwe. **acclamation** *n* shangwe *he was elected by ~* alichaguliwa kwa kauli moja.
acclimatize *vt (fig)* zoea (mambo mageni, mazingira).
acclivity *n* mwinuko.
accolade *n* himidi, sifa kuu.
accommodate *vt* 1 patia mahali pa kuishi. 2 patia nafasi *the house ~s ten people* nyumba ina nafasi ya watu kumi. 3 *(adapt)* rekebisha. 4 *(oblige)* fadhili, kirimu, -pa *to ~ somebody with a loan* fadhili kwa kumpa mkopo mtu. **accommodating**

adj -a hisani, -enye hisani, maridhia. **accommodation** *n* 1 *(board)* nyumba/ vyumba vilivyo tayari kukaliwa/kupangishwa. 2 marekebisho 3 *(kindness)* fadhila, hisani. 4 maafikiano.

accompany *vt* 1 enda na, fuatana na. 2 andamana na *fever~ ed with delirium* homa iliyoandamana na kuweweseka. 3 *(mus)* kupamba. **accompaniment** *n* 1 kifuasi, kiambata. 2 *(mus)* ala saidizi. **accompanist** *n (mus)* mpiga ala saidizi. **accomplice** *n* mshiriki (jinai).

accomplish *vt* maliza, timiza, fanikisha. **~ment** *n* 1 utimilifu, ufanikishaji. 2 ustadi. **~ed** *adj* hodari, stadi *an ~ed dancer* mcheza ngoma hodari.

accord[1] *n* 1 makubaliano, maafikiano. 2 mkataba. 3 uwiano. 4 *(phr)* **of her own ~** kwa hiari yake, bila kulazimishwa.

accord[2] *vi* 1 *(with)* patana (na), lingana (na); kubaliana (na) *vt (formal)* jalia, pa, toa *~ permission* toa ruhusa, -pa ruhusa *~ a warm welcome* karibisha kwa shangwe. **~ance** *n* kukubaliana **in ~ance with** kwa mujibu wa, kwa kufuatana na. **~ant** *adj* -enye kupatana (kulingana) na. **~ing** *conj you will be paid ~ing as you work hard or poorly:* utalipwa kwa kadiri ya utendaji kazi wako. **~ing** *prep he will be paid ~ing to his work* atalipwa kufuatana na kazi yake. **~ingly** *adv*.

accordion *n* kodiani.

accost *vt* kabili, laki *I was ~ed by a stranger* nilikabiliwa na mtu mgeni.

account[1] *n* hesabu; akaunti **current ~** akaunti ya hundi **savings ~** akaunti ya akiba **deposit ~** akaunti ya amana **final ~** hesabu za mwisho. **~ancy** *n* uhasibu **~ant** *n* mhasibu

account[2] *vi* 1 fikiria *He is ~ed innocent until he is proved guilty* anafikiriwa kuwa hana hatia mpaka atakapotiwa hatiani. 2 eleza sababu ya. 3 -wa sababu yaangamiza, teka. **~able** *adj* -enye kuwajibika, -enye kuhusika. **~ability** *n* 1 mkokotoo. manufaa. 2 **put sth to good ~** tumia kitu kwa manufaa. 3 maelezo. **call somebody to ~** taka mtu ajieleze. 4 *(phr)* **give a good ~** fanya vizuri. 5 *(phr)* **take something into ~** zingatia sababu. 6 **on ~ of** kwa sababu ya.

accoutrement *n* 1 vikorokoro, vitu vidogovidogo vinavyotumika katika shughuli fulani, hasa safari. 2 vifaa vyote vya askari isipokuwa mavazi na silaha.

accredit *vt* 1 teua kuwa mwakilishi. 2 tambua *~ed part adj* kutambuliwa rasmi.

accretion *n* 1 uongezekaji au ukuaji wa kitu utokanao na kuongezewa au kulimbikiziwa vitu vya nje. 2 ongezeko (hasa la polepole).

accrue *vi* ongezeka, tokana na *the profits which ~ from work* faida zinazotokana na kazi.

acculturation *n* uzoeaji wa utamaduni/tabia ya kigeni.

accumulate *vt* kusanya, limbika. *vi* ongezeka, jikusanya. **accumulation** *n*.

accumulator *n* 1 kilimbikizi umeme. 2 *(computer)* kilimbikizi namba.

accurate *adj* 1 -angalifu, barabara. 2 isiyo na hitilafu, sahihi. **accuracy** *n*. **~ly** *adv* sawasawa.

accursed *adj* -liolaaniwa.

accuse *vt* shtaki, laumu, kengemeka, shutumu *~ somebody of commiting a crime* shitaki mtu kwa kuvunja sheria. **accusation** *n* mashtaka, lawama, shutuma, mkengemeko. **~r** *n* mshtaki. **~d** *n* mshtakiwa. **accusingly** *adv* kwa shutuma.

accustom *vt* zoea, zoeza **~ oneself to** jizoeza. **~ed** *adj* 1 *(phr)* **be ~ed** zoea. 2 siku zote, *his ~ place* mahala pake pa kawaida.

ace *ji* 1 *ree* (karata ya kuchezea yenye ng'anda moja au dadu yenye alama moja). 2 *(colloq)* mtu hodari kabisa. k.m. mchezaji hodari wa mpira.

3 *(phr)* **within an ~ of** chupuchupu, nusura.
acerbity *n* ukali, uchungu (wa kitu, moyo au maneno). 2 *(pl)* **acerbities** maneno makali.
acetate *n (chem)* asetati.
acetic *adj* -a siki, -a asetiki.
acetylene *n* asetilini: gesi inayotumika kuwashia taa na kulehemia.
ache *n* mchonyoto, maumivu (yanayoendelea). *part adj vi* uma, wanga, ehanga, chonyota, *my head~s* kichwa kinaniuma; *(fig) my heart ~s* moyo unaniuma; *(fig)* tamani sana *my heart ~d for her* nilikufa juu yake.
achieve *vt* maliza, timiza, faulu, fanikisha ~ one's purpose: timiza lengo. **achievable**. *adj*. **~ment** *n* mafanikio.
Achilles *n (fig)* ~ **heel** udhaifu. *spelling is my ~ heel* udhaifu wangu uko katika tahajia.
acid[1] *adj* -kali, chachu, -a asidi *(fig)* -a kubeza. *adv* kwa bezo.
acid[2] *n* asidi .**~ify** *vt.* 1 *(chem)* fanya asidi. **~ity** *n* 1 uasidi. 2 *(heart burn)* kiungulia. **~ic** *adj* -enye asidi.
acidulous *adj (fig)* 1 -enye chachu, kali. 2 -enye tabia ya ukali.
ack-ack *n (sl)* kombora la kutungulia ndege.
acknowledge *vt* 1 kiri, kubali. thibitisha *he didn't ~ defeat* hakukiri kushindwa; *(receipt of) I ~ your letter* ninathibitisha kupokea barua yako. 2 shukuru. 3 *(regard as)* tambua *he is ~d to be an expert of this subject* anatambulikana kuwa ni bingwa katika fani hii. 4 onyesha ishara ya kutambua *I passed her in the street but she didn't ~ me* nilipishana naye barabarani lakini akajifanya hakunitambua. **~d** *adj* -naetambuliwa. **~ment** *n* 1 kukubali, kukiri. 2 shukrani.
acme *n* 1 upeo, kilele, kikomo *he reached the ~ of his ability* alifikia upeo wa uwezo wake.
acne *n* chunusi.
acolyte *n* 1 mtumishi (kanisani). 2 mfuasi.
acorn *n (bot)* mbegu au tunda la muoka.
acoustic *adj* -a akustika, -a sauti, -a elimu ya sauti na kusikia. **~s** *n* 1 akustika, taaluma ya sauti. 2 mazingira sikizi the ~s of this room are good mazingira sikizi ya chumba hiki ni mazuri.
acquaint *vt* 1 julisha, pasha habari, fahamisha. 2 fahamiana na, zoeana na. 3 jizoeza ~ *oneself with one's work* jizoesha kazi be ~ed with *someone* fahamiana na mtu fulani. **~ance** *n* 1 uzoefu, ujuzi, maarifa. 2 mtu unayemfahamu, jamaa.
acquiesce *vi* 1 kubali, ridhia (kimya kimya), ridhaa. **~nt** *adj*.
acquire *vt* pata, jipatia kitu (hasa kwa kujifunza au kujizoeza au kwa jitihada); *~d taste* upendeleo zoefu. ~ **ment** *n.*
acquisition *n* 1 kupata. 2 pato, kitu kipatikanacho. **acquisitive** *adj* -enye uchu, tamaa ya kupata. **acquisitiveness** *n.*
acquit *vt* 1 *(leg)* achilia ~ **somebody of an offence** hukumu mtu kuwa hana hatia. 2 tenda ~ *oneself well (of a task n.k.)* tenda vizuri, vyema. **~tal** *n* kuachiliwa.
acre *n* ekari, eka *fig* **God's~** makaburini **~age** *n.*
acrid *adj* -chungu, -kali (hasa kwa ladha au kwa harufu); -a ukali wa tabia au mwenendo. **~ity** *n.* **~ness** *n.*
acriflavine *n (chem)* akrifilavini.
acrimony *n* ukali (wa tabia/maneno). **acrimonious** *adj.*
acrobat *n* mwanasarakasi. **~ic** *adj* -a kisarakasi. **~ics** *n* michezo ya sarakasi.
acronymy *n* akronimi: neno linaloundwa kutokana na herufi za mwanzo za majina k.m. **UNO** - United Nations Organisation.
acrophobia *n* woga wa kina.
across *prep* 1 (vuka) toka upande mmoja hadi upande mwingine *walk ~ the street* vuka barabara.

2 ng'ambo (ya), upande wa pili.
acrostic *n* aina ya chemshabongo.
acrylic *n* ~ **fibre** utembo bandia unaotumiwa kutengeneza nguo.
act *vt, vi* 1 *(take action)* tenda, fanya. 2 *(of stage)* cheza, igiza. 3 jifanya *feign* ~ *for (represent)* wakilisha ~ **(up) on** 1 (a suggestion/ advice) fuata, fuatilia. 2 athiri *this medicine ~s upon heart* dawa hii inaathiri moyo. ~ **as** fanya kazi ya *he ~ as interpreter* anafanya kazi ya ukalimani. ~ **up** 1 jifanya, jifaragua. 2 leta maumivu au maudhi. *n* 1 tendo, kitendo, amali *in the* ~ katika kutenda, kitendo. 2 sheria (iliyopitishwa na Bunge). 3 onyesho (katika tamthiliya). 4 *(pretence)* kujifanya, kujifaragua. ~ **of God** kudura. **actor** *n* 1 mtenda, mtendaji, mhusika. 2 *(player)* mchezaji. ~**ress** *n (actor)* wa kike. **action** *n* 1 tendo, kitendo, amali. **take** ~ anza kutenda, chukua hatua **out of** ~ mbovu. 2 *(gesticulation)* ishara za maungo. 3 *(effect)* athari, matokeo ~ *of medicine, salt n.k.)* matokeo ya kutumia dawa (chumvi n.k.). 4 *(fighting)* mapigano. 5 *(leg)* madai; mashtaka, daawa criminal~ mashtaka ya jinai. **actionable** *adj (leg)* -a kuchukuliwa hatua. 6 *(lit) (action of a play)* onyesho
active *adj* 1 -tendaji. 2 mashughuli. 3 hai ~ *members* wanacha ma hai. ~ **volcano** volkenohai. 4 *(gram)* tendi/ ~ **voice** kauli tendi.
activate *vt* amsha, chochea. **activism** *n (polit)* uhamasishaji kwa vitendo. **activist** *n* mhamasishaji mtendaji.
activity *n* 1 hali ya utendaji, kushughulika, bidii, juhudi. 2 shughuli, utendaji, amali.
actual *adj* halisi, -liopo ~ *situation* hali halisi. ~**ity** *n*. ~**ly** *adj* kwa kweli. **actualize** *vt* 1 maliza, timiliza. 2 hakikisha. 3 thibitisha.
actuary *n* mtakwimu bima. **actuarial** *adj*.
actuate *vt* 1 anzisha, washa (mashine). 2 chochea, shawishi *be ~d by (love, jealousy etc)* sukumwa na (mapenzi, wivu, n.k.).
acuity *n* welekevu, ukali, wepesi.
acumen *n* busara, upevu wa akili, welekevu.
acupuncture *n* tiba vitobo. **acupuncturist** *n* mtaalamu wa tiba hiyo.
acute *adj* kali. ~ **angle** pembekali. **accent** alama ya lafudhi. *(phr)* ~ *condition* mahututi. ~ ly *adv*. ~**ness** *n*.
ad *(colloq)* tangazo la biashara (kifupi cha *advertisement*).
adage *n* methali, msemo wenye hekima.
adagio *adj (mus)* kipande cha muziki (kinachopigwa taratibu).
Adam *n* Adamu. *(fig)* **Adam's apple** kikoromeo, zoloto, kongomeo.
adamant *n* 1 jiwe linalosemekana kuwa haliwezi kukatika wala kuvunjika. 2 *(fig)* shika kani, kaidi, kataa katakata. **adamantine** *adj*.
adapt *vt* 1 rekebisha, badili, tengeneza, tohoa (ili kufaa matumizi fulani) ~ *ed from* iliyotengenezwa kutokana na iliyotoholewa *the play has been ~ed from English* mchezo umetoholewa kutoka Kiingereza. ~**ability** *n*. ~**ation** *n* 1 mabadiliko, marekebisho. 2 utohozi. ~**able** *adj* 1 -enye kurekebishika. 2 epesi kubadilika (kufuatana na mazingira). ~**er** *n* adapta; kirekebishi.
add *vt* jumlisha, ongeza, unga. ~ **up** jumlisha, ~ *things*. ~ **in** tia *vi* ~ **to** ongeza. ~**ed** *adj* ilioongezwa. ~**ition** *n* 1 ongezeko. 2 kuongeza. ~**itional** *adj* -a ziada.
addendum *n* nyongeza.
adder *n* kifutu.
addict *vi, vt* **be ~ed to** zoea, pendelea, tawaliwa na (hasa ubaya k.m. ulevi) *n* mtawaliwa (hasa wa ulevi ama desturi mbaya) *morphia* ~ mtawaliwa wa afyuni. ~**ion/** ~ **edness** *n*. ~**ive** *adj* ~enye kuzoesha tabia mbaya.

additive *n* -vingio, nyongeza.
addle *vt, vi* 1 vuruga, kanganya, changanya. 2 *(of eggs)* oza, ozesha. adj 1 -enye kukanganyikiwa. 2 viza. ~ **brained** mtu aliye changanyikiwa.
address[1] *n* 1 *(postal)* anwani. 2 *(home)* maskani. 3 *(speech)* hotuba, mahubiri. 4 *(arch) (manners)* adabu, mwenendo. **form of** ~ mtindo (wa mawasiliano au kuitana). **~ee** *n* mpelekewa barua.
address[2] *vt* 1 andika anwani. 2 hutubia. 3 ita kwa jina na cheo. *(phr)* ~ **oneself** to *(a piece of work)* jishughulisha na.
adduce *vt* toa, leta (ushahidi, sababu n .k.). **adduction** *n*
adeem *vt (leg)* batilisha *the legacy is ~ed* hiba imebatilshwa. **ademption** *n (leg)* batilisho, batiliko ~ *of legacy* batilisho/batiliko la hiba.
adept *adj n* stadi, -bingwa, hodari.
adequate *adj* -a kutosha,-a kufaa kwa kusudi fulani. **adequacy/ adequateness** *n* utoshelevu.
adhere *vi* 1 nata, gandama. 2 *(to be faithful to)* shika ~ *to a promise* shika ahadi. **~nce** *n* ufuasi, uaminifu. **adherent** n mfuasi.
adhesion *n* 1 mnato, unataji, wambiso. 2 *(path)* mng'ang'aniano, muunganiko. **adhesive** *adj* -enye kunata/kung'ng'ania; *n* kitu kinachonata k.m. plasta.
adhibit *vt* 1 ingiza, anzisha, tumia. 2 tia dawa. 3 ambatisha. **~ion** *n* 1 kuingiza mwanzo; matumizi. 2 kutia dawa. 3 ambatisho.
ad hoc *(lat)* kwa kusudi maalum ~ *committee* kamati ya dharura (maalum).
ad infinitum *(lat)* bila kikomo, milele, daima. **ad interim** *adv* kwa muda huu.
adipose *adj* shahamu (mafuta ya mnyama). **adiposity** *n* unono, shahamu ~ *tissue* tishu ya shahamu.
adit *n* mlango, hasa wa kuingilia katika mgodi n.k. kujongea, kusogea.
adjacent *adj* -a kupakana, -a karibu; -a jirani. adjacency *n* kupakana, ujirani, kukaribiana.
adjective *n (gram)* kivumishi. **adjectival** *adj* -a kivumishi *~phrase* kikundi vumishi; *~clause* kishazi vumishi.
adjoin *vt, vi* pakana na. **~ing** *adj* -a kupakana na, -a kuungana *~ing rooms* vyumba vinavyopakana.
adjourn *vt, vi* 1 ahirisha. 2 acha, funga (mkutano). **~ment** *n* uahirishaji.
adjudge *vt* 1 hukumu, amua, kata kesi. 2 amuru (mtu apewe kitu kisheria).
adjudicate *vt, vi* 1 hukumu, amua. 2 sikiliza kesi. 3 tamka to ~ *somebody bankrupt* kutamka kuwa fulani mufilisi. **adjudicator** *n* 1 hakimu, jaji. 2 mwamuzi. **adjudication** *n* 1 hukumu. 2 tamko la ufilisi.
adjunct *n* 1 kiongezo, kiungo (kilichoongezewa) 2 *(gram) (in clause)* kijalizo.
adjure *vt* 1 apisha. 2 *(implore)* taka mtu afanye jambo fulani. **adjuration** *n* 1 kiapo, tendo la kuapisha. 2 kusihi kwa moyo.
adjust *vt* rekebisha, weka sawa ~ *oneself to the climate* jizoeza na mazingira mapya. **~er** mkadiriaji wa madai ya bima. **~ment** *n* 1 urekebishaji. 2 zana za kurekebishia (virekebishio). **~able** *adj* -enye kurekebishika.
adjutant *n* 1 mfawidhi. **adjutancy** *n* cheo cha usaidizi, ufawidhi, upambe.
adjuvant *adj* -enye msaada, -enye kusaidia *n* msaidizi.
ad lib *adv (colloq) (abbr of ad libitum)* huru, iso kipingamizi. vi, iga, rekebisha utakavyo.
ad libitum *adv* 1 huria. 2 (katika sanaa utendi) kwa kuongezea tendo. 3 *(music)* kwa kuongeza sehemu mojawapo katika mwongozo wa muziki (ambayo ni huria).
adman *n (US sl)* mtunzi wa matangazo ya biashara.
admass *n* watu wanaovutwa upesi na matangazo ya vyombo vya habari.
administer *vt* 1 tawala, simamia, endesha. 2 toa, lisha ~ *an oath to*

lisha kiapo, apisha ~ *punishment* toa adhabu, adhibu, tia adabu. **administration** *n* utawala; himaya; uendeshaji; usimamiaji; ~ *of justice* utoaji wa haki. 2 sehemu ya uendeshaji katika serikali. **administrative** *adj*. **administrator** *n* msimamizi, mtawala, kabidhiwasii.

admirable *adj* -a ajabu, -zuri, -a kusifiwa, -a haiba. **admirably** *adv* kwa mshangao.

admiral *n* mkuu wa jeshi la wanamaji.

admire *vt* 1 tazama na kupendezwa; stahi, penda. 2 *(wonder at)* staajabia, shangilia. **admiration** *n* upendezewaji, uvu tiwaji; mshangao, ajabu, tendo la kupenda (kustahi, kusifu, kushangaza, kustaajabu). **~r** *n* ashiki (wa mwanamke). **admiring** *adj* -enye kuonyesha kustaajabia, kusifu; -enye kuvutiwa, -enye kushangilia. **admiringly** *adv* kwa kustaajabu, kwa kusifu.

admit *vi, vt* 1 ruhusu kuingia, ingiza, pitisha ~ *into a house* ruhusu mtu kuingia ndani ya nyumba. 2 chukua, kuwa na nafasi ya *the hotel ~s only 50 people* hoteli inachukua watu 50 tu. 3 laza. *be ~ted into hospital* lazwa hospitali. 4 *(acknowlege)* kiri, ungama, kubali ~ *(to) guilt* kubali kosa. 5 ruhusu; acha nafasi kwa *it ~s of no doubt* haina shaka hata. **~tedly** adv hakika. **admissible** *adj* 1 (leg) -a kukubalika, kubalifu, halali *admissible evidence* ushahidi wa kukubalika. 2 *(formal)* -a kufaa. **admissibility** *n* kukubalika, ukubalifu. **admission** *n* 1 ruhusa ya kuingia, kiingilio. 2 kukiri, kukubali, kuungama. *on his own admission* kwa kukiri mwenyewe. **admittance** *n* ruhusa ya kuingia, haki ya kuingia. *no* si ruhusa kuingia.

admix *vt, vi* changanya, changanyika. **~ture** *n*. mchanganyiko.

admonish *vt* onya, rudi, asa. **admonition** onyo dogo. **admonitory** *adj* -a onyo, -a kuasa.

ad nauseam *adv* kwa kiasi cha kuudhi. kwa kiasi cha kuchusha.

ado *n* udhia, fujo, ghasia, matata *much ~ about nothing* fujo za bure.

adobe *n* matofali ya udongo (yasiyochomwa) na nyasi.

adolescent *adj* -a balehe, *n* 1 kijana (kuanzia kubalehe hadi miaka 18). 2 mzulufu, mzee kijana. **adolescence** *n* ujana (kipindi kati ya utoto na utu uzima).

adopt *vt* 1 panga utoto ~ *a child* panga mtoto ~ *ed child* mwana wa kupanga. 2 kubali ~ *a resolution/an idea* kubali azimio/wazo. 3 chukua/twaa na tumia *we have ~ted the British legal system* tumechukua mfumo wa sheria wa Kingereza. **~ion** *n* 1 kitendo cha kupanga mtoto. 2 kukubali. 3 kuchukua/kutwaa. **~ive** *adj* -a kupanga.

adore *vt* 1 abudu, sujudu. 2 *(colloq)* penda mno, husudu, heshimu sana. **adorable** *adj* -a kupendeka mno, mahabuba. **adorably** *adv*. **adoration** *n* 1 kuabudu. 2 tendo la kusujudu. 3 *(rel)* ibada ya kuabudu. **~r** *n*.

adorn *vt* pamba, remba. ~ **ment** *n* 1 pambo, urembo. 2 upambaji, urembaji.

adrenalin *n* adrenalini. **adrenal** *adj*

adrift *adj, adv* -a kuyoyoma, -a kuelea ovyo. 2 *(fig) he cut himself ~from us* alijitenga nasi.

adroit *adj* stadi, bingwa. **~ly** *adv* kwa werevu, kwa ustadi. **~ness** *n*.

adulate *vt* sifu mno (hasa kwa kujipendekeza), vika kilemba cha ukoka. **adulation** *n*. **adulator** *n* msifu, asifuye. **adulatory** *adj*.

adult *n* mtu mzima, ngumbaru; mnyama aliyekua *adj* **~hood** *n* utu uzima, ukubwa. **adulterate** *vt* ghushi, changanya na kitu duni. **adulterant** *n* kighushi. **adulteration** *n* ughushi.

adultery *n* uzinzi, zinaa *commit ~* zini. **adulterer** *n* mgoni, mzinzi. **adulterous** *adj*.

adumbrate *vt* 1 dokeza, gusia. 2 bashiri. **adumbration** *n*.

ad valorem *adj, adv ~ (tax)* (kwa)

kufuatana na thamani ya kitu.

advance *n* 1 maendeleo. 2 *(finance)* chambele, mkopo. 3 *(pl)* kujipendekeza *he made ~* alitongoza. 4 mapema, kabla ya, rubuni *he saw me in ~ of the meeting* aliniona kabla ya mkutano *he booked in ~* alirubuni. *vt, vi* 1 endelea mbele, songa mbele, sogea. 2 toa *~ an opinion* toa (kauli, shauri). 3 sogeza *the date was ~d* tarehe ilisogezwa mbele. 4 *(finance)* kopesha, toa karadha. 5 *(rare) (price/rent)* (kodi) zidisha, pandisha. **~d** *adj* 1 -liotangulia, -lioko mbele. 2 *(of people and ideas)* -enye kuona mbele. *~d studies* masomo ya juu. 3 -lioendelea. 4 *(in years/age)* -zee. 5 -lioongezeka. **~ment** *n* 1 maendeleo. 2 *(position/rank)* kupanda.

advantage *n* 1 heri, nafuu. 2 faida, manufaa, mafao. **take ~ of** tumia (kitu fulani) kwa manufaa ya; jinufaisha; danganya. 3 **have (gain/win) an ~ (over)**, piku, kuwa na hali bora kuliko *vt* nufaisha. **~ous** *adj* -a manufaa -a kuleta faida. **~ously** *adv*.

advent[1] *n* 1 *(of important events, person etc)* majilio, kufika *the ~ of independence* majilio ya uhuru.

Advent[2] *n (rel)* muda wenye Jumapili nne unaotangulia Krismas; kuja kwa Kristo; kuja kwa Kristo kwa mara ya pili. **~ist** *n* mtu anayeamini kuwa Kristo atakuja tena hivi karibuni *Seventh Day Adventist* Msabato.

adventitious *adj* -a bahati, -a nasibu.

adventure n tukio; tukio lisilo la kawaida, la hatari, la ajabu *a life of ~* maisha yenye vituko. **~r/ress** *n* mpenda vituko. **adventurous** *adj* 1 -enye kuthubutu. 2 -a hatari. **adventurism** *n* ujasiri, bahatisho, jusura.

adverb *n (gram)* kielezi. **~ial** *adj*

ad verbum *adv* neno kwa neno.

adversary *n* adui, mshindani.

adverse *adj* -a kinyume; -baya, -siofaa *~ effect* athari mbaya **~ly** *adv* vibaya. **adversity** *n* 1 shida, dhiki, taabu. 2 mkasa, maafa.

advert[1] *vi* 1 *(pay heed)* taja, gusia. 2 rejea.

advert[2] see **advertisement**.

advertise *vt, vi* tangaza, eneza habari **~ment** *n (abbr. advert)*. **~r** *n* mtangazaji, **advertising** *n* matangazo (hasa ya biashara), utangazaji.

advice *n* 1 ushauri, nasaha, mawaidha *seek ~* tafuta ushauri. 2 *(pl) (comm)* taarifa (kutoka mbali).

advise *vt, vi* 1 shauri, nasihi, waidhi. 2 *(inform)* arifu, julisha. **~r** *n* mshauri *spiritual ~* muaidhi. **~d** *adj well ~* -a busara, *ill ~* si -a busara. **~dly** *adv* baada ya kutafakari sana, kwa makusudi. **advisory** adj -a ushauri *~ committee* kamati ya ushauri. **advisable** *adj* bora, -a kufaa, -a busara.

advocate *n* 1 *(general)* mtetezi. 2 *(legal)* wakili. *vt* tetea, pigania. **advocacy** *n* utetezi, uteteaji.

adze *n* tezo.

aegis, egis *n* himaya, uangalizi usimamizi *under the ~ of* chini ya uangalizi usimamizi wa.

aegrotat *n* igrotati: hati ya kuthibitisha kwamba mwanafunzi hawezi kuhudhuria mtihani kwa kuwa mgonjwa. ~ **degree** shahada igrotati.

aeon, eon *n* dahari, kipindi kirefu cha wakati kisichopimika.

aerate *vt* 1 ingiza hewa au gesi (katika uoevu, udongo n.k.). 2 safisha kwa hewa (k.m. damu). **aeration** *n*.

aerial *adj* 1 -a angani, -a hewani. 2 *(arch)* -a hewa, -a kama hewa. 3 *(lit) (immaterial)* -isoumbo. 4 -a ndege *~ photograph* picha toka angani *n* erio, kipokea mawimbi.

aerie, aery/eyrie, eyry *n* 1 kiota cha tai.

aerobatics *n* sarakasi.

aerobic *adj* -a hewa, -enye kutaka oksijeni. **~s** *n* mazoezi ya viungo vya kuongeza hewa.

aerodrome *n* kiwanja cha ndege

(kidogo).
aerodynamics *n* elimu mwendo (hewani).
aerogram *n* karatasi ya ndege.
aeronaut *n* mwanaanga, mwanahewa.
aeronautics *n* elimu ya usafiri anga.
aerophotography *n* upigaji picha angani.
aeroplane *n* ndege.
aerosol *n* 1 erosoli, upulizaji (wa uturi, rangi, dawa ya mbu n.k.). 2 kipulizaji.
aerospace *n* anga.
aery see **aerie**.
aesthete, esthete *n* mjumi, mpenda uzuri (hasa katika sanaa). **aesthetic** *adj*. **aesthetics** *n* ujumi.
aether see **ether**.
aetiology see **etiology**.
afar *adv* mbali. **from ~** kwa mbali, kutoka mbali.
affable *adj* bashasha. **affably** *adv* **affability** *n* ubashasha, uchangamfu.
affair *n* 1 shauri, jambo, shughuli, neno *urgent ~* amara, jambo muhimu. 2 *(pl)* mambo *state ~s* mambo ya dola. **foreign ~s** mambo ya nchi za nje. 3 *have an ~ with* tembea, fanya mapenzi na. 4 tukio.
affect[1] *vt* 1 athiri; gusa hisi *our position will not be ~ed by these events* msimamo wetu hautaathiriwa na matukio haya. **~ing** *adj* -enye kuathiri, -enye kuchoma moyo. **~ed** *adj* 1 *(diseased; injured)* -lioumia, -lioathirika, -lioshikwa na ugonjwa, maumivu. 2 -lioguswa (na sikitiko, furaha, huzuni n.k.).
affect[2] *vt* jifanya, jisingizia, jitendekeza, jitia *~ ignorance* jitia hamnazo, jitia mwapuza .**~ed** *adj*. **~ation** *n* tabia ya kujifanya. **~edness** *n*. **affection** *n* *(love)* upendo, huba *mutual ~* kupendana, urafiki. **gain/win somebody's ~s** pendwa na. **~ate** *adj* -enye moyo wa kupenda, -a kupenda, mpenda. **~ately** *adv* *yours ~ately* akupendaye.
affidavit *n* *(leg)* hati ya kiapo.
affiliate *vt, vi* shirikisha, jumuisha, kuwa sehemu ya. **be ~d to/with** shirikishwa na *n* mshirika, majumui. **affiliation** *n* ushirikishaji, kushirikishwa, kushirikisha, ushirikishwaji.
affinity *n* 1 udugu, ukoo. 2 uhusiano (baina ya mimea, wanyama, lugha n.k.). 3 *(attraction)* mvuto.
affirm *vt* kiri, tamka kwa dhati; thibitisha. **~ant** *n* mthibitishaji. **~ation** *n* uthibitisho. **~ative** *adj* -a kukubali, -a ndiyo *he answered in the ~ative* alikubali.
affix[1] *vt* funga, bandika, gandisha.
affix[2] *(gram)* *n* kiambishi.
afflatus *n* wahayi (ufunuo wa kidini).
afflict *vt* umiza, tesa, (kimwili/kiakili) *the ~ed* walio matesoni, wanaoteseka. **~ing** *adj* teso. **~ion** *n* mateso, huzuni. **~ive** *adj* huzunishi.
affluence *n* ukwasi, wingi, utajiri. **affluent** *adj* -a ukwasi.
affluent *n* kijito.
afford *vt* 1 mudu, kuwa na uwezo *he can ~ to pay* anamudu kulipa. 2 diriki, thubutu *I can't ~ to displease him* sithubutu kumuudhi. 3 toa, pa *he ~ed me no chance* hakunipa nafasi. **~able** *adj* -enye kumudika.
afforest *vt* panda miti (ili kufanya msitu). **~ation** *n*.
affranchise *vt* toa utumwani, komboa utumwani. **~ment** *n* ukombozi wa mtumwa.
affray n fujo, ugomvi hadharani.
affront *vt* tukana, adhiri, fedhehesha *n* izara, tusi, kashifa. **~ed** *adj*. -liochukiwa/chukia.
Afghan *n* 1 Mwafghan 2 ukaya au blanketi la sufi.
aficionado *n* mshabiki.
afield *adv* **(far ~)** (phr) mbali na nyumba, lengo n.k.
afire *adv, adj (poet)* -a kuwaka- a kubimbirika moto *he was ~with rage* aliwaka kwa ghadhabu.
aflame *adv, adj* -a kuwaka, -a moto. 2 -ekundu kama moto. 3 *(fig) be ~d with* jawa na, shikwa na.
afloat *adj, adv* 1 *(floating)* -a kuelea 2 *(on ship)* chomboni, melini.

3 *(awash)* -liojaa maji. 4 *(out of debt)* -sio na deni. 5 (of rumour) -lioenea (k.m. uvumi).
afoot *adv, adj* 1 -nayotayarishwa, -nayopikwa. 2 *(arch)* kwa miguu.
afore *adv, prep (naut)* mbele ya, lio tangulia. **~-said** *adj* -liotajwa. *(leg)* **~ thought** kwa kusudi.
afortiori *adv (lat)* bila shaka, ni dhahiri.
afoul *adv* katika kugongana na.
afraid *adj* -oga, -a hofu *be ~* ogopa, sikitika *I'm ~ I can't come* nasikitika sitakuja.
afresh *adv* tena, upya, kwa namna mpya.
Africa *n* Afrika ~ *n, adj* -a Mwafrika, Kiafrika.
Afrikaans *n* Kiafrikana. **Africaner** *n* Mwafrikana. **~nization** *n* Afrikanaizesheni: siasa ya kuwapa Waafrika kazi za madaraka. **~nize** *vt.*
Afro- *adj* -a Kiafro, -a kiafrika.
aft *adv* 1 nyuma; *(naut)* tezini. 2 -a tezini.
after *adj* -a baadaye, -a nyuma, -a kufuata *in ~ years* miaka inayofuata; *adv* baadaye, halafu, *conj; prep* baada ya, nyuma ya *(phr) ~all* hata hivyo; ingawaje *pref* -a baadaye alasiri. **do something ~a fashion** fanya kitu kwa namna moja au nyingine. **a man ~ my own heart** mtu ninayefanana naye kitabia; *(phr) be/get ~somebody* andama mtu.**~ birth** *n* kondo la nyuma. **~ care** *n* utunduizi baada ya kupona ugojwa au kutoka gerezani. **~clap** *n* 1 itiko. 2 matokeo yasiyotarajiwa (agh mabaya). **~piece** *n* fasi, mchezo mdogo baada ya tamthilia maalum. **~ cabin** *n (naut)* chumba cha sitaha ya nyuma. **afters** *n (colloq)* visindikizo (baada ya mlo).
afterwards *adv* baadaye, halafu, hatimaye.
again *adv* 1 tena, mara nyingine. **~ and ~** tena na tena. **now and ~** mara kwa mara, **never ~** kamwe, abadani. 2 vilevile.
against *prep* 1 kwa kupingana/ kushindana, dhidi ya. 2 pinga. 3 kinyume cha; hitilafu ya. 4 jitahadharisha na. 5 egemeza. 6 **over ~** kabiliana.
agape *pred adj* -a kuachama.
agar-agar *n* jeli ya mwani.
agaric *n (bot)* kiyoga tembo.
agate *n* 1 ageti: aina ya jiwe gumu lenye shondo.
agave *n (bot)* mkongepori.
agaze *adv* kwa kukodolea macho, kwa kutumbua macho.
age[1] *n* 1 umri. *(leg)* **~ of consent** umri wa idhini. **over ~** kuzidi umri uliowekwa. **under~** umri pungufu wa uliowekwa. **old ~** uzee, ukongwe. **~ group** hirimu, rika. **be of an ~** -wa na umri wa kufanya jambo. 2 kipindi, zama *stone ~* kipindi cha zana za mawe. 3 *(period)* kwa muda mrefu.
age[2] *adj (of persons)* -zee, -kongwe *an ~d man* mzee; *(of things)* kuukuu, -a kale, -a zamani. **~ ing** *n* kuzeeka. **~less** *adj* -a milele, -a kudumu mpaka mwisho, -siozeeka, **~ long** -a umri mrefu **~ old** -a miaka mingi.
agenda *n* ajenda.
agent *n* 1 wakala, ajenti. 2 nguvu za asili au mtu anayetenda kupata matokeo fulani *rain and wind are ~s that wear down rocks* mvua na upepo ni nguvu za asili zinazomomonyoa miamba. **agency** *n* wakala, uajenti. 2 nguvu, njia ya kufanya kitu. 3 sehemu/ofisi ya biashara.
agglomerate *vt* kusanya kwa wingi, rundika *vi* kusanyika, songamana. **agglomeration** *n.*
agglutinate *vt* ambatisha, bandika.
agglutination *n* uambatishaji, uambishaji. **agglutinative** *adj (ling)* -enye kiambishi, -enye kuambishika *language* lugha ambishi bainishi.
aggrandize, aggrandise *vt* jiongezea/jitwaza/jitwalia zaidi (hasa madaraka, cheo, utajiri, umaarufu n.k.). **~ment** *n* kujiongezea, kutwaza, kujitwalia zaidi.

aggravate *vt* 1 kuza, ongeza ubaya (wa kosa, maumivu, jambo, taabu n.k.). 2 *(provoke)* kera, kasirisha, udhi. **aggravating** *adj* -a kukasirisha, -a kuudhi. **aggravation** *n.*

aggregate *vt* kusanya *vi* jikusanya, kusanyika, jumlika, jumuika *n* jumla, mkusanyiko **in the ~** -ote pamoja, kwa jumla; *(in construction)* vifaa vigumu kama vile mawe, mchanga, **aggression** kokoto n.k. vinavyochanganywa na saruji. **aggregation** *n* 1 kusanyiko (la vitu).

aggression *n* uchokozi, ushari (wa maneno au vitendo). **aggressive** *adj* 1 shari, -gomvi, chokozi, jeuri. 2 -a kutaka maendeleo, -a hima *~ salesman* mwuzaji mwenye hima. **~ness** *n* uchokozi, ushari, hima.

aggressor *n* mchokozi, mshari.

aggrieve *vt (usu passive)* 1 tia uchungu, sikitisha, udhi, kera. 2 *(leg)* dhulumu. **~d** *adj.*

aggro *n (GB sl)* uhasama, uchokozi.

aghast *adj* -lioshikwa na woga au mshangao, liopigwa butwaa.

agile *adj* -nyumbufu, -epesi (wa mwendo). **agility** *n.*

aging *see* **ageing.**

agitate *vt* 1 tikisa /tingisha, koroga. 2 hamakisha, fadhaisha, chochea. 3 *vi* tikisika, hamasika; *(~ for)* shawishi, hamasisha, pigania. **~d** *adj* -enye wasiwasi, -enye kutia wasiwasi. **agitation** *n* 1 mkorogo, mtikiso/mtingisho. 2 *(perturbation of mind)* msukosuko, wasiwasi, fadhaa. 3 *(discussion for)* majadiliano, mabishano; uchochezi. **agitator** *n* mchochezi (hasa wa kisiasa); mfitini.

aglow *adj* -enye kumeremeta, -enye kuwaka, *be ~* waka, ng'aa, meremeta.

agnail *n* kigozikucha (kigozi kilichochanika ukingoni mwa ukucha)

agnate *n* ndugu wa kuumeni *adj* 1 -a kuumeni, -a upande wa baba. 2 *(fig)* -a damu moja, -a asili moja, -a kutoka taifa moja, -enye udugu. 3 -a kufanana, -a kushabihiana.

agnostic *n* agnostiki: asadikiye kuwa hatuna habari za Mungu wala hatuwezi kuzijua. *adj.* **~ism** *n*

ago *adv* zamani, kale, kitambo,-liopita *long ~* zamani sana *a little while ~* punde hivi, kitambo kidogo.

agog *adj* kwa shauku *be ~ for sth* ngoja kwa hamu, *set ~* tia hamu moyoni *be all ~* jawa na hamu shauku.

agony *n* masumbuko makali, maumivu makubwa. **agonize. agonise** *vi* umia vibaya, -wa na maumivu makali, sumbuka, teseka sana (moyoni) *vt* umiza vibaya, sumbua, tesa. **agonizing** *adj* -a kuumiza sana. -a mateso, gumu sana.

agoraphobia *n* woga wa nafasi kubwa za wazi. **agoraphobic** *n/adj.*

agrarian *adj* 1 -a kuhusu ardhi, mashamba, nchi na umilikaji ardhi. 2 -a wakulima.

agree *vi* 1 kubali. 2 patana, kubaliana, ridhiana, afikiana. 3 *(with)* lingana, fanana. 4 *(with)* chukua, afiki *the climate does not ~ with me* hali ya hewa hainichukui. 5 *(of sums, accounts etc)* oana, kuwa sawa. **~d** *adj* -liokubaliwa, **be ~d with somebody on (about) something** kubaliana juu ya *~d upon* iliyokubaliwa *that's ~d!* imekubalika! sawa. **~able** *adj* 1 -a kupendeza, -zuri, -tamu, -latifu. 2 -a maridhia. **be ~able to** ridhiana na. **~ ableness** *n* 1 kupatana, kukubaliana. 2 adabu. **~ment** *n* 1 maafikiano 2 *(contract)* mapatano, kondrati, kandarasi, mkataba **come to/arrive at/make/reach an ~ment (with) somebody** patana na. 3 *(gram)* upatanifu.

agribusiness *n* viwanda vya huduma za kilimo.

agriculture *n* kilimo, ukulima, elimu ya kilimo. **agriculturist**. *n.* **agricultural** *adj officer* bwana shamba/afisa kilimo.

agronomy *n* agronomia: sayansi ya uchumi wa kilimo. **agronomic** *adj* -a (kuhusu)ukulima, -a mashamba,

-a kilimo. **agronomist** *n* mtaalamu wa kilimo.

aground *adj, adv (of ship)* -lio pwelewa/kwama *run* ~ pwelewa/ kwama miambani.

ague *n (arch)* homa. **aguish** *adj* 1 -a homa. 2 *(of person)* -enye-homa.

ah *interj* aa! (sauti ya kustaajabu, ya furaha au ya kuhurumia) salale! Masalale!

aha *interj* enhe! sauti ya kustaajabu, kufurahi au kukubali.

ahead *adj, adv* mbele, kabla. **go** ~ endelea, tangulia. ~ **of** mbele ya. **look** ~ jiandaa, jitayarisha. **get** ~ faulu *the years* ~ miaka ijayo.

ahem *interj* ukohozi au mgumio maalum wa ishara au onyo.

aid *vt* saidia, auni *(leg)* ~ **and abet** saidia katika jinai *n* 1 msaada, amara ~ *without strings* msaada bila masharti **first** ~ huduma ya kwanza. 2 *(pl)* visaidizi **visual** ~**s** vielelezo.

aide-de-camp *n* mpambe.

aide-memoire *n* kidokezi, kisaidizi cha ukumbusho,ardhi hali.

AIDS *n* Ukimwi (Ukosefu wa Kinga Mwilini).

ail *vt, vi (arch)* 1 taabishwa, sumbuliwa. 2 ugua, umwa *what ~s him?* anasumbuliwa na nini?/anaumwa nini? ~**ment** *n* ugonjwa, uele, maradhi.

aim *vt, vi* 1 piga shabaha, lenga. 2 elekeza, azimia. *n* shabaha, lengo, kusudi, azma. ~**less** *adj* siyo na sababu, -siyo na lengo maalum. **lessly** *adj.*

ain't *(infml)* mkato wa maneno *are/is/ am have/ has not.*

air *n* 1 hewa, upepo. **in the** ~ -sio na hakika, -vumayo; hewani. **clear the** ~ safisha hewa *(fig)* ondoa mashaka (kwa kusema ukweli). 2 **by** ~ kwa ndege. 3 *(radio)* **on the** ~ redioni, (sikika) hewani. 4 upepo mwanana 5 umbo, mandhari *has an ~ of importance* onekana kuwa mtu maarufu *(usu pl)*. **give oneself/put on ~s** jidai, jitwaza, jifanya mtu wa maana, ringa *vt* 1 anika, kausha. 2 achia hewa ipite. 3 toa (mawazo n.k.). ~**ing** *n* 1 kuanika *give an ~ing* anika kitu. 2 kupunga hewa *go for an ~ing* punga hewa. ~**less** *adj* -enye fukuto, bila hewa, kutokuwepo upepo kabisa. **airy** *adj* 1 -enye wingi wa hewa. 2 *(trifling)* -epesi.

air-base *n* kituo cha ndege(za jeshi la anga).

air-bed *n* godoro la upepo/hewa **air-bladder** *n* kibofu hewa.

airborn *adj (of plane)* -liokwisha ruka hewani; *(of people etc)* -liosafirishwa kwa ndege.

air brake *n* breki za upepo.

air-brick *n* matofali yenye matundu.

air-bus *n* ndege kubwa isafiriyo masafa mafupi.

air-conditioner *n* kiyoyozi, kisafisha hewa.

air-conditioned *adj (of houses, cars)* -lioyoyozwa.

air-cooled *adj* -liopozwa kwa hewa.

aircover *n* ulinzianga (ulinzi wa ndege za kivita kwa majeshi ya nchi kavu).

aircraft *n* ndege. ~ **carrier** *n* manowari yenye kituo cha ndege.

air-crew *n* watumishi wa ndege.

air-cushion *n* mto wa upepo/hewa.

air-drop *n* kudondoshwa kwa watu, chakula, vifaa n.k. kwa kutumia miavuli. **air-field** *n* see **aerodrome**.

air-force *n* jeshi la anga.

air-freight *n* uchukuzi wa mizigo kwa ndege.

air-gun *n* bunduki ya upepo.

air-hole *n* 1 tundu la kuingizia hewa. 2 povu la hewa.

air-hostess *n* mhudumu wa kike wa ndege.

air-jacket *n (naut)* vazi la kujiokoa.

airletter *n see* **aerogram**.

air-lift *n* uchukuaji wa watu au vifaa kwa ndege (aghalabu katika dharura) *vt* chukua askari na vifaa kwa ndege.

air-line *n* shirika la ndege (za kuchukua abiria na bidhaa). ~**r** *n* ndege ya abiria.

air-lock *n* 1 zuio la hewa, kizuizi cha hewa. 2 mvungu wa hewa.
air-mail *n* barua za ndege ~ *edition* toleo la gazeti la kupelekwa kwa ndege.
airman *n* mwanahewa, mwanaanga
air-mass *n* masi hewa.
air-passage *n* koromeo, njia ya pumzi.
airpillow see **air cushion**.
air-plane *n* ndege.
air-pocket *n* kiriba hewa: kifuko cha hewa kinachosababisha ndege kushuka ghafla.
air-port *n* uwanja wa ndege.
air-pressure *n* kanieneo ya hewa.
air-raid *n* shambulio la ndege.
air-route *n* njia ya ndege.
air sea rescue *n* uokoaji wa watu kutoka kwenye ndege iliyoangukia baharini.
air-shaft *n* bomba la kuingizia hewa mgodini.
air-shed *n* banda la ndege.
airship *n* chombo anga.
air-sick *adj* -liyechefukwa angani. **~ness** *n*.
air-space *n* 1 anga ya nchi (yaani iliyo ndani ya mipaka yake). 2 anga hewa.
air-terminal *n* kituo cha abiria wa ndege.
air-tight *adj* 1 -sioruhusu hewa kuingia au kutoka. 2 *(of an argument etc)* -lio thabiti.
air-umbrella *see* **air-cover**.
airway *n see* **air route**.
air-worthy *adj (of plane)* -nayofaa kusafiri angani.
aisle *n* njia baina ya viti katika majengo maalumu (k.m.) kanisa, sinema, bunge).
ajar *adj* (*of door*) -lio wazi kidogo, -liofunguliwa kidogo.
akimbo *adj, adv (phr)* **with arms ~** kwa kuweka mikono kiunoni/nyongani.
akin 1 *adj* ~ **(to)** -a kufanana na. 2 -liohusiana na.
alabaster *n* jasi, alabasta: jiwe jeupe laini lililofanana na marumaru.
a la carte *adj, adv* alakati: kwa mchaguo wa chakula kutoka katika orodha ya vyakula.
alacrity *n* wepesi, hima, pamoja na bashasha *do sth with ~* fanya upesi sana.
a la mode *adv* kwa mtindo wa kisasa.
alarm *n* 1 kamsa, king'ora; onyo la hatari; yowe. **raise the ~** piga mayowe/king'ora, hadharisha. 2 hofu, wasiwasi (ilioletwa kwa hatari iliyokaribu), mshituko wa hofu *vt* shitua, kamsisha, ogofya *be ~ed at sth* ogopa, shtuka, **~ clock** saa ya kengele. **~ing** *adj* -a kutia hofu, -a kutisha, -a kuogogofya. **~ist** *n* mvumishaji (wa mambo ya kutisha).
albeit *conj* ingawa, ijapokuwa.
albino *n* zeruzeru, albino.
album *n* albamu: kitabu cha picha (majina ya watu, mashairi, stempu za posta n.k.).
albumen, albumin *n* uteyai.
alchemy *n* alkemia: kemia ya karne za kati iliyokusudia kugeuza metali ya kawaida kuwa dhahabu. **alchemist** *n* mualkemia.
alcohol *n* kileo: dawa inayotokana na sukari au vitu vyenye sukari vinapochacha, pombe, spiriti. **~ic** *adj* -a kileo, -a kulevya, -enye asili ya kulevya *n* mlevi sugu. **~ism** *n* taathira ya ulevi; dalili na hali ya ugonjwa uletwao na ulevi.
alderman *n (GB)* mjumbe; diwani mshauri wa Baraza la Jiji au mji.
ale *n (GB)* aina ya bia. ~ **house** kilabu ya pombe.
alert *adj* -a macho, -changamfu, tayari *n* tahadhari. **on the ~** wa katika tahadhari, -wa macho, -wa tayari *vt* tahadharisha. **~ness** *n* hadhari, kuwa macho, kuwa tayari.
alfalfa *n (bot)* alfalfa: majani ya kulisha ng'ombe.
alfresco *adj (of meals)* -a kuliwa nje *adv* nje.
alga *n* mwani, mchipwi.
algebra *n* aljebra. **~ic** *adj* -a kialjebra. **~ ically** *adj* kwa aljebra; kialjebra.

Algerian *n* Mwaljeria *adj* -a Aljeria, -a Kialjeria.
alias *adv* pia aitwaye, kwa jina jingine *n* lakabu, jina la kupanga, jina bandia.
alibi *n* 1 *(leg)* udhuru (madai kuwa mtu aliyeshtakiwa japo hakuwako pale jambo lilipotendeka). 2 kisingizio.
alien *n* mgeni *adj* -geni. ~ **to** -enye tabia zisizo sawa na, -a namna mbali, -siopatana na ~ *-environment* mazingira ya kigeni.
alienable *adj (of property)* -a kusikika, kuuzika au kuhamishika.
alienate *vt (from)* 1 *(of people)* farakisha, tenga, tenganisha. 2 *(of property)* sihia, twaa, nyang'anya. **alienation** *n* 1 utenganishaji, mfarakano. 2 kunyang'anya. 3 mkengeuko.
alight[1] *vi* 1 shuka, teremka (kutoka kwenye farasi, motokaa n.k.). 2 tua *the bird ~ed on the branch* ndege alitua tawini. 3 *(fig)* ~ **on** pata kwa bahati.
alight[2] *adj (be)* -inayowaka, inayong'aa, inayomeka *(fig) their faces were ~ with happiness* nyuso zao ziling'aa kwa furaha.
align *vt, vi* weka (panga) katika mstari ulio sawa, linganisha. 2 fungamana. **~ment alinement** mfungamano, mfuatano. **~ed** *adj* fungamanifu. **non aligned** -sio fungamana.
alike *adj* sawasawa,-enye kufanana, -a kulandana, *adv* kwa namna ile ile, kwa namna moja *treat everybody ~* mtendee kila mtu sawa.
alimentary *adj* -a chakula, **the ~ canal** njia ya chakula (mwilini).
alimony *n* masurufu (baada ya mume kumwacha mke).
alive *adj* 1 -zima, hai. 2 -a kuendelea, -a kukumbusha *keep the discussion ~* endeleza mjadala *the microphone is ~* maikrofoni inafanya kazi. 3 ~ **to** -enye kuelewa (fikra, wazo). 4 changamfu. **look ~** changamka. 5 ~ **with** jaa ~ *with lice* amejaa chawa.
alizarin *n (chem)* alizarini.
alkali *n* alikali (k.m. magadi, potasi, amonia). **~ne** *adj* -a alikali. **alikaloid** *n (chem)* alikaloidi
all[1] *adj* 1 -ote, kila ~ **Saints' Day** 1 Novemba siku ya watakatifu wote ~ **Souls' Day**, 2 Novemba, siku ya Marehemu wote. ~ *the people* watu wote. 2 -o -ote beyond ~ doubt bila shaka yoyote.
all[2] *adv* kabisa, -ote *she was ~ excited* alisisimkwa, ~ *alone* peke yake, bila msaada wa mtu yeyote. ~ **along** -ote -zima, ~ *along the road* barabara nzima; *(colloq)* muda wote, tokea mwanzo. ~ **the same** lakini, hata hivyo, ~ **the same to/** ~ **one to** mamoja, sawa haidhuru *(colloq)* choka sana ~ **out** *(colloq)* jitihada zote. ~ **over** kila mahali, pote; -kwisha. ~ **right** sawa, ~ **told** kwa jumla. ~ **up (with)** kwisha, malizika.
all[3] *n* **my/his/their etc** ~ kila kitu, mali yote, *he has lost his ~* amepoteza kila kitu.
all[4] *(in compounds)* 1 *adj prefix* -a kiwango cha juu kabisa; siyo na mipaka. ~ **merciful** mwenye rehema zote. 2 *(of radio)*. ~ **-mains** volteji zote. ~ **-round** -a kila kitu; stadi katika kila fani. ~ **time high/low** *(colloq)* rekodi ya juu/chini/ kabisa. *(of an aircraft) (phr)* ~ **up weight** uzito wa jumla wa ndege angani.
all[5] *pron* 1 -ote, kila kitu *he wanted ~ or nothing* alitaka kupata yote au kukosa yote ~ **(of)** kila mtu, -ote ~ *ofus want to go* sisi sote tunataka kwenda. **(not) at** ~ kwa vyovyote; kabisa *if you are at ~ worried* ikiwa una wasiwasi wowote *he is not at ~ suitable* hafai kabisa. **not at** ~ si kitu. **once (and) for** ~ kwa mara ya mwisho; kwa jumla. ~ in ~ kwa jumla ~ *in ~it was a good seminar* kwa jumla semina ilikuwa nzuri; tegemeo, *she is ~ in ~ to him* yeye (mke) ndiye tegemeo lake (mume).
Allah *n* Mwenyezi Mungu (katika Uislamu).

allay *vt* tuliza, punguza (maumivu matatizo, wasiwasi n.k.).
allege *vt* dai ~ *that somebody is a thief* dai kuwa fulani ni mwizi. **allegation** *n* dai, **~dly** *adv* kama inavyodaiwa.
allegiance *n* utii. wajibu, **oath of ~** kiapo cha utii,
allegory *n* istiari. **allegoric(al)** *adj* -a kiistiari.
alleluia *interj* see **halleluyah**
allergy *n* mzio, *she has an ~ to coffee* ana mzio wa kahawa. **allergin** *n* kizio. **allergic** *adj*. -a kuziza/kuzia. **be allergic to** -wa na mzio.
alleviate *vt* tuliza, punguza (ukali au uzito wa maumivu n.k.), fariji. **alleviation** *n* faraja, tulizo.
alley *n* **(also alley way)** 1 kichochoro, **blind ~** *(dead-end)* kichochorofunge: kichochoro kisichotoka. *(fig)* kazi ya kijungujiko. 2 njia nyembamba, njia.
alliance *n* 1 ushirikiano. 2 mwungano.
allied *see* **ally** *v*.
alligator *n* mamba, (wa Marekani). **-pear** *n* parachichi.
alliteration *n* takriri: marudio ya silabi za mwanzo k.m. kuno kunena kuno kwa nini. **alliterative** *adj* -enye takriri. **alliteratively** *adv*.
allocate *vt* 1 gawia, tenga, gawanyia. 2 wekea ~ *funds* tenga fedha. **allocation** *n* 1 ugawaji, mgawanyo. 2 fungu, sehemu iliyotengwa.
allocution *n* hotuba rasmi, mahubiri, mawaidha.
allomorph *n (ling)* alomofu: umbo jingine la mofimu moja.
allophone *n* alofoni; umbo jingine la fonimu moja.
allot *vt* gawa, gawanya, tenga ~ *duties* gawa kazi. **~ment** *n* 1 mgao. 2 *(ground)* kikataa, kitalu.
allow *vt* 1 ruhusu, kubalia. 2 *(acknowledge, admit)* kiri, tambua. 3 *(money)* toa *the bank ~s 5% interest* benki inatoa riba ya asilimia tano (5%). 4 ~ **for** zingatia, fikiria ~ *for damages* zingatia uharibifu. **~able** *adj* halali, -enye kuruhusiwa, -a kujuzu.
allowance *n* 1 kukubali, kukiri; ruhusa. 2 posho, ruzuku, marupurupu. 3 kipunguzi.
alloy *n* aloi: mwungano wa metali zaidi ya moja kufanya aina mpya ya metali *vt* 1 changanya metali bora na fifi. 2 *(fig)* dhoofisha, punguza thamani/ubora.
allude *vi* **(to)** dokeza, gusia, taja juujuu tu. **allusion** *n* **(to)** dokezo. **allusive** *adj* -enye vidokezo.
allure *vt* vutia, shawishi, tamanisha *n* mvuto, ushawishi. **~ment** *n* kivutio, kitamanishacho. **alluring** *adj* -a kuvutia, -a kutamanisha.
alluvium *n* kitope: udongo unaoachwa na mto/mafuriko n.k. **alluvial** *adj* -a kitope, -a aluvia.
ally *vt* **(oneself) with/to** ungana na; -wa na urafiki; shirikiana na. **allied** *to (of things)* husiana na, patana na, fanana na, fungamana na. **allied** *adj* -nayohusiana *n* rafiki *(person or state)* msaidizi.
alma mater *n* shule/chuo alichosomea mtu.
almanac *n* shajara ya mwaka; shughuli maalum katika mwaka
almighty *adj* -enye nguvu zote, -enye enzi *n (rel)* **The ~** Mwenyezi Mungu, Mweza.
almond *n (bot) (tree)* mlozi, *(fruit)* lozi, badamu *adj* -a lozi/badamu, -liotengenezwa kwa badamu, ~ *sweet* halua ya lozi. **~-eyed** *adj* -enye macho ya lozi.
almost *adv* takriban, karibu, nusura.
alms *n* sadaka. (itolewayo kwa maskini). **~box** *n* sanduku la sadaka. **~giving** *n* utoaji sadaka, **~house** *n* nyumba ya mafukara. **almoner** *n* 1 *(arch)* mtoaji sadaka. 2 *(hospital)* afisa ustawi wa jamii.
aloe *n* 1 mshubiri 2 *(also* **bitter ~s***)* shubiri.
aloft *adv* juu sana.
alone *adj* 1 pekee, pweke, -enyewe *do it ~* ifanye peke yako *adv* peke yake. 2 **let ~** sembuse, kefu. **let well ~** -siingilie, -siguse, siendeleze,

basi. **let somebody ~** achana naye.

along *adv* 1 **all ~** siku zote, wakati wote. 2 **move ~** *(of movement)* songa mbele. 3 **~ with** pamoja na. 4 **get ~ with** kubaliana na, patana na, elewana na. 5 **~ side** kandokando, ubavuni.

aloof *adv* mbali, -liojitenga, **hold/stand keep (oneself) ~** -jitenga, -jitoa, kaa peke, *adj* -a kujitenga, peke *He is ~ in character* ana tabia ya kujitenga. **~ness** *n.*

aloud *adv* kwa sauti (ya kusikika, bila kunong'ona).

alp *n* 1 alpu: mlima mrefu. 2 *(in Switzerland)* malisho ya milimani. 3 **the Alps** safu za milima mirefu baina ya nchi za Ufaransa na Italia n.k.

alpenstock *n* mkongojo mrefu (watumiao wapanda milima).

alpha *n* alf,. herufi ya kwanza ya alfabeti, ya Kiyunani **A~ and Omega** mwanzo na mwisho. **~ rays** miali alfa. **~ plus** -zuri kabisa.

alphabet *n* alfabeti, abjadi. **~ically** *adv*. **~ical** *adj* -a (kufuata) alfabeti, in *~ical order* kwa taratibu ya alfabeti.

already *adj* tayari, *it is done ~* imekwishafanyika, imefanyika tayari.

Alsatian *n* mbwa (kama bweha) mlinzi (wa polisi) *adj*.

also *adv* na, tena, vilevile, pia. **~ ran** *n* mshinde.

altar *n (rel)* 1 madhabahu, meza ya kutolea dhabihu au kafara. 2 *(chritstian)* altare: meza panapopokewa ushirika Mtakatifu. *(phr)* **lead (a woman) to the ~** oa ~ - *cloth n* tandiko la **altare**. **~-piece** *n (rel)* picha au sanamu nyuma ya altare.

alter *vt* badilisha, geuza *that ~s matters* hiyo inabadilisha mambo. **~ation** *n* mabadiliko. **~able** *adj* -a kuweza kubadili/kubadilishwa.

altercate *vi* gombana, bishana vikali, zozana. **altercation** *n* mzozo, ugomvi, mabishano makali.

alterego *n (lat)* mwandani, mwenzi, sahibu.

alternate *vt,vi* *(of two things)* 1 kuja/fanya kwa zamu (moja baada ya moja), badilishana, pokezana *wet days ~d with sunny days* siku za mvua zilibadilishana na siku za jua. 2 **~ between** geuka kati ya hali na hali. 3 **~ with** fuatana, moja baada ya jingine *adj* -a moja baada ya moja, -a mpokezano, *(of dates)* -a kwanza, -a tatu n.k. *they met on ~ days* walikutana kila baada ya siku moja ~ member mwanachama mbadala. **~ ly** *adv* kwa zamu, kwa mpokezano. **alternating** *adj* -a moja baada ya moja **~ current** mkondogeu: mkondo (wa umeme) unaogeuza mwelekeo baada ya kitambo fulani.

alternation *n* matukio ya zamu ubadilishaji duru; **alternative** *n* 1 uchaguzi badili: fursa ya kuchagua kati ya mambo mawili au zaidi. 2 mbadala, kibadala *I have no ~* sina uchaguzi/ hiari *is there no ~* hakuna njia nyingine? *adj* -ingine, -a pili, -enye hiari kati ya mambo mawili, enye fursa ya kuchagua baina ya vitu viwili. **~ly** *adv* badala yake.

alternator *n* altaneta: jenereta (inayogeuza mkondo wa umeme).

although *conj* ijapo (kuwa), ingawa.

altimeter *n (phy)* altimeta: chombo cha kupimia urefu juu ya usawa wa bahari.

altitude *n* 1 mwinuko (kutoka usawa wa bahari) *at high ~* juu kutoka usawa wa bahari. 2 palipo juu kulingana na bahari.

altogether *adv* 1 pamoja, kwa pamoja, pia, kwa jumla *I will take them ~* nitavichukua pamoja. 2 kabisa *it is ~ untrue* ni uwongo kabisa *n in the ~* uchi.

altruism *n* ubinadamu; uungwana; utu: tabia ya kufikiria wengine kuliko nafsi yako au kuishi na kutenda mambo kwa ajili ya manufaa ya wengine. **altruist** *n* mwungwana, mwenye ubinadamu, mwenye utu.

altruistic *adj* - sio na ubinafsi/choyo. **altruistically** *adv* kwa utu.
alum *n* shabu.
aluminium *(us)* **aluminum** *n* aluminiamu *(chem)* alumini.
alumna *n* alumna: mwanafunzi wa kike aliyepitia chuo fulani.
alumnus *n* alumnasi: mwanafunzi wa kiume aliyepitia chuo fulani
alveolar *n adj (phon)* -a ufizi.
always *adv* daima, sikuzote, kwa kawaida, kila mara.
a.m. *(abb) (lat) ante meridiem* asubuhi, baada ya saa sita usiku na kabla ya adhuhuri.
amah n yaya.
amalgam *n* 1 mchanganyiko. 2 aloi ya zebaki. 3 *(dental)* aloi risasi.
amalgamate *vt, vi (of classes, societies, races people, business companies)* changanya, unganisha, ungana. **amalgamation** *n* muungano, muunganisho, mchanganyiko, mchanganyo.
amanuensis *n* karani wa imla, mnakili, katibu.
amaryllis *n* nargisi.
amass *vt* kusanya, rundika, limbika.
amateur *n* 1 ridhaa: hali ya kujishughulisha na sanaa, michezo au utendaji wowote kwa kupenda bila kutegemea malipo. 2 mwanaridhaa *adj* -a ridhaa, -siostadi. **~ish** *adj* sio kamili, -sio stadi. **~ishness** *n* uanagenzi.
amaze *vt* staajabisha, shangaza *be ~d* staajabu, shangazwa. **~ment** *n* mshangao, mastaajabu. **blank ~ment** bumbuazi, hali ya kuduwaa, butwaa. **amazing** *adj* -a kushangaza, -a kustaajabisha. **amazingly** *adv* kwa mshangao.
Amazon *n* 1 Amazoni: mto mkubwa wa Amerika ya Kusini. 2 jikedume: mwanamke mwenye nguvu na tabia kama za mwanaume.
ambassador *n* balozi. **~rial** *adj* -a kibalozi. **~ship** *n* ubalozi **ambassadress** *n* balaozi wa kike.
amber *n* kaharabu *adj* -a rangi ya kaharabu.
ambergris *n* ambari.
ambidextrous *adj* -enye kuweza kutumia mikono miwili kwa ustadi ulio sawa. **ambidexterity** *n* ustadi wa kutumia mikono yote miwili sawa.
ambience *n* mazingira, hali, mandhari. **ambient** *adj* -a mazingira, -a pande zote.
ambiguity *n* utata: hali ya kuwa na maana nyingi -enye maana nyingi.
ambiguous *adj* tata, -enye maana nyingi.
ambit *n* eneo, mipaka au viwango vya mamlaka na madaraka.
ambitious *adj* -enye nia au tamaa ya makuu, -a kutaka makuu. **~ly** *adv* kwa tamaa ya makuu. **ambition** *n* 1 tamaa ya makuu. 2 lengo *I have achieved my ~* nimetimiza lengo langu.
ambivalent *adj* kinzani, -enye hisia/maana za kugongana k.m. "kupenda na kuchukia sawia." **ambivalence** *n* hisia kinzani.
amble *vi* enda dalji *n* dalji.
ambrosia *n* ambrosi: chakula cha miungu *(fig)* kitu kitamu chenye harufu ya kupendeza.
ambulance *n* gari la wagonjwa.
ambulatory *adj* -a kusogezeka, -a kuhamishika; *(leg)* -a kubadilika. **~ will** wasia wa kubadilika; -enye nguvu ya kwenda.
ambuscade see **ambush**.
ambush *n* uvamizi, mavizio *lay an ~* tayarisha uvamizi *vt* vamia.
ameba *n* see **amoeba**.
ameer *n* see **emir**.
ameliorate *vt, vi* tengeneza, fanya zuri zaidi. **amelioration** *n*
amen *n (rel)* amina, amin, na iwe hivyo.
amenable *adj (to)* 1 *(of people)* -sikivu, -epesi kuongozwa, tiifu. 2 *(of cases, situations)* -a kufuata kawaida *this case is ~ to ordinary rules* shauri hilo lafuata kanuni za kawaida *~ to jurisdiction* -a

kuwajibika. **amenability** *n (leg)* dhima.

amend *vt, vi* sahihisha, fanya zuri zaidi tengeneza, rekebisha. **~able** *adj* -a kurekebishika. **~ment** *n* marekebisho.

amends *n* fidia **make ~ to somebody** fidia.

amenity *n* uzuri (wa mahali na mazingira) (pl) vistawishi: huduma zinazofanya maisha kuwa mazuri.

America *n* Marekani, Amerika *~n adj* - -a Kimarekani *n* Mmarekani. **~ism** *n* Umarekani.

amethyst *n* ametisti: kito cha thamani chenye rangi ya zambarau.

Amharic *n* Kiamhari: lugha mojawapo ya wahabeshi.

amiable *adj* maridhia, -pole, -ema, latifu. **amiability** *n* urafiki, usuhuba. **amiably** *adv* kwa upole, kisuhuba.

amicable *adj* -a amani, -a urafiki *~ relationship* uhusiano wa amani. **amicably** *adv* kwa amani, kwa urafiki. **amicability** *n.*

amid *see* **amidst**.

amidst *also* **amid** *prep (poet)* kati ya, katikati ya, miongoni mwa, baina ya.

amidships *adv (naut)* katikati ya chombo.

amir *n see emir.*

amiss *adj, adv* -enye kasoro, -sio sawa **take sth ~** chukizwa, udhika, onea chuki (uchungu) (arch.) *(phr) what is ~?* kuna nini?

amity *n* urafiki, uhusiano mwema.

ammeter ameta: chombo cha kupimia mawimbi ya umeme kwa kutumia ampea.

ammonia *n (chem)* amonia: gesi yenye harufu kali ya kuchoma (mtu akiinusa huumia puani). **ammoniated** *adj (chem)* -enye amonia, -enye kuchanganyikana na amonia.

ammunition *n* risasi, baruti n.k. (zinazotumika katika silaha k.v. bunduki, kombora).

amnesia *n* usahaulifu.

amnesty *n* msamaha (hasa kwa makosa ya kisiasa/kiserikali) **grant ~** toa msamaha.

amoeba *n (biol)* amiba: jamii ya vijidudu vidogo sana visivyoonekana kwa macho, ambavyo huishi katika maji na udongo. **amoebic dysentry**: kuhara damu kunakosababishwa na vijidudu hivyo.

amok *adv (phr)* **run ~** charuka.

among(st) *prep* miongoni mwa, kati ya *I'm ~ many* mimi ni miongoni mwa wengi.

amoral *adj* potovu, siojali maadili.

amorous *adj* -enye ashiki nyingi, -a kuhusu/kuonyesha mapenzi. **~ly** adv .**~ness** *n.*

amorphous *adj* -sio na umbo wala sura maalum.

amortize/amortise *vt* weka akiba, tenga fedha (kwa ajili ya kulipia deni). **amortization** *n*

amount *vi* fikia, pata, -wa sawa (na) *his debt ~s to 100,000 shs.* deni lake linafikia shilingi laki moja; *it ~s to the same thing,* ni sawa tu *n* 1 idadi, jumla, yote pamoja *the ~ of books* idadi ya vitabu. 2 *(quantity)* kiasi, kadiri *he paid only a small ~ of money* alilipa kiasi kidogo tu cha fedha.

amour *n* mapenzi.

amour-propre *n* 1 kujistahi. 2. majivuno, majisifu.

amp *see* **ampere**.

ampere *n* ampea: kizio cha kupimia mkondoumeme. **amperage** *n* nguvu za umeme kwa ampea.

ampersand *n* alama ya & (= na).

amphetamine *n* amfetamini: aina ya dawa ya kulevya.

amphibia *n (zoo)* amfibia: ngeli ya wanyama wanaoweza kuishi nchi kavu na majini pia. **~n** *n* 1 *(zoo)* amfibia: mnyama anayeishi nchi kavu na majini. 2 *(aircraft)* ndege inayoweza kutua nchi kavu na majini. 3 *(mech)* gari linaloweza kutembea nchi kavu na majini. **amphibious** *adj* -a kiamfibia. **amphibiology** *n* amfibiolojia: taaluma ya elimuwanyama

inayoshughulikia amfibia.
amphitheatre *n* 1 uwanja duara (wenye safu za viti kwa watazamaji). 2 safu za viti vilivyopangwa nusu-duara (kwenye jumba la maonyesho) *natural* ~ uwanda uliozungukwa na vilima.
ample *adj* 1 kubwa; -enye nafasi. 2 -ingi, tele. 3 -a kutosha, maridhawa *a thousand elfu moja shillings will be* ~ *for my needs* shilingi zatosha kabisa kwa haja zangu. **amply** *adv* -vya kutosha na zaidi. **~ness** *n.*
amplify *vt* 1 kuza nguvu; pazasauti. ukuzaji nguvu, upazaji sauti.
amplifier *n* amplifaya. 2 ukuzaji, ziada, ongezeko. 3 eleza zaidi, zidisha, kuza, ongeza.
amplitude *n* 1 tambo: upepo wa mbembeo. 2 ukubwa, upana, wingi.
ampoule *n (med)* kitabakero: kichupa kidogo cha dawa ya sindano.
amputate *vt* kata kiungo cha mwili (k.m mguu au mkono. **amputation** *n* kukata/kukatwa kiungo cha mwili.
amputee *n* aliyekatwa kiungo cha mwili.
amuck *see* **amok**.
amulet *n* hirizi.
amuse *vt* chekesha, burudisha, furahisha ~ *oneself* jifurahia. **~ment** *n* kiburudisho, burudani, kichekesho, furaha *places of ~ment* sehemu za burudani. **amusing** *adj.* **amusingly.**
an see **a** *adv.*
anabolism *n* (zoo) uanaboli: hali ya jumla ya ujenzi wa kemikali mwilini.
anachronism *n* 1 jambo lililopitwa na wakati. 2 kosa la kikronolojia (k.m. *Mkwawa* alitazama saa yake wakati asingeweza kuwa na saa).
anachronistic *adj* -a kizamani; -a kukosewa tarehe.
anaconda *n (zoo)* chatu (wa Amerika ya Kusini).
anaemia *n (med)* anemia: upungufu wa damu. **anaemic** *adj* -enye anemia, -enye kupungukiwa damu.
anaerobe *n (bio)* anerobi: viumbe vyenye kuishi bila oksijeni katika mazingira yao. **anaerobic** *adj* -a anerobi.
anaesthesia *n* 1 *(med)* unusukaputi: hali ya kutokuwa na hisia; ganzi (za maumivu, baridi). 2 *(chem) general* ~ usukaputi, *local* ~ ganzi. **anasthetic** *n* nusukaputi, ganzi tawi la kemia lishughulikalo na dutu zenye kutoa unusukaputi. **anaesthetist** *n (med)* mtaalamu wa usukaputi. **anaesthetize** *vt. (med)* tia nusukaputi, tia ganzi.
anagram *n* anagramu: neno liundwalo kwa kubadilisha herufi za neno jingine k.m. sukuma - sumaku.
anal *adj. see* **anus**.
analgesia *n* hali ya kutosikia maumivu.
analgesic *adj (med)* -a kutuliza maumivu *n* kituliza maumivu.
analogy *n* analojia: hali au tabia ya kitu kufuata mkondo au sura ya kitu kingine kilichotangulia. **analogize** *vi* linganisha kwa kufananisha. **analogical** *adj* -a mfanano; -a ulinganifu. **analogous** *adj* -a kulingana, -a kufanana, a kushabihiana. ~ *conditions* hali zinazofanana. **analogue** *n* kifanani: kitu kinachofanana na kitu kingine (ingawa si cha asili moja nacho) mshabaha.
analyse *vt* 1 changanua, chambua. 2 chunguza ~ *the cause of failure* chunguza sababu za kutofaulu 3 (*gram*) tenga sentensi katika sehemu mbali mbali za kisarufi. **analysis** *n* uchanganuzi; uchambuzi: utafiti wa asili ya vitu ili kuvumbua sheria zinazotawala nguvu zake mbalimbali. **analytical** *adj.* **analytically** *adv.* **analyst** *n* mchanganuzi, mchambuzi. **analytics** *n* taaluma/sayansi ya uchanganuzi.
anapeast *n (poet)* kipande cha mstari wa shairi chenye silabi fupi mbili na ndefu moja.
anarchy *n* 1 hali ya utawala huria. 2 kutokuwepo na serikali. 3 vurugu. **anarchism** *n* utawala huria; nadharia

ya kisiasa inayosema kuwa serikali na sheria havitakiwi. **anarchist** *n* 1 mfuata utawala huria. 2 mpinzani wa aina yeyote ya serikali. **anarchical** *adj* -enye machafuko ya mambo ya kisiasa, -liojaa fujo.

anathema *n* apizo la kanisa, laana. 2 kitu kichukiwacho sana. *vt (rel)* laani, apiza.

anatomy *n* 1 anatomia: sayansi inayohusu mwili na viungo vyake jinsi vilivyo. 2 *(slang)* mwili. 3 *(fig)* uchambuzi, uchanganuzi. **anatomical** *adj* -a anatomia. **anatomist** *n* mwana anatomia, mchangua maiti.

anatomize *vt.* 1 tenga sehemu (za mwili n.k.), katakata. 2 *(fig)* chambua, changanua.

ancestor *n* mhenga, babu/mababu (wa zamani) *common ~* jadi moja. **ancestral** *adj* -a mababu, -a nasaba. **ancestress** *n* **ancestry** *n* ukoo, jadi, kizazi cha mtu.

anchor *n* nanga, *~ rope* amari: kamba ya nanga. **let go (drop/cast) the ~** tia nanga, tosa nanga *vt, vi* 1 tia/toa nanga. 2 funga/kaza barabara *drop ~* tia nanga. **~age** *n* 1 maezi/melezi; mahali pa kutia nanga. 2 *(fig)* kivuli. jambo ambalo mtu analitegemea kwa hifadhi. 3 ushuru: gharama ya kutia nanga bandarini. ~ **man** *n* mratibu wa kazi ya kikundi, mkuu wa kikundi.

anchorite *n* 1 sufii: mtu aliyejitenga na malimwengu, hasa kwa ajili ya dini. 2 mtu wa pekee.

anchoress *n* sufii (wa kike).

anchovy *n* aina ya dagaa wa maji chumvi.

ancient *adj* si -a siku hizi, kongwe *n* mkongwe *the ~s* watu wa kale *~ monuments* magofu, majengo ya zamani.

ancillary *adj.* 1 -dogo (kwa cheo/madaraka) *~ road* barabara ndogo. 2 -saidizi *~ staff* wafanyakazi wasaidizi.

and *conj* na: neno linalounganisha na kuendeleza sentensi *he came ~ ate food* alikuja na kula chakula.

andante *adj (of music)* -a mwendo wa taratibu kiasi, polepole.

andiron *n* kishika vijinga (cha chuma).

androgen *n (bio)* androjeni: jamii ya homoni inayoleta hali ya uume katika kiumbe.

androgynous *adj* 1 *(bio)* -a huntha, -a kiume na kike.

anecdote *n* mchapo, hadithi fupi (juu ya mtu au tukio la kweli). **anecdotal** *adj*.

anemia *see* **anaemia**.

anemometer *n (met)* anemometa: kipimaupepo.

aneurism, aneurysm *n (med)* perema: ugonjwa wa kuvimba tezi.

anesthesia *see* **anaesthesia**.

anew 1 *adv* tena, upya, kwa mara nyingine.

angel *n* 1 malaika. 2 *(fig)* mtu mzuri, mtu mpole na mwema. **~ic** *adj* -a malaika, -ema sana, takatifu.

angelica *n (bot)* mzizi wenye harufu nzuri unaotumika katika dawa na upishi.

angelus *n (rel)* (kengele ya) Sala ya Bikira Maria.

anger *n* hasira, ghadhabu, hamaki. *vt* hamakisha, ghadhibisha, kasirisha.

angina (pectoris) *n (med)* angina: ugonjwa wa moyo unaosababisha maumivu kifuani.

angle[1] *n* 1 pembe *from all ~s* kutoka kila sehemu (pembe). 2 pembenukta: sehemu baina ya mistari miwili ikutanayo *corresponding ~* pembe mshabaha *right ~* pembe mraba *acute ~* pembe kali. *straight ~* pembe mstari *reflex ~* pembe kuu. 3 *(fig)* mtazamo *look at something from all ~s* angalia jambo kuzingatia mitazamo yote *vi, vt* 1 geuka kipembe, pinda. 2 mili. **angular** *adj* -enye pembe au kona kali. 2 *(of a person)* king'onda, embamba sana na -enye mifupa iliyotokeza. 3 -gumu, -zito kufanya jambo. **angularity** *n* hali ya kuwa na pembe.

angle[2] *vi* vua samaki kwa mshipi. *n* **~r** mvuvi wa mshipi. **angling** *adj*

uvuvi wa mshipi. ~ **for something** *(fig)* pembeja: tumia mbinu/hila/ ujanja kupata kitu.
Anglican *n* Anglikana *adj* -a Kianglikana.
anglicize *vt* fanya kuwa kama Kiingereza. **anglicism** *n* umombo: msemo wa Kiingereza unaotumika katika lugha nyingine.
anglo *adj* -a Kiingereza. **Anglophone** *adj* Anglofoni:-enye kutumia Kiingereza.
angora *n* 1 angora: paka, mbuzi au sungura mwenye manyoya marefu. 2 kitambaa kilichotengenezwa kutokana na manyoya ya angora.
angry *adj* 1 -enye hasira, -enye chuki, -enye hamaki *be* ~ kasirika. 2 *(of a cut, wound)* -enye kupwita. 3 *(sea, sky, clouds)* -a kutisha, iliochafuka., **angrily** *adv* kwa hasira/ghadhabu chuki.
angst *n* hofu kubwa (inayosababishwa na hali ya ulimwengu).
anguish *n* maumivu makali (ya moyo au akili), uchungu. **~ed** *adj* a kuonyesha/ kusikia uchungu.
anima *n* 1 undani wa mtu. 2 hulka ya kike aliyonayo mwanamume.
animal *n* 1 mnyama *domestic* ~ mnyama afugwaye. 2 kiumbe mwenye uhai anayeweza kuhisi na kujongea k.m. mtu, mbwa, samaki n.k. 3 hayawani *adj* -a kinyama; -enye tamaa nyingi za kimwili. **~ism** 1 *n* unyama, uhayawani. 2 imani ya kuwa binadamu ni mnyama tu. **animality** *n* unyama.
animate *vt* 1 huisha. 2 changamsha, sisimua *the debate was ~d* majadiliano yalikuwa ya kusisimua. *adj* hai, -enye uhai, -a kuchangamka, -a kusisimua. **~ed** *cartoon* katuni hai (wa sinema). **animation** *n* 1 uhai. 2 bidii, shauku. 3 utengenezaji wa katuni.
animism *n* imani kuwa vitu vyote (miti, mawe upepo n.k.) vina roho.
animosity *n* chuki, uadui, uhasama.
animus *n* 1 chuki. 2 hulka ya kiume aliyonayo mwanamke.
ankle *n* kifundo au tindi ya mguu ~ *deep* mpaka miguuni. ~ **socks** soksi. **anklet** mtali, furungu.
annals *n* kumbukumbu za kihistoria (mwaka hadi mwaka). **annalist** *n* mwandishi wa matukio ya mwaka hadi mwaka.
annex *vt* 1 teka, nyang'anya, pokonya, twaa kwa nguvu (nchi au shamba). 2 unga, ambatisha, jaliza. **~ation** *n* 1 kutwaa kwa nguvu, kunyang'anya, kupokonya, utekaji. 2 kuunga, kuambatisha. **annexe** *n* 1 jengo dogo (lililounganishwa kutoka jengo jingine). 2 *(document)* kiambatisho.
annihilate *vt* hasiri, angamiza, teketeza. **annihilation** *n* maangamizo, kuteketea.
anniversary *n* 1 siku ya ukumbusho (wa jambo kila mwaka). 2 maadhimisho ya siku ya ukumbusho (yaani baada ya kuzaliwa Kristo).
Anne Domini *adv* katika mwaka wa Kristo.
annotate *vt* fafanua, ongeza maelezo, fasili, eleza. **annotation** *n* maelezo, ufafanuzi.
announce *vt* 1 tangaza, piga mbiu. 2 fahamisha. 3 tambulisha. **~ment** *n* tangazo, mbiu. **~r** *n* mtangazaji.
annoy *vt* udhi, sumbua, kera, kefya. **~ance** *n* udhia, usumbufu, kero *a look of ~ance* jicho kali. **annoying** *adj* -a kuudhi, -a kusumbua, -a kukera. **~ingly** *adv*.
annual *adj* 1 -a kila mwaka ~ *public holiday* sikukuu ya kila mwaka. 2 -a mwaka ~ *income* mapato ya mwaka. 3 *(of plants)* a mwaka mmoja tu. *n* toleo maalum la kitabu la kila mwaka; tukio la kila mwaka; mmea wa msimu. **annually** *adv* kila mwaka.
annuitant *n* mlipwa malipomwaka. **annuity** *n* 1 malipomwaka. 2 haki ya kupata au kulipwa malipomwaka. 3 bima ya malipomwaka.
annul *vt* batilisha, futa, tangua, sitisha.

annunciate *vt* 1 tangaza, taja, bashiri. **Annunciation** *n* 1 *(rel) the ~* Kupashwa habari Bikira Maria na Gabrieli kwamba atamzaa Yesu Kristo. 2 sikukuu ya kukumbuka tangazo hilo.

anode *n* anodi: ncha chanya ambapo mkondoumeme huingilia kichanganuziumeme.

anodyne *n (med)* anodini: dawa itulizayo maumivu.

anoint *vt (rel)* paka mafuta. **~ment** *n.*

anomalous *adj* -siokawaida; -a kipekee. **anomaly** *n* kioja: kitu kisicho kawaida.

anon *adv (arch)* punde, halafu kidogo. **ever and ~** mara kwa mara.

anonymous *adj* bila jina, -siyotiwa jina, -enye jina lisilojulikana *an ~ letter* barua bila jina *the author remains ~* mwandishi hajulikani.

anopheles *n* anofelesi: mbu aambukizaye ugonjwa wa malaria.

anorak *n* anoraki: koti fupi (la baridi/mvua) lenye kofia.

anorexia *n* ugonjwa wa kukosa hamu ya chakula. **anorexic.** *n* mtu mwenye ugonjwa huo.

another *adj (additional)* -ingine *~ thing* kitu kingine *give me ~ shirt* nipe shati jingine *(difference) come ~ time* njoo wakati mwingine *(similarity) he will be ~ Shaaban Robert* atakuwa kama Shaaban Robert *one way or ~* kwa njia moja au nyingine.

anoxia *n* unyongeo: hali ya kukosa oksijeni hata ukapata ugonjwa wa nyongea (hasa kwa watoto wadogo).

answer *n* 1 jibu, itiko. 2 *(maths)* jawabu. 3 *(leg)* utetezi. *vt, vi* 1 jibu, itika. *~ the door* itikia hodi. 2 *(satisfy)* ridhisha, tosheleza. 3 *(solve)* toa jawabu, tambua. 4 *(be useful)* faa *~ somebody's purpose faa mtu. (idm) ~ to a description* (of somebody/something *fanana na.* 5 *(correspond)* lingana. 6 *~ for* wajibika, kubali lawama *no case to ~* hakuna kesi. 8 *~ somebody back* jibu, jibiza. **~able** *adj* -a kuweza kujibiwa; -a kuwajibika, *he is ~ for his son's actions* anawajibika kwa matendo ya mwanawe.

ant *n (soldier)* chungu; *(termite, white ant)* mchwa; *(brown)* siafu; *(red)* maji moto; koyokoyo; *(small black)* sisimizi, nyenyere *~ hill* kichuguu.

antacid *n* kizimaasidi: dawa izimayo asidi, dawa ya kutuliza kiungulia.

antagonize *vt* chokoza, sababisha uhasama/adawa. **antagonism** *n* uhasama, utesi, uadui, chuki, adawa. **antagonistic** *adj.* **antagonist** *n* mpinzani, adui.

antarctic *adj* -a ncha ya kusini (ya dunia) *n* Antaktiki.

ante[1] *n* dau, chambele.

ante[2] *adj* -a kutangulia, -a kabla.

antecedent *adj* -liotangulia. *n* 1 *(of event, circumstance)* kitangulizi. 2 *(gram)* nomino/ kishazi/sentensi tangulizi: nomino, kishazi au sentensi inayorejewa na kiwakilishi au kielezi. 3 *(pl)* mababu, wahenga; historia ya mtu au watu. **antecedence** *n* aula, kipaumbele, utangulizi.

antechamber *n* chumba cha kungojea.

antedate *vt* 1 weka/toa tarehe ya nyuma (hasa kurudisha nyuma tarehe ya hati n.k.) 2 tangulia, tokea kabla ya.

antediluvian *adj* 1 -a zamani sana, kongwe. 2 -liotangulia gharika kuu *n* mtu wa kizamani.

antelope *n* paa, palahala.

antemeridiem *adj* -a wakati kati ya saa 6 usiku na saa 7 adhuhuri.

antenatal *n* -a kabla ya kuzaliwa au kuzaa.

antenna *adj* 1 kipapasio. 2 *(of redio)* antena: waya za kupokelea mawimbi ya sauti; erio.

antenuptial *adj* -a kabla ya ndoa.

antepenultimate *adj* -a tatu toka mwisho.

anterior *adj* -a kutangulia, (tech) mbele ya.

anteroom *n see antechamber.*

anthem *n* 1 *(of nation)* wimbo wa taifa/

nchi. 2 *(rel)* wimbo wa kanisa (aghalabu wa kwaya na kinanda).
anther *n (bot)* chavulio: sehemu za stameni katika ua ambapo chavuo hutengenezwa.
anthill *n see ant.*
Anthology *n* diwani, koja (la kazi ya fasihi).
anthrax *n* kimeta.
anthropoid *adj* -a kufanana na mwanadamu au sokwe *n* sokwe (k.m. gorila).
anthropology *n* anthropolojia: elimu ya binaadamu (hasa elimu ihusuyo habari zinazohusu asili na maendeleo yake ya awali). **anthropologist** *n* mwana anthropolojia. **anthropological** *adj.*
anti- *(pref)* -sopendelea; dhidi ya: kinyume na.
anti- aircraft *adj* -a kutungua ndege.
antibiotic *n* kiuavijasumu.
antibody *n* zindiko, kingamwili.
antic *n (usually pl)* tendo/mwendo chekeshi.
Antichrist *n (rel)* mpinga Kristo, adui wa Kristo (hasa anayesadikiwa kuwa atakuja muda mfupi kabla ya Kiyama).
anticipate *vt* 1 tangulia. 2 *(expect)* tumaini, dhani. 3 tazamia, tarajia. **anticipation** *n.* **anticipatory** *adj* -a kungojea, -a kutazamia, -a kuwaza ya mbele.
anticlerical *adj* dhidi ya ukasisi ~ *laws* sheria dhidi ya ukasisi.
anticlimax *n* 1 mpomoko: upeo wa chini. 2 *(of speech/story)* kupwaya kwa ghafla.
anticlockwise *adv* kinyume saa.
anticyclone *n* kitanguakimbunga, kinga ya kimbunga.
antidote *n* kiuasumu: dawa ya kupoza nguvu ya sumu.
anti-freeze kishushamgando.
antigen *n* antijeni.
anti-hero *n* shujaa pwaya.
anti-knock *n (of engine)* kizuianoki.
antimacassar *n (arch)* foronya ya kiti.
antipathy *n* uhasama, chuki, uadui.
antipathetic *adj.*
anti-personnel *adj* -a kuumiza au kuangamiza watu.
antipode *n* 1 kinyume kabisa. 2 *(usu (pl) n ~ to)* **antipode's** upande wa pili wa dunia (aghalabu kutoka hapo ulipo).
antipoison *n see* **antidote**
antiquary *n* mkusanya mambo ya kale. **antiquarian** *adj* -a kuhusu wakusanya mambo ya kale. **antique** *n* kitu cha kale (tunu) ~ *shop* duka la vitu na sanaa za kale *adj* -a kale. **antiquated** *adj* kuukuu, -sotumika. **antiquity** *n* 1 zamani za kale. 2 *(pl)* mambo ya kale k.v. nyaraka, majengo magofu n.k.). **antisepsis** *n* zindiko.
antiseptic *n* antiseptiki: aina ya kemikali inayozuia kukua kwa bakteria kwenye jeraha, ngozi, n.k.
anti-social *adj* -a kupingana na jamii. 2 -enye kuelekea kuvuruga ustawi wa jamii. 3 -sopatana na watu.
anti-tank *adj (milit)* -a kupigia vifaru ~*gun* mzinga wa kupigia vifaru.
antithesis *n* tabaini. **antithetical** *adj.* **antithetically** *adv.*
antitoxin *n* antitoksini: dawa au kemikali ya kuzuia au kuzimua sumu mwilini. **antitoxic** *adj.*
antitradewind *n* upepo (wa magharibi unaovuma kaskazini ya nchi za tropiki).
antler *n* pembe (ya paa).
antonym *n* kinyume.
anus *n* mkundu. *adj* -a mkundu.
anvil *n* 1 fuawe. 2 *(anat)* kifuawesikio.
anxiety *n* 1 wasiwasi, dukuduku. 2 hamu. **anxious** *adj* -a wasiwasi, -a dukuduku *be* ~ pata wasiwasi. dukuduku. **~ly** *adv.*
any *pron/adv* -o ote **in ~ case/at ~ rate** kwa vyo vyote vile *the patient is not ~ better* mgonjwa hana nafuu. ~ *body/ ~* ***one*** *will tell you* yeyote atakuambia. **is there ~body?** kuna mtu yeyote ~ **how/ ~way** *adv* 1 vyovyote vile. 2 ovyo ovyo. 3 kwa njia yoyote. **~thing** *pron* kitu

chochote *she does not do ~thing* hafanyi chochote. ~ **place/ ~where** *adv* popote. **~wise** *adv* kwa kadiri yoyote, kwa namna yoyote.

aorta *n (bio)* mkole: mshipa mkubwa wa damu wa upande wa kushoto wa moyo.

apace *adv* kwa haraka, kwa kasi, hima, chapuchapu

apanage *n* 1 mirathi: mali anayopata mtu kutokana na urithi au cheo. 2 vifuasi asilia vya mtu au kitu.

apart *adv* 1 mbali. 2 pembeni, faraghani; chemba. 3 *(separately)* tofauti *a thing ~* kitu tofauti. 4 *(asunder, parted)* mbalimbali. 5 *(out of consideration) ~ from* isipokuwa *set ~* weka mbali, tenga *force (draw) ~* mamanua.

apartheid *n* siasa ya ubaguzi wa rangi.

apartment *n* 1 chumba, fleti *US ~ house* fleti. 2 *(pl)* ~s vyumba vya kuishi (aghalabu hupangishwa).

apathy *n* hali ya kutojali. **apathetic** *adj* -siojali. **apathetically** *adv*.

ape *n* 1 sokwe. 2 mwigaji (wa sauti na matendo ya wengine). 3 *(colloq)* mjinga, -sio na umbo au adabu nzuri *vt* iga. **apish** *adj* 1 -a kisokwesokwe. 2 -a kuiga kipumbavu. **apishness** *n*.

aperient *n (medicine)* haluli: dawa ya kuharisha, *adj* -a kuharisha.

aperitif *n* kiamshahamu: kinywaji cha alkoholi kinywewacho kabla ya kula ili kuamsha hamu ya kula.

aperture *n* kitundu, kiupenyo, uwazi mfinyu k.m. wa kupitishia mwanga katika kamera.

apex *n* kilele, ncha, kipeo.

aphasia *n (path)* afasia: ukosefu wa uwezo wa kusema au kuelewa lugha kwa sababu ya kuumia ubongo.

aphorism *n*. methali, maneno: msemo mfupi wa busara.

aphrodisiac *n* mkuyati: dawa ya kuamsha tamaa (ya kiume au kike).

apiary *n* mahali penye mizinga ya nyuki; mahali pa kufugia nyuki. **apiarist** *n* mfuga nyuki. **apian** *adj* -a kuhusu nyuki. **apiculture** *n* ufugaji nyuki.

apiece *adv* kila moja, kila mojawapo *it costs two shillings ~* inagharimu shilingi mbili kila moja.

aplomb *n* kujiamini.

apocalypse *n (rel)* ufunuo, (hasa wa maarifa kutoka kwa Mwenyezi Mungu). *the A~* kitabu cha mwisho cha Agano Jipya chenye Ufunuo wa mtakatifu Yohana. **apocalyptic** *adj* -a kutabiri hali ya maafa makubwa; -a kiyama.

apocryphal *adj* -a wasiwasi; -a kubuniwa, siyothibitishwa.

apogee *n* 1 upeo wa sayari ikiwa mbali kabisa na dunia. 2 upeo wa juu kabisa.

apologia *n* utetezi wa kimaandishi.

apology *n* 1 kuomba radhi *unconditional ~* kuomba radhi bila masharti. 2 utetezi (wa imani, vitendo, maisha n.k.). 3 *(fig)* mfano mbaya *~ for a meal* mfano mbaya wa mlo. **apologize** *vi* omba radhi, kiri kosa *I beg to ~* kumradhi, niwie radhi. **apologetic** *adj*. **apologetically** *adv*. **apologist** *n* mtetezi.

apophthegm *n see* **apothegm**.

apoplexy *n (med)* kiharusi. **apopleptic** *adj* 1 -a kiharusi. 2 -lioghadhibika sana (kiasi cha kubadilika rangi).

apostasy *n* ukanaji, uasi (wa dini, imani, siasa). **apostate** *n* mwasi. **apostatize** *vi* asi.

a posteriori *adv, adj (lat) (reasoning)* mkasakisa (kupata sababu kutokana na matokeo/athari).

apostle *n* 1 *(rel)* mtume (mmojawapo wa mitume kumi na wawili wa Yesu Kristo). 2 kiongozi (wa imani mpya au tapo la kurekebisha dini fulani). **~s creed** Imani ya Mitume *adj* 1 -a kitume 2 -a Papa.

apostrophe *n* 1 apostrofi: alama ya kifupisho k.m. *can't* (badala ya *cannot*) Moh'd (badala ya Mohamed). 2 alama ya herufi k.m. ng'ombe.

apothecary *n (arch)* mfamasia: mtu anayechanganya na kuuza madawa.

apothegm msemo mkali.
apotheosis *n.* 1 ugeukaji mungu au mtakatifu. 2 uondokanaji na maisha ya kilimwengu. 3 kilele cha heshima au fahari. 4 mfano kamili, mfano bora sana *she is the ~ of womanhood* yeye ni mfano bora wa wanawake.
appal *vt* tisha, ogofya, shtua **~ling** *adj* 1 -a kutisha, -a kuogofya. 2 -a hali mbaya sana. **~lingly** *adv.*
appanage *see* **apanage**.
apparatus *n* 1 (seti ya) zana za kazi, vifaa; mashine (yenye kazi maalum). 2 ogani za mwili, sehemu za mwili zinazokamilisha mfumo wa kawaida mwilini *the breathing ~* ogani zote zinazohusiana na kupumua.
apparent *adj* 1 dhahiri, wazi heir ~ mrithi dhahiri. 2 -a kuonekana *the ~ cause* sababu inayoonekana. **~ly** *adv* inavyoonekana.
apparition *n* 1 shani la ajabu. 2 kivuli cha mfu (kionekanacho), mzuka.
appeal *vi* 1 omba, sihi. 2 kata rufaa. 3 vutia, pendeza *n* 1 *(for mercy)* ombi. 2 *(petition)* maombi, rufaa *allow an ~* kubali rufaa. 3 mvuto, tamanisho. **~ing** *adj* 1 -a kusihi. 2 -a kuvutia. **~ingly** *adv* **appellant** *n* mkata rufaa. **appellate** *adj* -a kukata rufaa. **appellate court** mahakama ya kukata rufaa.
appear *vi* 1 tokea, onekana; jitokeza. 2 hudhuria, enda mbele ya (k.m. mahakama). 3 elekea, onekana *he ~s to be a hard worker* anaelekea kuwa mchapakazi. **appearance** *n* 1 kujitokeza, kuhudhuria *put in an ~* hudhuria, (agh kwa muda mfupi). 2 sura, wajihi, umbo. 3 *(pl) to all ~* kadiri ionekanavyo.
appease *vt* tuliza, ridhisha. **~ment** *n* kuridhisha (hasa adui kwa kulegeza msimamo).
appellant *n see* **appeal**.
appellation *n* jina, cheo.
append *vt* ambatisha: ongeza mwishoni. **~age** *n* 1 kiambatisho. 2 nyongeza.
appendix *n* 1 kiambatisho. 2 *(med)* kidole tumbo, kibole. **appendicitis** *n* ugonjwa wa kidole tumbo/ kibole. **appendectomy** *n* upasuaji wa kuondoa kidole tumbo/kibole.
appertain *vi (to)* husu, husiana na. **~ing** *adj.*
appetite *n* 1 hamu (ya chakula, kinywaji n.k.) *the cook has no ~ for food* mpishi hana hamu ya chakula. 2 tamaa, uchu. **appetizer** *n* kiamsha hamu: zoezi, kitafunio, kinywaji (kinachoongeza hamu ya chakula). **appetizing** *adj* -a kutamanisha; a kuchapukia.
applaud *vt* 1 piga makofi (kwa kushangilia). 2 unga mkono.
applause *n* makofi; kusifu (kwa makofi, vifijo n.k.).
apple *n* tufaha *of the ~ eye* kipenzi. *Adam's ~* kikoromeo, zoloto *upset the ~cart* vurunga mipango.
appliance *n* chombo, kifaa *household ~s* vifaa vya nyumbani k.m. pasi, jiko la umeme n.k. *fire ~* kifaa cha kuzimia moto.
applique *n* nguo ya mapande, kipambio (juu ya kitambaa kingine).
apply *vt, vi* 1 tia, tumia. 2 (*of med*) paka, bandika, funga *~ a bandage* funga bendeji. 3 *(for)* omba *~ for a job* omba kazi. 4 *(refer to)* husika na, nenea, fanyia bidii, zamia (k.m. kimawazo). **applicable** *adj* -a kutumika, -faayo, -husikayo. **applicant** *n* mwombaji. **application** *n* 1 kutumia, kutumika. 2 mpako, mbandiko. 3 ombi, maombi *~ form* fomu ya maombi. 4 *(use)* matumizi. 5 *(hardwork)* bidii.
applied *adj* -a matumizi.
appoint *vt* 1 ajiri, teua, *~ a minister* teua waziri. 2 panga (saa, siku au mahali pa kukutana). 3 *(formal)* amuru, agiza. **~ee** *n* mteule, mteuliwa. **~ed** *adj* 1 -lopangwa, -a miadi. 2 -loteuliwa, -loajiriwa. 3 *(of room)* -enye vyombo,- enye samani. **~ment** *n* 1 miadi: ahadi ya kuonana. 2 uteuzi, kuteua. 3 cheo cha kazi, wadhifa. 4 samani (fanicha).
apportion *vt* gawa, gawanya, kasimu,

~ment *n.*

apposite *adj* mwafaka, -a kufaa kabisa. **~ly** *adv.*

apposition *n (gram)* mrejeosawa

appositive *n (gram)* kijalizo.

appraise *vt* tathmini, kadiria thamani, panga bei. **~r** *n* mthamini. **appraisal** *n* tathmini.

appreciable *adj* -a kuonekana, -a kutambulikana, -a kupimika. **appreciably** *adv.* kwa kiasi kikubwa. **appreciate** *vt, vi* 1 (*understand*) fahamu, tambua vyema. 2 *(enjoy)* furahia, pendezewa na. 3 *(estimate highly)* thamini sana. 4 *(thank)* shukuru *he ~ his help* alimshukuru kwa msaada wake. 5 *(of land, property etc)* ongezeka thamani. **appreciation** *n* tathmini *write an appreciation of this poem* andika tathmini ya shairi hili. 2 kuthamini. 3 shukrani. 4 ongezeko la thamani. **appreciative** *adj* -a kuonyesha shukrani; -a kuelewa, -a kufurahia.

apprehend *vt (leg)* 1 kamata (mwizi n.k.), shika, tia mbaroni. 2 *(arch) (understand)* fahamu, elewa, tambua. 3 *(formal) (fear)* hofia. apprehensible, *adj* -a kukamatika. **apprehensive** *adj* -enye hofu, -enye wasiwasi. **apprehension** *n* 1 welewa. 2 hofu, wasiwasi. 3 ukamataji.

apprentice *n* mwanagenzi: mwanafunzi wa ufundi (k.m. useremala, uashi n.k.). **~ship** *n* 1 uanagenzi. 2 muda wa kujifunza.

apprise *vt (formal)* arifu, pasha habari, *be* **~d** *of* arifiwa juu ya.

approach *vt, vi (come nearer)* 1 karibia, sogea, sogelea, jongelea. 2 *(go to)* endea *~ ones employer for higher pay* endea mwajiri na kuomba nyongeza ya mshahara *n* 1 kukaribia. 2 njia, mlango wa kufikia. 3 kuongea (na mtu kwa mara ya kwanza). 4 mtazamo. **~able** *adj* 1 -kunjufu, -a kuingilika. 2 -a kufikia.

approbate *vt (formal)* kubali, idhinisha.**approbation** *n* 1 kukubali, idhini, kibali.2 sifa. **approbatory** *adj* -a kusifu.

appropriate[1] *adj* -a kufaa. **~ness** *n.* **~ly** *adv.*

appropriate[2] *vt* 1 jitwalia, iba. 2 *(set apart)* tenga; tengea, weka upande (kwa kazi muhimu).

appropriation *n* 1 kutenga *wrongful~* matumizi songo, kitengo songo *~ bill* muswada wa matumizi ya fedha. 2 fungu (la fedha n.k.). 3 (tendo la) kujitwalia, wizi.

approve *vt, vi* 1 sifu, penda. 2 *(sanction)* afiki, kubali, thibitisha, idhinisha *~ the minutes of the meeting* thibitisha kumbukumbu za mkutano. **approving** *adv.* **approvingly** *adj.*

approval *n* kibali, idhini; kukubali.

approximate *vt, vi* 1 karibia. 2 leta karibu na (k.m. bei) *adj ~* ***(to)*** -a kukaribia, karibu sana. **approximation** *n* kisio, kadirio. **approximately** *adv* takriban, karibu sawa na.

appurtenance *n (usu pl) (legal)* kiambato, kifuasi, kiongezo. **appurtenant** *adj* -a kuambata, -a kuhusu.

April *n* Aprili; mwezi wa nne. *adj* -a Aprili.

a priori *adv* kisamkasa (kupata matokeo kutokana na sababu).

apron *n* 1 kimori, aproni: nguo maalum inayovaliwa hasa wakati wa shughuli za uchafu *tied to mother's (wife's) ~ strings* anayetawaliwa na mama yake/mkewe. 2 sehemu iliyosakafiwa kwenye uwanja wa ndege kwa ajili ya kupakia, kupakua na kugeuzia ndege. 3 ~ **stage** jukwaa chomozi: sehemu ya jukwaa kwenye thieta inayochomoza kuelekea watazamaji.

apropos *adv, adj* -a kufaa *his points were very ~* hoja zake zilifaa sana. 2 ~ **of** *prep* kuhusu.

apse *n* sehemu ya kanisa yenye umbo la mviringo.

apt *adj* 1 -a kufaa *an ~ word* neno la kufaa. 2 -epesi (kwa kujifunza n.k.), hodari. 3 -a kuelekea, -epesi wa *he is*

~ *to forget* ni mwepesi wa kusahau. **~ ness** *n*. **~ly** *adv*.

aptitude *n* 1 *(for)* kipaji ~ *test* mtihani wa kupima vipaji.

aqualung *n* kipafumaji: chombo cha kupumulia kinachotumiwa na wapiga mbizi.

aquamarine *n* 1 zumaridi: kito cha thamani chenye rangi ya kijani iliyopauka. 2 rangi ya kijani iliyopauka.

aquanaut *n* mzamiaji, mpigambizi (anayeishi na kufanya kazi chini ya maji kwa muda).

aquaplane *n* ubaomaji: ubao maalum unaotumiwa katika mchezo wa kuvutwa na boti *vi* 1 fanya mchezo huu. 2 teleza (kama gari juu ya barabara iliyojaa maji).

aquarium n tangisamaki, hodhisamaki: tangi la maji la kuwekea na kuonyeshea samaki na mimea ya bahari.

Aquarius *n* Ndoo: alama ya kumi na moja ya buruji.

aquatic *adj* -a majini, -a kuishi majini ~ *sports* michezo ya majini.

aquatint *n* 1 uchoraji kwenye shaba. 2 picha ya aina hii.

aqueduct *n* mfereji wa maji (agh. hujengwa na mawe juu ya ardhi).

aqueous *adj* -a maji, -a majimaji.

aquiline *adj* -a tai, -enye kufanana na tai ~ *nose* pua kali (iliyopindika kama ile ya tai).

Arab *n* Mwarabu *adj* -a Kiarabu. -a Uarabu, Arabuni. **~ian** *adj* -a Kiarabu the ~ *Nights* Alfu lela ulela. **~ic** *adj* -a Kiarabu *n* Kiarabu. **~ist** *n* mwanafunzi au mtaalam wa mambo ya Waarabu.

arabesque *n (art)* mchoro maalum (wenye nakshi nyingi). 2 miondoko maalum (ya aina ya mchezo wa bale).

arable *adj* -nayolimika ~ *land* ardhi inayolimika.

arachnid *n* araknida: jamii ya anthropoda inayojumuisha nge, buibui, chawa, kupe, n.k.

arbiter *see arbitrator*.

arbitrary *adj* 1 holela, -sio na mantiki, -sio na misingi maalum. 2 *(despotic)* -a kidikteta, -dhalimu.

arbitrate *vt, vi* 1 toa uamuzi. 2 patanisha, suluhisha. **arbitration** *n* maamuzi, usuluhishi. **arbitrator** *n also* ***arbiter*** msuluhishi, mpatanishi.

arbor, arbour *n* mahali penye kivuli cha miti (katika bustani). **~eal** *adj* a miti, -a mtini. **~eous** *adj* 1 penye miti mizima 2 -a mitini *~animals* wanyama wa mitini. **~escent** *adj* -kama mti, -enye matawi. **~tum** mahali penye mkusanyo wa miti kwa ajili ya maonyesho na mafunzo. **~culture** *n* ukulima wa miti.

arc *n* tao: sehemu ya duara au pindo ~ *welding* kulehemu kwa umeme *vi* fanya tao.

arcade *n* njia tao (njia yenye paa la tao). **~d** *adj*.

Arcadia *n* Arkadia: eneo mashambani ambapo watu wanaishi raha mustarehe. ~ **n** adj, n.

arcane *adj* -a kunga.

arch[1] *n* 1 tao; jengo la tao (lenye njia juu yake) *a bridge with three* **~s** daraja lenye matao matatu. 2 *(also ~ way)* lango.

arch[2] *adj* 1 tundu. 2 chepe. **~ly** *adv* kitundu; kichepe. **~ness** *n*.

arch[3] *(pref)* -kuu; *see* **archangel** n.k.

archaeology *n* akiolojia, elimukale. **archeologist** *n* mwanaakiolojia. **archaeological** *adj*.

archaic *adj* -a zamani, -a kale, -siotumika sasa. **archaism** *n* kikale: neno au msemo wa kale (usiotumika sasa).

archangel *n (rel)* malaika mkuu.

archbishop *n (rel)* askofu mkuu. **~ric** cheo (cha askofu mkuu); jimbo (la askofu mkuu).

archdeacon *n (rel)* kasisi mkuu.

archdiocese *n* jimbo la askofu mkuu.

arch-enemy *n* 1 adui mkuu. 2 *(rel)* Shetani.

archer *n* mpiga mishale. **~y** *n* upigaji mishale, ufundi/mchezo wa kupiga mishale.

archetype *n* chapaasili, umboasili, kielelezoasili.
archipelago *n* funguvisiwa: mkusanyiko wa visiwa vingi pamoja au bahari yenye mkusanyiko huu.
architect *n* 1 msanifu majengo. 2 muasisi (wa mipango maalum) *the ~ of our victory* muasisi wa ushindi wetu. **architecture** *n* usanifu majengo. **~ural** *adj*.
archives *n* 1 nyaraka. 2 hifadhi za nyaraka. **archivist** *n* mhifadhi nyaraka.
archway *n see* **arch**.
arctic 1 *adj* -a akitiki, -a kaskazini ya dunia. 2 baridi sana.
ardent *adj* motomoto, -a shauku. **ardency** *n*.
ardour *n* shauku, hamasa.
arduous *adj* 1 *(of work)* -a sulubu, ihitajiyo nguvu, gumu. 2 *(of road)* -enye mwinuko mkali. **~ly** *adv*.
are *see* **be**.
area *n* 1 eneo, kipimo cha eneo. 2 sehemu ya dunia. 3 *(subject)* mawanda (ya shughuli za kitaalam).
areca *n* 1 (mti) mpopoo. 2 (tunda) popoo.
arena *n* uwanja (wa michezo, maonyesho n.k.) *~ of war* medani.
aren't = *are not, see* **be**.
arete *n* ukingo mkali wa mlima.
argent *adj* -a rangi ya fedha.
argon *n* agoni: gesi iliyomo hewani, hutumika kwenye baadhi ya taa za umeme.
argot *n* msimo wa kikundi maalum.
argue *vi, vt* 1 toa hoja (sababu, maneno, yakuthibitisha au kukanusha). 2 shindana kwa maneno, hojiana, bishana, gombana. *~ somebody into/ out of sth* shawishi mtu afanye/ asifanye jambo. 3 jadili. **argument** *n* 1 hoja. 2 mabishano, mashindano, majadiliano. 3 muhtasari wa habari zilizo katika kitabu. **argumentative** *adj* -bishi. **arguable** *adj* 1 -a kujadilika. 2 -wezayo kujengewa hoja/ushahidi. **argumentation** *n* kubishana, kutoa hoja, kuhojiana.
Argus *n* zimwi lenye macho mia moja. **~ eyed** *adj* -enye kutazama sana, -angalifu, makini.
argy-bargy *(colloq) n* mabishano.
aria *n* wimbo wa sauti moja katika opera.
arid *adj* -kavu sana, yabisi, kame *(fig)* -siovutia. **~ity** *n* ukame. **~ness** *n* hali ya ukame.
Aries *n* Kondoo (alama ya kwanza ya buruji).
aright *adv* (*arch*) sawasawa, barabara. sahihi, kwa jinsi iliyopasa.
arise *vi* 1 tokea, tukia. *(arch)* inuka.
aristocracy *n* 1 tabaka/utawala wa makabaila. 2 waungwana. 3 *(fig)* walio bora katika shughuli fulani. **aristocrat** *n* mtoto wa watu, mtu wa ukoo bora. **aristocratic** *adj* -a kikabaila, -a jamii ya watu wakuu **aristocratically** *adv*.
Aristotelean -a Aristotle.
arithmetic *n* sayansi ya namba. **~al** *adj*.
ark *n* 1 safina: chombo kikubwa alichounda Mtume Nuhu kabla ya gharika *Noah's ~* safina ya Nuhu. 2 sanduku kubwa, *(rel), the A~ of the Covenant* Sanduku la Agano.
arm[1] *n* 1 mkono. **an infant in ~s** mtoto mchanga. **keep somebody at ~s length** epukana na, epuka urafiki au kuzoeana na. **with open ~s** kwa mikono miwili. 2 chochote kitokacho kama mkono, k.m *~ of the sea* mkono wa bahari, ghuba. 3 tawi kubwa (la mti). 4 sehemu ya vazi inayofunika mkono. 5 **~chair** *n* kiti cha mikono adj *(fig)* -a kinadharia **~ chair critic** mhakiki wa kinadharia. 6 **~pit** kwapa. 7 *the (long) ~ of the law* mamlaka ya sheria. 8 **~ hole** *n* mkono wa vazi. 9 **~let** *n* 1 kikuku. 2 kitambaa kinachovaliwa mkononi juu karibu na bega (hasa wakati wa msiba au kuonyesha cheo).
arm[2] *n* 1 *(usu pl)* silaha, zana za vita. **in ~s** -enye silaha. **lay down ~s** salimu amri. **take up ~s** jiandaa-kupigana. **2** ***up in ~s (about)*** pinga

sana na kuwa tayari kupigana. 3 **~s** ngao ya heshima. 4 **coat of ~s** nembo. 5 tawi la jeshi, k.m. *the air ~* jeshi la anga. **amorial** *adj* -a nembo, -a shajara ~ *bearings n* nembo; *n* shajara.

arm[3] *vi, vt* pa silaha, pa kitu cha kulinda, tega bomu ~ *with answers to likely questions* tayarisha majibu ya maswali yanayoelekea kuulizwa. **~ed** *adj* enye silaha *~ed robbery* unyang'anyi wa kutumia silaha *~ed forces* majeshi.

armada *n* armada: kundi kubwa la manowari.

armadillo *n* armadilo: mnyama kama kakakuona

Armageddon *n* amagedoni: (medani ya) vita; vita vya mwisho kati ya wema na waovu. (fig) mapambano makali ya vita.

armament *n (usu pl)* 1 zana za vita (hasa mizinga ya manowari). 2 jeshi lenye silaha. 3 matayarisho ya vita. **~s-race** mashindano ya silaha.

armature *n* 1 deraya. 2 *(in motor cars)* amecha: misuko ya waya katika jenereta au mota ya umeme ambayo huzunguka katika uga sumaku.

armistice *n.* mapatano ya kusimamisha vita kwa muda.

armoire *n (Fr)* kabati kubwa (aghalabu la nguo).

armour (U.S. armor) *n* 1 vazi la kujihami wakati wa mapigano. 2 ngao chombo: bamba la metali liwekwalo kwenye chombo ili kukihami kisitobolewe na risasi au mizinga ya adui. 3 vyombo vya kivita (magari, vifaru, manowari, n.k.) vilivyowekewa mabamba ya chuma *adj* -enye vazi la kivita la chuma, -enye dereya. ~ **plate**, dereya, bamba la chuma. **~er** *n* mtengeneza silaha; mtunzaji silaha za jeshi.

armoury *n* 1 ghala ya silaha. 2 *(US)* kiwanda cha silaha.

army *n* 1 jeshi. 2 jumuiya ya watu wenye madhumuni maalum *The Salvation ~* Jeshi la Wokovu. 3 kundi kubwa *an ~ of helpers* kundi la wasaidizi *an ~ of red ants* kundi la siafu.

aroma *n* 1 harufu nzuri. 2 *(fig)* hali au mazingira fulani maalum. **~tic** *adj* -enye kunukia vizuri, -enye kukolea viungo.

arose *see* **arise**.

around *adv* 1 pande zote (za) kuzunguka, kandokando, pote, kila mahali *I have been ~* nimeona mengi. 2 mnamo ~ *two o'clock* mnamo saa nane. 3 karibu.

arouse *vt* 1 amsha, shitua. 2 tia nguvu, tia ashiki, tia shonga.

arraign *vt* 1 shtaki. 2 laumu, kosoa. **~ment** *n.*

arrange *vt, vi* 1 *(put in order)* panga, weka kwa utaratibu, safidi. 2 *(organize)* panga (kwa baadaye) ~ *a date for a meeting* panga tarehe ya mkutano. 3 tayarisha ~ *a meeting* tayarisha mkutano. 4 *(with/ for)* afikiana, kubaliana. 5 suluhisha, patanisha. **~ment** *n* 1 mpango, utaratibu. 2 *(pl)* **~ments** matayarisho, mipango *I made ~ments to send books* nilifanya mipango ya kupeleka vitabu. 3 (music) *see* **adaptation**.

arrant *adj (always of sth or somebody bad) (derog)* -a hali ya juu, -a kupindukia *an ~ thief* mwizi wa kupindukia, mwizi mkubwa/ aliyekubuhu.

arras *n (arch)* mkeka wa kiwambazani, (namna ya) zulia la kupamba ukutani, kihangaisho.

array *vt* 1 panga askari tayari kwa vita. 2 valia *~ed in professorial attire* amevalia kiprofesa *n* 1 upangaji wa askari kwa ajili ya vita. 2 vazi *in ceremonial ~* katika vazi la sherehe.

arrears *n* 1 karisaji. 2 kiporo: kazi iliyopaswa kuwa imefanywa lakini haijafanywa.

arrest *vt* 1 *(stop)* simamisha, zuia. 2 (*seize*) kamata, bamba, shika, tia mbaroni. 3 *(catch attention)* vuta nadhari *n* 1 kukamata *resist an ~* goma kukamatwa *under ~* chini ya

ulinzi. 2 *(stoppage)* kizuizi *cardiac* ~ shituko la moyo. **~ing** *adj* -a kuvuta.
arriere pensee *n (Fr)* nia ya undani katika fikra.
arrive *vi* fika, wasili. 2 ~ **at** fika mahali, fikia ~ *at a conclusion* fikia tamati/hitimisho. 3 tokea, fanyika. **arrival** *n* 1 ufikaji, majilio, mjo, ujaji. 2 *(pl)* wanaowasili.
arrogance *n* kiburi, majisifu, ufidhuli. **arrongant** adj -enye kujisifu/kujigamba, -enye kupenda makuu, fidhuli, -enye kiburi. **arrogantly** *adv*.
arrogate *vi, vt* 1 jitwalia bila haki, jipatia (hasa kwa ujeuri), jitwaza, jipachika. 2 *(fig)* twaza, ambika, pachika.
arrow *n* 1 mshale. 2 alama ya mshale ~ *head n* chembe.
arrowroot *n* 1 aina ya chakula chenye wanga kinachotokana na mimea.
arse *n (sl)* mkundu, matako. **silly** ~ /~**hole** pumbavu ~ *around/ about* poteza muda.
arsenal *n* 1 ghala, silaha. 2 kiwanda cha zana za vita. 3 *(fig)* hifadhi ya nguvu.
arsenic *n* aseniki: kemikali (ngumu) ya sumu yenye maumbile mengi *white* ~ aseniki nyeupe (namna moja ya sumu inayotumika pamoja na kemikali nyingine) 2 *adj* -a kiaseniki.
arson *(legal)* uchomaji wa mali kwa makusudi *commit* ~ choma kwa makusudi.
art *n* 1 sanaa **Theatre A~s** Sanaa za Maonyesho. 2 ustadi/ ufundi (k.m. wa kupiga muziki, kupiga picha, kuchora sanamu n.k.). 3 *(pl)* **~s** fani **fine ~s,** sanaa, *faculty of ~s* kitivo cha fani ~ *exhibition* maonyesho ya sanaa ~ *school* chuo cha sanaa *work of* ~ kazi ya sanaa. 4 *(cunning)* werevu, ujanja. 5 **~ist** *n* msanii. **~iste** *n* msaniitendi, mwanasanaa. **~istic** *adj* -a sanaa, -stadi, -sanii, -zuri. **~istically** *adv*. **~istry** *n* ustadi, urembo, usanii.
artefact *see* **artifact**.
arterial *adj* 1 -a kiateri, -enye kufanana na ateri. 2 *(fig) (of road)* barabara kuu.
arteriosclerosis *n (med)* mkakamo ateri: hali ya mkauko wa vikole vya damu.
artery *n* 1 ateri: mshipa mkubwa upelekao damu moyoni mpaka kila sehemu ya mwili. 2 *(road)* njia kuu, barabara kuu. **arteriole** *n* kiateri, tawi la ateri.
artesian well *n* kisima cha chemchem.
artful *adj* janja, erevu/ enye ustadi, -enye hila. **~ness** *n* ujanja, udanganyifu, hila. **~ly** *adv*.
arthritis *n* ugonjwa wa baridi yabisi.
artichoke *n (bot)* ua la rubaruti, rubaruti.
article *n* 1 makala. 2 *(legal)* ibara, kifungu. 3 kikorokoro *household ~s* vikorokoro vya nyumbani. 4 kibainishi.
articulate *vt* 1 eleza kwa ufasaha. 2 fungamana viungo. 3 tamka *adj* semi, -enye kueleweka. **~ness** *n* ufasaha. **articulation** *n* 1 hali ya kujieleza kwa ufasaha. 2 *(bio)* kiungo (cha goti n.k.), uungaji. **articulator** *n* kitamka.
artifact *n* 1 kitu kilichobuniwa, chombo/ silaha) aghalabu cha kale, ughushi.
artifice *n* 1 ustadi. 2 hila, ulaghai, ujanja. **~r** *n* msani.
artificial *adj* 1. bandia 2. -a kinafiki. ~ **respiration** *n* uvutishaji hewa, upumuaji bandia: ~ **insemination** uhimilishaji kibandia: utiaji shahawa za tovi (dume lililochaguliwa) kwenye uterasi ya mnyama ili atunge mimba. **~fertilizer** mbolea ya chumvi chumvi. **~lly** *adv* kwa kughushi. **~ity** *n* ubandia, tabia ya kughushi.
artillery *n* 1 mizinga mikubwa. 2 jeshi lenye kutumia mizinga ya namna hii. ~ **wagon** *n* gari la kukotoea mizinga.
artisan *n* msanii, fundi mchundo.
artless *adj* -so hila. **~ly** *adv*. **~ness** *n*.
arty *adj* -a kujifanya/kujidai kuwa mpenda sanaa.
as *adv, conj* 1 *(in that degree, in like*

manner) hivyo hivyo *do ~ I do* fanya hivyo hivyo *such ~* kama *such things ~ chairs* vitu kama viti *he did the same ~ so and so* alifanya kama alivyofanya fulani. 2 *(since, because)* kwa sababu, kwa maana, kwa kuwa.3 *(when, while)* wakati, pale, -po-, -poki- *~ he was going (when he was going)* alipokuwa akienda. 4 *~ for instance* kwa mfano. 5 *(so ~ to)* ili *he ran so ~ to overtake him* alipiga mbio ili kumpita. 6 **as...as** almradi, madhali, kwa wakati wote. ~ **long** ~ *you are here let's finish the work* almradi uko hapa njoo tumalize kazi. ~ **far** ~ *(ever) I can* kwa kadiri niwezavyo *this ~ well ~ that* hiki na kile pia, hiki pamoja na kile *men ~ well ~ women* wanaume kwa wanawake. ~ **to,** ~ **for** kwa mintarafu ya, ~ **yet** hadi sasa. ~ **from** kuanzia. ~ **if/though** kana kwamba. **same** ~ sawa na.

asafoetida *n* mvuje.

asbestos *n* asbesto.

asbestosis *n* uasbesto: ugonjwa uletwao na asbesto.

ascar *n (pl) (bio)* minyoo mviringo, askari.

ascend *vt, vi* panda, paa *~ the throne* kuwa mfalme. **~ancy/~ency** *n* mamlaka. **~ant/~ent** *adj.*

ascent. upaaji, upandaji *the ~ of mountain* upandaji mlima.

ascension *n* 1 *see ascent.* 2 mpao, kupaa. 3 **The A** ~ sikukuu ya kupaa Yesu Kristo mbinguni.

ascertain *vt* hakikisha, yakinisha. **~able** *adj.* **~ment** *n.*

ascetic *n* mtu anayejinyima raha na anasa *adj* -a kujinyima anasa za mwili. **~ally** *adv.* ~ **ism** *n.*

ascorbic *adj* -enye vitamini **c** ~ **acid** asidi askobiki, vitamini **c**.

ascribe *vt* dhani kuwa sababu ya *he ~d his failure to bad luck* alidhani alishindwa kwa bahati mbaya. 2 -pa, patia, pachika. **ascription** *n.*

asdic *n* kipeleleza nyambizi.

aseptic *adj* -sio na bakteria. **asepsis** *n.*

asexual *adj* 1 -sojinsi. 2 -so na nyege. **~ity** *n.*

ash[1] *n (bot)* mjivujivu (aina ya mti).

ash[2] *n* jivu *(fig) reduce* to **~s** teketeza. **~y** *adj (fig)* -eupe kwa uso. **~-bin/~-can** *n* pipa la taka *adj (bot)* -a mjivujivu; -a (rangi ya) majivu, kijivu. **~-pit** *n* shimo la kufukia majivu. **~-tray** *n* kisahani cha majivu. **A~-wednesday** *n (rel)* Jumatano ya Majivu, siku ya kwanza ya Kwaresima.

ashamed *adj* enye kuona haya, enye kutahayari *be ~ of somebody/ something* aibishwa na, onea haya *I am ~ of you* unaniaibisha.

ashlar *n* jiwe la pembe mraba (lililochongwa).

ashore *adv* pwani, ufukweni *go ~* shuka pwani.

Asia *n.* Asia, **~ian** *adj* Mwasia. **~tic** *n adj.*

aside *adv* 1 upande, kando, pembeni. 2 *(in private)* faraghani, kwa siri *set ~ (judgement)* futa, tangua hukumu *n* 1 maneno ya pembeni *an ~* maneno (hasa katika tamthiliya) ambayo waigizaji wengine hawapaswi kuyasikia. 2 *(of speech)* mchepuko: maneno yanayoingizwa katika hotuba ambayo yako nje ya hotuba.

asinine *adj* 1 -a punda, -a kama punda. 2 *(fig)* -pumbavu sana.

ask *vt, vi* 1 *(question)* uliza, hoji. *~ after* ulizia hali, *~ the way (the time)* uliza njia (saa). ~ **for** tafuta *don't ~ for trouble* usitafute balaa. 2 *(request)* taka, omba, sihi. 3 *(invite)* alika, karibisha. **~ing** *n it's yours for the* **~ing** ukiomba utapewa.

askance *adv (only in) look ~ at a person* tazama (mtu) kichongochongo, tazama kwa shaka/kwa wasiwasi.

askew *adv* mshazari, upande *her nose was ~* pua yake ilikuwa ya mshazari.

aslant *adv, prep.* upande, mshazari.

asleep *adv, pref, adj* usingizini *(be) ~* lala *(sound/fast ~)* lala fofofo.

2 *(of joints of the body)* -fa ganzi.
aslope *adj* -a (kwa) kuinama.
ASP *abbr. of* Afro-Shirazi Party (Muungano wa chama cha Waafrika na Washirazi).
asp *n (bot)* nyoka sumu(wa Misri na Libya).
asparagus *n (bot)* asparaga: namna ya mboga.
aspect *n* 1 *(of people or things)* sura. 2 kipengele. 3 *(of house, thing etc)* mwelekeo *a house with a southern ~* nyumba inayoelekea kusini. 4 *(gram)* hali. **~ual** *adj.*
asperity *n* ukali, hamaki, harara *(pl)* **asperities** makali (k.m. maneno, hali ya hewa, ya maisha).
asperse *vt* kashifu, singizia, zulia jambo, sengenya; shutumu. **aspersion** *n* 1 kitendo cha kumkashifu mtu *(only in) cast~* kashifu. 2 unyunyiziaji maji ya baraka.
asphalt *n* lami *vt* tandaza lami.
asphodel *n (bot)* asfodeli: aina ya myungiyungi.
asphyxia *n* hali ya kukosa hewa ya kutosha. **asphyxiate** *vt* kaba, nyima pumzi. **~tion** *n.*
aspic *n* nyamaute.
aspiration *n* 1 *(gram)* mpumuo. 2 hamu ya kupata (kitu bora n.k.).
aspirator *n (tech)* aspireta: kisharabu.
aspire *vi* gombea, tamani, weka lengo la kupata kitu fulani. **aspirant** *n* mgombea, mtamani.
aspirin *n* aspirini.
ass[1] *n* 1 punda/ kihongwe. 2 *(fig)* mjinga, baradhuli *don't make such an ~ of yourself* usiwe mjinga kiasi hicho *a perfect ~* mpumbavu mkubwa.
ass[2] *see* **arse**.
assagai *see* **assegai**.
assail *vt* 1 *(with)* shambulia vibaya, chokoza, sumbua *~ somebody with questions* shambulia kwa maswali *~ed with the worries* sumbuliwa na mawazo. 2 *(fig) he ~ed the question* with vigour alilikabili swali kwa uthabiti. **~able** *adj* -a kushambulika.
~ant *n* mshambuliaji.
assasin *n* mwuaji. **~ation** *n* mauaji ya namna hiyo. **~ate** *vt* ua (aghalabu kwa kukodiwa na kwa sababu za kisiasa au dini).
assault *n* 1 uvamizi, shambulio (lolote la maombi, n.k.). 2 **~ (on, upon)** shambulio la ghafula (k.m. katika vita), uvamiaji, *(leg) ~ and battery* mashambulio ya nguvu, mapigo *vt* 1 vamia. 2 najisi.
assay *vt* 1 pima ubora wa metali (uliomo katika mawe yenye madini). 2 changanua kiasi cha dutu n.k. *n (chem)* uchanganuzi wa kiasi cha dutu (iliyomo katika mawe ya madini). **assegai** *n* sagai, mkuki (wa Wazulu).
assemble *vt* 1 kusanya, leta pamoja. 2 *(mech.)* unga pamoja sehemu za mashine *vi* kusanyika, kutana pamoja. **assemblage** *n* 1 *(of people/ things)* mkusanyiko, kongamano; *(art)* kitu kilichoungwaungwa k.m. mashine. 2 kuweka pamoja, kuunganisha. **assembly** *n* 1 kusanyiko, mkutano. 2 baraza **National ~** Bunge. 3 uunganishaji pamoja wa sehemu za (mashine n.k.) *~shop/plant* karakana ya kuunganishia *~ hall* bwalo, ukumbi wa mkutano *~ line* mashine na/au watu wanaofanya kazi hatua kwa hatua katika kuunda au kutengeneza kitu. 4 *(mil)* kuita askari (kwa ngoma au tarumbeta).
assent *vi (to)* kubali, idhinisha *n* idhini, kibali, ikibali, ruhusa *by common ~* kila mtu akikubali *with one ~* kwa kauli moja.
assert *vt* 1 dai, tetea (haki) kwa dhati. 2 tangaza, sema. **~ oneself** onyesha madaraka, jionyesha haki. **~ive** *adj.* **~vely** *adv.* **~tion** *n* utetezi wa haki; dai thabiti; *mere ~tion* maneno matupu *~ion of his rights* dai la haki yake.
assess *vt* 1 kadiria, panga kiasi (cha kodi, faini n.k.). *~ing officer* mkadiriaji, **~able** *adj.* 1 **~ment** *n*

ukadiriaji, makadirio, **~or** *n* 1 mkadiriaji. 2 *(leg)* mzee wa baraza.
asset *n* 1 *(usu pl)* **~s** raslimali, mali. 2 sifa au kitu chenye manufaa (k.m. ujuzi, elimu, kipaji, n.k.).
asseverate *vt (formal)* nena kwa uthabiti. **asseveration** *n*
assiduity *n* 1 uangalifu katika utendaji. **assiduous** *adj* -angalifu. **assiduously** *adv*.
assign *vt* 1 toa, -pa, gawia (vitu, kazi) *~ the task to Ali* mpe kazi Ali. 2 teua, taja *~the professor to the presidency* teua profesa kwa uraisi. 3 weka/panga (tarehe, siku ya kufanyika jambo). 4 *(leg)* hawilisha. **~able** *adj*. **~ment** *n* 1 utoaji. 2 uteuzi. 3 upangaji. 4 uhawilishaji. **~ation** *n* ahadi ya kukutana (aghalabu wapenzi), kuonana, miadi.
assimilate *vt, vi* 1 lishiza (chakula) baada ya mmeng'enyo *food that ~s easily* chakula kinacholishizwa kwa urahisi. 2 -wa/fanya mwenyeji; staarabika/staarabisha. 3 silimisha. 4 chukua, pata (maarifa, fikra n.k). **assimilation** *n* 1 mlishizo. 2 usilimishaji: sera ya Wareno na Wafaransa ya kuwageuza wenyeji wafanane kama wao. **assimilative** *adj*.
assist *vt, vi* saidia, auni. **~ance** *n* msaada/ muawana. **~ant** *n* msaidizi.
assize *n* kesi inayoongozwa na jaji na wazee wa baraza.
associate *vt* husisha, shirikisha, unganisha (watu au mambo katika fikira) *~ Egypt with the Nile* husisha Misri na mto wa Nile *vi* shirikiana na, ongea na, fanya urafiki na *a person to ~ with* mtu wa kushirikiana naye *n* mshiriki, mwenzi, rafiki *adj* -lioshiriki, -shiriki *~judge* jaji mshiriki. **association** *n* 1 ushirikiano, mwungano *~ of ideas* mwungano wa mawazo. 2 *(society)* ushirika, jumuiya, shirikisho, chama *articles of ~* kanuni ya kampuni *form an ~* unda chama. 3 *(meaning)* maana, ukumbusho, *it has many old ~ for us* inatukumbusha mambo mengi yaliyopita. **associative** *adj*.
assonance *n (ling & lit)* mshabaha wa irabu za shadda katika maneno mawili au zaidi. **assonant** *adj*.
assort *vt* gawanya, panga namna mbalimbali *vi*patana, afiki, chukuana na *~well with something* patana/chukuana vyema na. **~ed** *adj* 1 anuwai, -a namna mbalimbali. 2 -liochanganyika, -liopangwa vizuri, -enye kupatana. **~ment** *n* mkusanyiko wa vitu anuwai.
assuage *vt* tuliza, punguza, poza (maumivu, hamu) *~ thirst* tuliza kiu. **assuasive** *adj* -a kupoza.
assume *vt* 1 sadiki, ona, (bila ushahidi/uthibitisho), (ji)chukulia. 2 twaa, chukua *~office* twaa ofisi. 3 jifanya. **assumption** *n* 1 wazo, dhana, neno lisilohakikishwa **on the ~that** kwa kuamini kuwa 2 utwaaji. 3 *(rel) The ~ of Our Lady* Kupazwa kwa Bikira Maria Mbinguni.
assurance *n* 1 *(confidence)* imani, moyo wa kujiamini. 2 ahadi, uhakika. 3 *(rare)* majivuno/ ufidhuli. 4 *(guarantee)* bima/ dhamana *life ~* bima ya maisha. 5 yakini, uhakikisho.
assure *vt* 1 ahidi. 2 thibitisha hakikisha. 3 aminisha. 4 dhamini, wekea bima **rest assured (that)** ondoa wasiwasi, poa, amini kuwa. **assuredly** *adv* kwa yakini, kwa hakika.
asterisk *n*. kinyota: alama ya nyota ambayo hutumika kuashiria jambo katika maandishi.'
astern *adv* 1 (*naut*) shetrini. 2 (kwa) nyuma *fall ~ (of)* baki nyuma.
asteroid *n* asteroidi: gimba dogo, sayari ndogo.
asthma *n* pumu. **~tic** *adj* -enye pumu.
astigmatism *n (med)* 1 uastigmati dosari katika jicho/lenzi inayozuia fokasi sahihi. **astigmatic** *adj*.
astir *adj*, 1 -enye kusisimkwa, -a kufuruka. 2 *(dated)* -a macho, -lio amka. *adv* kwa msisimko, kwa kufurika.
astonish *vt* staajabisha, shangaza.

~ed -lioduwaa, -lioshangazwa. **~ing** *adj*. **~ingly** *adv*. **~ment** *n* mastaajabu, mshangao, mduwao.
astound *vt* shangaza, staajabisha, tia bumbuazi, shtusha. **~ing** *adj*.
astraddle *adv, adj see* **astride**
astral *adj* -a nyota, -a kutoka kwenye nyota.
astray *adv*, nje ya *go* ~ potea, nje ya mstari, potoka *lead* ~ potosha, poteza.
astride *adv* kwa kutagaa, kwa kumagamaga, kimagamaga.
astringent *n* kunyasi: kitu kinachosababisha tishu laini kujikunyata na kubana mishipa ya damu *adj* 1 -a kunyasi. 2 *(fig)* kali ~ *remarks* maneno makali.
astro *(pref)* -a nyota,-a anga la juu.
astrodome *n* dirisha dogo (juu ya ndege linalotumiwa na rubani).
astrolabe *n* astrolabu: chombo kilichotumiwa zamani kupimia urefu wa jua, nyota n.k.
astrology *n* unajimu. **astrological** *adj*. **astrologer** *n* mnajimu.
astronaut *n* mwanaanga.
astronomy *n* falaki. **astronomer** *n* majusi, mwanafalaki. **astronomical** *adj* -a kifalaki/elimu ya sayari; *(fig)* -ingi mno.
astrophysics *n* astrofizikia: sayansi ya hali ya nyota kikemikali na kimaumbile.
astute *adj* 1 -erevu, -epesi wa kung'amua. 2 -janja. **~ly** *adv*. **~ness** *n*.
asunder *adv* 1 *(of two or more things)* mbalimbali *they were split* ~ walitenganishwa mbalimbali. 2 vipande vipande *come* ~ vunjika vipande vipande *tear* ~ chana vipande vipande.
asylum *n* 1 kimbilio; mahali pa amani na usalama; *political* ~ kimbilio la hifadhi ya kisiasa. 2 *(old use)* hospitali watunzwapo wenda wazimu.
asymmetry *n* isopacha. **asymmetrical** *adj* kwa namna isopacha.
at prep 1 *(indicating place)* -ni, kwa ~ *home* nyumbani ~ *someone's* kwa fulani. **at-home** *n* tafrija inayofanyika nyumbani kwa wakati uliopangwa. 2 *(indicating direction or goal)* *aim* ~ lenga; *throw* ~ rushia. 3 *(indicating action)* ~*work* kazini *the children are* ~ *playing* watoto wanacheza *she is good* ~ *athletics* yeye ni hodari katika riadha. 4 *(indicating time)* ~ *once* mara moja ~ *five* saa kumi na moja ~ *first* mwanzoni ~ *last* hatimaye, mwishoni. 5 *(value)* bei ~ *two shillings a kilo* shilingi mbili kwa kilo ~ *a loss* kwa hasara. 6 ~ *war* vitani ~ *rest* mapumzikoni ~ *length* kwa kirefu *(Idiom) not* ~ *all* sivyo kabisa; si kitu ~ *any rate* kwa vyo-vyote.
atavism *n* uibukaji wa tabia, sura, umbo n.k. la zamani au ambalo halikutokea kwa vizazi vingi. **atavistic** *adj*.
ate *see* **eat**.
atelier *n. (Fr)* 1 studio. 2 karakana.
atheism *n* ukanaji Mungu: imani kwamba hakuna Mungu. **atheist** *n* mkanamungu. **atheistic** *adj* -a kukana Mungu.
athirst *adj (for)* -enye kiu, -enye shauku ya/ -enye uchu wa.
athlete *n*. mwanariadha. **athletic** *adj* 1 -a riadha. 2 aliyekakawana, shupavu wa mwili; -a miraba minne. **athletics** *n* riadha.
athwart *adv (naut)* kwa kukingama.
atilt *adj* -a upande, -liokaa upande *run or ride* ~ shambulia kwa farasi na mkuki *(for hat) with one's hat* ~ akiwa na kofia upande.
Atlantic *adj* -a Atlantiki ~ *Ocean* Bahari ya Atlantiki.
atlas *n* atlasi: kitabu cha ramani.
atmosphere *n* 1 angahewa. 2 hewa ya mahali. 3 *(surroundings)* mazingira, hali ~*of peace and calm* hali ya amani na utulivu. **atmospheric** *adj* -a hewa ~*condition* hali ya hewa, -a angahewa. **~pressure** kanieneo ya angahewa. **atmospherics** mikwaruzo

(ya redio).
atoll *n* kisiwa cha matumbawe.
atom *n* 1 atomu. 2 kipande kidogo mno, chembe *not an ~* hakuna hata chembe *smashed to ~s* imepondwa kabisa. **~ic** *adj* -a atomu. **~ic bomb** bomu la atomu. **~ize** *vt* 1 fanya kuwa chembechembe. 2 puliza manukato kwa mrashi. **~zation** *n* .**~zer** *n* mrashi, kirashi.
atonal *adj (mus)* -siofuata mfumo maalum wa sauti. **~ity** *n.*
atone *vt (for)* lipia kosa. **~ment** *n the Atonement (rel)* upatanisho wa Mungu na binadamu kwa maisha na kifo cha Yesu; mateso na kifo cha
atonic *adj (phon)* -sio -a toni.
atop *adv* ~ **(of)** juu ya.
atrabilious *adj (rare)* -a huzuni, -a majonzi.
atrocious *adj* 1 -ovu, -a kikatili, -baya mno. 2 *(colloq)* -baya sana. **~ness** *n.* **~ly** *adv.* **atrocity** *n* 1 uovu, ukatili. 2 *(pl)* maovu.
atrophy *n. (med)* kufifia, kupungua, kupotewa na nguvu mwilini; *(fig)* kuharibika kwa tabia *vt* fifisha (mwili) *vi* fifia, pungua, potewa na nguvu (mwilini).
attaboy *int. (sl)* heko!
attach *vt/ vi* 1 fungia, shikiza. 2 *(of documents etc)* ambatisha *no suspicion* **~es** *to them* hawatiliwi shaka. 3 *(passive) be* **~ed** *to someone* penda mtu sana, ganda. 4 ~ **oneself to** jitia, jiingiza *~ oneself to a party* jiingiza katika chama. 5 *(mil)* **~ed to** teuliwa kuwa kwenye kikosi kingine kama mtaalam. 6 *(seize)* tilia maana, ona, dhani *~ much importance to* tilia maanani sana. 7 *(leg)* shika, kamata, chukua kisheria. **~ment** *n* 1 uambatishaji. 2 kiambatisho, kifuasi. 3 penzi, upendo. 4 kushika mali ya mtu kisheria. 5 **an ~ment to** kuteuliwa kufanya kazi fulani. attache' *n* mwambata **cultural ~** mwambata wa utamaduni. ~ **-case** mkoba (wa hati n.k).
attack *vt* 1 shambulia. 2 *(of words)* suta. 3 *(of disease)* pata, shik(w)a. 4 anza *n* 1 shambulio. 2 masuto. 3 kupat(w)a. 4. uanzaji. **~er** *n* mshambuliaji.
attain *vt,vi* 1 *(to)* fikia, fika *~ to perfection* fikia ukamilifu/ upeo. 2 pata *~ power etc.* pata mamlaka n.k. **~able** *adj.* **~ment** *n.* 1. kupata *easy difficult of* **~ment** rahisi/-gumu kupatikana. 2 *(pl)* **~ments** elimu, ujuzi.
attainder *n (leg)* upotezaji wa haki za uraia na umilikaji wa mali (kufuatia hukumu ya kifo au kuharamishwa). **attaint** *vt (leg)* hukumiwa kukosa haki za uraia na umilikaji wa mali.
attar *n* halwaridi: manukato ya maua ya waridi.
attempt *vt* jaribu *n* jaribio. **an ~ on/upon somebody's life** jaribio la kuua mtu. 2 ~ **to do sth/at doing sth** jaribio la kufanya kitu. 3 **an ~ at** babio.
attend *vt, vi* 1 shughulikia, sikiliza, tumikia. 2 *(on/upon)* uguza/ hudumia, lea. 3 hudhuria. 4 *(formal) (accompany)* fuatana/ ambatana na *a method ~ed by great difficulties* njia inayoambatana na shida kubwa. **~ance** *n* 1 kuhudumia **be in ~ance on** ngojea, fuatana na, hudumia. 2 mahudhurio. 3 mkusanyiko. **~ant** *adj* 1 -a kufuatana na, -a kuambatana na. 2 -a kungojea, -uguzi *n* 1 mtumishi, mhudumu *library ~* mhudumu wa maktaba. 2 *(pl)* msafara, wajumbe wa mtu mashuhuri *Premier and his* **~ants** Waziri Mkuu na msafara wake.
attention *n* 1 uangalifu, usikivu, usikizi *pay (give) ~ to* angalia, zingatia sikiliza, fanya kwa makini **attract** ~ vuta macho, fanya *draw ~* vuta nadhari. 2 *(pl)* wema. *~ Mr. X,* aione X. 3 *(mil.) ~ !* mguu sawa! *come to /stand at ~* tulia, bakamaa. **attentive** *adj (to)* sikivu, angalifu. **~ly** *adv.* **ness** *n.*
attenuate *vt (formal)* fanya -embamba, kondesha, dhoofisha, punguza.

attest *vt, vi* 1 shuhudia, thibitisha ~ **a signature**. rasimisha sahihi. *~ed* mjarabu *~ed milk* maziwa mjarabu: yaliyothibitishwa kuwa hayana ugonjwa). 2 apa, apisha. 3 jiunga na jeshi. ~ **to** shuhudia. **~ation** *n* uthibitisho.

attic *n* darini.

attire *vt* vaa, vika, visha *n* mavazi, nguo.

attitude *n* 1 (*position*) jinsi (namna) ya kusimama au kukaa, mkao. 2 mtazamo, fikra, msimamo, mwelekeo *a negative* ~ mtazamo hasi dhidi ya mtu fulani. **attitudinize** *vi* jifanya, jifaragua (kwa kuchukua tabia na vitendo vya mwingine)/ sema, andika, tenda kwa namna ya kuathiriwa.

attorney *n* 1 wakili, mwanasheria, *power of* ~ uwakili. 2 **A~-General** Mwanasheria Mkuu. 3 ***State A*** ~ Wakili wa Serikali.

attract *vt* 1 vuta *a magnet ~s iron* sumaku huvuta chuma. 2 pendeza, vutia **feel ~ed to somebody** jihisi kuvutiwa (kupendezwa) na mtu fulani. **~ion** *n* 1 mvuto. 2 kivutio **~iveness** *n* uvutivu. **~ive** *adj*. **~ively** *adv*.

attribute *vt* ona/dhani ndiyo sababu ya, fikiria kuwa tabia/matokeo ya *I ~ his illness to the rain* naona mvua ndiyo sababu ya ugonjwa wake *n* 1 tabia, sifa ya kiasili ya *Mercy is an ~ of God* Huruma ni sifa ya Mungu. 2 ishara ya mtu au cheo chake. **attributable** *adj*. **attribution** *n*. **attributive** *adj (ling)* vumishi ~ *adjective* kivumishi angama.

attrition *n* 1 msuguano. 2 kulika kwa kusuguana *war of* ~ vita ya msuguano: (ambapo kila upande unasubiri vita idhoofishe kabisa upande mwingine). 3 *(Theol)* majuto.

attune *vt (to)* oanisha, patanisha; zoeza. **~ment** *n*.

atypical *adj* -iso kawaida.

aubergine *n (bot)* biringani.

auburn *adj* (of hair) hudhurungi /kahawia.

auction *n* mnada *public* ~ mnada wa hadhara *vt* nadi *put up to* ~ piga mnada. **~eer** *n* dalali, mnadi.

audacious *adj* 1 jasiri, shupavu. 2 fidhuli, safihi. 3 shujaa pite. **audacity** *n*. **~ly** *adv*.

audible *adj* -a kusikika *his speech was* ~ hotuba yake ilisikika. **audibly** *adv*. **audibility** *n*.

audience *n* 1 hadhira *have an ~ with the President* kutana na Rais (kwa mazungumzo rasmi). 2 wasikilizaji (wa pamoja na waliosambaa). 3 *(of a book)* wasomaji.

audio *pref/ adj* -a kusikia. ~ **visual aids** vielelezo (vya kusikia na kuona).

audit *n* ukaguzi wa mahesabu *vt* kagua mahesabu. **~ing** *n* ukaguzi. ~ *n* mkaguzi wa mahesabu.

audition *n* 1 uwezo wa kusikia. 2 majaribio ya sauti/uigizaji/utumiaji wa ala n.k. *vt give an ~ to* jaribu/pima sauti n.k. (kwa ajili ya kuajiriwa).

auditor *n* msikizi. **~ium** *n* bwalo /ukumbi (wa mikutano, maonyesho n.k.). **~y** *adj* -a kusikia, -a kusikizia.

au fait *adj (Fr)* -juzi, -stadi, -zoefu.

au fond *adv (Fr)* kimsingi.

auger *n* kekee.

aught *n (arch)* chochote, kitu chochote *for ~ I care/know* sijali chochote /sina habari.

augment *vt/ vi* kuza, ongeza, zidisha, ongezeka. **~ation** *n* kuongeza, kuongezeka, ongezeko.

augur *n* mbashiri, mtabiri *vi, vt* bashiri, tabiri ~ *well/ ill* ashiria uzuri/ ubaya wa jambo. **~y** *n*. ubashiri; (*omen*) ndege, ishara.

august *adj* -tukufu, adhimu.

August *n* Agosti: mwezi wa nane.

aunt *n* shangazi, mama mdogo /mkubwa, mke wa mjomba au mke wa baba mdogo au mkubwa.

au pair *n* mtumishi wa nyumbani wa kike (wa kutoka nchi nyingine ambaye ujira wake ni chakula, mavazi/ malazi na masomo.

aura *n* hali inayoashiria wema au ubaya wa mtu.

aural *adj* -a sikio, -a kusikika ~ *surgeon* daktari wa masikio. **aurist** *n* mtaalam wa magonjwa ya masikio.
aureole, aureola *n* 1 *(rel)* duara (inayochorwa kuzunguka vichwa vya watakatifu katika picha, kuonyesha utukufu wao, taji ya dhahabu). 2 taji takatifu. 3 duara linalozunguka (mwezi).
au revoir *int (Fr)* kwa heri ya kuonana.
auric *adj* -a dhahabu.
auricle *n* 1 orikali: sehemu ya nje ya sikio. 2 mojawapo ya chemba mbili za juu katika moyo.
auricular *adj* 1 -a kuhusiana na sikio, -liopatikana kwa kusikika. 2 -liofahamika kwa kutolewa taarifa.
auspice *n (pl)* 1 mtabiri anayetumia nyendo za ndege/ishara. 2 bahati njema. **auspicious** *adj* -heri -a bahati, -a ndege njema. **auspiciously** *adv*. **auspiciousness** *n* msaada, himaya, fadhili, *under the ~ of* kwa msaada wa.
Aussie *n (sl)* Mwaustralia.
austere *adj* 1 *(of person, his behaviour)* -a kushikilia maadili, -kali. 2 *(of a way of living, places, styles)* -a kawaida, sahili. **~ ly** *adv*. **austerity** *n*.
Australian *n* Mwaustralia *adj* -a Kiaustralia; -a Australia.
autarchy *n* mamlaka kamili, udikteta.
autarky *n* kujitosheleza (hasa kwa uchumi wa nchi).
authentic *adj* halisi, thabiti, -a kweli, hakika. **~ally** *adv*. **~ity** *n* uhalisi. **~ate** *vt* hakikisha, thibitisha (kuwa ni kweli). **authentication** n.
author *n* 1 mtunzi, mwandishi. 2 muumbaji. **~ship** *n* 1 utunzi. 2 utambulishi wa mwandishi wa kazi ya sanaa. **~ess** *n* mwandishi mwanamke.
authority *n* 1 mamlaka: uwezo wa kisheria wa kutenda jambo *lawful ~* mamlaka halali. 2 mtu mwenye mamlaka/amri mkuu *he is the ~ here* yeye ndiye mwenye mamlaka hapa. 3 serikali *local ~* serikali za mitaa. 4 bingwa *he is an ~ on Kiswahili* yu bingwa wa Kiswahili. ***authoritarian*** *adj* -enye kulazimisha utii, -a mabavu, -enye kuunga mkono mfumo wa namna hii. **~ism** *n*. **authoritative** *adj* 1 -enye mamlaka. 2 -a amri 3 -a kuaminika. **~ly** *adv*.
authorize *vt* 1 *(give leave)* toa idhini, ruhusu. 2. *(order)* amuru, toa mamlaka. **~d** *agent* ajenti mwenye mamlaka. **authorization** *n*.
autism *n (psych)* ugonjwa wa akili wa watoto. **autistic** *adj*.
auto *pref* -enyewe. **~car** *n* motakaa. **~biography** *n* tawasifu, habari za maisha ya mtu zilizoandikwa na yeye mwenyewe. **~biographic, ~biographical** *adj*. **~biographer** *n* mwandishi wa tawasifu.
autocracy. *n* udikiteta: utawala wa mtu mmoja. **autocrat** *n* dikteta, mtawala pekee. **autocratic** *adj*. **autocratically** *adv*.
auto-dafe *n (pl)* **autos-dafe**: hukumu za mazishi ya kidini - (agh. huchomwa moto), kitendo cha imani.
autograph *n* 1 mwandiko binafsi, sahihi halisi ya mtu. 2 *(book/album)* kitabu chenye sahihi, agh. za watu maarufu. **~y** *n* sayansi ya miandiko ya watu.
automatic *adj* 1 -a kujiendesha. 2 *(actions)* -liofanywa bila kufikiri *breathing is ~* kuvuta pumzi hufanywa bila kufikiri *n* mashine ya kujiendesha. **~ally** *adv*. **automate** *vt* fanya ijiendeshe yenyewe.
automation *n* utumiaji wa mitambo inayojiendesha. **automatism** *n*.
automaton/automate *n* 1 roboti: kitu kiendacho chenyewe au kwa mashine iliyowekwa ndani yake. 2 *(fig)* mtu atendaye kama roboti.
automobile *n (US)* motakaa.
autonomy *n* kujitawala. **autonomous** *adj* huru.
autopsy *n see* **postmorterm**.
autumn *n* majira ya kupukutika kwa majani. **~al** *adj* -a wakati wa kupukutika.
auxiliary *adj* saidizi, -a kuongeza nguvu/ msaada ~ *workers*

wafanyakazi wasaidizi ~ *verb* kitenzi kisaidizi *n* 1 msaidizi/kisaidizi. 2 *(pl)* jeshi (askari) lisaidialo.

avail *vt, vi* 1 (lit) saidia, nufaika. 2 *(phr)* ~ ***oneself of*** tumia, jipatia ~ *yourself of every opportunity* tumia kila nafasi. *n* 1 mafanikio, faida, manufaa *it is of little* ~ ina faida ndogo *it was of no* ~ ilikuwa ya bure *to no* ~ bila mafanikio. **~able** *adj* 1 -a kupatikana *the book is not* **~able** kitabu hakipatikani *your ticket is* **~able** *for one week only* tikiti yako ni halali (inaweza kutumika) kwa juma moja tu. 2 (*of person*) -wa na nafasi *are you* **~able** *tomorrow?* una nafasi kesho? **~ability** *n.*

avalanche *n* 1 poromoko theluji (mlimani). 2 *(fig)* lundo (k.m. la barua).

avant garde *(Fr) n* watu wanaovumbua na kujaribia mawazo mapya kabisa yasiyokubalika kwa urahisi; *(fig)* viongozi wanamapinduzi *adj* -a majaribio.

avarice *n* ulafi wa mali, uchoyo, hamu kubwa mno ya kupata kitu. **avaricious** *adj.*

avenge *vt* lipiza kisasi. ~ **oneself** - lipa kisasi. **avenging** *adj.*

avenue *n* 1 barabara yenye miti kando kando. 2 mtaa mpana wenye majengo pembeni. 3 *(fig)* njia ya kufikilia jambo au lengo fulani (usitawi, utajiri n.k.)

aver *vt* 1 nena kwa uthabiti. 2 (*leg*) thibitisha.

average *n* wastani, kadiri *general* ~ wastani wa jumla *adj* -a wastani, -a kadiri, -a katikati, -a kawaida. *vt, vi* 1 tafuta wastani (kwa kuhesabu). 2 fikia wastani fulani *the rainfall ~s 40 inches a year* mvua hufikia wastani wa inchi 40 kwa mwaka.

averse *adj* -ona karaha, -wa na chuki ya *he is ~ to it* akirihishwa nacho. **~ness/ aversion** *n* 1 chuki kubwa. 2 kitu kinachochukiwa *my* **pet aversion** away is nichukiacho sana ni.

avert *vt* 1 zuia, kinga. 2 *(from)* kengeua/geuza (macho, fikra n.k.) mbali na.

aviary *n* tundu kubwa, mahali pa kufugia ndege (hasa katika bustani ya wanyama).

aviation *n* sayansi na ufundi wa vyombo vya anga. **aviator** *n* rubani.

avid *adj (for)* -enye shauku, -enye uchu. **~ity** *n.* **~ly** *adv.*

avocado *n* parachichi.

avocation *n* shughuli za ziada.

avocet *n (bio)* chokowe.

avoid *vt* epa, epuka, ambaa. **~able** *adj.* **~ance** *n.*

avouch *vt (arch)* 1 thibitisha. 2 kiri, ungama, ahidi.

avow *vt* kiri, sema kwa waziwazi, kubali. **~al** *n.*

avuncular *adj (for)* -a mjomba.

await *vt* 1 ngoja, ngojea, subiri. 2 tarajia.

awake/awaken *vt,vi* 1 amka, amsha, toa usingizini. 2 *(to)* tambua, zinduka *adj* -enye kuwa macho *he is* ~ yu macho, *be* ~ fahamu, jihadhari, changamka. **awakening** *n* 1 kuzinduka. 2 utambuzi wa jambo (hasa baya) kwa mara ya kwanza.

award *vt* 1 zawadia/ tunza. 2 lipa, toa ~ *damages* lipa fidia *n* 1 tunzo, zawadi. 2 ruzuku ya masomo. 3 hukumu, uamuzi.

aware *adj* fahamivu, tambuzi, -enye kuwa macho, -wa -enye habari *be* ~ jua, fahamu *I am ~ that* ninafahamu kuwa, nina habari kuwa. ~ **ness** *n* kutambua *self~ness* kujitambua.

awash *adj* jawa na maji; elea.

away *adv* 1 *(kwa)* mbali, kutoka *I saw him some distance* ~ nilimwona kwa mbali *go* ~ ondoka *be* ~ -tokuwepo *he has gone* ~ amekwenda zake *he is* ~ hayuko, amekwenda zake. 2 *(onward, forthwith)* mara moja *right* ~ sasa hivi. 3 *(phr) take ~ with him!* mchukue, mwondolee mbali! *~with you!* toka hapa. 4 *(continuously)* bila kuacha. 5 *make ~ with* iba. 6 do ~ with achana na, futa, *(sl)* ua. 7 mbele ~ *across the horizon* mbele kupita upeo wa macho. 8 *pass* ~ kufa. 9 ~ *match* mechi ya nje ya nyumbani.

awe *n* 1 heshima (iliyochanganyika na hofu). 2 kicho, hofu, woga *keep somebody in* ~ tisha *stand in* ~ *of somebody* heshimu, stahi sana ~ *stricken* ingiwa na hofu.

awful *adj* 1 -a kutisha, -a kuogopa, -a kicho, -baya sana. 2 -a kuogofya *he is an* ~ *scoundrel* yeye ni mtu mbaya sana *I am in* ~ *pain* naumwa sana. **~ly** *adv*. sana.

awhile *adv* kwa muda mfupi, kitambo.

awkward *adj* 1 *(clumsy)* -so stadi, -zito kuelewa au kutenda; *(embarass)* -enye kufedhehesha. 2 gumu, si rahisi. 3 baya ~ *corner* kona mbaya. 4 (of person) korofi *an* ~ *customer* mteja mkorofi. 5 *(embarrassed)* -a kuleta mfadhaiko ~ *silence* ukimya wa kuleta mfadhaiko. **~ness** *adj*. **~ly** *adv*.

awl *n* msharasi.

awning *n* mfuniko (agh, wa turubai juu ya mlango/dirisha kuzuia jua, mvua n.k.).

awry *adj* 1 -liopinda. 2 kombo *go* ~ enda kombo.

ax/axe *n* shoka *he has an* ~ *to grind* ana sababu zake *vt* 1 punguza (gharama, huduma, ajira). 2 fukuza (kazini) (*phr*) *get the* ~ fukuzwa kazi.

axes *see* **axis**.

axil *n* 1 kwapa. 2 (*bot*) kwapajani: sehemu iliyo kati ya kikonyo cha jani na shina. **axillary** *adj (bot)* -a kwapajani ~ *bud* tumbakwapa: chipuko iliyoko kwenye kwapajani.

axiom *n* usemi unaochukuliwa kuwa kweli bila uthibitisho wala hoja. **~atic** *adj*. **~atic (al)***adj* -enye hakika dhahiri (bila uthibitisho).

axis *n* 1 *(math)* jira. 2 *(geo)* mhimili

axial adj 1 -a jira. 2 -a mhimili.

axle *n* ekseli **~-tree** ekseli ya gari inayovutwa na ng'ombe, punda n.k.

ayah *n* yaya, mlezi wa watoto,

aye *adv* 1 ndiyo, naam. 2 *n* (*Parliament*) (*pl*) kura za ndiyo. 3 *(old)* daima.

azure *adj* -a samawati, -a buluu *n* samawati, buluu, rangi ya samawi.

B

B,b be: herufi ya pili katika alfabeti ya Kiingereza.
baa *n* mlio wa kondoo vi lia kama kondoo. **baas** *n (S. Africa)* bwana, bosi.
babble *vi* 1 bwabwaja, tamka sauti zisizo na maana au zisizozoeleka; ropokwa. 2 *(of water)* bubujika: toa sauti kama maji ya kijito. **~r** *n* mropokaji.
babe 1 *n (liter)* mtoto mchanga. 2 *(colloq)* -so na ujuzi/uzoefu, -liye rahisi kudanganyika. 3 *(US. sl)* msichana au mwanamke mdogo.
babel *n* 1 *(rel)* **the Tower of ~** mnara wa Babeli. 2 ghasia, fujo, makelele (hasa ya sauti nyingi pamoja) *what a ~!* makelele gani haya!
babir(o'ussa) *n (bio)* aina ya nguruwe mwitu wapatikanao Sri Lanka.
baboon *n* aina ya nyani.
baby *n* 1 mtoto mchanga, mdogo katika familia au kikundi. **~ carriage** gari la mtoto ~ *talk* lugha ya kitoto. 2 *(prov) throw out the ~ with the bath water* tupa jongoo na mti wake. 3 *(sl)* kidosho, kisura, mrembo. **~hood** *n, adj* -a kitoto *~ish behaviour* tabia ya kitoto. 4 ~ **sit** angalia mtoto wakati wazazi hawapo. **~-sitter** *n* mlezi wa muda. ~ **farmer** *n* mlezi wa watoto wa nje ya ndoa.
baccalaureate *n* 1 (Fr) mtihani wa mwisho wa Elimu ya Sekondari. 2 shahada ya kwanza.
baccarat *n (Fr)* kamari ya karata.
baccate *adj* -a mforsadi.
bacchanal *n* 1 mfuasi wa Bacchus. 2 sherehe ya walevi. *adj* -a kufanana na *Bacchus*, -a kulewalewa. **~lian** *adj* -enye kelele na levi.
bacciferous *adj* -enye kuzaa matunda.
baccivorous *adj* -a mla matunda.
bachelor *n* 1 kapera: mtu ambaye hajaoa. 2 aliyehitimu shahada ya kwanza *adj* -a kumstahili mtu asiyeoa. **~hood**. **~ship** *n* ukapera.
back[1] *n* 1 *(of human body)* nyuma; mgongo: sehemu ya mwili kuanzia shingoni hadi mwisho wa uti wa mgongo. **~bone** uti wa mgongo. **~ ache** maumivu ya mgongo. **~ to front** mbele nyuma. **talk behind someone's ~** sengenya. **lie on one's ~** lala chali. **break ones ~** vunja uti wa mgongo *(fig)* menyeka (na kazi). **break the ~ of** maliza sehemu kubwa/ ngumu ya kazi. **get off someones ~** acha kumsumbua. **put ones ~ into** zamia/ fanya kwa nguvu zote. **turn one's ~ on** kana, kwepa. **with one's ~ to the wall** kabiliwa na hali ngumu, zongwa na maadui. 2 egemea. 3 sehemu ya kitu isiyotumika sana au kuonekana kwa urahisi. 4 *(sport)* beki.
back[2] *adv* 1 nyuma. **go ~ (up) on/from one's word** vunja ahadi, *~ and forth* nenda rudi, huku na huko, mbele na nyuma. 2 (hali/mahali) -pa awali *put ~ the book* rudisha kitabu mahali pa awali. 3 jibu, rudishia *If I hit you, would you hit me ~?* kama nikikupiga utanirudishia. **have/get one's own ~ (on sb)** *(colloq)* jibu mapigo, lipiza kisasi. 4 zamani, zama za zama, -liopita.
back[3] *vt,vi* 1 rudi(sha) nyuma. **~ the oars. ~ the water** rudisha chombo nyuma kwa kasia. 2 ~ **(up)** unga mkono. 3 wekea dau. 4 ~ **down (from)** ghairi. ~ **out of** jitoa. 5 bambia, funika. **~er** *n* mweka dau, mfadhili. **~ing** msaada, wafadhili; ala, waitikiaji. **~ache** *n see back*[1]. **~bencher** *n* mbunge (asiye na cheo kingine bungeni). **~bite** *vt, vi* sengenya, teta. **~r** *n*. **~board** *n* 1 mwegamo. 2 kiegemeo. **~bone** *n* 1 *see back*[1]. 2 *(fig)* nguzo, tegemeo. 3 *(releability)* utumainifu, uhodari *he has no ~* yu dhaifu, yu legelege (wa tabia). **~breaking** *adj* (of work) --a sulubu. **~chat** *n* ufyosi, majibu ya karaha (kijeuri). ~ **date** *vt* weka tarehe ya nyuma. **~door** *n* mlango wa nyuma. ~ **drop** *n* pazia la nyuma (la jukwaa lililorembwa kuonyesha mandhari). **~fire** *vi* lipuka (mapema ndani ya injini. 2 *(fig)* enda kinyume cha matarajio, enda upogo *n* mlipuko

katika eksozi. **~ground** *n* 1 usuli. 2 mahali pa nyuma (sehemu ya sanamu, picha n.k.). 3 mahali pa kufichia. 4 muziki wa chinichini. **~hand** *n* kitengelenyuma **~handed** *adj* a (kutumia) kitengelenyuma ~ **hander** *n* kofi la kitengelenyuma, kofi ya kelfu. **~lash** *n* 1 uduto wa gurudumu. 2 upinzani (hasa dhidi ya siasa au sera iliyoonekana kuungwa mkono awali). **~log** *n* kiporo, limbikizo: kazi ambayo haikumalizika. ~ **number** *n* toleo la nyuma (la gazeti); kitu (chochote) cha zamani; mtu mwenye mawazo ya kizamani. **~pay** *n* karisaji: malipo ya(fedha) nyuma. ~ **seat** *n* kiti cha nyuma chaari. **take a~** jiweka nyuma nyuma. ~side *n* (colloq) makalio, matako. **~slide** *vi* 1 rudia mazoea mabaya. 2 kengeua. **~space** *n* *(of typewriter)* kurudisha nyuma. **~stage** *n* nyuma ya jukwaa (la za. maonyesho *(pl)* ngazi ya nyuma. **~stays** *n (naut) (pl)* kamba za kikono cha mlingoti (zinazoelekea tezi). ~ **street** uchochoro *(pl)* mitaani. ~ **stroke** *n* 1 pigo la nyuma. 2 mtindo wa kuogelea kimangalimangali /kichali. ~ **sword** *n* upanga. ~ **track** *vi* 1 rudi ulikotoka. 2 badilisha/legeza msimamo. **~wash** *n* mkondo wa maji.

backward 1 -a (kuelekea) nyuma. 2 *(dull)* -enye maendeleo kidogo mno a ~ **child** mtoto mzito. 3 -a kurudi ~ *journey* safari ya kurudi. 4 -lo nyuma kimaendeleo ~ *country* nchi iliyo nyuma kimaendeleo. 5 -sojiamini, -enye aibu. **~s** *adv* 1 kinyumenyume *he walked ~s* alitembea kinyumenyume. 2 kabisa, fika *He knows it ~s* anaifahamu fika. **~ness** *n* hali ya kuwa nyuma. **~ly** *adv*.

bad 1 -baya *he has a ~ character* ana tabia mbaya ~ *news* habari mbaya from ~ to worse zidi kuwa baya *a ~ leader* kiongozi mbaya *it's ~ luck/ too* ~ bahati mbaya. 2 -bovu ~ *teeth* meno mabovu *he speaks ~ English* anaongea Kiingereza kibovu. 3 -ovu *a ~ man* **(also fig bad hat/egg/lot)** mtu mwovu. 4 -chafu ~ *language* lugha chafu. 5 -tundu ~ *child* mtoto mtundu. 6 hafifu ~ *light* mwanga hafifu. 7 **go** ~ oza, vunda. 8 **with ~ grace** shingo upande. 9 It wouldn't be a ~ thing isingekuwa vibaya, ingefaa. 10 have a ~ conscience juta, sutwa na dhamira. 11 **~ blood** uadui, chuki. 12 ~ **debt** deni lisilotegemewa kulipwa. 13 **be taken** ~ ugua, ugua zaidi. 14 **feel** ~a) jisikia vibaya/mgonjwa b) sikitika *I feel ~ I can't come* nasikitika kwamba siwezi kuja. 15 **call sb ~ names** tukana, tusi. 16 *be on ~ terms with* toelewana na. 17 ~ **tempered** -enye hasira *n* ubaya, uovu; ubovu. **go to the** ~ potoka, haribika. **~ness** *n* ubaya, uovu, ubovu. **~ly** *adv* 1 vibaya *he's ~ly wounded* amejeruhiwa vibaya. 2 sana *I ~ly want that dress* nataka lile gauni sana. 3 ovyo. 4 **~ly off** maskini.

bade *see* **bid**.

badge *n* 1 tepe, beji. 2 *(fig)* ishara.

badger[1] *n* 1 melesi. 2 ngozi ya melesi.

badger[2] *vt* sumbua, udhi.

badinage *n* mzaha, masihara.

badminton *n* mpira wa vinyoya.

baffle[1] *vt* kanganya, changanya *it ~s description* haielezeki. **baffling** *adj* -a kukanganya/ kukanganyikiwa. **~ment** *n* kuchanganyikiwa.

baffle[2] *n* kizibo: chombo cha kudhibiti mwendo wa gesi, uoevu, au sauti.

bag *n* 1 mfuko. **hand~** mkoba, kibogoshi. **kit** ~ shanta **mail** ~ mfuko wa barua. **sleeping** ~ fumba. **travelling** ~ mkoba wa safari. 2 *(of fishing)* mvuo. 3 *(of hunting)* mawindo. 4 *(pl) (of)* tele. 5 *(sl derog)* mwanamke mbaya. **a ~ of bones** *(of people, animals)* -kondefu sana. ~ **and baggage** vikorokoro. **let the cat out of the** ~ toa siri nje (bila kukusudia). ~ **under the eyes** uvimbe *he has ~under the eyes* macho yake yamevimba *vt,vi* 1 tia katika mfuko, gunia n.k. 2 *(of hunting)* ua, kamata. 3 *(colloq)* chukua *she ~ged the best*

chair alichukua kiti kizuri zaidi. **~gy** *adj* -a kupwaya, -liolegea.
baggage *n* mizigo; vikorokoro. 2 *(colloq)(arch)* msichana(mwanamke) mfidhuli. 3 hema na zana za jeshi. ~ **room** chumba cha mizigo *(of dhow)* feuli. ~ **check** hati ya mizigo/ msafara.
bah *int* puu! neno la kuonyesha dharau/ chukizo.
bail[1] *n (leg)* dhamana. **forfeit one's** ~ poteza dhamana. **~bond** hati ya kudhaminiwa. *vt* ~ **up (out)** dhamini.
bail[2] *see* **bale.**
bailiff *n* 1 *(leg) (Eng)* afisa wa mahakama (hasa anayetwaa mali ya mdeni). 2 *(estate)* msimamizi wa mali. 3 *(leg) (Am)* mfanyakazi wa mahakama hasa tarishi au mlinda mlango. 4 msimamizi/meneja wa shamba.
bairn *n (Scot)* mtoto.
bait *n* 1 chambo. 2 ubembe (kitu kimvutacho mtu afanye jambo) *vt,vi* 1 tia chambo (katika ndoana), ambika. 2 chokoza.
baize *n* kitambaa cha sufi (agh. cha kijani na hutumika kwa kufunika meza).
bake *vt,vi* 1 oka (mkate, nyama n.k.). 2 kausha (kauka); choma (kwa joto la jua au la moto) *~d bricks* matofali ya kuchoma, fukutwa. **~r** *n* mwoka mikate. **~ry** *n* tanuri mikate. **baking powder** *n* hamira. **~r's dozen** kumi na tatu. **baking hot** *adj* -a joto mno. **half ~d** -sio na busara, -a kipumbavu.
baksheesh *n* bahashishi.
balance *n* 1 mizani, kapani. 2 usawa, (wa uzito, nguvu n.k.). 3 baki, sazo. ~ *due* baki inayotakiwa ~ *brought down* baki ya kuanzia. ~ *in hand* masalio, faida tupu. 4 urari *trial* ~ urari, mlinganisho wa hesabu. ~ **of trade** urari wa biashara. 4 **strike a** ~ fikia mapatano ya haki. ~ **sheet** mizania *vt,vi (weigh)* pima katika mizani. 2 *(consider)* angalia pande zote za. 3 *(make equal)* sawazisha ~ *the accounts* sawazisha hesabu. 4 lingana. ~d *adj* sawasawa ~*d diet* mlo kamili. 5 **in the** ~ mashakani. 6 *keep one's* ~ simama bila kuanguka; -toyumba. 7 *on* ~ baada ya kufikiria yote. 8 *off* ~ -a kutetereka.
balcony *n* 1 roshani: ubaraza wa ghorofani. 2 *(in theatre)* viti vya juu.
bald *adj* 1 -enye upaa (upara). 2 ~ **headed**. ~ **pate** mtu mwenye upara. 2 -sio na nywele wala nyoya. 3 -sio na majani. 4 *(fig)* -kavu *a* ~ *statement* tamko bayana. **~ness** *n*. **~ly** *adv (always fig)* waziwazi, bila kuficha, kinaganaga.
balderdash *n* upuzi, upumbavu (wa maneno).
bale[1] *n* mtumba, robota, *vt* fungasha (katika mitumba/robota).
bale[2] *vt* 1 (also **bail**) ~ *out* fua maji (katika chombo). 2 **~out (of)** chupa kwa mwavuli (kutoka kwenye ndege inayotaka kulipuka au kuanguka).
baleful *adj* -ovu, -a chuki -a kutaka kuumiza a ~ look jicho la chuki. **~ly** *adv*.
balk, baulk *n* 1 boriti kubwa. 2 *(hindrance)* kizuizi *vt,vi* 1 zuia (kufikia lengo fulani). 2 sita. 3 simama.
ball[1] *n* 1 mpira *throw the* ~ tupa mpira. **the ~ is in your court** mpira uko kwako. 2 bonge, donge ~ of mud bonge la matope. **meat** ~ kababu. 3 *pl sl* (a) mapumbu, makende (b) *(int)* mavi, upuuzi mtupu. 4 *(arch)* risasi. 5 **eye** ~ mboni ya jicho. 6 ~ *of the foot* sehemu ya wayo chini ya kidole gumba. 7 ~ **bearing** gololi. 8 **on the** ~ *(infront)* hodari. 9 **play** ~ shirikiana. 10 **set the** ~ **rolling** anzisha (jambo, mazungumzo n.k.). 11 ~ **cok** mtungi (wa tangi ya maji). 12 ~ **pen**. ~ **point pen** bolpeni *vt,vi* 1 tengeneza donge, fanya donge. 2 *(vulg)* lalana. 3 *(up)* boronga. **~s up** vurugu tupu.
ball[2] *n* dansi rasmi. ~ **dress** *n* gauni rasmi la dansi. ~ **room** bwalo la dansi **have a** ~ starehe sana.

ballad *n* wimbo-pendwa, utumbuizo: wimbo upendwao sana (hasa wa asili) wa mapenzi au masimulizi.
ballast *n* 1 *(of ship)* farumi. 2 *(of railway, road)* kokoto. 3 *(fig)* uthabiti wa akili *vt* weka farumi; weka kokoto.
ballet *n* 1 bale: dansi yenye maigizo (bila maongezi wala nyimbo). 2 kundi la wacheza bale. ~ **dancer** *n* mcheza bale. ~**erina** *n* mcheza bale wa kike ~ **mane** *n* shabiki wa bale.
ballistic *adj* -a kuhusu mwendo wa risasi, makombora n.k. ~**s** elimu ya mwendo huu.
ballocks *n (vulg)* see **bollocks**.
balloon *n* 1 ~ **barrage** kizuio cha maputo. **hot air** ~ puto la hewa ya joto. 2 *(of cartoon)* sehemu inayobeba maneno ya wahusika. *vi (swell)* vimba, kama puto. *n* mwanaputo. ~**ist** mrukaji katika puto.
ballot *n* kura, *secret* ~ kura ya siri. ~-**box** sanduku la kura *vi (for)* pigia kura.
ballyhoo *n (colloq)* 1 utangazaji (wa vitu au watu) wa fujo na makelele. 2 fujo, makelele.
balm *n* 1 malhamu. 2 *(fig)* kitulizo, faraja. ~**my** *adj* 1 *(of air)* mwanana, -enye kutuliza. 2 -nayoleta nafuu. 3 -a kunukia. 4 see **barmy**.
baluster *n* see **banister**
balustrade *n* uzio: safu ya viguzo vyenye ubao (juu ukingoni mwa roshani au ukingoni mwa ngazi ya kupandia).
bambino *n* 1 *(It)* mtoto mchanga. 2 picha/sanamu ya mtoto Yesu.
bamboo *n* mwanzi.
bamboozle *vt (colloq)* laghai, danganya, ghilibu.
ban *n* amri ya kupiga marufuku *There is a ~ on smoking* ni marufuku kuvuta sigara *vt* 1 kataza, piga marufuku. ~**ed** marufuku. ~**ning order** amri ya kupiga marufuku.
banal *adj* -a kawaida mno, -siovutia. ~**ity** *n* 1 hali isiyovutia. 2 *(pl)* maneno yasiyo na maana; jambo duni (hafifu).
banana *n* 1 ndizi. 2 ~ **tree** mgomba *bunch of* ~ chane *stalk of* ~ mkungu ~ *republic* nchi inayoendelea (hasa za Marekani ya Kati na Kusini) yenye siasa isiyo imara.
band[1] *n* 1 ukanda, ugwe. ~ **saw** msumeno wa ukanda. 2 utepe. 3 *(stripe)* mstari, mlia. 4 *(of radio)* bendi. 5 **rubber/elastic** ~ elastiki *vt* tilia ukanda/mstari.
band[2] *n* 1 jamii, kundi, kikosi. 2 bendi, beni: kikundi cha wapigaji ngoma au wanamuziki. ~**master** *n* kiongozi wa bendi. ~ **man** *n* mwanabendi. ~ **stand** *n* jukwaa *(phr)*. **jump on the ~ wagon** fuata upepo vi (together/with ungana, jiunga pamoja.
bandage *n* bendeji, kitambaa. *vt* fungia bendeji.
bandana,bandanna *n* leso ya rangi ivaliwayo shingoni au kichwani yenye madoadoa mekundu au ya njano.
bandit *n* gaidi, jahili, mnyang'anyi, haramia. ~**ry** *n*
bandoleer, bandolier *n* ukanda wa risasi uvaliwao mabegani.
bandy[1] *vt* 1 rushiana, tupiana, peana. 2 *(about) (often pas)* sambaza; tajataja.
bandy[2] *adj (of legs)* -a matege. ~-**legged** *adj* -enye matege.
bane *n* 1 chanzo cha madhara *alcohol was the ~ of life* pombe ilikuwa chanzo cha madhara katika maisha yake. 2 *(in compound)* sumu *rat's ~* sumu ya panya. ~**ful** *adj* -ovu, baya -a kuleta madhara. ~**fully** *adv*.
bang[1] 1 n mshindo, mgoto. 2 kishindo. 3 *(sl US)* shauku kubwa. **go off/over with a** ~ fanikiwa sana *vt* 1 piga sana, gonga/ gogota. 2 piga kelele. 3 *(sl vulg)* kaza. 4 ~ **away** fanya kazi kwa juhudi. 5 ~ **into** kutana na *adv. int. go* ~ lipuka, kwa mlipuko.
bang[2] *n* kuchega nywele usoni *vt* chega nywele usoni.

bang[3] *adv* sawa kabisa, hapohapo *Your answer's ~ on* jibu lako ni sawa kabisa.

banger *n (sl)* 1 soseji. 2 fataki. 3 mkweche.

bangle *n* bangili, kikuku; kekee.

banian/banyan *n* 1 ~ **-tree** mbaniani. 2 baniani; mfanyabiashara wa Kihindu.

banish *vt* 1 fukuza nchini au sehemu ya nchi. 2 *(of emotions)* ondoa, fukuza, toa maanani. **~ment** *n.*

banister *n* mhimili wa mkono wa ngazi *(pl)* uzio wa ngazi.

banjo *n* gambusi.

bank[1] *n* 1 tuta. 2 *(of river)* ukingo, ufuko (wa mto n.k.). 3 mkusanyiko, lundo la mawingu, matope n.k. 4 **sand** ~ fungu la mchanga *vt,vi* 1 *(of aircraft)* ruka kiubavuubavu. 2 *(up)* fanya fungu, lundo, tuta.

bank[2] *n* benki *The ~ of Tanzania* Benki Kuu. 2 hifadhi. **blood** ~ hifadhi ya damu. 3 *(gambling)* fedha alizonazo mchezeshaji kulipia washindi *break the ~* filisi *vt* weka (fedha n.k.) benki *vi* 1 *(colloq) (on)* tegemea sana. **~er** mwenye benki; mkurugenzi wa benki; mbia wa benki. **~er's card** kadi ya mteja wa benki (inayotaja kuwa benki itawajibika kulipia cheki zote hadi kiasi fulani).

bank[3] *n* 1 *(of boats)* ubao (wa mpiga makasia). 2 mstari wa mashine aghalabu tapureta. ~ **draft** hati ya benki ya kuidhinisha malipo. ~ **rate** kiwango cha riba ya benki.

bankrupt *n* muflisi/ suta *become ~* filisika *vt* filisi *adj* -a kufilisika, muflisi *~ of ideas* muflisi wa mawazo **bankruptcy** *n* taflisi.

banner *n* 1 bendera, beramu. 2 bango *join/follow the ~ of* unga mkono *adj (US)* bora. ~ **headline** kichwa cha habari kikubwa; uzito (muhimu) wa kwanza.

bannister *n.* see **banister**.

banns *n (pl)* tangazo la ndoa (hasa kanisani).

banquet *n* dhifa *vt,vi* andaa dhifa. shiriki katika dhifa.

banshee *n* kizimwi (ambacho kilio chake chafikiriwa kuashiria kifo).

bantam *n* aina ya kuku mdogo. ~ **weight** mwanamasumbwi wa uzito wa kati ya kilo 51 na 54.

banter *vt* fanyia mzaha, masihara *n* mzaha, utani/ masihara. **~ing** *adj.* **~ingly** *adv.*

Bantu *n* Bantu *adj* -a Wabantu, -a Kibantu.

banyan *n* see **banian**.

baobab *n* mbuyu.

bap *n* mkate mdogo.

baptism n / ubatizo, tendo la kubatiza, ubatizaji. 2 kitu cha mara ya kwanza ~ *of fire (of soldiers)* mapigano ya mwanzo *adj* -a ubatizo **baptist** *n* baptisti. **~ry** *n* mahali pa kubatizia. **baptise/ize** *vt* batiza.

bar *n* 1 pao, ufito, mche *~of soap* mche/mnara/kinoo cha sabuni. 2 mti, nguzo. 3 *(of door)* nondo, kipinga, pingo. 4 *(of gold)* mkuo. 5 (-dogo) komeo, kiwi. 6 ukanda mwembamba. 7 *(obstruction)* kikomo, kizuizi. 8 fungu la mchanga, matope (mlangoni mwa mto au mwa bandari). 9 mhimili. 10 *(of music)* mstari ulalo wa nota ya muziki. 11 *(leg)* kizimba. 12 uwakili. **be/called to the ~** kubaliwa uwakili. **case at ~** kesi inayosikilizwa. **the ~** jamii ,ya mawakili. **read for the ~** soma sheria. 13 baa: mahali pa kuuzia na kunywa pombe, mvinyo, n.k. ~ **maid/man/ tender** mhudumu wa baa *coffee ~* mkahawa. 14 *(of sunlight)* mwonzi. 15 *(military)* tepe la nishani *vt* 1 *(obstruct)* zuia **be time ~red** - kinzwa na wakati.

barb *n* 1 *(bio)* kizari: kishore kidogo kwenye kikonyo cha unyoya. 2 chembe (cha mshale au ndoana). **~ed** *adj* 1 -a chembe. **~ed wire** seng'enge. 2 -a bezo a *sold* **~ed remark** msemo wa bezo.

barbarity *n* 1 ukatili; ushenzi. 2 *(pl)* vitendo vya ukatili. **barbarian** *n* mshenzi. **barbaric** *adj* -shenzi; katili. **barbarism** *n* 1 ushenzi.

2 matumizi mabaya ya lugha.

barbarous *adj* 1 -shenzi,-a kishenzi. 2 *(cruel)* -katili. **~ly** *adv*.

barbecue *n* ikari (nguruwe, ng'ombe n.k.). aliyebanikwa bila kuchanguliwa. 2 *(frame)* uchaga. 3 sherehe ya kula ikari.

barbel *n* samaki wa maji baridi.

barber *n* kinyozi, **~'s itch (rash)** mwacho wa vipele (kutokana na kunyoa).

barbiturate *n (chem)* aina ya dawa ya usingizi.

bard *n* mshairi, mtunga mashairi, malenga.

bare *vt* funua, vua, bambua, weka wazi, bainisha ~ *one's head* vua kofia. ~ **the teeth** kenua meno. ~ **one's heart** weka wazi hisia za ndani *adj* 1 wazi, pasipo kitu. ~ **headed** kichwa wazi. ~ **footed** pekupeku. **in one's ~ skin** uchi. ~ **backed** mgongo wazi *~faced lie* uwongo wa wazi ~ *chested* kifuawazi. 2 tupu, karibu tupu ~ *shelves* marafu matupu. 3 -sio zaidi ya, akali ~ *living* maisha ya kijungumeko. **~bones** *n* king'onda.

barely *adv* kwa shida *he can ~ read* anasoma kwa shida.

bargain *vt,vi* 1 jadiliana juu ya bei/malipo *they ~ed with the fisherman for a supply of fish* walijadiliana na mvuvi kuwapatia samaki. 2 kubaliana, afikiana, patana *they ~ed on the price of sugar* walipatana (juu ya) bei ya sukari. 3 ~ **for** tazamia, tegemea *we didn't ~for Ali getting married so soon!* hatukutegemea Ali angeoa mapema kiasi hicho. 4 wekea masharti *the workers ~ed they should not have to work on Sundays* wafanyakazi waliweka masharti kwamba wasifanye kazi siku za Jumapili. 5 uza *he ~ed away his freedom* aliuza uhuru wake *drive a hard ~* lazimisha mapatano kwa kuvutia upande wako *into the* ~vilevile *it's/that's a ~* nakubali, sawa. *n* 1 maafikiano, (ya kununua /kuuza au kubadilisha kitu), mapatano. **make a ~/ get the best of the ~** usipunjwe. **strike a ~** fikia mapatano. 2 kitu kilichonunuliwa /kilichopatikana kwa bei nafuu *~sale* seli ya bei nafuu ~ *price* bei ya uhafifu. **~ing** *n*

barge[1] *n* 1 tishali: mashua kubwa ya bapa itumiwayo kupakulia na kupakilia mizigo (na watu) bandarini, mitoni na kwenye mifereji. ~ **man** mwendesha tishali. 2 mashua ya meli ya vita itumiwayo na maofisa. 3 mashua kubwa ya makasia itumiwayo kwa shughuli za sherehe.~ **pole** *n* upondo. *(colloq)* **I wouldn't touch him ~ with a pole** namchukia sana au simwamini kabisa.

barge[2] *vi,vt* 1 *(colloq)* gonga, gongana, ingia ghafla na kwa vishindo *he ~ed into a wall* aligonga ukuta *they ~ed into each other* waligongana *he ~ed in on them while they were in a meeting* aliwaingia ghafla wakiwa mkutanoni. 2 *(about)* enda kwa haraka na ovyo ovyo. 3 ingilia *he ~ed into our discussion* aliingilia mazungumzo yetu.

barium *n* 1 bari: metali laini yenye weupe unaofanana na fedha. 2 ~ **meal** kemikali inayoingizwa katika utumbo kabla haujapigwa eksirei.

bark[1] n 1 gome, ganda. 2 ngozi *vt* 1 bambua, gomoa. 2 chubua.

bark[2] *vi,vt* 1 bweka, toa sauti kama ya mbwa. 2 foka, sema kwa sauti fupi, kali na yenye hasira. ~ **up the tree** 1 laumu/lalamika kwa makosa. 2 kosea, fanya kwa makosa. 3 banja, kohoa. 4 *n adj (fig)*. **~up the wrong tree** shambulia/laumu kwa makosa (yasiyo na sababu). **his ~ is worse than his bite** maneno yake ni makali kuliko matendo yake *n* mbweko, mlio kama wa mbwa (au mnyama wa aina yake). **~er** *n* mtangazaji (wa burdani), mnadi.

bark/bargue *(naut)* 1 jahazi lenye milingoti mitatu, merikebu ya matanga matatu. 2 *(poet)* jahazi au chombo chochote cha kusafiria

majini.
barker *n* 1 *(colloq)* mnadishaji. 2 *(sl)* bastola.
barley *n* shayiri **pearl** ~ shayiri iliyosagwa. ~-**sugar** *n* gubiti. ~ **water** *n* maji ya shayiri.
barm *n* hamira, chachu.
barmy *adj (GB colloq)* punguani, -pumbavu.
barn *n* kihenge: ghala ya nafaka, nyasi za kulishia wanyama. ~ **door** mlango mkubwa wa nyumba ya kuwekea nafaka au nyasi *(colloq fig)* dango la wazi. 2 *(derog)* jengo lolote kubwa lisilo na kurubakuruba au madoido. 3 banda, shedi. ~ **yard** *n* eneo la shamba lililozungukwa na nyumba.
barn-owl *see* **owl**.
barnstorm *vt,vi* 1 zunguka ukionyesha michezo ya kuigiza. 2 pita haraka ukitoa hotuba fupi katika sehemu nyingi, hasa wakati wa uchaguzi.
barometer *n* kipimahewa. **barometric** *adj*.
barouche *n* gari la farasi.
barrack[1] *vt* zomea.
barrack[2] *n* 1 *(usu pl)* kambi ya muundo maalumu ya jeshi. 2 jengo lolote lisilo na muundo maalumu wa kuvutia, banda.
barracuda *n* samaki mkali wa jamii ya kolekole apatikanaye katika sehemu za Carribbean.
barrage *n* 1 boma la kuzuia maji mtoni. 2 *(mil) (fig)* ukuta wa mizinga ipigwayo mfululizo katika sehemu fulani. 3 vitu mfululizo *a ~ of questions* mfululizo wa maswali.
barred *see* **bar**.
barrel *n* 1 pipa. ~**roofed** -enye paa la mviringo. 2 mtutu, kasiba, mwanzi, *single ~led* -enye mtutu mmoja *double ~led* -enye mitutu miwili. 3 kiasi kikubwa *a ~/~s of money* pesa tele 4 *(for fountain pen)* kineli cha wino vt,vi 1 tia (miminia) katika pipa. 2 *(sl) (along)* enda kasi. ~ **vault** *n* kuba yenye paa la mviringo.
barren *adj* 1 *(of land)* kame, jangwa. 2 *(of plants, female animals)* gumba, tasa. 3 *(fig)* -sokuwa na faida, bure. ~**ness** *n*.
barricade *vt* weka kizuizi *n* kizuizi.
barrier *n* kizuizi. ~ **reef** tuta, tumbawe.
barrister *n* wakili.
barrow[1] *n* 1 mkokoteni (wa gurudumu moja). 2 mkokoteni mdogo wa magurudumu mawili.
barrow[2] *n* kiduta, kilima (kilichojengeka kwenye eneo la makaburi).
barter *vt,vi* badilisha/badilishana (mali, bidhaa n.k.). ~ **away** badilisha kitu kwa kitu kingine bila kujali thamani halisi ya kitu. ~ **down** teremsha thamani ya kitu. *(fig)* ~ **away ones freedom** uza uhuru kwa kuubadilisha na kitu kingine *n* mali kwa mali.
bascule *n* bembea. ~ **bridge** daraja la bembea.
base[1] *n* 1 msingi, kitako, sehemu ya chini. 2 *(math)* kizio (cha kuhesabia). 3 *(chem)* besi, aina ya alkali. 4 *(mil) military* ~ kituo cha jeshi. 5 ~ **ball** kituo kimojawapo katika vituo vine vya mchezo wa besiboli. ~**less** *adj* -sokuwa na msingi, -sothibitishwa. ~**ness** *n*. **basement** *n* sehemu ya nyumba iliyo chini ya ardhi. *vt* weka msingi, tegemeza, ~ *taxation on income* kadiria kodi kutokana na mapato. **basal** *adj* -a msingi -a muhimu.
base[2] *adj* 1 *(of persons, their behaviour thoughts etc)* -a chini -ovu, -baya. 2 *(arch) (of minerals)* -a thamani ndogo. 3 *(of money)* -a bandia. 4 *(arch)* ~ **born** duni kwa asili, aliyezaliwa nje ya ndoa.
basic *adj* 1 -a msingi. 2 *(chem)* -enye besi.
baseball *n (US)* besiboli: aina ya mchezo wa mpira wa gongo unaochezwa na timu mbili za watu tisa kila upande.
bash *vt (colloq)* piga sana, gonga, ponda *n* 1 kipigo cha nguvu.

2 *(sl) have a ~ at* jaribu jambo. **~ful** *adj* -enye haya/aibu/soni. ~ness *n.* **~ly** *adv.*

basil *n* mrihani (mrehani).

basilica *n* basilika (kanisa la mtindo wa Kirumi).

basin *n* 1 beseni. 2 kibia, bunguu. 3 kilindi. 4 bonde lililotokana na mto. 5 kidimbwi.

basis *n* 1 dutu itumiwayo kuchanganyia vitu, sehemu muhimu ya mchanganyiko asili. 2 msingi *on a sound ~* kwenye msingi thabiti.

bask *vi* 1 ota jua. 2 *(fig)* furahia (sifa na maneno mazuri).

basket *n* 1 kikapu, pakacha, tenga, dahani, jamanda. **~ry** *n* 1 usukaji wa vikapu. 2 sanaa ya utengenezaji vikapu. **~ful** *n.* **~like** *adj.* **~-ball** *n* mpira wa kikapu. **~-chair** *n* kiti cha henzirani. **~-work** *(also basketry) see* **basket** 1.

bas-relief *n* sanamu za kuchonga (zinazojitokeza kutoka msingi wake).

bass *n* 1 besi; sauti ya nne. 2 sauti nene, sauti nzito, sauti ya chini. 3 mwenye besi *adj* -enye besi. **basso** *n* baso, mwanabesi *adj* -enye sauti nene.

bassinet *n (arch)* tenga la mtoto.

bast *n* nyuzinyuzi, utembo, ufumwele.

bastard *n* 1 mtoto wa nje ya ndoa. 2 mkatili, mshenzi. 3 asiye na bahati. 4 kitu bandia *vt* **~ize** 1 tamka au thibitisha mtu fulani ni wa nje ya ndoa. 2 potosha *~ized story* hadithi iliyopotoshwa. **~y** *n (leg)* hali ya kuzaliwa nje ya ndoa.

baste[1] *vt* shikiza, shulu, piga bandi *n* shikizo, mshono wa shulu.

baste[2] *vt* rudishia (mafuta, mchuzi) kwenye nyama.

baste[3] *vt* piga sana, tandika, ponda twanga.

bastinado *n* pigo la nyayoni *vt* chapa/piga nyayoni.

bastion *n* 1 *(often five-sides)* mojawapo ya pande za ngome ambayo hujitokeza zaidi kuliko nyingine. 2 *(fig)* ngome ya jeshi (karibu na nchi ya maadui). 3 *(fig)* jambo (kitu) lililohifadhiwa.

bat[1] *n* popo. *(sl)* **have ~s in the belfry** -wa punguani. **as blind as a ~** kutoona kabisa *(fig)* kutotilia manani yanayotokea. **~s/ ~ty** kichaa.

bat[2] *n* 1 mwendo *(sl)* **go off at a rare ~** piga mbio. 2 *(fig) he went on a ~* alichapa maji sana.

bat[3] *vt* 1 *(Phr) ~ the eyes* pepesa macho. **he never ~ed an eyelid** hakushangaa hata kidogo; hakulala hata kidodo. 2 *(of cricket)* piga mpira kwa kutumia gongo. *n* 1 *(cricket)* gongo la kriketi *(fig) off the ~* tenda bila fikra. *(fig)* **do something off one's own ~** kufanya kitu bila msaada. 2 **~s man** mchezaji wa kriketi mwenye zamu ya kupiga mpira.

batch *n* 1 bechi: idadi ya mikate, keki, na vyakula vingine vya kuokwa/ vilivyookwa kwa mkupuo mmoja. 2 jumla ya watu au vitu vinavyoshughulikiwa kama kundi.

bate *vt* punguza, fanya dogo. **with ~d breath** kwa kushika pumzi *n (fig)* kisirani, ghadhabu *he was in an awful ~* alikuwa ameghadhabika sana.

bath *n* 1 kuoga. 2 maji ya kuoga. 3 birika, bafu chombo cha kuogea/ kusafishia. **hypo~** chombo cha kusafishia filamu. 4 *(pl)* **swimming ~** bwawa la kuogelea *vapour ~s* mafusho, mafukizo *public ~s* hamamu. **~ chair** *n* gari la kuchukua mgonjwa. **~robe** *n* nguo ya kushindia nyumbani. **~room** *n* chumba cha kuogea, bafu, hamamu. **~ tub** *n* hodhi, bafu *vi,vt* oga, ogesha.

bathe *vt* 1 ogesha. 2 chovya, tia maji (au chochote kama maji), osha *be ~ed in* tota *be ~ed in tears* lowana machozi *vi* oga katika bahari, mto, kidimbwi ogelea. **bathing** kuogelea. **~cap** kofia ya kuogelea. **~costume/suit** nguo ya kuogelea.

bathos *n (rhet)* mpomoko wa uandishi au hotuba.

bathysphere *n* batisfia; chombo cha

utafiti baharini; kizamia lindi.
batik *n* batiki, uchapaji urembo kwenye nguo kwa kutumia rangi na nta.
batiste *n.* melimeli.
batman *n (GB mil)* mtumishi/ askari anayemhudumia ofisa wa jeshi.
baton *n* 1 *(police)* kirungu, kifimbo. 2 *(mus)* kifimbo (cha mwimbishaji).
battalion *n* batalioni: kikosi cha askari ambacho kina kombania kadhaa na ambacho ni sehemu ya brigedi au rejimenti.
batten *n* taruma: kipande cha mti kitumiwacho kuvifanya vipande vingine vikae mahali pake *vt,vi* 1 kaza kwa taruma ~ *down the hatches* funga milango ya kushukia ndani ya meli. 2 ~ *on/ upon* nenepa kwa kuwanyonya wengine.
batter[1] *vt,vi* 1 gongagonga sana. 2 ponda ponda. 3 *(mil)* piga makombora *(phr)* ~ *about* umiza sana, bomoa ~ *down* bomoa, vunja, tokomeza ~ *in* vunjavunja, haribu kabisa. **~ing-ram** *n* gogo la kuvunjia (kuta, milango n.k.) (fatuma).
batter[2] *n* 1 rojo ya ngano.
battery *n (mil)* 1 kikosi cha askari wa mizinga. **assault and** ~ shambulio. 2 kundi la mizinga mikubwa katika meli ya vita. 3 betri: seliumeme zaidi ya moja zilizoungwa pamoja. 4 seti ya vyombo au ala zitumikazo pamoja. 5 msururu wa viota vya kutagia/ kunenepeshea kuku.
batting *n* pamba ya kutengenezea tandiko la kitanda.
battle *vi* pigana, shindana, pambana. *n* 1 mapigano baina ya majeshi, vita 2 mashindano, mapambano. 3 ushindi *youth is half the* ~ ujana ni nusu ushindi. **~-axe** *n* shoka la vita *(sl)* mwanamke jabari. **~-cruiser** manowari. **~-dress** *n* vazi la kivita. ~ **field/ ground** *n* medani, uwanja wa vita. **~ship** manowari kubwa. **~-array** *n* mpango wa vita.
battlement(s) *n* buruji.
bauble *n* kitu kizuri chenye thamani ndogo k.m. pambo la jaribosi.
bauxite *n* boksiti: madini ya asili inayotoa alumini.
bawd *n (arch)* mwanamke mwenye danguro. **~y** *adj* -pujufu *n* **~y house** danguro. **~ly** *adv.*
bawl *vt* piga kelele, lia (kwa sauti kubwa), guta, ~ *abuse at sb* tukana kwa makelele *vi* ~ **sb out** karipia *n* ukelele, guto.
bay[1] *n* ghuba, hori, ~ *of Mexico* Ghuba ya Mexico.
bay[2] *n* 1 kidaka, kishubaka. 2 **~window** dirisha la kutokeza nje.
bay[3] *vi* gumia, bweka, lia (kama mbwa). *(idiom)* ~ **at the moon** lilia kitu usichoweza kupata *n* mlio wa mbwa, mbweko. **keep (hold) at** ~ simamisha (adui), zuia, kinga.
bay[4] *adj n* -enye damu ya mzee, farasi wa rangi ya damu ya mzee.
bayonet *n* singe *vt* choma kwa singe.
bayou *n (US)* kinamasi, mbuga yenye kinamasi (-enye tope la kunata).
bazaar *n* 1 *(of Iran, India & other Eastern countries)* mtaa wenye maduka na karakana; mahali penye maduka na soko. 2 duka lenye bidhaa rahisi, duka lenye vikorokoro. 3 (mahali pa) seli/mnada uliokusudiwa kupata fedha za kuwafadhili wasiojiweza.
bazooka *n* bazoka: aina ya silaha inayotumika kufyatulia guruneti.
be *vi 1 (irreg)* kuwa. *(indicating wish/hope/intention) I want to ~ a doctor* nataka kuwa daktari *he will ~ my savior* atakuwa mkombozi wangu *I intend to ~ with you on Sunday* nakusudia kuwa nanyi siku ya Jumapili. 2 *(with n/pron) (present: is, am, are)* ni *Saidi is a farmer* Saidi ni mkulima *I am his teacher* mimi ni mwalimu wake *they are sick* wao ni wagonjwa; *(past: was/ were)* -likuwa *I was a mechanic* nilikuwa makanika *they were good friends* walikuwa marafiki wazuri; *(perfect ~en)* -mekuwa *she has ~en* sick amekuwa mgonjwa, *she has ~en*

in Zambia amewahi kuwa Zambia. 3 *(with adj is, was, am, are were) the sea is red* bahari ni nyekundu *the food was good* chakula kilikuwa kizuri *the boys are poor* wavulana ni masikini *they were foolish* walikuwa wajinga. 4 *(with adv) the eggs were on the table* mayai yalikuwa juu ya meza. 5 *(with n or prep indicating possession) the book is mine* kitabu ni changu. 6 *(indicating change from one quality to another) she is a teacher but she wants to ~ a doctor* yeye ni mwalimu lakini anataka kuwa daktari. 7 *(indicating existence) there is life on the moon* kuna uhai mwezini *there are ten children* kuna watoto kumi. 8 *(go, come) I have been to see my uncle* nimekwenda/ kuja kumwona mjomba. 9 *(indicating unreal condition) If I were a king I would let you live* ningekuwa mfalme ningekuacha ukaishi *if I were to come* ningekuja. 10 *(purpose) the seminar was to enlighten the villagers* semina ilikusudiwa kuwaelimisha wanakijiji. 11 *(phr) ~ tired* choka, *~ angry* kasirika, *~ quiet* nyamaza, *~ available* patikana, *~ lost* potea, *~ off* ondoka, *~ about to* karibia, *~ over* kwisha, *~ for* unga mkono. 12 *(indicating obligation) you are to finish this work* lazima umalize kazi hii. 13 *pref* 1 kila mahali *~smear* pakaza kila mahali, *~dew* enea umande kote. 2 elekeza (kisarufi) *~mean* fanya omboleo, ombolezea. 3 vaa *~jewelled* pambwa vito. 4 shadidisha **~ labour** sisitiza jambo.

beach *n* pwani, ufukoni *lower part of the ~* pwani *dry/upper part of the ~* ufuko, ufuo; *sandy ~* mchanga, *vt* pweleza, pandisha pwani. **~ comber** *n* 1 mtarazaki pwani, mgaagaa na upwa. 2 wimbi kubwa linalomalizikia pwani. **~ head** *n* kituo cha jeshi la uvamizi ufukoni.

beacon *vt* ongoza, tangaza kwa mnara wa taa. *n* 1 kioleza: kilichowekwa kuonya hatari n.k., chungu ya mawe, mlingoti, nguzo, mnara. 2 mwanga mkubwa wa kujulisha habari (ya hatari, furaha n.k.).

bead *vt,vi* pamba kwa vilulu, shanga, n.k.; *(to pearl)* kutoa povu, matone n.k. *n* 1 ushanga. 2 tone (la jasho, la maji). 3 povu. 4 (idiom) ***draw a ~ on*** lenga. 5 *(pl)* **~s** *n* shanga *(rosary)* tasbihi. **tell one's ~s** sali kwa kutumia tasbiha, rozari *belt of ~s* kundavi *(circlet)* kogo. **~ ing** *n* nakshi, shanga. **~ed** *adj*. **~y** *adj* kama ushanga kwa udogo, -enye kung'aa sana *~y eyes* macho madogo tena ya umbo la mviringo.

beadle *n* bawabu wa kanisa.

beagle *n* 1 aina ya mbwa wa kuwindia. 2 *(GB) (arch)* mpelelezi; jasusi.

beak[1] *n* 1 mdomo wa ndege (hasa uliochongoka na mgumu). 2 *(informal)* pua kama mdomo wa ndege. 3 silaha (kama panga) inayojitokeza kama mdomo wa ndege mbele ya jahazi.

beak[2] *n (sl)* 1 hakimu. 2 *(arch)* mwalimu.

beaker *n* 1 *(science)* bika. 2 kikombe kikubwa.

beam *n* 1 mhimili, boriti. 2 mwali wa mwanga. 3 *(naut)* mkalio. 4 *(sl of person)* **be on one's ~ ends** ishiwa fedha. 4 ishara ya kuelekezea ndege **be on/off the ~** 1 *(aircraft)* fuata/potoka njia. 2 *(of a ship)* **on her ~ ends** lalia upande mmoja, karibia kuzama *vt,vi* 1 *(of the sun, moon, stars)* toa mwanga na joto. 2 *(fig)* tabasamu, furahia, changamka, kenua meno. 3 **~ sth (to)** tangaza (kuelekea), elekeza.

bean *n* 1 haragwe, mbegu ya jamii ya kunde *(sl)* **be full of ~s** -enye kuchangamka sana. **give sb ~s** adhibu, kemea *(sl)* **be without/not have a ~** kutokuwa na fedha. **spill the ~s** fichua, toa siri. **~pod** *n* ganda la maharagwe, mmea jamii ya kunde. **~stalk** *n* kikonyo cha mharagwe *(arch)* **old ~** rafiki, mzee.**~ feast** *(old* *use, Colloq)* sherehe, dhifa *(phr)* **I havent a ~** sina hata senti.

bear[1] *n* 1 dubu. 2 mtu mkali, asiye na adabu, mtu wa ovyo, mjeuri. **~ish** *adj* -a kijeuri -a -ovyo, -zembe, -a dubu.

bear[2] *vt* 1 chukua/ beba *~ a heavy load* chukua/beba mzigo mzito *~ away palm* shinda sana na kupata zawadi *~ away the prize* nyakua zawadi. 2 *(endure)* vumilia, stahimili *she can't ~ cats* hawezi kuvumilia paka *I cannot ~ him* simpendi kabisa *he can't ~ the pain* hawezi kustahimili maumivu. 3 *(produce)* zaa *~ fruits* zaa matunda. 4 onyesha kuwa na *~ signs of* onyesha alama za *the letter ~s your address* barua ina anwani yako. 5 **~ oneself** kuwa kama *~ oneself like a Professor* kuwa kama Profesa; jiheshimu, kuwa na adabu. 6 toa. **~ witness** toa ushahidi. **~ a hand** toa msaada *vi* 1 **~ on** husiana na. 2 elekea, enda, geuka *~ to the right* elekea upande wa kulia. 3 **~ with sb** vumilia mtu *~ with me* niwie radhi, nivumilie. 4 **~ down** shinda. **~ up** stahilimi, vumilia. **~ out** unga mkono, thibitisha. **~ on/upon** husiana; athiri **~ in mind** kumbuka, zingatia. **~ hug** kumbatia sana. **~able** *adj* -a kuvumilika, -a kustahimilika. **bearer** *n* mchukuaji, mjumbe, mwenye kuleta *payable to ~* -a kulipwa kwa mwenye kuchukua. 2 mtu asaidiaye kubeba jeneza; mbeba machela, bendera n.k. 3 mpagazi, hamali. 4 **office ~ er** mwenye cheo. 5 *(of trees) good/bad ~* mti unaozaa vizuri/ vibaya.

beard[1] *n* 1 ndevu. 2 kidevu (suke la nywele za kidevuni). 3 *(of maize)* kireri.

beard[2] *vi* **~ed/~less** *adj (fig) ~ the lion in his den* mchokoze simba katika pango lake, chokoa pweza mwambani.

bearing *n* 1 *(behaviour)* mwenendo; namna ya kusimama au kutembea. 2 *(patience)* saburi, uvumilivu *it's beyond ~* haistahimiliki. 3 *(production)* uzazi; zalisho. 4 *(meaning)* uhusiano, pande zote *consider the matter in all its ~s* angalia jambo kwa marefu na mapana. 5 *(position/condition)* mahali, hali, kikao; uelekeo, nyuzi *take one's ~s* tafuta uelekeo *I have lost my ~s* nimepotea, nimepoteza uelekeo; sijui niko wapi. 6 *(tech)* gololi. **armorial ~s** ngao ya heshima. **~ skin** *n* 1 ngozi ya dubu. 2 kofia za manyoya (za jeshi la kifalme).

beast *n* 1 mnyama. 2 *(farming)* ng'ombe, fahali, mnyama anayebeba mizigo. 3 mtu katili, mtu mwenye mwenendo/tabia mbaya. **~ly** *adj* -a kinyama, -siofaa kutumiwa na watu; kama mnyama, *(colloq)* baya; *(colloq)* mno *It is ~ly hot* kuna joto mno. **~ness** *n* 4 mshenzi. **~ly** *adj* 1 -a kinyama. 2 baya *adv* mno, sana.

beat[1] *vt* 1 *(strike)* piga, gonga, chapa, bubuta. **~ing** *n* adhabu (hasa kwa kupiga. *(colloq)* kushindwa. **~ the record** vunja rekodi *(fig) ~ the air* shindana bure **~ one's brains** fikiria sana. 2 *(surpass)* shinda, pita, tia fora. 3 *it ~s me* ninashangaa, sielewi hilo, gumu. 4 *(metal)* fua. 5 koroga barabara kwa nguvu (ili hewa iingie) *~ eggs* piga/vuruga/koroga mayai. 6 *(various uses)* **~ one's breast** sikitika, sononeka sana *(a retreat)* (toa ishara ya kurudi nyuma) jirudi. **~ down price** fanya bei ipunguzwe, punguza bei *~ in* vunja, ponda. **~ hollow** shinda. kabisa. **~ off (back)** shinda, fukuza. **~ it!** toka hapa! nipishe *vi* **~ about the bush** tangatanga, hangaika, zungukazunguka.

beat[2] n 1 pigo *heart ~s* mapigo ya moyo; **dead ~** taabani, hoi. 2 kipimo cha muziki/shairi. 3 njia au mapito ya mara kwa mara *(slang)* **the ~ of** kitu kilichozidi zaidi. *(fig)* **be off/out of one's ~** fanya jambo ambalo huna mazoea nalo.

beat[3] *attrib. adj* -a au kama wapinzani wa madili ya jamii. ***~en***

adj (esp) 1 -liotiwa umbo au sura kwa kugongwagongwa. 2 *(of path)* -liochakazwa kwa matumizi. **go off/ keep to the ~en track** fanya /tofanya kitu kisicho/cha kawaida. **be off the ~** choka; **beck** shindwa.

beater *n* 1 kifaa cha kupigia k.m. zulia **(carpet ~)**, yai **(egg ~)**. 2 mswagaji, msakaji/mwingaji ndege (wanaowindwa kwa bunduki).

beatify *vt* 1 tangaza utakatifu, tangaza kuwa marehemu ni mbarikiwa; tangaza mtu kuwa mwenye heri. 2 furahisha. **beatification** *n*. **beatific** *adj* -enye kuonyesha furaha kubwa, -a kufurahisha mno, -enye kubarikiwa. **beatitude** *n* 1 hali ya heri. 2 the **Beatitudes** Ibada ya kubarikiwa kwa Kristo.

beatnik *n* 1 mpinzani wa maadili ya jamii. 2 mwigaji wa tabia au mavazi (yasiyo ya kawaida) yanayopingana na maadili ya jamii.

beau *n (arch)* 1 mzee ambaye anapenda sana mtindo wa nguo zake. 2 shabiki wa wanawake. 3 mhusudu/ mpenzi wa msichana. 4 **~ ideal** wazo la mtu kuhusu uzuri na ubora. **the ~ monde** jamii/tabaka la juu lenye kupenda ulimbwende.

beauty *n* 1 uzuri, urembo. **a ~** mrembo, mwanamke mzuri sana, kizuri; *(sl)* toto shoo. **~ salon/parlour** duka la kurembea. **~ queen** msichana mshindi katika mashindano ya uzuri *~ sleep* usingizi kabla ya saa sita usiku. **~-**spot *n* 1 mandhari uzuri. 2 kidoto kwenye uso (inasemekana kinaongeza uzuri). **beauteous** *adj (poet)* = **beautiful**. **beautician** *n* mrembeshaji. **beautiful** *adj* -zuri, -a urembo. **~ ly.** *adv* **beautify** *vt* fanya zuri, pamba, rembesha.

beaver *n* 1 buku. 2 manyoya yake. 3 nguo ya sufu (kama ya manyoya ya buku). 4 mtu mwenye nguvu afanyaye kazi sana *(colloq)* **~ away (at sth)** fanya kazi kwa bidii.

becalm *vt* tuliza, nyamazisha. **~ed** -wa shwari, simamishwa *vi (of sailing ship)* **be ~ed** shindwa kwenda mbele (kwa sababu ya kukosa upepo) *~ed (pred) adj*.

became *see* **become**.

because *conj* kwa sababu; minajili ya, kwa kuwa. **~ of** kwa sababu ya.

beck *n* ishara (ya kichwa/mkono) **at one's ~ and call** chini ya amri ya wakati wote.

beckon *vi* pungia mkono, ashiria, ita/ karibisha kwa kupunga mkono *vt ~ in* karibisha kwa kupungia mkono.

become *vi* 1 geuka, -wa; anza kuwa *~ old* zeeka, konga, -wa mzee *~ thin* konda, sinyaa -wa mwembamba. 2 **~ of** tokea, kuwa *what has ~of him* kimemtokea nini? *~ ill* -wa mgonjwa *~ interested* vutiwa, pata hamu *~ known* julikana. 3 *vt* faa, pendeza, shamiri, falia. 4 chukua, pendeza, kaa *that hat ~s you* kofia ile inakukaa; inakupendeza sana. **becoming** *adj* -a kufaa, -a kupendeza. **becomingly** *adv*.

bed[1] *n* 1 kitanda, *go to ~* enda kulala *make a ~* tandika *(fig) a ~ of roses* maisha ya starehe/anasa *a ~ of thorns* maisha ya taabu. **as you make your ~ so you must lie in it** *(prov)* utavuna ulichopanda *(arch) be brought to ~* zaa; ugua **take to ~/ keep to one's ~** -wa mgonjwa, *put a child to ~* -laza mtoto; **get out of ~ on the wrong side** amka vibaya. **~ post** *n* besera. *between you and me and the ~* kati yangu mimi na wewe tu (siri). **~-ridden** *adj* -gonjwa kitandani **~-rock** *n* msingi wa mwamba *(fig)* kiini cha jambo. **~ price** bei ya mwisho (ya kwisha), rahisi mno *adj* -a chini kabisa. **~ roll** *n* 1 vikorokoro vya kitanda vinavyoweza kubebeka (safarini). 2 *(foundation)* msingi. 3 godoro, matandiko *vt* 1 patia kitanda/mahali pa kulala. *(fig)* **go to ~ with** jamiana, lalana. **~room** *n* chumba cha kulala. **~-side** *n* kando ya kitanda cha mgonjwa *at sb's ~* pamoja na mgonjwa ~ *side/ manners* tabia ya mganga katika kufariji wagonjwa *Dr Shija has good ~ side manners* Dkt Shija anajua kuwafariji wagonjwa. **~-sore** *n* kidondamalazi (kutokana na kulala sana kitandani kwa mgonjwa). **~-spread** *n* shuka ya kitanda. **~-stead** *n* matendegu. **~-time** *n* saa ya kulala; ~ *stories* hadithi za kusimulia kitandani.

bed[2] n 1 *(of plants)* tuta. 2 udongo ulio chini ya bahari (mto au ziwa) ~ *of sand* mahali penye mchanga, fungu la mchanga *vt* **bed (in/out)** pandikiza miche. ~ **(in)** weka au ingiza (kutoka/kwenye msingi n.k.) *the bullet ~ded itself in the wall* risasi iliingia ukutani. **~ding** *n* matandiko. **~ded** *adj*.

bedaubed *vt* ~ **with** paka, rashia (kwa uchafu). **~ed** *adj*.

bedeck *vt* pamba, tia urembo, rembesha. **~ed with** *pred,adj*.

bedevil *vt* tatiza, sumbua. **~ment** *n*.

bedew *vt (arch)* tia umande, nyunyuzia/rashia maji *~ed with* lowanishwa na *pred adj* loa, *a face ~ with tears* uso ulioloa machozi.

bedim *vt (arch)* tia giza (macho). **~med** *pred adj* -liotiwa giza, -liofifizwa.

bedlam *n* 1 *(arch)* hospitali ya vichaa. 2 *(fig)* ghasia, zahama, machafuko makelele.

Bedouin *n* **Bedui**.

bee *n* 1 nyuki *(fig)* **have a ~ in his bonnet** shikilia sana jambo fulani. **make a ~-line for** nenda moja kwa moja kwa njia iliyo fupi kabisa. **beehive** *n* 1 mzinga. 2 *(US)* mkusanyiko wa majirani (kwa ajili ya kazi ya burudani). 3 mashindano ya kirafiki. **~-eater** *n* keremkeremu. 2 ~ **bread** *n* mchanganyiko wa asali na chavua (chakula cha watoto) *n* **~'s wax** nta; polishi ya sakafu.

beech *n* mti kama mfune.

beef *n* 1 nyama ya ng'ombe *roast ~* nyama ya kubanika. 2 *(of people)* misuli nguvu. 3 *(US) (pl)* **beeves** ng'ombe walionona (agh. huchinjwa kwa chakula). *vi (sl)* kuwa na dukuduku, lalamika *stop ~ing* acha kulalamika. ~ **up** imarisha. **~ eater** *n* mlinzi wa *(Tower of London)*. ~ **steak** *n* steki ya nyama ya ng'ombe. ~ **cattle** *n* ng'ombe wa nyama. ~ **-tea** *n* supu ya nyama ya ng'o mbe (hasa kwa wagonjwa). **beefy** *adj (of a person)* -enye nguvu, -nene.

beefwood *n* mvinje.

beep *n* mwito, mlio wa moja kwa moja (k.m. kwenye simu).

beer *n* bia, pombe *local ~* pombe ya kienyeji k.m. ulanzi, buza, kangara n.k. **small** ~ *(sl)* kitu kisicho muhimu. mambo hafifu; vikorokoro. **~y** *adj (of air)* -enye harufu ya bia (pombe); *(of person)* -levi. ~ **money** fedha za kichele.

beet *n* kiazisukari. **red** ~ kiazisukari chekundu. **white** ~ kiazi sukari cheupe. ~ **sugar** sukari inayotokana na kiazisukari.

beetle[1] *n* kombamwiko, mende.

beetle[2] *(arch) n* nyundo ya mti, mtambo wa kubomolea *vt* ponda kwa mchi.

beetle[3] vt 1 ondoka haraka. ~ **off** ambaa. 2 *adj* -a kutokeza; -a kuning'inia. **~-browed** -enye nyusi zinazotokeza/ nzito.

befall *vi (arch) (used only in 3rd person)* tokea, tukia kuwa *what has ~en him?* amefikwa na maafa gani?

befit *vi* stahiki, stahili, faa, pasa. **~ting** *adj*. **~tingly** *adv*.

befog *vt* 1 funika kwa ukungu. 2 fumba, tia wasiwasi. **be ~ged** fadhaika, kanganyika, -funikwa na ukungu, *(fig)* -wa na wasiwasi, babaishwa, tatanishwa, kanganywa.

before *adv* 1 kabla (ya), awali ya ~ *everything else* awali ya yote ~ *me* mbele yangu *two days ~ he died* siku mbili kabla hajafariki ~ *my time* kabla ya wakati wangu *he arrived ~ time* alifika mapema. 2 mbele ya) *she stood ~ him* alisimama mbele yake he was brought ~ the judge aliletwa mbele ya hakimu. 3 kuliko *death ~ defeat* aheri kufa kuliko kushindwa. 4 *come/go ~* tangulia *the day ~ yesterday* juzi **carry all ~ one** fanikiwa katika yote unayofanya. **~ hand** *adv* mbele, kwanza, kabla, awali *pay ~* lipa kwanza, lipa kabla.

befriend *vt* 1 fanya urafiki na. 2 fadhili, saidia, tendea wema.

beg *vi* 1 omba, sihi *he ~ged me to go* alinisihi niende. 2 ombaomba *he lives by ~ging* anaishi kwa kuombaomba. 3 toa udhuru. 4 **go ~ging** -totakiwa *these things are going ~ging* vitu hivi havitakiwi. 5 (polite phr) *I ~ your pardon* naomba msamaha *I ~ to differ* nina wazo tofauti *we ~ to inform* you tunakuarifu. **~gar** *n* 1 mwombaji, ombaomba *~gars cannot be choosers* maiti hachagui sanda. 2 *(colloq playful or friendly use)* mtu. **~garly** *adj* maskini, nyonge, duni. ~gary *n* umasikini mkubwa, ufukara. *vt* 1 fukarisha, filisi. **be ~gared** fukarika, filisika. 2 **~gar** (*description*) fanya maelezo kuwa duni na kutotosheleza.

beget *vt* 1 *(arch)* zaa (kama baba). 2 *(cause)* sababisha, wa sababu ya tukio fulani. **~ter** *n.*

begin *vi* 1 anza *~ with* anza na **~ on** sth anza kufanya kitu. 2 *(start)* anzisha. **~ner** *n* mwanzishi, mwanzilishi, mwanafunzi. **~ning** *see* **begin** *n* mwanzo, awali, asili, chanzo *a good ~ning is half the battle* mwanzo mzuri ni nusu ya ushindi.

begone *vt(arch)* ondoka!nenda! *~ with you!* potelea mbali!

begrime *vt* chafua sana. **~d** *pred adj* -liochafuka sana.

begrudge *vt (envy)* onea chuki au kijicho (kwa ajili ya mtu kuwa na mali, kitu n.k.), onea wivu, husuda; -wa na inda.

beguile *vt* 1 **~ sb (into)** danganya, laghai, ghilibu, ghuri. 2 **~ (with)** changamsha, furahisha, ondoa uchovu burudisha. 3 **~ (with)** pitisha wakati n.k. kwa furaha. **~ment** *n.* **~r** *n* mdanganyifu, mlaghai.

behalf *n* kwa niaba ya; kwa sababu ya *he came here on my ~* alikuja hapa kwa niaba yangu *we were uneasy on your ~* tulikuwa na mashaka/ wasiwasi juu yako.

behave *vi, vt* 1 tenda, -wa na tabia *~ yourself* jiheshimu, shika adabu. ~ed *adj* **well ~ed** enye mwenendo mzuri. 2 (*of machine)* fanya kazi.

behaviour *n* mwenendo, tabia, mazoea,silika *good ~* adili, mwenendo mzuri, mazoea mazuri, matendo mema kwa wengine **be on one's best ~** shika adabu sana *insubordinate ~* tabia ya kutotii, kutojali, kudharau. **~ist** *n.* **~ism** *n (psych)* nadharia ya mwenendo inayohusu kiamshi na mwitikio.

behead *vt* kata kichwa.

beheld see **behold**.

behest *n (old use; only in)* **at sb's ~** kwa amri ya.

behind *(prep)* nyuma (ya) *he hid him self ~ the tree* alijificha nyuma ya mti *~ the scenes* kisirisiri *~ one's back* bila mtu kufahamu, sengenya. 2 nyuma kimaendeleo *he was ~ the other children in the class* alikuwa nyuma ya watoto wengine kimaendeleo darasani. 3 **leave ~** acha nyuma, bakiza. 4 be ~ one *(of time)* wa nyuma. *n (colloq)* matako kick sb's ~ piga teke. *adv* nyuma *be ~* 1 baki nyuma. **~ the times** -a zamani, chelewa, kawia. 2 *(support,* unga mkono. **~ hand** *(pred) adj* 1 nyuma (ya). 2 -wa nyuma, chelewa *be ~ hand with sth* kawia, -wa na karisaji (deni) *not to be ~ hand in sth* kutojicheleweshа.

behold *vt (arch)* ona (hasa kitu cha kuvuta macho au kisicho cha kawaida), tazama, angalia. *and ~!* tazama, kumbe! **~er** *n* aonaye, aangaliaye, shahidi.

beholden *adj* wiwa na (shukurani).

behove *vt* pasa, wajibika, -tokuwa na budi *it ~s us* yatupasa, hatuna budi *it ~s you to say that* inakupasa kusema hivyo.

beige *n* rangi ya mchanga.

being see **be** *n* 1 kiumbe, kitu chenye uhai *a human* ~ mtu, binadamu, mwanadamu **a restless** ~ asiyetulia. 2 asili, hali. 3 kuwa, -enye kuwa *bring sth into* ~ umba, tukia, wa *adj for the time* ~ kwa wakati uliopo *that* ~ *the case* kama ni hivyo.

bejewell *vt* pamba kwa vito. **~ed** *adj*

belabour *vt*. 1 sisitiza sana. 2 shambulia. 3 piga sana.

belated *adj* 1 -liolimatika, -liochelewa. **~dly** *adv*.

belay *vt (naut and mountainering* funga ~ *there!* basi. 2 weka salama, kaza.

belch *vi (eructate)* teuka, piga mbweu *vt (eject violently)* foka, toa kwa nguvu *n* 1 *(eructation)* mbweu. 2 *(spurt)* mbubujiko.

beldam(e) *n (arch)* 1 *(old use)* ajuza. 2 bibi kizee mkorofi.

beleaguer *vt* zingira, shambulia, kutoka pande zote.

belfry *n* mnara/chumba mnarani cha kengele.

Belial *n* shetani, jini baya, afriti.

belie *vt* 1 singizia, ingiza yasiyo kweli. 2 onyesha kwa jinsi isiyostahili (isiyo kweli) *that action ~s him* tendo hilo halionyeshi tabia yake ilivyo, si stahili yake, si laiki yake.

belief *n* 1 imani, . 2 dhana, wazo.

believe *vt* amini, sadiki. *vi* 1 tumaini, tegemea, 2 jisingizia, jifanya. **make** ~ *(that I am right)* ninaamini kwamba sikukosea (kwa jibu) *I* ~ *so (not)* naamini (siamini) hivyo, nadhani (sidhani) hivyo ~ *in total abstinence* amini katika kufunga *adj* -a kuaminika, -a kutumainika **~r** *n* muumini. **~ing** *adj* -enye imani, -tumainifu.

belittle *vt* dunisha, dhalilisha.

bell *n* 1 njuga, *(of cattle)* kivumanzi, mbugi, kengele *ring the* ~ piga kengele. **as sound as a** ~ *(fig)* imara. kabisa, *(colloq) ring a* ~ kumbusha. 2 *(naut)* (migongo ya) saa. 3 ~ **boy/** ~ **hop** *n (US) (in hotels)* mwandazi, mhudumu. ~ **bottomed** *adj (of trousers)* iliyo pana sana chini. ~ **bottoms** *n* bugaluu: suruali pana sana chini. ~ **bouy** *n* boya lenye kengele. ~ **tent** *n* hema lenye umbo la kengele. **~-founder** *n* mfua kengele. ~ **wether** *n* kondoo kiongozi (anayevishwa kengele shingoni); *(fig)* kiongozi wa mzozo *vt (fig)* ~ **the cat** jihatarisha, fanya jambo la hatari.

belladonna *n (drug prepared from)* dawa inayotokana na mbeladona.

belle *n* mrembo *the* ~ *of the ball* mrembo kuliko wote katika kikundi.

belles-lettres *n (Fr) (pl)* taaluma za fasihi.

bellicose *adj (liter)* -gomvi, -shari,

belligerent *n (nation, person)* mpigana vita; mchokozi *adj* -enye kupigana vita, chokozi. **belligerency** *n*

bellman *n (pl: bellmen)* mpiga mbiu.

bellow *vi* 1 lia (kama fahali), nguruma. 2 tamka kwa makelele au kwa hasira *n* ngurumo, mvumo, mlio (wa ng'ombe).

bellows *n (pl)* kiriba/viriba *a pair of* ~ jozi ya viriba.

belly *n* 1 *(colloq)* tumbo, kitambi. ~ **flop** *n (colloq)* upigaji mbizi (wa kutanguliza tumbo). **~-laugh** *n* kicheko kikubwa *vi* cheka kwa sauti kubwa. **~-button** *n (colloq)* kitovu. ~ **landing** *n (of aircraft)* kutua kwa tumbo (bila kutumia magurudumu). ~ **land** *vi* tua kwa tumbo. *(colloq)* lalamika bila sababu. **~-ache** *n* 1 *(colloq)* msokoto wa tumbo *vi* 2 mbinuko, kivimbe. **~ful** *n (colloq)* kinaa; kifu *I have had a ~ful of fighting* nimepigana kifu yangu *vi, vt* ~ *(out)* tuna, vimba (kama tanga lililojaa upepo), tokeza.

belong *vi (to)* 1 -wa mali ya, -wa kitu cha *the house ~s to May* nyumba ni (mali) ya May. 2 -wa -a, stahili kuwa, -wa/ishi (mahala), husu *put the book where it ~s* weka kitabu mahali pake, *he does not* ~ *here* si wa hapa, haishi hapa. **~ing** *n (pl)* mali inayohamishika *personal ~ings* mali ya mtu binafsi.

beloved *adj* muhibu, -penzi, -pendwa *adj (be) ~ by all* pendwa sana na wote *n* mpenzi, kipenzi, mpendwa, muhibu.

below *adv* 1 chini (ya) *she called from ~* aliita kutoka chini *~ the average* chini ya wastani *be/go ~ (in a ship)* teremka chini, n.k. *be ~ my dignity* -wa chini ya hadhi yangu. 2 mwishoni *affix the stamp ~* bandika stempu mwishoni/chini. 3 **down ~ in the valley/down ~** bondeni **here ~** hapa duniani **(speak) ~ one's breath** nong'ona.

belt *n* 1 mkanda, mshipi, ukanda *fasten the ~* funga mkanda. **hit below the ~** fanya faulo/ kosa. 2 **tighten one's ~** kaza mkanda, vumilia shida, jinyima *(Geog)* ukanda, safu, mstari, eneo *~ of trees* safu au mstari wa miti. **green-~** *n* ukanda/eneo la mashamba. **maize ~** *n* eneo/ ukanda wa mahindi. 3 mkanda duara. **fan-~** *n* mkanda wa feni. **conveyer ~** mkanda wa mizigo. **-line** *n* barabara au reli inayozunguka mji *vt* 1 funga mkanda. 2 chapa kwa mkanda *(colloq)* zibua kwa masumbwi. **~ing** *n* mcharazo *give a good ~ing* charaza barabara. 3 **~ along** *(colloq)* chapuka. 4 **~ out** amba kwa makelele. 5 **~ up** *(sl)* nyamaza.

bemoan *vt (poet)* lilia, sikitikia, huzunikia, ombolezea.

bemuse *vt* fadhaisha, shangaza. **~d** *adj* -liofadhaishwa, -lioshangazwa, -enye fadhaa, -enye kuchanganyikiwa.

bench *n* 1 benchi, fomu, ubao wa kukalia, kiti kirefu, *(of stone)* ufunga. **~ mark** alama teule. **back ~es** viti vya wabunge wasio na wadhifa. **cross ~es** viti vya wabunge huru. **front ~es** viti vya wabunge wenye wadhifa. **~ seat** *(in a car)* -a watu wawili au zaidi. 2 **the B~** majaji, mahakimu; kiti au ofisi ya jaji; mahakama. **King's ~** Mahakama (ya Kiingereza). **raise to the ~** fanya hakimu/askofu *~ warrant n* hati ya hakimu. 3 meza ya kazi (ya seremala n.k.), meza ndefu ya kufanyia kazi *vt to ~ a player* kumtoa nje, kumpumzisha mchezaji.

bend *n* 1 mzingo, kuruba, kona. **round the ~** kichaa. 2 *(in a rope)* fundo. 3 **the ~s** maumivu (ya maungo yatokanayo na kuibuka haraka baada ya kupiga mbizi) *vt, vi* 1 pinda, kunja, zinga. **~ the knee (to)** *(rhet)* inama, sali. **on ~ed knees** *(liter)* (kwa) kupiga magoti, katika ibada. **~ a rule** *colloq)* legeza kanuni/sheria pinda sheria. 2 inama, nepa, nesa *branches bent under the weight of leaves* matawi yalinesa kwa uzito wa majani. 3 *(direct)* elekeza, ongoza (akili, macho n.k.) *~ one's mind to one's work* elekeza akili zote kazini. 4 **be bent on** dhamiria, nuia, jibidiisha. 5 **~ sb to** salimu amri; tiisha. 6 inika, funga. **~ sail** funga tanga. **bent** *adj* danganyifu; ovu; kichaa.

beneath *adv* 1 chini ya. 2 -siostahili *he is ~ contempt* ni mtu duni, wa kudharauliwa *it is ~ him* haimfai kufanya.

benedick *n* mwanamume aliyeoa karibuni.

Benedictine *n* 1 Benediktini (mtawa), mbenediktini. 2 kileo cha kibenediktini.

benediction *n* baraka, dua (hasa baada ya ibada).

benefaction *n* ufadhili, fadhila, jamala, sadaka. **benefactor** *n* mfadhili, mtenda mema. **benefice** *n* wakfu. **beneficence** *n* ukarimu, upaji, wema. **beneficent** *adj* -karimu, -paji -ema, -fadhili.

beneficial *adj* -a kufaa, -a msaada, -enye manufaa.

benefit *n* 1 faida, msaada, fadhila. **~ of the doubt** -totia hatiani kwa kukosa. **~ performance/concert/match** onyesho la hisani *public ~* manufaa ya umma. 2 wema, upendeleo, manufaa. 3 ruzuku, posho *vi, vt* fadhili, nufaisha, faa, faidi.

n mnufaishwa, mfadhiliwa.
beneficiary *n* mnufaishwa, mfadhiliwa.
benevolence *n* ukarimu, wema.
benevolent *adj I* -karimu, -saidizi. 2 -a kukirimu. ~ **to/towards** karimi, saidizi kwa. **~ly** *adv.*
benighted *adj (liter or old use)*- 1 -a kuchwelewa, ingiwa giza we *were* ~ tulichelewa hadi usiku. 2 *(unenlightened)*-jinga, -shenzi, -siojua mambo.
benign *adj* 1 *(of persons)* -ema, pole. 2 *(of disease)* hafifu, -epesi, -sio hatari. 3 *(of soil, climate)* -a kufaa, -anana. **~ity** *n* wema.
benignant *adj (formal)* -ema, fadhili. **~ly** *adv.*
bent *n* kipaji, uwezo wa mtu *she has a ~ for sewing* ana uwezo mkubwa wa kushona.
benumb *vt (arch)* tia ganzi, fifisha, poozesha. **~ed** *adj* -fa ganzi, pooza.
benzine *n* benzini.
bequeath *vt* ~ *to* rithisha. 2 *(fig)* achia *traditions ~ed to us* mila tulizoachiwa. **~al** *n* urithisho.
bequest *n* wasia, urithi, mapokeo.
berate *vt* karipia, kemea.
bereave *vt (of)* 1 ondolea, twalia, tolea. ~ **of hope** ondolea matumaini. 2 *(of death)* fiwa, acha katika hali ya ukiwa, nyang'anya. **~d** *n.* **the ~d** mfiwa, wafiwa. **~ment** *n* 1 (tendo au hali ya) kufiwa. 2 msiba.
bereft *v* see **bereave**.
beret *n* bereti: aina ya kofia.
berg see **iceberg.**
beri-beri *n* beriberi (ugonjwa uletwao na ukosefu wa vitamini B_1 mwilini).
berry *n* tunda dogo lolote (kama forosadi, fuu, kunazi). 2 mbegu au kokwa ya tunda k.m buni.
berserk *adj* **go** ~ pagawa.
berth *n* kitanda (ndani ya meli, treni, ndege au gari). 2 *(in a port)* bandari: mahali pa meli kutia nanga na kukaa gatini *(fig)* **give a wide ~ to** epa, ambaa kwa usalama, jiepusha na. 3 *(colloq)* mgodi, kazi *find a snug ~* pata mgodi/kazi/ rahisi *vt* 1 funga gati. 2 tafuta/malazi (melini n.k.)
beryl *n* kito (aghalabu cha ahdhari).
beseech *vt* sihi, omba sana. **~ing** *adj* -enye kuomba. **~ingly** *adv.*
beset *vt* 1 zunguka na kushambulia. 2 zonga, sumbua. **~ting sin** tatizo la kudumu.
beside *prep (by side of)* kando ya, karibu ya/na ~ *the lake* kando/karibu ya/na ziwa *he is fat ~ me* yeye ni mnene akilinganishwa nami **be ~ oneself with joy** zuzuliwa na furaha.
besides *adv prep* aidha, vilevile, tena, zaidi ya hayo, licha ya hayo ~ **nothing** siyo zaidi ya.
besiege *vt* 1 zingira (mji) vitani; zunguka, husuru. 2 ~ **with** songa sana, songa pande zote *(fig) ~d with requests* ombwa na watu wengi mara nyingi. **~er** *n.*
besmear *vt* ~ **with** pakaza kote.
besmirch *vt* chafua; *(fig)* chafua jina.
besom *n* ufagio uliotengenezwa kwa fito na kufungwa katika kishikio kirefu.
besotted *adj* ~ **by/with (be)** pumbazwa (na ulevi, mapenzi, furaha nyingi n.k.).
besought *see* **beseech.**
bespangled *adj* -liopambwa kwa zari.
bespattered *pred adj* ~ **with** -liochafuliwa kwa kurushiwa matope, maji, mafuta; -liojaa madoa.
bespeak *vt* 1 agiza mapema, omba kabla. 2 ashiria, -wa ishara ya. 3 hutubia. 4 agiza (vifaa) *adj* -liofanywa kwa maagizo. **bespoke tailor/shoe maker** fundi wa kupima.
bespectacled *adj* -enye miwani, -enye kuvaa miwani.
best[1] *adj (independent superl) see* **good**, 1 bora kabisa, aali, -ema sana, -ote *the ~ student in the class* mwanafunzi bora kabisa darasani. **the ~ part of** takriban, sehemu kubwa kabisa ya *the ~ thing to do* jambo litakaloweza kuleta mapato maridhawa *make the ~use of* tumia jambo fulani kwa ufanisi (mkubwa).

put one's ~ foot foward kazana, fanya chapuchapu. **with the ~ will** kwa nia njema kabisa. **~ man** msimamizi wa bwana harusi.

best[2] *adv (independent superl see* **well, better)** 1 vizuri kabisa *she was the ~ dressed woman in town* alikuwa mwanamke mvaa vizuri kabisa mjini. **as ~ one may/can** kadiri inavyowezekana, kwa namna inavyowezekana. **think ~** amua njia bora kabisa *do as you think ~* fanya kwa namna unavyoona ni bora. 2 kabisa, sana, kuliko *he is the ~ hated man in the village* yeye ni mtu anayechukiwa sana kijijini. **~ seller** kitabu kinachouzwa sana *his new novel is one of the season's ~ sellers* riwaya yake ni kitabu kinachouzwa sana msimu huu. 3 **had ~** -yapasa, afadhali *you had ~ come home early* afadhali urudi nyumbani mapema.

best[3] *n (pron.) (independent superl see* **better)** 1 watu wenye uwezo, hadhi au sifa -wa bora *he is the ~ in his profession*ana uwezo mkubwa kuliko wote katika kazi yake *we are the ~ of friends* sisi ni marafiki sana. 2 kitu, hali, mazingira, tendo bora. **be at one's ~** kuwa katika hali, afya njema. **be all for the ~** kuwa na matokeo mema mwisho (ingawaje mwanzoni hapakuwa na matazamio mema). **do sth all for the ~** tenda jambo kwa nia njema (ingawa huenda isionekane hivyo). **be/dress in one's (Sunday) ~** valia nguo nzuri kabisa. **(even) at the ~ of times** (hata) pale mambo yanapoitika. **have/get the ~of it/of the quarrel deal/bargain** shinda, nufaika, faidi. **have/get the ~ of everything** faidi kila kitu. **with the ~** na mtu yeyote yule. **with the ~ of intentions** kwa nia njema kabisa. **do one's ~/the ~ one can** fanya liwezekanalo. **make the ~of a bad job/ business** jitahidi dhidi ya vikwazo. *make the ~ of one's way home* rudi haraka nyumbani licha ya matatizo. **make the ~ of things** ridhika (hata kama mambo hayaridhishi). **to the ~ of my knowledge** kadiri nijuavyo.

best *vt (colloq)* shinda.

bestial *adj* -a kihayawani, -a kinyama, -a kuchukiza. -a kikatili. **~ly** *adv* kikatili. **~ty** *n* 1 unyama, tendo la kikatili, uhayawani. **commit ~ity** tenda kikatili. 2 ingilia mnyama. **bestiary** *n* makusanyiko ya hadithi za wanyama za maadili.

bestir *vt* **~ oneself** jishughulisha, changamka.

bestow *vt* 1 tawaza, weka katika wadhifa. 2 **~ on/upon** toa, pa zawadi/msaada *~ a favour on sb* fadhili, kirimu *~ ones's hand on sb* olewa. **~ al** *n*

bestrew *vt* **~ (with)** *(poet)* tawanya, tapanya. **~ed** *adj* -liotawanyika.

bestride *vt* kaa/simama magamaga.

bet *n* 1 dau; mapatano ya kupinga au kuwekeana. 2 fedha au kitu kilichowekwa kwa mapatano hayo *vt* pinga, wekeana dau, pingana. **~ter** *n* mweka dau.

beta *n* beta (herufi ya pili ya alfabeti ya Kigiriki). **~ rays** miali ya beta.

betake *vt* **~ oneself** endea.

betel *n* 1 tambuu. 2 mtambuu. 3 majani ya tambuu.

bethink *vt* **~ oneself of** jikumbusha *~ oneselfto do* jishauri kufanya jambo.

betide *vt* pata. **woe ~ you** msiba ukupate, ole wako.

betoken *vt (arch)* wa dalili ya, ashiria.

betook *see* **betake**.

betray *vt* 1 saliti, haini, danganya, ghilibu. 2 **~ (to)** fichua siri. 3 onyesha dhahiri, fichua. 4 toa ishara, onyesha. **~al** *n* usaliti. **~er** *n* msaliti, haini.

betroth *vt (old formal use)* funga uchumba. **~al** *n* uchumba, ndoa. **~ed** *adj*

better[1] *(see good) adj* 1 bora, (zuri) zaidi, aula, -a kufaa zaidi. **~ than one's word** bora kuliko matarajio. **do (sth) against one's ~ judgement** fanya jambo shingo upande. **no**

~**than** ni hayo hayo. **the ~ part of** sehemu bora/kubwa zaidi. **see ~ days** -wana maisha bora zaidi. **one's ~ feelings** utu bora, idili. **his ~ half** *(colloq)* mkewe. 2 ahueni, afadhali, nafuu **be ~ off without** -wa na furaha zaidi bila ya **know ~** -wa mweledi zaidi; kataa jambo (kwa kujua kwamba halina ukweli). **but I know ~** lakini najua sana (kuwa si kweli). **think (all) the ~ of sb** enzi sana, heshimu sana. **think ~ of sth** ghairi, fikiri tena (dhidi). 2 **had ~** (ni) bora/vyema.

better[2] *n* **one's ~s** wakubwa wetu, watu wenye busara. **get the ~ of sb or sth** shinda, fanikiwa. **for ~ (or) for worse** kwa mema na mabaya, kwa vyovyote vile.

better[3] *vt* 1 fanya vyema zaidi *striving to be ~ of* kujitahidi kupata kilicho bora. 2 shinda. ~ **oneself** jiendeleza (kiuchumi, kielimu, kicheo) zaidi ~**ment** *n* maendeleo, hali bora.

better[4] *n see* **bet**.

between *prep* baina (ya), kati (ya). ~ **ourselves** kati yetu wenyewe *I rushed ~ them* nilijitoma kati yao. *adv* **(in) ~** katikati (ya). **few and far ~** moja moja, chache na zilizotawanyika. *n* **a go ~** mshenga. **come/stand ~** tenganisha. **little to choose ~ them** hakuna tafauti. **~ and between** katikati, si hiki wala kile.

bevel *n* matemo, ukingo wa ubao *(for carpentry)* piga ukingo wa ubao. **~-gear** *n* gia ya matemo, gia ya terebesha.

beverage *n (formal)* kinywaji chochote isipokuwa maji.

bevy *n* 1 *(of people)* umati. 2 *(of animals)* kundi.

bewail *vt (poet)* lilia, omboleza, sikitikia.

beware *vt,vi* **~ (of)** angalia, -wa macho, tahadhari,-wa na hadhari *~ lest you fall* angalia usije ukaanguka.

bewilder *vt* kanganya, tatiza. **~ment** *n* mkanganyiko, utatanishi.**~ed** *adj* -lio kanganyik(iw)a. **~ing** tatanishi.

bewitch *vt* 1 roga, fanyia uchawi, sihiri. 2 *(fascinate)* pagaza, duwaza. **~ing** *adj*. **~ingly** *adv*.

beyond *adv* ng'ambo ya pili (ya), upande wa pili (wa), mbele ya *the forest and fields ~* msitu na mashamba upande wa pili *prep* 1 mbele (ya). 2 kupita kiasi. ~ **measure** kupita (kadiri). 2 -wa nje. 3 kushinda, kupita *it is ~ his powers* iko nje ya uwezo wake ~ *belief* isiyosadikika ~ *recall*-siokumbukika ~*recovery*-sioponyeka, isiyopatikana tena ~ *compare* -siolinganishika. ~ **all reasonable doubt** bila shaka yoyote. 4 ila, isipokuwa *she has nothing ~ her beauty* hana zaidi ya/ila uzuri wake *n* pasipojulikana, ahera *the back of ~* mahali pa mbali sana.

bhang *n* bangi.

bi- *pref* -enye vitu viwili, -a kugawika kwa mbili, -a mbili, -a njia mbili.

bias *n (dress-making)* mshazari. **cut on the ~** kata mshazari. 2 upendeleo, upendelevu *have a ~ towards* pendelea **~(s)ed** *adj adv* -a chuki, baguzi *vi* athiri.

bib *n* bibu: kitambaa cha mtoto afungwacho shingoni alapo *(fig)* **put on one's best ~ and tucker** vaa nguo nzuri, toka.

Bible *n* Biblia. **biblical** *adj*.

bibliography *n* bibliografia. **bibliographer** *n* mwandishi wa bibliografia. **bibliographic (al)** *adj*.

bibulous *adj* -levi, -a kupenda ulevi.

bicameral *adj* -enye mabunge mawili (k.m. Uingereza, House of Commons na House of Lords).

bicarbonate *n (chem)* bikabonati. ~ **of soda** magadi.

bicentenary *n* 1 miaka mia mbili. 2 sikukuu ya kuadhimisha miaka mia mbili. **bicentennial** *adj n*.

bicephalous *n* -enye vichwa viwili.

biceps *n* musuli za mkono.

bicker vt bishanabishana, gombanagombana.

bicuspid *n* sagego.

bicyclist *n see* **bicycle**.
bid[1] *vt, vi (arch or lit)* 1 ambia *do as you are ~en* fanya unavyoambiwa. 2 takia *~ farewell* takia heri, aga. 3 alika *the ~den guests* wageni walioalikwa. **~ding** *n* amri. **~dable** *adj* -tiifu.
bid[2] *vt, vi* 1 *(for) (on)* zabuni. 2 *(against)* shindana na (katika kuzabuni). 3 tafuta, jaribu kupata *politicians ~ for support* wanasiasa wanatafuta kuungwa mkono. 4 *(fair to)* elekea. **today ~s fair to be fine** leo yaelekea kuwa nzuri. 5 *(of cards)* otea, arifia *n* 1 zabuni. 2 jaribio *the army made a ~ for power* jeshi lilijaribu kutwaa madaraka. **~der** *n* mzabuni.
bide *vt (lit arch)* ngoja, subiri. ~ **one's time** subiri wakati mzuri.
bidet *n (Fr)* chambio.
biennial *adj* -a miaka miwili; -a kila mwaka wa pili. **~ly** *adv*.
bier *n* tusi; kilili cha jeneza.
biff *sl n* konde, mdukuo *vt* piga makonde.
bifocal *adj* -enye lenzi mbili. **~s** *n* miwani yenye lenzi mbili (ya kuwezesha kuona mbali na karibu).
bifurcate *vi, vt (of roads, rivers etc)* fanya panda. **~d** *adj* -a panda, -a ncha mbili. **bifurcation** *n* panda.
big *adj* 1 kubwa ~ *house* nyumba kubwa. ~ **shot/wig** kizito, bwana mkubwa. ~ **words** majivuno. **talk** ~ jidai, jisifu. ~ **hearted** -karimu sana. **get/grow too ~ for one's boots** vimba kichwa. **think** ~ -wa na mipango mikubwa. ~ **game** wanyama (wakubwa) wa porini (k.v. tembo, simba n.k.). ~ **head** mtu anayejivuna sana. **have ~ ideas** taka makuu. 2 maarufu *he's a ~ name* yeye ni maarufu. 3 -enye mimba pevu. **~ness** *n*.
bigamy *n (leg)* kosa (katika nchi kadhaa) la kuwa na wake/waume wawili. **bigamist** *n*. **bigamous** *adj*.
bight *n* 1 kitanzi. 2 *(bay)* ghuba
bigot *n* mtu mwenye kushikilia itikadi yake, mlokole: mtu anayeng'ang'ania mawazo au imani yake kupita kiasi **~ed** *adj*.~ **ry** n.
bijou *n (Fr)* kito, jiwe la thamani *adj* -dogo na -a fahari.
bike *n vi see* **bicycle**.
bikini *n* bikini (aina ya vazi la kike la kuogelea lenye vipande viwili).
bilabial *adj (phon)* -a midomo.
bilateral *adj* -a pande mbili ~ *symmetry* uenzipacha ~ *agreement* mapatano kati ya pande mbili (k.m. nchi mbili). **~ly** *adv*. **ism** *n* sera ya kusisitiza mapatano kati ya nchi mbili (si zaidi).
bile *n* 1 nyongo. 2 *(ill humour)* chuki, hasira. ~ **duct** *n* kifuko cha nyongo.
bilious *adj* -a nyongo; -epesi wa kukasirika, -enye hasira. **biliousness** *n*.
bilge *n* 1 *(naut)* banduru *rest on its ~* sinika dau. 2 *(sl) (nonsense)* upuuzi; takataka *talk~* ongea upuuzi.
bilharzia *n* kichocho.
bilingual *adj* -enye kusema lugha mbili (hasa kutoka utotoni), -a lugha mbili.
bilk *vt* danganya/kwepa kulipa.
bill[1] *n* 1 hati ya madai ya fedha. **foot the** ~ lipa gharama zote. 2 *(US)* noti ya benki. ~ **fold** pochi ya fedha. 3 *(leg)* mswada. 4 tangazo, ilani. **fit/fill the** ~ faa sana. ~ **of fare** menu: orodha ya vyakula hotelini. ~ **board** bango la kuwekea matangazo. 5 cheti cha idhini. ~ **of lading** hati ya mizigo (melini). **clean ~ of health** cheti cha kuthibitisha afya. **~of rights** sheria ya haki za binadamu *vt* 1 andikia bili. 2 tangaza.
bill[2] n 1 mdomo wa ndege (mgumu na uliochongoka). 2 *(geog)* fungu, rasi *vi (of birds)* busu. ~ **and coo** *(of lovers)* busiana na nong'onezana.
bill[3] *n* **(also ~ hook)** mundu.
billet *n* 1 nyumba ya kupanga (kwa wanajeshi tu). 2 *(colloq)* kazi, cheo *vt (on)* pangisha nyumba za kukaa (za watu binafsi).
billet-doux *n (pl) (Fr)* barua ya

mapenzi.
billhook *n* **see bill**[3].
billiards *n* biliadi: aina ya mchezo wa kugonganisha mipira midogo kwenye meza maalumu. ~ **table** *n* meza ya biliadi ~ **room** n chumba cha biliadi. ~ **player** *n* mcheza biliadi. ~ **ball** *n* mpira wa biliadi. ~ **cloth** *n* kitambaa cha biliadi.
billngsgate *n* soko.
billion *n* bilioni (katika mfumo wa Amerika na Ufaransa mamilioni elfu, katika Uingereza mamilioni milioni).
billow *n* wimbi kubwa. *(pl) (poet)* **~s** bahari *vi* jongea kama wimbi. **~y** *adj* -enye mawimbi, -a kama mawimbi.
billy *n* 1 *(esp in Australia)* kopo la kupikia(kinachotumiwakamabirika).
billy-goat *n* beberu.
billy-(h)o *n (old sl)* **like ~** sana *he ran like ~* alikimbia sana.
biltong *n (of meat)* mtanda.
bimonthly *adj/adv* 1 (-a) kila miezi miwili. 2 (-a) mara mbili kwa mwezi.
bin *n* pipa, kilindo: chombo cha kuhifadhia nafaka, vyakula, takataka n.k. *dust/litter~* pipa la takataka.
binary *adj* -a jozi ~ *operation* tendo jozi ~ *expansion* ufafanuzi jozi.
bind *vi,vi* 1 **(up)** funga. 2 *(of books)* jalidi. 3 gandisha,unganisha. 4 *(constipate)* funga choo. 5 **(over)** tia sharti, shurutisha, pasi. ~ **oneself to do sth** ahidi kufanya. 6 **(on)** *(old sl)* lalamalalama. 7 *(gram)* ambatisha, funga. **~er** *n* 1 mjalidi; mashine ya kujalidi. 2 jalada jepesi la kuwekea magazeti. 3 dutu ya kugandishia (k.m.lami). **~ery** kitengo cha ujalidi. **~ing** *adj* -a lazima kutiiwa/kufuatwa *a ~ing agreement* makubaliano *n* jalada.
binge *n (sl)* ulevi.
bingo *n* aina ya mchezo wa kamari.
binnacle *n (naut)* sanduku la dira melini.
binocular(s) *n (pl)* darubini.
binomial *n (maths)* vipeo: iliyoundwa na namba mbili zilizounganishwa na alama za (+) (-) (k.m $x_2 - {}_4$)
bio *pref bio,* -a kuhusu uhai.
biochemistry *n* biokemia.
biodegradable *adj* -a kuweza kuvundishwa na bakteria.
biography *n* wasifu: kitabu kinachoelezea maisha ya mtu. **biographer** *n* mwandika wasifu. **biographic(al)** *adj* -a kuhusu wasifu.
biology *n* biolojia, elimu viumbe.
biologist *n* mwana biolojia.
biological *adj* -a biolojia. ~ **warfare** vita vya kutumia bakteria haribifu.
biosphere *n* sehemu ya dunia ambapo uhai wawezekana kuwepo.
bipartisan *adj* -a vyama viwili (vya siasa).
bipartite *adj* -a sehemu mbili, -a pande mbili ~ *agreement* makubaliano ya pande mbili.
biped[1] *n* mnyama mwenye miguu miwili *adj* -enye miguu miwili (kama mtu, ndege n.k.).
biped[2] *adj (zool)* kiumbe mwenye miguu miwili.
biplane *n* ndege yenye mabawa mawili kila upande.
birch *n* 1 *bot* mbetula. 2 *(twigs)* **(also - rod)** fimbo za kutolea adhabu *vt* adhibu kwa kuchapa fimbo.
bird *n* 1 ndege, nyuni *~s of a feather* watu wa tabia moja. **~s of a feather flock together** *(prov)* Waswahili wa Pemba hujuana kwa vilemba. **a ~'s eye view** mtazamo kutoka juu (angani), mtazamo wa jumla. **a ~ in the hand is worth two in the bush** heri kenda shika, kuliko kumi nenda uje. **early** ~ *n* mtu aamkaye au afikaye mapema. ~ **cage** *n* tundu la ndege. ~ **watcher** *n* mpenda kuangalia ndege. ~ **lime** *n* ulimbo. ~ **fancier** *n* mpenda ndege (hasa anayewafuga). ~ **call** *n* sauti ya ndege *(colloq)*. ~ **brained** *adj* -jinga. 2 mtu. 3 *(sl)* msichana, bibie. 4 kuzomea *get ~* zomewa.
biretta *n* bireta (aina ya kofia ya mapadre).

birth *n* 1 uzazi, kuzaliwa. **give ~ to** zaa, jifungua. **~ place** mahali pa kuzaliwa. **~ mark** alama ya kuzaliwa **~ rate** kima cha uzazi. **~ control** uzazi wa majira; udhibiti wa uzazi. 2 *(origin)* asili; ukoo, nasaba *Tanzanian by ~* Mtanzania wa asili. **~ right** haki kutokana na asili, haki ya mtu kutokana na uzawa wake, urithi *a man of high ~* mtu wa nasaba bora, mtoto wa watu. 3 *(beginning)* mwanzo, chanzo, chimbuko. **~ day** *n* siku ya kuzaliwa.

biscuit *n* 1 biskuti. 2 *(US)* mkate mdogo mkavu. 3 *(of colour)* hudhurungi. **take the ~** *(sl)* vunja rekodi.

bisect *vt* kata sawa, gawa kati. **~ on** *n* kukata sawa, kugawa kati. **~or** *n* 1 mstari wa katikati, mstari wa kugawa kati.

bisexual *adj* 1 -a jinsi mbili; -enye uke na ume, -a huntha. 2 -enye kutamani kufanya mapenzi na jinsi zote mbili *n* huntha; mpenda jinsi zote mbili. **~ity** *n*.

bishop *n* askofu, **auxiliary ~** askofu msaidizi *(chess)* sataranja. **~ric** *n* jimbo la askofu, dayosisi.

bison *n* baisani: aina ya nyati (wa Marekani na Ulaya).

bistro *n* baa ndogo; mkahawa; klabu ya usiku.

bit[1] *n* 1 lijamu. *(phr)* **champ at the ~** -wa na hamasa ya kuanza shughuli. **take the ~ between one's teeth** a) *(of horse)* toroka b) makinika (katika kazi ngumu). 2 *(of tool)* msumari wa kekee.

bit[2] *n* 1 sehemu, kipande kidogo sana. chembe kidogo *a ~ of bread* kipande cha mkate. **tear to ~s** chana vipande vipande. 2 muda mfupi, kidogo. **wait a ~** ngoja kidogo *I don't care a ~* sijali hata kidogo. **a ~ at a time/ ~ by ~** kidogo kidogo, polepole. **~s and pieces** vikorokoro. 3 **do one's ~** timiza wajibu. 4 **every ~ as** sawasawa na. 5 **not a ~ (of it)** si kitu, usijali. 6 (US) **two ~s** senti ishirini na tano. 7 **a nice ~ of goods/fluff/stuff** *(sl)* msichana mzuri.

bitch *n* 1 mbwa jike. 2 *(vulgar, derog)* mwanamke *vi* lalama. **~y** *adj* -korofi. **~iness** *n*.

bite *vt* 1 uma, ng'ata, mega kwa meno. **~ one's lips** uma meno, uma kidole (kwa kuficha hasira), uma chanda. **~ the dust** anguka, uawa (hasa katika pigano). **~ off more than one can chew** jaribu kufanya mambo yanayozidi uwezo wako. **~ sb's head off** karipia/kemea sana. **~ the hand that feeds one** nyea ago, nyea kambi. epukana na. **be bitten with** -wa na shauku ya. *(pro)* **once bitten twice shy** aliyeumwa na nyoka akiona ung'ongo hushtuka. 2 kamata, shika (k.m magurudumu). 3 umiza, penya. 4 *(of fish)* shika chambo *n* 1 kuuma kwa meno; umo. 2 kipande. 3 chakula; kitafunio. 4 kushika chambo. 5 ukali, uchungu. **the ~r bitten** mwinda mwindwa. **biting** *adj* -kali, -a kuumiza, -a kuchoma. **biter** *n* mwenye kuuma, mdanganyifu.

bitten *see* **bite**

bitter *adj* 1 -chungu, -kali. 2 -a kuleta huzuni gumu kuvumiliwa. **to the ~ end** hadi mwishoni, hadi kifo. **~sweet** chungutamu *n* 1 uchungu *we must take the ~ with the sweet* tukipenda damu na usaha papo. 2 aina ya (bia) chungu, *(pl) (med)* dawa ya kusaidia umeng'enyaji; chuki, uhasama. **~ness** *n* uchungu, ukali.

bitumen *n* lami. **~ize** *vt* geuza kuwa lami; funika kwa lami. **bituminous** *adj* -a lami.

bivalve *n adj* 1 valimbili; -a valimbili. 2 *(zool)* koambili.

bivouac *n* kambi ya muda (bila kupiga hema n.k.) *vt* piga kambi ya muda.

bizarre *adj* -a kioja, -siokuwa -a kawaida, -a ajabu (kwa kuwa geni au kupita kiasi). **~ly** *adv*.

blab *vi,vt* payapaya, payuka, bwabwaja. **~ out secret** toa siri. **~ber ~ mouth** *n* domokaya, mmbea.

black *adj* 1 -eusi ~ *shoes* viatu vyeusi.2 -chafu *your hands are* ~ mikono yako michafu. 3 -baya, ovu *he's not as* ~ *as you say* si mbaya kama unavyosema *today is a* ~ *day* leo ni siku mbaya. **be in someone's ~ books** chukiwa na fulani. 4 -a giza, -a utusitusi *n* 1 *(colour)* weusi, kiwi. 2 *(person)* mweusi. 3 **in the** ~ -wana pesa, -tokuwa na deni. 4 **in ~ and white** -loandikwa; *(of films and photographs)* so rangi *vt* 1 fanya weusi (viatu n.k). 2 *(of strikes)* susa, kataa kushughulikia. **~en** *vt* 1 fanya weusi. 2 *(someone's name)* chafua jina, kashifu. **~ing** *n* dawa nyeusi ya kupiga viatu. **~ish** *adj* -eusi kidogo, -eusi -eusi. **~ness** *n* weusi; giza, ubaya. **~ art/magic** *n* uchawi, uramali, ulozi. **~ ball** *vt* piga kura kumkataa mtu asiingie kwenye kikundi/chama. **~ board** *n* ubao (darasani). **~ box** *n* kisanduku cheusi: chombo maalum (agh ndani ya ndege kinachorekodi mambo yote yanayotokea, kinatumika hasa kujua chanzo cha ajali au maafa). **B~ Death** *n* tauni (iliyoua maelfu ya watu katika karne ya 14) .**~ eye** *n* kuvia, kuvilia. **give someone a ~ eye** kumviliza mtu. **~d** -enye macho meusi. **~ guard** *n* mwovu, baa, ayari, fasiki *vt* tukana, tusi. **~ly** *adj* ovu, laghai. **~ head** *n* chunusi. **~-lead** *n* risasi (katika kalamu ya risasi). **~ leg** *n (of strikes)* msaliti: anayeendelea kufanya kazi wakati wenzie wamegoma *vi* saliti wafanyakazi. **~ list** *n* orodha ya watu/mashirika/ nchi n.k wanaofikiriwa kuwa wabaya au wataabidhibiwa *he can't get a job because he's on the employers'* ~ hawezi kupata kazi maana yuko kwenye orodha ya watu wabaya *vt* weka mtu kwenye orodha hii. **~ mail** *vt* saliti; tisha mtu kwamba utafichua siri/maovu yake ili akupe fedha/ upendeleo *n* kupata pesa/ upendeleo kwa njia hii. **~er** *n* **~mark** *n* alama mbaya (shuleni au kazini) msaliti. **~ market** *n* magendo. **~eer** mfanya magendo. **~ Muslims** *n* Waislamu Weusi: kikundi cha watu weusi hasa Marekani ambacho, pamoja na kufuata Uislamu kinataka kujitenga na Wazungu na kuanzisha dola yao peke yao. **~out** *n* 1 giza tupu (kutokana na kuzimika kwa umeme ama kwa sababu ya hitilafu ya umeme ama kwa makusudi wakati wa vita). 2 *(plays)* kuzimika taa zote jukwaani. 3 kuzirai/kuzimia kwa muda mfupi. 4 *(of journalism)* kuzima kutangazwa kwa habari fulani *vt,vi* fanya giza; ficha kabisa; zimia. **~ power** *n* siasa kali ya kudai haki za watu weusi (hasa Marekani). **~ pepper** *n* pilipili manga. **~ sheep** *n* mtu anayetia aibu (katika familia, kikundi n.k.). **~smith** *n* mhunzi. **~spot** *n* mahali pa hatari (barabarani panapotokea ajali mara kwa mara).

bladder *n* 1 kibofu (cha mkojo). 2 mfuko (wa ngozi, mpira n.k. unaoweza kujazwa hewa au kioevu).

blade *n* 1 *(of plants)* jani, kijani. 2 (of sword) ubapa, kengee. 3 bapa la kasia. 4 *(fig) (arch)* mtanashati.

blah(blah-blah) *n (colloq)* blaablaa; maneno matupu.

blame *vt* 1 *(accuse)* laumu, shtaki, kengemeka, shutumu *I don't ~ you* sikulaumu *he is to* ~ yeye ni wa kulaumiwa *they are to* ~ wao ndio wa kulaumiwa. 2 **be to** ~ -wa na hatia, stahili lawama *n* shutuma, lawama. **lay (put, cast) the ~ on sb/at sb's door** laumu mtu. **~less** *adj* -so na lawama, -so na hatia. **~ worthy** *(also* **~able)** *adj* -a kulaumiwa, -a kustahili lawama.

blanch *vt, vi (also blench)* 1 ondoa rangi, fanya kupauka. 2 pauka, geuka -eupe *fear has ~ed his face* hofu imempausha uso. 3 *(of cooking)* chemsha kidogo tu.

blancmange *n* jeli nyeupe ya maziwa iliyotiwa katika chombo ili kuipa umbo maalum ~ *powder* mchanga-nyiko wa maziwa ya unga, gelatini ya unga, n.k.

bland *adj* 1 *(of person)* mwanana, mpole, shwari, mtulivu. 2 *(of food, drink)* -chapwa -so na ladha. 3 *(of climate)* nzuri. 4 *(of story, character, etc.)* -sokuwa na mvuto. **~ly** *adj*

blandish *vt* bembeleza, shawishi, sifusifu,rairai. **~ment** *n* ubembelezaji, ushawishi.

blank *adj* 1 tupu; -sioandikwa kitu chochote. **~ cheque** cheki/hundi ilowazi, cheki isiyoandikwa kiasi cha fedha. **~ space** nafasi tupu. **~ cartridge** baruti tupu. 2 *(fig)* **give someone a ~ cheque** -pa mtu madaraka kamili *(of face, look)* -soonyesha hisia, -lofadhaika, -a kushangaa, bila jambo lolote la kuvutia. 3 *(fig)* **~ wall** patupu **come up against a ~ wall** shindwa kupata habari, maelezo, maoni n.k. 4 **~ verse** ushairi usio na vina. 5 kabisa. **~ despair** kata tamaa kabisa *n* 1 pengo, nafasi tupu, nafasi wazi, uwazi. 2 *(in lottery)* tikiti isiyoshinda. *(fig)* **draw a ~**topata yaliyotumainiwa. 3 **~ ness** *n*. **~ly** *adv* 1 (*in refusing*) kabisa. **point ~** kabisa, katakata. 2 bila kuonyesha mawazo, hisia, uelewa n.k.

blanket *n* 1 blangeti *(fig)* **born on the wrong side of the ~** mtoto wa nje ya ndoa *get between the ~s* lala kitandani. *(fig)* **a wet ~** mtu anayefanya wenzake wasifurahie mambo kwa kuonekana mwenye huzuni au mnyonge. 2 maki nene inayofunika kitu; pazia la ukungu au wingu la moshi *adj* -enye kuhusu watu wote/ makundi yote/tabaka zote/ hali zote/namna zote *vt* 1 funika kama lifanyavyo blangeti. 2 zuia; fanya kitu kisionekane, zima.

blare *vi,vt (also ~* **out (forth))** *(of trumpets, horns etc.)* lia sana *(of person)* toa sauti, piga kelele *n* mlio (kama ule wa tarumbeta n.k.).

blarnely *n (colloq)* maneno ya kulaghai; udanganyifu.

blase *adj* **~ (about)** -sioonyesha kufurahishwa na jambo fulani (agh. kwa sababu ya kutosheka nalo sana), kinaifu; -siochangamkia jambo.

blaspheme *vt* kufuru *n* mjadhambi. **blasphemous** *adj* -a kukashifu Mungu, (dini n.k.). **blasphemy** *n* maneno ya kumtukana Mungu, dini; kufuru. **blasphemously** *adv*.

blast *vt* 1 pasua kwa baruti, lipua. 2 haribu, angamiza. 3 karipia, chachafya. 4 *(curse)* laani. 5 **of ~** *(of space craft etc.)* fyatuka kuelekea juu kutokana na kusukumwa na gesi. *n* 1 upepo mkali wa ghafla, upepo wa kishindo. 2 mkondo hewa mkali unaovukuta moto katika tanuri, (of a furnace) **in/out of ~** inafanya kazi/ haifanyi kazi. 3 sauti ya ala za upepo, k.m tarumbeta. 4 mlipuko, mpasuko (wa baruti n.k.). **at full ~** *(colloq)* kwa nguvu/uwezo wote; mlio (wa baruti) *adj* -lioangamizwa, -loharibiwa, -liolaaniwa. **~-furnace** *n* kalibu, tanuri. **~ing** *n* mpasuko (wa baruti n.k.). **~ing-powder** *n* baruti.

blatant *adj* 1 dhahiri, wazi. 2 *(of action)* -enye makelele, -enye vishindo, -enye fujo, -a kujitokeza, kwa majivuno. **~ly** *adv*.

blather *n,v* see **blether**.

blaze[1] *n* 1 mwako, mmeko, ndimi za moto, mbimbiriko wa moto *in a ~* katika ndimi za moto; *burst (out) into a ~* lipuka moto ghafla *in the ~ of day* wakati wa jua kali. 2 moto; jengo au nyumba inayowaka. 3 mng'aro wa rangi. 4 hasira ya ghafula. 5 *(pl) (sl)* motoni. **Go to~s!** potelea mbali! *vi* 1 waka. 2 ng'aa, meka. 3 onyesha hasira ya ghafula *~ with anger* waka kwa hasira. **~ away** piga mizinga, bunduki upesi na kwa mfululizo. 4 *(of news)* tangaza, eneza habari zikafika mbali *adj* 1 -a kung'aa. 2 -angavu. 3 dhahiri. 4 -a mnga'ro. 5 *he was working like ~s* alikuwa anafanya kazi kama punda.

blaze[2] 1 kata, weka alama (kwenye mti) ya utambulisho wa njia au mpaka. 2 *(fig) ~ a trail* onyesha njia kwa kuweka alama, -wa wa kwanza kufanya kitu na kuonyesha wengine jinsi ya kukifanya *n* alama kwenye mti (iliyofanywa kwa kukata gome lake); alama nyeupe kwenye uso wa mnyama (k.m.) farasi au ng'ombe.

blazer *n* bleza: koti lenye kupwaya kidogo na mara nyingine huwa lina alama ya skuli au klabu ya watu.

blazon *n* nembo (hasa kwenye ngao). **~ry** *n* 1 sanaa ya kuchonga nembo. 2 maonyesho ya kuvutia *vt* remba (ngao, bango na nembo).

bleach *vt,vi (of colour)* pausha; fanya kuwa nyeupe (kwa nguvu za madawa au za jua). **~ing-powder** *n* 1 dawa ya kung'arisha au kuondoa madoa kwenye nguo (namna ya chokaa yenye harufu kali). 2 dawa ya klorini.

bleachers *n (pl) (US)* mabenchi (viti na mbao za kukalia kwenye majukwaa ya viwanja vya michezo visivyoezekwa).

bleak *adj* 1 *(of weather or country)* baridi, -a kufanya watu wajikunyate. **a ~ wind** upepo wa baridi. 2 *(of place)* wazi, -a kuvumiwa na upepo mwingi. 3 *(fig)* pasipo matumaini; -a kutokuwa na wema. **~ly** *adv*. **~ness** *n*.

bleary *adj* 1 *(of eyes)* -enye utando, isiyoona vizuri. 2 *(of photograph)* si dhahiri. **~-eyed** *adj* -enye macho mekundu (kwa sababu ya usingizi, moshi, kulia sana n.k.).

bleat *vi* 1 lia kama kondoo, mbuzi au ndama. 2 sema kwa kudeka *n* mlio kama wa kondoo, mbuzi au ndama.

bleed *vt, vi* 1 *(draw blood)* toa damu, tokwa na damu. ~ **freely** tokwa na damu chapa. 2 *(extort)* toza fedha mno. ~ **someone white** chukua fedha zote za mtu. 3 ~ **for** onea imani/huruma *my heart ~s for him* namwonea huruma sana. 4 *(of plant)* toa utomvu. 5 *(of dye)* chururika, churuzika. 6 *(of air, water, gas etc.)* toa upepo, maji gesi n.k. kutoka katika chombo. **~ing** *n (of plants)* machozi ya mti, utomvu. **~er** *n* 1 mtu mwenye mhina (ugonjwa wa kutokwa damu). 2 *(sl)* mshenzi. 3 *(sl)* jamaa. **~ing-heart** *n* 1 mtu mwenye huruma nyingi mno. 2 aina ya mimea (hasa bustanini) yenye maua yaliyo na umbo la moyo.

bleep *n* sauti kali itolewayo na redio au rada (kuashiria jambo au kutahadharisha).

blemish *n* ila, baka, dosari, waa. **without ~** bila dosari *vt* tia dosari.

blench[1] *vi* nywea, (sita) kwa woga. **without ~ing** bila kushtuka.

blench[2] see **blanch**.

blend *vi,vt* patana, changanya *these things do not ~* vitu hivi haviwezi kuchanganywa, havipatani *n* mchanganyiko; aina *~ of coffee* aina ya kahawa. **~er** *n* mashine itumiwayo jikoni kusaga mboga, matunda, n.k.

bless *vt* bariki. **God ~ you!** Mungu akubariki. 2 takia heri. 3 tukuza. 4 *~ oneself with sign of the cross* fanya ishara ya msalaba. 5 **be ~ed with** wa na baraka. 6 *(colloq)* kuonyesha mshangao eg. **~ me! ~ my soul** Mungu wangu!, Mtume! **~ed** *adj* takatifu, -enye heri, -enye baraka, -lobarikiwa. **the ~ed Virgin** Bikira Maria. **~ness** *n* hali ya kubarikiwa, uanaheri. **~ing** *n* 1 baraka, mbaraka. 2 radhi, chochote kiletacho furaha, usitawi n.k. **a ~ing in disguise** bahati njema isiyotazamiwa. **what a ~ing** bahati gani hii! 3 dua la kumwomba Mungu alete heri, abariki mtu/ kitu. 4 *(pl)* **~ings** idhini, ruhusa.

blether *vi* toa porojo, ropoka, porojo. **~ing** *adj*.

blew *see* **blow**.

blight *n* 1 baka: maradhi ya mimea yanayosababishwa na kuvu. 2 pepo mbaya aharibuye matumaini, raha n.k. 3 *a ~ upon my hopes/plans etc.* kisirani katika matumaini yangu *vt* haribu, umbua, fisha, angamiza. **~er** *n* 1 mtu mwenye kuleta maudhi. 2 jamaa *(sl) you lucky ~!* una bahati sana.

blimey *int (sl, vulg)* -a kushangaza.

blind *adj* 1 *(of sight)* -pofu, -soona a ~ person asoona, *~ of one eye* -enye chongo. **~ spot** sehemu ya mboni isiyoona; sehemu isiyoonekana vizuri; kushindwa kuelewa jambo. 2 *(fig) be ~ to sth* kutoweza kutambua kitu; *turn a/one's ~ eye to sth* puuzia jambo, jifanya kwamba huoni. 3 -jinga, -zembe, -a harara, -sofikiri *in ~ haste* kwa haraka, pasipo kufikiria *~ rage* ghadhabu ya kijinga. 4 **a ~ corner** kona bubu, kali. 5 **a ~ alley** uchochoro usotoka. ~ **flying** urushaji ndege kwa kutumia vyombo (k.m. katika mawingu mazito, ukungu n.k.). ~ **turning** kona katika barabara isiyoweza kuonekana kwa urahisi. 6 **a ~ side of sb/sth** penye ubovu. 7 ~ **date** kukutanishwa na msichana/mvulana (bila kuwa mmepanga) kwa mara ya kwanza. ~ **drunk** -lolewa sana. **~er** *(colloq) vt* 1 pofusha. 2 danganya, ondolea uwezo wa kuamua kwa urazini, tia kiwi cha macho. ~ **fold** *adv, vt* 1 funga kidoto. 2 pumbaza *n* 1 pazia (ya kukingia jua dirishani); ukingo wa kutiwa katika madirisha. **Venetian ~**-luva (agh. za plastiki) za kuzuia mwanga. 2 udanganyifu, hila, hadaa, ghiliba. **~ness** *n* upofu; hali ya kutoweza kuona kitu/ jambo. **~ers** *(GB = blinkers) n (pl)* vinga vya macho (kuzuia farasi asione pembeni). **~-stitch** *n* mshono usioonekana.

blink *vi,vt* 1 pepesa, kopesa. 2 ~ **(at) the fact that** -tojali *he ~ed (at) the fact that* hakujali ukweli kwamba. 3 mwekamweka. 4 ~ **at** shangaa. **~ers** *see* = **blinders.**

blip *n* mweko (k.m. wa rada).

bliss *n* upeo wa furaha, furaha kamili. ~ **fully** *adv.*

blister *n* 1 lengelenge. 2 *(eruptive disease)* uwati. 3 *(plaster)* maturuturu kwenye mpako *vt* 1 sababisha/ tokeza lengelenge. 2 *(fig)* pinga vikali.

blithe, blithesome *adj (chiefly poet.)* -enye furaha, -kunjufu, -epesi wa moyo. **~r** *n* porojo *vi* porojoa, piga domo. **~ly** *adv.*

blitz *n* 1 shambulio kali la ghafula (hasa kwa ndege za vita) *vt* shambulia kwa ndege za vita; tupia makombora/ mabomu kutoka hewani.

blizzard *n* dhoruba kali ya theluji.

bloat *vt* vimba sana, fura. **~ed** *adj* -lovimba sana, nene mno *~ed corpse* maiti aliyevimba sana *~ed with pride* -lovimba kichwa.

bloater *n* aina ya samaki aliyekaushwa kwa moshi na kutiwa chumvi.

blob *n* tone au kibonge cha kitu chororo au cha majimaji; waa la rangi *vt* tia waa (la wino, rangi n.k.).

bloc *n* jumuiya, shirika.

block *n* 1 pande kubwa (la mti, jiwe, n.k.). 2 bloku: jengo kubwa lenye fleti, ofisi, maduka n.k. 3 kizuizi **traffic ~ /jam** msongamano wa magari barabarani. **road ~** kizuizi cha barabarani. 4 eneo lililo kati ya barabara nne zinazokutana. 5 vipande vya matofali ya saruji au mawe vya kujengea. 6 *(pulley)* kapi, gofia, roda. 7 kibao (kipande cha mti au chuma chenye herufi) sanamu zilizochorwa juu ya kipande hicho zikiwa alama ya chapa. 8 sehemu kuu ya injini ya petroli yenye silinda na vali. **have a ~ against sth** pata kizuizi katika kufanya jambo. 9 mgawanyo wa viti katika jengo la maonyesho ya tamthilia, sinema n.k. 10 kichwa (k.m. kichwa cha mtu) *I'll knock your ~ off* nitakukata kichwa chako. 11 kiolezo cha kofia zinapotengenezwa *vt* ~ **(up)** zuia, ziba. ~ **in** chora umbo, mpango wa sanamu au ramani bila kuchora kila kitu; funga. **~-chain** *n* mnyororo (wa baiskeli). **~ade** *n* uzio wa kuzunguka jeshi; zingio *run a ~ade* epuka/penya. 2 *(US)* zuio, kizuizi. *vt* 1 husuru, zunguka kwa vita 2. zingia, zingira na zuia (mji au ngome). **~age** *n* 1 hali ya kuzuia. 2 kikwazo. ~ **head** *n (colloq)* mjinga, kichwangumu, baradhuli. ~ *house* n ngome yenye matundu ya kupenyeza bunduki. **~-letters** *n* herufi kubwa zilizotengwa.

bloke *n (sl) (GB)* mtu, mvuli, jamaa.

blond(e) *n* 1 (mzungu) mwenye nywele zenye rangi ya shaba au rangi ya kimanjano *adj* 1 -enye rangi ya shaba au kimanjano. 2 *(of person)* -enye nywele nyeupe za rangi ya shaba au ya kimanjano.

blood *n* 1 damu. ~ **bank** benki ya damu *soldiers shed their ~ for their country* wapiganaji walikufa kwa ajili ya nchi yao. 2 *(temperament)* **in cold** ~ kwa makusudi. **hot ~ed** yenye hamaki, mori. **make bad ~ between persons** chonganisha, gombanisha. 3 undugu, ukoo. ~ **is thicker than water** damu ni nzito kuliko maji. **one's own flesh and** ~ watu wa ukoo mmoja. **blue** ~ ukoo bora. 4 ukoo wa kifalme *prince of the royal* ~ mwana wa mfalme. 5 *(arch)* kijana *vt* 1 onjesha mbwa damu ya mawindo kwa mara ya kwanza 2 -pa mtu zoezi kwa mara ya kwanza. ~ **curdling** *adj* -enye kutia hofu. **~ed** *adj* 1 -enye damu. 2 -a ukoo bora. **~-donor** *n* mtoaji damu. **~-group** *n* aina ya damu. ~ **heat** *n* joto la kawaida la damu. ~ **hound** *n* 1 aina ya jibwa liwezalo kumtafuta mtu kwa kunusa harufu yake. 2 *(fig)* mpelelezi. **~ily** *adv* 1 kwa damu. 2 kiibilisi. **~less** *adj* 1 -siokuwa na damu. 2 -liopauka. 3 bila nguvu, bila kuchangamka. **~-letting** *n* kuumika, kutoa damu kwa ajili ya kutibu. **~-money** *n (informal)* malipo ya kuua ama kumsaliti mtu. 2 fidia (kwa ndugu waliopoteza ndugu zao). ~ **poisoning** *n* kusumu damu. **~-red** *adj* -ekundu kama damu ~- **relation** *n* ndugu. ~ **relationship** udugu wa damu. **half-~ relation** ndugu wa mzazi mmoja. **~ed** *adj* uaji, -a mauaji, mwangaji damu. ~ **shot** *adj (of eyes)* -ekundu kwa damu. ~ **stain** *n* doa la damu. ~ **stock** *n* ukoo bora. **~-sucker** *n* mnyonyadamu, kupe. **~-thirstiness** *n* hamu ya kuua, ukatili, kupenda kuua. ~ **sports** *n* kuwinda wanyama na ndege. ~ **thirsty** *adj* -enye hamu ya kumwaga damu, katili. **~-vessel** *n* mshipa wa damu. **~y** *adj* 1 -a damu, -enye damu. 2 *(cruel)* -kali, katili -a kiuaji. 3 *(sl) adj, adv* mno, kabisa *it's ~y hot* kuna joto kali.

bloom[1] *n* 1 ua lolote. 2 hali ya mmea kutoa maua, kuchanua. 3 upeo wa afya au ukamilifu wa mtu au wa kitu; kipindi cha kukamilika. **in** ~ chanuka *in full* ~ katika kupevuka, katika upeo wake *in the ~ of youth* katika upeo wa ujana *it has lost its ~* imepoteza uzuri wake *vi* 1 toa maua, chanua. 2 kuwa na hali kamili (yaani sura nzuri ya afya kamili); sitawi. **~y. ~ing** *adj.*

bloom[2] *n* kipande kinene cha chuma.

bloomer *n (sl)* kosa *make a* ~ boronga, vuruga, koroga, kosea *n (pl arch)* suruali fupi (ya wasichana kwa kupandia baiskeli).

blossom *n* maua mengi (hasa ya miti ya matunda). **in** ~liochanua *vi* toa maua, chanua. ~ **out** sitawi *he ~ed into a statesman* ameinukia kuwa mwanasiasa mashuhuri.

blot *n* 1 waa, doa. 2 ila, kasoro, aibu *vt* 1 tia waa. 2 *(spoil)* hasiri, umbua, aibisha. 3 kausha kioevu (k.m wino, maji n.k.). **~ter. ~ting paper** *n.* kikausho. 2 *(police)* kitabu cha matukio. **police** ~ kitabu cha polisi cha matukio. ~ **one's copy book** haribu sifa yako.

blotto *adj (sl)* -liokuwa chakari; -liolewa kabisa, -sio na fahamu sababu ya ulevi.

blotch *n* doa.

blouse *n* 1 blauzi. 2 gwanda la kazi (aghalabu lenye mkanda kiunoni). 3 koti (kama avaalo askari kuzuia mvua au baridi).

blow[1] *vi, vt* 1 *(of air/wind)* vuma *it was ~ing hard* upepo ulikuwa unavuma sana. 2 tweta, hema. 3 *(of a bulb, fuse)* lipuka. 4 toa pumzi, pulizia, vivia, vuvuia ~ *a trumpet* piga tarumbeta, piga panda. ~ **one'sown trumpet** jigamba. ~ **one's nose** penga. ~ **hot and cold** sitasita, kutaka shauri, ghairighairi.

5 *(of flies)* taga mayai. 6 *(sl) (of money)* haribu, fuja. 7 ~ **about** peperusha, peperuka. ~ **away** peperusha, ondolewa, chukuliwa kwa nguvu za upepo. ~ **in** ingia kwa ghasia, macheche au furaha kubwa. 8 *(fig)* oza. ~ **out** zima kwa kupuliza, yeyuka (kwa sababu ya nguvu za umeme kupita kiasi). ~ **out one's brains** jipiga risasi. ~ **up** lipua, lipuka *(fig)* kasirika, kuza ~ *up a picture* kuza picha. ~-**hole** *n* 1 pua la nyangumi. 2 shimo la kutolea hewa. ~-**out** *n* 1 mpasuko. 2 kupasuka (k.m. mpira).~-**pipe** *n* kipulizo. ~-**torch** *n* kitambulio, stovu pulizi. ~ **one's stock/stuck** lipuka kwa hasira. ~ **someone's mind** staajabisha, fadhaisha. ~ **down** angusha kwa upepo. ~ **off** steam payuka.

blow[2] *n* 1 pigo, kipigo, kishindo, dharuba. **at a single** ~ kwa (dharuba) pigo moja. **come to ~s; exchange ~s** pigana. **without striking a** ~ bila kupigana *~s fell thick and fast* ngumi zilimiminika. 2 *(disaster)* msiba, maafa, masaibu. 3 kupunga upepo, kubarizi.

blow[3] *vi* chanua, toa maua *n* kuchanua *in full* ~ kwa usitawi kamili.

blower *n* 1 blowa: chombo cha kusukumizia hewa ndani ya chombo kingine. 2 mtengeneza vifaa vya glasi *(colloq)* simu. ~**ing** *n* kupuliza. ~**ing engine** mashine ya kupulizia.

blowzy *adj (usu of a woman)* 1 -enye sura nyekundu. 2 chafu, -a ovyoovyo.

blubber[1] *n* shahamu (ya nyangumi na wanyama/samaki wengine wakubwa wa baharini).

blubber[2] *adj (of lips)* nene, -liovimba.

blubber[3] *vt,vi* lia kwa sauti kubwa.

bludgeon *vt* 1 piga kwa rungu. 2 *(fig) ~ sb into doing sth* lazimisha mtu kutekeleza jambo *n* rungu.

blue *adj* 1 bluu, buluu, -a rangi ya samawati; kama maji ya bahari *dark~; navy ~*. -a rangi ya nili; -a matusi. films filamu za matusi. ~ **jokes** utani wa matusi. ~ **laws** sheria ngumu (ya kikanisa n.k.). ~ **ribbon** nishani ya ushindi wa kwanza. **once in a ~ moon** kwa nadra. 2 **be** ~ wa na moyo mzito; huzunika, udhika. **out of the** ~ ghafla; bila kutegemea. 3 mfuasi mwaminifu. **a true** ~ mfuasi mwaminifu. 4 *(pl)* **the ~s** 1 hali ya kuwa na huzuni/ moyo mzito. 2 *(arch)* aina ya muziki wa jazi wa wawindaji *vt* fanya kuwa buluu. 2 ~ **one's money** fuja fedha, tumia ovyoovyo fedha. ~ **bell** *n* ua la buluu lenye umbo la kengele. ~-**book** *n* 1 taarifa rasmi ya serikali au hati zilizojalidiwa kwa jalada la buluu. 2 *(US)* orodha ya majina ya watu maarufu kijamii. 3 kitabu cha mitihani. ~-**bottle** *n* nzi wa chooni, nzi choo. ~-**collar** *adj* -a kuhusu kazi za viwandani. ~-**jacket** *n* baharia. ~-**pencil** *vt* 1 hariri. 2 kagua *(censor)*. ~-**peter** *n* sero: kibendera (cha meli) cha buluu, alama ya kuondoka meli. ~-**print** *n* 1 karatasi ya kuchorea picha/ramani ya jengo. 2 mpango makini. ~**stocking** *n* *(derog)* mwanamke msomi. ~ **bluish** *adj* -a kibuluubuluu.

bluff[1] *adj* 1 *(of person)* raufu lakini -sio na simile, -nyoofu. 2 *(steep)*- enye kuinuka ghafula. ~**ly** *adv.* ~**ness** *n* gengetao.

bluff[2] *vt,vi* danganya (kwa kujifanya). ~ **sb into doing sth** hadaa/danganya mtu afanye kitu. ~ **it out** shinda majaribio/hali ngumu kwa kudanganya. ~ **one's way out of sth** epuka jambo kwa kujifanya *n* hila. udanganyifu, matumizi ya vitisho kupata mradi (bila kuvitekeleza). **call sb's** ~ chokoza mtu atekeleze vitisho vyake. ~**er** *n.*

blunder *vt,vi* 1 enda kwa taharaki. 2 kosa (kijinga), boronga; yumba. ~ **along** sitasita *n* kosa la kijinga. ~**rer** *n* mborongaji.

blunt *adj* 1 butu, -dugi, gutu *this knife is* ~ kisu hiki kibutu (kimesenea) *be* ~ senea. 2 (*plain spoken*) -a kusema waziwazi, bila kuficha *vt* 1 fanya butu, seneza. 2 punguza nguvu (ukali n.k.) ~ *the appetite* toa hamu. **~ness** *n* 1 ubutu. 2 unyoofu. **~ly** *adv* waziwazi, bila kuficha. **~-witted** *adj* -jinga, -zito wa akili.

blur *n* 1 waa, doa. 2 kiwi, uluwihuwi, ukungu *vt,vi* 1 fanya kiwi, tia ukungu. 2 tia waa.

blurb *n* blabu: maelezo ya mkato ya mchapishaji kuhusu kitabu (nyuma ya kitabu).

blurt *vt* ~ **sth out** ropoka.

blush *n* 1 wekundu wa uso (dalili ya fadhaa, haya, hasira 2 rangi nyekundu, k.m ya ua, jua *the ~ of dawn* nuru nyekundu ya mapambazuko. 3 *(fig)* ua (la ujana n.k.) *vi* ona haya, tahayari *I ~ed for him* nilitahayari, alimtahayarisha. **~ing** *adj* 1 *(of person)* mwenye kuona haya, aibu. 2 -a rangi ya waridi. **~ingly** *adv*.

bluster *vt,vi* 1 *(of person)* foka, nenda kwa kiburi. 2 *(of wind and waves)* chafuka. 3 ~ **out** tishia kwa kujigamba. ~ **out threats** toa vitisho, tishia, tia hofu. **~ing** *adj* -a kujivuna, -a makeke, -a vitisho *n* 1 mirindimo ya gharika, mivumo ya upepo mkali. 2 vitisho, makeke. **~y** *adj*.

boa *n* 1 chatu. 2 *(arch)* skafu ya manyoya.

boar *n* 1 nguruwe dume (asiyehasiwa). 2 nguruwe mwitu.

board[1] *n* 1 ubao. 2 *(pl)* **~s** jukwaa. 3 *(for advertisement)* ubao. **notice ~** ubao wa matangazo *chess ~* ubao wa sataranji. 4 *(stiff paper)* jalada, bango: karatasi nene ngumu *bound in (cloth) ~s* -liojalidiwa kwa bango. 5 chakula. ~ **and lodging** chakula na malazi. 6 *(fig)* **above ~** wazi, bila kuficha kitu, dhahiri. **sweep the ~** pata karibu kila kitu, shinda sana *(fig)* faulu sana. 7 halmashauri, kamati, bodi *the ~ of directors* bodi ya wakurugenzi. ~ **of inquiry** kamati ya uchunguzi. 8 **on ~** merikebuni, melini, ndani ya ndege. **go on ~** ingia melini. **go by the ~** *(of masts)* angukia chomboni *(of plans)* acha kabisa, telekeza. 10 *(compounds)*. ~ **room** chumba cha mikutano. ~ **walk** mbao za kutembelea.

board[2] *vt,vi* 1 funga/funika/ziba kwa mbao. 2 lisha/lishwa kwa mkopo (wa muda maalum) ~ *people* lisha watu. ~ **out** la chakula nje ya mahali pa kulala. 3 ingia, panda (merikebuni, melini, garini, n.k.). **~ing card** cheti cha kuingilia chomboni *be ~ed* pakiwa, -lishwa. **~er** *n* mtu anayelishwa, mwanafunzi wa bweni/dahalia. **~-over/~up** funga kwa mbao. **~ing-house** nyumba ya kupanga yenye huduma za malazi na chakula, nyumba ya wageni. **~ing-school** *n* shule ya bweni, dahalia.

boast *vt, vi* 1 jisifu, jiona, jigamba, jinata *that's sth to ~ of* hicho ni kitu cha kujivunia *without wishing to ~* bila kutaka kujisifu. 2 jisifia, jivunia jambo. *n* 1 majivuno, majisifu. 2 sababu ya kujisifia, kujinata. **~er.** *n* **~ful** *adj*. **~fulness** *n* hali ya kujinata.

boat *n* 1 mashua, boti. **ship's ~** hori. *(fig)* **be (all) in the same ~** -wa katika hali ileile. **burn one's ~** kata shauri, -torudi nyuma, piga moyo konde. 2 *(of gravy)* kibakuli cha mchuzi *vi* safiri kwa mashua. **go ~ing** safiri mashuani kwa kujifurahisha. **take to the ~s** *(of the crew and passengers)* kimbilia mashuani wakati wa ajali. **~-hook** *n* upondo wenye kulabu. **~-house** *n* banda la kuhifadhia, kuundia au kukalafatia mashua. **~ man/ ~-keeper** baharia. **~-race** *n* mashindano ya mashua. ~ **swain** *n* *(naut)* serahangi.

bob[1] *vt* kata, punguza, fupisha nywele (za mwanamke au msichana), *(of horse)* tia fugutu, fupisha mkia. ~ **tail** *n* mkia kipande, fugutu.

bob[2] *vi* rukaruka, ingia na kutoka. ~ **up** zuka, ibuka. **bob up and down** jitokeza, tinga *n* 1 mzuko. 2 salamu/kutoa heshima kwa kukunja

goti moja.
bob[3] *n (sl)* sarafu ya zamani ya Kiingereza ya shilingi moja.
bobbin *n* kibiringo.
bobby *n (sl) (GB colloq)* polisi.
bobby pin *n (US)* chupio.
bob-cat paka shume.
bod *n (infm)* jamaa, mtu.
bode *vt,vi* 1 bashiri. 2 ~ **well/ill** takia heri/maovu, -wa na ndege mbaya. **boding** *n* hisia ya ndege mbaya.
bodkin *n* shazia (butu ya kushonea tepe).
body *n* 1 mwili. **keep ~ and soul together** ishi. 2 **a dead** ~ maiti, mfu, mzoga, kimba. 3 *(trunk)* kiwiliwili. 4 *(person)* mtu. **some~** mtu fulani. **any~** mtu yeyote. **every~** kila mtu. 5 **heavenly** ~ sayari za juu, nyota, jua, mwezi. ~ **odour** gugumu, kutuzi, kikwapa. 6 *(company)* jamii, shirika; *(of troops)* kikosi, kundi, jeshi *the ~ of a concert hall* sehemu inapokaa hadhira *governing ~* baraza linalotawala *legislative ~* baraza la kutunga sheria *the diplomatic ~* kikundi cha mabalozi. 7 jumla, mkusanyo (wa habari, maarifa n.k.) *a ~of knowledge* jumla ya maarifa. 8 nguvu halisi *wine of good ~* divai halisi. 9 (compounds). **~guard** *n* mpambe; mlinzi binafsi. ~ **servant** hadimu (dobi). **~snatcher** *n* mfukuaji maiti kwa uchunguzi wa elimumwili. **~-work** *n* bodi ya gari,matengenezo a bodi ya gari. **bodiless** *adj* -sio na umbo, (-sio na) msingi. **bodied** *adj (able)* -enye nguvu, *(full)* -a miraba minne. **bodily** *adj* -a mwili, -a mfano wa mwili. **in bodily fear** katika hofu ya maisha. **bodily harm** madhara ya mwili *adv* 1 -zima, kwa pamoja. 2 kimwili, binafsi.
Boer *n* Kaburu.
boffin *n (sl)* fundi au mwana sayansi (hasa mchunguzi).
bog *n* 1 kinamasi. 2 *vt,vi* ~ **down** kwama. *(fig)* **~gy** *adj.*
bogey *see* **bogy**.
boggle *vi* sita, wa na shaka, staajabu.
bogie *n* **see** *bogy*.
bogus *adj* -a uwongo, -a bandia, -somakinika, -sohalisi.
bogy/bogey/ bogie *n* 1 zimwi, dubwana. 2 kitu kinachotisha. 3 toroli; bogi.
bohemian *n, adj* 1 mgaagaa na njia. 2 mtu (hasa msanii) asiyefuata desturi za kawaida.
boil[1] *n* jipu, uvimbe, kirasa.
boil[2] *vt, vi* 1 chemka. *(fig)* **keep the pot ~ing** pata riziki. ~ **point** kiwango mchemko *reach ~ing point* chemka. **~ing hot** *(colloq)* joto sana. 2 *(of the sea, person's feelings)* tutuma *(fig)* kasirika sana, shikwa na ghadhabu, fura kwa hasira, panda hamaki. 3 tokosa, chemsha ~ *eggs* tokosa mayai. ~ **away** endelea kuchemka; chemka mpaka imekauka kabisa. ~ **down** punguza kadiri ya kitu kwa kukichemsha, *it ~s down to this* matokeo yake ni; kiini chake ni. ~ **over** furumia, fufurika, furika *n* **the~**, hali joto ya kuchemsha *(fig) reach a ~ing* fikia kikomo cha uvumilivu, -tovumilia tena. **be on the ~** chemka. **bring sth to the ~** pika hadi kuchemka. **come to the ~** anza kuchemka.
boiler *n* 1 bwela. **~-suit** bwelasuti, ovaroli, msurupwete. 2 mchemshaji.
boisterous *adj* 1 *(of person)* -a makeke, -a machachari, -enye kelele na furaha. 2 *(of wind)* -a nguvu. 3 *(of sea)* -a kuchafuka, -enye mawimbi makali. **~ly** *adv*. **~ness** *n.*
bold *adj* jasiri, -shujaa, -kakamavu thabiti. **make ~ (free) with sth** tumia kitu bila ruhusa. 2 safi, -a waziwazi. **in ~ relief** -lioelezwa kinaganaga. 3 -a fidhuli, shupavu, -jeuri, -sioona haya. **as ~ as brass** fidhuli. **make ~** thubutu. **~-face** *n (in printing)* herufi nzito. **~-faced** *adj* -so na haya, -enye macho makavu, -shupavu. **~ly** *adv*. **~ness** *n.*
bole *n* shina la mti.
bolero *n* 1 bolero (dansi ya Kihispania). 2 bolero: kizibau

kisicho na vifungo.

boll *n* tumba (ya pamba). **~-weevil** *n* *(bio)* fukusitumba.

bollard *n* kizuizi, kizingiti, kigingi.

bollocks *n (pl) see* **ballocks** *(vulg)*. 2 upuuzi huo! mavi!

boloney *also* **baloney** *(US sl) n* 1 soseji. 2 upuzi.

bolshy *adj (sl)* asi, jeuri.

bolster *n* 1 mto mrefu (wa kulazia kichwa). 2 kiegemeo, egemeo *vt* 1 tegemeza, gadimu. 2 **~ (up)** tegemeza, shikilia, unga mkono.

bolt[1] *n* 1 komeo, kia. 2 radi. **a ~ from (out of) the blue** shani. 3 mshale. **shoot one's last ~** fanya jaribio la mwisho. 4 *(screw)* bolti *vt* komea, funga, kaza.

bolt[2] *vi,vt* 1 kurupuka, kimbia upesi. 2 meza (chakula) upesi. 3 *(of plants)* kua haraka sana *n* kukurupuka. **make a ~ for it** kimbia upesi (kwa nia ya kujificha). **~ hole** mahali pa kujificha.

bolt[3] *adv* **~ upright** wima kabisa.

bolt[4] *vt* chekecha, chunga.

bomb *n* kombora, bomu. **~ bay** chumba cha kuwekea mabomu (katika ndege). **~ disposal** uteguaji mabomu. **~ proof** *adj* -enye kinga ya mabomu, -solipulika. **~ shell** *n (fig)* mastaajabu, fadhaa, mshangao. **~ sight** kilengea shabaha ya bomu (katika ndege). **~ site** -eneo lililolipuliwa na mabomu. **go like a ~** *(sl)* fanikiwa sana, fana mno *it costs a ~* ni ghali sana *vt,vi* 1 shambulia kwa mabomu. **~ out** fukuza kwa mabomu toka katika jengo. 2 **~ up** pakia (ma) bomu. **~er** *n* 1 ndege ya mabomu. 2 mtupaji mabomu. **~ard** *vt* shambulia kwa mabomu, piga mizinga, tupia makombora *(fig)* shambulia, fululiza *~ard with questions* hoji sana, fululizia maswali, shambulia kwa maswali. **~ardment** *n*. **~ardier** *n* *(mil)* mtupa/mpiga makombora, mtega makombora.

bombast *n* maneno ya makeke, maneno matupu. **~ic** *adj* -a maneno matupu. **~ically** *adv*.

bonafide *adj (Lat)* halisi. *adv* kwa uaminifu, kwa nia njema. **bona fides** *n (leg)* uaminifu, nia njema.

bonanza *n* 1 bahati kubwa (k.m. kupata madini n.k.). 2 mafanikio; mwaka wenye mafanikio makubwa.

bonbon *n (Fr.)* peremende, pipi, lawalawa.

bond[1] *n* 1 kifungo, chochote kifungacho (k.m kamba, mnyororo, pingu (n.k.). 2 mapatano, sharti, mkataba *his word is as good as his ~* yu mwaminifu sana. 3 hati/ dhamana. **debenture ~** hati ya ukopeshaji. **~holder** mwenye hati/dhamana (ya serikali). 4 kitu kinachounganisha *(fig) joined in the ~s of friendship* -unganishwa kirafiki. 5 *(com.) in ~ (of goods)* bidhaa zilizo forodhani ambazo bado hazijalipiwa ushuru. 6 *(pl)* minyororo *(fig)* utumwa. **in ~s** -liofungwa, -lio katika hali ya utumwa. **break one's ~s** jikomboa. *vt* 1 gundisha. 2 weka bidhaa katika bohari ya ushuru. **~ed** *adj* -lozuiwa *~ed goods* bidhaa zilizozuiwa ili zilipiwe ushuru.

bond[2] *pref* -a utumwa. **~age** *n* utumwa; hali ya kufungwa. **~sman/servant** mtumwa, -lo katika utumwa. *n (pl)* **bondsmen** mdhamini/wadhamini.

bone *n* 1 mfupa. *(fig)* **a ~ of contention** kisa cha ugomvi *(of a person) he is a bag of ~s* mifupa mitupu, gofu la mtu. **have a ~ to pick with sb** -wa na neno/shauri na mtu. **make no ~s of** -toogopa, -tosita, -tojizuia, fanya bila wasiwasi. **make old ~s** ishi muda mrefu *feel cold to the ~* ona baridi kabisa *feel sth in one's ~s* -wa na hisia fulani juu ya. 2 *(of fish)* mwiba. **~less** *adj* -so mifupa. *vt* 1 *(to bone meat, fish)* kutoa mifupa/miiba kwenye nyama, samaki. 2 *(sl)* iba. **~ up on** jifunza sana. **~ head** *(sl)* mpumbavu. **~-dry** *adj* -kavu kabisa. *(fig)* **~-lazy/idle** *adj* mvivu kabisa. **~-meal** *n* mbolea ya mifupa. **~-setter** muunga mifupa. **~ shaker** *n (sl) (of motor vehicle/*

bicycle) mkweche, spana mkononi, -iliochakaa sana. **big/strong ~d** -enye mifupa mikubwa/imara.

boner *n (sl)* kosa la kijinga.

bonfire moto mkubwa aghalabu wa kuchoma takataka au wa sherehe.

bongo *n* **~ drum** kidogori, bongo.

bonhomie *n (Fr.)* ukunjufu, uchangamfu, ucheshi.

bonkers *adj (sl)* punguani.

bon mot *n* msemo wa kuchekesha.

bonny *adj (Scot)* 1 -zuri, -enye kuvutia. 2 -enye afya. **bonnily** *adv*

bonus *n* bonasi; malipo ya ziada, kifutajasho. **no claim ~** bonasi ya kuendesha bila ajali.

bony *adj* 1 -enye mifupa/miiba (ya samaki) mingi. 2 -embamba, -liokonda sana. 3 -enye mifupa mikubwa.

bon voyage *(Fr)* safari njema, kwa heri, buriani.

bonzer *adj (Ausl)* -zuri kabisa, -a kupendeza sana.

boo *n* sauti ya kushtusha au kuonyesha dharau *he can't say ~ to a goose* yu mwoga na mwenye aibu sana *vt,vi* zomea.

boob[1] *n* 1 mjinga. 2 *(colloq)* kosa la kijinga *vi (colloq)* fanya kosa la kijinga.

boob[2] *n (vulg. sl)* titi.

booby *n* 1 mjinga. 2 **~ prize** zawadi ya ushinde **~-trap** *n* mtego.

boode *n (sl US)* mapesa mengi, michuzi.

boogie-woogie *(also* **boogy-woogy**) *n* bugibugi (aina ya muziki wa densi).

book *n* 1 kitabu *read a ~*soma kitabu. **cheque~** kitabu cha cheki/hundi *exercise ~* daftari *go by the ~* shikilia mno sheria. 2 **the B~** Biblia *swear on the B~* apa, kula kiapo. 3 kitabu, bunda (la tiketi, stempu n.k). **bring to ~** toa hesabu, shtaki, patisha adhabu kwa kosa *bring sb to ~* adhibu; -taka ajieleze vitendo vyake. 4 *(pl)* hesabu, kumbukumbu za biashara. **keep the ~s** weka hesabu. **be in sb's good/black/ bad ~s** pendeza/topendeza mtu fulani *take sb's name off the ~s* futa jina lake katika orodha ya wanachama *read a person like a ~* tambua vema nia ya mtu *speak by the ~* -wa na tarifa sahihi *speak without ~* eleza habari kutokana na kumbukumbu *take a leaf out of a person's ~* iga (matendo ya) mtu fulani, *that suits my ~* inanifaa. 5 **~ case** *n* kabati ya vitabu, kasha la vitabu. **~-keeping** *n* uwekaji hesabu. **~keeper** *n.* **~-maker** *n* 1 mtengeneza vitabu. 2 mpokeaji fedha za bahati nasibu/dau/mashindano ya farasi. **~ marker** kalamu, kifaa cha kuwekea alama katika kitabu. **~ -seller** *n* mwuza vitabu. **~-shop** *n* duka la vitabu. **~-stall** *n* genge au kibanda cha kuuzia vitabu, magazeti (n.k.). **~ stand** *n* see **~ stall**. **~-store***n* *(US)* duka la vitabu. **~-worm** *n* 1 siridado. 2 *(fig)* mpenzi wa vitabu, msomaji sana, mbukuzi. *vt* 1 andika katika kitabu. 2 *(of the police, traffic wardens)* fungua mashtaka *~ sb for loitering* fungulia mashtaka kwa kuzurura. 3 weka/shika nafasi (kwa ajili ya safari, michezo n.k.), weka nafasi (of hotel) chumba *~ through to* kata tiketi ya moja kwa moja. **fully ~ed up** imejaa. **~ing office** *n* ofisi ya tiketi. **~able** *adj* -a kushikika, a kununulika. **~ing** *n* mpango wa kushika/kuweka nafasi (ya safari, mchezo n.k.) adj -a kuagiza (au kuagizwa kutoa) tiketi. **~ing-clerk** karani auzaye tiketi (za safari). **~ binding** *n* ujalidi, kujalidi vitabu. **~ binder** *n.* **~-end** *n (pl)* kishikiza vitabu. **~ish** *adj* 1 -a kuhusu vitabu, *(of person)* -a kupenda kusoma vitabu, -a kujua maarifa ya vitabuni tu. 2 *(of style)* mtindo wa lugha ya vitabuni. **~plate** *n* utepe wenye jina la mwenye kitabu. **~-post** *n* upelekaji vitabu kwa posta (kwa gharama ndogo). **~-rest** *n* kitegemezi cha vitabu mezani. **~ie** *n (sl)* see **~-maker**.

boom[1] *n* 1 boriti (inayoshikilia tanga

kwa chini). 2 kishikizo cha kamera, au (mkono wa) makrofoni. 3 *(at mouth of river, harbour)* kizuio.

boom[2] *vt* nguruma, vuma ~ **out** nena kwa sauti nzito. *(of commerce)* sitawi ghafla, tangaa au shamirisha kwa ghafla *n* ngurumo, ukuaji (wa ghafla wa biashara), ustawi wa haraka. ~ **town** mji uliostawi ghafla.

boomerang *n (Australia)* bumarengi *(fig) (action which recoils)* hoja au pendekezo ambalo humrudia mtoaji na kumdhuru *vi* rudia na kudhuru *his plan ~ed* mpango wake ulimrudia mwenyewe.

boon[1] *n* ombi, fadhila, upendeleo, faida, baraka, jamala.

boon[2] *adj (only in)* ~ **companion** mwandani.

boor *n* fidhuli, chepe. **~ish** *adj* -a kifidhuli. **~ishness** *n.* uchepe.

boost *vt* 1 piga jeki, sukuma juu, saidia. 2 *(electric)* ongeza nguvu ya umeme. 3 ongeza hadhi, thamani (ya mtu, kitu au mpango) *n* tendo la kuongeza nguvu, matangazo, hadhi au thamani. **~er** kiongeza nguvu (ya umeme au dawa), jenereta saidizi.

boot *n* 1 buti *my heart was in my ~s* niliogopa mno. **put the ~ in** piga mateke, chukua hatua kali *the ~ is on the other leg* mambo yamegeuka, ukweli haupo *(sl) get the ~* fukuzwa kazini. **~licker** barakala. **~leg** tengeneza pombe haramu. **~legger** mwuza pombe haramu, aghalabu mfanya magendo *too big for one's ~s* -enye kiburi sana. 2 sanduku; *(of motor car)* mahali pa mizigo nyuma au katika mvungu wa gari *vt* 1 piga teke. 2 *(sl)*. ~ **(out)**- fukuza, achisha (mtu) kazi. **~ee** *n* buti ya mtoto (iliyotengenezwa kwa sufu), buti fupi ya kike. **~lace** *n* gidamu, kamba ya kufungia viatu. **~less** *adj 1 (liter)* -a bure, bila faida, -sofaida. 2 bila viatu *(sl)* mtu atembeaye bila viatu. **~maker** *n* mshona buti. ~ **straps** *n* juhudi za mtu *he pulled himself up by own ~straps* aliinuka tena kwa juhudi zake mwenyewe. **~s** *n* mtumishi wa hoteli anayepiga rangi viatu, anayebeba mizigo n.k.

booth *n* 1 kibanda. 2 *(US)* kibanda cha simu. 3 *polling ~* kituo cha kupigia kura.

booty *n* mateka, nyara, mali ya wizi.

booze *vi (sl)* -nywa sana pombe *n (sl)* pombe. **~r** *n* mpenda pombe. ~ **up** sherehe na pombe nyingi,nafasi ya kulewa. **boozy** *adj.* **boozily** *adv,n* **booziness** n *(sl)* -levi.

bop *v* 1 gonga, piga, dunda. 2 cheza dansi huria.

bordello *n* danguro.

border *n* 1 mpaka *national ~* mpaka wa (nchi) taifa ~ *town* mji wa mpakani. 2 ukingo. 3 pindo, utarazo *vi* 1 pakana na, karibia. 2 ~ *on/upon* fanana na, landa, -wa kama, karibiana na *vt 1* pinda upindo. 2 tia ukingo *~-land n* 1 eneo la mpakani (linalozunguka mpaka wa nchi zote). 2 hali kati ya vitu viwili (k.m. kati ya usingizi na kuamka). **~-line** *n* mpaka, kuweka mpaka. **~line case** jambo lenye wasiwasi. ~ **on/upon** *(fig)* pakana na.

bore[1] 1 toboa, pekecha, chimba. 2 bungua *n* 1 *(calibre)* kipimo cha mtutu (wa bunduki, mzinga n.k.). 2 kitobo. **~r** *n* 1 mdudu anayepekecha. **grain ~r** dumuzi. 2 kekee **boring** *adj.* ~ hole *n* kisima, shimo lililochimbwa. **borings** *n (pl)* chembechembe (zitokazo katika tundu linalotobolewa).

bore[2] *vt* chosha, sumbua, (kwa mazungumzo yasiyovutia). ~ **to death/stiff** chosha kabisa. **~dom** uchoshi. **boring** *adj* -a uchoshi *n* mchoshi. **~r** *n.*

bore[3] *n (tidal wave)* wimbi kubwa sana la kuchanua.

boric *adj* -a boriki ~ *acid* asidi boriki.

born see **bear** *adj (sl)* zaliwa, -lozaliwa *first ~child* kifungua mimba *last ~child* kitinda mimba ~ *again* Mkristo aliyeokoka *in all my ~ days* enzi zangu *Arusha ~* mzaliwa wa

Arusha *a gentleman* ~ mwungwana halisi *a ~ poet* mwenye kipaji cha ushairi.

borne see **bear**.

borough *n* mji au sehemu ya mji iliyo na mwakilishi bungeni.

borrow *vt* 1 azima, kopa. 2 *(receive)* pokea, chukua. 3 *(imitate)* igiza, fuatisha. *(fig)* **~ed time** kipindi cha maisha baada ya almanusra. **~ed** *adj* 1 -lioazimwa. 2 *(assumed)* -a kuiga -a kujipa. **~er** *n* mkopaji.

borstal *n (GB)* chuo cha mafunzo kwa vijana wahalifu.

bort *n* vipande vya almasi.

bosh *n* upuzi, porojo, maneno matupu.

bosky *adj (liter)* kichaka.

bosom *n (arch)* 1 kifua cha mtu (hasa mwanamke) matiti (ya mwanamke). 2 sehemu ya wazi inayofunika matiti. 3 *(fig)* ndani ya moyo (hisia za ndani za furaha au majonzi). **a ~ friend** mwandani, sahibu. 4 katikati, baina *in the ~ of one's family* miongoni mwa ndugu zako.

boss[1] *n* 1 nundu, kinundu (k.m: kwenye ngao). 2 pambo (la ukutani, mlangoni, n.k.) lililoinuka, la vinundu.

boss[2] *n (colloq) (master)* bosi, mzee, *vt* tawala, amuru, simamia, ongoza ~ *the show* fanya mipango yote. **~y** *adj*.

bosun/bos's *n* see **boatswain**.

botany *n* botania: sayansi ya muundo wa mimea. **botanic** *adj*. **botanist** n mwanabotania. **botanize** *vi* botanisha (chunguza na kusanya mimea). **botanical garden** bustani ya mimea.

botch *n* 1 kazi mbovu *vi* **~ sth (up)** tengeneza ovyo, haribu kazi, vuruga, boronga. **~er** *n* mborongaji.

both *adj* -ote, -wili (mbili) ~ *of us* sisi sote, wote wawili *they are ~ alike* wote wawili wanafanana *you can't have it ~ ways* amua/chagua moja. *adv* **~ ... and** wote wawili ~ *the mother and the child* wote wawili mama na mtoto.

bother *vt* 1 sumbua, udhi, chokoza, kera. **I can't be ~ed** siwezi kusumbuliwa/kujisumbua. 2 ~ (about) sumbua, hangaika, jisumbua *vi* hangaika, ona wasiwasi, jikalifu, jitaabisha *n* udhia, taabu, matata, usumbufu. **~ation** *n*. **~some** *adj* -enye udhia, -chokozi, -a kuudhi.

bottle *n* chupa. **~fed** -liolishwa kwa chupa. *(of a child)* **brought up on the ~** -liyekuzwa kwa maziwa ya chupa. **too fond of the ~** -nayopenda sana ulevi. **hit the ~** anza kuwa mlevi *vt* tia /hifadhi chupa. **~ up one's anger** futika, zuia/ ficha hamaki. **~-green** *n*. kijani kiwiti. **~-neck** *n* 1 *(manufacturing process)* kikwazo; tatizo katika uzalishaji au utekelezaji wa kitu (jambo). 2 sehemu nyembamba ya barabara pana. **~-nose** *n* pua iliyovimba. **~-party** *n* tafrija (ambako kila mmoja huenda na pombe yake).

bottom *n* 1 chini, upande, sehemu ya (ndani au nje ya kitu) *look at the ~ of the page* angalia chini ya ukusara *the ship went to the ~* meli ilizama. 2 nchani, mwisho, nyuma, isoheshimika *at the ~ of the garden* sehemu ya mwisho ya bustani. 3 *adj* kikalio matako. *(sl)* **kick sb's ~** piga mtu teke la matakoni. 4 msingi, asili, chanzo, *get to the ~ of the trouble* gundua chanzo/msingi wa tatizo. 5 *(fig uses) the ~ has fallen out of the market* biashara imeshuka sana, imefikia kiwango cha chini sana ***at ~*** kimsingi *he is a good fellow at ~* yu mtu mzuri kimsingi *from the ~ of my heart*, kwa dhati kabisa, *start at the ~of the ladder* anzia ngazi za chini *knock the ~ out of (an argument etc)* thibitisha kuwa haina maana. 6 *(attrib)* -a chini kabisa, -a mwisho *what's your ~ price* bei yako ya mwisho ni ipi? *vi* **~ out** *(econ)* anguka; fikia kiwango cha chini na baki palepale. **~less** *adj* 1 -a kwenda chini mno *(of chair)* -sio na kikalio a kina kirefu; bila nguo za chini (chupi n.k.). **~s up** maliza vinywaji. **~up** chini juu.

botulism *n* ubotuli: ugonjwa unaotokana na sumu inayotokea kwenye chakula kisichohifadhiwa vizuri.

boudoir *n (arch)* chumba cha faragha cha mwanamke (k.m. chumba cha kuvalia).

bough *n* tawi (la mti).

bought see **buy**.

boulder *n* jabali.

boulevard *n (Fr/US)* njia pana (mjini aghalabu yenye safu ya miti pande zote).

bounce *vt,vi* 1 ruka (kama mpira), duta. 2 rushwa, tupwa kurudi nyuma au mahali ulipotokea *~ in at the door* ingia kwa nguvu/fujo/ ghafla *~ out of a room* toka chumbani ghafla kwa hasira. 3 laghai *~ sb into doing sth* shawishi mtu afanye jambo fulani. 4 *(colloq) (of cheque)* rudishwa (na benki kwa kutokuwa na fedha za kulipwa). 5 ~ **(back)** 1 rudishwa nyuma; jirudisha nyuma. 2 rudi na nguvu mpya *n* 1 pigo la ghafla, mruko *catch the ball on the ~* daka mpira unapodundwa. 2 *(of person)* uchangamfu, makeke. **~ing** *adj (colloq) (of person)* -enye nguvu na afya. **~r** *n* mzuia fujo katika kilabu, mbabe.

bouncy *adj* enye uchangamfu.

bound[1] *vi* ruka; kimbia kwa kurukaruka *his heart ~ed with joy* moyo wake ulinang'anika kwa furaha *n* kuruka mbele, mruko. **by leaps and ~s** kwa mbio sana, upesi sana. **at a ~** kwa mruko mmoja.

bound[2] *n (usu pl)* 1 *(limit)* mpaka, mipaka, kiasi *it is beyond ~s of my powers* ni nje ya mipaka ya uwezo wangu *beyond all ~s* pita kiasi. 2 upeo, kikomo, mwisho. **out of ~s** marufuku kuingia; -liokatazwa kuingia *vt* 1 pakana na. 2 *(surround)* zunguka, -wa pande zote *it is ~ed by* imezungukwa na, imepakana na. **~less** *adj*.

bound[3] *adj (for)* tayari kuanza /kuelekea/kwenda *the ship is ~ for Bombay* meli inakwenda /inaelekea Bombay *be ~ for* enda/ elekea *outward ~* kwenda nje.

bound[4] see **bind** 1 lazimika *I am ~ to go* sina budi kwenda. **be ~ up in** shughulika sana (na). **~ up** -wa na shughuli nyingi. **~ up with** fungamana na.

boundary *n* mpaka.

bounden *adj (arch) (only in)* **~ duty** wajibu wangu.

bounder *n (GB) (arch) (colloq)* ayari, safihi.

bounteous *adj* -karimu, -ingi *a year of ~ harvest* mwaka wa neema. **~ly** *adv.* **bountiful** see **bounteous.**

bounty *n* 1 ukarimu. 2 *(gift)* zawadi. 3 sadaka. 4 *(premium)* bonasi **bountifully** *adv*.

bouquet *n* 1 shada la maua. 2 harufu ya divai. 3 *(fig)* sifa.

bourgeois *n* bwanyenye *adj* -a kibwanyenye. **~ie** *n.* **the ~ie** tabaka la mabwanyenye.

bourne *n (arch)* 1 mpaka, mwisho. 2 nia, lengo.

bout *n* 1 *(of illness)* kuumwa sana ghafla, kushikwa (na ugonjwa) *I had a ~ of malaria* nilibanwa na malaria. 2 kipindi cha zoezi/ kazi/shughuli. 3 pambano.

boutique *n* duka la nguo na urembo.

bovine *adj* 1 -a kuhusu ng'ombe. 2 -a kama ng'ombe. 3 -enye akili nzito.

bow[1] 1 *vt,vi* 1 inamisha kichwa (au mwili). **~ and scrape** nyenyekea mno, jidhalilisha. 2 *(worship)* sujudu. 3 *(usu. pass)* kunja, pinda *his grandfather is ~ed with age* babu yake amepinda kwa uzee. 4 ~ **(down to)** salimu amri, kubali kutii *~ to nobody* -tokubali kutawaliwa, dai nafasi ya juu. 5 *(to sb's opinion)* kubali. 6 *(out of)* jitoa *n* kuinamia. **~line** *n (naut)* aina ya fundo la kibaharia.

bow[2] *n* 1 upinde, uta. **rain~** upinde wa mvua. **~legs** matege. **~ legged** -enye matege. **~ man** mpiga upinde. 2 fundo, kifundo. 3 *(fig)* **have two**

strings to one's ~ -wa na njia mbili za kufanya kitu. 4 uta wa kupigia zeze *vt* pinda ~ *a string* piga upinde. **~ing** see **bow** *v, n.*

bow[3] *n (naut)* gubeti, omo.

bowdlerize *vt* dhibiti kitabu kwa kuondoa mambo yanayofikiriwa hayafai.

bowel *n* 1 uchengelele. 2 *(pl)* matumbo. **~s are loose** ninaendesha. **have the ~s open** pata choo. **keep your ~s open** usivimbiwe. 3 *(fig)* huruma *the ~s of compassion (mercy)* hali ya kuonea huruma (samehe) *the ~s (of the earth)* chini kabisa ya ardhi (dunia). **bower** *n* 1 nyumba (nzuri) iliyojengwa maalum kama mahali pa kupumzikia. 2 banda lililojengwa kwa matawi na majani yaliyosukwa. 3 *(poet)* chumba maalum (cha mwanamke) cha kufanyia shughuli zake za kibinafsi k.m. kujipodoa.

bowie-knife *n* shembea, sime.

bowl[1] *n* bakuli.

bowl[2] *(for the game of bowls)* tufe. 2 *(pl)* mchezo wa kuvingirisha matufe chini.

bowl[3] *vi,vt* 1 vingirika, tupa mpira/tufe (katika mchezo wa kriketi au tufe). 2 ~ **along** enda upesi, enda mbio (kama kwa magurudumu) *vt* vingirisha, tupa mpira (tufe) wa kriketi. ~ **over** 1 angusha. 2 shinda. 3 staajabisha sana. ~ **out** toa mchezaji katika kriketi. **~er** *n* 1 mchezaji wa tufe; mtupaji mpira katika mchezo wa kriketi. 2 aina ya topi. **~ing** *n* 1 mchezo wa kuviringisha tufe. 2 kitendo cha kutupa mpira katika kriketi. **~ing alley/green** kiwanja cha kuchezea tufe.

bowsprit *n* mlingoti wa maji, dasturi; bulina.

bow-window see **bay-window**.

bow-wow *vi* bweka kama mbwa *n* 1 bweko. 2 *(of children's language)* mbwa.

box[1] *n* 1 kasha, bweta, sanduku. **letter** ~ sanduku la barua. 2 kijaluba. 3 kiti cha dereva katika gari (linalovutwa na farasi). 4 *(in courts) witness* ~ kizimba. 5 kibanda kidogo *sentry* ~ kibanda cha mlinzi. 6 *(sl)* televisheni *vt* 1 tia ndani, fungia (ndani ya kasha). 2 *(off)* tenga. ~ **in/ up** bana sana *we were ~ed up* tulibanana. **~-office** *n* sehemu ya kukatia tiketi (katika sinema n.k.).

box[2] *n* pigo *vi,vt* piga ngumi. **(~ with)** pigana ngumi, pigana ndondi. **~ing** mchezo wa ngumi. **~er** *n.* ~ing-gloves *n (pl)* glovu za ndondi. **~ing-match/bout** *n* pambano la ndondi/ ngumi. **~ing-weight** *n* uzito wa mwanandondi **Boxing-day** *n* tarehe 26 Desemba.

boy *n* 1 mtoto mwanamume, mvulana *I have known him from a* ~ ninamjua tangu utotoni *I have two ~s* nina wavulana/watoto wa kiume wawili. 2 mtu *he is a local* ~ ni mwenyeji wa hapa. **old/dear** ~ rafiki *oh boy!* do!, da!, du!, lo! 2 *(derog)* boi, mtumishi mwanamume. ~ **hood** *n* utoto, ujana. **~ish** *n* -a kivulana, -a mtoto wa kiume. **~ishness** *n* uvulana, tabia ya uvulana. **~friend** kipenzi (wa kiume). **~scout** skauti (wa kiume).

boycott *vt* susa, susia, gomea ~ *trade* susa biashara *n* kususa, kugomea, ususaji.

bra *see* **brassiere**

brace *n* 1 kitu cha kufungia, kukazia. 2 *(clamp)* gango. 3 ~ **and bit** keikei. 4 *(pair)* jozi *five ~ of partridges* kwale kumi. 5 *(naut)* amrawi, shauti, baraji. 6 *(pl)* kanda za kushika suruali *vt, vi* 1 changamsha, tia nguvu, kaza, kita, tegemeza. 2 saidia. ~ **up** jiimarisha. ~ **oneself up** jikaza. 3 *(naut)* sogeza, vuta tanga kwa amrawi **bracing** adj (of climate) -a kuleta afya.

bracelet *n* 1 kikuku, bangili. 2 kekee. 3 *(pl) (hand cuffs)* pingu.

bracket *n* 1 mwango, kiango (cha mti au chuma). 2 mabano, kikundi. **age** ~ kikundi cha watu wenye umri fulani, rika moja *vt,vi* 1 weka mabano; fungua mambano. 2 weka

pamoja.
brackish *adj (of water)* -a chumvi kidogo, -a chumvi chumvi.
brad *n* msumari bapa (usio na kichwa).
bradawl *n* kipatasi.
brag *vi* jigamba, jivuna, jisifu. *n* majivuno, majisifu makeke. ~ **gart** *n* mjigambi, mjisifu.
braid *vt* sokota, suka. *n* 1 kigwe, utepe, almaria. 2 zari, msuko, msongo. ~**ing** *n,adj*.
brail *n (naut)* demani *vt* teremsha/ tua tanga.
braille *n* breli: mfumo wa maandishi yenye vidutu yatumiwayo na vipofu.
brain *n* 1 ubongo. **blow out ones ~s** jiua kwa kujipiga risasi kichwani. 2 *(sense)* akili *use the* ~ tumia akili have a good ~ -wa na akili nyingi *beat/ rack ones ~s about sth* fikiri sana *have sth (eg. money) on the* ~ fikiria daima juu ya (fedha). **pick sb's ~(s)** chukua na tumia mawazo yake *it turned his* ~ ilimvimbisha kichwa. 3 *(pl)* akili *a person of (with) ~s* mwenye akili *~s trust* paneli ya wataalamu *the ~s of a canary* mpumbavu. 4 *(compounds)* ~ **-box** fuvu la kichwa. ~ **child** uvumbuzi, wazo jipya. ~ **fag** kuchoka kwa akili. ~ **teaser** chemsha bongo, fumbo. ~**wash** *(derog)* tia kasumba. ~ **drain** uhamaji wa wataalamu. ~ **storm** 1 dalili za ugonjwa wa akili. 2 kupeana mawazo ili kutafuta njia mpya za kufanyia kitu. 3 mbinu ya kutatua tatizo/ kujibu swali kwa kuchangia mawazo papo kwa papo kutoka kwa wote waliopo *(colloq)*. ~ **wave** wazo zuri la ghafla. 4 *(of food use (pl))* ubongo. ~**-fever** *n* homa ya ubongo, joto la kichwani. ~**-stem** *n* shina bongo. ~**less** *adj* pumbavu, asiye na akili, baradhuli. ~**y** *adj* -enye akili. *vt (sl)* vunja kichwa na kumwaga ubongo.
braise *vt* pika (nyama, mboga n.k.) kwa mvuke.
brake[1] *n* breki, *vt* 1 *apply the* ~ funga breki *put the ~s on* zuia. ~**-van** *n* behewa la breki.
brake[2] *n* gari linalokokotwa na farasi.
bramble *n* mkwamba.
bran *n* kapi, kumvi, wishwa.
branch *n* 1 tawi, ~ *of a tree* tawi la mti, utanzu, utagaa. ~ *office* ofisi ya tawi ~ *road* njia panda inayochepuka. *vi* gawika, fanya panda. ~ **off** acha barabara kuu na fuata barabara ndogo. ~ **out** *(of a person or business)* enea (kama matawi n.k.) panua, ongeza, panuka, ongezeka. ~ **forth** sitawi, matawi, shamirisha. 2 sehemu. 3 mkono wa mto (bahari).
brand *n* 1 *(of fire)* kijinga. 2 *(of trade)* rajamu, chapa. 3 *(stamp)* chapa
(ya chuma yenye moto n.k.), mhuri. ~ **iron** chuma chenye moto (kitumiwacho kwa kuchapa alama ng'ombe n.k.) alama (ichapwayo, itumiwayo katika kufanya biashara), *(fig)* alama ya aibu. 4 *(sort)* aina, namna *the best ~s of coffee* aina bora ya kahawa. 5 *(of plants)* maradhi ya mimea. 6 *(poet)* 1 upanga. 2 *(disgrace)* tia alama ya aibu, aibisha, -pa jina baya *be ~ed as a coward* -itwa mwoga. 3 ~ *new* mpya kabisa.
brandish *vt* tia tahabibu.
brandy *n* brandi, kilevi cha brandi.
brash *adj (colloq)* safihi, jeuri, fidhuli.
brass *n* 1 shaba nyeupe. ~ **plate** kibao cha shaba cha mlangoni (agh. huandikwa jina) ~ *tacks* pini *(fig)* kiini cha jambo. **get down to ~ tacks** anza kuzungumza/jadili kwa uwazi/ ukweli. **top** ~ maofisa viongozi wa ngazi za juu kabisa. ~ **hat** *(army sl)* afisa mwandamizi. 2 ~**es** vitu vya shaba nyeupe. 3 *the ~ (collective) (mus)* ala za muziki za shaba nyeupe. ~ **band** bendi ya matarumbeta. 4 *(impudence)* ufidhuli, ujuvi. 5 *(GB sl)* fedha. ~**y** *adj* 1 fidhuli. 2 -a shaba nyekundu. 3 *(of voice)* -a kikengele. 4 -a kelele.
brassard *n* utepe wa mkononi.

brasserie *n* mgahawa wenye pombe.
brassiere *n* sidiria, kanchiri.
brat *n (sl)* toto tundu: mtoto aliye mtovu wa adabu.
bravado *n* ujasiri/ushujaa (wa kujionyesha) *do sth out of ~* fanya jambo ili kuonyesha ushujaa.
brave *adj* 1 jasiri, -shujaa, -shupavu. 2 *(arch)* -zuri sana *vt* kabili bila woga. *n* 1 morani wa wahindi wekundu. 2 *(arch)* mtu katili, muuaji. **~ery** *n* ujasiri.
bravo *n (interj)* heko, oyee, hongera.
bravura *n* maonyesho/muziki wenye madoido sana.
brawl *n* ugomvi wa kelele, ghasia, mzozo, mapigano *vi* 1 gombana (kwa ghasia), zozana, pigana. 2 *(of streams)* vuma. **~er** *n* mgomvi, mchokozi.
brawn *n* 1 musuli ngumu, nguvu ya musuli. 2 nyama ya nguruwe ya kumimina. **~y** *adj*.
bray *n* 1 mlio wa punda. 2 sauti kali (kama ya tarumbeta) *vi* lia kama punda/tarumbeta.
braze *vt* lehemu kwa shaba.
brazen *adj* 1 -a kutokana na shaba nyeupe. 2 -enye mlio mkali kama wa ala ya shaba nyeupe. 3 -enye rangi ya shaba nyeupe iliyofuliwa. 4 -a kutokuwa na haya. **~faced** -enye kujikausha, bila haya *vt (out)* jikausha, shupaa. **~ness** *n*.
brazier *n* seredani, jiko la mkaa.
breach *n* 1 uvunjaji *~ of contract* uvunjaji mkataba *~ of promise* uvunjaji ahadi ya ndoa *~ of the peace* uvunjaji amani, upiganaji barabarani *~ of confidence* kufunua siri. 2 tundu, upenyu, ufa (kama katika ukuta au boma palipobomoka) *the waves made a ~ in the sea wall* mawimbi yalisababisha ufa katika ukuta wa bahari *step into/fill the ~* jitokeza kusaidia *vt* toboa, vunja.
bread *n* 1 mkate. 2 chakula, riziki. 3 *(sl)* pesa. **~ and butter** *n* mkate na siagi. *(sl)* njia ya kupatia fedha. **~ and butter letter** barua ya shukrani kwa ukarimu; *quarrel with one's ~ and butter* gombana na mkuu/ mwajiri. **~ and butter issue** suala linalohusu mambo muhimu katika maisha. **take the ~ out of sb's mouth** ondolea/ nyang'anya riziki. **~ winner** mkimu familia. **~ basket** *n* 1 kikapu cha mkate. 2 eneo la nchi linalozalisha nafaka kwa wingi. 3 *(sl)* tumbo. **~-crumbs** *n* chembe za mkate *(political sl)* makombo, masalia *~ line* foleni ya watu maskini wanaongoja mkate au chakula bure. **~-fruit** *n* shelisheli. **~-stuffs** *n (pl)* nafaka, unga wa mkate.
breadth *n* 1 upana, mapana *~ of mind* uwezo wa kupokea na kuvumilia fikra tofauti. **~ ways. ~ wise** *adv* kwa upana.
break *vt,vi* 1 vunja, pasua; vunjika, katika *he broke the cup* alivunja kikombe *the rope broke* kamba ilikatika *it broke in two* ilipasuka vipande viwili. **~ the law/one's word** vunja sheria/ahadi *~ a journey* vunja safari. 2 haribu. **~ a radio** haribu redio *his health broke* afya yake iliharibika. 3 *(of dog, horse etc)* tia adabu, zoesha, fundisha, fuga *a well broken horse* farasi mwelekevu. 4 **~ the back of** maliza sehemu ngumu. 5 **~ the bank** filisi. 6 *(mil)* **~ bounds** toka bila ruhusa. 7 **~ cover** jitokeza (baada ya kujificha). 8 **~ even** fanya biashara bila hasara wala faida. 9 **~ faith** saliti. 10 **~ new/fresh ground** lima sehemu mpya *(fig)* anza kazi/mwelekeo mpya. 11 **~ heart** vunja moyo, katisha tamaa. 12 **~ the ice** anza urafiki, ondoa ubaridi. 13 **~ a man** dhili, vunja, lazimisha kutoa siri. 14 **~ the news** tangaza/toa habari. 15 **~ an officer** fukuza afisa. 16 **~ open** vunja, fungua kwa kutumia nguvu. 17 **~ short** vunja. 18 **~ step** -tofuata mipigo, paraganya mwendo. 19 **~ wind** jamba, shuta *n* 1 mpasuko, mpasuo, mvunjiko. 2 *~ of day/day ~* mapambazuko. 3. mapumziko *without a ~* bila kupumzika.

4 tofauti, badiliko, usumbufu *~in one's way of life* mabadiliko katika mwenendo wa maisha ya mtu. 5 nafasi, wasaa *give sb a ~* mpa mtu nafasi. 6 *(colloq)* bahati *a lucky ~* bahati njema. 7 *(make a) ~ for it* toroka. **~fast** *n* kustaftahi, kifungua kinywa, kisebeho. **~water** *n* ukuta wa kuvunja nguvu ya mawimbi. **~ neck speed** mwendo wa hatari. **~er** *n* wimbi kubwa lenye povu (linaloishia mwambani au pwani). **circuit ~er** *(elect)* kikate. **~age** *n* 1 mvunjiko. 2 mahali/sehemuiliyovunjika. 3 *(usupl)* vitu vilivyovunjika, hasara inayotokana na kuvunjika kwa vitu. **~able** *adj* pekechu, -a kuvunjika (kwa urahisi). **~ away** *vi* 1 *(prisoner)* toroka. 2 *(politics)* jitoa, jitenga. 3 *(habits)* acha. **~ down** *vt,vi* 1 vunja, bomoa, haribu; haribika, *my car has broken down* gari langu limeharibika *peace talks have broken down* mazungumzo ya amani yamevunjika. 2 *(of person)* vurugikiwa, changanyikiwa. 3 ainisha *~ down expenditure* ainisha matumizi. 4 meng'enyuka, sababisha mabadiliko ya kikemikali. *n* 1 kuharibika. 2 uainishaji takwimu. 3 *nervous ~down* kurukwa na akili. **broken down** *adj* -lokwisha. **~ in** *vt* 1 ingia jengo kwa nguvu. 2 *(on, upon) (interrupt)* ingilia. 3 funza, tia adabu *n* wizi ndani ya nyumba. **~ into** *vt* 1 see **~ in** 2 anza (ghafla) *he broke into a run/song* alianza kukimbia/ kuimba. 3 tumia sehemu *~ into one's savings* tumia sehemu ya pesa zilizohifadhiwa. **~ off** 1 *(as vt,vi)* 1 acha kusema, katiza maneno. 2 pumzika. 3 vunja. **~ off relations** vunja uhusiano. 4 *(of food)* mega. **~ out** *vi* 1 tokea ghafla. 2 toroka. *n* kutoroka. **~ through** *vt,vi* 1 penya, tengua. 2 shinda. 3 songa mbele (licha ya upinzani). *n* 1 kupenya. 2 mwelekeo mpya. 3 *(of discovery)* uvumbuzi. 4 mafanikio mapya. **~ up** *vt,vi* 1 vunja, vunjika. 2 *(of persons)* fifia. 3 *(of school)* anza likizo. 4 *(of work)* gawanya. 5 *(of gatherings)* tawanya. 6 *(of marriage)* tengana. 7 *(US)* chekesha sana *n* kuvunjika; mgao.

breast *n* 1 *(of huma n)* 1 kifua. 2 *(of women)* ziwa, titi. 3 *(of animals)* kidari *vt* 1 kabili. 2 **~ the tape** gusa kamba. **make a clean ~ of** kiri, ungama. **beat one's ~** omboleza sana. **~ feed** *v* nyonyesha. **~ bone** *n* mfupa wa kidari. **~-high** *adv* kwa kufikia kifuani. **~-pin** *n* bruchi ya tai. **~-plate** *n* dera ya kifua. **~ stroke** mtindo wa kichura/kifua: mtindo wa kuogelea. **~ work** *n* ukingo, kizuizi; ukuta wa udongo wa kujihami wenye urefu unaofikia kifuani.

breath *n* 1 pumzi *in one ~* kwa pumzi moja *bad ~* kunuka mdomo *I caught my ~* nilishika/ nilikata pumzi (kwa muda). **catch/hold one's ~** zuia pumzi *(fig)* ngoja kwa hofu kubwa. **take ~** vuta pumzi. **waste one's ~** ongea bure. **take sb's ~ away** shtusha, shangaza. **under the ~** kwa kunong'ona, polepole. **with bated ~** kwa hofu kubwa 2. upepo mwembamba. 3 *(instant)* dakika moja, kufumba na kufumbua. **in the same ~** hapohapo *(fig) not a ~ of suspicion* hakuna hata chembe ya tuhuma. 5 *(pl) (in consonants)* hafifu, kavu. **~ less** *adj* 1 -a kutwetatweta, -a kuhema. 2 -a kukata pumzi, -a haraka, -a kushinda roho. 3 *(of night)* -tulivu. **~y** *adj (of voice)* dogo. **~ily** *adv*. **~alyse** *vt* pima ulevi wa mtu (hasa dereva). **~alyser** *n* chombo cha kupimia ulevi (mtu akitoa pumzi, chombo kinachoonyesha amekunywa kiasi gani). **~ taking** *adj* -a kustaajabisha, -a ajabu. **~e** *vi,vt* 1 vuta pumzi pumua. **~e in** vuta pumzi. **~e out** toa pumzi. **~e hard** kokotoa roho, tweta, korota, koroma. 2 *(live)* ishi, -wa na uhai. **~e one's last** kata roho, -fa, fariki. 3 *(reveal)* toa *dont ~e a word* usimwambie mtu.

~ er/~ing space nafasi ya kupumzika. **~ed** *adj (phon)* kavu, hafifu.

breech *n* tako, nyuma *load by the ~* shindilia kwa nyuma. ~ **birth** uzazi wa kutanguliza matako.

breeches *(also britches) n (arch) pl* suruali *(fig) (of woman) wear the ~* tawala nyumbani *too big for one's ~* -enye majivuno.

breed *vi,vt* 1 zaa, zalisha. 2 fuga. 3 lea, adilisha, elimisha *a well-bred child* mtoto mwadilifu, mtoto aliyelelewa vyema. 4 leta *war ~s poverty* vita huleta ufukara. *n* 1 kizawa. 2 jamii ya wanyama. **half ~** chotara. **~er** *n* 1 mfugaji/ mkuza kizazi bora cha wanyama. 2 (*of animals*) mzalishi. 3 kizalisha nguvumionzi. **~ing** *n* 1 uzazi. 2 ufugaji bora. 3 malezi mema; tabia njema. **~ing season** majira ya kuzaa.

breeze *n* 1 upepo mwanana *land ~* mwanashanga. **sea ~** matlai. 2 *(sl)* kazi rahisi. **in a ~** *(sl)* kirahisi. **shoot the ~** *(sl)* sogoa, piga soga *vt* **~ in/out** ingia/toka ghafula. **~ through** *(test etc)* pita bila matatizo. **breezy** *adj* 1 -a upepo. 2 -changamfu, -a furaha, bashashi. **breeziness** *n* ubashashi.

Bren-gun *n* bunduki ya Bren: aina ya bunduki inayotema risasi.

brer *n (US) (esp. in fables)* kaka, ndugu.

brethren *n (formal)(pl)* 1 ndugu. 2 wanachama (wa shirika au weledi/ utaalamu, umaalumu).

brevet *n (mil)* hati ya kumpandisha afisa cheo bila kuongeza mshahara.

breviary *n (rel. R.C.)* breviari: kitabu cha sala za kila siku zinazosemwa na mapadre.

brevity *n* 1 ufupi. 2 uchache wa maneno.

brew *vt,vi* 1 pika (pombe, chai) *(fig) they are ~ing trouble* wanapika majungu/ghasia. 2 tayarisha, andaa *a storm is ~ing* dhoruba inajikusanya *n* mpiko *local ~* pombe ya kienyeji. **~er** *n* mpika pombe, mtengeneza pombe. **~ery** *n* kiwanda cha pombe/bia.

briar *n* 1 mtemba (unaotengenezwa na mzizi wa waridi mwitu). 2 waridi mwitu.

bribe *n* hongo, rushwa, mrungura, chai. *accept a ~* pokea rushwa *vt* honga, toa rushwa/hongo. **bribable** *adj*. **~ry** *n* utoaji rushwa/hongo n.k.

bric-a-brac *n* vikorokoro.

brick *n* 1 tofali *a ~ house* nyumba ya matofali. *(fig)* **drop a ~** kosa. **make ~s without straw** jaribu kufanya kazi isiyo na mafanikio. 2 *(colloq)* rafiki. 3 kipande (chenye umbo la tofali) cha jibini *vt* ziba kwa matofali *~ up a window etc.* jaza ukuta. **~ bat** *n* kipande cha tofali *(fig)* maneno ya shutuma. **~-field ~-kiln** *n* tanuru la kuchomea matofali, kiwanda cha matofali. **~ layer** *n* mwashi. **~ laying** *n* uashi. **~ work** *n* ujenzi wa matofali.

bride *n* bibi arusi, bi-arusi. **~ price/ wealth** mahari. **bridal** *n* arusi *adj* -a arusi, -a bibi arusi. **~groom** bwana arusi. **~smaid** msindikizaji wa maarusi (wa kike).

bridge *n* 1 daraja, kantara, tingatinga. 2 *(naut)* jukwaa (juu ya sitaha ya meli ambapo nahodha/ maafisa hutoa amri zao. 3 sehemu ya juu ya pua. 4 kishikizi cha meno bandia. 5 mchezo wa karata. **~ head** *n* sehemu ya mbele ndani ya ardhi ya adui ambayo itatumika kumshambulia *vt* 1 unganisha kwa daraja, jenga daraja la kuvukia. 2 shinda, tatua (angalau kwa muda). 3 saidia. 4 *~ gap* ziba pengo. **bridging loan** mkopo wa kuziba pengo kwa muda maalum *a lot of water has flowed under the ~ since then* mambo mengi yametokea tangu wakati huo.

bridle *n* 1 *(reins)* hatamu, ugwe, kigwe (cha kuongoza punda, farasi, n.k.). **~ path** kijia (kwa ajili ya wapanda farasi) *vt,vi* 1 valisha hatamu. 2 zuia, dhibiti, tawala *~ your tongue* chunga mdomo wako. 3 onyesha hasira/kiburi (kwa kuinua kichwa).

brief[1] *n* 1 muhtasari (hasa wa kesi mahakamani) *hold a ~ for (sb)* tetea/unga mkono. 2 maagizo. ~ **case** *n* mkoba *vt* 1 eleza, -pa maelezo/maagizo. 2 *(comm)* toa muhtasari. **~ing** *n* maagizo maelezo, taarifa n.k. (itolewayo mapema k.m. kabla ya ndege kuruka).

brief[2] *adj* -fupi, -a muda/tukio/maelezo mafupi; -a kupita upesi *in ~* kwa ufupi, kwa muhtasari. **~ly** *adv*. **~ness** *n*.

briefs *n* chupi.

brier *see* **briar**[2].

brig (also brigantine) *n* 1 *(naut)* merikebu ya matanga (yenye milingoti miwili), baghala, kotia.

brigade *n* 1 brigedi (kikosi cha jeshi chenye askari wapatao 5,000). 2 kikundi/ kikosi cha kazi maalum *building ~* kikosi cha ujenzi. **fire ~** kikosi cha zima moto.

brigadier *n* brigadia. **brigadaier-general** brigedia jenerali.

brigand *n* mnyang'anyi (hasa aibaye vitu vya wasafiri katika misitu na milima).

brigantine *n see* **brig**.

bright *adj* 1 -enye kung'aa, ng'avu bashashi. 2 -a furaha, -changamfu, -kunjufu. 3 -elekevu, -enye akili. 4 *(of colour)* kali. 5 maarufu *look on/at the ~ side (of things)* -wa na matumaini, -tokata tamaa (licha ya matatizo). **~en** *vt,vi* 1 ~ **(up)** ng'arisha, changamsha, changamka. **~ness** *n*. **~ly** *adv*.

brilliant *adj* 1 -a kung'aa/kumetameta. 2 -zuri sana, tukufu, adhimu, -enye akili sana *he is ~* ana akili sana. *n* kito chenye pembe/pande nyingi. **brilliance, brilliancy** *n* mng'aro, uzuri, akili. **~ly** *adv*.

brilliantine *n* aina ya mafuta mazito ya nywele.

brim *n* 1 *(of hat)* ukingo. 2 *(of container)* mdomo, juu. **up to the ~** furifuri, pomoni, -a kujaa kabisa *vi* ~ **(over)** jaa sana, furika ~ *over with happiness* jaa furaha tele *her eyes ~ed with tears* machozi yalimlenga. **~ful** *adj*.

brimstone *n* 1 *(arch)* salfa, kibiriti. 2 **fire and ~** moto wa jahanamu.

brindled *adj (of animal)* -enye madoa, -enye mabaka.

brine *n* 1 maji yaliyokifu chumvi. 2 maji ya bahari. **briny** *adj n* **the ~** *n* bahari.

bring *vt* 1 leta ~ *me a book* niletee kitabu. 2 *(induce)* shawishi, vuta ~ *him to agree* mshawishi akubali ~ *oneself* shawishika ~ *to his notice* mfahamishe ~ *an action against* shtaki, dai, anzisha mashauri ~ *to bear (on)* tumia. ~ **low** dhalilisha, fedhehesha ~ *home* dhihirisha ~ *into question* tilia shaka ~ *tears to sb's eyes* liza. ~ **about** 1 sababisha. 2 *(of boat)* geuza. ~ **back** 1 rudisha. 2 kumbusha. ~ **down** 1 *(of prices etc)* shusha, telemsha. 2 *(of aircraft in war, government etc)* angusha. 3 *(of arith)* chukua. 4 ~ *(on)* sababisha (upana n.k.). 5 *(arch)* ~ **forth** (creature) zaa; toa matunda. ~ **forward** 1 onyesha. 2 *(of meeting etc)* wahisha, tanguliza. 3 *(bookkeeping)* peleka mbele. ~ **in** 1 anzisha. 2 leta faida, zaa, zalisha. 3 tumia. 4 toa uamuzi mahakamani. ~ **into** anzisha ~ *into force/effect*anza kutekeleza ~ *into contempt* dharaulisha. ~ **off** 1 okoa. 2 fanikisha *he brought it off* amefaulu. ~ **on** 1 sababisha. 2 stawisha, saidia. ~ **out** 1 sababisha kuonekana. 2 toa, anzisha. 3 *(of book)* chapisha. 4 *(of workers)* sababisha kugoma. ~ **over** geuza mawazo/ mtazamo. ~ **round** 1 amsha, tia mtu fahamu (baada ya kupoteza fahamu). 2 geuza. 3 ~ *(to)* elekeza. ~ **through** 1 *(in illness)* ponya. *(naut)* simamisha. 2 *see* ~ **round(1)**. ~ **together** leta pamoja, funganisha, kutanisha *chance brought us together* tulikutana kwa bahati. ~ **under** 1 tiisha. 2 jumlisha, weka pamoja. ~ **up** 1 lea funza. 2 tapika.

3 taja. 4 *(mil)* ~ *up the rear* peleka mbele tokea mwisho. 5 *(court)* leta mahakamani. 6 *(against) (usu pass)* kabili, tumiwa dhidi ya.

brink *n* ukingo, kando *be on the ~ of* -wa kando ya, -wa karibu kabisa (na hatari) *the ~ of death* chungulia kaburi. **~manship** *n* tabia ya kupenda kucheza na hatari hadi karibu kabisa.

briquette *n* tofali (lililotengenezwa kwa mavumbi ya mkaa kwa ajili ya kuchoma).

brisk *adj (of persons, movement)* -changamfu, -epesi (wa mwendo) ~ *walk* kutembea haraka. 2 *(of weather)* -nayochangamsha; enye ubaridi na upepo kiasi. **~ly** *adv*. **~ness** *n*.

brisket *n*. kidari.

bristle *n* 1 *(of animals)* unywele, laika. 2 *(of brush)* uywele mfupi tena mgumu; ufumwele, utembo *vi* 1 *(of hair)* ~ **up** simama (kwa hofu). 2 *(fig)* kasirika, pandwa hamaki. 3 ~ **with** onyesha (hasira); jaa tele *this job ~s with difficulties* kazi hii imejaa matatizo. **~ly** *adj*.

Britain *n* Uingereza. **British** *adj* -a Uingereza, -a Kiingereza *n* Mwingereza. **~er** *n (US)* Mwingereza. **Briton** *n* raia wa Uingereza, Mwingereza.

brittle *adj* -gumu lakini epesi kuvunjika (kama chungu n.k.) *(fig) He has a ~ temper* yu mwepesi kukasirika. **~ness** *n*.

broach[1] *n* 1 *(arch)* waya wa kuchomea mshikaki. 2 ncha (mnara uliochongoka juu). 3 msharasi.

broach[2] *vt* 1 fungua (chupa); toboa (kasiki) na tia mrija ndani yake ili kutoa mvinyo nje. 2 fanya kitu kijulikane kwa mara ya kwanza. 3 *(fig)* anzisha mazungumzo (ya mada fulani).

broach[3] *vi,vt (naut)* ~ **to** enda joshi/ kwa upande.

broad[1] *adj* 1 pana. 2 -nayoshika eneo kubwa mno, -enye kuenea mahali pakubwa mno. ~ **plains** nyanda. 3 kabisa. ~ **daylight** kweupe kabisa. ~ **hint** dokezo dhahiri la wazi. 4 -a jumla. **in ~ outline** kwa jumla. 5 *(of the mind and ideas)* -pana, -nayokubali mawazo ya wengine. **a ~minded person** mtu anayekubali kusikiliza mawazo ya wenzake japo si lazima akubaliane nayo *a man of ~ views* mtu mvumilivu mwenye kuheshimu mawazo ya wengine. 6 *(of speech)* -enye lafudhi/mkazo unaoonyesha wazi athari za kimazingira (zinazoathiri kisanifu). 7 *(phrase)* **It's as ~ as it is long** hakuna tofauti, ni mamoja. 8 *(compounds)* ~ **beans** maharage **~en** *vt, vi* (~ **out)** panuka,panua. **~-sheet** *n* laha: karatasi pana lililochapwa au kuandikwa upande mmoja tu. **~ly** *adv* **~ness n**

broad[2] *n* 1 sehemu iliyo pana (ya kitu fulani). 2 *(US slang)* mwanamke.

broadcast *vt,vi* 1 tawanya, eneza (k.m. habari, taarifa) pande zote kwa redio au televisheni. 2 zungumza, imba n.k. kwa ajili ya kuenezwa kwa redio au televisheni) *the President will ~ this evening* Rais atazungumza kwa njia ya redio/televisheni leo jioni. 3 tangaza. 4 panda mbegu kwa kuzitawanya *n* 1 tangazo, kipindi cha redio/televisheni). 2 **~ter** mtangazaji. **~ing** *n,adj*.

broadside *n* 1 ubavu wa meli juu ya maji. 2 shambulio la mizinga yote ya upande wa manowari. 3 *(fig)* shambulio kali la maneno. 4 karatasi pana. *adv* ~ **on (to)** kwa kuelekeza upande mmoja katika sehemu au lengo fulani. ~ **sword** *n* upanga wa bapa. ~ **ways** *adv* kwa kuelekea upana.

brocade *n* 1 hariri ya kimashariki iliyotariziwa. 2 nguo yoyote iliyo na taraza. **~d** *adj*.

broccoli *n* brokoli: aina ya mboga za majani zilizomo katika spishi ya kabichi ambazo maua yake huliwa.

brochure *n* brosha: kijitabu chenye maelezo mafupi ya kimatangazo.

brogue *n* buti: kiatu kigumu cha ngozi

chenye wayo mnene na mgumu.
broil[1] *n* ugomvi, mzozo.
broil[2] *vt,vi* 1 banika; *(fig)* -wa na joto kali; chemka *a ~ing day* siku yenye joto kali. **~er** *n* 1 kuku wa nyama. 2 siku yenye joto kali. 3 mgomvi.
broke *vt see* **break** *(sl)* **stony flat/dead ~** bila fedha, -liofilisika, -liowamba kabisa.
broken *adj* -liovunjika, -liokatika. **~ marriage** ndoa iliyovunjika *~ spirit* moyo uliovunjika. 2 *(of languages)* -baya, -bovu, -sio fasaha. *~ English* Kiingereza kibovu/ kisicho fasaha. **~ man** mtu aliyekatishwa tamaa kabisa. **~ ground** ardhi isiyo sawasawa. **~ hearted** -enye huzuni nyingi, -enye majonzi.
broker *n* 1 wakala. 2 dalali. **~age** *n* 1 ushuru wa dalali. 2 kazi au uanzishaji wa udalali.
brolly *n (colloq)* mwavuli.
bromide *n* 1 bromidi: dawa ya kutuliza. 2 *(colloq)* maneno mwanana. 3 mtu mchoshi.
bronchus *n* kikoromeo. **bronchial** *adj*.
bronchitis *n* mkamba.
bronco *n (US)* farasi asiyefunzwa utii.
bronze *n* shaba (nyeusi); rangi ya shaba (nyeusi) *vt* tia shaba nyeusi *adj* -a shaba nyeusi; -enye rangi ya shaba. **~d** *adj* -lobadilika rangi (kuwa kama shaba) kutokana na jua. **~age** enzi ya shaba.
brooch *n* bruki, bruchi, bronki, bizimu.
brood *n* makinda (vifaranga) yalioanguliwa pamoja; vitoto vya wanyama wengine vilivyoanguliwa kwa pamoja *(joc)* kundi la watoto. **~-hen** koo la kuku. **~-mare** farasi jike *vi* 1 *(of birds)* atamia. 2 **~ (over/on)** *(fig)* waza sana, fikiri sana, tafakari. **~y** *adj (of hens)* -nayo kokoreka *(fig) (of persons)* -lio kanyaga chechele. **~er** *n* koo la kuku.
brook[1] *vt* vumilia, stahimili *the matter ~s no delay* mambo hayastahimiliki.
brook[2] *n* kijito cha maji baridi. **~let** *n* kijito kidogo.
broom *n* 1 ufagio. *(fig)* **new ~** kiongozi mpya (mwenye kurekebisha maovu aliyoyakuta). **iron ~** fagio la chuma. 2 *(bot)* mfagio. **~stick** *n* mpini wa ufagio.
broomcorn *n (bot)* jamii ya mmea wa mtama.
broth *n* mchuzi wa nyama *(fig) a ~ of a boy* mvulana mzuri.
brothel *n* danguro.
brother *n* 1 ndugu mume, ndugu (wa tumbo moja) *older ~* kaka *husband's ~* shemeji, mwamu *~'s wife* wifi; shemeji *younger ~* mdogo wa (wa kiume) *mother's ~* mjomba. 2 *(rel)* mtawa, bruda. 3 *(int)* mwenzi. **~-in-law** *n* shemeji, mlamu, mwamu/muamu. **~liness** *n* undugu. **~ly** *adj* -a ndugu, -a kidugu.
brouhaha *n* ghasia, makelele.
brow *n* 1 nyusi. 2 paji *knit the ~s* kunja uso. 3 *(poet)* uso wa kilima, ukingo wa mteremko mkali.
browbeat *vt* onea, ogofya. **~ sb into doing sth** lazimisha mtu kufanya jambo.
brown *adj* hudhurungi, -a kahawia. **light ~** -a kahawia nyepesi *dark ~* -a kahawia iliyoiva. **~ shirts** wanazi (wanachama wa chama cha Nazi). **in a ~ study** katika hali ya kufikiri sana (hata kusahau vingine), -liozama katika mawazo. **~ paper** karatasi ya kaki ya kufungia vitu *~ bread* mkate (wa unga usiokobolewa) kahawia. **~ed off** *(slang)* -liochoshwa, lioudhika. *n* 1 rangi ya kahawia. **~s out** *n* kufifia kwa mwanga wa umeme. **~ tone** *n* jiwe la mchanga.
brownie *n* 1 kijini kidogo kisemwacho kuwa chafanya kazi ya kusaidia kazi za nyumbani. 2 **B~ (Guide)** skauti mdogo wa kike.
browse *vi,vt* 1 tafuna majani. 2 jilisha, chunga (kama wafanyavyo wanyama wala majani). 3 soma soma, pitiapitia kitabu, gazeti, n.k. bila lengo maalumu. *n* 1 malisho (majani laini, n.k.). 2 hali ya kuchunga mnyama.

bruin *n (fairy tales)* dubu (hasa katika hadithi za watoto).

bruise *vi* vilia *he ~s easily* anavilia kwa urahisi. *n* vilio la damu, alama ya pigo. **~r** *n (sl)* bondia apigaye ngumi kikatili.

bruit *n* 1 *(arch)* uvumi, mnong'ono. 2 sauti nyingi zisizo za kawaida zisikikazo (katika uchunguzi wa kiganga) katika mwili wa binadamu *vt* eneza uvumi, vumisha.

brunch *n (colloq)* chakula cha saa tano asubuhi badala ya kifungua kinywa na chakula cha mchana.

brunette *n* mtu (hasa kijana wa kike) mwenye nywele nyeusi na ngozi nyeusi kidogo *adj* -enye rangi ya kahawia au nyeusi.

brunt *n* 1 pigo kuu, nguvu kubwa, mshutuko mkubwa. 2 sehemu kubwa.

brush *n* 1 burashi, ufagio *tooth ~* mswaki. 2 kichaka. 3 mkia wa mbweha. 4 usafishaji kwa kutumia burashi. 5 pambano kali la muda mfupi *vt* 1 piga burashi; fagia, pangusa, sugua. 2 ~ **up** safisha kwa burashi; jikumbusha (masomo) *~ sth aside/away* puuza ~ **sb/sth off** ondoa, fukuza, kataa *~ down* safisha kwa burashi *~ out* fagia (chumba), chambua kwa kitana *~ over* tia (rangi n.k.) kwa burashi. *vi* ~ **by/** ~ **past** pita upesi sana *~ wood n* kichaka *~-work n* ufundi wa kupiga rangi; mtindo wa kuchora picha ya rangi. *my coat needs a ~* koti langu linahitaji kupigwa brashi.

brusque adj 1 -a ghafla na fupi. 2 -kali, -siyo na adabu, -a kukatiza. **~ness** *n.*

brutal *adj* katili, -a kinyama, -a kihayawani. **~ity** *n.* **~ize** *vt* fanya kuwa katili; geuza hayawani. **~ly** *adv.*

brute *adj* -a kinyama, katili *~ force n* 1 mbavu, ubabe. 2 upumbavu *n* 1 mnyama, hayawani. 2 mtu mbaya, baa, katili. **brutish** *adj.* **brutishness** *n.*

bubble *n* 1 kiputo: tone la hewa katika kioevu, povu. 2 kisoimara: kitu ambacho hakina uimara wa aina yoyote; kisothabiti: kitu kisicho na ukweli wa aina yoyote. 3 sauti ya mbubujiko. 4 ~ **tube** pimamaji. 5 **~gum** ubani, chingamu. *vi* 1 toa povu. 2 umuka. 3 chemka, toa kiputo *~ over* furika, fura (kwa furaha, hasira n.k.).

bubbly *n* shampeni *adj* 1 -lojaa viputo. 2 bashasha.

bubo *n* mtoki, uvimbe manenani/ kwapani. **~nic** *adj* -enye mitoki. **~ic plague** tauni.

buccaneer *n* 1 haramia wa bahari. 2 jambazi.

buck *n* 1 dume (la wanyama jamii ya paa, mbuzi, sungura, n.k.). 2 kifaa cha kuchezea sarakasi. 3 egemeo la mti wakati wa kupasua mbao. 4 mnyama aina ya paa (hupatikana zaidi Afrika Kusini). 5 *(colloq)* mtu wa miraba minne. 6 *(US)* dola *(arch)* kijana maridadi. ~ **fever** *n* homa ya kutetemeka, wasiwasi unaomwingia mtu anapokabiliwa na jambo geni (k.m. anapoanza madaraka mapya, anapokumbana na tatizo gumu n.k.) *vi* 1 *(of horse/mule)* ruka hewani na kutua chini kwa kutanguliza miguu ya mbele huku kichwa kimeinama. 2 enda au simama ghafla kwa mtikisiko au mshtuko. 3 gonga au gongana na kitu kwa ghafla. **pass the ~** kwepa wajibu. ~ **up** 1 fanya haraka. 2 tia moyo. ~ **skin** ngozi laini (k.m. ya paa/mbuzi) inayotumika kutengenezea glovu, mikoba n.k.). ~ **short** aina ya risasi. ~ **tooth** jino lililotokeza.

bucket[1] *n* 1 ndoo. *(sl)* **kick the ~** aga dunia. **~-shop** *(sl)* mwuza tikiti za kusafiria (agh. kwa ndege) kwa bei iliyopunguzwa. 2 **~ful** *n* ndoo tele.

bucket[2] *vt* 1 *(of horse)* endesha shoti. 2 *(of rain)* nyesha kwa nguvu.

buckhound *n* mbwa mwinda.

buckle *n* kishikizo, bakoli; bizimu. *vt,vi* 1 ~ **(on)** funga kwa bakoli. 2 *(of shoe, belt, etc)* funga (kwa namna

fulani). 3 ~ **to/down to** anza (kazi) kwa nguvu. 4 *(of metal work, etc)* pinda, pindika, kunjamana kwa sababu ya joto.
buckler *n* ngao ndogo, kikingio.
buckram *n* kitani nzito (namna ya kitambaa kigumu) kinachotumika kujalidi vitabu.
bucksaw *n* msumeno (agh wa kutumiwa na watu wawili).
buckshee bure, bila malipo.
buckwheat *n* nafaka inayofanana na ngano.
bucolic *adj* 1 -a mashambani, kishamba. 2 -a wachungaji *n (pl)* mashairi yaelezayo maisha ya vijijini/mashambani.
bud *n* 1 jicho (la ua), tumba. 2 chipukizi, kichomoza. 3 kizizi mbegu. **nip in the** ~ komesha upesi mwanzoni (mwa shauri n.k.) *vi, vt (-dd-)* chomoza, chipuka, mea, kua. **~ding** *adj*. **~ding artist** *n* msanii chipukizi.
Buddhism *n* Ubudha. **buddhist** *n* mfuasi wa Budha.
buddy *n* 1 *(sl)* ndugu, rafiki. 2 *(as address)* yakhe.
budge *vi,vt* 1 jongea, sogea, enda, mudu *it won't* ~ haijongei hata kidogo *I can't* ~ *it* siwezi kuijongeza. 2 *(fig)* badili (mawazo).
budget *n* 1 bajeti. 2 *(arch) (bundle)* kipeto (cha nyaraka, hati n.k.) *vi* ~ **for** wekea bajeti. **~ary** *adj* -a bajeti.
buff *n* 1 ngozi nene, imara na laini. 2 bila nguo, uchi. **in the** ~ uchi, bila nguo. **stripped to the** ~uchi wa nyama. 3 rangi ya kimanjano. 4 *(colloq US)* shabiki *vt* ng'arisha.
buffalo *n* nyati, mbogo.
buffer *n* 1 bafa: kifaa kitumiwacho katika kupunguza athari ya nguvu ya msukumo wakati gari inapogonga kitu. ~ **zone** eneo la amani. 2 kinga: kitu au mtu anayemkinga mtu mwingine au kitu kingine kisipate mshtuko. 3 *(sl)* **old** ~ mtu aliyepitwa na wakati au mjinga. 4 sehemu ya hifadhi ya muda (hasa katika kompyuta). ~ **state** *n* taifa kati: taifa dogo lisilopendelea upande wowote ambalo liko kati ya mataifa mawili yaelekeayo kuchukiana. ~ **stock** *n* akiba: hifadhi ya kitu inayonunuliwa wakati bei ni nafuu na kuwekwa ili itumiwe wakati bei yake itakapokuwa ghali *vt* 1 punguza mshtuko; punguza athari ya mgongano. 2 zuia kupata maumivu.
buffet[1] *n 1* bafe: kaunta ya kuuzia vyakula au vinywaji (k.m. katika treni). 2 kabati ya kuonyeshea vyombo vya kauri. 3 chakula ambacho kimewekwa kwenye meza ili walaji wajihudumie wenyewe. 4 mgahawa ambamo walaji hujihudumia wenyewe.
buffet[2] *n* 1 konde: pigo la mkono. 2 kitu kipigacho kwa nguvu kubwa *vt* 1 piga kwa nguvu. 2 gongagonga juu ya kitu. 3 tumia vibaya; fanyia ukatili. 4 ~ **(about)** rusha kwa nguvu toka upande mmoja hadi mwingine (k.m. katika ndege au treni).
buffoon *n* 1 mchekeshaji, mpumbavu. 2 mtu mpumbavu mwenye fujo na makelele *vi* chekesha, jipumbaza. **~ery** *n* upuzi, upumbavu, uchekeshaji.
bug *n* 1 mdudu *bed* ~ kunguni. 2 *(esp. US)* kijidudu. 3 *(sl)* **big** ~ mtu mashuhuri, mwenye cheo kikubwa, kizito, bwana mkubwa. 4 *(colloq)* virusi, chembe-maradhi. 5 *(sl)* ubovu, kasoro. 6 kinasasauti (kilichofichwa cha kusikilizia au kunasia mazungumzo ya siri) *vi* 1 *(colloq)* tumia kinasasauti kusikilizia siri. 2 *(US sl)* chukiza, udhi *adj* -enye kunguni (au wadudu wengine wa aina yake).
bugaboo *n* 1 usumbufu. 2 chanzo cha woga/hasira.
bugbear *n* kitu kinachoogopwa/ kisichopendwa (kinachofikirika tu).
bugger *n* 1 *(leg)* mlawati *(sl)* basha, mende. 2 *silly*~ mjinga. 3 *~y* ulawiti *vt* 1 lawiti. 2 ~ **up** haribu kitu (hasa kutokana na ujuzi mdogo). 3 ~ **off**

ondoka, ambaa, toka. ~ **about** fanya kijinga, sumbua.

buggy *n* kigari (cha farasi cha magurudumu mawili).

bugle *n* tarumbeta ndogo, buruji *vi* piga baragumu/tarumbeta.

build *vt* 1 jenga, ~ *a house* jenga nyumba. 2 unda. 3 anzisha na kuendeleza kitu. 4 fanya kitu kiongezeke polepole. 5 ~ **in** jengea ndani ya kitu kingine. 6 ~ **up** ongeza, ongezeka polepole; jaa majengo *built up areas* maeneo yaliyojaa majengo. 7 ~ **upon/on** tegemea, tumia kama msingi *n* 1 umbo *a man of powerful* ~ mtu mwenye umbo la nguvu. 2 uumbaji *n*. ~**ing** *n* 1 ujenzi *~ing materials* vifaa vya ujenzi. 2 jengo. 3 *(naut)* uundaji ~**up** *n* 1 ujengekaji, ongezeko. 2 kitu kitokanacho na ujengaji au uundaji. ~**er** *n,adj* -lojengeka *a well built person* mtu mwenye umbo zuri.

bulb *n* 1 tunguu. 2 balbu, glopu. ~**ous** *adj*.

bulbul *n* shore, teleka.

bulge *n* 1 uvimbe, mtokezo (wa mviringo juu ya uso wa kitu hasa kutokana na kanieneo iliyoko chini yake). 2 ongezeko (la ghafla na la muda) katika namba au ujazo *vi* 1 tokeza, vimba, benuka, fanya mgongo. 2 panuka, ongezeka ghafla, jaa. 3 **bulging** *adj* .

bulk *n* 1 wingi, ukubwa. 2 *(chief part)* sehemu iliyo kubwa ya. 3 *(cargo)* jumla ya shehena *load in* ~ pakia shehena zilizofunguka *sell in* ~ uza kwa mafungu, uza kwa jumla. **break** ~ toa shehena *vi,vt* -wa kubwa~ large -wa muhimu. 2 weka yote pamoja. ~**y** *adj*.

bulkhead *n (of ship or aeroplane)* kiambaza cha kukingama; ukuta unaotenga sehemu mbili.

bull[1] *n* 1 fahali, ng'ombe dume. 2 dume la mnyama mkubwa kama tembo au nyangumi. **take the ~ by the horns** jasiri, kabili kwa ujasiri. 3 mlanguzi, katika soko la hisa. 4 ~ **fight** mchezo wa kupigana na ng'ombe *vi* 1 songa mbele kwa nguvu. 2 jaribu kupandisha bei *adj* -a kidumedume, -a kufanana na dume la ng'ombe. ~**shit** mavi! upuuzi! ~ **head** *n* 1 bakarikichwa (samaki). 2 *(sl)* mjinga. ~ **headed** *adj* -kakamizi. ~**ock** *n* 1 fahali mdogo. 2 maksai. ~**-ring** *n* uwanja wa mchezo wa ng'ombe. ~**s-eye** *n* 1 katikati kabisa (hasa ya shabaha). 2 dirisha la mviringo.

bull[2] *(RC)* amri/tangazo la Papa.

bulldoze *vt* 1 sawazisha ardhi kwa buldoza. 2 lazimisha, shurutisha (mt u kufanya jambo). ~ **r** *n* buldoza.

bullet *n* risasi (ya bunduki). ~ **headed** *adj* 1 -enye kichwa cha mviringo. ~ **-proof** *adj* -siopenya risasi.

bulletin *n* taarifa rasmi ya habari.

bullion *n* kinoo au mkuo wa dhahabu au fedha.

bully[1] *n* 1 mwonevu, mkatili, dhalimu, mkandamizaji. 2 kuwadi (atongozaye wanawake kwa ajili ya wengine); mtu anayetetea malaya na kuwawekea kifua. 3 mpigo wa fimbo mbili mara tatu ili kuanza mchezo wa hoki *vt* onea, dhulumu, tisha.

bully[2] *adj (sl)* -zuri. **it's ~ for you!** oyee!

bully[3] *n* (*usu* ~**-beef**) nyama ya kopo.

bulrush *n* aina ya unyasi. ~ **millet** uwimbi.

bulwark *n* 1 boma, (hasa la ardhi). 2 *(fig)* kinga, ngao, kizuizi. 3 ukuta mdogo wa kuzungusha sitaha ya merikebu; ukingo wa mbavu za meli utokezao juu. 4 *(of small boat)* manjali *(of boat)* talibisi.

bum[1] *n (colloq)* matako.

bum[2] *n (colloq)* mdoezi, ombaomba. ~ around gaagaa, dusa. ~ **rap** kifungo cha uonevu. ~**'s rush** kufukuza kwa nguvu *vi* 1 doea, dusa. 2 ishi kikupe. **bummer** *n (US)* 1 lofa, mkunguni, mvivu. 2 kitu kisicho na thamani. 3 hali mbaya isiyopendeza aihisiyo mtu.

bumble-bee *n* nyukibambi, nyuki manyoya.

bumble *vi* 1 vuma. 2 tapatapa.
bumboat *n* 1 mashua ya kupeleka posho.
bump *vi,vt* 1 gonga, gongana na, kumbana na *I have ~ed my head* nimejigonga kichwa. ~ **along** gonga. 2 ruka; rusha/rushwa. ~ **off** *(sl)* ua. ~ **into** kutana na (kwa bahati). ~ **up** pandisha, ongeza. **~y** *adj,n* 1 pigo kama kwamba vitu viwili vimegongana. 2 mgongano, chubuko. 3 uvimbe. 4 *~s in the road* matuta ya barabarani. **~er** *n* 1 dafrau; bamba. 2 kikombe kilichojazwa divai pomoni. 3 kitu kilichopo kwa wingi sana ~ *harvest* mavuno makubwa mno *~er to ~er* msongamano wa magari.
bumpkin *n* mjinga, zuzu, mshenzi, mshamba.
bumptious *adj* -enye kiburi/ majivuno/makelele; -akujitokeza. **~ly** *adv*. **~ness** *n*.
bun *n* 1 mkate mdogo wa mviringo namna ya keki, andazi. 2 **have a ~ in the oven** -wa na mimba. 3 *(of woman's hair)* fundo la nywele za kusokotwa kisogoni.
bunch *n* 1 kicha cha matunda, mkungu ~ *of banana* mkungu wa ndizi. 2 *(informal)* kikundi cha watu *vi,vt* songana, fungamana, kunjamana kusanya, funga pamoja, tunga pamoja (k.m. shada la maua).
bundle *n* kifurushi, kipeto, fungu, kitita, mzigo *vt* 1 funga vitu vingi kwa pamoja. 2 tupa/weka bila mpango; tumbukiza. 3 ~ out (**off**) ondosha kwa haraka (kwa fujo), tupatupa. ~ **up** tupa ovyo; vaa nguo nyingi ili kujikinga na baridi.
bung *n* 1 kizibo au kifuniko (kilichotengenezwa kutokana na raba, plastiki n.k.). 2 *(of nose)*. ~ed up -lojaa makamasi *vt* 1 ziba. 2 tupa hewani.
bungalow *n* nyumba isiyo na ghorofa.
bungle *vt* 1 vuruga, boronga. 2 fuja, tia fujo, chafua. 3 fanya kazi ovyo ovyo. **~r** *n*.
bunion *n* kivimbe (hasa cha kidole gumba cha mguu).
bunk[1] *n* kitanda (chembamba kilichofungwa kwenye ukuta wa chumba melini au katika treni). ~ **beds** jozi ya vitanda vilivyobebana (viwili- viwili) *vi (US)* 1 lala; chukua kitanda katika meli au treni.
bunk[2] *vi* toroka, toweka haraka haraka.
bunk[3] *abbr. of* **bunkum**
bunker *n* 1 ghala ya mkaa au fueli melini. 2 *(mil)* handaki la kudumu. 3 *(of golf)* tuta (la kuzuilia) *vt* jaza ghala ya mkaa/fueli melini 2. *(fig)* kuwa matatizoni.
bunkum *n* upuuzi.
bunny *n* 1 (jina la kitoto la) sungura. 2 ~ **girl** kisungura: msichana anayevalia kama sungura (anayehudumia kwenye baa).
Bunsen *n* ~ **burner** stovu ya Bunsen ya gesi.
bunt *n* 1 sehemu ya kati ya tanga mraba. 2 mfuko (wa mshipi wa kuvulia samaki) *vt, vi* piga/ sukuma kwa kichwa au pembe.
bunting *n* aina ya vitambaa vya rangi-rangi kwa ajili ya bendera na mapambo (kwenye barabara na majumba wakati wa sikukuu).
buoy *n* 1 boya. 2 **life** ~ chelezo, boya au kifaa cha kuokolea maisha *vt* tia boya, weka vyelezo, funga pungu. 2 ~ **up** changamsha, tia moyo, eleza mtu au kitu majini kisizame. **buoyancy** *n* 1 uelezi. 2 *(cheerfulness)* ukunjufu, uchangamfu. 3 *(the stock market)* bei kuendelea kupanda. **buoyant** *adj*.
bur *n* kichomanguo. 2 *(fig)* mng'ang'aniaji.
burble *vi* bwabwaja, ongea kijinga; nong'ona.
burbot *n* 1 gadidi, mkunga wa majibaridi. 2 kambare mamba, kamongo.
burden *n*. 1 mzigo (mzito), **beast of ~** mnyama wa kuchukua mizigo (farasi,punda, ng'ombe, nyati, ngamia) *(fig)* hamali. 2 **the ~ of**

proof wajibu wa kuthibitisha. 3 shehena, bari. 4 kiitikio. 5 kiini, maana hasa ya jambo vt ~ **sb** twisha mizigo, sumbua, gandamiza.

bureau *n* 1 *(GB)* dawati, deski lenye mtoto wa meza. 2 *(US)* kabati la nguo lenye watoto wa meza. 3 ofisi (ya serikali au biashara hasa kwa ajili ya kuhifadhi taarifa) ~ *of Standards* Shirika la Viwango vya Bidhaa.

bureaucracy *n* urasimu. **bureaucrat** *n* mrasimu. **bureaucratic** *adj* -a kirasimu. **bureaucratically** *adv*.

burette *n* bureti.

burg *n (US sl)* mji, jiji; **~ess** *n* mwenyeji wa mji, raia; mpiga kura.

burgeon *vi* chipua, kua.

burglar *n* mwizi wa kuvunja nyumba. ~y *n* wizi. **~-proof** *adj* -lioimarishwa dhidi ya wizi. ~ **alarm** chombo cha kutoa tahadhari ya wizi.

burgle *vt, vi* vunja nyumba kwa sababu ya kuiba.

burgomaster *n* mkuu wa mji, meya (wa mji wa Uholanzi au Ujerumani).

burial *n* maziko, mazishi, kuzika *requisites for* ~ vifaa vya mazishi. **~-ground** *n*. makaburini, maziarani, mavani ~ *service n* ibada ya kuzika; talakini *say* ~ *service* soma talakini.

burlap *n* turubai.

burlesque *n* uigaji (wa mambo ya kuchekesha) *adj* -a kuchekesha *vt* igiza kwa namna ya kuchekesha.

burly *adj* -enye miraba minne, -enye maungo ya ukakamvu.

burn[1] *n (Scot)* kijito.

burn[2] *vt* 1 choma, unguza *~t bricks* matofali ya kuchoma. ~ one's fingers jiponza, bahatisha, yote kwa kutumaini kufaulu. 2 washa, waka. 3 *the fire is ~ing* moto unawaka ~ *with anger* kasirika sana. **~ing glass** lensi ya kuwashia (kwa kutumia mionzi ya jua). 4 ~ **down** teketeza, angamiza. ~out pofu, choka sana (kwa ajili ya jitihada ya muda mrefu; kwa mwanga mkali) *vi* 1 ungua, waka, teketea, ona jingi ~ *easily (of skin)* zingia kwa jua. 2 ~ **into** *(a metal etc.)* tia alama /mkato, mchoro kwa moto. ~ **up** kasirika. ~ **someone's ears** *(sl)* kemea sana *n* kuchomwa. **~ing-hot** -enye kuungua sana. **~er** *n* 1 mchomaji 2 buna. **burning** *n* 1 mwako, mchomo. 2 *(of brick)* kuchoma. 3 *(of stomach)* mchomo *adj* 1 -ingi, -kali *a ~ing thirst* kiu kali. 2 -enye kukera, -lio muhimu *a ~ing question* swali muhimu. 3 -baya, -a aibu, kubwa *a ~ing shame* -a aibu kubwa.

burnish *vt* kwatua, ng'arisha.

burnouse *n* juba.

burp *n* mbweu *vt,vi* piga mbweu, teuka, chemka.

burr[1] *n* sauti ya kimadende, tamko la kukwaruza konsonanti **R** *vt* tamka kimadende/ konsonanti **R**.

burr[2] *n see* **bur.**

burr[3] *n* 1 kinoo. 2 *(med)* ~ **drill** kekee ndogo.

burro[1] *n (US)* punda mdogo.

burrow[2] *n* kishimo (cha wanyama), kitundu (kipenyacho chini) *vi,vt* fukua, ingia, (kaa) shimoni *(fig)* chungua sana ~ *one's way* fuatisha njia. **~er** *n*.

bursar *n* 1 *(for schools and colleges)* msarifu. 2 mtu aliyepata msaada kwa kulipiwa masomo. **~y** *n* msaada wa masomo.

burst *vt* 1 pasua, vunja. 2 toka, penya, ingia kwa ghafla ~ *its banks* furika *he ~ a blood vessel* kapilari ilimpasuka *(fig)* ~ *one's sides with laughter* angua kicheko, vunjika mbavu *vi* pasuka, lipuka *the bomb* ~ bomu lililipuka; funguka ghafla ~ *asunder* pasuka *his heart will ~ with envy* moyo wake utapasuka kwa wivu *~into tears* angua kilio, toka machozi ghafla. ~ **on** *(appear suddenly)* zuka ~ **with** *(corn)* jaa tele (kwa nafaka). *(of person)* ~ *with envy etc.* -wa na husuda kubwa ~ with joy (pride etc) jaa tele, jawa na furaha kubwa (ona fahari kubwa n.k.) ~ *upon sb's sight* jitokeza ghafla ~ *sb's ears* lialia; jipenyeza kwa nguvu. **~out** toka kwa nguvu; bubujika, buguika, foka. **be ~ing to -** wa na shauku sana. **~ in (up) on** ingilia ~ *(up) on* fikia, tokeza *n* 1 mlipuko, mshindo, kuangua kicheko. 2 *a ~ in the water main* kupasuka kwa bomba la maji. 3 jitihada ya muda mfupi.

bury *vt* 1 zika *he buried two children* amefiwa na watoto wawili. 2 fukia, ficha, setiri, futia mbali. **buried in thought** zama katika fikra fulani. 3 tupilia mbali sahau. **~ the hatchet** sameheana. 4 *(cover, overwhelm)* funikiza, angamiza. 5 funika kwa ardhi *~ a dagger in sb's chest etc.* choma sime kifuani.

burying-beetle *n (zool)* tuta.

burying-ground *n see* **burial ground**

bus *n* basi *he took a ~* alipanda basi *miss the ~* kosa kitu, shindwa kutumia nafasi. **~ man** dereva wa basi. **~ man's holiday** mapumziko/likizo ya kufanya shughuli zinazofanana na zile za kazini. **~ stop** kituo cha basi *vt, vi* safiri/safirisha kwa basi.

busby *n* kofia ndefu ya manyoya ya askari-farasi.

bush[1] *n* 1 mti mfupi, kichaka, kituka, pori. **take to the ~** torokea msituni. **~ fighter** mpigania uhuru wa msituni. **~ lawyer** wakili wa mitaani. **~ telegram** ueneaji haraka wa uvumi; upelekaji habari kwa kutumia ngoma, moshi n.k. **~ whacker** mfyekaji vichaka. **~ whack** vt 1 ishi porini. 2 shambulia *beat about the ~* zungusha maneno, sema kwa kuzunguka zunguka bila kufikia shabaha ya mazungumzo . 3 **good wine needs no ~** chema chajiuza kibaya chajitembeza. **~ed** *adj (colloq) (US)* choka sana *(colloq)* Austral & N.Z.) potea msituni.

bush[2] *n* bushi/sandarusi/ bitani ya chuma. **~ing** *n* 1 bitani, kihani. 2 *(mech)* bushi.

bushbuck *n* mbawala, kulungu.

bushel[1] *n* kipimo, kadiri ya pishi tisa, **light under a ~** ficha kipaji chako.

Bushman *n* mwenyeji wa Kusini mwa Afrika katika mbari kuu ya wawindaji-wahamaji. 2 mtu wa msituni. **~veld** *n* mbuga (Afrika Kusini). **~y** *adj* 1. -enye msitu mkubwa, -lojaa miti/vichaka. 2 -a vitawi vingi; -a manywele/madevu, -enye kivunga.

busily *adv see* **busy**.

business *n* 1 biashara, kufanya biashara *he is in the timber ~* anafanya biashara ya mbao *start a ~* anza biashara. **~ address** anwani ya biashara au ofisi. **~ hours** saa za kazi. **~ like** -epesi; chapa kazi. -angalifu. **~ man** mfanyabiashara. 2 kazi, shughuli. **on ~** -wa katika shughuli. **I 'am here on ~** nipo hapa kwa shughuli. 3 kazi, wajibu, jambo linalopasa *It is my ~ to advise you* ni wajibu wangu kukushauri. **get down to ~** anza kufanya kazi iliyokusudiwa. **mind your own ~!** si shauri lako! haikuhusu! *mean ~!* jali, -wa makini *send sb about his ~* fukuza na onya (mtu) asiingilie mambo. 4 madaraka haki, *you have no ~ to interfere* usiniingilie. 5 jambo gumu, tatizo *what a ~ it is* tatizo gani hili. 6 jambo (la kukifu, kukera, kuchosha) *I am sick of the whole ~* jambo hili limenikifu. 7 *(colloq) the ~ end of a pin/a chisel etc* ncha ya kitu/chombo (inayotumika kufanyia kazi). 8 *(theatre)* ishara za uso/kuelezea, kufasili sehemu/kuelezea sehemu wanazoigiza (tofauti na wasemavyo). 9 **like nobody's ~** vizuri/haraka sana.

busk *vt* piga muziki/imba barabarani (kwa ajili ya kupata fedha). **~er** *n.*

bust[1] *n* 1 kifua cha mtu; maziwa ya mwanamke. 2 sanamu ya kichwa na mabega ya mtu.

bust[2] *vt,vi* 1 pasua, pasuka, vunja, vunjika. 2 filisika. 3 **go ~** filisika, shushwa/shusha cheo. 4 *(of police)* kamata, sachi, pekua. 5 **~ up** gombana; achana *n* ugomvi, kuvunjika (kwa ndoa) *n* 1 kukamata, kusachi. 2 kushindwa kabisa.

bustard *n* ndege wa jamii ya korongo.
buster *n* 1 (*in compounds*) kombora linaloangamiza kila kitu *tank ~* kombora lenye kuharibu kabisa kifaru. 2 *(US sl.)* namna ya kusalimiana, yahe! yakhe!
bustle *vt, vi* harakisha, harakia. ~ **sb out** sukuma nje, toa nje *n* 1 kukurukakara, pilikapilika. 2 *(arch)* kipanua-sketi (kwa nyuma).
busy *adj* 1 *(of person)* -enye kazi, mashughuli, -a shughuli (nyingi) *keep oneself~* jishughulisha. 3 *(of a road)* -enye magari mengi, kupitapita kwa magari (watu) mengi *(of business)* -a shughuli nyingi *the ~ hours* saa za kazi. **get** ~ anza *get ~ eating* anza kula *this is a ~ street* mtaa huu una magari/watu wengi. 4 *(of a telephone)* inatumika *the telephone line is ~* simu inatumika/ inaongea *vt* ~ **oneself (with)** jishughulisha, shughulisha. **~ness** *n.* ~ **body** *n* aingiliaye kati ya mambo ya wengine, duzi. **busily** *adv.*
but *adv* 1 tu *he left ~ an hour ago* ameondoka saa moja iliyopita tu *she is ~ a child* yeye ni mtoto tu *can not ~ + inf* lazimika; isipokuwa, ila *all ~ me* wote isipokuwa mimi. ~ **for** bila *~ for your help* bila msaada wako, kuwa, ila kwa *(conj)* 1 lakini, isipokuwa *Juma was there ~ his father was not* Juma alikuwepo lakini baba yake hakuwepo. 2 *no man is so old ~ that he may learn* hakuna mtu aliye mzee ambaye hawezi kujifunza *I cannot ~ believe* siwezi kufanya jingine isipokuwa kuamini *anything~* chochote isipokuwa.**~then** lakini pengine. ~ **that** hata hivyo, isipokuwa *adv ~ yesterday* jana tu *he all ~ fell* karibu alianguka *vi,n* ~ **me/ no ~s** usibishane na mimi *n there are no ~s about it* hakuna shaka.
butane *n* butani (gesi ya kuwashia).
butch *adj (colloq)* 1 *(of woman)* -enye tabia ya kiume *(of a man)* -enye kujifanya mbabe *n* jike dume.
butcher *n* 1 bucha. **~'s shop** bucha, duka la nyama. 2 *(murderer)* mwuaji, mkatili *vt* 1 chinja (mnyama kwa chakula). 2 ua kwa ukatili. **~y** n 1 uchinjaji nyama (kwa ajili ya kuuza). 2 mauaji ya binadamu kikatili. 3 madhabahu/machinjioni.
butler *n* mhudumu mkuu atunzaye vileo na maandalio ya meza n.k.); mtumishi mkuu (wa kiume) katika nyumba binafsi.
butt[1] *n* pipa kubwa.
butt[2] *n* 1 tako, kitako (k.m. cha bunduki). 2 *(of cigar or cigarette)* kichungi; kipande cha mwisho cha mshumaa/sigara iliyowashwa.
butt[3] *n* 1 *(usu pl. with def art)* renji, lengo, kusudio, shabaha. 2 mtu anayedhihakiwa au kutaniwa sana.
butt[4] *vt,vi* 1 sukuma kwa kichwa, kumba *(of horned animals)* piga pembe. 2 ~ in *(colloq)* jiingiza, ingilia, jidukiza. ~ **into** gonga kwa kichwa, gonga kwa mbele.
butter *n* siagi *look as if ~ would not melt in one's mouth* anaonekana kuwa ni mnyamavu na asiye na hatia *vi* paka siagi. *(fig)* **know which side one's bread is** ~ jua pweza alipo *bread ~ed on both sides* usitawi, utajiri. **~sb up** paka mtu mafuta kwa mgongo wa chupa. **~y** *adj ~-bean n* haragwe njano. **~cup** kombe-mtindi *~-dish (also ~-boat) n* kidishi cha siagi. **~-fingers** *n* mtu asiyeweza kushika/kudaka kitu vizuri. **~milk** *n* 1 mtindi. 2 maziwa majimaji. ~ **scotch** *n* namna ya peremende (tofi). **cocoa** ~ *n* siagi ya kakau. **~y** *n (GB)* ghala za vyakula katika vyuo.
butterfly *n* kipepeo. **have butterflies in the stomach** ogopa sana. **~-nut** *n* kikazio, nati masikio.
buttock *n* tako.
button *n* 1 kifungo. ~ **hole** tundu la kifungo. 2 swichi, kitufe *you've only to press the ~* unahitaji kubonyeza kitufe tu. 3 uyoga mdogo ambao haujafunuka. 4 *(colloq) (pl)* mtumishi wa hotelini *vt* 1 ~ **up** funga kwa vifungo. 2 kamilisha salama.

3 *(sl)* funga mdomo. **on the ~** safi kabisa *vi* fungika (kwa vifungo) *vt* sumbua, pekecha tundu la kishikizo. **~-loop** *n* kitanzi cha kishikizo. **~ up** *(colloq)* salama kabisa. **~ed up** *adj (of person)* -kimya.

buttress *n* gadi; kiegemezo *vt* egemeza, gadimu, shikiza.

buxom *adj (of women)* -zuri tena tipwatipwa.

buy *vt* nunua. **~ back** nunua tena (kitu ulichouza). **~ in** nunua kwa matumizi ya baadaye; nunua mwenyewe kitu ulichonadi **~** *off the judge* honga hakimu, zabuni na nunua kitu chako kwa bei ya juu zaidi kwa kulipa fedha **~** *it off* ondoa/maliza (madai yasohaki) kwa kulipa. **~ out** 1 tawala kwa kununua (kampuni). **~ sb over** honga. **~ up** nunua bidhaa yote. 2 pata kwa kujitoa mhanga/kukosa jingine *n* ununuzi. **~er** *n* mnunuzi, mshtiri. **~ers' market** soko la mnunuzi/mteja.

buzz *vi,vt* 1 vuma (kama nyuki). 2 enda, tembea kwa haraka na kwa msisimko. **~ off** *(sl)* ondoka, ambaa. 3 *(of the ears)* jawa na mvumo. 4 *(of an aircraft)* ruka karibu na ndege nyingine kwa namna ya kuitishia *n* 1 mvumo (k.m wa wadudu, mazungumzo ya watu, au mashine). **give sb a ~** *(sl)* pigia simu mtu. **~er** *n* mtambo uanzishao mvumo (umeme unapopita).

buzzard *n* aina ya mwewe.

by[1] *adv part* 1 karibu *there was nobody ~ when he hid the money* hapakuwepo na mtu yeyote karibu alipoficha pesa. 2 kupita *I can't get ~* siwezi kupita. 3 *lay/put/set sth ~* weka kitu kwa matumizi ya baadaye. 4 (*in phrases*) **~ and ~** baadaye. **~ the ~(e), ~ the way** licha ya hayo. **~ and large** kwa jumla.

by[2] *prep* 1 karibu na, kando ya, pembeni mwa *sit ~ me/ ~ my side* kaa karibu yangu, kando yangu. **(all) ~ oneself** peke yako, mwenyewe tu. **have sth ~ one** -wa na kitu karibu/tayari, weza kukipata kwa urahisi (ukikitaka). **stand ~ sb** unga mkono, -wa na. 2 *(in reading the cardinal points)* kuelekea upande wa..... 3 *(showing direction of movement)* kupita, kupitia *we came ~ the forest* tumepitia (njia ya) porini. 4 kupitia *I go ~ the post office every morning on my way to work* ninapitia posta kila asubuhi niendapo kazini kwangu. 5 *(of time, esp. to indicate conditions and circumstances)* wakati wa *do you prefer travelling ~ night or ~ day*? unapendelea kusafiri (wakati wa) usiku au (wakati wa) mchana? 6 *(of time)* sio zaidi ya, ufikapo muda fulani *I'll finish writing ~ 2.00 p.m.* nitamaliza kuandika ifikapo saa nane mchana. 7 (*to form adverbial phrases of time, length, weight, number)* kwa *hire a car ~ the day* azima gari (dogo) kwa siku mojamoja *sell eggs ~ the dozen* uza mayai kwa dazani. 8 *(as agency)* kwa kupitia, kwa kusababishwa na *he makes a living ~ teaching* anaishi kwa kufundisha *he was killed ~ lightning* aliuawa na radi. 9 *(phrasal words) (indicating path or means of travel transport, conveyance) travel, ~ bus/ship* safiri kwa basi/meli *send sth ~ post/hand* peleka kitu kwa posta/mkono. 10 *(indicating a part of body that is touched etc) take sb ~ the hand* shika mkono wake. 11 **know/learn ~ heart** kariri. **know sb ~ name/ reputation/sight** jua mtu kwa jina/ kumsikia (bila kufahamiana naye kabisa). 12 *(in adverbial phrases of manner) ~ accident/ mistake* kwa bahati mbaya, kwa makosa. **~ chance/good fortune** kwa bahati tu. **~ oneself** bila msaada, bila kusaidiwa. 13 kwa kufuatana /kulingana na *~ the Agreement* kwa kufuatana na Mkataba *~ my watch it is 2 o'clock* kwa kufuatana/kulingana na saa yangu sasa ni saa nane. 14 kwa kiwango cha *it needs to be increased ~ two feet* inatakiwa iongezwe kwa futi mbili. 15 *(to expresssquare or cubic measurement) a carpet 30 metres ~ 20 metres* zulia mita 30 kwa 20 *(arith)(to express division, = divided by)* gawanya kwa 15 divided ~ 3 *equals 5* 15 gawanya kwa 3 sawa na 5.

bye *n* 1 kitu kisicho muhimu (cha chini kihadhi). **by the** ~ juu ya, zaidi ya. 2 *(of game)* kuingia duru nyingine bila mpinzani, bila mshiriki. 3 *(also **bye bye**)* pita kwa heri. ~**s go to** ~ enda kulala.

by-election *n* uchaguzi mdogo.

bygone *adj* -a zamani, -liopita *n (pl) let ~ be ~* tuyasahau, yaliyopita yamepita, ya kale hayapo.

by-law *n* 1 sheria ndogo (za mji, kijiji, chama). 2 *(pl)* ~**s** taratibu, kanuni maagizo.

by-line *n* jina la mwandishi mwanzo wa makala (katika magazeti).

by-pass *n* barabara ya kando (inayozunguka mji/kijiji) *vt* kwepa (kwa kupita pembeni).

bypath *n* njia ndogo.

by play *n* maonyesho bubu.

by-product *n* pato la ziada.

byre *n* zizi la ng'ombe.

by-road *n.* barabara ndogo

bystander *n* mtazamaji.

by-way *n* 1 barabara ndogo. 2 *(usu.pl)* sehemu zisizofahamika vizuri.

byword *n* 1 mithali. 2 mtu, kitu au mahali maarufu panapovuma kwa ubaya *his action became a ~ in the town* kitendo chake kilivuma mji mzima *a ~ of iniquity* tendo la kudharauliwa.

C

C,c *n* herufi ya tatu katika alfabeti ya Kiingereza. 2 (*mus*) noti ya kwanza ya skeli ya kawaida. 3 mia (katika namba za Kirumi).

cab *n* 1 teksi, gari la kukodisha. **taxi~** teksi. **~-man** dereva wa teksi. **~-rank** *(also* ~ **-stand)** kituo cha teksi. 2 chumba cha mwendeshaji (katika gari-moshi au katika lori kubwa).

cabal *n* njama, siri (kikundi kidogo cha siri, cha kula njama). **~istic** *adj*. **~ler** *n* mla njama; wasiri.

cabaret *n (also cabaret show)* tumbuizo (la nyimbo au dansi) mkahawani wakati wa chakula.

cabbage *n* kabichi. *(bio)* ~ butterfly kipepeo mweupe. *(bot)* ~ **rose** waridi,taji.

cabin *n* 1 kibanda, kijumba cha makuti na magogo. 2 dambra; chumba katika ndege. 3 **~boy** mhudumu melini. 4 **~class** daraja la II (melini). **~-cruiser** *n* motaboti kubwa yenye dambra.

cabinet *n* 1 chumba kidogo, almari au sefu ya kuwekea ama kuonyeshea vitu, kabati. **medicine** ~ kabati la kuwekea madawa. **filing** ~ kabati yenye saraka za kuhifadhia mafaili. 2 baraza la mawaziri. **C ~ Minister** Waziri katika Baraza la Mawaziri. ~ **maker** fundi samani.

cable *n* 1 kebo; kamba nene (ya katani au ya waya). 2 *(naut)* amari, utari, waya wa kushikia daraja /kuvutia vigari. **~car** kigari cha kamba (milimani). 3 waya nene la kupelekea habari/umeme kupita chini ya bahari. 4 habari ichukuliwayo kwa sauti. **~gram** *n* kebo, simu. *vt* 1 peleka habari kwa simu (kupita baharini n.k.).

caboodle *n (sl)* kundi,jamii yote. **the whole** ~ watu wote,vitu vyote; kila kitu.

caboose *n* 1 jiko kwenye staha ya meli. 2 *(US)* behewa la gadi (katika gari moshi la mizigo).

cabotage *n* 1 biashara ya pwani. 2 haki ya kushiriki katika biashara hiyo.

ca'canny *n* 1 mgomo baridi. 2 uangalifu.

cacao *n* kakao. **~-tree** *n* mkakao.

cache *n* maficho ya vitu (k.m. dafina, silaha n.k.) *vt* ficha (fedha, vyakula n.k.), hifadhi mafichoni.

cachet *n* alama teule (ya ubora/ uhalisi).

cachou *n* kachu au lozenji, kipoteza harufu (peremende kwa ajili ya kupoteza harufu ya mdomoni).

cackle *n* 1 mteteo wa kuku. 2 kicheko cha sauti kubwa. 3 mpayuko. *(sl)* **cut the** ~ funga mdomo *vt (of hen)* 1 tetea. 2 payuka. **~r** *n* mpayukaji.

cacography *n* mwandiko au tahajia mbaya.

cacology *n* 1 uchaguzi mbaya wa maneno. 2 ukosefu wa matamshi.

cacophony *n* makelele, sauti kali zisizokubaliana, ukosefu wa ulinganifu katika sauti. **cacophonous** *adj*.

cactus *n (pl)* dungusi kakati, (jamii ya mimea kama mpungate n.k.).

cad *n* mhuni. **~dish** *adj*.

cadaver *n (med)* maiti. **~ous** *adj* kama maiti; dhaifu, ng'onda, -a kukonda sana.

caddy[1] kadi: kikopo cha kuwekea majani ya chai.

caddy[2], **caddie** *n (in golf)* mbeba vingoe. ~ **car**/ ~ **cart** kigari cha kubeba vingoe *vt* bebea vingoe.

cade *adj (of young animals)* -liyelelewa na binadamu (baada ya kumpoteza mamake).

cadence *n* 1 *(of music)* kiimbo mpandoshuko.

cadet *n* kadeti: mwanafunzi katika shule ya maofisa wa jeshi.

cadge *vt,vi* ~ **from** ombaomba vitu (hasa kwa rafiki, ndugu), doea, dusa, pandia. **~r** *n* mdoezi.

cadi *n* kadhi.

cadre *n* 1 kada. 2 maofisa wa jeshi.

caduceus *n* nembo ya uganga.

caecum *n (anatomy)* sikamu: tawi butu la utumbo kati ya utumbo mpana na utumbo mwembamba.

Caesar *n* Kaizari. **~ean operation /**

section kuzaa kwa kupasuliwa/ kisu.
caesura *n* kituo katika ushairi hasa katikati ya mstari.
cafe *n* 1 mkahawa. 2 kahawa. ~ **au lait** kahawa ya maziwa.
cafeteria *n* kafeteria; hoteli, mkahawa (ambamo wateja wanajihudumia wenyewe).
caffeine *n (chem)* kafeini.
caftan *n* kaftani; *(for males)* aina ya kanzu yenye masombo kiunoni, *(for females)* aina ya kanzu isiyokaza mwilini.
cage *n* 1 kizimba, tundu. ~**d bird** ndege afungiwaye tunduni. 2 *(fig)* gereza *vt* fungia tunduni.
cagey *adj (colloq)* -enye hadhari/siri. **cagily** *adv* kwa hadhari.
cagoule *n* koti la mvua (lenye kofia na mikono mirefu).
cahoots *n (sl)* **be in ~ with** -la njama, shirikiana na/panga na (hasa katika maovu).
caiman, cayman *n (bio)* kaimani: mamba wa Amerika kusini.
cain *n (rel)* kabili, kaini. **raise** ~ *(sl)* fanya fujo.
cairn *n* haram, rundo, chungu (ya mawe kama alama au kumbukumbu).
caisson *n* 1 *(mil)* kasha la kigari cha makombora. 2 keisoni: kitundu cha kuzuia maji yasiingie ambacho wajenzi wa majini hutumia ~ **disease** maumivu ya viungo yasababishwayo na kufanya kazi ndani ya hewa iliyobanwa/nzito.
caitiff *n (poet) (arch)* 1 mtu mbaya, mtu mnyonge. 2 mwoga *adj* -baya, -a woga.
cajole *vt* 1 ~ **sb into doing sth** bembeleza, vuta kwa werevu, danganya kwa kusifusifu, rairai fulani apate kufanya ulitakalo. 2 ~ **sth out of sb** pata taarifa kwa hila, ujanja au werevu. ~**ry** *n.*
cake *n* 1 keki. *(selling)* **like hot ~s** (nunulika) sana na kwa haraka. **take the** ~ -wa wa kwanza, anza. **you can't have your ~ and eat it** amua moja. **piece of** ~ rahisi, nyepesi. 2 mseto, mchanganyiko wa mapishi (vyakula). **fish ~s** keki/mseto wa samaki. 3 kipande, donge, bumbaa. ~ **of soap** kipande cha sabuni *vi* ganda, gandamana.
calabash *n* 1 kibuyu; mboko. ~ **pipe** buruma.
calaboose *n (US sl)* gereza, korokoro, mahabusi.
calamary *n (bio)* kalamari: ngisi mkubwa.
calamine *n* kalamini: aina ya mawe yenye zinki. ~ **lotion** kimiminiko cha kalamina.
calamint *n* mkalaminti: aina ya mnanaa.
calamity *n* 1 janga, balaa, msiba mkubwa; maafa. **calamitous** *adj.*
calcareous *adj* -enye chokaa, -enye kufanana na chokaa.
calcify *vt,vi* fanya (kuwa) chokaa; geuza/geuka kuwa chokaa.
calcine *vt,vi* 1 choma chokaa. 2 choma kwa moto mkali.
calcination *n* 1 uunguzaji: uchomaji kwa nguvu kitu chochote. 2 mgeuko chokaa.
calcium *n* kalisi: metali laini nyeupe (hutokea kwenye mifupa, meno, na sehemu ya chokaa, marumaru n.k.).
calculate *vt,vi* 1 kokotoa. 2 dhani, ona, fikiri; pima. 3 *(intend, plan)* kusudia, kisia, azimia. ~ **up (on)** *(US)* tumainia. 4 pangwa. **calculating** *adj.* **calculation** *n.* **calculator** *n* kikokotoo.
calculus *n* 1 kijiwe. 2 *(maths)* kalkulasi.
calendar *n* 1 kalenda. 2 orodha ya kesi mahakamani, miswada bungeni n.k. inayofuata kalenda *vt* orodhesha.
calender *n* 1 mashine ya kunyoosha nguo. 2 *(textile)* kukuto *vt* nyoosha, fingirisha.
calf *n* 1 ndama, mtoto wa mnyama. **cow in (with)** ~ ng'ombe mwenye mimba. **slip her** ~ avya. **the golden** ~ kuabudu mali, kuandaa kwa shangwe. ~**-love** mapenzi ya kitoto.
calibrate *vt* kadiria au rekebisha chombo cha kupimia au geji.

calibration *n* alama za vipimo/nyuzi (kwenye chombo).

calibre, caliber *n* 1 kipenyo cha mwanzi (wa bunduki au bomba lolote). 2 ubora wa tabia au akili. 3 *(capacity)* ukubwa; uhodari.

calico *n* kaliko: kitambaa kigumu cha pamba kama marekani au gamti.

caliph, calif *n* khalifa. **~ate** *n* milki ya khalifa.

calk[1] *n* 1 *(of horse)* njumu. 2 msumari wa kisigino cha kiatu *vt* tia njumu.

calk[2] *see caulk.*

call *n* 1 mwito. **within ~** karibu (karibu). 2 *(cry/shout)* yowe, mlio, ukelele (kilio cha mnyama au ndege). 3 matembezi, maamkio, ziara fupi. **port of ~** bandari ya kupitia tu. 4 *(vocation)* wito. 5 *(demand)* jambo la kupasa (la kubidi), dai. **~ loan/money, money on ~** mkopo unaoweza kudaiwa mara moja bila taarifa ya awali. 6 ujumbe. **~-bell** *n* kengele ya hatari; kengele ya kuita. **~ box** *n* kibanda cha simu. **~ boy** *n* tarishi (kijana). **~ girl** *n* malaya (atongozwaye kwa simu). **~-house** *n* danguro. 7 haja. *there is no ~ to blush* hakuna haja ya kuona haya. 8 *(radio)* **~ sign** alama ya kuitia. **~-over/roll-~** kuita majina (shuleni,jeshini n.k.). **~ing** *n* wito, weledi. **~er** 1 mgeni. 2 mpiga simu *vt* 1 ita kwa sauti; piga mayowe. 2 zuru, pitia, tembelea, amkia. *I ~ed on him* nilimtembelea *this train ~s at Mpanda Station* treni hii inapitia Mpanda. 3 ita, taja kwa jina la *we ~ him boss* tunamwita bosi *it is ~ed* inaitwa. **~ sb names** tusi, tukana. **~ sth one's own** dai (kitu) kuwa mali ya. **~ into being** buni, unda, umba, jaalia. **~ it a day** funga kazi, pumzika. **~ into play** ingiza, shirikisha, ita. 5 fikiria, chukulia. **~ it a deal** jichukulie kuwa umebarikiwa. 6 *(compounds)* **~ a halt (to)** simamisha. **~ a strike** itisha mgomo. 7 *(of cards)* otea; ita. 8 *(phrases)* **~ sb to account** ita mtu ajieleze. **~ attention to** vuta nadhari ya **~ into question** shuku, tilia (ma)shaka **~ a meeting to order** anzisha mkutano. 9 *(with adverbial particles and preps)* **~ by** (colloq) pitia. **~ sb down** karipia. **~ sth down** ita, ombea. **~ for** dai, hitaji. **~ for prayer** adhini. **~ sth forth** sababisha; tumia, changia. **~ sth in** taka kitu kirudishwe. **~ sth off** shikisha adabu; simamisha. **~ sb out** ita (haraka); toa amri ya kuanzisha mgomo. **~ over** ita/soma (majina). **~ sth/sb up** pigia simu; kumbuka jambo, ita/andikisha jeshini. **~ up** mwito, kuitwa jeshini. **~ on/upon** agiza, shurutisha; sihi, omba msaada. **~ up** kumbusha; ita juu. **~ off** vunja, simamisha, ondoa; ita kwingine *please ~ off your dog* zuia mbwa wako.

calligraphy *n* kaligrafia: sanaa ya kuandika vizuri.

callipers *n* 1 kalipa: namna ya bikari ya kupimia. 2 vyuma vya miguu vya kumsaidia kilema.

callisthenics *n* mazoezimwili (ya kutia viungo nguvu na uzuri).

callosity callus *n (med)* sugu, sagamba.

callous *adj* 1 -gumu, sugu. 2 *(of person)* -sio hisia, baridi, -siojali.

callow *adj* -siyo na manyoya; -siyo na ndevu; -changa *a ~ youth* kijana asiyepevuka. **~ness** *n.*

calm *adj* 1 *(of weather)* shwari, -tulivu. 2 pole, kimya, makini, -nyamavu. **~ water** maji matulivu. **pretty ~ about it** baridi, hata mshipa haumgongi *n* 1 utulivu, amani, raha. 2 shwari *a dead ~* utulivu mkubwa. *vi* tulia, nyamaza. **~ down** tulia *vt* tuliza, nyamazisha, fariji. **~y** *adv.* **~ness.** *n* **~ative** *adj (med)* -a kutuliza, -a kupoza *n* kipozamaumivu.

calomel *n* kalomeli: dawa ya kuharisha, aina ya haluli.

calorie/calory *(also calory) n* 1 kalori: kizio cha joto. 2 kizio/kipimo cha joto litolewalo na chakula. **calorific** *adj.*

calumniate *vt* zushia, zulia:

calumny *n (formal)* uzushi, usingiziaji (wenye lengo la kuharibu jina).
Calvary *n (rel)* 1 Kalivari: kilima nje ya Jerusalem aliposulubiwa Yesu. 2 uwakilishi wa kusulubiwa kwa Yesu. 3 mateso makubwa.
calve *vi* 1 *(of cow etc)* zaa. 2 *(of a piece of ice)* meguka.
Calvinism *n (rel)* mafundisho ya Calvi: kwamba kila kitu kilikwisha amuliwa na Mungu, amri ya Mungu. **Calvinist** *n.*
calypso n kalipso: nyimbo ya ki-West Indies.
calyx *n* kalisi: sehemu ya nje kabisa ya ua iliyojengwa na sepali.
cam *n (mech)* kemu: kibadili mwendo.
camaraderie *n* urafiki; udugu.
camarilla *n* kikundi cha njama.
camber *n* mbinukotuta, mbinuko *vt* binua, tia.
cambiat *n* mlanguzi wa fedha.
cambium *n (bio)* kambi: seli kuzi.
cambric *n* kambriki: kitambaa chororo cha lineni au pamba.
came *n* risasi ya fremu ya dirisha.
camel *n* 1 ngamia. **~ ('s) -hair** manyoya laini aghalabu ya ngamia. 2 chelezo. 3 rangi ya madafu. 4 **~ -back** kiraka, mpira hafifu wa kutengenezea tairi. **~eer** *n* mtunza ngamia.
cameo *n* 1 kito, sanamu. 2 taswira ya kitu, mtu au mahali.
camera *n* 1 kamera. **on ~** inapigwa picha. 2 *(leg)* chumba cha mkuu wa mahakama. **in ~** katika chumba cha hakimu; faraghani, si mbele ya watu; *(see in chambers)* kwa siri. **~ -man** *n* mpiga picha.
camisole *n* shimizi.
camlet *n* 1 *(arch)* kitambaa chepesi cha hariri na manyoya ya ngamia. 2 nguo ya kitambaa hicho.
camouflage *n* kamafleji, majificho *vt* ficha kwa njia ya kudanganya.
camp[1] *n* 1 kambi; kituo; kigono. 2 *(fig)* kundi la watu wenye msimamo/imani/ itikadi moja. **~-meeting** *n (US)* mkutano wa kidini unaofanyika nje. **eye -~** kambi ya matibabu ya macho. **~ -stool** *n* kiti cha kukunja; kiti cha safari. **~-follower** *n* raia anayefuatana na jeshi wakati wa vita (hasa malaya). 2 barakala *vi ~ (out)* fanya kambi, tua safarini, piga hema *vt (mil)* weka kambini. **~ing- ground** *n* uwanja wa kupigia kambi.
camp[2] *n* 1 basha; msenge. 2 tabia/sura ya mwanamke.
campaign *n* 1 kampeni. 2 mapambano ya kijeshi *vi* 1 fanya kampeni. 2 gombea uchaguzi. **~er** *n* mfany(i)a kampeni.
campanile *n* mnara wa kengele.
campanulate *adj* -a mfano wa kengele;-enye umbo la kengele.
camphor *n* kafuri, kafuri maiti.
campus *n* kampasi: eneo la shule kubwa au chuo.
camshaft *n (mech)* mtaimbokemu, kemshafti.
can[1] *n* 1 kopo, debe, mkebe. *a ~ of sardines* kopo la dagaa. *milk ~* chombo cha maziwa. 2 *(US)* pipa la taka. 3 *(US sl)* gereza; choo; filamu iliyowekwa tayari kwa kutumia *carry the ~* wajibika *vt* 1 tia koponi *~ned fruit/vegetables* matunda/ mboga za kopo. 3 *(US sl)* fukuza, toa kazini. 4 *(US sl)* acha *~ that noise* acha kupiga kelele. **~nery** *n* kiwanda cha kutia vyakula makoponi. **~-opener** kiboko, kifungua kopo.
can[2] 1 weza, fahamu *he ~ read* anaweza kusoma *I ~ not understand* sifahamu, sielewi. 2 wezekana *it ~ not be true* haiwezi kuwa kweli *the food ~ be eaten* chakula kinalika *as often as I (possibly) ~* kila niwezapo. 3 *(colloq)* ruhusiwa *~ I leave now?* naruhusiwa kuondoka?
canal *n* 1 mfereji. **Suez ~** mfereji wa Suez. 2 *(bio)* mfereji wa chakula. **~ize** *vt* chimba mfereji; *(fig)* elekeza.
canap'e *n* kitafunio.
canard *n* taarifa ya uwongo.
canary *n* kurumbiza.
canasta *n* kanasta (mchezo wa karata).
canaster *n* 1 *see* **canister** 2 *(arch)* tumbaku ya mnoga.

cancel *vt,vi* 1 futa. 2 batilisha. 3 ~ **out** sawazisa. ~**lation** *n.*
cancer[1] *n* 1 *(astro)* kaa. 2 *(geog)* **Tropic of** ~ Tropiki ya Kansa.
cancer[2] *n (med)* 1 kansa. **lung** ~ kansa ya mapafu. 2 *(fig)* uovu 3 *(sl)* ~ **stick** sigara. ~**ated, cancerous** *adj* -a kansa. **cancroid** *adj* 1 *(med)* -a kufanana na kansa. 2 *(bio)* - a kufana na kaa *n* kansa ya ngozi.
candelabrum *n* kinara cha mishumaa mingi. ~ **tree** mti wenye umbo la kinara cha mishumaa.
candescent *adj* -nayong'aa.
candid *adj* 1 wazi. 2 *(of photo)* bila kupanga. ~ **camera** *n* kamera ya picha zisizopangwa. ~**ly** *adv.* ~**ness** *n.*
candidate *n* 1 *(of election)* mgombea uchaguzi; mteuliwa; mtaradhia. 2 *(of examination)* mtahiniwa. candidacy, **candidature** *n* ugombea uchaguzi.
candle *n* mshumaa *the game is not worth the* ~ jambo halina maana/ faida *burn the* ~ *at both ends* jichosha kwa kazi *he cannot hold a* ~ *to you* si kufu yako. ~ **stick** kinara cha mshumaa.
candlemas *n (rel)* mweuo.
candour *n* 1 unyofu, uwazi: tabia ya kunena bila kupendelea; tabia ya kunena ukweli.
candy *n* 1 pipi, peremende, lawalawa *vt* hifadhi kwa kuchemsha na kupika na sukari.
cane *n* henzerani; ufito wa mwanzi. ~-**brake** kichaka cha mwanzi. ~ **chair** kiti cha henzerani. ~ **furniture** samani/fanicha ya henzerani; ~-**sugar** muwa *vt* 1 piga na fimbo ya henzerani. 2 suka kiti cha henzerani.~ -**sugar** *n* sukari muwa.
canine *adj* -a mbwa, kama mbwa *n* 1 ~ **tooth** chonge. 2 mbwa. 3 mnyama wa jamii ya mbwa (k.v. fisi bweha n.k.).
canister *n* 1 kopo (la kuwekea majani ya chai, unga n.k.) 2. kombora (k.m. ya gesi ya machozi).
canker *n* 1 *(med)* ugonjwa wa vidonda, (kinywani, masikioni), kidonda cha kinywani. 2 *(of plants)* kikwachu. 3 *(fig)* uovu *vt* ozesha, haribu. ~**ous** *adj.*
cannabis *n* bangi.
cannibal *n* mtu mla watu; mnyama alaye wenziwe. ~**ism** *n* ~**istic** *adj.* ~**ize** *vt* toa vipuli (kutoka kwa mashine iliyoharibika au kuukuu) ili kutengeneza nyingine.
cannon *n* 1 mzinga. ~-**ball** *n* tufe la mzinga. ~-**bone** *n (of horse)* mfupa baina ya goti na kwato. ~-**fodder** askari wanaofikiriwa si muhimu hivyo waweza kuteketezwa bila wakuu wao kujali. 2 mgongano katika mchezo wa biliadi (mpigo mmoja unaogusa mipira miwili) *vt* gonga kwa nguvu. ~**ade** *n* mpigo wa mizinga mingi; mfululizo wa risasi.
canny *adj* -erevu, -janja, -enye hadhari, -angalifu. **cannily** *adv.*
canoe *n* mtumbwi, kiperea, nchoro. **outrigger** ~ ngalawa *vi* endesha kiperea. ~**ist** mpiga makasia.
canon *n* 1 *(rel)* sheria/kanuni ya kanisa. ~ **law** kanuni/sha za kanisa. 2 kigezo. 3 vitabu vinavyotambulika (hasa vitabu ya Biblia ambavyo vinatambuliwa na kanisa). 4 orodha rasmi. 5 padri wa kanisa kuu. 6 sehemu kuu ya misa. ~**ical** *adj* -a kuhusu sheria za kanisa. ~**ical hours** saa za sala. ~**icals** mavazi rasmi ya ibada *(gram)* kuhusu msingi wa neno. ~**ize** *vt* 1 takatifuza: dumisha /tangaza kuwa mtakatifu. 2 idhinisha moja kwa moja. ~**ization** *n.*
canopy *n* 1 kanopi: kitambaa/kipaa kinachoning'inizwa juu ya kiti, kitanda n.k. 2 *(aircraft)* mfuniko wa chumba cha rubani 3. *(fig)* mwavuli; kivuli chochote kinachoning'inia *the* ~ *of the sky* anga, mbingu.
cant[1] *n* 1 mwinamo. 2 msukumo wa ghafula unaosababisha kuinama. *vt,vi (over)* laza upande; pindua; pinduka.
cant[2] *n* 1 ulaghai, unafiki. 2 misimu (ya tabaka/kikundi fulani).
cantaloup(e) *n* aina ya tikiti.
cantankerous *adj* -gomvi, -enye hasira.

canteen *n* 1 kantini. 2 bweta/sanduku la vyombo vya kulia. 3 *(mil)* vyombo vya chakula/maji vya askari.
canter *n (of horse)* mwendo wa matao *win in a* ~ shinda kwa urahisi *vt,vi* enda kwa matao.
canticle *n (rel)* wimbo mfupi wa kidini hasa unaotokana na Biblia.
cantilever *n* shikizowenza. ~ **bridge** daraja shikizowenza.
canto *n* sehemu kuu ya shairi refu.
canton *n* jimbo, mkoa (hasa Uswisi). ~**al** *adj*.
cantonment *n* kambi, makao ya wanajeshi.
cantor *n (rel)* kiongozi wa waimbaji katika kanisa au sinagogi.
canvas *n* 1 turubai. 2 *(sacking)* gunia. 3 *(of painting)* turubai ya kuchorea *under* ~ kambini, hemani *win by a* ~ shinda kwa nafasi ndogo.
canvass *vt,vi* 1 *(for)* pita na kuomba (kura, michango n.k.); jadili kwa undani. ~**er** *n*.
canyon *n* korongo kuu (lenye mto), genge kuu.
cap *n* 1 chepeo (aina ya kofia) *put on one's thinking* ~ fikiria jambo kwa makini. ~ **and gown** *(for University)* bushuti na kofia ya mahafali. ~ **in hand** kwa unyenyekevu *if the* ~ *fits* ukiona kwamba yanakuhusu. ~ **a pie** *adv (arch)* tangu kichwani hadi miguuni, kabisa *set one's* ~ *at sb (of girl)* jaribu, vutia mwanamume *a feather in one's* ~ kitu cha kujivunia. 2 fataki. 3 *(of bottle)* kifuniko. ~ **block** faruma. 4 *(biol)* kikungu cha uyoga. 5 **Dutch** ~ *(see diaphragm) vt* 1 vika chepeo. 2 funika. 3 shinda, pita, -wa bora kuliko. ~ **a joke** toa utani unaochekesha zaidi. **to** ~ **it all** mwisho wa hayo. 4 tunuku.
capability *n* 1 uwezo, uwezekano. **nuclear** ~ uwezo wa kupigana vita vya nuklea. 2 *(pl)* vipaji (vinavyoweza kuendelezwa) *that boy has great capabilities* mtoto yule ana vipaji vingi *adj* 1 hodari, -stadi, -enye akili. 2 *(of persons)* -enye uwezo. *3 (of things/situations)* -enye uwezekano. **capably** *adv*.
capacity *n* 1 nafasi, ujazo, ukubwa *filled to* ~ *(of a room etc.)* -liojaa kabisa, liojaa pomoni, tele *seating* ~ idadi ya viti. 2 *(of person)* uwezo (wa kukumbuka au kujifunza) *show one's* ~ onyesha uwezo wako. 3 wadhifa, cheo *in my* ~ *as Director* nikiwa ni Mkurugenzi.
capacious *adj* -enye nafasi kubwa ndani. ~**ness** *n*.
caparison *n (of horse)* matandiko yaliyopambwa *vt* tandika (farasi) matandiko yaliyopambwa.
cape[1] *n* juba.
cape[2] *n* rasi: **The** ~ **(of Good Hope)** Rasi ya Tumaini Jema.
caper *vi* rukaruka kwa furaha, chachawa *n* 1 kurukaruka kwa furaha, kuchachawa. 2 utundu. **cut a** ~/~**s** rukaruka kwa furaha; tenda kama mwenda wazimu.
capita see **per capita**.
capillary *adj* -a kapilari ~ *attraction* mvuto wa kapilari ~ *repulsion* msukumo wa kapilari *n (anat)* kapilari: mshipa mdogo wa damu. **capillarity** *n* ukapilari: uwezo wa kushuka au kupanda kwa kioevu katika neli kutokana na kani za mshikamano na mng'ang'anio kusukuma kwa nguvu za unywele.
capital[1] *n (arch)* kombe ya nguzo.
capital[2] *n* 1 makao makuu. 2 *(of letters of the alphabet)* herufi kubwa (eg. A,B,C.). 3 mtaji; raslimali; fedha. **floating** ~ mtaji geu. **fixed** ~ mtaji wa kudumu. **make** ~ **of** tumia kwa faida *adj* 1 *(arch colloq)* -zuri sana. **a** ~ **speech** hotuba nzuri sana. 2 -kuu. ~ **city** Makao Makuu, jiji kuu, mji mkuu. 3 -a kifo. ~ **punishment** adhabu ya kifo. ~ **offence** kosa linaloadhibiwa kwa kifo. 4 -a mtaji. ~ **levy** kodi ya mtaji. ~ **goods** bidhaa zinazotumika kuzalisha mali. ~ **expenditure** matumizi ya mitambo/ajengo. ~ **gain** faida tokana na mauzo ya raslimali.

capitalism *n* ubepari. **capitalist** *n* **capitalize** bepari *adj* -a kibepari.
capitalize *vt,vi* 1 andika kwa herufi kubwa. 2 geuza kuwa mtaji. 3 *(fig)* ~ **(on)** tumia kwa faida yako. **capitalization** *n.*
capitation *n* kodi ya kichwa. ~ **grant** ruzuku maalum kwa kila mtu mzima.
capitulate *vi* salimu amri kwa masharti, jisalimishe (kwa masharti). **capitulation** *n.*
capon *n.* jogoo (aliyehasiwa).
cappuccino *n* kapuchino: kahawa ya maziwa yenye povu.
caprice *n* 1 (mwelekeo wa) kubadilisha wazo/msimamo/ tabia ghafla. 2 kipande cha muziki mwanana.
capricious *adj* -geugeu.
caps *abbr of capital letters. see capital*[2].
capsize *vt,vi (esp of a boat in water)* pinduka, pindua.
capstan *n (naut)* roda/kapi kubwa; kitu kama gogo la kuzungusha kamba ya nanga n.k. na kuivuta.
capsule *n* 1 *(bot)* fumbuza. 2 *(med)* kapsuli, kidonge. 3 kapsuli: sehemu ya roketi yenye ala ambayo inaweza kutenganishwa. **capsular** *adj.*
captain *n* 1 *(mil)* kapteni. 2 *(of games)* kapteni, nahodha. 3 *(of ship)* nahodha. 4 (aviation) rubani *vt* ongoza. ~**cy** *n.*
caption *n* 1 maelezo mafupi (ya habari katika kitabu, gazeti au chini ya picha). 2 kichwa cha makala.
captious *adj* 1 *(formal)* -epesi kulaumu/ kukosoa. ~**ness** *n.*
captivate *vt* 1 pendeza mno, vuta kwa uzuri. **captivation** *n* mvuto.
captive *n* mfungwa; mateka *adj* fungwa, -a kutekwa. ~ **state** hali ya kufungwa. ~ **audience** hadhira tekwa: isiyoweza kuondoka (hivyo rahisi kushawishiwa). **take** ~ chukua mateka, teka nyara. **captivity** *n.*
capture *vt* 1 *(of people)* kamata, teka. 2 *(of land)* twaa. 3 *(of mind)* vutia, teka. 4 *(of photograph)* hifadhi *n* kukamata, kuteka kukamatwa, kutekwa.

car *n* 1 gari, motokaa. ~ **park** maegesho ya magari. ~ **port** banda la kuwekea motokaa. 2 behewa; kiberenge. **dining** ~ behewa la chakula.
carafe *n* chupa ya maji/divai (ya mezani).
caramel *n* karameli: sukari iliyounguzwa, gubiti.
carapace *n* gamba, ng'amba (la wanyama kama kobe, kaa, kasa).
carat *n* karati: kipimo cha kupimia usafi wa dhahabu, cha kupimia uzito wa vito vya thamani.
caravan *n* 1 msafara. 2 gari linalotumiwa kama nyumba *vi* ishi/ safiri kwenye msafara. ~ **serai** *n Asia*) nyumba ya wageni (yenye ua mkubwa wa kuhifadhi ngamia, farasi, magari n.k. ya misafara).
caravel *n (arch)* jahazi.
caraway *n* kisibiti.
carbine *n* karabini:bunduki fupi.
carbohydrate *n* 1 kabohaidreti. 2 *(pl)* vyakula vya wanga (k.v. viazi, muhogo, mkate n.k.).
carbolic *adj* -a kaboliki. ~ **acid** asidi kaboliki: dawa ya sumu itokayo katika makaa ya mawe, hutumika sana kusafisha vidonda na vyombo vya nyumbani au hospitalini.
carbon *n* 1 kaboni. ~ **dioxide** dioksidi ya kaboni. 2 *(electrode)* elektrodi ya kaboni. 3 ~ **paper** kaboni. ~ **copy** nakala halisi. ~ **copying** kunakili kwa kaboni. ~ **dating** njia ya kupima umri wa vitu vya kale kwa kupima kiasi cha kaboni. **carbonize** *vt* kabonisha, geuza kuwa kaboni. ~**iferous** *adj.* **carbonated** *adj* -enye dioksidi ya kaboni. ~**ation** *n.*
carboy *n* chupa kubwa ndani ya jamanda, chupa ya ubapa.
carbuncle *n* 1 kito chekundu. 2 jipu kubwa.
carburettor *n* kabureta: kifaa kinachochanganya hewa na petroli kutoa msombo ulipukao.
carcase, carcass *n* 1 mzoga. 2 *(sl)* ~ **meat** nyama mbichi. 3 gofu

la kitu (k.v.jengo, chombo n.k.). 4 *(sl)* mwili wa mtu. **save one's** ~ jiokoa maisha.

carcinogen n *(med)* kisababisha kansa.

card[1] *vt* chambua (sufi au katani) *n* chombo cha kuchambua sufi.

card[2] 1 kadi. **wedding** ~ kadi ya arusi. **post** ~ *n* postakadi. **membership** ~ kadi ya uanachama. **library** ~ kadi ya maktaba. 2 mtu wa mizaha, mcheshi. 3 **playing** ~ karata *put one's ~s on the table* julisha mambo, nia *play one's ~s well* cheza vizuri, tumia akili *on the ~s* wezekana *have a ~ up one's sleeve* -wa na mpango wa siri. **~index** faharisi *vt* weka faharisi, tia faharisi. **~sharp/~sharper** mfyatuzi, mlaghai katika mchezo wa karata.

cardamom *n* iliki.

cardboard *n* kadibodi (karatasi nene kama ubao mwembamba).

cardiac *adj* -a kuhusu moyo. ~ **arrest** *n* shtuko la moyo. **cardiogram** *n* kadiogramu. **cardiograph** *n* kadiografu. **cardiology** *n* kadiolojia: taaluma (ya) moyo. ~ **muscle** msulimoyo.

cardigan *n* sweta, fulana yenye vishikizo upande wa mbele.

cardinal[1] *n* *(rel)* kadinali: askofu mwenye cheo cha juu. **~ate/~ship** *n*.

cardinal[2] *adj* -kuu, -a maana, -a kiini cha jambo. ~ **numbers** namba kamili. ~ **points** sehemu kuu za dira (Kaskazini, Kusini, Mashariki, Magharibi). ~ **vein** vena kuu.

care[1] *n* 1 *(attention)* uangalifu, utunzaji. **take** ~ **of** angalia, tunza, shughulikia. **take** ~ angalia, tahadhari, jihadhari. 2 *(responsibility)* uangalizi, wajibu, usimamizi. ~ **of** *(of letter)* kupitia kwa *(k.k)*. **~taker** *n* mwangalizi; mlinzi; msimamizi; kabidhi. **~taker government** serikali ya muda. 3 mashaka, taabu, wasiwasi *he is free from* ~ hana taabu. **~laden** *adj* enye wasiwasi/mawazo mengi. 4 *(us pl)* mzigo, tatizo *the ~s of bringing up a large family* matatizo ya kulea familia kubwa. **~free** *adj* bila mawazo, changamfu; *(derog)* siojali; purukushani *vi* 1 ~ **(about)** jali I, don't ~, I couldn't ~less, *who ~s*! nani anajali. 2 ~ *(for)* *(like)* penda; *(look after)* tunza *would you ~ to come*? ungependa kuja; karibu. **careful** *adj* - angalifu, -a makini, -enye kujali. **carefully** *adv* kwa uangalifu, kwa hadhari, kwa makini. **~fulness** *n*. **~less** *adj* -zembe, vivu, -a ovyo ovyo. **~lessness** *n*.

careen *vt,vi* laza upande, (chombo au meli) ili itengenezwe; chini, inika; pindua. *vi* lala upande (ubavuni). **~age** *n* *(naut)* ulazaji upande wa chombo; gharama zake; mahali pa kufanyia kazi hiyo.

career *n* *(profession)* 1 kazi, amali. ~ **master/mistress** mwalimu, mshauri kuhusu maisha/kazi baada ya kumaliza masomo. ~ **girl** mwanamke anayejali sana kazi yake (k.m. kuliko kuolewa). 2 (matendo ya) maisha (ya watu). 3 mkurupuko. **in full** ~ kwa mwendo wa kasi sana *vi* kurupuka. ~ **along through** kwenda ovyo. **careerist** *n* mtu anayejali kusonga mbele katika amali.

caress *vt* papasa (kwa mahaba) *n* mpapaso (wa mahaba). **~s ing** *n*.

caret *n* kareti: alama katika mstari wa maandishi inayojulisha kuwa neno lililosahauliwa limeandikwa juu yake.

cargo shehena, kago, mizigo. **~-ship/ plane** meli/ndege ya mizigo.

caribou, cariboo *n* kuro, (wa Amerika ya Kaskazini).

caricature *n* karagosi: picha/sanamu iliyokuzwa mno kuliko kawaida yake kwa nia ya kuchekesha. 2 kuiga mtu kwa kusisitiza mambo fulani kwa nia ya kuchekesha; igiza fuatisha na kugeuza picha (tendo, jambo) hata lichekeshe. **caricaturist** *n* mchora vikaragosi.

caries *n* karisi: kuoza kwa jino/mfupa. **carious** *adj* enye (ugonjwa wa) karisi, -liooza (hasa jino). **cariosity** *n*.

carillon *n* seti ya kengele kwa ajili ya

kutoa ghani.
carmine *n adj* -ekundu.
carnage *n* mauaji ya watu wengi umwagaji damu.
carnal *adj* 1 -a mwili, -a kuhusu mwili; -a tamaa za mwili. ~ **knowledge** ngono. ~**ly** *adj*.
carnation *n* 1 aina ya ua.
carnival *n* 1 kanivali, sikukuu kubwa. 2 kipindi chenye sikukuu hizi kabla ya kwaresima.
carnivore *n (pl)* (of animals) wala nyama.
carob *n* karuba: mbegu zinazotumika badala ya kakao kutengeneza chakleti n.k.
carol *n* 1 *(rel)* wimbo wa Krismasi. 2 *(lit)* wimbo wa furaha *vi* 1 imba kwa furaha. 2 imba nyimbo za Krismasi. ~**ler** *n* mwimbaji wa nyimbo za namna hii.
carotene (also carotid) karotini.
carouse *vi* sherehekea, fanya karamu (ya ulevi) **carousal** *n*.
carp[1] *n* kambare mamba, kamongo wa maji baridi; samaki mrefu, mkubwa na hufanana na mamba.
carp[2] *vi* ~*(at)* kemea, karipia, lalamika, lalamalalama (kwa makosa madogomadogo yasiyo na msingi).
carpel *n* kapeli.
carpenter *n* seremala *vi* fanya kazi ya seremala. **carpentry** *n* useremala.
carpet *n* 1 zulia. *(colloq)* **be on the ~** karipiwa, kemewa. **sweep sth under the ~** sukumizia kando, ficha, weka pembeni (ili kuchelewesha utekelezaji/kukwepa lawama). **stair~** zulia la ngazini. ~ **sweeper** kifagia zulia *vt* tandaza, tanda ~ *with fallen leaves* tanda na majani makavu; laumu, karipia.
carpology *n* kapolojia: tawi la elimu mimea linaloshughulikia matunda na mbegu.
carpus *n (anat)* kiungo cha kiganja na mkono.
carpal *adj* (*anat*) -a kiungo cha kiganja na mkono.
carriage *n* 1 gari la farasi. **baby ~** (*US*) gari la mtoto. 2 behewa la garimoshi. 3 uchukuzi, upagazi. ~**forward** gharama za usafirishaji zinazolipiwa na mpokeaji bidhaa. ~ **free/paid** gharama zilizolipwa na mpelekaji bidhaa. 4 gurudumu bebaji. 5 sehemu ya mashine inayohamishika na inayoshikilia sehemu nyingine. 6 mkao wa mwili, mwendo wa kutembea. 7 ~ **way** *(part of road)* sehemu ya barabara inayotumiwa na magari. 8 **dual ~ way** njia mbili: barabara iliyogawanywa sehemu mbili (kwa tuta, majani n.k.). ~**able** *adj* (of roads) -a kuweza kupitika kwa magari.
carrick *n (naut)* ~ **bend** fundo linalounganisha kamba mbili.
carrion *n* mzoga, nyama iliyooza; chochote kichukizacho *adj* -liyooza; -a kuchukiza. ~ **crow** *n (bio)* kunguru mla mizoga.
carrot *n* 1 karoti; *(fig)* kishawishi, kivutio. 2 *(pl)* nywele nyekundu; mtu mwenye nywele nyekundu. 3 rangi ya karoti. ~**y** *adj*. **the stick and the ~** vitisho na hongo; tunzo au faida inayoahidiwa (na mara nyingi isiyokuwa yakini). **hold out/offer a ~ to sb** shawishi kwa kutoa tunzo au kufaidika na kitu.
carry *vt,vi* 1 beba, chukua, eleka *she carried the child on her back* alimweleka mtoto *he is ~the load on his head* ameubeba mzigo kichwani mwake. 2 peleka, pitisha *the pipes ~ water to the town* mabomba hupeleka maji mjini *copper carries electricity* shaba hupitisha umeme. 3 *(conquer)* shinda, faulu *our team carried the day* timu yetu ilishinda timu zote. ~ **everything before one** fanikiwa kila kitu, shinda kabisa. ~ **one's point** ungwa mkono. 4 himili *these pillars ~ the weight* nguzo hizi zinahimili uzito. 5 *(be pregnant) she is ~ing a child* yu mjamzito. 6 refusha, zidisha, endeleza ~ *the wall to ten feet* zidisha ukuta kufikia futi kumi.

7 (*with phrases*) ~ **weight** -wa na uzito *your reason ~ no weight* sababu zako hazina uzito. 8 simama/ tembea they ~ themselves like *soldiers* wanatembea kama askari. 9 *(of guns)* enda mbali, fikia mahali, masafa. 10 *(of disease)* eneza. 11 ~ **too far** zidi; vuka mpaka. ~ **about** tembea na, enda na (kila mahali). ~ **away** beba. **be carried away** jisahau. ~ **off** nyakua, shinda; ua. ~ **it off** fanikiwa (katika hali ngumu) *cholera carried off 10 people* kipindupindu kiliua watu 10. ~ **on** endelea (licha ya matatizo); lalama. ~ **(with)** fanya mapenzi na. ~**ings on** vitendo vya kijinga/ajabu. ~ **out** maliza, tekeleza. ~ **through** kamilisha. ~ **back** kumbusha *I was carried back to my youth* nilikumbuka ujana wangu *their courage will ~ them through* ujasiri wao utawasaidia *n* 1 *(of a gun range)* masafa. 2 uchukuzi, ubebaji. **carrier** *n* 1 mchukuzi *common carrier* uchukuzi wa aina yoyote; mpagazi; hamali; kampuni ichukuayo bidhaa. 2 **aircraft carrier** manowari ya kuchukulia ndege (agh. za vita). 3. keria: kiungo cha chuma cha kuchukulia mizigo n.k. katika baiskeli au motokaa. 4 **electric carrier** kipitisha umeme. 5 *(biol)* kichukuzi. 6 *(of disease)* mwenezaji. ~**-bag** *n* mfuko wa karatasi au plastiki. ~**-pigeon** n njiwa-kijumbe.

cart n mkokoteni, rukwama. **put the ~ before the horse** pindua jambo, fanya visivyo, fanya kinyume cha mambo. ~ **away** ondolea mbali. ~ **bad** mzigo wa kujaa rukwama vitu vingi. ~ **wright** mtengeneza rukwama. *n* mwendesha rukwama. *vt,vi* 1 beba/chukua kwa mkokoteni. 2 *(colloq) (around)* beba kwa mkono. 3 *(derog)* swaga. ~ **wheel** *n* 1 gurudumu (la mkokoteni). 2 kuvingirika kisarakasi.

carte blanche *(F)* *n* mamlaka kamili. **give a person** ~ pa mtu mamlaka afanye apendavyo.

carte du jour (F) *n* menyu (ya siku ile).

cartel *n* 1 muungano wa wakiritimba (ili kudhibiti biashara).

cartilage *n* gegedu, tishu.

cartography *n* usanifu wa ramani **cartographer** *n*.

carton *n* katoni.

cartoon *n* 1 katuni. 2 picha ya kuchekesha. ~**ist** *n* mchora katuni hasa ya kuigiza mambo yanayotendwa na watu *vi,vt* chora picha ya kuchekesha kama kiolezo. 3 filamu ya sinema ambayo wahusika wake ni picha zilizochorwa; ashiria mtu maalum katika picha ya kuchekesha.

cartouche *n* katushi: 1 kibamba cha madini chenye maandiko. 2 ganda la risasi lililotengenezwa kwa karatasi.

cartridge *n* 1 ganda, kibweta cha risasi. **ball** ~ risasi bila baruti. 2 kikuto cha filamu, ukanda (wa kunasia sauti n.k.). 3 kibweta cha wino (katika kalamu za wino). ~**-belt** ukanda wa risasi.

carve *vt* 1 chonga. 2 kata nakshi. 3 piga mtai; kata nyama (iliyopikwa) mezani. ~ **out** bandua; gawanya katika vipande vingi; *(fig)* fanikiwa kwa juhudi kubwa *he ~d out a career for himself in the army* alifanikiwa (baada ya jitihada kubwa) kupanda cheo jeshini. ~r *n* mchongaji; mkata nyama.

caryatid *n* kariatidi: sanamu ya mwanamke iliyotumika kama nguzo.

cascade *n* 1 maporomoko (makali lakini madogo) ya maji. 2 kitu kilichopangwa katika mfululizo wa matukio. 3 kitu kitokeacho ghafula na kwa vurumai; kitu kiangukacho kwa wingi.

case[1] *n* 1 *(affair)* jambo, kadhia *it is a ~ of stupidity not negligence* ni suala la ujinga si uzembe. **a ~ in point** mfano. **a ~ study** uchunguzi kifani. 2 **it is the** ~ ndiyo, naam, ni kweli. **in any ~/in no** ~ kwa vyovyote. 3 *(med)* mgonjwa anayeuguzwa; *five*

~*s of malaria* wagonjwa watano wa malaria. 4 *(of grammar)* uhusika. 5 *(leg)* kesi, daawa. ~ **at bar** kesi inayosikilizwa. **make out a ~ (for)** jengea hoja za kutetea jambo fulani ~ *for the defence/ prosecution* hoja ya mshitakiwa/mshitaki. ~**-law** sheria a desturi.
case[2] 1 kasha, sanduku, bweta, jamanda. 2 *(covering)* kifuniko. **pillow ~** foronya. 3 *(printing)* **upper-~** herufi kubwa. **lower-~** herufi ndogo *vt* 1 tia, weka bwetani, kashani; fungia ndani. 2 *(US sl)* chunguza kabla ya kuiba.
casing *see case n* kifuniko, kizingio. ~ **of rubber** kizingio cha mpira *vt* tia matiki *adj* ~**-hardened** *(fig)* sugu (kutokana na maisha,.
casein *n (chem)* kaseni: proteni kuu ya maziwa.
cash *n* pesa, fedha (noti na sarafu). **hard (spot)** ~ fedha, taslimu. ~ **sale** kuuza kwa fedha taslimu, fedha mkononi. ~ **on delivery/~ down** malipo wakati wa kupokea bidhaa. ~ **discount** aheri.~ **customer** mnunuzi anayelipa fedha taslimu. **petty ~ book** daftari ya matumizi madogomadogo. ~ **book** daftari ya fedha taslimu. ~**-desk** kaunta ya keshia. ~ **flow** mapato halisi.~**-register** mashine ya kuhesabia fedha. ~ **dispenser** mashine maalumu inayotunza na kutoa fedha *vt,vi* 1 lipa/pata fedha. ~ **a check** lipwa fedha (kwa kutoa cheki). 2 faidi; tumia kwa faida. **cashier** *n* keshia.
cashew 1 *n* korosho, kanju. 2 mkorosho, mkanju.
cashier *vt* fukuza jeshini.
cashmere *n* kashimiri: kitambaa cha sufi/ manyoya ya mbuzi wa Kashmiri.
casino *n* kasino: jengo la starehe hasa ya kamari.
cask *n* pipa, kasiki. **casket** *n* 1 kibweta, kijaluba, kikasha *(US)* jeneza.
cassava *n* muhogo. **dried ~** makopa. ~ **leaves** kisamvu.
casserole *n* 1 maziga. 2 chakula kilichookwa kwenye maziga.
cassette(s) *n* kaseti, kanda.
cassock *n (rel)*, kanzu/vazi la makasisi, wahudumu na waimbaji wa kanisani.
cast[1] *vt* 1 tupa, rusha. ~ **a dice** tupa dado. ~ **an anchor** tupa/ tia nanga. ~ **a vote** piga kura. ~**ing vote** kura makata. ~ **sth in sb's teeth** laumu. 2 kalibu, subu; mimina katika kalibu. 3 *(of snake)*, jinyonyoa jichuna, jiambua. 4 ~ **up** jumlisha, kokotoa. 5 geuza, elekeza (macho). ~ **about for** angaza, tafutatafuta. ~ **an eye over** tupia jicho. 6 *(theatre)* pangia wahusika dhima katika mchezo. 7 *(naut)* legeza (kamba). 8 *(printing)* kadiria nafasi (itakayohitajiwa). 9 *(knitting)* ~ **on** fuma safu ya kwanza ya vitanzi. ~ **a net** tupa wavu. ~ **a horoscope** piga falaki, bao ~ *a new light on a problem* leta mtazamo/ mwanga mpya (juu ya jambo). ~ **sb aside** achana na mtu, telekeza. ~ **away** *(usually pass)* acha (kutokana na kuvunjika kwa meli). ~ **down** sononesha ~ *(in one's lot) with sb* jiunga pamoja na. ~ **off** anza safari. ~ **off clothes** tupa nguo. ~ **offs** mitumba. ~ **off** legeza, fumua. ~ **out** toa, fukuza. ~ **out devils** fukuza pepo. ~ **away** *n* mtu aliyevunjikiwa na meli *adj* -enye kuvunjikiwa na meli. *n (throw)* 1 mtupo, mrusho. 2. kalibu. ~ **iron** kalibu ya chuma *adj (fig)* kaidi, bishi, gumu. 3 kitu kilichoumbwa katika kalibu. 4 *(squint)* kengeza kidogo. **a ~ in the eye** kuwa na kengeza kidogo. 5 wachezaji: seti ya wachezaji (k.m. katika filamu ya sinema) aina, sifa.
castanet(s) *n* kitoazi, namna ya kayamba.
caste 1 (*Ind.*) tabaka (litokanalo na kazi, vyeo, weledi, n.k.). 2 *(fig)* hadhi, nafasi, katika jamii. **lose ~** shuka hadhi.
castellan *n* liwali.
castellated *adj* -enye buruji; -enye ngome.

castigate *vt* 1 adhibu vikali (kwa kupiga au kukemea). 2 rudi. **castigation** *n*. **castigator** *n*.
castle *n* ngome, husuni, nyumba yenye boma; kasri. **~s in the air/~s in Spain** njozi, ndoto za mchana; mawazo ya tamaa isiyowezekana.
castor[1] *n* 1 gurudumu (la samani): gurudumu lifungwalo kwenye miguu ya samani (kiti, meza n.k.) kurahisisha mjongeo wa samani 2. kijaluba cha chupa au bati cha kuwekea sukari, chumvi, n.k.
castor[2] *n* 1 *(bot)* mbarika, nyoyo, mbono. ~ **oil** mafuta ya mbarika, kastoroli. ~ **bean** mbegu za mbarika, nyonyo. ~ **sugar** sukari laini.
castrate *vt* hasi; hanithisha. **castration** *n*.
casual *adj* 1 *(accidental)* -a bahati, -a nasibu; -a ajali. 2 *(occasional)* -a nadra, -siyo -a kudumu. ~ **labourer** kibarua. 3 *(informal)* -a kawaida, -sio rasmi. ~ **clothes** nguo za kawaida. ~ **friendship** urafiki wa kawaida, usio wa karibu; -liotokea bila mpango au bila kutegemewa. **~ness** *n*.
casualty *n* 1 ajali (agh. mbaya inayosababisha kifo. 2 majeruhi; mtu aliyejeruhiwa au aliyeuawa, aliyepotea vitani. ~ **ward** wadi ya majeruhi.
casuarina *n* mvinje.
casuistry *n (derog) (fig)* ulaghai: kupindua mambo kwa kutumia hoja za ulaghai. **casuist** *n*.
casus belli *(latin)* kisa cha vita (mapigano, ugomvi).
cat *n* 1 paka, nyau. **wild ~** gwagu, paka shume, paka nunda. **let the ~ out of the bag** fichua siri (bila kukusudia) *its raining ~s and dogs* mvua inanyesha kwa wingi. **wait for the ~ to jump** bana, tulia kwanza (mpaka uone upepo unaelekea wapi). **see which way the ~ jumps** ngojea fikira za watu wengine kabla ya kutoa shauri lako. **like a ~ on hot bricks** -enye wasiwasi sana. **set/put the ~ among the pigeons** leta vurugu sababisha wasiwasi. **~-and-dog life** maisha ya ugomvi. **has the ~ got your tongue** *(sl)* bana kimya. **it makes a ~ laugh** inafurahisha sana. even a ~ may look at the King hata watu wa chini wana haki zao. **when the ~ is away the mice will play** paka akiondoka panya hutawala (*compounds etc.*). ~ **burglar** *n* mwizi wa kuparamia kuta. ~ **call** zomea. ~ **fish** kambare. ~ **nap/ sleep** *n* usingizi (wa kuiba). ~ **walk** ujia, uchochoro (hasa kwenye daraja). **~er waul** *vi* lia kama paka *n* mlio kama wa paka. **~'s eye** *n* 1 kiashiria njia. 2 aina ya kito ambacho huonyesha mwale wa mwanga ndani yake. ~ **'s pan** *n* 1 kibaraka, kikaragosi. 2 *(naut)* upepo mdogo ufanyao viwimbi vidogo juu ya maji wakati bahari imetulia. **~gut** *n* uzi wa utumbo wa mnyama, kano.
catabolism *n (biol)* ukataboli.
cataclysm *n* 1 gharika, mafuriko ya maji. 2 maafa makubwa (badiliko la ghafla k.v. mafuriko, vita, n.k.). 3 mabadiliko ya ghafla ya mambo.
catafalque *n* jukwaa lililopambwa kwa ajili ya jeneza (agh la mtu mashuhuri).
catalepsy *n* mkakamao (wa miguu na mikono). **cataleptic** *adj*.
catalogue *n* 1 katalogi. 2 orodha ya vitu. *vt* andika katalogi; ingiza katika katalogi.
catalysis *(chem)* uchocheaji. **catalyst** *n* kichocheo **catalytic** *adj*.
catamaran *n* 1 *(naut)* chelezo au muunganisho wa mitumbwi miwili pamoja.
catapult *n* 1 manati, panda, fyata. 2 *(in ancient times)* mtambo wa kutupia mawe katika vita. 3 chombo cha kurushia ndege katika manowari ndege nyingine *vt* rusha ndege.
cataract *n* 1 maporomoko ya maji. 2 *(of the eye)* mtoto wa jicho: aina ya ugonjwa wa macho.
catarrh *n* 1 mafua; ugonjwa wa makamasi mengi. 2 makamasi. **~al** *adj*.
catastrophe *n* msiba mkuu,

machachafuko, maangamizi, balaa. **catastrophic** *adj.*

catboat *n* mashua ya mlingoti na tanga moja.

catch *vt,vi* 1 kamata, gwia, bamba ~ *a thief* kamata/bamba/ gwia mwizi. 2 shika, daka ~ *the ball* daka mpira ~*a knife* shika kisu. 3 *(fig)* pata, shikwa na ~ *a cold* pata mafua. ~ **fever** shikwa na homa. 4 kuta, fuma *I caught the boys stealing* niliwakuta watoto wakiiba. ~ sb in the act of doing sth gundua mtu kosa lake. 5 wahi. ~ **a train** wahi treni. ~ **sb** fuma mtu akifanya jambo. 6 ~ **(up)** fikia aliye mbele *you have to work hard to ~ up with the rest* huna budi kufanya kazi sana uwafikie wenzako. 7 nasa, kwama *the nail caught her dress* msumari ulinasa nguo yake. 8 fahamu, tambua, sikia *I ~ your meaning* nafahamu maana yako. 9 ~ **sight of** ona kwa kitambo kidogo. 10 piga *he caught me on the nose* alinipiga pua. 11 pata *you will ~ it* utaipata; *(of woman) (sl)* pata mimba. 12 jaribu kushika. **a drowning man ~es at straws** mfa maji haachi kutapatapa *n* 1 kudaka. 2 hila; mtego *there's a ~ in it* pana mtego. 3 vuo. 4 mwindo; pato la bahati. ~ **one's breath** ziba pumzi (kwa mshtuko). ~ **fire** shika moto. ~**er** *n* (basketball) mdakaji. ~**ing** *adj* 1 *(esp. of disease)* -a kuambukiza. 2 *(attractive)* -a kuvutia -a kuwaka. ~ **crop** *n* mazao yanayokua kwa haraka sana yanayopandwa kati ya mimea mingine (k.m. maharage kati ya mahindi).

catchment *n* eneo lililo chanzo cha maji ya mto/bwawa. ~ **area/basin** *(of school)* eneo ambamo wanafunzi wa shule moja wanatoka.

catchpenny *adj* 1 *(derog)* zuri nje tu lakini hafifu sana. 2 -lotengenezwa kwa madhumuni ya kuuza haraka bila kuweka makini.

catchword *n* 1 kidahizo. 2 *(mil) (password)* neno la siri. 3 neno linalorudiwarudiwa. ~ **phrase** msimu.

catchy *adj* 1 -a kusikiza, -a kuvuta masikio (sauti, wimbo n.k.). 2 *(tricky)* -danganyifu, -a hila; -erevu.

catechism *n (rel)* katekisimu. **catechist** mkatekista. **catechetic(al)** *adj* -a kujibizana. **catechize** *vt (rel)* fundisha, pima ujuzi wa dini kwa maswali na majibu; fundisha katekisimu. **catechumen** *n* mkatekumeni: mwanafunzi wa dini ya Kikristo (anayetaka kubatizwa).

category *n.* aina, namna jinsi, jamii, kundi. **categorical** *adj* dhahiri, -a hakika, halisi, pasi shaka. **caregorically** *adv* **categorize** *vt* ainisha, pambanua, bainisha.

cater *vi* andaa; patia. ~ **for** patia (chakula, michezo, mazungumzo n.k.). **caterer** mwandazi, mchukuzi wa chakula. ~**ring** *n.*

caterpillar *n* 1 kiwavi. 2 katapila, tingatinga.

catharsis *n* 1 *(med)* kuharisha, kuendesha. 2 *(psych)* kutoa/ kupoza hisia zilizochemka, mtakaso hisia. **cathartic** *n* aina ya haluli.

cathedral *n* kanisa kuu la dayosisi.

catheter *n (med)* katheta: neli ya kuingiza uoevu katika mishipa ya mwilini.

cathode *n (phys)* kathodi.

catholic *adj* 1 pana (wa mawazo, mitazamo n.k.). **the ~ church** Wakristo wote. **Roman C ~** Mkatoliki. **Catholicism** *n* ukatoliki, mafundisho na imani ya dini ya Katoliki.

ca-o'nine-tails *n* kato la ncha tisa; kiboko, mjeledi.

catsup *see ketchup*

cattle *n (pl oxen)* ng'ombe *(sl)*. **head of ~** kundi la ng'ombe. ~ **cake** mashudu. ~ **grid** kizuio cha ng'ombe: shimo barabarani linalofunikwa na vyuma linaloruhusu gari kupita lakini si ng'ombe. ~ **trespass** kuingia kwa mifugo (kusiko halali). ~ **man** *n* mchungaji wa ng'ombe. ~ **pen/~ shed** zizi, boma la ng'ombe. *adj (used esp. of a woman)*

-enye chuki ya kichini chini. **cattiness** *n.*

Caucasian *n* wa jamii/asili ya Kihindi - Kizungu.

caucus *n* 1 mkutano (wa siri) wa wanachama wa kuchagua wagombea viti.

caul *n (physiol)* tandabui, zalio. **born with a ~** *(fig)* -enye bahati.

cauldron *n* sufuria kubwa, jungu kubwa.

cauliflower *n* koliflawa: aina ya kabichi.

caulk *vt (naut)* kalafati.

cause[1] *n* 1 asili, chanzo *the ~ of the fire was carelessness* chanzo cha moto ule kilikuwa ni uzembe. 2 sababu *there is no ~ for anxiety* hakuna sababu ya kuwa na wasiwasi. 3 kusudi, ajili *fight in the ~ of justice* pigana kwa ajili ya haki. 4 *(leg)* kesi, daawa. **~-list** *n (leg)* orodha ya kesi *vt* sababisha. **~less** *adj* bila sababu. **causation** *n* 1 usababisho, kusababisha. 2 wiano wa sababu. **causative** *adj* -a kuleta, -a kufanyiza, -a kutendesha, -a kusababisha.

causerie *n* 1 mjadala usio rasmi.

causeway *n* barabara iliyoinuka juu kidogo (hasa kupitia maji au kinamasi).

caustic *adj* 1 -enye kuchoma kama moto, -a kuunguza *~ soda* magadi. 2 *(of words)* -kali, -chungu, -a dhihaka *n* namna ya dawa ichomayo bila moto, kwa mfano magadi. **~ally** *adv.*

cauterize *vt (med)* choma kwa chuma au dawa kali (ili kuondoa vijidudu mwilini), tia pisho; unguza. **cautery, cauterization** *n.*

caution *n* 1 uangalifu, hadhari, tahadhari. 2 onyo, shauri. 3 *(sl)* mchekeshaji *~ money* arubuni *vt* onya, tahadharisha. **cautious** *adj* -angalifu, -enye hadhari. **cautiousness** *n.* **cautiously** *adv.* **~ary** *adj* -a kushauri/onya.

cavalcade *adj* maandamano ya wapanda farasi.

cavalier *n (arch)* mpanda farasi mvulana *adj* 1 -fidhuli, -a kiburi, -a kutakabari. 2 *(arch)* kunjufu.

cavalry *n* 1 askari farasi. 2 kikosi cha magari ya deraya n.k.

cave *n* 1 pango, shimo (kwenye mwamba/kilima). 2 tundu *vi ~* **in** 1 achia, poromoka, poromosha, bomoka. 2 *(surrender)* shindwa, salimu amri. **~-dweller** *n.* mtu aishiye mapangoni agh. wa zamani. **~ -man** *n* mkazi wa mapangoni; mshenzi.

caveat n 1 *(leg)* uahirishaji wa kesi. 2 *(formal)* tahadhari; kivuo.

cavern *n (lit)* pango, shimo. **~ous** *adj.*

cavil *vi ~* **(at)** lalamika, laumu, kosoa bila msingi. **~ler** *n.*

cavity *n* pengo, kijishimo, mvungu.

cavort *vi (colloq)* chacharika, rukaruka.

caw *vi* lia (kama kunguru) *n* mlio wa kunguru.

cayenne, (cayenne pepper) *n* pilipili kichaa, mwachaka.

cease *vi,vt* koma; isha, acha, hulu. **~ from** komesha, simamisha. **without ~** kwa mfululizo. **~-fire** *n* kusimamisha mapigano, vita; koma kwa vita. **~less** *adj* -isiyo na/bila mwisho, -a daima. **~ lessly** *adv.*

CCM *n (abbr of)* Chama Cha Mapinduzi.

cedar *n* seda: mti wa mbao aina ya mkangazi.

cede *vt* toa kwa mwingine (haki, ardhi n.k.) achia.

ceiling *n* 1 dari; *(of boat)* darumeti. 2 kikomo cha juu (bei, mshahara, kuruka kwa ndege).

celebrate *vt, vi* 1 adhimisha, sherehekea. 2 sifu, heshimu, tukuza. 3 ainisha (misa). **~d** *adj* maarufu. **celebrant** *n (rel)* padri (aongozaye misa maarufu), kasisi afanyaye Ushirika Mtakatifu. **Con~** (mapadri) kusoma misa kwa pamoja. **celebration** *n* maadhimisho, sherehe. **celebrity** *n.* umaarufu, umashuhuri; mtu maarufu, mashuhuri.

celerity *n* wepesi.

celery *n* figili.

celestial *adj* -a mbingu;-a peponi. **the ~ Empire** Ufalme wa China.
celibacy *n* useja, ujane (hasa kwa misingi ya dini). **celibate** *n* mjane, mseja, mtu asiyeoa, (hasa kasisi) *adj* kapera; -a ujane.
cell *n* 1 seli, chumba kidogo (hasa katika gereza n.k.). 2 kijumba cha sega. 3 seli, chembe ya uhai *living ~* chembe hai *single living ~* chembe moja hai *the brain ~s* ubongo. 4 *(electricity)* betri, jiwe. **dry ~** seli umeme kavu. **electric ~** seli umeme. 5 *(of a party)* shina *~ leader* mjumbe, balozi. **~ular** *adj* 1 -enye seli. 2 -enye vitundu vitundu vidogo; -a vitundu tundu; -enye kipape maji.
cellar *n* sela: ghala iliyo chini ya ardhi. **~age** *n* 1 ushuru wa kukodi sela. 2 ukubwa wa sela. **~er** *n.*
cello *n* selo: vailini kubwa. **~ist** *n* mpiga selo.
cellophane *n* selofeni: aina ya karatasi ya plastiki.
celluloid *n* 1 seluloidi; aina ya plastiki. 2 filamu.
cellulose *n* selulosi: tishu iundayo sehemu kubwa ya mti na mmea.
Celsius *n* selisiasi.
cement *n* 1 saruji. 2 *(in teeth etc)* sementi *vt* tia sementi juu/ndani ya; unga kwa sementi; *(fig)* imarisha, unganisha. **~friendship** imarisha urafiki. **~ation** *n.* **~ mixer** kichanganya saruji.
cemetery *n* makaburini, mavani, maziara.
cenotaph *n* mnara wa kumbukumbu ya wafu (waliozikwa kwingine).
cense *vt* 1 fukiza. 2 fanya ibada kwa kufukiza. **~r** *n* chetezo.
censor *n* 1 mkaguzi (wa vitabu, filamu n.k.). 2 mdhibiti. 3 *(ancient Rome)* afisa anayehesabu wafu na kusimamia maadili ya taifa. *vt* kagua, ondoa sehemu za kitabu n.k. ambazo zinadhaniwa zina walakini. **~ial** *adj.*
censorship *n* ukaguzi, udhibiti.
censorious *adj* -kali, dodosi, -a kutafuta makosa/kasoro.
censure *n* lawama, karipio *motion of ~* hoja ya lawama *pass ~* laumu *vt* laumu, karipia, kosoa. **~ (for)** laumu kwa. **censurable** *adj.*
census *n* sensa; hesabu ya idadi ya watu.
cent *n* 1 senti. 2 **per ~** asilimia *five per ~* tano kwa mia; asilimia tano *agree one hundred per ~* kubali kabisa.
centaur *n* kentauro: mnyama wa hadithi aliye nusu binadamu nusu farasi.
centenary/centennial *n* miaka mia; si kukuu ya ukumbusho ya kila mwaka wa mia; kipindi cha miaka mia *adj* -enye miaka mia; -a baada ya miaka mia. **centenarian** *n* mzee mwenye umri wa miaka mia au zaidi *adj* -enye miaka mia au zaidi.
center see **centre**.
centering/centring *n* kishikiza tao.
centigrade *adj* sentigredi, -enye digrii 100.
centimetre/centimeter *n* sentimita: kipimo cha sehemu moja kwa mia ya mita.
centipede *n* tandu.
centre *n* 1 kati, katikati: *at the ~ of the town* katikati ya mji; *(fig)* sehemu muhimu sana. **~ of gravity** kitovu cha mvutano. 2 kituo; kitovu. **health ~** kituo cha afya. 3 kiini *~ of the question* kiini cha swali *~ of the fruit* kiini cha tunda. 4 *~ of interest* mtu anayevutia au mahali panapovutia. 5 msimamo wa kati; wale wenye msimamo wa kati (kisiasa, kidini, kifalsafa) *vt* 1 weka/chukua katikati, -wa katikati. 2 tenga, waza *all eyes were ~d on the teacher* macho yote yalimlenga mwalimu *~ one's hopes on sth* weka matumaini yote juu ya jambo fulani. 3 -wa katikati. **centric(al)** *adj.* **centricity** *n (tech).* **~-bit** kitoboleo, kekee. **~-fold/ ~ spread/ ~-piece** *n* pambo la katikati ya meza. **~ -spread** *n* kurasa mbili za katikati za gazeti.
central *adj* 1 -a katikati; hasa, -a katikati, karibu na katikati *(principal)*

-kuu; -a maana *central registry* masijala kuu *central heating* upashaji joto katika mabomba (kutoka kituo kikuu) *central committee* kamati kuu. **the central government** *n* serikali kuu *(US)* kituo cha simu. **centralism** *n* mfumo wa mamlaka kutoka sehemu moja, mfumo katikati, ukatikati. **centralize** *vt,vi* leta/weka katikati; weka chini ya makao makuu. **centralization** *n*.

centrifugal *adj* pewa; kirukia pewa: mwendo unaoelekea nje. ~ **force** kani nje, -enye kuelekea nje ya nukta.

centrifuge **n** mashinepewa.

centripetal *adj* tovu ~ **force** kani tovu -enye kuelekea ndani ya nukta . ~ acceleration mchapuko kitovu.

centring *see* **centering**.

centrist *n* mwanasiasa mwenye msimamo wa kati.

century *n* 1 karne. (muda wa miaka mia). 2 *(in cricket)* mabao 100.

ceramic *adj* -a ufinyanzi,-a vyombo vilivyofinyangwa: -a kauri. **~s** *n* 1 vyombo vya udongo. 2 sanaa ya ufinyanzi. **ceramist** *n* mfinyanzi.

cereal *n* 1 nafaka k.v. mahindi, ngano n.k. 2 chakula cha nafaka, hasa (cha kifungua (kinywa) *adj* -a nafaka.

cerebral *adj* 1 -a ubongo. 2 -enye kutumia akili tu. ~ **palsy** *n (med)* ugonjwa wa kupooza.

cerebellum *n* ubongonyuma.

cerebration *n* ufanyaji kazi wa ubongo, kufikiri. **cerebro- spinal** *adj (anat)* -a ubongo na uti wa mgongo. **cerebro-spinal meningitis (fever)** homa ya uti wa mgongo. **cerebrum** *n* ubongombele.

ceremonious *adj* 1 -a sherehe; -a ibada, -a mviga. 2 -a kupenda utaratibu/ itifaki/ uungwana. **stand on** ~ shikilia mno utaratibu. **ceremony** *n* 1 mviga, utaratibu, vitendo maalumu (agh. vinavyoambatana na dini/ ibada n.k.) katika sherehe (k.v. arusi, maziko, uzinduzi wa jengo, tambiko nk.). 2 kawaida za desturi na kiungwana. **Master of ceremonies** Mfawidhi wa sherehe. **ceremonial** *adj* -a kufuata utaratibu maalum (hasa wa dini, ibada n.k.) rasmi, -a sherehe *n* utaratibu rasmi, sherehe n.k., taadhima, utaratibu. **~ness** *n*.

cerise *adj* -enye rangi nyekundu isiyoiva.

cert *n (sl)* kitu chenye uhakika. *see* **certain**.

certain *adj* 1 yakini, -a hakika, bila shaka *make* ~ hakikishia *feel* ~ -wa na uhakika *for* ~ kwa yakini, hakika. 2 fulani *a* ~ *place* mahali fulani *a* ~ *man* mtu mmoja (fulani). 3 kidogo, kiasi *there was a* ~ *doubt about his health* kulikuwa na shaka kidogo kuhusu afya yake *to a* ~ *degree* kwa kiwango fulani. 4 *(fixed)* maalum. 5 (inevitable) -a hakika; hapana budi *he is* ~ *to go* ana uhakika wa kwenda *he is* ~ *to die* ni lazima afe. **~ly** *adv* bila shaka. **~ly not!** la hasha, katu! hata! **~ty** *n* 1 hakika, yakini *it is a dead* *~ty* ni hakika kabisa, hakuna shaka yoyote. 2 jambo linalokubalika; jambo linaloelekea kuwa hakika. **for a ~ty** kwa hakika.

certifiable *adj* 1 -a kuthibitika (agh.kwa kutoa hati) ~ *as a lunatic* -a kuweza kuthibitika kuwa na wazimu.

certificate *n* 1 hati (ya uthibitisho)/ cheti ~ of birth, marriage etc. cheti cha kuzaliwa, ndoa n.k. **degree ~** shahada. *vt* -toa cheti/hati n.k. **certificated** *adj* iliyohitimu.

certify *vt,vi* hakikisha, thibitisha *this is to* ~ *that* hii ni kuthibitisha kwamba. **certified cheque** hundi halali *he was certified insane* alithibitishwa kuwa mwenda wazimu *vi* **(to)** ~ toa ushahidi kuwa kitu ni sahihi.

certitude *n (formal)* yakini,uhakika.

cerulean *adj (formal)* -a (rangi ya) samawati, -a buluu.

cervix *n (anat)* mlango wa kizazi. **cervical** *adj*.

cess *n* kodi, ushuru, (agh. wa mazao).

cessation *n* kukoma; kuacha (kwa muda) ~ *of hostilities* kuacha

kupigana.
cession *n (leg)* 1 kutoa, kuachia, kwa mapatano. 2 kilichoachiliwa, kilichotolewa.
cesspit (also cesspool) *n* 1 shimo la maji machafu. 2 *(fig)* mahali pachafu ~ *of iniquity* mahali palipojaa maovu.
chafe *vt* 1 chua, sugua (ngozi n.k. ili kupasha moto). 2 chubua, kwaruza *vi (fig)* ona udhia, ghadhabika, -wa na hasira ~ *under insults* udhika kwa sababu ya matukano *n* hasira, uchungu.
chaff[1] *n* 1 kapi, kumvi, wishwa. 2 majani yaliyokatwa na kukaushwa kwa chakula cha ng'ombe, farasi n.k. 3 kitu cha bure *vt* kata majani kwa ajili ya chakula cha mifugo. ~**-cutter** kikataukoka.
chaff[2] *n* utani, mzaha *vt* tania, fanyia mzaha.
chaffinch *n* kurumbiza: aina ya ndege aimbaye.
chafing-dish *n* kipashamoto.
chagrin *n* hangaiko/ uchungu wa moyo (kwa sababu ya kushindwa, kufanya kosa n.k.) *vt* huzunisha.
chain *n* 1 mnyororo, mkufu. **in ~s** kifungoni au utumwani. 2 mfuatano/ mfululizo/mtungo, mlolongo wa mambo, vita, matukio n.k. ~ *of mountains (lakes, villages etc)* safu ya milima, maziwa, miji n.k. 3 kipimo cha urefu wa futi 66 *vt* funga (kwa mnyororo). ~**-gang** *n.* kikundi cha wafungwa (waliofungwa minyororo wakifanya kazi). ~ **letter** *n* barua - mkufu: barua maalum ambayo mpokeaji huombwa kutoa nakala na kuzipeleka kwa watu wengine ambao nao hufanya vivyo hivyo. ~**-mail** *n* deraya. ~**-smoker** *n* mvutaji sigara kwa mfululizo (akizima anawasha nyingine). ~ **stitch** *n* mshono - mkufu. ~**-stores** *n* mtungo wa maduka (ya tajiri mmoja). ~ **reaction** mlipizano/ mjibizano. ~ **saw** msumeno wa mnyororo.
chair *n* 1 kiti. 2 kiti, mahali au cheo; mwenyekiti; uenyekiti *address (appeal to) the* ~ elekeza mazungumzo kwa mwenyekiti. **take the** ~ shika uenyekiti; -wa mwenyekiti. 3 nafasi na kazi ya profesa. 4 *(US) electric* ~ kiti cha kuua *vt* 1 ongoza (mkutano). 2 chukua mtu kitikiti (agh. kwa shangwe); beba juu. **~man/ ~ person** *n* mwenyekiti, kinara. **~manship** uenyekiti.
chalet *n* 1 nyumba ndogo hasa katika milima ya Uswisi. 2 nyumba ndogo katika kambi ya kupumzikia.
chalice *n (rel)* 1 kalisi: kikombe maalum cha divai kitumiwacho wakati wa ibada ya Kikristo. ~ **veil** kifuniko cha kalisi.
chalk *n* 1 chaki; chokaa. ~**-pit** shimo la chokaa. **he does not know ~ from cheese** mbumbumbu. **better by a long ~** bora zaidi. as different/like as **~and cheese** tofauti kabisa *vt* 1 paka chaki, fanya alama kwa chaki. 2 ~ **up** weka rekodi; *(of sport)* pata. 3 ~ **out** eleza kwa jumla. **by a long ~** kwa mbali sana. **~y** *adj.*
challenge *vt* 1 ita kuja kushindana (katika michezo n.k.), karibisha kwenye mashindano. 2 *(mil)* simamisha na kudai jina. 3 *(leg)* pinga, kana, bisha. 4 taka sababu za kuthibitisha shauri au neno. 5 tania, toa changamoto *this situation is a ~ to the government* hali hii ni changamoto kwa serikali *n* 1 mwito wa kuja kushindana *issue a* ~ ita kuja kushindana. 2 neno la kukaidi, kubishana. 3 ulizo la mlinzi (k.m. Ni nani anayekuja?). 4 kichocheo. 5 chochezi. **~r** *n* mpinzani.
chamber *n* 1 *(arch)* chumba (hasa cha kulala). 2 *(pl)* chumba cha jaji (cha kusikizia kesi); *(not US)* vyumba vingi katika jengo kubwa. 3 baraza la wabunge. **Upper C~** baraza la juu (seneti). 4 Ofisi za wanasheria (hasa katika mahakama). 5 chama C~ *of Commerce* chama cha wafanya biashara. 6 chemba (nafasi ndani ya mwili wa mnyama au mmea) *nasal* ~

mba ya pua. **~lain** *n (old use)* msimamizi mkuu wa nyumba ya mfalme; mtunza mali. ~ **of horrors** chumba cha maonyesho ya vitu vya kuogofya. **~-maid** *n* mhudumu wa kike (aandaliaye vyumba vya kulala hotelini). ~ **-pot** chombo cha kuendea haja.

camelion *n* 1 kinyonga, lumbwi. 2 kigeugeu.

chammy-leather see **chamois leather**.

chamois *n (pl chamois)* swala. ~ **leather** *(also chammy/shammy leather)* ngozi laini (ya swala, mbuzi kondoo) (agh. hutumika kung'arishia vitu, hasa magari).

champ *vt,vi (of horse)* tafunatafuna chakula au lijamu kwa sauti. *(fig)* ~ **(at the bit)** -tokuwa na subira, -wa na harara. *n (sl) see* **champion.**

champagne *n* shampeni.

champaign *n* mbuga, tambarare.

champion *(also champ) n* 1 bingwa, mshindi (wa mashindano ya mbio, ngumi n.k.); shujaa. 2 mtetezi, mgombea *vt* tetea, pigania, saidia, linda *adj (colloq)* bora, -a kwanza, -a kupita ingine. **~ship** ubingwa, ushindi, mashindano.

chance *n* 1 bahati *by (any)* ~ kwa bahati *a happy* ~ bahati njema. 2 nasibu *a game of* ~ bahati nasibu. 3 *(opportunity)* nafasi *he lost his* ~ alipoteza nafasi yake *the ~s are against me* inaelekea nitashindwa. 4 *(probability)* uwezekano: *there is no~ of it* haiwezekani; si yumkini *an off*~ matumaini kidogo. **take one's** ~ jaribu bahati. **the main** ~ nafasi ya kupata pesa *vt* 1 *(risk)* bahatisha; jaribu *I'll ~ it* nitabahatisha. 2 tukia. kuta kwa bahati ~ *upon* kuta *if I ~ to see him* nikibahatika kumwona *it ~d that* ilitokea kwamba. **chancy** *adj (colloq)* -a hatari; mashaka; -sio ya uhakika.

chancel *n (rel)* sehemu ya wanakwaya na makasisi kanisani.

chancellery 1 nafasi/idara/nyumba ya Mkuu. 2 ofisi ya ubalozi.

chancellor *n* 1 Mkuu wa Serikali, Waziri Mkuu (k.m. katika Shirikisho la Ujerumani). 2 Mkuu wa Chuo Kikuu *the C~ of the Exchequer (GB)* Waziri wa Fedha *the Lord High C~* Jaji Mkuu wa nchi (katika Uingereza). 3 *(GB)* Katibu Mkuu wa Ubalozi. **~ship.** **~ry** *n.*

chancery *n* 1 mahakama kuu katika Uingereza inayoshughulikia haki na usawa. 2 masijala ya nyaraka za umma.

chancre *n* kidonda (agh.cha kaswende). **chancrous** *adj.*

chandelier *n* shada la taa zenye mapambo linaloning'inia.

chandler *n* mwuzaji (au mtengenezaji) mishumaa, sabuni, mafuta n.k. *ship's* ~ mwuza kamba na zana za meli.

change *vt,vi* 1 badili; badilisha; geuza; geuka. ~ **step** badili mwendo, badili hatua ~ *one's mind* ghairi. **the property ~d hands** mali iliuzwa kwa mwingine. 2 vunja; chenji ~ a 100 *shillings note* vunja noti ya shilingi mia moja. 3 ~ **up/down** badili gia. **~into** geuka *n* 1 mageuzi, mabadi liko, mabadilisho, badiliko ~ *of administration* mabadiliko ya utawala. 2 kitu cha lazima ili kugeuza, kubadili; kitu cha kubadilisha *take a ~ of clothes with you* chukua nguo za kubadili *for a* ~ kwa kubadilisha hali/mambo *get no ~ out of (sb) (colloq)* kutopata msaada wowote. 3 *(coins)* senti, kichele *(fig) get ~ out of sb* -mlipia/lipiza kisasi. 4 baki *no ~ given* hakuna chenji. **~able** *adj* -a kigeugeu, -a kuweza kubadilika badilika, badilifu, -a kuelekea kubadilibadili. **~less** *adj.* **~ableness. changeability** *n* ugeuzo, ugeukaji. **~ful** *adj.* **changeling** *n* 1 kubadilisha mtoto mzuri kwa mbaya (kwa siri). 2 *(in traditional stories)* mtoto mbaya/mjinga, kioja aliyebadilishwa na mwingine aliyeibiwa.

channel *n* 1 mlangobahari. 2 mlizamu, mfereji mfumbi. 3 njia (ambayo kwayo habari, mashauri n.k.) yaweza kupitia *follow the proper ~s* fuata ngazi (zilizowekwa). 4 mkanda. 5 (radio, TV) idhaa,bendi *vt* 1 chimbua/ elekeza mfereji. 2 *(fig)* elekeza *he ~ed his abilities into business* alielekeza uwezo wake kwenye biashara.

chant *vt* 1 imba *~ sb's praises (fig)* sifia, sifu fulani kila mara *n* 1 mkarara, uimbaji wa zaburi. 2 *(of crowd)* kurudia kuimba.

chantry *n* wakfu.

chanty *n (also shanty)* wimbo wa kuvutia makasia.

chaos *n* machafuko, vurumai, vurugu, fujo. **chaotic** *adj*. **chaotically** *adv*.

chap[1] *vi,vt* chubuka, pasuka; chubua, pasua *the skin of my hands is ~ped* ngozi ya mikono yangu imepasuka *n* mchubuko.

chap[2] *n (sl)* mtu (mwanamme), jamaa *a funny/queer ~* mtu wa ajabu *young ~* kijana *a good ~* mtu mwema.

chap[3] *n* taya ya chini (hasa ya mnyama k.m. nguruwe); mashavu. **lick one's ~s** ngojea kwa shauku/hamu kubwa. **~/crest fallen** *adj* -lokata tamaa, -sohali.

chapel *n* 1 kanisa dogo. 2 *(arch)* kanisa la wasio Waanglikana au Wakatoliki; ibada katika kanisa hilo. 3 tawi la chama cha wafanyakazi wapiga chapa. **~goer** *n*.

chaperon *n* mchunga/mtunza mwari, somo *vt* fuatana na msichana mahali asiporuhusiwa kwenda peke yake.

chaplain *n* kasisi (wa jeshi, Chuo Kikuu n.k.). **~cy** *n*.

chaplet *n* 1 taji la maua. 2 tasbihi.3 mtungo wa shanga.

chapman *n* mchuuzi.

chapter *n* 1 sura; mlango, somo *a ~ of accidents* mfululizo wa ajali *to the end of the ~* mpaka mwisho kabisa wa mlango. **~ and verse** rejeo kamili. 2 *(rel)* mkutano wa mapadri. 3 tawi, kikundi cha chama n.k. 4 enzi.

char[1] *vi* safisha nyumba, ofisi n.k. kwa malipo ya saa au siku. **~-woman. ~-lady** *n* mwanamke mnadhifishaji: mwanamke anayelipwa kusafisha nyumba *vt* unguza *vi* ungua mpaka kuwa mkaa, fanya/kuwa nyeusi kwa kuungua.

char[2] *n (sl)* chai.

charabanc *n* basi (linalotumika kwa safari za burudani).

character *n* 1 tabia, moyo, silika ya mtu, hulka. **in/out of ~** ilio/isio kawaida (ya mtu fulani) *he has a bad ~* ana tabia mbaya. 2 sifa bainifu. 3 unyoofu, ukunjufu wa moyo *takes ~ to speak the truth always* inahitaji unyoofu kusema kweli daima. 4 mtu wa ajabu; wa tabia za kiajabu/ kipekee *that man is a real ~* mtu yule ni wa ajabu. 5 mhusika (katika riwaya, tamthiliya n.k.). 6 herufi *in large ~s* kwa herufi kubwa. 7 *(arch)* uthibitisho wa sifa zilizobainishwa. ~less *(derog)* bila sifa; -a kawaida. **~istic** *adj* -a kawaida/tabia (ya mtu, kikundi) *it is ~istic of him to ask for money* ni kawaida yake kuomba hela n sifa bainifu what are the ~istics of *a savannah plain*? Ni nini sifa bainifu za ukanda wa savana? **~rization** *(lit)* uchoraji, uumbaji wa mhusika (katika riwaya n.k.); ubainishaji wa tabia. **~ize** *vt* 1 eleza sifa (tabia, kawaida), ainisha. 2 -wa kawaida ya, -julikana kwa *his work is characterized by sloppiness* kazi yake huonyesha uzembe, *the indigenous cow is ~ized by its hump* ng'ombe wa kienyeji ajulikana kwa nundu yake.

charade *n (usu pl)* **~s** mchezo wa kukisia neno kutokana na viigizo bubu; *(fig)* kitendo kisicho cha maana, kitendo cha kupotosha ukweli/cha uongo.

charcoal *n* 1 mkaa, makaa. **~ burner** mchoma makaa; sigiri.

chard *n* **Swiss ~** mchadi aina ya kiazi sukari ambacho majani na shina lake huliwa.

charge[1] *vt,vi* 1 shtaki. **~ sb (with)** shtaki mtu kwa. 2 *(attack)*shambulia, rukia, endea kwa nguvu. 3 *(load)* shindilia fataki, pakia chomboni, tilia, jaza (pomoni). 4 *(demand price)* toza, dai malipo. **he ~ed me twenty shillings** alinitoza shilingi ishirini. 5 *(with responsibility)* kabidhi, dhaminisha, -pa jukumu au wajibu, -wa na dhima *he ~d himself the task of looking after our school* alichukua dhima ya kuiangalia shule yetu. 6 *(command, instruction)* amuru, lazimisha, agiza *the judge ~d the jury* jaji aliwaamuru wazee wa baraza. 7 *(of battery)* chaji. 8 dai *he ~d that I don't work* alidai kwamba sifanyi kazi. 9 ~ **up to** rekodi, weka. **~able** *adj* -a kutozwa; -a kushtakiwa; -a kuweza kulaumiwa. **~d** *adj* -liochemka; nyeti *face a ~* jibu mashtaka, kabiliwa na mashtaka. **~-sheet** *n* kitabu cha mashtaka.

charge[2] *n* 1 shtaka *bring a ~* fungulia shtaka, shtaki. 2 shambulio *the soldiers made a sudden ~* askari walifanya shambulio la ghafla. 3 bei, malipo. ~ **account** akaunti ya malipo. 4 mshindilio, fataki, kiasi cha baruti au cha umeme katika chombo cha kuwekea nguvu za umeme; marisau. 5 wajibu, madaraka. **put sb/be in ~ (of)** kabidhi pesa madaraka. **take ~** twaa madaraka. 6 maagizo, maelekezo. 7 **take/give sb in ~** peleka mtu polisi/ shtaki.

charge' d'affaires *n* balozi mdogo, kaimu balozi.

charger[1] *n* 1 *(arch)* farasi (wa ofisa mwanajeshi).

charger[2] *n (arch)* sahani kubwa, sinia.

chariot *n* kibandawazi (cha kukokotwa na farasi). **~eer** dereva wa kibandawazi.

charisma *n* 1 haiba kubwa. 2 kipaji (kitolewacho na Mungu). **~tic** *adj.*

charity *n* 1 sadaka. **live on ~y** ishi kwa sadaka. **a ~ ball** densi la kuchangisha fedha kusaidia maskini. **~ walk.** matembezi ya hisani (ya kuchangia fedha). 2 wema, fadhila, hisani, huruma. **out of ~** kwa moyo, kwa wema. 3 shirika au chama cha kusaidia wenye shida. **~ begins at home** *(prov)* wema wa mtu huanza kwao. **charitable** *adj* 1 -enye huruma, -enye fadhila, -enye hisani. 2 *(of institutions etc.)* -a kutoa msaada. **charitably** *adv*.

charivari *n* kelele nyingi (za sauti mchanganyiko).

charlady *n see* **char**[1]

charlatan *n* tapeli, laghai, mjuvi. **~ry** *n.*

charlock *n (bio)* mharadali mwitu.

charm *n* 1 ucheshi, uzuri, haiba, mvuto. 2 hirizi, talasimu, kago, fingo *vt* 1 *(attract)* vuta kwa uzuri/mapenzi n.k.; sisimua, furahisha, pendeza kwa wema. **I'm ~ed to see you!** nimefurahi sana kukuona. 2 roga, fanyia uchawi. **~er** *n* 1 mchawi. 2 mtu mcheshi, mtu mwenye haiba. **snake ~er** mcheza na nyoka. charm**ing** *adj* -cheshi, changamfu. **~ingly** *adv.*

charnel-house n nyumba ya kuhifadhia maiti au mifupa.

chart *n* 1 ramani (inayotumiwa na mabaharia), chati. 2 chati (yenye michoro, jedwali n.k.) *vt* 1 chora ramani; onyesha katika chati. 2 chunguza hali ya safari baharini. 3 sawiri mawazo.

charter *n* 1 hati, mkataba, idhini. **~ member** mwanachama mwanzilishi *the Great C ~ (Magna Carta)* Hati ya Haki za Binadamu. **~ed accountant** *(GB)* mhasibu msajiliwa. **~ed bank** benki yenye idhini. 2 kukodi meli, ndege n.k. *vt* kodi chombo, idhinisha. **~-party** *n (comm)* mapatano ya kukodi (chombo, meli n.k.).

charterhouse *n* nyumba ya watawa.

charwoman *see* **char**[1].

chariness *n* hadhari. **charily**/ **chary** *adj* -enye hadhari, -angalifu **chary (of)** -woga (wa).

chase[1] *vt,vi* 1 fukuza, kimbiza. **give ~ (to)** kimbilia, saka, fuata, kimbiza, fukuza, fuata. 2 ~ **away/off** fukuza. 3 **~down/up** jaribu kupata. 4 ~

about kimbiakimbia *(colloq)* *n* msako. **go on a wild goose ~** tafuta kitu bure (bila tumaini la kufaulu), ufukuzaji. **chaser** *n* 1 msakaji. **woman ~r** mfukuzia mabibi. 2 farasi mruka viunzi.

chase[2] *n* 1 fremu, nakshi, mfuo. 2 *(of gun)* kasiba *vt* tia temsi/ nakshi.

chasm *n* shimo kubwa, genge, ufa mkubwa, korongo; *(fig)* tofauti kubwa iliyopo baina ya hisia za watu.

chassis *n (pl)* 1 chesisi kiunzi, fremu ya chombo km. gari, redio n.k.

chaste *adj* 1 -siozini, bikira, safi. 2 -siyopambwa, sahili. **~ly** *adv*. **chastity** *n* .

chasten *vt* 1 *(discipline)* rudi, hidi, taadibu. 2 pambua, zima, nyosha.

chastise *vt* adibu, tia adabu. **~ment** *n*.

chasuble *n (rel)* kasula.

chat *vi* 1 ongea, piga soga/ gumzo, porojo. 2 **~ sb up** tongoza; piga porojo. **~ty** *adj* -ongezi, -gumzi *n* maongezi, mazungumzo, soga, porojo *have a ~* zungumza.

chateau *n* kasri, ngome.

chattel *n* mali inayohamishika (km. viti, gari n.k.).

chatter *vi* 1 payapaya, bwabwaja, payuka, ropoka. 2 lia/toa sauti kama tumbili. ndege n.k. 3 tatarika (k.m meno kwa baridi au hofu) *n* 1 mpayuko, mbwabwajo *be involved in idle ~* piga domo. 2 *(of machine)* mtatariko. **~box. ~er** mpayupayu, mpayukaji, mlimi.

chauffeur *n* dereva, mwendeshaji wa motokaa (wa mtu binafsi).

chauvinism *n* 1 uzalendo pofu. 2 ujinsia. **chauvinist** *n*. **chauvinistic** *adj*.

chaw *vt (vulg)* tafuna. **~-bacon** *n* mshamba.

cheap *adj* 1 rahisi, bahasa. **go ~** uzwa rahisi. **on the ~** *(colloq)* rahisi, bila shida, kwa bei tupa. 2 hafifu, isiyo na thamani, duni. **~jack** *adj* hafifu, duni. 3 -sio ungwana; -sio staarabu; -sio aminifu. **feel ~** ona haya/aibu. **hold ~** dharau, dunisha. **make oneself ~** jihakirisha, jishusha hadhi, jidhalilisha. 4 -a kilemba cha ukoka. ~ flattery kilemba cha ukoka. 5 **~ gibe** utani mbaya *n* urahisi *(of price)* **dirt ~** rahisi mno. **~ly** *adv* kwa urahisi *he got off ~ly* aliupatia. **~ness** *n*. **~en** *vt, vi* shuka/shusha thamani, pungua/ punguza bei. 2 vunja heshima, dhalilisha, fakirisha *don't ~ yourself* usivunje heshima yako, usijivunjie heshima, usijidhalilishe. **~skate** *n (sl)* bahili; mnyimi.

cheat *n* 1 mdanganyifu, laghai. 2 udanganyifu, hila *vt,vi* 1 danganya, laghai, hadaa, kenga. 2 *(of shopkeeper)* punja. 3 *(in exam)* iba, ibia.

check[1] *vt* 1 cheki, pima usahihi, peleleza, angalia kwa makini. 2 zuia, simamisha. 3 **~ sth off** tia alama ya kuonyesha usahihi, usawa. **~ sth up. ~ up on sth** kagua au linganisha kupata usahihi. **~ up on sb** chunguza usahihi wa sifa/madai ya mtu. 4 *(US)* weka, hifadhi (mzigo, bahasha, koti) chini ya ulinzi. 5 **~ in** jiandikishe (hotelini, kazini) kwamba umefika. 6 ~out ondoka, aga; toa (kwa mfano kitabu maktabani). **~ over** kagua, angalia. **~er** *n* 1 kitu, mtu anayecheki. 2 mtu anayepokea mizigo n.k. 3 mpokea hela (dukani n.k.). 4 *(US) (pl)* dama. **~er-board** *n* *(US)* bao la mchezo wa dama au sataranji *n* 1 zuio, kizuio; udhibiti. **hold sb in ~** zuia. **~s and balances** taratibu za vyombo vya dola kudhibitiana ili kuzuia matumizi mabaya ya madaraka. 2 usahihi, kupima, kusahihisha; kuhakiki. **~ list** orodha ya kupimia/ kukagulia. **~point** kituo cha ukaguzi wa magari/mashindano n.k. **~ up** *(med)* kupimwa. 3 tikiti, cheti, risiti, stakabadhi ya uthibitisho wa kuwekea kitu. **~room** chumba cha mizigo. 4 hundi. **bad ~** hundi batili. **~ book** kitabu cha hundi. 5 *(chess)* **~ mate n** kushindwa kabisa *vt shinda (fig)* zuia na shinda.

check[2] *n* mirabaraba; kitambaa cha kunguru *adj* -a milia, -a miraba
cheek *n* 1 shavu. ~ **by jowl** iliokaribiana; -naoshirikiana. **turn the other** ~ -tolipiza kisasi. ~**bone** *n* kituguta, kitefule. 2 tako. 3 *(impudence)* usununu, ufidhuli, usafihi. ~**y** *adj* -enye kiburi, fidhuli, safihi. ~**ly** *adv* kitefute *vt* safihi, fanyia ufidhuli.
cheep *vi* lia (kama makinda ya ndege yaliavyo) *n* mlio wa namna hii.
cheer *n* 1 *(arch)* hali ya kuwa na matumaini, furaha *be of good* ~ furahia, changamka. 2 *(old use) good* ~ vyakula na vinywaji vizuri. 3 ukelele wa kufurahia, kushangilia, kusifu, kutia moyo au bidii. ~ **leader** *n* kiongozi wa mashabiki (wakati wa mashindano). 4 kwa afya yako: msemo wa kunywa na kutakia heri/afya. ~**y** *adj* -a furaha, -changamfu, -kunjufu, -a bashasha *vt, vi* 1 ~ **sb (up)** changamsha, fariji. 2 ~ **(on)** shabikia kwa nguvu. ~**ful** changamfu. ~**fulness** *n.* ~**less** *adj* -a huzuni, bila chochote cha kufurahisha, -liosonona.
cheerio *(int) (at parting)* kwa heri, buriani.
cheese[1] *n* jibini, chizi. 2 *(sl)* picha ya mwanamke mzuri. ~**cloth** *n* shashi. ~**monger** *n* mchuuza jibini. ~ **paring** *n* ubahili uliokithiri. **cheesy** *adj* -a jibini, -enye jibini, kama jibini; *(sl)* duni; hafifu. ~ **cake** keki ya jibini; *(sl)* picha ya umbile la kiwiliwili cha mwanamke.
cheese[2] *vt (sl)* ~**off** chosha, udhi sana. **say** ~ cheka.
cheetah *n* duma.
chef *n* mpishi mkuu (katika hoteli).
chef- d' oeuvre *n* kazi bora kabisa (ya msanii n.k.).
chemical *adj* -a kemia; kemikali; madawa.
chemise *n (arch)* shimizi.
chemist *n* 1 mkemia; mtaalam wa kemia. 2 mfamasia.
chemistry *n* kemia
chemotherapy tibakemikali.
chenille *n* uzi wa mahameli (unaoshonewa kupambia mavazi na samani).
cheque *n* cheki, hundi, *(draft)* hawala. **cross a** ~ funga hundi. **travellers** ~ hundi ya wasafiri. **dishonoured** ~ cheki iliyokataliwa. ~**-book** *n* kijitabu cha hundi.
chequer *n* 1 ruwaza yenye miraba ya rangi tofauti. 2 ~**ed cloth** *n* guo yenye mirabaraba *vt* 1 tia, andika mirabaraba kwa rangi tofauti. ~**ed career** maisha ya kupanda na kushuka.
cherish *vt* 1 tunza, lea hifadhi, kwa upendo mkubwa. ~ **illusions** fuga/ishi na matumaini/hisia/njozi.
cheroot *n* biri iliyo wazi pande zote.
cherry *n (tree)* mcheri; *(fruit)* cheri. *adj* -ekundu. ~ **lips** midomo myekundu.
cherub *n* 1 malaika mdogo: mmoja wa makerubini. 2 *(of child)* mtoto mzuri. ~**ic** *adj.*
chess *n* sataranji, chesi. ~**man** kisanamu cha sataranji. ~**board** *n* ubao wa sataranji.
chessel *n* kalibu ya jibini.
chest *n* 1 kasha, sanduku, (la kuhifadhia nguo, fedha, madawa n.k.). ~ **of drawers** almari. **medicine** ~ sanduku la madawa. 2 kifua; *(of animals)* kidari. ~ **complaint** maumivu ya kifua. **get sth off one's** ~ toa dukuduku. **keep/hold one's cards close to one's/** ~ -wa msiri, bania siri.
cheval-glass *n* kioo kikubwa (kilichotundikwa).
chevron *n* tepe ya V (ionyeshayo cheo cha askari cha koplo au sajini).
chew *vt vi* 1 ~ **(up)** tafuna. ~**ing gum** chingamu. **bite off more than one can** ~ jaribu kuliko uwezo. 2 ~ **over.** ~ **(up) on** fikiria, tafakari. ~ **the rag** *(dated sl)* jadili mambo (hasa ya magomvi au tofauti za zamani); lalamika. ~ **the cud** cheua. ~ **out** *(colloq)* karipia *n* 1 kutafuna. 2

kipande cha tumbako. **~ed up** *adj* enye wasiwasi sana.
chiaroscuro *n* msambazo wa mwanga wa vivuli (hasa katika uchoraji).
chic *n* ulimbwende, umaridadi *adj* maridadi, -a kufuata mtindo.
chicanery *n* 1 ulaghai wa kisheria, hila, werevu, udanganyifu; hoja potofu.
chick *n* kifaranga (cha kuku), kinda (la ndege); *(sl)* msichana, kijana.
chicken *n* 1 kifaranga *don't count your ~s before they are hatched* usinunue mbeleko na mwana hajazaliwa. 2 *(fig)* **(also spring ~)** msichana mzuri. **she is no ~** amezeeka, si kijana. 3 *(used mainly by children)* joga. **~ hearted/livered** joga. **~ out of** acha kufanya kwa sababu ya woga. 4 nyama ya kuku. **~ feed** *n* chakula cha kuku; *(fig)* kitu kisicho na thamani. **~pox** *n* tetekuwanga. **~ -run** *n* uga wa kuku.
chicle *n* ubani.
chide *vt* **~ sb (for)** karipia, kemea.
chief *adj* -kuu, -enye cheo cha juu kabisa. **C~ Justice** Jaji Mkuu; -a kwanza (kwa umaarufu). **the ~ idea** wazo kuu. **~ly** *adv* hasa, aghalabu. *n* 1 mkuu wa kundi; idara au shirika n.k. 2 mtemi, kiongozi, chifu. Commander -in- C~ Kamanda Mkuu, Amiri Jeshi. **C~ of Staff** Mnadhimu Mkuu. **in ~ /~ly** hasa, aghalabu. **~tain** *n* mtawala wa jadi, mtemi. **~taincy** *n* utemi.
chiffon *n* shifoni.
chiffonier *n* almari, saraka.
chignon *n* julfa/shungi la kisogoni.
chigoe/chigger *n see jigger*
chilblain *n* uvimbe unaotokana na baridi kali (hasa mikononi na miguuni). **~ed** *adj.*
child *n* 1 mtoto, kijana. **~'s -play** *n* *(fig)* kazi rahisi *be with ~ (arch)* -wa mjamzito *have a ~* zaa, jifungua. **~ welfare** usitawi wa watoto. **~-bearing. ~ birth** *n* kuzaa, kujifungua. **~ hood** *n* utoto. second ~hood ukongwe. **~ish** *adj* -a kitoto; -puzi, jinga. **~ishness** *n* utoto, upuuzi, upumbavu, ujinga. **~less** *adj* bila mtoto, gumba, tasa. **~like** *adj* -a kama mtoto -nyofu, tiifu, -sikivu. 2 *(follower)* mfuasi. 3 zao.
chile, chili *see chilli.*
chiliad *n* elfu; miaka elfu moja.
chill *n* mzizimo *take the ~ off sth* pasha moto kidogo. 2 homa ya baridi. 3 *(fig)* fadhaa, kuvunjika moyo *cast a chill over* vunja moyo, poozesha *adj* 1 -a mzizimo *a ~ breeze* upepo wa baridi. 2 sio -a kirafiki *a ~ welcome* makaribisho yasomlahaka *vt, vi* 1 tia baridi, zizimisha. 2 *(depress)* vunja moyo, fadhaisha. 3 zizima, geuka kuwa baridi. *~y adj* 1 -a mzizimo. 2 *(of person)* -baridi, asiye rahisi kufanya naye urafiki.
chilli *n* (*also chilly, chile, chili*) pilipili, pilipili hoho.
chime[1] *n* 1 *(usu pl)* sauti za seti ya kengele. 2 sauti ya kengele *vt,vi* 1 lia; liza kengele, piga kengele; tambulisha saa kwa kugonga. 2 **~ in** ingilia mazungumzo (kwa kukubali) au kuunga mkono *~ in with* patana na, lingana na.
chime[2] *n (of cask etc.)* ukingo uliojitokeza.
chimera *n* 1 *(myth)* kimaira: mnyama katika hadithi mwenye kichwa cha simba, mwili wa mbuzi na mkia wa nyoka, atokaye moto kinywani. 2 zimwi. 3 wazo/ndoto yoyote ya ajabu sana. **chimerical** *adj* -a kubuniwa tu.
chimney *n* 1 dohani. **~-sweep** msafisha dohani. 2 *(of lamp)* yai, chemli; *(mountaineering)* mwanya.
chimpanzee/chimp *n* sokwe.
chin *n* kidevu *keep one's ~ up (colloq)* piga moyo konde *~-wag n (colloq)* mazungumzo; soga; umbea.
china *n* 1 kauri. **~ closet** kabati la vyombo. **~ware** vyombo vya udongo. **~-clay** *n* udongo laini mweupe wa mfinyanzi, wa kauri. 2 vyombo (vikombe, sahani, mabakuli) vya kauri.
chine *n* 1 uti wa mgongo (wa

mnyama). 2 sarara.
chink[1] *n* tundu, upenyu/ufa mwembamba, mwanya (wa ukuta).
chink[2] *n* mlio (kama wa fedha, glasi n.k. zikigongana) *vt,vi* toa mlio (wa fedha, glasi n.k. kwa kuzigonganisha).
chintz *n* kaliko: kitambaa cha pamba kilichotiwa rangi (agh. hutumika kwa mapazia na kufunikia samani).
chip *vt,vi* 1 ~ **(off/from)** bambua, bambuka, banja. 2 kata vibanzi, chonga. 3 ~ **away** banduka, meguka. 4 ~ **in** ingilia kati (mazungumzo); changa, toa mchango *n* 1 kibanzi. ~ **board** ubao wa vibanzi. 2 kokoto. **a ~ of the old block** mwana anayemshabihi sana baba yake. **have a ~ on one's shoulder** -wa -kali kutokana na kuogopa/kujiona kudharauliwa/kudhalilishwa. 3 *(gambling)* kibao. **when the ~s are down** mambo yakiiva, mambo yakiwa magumu sana 4. *(usu pl)* chipsi *fish and ~s* chipsi na samaki. 5 *(electr)* kisilikoni. 6 kindu, upapi. ~**ping** *(usu pl)* kokoto, vibanzi.
chiromancy *n* utabiri (wa kuangalia kiganja/kitanga cha mkono, kupiga ramli (kwa kiganja).
chiropody *n* utabibu wa vitengele vya mguu. **chiropodist** *n* tabibu wa vitengele vya mguu. **cartographer**
chiropractor *n* tabibu maungo: mtaalam wa kurekebisha maungo.
chirp/chirrup *n* mlio mwembamba (wa ndege au mdudu) *vi* 1 lia kama ndege au mdudu. 2 ongea kwa uchangamfu. ~**y/chirrapy** *adj* -changamfu, -a furaha. ~**ily** *adv*. ~**iness** *n*.
chisel *n* patasi; juba *vt* 1 kata, chimba, umba (kwa patasi). 2 *(sl)* danganya, laghai, ghilibu. ~**ler** *n* mdanganyifu, tapeli.
chit[1] *n (sl)* 1 kitoto. 2 kisichana.
chit[2] *n* cheti, kinoti, barua ndogo.
chitchat *n* porojo, soga,mazungumzo, maongezi.
chitterlings *n* utumbo wa nguruwe n.k. unaopikwa.
chivalry *n* 1 uungwana, adabu,uadilifu. 2 *(arch)* mila, desturi (za waungwana wa Enzi za Kati). **chivalrous** *adj*.
chive *n* kitunguu jani.
chivy/chivvy *vt* fuatafuata; sumbua, kera.
chloride *n* kloridi ~ *of lime* shabu (hutumika kusafishia maji na kuua vijidudu).
chlorinate *vt* tia klorini (hasa kwenye maji). **chlorination** *n*. **chlorine** *n (chem)* klorini.
chloroform *n* klorofomu; nusu kaputi. *vt* tia nusukaputi.
chlorophyll *n* klorofili: kemikali ya rangi ya kijani ipatikanayo katika mimea.
chock *vi* kaza kwa kabari; *(boat)* zuia kwa kipande cha ubao. ~ **up** kaza kwa kabari/jaza pomoni *n* kigingi, kipande, kabari ya kukuzia. ~**-a-block full (of)** *adj* -a kujaa kabisa, pomoni.
chocolate *n* chokoleti *adj* 1 -a chokoleti. 2 *(colour)* kahawia *hot ~* kinywaji moto cha chokoleti.
choice *n* 1 chaguo, uchaguzi *my ~* chaguo langu. **Hobson's ~** chaguo lisilo chaguo (kwa sababu hakuna hiari nyingine). 3 haki au uwezo wa kuchagua *adj* 1 -zuri, bora- -teule, -liochaguliwa kwa uangalifu. 2 *(of language)* -a matusi. ~**ness** *n*.
choir 1 kwaya. 2 eneo la wanakwaya kanisani. ~**-boy, chorister** mwanakwaya. ~**master** kiongozi wa kwaya. **choral** *adj* -a kuimba au waimbaji ~ *service* ibada ya kuimba. **choral(e)** *n* 1 wimbo rahisi wa kanisani unaoimbwa na kwaya pamoja na waumini. 2 kiitikio, mkarara. 3 kwaya.
choke *vt,vi* 1 kaba/songa roho, zuia pumzi, tia kabali. 2 kabwa, paliwa *a voice ~ed with sobs* sauti ya kwikwi. 3 ~ **(up)(fill up)** zibwa, jaa kabisa *the pipe is ~d up with rubbish* bomba limezibwa na takataka. 4 ~ **back** zuia, ficha (hasira, masikitiko n.k. kwa shida). 5 ~ **down** meza haraka au kwa shida. 6 ~ **off** *(fig)*

epua; kemea, karipia *n* 1 kukabwa, kupaliwa. 2 *(of vehicle)* choki. ~-damp *n* gesi ya kaboni (migodini).
choker *n* 1 kola iliyosimama. 2 ushanga wa skafu ya kubana shingo.
choky *n (sl)* jela, korokoro.
choler *n* (*arch, lit.*) hasira. **~ic** *adj*.
cholera *n* kipindupindu, waba.
choose *vt,vi* 1 chagua, hitari, pambanua *pick and ~* chagua.2 amua (baina ya kitu kimoja na kingine). 3 taka, hiari, kusudia *whether he ~s or not* akitaka asitake. **choos(e)y** *adj* angalifu katika kuchagua, gumu kupendeza.
chop[1] *vt,vi* 1 kata, katakata. 2 *(of wood)* chanja, changa, tema (kuni) *~ping block* gogo la kuchanjia kuni. 3 *(strike)* piga (kuelekea chini). 4 ~ **away/off** kata; katilia mbali. 5 ~ *down* chengua. 6 ~ **out** toa ~ *out part of the play* toa sehemu ya tamthilia. 7 ~ **up** katakata,kata vipandevipande. 8 *(of wind)* badili mwelekeo ghafla. ~ **and change** badili kila mara (mipango, mawazo n.k.). ~ **logic** bishabisha (juu ya vitu vidogo) *n* 1 pigo la kukata. 2 kipande cha nyama chenye mfupa wa mbavu. 3 pigo (la mkono). 4 kishindo cha maji yakirushwa. **choppy** *adj (of the sea)* -a mawimbi mawimbi *(of wind)* -nayobadilika- badilika. **chopper** *n* 1 shoka. 2 *(sl)*helikopta. 3 *(pl)* meno: ~ **house**hoteli/mkahawa(hasaunaopika nyama). **be for/get the** ~ fukuzwa
chop[2] *n* muhuri; rajamu.
chopchop *adv* chapuchapu.
chopper *n* (in India) paa, kipaa, kisusi.
chop-sticks *n pl* vijiti (wanavyotumia Wachina kwa kulia chakula).
chop-suey *n* chopsue (chakula cha kichina cha nyama ya kukaanga kwa wali na vitunguu).
chord[1] *n* 1 utari. 2 upote. 3 mtambuko (mstari unaounga nukta mbili za kivimbe). 4 *(anat.)* ukano, mshipi, ugwe.
chord[2] *n (mus)* kordi: noti za msingi zinazoafikiana zikipigwa kwa wakati mmoja au pamoja. **touch the right** ~ gusa hisia. **strike a** ~ kumbusha.
chore *n* 1 kazi ya kuchosha. 2 kazi ndogo ndogo za kila siku.
choreography *n* koregrafia: elimu ya miondoko ya dansi/ngoma jukwaani **choreographer** *n*.
chortle *vi* chekelea *n* kuchekelea.
chorus *n* 1 kiitikio, kibwagizo, mkarara, kipokeo. 2 kwaya. 3 mlio/ sauti za umati wa watu/watu wengi pamoja. **in** ~ wote kwa pamoja *a ~ of approval* mlio wa kukubali/kuitikia. 3 *(drama)* wazumi. 4 kikundi cha waimbaji na wachezaji katika tamthilia/filamu *vi* imba/sema kwa pamoja. ~-**girl** *n* msichana (wa kikundi) aimbaye na kucheza katika tamthilia/filamu/maonyesho.
chow *n (sl)* chakula.
chowder *n (US)* mchuzi wa samaki au chaza na mboga.
chrism *n (rel)* krisma: mafuta matakatifu ya ibada nyingine za Kikristo.
Christ *n (rel)* Kristo **Jesus** ~ Yesu Kristo ~ *Child* Mtoto Yesu. **Christian** *n* mkristo *adj* -a kikristo *~ian name* jina la ubatizo *~ian era* enzi ya ukristo (tangu kuzaliwa kwa Kristo), zama za ukristo. **~anity** *n* ukristo. **C~ endom** *n* wakristo, mataifa ya Kikristo. **~en** vt 1 batiza. 2 -pa jina la kubatiza. **~ening** *n*. **C~ mas** *n* (*also Xmas*). C~mas day Noeli, Krismasi: siku ya kuzaliwa kwa Yesu, tarehe 25 Desemba *a merry/happy C~mas* heri/salam za Krismasi *Father C~mas* Baba Krismasi: mtu ambaye anaaminiwa hutoa zawadi kwa watoto wakati wa Krismasi. **~mas box** zawadi ya Krismasi (itolewayo kwa watu ambao wamehudumia mwaka mzima k.m. wazoa takataka. **~mas carol** wimbo wa Krismasi. **~mas eve** mkesha wa Krismasi. **~mas tree** mkrismasi, mvinje.
chrome *n* kromu: chumvichumvi inayotumiwa kutoa rangi ya manjano. ~ **steel** aloi ya chuma cha

pua na kromiamu. **chromatic** *adj* -a rangi, enye rangi nyingi.

chromium *n (chem)* kromiamu.

chromosome *n (biol)* kromosomu: nyuzinyuzi katika kiini cha seli zenyejeni; uwezo wa/ programu ya kurithisha tabia na maumbile.

chronic *adj* 1 -a kudumu, -a kuendelea siku nyingi, -a donda ndugu, -a kuselelea (kama ugonjwa au mazoea) ~ *invalid* mgonjwa wa siku zote. 2 *(sl)* kali mno. **~ally** *adv*.

chronicle *n* tarihi, wendo *vt* andika (tarihi).

chronology *n* 1 wendo, utaratibu wa kupanga miaka na matukio. 2 elimu wendo. **chronological** *adj* -a wendo ~ *age* umri makuzi.

chronometer *n* kipimawakati, kronometa, saa.

chrysalis *n* buu.

chubby *adj* nenenene, tipwatipwa, -liojaa.

chuck *n* 1 kofi la mahaba. 2 mtupo; kuacha kazi. **give sb the ~** fukuza *vt* 1 tupa ~ *me the ball* nitupie mpira. 2 **~ under the chin** papasa/piga kimchezo/mahaba chini ya kidevu. 3 ~ *away* tupa. 4 ~ **in/up** acha. ~ **up ones job** acha kazi ~ *it (in,* Acha! 5 ~ **out** fukuza. **~er out** *n* mbabe *n* 1 kufukuzwa kazi *he got the ~* alifukuzwa kazi. 2 kofi la mahaba (chini ya kidevu).

chuckle *n* kicheko cha chinichini *vi* jichekea, chekelea. **~-head** *n (sl)* mpumbavu, bwege.

chug *vi* titima.

chum *n* 1 rafiki.2 *(US)* mwenzi katika chumba *vi* 1 ~ **up with** jenga urafiki na; suhubiana. 2 kaa chumba kimoja na. **chummy** *adj* kirafiki, kama rafiki.

chump *n* 1 kigogo. 2 pande la nyama ~ *chop* pande la nyama ya paja la kondoo. 3 *(sl)* mpumbavu, mjinga. **silly** ~ mpumbavu. 4 *(sl)* kichwa. **off one's ~** wazimu.

chunk *n* 1 kipande kinene (cha kitu chochote, k.m. cha mkate, jibini n.k.). **~y** *adj*.

church *n* 1 kanisa. ~ **register** rekodi za uzazi, harusi, na vifo katika parokia. ~ yard sehemu ya makaburi katika eneo la kanisa. 2 ibada katika kanisa. ~ **goer** mwenda kanisani mara kwa mara. 3 jamii ya makasisi *go into the ~* -wa kasisi, ingia ukasisi. 4 **the C~ Christ** Wakristo wote, kundi zima la wakristo. **the C~ of England** kanisa la Anglikana. ~ **service** ibada ya kanisa.

churl *n* 1 mtu asiye na adabu, mshenzi; mtu wa hasira. 2 (*arch*) mtu wa tabaka la chini (hasa mkulima). **~ish** *adj*. **~ishness** *n*.

churn *n* 1 chombo cha kusukia maziwa, tungu. 2 gudulia kubwa la maziwa *vt,vi* 1 ~ **up** tengeneza siagi kwa kusuka maziwa. 2 vurugavuruga (kama upepo unavyovuruga bahari). 3 charuka, vurugika. 4 ~ **out** tengeneza/toa kwa wingi bila ubora.

chute *n* 1 njia ya kuteremshia magogo, makaa n.k. 2 poromoko la maji. 3 *(colloq abbr. of parachute)* mwavuli.

chutnee, chutney *n* achari.

cicada *n* nyenje.

cicatrice/cicatrix *n* kovu.

cicerone *n* gambera, kiongozi (wa kuonyesha na kuelezea sehemu za kuvutia/kitalii).

cider *n* sida: kinywaji/pombe ya matufaha. **~press** kikamua tufaha.

cigar *n* biri. **~ette** *n* sigara, sigareti. ~ **holder** *n* kishika sigara. ~ **lighter** kiberiti cha sigara.

cilia n *pl* (*anat)* kope (*bot bio)* vijisinga, vinywele vya jani. **~ry** *adj* *~ry muscles* visuli lensi.

cinch *n* 1 (*of horse*) mkanda wa tandiko. 2 *(sl)* jambo la uhakika/ yakini *vt* hakikishia.

cinchona *n* (*bot*) mkwinini: jamii ya miti ambayo magome yake hutumika kutengenezea dawa kama kwinini n.k.

cincture *n* (*arch.lit*) mshipi, ukanda *vt* zungusha ukanda/ mshipi.

cinder *n* 1 kipande cha mkaa/kuni ambacho kimeungua kiasi. 2 kipande

cha lava. 3 mabaki baada ya kutoa chuma chenye matapo. 4 (*pl*) majivu. ~ -track *(athletics)* uwanja wa kukimbia (uliotengenezwa na majivu).
cinderella *n* 1 kisonoko. 2 (*metaph.*) mtu au kitu ambacho uzuri/uwezo wake haujatambulika.
cine *pref* (*used for cinema in compounds*) ~ **camera** *n* kamera senema.
cinema *n* 1 jumba la kuonyeshea filamu. 2 filamu, sinema. **~tograph** *n* chombo cha kupigia picha za sinema. **~tography** *n* elimu/sanaa ya upigaji picha za sinema.
cinnamon *n* mdalasini *adj* -a kahawia isiyoiva.
cipher, cypher *n* 1 tarakimu 0, sifuri. 2 tarakimu ya kiarabu (yoyote toka 1 hadi 9). 3 (*secret writing*) maandishi ya kimafumbo ~ *key* kifumbuzi. 4 *(fig)* mtu/kitu duni, yahe, hohehahe *vt, vi* (*colloq*) 1 jumlisha, fanya hesabu, gawa. 2 andika maandishi ya kimafumbo.
circa *adv, prep* (*lat.*) mnamo (mwaka fulani). ~ **1500** mnamo mwaka 1500.
circle *n* 1 duara; mviringo (kama wa sahani), kitu mfano wa duara; familia moja *have black ~s under the eye* kunjana kwa ngozi za macho na kuwa nyeusi zaidi achokapo mtu. 2 (ring) pete, taji. 3 mfululizo kamili *come full ~* malizia, rudia mahali pa kuanzia. 4 jamii ya watu wenye mawazo /kazi zinazofanana *he was praised in academic ~s* alisifiwa na jamii ya wanataaluma. **in business~s** miongoni mwa wafanyabiashara *vi* zungusha, zunguka, enda mwendo wa duara. **~t** *n* 1 kiduara. 2 kitaji. **circular** *adj* kiduara, -a duara, -a mviringo. **circular saw** msumeno gurudumu *n* waraka, ilani (kwa wote wanaohusika). **circularize** *vt* peleka kwa watu wengi.
circuit *n* 1 duru, mzunguko, njia ya kuzunguka *you have to make a wide ~* inakupasa uzunguke mbali. 2 ziara: safari ya kutembelea eneo maalumu (k.v. jaji anayetembelea mahakama na walio chini yake). 3 (*electricity*) mzunguko umeme, saketi *a short ~* mkato wa mzunguko wa umeme. 4 kundi la sinema, chini ya utawala/ kampuni moja *vt* zungusha *vi* zunguka. **circuitous** *adj* -a kuzunguka zunguka. **~ously** *adv*.
circulate *vt,vi* 1 zunguka *blood circulates in the body* damu inazunguka mwilini. 2 *(spread)* enea; eneza, vumisha *the news ~d rapidly* habari zilienea haraka *circulating library* maktaba (ya kuazimisha vitabu). **circulation** *n* 1 mzunguko (agh wa damu). 2 uenezaji, usambazaji. 3 jumla ya magazeti yanayouzwa kila toleo. **circulatory system** *n* mfumo wa mzunguko wa damu.
circumcise *vt* tahiri, tia jando, tia kumbi. **circumcision** *n* 1 tohara. **circumcision rites** jando, kumbi.
circumference *n* mzingo, kivimbe.
circumlocution **n** maneno ya kuzungusha, maneno mengi.
circumnavigate *vt* zunguka kwa meli ~ *the globe* zunguka dunia kwa meli. **circumnavigation** *n*.
circumscribe vt 1 zungushia mstari. 2 wekea mipaka; zuia. **circumscription** n 1 kuweka/wekewa mipaka. 2 (*coins*) mwandiko (unaozungukia sarafu).
circumspect *adj* 1 -enye hadhari, -a kuangalia kila upande, -angalifu. **~ion** *n* uangalifu, hadhari. **~ly** *adv*.
circumstance *n* (*usu pl*) 1 hali, hali ya mambo *the ~s do not permit it* hali hairuhusu. **under good ~ you can see the island** hali (ya hewa) ikiwa nzuri unaweza kuona kisiwa. **in/ under the ~s** kwa hali ilivyo *under no ~s* kamwe, kwa hali yoyote ile. 2 mazingira *you must know the ~s of the crime* huna budi kufahamu mazingira ya jinai. 3 jambo *you have overlooked one ~* umesahau jambo moja. **circumstantial** *adj* 1. (*of description*) -enye kueleza habari

zote. 2 ~ *evidence* ushahidi usio kizibiti. **~ly** *adv*.

circumvent *vt* 1 (*formal*) zuia (mpango) usitekelezwe. 2 epuka (tatizo, sheria) kwa ujanja, ghilibu. **~ion** *n*.

circus *n* 1 sarakasi. 2 kiwanja mfano wa duara cha kuonyeshea michezo. 3 wachezaji wazungukao mjini kuonyesha michezo yao; tamasha. 4 makutano: sehemu ambapo barabara nyingi hukutana.

cirrus *n (Meteorol)* mavundevunde; mawingu mepesi mepesi ya juu sana.

cissy *n adj see* **sissy**.

cistern *n* tangi la maji (k.m.juu ya choo au nyumba).

citadel *n* ngome (ya kulinda mji). 2 *(fig)* mahali pa usalama, mahali pa kukimbilia (wakati wa hatari).

cite *vt* 1 dondoa kama mfano (kutoka kitabuni n.k.) ili kuthibitisha hoja. 2 (*US*) taja (mtu) kwa ujasiri wake vitani. 3 (*leg*) ita shaurini (mahakamani). **citation** *n* 1 dondoo. 2 mtajo. 3 hati inayoambatana na tamko la tuzo. 4 *(US)* tamko katika kutaja kumbukumbu rasmi (k.m. ushujaa katika vita).

citizen *n* 1 raia; mwananchi born ~ raia wa kuzaliwa *naturalized* ~ raia wa kuandikishwa. **~ of the world** mlimwengu: mtu afurahiaye popote atakapoishi. **~ship** *n* 1 uraia. 2 mambo yampasayo raia bora. **~ry** kundi zima la wananchi/raia.

citrus *n adj* mti wa jamii ya mchungwa, mlimau, mdimu, n.k.

citric *adj* sitriki. **citric acid** asidi sitriki: asidi itokanayo na matunda ya jamii michungwa, milimau n.k., mbalungi; balungi.

citron *n,adj* -a mti wa jamii ya michungwa, milimao n.k.

city *n* 1 jiji, mji mkubwa. 2 mji uliopewa haki maalum za kujitawala ~ *centre* katikati ya mji. ~ **fathers** madiwani wa jiji. ~ **slicker** jambazi au mhuni (aghalabu wa jijini). 3 raia wa jiji.

civet *n* 1 ~ *cat* ngawa. 2 fungo.

civic *adj* 1 -a kiraia, -a uraia. 2 -a jiji; -a kuhusu mji au wakaao mjini ~ *centre* mahali palipo na ofisi za jiji na majengo ya serikali. **~s** *n* uraia: elimu ya utawala wa mji kazi na haki za raia.

civil *adj* 1 -enye kuhusu raia. ~ **servant** mtumishi wa serikali. **the ~ service** utumishi wa serikali. ~ **marriages** ndoa za kiserikali. ~ **rights** haki za raia (kisiasa, kisheria, kijamii). ~ **war** vita vya wenyewe kwa wenyewe. 2 -a madai. ~ **case** kesi ya madai. ~ **Defence Corps** ulinzi wa raia (dhidi ya shambulio la adui hasa kutoka angani). ~ **defence corp** mgambo. ~ **disobedience** uasi, uvunjaji sheria. 3 -a kuhusu ujenzi. ~ **engineer** mhandisi ujenzi (barabara, daraja, n.k.). **civilly** *adv* kwa adabu, kwa unyofu, kwa unyenyekevu. **civility** unyenyekevu, adabu heshima, uungwana. **civilian** *n* raia (asiye askari) *adj in ~ian clothes* -enye kuvaa nguo za kiraia.

civilization *n* ustaarabu; hali bora ya kuishi *the ~ of Egypt* ustaarabu wa Misri. **civilize** *vt* staarabisha.

civies/civies *n pl (sl)* nguo za kiraia *adj* **in ~** -liovaa nguo za kiraia.

clack *vi* fanya kishindo; alika *n* 1 kishindo. 2 mwaliko.

clad *old pp. of clothe adj poorly ~* -liojiambika maguo, -lovalishwa, -lofunikwa.

claim *vt* 1 dai, taka haki. 2 *(assert oneself)* nena kwa dhati (ili kuthibitisha ukweli); taja. 3 stahili, hitaji *n* 1 dai, madai ~ *of right* madai ya haki *statement of ~* maelezo ya madai *a ~ for damages* madai ya gharama *lay ~ to sth* dai ujira au ushuru *a legal ~ to sth* daawa. 3 kilichodaiwa. 4 machimbo/miliki ya mtu. **~ant** *n* mdai.

clairvoyance *n* ubashiri. **clairvoyant** mbashiri.

clam *n* 1 chaza; *(sl)* mnyamavu. ~ **bake** (*US*) mandari ya ufukoni ambapo chaza na vyakula vingine huokwa; tafrija; mkutano wa siasa *vt*1 chimba chaza, enda kutafuta chwago. 2 ~ **up** *(colloq)* nyamaza (ghafla), kataa kuongea.

clamber *vi* panda, kwea kwa shida (hasa kwa kutumia mikono na miguu), paramia, sombea *n* mpando, mparamio, usombeaji.

clammy *adj* 1 -a kunata *a face ~ with sweat* uso unaonata jasho. 2 -a unyevu, -a baridi na -enye kunata, ~ *hands* mikono baridi. **clammily** *adv*.

clamour *n* makelele, ghasia, (hasa ya watu wanaolalamika kwa hasira au wanaodai haki) *vi*, *vt* fanya makelele/ghasia. ~ **for** piga kelele kwa ajili ya kitu fulani *the troops were ~ing to go home* majeshi yakipiga makelele kutaka kwenda nyumbani. ~ **against sth** pinga jambo kwa kupiga kelele. **clamorous**. *adj* -a makelele, -a ghasia.

clamp[1] *n* klempu, kibanio; (*naut.*) kipingo *vt* bana, kaza, funga kwa gango. ~ **down (on)** *(colloq)* bana, tia shinikizo (ili kuzuia kitu); -wa mkali. ~ **down** *n* kubanwa.

clan *n* 1 ukoo, uzawa; mbari; jamii ya watu wa mlango mmoja. **~ish** *adj (derog)* -a kupenda ukoo, -a kulindana kiukoo; -a kukaa kiukoo. **~s man** *n* mtu wa ukoo. **~ishness** n.

clandestine *adj* (*formal*) -a siri, -a kificho. **a ~ marriage** *n* ndoa ya siri. **~ly** *adv*.

clang *vi,vt* fanya sauti kubwa (k.m. vyuma vikigongana) *he ~ed the bell* alipiga kengele *n* sauti kubwa (ya kengele, tarumbeta au ndege). **~er** *n (sl)* **drop a ~er** sema kitu cha aibisha; kashifu. **clangour** *n* sauti kubwa ya mfululizo. **~rous** *adj*.

clap[1] *vt, vi* 1 piga makofi (kwa kushangilia) ~ *one's hands* piga makofi (ya shangwe) ~ *in prison* tia mtu jela ~ *duty on goods* toza ushuru. ~ **eyes on sb** *(colloq)* ona. 3 pigapiga kwa kiganja kuonyesha upendo.**~per** *n* 1 mtu/kitu kifanyacho mlio/sauti ya mpasuko (k.v. ulimi wa kengele). 2 mtu ashangiliaye. 3 ulimi wa mtu anayesema sana *n* 1 sauti ya mpasuko kama wa radi. 2 kofi.

clap[2] *n* (*sl*) kisonono.

claptrap *n*. (*colloq*) maneno matupu, mapuo (hasa ya kujipendekeza ili kuwavuta watu).

claque *n* 1 washangiliaji wa kukodishwa. 2 kundi la watu wanaowarairai watu wengine kwa ajili ya manufaa yao. 3 upuuzi, jambo lisilo na maana.

claret *n* 1 bordo (namna ya divai nyekundu). 2 (*sl*) damu. **tap sb's ~** toa damu ya pua kwa kumpiga mtu konde. 3 rangi nyekundu; ngeu.

clarify *vt* 1 eleza wazi, bainisha. 2 safisha, safika; chuja. **clarification** *n*. **clarity** *n* uwazi, ubayana.

clarinet/clarionet *n* (*mus*) zumari. **clarinetist** *n* mpiga zumari.

clarion *n* 1 panda, parapanda, baragumu *(attrib)* -a sauti kuu na -lio wazi; *(fig)* ~ *call* wito ulio wazi.

clarionet *see* **clarinet.**

clash *n* 1 mgongano. 2 mapigano, makinzano, mabishano, mapambano *vt,vi* 1 gonganisha, pambanisha gongana, pambana; ingiliana. **the two weddings ~ed** harusi hizo mbili ziliingiliana. 2 *(oppose)* ~ *with* kinzana (na), umana (na) *colours that* ~ rangi zisizooana.

clasp *n* 1 kifaa (chenye sehemu mbili) cha kufungia au kushikia vitu pamoja (k.m. kifungo, bizimu). 2 kipande cha madini ya fedha, n.k. kwenye medali chenye jina la vita (kwa askari) au kampeni inayofanywa. 3 kushika kwa nguvu (kwa vidole au mikono). 4 kupeana mkono. 5 mkumbatio *vt* 1 funga (k.m. kwa kifungo au bizimu). 2 *(embrace)* kumbatia. 3 kamata, shika. 4 fumbata ~ *hands* shikana/ peana mikono ~ *knife n* kisu cha kukunja.

class *n* 1 (*social*) tabaka *working* ~ tabaka la wafanyakazi. ~ **consciousness** hisia za kitabaka.

~ **struggle** mapambano ya kitabaka, harakati za kitabaka. 2 (*of travel*) daraja. 3 (*of school*) darasa (la watu wafundishwao pamoja). **~room** darasa. **~mate** mwanafunzi mwenza. 4 jamii ya vitu vya namna moja *more in a ~* (*of its own*) -a pekee. 5 (*milit*) marika. 6 *(gram)* ngeli *vt* **~fy** 1 tabakisha. 2 ainisha. **~fied** adj 1 -loanishwa. **~ified ad** tangazo dogo (katika gazeti la biashara). 2 -a siri *~ified information* habari za siri. **~ification** *n* 1 upambanuzi; uainishaji. 2 mpango wa aina mbalimbali; mgawanyo wa aina mbalimbali. **~ism** *n* 1 urasimi. 2 fani, kauli bora; usomi wa fasihi (sanaa) iliyothaminiwa kuwa bora. **~y** *adj* (*colloq)* -a mitindo, -a tabaka/daraja la juu. **~ess** *adj* -siyo na tabaka.

classic *n* 1 sanaa au kazi ya kiwango cha juu sana (inayotambuliwa na kutumiwa kama mfano bora). 2 fasihi, historia na falsafa ya Wayunani na Warumi. **the C~s** maandishi/maandiko bora (hasa ya Wayunani na Warumi wa zamani) *adj* 1 -lio bora kabisa; -lio maarufu sana. 2 (*of style in costume, etc.)* -a jadi, -a kimapokeo. 3 -siopambwa sana; -sionakshiwa. **~ist** *n.* **classical** 1 *adj* -a kuhusu utamaduni na elimu ya Wayunani na Warumi wa zamani. **a ~al scholar** mwanazuoni wa elimu na lugha. 2 (*music)* muziki dhati.

clatter *n* 1 sauti ya vitu vinavyogongana. 2 makelele, maongezi yenye makelele *vt vi* fanya makelele, gonganisha ~ *down* anguka kwa kishindo, teremka kwa kishindo.

clause *n* (*gram*) kishazi. 2 (*leg*) sharti; mlango, sura moja katika mapatano au sheria, ibara *attestation~* ibara ya ushuhuda.

claustrophobia *n* 1 (*med*) klaustrofobia: woga aupatao mtu awapo shimoni/pangoni. 2 chumba kidogo; mahali (popote) palipofinywa/palipobanwa.

clavicle *n* mtulinga.

claw *n* 1 kucha (la mnyama au ndege). 2 (*of crab, lobster etc.*) gando/koleo. 3 *vt, vi* 1 papura; piga makucha. 2 shika kwa kucha au kwa vidole. ~ **away (off)** (*of ship*) acha bandari. ~ **at/back** *(colloq)* pata kitu tena kwa jitihada. ~ **hammer** *n* nyundo/koleo.

clay *n* 1 udongo wa mfinyazi. 2 *(arch)* mwili wa mwanadamu; maiti *we are but ~* sisi ni udongo tu *~-cold adj* -a baridi sana (hasa kwa maiti). **~ed** *adj* -enye/-lofunikwa na/; -a udongo wa mfinyanzi.

clean *adj* 1 safi, -eupe. 2 -sio na waa, -sio na hatia *have ~ hands* wa bila kosa wala hatia. 3 -enye udhu, tohara. **make a ~ breast of sth** ungama. 4 mpya, -sotumika bado *start a ~ slate* anza upya 5 -enye kupendeza. ~ **-limbed** *adj* -a maungo mazuri. 6 stahifu *have a ~ tongue* -wa na lugha stahifu. 7 kamilifu kabisa. 8 *(of tree)* bila mafundo. 9 aminifu. 10 stadi *a ~ boxer* mwanamasumbwi stadi. 11 -enye kufaa kwa chakula *un ~ animals* wanyama wasioruhusiwa na dini kuliwa (k.m. nguruwe) *adv* kabisa, pia *we forgot you were coming* tulisahau kabisa kuwa unakuja *come ~* jitakasa kabisa ~ *cut adj* -lotengenezwa vizuri *~living adj* bikira *~shaven adj* lonyolewa vizuri. ~ **through** katikati, kote *vt,vi* 1 safisha, takasa; osha. 2 fua. 3 *(sl)* **be ~ed out** filisiwa. **~out** *adj* 1 safisha. 2 chukua fedha zote (kwa kushinda au kuiba). **~up** safisha sana *(fig) ~up the city* safisha mji (kwa kuondoa wahalifu). **cleaner** *n* mnadhifishaji. **take sn to the ~er's** filisi. **dry ~er** *n* dobi ~ *fingers (fig)* -siopokea wala kutoa hongo. **cleanly** *adj* nadhifu *adv* kwa unadhifu. **~liness** *n.*

cleanse *vt* 1 safisha sana; eua. **~r** *n* kifaa cha kusafishia.

clear *adj* 1 -eupe, angavu. 2 dhahiri, wazi *make ~* eleza wazi; dhihirisha, funua. **~cut** dhahiri kabisa ~

headed/sighted -enye kuelewa haraka *a ~ case* jambo la wazi, dhahiri. 3 bila kizuizi wala shida; bila shaka. **it's ~ sailing** hakuna taabu yoyote *the coast is ~* hakuna hatari yoyote. 4 bila hitilafu, bila hatia/lawama, bila mgogoro. 5 kamili *three ~ days* siku tatu kamili *~ voice* sauti wazi (isikikayo vizuri *~ speaker* msemaji asikikaye vizuri. *~* **about/on** -enye hakika. **in the ~** -siotuhumiwa *adv* 1 kwa wazi, kwa dhahiri. 2 kabisa *the prisoner got ~ away* mfungwa alitoroka kabisa. 3 ~ **(of)** pasipo, bila, mbali na *vi,vt* 1 safisha, takasa, safika, takata, ondolea (vizuizi, shida, mashaka, hatia). 2 epuka, jihadhari. **keep ~ of sth** jitenga. 3 weka wazi. ~ **the way!** acha njia (iwe) wazi *~ the ground for negotiations* ondoa vikwazo ili kurahisisha mazungumzo. 4 *(of liquids etc.)* chuja. 5 fyeka *~ the bush* fyeka magugu/gugu. 6 kiuka, pita juu ya au kando ya bila kugusa kitu. 7 pata faida ya **we ~ ed** shs 50,000 tumepata faida ya sh. 50,000. 8 (tax etc.) lipa *he ~ed his debts* alilipa madeni yake. 9 ~ **away** ondoa *~ away the plates* ondoa sahani; (*of mist*) tanzuka *the clouds have ~ed away* mawingu yametanzuka ~ *(sth) off* ondoa, maliza (ote); uza rahisi; potelea mbali; (*fig*) penya, puruka. ~ **out** kumba, ondoka, ondoa. **~(sth) up** tengeneza, panga vizuri *(of weather)* takata; fumbua, tatua *they ~ed their problems* walitatua matatizo yao; safisha. **clearly** *adv* kwa dhahiri *he is not ~ly intelligent* ni dhahiri kwamba hana akili. 10 *(pass over)* pitisha *(for cargo, ship)* maliza taratibu za kuondoa (mizigo, meli) bandarini. 11 pata idhini (ya kuingia bandarini, kutua uwanjani). **~nce** *n* 1 kusafisha, kuondoa (vizuizi, shida n.k.). **~ance sale** seli ya kumaliza vitu. 2 ruhusa *~ance certificate* hati ya ruhusa (ya kuondoa mizigo). 3 nafasi (iliyoachwa baina ya vitu viwili). 4 *(mil)* kibali cha kujiuzulu jeshini, kibali cha kusoma nyaraka za siri. **~ing** *n* 1 mahali peupe (pasipo miti katika mwitu); palipofyekwa, chenge, tendo la kusafisha. **~ing house** ofisi ya kubadilishia hundi za benki.

cleat *n* 1 (*naut*) makari *anchor~* mangili. 2 njumu: msumari unaojitokeza kwenye kiatu cha mwanariadha.

cleave *vt* 1 pasua, kata, (vipande viwili), tenga kwa nguvu, chana chana. 2 (*penetrate*) penya *~ ones way through the crowd* penya katikati ya watu *cloven hoof* kwato yenye pande mbili (k.v. ng'ombe mbuzi etc); (*fig*) kwato ya shetani. **cleavage** *n* 1 mpasuo; mpasuko. 2 mfarakano, mgawanyo. 3 *(colloq)* nafasi katikati ya matiti *vi (arch)* nata, shikamana na, ganda *~ to one's opinion* shikilia mawazo (yake). **~r** *n* shoka au kisu kikubwa agh. cha kukatia nyama.

clef *n (music)* kitambulisho (cha mistari ya noti).

cleft[1] *n* ufa, mwanya.

cleft[2] *see cleave ~ palate* kaakaa lililopasuka *in a ~ stick* katika hali ya kutokuwa na njia, katika hali ya kutokuwa na tamaa.

clemency *n* 1 huruma, upole. 2 (of atmosphere *etc)* hali nzuri; joto kidogo; hali mwanana. **clement** *adj* -anana, -pole, -enye huruma, -ema.

clench *vt* 1 kaza msumari kwa kuukunja na kuugandamiza. 2 funga sana, shika sana, kaza sana (k.m. meno, ngumi), fumba sana (mikono)

clergy *n (collective) n* 1 mapadri, wachungaji, makasisi wa kanisa. **~man/cleric** *n* mhudumu wa kanisa, padri; kasisi *~ in holy orders,* padri.

clerical *adj* -a kuhusu mapadri, wachungaji na makasisi *n* mbunge, mfuasi (mjumbe) wa chama cha dini.

clerihew *n* (*liter*) kipande cha ubeti chenye mzaha.

clerk *n* 1 karani **clerical** -a kuhusu makarani *a clerical error* kosa la maandishi, kosa katika kunakili (kufuatisha) *town* ~ katibu wa mji *chief* ~ karani mkuu ~ *of the works* msimamizi wa majengo ~ *to the cabinet* karani wa baraza la mawaziri. 2 (*US*) (*of shop*) mwuzaji.

clever *adj* 1 stadi, mahiri, -juzi *be ~ with one's hands* wa hodari kwa kazi ya mikono *a ~ workman* fundi, stadi, waria. 2 -enye akili, hodari *be ~ at sth* wa hodari kwa jambo fulani ~ *dick* mtu anayetambia akili yake. 3 janja. **~ness** *n*.

clew (*US clue*) *n* 1 bonge la uzi. 2 (*naut*) kitanzi *vt,vi* 1 (*of ball of e.g. thread*) zonga zonga, kunjakunja. 2 (*naut*) ~ *up* kunja tanga, maliza kazi; pambana na kazi.

cliche *n* mchuuko, istiari iliyochakaa.

click[1] *n* 1 mwaliko sauti: sauti ya kualika kama vile kidole, mtambo wa bunduki, n.k. 2 kidoko. 3 (*of horse*) mwaliko wa kwato (wa miguu ya mbele na nyuma inapokutana) *vt* alisha, liza kidoko, piga kidoko ~*one's tongue* piga kidoko ~ *one's heels* gonganisha visigino (vya miguu).

click[2] *vi* (*sl*) 1 eleweka *the point suddenly ~ed up* wazo lilieleweka. 2 elewana mara moja.

client *n* mteja ~ **ele** wateja.

cliff *n* jabali, mteremko wa ghafula agh. wa mwamba (wa mlima au mahali palipochongoka), genge, (hasa ukingoni mwa bahari) ~ *-hanger* tukio la taharuki sana. **~y** *adj*.

climacteric *n (med)* mabadiliko muhimu katika maisha ya mwanadamu (kati ya miaka 45 na 60).

climate *n* 1 tabia ya nchi (yaani joto, baridi, upepo, mvua n.k.); hali ya mambo ilivyo *political*~ hali ya siasa ilivyo. **climatic** *adj*. **climatology** *n* taaluma ya hali ya nchi. **climatologist** *n*.

climax *n* upeo, kilele *vt,vi* fikia/fika/fikisha kilele(ni). **climactic** *adj* -a juu kabisa, -a upeo, a kileleni.

climb *vi,vt* 1 (*slope upwards*) kwea, panda. 2 (*of plants*) tambaa. **~ing plant** mmea mtambazi. ~ **up** 1 paramia, panda, sombera. ~ **down** shuka; kubali kosa. 2 paraga *n* 1 upandaji, uinukaji. 2 ukwezi; *(fig)* -ja kwa matao ya chini (kiri kosa) *~ing irons* pingu za mkwezi. **~er** *n* mkwezi; mtu anayejiendeleza; mmea unaotambaa.

clime *n* (*poet*) tabia ya nchi.

clinch *vt* 1 *see clench*. 2 kaza msumari kwa kuugongomea. 3 *(of boxers)* shikana, kamilisha ~ *a deal/an agreement* fikia/kamilisha mapatano. 4 (*colloq*) kumbatiana *n* mshikamano, mkazo. **clincher** *n* jambo/neno mkata.

cling *vi* ~ **to/together** shikilia, ng'ang'ania, gandama, ambatana. ~**y** *adj*.

clinic *n* 1 kliniki. 2 hospitali maalumu. 3 mahali pa ushauri (wa kiganga) au matibabu. **~al** *adj* 1 -a hospitali, -a kuhusu mafundisho ya utibabu (uganga) yanayotolewa katika hospitali. **~al thermometer** kipima joto. 2 adilifu.

clink[1] *n* sauti ya mgongano wa kauri au glasi *vt,vi* fanya/ fanyiza sauti ya mgongano wa kauri au glasi.

clink[2] *n* 1 (*sl*) gereza, jela *be in* ~ -wa gerezani *go to* ~ nenda jela.

clinker[1] *n* mabaki ya mkaa.

clinker[2] *n* (*sl*) kosa kubwa.

clip[1] *vt* shikiza, bana, funga weka pamoja kwa kibao (n.k.) *n* kishikizo, kibano.

clip[2] *vt* 1 kata (kwa makasi), dira, punguza, fupisha ~ *a hedge* (*or the wool from a sheep's back*) dira, (kata) uga wa mimea, manyoya mgongoni mwa kondoo). 2 ~ *sb's wings* fanyia mtu inda asifikie lengo lake. 3 (*of ticket*) toboa. 4 (*colloq*) piga vizuri, ruka au fupisha sauti mwishoni mwa neno *n* 1 kukata; mkato. 2 (*for hair*) kudira. 3 (*of sheep*) kunyoa. 4 pigo. 5 (*colloq*) mwendo wa kasi. **clipping** *n* makala iliyokatwa kutoka gazetini. ~per *n* 1 (*of person*) mkataji manyoya. 2 (*pair of*) **clippers** mkasi. 3 merikebu iendayo kasi sana (kwa matanga) .

clique *n* genge: kikundi cha watu wenye mawazo yanayofanana. **cliquish** *adj*.

clitoris *n* kinembe, kisimi.

cloak *n* 1 joho. 2 kifuniko; pazia; kitu kinachoficha sababu/mawazo ya ukweli *vt* ficha; setiri, valisha; funika. **~and dagger** -a kuhusu upelelezi, -wa siri. **~-room** *n* 1 chumba cha kuwekea makoti, mizigo n.k. 2 (euphem) choo.

clobber[1] *n* (*GB sl*) mavazi na vifaa.

clobber[2] *vt* 1 *(sl)* twanga, umiza vibaya. 2 shinda vibaya.

clock[1] *n* 1 saa (kubwa ya mezani, ukutani, au mnarani) *put the ~ back* rudisha nyuma; rudia mambo ya zamani. *(arch)* **against the ~** kabla ya saa iliyopangwa. *(sl)* **sleep/work around the ~** lala/fanya kazi saa 24 *vt,vi* 1 pima muda unaotumiwa kwa jambo. 2 (*GB sl*) piga. 3 **~ in (out)** ripoti, jiandikisha saa ya kufika (kutoka) kazini. **~ up** fikia. **~wise** *adv* kwa mzunguko wa akrabu, kisaa *turn the handle ~wise* zungusha mkono upande wa kulia. **anti ~wise** kinyume saa. **~work** *n* mtambo wa saa, chombo cha aina hiyo *like ~work with ~ work* kwa taratibu, kwa mpango uliowekwa, bila tatizo lolote. **~ watching** *n* tabia ya kungoja saa ya kufunga kazi ifike.

clock[2] *n* kipambo kinacho fumwa kwenye soksi.

clod *n* 1 bonge, donge (hasa la udongo). 2 (*colloq*) mjinga, mshamba. **~hopper** mtu mzito wa mwili, mshamba. **~hoppers** (*colloq*) viatu vizito kama vya mkulima. **~dish** *adj*.

clog[1] *n* 1 kizuizi, kizibo *vt* ziba (agh. kwa uchafu), zuia, zibika, zuilika.

clog[2] *n* 1 mtalawanda, kiatu cha gongo (kiatu chenye soli ya mti). 2 kibao kinachofungwa miguuni mwa mnyama ili asizurure; (*fig*) kizuizi *vt* 1 ziba (bomba nk.). 2 zuia. **~gy** *adj*

cloister *n* 1 makazi ya watawa. utawani. 2 ujia (mrefu, mwembamba) wenye matao, (agh. wa nyumba ya watawa) *vt* 1 weka/ishi kwenye nyumba ya watawa. 2 (*fig*) **live a ~ed life** ishi maisha ya kutengwa kama watawa.

clone *n* (*bio*) aina ya kiumbe kilichoumbwa na kiumbe kimoja bila kujamiiana.

close[1] 1 *adj* (*arch*) karibu *~ to the house* karibu na nyumba. **a ~ call/thing/shave** kuponea chupuchupu. **~ up** picha ya karibu *~ friends* marafiki sana. 2 -liopangwa karibu karibu; -liosongana. **~ weave** mfumo wa karibu. 3 kali *in ~ confinement* chini ya ulinzi mkali *keep a ~ watch* chunga vikali. 4 -a makini *make a ~ inspection* kagua kwa makini. 5 -a siri; -a faragha: -liofichwa *she is very ~ about her life* ni msiri sana kuhusu maisha yake. 6 **~fisted** bahili, -nyimifu, -choyo. 7 (*sports games*) karibiana sana *it was a ~game* walikaribiana sana (katika mashindano). 8 (*weather*)-enye jasho na joto; -inayobana; zito sana; inayokaza *the sweater is a ~ fit* sweta inabana *~friend* mwandani, -a kusafiana nia. 10 (*phonetics*) (*of vowels*) -a juu. **~d** funge (*season*) **~ season** wakati ambapo uwindaji ni marufuku (ili wanyama wazae) *adv* karibu karibu sana. **~ at hand** hapa hapa, **~ by/to** karibu na; **~ upon** karibia. **~ up to** karibiana na. **~ness** *n*. **~ly** *adv* kwa makini, karibukaribu sana.

close[2] *n* 1 uwanja, uga (wa kanisa/shule). 2 njia iliyofungwa *break ~* kumwingilia mtu katika ardhi yake. **~ cropped** *adj* (*hair, grass*) fupi sana. **~ together** karibu karibu *adv* **sail ~ to the wind** karibia kuvunja sheria/ mila/miiko. **~hauled** *adj* -lioenda joshi.

close[3] *vt,vi* funga *~ the doors* funga milango; (*fig*) -fa. **~ed book** fumbo, jambo lisiloeleweka, uchawi; jambo lililokwisha. **~ accounts** funga hesabu. 2 ~ *one's eyes* funga, fumba macho, -totia maanani, jifanya huoni ~ a debate maliza mjadala. ~ **down** funga (duka n.k.). ~ **up** sogeza/ ziba kabisa. 3 fungika, fumbika, jifunga *the theatre ~es on Monday* thieta hufungwa kila Jumatatu. 4 songa, kubali. ~ **with (agree)** kubali, patana, -wa karibu; (*of war*) ~ *with the enemy* anza kupigana. ~ **with the land** karibia pwani. **~d circuit** -a nyaya maalum. **~d shop;** wanachama (tu); (*of a shop etc*) fungwa. ~ **in** -wa fupi *the days are closing in* siku zinakuwa fupi (of radio) maliza matangazo. ~ **in/on/~ upon** zingira na shambulia *the enemy ~ upon us* adui alituzingira na kutushambulia *n* mwisho, hitimisho *at the ~ of the day* jioni *at the ~ of this century* mwisho wa karne hii *draw/bring sth to a ~* maliza.

closed *adj* (*of society, system*) -liojitenga, -liotengwa kwa shughuli maalum; -a siri. ~ **session** mkutano wa siri, wa faragha .

closet *n* 1 chumba cha faragha. 2 (*US*) chumba cha kuhifadhia vitu; kabati. 3 (*arch*) *water ~* choo, msala *vt ~ oneself* jitenga; jifungia. **be ~ed with sb (together)** kutana faraghani (kwa shauri, kwa kusoma n.k.) *adj* -a siri *come out of the ~* tangaza kwamba ni msenge/msagaji/basha.

closure *n* 1 ufungaji. 2 (*Parl*) uamuzi (wa kufunga kwa kura). **move the ~** toa hoja ya kumaliza mkutano (kwa kupiga kura) funga mkutano.

clot *n* 1 donge (la damu). 2 (*sl*) jinga, pumbavu *vi* ganda *the blood is ~ted* damu imeganda.

cloth *n* 1 nguo, kitambaa cha namna yoyote; (*woollen*) sufu; (*linen*) kitani, bafta; (*calico*) marekani, ulaiti, gamti; (*black*) kaniki; baibui; (*of gold*) zari; (*loin-cloth*) shuka, kikoi, kitambi, (*table cloth*) kitambaa cha meza *turban ~* kilemba. 2 (*naut*) tanga, gamti, maradufu. 3 (*rel*) *a man of the ~* kasisi. **~es** *n* 1 mavazi, libasi, nguo *in plain ~es* katika nguo za kiraia *put on* (*take off*) *one's ~es* vaa/vua. 2 (*bed-clothes*) nguo za kitandani. **~es -basket** *n* tenga la kuwekea nguo za kufua. **~es -horse** *n* ubao wa kuanikia nguo. ~ **es-line** *n* kamba ya kuanikia nguo. **~es -man** *n* mchuuzi wa mitumba/nguo kuukuu. ~ **es-moth** *n* nondo mla nguo. **~es -peg** *n* kibanio. ~ **es-prop** *n* (*also* **~es-post)** mwegamo (wa kamba ya kuanikia nguo). **~ier** *n* (*arch*) mchuuza nguo au vitambaa. **~ing** nguo, mavazi, libasi *articles of ~ing* mavazi. **the ~ing trade** biashara ya nguo.

clothe *vt* 1 vika, visha. ~ **oneself** vaa, jivisha. 2 (*fig*) fumba, eleza ~ *in a sweet language* fumba/eleza kwa lugha tamu.

cloture (US) *closure.*

cloud *n* 1 wingu; mavundevunde. ~ **bank** mawingu mazito yaliyo chinichini. **~-burst** tufani ya mvua. **~capped** -lofunikwa na mawingu. 2 (*of mass of things moving together*) kundi. ~ **of bees** kundi la nyuki. 3 (*of smoke, dust, sand*) ghubari. 4 jambo linalotia hofu, wasiwasi, tishio: n.k. *the ~ of hunger* tishio la njaa. 5 utusitusi ulio kwenye uoevu au kioo. **have one's head in the ~s** (*fig*) wa ndotoni, -wa mbali kimawazo. 6 fifisha *age has ~ed his memory* umri umefifisha kumbukumbu yake *vt* 1 tia kivuli (giza), ficha mwangaza *it has ~ed over* kumetanda. ~ **up (over)** tanda, funika (na mawingu) *~ed her eyes* machozi yalimlengalenga. 2 (aggrieve) kanganya, vunga, huzunisha. 3 (*defame*) aibisha, tweza, pata huzuni. **~y** *adj*. **~less** *adj*. **~iness** *n*.

clout *n* (*arch*) 1 (*colloq*) pigo (hasa la mkono). 2 kitambaa, hasa cha kusugulia au kusafishia. 3 (*of shoe*) njumu. 4 (*US sl*) uwezo wa kushawishi /kutenda hasa kisiasa *vt* 1 (*colloq*) piga. 2 pigilia njumu ya kiatu.

clove[1] *n* **garlic** ~ kidole cha kitunguu saumu.
clove[2] *n* 1 mkarafuu. 2 karafuu,
clover *n* (*bot*) klova: jamii ya mimea yenye majani ya pande tatu (hupendwa sana na ng'ombe, mbuzi n.k). **live in** ~ kaa katika hali ya neema.
clown *n* 1 chale, damisi/ mcheshi. 2 mpumbavu. 3 mtovu wa adabu *vi* chekesha.
cloy *vt* kinaisha, kifu. ~ **the appetite** toa hamu ya kula.
club *n* 1 rungu. ~ **footed** -enye miguu iliyopindika. 2 (*in cards*) pau, mavi ya mbuzi. 3 chama, shirika la watu (kwa michezo n.k.), klabu *vt* 1 piga kwa rungu. 2 ungana, shirikiana. ~ **together** shirikiana. ~**bable** - kunjufu; **in the** ~ mjamzito.
cluck *n* 1 kidoko. 2 mlio (wa kuku anayeita vifaranga vyake) *vi* 1 piga kidoko. 2 lia, fanya mlio kama kuku.
clue *n* 1 alama, dalili, dokezo, ishara (ya kuonyesha njia, maana n.k.) *give sb a* ~ dokeza, ashiria *be without a* ~ wa gizani (kutokuwa na habari). ~**in/up** (*sl*) arifu. ~**less** jinga.
clump *n* 1 kichaka. 2 bonge (la udongo). 3 fungu. 4 soli (nene), kishindo *vt, vi* 1 tembea kwa kishindo. 2 panda pamoja.
clumsy *adj* 1 (*of person*) -zito, -si stadi, si -elekevu. 2 -a ovyo, -jinga, goigoi. clumsily *adv*. **clumsiness** *n*.
clung *pt, pp of* **cling.**
clunk *vi n* (fanya) sauti ya mgongano wa metali nzito.
cluster *n* 1 kishada. 2 (*of people, things etc*) fungu, kundi *vi* kusanyika, zunguka. ~ **together/round** zunguka, kusanya, konga.
clutch[1] *vt* ~ **(at)** 1 kamata imara, fumbata, shika. 2 ~ **at** jaribu kukamata *a drowning man will ~at any straw* mfa maji haachi kutapa *n* 1 kukamata, mfumbato. 2 kłachi.
clutch[2] *n* jumla ya mayai yanayoatamiwa; idadi ya makinda yaliyototolewa.
clutter *n* mparaganyo, vurugu, mkusanyiko wa ovyo wa vitu *vt* ~ **up** panga ovyoovyo, paraganya, vuruga. ~ **up the paths** zagaa njiani.
co- *pref* 1 mshiriki katika kazi, mwenzi ~ *editor* mhariri mshiriki ~*wife* mke mwenza. 2 pamoja na, -a mchanganyiko wa vitu viwili ~*education* shule ya mchanganyiko ~*adjutor n* 1 mshirika katika kazi; msaidizi, mwenzi. 2 (*rel*) msaidizi wa askofu ~*axial adj* -enye mhimili wa pamoja.
coach *n* 1 matwana farasi. **drive a** ~ **and horses through sth** kwamisha jambo kwa kufichua upungufu wake, onyesha kasoro zake. 2 behewa la abiria. 3 (motor~) basi (liendalo safari ndefu). 4 kocha, mwalimu wa michezo. 5 (*US*) daraja la pili (katika vyombo vya usafiri) *vt* zoeza, fundisha kwa undani (hasa kwa kuandaa).
coagulate *vt* gandisha *vi* ganda, tungamana. **coagulant** dutu inayogandisha kioevu. **coagulation** *n*.
coal *n* makaa ya mawe. **live ~s** makaa ya moto. **dead ~s** makaa baridi. **carry ~s to Newcastle** rudisha tende Manga. **haul sb over the ~s** kemea, karipia. **heap ~s of fire on sb** lipa mema kwa maovu *vi,vt* pakia makaa melini. ~ **field** bondemakaa, machimbo ya makaa (mahali penye machimbo ya makaa). ~ **gas** gesi ya makaa. (*arch*) ~**ing station** (*for ships*) stesheni ya makaa. ~ - **mine/pit** mgodi wa makaa. ~ **scuttle** ndoo ya makaa. ~ **face** kiambaza cha makaa. ~ **tar** lami.
coalesce *vi* ungana, changanyika. ~**nce** *n*.
coalition *n* muungano, mseto ~ *government* serikali ya mseto.
coaming *n* kizibalango: ukingo ulioinuka kuzuia maji yasiingie melini.
coarse *adj* 1 (*rough*)-a kukwaruza; (nguo) isiyo laini. 2 (*inferior*) duni, hafifu. 3 (*rude*) -shenzi, bila adabu -sio na adabu; ~ *language* lugha ya

matusi. 4 -enye chengachenga. **~n** *vi* kwaruza; potosha. **~ness** *n*.

coast *n* 1 pwani; mwambao, ufuko. 2 *(US)* mtelemko (ambapo unaweza kushuka kwa kuteleza *the ~ is clear* hamna hatari *vi* ~ **(along)** 1 pita pwani pwani kwa, ambaa pwani, sairi. 2 (*of cars, bicycles etc*) telemka mlima bila kutumia nishati. ~ **guards** *adj* walinzi wa pwani. **~-line** ukanda wa pwani. **~-wise** *adj* & *adv* (a) pwani pwani. **~er** *n* 1 chombo cha mwambao. 2 chombo cha kuteleza kisicho na magurudumu. 3 kikalio cha glasi/sahani/sinia(kuzuia meza isipate unyevu/maji). 4 mkeka mdogo wa kuwekea glasi.

coat *n* 1 koti ~ *hanger* kitundika nguo, kitundika koti. **turn one's ~** badili msimamo/chama n.k; jiunga na adui au kundi jingine. **you must cut your ~ according to your cloth** fanya jambo kulingana na uwezo wako. **trail one's ~ (-tails)** zusha ugomvi. **on someone's ~ tails** *(US)* kwa msaada wa mwingine. 2 kitu chochote kinachofunika (k.m. manyoya/sufu/nywele n.k.). 3 mpako *give something a ~ of paint* paka rangi *vt* 1 funika. 2 paka (kwa rangi). ~ **tail** sehemu ya chini ya koti iliyo pana. **~ing** *n* 1 mkono. 2 kitambaa cha kutengenezea koti. **~tee** *n* kikoti.

coax *vt* bemba, bembeleza, rairai, shawishi; (*of fire*) vuvia ~ *sb into doing sth* bembeleza mtu afanye jambo fulani ~ *sth out of sb* pata kitu kwa kumbembeleza mtu. **~er** *n*. **~ing** *n*. **~ingly** *adv*.

cob *n* 1 (*corn*) bunzi, guguta. 2 farasi mfupi mnene. 3 kotwe dume.

cobalt *n* kobalti: aina ya chuma ~ *blue* rangi ya nili iliyoiva.

cobble[1] *n* (*also ~stone*) (jiwe) mango *vt* tandaza mawe chini (wakati wa kujenga barabara).

cobble[2] *vt* shona (hasa viatu vilivyoharibika), tia kiraka. 2 weka ovyo ovyo. **~r** *n* 1 mshona viatu. 2 mlipuaji. 3 kinywaji baridi cha divai, sukari na malimau. 4 aina ya pai ya matunda.

cobra *n* swila, firi.

cobweb *n* utando wa buibui.

coca *n* (bot) 1 koka: mojawapo ya magugu yapatikanayo Amerika ya Kusini yenye majani yanayofanana na majani ya chai. 2 majani yaliyokaushwa ya mikoka.

cocaine *n* kokeini: aina ya dawa ya kulevya.

coccyx *n* (*anat*) kifandugu, kitokono.

cochineal *n* kochinili: rangi nyekundu inayotokana na kochinili jike.

cochlea *n* (*anat*) komboli: sehemu iliyoko ndani kabisa ya sikio ambayo inafanana na kitu kama springi ambamo mawimbi ya sauti hufasiriwa kuwa fahamu).

cock[1] *n* 1 jogoo, jimbi; kikwarakucha. ~ **and bull story** hadithi ya kipuuzi isiyo ya kuaminika. ~ **-a doodle -doo** kokoriko, mlio wa jogoo. ~ **-a hoop** *adj* -a kufurahi sana, -enye kujigamba *adv* kwa kujigamba. ~ **crow** *n* alfajiri. **~-fight** *n* mashindano ya kuchi. **live like fighting ~s** -ishi kama lodi. ~ **of the walk (often derog)** kiongozi, mtu anayetawala/ kandamiza wengine. **~erel** *n* kijogoo, pora. 2 ndege dume. 3 *(of water tap)* bilula, chombo/ vali ya kufungulia na kufunga k.v. maji n.k. 4 (*of gun*) kibiri. **position of ~** iliyopangwa tayari kufyatuliwa. **go off at half ~** anza (sherehe/ mipango) kabla matayarisho hayajawa sawa. 5 (*vulg sl*) mboo. **~up** simamisha. ~ **up one's ears** tega masikio. **~ed to one side** iliyokaa, -simama. 6 ~ **up** (*sl*) haribu, chafua, udhi *they completely ~ed up our plans* waliharibu mipango yetu *vi* (*colloq*) tambatamba; injika risasi. ~ **up** weka upande (kofia/ kichwa). **~ed** *adj*. **~-eyed** *adj* 1 (*sl*) -enye makengeza, -a upogo. 2 (*sl*) -pumbavu, puzi. **~y** *adj* -enye majivuno, -enye kiburi -enye sodai, -a kujiamini mno.

cock[2] *n* rundo (la majani makavu; samadi n.k.) *vt* rundika.

cockade *n* 1 kishada cha kasha la kofia. **cockatoo** *n* 1 kasuku kishungi. 2 (*Aust. & NZ colloq*) mkulima mdogo. **cockchafer** *n* tutu.

cock-horse *n* kinyago cha farasi wa kuchezea watoto.

cockle *n* 1 (*Phr.*) **~s of the heart** hisia za moyo. **warm the ~s of one's heart** pendeza sana. 2 mashua, boti ya bapa. 3 *(of shell fish)* kamba, kaa, chaza.

cockney 1 mkukni: mtu wa London (hasa sehemu ya mashariki). 2 lafudhi ya kikukni.

cockpit *n* 1 (*of aeroplane*) dungu, chumba cha rubani; (*fig*) eneo ambapo vita vimewahi kupigwa mara nyingi. 2 kiwanja cha kupiganishia kuchi.

cockroach *n* mende, kombamwiko.

cockscomb/coxcomb *n* 1 undu, kilemba, upanga wa jogoo. 2 mmea kishungi (mmea wenye vishada vya maua ya njano na mekundu). 3 chepeo ya mchekeshaji.

cocksparrow *n* shoredume (*fig*) mgomvi, kijana mgomvi; mwenye kujiona.

cock-sure *adj* 1 hakika kabisa. 2 -juvi tena -enye majivuno; -enye kujiamini sana.

cocktail *n* 1 kokteli: kileo kikali cha mchanganyiko wa divai n.k. 2 mchanganyiko wa maji ya matunda. 3 mseto wa saladi na matunda.

coco *n (also* **~ palm, ~nut palm**) mnazi. **(~nut)** nazi. **green ~nut** dafu, koroma ~ *leaf* kuti; *(for thatch)* makuti ya mbale, makuti ya viungo; *(for screen, enclosure)* makuti ya kumba, makuti mazimi *fibre,* ~ *coir* makumbi *(cleaned fibre)* usumba ~ *shell* kifuu ~ *oil* mafuta ya nazi *shoot* ~ kitale ~ *grate* chicha, ~ *milk* tui *which accounts for the milk in the* ~ *nut (joc)* sasa yote imeelezwa.

cocoa *n* kakao. ~ **bean** kokwa za kakao. ~ **nib** kotiledoni ya kakao.

cocoon *n* kifukofuko.

cod[1] *n (also* **~-fish**) chewa. **~-liver oil** mafuta ya chewa. **~ling** *n* chewa mdogo.

cod[2] *vt, vi (arch. colloq)* fanyia mzaha, cheza shere.

coddle *vt* 1 ivisha taratibu (kwa joto lisilo kali sana). 2 engaenga, tendekeza, dekeza, endekeza.

code *n* 1 mkusanyiko wa sheria zilizopangwa kwa mfumo maalum. **penal ~** kanuni ya adhabu. 2 mfumo wa kanuni na taratibu zilizokubaliwa na jamii/ tabaka /kikundi cha watu. 3 ishara (mfumo wa alama zinazotumiwa katika maandishi ya siri au yaliyofupishwa; alama ya siri. **break a ~** gundua jinsi ya kufumbua siri *vt (also* **en~**) andika kwa kutumia alama za maandiko ya siri; simba.

codify *vt* panga kanuni, weka katika mpango ulio wazi. **codification** *n.*

codeine *n* kodeini: kitulizaji kitengenezwacho kutokana na kasumba.

codex *n* kodeksi: kitabu cha miswada ya kale.

codger *n (colloq)* mzee wa vituko; jamaa.

codicil *n* kiambatisho cha wasia (kinachofafanua zaidi au kutangua sehemu ya wasia huo).

codling *n* tofaa la kupikwa.

coefficient *n* 1 kizigeu wiano kati ya vipimo viwili. 2 *(maths)* kizidishi.

coequal *adj,n* sawasawa (hasa kwa umri, cheo, uwezo n.k.).

coerce *vt* 1 shurutisha, lazimisha, gagamiza. 2 *(often pass)* dhibiti, onea. **coercion** *n.* **coercive** *adj.*

coeval *adj* 1 -enye hirimu, rika moja. 2 -a wakati mmoja.

coexist *vi* ishi pamoja chanjari (kwa amani). **~ence** *n* .**~ent** *adj.*

coffee *n* kahawa. **~-bean** *n* buni. **~cup** *n* kikombe cha kunywea kahawa. **~-grounds** *n (pl)* machicha ya kahawa. **~-house** *n* mkahawa. **~-mill/ grinder** *n* kinu cha kusagia kahawa (buni iliyokwisha kukaangwa). ~-**pot** *n* mdela. ~-**room** mkahawa mdogo. ~-**set** *n* seti ya vyombo vya kahawa. ~-**stall** *n*. genge la kahawa. ~-**tree** *n* mbuni.

coffer *n* 1 sanduku, kasha kubwa (hasa la kuwekea fedha au vito). 2 *(pl)* mahali pa kuhifadhia dafina. **the C~s of the State** Hazina ya Serikali. 3 kibao cha nakshi,dariri. ~ **dam** *n see caisson.*

coffin *n* jeneza. *(fig)* **a nail in one's ~** kitu kinachoharakisha kufa mtu *vt* tia maiti katika sanduku.

coffle *n* mlolongo wa wanyama, watumwa n.k. waliofungwa pamoja.

cog *n* 1 jino la gurudumu (agh. gia). **be a ~in the machine** *(fig)* mtu/kitu kisichokuwa muhimu katika shirika, serikali, tasnia n.k. ~ **-wheel** *n* gurudumu meno.

cogent *adj (of arguments)* -zito na kubalifu; -a maana. **cogency** *n*.

cogitate *vi,vt* tafakari **cogitation** *n* 1 kutafakari. 2 *(pl)* mawazo, mafikara, tafakari. **cogitative** *adj*. **cogitatively** *adv*.

cognac *n* brandi (ya Kifaransa).

cognate *adj* 1 ~ **(with)** -enye asili au chanzo kimoja (k.m. viumbe, lugha). 2 inayohusiana (na) *n* 1 neno lenye uhusiano na neno jingine. 2 *(pl)* ~**s** jamaa wa damu. 3 *(gram)* ~ **object** shamirisho yenye mzizi mmoja na kitenzi (k.m. ota ndoto).

cognition *n* utambuzi, ufahamu, ujuzi. **cognitive** *adj*. tambuzi. **cognizable** *adj* -a kutambulikana. **cognizance** *n* 1 *(leg)* utambuzi, uzingatifu; kutambua. **take cognizance of** tambua, zingatia 2. haki/mamlaka ya kushughulikia jambo kisheria *fall within one's cognizance* -wa ndani ya uwezo wa ... (kushughulikia). 3 nembo. **cognizant** *adj*.

cognomen *n* 1 *(surname)* jina la ukoo. 2 jina la kupachikwa.

cohabit *vi* kaa kinyumba. ~**ation** *n*.

cohere *vi* 1 *(of parts or whole)* ambatana, shikamana, fungamana. 2 *(of arguments)* fuatana kwa taratibu, chukuana, patana. ~**nce** *n*. ~**nt** *adj* 1 -a kuambatana, -a kufungamana. 2 -a kuchukuana *(of speech)* -a wazi,-enye kueleweka. **cohesion** *n* mwambatano, mshikamano; hali ya kuendelea kushikana pamoja. **cohesive** *adj*.

cohort *n* 1 *(in ancient Roman Armides)* divisheni. 2 kundi la watu waliofungamana. 3 mwenzi, rafiki.

coiffeur *n (fr)* mtengeneza nywele.

coiffure *n (fr)* mtindo wa utengenezaji nywele; mchano wa nywele.

coign *n (US fig)* ~ **of vantage** mahali pafaapo kuonea kitu vizuri.

coil *vt,vi* zungusha, zongomeza, kunja, viringisha *n* 1 koili: sukepindi la nyaya (za umeme). 2 mzingo, mkunjo. *n* **ignition** ~ koili mwasho 3 *(of contraceptive)* koili, kidude.

coin *n* 1 sarafu. **false** ~ sarafu za bandia *the other side of the ~ (fig)* kwa upande mwingine *pay sb back in his own ~* tendea mtu kama alivyokutendea, akutendaye mtende, mche asokutenda *vt* 1 tengeneza sarafu. ~ **money** *(fig)* pata donge kubwa. 2 *(of new words)* buni, tunga *~ a new terminology* unda istilahi mpya. ~**age** *n*. ~**er** *n* mtengeneza sarafu bandia.

coincide *vi* 1 ~ **(with)** *(of two or more objects)* lingana, fanana (kwa eneo au umbo). 2 *(of events)* tukia, sawia/ wakati mmoja. 3 *(of ideas etc)* patana, oana, afikiana. ~**nce** *n* 1 ulinganifu, upatanifu, utukizi. 2 jambo litukialo kulingana na jingine (kwa nasibu au ajabu). ~**nt**. ~**ntal** *adj* -a nadra, tukizi.

coir *n* makumbi ya nazi; *(cleaned)* usumba.

coitus/coition *n* ngono, mtombo, mtombano, mlalano. ~**interruptus** azili, katiza kujamiiana, chomoa kumwaga nje.

coke[1] *n* mkaazimawe: makaa ya mawe yasiyo na gesi.

coke[2] *n* koka-kola.

coke[3] *n (sl)* kokeini.
col *n* mwegama, genge (la mlimani).
cola *n (bot)* mkola, kola.
colander *n* kung'uto; chujio.
cold[1] *adj* 1 -a baridi ~ *weather* hali ya (hewa) ya baridi. ~ **storage** chumba cha baridi. **give sb the ~ shoulder** *(fig)* -tothamini, dharau *have ~ feet* -wa na hofu ya kufanya jambo *leave one ~* -tovutwa na. **in ~ blood** kikatili. ~ **-chisel** patasi ya kukatia metali baridi. ~ **-fish** mtu asiyechangamkia watu. ~ **-snap** kipindi (kifupi) cha baridi. ~ **-sore** kidonda cha homa (mdomoni). ~ **-steel** silaha ya kukatia au kuchomea. ~ **-sweat** kijasho chembamba. ~ **-war** vita ya maneno na propaganda. ~ **-blooded** *(fig) (of persons, actions)* katili; -a damu baridi: -enye damu inayobadilika kufuatana na hali ya hewa. ~ **hearted** -sio na huruma, -siostuka; baridi. 2 *(fig)* sio -ema, hasimu; *(of sex)* -sionyegereka/ashiki. 3 *(of colours)* -a giza. **~ly** *adv*. **~ness** *n* 1 baridi *(be left) out in the ~* dharauliwa, sahauliwa kabisa. 2 mafua. **catch a ~** shikwa na mafua. 3 *(phys)* kiwango cha kuganda.
cole, slaw *n* kachumbari ya kabichi.
colic *n* mchango: msokoto wa tumbo (bila kuharisha). **~ky** *adj*.
coliseum *n* uwanja mduara.
colitis *n (med)* uvimbe wa utumbo mpana.
collaborate *vi* 1 shiriki katika kazi. 2 shirikiana kisaliti na adui. **collaboration** *n* **collaborationist** *n* mshiriki katika usaliti. **collaborator** *n* mshiriki, kibaraka.
collage *n* kolagi: picha itengenezwayo kwa kugandishwa vipande vipande vya karatasi, nguo, metali n.k.
collapse *vi,vt* 1 vunjika, anguka, poromoka, gwa. 2 zimia, zirai, poteza fahamu/ nguvu/uwezo/moyo. 3 *(apparatus)* kunjana, kunjamana. 4 kunjisha, fanya -jikunje. **collapsible** *adj* -a kukunjika *n* 1 poromoko, uangamio. 2 mzimio, kukata tamaa.
3 ~ **of the lung** mzimiko wa pafu. **~of the dollar** kuporomoka kwa (thamani) ya dola.
collar *n* 1 ukosi, kola. 2 ukanda wa shingo ya farasi/mbwa. 3 mkwiji, skafu, kashda. ~ **-stud** kifungo, kibanio. 4 kiungo cha chuma cha kuungia mabomba. 5 ~ **-bone** mtulinga *vt* 1 kamata *the police ~ed the thief* polisi alimkamata mwizi. 2 *(dated, colloq)* chukua bila ruhusa.
collate *vt* 1 linganisha, pambanisha (hasa maandiko). 2 *(arrange)* panga kwa taratibu (k.m. kurasa za vitabu tayari kutiwa jalada). 3 weka pamoja (habari). 4 *(rel)* teua, chagua (kiongozi wa dini). **collation** *n* 1 ulinganisho. 2 chakula chepesi.
collateral *adj* 1 sambamba, bega kwa bega. 2 -enye asili moja lakini wazazi mbalimbali (k.m. watoto wa ndugu wawili). 3 -a ziada, -a nyongeza. ~ **-evidence** ushahidi wa nyongeza *n* dhamana ya mkopo.
colleague *n* mwenzi, mshiriki (mmojawapo wa watu wawili au zaidi wafanyao kazi pamoja).
collect[1] *n (rel)* sala fupi ambayo inabadilika kufuatana na siku.
collect[2] *vt vi* 1 kusanya, leta pamoja, changa. 2 chukua, zoa *~-a child* chukua mtoto. 3 kusanyika, kutanika; konga. 4 ~ **oneself** jitayarisha; jikusuru. 5 hifadhi, pata nakala/sampuli (ya kitu). **~ed** *adj* tulivu, makini. **~edly**. *adv* **~ion** *n* mkutano, halaiki, mkusanyiko/ ukusanyaji. 2 mchango (wa fedha)/ sadaka. 3 *(of poems)* diwani. 4 lundo. **~tor** *n* mkusanya. ~ **of customs** mtoza ushuru/kodi. **~ive** *adj* 1 -a pamoja *n* kundi, shirika linalomilikiwa na wafanyakazi wake. **~ive leadership** uongozi wa pamoja. 2 -a umma. **~farm** shamba la umma/ujamaa. 3 *(gram)* **~noun** nomino wingi. **~ly** *adv*. **~ivism** *n* ujima: mfumo wa ujamaa ambamo nyenzo/zana kuu za uzalishaji mali humilikiwa na dola au umma. **~ize** *vt*

unganisha; jumuisha; weka chini ya mamlaka moja; fanya jamaa. **~ivization** *n* ujima, ujumuishaji.

colleen *n (Irish)* msichana.

college *n* 1 chuo cha elimu (agh sehemu ya chuo kikuu); walimu na wanafunzi wanaofanya sehemu ya Chuo Kikuu. **C~ of Agriculture** Chuo cha Kilimo. 2 baraza, chama; jamii ya watu wenye nia moja. **Sacred C ~, the C~ of Cardinals** baraza la makadinali. **collegiate** *adj*. **collegian** *n* 1 mwanachuo.

collide *vt* ~ **(with)** gongana, pambana *the ships ~ed in the fog* meli ziligongana katika ukungu. **collision** *n* mgongano, dafrao, mapambano *be in/come into ~ (with)* pingana, pambana, gongana. head-on ~ mgongano wa uso kwa uso.

collier *n* 1 mchimba makaa (ya mawe). 2 meli (ichukuayo shehena) ya makaa ya mawe. **~y** *n* mgodi wa makaa ya mawe.

colligate *vt,vi* 1 unga, unganisha, jiunga, jihusisha. 2 leta, weka pamoja (matukio au habari).

collocate *vt (with) (of words)* tangamana, tokea/enda pamoja. **collocation** *n* tangamano, utokeaji/uendaji pamoja wa maneno.

colloquial *adj (of words, phrases, style)* kimazungumzo; -a simo. **~ly** *adv*. **~ism** *n*

colloquium kongamano, semina ya wataalamu. **colloquy** *n (formal)* mazungumzo, maongezi. engage in ~ zungumza.

collude *vi (arch)* kula njama, shirikiana, saidiana (hasa katika hila au udanganyifu). **collusion** *n* njama, ushirika, mapatano (hasa katika udanganyifu); maafikiano ya siri (ya hila, ujanja). **collywobbles** *(pl) (colloq)* kuumwa tumbo; woga, wasiwasi.

colon[1] *n* utumbo mpana.

colon[2] *n* koloni, nukta pacha.

colonel *n* kanali. **~ship** *n* ukanali, cheo cha kanali.

colonnade *n* safu ya nguzo.

colony *n* 1 koloni. **colonist** *n* mlowezi, setla. 2 *(collection)* jamii/kundi la wanyama/mimea, watu wa maslahi moja *a ~ of plants/ insects* kundi la mimea/ wadudu wanaoishi pamoja. colonial *adj* -a kikoloni: *(Hist)* **Colonial Office** *(GB)* Wizara ya Makoloni. ~ **hangover** kasumba ya kikoloni *n* mkazi wa koloni. **colonialism,** *n* ukoloni. ukoloni mkongwe. **neo-** ~ ukoloni mamboleo. **colonist** *n* mkoloni. **colonize** *vt* tia ukoloni, anzisha koloni, tamalaki/twaa nchi ya wengine. **colonization** *n* ukoloni. **colonizer** *n* mkoloni, mtwaa nchi ya wengine.

color *(US) see* **colour**.

colorimeter *n* kipimarangi, kibainisha rangi.

colossal *adj* -kubwa mno; -enye nguvu kubwa. **colossus** *n* 1 sanamu kubwa mno. 2 *(giant)* jitu, pandikizi la mtu, sifa za mtu zilizozidiana.

colostrum *n* dang'a.

colour[1] *n* 1 rangi *there isn't enough ~ in the picture* picha haina rangi ya kutosha ~ *blind* kipofu rangi. ~ **blindness** *n* upofu rangi. ~ **scheme** mpangilio/ mchanganyo/mfumo wa rangi. ~ **-wash** rangi (za maji) za kupaka kuta. 2 rangi za wasanii. **powder** ~s rangi za unga. **oil** ~ rangi ya mafuta. **water** ~ rangi ya maji. 3 *(of events, descriptions)* sura, maana, maono. **give (lend) ~ to** elekea kuthibitisha jambo fulani *give false ~ing to* sema uwongo, danganya. 4 *(of facial expression)* **high** ~ uso wa kunawiri/ mwekundu. **~ful** *adj* -liosharabu rangi, changamfu, -a kupendeza. **~less** -sio na rangi/ -angavu; *a ~less person* mtu baridi, asiyechangamka. **be off** ~zingia. **change** ~ geuka rangi. 5 *(of skin)* rangi ya mtu. ~ **bar** *(line)* kalabaa: ubaguzi wa rangi. ~ **problem** tatizo la ubaguzi. 6 *(pl)* bendera, beramu *called to the ~s* -itwa jeshini nail one's ~ s to the mast amua, tangaza/ ng'an g'ania/ shikilia msimamo *sail under false ~s (fig)* -wa mnafiki *show oneself in one's true ~* bainisha tabia halisi ya mtu ilivyo *come off/pass an examination with flying ~s* fanikiwa vizuri kabisa stick to (one's) ~ kataa kabisa kuacha imani yako/shikilia imani yako. 8 **local** ~ *(lit)* maelezo ya kina/kinaganaga kuonyesha hali halisi ya mahala au wakati. ~ **ful** *adj*.

colour[2] *vt,vi* 1 paka/tia rangi, -wa mwekundu. 2 *(up)* pata rangi; *(blush)* iva uso, geuka rangi. 3 *(exaggerate)* piga chuku, tia chumvi, potosha *his hate ~ed his account* chuki yake iliathiri maelezo aliyoyatoa; *(misrepresent)* potosha, singizia. ~ **in** jaza rangi. ~**ing** *n* kitu kinachotia rangi, rangi (ya ngozi) ya uso; mtindo wa utiaji rangi wa msanii. **coloration** *n* 1 mpangilio wa rangi. 2 jumla ya imani/ misimamo n.k. ya mtu/kundi/ taifa. **colorific** *adj* 1 -a rangi nyingi. 2 -enye kutoa rangi.

colt[1] *n* 1 mwana farasi dume. 2 *(youth)* kijana mdogo asiye na uzoefu. ~**ish** *adj* 1 -a mwana farasi. 2 -enye ujuzi mdogo.

column *n* 1 nguzo, mhimili, mnara. 2 kitu chenye umbo la nguzo. **spinal** ~ uti wa mgongo. 3 safu ya chapa. 4 mpango wa vitu kwa safu safu. 5 mlolongo. **a ~ of cars/ships** mlolongo wa magari/meli. ~ **of figures** safu ya tarakimu. ~**ist** *n* mwandishi wa habari anayeshughulikia mada au makala maalum.

coma *n* 1 usingizi mzito; hali ya kuzimia. **be in a ~. go into a** ~ wa katika usingizi mzito, poteza hisia/fahamu, zirai, zimia kwa muda mrefu *adj* 1 -enye kuzimia. 2 -enye usingizi/kusinzia.

comb *n* 1 kitana; chanuo. 2 undu wa jogoo. 3 *honey* ~ sega la nyuki.
4 kichambuzi, kichaguzi (mashine inayochagua k.v. pamba). 5 kuchana *give one's hair a ~* chana nywele *vt,vi* 1 chana. ~ **one's hair** chana nywele. 2 *(for wool, cotton etc.)* chambua kwa chanuo au kichambuzi. 3 chakura, tafuta kila mahali. 4 ~**out** *(fig)* ondoa (vitu, watu wasio takiwa). 5 *(of waves)* kunjamana na inuka, vimba.

combat *vt,vi (against/with)* 1 pigana, shindana na *n* mapambano, mapigano. **single** ~ mapigano kati ya watu wawili tu. ~**ant** enye kupigana *n* mpiganaji *adj* -a kupigana, -a kushindana, -a vita. ~**ive** *adj* chokozi, -enye uchu wa kupigana. ~**iveness** *n* upiganaji, tabia ya ugomvi. ~**ively** *adv*.

combine[1] *n* 1 shirika la makampuni ya biashara. 2 ~ **harvester** kivuna nafaka (kinachovuna na kupurura sawia).

combine[2] *vt,vi* ~ **(with)** ungana; unga, unganisha; changanya, shirikisha. ~**d operations/exercises** shughuli mchangamano. **combination** *n* 1 mchanganyo; muungano; uunganishaji. 2 - mchanganyiko ushirikiano *enter into with* ungana na. 3 **room** *see* **common room** chumba (kitumi-wacho na wanafunzi na walimu shuleni/chuoni) cha kupumzikia. 3 *(pl)* ~ nguo ya ndani (inayovaliwa mwili mzima). 4 pikipiki yenye kigari ubavuni. 5 fomula, ~**lock** kufuli la kufunguliwa kwa namba.

combustion *n* mwako. **internal ~ engine** injini ya mwako wa ndani. **combustible** *adj* 1 -a kuweza kuwaka.2 *(excitable)*-a harara *n* kitu chenye mwako. **combustibility** *n* *(physics)* uunguzaji, mwako.

come *vi* 1 ~ **(to/from) (with)** jai, wasili, fika ~ *and see me* njoo tuonane ~ *this way* pita huku. 2 ~ **(into/ onto/in/on etc)** ingia. ~ **into the room** ingia/karibu chumbani. 3 ~**to sth** fikia *the number of his children ~s to thirty* idadi ya watoto wake inafikia thalathini ~ *to little/nothing* tofanikiwa, -wa kazi bure *she never came to much* hakufanikiwa. ~ **to this/ that** maanisha, wa na maana ya -wa hivyo (ilivyo). **if it ~s to that** kama mambo ndiyo hayo *(with fixed phrases)* ~ **to an agreement** afikiana. ~ **to blows (with)** anza kupigana. ~ **to a decision** amua. ~ **to an end** isha; malizika. ~ **to fruition** iva, komaa, zaa matunda. ~ **to halt/standstill** simama. ~ **to light** julikana, tangazwa ~ *to one's notice/attention* tambuliwa, fahamika ~ *to one's senses/oneself* zinduka pata fahamu; jirudi. ~ **to terms (with sb)** fanya suluhu, kubaliana, afikiana. 4 (tokea) (anza) kuwa. ~ **into flower** tokea/anza kuwa ua, chanua. ~ **into bud** chipua; ~**into contact** kutana, gusa,wasiliana. ~ **into focus** jitokeza, jiengua. ~ **into money/ a fortune /legacy etc** rithi/ pata/pesa. ~**into operation** anza kufanyakazi. ~ **into one's own** stahiki, pata heshima/sifa. ~ **into power** twaa madaraka.~ **into sight/ view** tokeza, onekana. 5 ~ **to sb (from sb)** achiwa, rithi (shwa). 6 ~ **to sb** tukia, tokea, -ja *nothing will ~to you* hutadhurika. 7 elewa/tambua/ ona hatimaye. ~ **to realize** -ja kung'amua. 8 **how ~ (that)** vipi, imekuwaje. 9 ja, jia, tokea, wa (mahala) her decision came as a surprise uamuzi wake ulitushangaza. 10 -wa, tokea kuwa, -ja kuwa *be as clever/stupid as they ~* kuwa hodari/ mpumbavu sana. 11 *(colloq)* jifanya, jitia *don't ~ the bully* usijitie ungambi/ubabe/ umwamba. 12 **to ~** baadaye *the life to ~* maisha ya baadaye. 13 *(colloq uses)* ifikapo, ijayo *she will be 15 ~ December* atakuwa na miaka 15 ifikapo Desemba. 14 *(colloq) (of sex)* mwaga/ tema/kojoa (*with adverbials and preps*) *1 ~ about* fanyika, tukia, jiri. 2 ~ **across** kuta, kutana na; ona kwa bahati; tokea (kwa) *I ~across John in the market* nilikutana na John sokoni. 3 ~ **after sb** fuatia, fukuzia, fuata kwa kukimbilia. 4 ~ **again** rudi. **please ~ again** karibu tena. 5 ~ **against** kuta, gongana; shambulia. 6 ~ **along** fanya haraka, jitahidi, endelea, fika ~ along now you know the answer jitahidi, unalijua jibu. 7 ~ **alongside** egeka, egemea. 8 ~ **apart** vunjika, katika, pasuka. 9 ~ *at sb/sth* fikia, pata, shambulia. 10 ~ **away** *(from)* achia, ondoka. 11 ~ **back** rudi, kumbuka *his name came back to me* nilikumbuka jina lake. ~ **back at** jibu, lipiza (kisasi). 12 ~ *before sb/sth* sikilizwa na, shughulikiwa na; tanguliwa na. ~ **back** *n* kurudi (tena); majibu; fidia *his case will ~ before Judge Nyalali* kesi yake itasikilizwa na Jaji Nyalali. 13 ~ *between (interfere)* ingilia kati; zuia *it is not good to ~ between a man and his wife* haifai kuingilia kati ya mume na mke. 14 ~ **by** pita; jia; pata kitu (kwa juhudi/bahati). ~ **by house** pita nyumbani kwangu. 15 ~ *down (collapse)* anguka, poromoka; *(of rain, snow etc)* nyesha, -nya; *(of prices)* shuka, teremka; *(be reduced)* pungua. ~ **down a peg** shuka cheo. ~ **down in the world** angamia, shuka cheo. ~**s /boils down to** ~ ishia; maanisha; *(of tradition)* pokewa, rithishwa. ~ **down upon** kemea, adhibu, wia mkali. ~ **down on the side of sb** unga mkono. ~ **down to earth** amini kama ilivyo, acha ndoto, tambua hali ilivyo. 16 ~ **forth** jitokeza, tokea mbele. 17 ~ **forward** karibia; jitokeza, jongea karibu, patikana. 18 ~ **from** zaliwa, chimbuka, tokea. 19 ~ **in** *(of the tide)* jaa *(become seasonable)* anza (kupendwa) *when do mangoes ~ in* maembe yanapatikana lini? *(fashionable) how does this style ~ in* mtindo huu unapendelewaje/ unapokelewaje? ~ **in handy/ useful** faa, -wa na manufaa. ~ **in for**, pata, vuta *you'll ~ in for a scolding* utakaripiwa *she's ~ in for a large amount of money* amerithi fedha nyingi. ~ **in on** shiriki, jiunga.

20 ~ **near** jongea, karibia *he came near to failing* alikaribia kushindwa. 21 ~ **of** -wa -a nasaba; tokana na; tokea *she ~s of a given family* -wa -a ukoo/ nasaba fulani *what ~ of your conversation* mazungumzo yenu yalikuwa na matokeo gani? 22 ~ **off** toka; tukia, fanyika; fanikiwa. ~ **(sth)** dondoka; kimbia, okoka, banduka. ~ **off a winner/loser** shinda/shindwa. ~ *off victorious/badly* pata ushindi/ hasara *(colloq)* ~ **off it!** acha! 23 ~ **on** fuata *you go first I'll ~ on later* tangulia nitakufuata baadaye; endelea *his child is ~ing on fine* mtoto wake anaendelea vizuri; kuta, vumbua, gundua. ~ **on!** njoo! endelea! (kwa mchezaji) anza kucheza ~ *on let's have game* njoo tucheze. 24 **~out** tokea wazi, tangaa/bainika *his book has ~ out* kitabu chake kimechapishwa *the whole affair has ~ out* jambo lote limejulikana ~ *out with a remark* sema ghafula *the workers will ~out again* wafanyakazi watagoma tena. **~out first** -wa wa kwanza ~ *out in a rash* pata vipele ~ *out at so much* afiki jumla *(of stains etc.) these ink stains won't ~ out* madoa haya hayatoki. **~out against/ for** pinga/unga mkono. 25 ~ *over (from a distance)* fika; *(change)* geuka, enda upande mwingine, badili mawazo *what has ~ over you* limekutokea jambo gani ~ *over funny/ dizzy/ faint* jisikia vibaya, taka kuzimia. 26 ~ **round** zunguka; *(visit)* zuru, tembelea; *(recover)* pata fahamu ~ *round to sb's way of thinking* badili mawazo. 27 ~ **short of** pungukiwa na; -wa na upungufu wa. 28 ~ **through** *(recover from illness)* pata nafuu, pona; pita *your posting has just ~ through* ajira yako imepitishwa. 29 ~ **to** pata fahamu ~ *to one's senses* pata fahamu baada ya kuzimia; husu *when it ~s to politics* inapohusu siasa; *(colloq)* jitambua. ~ **to grief** patwa na ajali (matata n.k.). ~ **to a head** iva. ~ **to pass** fanyika, -wa, tukia, jiri. 30 ~ *under sth* -wa chini ya. 31 ~ **up (grow)** mea, ota, kua; fikia; *(appear)* tokea, zuka, onekana ~ *up against sb* pambana, gongana, kutana *your work has not ~ up to expectations* kazi yako hairidhishi. **~up with** fikia 32. ~ **upon sb** shambulia ghafla.

comedy *n* 1 futuhi; tamthiliya kuchekesha. 2 tukio au mkasa unaochekesha *musical~* futuhi yenye muziki. **comedian** *n* chale, mtu wa mikasa/mizaha; mchekeshaji. **comedienne** *n* chale wa kike.

comely *adj (old) (arch) (usu of person)* -zuri, -enye sura, maungo ya kupendeza. **comeliness** *n.*

comer *n* mjaji, anayekuja. **all ~s** wajaji wote. **first** ~ mja awali, anayekuja kwanza. **late-~** mchelewaji.

comeuppance *n* adhabu/maafa stahilifu.

comestible *n (formal, usu pl)* chakula, kitu cha kula, kitu kinachofaa kuliwa.

comet *n* kimondo.

comfit *n (old (arch)* 1 haluwa. 2 tunda lililogandishwa kwa sukari. 3 kashata.

comfort *vt* fariji, liwaza, ondolea, majonzi *n* 1 faraja, maliwazo, jamala. **cold** ~ maliwazo yasiyoridhisha. **take** ~ *(from)* jifariji. 2 tumbuizo, burudani. 3 raha, hali njema, starehe, anasa. **creature ~s** mambo ya anasa *(US)* ~ **station**. *(US)* choo cha umma. **~able/also comfy** *adj* -a kustarehesha, -a raha *it's so ~able here* hapa pana starehesha kweli. 2 -a kufariji, kutuliza *be ~able about sb,* ridhika na. **~ably** *adv.* **be ~ably off** -wa na pesa za kutosha. **~er** *n* 1 mfariji. **the C~er** Roho Mtakatifu. 2 *(GB)* shali/ skafu/kashida ya sufu ya kuvaa shingoni. 3 *(GB)* chuchu (cha mtoto). 4 *(US)* blanketi zito.

comic *adj* 1 -a kuchekesha, -chekeshaji,-a mzaha. 2 -a futuhi *n* 1 chale (katika sanaa za maonyesho (muziki). 2 ~ **book** gazeti lenye hadithi za katuni.~**al** *adj* -a kuchekesha -a kimzaha. ~**ally** *adv*.

coming see **come** *adj* -a kuja; -naokuja; baadaye. *n* 1 majilio *the Second Coming* Majilio ya Pili ya Yesu Kristo.

comity *n* uhusiano wa kirafiki ~ *of nations* uhusiano wa kirafiki kati ya mataifa.

comma *n* mkato, koma. **inverted ~s** alama za kufungua na kufunga usemi, yaani ("....") au ('....').

command *vt* 1 amrisha, amuru. 2 *(control) (govern)* tawala ongoza; -wa na amri juu ya (watu mali n.k.). 3 *(emotions)* zuia, tawala. 4 -wa na uwezo juu ya. 5 stahili, kuwa na ~ *respect and sympathy* stahili kupewa heshima na huruma. ~ **a high price** stahili kuuzwa kwa bei ya juu. 4 *(front, overlook)* tawalia/dhibiti uwanda (kwa sababu ya kuwa juu) *the hill ~s the plains* kilima kinadhibiti uwanda *n* 1 *(order)* agizo, amri. 2 utawala, ukuu *I'm at your ~* niko chini ya amri yako ***at the word of*** ~amri inapotolewa. 3 uwezo *have a ~ of several languages* fahamu lugha kadhaa ***have ~ over oneself*** jitawala. ~ **post** kituo cha kamanda. ~**ing** *adj* 1 -kuu, -nayotawala *~ing heights of the economy* nguzo kuu za uchumi; nayostahili heshima. ~**ant** *n (mil)* mkuu (wa boma, ngome, kikosi, kambi n.k.). ~**eer** *vt* twaa (magari, nyumba) kwa matumizi ya jeshi. ~**er** *n* kamanda, mkuu wa kundi la askari au manowari, amiri jeshi. **C~er- in -Chief** *n* Amiri Jeshi Mkuu. ~**ment** *n* 1 amri ya Mungu. **the Ten C~ments** amri kumi za Mungu. 2 amri, agizo.

commando *n* komando: kundi la jeshi kwa kazi maalum.

commemorate *vt* fanya ukumbusho wa, fanya kumbukumbu ya, adhimisha sikukuu ya kukumbuka mtu (jambo fulani). **commemorative** *adj*. **commemoration** *n* ukumbusho (kwa sala, heshima, sikukuu, mchezo, karamu n.k.) **in ~ of** kwa ukumbusho wa, kwa kumbukumbu ya.

commence *vt,vi* anza, amiri, anzisha. ~**ment** *n* 1 mwanzo. 2 *(in US Universities, and at Cambridge and Dublin)* sherehe ya mahafali ya kutunuku shahada/stashahada.

commend *vt* 1 *(praise)* sifu, tukuza. 2 *(entrust)* weka amana, weka mikononi mwa. **he ~ed his soul to God** aliweka roho yake mikononi mwa Mungu. 3 ~ *me to so-and-so* nisalimie fulani. 4 ~ *oneself/itselfto* pendwa na; kubaliwa na. ~**ble** *adj* -a kustahili kusifiwa. ~**ation** *n* sifa.

commensurable *adj* -a kupimika kwa jinsi moja; -a kulingana, -a kadiri moja. **commensurate** *adj* 1 -a kipimo/kadiri iliyo sawa. 2 -a kufaa.

comment *n* neno, fasiri, wazo, maoni. **no** ~ sina neno *vt* ~ **(on/upon)** toa mawazo/maoni. ~**ary** *n* 1 sherehe. 2 tangazo mfululizo (juu ya tukio) wakati likitendeka *broadcast ~ on a football match* tangazo la mchezo wa kandanda. ~**ate** *vi* toa maoni juu ya jambo fulani. ~**ator** *n* 1 mtoa maoni. 2 mtangazaji (wa tukio).

commerce *n* 1 biashara, (hasa baina ya mataifa); ubadilishanaji na ugawaji wa bidhaa *Chamber of C~* chama cha wafanyabiashara. **Faculty of ~** Kitivo cha Biashara. **commercial** *adj* 1 -a biashara ~ *radio,* redio ya biashara (inayojigharamia kutokana na malipo yatozwayo kwa vipindi vya biashara). ~ **traveller** mchuuzi msafiri: mtu asafiriye kuonyesha vitu vya biashara na kupokea maagizo juu yake. 2 nayoweza kuleta faida. 3 -a kupenda faida tu *n* tangazo la biashara (katika vipindi vya TV au redio). **commercially** *adv*. **commercialize** *vt* geuza -a biashara ili kupata faida ~ *sports* geuza michezo iwe biashara. **commercialism** *n* commination *n* 1 tishio la kulipiziwa kisasi na Mungu (hasa kwa wafanyao dhambi). **comminatory** *adj*. .

commingle *vt,vi* changanya,

changanyika.

commiserate *vt,vi (with)* -pa mtu pole, sikitikia, hurumia. **commiseration** *n.*

commissar *n* 1 kamisaa. **Political C~** kamisaa wa siasa: afisa wa chama, Wizara, Shirika, Jeshi n.k. katika jeshi la Urusi. **commissariat** *n* 1 *(out of use)* idara ya jeshi kwa ajili ya ugawaji wa chakula. 2 ugawaji wa chakula. **commissary** *n* 1 naibu, mjumbe, wakili; kamisaa wa jeshi (anayehusika na ugawaji wa chakula). 2 duka la chakula (la jeshi, kampuni n.k.). **~ial** *adj.*

commission *n* 1 tume. **Presidential C~** Tume ya Rais. 2 utoaji mamlaka/ wajibu (kwa mtu au kundi la watu); agizo, amri. 3 *(crime)* tendo, utendaji. **~ of a crime** tendo la jinai. 4 hati ya kibali cha kupewa cheo katika jeshi. **get one's ~** pata cheo cha ofisa. 5 asilimia ya faida (anayopewa mwuza bidhaa) *sell goods on ~* uza bidhaa na kupata asilimia ya faida yake. 6 kazi (yenye ujira wake maalum) *she received the ~ to paint the President's picture* alipewa kazi ya kuchora picha ya Rais. 7 **in ~ (of ship)** -wa tayari kusafiri (yenye mabaharia na vyakula vyote vinavyohitajika). 8 **out of ~** iliyoharibika, isiyofanya kazi tena *my radio is out of ~* redio yangu imeharibika *vt* 1 teua, agiza kazi kwa malipo maalum. 2 *(mil)* pa mtu cheo cha ofisa. 3 (of warship) tayarisha kwa pigano. **~ed** *adj* -enye cheo cha ofisa. **~er** *n* 1 mwanatume. 2 mkuu, kamishna. **District ~er** Mkuu wa Wilaya. **Regional ~er** Mkuu (kamishna) wa Mkoa. 3 wakili wa serikali, mwenye kuagizwa, mwenye amri. **~ for oaths** wakili wa kuapisha. **High ~er** Balozi (katika nchi za Jumuiya ya Madola).

commissionaire *n* bawabu (wenye yunifomu maalum wa hoteli, senema n.k.).

commit *vt* 1 tenda, fanya. **~ adultery** zini. **~ a crime** fanya kosa la jinai. **~ murder** ua. **~ suicide** jiua. 2 peleka; kabidhi; tia. **~ sb for trial** peleka mahakamani ~ a child to someone's care kabidhi mtoto kwa mwingine ili amtunze. **~ to writing** tia katika maandishi. **~ to memory** jifunza kwa ghibu, hifadhi kwa moyo. **~ to the flames** unguza ~ *to the earth* zika. 3 **~ oneself** jipa sharti, ahidi *he has ~ted himself* amejipa sharti, ameahidi *without ~ting myself* bila ya kujifunga. 4 *(oneself to)* diriki, kubali wajibu. **~tal** *n* 1 upelekaji, uwekaji the ~tal of a body to the *earth* kuzika. ***~tal*** *of sb to jail* kupeleka mtu gerezani. **warrant of ~tal** hati ya kifungo. **~ted** *adj* 1 -enye msimamo. 2 -a kujitolea nafsi. **~ ment** *n* 1 sharti, ahadi *honour your* **~ments** heshimu ahadi zako. 2 wajibu. 3 moyo, msimamo. **political ~ment** msimamo wa kisiasa. 4 tendo la kupeleka (kifungoni n.k.).

committee *n* kamati. executive ~ kamati ya utendaji. **steering~** kamati ya uendeshaji *member of ~* mwanakamati.

commode *n* 1 almari. 2 kibago cha kuwekea kibakuli cha haja cha chumbani. 3 *(US)* choo.

commodious *adj* -enye nafasi (ya kutosheleza), -a kufaa, -kubwa, enevu. **~ness** *n.*

commodity *n* bidhaa, kifaa. **essential~** bidhaa muhimu.

commodore *n* kamadori: ofisa wa jeshi agh. la majini au angani mwenye cheo cha juu ya kapteni; kapteni mwandamizi wa meli za biashara.

common *adj* 1 -a pamoja,-a wote. **a ~ land** ardhi ya wote, ardhi ya umma. **~ consent** makubaliano ya pamoja/wote. **~ knowledge** habari inayojulikana na wote. **~ ground** *(fig)* hoja inayokubaliwa na wote katika majadiliano. **~ room** (*in schools, college*) chumba cha mapumziko. 2 -a kawaida. **~ soldier**

askari wa kawaida, kuruta. ~ **sense** maarifa ya kawaida. ~ **practice** jambo la kawaida (kutendwa). 3 *(Math)* -a shirika ~ *factor/ multiple* kigawo/kigawe shirika. *(GB)* ~ **Law** sheria zisizoandikwa. ~-**law wife** kimada. ~ **market** *n* soko la ushirikiano/ pamoja. 4 ~ **noun** *(gram)* nomino ya jumla. 5 *(colloq) (of persons, their behaviour and possessions)* hafifu, -baya. ~ **manners** tabia mbaya. ~**ly** *adv n* 1 eneo la ardhi lisilo na mwenyewe, ardhi ya jumuiya yote. 2 **in** ~ kwa ajili ya wote, kwa wote. **in** ~ **with** pamoja na; sawa na *out of the* ~ si -a kawaida. ~**er** *n* mwanachi wa kawaida. ~**s** *n (pl (arch)* 1 umma. 2 the ***House of C~*** (sometimes the *Commons*) Bunge la Uingereza lililochaguliwa na wananchi). 3 **short** ~**s** uchache/upungufu wa chakula *be on short* ~**s** -topata chakula cha kutosha. ~**alty** *n* watu wa kawaida, makabwela. ~**wealth** *n* 1 dola; jumuiya ya madola. 2 *The C~wealth (also ~wealth of Nations)* Jumuiya ya Madola: jumuiya ya nchi huru zilizokuwa chini ya utawala wa Kiingereza.

commotion *n (disorder, uproar)* vurugu, ghasia, makelele, vurumai, rabsha. **make a** ~ piga kelele, fanya ghasia *in a state of* ~ katika hali ya ghasia.

commune[1] *n* 1 wajima: kikundi cha watu wanaoishi pamoja na kugawana mali zao. 2 kikundi cha watu wanaofanya kazi pamoja kwa faida ya wote. 3 eneo la kikundi. 4 *(in France etc)* Halmashauri.

communal *adj* 1 -a jumuia; -a kutumiwa na watu wote. 2 -a kuhusu vikundi mbalimbali katika jamii *communal disturbances* fujo kati ya vikundi mbalimbali (kwa sababu ya dini, taifa, rangi n.k.). **communalism** *n* ujima.

commune[2] *vi* 1 *(with)* jisikia kuwa pamoja. ~ **with the night** vaa usiku. 2 *(together)* badilishana mawazo n.k. 3 *(rel)* pokea komunyo/ushirika mtakatifu.

communicant *n* 1 *(informer)* mpasha habari. 2 *(rel)* mpokeaji wa komunyo.

communicate *vt,vi* 1 *(share, pass)* toa, pasha, pitisha (habari n.k.). 2 *(with)* wasiliana na. 3 ungana na (kama nyumba, bustani, chumba kwa njia ya mlango, geti n.k.). 4 *(rel)* pokea Ushirika Mtakatifu/komunyo. 5 jieleza *that student can't* ~ *well* yule mwanafunzi hawezi kujieleza vizuri. **communication** *n* 1 mawasiliano. 2 njia za mawasiliano (k.m. simu, reli n.k.). 3 habari, taarifa ~ *from the chair* taarifa ya mwenyekiti. ~ **cord** *(in train)* mnyororo ya tahadhari. **communicable** *adj* 1 -enye kuwezekana kuelezwa. 2 *(of disease)* -a kuambukiza. **communicable disease** maradhi ya kuambukiza. **communicative** *adj* -enye kupenda kuwasiliana. **communicativeness** *n.* **communicator** *n.*

communion *n* 1 *(sharing)* ushirikiano, umoja. 2 kupeana/kushirikiana (mawazo, n.k); urafiki. 3 ushirika: jamii ya watu wenye kanuni zile zile za imani. 4 *(rel)* **(Holy) Communion** Komunyo: Karamu Takatifu, Ushirika Mtakatifu.

communique *n* taarifa. **joint** ~ taarifa ya pamoja.

communism *n* ukomunisti. **communist** *n* mkomunisti. ~ **party** chama cha kikomunisti.

community *n* 1 jumuia *religious* ~ jumuia ya watawa/mapadre. 2 umoja, usawa *a* ~ *of interests* watu wenye mawazo sawa. **C~ Centre** Jumba la Starehe. ~ **chest** akiba ya fedha ya jumuiya za kuwasaidia wenye dhiki. ~ **singing** uimbaji wa pamoja. **in** ~ pamoja.

commute *vt,vi* 1 badilisha (aina ya malipo k.m. pesa badala ya huduma). 2 punguza adhabu, toa tahafifu. -pa tahafifu. 3 badilisha (mkondo umeme). 4 safiri kila siku mjini (kwa treni/gari n.k.). **~r** msafiri wa aina hii. **commutable** *adj* -a kuweza kubadilishiwa/kupunguzwa au kusahilishwa . **commutation** *n* 1 ubadilishaji. 2 *(of punishment)* tahafifu. 3 *(US)* ~ **ticket** tiketi ya muda. **commutator** *n* komutata: chombo cha kugeuzia mwelekeo wa mkondo umeme.

compact[1] *n* mapatano, maafikiano, mkataba.

compact[2] *n* bweta la poda (daima huwa na kioo).

compact[3] *vt* unganisha, gandamiza; gandisha, *adj (firm)* -gumu, -a kubanana, imara, thabiti. 2 *(close)* -a karibukaribu. 3 *(brief)* fupi, -lioshikamana vizuri. **~ness** *n*.

companion[1] *n* 1 mwenzi, rafiki, mwandani. ~ **in distress** mwenzi katika shida. 2 ~ **volume** kitabu cha rejea/ mwongozo. **~able** *adj*. **~ship** *n*.

companion[2] *n (naut)* 1 dirisha la kupitisha mwangaza chini melini. 2 ~ *ladder way* ngazi ya ndani ya meli.

company *n* 1 kuwa pamoja na wengine *I shall be glad of your* ~ nitafurahi kuwa pamoja nawe. **sin in good** ~ watu bora zaidi wamefanya vile vile keep ~ with kuwa na urafiki na (hasa mwanamume kwa mwanamke) *keep (bear) sb* ~ enda naye, kaa naye. **part** ~ achana (na) *two's ~ three's a crowd* wawili ni sawa akiongezeka mmoja ni vurugu. 2 wageni walioalikwa *a man is known by his* ~ tabia ya mtu hujulikana kutokana na marafiki zake. **in** ~ mbele ya watu. 3 mwenzi *he is good* ~ ni mwenzi mzuri. 4 Kampuni. **private** ~ kampuni ya binafsi. 5 *(mil.)* kombania. 6 kundi la watu wafanyao kazi pamoja (k.m. wasanii, mabaharia).

compliance *n* 1 tendo la kukubaliana, kuafikiana na; kulingana na, kufuatana na. **in ~ with** kulingana na. 2 radhi, ridhaa, ikibali, ukubalifu. **compliant** *adj* 1 -enye ikibali/ ridhaa; tiifu, sikivu, maridhia. 2 *(of yield)* -a kufuata wengine.

compare *vt,vi* 1 **~(with)** linganisha ~ *these poems* linganisha mashairi haya *this is large ~ed with that* hii ni kubwa ikilinganishwa na ile. ~ **notes** badilishana mawazo. 2 *(to)* tofautisha/ fananisha, mithilisha *it is not to be ~ed to mine* isifananishwe na yangu *he ~ed music to food* alifananisha muziki na chakula. 3 *(gram)* linganisha *n beyond/without/ past* ~ -sio kifani, bila mfano. **comparable** *(to with) adj* -a kuweza kulinganishwa na, -a kufananishwa na. **comparative** *adj* 1 linganishi. **comparative linguistics** isimu linganishi. 2 -a kulinganisha *live in comparative luxury* ishi maisha ya anasa ukilinganisha na. 3 *(gram)* linganishi **comparative adjective** kivumishi linganishi. **comparatively** *adv*. **comparison** *n* 1 ulinganishi; mlingano. 2 *(likeness)* mfano, mithili, kifani *there is no ~ between them* havifanani hata kidogo, havilingani. 3 *(gram)* **degrees of** ~ viwango linganishi *make/ draw a ~ between A and B* linganisha baina ya A na B *stand (bear) ~ with* weza kulinganishwa na *by* ~ kwa kulinganisha. ~ **are odious** si vizuri kulinganisha.

compartment *n* chumba (agh. behewa au ofisi iliyogawanywa katika sehemu kadhaa). **~alize** gawa katika vyumba; tenganisha.

compass *n* 1 *(magnetic)* dira. 2 *(circle)* duara, mzingo. 3 *(pl) also a pair of* **~es** bikari. **string** ~ bikari ya uzi. 4 *(extent)* eneo, *(limit)* upeo, kikomo, mpaka. **~-window** dirisha roshani *vt* see **encompass**.

compassion *n* huruma, kite *have ~ on sb* onea (fulani) huruma. **~ate** *adj* -enye huruma, -pole. **~ate leave** likizo ya huruma.

compatible *adj (with)* 1 *(of ideas, arguments principles etc)* -a kupatana; -a kulingana. 2 *(of people)*

-a kutangamana,-a kuweza kuchukuana. **compatibility** *n* upatanifu, ulinganifu, hali ya kuchukuana.

compatriot *n* ndugu wa kwetu, wa nyumbani.

compeer *n (arch)* 1 mwenzi. 2 mtu aliyelingana na mwingine (kwa cheo au uwezo).

compel *vt (-ll-)* 1 **(to sth)** lazimisha, shurutisha, juburu. **~ling** -a kuvutia sana. **a ~ling film** filamu ambayo inavutia sana.

compendious *adj (of authors, books etc).* -enye ufupisho kamili/makini. **compendium** *n* ufupisho kamili/makini.

compensate *vt,vi* fidia, toa fidia, lipia *~ for the lost book* fidia kitabu kilichopotea. **compensatory** *adj.* **compensation** *n* 1 fidia, dia.

compere *n (F)* mtangazaji (wa sanaa za maonyesho, kipindi cha TV n.k.) *vt* tangaza.

compete *vi* shindana.

competent *adj* 1 -enye ustadi/uwezo/uhodari. 2 *(legitimate)*halali,-a sheria. 3 -a kutosha -a kuridhisha.

competition *n* mashindano *open ~* mashindano ya wazi *throw sth open to ~* tangaza ili kushindaniwa *business ~* mashindano ya biashara. **competitive** *adj* 1 -a ushindani, -a mashindano *~ examination* mtihani wa mashindano. 2 *(of people)* -a kupenda kushindana. **competitor** *n* mshindani.

competence/competency *n* 1 uwezo, ustadi, uhodari; ufarisi. 2 *(lit) (moderate means)*, riziki, mali (si nyingi ila) za kutosha. 3 *(of a court, a magistrate)* uwezo wa kisheria.

compile *vt* 1 tunga; kusanya (maarifa, habari n.k.) *~ a dictionary* tunga kamusi. **compilation** *n* mkusanyiko, mtungo. **~er** *n.*

complacence/complacency *n* ridhaa (kupita kiasi). **complacent** *adj* 1 -a kuridhika, mno, -a kupendezwa. 2 **complacently** *adv.*

complain *vi* 1 nung'unika, lalamika. 2 *(accuse)* shtaki. **~ant** *n (leg)* mlalamikaji, mshtaki. **~t** *n* 1 *(lament)* malalamiko. 2 *(grumbling)* manung'uniko. 3 *(illness)* ugonjwa. **children's ~ ts** magonjwa ya watoto. 4 *(leg)* mashtaka. **lodge a ~t** andikisha shitaka.

complaisance *n* hulka ya kupendezesha/kuridhisha watu wengine; uelekevu. **complaisant** *adj.*

complement *n* 1 kijalizo, kitimizo, kikamilisho, kiasi kamili. *(maths)* **~ of a set** kikamilisho cha seti. 2 *(gram)* shamirisho *vt* kamilisha, timiza, shamirisha. **~ary** *adj* 1 -a kutimizana, -a kukamilishana, -a kufanya kamili; -a -ote pamoja *farming and industry are ~ary* kilimo na viwanda hukamilishana. 2 *(maths)* **~ary angles** vikamilisho vya pembe mraba.

complete *adj* 1 kamili, -zima, kamilifu, -timilifu. 2 kabisa *a ~ stranger* mgeni kabisa. **~ surprise** jambo lisilotegemewa kabisa *vt* timiza, maliza *~ ones education* maliza masomo/kamilisha, ishiliza. **~ly** *adv* kabisa *my watch is lost ~ly* saa yangu imepotea kabisa. **~ness** *n* ukamilifu. **completion** *n* ukamilishaji, umalizaji; ukamilisho *you will be employed on completion of your studies* utaajiriwa umalizapo (ukamilishapo) masomo yako.

complex *adj* 1 -enye sehemu/tabia nyingi, changamani. 2 -gumu kufahamika,-sioelezeka kwa urahisi, *(gram)* changamano. **~ sentence** sentensi changamano *(commerce) ~ interest* riba changamano *(Bio) ~* **sugar** sukari changamano. **~ situation** hali ngumu isiyoelezeka kwa urahisi. *(Psy) n* **inferiority ~** hisia za udhalili. **superiority ~** majikwezo. **~ity** *n.*

complexion 1 rangi ya uso, (ya asili), takaso *~ cream* krimu ya uso. 2 *(disposition, quality)* sura, hali *that puts a new ~ on the matter* hiyo inalipa sura mpya jambo hilo/hili.

complicate *vt* tatiza, tatanisha, fumba; fanya kuwa changamano. **~d** *adj* 1 -enye utata, mashaka, mafumbo, changamano *a ~d machine* mashine yenye muundo tata *~d business deals* mambo changamani. 2 gumu *~d questions* maswali magumu. **complication** *n* 1 hali ya kuwa tata; ugumu, kitu kiongezacho utata/ ugumu. 2 ugonjwa ziada; *(med)* ugonjwa mpya au unaotokea zaidi ya ule mtu alionao (na kufanya matibabu kuwa magumu) measles with eye and ear ~ surua inayoambatana na matatizo ya macho na masikio.

complicity *n* **~(in)** ushiriki (katika mabaya); tendo la kula njama.

compliment *n* 1 sifa, maneno ya kusifu *pay (make) sb a ~* sifu; taadhimu *fish/angle for ~s* tafuta kusifiwa. 2 *(formal)* salamu *return the ~* rudishia sifa. **my ~s to so and so** nisalimie fulani. **with ~s** pamoja na salamu za ... *pay one's ~s to sb* enda kuamkia (n.k.) *~s (of the season)* heri ya Krismasi na mwaka mpya 1 *vt* toa heshima, sifu. 2 salimu. **~ary** *adj* 1 -a kusifu, -a kusalimu,-a kuheshimu; -enye kutoa heshima. 2 -a dibaji ~ *title (in letter, book)* dibaji. 3 -a bure, -a hisani, -a heshima. ~ **ticket** tikiti iliyotolewa bure.

complin(e) *n (rel) (RC and AC)* sajio: sala za mwisho jioni.

comply *vi,vt* tii, fuata, kubaliana. ~ **(with)** timiza, tekeleza (matakwa ya mtu au kitu fulani).

component *adj* -lio sehemu *n (component part)* kijenzi; kitu kisaidiacho kukamilisha kitu kingine.

comport *vi,vt* 1 heshimu, stahi, ~ *oneself with dignity* jiheshimu, jistahi. 2 patana na, faa, chukuana na *his conduct does not ~ with his rank* tabia yake haichukuani na madaraka yake. ment *n* mwenendo mzuri, staha.

compos *adj (also compos mentis)* *(colloq)* -enye akili timamu, -enye welekevu kamili *non compos mentis* afkani, mwendawazimu, punguwani.

compose *vt,vi* 1 fanyiza, tengeneza. be ~d of -wa na sehemu (nyingi); tengenezwa kwa; umbwa kwa *it is ~d of rock* -metengenezwa kwa jiwe. 2 tunga, buni, andika (wimbo, shairi, mawazo, hotuba). 3 *(printing)* panga herufi za chapa ili kuunda maneno au sentensi. 4 tuliza. ~ **oneself** jituliza, -wa makini. **~d** *adj* tulivu. **composedly** *adv*. **composer** *n* mtungaji. **composing frame** *n* fremu ya kupanga herufi. **composing machine** *n* mashine ya kupanga herufi. **composing stick** *n* chombo cha kuwekea herufi. **composition** *n* 1 utungo, insha, kitu. 2 kazi ya sanaa k.v. kitabu, maandiko, nyimbo n.k. 3 utungaji/usanii wa kitu. 4 *(agreements)* mapatano. ~ **of creditors** mapatano ya wawia. 5 *(mixture)* mchanganyiko. 6 *(ingredients)* vijenzi, sehemu mbalimbali, asili za kitu. 7 kupanga herufi za chapa. 8 *(Maths; Physics)* kivungo. **composite** *adj* -enye sehemu (vitu, tabia) zaidi ya moja, -liofanywa na sehemu nyingine au na vitu mbalimbali. **compositor** *n* mpanga herufi za chapa. **composure** *n* utulivu, makini.

compost *n* mchanganyiko (hasa wa mimea kufanya mbolea), mboji, mbolea mkusanyiko *vt* fanya mboji/ mbolea mkusanyiko.

compound[1] *vt* 1 *(mix)* changanya pamoja ili kupata kitu kipya na tofauti; unga. 2 *(settle)* tatua (tatizo), maliza ugomvi/deni. 3 *(add to, increase)* ongezea (tatizo, kosa, n.k.) *adj* 1 iliyotengenezwa kwa kuchanganya vitu viwili au zaidi; -lioungwa. 2 *(gram)* ambatani. ~ **noun** nomino ambatani. 3 *(make)* -enye sehemu nyingi ~ *interest* riba mchanganyiko. ~ **fracture** mvunjiko mkuu. ~ **sentence** sentensi ambatani.~ **word** neno ambatani *n* 1 mchanganyiko/msombo: kitu kilichochanganywa au kutengenezwa na vitu viwili au zaidi.

compound[2] *n* 1 eneo maalumu (pengine hujengwa boma) lenye majengo, viwanja n.k. **a school** ~ eneo la shule. **a factory** ~ eneo la kiwanda. 2 ua, uga, kiwanja cha nyumba. 3 kambi ya wafanyakazi.

comprador *n (arch)* wakala wa kampuni au shirika la kigeni katika nchi. *(fig)* ~ **bourgeoisie** bwanyenye kibaraka.

comprehend *vt* 1 fahamu, tambua, jua. 2 -wa na, ingiza, jumuisha. **comprehensible** *adj* -a kufahamika, -a kueleweka, -a maana, -a kutambulika. **comprehension** *n* 1 uwezo wa kufahamu, ufahamu, ujuzi, akili tambuzi *it is beyond my* ~ siifahamu, siielewi, nashindwa kuelewa, inanizidi kimo, iko nje ya uwezo wangu wa kutambua. 2 eneo kubwa la maana au matumizi *a term of wide* ~ neno lenye maana na matumizi mengi. 3 *(of exercise)* (zoezi la) ufahamu. **comprehensive** *adj* 1 pana *the* ~ *faculty* uwezo wa kufahamu, akili tambuzi. 2 -enye vitu/ maarifa/ mambo mengi *he took a* ~ *view of the subject* alichungua (alielewa) habari zote za jambo hilo *a* ~ *school* shule ya sekondari kwa wote (bila vipaji au tabaka). ~**ness** *n*. ~**ly** adv

compress *vt* 1 gandamiza, bana, shinikiza. 2 *(of ideas, words, etc)* fupisha. ~**ible** *adj* -a kushindilika, -a kupunguzika kwa kugandamizwa/ kwa kushindiliwa *n*. kigandamizo: kipande cha nguo kilichobandikwa katika sehemu ya mwili kuzuia damu kutoka, kutuliza homa, n.k. ~**ion** *n* 1 mgandamizo, mbano, msongo, shinikizo. 2 ufupisho. ~**or** *n* kishinikizi: kitu chochote kinachokaza kwa kushindilia (au kubana, au kugandamiza); kompresa: mashine itumikayo kubana hewa au gesi.

comprise *vt* -wa na... ndani yake the book ~s all sort of knowledge kitabu kina maarifa ya namna mbalimbali.

compromise *n* mwafaka, masikilizano, maafikiano (ambapo kila upande hulegeza masharti/madai yake) *vt* 1 patana, ridhiana, afikiana, kubaliana) juu ya jambo. 2 *(endanger)* tia hatarini, tia matatani. 3 tuhumisha vibaya. ~**oneself** jiaibisha, jikashifu.

comptroller *n (accounts) (also controller)* mdhibiti fedha.

compulsion *n* 1 shurutisho, ulazimishaji, sharti. **under** ~ kwa kushurutishwa. **compulsive** *adj* -siyoweza kudhibitika: -a lazima, -a kulazimisha. ~**e -liar** mwongopaji (aliyekubuhu).~ smoking uvutaji ulokithiri. **compulsory** *adj* -a lazima, -a sharti *mathematics is a compulsory subject* hisabati ni somo la lazima.

compunction *n* majuto; haya, aibu. **compunctious** *adj*.

compute *vt* kokotoa, fanya hesabu.

computation *n* mkokotoo.

computer *n* kompyuta. ~ **services division** idara ya huduma za kompyuta. ~**ise** hifadhi kwenye kompyuta, tumia kompyuta.

comrade *n* 1 rafiki, mwenzi, sahibu, mwandani. 2 ndugu, komredi. ~ **in arms** mwanajeshi mwenza. ~**ship** *n*.

con[1] *adv* **pro and** ~ pande zote (hasi na chanya) *n* **the pros and** ~**s** hoja za pande zote.

con[2] *vt (naut)* shika usukani wa chombo.

con[3] *vt (forml)* chunguza kwa makini; jifunza kwa ghibu sana. ~ **over** sema kwa akili.

con[4] *n* mfungwa.

con[5] *vt (colloq)* danganya mtu. ~**man** *n* tapeli.

conation *n (philos)* uelekeo hiari: nia ya kutenda kwa hiari.

concatenate *vt* unganisha (kwa mfuatano), fuatana. **concatenation** *n*.

concave *adj* -a kubonyea, -enye shimo.

~ lens lenzi mbonyeo. **concavity** *n* mbonyeo; ubonyevu.

conceal *vt* ficha, setiri ~ *sth from sb* ficha mtu jambo/kitu fulani. **~ment** *n*. maficho. **a place of ~ment** mafichoni.

concede *vt,vi* 1 *(admit)* kubali, kiri, jitoa ~ *a point in an argument* kubali hoja katika majadiliano. 2 *(grant)* toa ruhusa, achia. 3 jitoa, jiweka chini (bila pambano). ~ **defeat** kubali kushindwa; salimu amri.

conceit *n* 1 majivuno, kiburi, makuu. 2 wazo/kauli chekeshi. **~ed** *adj* -enye makuu/kiburi/majivuno.

conceive *vt,vi* pata/tunga/shika/chukua mimba. 2 ona, waza, dhani, fahamu *~a liking for sb* -mtia moyoni. ~ **an idea** tunga wazo. **conceivable** *adj* -a kuweza kubuniwa/kufikiriwa, -a kuwezekana. **conceivably** *adv* yawezekana. **conception** *n* 1 utungaji mimba; utungaji dhana. 2 wazo, dhana. **concept** *n* wazo, fikra, dhana. **conceptualism** *n (philos)* umawazo, udhanifu. **(also conceptive, conceptual)** *adj* -a maana, -a akili, -a kuwaza moyoni, -a mawazo. **conceptualize** *v* -buni.

concentrate *vt,vi* 1 kusanya mahali pamoja; leta pamoja, unganisha. 2 *(condense)* fanya -zito kwa kukausha maji/ kushindilia/kugandamiza au kubana; ongeza nguvu ya kitu. 3 kolea *~d solution* mmumunyo kolezi. 4 makinikia ~ *upon (on) sth* makinikia jambo. **~d** *adj*. kali; -lokolea. **concentration** *n* kikoleza, mkusanyo wa mahali pamoja. **~camp** kambi ya wafungwa wa siasa /wakimbizi/ mateka wa vita. 2 ukolezi. 3 umakinifu.

concentric *adj* -a kati moja, -enye kitovu shirika *a system of ~ circles* mfumo wa duara za kati moja. **~ity** *n*.

concern *vt,vi* 1 **(with/in/ about)** husu *it doesn't ~ you* haikuhusu. 2 shughulisha; hangaisha *don't* yourself with minor issues usijishu- ghulishe na vitu vidogo. 3 sikitisha *his very* poor health ~s us afya yake mbaya sana inatusikitisha *n* 1 uhusiano, ipasayo; ihusuyo *it's no ~ of mine* hainihusu. 2 jambo, shughuli. 3 ushirika, shirika, kampuni. **a going ~** kampuni inayofanyakazi, kampuni hai. 4 *(interest)* hisa *he has a ~ in business* ana hisa katika biashara. 5 masikitiko, *(anxiety)* shaka, hangaiko, tatizo, shauku. **~edly** *adv*.

concert *n* 1 *(mus)* burudani/ maonyesho ya muziki. 2 umoja wa shauri *acting in ~* tenda kwa pamoja. **in ~ with** pamoja na *vt,vi* fanya shauri pamoja, tengeneza kwa mapatano. **~ed** *adj* 1 -enye kufanywa kwa pamoja. 2 kali.**~ed action** tendo lililofanywa kwa pamoja.

concertina *n (mus)* konsertina: aina ya ala ya muziki mithili ya kinanda cha mivukuto; kodiani.

concession *n* 1 kukubali. 2 tahafifu. 3 milki. **concessive** *adj* 1 -enye kuruhusu. 2 -a ridhaa, -tulivu, -sikivu. 3 *(gram)* -a kuridhia. **~aire** *n* miliki, mwenye hati ya kumiliki.

concerto *n* koncheto (muziki wa ala moja unaojitokeza zaidi katika okestra kuliko ala nyingine).

conch *n* kombe. **~ology** *n* elimukombe; elimu ya konokono na kombe za pwani.

concha *n* 1 *(bio)* sikio la nje, mvungu wa sikio. 2 *(arch)* paa la duara.

conchy *(sl)* **conscientious objector** *see* **conscientious**.

concierge *n (Fr.)* bawabu, mlinda mlango.

conciliate *vt* 1 patanisha (hasa mtu asiye rafiki), suluhisha. 2 tuliza (hasira ya fulani). 3 ungwa mkono. **conciliation** *n* usuluhishi, upatanisho *court of ~* baraza la usuluhishi. **conciliatory** *adj*.

concinnity *n* ufasaha (wa maneno); umbuji.

concise *adj (speech or style of writing)* fupi, -enye habari nyingi katika maelezo machache; -dogo; -a muhtasari. **~ly** *adv.* **~ness** *n.*

conclave *n* 1 baraza la siri la makadinali linalomchagua papa; *(fig)* mkutano wa faragha.

conclude *vt,vi* 1 *(make an end)* hitimisha, maliza. 2 *(agreement)* fikia, panga, mapatano. **~ a treaty** kamilisha mkataba. **~ a bargain** fikia mapatano; patana. 3 *(come to an end)* isha, fika mwisho, koma. 4 fikia uamuzi. **conclusion** *n* 1 hitimisho. 2 *(judgement)* uamuzi, hukumu, maoni (yanayotokana na kuzingatia suala zima) *jump to ~* amua jambo upesi bila kuzingatia suala zima. **in ~** mwishowe, hatimaye. **buy ~ with** shindana na. **a foregone ~** kitu cha wazi kabisa; kitu kilicho-kwishaamuliwa. **conclusive** *adj* -enye kuthibitisha, -enye kuondoa shaka, -a mwisho. **~ evidence** ushahidi unaothibitisha. **~ness** *n.*

concoct *vt* 1 tengeneza kwa kuchanganya pamoja *~ a new kind of soup* changanya namna mpya ya supu. 2 buni, tunga shauri/maneno ya uwongo/ hadithi. **~ion** *n.*

concomitant *n* kiambata *adj* ambatani. **concomitance** *n* hali ya kuambatana au kufuatana na (kitu kingine).

concord *n* 1 mapatano, maelewano, upatanishi, itifaki. 2 mpangilio wa kialfabeti (wa maneno muhimu ya kitabu k.m. biblia). 3 mkataba na. **~ance** *n* upatano. **~ant** *adj* (*with*) -enye kupatana. ~ *n* mapatano (kati ya dini na dola kuhusu dhima ya dini katika jamii).

concourse *n* 1 mkusanyiko, kundi, umati. 2 makutano: sehemu ya wazi ambapo barabara na njia hukutana. 3 (*place*) uwanja wa mikutano, riadha n.k.; ukumbi wa stesheni ya gari moshi.

concrete *adj* 1 -a kushikika, -a kuonekana (wala si -a kuwazika tu); thabiti *~ example* mfano thabiti *~ noun* nomino mguso. 2 -a saruji. **~ block** tofali la saruji. *n* **~ mixer** kichanganya zege *reinforced~* zege imara *vt,vi* tia saruji, paka saruji; ganda (kama saruji).

concubine *n* 1 hawara, kimada. 2 mke mdogo (katika ndoa za mke zaidi ya mmoja). **concubinage** *n* uhawara.

concupiscence *n* ashiki, nyege.

concur *vi* 1 tokea/tukia tendeka kwa wakati mmoja. 2 (*agree in opinion*) afiki, kubali. **~rence** *n.* **~rent** *adj* 1 -enye kulingana/kupatana; -enye kutendeka, kuwapo au kufuatana pamoja. **~rently** *adv.*

concuss *vt* (*often passive*) jeruhiwa ubongo (kutokana na kupigwa/ kishindo/mtikisiko kali). **~ion** *n* 1 jeraha la bongo linalotokana na kupigwa/kugongwa). 2 (*shock*) mshtuko, mtikiso (wa nguvu).

condemn *vt* 1 laumu, shutumu; laani *we ~ed his bad behaviour* tulilaani tabia yake mbaya. 2 (*to convict*) hukumu, tia hatiani. 3 weka, tuma, agiza fulani kuishi katika hali ya taabu au maumivu. **~ation** *n* shutuma; laana; lawama. 4 (*reject*) kataza, tupa ~ed house nyumba iliyopigwa marufuku kukaliwa na mtu (kwa sababu ya ubovu). 5 (*arch*) twalia, taifisha k.v. (mali ya magendo).

condense *vt,vi* 1 fanya zito; fanya umande/wingu; punguka na kuwa zito zaidi. 2 (**of steam**) tonesha: geuza mvuke uwe maji. 3 (*shorten*) fupisha, fanya muhtasari *a ~ed account of an event* muhtasari wa habari. *n* 1 kijazi, kondensa: chombo cha kukusanyia au kugeuzia nguvu ya umeme. 2 kitoneshi: chombo cha kugeuza hewa kuwa majimaji.

condensation *n* 1 mtonesho. 2 ufupisho.

condescend *vi* **~ to sb/sth; ~ to do sth** 1 (*in a good sense*) fanya kitu, kubali kazi, cheo kilicho chini ya hadhi yako. 2 (*in a bad sense*) jishusha hadhi. 3 tenda wema (kwa lengo la kusimanga/kujionesha bora). **condescension** *n.*

condign *adj* (*of punishment*) kali, iliyostahili.
condiment *n* kiungo, kikolezo cha kutia ladha katika chakula k.m. chumvi/ pilipili.
condition *n* sharti *on no ~* bila ya sharti/mapatano *on ~ that* ikiwa/endapo kwamba *contrary to the ~ we agreed upon* kwa kinyume cha mapatano yetu. 2 (*state*) hali, tabia; (*pl*) **~s** hali ya mambo muhimu kwa uhai. **under existing ~s** katika hali ya mambo ilivyo. 3 (*health*) afya, siha, rai, zima *out of ~* katika hali mbaya, -lioharibika *the ~ of my health* hali ya afya yangu *be in no ~ to do something* -toweza kufanya (jambo). 4 nafasi (ya kitabaka) katika jamii *people of all ~s attended* watu wa matabaka yote walihudhuria.
condition *vt* 1 shurutisha, lazimisha *be ~ed* tawaliwa *my expenditure is ~ed by my income* matumizi yangu yanatawaliwa na mapato yangu. **~ed** *adj* 1 -enye masharti *~ed reflex* tendo la kujiendea *~ed reaction* mlipizo zoevu. 2 -enye hali fulani nzuri/mbaya n.k.. **~ed** *adj*. **~al** 1 sharti, -enye masharti, kutegemeana na. **~al sale** uuzaji kwa masharti. 2 (*gram*) **~al sentence** sentensi sharti.
condole *vi* (*grieve with*) hani, toa (salamu za) mbirambi, -pa mkono wa pole. **~nce** *n* mbirambi, rambirambi, liwazo. **letter of ~nce** barua ya rambirambi.
condom *n* kondomu, mpira wa kiume.
condominium *n* 1 miliki bia, utawala bia (wa nchi mbili au zaidi); mamlaka bia. 2 (*US*) nyumba ya majumui imilikiwayo na wakazi.
condone *vt* 1 samehe, jifanya kutoona, puuza. 2 *(of an act)* toa kafara, fidia. **condonation** *n*.
condor *n* aina ya tai mkubwa (wa Marekani ya Kusini).
conduce *vi* faa, saidia, elekea kuleta, changia. **conducive** *adj*.
conduct[1] *n* 1 mwenendo, tabia (nzuri au mbaya), maadili mema. **code of ~** kanuni za maadili mema. 2 usimamizi, uongozi, uendeshaji, ufuataji maadili mema. **~ of business etc** utaratibu wa shughuli n.k. **~ -money** gharama za shahidi.
conduct[2] *vt* 1 (*lead*) ongoza, peleka, chukua *~ed tour* ziara iliyoongozwa. 2 (*manage*) endesha. 3 (*phys*) pitisha/ ruhusu *iron ~s heat* chuma hupitisha joto. 4. **~ oneself** (*behave*) tenda. 5 *(mus)* ongoza, imbisha. 6 fanya kazi ya kondakta. **~ oneself towards sb** jiweka kwa jambo la mtu fulani. **~ion** *n* upitishaji (k.m. umeme katika waya). **~ion of heat** upitishaji wa joto. **~ion system** mfumo wa upitishaji joto, umeme, maji **~ive** *adj* -enye uwezo wa kupitisha. **~ivity** *n*.
conductor *n* 1 (*guide*) mwongozaji, kiongozi. 2 (*US*) msimamizi; mwangalizi wa abiria, kondakta anayekusanya nauli. 3 (*phys*) kipitishi (cha joto au umeme) *~ rail* reli inayopitisha umeme. **conductress** kondakta wa kike.
conduit 1 mfereji, bomba (la maji); bomba la kupitishia waya/nyaya za umeme.
cone *n* 1 pia. 2 (*bio*) sonobari. 3 koni. 4 (*of ice cream*) koni. **~-pulley** *n*. kapi ya pia.
coney *n see cony.*
confabulate *vi* (*also inform confab*) zungumza, ongea. **confabulation** *n* mazungumzo (ya kirafiki, faragha).
confection *n* 1 tamutamu. 2 vazi (agh. kwa wanawake). 3 mchanganyo; (*of clothes*) tayari kwa kuuza. **~er** *n* mtengezaji/mwuzaji vitamutamu. **~ery** vitamutamu, kiwanda/duka la vitamutamu.
confederacy *n* 1 shirikisho; mwuungano (wa majimbo, nchi, vyama au watu). 2 njama. **be in ~** kula njama (na). **confederate** *adj* -liounganana pamoja kwa mapatano au mkataba *n* 1 mwenzi. 2 mshirika, msaidizi katika uovu *vt,vi* 1 ungana kwa mapatano. 2 fanya njama.

confederation *n.*
confer *vt,vi* 1 ~ **sth on/upon** tunukia, tunza (shahada; heshima; n.k.). ~ **a degree** tunukia shahada. ~ **(with sb) (on/about sth)** shauriana, jadiliana na ~**ment** *n.*
conference *n* mkutano.
confess *vt,vi* 1 kiri, kubali kosa *he ~ed that he stole the money* alikiri kuwa aliiba zile fedha. 2 tubu, ungama. ~**edly** *adv.* ~**ion** *n* 1 kukiri, kukubali. 2 ungamo. 3 (*creed*) tangazo la imani, ushuhuda. 4 (*rel*) maungamo, *adj* -a maungamo -a imani. ~**ional** *adj, n* (*rel*) kizimba cha maungamo ~**or** *n* (*rel*) 1 mwungamishi (padri mwenye mamlaka ya kusikiliza maungamo). 2 muungamaji. 3 shahidi (mtu anayejitolea kuteswa au kufa kwa ajili ya dini yake).
confetti *n (pl)* chengechenge za rangi mbalimbali (ambazo hutupiwa maarusi n.k.).
confide(e) *vt,vi* 1 ~ **to** ambia siri. 2 kabidhi *they ~d their children to the neighbour* walikabidhi watoto wao wa jirani. 3 ~ **(in)** -wa na imani. **confiding** *adj* -a kweli, -a kuaminika, -a kuamini wengine. **confidingly** *adv.* **confidant** *n* msiri (agh. wa mambo ya mapenzi). ~**nce** *n* 1 matumaini, imani *put one's ~ ence in sb* wa na imani naye. **have in ~nce** tegemea, tumainia. 2 maneno ya siri, siri iliyotolewa kwa mtu mwingine *give a ~nce to sb* dokolea siri **take into ~nce** mwamini. ~**ence trick/ ~ ence game** kuiba kwa ghiliba kimachomacho, ulaghai, utapeli. 3 hakika *I had every ~nce that we should win* nilikuwa na hakika kwamba tutashinda. ~ **nt** *adj* 1 -tumainifu, -enye imani. 2 -enye hakika, -enye kujiamini. ~**ntly** *adv.* ~**ntial** *adj* 1 (*of information*) -a siri. 2 *(of a person)* -enye kuamini mno. ~**ntiality** *n.* ~**ntially** *adv.*
configuration *n* umbo, sura; namna ya kupanga.
confine *vt* 1 wekea mipaka ~ *your remarks to the subject* usitoke/ usizungumze nje ya mada. 2 fungia, zuia *she is ~d to her room* amezuiliwa chumbani mwake. 3 **be ~d** (*passive only*) (*old use*) jifungua, zaa; -wa kitandani tayari kwa kujifungua. ~**d** *adj.* ~**ment** *n* 1 kifungo. 2 uzazi, kuzaa, kujifungua. ~**s** *n* 1 mipaka *beyond the ~s of human knowledge* nje ya mipaka ya ujuzi wa binadamu.
confirm *vt* 1 (*strengthen*) thibitisha, imarisha (nguvu, maoni, haki n.k.); tia nguvu, tegemeza. 2 (*ratify*) idhinisha, sahihisha, yakinisha. 3 (*rel*) tolea kipaimara, tia (bandika) mikono baada ya ubatizo. ~**ed** *adj* imara; kabisa, -a siku nyingi. ~**ation** *n* 1 uthibitisho; shahada, ushahidi, hakika. 2 (*rel*) kipaimara.
confiscate *vt* (*as punishment*) nyang'anya, chukua ngawira; taifisha. **confiscation** *n.*
conflagration *n* moto mkubwa, (hasa unaoteketeza majengo na misitu).
conflict *n* 1 mapigano; vita; mapambano; ugomvi. 2 (of opinions, desires etc) mgongano. ~ **of law** mgongano wa sheria. **be in ~ with** pingana na, -tokubaliana na. **a wordy** ~ ushindani wa maneno, ubishi mkali, mzozano, mgogoro *vi* (~ **with**) pingana au -tokubaliana na. ~**ing** *adv.*
confluence/conflux *n* ndagano: mahali mito miwili inapoungana. **confluent** *adj.*
conform *vt,vi* 1 ~ **(to)** fuata, kubali (sheria, kanuni, viwango vilivyokubaliwa), tii, patana na. ~ **oneself** kubali kupatana na. 2 ~ **(to)** fanya sawa na. ~**able** *adj* tiifu, kubalifu, -a kukubaliana na. ~**ity** (*also conformance*) *n* usawa, ulinganifu, ukubalifu, tendo au tabia inayokubaliana na. **in ~ity with** kwa kupatana na, kwa kufuata. ~**ist** mfuata kanuni/desturi n.k.
confound *vt* 1 (*perplex*) shangaza, fadhaisha, staajabisha, tunduwaza.

2 (*arch*) ~ **(with)** changanya (mawazo n.k.). 3 angamiza, shinda (mpango, tumaini). 4 aibisha. **~ed** *adj* 1 -lostaajabu, -lofadhaika. 2 -a laana. **~edly** *adv*. **~ly** *adv* sana.
confraternity *n* kundi la kidini linalotenda jamala na kutoa sadaka kwa jamii.
confrére *n* mwenzi (wa kazi, wa chama).
confront *vt* 1 (*oppose*) ~ **sb with** kabili. 2 (*set opposite , bring before*) kabiliana ana kwa ana. 3 -wa mkabala na. **~ation** *n*.
Confucian *adj n* -enye kumfuata Konfyushasi (mwana falsafa na mwalimu wa maadili wa Kichina). **~ism** *n*.
confuse *vt* 1 ~ **(with)** changanya, tinga, tanza. 2 (*perplex*) hangaisha, tia wasiwasi, tatiza, tatanisha. 3 (*fail to distinguish*) kanganya *don't ~ me with Joseph* usifikiri mimi ni Joseph. **~dly** *adv*. **confusion** *n* 1 mchafuko, kakara, shaghalabaghala. 2 rabsha, ghasia. 3 kiwewe.
confute *vt* bainisha/dhihirisha kosa, onyesha, bainisha ukweli. **confutation** *n*.
congeal *vt,vi* ganda, gandisha, -wa ngumu *his blood ~ed* (*fig*) mwili ulimsisimka (kwa hofu), kacha.
congenial *adj* 1 (*of persons*) -enye hulka moja. 2 (*of things, occupation etc.*) -inayofanana/kukubaliana na matakwa, hulka ya mtu *a ~ job* kazi inayochukuana na hulka ya mtu. **~ity** *n*. **~ly** *adv*.
congenital *adj* (*esp disease or defect*) -a kuzaliwa na, kizaliwa *a ~ disease* ugonjwa wa kuzaliwa nao. ~ **idiot** mpumbavu; (*fig*) mpumbavu kabisa.
conger (*also ~ eel*) *n* mkunga wa baharini.
congest *vt* 1 songa, jaza sana, banana. 2 (*med*) jaa/jaza uoevu *his lungs are ~ed* mapafu yake yamejaa *vi* 1 -wa na damu nyingi mno. 2 fanyiza msongano. **~ed** *adj* 1 (*over crowded*) -a kusongana mno, -a kujaa sana *the streets were ~ed with people* kulikuwa na msongamano wa watu barabarani. 2 (*of parts of the body eg. brain*) -enye mavilio ya damu, -enye damu nyingi kuliko kiasi *his lungs were ~ed* mapafu yake yalikuwa na damu nyingi. **~ion** *n*.
conglomerate 1 *adj, n* -liyoundwa katika bonge. bonge. 2 mkusanyiko wa vitu. 3 (*comm*) shirikisho; makampuni *vt,vi* kusanya/unda katika bonge/kitu kimoja. **conglomeration** *n*.
congratulate *vt* 1 pongeza, -pa mkono wa tahania, -pa hongera, hongeza. 2 ~ (*oneself*) jipongeza; (*after accident/ danger*) shukuru. **congratulatory** *adj*. **congratulation** *n* (*often pl*) hongera, pongezi, mkono wa tahania.
congregate *vt,vi* kusanya, kusanyika, kutana, kutanika *people quickly ~d around the speaker* watu walikusanyika haraka na kumzunguka msemaji. **congregation** *n* 1 mkusanyiko wa watu; mkutano, usheha. 2 (*rel*) mkusanyiko wa waumini, usharika. 3 (*of a University*) mahafali. **congregational** *adj*.
congress *n* 1 mkutano wa watu (wa shughuli maalum). 2 *(US)* Bunge la Marekani; (India) chama cha siasa cha Kongresi. **~ional** *adj*. **~man/woman** *n*. mbunge.
congruence/congruency *n* mlingano, ulinganifu. **congruent** *n*. **congruous** *adj* 1 -a kupatana, -a kulingana. 2 (*geom*) -a mlingano, -liolingana. ~ **lines** mistari iliyolingana. **congruity** *n*.
conic(al) *n* **coniform** *adj* kama pia, -enye umbo la pia.
conifer *n* aina ya msonobari, mpia ~**ous** *adj*.
conjecture *vt* bahatisha, kisia, dhani, bunia *n* kisio, bahatisho. **conjectural** *adj*.
conjoin *vt* unga, unganisha *vi* ungana. ~t *adj*. **~tly** *adv*.
conjugal *adj* -a ndoa; -a mume na

mkewe, -a unyumba. ~ **rights** haki za unyumba/ndoa.

conjugate *vt* (*gram*) nyambua kitenzi *vi* (*biol*) ungana. **conjugation** *n*.

conjunct *adj n* -a kuunga, -liounganika; muungano. **~ly** *adv*. **~ion** *n* 1 mwungano. **in ~ion with** pamoja na, kwa kuungana na. 2 (*gram*) kiungo (k.m. na, ya, wa). 3 mwingiliano, mchanganyiko. **~ion of circumstances** mwingiliano wa mambo. **~ive** *adj* 1 -a kuunganisha, -a kiunganishi *n* kiunganisho. **~ively** *adv*. **~ure** *n* mwungano wa matukio that ~ure of flood and drought resulted in famine mwungano wa mafuriko na ukame ulisababisha njaa.

conjuration *n* 1 maneno ya kunuizia uchawi; matabano, matagonya.

conjure *vt, vi* 1 fanya mizungu, kiinimacho, mazingaombwe. 2 omba, sihi sana. 3 ~ **up** (*of spirits*) ita; (*fig*) buni, vuta picha, kumbusha; (*of meal*) tengeneza. **a name to ~ with** mtu muhimu. **~r/conjuror** *n* mfanya kiinimacho, mazingaombwe, mizungu.

conk[1] *n* (*GB*) (*sl*) pua.

conk[2] *vi* ~ **out** 1 (*colloq*) (*of machine*) haribika, shindwa (kufanya kazi ipasavyo) *the engine ~ed out* injini iliharibika/imenoki.

conman *n* tapeli.

connect *vt, vi* 1 unganisha; unganika *the two towns are ~ ed by a railway* miji miwili hii imeunganishwa na reli. 2 (*associate*) husu; husisha *the subjects are ~ed* mambo haya yanahusiana, yanafungamana. ~ **with** husiana na. **well ~ed** husiana na watu maarufu. **~er** *n*. **~edly** *adv*. **~ion. connexion** *n* 1 uhusiano/mwunganisho, (*coherence*) uwiano *these affairs have no ~ion with each other* mambo haya hayawiani, hayahusiani. 2 kuunganisha kiungo. 3 (*relation*) ndugu; jamaa, ahali. 4 kuunganisha safari kwa kubadili vyombo vya usafiri. 5 (*context*) muktadha, mintaarafu ya. **in ~ion with this** kwa mintarafu ya. 6 (*rel*) madhehebu. 7 (*in business*) mbinu, washiriki katika biashara. 8 (*collection*) wateja. **~ive** *adj* 1 -a kuunganishia. 2 (*gram*) kiunganisho. 3 kiangama cha ushirikisho.

conning-tower *n* (*on warship*) mnara wa rubani wa manowari.

connive *vi* ~ **at sth** 1 fumbia macho, achilia kwa makusudi (kosa lifanyike), jitia mwapuza. 2 kula njama. *(abet)* shiriki katika tendo kwa siri ~ *at a crime* kula njama. **connivance** *n* **~r** *n*.

connoisseur *n* mwonjaji, mjuzi, mfahamivu, mmaizi.

connote *vt* maanisha kwa maana nyingine, ashiria **connotative meaning** maana matilaba **connotation** *n* kidokezo.

connubial *adj* -a mke na mume, -a unyumba.

conquer *vt* 1 shinda (adui, tabia au mazoea mabaya). 2 kamata, twaa (kwa nguvu hasa wakati wa vita). **~or** *n* mshindi. **conquest** *n* 1 ushindi; ushinde. 2 (*spoils*) mateka, nyara, nchi zilizotekwa. 3 kipenzi *make a ~* (*of*) vutia mtu (kwa mapenzi), pata, pendwa.

consanguinity *n* udugu wa nasaba.

conscience *n* dhamiri. **good (bad)** ~ dhamiri njema/mbaya; moyo wenye raha/wasiwasi kwa ajili ya matendo. **have a clear** ~ -wa na moyo safi. **guilty** ~ shitakiwa na dhamiri. **for ~ sake** tosheleza dhamiri *I would not have the ~ to do that* nisingalikuwa na moyo wa kufanya hivyo. **in all ~/upon my ~** kwa dhamiri yangu/kwa mawazo yangu. **have no ~** -toweza kutofautisha mema na mabaya. ~ **money** *n* malipo ya ria. **~-stricken** jawa na majuto. **conscientious** *adj* -a kufanya kwa makini, -angalifu sana. **conscientious objector** mtu akataaye kufanya kitu (k.m. huduma ya jeshi) kwa sababu hakipatani na maadili yake. **conscientiousness** *n*.

conscious *adj* 1 -a kuona, -a kufahamu,

-a kusikia *he was ~ of a smell* alisikia harufu *become ~ of sth* tambua jambo *the man who was hurt was still ~* yule mtu aliyeumia alikuwa bado na fahamu zake. 2 (*of others, feelings*) -a kujua, -a kufahamu moyoni (nafsini). 3 -a kuweza kufikiri na kuamua. 4 -a makusudi. **~ly** *adv*. **~ness** *n* 1 fahamu, utambuzi. 2 (*perception*) akili. **he lost ~ness** alizimia, alizirai. **he regained ~ness** alipata fahamu tena.

conscript/conscribe *n* (*US* **conscriptee**) mwanajeshi kwa mujibu wa sheria *vt* andikisha jeshini kwa mujibu wa sheria. **~ion** *n*.

consecrate *vt* ~ **(to)** 1 weka wakfu. 2 toa (tenga) kwa ajili ya dini, Mungu au kusudi fulani. 3 tukuza, fanya takatifu. 4 (*inaugurate*) zindua *adj* **~d** -liofanywa takatifu, wakfu. **consecration** *n* 1 ufanyaji wakfu, kuweka wakfu. 2 ~ in Mass mageuzo. **consecrator** *n* mweka wakfu. **consecratory** *adj*. -a kutunzwa, -enye kuwekwa wakfu.

consecutive *adj* 1 mfulizo, -a kufuatana/kufuata, moja baada ya moja *three ~ days* siku tatu mfulizo. 2 (*gram*) (*of a sentence*) -enye matokeo yaliyofuatana. **~ly** *adv*. **consecution** *n* mfululizo, mfuatano wa matukio.

consensus *n* muafaka, makubaliano (juu ya shauri). **consensual** *adj* 1 -enye muafaka, -a kuridhiana, -a kukubaliana, pamoja. 2 (*phys*) -a kisilika (kwa mwendo).

consent *vi* ~ **(to)** ridhia, kubali, wafiki, toa idhini *n* ridhaa, idhini, ruhusa, radhi. **age of ~** umri wa utu uzima. **with one ~** kwa kauli moja.

consequence *n* 1 matokeo (ya jambo). **in ~ (of)** kwa sababu hiyo. **in ~ of sth** kwa ajili ya jambo fulani. **bear the ~s** kubali matokeo. 2 umuhimu, umaarufu, cheo. **it is of no ~** sio muhimu. **a person of ~** mtu maarufu. consequent *n* 1 tokeo la jambo, mfululizo; (*gram*) kishazi kifuasi *adj* 1 **consequent on/upon** -a kufuata, -a kufuatana na. (*law*) **consequent damage** hasara inayofuatia. 2 (*maths*) *consequent number* namba fuasi katika uwiano. **consequential** *adj* -a kufuata. **consequential loss** hasara inayoandamana na. 2 (*pompous*) -enye majivuno, -enye makuu. **consequently** *adv* kwa hiyo, hivyo.

conservatoire *n* (*esp. in Europe*) chuo cha muziki.

conservatory *n* (*US*) 1 kibanda cha kukuzia miche. 2 (*mus*) chuo cha muziki.

conserve *vt* linda, tunza, hifadhi, weka vizuri *n*. (*usu pl*) **~s** matunda ya kopo; jamu. **conservation** *n* 1 hifadhi; (*of game, forest*) hifadhi ya wanyama/misitu; (*mech*) *conservation of momentum* hifadhi ya nguvu mwendo. **conservancy** *n* 1 tume ya hifadhi ya mali asili. 2 hifadhi rasmi ya mali asili. **conservatism** *n* ushikiliaji (wa) ukale/mfumo uliopo; kutopenda mabadiliko. **conservator** *n* 1 mhifadhi. 2 mwangalizi (wa makumbusho n.k.). **conservative** *adj* 1 -enye kushikilia ukale; -siyependa kubadili mambo *The Conservative Party* Chama cha *Conservative*. 2 -a kulinda, -a kutunza. 3 -enye hadhari, -a kiasi *n* mtu asiyependa mabadiliko.

consider *vt* 1 (*deliberate on*) fikiria, dhukuru, angalia. **one's ~ed opinion** wazo la mtu baada ya kufikiria sana. 2 *(take into account)* zingatia, kumbuka, pima. **all things ~ed** baada ya kufikiria yote. 3 wazia, dhania, fikiria, ona. **~able** *adj* kubwa, -ingi. **~ably** *adv* mno, sana. **~ate** (*important*) -a kustahili kufikiriwa -enye kufikiria wengine, -enye huruma, -enye busara *it was ~ of him* alifanya busara. **~ately** *adv* **~ateness** *n* ~ation *n* 1 (*deliberation*) fikira, shauri, nadhari **take into ~ation** angalia. **under ~ation** inayofikiriwa.

in notion **of ~ation** kwa sababu ya *give sth careful ~* fikiria kwa makini. **leave out of ~ation** sahau, shindwa kufikiria. 2 *(kindness)* huruma, wema. 3 (*motive, reason*) sababu, kisa, jambo, hoja *these are the ~ations which influenced him in making his plans* haya ndiyo mambo ambayo yalimwathiri sana katika kufanya mipango yake. **on no ~ation** (isiwe) kwa vyovyote vile, hapana kabisa. 4 (*rare use*) umuhimu. 5 (*compensation, reward*) tuzo, malipo. **~ing** *prep* -a kuzinga tia, -a kulinganisha *he scored highly ~ing his long illness* amefaulu sana ukilinganisha na kipindi kirefu alichokuwa mgonjwa.

consign *vt* (*to*) 1 peleka, pelekea, safirisha (mizigo, bidhaa n.k.). 2 toa, tokea, pa, aminisha. **~ee** *n* wakili. **~er**, **~or** mwakilishaji. **~ment** *n* mali. **~ment note** hati ya mali.

consist *vi* 1 (*of*) -wa na. 2 (*in*) tegemea. **~ence**/ **~ency** *n* 1 kuwa na msimamo, hali ya kuwa na fikira (desturi, tabia n.k.) zile zile daima. 2 uthabiti. 3 uzito, ugumu *mix flour and milk to the right ~ency* koroga pamoja unga na maziwa ili kupata uzito (ugumu) ufaao. **~ent** *adj* (*of person, his behaviour, principles etc)* -enye msimamo, thabiti, -aminifu, -a kulingana, sawa. 2 **(with)** kwa kupatana/kukubaliana, -a kushikilia jambo; -nyofu. **~ly** *adv.*

consistory *n* (*rel- R.C.*) (*also C~ Court*) Baraza linaloundwa na Papa na Makadinali (kwa shughuli za kanisa). **consistorial** *adj.*

console[1] *vt* fariji, tuliza, liwaza, poza moyo *~ sb for a loss* tuliza mtu kwa hasara aliyoipata. **consolable** *adj* -enye kuweza kufarijika. **consolation** *n* faraja, maliwazo, kitulizo; (*of person*) mfariji; (*sports*) ~ **prize** zawadi ya kufariji/ kufuta jasho. **consolatory** *adj* -enye faraja, -a kufariji.

console[2] *n* kiweko ~ *mirror* kioo chenye kiweko ~ *table* meza yenye kiweko. 2 chumba cha vifaa vya elektroniki. 3 redio au TV ya kabati.

consolidate *vt,vi* 1 (*make firm*) imarisha, (ji)zatiti. 2 (*unite*) unganisha, fanya moja *~d funds* mfuko wa jumla. **consolidation** n.

consomme *n* supu nyepesi ya nyama.

consonance *n* 1 upatanifu. 2 ulinganifu *be in ~ with* lingana na; (*mus*) ulinganifu wa sauti. 3 konsonanti: upacha wa konsonanti za mwisho za maneno tofauti (k.m. *t* katika maneno *fit, hot, bet* ya Kiingereza). **consonant** *adj* 1 -a kupatana, -a kulingana, sawa. **consonant with** -enye kuchukuana na. **consonant to** muwafaka, kubalifu, kabuli. **consonant** *n* konsonanti **consonantal.** *adj.*

consort[1] *n* 1 mume au mke (hasa) wa mtawala *the queen ~* mke wa mfalme *the prince ~* mume wa malkia. 2 meli inayofuatana na nyingine (hasa kwa ajili ya ulinzi wakati wa vita).

consort[2] *vi* ~ **with** 1 andamana na, fuatana na. 2 patana, afikiana. **~ium** *n* ubia (wa mashirika, mabenki n.k.).

conspectus *n* muhtasari; maelezo ya jumla, vidokezo.

conspicuous *adj* 1 -enye kuonekana waziwazi, -enye kuvutia. **be** ~ onekana wazi *make oneself ~* jionyesha. ~ **consumption** matumizi ya ufahari/kujichana. **~ly** *adv*. **ness** *n*.

conspire *vt,vi* 1 -la njama. 2 (*of events*) unganisha, jumuisha, ungana *events ~d to bring about his failure* kushindwa kwake kumetokana na mambo mengi. **conspirator** *n* mla njama, haini. **conspiracy** *n* njama, kigwena. **conspiratorial** *adj.*

constable *n (GB)* 1 konstebo; polisi (wa daraja la chini) *special ~* raia afanyaye kazi ya polisi wakati maalumu. 2 *(hist)* ofisa mkuu wa kifalme. **constabulary** *n* jeshi la polisi.

constant *adj* 1 -a siku zote, -a daima, -a kawaida. 2 (*firm*) thabiti, imara *n* (*maths*) kisobadilika. ~ **rate** kima kisichobadilika. **~ly** *adv*. **constancy** *n* 1 uthabiti. 2 uaminifu.

constellation *n* kilimia; (*fig*) kundi.

consternation *n* fadhaa, hofu kuu na mshangao.

constipate *vt* funga choo. **~d** *adj*. **constipation** *n* kufunga choo, hali ya kufunga choo (ya kutopata choo barabara); uyabisi wa tumbo (choo).

constituent *adj* 1 -a sehemu ya kitu kizima. 2 (*of assembly*) -enye haki na uwezo wa kufanya au kubadilisha katiba *n* 1 mpiga kura. 2 sehemu ya kitu kizima. 3 (*gram*) ~ *part* kiamba jengo. **constituency** *n* jimbo la uchaguzi.

constitute *vt* 1 (*establish*) anzisha (shirika), toa madaraka kwa (kamati n.k.). 2 (*form, compose*) fanya, fanyiza; -wa na; -wa na afya nzuri/ udhaifu. 3 (*appoint*) teua, weka madarakani. **constitution** *n* 1 katiba ya nchi, chama n.k. 2 (*of a person*) gimba, tambo, zihi. 3 (*of a thing*) umbile; (*act/ manner*) *the constitution of the solar* mjengo wa mfumo wa jua. **constitutional** *adj* 1 -a kikatiba ~ *law* sheria ya katiba. 2 (*lawful*) halali, -a kutii sheria. 3 -a asili, -a umbile, -a afya *n* (*dated colloq*) matembezi mafupi kwa ajili ya afya **take a ~ walk** tembea, nyosha miguu, (kwa ajili ya afya). **~ism** *n* imani kwamba serikali sharti ifuate misingi ya katiba. **~ly** *adv* kwa mujibu wa katiba. **constitutive** *adj* 1 jenzi. 2 (*original*) -a asili. 3 -a sehemu ya kitu.

constrain *vt* 1 lazimisha, shurutisha. 2 bidi. 3 (*limit*) zuia. **~ed** *adj* -lobanwa. **~t** *n* kikwazo, kizuizi, kigingi. **~edly** *adv*.

constrict *vt* 1 bana, songa, minya, binya. 2 zuia ukuaji, dumaza; (*fig*) finya. **~ed** *adj a ~ed outlook* mtazamo finyu. **~ion** *n*. **~or** *n* 1 (*surgical*) kibano. 2 (*anat*) msuli bana. 3 chatu.

construct *vt* 1 jenga. 2 fanya, fanyiza, unda. 3 buni. **~ion** *n* 1 ujenzi, uundaji. 2 jengo, nyumba (chochote kilichojengwa au kuundwa). 3 mjengo. 4 (*gram*) muundo wa maneno au sentensi. 5 tafsiri, maana *his statement does not bear such a ~ion* maelezo yake hayana maana hiyo. **~ive** *adj* -a kutoa maoni yanayosaidia; jenzi.

construe *vt,vi* 1 fasiri, tafsiri, eleza maana, chambua; (*infer*) fahamu maana yake *he was mis ~d* alieleweka vibaya. 2 changanua, chambua; unda, unganisha kisarufi ~ *a sentence* chambua sentensi. 3 (*of sentence*) wezekana kuchambuliwa au kutafsiriwa.

consubstantiation *n* (*rel*) imani kuwa damu na mwili wa Yesu Kristo upo pamoja na divai na mkate (katika Ekaristi Takatifu). **consubstantial** *adj* -enye asili moja.

consul *n* 1 balozi mdogo. **~ar** *adj*. **~ship** *n* Ubalozi Mdogo. **~ate** *n* 1 ofisi ya balozi mdogo. 2 Ubalozi Mdogo.

consult *vt,vi* 1 taka shauri. 2 tafuta maoni (katika kitabu n.k.). 3 shauri, elekeza, fanya shauri. ~ **in** toa shauri ~ **with** shauriana. **~ant** *n* mshauri, mwelekezi; bingwa. **~ation** *n* 1 ushauri, uelekezi, mashauriano. 2 mkutano wa kushauriana. 3 kitendo cha kushauriana. **~ative** *adj*.

consume *vt,vi* 1 -la, -nywa. 2 (*of fire*) teketeza, tumia, maliza. 3 haribu, fuja ~ *away* haribika, oza. **consumable** *adj*. **consuming** *adj*. **~r** *n* mlaji, mnunuzi, mtumiaji. **~r goods** bidhaa zitumiwazo (chakula, nguo, gari n.k.) *~r cooperative shop* duka la ushirika la walaji *~r wants* mahitaji ya wanunuzi *~r sales resistance* uzito wa kununua bidhaa (wa wateja). **consumption** *n* 1 ulaji. 2 utumiaji; ufujaji. 3 (*med*) kifua kikuu. **consumptive** *adj* 1 -enye kifua. 2 -haribifu; -a kutumia *n* mgonjwa wa kifua kikuu. **~ness** *n*.

consummate *vt* kamilisha, timiliza, maliza, isha. 2 kamilisha/timiliza ndoa kwa ngono **~d marriage** ndoa iliyokamilishwa, ndoa kamilifu. **~ly** *adv,adj* 1 -kamili, -timilifu, bora; stadi. **consummation** *n* 1 kilele, ukamilisho; tendo la kumaliza kutimiza/kukamilisha. 2 *~ of marriage* mfumo wa kukamilisha ndoa kwa ngono; kukamilishwa kwa ndoa.

contact *n* 1 mgusano, mawasiliano, mpambano *come into ~* kutana, wasiliana; gongana, pambana. **be in ~ with** gusana *be in ~ with sb* wasiliana na mtu, gusana na mtu, kabiliana na mtu. ~ **lens** lenzi (ya plastiki) inayoambatanishwanamboni (kuonea vizuri). 2 *(med)* mtu aliyekutana na/kuwa na mgonjwa mwenye maradhi ya kuambukiza *~ infection* uambukizaji kwa kugusana *~ poison* sumu mgusano. 3 (*elect*) kiungo cha umeme (*device*) kipitishio *make ~* unganisha waya za umeme (ili nguvu ya umeme iweze kupita) *break ~* kata umeme. 4 (*pl*) **~s** mwunganisho; (*of people*) uhusiano miongoni mwa watu *~s man* mpatanishi (wa kesi ya kampuni na serikali); mtu wa kati, msuluhishi. **~s** wahusika, washirika. **business ~s** watu unaohusiana nao kibiashara *vt, vi* kutana, gusana, wasiliana, ungana.

contagious *adj* (*of people or disease*) -a kuambukiza. ~ **disease** ugonjwa wa kuambukiza; (*fig*) -a kuenea upesi kwa kuigana, -a kuathiri. **contagium** *n* kiambukizi (k.m. virusi).

contagion *n* 1 uambukizaji (kwa kugusana, kukaribiana). 2 ugonjwa wa kuambukiza; *(fig)* uenezaji wa mawazo potofu/mashauri maovu/ umbeya/uvumi.

contain *vt, vi* 1 -wa na (vitu) ndani *this cup ~s water* kikombe hiki kina maji ndani yake. 2 -wa kadiri ya, -wa sawa na *a gallon ~s eight pints* galoni ni sawa na painti nane. 3 chukua/weka *how much does this bottle ~?* chupa hii huchukua kadiri gani? 4 dhibiti, zuia (uharibifu) *contain oneself* jizuia. 5 (*geom*) -wa mpaka wa. 6 *(maths) ~* a number gawanyika. **~er** *n* 1 chombo (agh. sanduku, chupa n.k.) cha kutilia vitu. 2 kontena: kasha kubwa la chuma la kusafirishia mizigo.

contaminate *vt* chafua, tia uchafu, najisi (k.m. kwa kugusa). **contamination** *n.*

contemn *vt* (*liter*) dharau, tweza, hizi, beza.

contemplate *vt,vi* 1 tazama sana (kwa macho au kwa kufikiri) *it is ~d* inafikiriwa. 2 tafakari, zingatia. 3 (*intend*) kusudia, azimu, nuia. 4 (*look forward*) tazamia. 5 taamali, dhukuru. **contemplation** *n*. **comtemplative** *adj* 1 -enye kufikiri sana; -a kutafakari. 2 (*rel*) -a kisufii *n* sufii, usufii.

contemporary *adj* 1 -a wakati ule ule. 2 -a kisasa, -a siku hizi *n* 1 mtu wa hirimu au rika lilelile (la mwingine). 3 (*persons, newspaper etc*) wakati ule ule *we were contemporaries at school* tulisoma wakati uleule mmoja chuoni (*pl*) *our contemporaries* wenzetu wa kisasa/siku hizi. **contemporaneous** *adj* (*with*) -a kutokea/kuanza/kuishi wakati mmoja.

contempt *n* 1 (*scorn*) dharau, twezo, bezo *treat with ~* dharau, beua, tweza, hakiri *beneath ~* hastahili hata kudharauliwa; hata tusi ghali. 2 aibu. 3 *~ of court* kudharau mahakama. **~ible** *adj* -a kudharauliwa, duni, hafifu. **~uous** *adj*.

contend *vt,vi* 1 pambana, shindana, pingana, bishana *~ for/with* shindania. 2 shikilia kauli, dai. **~er** *n*. **~ing** *adj*.

content[1] *n* 1 kadiri *the gold ~ of the ring* kadiri ya dhahabu ndani ya pete. 2 (*pl*) yaliyomo, fahirisi *table of ~s* fahirisi. 3 (*subject matter*) maudhui. 4 ujazo, uwezo (wa kuchukua).

content[2] *adj* 1 (**with**) ridhi, ridhika. 2 (**to**) -wa radhi/ tayari (kufanya n.k.) *I am ~ to work in Mtwara* niko tayari/ nafurahi kufanyia kazi

Mtwara *n* radhi, ridhaa, kinaa *to one's heart's* ~ kwa kutoshelezeka, ridhika. *vt,vi* ridhisha. **be ~ed** ridhika, -wa radhi. **be self ~ed** kinai. **~ed** *adj*. **~edly** *adv*. **~ment** *n*.

contention *n* 1 ushindani, ugomvi, ukinzani *bone of* ~ chanzo cha ugomvi. 2 hoja. **contentious** *adj* -gomvi; -shindani, -bishani, -a kuleta ubishi. **contentiousness** *n*.

conterminous *adj* 1 (*see* ***coterminous***) -a jirani; -liopakana. 2 -lioafiki.

contest *vt,vi* 1 jadili, toa hoja, bisha. 2 ~ *a seat in Parliament* gombea kiti cha Bunge (*strive for*) shindana, shindania, gombea; pinga ~ *an action* pinga madai *n* 1 shindano, pambano. **~able** *adj* -a kujadilika. **~ant** *n* mgombea, mshindani. **~ed** *adj* -a kugombewa.

context *n* 1 muktadha. 2 mazingira ambamo jambo hutokea. **~ual** *adj*. **~ure** *n* 1 taratibu, mtindo. 2 ufumaji.

contiguous *adj* **~(to)** -a kugusana, -a kupakana, -a karibu, -a jirani; (*geom*) -liotangamana. **contiguity** *n* ujirani; hali ya kuwa karibu.

continence *n* kujizuia/kutawala tamaa (hasa ashiki).

continent[1] *adj* 1 kujizuia, -enye kutawala tamaa (hasa ashiki).

continent[2] *n* bara, kontinenti. **~al** *adj* -a bara, -a kontinenti *n* 1 mkazi wa bara la Ulaya. **~al breakfast** kifungua kinywa cha chai/kahawa na mkate tu.

contingency *n* 1 tukio la nasibu/bila kutarajiwa *in such a* ~ *we cannot agree* mambo yakitokea hivi hatuwezi kukubali. 2 (*pl*) **contingencies** matumizi yanayotokea/ya dharura, matumizi mengine *be prepared for all* ~ -wa tayari kwa lolote litakalotokea. **contigent** *adj* 1 -sio hakika, -a bahati, -a kuwezekana (lakini hakuna hakika kwamba itatokea). 2 ~ **upon** yamkini; -a kutegemea jambo jingine *n* (*mil*) kikosi cha ziada/saidizi.

continuant *n* (*gram*) kifulizwa: sauti ambazo hutamkwa kwa mwendelezo.

continue *vt,vi* 1 endeleza, fuliza, zidi, sedeka ~ *the debate* endeleza mjadala. 2 anza upya/baada ya/tena. 3 dumu, kaa, shinda ~ *in (at) a place (office etc.)* endelea kukaa. **~d** *adj*. **continual** *adj* -a moja kwa moja, -a mfulizo; -a siku zote, -a kila siku, -a daima, -a kuendelea n **continually** *adv*. **continuance** n 1 kudumu, kuendelea *of long* ~ -a kudumu, -a muda mrefu. 2 ufulizaji, wakati ambapo jambo linaendea. 3 (*leg*) kuahirisha ~ *of drought* kuendelea kwa ukame. **continuation** *n* 1 mfulizo. 2 mwandamano, mwendelezo. **continuity** *n* 1 mwendelezo, mfululizo, mfulizo. 2 maneno ya kuendelea/kuunganisha sehemu za kipindi. 3 uendelezaji, hali ya kuendeleza. **continuous** *adj* -a moja kwa moja, -a siku zote; isosita ~ *furnace* tanuu isiyozimika (*math)* ~ *function* husisho endelevu; ~ *numbers* nambari endelevu. *~ly adv*. **continuum** *n* mwendeleo (*phys. math*) endelezo.

contort *vt* 1 umbua, potoa, nyonganyonga. 2 (*of face*) kunja, finya, kunyata. **~ion** *n* 1 upotozi, mageuzo. 2 (*of face*) finyo, kasikasi, kunjo. **~ionist** *n* mpindaviungo.

contour *n* 1 umbo, sura, namna. 2 (*geog*) kontua, (~ **line**) kontua ~ *interval* nafasi kati ya kontua *vt* piga kontua. **~-farming** *n* kilimo cha kontua. **~-map** *n* ramani ya kontua.

contra (*pref*) dhidi ya, kinyume cha.

contraband *n* 1 uingizaji au utoaji wa magendo. 2 bidhaa za magendo.

contraceptive *n* kuzuia mimba; dawa ya kuzuia mimba, kingamimba *adj* -a kuzuia mimba. **contraception** *n* uzuwiaji mimba.

contract[1] *vt* ~ **(with)/(for)** fanya mkataba; fanya mapatano; afikiana. 2 ~ **out (of)** kataa, tupilia mbali (masharti ya mkataba). 3 (*illness*) pata/patwa na, shikwa na. 4 (*of debts*) wiwa, daiwa. **~or** *n* kontrakta. **~ual** *adj* -a mkataba. *n* 1 mapatano, maafikiano, maagano, mkataba;

kondrati *breach of* ~ kuvunja mkataba ~ *of carriage* mkataba wa uchukuzi. 2 (*of marriage*) ahadi ya ndoa.

contract[2] *vt,vi* 1 punguza, fupisha; punguka, nywea *iron ~s when it cools* chuma hunywea kinapopoa. 2 bana, kacha, -wa -embamba, fanya kunyazi. **~ile** *adj* -a kuweza kunywea. **~ility** *n*. **~ion** *n* 1 mpunguo; ufupisho, mnyweo, kunywea. 2 (*wrinkle*) mfinyo/mkunyato *muscle ~ion* kukaza/kubana kwa misuli, maumivu ya misuli. 3 (*gram*) kufupisha, mkato.

contradict *vt* 1 kana, kanusha, pinga, bishia (jambo lililotajwa). 2 (*of facts*) hitilafiana, pingana, ukinzani, kujipinga; kupingana *be in ~ion with* hitilafiana na *~ion in terms* mikingamo; maelezo yanayopingana yenyewe. **~ory** *adj*.

contradistinction *n* tafautisho linganishi. **contradistinguish** *vt ~ from* tofautisha kwa kulinganisha.

contralto *n* sauti ya chini ya kike; mwanamke mwenye sauti ya chini.

contraption *n* (*colloq*) dude, dubwana.

contrary *adj* 1 -a kinyume, -a namna nyingine kabisa. 2 (*of the wind*) -sio faa, hasimu, kingamo. 3 bishi, kaidi *n* kinyume ~ *to* kinyume cha *to the* ~ kinyume *on the* ~ hata, sivyo, hasha *have you just come? on the ~ I came a long time ago* ndio kwanza umekuja? hasha, nimekuja kitambo *to the* ~ kinyume cha, vinginevyo *advise to the* ~ shauri vinginevyo. 3 *by contraries* kinyume cha mategemeo; kinyume. **contrariety** *n* (*formal*) ukinzani, uhasama (wa asili n.k.). **contrariwise** *adv* kinyume, kwa namna nyingine.

contrast *vt,vi* ~ **(with) and** -wa mbalimbali na; -wa kinyume cha, -wa namna nyingine kabisa; tofautisha ~ *with* onyesha tofauti kwa kulinganisha *n* 1 utofautishaji; tofauti, hitilafu, kinyume. *by/in ~ with* hitilafiana na, kinyume cha, tofauti na *sharp* ~ hitilafu kubwa sana, tofauti kubwa.

contravene *vt* 1 vunja (sheria n.k.) halifu, asi. 2 pinga **contravention** *n* uasi, uhalifu, uvunjaji wa sheria.

contretemps *n* (*Fr*) mgogoro; bahati mbaya.

contribute *vi,vt* **to** 1 saidia, toa. 2 changa; changia, shiriki. 3 (*of newspaper*) andikia (makala). **contributor** *n*. **contribution** *n* 1 msaada, sadaka. 2 mchango, hisa. 3 habari, makala za gazeti. 4 malipo ya lazima *lay under contribution* lazimisha mtu/nchi kulipa mchango. **contributory** *adj* -enye kusaidia; -enye kusababisha ~ *negligence* uzembe unaosababisha.

contrite *adj* -enye toba, -enye majuto. **~ly** *adv*. **contrition** *n* majuto, toba *perfect* ~ majuto kamili.

contrive *vt,vi* 1 panga kwa ustadi, simamia. 2 tunga, buni, vumbua, fanya *n* mvumbuzi; msimamizi. **contrivance** *n* 1 hila. 2 uwezo wa kuvumbua. 3 kitu kilichovumbuliwa. **~d** *adj* a ku(ji)lazimisha.

control *n* 1 madaraka au mamlaka ya kuongoza, kuamuru au kuzuia *be in ~ of* -wa na amri juu ya *get/be/come/bring under* ~ dhibiti, zuia *get out of* ~ shindikana kutawala, asi *your children are out of* ~ wanao hawaambiliki/hawakanyiki *have/keep/get ~ over* tawala, -wa na mamlaka juu ya, amirisha *have ~ over your children* tawala wanao *lose* ~ shindwa kuzuia hasira *take ~ of this project* chukua uongozi wa mradi huu. 2 usimamizi udhibiti, uongozaji ~ *of finance* udhibiti wa fedha *birth* ~ upangaji (wa) uzazi. 3 kuzuia, kurekebisha *a ~ over sth* kuzuia jambo (lisifanyike). 4 (*of experiments etc.*) kigezo/kiwango cha jaribio. 5 (*of machines etc.*) virekebishi, kidhibiti, viendeshi *volume* ~ urekebishaji wa sauti *aircraft ~ tower* mnara wa kuongozea ndege. 6 kituo cha magari ya mashindano *vt* 1 tawala, amrisha, zuia, simamia, dhibiti ~ *oneself* jitawala/jiheshimu

*~ing interest*umilikaji hisa kubwa wa kumwezesha mtu kuwa na kauli kubwa juu ya sera (katika kampuni). 2 chunguza, hakiki. 3 (*of prices*) rekebisha. **~able** *adj*. **~ler** *n* msimamizi, mtawala/mdhibiti.

controversy *n* ubishani, mabishano *without/(beyond)* ~ bila kupingwa. **controversial** *adj* -a kuelekea kuleta mabishano; *(of person)* -enye kupenda ubishani. **controversialist** *n* mbishani. **controversially** *adv*.

controvert *vt* (*rare*) pinga, bishania, kanusha, kana.

contumacy *n* ukaidi, ubishani wa kupita kiasi. **contumacious** *adj* -kaidi, bishi mno.

contumely *n* 1 ufidhuli, ujuvi, twezo. 2 matusi. **contumelious** *adj* -a ufidhuli, juvi, -a kutweza.

contuse *vt* viliza, vilisha damu. **contusion** *n* mavilio (ya damu).

conundrum *n* kitendawili, fumbo, chemsha bongo (la kuchekesha) *set ~s* tega vitendawili, mafumbo.

conurbation *n* muunganomiji: mwingiliano wa miji ambayo hapo awali ilikaa mbalimbali kuunda jamii moja kubwa.

convalesce *vi* pata ahueni, pata ashekali. **~nce** *n* muda wa kupata ahueni. **~nt** *adj* -enye ashekali *n* ahueni. **~nt home** nyumba ya mapumziko. **~nt period** kipindi cha ahueni.

convection *n* myuko (upitishaji wa joto katika uoevu). **convector** kifaa cha kupitisha joto (chumbani n.k.).

convene *vt,vi* ita/itisha/fanya mkutano; kusanyika kwa mkutano. **~r** *n* mwitishaji.

convenience *n* 1 hali inayofaa, isiyo na taabu au wasiwasi. **at your ~** kwa nafasi yako *at your earliest ~* mapema iwezekanavyo *a marriage of ~* ndoa ya kufaana. **a public ~** choo cha umma. **make a ~ of** tumia huduma ovyo. **~ food** chakula kilicho rahisi kutayarisha. **convenient** *adj* 1 -a kufaa. 2 -enye kufikika kwa urahisi, karibu *be ~ for sb* -mfalia *would it be ~ for you to come tomorrow* unaweza kuja kesho *(colloq)* -lioko mahali panapofikika kwa urahisi. **~ly** *adv* kwa kufaa/ urahisi/manufaa; bila matata/shida.

convent *n (rel)* 1 jumuia ya watawa wanawake. 2 makazi ya watawa wanawake. **enter a ~** -wa mtawa.

conventicle *n (rel)* 1 (jengo la) mkutano wa siri wa dini.

convention *n* 1 mapatano, maagano, makubaliano. **the Hague C~** Mapatano ya Hague. 2 mkutano (wa siasa, dini n.k.) wa wanachama kwa kusudi maalum k.m. uchaguzi. 3 jambo la desturi, kawaida, mila. **~al** *adj* 1 *(often derog)* -a desturi, -a kawaida, -a mazoea. **a ~al greeting** salamu ya kawaida. 2 -enye kufuata mila, jadi n.k. **~alist** *n* mwanadesturi.

converge *vi* **(at, on, upon)** kutana, elekea. **~nce** *n (maths)* kukutana. **convergent** *adj (maths)* -enye kukutana.

conversant *adj* -zoefu, -enye kujua/ kufahamu vizuri. **be ~ with a subject** -fahamu vema mada. **conversance** *n*.

converse[1] *vi* zungumza, ongea, sema, semezana *n (arch)* mazungumzo, maongezi. **conversation** *n* mazungumzo, maongezi. **enter into ~** anza kuzungumza *hold (have) ~* wa na mazungumzo. **~al** *adj* 1 -a maongezi, -a mazungumzo *in a ~al tone* kwa sauti ya maongezi. 2 *(of words)* -a kawaida. *~alist* msemaji sana, mtu anayejua sana kuzungumza.

converse[2] *adj* 1 a kinyume cha, -a upande wa pili; -liogeuzwa au kubadilika. *(logic) n* kinyume chake. **~ly** *adv*.

convert *n* mtu aliyebadili dini, msimamo. **make a ~** ingiza mtu katika imani nyingine (dini, siasa n.k.) *vt* 1 *(change)* geuza, badili (hali, dini, fedha matumizi n.k.). 2 *(of religion)* badili. **~ to Islam**

silimu. ~ **from Islam** itadi. ~ **from Islam to Christianity** tanasari. 3 *(Rugby football)* kamilisha (jaribio) kwa kufunga goli **~ed** *adj*. **~ible** *adj* 1 -a kuweza kubadilika, -a kugeuka, -a kubadilika -a *~ible (car)* kigeukaumbo, kibandawazi. 2 **~ible currency** fedha yenye kubadilishika/ kusarifika. **conversion** 1 ubadilishaji, kubadili, ugeuzaji ~ *of sth into sth else* ubadilishaji wa kitu kuwa kitu kingine. 2 *(rel)* kibadili dini. **~er** *n* 1 tanuri ya kutengeneza chuma. 2 chombo cha kubadilisha mwelekeo wa umeme. 3 chombo cha kubadilisha masafa. 4 chombo cha kubadilisha umbo la habari.

convex *adj* 1 -a mbinuko/ -a mbenuko, -a kubinuka. ~ **lens** lenzi mbinuko. **~ly** *adv*. **~ity** *n*.

convey *vt* **(to) (from)** 1 chukua, beba, peleka. 2 wasilisha, fikisha, julisha, eleza *words cannot ~ my feelings* maneno hayatoshi kueleza hisia zangu *~ one's meaning* beba maana yake *this ~s nothing to me* hii haina maana kwangu. 3 *(leg)* hawilisha. ~ **land** hawilisha ardhi. **~or/~er** mchukuzi/ kichukuzi. **~er belt** mkanda wa kuchukulia. **~ace** *n* 1 gari, chombo cha uchukuzi. 2 uchukuzi, upelekaji. 3 *(leg)* uhawilishaji; hati ya kuhawilisha (mali). **~ancer** *n* mwanasheria anayeandaa hati ya kuhawilisha. **~ancing** *(leg) n* kuhawilisha.

convict *vt* 1 tia hatiani, ona na hatia. **be ~ed** onekana na hatia *n* mfungwa. **~ion** *n* 1 kupatikana na hatia. 2 kusadikisha, kusadiki sana *carry~ion* sadikisha kabisa, ondoa shaka *be open to ~ion* tayari kuthibitishiwa. 3 imani, msimamo *it is my own ~ion* ni imani yangu, ndivyo ninavyoamini.

convince *vt* thibitishia, ridhisha *we couldn't ~ him of his mistake* tulishindwa kumridhisha kwamba amekosea *I am ~d that he is honest* nimeridhika kabisa kwamba ni mwaminifu. **~d** *adj*. **convincing** *adj* a raha/anasa; -a kupenda raha.

convivial *adj* 1 anisi, changamfu, kunjufu. **~ity** *n*.

convoke *vt* ita, itisha (mkutano).

convocation *n* 1 mkutano. 2 *(rel)* baraza la wakuu wa kanisa. 3 baraza la watu waliohitimu kutoka chuo kimoja.

convoluted *adj* 1 *(bio)* -lioviringika. 2 *(of argument etc)* -gumu kueleweka. **convolution** *n* mzingo.

convoy *vt* sindikiza kwa ajili ya ulinzi *n* 1 ulinzi wa njiani. 2 *(guard)* walinzi wa msafara. 3 msafara wenye walinzi.

convulse *vt* sukasuka, tikisa sana *the country was ~d by civil war* nchi ilitikiswa na vita vya wenyewe kwa wenyewe *be ~d with laughter* angua kicheko *be ~d with anger* fura kwa hasira. **convulsion** *n* 1 *(violent disturbance)* msukosuko, machafuko. 2 kicheko cha kuvunja mbavu. 3 mtukutiko wa maungo (kwa kifafa, dege, mashetani n.k.). **convulsive** *adj*.

cony/coney *n* 1 sungura kwanga, pelele, wibari. 2 ngozi ya sungura.

coo *vi* lia polepole (kama njiwa); sema kwa sauti ya chini *n* kulia polepole (kama njiwa).

cook *vt,vi* 1 pika; pikwa; pikika, iva ~ *sb's goose* -komesha mtu. 2 andika kwa uongo ~ *the books/ accounts* andika hesabu za uongo. 3 ~ **up** buni, zua habari *n* mpishi ***too many ~s spoil the broth*** manahodha wengi chombo huenda mrama. **~house** jiko la kambi/meli. **~er** *n* jiko, chombo cha kupikia. **~ery** *n* upishi. **~ery book** *(also ~ book)* kitabu cha mapishi.

cookie(cooky) *n (US)* biskuti.

cool *adj* 1 -a baridi kidogo. **get** ~ poa. 2 -tulivu *as ~ as a cucumber (fig)* tulivu kabisa, asiyetaharuki kabisa. **keep** ~ *(fig)* tulia. 3 ~ **it cool** shughulika bila kuhangaika *it cost me a ~ hundred shillings* imenigharimu takribani shilingi mia *me a ~ hundred shillings* imenigharimu takribani shilingi mia moja. 4 *(impudent)* -shupavu, -fidhuli, -safihi. 5 baridi, -so -a kirafiki. 6 *(sl)* -zuri *you look real* ~ unapendeza sana *vt,vi* 1 poa, poza, zimua. 2 tulia, tuliza. ~ **it** tulia. 3 ~ **down/off** tulia, poa. **a ~ing off period** kipindi cha kutulizana (wakati wa ugomvi kati ya wafanyakazi na menejimenti). 4 ~ **one's heels** ngojeshwa. **~ing tower** mnara poza *n* 1 baridi. 2 utulivu. **~ness** *n*. **~ant** *n* kimiminiko cha kupozea. **~er** *n* 1 kipozaji. 2 *(sl)* jela.

coolie *n (sl. derog)* kibarua, kuli.

cooly see coolie *n* 1 *(bot)* kuuni (mnyama mdogo alaye wenzake huko Amerika ya Kaskazini). 2 *(sl)* mjanja.

coop *n* tundu, kizimba (cha kuku n.k.) *vt* funga, zuia (katika tundu au kizimbani).

co-op *n (colloq) see* **cooperative**.

cooper *n* mtengeneza mapipa.

cooperate *vi* shirikiana. **co-operation** *n* ushirikiano *in cooperation with* kwa kushirikiana na. **co-operative** *adj* -a kushirikiana, -a ushirika, -a kupenda kusaidia *a ~ spirit* moyo wa kushirikiana. ~ **societies** *(also coops)* vyama vya ushirika. ~ **shop** duka la ushirika. **co-operator** *n* mshiriki.

co-opt *vt (of a committee)* shirikisha. **~ed member** mjumbe mshirikishwa.

co-ordinate *adj* 1 -a namna sawa, adiri, cheo kile kile. 2 -a kulingana sawa. 3 ambatanisha. ~ **clause** kishazi ambatani *vt* ratibu *n* watu/vitu sawa. **co-ordination** *n* 1 uratibu. 2 hali ya kuwa namna/kadiri/cheo sawa. ~point kituo cha uratibu. 3 *(of muscles)* kupatana, kukubaliana. **co-ordinator** *n* mratibu.

coot *n* 1 aina ya ndege anayeishi mjini. 2 *(sl)* mjinga/mpumbavu *as bald as a* ~ -enye upara kabisa.

cootie *n (army sl)* chawa.

cop[1] *see* **cooper**[2]

cop[2] *vt,vi* 1 ~ **it** adhibiwa. 2 ~ **out (of)** kwepa, acha (jambo/wadhifa n.k.). ~-out *n* kukosa/kukwepa kuwajibika. 3 ~ **a plea** kiri kosa na kuomba radhi *n* (sl) kushika, kukamata *it's a fair* ~ ni kukamatwa kihalali/palepale unapokosea. **not much** ~ sio na maana, bure.

copal *n* sandarusi.

cope *vi (with)* weza, vumilia.

copeck/kopek *n* kopeki: senti ya Kirusi.

coping *n (archit)* kigongo cha ukuta. ~ **stone** *n (fig)* kiishilizo.

copious *adj* 1 ingi, furufuru, tele, -a kufurika. 2 *(of writer)* -lioandika sana. **~ly** *adv*. **~ness** *n*.

copper[1] *n* 1 shaba nyekundu. *(attrib)* ~ **wire** udodi. ~ **cable** kebo ya shaba. 2 *(vessel)* sufuria kubwa (hasa ya kuchemshia nguo). 3 *(coin)* senti, fulusi, sarafu ya shaba. 4 ~ *beech* mti (wa) shaba: mti wenye majani ya rangi ya shaba. ~ **bottomed** *adj* meli iliyopakwa shaba kwenye kitako; *(fig)* salama kabisa, -enye uhakika. ~ **plate** bamba la shaba (lililonakshiwa) ~ *plate hand writing* mwandiko mzuri. ~ **smith** mfua shaba *vt* paka shaba kitako cha meli.

copper[2] *(also cop) n (sl)* polisi.

copra *n* mbata.

coppice/copse *n* msitu mdogo.

Copt *n* Mkhufti: mtu wa asili wa Misri.

copula *n* 1 *(gram)* kitenzi shirikishi, kopula. 2 *(med)* kiungo.

copulate *vi* ~ **(with)** jamiiana (of animals) pandana. **copulation** *n*. **~copulative** *adj* 1 *(formal)* -a kuunga, -a kuunganisha. 2 *(gram)* shirikishi. **verb** kitenzi shirikishi *n (gram)* kishirikishi.

copy *vt,vi* 1 *(out)* nakili *make a ~ of sth* nakili. 2 iga, fuatisha. 3 ~ **from/off** ibia (mitihani n.k.) *n* nakala. **attested** ~ nakala iliyoshuhudiwa. **certified** ~ nakala iliyothibitishwa *fair* ~ nakala safi *did you get your ~ of the book/ newspaper?* ulipata nakala yako ya kitabu/gazeti?. 2 maandiko (tayari kuchapwa). **good** ~ habari za kuvutia. **~-cat** *n* mwigaji. **~ist** *n* sifa yako. ~-**boy/girl** *n* kijana tarishi (katika ofisi ya gazeti). ~-**desk** *n* meza ya mhariri. **copyhold** *(GB)* n ukodishaji wa ardhi; ardhi iliyokodishwa *n* mkodishaji wa ardhi. ~**right** *n* haki ya kunakili *vt* pata haki ya kunakili. ~**writer** *n* mwandishi wa matangazo (agh ya biashara).

coquette *vi* piga ubembe, bemba. tia ashiki kwa kujishaua. **coquetry** *n* ubembe; tabia ya kushawishi/vutia/tamanisha wanaume *n* mbembe. **coquettish** *adj*. **coquettishly** *adv*.

coracle *n* mashua ndogo ya fito na ngozi.

coral *n* 1 *(red)* marijani, fedhaluka; *(white)* matumbawe ~ **reef** mwamba tumbawe *adj* -enye rangi ya waridi au nyekundu. ~ **lips** midomo myekundu.

cord *n* 1 kamba, mshipi, ugwe. 2 kiungo cha mwili kilicho kama mshipi. **the vocal** ~**s** vitunga mlio, vitunga mito *umbilical* ~ kitovu. **spinal** ~ uti wa mgongo. 3 *(elec)* waya, uzi. 4 *see corduroy (pl) vt* funga kamba. ~**age** *n* 1 kamba. 2 kamba zitumiwazo melini.

cordial adj 1 -kunjufu, -changamfu *give a ~ welcome* pokea kwa furaha, karibisha vizuri. 2 -kali, -enye nguvu. **a ~ hatred** chuki kali *n* kinywaji (hasa cha matunda cha kuchangamsha mwili). ~**ly** *adv*. ~**ity** *n*.

cordite *n* baruti (isiyotoa moshi).

cordon *n* 1 kizuizi cha askari. **a sanitary** ~ kizuizi cha askari cha karantini.

corduroy *n* 1 kodrai. 2 *(pl) (also cords)* suruali za kodrai. ~ **road** njia ya miti (kupita matope n.k.).

core *n* 1 *(of frut)* kokwa. 2 kiini, maana *get to the ~ of the subject* fikia kiini, gusa kiini/maana *rotten to the ~* -liooza kabisa *vt* toa kokwa. ~**r** *n* kisu cha kutolea kokwa.

co-respondent *n* mshitakiwa mwenzi (kwa kuzini na mume/mke wa mshitaki katika daawa ya talaka).

coriander *n* giligilani. ~ **leaves** kitimiri.

cork *n* 1 koki, gome muoki, gome jepesi la muoki. 2 kizibo (cha gome muoki) *vt (up)* 1 ziba; *(feelings)* zuia kabisa. ~**ed** *adj* 1 -enye ladha mbaya (kutokana na koki iliyooza). 2 *(sl)* liolewa sana. ~**screw** kizibuo. ~**age** *n* malipo ya huduma kwa ajili ya vinywaji vilivyoletwa na wanywaji wenyewe mkahawani.

corker *n (dated sl.)* 1 jambo la ajabu. 2 wazo lisilopingika.

cormorant *n* mnandi.

corn[1] *n* 1 *(grain)* nafaka (hasa mhindi, mchele, ngano na mtama) ~ *meal* unga wa sembe n.k. ~ *flour/starch* unga wa mahindi n.k. ~-**cob** konyo au gunzi la hindi. ~ **pone** mkate wa mahindi. 2 punje moja ya nafaka au pilipili manga. ~**crake** *n* kwekakweka (ndege).

corn[2] *n* sugu/sagamba katika kitengele cha mguu hasa katika kidole cha mguu *tread on sb's ~s* udhi mtu.

corn[3] *vt* hifadhi nyama kwa chumvi. ~**ed beef** nyama ya kopo, bifu (iliyohifadhiwa kwa chumvi).

cornea *n* konea: sehemu ya mbele ya jicho (iliyo ngumu) inayowezesha miali ya mwanga kupenya.

cornelian *n* akiki.

corner *n* 1 pembe, kona *standing at a street~* kusimama kwenye pembe ya barabara *just round the ~* nyuma (hapo) kwenye kona; karibu sana *turn the ~* kata kona; *(fig)* pata ahueni/ nafuu (baada ya maradhi/ kipindi kigumu) *cut off a ~* pita moja kwa moja (badala ya kuzunguka). **cut ~s** tumia njia za mkato, pinda sheria (ili kufanikisha kitu) *drive sb into ~* tia mashakani *be in a tight ~* -wa hatarini, -wa katika hali ngumu. 2 *(secret or remote places)* mahali pa siri *they searched all ~s* walitafuta kila kipembe. 3 *(region quarter)* sehemu *to the four ~s of the earth* pote duniani, pembe zote za dunia. 4 *(comm)* kununua bidhaa zote za aina fulani (kwa ajili ya kuhodhi na kudhibiti bei). 5 *(foot- Hockey)* kona. ~ **kick** mpira wa kona. ~ **stone** jiwe la msingi *(fig)* msingi/kiini cha jambo *vt, vi* 1 sukumia kwenye pembe/ kona *(fig)* weka katika hali ngumu. **~ed animal** mnyama aliyezingwa. 2 dhibiti (kwa kununua bidhaa zote). 3 *(of vehicles)* kata/ pinda kona.

cornet *n* buruji.

cornucopia *n* 1 *(myth)* pembe itoayo chakula na vinywaji bila kikomo. 2 alama (ya pembe hii) inayoonyesha wingi wa neema.

corny *adj (sl)* -a kale, -liochakaa. **~joke** mzaha uliochakaa.

corolla *(bot)* korola: jumla ya petali katika ua.

corollary *n* matokeo.

corona *n (pl.)* taji la nuru, kitanga cha mwezi; jua.

coronal *adj* -a korona/kaakaa.

coronary *adj (med)* -a moyo. ~ **arteries** ateri za moyo. ~ **thrombosis** kitomoyo, shtuko la moyo.

coronation *n* kutawaza/kutawazwa.

coroner *n (leg)* afisa mchunguzi wa vifo(vya ghafla/visivyo vya kawaida). **~'s inquest** baraza la utafiti wa sababu ya kifo.

coronet *n* 1 kitaji, shada la maua, taji dogo, pambo la kichwa 2 *(bot)* shada.

corporal[1] *n (mil)* koplo.

corporal[2] *adj* -a mwili, -a kuhusu mwili ~ *punishment* adhabu ya kutandikwa. **corporeal** *adj* -a kimwili (badala ya kiroho). ~ **needs** mahitaji ya mwili.

corporate *adj* -a shirika, -a pamoja ~ *body* shirika ~ *name* jina la shirika ~ *responsibility* madaraka ya pamoja. **corporation** *n* 1 ushirika, shirika *public* ~ shirika la umma. 2 madiwani, *manispaa the mayor and* ~ meya na madiwani wake. 3 *(colloq)* kitambi. 4 *(US)* kampuni, shirika ~ *tax* kodi ya shirika.

corps *n* 1 kundi la wanajeshi (agh wa kazi). **carrier** ~ kikosi cha wachukuzi. 2 jeshi la askari. 3 **diplomatic** ~ jamii ya mabalozi. 4 kundi.

corpse *n* maiti, mzoga.

corpulent *adj* -nene sana. **corpulence** *n.*

corpus *n* 1 mkusanyo (wa maandishi yote ya mwandishi mmoja/aina moja/ mada moja). 2 mwili. 3 *(leg) writ of habeas* ~ amri ya kufikisha mfungwa kortini. 4 *(rel) C~ Christ* Sikukuu ya Ekaristi Takatifu.

corpuscle *n* chembechembe za damu, chembedamu. **corpuscular** *adj* -a chembe za damu.

corral *n* 1 zizi. 2 boma vt 1 tia zizini. 2 *(sl)* teka, kusanya; fungia zizini, tengeneza boma.

correct *vt* 1 rekebisha, sahihisha, kosoa. 2 *(punish)* rudi, tia adabu. 3 rekebisha, ondoa kasoro ~ *a malformity/disorder* ondosha kilema cha mwili; ponyesha *adj* 1 sahihi, fasaha ~ *(clear) style* mtindo fasaha. 2 *(of manner, conduct)* muwafaka, barabara; bila kosa. **~ly** *adv.* **~ness** *n.* **~ion** *n* 1 usahihishaji, utoaji makosa, sahihisho, rekebisho. 2 *(arch) a house of ~ion* chuo cha mafunzo, jela *speak under ~ion* sema kwa sharti (kwamba unaweza kusahihishwa). 3 *(punishment)* adhabu, marudi, rada. 4 *(improvement)* matengenezo. **~ional** *adj.*

correlate *vi,vt* ~ *(with)* wiana, husiana, patana; patanisha. **correlation** *n* uwiano, uhusiano.

correlative *adj* 1 *(word or thing)* -a uwiano, -enye uhusiano. 2 *(gram)* ~ *conjunction* kiunganishi wiani.

correspond *vi* 1 ~ *(with)* fanana, kubaliana, tangamana, lingana. 2 ~ **(to)** -wa sawasawa, fanana na. 3 ~ *(with)* andikiana barua; wasiliana (kimaandishi). **~ingly** *adv.* **~ing** *adj the ~ing time last year* ikilinganishwa na) mwaka jana wakati kama huu. **~ence** *n* 1 ulinganifu, tangamano, kukubaliana, uhusiano *one-to-one ~ence* uhusiano wa moja kwa moja. 2 barua; mawasiliano (ya kimandishi);

kuandikiana barua *~ence education* elimu kwa njia ya posta. **correspondent** *n* 1 mwandishi wa makala (katika magazeti n.k.); mleta habari. 2 mtu anayeandikiana barua na mwingine. 3 *(comm)* vyombo vinavyohusiana (k.m. benki, mashirika).

corridor *n* ushoroba. ~ **train** garimoshi lenye ujia wa kuingilia vyumbani. **~s of power** mahali panapofanyiwa kampeni zisizo rasmi; mlango wa nyuma.

corrigendum *n* korijenda: orodha ya makosa na masahihisho katika kitabu. **corroborate** *vt* thibitisha, (kwa kutoa ushahidi wa ziada). **corroboration** *n* uthibitisho, ushuhuda *in corroboration (of)* kwa ithibati. **corroborative** *adj* -a kuthibitisha, -a kuelekea kuthibitisha. ~ **evidence** ushahidi wenye ithibati.

corrode *vt, vi* -la, haribu, lika. **corrosion** *n* uharibifu, ulikaji (k.m. wa kutu). **corrosive** *adj (substance)* -enye ukali wa kuharibu, kubabua *n* dawa yenye ukali.

corrugate *vt,vi* kunjakunja (kama migongogongo midogo), kunjamana, weka matuta. **~d** *adj* -enye mikunjo *~d iron (sheets)* mabati (ya kuezekea). **corrugation** *n* migongogongo, mikunjokunjo, makunyanzi.

corrupt *vt,vi* 1 potosha, shawishi kufanya mabaya *he was ~ed by the life in the city* alipotoshwa na maisha ya mjini. 2 toa rushwa/hongo. 3 haribu, chafua. 4 oza, ozesha. **~ible** *adj*. **~ibility** *n, adj* 1 *(of persons, their actions)* -ovu, -so na maadili, -- soaminika, -enye kupokea/kutoa rushwa. ~ **practices** vitendo vilivyo-potoka, matendo maovu; *(of language)* potovu *this is a ~ text* haya ni matini yaliyoharibiwa/ ghushiwa. **~ion** *n* 1 utoaji/ulaji rushwa/hongo/mlungura, ufisadi, upotovu. 2 uozo, ubovu, uchafu. 3 uharibifu.

corsage *n* 1 badisi. 2 *(US)* shada (la kifuani).

corsair *n (hist)* 1 haramia wa baharini. 2 meli ya haramia wa baharini.

corse *n (arch or poet)* maiti.

corset *n* koseti (nguo ya ndani ya kubana kuanzia kiunoni hadi mapajani).

cortege *n* wasindikizaji, waandamanaji wa sherehe maalum (ya rais, mfalme n.k.) agh. kwa ajili ya mazishi, n.k.

cortex *n* gamba, ganda, gome, tabaka la nje ya ubongo. **cortical** *adj*.

coruscate *vi* metameta, memeteka, ng'aa. *(fig)* **~ing wit** uchekeshaji werevu. **coruscation** *n*.

corvee *n (arch)* shokoa.

corvette *n* manowari ndogo (ya kusindikiza meli ya shehena).

cosh *n (GB sl)* rungu vt *(GB sl)* piga kwa rungu.

cosher *adj, n see* kosher.

co-signatory *adj, n* mtiaji sahihi mwenzi.

cosmetic *adj* -a kipodozi. *n (usul. pl)* kipodozi. **~ian** *n* mtaalamu wa vipodozi.

cosmopolitan *adj* 1 -a kuhusu/kutoka sehemu zote za dunia. 2 -a kidunia; pana (kutokana na uzoefu wa sehemu nyingi za dunia) *a ~ outlook* mtazamo wa kidunia *adj (person)* -enye mtazamo wa kiulimwengu *n* 1 msafiri wa dunia. 2 mlimwengu: mtu mwenye mtazamo wa kimataifa. 3 kiumbe/mmea wa duniani pote. **cosmopolitism** *n*.

cosmos *n* ulimwengu. **cosmic** *adj* -a (kuhusu) ulimwengu mzima. **cosmic rays** miali ulimwengu. **cosmogony** *n* nadharia kuhusu chanzo cha ulimwengu. **cosmography** *n* kosmografia: maelezo ya sura ya dunia katika ramani.

cosmology *n* 1 kosmolojia: sayansi kuhusu ulimwengu. 2 tawi la sayansi lishughulikalo na muundo na umbo la ulimwengu. **cosmonaut** *n also astronaut* mwanaanga (wa Kirusi).

cosset *vt* engaenga, endekeza; dekeza.

cost[1] *vt,vi* 1 *(cost)* gharimu,

patikana kwa bei/gharama fulani *the house ~s 4ml shs to build* nyumba inagharimu shs mil 4 kujenga *dictionary making ~s much time* kutunga kamusi huchukua muda mwingi. 2 *(result in the loss of)* patisha/ingiza hasara; hasiri *careless driving may ~ you your life* uzembe katika kuendesha gari unaweza kuhasiri maisha yako. 3 *(industry and comm)* kadiria bei (kwa kuzingatia gharama za uzalishaji). **~ing** *n (Industry)* upangaji/uwekaji/ukadiriaji bei *the ~ing department* idara ya kupanga bei *n* 1 bei, gharama *the ~ of living* gharama za maisha *the ~ of a house* gharama/bei ya nyumba *the ~ price of an article* gharama za kutengeneza kitu; bei ya kununulia (itolewayo na mfanyabiashara). ~ **accounting** hesabu za kuonyesha gharama. 2 **~s** *(leg)* gharama za kesi (zitolewazo na aliyeshindwa kesi). **at all ~s** kwa vyovyote vile *at the ~ of* kwa kupoteza *count the ~* kadiria hasara. **~ly** *adj* 1 -a gharama kubwa, -a thamani kubwa. 2 -enye kufanywa kwa gharama kubwa.

co-star *vt* 1 -wa nyota pamoja (na), shiriki na wengine kama mababe. 2 ingiza mababe wawili katika filamu *n* mbabe mwenzi.

coster monger *n* mchuuzi anayeuza matunda/mboga mitaani.

costive *adj (liter)*-enye kufunga tumbo; -a kufunga choo, -enye uyabisi wa tumbo. **~ness** *n*.

costume *n* 1 mavazi (maalum) (agh. kwa kipindi, nchi, cheo maalum au taifa fulani) *national ~* vazi la taifa. 2 maleba: mavazi ya shughuli/majira maalumu *vt ~ a theatre etc.* leta/shona maleba n.k. kwa ajili ya michezo. 3 suti ya mwanamke. *swimming ~* vazi la kuogelea ~ jewellery vito bandia. **costumier** *n* mtengenezaji, muuzaji na mwazimishaji wa mavazi ya sherehe mbalimbali.

cosy[1] *adj* -a kufurahisha/kuburudisha na kuleta raha *it's very ~ here* mahali hapa pazuri/pana burudisha. **a ~ little job** kazi ndogo ya malipo makubwa *adv* kwa furaha/raha.

cosy,[2] **cosey** *n* kifuniko (cha birika la chai) au yai lililochemshwa.

cot[1] *n* 1 *(poet)* kibanda. 2 kifuniko (hasa kinachofunika kidole ili kisiumie).

cot[2] *n* 1 kitanda kidogo chembamba (kinachoweza kubebwa kwa urahisi) cha mtoto mdogo. 2 kitanda cha safari. ~ **death** kifo cha ghafla cha mtoto mchanga (agh usingizini bila kuugua).

cotangent *n (maths)* kotanjiti.

cote *n* kibanda (kwa ajili ya kuku, njiwa n.k.).

coterie *n* genge (watu wenye mawazo mamoja).

cottage *n* nyumba ndogo hasa ya kijijini/shambani. ~ **hospital** hospitali ndogo ya kitongojini. ~ **industry** kiwanda kidogo. **cotter** *n* mkazi katika nyumba ndogo mashambani. **~r** *n* mtu aishie kwenye nyumba ndogo (mkulima; kibarua wa mashambani).

cotton[1] *n* pamba. ~ **wool** pamba. **~-cake** mashudu ya pamba agh. hutumiwa kama chakula cha ng'ombe. **~-gin** kinu cha kuchambulia pamba **~-grass** pamba mwitu. **~-mouth** nyoka wa majini mwenye sumu. **~-tail** *(US)* mnyama aina ya sungura.

cotton[2] *vi (sl)* 1 kubaliana. 2 -wa na urafiki *~ on (to) (colloq)* fahamu, elewa *~ up to* jenga urafiki; jaribu kufanya urafiki.

cotyledon *n* kotiledoni.

couch *vt,vi* 1 jilaza (kwa ajili ya kupumzika au kulala). 2 lala kwa kuvizia; weka mahali pa maficho au pa kuvizia. 3 *(of animals)* jikunyata na kulala usingizi. 4 fuma, tarizi. 5 kuweka maelezo katika mtindo maalumu. 6 shusha (mkuki, panga, n.k.) tayari kwa kushambulia *n* 1 kochi: samani itumiwayo kwa kukalia au kulalia. 2 kitanda cha mgonjwa wakati anapofanyiwa uchunguzi.

couchant *adj (heraldry, of animals)* -liolalia miguu na kuinua kichwa juu (kama afanyavyo paka).

couch-grass *n (bot)* ukoka.

cough *vi, vt* 1 kohoa. ~ **out** kohoa, toa kohozi. 2 *(draw attention)* jikohoza ~ *down a speaker* nyamazisha msemaji. ~ **up** ondoa kooni kwa kukohoa. ~ *up a fish bone* toa mwiba wa samaki kwa kukohoa. ~ **up** *(sl)* toa, changa, kabidhi bila kupenda. ~**-drops** vidonge (peremende) vya kikohozi.

council *n* 1 halmashauri; baraza **City C~** Halmashauri ya Jiji *Revolutionary C~* Baraza la Mapinduzi *Executive C~ (Cabinet)* Baraza la Mawaziri. **Legislative C~** Baraza la Kutunga Sheria. 2 mkutano. ~ **of war** mkutano wa kushauriana mambo ya vita. ~ **board** *n* meza ya mkutano ya halmashauri. ~ **chamber** *n* chumba cha mikutano ya halmashauri *~lor (also ~-man) n* diwani, mjumbe wa baraza.

counsel *n* 1 *(also advice)* ushauri, mawaidha, wasia. **give** ~ shauri, toa ushauri/wasia *take/ hold ~ with sb* pata ushauri kutoka kwa mtu *keep one's own ~* setiri siri. 2 *(with indef. art or in pl but not with numerals) a ~ of perfection* ushauri mzuri kabisa ambao hauwezi kufuatwa. 3 mshauri; wakili, mwanasheria *~ for defence* wakili wa utetezi *~ for prosecution* wakili wa mashitaka. **King's (Queen's)** ~ wakili mwandamizi (wa serikali) *vt* shauri, nasihi/usia. ~**lor** *n* 1 mshauri. 2 *(US)* wakili.

count[1] *n* aina ya lodi (katika Bara la Ulaya isipokuwa Uingereza). ~**ess** *n* mke wa lodi.

count[2] *vt, vi* 1 ~ *(from) (to)* hesabu, taja mlolongo wa idadi. *(colloq)* ~ **noses** hesabu idadi ya watu. ~**less** *adj* bila idadi, -ingi mno, -siohesabika, pasi na idadi *there are ~less examples etc.* kuna mifano chungu mzima *there are 10 ~ without the visitors* wako 10 tukiacha wageni *~able noun* nomino ya idadi. 2 jumlisha, ingiza. 3 *(fig)* (ji) hesabu. 4 -wa na thamani/maana *he doesn't ~* hana maana *every minute ~s* kila dakika ina thamani. ~ **against** athiri, fanya mtu afikiriwe vibaya. ~ **among** fikiriwa. ~ **down** hesabu kurudi nyuma. ~ **in** ingiza, ongeza/ jumuisha. ~ **me in** nimo. ~ **on** tegemea, tumainia *may ~ on you* naweza kukutegemea. ~ **out** hesabu moja moja; *(boxing)* hesabia muda; ondoa; *(of parliament)* tangaza kuwa hakuna akidi. ~ **up** jumlisha *it ~s for much* ina maana sana/kubwa *n* 1 hesabu, kuhesabu *ask for a ~* omba kuhesabu kura *keep ~ of sth* weka hesabu ya. **lose** ~ shindwa kuhesabu *take the ~/be out for the ~* hesabiwa muda. 2 kujali *take no ~ of* -tojali. 3 shitaka.

countenance *n* 1 uso, sura *a person with a fierce ~* mtu mwenye sura ya ukatili. 2 fikra zilizotulia, utulivu, udhibiti wa nafsi *put out of ~* fadhaisha, tahayarisha *keep one's ~* tulia, -toonyesha hisia, kaza uso kuzuia kicheko n.k. *give ~ to a plan* kubali shauri *vt* kubali, unga mkono *I cannot ~ it* siikubali.

counter[1] *n* 1 kaunta: sehemu ya mfuto k.m. meza, ambapo vitu hununuliwa/huuziwa *sell under the ~* uza kwa mlango wa nyuma. 2 kipande, sarafu (ya kuhesabu katika michezo fulani). 3 mtu ahesabuye. 4 *(math.)* kihesabio.

counter[2] *adv* kinyume, kwa kubadili *run ~ to* shindana na; enda kinyume na, pinga *adj* -a kinyume; -a kukabili *vt, vi* 1 kabili, jibu mapigo, pinga *(pref)* 1 kinyume cha. 2 jibu la. 3 lingana na. 4 dhidi ya.

counteract *vt* kinza, zuia, shinda. ~tion *n*. ~**tive** *adj*.

counter-appeal n rufani dhidi ya rufani *vt* kata rufani dhidi ya rufani.

counter-attack *n* jibu la mapigo *vt* rudishia shambulio/pigo.

counter-attraction *n* mvuto shindani; mivutano.
counterbalance see **counterpoise** *vt* sawazisha. *n* usawazisho (uzito ulio sawa na uzito mwingine k.m. mizani).
counterblast *n* jibu kali na lenye nguvu, upepo mshindani.
counterblow *n* pigo linalojibu pigo jingine; midundano.
counter-change *n* kubadilisha (nafasi/ sehemu/vifaa n.k.); mabadilishano.
counter charge *(leg)* shitaka la mshitakiwa (dhidi ya mshitaki).
countercheck *n* 1 kuzuia kinachopinga. 2 kaguo *vt* 1 kagua tena. 2 zuia kinachopinga.
counter-claim *n* dai kinzani. *vt* leta dai juu ya dai.
counter-clockwise *adv see* **anti clockwise**.
counter-espionage *n* ujasusi pinzani: ujasusi dhidi ya ujasusi.
counterfeit *vt* ghushi, buni; iga, (kwa nia ya kudanganya) *n* bandia,mfano *adj* -a bandia, -a kubuni -a kughushi; -a kuiga. **~er** *n*. **~ing** *n*.
counterfoil *n* kishina (cha stakabadhi, barua ya fedha, hawala n.k.)
counter-irritant *n* kipoza maumivu.
countermand *vt* 1 tangua amri, (kwa kutoa amri ya kinyume). 2 kurudisha nyuma (k.m. kundi la askari) kwa kutoa amri kinyume na ile iliyotolewa kwanza *n* utoaji amri inayotangua amri ya awali.
countermine *vt, vi* 1 tega bomu dhidi ya bomu lingine. 2 zuia pigo kwa kulivuruga kabla ya kutokea kwake *n* mpango wa kupinga shambulio; mpango dhidi ya shambulio la adui lililopangwa.
counteroffensive *n* kujibu (mapigo/shambulio).
counterpane *n* firashi.
counterpart *n* 1 nakili. 2 *(of a person)* mwenzi. 3 *(of a thing)* kifanani.
counter offer *n* fadhila ya kujibu fadhila.
counterplot *n* hila ya kupindua hila, hila dhidi ya hila.
counterpoint *n (mus)* 1 utumbuizo; kijalizo cha wimbo. 2 ujalizaji wa wimbo.
counterpoise *vt* sawazisha, tia uzito upande ulio mwepesi ili kusawazisha pande zote mbili *n* 1 (jiwe lenye) uzito ulio sawa na uzito mwingine. 2 hali ya urari /mizani/ usawazisho.
counterpoison *n* dawa inayozuia sumu.
counter revolution *n* kupinga mapinduzi. **~-revolutionary** *n, adj*.
countersign *vt* 1 tia sahihi (hati n.k.) iliyokwisha tiwa sahihi na mwingine. 2 thibitisha kwa kutia sahihi *n* 1 *(mil)* neno, ishara, itikio la siri (ya kupishwa askari walindao zamu). 2 utiaji/uwekaji sahihi.
countersink *vt* 1 *(tech)* panua tundu la kuingizia skrubu. 2 shindilia skurubu ndani ya tundu.
countervail *vt, vi* 1 sawazisha, tumia nguvu dhidi ya kikinzani chenye athari mbaya au chenye hatari. 2 -wa/pata nguvu sawa ya kufidia. 3 pata/lipwa sehemu ya ushuru juu ya maduhuli (yaliyofidiwa na nchi iingizayo bidhaa).
counterweight *n* uzito wa kusawazisha.
country *n* 1 nchi. 2 shamba *in the ~side* mashambani. **~life** maisha ya shamba. **town and ~ planning** mpango wa miji na vijiji. **go up ~** enda bara. 3 **the ~** wananchi; taifa kwa jumla. **go to the ~** itisha uchaguzi mkuu (kwa haki ya kuunda serikali mpya). 4 *(as attrib.)* **~ club** klabu ya kiungani. **~ cousin** *(colloq)*. jogoo la shamba, mshamba **~-folk** *n* wenyeji wa mashambani, wanavijiji, watu wa vijijini. **~gentleman** mwinyi. **~ party** chama cha maslahi ya wakulima. **~ house** *n* nyumba ya shamba. **~man/women** *n* 1 mwananchi. 2 mkazi wa shamba. **~ seat** *n* nyumba kijijini (agh. ya mtu tajiri). **~side** *n* shamba. **countrifield** *adj* -a kimashamba, -enye desturi za kishamba.
county *n (GB)* mkoa; *(US)* wilaya. ~ *family* ukoo wa asili (katika mkoa/

wilaya).

coup *n* mapinduzi. **~d'etat** *n* mapinduzi ya serikali. **~de grace** pigo la kifo.

coupe *n* 1 gari la farasi la abiria wawili. 2 *(US)* motokaa ya watu wawili yenye milango miwili.

couple *n* 1 vitu au watu wawili wanaohusiana (mtu na mkewe); wachumba, maharusi. 2 *(fig) they go in ~s* huenda wawili wawili. 3 mbilitatu, kadhaa *vt,vi* 1 *(on)* unga, unganisha, ungana (fikirani). 2 oana; jamiiana. 3 *(of animals)* pandana. 4 **~ with** unganisha, husisha. **~d with this** pamoja na hayo. **~r** *n* kiunganisho. **coupling** *n* 1 kiungo. 2 uunganishaji; uunganaji. 3 njia inayounganisha mizunguko miwili ya umeme ili umeme upite kati yake. **coupling-pin** *n (tech)* pini ya kiungo.

coupon *n* 1 kuponi: hati itolewayo kumwezesha mtu kupata kitu, huduma au malazi. 2 kipande cha tangazo lililochapishwa kinachokatwa na kutumiwa kama fomu ya kuagizia kitu au maelezo. 3 sehemu ya/kipande cha hisa kinachoonyesha kiasi na tarehe ya riba.

courage *n* ushujaa, ujasiri, ushupavu. **take ~** jipa moyo. **take one's ~in both hands** jipiga moyo konde *have the ~ of one's convictions* -wa na moyo wa kufanya unaloamini. **~ous** *adj*.

courier *n* 1 mjumbe; tarishi. 2 mtu anayesindikiza na kuwafanyia watalii mipango ya safari.

course[1] *n* 1 mwendo *the ~of events* jinsi mambo yanavyoenda *in the ~ of his childhood* wakati wa utoto wake *in the ordinary ~ of nature* kwa kawaida *in (the) ~ of time* hatimaye *in the ~ of the conversation* wakati wa mazungumzo *in due ~* kwa wakati wake *let nature take her ~* yaache mambo yalivyo. 2 njia, uelekeo *(naut) a northerly ~* uelekeo wa kaskazi *there is no other ~ open* hapana njia nyingine *take a middle ~* fuata njia isiyoelemea upande mmoja *take a different ~* fanya vingine *as a matter of ~* mambo kama yalivyo/yanavyotarajiwa kuwa. 3 *(series of lectures, treatments etc.)* kozi: mfulizo wa masomo; mfululizo wa matibabu. 4 *(part of meal)* sehemu ya mlo. 5 uwanja (wa kushindania mbio za farasi n.k.). **stay the ~** endelea hadi mwisho (licha ya matatizo); -tokata tamaa. 6 tabaka, mstari (wa matofali au mawe katika nyumba). 7 **on/off ~** sawa/mrama.

course[2] *vt,vi* 1 kimbiza, fukuza (hasa sungura) kwa kutumia mbwa. 2 *(of liquids)* tiririka.

courser *n (poet)* farasi mwenye mbio.

court[1] *n* 1 kitala. 2 mahakama, korti. **appellate ~** mahakama ya rufani. **civil ~** mahakama ya madai. **high ~** mahakama kuu. **primary ~** mahakama ya mwanzo *contempt of ~* kudharau mahakama *open ~* mahakama ya wazi, (ambapo wasikilizaji wowote wanaruhusiwa). *be ruled/put out of ~* kataliwa mahakamani *take to ~* shitaki. 3 ua (wa nyumba). **~yard** uga, uwanja. 4 kiwanja cha michezo. **~card** karata ya mzungu (katika mchezo wa karata). **~ier** *n* mtumishi wa kitala. **~ martial** *n* mahakama ya kijeshi *vt* shtaki kijeshi. **be ~ martialled** shtakiwa kijeshi.

court[2] *vt* 1 jipendekeza kwa heshima. 2 bembeleza *pay ~ to (a woman)* fanya urafiki, posa (mwanamke), bemba. 3 karibisha/chokoza (hatari, maafa, n.k.).

courtesan *n* malaya, kahaba (hasa wa matajiri).

courtesy *n* 1 adabu, heshima, ustahifu, uungwana *treat with ~* stahi, heshimu. 2 kuheshimu, kitendo cha heshima. 3 *~ title (GB)* cheo cha heshima. 4 **by ~ of** kwa fadhila ya.

courteous *adj* -a adabu, -a heshima, stahifu. **courteousness** *n*. **courtly** *adj* -enye adabu, -a heshima, stahifu. **courtliness** *n*.

courtship *n* 1 posa, uchumba,

ubembelezi. 2 kipindi cha posa.

cousin *n* binamu: ndugu (waliozaliwa na ndugu wa baba na mama). **~ly** *adj.*

cove[1] *n* ghuba ndogo.

cove[2] *n (GB dated sl.)* jamaa.

coven *n* mkutano wa wachawi.

covenant *n* 1 *(leg)* mkataba, hati, mapatano. **deed of ~** hati iliyothibitishwa kisheria (agh.) kuhusu mali). 2 ahadi ya maandishi ya kutoa malipo ya ufadhili kwa vipindi vilivyopangwa *vt,vi* agana, patana, kubaliana, andikiana mkataba. **~ed** *adj* liofungwa na mkataba.

coventry *n (phr)* **send a person to ~** tenga mtu kabisa (kwa kukataa kuongea naye).

cover *vt* 1 funika; funikiza. 2 ~ **over** tandaza. ~ **up** fungia, ficha, funika kabisa *n* kuficha; mbinu/namna (ya kuficha) *vi* danganya; enea, tanda *the water ~s the whole plain* maji yameenea uwanda mzima. 3 **be ~ ed with** pambwa na; jaa; rashia; pakaza (tope). 4 *(of money)* tosha *100 shs will ~ my needs* shilingi mia zitanitosha/tosheleza. 5 *(protect)* kinga, wekea bima, tetea, linda. 6 *(of guns/fortress)* tawala. 7 safiri; maliza *~ ten miles in an hour* safiri maili kumi kwa saa moja. 8 *(sports)* linda; kaba. 9 *(comprise)* jumlisha, -wa na *the speech ~ed all the main issues* hotuba ilikuwa na mambo yote muhimu. 10 *(of a journalist) he ~ed the meeting* alielezea habari za mkutano *he ~s sports* yu mwandishi wa habari za michezo. **~ing letter** barua iliyoambatishwa ya maelezo (ya ziada). 11 ~ **in** fukia kabisa (shimo n.k.); funika. 12 jiingiza; jitetea. ~ **oneself with disgrace** jiingiza fedhehani *n* 1 kifuniko, kawa. 2 nguo (kitambaa cha maandalizi) ya meza. 3 kinga, maficho. **take** ~ jificha. break ~ jifichua. 4 jalada. **read a book from ~ to ~** soma kitabu chote. ~ **girl** msichana anayepigwa picha za kuwekwa kwenye majalada ya magazeti. 5 *(insurance)* fedha za fidia (dhara likitokea). ~ **note** hati ya bima ya muda. 6 *(comm)* fedha, dhamana. 7 **under ~of** kwa kisingizio cha. 8 bahasha. **under separate ~** ndani ya bahasha nyingine. 9 **under plain ~** isiyo na kitambulisho/alama. 10 magugu. **~age** *n* taarifa za matukio. **~let** *n* firashi.

covert[1] *n* maficho, kichaka.

covert[2] *adj* -a siri, -liofichwa, -a hila. ~ **glances** kutupa macho kwa siri. **~ly** *adv.*

covet *vt* tamani (hasa mali ya mwingine), taka sana; ona shauku ya (kitu kisicho halali au kisicho chako). **~ous** *adj* ~ **(of)** -enye tamaa (shauku, uchu) (hasa ya mali ya mwingine). **~ousness** *n.*

covey *n* kundi (la ndege).

cow[1] *n* 1 ng'ombe jike. 2 jike la mnyama (kama tembo, kiboko n.k.). 3 *(derog sl)* mwanamke *till the ~s come home* daima. **~-bell** *n* kengele inayofungwa ng'ombe. ~ **boy** *n* 1 mchunga ng'ombe (katika tambarare za Amerika). 2 mfanyabiashara asiye mwaminifu. 3 mhuni, mdanganyifu. **~-catcher** *n* ngao (ya gari), fremu ya chuma iliyofungwa mbele ya injini ya garimoshi inayoondoa vizuizi vya relini. **~-fish** *n* samaki-ng'ombe (samaki mwenye kichwa kama cha ng'ombe). **~herd** *n* mchunga ng'ombe, mchungaji wa ng'ombe. **~hide** *n* ngozi ya ng'ombe. **~man** *n (pl)* **~men** mkama ng'ombe. **~shed/~-house** zizi la ng'ombe. **~-pox** *n* ndui ya ng'ombe.

cow[2] *vt* ogofya, tisha.

cowage *n* upupu, kiwavi.

coward *n* mwoga *adj* -oga,-enye hofu. **~ly** *adj.* **~ice** *n* woga.

cower *vi* nywea, jikunyata; jikunja (ili kujificha au kwa hofu).

cowl *n* 1 ukaya (namna ya kofia); kifuniko cha bomba la moshi. 2 kifuniko (cha injini ya gari). 3 kanzu yenye kofia. **~ing** *n* kifuniko (cha mashine n.k.).

cowpea *n* kunde.

cowrie, cowry *n* kauri.
coxa *n (anat)* nyonga. **~l** *adj*.
coxcomb *n* fidhuli; mfuauji, mtanashati.
coxswain *n* sarahangi.
coy *adj* -enye haya,-enye soni, -enye kudai kuona haya. **~ly** *adv*. **~ness** *n*.
coz *n (arch) (sl)* binamu.
cozen *vt* danganya, laghai, ghilibu, nyenga ~ *sb into doing sth* danganya mtu afanye jambo ~ *sth out of* chukua kitu kwa hila. **~age** *n* udanganyifu.
cozy *see* **cosy**.
crab[1] *n* 1 kaa. *(fig)* **catch a ~** piga kasia vibaya. ~ **wise** *adj* upogoupogo *n (also* **~-apple**). 2 tofaa pori.
crab[2] *vi (colloq)* lalamika; nung'unika; kosoa, laumu. **~bed** *adj* 1 -epesi kughadhabika. 2 *(of hand writing)* -siosomeka kwa urahisi. 3 *(of writings/authors)* -sioeleweka kwa urahisi.
crack[1] *vt,vi* 1 tia ufa, fanya upenyu. **the ~ of dawn** *(colloq)* wakati wa mapambazuko. 2 alisha; alika, fanya mwaliko; *(of voice)* wa kali; kwaruza. 3 banja; kwaruza. 4 *(chem)* safisha; yeyusha mafuta mazito. 5 *(colloq and sl. uses)*. **~ down on** chukulia hatua kali (za kinidhamu). ~ **up (to be sth)** sifu mno, kuza. ~ **up** kosa nguvu (kwa uzee); pata kichaa; *(of a vehicle)* haribu; haribika, vunjika. ~ **a bottle** fungua chupa na nywa kilichomo. ~ **a joke** toa mchapo, piga porojo.
crack[2] *n* 1 ufa, mwatuko. 2 kishindo, mwaliko. **the ~ of doom** siku ya kiyama. 3 kipigo cha ghafula. **give sb a ~ on the head** piga kichwani. 4 mzaha, dhihaka, jibu la kuchekesha. 5 *(sl)* stadi, mwenye akili, bora, bingwa. 6 *(sl)* majaribio. **have a ~ at sth** jaribu kitu. 7 **~-brained** *adj* -enye kichaa/wazimu; pumbavu. **~ed** *adj* -enye wazimu. **~er** *n* 1 biskuti/mkate mkavu. 2 fataki ya kuchezea (ialikayo ikipasuka). 3 kibanguzi: chombo cha kubangulia (mathalani korosho, nyonyo n.k.). **~-jack** *n* 1 *(sl)* mtu stadi, bora kabisa. 2 kitu bora kabisa. **~ers** *adj (GB sl)* -enye wazimu.
crackle *vi* lia, data, chakarika; alikaalika (kama fito zikipasuka au kuchomwa moto) *n* mwaliko. **crackling** *n* 1 *(see crackle)*. 2 ngozi ya nguruwe (iliyookwa).
crackpot *n* mtu mwenye mawazo ya ajabu; pumbavu. ~ **ideas** mawazo ya ajabu.
cracksman *n* mwizi (wa kuvunja nyumba).
cradle *n* 1 susu, kitanda kidogo cha mtoto; mlezi. 2 *(fig)* chanzo, chimbuko *Lamu is the cradle of Swahili poetry* Lamu ni chanzo cha ushairi wa Kiswahili. 3 *(naut)* kiunzitegemeo. 4 farasisimu *vt* 1 laza, weka (katika kitanda n.k.). 2 *(hold)* lea; shika ~ *the telephone receiver* rudisha simu.
craft *n* 1 ufundi, ustadi. 2 hila; werevu, ujanja; udanganyifu. 3 *(handicraft)* kazi ya mikono. **arts and ~s** sanaa na kazi za mkono. 4 *(pl craft)* chombo, mashua, jahazi, meli; muundo. **~ly** *adv*. **~iness** *n*. **~y** *adj* janja. **~sman** *n* fundistadi. **~smanship** ufundistadi.
crag *n* jabali, mwamba uliochongoka. **~giness** *n*. **~gy** *adj*. **~sman** *n* fundi wa kupanda majabali.
cram *vt,vi* 1 jaza kabisa, shindilia, songa, sokomeza. 2 bukua. **to ~ (up) a subject** kariri, hifadhi, andaa kwa mtihani (kwa kufundisha harakaharaka). **~mer** *n* mbukuzi. **~full** *adj* pomoni.
cramp *n* 1 *(also* ~ **iron)** gango, jiriwa. 2 mkakamao (wa ghafla hasa kutokana na baridi au kazi) *vt* 1 bananisha, weka katika nafasi ndogo; viza. 2 sababisha mkakamao misuli. 3 tia gangoni. **~ed** *adj* 1 -enye nafasi ndogo. 2 -liyobanwa.
crampon *n* upanga njumu (unaowekwa kwenye viatu ili kupanda milima/kutembelea kwenye barafu).
crane *n* 1 korongo. 2 winchi *vt,vi* nyosha (shingo).
cranial *adj (anat)* -a fuu la kichwa.
craniology *n* kraniolojia: elimu ya fuu

la kichwa. **cranimerty** *n* upimaji wa ukubwa wa fuu la kichwa. **cranium** *n* fuu la kichwa.

crank[1] *n* kombo. **~shaft** *n* fito kombo *vt* 1 komboa. 2 hendeli. ~ **up** anzisha kazi ya mashine kwa kuzungusha mpini wake.

crank[2] *n* mtu mwenye mawazo ya ajabu na kuyashikilia sana *a fresh air ~* mtu apendaye kuwa na madirisha wazi hata kama kuna baridi kiasi gani. **~y** *adj (of people)* -enye mambo ya ajabu; -enye wazimu; *(of machines)* -sio imara; *(naut)* -enye uwezekano wa kupinduka. **~y** *adj.*

cranny *n* ufa mdogo, mwanya. **crannied** *adj* -enye nyufa nyingi.

crape *n* kitambaa cheusi chenye mikunjo (kilichotumiwa zamani kushonea nguo ya mfiwa) *vt* funika, visha kitambaa hicho.

crap *vt* nya *n* 1 mavi. **have a ~** nya. 2 *(sl)* upuuzi.

craps *n* mchezo wa kamari unaochezwa kwa dadu. **shoot ~** cheza mchezo huu.

crash[1] *n* 1 kishindo (cha kuanguka au mpasuko). 2 mgongano. ~ **barrier** kizuizi cha hatari. **~-dive** uzamaji ghafla wa nyambizi kuepa shambulio *vi* 1 tua/zama kwa haraka. 2 anguka/vunjika vipande kwa kishindo. 3 gonga; gongana. 4 pata kwa nguvu. **gate ~** ingia kwa nguvu. **~-landing** *n (of aircraft)* kutua/anguka (kwa nguvu na kwa kishindo). ~ **helmet** kofia ya kinga. ~ **pad** *(sl)* mahali pa kulala wakati wa dharura. **~-programme** mpango wa dharura. 5 *(of company)* filisika. **~ing** *adv (sl)* sana, kabisa. **a ~ing fool** mpumbavu kabisa.

crash[2] *n* kitambaa cha kitani.

crass *adj* 1 (*of such qualities as ignorance, stupidity etc*) sana, kabisa. ~ **ignorance/stupidity** kipeo cha ujinga/upumbavu. ~ **behaviour** vitendo vya kijinga. **~ness** *n.*

crate *n* 1 sanduku/kasha la kuchukulia bidhaa. 2 *(of fish etc)* tenga. 3 *(of beer)* kreti. 4 *(sl)* mkweche, ndege au gari la zamani lililochakaa *vt* funga ndani ya kasha n.k.

crater *n* 1 kasoko: shimo la katikati ya mlima, zaha/ volkeno. 2 shimo (baada ya mpasuko).

cravat *n* skafu.

crave *vt,vi* 1 ~ **(for)** sihi, omba. 2 tamani sana, taka sana, onea shauku (uchu); hitaji. **craving** *n.*

craven *n* mwoga *adj* -oga.

craw *n* tumbo la kuku.

crawfish *n see* **crayfish**.

crawl *vi* 1 tambaa; jikokota. ~ **to sb** jipendekeza. 2 enda polepole. 3 jaa viumbe watambaao *~ with vermin etc.* jaa wadudu n.k. 4 *(of skin)* sisimka *n* 1 kutambaa, mtambao. 2 kuogelea kipaka. **~y** *adj.* **~y feeling** msisimko. **~er** *n* mtambazi. 2 *(of baby)* ovaroli ya kutambalia. 3 *(GB sl.)* mtu mwenye kujidhalilisha.

crayfish (*also* **crawfish**) *n* kamba wa maji baridi.

crayon *n* 1 chaki/penseli laini ya rangi. 2 picha/mchoro wa chaki/penseli ya rangi au mkaa *vt* chora kwa chaki/makaa.

craze *vt,vi* 1 tia kichaa, tia wasiwasi, rusha akili. 2 pata wazimu *n* 1 wazimu, kichaa. 2 mtindo (unaopendwa sana na kudumu kwa muda mfupi).

crazy *adj* 1 **crazy (about)** 1 -enye kupenda/kutamani sana. 2 jinga; -enye wazimu (kichaa, mafuu). **go ~** pata wazimu *drive sb ~* 1 tia wazimu. 2 -liochangamka, -enye kupenda sana kuliko kiasi *he is crazy about the cinema* mshabiki wa sinema. 3 *(of buildings etc.)* -sio salama, karibia kuvunjika au kuanguka; *(of a ship)* -lioharibika, isiyofaa kwa safari. ~ **bone** see funny bone. **craziness** *n.* **crazily** *adv.*

creak *vi* 1 toa sauti ya mkwaruzo, kereza *n* mkwaruzo, mkerezo. **~y** *adj.* **~ily** *adv.*

cream *n* 1 malai. 2 sehemu iliyo bora ya kitu au jambo lolote *the ~ of the students* wanafunzi bora. 3 dawa ya viatu (ifananayo na malai). 4 *(chem)* ~ *of tartar* hamira, soda *vt* engua malai, fanya kama malai. **~y** *adj* -enye rangi ya malai. **~er** *n* 1 mashine ya kutenga malai. 2 mwiko au chombo cha kukusanyia malai. **~ery** *n* 1 duka la kuuza siagi, maziwa, jibini. 2 kiwanda cha kutengenezea siagi.

crease *n* 1 *(on cloth)* mkunjo, mfinyo, upanga. 2 *(cricket)* mstari katika kiwanja cha kriketi *vt,vi* 1 kunja. 2 chekesha sana, vunja mbavu.

create *vt* 1 umba, huluku. 2 sababisha, onyesha. 3 *(invent)* buni, vumbua, tunga, anzisha. **creation** *n* 1 uumbaji, kuhuluku. 2 vitu vyote vilivyoumbwa. 3 kazi za sanaa *the women were wearing the newest ~s of the Paris dress designers* wanawake walikuwa wakivaa mitindo mipya kabisa ya washonaji wa Paris. **creative** *adj* -a kubuni; bunifu. **creativity** *n* kipaji cha kubuni/ kutunga. **creator** *n* muumba, mwumbaji; *(rel)* Mwenyezi Mungu.

creature *n* 1 kiumbe *dumb ~s* wanyama *poor ~* maskini! *lovely ~* mrembo/mtu mwenye sura nzuri. 2 kibaraka, kikaragosi.

creche *n (GB)* kituo cha kulelea watoto wachanga.

credence *n* 1 imani. **give ~ to** amini, sadiki. **letter of ~** hati ya utambulisho. **credentials** *n* hati ya utambulisho, sifa.

credible *adj* -a kusadikika, -a kustahili kusadikika, -a kuaminika. **credibility** *n*.

credit *n* 1 muamana 2 mkopo, karadha. **buy/sell on ~** nunua/ uza kwa mkopo. **~ account** *(US charge account)*. **~ card** kadi ya mkopo. **~ note** hati ya kudai. **letter of ~** hati ya muamana. ~ squeeze sera ya kubana utoaji mikopo. **~ balance** baki ya upande wa malipo. 3 *(book-keeping)* mpe: maingizo ya fedha zilizotolewa. 4 sifa njema, heshima. **give ~ (to)** sifia, tambua. **do/reflect ~** ongezea sifa. 5 imani *the rumour is gaining ~* uvumi unazidi kuaminika *she has five books to her ~* ameandika vitabu vitano *vt* 1 amini. 2 kopesha. 3 fanya maingizo ya. **~able** *adj*. **~or** *n* mwia. **ably** *adv*.

credulity *n* 1 wepesi wa kuamini (kusadiki) bila ushuhuda. 2 ujinga.

credulous *adj* 1 -epesi kuamini (kusadiki) bila ushuhuda. 2 -jinga.

creed/credo *n* imani, kanuni za imani.

creek *n* 1 *(GB)* hori. 2 kijito. **be up the ~** wa taabuni.

creel *n* tumbi.

creep *vi* 1 tambaa. 2 *(of age, time)* enda polepole, fikia/ ingia polepole. 3 nyata, nyapa. ~ **up to** nyatia, nyemelea *n the ~s (sl)* mtu anayejipendekeza; msisimko, hali ya damu kusisimka *it gave me the ~s* ilinisisimsha damu kwa hofu. **~er** *n* 1 kiumbe mwenye kutambaa, mtambaa. 2 (kwa nafaka) mtambo wa uchukuzi. **~y** *adj* -enye msisimiko.

cremate *vt* unguza/choma maiti (badala ya kuzika). **cremation** *n*. **crematorium/crematory** *n* tanuu ya kuchomea maiti.

creole *n* 1 chotara. 2 *(ling)* krioli: lugha ya machotara/ vizalia.

creosote *n (chem)* kresoti: aina ya mafuta mazito yatokanayo na lami (hutumika kuhifadhia mbao) *vt* paka kresoti.

crepitate *vt,vi* alika; alisha. **crepitation** *n*.

crepusular *adj* tusitusi; *(zool)* -a kuonekana au kusikika wakati wa utusitusi.

crescent *n* 1 hilali, mwezi mwandamo, mwezi kongo. 2 safu ya nyumba yenye umbo la hilali. **the ~** *(fig)* Uislamu *adj* -a hilali, -enye umbo la mwezi mwandamo.

crest *n* 1 *(tuft)* shungi, kishungi, kilemba, kishada. 2 *(top)* kilele, ncha ya juu *on the ~ of a wave* wakati wa nyota ya jaha. 3 upanga wa jongoo, undu. 4 nembo ya kinasaba. 5 kufika kileleni. **~ed** *adj*. **~fallen** *adj*

-liovunjika moyo, -a huzuni, -sio na raha.

cretaceous *adj (geol)* -a chaki .~ **age** kipindi ambapo miamba ya chaki iliumbika.

cretin *n* 1 mdumavu wa akili. 2 *(sl)* mpumbavu. **~ism** *n.* **~ous** *adj* -liodumaa.

crevasse *n* mwanya, ufa mkubwa (hasa katika mto wa barafu).

crevice *n* ufa mdogo, mwanya (kwenye mwamba, ukuta n.k.).

crew[1] *n (collective noun)* 1 wafanyakazi melini, katika ndege au gari moshi. **ground** ~ mafundi ndege (katika kiwanja cha ndege). 2 kundi la watu wafanyao kazi pamoja. **~-cut** mtindo wa kukata nywele na kuwa fupi sana. ~ **list** koli *vi I'll ~ for you next week* nitakuwa baharia wako wiki kesho.

crew[2] *pt of crow*[2].

crib[1] *n* 1 hori (ya kuwekea chakula cha mfugo). 2 mlezi. 3 *(US)* tangi, boksi, kasha (la kuhifadhi mahindi n.k.).

crib[2] *n* kazi iliyonakiliwa kwa kuibiwa, maandishi yaliyoghushiwa, maandishi yaliyokaririwa *vt,vi (of students)* ibia (kazi ya mwingine kwa kunakili), ghushi, nakili.

crick *n* kishingo.

cricket[1] *n (bio)* nyenje, chenene.

cricket[2] *n* kriketi. *(colloq)* **not** ~ si desturi, si haki. **~er** *n* mcheza kriketi.

crier *n* 1 mnadi. **town** ~ mpiga mbiu. 2 *(of a young child)* mlia ovyoovyo.

crikey *(int) (colloq)* loo!, lahaula.

crime *n* 1 jinai, uhalifu, kosa. ~ **fiction** riwaya za jinai *commit a ~* tenda kosa la jinai. 2 manza, kosa la kijinga. 3 *(in the army)* uvunjaji kanuni; kuvunja sheria. 4 aibu, jambo la kutia huruma, dhambi. ~ **sheet** rekodi ya makosa ya askari. **criminal** *adj* -a jinai, halifu. ~ **court** mahakama ya jinai. ~ **record** historia/ kumbukumbu ya jinai. ~ **procedure** taratibu za kesi ya jinai. **of a ~ nature** -a jinai, -a kijinai *institute ~ proceedings against sb* shtaki mtu *C~ Investigation Department* Idara ya Upelelezi wa Jinai *n* mhalifu, mvunja sheria. **habitual** ~ mhalifu sugu. ~y *adv.* **criminology** *n* elimu jinai.

crimp *vt* sokota, tia mawimbi (agh. katika nywele).

crimplene *n* krimplini.

crimson *n* nyekundu iliyoiva, damu ya mzee *adj* -ekundu iliyoiva. **turn** ~ geuka rangi kuwa nyekundu iliyoiva *vt,vi* -wa nyekundu iliyoiva.

cringe *vi* 1 ~ **(at)** nywea, jikunyata. 2 nyenyekea, jifanya kama mtumwa. 3 ~ **(at)** udhika *n* kujikunyata; unyenyekevu.

crinkle *vt,vi* vungavunga, kunjakunja, nyonganyonga. *n* mkunjo. **crinkly** *adj (of materials)* -enye mkunjo; *(of hair)* -enye kusokotana.

crinoline *n* 1 nguo nzito na ngumu. 2 *(arch)* skuta (kitanua sketi).

cripes *int (expressing astonishment etc)* mshangao, mstuko, lahaula! Mungu Wangu! Yesu! Mtumee!

cripple *n* kiwete *vt* 1 fanya mtu kiwete. 2 haribu, dhoofisha kabisa, hasiri, vunja *adj* -a kiwete, -a kwenda chopi. **~dom.** **~hood** *n.*

crisis *n* 1 kipeo, upeo wa mgogoro; kilele cha hatari, ugonjwa n.k. 2 hali ya hatari, hali ya wasiwasi mkubwa *reach a ~* fikia upeo wa tatizo.

crisp *n* kaukau *adj* 1 *(esp. of food)* ngumu, kavu, -a kuvunjika kwa urahisi. 2 *(of hair)* -a pilipili,-a kipilipili. 3 *(of weather)* -a baridi. 4 *(of style, manners)* -epesi, thabiti, bila shaka. 5 *(firm)* -gumu kidogo, -bichi *vt,vi* 1 sokota, sokoteka. 2 kausha; wa kavu. **~ly** *adv.* **~ness** *n.* **~y** *adj.*

criss-cross *n* mistari mkingamo *adj (of lines)* -liokingama *vt,vi* kingama *adv* kinyume.

criterion *n* kigezo.

critic *n* 1 mhakiki. 2 *(fault finder)* mkosoaji. **~al** *adj* 1 *(of a crisis)* -a kipeo (cha matatizo n.k.). 2 *(of the work of art)* -a kihakiki.

~al thinking umakinifu. 3 *(of fault finding)* -a kukosoa. **~ally** *adv she is ~ally ill* yu mgonjwa taabani.

criticism *n* 1 kazi ya mhakiki, ufundi wa kutoa maoni kuhusu sanaa, fasihi n.k. 2 uhakiki. 3 ukosoaji. **criticize** *vt vi* ~ **(for)** 1 hakiki. 2 kosoa.

critique *n* tahakiki, uhakiki.

croak *vi* 1 ~ **(out)** koroma, lia kama chura au kunguru), kwaruza *his voice was ~ing* sauti yake ilikuwa ikikwaruza. 2 *(grumble)* nung'unika, guna. 3 bashiri mabaya. 4 *(sl)* -fa *n* 1 mlio kama wa chura/ kunguru. 2 mkoromo, mkwaruzo.

croceate *adj* -a zafarani.

crochet *n* kroshia. **~-hook**. **~-needle** kulabu *vt,vi* fuma kroshia.

crock[1] *n* mtungi, chungu/gae. **~ery** *n* vyombo vya udongo (vikombe n.k.).

crock[2] *n* 1 *(colloq)* farasi mkongwe. 2 *(of motorcar)* mkweche. 3 *(colloq)* mkongwe (dhaifu, asiyejiweza) *vt, vi* 1 ~ **up** dhoofisha, dhoofika, kongoka. 2 zeeka; zeesha.

crocodile *n* 1 mamba, ngwena. (*idiom*) ~ **tears** majonzi ya uongo. 2 *(GB-colloq)* mlolongo wa watu katika safu mbili.

croft *n (GB)* shamba dogo (agh. lililozungushiwa uzio). **~er** *n* mpangaji wa mwenye shamba dogo.

cromlech *n* kaburi la kale.

crone *n* ajuza, bikizee.

crony *n* mwandani, shoga.

crook *n* 1 bakora. 2 mapindi (ya mto, njia). **~-back(ed)** kibiongo. 3 *(colloq)* mkora, jambazi, mdanganyifu. 4 *on the ~ (sl)* kwa ukora *vt vi* pinda, potoa; pindika, potoka. **~ed** *adj* -sionyooka, -enye matege, -a upogoupogo; halifu, -sio aminifu.**~edly** *adv*. **~edness** *n*.

croon *vt,vi* imba (bila kutamka maneno au kwa sauti ndogo). **~er** *n* mwimbaji atumiaye sauti ndogo.

crop[1] *n* 1 zao. **cash** ~ zao la biashara. **food ~s** mazao ya chakula. **forage ~s** mazao ya malisho. ~ **rotation** mbadilisho wa mimea. 2 *(pl)* mavuno. 3 kundi la watu au vitu vinavyoonekana au kutengenezwa pamoja *vt,vi* 1 nyoa, kata fupi (nywele n.k.). 2 *(of animals)* -la machipukizi/vilele vya mimea. 3 ~ **(with)** otesha, panda mazao. 4 zaa *the peas ~ped well* njegere zimezaa vizuri. 5 ~ **up** onekana kwa ghafula, tokea, onekana, zuka. ~ **out** tokeza juu ya ardhi. **~-eared** *adj* -enye masikio yaliyofupishwa, yaliyokatika kidogo.

crop[2] *n* 1 gole. 2 mpini wa mjeledi/ mchapo. 3 mkato mfupi wa nywele. **~per** *n* 1 mmea utoao mazao *a good/bad/heavy ~per* mmea unaotoa mavuno mazuri/ mabaya/mengi. 2 mtu au chombo cha kuchengea. 3 **come a ~per** *(colloq)* anguka sana, shindwa (k.m. katika mtihani).

croquet *n (sports)* krokei (mchezo wa kupitisha tufe za mti kwenye duara za chuma kwa kuzipiga kwa nyundo *vi* cheza tufe za miti.

croquette *n* kababu, chopsi.

crosier,crozier *n (rel)* fimbo ya kiaskofu.

cross[1] *n* 1 msalaba *pectoral ~* msalaba wa kifuani. 2 alama ya msalaba (k.m. x, +) *make one's ~* tia dole. 3 *(fig)* jaribu/taabu, majonzi. **bear one's ~** beba msalaba/mzigo wako. 4 mchoro/mstari unaokata herufi (k.m. katika herufi 't'); *(bot, bio)* uzazi mchanganyiko. 5 njia panda. 6 (*dress making)* mshazari, mshono kingama. 7 nishani ya ushujaa (e.g. **Victoria~**).

cross[2] *vt,vi* 1 pitana; kingama, kingamana, kunja (mikono, miguu). ~ **sb's palm with silver** patia hela (hasa mtabiri). ~ **words with sb** pigana/bishana na mtu. keep one's fingers *~ed (fig)* tumaini (kuwa kila kitu kitakwenda sawa). ~ **my heart!** kweli! haki ya Mungu. 2 ~ *(off/out/ though)* kata kwa mistari. ~ **a cheque** funga cheki. **~ed cheque** cheki iliyofungwa. ~ **one's t's and dot one's i's** wa sahihi na mwangalifu sana. 3 *(of river, road* *etc)* ~ *(from)*, ~ *(to)* vuka, enda ng'ambo ya pili ~ *sb's path* kutana na; *(pass)* pita; kata ~ *one's mind* kumbuka, jiwa na wazo, ingia ghafula katika fikira. 4 zuia, kingama, pinga. 5 kutana njiani, pishana. **~ed line** kuingiliana kwa makosa katika simu. 6 *(be athwart)* kata, kingamiza. 7 ~ (**with**) zalisha kwa kuchanganya (mbegu n.k.). 8 *(rel)* ~ **oneself** fanya/onyesha alama ya msalaba. 9 ~ **off/out** futa.

cross[3] *adj* 1 *(colloq)* -kali, -a hasira, -a chuki, -a kuchacha *as ~ as two sticks* -enye kukasirika sana, -enye hamaki mbaya. **be** ~ fanya chuki. 2 -a kwenda upande, -a mshazari, -a kingamizi. 3 -a kukabili, -a kuelekea. 4 -a kukingama, -a kupandana, -a kupinga njia; *(of winds)* mbisho, tanga mbili. **~ness** *n*. **~-bones** *n (pl (of a sign)* mifupa ya paja iliyopandana inayochorwa chini ya fuvu la kichwa kuashiria mauti au hatari. **~-breed** *n* uzalishaji mtambuka *vt* zalisha kwa mtambuka. **~-bred** *adj*. **~-current** *n* mikondo pishani; *fig)* maoni tofauti na (maoni) ya wengi. **~-fertilization** *n* uchavushaji mtambuko. **~-fire** *n (mil)* mashambulio ya risasi kutoka pande mbili; *(fig)* hali ya kuulizwa maswali na watu mbalimbali *be caught in ~ fire* jikuta katikati ya mambo/mzozo. **~-grained** *adj* 1 *(of wood)* -enye nyuzi zinazopishana. 2 *(fig)* -kaidi, -a chuki, korofi. **~-index** *see cross reference*. **~-legged** *adj* -a kukaa kimarufaa. **~-over** *n* 1 kipito cha reli. 2 koti lenye kufunga. 3 mbadilishano wa jeni kati ya kromosomu. **~-pollination** *n (bio)* uchavushaji mtambuko. ***~-purpose*** *n* (*of persons*) kuwa na malengo yanayopingana; hali ya kutoelewana, suitafahumu *they were talking at ~ purpose* kila mtu alikuwa akiongea vyake. **be at ~ purpose** -toelewana, pingana. ~ **-reference** *n* marejeo mtambuko (ili kupata maelezo zaidi). **~-roads** *n (pl)* njia panda; *(fig)* (in life) kipindi cha kufanya maamuzi muhimu ya maisha. **~-stitch** *n* mshono kingama. **~-word** *n (also cross-word puzzle)* chemsha bongo, fumbo la maneno (katika jedwali mraba).

cross-beam *n* boriti ya kukingama, mtambaapanya.

cross-bench *n (in U.K Parliament)* benchi la wabunge huru wasiopigia kura chama chochote.

crossbow *n* uta, upinde.

cross-check *vt vi* thibitisha tena (kwa njia nyingine).

cross-country *adj* -a kukatambuga.

crosscut *n* mkato; njia ya mkato *vt* kata toka upande huu mpaka upande wa pili wa *adj (of a saw)* -enye meno maalum ya kukata nyuzi za mbao.

cross-examine *vt (also cross-question)* dodosa, dadisi, hoji, saili (ili kuthibitisha ushahidi uliotolewa). **~-examination** *n*.

cross-eyed *adj* -enye (macho ya) makengeza.

cross-heading *n (in a newspaper)* kichwa kidogo cha habari kinachodokeza yaliyomo.

crossing *n* 1 kivuko; *(of roads) zebra ~* kivuko cha miguu. 2 makutano ya barabara na reli, tambukareli. 3 safari ya meli *did you have a good ~* ulikuwa na safari nzuri?

cross-patch *n* 1 *(colloq)* mtu mwenye hasira. 2 hasira, ghadhabu.

crossquestion *see* **cross -examine**.

cross-section *n* 1 picha ionyeshayo sehemu za ndani ya kitu. 2 *(fig)* kiwakilishi; kundiwakilishi, mfano halisi wa kitu au jambo ~ *of the voters* kundi wakilishi la wapiga kura.

cross-walk *n* kivuko cha barabara, kivuko milia.

cross-wise *adv* kwa kukingama.

crotch *n* 1 *(of a tree)* panda. 2 pachipachi (ya suruali, kaptura, miguu n.k.). 3 *(of person)* msamba.

crotchet *n* 1 mawazo ya ajabu na kijinga. 2 ulalamishi. 3 *(music)* robo noti. **~y** *adj* lalamishi, -enye hasira.

crouch *vi* jikunyata; jikunja; chutama *n* hali ya kujikunyata; kujikunja; kuchutama.

croup[1] *n* kifaduro. **~y** *adj*.

croup[2] *n (of certain animals)* tako.

croupier *n* mhazini, mkusanyaji na mlipaji pesa katika mchezo wa kamari.

crow[1] *n* 1 *(of a cock)* kuwika. 2 *(of a baby)* kucheka *vi* 1 wika. 2 cheka, lia kwa furaha. 3 ~ *about/over* jivunia. 4 cheka, shangilia.

crow[2] *n* 1 kunguru. **as the ~ flies** kwa mwendo wa moja kwa moja. **to eat ~** salimu amri kwa lazima; dhilishwa, twezwa. **have a ~ to pick (to pluck) (with sb)** kamia, -wa na jambo baya la kuzungumza na mtu. 2 *see* ~ **bar**. ~ **'s-foot** *n* kijikunjo kwenye pembe la jicho. **~'s -nest** *n* kidungu juu ya mlingoti wa chombo.

crowbar *n* nondo.

crowd *n* 1 kundi, halaiki, umati, kaumu. 2 watu, umma *follow the ~* fuata mkumbo/mkondo. 3 *(colloq)* genge. 4 lundo *vt,vi (colloq)* songa, jaza sana; jaa, songamana. ~ **round** zunguka, songa. ~ **on sail** tweka matanga yote. ~ **in** penya/penyeza kwa wingi. ~ **through** gagamiza, penyeza kwa wingi. ~ **out (of a group)** toka, zuia *your article was ~ed out* makala yako haikupata nafasi/ilizuiliwa. **~ed** *adj* -liojaa, -liosongamana.

crown *n* 1 taji la mfalme/malkia; uwezo/amri ya mfalme/utawala wa mfalme; mfalme. ~ **colony** koloni la kifalme. ~ **ed head** mfalme/malkia. ~ **lands** milki za kifalme. ~ **prince** mwana wa mfalme atakayerithi ufalme. ~ **witness** shahidi upande wa serikali. 2 utosi, sehemu ya juu ya kofia, kileleta; sehemu ya jino inayoonekana. 3 uzuri; ukamilifu, utimilifu. 4 taji la maua la kichwani kama dalili ya ushindi. 5 *(arch)* sarafu ya Kiingereza ya thamani ya shilingi tano *vt* 1 visha taji, tawaza. 2 (reward) tuza. 3 kamilisha. 4 tukuza. 5 -wa matokeo ya; fanikisha *success will ~ his efforts* ushindi utakamilisha/utapamba jitihada zake; atafanikiwa katika juhudi zake. **that ~s it all** hiyo inakamilisha yote. 6 -wa juu ya *a hill ~ed with trees* kilima chenye miti kileleni. 7 ziba jino. **~-wheel** *n (tech)* gurudumu lenye meno.

crozier *n see* **crosier**.

crucial *adj* -a maana sana; *(colloq)* -a muhimu sana.

crucible *n* 1 kalibu, kikalibu. ~ **steel** chuma cha pua cha kalibu; chungu cha kuyeyushia madini. 2 *(colloq)* majaribio makali. ~ **of suffering** majaribio ya matuo (maumivu n.k.).

crucify *vt* 1 sulubisha, sulubu. 2 *(torment)* tesa. **crucifixion** *n*. **crucifix** *n (rel)* msalaba (wenye sanamu ya Yesu Kristu).

crude *adj* 1 -bichi, -siosafishwa (k.m. kama sukari guru)/ghafi. **~oil** mafuta yasiyosafishwa. 2 *(rude)* -sio adilifu. 3 -sio stadi, -siokamilishwa vema au -liofanywa ovyoovyo. 4 *(of statistics)* -siorekebishwa, -siosahihishwa, -sioficha. **~ly** *adv*. **~ness** *n*. **crudity** *n*.

cruel *adj* -katili, jahili, -dhalimu. **~ly** *adv*. **~ty** *n*.

cruet *n* 1 ndiani (kichupa cha kuwekea viungo k.v. pilipili, chumvi n.k. mezani). 2 *(rel)* chombo kidogo chenye divai au maji. ~ **stand** *n* kiweko cha ndiani.

cruise *vi* 1 *(of ships)* vinjari, enda huko na huko, zunguka. 2 *(of vehicle)* enda kwa kadiri. 3 tafuta mpenzi barabarani. 4 linda doria *n* safari za burudani/kutalii. **~r** 1 manowari ya kasi. 2 *(of a police vehicle)* gari la doria. **cabin ~r** motaboti yenye nafasi ya kulala.

crumb *n* 1 chembe ya mkate. 2 **the ~** *(of a loaf)* nyama ya mkate. **pick up the ~** okota/ lamba makombo. 3 *(fig)* kiasi kidogo *vt* 1 funika kwa chembechembe za mkate. 2 fikicha.

~y *adj*.

crumble *vt,vi* 1 fikicha, vunja, meng'enya. 2 *(fig)* **hopes that ~d to dust** matarajio yaliyoshindikana kabisa. **crumbly** *adj*.

crummy *adj (sl)* chafu; hafifu, -a thamani ndogo.

crump *n (army sl.)* pigo kubwa, mlio wa kombora lipasukalo *vt (colloq)* piga kombora.

crumpet *n* 1 *(cookery)* mkate laini wa hamira. 2 *(US) sl* kichwa. 3 *(sl) (female)* mtia ashiki.

crumple *vt,vi* 1 kunjakunja. 2 ~ **(up)** kunjakunja, vunjavunja, kunjamana.

crunch *vi,vt* 1 saga kwa meno, chakacha, tafuna kwa kelele/ kishindo. 2 kanyaga/vunjavunja changarawe, theluji kwa miguu/ gurudumu *n* 1 kusaga kwa meno *when it comes to the ~ (colloq)* wakati wa kukata shauri ukifika..., mambo yakiiva.

crupper *n* 1 mtafara, kitanzi cha mkiani cha tandiko la punda (farasi n.k.). 2 tako (la farasi).

crusade *n* 1 vita vya msalaba, vita vya dini (vya zamani), vita vitakatifu. 2 harakati au mapambano yoyote dhidi ya yale yanayoaminika kuwa maovu *vi* ~ **(for/against)** shiriki katika vita takatifu kwa/dhidi ya. **~r** *n*.

crush *vt,vi* 1 seta, ponda, vyoga, gandamiza; kunjika, pondeka. ~ **ruthlessly** ponda. 2 tiisha, vunja nguvu ya *(ruin)* angamiza ~ *one's way through* penya, swaga. ~ **out** kamua *n* 1 msongano (wa watu), ghasia. 2 mbano, msongo. 3 *(colloq) have a ~ on sb* husudu mtu; tamani mtu. 4 *(biol)* kilingo. 5 sharubati/kinywaji cha matunda. **~ing** -a ushindi/ushinde; -baya mno. ~ing blow pigo angamizi.

crust *n* 1 gamba la mkate. 2 *(on rice)* matandu. 3 *(on teeth)* ukoga. 4 *(on water)* ukoga, gaga. 5 umbo/uso wa dunia. 6 *(of salt)* chunyu. 7 *(biol)* ganda, kigaga *vt,vi* gandamanisha; gandamana. **~y** *adj* 1 -enye gamba. 2 kali, -enye ghadhabu.

crustacea *n* krasteshia: wanyama wenye magamba kama kaa, kamba, uduvi.

crutch *n* 1 gongo (la kutembelea mgonjwa au kilema). 2 *(support)* tegemeo; *(fig)* msaada wa hali. 3 pachipachi ya suruali, kaptura na miguu; kiraka *(see crotch)*.

crux *n* 1 sehemu ya jambo ambayo ni ngumu kutatuliwa. 2 kiini (cha jambo) ~ *of the matter* kiini cha jambo.

cry *vi,vt* 1 toa sauti, guta, paza sauti, piga yowe. 2 lalama, lalamika. ~ **for the moon** omba miujiza. 3 lia, toa machozi. ~ **one's eyes/heart out** lia sana. ~ **oneself to sleep** lia mpaka kupatwa usingizi. **give a child sth to ~ for/about** adhibu mtoto kwa kulia pasi sababu. 4 tangaza. 5 ~ **at** lilia, pigia kelele. ~ **down** dharau, shusha heshima, punguza thamani. ~ **off** jitoa (katika jambo uliloahidi au kupatana juu yake) *n* 1 kilio, mlio, ukelele, ukemi. **give a ~** piga kelele. **in full ~** *(of dogs)* bweka wote pamoja; *(of peoples) (fig)* shambulia (mtu) **much ~ and little wool** *(prov)* mwenye kelele hana meno. **within ~ (of)** hapa hapa, kando. 2 *(of sorrow)* yowe, unyende. 3 *(of happiness)* kigelegele, hoihoi. 4 *(of complaint)* lalamo. 5 kugutia. *(fig)* **a far ~** mbali sana; tofauti sana. 6 kilio *have a good ~* lia sana ili kupata tulizo *have one ~ out* acha alie mpaka atulie. **~ing** *n, adj* kubwa sana. **~ing need** haja kubwa sana. **~-baby** *n* mlialia.

crypt *n* chumba chini ya ardhi (hasa chini ya kanisa). **~ic** *adj* -a siri, -a fumbo, -a kufichwa. **~ically** *adv*.

crypto *adj* -a siri, -a mficho. **a ~ fascist** mtetezi wa siri wa mafashisti. **~gram** *n* maandiko ya mficho (ya siri). **~grapher** *n*.

crystal *n* 1 fuwele. 2 chembechembe (jiwe kama kioo). **as clear as ~** angavu kabisa, dhahiri kabisa *adj* -angavu, -a kung'aa. **~line** -liotengenezwa kwa fuwele; kama fuwele, angavu mno. **~lography** elimu ya fuwele. **~-gazing** *n* utabiri wa kutumia tufe la kioo. **~lize** *vt, vi* 1 ganda/gandisha; fanya, fanyika kitu kama kioo. 2 dhihirika/dhihirisha (kwa mawazo n.k.). 3 gandisha kwa shata la sukari. **~lization** *n*. **~lized fruits** matunda yaliyogandishwa kwa sukari, kashata za matunda.

cub *n* 1 mtoto wa wanyama fulani wa mwitu (kama simba, chui, mbweha). 2 *(of a person)* limbukeni; safihi. 3 chipukizi, kijana anayejifunza ufundi fulani, mkurufunzi ~ *(scout)* skauti chipukizi ~ *reporter* mwandishi wa habari chipukizi *vt,vi* 1 *(of animals)* zaa. 2 saka watoto hasa wa dubu. **~bing** *n*. **~by hole** *n* 1 kijichumba. 2 mahali padogo.

cube *n* 1 mchemraba, mchemrabasawa. ~ **root** kipeo cha tatu. 2 *(of sugar n.k.)* kidonge cha sukari *vt* 1 *(math)* peua mara tatu. 2 *(cookery)* kata vipande vidogo vidogo vya kimraba. **cubic** *adj* -a mchemraba. **cubic unit** kizio cha ukubwa. **cubism** *n* uchoraji wa kutumia maumbo ya jometri. **cubist** *n*. **cubital** *adj*. **cuboid** *adj* kimchemraba

cubicle *n* 1 kijichumba agh hutengwa kwa bango. 2 behewa dogo.

cubit *n* dhiraa.

cuckold *n (arch)* mume wa mke aliyezini *vt* zini.

cuckoo *n* kukuu *adj (sl)* mjinga, kichaa.

cucumber *n* tango, tangopepeta.

cud *n* cheua *chew the* ~ cheua, tafuna-tafuna (kama ng'ombe, mbuzi); *(fig)* fikirifikiri, dhukuru.

cuddle *vt,vi* 1 kumbatia. 2 ~ **up (to/together)** kumbatiana, lala karibu/unono, jongele(an)a, pakana *n* kukumbatiana; kupakatana. **~some, cuddly.** zuri kwa kukumbatia.

cudgel *n* kigongo, kirungu *take up the ~s for* pigania, tetea *vt* 1 piga kwa gongo. 2 *(fig)* ~ **one's brains** fikiri sana, tafuta sana shauri la kufaa, jaribu kukumbuka.

cue[1] *n* 1 ishara (k.m. maneno ya mwisho ya mwigizaji katika tamthiliya) inayoonyesha jambo la kufanywa na mwenzake. 2 kidokezi *take one's ~ from sb* fuata nyayo. ~ **in** *(fig)* toa habari kwa, fuata msimamo wa mwingine.

cue[2] *n* fimbo ya kuchezea biliadi.

cuff[1] kofi *vt* piga kofi.

cuff[2] *n* 1 sijafu (la mkono au mguu). **off the** ~ papohapo, bila kujiandaa, kiurafiki *an off the ~ speech* hotuba isiyoandaliwa *play it off the ~* faragua (kufuatana na hali ilivyo). 2 *(pl)* **~s** pingu. **~-links** vipingu vya sijafu.

cuirass *n* deraya (vazi la kiaskari kama kizibau cha ngozi ngumu au chuma). **~ier** *n (mil)* mpanda farasi aliyevaa deraya.

cuisine *n* upishi, mapishi.

cul-de-sac *n see* **blind alley**.

culex *n* kuleksi: aina ya mbu.

culinary *adj* -a jikoni, -a upishi, -enye kupikika.

cull *vt* 1 chuma, chagua, kusanya, tenga. 2 ua (wasiohitajika kudhibiti ustawi). ~ **elephants** punguza/ua tembo *n* kitu kilichotengwa, takataka.

cullender *see* **colander**.

cullet kipande cha kioo.

culminate *vt* ~ *in (of hopes, careers etc)* fikia kilele upeoishia. **culminant** *adj*. **culmination** *n*.

culottes *n (pl)* sketi; kaptura.

culpable *adj* -a kulaumika; -a kustahili adhabu. ~ **negligence** uzembe unaostahili adhabu. **culpably** *adj*. **culpability** *n*.

culprit *n* mkosaji, mhalifu, mkosefu.

cult *n* 1 *(also religion)* madhehebu. 2 upendo wa mtu (kwa kitu, kazi mchezo n.k.). 3 kikundi cha watu wanaopenda sana vitu vya kisasa, mitindo ya kisasa n.k.

cultivate *vt* 1 lima, palilia. 2 *(improve)* endeleza, kuza (mtu, tabia); -wa makini, lea, kwa wema. 3 jenga urafiki. **cultivable** *adj*. **cultivation** *n*.

cultivator *n* mkulima; kaltiveta. **~d** *adj* 1 -enye elimu na adabu njema. 2 -liolimwa.

culture *n* 1 utamaduni. 2 kukua na kukomaa (kwa akili na mwili wa binadamu kutokana na mafunzo au uzoefu wa kutenda kazi). 3 hali ya maendeleo ya maarifa, elimu ya watu. 4 ulimaji, utunzaji (wa nyuki n.k.). 5 ustaarabu: fani zote, imani, mila na desturi, asasi za kijamii zitambulishazo jamii/mbari. 6 *(bio)* ukuzaji wa bakteria (kwa ajili ya matibabu au uchunguzi wa kisayansi). **~d** *adj (of persons)* 1 -lioelimika, -liostaarabika. 2 *(of artifact)* -liosanifiwa/tengenezwa na binadamu. **cultural** *adj*.

culvert *n* kalvati, mtaro (chini ya ardhi) wa kupitishia maji au kebo za umeme.

cumber *vt* (**with**) zuia; pinga; sumbua, elemea *n* kipingamizi, kizuizi. **~some** *adj* -zito, -a kulemea, -a udhia, -sumbufu.

cumbrous *adj see* **cumbersome**.

cummerbund *n* mahazamu, masombo.

cumulative adj -a kukusanywa kidogo kidogo, -a kulimbikiza. ~ **records** kumbukumbu za kulimbikiza/ limbikizi.

cumulus *n* kumulasi: wingu zito kiasi.

cuneiform *adj* -a kikabari.

cunning *adj* 1 -erevu, -janja, -a hila, baramaki, karamshi. 2 *(arch)* hodari, -stadi. 3 *(US)* -a kuvutia *n* 1 werevu, ujanja; hila. 2 *(old use)* ustadi, ufundi.

cunt *n* 1 kuma. 2 kujamiiana. 3 *(vulg) (of woman)* malaya. 4 *(of person)* korofindo.

cup *n* 1 kikombe *he is in his ~s* amelewa. 2 *(fig)* kufikwa, kitu kinachomjia mtu *his ~ was full* uchungu, furaha yake ilikamilika *between ~ and lip* kitambo kidogo kabla ya kupata. **the parting** ~ kinywaji cha mwisho kabla ya kuagana. **one's ~ of tea** kitu kimpendezacho. 3 *(of sports)* kombe *World ~* Kombe la Dunia *vt* fanya umbo la kikombe; umika, piga chuku. **~ping** *n* mwumiko, umiko ~ *glass* chuku, ndumiko. **cup final (football)** fainali ya mashindano (ya kugombea kikombe). ~ **bearer** mwandazi divai katika karamu kitaluni au makao ya mfalme.

cupboard *n* kabati ~ *love* mapenzi njaa, mapenzi tumbo.

cupel *n* kupeli (chombo cha kuchuja, kujaribu dhahabu, fedha n.k.).

cupid *n* 1 Mungu wa mapenzi (wa Kirumi). 2 picha/sanamu (ya mvulana mzuri) ya alama ya mapenzi.

cupidity *n* uchu, tamaa (hasa ya fedha au mali).

cupola *n* 1 kuba. 2 ~ *furnace* tanuri la kuba.

cuppa *n* (*sl*) (*GB*) kikombe cha chai.

cupping *n* see **cup**.

cupric *adj* enye kupri.

cur *n* 1 mbwa (koko), kijibwa. 2 mtu mwoga; safihi. **~rish** *adj*.

curate *n* padre/kasisi msaidizi.

curacy *n* ofisi/kazi ya padre msaidizi.

curator *n* afisa mwangalizi (wa jumba la makumbusho/sanaa n.k.).

curb *n* 1 lijamu. 2 (*fig*) kizuio, udhibiti. 3 *see kerb*. 4 sugu lililoota katika kifundo cha mguu (wa nyuma) wa farasi *vt* 1 dhibiti, zuia (hasira, matumizi ya fedha n.k.). 2 tawala (farasi).

curd *n* magandi, maziwa ya mgando, mtindi *vt,vi* 1 (*curdle*) gandisha; ganda; gandamana. 2 (*fig*) ogofya, ogopesha, tisha *his blood ~led* mwili ulimsisimka, alijaa hofu.

cure[1] *n* dawa *this disease has no ~* maradhi haya hayana dawa. 2 matibabu *his ~ took a year* matibabu yake yalichukua mwaka *no ~ for the disease* maradhi haya hayana dawa. 3 kupona *I can't guarantee you a ~* sikuhakikishii kuwa utapona. 4 (*rel*) nafasi/kazi ya upadre; kasisi *vt,vi* 1 ponya, ponyesha *~-all* kiponya madhila/maradhi yote. 2 hifadhi (nyama, samaki n.k. kwa kutia chumvi au dawa asioze), kausha; koleza. 3 ondolea mbali; tatua tatizo, ondoa. ~ **poverty** ondoa ufukara.

curative *adj* -a kuponya, -a kuweza kuponya (ugonjwa) *n* dawa *what can't be ~d must be endured* lililovia limevia. **curable** *adj* -a kuponyeka, -a kuweza kuponyeshwa. **curability** *n*.

curette *n* chombo cha madaktari cha kuchunia au kukwangulia.

curfew *n* 1 amri ya kutotembea wakati fulani (agh usiku fulani). 2 ishara ya kuanza kutotembea. 3 kipindi cha kutotembea.

curio *n* kazi ya sanaa (yenye thamani kutokana na upekee wake). **~shop** duka la sanaa.

curious *adj* 1 chunguzi, -enye kutaka kujua. 2 (*inquisitive*) dadisi it was a ~ situation ilikuwa hali ya ajabu. 3 -a tunu, -a kipekee. **~ly** adv.

curiosity n 1 (*inquisitiveness*)upekuzi, udadisi, uchunguzi, utafiti. 2 kitu cha pekee, tunu, udaku *as a matter of ~* ningependa kujua.

curl *vt,vi* 1 (*of hair*) kunja, pinda, pota, tia mawimbi. 2 jipindapinda. 3 jinyonganyonga. 4 ~ **up** anguka, kunjamana. **~er** *n* kitia mawimbi. **~ing irons/tongs** (*arch*) vifaa/vikoleo vya kunyoshea/kutilia mawimbi nywele. **~y** *adj* a mawimbi *~y kit* seti ya kutengeneza nywele.

curmudgeon *n* (*colloq*) mtu mwenye hamaki; bahili.

currant *n* 1 zabibu kavu 2. tunda dogo kama zabibu la rangi ya zambarau.

current[1] *adj* 1 -a desturi, -a kawaida. 2 -liyopo, -a wakati uliopo, -a sasa, -a kukubaliwa na wengi ~ *events/affairs* mambo leo ~*periodical* jarida la sasa. 3 (*of money*) zinazotumika ~ *assets* raslimali ~ *account* akaunti ya hundi. **~ly** *adv* **currency** *n* 1 desturi, matumizi, kuenea *give ~ to a rumour* eneza uvumi. 2 sarafu, fedha ~ *note* noti *foreign ~* fedha za kigeni.

current[2] *n* 1 mkondo (wa maji, hewa, gesi, umeme n.k.). 2 mfulizo wa mambo, mfuatano (wa mambo).

curriculum mtalaa. ~**developer** mkuza mitalaa. ~ **vitae** maelezo binafsi ya mtu (kuhusu elimu, ujuzi n.k.).

curry[1] *vt* 1 chana nywele za farasi n.k. 2 tengeneza ngozi iwe laini, isioze ~ *favour* jipendekeza.

curry[2] *n* mchuzi wa viungo. ~**-powder** bizari *vt* unga (mchuzi) na viungo.

curse *n* 1 laana, apizo, hizaya *be under a ~* laaniwa, teseka kwa laana. 2 sababu ya hasara, nuksi *gambling is often a ~* kucheza kamari ni nuksi. 3 tusi. 4 (*colloq*) **the** ~wakati wa hedhi. 5 **not give/ care a (tinker's) ~** -tojali kabisa *vt,vi* 1 laani, apiza. 2 **~d with** teseka na, sumbuliwa na. 3 tukana sana, tolea matusi. **~d** *adj* (*also curst*) -laanifu, -liolaniwa; -a kuchukiwa, -a kuchukiza mno. **~ly** *adv*.

cursive *adj* (*of handwriting*) ulioviringwa na kuunganishwa.

cursory *adj* -a haraka, -a juu juu tu *give a ~ glance to* tupia macho.

curt *adj* (*of speech*) -a maneno ya mkato, -a kukatiza; -sio adabu.

curtail *vt* katiza, fupisha, punguza, kata. **~ment** *n*.

curtain *n* pazia *draw a ~ over sth* (*fig*) -tozungumzia tena jambo hilo ~*-call n* kuita mchezaji mbele ya pazia apigiwe makofi. ~ **raiser** *n* mchezo mfupi kabla mchezo halisi. **~s** (*sl*) mwisho *it'll be ~s for you* itakuwa mwisho wako *vt* funika kwa pazia. ~ **off** kata/gawanya (k.m. chumba) kwa pazia.

curts(e)y *n* heshima (itolewayo kwa kukunja goti) vt toa heshima (kwa kukunja goti).

curve *n* 1 kizingo, tao pindi. 2 (*math*) mchirizo *vt vi* kunja, pinda, peta ~ *to the right* pinda kulia. **curvature** *n* mpindo, mpindiko.

cushion *n* 1 mto. 2 takia *vt* 1 tia mto chini. 2 linda (kutokana na dhiki) mabadiliko mabaya. 3 punguza nguvu.

cushitic *n* Kikushi: mojawapo ya lugha za kundi la Afro-Asia.

cushy *adj* (*sl*) (*of a job etc.*) -siohitaji juhudi kubwa; -enye raha, -a dezo.
cusp *n* ncha (agh. ya jani/jino).
cuspidor *n* chombo cha kutemea mate.
cuss *n* 1 (*sl*) laana *not give/care a* ~ -tojali kabisa *not worth a tinker's* ~ bure kabisa. 2 mtu. **~ed** *adj* kaidi. **~ness** *n*.
custard *n* faluda, kastadi.
custard-apple *n* 1 (*tree*) mtopetope, mtomoko. 2 (*fruit*) topetope, tomoko.
custody *n* 1 ulinzi, utunzaji/usimamizi, uangalizi. 2 ulezi, malezi. 3 kifungo *take sb into* ~ funga/ kamata *give into* ~ peleka polisi. **be in** ~ -wa rumande. **custodian** *n* mtunzaji, mlinzi; mwangalizi, msimamizi.
custom *n* 1 desturi, mila *native law and* ~ sheria na mila za kienyeji. 2 kawaida, mazoea, ada. 3 uteja fulani *I shall take my* ~ *elsewhere* nitanunua mahali pengine. 4 (*pl*) ushuru (wa nje). **~s house** forodha. **~s clearance** hati ya utakaso (wa ushuru). **~s duty** ushuru wa forodha the *Customs* idara ya Forodha. 5 **~built** -a matakwa ya mteja. **~made** -a kupima. **~ary** *adj* 1 -a desturi, -a mazoea, -a kawaida. 2 -a mila *~ary law* sheria ya mila. **~arily** *adv*. **~er** *n* mteja mnunuzi, mshitiri; (*colloq*) jamaa, mtu.
cut[1] *vt,vi* 1 kata; (*of minor cuts*) chanya, kwaruza; (*of grass*) fyeka; (*of nails*) punguza; (*of parts*) mega; (*of time, story etc.*) fupisha; (*of inscription*) chonga, toboa. 2 (*suitability for use*) kata *the matchet ~s well* panga linakata vyema; (*of material*) katika. 3 (*of class, lecture etc.*) kacha. 4 (*of lines*) kata, pishana. 5 (*of sport*) betua. 6 choma moyo, umiza *his words ~ me deeply to the quick* maneno yake yaliniumiza sana. 7 (*with nouns or pronouns*) *~firewood* tema/chanja/changa kuni. **~planks** pasua mbao ~ *the cards/ pack* kata karata. ~ **one's coat according to one's cloth** tumia kulingana na mapato; -tokuwa na tamaa mno katika mipango. ~ **(off) a corner** katiza. ~ **a disc/record** rekodi kwenye sahani ya santuri ~ *the ground from under someone's feet* bomoa misingi yake (ya hoja, mipango n.k.). ~ **no/not much ice** tovutia, -tostua. ~ **one's losses** acha mpango kabla ya kula hasara zaidi ~ *a tooth* ota jino. ~ **one's teeth on** jifunza; pata uzoefu. ~ **both ways** -wa msumeno *the law ~ both ways* sheria ni msumeno. ~ **sb to ribbons** adhiri, umbua kabisa. 8 (*with an adj as comp*) ~ **sb dead** -pa kisogo, jifanya huoni. ~ **it fine** (*colloq*) acha hadi dakika ya mwisho. ~ **open** tumbua, pasua. ~ **short** fupisha *to ~ a long story short* kwa kifupi. 9 **C~!** ingilia; wacha, simamisha (kupiga picha). 10 (*with pp*) ~ **and dried** -lokwisha amuliwa. ~ **flowers** maua ya mapambo. ~ **glass** gilasi zilokatwa nakshi **~place/rate** bei poa/tupa, bwerere, dezo. ~tobacco tumbaku iliyo katwakatwa. 11 (*with adv and prep*) ~ **across** katiza; pinga; vuka mipaka. ~ **at** lenga kupiga. ~ **away** ondoa kwa kukata. ~ **back** punguza ~ *back expenses* punguza gharama. ~ **down** angusha, ua, jeruhi (kwa silaha ya kukata); punguza kuvuta sigara *~sb down to size* punguza majivuno/ujeuri, onyesha kuwa mtu hastahili anachodai.
cut[2] *n* 1 ukataji, mkato. ~ **and thrust** (*fig*) mabishano makali. 2 upunguzaji. 3 makato. 4 pande, kipande. 5 (*of clothes*) mtindo, mshono. 6 mbetuo, mchinjo. 7 simango. 8 msuso. 9 **short** ~ njia ya mkato. 10 **a** ~ **above** bora zaidi. 11 tambuka reli, tambuko. 12 mchongo, kinyago. **~out** kidhibiti umeme. ~ **in** ingilia; (*of cars*) jipachika. ~ **into** katiza. ~ **into pieces** gawanya. ~ **off (from)** ondoa kwa kukata; zuia; ingilia; tenga; gawanya; nyima urithi; (*mil*) zingira. ~ **out** kata; (*of engine etc.*) acha kufanya kazi, simama; (*omit/stop*) acha; (*of competition*) shinda. ~ **it/that out!** acha

magomvi/maneno. **be ~ out for** toa kwa *have one's work ~ out for one* kabiliwa na kazi kubwa. **~ up** katakata; (*mil*) teketeza (*usu pass*) umia; (*sl*) kosoa, lima. **~up rough** -wa mgomvi. 12 (*in compounds*) **~purse** *n* mchomozi, mwizi wa mfukoni. **~throat** *n* mwuaji *adj* kali sana; katili *~ throat competition* mashindano makali sana. **~throat razor** kisuwembe. **~ting** *n* 1 korongo maalum. 2 (*of newspaper*) kipande cha gazeti (kilichokatwa na kuhifadhiwa). 3 (*of plants*) kipandikizi, kitawi. 4 (*of films etc.*) uhariri (kwa kuondoa sehemu zisizotakiwa *adj* kali, -a kuumiza, -a kuchoma. **~ter** *n* 1 dau. 2 kikata. 3 mkataji. **tailor's ~ter** mkataji wa nguo.

cutaneous *adj* -a ngozi.

cute *adj* 1 -erevu, -enye akili. 2 (*US colloq*) bashashi, -zuri, -a kuvutia. **~ness** *n*. **~ly** *adv*.

cuticle *n* (*bio*) ukaya wa ukucha.

cutlass *n* 1 panga. 2 jambia.

cutler *n* mjumu: mfua na mwuza visu, nyembe n.k. **~y** *n* 1 biashara ya mjumu. 2 vilia (vyombo vitumiwavyo kulia mezani k.m. kisu, uma, kijiko).

cuttlefish *n* ngisi.

cutworm *n* sota.

cwt see hundred weight.

cyanide *n* (*chem*) sianidi: aina ya sumu kali.

cybernetics *n* saibenetiki: sayansi ya mfumo wa mawasiliano na nadharia ya udhibiti wake (katika wanyama na mashine).

cycle *n* 1 muhula mzima, kipindi au mambo yanayojirudia (k.m. majira), mbembeo. 2 duru, mzunguko wa kitu, mafuatano *the ~ of the seasons of the year* mafuatano ya nyakati za mwaka *the life-~ of bee* mzunguuko wa maisha ya nyuki. 3 (*of woman*) hedhi. 4 mkusanyiko wa mashairi/nyimbo (agh. unaohusu tukio moja au mtu mmoja) *vi* panda baisikeli.

cyclic *n,adj*. **cyclical** *adj*. **cyclist** *n* mpanda baiskeli.

cyclone *n* tufani, kimbunga.

cyclopaedia *see* **encyclopaedia**

cyclops *n* (*myth*) zimwi lenye jicho moja tu, kashkash.

cyclostyle *n* 1 mashine ya kurudufu. 2 (*of a pencil*) kalamu ya kuandikia stensili *vt* rudufu.

cygnet *n* mtoto wa bata maji.

cylinder *n* 1 (*geom*) silinda. 2 mcheduara, mwanzi; (*tech*) silinda *two ~s* silinda mbili. 3 (*of a pistol*) silinda ya risasi *working on all ~s* kwa nguvu/bidii zote. **cylindric(al)** *adj*.

cymbal *n* matuazi, tasa.

cynic *n* mbeuzi. **~al** *adj* beuzi. **~ism** n ubeuzi. **~ally** *adv*.

cynocephali 1 (*myth*) mtu mwenye kichwa cha mbwa. 2 nyani mwenye kichwa cha mbwa.

cynosure *n* 1 kivutio kikuu *he was the ~ of every eye* kila mtu alivutiwa naye (na uzuri wake).

cypher *see* **cipher**.

cypress *n* mvinje (wenye majani ya rangi nzito ya chanikiwiti).

cyst *n* uvimbe (uliojaa maji). **~its** *n (med)* kuvimba kibofu.

cytology *n* sitolojia: tawi la biolojia linaloshughulikia mambo yote yanayohusu seli.

cytoplasm -sitoplazimu: sehemu izingirayo kiini cha seli na iliyozungukwa na kiwambaseli.

Czar(also tsar) Zari (mfalme wa Urusi kabla ya mapinduzi). **C~ina** Zarina.

D

D, d herufi ya nne katika alfabeti ya Kiingereza. 2 *(Roman numeral) 500/* *'d (abbrev. of had, should, would) I'd rather go today* ningependa kwenda leo.

dab[1] *vt, vi* 1 tona, tonea. ~ **with a sponge** tona kwa sifongo. 2 pangusa kidogo. 3 ~ **at** gusia, gusa *n* kutona.

dab[2] *n also* ~ **hand** *(colloq)* bingwa (katika michezo n.k.).

dabble *vt,vi* 1 chovyachovya. 2 ~ **at/in** *(art, politics etc)* fanyafanya, jifunza juujuu, jifanyia. ~**r** *n.*

dactyl *n (lit)* silabi tatu (ndefu zikifuatiliwa na mbili fupi).

dad; ~dy *n (colloq)* baba. ~**long legs** aina ya mdudu (mwenye miguu mirefu).

dado *n* 1 kiweko cha ukuta (chenye rangi tofauti).

daemon *see* **demon**.

daffodil *n* ua la rangi ya manjano.

daft *adj* -pumbavu, bozibozi.

dagger *n* 1 hanjari; sime; *(curved)* jambia. **at ~s drawn** tayari kupigana. **look ~s** tazama kwa chuki/uadui sana. 2 *(printing)* alama ya kurejea.

Dail Eireann *n* Bunge la Ireland.

daily *n* 1 gazeti la kila siku. 2 *(colloq)* mtumishi wa nyumbani (ambaye hakai pale anapofanya kazi) *adj* -a kila siku. **one's ~ bread** riziki. ~ **dozen** mazoezi ya maungo (ya kila siku) *adv* kila siku.

dainty *n* kitafunio, kitafunwa; *(pl)* mapochopocho *adj* 1 -rembo, tanashati. 2 *(fastidious)* -teuzi, chaguzi, -enye machagu; -enye kidomo. 3 *(of things)* zuri, laini, rahisi kuharibika. 4 *(of food)* ladhidhi, tamu, tamanishi. **daintiness** *n.*

dairy *n* 1 banda la kuhifadhi maziwa na kutengenezea bidhaa za maziwa. 2 duka la kuuzia maziwa na bidhaa zake. 3 kiwanda cha maziwa na bidhaa zake. ~ **farm** *n* shamba la kufugia ng'ombe wa maziwa. ~ **cattle** *n* ng'ombe wa maziwa. ~**maid** *n* mwanamke anayefanya kazi kwenye banda la ng'ombe wa maziwa. ~**man** *n* mwuza maziwa na bidhaa zake; mfanyakazi katika shamba la kufugia ng'ombe. ~ **products** *n* bidhaa za maziwa.

dais *n* kikwezeo.

dale *n (esp in N. England and in poetry)* bonde. ~**sman** mkazi wa mabondeni.

dally *vt,vi* 1 **(with)** chezacheza, tongozatongoza, fanya ubembe. 2 ~ **with an idea** fikiriafikiria. 3 poteza wakati (kwa uvivu, uzembe), chelewa, kawia, faitika.

dalliance *n* utongozaji (wa mzaha/utani).

dam[1] *n* lambo, bwawa, boma la kuzuia maji (mtoni, baharini n.k.); *(of irrigation channels)* kuko *vt* ~ **(up)** tengeneza bwawa, zuia maji; *(fig)* zuia (hisia n.k.)

dam[2] *n* mvyazi (hasa mnyama).

damage *n* 1 hasara, madhara. **cause ~s to sb** tia hasara. 2 *(pl legal)* fidia *vt* haribu, hasiri, vunja. **be ~d** haribika, vunjika.

dame *n* 1 *(arch)* mwanamke (hasa aliyeolewa). 2 *(US sl,)* mwanamke. 3 *(GB)* cheo cha heshima ya juu cha mwanamke. 4 mke au binti wa Lodi. 5 jina (la kitu kinachofananishwa na mwanamke). **D~ Nature** Asilia. **D~ Fortune** Bahati.

damfool *adj (also* **damned fool)** pumbavu kabisa/sana.

dammit/damnit *interj* al-la!; potelea mbali! *as near as ~* karibu sawa kabisa!

damn *vt* 1 laani, apiza. 2 *(of God)* hukumu kwenda motoni, tia/takia adhabu ya milele. 3 sema kuwa kitu fulani ni hafifu; shutumu; puuza, toa thamani *a book ~ed by the critics* kitabu chapwa (kwa maoni ya wahakiki) ~ *with faint praise* sifu kidogo (kiasi cha kuonyesha kuwa hupendi). 4 (*as interjectionto express strong emotion) I'll be ~ed if I accept your order* sikubali kamwe/ng'oo! maagizo/amri zako ~ *you* mshenzi we! ~ *his impudence* ufidhuli wake ulaaniwe *n* 1 matusi. 2 **I don't give/care a ~** hainiumi sikio wala ndewe; sijali kabisa. **not worth a ~** bila thamani. **~able** *adj (also* **~ed)** 1 -a kuchukiza mno; *(colloq)* baya sana sana *he spoke ~ well* aliongea vizuri sana *you 'll get ~ all* hupati kitu. 2 -a kustahili laana, -enye kulaniwa milele; maluuni. **~ation** *n* 1 kulaani/ kulaaniwa, ulaanifu. 2 laana: adhabu ya kutengwa na Mungu. **eternal ~ation** laana ya milele.

Damocles *n sword of* ~ tishio (linaloweza kutokea wakati wowote).

damp *vt,vi (also* **dampen)**. 1 fifiza kazi/nguvu ya kitu; punguza mbembeo polepole hadi kusimama kabisa. 2 tilia gesi yenye sumu; palia kooni. 3 fanya kuwa na unyevunyevu ~ *sb's spirits* punguza ari ya mtu ~ *down a fire* kupunguza mwako wa moto (kwa kutia majivu); *(fig)* punguza (furaha, raha, n.k.). 4 *(of voice or musical instrument)* punguza sauti. 5 ~ **off** *(of plants)* oza kwa unyevu mwingi. 2 harufu mbaya ya hewa au gesi yenye sumu (hasa katika mgodi wa makaamawe). 3 hali ya kukatisha tamaa *adj* 1 pwetepwete, -a majimaji, -a chepechepe kidogo, -bichi kidogo. ~ **clothes** nguo zenye unyevunyevu. 2 -enye ari ndogo; -enye hali kupombogea, kutia majonzi, masikitiko. **cast a ~ over** *(fig)* tia mashaka/masikitiko/ wasiwasi; punguza matumaini. 3 *(also fire ~)* -a gesi ya sumu/hatari. **~ness** *n* unyevunyevu, umajimaji, upwetepwete *n* unyevu, umajimaji.

damper *n* 1 valvu ya kudhibiti uingizaji wa hewa katika moto. 2 **put a ~ on** punguza furaha/starehe. 3 kizingiti.

dance *vt,vi* 1 dansi, cheza ngoma. 2 chachawa; rukaruka *the children ~ed for joy* watoto walichachawa. 3 *(of a child)* vinyavinya, chezesha. ~ **attendance upon sb** sikiliza na fuata (matakwa ya mtu) kwa makini. ~ **to sb's tune** tii. **~r** *n* mcheza ngoma *n* 1 *(series of movements and steps)* dansi. **lead sb a (pretty)** ~ endesha mtu; -pa mtu matatizo. 2 mkusanyiko wa wacheza dansi. **~ing.** *adj* **~ing-master** -a kudansi/ mwalimu wa dansi. **dancing place** batobato.

dander *n (colloq only) get one's ~up* pandisha hasira. **get sb's ~ up** kasirisha mtu, udhi. 2 *(of hair)* mba; magamba (madogomadogo kutoka kwenye ngozi au manyoya ya ndege).

dandle *vt* 1 vinyavinya. 2 chezesha (k.m. mtoto mikononi).

dandruff *n* mba.

dandy *n* 1 mlimbwende, mmbuji, mtanashati, mfuauji *adj (sl)* bora sana, safi sana. **dandified** *adj* -lovalia kitanashati/kimaridadi.

dandify *vt* fanya maridadi.

danger *n* 1 hatari, janga, baa. 2 jambo/ kitu kisababishacho hatari. **put in** ~ hatarisha, tia hatarini *he is out of* ~ ameanza kupona, amenusurika. 3 alama/rangi ya hatari. **the signal is at** ~ ishara inaonyesha hatari. ~ **point** sehemu ya hatari. ~ **zone** eneo la hatari. ~ **money** malipofidia: malipo ya ziada yatolewayo kwa ajili ya kazi ya hatari. **~ous** *adj.* ~ **(to/ for)** -a hatari; -enye kudhuru. **be on ~ous ground** -wa mahali pa hatari. **~ously** *adv*.

dangle *vt,vi* 1 ning'inia, ning'iniza *keep someone dangling* mwache mtu hewani. 2 *(fig)* shawishi. 3 ~ **round/about** nyemelea.

Daniel *n* 1 hakimu mwadilifu. 2 mtu mwenye busara nyingi.

dank *adj* -enye unyevunyevu unaotia kinyaa.

dapper *adj (usually of a small person)* nadhifu; chapuchapu.

dappled *adj* -enye madoadoa, -enye

mabaka, paku *vt* tia madoadoa ya mviringo ya rangi mbalimbali. **~grey** *n (horse)* farasi mwenye rangi ya kijivu na madoadoa yaliyoiva.

Darby and Joan *n (married couples)* wazee (mke na mume) wapendanao.~ **club** klabu ya wazee.

dare *vi,vt* thubutu, jusuru, jasiri; *(defy challenge)* pinga *I wont ~ do that again* sitathubutu kufanya hivyo tena. **I ~ say** bila shaka! nathubutu kusema. ~ **devil** *n* jasiri, jahili (asiye mwangalifu). **daring** *adj* hodari, jasiri, -sio na hofu *n* ujasiri.

dark[1] *n* 1 giza. ~ **room** chumba cha kusafishia picha. 2 utusitusi, weusi; mazimbwe- zimwe; *(fig)* ujinga. **be in the ~about sth** -tokukijua kitu; -wa gizani. 3 machweo. **before** ~ kabla ya kuchwa. **after** ~ baada ya kuchwa *adj* 1 -a giza. **The ~ Continent** Bara la Giza, -a zama za giza. **a ~ horse** mtu asiyetegemewa kushinda. 2 -eusi. 3 *(of colour)* -sio na mwanga mkali, -nayokaribia nyeusi. ~ **blue** buluu nzito, buluu iliyokoza. 4 *(secret)* -a siri -a mafambafamba. **keep sth ~** tunza, sitiri. 5 *(difficultto understand)* -a fumbo, -gumu. 6 *(wicked)* -ovu. 7 *(unenlightened)* -jinga, -shenzi *look on the ~ side of things* ona mabaya tu. **~en** *vt,vi* 1 tia giza, fifiza, tia kivuli, tanda (mawingu). **~n sb's door** *(facet)* tembelea mtu. 2 *(sadden)* huzunisha. **~y, ~ey** *(derog)* mtu mweusi.

darling *n* mahabubu, mpenzi, kipenzi *adj* -penzi.

darn *vt* tililia, shona (kufuata nguo namna ilivyofumwa) *n* 1 mtililio, mshono wa kutililia. 2 kiraka. **~ing -ball/ ~ing-egg** dopa. **~ing needle** sindano ya utililiaji. **~er** *n*

dart *vi* 1 kupuka, (toka, enda) upesi kwa ghafula. ~ **in** kupukia ndani. ~ **out** kupukia nje, tokeza kwa ghafula (kama ulimi wa nyoka). 2 tupa (piga, vurumisha) kwa ghafla na haraka *n* 1 kigumba (hasa kitumiwacho katika mchezo wa datsi). 2 mruko, mchupo wa ghafula. **~s** *n* mchezo wa datsi. **~s board** *(of game)* ubao wa datsi.

dash *n* 1 mvumburuko: mwendo wa kukurupuka; mfyatuko *make a ~ for shelter (safety)* kimbilia kivulini/ mahali pa salama. 2 mwatuko. 3 mshindo wa mawimbi yakatikapo. 4 *(small quantity)* kiasi kidogo (lakini muhimu). **add a ~ of pepper** ongeza kiasi kidogo cha pilipili. 5 *(line)* kistari, dashi. 6 *(vigour)* bidii; ujasiri; nguvu; wepesi; hima. **cut a ~** onyesha uhodari/ufundi n.k. 7 **the ~** mbio fupi (hasa meta 100). 8 (*W. Africa*) rushwa, mlungura *vt* 1 *(throw violently)*fyatua/tupa/gea kwa nguvu. 2 *(destroy)* haribu ~ *a person's hopes* vunja matumaini ya fulani. 3 tia kwa haraka; fanya kwa haraka. ~ **along** pita mbio. ~ **away** toweka haraka, kurupuka. 4 *(usu a/the ~ of) (sound of waves)* pigapiga; rukaruka. **~ing** 1 changamfu, -enye uhai. 2 mtanashati. **cut a ~** vutia sana. **~ed** *adj* 1 -lovunjika moyo. 2 *see* **damned.** **~-board** *n* 1 kinga matope/maji/upepo/ theluji/ n.k.; kioo (cha mbele). 2 dashibodi: ubao/paneli ya gari inayoshikilia mita na vipimo vingine.

dastard *n (arch)* mwonevu; mwoga, (afanyaye ukatili mahali ambapo yu salama). **~ly** *adv.*

data *n* data: habari, vitu, n.k. vitumiwavyo katika kufikia hitimisho fulani.

date[1] *n* 1 tarehe *what ~ is it* tarehe ngapi. 2 kipindi maalumu (cha jambo fulani). **out of ~** -a zamani, -a kale. **up to ~** -a siku hizi, -a sasa, -pya, -enye kwenda na wakati *his books are up to ~* mahesabu yake hayakucheleweshwa. **to ~** adi leo. 3 miadi. **make a ~** weka miadi *vt,vi* 1 tia tarehe, andika mwaka, mwezi na siku ya jambo fulani. 2 ~ **from** anzia (enzi, karne, mwaka). **bring up to ~** fanya kuwa -a kisasa/kileo. **dating from** tangu. **it ~s from** -lianzia. ~ **back to a period** rejea kipindi. 3 anza kupitwa na wakati. **be out of ~**

-wa -a zamani. 4 -pa miadi, weka miadi. ~ **less** *adj* 1 sio na tarehe, (siku, mwezi na mwaka). 2 -sio na mwanzo, -isiyokumbukwa chanzo chake. **~ed** *adj* lopitwa na wakati. ~ **line** *n* mstari wa tarehe. **international ~line** mstari wa tarehe wa kimataifa, (mstari unaogawanya dunia katika sehemu mbili za kuhesabu siku na tarehe).

date[2] *n* tende. **~palm** *n* mtende.

datum *n* (*see* **data**)

daub *vt,vi* 1 kandika, paka, siriba (ovyoovyo). 2 chora picha zisizo nzuri. 3 tia uchafu, chafua *n* 1 picha iliyochorwa ovyovyo. 2 msiribo, mkandiko. **~er** *n* mkandikaji, mpakaji rangi, mchoraji asiye na ujuzi.

daughter *n* binti, mtoto wa kike. **~ly** *adj* -a binti; kama binti. **~-in-law** *n* mkwe; mke wa mwana wa kiume.

daunt *vt* 1 katisha tamaa. 2 ogofya, tia kitata, tisha, tia hofu. **nothing ~ed** bila kukata tamaa. **~less** *adj* hodari, jasiri, siyo na hofu, -shupavu. **~lessly** *adv*.

davenport *n* 1 *(GB)* dawati dogo lenye saraka.2*(US)* sofa kubwa (linaloweza kufanywa kitanda), kochi refu.

davit *n (naut)* manjanika, winchi (hasa ya melini ya kupandishia na kuteremshia mashua).

Davylamp *n* taa ya wachimba migodi (iliyozingirishwa wavu wa waya).

Davy-Jones *n* chini (ya bahari) *go to Davy Jones's locker* zama chini ya bahari

dawdle *vt,vi.* kawia, poteza wakati (kwa uchezacheza/kwa uzembe); ajizi, enda polepole, piga ubwete, susurika. **~er** *n.*

dawn *n* 1 mapambazuko, alfajiri, mawio, macheo; weupe wa alfajiri. 2 *(fig) (beginning)* mwanzo, asili chimbuko *vt,vi* 1 pambazuka. 2 *(begin)* anza. 3 ~ **(on/upon sb)** *(fig)* fahamika polepole. **it ~ed upon me** lianza kufahamu, ilinielea. **~ing** *n* 1 kupambazuka, kucha. 2 *(on/upon) (fig)* kuanza kufahamu/kuelewa.

day *n* 1. siku. ~ **off** siku ya kupumzika kazi. 2 *(time of daylight)* mchana, kutwa. 3 wakati, muda *all* ~ mchana kutwa. ~ **by** ~ kila siku. **the ~ after tomorrow** kesho kutwa. **the ~ before yesterday** juzi. **this ~ week** siku kama leo baada ya juma moja. ~ **after ~; from ~ to ~** siku kwa siku. **~ly** siku hadi siku. ~ **in ~ out** siku nenda rudi. **good ~** *(formal) (greeting)* hujambo. **one of these ~s** katika siku za karibuni/usoni. **the other ~** juzi juzi. **call it a ~** gotoka *let's call it a ~* tugotoke. **that will be the ~** kamwe siku hiyo haitatokea. **not to be one's ~** siku ya ndege mbaya. **win/ lose the ~** shinda/shindwa *we have won the ~* tumeshinda. **better ~s** siku za fanaka. **evil ~s** siku za nuksi. **fall on evil ~s** pitia wakati mgumu; pata mkosi. **in our ~s** katika enzi yetu. **to end one's ~s** kufa; kupitisha siku za mwisho za uzeeni. 4 kazi (ya kibarua cha kutwa). **work by the ~** kufanya kazi za kibarua. 5 tarehe *which ~ of the month is it?* ni tarehe ngapi? 6 mwisho, ukomo *everything has its ~* kila kitu kina siku yake *the theory etc has had its ~* umaarufu wa nadharia umegota. **~-boarder** *n* mwanafunzi (asiyekaa boda lakini hupata chakula cha mchana shuleni). **~-book** *n* 1 shajara: kitabu cha kumbukumbu za kila siku. 2 *(comm)* kitabu (cha mahudhurio ya kutwa). ~ **break** *n* mapambazuko, alfajiri, macheo. **~-care centre** *n* kituo cha chekechea, mahali pa kutunza watoto wadogo mchana. **~light** *n* 1 macheo, mchana; mwangaza wa mchana. **in broad ~light** mchana; hadhara *adj* 1 mchana kutwa, kutwa mzima 2 siku nzima *adv* kwa siku nzima. ~ **school** *n* shule ya kutwa. **~spring** *n (poet)* macheo. **~time** *n* mchana *in the ~time* wakati wa mchana. **~work** *n* 1 kazi ya mchana. 2 kazi ya kutwa.

kazi ya siku.
daze tunduwaza, tia bumbuwazi; changanyikiwa. **in a ~** -liotunduwaa. **~dly** *adv*.
dazzle *vt* fanya kutoona vizuri kwa sababu ya mwanga mwingi *n* mng'ao/mng'aro.
deacon *n* 1 shemasi. 2 mhudumu wa kanisa. **~ess** mhudumu wa kike.
dead *adj* 1 *(of plants, persons)* -liokufa. **the ~** wafu, marehemu. **D ~ men tell no tales** ya kale hayanuki. **wait for a ~ man's shoes** subiri kurithi cheo. **rise from the ~** fufuka. **~ march** wimbo wa mazishi *~ as a doornail* kufa fofofo. 2 *(matter)* -siowahi kuwa na uhai (k.m. jiwe). 3 kimya tuu, -liotulia kabisa. **the ~ hours of the night** usiku wa manane *be at/come to/reach a ~ end* fikia mwisho kabisa, kwama. 4 *(of languages, customs etc.)* -liokufa, -siotumika sasa (k.m. lugha ya Kiyunani). **~ letter** sharti/kanuni ambayo imepuuzwa, isiyo na nguvu tena; barua iliyowekwa na posta baada ya kumkosa mpelekewa na kushindika na kumrudishia mpelekaji. 5 *(of hand etc.)* -liopooza; -liokufa ganzi kwa baridi; *(colloq) ~ to the world;* liolala fofofo. 6 kamili, kabisa. **~ calm** utulivu kamili. **~ shot** -enye shabaha kali. **~ sleep** usingizi wa pono. **~ silence** kimya kabisa. **~ heat** suluhu katika shindano, sare. **go into/be in a ~ faint** zimia kabisa. **~ loss** bila fidia; hasara tupu; *(sl)* (mtu) asiye na msaada wotewote. **~ centre** katikati kabisa, kitovu. 7 -sioweza kutumika tena. **a ~ match** njiti ya kibiriti iliyokwishatumika. 8 *(of sounds)* -zito; *(of colours)* -siong'ara sana, -liochujuka. 9 *(various uses)* **~ ahead** mbele. **~ fall** mtego wa gogo. **~ slow** polepole kabisa. **~ sure** hakika kabisa. **~line** muda wa mwisho wa kutenda jambo. **~ pan** *(of face) adj* -enye kujikausha; -sioonyesha hisia. **~ weight** uzito wa jumla (wa chombo na mizigo). **~ wood** mti mkavu; *(fig)* mtu mjinga; -sioweza kitu, -lokwisha (vunyenge). **~lock** *n* 1 mkwamo; kushindwa kabisa (kufikia maafikiano). **break the ~lock** fanya hali ya kutokuafikiana itoke. **~en** *vt,vi* 1 punguza; *(of feelings)* tuliza; fifisha *drugs to ~en pain* dawa za kutuliza maumivu. **~ly** *adj* 1 -a kufisha, uaji, angamizi, -a kudhuru sana, -a kutilifu mwili, -a kuhatarisha. 2 chushi. 3 apizi/laanifu. 4 -a kama kifo. 5 *(colloq)* kali, -liozidiana. *(of aim)* **~ly shot** dango kali. **~liness** *n*.
deaf *adj* 1 -ziwi, -sioweza kusikia vizuri/kabisa *a ~ person* kiziwi. 2 -a kuziba masikio, -siotaka kusikiliza. **turn a ~ ear to sth** -pa kisogo jambo fulani *the ~* viziwi. **~ness** *n*. **~mute** *n* bubukiziwi *adv* kama kifo, mno. **~en** *vt* 1 hanikiza. 2 zuia msikiko/ vishindo. **~ening** *adj*.
deal[1] *n* ubao wa msonobari *~ furniture* samani ya msonobari. **~ table** meza ya msonobari.
deal[2] *n* 1 *(portion)* sehemu. 2 *(quantity)* kiasi, kiwango *a great ~ of* kiasi kikubwa sana, kiwango kikubwa, tele. **a good ~ of** kiasi fulani, -ingi kidogo *that's saying a good ~* inatosha, umesema vya kutosha.
deal[3] *vt,vi* 1 *(of cards etc)* gawa/ gawanya. **~ out** gawa, gawanya (kwa watu kadhaa) *~ out cards* gawa karata (kwa wachezaji). 2 *~ sb a blow/ ~ a blow at/to sb* piga; *(fig)* umiza, tafrisha. 3 *~ in sth* uza *the market ~s in assorted goods* soko linauza bidhaa za aina mbalimbali; tumia muda katika kufanya jambo *do not ~ in gossip* usishiriki umbea. 4 *~ with sb/at a place* fanya biashara (na). **(treat) ~ with** kuwa na muwasala na, la hiki; *(of affairs)* shughulikia; jihusisha na; *(of a book)* ongelea, husu. 5 **~ well/badly by sb** tendea/fanyia vyema, vibaya *n* 1 mgawo. 2 mpango, haki. **a new ~** mpango mpya wenye manufaa. **a square ~** haki halali. 3 mapatano

(katika biashara), maafikiano. **it's a ~** tumekubaliana *do a ~with sb* weka /fikia mapatano na. *n* **a raw/rough ~** maonevu. **~ing** *n.* **~er** *n* 1 mchuuzi, mfanyibiashara *~er in a commodity* muuza bidhaa. 2 mgawa karata.

dealt *vt see* **deal**.

dean[1] *n* bonde (jembamba lenye kijito na miti).

dean[2] *n* 1 paroko (mkuu wa makasisi wa parokia). 2 *(of faculty)* mkuu wa kitivo. 3 *(of students)* mshauri. 4 mkuu wa mabalozi (katika nchi moja). **~ery** *n* 1. ofisi/ nyumba ya padre mkuu. 2 parokia zilizo chini ya paroko mmoja.

dear *adj* 1 *(expensive)* ghali, -a thamani nyingi, -enye wakifu. **that's too ~** ni ya wakifu mkubwa; ni ghali mno 2. **~ (to)** *(beloved)* -penzi, mahabubu, -a kupendeza. **hold sb ~** penda sana 3. *(form of address)* **~ friend** rafiki mpendwa. **~Amina** mpendwa Amina. **~ Sir** Bwana *(exclamation) oh ~* maskini! **~ me!; ~ ~!** masalale! mama wee! *n* mpenzi, kipenzi, mhibu. **~ly** *adv.* **~ness** *n.* **~y/ ~ie** *n (colloq)* kipenzi (hasa mtoto kwa mama yake).

dearth *n* **~ (of)** upungufu, ukosefu, uhaba, uchache *a ~ of food* upungufu wa chakula.

deary *see* **dearie**.

death *n* 1 mauti, kifo, ufu. at ~'s door chungulia kaburi. **he's working himself to ~** anafanya kazi sana. **bore sb to ~/stiff** chosha mtu. **sick to ~ of sb** choshwa na mtu. **~-bed** kitanda cha mauti *on his ~-bed* karibia kufa. **~-bed confession** maungamo ya mwisho. **~ dut** ushuru wa mirathi. **~ rate** kiwango cha vifo. 2 kuua/kuawa, kifo. **accidental ~** kifo cha ajali. **~ by misadventure** kifo cha bahati mbaya. **~ sentence** hukumu ya kifo. **die a natural ~** -fa kipinda/kibudu; *(of person)* -fa kawaida. **be in jaws of ~** -wa hatarini, ingia kwenye mdomo wa mamba. **be in at/the ~** shuhudia kifo; *(fig)* shuhudia mwisho wa amali *put sb to ~* ua *to stone sb to ~* rujumu. **~roll** orodha ya watu waliouawa vitani. **~ trap** mazingira ya kifo; machinjioni. **~ -warrant** hati inayoruhusu kuua mhalifu. 3 **be the ~ of** sababisha kifo/ajali. **catch one's ~** *(of cold)* pata mafua makali. **~ blow** pigo la kufa; *(fig) that was a ~-blow to my hopes* hili lilikuwa pigo la wisho la matarajio yangu. *(of 14th c.)* **the Black D~** tauni *(a fate) worth than ~* a kutisha mno. 4 *(fig)* kuharibika, mwisho *the ~ of our plans* kuharibika kwa mipango yetu. **~ chamber** *n* chumba cha waliohukumiwa kifo. **~-cap** *n* uyoga wa sumu. **~ -house** *n*; **~s head** *n* fuvu (la kichwa) lenye mifupa iliyokingama ikiwa ni ishara ya hatari. **~ rate** idadi ya vifo kwa mwaka. **~rattle** mkoromo (wa kifo). **~toll** idadi ya watu waliokufa katika ajali. **~ watch** kukesha na mgonjwa aliyekaribia kufa. **~less** *adj* -a milele, -siyo na mwisho, -siokufa; -a azali/ aushi. **~less fame** sifa isiyokufa. **~like** *adj* kama kifo, kama mauti.

debacle *n* 1 mbio za kuhangarara, ghuma, haikahaika. 2 kuvunja kivangaito; maafa makubwa. 3 anguko (k.m. la serikali); gharika ya ghafula.

debag *vt* vua suruali kwa nguvu.

debar *vt* **~ sb from** pinga, zuia, kataza (mtu) kwa sheria.

debark *vt,vi* **debarkation** *n see*

debase *vt* 1 shusha hadhi, cheo, thamani, vunja bei. **~ currency** shusha thamani ya fedha za nchi. **~d** *adj* ioshushwa hadhi, cheo au thamani. **~ment** *n.*

debate *vt,vi* jadili, jadiliana; fanya mdahalo. *(consider)* **~ upon** fikiri, zingatia *n* mjadala, majadiliano; *(official)* hoja, mdahalo. **~r** *n* mjadili; mdahili. **debatable** *adj* -a mashaka, -sio thabiti, -a kuweza kujadiliwa.

debauch *vt* potosha; fisidi; zaini. rairai, (haribu) kwa zinaa/uasherati/ulevi *n* kipindi cha ufisadi. **~ed** *adj*. **~ee** *n* fisadi. **~ery** *n*.

debenture *n* 1 stakabadhi ya mkopo, hati ya malipo ya kurejeshewa kodi iliyokatwa kwenye bidhaa zilizotengenezwa/ zilizozalishwa au zilizoingizwa nchini. 2 karadha (iliyokopeshwa kwa dhamana ya raslimali). 3 dhamana ya ushirika. ~ **bond** karadha ya dhamana ya ushirika. ~ **issued at discount** karadha yenye turuhani/kipunguzo. ~ **issued at premium** mikopo yenye ziada. ~ **stock** jumla ya mikopo.

debilitate *vt* dhoofisha, ondolea nguvu, fanya dhaifu, sawijisha. **debility** *n*.

debit *n* mtoe, daiwa hesabu (iliyoandikwa upande wa madeni katika daftari) (kinyume cha mpe). ~ **balance** baki katika hesabu ya mtoe *enter a sum to the ~ side* ingiza fedha upande wa mtoe *vt* rajisi madeni. ~ **sb with a sum** sajili mtu na deni lake.

debonair *adj* -a bashasha, -kunjufu; -changamfu; -cheshi.

debouch *vi* 1 tokeza. 2 toka mafichoni na ingia hadharani.

de-brief *vt* uliza, hoji kupata taarifa (kutoka kwa mtu uliyemtuma).

debris *n* kifusi, mabaki ya mvunjiko, mabaki ya nyumba.

debt *n* deni. **be in** ~ wiwa, -wa mdeni, daiwa *have in one's ~s* wia. **run/get into** ~ wiwa, pata madeni. **bad** ~ *(written off)* deni lisiloweza kulipwa. **~or** *n* mdeni, mwiwa; mdaiwa. **~or-creditor relationship** uhusiano wa mwiwa na mwia.

debug *vt* 1 tafuta na ondoa kasoro, matatizo kwenye kompyuta au mashine. 2 tafuta na ondoa vinasa sauti kwenye kuta, chumba, nyumba n.k.

debunk *vt (sl)* 1 fichua maringo/ majivuno, dhihirisha ukweli kwa kuonyesha mambo yasiyo ya kweli yanayopamba kitu au mtu . 2 *(unmask to diclose, to renounce)* umbua.

debut *n* limbuko *vt* tokea/jitokeza/fanya kwa mara ya kwanza. 2 uingiaji rasmi katika chama. ~ **ant(e)** *n* limbukeni.

deca *pref.* kumi.

decade *n* muongo: kipindi cha miaka kumi.

decadence *n* kufifia, kushuka kiwango, kuharibika, uoza (kwa sanaa, fasihi, maadili). **decadent** *adj*.

decalcify *(chem) vt* 1 ondoa chokaa; ondoa chokaa kwa kemikali. **decalcification** *n*.

Decalogue *n* **the D~** Amri kumi za Mungu.

decamp *vi* 1 vunja (kambi, chama, ago). 2 ~ **(with)** ondoka ghafla na kwa siri. **~ment** *n*.

decant *vi* chingirisha, gida. **~er** *n* kigida (chupa au chombo cha kugidia divai n.k).

decapitate *vi* kata kichwa (hasa ikiwa ni adhabu). **decapitation** *n*.

decarbonize *vt* ondoa kaboni. **decarbonization** *n*.

decasyllable *n*. silabi kumi. **decasyllabic** *adj (poetic)* -enye silabi kumi.

decathlon *n* seti ya michezo kumi katika riadha.

decay *vi* 1 oza. 2 anguka. 3 dhoofu *n* uozo. 2 kuanguka. 3 kudhoofika.

decease *vi (formal) (of a person)* -fa, fariki dunia *n* kifo, mauti, kufa. **the ~d** *n (legal)* marehemu, hayati. **decedent** *n (US)* marehemu.

deceive *vt* ~ **(in/into)** danganya, hadaa, ghilibu, laghai. ~ **oneself** jidanganya. **~r** mdanganyifu, ayari. **deceiving** *adj*. **deceivingly** *adv*. **deceit** *n* ughushi, udanganyifu, ulaghai, kengo. **~ful** *adj*. **ulness** *n*. **~fully** *adv*. **deception** *n* udanganyifu; kudanganya; hila. **deceptive** *adj* -a kudanganya, -a hila, -a kutia mashaka, -danganyifu.

decelerate *vt,vi* punguza; pungua mwendo, punguka mwendo. **deceleration** *n* upunguzaji mwendo.

December *n* Desemba, mwezi wa

kumi na mbili.
decennial *adj* -a kila mwaka wa kumi.
decent *adj* 1 -a adabu, -a heshima ~ *dress* nguo ya heshima. 2 -zuri, -a kupendeza; stahifu, -a kufaa; ~ *weather* hali ya hewa inayofaa ~ *meal* chakula kizuri; *(colloq)* -a kupendeka, -a wastani. **~ly** *adv* kwa adabu, kwa heshima. **decency** *n* 1 adabu, heshima; ustahifu; mwenendo mwema *have the ~ to* stahi, onyesha heshima. 2 *(pl)* **the decencies** kanuni za adabu.
decentralize *vt* gatua madaraka; *(of go vt.)* toa madaraka mikoani. **decentralization** *n.*
deci- *(pref)* -a sehemu ya kumi.
decibel *n* kizio cha kupimia kiwango cha sauti.
decide *vt,vi* 1 kata shauri, amua ~ *a dispute* amua ugomvi, amua mabishano. 2 hukumu. **~d** *adj (in all senses)* 1 *(determined, resolute)* thabiti, imara, -a nguvu, -enye nia. 2 *(clear)* dhahiri, wazi. **~dly** *adv* bila shaka, kwa vyovyote. **decision** *n* 1 uamuzi, hukumu, maamuzi, mkataa. **binding ~** hukumu ya mkataa *come to ~* fikia uamuzi, azimia *final ~* uamuzi wa mwisho. 2 *(resolution)* uwezo wa kukata shauri, kuamua, kuhukumu *lacking decision* -siokuwa na uamuzi thabiti. **decisive** *adj* 1 *(clear)* -enye uwezo wa kuamua, -a mkataa *a ~ battle* vita vya kuamua mshindi na mshinde, mapambano ya mkataa, -a kukata shauri/maneno. 2 -enye uamuzi *a ~ man* mtu mwenye uamuzi. 3 -a wazi *a ~ victory* ushindi wa wazi. ~ **ly** *adv.* **~ness** *n.*
deciduous *adj (of trees)* -a kupukutika majani yake; *(of ants)* -a kupukutika mbawa zake.
decimal *adj* -a miongo; -a sehemu za kumi, -a desimali ~ *number* numerali ya desimali, ushuria *n* sehemu ya kumi, ushuria.
decimate *vt* 1 *(hist)* ua kila mtu wa kumi. 2 angamiza, ua idadi kubwa ya watu. **decimation** *n.*
decimetre *n* desimita.
decipher *vt* fumbua (fasiri) maandiko ya siri/ya fumbo; tambua maana ya maandishi yasiyosomeka. **~able** *adj.*
deck *n* sitaha *after ~* sitaha tezi. **clear the ~s** *(for action)* jitayarisha kwa jambo au mapambano ~ *hand* muhudumu sitahani. 2 *(US)* jozi ya karata. 3 *(comm)* mkusanyo wa kadi zenye matobo katika faili moja. **~-cargo** *n* shehena, mizigo iliyowekwa sitahani. **~- chair** *n* kiti cha stahani. **~- house** *n* kibanda, kijumba kilicho kwenye sitaha katika meli, kijumba cha sitahani. ~ **passenger** *n* abiria wa sitahani. **~er** *(in compounds)* -enye ghorofa maalumu ya sitaha. **a double ~er bus** basi la ghorofa. ~ **(with/out in)** *vt* 1 pemba, remba, pamba ~ *oneself out in fine clothes* jipamba kwa mavazi mazuri. 2 funika, tia sitaha chomboni.
declaim *vt* 1 sema kwa ukali. ~ **against** kemea, kengemeka, shambulia kwa maneno. 2 *(practisespeaking)* jifunza usemaji, kutongoa (mashairi), tongoa, hubiri. **declamation** *n* 1 usemaji; kuhutubia. 2 makelele, ugomvi; hotuba kali. **declamatory** *adj.*
declare *vt,vi* tangaza, tamka, arifu.~ **(to be) innocent** toa hatiani. ~ **war (on/ against)** tangaza vita. 2 nena kwa nguvu/uthabiti. 3 *(to customs officials)* onyesha mali mpya. 4 ~ **for/against** unga mkono/pinga. 5 *(int)* onyesha mshangao *well I ~* loo!! **~d** *adj* -a wazi. **~dly** *adv* kwa nguvu sana. **declarable** *adj.* **declaration** *n* 1 azimio, tamko, tangazo. **Arusha D~** Azimio la Arusha. 2 taarifa ~ *of the polls* taarifa ya matokeo ya uchaguzi. 3 hati ya kujulisha/kueleza habari. **declarant** *n* mtamkaji.
declassify *vt* tangua (agh habari iliyokuwa siri na kuifanya bayana). **declassification** *n.*
decline *vi,vt* 1 *(refuse)* kataa, kana. 2 *(slope)* inama. 3 *(go down)* shuka *a declining birthrate* kushuka kwa

kima cha uzazi. 4 pungua, punguka. 5 *(decay)* dhoofika; fifia *n* 1 mteremko. mwinamo. 2 kushuka, kupungua nguvu; kudhoofu; kufifia (hasa kwa kuugua kifua kikuu) *go into ~* dhoofika. **declination** *n* 1 mkengeuko wa mshale wa dira. 2 mwinamo. 3 *(US)* kukataa. **declinometer** *n* kipimo-mwinamo. **declivity** *n* mteremko. **declivitious** *adj*.

declutch *vi* tengua klachi (ya motokaa), kanyaga klachi.

decoct *vt* pata vijenzi halisi vya kitu kwa kukichemsha ili kuondoa vingine visivyo muhimu. **~ion** *n*.

decode *see* **code** vt simbua. **~er** *n* chombo cha kufasiria maandishi ya siri.

decoke *vt see* **decarbonize**.

decolonize *vt* ondoa katika ukoloni, toka katika ukoloni, toa uhuru. **decolonization** *n*.

decompose *vt, vi* 1 *(analyse)* changanua, vunja; changuka; geuza hali ya asili. 2 *(rot)* oza, ozesha, haribu, haribika. **decomposition** *n*.

decompress *vt* ondosha kani, punguza msukumo, gandamua. **~ion** *n*. **~or** *n* chombo cha kupunguzia msukumo (kipunguzi msukumo).

deconsecrate *vt* tangua wakfu.

decontaminate *vt* ondoa uchafu n.k., twahirisha. **decontamination** *n*.

decontrol ondoa udhibiti, acha huru.

decor *n* nakshi/mapambo, marembo na vitu vyote vinavyokamilisha (sura mandhari, chumba, jukwaa n.k.). **~ate** *vt* 1 pamba, remba, tia nakshi. 2 paka rangi; *(with badge or medal)* visha/tunuku nishani. **~ate with an order** tunukia nishani. **~ator** *n* mpaka rangi, mtia nakshi, mpambaji. **~ation** *n* 1 pambo, kupamba, urembo, kuremba. 2 *(medal)* nishani; cheo cha heshima. **~ative** *adj* -a kufaa kwa kupamba, -a mapambo, -a urembo. **~ative stitches** mishono ya mapambo, mishono nakshi (urembo); darizi.

decorticate *vt* ponoa, ambua gamba. **sisal is ~d to get fibre** katani huponolewa ili kupata nyuzi zake. **decorticator** *n* furutile.

decorum *n* adabu, heshima, staha. **with due ~** kwa adabu zote. **decorous** *adj* -a adabu, -a heshima, stahifu.

decoy *n* mtego; (*bait*) chambo *vt* tega, nasa, (kwa kudanganya, werevu) vuta *~ sb into doing sth* tega mtu afanye jambo.

decrease *vt, vi* 1 punguza; pungua, punguka, fifia *n* upunguaji, kupungua. **crime is on the ~** uhalifu unapungua.

decree *n* amri, agizo, makataa, hukumu. **~ absolute** makataa. **~ nisi** hukumu maalum ya talaka *vt* toa amri, amuru, agiza, tangaza mkataa.

decrepit *adj* -dhaifu (kwa sababu ya uzee au kuchakaa), -kuukuu, -kongwe, -chakavu. **~ude** *n* ukongwe; udhaifu; uchakavu; mtambariko.

decry *vt* tweza; laumu, tuzua, paka matope.

decumbent *adj* -a kulala chini.

dedicate *vt, vi* **~ to** 1 weka wakfu, (weka) kwa matumizi mema au kusudi jema (kama vile matumizi ya dini au utukufu wa Mungu); tabaruku, zindua. 2 (*devote*) toa (weka, funga kabisa) kwa ajili ya kusudi fulani maalumu. 3 andikia ukumbusho au heshima ya mtu (au kusudi maalumu) *this book is ~d to my children* kitabu hiki ni kwa heshima ya watoto wangu. 4 toa idaya; tunukia. 5 **~ oneself to** jitolea kwa dhati. **dedication** *n*. **~d** *adj*.

deduce *vt* fikia hitimisho (kutokana na ithibati iliyopo). **deducible** *adj*.

deduct *vt* toa, punguza, ondosha; kata. **~ion** *n* 1 kutoa; kukata, kukatia; kuchukua. 2 (*of salary*) makato. 3 mambo yaliyofasiriwa (au kukisiwa hivyo). **~ive** *adj* -liopatwa kwa kufasiri mambo mengine yalivyo. **~ively** *adv*.

deed *n* 1 tendo, kitendo *be rewarded for one's good ~s* pewa tuzo kwa kitendo chema *great ~* tendo kuu (la ushujaa, la ujasiri) *a foul ~* tendo ovu. 2 hati rasmi ya makubaliano/ mkataba. ~ **poll** hati (inayotiwa sahihi ya mtu mmoja) ya kumgawia mwingine ardhi, hati ya kubadilisha jina). **title** ~ hati ya kumiliki. ~ **box** kasha mnamowekwa hati hizi.

deem *vt* (*formal*) ona kuwa, chukulia kuwa, fikiria kuwa, amini kuwa ~ *it an honour to do sth* chukulia kuwa jambo la heshima kufanya kitu.

deep *adj* 1 -a kwenda chini, -enye kina, -enye uketo. ~ **water** kina, lindi *ten feet~ in water* kina cha futi 10 majini ~ *river* mto wenye uketo. **in ~ water(s)** (*fig*) -wa na matatizo makubwa. 2 -liowekwa ndani sana, -iokuwa nyuma sana, -a ndani. 3 -pana. 4 -sana, kabisa ~ *red* -ekundu sana ~ *secret* siri sana. **(be) ~ in thoughts (study** etc.) zama katika mawazo, -wa mbali kimawazo. 5 (*of voice*) -zito, nene, -a chini. 6 (*of feeling etc.*) -ingi; -zito; -kuu, kubwa ~ *sorrow* majonzi makuu ~ *mourning* huzuni kubwa ~ *sleep* usingizi mzito. 7 (*fig*) -gumu kueleweka *a ~ mystery* fumbo kubwa. 8 (*fig*) -enye kuzama, -siyo ya juujuu *a woman with ~insight* mwanamke mwenye mawazo yaliyozama. 9 siri. **he is a ~ one** msiri. **~ly** *adv*. **~ness** *n*. **~en** *vt,vi* 1 enda chini; -wa na kina; ongeza uketo. 2 zidisha *adv* chini sana; ndani. **still waters run ~** (*prov*) kimya kingi kina mshindo. ~ **freeze** *vt* gandisha chakula n.k. ili kuhifadhi *n* ~ **freezer** jokofu gandishi. ~ **mined** *(of coal)* -a kutoka machimboni. ~ **drawn** pumzi iliyoshushwa kwa nguvu. ~ **rooted** -siyo rahisi kutolewa; enye mizizi imara. ~ **seated** -iliyojijenga, -enye nguvu *n* (*poet*) **the ~** bahari.

deer *n* mbawala, paa, kulungu; ~ **skin** ngozi ya mbawala iliyohifadhiwa. ~ **stalker** mwindaji wa mbawala; kofia ya kitambaa yenye mikia miwili (mmoja mbele mwingine nyuma). ~ **stalking** mchezo wa kuwinda mbawala kwa kuwanyemelea.

de-escalate *vt* punguza eneo au nguvu ya vita n.k.

deface *vt* 1 umbua, (kwa kuandika/ kuchora juu yake), fuja. 2 fanya maandiko yasisomeke (k.m. juu ya jiwe la kaburi). **~ment** *n*.

defacto *adj* -siopingika, -enyewe, halisi *adv* kenyekenye: bila kupingwa, moja kwa moja.

defalcate *vi* fuja/badhiri amana.

defalcation *n* budhara, ubadhirifu wa amana.

defame *vt* kashifu, haribu jina. **defamation** *n*. **defamatory** *adj*.

default *n* 1 kushindwa kufanya jambo; kupuuza. 2 kosa (la kutofanya ipasavyo), mwepuza. **win a case (a game) by ~** shinda kesi (au mchezo) kwa kuwa washindani wamepuuza. **be in ~** kosekana. ~ **of** bila, kwa kukosa *vi* 1 shindwa kutekeleza wajibu/kufuata mkataba. 2 shindwa kulipa madeni. 3 shindwa kufika mahakamani. **~er** *n* 1 mwenye kosa la kutoonekana, kutolipa deni. 2 askari aliyehukumiwa kijeshi.

defeat *vt* 1 shinda, zidi nguvu, vota. 2 vunja, angamiza *n* 1 ushinde; kushindwa. 2 maangamizo. **~ist** *n* mtu anayetegemea kushindwa tu. **~ism** *n* hali ya kutazamia kushindwa tu.

defecate *vi* (*med*) kunya, -enda choo/ haja kubwa. **defecation** *n*.

defect[1] *n* dosari; kasoro; walakini; upungufu. **inherent ~** dosari ya kimaumbile. **latent ~** dosari iliyofumbika. **patent ~** dosari dhahiri. **~ive** *adj* -enye kasoro/ upungufu. **mentally ~ive** -enye upungufu wa akili.

defect[2] *vi* **(from/to)** asi, saliti. **~or** *n* mwasi, msaliti. **~ion** *n* uasi, usaliti.

defend *vt* ~ **(against/from)** 1 (*guard*) linda, kinga, hami. 2 (*speak for*) tetea. 3 (*sport*) linda (goli). **~er** *n* mlinzi; mtetezi. **defence** *n* 1 ulinzi, hali ya kulinda/kujihami/kujikinga. 2 kulinda usishambuliwe. 3 (*anything which protects*) ngome, ngao, kinga;

(*pl military*) ~*s* silaha, ulinzi ~ *area* ngome. 4 (*legal*) utetezi ~ *counsel* wakili wa utetezi. **defenceless** *adj* bila ulinzi/kinga; bila utetezi. **~lessly** *adv*. **~lessness** *n*. **~ant** *n* mshitakiwa; mdaiwa. **defensible** *adj* 1 -a kulindika. 2 (*capable of vindication*) -a kuthibitika. **defensive** *adj* 1 -enye mwelekeo wa kujilinda/kujitetea; -a kujikinga ~ *weapon* silaha za kujikinga/kujilinda. 2 (*often derog*) -tetezi *why is he always so* ~? kwa nini anajiteteatetea. *n* **be/act on the** ~ -wa katika hali ya kujilinda/jikinga/jihamijitetea. **~ly** *adv*.

defer[1] *vt* ahirisha *payment on ~red terms* kulipia kidogo-kidogo, kununua kwa kubandika. **~ment** *n*.

defer[2] *vi* (**to**) kubali kushindwa (hasa kwa sababu ya kuonyesha heshima); ridhi kwa kustahi, stahi. **~ence** *n* kukubali kushindwa (kwa kuonyesha heshima); ridhaa (ya kustahi); staha. **in ~ence to** kwa staha; kwa kustahi. **~ential** *adj* -enye kuonyesha staha. **~entially** *adv*.

defiance *n* uasi; ufidhuli; kutojali; ujasiri (wa wazi). **defiant** *adj*.

deficiency *n* upungufu, uchechefu, kasoro. ~ **disease** utapiamlo. **mental** ~ upungufu wa akili. **deficient** *adj*.

deficit *n* hasara; upungufu, (hasa kwa fedha au mali); nakisi, kasoro.

defilade *vt* (*mil.*)jilinda dhidi ya mashambulizi ya maadui, jihami, jikinga *n* mashambulizi, mapambano ya kivita.

defile[1] *vt,vi* najisi, chafua, tia taka, baka. **~ment** *n*.

defile[2] *n* 1 ushoroba, njia nyembamba ya mlimani. 2 korongo *vi* (*of troops*) enda katika mlolongo/msururu.

define *vt* 1 (*explain meaning*) fasili; (*duties etc.*) eleza wazi kabisa, baini, fafanua. 2 weka mpaka ~ *a country's boundaries* weka mipaka ya nchi. 3 eleza sifa bainifu (za kitu). **definable** *adj*. **definite** *adj* 1 -enye mpaka. 2 wazi. 3 -enye msimamo. **definitely** *adv* 1 -a waziwazi. 2 ndio! haswa! kabisa! **definition** *n* 1 fasili, ufafanuzi. 2 udhahiri/udhihirishaji wa umbo. 3 ubainifu wa taswira (katika lenzi, picha n.k.). **definitive** *adj* 1. -a mkataa, -a kumalizia, -a hakika 2. bora kabisa.

deflate *vt* 1 (*of tyre*) toa upepo. 2 (*fig*) punguza majivuno. 3 punguza jumla ya fedha zitumiwazo ili kudhibiti bei. **deflation** *n*. **deflationary** *adj*.

deflect *vt,vi* ~ *(from)* vuta upande, kengeusha; enda upande. **~ion** *n*. **~or** *n*.

deflower *vt* (*liter or old use*) bikiri. **defloration** *n*.

defoliate *vt* teketeza majani; pukuta. **defoliation** *n*. **defoliant** *adj*.

deforest *vt* fyeka/kata miti ya mwituni; haribu mwitu.

deform *vt* kashifu; haribu umbo/sifa; umbua. **~ed** *adj* -enye kwenda kombo, -lioumbuka; -enye kasoro. **~ation** *n* ugeuzi (kuwa baya); kilema; kombo, upotovu. **~ity** *n* ulemavu.

defraud *vt* 1 danganya; fanya hila, laghai, ghilibu.

defray *vt* lipa gharama, lipia, gharimia.

defrost *vt* yeyusha barafu, ondoa ukungu. **~er** *n* (*tech*) kiyeyusha barafu, kiondoa ukungu.

deft *adj* stadi. **~ness** *n*.

defunct *adj* 1 -fu, marehemu. 2 -liovunjwa, -liotenguliwa, -liofishwa. 3 -siotumika siku hizi, -lioachwa *n* marehemu, hayati, mfu.

defuse *vt* toa fyuzi; (*of a bomb*) tegua bomu; (*fig*) lainisha, tuliza.

defy 1 kataa katakata; taka shari; taka vita *I ~ you to do it* thubutu! fanya uone! 2 dharau; asi, -totii; -toogopa. 3 (*provoke*) chokoza, tolea ujuvi; kaidi; fanyia kiburi. ~ **sb to do sth** taka mtu afanye jambo ambalo ni muhali kwake/hatokubali kulifanya. 4 shinda, leta shida zisizoweza kuondolewa; shindikana kutatuliwa. **her boldness defies competition/description** ujasiri wake hauna kifani. **defier** *n*.

degauss *vt* tengua nguvu za sumaku.
degenerate *vi,vt*~ **(into)** haribika tabia, sawijika; potoa *adj* -lioharibika tabia; pungua (kiafya), -liosawijika, -liopotoka *n* mpotovu, asherati. **degeneration** *n* **degeneracy** *n* 1 upotovu, mtenguko wa maadili, ugeukaji vibaya, uharibifu wa tabia. 2 upungufu. 3 udhoofu.
degrade *vt,vi* 1 shusha daraja/cheo au hadhi, shusha. 2 ~ *oneself* jivunjia heshima/hadhi. **degradation** *n.*
degree *n* 1 (*for angles, temperature*) nyuzi, digrii. 2 (*rank*) cheo, hadhi, daraja, manzili. 3 hatua, daraja (ya maendeleo), kiasi. **by ~s** hatua kwa hatua. **to a high ~** sana, mno. **to what ~** (kwa) kiasi gani; hatua ya uzito (kwa jambo) *third ~* ulazimishaji wa mtu kukiri (wa mateso makali). 4 *(academic)* digrii, shahada. **Ph.D ~** shahada ya Udaktari wa Falsafa. 5 (*gram*) kiwango cha ulinganisho wa vivumishi na vielezi (k.m. *thin, thinner, thinnest*) 6. kiwango *they differ to a certain ~* wanatafautiana kwa kiwango fulani.
dehorn *vt* ng'oa pembe (ya mnyama).
dehumanize *vt* toa (ondoa) utu, dunisha, umbua, dhalilisha. **dehumanization** *n.*
dehumidify *vt* ondoa unyevunyevu.
dehydrate *vt* kausha, pweza. **~d** *adj* -liopwezwa, -lionyauka. **~d eggs** mayaipwea. **dehydration** *n* kuishiwa/ kukausha maji.
de-ice *vt* ondoa barafu; zuia kufanyika kwa barafu. **~r** *n* kiondoa barafu.
deicide *n* 1 muuaji wa mungu; mwangamizaji wa viwakilishi vya mungu. 2 tendo la kuua/au kuharibu sanamu ya mungu.
deictic *n* (*gram*) kionyeshi bainishi.
deify fanya mungu; abudu au heshimu kama mungu. **deification** *n* kufanya (kitu au mtu) Mungu, kuabudu au kuheshimu (kitu au mtu) kama Mungu.
deign *vi* ~ **to do sth** (jambo) kubali, ridhia, jidhili. ~ **to listen** -wa na idhilali ya kusikiliza *he did not ~ to answer* hata/wala hakujibu.
deism *n* (*rel*) imani ya uungu bila kukubali ufunuo wala mizengwe yake. **deist** *n* muumini asiyekubali ufunuo.
deity *n* 1 uungu, umungu. 2 mungu. **the D~** Mwenyezi Mungu.
deject *vt* huzunisha, vunja moyo, tia majonzi. **~ed** *adj* -enye huzuni. **~edly** *adv.* **~ion** *n* huzuni, majonzi, moyo mzito. **he left in ~ion** aliondoka na huzuni kubwa.
de jure *adv,adj* kwa sheria; -a halali; kisheria.
dekko *n* (*sl)* deku. **to have a ~** kudeku, kutupia jicho.
delate *vt* (*arch*) laumu; suta, sengenya, aili. **delation** *n* aili, lawama. **delator** *n* mtesi, mbea, mchonge.
delay *vt,vi* 1 kawiza/kawisha, cheleweshа, kawia, chelewa. 2 ahirisha, faitisha *n* kukawia; ucheleweshaji, usiri; taahira *without ~* bila kukawia *make no ~ in doing sth* usichelewe kufanya kitu.
delectable *adj* 1 -a bashasha, anisi. 2 tamu. **delectation** *n* furaha, anasa, bashasha, burudani *for the ~ of his guests* kwa ajili ya kuwafurahisha wageni wake.
delegate *n* mjumbe, mwakilishi *vt* 1 wakilisha. 2 tuma, agiza *~ authority* naibisha mamlaka *~ to* wekea; agizia. **delegation** *n* 1 ujumbe. 2 uwakilishi, uwakilishaji *lead a ~* ongoza ujumbe. **delegacy** ujumbe, uwakilishi.
delete *vt* (*from*) futa, ondoa, (herufi, neno, maandiko). **deletion** *n.*
deleterious *adj* (*formal*) -haribifu, -a kudhuru, -a kuumiza.
delft (*also delf*) *~-ware* vyombo vya udongo (vya Uholanzi) vyenye nakshi za buluu.
deliberate *vt,vi* ~ *(over/on/upon)* fikiri sana, taamali, shauriana, jadiliana *adj* 1 -a kusudi. 2 -angalifu, -a hadhari, bila haraka. **~ly** *adv* kwa makusudi/ kudhamiria. **deliberative** *adj* -a kufanya shauri. **deliberation** *n* 1

(*discussion*) mashauriano, majadiliano. 2 (*consideration*) fikira; uangalifu, hadhari, taamuli.

delicate *adj* 1 laini, -ororo, -epesi *her skin is ~* ngozi yake ni nyororo. 2 -zuri, -a kuvutia, -a kupendeza. 3 -epesi kudhuriwa, dhaifu, -epesi kuugua *he is in ~ health* hana afya nzuri *a ~ looking child* mtoto dhaifu (anayehitaji matunzo zaidi). 4 -a kutaka uangalifu mkubwa. 5 (*of colours*) -a kupendeza; -siokoza. 6 (*of the senses or instruments*) -kali, -a kuweza kupima tofauti ndogo sana *a ~ sense of smell* hisia nyingi za kunusa. 7 angalifu sana; -a adabu, -a kujali wengine; -a kutafakari. 8 (*of food, its flavour*) -tamu, -sio na ladha kali. **~ly** *adv*. **delicacy** *n* 1 uzuri, ulaini, wororo, mtiririko. 2 (*refinement*) adabu; malezi mema, murua. 3 (*care*) unyeti, uangalifu. 4 (*nice dish*) chakula kitamu, mapochopocho. **~ssen** *n* 1 duka la vitoweo, duka linalouza vyakula vilivyopikwa tayari, duka la mapochopocho.

delicious *adj* -a kupendeza sana (hasa kwa ladha, harufu n.k.), -tamu; -zuri. **~ly** *adv*.

delight *vt,vi* 1 pendeza sana; anisi furahisha sana; teremesha. 2 **~ed with** furahishwa, pendezwa na. 3 **(take) ~ in** furahia *she ~s in criticizing people* anafurahia kukosoa watu *n* 1 furaha; nderemo *give ~ to sb* furahisha. 2 kitu kiletacho furaha *javelin is my chief ~* kutupa mkuki kunanifurahisha. **~ful** *adj*. **~edly** *adv*.

Delilah *n* (*of a woman*) 1 Delila (Mwanamke katika Biblia aliyemshawishina kumsaliti Samson). 2 shawishi na habithi.

delimit/delimitate *vt* wekea mpaka. **delimitation** *n*.

delineate *vt* 1 onyesha kwa kuchora/kusawiri/kueleza; chora, sawiri. 2 fafanua kwa maneno, eleza kinaganaga. **delineation** *n*.

delinquency *n* 1 ukosaji, uhalifu; kutowajibika. 2 kosa, hatia *juvenile ~* uhalifu wa vijana. **delinquent** *n* mkosaji, mwenye hatia, mhalifu *juvenile ~* mtoto mhalifu *adj* -kosaji, -enye hatia; sowajibika. **delinquently** *adv*. **deliquescent** *adj* -lioyeyuka kuwa majimaji. **deliquescence** *n* mmumunyisho maji. **deliquesce** *vi* (*chem*) -wa majimaji kwa kuvuta maji hewani.

delirious *adj* zezeta, -a kupagawa, -enye kupayuka- payuka/kuweweseka kwa ugonjwa au ulevi, -a kupayuka; -a kuchachawa *be ~ with joy* jawa na furaha, pagawa kwa furaha. **delirium** n mapayo, weweseko; wazimu, mazezeta. ~ **tremens** mapayo ya ulevi.

deliver *vt* 1 peleka (barua, vifaa n.k.), wasilisha; (*fig*) ~ *the goods* tekeleza wajibu. 2 ~ **from** okoa, ponya, opoa, fanya huru (tokana na hatari, utumwa, kifungo, maumivu, mauti, dhambi n.k.). 3 toa ~ *oneself of an opinion* toa mawazo ~ *a speech/lecture* toa hotuba/mhadhara ~ *an order* toa amri. 4 (*give birth to*) zaa, jifungua; zalisha. 5 ~ **up/over (to)** kiri, toa, kabidhi. 6 anzisha (mpango); peleka dhidi ya. (*fig*) ~ **a blow** piga. **~er** *n* mwokozi, mkombozi. **~ance** *n* 1 ~ **from** wokovu, ukombozi, uhuru. 2 afua, nusura. 3 (*utterance*)kutoa mahubiri, hotuba. 4 (*leg*) (*sentence*) hukumu. **~y** *n* 1 uokoaji, ukombozi, kuopoa, kufanya huru. 2 kupeleka, kukabidhi, kuwasilisha, kutoa (barua bidhaa n.k.). 3 uwasilishaji. **on ~y** wakati wa kuwasilisha. **take ~y of** pokea. **~y note** hati ya kuwasilisha/kupokea. **~y van** gari la ugawaji. 4 kuzaa, kuzalisha. 5 namna ya kuongea/kutoa hotuba n.k. 6 pigo. 7 (*mode of speaking*) jinsi ya kusema.

dell *n* bonde; kibonde kilichopamba msitu.

delouse *vt* ondolea chawa.

Delphian, Delphic *adj* -tata, -siyoeleweka, -a fumbo.

delta *n* 1 herufi **d** ya alfabeti ya Kigriki. 2 (*of a river*) delta. 3 ~ *rays* miali delta ~ *metal* madini ya delta.
deltoid *adj* -a pembetatu *deltoid muscle* musuli wenye pembe tatu *n* umbo la pembe tatu.
delude *vt* ~ **with/into** danganya; laghai; tia mchanga wa macho ~ *sb with promises* -pa mtu ahadi za uongo; (*refl*) ~ *oneself* jidanganya. **delusion** *n* 1 kudanganya; kudanganywa. 2 madanganyo, ghiliba. 3 maono/imani za uwongo (hasa kama dalili ya wazimu) *he is a victim of* ~ anadanganyika sana, amerukwa na akili; majinuni. **delusive** *adj* danganyifu, -a kudanganya, -a uwongo.
deluge *n* gharika, mafuriko ya maji; mvua kubwa sana **the D** ~ gharika wakati wa Nuhu *vt* ~ **(with)** gharikisha; funikiza; nyeshea sana.
de luxe *adj* -a hali ya juu sana, -a fahari; -a anasa tupu.
delve *vt,vi* 1 (*old use*) chimba. 2 ~ **into** chungua/chunguza sana (kitabu, elimu, masomo).
demagnetize *vt* sumakua, ondoa nguvu za sumaku. **demagnetization** *n.*
demagogue *n* 1 mhemshaji/mhisishi, msukumizi: kiongozi wa kisiasa anayeshawishi watu kwa kutumia hisia badala ya fikra zao. 2 mfitini. **demagogic** *adj.* **~ry/demagogy** *n.*
demand *vt* 1 dai, taka (kwa nguvu au kwa haki). 2 (*require*) hitaji *this work ~s great care* kazi hii inahitaji uangalifu mkubwa *n* ~ **(for)** 1 dai, madai, kutaka kwa nguvu; kudai. 2 **on** ~ itakapohitajiwa *payable on* ~ (-a kulipwa) idaiwapo. ~ **(note)** hati ya madai. **in** ~ -enye kutafutwa/kupendwa sana *This ~ is fair* dai hili la haki. 2 *(need)* mahitaji, matilaba, tamaa. ~ **curve** mchirizo wa mahitaji. ~ **schedule** jedwali la mahitaji. *(pl)* ~s matakwa. 3 **~s on sb's good nature** kumhitajia mtu kwa wema wake *I have many ~s on my time* nina mambo mengi muhimu ya kutimiza. **~ing** *adj* -a kuhitaji uangalifu mkubwa/bidii nyingi.
demarcate *vt* 1 aua, weka mpaka/mipaka. 2 tenga. **demarcation** *n* 1 kuaua, kuweka mpaka/mipaka. 2 mpaka/mipaka; mwauo *line of* ~mpaka. 3 mtengano.
dèmarche *n* (*F*) 1 hatua au taratibu za kisiasa (hasa za kuanzisha sera mpya). 2 ujumbe wa kidiplomasia wa kutoa malalamiko.
demean *vi,vt* 1 (*debase*) ~ **oneself** jitweza, jidharau, jidhalilisha.
demeanour *n* mwenendo; mazoea; adabu.
demented *adj* -enye wazimu, kichaa. **be** ~ fadhaika; (*med*) -a kiendawazimu. **~ly** *adv*. **demential** *n* kichaa, ukichaa.
demerara *n* demerara: guru (kutoka Guyana). ~ **sugar** sukari-guru.
demerit *n* 1 kosa. 2 upungufu, kasoro, dosari, hitilafu.
demesne *n* 1 (*leg*) umilikaji ardhi *hold in* ~ -wa mwenye ardhi. 2 milki, shamba kubwa.
demi (*prefix*) nusu.
demijohn *n* chupa kubwa (iliyotiwa ndani ya mfuko wa mianzi).
demilitarize *vt* ondoa majeshi, kataza mambo ya kivita/ kijeshi. **~d zone** ukanda usio na majeshi, ukanda uliokatazwa mambo ya kivita/ kijeshi.
demise *n* 1 (*leg*) mauti; kufa; kifo. 2 uhawilishaji *vt* hawilisha.
demist *vt* ondoa unyevu (katika madirisha ya gari n.k.). **~er** *n.*
demit *vt,vi* ng'atuka, acha kazi, jiuzulu, **demision** *n.*
demo *n* (*colloq*) *see* **demonstration**. **demobilize/demob** *vt* changua (askari, manowari); ruhusu askari kwenda kwao (baada ya vita). **demobilization** *n.*
democracy *n* 1 demokrasia: mfumo wa serikali unaoshirikisha wananchi kupitia wabunge (waliochaguliwa). 2 nchi yenye kuhimiza na kuruhusu

haki za uraia kama uhuru wa kusema, kuabudu, kutoa maoni na kushiriki, kusisitiza utawala wa sheria, utawala wa walio wengi, pamoja na kuheshimu haki za wachache. 3 jamii ambamo watu wote ni sawa na hakuna hisia za kitabaka. **democratic** *adj* 1 -a demokrasi, -enye kuunga mkono demokrasi, -a kidemokrasi. **democrat** *n* 1 mwanademokrasia; mpenda demokrasia. **Democrat** (*US*) mwanachama wa Chama cha Democrat. **democratize** *vt* fanya iwe -a kidemokrasi; fanya -a demokrasi. **democratization** *n*.

démodé *adj* -a kale, -a zamani *it is ~* siyo ya kisasa, ni ya zamani, imepitwa na wakati.

demography *n* demografia: taaluma ya takwimu ya kima cha uzazi, vifo, maradhi n.k. kuonyesha hali ya jamii fulani.

demolish *vt* 1 (*of buildings*) bomoa, vunja. 2 (*of arguments*) tilifu, angamiza; bomoa; (*jocular*) -la. **demolition** *n*.

demon *n* 1 pepo mbaya; jini mbaya; shetani. 2 mtu katili/mwovu/ mharibifu/mwangamizi; (*colloq*) -enye juhudi, shababu *~ for work* hodari wa kazi. **~ic** *adj*. **~ism** *n*. **~ology** *n*. **~iac** *adj* 1 -enye pepo mbaya. 2 -a shetani. 3 katili, -ovu sana. **~iacal** *adj*. **~iacally** *adv*.

demonetize *vt* 1 ondolea fedha thamani. 2 acha kutumia madini fulani kama sarafu.

demonstrate *vt*, *vi* 1 fafanua kwa kutoa sababu dhahiri (mifano); thibitisha. 2 onyesha wazi, dhihirisha; (*manoeuvre*) onyesha mbinu (katika jeshi). 3 andamana. **demonstrator** *n*. **demonstrable** *adj* -a kuthibitishika, -a kudhihirika *it is ~ that* inathibitishika kwamba. **demostration** *n* 1 (*proof*) uthibitisho, ushahidi; mafafanuzi. 2 (*certainty*) uthabiti, hakika; 3 (*show*) maonyesho. 4 (*also demo*) maandamano. **demostrative** *adj* 1 -a kuonyesha wazi, -a kuashiria (maono, upendo, furaha, chuki, n.k.). 2 -a kuainisha. 3 (*gram*) kionyeshi. **~ pronoun** kiwakilishi kionyeshi. **demonstratively** *adv*. **demonstrativeness** *n*.

demoralize *vt* 1 vunja moyo (k.m. wa askari vitani). 2 chafua, haribu moyo/tabia/hali. **demoralization** *n*.

demote *vt* teremsha/shusha cheo, **demotion** *n*.

demotic *adj* (*of languages*) -a kila siku, -a kawaida, maujudi, -a umma, -a mitaani.

demur *vt* ~ **(to/at)** kinza, bisha; kataakataa; sita; onea shaka *n* makinzano, kani, ubishi, kusita *obey without ~* tii bila kusita *make no ~* usisite, usikaidi, usibishe.

demure *adj* 1 -nyamavu; -pole, -enye kumakinika, -kimya. 2 taratibu. 3 -enye haya. **~ly** *adv*. **~ness** *n*.

demurrage *n* 1 fidia ya kuchelewa. 2 faini ya kuchelewesha kukomboa mizigo; haka ya meli (kwa kuchelewa gatini).

demystify *vt* fichua, weka wazi, umbua.

den *n* 1 tundu (la mnyama wa mwitu); kitundu, pango. 2 majificho/ makutano ya waovu, (wevi n.k.). 3 chumba cha faragha cha kazi.

denary *adj see* **decimal**.

denationalize *vt* 1 ondoa utaifa. 2 rudisha kwa watu binafsi kilichotaifishwa. **denationalization** *n*.

denaturalize *vt* 1 geuza desturi za asili. 2 ondoa haki ya mtu kuwa na taifa (au nchi) fulani, nyima uraia. **denaturalization** *n*

denatured *adj* -siofaa kwa kula au kunywa, -lioharamishwa.

denature *vt* badilisha tabia, nyang'anya asili.

denrology *n* elimu (ya) miti.

dengue *n* (*med.*) kidingapopo, homa ya vipindi.

denier *n* denyi (kipima uzito agh. wa sufi, nailoni n.k. katika kitambaa).

denigrate *vt* paka matope, vunjia ulua, aziri. **denigration** *n*.

denim *n* denimu: kitambaa cha pamba kigumu agh. hutumiwa kushonea ovaroli, dangirizi.

denizen *n* (*of persons*) mkazi, mwenyeji; mlowezi. 2 (*of animals and plants*) kiselea.

denomination *n* 1 madhehebu. 2 (*currency*) kima, kiwango. **money of small ~s** fedha za kichele *reduce to the same ~* badili fedha kwa kima kile kile. **~al** *adj*. **denominate** *vt* taja, ita, -pa jina. **denominative** *adj*.

denominator *n* (*Math*) asili: namba ya chini ya mstari katika hesabu za sehemu ¾, ⅞.

denote *vt* 1 maanisha, onya; onyesha, -wa ishara ya. 2 -wa dalili ya, -wa ishara ya maana fulani. 3 -wa jina la. **denotation** *n* 1 maana halisi ya neno. 2 jina. **denotative** *adj*.

denouement *n* 1 sehemu ya mwisho ya hadithi/mchezo baada ya kilele (ambapo mambo yanawekwa wazi). 2 sehemu ya mwisho ya shani; mfululizo baada ya kilele.

denounce *vt* 1 shutumu; kana hadharani, suta. 2 tangaza kusudi la kufuta mkataba/mapatano. **~ment** *n*. **denunciation** *n* masuto, shutuma. **denunciator** *n*. **denunciatory** *adj*.

dense *adj* 1 (*of liquids, vapor*) -nene, -zito. 2 (*of people and things*) -ingi; -liosongamana. 3 (*colloq*) -pumbavu, -enye uzito wa kuelewa. **~ness** *n*. **density** *n* msongamano, uzito *~ of water* msongamano, uzito wa maji. 2 upumbavu, uzito wa kuelewa.

dent *n* kibonyeo *vt* bonyeza *vi* bonyea.

dentist *n* daktari wa meno. **~ry** *n* utaalamu wa meno. **dental** *adj* -a meno. **dentifrice** *n* dawa ya mswaki. **dentition** *n* 1 mpango wa meno. 2 kuota meno. **denture** *n* meno bandia.

denude *vt* acha wazi, acha rabana *a tree ~d of leaves* mti uliopukutika majani *a hill ~d of trees* kilima kisichokuwa na miti. 2 (*deprive*) twalia. **denudation** *n*.

deny *vt* 1 kana, kanusha. 2 (*refuse*) kataa. 3 (*withhold*) nyima, hini. **deniable** *adj*. **denial** *n* 1 kanusho *give a flat ~* kanusha, kataa kabisa. 2 *(withholding) ~ (of)* kunyima, kuhini, hiana.

deodorant *n* kiondoa harufu (agh. kutuzi/kikwapa). **deodorize** *vt* ondoa harufu.

depart *vi* 1 ~ **(from)** uka, ondoka, enda. 2 (*die*) fariki dunia, -fa, shikwa na faradhi *~ this life* fariki dunia. 3 (*deviate from)* acha, kengeuka *~ from old customs* acha desturi za zamani *~ from truth* sema uongo. **the ~ed** *n* marehemu (aliyefariki hivi punde). **~ure** *n* 1 kuondoka, kwenda *take one's ~ure* ondoka. **~ure platform** mahali pa kuondokea. 2 kuacha, kubadilika, mkengeuko *~ ure from a law* ukengeukaji sheria. **a new ~ure** jambo jipya, *a new ~ure in mathematics* mwelekeo/mtazamo mpya katika hesabu. 3 (*death*) kifo.

depasture *vt* chunga, peleka malishoni; (*of cattle*) -la/lisha majani.

depend *vi* ~ **on/upon** 1 tegemea *that ~s; it (all) ~s* inategemea -fungamana na, fuatana; inamia; elekea. 2 amini; tumainia; -wa na hakika juu ya. ~ **upon it** usiwe na shaka *the old man still ~s on his son* mzee bado anatumainia mwanae. **~able** *adj* -a kutegemea. **~ant, ~ent** *n* 1 mtegemea mtu, anayelelewa (mtoto, mtumishi). 2 mfuasi; *pl* watu wanaotegemea kulelewa na mtu mwingine. **~ence** *n* **(on/upon)** 1 (hali ya) kutegemea (mtu au kitu). 2 imani *I have a lot of ~ence on her* nina imani sana naye. 3 (*addiction*) uraibu. **~ency** *n* 1 koloni. 2 kitegemea. **~ent** *adj* 1 tegemezi. ~ent clause kishazi tegemezi. **~ent economy** uchumi tegemezi. **~ent on/upon** -a kutegemea *victory is ~ent on the weather* ushindi unategemea hali ya hewa.

depict *vt* 1 onyesha kwa mchoro, picha n.k.; sawiri. 2 eleza, fafanua. **~ion** *n*.

depilate vt ondoa nywele. **depilatory**

adj -a kuondoa nywele, -a kunyonyoa nywele *n* dawa ya kunyonyoa nywele.

deplane *vt* (*usu of troops*) toka, chupa kutoka kwenye ndege.

deplete *vt* 1 (*of*) punguza sana, tumia hadi karibu kumaliza. 2 (*rare*) maliza kabisa, toa vitu vyote hadi pasibaki kitu. **depletion** *n*.

deplore *vt* sikitikia, jutia; laani; laumu. **deplorable** *adj*. **deplorably** *adv*.

deploy *vt mil.*) eneza, sambaza, panga (tayari kwa mapigano); (*fig*) tumia *he ~ed his arguments* alitumia hoja zake. **~ment** *n*.

deplume *vt* nyonyoa, toa manyoya; (*fig*) uzua, vua nishani n.k.

deponent *n* (*leg*) shahidi wa maandishi.

depopulate *vt* 1 punguza sana idadi ya watu, angamiza watu *AIDS is depopulating some villages* ukimwi unaangamiza watu katika baadhi ya vijiji. **depopulation** *n*.

deport[1] *vt* fukuza nchini (mtu asiyetakiwa). **~ation** *n*. **~ee** *n*.

deport[2] *vt ~ (oneself)* -wa na tabia/mwenendo (wa namna fulani maalum) *~ oneself with dignity* -wa na adabu, jiheshimu, jichunga, jistahi. **~ment** *n* mwenendo; mwendo.

depose *vt,vi* uzulu, ondosha madarakani. ~ **(to** + *gerund)* (*leg*) toa ushahidi (hasa baada ya kuapa kortini), shuhudia, thibitisha (kwa kiapo). **deposition** *n*.

deposit *vt* 1 weka *~ the papers on the table* weka karatasi mezani *~ money in a bank* weka fedha benki. 2 (*of a river*) acha mashapo/tope *the river ~s mud on the fields* mto huacha matope katika mashamba. 3 lipa sehemu ya fedha kama amana/rubuni, weka amana/rubuni. *n* 1 amana; uwekaji amana *~ account* hesabu ya amana. ~ **slip** stakabadhi ya amana. 2 arbuni *he put a ~ on the car* aliliwekea gari arbuni. 3 (*sediment*) mashapo. 4 (*of drink*) machicha. **~or** *n fig* hazina. **~ory** *n (store)* depo, ghala, bohari.

depot *n* 1 (*store*) depo, ghala, bohari. 2 (*mil.*) kambi la kuruta. 3 (*US*) stesheni ya garimoshi au basi.

deprave *vt* haribu tabia; potosha, kengeusha. **depravation** *n*. ~ **depravity** *n* upotovu, uharibifu wa tabia, mkengeuko.

deprecate *vt* (*formal*) lalamika, pinga. **deprecation** *n*. **deprecating** *adj*. **deprecatory** *adj* 1 -a kulalamika. 2 -a kujihami dhidi ya lawama. **a ~ smile** tabasamu la kinafiki.

depreciate *vt,vi* 1 chakaa; chakaza, pungua thamani; punguza thamani. 2 (*disparage*) kashifu, shusha hadhi, dhalilisha. **depreciative/depreciatory** *adj*. **depreciation** *n* uchakavu, upunguzaji thamani.

depredation *n* (*usu pl*) 1 uharibifu mkubwa (wa mali). 2 unyang'anyi, ujambazi.

depress *vt* 1 (*lower*) inamisha; sukuma/vuta chini, kandamiza, bonyeza. 2 (*make dejected*) huzunisha, sikitisha, fadhaisha. 3 punguza nguvu, dhoofisha. 4 shusha (bei, mishahara n.k.). **~ed** *adj* -enye huzuni. **~ed classes** tabaka za chini (za watu wanaokandamizwa). **~ive** *adj*. **~ing** *adj* -a kufadhaisha/kuvunja moyo. **~ion** *n* 1 huzuni; *(psych)* majonzi; mfadhaiko. 2 bonde; mwinamo, mbonyeo. 3 mdororo wa shughuli za uchumi, mdodo. 4 upunguaji wa kanieneo ya angahewa.

deprive *vt ~ (of)* nyima, nyang'anya, poka. **deprivation** *n*. **~d** *adj*.

depth *n* 1 kina: urefu wa kwenda chini, uketo. **in ~** *adj,adv* barabara, kwa kina; -a kuzamia. **be (get) out of one's ~** -wa katika maji marefu kuliko urefu wako; (*fig*) fanya jambo linalokuzidi kipimo/uwezo wa kuelewa. 2 usomi/mawazo/maono yaliyobobea/topea. 3 **the ~ (s)** kina, lindi, ndani kabisa *~s of ignorance* lindi la ujinga *~ of night* usiku wa manane *~s of the sea* vilindi *in the ~ of my heart* moyoni kabisa *in the ~of the country* shambani kabisa. ~ **charge** *n* (*mil.*) bomu la majini.

~-**gauge** *n* pima kina.

deputation *n* 1 wajumbe, wawakilishi. 2 agizo, ujumbe.

depute *vt* kaimisha, naibisha, toa kazi/madaraka n.k. kwa mtu mwingine ili awakilishe; weka naibu/ makamu/kaimu. **deputize** *vi* **(for)** kaimu, fanya badala ya mtu mwingine, -wa naibu. **deputy** *n* 1 kaimu, naibu; makamu *she will be my ~ when I am away* atakuwa kaimu wangu wakati sipo ~ *minister* naibu waziri. 2 (*in some countries eg. France*) mbunge.

derail *vt,vi* angusha/anguka treni; toa katika reli *the train was ~ed* treni ilianguka.

derange *vt* 1 *(make mad)* tia kichaa/ wazimu. 2 haribu, vuruga.

derby *n* mashindano ya farasi *n* (*US*) pama.

derelict *n* 1 mali (meli, chombo) iliyotelekezwa/tupwa. 2 ombaomba, maskini, msikwao *adj* (*esp. of ship*) -lioachwa; -liotupwa ~ *vessel* chombo kihame ~ *old house* mahame. ~**ion** *n* hali ya kuachwa. ~**ion of duty** uzembe mkubwa, kutowajibika, kutotimiza wajibu.

deride *vt* kejeli, dhihaki, beza, beua. **derision** *n* kejeli, dhihaka; dharau *hold in ~* dhihaki, dharau. **derisory** *adj* 1 (*also derisive*) -a kudhihaki/ kukejeli. 2 -a kustahili dhihaka, -a kudharauliwa, -a kupuuza ~ *salary* mshahara wa dhihaka/kubeza.

de rigueur *adj* -a lazima.

derive *vt,vi* ~ **(from)** 1 zalisha, pata kutokana na, tokana na, chimbuka *it ~d from* asili/mwanzo/chimbuko lake ni. 2 (*math*) nyambua. 3 (*gram*) nyambulisha. **derivation** *n* 1 (*origin*) asili, mwanzo, chimbuko. 2 umbo na maana ya asili ya neno. 3 (*gram*) unyambulishaji: uundaji maneno mapya kutokana na viini au mashina. 4 (*Math.*) unyambuaji. **derivative** *adj* 1 zalika, kitokanacho; (*derog*) -sio asili, -sio na uasili, -enye kuigaiga *a ~ poem* shairi lisilo na uasili, shairi la kuigaiga. 2 (*Math.*) -nyambuo. 3 (*gram*) *n* kinyambuo: kitu kinachotokana na kitu kingine.

derm *adj.* -a ngozi. ~**atitis** ugonjwa wa ngozi. ~**atology** *n* elimu ya ngozi (hasa magonjwa yake). ~**atologist** *n* daktari wa ngozi.

derogate *vi* ~ **(from)** shusha/punguza, (hadhi, heshima, mamlaka n.k.). **derogation** *n*. **derogatory** *adj*. ~ **(to)** -a kushusha heshima/hadhi, -a kuaibisha. 2 -a matusi.

derrick *n* 1 ~-**crane** winchi, slingi, manjanika: mashine ya kuinua vitu vizito (hasa katika meli). 2 fremu za mashine za kekee.

derring-do *(old use)* tendo la ushujaa.

dervish *n* 1 darweshi: walii/muumini wa kiislamu anayeshikilia jadi na kutenda kufuatana na Hadithi bila kujali wakati wala mabadiliko; mwana tablighi. 2 mtu anayeji- sahau katika kucheza muziki.

desalinate *(also* **desalinize**) *vt* ondoa chumvi (toka kwenye maji ya bahari). **desalination** *n.*

escale *vt* kwangua/para mashapo/ makoko.

descend *vt, vi* 1 (*go or come down*) shuka, enda/-ja chini, teremka. 2 (*slope*) inama. 3 (*of origin*) **be ~ed from** toka, tokana na (babu fulani), zaliana, -wa katika ukoo wa... 4 rithishwa (na); rithiwa *his bravery ~s from his father* ameurithi ushujaa kwa baba yake. 5 ~ **(upon)** shambulia kwa ghafla; (*fig*) tembelea ghafla. 6 ~ **to** jishusha. ~**ant** *n* dhuria. ~**able** *adj* -a urithi. **descent** *n* 1 mshuko, mteremko, mwinamo. 2 (*ancestry*) nasaba, ukoo, uzazi. 3 urithi, kurithiwa. 4 ~ **on/upon** shambulio la ghafula; *(colloq)* kutembelea kusikotegemewa, ugeni usiotegemewa.

describe *vt* 1 eleza, toa wasifu. 2 chora, (hasa maumbo ya jiometri). 3 ~ **as** ita. **description** *n* 1 maelezo. 2 *(colloq)* jinsi, namna, aina.

descriptive *adj* -a kueleza, -a kutoa wasifu.
descry *vt* ona, weza kuona (kama mbali).
desecrate *vt* 1 najisi, kufuru; haramisha. **desecration** *n.*
desegregate *vt* ondoa ubaguzi (hasa ubaguzi wa rangi). **desegregation** *n.*
desensitize *vt* haribu/punguza fahamu (za mwanga au maumivu)/ milango ya fahamu; tia ganzi. **desensitization** *n.*
desert[1] *n* jangwa *adj* kame, -siolimwa.. 2 -siokaliwa na watu.
desert[2] *vt,vi* 1 acha; toka *the streets were ~ed* mitaa ilikuwa mitupu. **a ~ed village** mahame. 2 telekeza *he ~ed his wife* alimtelekeza mkewe. 3 toka *his courage ~ed him* ujasiri wake ulimtoka. 4 (*mil.*) toroka. **~er** *n* mtoro. **~ion** *n.*
deserve *vt,vi* 1 stahili. 2 *(idiom) ~ well/ill of* stahili kutendewa vizuri/ vibaya. **~d** *adj* -liostahili. **~dly** *adv.* **deserving** *adj* -a kustahili, -a stahilifu. **deserts** *n* ustahili; (*reward*) thawabu.
deshabille *n see* **dishabille**.
desiccate *vt* kausha kabisa (ili kuhifadhi). **~d fruit** tunda lililokaushwa. **desiccative** *adj.* **desiccator** *n.* **desiccant** *n (US)* kikausho.
desiderate *vt (want)* taka sana, hitaji.
desideratum *n* kitu kinachotakiwa sana.
design *vt,vi* 1 *(draw)* chora. 2 *(of book etc)* sanifu. 3 *(of ideas)* buni, panga. 4 *(intend)* kusudia, nuia, azimia *n* 1 mchoro, picha, kielelezo. 2 usanifu, ruwaza, nakshi. 3 mpango, plani, kielelezo. 4 kusudi, nia, madhumuni, maarubu. **have ~s on/against** -wa na kusudi baya/hila *He has ~s on that young girl (colloq)* anamtaka msichana yule. **~er** *n* 1 msanii mchoraji. 2 mbuni. **~ing** *adj* -erevu, -janja; -a hila *n* uchoraji, ubunifu (wa mashine n.k.). **~edly** *adv* makusudi.
designate *vt* 1 onyesha; dhihirisha *~ boundaries* onyesha mipaka. 2 *(denote)* taja; -wa dalili ya; -wa na maana fulani. 3 *(appoint)* teua (mtu) kwa kazi fulani *he ~d me as his successor* aliniteua niwe mrithi wake *adj* -teule. **the bishop ~** askofu mteule. **designation** *n* uteuzi (wa mtu kushika cheo fulani); jina, cheo; maelezo.
desire *vt* 1 taka sana, tamani *leaves much to ~d* hairidhishi kabisa. 2 *(sexual)* ashiki, tamani. 3 *(request)* omba. **I ~d her to sit down** nilimwomba aketi *n* 1 hamu, tamaa, uchu, shauku. 2 *(formal)* ombi. 3 kitu kinachotamaniwa/takiwa. **what is your heart's ~** kitu gani unachotamani kuliko vyote. 4 *(sexual)* ashiki. **desirable** *adj* 1 -a kufaa. 2 -a kutamanisha. **desirability** *n.*
desirous *adj (formal/official)(of)* -enye kutaka. **desirous of peace** -enye kutaka amani.
desist *adj (formal)* ~ **(from)** acha, hulu.
desk *n* 1 meza (ya kuandikia), dawati, deski. ~ **work** *(often derog)* kazi ya ofisi *reception ~* mapokezi, maulizo *~ clerk* karani wa mapokezi. 3 *(journalism)* meza ya mhariri.
desolate *vt (make sad)* uzunisha, tia majonzi, tia ukiwa *adj* 1 -a ukiwa; -enye huzuni, -enye majonzi. 2 -lioachwa, -liotelekezwa, -liotupwa, hame. **~ly** *adv.* **desolation** *n.*
despair *vi* kata tamaa; -fa moyo *n* kukata tamaa, kufa moyo. **be the ~ of** katisha tamaa. **~ing** *adj.* **~ingly** *adv.*
despatch *n,vt see* **dispatch**.
desperado *n* jahili.
desperate *adj* 1 -enye kukata tamaa, -liokata tamaa, bila tumaini, tayari kufanya lolote (kutokana na kukata tamaa), -sofuata sheria (kutokana na kukata tamaa/kutokuwa na matumaini tena) *~ criminal* jahili. 3 -baya sana, -a hatari *the country is in ~ state* nchi iko katika hali mbaya sana. 4 -enye kuwa na mahitaji makubwa ya kitu. 5 -a mwisho

kabisa *a last ~ effort* jaribio la mwisho kabisa. **~ly** *adv.* **desperation** *n.*

despicable *adj* -enye kustahili dharau/twezo; -enye kuleta hizaya.

despise *vt* tweza, dharau, hakiri.

despite *n, prep.* **~ of/in spite of** licha ya. **~ his wishes** licha ya matakwa yake. **~ful** *(arch. see* **spiteful. ~fully** *adv.*

despoil *vt* nyang'anya, pora, ghusubu. **~ation** *n.* **~ment** *n* uporaji. **~er** *n* mporaji.

despondency *n* hali ya kukata tamaa, ukataji tamaa. **despondent** *adj.* **be ~** kata tamaa, -fa moyo. **despondently** *adv.*

despot *n* 1 dikteta, mtawala mwenye mamlaka yote. 2 *(tyrant)* mdhalimu. **play the ~** fanya udhalimu, -wa dikteta. **~ie** *adj.* **~ism** *n.*

dessert *n* kitindamlo (tamutamu, matunda n.k.). **~ spoon** kijiko cha pudini.

destabilize *vt* yumbisha, chochea ghasia, vuruga amani.

destine *vt* kusudia, taka *I was ~d never to see her again* nilitakiwa nisimwone tena *this is ~d for Zanzibar* hii inakwenda Unguja.

destination *n* mwisho wa/kikomo cha safari; makusudio.

destiny *n* 1 *(power)* takdiri. 2 *(that which happens)* majaliwa, kudura, bahati.

destitute *adj* 1 hawinde, mkata, fukara. 2 **~ of** -a kukosa, sio kuwa na *~ of sympathy* kukosa huruma. **destitution** *n* ufukara.

destroy *vt* 1 haribu, bananga, vunja; *(completely)* angamiza, teketeza, tilifu. 2 *(usu of animal)* ua. **er~** *n* 1 mharabu; mwangamizi. 2 manowari (ya kulinda meli nyingine).

destruction *n* 1 uharibifu, uvunjifu, maangamizo. 2 uteketeaji, uangamiaji. **destructible** *adj.* **destructive** *adj* 1 -a kuharibu, -haribifu, -harabu, -a kutilifu. 2 -a shari. **destructiveness** *n.*

destructor *n* tanuri (la kuchomea takataka); kichomataka.

desuetude *n* 1 kutotumika. 2 **to fall into ~** kutotumika tena.

desultory *adj* -badilifu -siyo na taratibu, geugeu, -a kuchezacheza.

detach *vt* 1 tenga; bandua, kata. 2 peleka kikosi cha askari kutoka jeshi kubwa. **~able** *adj.* **~ed** *adj* 1 *(of the mind, opinion)* adilifu, siopendelea; -siyovutwa/sioshawishiwa na watu wengine. 2 -sio na hisia, sioonyesha hisia; *(aloof)* liokaa kando. 3 *(house)* nayokaa peke yake. **~ment** *n* 1 mtengo; mabanduko, mtego. 2 *(of soldiers, war-ships)* kikosi kinachotumika kwa kazi maalum. 3 *(impartiality)* uadilifu, hali/tabia ya kutokuvutwa na maneno au fikra za watu; *(aloofness)* upweke: kukaa kando.

detail *n* 1 kila kitu. 2 utondoti. **in the fullest ~** kwa utondoti, kinaganaga. **go/enter into ~s** chunguza kwa utondoti *explain in ~* eleza kinaganaga. 3 *(mil)* kikosi maalum cha askari *vt* 1 **~ (to/for)** tongoa; eleza kila kitu kwa ukamilifu, eleza kwa kusimulia habari yote. 2 tuma, agiza, amuru kufanya kazi maalum.

detain *vt* 1 kawisha, kawiza, chelewesha. 2 weka kizuizini, zuia. **~ee** *n* mtu aliye kizuizini. **detention** *n* 1 kizuizini *put in detention* weka kizuizini. **preventive detention** uzuizi wa hadhari. 2 uzuiliwaji (agh mtoto shuleni kama adhabu).

detect *vt* gundua;ona.**~ion** *n* ugunduzi; upelelezi. **~ive** *n* mpelelezi, askari kanzu, kachero *adj* -a upelelezi. **~or** *n* kigunduzi. **lie ~ or** kigundua uongo.

detente *n* maridhiano (hasa baina ya mataifa).

deter *vt* shusha/vunja moyo; zuia, punguza ari (kwa kutia shaka, hofu, vitisho n.k.). **~rent** *n* kizuio, kigingi.

detergent *adj* -a kusafisha *n* dawa kali ya kusafishia; sabuni (ya unga/maji).

deteriorate *vt,vi* pungua/punguza thamani/manufaa/matumizi; fifia, haribika; chakaa. **deterioration** *n.*

determine *vt,vi* 1 *(limit, define)* ukilia, amua. 2 ~ **to do sth; ~upon doing sth** kusudia, dhamiria. 3 tambulisha, tafuta, pata, bainisha. **~a number** tambulisha namba. 4 *(fix beforehand)* weka/panga muda (miadi, tarehe). 5 *(settle, decide)* amua, nuia, fanya uamuzi, kata shauri. 6 ~ **sb to do sth** fanya, shurutisha, sababisha *what ~d you to go to Morogoro* kitu gani kilikufanya kwenda Morogoro. 7 pambanua ~ *the meaning of a word* pambanua maana ya neno. **determinable** *adj.* **determinant** *n* 1 kiukilia, kitu (mtu) kinachodhihirisha tambulisha/yakinisha/onyesha manuizi. 2 kiamuzi, kitu (mtu) kinachoamua/maliza/kata/shauri. **determinate** *adj* thabiti, imara; -dhahiri; -enye mipaka. **determination** *n* 1 *(resoluteness)* uamuzi (mkata), azimio; kuamua; ushupavu. 2 *(resolve)* azma, kusudi, nia, dhamiri. 3 *(of word etc)* kupambanua. 4 *(of number etc)* utambuzi, upataji, utafutaji; kutambulisha. **~r** *n (gram)* kibainishi.

detest *vt* chukia sana, kirihi, sinya.

dethrone dethrone *vt* uzulu, ondoa (mfalme). **~ment** *n.* **~able** *adj* -a karaha, -enye makuruhu. **~ation** *n* chuki, karaha, makuruhu.

detonate *vt, vi* lipua; lipuka. **detonation** *n.* **detonator** *n.*

detour *n* njia ya mchepuo/mzunguko. **make a** ~ chepuka.

detract *vt* ~ *(from)* 1 punguza (thamani). 2 *(slander)* punguza sifa; dunisha; kashifu. ~ **ion** *n.* **~or** *n* mkashifishaji.

detrain *vi,vt (of troops etc.)* teremsha, shuka/shusha (toka garimoshi).

detribalize *vt* 1 tenga mtu kutoka kabila lake. 2 vunja mila au desturi za kabila/mbari. **detribalization** *n.*

detriment *n* hasara; dhara. **to the ~ of** -enye kuleta hasara/dhara. **~al (to)** *adj* -enye kuleta hasara/dhara.

detrition *n* kuisha/kupungua kutokana na msuguano.

detritus *n* mabaki/unga utokanao na kusagika kwa mchanga, mawe n.k. (ya kusugua).

detrop *adj* kisonoko, ziada mbovu.

deuce *n* 1 karata ng'anda mbili. 2 *(tennis)* sare. 3 *(devil)* shetani, ibilisi. **what the ~/the ~ to pay etc** *see* **devil. ~d** *adj,adv* -baya mno.

Deuteronomy *n* kumbukumbu ya Torati.

devalue *vt (also US devaluate)* shusha thamani. **devaluation** *n.*

devastate *vt* 1 teketeza, haribu, bananga. **devastating** *adj.* **devastation** *n.*

develop *vt,vi* 1 kuza; kua. **~ing country** nchi inayoendelea ~ *quickly* vuvumka. 2 jitokeza, funuka, dhihirika. 3 *(of films)* safisha. 4 *(of land)* endeleza (kwa kujenga). 5 *(explain)* fafanua, eleza. **~er** *n* 1 mwendelezaji. **land ~er** mwendelezaji ardhi. 2 *(of film)* developa. **~ment** *n* 1 *(augmentation)* kukuza; kuendeleza, kusitawisha. 2 *(growth)* maendeleo, usitawisho. **community ~ment** maendeleo ya jamii, usitawi wa jamii. **~ment Studies** Taaluma ya Maendeleo. 3 *(film)* kusafisha picha. 4 *(explanation)* ufafanuzi (wa wazo, mada, maana).

deviate *vi* 1 chepuka. 2 kengeuka, potoka (katika maadili). 3 hitilafiana. **deviation** *n* mkengeuko, mchepuko. **deviant** *n* mwachamaadili/desturi. **deviance** *n.* **deviationist** *n* mkengeuka, mtu anayekengeuka misingi ya kijamii au ya mfumo wa siasa uliopo. **deviationism** *n.*

device *n* 1 hila, mbinu, mpango. leave sb to his own ~s mwache afanye apendavyo; *(contrivance)* chombo, ala, kitu (cha kufikilia lengo/kufanyia jambo fulani). 3 *(emblem)* chapa, alama, sanamu, picha itumikayo kama nembo/ urembo/pambo. 4 kitu au usemi utumiwao kuleta athari fulani ya kisanii.

devil *n* 1 shetani, ibilisi; *(fig)* adui mbaya. **between the ~and the deep (blue) sea** katika hali ya atiati ukashindwa kuamua jambo; kimbia kufiwako kwenda kuliwako nyama. **give the ~ his due** mtendee kila mtu haki yake (hata kama ni adui). **go to the ~** nenda zako! haribika! kwisha! *play the ~ with* umiza, haribu. **the D~** shetani. **~'s advocate** mchochea mjadala kwa kuonyesha ila au kasoro ya kitu. **lucky ~** mwenye bahati. **speak/talk of the ~and he is sure to appear** hatajwi (akitajwa tu hutokea). 2 *(usu* **poor ~)** *(as interjection)* masikini! 3 *(arch)* **printer's ~** kijana atumiwae kama tarishi mwanagenzi katika ofisi ya uchapaji, mwanasheria mwanagenzi. 4 *(colloq)* msisitizo. **what/who/why/ where the ~** nini/ nani/kwa nini/wapi ... (kutegemea muktadha). **~ may-care** *adj (carefree)* asiyejali. 5 *(tech)* mashine ya kuchambua *vt* 1 *(spice a dish)* koleza chakula (hasa kwa viungo vyenye pilipili). 2 **~ for** fanya kazi kama mchapaji/mwanasheria mwanagenzi. **~ish** *adj* 1 kama shetani. 2 -baya mno; ovu sana; -uaji, -katili *adv* kikatili. **~ry** *(also* **~ ment)** *n* 1 ushetani, uibilisi. 2 -ukatili; -uovu. 3 uchawi. 4 *(rel.)* elimu ya mizimu.

devil-fish *n* karwe.

devious *adj* 1 -a mchepuko, -a uzunguka, -enye kuruba. 2 -janja, -a kichinichini. **~ness** *n.*

devise *vt* 1 tunga, buni. 2 **(~ to)** rithisha mali (hasa ardhi) *n* wasia (wa mali, ardhi, n.k.). **~e** *n* mtu anayerithishwa mali. **~r** *n* msimamizi wa mirathi. **devising** *adj.*

devisor *n see* **deviser** *n.*

devitalize *vt* ondoa nguvu, dhoofisha, fifiza, fifiliza. **devitalization** *n.*

devoid *adj* **~ (of)** pasipo, bila; -kosefu *he is ~ of sense (fear, shame etc.)* hana akili, hofu, haya, n.k. *a country ~ of inhabitants* nchi isiyo na wakazi.

devoir *n (arch)* 1 wajibu. **do one's ~** timiza wajibu wako. 2 *(usu pl)* **pay one's ~s** wekea heshima, stahi.

devolve *vt,vi* **~ (on/upon)** 1 kabidhi, hamishia (kazi, madaraka, zamu n.k.) kwa. **~ (to/upon)** kabidhiwa **~** *a responsibilityto sb* kabidhi madaraka kwa mwingine. 2 rithiwa.

devolution *n* 1 *(transfer of rights)* kukabidhi madaraka, kazi, haki, wajibu n.k.; ugatuzi. 2 urithishaji.

devote *vt* tenga (k.v. muda) kwa madhumuni maalumu; toa. **~oneself/ sth to** jifunga/jizatiti/jitolea kufanya kitu fulani. **~d** 1 -enye bidii, -a kushika kazi kwa moyo. 2 -aminifu. 3 -a kupenda sana, shabiki; -a kujisabilia. **be ~d to work** -wa na moyo katika kazi. **~d to good works** -a kujitoa kwa mambo mema/fadhila. **~e** *n* 1 *(rel)* **~e (of)** mfuasi wa dini (agh. mtawa, sufii, walii). 2 mpenzi wa michezo, shabiki n.k. **devotion** *n* 1 moyo wa ibada (wa dini, wa kumwabudu Mungu). 2 *(earnestness)* upendo, mapenzi *mother's ~ to her children* mapenzi ya mama kwa watoto wake. 3 bidii; moyo. 4 kujifunga. **~ to learning** moyo wa kupenda kujifunza. 5 *(pl)* ibada, sala. **devotional** *adj.*

devour *vt* 1 -la kwa ulafi/kwa harakaharaka. 2 meza/teketeza. 3 kuwa katika lindi la wasiwasi/ mawazo. **be ~ed by anxiety** jawa na wasiwasi. 4 zamia katika fikra. **~er** *n.* **~ingly** *adv.* **devout** *adj* 1 -enye kumcha Mungu *n* masalihina. 2 *(of prayers, wishes)* -a moyo, -a dhati. **~ness** *n.* **~ly** *adv.*

dew *n* umande. **~y** *adj* -enye umande. **~-drop** *n* tone (la umande). **~-fall** *n* umande (ulioanguka). **~ point** *n* kiwangoumande.

dewlap *n* shambwelele: ngozi inayoning'inia chini ya shingo ya ng'ombe.

dexter *adj* -a kulia, -lio upande wa kulia.

dexterity *n* 1 ustadi; ubingwa; umahiri; wepesi (aghalabu wa kutumia mikono au mwili). 2 wepesi wa akili (katika kujenga hoja au kuelewa jambo). **dexterous** *adj.*

dhobi *n* dobi.

dhoti *n* doti.

dhow *n* dau, jahazi.

diabetes *n (med)* (ugonjwa wa) kisukari. **diabetic** *adj* -enye kisukari.

diabolic(al) *adj* 1 -a shetani, -a ibilisi. 2 -ovu sana, -baya sana, -katili. **diabolism** *n* 1 umilikaji, uabudu, ushughulikiaji mashetani. 2 tabia ya kishetani.

diacritic *n* alama ya kutofautisha matamshi ya herufi. **~al** *adj.*

diadem *n* taji.

diaeresis *n (gram)* alama ya kutofautisha matamshi ya irabu mbili tofauti zinazofuatana.

diagnose *vt* tambua/baini ugonjwa/ matatizo n.k. (kwa kuangalia dalili zilizopo), zuza. **diagnosis** *n* utambuzi/ ubainishaji wa ugonjwa. **diagnostic** *adj* -a kuchunguza na kubainisha ugonjwa, -a uaguzi. **diagnostician** *n.* **diagnostics** *n* elimu ya uchunguzi wa aina na sababu za ugonjwa.

diagonal *adj* -a hanamu, -a kutoka pembe mpaka pembe iliyoielekea, -a kukata mraba pembe kwa pembe, -a mshazari *n* hanamu, mshazari.

diagram *n* mchoro, kielelezo. **~atic(al)** *adj.*

dial *n* 1 uso wa saa; diski yenye namba. 2 bamba linaloonyesha vipimo agh. kwa kutumia mkono. 3 kizungusho (kitu kinachozungushwa kupata namba, mita fulani k.m. ya redio). 4 chombo cha simu chenye nambari juu yake *vt* piga simu ~ *a number* piga namba: zungusha namba za simu (ili kupata namba fulani). **~ing code** namba ya kupiga. ~ **tone** mlio wa kupiga.

dialect *n* lahaja. **~al** *adj.*

dialectic(s) *n* upembuzi: kuhakiki ukweli wa nadharia au wazo kwa mjadala wa kimantiki. **~al** *adj* 1 -a kipembuzi. 2 ~al method mbinu -pembuzi. **~al meterialism** uyakinifu pembuzi. **~ian** *n* mpembuzi.

dialogue *n* 1 mazungumzo (agh. baina ya pande mbili/watu wawili). 2 maandiko (yaliyotungwa kama kwamba watu wanasemezana). 3 mabadilishano ya mawazo.

dialysis *n (chem)* 1 dialisisi: utenganishaji wa koloidi kutoka katika kitu kilichomo kwenye mmunyo na kukiacha kipenye katika kiwambo penyu. 2 usafishaji damu kwa mashine ya figo.

diameter *n* kipenyo. **diametrical** *adj* 1 -enye kupingana kabisa; -a kinyume kabisa *be in ~ opposition to sth* kuwa na msimamo tofauti kabisa. 2 -a/-enye kuhusu/-lio katika kipenyo. **diametrically** *adv.*

diamond *n* 1 almasi; *(fig)* **rough** ~ mtu anayeonekana mkatili lakini ana moyo mzuri. ~ **cut** chombo (chenye ncha ya almasi) cha kukatia kioo. 3 umbo la almasi *(of playing cards)* uru. 4 *(baseball)* kitovu cha uwanja wa besiboli. 5 **~back** nondo; *(US)* nyoka mwenye madoa ya almasi. **~drill** *n* kekee ya almasi. **~-field** *n* mgodi wa almasi. ~ **wedding** *n* ndoa ya miaka sitini. **~point** chombo chenye ncha ya almasi agh. hutumiwa kuchimbulia vitu; makutano ya reli.

diaper *n* 1 kitambaa chororo au cha pamba kitumikacho katika kutengeneza vitambaa vya meza na taulo. 2 nepi. 3 darizi ya almasi; nakshi *vt* nakshi, tarizi.

diaphanous *adj (of fabric)* -epesi na ororo; -a kupenya nuru, -enye kuona.

diaphragm *n* kiwambo (cha moyo, sikio n.k.); kitangaa. 2 kiwambo cha ngoma (simu n.k.). 3 kizuia mimba: chombo cha mpira kinachowekwa ukeni kuzuia mimba. 4 *(photography)* mboni mwanga. **~etic** *adj.*

diarchy *n* serikali thaniya: serikali ya watawala wawili.

dirrhoea *n* kuhara, kuendesha.

diary *n* 1 shajara: kitabu cha

kumbukumbu za kila siku. **diarist** *n.*

diaspora *n* 1 **the D~** kutawanyika kwa Wayahudi miongoni mwa watu wa mataifa. 2 upatiaji makazi kando ya Palestina kwa Wayahudi waliosambaa; makazi ya Wayahudi hao. **The Black ~** Waafrika weusi popote walipo duniani (kutokana na kutawanyika kwao).

diatribe *n* tahakiki ndefu yenye machungu, makemeo na matusi.

dibber *also* **dibble** *n* muo, (kijiti cha kuchimba makoongo ya kupandia mbegu). **dibble** *vt* 1 piga koongo kupandia. 2 panda mbegu kama kwamba umetumia koongo.

dice *n (pl) (sing formal)* **die** *(colloq dice)* 1 dadu. **The die is cast** uamuzi umekwishafanywa, mambo yameiva. *(sl)* **no ~** haifai kitu! *vt,vi* 1 cheza dadu; cheza kamari, tia mirabumirabu. **~ box** kikopo au kisanduku cha kuchezea dadu. **~ with death** *(colloq)* hatarisha maisha. 2 kata katika michemraba midogo midogo. **~y** *adj (colloq)* -a mashaka; -a hatari.

dichotomy *n* mgawo wa sehemu mbili; mwainisho wa uwili (agh. wenye kukinzana).

dick *n (sl)* 1 mboo. **take one's ~** apa, thibitisha. 2 askari kanzu, mpelelezi, kachero.

Dickensian *adj* -a Dickens; shabiki wa kazi za Dickens; mwanafunzi wa Dickens (mtunzi maarufu wa riwaya).

dicker *vt (trade bid)* shindania bei.

dickey *(also dicky) n* 1 **~ bird** (neno watumialo watoto) ndege. 2 **~ seat** kiti cha ziada cha nyuma cha kukunja katika gari la viti viwili. 3 sehemu ya shati ya mbele iliyogeuzwa.

dicky *adj* -siojisikia vizuri, dhaifu, -a wasiwasi.

dicotyledon *vt* dikotiledoni: mmea ambao mbegu yake ina kotiledoni mbili (k.m. harage).

dictaphone *n* diktafoni: kinasa sauti cha

dictate *vt* **~ (to)** 1 *(read aloud)* sema au soma kwa sauti ili mwingine aandike yaliyosemwa, toa imla. 2 toa masharti, amuru. 3 *(declare) I wont' be ~d to* sitaamrishwa *n (pl)* mwongozo:kanuni/amrizinazomwongoza mtu kutenda jambo. **dictation** *n* 1 maamuru. 2 imla. 3 *(orders)* amri nzito; maonyo makali *I will not submit to ~* sikubali kuamrishwa. **dictator** *n* dikteta: mtawala wa mabavu (hasa aliyejitwalia madaraka kwa nguvu). **dictatorial** *adj.* **dictatorship** *n.*

diction *n* uteuzi na matumizi ya maneno; mtindo na jinsi ya kuongea.

dictionary *n* kamusi: kitabu cha orodha ya maneno yaliyopangwa kwa kufuata utaratibu maalumu au kwa kufuata alfabeti pamoja na maana zake.

dictum *n* 1 tamko rasmi juu ya jambo fulani; tamko lenye mamlaka kuhusu kitu fulani. 2 msemo.

did *see* **do**.

didactic *adj* 1 -lokusudiwa kufundisha. 2 *(usu derog)* -enye kutaka kufundisha kila mahali; -enye kupenda kuhubirihubiri. **~ally** *adv.* **~s** *n* elimu ya kufundisha.

diddle *vt* **~ sb (out of sth)** *(colloq)* danganya, kenga, tapeli.

die[1] *n* 1 *see dice.* 2 *(pl) (stamp, punch)* chapa, kipande cha metali cha kupigia chapa sarafu, (nishani, karatasi n.k.).

die[2] 1 -fa, fariki, kata roho *~ of an illness* -fa kwa maradhi *~ of laughter* angua kicheko *~ by one's own hand* jiua. 2 *(phrases)* **~ in one's bed** kufa kwa uzee. **~ with one's boots on** kufa ukiwa bado ukingali na nguvu, ukingali unapigana. **~ in the last ditch** pigana kwa namna zote ili kutetea kitu/jambo fulani. **~ game** kabili kifo kishujaa. **~ hard** kufa tu baada ya mapambano makali. **~ in harness** kufa ukiwa bado ukifanya kazi. 3 **be dying for sth/to do sth** taka sana kitu. 4 acha kufahamika, potea *his fame will never ~* sifa yake kubwa haitapotea. 5 **~- hard** mkaidi, asiyependa mabadiliko; asiyekubali kushindwa. 6 *(used with adverbial particle)* ~ *away* isha, poteza nguvu, fifia. ~ **back** *(of plants)* kauka hadi kwenye mizizi ambayo baadaye huchipua. ~ **down** *(of fire in a fire place)* fifia; *(of excitement)* pungua. ~ **off** kufa moja baada ya nyingine.~ **out** toweka kabisa, fikia mwisho.

diesel *n* dizeli. ~ **engine** injini ya dizeli. **~electric locomotive** injini itumiayo dizeli yenye kutoa mkondoumeme.

diet[1] *n* 1 mkutano wa kujadili mashauri ya kitaifa, ya kimataifa au ya kikanisa. 2 *(in certain countries)* bunge (hasa la Japani).

diet[2] *n* 1 chakula, mlo. **balanced** ~ mlo kamili. 2 utaratibu maalumu wa chakula (agh. kwa mtu anayetaka kupunguza uzito/unene). **~ary** *adj* 1 -enye kuhusu chakula. 2 -a kuhusu mwiko, mzio, ugunga. **~etics** *n* ugunga, elimu-lishe. **~ician** *n* mgunga, mwanalishe *vt* gunga, kula kwa kufuata maelekezo, taratibu na miko iliyowekwa.

differ *vi* 1 tofautiana, hitilafiana, achana; -topatana. 2 **(from sb) (about/on sth)** -tokubaliana. **agree to** ~ kubali kutofautiana. **~ence** *n* 1 tofauti, hitilafu, hali ya kuwa mbalimbali. **~ence of opinion** tofauti za mawazo. **makes no ~ence** ni mamoja tu, ni sawa tu *that makes all the ~ence* hiyo hubadili hali ya mambo kabisa. 2 kutokukubaliana, mfarakano mdogo. 3 kiwango cha vitu kutofautiana. 4 kiasi, kadiri iletayo tofauti, hitilafu. **~ent** *adj* mbalimbali, sokuwa sawa na -ingine, tofauti. **~ently** *adv*. **~ential** *n, adj* 1 difrensha. 2 *(Math)* ~ential equations milinganyo tenguo. 3 *(wage)* tofauti (katika asilimia) za ujira kati ya wafanyakazi wenye ujuzi na wale wasio na ujuzi wa kiwanda kile kile. **~entiate** *vt* 1 tofautisha, pambanua, ainisha. 2 *(Math)* tengua. 3 **~entiate between** tendea tofauti. ~ **entiation** *n* utofautishaji, upambanuzi. 2 utenguzi.

difficult *adj* -gumu; -zito, -a shida; -a fumbo. **~y** *n* 1 shida, matatizo, dhiki, ugumu *the ~y is to make good choice* tatizo ni kufanya uchaguzi mzuri *I have ~y in saying* napata shida/ ninashindwa kusema. 2 *(pl)* **be in ~ies**, -wa na matatizo, wamba *get oneself into ~ies* jitia matatani *be in financial ~ies* wamba. **make ~ies** leta ubishi.

diffident *adj* -siojiamini, -enye haya. **diffidence** *n*.

diffract *vt (of a beam of light)* samba. **~ion** *n* msaambazo.

diffuse *vt,vi 1* eneza, tawanya. 2 enea, vavagaa, tawanyika. 3 *(of gases and liquids)* changamana polepole. **diffusible, diffusive** *adj*. **diffusiveness** *n* ueneaji, usambaaji. **diffusion** *n* mweneo, msambao. **diffuse** *adj* 1 -a kutumia maneno mengi zaidi. 2 -a kutawanyika pande zote. **~ly** *adj*. ~ **ness** *n* uenevu.

dig *vt* 1 chimba. 2 *(sl)* furahia; elewa. 3 *(with adv. particles & prep)* ~ **in/~ into sth** anza kula, kamata! ~ *sth in* chimbia, changanya. ~ **sth into sth** tia, choma, chocha. ~ **oneself in** jikita; jizatiti. ~ **sth/sb out** chimbua, chokonoa, fukia *n* 1 kikumbo, pigo. **~ger** *n* 1 *(usu in compounds)* mchimbaji. **gold** ~ mchimba dhahabu. 2 mashine ya kuchimbulia, eksikaveta. 3 *(sl)* Mu-Australia. **~ging** *n* 1 uchimbaji. 2 *(pl)* mahali ambapo panachimbwa metali agh. dhahabu. 3 *(pl, colloq)* **(also digs)** chumba/vyumba vya kupanga.

digest[1] *vt,vi* 1 *(of food)* meng'enya; meng'enyuka. 2 *(consider)* fikiria, waza. **~ible** *adj*. **~ibility** *n*. **~ion** *n* mmeng'enyo wa chakula. **~ive** *adj* -a mmeng'enyo wa chakula. **~ive system** mfumo wa mmeng'enyo wa chakula.

digest[2] *n* muhtasari, ufupisho ~ *of cases* muhtasari wa kesi.

digit *n* 1 kidole. 2 tarakimu. **~al** *adj* -a kidole, -a tarakimu. **~al clock/watch** saa isiyokuwa na mishale, saa ya tarakimu. **~al computer** kompyuta ionyeshayo mahesabu kwa tarakimu.

dignify *vt* ~ **(with)** tukuza, zidishia heshima. **dignified** *adj*. **dignitary** *n* mwadhamu, mheshimiwa, mtu mwenye cheo. **dignity** *n* 1 heshima, hadhi. **human** ~ hadhi ya utu. **beneath one's** ~ -siolingana na hadhi ya mtu. 2 *(greatness)* ukuu; ubora. 3 *(rank)* cheo, hadhi. **stand on one's** ~ ng'ang'ania kuheshimiwa. 4 utulivu na makini ya tabia au mtindo.

digraph *n* herufi mbili zinazowakilisha sauti moja k.m. sh/katika neno sheria.

digress *vi (of speech, writing)* toka nje ya mada. ~**ion** *n*. ~**ive** *adj*.

digs *n see* **dig**.

dike, dyke *n* 1 handaki, mfereji. 2 boma (la kuzuia maji yasienee yakifurika). 3 *(fig)* kizuio *vt* zuia kwa boma.

dilapidated *n* -liochakaa, bovu, gofu. **a** ~ **old car** mkweche. **dilapidation** *n*.

dilate *vt,vi* tanua, panua, vimbisha; tanuka, panuka vimba. 2 ~ **up on** sema/andika kwa mapana na marefu. **dilatable** *adj*. **dilatation, dilation** *n*.

dilatory *adj* 1 -vivu, -zembe, goigoi, si -epesi, si -tendaji. 2 *(delaying)* -a kukawia, -a kuchelewa, -a kukawilisha, -a kuchelewesha.

dilemma *n* mtanziko (hasa katika kuchagua moja katika mawili) *you are on the horn of a* ~ huna budi kuchagua, ukipenda usipende.

dilettante (*pl* **dilettanti**) *n* ajifunzaye kitu kijuujuu; mbabaishaji; mpenda sanaa wa ridhaa *adj* -a kijuujuu; -a ridhaa. **dilettantism** *n*.

diligence *n* bidii, uangalifu, jitihada, juhudi. **diligent** *adj*. ~ **(in)** -enye bidii, -angalifu, -enye juhudi, -enye jitihada. **diligently** *adv*.

dilly-dally *vi* sitasita; poteza wakati, fanya ajizi.

dilute *vt* 1 zimua. 2 *(fig)* fifilisha, fifiliza ~ *skilled labour* changanya vibarua na wataalamu badala ya kuajiri wataalamu peke yao. **dilution** *n*. **diluent** *adj* -a kuzimulia, zimulifu, -liozimuliwa *n* kizimuo.

dim *vt,vi* tia giza; fifiliza; punguza mwanga *adj* 1 -a gizagiza. 2 *(indistinct)* sio dhahiri, -sioonekana vizuri, -liofifia; -siosikilika vyema. 3 *(of eyes, eyesight)* -sioweza kuona vizuri, -iliyoingia giza. **take a** ~ **view of** *(colloq)* angalia vitu kwa upande wa ubaya; -toridhika na jambo; angalia vibaya, -topenda. 4 *(colloq) of persons)* -jinga, -sio na akili, -sio na maarifa. ~**ly** *adv*. ~**ness** *n*. ~-**wit** mjinga.

dime *n* sarafu ya Marekani na Kanada yenye thamani ya 1/10 ya dola.

dimension *n* 1 ukubwa; kadiri. 2 kipimo cha aina yoyote. 3 kivimbe. ~**al** *adj*.

diminish *vt,vi* punguza; pungua, punguka.

diminuendo *n (Mus.)* sauti ipungukayo polepole.

diminution *n 1* upunguaji; mpunguo, kipunguo. 2 mpunguzo. **diminutive** *adj* 1 -dogo sana. 2 *(gram, of a suffix)* -enye kuonyesha udogo *n* neno lililoundwa kwa kuongezwa kiambishi cha kuonyesha udogo.

dimple *n* kibonyo kidogo (hasa katika shavu au kidevu) *vt,vi* bonyea kidogo shavuni au kidevuni.

din *n* 1 kelele. 2 mshindo. 3 ghasia *vt,vi* fanya kelele (mshindo, ghasia), chagiza, fanyia ging'izo. ~ **sth into sb** chagiza.

dine *vt,vi (formal)* 1 -la chakula kikuu cha siku. ~ **out** -la chakula hotelini au kwa marafiki. 2 karibisha mtu kwa chakula kikuu cha siku; kirimu. **dining car** behewa la kulia chakula. **dining room** chumba cha kulia. **dining table** meza ya chakula. ~**r** *n* 1 mla chakula (kikuu hasa cha kutwa). 2 behewa la kulia chakula; *(US)* mgahawa wenye umbo la behewa la kulia chakula.

ding-dong *n* mlio wa kengele (agh. wa mfululizo) *adj*. ~ **struggle/battle** mapambano makali, vuta nikuvute *adv* kwa mshindo wa sauti

zinazofuatana mfululizo.
dinghy,dingey *n (naut)* kihori.
dingle *n* kibonde (hasa chenye uvuli wa miti).
dingy *adj* 1 -chafuchafu; -enye gizagiza; ovyoovyo. **dingily** *adv.* **dinginess** *n.*
dinky *adj* 1 -zuri, nadhifu. 2 *(derog)* dogo sana, -siomuhimu.
dinner *n* 1 mlo mkuu wa siku/kutwa; dhifa. 2 chakula rasmi kinachoandaliwa kwa ajili ya mgeni. **~-jacket** koti jeusi linalovaliwa na wanaume kwenye sherehe rasmi jioni. **~-service, ~-set** seti ya vyombo vya chakula.
dinosaur *n* dinosau pia dinosaria: mnyama mkubwa sana wa zamani (mwenye umbo la kenge).
dint *n* 1 *see dent.* 2 **by ~ of** kwa kufanya; kwa kutumia; kwa sababu ya *he succeeded by ~ of hard work* amefaulu kwa kufanya kazi kwa bidii.
diocese *n* jimbo (la askofu), dayosisi. **diocesan** *adj & n.*
dip *vt,vi* 1 **~ in/into** chovya, zamisha. **~ stick** kijiti cha kupimia oili/mafuta. 2 ogesha (kondoo, ng'ombe) kwa dawa katika josho. 3 teremsha na kutweka tena upesi. **~ a flag** amkia kwa bendera *~ the head lights* punguza nuru ya taa za gari. 4 inama, nepa, enda chini, teremka kidogo *the sun ~ped below the horizon* jua lilizama chini ya upeo wa macho. 5 **~ into** *(fig) ~ into one's purse* tumia pesa. **~ into the future** jaribu kufikiria yajayo *~ into a book* somasoma, angalia angalia kitabu. *n* 1 mchovyo; mzamo. 2 dawa ya kuogeshea mifugo. 3 mbetuko, mwinamo, mteremko. 4 mkao wa bendera inapoteremshwa au kutwekwa. 5 kuogelea (kwa muda mfupi).
diphtheria *n (med.)* dondakoo: ugonjwa wa koo unaoambukiza ambao husababisha kupumua kwa shida. **diphtheritic** *adj.*
diphthong *n (ling.)* irabu unganifu, irabu-pacha k.m. ai katika laiti.
diploma *n* diploma; stashahada, hati ya sifa.
diplomacy *n* 1 diplomasia. 2 upatanishi, usuluhishi. 3 *(cunning)* werevu/ujanja/ustadi wa kushughulika na watu wengine (ili mambo yote yafanikiwe); busara; hekima. **diplomat** *n* 1 mwanadiplomasia; balozi. 2 bingwa katika uhusiano na watu. **diplomatic** *adj* 1 -a kidiplomasia. **~ corps** maafisa wa ubalozi katika nchi. **~ immunity** huria kwa wanadiplomasia. **~ relations** uhusiano wa kibalozi. 2 -erevu; -a busara. -a hekima. **diplomatically** *adv.*
dipper *n* 1 kata; upawa. 2 *(US)* **the Big (Little) ~** Nyota Kuu za Kaskazini.
dippy *adj (sl)* -enye wazimu.
dipsomania *n* hamu/kiu ya ulevi. **~c** *n* mtu mwenye hamu kubwa ya ulevi; ugonjwa wa ulevi.
dire, ~ful *adj* 1 -a kutisha, -a kuogofya, -enye misiba, -baya. 2 kubwa sana.
direct[1] *adj* 1 nyoofu, -a moja kwa moja *a ~ hit* kupiga shabaha barabara *~ road* njia ya moja kwa moja. 2 -a kweli, -siotetereka. 3 -a wazi, -aminifu, bila kuficha *he gave a ~ answer* alijibu waziwazi. 4 *(various uses)* **~ action** migomo. **~ speech** kauli halisi. **~ tax** kodi ya dhahiri. **~ object** yambwa (tendwa). **~ current** mkondo fulizo *adv* moja kwa moja *the child went ~ to its mother* mtoto alikwenda moja kwa moja kwa mama yake. **~ness** *n.*
direct[2] *vt,vi* **~ (to)** 1 elekeza, ongoza, onyesha. 2 andika, peleka. 3 **~ sth to sb** elekeza, lenga, kusudia. 4 simamia, ongoza, dhibiti. 5 **~ to/ towards** geuza, badili; amuru, simamia, agiza. **~ion** *n* 1 *(course)* mwelekeo, uelekeo; jiha *in the ~ion of* upande wa, kuelekea. **in all ~ions** kila upande. 2 majira. **have a good/ poor sense of ~ion** weza/-toweza kutambua vizuri majira au uelekeo. 3 *(oftenpl)* maelekezo, maagizo. 4 *(pl)* anwani (ya barua, kifurushi). 5

uongozi, uratibu, usimamizi. **~ional** *adj*. **~ive** *n* agizo, maelekezo. **~ly** *adv* 1 moja kwa moja. 2 *(at once)* mara, mara moja, bila kuchelewa. 3 *(plainly)* wazi, bila kuficha. **~or** *n* mkurugenzi **managing ~or** mkurugenzi mwendeshaji. **Board of ~ors** Bodi ya Wakurugenzi. **film ~or** mwendeshaji filamu. **~orship** *n* nafasi ya/kipindi cha ukurugenzi. **~orate** *n* 1 kurugenzi. 2 bodi ya wakurugenzi. **~ory** *n* 1 kitabu chenye orodha ya majina, anwani, kazi na habari nyinginezo za watu (wa mtaa, mji n.k.). **a telephone ~ory** kitabu cha orodha ya simu.

direful *adj (liter) see* **dire**

dirge *n* wimbo wa maziko/maombolezo.

dirt *n* 1 uchafu, taka, ukoko *the compound was covered with ~* eneo lilitapakaa/jaa uchafu. 2 udongo, kifusi *a ~ road (US)* barabara ya udongo. **as cheap/common as ~**, duni, -a hali ya chini. **fling/throw ~at sb** haribu sifa za mtu, kashifu. **treat a person like ~** dharau mtu. **~ farmer** *(US)* mtu anayefanya kazi zake zote. **~ cheap** rahisi sana. 3 mawazo/mazungumzo machafu. **~y** *adj* 1 chafu, -enye taka. 2 *(of the weather)* -enye upepo mwingi, -a mvua nyingi. 3 -enye mawazo/mazungumzo machafu; -enye matusi. 4 choyo; -sio na heshima. **~ily** *adv*. **~y** *vt, vi* chafua, tia taka. **do the ~y on sb/play a ~y trick** fanyia vibaya/hila. **give a ~y look** angalia vibaya/kwa jicho kali. **wash one's ~y linen in public** fichua hadharani siri za ndani.

dis- *(pref)* 1 tenda kinyume cha. **~obey** -totii. **~arm** silaha. 2 sio *~honest* -sio aminifu.

disability *n* 1 udhaifu, upungufu, ulemavu *be under a ~* -wa na upungufu (fulani). 2 kilema *permanent ~* kilema cha kudumu; kutoweza *legal ~* kutoweza kisheria. **disable** *vt* 1 lemaza. **disabled** *adj* lemavu. **disabled soldier** askari mlemavu (aliyeumia vitani). 2 nyima/ondolea uwezo. **disablement** *n*.

disabuse *vt ~* **(of)** *(formal)* weka mtu sawa (kimawazo), elimisha; sahihisha.

disadvantage *n* 1 upungufu, kasoro, hitilafu. 2 hali ngumu, kizuizi (katika kufanikisha jambo) *at a ~* katika hali ngumu. **~ ous** *adj*. **~ ous (to)** inayoleta madhara. **~ously** *adv*.

disaffected *adj* -sioridhika, -a kukosa/kupoteza imani; asi. **disaffection** *n* chuki (hasa ya kisiasa), kukosa imani. **disagree ~ (with)** 1 -tokubaliana na, toafikiana, tofautiana. 2 dhuru; -tofaa *this food ~ with me* chakula hiki kinanidhuru. **~able** *adj* 1 -siopendeza, -enye kusumbua, baya. 2 -enye hasira, kali. **~ ableness** *n*. **~ably** *adv*. **~ment** *n*.

disallow *vt* kataa.

disappear *vi* 1 toweka, potea, didimia, fifia. 2 *(come to an end)* isha, koma, potea. 3 *(fig)* ambaa, tokomea. **~ance** *n*.

disappoint *vt* 1 -toridhisha, sikitisha. 2 vunja matumaini/matarajio (yanayotegemewa kutoka kwako), batilisha; *(fig)* angusha. **~ed** *adj*. **~ed (in/at) (with)** sikitishwa kwa jambo (na mtu). **~ing** *adj*. **~edly** *adv*. **~ment** *n* 1 masikitiko, maudhi. 2 hali nayovunja matumaini. 3 kitu/jambo/mtu anayevunja matumaini ya mwingine.

disapprobation *n (formal)* kutoridhia, rai katavu, kutounga mkono.

disapprove *vt,vi* 1 ~ **(of)** -tokubali, -toridhia, -topenda *my parents ~ of my leaving home* wazazi wangu hawakubali niondoke nyumbani. **disapproval** *n*. **disapprovingly** *adv*.

disarm *vt,vi* 1 nyang'anya silaha. 2 *(of a country)* punguza/acha kutumia silaha, punguza majeshi. 3 poza, vunja nguvu; zima. **~ament** *n* upunguzaji wa silaha za vita.

disarrange *vt* pangua, chafua, fuja, vuruga. **~ment** *n* mchafuko, fujo,

mtawanyiko, vurugu.
disarray *vt,n* vuruga, fanya kuwa mchafukoge. **in** ~ mchafukoge.
disassemble *vt* tenganisha, changua, bomoa.
disassociate *see* **dissociate.**
disaster *n* baa, msiba, maafa. **disastrous** *adj*.
disavow *vt (formal)* kana, kataa. **~al** *n*.
disband *vt,vi. (of organized groups)* vunja, tawanya, fumukana, tawanyika. **~ment** *n*.
disbar *vt* toa kwenye uwakili, fukuza, achisha uwakili.
disbelieve *vt,vi* ~ **in** -tosadiki, -toamini. **disbelief** *n* hali ya kutoamini, kutosadiki, ukosefu wa imani. **~r** *n*.
disbench *vt* achisha uhakimu.
disbud *vt* kata chipukizi.
disburden *vt* ~ **(of)** *(formal)* ondolea mzigo, matatizo; tuliza. ~ *one's mind* pumzisha akili.
disburse *vt,vi* toa fedha, lipa *disbursing official* ofisa mlipaji. ~ **ment** *n*.
disc (also disk) *n* kisahani, rekodi. ~ **brake** breki kisahani. ~ **jockey** diskojoka. 2 *(anat.)* gegedu. 3 diski. **floppy** ~ diski laini (inayohamishika). **hard** ~ diski ngumu (isiyohamishika). ~ **drive** kiendesha diski.
discard *vt* tupa, acha *n* 1 kitu kilichotupwa au kuachwa. 2 karata iliyotupwa.
discern *vt* tambua, maizi, ona, fahamu. **~ing** *adj* tambuzi. **~ible** *adj*. **ment** *n* utambuzi.
discharge[1] *vt,vi.* 1 *(dismiss)* ondoa, fukuza, toa (kazini). 2 *(of liquid, gas etc.)* toa, toka; foka. 3 *(let off)* piga, fyatua (bunduki), tupa (mshale). 4 *(release)* fungulia, ruhusu, achilia. 5 *(unload)* shusha, teremsha, pakua (shehena). 6 lipa, maliza (deni); feleti. 7 *(execute)* timiza, tekeleza *n* 1 mshuko. 2 kutoa. 3 mlipuo/ mfyatuko. 4 kuruhusiwa, kuachiliwa, kuachilia. 5 *(of a boil)* kutoka usaha. 6 *(of duty)* utimizaji.
disciple *n* mwanafunzi; mfuasi wa dini. **the Twelve D~s** wanafunzi kumi na wawili wa Yesu. **~ship** *n*.
discipline *n* 1 nidhamu. 2 ufundishaji wa nidhamu. 3 adhabu. 4 somo *vt* 1 fundisha nidhamu. 2 -pa adhabu, adhibu. **disciplinary** *adj*.
disciplinarian *n* mdhibiti nidhamu *be a good* ~ -wa mdhibiti nidhamu mzuri.
disclaim *vt* kana, kanusha; *(legal)* kataa haki. **~er** *n* 1 kanusho, katao la haki/ dai. 2 hati ya kukataa.
disclose *vt* ~ **(to)** funua, toa/toboa, arifu, fichua. **disclosure** *n*.
discolour *vt, vi* geuza (haribu) rangi, chujua, fichua; geuka (haribika) rangi; kwajuka, **~ation** *n*.
discomfit *vt* 1 fadhaisha, aibisha, bumbuaza, udhi. 2 *(baffle)* kanganya. 3 fanya mipango ya mtu ivie, tibua mipango. *(roust) (arch.)* shinda kabisa. **~ure** *n*.
discomfort *vt* sumbua, kera *n* 1 usumbufu, kero, adha. 2 aibu/soni (kidogo).
discommode *vt (formal)* sumbua.
discompose *vt* babaisha, vuruga akili, udhi, tia wasiwasi. **discomposure** *n*.
disconcert *vt* 1 tia wasiwasi, babaisha, kanganya, vuruga akili. **~edly** *adv*. **~ment** *n*.
disconnect *vt* ~ **(from)** vunja (muungano wa vitu), tenga, achanisha ~ *a plug* toa plagi ~ *a telephone* kata simu. **~ed** *adj* -sioungana, -siopangwa vizuri. *(of words or thoughts)* -siofungamana vizuri, -siofuatana barabara. **~ion, disconnexion** *n*.
disconsolate *adj* -enye huzuni majonzi/ sikitiko sana, -siofarijika, -sio na faraja, -sio na furaha. **~ly** *adv*.
discontent *n* 1 kutoridhika; ukosefu wa ridhaa, chuki *show* ~ nung'unika *vt* -toridhika, -totosheka, kutoridhisha *he was ~ed with his job* hakuridhika na kazi yake. **~ment** *n* kutotosheka, kutoridhisha.
discontinue *vt,vi* acha, komesha; achisha, maliza. **discontinuance** *n*.

discontinuous *adj* -sioendelea, -sioungana. **discontinuity** *n.*

discord *n* 1 kutokupatana, kutokuelewana, utesi. 2 *(music)* sauti zisizolingana. **~ant** *adj* 1 -a kutoelewana, -a kutopatana. 2 siooana. **~antly** *adv.* **~ance** *n.* **~ant** *adj.*

discotheque *n (colloq abbr disco)* disko; jumba la starehe ambapo watu hucheza muziki uliorekodiwa.

discount *n* kipunguzo, turuhani. *(of goods)* **at a ~** kwa bei nafuu, isiyopatikana kwa shida, aheri. **~ broker** dalali, mlanguzi; *(fig)* -sio na thamani *Is justice at a ~ these days* je haki haithaminiwi siku hizi *vt* 1 punguza bei. 2 lipa, pokea thamani ya sasaya hawala isiyotazamiwa kulipwa bado. 3 -toamini kabisa kabisa; puuza, chukulia ilivyo. **~ able** *adj.*

discountenance *vt* 1 nyima msaada/ idhini/ruhusa/upendeleo; -tokubali, -topendelea. 2 vunja moyo.

discourage *vt* 1 vunja moyo, katisha/ tamaa. **~ a person from doing sth** katisha tamaa (mtu) asifanye jambo. 2 pinga, wekea vikwazo. **~ment** *n.*

discourse *n* 1 hotuba, mhadhara; mahubiri *hold a ~ with (formal)* wa na mazungumzo ya makini na. *vi* **~ upon** hutubia, toa mhadhara, hubiri.

discourteous *adj* -sio na heshima, adabu, staha. **discourtesy** *n.*

discover *vt* gundua, tambua, funua, fichua. **~er** *n.* **~y** *n* 1 ugunduzi, ugunduaji. 2 jambo jipya, geni, lisilojulikana kwanza; ajabu; kitu kilichogunduliwa. 3 (*legal*) *order for ~y* amri ya kudhihirisha.

discredit *vt* 1 (*dishonour*) aibisha, punguza sifa, tahayarisha, tia fedheha. 2 (*disbelieve*) -toamini, -tosadiki, -tothamini. 3 tia shaka, onyesha uongo *n* 1 aibu. 2 shaka, kutoamini. **~able** *adj.* **~ ably** *adv.*

discreet *adj* 1 -makinifu. 2 -a tahadhari kubwa (kabla ya kutenda), angalifu, -enye hadhari, -teuzi maneno. **~ly** *adv.*

discretion *n* 1 busara, akili, makini, hadhari *he has reached years of ~* amefikia utu uzima, amekomaa. **D ~ is the better part of valour** *(prov)* busara ni bora kuliko ushujaa. 2 hiari *at your own ~* kwa hiari yako. **~ary** *adj.*

discrepancy *n* tofauti, hitilafu. **discrepant** *adj.*

discrete *adj* -sio ungana, peke. **~ness** *n.*

discriminate *vt,vi* 1 **~ (between/from)** tofautisha, tenga, ona tofauti, pambanua. **~ between so and so** ona tofauti, pambanua baina ya fulani na fulani. 2 **~ (against)** bagua, pendelea *laws which do not ~ against anyone* sheria zisizopendelea. **discrimination** *n* ubaguzi, upambanuzi. **disriminatory** *adj.*

discursive *adj* 1 -enye kutangatanga (kimatendo, mawazo) -sio na mpango, -sio na msimamo. 2 -enye kufuata mantiki au hoja maalum. **~ly** *adv.* **~ness** *n.*

discuss *n* kisahani. *vt* **~ (with)** jadili, zungumza. **~able** *adj.* **~ion** *n* majadiliano, mjadala, mazungumzo. **it is under ~ion** imo katika kujadiliwa, inajadiliwa.

disdain *vt* dharau, tweza, beza, bera, (kwa kiburi, dharau) *n* dharau, kiburi, makuu, usodai. **~ful** *adj.* **~ fully** *adv.*

disease *n* ugonjwa, maradhi, uele, ndwele. **communicable ~** maradhi ya kuambukiza. *~ of the mind/mental ~* ugonjwa wa akili. *adj* **~d** gonjwa.

disembark 1 *vt,vi* **~ (from)** shusha, teremsha, shuka, teremka (kutoka chomboni, melini). **~ation** *n.*

disembody *vt* tenga mwilini, toa (roho kutoka mwilini); achia huru. **disembodied spirit** pepo.

disembowel *vt* tumbua, toa matumbo.

disembroil *vt* toa katika matatizo, mkanganyiko, tanzua.

disenchant *vt* 1 zingua, opoa uchawi. 2 fumbuliwa macho, poteza imani *he is ~ed with the government* amepoteza imani na serikali. **~ment** *n* kupoteza imani.

disencumber *vt* ondolea mzigo.

disendow *vt* ondolea/twalia wakfu/ ruzuku.

disengage *vt,vi* kong'oa, namua, toa, ondoa. ~ **(from)** achanisha, nasuka. ~**d** *adj*. ~**ment** *n*.

disentail *vt* (*legal*) batilisha wakfu.

disentangle *vt,vi* ~ **(from)** 1 fundua, funua. 2 eleza, fumbua, dhihirisha, dadavua. ~**ment** *n*.

disequilibrium *n* ukosefu wa msawazo, ukosefu wa urari.

disestablish *vt* ondolea hadhi ya taasisi, vunja uhusiano (kati ya taasisi na serikali). ~**ment** *n*.

disfavour *n* 1 kutopendelea; chuki, kutokubali. 2 kuchukiwa *vt* -topendelea, -tounga mkono.

disfigure *vt* umbua, haribu sura, rembua *be* ~*d* umbuka; kwajuka; sawijika. ~**ment** *n*.

disforest *vt* fyeka/ondoa msitu.

disfranchise/(*also* **disenfranchise**) *vt* 1 nyima haki ya uraia (hasa haki ya kupiga kura). 2 nyima jimbo, haki ya kuchagua Mbunge. ~**ment** *n*.

disgorge *vt* 1 tapika, kokomoa; (*fig*) (*yieldup*) rudisha (kitu kilichotwaliwa kwa makosa). 2 (*of rivers etc.*) mimina.

disgrace *n* aibu, fedheha, tahayari, soni. ~**ful** *adj*. ~**fully** *adv* *vt* tia aibu, fedhehi, tahayarisha, tweza.

disgruntled *adj* ~ **(at/with)** -sioridhika, -siopendezwa na; -enye chukichuki.

disguise *vt* 1 ficha, funika ukweli. 2 geuza uso (umbo) ili kudanganya *n* mavazi ya kujigeuza (ya uigaji), umbo la uwongo, hila. **under the ~ of** kwa kujifanya. **blessing in ~** bahati iliyojitokeza kwanza kwa sura ya balaa, kufa kufaana.

disgust *n* ~ **(at/with)** karaha, ikirahi, maudhi, unyarafu *vt* chukiza, chafua moyo; kirihi. ~**ingly** *adv*. ~ **edly** *adv*. ~ **ing** *adj*.

dish[1] *n* 1 sahani, kombe, bunguu. **a ~ul** sahani tele. 2 (*food*) chakula **standing ~** chakula kinachoandaliwa kila siku. 3 **the ~es** vyombo vya udongo (sahani, bakuli, vikombe). ~ **washer** mashine ya kuoshea vyombo. ~ **water** maji yaliyooshea vyombo. ~ **cloth**, ~ **rag** kitambaa cha kufutia sahani. ~ **cover** kawa. 4 (*sl*) mtanashati (hasa msichana). ~**y** *adj*.

dish[2] *vt* ~ **up** pakua; (*fig*) tayarisha, toa hoja. ~ **out** gawa. 2 (*colloq*) vuruga. ~ **plans** vuruga mipango ya mtu.

dishabille *n* (*usu* **in** ~) (*usu of woman*) uvaaji wa nguo usiokamilika, kuvaa nguo ovyo ovyo.

disharmony *n* kutotangamana; kutokuwa na mwafaka. **disharmonious** *adj*.

dishearten *vt* vunja moyo, ondoa *become ~ed* vunjika moyo.

dishevelled *adj* (*of hair*) timtimu, chafu, -sio safi; (*of appearance*) -sio nadhifu.

dishonest *adj* 1 -sio aminifu, -danganyifu ~ *person* ayari, mwizi. ~**ly** *adv*. ~**y** *n*.

dishonour *vt* 1 aibisha, fedhehesha, tahayarisha. 2 (*refuse to redeem*) -totekeleza (ahadi, deni); kataa kulipa (hundi, hawala); (*of a bank*) ~ *a cheque* kataa kulipa fedha ya hundi, -totambua hundi *n* 1 aibu, hizaya, fedheha. 2 kukataa *notice of* ~ notisi ya kukataa. ~**able** *adj*. ~**ably** *adv*.

disillusion *vt* ondosha fikra dhanifu/ njozi/ruya, ~**ed** *adj* -lioishiwa imani/ hamu, -lioachana na njozi. ~**ment** *n*. **disincentive** *n* kivunja motisha/ raghba/moyo; ukatishaji tamaa.

disincline *vt* 1 (*usu passive*) **be ~d for sth; be ~d to do sth** -tokuwa na hamu/ari ya kutenda jambo. 2 -tochangamkia jambo. **disinclination** *n* ~ **(for sth/to do sth)** ukosefu wa ari (ya kufanya jambo), kutotaka/ kutokuwa na ari/hamu ya kutenda jambo.

disinfect *vt* ua viini vya maradhi/ vijidudu, safisha, takasa. ~**ant** *n* kipukusi: kemikali ya kuzuia au kuua viini vya maradhi. ~**ion** *n*.

disinfest *vt* ondoa wadudu/vinyama

vidogovidogo (k.m. panya). **~ation** *n* ~ *officer* ofisa muua/mwondoa wadudu.

disinflation *n* udhibiti wa mfumuko wa bei (ambapo bei na mishahara havipandi na kushuka ovyoovyo).

disingenuous *adj* (*formal*) -enye hila, -danganyifu, laghai. **~ly** *adv*. **~ness** *n*.

disinherit *vt* toa katika urithi, nyima mrithi haki ya kurithi. **~ance** *n*.

disintegrate *vt,vi* 1 changua, vunja, vunjika, changanua. 2 tenga sehemu mbalimbali. **disintegration** *n* uchangukaji.

disinter *vt* (*formal*) 1 fukua, chimbua (kitu kilichozikwa). 2 *(bring into view)* (*fig*) vumbua, gundua. **~ment** *n*.

disinterested *adj* 1 -sio na raghba, -siopendelea, -enye haki. 2 siojali, -siotaka faida. **~ly** *adv*. **~ness** *n*.

disjoin *vt* kongoa, tenganisha, achanisha.

disjoint *vt* 1 vuruga mpango, pangua. 2 tenga viungo, changua, ambua, tangua. **~ed** *adj* (*of speech and writing*) -sio na mtiririko, -siofuatana, -sio ungana, -sio na mantiki. **~edly** *adv*. **~edness** *n*.

disjunctive *adj* -a kutenganisha, -a kuachanisha, -a kutengua; *(gram)* -enye kueleza tafauti, ukinzani, uteuzi kati ya mambo mawili (mfano ama -au-).

disjunction *n* 1 mwachano, kutenganisha, kuachanisha. 2 (*maths*) funduo. **disjunctively** *adv*.

dislike *vt* chukia, -topenda, -totaka *n* chuki. **take a ~to sb** chukia mtu, anza kuchukia mtu. **likes and ~s** mapendezi na machukizo; raha na karaha.

dislocate *vt* 1 tegua, tengua. 2 (*disturb*) vuruga; fuja, chafua, haribu *constant power cuts may ~ business* ukatizaji umeme wa mara kwa mara huenda ukavuruga biashara. **dislocation** *n*.

dislodge *vt* **(from)** 1 ng'oa, ondoa (kwa kutumia nguvu) toka mahali pake. 2 fukuza (toka mafichoni).

disloyal *adj* ~ **to** -asi, -sio -aminifu. **~ly** *adv*. **~ty** *n*.

dismal *adj* 1 -a kuhuzunisha, -a majonzi, -a kusikitisha, -sio na raha. 2 -a ovyo; baya. **~ly** *adv*.

dismantle *vt* 1 pambua, kongoa. 2 vunja, bomoa. **~ment** *n*.

dismast *vt* ondoa, vunja milingoti ya chombo (kwa dhoruba, tufani, mzinga n.k.).

dismay *n* hofu, fazaa; mvunjiko wa moyo. **stricken with ~** -lioshikwa na hofu, -liofadhaishwa.

dismember *vt* 1 kata kiungo, changua; rarua. 2 (*fig*) gawa, gawana (dola/ nchi). **~ment** *n*.

dismiss *vt* ~ **(from)** 1 fukuza, ondosha (hasa katika kazi). 2 (*allow to go*) ruhusu, fungulia. 3 toa fikrani, puuza; (*leg*) futa, tupilia mbali *the judge ~ed the case* jaji alifuta kesi. 4 (*of cricket*) toa. **~al** *n*. **~ible** *adj*.

dismount *vt,vi* ~ **(from)** 1 shuka, teremka. 2 shusha, teremsha, toa *~from one's horse* shuka juu ya farasi. 3 angusha, (toka kwenye farasi, pikipiki, n.k.).

disobey *vt,vi* asi, kaidi, -totii, puuza (amri). **disobedience** *n* **(to)** kutotii, uasi *disobedience to orders* kutotii amri. **disobedient** *adj*. **disobediently** *adv*.

disoblige *vt* (*formal*) 1 kataa kusaidia/ kufikiria wengine. 2 bughudhi, -tojali (matakwa, haja) ya mwingine. **disobligingly** *adv*.

disorder *vt* chafua; fuja, vuruga *n* 1 fujo, vurugu; machafuko, ghasia. 2 (*illness*) ugonjwa, maradhi. **~ed** *adj* -liovurugika *~ed mind* akili iliyovurugika. **~ly** *adj* 1 -sio taratibu, -sio na mpango, -a mvurugiko, -liochafuka. 2 (*riots*) -a ghasia. ~ly house danguro; kasino. **~ly person** mkorofi. **~liness** *n*.

disorganize *vt* vuruga, pangua, tangua. **disorganization** *n*.

disorientate/*(US)* **disorient** *vt (lit, fig)* kanganya. **disorientation** *n*.

disown *vt* 1 kana, kataa. 2 achia radhi, kanusha.

disparage *vt* umbua, aziri, shushia hadhi. **~ment** *n*. **disparagingly** *adv*.
disparate *adj* -lio tofauti kabisa, sio linganishika *n (pl)* vitu tofauti. **disparity**. *n* tofauti, hali ya kutofautiana kabisa.
dispassionate *adj* -siopendelea; -sioathirika na jazba, -siohemkwa. **~ly** *adv*. **~ness** *n*.
dispatch,despatch *vt* ~ **to** 1 *(of errand)* tuma; (*of material*) peleka. 2 maliza (k.m. kazi chakula n.k.) haraka. 3 ua; fisha, nyonga *n* 1 haraka; kufanya upesi, wepesi; ufanisi. 2 barua, waraka, ripoti inayopelekwa na kijumbe. 3 upelekaji, utumaji (wa barua, waraka, ripoti). 4 uuaji, ufishaji. **~er** msimamizi wa usafirishaji ~ *boat* mashua ya kupelekea barua ~ *book* kitabu cha barua za mkono ~*-box* sanduku la kuchukulia nyaraka za serikali ~*-rider* mtu apelekaye habari kwa pikipiki
dispel *vt* ondoa, fukuza, tawanya, (fikra, mashaka n.k.).
dispensable *adj* si -a lazima; si -a muhimu.
dispense *vt,vi* 1 gawa, toa (haki, msaada n.k.). 2 ~ **(with)** acha kutumia, achana na, fanya bila ya, achilia. 3 changanya na toa dawa. **~r** *n* 1 mgawanyaji wa dawa. 2 kimiminio. **dispensary** *n* 1 zahanati. 2 (*in hospitals*) chumba cha dawa. **dispensation** *n* 1 mgawanyo, mgawo. 2 (*divine*) mpango wa Mungu. 3 (*special leave*) ruhusa, kibali (cha kuvunja kanuni). 4 mfumo wa dini (katika kipindi fulani maalum).
disperse *vt,vi* 1 tawanya, tawanyisha; tawanyika, enea, eneza. 2 toweka *the fog ~d* ukungu ulitoweka. **dispersal** *n*. **dispersion** *n*. **dispersive** *adj*. **the Dispersion** *see* **Diaspora**.
dispirit *vt* vunja moyo; katisha tamaa; huzunisha. **~ed** *adj*. **~edly** *adv*.
displace *vt* 1 hamisha, ondoa mahali pake (makazi, nchi, ofisi). **~d persons** wakimbizi: watu waliolazimishwa kuhama (kwa sababu ya vita n.k.). 2 shika nafasi ya mwingine. **~able** *adj*. **~ment** *n* 1 kutwaa mahali pa mwingine. 2 uhamisho. 3 nafasi ya maji iliyotwaliwa na chombo/kitu kinachoelea; maji ya kujaza nafasi hiyo.
display *vt* 1 onyesha. 2 tandaza, pamba (ili kitu kionekane waziwazi) *n* 1 maonyesho. 2 (*show off*) takabari, kukoga, mikogo.
displease *vt* chukiza, kasirisha, udhi, kera. **be ~d with sth** topendezwa/ kerwa na jambo fulani. **displeasing (to)** *adj* -a kero, -a chuki, -a maudhi. **displeasure** *n* chuki, maudhi, kero.
disport *vt* ~ **oneself** (*formal*) chezacheza, jifurahisha, jiburudisha (majini, juani n.k.).
dispose *vt,vi* 1 panga ~ *the boats in port* panga mashua bandarini. 2 ~ **of** tupa, maliza, angamiza, ondoa ~ *of vehicles* ondosha/tupilia mbali mikweche. 3 ~ **to** elekeza, tayarisha. **be ~d to** taka, penda, elekea. 4 amuru ~ *of* amuru. **man proposes, God ~s** (*prov*) mja hutaka, Mola hujaalia/huamuru. **disposable** *adj* -a kutupika, -a kutupa (baada ya kutumika). **disposal** *n* **(of)** 1 utumiaji, utupaji ~ *of waste* utupaji wa uchafu. 2 udhibiti, mpangilio, upangaji. 3 haki ya kutumia kitu, mamlaka, idhini. **at your** ~ chini ya mamlaka yako *means at my* ~ uwezo nilionao. 4 uuzaji, utoaji. **disposition** *n* 1 (*character*) tabia, silika, moyo, welekea. 2 (*inclination*) elekeo. 3 mpangilio, mpango. 4 madaraka, mamlaka.
dispossess *vt* nyang'anya, pokonya, pora. ~ **sb of sth** nyang'anya mtu kitu. **~ion** *n*.
disproportion *n* kutolingana, kutowiana, ukosefu wa urari. **~ate** *adj* -siolingana.
disprove *vt* kanusha, kana, bainisha uwongo. **disproof** *n* kanusho, ushahidi unaokanusha.
dispute *vt,vi* 1 ~ **(with/against sb)** bishana; jadiliana. 2 jadili, pinga,

saili (ukweli wa...). 3 shindana, tetea. **disputable** *adj* -enye mashaka, si hakika, si yakini, -enye kuzua mjadala. **disputant** *n* mshindani, mbishani, mkaidi. **disputation** *n* mashindano, majadiliano, mabishano. **disputatious** *adj* -kaidi, -gomvi, -bishi, -shindani *n* shindano (la maneno); mabishano, mzozo, ugomvi. **in** ~ inayogombaniwa *trade* ~ mgogoro wa kazi. **beyond/past all** ~ si jambo la kushindania, jambo linalokubaliwa, lisilo mjadala. **without** ~ bila mgogoro/ubishi.

disqualify *vt* 1 ~ **sb (for sth/from doing sth)** (*debar*) futa, ondolea haki, harimisha, batilisha. 2 (*render unfit, incapacitate*) zuia, -tostahilisha, ondoa ustahili, ondolea nguvu. **disqualification** *n.*

disquiet *vt* fadhaisha, tia wasiwasi, hamanisha, sumbua *n* fadhaa, wasiwasi, hamaniko, hangaisho. **~ing** *adj* hamanishi. **~ingly** *adv*. **~ude** *n* wasiwasi.

disquisition *n* ~ **on sth** hotuba ndefu; maandiko marefu (yaliyofafanuliwa sana au kutiwa madoido).

disrate *vt* (*naut.*) shusha/teremsha (baharia) cheo.

disregard *vt* -tojali, puuza, dharau, bekua *we may ~ this item* tunaweza kuacha jambo hili *n* dharau, kupuuza, mbekuo.

disremember *vt* (*US*) -tokumbuka, sahau *I ~ed the fact* sikukumbuka jambo lile.

disrepair *n* uchakavu.

disrepute *n* tabia/sifa mbaya, utovu wa heshima *bring into ~* aziri *fall into ~* poteza heshima/sifa njema. **disreputable** *adj* -enye tabia/sifa mbaya; -a ovyo *he is ~ looking* ni mtu ovyo. ~ **to** -enye kuashiria vibaya kwa.

disrespect *n* utovu wa heshima/adabu, ufidhuli, usafihi, ujuvi *treat sb with ~* -tomheshimu mtu, vunjia mtu heshima. **~ful** *adj*. **~fully** *adv*.

disrobe *vt,vi* vua (hasa mavazi rasmi).

disrupt *vt* 1 vunja, vuruga. 2 (*discussion*) katiza, ingilia kati, dakiza; tenganisha. **~ion** *n*. **~ive** *adj*.

dissatisfy *vt* -totosheleza, -toridhisha *to be dissatisfied with living condition* kutoridhika/kutoridhishwa na hali ya maisha *dissatisfaction n* ~ **(with sb/ sth)/(at doing sth)** kutoridhika, kututosheka.

dissect *vt* 1 changua, kata vipande vipande; tenga sehemu mbalimbali za mnyama, mimea n.k. (ili kuchunguza muundo wake). **~ed plateau** uwanda uliogawanyika (katika milima na mabonde). 2 (*fig*) chambua, hakiki kwa makini au kwa undani kila sehemu. **~ing room** chumba cha kufanyia mazoezi ya upasuaji viumbe. **~ion** *n* uchunguzi; sehemu.

dissemble *vt,vi* (*formal*) ficha (hisia, kitu, nia, maono n.k.). 2 danganya, ghilibu, fanya unafiki. **~r** *n* mdanganyifu, mnafiki.

disseminate *vt* eneza, tawanya, sambaza (maoni, imani n.k.). **dissemination** *n.*

dissent *vi* 1 ~ **from** -wa na maoni tafauti, -tokubali, -towafiki. 2 kataa (imani ya kanisa la Kianglikana) *n* mfarakano wa mawazo, kutokubaliana, kutowafiki. **dissension** *n* mfarakano, ugomvi. **~ient** *adj* -enye kuona vingine, -siokubali *a ~ient voice* -a kukataa, -a kupinga, -enye kukaidi, -enye shauri tafauti *n* mbishi.

dissertation *n* 1 tasnifu: andiko au maelezo marefu ya mada fulani (yanayohudhurishwa kwa digrii ya chuo kikuu). 2 insha, hotuba.

disservice *n* **(a)** ~ **(to)** tendo linalodhuru/lisilosaidia.

dissever *vt* (*formal*) tenga, kata vipande vipande; achana, katika.

dissident *adj* -a kupinga, -pinzani *n* mpinzani. **dissidence** *n.*

dissimilar *adj* ~ **(from/to)** -siofanana, -enye kutofautiana na. **~ity** *n*. **dissimilitude** *n* tofauti, umbalimbali. **dissimilation** *n* (*ling.*) msigano:

kutofautiana kwa sauti zilizofanana kiasi hapo awali.

dissimulate *vt,vi* *see* **dissemble**. **dissimulation** *n*

dissipate *vt,vi* 1 tapanya, tawanya; tawanyika; sambaza; sambaa. 2 (*waste by extravagence*) badhiri, fuja, fanya ubadhirifu/ufasiki. **dissipation** *n* utapanyaji; ubadhirifu. **~d** *adj* -a uasherati; badhirifu.

dissociate (*also* **disassociate**) *vt,vi* ~ **(from)** tenga, jitenga, kata, weka mbali. 2 (*repudiate connection*) kaidi, kanusha, kana, jitoa. **dissociation** *n* 1 kutenga; kujitenga. 2 kukanusha, kukaidi.

dissolute *adj* fisadi, -potovu; -asherati; -levi; -ovu. **~ly** *adv*. **dissolution** *n* 1 ~ **(of)** (*disintegration*) mvurugiko, kuoza, kuharibika. 2 mwisho, kikomo; mauti. 3 utanguzi. 4 kuvunjika (kwa chama, ushirika au ndoa). ~ **of partnership** utanguzi wa ubia. ~ **of Parliament** kuvunja Bunge.

dissolve *vt,vi* 1 (*melt*) yeyusha. **~in (to)** yeyuka. ~ **in (to) tears** angua kilio. 2 vunja, vunjika, komesha, tangua, tanguka, isha ~ *a marriage* vunja ndoa ~ *a committee* vunja kamati. 3 toweka polepole, fifia, potea. **dissoluble, dissolvable** *adj*. **~nt** *n* kiyeyushi *adj* -enye kuyeyusha.

dissonant *adj* 1 -a sauti tafauti (zisizoafikiana, zisizo nzuri); -a makelele. 2 -enye hitilafu. **dissonance** *n* 1 sauti zisizolingana; ukosefu wa muwafaka, makelele. 2 tofauti, hitilafu (za imani, vitendo n.k.).

dissuade *vt* ~ **sb (from)** shawishi (mtu) asifanye jambo, vuta, shauri dhidi ya, geuza mawazo (ya mtu mwingine). **dissuasion** *n*. **dissuasive** *adj*.

dissyllable (*US*) *see* **disyllable**.

dissymetry *n* hali ya kutokuwepo na ulinganifu/ urari. **dissymetric(al)** *adj*.

distaff *n* kijiti cha kukunjia uzi (chenye bonge la uzi) unaokunjwa kwa mkono. **on the ~ side** kukeni.

distance *n* 1 umbali; masafa, kitalifa *part of the* ~ sehemu ya umbali (fulani) *a good ~off* mbali kidogo na hapo *a short ~ from* karibu na. **at a** ~ kwa mbali *within calling* ~ karibu vya kutosha kusikika/kuitika, kitambo kidogo. **in the** ~ huko mbali. **keep sb at a** ~ fanya mtu asikuzoee. **keep one's** ~ (*fig*) kaa mbali, jitenga usizoeleke. **some** ~ mbali kiasi *within walking* ~ karibu tu. **long** ~ *adj* (*of races, journeys*) -a masafa marefu, mbio ndefu, safari ndefu; (*of telephone calls*) simu kutoka/kwenda mbali. **middle** ~ (*of races*) mbio za umbali wa kati. 2 (*space of time*) muda, kitambo *vt* ~**(from)** weka/kaa mbali na, pita mbali kabisa, acha nyuma. **distant** *adj* 1 ~ **(from)** -a mbali *have a ~ recollection* kukumbuka kwa mbali *a ~ relative* ndugu wa mbali. 2 (*of degree of similarity*) -siofanana sana, -a kufanana kidogo sana. 3 (*cold, reserved*) -siozoeleka, baridi, si -kunjufu *we are on ~ terms* hatukuzoeana sana. **distantly** *adv*.

distaste *n* **(a)** ~ **(for)** kutopenda, kuchukia, maudhi, chuki *he looked at me in ~s* aliniangalia kwa chuki *adj* ~ **(to)** -a maudhi, -a chuki. **~fully** *adv*. **~ness** *n*.

distemper[1] *n* (upakaji) rangi ya maji *vt* paka rangi ya maji.

distemper[2] *n* ugonjwa wa mbwa na baadhi ya wanyama (wa kukohoa na kukosa nguvu).

distend *vt,vi* vimbisha, vimba; tanua, tanuka; futuka. **distensible** *adj*. **distension** *n*.

distil *vt,vi* 1 ~ **sth (from sth)**; ~ **sth off/out** tonesha, tona, geuza kuwa mvuke. 2 tiririsha; dondoka (kwa matone). **~lation** utoneshaji. **~ler** toneshaji. **~lery** *n* kiwanda cha kutonesha.

distinguish *vt,vi* 1 ~ **from** pambanua, bainisha, weka mbali. 2 tofautisha. ~ **between two things** tofautisha vitu viwili. 3 (*perceive*) ona, tambua. 4 ~

oneself jipatia sifa *he greatly ~ed himself* alijipatia sifa bora. **~able** *adj* -a kutambulikana; -a kuonekana dhahiri. **~ed** *adj* maarufu, -a heshima, mashuhuri, bora *look ~ed* onekana mtu wa heshima.

distinct *adj* 1 (*different*) ~ **(from)** tofauti na *these matters are entirely ~ from each other* mambo haya yanatofautiana kabisa. 2 (*clear*) dhahiri, wazi, losikika kwa urahisi. **~ness** *n*. **~ly** *adv*. **~ion** *n* 1 kutofautisha; utofautishaji *a ~ion without difference* utofautishaji usio halisi. 2 tofauti. 3 (*honour*) heshima, sifa; hali ya kuwa bora *a man of ~* mtu wa sifa/heshima maalum *gain ~ion* pata sifa. 4 alama ya heshima, zawadi, nishani. **~ive** *adj* -a kutofautisha; -a pekee *~ive features* sifa bainishi.

distort *vt* 1 geuza/badili umbo (hali ya kawaida). **a face ~ed by pain** uso uliobadilika kwa maumivu. 2 potosha habari/ukweli. **~ion** *n*.

distract *vt* ~ **(from)** 1 (*draw attention*) vuta (mawazo, fikra), vuruga (mawazo); ondoa katika shughuli. 2 (*occupy*) shughulisha. **~ed** *adj* **~ed (with/by)** -liochanganyikiwa, -enye wasiwasi. **~edly** *adv*. **~ion** *n* 1 (*attention*) kuvuta mawazo, kuondoa katika shughuli. 2 (*unsettlement*) fadhaa, mashaka, wasiwasi, hangaiko, wazimu *you drive me to ~ion* unanitia wazimu. 3 *(rest)* pumzisho, kitulizo, mchezo, burudiko.

distrain *vt* ~ **(upon)** (*leg*) piga tanji; shika/zuia mali ya mtu (kumlazimisha alipe deni), lipisha *~ upon sb's property* piga tanji *n* tanji.

distraught *adj* -enye kuhangaika, -enye wasiwasi, -liochanganyikiwa, -liofadhaishwa.

distress *vt,vi* dhikisha, tesa, huzunisha, tia wasiwasi. ~ **oneself** jitesa, ona wasiwasi *be much ~ed* huzunishwa/ sikitishwa na. **~ed area** eneo la dhiki/ lisilo na kazi. **~ing** *adj*. **~fully, ~ingly** *adv* *n* 1 dhiki; majonzi, huzuni *companion in ~* rafiki katika dhiki *~ committee* kamati ya wenye shida, wasio na kazi. 2 hali ya hatari; tatizo/shida kubwa. ~ **signal** alama ya hatari. 3 maumivu, mateso, uchungu.

distributary mkono wa mto.

distribute *vt* ~ **(to/among)** 1 gawanya; gawa. 2 tandaza, sambaza. **distributor** *n* mgawaji; (*electr*) kigawi, distribyuta. **distribution** *n* 1 mgawanyo, ugawaji, maenezi, usambazaji. 2 (*Maths*) uenezaji. **distributive** *adj* -a kugawanya, -a kusambaza, -a kueneza. ~ **share** hisa mgawanyo.

district *n* 1 wilaya *~ magistrate* hakimu wa wilaya. 2 (*of town*) mtaa, kiambo. **the D~ of Columbia** jiji la Washington, eneo la serikali ya Muungano ya Marekani. 3 jimbo la uchaguzi.

distrust *vt* shuku, tuhumu, *n* ~ **(of)** shaka. **~ful** *adj* -a kushuku, -enye mashaka, -sioamini. **~fully** *adv*. **~fulness** *n*.

disturb *vt* 1 (*disarrange*) chafua, fuja, vuruga. ~ **the peace** vuruga/vunja amani. 2 sumbua *do not ~ me* usinisumbue. **~ance** *n* 1 ghasia, usumbufu, machafuko, vurugu. 2 (*emotional*) kuchanganyikiwa *mental disturbance* mvurugiko wa akili.

disunite *vt,vi* tenganisha, farakanisha; tengana, farakana. **disunity** *n*. **disunion** *n* 1 mfarakano, utengano. 2 (*discord*) kutopatana, ugomvi.

disuse *n* kutotumika *this path has fallen into ~* njia hii haitumiki. **~d** *adj* -siotumika tena.

disyllabic *adj* -enye silabi mbili.

disyllable *(US)* **(dissyllable)** silabi mbili.

ditch *n* handaki, mtaro, mfereji *make a last ~stand* linda/pigana mpaka mwisho; endelea mpaka mwisho. **dull as ~ water** -jinga kabisa *vt* 1 tengeneza/chimba/safisha handaki. 2 *(sl)* telekeza, acha, tupa *he ~ed his old car* alitupa mkweche wake. 3

tupa handakini.
dither *vi* 1 (*arch*) tetemeka. 2 (*colloq*) tapatapa, sita, shindwa kuamua la kufanya *n* mtetemeko; (*colloq*) hali ya kutapatapa, hali ya kushindwa kuamua la kufanya.
ditto *n* (*abbr*. **do)** 1 mshabaha ule ule. 2 kama kwanza, sawa sawa ~ *marks* alama za mshabaha. ~ **sb** kubaliana na fulani, afiki hoja yake; sema kitu kilekile kama fulani. **say ~ to** (*colloq*) sema kitu kilekile kama; kubaliana na.
ditty *n* wimbo mfupi mwepesi.
diuresis *n* (*med*) ongezeko la mkojo. **diuretic** *adj* -a kuongeza mkojo, -a kukojoza *n* dawa ya kukojoza.
diurnal *adj* 1 (*of daylight*) -a mchana. 2 (*daily*) -a kila siku. 3 (*astron*) -a siku nzima.
divagate *vi* 1 tangatanga. 2 ~ **from** acha (njia/lengo n.k.), kengeuka; zungukazunguka.
divan *n* 1 kiti kisicho na egemeo. 2 (*also* ~ **bed**) kochi kitanda. 3 (*in Muslim countries*) baraza.
dive *vi* 1 zamia majini; *person*) piga mbizi. 2 tia mkono ghafla (mfukoni, chomboni n.k.). 3 (*go deeply into*) jitia kabisa, zamia. 4 (*of aeroplanes etc.*) piga, mbizi, shuka, ghafla. ~ **bomb** *vt,vi* shuka ghafla na kudondosha mabomu *n* 1 mzamo, mzamio; kupiga mbizi *make a ~ into one's pocket* tia mkono mfukoni. 2 (*colloq*) mkahawa/baa isiyo ya heshima. **diving-bell** *n* chombo cha mpiga mbizi. **diving-board** *n* ubao wa kupiga mbizi. **~bomber**. **~r** *n* mpiga mbizi. **pearl ~ r** mzamia lulu.
diverge *vi* achana, fuata njia mbalimbali. **~nce** *n* muachano; tofauti. **~nt views** mawazo yanayotofautiana.
divers *adj* (*arch*) kadhaa; zaidi ya moja.
diverse *adj* -a namna mbalimbali, anuwai. **diversify** *vt* 1 fanya tofautitafouti/anuwai/mbalimbali. 2 (*of business etc.*) panua biashara kwa kutengeneza/kuuza bidhaa za aina nyingine. **diversity** *n* hali ya kuwa anuwai, tofauti. **~ly** *adv*.
divert *vt* ~ (*from*) 1 chepua. 2 (*relieve, amuse*) liwaza, burudisha. 3 potosha, vuta kwingine. **diversion** *n* 1 njia ya mchepuko. 2 (*passtime*) mchezo, liwazo, pumzisho. 3 (*stratagem*) mbinu (ya kuvutia macho kwingine), hila (ya kudanganya adui). **diversionist** *n*. **diversionary** *adv*.
divest *vt,vi* (*formal*) 1 ~ **sb of** vua, vulia, twalia. 2 uzulu, vua madaraka, nyang'anya. 3 ~ **oneself** achana na.
divide *vt,vi* 1 gawa, gawanya, gawanyika, tenga *the road ~s the village* barabara inagawa kijiji. 2 ~ **into/by** gawa kwa ~ *6 by 3* gawa 6 kwa 3. 3 (*set at variance*) gombanisha, gawanya, leta kutokukubaliana. **opinions are ~d on this matter** watu hawakubaliani kuhusu swala hilo. 4 (*classify*) pambanua, ainisha. 5 (*in parliament*) piga kura. 6 ~ **up** gawana *they ~d up the money* waligawana pesa. **the Great** ~ *n* mpaka kati ya uhai na mauti.. **division** *n* 1 (*separation*) kutenga, mtengo. 2 (*Math*) ugawanyaji ~ *sign* alama ya kugawanya. 3 (*distribution*) mgawo, kigawe, mgawanyiko, mgawanyo ~ *of labour* mgawanyo wa kazi. 4 (*partition*) mpaka, kitu cha kutengea. 5 (*part*) sehemu ya kitu kilichogawanyika au kilichojitenga. 6 kutoafikiana; kutofautiana mawazo. 7 (*mil*) divisheni. 8 (*Parliament*) kugawanyika makundi mawili kwa ajili ya kuhesabu kura. ~ **bell** kengele ya kuwaashiria wabunge kuwa kuna kupiga kura. 9 (*in govt. establishments*) idara *budget* ~ idara ya makadirio ya fedha. **~al** *adj*. **divisive** *adj* -enye kugawa/kutenganisha. **~ness** *n* **divisor** *n* (*Maths*) kigawanyo. **divisible** *adj* -a kugawanyika. **divisibility** *n* 1 (*Geog.*) kigawa mito.
dividend *n* 1 (*comm*) gawio. 2 (*Math.*) kigawanyo, hesabu yenye k

kugawanyika. 3 **pay ~s** leta faida.
dividers (*Maths*) kigawanyi; (*compass*) bikari.
divine[1] *vt,vi* agua; bashiri, tabiri. divination *n* uaguzi, ubashiri, utabiri. **~r** *n* mwaguzi. **~-rod** *n* fimbo ya mwaguzi.
divine[2] *adj* 1 -a Mungu, kama Mungu; takatifu *~ service* ibada takatifu. 2 (*surpassing*) (*colloq*) bora sana, -tukufu, -a fahari *n* mjuzi wa mambo ya Mungu (dini). **divinity** *n* 1 Uungu; Umungu, utukufu wa Mungu. 2 **D~** Mungu. 3 tawhidi, theolojia.
divorce *n* 1 talaka *grounds for ~* sababu za talaka. 2 mtengano, mwisho wa ushirikiano (wa vitu viwili vilivyoshikamana) *vt ~* **(from)** 1 taliki, tangua ndoa. 2 (*fig*) (*separate*) tenga; tenganisha. **~e** mtalaka.
divot *n* majani yaliyong'olewa na udongo wake.
divulge *vt* funua, toa wazi, toboa, fumbua (siri). **~nce** *n*.
divvy *n* (*colloq abbr. of* **dividends**).
dixie *n* sufuria kubwa ya chuma (itumiwayo na majeshi au kambini).
dizzy *adj* 1 -enye kizunguzungu/kisulisuli; -a kutia kizunguzungu. 2 (*perplexed*) -enye -kuchanganyikiwa, -enye wasiwasi; (*sl*) -jinga, -pumbavu *vt* tia kizunguzungu; tia wasiwasi. **dizzily** *adv*. **dizziness** *n*.
djin *n* jini.
do *vt,vi* 1 fanya, tenda *what are you ~ing tomorrow*? unafanya nini kesho *I'll ~ my best/all I can/all in my power* nitafanya kila niwezalo. **when in Rome ~ as the Romans** ~ *(prov)* ukiwa Roma tenda kama Warumi *she is ~ing her homework* anafanya zoezi (la nyumbani). **what's done can't be undone** *(prov)* maji yakimwagika hayazoleki. **no sooner said than done** fanyika mara moja. **well begun is half done** *(prov)* mwanzo mzuri ni nusu ya kufanikiwa. **easier said than done** rahisi kusema kuliko kutenda. 2 tengeneza *I have done 10 copies* nimetengeneza nakala 10. **~ it yourself** *(abbr* **DIY**) fanya mwenyewe (hasa ujenzi, useremala, ukarabati n.k. bila kuajiri wafanyakazi). 3 soma, jifunza *I am ~ing zoology at the University* nasoma zoolojia Chuo Kikuu. 4 (*Maths*) pata jawabu *she can ~ this sum* anaweza kupata jawabu la hesabu hii. 5 (*attend to*) shughulikia *I'll ~ you now* nitakushughulikia sasa. 6 (*with nouns*) *~ one's teeth* piga mswaki *~ one's hair* chana nywele *~ the dishes* safisha vyombo *~ the flowers* panga maua *~ one's duty* timiza wajibu. **patience and perseverance will ~ wonders** *(prov)* mstahimilivu hula mbivu *~ time* (*sl.*) fungwa jela *~ good* tenda wema; saidia *this medicine will ~ you good* dawa hii itakusaidia. 7 (*with gerunds*) *~ the cooking* pika *~ the washing* fua. 8 (*with the pp and perfect tenses*) maliza; timiliza, isha *it is done* imemalizwa, imetimizwa. 9 ~ **(for)** faa, tosha *will it ~ for you*? itakufaa? *this will never ~* haifai kabisa *it is not done to talk with your mouth full* si vizuri/haifai kuzungumza na chakula kinywani. 10 (*with passive force colloq*) *what's ~ing*? kuna nini? *Nothing ~ing*! Hamna! endelea *the patient is ~ing well* mgonjwa anaendelea vyema (*for vehicles etc.*) enda, safiri *this old car only does 40 kilometres an hour* mkweche huu unaenda kilomita arobaini tu kwa saa. 12 ~ **sb (out of sth)** (*colloq*) tapeli, punja, rubuni, iba. 13 iga, igiza *he ~es Kinjeketile well* anaiga Kinjeketile vizuri. 14 ~ **sb/oneself well** *(colloq)* kimu, hudumia (kwa chakula malazi n.k.). 15 (*colloq*) zuru, tembelea *she did Tanzania in two weeks* alitembelea Tanzania kwa wiki mbili. 16 iva, ivisha *the beef was done to a turn* nyama iliiva barabara. 17 husika na; tokana na *~n't have anything to ~ with him* usihusike na huyu *have a*

great deal to ~ with husika sana na. 18 (*in greetings*) *how ~ you ~ (formal)* u hali gani? *how (are) you ~ing*? vipi mambo? 19 *~ oneself proud* furahisha, ridhisha. 20 *~ to death* ua; (*fig*) haribu, chusha. 21 *make ~ with* tumia (ingawa haitoshi/ hairidhishi), jishikiz(i)a. 22 *~ your own thing* (*sl.*) shika taimu yako, shika hamsini zako. 23 (*with adv particles and preps*) ~ **away with** futa, tangua; ua. ~ **well/badly by sb** tendea wema/mabaya. **be hard done by** onewa. ~ **as you would be done by** (*prov*) tenda upendavyo kutendewa. ~ **sb down** (*colloq*) laghai, danganya; sengenya, teta. ~ **for** fanyia kazi za nyumbani; fanya mpango ya. **be done for** haribika, kwisha. ~ **in** (*sl*) ua. **be done in** choka sana. ~ **out** fagia, safisha; panga. ~ **over** piga rangi upya; piga; umiza. ~ **up** karabati, tengeneza, fufua; (*of dress etc.*) funga (na vifungo n.k.); fanya kifurushi; chosha. ~ **with** hitaji, taka; (*tolerate*) vumilia; (*pass time*) fanya *what did you ~ with yourselves yesterday* mlifanya nini jana? mudu/weza/ishi bila *we will ~ without his help* tutamudu bila msaada wake *n* 1 *(sl)* (*swindle*) hila, ujanja, kuiba. 2 (*colloq*) (*party*) tafrija. 3 desturi, kanuni. 4 **fair dos/do's** (*GB*) *(as an exclamation)* haki, tutendeane haki (katika kugawana). **~ings** *n* 1 (*sl*) shughuli; mishughuliko, mambo. **~er** *n* mtendaji. **wrong-~er** mkosaji.

do,doh[1] *n* noti ya kwanza na ya nane katika skeli.

do[2] (*abbr. of*) ditto.

doc (*colloq abbr of*) doctor.

docile *adj* 1 -tiifu, -sikivu, -elekevu. **docility** *n.*

dock[1] *vt* ~ **(off)** (*of tail)*, fupisha, punguza. 2 kata, punguza (mshahara, chakula).

dock[2] *n* (*of court*) kizimba.

dock[3] *n* 1 gati, bunta. **dry** ~ guda. **~yard** gatini. 2 *(pl)* bandari *vt,vi* 1 (*of ship*) pandisha gudani; funga gatini. 2 unganisha vyombo viwili vya anga. **~er** *n* hamali, kuli.

docket *n* 1 muhtasari (wa barua, hati n.k). 2 (*comm*) orodha (ya bidhaa, kazi zilizofanywa). 3 lebo (juu ya bidhaa iliyofungwa kueleza vitu vilivyomo, matumizi au jinsi ya kuunganisha) *vt* 1 andika (muhtasari wa barua, hati n.k.). 2 orodhesha (bidhaa; kazi zilizofanywa). 3 andika lebo.

doctor *n* 1 daktari, tabibu, mganga. 2 daktari (wa falsafa): mtu mwenye shahada ya juu kabisa katika somo. ~ **of laws** daktari wa falsafa katika sheria *vt* 1 (*colloq*) ganga, tibu. 2 (*mend, repair*) tengeneza. 3 ghushi. ~ **food** ghushi chakula: fanya chakula/kinywaji kiwe kibaya kwa kuongeza kitu kingine. ~ **the accounts** ghushi hesabu. 4 (*of animals*) hasi. **~ate** *n* shahada ya udaktari. **~ial** *adj* -a udaktari.

doctrine *n* 1 kanuni, mafundisho (ya dini, vyama vya siasa n.k.), imani *it is his ~* ndiyo imani yake. **doctrinaire/doctrinar** *n* mnadhariasugu *adj* -a kanuni/ nadharia tupu *doctrinaire socialism* ujamaa wa nadharia tu. **doctrinal** *adj* -a kanuni, -a mafundisho; -a madhehebu (ya dini).

document *n* hati, nyaraka *vt* thibitisha kwa kutoa hati/-pa hati, toa hati. **~ation** *n* uandikaji wa hati; hifadhi ya hati. **~ary** *adj* 1 -a hati, -enye kuandikwa. **~ary evidence** ushahidi ulioandikwa 2. (*of film*) -a mambo yasiyokuwa ya kubuni; -a maisha halisi *n* filamu ionyeshayo hali halisi.

dodder *vi* (*colloq*) jikongoja, enda mwendo wa kutetemeka (kwa udhaifu, uzee, ugonjwa). **~er** *n.* **~y** *adj.*

dodeca (*pref.*) kumi na mbili. **~gon** *n* pembe kumi na mbili. **~hedron** umbo lenye sura kumi na mbili **~syllable** *n* mstari wenye silabi kumi na mbili.

dodge *vt,vi* 1 (piga) chenga, kwepa (ili

usionekane, au usikamatwe). 2 tumia hila (werevu) ili kukwepa jambo *n* 1 chenga. 2 hila, ukwepaji. **~r** *n.*

dodgy *adj.* 1 -a hatari 2 -enye hila.

doe *n* sungura/swala/digidigi jike. **~s kin** ngozi ya sungura, swala, digidigi.

doff *vt* (*old use*) vua (kofia, nguo, mavazi). **~ one's hat** kuamkia mtu kwa kuvua kofia.

dog *n* 1 mbwa; mbwa dume. 2 (*in phrases*) **every ~ has his day** kila mtu ana siku yake, iko siku. **give a ~ bad name (and hang him)** paka mtu matope/haribu jina la mtu (na watu wataendelea kumfikiria vibaya). **help a lame ~ over a stile** saidia mtu wakati wa dhiki/matatizo. **let sleeping ~s lie** acha mambo kama yalivyo, usimwamshe aliyelala, ukimwamsha utalala wewe. **love me love my ~** ukimpenda baniani upende winda wake. **he doesn't stand/have (even) a ~'s chance** hana uwezo wowote (wa kushinda, kushiriki). **go to the ~s** potoka, haribika; haribikiwa, kwisha. **throw/give to the ~s** tupa (kama takataka), sukumia. **lead a ~s life** ishi maisha ya taabu. **lead sb a ~'s life** sumbua/ghasi mtu kila wakati *treat sb like a ~* tendea vibaya, dhalilisha **a ~ in the manger** mtu mwenye inda (anayewazuia wengine wasifaidi kitu fulani ambacho hakimsaidii yeye). **be the under ~** -wa mtu wa kushindwa tu. **be top ~** (*colloq*) -wa kiongozi, -wa mwenyewe. **die a ~'s death/die like a ~** -fa kifo cha aibu/dhiki. **dressed like a ~'s dinner** (*colloq*) amevalia maridadi sana/kufuata mitindo mipya kabisa. **look like a ~'s breakfast/dinner** onekana shaghala-baghala. **a case of ~ eat ~** hali ya unyang'au. **you can't teach an old ~ new tricks** (*prov*) si rahisi kumbadilisha mzee. 2 (*colloq*) jamaa. **a sly ~** mtu mjanja. 4 **a hot ~** mkate wenye soseji. 5 (*in compounds*). **~ biscuit** *n* biskuti za mbwa. **~s body** *n* mtu wa chini (afanyaye kazi za ovyo). **~collar** *n* mkanda wa mbwa; (*colloq*) kola ya padre. **~days** *n* siku za jua kali. **~-eared** *adj* (*of book*) -enye visikio, -enye vikunjo. **~fight** *n* mapigano baina ya ndege za kivita. **~house** kibanda cha mbwa. (*sl*) **be in a ~ house** aibika. **~-paddle** *n* mtindo wa kuogelea kama mbwa. **be~-tired** -wa taabani kwa uchovu/kuchoka sana. **~-watch** (*naut*) zamu ya saa mbili katika meli. **~vane** (*naut*) kibendera. **~ eat ~** *adj* katili -a unyang'au. **~like** *adj* a kama mbwa. **~gy/ ~gie** (*child's word for*) mbwa *vt* fuata karibu sana, andama. **~ sb's footsteps** fuata mtu kila aendapo. **~ged** *adj* (*obstinate*) -kaidi, shupavu, -gumu. 2 (*firm*) kakamavu, -siokata tamaa, thabiti.

doggerel *n* mashairi hafifu.

doggo *adv* **lie ~** (*sl*) lala kimya kabisa; jificha.

doggone (*US sl*) neno la mshangao kama salale! **that ~ cat** yule paka mshenzi.

dogie *n* ndama mkiwa (asiye na mama).

dogma *n* 1 imani, mfumo wa imani unaofundishwa na kanisa. 2 (*usu derog*) imani (ambayo watu wanatakiwa kukubali bila kusaili). **~tic** *adj* 1 -enye kutangazwa kama imani ya kanisa. 2 *(of a person)* -enye kulazimisha kauli (bila kutaka kusailiwa). 3 *(of statement)* -liotolewa/lazimishwa bila kuthibitishwa. **~tics** *n* elimu ya imani za dini. **~tism** *n* kung'anga'nia/ kulazimisha kauli/imani/tabia. **~tize** *vi, vt* shikilia/lazimisha kauli, shauri, maneno.

doh *see* **do**.

doily *n* kitambaa cha mapambo (kinachowekwa chini ya sahani, glasi n.k.).

doldrums *n* 1 mahali baharini karibu na ikweta ambapo kwa kawaida hakuna upepo kabisa. 2 (*colloq*) **in the ~** katika hali ya huzuni, kusononeka.

dole *vt* **(out)** gawia (chakula, fedha kidogo kidogo watu wenye shida) *n* **the ~** (*colloq*) posho ya serikali kwa wasio na kazi. **be/go on the ~** anza kupata posho hii kwa sababu ya kukosa kazi. **~ful** *adj* -a huzuni, -a majonzi, -enye moyo mzito.

doll *n* 1 mwanasesere; mtoto wa bandia. 2 *(sl)* kidosho *vt,vi* ~ **up** jipamba, jipara. **~y** *n* 1 (*child's word for*) mwanasesere. 2 toroli. 3 (*also* **~y bird**) (*sl*) kidosho.

dollar *n* 1 dola. **American ~** dola ya Marekani.

dollop *n* (*colloq*) chakula kilichopakuliwa.

dolour *n* huzuni; majonzi. **~ous** *adj* -a huzuni, -zito, -a kuhuzunisha.

dolphin *n* (*bio*) pomboo (mnyama kama nyangumi mwenye urefu wa futi 8-10).

dolt *n* mjinga, baradhuli; zuzu. **~ish** *adj*.

domain *n* miliki. 2 (*fig*) uwanja (wa elimu n.k.) *that is my domain* huo ni uwanja wangu. 3 (*maths*) kao.

dome *n* 1 kuba. 2 (*US sl*) kichwa (hasa kipara). 3 **~d** -enye umbo la kuba, -liofunikwa na kuba.

domestic *adj* 1 -a nyumbani, -a jamaa *a ~ person* mtu anayependa kukaa nyumbani, mkaa nyumbani *~ science* sayansi kimu, maarifa ya nyumbani. 2 -a nchini, -a ndani, -a kienyeji. **~ flights** safari za ndege za ndani. **~ news** habari za nchini. 3 (*of animals*) -liofugwa na binadamu; -enye kukaa na binadamu. **a ~ animal** mnyama anayefugwa *n* mtumishi wa nyumbani. **~ally** *adv*. **~ate** *vt* (*chiefly in pp*) 1 idilisha, zoeza kazi za nyumbani *she's not at all ~ated* hapendi/hawezi kazi za nyumbani. 2 (*of animals*) fuga. **~ation** *n*. **~ity** *n* 1 (kupenda) maisha ya nyumbani, maisha ya familia. 2 (*pl*) mambo ya nyumbani.

domicile *n* (*formal*) makao, makazi; nyumba, maskani *vi* fanya maskani, anzisha makazi. **domiciliary** *adj* (*formal*) -a kimakazi *~ visit* ziara ya afisa wa serikali/mganga nyumbani kwa kufanya upekuzi/matibabu.

dominate *vt,vi* ~ **(over)** 1 (*rule*) tawala, -wa na amri juu ya, amuru. 2 (*of a place esp. a height*) -wa refu kuliko, tawalia, angalia kutoka juu. **domination** *n*. **dominant** *adj* 1 -a nguvu, -a kutawala. 2 (*of heights*) -lio juu ya *n* noti ya tano katika skeli. **dominantly** *adv*. **dominance** *n*.

domineer *vi* ~ **(over)** fanya jeuri; kandamiza, onea. **~ing** *adj* -jeuri, -onevu. **~ingly** *adv*.

dominie *n* (*Scot*) mwalimu.

dominion *n* (*over*) 1 mamlaka, utawala *be under the ~ of* tawaliwa na, -wa chini ya. 2 miliki. 3 (*old use*) moja ya nchi za madola zilizokuwa zikijitawala k.m. (Kanada na Australia).

domino *n* dhumna, dadu, domino.

don[1] *(old use)* vaa nguo.

don[2] *n* (*SP*) bwana, mwungwana. 2 (*GB*) mhadhiri, mwalimu wa chuo kikuu. **~nish** *adj* -a kama mhadhiri; -a kinadharia tu.

donate *vt* toa/-pa msaada (kwa fedha n.k.), changa. **donation** *n* utoaji msaada; msaada, mchango. **donor** *n* mfadhili, mhisani, mtoa msaada/mchango. **blood ~** mtoaji damu; mtu anajitolea tamu.

done *see* **do**.

donga *n* (*S. Africa*) korongo.

donkey *n* 1 punda. **~ engine** injini ndogo ya mvuke (hasa kwenye meli). **~ jacket** koti fupi zito la mfanyakazi. **~work** kazi ya sulubu. **~'s years** muda mrefu. 2 **that was ~'s ago** ilikuwa zamani sana (*stupid person*) mpumbavu; mpuuzi. 3 (*fig*) *talk the hind leg off a ~* bwabwaja.

don't, do not. 1 *see* **do**. 2 **do's and ~s** masharti na miiko.

doodle *vi* (*colloq*) chorachora.

doodlebug *n* (*colloq*) kombora (katika vita kuu ya pili).

doom *n* 1 maangamizi, kifo, hukumu *to go to one's ~* kufa, kuangamia. 2 (*also* **~'s day**) siku ya hukumu ya mwisho, mwisho wa dunia, siku ya

Kinyama. **till ~sday** milele *vt* ~ **(to)** (*usu, passive*)hukumu. **~ed to misery** -lioandikiwa tabu *stories ~ed to oblivion* hadithi za kusahaulika.

door *n* 1 mlango; *(of two halves)* tarabe. **back** ~ mlango wa nyuma, mlango wa uwani. **front** ~ mlango wa mbele, mlango mkubwa *be on the* ~ kusanya tikiti mlangoni; simama mlangoni. 2 *(fig)* nyumba. **next** ~ **(to)** nyumba ya pili (jirani). **next** ~ **to** *(fig)* karibu na. **two/three ~s away/down/off** nyumba ya pili/tatu kutoka--. ~ **to** ~ nyumba hadi nyumba. **out of ~s** nje (ya nyumba). **within ~s** ndani (ya nyumba). **at death's** ~ karibu ya kufa. **lay sth at sb's** ~ sema kuwa fulani anawajibika kwa jambo fulani, laumu, shutumu. **show sb to the** ~ sindikiza mgeni *show sb the* ~ fukuza, toa nje. 3 *(fig)* namna ya kupata (kufikia) kitu. **a ~ to success** njia ya kupata mafanikio. **close the ~ against sb** zuia mtu kufanya jambo, vunja uwezekano. **send the ~ in someone's face** zuia mtu asiingie, zuia mpango wa mtu. *(compounds)* ~ **bell** kengele ya mlango. ~ **case/frame** fremu ya mlango. ~ **handle** mkono wa kitasa cha mlango. **~keeper** bawabu. **~knob** kitasa cha rungu/nundu. **as dead as a ~nail** kufa fofofo. **~plate** kibandiko cha kutia jina (namba) la mwenye nyumba, kipande cha anuani. **~post** mhimili, mwimo. **as deaf as ~post** kiziwi kabisa. **~step** ngazi za mlangoni. **~stopper** kishikizi/kizuizi cha mlango. ~ **way** mlangoni.

dope *n* 1 rangi ya kung'arisha, vanishi. 2 *(colloq)* dawa ya kulevya (k.m. afyuni, kasumba, bangi). 3 *(sl)* maelezo, habari. 4 mpumbavu *vt* 1 -pa dawa (hasa inayolevya). 2 changamsha kwa dawa ya kulevya (k.m. farasi au mbwa katika mashindano). 3 laza kwa dawa. **~y** *adj* 1 jinga. 2 -liolala nusu, levi; *(sl)* -liopumbazwa na dawa ya kulevya (bangi n.k.). **~-fiend** *n (sl)* mtumwa wa dawa za kulevya.

dormant *adj* -a kulala, -siotumika kwa muda, -liolala, bwete (-enye uwezo wa kuamka/kukua/kuendelezwa baadaye) *a ~ volcano* volkano bwete: volkano ambayo haijalipuka. **dormancy** *n* ubwete.

dormitory *n* bweni, dahalia. ~ **town** mji wa makazi (ambapo watu huishi lakini wanakwenda kufanya kazi mji mwingine).

dorsal *adj (anat)* -a mgongoni, -a nyuma ~ *sound* sauti za nyuma ya ulimi.

dory *n* boti ndogo ya makasia yenye tako bapa.

dosage *n* kipimo na masharti ya matumizi ya dawa.

dose *n* 1 kipimo cha dawa. 2 *(sl)* ugonjwa wa zinaa *vt* 1 nywesha dawa, -pa dawa, -nywa dawa.

doss *n* ~ **house** nyumba ya kulala wageni ya bei nafuu; hoteli ndogo; usingizi mfupi *vi (sl)* lala katika hoteli. ~ **down** enda kulala. ~ **out** lala nje! **~er** *n* mzururaji.

dossier *n* jalada la hati/nyaraka zenye habari za mtu au tukio.

dot[1] *n* 1 nukta, alama ndogo, kitone. **on the** ~ *(colloq)* juu ya alama *come at five on the* ~ njoo saa 11 juu ya alama. 2 kitu kionekanacho kama tone. **the year** ~ zama za kale *vt* 1 tia (alama ya) tone/nukta. **one's i's and cross one's t's** *(fig)* fanya kuwa wazi na -a uhakika, kamilisha kila kitu. 2 fanya/funika kwa nukta. ~ **about** tia nukta huko na huko. **be ~ted about** tapakaa, tawanyika. **sign on the ~ted line** *(fig)* kubali bila kukawia au upinzani. **~ty** *adj* 1 -liotapakaa madoa. 2 *(colloq)* punguani, -pumbavu, -jinga.

dot[2] *n (Fr)* mahari.

dotage *n* uzulufu: kipindi cha upungufu wa akili kutokana na uzee. **dotard** *n* mtu katika hali hii.

dote *vi* ~ **(on/upon)** penda sana, pendelea, tunuka.

dottle *n* bumba la tumbaku lililobakia

kwenye kiko.

double *adj* 1 maradufu. 2 *(in pairs)* -wili, kwa- jozi. 3 tengenezwa kwa ajili ya watu au vitu viwili. 4 *(of flowers)* -enye zaidi ya duara moja ya petali. 5 -enye kazi/faida mbili. ~ **dealing** *n,adj* (u)janja, (u)kauleni, (u)danganyifu, (u)ndumakuwili. ~**dealer** *n* mdanganyifu, ndumakuwili, kauleni *n* kitu kilicho mara mbili (ya kubwa/nguvu/mwendo, n.k. wa kawaida). 2 (*counterpart*) mwenzi wa mtu/kitu kingine, nakala, rupia kwa nyenziye ~ *of his father* anafanana na baba yake. 3 *(Tennis)* mchezo wa watu wawili kila upande. 4 **at/on the** ~ chapuchapu, shoti, haraka. 5 mwigizaji badili. ~**or quits** pata potea *adv* 1 mara mbili **cost** ~ gharimu mara mbili. 2 kwa jozi *vt,vi* 1 rudufu, zidi/zidisha mara mbili, ongeza/ongezeka. ~ **up in a room** weka watu wawili katika chumba kimoja. 2 ~ **up/over/across** kunja/ kunjika, pinda/pindika mara mbili; *(of a pair of trousers)* sega, pania. 3 *(naut)* zunguka, badili mwelekeo haraka (pitia rasi). 4 fumba. 5 ~ **back** rudi mbio haraka ~ *up (with pain)* jikunja (kwa maumivu); (*with laughter*) angua kicheko ~ *as (play)* igiza wahusika wawili; fanya kazi mbili; *(in room/ bed)* lala wawili wawili *adj, adv (in compounds)* ~**barrelled** *(of a gun)* -enye mitutu miwili ~*-barrelledgun* bunduki yenye mitutu miwili; *(fig, of a compliment, etc)* -enye utata. ~ **bass** *n (music)* zeze chini. ~-**bedded** (*of a room*) -enye vitanda viwili; chumba cha watu wawili. ~-**bind** *n* kuwa katika ugumu wa kuamua; shaka. ~ -**breasted** *(of a coat)* -enye safu mbili za vifungo. ~-**check** *vt* kagua/ chunguza maradufu; saliti; danganya. ~-**cross** *n* tendo la kudanganya au kusaliti. ~**decker** meli/basi/kitanda cha ghorofa. ~ **take** chelewa kung'amua/kutambua jambo. *n* ~ **talk** kusema kinyume. ~ **think** uwezo wa kuamini mambo mawili yanayopingana. ~-**edged** *adj* -enye sehemu mbili za makali; *(fig, of an argument, compliment)* -enye utata. ~-**entry** *adj (of a cash book)* maingizo mawili. ~-**entry system** mpango wa maingizo mawili. ~-**faced** *adj* -nafiki; *(of a cloth)* -enye nyuso mbili. ~ **first** *n* shahada ya daraja la kwanza kwa ajili ya kufaulu masomo mawili kwa wakati mmoja. ~**jointed** *adj* -enye viungo vinavyokunjika isivyo kawaida. ~ **park** *vt, vi* egesha gari njiani kando ya gari lingine. ~-**quick** *adj* -a mbio, -a haraka *adv* upesi sana, haraka sana. ~-**stop** *n (music)* sauti mbili kwa pamoja (za noti). **doubly** *adv* 1 mara mbili. 2 *to be doubly faithful* kuwa -aminifu sana.

doublet *n* 1 jaketi la kubana. 2 jozi ya kufanana. 3 nenokikoa: neno moja kati ya jozi yenye asili moja lakini maana tofauti.

doubt *n* shaka, wasiwasi, tashwishi, tuhuma. **beyond all reasonable** ~ bila shaka yoyote. ~ **as to sth** tilia shaka. **be in** ~ kuwa katika shaka/ wasiwasi *make no* ~ usiwe na shaka, usitie shaka *there is no* ~ *about it* hapana shaka juu jambo hili *throw* ~ *upon sth* (jambo) tilia jambo shaka *vt, vi* -wa na shaka, ona shaka; shuku, tuhumu, -tosadiki ~ *sb's word* -toamini maneno yake. ~**ful** *adj* (*about/of*) 1 *(irresolute)* -enye wasiwasi, -a shaka. 2 *(uncertain)* si hakika, si yakini, -siojulikana, si dhahiri. ~**fulness** *n.* ~**less** *adv* bila shaka, hakika, kwa yakini.

douceur *n* 1 zawadi, bahashishi. 2 rushwa.

douche *vt (of medicine)* piga bomba (ya kusafisha, ya kuogesha) *n (of medicine)* 1 msukumo wa maji ya kupiga bomba.

dough *n* kinyunya. 2 *(sl.)* pesa, ngamia.

dough-nut *n* donati, aina ya maandazi. ~**y** *adj* laini, kama kinyunya.

doughty *adj (old use or joc.)* 1 shujaa.

2 madhubuti.
dour *adj* 1 kali. 2 -kaidi. 3 sononi: -enye kusononeka. **~ly** *adv*. **~ness** *n*.
douse/dowse *vt* 1 lowesha, mwagia maji; chovya majini; zamisha. 2 *(naut)* teremsha tanga; funga kishubaka; anguka majini; tua tanga. 3 zima (taa).
dove *n* 1 njiwa (wadogo zaidi kuliko wafugwao); alama ya amani. 2 mpatanishi (katika utesi). 3 *(fig)* mpenzi. 4 *(colour)* mpigania amani, mwanachama wa watetezi wa amani. **~coloured** *adj* -a rangi ya njiwa. **flutter the ~ cotes** shtua watu wapole/wakimya. **~-cote** *n* tundu la njiwa. **~eyed** *adj* -enye macho ya njiwa (kwa upole na usafi). **~hawk** *n* mwewe. **~tail** *vt,vi (mortise)* unganisha (mbao) kwa kufanya vipande viwili viumane; *(fig)* umana, kubaliana *n* kiungo cha mbao; kuumana. **~-joint maker** mtengeneza viungo vya kuumana.
dowager *n* 1 mjanekike mrithi (wa mali au cheo cha mumewe). 2 *(colloq)* mwanamke wa makamo mwenye hadhi kubwa.
dowdy *adj* 1 -enye kuvaa ovyo, asiyevutia. 2 -a kizamani (kitabia, kimavazi, kimatendo).
dowel *n (dowel-pin)* kiwi, pini isiyo na kichwa, kijiti kiingizwacho ndani ya tundu kuviweka vitu pamoja.
dower *n* 1 haki ya mke mfiwa (kutokana na mali ya mumewe), sehemu ya urithi (wa mali ya mumewe) apewayo mjane mwanamke. 2 mahari. 3 kipaji (k.m. akili) *vt* 1 lipa mahari. 2 -pa kipaji.
down[1] *n (fine hair)* laika, malaika; manyoya laini (ya makinda ya ndege); ndevu laini (za kwanza za kijana). **downy** *adj* laini, -ororo, -a laika.
down[2] *adv* 1 *(with vv of motion)* chini *the flag was hauled ~* bendera ilishushwa chini *come ~* shuka. 2 *(with vv of motion)* lala, anguka chini *the boxer knocked his opponent ~* mwanamasumbwi alimwangusha chini mpinzani wake. 3 *(with vv indicating change of stance but not of position in space)* kuelekea/kwenda *sit ~* kaa chini kitako *bend ~* inama. 4 *(with vv indicating position or state)* kuwa katika hali ya kushuka *Juma isn't ~ yet* Juma hajawa tayari kushuka *there are no lights in the streets because the lamp posts are ~* taa za mitaani haziwaki kwa sababu nguzo zote zimeanguka chini. 5 kutoka sehemu maarufu zaidi kwenda sehemu isiyo maarufu. 6 *(with vv to indicate reduction to a smaller volume, less degree etc.) the tyre is ~* tairi halina upepo *the storm has died ~* dhoruba imetulia *the fire is burning ~* moto unafifia *the price of fish is ~* bei ya samaki imeshuka. 7 *(with reference to writing) write the address ~* andika anwani (kwenye karatasi) *put me ~* andika jina langu, niandikishe. 8 kuanzia wakati wa nyuma hadi baadaye *the history of phonology ~ to Chomsky* historia ya fonolojia hadi kufikia wakati wa Chomsky. 9 *(include the lower limit in a series)* kuanzia kiwango cha chini katika mfululizo *from old men ~ to small children* kuanzia wazee hadi watoto wadogo. 10 *(used in various phrases)* **D ~ with** hatutaki. **up and ~** huku na huko. **money/cash ~** arubuni. **~ payment** malipo ya kwanza (arubuni). **be ~ and out** *(colloq)* tolewa nje kwa kuangushwa chini (katika masumbwi), shindwa kurudi katika pambano la masumbwi. **get ~ to business** anza kuchangamkia kazi. **be ~ on sb** chukia mtu. **~ in the dumps** *(colloq)* katika sura ya majonzi. **~ on one's luck** patwa na mikasa. **come ~ in the world** shuka hadhi. **come ~ on sb** karipia. **~ to earth** -enye kuhusika na mambo halisi. **turn upside ~** geuza juu chini. **hunt/track ~** winda, saka. **~ with** umwa, ugua. **be ~ for** andikishwa kwa *prep* 1 *(direction)* chini *tears ran ~ his face* machozi

yalimtiririka usoni. 2 *(position)* mbele *Kilwa is further ~ the coast* Kilwa iko kusini zaidi ya mwambao. 3 *(time)* **all ~ the ages** toka zamani. *(fig) (colloq)* **all ~ the line** pote *fall ~ a hole* anguka kwenye shimo *run ~ the hill* shuka mlima (kwa kukimbia) *cut ~ the middle* kata katikati *pace up and ~ the room* tembea huku na huko chumbani *n* **ups and ~s** mema na mabaya. **have a ~ on him** mchukie. *vt (a drink)* gugumia. **~ tools** -goma kazi. **~ beat** *n (music)* pigo la kwanza. **~ cast** *adj* 1 -enye huzuni, -zito *be ~ cast (of eyes)* vunjika (moyo). 2 -a kutazama chini. **~-draught** *n* mjongeo wa gesi, hewa kuelekea chini. **~fall** *n* 1 maanguko, maangamizi; *(~ of rain)* mvua nyingi. 2 ushinde. **~-grade** *vt* teremsha cheo/ hadhi/umuhimu. **~-hearted** *adj* -enye huzuni,-enye kuvunjika moyo. **~hill** *adj* -a kuja (kwenda) chini, -a kuteremka mlima chini. *(fig) adv* **go ~hill** haribikiwa. **~pour** *n* mvua kubwa. **~ town** *adv (US)* mjini; katika/kuelekea sehemu ya chini ya mji; sehemu iliyo na shughuli nyingi za kibiashara. **~trodden** *adj* -a kudhulumiwa, -a kuonewa, -a kudhalilishwa. **~ward** *adj* 1 -a kwenda chini, -a kuteremka. 2 *(of price)* -a kushuka; *(of a commodity)*-a kushuka thamani. **be on the ~ path** elekea uharibifu; fifia. **~-at-heel** *adj* 1 *(of shoes)* -livyochakaa. 2 (kwa mtu) liyevaa nguo zilizochanika.

Downing Street *n* mtaa wa London ambapo ni makazi ya waziri mkuu; *(colloq)* Serikali ya Uingereza.

downright *adj* kweli, -enye kuwa wazi *adv* kwa wazi, kabisa, sana; dhahiri. **~ness** *n.*

downs *n* nchi ya vilima vyenye majani mafupi; ukanda wa juu usio na miti.

downstairs *adj* -a kwenda chini; -a ghorofa ya chini zaidi *adv (of place)* chini, chini kwa kushuka ngazi, kwenda chini.

dowry *n* mapambo (vitu vitolewavyo na bibi arusi kwenda kwa bwana arusi).

dowse *see* **douse**.

doxology *n* wimbo wa kumsifu Mungu.

doyen *n* kiongozi wa mabalozi.

doyley *see* **doily**.

doz *abbr. of dozen.*

doze *vi* sinzia. **~ off** pata usingizi wa kimang'amung'amu *n* usingizi mwepesi *have a ~* lala kidogo. **~ (at)** gona *n* gonezi.

dozen 1 dazeni: fungu la vitu kumi na viwili. **talk nineteen to the ~** porojoa. 2 **~s of** idadi kubwa ya.

draconian *adj* -kali sana, -katili, -onevu; -a dragoni. -a zimwi.

draft[1] *n* 1 kundi dogo la askari (lililotolewa katika kundi kubwa kwa kazi maalumu). 2 *(US)* kikundi cha watu wanaoitwa jeshini; kuitwa jeshini. **~ card** barua ya kuitwa jeshini. 3 *(sketch, design)* kielezo, kielelezo, rasimu, ramani; mfano (wa kazi). 4 mswadajaribio la kwanza, mchoro wa kwanza; mwandiko wa upesi (wa kujaribia, wa kufikiria) wa hati. 5 hati ya malipo itolewayo na benki; ulipwaji wa fedha kwa kutumia hati hiyo *vt* 1 *(select, separate)* tenga (chagua) kundi dogo (katika kundi kubwa la askari); ita jeshini. 2 *(design)* andika (piga) sanamu ya; sawidi, chora jaribio la awali.

draft[2] *adj* 1 -enye kufanya kazi ya kubeba. **~ animals** wanyama wavutao mizigo (k.m. punda). 2 -lotoka pipani. **~ beer** bia inayotolewa katika pipa.

draftsman *n see draughtsman* 1 *(legal)* msawidi.

drafty *adj (US) see* **draughty**.

drag[1] *vt,vi* 1 kokota, buruta. 2 enda pole na kwa shida; kawia, chelewa. **~ one's feet** vuta miguu; *(fig)* fanya shingo upande. **~ sb into doing sth** lazimisha/fanya mtu afanye jambo bila hiari. **~ up (a child)** lea vibaya mtoto. **~ up** leta, ingiza (swali/hoja). 2 *(search)* tafuta majini kwa kutumia wavu. 3 vuta (nanga). 4 vuta kiubavubavu mshipi wa kuvulia. 5 ~ **about** vuta popote. ~ **down** shusha hadhi, fanya nyonge. ~ **in** (*colloq*) vuta ndani, ingiza. ~ **on** endelea na jambo hilohilo kwa namna isiyopendeza/kwa kuchosha ~ *on a miserable existence* endelea katika maisha ya dhiki. ~ **out** vuta, endeleza kwa muda mrefu; refusha bila sababu.

drag[2] *n* 1 *(hindrance)* kizuio, mgogoro, mzigo; *(net)* jarife, juya. 2 *(colloq)* mzigo, mtu anayechosha. 3 *(sl)* mavazi ya kike yanayovaliwa na mwamume. 4 *(sl)* mkupuo wa sigara. ~ **chain** *n* mnyororo wa kuburura. **~y** *adj (colloq)* -enye sura mbaya, -siopendeza, -nayochosha.

draggled *see* **bedraggled**.

dragoman *n* mkalimani (wa Kiarabu, Kituruki, Kiajemi).

dragon *n* dragoni; zimwi; mnyama mtambaachi mkubwa wa kubuni (mwenye mbawa na kucha, na daima hupumua moto). **~'s blood** *n* gundi nyekundu; *(colloq)* mtu mkali. **~-fly** *n* kerengende.

dragonnade *n* mateso kwa kutumia jeshi.

dragoon *n* askari mpanda farasi *vt* ~ **into** lazimisha, tisha kwa nguvu, sumbua. ~ **sb into doing sth** lazimisha mtu kufanya jambo.

drail *n* ndoana kubwa yenye mshipi na chubwi.

drain *vt* 1 ~ **away/off** toa maji kwa mifereji/bomba. 2 kausha. **~ing board** kichanja cha kukaushia vyombo. 3 *(drink)* -nywa yote. 4 ~ **(away/off)**, ~ **(of)** *(fig)* fifisha, dhoofisha, nyonya ~ *sb of his strength etc.* chosha mtu. 5 nyonya usaha, unyevu (kwa bomba). 6 nywa/maliza kunywa (agh. ndani ya glasi). 7 ~ **the cup of** pitia (hasa matukio/maisha mabaya) *n* 1 mfereji, mfumbi, bomba la kutoa maji. **throw money down the** ~ ponda mali, tumia pesa vibaya. **go down the** ~ potea bure, teketea, haribika. 2 jambo linalofifilisha/ nyonya. **brain** ~ uhamaji wa wasomi/mabingwa toka nchi moja hadi nyingine (wakitafuta maslahi). 3 kinywaji kidogo, tone. **~age** *n* 1 mtiririsho. 2 *(sewers)* mfereji, bomba la maji machafu. ~ **system** mfumo wa kuchukua maji machafu. **~age-area/~basin** *n* eneo ambalo maji ya mto hutokea. **~age-tube** *n (med)* neli ya usaha.

drake *n* bata dume.

dram *n* 1 dramu (kipimo cha uzito); 1/8 ya wakia. 2 kiasi kidogo sana cha ulevi. **take a** ~ nywa kidogo.

drama *n* 1 drama; tamthiliya. 2 mfululizo wa mambo/matukio ya kuvutia. **~tic** *adj* -a drama; -a kutia shauku/kuvutia; *(of a person bahaviour)* -enye kuonyesha hisia kwa namna ya kuvutia/mno, -enye kupenda kuigiza. **~tically** *adv*. **~tics** *n usu with sing* 1 sanaa ya kuandaa na kuonyesha tamthiliya. 2 tabia ya kujionyesha. **~tist** *n* mwandishi wa tamthiliya/drama. **~tis personae** *n pl (lat)* (orodha ya) wahusika wa tamthiliya. **~tize** *vt* 1 igiza tamthilia/ drama; geuza hadithi kuwa ya kidrama; -wa na tabia ya kidrama. 2 geuza. 3 tia chumvi, igiza. **~tization** *n*. **~turgy** *n* sanaa ya kutunga tamthiliya.

drank *pt of* **drink**.

drape *vt* 1 ~ **(around/over)** funika na kitambaa. 2 ning'iniza nguo kuzunguka au juu ya kitu. 3 ~ **(with)** funika/pamba. 4 pumzisha, laza, bwaga. **~r** *n (GB)* mwuza nguo *a ~r's shop* duka la nguo. **~ry** *n* 1 biashara ya kuuza nguo. 2 nguo. 3 nguo zinazoning'inia, mapazia.

drastic *adj (of actions, methods, medicines)* kali, -enye athari kubwa, -enye matokeo ya haraka ~ *steps* hatua kali. **~ally** *adv*.

draught(*US* **draft**) *n* 1 *(current of air)* upepo, hewa ipitayo katika chumba. 2 mvuo wa samaki kwa wavu. 3 kina cha maji chenye kuwezesha meli ielee. 4 mnywo, funda, mvuto, mfyonzo; kuvuta/kunyonya uowevu kutoka katika chombo (mf. pipa). ~

beer bia ya kasiki. 5 funda *a ~ of water* funda la maji. 6 *(pl) (US)* drafti *vt see* **draft**. ~ **horse** farasi avutaye mizigo mizito. **feel the** ~ *(sl)* -ishiwa; sikia upepo. **~-board** *n* ubao wa drafti. **~sman** *n* mrasimu, msawidi. **~smanship** *n* urasimu.

draw *n* 1 kuvuta. 2 *(of lottery)* kuchezesha bahati nasibu *when will the ~ take place*? bahati nasibu itachezeshwa lini? 3 suluhu, sare *the game ended in a ~* mchezo ulikuwa sare. 4 kivutio, mvutiaji *Mr Mrema is a great ~ at meetings* anavutia sana watu kuja mkutanoni. 5 kufuta **be quick on the** ~ -wa mwepesi kufuta/kuchomoa (upanga, bastola); *(fig)* mwepesi kuelewa mambo *vt,vi* 1 vuta. ~ **aside** chukua mtu pembeni. ~ **the curtains** vuta/funga pazia. 2 kokota. **plough ~n by the tractor** plau linalokokotwa na trekta. ~ **(out)**; **(from/out of)** ondoa kwa kuvuta; zidua; zibua ~ *a cork* zibua kizibo ~ *a nail* zidua msumari; *(in card games)* kata ng'anda. **to ~ a winner** kupata tiketi ya ushindi; tafuta/bahatisha mshindi. ~ **a blank** -topata chochote. ~ **sb's teeth** poza mtu, maliza ukali wake. 4 ~ **(from/out of)** chota ~ *water from a well* teka/chota maji kisimani; *(of money/from one's account)* chukua *to ~ rations* kuchukua posho. ~ **it mild** *(fig)* -wa wa kiasi; -totia chumvi nyingi, -wa taratibu. ~ **tears/applause** sababisha machozi/makofi *the news drew tears* habari ile ilimliza. 5 ~ **(to)** vuta, vutia *he drew my attention to* alinionyesha *I don't feel ~n to him* sivutiwi naye. 6 vuta, ingiza ndani *to ~ a deep breath* vuta pumzi kubwa. ~ **one's first/last breath** zaliwa/-fa. 7 *(of a chimney)* acha nafasi ya hewa kupita; -jengwa ili kupitisha hewa/moshi. 8 **~(out)** sababisha/shawishi (mtu) kuongea, kuonyesha hisia zake. 9 enda karibu, karibia *Republic day is ~ing near* siku ya Jamhuri inakaribia. ~ **near** karibia. ~ **ahead** enda mbele ~ *ahead from others* enda mbele kuliko wengine. ~ **off/back** rudi nyuma *he drew himselfup* alisimama wima. 10 sababisha kusogea/kuja. 11 chora ~ *a line* piga mstari ~ *picture (fig)* eleza kwa maneno. ~ **the line** weka mpaka, kataa, weka kiwango, kataza. ~ **a distinction (between)** onyesha tofauti. ~ **a parallel/comparison/analogy between**. linganisha; onyesha ulinganifu. ~ **the line (at)** weka kikomo; eleza jambo lisiloruhusiwa; kataa kuendelea. 12 andika ~ *a cheque (on a bank for a sum of money)* andika cheki; *(of writers)* chota, sawiri. 13 *(of a ship)* -hitaji kina (ili kuelea) *the ship ~s six metres of water* meli yahitaji kina cha mita sita za maji ili ielee; *(of competition)* toka sare, fungana. 14 *(of the features)*kunjamana, umbuka, umbua, rembua. 15 *(special uses with prep and adv particles)* ~ **apart** tengana. ~ **away** zidi kutangulia. ~ **back** kaa mbali; *(fig)* sita; onyesha kutotaka *n* kizuizi, dosari, kipingamizi. ~ **in** *(of a day)* fikia mwisho wake; -wa fupi zaidi. ~ **down** vuta. ~ **for** jaribu bahati, pigia kura. ~ **into** shawishi kujiunga. ~ **on** *(of a period of time)* karibia, ingia *night drew on* usiku ulikaribia. ~ **off** ondoa. ~ **on sb** tumia. ~ **sb on** vutia, shawishi. ~ **on sb** tishia kwa silaha. ~ **out** *(of a day)* -wa refu, refuka; nyosha, refusha. ~ **up** *(of vehicle)* simama/simamisha; tayarisha, tunga; *(US passive) (of troops etc.)* panga, simama hima. **~back** *n* 1 kizuizi, kipingamizi. 2 marejesho (ya kodi/ushuru). ~ **bar** *n* kifungo kitenganishacho mabehewa. **~bridge** *n* daraja (ulalo, mtatago) ya kuinuliwa. **~er** *n* 1 mtoto wa meza. 2 *(daughtsman)* mrasimu, mchoraji, mwandika hundi. **~ers** chupi (ya zamani). **~ing** *n* 1 uchoraji (picha, ramani, vielelezo n.k.). 2 *(picture)* picha, mchoro, kielelezo, taswira. **out of** ~ liochorwa vibaya. ~

board ubao wa kuchorea (k.v. wa mrasimu). **~room** *n (US)* sebule, ukumbi.

drawl *vt,vi* kokota/kokoteza/vuta maneno (sauti) *n* usemi wa kukokoteza maneno, uvutaji maneno.

dray *n* rikwama: mkokoteni wa magurudumu manne kwa ajili ya kuchukulia mizigo mizito.

dread (*also* **a ~ of**) *stand in ~ of* ogopa sana, hofia *n* woga *vt,vi* ogopa, hofia. **~ed part** *adj* -enye kuhofiwa sana. **~ful** *adj* -a kuogopesha; *(colloq)* -siopendeza *stand in ~ of sb* kuwa katika hofu. **~fully** *adv*. **~fulness** *n*.

dream *n* 1 ndoto, njozi, ruya *I had a ~* niliota. **~-land** ulimwengu wa njozi. 2 usingizi. **go about in a ~** (*colloq*) tembea kama unaota, tangatanga ndotoni. 3 *(colloq)* mtu mzuri anayevutia. **sweet ~s**! lala unono, **~like** *adj* kama ndoto. *vt,vi* 1 ~ **(about/of)** ota ndoto. 2 waza, -wa na taswira. ~ **away** poteza wakati. 4 ~ **up** *(colloq)* fikiria, buni (mpango). **~er** *n*. **~y** *adj* 1 -a kama ndoto, -enye kuota ndoto, -enye kusinzia *~ eyes* macho ya kusinzia *a ~ person* mtu afanyaye mambo kama kwamba anasinzia; awazaye sana mambo yasiyoweza kuwa. 2 *(of things, experiences)* -sio dhahiri; -sio ya kweli; *(colloq)* -a kupendeza; -a kutuliza, -a kufariji. **~ily** *adv*.

dreary/drear *adj* 1 -a kuchosha. 2 -a kutia huzuni, -a kufanya moyo mzito. **drearily** *adv*.

dredge[1] *vt* nyunyizia *~ meat with flour* nyunyiza unga juu ya nyama. **~r** *n* chombo cha kunyunyizia unga, sukari n.k; kinyunyizio, mrashi.

dredge[2] *n* kizoa taka (chini ya maji) *vt* ~ **(up)** zoa taka (chini ya maji mtoni n.k.) kwa wavu. 2 vua kwa wavu. **~r** *n* merikebu ya kuvua/kuzoa/kuvuta takataka.

dregs *n* 1 masimbi, mashapo, makapi, machicha. **drink to the last ~** pasipo kusaza. 2 *(fig)* kitu kisichofaa, takataka.

drench *vt* rowesha, mwagia maji *get ~ed (to the skin)* rowana kabisa. **~ing** *n* chepechepe.

dress[1] *vt,vi* 1 visha/vaa nguo. **be ~ed in** vaa *she was ~ed in red* alivaa nguo nyekundu. 2 ~ **up** valia (vizuri/rasmi); vaa nguo za kutokea. 3 visha *~ your children* visha wanao, patia mavazi. 4 tayarisha (kwa matumizi) *to ~ a chicken* kumtayarisha kuku (kwa kupika). 5 tengeneza nywele. ~ **down** *(fig)* karipia, kemea. 6 funga (kidonda). 7 vutia. 8 panga (askari). **~er** *n* 1 meza (kabati) ya jikoni. 2 *(US)* kabati la kujipambia. 3 muuguzi msaidizi anayesaidia kufunga vidonda. 4 mtu anayewasaidia waigizaji kuvalia rasmi kabla ya mchezo kuanza. *n* nguo, mavazi. **evening ~** vazi la jioni. **morning ~** vazi la asubuhi. ~ **coat** koti jeusi wavaalo wanaume jioni. ~ **rehearsal** zoezi la mwisho (la mchezo/tamthiliya ngoma) ambapo wahusika wanavaa mavazi yao ya mchezo. **full ~** mavazi rasmi. **~maker** mshonaji magauni. **~ing** *n* 1 uvaaji. 2 *(med.)* kufunga vidonda; bendeji ya vidonda. 3 masala; chatne, siki. 4 dondo/wanga. 5 *(manure)* mbolea, samadi. **~-case** *n* kishubaka cha kuwekea vyombo vya safari. **~-gown** *n* vazi livaliwalo wakati mtu anapopumzika. ~ **-room** *n* chumba cha kuvalia nguo. **~-table** *n* meza ya kujipambia. **~y** *adj (colloq of persons)* -enye mavazi mazuri, maridadi, mtanashati.

drew *pt. of* **draw**.

dribble *vi* 1 tiririka, dondoka. 2 toa kidogo kidogo udenda/uderere/mate; *(football)* chenga, piga chenga. **~r** *n*.

driblet *n* tone linaloanguka; kiasi kidogo *by ~s* kidogo kidogo.

dribs and drabs *(colloq)* kiasi kidogo.

dried *pt, pp* **dry**.

drift[1] *n* 1 mkondo (k.m. wa maji); mwelekeo wa mkondo; mvuto wa meli (chombo nje ya uelekeo wake kwa mkondo). 2 *(heap)* lundo, chungu (ya majani, mchanga n.k.) iliyofanywa kwa upepo/bahari n.k. 3 maana, mwelekeo *I see his* ~ naelewa maana yake. 4 hali ya kwenda bila malengo wala mwelekeo. 5 mwelekeo (usio na mpango) *the ~ is towards war* tunaelekea kwenye vita *n* 1 kwenda pepe. 2 mvuto, mwelekeo. 3 vitu vilivyopwelewa. **~-anchor** *n* nanga ya pepe. **~-ice** *n* mabonge ya barafu yanayochukuliwa na mkondo. **~-net** *n* jarife (la kusambaza). **~-sand** *n* mchanga unaopeperushwa. **~-wood** *n* mbao zilizopwelewa *vt* 1 chukuliwa. 2 tangatanga hapa na pale, zurura. 3 -enda pepe/kombo/mrama; fuata upepo. **~er** *n* mzururaji; boti ya kuvulia.

drill[1] *n* keekee *vt, vi* toboa shimo kwa keekee.

drill[2] *n* 1 mafunzo ya wanajeshi juu ya matumizi ya silaha; kwata. 2 mafunzo kamili yenye mazoezi mengi ya kurudiarudia. 3 taratibu (k.m wakati wa dharura).

drill[3] *n* mfuo (wa kupandia mbegu) *vt* panda mbegu katika mfuo.

drill[4] *n* dreli (aina ya kitambaa kigumu).

drink[1] *vt,vi* 1 -nywa. 2 ~ **down/off/ up** -nywa yote. 3 ~ **in/up** pokea (sikia/ ona) kwa furaha; pokea akilini; *(of plants)* nywa. 4 kunywa sana. 5 ~ **(to)** takia heri, kwa afya ya.

drink[2] *n* kinywaji, kileo *soft~* kinywaji baridi. 2 ulevi, kileo, pombe *strong~* pombe kali *have a ~* kunywa (kinywaji). **be in ~/the worse for ~/ under the influence of ~** wa katika hali ya kulewa. **take to ~** ingia ulevini. 3 *(colloq)* **the ~** bahari; ziwa, mto. **~able** *adj* -a kunyweka; *~ (pl)*. **~ables** vileo. **~er** *n* mnywaji; mlevi. **~ing** *n* unywaji. **~i-bout** *n* mfululizo wa kulewa. **~-fountain** *n* mashine inayorusha maji ya kunywa. **~water** maji ya kunywa.

drip *vt,vi* 1 dondoka, tona; dondosha, tonesha. **~ping-wet** iliyorowa chepechepe. **~dry** *(of fabric) adj* inayokauka haraka bila kukamuliwa *vt* 1 anika bila kukamua. 2 nyonyota *n* 1 tone, ndondondo, kutona. 2 *(sl)* (mtu) asiyevutia watu. **~ping** *n (of meat)* mafuta ya nyama iliyobanikwa. ~ **pan** *n* sinia la kukusanyia matone.

drive[1] *vt* 1 swaga. ~ **sb into the corner** *(fig)* weka mtu katika hali ngumu, bana sana. 2 endesha (motokaa, garimoshi n.k.). **driving licence** liseni ya kuendeshea gari. **driving school** shule ya udereva. **driving test** mtihani wa udereva. **driving lessons** mafunzo ya udereva. 3 chukua/peleka kwa gari *~ a friend to town* mchukue rafiki mjini (kwa gari). 4 enda/tembea kwa gari. ~ **in** *n (and attrib.)* mgahawa, sinema n.k. ambako watu huingia na magari yao. 5 *(usu passive)* endesha. **driving belt** ukanda wa kuendeshea. 6 *(of wind, water)* peleka/tupa/ sukuma. 7 *(of rain, ship)* enda upesi au kwa nguvu/ kwa kasi. 8 ~ **in; ~into** pigilia, kongomea. 9 piga kwa nguvu. ~ **home** *(fig)* elewesha barabara. **let ~ at** piga, rushia kombora, lenga. 10 sababisha; fanya (kitu kitokee), lazimisha. 11 sulubisha, fanya/ fanyisha kazi sana. ~ **away at (one's work)** fanyia kazi sana. 12 fukua; toboa (kwa nguvu) (shimo, tundu). 13 endesha shughuli (agh. biashara). ~ **a hard bargain** -wa mkali kwenye biashara, -wa mgumu. 14 ~ **at** -wa na maana ya; maanisha; kusudia. 15 ahirisha. 16 ~ **off** fukuza, rudisha nyuma *n* 1 *(in US also* ~ **way)** njia ya binafsi ya kwenda nyumbani. 2 matembezi kwenye gari ya binafsi *to take for a ~* kutembeza ndani ya gari (ya binafsi). 3 nguvu ya kupiga/ kurusha mpira; mpigo. 4 bidii, nguvu, wepesi; uwezo wa kuendesha mambo, msukumo. 5 kampeni. 6 mashindano. 7 *(mech)* chombo cha kuendeshea. **right hand ~** kuendeshea kulia. **four wheel ~** endesha kwa magurudumu manne. **~r**

n 1 dereva *be a good (bad) ~r* kuwa dereva hodari (asiyefaa). 2 msimamizi (wa gari, farasi, watumwa). **in the ~r's seat** kwenye uongozi; *(mech)* kiendesha mitambo. 4 *(golf)* rungu ya kupigia mpira mbali, kingoe. **driving** *adj* -enye nguvu/uwezo.

drive[2] *vi* payuka, payapaya, bwabwaja *n* upuuzi, mapayo, mapiswa. **~ler;** *(US)* **~er** mpayukaji.

drizzle *n* manyunyu, mvua ya rasharasha *vi* nyunya, nyonyota. **drizzly** *adj*.

drogue *n* 1 *(naut)* nanga ya majini. 2 dango (kilengwa shabaha) (katika mazoezi ya ndege za vita). 3 **~ parachute** parachuti ndogo itumikayo kuitia kubwa kwenye mfuko wake.

droll *adj* -a kuchekesha *n* mchekeshaji. **~ery** *n* kichekesho, shere ya kufurahisha, uchekeshaji.

dromedary *n* ngamia (mwenye nundu moja).

drone *n* 1 nyuki dume. 2 mvivu; *(colloq)* kupe. 3 mvumo. 4 msemaji hotuba isiyosisimua *vt,vi* 1 vuma. 2 ongea bila kusisimua/kuchangamka. 3 **~ on** endelea kuchosha *the meeting ~ on for hours* mkutano uliendelea kwa saa nyingi.

droop *vt,vi* 1 inama, inamisha, fifia (kwa uchovu). 2 huzunika, nyong'onyea *n* kuinama. **~ingly** *adv*.

drop[1] *n* 1 tone **have a ~** kunywa pombe. **in ~s** kidogo kidogo. 2 pombe (kidogo). **take a ~ too much** lewa. 3 kiasi kidogo. **only a ~ in the ocean** kiasi kidogo sana. 4 *(med)* dawa ya matone. 5 *(decrease)* kipunguo *~ in price* kipunguo cha bei. 6 kitu kiangukacho/kiteremshwacho. **~ curtain** pazia zinazoteremshwa katika mchezo **at the ~ of a hat** mara moja. 7 peremende (ya mviringo).

drop *vt, vi* 1 anguka, ponyoka, poromoka; poromosha. **~ out of sb's hands** angusha; ponyoka. **~ into a habit** zoea, ingia katika tabia. **~ anchor** shusha nanga. 2 tona, dondosha, dondoka. 3 koma, isha, malizika *the matter ~ed* jambo hilo likamalizika. 4 *(utter)* toa (neno); ambia. 5 acha, achia, toa. **~ a hint** dokeza *~ a line* andika barua fupi. 6 *(of leaves)* pukutika. 7 pungua, punguka; tulia ghafula. 8 *(with adv. particles & preps) (in car)* teremsha *~ me at the office* niache/nidondoshe ofisini. **~ away** ondoka, pungua toweka. **~ back** rudi, baki nyuma. **~ behind** chelewa, fuata nyuma (kwa kuwa huwezi kumudu mwendo). **~ down** anguka, zuru. **~ off** pungua; acha, teremsha, sinzia. **~ on sb** angukia mtu fulani. **~ into** tumbukia. **~ out of** acha kushiriki, jitoa, kana. **~ out** *n* mtu anayejitoa/anayeacha kushiriki. 9 *(colloq.)* poteza fedha (katika kamari n.k). **~ a brick** fanya kosa, sema kwa makosa. **~ dead** *(sl)* potea, ambaa, ondoka. **~ sth like a hot potato** acha mara moja (kwa sababu ya matatizo/unyeti). **~let** *n* kitone.

dropsy *n* jongo.

dross *n* 1 mavi (ya chuma, ya madini). dongo la chuma. 2 *(fig)* takataka, kisichofaa; kilichochanganywa na kitu kingine (hivyo kufanya kisifae). **~y** *adj*.

drought *n* 1 ukame, ukavu.

drove[1] *pt of* **drive**.

drove[2] 1 kundi (la ng'ombe, kondoo n.k.) linaloswagwa. 2 umati, halaiki. 3 juba; patasi (ya mwashi). **~r** *n* mchuuza ng'ombe; mswaga mifugo mnadani/gulioni.

drown *vt,vi* 1 zama majini, -fa maji; zamisha majini, fisha maji. 2 **~ (out)** *(of sound)* hanikiza. 3 *(fig) a face ~ in tears* uso uliorowana machozi; *~ in sleep* -wa katika usingizi mzito (hasa kutokana na uchovu; lala fofofo *to ~ one's sorrows in drink* kufifilisha huzuni kwa kunywa pombe, kusahau matatizo kwa kulewa.

drowse *vt,vi* **~ (away/off)** sinzia, shikwa na usingizi *n* lepe la usingizi. **drowsy** *adj* -enye kusinzia, -enye lepe, -zito kwa usingizi. **drowsily** *adv.* **drowsiness** *n.*

drub *vt* piga mfululizo (kwa mkono/ fimbo); *(fig)* sisitiza jambo, lazimisha mtu akubali/aseme. **~bing** *n* kipigo *give a good/sound ~* piga mtu barabara; shinda sana.

drudge *vi* ~ **at** fanya kazi ya kuchosha *n* mfanya kazi ya sulubu na yenye kuchosha. **~ry** *n* kazi ngumu.

drug *n* 1 dawa (itumiwayo kwa matibabu). **dangerous ~** dawa za hatari. 2 dawa ya kulevya *trafficking in ~s* upitishaji wa madawa ya kulevya *the ~ habit* tabia ya kutumia madawa ya kulevya. **a ~ on the market** biashara iliyochina, bidhaa zisizonunulika. **~-pedlar** *n* muuza madawa ya kulevya. **~ addict** *n* mlevi wa na madawa *~ dealer/pusher n* mwuza madawa *vt* 1 nywesha dawa (hasa mbaya, sumu, kileo). 2 tia dawa/ghoshi (chakula na vinywaji). **~gist** *n* 1 *(GB)* muuza madawa. 2 *(US)* muuza madawa, vyakula na vinywaji. **~ store** *n (US)* duka la madawa na vinywaji vya kulevya (bangi, marijuani, mirungi).

drugget *n* zulia la sufu.

drum *n* 1 ngoma. **~fire** mfululizo wa milio/milipuko ya mizinga vitani. **~head court-martial** mahakama ya kijeshi wakati wa mapambano. **~ major** kiongozi wa bendi ya jeshi. **~ stick** mkwiro; *(fig)* mguu wa kuku/ bata. 2 pipa. *vt,vi* 1 piga ngoma, lia/liza/ ngoma. 2 ~ **(on)** lizaliza sauti kama za ngoma k.m. kugongagonga meza, chezeshachezesha miguu sakafuni. 3 ~ **up** ita kwa ngoma, piga chando; *(fig)* fanya kampeni. 4 ~ **into** sisitizia mtu jambo. 5 ~ **out** fukuza; tuma (ujumbe) kwa ngoma. **~mer** *n* mpiga ngoma; *(colloq) (US)* mfanyabiashara msafiri.

drunk *pp of* **drink** *adj* -liolewa **get ~** lewa. **~ with sth** *(fig)* jawa na *~ with joy* jawa na furaha *n* mlevi. **~ard** *n* mlevi. **~en** *adj* 1 -a kulewa; levi, -a ulevi. 2 -a kusababishwa na ulevi, -enye kuonyesha ulevi/kulewa. **~enness** *n.* **~enly** *adv.*

drupe *n (bot)* tunda lenye nyama yenye majimaji na kokwa katikati k.m. tunda damu, embe.

dry *adj* 1 -kavu. **~ as a bone/bone ~** kavu kabisa *~maize* mahindi makavu. 2 *(waterless)* kame. 3 -liokauka *a ~ well* kisima kilichokauka. 4 *(of wine)* -chungu, -siyo tamu. 5 *(colloq)* -enye kuleta kiu. 6 -siosisimua, -a kuchosha. **~ as dust** isiyosisimua, isiyovutia. 7 -sioonyesha hisia. 8 waziwazi, dhahiri *~ facts* ukweli dhahiri. *(compounds)* **~ battery; ~ cell** betri. **~ clean** safisha kwa mvuke au petroli. **~ cleaner** *n* dobi. **~ cleaning** *n* kusafisha kwa dawa. **~ eyed** macho makavu. **~ dock** gudani. **~ goods** bidhaa kavu. **~ nurse** yaya. **~ rot** uozo unaofanyika bila unyevu (hasa wa mbao/miti mikavu); *(fig)* upotovu wa jamii usio dhahiri. **~shod** *adj, adv* bila kulowanisha miguu, miguu au viatu vikavu. **~ walling** kujenga ukuta wa mawe. **drily** *adv.* **~ out** *vt,vi* kauka; kausha; anika; *(of hands)* futa; acha ulevi. **~ off** kausha. **~ up** kauka, sahau kiini cha usemi; *(fig)* **~ up!** nyamaza! kaa kimya! **~ness** *n.* **~ing** *adj.* **~ly** *adv.*

dual *adj* -a mbili, -enye mbili *~ control* udhibiti wa watu wawili *~ ownership* umilikaji wa watu wawili *~ purpose* -enye matumizi mawili (k.m. gari kwa mizigo na abiria) *~ economy* uwekevu. **~ity** *n.*

dub *vt* 1 -pa cheo cha uungwana. 2 -pa jina la utani. 3 paka ngozi mafuta (ili ilainike). 4 *(of film)* weka/badili sauti nyingine (hasa ya lugha nyingine). 5 nakili. **~bin** *n* mafuta mazito ya kulainishia ngozi.

dubious *adj* 1 ~ **(of/about)** *(of persons)* -a wasiwasi na, -enye mashaka. 2 *(of persons)* -a kutia wasiwasi, -sioaminika, -a kutia mashaka. 3 *(of things/actions etc.)* -iletayo wasiwasi, -sioaminika. **~ly** *adv.* **~ness** *n.* **dubitative** *adj* -enye shaka, -enye kusitasita, -a wasiwasi. **dubiety** *n* shaka.

duchess *n* mke (au mjane) wa mwana mfalme.

duck[1] *n* 1 bata, salili; *(white backed)* kotwe. **a lame ~** mlemavu, kitu kisicho na faida; shirika lenye matatizo kifedha. **play ~s and drakes with** ponda mali, -wa mwepesi kuzoea jambo fulani. **take to it like a ~ to water** jifunza, zoea bila matatizo. **like water off ~'s back** bila kuleta matokeo yoyote, bila ya hofu, -sio na athari. **~s and drakes** mchezo wa kurusha mawe majini. **~ling** *n* mtoto wa bata. **an ugly ~** mtoto mzito (kiakili) ambaye baadaye hubadilika na kuwa na akili sana.

duck[2] *vt,vi* 1 kwepa. 2 zama/zamisha majini kwa muda mfupi *n* kuzama; kuzamisha. 2 kukwepa. **~ing** *n*. **give a ~** sukumiza majini.

duck[3] *n* kitambaa kizito cha pamba (kitani).

duck[4] *n (sl)* kipenzi, muhibu.

duct *n* mchirizi, kichirizi, kifereji minyweleo.

ductile *adj* 1 (*of metal*) -a kufulika uzi. 2 (*of clay, etc*) -a kunyumbuka, -a kufinyangika, -a kunama; -a kinamo ~ *clay* udongo wa kinamo; (*of a person*) -enye kuathiriwa/ kutawaliwa/ kushawishika kwa urahisi. **ductility** *n*.

dud *n adj* 1 (*sl*) (*of thing or person*) -siofaa/sio na faida, bunga, dude.

dude *n* (*US*)(*sl*) mlimbwende, mtanashati. **~ ranch** (*US*) ranchi kwa ajili ya utalii.

dudgeon *n* mfundo. **in high ~** -wa na mfundo mkubwa.

duds *n* tambara, (*sing only*) rapurapu.

due *n* (*sing only*) 1 haki, stahili *give sb his ~* mpe mtu sifa/haki yake hata kama humpendi. **give the devil his ~** (*prov*) uwe adili hata kwa mtu mbaya. 2 (*tax*) (*pl*) kodi, ushuru, ada *adj* 1 -a haki, stahili; (*befitting*) -a kupasa. **with ~ respect** kwa heshima ipasayo, pamoja na kuheshimu. **in ~ time; in ~ course** kwa wakati upasao. 2 ~ (**to**) -a kulipwa *the debt ~ to him will be paid today* deni lake atalipwa leo. 3 (*expected*) -tazamiwa; *the ship is ~ today* meli inatazamiwa kufika leo. 4 **~ to** kwa sababu ya, sababishwa na *it is ~ to the sun* ni kwa sababu ya jua *his death was ~ to an accident* kifo chake kilisababishwa na ajali *adv* moja kwa moja, barabara, sawasawa. **the ship will sail ~ South** meli itasafiri kusini moja kwa moja. **duly** *adv* ipasavyo, kwa wakati wake.

duel *n* 1 *(hist)* mapigano rasmi ya watu wawili mbele ya mashahidi (agh. ya bastola au panga) kwa madhumuni ya kuamulia ugomvi/kutetea hadhi. 2 mapambano kati ya watu wawili wenye uwezo sawa, wenye kutofautiana mawazo/msimamo n.k. **~list**; **~ist** *n* mpambanaji wa shindano la aina hii.

duenna *n* (*esp in a Spanish or Portuguese family*) mwanamke ajuza mtunza wasichana.

duet *n* 1 muziki wa sauti mbili au watu wawili. 2 (*fig*) mazungumzo ya watu wawili.

duffer *n* 1 (*colloq*) bozi, mzito wa akili, zebe.

duffle, duffel *n* kitambaa kigumu cha sufu. **~ coat** koti refu la sufu lenye vifungo vya mbao.

dug[1] *n* 1 kiwele, chuchu.

dug[2] *pt,pp of* **dig**.

dugong *n* nguva.

dug-out *n* 1 mtumbwi. 2 handaki la vita.

duiker *n* (*Abbotts*) mindi; (*common*) funo.

duke *n* 1 mwinyi. 2 mwana mfalme mtaala (huru) wa jimbo. **~dom** *n* *see* **duchy**.

dulcet *adj* (*usu of sounds*) -tamu, -ororo

dulcify *vt* fanya kuwa -tamu na ororo.

dull *adj* 1 (*of colour, sound*) -liofifia. 2 -a mawingu *a ~ day* siku ya mawingu *~ weather* hali ya mawingu. 3 goigoi *a ~ pupil* mtoto goigoi. 4 -a kuchusha, -a kuchosha,

-siopendeza *a ~ play* mchezo usiopendeza/furahisha, *a ~ speech* hotuba ya kuchusha. 5 butu, sio kali *a ~ knife* kisu kibutu *a ~ pain* maumivu hafifu yasiyo makali. 6 (*of trade*) -liolala, -siochangamka, -siotoka, iendayo polepole; (*of goods*) -liododa *vt, vi* 1 fifisha, chujusha. 2 fanya zito/ goigoi. 3 chukiza, chosha akili. 4 poza, tuliza. 5 fanya butu. 6 tia giza, tia utusiutusi. ~ **ness** *n*. **~ard** *n* bozi; mzito wa akili.

dumb *adj* 1 bubu ~ *animal* mnyama bubu. **strike** ~ shitua mtu asiweze kusema, pigwa bumbuazi. ~ **show** mchezo wa kibubu. 2 (*silent*) -a kimya, -a kunyamaa. 3 (*US*) (*colloq*) -pumbavu, bozi ~ *blonde* msichana mrembo mpumbavu. **~ly** *adv*. **~ness** *n* ububu. **~bell** *n* 1 (*of gymnastics*) chuma chenye uzito cha mazoezi ya viungo vya mwili. 2 (*sl*) (*US*) mjinga. **~found/be ~ed** *vt* pigwa na bumbuazi. ~ **waiter** *n* 1 meza yenye rafu zinazozunguka itumikayo kugawia chakula. 2 (*US; in GB food lift*) kasha lenye vyakula lichukuliwalo kwa kambarau kutoka jikoni hadi chumba cha chakula.

dum-dum *n* ~ **bullet** risasi ifanyayo uwazi/uharibifu mkubwa.

dummy *n* 1 mwigo (utumikao badala ya kitu halisi) a *baby's* ~ chuchu bandia, nyonyo. 2 (*attrib*) bandia. **a ~ gun** bunduki (ya) bandia. 3 (*in card games esp. bridge*) mchezaji ambaye karata zake zimewekwa wazi mezani. 4 mchezaji wa akiba. 5 mpumbavu. 6 (*publishing*) mfano wa kitabu. 7 (*attrib*) ~ **run** jaribio/mazoezi (ya kupigana, kulenga shabaha n.k.) *adj* -a kuigiza, -a bandia.

dump *vt,vi* ~ **(down)** 1 tupa, weka ovyoovyo; tupa (takataka) jalalani; anguka ghafula (kwa kishindo). 2 uza kwa bei nafuu katika nchi nyingine bidhaa zisizotakiwa katika soko la nyumbani ~ *goods on the market* jaza bidhaa sokoni *n* 1 jaa la taka, dampo. 2 lundo la taka. 3 ghala (akiba) kubwa (hasa ya zana za vita). 4 (*sl*) genge, sehemu au mahali pachafu k.m. mji au kijiji. ~ **cart, ~er** (~ **truck**) *n* gari la taka, lori la taka, tipa: gari libebalo na kumwaga mchanga, kokoto n.k.

dumpling *n* 1 andazi la kinyunya kilichopikwa kwa mvuke au kuchemshwa lenye nyama au matunda ndani. 2 pudini ya kinyunya iliyookwa yenye matunda ndani.

dumps *n* (*pl*) **(down) in the** ~ -a kujisikia vibaya vibaya, -sio na raha.

dumpy *adj* -fupi na -nene.

dun[1] *adj* kahawia, jivujivu *n* chambobandia.

dun[2] *vt* dai deni/madeni kwa nguvu *n* mdai madeni; mtu anayekusanya malipo ya madeni.

dunce *n* zuzu, mbumbumbu. **~'s cap** kofia ya karatasi (aliyokuwa akivishwa zuzu darasani kama adhabu).

dunderhead *n* mpumbavu. **~ed** *adj*.

dune *n* chungu ya mchanga.

dung *n* 1 mavi/kinyesi cha mnyama (hasa ng'ombe). 2 samadi. ~ **cart** gari la (kubebea) samadi. **~hill** lundo la samadi (shambani).

dungaree *n* 1 kitambaa cha dangirizi. 2 (*pl*) *~s* dangirizi.

dungeon *n* (*hist*) gereza la chini ya ardhi.

dunk *vt* chonya, chovya (mkate, ugali) ndani ya mchuzi, maziwa.

duo *adj* wili *n* jozi, mbili; wanamuziki wawili.

duodunary/duodecimal *adj* -a kumi na mbili; iendeleayo kwa kumi na mbili; kumi na mbili; *(pl)* (*maths*) mfumo wa kumi na mbili.

duodenum *n* (*anat*) duodeni, mbuti.

duologue *n* mazungumzo baina ya watu wawili (hasa katika mchezo).

dupe *vt* danganya. *n* mtu anayedanganywa. **~ry** *n* udanganyifu, ulaghai.

duplex *adj* -a mara mbili, -a mara dufu *n* (*US*) nyumba yenye kuishi familia mbili; nyumba yenye ghorofa mbili.

duplicate *adj* -a nakili, -a maradufu. ~ **key** ufunguo wa nakili/ziada *n* nakala, kifani *made in* ~ imerudufiwa *vt* 1 nakili. 2 rudufu, andika/fanya -ingine. 3 (*increase*) zidisha kwa mbili. **duplicator** mashine ya kurudufia. **duplication** *n*.

duplicity *n* 1 unafiki. 2 undumakuwili.

durable *adj* -a kudumu sana, -a aushi *n* (*usu pl*) vifaa vinavyodumu k.v. friji. **durability** *n*.

durance *n* 1 kifungo. **in** ~ (*old use*) kifungoni.

duration *n* muda, kitambo *for the* ~ *of the war* kwa muda wote wa vita.

duress *n* vitisho (k.m. vya kufungwa au kupigwa).

during *prep* wakati (wa), muda wote kwa kipindi cha.

dusk *n* magharibi, utusitusi. **~y** *adj* -enye rangi nyeusi, -a utusitusi. **~iness** *n*.

dust[1] *n* 1 vumbi; tifutifu. **bite the** ~ uawa, jeruhiwa; shindwa kabisa. **(humbled) in (to) the** ~ nyanyaswa, dhalilishwa. **shake the** ~ **off one's feet** ondoka kwa ghadhabu au dharau. **throw** ~ **in a person's eyes** laghai, danganya mtu. ~ **bowl** jangwa (lililotokana na kulima ovyo). **~-coat** *n* vazi la kuzuia vumbi. ~ **jacket** *n* ganda (la kitabu) la vumbi *also* **~-cover**. **~pan** *n* kibeleshi (cha kuzolea vumbi/taka). ~ **sheet** *n* shuka la kuzuia vumbi (la samani zisizotumika). **~storm** *n* dhoruba ya vumbi. **~-wrapper** *n* see **~-jacket**. 2 **a** ~ kiwingu cha vumbi. **what a** ~ (*fig*) vurumai. **kick up/ make/raise a** ~ (*sl, fig*) fanya fujo/ghasia. 3 (*in compounds*) **~bin** pipa la taka. 4 *pl* mabaki ya mwili wa binadamu. **~-cart** *n* gari la (kuchukulia) taka. **~man** *n* mwondoa/mzoa taka (katika mapipa).

dust[2] *vt* 1 ~ **sth (down/off)** pangusa, futa meza n.k; kung'uta (nguo). 2 nyunyizia kitu kama unga (vumbi, sukari; mchanga, dawa ya unga n.k.). **~er** *n* kifutio, dasta, kitambaa cha kufutia vumbi. (*fig*) ~ **a person's jacket** piga mtu. **~-up** (*colloq*) mapigano, mzozo. **~y** *adj* 1 -enye mavumbi; -a kama vumbi. 2 -siovutia. 3 (*colloq*) **it's not so** ~ siyo vibaya.

dust[3] *n* debe/pipa la taka.

Dutch *adj* -a Kiholanzi; -enye kutoka Uholanzi. ~ **auction** mnada wa kushusha bei. ~ **courage** ujasiri wa kilevi. **~oven** jiko la bati la kuweka mbele ya moto. ~ **treat** karamu ya kujilipia. **go** ~ **(with sb)** gawana matumizi, changizana. **talk like a** ~ **uncle** asa *n pl* 1 **the** ~ Waholanzi. 2 (lugha ya) Kiholanzi; (*colloq*) **double** ~ Kichina; lugha isiyoeleweka.

duty *n* 1 wajibu *it is my* ~ ni wajibu wangu. 2 kuwajibika. ~ **call** ziara ya wajibu. 3 zamu. **on** ~ kuwa kwenye zamu. **off** ~ kuwa mapumzikoni. **(as) in** ~ **bound** kama (ilivyo) ada. **do** ~ **for** shikia zamu, tumika badala ya. 4 ~ **(on)** ushuru; kodi. **~free** *adj* -siolipiwa ushuru. **dutiful** *adj*. ~ **(to)** tiifu, -sikivu; -a kufanya wajibu (ipasavyo). **dutifully** *adv*.

duvet *n* mfarishi.

dwarf *n* kibete, kibushuti. **~ish** *adj* -liovia, -liodumaa *adj* -dogo; -fupi (kuliko -a kawaida) *vt* 1 fanya kuonekana kama kwamba ni -dogo (kwa kupambanua, kwa kulinganisha). 2 (*hinder growth*) kundaalisha, dumaza.

dwell *vi* 1 ~ **in/at** kaa, ishi. ~ **on/upon** fikiri sana, eleza sana, andika sana; (*music*) ~ *on a note* refusha noti. 3 (*of a horse*) simama (kabla ya kuruka). 4 (*tech*) simama (mtambo wa mashine n.k.). **~er** *n* mkazi. **~ing house** nyumba ya kukaa. **~ing-place** *n* makazi.

dwelt *pt of* **dwell**.

dwindle *vi* (*also* ~ **away**) pungua, fifia.

dyarchy *see* **diarchy**.

dye *vt,vi* 1 tia rangi. ~ **in the wool/ grain** tia rangi (nguo n.k.) ikiwa ingali ghafi (ili ikolee). **~d in the**

wool *adj* (*fig*) kabisa, kamili. 2 remba, tia rangirangi/nakshi. 3 chukua rangi, kolea, pata rangi *n* 1 rangi, (za nguo). **fast** ~ rangi isiyochujuka. 2 kubuhu, makuruhu. **a scoundrel of the deepest** ~ mhalifu mkubwa mno. **~r** *n* mtiaji rangi nguo, mtia rangi. **~stuff** *n* dawa ya rangi. **~-wood** *n* mtirangi (unatoa rangi). **~-works** *n* kiwanda cha kutia rangi.

dying *pre cont. of* **die**.

dyke *see* **dike**.

dynamic *adj* -a elimumwendo; (*of person*) -enye nguvu. **~al** *adj*. **~ally** *adv*. **dynamism** *n* 1 nguvu. 2 (*pl*) uwezo wa mtu/kitu. **~s** *n* elimumwendo.

dynamite baruti kali *vt* lipua kwa baruti.

dynamo *n* dainamo: chombo cha kuzalisha umeme mfululizo. **~meter** *n* kipimanguvu.

dynast *n* mtawala wa kinasaba, Lodi. **~y** *n* nasaba (jamaa, jadi, ukoo) ya mfalme.

dyne *n* daini: kizibo cha kani (katika mfumo meta).

dys (*pref*) -baya, -a shida **~raphia** -sioweza kuandika vizuri. **~menorrhoea** maumivu makali ya hedhi.

dysentery *n* ugonjwa wa kuhara damu. **dysenteric** *adj*.

dyslexial *n* kutoweza kusoma vizuri.

dyspepsia *n* 1 kutomeng'enya chakula (tumboni). 2 (*heartburn, eructation*) kiungulia. **dyspeptic** *adj & n*.

dysuria *n* (*med*) kukojoa kwa maumivu.

E

E,e *n* herufi e; herufi ya tano ya alfabeti ya Kiingereza.

each *adj* 1 kila moja ~ *person* kila mtu. 2 (*pron*) 1 kila (mtu, kitu, jambo, n.k.). 2 (*used in apposition*) -ote, pamoja *we ~ helped the minister* sote tulimsaidia waziri. 3 (*used adverbially*) kila moja/ kipande *~of the members* kila mwanachama. 4 (*as reciprocal object*) **~ other** wao kwa wao, sisi kwa sisi/nyinyi kwa nyinyi *they help ~ other* wanasaidiana *they see ~ other* wanaonana.

eager *adj* ~ **(for sth/to do sth)** -enye hamu/shauku/moyo *be ~ to leave* -wa na hamu ya kuondoka. **~ beaver** (*colloq*) mchangamkia kazi. **~ly** *adv*. **~ness** *n*.

eagle *n* 1 tai. **~ eyed** -enye macho makali. **~t** *n* kinda la tai.

ear[1] *n* 1 sikio. **be all ~s** sikiliza kwa makini/shauku. **fall on deaf ~s** tosikilizwa, pita kienyeji. **feel one's ~s burning** hisi/ona mtu anakuteta. **give one's ~s (for sth/to do)** jitoa mhanga, fanya liwezekanalo. **go in (at) one ~ and out (at) the other** haisikilizwi, haitiwi maanani. **have an ~ to the ground** tahadhari, kaa macho. **(have) a word in sb's ~** nong'oneza, -pa siri. **have/ win sb's ~** sikilizwa, pokelewa vyema. **over head and ~s** sana *over head and ~ in debt* daiwa kope (si zako), lemewa madeni. **pick up one's ~** sikiliza/ shughulika mara, tega sikio. **turn a deaf ~ (to)** kataa kusaidia. **up to the one's ~s in (work, etc)** shughulika sana, lemewa sana. **be wet behind the ~s** -wa mshamba. **out on one's ~** fukuzwa kazi, timuliwa. **~ache** *n* maumivu ya sikio. **~drop** *n* 1 dawa ya sikio (ya kutiririsha ndani). **~drum** *n* kiwambo cha sikio. 2 herini, ' kipuli. **~ful** karamu ya maneno; karipio. **~ lobe** *n* ndewe. ~ mark (*of cattle*) alama; kipuli; *(fig)* tabia, mwenendo, kawaida maalumu inayotambulisha *vt* 1 tia, wekea alama. 3 (*set aside*) tenga kwa ajili ya. **~piece** *(see ~ phone)*. **~phone** *n* chombo cha kusikilizia. **~-place** *n* sehemu ya kofia inayofunika masikio. **~-log** *n* kiziba sikio (cha kujikinga na kelele au maji). **~-ring** *n* hereni. **~shot** *n* umbali wa kuweza kusikia sauti. **~trumpet** *n* kineli kama tarumbeta kisaidiacho watu wasiosikia vizuri. **~ wax** *n* nta/taka za masikio. 4 uwezo wa kusikia. 5 kitu chenye umbo la sikio (k.m. mkono wa birika, bilauri, n.k.). **~ed** -a masikio. **long-~ed** -enye masikio marefu.

ear[2] (*of corn, etc*) *n* shuke.

earl *n* cheo cha mtu mashuhuri wa Uingereza. **~dom** *n* cheo cha mtu mashuhuri wa heshima wa Uingereza.

early *adj,adv* 1 mapema. **bright and ~** asubuhi na mapema ~ *in life* katika ujana, siku za ujana *an ~ riser* mraukaji ~ *fruit* matunda ya mlimbuko (*to*) *keep ~ hours* wahi kulala na kuamka *at the earliest possible moment* mapema iwezekanavyo *eat an ~-dinner* -la chakula cha jioni mapema. 2 *(ancient)* -a kale, -a zamani. 3 (*near the beginning*) mwanzo, mwanzoni ~ *in the year* mwanzoni mwa mwaka. **The ~ bird gets/catches the worm** (*prov*) aamkaye mapema huvuna neema. **~days (yet)** mapema mno (kusema, kujua). **earlier on** mwanzoni. **~warning** *adj* -a (kuashiria) mapema.

earn *vt* 1 chuma, pata (kwa kazi). 2 (*deserve*) stahili. **~ing** *n* (*pl*) **~ings** mapato *~ing capacity* uwezo wa kuchuma. **~ings yield** (*comm*) urari kati ya faida ya mwaka na mtaji.

earnest[1] *adj* -enye ari, -enye bidii, -a moyo *n* **in ~** kwa bidii, kwa moyo *do/say in ~* fanya/sema kwa dhati.

~**ly** *adv*. ~**ness** *n*.

earnest[2] *n* arbuni.

earth *n* 1 **the** ~ dunia; ulimwengu; ardhi. **come down/back to** ~ ondoka ruuyani/ndotoni. 2 uso wa dunia (*to*) *drop to* ~ tua ardhini; (*dry land as opposed to sea*) nchi kavu. **move heavens and** ~ (to do sth) fanya juu chini kupata jambo. **how/why/ where/who, etc on** ~ vipi tena/ mbona/wapi sasa/nani tena. 3 (*soil*) udongo. ~ **closet** choo, lindi. ~ **nut** karanga. ~ **work** *n* boma la udongo. ~ **worm** *n* nyungunyungu. 4 (*animal's hole or lair*) pango, shimo (la mnyama). **run/go to** ~ (*of a fox*) kimbilia shimoni. **run sth/sb to** ~ (*fig*) saka, gundua baada ya kutafuta sana. 5 (*electr*) waya au njia ya kugusia kukamilisha mzunguko wa umeme *vt* 1 ~**up** funika kwa udongo, fukia. 2 (*electr*) tia waya wa umeme ardhini. 3 (*of fox*) jificha pangoni. ~**born** *adj* -liozuka ardhini; -liozaliwa duniani, -a binadamu. ~**bound** *adj* (*fig*) -enye mwanzo wa kilimwengu, -enye kuelekea duniani; -sioweza kuacha dunia; -sio bunifu. ~**en** *adj* -a udongo, -liofinyangwa. ~**enware** *n* vyombo (vitu) vya udongo. ~**ly** *adj* -a dunia hii. 2 (*colloq*) -a kuwezekana; -enye kufikirika. **no** ~ **use** (*colloq*) haifai hata kidogo *there is no* ~ *chance* (*sl*) hakuna uwezekano. ~**quake** *n* zilizala: tetemeko la ardhi. ~ **shine** *n* mwako wa dunia: mwangaza unaotoka duniani na kuonekana kwenye sehemu ya kiza ya mwezi. ~**y** *adj* 1 -a udongo. 2 (*fig*) fidhuli.

ease *n* raha, utulivu, amani. **at** ~ starehe, poa, tuli; kwa utulivu/ starehe; (*after pain*) faraja. **be ill at** ~ taharaki, tahayari. **be/feel at** ~ tabaraki, tabaradi. **put at** ~ starehesha, poza, tuliza. **stand at** ~ (*as a mil command*) mguu upande. **take one's** ~ tulia, acha kufanya kazi. **with** ~ bila kuhangaika *vt,vi* 1 ~ **(of)** fariji; (*of pain*) tuliza, punguza maumivu; (*make easy*) rahisisha ~ *oneself* enda chooni ~ *down* punguza mwendo, legeza mwendo; (*make loose*) legeza. ~ **off/up** punguza hali ya wasiwasi; tulia; punguza makali. ~**fully** *adv*. ~**fulness** *n*.

easy *adj* 1 rahisi, epesi *people who are* ~ *to get on with* watu ambao ni rahisi kuelewana nao ~ *victim* mtu ambaye ni rahisi kudanganyika. 2 (*quite, comfortable*) -a raha, tulivu, radhi, siyo na taabu *an* ~ *chair* kiti cha raha *an* ~ *life* maisha yasiyo na taabu ~ *money* pesa ipatikanayo bila jasho *on* ~ *terms* -a kulipia kidogokidogo *by* ~ *stages* (*of journey*) kwa awamu ndogondogo *within* ~ *reach* -a kufikika kwa urahisi; karibu *woman of* ~ *virtue* mwanamke mtembezi *I'm* ~ (*colloq*) sina ubishi, sina neno *adv* kwa urahisi ~ *come* ~ *go* kinachopatikana kwa urahisi hupotea kwa urahisi *go* ~ punguza kazi/kasi. **go** ~ **on with** -wa mwangalifu *take it/things* ~ -tofanya kazi kwa bidii sana, -tojisumbua. **easier said than done** kusema ni rahisi kuliko kutenda. **stand** ~ (*mil*) legeza mwili. **easily** *adv* 1 kwa urahisi. 2 bila shaka, kwa mbali sana *he is easily the best singer* yeye ni mwimbaji bora kwa mbali sana. **easiness** *n*. **easygoing** *adj* 1 (*of persons*) pole, si gumu, si kali; radhi. 2 (*careless*) zembe, vivu, -siojali.

easel *n* kiegemeza picha/sanamu, kiegemeza ubao (wa kuandikia).

easement *n* (*leg*) haki ya njia katika ardhi (ya mtu mwingine).

east *n* **the** ~ mashariki, matlai. **the F ar** ~ Mashariki ya Mbali. **the Middle** ~ Mashariki ya Kati *adj* -a mashariki. ~ **End** mtaa wa mashariki ya London wenye magati (maskani ya wakukni) *adv* mashariki. ~**ward**/~**bound** *adj* kuelekea mashariki ~ *wind* pepo za matlai. ~**erly** *adj* -a mashariki. ~ **winds** pepo za matlai. ~**ern** *adj* -a mashariki (nchi, jimbo, wilaya, tarafa, kata, mji, n.k.). ~**erner** *n* mtu wa mashariki. ~**ernmost** *adj* -a mashariki kabisa.

Easter *n* Pasaka. ~ **egg** yai lililopakwa rangi; yai lililotengenezwa kwa chokuleti (kwa ajili ya Pasaka).

eat *vt,vi* 1 ~ **(up)** -la. ~ **it's head off** (*a horse*) kula mno, gharimu zaidi kumlisha kuliko thamani yake. ~ **one's heart out** umia kimoyomoyo. ~ **one's words** futa usemi; omba radhi. ~ **out of sb's hand** mtii sana, mkubalia sana ~ *sb out of house and home* kula sana kwa gharama ya mwingine; (*destroy*) -la na haribu, mong'onyoa *be ~en up with (jealousy, etc.)* jaa (wivu, n.k.). 2 ~ **into** tumia/maliza sehemu. ~**ing house/place** mkahawa, hoteli. ~**ing apple** tufaha linaloliwa bila kupikwa. ~**s** *n* (*sl*) chakula, maakuli. ~**able** *adj* -a kulika. ~**ables** *n* vyakula.

eaves *n* (*pl*) pembe la paa linaloning'inia, upenu, mchirizi, mdoya.

eavesdrop *vi* sikiliza kwa siri mazungumzo ya watu. ~**per** *n* dukizi.

ebb *vi* 1 (*of tide*) pwa. 2 (*fig*) (*lessen*) pungua, fifia; dhoofika *n* 1 maji kupwa/mafu *the tide is on the ~* maji yamekupwa. 2 (*fig*) hali duni, kudhoofika; kupungua *be at a low ~* kuwa katika hali duni. ~**-tide** *n* kupwa.

ebony *n* (*poet*) 1 mpingo. 2 (*of colour*) *adj* -a mpingo; -eusi kabisa *the ~ keys of a piano* vipande/funguo nyeusi za kinanda.

ebullient *adj* 1 -enye kububujika. 2 -enye kujaa furaha. **ebullience** *n* mchemko.

eccentric *adj* 1 (*of person*) -a pekee, si -a kawaida. 2 (*of circles*) sio duara *n* 1 mtu wa kipekee. 2 chombo cha kubadilisha mwendo duara uwe mwendo wa kurudi nyuma na kwenda mbele. ~**ity** *n* 1 upekee wa tabia, tabia ya kipekee. 2 kitendo au tabia ya ajabu, isiyo ya kawaida.

ecclesiastic *n* kasisi, padri *adj* -a padri, -a dini. ~**al** *adj* -a kanisa la Kikristo, -a padri. ~ **history** historia ya kanisa. ~**lly** *adv*.

echelon *n* 1 mpango (wa ngazi unaotumika na vikundi vya askari jeshi), ndege za vita, manowari, n.k. 2 (*often pl with sing meaning*) ngazi. **the upper ~s of the government** ngazi za juu za serikali.

echo *n* 1 mwangwi. ~ **chamber** mahala pa mwangwi. ~ **sounding** -pimaji masafa kwa mwangwi. ~ **sounder** kipima kina/masafa. 2 (*likeness*) kifano; mtu anayefanana na mwingine *vi,vt* ~ **sth (back)** 1 (*of places*) rudisha mwangwi. 2 -wa mwangwi wa. 3 rudia maneno, n.k. ya wengine.

eclat *n* mafanikio ya kusifika, mafanikio ya wazi; sifa kutoka kwa watu wote.

eclectic *adj* (*of persons, methods, etc*) -siofuata mfumo/msimamo mmoja (wa mawazo, nadharia, n.k.). ~**ism** *n*.

eclipse *n* 1 kupatwa mwezi au jua. 2 (*fig*) kupoteza nguvu/umaarufu, n.k.*vt* 1 (*of the moon, a planet, etc*) patwa; zuia mwanga. 2 (*fig*) zima; pita kwa mbali sana, fanya wengine waonekane hawana kitu. 3 (*of feelings*) maliza. ~ **ecliptic** *n* njia ya jua.

eclogue *n* shairi fupi (juu ya maisha mazuri ya shambani).

ecology *n* ikolojia: elimu ya uhusiano wa viumbe na mazingira. **ecological** *adj* ~ *system* (*also* **ecosystem**) mfumo wa ikolojia. **ecologically** *adv*. **ecologist** *n*.

economy *n* 1 uwekevu, iktisadi, ukabidhi. 2 uchumi. **economic** *adj* 1 -a kiuchumi ~ *assistance* msaada wa kiuchumi. 2 -enye kufidia gharama ~ *rent* kodi yenye kufidia gharama.

economics *n pl* uchumi: sayansi ya uzalishaji, usambazaji na utumiaji bidhaa. **economist** *n* 1 mtaalam wa uchumi, mchumi. 2 msarifu. **economical** *adj* wekevu, -enye kupunguza gharama, angalifu katika matumizi; kabidhi; (*cheap*) rahisi.

economize *vt,vi* punguza gharama, sarifu, bana matumizi.

ecstasy *n* 1 upeo wa hisi (hasa furaha) *she was in ~ about her new job* amefurahia mno kazi yake mpya. 2 (*rel*) hali ya roho kuungana na Mungu katika upeo wa kumwombea, n.k.). 3 (*frenzy*) hali ya kurukwa na akili; kurusha akili; kurukwa na akili. **ecstatic** *adj* -liojaa furaha/huzuni. **ecstatically** *adv*.

ecumenical *adj* 1 -a ekumeni *~ Council* (RC) Mtaguso wa kanisa (unaoitwa na Papa). 2 -a kupenda muungano wa madhehebu yote ya Ukristo. **~ism** (*also* **ecumenism**) imani au tapo la kuleta umoja wa wakristo wote. **~ly** *adv*.

eczema *n* ukurutu.

eddy *n* 1 (*of wind, smoke, fog, mist, dust, water etc*) mzunguko, mzingo, mkondo wa maji unaozunguka zunguka. 3 chamchela, kinyamkela *vi* enda kwa kuzungukazunguka; zungukazunguka.

Eden *n* (*Bible*) bustani ya Edeni; (*fig*) mahali pa raha, peponi.

edge[1] *n* 1 (*of a weapon*) machinjioni, makali. **give an ~ to** tia makali, noa. **set one's teeth on ~** tia meno ganzi; (*give offence*) udhi. **on ~** wahaka, -enye kiherehere. **take the ~ off sth** punguza makali; (*fig*) utamu, furaha, maana. **give sb the ~ of one's tongue** karipia vikali. **have the ~ on** zidi (kidogo). 2 (*of a river, rock*) ukingo *the ~ of a cliff* ukingo wa mwamba. 3 (*of a cloth*) upindo. 4 (*of a place*) mpaka *vt* 1 tia makali, noa. 2 (*of a cloth*) tia upindo. 3 (*of a road, etc*) tia ukingo/mpaka. 4 penya; penyeza *he ~d through the crowd* alipenya katikati ya umati wa watu. 5 **~ away** toka/jitoa polepole/kwa hadhari *~ one's way into the room* jipenyeza pole pole chumbani. **~ out** 1 ondosha polepole. 2 shinda/zidi kidogo. **~ways**, **~wise** *adv*. upande, ubavuni *I could not get a word in ~ways* sikuweza kusema hata neno moja. **edging** *n* ukingo; (kwa nguo) upindo *~-shears* mkasi wa majani. **edgy** *adj* -enye wahaka, -enye wasiwasi sana. **edgily** *adv*.

edible *adj* -a kulika *n* (*pl*) vyakula, chakula. **edibility** *n*.

edict *n* amri; sheria.

edifice *n* jumba; (*fig*) ruya, ndoto.

edify *vt* adilisha, rekebisha maadili. **edification** *n* ujenzi wa maadili.

edit *vt* 1 (*book, film, etc.*) hariri. 2 ongoza/simamia kazi ya uhariri. 3 panga data ili ziingizwe kwenye kompyuta. 4 **~ out** ondoa maneno wakati wa kuhariri. **~ion** *n* toleo. **~or** *n* 1 mhariri. **~orial** *adj* -a mhariri *~ staff* wahariri *n* tahariri. **~orship** *n*. **~orialise/ize** *vt* andika tahariri; (*often derog*) changanya mawazo binafsi na mambo ya kweli.

educate *vt* elimisha, funza, fundisha, somesha *an ~d person* (*a person of education*) msomi, mtu aliyeelimika; mjuzi. **educator** *n* mwalimu, mwelimishaji. **education** *n* 1 elimu. 2 maadilisho, malezi. **educational/educative** *adj*. **educationist/educationalist** *n* mtaalamu wa elimu.

eel *n* mkunga *as slippery as an ~* -sioshikika; (*fig*) (*of a person*) asiyeaminika, asiyechukulika.

eerie,eery *adj* -a kutia hofu, -a kioja, -a kutisha. **eerily** *adv*. **efface** *vt* 1 futa, futilia mbali *~ memories* sahau, sahaulisha. 2 **~ oneself** jificha, jifanya si mashuhuri *a self-effacing person* mtu mpole, mwenye haya. **~ment** *n*.

effect *n* (*result*) athari, matokeo. **the ~s of drought** athari za ukame. **of no ~** bure, -siofaa. **in ~** kwa kweli; (*of a rule, law, etc*) inayotumika *the rule is still in ~* kanuni bado inatumika. **bring/carry/put sth into ~** tekeleza; fanya itumike. **come into ~** tumika. **give ~ to** fanya iwe na maana/matokeo/taathira. **take ~** toa matokeo yanayotakiwa; fanya kazi *the medicine is taking ~* dawa inafanya kazi; anza kutumika/kutekelezwa. 2 mawazo/hisiaanayoyapatamtazamaji, msikilizaji, msomaji, n.k. 3 **to this/that ~** kwa maana hii/ile. **to the ~ that ...** inayosema kuwa. **to the same ~** inayotoa habari hiyohiyo. 4 (*effects*) (*pl*) (*property*) vyombo, mali. **no ~s** (*written often N/E by banker*) hundi iliyokataliwa *vt* timiza, tekeleza; (*to*) *~ an insurance* anzisha bima. **~ive** *adj* 1 -a kufaa, -enye nguvu, -enye matokeo yanayotarajiwa. 2 -a kupendeza, -a kufaa -enye kufaa kazi, kupigana. **~ively** *adv*. **~iveness** *n*. **~ual** *adj* (*not used for persons*) -enye kuleta matokeo yanayotakiwa. **~ally** *adv*. **~ness** *n*. **~uate** *vt* tekeleza, timiza, fanya. **~uation** *n*.

effeminate *adj* (*of man, derog*) -a (kama) kike. **effeminacy** *n*.

effervesce *vi* 1 toa gesi; (*fig of persons*) changamka. **~nce** *n*. **~nt** *adj*.

effete *adj* -liochakaa, -liyokwisha, haifu. **~ness** *n*.

efficacious *adj* (*not used of persons*) -a kufaa, -enye kuleta matokeo yanayotakiwa. **~ly** *adv*. **efficacy** *n*.

efficient *adj* -a kufaa, madhubuti, fanisi. 2 (*of persons*) hodari, stadi, -enye ufanisi. **~ly** *adv*. **efficiency** *n* utendaji bora, ustadi; ufanisi.

effigy *n* sanamu, kinyago *in effigy* katika sanamu. **burn/hang sb in ~** choma/nyonga sanamu ya mtu (kama ishara ya chuki).

efflorescence (*formal*) *n* 1 uchanuaji (maua). 2 (*crystals*) chunyu. **efflorescent** *adj*.

effluent *n* 1 mto, mfereji utokao katika mto mkubwa zaidi. 2 maji machafu yanayotoka kwenye kiwanda.

effluvium *n* uvundo, harufu mbaya.

efflux *n* utoaji; utokaji (wa gesi au kioevu) *~ of time* kupita wakati.

effort *n* 1 bidii, juhudi, jitihada, nguvu *make an ~* jitahidi, fanya bidii, tumia nguvu. 2 (*colloq*) matokeo ya jitihada/nguvu; kitu kilichofanywa kwa jitihada/nguvu *that's a good ~* umejitahidi. **~less** *adj* pasipo na haja ya bidii/jitihada/nguvu *he is an ~less singer* ni mwimbaji stadi (asiyehitaji kufanya bidii).

effrontery *n* ujuvi, usafihi, usodai; kiburi (*to*) *have the ~ to* kutokuwa na soni; kuthubutu.

effulgent *adj* (*liter*) -a kuang'aa, -enye kutia nuru, mwangaza, mng'ao *be ~ with joy* ng'aa kwa furaha. **effulgence** *n* mng'ao.

effusion *n* 1 utoaji, utokaji (wa gesi au kioevu); kumwaga, kumwagika, n.k. 2 (*derog*) maneno mengi yaliyojaa hisia. **effuse** *vt* toa (hewa, kioevu, gesi, n.k). **effusive** *adj* kunjufu; -ingi wa maneno, (katika kuonyesha upendo, shukurani). **effusively** *adv*. **effusiveness** *n*.

eft *n see* **newt**.

e.g. (*abbr of* **for example**)

egalitarian *n adj* (*person*) -enye kupenda usawa; -enye usawa. **~ism** *n*.

egg[1] *n* 1 yai. **a bad ~** yai viza; (*colloq*) mtu wa ovyo, mhalifu. **as sure as ~s is ~s** dhahiri, wazi kabisa; bila shaka. **in the ~** changa, bado kukua. *put all one's ~s in one basket* weka matumaini yote katika jambo moja *walk on ~s* enda kwa uangalifu. **teach one's grandmother to suck ~s** kufunza sogora jambo alijualo *have ~ on one's face* onekana mjinga/bwege *~ cup* kikombe cha yai. **~ nog** *n*. kileo kilichoongezewa maziwa, yai na viungo yai. **~ white** ute wa yai. **~ yolk** kiini cha yai. **~ shell** kaka la yai. **~ head** (*colloq*) (*usu derog*) msomi, mtoa nadharia. ~ **plant** mbilinganyi/biringanya. ~**whisk** chapo.

egg[2] *vt* ~ **on** sukuma, chochea, himiza.

ego *n* nafsi. ~ **trip** kitendo/vitendo vya kufurahisha nafsi. ~**centric** *adj* -enye ubinafsi. ~**ism** *n* 1 nadharia ya ubinafsi. 2 ubinafsi ~**istical** *adj*. ~**tism** *n* majisifu; ubinafsi. ~ **ist** *n*. ~**tistic** *adj*. ~**tistically** *adv*.

egregious *adj* -a kupita kiasi upeo (kwa ubaya) ~ *folly* ujinga kupita kiasi; baya sana. ~**ness** *n*.

egress *n* 1 uhuru/haki/uwezo wa kutoka. 2 njia ya kutokea.

Egypt *n* Misri. ~**ian** *n* Mmisri *adj* -a Misri, Kimisri. ~**ology** *n* elimu ya mambo ya kale ya Misri. ~**ologist** *n*.

eh *int* lo, nini, ati; au siyo; ulisemaje?

eider/~**duck** *n* somateria: aina ya bata mkubwa. ~ **down** manyoya ya kifuani mwa somateria; (*quilt*) mfirashi.

eight *adj* nane *he is* ~ ana miaka minane. **have one over the** ~ lewa sana *n* nane. ~**teen** *adj,n* kumi na nane. ~**teenth** *adj* -a kumi na nane. ~**some** wachezaji wanane. ~**ty** *n* themanini. ~**ies** *n* miaka ya themanini. ~**ieth** *adj* -a themanini.

either *adj* -o-ote, mojawapo ~ *answer is correct* jibu lolote ni sawa *choose* ~ *basket* chagua kikapu kimojawapo *pron* ~ (**of**) -ote mbili, -o -ote, mojawapo *I don't like* ~ sipendi chochote/vyote viwili *conj* ~ ... **or** ama ... au ~ *do this or that* ama fanya hili au lile *adv* (*with neg*) wala *he is not clever or wise* ~ si mwerevu wala si mwenye busara *I shall not go* ~ wala siendi *I can't* ~ hata mimi.

ejaculate *vt* 1 toa neno ghafla, tamka (ghafla). 2 kojoa, mwaga (agh manii). **ejaculation** *n*. **ejaculatory** *adj*.

eject *vt* 1 ~ **from** fukuza, toa kwa nguvu. 2 (*of volcano, etc.*) tupa. 3 (*of eroplane)* toka kwa dharura. ~**ion** *n*. ~**or** *n*. ~ **seat** kiti cha dharura.

eke *vt* 1 ~ **sth out** fanya kitu kidumu zaidi kwa kutumia uangalifu mkubwa au kukiongezea ili kitosheleze. 2 ~ *out a living* pata riziki kwa shida sana.

elaborate *adj* -liochanganuliwa, -liofanywa kwa uangalifu; -liofafanuliwa kwa undani; (*of artwork*) -lionakishiwa sana *vt* eleza kinaganaga, fafanua. ~**ly** *adv*. ~**ness** *n*. **elaboration** *n*.

e'lan *n* (*Fr*) uchangamfu; ukunjufu, bidii.

eland *n* pofu.

elapse *vi* (*of time*) pita.

elastic *adj* 1 nyumbufu, -a kunyumbulika, -a kunapukia. ~ **bands** mipira (ya kunyumbulika). 2 -a kubadilika ~ *temperament* tabia ya kubadilika ~ *rules* kanuni nyumbufu/za kubadilika *n* mpira. ~**ity** *n* unyumbuko ~ *of demand* mnyumbuko wa mahitaji.

elate *vt* (*usu pass*) furahisha, sisimua. 2 *adj* (*arch*) -a furaha. **elation** *n* furaha.

elbow *n* kiwiko, kivi. **out at** ~ (*of clothes*) tambara; (*of a person*) aliyevaa matambara *up to the* ~*s in work* kuwa na kazi kupindukia. **at one's** ~ karibu na *vt* jisukuma, jiingiza kwa nguvu/mabavu katika kundi la watu; toma, piga kikumbo, jipenyeza. ~**-grease** *n* msuguo wa nguvu, kazi ngumu (*to*) *put* ~*-grease into a piece of work* fanya kazi kwa nguvu. ~**-joint** *n* kiungo cha kiwiko (cha mkono). ~**-room** *n* nafasi a kutosha.

elder[1] *adj* -enye umri mkubwa kuliko; kubwa ~ *brother* kaka mkubwa *n* mzee. 1 **the** ~**s** wazee. 2 mzee wa kanisa. ~**ly** zee, -enye kuzeeka.

elder[2] *n* msambuku (mti mdogo unaozaa fuu nyekundu au nyeusi zitumikazo kutengeneza mvinyo).

eldest *n* 1 mkubwa kwa umri. 2 ~ **child** kifungua mimba.

El Dorado *n* El Dorado; nchi ya kufikirika ya utajiri hasa wa madini.

elect *vt* 1 chagua kwa kupiga kura. 2 chagua, amua *adj* teule. **President ~** Rais mteule *n* **the ~** wateule. **~ion** *n* uchaguzi. **by ~ion** uchaguzi mdogo. **general ~ion** uchaguzi mkuu ~ *campaign* kampeni ya uchunguzi. **~ioneer** *vi* pigia/fanyia kampeni (ili mtu fulani achaguliwe). **~ioneering** *n* ufanyaji kampeni. **~ive** *adj* 1 -enye uwezo wa kuchagua. 2 nayochaguliwa kwa kupigiwa kura. 3 (*US*) -a hiari, -a ziada. **~or** *n* mpiga kura. **~oral** *adj* -a kupiga kura. **the ~ roll/register** rejesta ya orodha ya wapiga kura. **~orate** *n* wote wenye sifa ya kupiga kura.

electric *adj* 1 -a umeme ~ *current* mkondo wa umeme ~ *chair* kiti cha umeme (cha kufisha wahalifu) ~ *motor* mota ya umeme. 2 (*of speech, personality, etc.*) -a kuchangamsha sana. **~al** *adj* -a umeme. **~ engineer** mhandisi umeme. 2 (*fig*) (*e.g. of news*) -a kushtusha sana, -enye kuleta wasiwasi. **~ally** *adv*. **~ian** *n* fundi umeme **~ity** *n* 1 umeme. 2 elimu umeme na asili yake. **electrify** *vt* 1 tia umeme (ili kuendesha mashine, kuwasha taa); peleka umeme. 2 (*fig*) (*astonish*) shtusha sana. **electrification** *n*.

electro *pref* (*in compounds*) -a kuhusu umeme *~-cardiogram* *n* elektrokardiogramu. **~-chemistry** *n* elektrokemia, kemia ya umeme. **~-dynamics** *n* nguvu za umeme. **~magnet** *n* sumaku umeme. **~meter** *n* elektromita: kipimo cha nguvu umeme. **~plate** *vt* paka madini (mf. fedha) kwa elektrolisisi. **~cute** *vt* ua kwa umeme. **~cution** *n*. **~de** *n* elektrodi. **~lysis** *n* elektrolisisi: uchanganuaji dutu kwa nguvu za umeme. **~n** *n* elektroni. **~ flow** mtiririko wa elektroni. **~ic** *adj* -a elektroni. **~ics** *n* sayansi na teknolojia ya elektroni (mf radio, TV). **~scope** *n* elektroskopu. **~therapy** *n* utabibu wa umeme.

eleemosynary *adj* (*formal*) -a kutegemea msaada/sadaka.

elegant *adj* -a jamala, -a madaha, -a sanaa, sanifu. **~ly** *adv*. **elegance** *n*.

elegy *n* shairi/wimbo wa huzuni, maombolezo. **elegiac** *adj* 1 (*of metre)* -enye huzuni, -a msiba. 2 -a kuomboleza, -enye maombolezo.

element *n* 1 (*science*) elementi. 2 (*according to the ancient philosophers)* vitu vya asili: ardhi, hewa, moto, maji. **out of one's ~** sio mahali pake. 3 (*pl*) **the ~s** nguvu za asili; hali ya hewa. 4 (*pl)* mwanzo, madokezo ya awali. 5 msingi, sifa ya lazima na muhimu (ya kitu fulani). 6 dalili, ishara *there is no ~ of truth in his statements* hakuna dalili zozote za ukweli katika maneno yake. 7 (*maths*) memba; (*electric)* waya kinzi (wa umeme). **~al** *adj* 1 -a vitu/nguvu ya asili. 2 -enye hisia kali. **~ary** *adj* -a asili, -a mwanzo. **~ colours** rangi za msingi. **~arily** *adv*.

elephant *n* tembo, ndovu. **a white ~** mzigo; mali ya gharama kubwa isiyo na faida/matumizi. **~iasis** matende. **~ine** *adj* -kubwa mno, -a kama tembo, nzito *an ~ memory* kumbukumbu ya kuaminika.

elevate *vt* ~ **(to)** (*formal)* nyanyua, ongeza, inua; (*fig)* kuza, adilisha, pandisha ~ *the voice* ongeza sauti, sema kwa sauti kubwa. **~d railway** reli inayopita juu kwa juu (hewani). **elevation** *n* 1 upandaji cheo/hadhi. 2 (*height)* urefu wa kwenda juu, kipeo, kimo. 3 (*hill)* kilima, mwinuko. 4 (*drawing)* picha/ramani ya upande mmoja wa jengo. 5 pembe (mwinuko). **elevator** *n* 1 *grain ~* ghala ya nafaka. 2 *(US)* lifti, kambarau. 3 kipandishi.

eleven *n adj* 1 kumi na moja. 2 timu ya wachezaji/wanachama kumi na mmoja. **~th** -a kumi na moja. **at the ~th hour** dakika za mwisho.

~**ses** *pl (GB)* kitafunio na kinywaji cha asubuhi (mnamo saa tano).

elf *n* kibwengo; *(mischievous child)* mtundu. ~**in** *adj* -a kibwengo, tundu, tukutu. ~**ish** *adj* cheshi.

elicit *vt* ~ **sth (from sb)** vuta/shawishi/bembeleza mtu ajibu ~ *the truth* shawishi mtu aseme kweli. ~**ation** *n*.

elide *vt* dondosha irabu/silabi katika kutamka k.m. Mungu badala ya Muungu. **elision** *n (from elide)* ufupisho wa matamshi ya neno.

eligible *adj* ~ **(for)** -a kufaa, -akustahiki, -stahilifu. **elegibility** *n*.

eliminate *vt* 1 ~ **(from)** futa, ondosha, acha. ~ **sb (from sth)** toakatika mashindano. 2 *(inform or euph)* ua. **elimination** *n*.

elite *n* kikundi/tabaka aali la watu wenye uwezo (kipaji au nafasi nzuri katika jamii); *an educated* ~ mwanazuoni; tabaka la wasomi. **elitism** *n* imani kuwa tabaka aali linapaswa kutawala. **elitist** *n, adj*.

elixir *n* 1 maandalizi ambamo wanasayansi wa zamani walitaka kubadili chuma kuwa dhahabu. 2 tiba inayoponyesha magonjwa yote ~ *of life* kioevu cha maisha (ambacho humfanya mtu aishi milele).

Elizabethan *adj* -a wakati wa malkia Elizabeth I wa Uingereza *n* mtu aliyeishi wakati wa malkia Elizabeth I (k.m. Shakespeare).

elk *n* kulungu wa kaskazini Ulaya na Asia.

ellipse *n* umbo yai; duaradufu. **elliptic/elliptical** *adj* -a umbo la yai.

ellipsis *n* udondoshaji wa maneno. **elliptical** *adj (of a sentence)* -liodondosha maneno.

elocution *n* ufasaha. ~**ary** *adj*. ~**ist** *n* mtu azungumzaye kwa ufasaha.

elongate *vt,vi* refusha; refuka *adj (Bot, zool)* refu. **elongation** *n* mwongezeko wa urefu; *(of a line, etc)* kipande kilichorefushwa.

elope *vi* ~ **with** hala, toroka, hasa mtu na mchumba ili waoane bila idhini ya wazee. ~**ment** *n*.

eloquence *n* umbuji, lugha ya kushawishi. **eloquent** *adj*. **eloquently** *adv*.

else *adj (with indef or interr pron)* 1 *(besides)* tena, juu ya hayo, zaidi *what ~ shall I say?* nitasema nini tena (zaidi)? *did you see anybody* ~ ulimwona mtu mwingine (zaidi)? 2 *(otherwise)* **(or)** ~ ama sivyo, au, la sivyo; vinginevyo *take care or ~ you will fall* jihadhari, ama sivyo/la sivyo utaanguka *he's joking (or) ~ he's mad* anatania ama sivyo ni kichaa/mwehu. ~**where** *adj* penginepo, mahali pengine.

elucidate *vt (formal)* eleza, fafanua, fumbua. **elucidation** *n*.

elude *vt* 1 epuka kwa hila/mbinu. 2 *(baffle)* fumba, tatiza. **elusion** *n*. **elusive** *adj* -a kuepuka kwa hila; telezi. ~**ness** *n*. **elusory** *adj*.

Elysium *n (GK myth)* 1 *(final bliss)* peponi, ahera; *(happiness)* raha mustarehe, nderemo. **Elysian** *adj* -a peponi, -a raha mustarehe.

em *n (pron)(colloq)* 1 herufi m. 2 *(of a print)* kipimo cha kupimia idadi ya chapa katika mstari.

emaciate *vt (usu passive)* dhoofisha, kondesha *He is ~d by hard work* amedhoofishwa na kazi ya sulubu. **emaciation** *n*.

emanate *vi* ~ **(from)** *(formal)* anzia; tokea. **emanation** *n*.

emancipate *vt* ~ **(from)** komboa. **emancipator** *n*. **emancipatory** *adj*. **emancipation** *n* ukombozi *women's* ~ ukombozi wa wanawake.

emasculate *vt* 1 hasi, hanithisha. 2 *(weaken)* dunisha, dhoofisha sana. **emasculation** *n*.

embalm *vt* 1 *(of corpse)* tia dawa (maiti) ili isioze. 2 *(preserve carefully)* linda/hifadhi isisahaulike. 3 *(perfume)* tia harufu nzuri. ~**er** mtu atiaye dawa (maiti) ili isioze. ~**ment** *n*.

embankment *n* ukuta/tuta lililojengwa kando ya mtaro, barabara, handaki, mto, n.k. **embank** *vt* jengea/fanya tuta kando ya mtaro, barabara, handaki, mto, n.k.

embargo *n* 1 kikwazo. 2 *(fig)* kizuizi. **lift/raise/remove an ~ (from sb)** ondoa kikwazo; anza kufanya biashara na. **place/lay sb under (an) ~; put an ~ on sb** wekea kikwazo mtu fulani, acha kufanya biashara na. **~ed** *adj* -liowekewa kikwazo/kizuizi na mtu fulani.

embark *vi,vt* 1 panda, ingia, pakia. 2 **~ on/upon** anza, anzisha. **~ation** *n* upakiaji chomboni.

embarrass *vt* 1 tahayarisha, aibisha. 2 *(old use)* zuia, sumbua. **~ing** *adj*. **~ingly** *adv*. **~ment** *n* 1 aibu. 2 shida *financial ~s* shida ya fedha; *an ~ of riches* mali nyingi kupita kiasi.

embassy *n* ubalozi, ofisi/kazi ya/balozi; balozi na wafuasi wake *(to) send sb with an ~* kumtuma mtu na mabalozi au wajumbe.

embattle *vt* andaa askari kwa vita. **~ed** *adj (of an army)* -liowekwa tayari kwa vita; *(fig)* kujihami; *(of a tower or building)* -enye ukuta juu wenye nafasi za kupigia risasi.

embed *vt (usu passive)* **~ (in)** tia ndani ya.

embellish *vt* **~ with** pamba; rembesha, tia nakshi; *(of a story)* piga chuku, tia chumvi. **~ment** *n* mapambo, urembo, kupiga chuku, kutia chumvi.

ember *n (usu pl)* 1 kaa la moto, kijinga cha moto. 2 *(pl)* majivu.

embezzle *vt* badhiri amana. **~ment** *n*. **~r** *n* mbadhiri amana, mbadhirifu.

embitter *vt* chukiza, tia uchungu sana.

emblazon *vt* **~ (with)** 1 pamba (ngao, bendera, n.k.) kwa nembo mbalimbali. 2 sifu mno. **~ment** *n*.

emblem *n* nembo, ishara. **~atic** *adj* -wa (kama) ishara ya. **~ (of)** -wa kama nembo. **~atize** *vt* tumia/tumika kama nembo.

embody *vt* **~ (in)** 1 pamba, mawazo/maono. 2 jumuisha, unganisha. 3 -pa pepo mwili.

embodiment *n he is the ~ of goodness* ni mfano halisi wa wema.

embolden *vt* tia moyo, -pa moyo, tia hamasa.

embonpoint *n (F, usu euphem)* unene.

embosom *vt (poetic)* kumbatia, tia moyoni.

emboss *vt* **~ with** (chora) tunisha kwa kugandamiza. **~ed** *adj* -liogandamizwa/tunishwa.

embouchure *n* 1 mlango wa mto; *(of mus instruments)* kilimi, mtapa.

embowel *vt (arch)* tumbua, toa matumbo.

embrace *vt* 1 kumbatia, kumbatiana, piga pambaja. 2 *(accept)* kubali, pokea kwa moyo, tumia kwa bidii. 3 *(include)* jumuisha, ingiza. 4 *(take in)* fahamu, tambua. 5 *(of religion)* fuata *n* kumbatio, pambaja. **~able** *adj*. **~ment** *n*.

embrangle *vt* tatanisha.

embrasure *n* 1 tundu ukutani (la kupenyeza mzinga au bunduki). 2 buruji, agh. katika jumba.

embrocation *n* fututa, dawa ya kuchua.

embroider *vt,vi* 1 tarizi, nakshi, tia almaria. 2 *(fig) (a story)* piga chuku, tia chumvi. **~y** *n* 1 almaria, nakshi, *(stitches)* taraza. 2 *(of story)* kupiga chuku *adj ~y stitches* mshono tarizo. **embroil** *vt* **~ sb/oneself (in)** gombanisha, chochea, husisha na ugomvi. **~ment** *n*.

embryo *n* 1 kiinitete. 2 kitu kilicho katika hatua za mwanzo. **~nic** *adj*. **~logy** *n* embriolojia: taaluma ya maisha ya kiinitete.

embus *vt,vi (mil)* tia/pakia/panda gari.

emend *vt* sahihisha, rekebisha (maandiko). **~ation** *n*.

emerald *n* zumaridi.

emerge *vi* **~ (from)** 1 ibuka, zuka. 2 *(of facts, ideas)* jitokeza, julikana, dhihirika; *(after defeat)* fufuka. **~nce** *n*. **~nt** *adj*. **emersion** *n* mwibuko, mzuko, utokezi.

emergency *n* dharura. **~ brake** breki za dharura *~ leave* likizo ya dharura *state of ~ncy* hali ya hatari. 3 tukio *be ready for any ~* jiandae kwa tukio lolote. 4 *(attrib use)* -a kutumika wakati wa dharura *an ~ exit* mlango wa dharura.

emeritus *adj* -liostaafu na kubaki na cheo/heshima *professor ~* profesa wa heshima (baada ya kustaafu).

emery *n* msasa.

emetic *n* tapisho *adj* -a kutapisha.

emigrate *vt* **~ (to/from)** hama, hajiri. **emigrant** *n* mhamaji, mhajiri. **emigration** *n*. **emigratory** *adj*. **emigre** *n* mhamaji wa kisiasa, mkimbizi (agh wa kisiasa).

eminent *adj* tukufu, adhimu, maarufu. **~ly** *adv*. **eminence** *n* 1 mwadhama; ukuu, ubora, utukufu (wa daraja, cheo,tabia, sifa, uwezo). 2 kilima, mwinuko. 3 *(R.C.)* **His/Your E~** Mhashamu/mwadhamu Kadinali.

emir *n* kadhi, sheikh.

emissary *n* mjumbe.

emit *vt* toa. **emission** *n* **~ (of)** kutoa, kutokeza, utokezaji (wa mwanga, joto, harufu, n.k.).

emollient *n* dawa ya kulainisha ngozi; dawa ya kutuliza maumivu *adj* -a kulainisha, -a kutuliza.

emolument *n (usu pl formal)* mshahara, ujira.

emotion *n* 1 mhemuko, hisia kubwa, jazba, mshtuko, mchomo wa moyo *(to) appeal to the ~s* gusa hisia. **~al** *adj* 1 -enye mhemuko/jazba *(psych) ~ disturbance* mvurugiko wa akili. 2 ilioelekezwa kwenye mhemuko. **~less** *adj* bila hisia kubwa/ mhemuko. **~ally** *adv*. **emotive** *adj*. -enye kuamsha hisia. **~alism** *n* hali ya kuhemkwa mno.

empanel/impanel *vt* orodhesha (jina la mtu) katika jopo/baraza la wazee.

empathy *n (psych)* uwezo wa kuhisi maono ya mwingine.

empennage *n* sehemu ya mkia wa ndege/eropleni.

empire *n* ufalme, milki, *(sovereignty)* enzi kuu *British ~* Falme ya Uingereza.

emperor *n* mfalme mkuu (hasa atawalaye falme mbili au zaidi). **empress** *n* mfalme wa kike.

emphasize *n* mkazo *vt* tia mkazo, kaza, sisitiza. **emphatic** *adj* -a nguvu, -a mkazo; *(distinct)* dhahiri, waziwazi. **emphatically** *adv*.

emphysema *n (med)* ugonjwa wa kuvimba mapafu na kupumua kwa shida.

empirical *adj* jarabati, -a kutegemea majaribio, (si ya kutegemea nadharia/si -a kubahatisha). **empiricism** *n* matendo jarabati. **empiricist** *n* mwanafalsafa jarabati. **~y** *adv*.

emplacement *n (mil)* mahali pakuwekea mizinga, n.k.

emplane *vt,vi* panda/pakia kwenye ndege (eropleni).

employ *vt* 1 ajiri. 2 *(make use of)* tumia. 3 **~ in** *(often pass)* shughulika; (ji)shughulisha *n* kazi *I am in his ~* nafanya kazi kwake. **~able** *adj*. **~ee** *n* mwajiriwa, mfanyakazi. **~er** *n* mwajiri. **~ment** *n* 1 ajira *thrown out of ~* fukuzwa kazi. **be in/out of ~** -wa na/kuwa bila kazi. **~ agency** wakala wa ajira. 2 *(use)* matumizi.

emporium *n* 1 chete kuu, gulio. 2 mahali penye biashara nyingi; duka kubwa.

empower *vt* wezesha, -pa idhini/ mamlaka.

empty *adj* tupu *an ~ bottle* chupa tupu; *(colloq) on an ~ stomach* bila kula chakula *~words* maneno matupu yasiyo na maana; *(math) ~ set* seti tupu *n (pl)* vitu visivyo na kitu ndani k.v. chupa za bia. **~handed** *adj* mikono mitupu. **~headed** *adj* pumbavu *vt,vi* **~ (out)** mwaga, mimina mbali, toa; toka -ote -aliyomo, -wa tupu *the river empties into the sea* mto unaingia baharini. **emptiness** *n*.

empurple *vt* tia rangi ya zambarau. **~d** *adj* -liojaa rangi ya zambarau.

empyrean *n* mbingu, mbinguni *adj* -a

mbinguni.

emu *n* emu (ndege wa Australia mfano wa mbuni).

emulate *vt* 1 igiza, iga, fuatisha; husudu; jaribu kushinda mwingine (kwa ustadi, tabia, akili, uwezo, ushujaa), shindana na. **emulation** *n*. **emulative** *adj*. **emulator** *n*.

emulous *adj* -enye moyo au shauku ya kufaulu/kupata (kuendelea, kusitawi) *with ~ zeal* kwa shauku ya kufaulu.

emulsion *n* emalshani: ugiligili au weupe *~ paint* rangi ya maji. **emulsive** *adj*. **emulsify** *vt* gandisha.

enable *vt* wezesha, -pa uwezo. **enabling part** *adj* -enye kuwezesha.

enact *vt* 1 fanya kuwa sheria, toa *as by law ~ed* ilivyotungwa kisheria. 2 tenda kama kwenye maigizo. **enactment** *n*.

enamel *n* 1 enameli: rangi ngumu ya kupaka *~ ware* vyombo vya enameli. 2 tabaka ngumu ya nje juu ya jino, gamba la jino *vt* paka enameli.

enamoured *vt (usu in passive)* **be ~ed of** tamanisha, penda, pendezwa na; vutiwa na, furahia na taka kutumia.

enbloc *adj (Fr)* kwa jumla; kwa pamoja.

encage *vt* funga tunduni.

encamp *vt* piga kambi. **~ment** *n* kambi (hasa ya jeshi).

encase *vt* ~ **(in)** funga katika kasha, sanduku, funika pande zote. **~ment** *n*.

encaustic *adj* -a kuokwa, -a kutia rangi kwa kuchoma pamoja na rangi.

enceinte *n, adj* 1 *(arch) (of woman)* mjamzito. 2 *n* uzio (katika ngome).

encephalic *adj* -a ubongo. **encephalitis** *n* uvimbe wa ubongo.

enchain *vt* 1 vuta; funga minyororo; *(fig)* shika, shikilia. **~ment** *n*.

enchant *vt* 1 *(delight)* pendeza mno, furahisha. 2 roga, sihiri, fanya mazingaombwe. **~er** mchawi wa kiume. **~ess** mchawi wa kike. **~ingly** *adv*. **~ment** *n* 1 uchawi; maliwazo. 2 kurogwa. 3 furaha, raha.

enchase *vt* 1 tia (kama kito) katika kiunzi k.m. pete; tia nakshi.

encircle *vt* zunguka, zingira; fanya duara. **~ment** *n*.

enclair *adv phrase (F)(used in telegrams, official dispatches, etc)* katika lugha ya kawaida, -sio katika lugha ya mficho.

enclasp *vt* kumbatia.

enclave *n* nchi iliyozungukwa na nchi nyingine k.m. Lesotho.

enclitic *n* kiangama (k.m. -we katika mwanawe au -pi katika wendapi?).

enclose *vt* ~ **(with)** 1 zunguka kabisa, zungushia ukuta au boma. 2 tia/funga (kitu) ndani (ya kasha, bahasha, furushi). **enclosure** *n* 1 kiwanja kilichozungushiwa ua au boma *the enclosure of common land* kuzungushia ua ardhi ya wote (kijiji, n.k.) kwa faida ya mtu binafsi. 2 *(thing enclosed)* kitu kilichotiwa ndani ya kingine (kama barua katika bahasha).

encode *vt* simba, andika katika lugha mficho.

encomium *n (formal)* sifa za juu kabisa. **encomist** *n*.

encompass *vt* zingira, zunguka, funika; jumuisha.

encore *int*. Rudia! Tena! *vt (of a song, etc)* taka kurudiwa au kuendelea kwa wachezaji wale wale *the audience ~d the singer* hadhira ilimtaka mwimbaji arudie tena *n* kurudia tena wimbo/mchoro, n.k. kwa mwito wa wasikilizaji.

encounter *vt* 1 kabiliwa na (adui, hatari, matatizo, n.k.). 2 kutana na (rafiki) bila kutegemea *n* ~ **(with)** pambano.

encourage *vt* ~ **sb in sth/to do sth** tia moyo, tumainisha *feel ~d by his progress* tiwa moyo na maendeleo yake. **~ment** *n*.

encroach *vi* ~ **on/upon** 1 twaa isiyo haki. 2 ingilia mali ya mwingine *~ on sb's land* ingilia ardhi ya mwingine. **~ment** *n*.

encrust,incrust *vt* ~ **(with)** funika

kwa gamba; funika kwa vito au madini yenye thamani *vi* tanda. **~ment** *n*.

encumber *vt* **~ (with)** 1 zuia, tatiza, -wa mzigo kwa, elemea *be ~ed with many responsibilities* sumbuliwa na majukumu mengi. 2 jaza, lundika *a hall ~ ed with useless things* bwalo lilojazwa vikorokoro. **encumbrance** *n*.

encylic(al) *n* waraka wa Baba Mtakatifu *adj* -a waraka wa Baba Mtakatifu.

encyclopaedia, encyclopedia *n* ensaiklopidia: kitabu au seti ya vitabu vinavyotoa taarifa kuhusu mambo mengi. **encyclopedicpedic** *adj*. -a ensaiklopidia.

end *n* 1 mwisho, kikomo *the ~ of the road* mwisho wa barabara. **begin/start at the wrong ~** anza vibaya. **get hold of the wrong ~ of the stick** elewa vibaya. **keep one's ~ up** *(GB)* endelea/wa na uso mkunjufu hata katika matatizo. **at a loose ~** bila chochote cha kufanya. **on ~** wima *place the box on its ~* simamisha kasha wima; mfululizo, bila kukoma *four hours on ~* saa nne bila kukoma. **~ on** ncha zinapokutana. **~ to ~** kutana/kutanisha ncha kwa ncha. **go (in) off the deep ~** chukua bila kujizuia, shindwa kujizuia. **make (both) ~s meet** ishi kulingana na kipato chako. **(reach) the ~ of the line/road** *(fig)* fikia mahali ambapo huwezi tena kuendelea. 2 kipande kilichobakia *a cigarette ~* kipande cha sigara kilichobakia. **~ papers** kurasa tupu za mwisho wa kitabu. **~point** hatua ya mwisho ya jambo. 3 mwisho, kikomo, hatimaye *the ~ of the month* mwisho wa mwezi *the ~ of the story* mwisho wa hadithi. **(be) at the ~; at the ~ (of)** mwisho *the fighting was at an ~* mapigano yalifikia kikomo. **come to an ~** kuisha *the conference came to an ~* mkutano uliisha. **come to a bad ~** isha vibaya; adhirika *if you don't stop racketeering you will come to a bad ~* usipoacha ulanguzi mwishowe utaadhirika, utafungwa jela. **draw to an ~** karibia mwisho. **make an ~ of sth, put an ~ to sth** komesha. **in the ~** hatimaye. **no ~ of** *(colloq)* mno, sana *he thinks no ~ of himself* anajiona sana. **without ~** pasipo kufikia mwisho, bila mwisho. 4 kifo *she is nearing her ~* anakaribia kufa. 5 kusudi, madhumuni, lengo *gain one's ~* pata kitu mtu alichokusudia *to no ~* bila mafanikio. **the ~ justifies the means** *(prov)* kusudi zuri huhalalisha njia ya kulifikia, bora kufika *vt,vi* maliza, isha *the game ~s here* mchezo unaishia hapa *~ your argument* malizeni ubishi wenu. **~ in sth** -wa matokeo ya; ishia *the plan ~ed in failure* mpango haukufaulu. **~ off** maliza *he ~ed off teaching at 2.00 pm* alimaliza kufundisha saa nane mchana. **~ up** ishia, maliza, hitimisha *if you go on stealing you will ~ up in jail* ukiendelea kuiba utaishia kifungoni. **~ng** mwisho, kikomo. **~ less** *adj* -siokuwa na mwisho, -enye kuendelea *~ chain* mnyororo usiokuwa na mwisho (ambao mwisho wake umeunganishwa). **~most** *adj* mwisho kabisa. **~ways/ ~wise** *adv* pembe hadi pembe, mwishoni, kwa (kutanguliza) mwisho.

endanger *vt* hatarisha, ponza.

endear *vt* **~ sb/oneself to sb** fanya upendeke *his kindness ~ him to all* ukarimu (wema, upaji) wake ulifanya watu wote wampende. **~ oneself to** jifanya upendwe na mtu. **~ingly** *adv*. **~ment** *n* ubembelezi; neno, usemi wenye kuonyesha upendo k.m. mpenzi, mahabubu.

endeavour, (*US* **endeavor**) *vi (formal)* jaribu, jitahidi *n* juhudi, bidii, jitihada. **(to) make an ~** fanya bidii *(to) make every ~ to* fanya kila jitihada.

endemic *n, adj* ugonjwa ulioenea

unaowapata watu fulani mara kwa mara k.m. malaria hapa Afrika Mashariki.

endogamy *n* ndoa ndani, ndoa kati ya watu wa ukoo mmoja.

endorse,indorse *vt* 1 andika jina nyuma ya/katika cheki au hati fulani, wekea mkono/sahihi (kama uthibitisho). 2 *(accept)* idhinisha, unga mkono. 3 *(usu pass)* andika kwenye leseni kwamba dereva amevunja sheria. **~ment** *n*.

endow *vt* ~ **(with)** 1 toa fedha, mali, n.k. kuwa wakfu. 2 **be ~ed (with)** jaliwa *he is ~ed with great gifts* amejaliwa vipaji vingi (akili, maarifa, karama, n.k.). **~ment** *n* 1 mali iliyowekwa wakfu. 2 kipaji, majaliwa *~ policy* bima ya maisha.

endue *vt (usu pass)* **be ~d with** jaliwa na, patiwa.

endure *vt,vi* 1 *(last)* ishi, dumu, endelea. 2 *(remain firm)* vumilia, stahimili. **endurable** *adj* -a kuvumilia, -a kustahimilika; -a kuchukulika. **enduring** *adj*. **enduringly** *adv*. **endurance** *n* uvumilivu, ustahamilivu, jambo la kuvumilia. **beyond ~** -siovumilika. **~ test** kipimo cha uvumilivu.

enema *n* 1 enema: uingizaji wa maji mkunduni. 2 bomba la kuingizia maji mkunduni.

enemy *n* 1 ~ **(of/to)** adui. 2 **the ~** majeshi ya adui. 3 mwanajeshi adui. 4 jambo linalodhuru. **enmity** *n* uadui, uhasama *be at ~ with* wa adui na.

energy *n* 1 nguvu, bidii. 2 nishati. **energize** tia nishati, changamsha. **binding ~** nishati babadu. **kinetic ~** nishati mwendo. **potential ~** nishati tuli. **thermal ~** nishati joto. **energetic** *adj* -enye nguvu, bidii, juhudi. **energetically** *adv*. **energetics** *n* elimunishati.

enervate *vt* dhoofisha, legeza. **enervation** *n*.

enfamille *adj (F)* nyumbani.

enfant terrible *n (F)* mtoto/kijana mkorofi.

enfeeble *vt* dhoofisha, ondolea nguvu, nyong'onyeza.

enfetter *vt* tia pingu, zuia kama mfungwa.

enfilade *vt* -pigia bunduki/mizinga mstari mzima. 2 panga bunduki/ mizinga ili ziweze kupiga mstari mzima *n* kupiga mstari mzima.

enfold *vt* ~ **(in)** 1 funga kwa kuzungushia. 2 kumbatia.

enforce *vt* ~ **(on, upon)** 1 lazimisha, tiisha, shurutisha utiifu; *(of law)* tekeleza sheria. 2 tia nguvu. **~able** *adj*. **~ment** *n*.

enfranchise *vt* -pa wananchi haki ya kushiriki katika uchaguzi k.m. wa wabunge, wajumbe wa halmashauri, n.k. 2 weka huru, toa katika utumwa. **~ment** *n*.

engage *vt,vi* 1 ajiri *~ an accountant* ajiri mhasibu. 2 ahidi, jipa sharti, hakikishia. 3 ~ **in** shiriki katika, jishughulisha na *~ in politics* jishughulisha na siasa. 4 **be ~ to marry** chumbia, chumbiwa. 5 *(usu pass)* vutia *nothing ~s her* havutiwi na chochote. 6 *(mil)* shambulia, anza kupigana. 7 ~ **(with)** *(of parts of a machine)* fungamana, funganisha pamoja; *(motoring) ~ the first gear* weka/ingiza gea ya kwanza. 8 ~ **upon** anza; anzisha. **engaging** *adj* cheshi; -a kuvutia. **engagingly** *adv*. **~ment** *n* 1 *(promise)* ahadi, miadi. 2 shughuli. 3 *(betrothal)* ahadi ya ndoa, uchumba. **~ ring** pete ya uchumba. 5 mapigano, vita. 6 kuingia kwa gea. **~d** *adj* 1 -enye kazi. 2 *(telephone)* inatumika inaongea.

engender *vt* sababisha *crime is often ~ed by poverty* uhalifu agh husababishwa na umaskini.

engine *n* injini. ~ **driver** dereva (hasa) wa treni. 2 *(old use)* mashine au zana. **~er** *n* 1 mhandisi. 2 *(US)* dereva wa treni. 3 **the ~ers** kikosi cha ufundi/uhandisi *vt* 1 handisi. 2 panga au anzisha jambo fulani. **~er a project** panga na anzisha mradi.

~ering *n* uhandisi.
English *adj* -a Kiingereza, -a Uingereza *n* 1 Kiingereza. **the Queen's/King's ~** Kiingereza sanifu *in plain ~* kwa Kiingereza chepesi. 2 *(pl)* **the ~** Waingereza.
engorge *vt* -la kwa wingi na kwa pupa. **~ment** *n*.
engraft *vt* **~ (into/upon)** pandisha/unganisha (mche katika shina la mmea mwingine). **~ (in)** *(fig)* zoeza mwingine mawazo fulani, ingiza (moyoni/akilini mwa mwingine).
engrave *vt* **~ on/upon**. 1 chonga, tia/kata nakshi. 2 **~ with** chonga maandishi. 3 **~ on/upon** sisitiza sana ili mtu apokee na kukumbuka; *(fig)* kaa/weka katika kumbukumbu. **engraving** *n* sanaa ya utiaji nakshi; picha, sanamu iliyonakshiwa.
engross *vt* 1 *(occupy, absorb) (usu pass)* jishughulisha sana na *he was ~ed in his work* aliizamia kabisa kazi yake; *(active)* shughulisha, vuta. 2 *vt (legal)* andika (k.m. hati ya kisheria) kwa maandishi makubwa au kwa mtindo rasmi wa kisheria. **~ment** *n*. **~ing** *adj* -a kuvutia sana.
engulf *vt* meza (kama mawimbi yamezavyo mashua). **~ment** *n*.
enhance *vt* ongeza, zidisha, (ubora, moto, nguvu, n.k.). **~ment** *n*.
enigma *n* fumbo, swali, mtu kitu/hali inayotatanisha. **~tic** *adj* -a kutatanisha, -a fumbo. **~tically** *adv*.
enjoin *vt* **~ (on sb)** agiza; amuru. **(to) ~** amuru. 2 **~ from** kataza.
enjoy *vt* 1 faidi, furahia. 2 faidika na *vi* 1 **~ oneself** furahia, furahi. 2 -wa na. 3 ona raha, furahi. **~able** *adj*. **~ ably** *adv*. **~ment** *n* 1 raha, furaha, ridhaa. 2 milki na matumizi -kuwa na *the ~ of good health* kuwa na siha.
enkindle *vt* washa, amsha, chochea.
enlarge *vt,vi* 1 kuza, ongeza, ongezeka, tanua. **~ on/upon** elezea zaidi. **~ment** *n ~ of photograph* kukuza picha.
enlighten *vt* elimisha, taalamisha, ongoa. **~ed part** *adj*. -enye kuelimika, -enye kutaalamika, -ongofu. **~ment** *n*.
enlist *vt,vi* 1 **~ (in)** andika/jiandikisha, andikisha (jeshi). **~ed man** askari. 2 **~ (in, for)** pata msaada, saidia. **~ment** *n*.
enliven *vt* changamsha.
en masse *adj (F)* kwa jumla, -ote pamoja, kwa pamoja.
enmesh *vt* **~ (in)** tatiza, tega, kamata, zonga.
ennoble *vt* 1 fanya mtu awe muungwana. 2 adilisha, kuza (hadhi).
ennui *n* uchovu (wa akili).
enormous *adj* -kubwa mno; -a kupita kiasi. **~ly** *adj*. **~ness** *n*.
enormity *n* 1 uovu uliokithiri. 2 uhalifu mkubwa. 3 ukubwa uliopita kiasi.
enough *adj* -a kutosha. **more than ~** mno, zaidi ya kiasi cha kutosha *n* kadiri ya kutosha *have ~* shiba, tosheka, kinai *~ is as good as a feast* shibe ni sawa na karamu. **be ~** tosha *adv* kiasi cha kutosha/kufaa *has been good ~ to give me* kwa hisani yake amenipa *it is ~* basi! *sure ~* kama tulivyotazamia. **oddly/strangely ~** kwa ajabu, ni ajabu kwamba.
enquire, enquiry *n see* **inquire, inquiry**.
enrage *vt* kasirisha, ghadhibisha.
enrapture *vt* pendeza mno, furahisha sana.
enrich *vt* **~ (with)** 1 tajirisha, sitawisha. 2 *(of soil)* rutubisha. **~ment** *n*.
enrol *vt,vi* **~ (in)** 1 andikisha, jiandikisha *~ for a course* jiandikisha kuchukua kozi. **~ment** *n*.
en route *adv*. **~ (from/to)** njiani, katika safari, kupitia kwenda mahali.
ensconce *vt* weka *he ~d himself on the couch* alikaa kwenye kochi.

ensemble *n (F)* 1 jumla. 2 *(music)* kipande cha muziki kinachoshirikisha wote, kikundi cha wanamuziki wapigao pamoja (kidogo kuliko bendi). 3 *(trade use)* suti ya kike.
enshrine *vt* ~ **(in)** *(formal)* tunza, hifadhi sana.
enshroud *vt* funika kabisa.
ensign *n* 1 *(esp naval)* bendera. 2 (*US*) cheo cha chini cha askari wa majini. 3 *(old use)* tepe (inayoonyesha cheo), askari aliyebeba bendera ya kikosi.
enslave *vt* tia utumwani; tawala kabisa (moyo, tamaa, akili) *be ~ by one's passions* tawaliwa kabisa na tamaa za mwili. **~ment** *n*.
ensnare *vt* ~ **(in)** tega, kamata kwa hila/werevu.
ensue *vi* ~ **(from)** tokana na, tokea/ tukia kwa sababu ya, fuatia, tokea baadaye. **ensuing** *adj* liyofuata.
ensure *vt,vi (US = insure)* 1 hakikisha. 2 ~ **against** salimisha, okoa, linda, hami. 3 -pa, pata. 4 *(formerly) see* **insure**.
entail *vt* ~ **(on)** lazimisha, fanya iwezekane, hitaji, taka; (*leg*) weka wakfu *n* wakfu.
entangle *vt* ~ **(in)** tega, tatanisha, tatiza, zongomeza; (*fig*) ingia au ingiza matatizoni, katika hali ngumu. **~ment** *n* 1 mtego, tatizo. 2 *(pl)* mtego wa seng'enge.
entente *n (F)* maelewano. ~ **cordiale** *n* maelewano (hasa kati ya serikali mbili).
enter *vt,vi* 1 ingia; *(stage direction in a printed play) ~ Hamlet/Kinjeketile* Hamlet/ Kinjeketile anaingia. 2 jiunga na shiriki, -wa mwanachama/ mshiriki wa. 3 ~ **into (with)** anza, fungua, fungulia. ~ **into** anza kushughulika na ~ *into details* anza kushughulika kwa undani. ~ **into sb's feelings** hurumia, elewa kwa ndani ~ *into the spirit of the occasion* jiingiza kikamilifu katika shughuli, -wa sehemu ya. 4 ~ **(in/up)** ingiza/orodhesha (majina, taarifa kitabuni). 5 ~ **for;** ~ **sb for** jiandikisha; andikisha kwa mashindano. 6 ~ **on/ upon** ingia, anza kumiliki.
entrance *n* 1 mlango/lango/njia ya kupitia, kuingia, kutokea kwa mchezaji katika jukwaa. 2 kuingia *(to) force ~* ingia kwa nguvu. 3 haki ya kuingilia. ~ **fees** malipo, kiingilio. ~ **examination** mtihani wa kuingilia. **entrant** *n* 1 mwingiaji. 2 mshindani. **entry** *n* 1 kuingia. 2 mlango; ruhusa ya kuingia. **no ~** hakuna ruhusa kuingia. 3 ingizo. 4 *(of a dictionary)* kitomeo. 5 orodha/idadi ya washiriki katika mashindano.
enteric *adj* -a matumbo ~ *fever* homa ya matumbo, taifodi. **enteritis** *n* mwako wa tumbo.
enterprise *n* 1 jambo kubwa (hasa la ujasiri). 2 moyo wa utendaji, uhodari *he has no ~* hana bidii. 3 shughuli *commercial ~* shughuli za biashara. **enterprising** *adj* jasiri, hodari. **enterprisingly** *adv*.
entertain *vt* 1 ~ **(to)** kirimu, karibisha. 2 burudisha *(to) ~ angels unawares* kuwakaribisha wakuu bila kuwafahamu. 3 ~ **(with)** pendeza, furahisha. 4 *(consider)* wa tayari kufikiria, kuridhia, kuwazia ~ *an appeal* kubali kusikiliza rufani ~ *an illusion* kuwaza na kuwazua juu ya jambo lisilowezekana, kufurahia kama kwamba linawezekana. ~ **allowance** jamala/takrima. **~ing** *adj* -a kupendeza, -a kufurahisha. **~ingly** *adv*. **~ment** *n* burudani. **~er** *n*.
enthral *vt* 1 vutia sana/kabisa furahisha sana. 2 fanya mtumwa, tia utumwani; *(usu fig)* teka *~led by woman's beauty* tekwa na uzuri wa mwanamke.
enthrone *vt (of king or bishop)* tawaza, simika; *(fig)* taadhimu. **~ment** *n*.
enthuse *vi* ~ **over** *(colloq)* onyesha shauku. **enthusiasm** *n* shauku. **enthusiast** *n* mwenye shauku *a*

sports ~ shabiki, mpenzi wa michezo (riadha). **enthusiastic** *adj* -a shauku *(to) become ~ over sth* -wa na shauku kubwa kuhusu kitu. **enthusiastically** *adv*.

entice *vt* laghai, shawishi. **(to) ~ away from** shawishi aache jambo moja ashike jingine. **~ment** *n*.

entire *adj* zima, ote *the ~ village was destroyed* kijiji kizima kiliharibiwa *n* mnyama asiyehasiwa. **~ly** *adv*. **~ty** *n*.

entitle *vt* 1 **(be ~d)** itwa, -wa na jina *a book ~d "Mashetani"* kitabu kinachoitwa Mashetani. 2 **~d to do sth** -pa haki (ya) *you are not ~d to have an office car* huna haki ya kuwa na gari la kazini. **~ment** *n*.

entity *n* 1 kitu/chombo kamili. 2 kuishi, kuwepo.

entomb *vt* zika, -wa kaburi la **~ment** *n*.

entomology *n* entomolojia: elimu wadudu. **entomological** *adj*. **entomologist** *n* mwanafunzi/bingwa wa elimu wadudu.

entourage *n* msafara (wa kiongozi mashuhuri) *Presidential ~* msafara wa Rais.

entr'acte *n* mapumziko (katikati ya mchezo).

entrails *n* 1 matumbo, utumbo.

entrain *vt,vi (of troops)* pakia, ingia (katika gari la moshi).

entrance *vt* **~ (at, with)** vutia/pendeza/furahishana.

entreat *vt* sihi. **~ing** *adj*. **~ingly** *adv* **~y** *n* kusihi.

entree *n (F)* 1 ruhusa/haki ya kuingia. 2 *(course of meal)* chakula kinacholetwa baada ya kula samaki na kabla ya nyama.

entrench *vt* 1 zungushia handaki, zungushia boma (la kulinda maji, kambi, jeshi). 2 fanya madhubuti. **~ed clauses** vifungu (vilivyofungwa) vya katiba, fungu madhubuti. **~ment** *n*.

entrepot *n* 1 bohari. 2 eneo la biashara (ndani na nje), kituo cha kuhifadhi na kusambaza bidhaa.

entrepreneur *n* mjasiriamali, mwekezi, mwaminishi. **~ship** *n*.

entrust *vt* amini, aminisha (kukamilisha au kulinda kitu), kabidhi.

entwine *also* **entwist** *vt* **~ (with/round)** sokota, pota, nyonga (kamba).

enumerate *vt* taja moja moja, hesabu. **enumeration** *n*.

enunciate *vt,vi* 1 taja, tamka wazi, tangaza, hubiri. 2 elezea nadharia wazi au kwa uwazi. **enunciation** *n*.

envelop *vt* **~(in)** funga, gubika, funika.

envelope *n* 1 bahasha. 2 gubiko la baluni au chomboanga.

envenom *vt* 1 tia sumu (uchungu, ukali). 2 *(fig)*chukiza.

environs *n* 1 maeneo yanayozunguka mji. 2 mwanamazingira. **environ** *vt* zunguka, zingira. **environment** *n* mazingira, hali. **environmental** *adj* **environmentally** *adv*. **environmentalist** *n*.

envisage *vt* taamali, hisi, fikiria *~ a danger* hisi hatari.

envoy *n* mjumbe (wa serikali), balozi mdogo.

envy *n* husuda, wivu, kijicho *out of ~* kwa wivu, kwa uhasidi *filled with ~ of me/at my success* jaa kijicho kwa mafanikio yangu, wanatoa kashfa yote kwa ajili ya kijicho tu *vt* onea husuda, husudu, onea wivu; tamani (mali au haki ya mwingine) *I ~ you* nakuonea wivu *I ~ your good fortune* nakuonea kijicho kwa bahati yako nzuri, ninahusudu bahati yako. **envious** *adj* -enye kijicho *(to) make sb ~* fanya aone kijicho. **enviable** *adj* 1 -a kuleta wivu, -a kulilia ngoa. 2 -a kufanikiwa sana, a kuhusudiwa. 3 -enye husuda; hasidi.

enzyme *n* kimeng'enya.

eon *n see* **aeon**.

epaulet, epaulette *n* mapurendi; nyota za mabegani (kwa wanajeshi).

epenthesis *n* kuongeza herufi au sauti katika neno. **epenthetic** *adj*.

epergne *n* bakuli la kuwekea maua mezani.
ephemeral *adj* -a muda mfupi, -a kupita.
epic *n* utendi *adj* -a utendi; *(colloq)* -nayofaa kusherehekewa, -a kishujaa, -a kama utendi *of ~ proportions* kubwa mno.
epicentre *n* kitovu cha zilizala.
epicure *n* mteuzi, machagu, kidomo.
epicurean *adj (person)* -enye kupenda anasa. **epicurianism** *n*.
epicycle *n (geom)* duara linalozunguka nje ya duara jingine.
epidemic *n* magonjwa ya mlipuko *adj* (magonjwa) -a mlipuko. **epidemiology** *n* elimu ya magonjwa ya mlipuko.
epidermis *n* ngozi ya nje. **epidermic** *adj*.
epiglottis *n* kidakatonge, kimio.
epigram *n* shairi fupi au usemi unaochekesha. **~atic** *adj (of a person)* -enye mafumbo.
epigraph *n* mchoro, maandishi (juu ya sanamu, sarafu n.k).
epilepsy *n* kifafa. **epileptic** *adj* -a kifafa *n* mtu mwenye kifafa.
epilogue *n* hitimisho la kazi ya sanaa agh. shairi.
Epiphany *n* Epifania, sikukuu ya Majusi.
episcopal *adj* -a maaskofu, -a kuhusu maaskofu. **the ~ church** *(esp US, Scot)* Kanisa la Kianglikana. **~ian** *adj* mfuasi/mwumini wa Kanisa hili. **episcopate** *n* 1 kazi ya uaskofu, ofisi/ enzi/kipindi cha uaskofu. 2 *(bishops)* jamii ya maaskofu.
episode *n* tukio (kisa) katika mfululizo wa matukio. **episodic** *adj*.
epistemology *n* epistemolojia: elimu ya ufahamu.
epistle *n* 1 *(old use or joc)* barua, waraka. **the E~s** Nyaraka za Mitume katika Agano Jipya. **epistolary** *adj* -a waraka.
epistrophe *n* neno linalorudiwa mwisho wa kila fungu la maneno.
epitaph *n* wasifu wa marehemu (agh. huandikwa kaburini).
epithet *n* wasifu, sifa (maelezo) inayoongezwa katika jina la mtu (kitu) kuashiria tabia yake.
epitome *n* 1 kifano. 2 muhtasari, ufupisho wa habari. **epitomize** *vt* 1 fanya muhtasari. 2 -wa kifano cha.
epoch *n* (mwanzo wa) kipindi maalum katika historia **~ making** *adj* -enye kuanza kipindi kipya cha historia. **~al** *adj*.
eponym *n* jina la mtu/shetani/kitu litolewalo kwa mtu/kitu mahali fulani.
epsilon *n (Greek)* epsiloni (herufi E,e).
Epsom salts *n* haluli ya chumvi.
equable *adj* 1 *(of climate)* sawasawa, -siobadilikabadilika *an ~ climate* hali ya hewa isiyobadilikabadilika. 2 *(of persons) he has an ~ temper* habadilikibadiliki (kitabia). **equably** *adv*.
equal *adj* 1 sawa, sawasawa, -a kulingana *twice three is ~ to six* mbili mara tatu ni/sawa na sita *all things being ~* mambo yote yakiwa sawa. **on ~ terms** kwa usawa *(to) get ~ with sb* kulingana na fulani. 2 **~ to sth/to doing sth** -enye uwezo/ ujasiri *be ~ to the ocasion* weza, mudu, toshindwa. **are you ~ to it?** waiweza? *n* 1 *(in age)* hirimu, marika. **live as ~s** ishi kama marika kwa usawa. 2 *(in condition, quality)* mwenzi *she has no ~* hana kifani *vt* -wa sawa na, lingana na, landana. **~ity** *n*. **~itarian** *n see* **egalitarian**. **~ize** *vt* sawazisha.. **~ization** *n* ulinganifu, usawazishaji. **~izer** *n* kisawazishaji. **~ly** *adv*.
equate *vt* ~ **(with)** linganisha na, sawazisha. **equation** *n* 1 **equation (with)** kusawazisha, kulinganisha. 2 *(maths)* mlinganyo equation of a circle mlinganyo wa duara.
equanimity *n* utulivu (wa moyo, tabia), upole.
equator *n* ikweta, istiwai. **~ial** *adj* -a ikweta, -a karibu na ikweta.
equerry *n* mpambe/katikiro wa

mfalme (rais, malkia).

equestrian *adj* -a kupanda farasi. **~ skill** ustadi wa kupanda farasi *equestrian statue* sanamu ya mawe ya mpanda farasi *n* mpanda farasi stadi.

equi *(prefix)* sawa. **~angular** *adj* -enye pembe sawa. **~distant (from)** *adj* -enye umbali sawa *n* *(maths)* umbali sawa. **~lateral** *adj* -enye pande zote sawa. **~ triangle** pembetatu sawa. **~librate** *vt* sawazisha, linganisha. **~libration** *n*. *(in circus)* **~librist** *n* mnegaji (juu ya kamba), msawazishaji, mtu mwenye ujuzi wa kusawazisha katika mizani. **~librium** *n* 1 ulinganifu, usawa. **be in ~librium** simama sawa, -wa na ulinganifu, tulia. 2 *(maths)* msawazo. **~librium price** bei sawa (ambapo bidhaa na mahitaji vinalingana).

equine *adj* *(formal)* -a farasi, -a kama farasi.

equinox *n* ikwinoksi: siku mlingano (ambapo jua huvuka mstari wa ikweta na usiku na mchana kuwa sawa). **equinoctial** *adj* -a (karibu ya) ikwinoksi.

equip *vt* **~ (with)** tayarisha, andaa, zatiti. **~age** *n* *(former times)* zana za safari, gari na masaisi. **~ment** *n* 1 *(collective noun)* vifaa. 2 uwekaji/maandalizi ya vifaa.

equipoise *n* 1 ulinganifu, mlingano. 2 kilinganishi.

equitation *n* *(usu joc)* upandaji farasi. **~ school** shule ya upandaji farasi.

equity *n* 1 usawa, sawa, haki. 2 *(often pl)* hisa zisizo na riba ya kudumu. **equitable** *adj* -a sawa, -a haki *~ interest* masilahi ya haki *~ distribution* mgawano sawa. **equitably** *adv*.

equivalent *n adj* 1 **~ (to)** -a kulingana, sawa, -linganifu, mamoja. **~ equations** milinganyo sawa. **~ sets** seti sawa. 2 kisawe. **equivalence** *n* usawa, ulinganifu.

equivocal *adj* 1 *(of words)* -a kauleni, -enye maana mbili au zaidi. 2 -a shaka. 3 *(of character)* -enye kupotosha, babaishi. **equivocate** *vi* tatiza maneno, sema maneno yenye maana isiyo dhahiri (hasa kwa kusudi la kutatiza au kudanganya). **equivocation** *n* 1 matumizi ya kauli tata. 2 kupotosha watu. 3 misemo isiyo dhahiri.

era *n* enzi.

eradicate *vt* ng'oa, futa, komesha. **eradicable** *adj*. **eradication** *n*.

erase *vt* futa, pangusa. **erasable** *adj* -enye kufutika. **~r** *n* kifutio. **erasure** *n* mfuto.

ere *adv, prep (old use, or poet)* kabla. **~ long** kabla ya muda mrefu. **~ now** kabla ya sasa.

erect *adj* -a kusimama wima. **~ly** *adv*. **~ness** *n*, *vt* 1 *(construct)* jenga, unda. 2 simamisha, simika. **~ile** *adj* *(physiol)* -a kuweza kusimika/kudinda/kusimama/kuwa gumu/kutanua mishipa ya damu. **erection** *n* 1 usimikaji, usimamishwaji; *(physiol)* kusimika/kudinda dhakari/kinembe. 2 ujenzi; jengo. **erector** *n* mtu/chombo kinachosimika/simamisha kitu fulani.

eremite *n see* **hermit**.

erg *n (phys)* egi: kizio cha kazi (kipimo cha metriki cha kani au nishati).

ergo *adv (Lat) (usu hum)* basi, kwa hiyo, hivyo.

ergonomics *n* taaluma ya mazingira, hali na ufanisi wa wafanyakazi (wanaohusika na mashine).

ermine *n* 1 jamii ya kicheche wa Ulaya. 2 ngozi ya kicheche. 3 vazi la ngozi ya kicheche (agh vazi la jaji).

erode *vt,vi* *(of acids, rains etc)* momonyoa. **erosion** *n* *soil erosion* mmomonyoko wa udongo. **erosive** *adj*.

erogenous *adj* -enye kutia nyege. **~ zone** sehemu za unyegevu/nyegereshi.

erotic *adj* -a ashiki *n pl* vitabu, picha, mashairi ya kutia ashiki/nyege. **~ism** *n* ashiki. **erotomania** *n* wehu wa mapenzi.

err *vi (formal)* kosa, potoka *it is better to ~ on the side of mercy* afadhali kuwa mwingi wa huruma kuliko kuwa mwingi wa mateso. **~oneous** *adj* -enye kosa, -sio sahihi. **~oneusly** *adv*. **~oneusness** *n* kosa. **spelling ~ors** makosa ya tahajia *clerical ~* kosa la maandishi. **~or less** *adj* -siokosa/waa. **in ~or** kwa makosa.

errand *n* 1 safari fupi k.m. kwenda benki na kurudi.**to run ~s/to go on ~s for sb** tumwa na mtu. **~ boy** tarishi. 2 nia/madhumuni ya safari hiyo *what is his ~?* ameendea nini? **a fool's ~** safari ya kuzurura.

errant *adj, n* 1 -enye kuvinjari, -a kutembeatembea kutafuta mambo ya ujasiri (uhodari n.k.). 2 -enye kwenda ovyo/kupotea; -bembe; tembezi. 3 -a kukosea, -enye kupotoka. **~ly** *adv*.

erratic *adj* 1 *(of person or his behaviour)* -siotabirika, -enye kukosakosa. 2 -potovu; *(of things, e.g. a clock)* -enye mwendo usioaminika. **~ally** *adv*.

erratum *n* kosa (katika uandikaji au uchapaji) *an ~ slip* karatasi yenye orodha ya makosa katika kitabu.

erstwhile *adv* zamani, kale.

eructation *n (formal)* kokomoko, cheuo, mbweu agh. ya volkano.

erudite *adj (formal)* alimu, -enye maarifa, -enye elimu, juzi. **~ly** *adv*. **erudition** *n* maarifa, elimu, ujuzi.

erupt *vi* fumuka, ripuka, foka, (hasa kwa volkano). **~ion** *n* kufoka kwa volkano; *(fig)* kuzuka (kwa vita, magonjwa, n.k.), kutokwa na upele, meno. **~ive** *adj*.

erysipelas *n (Med)* erisipela: ugonjwa wa ngozi uletao homa na ngozi kuwa nyekundu.

escalate *vt,vi* ongeza, endeleza, shadidisha hatua kwa hatua. **escalation** *n*. **escalator** *n* eskaleta: ngazi za umeme katika jengo.

escalope *n* kipande cha mnofu (bila mfupa).

escapade *n* tendo la ujasiri, utundu, utani linalosababisha maneno au matata.

escape *n* 1 kutoroka, utorokaji. 2 kuokoka, kuponyoka; njia/chombo cha kuokolea/kutolea kitu/mtu *he had a narrow ~* aliponea chupuchupu. **~ velocity** kasi mwelekeo ya kuponyokea: kasi inayohitajika kukiwezesha chombo fulani (hasa cha anga) kujitoa kwenye eneo la nguvu za mvutano fulani; *(of gas, smoke, etc)* mvujo, kuvuja; chombo cha kutolea mvuke, gasi, n.k. *an ~ pipe* bomba la kutolea moshi, mvuke n.k. *an ~ valve* vali ya kutolea hewa, kupumulia n.k. 3 kimbilio: kitu kinachobadilisha/sahaulisha mawazo kwa muda, mfano muziki, michezo, kileo, n.k. **~e** *n* mtoro, mfungwa aliyetoroka. **escapism** *n* ukwepaji (wa matatizo). **escapist** *n* mkwepaji, mtu mwenye tabia ya kukwepa/ kukimbia (mambo) *vt,vi* 1 *~ (from)* toroka, kimbia, toka *the prisoner has ~d* mfungwa ametoroka *gas ~s from an open pipe* gasi hutokea kwenye bomba lililo wazi. 2 okoka, nusurika, epa *he ~d from injury* amenusurika. 3 -toangaliwa, -totambuliwa; sahauliwa, pitiwa *this issue ~d my notice* suala hili limenipitia.

escarpment *n* mharara, genge.

eschatology *n (rel)* tawi la theolojia linalojishughulisha na kifo, hukumu, pepo na jehanam.

eschew *vt (formal)* epukana na, kwepa.

escort *n* 1 mlinzi, kikundi cha walinzi. 2 msindikizaji *vi* fuatana na, sindikiza.

escritoire *n* dawati, meza yenye saraka.

escutcheon *n* 1 ngao yenye nembo ya cheo au nasaba ya mtu. **a blot on one's ~** doa/waa kwenye sifa ya mtu. 2 *(of a padlock)* kifuniko cha tundu la ufunguo.

esophogus *n (also* **oesophagus***)* umio.

esoteric *adj* -a ndani, -a siri, -a kuhusu kikundi fulani tu, faragha (k.m. siri za jandoni).
espalier *n* 1 mitambazi; mimea inayotambaa kwenye uchaga. 2 uchaga ambamo mimea hutambaa.
especial *adj* -a kipekee, mahsusi, maalumu *for your ~ benefit* kwa faida yako mahsusi. **~ly** *adv* zaidi, hasa, hususa.
esperanto *n* esperanto (lugha bandia iliyoundwa kutumiwa na watu wote duniani).
espionage *n* ujasusi.
esplanade *n* uwanja, barabara pana, hasa kando ya bahari, kwa watu kutembelea.
espouse *vt (of man)* 1 oa. 2 *(support)* unga mkono. **espousal** *n* 1 utetezi. 2 *(old use usu pl)* **espousals** posa, ndoa.
espresso *n* **~ coffee** kahawa inayotengenezwa kwa mvuke mkali, spreso.
esprit *n (F)* uchangamfu, werevu. **~ de corps** moyo wa mshikamano, kupenda, kusitawisha na kuheshimu jamii au shirika.
espy *vt (usu joc)* chungulia, gundua (kosa), ona.
esq *(abbr)* **Esquire**.
Esquire *n (GB)* cheo cha heshima kinachoandikwa baada ya jina la ukoo, huandikwa **Esq**. baada ya jina k.m. *John Smith Esq.*, badala ya Mr. John Smith.
essay[1] *n* insha. **~ist** *n* mwandishi wa insha.
essay[2] *n (effort)* juhudi, jaribio *vt* 1 aribu, jitahidi. 2 *(arch) (try, prove)* hakiki, pima.
essence *n* 1 asili, nafsi, dhati, hali. 2 *(extract, perfume)uto,uturi,marashi; (domestic science)* ariki. 3 moyo, kiini, kitovu *~ of the matter* kiini/kitovu cha jambo *time is the ~ of the contract* muda au wakati ndio kiini cha mkataba. **essential** *adj* 1 -a lazima, muhimu *it is ~ that* ni muhimu kwamba. 2 -a msingi. 3 -a uto *n (usu pl)* **~s** mambo ya msingi (muhimu). **essentially** *adv* kimsingi.
establish *vt* 1 weka, anzisha, unda, asisi. 2 *(make firm)* imarisha, weka imara, zatiti, rasimisha; thibitisha. 3 *(appoint)* weka, amuru, taifisha (kanisa) *he ~ed his son in his farm* alimweka mtoto wake katika shamba lake. 4 *(prove)* kubalisha, shuhudia, sadikisha *~ a reputation for* jenga jina la. **~ed** *adj* imara, thabiti, madhubuti. **~ment** *n* 1 kuimarisha, kuweka, kuanzisha. 2 serikali, shirika, kampuni, n.k., dini ya taifa kisheria; *(of a department)* idara na ikama. 3 **E ~ment** *(GB)* wenye nchi, wenye madaraka.
estaminet *(US) n* kijimkahawa cha bia, mvinyo, kahawa, n.k.
estate *n* 1 shamba. **~ agent** mkadamu, wakala: mnunuzi/mwuzaji wa kati. **housing ~** eneo la makazi. **industrial ~** eneo la viwanda. **fourth ~** (waandishi wa) habari. 2 milki, mali. **personal ~** mali ya mtu binafsi. 3 tabaka la watu. 4 *(old use)* hali. 5 stesheni wagoni: gari dogo lenye nafasi ya abiria na mizigo ndani.
esteem *vt* 1 *(formal)* sharifu, enzi, tukuza. **your ~ed letter** barua yako tukufu. 2 *(consider)* ona, chukulia *~ it a privilege* ona/chukulia jambo kuwa ni heshima *n* taadhima, enzi.
estimable *adj* -a kusifiwa.
estimation *n* 1 heshima, sifa *be held in high ~* tukuzwa, heshimiwa sana. 2 *(judgement)* maoni, tafkira *in my ~* kwa maoni yangu.
esthetic *adj see* **aesthetic**.
estimate *vt,vi* **~ (at)** kadiria, kisia. **make ~** fanya makadirio. **estimative** *adj n* makadirio. The **E ~s** makadirio ya matumizi na mapato ya Serikali *at a rough ~* kwa kukadiria/kukisia. **estimator** *n*.
estop *vt (leg)* kataza, zuia, zibia. **be ~ped** zibiwa. **~pel** *n (leg)* katazo, zuio, kuzibia, kuzibiwa: kanuni ya sheria inayomzuia mtu kukana au kukanusha ushahidi aliokwishatoa na

kusema kuwa ni kweli.

estrange *vt* ~ **(from)** farikisha, tenganisha. **become** ~**d from** tenganishwa na, farakana na. ~**ment** *n.*

estuary *n* mlango wa mto.

et al *adv* (pamoja) na wengine.

et cetera *(Lat usu shortened to etc.)* 1 na kadhalika. 2 *(pl)* ~s mengineyo, vitu vya ziada.

etch *vt* 1 chora juu ya metali kwa kutumia asidi kwa ajili ya kutolea nakala; tengeneza picha kwa asidi; *(fig)* ganda akilini. ~**ing** *n* sanaa ya uchoraji wa kutumia asidi; nakala ya picha iliyochorwa na asidi. ~**er** *n* mchoraji asidi.

eternal *adj* 1 -a milele, -a daima ~ *life* uzima wa milele. 2 *(colloq)* isiyoisha. **the** ~ **triangle** mgogoro wa mapenzi ya wawili kwa mmoja *n* 1 **the E**~ Mungu. 2 kitu kinachodumu milele. ~**ly** *adv*. **eternity** *n* 1 milele, daima dawama, *(the next world)* ahera, kuzimuni. 2 **an** ~ muda mrefu. 3 *(pl)* ukweli wa milele.

ether *n* 1 *(phy, chem)* etha: aina ya nusu kaputi. 2 *(poet)* anga ya juu. ~**eal** 1 *(chem)* -a etha. 2 *(poet)* -a mbinguni, -a peponi, kuliko -a duniani.

ethic *n* **an** ~ mfumo wa maadili. ~s *n (pl)* 1 maadili. 2 elimuadili. ~**al** *adj.*

Ethiopian *n* 1 Mhabeshi. 2 *adj* -a kihabeshi.

ethnic *adj* 1 -a kabila/mbari au makabila ya walimwengu; *(colloq)* -a kikundi cha utamaduni fulani. ~**ally** *adv*. **ethnography** *n* ethnografia: maelezo ya kisayansi kuhusu mbari, mila, utamaduni n.k. ya binadamu. **ethnographer** *n*. **ethnographic** *adj*. **ethnology** *n* ethnolojia: sayansi ya makabila/mbari za binadamu, mahusiano kati yao. ~**logist** *n* Mwethnolojia.

ethos *n* maadili ya jamii au taifa.

ethyl *n* ethili: radikali ya kikaboni itokanayo na ethani. ~ **alcohol** *n* alkoholi ethili.

etiology *n (med)* elimu ya chanzo cha magonjwa; utoaji wa sababu za magonjwa.

etiquette *n* adabu, taratibu za itifaki/mahusiano, miiko ~ *of the bar* adabu ya uwakili *professional* ~ adabu ya weledi/utaalamu, miiko ya kazi.

etude *n (mus)* utungo wa muziki unaotumiwa kama zoezi.

etymology *n* etimolojia: elimu ya asili na historia ya neno; maelezo ya asili na historia ya maneno. **etymologist** *n*. **etymologic (al)** *adj.*

eucalyptus *n (bot)* kalitusi, mkalitusi.

Eucharist *n (rel)* Ekaristi. **Holy** ~ Ekaristi Takatifu; Karamu ya Bwana. ~**ic(al)** *adj.*

eugenics *n* yujeniki, udhibiti hali: sayansi ya uzalishaji watoto wenye afya (kwa nia ya kustawisha hazina ya jeni ya watu).

eulogize *vt* sifu sana katika hotuba au maandishi. **eulogist** *n*. **eulogistic** *adj.*

eulogy *n* maneno ya kusifu; taabini.

eunuch *n* towashi.

eupeptic *adj* -enye mmeng'enyo mzuri (wa chakula tumboni). **eupepsia** *n.*

euphemism *n* usafidi, tasifida: (mifano ya) matumizi ya maneno ya staha badala ya yale yenyewe k.m. aga dunia badala ya kufa. **euphemistic** *adj*. **euphemistically** *adv.*

euphony *n* utamu wa sauti; sauti ya kupendeza. **euphonic. euphonious** *adj.*

euphoria *n* wingi wa furaha, hali ya kufurahia. **euphoric** *adj.*

euphuism *n* mbwembwe katika mwandiko na kusema.

Eurasian *n* chotara wa Mzungu na Mwasia, -enye wazazi wa Kizungu na Kiasia *adj* -a Ulaya na Asia.

eureka *(int)* nimeipata!

eurhythmics *n* ulinganishaji wa mwendo wa mwili hasa kwa mfumo wa kufanya mazoezi ya mwili kwa muziki.

Europe *n* Ulaya. **Eurodollar** *n* dola ya Marekani iliyo katika benki za Ulaya. **European** *n* Mzungu *adj* -a kizungu. **europeanize** *vt* fanya kizungu **E ~ an Economic Community** Jumuiya ya Uchumi ya Ulaya.

Euro-vision *n*. mfumo wa televisheni ya Ulaya.

euthanasia *n* 1 eutanasia: kifo cha huruma (kwa mgonjwa aliyeteseka sana kwa maradhi yasiyotibika).

evacuate *vt,vi* 1 hama. 2 ~ **sb** hamisha. 3 *(of bowel)* nya. **evacuation** *n*. **evacuee** *n* mtu anayehamishwa/anayenyeshwa.

evade *vt* 1 *(of a blow, attack, obstacle)* epa, epuka. 2 *(of duty)* kwepa, tega. ~ **paying tax** kwepa kulipa kodi.

evasion *n* 1 kuepa, kukwepa, werevu. 2 kisingizio, maneno ya kukwepa *resort to ~s* chenga, danganya. **evasive** *adj* -a kuepaepa, -a kukwepa. **evasively** *adv*. **evasiveness** *n*.

evaluate *vt* tathmini. **evaluation** *n* tathmini. **evaluator** *n* mthamini.

evanescent *adj* -enye kusahaulika upesi; -a kufifia; -a kupita. **evanescence** *n*.

evangelical *adj* 1 -a kiinjili. 2 -a kiprotestanti, -a kilokole *n* mlokole. **evangelist** *n* mwinjilisti, mmoja kati ya waandishi wa injili (John, Luka, Matayo, Marko). **evangelism** *n*. uinjilisti; ulokole. **evangelistic** *adj*. **evangelize** *vt* fundisha Injili; shawishi mtu kuingia ukristu.

evaporate *vt,vi* 1 vukiza; *(be absorbed)* nywewa. 2 toweka; fariki dunia. **evaporation** *n* mvukizo.

Eve *n (in the Bible story of the Creation)* Hawa, Eva, mwanamke wa kwanza.

eve *n* mkesha *Christmas Eve* Mkesha wa Noeli.

even[1] *adj* 1 *(level)* sawasawa, bapa. 2 linganifu, -enye urari. 3 *(of temper)* tulivu, -siokasirika kwa urahisi. 4 *(of amounts, distances, values)* imara, isiyobadilika *be/get ~ with sb* lipiza kisasi. ~ **odds** matumaini sawa *at an ~ pace* kwa muda/mwendo usiobadilika. **break** ~ *(colloq)* -topata faida wala hasara. 5 sawa. **an ~ chance** fursa sawa. ~ **handed** -a haki. 6 *(of numbers)* shufwa. ~ **numbers** namba shufwa. ~ **powers** vipeo shufwa *vt* sawazisha. **make ~/~ up** linganisha, sawazisha. **~ly** *adv*. **~ness** *n*.

even[2] *adv (used to invite a comparison between what happened and what might have happened) He never ~ opened the letters* hata barua hakuzifungua kamwe ~ *now she does not believe me* hata sasa haniamini. ~ **so** hata hivyo. 2 ~ **if/though** *(to call attention to the extreme nature of what to follow)* hata kama ~ *if you die* hata ukifa ~ *if you go, it is all the same to me* hata kama ukienda ni mamoja kwangu.

even[3] *n (poet)* jioni. **~song** *n* Sala ya Jioni (kwa kabila la Kiingereza). **~tide** *n (poet)* jioni.

evening *n* 1 jioni. 2 *(attrib)* ~ **dress** vazi la jioni. ~ **paper** gazeti la mchana/jioni. ~ **prayer** sala ya jioni.

event *n* 1 tukio. **in the natural/normal/usual course of ~s** kwa mfuatano wa mambo. 2 kutokea. 3 matokeo. **at all ~s** chochote kile kiwacho. **in that ~** kama hivyo ndivyo. **in the ~** kama inavyotokea. 4 shindano. **~ful** *adj*.

eventual *adj* -a badaye; hatimaye. **~ly** *adv* mwishowe.

ever *adv* 1 *(any time)* wakati wowote *nothing ~ happens here* kwa wakati wowote hakuna kinachofanyika hapa. 2 wakati wowote hadi sasa *have you ~ been there* umepata kufika mahali pale. 3 kuliko wakati wowote *it is darker than ~* kuna kiza kuliko wakati wowote mwingine. 4 *(chiefly in phrases)* daima, kila mara. **for ~ and ~** dumu daima, daima dawamu ~

since I was a boy tangu nilipokuwa kijana. 5 *(colloq) run as fast as you ~ can* kimbia kasi kadiri unavyoweza. 6 *how did you ~ manage?* uliwezaje kweli? *did you ~ !* Loo! *did you ~ hear such a story* umewahi kusikia hadithi ya aina hii. 7 *(old use)* daima *I shall ~ be at your service* nitakuwa daima tayari kukutumikia. 8 *yours ~ (used at the end of the letter)* wako daima. 9 ~ **so, ~ such a** sana. **~green** *adj (tree, shrub)* -siokauka, -enye majani mwaka mzima *n* mmea wenye majani mwaka mzima. **~lasting** *adj* 1 -a milele, -a kudumu ~ *life* uzima wa milele. 2 -sioisha ~ *quarrels* ugomvi usioisha *n* **the E~** Mungu. **~lastingly** *adv* kila wakati. **~more** *adv* milele *for ~* hata milele.

every *adj* 1 kila. ~ **thing** kila kitu *you have ~ reason to be happy* una kila sababu ya kufurahi. 2 -ote *she used ~ cent* alitumia fedha zote *he ate ~ single/last bit of the food* alikula chakula chote. 3 ~ **time** kila mara. **he comes late ~ time** anachelewa kila mara. ~ **one of them** kila mmoja, wote (kwa jumla). **in ~ way** kwa kila hali. **~body/one** kila mtu. ~ **day** *pron* kila siku *adj* -a kawaida *my ~ day clothes* nguo zangu za kawaida. ~ **where** *adv* kila mahali. ~ **now and again/ ~ now and then/ ~ so often** mara moja moja. ~ **bit as** sawasawa kwa kila hali *she's ~ bit as intelligent as you* ana akili sawasawa na wewe kwa kila hali.

evict *vt* ~ **(from)** fukuza mpangaji (kutoka shamba/nyumba kwa kutumia sheria). **~ion** *n*. ~ **order** hati ya kumfukuza mpangaji.

evidence *n* 1 ushahidi, ushuhuda. **give ~** toa ushahidi. **(be) in ~** onekana wazi au kwa urahisi *Hamisi was no where in ~* Hamisi hakuonekana popote. **turn Queen's/ King's/***(US)* **State's ~** *(of a criminal)* toa ushahidi dhidi ya washitakiwa wenzako. 2 *(usu in pl)* alama, ishara. **bear/give/ show ~ of** onyesha ishara za *vt (rare)* shuhudia/ thibitisha, onyesha.

evident *adj* dhahiri, wazi. **~ly** *adv*.

evil *adj* 1 ovu, fisadi, baya. ~ **minded** -enye mawazo maovu ~ *tempered* -enye hasira mbaya *the ~ one* Shetani, Ibilisi. ~ **spirits** pepo wabaya. 2 *(unfortunate)* -enye kisirani, -a ndege mbaya. ~ **eye** kijicho *fall on ~ days* pata visirani *n* uovu, ubaya. **~-doer** mwovu. **choose the lesser of two ~s** chagua -lio afadhali (ingawa yote mawili ni mabaya). **~ly** *adv* vibaya.

evince *vt (formal)* dhihirisha.

eviscerate *vt* tumbua, toa matumbo.

evoke *vt* 1 ita. ~ **spirts** ita pepo. 2 amsha, leta. ~ **feelings** amsha, leta hisia. **evocative** *adj*. **evocation** *n*.

evolve *vt,vi* 1 kua, geuka *my feelings have ~d* hisia zangu zimekua. 2 endeleza taratibu/ kiasili; *(of plan)* zindua kiasili *vi* funuka. **evolution** *n* 1 mageuko/ mabadiliko (ya polepole au yasiyoingiliwa kati). 2 nadharia ya mageuko kutoka sahili kuwa tata. 3 mwendo uliopangwa/ maalum (wa majeshi, wacheza dansi, n.k.). **evolutionary** *adj*.

evulsion *n* kutoa kwa nguvu.

ewe *n* kondoo jike.

ewer *n* chungu kikubwa (chenye kishikizo kwa ajili ya kuhifadhi maji).

ex *(pref)* -a zamani. **~-president** rais wa zamani.

exacerbate *vt (formal)* 1 zidisha (maumivu, ugomvi, hasira, chuki, uchungu, n.k.). 2 *(irritate)* kasirisha, chukiza. **exacerbation** *n*.

exact[1] *adj* 1 sahihi, hasa, barabara, kamili *his ~ words* maneno yake hasa. 2 -enye uwezo kamili. **an ~ memory** kumbukumbu iliyo barabara. **~ly** *adv* 1 kabisa, kamili *that's ~ right* ni sawasawa kabisa *it's ~ two o' clock* ni saa nane kamili; *(answer or confirmation)* sawa, kabisa, hasa. **~ness, ~itude**

n.

exact[2] *vt* ~ **(from)** 1 toza, lipisha kwa nguvu. 2 hitaji, taka *this work ~s closest attention* kazi hii inataka/inahitaji uangalifu sana. 3 *(compel)* shurutisha, lazimisha, sisitiza ~ *obedience* tiisha, shurutisha/lazimisha kutii. **~ing** *adj*. **~ion** *n* 1 kutoza, kulipisha kwa nguvu. 2 kitu kinacholipwa k.m. kodi.

exaggerate *vt,vi* kuza, piga chuku, tia chumvi. **exaggeration** *n*.

exalt *vt* 1 *(promote)* pandisha (cheo, hadhi). 2 *(praise)* tukuza sifu sana, kuza. **~ation** nderemo, furaha.

examine *vt* 1 ~ **(for)** chunguza. 2 ~ **in** tahini, pima, pimwa. 3 kozi. **examination/exam** *n* 1 mtihani *pass an examination* pasi/faulu mtihani. 2 uchunguzi. **under** ~ katika kuchunguzwa *medical examination* uchunguzi wa kitabibu. 3 *(leg)* kuhoji kwa wakili. **examinee** *n* mtahiniwa. **examiner** *n* mtahini, mchunguzi.

example *n* 1 mfano. **set an** ~ onyesha mfano. **for** ~ kwa mfano, mathalani. 2 kielelezo. 3 funzo, fundisho *let this be an ~ to you* liwe fundisho kwako *make an ~ of sb* adhibu kama fundisho/mfano kwa wengine. **exemplar** *n* sampuli, mfano. **exemplary** *adj*. **exemplify** *vt* onyesha kwa mfano, -wa mfano.

exanimate *adj* -sio na uhai.

exasperate *vt* udhi, kasirisha, ghadhibisha, kera. **exasperation** *n*.

excavate *vt* chimbua, fukua (hasa kwa ajili ya utafiti wa vitu vya kale). **excavator** *n* mtu au mashine inayochimbua. **excavation** *n*. uchimbuaji, sehemu inayochimbuliwa au iliyochimbuliwa (yaani shimo).

exceed *vt* 1 zidi, -wa zaidi ya. 2 vuka/pita (kiwango kilichowekwa). **~ingly** *adv* mno.

excel *vt,vi* ~ **(in/at)** fanya vizuri kuzidi wengine, -wa bora kabisa, tia fora. **~lence** *n* ~ **(in/at)** ubora, uzuri. **~lent** *adj* bora sana, aali. **~lently** *adv*.

Excellency *n* Mheshimiwa, Mtukufu. **Your** ~ Mheshimiwa.

excelsior *n*. *(US)* 1 alama ya ubora wa bidhaa. 2 takataka za randa (za kufungia vitu vinavyovunjika kwa urahisi k.m. kauri).

except *(prep)* isipokuwa, ila *vt* ~ **from** acha, -tohesabu. **present company ~ed** ukiacha waliopo hapa. **~ing** *(prep) (used after not, always and without)* kuacha, kutoa *not* ~ bila kuacha/kutoa. **~ion** *n* 1 jambo la pekee, jambo lisilofuata kawaida. *with the ~ of* isipokuwa. 2 *(objection)* kinzano, maudhi, kikwazo. **take ~ to** udhiwa/kerwa na, kinza. **~ionable** *adj* -nayochukiza. 3 *(gram)* -siofuata kanuni. **~ional** *adj* -sio -a kawaida, -a pekee, bora sana. **~ionally** *adv*.

excerpt *n* dondoo *vt* dondoa.

excess *n* 1 ziada. **an ~ of** ziada ya. **in ~ of** zaidi ya kupindukia, kuzidi. **to** ~ mno, -a kupindukia. 2 *(pl)* **~es** maovu/matendo mabaya ya kupindukia; kujiachia. **~ive** *adj* -a ziada, -liozidi ~ *luggage* mizigo yenye uzito uliozidi. **~ively** *adj*.

exchange *n* 1 kubadilishana *an ~ of views* kubadilishana mawazo *in ~ for* badala ya. 2 *(of money)* kubadilisha/mabadilishano ya fedha *rate of ~* kima cha mabadilishano ya fedha *foreign ~* fedha za kigeni. ~ **Control** Udhibiti wa fedha za kigeni. 3 ofisi. **labour** ~ ofisi ya kazi, leba *telephone* ~ ofisi ya simu. 4 soko *Stock E* ~ Soko la Hisa *vt* badilishana ~ *presents* peana zawadi ~ *greetings* salimiana, amkiana. ~ **blows** pigana. ~ **words (with)** bishana. **~able** *adj*.

exchequer *n* 1 **the E~** *(GB)* Wizara ya F(edha. **Chancellor of the E~** *(GB)* Waziri wa Fedha. 2 ugavi wa fedha; hazina.

excise[1] *n* ushuru. ~ **duty** *(leg)* ushuru. ~ **officer** afisa wa ushuru. ~ **revenue** mapato ya ushuru.

excise[2] *vt* kata (sehemu ya mwili, kitabu, n.k.); ondoa, toa. **excision** *n*.

excite *vt* 1 sisimua, chochea *an exciting book* kitabu cha kusisimua *the freedom fighters ~ d the peasants to rise against the colonialists* wapigania uhuru waliwachochea wakulima kupigana na wakoloni. **be ~d** sisimka *don't ~ yourself* tulia. 2 *(cause)* amsha *~ attention* tazamisha, vuta macho *~ desire* tamanisha, tia shauku/ashiki/tamaa, sisimua *drugs that ~ the nerves* madawa yaamshayo neva. **~ment** *n* msisimko, taharuki, mpwitompwito *be in a state of ~* sisimkwa, taharuki, -wa na mpwitompwito. **excitable** *adj*. **excitability** *n*. **~dly** *adv*.

exclaim *vt,vi* 1 guta (kwa mshangao, maumivu/hasira n.k.), tamka ghafla (kwa mshangao (hasira, maumivu). 2 **~ against** shutumu, pinga vikali. **exclamation** *n* tamko/neno la mshangao; usiyahi *~ mark (US ~ point)* alama ya mshangao (!). **exclamatory** *adj* -a mshangao. **~ sentence** sentensi ya mshangao.

exclude *vt* **~ (from)** 1 *(remove) shut out* toa, acha, tenga *~ him from the list* mtoe katika orodha. *be ~d from* achwa *~ from the mind* ondoa katika mawazo. 2 *(refuse)* zuia *~ from membership of a club* zuia mtu asiingie katika kilabu. **exclusion** *n*. **excluding** *prep* mbali na, kuondoa, bila ya *~ the children there were 20 people* mbali na watoto kulikuwa na watu 20. **exclusive** *adj* 1 *(of persons)* nayejitenga (kwa kujiona bora), -siyechanganyika na wengine, pweke. 2 *(of a group/society)* maalum (kwa watu fulani tu). 3 -a pekee *Dictionary making is not his ~ employment* utungaji kamusi si kazi pekee anayoifanya. 4 *~ of* pasipo, bila kuhesabu, mbali na. **exclusively** *adv*.

excogitate *vt (formal or hum)* handisi, fikiria, buni (mpango). **excogitation** *n*.

excommunicate *vt (rel)* tenga na kanisa. **excommunication** *n*.

excoriate *vt (formal)* chubua, chuna (ngozi); *(fig)* kosoa sana. **excoriation** *n*.

excrescence *n* tezi, kinundu (kitu kisicho cha kawaida kinachojitokeza katika mwili au mmea).

excrescent *adj* -a kuzidi kadiri inayotakiwa, -a zaidi.

excreta *n* takamwili (zitokazo kama kinyesi, mkojo, jasho). **excrement** *n* kinyesi. **excremental** *adj*. **excretion** *n*. **excrete** *vt* -nya, toa takamwili.

excruciating *adj (of pain, bodily or mental)* -a kutesa sana, kali sana.

exculpate *vt* **~ (from)** toa katika hatia/lawama, burai, ondolea tuhuma. **exculpation** *n*. **exculpatory** *adj*.

excursion *n* 1 matembezi, matembezi/safari fupi (agh. ya kikundi cha watu). **~ ticket** tikiti ya bei nafuu. 2 *(Astron)* mchepuko kutoka njia kuu.

excuse *n* 1 udhuru, sababu; kisingizio. **in ~ of** kwa kisingizio cha *vt* 1 *(pardon)* samehe, wia radhi. **~ me** kumradhi, niwie radhi, samahani *~ my coming late* nisamehe kwa kuchelewa. 2 **~ from** ruhusu, achilia. **excusable** *adj*. **excusably** *adv*.

ex-directory *adj (of telephone numbers)* isoyoorodheshwa (kwa faragha/usalama).

execrate *vt* chukia mno, kirihi, laani, apiza. **execration** *n*. **execrable** *adj* karaha, makuruhu; *(of weather)* mbaya sana.

execute *vt* 1 tekeleza, fanya, timiza. 2 *(leg)* tekeleza; funga/bana kisheria *~ a will* tekeleza wasia; tia sahihi *~ a legal document* tia sahihi mkataba wa kisheria. 3 adhibu kifo, ua *~ a criminal* ua mhalifu (kwa sheria). 4 *(of concert)* cheza, onyesha (jukwaani). **executant** *n* mtekelezaji mpango, mpiga muziki. **execution** *n* 1 *(performance)* utekelezaji, utimizaji (wa jambo).

put/carry sth into ~ tekeleza, timiza jambo. 2 ustadi katika uchezaji/upigaji (mf. muziki). 3 *(of weapons)* uharibifu, uangamizaji. 4 kuua (kisheria). **executioner** *n* chakari. **executive** *adj* 1 -a utendaji. ~ **duties** kazi za utendaji ~ *secretary* katibu mtendaji. 2 -enye mamlaka/madaraka ya uamuzi. ~ **order** amri ya Rais *n* 1 *the* ~ serikali. **E ~ committee** Halmashauri Kuu. 2 *(in the civil service)* mtendaji, mtekelezaji. 3 *(business)* bosi, meneja.

executor, executrix *n* kabidhi wasii: msimamizi wa mirathi.

exegesis *n* ufafanuzi/fasili ya maandiko (hasa matakatifu). **exegete** *n*. **exegetic(al)** *adj*.

exempt *vt* ~ **(from)** samehe (kodi, kazi), achilia, ruhusu. ~**ion** *n* ruhusa (ya kutofanya), kusamehewa, ondoleo, msamaha.

exequies *n (pl)* maziko.

exercise[1] *n* 1 *(use)* matumizi; kutumia *the ~ of the imagination* matumizi ya ubunifu *the ~ of his duty shows his zeal* utekelezaji wa wajibu wake unaonyesha bidii aliyonayo ~ *of patience* subira. 2 *(practice)* mazoezi *he does ~s every morning* anafanya mazoezi kila siku asubuhi. 3 jaribio, shindano, zoezi *the pupils were given an ~ by their teacher* wanafunzi walipewa zoezi na mwalimu wao. ~ **book** daftari (la mazoezi). 4 *(usu pl)* mazoezi ya kijeshi, drili. 5 *(US pl)* sherehe *graduation ~* mahafali.

exercise[2] *vt,vi* 1 tumia ~ *authority* tumia madaraka. ~ **patience** fanya subira. 2 fanya mazoezi, zoeza, jizoeza *you don't ~ enough* hufanyi mazoezi ya kutosha. 3 *(usu passive)* sumbua, hangaisha (moyo) *this problem is exercising our minds* tatizo hilo linasumbua akili zetu.

exercitation *n (arch)* 1 mazoezi. 2 onyesho la umahiri.

exert *vt* ~ **(on/upon)** tumia, weka/ wekea. ~ **pressure** tumia nguvu, gandamiza. ~ **oneself** fanya jitihada, jitahidi. ~**ion** *n* 1 bidii, juhudi. 2 matumizi ~ *of authority* kutumia madaraka. 3 *(difficulty)* ugumu.

exeunt *(Lat) see* **exit**.

exfoliate *vt vi* 1 *(of bark, skin, minerals, etc)* bambua. 2 para, parura (magamba, n.k.). 3 achana; jigawa katika tabaka, fanya tabaka. 4 (ji) tandaza. **exfoliation** *n*.

exgratia *n (lat)* ~ **payment** malipo ya hiari (yasiyowajibu kisheria).

exhale *vt,vi* toa pumzi, toa mvuke (harufu, uvundo) ~ *air from the lungs* toa hewa mapafuni. **exhalation** *n*.

exhaust[1] *n* ekzosi. ~ **pipe** bomba la ekzosi.

exhaust[2] *vt* 1 chosha kabisa ~ *oneself by hard work* jichosha kwa kazi ngumu. 2 tumia -ote, ondoa -ote, maliza -ote. ~ **a drum** maliza pipa zima. 3 sema yote ~ *a subject* sema yote kuhusu mada fulani. ~**ion** *n* 1 kuishiwa nguvu, uchovu kabisa, mavune. 2 kutumia -ote. ~**ive** *adj* kamilifu, -a kumaliza kabisa. ~**ively** *adv*.

exhibit *n* 1 maonyesho. 2 *(leg)* kizibiti, ushahidi. 3 *(US)* maonyesho *vt* 1 onyesha hadharani (kwa mnada au kwa mashindano). 2 dhihirisha, onyesha (uwezo, n.k. wa mtu). ~**or** *n* mwonyeshaji. ~**ion** *n* 1 maonyesho. 2 kuonyesha, (tabia, maarifa n.k.). **make an ~ of oneself** fanya vituko hadharani, jiaibisha. 3 *(GB)* ruzuku ya fedha (apewayo mwanafunzi shuleni au chuoni). ~**ioner** *n* mwanafunzi apokeaye ruzuku shuleni/chuoni. ~**ionism** *n* 1 tabia ya kujitangaza, (kujitwaza); kuonyesha sehemu za siri za mwili hadharani. 2 ~**ionist** *n* mjitwazaji; mtu anayeonyesha sehemu za siri hadharani.

exhilarate *vt (usu passive)* sisimka sana, jaza matumaini/furaha, furahisha sana. **exhilarating news**

habari za kusisimua. **exhilation** *n* ukunjufu, ubashasha.

exhort *vt* ~ **sb to sth/to do sth** *(formal)* sihi, shawishi ~ *sb to vacate an old building* sihi mtu kuhama kutoka jumba kuukuu. **~ation** *n*. **~ative** *adj*.

exhume *vt* 1 *(dig up)* fukua, chimbua (hasa maiti kaburini). **exhumation** *n*.

exigency *n* dharura, hali ya kuhitaji sana. **exigent** *adj* 1 -a kuhitaji kushughulikiwa haraka. 2 *(derog)* -enye madai mno.

exiguous *adj (formal)* dogo mno, si -a kutosha. **exiguity/~ness** *n*.

exile *n* 1 kuhamisha; kufukuzwa mbali na kwao. 2 mkimbia kwao. **in** ~ mbali na kwao (sababu ya siasa, n.k.) *go into* ~ enda uhamishoni *vt* fukuza, hamisha (kwa nguvu).

exist *vi* -wa hai, ishi, kuwepo *he ~ed on grass* aliishi kwa kula majani *where does it* ~ huishi/hupatikana wapi? makao yake wapi? *do spirits ~?* mizimu ipo? **~ence** *n* 1 kuweko, kuishi *there is no such thing in* ~ hakuna kabisa kitu cha namna hiyo *come into* ~ kuwepo. 2 **an** ~ maisha *lead a happy* ~ kuwa na maisha mazuri. **~ent** *adj* -a wakati huu, nayobaki. **~ential** *adj* -enye kuhusu maisha. **~entialism** *n* falsafa inayokiri kwamba dunia haina mantiki na binadamu yu peke yake, hivyo binadamu yu huru kuchagua mwenyewe na anawajibika kwa vitendo vyake. **~entialist** *n* mfuasi wa falsafa hiyo.

exit *n* 1 kutoka kwa mchezaji jukwaani *make one's* ~ ondoka. 2 mlango wa kutoka (kwenye ukumbi wa sinema, n.k.) *vi* 1 toka, ondoka. 2 *(drama) Pl* **exeunt)** toka jukwaani. **E ~ Ayubu** Ayubu anatoka. **exodus** *n (sing only)* kutoka, kuhama, kuondoka kwa watu wengi pamoja. *(rel.)* **Book of E ~** Kitabu cha Kutoka. **the Exodus** Kutoka kwa Waisraeli Misri (1300 KK).

ex-officio *adv, adj (Lat)* kwa cheo, kwa wadhifa wake.

exogamy *n* ndoanje: desturi ya kuoza watu wasio wa kabila/taifa moja. **exogamic** *adj*.

exonerate *vt* ~ **sb (from)** toa katika lawama/hatia, achilia huru. **exoneration** *n*.

exorbitant *adj (of a price, charge or demand)* -a kupita kiasi, kubwa mno, ingi mno *the price of this is* ~ bei ya hiki ni kubwa mno, ni ghali sana. **~ly** *adv*.

exorcise *vt* ~ **(sth from), (sb of)** punga pepo, lema. **exorcism** *n*. **exorcist** *n* mpungaji pepo.

exoteric *adj (of doctrines, modes of speech)* -a watu wote, -a kufahamikana na watu wote.

exotic *adj (of plants, fashions, words, ideas)* 1 -a kigeni, -a kutoka nchi za nje. 2 geni, sio -a kawaida -a ajabu. ~ **fashions** mitindo ya ajabu. **exotism** *n*.

expand *vt,vi* 1 panua, tanua, panuka, kuza *the farm was ~ed by 100 hectares* shamba lilipanuliwa kwa hekta 100. 2 kunjua, funua. 3 *(of a person)* -wa mkunjufu. 4 ~ *on* fafanua, eleza zaidi. **~ed** *n (maths)*. **~ed form** ufafanuzi. **~ible** *adj*. **expanse** *n* eneo pana na wazi. **expansion** *n* 1 *(tech)* mtanuko. 2 uenezi, upanuzi. ~ **pipe** bomba panuzi. ~ **policy** sera ya upanuzi. **expansive** *adj* 1 -enye kutanua, -enye kutanuka, kuvimba, -a mtanuko. 2 *(of persons, speech)* kunjufu, wazi. **expansively** *adv*. **expansiveness** *n*.

exparte *adj (leg)* -a kupendelea kufadhili, kusaidia, kufaidi upande mmoja tu *adv* kwa kupendelea kufadhili, kusaidia, kufaidi upande mmoja.

expatiate *vi* ~ **upon** simulia kwa maneno mengi, eleza/andika kwa kirefu. **expatiation** *n*. **expatiatory** *adj*.

expatriate *vt* 1 ~ **oneself** hama/ondoka kutoka nchini mwako; ishi nje ya nchi yako, kataa uraia wako. 2 kanusha, fukuza nchini *n* 1 mtu akaaye nje ya nchi yake. 2 mtaalamu kutoka nchi ya kigeni. **expatriation** *n*.

expect *vt, vi* tazamia, tarajia *when do you ~ him* mnamtazamia lini? *we were ~ing some money from him* tulitarajia kupata fedha kutoka kwake *I ~ not* sitegemei. **I ~ so** natumaini. *(of woman)* **be ~ing (a baby)** wa mja mzito. **~ancy** *n* 1 kungojea, matazamio, matarajio, mategemeo. **state of ~** hali ya matazamio. **life ~** matarajio ya muda wa kuishi. **~ant** *adj* -a kungojea *an ~ mother* mja mzito *n (candidate)* mgombea. **~antly** *adv*. **~ed** *adj* liotegemewa. **~ income** mapato yanayotegemewa. **expectation** *n* 1 mategemeo, matarajio. **contrary to ~s** kinyume cha matarajio. **fall short of/not come up to one's ~s** kuwa pungufu ya matarajio. 3 *(pl)* matazamio ya urithi. **expextative** *adj* -a kutazamiwa.

expectorate *vt,vi* 1 kohoza. 2 *(formal)* tema makohozi/damu balaghamu. **expectorant** *n* dawa ya kikohozi.

expedient *adj (usu pred)* -a kufaa, -a manufaa kwa lengo fulani *~ plan* mpango wa kufaa kwa lengo fulani. **expedience/expediency** *n* 1 manufaa. 2 *(derog)* kuangalia faida yako tu.

expedite *vt (formal)* himiza, harakisha. **expeditious** *adj (formal)* -a haraka, -enye kuwahi. **expeditiously** *adv* kwa wepesi, kwa haraka. **expedition** *n* 1 *(formal)* wepesi, haraka, hima. **with ~** upesi (safari yenye lengo maalumu). 2 **expeditionary force** kikosi cha jeshi kinachopelekwa vitani ugenini.

expel vt 1 **~ (from)** fukuza, ondosha *~ from a community/society* fukuza kutoka jamii/chama. 2 toa (pumzi, hewa, n.k.).

expend *vt* 1 **~ sth on/upon sth/in doing sth** tumia (fedha, nguvu, akili, fikira, n.k.). 2 maliza, tumia yote. **~able** *adj* -enye kutolewa mhanga *the general considered his troops ~able* jenerali aliona kwamba majeshi yake yanaweza kutolewa mhanga. **~iture** *n* 1 matumizi, harija, gharama. **capital ~** matumizi *recurrent ~* matumizi ya kawaida. **revenue ~** matumizi ya mapato. 2 kiasi cha matumizi. **expense** *n* 1 gharama, harija. **at the ~ of** kwa kusabilia/kuchuuza *spare no expense* fanya bila kujali gharama, usijali gharama! **at sb's ~** kwa gharama/ fadhila ya; *(fig)* dhidi ya *we had a good laugh at his ~* tulicheka dhidi yake. **put sb to the ~ of** hasiri, ingiza gharama. **at the ~ of** kwa hasara ya, kwa gharama ya *free of expense* isiyo gharama *expense account* hesabu ya matumizi. 2 *(pl)* *~* gharama *trading ~s* gharama za biashara *preliminary ~s* gharama za mwanzo *supplmentary ~s* gharama za ziada. **expensive** *adj* -ghali, -a bei kubwa. **~ly** *adv* **~ness** *n*.

experience *n* 1 uzoefu (wa mambo ya maisha), tajriba *he has much ~ in leading young people* ana uzoefu mkubwa katika uongozi wa vijana. 2 tukio (linaloathiri maisha ya mtu) *vt* pitia, pata uzoefu katika jambo fulani *I have ~d many problem in my life* nimepitia matatizo mengi katika maisha yangu. **~d** *adj* -enye uzoefu; mjarabu *an ~d driver* dereva mwenye uzoefu. **experiential** *adj* -nayotokana na uzoefu wa mtu; -a tukio/hisia.

experiment *n* jaribio, jaribu *by way of ~* kwa majaribio. **make ~s** fanya majaribio *vi* jaribu. **~ation** *n*. **~al** *adj* -a kujaribia, -a majaribio *an ~ school* shule ya majaribio. ~ally *adv*.

expert *n* bingwa, stadi. **~ witness** shahidi bingwa *adj* stadi, mahiri. **~ise** *n* 1 ubingwa. 2 *(comm)* ripoti ya tathmini. **~ly** *adv*. **~ness** *n*.

expiate *vt* 1 lipia, fidia kosa.

expiation *n*.

expire *vi* 1 *(of a period of time)* isha, malizika, fikia mwisho *his duty ~s today* zamu yake inaisha leo. 2 *(liter)* fa. **expiration** *n* 1 *(formal)* upumuaji, utoaji pumzi. 2 ~ **(of)** mwisho, kwisha, kumalizika (kwa). **expiratory** *adj* -a kupumulia. **expiry** *n* ~ **(of)** mwisho, kwisha, kumalizika (kwa muda fulani). ~ **date** tarehe ya mwisho kutumika.

explain *vt* 1 ~ **sth to sb** eleza; fafanua; fasili ~ *the riddle to him* mfumbulie fumbo. 2 dhihirisha, toa sababu. ~ **sth away** eleza vinginevyo (kumtoa mtu hatiani), (ji)tetea *I can ~* naweza kuelezea. **explanation** *n* 1 maelezo; ufafanuzi; fasili *say sth in ~ of one's conduct* toa maelezo ya mwenendo wake. 2 *(reason)* sababu, kisa, hoja (za kuelezea). **explanatory** *adj* fafanuzi, -a kueleza *this statement is self ~* hoja hii inajieleza.

expletive *n* mapayo (k.v. matusi, viapo, n.k.).

explicate *vt (formal)* eleza na fafanua kwa undani, chambua. **explicable** *adj (formal)* -a kuelezeka, -a kufafanulika. **explication** *n*. **explicatory** *adj* -a kuelezea. **explicit** *adj* 1 wazi, dhahiri. ~ **faith** imani kamilifu. 2 *(of a person)* -nyofu, msema kweli. **explicitly** *adv*. **explicitness** *n*.

explode *vt,vi* 1 *(blow up)* lipua; lipuka. 2 *(of feelings)* bubujik(w)a ~ *with anger* hamaki ~ *with joy* bubujikwa na furaha. 2 *(of an idea, theory)* tangua, lima, haribu. **explosion** *n* 1 mlipuko *gas ~* mlipuko wa gesi. 2 ~ **(of)** *(of feelings)* kupandwa (na jazba; uanguaji kicheko, n.k.). 3 mfumuko, ongezeko kubwa la ghafla (agh. la watu, magonjwa n.k.). **explosive** *adj* 1 -enye kulipuka ~ *issue* suala nyeti *n* kilipukaji *high ~* baruti kali. **explosively** *adv*.

exploit[1] *n* tendo (la ujasiri, ushujaa, sifa, n.k.).

exploit[2] *vt* 1 chimba (madini, mgodi); tumia/endeleza (nguvu za maji/za asili) 2 *(derog)* nyonya. ~**er** *n* mnyonyaji; mchimbaji, mtumiaji, mwendelezaji. ~**ation** *n* unyonyaji; utumiaji, uendelezaji.

explore *vt* 1 talii, tafiti, peleleza. 2 chungua, gundua, chunguza. ~**r** *n* mpelelezi, mgunduzi, mchunguzi, mtafiti *the explorers preceded the colonialists* wapelelezi waliwatangulia wakoloni. **exploration** n upelezi, ugunduzi, uchunguzi. **exploratory** *adj*.

expo *n see* **exposition**.

exponent *n* ~ **(of)** 1 mfasiri mwakilishi, mtetezi. 2 *(alg)* namba kipeo. ~ **function** kipeo husisho. ~**ial** *adj*.

export *n* 1 biasharanje. 2 mahuruji, bidhaa nje *vt* uza/toa nje ya nchi kuuzwa. ~**er** *n* muuzaji bidhaa za nje. ~**able** *adj*. ~**ation** *n*.

expose *vt* 1 *(uncover)* weka/acha/wazi/ funua ~ *to danger* hatarisha ~ *food* funua chakula. 2 *(disclose)* fichua, kashifu. 3 *(display)* onyesha (bidhaa, n.k.). 4 *(photo)* ingiza mwanga. 5 ~ *oneself* onyesha sehemu za siri za mwili hadharani *n* 1 muhtasari wa jambo fulani. 2 ufichuaji kashfa. **exposition** *n* 1 ufafanuzi, ufasiri; maelezo. 2 *(abbr* **expo)** maonyesho ya kimataifa. **expositive** *adj*. **exposure** *n* 1 mfichuo. 2 kuwa wazi *indecent ~* kuwa uchi hadharani. 3 *(photo)* picha ~ *meter* kipima mwanga. 4 mwelekeo (wa chumba au nyumba).

expostulate *vi* ~ **(with sb) (on/about sth)** pinga, lalamikia (kiungwana). **expostulation** *n*.

expound *vt* ~ **(to)** eleza, fasili, eleza kinaganaga.

express[1] *adj* 1 halisi, dhahiri, wazi. ~ **condition** sharti dhahiri *an ~ command* amri dhahiri. 2 *(speedy)* -a kwenda mbio sana, isio simama mara kwa mara, -a haraka *an ~ letter* barua ya haraka *an ~ train* treni ya moja kwa moja; treni kasi. **~ way** *(US)* barabara pana (kwa ajili ya magari yaendeshwayo kwa kasi) *n* 1 treni kasi. 2 *(US)* kampuni ya kusafirisha mizigo kwa haraka na usalama. 3 huduma za haraka (zitolewazo na posta, reli na barabara za kusafirisha mizigo, n.k.). **~ly** *adv* 1 kabisa, kwa dhati, kwa hakika *you are ~ forbidden to go* huruhusiwi kabisa kwenda. 2 hasa, kwa madhumuni ya *the function was ~ for children only* tamasha ilikuwa hasa kwa watoto tu.

express[2] *vt* 1 peleka kwa njia ya haraka barua, mzigo eleza, dhihirisha, onyesha, simulia. **~ oneself** jieleza n.k. 2 **~ (from/out of)** *(formal)* kama, kamua. **~ion** *n* 1 *(facial)* sura *she had an ~ of sorrow* alikuwa na sura ya huzuni. 2 *(words)* neno, usemi, msemo. **beyond/past ~** isiyoelezeka (to) *give ~ion to sth* dhihirisha/eleza jambo fulani. **find ~ in** jitokeza katika, jidhihirisha kwa. 3 *(feeling)* kuonyesha hisia *she sang with ~* aliimba kwa kuonyesha hisia. 4 *(Maths)* uonyesho. 5 *(pl)* **cognate ~ions** misemo ya mshabaha, misemo inayoshabihiana, misemo inayofanana. 6 kusema *freedom of ~ion* uhuru wa kusema/kutoa mawazo. **~ionless** *adj.* **~ive** *adj.* **~ (of)** -enye maana, -enye kuelezea, -enye kuonyesha hisia. **~iveness** *n.* **~sionism** *n (of painting, part, etc)* fasihi halisia-nafsi. **~ionist** *n.*

expropriate *vt* **~ (from)** pokonya, nyang'anya; taifisha. **expropriation** *n.*

expulsion *n* **~ (from)** ufukuzaji, utoaji *the ~ of students from this college* ufukuzaji wa wanachuo kutoka kwenye chuo hiki.

expunge *vt* **~ (from)** *(formal)* futa maandishi n.k. (toka kitabuni n.k.). **expurgate** *vt* ondoa maneno machafu n.k. katika kitabu. **expurgation** *n.*

exquisite *adj* 1 bora sana, -zuri sana. 2 *(of pain, pleasure, etc)* kali, tamu. **~ly** *adv.* **~ness** *n.*

ex-service *adj.* **~ man** mwanajeshi aliyeacha kazi.

extant *adj* -liopo hadi leo, -enye kuwapo (hasa nyaraka, n.k.).

extempore *adv (spoken or done)* bila kujiandaa, papo hapo *speak ~* sema bila kuandaa *adj* -enye kutungwa na kusemwa papo hapo *an ~ speech* hotuba ya papohapo. **extemporaneous, extemporary** *adj.* **extemporize** *vi* ongea bila kujiandaa, faragua.

extend *vt,vi* 1 *(stretch out)* nyosha, tandaza (mwili, mikono, n.k.). 2 *(stretch)* vuta, endeleza, eneza (waya, kamba, n.k.). 3 *(prolong)* ongeza, refusha *~ a line* refusha mstari. **~ credit** ongeza muda wa mkopo. **~ time** ongeza muda. 4 *(reach)* -enda hadi, fikia *the region ~s as far as that river* mkoa unafikia mto ule. 5 **~ sth (to sb)** toa, -pa (msaada, mwaliko, salamu n.k.) kwa mtu fulani *~ a welcome* karibisha. 6 *(usu passive)* fanya kutumia nguvu *he won without being fully ~ed* alishinda bila kutumia nguvu zote. **extension** *n* 1 upanuzi, uenezi *the ~ of trade* upanuzi wa biashara. 2 nyongeza *an extension to a hotel* nyongeza ya hoteli. **~ education** elimu ya nje ya vyuo. 3 *(of telephone)* mkondo. 4 *(gram.)* mnyambuliko. **extensive** *adj* 1 -a kuenda mbali, -enye eneo kubwa, -kubwa. **~ farming** kilimo chenye eneo kubwa. 2 kubwa sana *the storm caused ~ damage* kimbunga kilisababisha hasara kubwa sana. **extensiveness** *n.* **extensively** *adv.* **extent** *n* 1 **~ (of)** urefu, eneo, ukubwa. 2 *(degree)* kadiri *to a certain/to some ~* kwa kiasi fulani *to what ~?* kwa kiasi gani? *to such an ~ that* kiasi kwamba. **extensor** *n (biol)* musuli wa mpanuko.

extenuate *vt* punguza/poza ubaya/ukubwa/makali ya kosa. **extenuating** *adj.* **~ circumstances** mambo ya kupunguzia ukubwa wa kosa/hatia. **extenuation** *n*. **extenuatory** *adj*.

exterior *adj* -a nje. *(maths)* ~ **angles** pembe za nje *n* 1 nje, sura, umbo la nje. **on the** ~ kwa nje, kwa juu juu. 2 picha ya maisha ya nje. ~**ize** *vt see* **externalize**.

exterminate *vt* angamiza, teketeza, maliza; ua wote. **extermination** *n*. **exterminatory** *adj*.

external *adj* 1 -a nje, lio nje. ~ **examiner** mtahini wa nje. ~ **auditing** ukaguzi hesabu wa nje ~ *economy* uchumi wa nje, iktisadi za nje. 2 *(med)* **for** ~ **use** -a kutumika kwenye ngozi tu; *(foreign)* -a nchi nyingine, -a kigeni -a nje. ~ **affairs** mambo ya nje. 3 *(unessential)* -a juu juu *n* *(sl)* ~**s** sura ya nje, maonekano, -sio -a kiini. ~**ize/ exteriorise** *vt* fanya -a nje/geni. ~**ly** *adv*.

exterritorial *adj* -a nje ya sheria za nchi (k.m. mabalozi n.k.). ~**ity** *n*.

extinguish *vt* 1 zima. 2 komesha, fisha. 3 futa. ~ **debt** futa deni. **fire** ~**er** *n*. kizimamoto.

extinct *adj* 1 *(of species, ect)* -liokufa, -liokwisha, siopo sasa. 2 -liozimika ~ *volcano* zaha/volkano zimwe. ~**ion** *n* 1 kufa, kukomesha, kufisha. 2 kuzimika, kuzima.

extirpate *vt* 1 *(root out)* ng'oa. 2 *(destroy)* haribu kabisa, komesha kabisa, angamiza. **extirpation** *n*. **extirpator** *n*.

extol *vt* sifu sana, tukuza ~ *sb to the skies* tukuza mtu sana.

extort *vt* ~ **(from)** pata kwa kutumia nguvu, pokonya, ghusubu. ~**ion** *n* kutoza (kupata) kwa nguvu, kutaka bei kubwa sana kwa kitu, kughusubu. ~**ionate** *adj* -a kupokonya, -a kughusubu. 2 *(of price)* ghali mno.

extra *adj* -a ziada, -a nyongeza. ~ **fare** nauli ya ziada *adv* zaidi sana, zaidi na zaidi. ~ **special** zuri mno *try* ~ *hard* jitahidi zaidi na zaidi (kuliko kawaida) *n* 1 ziada *music is an* ~ *at our school* muziki ni somo la ziada shuleni kwetu. 2 *(film)* mwigizaji mdogo, mwigizaji wa ziada. 3 *(of newspaper)* toleo maalum *pref*. -a nje, -a ziada.

extract *vt* 1 toa; *(tooth, root)* ng'oa; *(nails, etc)* kongoa, zidua; *(from bundle etc)* chopoa. *(fig)* ~ **information** pata habari (kwa hila/ vitisho). 2 *(of liquid)* zidua. 3 *(from a book, speech, etc)* dondoa *n* kiziduo; dondoo, sehemu. ~**ion** *n* 1 kutoa, uziduaji. 2 *(crushing)* kusindika. 3 *(lineage)* asili. **of Tanzanian** ~ -a asili ya Tanzania. ~**ive** *adj*. ~**or** *n*.

extracurricular *adj* nje ya masomo, nje ya mihutasari.

extradite *vt (leg)* rejesha (mkosaji) ahukumiwe katika nchi aliyofanya makosa. **extradition** *n*.

extrajudicial *n* *(leg)* -a nje ya mahakama ~ *statement* maelezo nje ya mahakama.

extramural *adj* 1 *(of a town/city)* -a nje ya mipaka. 2 -a nje ya chuo ~ *students* wanafunzi wa jioni wanaochukua mafunzo ya Chuo Kikuu. ~ **prisoner** mfungwa wa nje.

extraneous *adj* -a nje, -siofungamana na, -siohusiana na.

extraordinary *adj* 1 -a ajabu, -a pekee, -sio -a kawaida. ~ **beauty** uzuri wa pekee. 2 *(irregular)* -a dharura. ~ **meeting** mkutano wa dharura. 3 maalum. **ambassador** ~ balozi wa ziada. **extraordinarily** *adv*.

extrapolate 1 *(math)* bashiri thamani ya tarakimu (kwa kutumia tarakimu zilizopo). 2 tabiri (mambo ya baadaye kutokana na habari zinazofahamika tayari). **extrapolation** *n*

extrasensory *adj* -a nje ya hisia. ~ **perception** *(abbr ESP)* maono ya mambo bila kutumia hisia zo zote.

extra-territorial *adj see* **exterritorial**.

extravagant *adj* 1 badhirifu. 2 *(of ideas, speech, behaviour)* -a

kupita kiasi. **extravagance** *n* budhara, ubadhirifu. **~ly** *adv*.
extravaganza *n* *(arts)* maonyesho yenye madoido mengi.
extreme *adj* 1 kabisa, mno ~ *cruelty* ukatili mno *to the ~ left* kushoto kabisa. 2 *(fig)* -a kuzidi kiasi, bila kadiri ~ *views* mawazo yasiyo na kadiri *n* 1 mwisho, kipeo. **E~ unction** Mpako wa Mwisho. 2 *(pl)* sifa zenye kutofautiana sana *love and hate are ~* upendo na chuki ni sifa zinazotofautiana sana. **go to ~s** vuka mpaka, zidi. **~ly** *adv*. **extremist** *n* mtu asiye na kadiri, mtu mwenye siasa kali sana. **extremism** *n* siasa isiyo na kadiri. **extremity** *n* 1 ncha, kikomo, mwisho. 2 upeo (hasa wa mateso au huzuni). 3 *(pl)* mikono na miguu. 4 *(pl)* vitendo vya kikatili (vya kulazimisha utii, kulipiza kisasi, n.k.).
extricate *vt* ~ **(from)** nasua, toa. **extricable** *adj*. **extrication** *n*.
extrinsic *adj* -a nje, si -a kiini, si -a msingi.
extrovert *n* 1 *(psych)* msondani. 2 bashashi, mcheshi. **extroversion** *n*.
extrude *vt,vi* 1 toa/toka/sukumia/tokeza nje. 2 *(tech)* subu kwa kalibu. **extrusion** *n*. **extrusive** *adj*.
exuberant *adj* 1 -enye kusitawi sana, tele. 2 changamfu sana, kunjufu sana, -enye kufurahia maisha *in ~ health* -enye afya nyingi. **exuberance** *n*. **~ly** *adv*.
exude *vt,vi* toa, toka (maji, jasho, n.k.); rishai, rishaika. **exudation** *n*.
exult *vi* 1 ~ **(at, over)** furahia sana, shangilia sana. **~ation** *n*. **~antly** *adv*.
eye *n* 1 jicho *where are your ~s* huoni? **an ~ for an ~** jicho kwa jicho; kulipiza kisasi. **~s right/left/front** macho kulia/kushoto/mbele *as far as the ~ can see* upeo wa macho *if you had half an ~* ungekuwa na akili kidogo. **in the ~s of the law** kufuatana na sheria **in my ~s** kwa mawazo yangu. **under/before my very ~s** mbele yangu kabisa; bila kuficha. **up to the ~s in (work, etc)** tingwa na. **with an ~ to** kwa kutazamia *I can do it with my ~s closed* ni rahisi sana kwangu. **be all ~s** tazama kwa makini. **be in the public ~** fahamika/julikana, onekana mara kwa mara hadharani. **close/shut one's ~s** fumba macho. **close/shut ones's ~s to** fumbia macho; jifanya kutoona. **give sb a black ~/black sb's ~** tia ngeu. **have an ~ for** jua, kutambua/kuelewa. **have an ~ to** lenga. **keep an ~ on,** angalia kwa makini *keep one's ~s open/skinned/peeled* angalia/chunga sana. **make ~s at** angalia kwa mapenzi. **make sb open his ~** shtua. **Mind your ~!** *(infomal)* Angalia! *open the ~s* fumbua jicho. **open sb's ~s to** onyesha, elewesha, fahamisha. **see ~ to ~** patana na, elewana na. **see sth with half an ~** ona mara moja. **set/clap ~s on** ona. **never take one's ~s** angalia kwa makini sana. 2 tundu, kitundu ~ *of needle* tundu la sindano. 3 *(of a storm)* kiini. *(in compounds)* **~ball** mboni ya jicho. **~-ball to ~-ball** ana kwa ana. **~-bath/~-cup** chombo cha dawa ya macho. **~-brow** nyusi. **raise one's ~-brows** onyesha mshangao *up to one's ~ brows in work* -wa na kazi nyingi mno, tingwa na kazi. **~-full** upeo wa macho. **have an ~-full (of)** tazama kwa muda mrefu. **~-glass** rodi; *(pl)* miwani. **~lash** ukope. **~let** tundu, kitundu. **~lid** kigubiko cha jicho. **hang on by the ~lids** ning'inia, shikiza kwa shida. **~-opener** kitu kinachozindua. **~-piece** lenzi ya kukuzia (darubini, n.k.). **~-shade** kinga ya macho. **~-shadow** rangi ya kupambia macho. **~shot** upeo wa macho. **~sight** uwezo wa kuona kwa macho. **bad ~sight** kiwaa. **~-socket** tundu la kishimo cha jicho. **~sore** chukizo. **~ strain** uchovu

wa macho. ~**tooth** jino chonge *give one's ~teeth (for)* fanya lolote (ili kupata kinachotamaniwa). ~**wash** 1 dawa ya kukoshea macho. 2 *(colloq)* ghiliba. ~ **witness** shahidi aliyeona. ~**d** *(suff)* -a macho. **brown ~d girl** msichana mwenye macho ya kahawia *vt* tazama, angalia.

eyrie, eyry *see* **aerie**.

F

F,f *n* herufi ya sita katika alfabeti ya Kiingereza.

fa *n* (*mus*) noti ya nne katika mfumo wa Solfa.

Fabian *adj* (*of person*) -enye kukawilisha kwa hila ili kumchosha adui *n* (*GB*) (mfuasi) mwenye kuleta mabadiliko ya Kijamaa taratibu.

fable *n* 1 hekaya (za kufunza maadili). 2 kauli za uwongo. 3 ngano fupi *adj* -a kubuniwa. **~r** *n.* **fabulist** *n* 1 mtungaji ngano, mwandishi wa kisa. 2 mwongo *vt* (*arch*) 1 simulia hadithi za kubuni. 2 eleza uwongo.

fabric *n* 1 (aina ya) kitambaa. 2 (*arch*) jengo. 3 (*of a building*) kiunzi; (*of a society*) mfumo.

fabricate *vt* 1 (*construct*) tengeneza, jenga. 2 (*invent*) buni, tunga, zua (jambo la uwongo), ghushi (hali). **fabrication** *n.* **fabricator** *n.*

fabulous *adj* 1 -a uwongo; -a kubuniwa; -a kuishi katika ngano tu; -a ajabu. 2 (*colloq*) -zuri sana. **~ly** *adv* sana!

facade *n* upande wa mbele wa nyumba; (*fig*) sura ya kinafiki.

face *n* 1 uso, wajihi *fall on one's ~* anguka kifudifudi. **bring two parties ~ to ~** kutanisha pande mbili ili zikabiliane. **come ~ to ~ with sb** kutanisha uso kwa uso. **look sb in the ~** kazia mtu macho. **be unable to look sb in the ~** shindwa kumtazama mtu kwa sababu ya aibu au woga. **set one's ~ against sb** pinga sana. **show one's ~** tokea, onekana jitokeza ili kuonekana. **in (the) ~ of** kabiliwa na licha ya *I could do nothing in the ~ of these problems* sikuweza kufanya lolote nilipokabiliwa na matatizo haya. **fly in the ~ of** pinga waziwazi. **in one's ~ ; in the ~** usoni, pajini; pasipo kujaribu/kuficha *death stared at him in the ~* alijikuta kwenye mauti. **to one's ~** bayana (bila kuficha au kuogopa) *tell him so to his ~* mweleze bayana. 2 (*compounds*) **~ ache** kipanda uso. **~ card** karata ya sura ya mzungu. **~ cloth** taulo ndogo ya kunawia uso. **~ cream** krimu ya uso. **~ lift(ing)** operesheni ya ngozi ya uso (kufanya uonekane laini/wa kijana). **~ powder** poda ya uso. 3 *(expression/look)* sura. **keep a straight ~** -toonyesha hisia. **make/pull ~s** geuza/finya uso. **put on/wear a long ~** onekana mwenye kufikiri sana au kuhuzunika. 4 (*various senses)* **have the ~ (to do sth)** thubutu. **lose ~** adhirika. **put a good/bold/brave ~ on** fanya ionekane kuwa nzuri, -wa na ujasiri wa kukabili jambo. **put a new ~ on** badili sura ili ionekane tofauti. **save (one's) ~** jiepusha na aibu. **~ saver** *n* tendo la kuepusha aibu . **~ saving** *n part adj.* **on the ~ of it** kama inavyoonekana. 5 sura, sehemu ya mbele *north ~ of the mountain* upande wa kaskazini wa mlima *a diamond has many ~s* almasi ina sura nyingi. **~ value** thamani iliyoandikwa. (*fig*) **at ~ value** bila kuangalia kwa undani; (*fig*) jinsi kitu au mtu anavyoonekana kijuu juu. 6 ukubwa na mtindo wa sura ya kalibu ya kuchapa. **~less** *adj* (*fig*) -sojulikana/tambulika *vt* 1 elekea, tazama, kabili *the house ~s the bank* nyumba inatazamana na benki. **About/Left/Right ~** (*US mil. commands*) = *(GB)* **About/ Left/ Right turn**) nyuma/kushoto/kulia geuka. 2 kabili (kwa kujiamini). **~ it out** kabili kishujaa. **~ the music** kabili matatizo/hatari n.k. (bila kuogopa). **~ up to** kubali hali ilivyo. **let's ~ it** (*colloq*) lazima tukiri. 3 tambua kuwepo kwa. 4 kabili *the problem that ~s us* tatizo ambalo linatukabili. 5 ~ **(with)** funika kwa tabaka la kitu kingine *n* (*GB dated, colloq*) tatizo kubwa linalomkabili mtu ghafla au pasipo kutegemea. **facial** *adj* -a uso. *n* **~ massage** kukanda na kupodoa uso. **facing** *n* 1 kibandiko. 2 mkono, mpako (wa rangi au kitu tofauti) k.m. kwenye ukuta.

facet *n* uso/sehemu: upande mmoja wa jiwe au kito kilichokatwa; (*fig*) kipengere.

facetious *adj* -chekeshi, kebehi.

-a mzaha, -a utani (mbaya). **~ly** *adv*. **~ness** *n*.

facile *n* 1 -epesi kufanyika au kupatikana, -sio na maana, -epesi mno; (*of speech, of writing*) -a kufanyika kwa urahisi pasipo kujali ubora wake.

facility *n* 1 (*ease*) urahisi, wepesi, hali iwezeshayo mtu kujifunza kitu kwa urahisi. 2 (*pl*) vifaa, nyenzo. **facilitate** *vt* (*of an object, process*) rahisisha, punguza shida, saidia.

facsimile *n* nakala halisi ya mwandiko, mchoro, picha.

fact *n* 1 tendo, jambo ambalo limetendeka au limefanywa. **accessary before the ~** (*leg*) mtu aliyemsaidia mhalifu kabla ya tendo kufanyika. **accessary after the ~** (*leg*) mtu aliyemsaidia mhalifu baada ya tendo. 2 ukweli, jambo la hakika. **a ~ of life** ukweli usioepukika. **the ~s of life** (*colloq, euphem*) maelezo kuhusu jinsi watu wanavyozaliana (kama wanavyosimuliwa watoto). **~ finding** *adj* -enye kutafuta/kuchunguza ukweli. **in ~, in point of ~, as a matter of ~** kwa kweli. **~ual** *adj* -enye ukweli. **~um** *n* (*leg*) kanuni, taarifa ya kweli.

faction *n* 1 kikundi kidogo ndani ya kundi zima. 2 ugomvi baina ya vikundi tofauti vya chama au jumuiya moja. **factious** *adj*.

factitious *adj* (*formal*) -liobuniwa, bandia, -si -a asili.

factor *n* 1 (*arith*) zao mtiririko, namba kamilifu. 2 kweli/hali inayosaidia kuleta matokeo, kipengele 3. wakala; mtu anayenunua na kuuza kwa riba. **~ize** tafuta zao mtiririko.

factory *n* 1 kiwanda. 2 (*hist*) kituo cha biashara katika nchi ya kigeni.

factotum *n* **(general)** ~ mtumishi wa kazi zote.

faculty *n* 1 welekevu (ustadi, uwezo) wa kufanya tendo lolote *be in possession of all one's faculties* wa na akili timamu. 2 weza kusikia, kusema, kuelewa, kuona n.k. 3 (*university*) kitivo cha chuo kikuu. 4 (*US*) wahadhiri wote katika chuo kikuu, wahadhiri, maprofesa wa kitivo.

fad *n* mtindo wa muda; kivutio. **~dy** *adj* -enye mambo mengi ya kupenda na kutopenda; chaguzi. **~dily** *adv*. **~dist** *n*.

fade *vt,vi* 1 **~ (away)** fifisha; fifia, chujusha; chujuka. 2 (*of colour*) pauka; pausha *the colour of the dress ~ed* rangi ya gauni ilichujuka. 3 (*cinema/radio/broadcasting*) punguza/pungua sauti. ~ *up/in* ongeza sauti.

faeces/(*US*/**feces**) *n* (*pl*) mavi, kinyesi.

faerie, **faery** *n see* **fairy**.

fag *n* (*colloq*) 1 kazi ya kuchosha/ngumu. 2 (*sl*) sigara. 3 (*US, sl derog*) mende, mfiraji; mmendewa, mfirwaji *vt,vi* 1 **~ (at)** (*colloq*) fanya kazi ya kuchosha. 2 **~ (out)** (*colloq*) (*of work*) chosha sana *the work ~ged him out* kazi ilimchosha sana. **~ged (out)** *adj* -liochoka kabisa. **~-end** *n* 1 (*colloq*) mabaki, kitu kilichosalia/kisichofaa. 2 kipande cha sigara kilichotupwa, kichungi. **~got**/(*US* also -~ot) *n* 1 tita (la kuni, la pao za chuma). 2 maini yaliyotiwa viungo. 3 (*US sl. derog*) mende, mfiraji.

Fahrenheit *n* farenhaiti: pimajoto (yenye kuonyesha maji kuganda katika digrii 32 na kuchemka katika digrii 212).

faience *n* (*F*) vyombo vya udongo vilivyotiwa nakshi.

fail[1] *n* (*only in*) **without ~** bila kukosa.

fail[2] *vi,vt* 1 **~ (in)** shindwa, feli, -tofaulu *they ~ed the examination* walifeli/walishindwa/hawakufaulu mtihani. 2 (*of examiners*) felisha, angusha *the examiners ~ed the whole class* watahini walifelisha darasa lote. 3 (*often with an indirect object*) haribika, kosekana, -totosheleza *the crops ~ed because of cold* mazao yaliharibika kwa sababu ya baridi *the rain ~ed this year* mvua hazikuwa za kutosha mwaka huu. ~ **safe** (*attrib* *adj) (of a mechanical device)* kinga, chombo chenye uwezo wa kuepusha hatari. 4 (*of health, eyesight etc*) dhoofika, pungua nguvu. 5 acha, sahau, kosa; (*in many cases with the inf. making a neg. of an affirm*) *we never ~ to write* hatusahau/hatuachi kuandika *his hopes ~ed to materialize* matumaini yake hayakufanikiwa. 6 filisika *the parastatals ~ed* mashirika ya umma yamefilisika. 7 ~ **in** -tokuwa imara, tokamilika *Juma is strong but ~s in endurance* Juma ana nguvu lakini sio mvumulivu *words ~ me* nashindwa kujieleza. **~ing** *n* kasoro, dosari (la tabia) *prep* bila. **~ure** *n* 1 kushindwa, kutofaulu. 2 hali ya kutofanyika kwa jambo *heart ~ure* kushindwa kwa moyo kufanya kazi kama kawaida yake. 3 ushinde; jaribio au jambo lililoshindikana, mshinde. 4 (*bankruptcy*) kufilisika. 5 kudharau, kuacha au kutoweza (kufanya jambo).

faint *adj* 1 (*of things perceived through the senses*) dhaifu, hafifu, -enye hofu. 2 (*of things in the mind*) -a mashaka, si dhahiri *I haven't the ~est idea* sina habari hata kidogo, sielewi kabisa. 3 (*of the body's movements and functions*) -nyonge, nyong' onyevu. 4 (*pred only*) (*of persons*) -a kizunguzungu; -enye kuelekea kupoteza fahamu. 5 (*pred only*) (*of persons*) -liochoka/dhaifu sana. 6 (*of actions*) dhaifu. 7 ~ **heart** woga ~ *hearted adj* -oga. **~ly** *adv*. **~ness** *n,vi* 1 zirai, ghumiwa. 2 fifia, dhoofu. 3 kuwa dhaifu, fifia *n* kuzirai. **in a (dead)** ~ zirai kabisa.

fair[1] *adj* 1 (*just*) -a haki, -a kutopendelea. **give/get a ~ hearing** sikilizwa, -pa/pata nafasi ya kujitetea. ~ **minded** -sopendelea upande wowote. 2 -a kadiri, -a watani, -zuri kiasi, -zuri vya kuridhisha ~ *condition* hali nzuri *the goods arrived in ~ condition* bidhaa ziliwasili katika hali nzuri vya kutosha. 3 *(of the weather)* -zuri na kavu. ~ **weather friend** rafiki wakati wa neema tu. 4 maridhawa, -a kuridhisha, -ingi; (*of the skin/hair*) -eupe; nywele nyeupe/za dhahabu. 6 safi, -sio doa/alama ~ *copy* nakala safi. 7 (*of speeches, promises*) tamu, -a kupendeza. 8 (*old use*) -zuri, -rembo. **the ~ sex** wanawake. **~ness** *n*. **~ish** *adj*, *adv* 1 kwa haki/idili *play ~* cheza kwa haki. ~ **enough** (*colloq*) sawa, vizuri, kwa usafi. 2 (*old use*) kwa upole, kwa heshima. **~ly** *adv* 1 kwa kiasi *speaks English ~ly well* ana sema Kiingereza vizuri kidogo. 3 (*colloq*) kabisa.

fair[2] *n* 1 soko (ambalo agh. hufunguliwa katika vipindi maalum na hutoa pia huduma za starehe). **a day before/after the ~** mapema mno/kwa kuchelewa mno. 2 maonyesho. ~ **ground** uwanja wa maonyesho. **International Trade F~** Maonyesho ya Biashara ya Kimataifa. **book ~** maonyesho ya vitabu. **~ing** *n* zawadi iliyonunuliwa kwenye maonyesho.

fairway *n* 1 (*of ship*) mlango bahari unaopitika; (*golf*) njia safi (kati ya vishimo vya gofu na majani marefu).

fairy *n* 1 kichimbakazi. ~ **lamps/lights** vitaa vidogovidogo vya rangi vitumiwavyo kwa mapambo. ~ **land** *n* nchi ya vichimbakazi, hadithi za vichimbakazi, uongo hasa wa mtoto. 2 (*sl.derog*) msenge.

fait accompli *n (F)* jambo lililokwisha fanywa na kuhitimishwa.

faith *n* 1 imani. ~ **cure** kuponya kwa imani. ~ **healing** kuganga kwa imani. 2 (*promise*) ahadi, miadi. 3 dini, itikadi. 4 utiifu, uaminifu. **in good ~** kwa nia njema. **in bad ~** kwa nia ya kudanganya. **give/pledge one's ~ to** ahidi kusaidia. **keep/break ~ with** kuwa/tokuwa mwaminifu. **~ful** *adj* 1 -aminifu. 2 -a kweli, halisi. 3 *the ~ n* (*pl*) waumini (agh. Kiislamu au Kikristu). **~fully** *adv* kwa uaminifu. **yours ~fully** wako mwaminifu. **~fulness** *n*. **~less** *adj*. -danganyifu -wongo, -sioaminika. **~lessly** *adv*. **lessness** *n*.

fake *vt* ~ **(up)** igiza kazi ya sanaa kwa udanganyifu, buni *n* mwigo, bandia *adj* -a bandia.

falcon *n* 1 kipanga. **~er** *n* mfugaji vipanga. 2 mwindaji awindaye kwa msaada wa vipanga waliofugwa. **~ry** ufugaji/uwindaji wa vipanga.

fall *n* 1 kuanguka, kuporomoka, maanguko. 2 *(decrease)* kupungua, kushuka. 3 (*error*) kosa, dhambi. **The ~ of Man** dhambi ya Adam na Hawa, Dhambi ya Asili. ~ **guy** *n* (*colloq*) -mwenye kuonewa, mwenye kusukumiziwa mabaya. 4 (*ruin*) maangamizi. 5 *(death)* mauti. 6 (*defeat*) kushindwa, kutekwa (mji). 7 *(descent)* mteremko. 8 kiasi cha mvua iliyonyesha *a heavy ~ of rain* mvua kubwa. 9 maporomoko ya maji. 10 mshuko, mpunguo wa sauti. 11 (*US*) majira ya majani kupukutika *vi* 1 ~ **(down/over)** anguka, -gwa; (*with force in a mass*) poromoka. **~on one's feet** (*fig*) -wa na bahati. ~ **short** tofika. ~ **short of** -tofikia, punguka; *(of lambs)* zaliwa. ~ **flat** pooza, -topendeza; lala/angukakifudifudi; *(of leaves)* pukutika; (*of rain*) -nya, -nyesha; (*in drops*) dondoka. ~ **into (a river, hole)** tumbukia *let ~* angusha, bwaga. ~ **in love with** penda/husudu kitu au mtu fulani. **(to) ~ into sections** fanya katika makundi madogo. **(to) ~ on (the enemy etc.)** endea, shambulia, rukia (adui n.k.). **(to) ~ over one another for** gombania au pigania kitu kimoja. **(to) ~ under** -wa chini ya (katika). 2 *(be ruined)* angamia, haribika. 3 (*error*) kosa. 4 (*from hand, slip*) ponyoka. 5 (*diminish*)punguka, pungua; (*mercury etc. in thermometer*) shuka; (*of temperature*) zidi kuwa baridi. 6 (*slope*) teremka, shuka. 7 *his face fell* alionyesha huzuni. **(to) ~ in esteem** shikwa na butwaa, pigwa na bumbuwazi. ~ **sick** ugua. ~ **vacant** wazi. 8 (*special uses*) ~ **about (laughing/with laughter)** (*colloq*) angua kicheko, cheka sana. ~ **away** acha, potea, -toonekana. ~ **among** angukia; kutana na. ~ **asleep** shikwa na usingizi, sinzia. ~ **away** konda; asi; (*be lost*) potea; (*lapse*) kufuru, kosa. ~ **back** enda nyuma, rudi. ~ **back on** tegemea; (*decrease*) punguka. ~ **down on sth** (*colloq*) shindwa. ~ **foul of** kosana na. ~ **in** tumbukia; (*of walls*) bomoka; (*soldiers*) jipanga. ~ **off** punguka. ~ **out (with sb)** kosana, gombana; (*soldiers*) tawanyika. **~-out** *n* cheche za mnururisho zinazotokana na mlipuko wa bomu la nyuklia. ~ **through** shindwa; shindikana; (*of religion*) asi. ~ **to** shika kazi; (*be allotted to*) -wa mali ya (kazi ya). 9 angukia *Workers' day ~s on Saturday this year* Sikukuu ya Wafanyakazi itaangukia Jumamosi mwaka huu. 10 tamkwa. **the ~en** waliofia vitani. **~en woman** *(old use)* mwanamke aliyepoteza ubikira wake, asherati.

fallacy *n* dhana yenye kosa; hoja ya uwongo, kosa, uwongo. **fallacious** *adj*. **fallaciousness** *n*.

fallen *pp of* **fall.**

fallible *adj* -a kuweza kukosa, -a kuweza kuwa na kosa. **fallibility** *n*.

fallow *n* ardhi/shamba lililolimwa na kuachwa bila kupandwa mbegu *adj* -a kulimwa na kuachwa bila kupandwa mbegu.

false *adj* 1 si kweli, -a uongo, si halisi. 2 nafiki, -danganyifu, -ongo, -mbea. 3 (*artificial*) si -a asili. 4 -a bandia. **a ~ bottom** kitako-bandia. **under ~ pretences** kwa udanganyifu. **sail under ~ colour** 1 *sl* (*of a ship*) safiri na bendera isiyo halali. 2 (*fig*) jifanya kuwa tofauti na ulivyo *adv* kwa udanganyifu. **(to) play ~** danganya. ~ **hood** *n* 1 uwongo. 2 kusema uongo *guilty of ~hood* kosa la kusema uongo. **~ly** *adv*. **~ness** *n*.

falsify *vt* 1 danganya. 2 potosha. **falsification** *n*. **falsity** *n* 1 uwongo, udanganyifu. 2 uhaini.

falsetto *n* sautikike (sauti ya

mwanamume ya juu inayofanana na ya kike).

falsies *n* (*pl*) (*colloq*) sidiria iliyojazwa ili kukuza matiti.

falter *vi,vt* 1 sita. 2 (*of the voice*) gugumia. **~ingly** *adv*.

fame *n* see **famous**.

familiar *adj* 1 ~ **with** -zoefu. 2 (*well known*) -a kujulikana; (*of a person*) mashuhuri. 3 -a siku zote, -a kawaida. 4 -a kusuhubiana sana, -a karibu. 5 -enye kujipendekeza/kujikomba *n* rafiki, mwenzi. **~ly** *adv*. **~ity** *n* 1 mazoea, uzoefu. 2 urafiki; utani. 3 (*knowledge*) kujua sana, ujuaji. ~ **breeds contempt** (*prov*) ukicheza na mbwa utaingia naye msikitini. 4 (*pl*) vitendo vya kirafiki (sana). **~ize** *vt* 1 jizoeza. ~ **oneself with** zoeza. 2 eneza, tangaza.

family *n* 1 familia. 2 watoto (wa mtu fulani). 3 ahali, jamaa, aila *extended* ~ jamaa *nuclear* ~ ndugu wa karibu. 4 ukoo, nasaba. 5 kundi (la viumbe vya aina moja). 6 (*attrib*) -a jamii/ jamaa/familia. ~ **doctor** daktari wa familia. ~ **hotel** hoteli yenye bei nafuu kwa familia. ~ **likeness** kufanana kwa watu wa familia moja. ~ **man** mtu apendaye kukaa nyumbani na familia yake; mwenye familia. ~ **name** jina la ukoo. ~ **planning** uzazi wa majira, upangaji (wa) familia . ~ **tree** chati ionyeshayo uhusiano wa aila; shajara. **in the ~ way** (*sl*) mja mzito. **familial** *adj* -a kifamilia, -a jamii, -a ukoo.

famine *n* njaa, gumba; (*attrib*) -a njaa.

famish *vi,vt* taabika kwa njaa, -wa na njaa, taabisha kwa njaa *I am ~ed* (*colloq*) nina njaa sana.

famous *adj* 1 maarufu, mashuhuri *make* ~ fanya maarufu. 2 (*colloq*) zuri sana; -a kutosha. **~ly** *adv*. **fame** *n* umaarufu. **famed** *adj* mashuhuri.

famulus *n* katibu myeka, msaidizi wa profesa, hadimu.

fan[1] *n* (*colloq*) shabiki.

fan[2] *n* pepeo, feni *vi,vt* (*fig*) tia mshawasha. ~ **belt** mkanda wa feni. ~ **light** dirisha juu ya mlango lenye umbo la feni *vi,vt* 1 pepea, punga. 2 (*grain*) pepeta, peta. 3 ~ **up** puliza moto; fukuta. 4 ~ **out** tanda.

fanatic *n* mlokole (hasa wa dini), mtu ashikiliaye sana jambo bila akili *adj* (*also* **~al**) -a kilokole, -a mno, -a kukithiri. **~ally** *adv*. **~ism** *n*.

fancier *n* shabiki/mpenzi wa (jambo, mtu, mnyama fulani).

fancy *n* 1 ubunifu *mere* ~ wazo tu, ndoto tu. 2 fikira, wazo, ndoto *the ~ took him* wazo lilimjia. 3 **a ~ (for)** mapenzi, upendeleo. **take a ~ to** penda. **take/catch the ~ of** furahisha, vutia. **a passing** ~ kitu kivutiacho kwa muda mfupi. ~ **free** *adj* siopenda, -a utani/kutania, a mzahamzaha *adj* 1 -a kupendeza. 2 (*esp of small things*) -liorembwa; -a kupendeza macho; -a urembo. 3 (*extravagant*) -a mno, ghali sana. ~ **dress** nguo iliyorembwa inayovaliwa kwenye sherehe maalum. ~ **work** mashono ya urembo. 4 (*sl derog*) ~ **man** kuwadi wa malaya. ~ **woman** (*derog*) kimada; kipenda roho. 5 -liofugwa kwa ajili ya uzuri/urembo. 6 (*US, of goods*) bora. 7 -liobuniwa, -liowazi. **fanciful** *adj* 1 (*of persons*) bunifu sana, dhanifu, nayofuata ndoto tu. 2 -a njozi, -a kutunga; -enye umbo la ajabu. ~ **drawings** michoro ya ajabu. **~ly** *adv*, *vt* 1 (*imagine*) waza, tunga moyoni, dhani *just ~/~ that* ona! ajabu! zuri. 2 (*like*) penda, vutiwa na *I don't ~ his looks* sivutiwi na sura yake. 3 hisio, fikiri, labda *I ~ he is out* nadhani ametoka *I ~ so* naona hivyo. 4 taka. 5 ~ **oneself** jiona.

fanfare *n* (*music*) mshindo wa matarumbeta.

fang *n* 1 chonge, jino la mnyama (hasa kwa wala nyama): jino lenye sumu (la nyoka). 3 shina la jino.

fanny *n* (*US sl*) matako; (*GB*) kuma.

fantastic *adj* 1 -a kutisha; -a ajabu ~ *dreams* ndoto za ajabu. 2 (*of ideas, plans*) -a kuwazika tu; -siowezekana;

pumbavu. 3 (*sl*) safi *John is a really ~ boy* John ni mvulana safi sana! **~ally** *adv.*

fantasy *n* 1 uwezo wa kubuni/kuwaza/ kutunga taswira; matokeo ya mawazo ya kinjozi. 2 ndoto, njozi, ruya. **fantasize** *vt,vi* ~ **(about)** ota (ukiwa macho), waza.

fantasia *n* sanaa ambamo mtindo na fani ni muhimu kuliko muundo.

far *adj* 1 -a mbali. **be ~ (from)** -wa mbali sana (kutoka); (*fig*) tofauti kabisa na. 2 **the Far East** Mashariki ya Mbali. 3 chokomeani. **the ~ end** mwisho, chokomeani *adv* 1 mbali *we did not go ~* hatukwenda mbali. ~ **between** mara chache. **as ~ as** hata, mpaka, hadi. ~ **and wide** kotekote *as ~ as the eye can reach* upeo wa macho *he is not ~ off sixty* yeye anakaribia (miaka) sitini. **how ~?** umbali gani? ~ **from** (*let alone, not to mention, not only*) licha ya, sembuse. ~ **from it** hasha, sivyo. ~ **be it from me** siwezi; sipendi, mbali, sithubutu *in so ~ as I am concerned* kwa kadiri inavyonihusu mimi *so ~ so good* mpaka hapo sasa mambo ni mazuri. **(to) go ~ to** 1 enda mbali *it won't go very ~* haifiki mbali sana *that's going too ~* hilo linavuka mpaka. **as ~ back as** tangu ~ *into the night* hadi usiku wa manane. 2 (*compounds*) ~ **fetched** *adj* -sioaminika. ~ **flung** *adj* (*rhet*) -lioenea sana, -liotapakaa, liotawanyika. ~ **reaching** -enye athari nyingi. ~ **seing** -enye kuona mbali. ~ **sighted** -enye kuona mbali; (*fig*) -enye kuzingatia ya mbele, angalifu. ~ **famed** *adj* -enye kufahamika sana, maarufu. ~ **gone** -lioingiliwa sana,lio zama (na ugonjwa, ulevi n.k.). ~ **out** tofauti kabisa, -a ajabu. 3 (*with other adv & preps*) ~ **away** mbali sana ~ *beyond the river* mbele sana ya mto. ~ **from** hata kidogo. ~ **off** mbali sana. **by ~** kwa mbali. **go ~** (*of persons*) enda mbali, penda sana; (*of money*) weza kununua bidhaa/huduma. **go/ carry too ~** vuka mpaka, zidi. **as/so ~ as** hadi, hata mpaka, kwa kadiri; (*with qualifying adj & adv*) sana, kwa kiasi kikubwa *this is ~* hii ni afadhali sana. ~ **and away** (*with comp and super*) kwa mbali. ~ **away** *adj* -a mbali, -a zamani. **~ther** *adj* -a mbali zaidi *at the ~ end* mbali zaidi ~ *back* nyuma zaidi; (*later*) mbele; (*additional*) -a zaidi *adv* mbali zaidi ~ *off* si zaidi ya *nothing is ~ from my thoughts* mawazo yetu hayatofautiani sana. ~ **most** *adj* mbali kabisa *on the ~ side of the street* upande wa pili wa mtaa. **~thest** *adj & adv* mbali sana, mbele kabisa, mbele kupita kina kikuu. **at the ~** 1 mwisho kabisa. 2 (*of time*) kwa kuchelewa kabisa.

farce *n* 1 kichekesho; mchezo (jambo, hadithi) wa kuchekesha sana; (*joke*) utani; upuuzi. 2 matukio halisi ya upuuzi/kuchekesha. **farcical** *adj.* **farcically** *adv.*

fare[1] *n* nauli, uchukuzi *what is the ~?* nauli ni kiasi gani?; (*passenger*) msafiri, abiria.

fare[2] *n* (*food*) mlo. **bill of ~** orodha ya vyakula (vya karamu hotelini). **be fond of good ~** penda sana kula *vt,vi* 1 (*proceed*) (*old use*) enda, safiri, endelea *how did you ~?* uliendeleaje? **he ~d well** alifanikiwa. **you may go farther and ~ worse** unaweza kuendelea na kupata shida zaidi. 2 (*happen*) tukia, tokea. 3 (*get on*) -wa na hali, patwa na mambo. 4 (*be entertained*) tendewa, lishwa. 5 ~ **forth** anza safari. **~well** *int.* kwaheri, buriani *n* kuaga, maagano. **say/bid well to** aga, sema kwaheri *adj ~ well speech/dinner* hotuba/karamu ya kuagana.

farina *n* unga wa nafaka. **~ceous** *adj* -a wanga.

farm *n* 1 shamba. ~ **hand**/~ **worker** kibarua wa shamba. ~ **yard** uwanja baina ya majengo shambani. 2 ~ **house or ~ stead** nyumba ya mkulima shambani *vt,vi* 1 (*land*) lima; (*animals*) fuga. 2 ~ **out (to)** toa kazi ikafanywe na wengine; kabidhi mtoto alelewe na mlezi. **~er** *n* mkulima, mfugaji. **~ing** *n* ukulima.

farrago *n* 1 mchanganyiko wa vitu, mparaganyo. 2 mchuuzi wa vitu mchanganyiko.

farrier *n* 1 mfua njumu za farasi. 2 mganga wa farasi.

farrow *vi* (*of pigs*) zaa *n* vitoto vya nguruwe; uzaaji.

fart *vi* (*not in polite use*) sura, shuta, jamba *n* ushuzi.

farthing *n* (*formerly* sarafu yenye thamani ya robo ya peni *it is not worth a brass ~* haina thamani yoyote; bure ghali *without a ~* bila fedha mfukoni. **it does not matter/ he does not care a ~** haitishi/hajali.

fascia *n see* **dash board**.

fascinate *vt,vi* 1 vutia sana. 2 pumbaza kwa kukazia macho. **fascinating** *adj*. **fascination** *n*.

fascism *n* 1 ufashisti. 2 serikali ya mrengu wa kulia inayogandamiza watu. **fascist** *n* fashisti *adj* -a kifashisti.

fashion *n* 1 **a/the ~** mtindo. **after/in a ~** kwa kadri/kiasi fulani. **after the ~ of** kwa mtindo wa. 2 mtindo wa kisasa. **be all the ~** pendwa sana. **come into/go out of ~** kuingia/ kutoka kwa mitindo. **follow/be in the ~** fuata mtindo. **set the ~** anzisha mtindo. **a man/woman of ~** shabiki wa mitindo. **~ plate** picha ionyeshayo mtindo wa nguo *vt* unda. **~able** *adj* -a mtindo/-a siku hizi. **a ~able hotel** hoteli ya kisasa.

fast[1] *vi* funga (chakula n.k.) *n* 1 (*period of*) mfungo, saumu. 2 siku ya kufunga. **break one's ~** futuru.

fast[2] *adj* 1 imara, kikiki, madhubuti. **hard and ~ rules** sheria ngumu na imara. 2 amini, aminifu *a ~ friend* rafiki mwaminifu. 3 (*of colours*) -a kudumu, -siochujuka *adv* imara, thabiti. **stand ~** simama imara (kataa kuyumbishwa). **stick ~** simama imara; kwama. **~ bind, ~ find** (*prov*) kilichofungwa imara si rahisi kupotea. **play ~ and loose with** badilisha msimamo mara kwa mara. **~en** *vt&vi* 1 ~ **(up/down)** kaza, komea *~en all the doors* komea milango yote. 2 ~ **(on/upon) a nick name** tunga, pachika, -pa mtu jina la utani. **~en an accusation on/upon sb** tuhumu mtu. 3 funga *the window won't ~en* dirisha halitafunga. 4 ~ **on/upon** shikilia *he ~ened on her argument* ameshikilia hoja yake. **~ener** *n* kishikizo *a zip ~* zipu. **~ening** *n*.

fast[3] *adj* 1 -a upesi, -a haraka *a ~ trip* safari ya haraka. 2 (*dated*) (*of person, his way of living*) -a anasa, fujaji *a ~ man* mwanamume mfujaji mali, fisadi. 3 (*of a watch/clock*) -enye kukimbia *my watch is ~* saa yangu inakimbia. 4 (*of a surface*) -enye kufanya iwe haraka/iwe na mwendo. 5 (*of photographic film*) -a muda mfupi *adv* haraka, upesi *he speaks ~* anasema upesi. 2 **live ~** ishi kifisadi; (*old use*) *she lives ~ by* anaishi karibu.

fastidious *adj* (*in matters of food*) -enye machagu, gumu kuridhisha, haraka kukosoa. **~ly** *adv*. **~ness** *n*.

fat *adj* 1 -a mafuta, nene; (*of animals*) nono *a ~ man* mtu mnene. **~ head** *n* mpumbavu. 2 -liojaa *a ~ wallet* pochi iliyojaa noti. **a ~ lot** (*sl*) nyingi sana; *(ironic)* kidogo sana *n* 1 mafuta. 2 *(animal)* shahamu. **chew the ~** endelea kunung'unika. **live off the ~ of the land** ishi maisha ya anasa. **the ~s in the fire** mambo yameharibika. **(to) put on ~** nenepa. 3 -enye rutuba *~ lands* ardhi yenye rutuba. **~-tish** *adj* -nene nene. **~ness** *n,vt* nenepesha. **kill the ~ted calf** (*fig*) karibisha kwa furaha kubwa (mtu aliyerudi). **~ten** *vt* **~ ten (up)** nenepesha; nonesha. **~ty** *adj* -a mafuta, shahamu *n* (*colloq*) mnene.

fate *n* 1 jaala , majaliwa. **as sure as ~** hakika. **the F~s** miungu wa kike watatu wa Kigiriki (wa majaliwa). 2 kifo, mauti; maangamizi *vt* (*usu pass*) andikwa. **it was ~d**

imeandikwa (na Mungu); tabiriwa kuwa. **fatal** *adj* ~ **(to)** -a kufisha, -a mauti -baya *fatal accident* ajali ya kufisha *his long absence was fatal to our plans* kutokuwepo kwake kwa muda mrefu kuliharibu mipango yetu. 2 -a jaala. **~ly** *adv*. **~ism** *n* falsafa ya jaala/majaliwa. **~ist** *n* muumini wa falsafa ya jaala. **~istic** *adj* -a jaala/ majaliwa. **~ity** *n* 1 msiba, baa. 2 kifo cha ajali/vita n.k. 3 mauti, athari mbaya (ya ugonjwa). **~ful** *adj* 1 -a jaala, -a majaliwa. **~ful events** matukio ya majaliwa. 2 -enye kutabiri.

father[1] *n* 1 baba *adoptive* ~ baba wa kupanga *putative* ~ baba wa kudhaniwa *step* ~ baba wa kambo. **the child is ~ to the man** (*prov*) matendo ya utotoni yatajidhihirisha ukubwani. **the wish is ~ to the thought** (*prov*) imani yetu ni kwa yale mambo tunayotaka kuwa kweli. **~-in law** baba mkwe. **~-figure** mzee anayeheshimika (kwa ushauri wake wa kibaba). 2 (*usu pl*) mababu *sleep with one's ~s* zikwa pamoja na mababu. 3 mwanzilishi, kiongozi wa kwanza. **F~s of the Church** waanzilishi wa kwanza wa Kikristo katika (karne tano za mwanzo). **F~ of the Nation** Baba wa Taifa. **City F~s** madiwani. 4 **Our (heavenly)** ~ Mungu (Baba). 5 padre, kasisi; kiongozi katika nyumba ya mapadre *the Holy* ~ Baba Mtakatifu. 6 jina la kupanga ~ *Christmas* Baba Noeli. **~-hood** *n* ubaba. **~-land** *n* nchi ya kuzaliwa kwetu. **~less** -liofiwa na baba, yatima. **~ly** *adj* *~ly love* mapenzi ya baba *vt* 1 asisi jambo/ wazo. 2 kubali kuwa baba (wa mtoto/ mwandishi wa kitabu n.k). 3 ~ **on/ upon** -pa ubaba wa mtoto; twisha mzigo.

fathom *n* kina cha maji (futi sita, au mita 1.8), wari mbili *vt* 1 pima kina cha; elewa. **~less** *adj* -siopimika kina; -sioeleweka.

fatigue *n* 1 uchovu, mavune. 2 (*of metals*) kuchoka (kutokana na matumizi mengi). 3 kazi ya sulubu; (*of soldiers*) kazi zisizo za kijeshi (kupika, kulima). **~-party** *n* kikosi cha wanajeshi n.k. kinachopewa kazi hizo. (*pl*) **~s** *n* nguo za wanajeshi *vt* chosha.

fatuous *adj* -pumbavu, -sio na maana. ~ **reply** *n* jibu la kipumbavu. **~ly** *adv*. **fatuity/~ness** *n*.

faucet *n* (*esp. US*) bilula, mfereji.

faugh *int* Yeh! sauti ya kuonyesha hasira au kinyaa.

fault *n* 1 kosa, hatia, taksiri, dosari. **at** ~ -enye hatia/makosa; katika hali ya kutatizwa. **to a** ~ kupita kiasi. **find ~ (with)** lalamika. **~-finder** mtu asiyeridhirika. ~ **finding** kutafuta makosa. 2 kosa, lawama *the ~ lies with you* lawama ni yako. 3 jambo lililofanywa kwa makosa; (*of tennis*) mpira uliopigwa vibaya. 4 (*of rocks*) ufa, muatuko *vt* kosoa, laumu *no one could ~ his implementation* hakuna ambaye angeweza kukosoa utekelezaji wake. **~less** *adj*. **~lessly** *adv*. **~y** *adj* -enye kosa, -baya, ovyo *the work was done in a ~ manner* kazi ilifanyika ovyo. **~ily** *adv*.

faun *n* (*Roman myth*) mungu wa mashambani mwenye pembe na miguu ya mbuzi.

fauna *n* fauna: mkusanyiko wa wanyama wote katika mazingira fulani.

faux pas *n* tendo/neno linalovunja heshima k.m. kujamba.

favour/favor *n* 1 fadhila *win a person's* ~ pata fadhila za fulani. **be/stand high in sb's ~** pendwa na mtu fulani. **be in/out of ~ (with sb)** pendwa/ -topendwa na. **find/lose ~ with sb/in sb's eyes** pata/kosa fadhila mbele ya fulani. 2 msaada, kuunga mkono, kukubali kusaidia. **in ~ of** (kwa) upande wa, niaba/kuunga mkono/ faida ya; kwa ajili ya. 3 upendeleo. **without fear or ~** kwa haki kabisa, bila kuogopa au kupendelea. 4 msaada, wema. **do sb -a ~** tendea mtu wema. **do a ~ for sb** fanya wema/toa msaada kwa mtu fulani. 5 pambo, tunu *vt,vi* 1 unga mkono, fadhili, pendelea *fortune ~s the brave* bahati humwendea shujaa. 2 pendelea. 3 ~ **sb with sth** (*old use or formal*) -pa fursa; fanyia jambo *the child will ~ us with a song* mtoto atatuimbia. 4 (*of circumstances*) wezesha, rahisisha. 5 (*old use*) fanana na, landana na *the girl ~s her mother* msichana yule anafanana na mama yake. **ill/well ~ed** *adj* -enye sura mbaya/nzuri. 6 ~ **with** -pa, tolea, wezesha. **~able** *adj* -enye kufaa, -enye kusaidia. **~ably** *adv*. **~ite** *n* 1 kipenzi, mpenzi. 2 **the ~ite** (*racing*) farasi anayetegemewa kushinda. 3 mtu anayependelewa *adj* **~tism** upendeleo. pendezi, penzi.

fawn[1] *n* 1 mtoto wa paa, paa mdogo (asiye na umri wa zaidi ya mwaka). 2 (*colour*) rangi ya paa kama hudhurungi, madafu.

fawn[2] *vi* (**on**) (*of dogs*) 1 onyesha furaha na upendo (kwa kurukaruka na kutikisa mkia). 2 (*of persons*) jipendekeza, jikomba; bembeleza.

faze *vt* (*usu with a neg*) shtua, hangaisha, sumbua *It doesn't ~ a bit* hainisumbui hata kidogo.

fealty *n* (*in feudal times*) kiapo, ahadi ya kumtumikia mtu *take an oath of ~* kula kiapo cha uaminifu kwa bwana.

fear (*dread*) 1 hofu, woga. **for ~ of** kwa hofu ya. **for ~ that/lest** kwa kuhofia ili kwamba jambo lisitokee. 2 wahaka *he is in ~ of his life* ana wasiwasi juu ya maisha yake. 3 uwezekano *no ~* (*colloq*) haiwezekani. 4 kicho, uchaji *the ~ of God* uchaji wa Mungu. **~ful** *adj* -a kutisha, -a kuogofya *a ~ful story* hadithi ya kutisha. **~fully** *adv*. **~fulness** *n*. **~less** *adj* jasiri, shupavu. **~lessly** *adv* bila hofu. **~lessness** *n*. **~some** *adj* (*usu jokingly*) -enye sura ya kutisha, -a kuogofya *vt,vi* 1 ogopa, hofu. 2 chelea. 3 ~ **for** -wa na wasiwasi wa ~ *the worst* -wa na wasiwasi kuwa jambo baya limetokea au litatokea. 4 -cha, ogopa ~ *God and obey your parents* ogopa Mungu na watii wazazi wako.

feasible *adj* 1 a kuwezekana, -a kutendeka. 2 (*colloq*) yamkini, -a kuaminika. **feasibility** *n* uwezekano ~ *study* uchunguzi wa uwezekano/ hali halisi.

feast *n* 1 (**~day**) sikukuu; sherehe. 2 karamu. 3 (*fig*) kitulizo cha akili au hisi *vt,vi* 1 (*entertain*) kirimu, karibisha; (*delight*) furahisha; (*enjoy*) jifurahisha. **(to) ~ one's eye on sth** furahisha macho kwa kuangalia jambo fulani. 2 shiriki/shirikisha katika karamu; -la, lisha sana (na kusaza).

feat *n* tendo gumu (la ajabu, la ujasiri, la uhodari, la nguvu) lifanywalo vizuri; tendo kubwa.

feather *n* 1 unyoya. **a ~ in one's cap** kitu cha kujivunia. **as light as a ~** epesi sana. **in full/high ~s** kuwa katika furaha/hali/ afya nzuri. **(to) show the white ~** onyesha woga. **birds of a ~ (flock together)** Waswahili wa Pemba hujuana kwa vilemba. **~-bed** godoro la manyoya *vt* penda mno, fanyia huruma/karimu; saidia. **~-bed the farmers** toa misaada kwa wakulima. **~-brained; ~ headed** *adj* -jinga, pumbavu; -enye mawenge. **~weight** *n* (*boxing*) uzito wa unyoya. **~y** *adj* -a laini na epesi kama unyoya *vt* 1 pamba (kwa manyoya), tia manyoya. **~ one's nest** 1 jitajirisha, jiletea raha, jianisi. 2 elea, pepea kama unyoya. 3 ~ *one's oar* pindisha kasia ili bapa likae juu ya maji.

feature *n* 1 sehemu ya uso (pua, midomo n.k.). 2 (*pl*) sura, uso. 3 sifa/sehemu muhimu *the geographical ~s* sura ya nchi (k.m. milima, maziwa, mabonde n.k.). 4 makala/habari maalum katika gazeti. 5 filamu (ndefu ya hadithi) *vt* 1 -wa sifa/sehemu muhimu ya. 2 fanya kuwa muhimu, maarufu. 3 onyesha *a film that ~ a new singer* filamu inayomwonyesha mwimbaji mpya . **~less** *adj* -sio pendeza, sio na umuhimu, -sio na sifa muhimu.

February *n* Februari: mwezi wa pili.

feces *see* **faeces**.

feckless *adj* -zembe; -sojali wajibu, -sofanikiwa. **~ness** *n.* **~ly** *adv.*

fecund *adj* -a kuzaa sana, -enye kizazi kikubwa. **~ity** *n* kizazi kikubwa, uzaaji.

fed *pt, pp of* feed.

federal *adj* 1 -a shirikisho 2. -a kuhusu serikali ya shirikisho. **~ist** *n.* **~ism** *n.* **federate** *vt,vi* (*of State, Society, Organizations*) unganisha, ungana kuwa shirikisho. **federative** *adj.* **federatively** *adv.* **federation** *n* 1 shirikisho. 2 uundaji wa shirikisho. 3 kitendo cha kuungana.

fee *n* 1 ada, karo, kiingilio. 2 (*legal*) mali ya kurithi *estate in ~ simple* mali inayorithiwa na mrithi yeyote *~ tail* mali inayorithiwa na warithi wa aina fulani tu *vt* 1 lipa ada/karo/kiingilio. 2 weka mtu kwa malipo (k.m. wakili).

feeble *adj* dhaifu, hafifu, nyonge. **~ -minded** *adj* punguani. **feebly** *adv.* **~ness** *n.*

feed *n* 1 chakula; malisho *be off one's ~* -tokuwa na hamu ya chakula. 2 bomba la kupelekea vitu (malighafi) kwenye mashine; mali ghafi inayopelekwa kwenye mashine kwa bomba. **~-back** *n* 1 majibu ya utekelezaji wa maazimio. 2 mwangwi katika redio. 3 (*colloq*) habari azitoazo mtumaji wa bidhaa kwa mtengenezaji n.k.; majibu, maoni *vt,vi* 1 **~ on** lisha; -la *lions ~ chiefly on meat* simba hula nyama *~ one's face* kula kila mara. **~ oneself** jilisha chakula. **~ up** lisha chakula bora. **be fed up (with)** (*fig,sl*) choshwa na. **~ing-bottle** chupa ya kunyonyeshea. 2. **~ to** lisha/-pa chakula. 3 (*chiefly of animals, colloq or hum of persons*) -la chakula. 4 (*of a belt*) tawanya, gawa mali ghafi kwenye mashine. **~on** -la (kama chakula). **~er** *n* 1 (*of plants and animals)* mlaji *be a large ~er* wa mlishaji. 3 kitu kizidishacho au kitia nguvu kitu kingine. 4 (*often attrib.*) njia za reli, n.k. zinazoingia katika njia kuu. 5 chupa ya kunyonyeshea; bibu.

feel *n* (*sing only*) 1 *the ~* hisia za kugusa (mfano ugumu, ulaini, uororo n.k.). 2 *the ~* msisimko unaotokana na kuguswa au kupapaswa. 3 kugusa. 4 **get the ~ of** anza kuzoea *vt,vi* 1 hisi, jua kwa kugusa/kushika n.k. *~ the pulse* hisi/pima mapigo ya moyo. **~ one's way** tembea kwa uangalifu (kama katika giza au kipofu afanyavyo), papasa; tahadhari katika kutenda mambo fulani. 2 **~ (about) (for)** papasa papasa, tomasa, sunza *he felt about in the dark for his bed* alisunza ili aone kitanda chake. 3 (*through contact*) sikia *I can ~ a thorn in my* shoe nasikia mwiba ndani ya kiatu changu. 4 (*not through contact*) ona. **(to) ~ the weight of sth** fahamu umuhimu wa jambo fulani *I ~ it my duty to* natambua ni wajibu wangu *the chairman felt the force of his argument* mwenyekiti aliona uzito wa hoja yake. **~ sb out** jaribu kujua maoni ya mtu kwa uangalifu. 5 -jisikia, -jiona, -ona *I ~ ill* na jisikia mgonjwa. **to ~ quite oneself** kujiona barabara *~ cold/happy/* -ona baridi/ furaha. 6 -wa na uwezo wa kuhisi *a corpse does not ~* maiti hana uwezo wa kuhisi. 7 **~ for/with one; ~ pity for sb** onea huruma, hurumia. 8 **~ as if/though** hisi/jihisi kana kwamba *he felt as if he was flying* alijiona kana kwamba alikuwa anapaa. 9 onekana, onekana kama *it ~s like wood* inaonekana kama ubao *it ~s soft* inaonekana ororo. 10 **~ like** (*of persons*) jisikia, taka, penda, pendelea *we shall go together if you ~ like it* tutakwenda wote ukipenda. **~ equal to** jihisi sawa na; (*colloq*) **~ up to** -wa na nguvu/uwezo wa. 11 patwa na, sumbuliwa na *she ~s the loss of her father* msiba wa baba yake unamhuzunisha *he does not ~ the cold at all* baridi haimsumbui. 12 fikiria kwamba, waza kuwa, onelea *the committee felt the project to be feasible* kamati imefikiria kwamba mradi unawezekana kutekelezwa. 13 furahia, changamkia, elewa vizuri. ~ **er** *n* (*of insects, animals*) 1 papasi. 2 (*test*) hoja itolewayo ili kupima mawazo ya watu wengine. **put out ~s/a ~** pima mawazo ya wengine kwa kuwapa maswali maalum. **~ing** *n* 1 uwezo wa kuhisi *the ~ in his legs is weak* uwezo wa kuhisi katika miguu yake ni dhaifu.2 hisia *a ~ of hunger* hisia ya njaa. **a ~ing of joy** hisia ya furaha; (*of an opinion*) (*usu sing*) wazo la wote. 3 (*pl*) hisia za mtu *hurt a man's ~s* udhi mtu, tia uchungu wa moyo. 4 huruma; uelewano *he does not show much ~ for the sufferings of others* hana huruma na wenziwe, haonei huruma wenzake. **good ~** urafiki, uelewano. **ill/bad ~** chuki, uhasama. 5 chuki; hasira *his failure aroused strong ~s in teachers* kufeli kwake kumeibua chuki kubwa miongoni mwa walimu wake. 6 mapenzi *he has much ~ for (art, beauty etc.)* ana mapenzi makubwa ya (sanaa, uzuri n.k.) *adj* -enye huruma; -ema; -enye kuonyesha hisia zake. **~ingly** *adv*.

feet *n, pl of* **foot**.

feign *vt* (*arch*) 1 tunga, buni, zua *~ a story* tunga hadithi. 2 jifanya, jisingizia. ~ **madness** jifanya kichaa.

feint *n* kisingizio, mwigo, hila, uwongo *(to) make a ~ of doing sth* singizia kufanya jambo fulani *vi* fanya shambulio la uongo (katika vita, ngumi ili kupoteza lengo/ kudanganya adui).

felicitate *vt* ~ **sb (on/upon sth)**(*formal*) pongeza, -pa hongera. **felicitation** *n*. **felicitous** *adj* (*formal*) (*of words/ remarks*) fasaha,teule; -a kufurahisha, -a heri, zuri. **felicity** *n* 1 (*formal*) furaha kuu, nyemi. 2 sudi, baraka. 3 ufasaha, maneno fasaha.

feline *adj* -a (kama) paka, -a jamii ya paka. ~. **felinity** *n*.

fell[1] *pt of* **fall**

fell[2] *n* ngozi ya mnyama yenye manyoya.

fell[3] mbuga yenye majabali na vilima.

fell[4] *adj* -kali, -katili, jeuri *with one ~ swoop* kwa pigo moja kali.

fell[5] *vt* angusha; kata (mti) *~ a seam* (*in sewing*) shona jongo mlazo *n*. **flat ~ seam** jongo mlazo. **~er** *n* mkata miti; (*of machine*) kata miti.

fellah *n* mkulima (katika nchi za Kiarabu).

fellow *n* 1 (*colloq*) mtu, jamaa (mwanaume au mvulana) *a good ~* mtu mzuri *lucky ~* mtu mwenye bahati *my good ~* rafiki yangu! *old ~!* rafiki! *poor ~!* masikini! *what do you ~s think*? vipi jamani? mwambaje? 2 mwenzi, mshiriki. **be hail ~ well met with sb** -wa na urafiki wa juu juu/wa unafiki. 3 (*attrib*) wa aina moja. ~ **country man** mwananchi mwenzio; mpenzi wa chama/ushirika (lakini si mwanachama). 4 mwanazuoni, msomi. **Research ~** Mchunguzi. 5 (sehemu) moja ya jozi. ~ **feeling** *n* huruma. **~ship** *n* 1 urafiki. 2 uanachama, ushirika. 3 uanazuoni.

felony *n* jinai (kuua, kuunguza nyumba ya mtu n.k.). **felonious** *adj*. **felon** *n* mkosaji.

felt[1] *n* 1 kitambaa gandamizo; (*tarred*) -a kuezekea *vt* tengeneza kitambaa gandamizo.

felt[2] *pp of* **feel**

female *adj* -a mwanamke, -a kike *n* 1 mwanamke, jike. 2 (*tech*) parafujo pokeaji.

feminine *adj* 1 -a kike, -a wanawake. 2 (*gram*) -a (jinsi ya) kike. **femininity** *n* ujike: hali ya kuwa mwanamke. **feminism** *n* tapo la kupigania ukombozi, haki, na usawa wa wanawake; nadharia ya usawa wa wanawake. **feminist** *n* mtetezi wa nadharia ya haki na usawa wa wanawake. **feminize** *vt,vi* 1 fanya/

kuwa -a kike. 2 pa/pata/chukua tabia ya kike.

femur *n* fupa la paja.

fen *n* mbuga yenye kinamasi.

fence *n* 1 ua. **come down on one side or the other of the ~** unga mkono upande mmoja au mwingine. **come down on the right/wrong side of the ~** kuwa upande wa mshindi/mshinde. **mend one's ~s** patana na, leta suluhu. **sit on the ~** (*usu derog*) kaa chonjo/kando, jivuta; -tojitia upande huu wala ule. **~-sitter** asiyejiingizakokote. 2 ukingo. 3 upokeaji/mpokeaji wa mali iliyoibwa *vt,vi* 1 tenga na zungushia ua. 2 zuia kwa ukingo. 3 pokea mali iliyoibwa. 4 shindana kwa kitara; (*fig*) epuka kujibu swali. **fencing** *n* vifaa vilivyotumiwa kujenga kitalu; mchezo/ufundi wa kushindana kwa vitara. **~r** mtumiaji kitara/upanga/sime. **~less** *adj* bila kitalu.

fend *vt,vi* **~(off)** jikinga/linda/jilinda, dhidi ya. **~ for oneself** jitegemea, jikimu. **~er** *n* 1 kinga. 2 bamba.

fennel *n* shamari (kiungo jamii ya karoti)

fenugreek *n* uwatu.

feral *adj* 1 (*of an animal*) -kali, -siofugwa, -a mwituni.

ferment *n* 1 uchachu chachu, hamira. 2 msisimko. **be in a ~** sisimkwa; umuka *vt,vi* 1 vundika, chachusha; chachuka; umua. 2 (*stir up*) chochea, leta mkoroganyo. **~ation** *n*.

fern *n* kangaga, dege la watoto, madole matano. **~y** *adj*. **~ery** *n*.

ferocious *adj* -kali, -katili. **ferocity** *n* ukali, ukatili.

ferret *n* 1 aina ya nguchiro. 2 chunguzi. **~y** *adj,vt* 1 winda na cheche/nguchiro; tafutatafuta, peleleza, chunguza. 2 **~ sth out/ ~ about (for sth)** gundua kwa kuchunguza, chunguza.

ferro (*pref*) -enye chuma.

ferro-concrete *n* zege madhubuti/kali. **~ous** *adj* -enye (kuhusu) chuma.

ferrule *n* 1 (*ring*) pete. 2 kifuniko chani mwa bakora/ mwavuli n.k.

ferry *n* kivuko *vt,vi* 1 vusha. 2 safirisha; vuka. **~ boat** *n* mashua ya kuvushia. **~ man** *n* mvushaji. **~ pontoon** *n* pantoni.

fertile *adj* 1 -enye kuzaa sana, -enye rutuba. 2 -enye uwezo wa kuzaa. 3 -enye mawazo, mipango mingi. **fertility** *n*. **fertilize** *vt* 1 rutubisha. 2 tungisha mimba. **fertilizer** *n* mbolea (k.m. ya chumvichumvi, samadi, mboji n.k.). **fertilization** *n* 1 rutubisho. 2 utungisho.

ferule *n* rula bapa ya kuwachapia watoto shuleni.

fervent *adj* 1 (-enye) moto, -enye kuwaka. 2 -enye ari, -enye hamasa; (*of feeling*) kali. **fervency** *n*. **fervid** *adj* -enye ari, hamasa; -enye bidii. **fervour** *n* ari, hamasa; bidii.

fester *vi* 1 tunga usaha. 2 (*fig*) kereketa/ choma (moyo).

festival *n* 1 sikukuu, sherehe. 2 tamasha (la muziki, filamu n.k.). **festal** *adj* -a sikukuu, -a sherehe; -enye kuchangamka. **festive** *adj* 1 -a sikukuu, -a sherehe. 2 -enye kuchangamka. **festivity** *n* 1 furaha/ shangwe ya sikukuu. 2 (*pl*) sherehe, sikukuu.

festoon *n* ushanga/utungo wa maua, karatasi za rangirangi, vitambaa vya rangirangi n.k. (kwa ajili ya mapambo) *vt* pamba kwa ushanga, utungo wa maua n.k.

fetch *vt,vi* 1 leta *go and ~* nenda kalete. **~ and carry (for)** fanyia mtu kazi ndogondogo; tumikia. 2 (*be sold for*) uzwa kwa; pata *the car will ~ a good price* gari litauzwa kwa bei nzuri. 3 (*colloq*) piga. 4 toa, toza (machozi, kite n.k.). **~ up** 1 toa; leta. 2 komesha. 3 tapika. 4 fik(i)a (kiwango) *n* 1 tendo la kwenda kuchukua kitu. 2 hila. **~ing** *adj* (*colloq*)-enye kuvutia, -a kupendeza.

fete *n* (*usu outdoor*) fete: sherehe za kuchangisha fedha kwa shughuli maalum *vt* sherehekea; laki kwa shangwe.

fetid *adj* -a kunuka, -enye uvundo,

-enye harufu mbaya.

fetish *n* 1 miungu ya masanamu. 2 kitu kinachopendwa na kuabudiwa mno. **~ism** *n*.

fetter *n* pingu za miguu, mnyororo; (*fig. usu pl*) kizuizi, kipingamizi. *vt* 1 tia pingu; (*fig*) zuia. 2 *make a ~ of* penda mno, husudu.

fettle *n*. **in fine/good ~** katika hali nzuri ya uchangamfu/uzima.

fetus *see* **foetus**.

feud *n* ugomvi mkubwa; uhasama wa muda mrefu baina ya watu wawili, familia, kikundi cha watu n.k.

feudal *adj* -a kikabaila *~ society* jamii ya kikabaila. **~ stage** hatua ya ukabaila. **~ system** *n* mfumo wa kikabaila, nyarubanja. **~ism** *n* ukabaila. **~ist** *n* kabaila. **feudatory** *adj* -enye kumtumikia kabaila *n* mtwana wa kabaila.

fever *n* 1 homa. **~ heat** joto la homa. **yellow ~** homa ya manjano. **typhoid ~** homa ya matumbo. 2 (*excitement*) msisimko. **at/to ~ pitch** kusisimka sana ~ *adj* -enye msisimko mkubwa. **~ sh** *adj* -enye dalili ya homa. **~ishly** *adv*.

few *adj* 1 chache *a man of ~ words* mkimya *every ~ days* kila baada ya siku chache *not a ~* si haba. 2 **no ~er than** -sio pungufu ya. 3 (*positively*) **a ~** kiasi kidogo. **some ~, a good ~, quite a ~, not a ~** kiasi cha kuridhisha, maridhawa, tosha. 4 **the ~** wachache. **a ~ of** (*positive*) baadhi, chache *I know a few of them* nawafahamu baadhi yao *have a ~* (*colloq*) -nywa pombe kiasi cha kutosha. **~ness** *n*.

fey *adj* 1 (*Scot*) -enye hisia ya kukaribia kufa. 2 -enye uwezo wa kutabiri. 3 -a kuzimu.

fez *n* tarbushi, kitunga.

fiancé (*feminine* **fiancée**) mchumba.

fiasco *n* kushindwa kabisa (kwa jambo); kazi bure, hasara (tupu).

fiat *n* 1 amri, agizo (litolewalo na mtawala).

fib *n* (*colloq*) uwongo (hasa wa jambo lisilokuwa muhimu) *vi* ongopa. **~ber** *n* mwongo. **~bing** *n* kusema uwongo.

fibre (*US* **fiber**) *n* 1 ufumwele, utembo, ung'ong'o, unyuzi. 2 bonge/donge/bao/bamba la nyuzinyuzi. **~ board** bamba (la) nyuzi, hadibodi. **~ glass** kioo nyuzi: bamba/bati/bodi la mseto wa glasi na nyuzi. 3 umbile, msuko; (*fig*) (*of person*) tabia. **of strong moral ~** adilifu. **fibrous** *adj*.

fibula *n* (*anat*) fibula, goko, muundi.

fickle *adj* (*of moods, the weather etc*) -a kubadilika badilika, -geugeu *a ~ lover* mpenzi (aliye na) kigeugeu. **~ness** *n*.

fiction *n* 1 (*untruth*) habari za kubuniwa. **a polite/legal ~** jambo linalofikiriwa kuwa kweli japokuwa laweza kuwa uwongo kisheria au kijamii. 2 tanzu ya fasihi inayojumuisha masimulizi ya kubuni. **fictitious** *adj* -a uwongo; -a kubuni.

fiddle *n* 1 (*colloq*) fidla. **fit as a ~** mzima sana. **have a face as long as a ~** -wa na sura ya masikitiko. **play second ~ (to)** chukua nafasi ya usaidizi. **~-faddle** *n* upuuzi, mambo madogomadogo. **~ stick** *n* upinde. **~sticks** *int* upuuzi. 2 (*colloq*) utapeli, ughushi, ubabaishaji *vt* 1 (*colloq*) piga udi/fidla. 2 **~ (about) (with)** chezacheza na, chezeachezea. 3 (*sl*) badilisha ili kuvuruga. **~er** *n* mpiga fidla; mghushi. **fiddling** *adj* (*colloq*) -siokuwa -a maana.

fidelity *n* **~ (to sb, sth)** 1 uaminifu. 2 usahihi.

fidget *vt,vi* **~ (about) (with)** fazaisha; riaria, hangaika, tukuta; hangaisha *stop ~ing* acha kuriaria, kutukuta *n* 1 **(usu the ~s)** hali ya kutukuta/kuriaria. 2 mtukutu. **~y** *adj* -siotulia; tukutu.

fie *int* aibu *~ on you* huoni aibu.

field *n* 1 mbuga ya malisho, shamba *a ~ of wheat* shamba la ngano. 2 (*usu in compounds*) uwanja *a landing ~* (*for aircraft*) uwanja wa ndege. **~ events** *n pl* mashindano ya kuruka/

kutupa (si ya kukimbia). ~ **glasses** *n* bainokula/darubini. ~**sports** *n* michezo ya nje, kuwinda, n.k. 3 (*usu in compounds*) eneo la machimbo, mgodi *gold* ~ mgodi wa dhahabu. 4 uwanja wa kitaaluma *this is in my* ~ hili lipo katika uwanja wangu (wa kitaaluma). ~ **work** utafiti ufanywao nje ya maabara/maktaba, utafiti/kazi ya uwandani. 5 eneo (la matumizi n.k.) *magnetic* ~ eneo la sumaku. 6 *(mil)* uwanja wa mapambano *battle* ~ uwanja wa vita. ~ **day** siku ya mazoezi ya kijeshi; (*fig*) siku maalum. **have a ~ day** (*fig*) fanya sherehe, -wa na ushindi. ~ **hospital** hospitali ya muda vitani. **F~ Marshal** Jemadari Mkuu. ~ **gun** mzinga. 7 (*sports and athletics*) washindani/washiriki wote, wasasi wote. **-~ed** *vt,vi* 1 (*cricket and baseball*) -wa tayari kudaka au kuzuia (mpira) *she ~ed the ball well* aliudaka mpira vema. 2 *(of football teams)* ingiza panga, chezesha timu uwanjani. **~er** *n*, **~sman** *n* (*cricket etc*) mdaka/mzuia mpira. 3 (*colloq*) jibu *he ~ed that question well* alijibu vizuri swali hilo.

fiend *n* 1 shetani, ibilisi. 2 katili, dhalimu, jeuri. 3 (*colloq*) mtu aliyeathiriwa sana na jambo/kitu fulani. **drug-~** mlevi wa madawa. **~ish** *adj*. **~ishly** *adv*.

fierce *adj* -a kali, katili; -a nguvu. **~ly** *adv*. **~ness** *n*.

fiery *adj* 1 -a moto; -a joto, -enye kuwaka. 2 (*fierce*) kali; -a harara. **fierily** *adv*. **fieriness** *n*.

fiesta *n* (*Sp*) sikukuu/tamasha la kidini.

fife *n* filimbi *vi,vt* piga filimbi. **~r** *n* mpiga filimbi.

fifteen *n, adj* kumi na tano. **~th** *adj* -a kumi na tano.

fifth *n, adj* (-a) tano. ~ **column** vibaraka wasaliti. **~ly** *adv*.

fifty *n* hamsini. **the fifties** miaka ya 50. **go ~-~ (with); be on a ~-~ basis (with)** pata/-wa nusu kwa nusu. **a ~-~ chance** tumaini la sawa kwa sawa/nusu kwa nusu. **fiftieth** *n, adj*.

fig *n* mtini; (*fruit*) tini. **not care/give a fig (for)** kutojali hata kidogo, kuona upuuzi mtupu!

fight *n* 1 pambano, mapigano. **put up a good/poor** ~ pigana kishujaa/ovyoovyo; (*brawl*) (*fig*) ugomvi. 2 ari na uwezo wa kupigana *they still had ~ left in them* bado walikuwa na ari na uwezo wa kupigana. **show** ~ onyesha/wa na moyo wa kupigana *vi,vt* 1 pigana, fanya vita, shindana. ~ **with (against) sb, sth** pigana na. ~ **for sth** pigania, shindania. ~ **to a finish** pigana mpaka kufikia uamuzi. ~ **shy of** epukana na. 2 (*of battle*) pambana; *(of election)* gombea. 3 ~ **sth down** shinda, kandamiza, zima. **to ~ one's way** sukuma/pita kwa nguvu, pigania. ~ **off** rudisha nyuma; zuia kwa nguvu. ~ **it out** pambana hadi suluhu ipatikane. **~ing chance** uwezekano wa kufanikiwa ikiwa unajitahidi sana. **~er** *n* 1 mpiganaji. 2 ndege ya kivita.

figment *n* kitu kilichobuniwa au kutungwa ~ *of one's imagination* kitu kilichobuniwa, ndoto.

figure *n* 1 (*number*) tarakimu (hasa kutoka 0 mpaka 9). **double ~s** makumi: tarakimu kuanzia 10 hadi 99. **single ~s** mamoja/epesi. 2 (*pl*) hesabu *quick at ~s* -elekevu wa kuhesabu. 3 (*appearance*) umbo. **have a fine** ~ -wa na umbo zuri. **cut a fine/poor/ sorry** ~ onyesha sura nzuri/mbaya/ya masikitiko. 4 mchoro (k.m. wa mtu, mnyama, ndege n.k.), sanamu. ~ **head** sanamu ya kuchonga (ya kichwa na kifua tu au umbo zima) inayotumiwa kama pambo juu ya gubeti; *(fig)* mkubwa wa jina tu, mtu mwenye cheo kikubwa lakini kisicho na madaraka hasa/ya haja. 5 bei *buy sth at a low* ~ nunua kitu kwa bei ndogo *what is your* ~? kiasi gani? wauzaje? 6 mtu, hasa tabia yake *dominating* ~ mtu mashuhuri sana. 7 ~ **of speech** tamathali ya usemi. 8 mchoro, kielelezo, chati n.k. *vt,vi* 1 fikiria/waza moyoni; onyesha.

2 ~ **(in)** onekana; jitokeza, wa mashuhuri *he ~s in Kiswahili* yu mashuhuri katika Kiswahili. 3 ~ **sth out** elewa, piga hesabu. ~ **sb out** elewa mtu *I can't ~ that man out* simwelewi mtu huyu. 4 ~ **(on)** (*US*) kisia, kadiria, dhani, tegemea *I ~ him (to be) honest* nadhani yu mwaminifu. 5 (*represent*) -wa mfano wa. **~d** *adj* -liotiwa nakshi.

figuration *n* ufanyizaji wa umbo; umbo; uumbaji wa taswira. **figurative** *adj* -a kitamathali, kistiari, -a methali. **figuratively** *adv*. **figurine** *n* sanamu ndogo.

filament *n* uzi, waya (ndani ya balbu).

filature *n* kiwanda cha kusokota nyuzi za hariri.

filch *vt* dokoa; sogeza.

file[1] *n* tupa *vt* piga tupa, kata kwa tupa; chonga. **filings** *n* cheche/punje za tupa.

file[2] *n* faili, jalada *vt* 1 faili, hifadhi jaladani. 2 andikisha jambo mahakamani, sajili.

file[3] *n* safu. **(in) single ~; (in) Indian ~** sanjari. **the rank and ~** askari (wasio maofisa); (*fig*) watu wa kawaida; akina kabwela/yahe *vi* fuatana, andamana katika safu. ~ **in/out** ingia/ toka kwa safu.

filial *adj* -a mtoto ~ *love* mapenzi ya mtoto kwa wazazi.

filibuster *n* 1 mberegezaji, mtu anayezuia upitishaji wa maamuzi katika mikutano, hasa bunge kwa hotuba ndefu. 2 hotuba ya namna hiyo *vi* beregeza.

filigree *n* temsi.

filings *n pl see* **file**!

fill *vt,vi* 1 ~ **(with)** jaa; jaza ~ *a tank with petrol* jaza tangi petroli. ~ **in** jaza (ili kukamilisha). ~ **in an application form** jaza fomu ya maombi. ~ **in for** (*colloq*) chukua nafasi ya (kwa muda). ~ **out** tanuka, vimba, nenepa; (*esp US*) ~ **in,** ~ **up** jaza au jaa kabisa ~ *up a tank* jaza kabisa tangi. **~ing station** kituo cha petroli. 2 jaza nafasi ya kazi (na tekeleza kazi hiyo); weka mtu katika nafasi ya kazi. ~ **the bill** kidhi haja, faa sana *n* 1 shehena kamili. **have one's ~ (of sth)** (*colloq*) choshwa na. 2 tosha kujaza, maridhawa. **~ing** *n* kijazi, kijazo (k.m. risasi ya meno)).

fillet *n* 1 utepe (wa nywele). 2 sarara; mnofu wa samaki *vt* 1 kata mnofu. 2 toa miiba ya samaki.

fillip *vt,vi* 1 piga kwa kidole. 2 amsha, shtua *n* 1 kipigo cha kidole. 2 (*fig*) motisha, kichocheo.

filly *n* 1 mwana farasi jike. 2 (*sl outdated*) msichana mchangamfu.

film *n* 1 utando; utando wa macho. 2 filamu, sinema. **the ~s** sinema. ~ **star** mchezaji sinema mashuhuri. **~y** *adj* -a utando, -a utusitusi *vt,vi* 1 piga picha za sinema. 2 ~ **(over)** tanda, tandaza. 3 tokea vizuri/vibaya katika picha. **~able** -enye kufaa kutolewa picha ya sinema.

filter *n* 1 chujio. 2 (*of camera*) kichujio. ~ **tip** kichungi *vt,vi* 1 safisha kwa chujio, chuja. 2 (*fig of a crowd, traffic, news, ideas etc.*) penya, sambaa, ingia. **filtrate** *vt,vi see filter v.* **filtration** *n* tendo la kupenya/kupita/kuchuja.

filth *n* uchafu, taka; kinyaa, najisi *adj* -enye kutia kinyaa; (*colloq*) -chafu sana. **~y rich** (*colloq*) tajiri sana. **~ly** *adv*. **~ness** *n*.

fin *n* pezi, chombo kilicho/kitumiwacho kama pezi. **tail-~** (*of an aircraft*) mkia wa ndege.

final *adj* 1 -a mwisho. 2 -a kukata maneno; makataa *n* (*often pl*) 1 fainali. 2 mtihani wa mwisho. 3 (*colloq*) toleo la gazeti litolewalo mwisho wa siku. **~ist** *n* 1 mshindani wa fainali. 2 mwanachuo wa mwaka wa mwisho. **~ly** *adv* 1 hatimaye, mwishowe. 2 kabisa *he was finally cured* alipona kabisa. **~e** *n* (*mus*) sehemu ya mwisho ya utungo; mwisho. **~ity** *n* makataa, mwisho. **~ize** *vt* hitimisha, kamilisha, maliza.

finance *n* 1 (sayansi ya) usimamizi wa fedha (hasa za umma) *expert in ~*

mtaalamu wa wa fedha *the Minister of ~ (G.B. Chancellor of the Exchequer)* Waziri wa Fedha. ~ **house/company** kampuni ya fedha/ karadha/mikopo. 2 (*pl*) fedha (hasa za serikali na kampuni) *vt* gharamia. **financial** *adj* -a fedha. ~ **year** mwaka wa fedha. ~**ly** *adv*. **financier** *n* bepari; stadi katika mambo ya fedha.

finch *n* aina ya shorewanda wadogo.

find[1] *n* ugunduzi; kitu cha thamani kilichopatikana agh. kwa bahati.

find[2] *vt* 1 ona, pata (baada ya kutafuta kitu kilichopotea). ~ **one's voice/ tongue** weza kuzungumza (baada ya kuwa kimya). 2 tambua, ng'amua ~ *a solution to the problem* ng'amua utatuzi wa tatizo. ~ **one's feet** anza kusimama na kutembea (k.m. mtoto); weza kufanya mambo bila kutegemea wengine. ~ **oneself** jitambua, jijua. 3 fika, fikia *water always ~ its own level* maji hufikia usawa wake. 4 gundua, kuta (kwa bahati). ~ **sb (out)** gundua. ~ **sb out** gundua mtu akifanya kosa. 5 ona, kuta, ng'amua *do you ~ that hard work brings rewards?* unaona kuwa bidii inalipa? *take us as you ~ us* tuchukulie kama tulivyo. 6 tafutia, toa; patia. ~ **sb/ oneself in** patia/jipatia (kitu). **all found** patiwa kila kitu *wanted a good cook, 6000 shillings a month and all found* anatafutwa mpishi mzuri, mshahara shilingi 6000 na atapatiwa chakula na malazi bure. 7 (*leg*) hukumu, amua. ~ **for** amua kutoa ushindi kwa ~ *for the defendant* upande wa utetezi umeshinda. 8 ona *how did you ~ the play*? uliuonaje mchezo? 9 ~ **out** chunguza, tafiti, tafuta ~ *out the price of coffee* tafuta bei ya kahawa. ~ **sb out** gundua, tambua. ~**er** *n* 1 mtu apataye/aonaye kitu kilichopotea. 2 (*of camera*) kitafuta kilengeo. ~**ing** *n* (*usu pl*) 1 matokeo. 2 uamuzi wa mahakama.

fine[1] *n* faini *vt* toza faini. ~**able** (*also* **finable**) *adj* inayotozeka faini.

fine[2] *n* (*only in*) **in** ~ (*old use*) kwa kifupi; mwishowe.

fine[3] *adj* 1 -angavu, -zuri *it is a ~ day* ni siku angavu. **one ~ day** (*in story telling*) siku moja *one of these ~ days* iko siku hapo baadaye. 2 -a kupendeza *a ~ view* mandhari ya kupendeza. ~ **art** sanaa za uchoraji, uchongaji, ufinyazi n.k. ~**-spun** -liosokotwa vyema. 3 ororo, laini; -liyofanywa kwa ustadi na epesi kuharibika. 4 (*slender*) -embamba sana, -dogo sana ~ *distinction* ubainisho mdogo, mkali. **not to put too ~ a point on it** eleza waziwazi/ bayana. 5 *(of metal)* safi ~ *gold* dhahabu safi. 6 (*healthy*) -a afya. 7 (*of speech or writing*) -liotiwa chumvi, -sio kweli. **call sb/sth by ~ names** taja kitu kwa kutumia tasifida; (*of sb*) vika kilemba cha ukoka. ~**ly** *adv* 1 kwa kupendeza, kwa uzuri. 2 katika vipande vidogo sana. ~**ness** *n adv* (*colloq*) zuri *that suits me ~* inanifaa sana. ~**ry** *n* umalidadi; mavazi mazuri *in all her ~* kwa umalidadi wake wote.

finesse *n* werevu, uwezo wa kufanya jambo kwa maarifa na upole; (*cards*) jitihada za kushinda kwa kutumia mbinu *vt* ~ **sb into doing sth** shawishi mtu kwa ujanja na upole kufanya kitu fulani.

finger *n* kidole, chanda. **little-~** kidole cha mwisho. **ring-~** kidole cha pete. **middle** ~ kidole cha kati. **index/fore** ~ kidole cha shahada. **sb's ~s are all thumbs** mtu mzito katika kutenda jambo, goigoi. **burn one's ~s** pata matatizo, ingia matatani kutokana na uzembe. **lay a ~ on** gusa *don't lay a finger on this book* usiguse kitabu hiki. **lay/put one's ~ on** tambua kiini cha kosa, tatizo n.k. **not lift/raise/ stir a ~ (to help sb)** -tosaidia mtu. **put the ~ on sb** *(sl)* fichua (mhalifu). **twist sb around one's litle ~** tawala mtu kabisa. **work one's ~s to the bone** chapa kazi sana. ~**-alphabet** *n* mfumo wa kutumia vidole kuzungumza na kiziwi, lugha ya viziwi wasiosikia. ~-**board** daraja la fidla. ~-**bowl** *n* tasa (la kunawia mikono). ~-**mark** alama za vidole (vichafu). ~-**nail** ukucha. ~-**plate** kizuizi cha uchafu katika kitasa cha mlango. ~ -**post** *n* ubao unaoelekeza njia kwa picha ya kidole. ~-**point** alama ya kidole. ~-**tip** ncha ya kidole. **have sth at one's ~ tips** jua sana, -wa na uzoefu mkubwa wa jambo fulani *pull your ~ out* (*sl*) fanya/chapa kazi. ~**stall** kifuniko/ kinga ya kidole (kilicho jeruhiwa) *vt* 1 gusa, papasa, tomasa, shikashika, tia vidole ~ *a piece of cloth* gusa kitambaa (cha nguo). 2 (*US sl*) taja (agh. mhalifu).

finial *n* umbo la nakshi juu ya jengo maalum k.m. mnara. **finical** *adj*. **finicking**, **finicky** -enye machagu.

finis *n* (*sing only*) (*Lat*) mwisho, tamati.

finish *vt,vi* 1 maliza, timiza, hitimisha, akidi *that long walk ~ed me* ile safari ndefu nusura inimalize. ~ **sb off** (*sl*) ua, teketeza. ~ **sth off/up,** ~ **up** maliza -ote. ~ **up with** maliza -ote, malizia na. ~ **with** maliza na; fikia mwisho wa; vunja urafiki. 2 ishiliza, kamilisha *the table is beautifully~ed* meza ilikamilishwa kwa ustadi. ~**ing school** shule binafsi ya kuwatayarisha wasichana kwa maisha ya utu uzima *n* (*sing only*) 1 mwisho. **be in at the** ~ kuwepo wakati wa mwisho *a fight to the* ~ pigana hadi mwisho. 2 ukamilifu. ~**ed** *adj*. ~**ing** *adj*.

finite *adj* 1 -enye kikomo/-enye kwisha/ mpaka. 2 (*gram*) -enye kukubaliana na kiima katika idadi na nafsi.

fiord, -fjord *n* fiodi: mkono wa bahari kati ya magenge, milima n.k.

fir *n* msonobari, mbao za msonobari. ~-**cone** tunda la msonobari.

fire[1] *n* 1 moto. **lay a** ~ koka moto. **light/make a** ~ washa moto. **set on** ~ choma moto, tia moto, unguza. **make up a** ~ chochea. **catch** ~ shika moto. **between two ~s** katikati ya hatari mbili. **set on** ~ choma moto. **strike** ~ **from** pekecha moto. **he never set the Thames on** ~ hatatia fora; hatafanya la ajabu. **there is no smoke without** ~ (*prov*) pafukapo moshi pana moto. **play with** ~ chezea moto/hatari. 2 (*blaze*) mwako, uteketezaji. ~ **and sword** mauaji na uteketezaji (vitani). ~ **risks(s)** visababisha moto. 3 (*brightness*) wangavu. 4 (*excitement*) juhudi, harara. 5 (*energy*) nguvu. 6 mshindo wa bunduki; kupiga bunduki. **open/cease** ~ anza/ simamisha mashambulio. **under** ~ shambuliwa. **running** ~ mfululizo wa mashambulio; (*fig*) mfululizo wa maswali, shutuma n.k. 7 (*comp. words*). ~-**alarm** king'ora (cha moto). ~ **arm** *n* silaha ya moto, bunduki, bastola, n.k. ~-**ball** *n* kimondo; (*mil.*) sehemu ya katikati ya bomu la atomi. ~**bird** *n* ndege wa kimarekani mwenye rangi ya manjano na nyeusi. ~**bomb** *n* bomu la moto. ~**box** *n* chumba cha fueli. ~**brand** *n* kijinga cha moto; (*fig.*) mchochezi wa mambo (katika jamii au kisiasa). ~**break** *n* kinga ya moto sehemu iliyolimwa na kukatwa miti kusudi kuzuia moto usiingie katika msitu. ~**brick** *n* tofali lisiloathiriwa na moto. ~ **brigade** *n* zimamoto: kikosi maalum cha kuzima moto. ~**bug** *n* (*sl*) mtu mwenye kuchoma nyumba kusudi. ~ **clay** *n* udongo usioshika moto, agh. hutumiwa kwa kutengenezea matofali ya kukinga moto. ~ **control** *n* udhibiti (wa) mapigo ya bunduki. ~ **cracker** *n* fataki. ~ **damp** *n* mitheni. ~ **dog** *n* *see* **andiron.** ~ **drill** *n* mazoezi ya utaratibu unaotakikana kufuatwa kama kumetokea moto. ~**eater** *n* mshari. ~ **engine** *n* gari la zima -moto. ~**escape** *n* ngazi/njia ya kinga (ya) moto, ngazi za wazimamoto za kuokolea watu (wakati wa hatari ya moto). ~**extinguisher** *n* kizima moto: kifaa cha kuzimia moto. ~**fighter** *n* mzimamoto (hasa moto wa misitu). ~**fly** *n* kimemeta, kimulimuli. ~**guard** *n* kiunzi cha waya wa metali cha kuzuilia moto. ~**hose** *n* bomba la mpira la kuzimia moto. ~**irons** *n* vichocheo, koleo ya moto. ~**light** *n* mwangaza wa moto; kijinga; tita la kuni la kuwashia moto. ~**man** *n* mwangalizi wa moto katika tanuu au injini ya moto; mzimamoto. ~**place** *n* mekoni; ukingo wa fito wa kuzuilia moto nyumbani; jiko. ~ **plug** *n* plagi, kiunganishio cha mpira wa zimamoto. ~**power** *n* uwezo wa kupiga silaha (unaopimwa kwa idadi na uzito wa milipuko kwa kila dakika). ~**proof** *adj* -sioungua, -sioshika moto. ~**raising** *n* uchomaji nyumba kwa makusudi. ~**side** sebule ya kuotea moto *sit at the ~ side* (*fig*) tulia nyumbani; ishi maisha ya nyumbani. ~**station** makazi ya zima moto na vifaa. ~**stone** jiwe lisoshika moto. ~**walking** tambiko au sherehe ya kukanyaga mawe ya moto kwa miguu mitupu. ~ **water** *n* (*colloq*) pombe kali hasa kama vile wiski, jini n.k.. ~**wood** *n* kuni. ~-**work** *n* fataki: chombo chenye baruti na kemikali kitumiwacho kwa kufanyia michezo *vt,vi* 1 tia moto, choma moto, unguza, teketeza. 2 kaanga, choma, oka katika tanuu. ~ **bricks** choma matofali. 3 chochea kuni. 4 piga bunduki ~ *a salute* toa salamu ya heshima (kwa kupiga mzinga). ~ **a shot** piga bunduki. ~ **at/ into/on/ upon sth/sb** piga risasi, fyatulia risasi. ~ **away** endelea kupiga risasi. **firing line** *n* mstari wa mbele wa mashambilizi. **firing squad/party** *n* kikosi cha wauaji/watoa salamu za rambirambi (jeshini) (*colloq*) anza mara moja. 5 fukuza kazini. 6 (kwa bunduki) lia. 7 lipuka; waka. ~ **up** *(usu flare up)* kasirika, hamaki, sisimua. ~ **sb with sth** sisimua, tia hamu, hamasisha.

firkin *n* kasiki dogo.

firm[1] *adj* 1 imara, thabiti, -gumu. **be on ~ ground** -wa na uhakika; -wa thabiti katika maoni *be ~ on one's legs* simama tisti. 2 (*resolute*) shupavu *be ~ in one's beliefs* shikilia. 3 (*of a person, his body, its movements, characteristics etc*) -siotetereka, madhubuti, -liotengamaa *vt,vi* (*make/become*) -wa imara, jikita; imarisha, kita, shupaza *adv* kwa imara *stand ~* (*lit or fig*) shupalia jambo. ~**ly** *adv*. ~**ness** *n*.

firm[2] *n* washirika, wabia (katika biashara, kampuni).

firmament *n* **the ~** anga, mbingu.

first[1] *adj* 1 (*abbr 1st*) kwanza; -a awali; -a mwanzo. **at ~ sight** ilivyoonekana kwa mara ya kwanza. **in the ~ place** kwanza kabisa. ~ **thing** jambo la kwanza. ~ **things** ~ -a muhimu kwanza, panga kufuatana na umuhimu wa jambo. **not to know the ~ thing about sth** kutofahamu chochote kuhusu jambo fulani. 2 (*special uses, compounds*) ~**aid** huduma ya kwanza. ~ **base** *(base ball)* kituo cha kwanza. **get to ~ base** (*fig*) anza vizuri. ~ **class** *n* daraja la kwanza *adj* safi sana; -a daraja la juu ~ *class entertainment* burudani safi kabisa *travel ~ class* safiri kwa daraja la kwanza. ~ **cost** *n* (*comm*) gharama bila faida. ~ **fruits** mlimbuko, mavuno ya kwanza ya msimu; (*fig*) matunda ya mwanzo ya kazi za mtu. ~ **hand** *adj,adv* -a asili, -a moja kwa moja, -liopatikana kutokana na chimbuko ~ *hand information* habari/ushahidi kutoka kwa mtu aliyekuwapo wakati jambo linatokea *at ~ hand* moja kwa moja. ~ **name** jina la kwanza (sio la ukoo). ~ **night** *n* usiku wa kwanza (wa mchezo). ~ **nighter** *n* mtazamaji wa mara kwa mara wa maonyesho hayo. ~ **offender** mhalifu wa mara ya kwanza. ~ **person** (*gram*) nafsi ya kwanza. ~ **rate** *adj* -a hali ya juu, bora, aali; (*colloq*) vizuri sana *she is getting on ~-rate* anaendelea vizuri sana. ~**ly** *adv*.

first[2] *adv* 1 kwanza. ~ **of all** kwanza. ~ **and foremost** awali ya yote. ~ **come first served** wa kwanza kwanza. ~ **and last** kwa jumla; zaidi ya yote;

mwanzo na mwisho. ~ **born** *n* kifungua mimba. 2 kwa mara ya kwanza *when did you ~ see this?* ulikiona lini kwa mara ya kwanza? 3 kuliko *he will resign ~* atajiuzulu kuliko *n* 1 **at ~** mwanzoni. **from the ~** tokea mwanzo. **from ~ to last** toka mwanzo hadi mwisho. 2 (*in examination, competitions*) nafasi ya kwanza; mwenye kushika nafasi ya kwanza. 3 (*at University*) digrii ya daraja la kwanza.

firth *n* hori nyembamba; (*esp in Scotland*) mlango wa mto.

fiscal *adj* -a hazina ya serikali. ~ **year** *n* mwaka wa fedha.

fish *n* 1 samaki, nswi. **a pretty kettle of ~** hali ya matata/vurumai. **have other ~ to fry** -wa na shughuli nyingine muhimu zaidi. **there's as good ~ in the sea as ever came out of it** (*prov*) iko siku *drink like a ~* kunywa pombe mno. 2 mlo wa samaki. ~ **and chips** chipsi na samaki. 3 (*compounds*) ~ **-ball/~ -cake** andazi la samaki na viazi vya kupondwa. ~ **bone** mwiba wa samaki. ~ **-hook** ndoana. ~**-knife** kisu cha kulia samaki. ~**-monger** mchuuzi/ muuza samaki. ~**-paste** lahamu ya samaki. ~**-slice** kisu cha kupakulia samaki mezani. ~**-wife** mwanamke muuza samaki; (*colloq*) mwanamke mwenye mdomo mchafu. ~**y** *adj* 1 -enye shombo. 2 (*colloq*) -sioaminika *vt,vi* 1 vua samaki. ~ **in the sea** (*fig*) jaribu kupata kitu kwa njia za kuzunguka. ~ **in troubled waters** jaribu kupata faida kutokana na machafuko fulani. 2 ~ **up (out of) (from)** toa, chomoa *~ from one's pocket* chukua sarafu kutoka mfukoni. 3 ~ **for compliments** (*informal derog*) tafuta sifa *~ for information* tafuta habari kwa njia za kuzunguka. ~**ing** *n* kuvua samaki. ~**-line** mshipi. ~**-rod** ufito wa kuvua, ~**-tackle** vifaa vya uvuvi. ~**er** mvuvi; mtu anayeishi kwa kuvua samaki. ~**man** *n* mtu anayeishi kwa kuvua, samaki, mvuvi. ~**ery** *n* 1 sehemu ya uvuvi (baharini, mtoni, ziwani n.k.) *in-shore ~eries* uvuvi wa karibu na pwani.

fish plate *n* taruma la reli.

fission *n* mgawanyo/mpasuko (mfano wa chembe hai au wa nguvu za atomu). ~**able** *adj* -a kuweza kugawanyika, -a kuweza kupasuka kwa nguvu za atomu. **fissile** *adj* -a kuweza kupasuka/kuchanika. **fissiparous** *adj* (*of cells*) -a kuongezeka kwa njia ya mpasuko/ kugawanyika. **fissure** *n* ufa.

fist *n* gumi, konde *hit with a ~* piga ngumi/konde *put up your ~* jitayarishe kupigana. ~**icuffs** *n* (*pl*) (*usu hum*) kupigana ngumi.

fistula *n* nasuri.

fit *adj* 1 ~ **(for)** -a kufaa; laiki, -enye kustahili *the meal is ~ to eat* chakula kinafaa kuliwa *that post does not ~ you* cheo/kazi ile si laiki yako *the proposed time is ~ for us all* muda uliopendekezwa unatufaa sote. 2 sawa, -a haki *it is not ~ that you should abuse your teacher so* sio haki kumtukana hivyo mwalimu wako. **think/see ~ (to do sth)** amua kufanya kitu fulani. 3 -wa tayari *feel ~ to do sth* -wa tayari kufanya jambo fulani; (*also colloq, as an adv*) *we laughed ~ to burst* tulivunjika mbavu kwa kucheka. 4 -enye afya nzuri *feel ~ as a fiddle* -wa mzima kabisa. ~**ly** *adv.* ~**ness** *n* 1 ubora wa. 2 siha, uzima *vt,vi* 1 kaa, enea, faa, tosha *his clothes ~ him* nguo zake zimemkaa *it ~s you like a glove* imekukaa; kama ulizaliwa nayo *it ~s me* inanitosha, imenienea *~ tight* saki, bana. 2 ~ **(on)** jaribu kuvaa (nguo, viatu ili kupima). 3 weka, kaza, pachika *~ a new door* weka mlango mpya. 4 ~ **(for)** andaa; kuwa barabara/laiki/imara. 5 ~ **in (with)** patana na *my outing must ~ in with yours* matembezi yangu lazima yapatane na yako. 6 ~ **sb/sth out/up** -pa matumizi, -pa vifaa vinavyo-hitajika *n* jinsi mavazi yakaavyo *be a* *good/bad* ~ nguo ikaayo vizuri vibaya mwilini. **~ment** *n* kifaa, zana. **kitchen ~ment** zana za jikoni. **~ter** *n* 1 fundi (cherehani) anayepimisha na kushonesha nguo. 2 fundi wa kuunganisha sehemu za mashine, injini, mitambo n.k. **~ting** *adj* -a kufaa; stahiki *n* 1 kujaribisha nguo kwa fundi. 2 zana, kifaa (cha kudumu). **electric light** ~ zana ya taa za umeme; (*pl*) samani, fanicha, vyombo.

fit[2] *n* 1 ugonjwa wa ghafla wa muda mfupi *a ~ of coughing* kushikwa na kikohozi (kwa muda); kikohozi *a fainting* ~ kuzirai.2 kifafa *epileptic* ~ kifafa *hysteria* ~ kulialia/ chekacheka ovyo. **have a** ~ (*colloq*) shtuka mno. **give sb a** ~ (*colloq*) kasirisha, shtua. 3 shambulio la ghafla la muda mfupi; mlipuko *a ~ of anger* hasira ya ghafla, ya muda. **in by ~s and starts** kwa vipindi vifupi mara moja moja. **~ful** *adj* -enye kutokea kwa vipindi; (*restless*) -a kugeuka geuka. ~ **fully** *adv*. 4 kujisikia *when the ~ was on him* alipojisikia.

five *adj,n* -tano *she is ~ (years old)* ana umri wa miaka mitano. ~ **figured** *adj* -a tarakimu tano. ~ **fold** *adj* -a mara tano *adv* mara tano. **~r** *n* 1 (*colloq*) (*GB*) noti ya pauni tano; (*US*) noti ya dola tano. **~s** *n* (*GB*) mchezo wa mpira uchezwao kwa mkono au kibao kwenye uwanja.

fix[1] *vt,vi* 1 kaza, kongomea, imarisha. 2 ~ **on** kazia, elekeza (macho, fikra n.k.) juu ya; kodolea (macho). 3 (*of objects*) vuta/vutia macho, tazamisha *the lady's dress ~ed his attention* gauni la mwanamke lilimvutia macho. 4 amua, panga *~ a date for a journey* panga siku ya safari. 5 tengeneza kwa/tia dawa (filamu, rangi) ili zisififie kwa mwanga wa jua. 6 ~ **up (with sth)**; ~ **sth up (with sb)**, pangia; panga, tayarisha *~ up a friend for the night* -pa rafiki malazi. 7 ~ **on/upon** chagua. 8 (*sl)* toa rushwa, honga *It's a major offence to ~ government officials* ni kosa kubwa kuwahonga maafisa wa serikali. 9 lipiza kisasi; tengeneza. 10 (*colloq*) tengeneza *~ one's hair* chana, nywele. ~ **a radio** tengeneza redio. **~ed** *adj* -a kudumu; thabiti; siobadilika/geuka/sogea. ~ **assets** rasilimali za kudumu. ~ **capital** mtaji wa kudumu. **~ed point** nukta tuli. ~ **price** bei moja. **~edly** *adv* kwa ukakamavu. **~edness** *n*.

fix[2] *n* 1 matatizo, matata, mkwamo. **get sb into a** ~ tia mtu matatani. **be in a** ~ kwama. 2 kutambua mahali kwa kuangalia nyota. 3 (*sl*) sindano ya dawa za kulevya. **~ate** *vt* 1 kodolea/ kazia macho. 2 **be ~ed (on)** (*colloq*) tawaliwa na tamaa ya. **~ation** *n* 1 (*of film etc*) kutengeneza kwa dawa. **~ation (on)** tamaa kuu (ya).**~ative** *n* dawa ya kutengeneza filamu n.k.; dawa ya kugandisha (meno, nywele n.k.). **~ity** *n* (*phyl*) uthabiti, ugumu, uimara. ~ **ture** *n* 1 chombo/zana iliyowekwa mahali pa kudumu (agh hununuliwa pamoja na nyumba). 2 (*colloq*) mtu/kitu kinachoonekana sana mahali/kinakuwepo kila wakati *he is a ~ at the bar* hakosekani kwenye baa. 3 (*of games*) (ratiba ya) pambano.

fizz *vi* 1 toa povu, toa sauti kama gesi (k.m. soda/bia inapofunguliwa). 2 (*colloq*) shampeni. **~y** *adj*.

fizzle *vi ~ out* fifia, malizia/malizika kwa unyonge/kinyonge.

fjord *see* **fiord**

flabbergast *vt* (*colloq*) shangaza; pumbaza, duwaza.

flabby *adj* 1 (*of the muscles flesh*) teketeke, dhaifu, tepetevu 2. (*fig*) nyonge, -sio imara, -sio thabiti, legelege. **flabbily** *adv*. **flabbiness** *n*.

flag[1] *n* 1 bendera, baramu. ~ **of convenience** bendera ya bandia (itumikayo kumficha mwenye meli ili aepuke kutoa ushuru). **lower/ strike one's** ~ teremsha bendera kama ishara ya kuonyesha kukubali ushinde. (*compounds*) **~-captain**

kapteni wa meli ya admeri. **~-day** siku ya kutoa michango ya kusaidia wenye shida. **~-officer** admeri. **~-pole/~-staff** mlingoti (wa bendera). **~-ship** manowari yenye bendera ya admeri *vt* 1 pamba kwa bendera. 2 simamisha gari, treni n.k. kwa bendera *vi* legea, tepeta; (*diminish*) fifia, pungua; (*fig*) nyong'onyea, choka.

flag[2] *n* (*also* **~-stone**) jiwe bapa linalotumiwa kusakafia.

flag[3] *n* (*bot*) kangaga.

flagellant *n* mtu anayejipiga mijeledi (kama malipizo ya dini). **flagellate** *vt* piga mijeledi. **flagellation** *n*.

flageolet *n* filimbi, zumari, nai.

flagon *n* kuzi la divai.

flagrant *adj* -baya na wazi, dhahiri, -sio na haya. **~ly** *adv*. **flagrancy** *n*.

flail *n* ala ya kuputia *vt* puta.

flair *n* kipaji, kipawa, wepesi, karama *(to) have a ~for sth* -wa na kipaji cha jambo fulani.

flak *n* (*G*) mzinga wa kupigia ndege.

flake *n* 1 chembe, sehemu ndogo ndogo *snow* ~ vipande vidogo vya theluji. 2 (*of metal*) mavi *vt,vi* banduka; (*fig*) ~ **out** zimia, anguka kwa uchovu. **flaky** *adj* **flakiness** *n*.

flambeau *n* mwenge.

flamboyant *adj* 1 -enye kumeremeta kuzidi kiasi, -a rangi inayong'ara sana. 2 *(of person)* mshaufu. **~ly** *adv*. **flamboyance** *n* ushaufu.

flame *n* 1 mwale, mwako wa moto, ulimi wa moto. 2 *(colloq)* mpenzi, mchumba. 3 mwako (wa upendo, wa hasira, wa shauku). **(to) fan the** ~ chochea moto *~-tree* kifabakazi *~-thrower* silaha ya moto *vt* 1 waka, lipuka, toa moto. 2 fanana na miale kwa rangi. 3 ~ **out (up)** waka kwa hasira. **flaming** *adj* -nayowaka, -a moto sana; *(vulg. colloq) see* **demn.**

flamingo *n* flamingo, korongo.

flammable *see* **inflammable**.

flange *n* kigingi, kipande (ulimi) kinachotokeza (katika gurudumu, boriti n.k.).

flank *n* 1 ubavu, upande wa mtu au nyama. 2 kando, upande (mlima, jengo, msafara). 3 sehemu ya pembeni ya jeshi *a ~ movement* mwendo wa kupita upande, mzunguko *vt,vi* zunguka pembeni; shambulia kutoka pembeni; (pita, weka) ubavuni kwa (upande wa, kando ya) *vi* -wa kandoni; pakana na. **~er** *n* mchezaji wa pembeni.

flannel *n* 1 fulana. 2 tambara (la kusafishia) *face* ~ tambara la uso. 3 (*pl*) suruali ya fulana (hasa ya michezo wakati wa joto); (*US sl*) upuuzi *adj* -a fulana.

flap *n* 1 pigo. 2 (*of cloth, paper etc*) kifuniko. 3 (*of aircraft wing*) upindo, lisani. (*fig*) **be/get in a** ~ hangaika, tapatapa *vt,vi* 1 pigapiga, piga (mabawa); punga. 2 tapatapa, papatika.

flapjack *n* keki (ya kukaanga katika samli); (*US*) gole.

flapper *n* 1 chombo cha kupigia nzi n.k. 2 pezi pana. 3 (*sl 1920's*) mrembo.

flare *vi* 1 waka, toa moto. 2 tanuka. **~d** *adj* -liyotanuka. ~ **skirt** sketi pana. **~d trousers** suruali pana. ~ **up** lipuka (moto, hasira n.k.) *n* 1 mwako. 2 mwako wa kuashiria hatari. **~-up** *n* 1 lipuko. 2 magomvi ya ghafula.

flash 1 mwako, nuru ya (mwanga wa) kumulika ghafula. (*fig*) **in a** ~ kufumba na kufumbua. **a ~ in the pan** limbuko. 2 ~ **light** *n* taa; (*naut*) mmuliko; (*US*) tochi; *(also* ~ **bulb**) taa ya picha. ~ **gun** tochi ya picha. ~ **point** (*of gas*) kiwango cha kuwaka mafuta; 1 (*fig*) mahali pa hatari (ambapo vita vinaweza kuzuka wakati wo wote). 2 **news** ~ taarifa motomoto/za ghafla (zinazopokelewa ili kutangazwa na vyombo vya habari). 3 (*mil*) medani ya utepe kwenye sare ya jeshi *vi* 1 waka, mulika ghafla na kuzimika. 2 (*fig*) -jia ghafla (akilini) *it suddenly ~ed upon him* ghafla yakamjia; pita upesi sana *the train ~ed past* treni ilipita haraka sana. 3 enda upesi *news ~ed across the world* habari zilitangaa upesi duniani pote. 4 ~ **back** rejea ghafula; kumbuka, kumbusha. ~ **back** *n* kumbusho (la ghafula). **~y** *adj* -shaufu, -a maringo, -a madaha. **~ily** *adv*.

flask *n* 1 chupa ndogo (ya maabara). 2 **powder** ~ pembe ya baruti. 3 kiriba cha mvinyo.

flat *adj* 1 sawasawa, bapa *the floor is ~* sakafu iko sawasawa. ~ **land** ardhi tambarare. ~ **bottomed** (*of boat*) bapa, -enye kitako. ~ **car** (*US*) behewa la mizigo (lisilo na bodi). ~ **fish** samaki wa jamii ya wayo. ~ **footed** *adj* -enye nyayo bapa; (*colloq*) thabiti, imara. **~foot** *n* polisi. **~racing/the F~** mashindano ya farasi bila kuruka viunzi. ~ **top** *n* (*colloq*) *see* **aircraft carriers.** 2 (*insipid*) baridi, dufu; -sio tamu, chapwa *the dance fell ~* ngoma haikufana *his speech fell ~* hotuba yake haikukolea. 3 (*of liquor*) siyo na gesi. 4 -a kuteremsha *sing ~* imba kwa kiteremsho. 5 (*depressed*)-enye moyo mzito. 6 -a wazi kabisa *he gave a ~ denial* alikana kabisa *that's ~* basi! 7 *(of a tyre/football)* -liokwisha pumzi. 8 (*comm*) **~rate** bei moja. 9 (*of colours*) -siyo vivuli, bapa. 10 (*of battery*) -lokufa, -siochaji. 11 (*of characters, lit.*) bapa. 12 ~ **spin** (*of aircraft*) kushuka kwa kasi; (*colloq*) (*of a person*) kuchanganyikiwa *adv* 1 kwa kutandazwa/kulaza *fall ~ on one's face/back* anguka kifudifudi/ chali *the earth quake laid the city ~* tetemeko la ardhi liliteketeza mji. 2 moja kwa moja. ~ **broke** kuchalala, kukaukiwa, mwambo. 3 ~ **out** kwa nguvu zote; hoi *n* 1 mahali sawa na papana; (*usu near sea*) wangwa. 2 *(of sword)* ubapa ~ *of the hand* kitanga cha mkono. 3 (*mus*) kiteremsho. 4 (*US*) pancha, gurudumu lililokwisha upepo. **~tish** *adj*. **~ly** *adv* kabisa, waziwazi; bila furaha *n* 1 (*US apartment*) nyumba ya ghorofa. **block of ~s** maghorofa. **~ten** *vt,vi* 1 ~ **out** sawazisha, laza, nyoosha, tandaza *I ~ed myself against the wall* nilijibana ukutani; (*of aircraft*) enda sawa baada ya kushuka; *(fig)* aibisha sana, maliza, dhalilisha, gonga.

flatter *vt* 1 sifu mno, jipendekeza, rai, bembeleza. 2 furahisha, pendeza *be ~ed by an invitation* pendezwa na mwaliko. 3 (*of picture, image*) fanya -zuri kuliko -a kweli. 4 ~ **oneself** jivuna (bila haki); jifurahisha. **~er** *n*. **~ry** *n* ubembelezaji, sifa isiyostahilika.

flatulence *n* 1 riahi, gesi tumboni. **flatulent** *adj*.

flatware *n* vyombo vya kulia, kupakulia chakula.

flaunt *vt,vi* 1 koga, ringa. ~ **oneself** jishaua, tamba, punga kwa madaha.

flautist *n* mpiga filimbi.

flavour/flavor *n* 1 ladha; *(fig)* namna; mtindo *vt* koleza, unga; tia viungo. **~ed** *adj*. **~ing** *n* ladha. **~less** -sio na ladha.

flaw *n* 1 (*crack*) ufa. 2 dosari, ila, hitilafu, upungufu *vt,vi* tia dosari; pata ufa *his character is ~ed* tabia yake ina dosari. **~less** *adj* -sio na dosari.

flax *n* kitani. **~en** *adj*. ~ **hair** nywele zenye rangi ya kitani.

flay *vt* chuna, sopoa; (*fig*) kosoa sana.

flea *n* kiroboto. **with a ~ in the ear** karipio kali. **~-bite** *n* 1 alama ya kuumwa na kiroboto; (*fig*) jambo dogo sana. **~-bitten** *adj* (*fig*) (*of an animal's colouring*) -a madoadoa. **~market** (*colloq*) gulio, mjajaro; soko la mitumba. ~ **pit** *n* (*colloq*) mahali pa starehe palipochakaa na pachafu.

fleck *n* 1 kipaku, kidoa. 2 chembe *vt* tia vipaku.

fledged *adj* (*of birds*) -enye mabawa ya kurukia, -enye nguvu ya kurukia *fully ~* (*fig*) -liofunzwa na -enye uzoefu wa muda mrefu. **fledg(e)ling** *n* kinda (kifaranga) la ndege; (*fig*) kijana asiye na uzoefu.

flee *vi* kimbia.
fleece *n* 1 manyoya ya kondoo; lundo la manyoya ya kondoo ya mkato mmoja. 2 kitu kilichofanana na manyoya ya kondoo k.m. mawingu. ~ **sb (of sth)** (*fig*) ibia mtu kwa ujanja; tapeli; (*by charging high prices*) gonga. **fleecy** *adj*.
fleet[1] *n* 1 kundi la manowari chini ya kamanda (kiongozi) mmoja; manowari zote za nchi moja. 2 kundi la meli, ndege, motokaa n.k. chini ya kiongozi mmoja au miliki moja.
fleet[2] *adj* (*poet. liter*) -epesi (katika mwendo); -enye kasi kubwa. **~ly** *adv*. **~ness** *n*. **~ing** *adj* upesi, -a muda mfupi tu, -a kupita, -a mara moja *pay sb a ~ visit* tembelea mtu kwa muda mfupi tu.
flesh *n* 1 nyama *lions are ~-eating animals* simba ni wanyama walao nyama. ~ **and blood** hali ya ubinadamu, utu; udhaifu. **it's more than ~ and blood can bear** imepita kiwango cha kuvumilia. **one's own ~ and blood** ndugu wa karibu. **in the ~** katika maisha, katika umbo la mwili *he is nicer in the ~* ni mzuri zaidi ukimwona. **go the way of all ~** kufa. **have/demand one's pound of ~** dai malipo bila huruma. **make a person's ~ creep** tisha/ogopesha mno mtu. **put on/lose ~** nenepa/konda. **~pots** *n* (*pl*) mahali pa starehe. ~ **wound** *n* kidonda kidogo, kidonda cha juu. 2 **the ~** matamanio ya kimwili. 3 mwili *in the ~* mwenyewe, nafsi yake *he was there in the ~* alikuwepo yeye mwenyewe. **the spirit is willing but the ~ is weak** nia ipo lakini nguvu hakuna. 4 nyama ya matunda/mboga. **~ly** *adj* -a mwili; -a tamaa za mwili. **~y** *adj* nene, nono, -a nyama. **fleshings** *n* (*pl*) nguo za rangi ya mwili (kama zile zinazovaliwa na wachezaji wa bale).
flew *pt of* **fly**.
flex[1] *n* kamba ya umeme (ya taa, pasi n.k.).
flex[2] *vt* kunja, nyumbua (mkono, mguu). ~ **one's muscles** nyumbua/chezea/nyoosha misuli. **~ible** *adj* -a kunyumbulika, -enye kupindika; (*fig*) -nayoweza kubadilika kwa urahisi kupokea mazingira mapya; (*of persons*)-enye uwezo wa kubadilisha (mipango, malengo). **~ibility** *n*.
flibbertigibbet *n* mpiga domo; mtu asiyetulia, kirukanjia.
flick *n* 1 papaso; pigo jepesi na la haraka. 2 mfyekuzo. **~-knife** kisu cha kukunjua kwa mshtuo. 3 (*sl*) filamu za sinema. **the ~** sinema *vt* 1 piga kidogo (mf. kwa kiboko n.k.); papasa. 2 ~ **sth away/off** pangusa.
flicker *vi* (*of light*; (*fig*) *of hopes, etc*) memeteka; wakawaka, tikisika, yumbayumba *n* 1 (*usu sing*) kutikisika, kuyumbayumba. 2 mwako wa mtetemeko *a ~ of the eyelid* mpepeso.
flight[1] *n* 1 kuruka *the art of ~* ufundi wa kuruka. 2 safari ya angani; masafa ya mruko. ~ **deck** *n* (*on an aircraft carrier*) sitaha ya kupurukia na kutulia; (*in an airliner*) chumba cha rubani, n.k.. 3 mwendo wa hewani. 4 kundi la ndege (au vitu virukavyo pamoja) hewani. **in the first ~** katika nafasi ya mbele, -enye kuongoza. 5 kupita kwa haraka. 6 *(of stairs)* ngazi. 7 kundi la ndege katika jeshi la anga la nchi. ~ **Lieutenant** Luteni wa jeshi la anga. **~y** *adj* -geugeu. **~iness** *n*.
flight[2] *n* 1 kukimbia; ukimbizi *put to ~* fukuza/kimbiza maadui. **take ~, take to ~** kimbia.
flimsy *adj* (*of material*) -sio na nguvu (kwa sababu ya kuwa -embamba, laini); -a kuharibika; -a kuvunjika kwa urahisi; (*fig*) *a ~ excuse/argument* udhuru/hoja hafifu, isiyoridhisha *n* karatasi nyepesi. **flimsily** *adv*. **flimsiness** *n*.
flinch *vi* ~ **(from)** 1 shtuka, jivuta kidogo (mwili shauri ya maumivu). 2 kwepa kidogo.
fling *vt,vi* 1 vurumiza, vurumisha, tupa kwa nguvu *(to) ~ caution to the*

winds fanya mambo bila kujali matokeo *be flung into prison* tupwa gerezani *she flung an angry look at him* alimtupia jicho la hasira ~ *oneself into* jishughulisha kwa nguvu. 2 rusharusha ~ *one; hands about* rusha rusha mikono. 3 ondoka kwa hasira/ nguvu *he flung off without saying goodbye* aliondoka kwa hasira bila kuaga *n* 1 kutupa/kurusha/ kuvurumuza. **have a ~ at** jaribu, jaribia. 2 aina ya dansi ya (Kiskoti). **have one's ~** starehe bila kifani.

flint *n* 1 namna ya jiwe gumu sana. 2 ~ *stone* jiwe la mango; (*of cigarette lighter*) jiwe la kiberiti. **~y** *adj* gumu sana; katili.

flip[1] *vt,vi* 1 shtua, rusha kwa kidole. 2 *(fig)* geuza, bingirika. 3 (*sl*) pata wazimu. 4 (*sl*) jaa shauku, sisimka sana (kwa ajili ya mtu/jambo). 5 ~ **through** soma juujuu, somasoma *n* 1 mrusho mdogo; kipigo cha haraka. 2 (*colloq*) mruko wa muda mfupi kwa eropleni (kwa kujifurahisha) *adj* -siokuwa na makini/ukweli. **the ~ side** *(colloq)* upande wa pili wa sahani ya santuri.

flip-flop (*colloq*) *n* ndara.

flippant *adj* -puuzi, -a purukushani; -a kejeli, -a mzaha. **~ly** *adv*. **~flippancy** *n.*

flipper *n* 1 kikono (cha nyangumi, pomboo n.k). 2 mpira ufungwao miguuni (wakati wa kuogelea) (kwa kujifurahisha tu); bemba.

flirt *vi* 1 ~ **(with)** onyesha mapenzi (kwa kuchezea). 2 chezea, fikiria (bila makini). ~ **with danger** chezea hatari *n* mbembe. **~ation** *n*. **~atious** *adj*.

flit *vi* 1 rukaruka, kwa wepesi na haraka ~ *to and fro* ruka huku na huko, pita kwa wepesi au kimya. 2 (*colloq*) hama/ondoka kimyakimya (kukwepa madeni n.k.) *n* (*colloq*) kuhama/kuondoka kwa siri.

float *n* 1 chelezo, boya. 2 jukwaa lenye magurudumu; gari lenye jukwaa *vt,vi* 1 elea. 2 fanya (kitu) kielee. 3 (*comm*) pata msaada (wa fedha)/mtaji kuanzisha jambo; anzisha shirika n.k (kwa kuuza hisa). 4 (*finance*) acha fedha ibadilikebadilike thamani bila kizuizi, ondoa udhibiti wa thamani ya fedha. 5 eneza ~ *a rumour* eneza uvumi. **~ing** *adj* 1 inayobadilika-badilika, geuzi; geugeu. 2 ~ **debt** deni ambalo sehemu yake sharti ilipwe inapotakiwa. ~ **rib** (*anat*) ubavu usioungana na kidari. **~ation** (upataji mtaji wa) kuanzisha kampuni n.k.

flock[1] *n* 1 (*usu sheep, goats*) kundi. ~ **and herds** kondoo na ng'ombe. 2 (*of people*) umati; kiasi kikubwa. 3 (mkusanyiko wa) waumini (wa kikristo); watu walio chini ya mtu mmoja *a priest and his ~* padre na waumini wake *vi* kusanyika; -ja/enda wengi pamoja *the children flocked to see the magician* watoto walikusanyika kumtazama mfanya mazingaombwe. ~ **out** toka kwa makundi.

flock[2] *n* kibonge cha sufu au nywele; (*pl*) taka za sufu au pamba zitumiwazo kujaza godoro n.k.

floe *n* pande kubwa la barafu linaloelea.

flog *vt* 1 tandika/chapa kiboko au mjeledi. ~ **a dead horse** poteza nguvu bure. ~ **sth to death** rudiarudia kitu hadi kinachusha. 2 (*sl*) uza (bidhaa kuukuu au za wizi). **~ging** *n* kuchapa kwa kiboko au mjeledi.

flood *n* 1 mafuriko *The Flood* (*rel*) gharika. 2 wingi, mbubujiko ~ *of tears* mbubujiko wa machozi. 3 ~ **tide** maji kujaa. ~ **gate** mlango wa kuzuia/kutoa maji. **~lights** *n* (*pl*) taa kubwa zenye mwanga mkali. **~light** *vt* angaza kwa taa kubwa *vt,vi* 1 furika. 2 (*of rain*) sababisha mafuriko. 3 ~ **out** furika; lazimisha kuhama kwa sababu ya mafurikio; (*fig*) ~ *the market* jaza/sheheneza bidhaa (ili kuteremsha bei). 4 ~ **in** -ja kwa wingi.

floor *n* 1 sakafu. **wipe the ~ with sth**

shinda mtu (k.m. kwenye ugomvi au mabishano). ~ **board** ubao wa sakafu, mbao. ~ **show** maonyesho (katika hoteli, mkahawa n.k.). 2 ghorofa. **ground** ~ (*GB*) ghorofa ya chini. **first** ~ (*GB*) ghorofa ya kwanza (*US*) ghorofa ya chini. 3 chini (ya bahari, pango n.k.). 4 sehemu ya bunge wanapokaa wajumbe. **take the** ~ ongea katika mdahalo/majadiliano. **the** ~ haki ya kuzungumza/ongea hadharani *the delegate has the* ~ mjumbe ana haki ya kuzungumza. 5 *(of prices)* bei ya chini kabisa. **~ing** *n* vifaa vya kutengenezea sakafu vt 1 sakafia. 2 angusha ~ *a man in a boxing match* angusha mtu kwenye ndondi. 3 (*of a problem, argument*) tatiza, shinda; changanya.

floozy, floozie *n* malaya.

flop *vt,vi* 1 enda/anguka kwa kishindo; jipweteka, jitupa. 2 ~ **down** weka/ angusha kizembe. 3 (*sl*) (*of a book, a play for the theatre etc*) shindwa, -tofanikiwa *n* 1 kishindo. 2 (*sl*) ushinde (wa kitabu, mchezo n.k.). **~py** *adj* laini sana. **~py disk** sahani/ diski laini/tepe *adv* kwa kishindo. **flop-house** *n* hoteli ya hali ya chini kabisa (agh ya wanaume).

flora *n* flora: mimea yote ya nchi fulani au ya kipindi maalum. **~l** *adj* -a maua. **florescence** *n* hali ya maua kuchanua; wakati mmea unapotoa maua. **floriculture** *n* kilimo cha maua. **florist** *n* muuza maua. **florid** *adj* 1 -liorembwa/nakshiwa sana; -enye mapambo na rangi nyingi mno; (*of music etc.*) -liotiwa madoido mengi mno. 2 (*of a person's face*) -ekundu (kwa asili). **floridly** *adv*.

floss *n* nyuzi za hariri juu ya kimvugu. ~ **silk** hariri iliyosokotwa kwa nyuzi hizo. **candy** ~ sukari laini iliyotengenezwa kwa mfano huo. **~y** *adj*.

flotation *see* **floatation**.

flotilla *n* msafara wa manowari ndogo.

flotsam *n* (*leg*) mabaki ya meli/shehena yanayoelea baharini.

flounce[1] *vi* jitupatupa, enda kwa vishindo/haraka/hasira/makeke ~ *out of the room* toka chumbani kwa makeke *n* kujitupatupa; kwenda kwa hasira/makeke.

flounce[2] *n* (*often ornamental*) lesi au pambo la kitambaa katika upindo wa nguo *vt* sawazisha kwa pambo la lesi/ kitambaa.

flounder[1] *vi* tapatapa; hangaika (kwa bidii bila mafanikio); (*fig*) sita, tatanika, -wa na wasiwasi ~ *through an explanation* tatanika katika utoaji maelezo.

flounder[2] *n* (aina ya) wayo.

flour *n* unga ~ *mill* mashine, kinu cha kusagia unga ~ *moth* nondo aharibuye unga *vt* funika kwa/ nyunyizia unga. **~y** *adj*.

flourish *vt,vi* 1 sitawi, fanikiwa, shamiri *his business is ~ing* shughuli/ biashara yake inafanikiwa. 2 pepea, punga, tikisa *she ~ed a knife* alipepea kisu. 3 *(of a famous person)* -wa mchangamfu na mwenye ari. 4 tia mapambo, nakshi, urembo (katika muziki, maandishi n.k.) *n* usitawi; mapambo, nakshi, madoido katika maandishi; milio na vishindo vya matarumbeta, chereko.

flout *vt* pinga; dhihaki, dharau *n* dhihaka, dharau.

flow *vi* 1 bubujika, tiririka *the river ~s into Lake Malawi* mto ule unatiririka katika ziwa Malawi. 2 *(of hair, articles of dress)* ning'inia. **~ing robes** magauni ya kuning'inia. 3 -wa matokeo ya, tokana na; *success ~s from hard work* mafanikio yanatokana na bidii katika kazi; *(of the tide)* jaa *n (sing. only)* 1 mtiririko, mbubujiko, mkondo. 2 *(abundance)* wingi kiasi *a good ~ of water* mtiririko wa maji mengi *a ~ of angry words* mbubujiko wa maneno ya hasira/makali ~ *chart/diagram* mchoro wenye kuonyesha hatua kwa hatua uhusiano au utaratibu wa vitu katika mfumo.

flower *n* 1 ua. **in** ~ -enye maua, -liochanua. **~-bed** kitalu cha maua.

~-bud tumba la ua. ~ **garden** bustani ya maua. ~-**girl** msichana muuza maua. ~ **children/people** *(colloq in the 1960's)* washabiki wa Mahipi, wahuni; washabiki wa upendo na amani. ~-**power** mawazo ya watu kama hao. ~-**pot** chungu cha (kuoteshea) maua. ~-**show** maonyesho ya maua. 2 **the** ~ **of** kipeo cha (uzuri/umuhimu) *the ~ of the nation's youth* -wa bora miongoni mwa vijana wa taifa. 3 ~ **of speech** misemo, mbinu na madoido. ~**ed** -liopambwa maua *vi* toa maua; chanua. **burst into** ~**s** pamba, tapakaa maua. ~**y** *adj* -enye maua mengi; *(fig)* -enye misemo mingi ya madoido. ~ **language** lugha ya madoido. ~**less** *adj* -sio na/toa maua.

flu *n (colloq abbr of)* **influenza**.

fluctuate *vi (of levels, prices etc)* panda na kushuka, badilikabadilika. **fluctuation** *n* kupanda na kushuka, mabadilikobadiliko.

flue *n* dohani.

fluent *adj (of a person)* -enye kusema lugha (bila shida); *(of speech)* sanifu, fasaha ~ *Swahili* Kiswahili fasaha. ~**ly** *adv*. **fluency** *n* ufasaha.

fluff *n* 1 kibonge cha sufi, manyoya, malaika. 2 *(colloq)* kosa (katika kutenda jambo) *vt* 1 ~ **(out)** kung'uta, timua. 2 *(colloq)* kosea (katika kutenda jambo n.k.). ~**y** *adj* -liopamba sufu/manyoya, kama sufu.

fluid *adj* -a ugiligili, -oevu, -a kuweza kumwagika (k.m. maji, hewa); *(of ideas etc)* -sio imara, -a kuweza kubadilika *n (chem)* ugiligili, uowevu; *(colloq)* giligili. ~**ity** *n* ugiligili.

fluke[1] *n* bahati njema (isiyotegemewa) *vt* bahatisha, -wa na bahati *he ~d* alibahatisha.

fluke[2] *n* 1 *(of anchor)* ncha ya nanga. 2 mkia wa nyangumi.

fluke[3] *n* mnyoo bapa (katika ini la kondoo).

flume *n* mfereji wa kupitishia maji kwenye kinu (mtambo, mashini); korongo lenye mto (wa matumizi ya kiwanda).

flummox *vt (colloq)* fadhaisha, duwaza.

flung *pp of* **fling**.

flunk *vt,vi (out) (US colloq)* feli, shindwa, -tofaulu (mtihani); felisha.

flunkey, flunky *n (derog)* 1 mtumishi (aliyevaa sare maalumu). 2 mtu anayejikomba.

fluorescent *adj (of substances)* -enye kuakisi mwanga. **fluorescence** *n*.

fluorine *n (chem) (symbol F)* florini.

fluoride *n (chem)* msombo, kampaundi yoyote ya floraidi. **fluoridate/ fluoridize** *vt* tia floraidi kwenye maji ili kuzuia kuoza kwa meno. **fluoridation/fluoridization** *n* **fluor** *n* aina ya kito cha thamani chenye florini. **flourspar** madini ya kalisiamu floraidi.

flurry *n* 1 mvumo wa upepo, mwanguko wa theluji/mvua (wa ghafla na wa muda mfupi). 2 *(fig)* kiherehere, haraka yenye wasiwasi, hangaiko *vt* hangaisha, fadhaisha *be fuurried* hangaika, ona wasiwasi.

flush[1] *adj* 1 ~ **(with)** -liosawazishwa, -a kulingana na. 2 *(pred)* -a kujaa mpaka juu; -enye wingi wa (fedha n.k.). ~ **with money** -enye fedha nyingi, -liojaa fedha.

flush[2] *n* 1 *(of water)* kufoka, kububujika. 2 bubujiko la damu; kuiva uso, wekundu usoni. 3 msisimko wa hisia (hasira, furaha n.k.). 4 ustawi, ukuaji. **the (first)** ~ machipukizi ya kwanza ya mmea *in the first ~ of youth* katika nyakati za ujana *in the full ~ of health* katika afya nzuri *vt,vi* 1 *(of a person, his face)* iva uso (-wa mwekundu) kwa sababu ya bubujiko la damu. 2 *(of heat, health, emotions etc)* iva uso kwa sababu hiyo; *(fig)* jawa na msisimko/hasira, furaha, majivuno. 3 *(of a latrine)* vuta maji.

flush[3] *n (in card games)* seti ya karata za aina moja *royal ~ (poker)* seti ya karata tano za juu za aina moja.

flush[4] *vt,vi* 1 *(of birds)* bumburusha. 2 ~ **from/out of** kurupusha, timua.

fluster *vt,vi* vuruga; tia msukosuko; ingia/tia wasiwasi *n* mvurugiko, wasiwasi, msukosuko *be in a ~* -wa na msukosuko/wasiwasi, hangaikahangaika.

flute[1] *n* filimbi; zumari *vi* 1 piga filimbi/zumari. **~ player** *n* mpiga filimbi/zumari.**flutist** *(US)* **flautist** mpiga filimbi/zumari.

flute[2] *vt* tia nakshi ya mifuo. **fluting** *n* nakshi ya mifuo.

flutter *vt,vi* 1 *(of birds)* pigapiga mabawa (bila kuruka), papatika, papatisha, rukaruka hewani. 2 pepesuka, yugayuga, hangaika; *(of loose material)* pepea; *(agitate)* tia wasiwasi, ogofya; *(of the heart)* dunda upesi *n* 1 fazaa, wasiwasi, msukosuko. 2 *(usu sing)* papatiko. 3 mtetemeko, mtikisiko (wa sauti) katika redio, kinasa sauti n.k. 4 *(colloq)* kamari; burudani.

fluvial *adj* -a mto/mtoni.

flux *n* mfululizo wa mabadiliko. 2 *(sing only)* mtiririko, mbubujiko. 3 dutu ya kurahisisha kuyeyusha vyuma.

fly[1] *n* 1 nzi. **a ~ in the ointment** dosari ndogo inayochafua sherehe/furaha. **there are no flies on him** *(fig sl)* mjanja, yu mwerevu. 2 *(compounds)* **~-away** *adj* *(of clothes)* -a kupwaya; *(of persons)* badhirifu, -liopoteza fikra. **~-blow** *n* yai la nzi. **~-blown** *adj (of meat)* -lioanza kuoza (kwa sababu ya mayai ya nzi ndani yake); *(fig)* chafu; bovu. **~-boat** *n* mashua ieleayo. **~book** *n* kijaruba cha kuwekea chambo (nzi) cha kuvulia samaki.**~-by-night** *n* mtu atembeaye usiku; mtu asiye mwaminifu. **~-catcher** *n* mtego wa nzi; shore kishungi, tiva. **~-fish** *vi* vua samaki kwa nzi bandia. **fly-fishing** *n* kuvua samaki kwa nzi bandia. **~ing-leaf** ukurasa mtupu usiopigwa chapa (mwanzoni au mwishoni mwa kitabu). **~-over** *n* (*US* = **over pass**) barabara, daraja n.k. ipitayo juu ya barabara nyingine. *(GB)* **~past** *n* gwaride la Wanaanga. **~-wheel** *n* gurudumu tegemeo. **~-paper** *n* karatasi yenye kunata ya kunasia nzi. **~-sheet** *n* waraka/sekula ya kurasa. **~-swatter**, **~-whisk** *n* mwengo, mgwisho. **~-trap** mtego wa kunasia nzi. **~-weight** *n (of boxing)* uzito wa chini. **~er,flier** *adj* 1 mnyama, gari n.k. liendalo kasi mno. 2 mfanyakazi ndani ya ndege hasa rubani. **~ing** *adj* 1 -a kuruka. 2 -a muda mfupi; -a haraka, -a mbio sana. 3 -siyokazwa, -a kupwaya. 4 *(compounds)* **~-ant** *n* kumbikumbi. **~ boat** ndege (eropleni) ya majini. **~-bomb** roketi yenye bomu la kupiga mbali. **~-club** chama cha watu wapendao mchezo wa kuruka (hewani). **~- colours** bendera za kupamba/kupepea (agh. wakati wa sherehe). **~ -column** *n (mil)* kikosi cha jeshi chenye uwezo wa kwenda haraka na kufanya mashambulizi chenyewe. **~-field** *n* uwanja wa ndege. **~-fish** *n* panzi la bahari: samaki wa nchi za tropiki awezaye kuruka. **~-fox** *n* nundu. **~-jump** *n* urukaji unaoanza kwa kukimbia. **~-saucer** kisahani kinachosemekana kilionekana kikipita angani. **~-squad** *n* kikosi cha polisi cha kufukuza wahalifu chenye gari za kasi sana. **~-visit** *n* ziara ya muda mfupi; kupitia.

fly[2] *vi,vt* 1 ruka, puruka. **~ high** -wa na tamaa ya (kuendelea, kukuza hali n.k.). **~ up** ruka angani. **the bird has flown** mtu anayetafutwa ametoroka. 2 endesha ndege (hewani n.k.); safiri, safirisha (kwa ndege) *every day people ~ to Zanzibar from Dar es Salaam* kila siku watu husafiri kwa ndege kwenda Zanzibar kutoka Dar es Salaam. 3 kimbia, kimbilia, enda mbio, pita upesi. **~ off** toka (enda) ghafla. **~ open** funguka (dirisha, mlango n.k.) ghafla. **(to) ~ at sb** rukia, shambulia. **~ in the face of** pinga, kana, katalia hadharani/ wazi; kuwa dhidi ya kinyume kabisa cha mambo. **~ into a rage/passion/**

temper pandwa na hamaki, hasira. ~ **to arms** twaa silaha kwa ari. ~ **to bits/~into pieces** pasuka na kutawanyika. vipande vipande. ~ **to the rescue** kimbilia kuokoa maisha. **make the feathers/fur** ~ sababisha fujo/ugomvi. **make the money** ~ fuja mali. **send sb ~ing** piga/gonga mtu ili aanguke kifudifudi au kwa mgongo. **send things ~ing** vurumisha vitu pande zote. 4 rusha (tiara, kishada) hewani; pandisha bendera. 5 hajiri.

fly[3] *n* 1 *(also colloq, pl. used with sing. meaning)* lisani, mhalibori. 2 kipande cha turubali kwenye mlango wa hema au gari. 3 ncha ya bendera iliyo mbali na mlingoti.

fly[4] *adj (sl)* -erevu, janja; -siodanganyika.

foal *n* mwana farasi/punda. **in/with ~ (of a mare)** -enye mimba *vi,vt (of horse)* zaa.

foam *n* 1 povu, ukafu. 2 *(also~-rubber)* sponji (agh. hutengenezea matakia, magodoro n.k.). **bath** ~ sabuni itowayo povu inayotiwa katika maji ya kuoga *vi* toa povu; *(fig) ~ing with rage* kutazama kwa hasira; kufoka kwa hasira. **~y** *adj*.

fob[1] *n* 1 mfuko mdogo wa kutia saa; ubindo wa saa. 2 kinyororo cha saa.

fob[2] *vt* ~ **sb off with sth/sth off** danganya mtu apokee kitu kisicho na thamani.

fo'c'sle *n* **forecastle**.

focus *n* 1 fokasi, kitovu: mahali miale ya nuru au moto ikutanapo; mahali kitu kionekanapo vizuri zaidi kwa macho. **out of** ~ -enye mauzauza. 2 kiini, mahali penye jambo hasa *vt* ~ **(on)** 1 weka fokasi, lenga. 2 ~ **on** lenga, sisitiza. **focal** *adj* -a fokasi, -lio kwenye fokasi; -liolenga. **focal-plane** 1 eneo la kutazamia. 2 *(shutter)* pazia la fokasi.

fodder *n* 1 chakula kikavu, nyasi kavu (kwa ajili ya kulisha mifugo) *vt* lisha (mifugo) kwa nyasi kavu.

foe *n (poet)* adui.

foetus,fetus *n* kijusi. **foetal/fetal** *adj*.

fog *n* 1 ukungu, mavunde, kungugu *be in a ~ (fig)* -toelewa -tojua, chaganyikiwa. **~-bank** *n* ukungu mzito juu ya bahari. **~-bound** *adj* -sioweza kuendelea na safari kwa sababu ya ukungu. **~horn** *n* parapanda ya kutangaza hatari ya ukungu baharini. ~ **signal** ishara ya ukungu relini. 2 hali ya ukunguukungu kwenye picha au filamu *vt,vi* funikwa, funika na ukungu; *(fig)* changanya, pumbaza. **~gy** *adj* 1 -enye ukungu. 2 *(fig)* -sioelewa/jua *I haven't the ~giest idea* sina hata fununu. **~giness** *n*.

foible *n* kosa/hitilafu ndogo (ya tabia, fikra za mtu) *one of his ~s is to think he can sing* moja ya kasoro zake ni kujiona kuwa anaweza kuimba (kumbe wapi).

foil[1] *n* 1 jaribosi. 2 mtu/kitu kinacho dhihirisha uzuri/ubora wa kingine kwa kuvilinganisha.

foil[2] *n* kitara kisicho na ncha kali (cha kufanyia mazoezi, kuchezea).

foil[3] *vt* zuia; kwamisha.

foist *vt* ~ **sth off on sb,** ~ **sb off with sth** ghilibu mtu akubali kitu kisicho na thamani.

fold[1] *vt,vi* 1 kunja, pinda. 2 *(the arms)* ~ **one's arms** kunja mikono/ kumbatia ~ *sb to one's breast* kumbatia, kunjamana, jikunjakunja. ~ **(up)** *(fig)* kumbatia mtu kifuani. 3 kunjikana, *(colloq)* filisika, shindwa kibiashara. 4 funga, kunja, funika. 5 changanya, koroga *n* kunjo, kibonde; *(of man's loin cloth used as a pocket)* kibindo. ~ **mountain** mlima kunjamano. **~er** *n* 1 folda (kifuko cha karatasi ngumu cha kubebea karatasi). 2 kijitabu cha matangazo, ratiba n.k., brosha.

fold[2] *n* 1 zizi, boma la mifugo. 2 *(fig)* kundi la waumini. **return to the** ~ rejea katika kundi la waumini nyumbani.

foliage *n* majani (ya mmea). **foliaceous** *adj* 1 -a jani, -enye viungo kama jani. 2 -enye tabaka nyembamba. **foliar** *adj (bot)* -a jani -enye kufanana na majani. **foliate** *vt* chanua *adj* -enye umbo la jani. **foliation** *n.*

folio *n* 1 ukurasa, folio, sahifa. 2 *(of ledger)* kurasa mbili za daftari zinazoelekeana,(upande mmoja wa matumizi na wa pili wa mapato). 3 namba ya ukurasa wa kitabu. 4 ukurasa mkubwa na karatasi iliyokunjwa mara moja, kitabu kikubwa chenye kurasa namna hii.

folk *n* 1 watu kwa jumla. 2 *(in compounds)* ~ **dance** ngoma ya jadi. ~**lore** elimu ya mila na desturi za jamii fulani, sanaa (ya) jadi. ~**medicine** madawa ya kienyeji, mitishamba. ~-**music** muziki wa jadi. ~ **tale** ngano, hadithi. 3 *(pl) (colloq)* ndugu wa familia moja, jamaa *my old ~s at home* ndugu zangu wa nyumbani. ~**sy** *adj (colloq)* cheshi; kunjufu.

follicle *n* kinyeleo, kinyweleo.

follow *vt,vi* 1 fuata, andama *don't ~ him* usimfuate. ~ **on** fuata baada ya muda. ~ **through** kamilisha pigo; maliza jukumu, timiza ahadi. 2 fuata/shika njia. 3 elewa, fahamu (hoja, jambo linalojadiliwa) *do you ~ my argument?* unaelewa hoja yangu. 4 fanya kazi fulani. ~ **the law** fanya kazi ya uanasheria. 5 iga, igiza, fuatisha vitendo ya mtu fulani, fuata nyayo. 6 tokana na *it ~s from what you say that* kutokana na unavyo sema inaonekana kwamba. 7 ~ **sth out** fuatia jambo hadi mwisho. ~ **sth up** fuatilia. ~-**up** *n* kitu (k.m. barua, waraka n.k.) kinachofuatilia kitu kilichotangulia; ufuatiliaji. ~**er** *n* 1 mfuasi, muunga mkono; *(disciple)* mwanafunzi. 2 mfuatiliaji. ~**ing** *adj* -nayofuata. **the** ~ *n* jambo linalofuata;kundi la wafuasi. **he has a large** ~ ana wafuasi wengi.

folly *n* upuuzi, upumbavu.

foment *vt* 1 kanda/chua kwa dawa/maji moto. 2 *(excite) (fig)* chochea, chokoza. ~**ation** *n* 1 majimoto/dawa ya kukanda/kuchua. 2 *(instigation)* uchochezi, uchokozi.

fond *adj* 1 *(pred only)* **be ~ of** penda. 2 -enye upendo *a ~ mother* mama mwenye upendo. 3 -nayopenda mno (hadi kuwa -jinga). 4 -a ndoto, matumaini, matarajio ambayo uwezekano wake wa kutimizika ni mdogo sana. ~**ly** *adv* 1 kwa upendo. 2 kwa matumaini ya kijinga. ~**ness n** upendo.

fondant *n* peremende laini yenye kuyeyuka mdomoni.

fondle *vt* papasa/tomasatomasa kwa mahaba, bembeleza *~ sb's hair* gusa nywele kwa mapenzi.

font[1] *n* 1 fonti: kisima cha maji ya ubatizo. 2 kitungi cha mafuta katika taa. ~**al** *adj* 1 -a asili. 2 -a chemchemi. 3 -a ubatizo.

font[2] see **fount**.

fontanel, fontanelle *n* utosi wa mtoto mchanga.

food *n* chakula, maakuli *~ chain* (mfuatano wa) mlishano; *~ crops* mazao ya chakula. ~-**stuff** vyakula *~ for thought* jambo la kuwazia. ~**less** *adj* bila chakula.

fool[1] *n* 1 mpumbavu. **be a ~ for one's pains** fanya jambo lisilokuletea pato wala shukurani. **be/live in a ~'s paradise** -wa na furaha ya kipumbavu isiyodumu. **be sent/go on a ~s errand** tumwa/fanya jambo lisilo na faida. **make a ~ of sb** danganya, ghilibu mtu; mfanye mtu aonekane mpumbavu. **play the ~** jifanye mpumbavu. **There is no ~ like an old ~** *(prov)* mzee mpumbavu ndiye mpumbavu hasa. 2 *(in the Middle Ages)* mchekeshaji (aliyeajiriwa na mtawala au muungwana). 3 **April ~** mtu aliyedanganywa kwenye sikukuu ya wapumbavu (yaani tarehe 1 Aprili). **All F~s' Day** Sikukuu ya Wapumbavu. 4 *(used attrib, colloq)* mpumbavu *vi,vt* 1 ~**(about/around)** -wa kama mpumbavu, chezacheza *stop ~ing (about!)* acha upuuzi. 2 ~

sth (out of sth) danganya. **~ery** *n* tabia ya kipumbavu, matendo/mawazo/ matamshi ya kipumbavu. **~-hardy** *adj* jasiri mno/pasi busara, -a kujihatarisha bure. **~-hardiness** *n* ujasiri (bila busara) wa kipumbavu. **~ish** *adj* pumbavu. **~ talk** upuuzi *he is ~* hana akili. **~shly** *adv*. **~ishness** *n*. **~proof** *adj* -sio na hitilafu.

fool[2] *n* aina ya chakula kitamu (kinachotengenezwa kwa matunda na malai au faluda).

foot *n* 1 mguu, kanyagio, wayo. **on ~** (kwenda) kwa miguu, kwa kutembea; *(fig)* -lioanzishwa tayari *the project is on ~* mradi umeshaanza (na sasa unaendelea). **be on one's feet** -wa wima; simama, inuka (ili kusema jambo fulani) *the Minister was on his feet at once to answer the charge* Waziri alisimama mara moja kujibu shitaka; *(fig)* -wa na afya njema baada ya kuugua. **fall on one's feet** *(colloq)* -wa na bahati, bahatika. **have feet of clay** -wa mnyonge au mwoga. **have one ~ in the grave** karibia kufa (k.m. kutokana na uzee), chungulia kaburi. **keep one's feet** -toanguka (k.m. wakati unatembea kwenye utelezi. **put one's ~ down** *(colloq)* kataa; pinga; shikilia msimamo. **put one's ~ in it** *(colloq)* sema au fanya kosa au upuuzi; boronga. **put one's feet up** *(colloq)*, pumzika huku miguu imenyooshwa, miguu juu. **put one's best ~ forward** tekeleza kazi yako haraka iwezekanavyo. **set sth/sb on its/his ~** wezesha mtu/kitu kijitegemee. **set sth on ~** anzisha kitu/jambo. **sweep sb off his ~** tia mtu ari/jazba, hamasisha sana. **under ~** chini, ardhini. 2 hatua, mwendo *swift of ~* mwendo wa haraka, mwendo mwepesi. 3 sehemu ya chini (ya kitu); tako *at the ~ of a hill* chini ya mlima. 4 sehemu ya mwisho ya mguuni mwa kitanda au kaburi. 5 *(measure)* futi. 6 kipimo cha mkazo katika mashairi. 7 *(mil. old use)* askari wa miguu. 8 *(compounds)* **~-and mouth disease** *n* shuna, ugonjwa wa midomo na miguu. **~-ball** *n* soka, kandanda. **~ bath** beseni la kunawia miguu. **~-board** *n* kibao cha mwinamo anachokanyaga dereva. **~-bridge** *n* daraja la waendao kwa miguu. **~-fall** *n* sauti ya hatua. **~-fault** *n (sport (tennis)* kosa la hatua (la kuruka msitari wakati wa kupiga mpira mara ya kwanza). **~-hills** *n* vilima vidogo chini ya mlima mkubwa au safu za milima mikubwa. **~-hold** *n (in climbing)* kidato; *(fig)* mahali pa usalama. **~-lights** *n* taa za chini za jukwaa. **the ~-lights** *(fig)* kazi ya uigizaji. **~ loose; ~ loose and fancy free** *adj* huru bila dhima. **~-man** *n* mtumishi wa kiume, mkaribishaji wageni, mtumishi anayekuwa mezani wakati wa chakula. **~-mark** see **~-print.** **~-note** *n* rejeo/tanbihi chini ya ukurasa. **~-path** *n* njia ya miguu. **~-plate** *n (of a train)* kijukwaa cha kusimamia dereva na mchochea moto. **~-pound** *n* kipimo cha kazi (cha kunyanyua ratili moja futi moja). **~-print** *n* wayo. **~-race** *n* mashindano ya mbio. **~-rule** *n* rula ya mti au metali (urefu wa inchi 12). **~-slog** *vi (colloq)* enda mbali kwa hatua kubwa na kishindo. **~-slogger** *n (colloq)* mwendaji wa miguu, mtu anayekwenda mwendo mrefu kwa miguu. **~-sore** *adj* -enye jeraha la miguu kutokana na kutembea. **~-step** *n* sauti ya hatua; wayo. **follow in one's father's ~ step** fuata vitendo vya baba; fuata nyanyo. **~-stool** *n* kibao cha kuwekea mguu. **~-sure** *adj* -siotetereka; -siochukua hatua potovu; imara. **~-wear** *n (tradesman term for)* viatu. **~-work** *n* namna ya kutembeza miguu kwenye dansi au mchezo wa ngumi *vt,vi* 1 fuma mguu wa soksi. 2 **~ it** *(colloq)* nenda kwa miguu, tembea. **~ the bill** *(colloq)* lipa (gharama). **~ed** *(in compounds)* -enye miguu kama ilivyoonyeshwa. **sure -~ed** -siotetereka, imara. **~ing** n *(sing only)* usimamaji; mahali pa kusimamia *he lost his* ~ aliteleza, alikunguwaa. 2 nafasi (katika jamii kikundi n.k.). **be on a friendly ~ with** *(your neighbours)* -wa na uhusiano mzuri na majirani zako. 3 hali *on a peace/war* ~ katika hali ya amani/vita. **~age** *n* urefu unaopimwa kwa futi (hasa filamu). **~er** *n* 1 *(colloq)* soka, kandanda. 2 *(compounds)* **a six-~en** mtu mwenye urefu wa futi sita. **footle** *vi,vt (colloq)* chezacheza, fanya upuzi, danganya. **~ling** *adj* -sio na maana au muhimu, -a upuzi.

fop *n* maridadi, mlimbwende, mno. **~pery** *n*. **~pish** *adj*.

for[1] *(prep)* 1 *(indicating destination or progress towards) set out ~ the beach* elekea pwani; *passengers ~ Mombasa* abiria waendao Mombasa. 2 *(indicating intention) built ~ rough roads* -lioundwa kwa barabara mbovu. 3 *(indicating ultimate possession) make some coffee ~ the guests* tayarisha kahawa kwa ajili ya wageni. **be ~ it** *(colloq)* weza kuadhibiwa au kupata shida, pata *you are ~ it now* utaipata sasa. 4 *(indicating preparation for) be ready ~ the long drought* jiandae kwa ukame wa muda mrefu. 5 *(indicating purpose) read ~ fun soma* kwa kujifurahisha. **what ~** kwa sababu/ kazi gani. 6 *(introducing complement) they were taken ~ crooks* walidhaniwa wahuni. **~ certain** kwa uhakika/ yakini. 7 *(with an object of hope, wish, search, inquiry etc) hope ~ the best* omba Mungu. 8 *(indicating endowment) an aptitude ~ mathematics* kipaji/ kipawa cha hisabati. 9 *(indicating liking) has a taste ~ wine* anapenda mvinyo. 10 *(indicating suitability) a man ~ the job* mtu anayefaa kazi. 11 *(after adj) too little ~ the day's wage* kidogo mno kwa ujira wa siku. 12 kwa kuzingatia *it is quite an achievement ~ a foreigner* ni mafanikio makubwa kwa mgeni. **~ all that** licha ya yote hayo. 13 *(representing)* mwakilishi, kwa niaba ya, badala ya, kwa/badala ya. **stand ~** wakilisha. 14 *(in defence or support of) she was ~ mult-partism* aliunga mkono/alitetea vyama vingi. 15 *(with regard to) ~ my part* kwa upande wangu *I am hard up ~ money* kuhusu fedha nimeishiwa kabisa. 16 kwa sababu ya *blame ~ the delay* laumu kwa (sababu ya) kuchelewa. 17 *(after a comparative) my shoes are the worse ~ wear* viatu vyangu vimezidi (kwa) kuchakaa. 18 licha ya, dhidi ya ~ *all you say, I still enjoy his company* bado nafurahia usuhuba wake licha ya yote usemayo. 19 kwa kiasi cha *reserve two seats ~ $ 50* weka/shika viti viwili vya (kiasi cha) $ 50. 20 *(in exchange for)* **plant two trees ~ every tree you cut down** panda miti miwili kwa kila mti unaoukata. 21 *(in contrast with) ~ one enemy she had a hundred friends* kwa kila adui mmoja alikuwa na marafiki mia moja. 22 *(duration) I shall be away ~ three weeks* nitakuwa sipo/nitaondoka kwa majuma matatu. 23 *(distance) we walked ~ twenty kilometers without meeting a soul* tulitembea kwa kilomita ishirini bila kukutana na mtu. 24 *(as part of the subject) ~ a man to chair a womens association is impossible* kwa mwanaume kuwa mwenyekiti wa chama cha wanawake ni muhali. *(conj.)* kwani, kwa kuwa *I asked her to join us ~ she was all alone* nilimtaka aungane nasi kwani alikuwa mpweke.

for[2] *conj* kwa kuwa, kwa maana, maana.

forage *n* 1 chakula cha farasi (punda, ng'ombe). 2 kutafuta chakula. *(mil)* **~-cap** kofia ya kazi ya askari *vt* ~ **(for)** tafuta chakula, tafuta (kitu chochote), nyang'anya. ~ **for oneself** jitegemea. **~r** *n* mtafutaji chakula.

foramen *n (anat)* tundu, shimo dogo,

kilango.
forasmuch as *adj conj* kwa kuwa, kwa sababu.
foray *n* uvamizi *vt* vamia.
forbad/farbade *pt. of* **forbid**.
forbear[1] *vt,vi* ~ **(from)** stahamili, vumilia; epuka. **~ance** *n.* **~ing** *adj.*
forbear[2] *n (US* **forebear)** *(usu pl)* mhenga.
forbid *vt* kataza, kanya, piga marufuku ~ *sb the house* kataza mtu nyumbani. **God** ~ Mungu apishe mbali! **~den** *adj* -liokatazwa, mwiko. **~den fruit** jambo linalotamaniwa sana lakini mwiko/marufuku. **~ding** *adj* -a kuogofya, -a kutisha, -kali. **~dingly** *adv.*
forby(e) *(arch. or Sc.) prep/adv* tena, zaidi ya.
force[1] *n* kani, nguvu *the ~ of a blow* nguvu ya pigo (kulipuka, mabishano maneno); *by sheer* ~ kwa nguvu tu. **in** ~ *(usu of people)* kwa wingi. **in full** ~ kwa nguvu zote. 2 *(energy)* bidii, juhudi, jitihada. **join ~s with** unganisha nguvu/juhudi. 3 *(violence)* jeuri, dhulumu. 4 **by** ~ kwa nguvu/ mashauri ya nguvu. 5 **the** ~ polisi. 6 *(pl)* **~s** majeshi. **join the ~s** jiunga na jeshi. 7 *(gram)* maana, *what is the ~ of 'for' here? 'for'* ina maana gani hapa? 8 *(leg)* amri, sharti, nguvu. **be in** ~ tumika. **put a law into** ~ fanya sheria itumike. *vt* 1 lazimisha; shurutisha, vunja/pasua kwa nguvu. ~ **a person's hand** shurutisha mtu kufanya kitu. ~ **entry** ingia kwa nguvu. ~ **landing** kutua kwa dharura. ~ **land** *vt,vi* tua kwa dharura. 2 *(fasten growth)* komaza mmea haraka (kwa kutumia joto n.k.); *(fig)* ~ *a pupil* fanya mwanafunzi ajifunze kwa muda mfupi kwa kumpa masomo ya ziada. 3 fanya jambo kwa kujilazimisha ~ *a laugh* cheka kwa kujilazimisha (wakati mtu hana furaha). **~-feed** *vt* **(~-fed)** lazimisha (mnyama, mfungwa, mgonjwa) kula au kunywa. **~ful** *adj (of person, his character, of argument)* 1 -enye nguvu; -enye kani. 2 -a kujitokeza; -a maana. **~fully** *adv* **~fulness** *n.* ~ **majeure** *n (leg)* jambo lisilozuilika, nguvu kubwa. **~-meat** *n* kima (nyama iliyokatwakatwa au kusagwa na kutiwa viungo, hutumika k.m. kujazia kuku kabla ya kumpika). **~meat balls** kababu. **forcible** *adj* 1 -liofanywa kwa nguvu, ~ **entry** kuingia kwa nguvu. 2 *(of a person, his acts words etc)* -enye kuvuta, -enye kushawishi. **forcibly** *adv.*
forceps *n* koleo (inayotumiwa na madaktari hasa wa meno).
ford *n* kivuko cha maji mafupi *vt* vuka mto kwa miguu/kwa gari. **~able** *adj.*
fore *adj (attrib only)* -a mbele, -a kutangulia, -a omo. **to the** ~ tayari kufanya jambo; papo hapo; maarufu. **come to the** ~ -wa maarufu *adv (naut)* mbele. ~ **and aft** tezini na omoni; kwa urefu wa meli ~ *and aft sails* tanga lisilo mraba *int (golf)* oha! (tamko la kutahadharisha walio mbele kuwa mchezaji anataka kupiga mpira). **~arm** *n* kigasha, mkono (tangu kiko mpaka kitanga). **~arm** *vt (usu passive)* -pa silaha kabla/ mapema weka tayari (kwa vita). **~bode** *vt (formal)* 1 -wa dalili ya. 2 agua, bashiri. **~boding** *n* ubashiri. **~cast** *vt* tabiri *n* utabiri *the weather ~* utabiri wa hali ya hewa. **~castle** *n (in some merchant ships)* sitaha ya gubeti. **~close** *vt,vi* **~close (on)** *leg)* chukua mali ya mkopaji aliyeshindwa kulipa kwa wakati uliokubaliwa. **~closure** *n.* **~court** *n* baraza (iliyojengewa) mbele ya nyumba. **~doom** *vt (usu passive)* **~doom (to)** panga kwa kudra, *an attempt ~doomed to failure* jaribio lililopangiwa kushindwa. **~father** *n (usu pl)* mhenga. **~-feet** *see* **fore-foot.** **~finger** *n* kidole cha shahada. **~foot** *n* mguu wa mbele wa mnyama *cross a ship's ~foot* kata njia ya meli. **~- front** *n* 1 sehemu ya mbele kabisa. 2 *(mil)* mstari wa mbele. **~gather** *see* **forgather.** **~ground** *n* 1

mbele, sehemu ya mandhari (hasa kwenye picha) iliyo karibu ya mtazamaji. 2 *(fig)* mahali penye kuonekana vizuri. **~head** *n* paji la uso *a broad ~* bapa la uso. **a projecting ~head** komo la uso. **~ knowledge** *n* kujua kitu kabla hakijatokea. **~land** *n* rasi. **~leg** *n* mguu wa mbele (wa mnyama). **~mast** *n (naut)* mlingoti wa mbele. **~most** *adj* -a mbele, -a kwanza, -kuu *adv*. kwanza; muhimu. **first and ~most** kwanza kabisa. **~name** *n (as used in official style)* jina la kwanza (sio la ukoo). **~ordain** *vt* amuru mbele; teua kabla. **~runner** *n* 1 mtangulizi, mtakadamu. 2 dalili/ ishara ya mambo yatakayotokea. **~sail** *n (naut)* tanga kuu la mbele. **~see** *vt* ona mbele, jua ya mbele/yajayo. **~able** *adj* -enye kutabirika. **~able future** kipindi cha karibuni ambacho matokeo yake yanatabirika. **~sight** *n* 1 uwezo wa kutabiri; uangalifu (katika kujitayarisha kwa mambo ya baadaye; busara ya kuganga yajayo. **~taste** *n*. limbuko. **~show** *vt* tabiri, onyesha dalili ya mwonjo wa awali *a ~ show of suffering* mwonjo wa kwanza wa mateso. **~tell** *vt* agua, tabiri, bashiri *~tell sb's success* tabiri ushindi wa fulani. **~thought** *n* mawazo/mipango ya busara kwa faida ya baadaye, kuona mbali. **~time** *n (arch)* nyakati za zamani; zama za kale. **~token** *vt* toa dalili/ ishara ya; onya mapema *n* ishara/dalili ya yajayo. **~told** *pt pp of ~tell*. **~warn** *vt* onya (asa, kanya) mapema. **forego** *see forgo*.

foreign *adj* 1 -geni, -a kigeni, -a nchi za nje. **~ affairs** mambo ya nchi za nje. 2 **~ to** -siohusu; -sio -ake *a ~ body in the eye* kitu kilichoingia jichoni (k.m. uchafu) *~ languages* lugha za kigeni. **~er** *n* mgeni anayeishi katika nchi.

forelock *n* kishungi, shore juu ya paji. **take the occasion by the ~** tumia wasaa barabara.

foreman *n* 1 msimamizi; mnyapara. 2 *(leg)* kiongozi wa baraza la wazee.

forenoon *n (old use)* asubuhi, mchana kabla ya saa sita.

forensic *adj* -a mahakama (na mambo, maneno yake); -a barazani, -inayohitajika na mahakama. **~ skill** ustadi unaohitajika na mahakama.

foreplay *n* unyegereshano/utianaji nyege (kabla ya tendo).

foreshadow *vt* -onyesha dalili/ishara ya *the clouds ~ rain* mawingu huwa dalili ya mvua.

foreshore *n* ufuko (ulioendelezwa).

foreshorten *vt (in drawing pictures)* chora picha kwa mlingano/uwiano na kitu chenyewe.

foreskin *n* govi.

forest *n* 1 msitu. **~ reserve** pori, hifadhi ya msitu. 2 mbuga. 3 *(fig)* mandhari inayofananishwa na msitu *a ~ of masts* msitu wa milingoti. **~er** *n* bwana miti/misitu. **~ry** elimu misitu.

forestall *vt* bananga, vuruga (mipango ya mtu) kwa kufanya jambo mapema bila kutegemewa/kuwahi.

foreswear *v see* **forswear**.

foretop *n (naut)* kishungi juu ya mlingoti wa meli.

forever *adj* milele, daima.

foremore *adv* milele na milele.

forewoman *n see foreman*.

foreword *n* dibaji.

forfeit *vt* 1 poteza, twaliwa, nyanganywa (kwa adhabu ya kosa). 2 toa haka *n* 1 haka, fidia, faini. 2 *(pl)* mchezo ambao mchezaji hutoa vitu kadha kwa kufanya makosa na kurudishiwa kwa kutoa faini ya kichekesho. **~ure** *n* utwaliwaji wa mali kama haka, usabiliaji.

forgather/foregather *vi* kutana, onana.

forgave *pt of* **forgive**.

forge[1] *n* 1 karakana ya kulehemu na kufua vyuma. 2 karakana yenye kalibu *vt* 1 unda kwa kulehemu na kuponda kwa nyundo *(fig) their friendship was ~d by shared adversity* urafiki wao ulitokana na matatizo yaliyowapata kwa pamoja. 2 bini, ghushi. **~r** *n* mdanganyifu, mbini. **~ry** *n* 1 ubini, ughushi, udanganyifu. 2 hati au maandishi yaliyobuniwa/ghushiwa. **forging** *n* kipande cha metali kilicholehemiwa au kupondwa.

forge[2] *vi* **~ahead** endelea mbele *(in a race etc)*, ongoza.

forget *vt,vi* ~ **(about)** 1 sahau, pitiwa *never to be forgotten* -siosahaulika *let's ~ our differences* tusahau tofauti zetu. 3 ~ **oneself** jichukua visivyo, jisahau, fikiria zaidi juu ya wengine kuliko binafsi. **~ful** *adj* -sahaulifu. **~fully** *adv* **~fulness** *n* usahaulifu.

forgive *vt,vi* 1 ~ **sb for doing sth** samehe, ghofiri ~ *me* niwie radhi, kumradhi, nisamehe ~ *each other* sameheana. 2 achilia, burai *do please ~ his debt* tafadhali mburaie deni lake. **forgivable** *adj* -a kusameheka. **forgiving** *adj* -enye huruma, -enye msamaha, -lio tayari kusamehe. **forgivingly** *adv*. **~ness** *n* msamaha, buraa. **ask for ~ness** omba msamaha.

forgo *vt* samehe, achilia.

forgone *pp of* **forgo**.

forgot *pt of* **forget**.

forgotten *pp of* **forget**.

fork *n* 1 uma. ~ **lunch/supper bufe** (mlo wa watu wengi). 2 *(for gardening)* rato. 3 *(of roads)* njia panda. 4 **~-lift truck** foko *vt,vi* 1 inua, beba kwa foko ~ *in manure* chimbia mbolea kwa reki/rato. 2 *(of a road, river)* gawanyika, fanya mikondo/ mikono katika, *(ofpersons)* geuka (kushoto au kulia). 3 ~ **sth out**, ~ **up/out** *(colloq)* lipa. **~ed** *adj* -enye kugawanyika sehemu mbili au zaidi; -a uzandiki.

forlorn *adj (poet or liter)* -pweke, -kiwa, -sio na mategemeo, -liotupwa. ~ **hope** shughuli isiyo na mategemeo ya kufaulu. **~ly** *adv*. **~ness** *n* upweke, ukiwa.

form *n* umbo, sura, jinsi *what is its ~?* ina umbile gani? *she has a good ~* ana umbo zuri. 2 *(prescribed order)* taratibu, desturi; mtindo *literary ~* fani, mtindo wa maandishi. **good/bad** ~ desturi njema/mbaya. 3 *(pattern)* muundo, aina ~ *of government* muundo wa serikali. 4 *(gram)* umbo la neno (katika matamshi au tahajia) *different in ~ but identical in meaning* yanatofautiana kwa umbo lakini yana maana sawa. 5 maadili, taratibu (za jadi); hali ya mwili. **in/ out of ~; on/off** ~ -wa katika hali nzuri/mbaya. *(esp. of horses and athletes)* **out of** ~ -sioelekea kushinda. *do sth for ~'s sake* fanya jambo kutimiza mradi/ada. 6 kawaida katika kufanya jambo (k.m. salamu, usemi). 7 fomu *application ~s* fomu za maombi. 8 uchangamfu, ubashasha *he was in great ~ at the party* alikuwa na ubashasha kwenye karamu. 9 *(seat)* fomu, benchi. 10 kidato. **~less** *adj* bila umbo, ovyo. **~lessly** *adv* *vt,vi* 1 unda, umba (sura), tunga ~ *words and sentences* unda maneno na kutunga sentensi. 2 fanya, fanyiza, tengeneza, panga ~ *two rows* panga/fanya mistari miwili. 3 anzisha ~ *a class of adults* anzisha darasa la watu wazima. 4 -wa sehemu ya, fanya *this building ~s part of the school buildings* jengo hili ni sehemu ya majengo ya shule. 5 ~ **into** *(mil)* enda/fuata mpango maalum *the section ~ed three ranks* kikosi kiliunda/kilifuata safu tatu. 6 fanyika, chukua, kuwa umbo/sura *the idea ~ed in his mind* wazo lilipata umbo akilini.

formal *adj* 1 *(prescribed)* rasmi, -a utaratibu uliozoeleka/kubalika ~ *dress* vazi rasmi. 2 *(of garden etc)* pacha. 3 -a sura au mbo la nje; -a fani. 4 ~ **grammar** sarufi maumbo. **~ly** *adv*. **~ism** *n* urasmi. **~ist** *n* mrasimu, mshika desturi. **~ity** *n* 1 urasmi, urasmi wa. 2 kanuni, urasimu. *(leg)* **~lities** urasmi wa kisheria. **~lize** rasimisha.

formaldehyde *n (chem)* gesi ya maji ya kidhuru bakteria.

format *n* 1 umbo na ukubwa wa kitabu (maandishi, karatasi, ujalidi). 2

muundo *the examination* ~ muundo wa mitihani. **~ion** *n* 1 uumbaji, utengenezaji *the ~ of characters* uumbaji wa wahusika. 2 muundo au mpango. **~ive** *adj* -enye kupatia umbo, -enye kuumba, -enye kutengeneza, -enye kujenga.

former *adj* 1 -a awali, -a kipindi cha mwanzo, -a zamani. 2 *(also as pron)* **the ~** *(contrasted with the latter)* -liotajwa mwanzo, -a mwanzoni.

formica *n* fomaika.

formidable *adj* 1 -a kuogofya, -a kutisha. 2 gumu; ngome. **formidably** *adj.*

formula *n* 1 virai vinavyotumika sana kwenye mazungumzo, k.m. *how d'you do ?* uhali gani? *excuse me* samahani *thank you* asante. 2 fomyula, k.m. H_2 0 (maji); 0 oksijeni. **~te** *vt* eleza kwa usahihi na kueleweka; unda/eleza kwa utaratibu. **~tion** *n.*

fornication *n* uzinzi. **fornicate** *vt* zini.

forrader *adv (colloq)* mbele zaidi *there is a sign of getting ~* kuna dalili ya kuendelea mbele.

forsake *vt* telekeza, tupa, toroka ~ *one's parents* telekeza/toroka wazazi.

forsooth *adv (old use) (used in irony)* kwa kweli, kwa hakika.

forswear *vt* 1 acha (kufanya jambo) ~ *smoking* acha kuvuta sigara. 2 ~ **oneself** sema uongo chini ya kiapo.

fort/~ress *n* ngome; husuni, boma.

forte[1] *n* kipaji, uwezo, *his special ~ is teaching* uwezo/ kipaji chake ni katika kufundisha.

forte[2] *adj,adv (mus)* kwa nguvu/sauti.

fortissimo *adj, adv* kwa sauti kubwa sana.

forth *adv* 1 *(formal)* mbele, kwa mbele *from this day ~* kutoka leo na kuendelea. **and so ~** na kadhalika. **back and ~** kwenda mbele na nyuma. 2 *(arch)* nje. **~coming** *adj* 1 -liokaribu kutokea. 2 *(pred)* patikana, -tayari kutumika/kuja. 3 *(of a person)* -lio tayari kusaidia/kutoa habari.

forthright *adj* kweli, wazi.

forthwith *adv* mara moja, bila kukawia.

fortify *vt* 1 ~ **(against)** imarisha (mahali) dhidi ya mashambulizi (kwa kuta, mahandaki, bunduki). 2 *(of a person)* jikinga na (baridi, maadui n.k.), jiimarisha. **fortification** *n* 1 kuimarisha, kutia nguvu. 2 kitu kinachoimarisha. 3 *(pl)* ngome.

fortitude *n* ushupavu, uvumilivu (wakati wa maumivu, shida, taabu, hatari n.k.), ustahimilivu.

fortnight *n* wiki mbili, siku kumi na nne *~'s rest* mapumziko ya majuma mawili *this day a ~* wiki mbili kuanzia leo. **~ly** *adj,adv* -a wiki mbili; kila wiki mbili.

fortuitous *adj (formal)* -a bahati, -a nasibu. **~ly** *adv.* **~ness** *n.* **fortuity** *n.*

fortune *n* 1 bahati **the ~ (s) of war** matokeo ya vita. **try one's ~** bahatisha, jaribu bahati. **tell sb his ~** bashiri, pigia ramli. **~teller** *n* mpiga ramli, mwaguzi. 2 ustawi, neema, baraka, mafanikio. 3 mali, utajiri, fedha nyingi. **come into a ~** rithi fedha nyingi. **marry a ~** oa mtu tajiri. **a small ~** fedha nyingi. **make a ~** pata/tengeneza fedha nyingi, tajirika. **~ hunter** *n* mtu atafutaye utajiri kwa ndoa. **fortunate** *adj* -a bahati, -enye bahati *I was ~ in finding* nilibahatika kugundua *how fortunate!* bahati iliyoje! **fortunately** *adv.*

forty *n, adj* arubaini *a woman of ~* mwanamke wa miaka arubaini. **fortieth** -a arubaini.

forum *n (in ancient Rome)* baraza.

forward[1] *adj* 1 -a mbele, -a kutangulia; -a kuendeleza/kuelekea mbele. 2 *(of plants, crops, seasons, children)* -liostawi, -liokua, -nayoendelea vizuri. 3 -a kimbelembele. 4 -enye shauku. 5 *(of opinions etc)* -a mbele ya wakati. 6 *(comm)* -a kutumika baadaye ~ *prices* bei za kutumika baadaye *n (in games)* fowadi. **~ness** *n* *vt* 1 himiza/sukuma mbele (mambo, kazi n.k.). 2 peleka, safirisha, tuma, (mizigo, barua n.k.)

~ **goods to sb** pelekea mtu mizigo ~ *my letters to the new station* peleka barua zangu kwenye kituo kipya (cha kazi). **~ing agent** *n* wakala wa usafirishaji mizigo. **~ing instructions** maagizo ya ufikishaji/usafirishaji mizigo. **~(s)** *adv* 1 mbele, kwa mbele *go* ~ sogea, nenda mbele. 2 kwa kuendelea mbele *from this day* ~ kuanzia leo na kuendelea. **look ~ to sth** ngojea/tarajia/tegemea kwa furaha. **bring ~** onyesha. **come ~** jitolea, jionyesha. 3 **backward(s) and ~s** mbele na nyuma.

fosse *n* handaki; shimo refu na jembamba (agh. kwa ajili ya ngome au maji).

fossil *n* 1 kisukuku. 2 *(colloq)* mtu asiyekubali kupokea mambo mapya, mtu wa zamani. **~ation** *n*. **~iferous** *adj*. **~ize** *vt,vi* -wa kisukuku.

foster *vt* 1 lea; kimu. **~brother/sister** *n* ndugu wa kulea. ~ **child** mtoto wa ziwa/kulea. ~ **parents** walezi. ~ **father/mother** baba/mama mlezi. 2 kuza, endeleza ~ *musical ability* kuza kipaji/uwezo wa muziki. **~er** *n*. **~age** *n* kukimu. **~ing** *n* mtoto wa kulea.

fought *pt, pp of* **fight**.

foul *adj* 1 -a kuchukiza, -a kirihi; *(of smell)* -a kunuka; (*taste*) -mbaya sana *a drink with a ~ taste* kinywaji chenye ladha mbaya *a ~ meal (sl)* chakula kibaya; *~ smelling latrine* choo kinachonuka. 2 -chafu, -a taka *a ~ market* soko chafu. 3 ovu, potevu, fasiki, *(of language)* -a matusi; *(of the weather)* -a dhoruba, -liochafuka. ~ **spoken/-mouthed** *adj* -enye maneno machafu. **by fair means or ~** kwa halali au dhuluma. 4 ~ **play** *(in sport)* dhambi, kosa; kuvunja sheria; *(crime)* mauaji, uhalifu wa kutumia nguvu *It is ~ play* ni kosa la jinai. 5 -liotatizwa, liozongomezwa *a ~ rope* kamba iliyozongomezwa. 6 *(of a flue, pipe, gun-barrel etc)* -lioziba, chafu. 7 **fall ~ of** *(of a ship)* gongana na zongomezwa na; *(fig)* pata msukosuko, andamwa na. 8 **through fair and ~** kwa mema na mabaya, kwa njia yoyote ile. **~ly** *adv*. **~ness** *n* *vt,vi* ~ **up** 1 tia taka, chafua. 2 pambana, gongana, tatiza, zongomeza. 3 fanya faulu/dhambi.

foulard *n* kitambaa cha hariri.

found[1] *pt,pp of* **find**.

found[2] *vt* 1 weka msingi wa, anzisha. 2 fadhili ili kianzishwe ~ *a new institute* fadhili taasisi mpya. 3 ~ **sth on/upon** weka juu ya misingi ya *a story ~ed on facts* hadithi inayotokana na ukweli. **~ation** *n* 1 uanzishaji (wa shule, mji, taasisi n.k.). 2 kitu kilichoanzishwa (k.m. taasisi, shirika, chuo, hospitali n.k.). 3 mfuko wa fedha kwa ajili ya kutoa misaada. 4 *(often pl.)* msingi wa jengo. ~ **stone** jiwe la msingi. 5 kanuni/msingi wa jambo, imani n.k. 6 ~ **cream** krimu ya usoni (inayotangulia kupakwa kabla ya vipodozi vingine). **~er**; **~ress** *n* mwanzilishi, mwasisi.

found[3] *vt* yeyusha madini na kuimimina ndani ya kalibu. **~ry** *n* kalibu; kiwanda cha kukalibu madini (cha mhunzi).

founder *vt,vi* 1 *(of a ship)* zama (kwa kujaa maji). 2 *(of a horse)* anguka/ kwama kwenye matope (kutokana na uchovu). 3 *(of a plan)* shindwa kabisa *n (of horses)* uvimbe (katika mguu).

foundling *n* mwana mkiwa aliyetelekezwa na wazazi wake, mtoto wa kuokotwa.

fount *n* 1 *(poet)* chemchemi. 2 *(poet or rhet)* chanzo, asili. 3 *(also* **font***)* *(printing)* fonti (seti ya herufi za aina fulani). **~ain** *n* 1 chemchemi (agh. iliyojengwa kwa kutumia bomba. **drinking-~** mashine/chemchemi ya maji baridi ya kunywa. **~pen** kalamu ya wino. 2 *(fig)* chanzo, asili. 3 *(of burst pipe etc)* mbubujiko. ~ **head** *n* chanzo, asili.

four *n,adj* namba 4 (nne) *a child of ~* mtoto wa miaka minne *on all ~s* kwa kutambaa. **be on all ~s with** -wa sawasawa na. ~- **figured** *adj* a namba 1000-9999. ~ **letter word** tusi. ~ **fold** mara nne. ~-**in-hand** *n* gari la farasi wanne *(US colloq)* tai ya shingoni. ~-**part** *adj* -lioimbwa na sauti nne. ~**pence** *adj* mapeni manne. ~-**ply** *adj* -enye tabaka nne. ~-**poster** *n* kitanda chenye miti ya chandarua, pazia n.k. ~-**pounder** *n* mzinga utupao risasi za ratili nne. ~ **score** *adj, n* themanini; -a themanini; korija nne. ~**some** *n* 1 mchezo wa wachezaji wanne. 2 watu wanne. ~**square** *adj* -enye umbo mraba; *(fig)* -nyofu. ~**teen** *n,adj* kumi na nne, -a kumi na nne. ~**teenth** *n* -a kumi na nne, kumi na nne. **one** ~**teenth** moja ya kumi na nne. ~**thly** *adv* nne. ~-**way** *adj* -enye njia nne. ~**wheel** *adj* -enye magurudumu manne. ~ **wheel drive** -enye kuendeshwa kwa magurudumu yote manne.

fowl *n* 1 *(old use)* ndege. 2 ndege wanaofugwa hasa kuku. 3 nyama ya kuku, ndege. ~**er** *n* mwindaji ndege. ~**ing-piece** *n* bunduki ya marisau (ya kupigia ndege). ~**pox** *n* ndui ~-**run** *n* uwanja wa kuku (agh. huzungukwa na kizuizi). ~ **typhoid** *n* kideri. ~**pest** mdondo, kideri.

fox[1] *n* 1 mbweha. 2 mjanja. ~**hole** *n* *(mil.)* handaki. ~**hound** *n* mbwa wa kuwindia mbweha. ~**hunt** *vi* winda mbweha *n* uwindaji mbweha. ~**y** *adj* 1 -a kama mbweha. 2 janja, -enye hila *vt (colloq)* 1 laghai; danganya. 2 tatanisha, kanganya *n (colloq)* mlaghai, ayari.

foyer *n* sebule, ukumbi.

fracas *n* tafrani, ugomvi wenye kelele.

fraction *n* 1 sehemu ndogo, kipande. 2 *(math)* sehemu. ~ **indices** vipeo sehemu; tarakimu isiyo kamili (k.v. ½, ⅝, (0.76). ~**al** *adj* 1 -a sehemu, -a hesabu ya sehemu. ~ **distillation** *n* mkeneko sehemu. 2 -dogo sana. ~**ate** *vt (chem)* tenganisha kwa kukeneka.

fractious *adj* gomvi; -enye hasira.

fracture *n* mvunjiko, kuvunjika *he has a ~ of the leg* amevunjika mguu *vt,vi* vunja; vunjika.

fragile *adj* -a kuvunjika upesi *(of a person)* dhaifu. **fragility** *n.*

fragment *n* kipande, sehemu; kigae. ~**ary** *adj* -a vipande vipande, -siokamilika, -a sehemusehemu. ~**ation** *n* kuvunjavunja katika vipande. ~ **bomb** bomu la kuvunjika vipandevipande.

fragrant *adj* 1 -a kunukia, -enye harufu nzuri; -tamu. 2 *(fig)* -a kupendeza. **fragrance** *n* harufu nzuri.

frail *adj* 1 *(of person)* dhaifu. 2 *(of things)* -a kuvunjika upesi; isio imara. 3 dogo *a ~ chance* nafasi ndogo. ~**ty** *n* udhaifu *(pl.* ~**ties)** kasoro.

frame *n* 1 kiunzi (agh. cha majengo). ~ **house** nyumba ya mbao. 2 *(of picture, window, glasses etc)* fremu (k.m.fremu ya picha au ya miwani). 3 mwili, umbo, gimba. 4 jengo la mbao na vioo la kulinda mimea dhidi ya baridi. 5 ~ **of mind** hali (ya muda) ya akili; hasira/furaha *in a cheerful ~ of mind* katika hali ya furaha. 6 *(more usu* ~**work)** mfumo. 7 *(photography)* sehemu ya picha moja katika filamu ~ *work* kiunzi, mhimili *vt,vi* 1 tengeneza; tunga, buni ~ *a sentence* tunga sentensi. 2 tia fremu (k.m. picha). 3 endelea, elekea kuendelea; endeleza; toa matumaini ya kuendelea. 4 *(sl)* singizia, zulia mtu uongo: ~-**up** *n* uongo uliozuliwa kumtia mtu hatiani, kusingiziwa; kusingizia.

franc *n* faranga.

France *n* Ufaransa.

Franco *pref (used in compounds)* -a Ufaransa, -a Wafaransa. *The ~-German War* Vita vya Wafaransa na Wajerumani. ~**phile** mshabiki wa Ufaransa. ~**phobe** mtu mwenye chuki dhidi ya Ufaransa, mtu aichukiaye Ufaransa. ~**phone** *adj* -nayotumia Kifaransa.

franchise *n* 1 **the** ~ haki kamili za uraia zinazotolewa na nchi au mji, (hasa haki ya kupiga kura kwenye uchaguzi). 2 *(chiefly US)* haki maalum inayotolewa na utawala kwa mtu au kampuni.

francolin *n* kwale.

frangipane *n* halua ya lozi.

frangipani *n* mjinga, msanapiti.

frank[1] *adj* -a kusema kweli, -a kusema wazi/bila kuficha *be quite ~* sema kweli, sema wazi. **~ly** *adv*. **~ness** *n*.

frank[2] *vt* weka stempu au alama; gonga barua kuonyesha kuwa gharama ya usafirishaji imeshalipiwa. **~ing machine** *n* mashine inayoweka bei ya stempu.

frankfurter, frankfurt *n* soseji ya ng'ombe na nguruwe.

frankincense *n* ubani, uvumba.

frantic *adj* -enye wayowayo (kwa hasira, maumivu, majonzi n.k.) *drive sb ~* fanya mtu akasirike; tia wazimu. **~ally** *adv*.

fraternal *adj* -a kidugu. **~ly** *adv*. **fraternity** *n* 1 udugu. 2 chama, shirika, jamii ya watu wenye hali moja. 3 *(US)* chama cha wanafunzi wanaume. **fraternize** *vi* **~ (with)** suhubiana (na). **fraternization** *n*. **fratricide** *n* *(person guilty of)* kuua/muuaji wa kaka/dada. **fratricidal** *adj*.

fraud *n* 1 udanganyifu, ulaghai, hila. 2 mdanganyifu, laghai. **~ulent** *adj* danganyifu, laghai. **~ulently** *adv*.

fraught *adj* 1 -liojaa, -enye kuleta hatari/maafa/huzuni n.k. 2 -liojaa vitisho; -enye wasiwasi.

fray[1] *n (lit, fig)* ugomvi; mashindano.

fray[2] *vt,vi* 1 *(of cloth, rope, etc.)* chakaa, chakaza (kutokana na msuguano wa muda mrefu). 2 *(fig)* choka/ chosha; ghadhibika/ ghadhibisha.

frazzle *n* hali ya kutambarika *vt,vi* tambarika.

freak *n* 1 kituko,kioja,shauri tendo/jambo lisilo la kawaida. 2 *(also ~* **of nature***)* mtu/mnyama au mmea usio wa kawaida (k.m. mbuzi mwenye miguu mitano), dubwana, dubwasha *vi,vt (sl)* ~ **out** -wa na mhemko, pandwa na mori (kama vile kutokana na madawa ya kulevya). ~ **out** *n* hali ya kupoteza akili kwa sababu ya madawa ya kulevya. **~ish** *adj* -a kioja. **~ishly** *adv*. **~ishness** *n*. **~y** *adj*.

freckle *n* 1 doa katika ngozi (kutokana na jua). 2 *(pl)* **~s** mabakabaka *vt,vi* pata/sababisha madoa katika ngozi.

free *adj* 1 *(of a person)* huru, -ungwana; -siofungwa. **~man** muungwana. ~ **born** mtu huru. 2 *(of a state, its citizens, and institutions)* huru, -nayojitawala. 3 -siozuiwa; huria, -lioachwa huru. **allow sb/give sb/have a ~ hand** -pa mtu/ruhusu mtu/-wa na uhuru wa kufanya jambo bila kushauriana na mwingine/ wengine. ~ **agent** *n* mtendaji huria (awezaye kutenda jambo bila kizuizi). **F~ church** *n* Kanisa Huria; Kanisa lisilo chini ya udhibiti wa dola/serikali. ~ **enterprise** uchumi huria. **~-and-easy** *adj* bila taadhima. ~ **fall** *n* kuanguka/kujirusha toka kwenye ndege bila mwavuli (mpaka unapohitajiwa). ~ **fight** mapigano ambayo yeyote aliyepo aweza kujiunga, mapigano yasiyo na kanuni. **~-for-all** ugomvi/ majadiliano huria (ambayo yeyote anaweza kutoa maoni bila kuzuiwa). ~ **hand** *adj (of drawings)* -liochorwa kwa mkono tu (bila kutumia vifaa kama rula, bikari); -a kukakata. ~ **handed** *adj* karimu; si mkono wa birika. ~ **hold** *n (leg)* umilikaji ardhi bila masharti. ~ **holder** mmilikaji ardhi asiyekuwa na masharti. **~house** *n (GB)* kilabu cha pombe za aina zote. ~ **labour** *n* wafanyakazi wasio wanachama wa vyama vya wafanyakazi. ~ **lance** *n (in middle ages)* mamluki; mwandishi/ mtengenezaji filamu huria (anayetoa huduma zake popote) *vi* fanya kazi ya uandishi huria. ~ **liver** *n* mwanisi: mtu ajiingizaye kwenye raha (hasa ya chakula na vinywaji) bila kizuizi. ~ **living** *n adj* maisha ya anasa. ~ **love** *n (old use)* uhusiano wa mapenzi bila kuoana; mapenzi huria. ~ **kick** *n (football)* mpira wa adhabu. ~ **port** bandari huria (ambayo wafanyibiashara wote wanaweza kuitumia bila vizuizi vya kodi n.k.). ~ **range** *adj (of poultry)* -a kienyeji; -siofungiwa ndani. ~ **speech** *n* uhuru wa kusema. ~ **spoken** *adj* bila kuficha mawazo; -liosemwa kwa bahati. ~ **standing** *adj* -siotegemezwa popote. ~ **stone** *n* jiwe mchanga. ~ **style** *n (swimming)* mashindano yasiyo na mkambi maalumu. ~ **thinker** *n* mtu asiyefuata mafundisho ya dini ya asili bali atumiaye mantiki. ~ **thinking** *adj* bila kufuata mapokeo ya vitabu vya dini. ~ **thought** *n* fikra zisizofuata mapokeo ya dini. ~-**trade** *n* biashara huria (bila vikwazo vya kodi, ushuru). ~-**translation** *n* tafsiri isiyo ya neno kwa neno. ~-**verse** *n* shairi guni. ~-**way** *n (US)* baraste. ~-**wheel** *vi* enda kwa baiskeli bila kupiga pedali, *(fig)* tenda/ishi kwa kujiamulia. ~-**will** *n* hiari (ya moyo), utashi. ~-**will** *adj* -a hiari. 4 ~ **from** bila. ~ **of** nje ya; bila. 5 bure, pasipo malipo *admission* ~ kiingilio bure ~ *of income tax* pasipo malipo ya kodi ya mapato *get for* ~ pata kitu bure. ~ **list** *n* orodha ya watu wa kuingia bure; orodha ya vitu vinavyoweza kuingia bila kulipiwa ushuru wa forodha; ~ **on board** *(abbr fob) (comm)* huduma hadi bandarini. ~ **pass** ruhusa ya kusafiri bure/bila kulipa nauli. ~-**loader** *(sl)* doezi. 6 *(of place or time)* bila shughuli; isiyotumiwa *(of persons)* bila kazi. **have one's hands** ~ -wa bila shughuli; -wa katika hali ya kuweza kujiamulia mambo. 7 -ja/toa kwa wingi *a ~ flow of water* mtiririko wa maji mengi. 8 bila aibu/kizuizi. **make ~ with** tumia kitu bila aibu (kama chako). 9 **make sb ~ of** -pa mtu haki ya uwanachama wa kikundi, uraia n.k.

~**man** *n* mtu aliyepewa haki ya uraia wa jiji *vt* ~ **(from/of)** 1 weka huru, komboa, okoa. 2 ondosha; komesha, batilisha ~ *a country of cholera* komesha kipindupindu katika nchi. 3 ondolea kizuizi/shida/matata. ~**d man** mtumwa aliyeachiwa huru. ~**dom** *n* 1 uhuru *the ~dom of the seas (international law)* haki ya meli kusafiri baharini bila kuingiliwa na manowari *give a friend the ~dom of one's house* -pa rafiki ruhusa ya kutumia nyumba kama yake. 2 hiari, chaguo. 3 **give/receive the ~dom of a town/city** -pa mtu/pokea haki zote za uraia wa mji/jiji. ~**fighter** *n* mpigania uhuru.

freebooter *n* haramia (wa baharini).

Freemason *n* mwanachama wa chama cha siri cha kusaidiana. ~**ry** *n* 1 mfumo wa chama hicho. 2 kuoneana huruma na kusaidiana baina ya watu wenye kazi moja na wa jinsi moja.

freeze *vt,vi* 1 ganda. **freezing point** *n* kiwango cha kuganda. 2 ~ **(over/up)** *(of liquids)* ganda. **make one's blood** ~ ogofya. 3 ona baridi sana. 4 ~ **(over/up)** ganda, fanya/tia baridi sana; gandisha, funika na barafu *frozen food* chakula barafu. **freezing mixture** mchanganyiko wa kugandishia. 5 dhibiti *price freezing (fin)* kusimamisha bei. 6 ~ **sb out** *(colloq)* ondosha/zima mtu kwenye biashara, jamii n.k. kwa mashindano/kutomjali n.k. 7 ~ **on to sth** *(colloq)* shikilia kitu kwa nguvu. 8 simama tuli, tulia k.m. mnyama ili kutoshtua. ~ **up** *(of an actor)* kutoweza kusema/kufanya kitu kwenye jukwaa *n* 1 kipindi cha majira ya baridi sana. 2 *(fin)* udhibiti mkali, usimamishaji wa mapato, mishahara n.k. 3 **deep**-~ sehemu ya friji ya kugandishia. ~**r** *n* friza; mashine ya barafu; chumba cha barafu.

freight *n* 1 (nauli ya) uchukuzi wa mizigo. 2 shehena, mizigo. ~ **liner** *n* meli ya mizigo. ~ **train** *(US)* treni ya mizigo *vt* ~ **with** pakia mizigo (melini); peleka/chukua mizigo. **~er** *n* meli/ndege ya mizigo.

French *adj* -a Kifaransa; -a Wafaransa; -a Ufaransa. **take ~ leave** jiondokea bila kutoa taarifa au kuruhusiwa. **~ chalk** jasi. **~ dressing** masala ya mafuta na siki. **~ fries** *n (pl. see* **chips** *n)*; **~ horn** tarumbeta sikio. **~ window** dirisha kubwa (liwezalo kutumika kama mlango) *n* Kifaransa. **the ~** Wafaransa. **~ man/woman** Mfaransa. **~ kiss** kufyonzana ulimi. **~ letter** mpira kondomu.

frenzy *n* wazimu, mhemuko *vt (usu in pp)* tia wazimu/kichaa/mhemuko.

frenzied *adj* -enye wazimu/ kichaa.

frenziedly *adv*.

frenetic *adj* -enye wayowayo, -enye msukosuko/kiherehere sana; -enye wazimu.

frequent *vt* enda (mahali) mara kwa mara; -wa/ onekana (mahali) mara kwa mara/kwa kawaida *frogs ~ wet place* vyura kwa kawaida huonekana mahali penye unyevunyevu *adj* -a mara nyingi; -a mara kwa mara, -a kawaida. **~ly** *adv*. **frequency** *n* 1 marudio, kufanyika mara kwa mara. 2 idadi ya marudio *~ meter* kipimo cha idadi ya marudio.

fresco *n* 1 fresko: uchoraji wa sanamu ukutani (wakati chokaa/lipu ingali mbichi). 2 picha/sanamu iliyochorwa namna hiyo *vt* chora sanamu kwa namna hiyo.

fresh *adj* -bichi, -pya *~ milk* maziwa mabichi. **~man** mwanafunzi mpya wa chuo kikuu. 2 *(of food)* -siotiwa chumvi; -siotiwa kwenye kopo/ kugandishwa; *(of water)* -baridi; -sio ya bahari *~ water fish* samaki wa maji baridi. 3 -pya au tofauti. **break ~ ground** *(fig)* anza kitu kipya; pata habari mpya. 4 *(of air, wind, weather)* safi; baridi; -anana. **~ breeze/wind** upepo mwanana. 5 -enye afya; -a nguvu; -a kupendeza *a ~ complexion* sura ya kupendeza (ionyeshayo afya). 6 *(US colloq)* safihi, fyosi *adv. (in hyphened compounds)* sasa hivi *~-caught fish* samaki aliyevuliwa sasa hivi. **~ly** *adv (only with pp, without hyphen)* sasa hivi *~ picked tomatoes* nyanya zilizochumwa sasa hivi. **~er** *n see* **~man**. **~ness** *n*. **~en** *vi,vt* 1 burudika; tia/pata nguvu. 2 zidi, kazana *the breeze ~ened* upepo ulizidi. **~et** *n* kijito kidogo.

fret[1] *vi,vt* 1 *(harass)* -wa na wasiwasi, jisumbua; -pa taabu, hangaisha. 2 chakaza, kwa kusugua au kutafuna *n* wasiwasi; wahaka. **~ful** *adj* -sio ridhika; -enye kiherehere. **~fully** *adv*.

fret[2] *vt* tia nakshi (kwa kuuchimba ubao). **~saw** msumeno wa nakshi. **~-work** *n* ubao uliotiwa nakshi kwa kuchimbwa.

fret[3] *n* vituta gitaa (vya kuelekezea mahali pa kubonyeza waya wa gitaa, gambusi n.k.).

Freudian *adj* -a nadharia za udodosi nafsi za Sigmund Freud. **~ slip** *(colloq)* kujikwaa, kuteleza ulimi.

friable *adj* -a kupukutika kwa urahisi. **friability** *n*.

friar *n* mtawa (wa kiume). **~y** *n* nyumba ya watawa hawa.

fricassee *n* nyama/kuku wa kupaka (anayekaangwa na kufanywa mchuzi).

friction *n* msuguano (wa vitu au mawazo).

Friday *n* Ijumaa **Good ~** Ijumaa Kuu. **man ~** mtumishi mwaminifu (kutokana na hadithi ya Robinson Kruso).

fridge *n see* **refrigerator**

fried *pp, pt of* **fry**.

friend *n* 1 rafiki, sahibu. **be ~s with/ make ~s/make a ~ of** fanya urafiki. **a ~ in need is a ~ in deed** akupendaye kwa dhiki ndiye rafiki. 2 tabia au kitu kinachosaidia. 3 msaidizi, mfadhili. 4 **F ~** *(rel)* mwanachama wa Ushirika wa Marafiki. **~liness** *n*. **~ly** *adj* -a kirafiki, -ema *be ~ to a cause* wa rahisi kukubali; wa tayari kusaidia. **~ nation** taifa rafiki *in a ~ way* kirafiki *F~ Society* Chama cha kusaidiana.

~**ship** *n* urafiki, usuhuba.
frieze *n* ukanda wa nakshi uwekwao kiambazani (agh. juu).
frigate *n (GB)* manowari sindikiza; *(US)* manowari ya ukubwa wa kati.
fright *n* 1 hofu, tisho. **get a** ~ shtuka. **give sb a** ~ shtusha mtu. 2 *(colloq)* mtu/kitu cha kuchekesha *vt (poet)* tisha. ~**en** *vt* ogofya, shtua, tisha. ~ **sb into sth** tisha mtu kufanya kitu ~ *away* kimbiza, fukuza. ~**ened** *adj* -liotishwa. ~**ful** *adj* 1 -a kutisha, -a kitisho, -a kuogofya. 2 *(unpleasant)* -baya, -a kuchukiza. ~**fully** *adv* sana.
frigid *adj* 1 baridi ~ *zone* ukanda wa baridi. 2 *(of a woman)* hanithi, -sio na ashiki. 3 *(of manner)* baridi, si -kunjufu. ~**ly** *adv*. ~**ity** *n*.
frill *n* 1 marinda ya pindo. 2 *(pl)* madoido *put on* ~*s* deka, fanya madaha *vt* tia, funga virinda vikunjo/kunjamana. ~**ing** *n* marinda. ~**ed** *adj* -enye virinda. ~ *adj (colloq)* -enye urembo/marinda mengi.
fringe *n* 1 matamvua; taraza. 2 shore. 3 ukingo, pembezoni, pembeni. ~ **area** mpakani. ~ **benefits** marupurupu. ~ **group** kikundi ndani ya kundi; *(fig)* sehemu isiyo muhimu sana *vt, vi* tia matamvua, tarizi; -wa mpaka/ukingo.
frippery *n* mavazi ya umaridadi kupita kiasi; takataka; *(pl)* mapambo hafifu/ya ovyo (kwenye nguo, nyumba n.k.).
frisk *vt,vi* 1 chachawa, randa, rukaruka. 2 papasa (kutafuta silaha n.k.) *n* mruko, mchezo (wa kurukaruka). ~**iness** *n*. ~**y** *adj*.
frisson *n (F)* msisimko.
fritter[1] *vt* ~**sth away/(down)** fuja, poteza.
fritter[2] *n* kaimati.
frivol *vt,vi* 1 fanya upuuzi, shughulika na mambo yasiyo na maana. 2 ~ **away one's time/money** poteza wakati/fedha kipuuzi. ~**ous** *adj* 1 -a kipuuzi. 2 *(of persons)* -sio na makini; -enye kupenda anasa; puuzi. ~**ity** *n* 1 upuuzi. 2 *(pl)* maneno/ mambo yasiyo na maana. ~**ly** *adj*.
frizz *vt (of hair)* sokota, sokoteka *n* hali ya kusokoteka. ~**y** *adj*.
frizzle *vt,vi* 1 toa sauti ya kukaanga kwa mafuta. 2 kaanga; chachatika.
fro *adv*. **to and** ~ kwenda na kurudi; mbele na nyuma.
frock *n* 1 gauni. 2 kanzu, vazi la mtawa.
frog[1] *n* chura. **have** ~ **in the throat** koroma. ~**man** mpiga mbizi. ~ **march** *vt* chukua (mfungwa) kifudifudi kwa kushikwa na watu wanne; sukuma mtu mbele (kwa kushika mikono yake nyuma). ~**gy** *adj*.
frog[2] *n* ala, kipande cha ukanda cha kuchomeka upanga au singe.
frolic *n* 1 kuchezacheza. 2 masihara, mzaha. ~**king** chezacheza, rukaruka. ~**some** *adj*.
from *(prep)* 1 *(from a place, starting point)* toka, kutoka *he is* ~ *Tarime* ametoka Tarime *he is* ~ *home* ametoka nyumbani *where are you* ~ umetoka wapi? 2 *(starting a period of time) in the past* tangu ~ *childhood* tangu utotoni ~ *that day* tangu siku ile ~ *the beginning to the end* tangu mwanzo hadi mwisho; *(in the future)* kuanzia ~ *tomorrow* kuanzia kesho. 3 *(showing giver, sender etc)* kutoka kwa *a letter* ~ *my mother* barua kutoka kwa mama yangu. 4 *(separation, removal, prevention, escape)* toka *released* ~ *prison* achiliwa kutoka gerezani *refrain* ~ *laughing* jizuia kucheka *a shelter* ~ *the rain* kinga ya mvua. 5 *(showing lower limit)* kuanzia *mangoes sell* ~ *shs 10/=* .embe zinauzwa kuanzia shilingi kumi. 6 *(source taken from)* -tokana na; kutoka kwa *ideas drawn* ~ *Shaaban Robert* mawazo yanayotokana na Shaaban Robert. 7 *(material used in process) the bridge is made* ~ *steel* daraja limetengenezwa kwa chuma *(change) the price has risen* ~ *20/= to 30/=* bei imepanda kutoka sh 20/= hadi 30/=. 8 *(distinction or*

difference) distinguish the good ~ the bad pambanua wema na ubaya *(reason, cause, motive)* kwa sababu ya *what does it stem ~?* sababu yake nini? ~ **fatigue** kutokana na uchovu. 9 *(judging by)* kwa kuangalia, kutokana na ~ *her appearance you would think she was young* kwa kuangalia umbo lake ungedhani ni kijana. 10 (with *adv & prep phrases)* ~ **above/ below** toka juu/chini. ~ **afar** toka mbali. ~ **over there** toka kule.

frond *n* kuti.

front *n* 1 **the** ~ mbele; upande ulio muhimu. ~ **page news** habari muhimu (ziwekwazo ukurasa wa kwanza wa gazeti). **(be) in the ~ rank** *(fig)* -wa mashuhuri; julikana. ~ **runner** anayeongoza. **come to the** ~ *(fig)* jitokeza; julikana, fahamika. **in** ~ *adv* mbele, **in ~ of** *prep* mbele ya. ~ **runner** *n (in elections etc)* -enye kuelekea kushinda. 2 *(war)* medani, uwanja. *(fig)* **domestic** ~ *(colloq)* nyumbani. 3 barabara ya ufukoni/ pwani. 4 **have the ~ (to do sth)** -wa juvi, thubutu (kwa ubaya). **put on/show/present a bold** ~ kabili jambo kwa ujasiri. 5 **(shirt)** ~ kifua. 6 *(theatre)* ukumbi. 7 *(met)* mpaka baina ya tungamo hewa ya baridi na ya uvuguvugu. 8 *(poet, rhet)* paji, uso. 9 kiongozi au kikundi cha watu kinachoficha njama za mtu fulani. 10 *(polit.)* umoja. *vt,vi* 1 tazama; elekea *the hotel ~s the ocean* hoteli inaelekea bahari. 2 *(old use)* kabili, pinga. **~age** *n* 1 upande wa mbele wa (nyumba, shamba). 2 upande unaoelekea barabarani (njiani n.k.). **~al** *adj* -a mbele ~ *attack* shambulio la ana kwa ana, pigo la usoni *n* mbele.

frontier *n* 1 mpaka ~ *disputes* ugomvi wa mpaka. **~(s) man** *n* mtu wa mpakani; mwanzilishi wa makazi karibu na mpaka. 2 *(fig)* kikomo; mpaka (kati ya yanayofahamika na yasiyofahamika).

frontispiece *n* picha ya mwanzo kitabuni.

frost *n* 1 jalidi. **~-bite** ugonjwa wa kuganda tishu kwa jalidi. **~-bitten** -enye ugonjwa wa jalidi. **~-bound** *adj (of the ground)* -enye jalidi. 2 theluji nyembamba. 3 *(colloq)* jambo lisilofanikiwa *vt,vi* 1 gandisha; *(of cake)* ikiza. 2 ua, haribu mimea kwa jalidi. 3 fifisha kioo kisione. 4 ~ **(over/up)** funika kwa theluji, jalidi. **~ing** *n* kuikiza. **~y** *adj* 1 -a baridi kali. 2 *(fig)* -sio kunjufu; baridi. **~ily** *adv*. **~iness** *n*.

froth *n* 1 povu, fuo. 2 *(folly)* upuuzi *vt,vi* toa povu, foka, umuka. **~y** *adj*. **~ily** *adv*. **~iness** *n*.

froward *adj (arch)* -kaidi, -korofi, -asi, -siosikia.

frown *vi* 1 kunja kipaji. 2 ~ **on/upon** chukia; sinya, -topendelea *gambling is very much ~ed upon here* kamari inakatazwa kabisa hapa. **~ing** *n*. **~ingly** *adv*.

frowsty *adj* -enye hewa nzito; -a kuvu.

frowzy *adj* 1 -a kunuka, -enye uvundo. 2 chafu, kuukuu.

froze *pp,pt of* **freeze**.

fructify *vt,vi* zaa (mmea), zalisha, rutubisha, (fanya) kutoa faida (mavuno), fanikisha. **fructification** *n*.

frugal *adj* ~ **(of)** wekevu, -angalifu (hasa katika matumizi ya chakula/ fedha); -a kudunduiza. **~ly** *adv*. **~ity** *n*.

fruit *n* 1 tunda, ~ **cake** *n* keki ya matunda. ~ **fly** nzi-tunda ~ *fritter (s) n* kaimati ya tunda. ~ **salad** *n* saladi ya matunda. **the ~s of the earth** mazao ya ardhi. *(fig often pl)* faida. 2 mafanikio; matokeo. 3 **~-machine** *n (GB colloq)* mashine (ya kuchezesha kamari ya sarafu). **~erer** *n* muuza matunda. **~ful** *adj* -a kuzaa matunda; -a faida; *(fig)* -enye matokeo mazuri. **~fully** *adv*. **~fulness** *n*. **~less** *adj* bure, -sio na matunda; *(fig)* -sio na mafanikio. **~lessly** *adv*. **~le(s)sness** *n*. **~y** *adj* 1 -a kama tunda. 2 *(colloq)* -a kuchekesha (agh kwa mambo ya ngono). 3 *(colloq)* kali, zito *He has a ~ voice* ana sauti nzito. **~ion** *n* 1 kufaulu; kupevuka. 2 kuzaa matunda, kupata mafanikio.

frumenty *n* uji wa ngano.

frump *n* mtu anayevaa mitindo ya zamani isiyovutia. **~ish** *adj*. **~ y** *adj*.

frustrate *vt* zuia mtu asifanye atakavyo, vunja moyo, katisha tamaa; pinga (mipango isifanyike). **frustration** *n*.

fry[1] *vt, vi* kaanga *fried chicken* kuku wa kukaangwa. **~ing-pan** *n* kikaango. **out of the ~ing-pan into the fire** toka katika tatizo moja na kuingia jingine kubwa zaidi, ruka majivu ukanyage makaa *fryer/frier* kuku mchanga afaaye kwa kukaanga.

fry[2] *n* 1 samaki wachanga. 2 **small ~** chekechea; watu wasio muhimu.

fuck *vt, vi (taboo word sl)* tomba. **~ about** zubaa, chezacheza. **~ (it)!** tamko la kuonyesha hasira, vuruga. **~ off** toka. **~ sth up** haribu. **~ all** *n* bure *I did ~ all* nilifanya kazi bure, sikufanya kitu *n* kutomba *I dont care/give a ~* sijali kitu/kabisa. **~er** *n* mpumbavu. **~ing** *adj*. **~ing well** hasa, hakika.

fuddle *vt* pumbaza, lewesha. **get ~d** lewa *n* ulevi, kuchanganyikiwa.

fuddy-duddy *(n (colloq)* mzee msumbufu, zee.

fudge *n* 1 peremende laini ya maziwa, sukari na chakleti. 2 *int (dated)* upuuzi. 3 udanganyifu katika kazi *vi, vt* 1 vuka mpaka; danganya, ibia. 2 -totimiza ahadi, shindwa; kwepa.

fuel *n* fueli (k.m. kuni, makaa, mafuta n.k.); *(fig)*kichochezi, kichochea *vt, vi* tia/pata fueli. **add ~ to the flames** chochea/palilia.

fug *n* ufukuto (wa hewa mbaya chumbani), hewa nzito. **~gy** *adj* -enye ufukuto.

fugacious *adj* -a kupita, -a kutoweka (baada ya muda mfupi). **fugacity** *n*.

fugitive *n* ~ **(from)** mtoro, mkimbizi *adj* 1 -a kupita. 2 -toro.

fulcrum *n* egemeo (la wenzo).

fulfil *vt* timiza, maliza, kamilisha. **~ment** *n*.

fulgent *adj (poet or rhet)* -a kung'aa, -a kuwaka, -enye mwangaza.

fuliginous *adj* -enye masizi, -a giza kidogo.

full[1] *adj* 1 ~ **(of)** -liojaa; tele. **~ up** pomoni; *(colloq) (from excessive eating)* liovimbiwa. 2 ~ **of** -liokaa akilini, -a kushughulisha/kufikiria mno *she was ~ of a trip* safari ilimkaa sana akilini; *he is ~ of himself* anajipenda, anajivuna. 3 nene, kibonge, tipwatipwa *a girl with a ~ figure* msichana tipwatipwa, -liojaa. 4 *(of clothes)* pana, -a kuvalika kwa urahisi. 5 -nayofikia kiwango kinachohitajika; -enye kukomaa, -zima. 6 kamili. 7 *(phrases and compounds)* **at ~ speed** kwa kasi zote. **in ~** kikamilifu. **in ~ career** -lio katika upeo wa maendeleo. **to the ~** kwa ukamilifu. **~ back** *n (in football)* mlinzi, beki. **~ blooded** *adj* shababi, -enye nguvu na uchangamfu; menyu. **~ blown** *(of flowers)* -liochanua. **~ board** *(in a hotel)* -enye kutoa malazi na chakula. **~ dress** *n* vazi rasmi *~-dress rehearsal* zoezi lenye mavazi rasmi. **~ face** *adj* uso kwa uso, uelekeano wa ana kwa ana **~ fashioned** *adj (trade use, of garments)* -a kupima, -liotengenezwa kwa kufuata gimba. **~ fledged** *adj (of a bird)* -enye kuweza kuruka; *(fig)* -liokubuhu, -liotopea. **~ grown** *adj* -liokomaa. **~ house** *n* kujaa kabisa. **~ length** *adj (of a portrait)* -zima, -nayoonyesha -ote; -a urefu wa kawaida. **~ marks** *n (pl)* alama zote. **~ moon** *n* mwezi mchimbu/mpevu. **~ page** ukurasa mzima. **~ scale** *adj (of drawings, plans etc)* -a kipimo sawa na kitu chenyewe; halisi; *(colloq)* kamili. **~ stop** nukta, kituo kikubwa. **come to a ~ stop** simama kabisa. **~ time** *n* kamili *adj* -a kudumu, -a muda wote. **~ time worker** mtumishi wa kudumu. **~y** *adv* 1 kwa ukamilifu;

kabisa. 2 angalau. ~**ness** *n*. **in the ~ness of time** kwa wakati uliopangwa/ tegemewa; mwishowe.

full[2] *vt* takasa nguo. ~**ler** *n* mtakasa nguo. ~**ers earth** udongo wa mfinyanzi (wa kutakasia vitambaa).

fulminate *vi* foka; vuvumka; lipuka. ~ **(against)** kemea, pinga vikali, shutumu. **fulminant** *adj* -enye kuvuvumka. **fulmination** *n*. **fulminator** *n*. **fulminatory** *adj*.

fulness *see* **fullness**.

fulsome *adj (of praise, flattery, etc)* mno, -enye kuvisha kilemba cha ukoka ~ *praise* sifa za kinafiki/ uongo. ~**ly** *adv*.

fumarole *n* ufa mdogo kwenye mlima wa volkano (unapopitia mvuke).

fumble *vt,vi* 1 papasa, tafutatafuta. 2 babaisha, babia; shughulikia jambo kwa wasiwasi, bila kujiamini. ~**r** *n*.

fume *n (US pl)* 1 harufu kali ya moshi, mvuke mzito, fukizo. 2 *(liter)* hangaiko, kiherehere. 3 hasira, ghadhabu *vt,vi* 1 ~ **(at)** toa mvuke, fuka moshi *pass away in ~s* kasirika; *(fig)* foka, onyesha hasira, kasirika. 2 *(of wood, etc)* tia moshi, fukiza. **fumigate** *vt* 1 fukiza, tia buhuri ~ *tomato plants* fukiza miche ya nyanya. **fumigation** *n* ufukizaji. **fumigator** *n*.

fun *n* 1 kujifurahisha, burudani, mchezo, raha *there is plenty of ~ out here* kuna burudani nyingi sana hapa *I don't see the ~ of it* ni kipi cha kuchekesha. **have ~** furahia; starehe. ~**-fair** *n* kiwanja cha michezo. ~ **and games** *(colloq)* mzaha, burudani za kuchangamsha. **make ~ of; poke ~ at** fanyia mzaha, tania; dhihaki. **for/in ~** kwa utani, kwa mzaha, kwa kujifurahisha. 2 jambo/mtu anayefurahisha, kichekesho. 3 *(attr. colloq)* -a kuchekesha *a ~ hat* kofia ya kuchekesha/ kufurahisha. ~**ny** *adj* 1 -a kuchekesha *he is trying to be ~* anajaribu kufanya mzaha. **a ~ man** mtu wa kuchekesha; mcheshi. 2 -geni, -a ajabu -sio sawa, -gumu kufahamika *there is sth ~ about this letter* kuna jambo lisiloeleweka katika barua hii. ~ **-bone** *n* mfupa wa kiko unaopitisha neva-ulna. ~ **business** *(sl)* udanganyifu. ~ **farm** *(sl)* hospitali ya magonjwa ya kichwa/ akili. **the ~nies** *(pl)* katuni. ~**nily** *adv* ~ *enough* ajabu ni kwamba. ~**niness** *n*.

funambulist *n* mwana sarakasi (anayetembea juu ya kamba).

function *n* 1 shughuli, kazi *~s of marketing* shughuli za mauzo. 2 *(ceremony)* tamasha, adhimisho. 3 *(maths)* namba tegemezi. 4 kazi *vt* fanya kazi, faa; shughulika *the telephone is not ~ing* simu haifanyi kazi. ~**al** *adj* -a kufaa kazi, -enye kuathiri/inayohusu kazi; -a kutenda, -a kazi maalum. ~ **head** kiongozi mtendaji. ~**alism** *n* utenzi, utendaji: kanuni/nadharia inayodai kuwa kazi ya kitu itawale muundo na vifaa vyake. ~**alist** *n*. ~**ary** *n (pl ~* **ries***) (often derog)* mtendaji (wa shughuli za kiofisi), mtenzi mrasimu.

fund *n* 1 *(of commonsense /humour/ amusing stories)* hazina *a ~ of funny stories* hazina ya hadithi za kufurahisha. 2 *(often pl)* mfuko wa fedha, hazina (kwa makusudi maalum) *school ~s* mfuko wa shule. **public ~s** mfuko wa serekali; fedha ya serikali *reserve ~s* mfuko wa akiba. ~ *raising* kuchangisha fedha. **no ~s** taarifa (ya benki) kuwa mwandika hundi hana fedha kwenye akaunti yake *vt* 1 fadhili, gharimia. 2 *(fin)* badili deni la muda mfupi kuwa la muda mrefu kwa riba maalum.

fundamental *adj* ~ **(to)** -a asili, -a msingi, -a muhimu *n* msingi, asili, kanuni. **the ~s** misingi na kanuni. ~**ly** *adv*. ~**ism** *n* hifadhi ya misingi ya dini ya Kikristo, ulokole. ~**ist** *n* mfuasi wa misingi ya kale ya dini ya Kikristo *religious ~ists* waumini wakereketwa.

funeral *n* 1 mazishi; maziko *provide a ~* zika *attend a ~* hudhuria mazishi *perform ~ service (Muslims)* soma talakini. 2 *(attr use)* kwa/-a mazishi/maziko *a ~ procession* msafara wa mazishi *a ~ parlor (US)* ofisi inayoshughulikia mazishi. **it's/that's my/your ~** *(colloq)* hilo ni shauri langu/lako. **funereal** *adj* 1 -a (kufaa) mazishi. 2 -a huzuni, -a kusikitisha.

fungus *n* **~es** 1 ukungu, kuvu. 2 *(mushroom like growth)* uyoga, kiyoga. **fungicide** *n* kiua kuvu, dawa ya kuvu. **fungoid** *adj* -a kuvu. **fungous** *adj* -a kuvu, -nayoletwa na kuvu. **fungal** *adj.*

funicular *adj* **~ (railway)** reli iliyo katika mwinamo/mteremko, (inayoendeshwa kwa waya na injini).

funk *n (colloq)* 1 hofu kuu, woga mkubwa *be in a ~* ogopa sana. 2 mwoga ~-hole *n* handaki, mbinu za kuepea kulitumikia jeshi *v,vi* 1 ogopa, onyesha woga; kwepa/ shindwa (kwa woga) *we ~ ed telling him the truth* tulikwepa/shindwa kumwambia ukweli. **~y** *adj (US sl) (of music)* -enye hisia na mdundo.

funnel *n* 1 bomba, faneli. 2 *(of ship etc)* dohani *two/three ~ed* -enye dohani mbili/tatu *vt,vi* penya/pita kama katika faneli/dohani.

fur *n* 1 manyoya (ya mnyama), nywele ndogondogo. **make the ~ fly** fanya fujo. **~ and feather** wanyama na ndege wa manyoya. 2 ngozi ya wanyama yenye manyoya (hasa iliyotengenezwa nguo) *(attr) a ~ coat* koti la manyoya. 3 utando (ukoga, uchafu) wa ulimi. **~ry** *adj* -enye manyoya; -enye utando. **~rier** *n* mwuzaji/mtengenezaji ngozi za manyoya.

furbish *vt* ng'arisha, sugua, safisha, fanya kama mpya.

furcate *adj* -a panda; -a kugawanyika. **furcation** *n.*

furl *vt,vi (of sails, flags, umbrellas etc)* kunja, kunjika.

furlong *n* yadi 220, mita 201, sehemu moja ya nane (⅛) ya maili moja.

furlough *n* likizo, livu (ya kupumzika kwa watumishi wanaokaa ughaibu).

furnace *n* 1 tanuu. 2 kalibu *blast ~* tanuu *house-heating~* tanuu la joto.

furnish *vt* **~ sth (to sb); ~ sb/sth with sth** toa/-pa/patia, pasha mtukitu/habari; nunua/weka samani, fanicha. **~ed with** -enye samani/fanicha. **~ed house** nyumba yenye fanicha. **~ings** *n (pl)* fanicha na vyombo.

furniture *n* fanicha, samani.

furore (US furor) *n* makelele, vifijo *create a ~* piga vifijo, tia msisimko.

furrow *n* 1 mfuo, mtaro, mkondo. 2 *(wrinkle, crease)* kunjo, finyo, kunyanzi *vt* tengeneza mfuo; tia makunyanzi *(fig) ~ one's brow* kunja uso.

furry *see* **fur**.

further *adv,adj* 1 *(often used for farther)* mbali, mbele zaidi *don't go ~ than here* usiende mbali zaidi ya hapa. 2 *(not interchangeable in this sense with farther)* zaidi, ziada *what ~ news do you have* una habari gani zaidi *until ~ notice* hadi baadaye. 3 *(also further - more)* zaidi ya hayo, pia *vt* saidia, endeleza *~ your studies* endeleza masomo yako. **~ance** *n* maendeleo, ukuzaji. **~more** *adv* juu ya hayo, zaidi ya hayo, zaidi. **~most** *adj* mbali kabisa.

furtive *adj* 1 -a siri, -a kufichaficha, -a kichini chini *a ~ glance* mtazamo wa siri. **~ly** *adv.* **~ness** *n.*

fury *n* 1 *(anger)* ghadhabu, kiruu. 2 harara. **furious** *adj* -a ghadhabu, -enye hasira, -kali mno, -a nguvu sana *the fun became fast and furious* mchezo ulipamba moto hasa *get furious* ghadhibika. **furiously** *adv.* 3 *(of wind)* dhoruba, tufani. 4 mwanamke mkali.

fuse *vt,vi* 1 yeyusha; yeyuka. 2 ungana, unganisha. 3 *(electric)* katika (waya wa fuzi) *n (electric) n* fyuzi. **time ~** fyuzi inayolipuka katika muda uliotegeshwa. **fusibility** *n.* **fusible** *adj.*

fusion *n* kuunganisha; kuyeyusha;

mchanganyiko. ~ **bomb** bomu (kama) la haidrojeni.
fuselage *n* kiunzi cha ndege/ eropleni.
fusillade *n (US)* mfululizo wa kupiga bunduki.
fuss *n* msukosuko, mhangaiko, wasiwasi, kiherehere. **make a ~** hangaika; lalamika; ingiwa na wasiwasi. **make a ~ of sb** sumbukia, hangaikia. **kick up a ~** leta fujo kwa ajili ya mtu. **~pot** *n (colloq)* machagu *vi,vt* hangaisha; tia wasiwasi; hangaika; sumbuka sana. **~y** *adj* 1 -enye kuhangaika; -enye kusumbuka mno, -enye kuchagua, -enye madoido mno, -enye mapambo mno. **~ily** *adv*. **~ iness** *n*.
fustian *n* 1 kitambaa kizito cha pamba. 2 *(fig)* makeke; mikogo *adj* -a maringo; bure.
fusty *adj* 1 -enye kunuka ubichi/ ukuvu/ukungu/unyevunyevu. 2 *(fig)* -enye mawazo ya kizamani. **fustiness** *n*.
futile *adj* 1 -isioleta manufaa, -sio na maana, -isiyofanikiwa chochote. 2 *(ofpersons')* -siyefanya lolote la maana. **futility** *n*.
future *adj* 1 -a baadaye, -takaokuja *the ~ life* ahera, kesho *n* 1 wakati ujao. **for the ~** wa siku za baadaye. 2 mategemeo ya baadaye *this job has no ~* kazi hii haina mategemeo. **in ~** tangu leo, hapo baadaye. 3 *(pl) (comm)* bidhaa zilizonunuliwa lakini zitakazolipwa baadaye. **~less** isio na mafanikio baadaye. **futurism** usasa: falsafa na mtindo wa sanaa unaokwenda na wakati/upingao mambo ya zamani na ya mapokeo. **futurist** *n* msanii wa tapo la kilele. **futuristic** *adj*. **futurity** *n (pl)* **futurities** wakati ujao, matukio ya baadaye.
fuze *see* **fuse**.
fuzz *n* 1 sufi, (kitu) timtimu. 2 **the ~** *(US) (sl)* polisi. **~y** 1 *adj* timtimu, -enye kutuna na kujifumba; -liofunikwa na nywele za kipilipili. 2 *(of image)* -sio dhahiri, -siobainika au kutambulika sawasawa. **~iness** *n*.

G

G,g herufi ya saba ya alfabeti ya Kiingereza; *(US sl)* dola elfu moja.

gab *n (colloq)* porojo. **stop your ~** *(sl)* nyamaza. **have the gift of the ~** -wa na kipaji cha kuzungumza *vt (colloq)* piga porojo. **~by** *adj* -enye porojo.

gabardine/gaberdine *n* gabadini: aina ya kitambaa cha sufu laini na imara.

gabble *vt,vi* sema upesi upesi bila kutamka vizuri maneno, tatanika; *(of traditional doctor)* rogonya *n* msemo usioeleweka; urogonyaji.

gable *n* ukuta wa pembetatu katikati ya paa la nyumba ya mgongo. **a ~ house** nyumba ya mgongo.

gad *vi* **~ about** *(colloq)* tangatanga, zurura kutafuta buruda. **~ about** *n* mzururaji.

gadfly *n* 1 nzi (anayeuma ng'ombe/ farasi), pange. 2 mtu anayeudhi wengine makusudi kwa chokochoko na uchokozi, mtu mwenye gubu.

gadget *n (colloq)* kifaa cha kazi kidogo, kidude. **~ry** *n* ala, zana (zote) pamoja.

gaff[1] *n* uloo *vt* vua kwa uloo.

gaff[2] *n* **blow the ~** *(sl)* toa siri; *(US) stand the ~* vumilia.

gaffe *n* kosa; tendo la kutia aibu.

gaffer *n* 1 *(colloq)* msimamizi, mnyapara. 2 mzee, shaibu.

gag *n* 1 kifaa cha kuweka mdomoni (ili kinywa kikae wazi). 2 maneno anayoongezewa mtu na mwigizaji, ufaraguzi wa ziada. 3 kichekesho, hadithi ya kuchekesha *vt,vi* 1 tia kifaa (tambara, pamba n.k.) kinywani; nyamazisha; *(fig)* nyima uhuru wa kujieleza/kusema. 2 ingizia maneno/ semea. 3 *(colloq)* tapika (kiuongo).

gaga *adj* punguani.

gage[1] *n (old use)* 1 dhamana; ahadi, amana. 2 glavu/changamoto ya kupigana (kushindana), mwaliko wa kupigana (kushindana). **throw down the ~ to sb** alika mtu kupigana *vt (old use)* weka amana, rehani; weka ahadi.

gage[2] *n* see **gauge**.

gaggle *n* 1 kundi la mabata Bukini. 2 *(hum)* kundi la wasichana/ wanawake wasemi.

gaiety *n* 1 uchangamfu; shamrashamra. 2 sherehe; maadhimisho; tafrija.

gaily *adv see* **gay**.

gain *n* 1 ongezeko la mali/uwezo/ nguvu; chumo, pato, faida. **ill-gotten ~s** faida/pato lisilo halali *a ~ in wealth* ongezeko la utajiri *a ~ in strength* ongezeko la nguvu. **~ful** *adj* -a pato, -enye kuzalisha mali/fedha. **~fully** *adv* -kwa manufaa, kwa faida *vt,vi* 1 pata; chuma; ongeza *~ experience* pata uzoefu *~ weight* nenepa *~ wealth* chuma mali. ~ **ground** piga hatua. ~ **time** chelewesha kwa hila kwa manufaa yako, vuta muda, pata muda zaidi wa kufanya jambo baada ya kuchelewa. ~ **the upper hand** shinda. 2 ~ **(from)** faidi *he ~ed a lot from his trip* alifaidi sana kutokana na safari yake. 3 *(of a watch or clock)* -enda haraka, kimbia *our clock ~s four minutes a day* saa yetu hukimbia dakika nne kwa siku. 4 ~ **on/upon** karibiana na, sogelea, pita, fika mbele kabla/mbele ya; enda kasi kuliko; *(of the sea)* momonyoa ardhi. 5 fika mahali (baada ya juhudi). **~ings** *n (pl)* tija; pato; ushindi.

gainsay *vt (liter) (chiefly in neg and interr)* kana, kaidi *there's no ~ing* haipingiki, hakuna upinzani, haikanikiki.

gainst *(poet) see* **against**.

gait *n* mwendo *an unsteady ~* mwendo wa kupepesuka, kuyumbayumba.

gal *n (dated colloq)* msichana.

gala *n* tamasha, shangwe *(attrib) a ~ day* siku ya shangwe/fete *~ week* wiki ya shangwe/fete.

galantine *n* nyama nyeupe ya mifupa (iliyoungwa, ikakunjwa, ikapikwa na kuliwa baridi).

galaxy *n (pl -xies)* 1 kundi la nyota. **the G ~** kundi la nyota na sayari ikiwemo yetu. 2 kundi la watu mashuhuri/wazuri. **galactic** *adj (astron)* -a galaksi, -a falaki kubwa angani.

gale *n* 1 upepo mkali, dhoruba *it is blowing a* ~ kuna dhoruba. 2 mpasuko wa kelele *a ~ of laughter* kicheko kikubwa.

gall[1] *n* 1 nyongo. ~ **bladder** *n* kibofu nyongo. ~ **stone** jiwe: ugumu unaoota kwenye nyongo. 2 uchungu, chuki. 3 *(colloq)* ufidhuli.

gall[2] *n (of an animal esp a horse)* lengelenge, kidonda, chubuko *vt* 1 chubua, kwaruza. 2 *(fig)* tweza, dhilisha; umiza.

gall[3] *n* kinundu cha mti kinachooteshwa na wadudu.

gallant *adj* 1 shujaa, hodari. 2 *(gay)* -zuri, bora, -a fahari. 3 *(chivalrous)* -enye kuheshimu/kujali wanawake *n* 1 maridadi, mshaufu (anayejali/ heshimu sana wanawake). ~**ly** *adv*. ~**ry** *n* 1 ushujaa. 2 kujali/kupendelea/ kuheshimu wanawake. 3 *(pl -ries)* matendo/maneno ya kupamba/ kubemba.

galleon *n* jahazi kubwa la zamani (la Kihispania).

gallery *n* 1 nyumba ya sanaa. 2 watu wakaao kwenye viti rahisi vya juu kwenye thieta. **play to the** ~ jipendekeza kwa umma. 3 *(in theatre, church etc)* orofa ya juu. 4 ujia (mrefu mwembamba) ulioezekwa juu. 5 chumba kirefu na chembamba. 6 njia (ya mlalo ndani ya machimbo ya madini).

galley *n* 1 *(hist)* manchani inayoendeshwa na watumwa au wahalifu. ~ **slave** *n* mtumwa aliyehukumiwa kuvuta makasia katika manchani. 2 trei ya kuwekea herufi. ~ **proof** *n* gali: chapa ya kwanza katika kipande kirefu cha karatasi.

Gallic *adj* -a Wafaransa; -a Ufaransa; -a Kifaransa. ~**ism** neno/msemo wa Kifaransa katika lugha ya kigeni.

gallivant *vi* ~ **about/off** *(not used in the simple tenses)* tangatanga, tembeatembea, zurura, chungachunga (kutafuta burudani).

gallon *n* galoni, lita 4½

gallop *n (of a horse, etc)* mwendo wa shoti *at full* ~ mbio sana *vt,vi* 1 enda shoti, endesha shoti. 2 fanya (soma, enda n.k.) kwa haraka, chapuka.

gallows *n (pl) (usu with sing v)* kiunzi cha miti cha kunyongea. ~ **bird** *n* mtu anayefikiriwa anastahili kunyongwa *send sb to the* ~ hukumu mtu kunyongwa.

Gallup poll *n* kura fatiishi; kura ya kupima mawazo ya watu juu ya masuala mbalimbali (kwa kuuliza kikundi kiwakilishi cha watu).

galore *adv* kwa wingi, teletele.

galoshes *n (pl)* **(pair of)** ~ mabuti ya mvua (yanayovaliwa juu ya viatu).

galumph *vi (colloq)* rukaruka kwa furaha kuu.

galvanize *vt* 1 paka madini (chuma, bati). ~**d iron sheet** bati. 2 ~ **sb (into doing sth)** shtua, amsha. **galvanization** *n*. **galvanometer** *n* galvanometa. **galvanism** *n* nguvu ya umeme kutoka kwenye betri. **galvanic** *adj* 1 -a nguvu ya umeme wa betri. 2 *(fig) (of smiles, movements, etc)* -liotokea ghafla.

gambit *n* 1 mwanzo wa mchezo wa sataranji. 2 *(fig)* mwanzo wa jambo (shughuli).

gamble *vi,vt* 1 cheza kamari; bahatisha. ~ **away one's fortune** poteza mali kwa kamari *n* kubahatisha *it's pure* ~ ni kubahatisha tu. **take a ~ (on sth)** jaribu bahati. ~**r** *n* mchezaji kamari; mtu anayebahatisha. **gambling** *n* kucheza kamari. **gambling den/house** *n* mahali pa kuchezea kamari/nyumba ya kamari.

gambol *n (usu pl)* mruko, kuchachawa *vi* rukaruka, chachawa.

game[1] *n* 1 mchezo (wenye sheria/ kanuni). **be off one's** ~ -tokuwa katika hali nzuri ya kucheza. **have the ~ in one's hands** -wa na hakika ya kushinda. **play the** ~ fuata kanuni ya mchezo; *(fig)* -wa wazi na mwaminifu ~*s master/mistress* mwalimu wa michezo shuleni.

~**smanship** *n (colloq)* mbinu ya kushinda michezo. 2 vyombo vya kuchezea bao n.k. 3 *(international contest)Olympic/Commonwealth/East African G~s* Michezo ya Olympiki/Madola/AfrikaMashariki.4 *(single round in some contests e.g. tennis)* raundi *win five ~s in the first set* shinda raundi tano katika seti ya kwanza. 5 *(scheme, plan)* hila, shauri *play a dangerous ~* -wa na shabaha yenye hatari/hila za kichinichini. **beat sb at his own ~** shinda mtu katika ujanja wake. **make ~ of sb** fanyia mzaha/dhihaki mtu *the ~ is up* mambo (njama) yamefichuka *don't play ~s with me* usinichezee, usinidanganye. **give the ~ away** toa siri/ nia. **play sb's ~** endeleza hila/ mpango wa mtu (bila kujua). 6 *(collective)* mawindo, wanyama/ ndege wa kuwinda. **big ~** wanyama wakubwa (agh. tembo, simba, nyati n.k.). **fair ~** wanyama wanaoruhusiwa kuwindwa; *(fig)* mtu/ shirika linaloweza kukosolewa/kushutumiwa. ~ **bag** mfuko wa mawindo. ~ **bird** ndege wa kuwinda. ~ **cock** kuchi. ~ **keeper** mlinzi wa wanyama/ndege wa kuwinda. ~**laws/act** sheria za kuhifadhi wanyama. ~ **licence** leseni ya kuwinda na kuua wanyama wa kuwinda. ~ **reserve** hifadhi ya wanyama. **gamy** *adj* -enye harufu ya wanyama pori.

game[2] *adj* shujaa. **be ~ for/to do sth** -wa tayari. ~**ly** *adv* kwa uhodari, kwa ushujaa.

game[3] *vi,vt* cheza kamari. **gaming house/room/table** nyumba ya kamari iliyokatiwa leseni.

game[4] *adj (of arm, leg)* -enye kilema.

gamete *n* gameti: seli pevu za uzazi.

gamma *n* gama: herufi ya tatu ya alfabeti ya Kigiriki. ~**-rays** miali gama.

gammon *n* paja la nguruwe (na sehemu ya mgongo); nyama ya nguruwe iliyokaushwa kwa moshi *vt* kausha kwa moshi nyama ya nguruwe.

gammy *adj (colloq)* lemavu.

gamp *n (colloq)* mwavuli (agh mkubwa, ovyoovyo).

gamut *n* **the ~** upeo wa kitu/jambo/ hisia. **run the ~ (of sth)** pitia mambo yote.

gander *n* bata dume la bukini.

gang *n* 1 kundi/jamii ya watu wafanyao kazi pamoja (agh. wahalifu), genge. 2 *(colloq)* kundi la wahuni *vi* **~ up (on)** piga maro, changia. ~**ster** *n* jambazi *~films* filamu za kijambazi. ~**er** *n* msimamizi, mnyapara.

gangling *adj (of a person)* mtu njorinjori, ngongoti.

ganglion *n* ganglioni: kifundo cha neva; *(fig)* kitovu cha kani/juhudi/ shughuli.

gang-plank *n* ubao wa kuingilia/ kushukia melini.

gangrene *n* 1 gangrini: uozo wa sehemu ya mwili kutokana na ukosefu wa damu. 2 *(fig)* uovu *vt, vi* ozesha, oza. **gangrenous** *adj*.

gangway *n* 1 njia, ulalo, ubao wa kuingilia melini. 2 *(US* **aisle***)* nafasi kati ya viti au safu za watu; *(GB in the House of Commons) members above the ~* wabunge mashuhuri *(int)* hodi! nipishe!

gannet *n* membe mweusi.

gantry *n* mhimili wa chuma wa kushikilia winchi au selo ya reli.

gaol,jail *n (usu jail in US)* gereza, kifungo *put in ~* funga jela *four years in ~* miaka minne kifungoni. ~ **bird** *n* mfungwa. ~ **break** *n* kutoroka gerezani. ~**er/jailer, jailor** mlinzi wa gereza, askari jela.

gap *n* 1 ufa, kipenyo, uwazi. 2 nafasi, pengo; hitilafu. **bridge/fill/stop a ~** ziba/zuia pengo. **credibility ~** kutoaminika, ukosefu wa kuaminiana. **generation ~** migongano ya kizazi. ~**-toothed** -enye mwanya. 3 mlango (kati ya milima).

gape *vi* ~ **(at sb/sth)** 1 achama. 2 piga miayo; *(of earth etc)* atuka, pasuka, fanya ufa *n* miayo, mwachamo wa

mdomo. *(pl)* **the** ~s miayo ya ugonjwa wa kuku; *(joc)* kushikwa na miayo.
garage *n* 1 gereji *vt* weka gereji.
garb *n* 1 *(style of)* vazi, nguo. 2 kuvaa mavazi, nguo maalum *in clerical* ~ katika mavazi ya kipadre *vt (usu passive)* valia, vaa *~ed as a sailor* -liovaa mavazi ya kibaharia.
garbage *n* 1 takataka za chakula, *(US)* takataka zozote. ~ **can** *(US)* pipa la taka. 2 *(colloq)* karatasi n.k zisizokuwa na maana, data isiyo na maana katika kompyuta *literary* ~ maandishi yasiyo na maana/machafu.
garble *vt* potoa wazo (kwa kutokamilisha au kuchagua upande fulani; changanya wazo *~d version of a story* mateuzi potofu ya hadithi.
garden *n* 1 bustani *market* ~ bustani (ya maua/matunda/mboga) ya biashara *kitchen* ~ bustani ya mboga (kwa matumizi ya nyumbani). **lead sb up the ~ path** *(colloq)* danganya mtu *common or ~ variety* aina ya kawaida. 2 *(pl)* ~**s** bustani kubwa kwa maburudisho ya wote, bustani ya hadhari. 3 *(compounds)* ~ **centre** mahali panapouziwa mbegu, mimea au vifaa vya kulimia bustani. ~ **city/suburb** mji/kitongoji chenye sehemu nyingi wazi zilizopandwa miti mingi. ~ **party** karamu bustanini *vi* lima bustani. **~er** *n* mkulima wa bustani. **~ing** *n* kilimo cha bustani.
gardenia *n* mgadenia.
gargantuan *adj* -kubwa sana.
gargle *vt,vi* gogomoa *n* dawa/maji ya kusukutua/kugogomoa; ugogomozi.
gargoyle *n* mlizamu ambao kinywa chake ni sanamu ya mtu au mnyama.
garish *adj* -shaufu, -a rangi nyingi sana, -enye marembo kupita kiasi. **~ly** *adv*. **~ness** *n*.
garland *n* shada la maua *vt* visha shada la maua.
garlic *n* kitunguu saumu *a clove of* ~ tumba la kitunguu saumu.
garment *n* vazi, nguo.
garner *n (poet, rhet)* ghala, bohari *vt* weka ghalani, hifadhi; kusanya.
garnet *n* ganeti; kito chekundu.
garnish *vt* ~ **with** pamba (hasa chakula mezani) *meat ~ed with vegetables* nyama iliyopambwa na mboga *n* kipamba chakula.
garret *n* upenu.
garrison *n* askari walinzi wa mji, ngome, boma *vt* weka askari walinzi (bomani/ mjini/ngomeni).
garrotte, garotte *vt* ua (mtu) kwa kukaba koo/ kutia kabali; nyonga *n* kunyonga; chombo cha kunyongea mtu.
garrulous *adj* semi, -enye kubwabwaja. **garrulity** *n*.
garter *n* ukanda (wa mpira) wa kushikiza soksi. **the G~** nembo ya/cheo cha heshima kubwa sana Uingereza.
gas *n* 1 gesi. ~ **bag** *n* mfuko wa gesi; *(colloq)* mtu anayebwabwaja. ~ **bracket** *n* kiango cha gesi. ~ **fire** *n* moto wa gesi (wa kutia joto chumba). ~ **fitter** fundi gesi, fundi wa kutia vifaa vya gesi katika jengo. ~ **helmet,** ~ **mask** *n* chombo/kofia/ helmeti la kuzuia gesi isiingie puani. ~ **holder/** ~ **meter** *n* mita ya gesi. ~ **main** *n* bomba kubwa la kugawia gesi majumbani. ~ **tar** *n* lami ya gesi. ~ **chamber** chumba chenye gesi cha kuulia watu/wanyama. **~cooker/stove/oven** *n* jiko la gesi. ~ **fittings** vifaa k.m. mabomba kwa ajili ya kuwashia gesi. **~light** mwanga utokanao na gesi. **~poker** kiwashia moto cha gesi. **~works** *(pl)* mahali gesi ya makaa inapotengenezwa. 2 *laughing* ~ nusu kaputi. 3 *(US colloq) (abbr of gasoline)* petroli. **step on the** ~ kanyaga eksileta; ongeza mwendo; *(fig)* harakisha. tia mwendo. ~ **station** *n (US)* kituo cha petroli. 4 *(fig) (colloq) n* mbwabwajiko, kuringa *vt,vi* ua/kufa kwa gesi. 2 *(colloq)* bwabwaja, piga soga. **~eous** *adj* -a gesi, kama gesi. **~ify** *vt,vi* geuza/geuka kuwa gesi ~**ification** *n*. **~sy** *adj* 1 -a gesi, -liojaa

gesi. 2 *(of talk etc)* -a kubwatabwataa mbwembwe. **~oline/~olene** *n (US)* petroli.

gash *n* jeraha kubwa *vt* jeruhi kwa kukata.

gasket *n* gasketi.

gasp *vi,vt* 1 tweta *I ~ed with surprise* nilitweta kwa kushtuka. 2 ~ **(out)** sema kwa kutweta ~ *out life* kata roho *n* kutweta; kuhema kwa shida kwa sababu ya maumivu au mshangao *beat one's last ~ (fig)* choka kabisa; karibia kufa; -wa hoi.

gastric *adj* -a tumbo ~ *fever* homa ya tumbo ~ *juice n* majitumbo ~ *ulcer* kidonda tumbo. **gastritis** *n* uvimbe -tumbo.

gastronomy *n* gastronomia: sayansi ya mapishi, uchaguzi, utayarishaji na ulaji bora. **gastronomic** *adj*.

gate *n* lango; kizuizi. ~ **crash** *vt* ingia (katika nyumba, tafrija au uwanja) bila idhini au kiingilio. ~ **crasher** *n* mpandiaji. ~ **house** *n* nyumba iliyo karibu na lango. ~ **keeper** *n* bawabu. **~legged table** meza ya miguu ya kukunjuka. ~ **money** *n* fedha za kiingilio. ~ **post** nguzo ya lango. **between you(and) me and the ~ post** kwa siri sana. ~ **way** *n* njia inayofungwa kwa lango; *(fig)* mbinu/njia ya kukabili/kufikia (jambo) *vt* zuia mwanafunzi abakie shuleni (kama adhabu).

gateau *n (F)* keki ya malai.

gather *vt,vi* 1 *(of people, things etc)* dunduliza, kusanya; kusanyika, konga ~ *crowd of people* kusanya umati wa watu *the clouds are ~ing* mawingu yanakusanyika. **be ~ed to ones fathers** fariki. 2 *(of flowers, berries etc)* chuma. 3 pata polepole ~ *rust* pata kutu ~ *information* pata habari kidogo kidogo, duduliza/kusanya habari ~ *speed* ongeza mwendo. 4 *(understand, conclude)* elewa, fahamu *what did you ~ from his statement?* ulielewa nini kutokana na usemi wake? 5 *(in sewing)* fanya marinda. 6 *(of a boil)* tunga usaha, iva. **~ing** *n* 1 kukutana, mkutano, mkusanyiko. 2 kutunga usaha.

gauche *adj* shamba. **~rie** *n* mshamba.

gaucho *n* mchunga ng'ombe (wa Amerika ya Kusini).

gaud *n* urembo. **~y** *adj* -a urembo mno. **~iness** *n*.

gauge, (US gage) *n* 1 geji *standard ~* geji ya kawaida *take sb's; (fig)* pima, tathmini, kisia tabia ya mtu. 2 kipimia mvua/nguvu ya upepo/ unene n.k. *rain ~* kipimia mvua. 3 *(railway)* geji: upana kati ya reli. 4 *(of wire etc)* geji: unene wa waya, bati n.k. *vt* pima, kadiria, kisia; *(fig)* kisia.

gaunt *adj (of a person)* ~ liokonda sana kwa dhiki. **~ness** *n*.

gauntlet[1] *n* 1 glavu ya chuma (iliyovaliwa na askari wa zamani sana). **throw down/ pick up/take up the ~** dai/kubali kupigana. 2 glavu ngumu ya kuendeshea gari n.k.

gauntlet[2] *n (only in)* **run the ~** kimbia kati ya safu mbili za watu na pigwa nao kadri upitavyo; *(fig)* kabiliwa na hatari/kashfa n.k.

gauze *n* 1 shashi; kitambaa chembamba sana kinachoona; wavu wa nyuzi (kama chandarua). 2 wavu wa nyuzi za madini *wire ~* wavu. **gauzy** *adj*.

gave *pt of* **give**.

gavel *n* nyundo ya dalali, mwenyekiti n.k. ya kunyamazishia watu/kutulizia fujo.

gawk *n* thakili, mtu mzito, mwenye aibu *vi (colloq)* kodolea macho. **~y** *adj*. **~iness** *n* uzito.

gawp ~ (at) *see* **gawk** *vi*.

gay *adj* 1 -changamfu, bashashi. 2 -a kufurahisha, -a kupendeza ~ *colours* rangi zinazofurahisha/zinazopendeza. 3 *(colloq)* hanithi, msenge; basha. **gaily** *adv* kwa uchangamfu. **~ness** *n*.

gaze *vi* ~ **(at)** angaza/kazia macho. ~ **(upon, on)** ona.

gazelle *n* swala.

gazette *n* gazeti la kiserikali (kuhusu ajira mpya, vyeo n.k.) *vt (usu passive)* **be ~d** chapishwa katika gazeti la serikali.

gazetteer *n* faharasa ya majina ya kijiografia.

gazump *vi,vt (colloq)* danganya kwa kuongeza bei (baada ya makubaliano na kabla ya kusaini mkataba).

gear *n* 1 gia (k.v. ya gari) *change* ~ badili gia. **high/low** ~ gia kubwa/gia ndogo. **in/out of** ~ katika gia/ bila gia. **top/ bottom** ~ gia ya juu/ ya chini. ~ **box** giaboksi. ~ **shift/lever/ stick** mkono wa kubadilishia gia. 2 zana zenye kazi maalum *the landing ~ of an aircraft* miguu ya kutulia ndege. 3 vifaa jumla *hunting* ~ vifaa vya kuwindia *(modern colloq)* nguo, mavazi *party* ~ nguo za sherehe *vt,vi* ~ **up/ down** weka gia ya juu/ ya chini. ~ **to** rekebisha kitu kikidhi matakwa ya wakati huo ~ *the country's economy to wartime requirements* rekebisha uchumi wa nchi kukidhi mahitaji ya wakati wa vita. **gecko** *n* mjusi kafiri.

gee[1] **(also ~ up)** *int (command to horse)* endelea; hamasisha~ ~*n* neno atumialo mtoto kwa farasi.

gee[2] *(also* **~-whiz)** *int (US)* mshangao unaoonyesha kupenda au kustaajabu, salaale! lo!

geese *n pl of* **goose**.

geezer *n (sl)* shaibu.

Geiger *n (esp* **G~-counter)** gaiga: kipima mnururisho.

geisha *n* geisha: msichana au wanamke wa Kijapani anayewaburudisha watu kwenye tafrija n.k. kwa kuimba na kucheza.

gel *n* kitu kitekcteke kama jeli *vi* fanya kuwa jeli; gandisha *it doesn't ~ (colloq)* haiji, haileti.

gelatin(es) *n* jelatini:gundi-gundi (ya mifupa, nyama n.k.). **gelatinous** *adj*.

geld *vt* hasi. **~ing** *n* maksai.

gelignite *n* baruti (ya asidi naitriki na gliserini).

gem *n* 1 kito johari. 2 kitu kinachothaminiwa sana kwa sababu ya uzuri wake. **~med** *adj* -liopambwa na vito.

geminate *adj* -a jozi *vt* gawa/panga katika jozi. **gemination** *n*.

Gemini *n* mapacha.

gen *(sl)* **(the)** ~ habari *vt* ~ **up** toa/ pasha habari, elewesha.

gendarme *n (in France and some other countries, but not in GB or US)* polisi. **~rie** *n (collective sing)* kikosi cha polisi.

gender *n* 1 jinsi (mume au mke); jinsia ~ *question* suala la kijinsia. 2 *(gram)* ngeli (za maneno) *feminine* ~ jinsi ya kike *masculine* ~ jinsi ya kiume *neuter* ~ jinsi isiyo ya kike wala ya kiume.

gene *n* jeni: sehemu ya DNA inayorithisha tabia au umbile fulani. **~tic** *adj* 1 -a jeni/-a jenetiki. 2 -a kinasaba/kijeni *a ~ defect* hitilafu ya kinasaba. **~s** *n* jenetiki.

genealogy *n* (elimu ya) nasaba, kizazi, ukoo. **~tree** shajara ya nasaba. **genealogical** *adj*. **genealogically** *adv*.

genera *n pl of* **genus**.

general *adj* 1 -a jumla; -a -ote; si maalum *a matter of ~ interest* jambo la kuhusu watu wote. ~ **knowledge** maarifa, malimwengu ~ *paper* karatasi ya maarifa. ~ **practitioner** daktari anayetibu magonjwa yote ~ *clauses* ibara za jumla. ~ **degree** digrii ya jumla; *(common)* -a desturi, -a kawaida, -a siku zote. **in ~; as a ~ rule** kwa kawaida/-desturi, mara nyingi *of ~ application* -a kutumika kwa kawaida. 2 -a kudokeza, -a jumla jumla ~ *idea/outline* dokezo, maelezo ya juujuu tu *a ~ statement* maelezo ya juu-juu tu. 3 *(chief, principal)* -kuu, -kubwa. ~ **election** uchaguzi mkuu. ~ **meeting** mkutano mkuu *n (milit)* jenerali. **~ization** *n* 1 jambo, shauri, neno, maono maarifa n.k. ya kijumla jumla (bila kuhoji au kufikiria mambo yote, jumuisho). 2 majumui. **~ize** *vi, vt* **~(from/about)** 1 fikia hitimisho la jumla; toa kauli ya jumla. 2 eleza jambo jumlajumla, jumuisha. 3 ingiza katika matumizi ya jumla, sambaza/ fanya itumike kote. **~ly** *adv* 1 mara nyingi, kwa kawaida/ desturi. 2 kwa jumla. **~ship** *n* 1 ujenerali. 2 maarifa ya vita. 3 ustadi wa usimamizi (wa shughuli n.k.). **~issimo** *n* jemadari mkuu wa majeshi yote (ya nchi kavu, anga na majini). **~ity** *n* 1 kauli ya jumla. 2 **the ~ (of)** idadi kubwa (ya); wengi *the ~ of students passed the examination* wengi wa wanafunzi walifaulu mtihani.

generate *vt* fanyiza; leta; zalisha *~ electricity* zalisha umeme. **generator** *n* jenereta. **generation** *n* 1 kizazi *~ generations* vizazi vitatu (baba na wanawe na mjukuu). 2 kufanyiza, kuzalisha. 3 kizazi: kipindi cha wastani cha umri wa mtu wa kuoa na kuwa na watoto. 4 rika, watu waliozaliwa wakati mmoja, wa rika moja. **generative** *adj* -zazi *~ organs* viungo vya uzazi *~ grammar* sarufi fafanuzi/zalishi.

generic *adj* -a jenisi, -a ainasafu, a kuhusu -ote.

generous *adj* 1 *(liberal)* karimu; paji. 2 ingi, kubwa *a ~ portion* fungu kubwa/-ingi. **~ly** *adv*. **generosity** *n* ukarimu.

genesis *n* 1 asili, mwanzo, chimbuko. 2 *(rel)* **G~** Mwanzo: kitabu cha kwanza cha Agano la Kale.

genial *adj* 1 -kunjufu, -changamfu -enye huruma. 2 -enye kupendeza, a joto. **~ly** *adv*. **~ity** *n* ukunjufu, uchangamfu.

genie *n* jini.

genital *adj* -a viungo vya uzazi *n (pl)* **~s** viungo vya uzazi.

genitive *adj* **~ (case)** *(gram)* -a chanzo; milikishi.

genius *n* 1 kipaji. 2 mtu mwenye kipaji hicho. 3 **a ~ for** kipaji/uwezo asilia wa *a ~ for languages* kipaji cha lugha. 4 **the ~ (of)** busara, roho ya namna fulani maalum. 5 **one's good/ evil/ ~** pepo mwema/mbaya anayetawala, anayelinda, anayeongoza mahali au watu wengine; mtu anayewaathiri sana wenzie *~ loci* mazingira ya mahala; *(evil)* afriti. 6 *(pl genii)* jini, zimwi.

genocide *n* uangamizaji wa kabila, taifa kwa mauaji au uwekaji wa masharti muhali kuishi.

genre *n (F)* 1 namna, aina, jinsi. 2 *(of liter)* tanzu. **~-painting** *n* uchoraji wa picha kutokana na mambo ya kawaida ya maishani.

gent *n (colloq abbr of gentleman)* mwanamume. **the/a G~s** *n (GB colloq)* choo cha wanaume.

genteel *adj (usu ironic in modern use; but serious in former use)* -a kiungwana; -a daraja kubwa *living in ~ poverty* jaribu kuishi maisha ya juu ingawa maskini sana; kufa kiofisa. **~ly** *adv*. **gentility** *n* uungwana; ubwana *living in shabby ~* jitwaza, iga maisha ya juu.

gentian-violet *n (med)* jivii.

gentile *n,adj* mataifa; -a mataifa; asiye Myahudi.

gentle *adj* 1 -pole, raufu; latifu, si kali *a ~ breeze* upepo mwanana *a ~ slope* mteremko usio mkali. 2 *(of a family)* ungwana. **~folk** *n (pl)* waungwana. **~ness** upole, uraufu; *n* chambo cha funza (wa nzi) *vt* 1 fundisha/ ongoza farasi kuwa mpole. 2 bembeleza, tuliza. **gently** *adv* 1 kwa upole, kinyerenyere; kwa uangalifu *hold it ~* shika kwa uangalifu.

gentleman *n* 1 muungwana, bwana, mwanaume. **~'s agreement** kuaminiana, mapatano ya kiungwana. 2 *(hist)* mtu wa daraja kubwa. **~ at arms** mlinzi wa mfalme. 3 *(hist)* mtu aliyeruhusiwa kuwa na silaha ingawa si wa daraja kubwa. 4 *(dated use)* mwinyi. 5 *(pl)* njia ya heshima ya kuwaita wanaume waliohudhuria *Ladies and Gentlemen* Mabibi na Mabwana. 6 njia ya kuanza barua rasmi. **~ly** *adj* -a kiungwana. **gentlewoman** *n (pl gentlewomen)* see **lady**.

gentry *n (pl)* **(the)** ~ watu wa daraja kubwa kidogo.

genuflect *vi* piga goti (katika kuabudu au kuheshimu). **~ion, genuflexion** *n*.

genuine *adj* -a kweli; halisi *~ article*

bidhaa halisi *a ~ purchaser* mteja halisi. **~ly** *adv.* **~ness** *n.*

genus *n* 1 jenasi: uainishi spishi zenye sifa zinazofanana; *(bio)* nasaba *~ Homo* wanadamu. 2 jinsi, namna, aina; jamii.

geo *pref* dunia. **~centric** *adj* -enye/-a kuwakilisha dunia kama kitovu. **~dess** *n* upimaji dunia. **~physics** elimu ya fizikia ya dunia. **~politics** *n (pl)* siasa ya nchi kama inavyoathiriwa na jiografia.

geography *n* jiografia. **geographer** mtaalam wa jiografia. **geographical** *adj.* **geographically** *adv.*

geology *n* jiolojia. **geologist** mtaalamu wa jiolojia. **geological** *adj.* **geologically** *adv.*

geometry *n* jiometri *analytical ~* jiometri changanuzi/chambuzi. **geometric, geometrical** *adj* -a kijiometri. **~ progression** mwendelezo jiometri. **geometrically** *adv.*

George *n* 1 **St ~** Mtakatifu George (mtakatifu mlezi wa Uingereza) *St ~s' cross* Msalaba mwekundu kama ule wa bendera ya Uingereza 2. *(sl) (aircraft)* kiendeshaji kinachojiendesha *int by ~ (dated)* aaa! lo!

georgette *n* hariri nyembamba.

Georgian *adj* 1 -a wakati wa mfalme George I, II na wa III wa Uingereza. 2 mkazi wa Georgia (ya Urusi na ya Marekani).

geriatric *adj* -a utibabu wa wazee. **~s** *n* utibabu wa wazee. **~ian** *n* daktari wa magonjwa ya wazee.

gerontology *n* jerontolojia: sayansi inayohusika na uzeekaji (hasa wa binadamu).

germ *n* 1 mbegu *~ cell* seli zazi; *(fig)* asili, chanzo cha wazo n.k. 2 kijidudu, kiini cha maradhi *vi (fig)* chipua, mea. **~icide** *n* kiua vijidudu (hasa bakteria) **~icidal** *adj.* **~inate** *vi,vt* chipua, mea, ota. **~ination** *n* uotaji, kuchipua, kumea.

German *n* Mjerumani; lugha ya Kijerumani *adj* -a Kijerumani -a Ujerumani. **~ic** -a kundi la lugha zinazohusiana na Kijerumani.

germane *adj* **~ (to)** -nayohusu kabisa.

gerrymander *vt* fanya hila katika uchaguzi (katika kupanga mpaka wa majimbo ya uchaguzi kwa ajili ya kupendelea mtu/chama/tabaka fulani *n* hila katika uchaguzi.

gerund *n* kitenzi nomino.

Gestapo *n* Gestapo: polisi wa siri wa Kijerumani wakati wa utawala wa Nazi.

gestation *n* 1 kuchukua mimba, ujauzito. 2 *also* **~ period** kipindi cha kuchukua mimba, ujauzito; *(fig)* kipindi cha kukua kwa wazo.

gesticulate *vi* ashiria, tumia mikono, kichwa n.k. wakati wa kuzungumza. **gesticulation** *n.*

gesture *n* 1 ishara ya mikono au kichwa (kutoa wazo, hisia n.k.). 2 tendo la kuonyesha hisia/mtazamo *as a ~ of friendship he gave us his new book* alitupatia kitabu chake kipya kama ishara ya urafiki; utumiaji wa ishara *vi* ashiria.

get *vi,vt* 1 *(obtain, receive)* pata *~ a present* pata zawadi. **~ an illness** pata ugonjwa. 2 -wa *~ wet* rowa *~ lost (sl)* ambaa! potea! ondoka! 3 fanya, sababisha *~ the food ready* andaa chakula. **~ sth done** kamilisha, maliza kufanya. 4 anza anzisha *~ going* anza *when the women ~ talking* wanawake wanapoanza kuongea. 5 pata (kujua, kusikia, n.k.) *when you ~ to know her you will like her* utakapomfahamu vizuri utampenda. 6 shawishi, leta *you'll never ~ him to understand* huwezi kumweleweshaa *I can't ~ him to talk* nashindwa kumshawishi aongee. 7 pewa adhabu *~ six months* pewa kifungo cha miezi sita. **~ told off** *(colloq)* semwa, karipiwa. 8 *(colloq)* elewa, pata *I didn't ~ the joke* sikuuelewa mchapo wenyewe *I don't ~ you* sikuelewi/ pati. 9 *(esp. in perfect tenses)* tatanisha, pata *I have got you there!* Nimekupatia! 10 -wa na, miliki *we have got a big house* tuna nyumba kubwa. 11 **have got to** paswa, lazima *I have got to finish this job* lazima nimalize kazi hii. 12 weza, fanikiwa. 13 *(non idiomatic intransitive uses with adverbial particles and preps)* enda. ~ **across** vuka. ~ **back** rudi. ~ **home** fika nyumbani. ~ **off** toka. ~ **a move on** fanya haraka *where can it have got to?* iko wapi/imepotelea wapi? ~**somewhere** piga hatua. ~ **nowhere/not ~ anywhere** -tofika popote. ~ **there** *(colloq)* fanikiwa. 14 *(non idiomatic transitive uses)* peleka. patisha: *I'll ~ you home before midnight* nitakurudisha kabla ya saa sita usiku ~ *your clothes on* vaa *I'll ~ you to the station early* nitakupeleka/fikisha stesheni mapema. 15 *(idiomatic uses with adverbial particles and preps)* ~ **about** *(of sb who has been ill)* tembeatembea, pata nafuu; *(of news, rumour, story)* enea; *(of a person infml)* safiri, zunguka. ~ **above oneself** jivunia, jiona. ~ **sth across (to sb)** *(colloq)* elewesha. ~ **ahead (of sb)** pita (mtu); fanikiwa zaidi. ~ **along** weza; endelea; ondoka. ~ **along with** elewana na/patana na. ~ **along with you!** *(colloq imper)* ondoka; acha! usiniambie! ~ **around** *see* ~ **round** ~ **at sb/sth** fikia; pata. ~**-table** *adj* -enye kufikika; -enye kupatikana. ~ **at sb** *(bribe)* honga, -pa rushwa; *(taunt)* chokoza, kera. ~ **at sth** gundua, pata ~ *at the truth* gundua/pata ukweli. **be ~ting at** *(colloq)* maanisha. ~ **away** toroka. ~ **-way** *n* kutoroka *make one's ~ away* toroka. ~ **away with sth** fanikiwa bila kugunduliwa (katika jambo ovu) *you'll never ~ away with it* watakugundua. ~ **back** rudia kwenye madaraka (baada ya kuyapoteza). ~ **back at sb/~ one's own back (on sb)** lipa kisasi. ~ **by** pita/kubalika, weza, ishi. ~ **down** *(of children)* ondoka mezani (baada ya kula); shuka, teremka; shusha. ~ **sb down** *(colloq)* sononesha, fadhaisha. ~ **sth down** *(swallow)* meza; *(write)* andika. ~ **down to sth** anza kufanya kitu kwa makini. ~ **home (to) sb** eleweka wazi. ~ **in** fika; *(to a car etc)* panda; *(of election)* chaguliwa. ~ **sb in** ita mtu (fundi, daktari n.k.) nyumbani (ili kutoa huduma). ~ **sth in** kusanya; jaliza, weka akiba. ~ **into** *(of clothes)* vaa; ingia katika hali fulani ~ *into trouble* ingia matatani. ~ **a girl into trouble** *(colloq)* tia msichana mimba. ~ **into bad company** shirikiana na waovu; jifunza, zoea. ~ **into one's head that** elewa kuwa. ~ **off** anza. ~ **off lightly/cheaply** -topata adhabu kali. **tell sb to ~ off/where he ~s off** *(colloq)* -pa mtu ukweli wake. ~ **sb/-sth off** tuma, peleka (barua n.k.). ~ **off** *(bus etc)* shuka, telemka. ~ **sb off** okoa (kwenye adhabu). ~ **sb off to sleep** laza. ~ **sth off** ondoa; vua. ~ **sth off (by heart)** kariri. ~ **off with sb** *(colloq)* fanya mapenzi na. ~ **off with sth** pata (adhabu ndogo) *he got off with a fine* alipata faini tu. ~ **on** endelea, songa mbele; *(of time)* pita. ~ **on sth** panda. ~ **on one's feet** simama; *(fig)* pata nguvu mpya; fufuka, inuka. **be ~ting on for** *(of time age)* karibia. ~ **on to sb** wasiliana na *(colloq)* tambua/gundua (ujanja, hila n.k.). ~ **on (with sb)** elewana/patana na. ~ **on (with sth)** endelea na. ~ **on with it!** fanya haraka! ~ **out** *(of secret etc)* julikana, fichuka. ~ **sth out** *(of words)* sema; *(of produce)* toa; chapisha; tawanya; *(of meeting etc)* ondoka. ~ **out of (doing) sth** kwepa; *(fig)* acha polepole. ~ **sth out of sb** pata jambo kutoka kwa mtu. ~ **over sb** *(colloq)* sahau. ~ **over sth** *(of ilness etc)* pata ahueni, nafuu, *(over come)* shinda. ~ **sth over (with)** maliza, fikia mwisho wa (kitu kibaya au chenye matatizo). ~ **sth over (to sb)** elewesha *I can't ~ over it* nashindwa kuamini. ~ **round sb** shawishi mtu. ~ **round sth** epa; zunguka. ~ **round to doing sth** pata muda wa kushughulikia jambo (baada ya mengine yenye maana kushughulikiwa). ~ **through (to)** fikia, fika, wasiliana na. ~ **through (sth)** pita, faulu, shinda ~ *through an examination* faulu mtihani. ~ **through (with) sth** maliza, fikia mwisho. ~ **through to sb that** elewesha mtu/pasha mtu habari kuwa. ~ **sb through (sth)** saidia mtu kushinda/kufaulu. ~ **sth through** hakikisha jambo linatekelezwa; *(of proposal, bill in parliament etc)* pitisha kuwa sheria; pitisha. ~ **to** fikia hali fulani. ~ **together** kutana (kwa dhifa, majadiliano n.k.). ~ **together** *n* kukutana, mkusanyiko (kwa ajili ya tafrija, mkutano n.k.). ~ **it/sth together** *(colloq)* panga, ratibu/ simamia jambo. ~ **oneself together** *(colloq)* weza kujizuia; jitawala. ~ **people/things together** kusanya. ~ **up** inuka; *(from bed)* amka; *(mount)* panda; *(of wind, sea)* anza kuchafuka/kucharuka. ~ **sb/sth up** inua; amsha, andaa vizuri (kitabu n.k.). ~ **up** *n* mtindo/mpango wa kitabu/jarida/mavazi (hasa usio wa kawaida). ~ **sth up** tayarisha, panga. ~ **up to sth** fikia; shughulika/fanya lisilo la kawaida. ~ **sb with child** *(arch)* tia mimba.

gewgaw *n* kishaufu, pambo.

geyser *n* 1 chemchemu ya maji moto. 2 chombo cha kupashia maji moto (hasa kwa kutumia gesi au umeme).

gharry *n* (*India*) gari (linalovutwa na farasi).

ghastly *adv* kama kifo *adj* 1 mahututi; -a kupauka *he was looking* ~ alionekana mahututi. 2 -a kutisha, -a kuogopesha *a* ~ *accident* ajali mbaya mno. 3 *(colloq)* -a ovyo, -siopendeza.

ghee *n* samli.

gherkin *n* namna ya tango dogo (la kutengenezea achari).

ghetto *n* 1 *(hist) (of a town)* mtaa wanakokaa Wayahudi. 2 sehemu ya jiji wanakokaa maskini au watu wanaobaguliwa.

ghost *n* 1 pepo, zimwi *there are ~s in the room* chumbani mna pepo/vizuka. **raise a** ~ ita/pandisha pepo *I don't believe in ~s* siamini mambo ya pepo. 2 roho. **give up the** ~ kata roho, -fa, fariki dunia. **the Holy G~** Roho Mtakatifu. 3 kivuli, kitu hafifu *a* ~ *of a smile* kicheko hafifu sana. **not have the ~ of a chance** -toweza kufanikiwa/kushinda kabisa. ~ **town** mahame, ganjo. 4 **~writer** mwandishi anayemtungia mwingine kazi (bila yeye kutajwa jina). 5 (*television)* taswira, rudufu *vt,vi* tungia mwingine. **~ly** *adj* 1 kivuli; hafifu; -a mzuka; -a kama mzuka. 2 *(spiritual) (arch)* -a kiroho. **~ly advice** ushauri wa kiroho.

ghoul *n* 1 *(in stories)* zimwi mla maiti. 2 mtu katili sana. **~ish** *adj*.

GI *n* askari wa jeshi la Marekani.

giant *n* 1 *(in fairy tales)* jitu. 2 pandikizi (la mtu/mnyama n.k.); *(fig)* mtu mwenye akili au kipaji kikubwa. 3 *(attrib)* -kubwa sana, -enye nguvu sana. **~ess** jitu la kike.

gibber *vi* tatarika; payapaya, bwata. **~ish** *n* payo; maneno ya kipuuzi.

gibbet *n* 1 kiunzi cha kunyongea. 2 kifo cha kunyongwa. 3 kiunzi cha kuonyesha walionyongwa *vt* nyonga kwa kitanzi; *(fig)* dharau.

gibbon *n* sokwe.

gibbous *adj* 1 -a mwezi mwandamo. 2 -enye kubenuka, -a kibyongo.

gibe (also jibe) *vi* ~ **(at)** kebehi, dhihaki; beza *n* bezo.

giblets *n* sehemu za ndani za ndege (nyuni).

giddy *adj* 1 -enye kizunguzungu. 2 -enye kupenda raha; -sio na makini; -sio na msimamo thabiti. **giddily** *adv*. **giddiness** *n*.

gift *n* 1 zawadi, hiba, tunu. 2 kipaji. ~ **from God** karama, kipawa. 3 uwezo/ mamlaka ya kutoa kitu *vt* tunukia, -pa zawadi. **~ed** *adj* -enye kipaji, -liojaliwa.

gig *n* 1 *(hist)* gari dogo la farasi lenye magurudumu mawili. 2 *(naut)* mashua ndogo (ya meli kubwa agh. kwa matumizi ya nahodha). 3 *(colloq)* onyesho la muziki.

gigantic *adj* -kubwa kabisa, -refu mno, -a kupita kiasi *he has a ~ appetite* yu mlaji sana.

giggle *vi* chekacheka *n* kicheko. **giggly** *adj.*

gigolo *n* 1 mwanamume anayekodishwa na mwanamke (kucheza naye dansa). 2 kijana kipenzi cha mwanamke mzee tajiri (anayetunzwa naye).

gild[1] *vt* chovya/paka dhahabu. ~ **the lily** haribu uzuri wa kitu kwa kukipamba sana. ~ **the pill** pendezesha kitu kinachochukiza. ~**ed youth** kijana maridadi na tajiri. ~**er** n. ~**ing** *n.*

gilt *n* mpako wa dhahabu. **take the ~ off the ginger bread** ondoa uzuri wa kitu. ~**-edged stocks/securities** vitegauchumi madhubuti.

gild[2] *see* **guild**.

gill *n* yavuyavu: shavu la samaki *vt* toa/tumbua mashavu (ya samaki).

gillie *n (Scot)* mhudumu wa mwindaji au mvuvi.

gimbals *n* vigango (vya dira, horometa n.k.); viungo viunganavyo katika mashine.

gimcrack *n* kinyangarika, kitakataka, kitu hafifu *adj* -a ovyo, bure. ~ **ery** *n.*

gimlet *n* kekee ndogo. ~ **eyes** macho makali.

gimmick *n (colloq)* hila/ujanja wa ku(ji)tangaza/kujitambulisha,vitimbi.

gin[1] *n* 1 mtego (wa wanyama). 2 **(cotton)** ~ kinu cha kuchambulia pamba *vt* 1 tega/mtego wa kufyuka. 2 chambua pamba kwa kinu.

gin[2] *n* jini: aina ya pombe kali.

ginger *n* 1 tangawizi. ~ **beer/ale** soda ya tangawizi. ~ **bread** keki/mkate wa tangawizi. 2 bidii; nguvu; uchangamfu *~group (in parliament)* kikundi cha kuchemsha/kuchangamsha serikali. 3 rangi ya hudhurungi nyekundu. ~**y** *adj.* ~**ly** *adv* kwa hadhari sana, kwa uangalifu sana, kwa makini sana. ~ **up** changamsha.

gingham *n* ging'amu.

gipsy, Gypsy *n* 1 **gipsy** mzururaji. 2 **Gypsy** mhamaji mzururaji (agh. mwenye asili ya kihindi apataye riziki yake kwa biashara ya farasi, kuuza vikapu, utabiri n.k.).

giraffe *n* twiga.

gird *vt (poet or rhet)* 1 ~ **on** vaa, funga (kiunoni). 2 ~ **up** funga (kwa shipi). ~ **up one's loins** jiweka tayari/jitayarisha (kwa kazi, vita); jifunga kibwebwe. 3 zunguka, zingira (mji, kisiwa, n.k.) *a town ~ed with mountains* mji uliozingirwa na milima.

girder *n* boriti, mhimili (wa mbao au chuma).

girdle[1] *n* 1 kanda; *(after child birth)* mkaja. 2 kitu kinachozingira kama mkanda *vt* ~ **about/around/with** zunguka, zingira.

girdle[2] *n (Scot)* see **griddle**.

girl *n* 1 msichana. 2 mwanamke, afanyaye kazi katika ofisi, dukani n.k.. **house** ~ msichana wa kazi. ~ **(friend)** rafiki wa kike, mpenzi. *(GB)* **G~ Guide** *(US)*. **G~ Scout** skauti wa kike. ~ **hood** n usichana. ~**ish** *adj* -a msichana, -a kisichana. ~**lishly** *adv.* ~**lishness** *n.*

giro *n* mfumo wa kuhawilisha fedha/mali, jiro.

girth *n* 1 kipimo cha mzingo *a circle/waist/barrel 30 metres in ~* duara/kiuno/pipa lenye mzingo wa mita 30 *his ~ is increasing* ananenepa. 2 *(in harness)* ukanda unaopitishwa tumboni mwa farasi (kufungia matandiko).

gist *n* **the** ~ kiini, mambo muhimu *the ~ of sb's remarks* kiini cha (maneno ya mtu), maana hasa *the ~ of the matter* kiini cha jambo.

give *vt,vi* 1 ~ **(to)** -pa, toa, patia, gawia *~ alms* toa sadaka *~ a message* toa/pa ujumbe *~ medicine* -pa dawa *the sun ~s us light* jua hutupa mwanga. 2 ~ **for sth; ~ to do sth** -lipa, lipia *How much did you ~ for your new farm?* ulilipa kiasi gani kwa shamba lako jipya? 3 ~ **(to)** kabidhi, wekesha, salimisha, -pa ~ *the customs officer your luggage* kabidhi mizigo yako kwa afisa wa forodha. 4 ruhusu, kubali, achilia, -pa. ~ **sb ten minutes** ruhusu mtu dakika kumi. ~ **sb trouble** sumbua; fanyia fujo/matata. 5 ambukiza *you have ~n me a rash* umeniambukiza upele. 6 jitolea. ~ **your life to the cause of God** jitolea maisha kwa ajili ya kazi za Mungu. 7 *(used in the imper to show preference)* ~ *us a proper salary or fire us* tupe mshahara halali ama sivyo tufukuze. 8 *(used with a noun in a pattern that may be replaced by one in which the noun is used as a verb)* ~ *a push* sukuma ~ *sb a ring* pigia mtu simu ~ *a smile* tabasamu. 9 *(in fixed phrases)* ~ **or take** kama/kiasi cha *he is forty years old, ~ or take a year* ana kiasi cha miaka arubaini. ~ **sb to best** *(old use)* kiri/kubali ubora (wa mtu) ~ *sb understand that* taarifu, fahamisha, hakikishia (mtu fulani) kuwa. ~ **it to sb to** *(colloq)* adhibu, karipia *G~ it to him!* Mpe! ~ **sb what for/a piece of one's mind** *(colloq)* adhibu, kemea, -pa ukweli wake. ~ **way** rudi nyuma; *(of support)* shindwa kuhimili. ~ **way (to sth/sb)** pisha; *(replace)* badiliwa na; *(abandon oneself)* jiachia; *(concede)* kubaliana na ~ *way to demands* kubaliana na madai. 10 legea; pinda, nepa, bonyea *the bow does not ~ well* upinde haupindiki vizuri *this matress ~s comfortably* godoro hili linabonyea vizuri. 11 **~n** *(pp) (in formal documents)* -liotolewa ~ *under my hand and seal on this tenth day of February, 1996* -liotolewa kwa idhini na muhuri wangu leo tarehe kumi mwezi Februari, 1996; *(in reasoning)* ikiwa, iwapo ~ *the opportunity he could make a good politician* ikiwa atapewa nafasi anaweza kuwa mwanasiasa bora; -liokubaliwa; -liopangwa *the ~ time and place* mahala na saa iliyopangwa *the ~ conditions* masharti tuliyo kubaliana. **be ~ to sth/doing sth** -wa na tabia ya, penda ~ *to gossiping* -enye tabia ya utetaji ~ *to drink* penda kunywa pombe. 12 **what ~s** *(colloq)* kuna nini? 13 *(uses with adv particles and prep)*.~ **sb away** kabidhi bibi arusi (kwa bwana arusi wakati wa arusi). ~ **sth away** toa sadaka, -pa mtu; *(lose unnecessarily* tupa; *(distribute)* gawa, toa bure ~ *away clothes* gawa/toa nguo bure; fichua, toa siri ~ *away a secret* fichua siri. **~away** *n (colloq)* vitu vitolewavyo bure *at ~ prices* rahisi sana *the examination was a ~* mtihani ulikuwa rahisi mno; kitu kifichuliwacho *the child's face was a ~ away* uso wa mtoto ulifichua kosa lake. ~ **sth back (to sb); ~ sb back sth,** rudisha ~ *the book back to the teacher* rudisha kitabu kwa mwalimu. ~ **sth forth,** *(old use or liter)* toa (moshi, hewa n.k.). ~ **in (to sb)** kubali kushindwa *terrorists gave in* magaidi walikubali kushindwa. ~ **sth in** kabidhi, wasilisha (ripoti, karatasi n.k.) *the commission gave in the report to the Minister* tume iliwasilisha ripoti kwa Waziri. ~ **one's name in (to sb)** julisha/tangaza nia/madhumuni (ya kugombea uchaguzi n.k.). ~ **sth off** toa (moshi, hewa n.k.). ~ **on to** elekea, chungulia. ~ **out** *(finish)* kwisha, malizika. ~ **sth out** gawa; peleka ~ *out tea* gawa chai. ~ **out to be; ~ it out that sb is** tangaza *The Minister ~s Mr Pandu out to be the Director* Waziri amemtangaza bwana Pandu kuwa Mkurugenzi. ~ **upon; ~ on to; ~ over** *(sl)* acha ~ *over gabbling* acha kubwata. ~ **sb/sth over (to sb)** kabidhi, peleka ~ *sb over to the police* peleka/kabidhi mtu polisi. **be ~n over to sth** jiachia, jikita, jishughulisha sana (katika tamaa, dhambi huzuni n.k.); *(set aside)* tengwa kwa shughuli maalumu *the last week before* *examinations was ~n over to revision* wiki ya mwisho kabla ya mitihani ilitengwa kwa ajili ya marudio. ~ **up** salimu amri. ~ **sb up** *(lose hope in)* achana na, pigia mahuru; *(colloq)* acha, achana na *she gave up her friend* ameachana na rafiki yake *(lose hope of seeing)* -tomtarajia mtu, kata tamaa *our mother arrived after we had ~n her up* mama yetu aliwasili baada ya sisi kukata tamaa. ~ **sb up for lost** kata tamaa (ya kumwona au kumwokoa). ~ **sb/one self/ sth up (to sb)** salimisha, kabidhi *the bandit gave himself up to the police* jambazi lilijisalimisha kwa polisi ~ *up ones seat to someone* pisha mtu. ~ **sth up** acha. ~ **up drinking** acha kunywa pombe. ~ **up the ghost** -fa, aga dunia *n* hali ya kunyumbuka/pindika/ nepa/bonyea *wooden chairs have no ~ in them* viti vya mbao havibonyei; *(fig) (of a person)* hali ya kujitoa/ kushindwa/kujisalimisha/kukubali. ~ **and take** maafikiano, makubaliano *there must be a ~ and take in settling any dispute* lazima kuwa na maafikiano katika kusuluhisha ugomvi wowote. **~r** *n* mpaji, mtoaji.

given *pp of* **give**.

gizzard *n* firigisi; finingi; *(fig, colloq)* koromeo *it ticks in my ~* ni wazo/ jambo nisilopenda kabisa.

glace *adj (of fruits)* -liotiwa sukari; *(of leather, cloth)* laini, iliyong'arishwa.

glacial *adj* 1 -a theluji, -a barafu, -a enzi ya barafu *the ~ era/epoch* kipindi ambacho eneo la kaskazini mwa dunia lilifunikwa na barafu; *(fig)* -a baridi sana ~ *manner* tabia baridi. **~ly** *adv*. **glaciation** *n*. **glacier** *n* mto (wa) barafu.

glad *adj* 1 *(pred only)* -enye furaha *they will be ~ to hear* watafurahi kusikia *make ~* furahisha. 2 -a kufurahisha *~news* habari za kufurahisha. **give sb the ~ eye** *(sl)* tazama kibembe, kwa macho ya kurembua. **give sb the ~ hand** *(sl)* karibisha, salimu kwa uchangamfu (hasa kwa lengo la kufaidi kitu). ~ **rags** *(sl)* nguo za sherehe/tafrija. **~den** *vt*. furahisha **~ness** *n*. **~some** *adj (liter)* -a furaha, -kunjufu. **~ly** *adv*.

glade *n* uwanja/uwazi (katika mwitu).

gladiator *n (in ancient Rome)* mtu aliyefunzwa kupigana na watu au wanyama kwa silaha kwa ajili ya maonyesho. **~ial** *adj*.

glamour (*US* **glamor**) *n* 1 heba/haiba, mvuto. 2 ubembe, uzuri unaovutia kimapenzi ~ *girl* msichana mwenye ubembe. **glamorize** -fanya kuwa zuri (kwa kupiga chuku). **glamorization** *n*.

glance *n vi,vt* 1 ~ **at** tupia jicho, angalia kidogo, chungulia, tazama mara moja *he ~d at his watch* alitazama saa mara moja. 2 ~ **at/ through/over/ down** pitia kwa haraka, pitisha macho. 3 ~ **aside/ off***(of weapon or blow)* paruza. 4 *(of bright objects, light)* mweka, metameta *n* 1 tazamo la haraka, mtupo wa jicho *loving ~* tazamo la mahaba/kimapenzi *cast a ~* tupia jicho. **at a ~** kwa tazamo la haraka; mara moja. **at first ~** kwa kuangalia mara ya kwanza; kwa kuangalia juujuu. 2 mweko (wa visu, mapanga, taa n.k.).

gland *n* 1 tezi *swollen ~ (in groin)* mtoki; *(in throat)* makororo, findofindo. **adrenal ~** tezi adrenali. 2 *(bot)* kitunga utomvu. **~ular** *adj* -a (kama) tezi. **~ule** *n* tezi ndogo.

glare *n* 1 mweko, mng'ao mkali. 2 jicho la hasira/ukali n.k. *(fig) in the full ~ of publicity* machoni mwa watu, hadharani *vi,vt* 1 mweka. 2 ~ **(at)** kazia macho. **glaring** *adj* 1 -a kutia kiwi. 2 kali. 3 -a waziwazi, dhahiri. 4 *(of colours)* -siovutia.

glass *n* 1 kioo *he has a ~ eye* ana jicho la bandia. 2 kitu kilichotengenezwa kwa kioo; gilasi, bilauri *give me a ~ of milk please* tafadhali nipe gilasi ya maziwa *he has had a ~ too much* amelewa; darubini *the captain looked through his ~* nahodha alitazama katika darubini yake; barometa. **the ~ is falling** kanihewa/anga inashuka; *(also looking ~)* kioo; *(pl) (rarely eye ~es)* miwani *I can't see without my ~es* sioni bila miwani yangu; *(binoculars)* darubini ya vioo viwili. **magnifying** ~ kioo cha kukuza kitu. 3 *(compounds)* **~-blower** mtengenezaji vyombo vya kioo agh chupa, bilauri n.k.. ~ **cutter** *n* mkataji vioo; kikata kioo. ~ **house** jengo la kioo, kibanda cha kioo, (kwa kuotesha mimea). *(prov)* **people who live in ~ houses shouldn't throw stones** usiwalaumu wenzio ilihali wewe unatenda vivyohivyo. **~ware** vyombo vya kioo. **~-wool** nyuzi nyembamba za kioo. **~-works** *n (pl)* kiwanda cha kioo *vt* ~ **(in)** tia kioo (madirishani n.k.). **~ful** bilauri tele, glasi nzima. **~y** *adj* 1 -a kama kioo. 2 *(of the sea)*. -eupe. 3 *(of a look/stare/ eye)* baridi.

glaucoma *n* glakoma: ugonjwa unaotanua mboni ya jicho na kutatiza kuona.

glaucous *n,adj* 1 -a kijani/buluu jivu. 2 *(of leaves, etc)* -enye mavumbi/ ukungu.

glaze *vt,vi* ~ **(in)** 1 tia/weka kioo. 2 ~ **(over)** ng'arisha; weka utando (wa kioo). 3 **~(over)** *(of the eyes)* kauka, -wa baridi, poteza hisia *n* mpako wa rangi ya kioo; ng'arisho. **glazier** *n* fundi wa kutia kioo (madirishani n.k).

gleam *n* 1 kimulimuli. 2 *(fig)* kiasi kidogo, dalili ndogo (ya kutumainisha, kufurahisha n.k.) *a ~ of hope* dalili ya matumaini *vi* ng'aa, mulika.

glean *vt,vi* 1 buga. 2 kusanya,pata kidogo kidogo (habari n.k.). **~er** *n* mbugaji. **~ings** *n (pl)* masazo ya mavuno; *(fig)* habari ndogondogo (zinazokusanywa hapa na pale).

glebe *n* 1 shamba lililowekwa wakfu (kwa matumizi ya dini au maskini). 2 *(poet)* shamba, ardhi.

glee *n* 1 raha (inayotokana na mafanikio). 2 wimbo wa kwaya. ~ **club** kwaya, chama cha waimbaji. **~ful** *adj*. **~fully** *adv*.

glen *n* bonde jembamba.

glib *adj* 1 *(of a person)* -epesi wa kusema (lakini si mkweli), -enye ulimi laini, -a maneno matamu (matupu). 2 *(of words)* rahisi *a ~ answer* jibu rahisi. **~ly** *adv*. **~ness** *n*.

glide *vi* nyiririka, teleza *n* 1 kunyiririka, kuteleza. 2 *(phonetics)* kiyeyusho. **~r** *n (aviation)* nyiririko. **gliding** *n* mchezo wa kunyiririka.

glimmer *vi* mulika kidogo kidogo *n* mwangaza hafifu (wa taa, mshumaa n.k.), kimeto; *(fig)* dalili *there's not a ~ of hope* hakuna dalili ya matumaini hata kidogo.

glimpse *n* tazamo la mara moja, kuona kidogo tu *vt* (*also ~ of)* ona mara moja.

glint *vi* metemeta; ng'aa *n* kimeto.

glissade *vi* teleza *n* kuteleza.

glisten *vi* nang'anika, mweka mweka, meremeta, waka *her eyes ~ed with tears* macho yake yalilengalenga machozi.

glitter metameta, ng'aa *n* kimulimuli, kimeto. **~ing** *adj* -a kuvutia, -a kumetameta.

gloaming *n (poet)* **the** ~ utusitusi wa jioni.

gloat *vi* ~ **(over sth)** angalia (kwa wivu/uchoyo/ubaya/husuda); chekelea/cheka (kwa bezo/inda). **~ingly** *adv*.

globe *n* 1 tufe, mviringo. **the** ~ dunia. 2 ramani ya tufe. 3 bakuli la mviringo la kioo.**~-fish** bunju. **~-trot** *vi* zunguka dunia, safiri nchi nyingi. **~-trotter** *n* msafiri duniani, mtembezi sana. **global** *adj* -a ulimwengu. (mzima); -a jumla. **globally** *adv*. **globule** *n* tone. **globular** *adj*; -enye umbo la tufe -enye umbo la tone.

glockenspiel *n* marimba ya chuma.

gloom *n* 1 utusitusi. 2 *(sorrow)* huzuni, majonzi, ghamu, sononeko *cast a ~ over* tia ghamu, sonenesha, huzunisha. **~y** *adj* 1 -a gizagiza.

2 -a huzuni,-a ghamu -zito *become ~* sononeka, kuwa na huzuni *see the ~ side of things* ona ubaya tu.

glory *n* 1 sifa kuu, adhama. 2 uzuri. 3 fahari *the glories of Zimbabwe* fahari za Zimbabwe. 4 hali ya kuwa tukufu; utukufu (wa Mungu na malaika) *G ~ to God in the highest* Utukufu kwa Mungu juu. 5 raha ya mbinguni *go to ~* fariki dunia. **~-hole** chumba/ dawati lenye vikorokoro *vi* jivunia, furahi.

glorify *vt* tukuza; adhimisha, faharisha, kuza. **glorification** *n.* **glorious** *adj* 1 -adhimu. 2 -a kuleta sifa kuu. 3 *(colloq)* -a kupendeza; -a kufurahisha *have a ~ time* furahi sana. 4 *(ironic)* ubaya sana *it's a ~ mess!* ni fujo tupu! **gloriously** *adv.*

gloss[1] *n* 1 mng'ao, king'aa uwongo. **~ paint** rangi inayong'aa. 2 sura (danganyifu) *vt* **~ over** sitiri, funika. **~y** *adj.* **~iness** *n.*

gloss[2] *n* maelezo, ufafanuzi *vt,vi* fasiri, fafanua. **~ary** *n* sherehe, faharasa.

glottis *n* koo. **glottal** adj -a koo/glota. **glottal stop** sauti ya koo/glota.

glove *n* glavu. **be hand in ~ with** kuwa chanda pete na. **fit like a ~** kaa sawasawa. **handle sb without ~s** bishana vikali/bila huruma *handle with kid ~s* shughulikia kwa hadhari sana. **~ compartment** kidawati/ kishubaka garini.

glow *vi* 1 ng'aa, waka (bila kutoa ndimi za moto). 2 *(fig)* waka, chachawa, sisimka *~ with pride* sisimka kwa fahari *n* mng'aro *the ~ of the sky at sunset* mng'aro wa jua wakati wa magharibi. **~-worm** *n* kimulimuli. **~ing** *adj* -a kung'ara; *(fig)* -enye shauku. **~ingly** *adv.*

glower *vi* **~ (at)** kunja uso, tazama kwa hasira au kwa kutisha. **~ingly** *adv.*

glucose *n* glukosi.

glue *n* gundi *vt* **~ (to)** ganda; gandisha, natisha (kwa gundi) *~ up a broken object* unga kwa gundi kitu kilichovunjika. 2 kazia, ambatana, ganda *his eyes were ~d to the picture* alikodolea macho picha *Mary is always ~d to her mother Mary* anamganda mama yake, habanduki kwa mama yake. **~y** *adj.*

glum *adj* -enye masikitiko, -enye uzito wa moyo/jitimai. **~ly** *adv.* **~ness** *n.*

glut *vt* **~ (with)** 1 sheheneza, furisha, jaza sana. 2 kula mno; shiba kupita kiasi *n* furiko, ulevi.

gluten *n* protini inayobaki baada ya kutoa wanga. **glutinous** *adj* -a kunata.

glutton *n* 1 mlafi. 2 mpenzi mkubwa wa kitu fulani *a ~ for work* mpenda kazi sana. **~ ous** *adj* lafi. **~ ously** *adv.* **~y** *n* ulafi.

glycerine *(US* **glycerin**) *n* gliserini.

gnarled *adj (of tree trunk)* -enye vifundo vingi, -a kupindapinda, -a vinundunundu; *(of hands/ fingers)* -a misuli iliyokakamaa, -liofinyangika, -liovingirika.

gnash *vt,vi (of teeth)* kereza, saga meno.

gnat *n* aina ya visubi; *(fig)* jambo dogo linaloudhi. **strain at a ~** sita kwa jambo dogo.

gnaw *vt,vi* **~ (at)** tafuna, guguna, ng'wenya *the rats ~ed a basket* panya waliguguna kapu. 2 **~ (at)** *(of feelings)* tesa, sumbua, udhi.

gnome *n (in tales)* kizimwi (kinachoishi chini ya ardhi na kulinda dafina) *the ~s of Zurich* wenye mabenki Uswisi.

gnu *n* kongoni.

go[1] *vi* 1 **~ (from to)** -enda, ondoka *she will ~ to Arusha* atakwenda Arusha *let them ~* waache waondoke. **~ away** nenda zako *all hope has gone* matumaini yote yameondoka. 2 kaa, -wa mahali pake pa kawaida *where does the book go?* kitabu kinakaa wapi?; ingia (ndani ya). 3 **~ (from/ to)** fika, fikia *the river ~es to the ocean* mto huu hufika baharini *the differences between the friends ~es back a long way* kutoelewana kwa hawa marafiki wawili ni kwa muda mrefu. **~ a long way** *(last)* dumu *he makes his wages ~ a long way* hutumia mshahara wake kwa uangalifu; *(endure) (colloq)* -wa kiasi cha kuvumilika. ~ **a long way/far towards doing sth** changia, saidia. ~ **(very) far** dumu; *(of a person, future tense)* fanikiwa. ~ **too far** vuka mpaka, zidi *you've ~ne too far!* umezidi. ~ **(any) further** pita/ kiwango fulani *I've ~ne as far as I can in this job I can't ~ any further* nimefikia kikomo changu katika kazi hii. ~ **as/so far as to do sth** thubutu. **as far as it ~es** kwa kiasi fulani *His views are valid as far as they ~* hoja zake ni za msingi kwa kiasi fulani. ~ **to great lengths/ trouble (to do sth)** jitahidi/hangaika sana; -wa mwangalifu kufanya jambo vizuri. ~ **as low/high as** *(of a price)* shuka/panda hadi, fikia kiwango fulani. ~ **one better (than sb)** fanya vizuri zaidi (kuliko mtu mwingine). 4 ~ **on a journey/trip/outing** safiri, fanya safari. ~ **for a walk/swim** enda kutembea/kuogelea. ~ walking tembea. 5 *(in the pattern ~ prep n)* enda (mahali palipodhamiriwa). ~ **to school** enda shule. ~ **to church** enda kanisani. ~ **to sea** -wa baharia. 6 ~**to sb** -wa mali ya mtu, rithiwa, gawiwa, enda kwa *when the man died his property went to his grand children* mtu yule alipokufa mali yake iligawiwa/ilirithiwa na wajukuu zake *the gold medal went to Michael* medali ya dhahabu ilienda kwa Michael. 7 -wa *he went red with rage* aliwiva kwa hasira *he will ~ mad* atakuwa kichaa. ~ **broke** ishiwa fedha; -tokuwa na fedha. ~ **flat** *(of liquid)* -tokuwa na gesi. ~ **native** iga maisha ya wenyeji. ~ **put** *(colloq of machines)* haribika *(fig) my project has gone put* mradi wangu umeharibika. ~ **scot-free/ unchallenged/unpunished** -toadhibiwa, -topingwa. 8 fanya kazi, enda *my watch is not ~ing* saa yangu haiendi, haifanyi kazi. **a ~ing concern** shughuli hai iliyostawi *I've been ~ing all day* nimekuwa nikifanya kazi siku nzima. 9 zoea, -wa katika hali fulani (kila mara) *you need not ~ armed while in town* huhitaji kuwa na silaha unapokuwa mjini *she is six months ~ne* ana mimba ya miezi sita. 10 *(after How)* endelea *How's the work ~ing?* Kazi inaendeleaje? *His plans are ~ing well* mipango yake inaendelea vizuri. ~ **easy (on/with sb/sth)** -tokuwa mkali, fanyia uungwana; wa mwangalifu; -wa mpole ~ *easy* asteaste! ~ **slow** *(of traffic)* sota, enda pole pole; *(of workers in factories etc)* fanya mgomo baridi. ~ **slow** *n* mgomo baridi. **be ~ing strong** endelea kusitawi, -wa na nguvu bado *Born in 1900 but still ~ing strong* alizaliwa 1900 lakini bado ana nguvu. 11 tumia, fanya kazi kwa *this car ~es by petrol* gari hili linatumia petroli. 12 *(in progressive tense only)* patikana *that's the best house ~ing* hii ndiyo nyumba bora inayopatikana. 13 ~ **(to sb) for** uzwa kwa bei (fulani) *the radio went cheap* radio iliuzwa kwa bei rahisi. 14 ~ **on/in** *(of money)* tumika kwa *half my income ~es on food* nusu ya pato langu hutumika kwa chakula. 15 telekezwa, potea *his sight is ~ing* uwezo wake wa kuona unapotea. 16 semekana, sadikiwa *the story ~es that....* inasemekana kuwa... 17 kwa wastani, kwa jumla, ilivyo. **as people** ~ watu walivyo kwa wastani *one hundred and fifty for a button is not bad as things ~ today* bei ya shilingi mia moja na hamsini kwa kifungo kimoja sio mbaya sana ukifikiria jinsi bei ya vitu ilivyo siku hizi. 18 anguka, poromoka, angamia *first the roof and then the walls went in the storm* paa liling'oka kwanza kisha kuta ziliporomoka *she is far gone* yu mahututi; *(colloq)* yu mwenda wazimu. **let oneself** ~ jifurahisha. 19 -fa *he has gone* amekufa. **dead and ne** amekufa na kuzikwa. 20 amuliwa *The election went in his favour* alishinda uchaguzi. 21 *(various phrases)* ~ **it** tenda kwa bidii; jiingiza katika ubadhirifu. ~ **it alone** fanya pekee (bila msaada). 22 *(of words, tune)* pangiliwa *I'm sure of how the words ~* nina hakika jinsi maneno yanavyo pangiliwa. 23 *(colloq as informal request)* enda ~ *and dust the table* nenda kafute meza *now you have ~ne and done it* ((sl) umeshaharibu. 24 toa mlio au sauti maalum *'Bang' went the door* mlango ulijifunga 'mba'. 25 *(of competitors in a race)* anza *ready, steady ~* kuwa tayari, kaa sawasawa, anza (kukimbia) *here ~es* haya tunaanza. 26 *(to express future)* -ta *I'm ~ing to live on campus* nitaishi chuoni *we are ~ing to have rain today* huenda mvua itanyesha leo *my son is ~ing to be ten tomorrow* mwanangu atatimiza umri wa miaka kumi kesho. 27 ~ **as you please** *(atrrib adv)* huru. 28 *(idiomatic uses)* ~ **about** tembea, randaranda; *(of rumours, stories)* enea; *(of a ship)* badili njia. ~ **about sth** anza kuifanya kazi. **please ~ about it more carefully** tafadhali ifanye kwa uangalifu zaidi. ~ **about one's business** jishughulisha na mambo yako. ~ **about with sb** fuatana na, -wa na mtu mwingine mara kwa mara. ~ **after/sth** jaribu kupata kitu fulani. ~ **against sb** pinga *do not ~ against your employer* usipingane na mwajiri wako; elekea/tokea vibaya *the game is ~ing against them* wanaelekea kushindwa. ~ **against sth** enda, -wa kinyume na *it will not ~ against my tastes* haitakuwa kinyume na vionjo vyangu. ~ **ahead** endelea *they are ~ ahead people* ni watu wanaopenda maendeleo *may I leave? yes ~ ahead* naweza kuondoka? ndiyo bila wasiwasi. ~ **ahead** *n* ruhusa ya kuendelea. ~ **along** endelea: *the lessons will be easy as you ~ along* masomo yatakuwa rahisi kadiri unavyoendelea. ~ **along with sb** sindikiza. fuatana na *she will ~along with her boy friend* atamsindikiza mpenzi wake *(agree)* kubaliana na *we can't ~ along with him on that argument* hatuwezi kukubaliana na yeye katika hoja ile. ~ **at sb/sth** shambulia, vamia *they went at it tooth and nail/hammer and tongs* walishambuliana vikali; shughulikia kikamilifu. ~ **away** ondoka. ~ **away with sb** ondoka na, chukua *she has ~ne away with my book* ameondoka na kitabu changu. ~ **back** rudi; rudi nyuma *our friendship~es back to the 1960s when we were at Makerere* urafiki wetu ulianza zamani katika miaka ya 60 tulipokuwa Makerere. ~ **back on/upon** vunja (*k.m.* ahadi). ~ **before (sth)** tangulia. ~ **behind** tafuta. ~ **behind sb's back** sengenya, fanyia mtu kitu pasipo yeye kujua. ~ **beyond sth** vuka mpaka, zidi *you are ~ing beyond your responsibility* umevuka mpaka wa madaraka yako *that's ~ing beyond a joke* imezidi. ~ **by** pita *he went by in a hurry* alipita haraka sana. ~ **by sth** fuata, ongozwa na *~ by the book* fuata sheria barabara. ~ **by/under the name** tumia jina (fulani) itwa (fulani). ~ **-by** *n.* **give sb/sth the ~-by** *(colloq)* puuza, dharau. ~ **down** *(of a ship)* zama; *(of the sun, moon)* tua; *(of food and drink)* telemka, mezwa *the piece of meat won't ~ down* siwezi kuimeza nyama hii; ondoka chuo kikuu (baada ya kuhitimu; *(of the sea, wind etc)* pungua, tulia; *(of prices)* poa, shuka *the price of meat has ~ne down* bei ya nyama imeshuka. ~ **down to the coast/village** tembelea pwani/kijijini n.k. ~ **down before sb** shindwa au pinduliwa. ~ **down (in sth)** andikwa; kumbukwa *you will ~ down in historyas a hero* utakumbukwa kuwa shujaa mkuu. ~ **down** to be endelea *the liberation of man ~es down to the present century* ukombozi wa binadamu umeendelea hadi karne hii.

~ **down (with sb)** *(of a story)* kubaliwa, pendwa (na msikilizaji) *the story won't ~ down with my son* mwanangu hatapenda hadithi hii *the idea of the second wife does not ~ down well with the first wife* fikra za kuoa mke wa pili hazikubaliwi na mke wa kwanza. ~ **down (with sth)** ugua; pata ugonjwa *the beggar has gone down with cholera* yule ombaomba amepata kipindupindu. ~ **for sb** -enda kumchukua (fulani) ~ *for the children* enda kuchukua watoto; shambulia *the audience went for me in the seminar* wasikilizaji walinishambulia katika semina; husu *what I said about your friends ~ es for you too* nilichosema kuhusu rafiki zako kunakuhusu na wewe pia; penda *I don't ~ for detective nowels* sipendi riwaya za upelelezi. ~ **for nothing/little** puuzwa; -tothaminiwa. ~ **forth** *(formal)* tolewa. ~ **forward** enda mbele; endelea. ~ **in** ingia *(of the sun, moon etc)* funikwa na mawingu; ingia mashindanoni. ~ **in for sth** fanya, shiriki katika (mtihani; mashindano n.k.). ~ **into sth** ingia ~ *into the army* ingia jeshini; *(investigate)* peleleza, chunguza kwa makini ~ *into fits of laughter* kauka kucheka. ~ **into mourning** vaa nguo nyeusi kama ishara ya msiba. ~ **off** *(explode)* lipuka; fyatuka; *(go bad)* poteza uzuri/ubora; *(of milk)* ganda; *(of meat etc)* oza; *(of fish)* china; *(sleep)* lala; poteza fahamu; *(sale of goods)* uzwa rahisi; *(of events)* enda/endelea (vema) *the discussion went off well* mjadala uliendelea vema; *(as a stage direction in a printed play)* toka jukwani. ~ **off sb/sth** chushwa na; kinai. ~ **off with sb/sth** iba, toweka na (kitu), torosha *He has ~ne off with your sister* amemtorosha dada yako. ~ **on** *(of time)* pita *As days went on* kadiri siku zilivyopita; *(behave)* endelea na tabia (hasa mbaya) *if she ~es on like this she will be divorced* akiendelea na tabia hii atatalikiwa; *(happen)* tokea, endelea kufanyika *there is nothing ~ing on there* hakuna lolote linalofanyika pale; *(theatre)* tokea jukwaani; *(take ones turn)* fanya zamu. **tell him to ~ on** mwambie afanye zamu yake. ~ **on sth** kubali, saidiwa na (k.m. ushahidi). ~ **on the dole/social security** *(US)* **welfare** lipwa posho na serikali wakati wa kukosa ajira. ~ **on the pill** anza kutumia vidonge vya kuzuia mimba. ~ **on about sth** ongea kirefu, bwata. ~ **on (at sb)** gombeza, kefyakefya, zoza. **be ~ing on (for)** *(of age/time)* karibia *I'm ~ing on (for) fifty* nakaribia miaka hamsini. **be ~ne on** *(sl)* pambazwa. ~ **on to sth/to do sth** endelea (na) ~ *on to the next item on the agenda* endelea na dondoo linalofuata katika ajenda. ~ **on (with sth/doing sth)** endelea, vumilia. ~ **on (with you)!** *(colloq)* ondoka hapa. **~ings-on** *n pl (colloq)* matukio, mambo (agh. ya ajabuajabu). **on ~ing** *adj* -enye kuendelea. ~ **out** toka, ondoka (chumbani, nyumbani n.k.); toka (kwenda kwenye burudani karamu n.k.; *(of fire, light)* zimika; *(of fashion)* -wa zilipendwa; *(of a government)* acha madaraka, jiuzulu (kutoka madarakani); *(as used by the workers)* goma. **we shall get better by ~ing out** tutapata mishahara mizuri zaidi kwa kugoma; *(of a year)* isha. ~ **out to** hama nchi yako; safiri. ~ **out to sb** *(of the heart, feelings)* hurumia, -wa pamoja na. ~ **out with sb** *(colloq)* -tembea na, -wa mpenzi wa. ~ **over** *(colloq)* pokelewa, furahisha *the game did not ~ over well with the spectators* mchezo haukuwafurahisha watazamaji. ~ **over sth** chunguza kwa makini; *(review)* rudia. **~ing over** *n (colloq)* kuchunguza; uchunguzi; *(sl)* piga; *(beating)* kung'uta *they gave him a thorough ~ing -over* walimkung'uta. ~ **over to sb/sth** badili kitu kimoja kwa kingine *he went over to Rex* amebadili sigara aliyokuwa akivuta kwa Rex. ~ **round** tosheleza wote *we don't have enough drinks to ~ round* hatuna vinywaji vya kuwatosheleza wote; zunguka. ~ **round (to a place/ to do sth)** zuru, tembelea, tembea. ~ **round the bend** *(colloq)* pata wazimu, kasirika, -wa mwehu. ~ **through** pitishwa, idhinishwa *the motion did not ~ through* pendekezo halikuidhinishwa. ~ **through sth** *(of discussion)* jadili kwa undani; *(paper, book etc)* pitia; *(search)* pekua, shiriki; *(suffer)* teseka, pitia *you 'll have to ~ through the hardships* utalazimika kuteseka; *(of a book, edition etc)* uzwa; maliza, tumia (fedha). ~ **through with sth** timiza, kamilisha, endelea hadi mwisho. ~ **to/towards sth** changia, saidia kufanya *the savings will ~ towards the car I want to buy* akiba itachangia fedha za kununulia gari nililokusudia. ~ **together** enda pamoja, ambatana *war and famine ~ together* vita na njaa huenda pamoja; endana, chukuana *the black coat and white shirt ~ together* koti jeusi na shati jeupe vinachukuana. ~ **under** zama; *fig)* shindwa; *(of business)* filisika. ~ **up** panda *the prices will ~ up* bei zitapanda; *(of buildings)* jengwa; *(explosion, fire)* lipuliwa, teketezwa; ingia chuo kikuu; -enda mjini (agh. mji mkuu). ~ **up sth** panda, kwea mlima, mti, ngazi). ~ **with sb/sth** ambatana; fuatana *~ with him* fuatana naye; *(of views etc)* kubaliana; *(together)* enda pamoja; ambatana *the table ~es with the dining chairs* meza inaambatana na viti vya kulia; *(match)* chukuana *this suit doesn't ~ with white shoes* suti hii haichukuani na vitu vyeupe; *(colloq) (of a young man and a girl)* tembea/fuatana. ~ **without (sth)** kosa, vumilia kutokuwa (na kitu fulani) *you will have to ~ without a breakfast* utalazimika kuvumilia kukaa pasipo kifungua kinywa *~ without saying* inafahamika pasi kuelezwa, bila kupingwa. **~ing** *n* 1 hali ya njia, barabara kwa matembezi n.k. *go while the ~ing is good* ondoka wakati hali inaruhusu. 2 kuondoka *(usu) (pl) (lit, and fig)*. **comings and ~ings** kuja na kuondoka. 3 mwendo, kasi *n (all uses colloq) all systems ~* mambo tayari (kuondoka). **all the ~** -enyewe, -a kisasa. **at one ~** kwa mpigo mmoja. **be full of ~; have plenty of ~** -wa na bidii/juhudi nyingi. **be on the ~** shughulika. **have a ~ (at sth)** jaribu. **near ~** ponea chupuchupu. **no ~** mwanzo mbaya; *(impossible situation)* hali isiyowezekana/mbaya *it's no ~ asking to ~ to the disco* haiwezekani kuomba kuenda disko. **no ~ area** eneo lililopigwa marufuku. ~ **between** msuluhishi; tarishi; *(of a marriage)* mshenga; *(of seduction)* kuwadi.

goad *n* 1 mkosha, fimbo (ya kuswaga ngo'mbe). 2 *(stimulus)* mchocheo, kichocheo *vt* swaga; chochea.

goal *n* 1 kikomo, mwisho (wa mbio). 2 *(football posts)* goli; *(score)* bao, goli. ~ **keeper** *n* **(~ie** *colloq) n* golikipa, mlinda mlango. ~ **line** *n* mstari wa goli. ~ **post** *n* nguzo ya goli. ~ **mouth** *n* golini. 3 *(in life etc)* lengo.

goat *n* mbuzi. **he-~** beberu; denge la mbuzi. **she ~ (or nanny ~)** mbarika. **get one's ~** *(sl)* udhi, kasirisha. **play/act the giddy ~** fanya upumbavu. **separate the sheep from the ~s** tenga wema na wabaya. **~ee** *n* ndevu (kama) za mbuzi (beberu). ~ **-heard** *n* mchunga mbuzi. **~skin** *n* 1 vazi lililotengenezwa kwa ngozi ya mbuzi.

gob^1 *n (vulg)* ute unaoteleza, fundo (la mate).

gob^2 *n (derog sl)* mdomo. **shut your ~** funga kidomo/bakuli lako.

gob^3 *n (US sl.)* baharia, mwanamaji.

gobbet *n* tonge; *(of meat)* chinyango.

gobble^1 *vt* ~ **up** -la kwa pupa.

gobble[2] *vt* gooka.
gobbler *n* bata mzinga dume.
gobbledygook Kichina; lugha isiyoeleweka.
goblet *n* bilauri (agh ya divai).
gobblin *n* zimwi, jini, afriti.
go-cart *n* gari la mkono.
god *n* 1 mungu. **the ~s** miungu. 2 **G~** Mungu, Mola, Allah, Muumba. **G~ willing** Mungu akipenda *G~ be with you* Mungu awe nanyi *G~ forbid! ~ preserve us!* Mungu aepushie mbali **G~'s truth!** haki ya Mungu! **thank G~!** shukuru Mungu. 3 mungu mdogo *he thinks he is a ~* anajifanya mungu mdogo. 4 *(theatre)* **the ~s** viti vya juu. 5 *(compounds)* **~child, ~ daughter/~son** *n* mtoto wa ubatizo. **~father/~mother**, baba/mama wa ubatizo. **~-damn (ed)**/*(US)* **~dam** *adv,adj (sl vulg)* mno, sana. **~ fearing** *adj* -chaji mungu, -cha mungu. **~forsaken** *adj* 1 *(of place)* -a ovyo, baya sana, la kukatisha tamaa. 2 **G~'s acre** *n (old use)* makaburini, uwanja wa kanisa. **~s end** *n* bahati kubwa (isiyotegemewa). **~speed** *n wish sb ~speed* takia mtu safari ya heri. **~dess** *n* Mungu wa kike. **~head** *n* uungu. **the G~head** mungu. **~less** *adj* kafiri, -siomjua/-siotambua Mungu, -ovu. **~like** *adj* -a kimungu, kama mungu. **~ly** *adj* -enye kucha mungu. **~liness** *n*.
godown *n* ghala, bohari.
go-getter *n (colloq)* mwenye bidii, jasiri.
goggle *vi* ~ **(at)** kodolea macho. **~-box** *n (sl)* televisheni. **~-eyed** *adj* -enye macho ya gololi/tunguja. **~s** *n* miwani mikubwa ya kuzuia upepo, maji, vumbi n.k.
goitre *n* tezi.
gold *n* 1 dhahabu. **worth one's weight in ~** -enye thamani kubwa, muhimu sana. 2 utajiri. 3 *(fig)* kitu cha thamani sana; tabia nzuri *a heart of ~* moyo mkunjufu/mkarimu. 4 rangi ya dhahabu. **~ beater** mtengeneza mabamba ya dhahabu, mfua dhahabu. **~-digger** *n* mchimba dhahabu; *(sl)* mwanamke anayetafuta mapenzi kwa sababu ya hela. **~ field** machimbo ya dhahabu. **~-dust** *n* mavumbi ya dhahabu. **~-foil, ~-leaf** *n* jaribosi/bamba/karatasi ya dhahabu. **~mine** *n* mgodi wa dhahabu; *(fig)* mradi wa utajiri/tija. **~-plate** *n* vyombo (vijiko, sahani n.k.) vya dhahabu. **~-rush** *n* kikaka cha kutafuta dhahabu iliyogunduliwa. **~ smith** *n* sonara, mfua dhahabu. **~en** *adj* 1 -a dhahabu, kama dhahabu, -enye rangi ya dhahabu. 2 -a thamani sana, -a tunu; -zuri mno *a ~en opportunity* nafasi ya kufaa sana. **the ~en age** (katika hadithi za kiyunani) zamani za ustawi, heri na furaha kubwa; kipindi cha upeo wa ustawi wa fasihi na sanaa. **~en handshake** *n* kiinua mgongo kikubwa anachopewa mtu wa cheo anapostaafu. **the ~en mean** *n* kanuni ya kutovuka mpaka/ya suluhu (katika tabia ya mtu). **the ~en rule** *n* kanuni ya muhimu/ya msingi/gezi (k.m. watendee wenzio kama unavyopenda kutendewa). **~en wedding** *n* maadhimisho ya miaka 50 ya ndoa.
golf *n* gofu *vi* cheza gofu. **~ball** *n* mpira wa gofu. **~-club** *n* 1 klabu ya gofu. 2 kigoe/kingoe cha gofu. **~-course** *n* uwanja wa gofu. **~er** *n* mchezaji wa gofu.
Goliath *n* Goliati; *(fig)* pandikizi la mtu.
golliwog *n* mwanasesere mweusi.
golly *int (sl)* loo! tamko la kuonyesha mshangao.
golosh *n see* **galosh**.
gondola *n* gondola (mtumbwi/mashua ndefu iliyotumika katika mifereji ya Venice) *~ car* jukwaa la bidhaa la reli. **gondolier** *n* mwendesha gondola.
gone *pp of* **go**.
goner *n (sl)* kitu kilichoharibika kabisa/liokwisha.
gong *n* upatu; *(sl)* nishani, medali *vt* ashiria kwa upatu.
goniometer *n* goniometa (kipima

pembe).
gonna *(US sl)* ~**ing to** *see* **go**.
gonorrhoea/rohea *n* kisonono.
good *adj* 1 -ema, -zuri *a ~ car* gari zuri *a ~ blade (i.e. sharp)* wembe mkali. 2 -a kufaa; -a maana. 3 -enye kumudu/ kuweza kutenda, hodari, bora *she is a very ~ teacher* yeye ni mwalimu hodari sana. 4 -a kupendeza, -a manufaa *the news he brought was ~* habari alizotupasha zilitupendeza. **have a ~ time** jifurahisha *(colloq) a ~ time girl* msichana mpenda starehe tu. **(all) in ~ time** kwa wakati unaofaa. **be a ~ thing** -wa jambo la manufaa *lower taxes are a ~ thing for all the people* kodi nafuu ni jambo la manufaa kwa watu wote. **be a ~ thing that** -wa na bahati kuwa. **have a ~ night** lala vizuri. **start/arrive/in ~time** anza/fika/ondoka mapema. **put in/say a ~ word for sb** tetea mtu. 5 fadhili, karimu *be ~ enough to* tafadhali. **be ~ to sb** fadhili mtu. *(in exclamations of surprise, shock etc)* **~God! ~ Heavens!** Mungu wangu! subuhana. 6 kamili, -a kutimiza, -mno *give sb a ~ scolding* mkaripie mno *he had a ~ excuse* alikuwa na kisingizio/sababu nzuri. **have a ~ mind to do sth** tamani, -wa na hamu kubwa kufanya kitu. **all in ~ time** wakati utakapowadia. 7 kakamavu, -enye nguvu *her hearing is still very ~* bado anasikia vizuri. 8 -a kuchekesha *she told us a ~ story* alitusimulia hadithi ya kuchekesha *as ~ as a play* kichekesho, senema ya bure. 9 -a kufaa kuliwa, -pya, -bichi *this meat is still ~* nyama hii bado inafaa kuliwa. 10 -a kuaminika, -ahakika *the brakes on this car are ~* breki za gari hili zinaaminika *~ for 1000/=* inayofaa kwa sh 1000/= *my car is ~ for another two years* gari langu litafaa kwa muda wa miaka miwili ijayo *be ~ for a ten mile walk* -wa tayari kutembea maili kumi *this ticket is ~ for one year* tiketi hii inafaa kwa muda wa mwaka mmoja. 11 *(of behaviour)* -enye adabu; -pole *a ~ child* mtoto mwenye adabu. **as ~ as gold** -ema sana/tulivu. 12 adilifu. **a ~ person** mtu mwadilifu. **~ works** misaada, fadhila kwa wasiojiweza. 13 sawa *I thought it ~* niliona sawa. 14 *(in forms of greetings)* **~ morning /afternoon/evening** hujambo? habari za asubuhi/mchana/jioni. **~ morning** subalkheri. **~afternoon** masalkheri. **~night** alamsiki, usiku mwema. 15 (*as a polite (but often ironical, patronizing or indignant form of address) my ~ man* mume wangu (we). **your ~ lady** mke wako. **the ~ people** malaika. 16 *(considerable)* -ingi *a ~ deal of money* fedha nyingi *it takes a ~ deal of time* inachukua muda mrefu. 17 zaidi ya, si chini ya *we waited for a ~ hour* tulingojea kwa zaidi ya saa moja. 18 mno *a ~ deal of money* fedha nyingi mno. 19 **as ~ as** sawa na *he is as ~ as called me a thief* aliyoyasema ni sawa na kuniita mwizi. 20 **make ~** faulu, shinda, fanikiwa *he made ~ as a mechanic* alifaulu katika kazi yake ya umakanika. **make sth ~** fidia *make ~ a loss* fidia hasara, timiza (shabaha, haja) *they made ~ their escape* walitimiza shabaha yao ya kutoroka *the wall will have to be made ~ before painting* itakubudi kutengeneza ukuta (kuziba nyufa n.k.) kabla ya kupaka rangi; thibitisha madai. 21 *(phrases and compounds)* **~ breeding** adabu, uungwana; jamala. ~ **fellowship** uhusiano mzuri, urafiki mwema; ukunjufu. **~ for-nothing** -onyo; nyangarika. **~ hearted** -pole. **~ humoured** *adj* changamfu, -enye uchangamfu. **~ looking** -enye sura ya kupendeza, jamili **~** *looks* sura ya kupendeza. **~ luck** bahati njema. **~ money** fedha halisi; *(colloq)* mshahara mzuri. **throw ~ money after bad** poteza fedha kwa kujaribu kunusuru zilizopotea **~** *natured* tulivu, -karimu. **~ neighbour** jirani

mwema. ~ **sense** busara. ~**-tempered** *adj* -pole *n* 1 (kitu) chema/adili/-a faida/-a thamani. **do** ~ auni, saidia. **for the** ~ **of** kwa manufaa/faida ya. **do sb** ~ nufaisha mtu. **be up to no** ~ tenda/jishughulisha na maovu. **be no/ not much/any/some** ~ (-wa) kazi bure, -tosaidia. 2 **for** ~ kabisa. 3 **to the** ~ faida. 4 *(pl)* wema, -wa bora. ~**-bye** *int n* kwa heri *say ~-bye to* aga, agana na. **G~ Friday** *n* Ijumaa Kuu. ~**ish** *adj* kubwa, mbali/zuri kidogo *a ~ distance away* mbali kidogo *~ food* chakula kizuri kiasi. ~**ly** *adj* 1 -zuri, -enye sura mwanana. 2 -ingi, kubwa. ~**ness** *n* 1 wema, uzuri, hisani. **have the** ~ **to** kwa hisani yako. 2 *(strength, quality)* nguvu, utamu *(in exclamations) G~ness Gracious/G~ me!* Mungu wangu! *Thank ~!* shukuru Mungu! ~ **knows!** sijui!; Mungu Shahidi! ~**will** *n* 1 urafiki, ukarimu, mapenzi. 2 *(of trade)* sifa njema, jina. ~**y** *n (colloq)* peremende; halua; kitu kizuri. ~- ~ *n* mtu ajifanyaye kuwa mtakatifu.

goods *n (pl)* 1 bidhaa, mali inayohamishika. ~ **and chattels** *(leg)* mali ya mtu. 2 shehena, mizigo (ichukuliwayo na garimoshi n.k.). ~ **train** *(US) (freight train)* gari (moshi) la mizigo *piece of ~ (colloq)* mtu.

goof *(sl) n* mjinga; mpumbavu *vt,vi* ~ **(of)** fanya jambo la kijinga, bananga.

goon *n (sl)* 1 mjinga; zebe. 2 *(US)* mtu anayeajiriwa kutisha watu.

goose *n* 1 bata bukini. **cook sb's** ~ zima mtu; komesha. **kill the ~ that lays the golden eggs** *(prov)* haribu cha baadaye kwa tamaa ya sasa, kula mbegu. **be unable to say boo to a** ~ -wa mwoga sana. **all one's geese are swans** chongo kuona kengeza, sifu mno kila kitu. ~**-flesh** *n* kimbimbi. ~**step** kwenda bila kukunja magoti. 2 mbumbumbu. **gosling** *n* mtoto wa bata maji/bukini.

gooseberry *n* zabibubata. **play ~berry** -wa kisikimtu wa wapenzi wawili.

Gordian *adj (only in)* ~ **knot** fundo/ fumbo gumu kufungua; jambo gumu (kutatua). **cut the ~ knot** tatua tatizo kwa nguvu au bila kujali masharti.

gore[1] *n* damu iliyoganda. **gory** *adj* -enye/-liotapakaa damu; -a kumwaga damu, -a kikatili.

gore[2] *n (of cloth)* kijambia; pembe; kipande cha pembe tatu cha nguo n.k. *vt* piga pembe, guta.

gorge[1] *n* 1 korongo. 2 umio; vilivyo kwenye matumbo *it made his ~ rise* kilimtia kichefuchefu; kilimuudhi.

gorge[2] *vi,vt* ~ **(oneself) (on/with sth)** lafua *n* ulafi, kuvimbiwa.

gorgeous *adj* 1 -zuri sana, -enye marembo (mapambo) mengi. 2 -a kufurahisha, -a kupendeza, tamu. ~**ly** *adv.*

Gorgon *n (Gk myth)* Gogoni: mmoja wa ndugu wa kike watatu wenye nywele za nyoka; mtu anayetisha; mwanamke anayechukiza.

gorilla *n* sokwe.

gosh *int (sl)* (*also* **by** ~) kumbe, loo.

gosling *n see* **goose**.

gospel *n* 1 **G~** injili. 2 *(doctrine, tenets)* imani. 3 ~ **truth** (jambo la) kweli kabisa.

gossamer *n* 1 utando. 2 kitambaa cha shashi nyepesi sana *(attrib) a ~ veil* veli ya shashi nyepesi.

gossip 1 umbeya, udaku. 2 uandishi wa habari za watu za binafsi k.m. katika gazeti. *(attrib)* **the ~ column** safu ya habari za binafsi. 3 *(chat)* soga, maongezi. 4 mbeya, mdaku *vi* sema/ andika habari za binafsi; piga domo/ umbeya.

got *pp, pt* **of get**.

Goth *n* 1 Mgothi (kabila mojawapo la Ujerumani); mshenzi. **G~ic** *adj* 1 -a Kigothi; -a Wagothi. 2 *(arch)* -a matao yaliyochongoka; *(of printing type)* -nene; -a kijerumani *n (of language)* Kigothi *(archit)* mjengo wa Kigothi.

gotta *(US sl have got to)* ni lazima.

gotten *(US) pp* of **get**.

gouache *n* rangi ya maji; upakaji wa rangi hiyo.

gouge *n* patasi, bobari, ukombo *vt* ~ **(out)** chimba kwa ukombe; toa, ngo'a. ~ **out sb's eye** toa jicho.
goulash *n* nyama na mboga iliyotokoswa na kutiwa pilipili hoho, supu (ya nyama).
gourd *n* kitoma, kibuyu.
gourmand *n* mlafi, mtu apendaye chakula. **gourmet** *n* kidomo (wa chakula); mjuzi wa kuchagua chakula kizuri, mvinyo n.k. **gormandize** *vi* lafua, -la sana
gout *n* jongo. **~y** *adj* -enye jongo.
govern *vi,vt* 1 tawala. 2 *(control)* zuia; dhibiti ~ *one's temper* zuia hasira. 3 *(usu passive)* ongoza *be ~ed by the opinions of others* ongozwa na mawazo ya watu wengine. 4 *(gram esp of verb or prep)* miliki, goeka. **~ing** *adj* -enye kutawala, -a utawala. **~ance** *n* utawala; uongozi; udhibiti. **~ment** *n* 1 serikali. **G~ House** Ikulu. **responsible** ~ serikali ya madaraka. 2 utawala *democratic* ~ utawala wa kidemokrasi *adj* -a kiserikali. **~or, guv'nor** *n* 1 gavana. **G~ General** Gavana Mkuu. 2 mjumbe wa bodi ya shule, hospitali n.k. 3 *(colloq)* mkuu; mwajiri, baba *(sl)* bosi. 4 kirekebisho kinachojiendesha (katika mashine, kudhibiti gesi, mvuke n.k) msimamizi. 5 *(tutor)* mlezi. **~ess** *n* mwalimu wa kike wa watu binafsi/ wa familia fulani.
gown *n* 1 gauni. 2 joho (linalovaliwa agh. na majaji, wahadhiri n.k.) *vt* visha. **~ed solicitor** mwanasheria mwenye joho.
grab *vt* ~ **(at)** nyakua, chopoa *n* 1 unyakuzi *make a ~ at sth* nyakua kitu. **up for ~s** *(US sl)* -enye kupatikana kwa urahisi. 2 kinyakulio. **~ber** *n* mpendapesa, mnyakuzi. **land** ~ mnyakuzi ardhi.
grabble *vi* tutusa, chakura, tambaa.
grace *n* 1 *(elegance)* uzuri, madaha, madahiro, matuko. 2 **airs and ~s** namna ya kusema/kutenda iliyokusudiwa kuleta mvuto. 3 huba, upendeleo, hisani, nia njema. **an act of** ~ jambo la hiari/bure/upendo. **days of** ~ muda wa nyongeza (unaoruhusiwa baada ya siku ya kudaiwa kupita). **be in sbs good ~s** ungwa mkono/pendelewa na. 4 **have the ~ to do sth** tambua kuwa ni haki na sawa kufanya jambo. **do sth with a good/bad** ~ fanya jambo kwa hiari/ shingo upande. 5 sala ya mlo. 6 Rehema na neema za Mungu. **in a state of** ~ katika hali ya neema *fall from* ~ kosa/jikosesha rehema. 7 *(title)* **His/Her Your G~** muhasham mtukufu *vt* pamba; tunuka. **~ful** *adj* 1 -zuri, -enye madaha. 2 -a upendeleo. **~fully** *adv*. **~less** *adj* 1 -baya, bovu. 2 bila adabu. 3 -a bila neema ya Mungu. **~lessly** *adv*. **gracile** *adj* -embamba, zuri. **gracious** *adj* 1 -fadhili; -zuri; -enye hisani; -enye neema. 2 *(of God)* rehema. 3 **Good ~!** lahaula; masikini wee! **graciously** *adv.* **graciousness** *n.*
gradation *n* 1 mgeuko wa polepole. 2 daraja la maendeleo (ustawi). 3 mabadiliko ya tabaka. 4 *(philol)* apofonia. **gradate** *vi,vt* panga katika madaraja, geuka polepole.
grade *n* 1 cheo, daraja, hadhi. 2 *(US)* darasa. 3 alama, maksi. **make the** ~ *(colloq)* fikia kiwango kinachotakiwa.4 *(US)* mteremko, mwinamo. **on the up/down** ~ kupanda/kushuka. ~ **crossing** njia panda (ya reli), tambukareli *vt* 1 panga katika madaraja. 2 sawazisha ardhi. 3 ~ **up** pandisha mbegu bora (ya ngo'mbe).
gradient *n* mteremko, mwinamo.
gradual *adj (of a slope)* -sio na mteremko mkali; -a polepole, asteaste. **~ly** *adv*. **~ness** *n*.
graduate *n* 1 mtu aliyepata digrii ~/ *post ~ student* mzamili. 2 *(US)* mtu aliyehitimu mafunzo katika taasisi ya elimu (chuo, shule n.k.) *vt,vi* 1 tia alama za vipimo. 2 panga kwa madaraja. 3 pata digrii, hitimu. 4 *(chiefly US)* toa digrii/diploma/cheti n.k.). **graduation** *n* mahafali.

graffito *n (usu pl)* grafiti: michoro ya mikwaruzo/maneno ukutani.
graft[1] *n* 1 kipandikizi: chipukizi lililopandikizwa katika mmea mwingine. 2 *(surg)* kipandikizi: kipande cha ngozi au cha mfupa n.k. cha mtu au mnyama kilichotiwa mwilini mwa mtu mwingine au katika sehemu nyingine ya mwili uleule *vt* pandikiza chipukizi/ngozi katika mti, mtu au mwili; unganisha.
graft[2] *n* rushwa *vi* 1 -la rushwa. 2 suka mpango, fuata desturi ya udanganyifu (mara nyingi katika biashara). **~er** *n* mla rushwa.
grail *n (usu* **the Holy G~)** kikombe ama sahani iliyotumiwa na Kristo wakati wa Alhamisi kuu/Karamu ya Mwisho.
grain *n* 1 *(collective sing)* nafaka. **~ elevator** ghala. 2 mbegu, punje. 3 chembe *~s of sugar* chembechembe za sukari *(fig)* kiasi kidogo. 4 kizio kidogo kabisa cha uzito. 5 mpangilio asili wa fumwale katika mbao. **be/go against the ~** fanya kinyume cha msimamo/ada.
gram[1] *n* choroko *green/black ~* choroko kijani/nyeusi.
gram[2] *n* gramu.
grammar *n* 1 sarufi. 2 kitabu cha sarufi. **~ school** *(GB)* shule ya sekondari (inayoelemea taaluma). **~ian** *n* mwanasarufi. **grammatical** *adj* -a kisarufi *~ error* kosa la kisarufi. **grammatically** *adv*.
gramme *n see* **gram**
gramophone *n* santuri gramafoni.
grampus *n* pomboo; mtu anayekoroma.
granary *n* ghala ya nafaka.
grand *adj* 1 -kubwa; -kuu *(official title) G~ Master* Mkuu, ashrafu; *(sports)* bingwa wa mchezo wa sataranji *G~ Vizier (arch)* Waziri Mkuu Uturuki *~ finale* kilele, mwisho maalum. **~ entrance** lango kuu. 2 muhimu; maalum. 3 -tukufu; -a fahari *~ clothes* nguo za fahari. 4 -enye kujiona, -a majivuno. 5 *(colloq)* -a kupendeza, zuri sana. 6 kamili *the ~ results of our efforts* matokeo kamili ya jitihada zetu. 7 -adilifu. 8 *(phrases)* **~ opera** opera: maigizo ya dhamira makini yatekelezwayo kwa kuimba. **~ piano** piano babu kuu. **G~ Prix** mashindano ya kimataifa ya (mbio za) magari. **~ stand** jukwaa maalum (lenye paa). **~ly** *adj*. **~eur** *n* fahari, ukuu, utukufu. **~iloquent** *adj* -a kujivuna maneno, -semi, -a kupiga domo. **~iose** *adj* 1 -a fahari, -a kujionyesha. 2 -a kujivuna; adhimu.
grand[2] *(pref)* **~ child** *n* mjukuu. **~ son/daughter** mjukuu wa kiume/kike. **~ parent** babu/bibi. **~ father/mother** babu/bibi. **~ nephew/niece** mjukuu wa mjomba/shangazi. **~uncle/aunt** mjomba/shangazi wa baba/ mama. **~ father clock** saa babu kuu. **~-dad/ grandad** *n (colloq)* babu. **~ma** *n (colloq)* bibi. **~pa** *n (colloq)* babu.
grandee *n (hist)* Mhispania au Mreno wa cheo cha juu.
grange *n* nyumba ya shamba.
granite *n* itale/matale.
granivorous *adj* -a kula nafaka.
granny,grannie *n (colloq for)* bibi, nyanya *~ knot* fundo la lifu lililofungwa vibaya.
grant *vt* 1 toa ruhusa, toa idhini, ridhia *~ sb permission/a request to do sth* toa idhini kwa mtu kufanya jambo fulani. 2 kubali (kuwa jambo fulani ni kweli) *~ the truth of what someone says* kubali ukweli wa mtu. **take sth for ~ed** chukulia jambo fulani kuwa la kweli au litatukia. **take sb for ~ed** ona wa kawaida, -totambua hadhi ya mtu *n* hiba.
granule *n* chembe ndogo, kijichembe. **granular** *adj* -a chembechembe. **granulate** *vt, vi* fanya chembechembe. **~ d** *adj* chembechembe *granulated sugar* sukari mchanga. **granulation** *n*. **granulator** *n*.
grape *n* 1 zabibu. **sour ~s** zabibu mbichi (kwa kuzikosa) *(comp)* **~-shot** marisau. **~-sugar** glukozi;

sukari matunda. **~-vine** mzabibu; *(fig)* mnong'ono, uvumi.

grape-fruit *n* balungi.

graph *n* grafu. ~ **paper** karatasi ya grafu. **~ic** *adj* 1 -a ishara/alama zinazoonekana (k.m. maandishi, michoro, vielelezo n.k.). 2 -a wazi, -a bayana, -enye kutoa picha wazi (akilini) *(comp)* **~ic arts,** sanaa za maandishi, kuchora, kunakshi n.k. *n* vitu vitokanavyo na sanaa hizo. **~ically** *adv* kwa kuandika au kuchora; *(fig)* bayana, waziwazi, dhahiri.

graphite *n* grafati: aina ya kaboni laini, nyeusi (ya kutengeneza penseli).

grapnel *n* 1 nanga ndogo (-enye makombe mengi). 2 chombo cha kushikia meli za adui.

grapple *vi* 1 ~ **(with)** kamatana na, ng'ang'ania, pambana na. 2 ~ **with** *(fig)* shughulikia, jitahidi sana kushinda/kukamilisha jambo fulani *n* **grappling-iron/grappling-hook** kulabu; ndoana.

grasp *vt,vi* 1 shika, fumbata kitu kwa nguvu; fahamu/elewa ~ *sb's hand,* shika mkono wa fulani ~ *sb's meaning* elewa hoja ya fulani. 2 ~ **at** jaribu kukamata/kuchukua; pokea/ kubali kwa moyo mkunjufu ~ *at an opportunity* jaribu kuchukua nafasi *a man who ~s at too much may lose everything* mtaka yote hukosa yote *n (power)* kushika kwa nguvu; uwezo wa kushika, umahiri, ufahamu *have a thorough ~ of the problem*, elewa vizuri tatizo *within/beyond one's ~* -enye kueleweka/sio eleweka. **~ing** *adj* -enye uchu/uchoyo wa (fedha n.k.).

grass[1] *n* 1 majani. **not let the ~ grow under one's feet** *(fig)* tekeleza jambo (bila kuchelewa), -tochelewesha jambo. 2 nyasi. 3 malisho ya wanyama; malishoni *put land under ~* geuza shamba liwe malisho. **turn/put, animals etc out to** ~ peleka wanyama malishoni. 4 *(comp)* **~roots**, *(polit)* umma. **~snake,** ukukwi. ~ **widow(er),** mjane wa muda; mwanamke anayeishi mbali na mume kwa muda. **~land** ukanda wa mbuga *vt,vi* 1 funika kwa majani/nyasi; lisha wanyama majani/ nyasi. 2 *(on sb) (GB sl)* chongea, toa habari, saliti. **~y** *adj.*

grasshopper *n* panzi.

grate[1] *vt,vi* 1 kuna, paruza ~ *coconut* kuna nazi. 2 ~ **(on)** kwaruza (kwa makelele) *(fig)* udhi, sumbua. **gratingly** *adv*. **~r** *n* kikalio/mbuzi. **coconut ~r** *n* mbuzi.

grate[2] *n* chanja ya chuma kwenye tanuri. **grating** *n* kiunzi cha nondo (agh. huwekwa dirishani kwa usalama).

grateful *adj.* ~ **(to sb) (for sth)** -a kushukuru, -enye shukurani *we are ~ to you for your help* tunakushukuru kwa msaada wako. 2 *(liter)* tamu, -a kupendeza *trees that afford a ~ shade* miti yenye kivuli cha kupendeza. **~ly** *adv.* **~ness** *n.*

gratitude *n.* ~ **(to sb) (for sth)** shukrani.

gratify *vt* 1 pendeza, furahisha, anisi *we were all gratified with/at the results* tulifurahishwa na matokeo. 2 tosheleza ~ *a child's thirst for knowledge* kidhi haja ya mtoto ya kutaka kupanua maarifa. **~ing** *adj* **gratification** *n.*

gratis *adv* bure *adj* -a bure.

gratuitous *adj* 1 -a bure, bilashi. 2 bila kisa/sababu *a ~ insult* matusi bila sababu.

gratuity *n* 1 kiinua mgongo. 2 bahashishi.

grave[1] *n* 1 kaburi. **have one foot in the** ~ chungulia kaburi. **~-clothes** sanda. ~ **stone** tofali linalowekwa juu ya kaburi likiwa na jina la marehemu. **~yard** makaburini, sehemu ya makaburi. ~ **digger** mchimba kaburi.

grave[2] *adj* -a kuhitaji makini, -kubwa; -a mashaka, -a hatari. ~ **offence** kosa kubwa *the situation is more ~* hali ni mbaya.

grave[3] *vt (arch or liter)* chora/chonga *~n image* sanamu ya kuabudika.

grave[4] *n* alama itumikayo kuonyesha

jinsi irabu inavyotamkwa katika neno fulani.

gravel *n* changarawe. **~-pit** shimo la changarawe. **~ly** *adj (of a voice)* madende/makwarukaru *vt* 1 mwagia changarawe. 2 kanganya.

graving-dock *n* gati kuu, jahabu.

gravitate *vi* ~ **to/towards** elekea, vutiwa *young people in the rural areas seem to ~ towards the urban areas* vijana wa vijijini wanavutiwa na maisha ya mijini. **gravitation** *n.*

gravity *n* 1 *(phys)* mvutano. 2 *(phys)* **specific ~** uzito halisi. 3 kiwango (cha juu) cha umakini. 4 *(of a situation)* uzito, ukubwa.

gravy *n* 1 mchuzi rojo. ~ **boat** bakuli la mchuzi. 2 *(sl)* marupurupu, michuzi. **~-train** chanzo cha fedha nyingi na za urahisi *get on the ~-train* ajiriwa katika sehemu kama hiyo.

gray *adj,n see* **grey**

graze[1] *vt,vi* 1 *(of cattle, sheep etc)* -la majani. 2 lisha, chunga. **grazingland** *n* malishoni, machungani. **grazier** mchungaji wanyama.

graze[2] *vt,vi* 1 paruza, chubua kidogo. 2 gusa, papasa *n* mchubuko, mkwaruzo.

grease *n* 1 shahamu iliyoyeyushwa. 2 grisi; bereu. **~-gun** chombo cha kuingizia grisi katika mashine. **~-paint** *n (of actors)* rangi iliyochanganywa na shahamu ya kupaka usoni *vt* paka, tia grisi (hasa katika viungo vya machine). ~ **one's palm** -pa rushwa. **~r** *n* mpaka/mtia grisi katika mashine. ~ **proof** *adj (of paper)* isiyoruhusu grisi ipite. **greasy** *adj* -enye shahamu, -enye grisi; -a kuteleza *a ~ path* njia ya kuteleza. **~-spoon** *(sl)* mkahawa mchafu. **greasily** *adv.* **greasiness** *n.*

great *adj* 1 kubwa, -ingi *a ~ enemy* adui mkubwa *a ~ deal of rain* mvua nyingi *~ with child (old use)* mja mzito; *(attr. only) she is a ~singer* yeye ni mwimbaji mkuu/mkubwa. ~ **coat** *n* 1 koti zito. 2 -enye/-a uwezo mkubwa, mashuhuri *~ men* watu mashuhuri. 3 adhimu, -kuu, muhimu. 4 *(colloq) (preceding another adj which is weakly stressed; implying surprise, contempt etc) what a ~ big lie from a child!* uwongo gani mkubwa huo kutoka kwa mtoto mdogo! 5 *(also G~er) used as a distinctive epithet of the larger of two.* **G~ Britain** *(abbr* **GB)** Uingereza, Wales na Scotland ukiondoa Ireland ya Kaskazini. **the G~ Lakes** mfululizo wa maziwa matano makubwa katikati ya mpaka wa Kanada na Marekani. **the G~ War** vita vikuu vya 1914-18. 6 *(with agent nouns; attrib only)* -enye umaarufu; -a umashuhuri sana *a ~ eater* mlaji sana ~ *landowner* kabaila maarufu. 7 *(combined with words indicating quantity) a ~ deal* -ingi sana *a ~ number of* idadi kubwa ya *a ~ while ago* zamani sana. 8 *(colloq)* -zuri, safi; -a kuridhisha **that's ~!** safi sana. 9 *(colloq pred only)* ~ **at** -enye uwezo wa. ~ **on** -enye weledi *(prefixed to a kinship words in* **grand** *to show further stage in relationship) ~-grandchild* kilembwe ~ *grandfather* babu wa baba/mama *~-grandmother* bibi wa baba/mama. **~ly** *adv* sana, kwa wingi. **~ness** *n* ukuu, ukubwa, umuhimu, umashuhuri.

greaves *n (pl)* deraya (za miguuni).

grebe *n* kibisi.

Greek *n* Mgiriki, Giriki; *(ancient)* Myunani; lugha ya Kigiriki, Kiyunani. **be ~ to one** -toeleweka *its all ~ to me* haieleweki kabisa *adj* -a Kigiriki/Kiyunani. **Grecian** *adj* -a Kigiriki, -a Kiyunani.

greed *n* ulafi, uroho. **~y** *adj* 1 **~y (for sth/to have sth)** -lafi, -enye uroho; -enye tamaa *~ for honours* -enye tamaa ya cheo. 2 **~y (to do sth)** -enye shauku. **~ily** *adv.* **~iness** *n.*

green *adj* 1 -a kijani, -a chanikiwiti *give sb/get the ~ light (colloq)* -pa mtu/pata ruhusa ya kuendelea na jambo fulani. 2 *(of fruit, wood)* -bichi *~ oranges* machungwa mabichi ~ *wood does not burn well* kuni mbichi haziwaki vizuri. 3 -sio na uzoefu; -sioendelea, mshamba, -sioelimika *he is still ~ at his job* hana uzoefu katika kazi yake. 4 *(fig)* -a kusitawi, -enye nguvu. 5 *(of the complexion)* -a kufifia, -gonjwa, -a kusawajika. **~-eyed** *adj* -enye wivu/ husuda, -a kijicho. **the ~-eyed monster** kijicho, husuda. **~ with envy** -enye kijicho sana. 6 *(special compounds)* **~-back** *n (US)* dola, noti ya fedha za Marekani. **~-fingers** *n (colloq)* ustadi katika shughuli za bustanini. **~-fly** *n* (aina ya) kidukari. **~-grocer** muuza duka la mboga na matunda. ~ **grocery** biashara/uuzaji wa mboga na matunda. **~-horn** *n* zuzu, mshamba. **~-house** nyumba ya kioo (ya kuhifadhi mimea). **greenroom** chumba (cha mapumziko). **~-stuffs, ~s** *n (pl)* mboga za majani. **~-tea** *n* majani ya chai yaliyokaushwa kwa mvuke. **~-wood** *n* mbuga (hasa wakati wa kiangazi); msitu uliostawi *n* 1 kijani, chanikiwiti. 2 *(pl)* mboga za majani (kabla au baada ya kupikwa) (US) *Christmas~s* matawi ya msonobari ya kupambia. 3 eneo linaloota majani kwa matumizi ya wote/kwa mchezo wa tufe kuzunguka shimo katika uwanja wa gofu. **~ery** *n* majani ya kijani, kijani cha mimea michanga. **~ish** *adj* -a kijanikijani *(in compounds)* **~ish-yellow** njano-kijani **~ishness** *n*. **Greenwich** *n* Griniwichi. **~ mean time** (*abbr* **GMT)** wastani wa majira ya jua; saa ya ulimwengu.

greet *vt* ~ **(with)** 1 salimu, amkia; pokea kwa kuonyesha hisia; *(in a letter)* andika maneno kuonyesha urafiki, heshima n.k. *the news was ~ed with dismay* habari zilipokewa kwa fadhaa. 2 *(of sights and sounds)* onekana, sikika. **~ings** maamkizi, salamu. **~ing-card** kadi ya salamu.

gregarious *adj* -a kuishi makundi-makundi; -enye kupenda kushirikiana na wengine. **~ly** *adv*. **~ness** *n*.

Gregorian *adj* 1 ~ **chant** -a muziki wa ibada wa Papa Gregory. 2 ~ **calendar** -a kalenda ya Papa Gregory (iliyopangwa kama ilivyo sasa).

gremlin *n* zimwi (linalosemekana linasababisha matatizo ya mitambo).

grenade *n* kombora. **grenadier** *n* *(formerly)* askari mtupa makombora; *(now)* askari wa kikosi cha miguu cha Uingereza.

grenadine *n* sharubati ya komamanga.

grew *pt of* **grow**.

grey/gray *adj* 1 -a rangi ya kijivu. 2 -enye mvi *she has ~ hair* ana mvi. **~-board** *n* shaibu. **~-headed** *adj* -zee, -a siku nyingi. ~ **matter** ubongo *n* kijivu *she is dressed in ~* amevaa nguo ya kijivu *vt,vi* -wa na rangi ya kijivu, ota mvi. **~ish** *adj* kijivukijivu. **greyhound** *n* mbwa mwindaji. **ocean ~** meli ya abiria iendayo kasi.

grid *n* 1 *(of electricity)* fito umeme (mfumo wa waya wa kupitisha umeme). 2 miraba fito, mstari ramani. 3 kiunzi cha fito (za chuma) zinazokingamana, chanja. 4 kiunzi cha waya za redio. 5 fitokaangio (za kukaangia nyama). **~dle** n kiokeo, chuma. **~iron** *n* 1 fito, kaango, chanja. 2 *(US)* kiwanja cha mpira wa miguu.

grief *n* 1 huzuni, ghamu. 2 kitu kiletacho huzuni. **bring to ~** tia nuhusi. **come to ~** pata maumivu, balaa, huzuni n.k.; angamia. **~-stricken** *adj* -liopatwa na msiba/ hasara, majonzi, -enye huzuni. **grievance (against)** *n* nung'uniko, lalamiko, dai *air one's grivance* toa manung'uniko *have a grievance against sb* -wa na kisa na, lalamikia mtu. **grieve** *vt,vi* 1 sikitisha, huzunisha. 2 sikitika, huzunika **grievous** *adj* 1 -a kuhuzunisha, -a kusikitisha *a ~ massacre* mauaji ya kuhuzunisha. 2 -a kali sana *~ pain* maumivu makali *~ punishment* adhabu kali. **grievously** *adv*.

griffin (*also* **griffon, gryphon**) *n* (*GK*

myth) mnyama (katika hadithi) mwenye mwili wa simba na kichwa na mbawa za tai.

grill *n* 1 chanja/wavu wa kuchomea nyama, samaki n.k. 2 nyama, samaki n.k. iliyochomwa. ~ **room** chumba cha kuuzia vyakula vilivyobanikwa katika hoteli. **mixed** ~ mchanganyiko wa nyama tofauti k.m. steki, maini n.k. *vt,vi* 1 choma nyama, samaki n.k.; jianika katika jua/joto kali sana. 2 *(of the police)* hoji mkosaji kwa ukali.

grille *n* dirisha lenye nondo.

grim *adj* 1 -kali, -zito, -katili. 2 *(ghastly)* baya, -a kutia hofu, -a kuogofya. **hold on like ~ death** shikilia kwa nguvu zote. **~ly** *adv*.**~ness** *n*.

grimace *n* mkunjo wa uso. **make ~s** finya uso *vi* kunja uso kwa maumivu au kuchekesha n.k.

grime *n* masizi, nongo, uchafu *vt* chafua kwa masizi, taka, uchafu. **grimy** *adj* -enye taka, -chafu, -enye masizi. ~ **faced** -enye uso mchafu. **griminess** *n*.

grin *vi,vt* 1 kenua. ~ **and bear it** vumilia maumivu, hasara n.k. bila kulalamika, jikaza kisabuni, kufa na tai shingoni. 2 eleza/jieleza kwa tabasamu *n* tabasamu.

grind *vt,vi* 1 ~ **(down) (to/into)** saga ~ *down to flour* saga mpaka kuwa unga. 2 sagika. 3 ~ **(down)** *(usu passive) (fig)* dhalilisha ~ *down the poor* onea watu maskini. 4 *(of tools etc)* noa ~ *a knife* noa kisu. 5 kereza, kwaruza; *(of teeth)* saga meno. ~ **to a halt** *(of a vehicle)* simama kwa breki za kukwaruza; *(fig) (of a process)* simama polepole *the scarcity of raw materials brought our industry ~ing to a halt* uhaba wa mali ghafi umesababisha kiwanda chetu kusimama polepole. 6 endesha kwa kuzungusha ~ *a coffee mill* endesha kinu cha kahawa kwa mkono. 7 ~ **(away) (at)** fanya kazi/soma kwa bidii na kwa muda mrefu ~ *away at one's work* fanya kazi kwa bidii sana ~ *for an examination* bukua *n (colloq)* kazi ya kuchusha ya muda mrefu. **~er** *n* mashine/kisagio, chego, gege *coffee* ~ mashine ya kusaga kahawa. 2 *(in compounds)* msagishaji/ mnoaji *a knife* ~ mnoa kisu. **~-stone** *n* kinoo, cherehe; *(for grinding grain)* kijaa. **keep one's nose to the ~stone** shurutisha kufanya kazi kwa bidii bila kupumzika.

grip *n* 1 kushika, kukamata sana kwa mkono n.k. **be at ~s with**; **come to ~s with the enemy** shambulia, shikamana, sana *have a strong* ~ shika imara; *lose one's ~ on sth* ponyokwa na kitu. 2 nguvu/uwezo wa kushika *have a good ~ of a problem (fig)* fahamu sana jambo. **take a ~ on oneself** *(colloq)* jikaza. 3 *(in a machine etc)* sehemu inayoshika/ bana; klachi. 4 **(also ~ sack)** *(US)* begi/mfuko wa msafiri *vt,vi* 1 shika, kamata sana. 2 vutia *the film ~ped the audience* filamu ilivutia hadhira. 3 fahamu jambo. 4 *(of tires)* shikamana, kwama.

gripe *vt,vi* 1 uma/umwa tumbo. 2 nung'unika, lalamika *n* malalamiko. **~r** *n* mlalamikaji. **(the) ~s** *(colloq)* maumivu makali ya tumboni, msokoto wa tumbo. ~ **water** dawa ya msokoto wa tumbo.

grippe *n* **the** ~ mafua.

grisly *adj* -a kutisha, -a kuogofya.

grist *n* nafaka ya kusagwa. **it's all ~ to the mill/all is ~ that comes to his mill** *(prov)* yote ni faida kwako, kila kitu kinaleta faida. **~-mill** mashine ya kusaga nafaka.

gristle *n* wamba-ngoma; nyama ngumu inayovutana.

grit *n* 1 mchanga, changarawe *throw ~ in the bearings* haribu mpango. 2 *(courage)* ujasiri na uvumilivu *he has no* ~ si jasiri *vt* ~ **one's teeth** kereza meno; *(fig)* jikaza kisabuni. **~ty** *adj* 1 -enye mchanga. 2 mtu jasiri/ imara. **grits** *n, pl* nafaka (aina ya shayiri) iliyokobolewa; unga wa nafaka (aina ya shayiri).

grizzle *vt (colloq) (esp of children)* lialia, nung'unika bila kuachа *n* kulialia *have a good ~* nung'unika.

grizzled *adj* -enye mvi; -a kijivu. **grizzly** -a kijivu, -enye mvi *n (also* **grizzly bear***)* dubu mkubwa na mkali wa Marekani ya kaskazini.

groan *vi,vt* 1 gumia, piga kite, koroma. 2 *(of things)* toa sauti ya kuelemewa. 3 ~ **(out)** simulia kwa sauti ya huzuni/maumivu. 4 ~ **down** zomea *n* kite, mgumio.

groats *n pl* unga wa nafaka zilizokobolewa (hasa aina ya shayiri).

grocer *n* mwuza duka (la vyakula na bidhaa ndogo ndogo). **~s (shop)** duka la bidhaa za vyakula na matumizi ya nyumbani (k.m. sabuni n.k.). **~y** *n* 1 biashara ya kuuza vyakula. 2 duka (la vyakula k.m. pilipili, -bizari). 3 *(pl)* **the ~ies** bidhaa za vyakula na matumizi ya nyumbani.

grog *n* pombe kali inayochanganywa na maji.

groggy *adj* dhaifu; legevu.

groin *n* 1 kinena. 2 *(archit)* ukingo katika paa. 3 *(US)* **see groyne** *vt* jenga kwa kuba.

groom *n* 1 saisi. 2 **bride~** bwana arusi *vt* 1 *(of horses)* tunza (kwa kulisha, kusafisha, kuchana). 2 *(of apes, monkeys)* safisha manyoya. 3 *(usu in pp, of persons) well ~ed* -liopunwa, nadhifu (hasa nywele, ndevu, nguo); *(colloq)* andaa/tayarisha mtu kwa wadhifa fulani.

groove *n* 1 mfuo. 2 *(routine)* mazoea, desturi. **be stuck in/get into a ~** fuata kawaida/desturi/mkondo. **in the ~** *(dated sl)* katika hali nzuri ya kufanya jambo; furahishwa *vt* tia mfuo. **~r** *n (sl)* mtu asiyepitwa na wakati. **groovy** *adj* -a sasa, kisasa, kileo.

grope *vi,vt* ~ **(about) (for/after)** *(lit or fig)* tafuta kwa kupapasa (kama kipofu au mtu aliye gizani), papasa *(in the dark)* tutusa ~ *one's way* tafuta njia kwa kupapasa. **gropingly** *adv*.

gross[1] *n* dazeni kumi na mbili.

gross[2] *adj* 1 -sio na adabu, chafu ~ *language* tusi. 2 *(of food)* -baya (kisichovutia); -enye mafuta mengi ~ *eater* mlaji anayependa chakula kibaya. 3 (of the senses) zito na -siochangamka. 4 wazi, dhahiri sana ~ *injustice* udhalimu dhahiri. 5 *(of vegetation)* -a kusitawi sana. 6 *(of persons)* -nene kupita kiasi, nono. 7 jumla, kamili/yote ~ *profit* faida ya jumla. ~ **national product (GNP)** Jumla ya Pato laTaifa. 8 **in (the) ~** jumla jumla *vt* leta kipato cha jumla *exports sales of cotton ~d one million last month* mwezi jana uuzaji wa pamba umechuma pato ghafi la shilingi milioni moja. **~ly** *adv*. **~ness** *n*.

grot *n (poet) see* **grotto**.

grotesque *adj* 1 -a ajabu (hata kuchekesha), -a kioja. 2 *(art)* -enye sura (za binadamu/wanyama n.k.) za ajabu *n* jambo la kuchekesha, kioja cha kuwazika. **~ly** *adv*. **~ness** *n*.

grotto *n* pango.

grotty *adj (sl)* -a kuchukiza, -a kutopendeza.

grouch *vi (colloq)* nung'unika, lalamika *n* 1 mnung'unikaji, mlalamikaji. **~y** *adj*.

ground[1] *n* 1 chini, ardhi *fall on the ~* anguka chini *(in compounds) ~ to air missiles* makombora ya kutungulia ndege *~ controlled* kuelekezwa/dhibitiwa kutoka chini. **above ~** hai. **below ~** -liokufa na kuzikwa. **fall/ be dashed to the ~** shindikana, fifia, shindwa, katishwa tamaa. **get off the ~** *(of an aircraft)* ruka; *(fig)* anza utekelezaji, zinduliwa. 2 nafasi, eneo. **cut off the ~ from under sb's feet** wahi/bashiri/gundua mipango ya mtu (na kumuaibisha). **cover (much) ~** safiri sana; *(fig. of lecture, meeting etc)* shughulikia mambo mengi. **gain ~** songa mbele, piga hatua; fanikiwa. **give/lose ~** rudi nyuma, rudishwa nyuma. **hold/stand/keep one's ~** simama imara, shikilia msimamo.

shift one's ~ geuza/badili msimamo. **suit sb down to the** ~ faa kikamilifu/ sana *common* ~ mwafaka. **forbidden** ~ mwiko. **meet sb on their own** ~ kutana na mtu mahali pake, kubaliana na masharti, ridhisha. 3 ardhi, udongo. **break fresh/new** ~ lima shamba jipya *(fig)* anza jambo jipya; chimbua kitu. 4 *(of sports)* eneo, kiwanja, uwanja; *(of fishing ~s)* mvuo; *(of hunting)* eneo. 5 *(pl)* bustani *the State House* ~ bustani inayozunguka Ikulu. 6 chini (ya bahari, mto n.k.) **touch** ~ *(of a ship)* pwelewa; *(fig)* fikia mambo muhimu baada ya mazungumzo ya juujuu tu. 7 *(pl)* punjepunje (agh. za kahawa), mashapo. 8 *(usu pl)* sababu. **on the ~s of** kwa sababu ya. **~s for divorce** sababu za kutoa/kudai talaka. **be/ give/have ~s for** -wa/-pa/-wa na sababu ya. 9 mji, sehemu wazi (isiyo na mapambo) *a dress with blue flowers on a white* ~ gauni lenye maua ya buluu na mji mweupe. 10 *(compounds)* **~-bait** chambo. **~-fish** samaki wa kilindi. ~ **-floor** orofa ya chini. **be/get in on the ~-floor** *(colloq)* wa waanzilishi. **~nut** (*also* **earthnut/peanut)** karanga. **~-plan** ramani ya nyumba ardhini. **~-rent** kodi ya kiwanja. **~sman** mtunzaji kiwanja cha mchezo. **~sheet** turubai la kutandika agh. chini ya hema. **~speed** *(aviat)* kasi ya ndege ardhini. **~crew/staff** *(aviat.)* wahudumu uwanjani. **~swell** mawimbi mazito (yanasabaishwa na dharuba ya mbali). **~work** *(usu fig)* maandalizi, matayarisho ya kazi *n (usu fig)* msingi *vt,vi* 1 *(of a ship)* kwama baharini, panda mwamba; *(of aircraft)* zuiliwa kuruka. 2 ~ **arms** *(mil)* weka silaha chini. 3 ~ **sth on sth** tumia kama msingi. 4 ~ **sb in sth** funda/-pa mtu (mafunzo ya) msingi; *(elect.)* unganisha waya n.k. wa umeme na ardhi. **~ing** *n* mafundisho hasa ya msingi. **~less** *adj* bila sababu/msingi maalum.

ground[2] *pt pp of* **grind** ~ *rice* unga wa mchele. ~ **glass** kioo kisichoona (kwa kusagwa).

group *n* 1 jamii, kundi, kikundi *so and so's* ~ kundi la akina fulani. 2 *(cultivating together)* chaa. 3 *(mil)* kikosi. **~-captain** *n* ofisa kiongozi wa jeshi la anga. 4 *(math)* kikundi. 5 *(mus)* bendi *vt,vi* panga/weka katika makundi *~ed data* data ya vikundi.

grouse[1] *n* kwale wa Ulaya.

grouse[2] *(colloq) vi* nung'unika, lalamika *n* manung'uniko, malalamiko.

grout[1] *n (construction)* niru, chokaa laini, rojo *cement* ~ machicha ya saruji *vt* paka nyiru, ziba kwa chokaa.

grove *n* kijisitu.

grovel *vi* tambaa, lala kifudifudi, *(abase oneself)* jidhili, pigia magoti, angukia ~ *in the dirt (fig)* nyenyekea kabisa, jifanya mnyonge. **~ler** *n.*

grow *vi,vt* 1 kua; mea, ota *the child is ~ing well* mtoto anakua vizuri *maize ~ well in Iringa* mahindi yanaota vizuri huko Iringa. ~ **out of** -wa kubwa kuliko/kua; zidi. 2 *(increase)* zidi, ongezeka. ~ **on/upon** zidi kupendeza *she ~s on you* anazidi kukupendeza *the book grows on me* kitabu kinaniteka, kinazidi kunipendeza; acha kufanya (kwa uzee) *I' ve ~n out playing football* nimeacha kucheza mpira; tokana na *his troubles ~ out of his laziness* matatizo yake yanatokana na uvivu wake. ~ **up** komaa, pevuka, -wa -zima *what do you want to do when you ~ up?* unataka kufanya nini utapokuwa mtu mzima?; kua *friendship grew up between the two students* urafiki ulikua kati ya wanafunzi hawa wawili. **~ing pains** *n pl* maumivu ya viungo; *(fig)* matatizo ya mwanzoni mwa shughuli fulani **~n up** *n* mtu mzima. 3 -wa ~ **older** konga, chakaa ~ *smaller* pungua ~ *taller* refuka. ~ **dark** -wa giza. 4 *(agrc.)* panda, lima, otesha *he ~s three crops a year* anapanda mara tatu kwa mwaka. 5 fuga, acha kitu kikue ~ *a beard* fuga ndevu, acha ndevu zikue. 6 ~ **to be/ like etc** zoea *I grew to like cheese when I lived in Germany* nilipokuwa Ujerumani nilianza kuzoea jibini. **~er** *n* 1. mwoteshaji 2. mmea (unaokua kwa njia fulani) *a fast/slow* ~ mmea unaokua upesi/polepole. **~th** *n* 1 kuzidi, kukua, ukuaji. 2 ongezeko. **~th rate** kima cha ongezeko. 3 *(vegetatition)* ulimaji, uotaji *this year's ~ of maize has been good* uotaji wa mahindi mwaka huu ulikuwa mzuri. 4 maendeleo; kuenea eneo. 5 maotea. 6 *(med)* kushika ugonjwa k.m. kansa, donda ndugu.

growl *vi,vt* 1 nguruma. 2 *(complain)* nung'unika. 3 ~ **(out)** sema kwa kunguruma *n* mngurumo; manung'uniko. **~ingly** *adj.*

grown *pp of* **grow**.

groyne *(US* **groin)** *n* bomazuizi, kinga (baharini).

grub[1] *n* 1 funza. 2 *(sl)* chakula. **~by** *adj* 1 -chafu, -enye taka. 2 *(of fruit)* -enye funza. **~bily** *adv.* **~biness** *n.*

grub[2] *vi,vt (sl)* -la pekua. ~ **about** chimbachimba. *(of soil)* ~ **up** tifua, fukua;

grudge *vt* sunza, toa shingo upande *n* mfundo, kinyongo *bear a ~ against* -wa na kisasi dhidi (ya), -wa na kinyongo na. **grudgingly** *adv.*

gruel *n (of rice)* ubwabwa, fuka, uji wa mapande; *(of milk and maize flour)* uji, farne.

gruelling *adj* gumu sana, -a kuchosha.

gruesome *adj* -a kutisha, -a kuogofya; kuchukiza. **~ly** *adv.* **~ness** *n.*

gruff *adj (of behaviour)* -a tabia mbaya; *(voice)* -nene, -a kukwaruza.

grumble *vt,vi* 1 **~(at/about/over sth)** lalamika, nung'unika ~ *over trivial issues* lalamika kwa mambo yasiyo na maana. 2 ~ **(out)** nung'unika. 3 vuma, nguruma, *n* lalamiko. **~r** *n.*

grumpy *adj* -enye harara, -enye hamaki; -enye chuki. **grumpily** *adv.*

grumpiness *n.*

grunt *vt,vi* 1 koroma. 2 *(of persons)* guna ~ *out an answer* mumunya jibu *n* mkoromo. **~er** 1 *n* mguno. 2 nguruwe.

gryphon *n* see **griffin**

guano *n* guano: mavi ya ndege wa baharini yatumikayo kama mbolea.

guarantee *n* **(in law guaranty)** 1 *(written promise)* dhamana. 2 mdhamana. 3 **(guarantor)** mdhamini. 4 **(in law guaranty)** *(sth offered)* rahani *he offered his house as a ~* aliweka nyumba yake rahani. 5 *(colloq) (assurance)* hakikisho *passing an examination is not always a ~ of getting a job* kufaulu mtihani hakumhakikishii mtu kupata kazi *vt* 1 dhamini, weka rahani, toa uhakikisho *he does not ~ habitual criminals* hadhamini wahalifu sugu. 2 *(colloq) (without legal obligation)* ahidi *we ~d to pay you well* tuliahidi kukulipa vizuri. **guarantor** *n* mdhamini. **guaranty** *n (leg)* dhamana, mdhamana; rahani.

guard *n* 1 ulinzi *you will be on ~ today* utakuwa mlinzi leo *the militia was orderd to keep ~* mgambo aliamriwa kulinda lindo. 2 tahadhari, kujihadhari, kujikinga. **be on/off one's ~** kujihadhari, kujikinga *he was on his ~ against pick pockets* alijihadhari na wezi wa mifukoni. 3 askari, kikosi cha askari walinzi, mlinzi. **change ~** *(mil)* badilisha walinzi. **mount ~** ingia lindoni (kama mlinzi). **relieve ~** chukua nafasi ya mlinzi aliyemaliza zamu. **stand ~** kuwa mlinzi, linda. 4 *(also called warder)* askari jela (wanaolinda jela). 5 *(GB) (of a railway train)* gadi. 6 *(pl)* **G~s** walinzi wa kiongozi wa nchi/mfalme. 7 gadi, askari (wenye kumlinda, kumpa heshima, kumsindikiza mtu) *the President inspected the ~ of honour* Rais alikagua gwaride la heshima. 8 *(compounds)* ~ **boat/ ship** n. mashua/meli ya doria. ~

house n *(mil)* nyumba ya walinzi; mahabusu. ~ **room** chumba cha walinzi, mahabusu *vt* 1 linda ~ *a bridge* linda daraja. 2 ~ **against** (ji) hadhari, (ji)linda kwa uangalifu ~ *against malaria* jikinge dhidi ya malaria. **~ed** *(of statements)* -a hadhari ya *~ed answer* jibu la hadhari. **~edly** *adv* kwa hadhari. **~ian** *n* 1 *(official or private legal use)* mlezi. 2 mwangalizi. **~ianship** *n* ulezi; ulinzi.

guava *n (tree)* mpera; *(fruit)* pera.

gubernatorial *adj (US, Nigeria)* -a gavana, -a kuhusu gavana.

gudgeon *n* samaki wadogo ambao hutumiwa kama chambo.

guerden *n (poet)* zawadi, tuzo, malipo *vt* toa zawadi, tuza.

guerrilla,guerilla *n* 1 askari wa msituni; mpiganaji wa kuvizia (agh. wa vita vya msituni), apiganaye katika vikundi vidogo msituni. **urban** ~ *n* mpiganaji wa kuvizia (wa mjini). ~ **warfare/war** vita vya msituni/vya askari wa msituni.

guess *vt,vi* 1 ~ **(at)** kisia, bahatisha *I should ~ your age as* kwa kukisia, kubahatisha umri wako ni. 2 *(think)* ona, dhani *I ~ you got it wrong (US colloq)* nadhani umekosea *n* dhanio, kisio. **it is any body's** ~ hakuna mtu mwenye hakika. **at a** ~ kwa kubahatisha. **make a lucky** ~ bunia, bahatisha *your ~ is as good as mine* ni vigumu kukisia. **by** ~ kwa kubahatisha. **~timate** *(modern colloq)* bahatisha kwa kukisia na kufikiri. ~ **work** kazi ya kubahatisha.

guest *n* 1 mgeni. ~ **room** chumba cha wageni. ~ **of honour** *n* mgeni wa heshima. ~ **house** *n* nyumba ya wageni. ~ **night** *n* usiku wa karamu (ya wageni wa klabu). **paying** ~ *n* mgeni alipaye kodi ya malazi na chakula (kwenye nyumba ya mtu).

guffaw *n* kicheko kikubwa *vt* angua kicheko.

guide *n (of a person or instruction)* 1 kiongozi. **Girl G~** skauti wa kike *teacher's guide* kiongozi cha mwalimu *railway ~* kiongozi cha safari za gari moshi. 2 kiashirio, kishawishi. **~lines** mwongozo (agh. kutoka kwa wenye madaraka). 3 ~ **book** kitabu cha kuongoza wageni/wasafiri. 4 kielekezi **~d missile** kometi inayoongozwa *vt* ongoza, elekeza, onyesha njia. **guidance** *n* 1 kuongoza; kuongozwa; uongozi *for your guidance* kwa mwongozo wako. 2 ushauri(kwa kazi).

guild *n* chama, ushirika (wa watu wenye matakwa au shughuli za namna moja). ~ **socialism** mfumo wa kuongoza kiwanda kwa baraza la wanachama.

guilder *n* gilda (sarafu ya Uholanzi).

guile *n* hila, ujanja *get it by ~* pata kwa ujanja. **~less** *adj*. **~ful** *adj*.

guillotine *n* gilotini: bamba la kukata kichwa (kwa wahalifu Ufaransa); kisu cha kukatia makaratasi; *(in parliament)* ukatishaji mjadala (wa kupinga mswada) *vt* kata (kwa bamba, kisu) kichwa, karatasi.

guilt *n* hatia. **~less** *adj* -tokuwa na hatia; -safi *~less of robbery* -siokuwa na hatia ya ujambazi. **~y** *adj* ~ **(of)** 1 liofanya kosa *plead ~ of on offence* kiri kosa. 2 -enye hatia, -enye kuonekana na hatia *~ look* -enye uso wa hatia *look ~* onekana kuwa na hatia *~ conscience* hisia ya hatia, majisuto *be found ~* onekana na hatia *find ~* ona/pata na hatia. ~ **or not** ~ una makosa au huna.

guinea *n* gini (sarafu ya zamani ya dhahabu yenye thamani ya shilingi ishirini na moja) **~-corn** *n* mtama. **~-fowl** *n* kanga; *(crested)* kororo; chepeo. **~-pig** *n* 1 nungubandia (agh. hutumiwa kwa majaribio). 2 mjaribiwa.

guise *n* 1 *(old use)* mtindo wa vazi. 2 **in/under the** ~ **of** kwa kusingizia, kwa kutumia/-kujifanya; -enye umbo la.

guitar/guitor *n* gita.

gulch *n (US)* bonde jembamba.

gulf *n* 1 ghuba. **Persian** ~ Ghuba ya

Uajemi. 2 *(cavity)* shimo kubwa; korongo refu *(fig)* tofauti kubwa bainishi.
gull[1] *n* shakwe.
gull[2] *n* *(simpleton)* mjinga, zuzu, mshamba *vt* danganya, ghilibu, laghai. **~ibility** *n.* **~ible** *adj* -enye kudanganywa.
gullet *n* umio; koo.
gully[1] 1 mvo, korongo. ~ **hole** *n* mfereji wa maji machafu, mtaro.
gulp *vt,vi* ~ **(down)** gugumia (maji, chakula); meza kwa pupa, bwia. ~ **back/down tears** *n* zuia machozi.
gum[1] *n* ufizi wa meno, sine. **~boil** jipu la ufizi.
gum[2] *n* 1 sandarusi; gundi, ulimbo. 2 *chewing* ~ ubani. 3 *(also ~ tree)* mkalitusi. **up a ~ tree** *(sl)* kwa shida sana. ~ **boot** buti ya mpira. ~ **shoe** *(US)* raba; *(sl)* mpelelezi *vt* gandisha, tia gundi, paka gundi. **~my** *adj.*
gum[3] *n (esp. N England) (in oaths etc)* Mungu.
gumption *n (colloq)* akili, busara.
gun *n* 1 bunduki. **be going great ~s** endelea vizuri sana. **blow great ~s of the wind** vuma kwa nguvu sana. **tand/stick to one's ~s** shikilia msimamo wako *(be) sure as a* ~ (-wa na) hakika kabisa ~ *barrel n* mtutu. ~ **boat** *n* manowari ndogo inayobeba mizinga. ~ **boat diplomacy** *(fig)* diplomasia ya vitisho ~ *cap n* fataki. ~ **carriage** *n* gari la mzinga. ~ **cotton** *n* baruti ya pamba iliyolowekwa kwenye asidi. ~ **fire** *n* mlio/mapigo ya bunduki/mzinga. ~ **man** *n* jambazi. **~metal** *n* mchanganyiko wa madini ya shaba na bati au zinki. ~ **powder** *n* baruti. ~ **room** *n (in a warship)* chumba cha maofisa wa ngazi za chini. ~ **running** *n* magendo ya silaha. ~ **runner** *n* mwendesha/ mfanya magendo ya silaha. ~ **shot** *n* mpigo wa bunduki; masafa ya bunduki. ~ **smith** *n* mfua bunduki, mwindaji. 3 *big ~ (colloq)* mtu maarufu au mwenye madaraka makubwa, mheshimiwa *vt* ~ **sb (down)** piga mtu risasi. **~ner** *n* mpiga mizinga; *(in the navy)* ofisa msimamizi wa silaha. **~nery** *n* utengenezaji/utumiaji wa mizinga.
gunny *n* gunia.
gunwale *n* ukingo wa juu wa meli/ mashua.
gurgle *vi* bubujika; sukutua; gugumia *n* mbubujiko wa maji.
guru *n* guru: mwalimu wa dini wa Kihindu; *(colloq)* mwalimu au mtu mashuhuri anayeheshimiwa.
gush *vi* 1 *(of water)* foka, mwagika. 2 *(talk too much)* bubujika, zungumza kwa shauku *n (outburst)* bubujiko, kufoka. **~er** *n* kisima cha mafuta yanayofoka. **~ing** *adj* **~ingly** *adv.*
gusset *n* upapi wa nguo, kijambia.
gust *n* dharuba (ya ghafla); mvua, moto n.k. wa ghafla *(fig) a ~ of passion* fumuko la hamaki, hasira/huba. **~y** *adj.*
gustation *n (formal)* kuonja.
gusto *n* kufurahia kufanya jambo fulani *eat with ~* kula kwa kufurahia.
gut *n* 1 *(colloq)* matumbo; utumbo. **hate sb's ~s** mchukia mno. 2 *(pl) (colloq)* yaliyomo (katika kitu/jambo fulani) *his speech had no ~s* hotuba yake haikuwa na lolote (la maana). 3 *(pl) (colloq)* ujasiri: *he has no ~s* yu mwoga. 4 uzi wa utumbo (utumikao kwa kutengenezea zeze n.k.) *vt* 1 *(remove ~s)* tumbua. 2 *(destroy)* teketeza *a house ~ted by fire* nyumba iliyoteketezwa kwa moto. **~less** *adj* -oga.
gutta-percha *n* (aina ya) mpira.
gutter[1] *n* 1 mchirizi, mfereji, mlizamu. 2 **the** ~ *(fig)* ufukara, ukata *the language of the ~* lugha ya matusi *take the child out of the ~* toa mtoto kwenye ufukara. **the ~ press** magazeti ya matusi na kashifa. ~ **snipe** *n* msikwao.
gutter[2] *vi (of a candle)* waka kwa vipindi (hata nta kutiririka upande mmoja).
guttural *adj (of sounds)* -a kooni.
guv'nor *n* bosi *see* **governor**.

guy[1] *n* 1 *(sl)* jamaa *vt* dhihaki; fanya/ onyesha sanamu ya mtu (kwa lengo la kubeza, kuchoma moto n.k.). 2 sanamu (inayovalishwa na kuchomwa moto siku ya Novemba 5 Uingereza). 3 mtu aliyevaa kiajabuajabu; kinyago.

guy[2] *(also* **~rope)** *n* kamba ya kukazia/ kuinulia hema n.k.

guzzle *vt,vi* la/ nywa kwa pupa. **~r** *n.*

gybe (US jibe) *vi,vt (naut) (of a sail or boom)* zinga, pembea toka upande mmoja wa tanga hadi wa pili.

gymkhana *n* tamasha ya michezo (agh. ya farasi, magari n.k.).

gymnasium (*also* **gym**) *n* 1 ukumbi wa michezo ya mazoezi ya viungo. 2 shule ya sekondari.

gymnast *n* mwanasarakasi. **~ics** *n* mazoezi ya viungo vya mwili, sarakasi. **gymnastic** *adj.*

gynaecology, gynecology *n* jinakolojia: elimuuzazi.

gynaecologist *n* mwana jinakolojia. **gynaecological** *adj.*

gyp[1] *n* danganyifu *vt* danganya.

gyp[2] *n* **give sb ~** *(sl)* karipia, adhibu (bila huruma); tesa.

gypsum *n* jasi.

Gypsy *see* **gipsy**.

gyrate *vi* zunguka katika duara.

gyration *n* mzunguko; kuzunguka. **gyratory** *adj.*

gyro *(pref)* giro (duara). **~compass** diragiro. **~scope** gurudumu tuzi.

H,h *n* herufi ya nane ya alfabeti ya Kiingereza. **drop one's h's** acha kutamka /h/ katika maneno k.m. kusema apana badala ya hapana.
ha *int lo,ha* (*when repeated in print*) (Ha! ha! Ha!) kicheko.
habeas corpus *n* (*Lat leg*) **(writ of)** ~ amri ya kumfikisha mfungwa kortini (hasa kuangalia uhalali wa kumfunga).
haberdasher *n* mwuzaji nguo (na vikorokoro vyake). **~y** duka la nguo.
habiliments *n* (*liter or hum*) mavazi.
habit *n* 1 mwenendo, tabia. **be in/fall into/get into the ~ of** -wa na tabia ya. **get sb into the ~ of** zoesha mtu tabia ya. **fall/ get out of the ~ of** acha tabia ya. **make a ~ of sth** zoea kufanya. 2 mazoea, desturi. **creature of ~** mtu wa mazoea. **do sth out of ~/from force of ~** fanya jambo kwa sababu ya mazoea/desturi. 3 *(old use)* hali (ya akili au mwili). 4 vazi la kitawa. **riding ~** vazi la mpanda farasi (koti na sketi). **~ual** *adj* 1 -a mazoea, -a desturi, -a kawaida. 2 -zoefu, -liokubuhu, ~ *thief* mwizi mzoefu. **~ually** *adv.***~uate** *vt*. **~uate sb/oneself to sth** (ji) zoeza. **~ude** *n* (*formal*) desturi, mazoea. **~ue** *n* mtu aliyezoea kwenda mahala fulani *a ~ of Cosy Cafe* mtu aliyezoea kwenda Cosy Cafe. **~able** adj -a kukalika (na watu). **~at** *n* (*of plants, animals*) mazingira, makazi ya asili; nyumbani. **~ation** *n* 1 kukaa, kuishi *houses fit for ~* nyumba zinazofaa kukaliwa. 2 (*liter*) makazi; nyumba.
hacienda *n* (*in Latin American Countries*) gunda (lenye nyumba).
hack[1] *vt,vi* ~ **(at)** katakata; tema. **~ing cough** kikohozi kikavu. **~saw** msumeno wa kukatia chuma.
hack[2] *n* 1 farasi wa kukodi. 2 mtu (anayepewa kazi ya kuandika iliyo ngumu na inayochusha, au ambaye anaandika kazi hafifu) *vt* tembea barabarani na farasi. ~ **work** *n* kazi ya uandishi wa kutafuta pesa tu.
hackles *n* 1 manyoya ya shingoni mwa jogoo. **have one's/get sb's ~ up** kasirika; kasirisha; -wa tayari kupigana.
hackney *n* 1 farasi wa kupandwa/ kukokota gari. **~ed** *adj* (*esp. of sayings*) -liochusha (kwa sababu ya kutumika mno).
had *pp of* **have**.
haddock *n* namna ya chewa mdogo.
Hades *n* (*Gk myth*) kuzimu.
Hadj, Hajji *n* Al-Haji, Haji.
haft *n* mpini.
hag *n* mchawi; ajuza mwenye sura mbaya (hasa anayedhaniwa kuwa mchawi). **~-ridden** anayeweweseka; anayesumbuliwa na mawazo.
haggard *adj* (*of a person, his face*) -liotambarajika, -liosawajika.
haggle *vi* ~ **(with sb) about/over sth)** bishana (hasa kwa ajili ya bei).
hagiology *n* hagiolojia: maandiko yanayoeleza maisha na hadithi za watakatifu.
haha *n* ua/ ukuta mfupi bustanini.
hail[1] *n* 1 mvua ya mawe. **~-stone** kijiwe (cha mvua ya mawe). ~ **storm** tufani ya mvua ya mawe. 2 (*fig*) wingi/mfululizo (wa matusi, ngumi n.k.) *vt,vi* 1 -nya mvua ya mawe. 2 ~ **(sth) down (on sb)** (*of blows etc*) angushia, piga, tolea kwa nguvu na haraka ~ *curses on sb* tukana mtu sana, tolea matusi mfululizo.
hail[2] *vt,vi* 1 ita (na kusalimu, kusifia kukaribisha, n.k.) ~ *a tax* ita teksi *he was ~ed as a hero* alisifiwa kama shujaa. 2 ~ **from** toka, tokea *where does the ship ~ from?* meli inatoka wapi? *n* salamu, wito. **~-Mary** (*rel*) Salamu Maria. **within** ~ (*esp of ship*) karibu kiasi cha kuweza kusikia wito. **be ~-fellow-well-met (with sb)** (*sometimes derog*) kunjufu (mno). **hair** *n* 1 nywele; usinga; (*of beard*) ndevu; (*of hand and arm*)(ma)laika; (*pubic*) (ma)vuzi; (*of animals*) singa, manyoya *comb* ~ chana nywele. **get in sb's** ~ udhi/kera

mtu. **get sb by the short ~s** (*sl*) weka mtu mkononi. **keep your ~ on** (*sl*) poa, tulia; usipandwe na mori. **let one's ~ down** (*of a woman*) achia nywele zianguke mabegani; (*fig*) jiachia (baada ya kipindi cha kubanwabanwa). **lose one's ~** pata upara; kasirika. **make one's ~ curl** (*fig*) shtua sana. **make one's stand on ~ end** ogofya. **put one's ~ up** tengeneza nywele (kwa kuzifunga utosini). **split ~s** ona/ jifanya kuona/shughulikia/sisitiza tofauti ndogo sana (za maana n.k.). **~-splitting** *n* kuona tofauti ndogo sana; mabishano ya bure. **tear one's ~** onyesha huzuni kubwa. **not turn a ~** -toonyesha kujali/wasiwasi *to a ~* (*of describing sth*) hasa, kabisa. 2 (*compounds*) **~ ('s) breadth** *n* chupuchupu; umbali mdogo sana (baina ya) *escape by a ~'s breadth* nusurika, ponea chupuchupu. **~-brush** *n* brashi ya nywele. **~-cloth** kitambaa chenye manyoya. **~-cut** *n* kunyoa; (mtindo wa) kukata nywele. **~-do** *n*. mtindo wa kutengeneza nywele. **~-dresser** *n* mtengeneza nywele (k.m. msusi, kinyozi). **~-dye** *n* rangi (ya kupaka) nywele. **~-line** *n* maoteo ya nywele kwenye ngozi (*attrib*) -embamba sana *a ~line space* nafasi nyembamba sana. **~-net** wavu wa kufungia nywele. **~-oil** *n* mafuta ya nywele. **~-piece** *n* kipande/kibandiko (cha nywele bandia), wigi. **~-pin** *n* chupio (ya nywele). **~-pin bend** kona kali hasa kwenye mwinuko mkali. **~-raising** *adj* -a kutisha, -a kuogofya. **~-shirt** shati lililoshonwa kwa kitambaa cha manyoya. **~-slide** *n* kibanio (cha nywele). **~-spring** *n* kamani, utumbo wa saa. **~ style** mtindo wa nywele. **~stylist** msusi. **~-trigger** kifyatuo cha bunduki (kinachotoa risasi hata kwa kuguswa kidogo tu). **~less** *adj* bila nywele; -enye upara. **~like** *adj*. **~y** *adj* -a kama nywele, -liojaa nywele. **~iness** *n*.

hake *n* aina ya chewa.

halberd *n* mkukishoka. **~ier** *n* askari anayetumia mkukishoka.

halcyon *adj* -a heri *~ days* siku za heri.

hale *adj* (*usu of old persons*) (*rare except in*) **~ and hearty** -enye nguvu na afya, -zima sana.

half *n,adj,adv* 1 nusu *~ of two is one* nusu ya mbili ni moja *cut in ~/into halves* kata nusu kwa nusu. **(do sth) by halves** (fanya jambo) ovyoovyo. **go halves (with sb) in sth** gawana nusu kwa nusu *too clever etc. by ~* erevu mno n.k. **one's better ~** (*colloq*) mke/mume (wa mtu). *adv* nusu; kwa kiwango kikubwa *~-cooked* bichi -sioiva sawasawa; **~-dead** (*colloq*) -iliochoka kabisa, hoi. **not ~-bad** (*sl*) si mbaya, nzuri vya kutosha. **not ~** sana, haswa *he didn't ~ swear* alitukana sana *was she annoyed*? *Not ~* alikasirika? Sana! mno! (*in compounds*) **~ a dozen** *n* sita. **~ and ~** *n* kitu kilichote ngenezwa kwa nusu mbili tofauti. **~-back** *n* (*in football/ hockey*) hafubeki. **~-baked** *adj* (*colloq*) -jinga; -sio na uzoefu *a ~-baked man* mtu mjinga *~ baked ideas* mawazo ya kijinga. **~-blood** *n* ndugu waliochangia mzazi mmoja, ndugu wa kambo. **~-breed/~-caste** *n* chotara. **~-brother** *n* kaka wa kambo. **~-cock** (*of a gun*) -liofunguliwa nusu. **go off at ~-cock** (*fig*) shindwa kufanya jambo kwa ajili ya haraka. **~-hardy** *adj* (*of plants*) -nayohitaji kinga kutokana na jalidi. **~-hearted** *adj* -a shingo upande. **~-heartedly** *adv*. **~-holiday** *n* nusu siku. **~ an hour, a ~-hour** *n* nusu saa, dakika thelathini. **~-hourly** *adj, adv* -a kila nusu saa. **~-length** *adj* (*of a portrait*) nusu. **at ~-mast** (*of a flag*) nusu mlingoti. **~-pay** *n* nusu mshahara *he is placed on half-pay* anapata nusu mshahara. **-penny** *n* nusu peni. ~ **penny-worth,** ~ **ha'p'orth** *n* -nayogharimu nusu peni. ~**-price** *adv* bei/kiingilio nusu. ~**-seas-over** *pred adj* (*colloq*) -liolewa kiasi. ~**-sister** dada wa kambo. ~**-size** *adj* -a nusu umbo la kawaida. ~ **term** *n* mapumziko/ likizo (katikati ya muhula wa shule). ~**- timbered** *adj* -liojengwa kwa mbao na matofali/mawe n.k.. ~**-time** *n* (*of work*) ya nusu siku; (*of sport*) hafutaimu, mapumziko. ~**-tone** *n.* picha isiyo ya rangi (agh. katika kitabu). ~ **track** *n* gari la askari lenye magurudumu ya minyororo nyuma. ~**-tracked** *adj*; ~**-truth** *n* usemi wenye ukweli nusu. ~**-way** *adj* nusu njia, katikati; (*incomplete*) -sio kamilifu, -a juujuu *adv* kwa kuafikiana *meet a person ~-way* -wa tayari kuafikiana. ~**-witted** *adj* -enye akili pungufu, -sio na busara. ~**-wit** *n* punguani. ~**-yearly** *adj, adv.* -a kutendeka/kutokea kila nusu mwaka, mara mbili kwa mwaka. **halve** *vt* 1 gawa nusu kwa nusu, punguza kwa nusu yake.

halibut *n* halibati: aina ya samaki mkubwa wa baharini aliwaye.

halitosis *n* harufu/pumzi mbaya (ya mdomo), kishuzishuzi.

hall *n* 1 ukumbi, bwalo *the Town/ City Hall* ukumbi wa Mji/Jiji. **dance** ~ ukumbi wa dansi. 2 (*in colleges at English Universities*)bwalo *dine in* ~ kula bwaloni. 3 ~ *(of residence)* bweni. 4 (*in England*) nyumba kubwa mashambani, (agh ya mtu mwenye ardhi nyingi). 5 sebule.

hall-mark *n* chapa inayopigiwa fedha au dhahabu kuonyesha ubora wake; (*fig*) sifa bainifu *vt* tia chapa.

hallelujah *n int* aleluya.

hallo int see **hullo**.

hallow *vt* (*usu passive*) fanya wakfu; *(reverence)* tukuza *n* (*only in*) **All H~'s Day** sikukuu ya watakatifu wote (1 Novemba). **~e'en** *n* mkesha wa sikukuu ya watakatifu wote (31 Oktoba).

hallucinate *vt* -ota njozi. **hallucination** *n* ndoto, njozi. **hallucinatory**, **hallucinogenic** *adj* (*of drugs*) (madawa) yenye kuleta njozi.

halo *n* duara ya mwangaza/nuru (hasa inayozunguka kichwa cha picha ya mtakatifu).

halt[1] *n* 1 kusimamisha (*chiefly mil, of soldiers*). **call a ~ (to)** simamisha kwa muda mfupi (safari/mwendo); (*fig*) kukomesha *it is time to call a ~ to vandalism* (*fig*) wakati umefika kukomesha uharibifu. 2 (*more general use*) **come to a** ~ simama, (kwa muda). 3 kituo kidogo cha treni *vt,vi* (*as a mil command*) simama, hima *the officer ~ed his troops for a rest* ofisa alisimamisha kikosi chake kwa mapumziko H ~ ! Hima! *vi* sita; tembea/sema kwa kusitasita *talk in a ~ing voice* zungumza kwa sauti ya kusitasita *adj* (*arch*) -a kusitasita; -a kuchechemea. **~ingly** *adv.*

halter *n* 1 hatamu:kamba ya kufungia/ kuongoza farasi. 2 kitanzi.

halyard *n* henza, jarari.

ham *n* 1 paja agh. la wanyama. 2 hemu: paja la nguruwe lililokaushwa ~ *and eggs* mayai yaliyokaangwa na hemu. 3 ~ *(actor)* mwigizaji mbovu *a radio* ~ mtangazaji/mpokeaji (ujumbe wa) redio wa ridhaa ~ *handed/fisted* zito (katika kutumia mikono). ~ **burger** *n* hambaga: kababu ya nyama iliyosagwa (agh inayoliwa ndani ya mikate miwili).

hamadryad *n* 1 kizimwi wa mitini. 2 koboko mkubwa wa India .

hamlet *n* kijiji, kitongoji.

hammer 1 nyundo. **be/go at it ~ and tongs** bishana/gombana kwa kelele nyingi, fanya kwa bidii sana. **throwing the** ~ mchezo wa kutupa nyundo (nzito). ~ **and sickle** nyundo na nyengo. 2 (*in a piano*) kinyundo. 3 (*of guns*) hama: kitu kinachopiga na kulipusha risasi. 4

nyundo (ya dalili). **be/come under the ~** uzwa mnadani. 5 (*bone of ear*) nyundo. 6 (*compounds*) **~-beam** kombamoyo **~-head** kichwa cha nyundo; (*shark*) papa-nyundo **~-lock** (*wresting*) maongonyo *vt,vi* **in/ out/down (at)** 1 piga nyundo *~ in* gongomea; (*nails*) pigilia *~ down the lid of a box* gongomea mfuniko wa sanduku *~ into shape* rekebisha. **~ sth into sb's head** sisitizia mtu jambo (kwa kurudia sana). **~ sth out** (*metal*) babatisha. **~-out** *(fig)* toa/ fanya kwa bidii, fikia kwa kujadili sana *~ out solution* fikia suluhisho kutokana na mjadala mkali *~ away at* endelea kufanya kazi. 4 piga mfululizo. 5 (*colloq*) shinda, twanga.

hammock *n* kitanda cha bembea.

hamper[1] *n* jamanda.

hamper[2] *vt* zuia.

hamster *n* buku (agh. hufugwa na watoto).

hamstring ukano wa mvungu wa goti *vt* lemaza (kwa kukata ukano wa mvungu wa goti); (*fig*) haribu, vuruga (uwezo au ufanisi).

hand[1] *n* 1 mkono, kitengele. **at ~** karibu. **at sb's ~s** kutoka kwa *I did not expect such treatment at your ~s* sikutarajia kitendo kama hicho kutoka kwako. **bind sb ~ and foot** funga mikono na miguu; (*lit. fig*) zuia mtu asiweze kufanya chochote. **serve/wait on sb ~ and foot** tumikia mtu sana. **by ~** kwa mkono *this sweater is made by ~* sweta hii imefumwa kwa mkono *this letter was sent by ~* barua hii imepelekwa kwa mkono. **bring up a baby/a calf by ~** lisha mtoto/ndama kwa chupa. **eat/feed out of one's ~** (agh. ndege) fugika; (*fig*) -wa tayari kutii lolote. **from ~ to ~** pokezana mkono kwa mkono. **fight ~ to ~** pambana, pigana kwa kukaribiana sana. **give/ land (sb) ~ (with sth)** saidia mtu. **give one's ~ on a bargain** kubaliana kwa kushikana mkono. **have one's ~ full** -wa na shughuli/ kazi nyingi. **~ in ~** kwa kushikana mkono kwa mkono. (*fig*) **H~s off!** Acha! Usiguse! **H~ up!** Mikono juu! **~ over ~** kwa kutumia mikono yote; (*fig*) kwa haraka na uthabiti. **in ~** tayari, mkononi *cash in ~* fedha taslimu; (*of work etc.*) -nayoshughulikiwa. *the matter is in ~* jambo linashughulikiwa. **in the ~s of** mikononi mwa; juu ya *the matter is in your ~s* ni juu yako. **in good ~s** salama, inayotunzwa vizuri *the child is in good ~s* mtoto anatunzwa vizuri. **not lift a ~, not do a ~s turn** -tosaidia kabisa. **lift/raise a/one's ~ against sb** tishia, shambulia. **live from ~ to mouth** ishi maisha ya kijungumeko; -wa maskini. **(get sth) off one's~s** jitoa (katika wajibu); achana na. **on ~** -liopo. **on one's ~** chini ya madaraka ya; mikononi mwa. **out of ~** -sioweza kudhibitiwa *the crowd was out of ~* umati ulikuwa haudhibitiki. **shake ~s (with)** shikana mikono. **take a ~ (in)** saidia, shiriki. **take sth/sb in ~** chukua madaraka ya. **be to ~** (*commerce*) pokelewa *your letter is to ~* barua yako imepokelewa. **wash one's ~ of** nawa mikono, jitenga na. **win ~ down** shinda kwa urahisi. **(rule) with a heavy ~** (tawala) kwa ukali. **win a lady's ~** kubaliwa uchumba. 2 (*pl*) uwezo, mamlaka, madaraka. **in sb's ~** chini ya madaraka ya mtu fulani *the house is no longer in my ~* sina madaraka tena. **change ~s** badili umiliki. 3 (*sing only*) mkono: *there's someone's ~ in this* pana mkono wa mtu. 4 (*sing only*) **at first ~** moja kwa moja *I received the news from him at first ~* nilipata habari toka kwake moja kwa moja. **at second ~** kwa kupitia njia nyingine *I received the news about him at second ~* nilipashwa habari zake kwa kupitia mtu mwingine. 5 (*sing only*) ustadi, weledi *he's a good ~ at sth* yu stadi wa kufanya kitu. **get one's ~ in** jizoeza (tena). **keep one's ~ in** dumisha umahiri (wa kufanya mambo). 6 mtendaji mzoefu; *(labourer)* kibarua, mfanyakazi, *(nautical)* baharia **all ~** watu wote, kila mtu. 7 mshiriki. **have a ~ in sth** -wamo (katika jambo fulani). 8 (*watch, clock etc*) mshale, akrabu. 9 upande *left ~* mkono wa kushoto *right ~* mkono wa kuume (wa kulia). **on every/either ~; on all ~s** toka/kila upande, pande zote. **on the one ~** kwa upande mmoja. **on the other ~** kwa upande mwingine. 10 (*sing only*) mwandiko *he writes a legible ~* mwandiko wake unasomeka. 11 (*formal*) sahihi *given under my ~ and seal* idhinishwa kwa sahihi na muhuri wangu. 12 (*cards*) karata (alizoshika mchezaji). **have a good/bad/poor ~** -wa na karata nzuri/ mbaya. **play a good/bad ~** cheza (karata) vizuri/vibaya. **play into sb's ~s** fanya jambo litakalo mnufaisha mtu mwingine; mchezaji (karata); mchezo mmoja (wa karata). **take a ~ at sth** shiriki; cheza karata. 13 kipimo kama inchi nne; nusu shubiri. 14 (*colloq*) makofi. **give sb a good ~** pigia makofi. 15 *(compounds)* **~bag** *n* begi, mkoba. *n* **~-barrow** mkokoteni unaosukumwa. **~bill** *n* tangazo (linalotolewa kwa mkono). **~ book** *n* kiongozi, kijitabu cha maelekezo. **~ brake** *n* breki ya mkono. **~clap** *n* (pigo la) makofi. **~cuff** pingu *vt* tia pingu. **~ful** *n* -chache; kiasi kidogo; konzi; ukufi *only a ~ of people attended the meeting* watu wachache tu walihudhuria mkutano; kiasi cha kuweza kujaza kitengele; (*colloq*) tukutu, sumbufu. **~-grenade** *n* kombora la mkono. **~-hold** *n* kishikizi; kitu cha kushika wakati wa kupanda. **~-luggage** *n* mizigo ya mkononi. **~ made** *adj* -a mkono; -liotengenezwa kwa mkono. **~ maid** *n* mjakazi, mtumishi wa kike. **~-me -down** n mtumba, kitu ambacho kimeshatumika, **~-picked** *adj* -liochaguliwa kwa makini. **~rail** *n* papi za ngazi. **~saw** *n* msumeno (wa mpini mmoja). **~shake** kupeana mikono. **~stand** kusimama kwa mikono. **~work** *n* kazi ya mkono. **~writing** *n* mwandiko, mkono. **~y** *adj* 1 fundi, -epesi. **~ly** kwa kazi (hasa za mikono). **~ man** mtu mwepesi wa kazi (hasa za mikono): wepesi kufanya kazi yoyote. 2 (*of things, place*) -a kuchukulika; (*useful*) -a kufaa kutumiwa kwa urahisi *come in ~* faa wakati mwingine. 3 karibu, tayari,-siokuwa mbali. **~ily** *adv* **~iness** *n*.

hand[2] *vt* 1 pa, leta, saidia kwa mikono *please ~ me that pencil* niletee kalamu hiyo. 2 **~ down (to)** rithisha *the house was ~ed down to his son* mtoto wake alirithi nyumba yake. 3 **~ sth on to sb** pitisha *please ~ this book on to Mary* tafadhali nipitishie kitabu hiki kwa Maria. 4 **~ out (to sb)** (*colloq*) toa sadaka. **hand-out** *n* taarifa iliyotayarishwa na mkuu na kutolewa (agh. kwa waandishi habari); (*of school*) kitini; sadaka kwa maskini. 5 **~ over (to sb)** peleka mtu kwa polisi n.k.. **~ sth over (to sb)** kabidhi. 7 **~ it to sb** (*colloq*) msifu mtu, -pa (mtu) haki yake.

handicap *n* 1 kikwazo. 2 kilema, upungufu *vt* 1 zuia. 2 lemaa *~ped people* vilema, walemavu.

handicraft *n* kazi ya mikono (kama kufuma, kusuka vikapu, kufinyanga n.k.).

handiwork *n* kazi ya mikono; kitu kilichofanyizwa kwa mikono agh. ya mtu fulani.

handkerchief *n* leso.

handle *n* 1 mpini; (*of a cup*) mkono; (*of a bucket*) utambo; *(of a door or box)* kipete. **~ bar** *n* (*often pl of a bicycle*) usukani. **fly off the ~**

(*colloq*) hamaki, pandisha. (*fig*) **give a ~ (to sb) (against sb)** toa nafasi, kisingizio kinachoweza kudhuru/ kuumiza. 2 (*sl*) cheo; jina la heshima *have a ~ to one's name* -wa na jina la heshima k.m. Alhaji. *vt 1* gusa, shika *~ the ball* gusa mpira kwa mikono. 2 simamia; shughulika; ongoza, tawala. 3 (*treat*) tendea. 4 (*comm*) nunua, uza *he does not ~ perishable goods in his shop* hafanyi biashara ya bidhaa zinazoharibika upesi. **handler** mtu afunzaye na kuwatunza wanyama k.m. mbwa wa polisi.

handsel *n* zawadi (kwa ajili ya kuanza maisha mapya, mwaka mpya) *vt* 1 toa zawadi. 2 zindua; takadamu.

handsome *adj* 1 -enye umbile zuri; (*of men*) -zuri, -enye sura nzuri; (*of women*) -enye umbo zuri. 2 (*of conduct*) kubwa. **H~is as/that ~ly does** (*prov*) mwungwana ni kitendo.

hang[1] *n* 1 (*sing only*) mning'inio, mkao *the ~ of a dress* mning'inio wa gauni. 2 **get the ~ of sth** (*colloq*) elewa jinsi ya kutumia (teknolojia, mashine, wazo n.k.); pata/ona maana au umuhimu wa kilichosemwa au kuandikwa. **not give/care a ~** (*colloq*) (*euphem for damn*) -tojali chochote *vt,vi* 1 tundika, angika, ning'iniza, ngoeka *~ the pictures on the wall* tundika picha ukutani *~ the towel on the line* angika taulo kwenye kamba. 2 (*pt, pp* **~ed**) nyonga *he ~ed himself* alijinyonga *he was ~ed for murder* alinyongwa kwa kuua 3 (*mild equivalent of damn-dated*) *I'll be ~ed if I come* sitakuja kabisa; wallahi siji! 4 (*various uses*) *~ a door* tia mlango bawaba. **~ by a hair/a single thread** (*of a person's fate*) -wa katika hali mbaya/ngumu, tegemea kitu kidogo, wa mashakani sana. **~ one's head** inamisha kichwa hasa kwa aibu. **~ fire** (*of a gun*) kawia kufyatuka; (*of events*) kawia kutokea/kuanza. **let things go ~** (*colloq*) puuza, -tojali. **~ in the balance** -wa na matokeo yenye mashaka, -wa mashakani. 5 acha *leave ~ing until the right time* acha mpaka wakati ufaao. 6 (*compound*) **~man** *n* chakari, mnyongaji. **~ dog** *adj* (*of sb's look*) -danganyifu na -liotahayari; -enye aibu. **~over** *n* kasumba; uchovu baada ya kulewa sana; mabaki ya habari, sheria za zamani; (*with adverbial particles and preps*) *colonial ~ over* kasumba ya kikoloni. **~ about/ a round** randaranda. **~ back** sita. **~ on** shikilia kwa nguvu; vumilia. **~ on (a minute)** (*colloq*) ngoja kidogo. **~ on/upon sb's words/lips** sikiliza kwa makini. **~ on to sth** ng'ang'ania; shikilia imara. **~ out** (*sl*) ishi; panga. **~ sth out** tundika, anika, angika (nguo mbichi) juani zikauke; onyesha. **~ together** (*of persons*) saidiana, shirikiana *if we dont ~ together we shall fail* tusiposhirikiana tutashindwa; patana, lingana *the evidence of the witnesses ~s together* ushahidi wa mashahidi unalingana. **~ up** kata simu. **~ up on sb** (*colloq*) kata simu kabla mtu mwingine hajamaliza kuongea. **be hung up** cheleweshwa, katishwa tamaa; fadhaika. **~-up** *n* 1 shida, matatizo. 2 fazaa. **~er** *n* kiango (cha kutundikia vitu) (*in compounds*) *clothes-/dress-~*kiango cha nguo. **~-on** mtu anayejitiatia, mdoezi. **~ing** *n* 1 kufa kwa kunyongwa. 2 (*usu.pl*) pazia.

hangar *n* banda la ndege.

hangnail *n* kigozikucha.

hank *n* kibonge, kidonge (cha uzi, hariri).

hanker *vi* ~ **after/for sth** taka sana, tamani sana *~ after wealth* tamani sana mali. **~ing** *n* tamaa *have a ~ing for power* -wa na tamaa ya madaraka.

hanky *n (child's word for* **hand-**

kerchief) leso.
hanky-panky *n* hila.
Hansard *n* kumbukumbu rasmi za mijadala ya bunge.
hap *n* (*archaic*) bahati; jaha *vt,vi* tukia. **~less** *adj* (*archaic*) -a bahati mbaya, -sio na bahati. **~ly** *adv* 1 kwa bahati; kwa nasibu. 2 huenda, labda.
haphazard *n* bahati *adj* -a ovyo *adv* ovyo ovyo, shaghalabaghala *~ attempt* jaribio la ovyoovyo/lisilo na mpango/la wasiwasi.
happen *vi* 1 (**to**) tukia, jiri, tendeka. **~ again** tukia tena *it so ~ed that* ilitokea kuwa. 2 -wa na bahati; bahatisha; bahatika *as it ~s* kwa bahati. 3 **~ on/upon** ona/pata kwa bahati. **~ on sb** pata mtu kwa bahati. **~ing** *n* (*often pl*) tukio.
happy *adj* -a furaha; -a bahati; -lioridhika. **as ~ as the day is long** -enye furaha kabisa. 2 fadhiliwa, furahishwa. 3 -enye kufaa, inayosibu *a ~ idea* wazo linalofaa. **~ go lucky** *adj* -siojali; -enye kuchukua maisha yalivyo. **happily** *adv*. **happiness** *n*.
hara-kiri *n* kujiua kwa kujikata matumbo kama ishara ya **samurai** ya kuwajibika.
harangue *n* makemeo, mahubiri *vt,vi* hubiri/kemea kirefu.
harass *vt* 1 sumbua, bughudhi. 2 shambulia mara kwa mara. **~ ment** *n*.
harbinger *n* dalili *heavy clouds is the ~ of rain* mawingu mazito ni dalili ya mvua.
harbour *n* 1 bandari. **~ dues** kodi ya kutia nanga. 2 (*fig*) mahala pa kinga/hifadhi *vt,vi* 1 hifadhi, linda, ficha. 2 hodhi (mawazo). 3 tia nanga bandarini. **~age** *n* mahala pa hifadhi.
hard (*contrasted with soft*) *adj* 1 -gumu *a ~ wood* mti mgumu *a ~ nut to crack* (*fig*) tatizo kubwa; mtu asiyechukulika. 2 (*contrasted with easy*) -gumu/isio rahisi (kueleweka) *~ words* maneno magumu *~subject* somo gumu *he finds it ~ to understand* anaona vigumu kuelewa. 3 -a dhiki, -a shida, -a tabu. **~ going** kazi ngumu. **~ times** siku za dhiki. **learn sth the ~ way** jifunza kwa tabu. 4 kali, korofi *a ~ father* baba mkali. **be ~ on sb** fanyia mtu ukali; tendea bila huruma. **take a ~line** -wa na msimamo mkali. 5 (*of the body*) -kavu, kakamavu, -liokakamaa *~ muscles* misuli mikavu. **as ~ as nails** -enye nguvu; (*fig*) katili. **~hearted** -enye moyo mgumu. 6 -enye bidii/juhudi *~ worker* mfanyakazi mwenye bidii. 7 (*of the weather, sound*) kali **a ~ winter** kipupwe kikali *a ~ drought* ukame uliokalifisha. 8 (*various uses*) **~ and fast (rules etc)** mkata, -siobadilishwa. **~ cash** *n* fedha taslimu; kichele *~ of hearing* -enye uziwi. **~ back/cover** *n* kitabu chenye jalada gumu (kinyume na jalada laini). **~ board** *n* hadibodi, bango. **~ core** *n* kifusi; msingi/kiini; sugu *~ core criminal* jambazi sugu. **~ court** *n* kiwanja cha sakafu. **~currency** *n* fedha isiyobadilika ovyo thamani/inayoaminika (kimataifa). **~ drug** *n* dawa ya kulevya (k.m. heroini). **~headed** *adj* -tendaji, -enye kutenda. **~ labour** *n* kazi ngumu. **~ liquor/drink** *n* kinywaji kikali. **~ luck/line** *n* bahati mbaya, -a kusikitisha. **~ luck story** *n* hadithi ya kusikitisha. **~ shoulder** *n* sehemu ya kando ya barabara ya dharura. **~ware** *n* vifaa vya bati vitumiwavyo nyumbani k.m. sufuria, vikaango, misumari military ~ zana za kijeshi *computer ~* zana za vifaa vya mitambo ya kompyuta. **~ water** maji ya chumvichumvi. **~ wood** mti/ubao mgumu k.m. mninga, mvule, mpingo n.k. **~ness** *n* *adv* 1 kwa nguvu, kwa bidii *work ~* fanya kazi kwa bidii *pull ~* vuta kwa nguvu. **~ hitting** *adj* -lioeleza waziwazi. **~working** *adj* -enye

kufanya kazi kwa bidii; chapa kazi. 2 kwa vikali sana *it is raining* ~ inanyesha sana. 3 kwa matatizo, kwa tabu *my ~ earned wealth* mali yangu niliyoipata kwa tabu. **be ~ hit** hasirika sana hasa kwa fedha. **be ~ pressed (for sth)** banwa sana na jambo. **be ~ put to it (to do sth)** -wia vigumu *I was ~ put to it to explain how I got the new car* iliniwia vigumu kueleza jinsi nilivyopata gari jipya. **be ~ up** wamba, -tokuwa na fedha. **be ~ up for (sth)** -wa mhitaji wa kitu, kosa kitu. ~ **boiled** gumu, yai lililochemshwa. 4 **~baked** *adj* -liookwa mpaka likawa gumu. ~ **bitten** *adj* (*of a person*) -enye kupigana kishupavu; *(fig)* sugu, -siojali. 5 karibu, mara *follow ~ after sb* fuata mtu karibu. ~ **by** karibukaribu, sio mbali, karibu. **run sb ~** kimbiza/fukuzia/fuata karibukaribu. **~ship** *n* taabu, shida, dhiki. **~en** *vt,vi* -wa/fanya/gumu, madhubuti, imara; shupaza; shupaa ~ *the heart* shupaza moyo. **be ~ to** -tojali jambo/kitu fulani, fanywa sugu. ~ **off** (*of young plants, esp. seedlings*) imarika, tayari kwa kupandikizwa mahali pengine. **~hood** *n* ujasiri, ushupavu. **~y** *adj* 1 -enye nguvu; -nayoweza kustahimili taabu. 2 (*of plants*) -sioharibika kwa baridi. 3 shupavu, jasiri, **~ness** *n*.

hardly *adv* 1 chache, kidogo tu *we had ~ rested* hatukudiriki/hatukuwahi kupumzika. 2 (*used to suggest that sth is improbable, unlikely or unreasonable*) *I can ~ give you a drink today* sidhani kama naweza kukununulia kinywaji hivi leo. 3 (*neg. in meaning*) chache, kwa nadra sana ~ *anybody came to the meeting* ni watu wachache sana waliofika mkutanoni. 4 vikali, kwa ukali *the child was scolded* ~ alikaripiwa kwa ukali sana.

hare *n* 1 sungura. 2 **start a ~** anzisha hoja, mjadala (usiohusiana na suala kuu). **first catch your ~ then cook him** usikate mbeleko na mwana hajazaliwa. **run with the ~ and hunt with the hounds** ridhisha kila upande; -wa ndumila kuwili *mad as a March* ~ kichaa kabisa. **~-brained** *adj* -a harara; pumbavu. **~lip** *n* mdomo uliojigawa (tangu kuzaliwa).

harem *n* 1 nyumba ya harimu. 2 harimu.

haricot *n* ~ **(beans)** maharage madogo meupe.

hark *vi* (*chiefly imper*). ~ **at** *(colloq)* sikiliza! msikilize! 2 ~ **back (to)** rejea/kumbuka jambo lililofanywa au lililosemwa.

harlequin *n* mchekeshaji, mtu wa mzaha. **~ade** mchezo wa kuigiza ambao sehemu kubwa inachukuliwa na mchekeshaji.

harlot *n* (*archaic*) malaya, kahaba.

harm *n* madhara *there is no ~ in doing so* hakuna madhara kwa kufanya hivyo. **do sb ~** umiza mtu. **out of ~'s way** mahali pa salama *vt* dhuru. **~ful** *adj* -a kudhuru. **~fully** *adv*. **~less** *adj* 1 si -a kudhuru, si-a shari, -pole. 2 -sio na hatia. **~lessly** *adv*.

harmattan *n* hamatani, kipupwe; upepo mkali wenye vumbi jingi uvumao katika pwani ya Afrika Magharibi.

harmonica kinanda cha mdomo.

harmonium *n* kinanda.

harmony *n* 1 upatanifu (katika maono, mtazamo n.k.), amani. 2 (*music*) mwafaka, ulinganifu wa sauti. **harmonic** *adj* (*of sound*) -a hamoniki, linganifu, -enye kuoana/kuchukuana. **harmonics** *n* sauti za hamoniki. **harmonious** *adj* 1 -enye mpangilio mzuri/wenye kuridhisha, linganifu. 2 patanifu. 3 *(of music)* tamu. **harmonize** 1 *vt* patanisha, linganisha. 2 *vi* lingana patana, chukuana. **harmonization** *n*.

harness *n* 1 lijamu na hatamu. **in ~** (*fig*) kufanya kazi ya kawaida *he* *died in* ~ alikufa angali akifanya kazi yake. **work/run in double** ~ shirikiana na mwenzi katika kazi. 2 (*in a loom*) sindano (ya kufumia) *vt* 1 funga/visha farasi lijamu na kigwe. 2 tumia mto, maporomoko ya maji agh. kutengeneza umeme.

harp *n* kinubi *vi* 1 piga kinubi. 2 ~ **on sth** (*fig*) zungumza kwa kurudiarudia na kuchosha ~ *upon the same thing* rudiarudia yale yale. **~er**. **~ist** *n* mpiga kinubi.

harpoon *n* chusa *vt* vua kwa chusa, piga chusa.

harpy *n* (*Gk myth*) 1 mwana mkendege: kiumbe mkali mwenye sura ya mwanamke na kiwiliwili cha ndege. 2 mwanamke katili na mchoyo.

harridan *n* ajuza/bibi kizee mkali sana.

harrier *n* 1 mbwa wa kuwindia sungura (*pl*) kundi la mbwa hao pamoja na wawindaji. 2 mkimbiaji wa mbio ndefu.

harrow *n* haro *vt* 1 piga haro. 2 (*fig*) huzunisha, tia uchungu.

harry *vt* 1 shambulia mara kwa mara; vamia na kupora. 2 sumbua, udhi.

harsh *adj* 1 (*of texture, voice etc*) kali, -siopendeza, -a kuchukiza. 2 kali, katili *a* ~ *punishment* adhabu kali, katili. **~ly** *adv*. **~ness** *n*.

hart *n* ayala.

hartebeest *n* kongoni.

harum-scarum *n* (*colloq*) mtu mwenye harara, msojali *adj* -a harara, -siojali.

harvest *n* 1 mavuno. ~ **festival** (*rel*) sikukuu ya mavuno. ~ **home** sikukuu inayofanywa na wakulima mwishoni mwa mavuno kwa ajili ya wafanyakazi wao. ~ **moon** mwezi mpevu. 2 (*fig*) matokeo *reap the* ~ *of your work* vuna matunda ya kazi yako/ulichopanda *vt* vuna. **~er** *n* 1 mvunaji. 2 mashini ya kuvunia. **has** *see* **have** **~-been** *n* (*colloq*) zilipendwa.

hash *n* 1 chinyango iliyopikwa na kupashwa moto. 2 (*muddle*) fujo. **make a** ~ **of sth** fanya (jambo) ovyoovyo, vuruga. **settle sb's** ~ komesha (mtu). 3 (*colloq*) bangi *vt* ~ *(up)* katakata (nyama).

hashish *n* bangi.

hasp *n* kipete.

hassle *n* (*colloq*) mabishano; ugomvi, mzozo *vt,vi* bishana, gombana.

hassock *n* takia la kupigia magoti (mf. kanisani).

hast (*arch*) *thou* ~ una.

haste *n* haraka, hima. **Make** ~ fanya hima. **More** ~ **less speed** *(prov)* haraka haraka haina baraka. **~n** *vi,vt* harakisha, fanya haraka, hima. **hasty** *adj* -a haraka *a* ~ *departure* kuondoka kwa haraka *speak* ~ *words* ropoka. **hastily** *adv*. **hastiness** *n*.

hat *n* kofia, chepeo, heti. **go/come** ~ **in hand** njoo/nenda kuomba msamaha. **pass/send round the** ~ changisha fedha. **talk through one's** ~ (*sl*) payapaya, bwabwaja *keep information under one's* ~ tunza siri, funika kombe *lift ones's* ~ *to sb* toa heshima. **take off one's** ~ **to** (*fig*) vulia kofia; shangilia. (*US*) **throw one's** ~ **into the ring** ingia/ ingiza kwenye mashindano/ ulingo. ~ **in hand** kwa unyenyekevu. ~ **off to**... (*fig*) makofi! tunashangilia...! **my** ~**!** ala! **a bad** ~ (*sl*) (mtu) mwovu. **~-band** *n* utepe wa kofia. **~-pin** *n* chupio ya kufungia kofia. ~ **trick** *n* magoli matatu mfululizo. **~less** bila kofia. **~ter** mtengeneza kofia. **as mad as a ~ter** kichaa kabisa.

hatch[1] *n* 1 mfuniko wa mlango. *(esp)* ~ **way** mfuniko wa sitaha; dirisha baina ya vyumba viwili (hasa jiko na chumba cha kulia). **under** ~ chini ya silaha. 2 sehemu ya chini ya mlango uliogawika.

hatch[2] *vt,vi* angua (yai). **don't count one's chickens before they're ~ed** (*prov*) usikate mbeleko na mwana hajazaliwa. 2 buni, tunga ~ *a plot* buni njama, kula njama. **~ery** mahali pa kuangulia (hasa mayai ya samaki).

hatch[3] *vt* chora/chimba mistari sambamba. **~ing** *n* mistari hiyo.

hatchet *n* kishoka. **bury the ~** patana, acha ugomvi. **~ face** uso wa upanga.

hate *vt* chukia, -wa na kinyongo na; (*colloq*) juta *n* chuki, kinyongo. **~ful** *adj* -a kuchukiza, -a kinyongo, -a kuchukia. **hatred** *n* chuki, kinyongo, kisirani.

haughty *adj* -enye kiburi; -enye maringo, -a majivuno/kujivuna. **haughtily** *adv*. **haughtiness** *n*.

haul *vt,vi* kokota, burura, buruta. **~ down one's flag/colours** salimu amri. **~ sb over the coals** karipia, kemea *n* 1 kukokota. 2 pato (linalopatikana kwa jasho/kukokota, hasa uvuvi wa samaki kwa nyavu) *a good ~ of fish* samaki wengi walipatikana. **~age** *n* usafirishaji (wa bidhaa) *road ~* usafirishaji wa barabara. 3 gharama ya usafirishaji. **~ier** *n* msafirishaji; mwenye magari ya kusafirisha bidhaa.

haulm *n* (*collective, sing*) mashina na matawi ya njegere, maharagwe, mbatata (hasa baada ya mavuno).

haunch *n* tako.

haunt *vt* 1 tembelea/ingilia/kalia/ rudia mara kwa mara. 2 (*esp of ghosts and spirits*) fanya maskani, makao. 3 (*of mind*) sumbua/tawala *n* makao *the ~ of criminals* makao ya wahalifu.

hauteur *n* majivuno, maringo.

Havana *n* biri ya Havana Cuba.

have *vt,vi aux* (*pres) I ~ he/she has we/you ~, pt,pp had*) 1 -wa na *April has thirty days* Aprili ina siku thelathini. 2 pata, patia, chukua; kubali *I didn't ~ much difficulty* sikupata shida sana. **let him ~ it** (*sl*) mwache akione. **~ had it** (*sl*) -wa na wakati ngumu. 3 **~ sth done** sababisha/amuru kitu kifanywe. 4 (-wa na) lazima, sharti *I ~ to go* lazima niende. 5 **~ sb do sth** taka mtu afanye jambo. 6 **~ sth done to you** wahi/pata kufanyiwa jambo *he had his pocket picked* aliwahi kuibiwa, alichomolewa. 7 (*colloq*) danganya *mind she doesn't ~ you* angalia asikudanganye; shinda; patia *you had me there*! umenipatia kwelikweli! 8 (*with it and a clause*) sema, eleza *as Marx has it...* kama asemavyo *Marx...* 9 (*used with adverbial particles and preps*). **~ sth back** rudishiwa *you'll ~ it back* nitakurudishia. **~ sb down** karibisha mtu. **~sb/sth in** -wa na mtu/kitu (chumbani, nyumbani n.k.). **~ it off/away (with sb)** (*sl*) jamiiana na, kazana, tombana na. **~ sb on** (*colloq*) danganya mtu. **~ sth on** (a) vaa (b) -wa na shughuli *I ~ nothing on tomorrow* sina shughuli yoyote kesho. **~ sth out** toa, ng'oa *~ a tooth out* ng'oa jino. **~ one's sleep out** maliza usingizi. **~ it out with sb** elewana kwa kuambizana ukweli, toa fundo. **~ sb over/round** -wa na mgeni. **~ sb up** pata mgeni (*usu passive*) (*colloq*) peleka mtu mahakamani; shitaki *he was had up for robbery* alishitakiwa kwa wizi *n pl* (*of people and countries*) *the ~s* matajiri. **the ~s and ~-nots** matajiri na maskini.

haven (*fig*) kimbilio; mapumzikoni, mahali pa usalama.

haversack *n* shanta.

havoc *n* maangamizi, uharibifu mkubwa, nakama; vurumai. **play ~ with/among; make ~ of** haribu, umiza; vuruga.

haw *vi,n see* **hum**.

haw-haw *n, int* kikwakwa.

hawk[1] *n* 1 mwewe. **~-eyed** *adj* -enye macho makali (yawezayo kuona upesi na mbali). 2 mwanamabavu: mtu apendaye matumizi ya nguvu za kijeshi katika siasa za nchi za nje.

hawk[2] *vt*'kohoa. **~ up** toa makohozi, safisha koo.

hawk[3] *vt* ~ **(about/around)** tembeza biashara; (*fig*) eneza ~ *news* eneza habari ~**er**. *n* mchuuzi, guoguo.

hawser *n* (*naut*) utari.

hay *n* nyasi kavu. **make** ~ kausha nyasi, geuza nyasi (ili zikauke). **make ~ of** vuruga. **make ~ while the sun shines** linalowezekana leo lisingoje kesho, tumia nafasi iliyopo. ~ **cock** *n* tita la nyasi kavu shambani. ~ **fever** *n* kikohozi/mafua yaletwayo na vumbi. ~ **fork** *n* uma wa kubebea nyasi kavu shambani. ~ **loft** ghala ya nyasi kavu. ~**maker** mkausha nyasi. ~ **making** *n* kukausha nyasi. ~**rick**, ~ **stack** *n* lundo la nyasi (lililofungwa tayari kuhifadhiwa ghalani). ~ **wire** *n* waya wa kufungia marobota ya nyasi kavu *pred adj* (*colloq*) -lio ovyo ovyo/ vurugika; -enye wasiwasi hamaniko, fadhaa/wazimu. **go ~wire** (*of persons*) hangaika, hamanika, pata wazimu; (*of sth e.g a plan*) vurugika.

hazard *n* 1 hatari *navigation ~s* hatari za usafiri (wa baharini). **at all ~s** licha ya hatari zote, lolote/liwe liwalo. 2 *game of* ~ mchezo wa dadu *vt* 1 jaribu, bahatisha, hatarisha *I'll ~ a guess* nitabahatisha. **~ous** *adj* -enye hatari *a ~ jump* mruko wa hatari.

haze[1] *n* 1 ukungu, (*thin*) utusitusi; (*fig*) kuchanganyikiwa, hangaiko, fazaa *vt* ~ **over** jaa/tia ukungu.

haze[2] *vt* (*US*) tesa, onea, dhalilisha. **hazy** *adj* 1 -enye ukungu. 2 (*fig*) si dhahiri; sio na uhakika; -enye wasiwasi. **hazily** *adv*. **haziness** *n*.

H-bomb *n see* **hydrogen**.

he *pron* 1 yeye (mwanamume) *that is ~! there ~ is*! ni yule! huyo! *it is ~, ~ is the man* ndiye. 2 (*as pref*) -a kiume ~ *goat* beberu. ~ **man** *n* dume. 3 (*liter style*) **who** yule ambaye, yeyote ambaye.

head *n* 1 kichwa; (*fig*) maisha *it costed him his ~* amepoteza maisha yake. 2 kipimo cha kichwa *~'s length* urefu wa kichwa *John is taller than Mary by a ~* John amempita Mary urefu kwa kichwa. **be ~ and shoulders above sb** (*fig*) pata/zidi sana (kwa uwezo au akili). 3 ~ **(s)** upande wa sarafu wenye kichwa. **~s or tails?** Kichwa au Mwenge? **be unable to make ~ or tail of sth** -toweza kuelewa kitu. 4 mtu *the entrance fee is 200/= per ~* kiingilio ni Shs 200/= kwa kila mtu. 5 (*pl unchanged*) moja katika kundi, idadi *fifty ~ of sheep* kundi la kondoo hamsini. 6 akili; uwezo wa kufikiri *he made it up out of his own ~* alitunga mwenyewe. 7 kipaji *he has a good ~ for leadership* ana kipaji cha uongozi. 8 (kitu kama) kichwa (kwa umbo, kazi au mahali) *the ~ of a nail* kichwa cha msumari *the ~ of a hammer* kichwa cha nyundo. 9 sehemu ya juu/mwanzo *at the ~ of the list* mwanzoni mwa orodha. 10 sehemu ya juu/ya mwisho wa kitu *the ~ of a bed* kichwani mwa kitanda. 11 (*of plants*) kishada cha majani au maua juu ya shina *a ~ of cabbage* kabeji. 12 (*often attrib*) mtawala, mkuu, kiongozi *the ~ of the school* mkuu wa shule *crowned ~s* mfalme na malkia. **H~ of State** Mkuu wa Nchi. 13 sehemu ya mbele (*of a ship*) omo *at the ~ of a queue* mwanzo/mbele ya mlolongo/foleni *at the ~ of a ship* omoni. 14 (*chiefly in proper names*) rasi. 15 kiasi cha maji kinachowekwa kwa sababu maalumu (k.m. ya kuzalisha nguvu za umeme) ~ *of a steam* nguvu ya mvuke. 16 kichwa cha habari *this essay has several ~s* insha hii ina vichwa vya habari kadhaa. 17 povu (agh. la maziwa, pombe n.k.). 18 ncha/mdomo/ kichwa cha jipu (lililoiva) *the boil came to a ~* jipu liliiva. **come to a ~** (*fig*) iva, fikia upeo (wa hatari) *misunderstanding has come to a ~* kutoelewana kumefikia hatua ya hatari. 19 (*various phrases*) a~/ **over one's ~** ngumu kuelewa.k **above their ~s** ongea pasipo kueleweka. **an old ~ on young shoulders** busara aliyonayo kij. **bite sb's ~ off** kemea kwa hasi jibu vikali. **eat one's ~ off** (*of a horse*) kula sana (na fanya kazi kidogo). **give sb his ~** ruhusu m afanye atakavyo. **go to one's ~** (*. liquor*) levya; lewesha, tia kiburi/majivuno. **have a good ~ o one's shoulder** -wa na uwezo wa kutenda/busara. **~ over heels** kichwangomba; (*fig*) kabisa **keep one's ~** tulia. **keep one's ~ above water** (*fig*) epuka madeni/matatizo n.k. **keep one's ~ down** epuka hatari/uharibifu. **laugh/scream one's ~ off** cheka/lia kwa nguvu sana. **lose one's ~** changanyikiwa! **(go) off one's ~** pata wazimu. **(stand etc) on one's ~** simama kichwagomba *I could do it* (*standing*) *on my ~* (*colloq*) ni rahisi mno; hainipi shida. **on one's own ~ be it** shauri hako. **over one's ~, above one's ~/ over another's ~/over the ~s of others** mbele ya mtu/watu waliotangulia/ stahili zaidi. **put our/your/their ~s together** shauriana. **put sth into a person's ~** endekeza/ shauri mtu. **put sth out of one's ~** sahau, acha kufikiria, acha wazo fulani. **put sth out of sb's ~** sahaulisha. **take sth into one's ~** amini kitu fulani. **talk one's head off** zungumza kupita kiasi. **talk sb's ~ off** chosha (mtu) kwa maongezi. **two ~s are better than one** (*prov*) penye wengi hapaharibiki neno. **turn sb's ~** pumbaza, tia kiburi; lewesha ajivune. **(be) weak in the ~** pungukiwa na akili. 20 (*compounds*) **~ ache** *n* maumivu ya kichwa (*sl*) tatizo, shida *it gives me a ~ahe* inanisumbua akili. **~ band** utepe/ ukanda wa kichwa. **~ dress** *n* ukaya, dusumali, kilemba. **~ gear** kofia, chepeo. **~ hunter** *n* muuaji anayehifadhi vichwa vya maadui zake; (*fig*) mtu anayeshawishi kwa nguvu ujiunge na shirika, jeshi n.k. **~ lamp/light** *n* taa ya mbele (ya gari, meli n.k.). **~ land** *n* rasi. **~ line** *n* kichwa cha habari (*pl*) habari kwa ufupi (agh katika radio). **~man** *n* (*pl men*) mjumbe. **~ master** *n* mkuu wa shule (mwanamume). **~mistress** *n* mkuu wa shule (mwanamke). **~ on** *adj,adv* (*of collisions*) uso kwa uso. **~phones** *n pl* vipokea sauti vinavyobanwa kichwani. **~piece** *n* kofia ya chuma; (*colloq*) bongo, akili. **~quarters** *n* (*sing or pl*) makao makuu. **~ rest** *n* msamilo. **~room** *n* nafasi. **~ set** *n see ~* **phones**. **~ship** *n* ukuu (agh. wa shule). **~stall** *n* sehemu ya hatamu inayovishwa kichwani. **~ stone** *n* jiwe linalowekwa kichwani mwa kaburi. **~ wind** *n* upepo wa mbisho. **~word** *n* kitomeo. **~ed** *adj* (*in compounds*) -enye kichwa *three ~* -enye vichwa vitatu *long ~* -enye kichwa kikubwa. **~less** *adj* -sio na kichwa *vt vi* 1 ongoza *Kimathi ~ed Mau Mau* Kimathi aliongoza Mau Mau. 2 -wa juu/mwanzo. 3 gonga kwa kichwa, piga kichwa. 4 **~sth/sb off** badilisha mwelekeo; rudisha (*fig*) zuia. **~er** *n* 1 kuanguka/kupiga mbizi kwa kutanguliza kichwa. 2 (*football*) kupiga mpira kwa kichwa. **~ing** *n* kichwa cha habari. **~long** *adv,adj* 1 -a kutanguliza kichwa *fall ~long* anguka kwa kutanguliza kichwa. 2 -a ubahau, bila kufikiri *a ~long decision* uamuzi bahau. **~strong** *adj* -kaidi, -bishi. **~y** *adj* (*of alcoholic drink*) -a kulevya haraka.

heal *vt,vi* 1 ponya, pona. 2 maliza *~ a quarrel* maliza ugomvi. **~er** *n*. **~ing** *adj*.

health *n* 1 afya, siha *dangerous to ~* -a kuhatarisha afya. **drink the ~ of sb/sb's ~** kunywa kwa afya ya *~ centre* kituo cha afya *~ food* chakula bora *World Health*

Organisation (WHO) Shirika la Afya Duniani. 2 uzima *in good ~* -enye uzima. **~ful** *adj* 1 -enye afya njema/nzuri. 2 zuri *a ~ climate* hali ya hewa nzuri. **~ily** *adv*.

heap *n* 1 fungu, rundo *a big ~ of books* rundo kubwa la vitabu. **be struck/knocked all of a ~** (*colloq*) pigwa na bumbuwazi; kanganyikiwa. 2 **~ (of)** (*colloq*) tele, -ingi *we have ~s of books* tunavyo vitabu vingi. 3 **~s** (*adv colloq*) sana *she is feeling ~ better* ana nafuu sana *vt* **~ (up)** 1 rundika; limbikiza. 2 **~ sth on/upon sb/sth; ~ sb/sth with sth** jazia; lundikizia, sheheneza (na).

hear *vt,vi* 1 sikia. 2 ambiwa, arifiwa, sikia (habari) *I ~ that he was ill* nimearifiwa kuwa yu mgonjwa. **~ about sth** pata habari juu ya jambo fulani. **~ from sb** pokea barua, habari n.k. toka kwa. **~ of sb/sth** jua. **~ tell of** sikia watu wakizungumzia. 3 sikiliza; (*of a judge in a law court*) sikiliza kesi. **~ sb out** sikiliza mpaka mwisho. **not ~ of** kataa kutoa ruhusa, kataa kufikiria. 4 **H~! H~!** Toboa! Sawa! (msemo wa kuonyesha kuafiki, wakati mwingine huonyesha kejeli). **~er** *n*. **~say** *n* tetesi, uvumi, fununu *know from ~* pata habari kutokana na uvumi *~ evidence is not accepted in law courts* uvumi haukubaliwi katika ushahidi mahakamani. **~ing** *n* 1 usikivu, uwezo wa kusikia *her ~ is poor* hasikii vizuri *hard of ~* kiziwi kiasi. 2 umbali wa kusikia/kusikiwa. **within/out of ~** karibu/mbali kuweza kusikia/kusikiwa. 3 nafasi ya kusikilizwa (katika mazungumzo). **gain a ~** pata nafasi ya kujitetea. **give sb/get a fair ~** sikiliza mtu bila upendeleo. 4 *(leg)* usikilizaji wa kesi mahakamani. **~ken** *vi (arch)* sikiliza.

hearse *n* gari la kuchukulia jeneza mazikoni.

heart *n* 1 moyo *~ attack* shtuko la moyo. 2 kiini cha hisia, (hususa mapenzi) undani wa tabia ya mtu *a man with a kind ~* mtu mwenye roho nzuri/huruma. **after one's own ~** -enye kupendeza nafsi; -a kuafikiana. **at ~** kimoyomoyo, kwa kweli; kimsingi. **have sth at ~** penda moyoni, vutiwa/ pendezewa na. **from (the bottom of) one's ~** kwa yakini, kwa dhati. **in one's ~ of ~s** moyoni. **to one's ~'s content** kiasi chake. **with all one's ~** kwa utashi/moyo wote *I love you with all my ~* nakupenda kwa moyo wangu wote. **~ and soul** kabisa *I am yours ~ and soul* mimi ni wako wa daima *break a person's ~* vunja moyo, sikitisha. **cry one's ~ out** wazia sana (agh kwa siri). **do one's ~ good** tia moyo. **get/learn/know sth by ~** kariri. **have a ~** onyesha huruma. **(have) a change of ~** badilisha mawazo/msimamo. **have the ~ to** (*usu neg*) -wa na moyo mgumu, -tokuwa na huruma. **have one's ~ in sth** vutiwa/pendezewa na kitu. **have one's ~ in one's boots** katishwa tamaa sana. **have one's ~ in one's mouth** ogopa sana. **have one's heart in the right place** -wa na moyo mzuri, -wa mkweli. **have one's ~ set on sth** taka sana. **lose ~** kata tamaa. **lose one's ~ to sb/sth** penda sana mtu/ kitu. **set one's ~ on sth/ having sth/doing sth etc** taka sana; -wa na shauku kupata/kufanya kitu. **take (fresh) ~ (at sth)** jiamini. **take sth to ~** athiriwa na jambo. **wear one's ~ on/upon one's sleeve** onyesha hisia kwa uwazi. 3 katikati ya (kitu); kiini (cha jambo) *in the ~ of the forest* katikati ya msitu *the ~ of the matter* kiini cha jambo. 4 (*of land*) rutuba *in good ~* katika hali nzuri *out of ~* katika hali mbaya. 5 (*cards*) kopa. 6 (*as a term of endearment to a person*) *dear ~* mpenzi *sweet ~* mpenzi. 7 (*compounds*) **~ache** *n* huzuni kubwa. **~beat** pigo la moyo. ~

breaking *adj* -a kuhuzunisha sana; -a kuvunja moyo. ~ **broken** *adj* -enye huzuni nyingi. ~**burn** *n* kiungulia. ~ **burning** *n* kijicho. ~ **disease** *n* afkani, ugonjwa wa moyo. ~-**failure** *n* moyo kusita/ kufa. ~**felt** *adj* -a dhati. ~ **rending** *adj* -a kuhuzunisha sana. ~**sick** *adj* -enye huzuni, -enye kusononeka. ~ **strings** *n* upendo, mapenzi. ~**ed** *adj (in compounds) hard* ~ -enye moyo mgumu *faint*-~ -oga. ~**less** *adj* -katili; -sio na huruma. ~-**searching** *n* -kujichunguza. ~**lessly** *adv*. ~**lessness** *n*. ~**en** *vt* tia moyo; changamsha. ~**y** 1 -a kweli, kunjufu. 2 zima, -enye nguvu, -enye afya njema. ~**ily** *adv* 1 kwa nia njema, kwa hamu. 2 sana *I am ~ glad that you sent me a letter* nimefurahi sana kwamba umeniletea barua. ~**ening news** habari za kutia moyo/ kuchangamsha.

hearth *n* 1 meko. 2 (*fig*) nyumba *fight for ~ and altar* tetea makazi na imani. ~-**rug** *n* zulia la meko. ~**stone** *n* figa.

heat *n* 1 joto, hari *the ~ is very tiring* joto linachosha sana. 2 **(the)** ~ (*fig*) shauku, mhemko, msisimko, harara *in the ~ of the argument* wakati mjadala ulipopamba moto. 3 (*sports*) mchuano; mchujano 4. (*of female animals*) nyege. **be in/on/at** ~ shikwa na nyege. 5 (*compounds*) ~-**capacity** *n* ujazojoto. ~-**flash** *n* joto kali (agh. kutokana na mlipuko wa bomu la atomiki). ~-**pump** *n* mashine ya kupitisha joto. ~ **shield** kinga-joto. ~-**spot** sehemu ya mwili inayoathiriwa zaidi na joto. ~-**stroke** *n* ugonjwa wa kuzirai ghafla kutokana na joto jingi. ~-**wave** wimbi la joto; kipindi cha joto kali *vt,vi* ~ **(up)** pasha moto. ~**ed** *adj* -enye mhemko, -a kusisimua, kali; -enye hamaki. ~**edly** *adv*. ~**er** kikanza. **a gas**-~ kikanza cha gesi. ~**ing** *n* kupashajoto *convection-~ing n* kupashajoto kwa myuko.

heath *n* 1 pori, nyika, mbuga. 2 (*plant*) mmeapori: namna ya mimea iotayo nyikani; ua lenye umbo la kengele.

heathen *n* 1 mpagani, kafiri. 2 (*colloq*) mshenzi. 3 (*attrib*) *a ~ country* nchi ya wapagani. ~**ish** *adj*.

heather *n* mmeapori (wenye maua madogo meupe au ya zambarau). **take to the** ~ (*in olden times*) -wa mhalifu, haramia, jahili. ~-**mixture** *n* (*of cloth*) nguo ya rangi inayofanana na mimeapori.

heave *vt,vi* 1 inua, nyanyua (kitu kizito); ng'oa ~ *the anchor* ng'oa nanga. 2 toa ~ *a sigh* shusha pumzi kwa nguvu. 3 (*colloq*) tupa, vurumisha ~ *a stone through a door* vurumisha jiwe mlangoni, tupia fatuma. 4 ~ **(at/on sth)** vuta. ~-**ho!** harambee! 5 (*of breath, waves etc.*) panda na kushuka kwa nguvu na utaratibu. 6 ~ **to** (*of sailing ship*) elea, tua(ma) bila kutia nanga. 7 ~ **in sight** (*naut*) onekana *n* unyanyuaji (kwa nguvu); uvurumishaji (kwa kishindo).

heaven *n* 1 pepo, mbinguni. 2 ~ Mungu *Good ~s!* Mungu Wangu! *H ~ forbid* Mungu apishe mbali. ~**set** *adj* -a bahati njema. 3 mahali pa raha zote. 4 *(often* **the** ~**s)** anga, mbingu. **move ~ and earth** fanya kila linalowezekana *the ~s opened* (*colloq*) mvua ilinyesha ghafla. ~**ward(s)** *adv* kuelekea mbinguni. ~**ly** *adj* 1 -a mbinguni. ~ **angel** malaika wa mbinguni. **the ~ bodies** jua, mwezi na sayari zote. **the ~ city** peponi, paradiso. 2 -a uzuri wa peponi. 3 (*colloq*) -a kupendeza mno, zuri mno.

heavy *adj* 1 -zito *that stone is very ~* jiwe lile ni zito sana. ~ **heart** moyo mzito. ~-**weight** *n* mwanamasumbwi wa uzito wa juu (kilo 79.3 au zaidi). 2 kubwa (kuliko kawaida), -ingi *~-guns* mizinga ~ *rain* mvua kubwa.~**duty** kazi ngumu sana. **find sth** ~

going ona ugumu (katika kutenda jambo). **find sb (rather) going** ona mchoshaji, choshwa na mtu. 3 (*of persons*) zito; (*of writing or painting*) -siovutia, -a kuchusha; (*of parts in a play for the theatre*) -zito; (*of bodily states*) -a kuzubaa. 4 (*compounds*) ~**-handed** *adj* -enye mkono mzito. ~**-hearted** *adj* -enye huzuni, -enye moyo mzito *adv* kwa zito. ~**-laden** *adj* -enye mzigo mzito; (*fig*) -enye moyo mzito. **heavily** *adv. a heavily loaded cart* mkokoteni uliopakiwa sana. **heaviness** *n.*

hebdomadal *adj* -a kila wiki ~ *Council* Baraza la kila wiki.

Hebrew *n* 1 Mwebrania; Myahudi. 2 (*language*) (*in Old Testament*) Kiebrania, (*modern*) Kiyahudi *adj* -a Kiyahudi. **Hebraif** *adj* -a Kiebrania.

hecatomb *n* (*in ancient Greece*) kafara; kafara (agh. ya kuchinjwa maksai 100).

heck *n (sl euph)* jahanamu (*used in exlamations*) ch! *what the* ~! Lo! mambo gani haya!

heckle *vt* hanikiza. ~**r** *n.*

hectre *n* hekta (eka 2.47).

hectic *adj* 1 -a wekundu uliokithiri; -a homa; -a kifua kikuu. 2 (*colloq*) -enye msisimko na shughuli nyingi; -enye mishughuliko mingi *a* ~ *life* maisha yenye msisimko na shughuli nyingi.

hecto *pref* (*in comb*) mia moja; *gramme* gramu mia moja.

hector *vt, vi* onea; fanya ufidhuli.

he'd *abbrev of he had/would* ange/ -ngali.

hedge *n* ua wa miti iliyooteshwa. ~ **hop** *vi* rusha ndege chinichini (k.m. wakati wa kunyunyizia mimea dawa). ~**-row** *n* safu ya miti inayofanya ua. ~**-sparrow** *n* shorewanda wa Uingereza na Amerika. 2 (*fig*) kinga *buy assets as a* ~ *against inflation* nunua rasilmali kama kinga ya wakati wa kushuka kwa thamani ya fedha *vt,vi* 1 weka/ zungushia ua, zingira kwa ua. 2 (*fig*) epa kutoa jibu la moja kwa moja. 3 (*colloq*) chukua tahadhari ya hasara. 4 chenga: ua.

hedgehog *n* nungunungu.

hedonism *n* imani ya kuwa anasa ni kitu muhimu katika maisha; maisha ya anasa. **hedonist** *n* muumini wa imani hiyo. **hedonistic** *adj.*

heed *vt* (*formal*) sikiza ~ *advice* sikiza ushauri *n* **pay/give** ~ **(to); take** ~**(of)** tilia maanani. ~**ful** *adj* -angalifu, tiifu. ~ **(of)** sikivu. ~**less** *adj* (*of*) -zembe -siosikivu, -siojali. ~**lessness** *n.*

heehaw *n* 1 mlio wa punda; kikwakwa.

heel *n* 1 kisigino. **at/on the** ~ **of sth, at/on sb's** ~ nyuma, karibu sana (kutoka nyuma) na kitu/mtu *the school children were at the* ~ *of the thief* wanafunzi walimkaribia kabisa yule mwizi. **bring/come to** ~ (*of a dog*) fuatisha/fuatana na bwana wake; (*fig*) tiisha, shikisha adabu. **down at** ~ (*of shoes*) -enye kisigino kilichochakaa; (*of a person*) anayevaa viatu vilivyochakaa; chafuchafu. **head over** ~**s** chini juu (*fig*) sana. **kick/ cool ones** ~**s** ngojeshwa, lazimishwa kusubiri. **lay sb by the** ~**s** funga. **show a clean pair of** ~ kimbia/toroka (kwa haraka sana). **take to one's** ~ kimbia. **turn on one's** ~ geuka ghafla. **under the** ~ **of** (*fig*) -liotawaliwa na.

hefty *adj* (*colloq*) bonge.

hegemony *n* hegemonia:/ mamlaka amri agh. ya dola moja juu ya dola nyingine.

Hegira/Hejira Hijra. **the** ~ mwanzo wa kalenda ya Kiislamu.

heifer *n* mtamba/mfarika wa ng'ombe; mnyama ambaye hajazaa.

heigh-ho *int* (*of worry, boredom etc.*) oh!

height *n* 1 urefu (wa kwenda juu), kimo *measure your* ~ pima kimo chako *this table is four feet in* ~

meza hii ina kimo cha futi nne. 2 sehemu ya juu; kilele, upeo *the fair was at its ~* maonyesho yalikuwa yamepamba moto hasa *the ~ of an argument* upeo wa majadiliano. **~en** *vt,vi* 1 refuka/refusha (kwa juu). 2 zidi/zidisha (kiwango) *the exam results ~ed his ambitions* matokeo ya mtihani yalizidisha matarajio yake.

heinous *adj* (*of crime*) -a kuchukiza; -baya sana, ovu sana. **~ly** *adv*. **~ness** *n*.

heir *n* mrithi *~ to the throne* mrithi wa ufalme. ~ **apparent** mrithi mstahiki. ~ **presumptive** mrithi mdhaniwa/asiyestahiki. **~ess** *n* mrithi (wa kike). **~loom** *n* kitu kinachorithiwa kizazi hadi kizazi.

Hejira *see* **Hegira**.

held *pt, pp of* **hold**.

helicopter *n* helikopta.

helio (*pref*) -a kuhusu jua. **heliacal** *adj* (*astron*) -enye kuhusiana/ kukaribiana na jua. **~graph** *n* heliografu: chombo kinachoashiria kwa kuakisi mionzi ya jua. **~scope** *n* shamsibini: chombo cha kutazamia jua bila ya kuumiza macho. **~therapy** *n* utabibu kwa kutumia jua. **~trope** *n* heliotropu: ua linalopenda kuelekea jua, lenye rangi ya zambarau nyeupe kidogo; rangi /harufu ya ua hilo.

heliport *n* uwanja wa helikopta.

helium *n* heliamu. **(He)**.

helix *n* 1 hesi. 2 *(arch)* msokoto. 3 mzingo ndani ya sikio. **helical** *adj* -enye hesi, -liosokotwa.

hell *n* 1 (*Rel*) jahanamu, motoni. 2 mahali/hali ya mateso *make your life a ~* fanya maisha yako yawe ya mateso *give sb ~* sumbua mtu. 3 (*colloq in exclamation, to express anger, or to intensify a meaning*) *a ~ of a noise* kelele nyingi mno *go to ~* potelea mbali *what the ~* baka gani? **for the ~ of it** bila sababu maalum. **ride ~ for leather** haraka iwezekanavyo. ~ **cat** *n* mtu mkali/ mwenye ghadhabu (hasa manamke). **~ish** *adj* -a kishetani; baya mno. **be ~ bent on sth** (*sl*) nuia kutenda kitu bila hadhari.

Hellene *n* Myunani halisi, Mgiriki wa kisasa. **Hellenic** *adj* -a Kiyunani; sanaa na utamaduni wao. **Helleniasm** *n* 1 utamaduni/ utaifa wa Myunani. 2 mafumbo, nahau (za Kiyunani). **Hellenist** *n* 1 mtu anayozungumza Kiyunani. 2 mtaalamu wa Kiyunani.

hello *int see* **hullo**.

helm[1] *n* (*archaic*) *see* **helmet**.

helm[2] *n* usukani wa boti/meli *the man at the ~* rubani, (*fig*) kiongozi *the ~ of state* Serikali. **~s man** rubani.

helmet *n* helmeti: kofia ya chuma/ plastiki gumu (agh. huvaliwa na wanajeshi, wazima moto, wapanda pikipiki n.k.). **~ed** *adj* -enye helmeti.

helot *n* 1 mtumwa. 2 (*fig*) hohehahe.

help *n* 1 msaada, auni, muawana. **be of ~ (to sb); be (of) any/much/ some ~ (to sb)** saidia mtu fulani it wasn't much ~ haikusaidia sana. **lend sb one's ~** -pa mtu msaada *his public lecture was a great ~ to us* mhadhara bayana wake ulikuwa (wa) msaada mkubwa kwetu. 2 **a ~** msaada/mtu anayesaidia, mtumishi wa kutwa wa nyumbani, msaidizi *my ~ is sick today* mtumishi wangu yu mgonjwa leo. 3 njia, dawa *there's no ~ for it* hakuna dawa/njia ya kuweza kusaidia, haikwepeki. **~ful** *adj* -enye msaada; -a kusaidia. **~fully** *adv*. **~fulness** *n*. **~less** *adj* 1 bila msaada. 2 -siojiweza. **~lessly** *adv*.**~lessness** *n*. **~er** *n*. msaidizi. **~ing** *n* mpakuo mmoja wa mlo *a ~ of rice and chicken* mpakuo wa wali na kuku *vt,vi* 1 saidia, auni *that won't ~* hiyo haisaidii *he knows how to ~ himself* anajua jinsi ya kujisaidia *~ sb across* saidia mtu kuvuka (mto n.k.). ~ **down** saidia kuteremsha/ endeleza. ~ **in** saidia kuingia (garini n.k.) *~ off/or with* *his coat* saidia kuvua/kuvaa koti. ~ **out** toa msaada, kwamua. ~ **up** saidia mtu (kupanda ngazi n.k.). 2 ~ **sb/oneself (to sth)** (ji)gawia chakula, vinywaji n.k. *he ~ ed me to some food* alinigawia chakula ~ *yourself to some drinks* jihudumie vinywaji mwenyewe (kwa kiasi chako). 3 zuia/jizuia; epuka/ epusha; acha *I could't ~ laughing* sikuweza kujizuia kucheka *I cannot ~ doing it* siwezi kuacha kufanya *it can't be ~ed* haizuiliki. 4 **So ~ me God** (*in an oath*) Mungu nisaidie. ~ **mate/meet** mwenzi (hasa mke na mume).

helter-skelter *adv* shaghalabaghala; harakaharaka *n* kitelezi msokoto kirefu (agh. katika uwanja wa maonyesho ya biashara).

helve *n* mpini (hasa wa shoka).

hem[1] *n* pindo. **~ming stitch** mshono mficho. ~ **stitching** pindo/rembo. **~ming line** *n* pindo hasa la gauni/ sketi. **~ming slip** *n* mshono mficho *vt* 1 pinda. 2 ~ **about/around/in** funga; zunguka, zingira; zuia *the street boys were ~med in by the police* watoto wazururaji walizingirwa na polisi.

hem[2] *int h'm* sauti ya kukohoa (ya kuonyesha wasiwasi au ubishi au kuvuta usikivu) *vi* 1 kohoa. 2 kohoa (kuvuta usikivu). 3 kokota maneno.

hematite, haematite *n* mtapo chuma.

hemi (*pref*) nusu. **~sphere** *n* 1 nusu ya mviringo. 2 nusu ya dunia. **the Eastern ~sphere** (Ulaya, Asia, Africa). **the Western ~sphere** Amerika Kaskazini na Kusini. **the Northern/Southern ~sphere** Kaskazini/Kusini mwa ikweta.

hemo/haemo *adj* -a damu. **~globin** *n* himoglobini. **~philia** *n.* hemofilia: ugonjwa wa damu kutoganda. **~philiac** *n.* **~rrhage** *n* hemoraji: kutoa/utokaji wa damu. **~rrhoids** *n* bawasiri, puru.

hemp *n* 1 katani. **Indian ~** bangi. **~en** *adj* -a katani ~ *rope* kamba ya katani.

hen *n* 1 kuku; (*ready to lay*) tembe; (*laying*) koo. **hen bane** *n* dawa ya usingizi. **~-coop** tundu la kuku. **~-house** *n* banda la kuku agh. la miti. **~-party** *n* (*colloq*) tafrija ya wanawake pekee. **~-pecked** *adj* mtu anayetawaliwa na mkewe. **~-roost** *n* 1 kituo cha kuku usiku. 2 ndege jike. **guinea-~** kanga jike. **pea ~** tausi jike.

hence *adv* (*formal*) 1 kuanzia hapa; tangu sasa *a month ~* mwezi mmoja tangu sasa. 2 kwa hiyo, kwa sababu hiyo. **~forth, ~forward** *adv* tangu sasa na kuendelea. 3 (*poet rhet*) toka! ondoka!

henchman *n* kibaraka, mfuasi bubu/ mnyenyekevu.

henna *n* 1 hina. 2 (*plant*) mhina. **~ed** *adj* -liopakwa hina.

hepatitis *n* (*med*) homa ya manjano (inayoashiriwa na ini kuvimba). **hepatic** *adj* -a maini.

hepta (*pref*) saba. **~gon** *n* pembesaba. **~gonal** *adj*.

her *pron* (*fem*) (*3rd p. sing obj*) *give ~ the pencil* mpe kalamu (*poss. adj*) -ake *that is ~ book* kile ni kitabu chake. **~self** (*refl pron*) yeye mwenyewe *she is ~ again* amerudia hali yake ya kawaida *she came by ~* amekuja mwenyewe *she lives by ~self* anaishi peke yake. **~s** (*poss. pron (fem.)*. *this book is ~s* kitabu hiki ni chake.

herald *n* 1 (*hist*) mpiga mbiu, mtabiri, kijumbe. 2 dalili, ishara *clouds are a ~ of rain* mawingu ni dalili ya mvua. 3 mhifadhi majina ya nasaba ya jamaa *vt* tangaza, ashiria, piga mbiu. **~ic** *adj* -a nasaba. **~dry** *n* elimu ya nembo, unasaba na historia ya koo za kale.

herb *n* mimea ya msimu/ viungo; mitishamba *medicinal ~s* mitishamba. **~sceous** *adj* -a mimea, -a mitishamba, -enye mimea. **~age** *n* majani mateke. **~al** *adj* -a mitishamba. **~alist** mtaalamu wa mitishamba. **~arium** *n* hebaria: mahali pa kuhifadhia mimea iliyokaushwa. **~ivorous** *adj* -enye kula majani.

herculean *adj* -enye kuhitaji nguvu/akili nyingi.

herd *n* 1 kundi la wanyama (agh. ng'ombe). 2 (*derog*) makabwela. 3 (*esp in compounds*) **cow~/goat ~** mchunga ng'ombe/mbuzi *vi,vt* chunga; kusanya katika makundi. **~sman** *n* mchungaji.

here *adv* 1 huku; humu, hapa *bring the book ~* leta kitabu hapa *come ~* njoo hapa. 2 (*point in time*) sasa, hapo *~ I would like to ask a question* sasa nataka kuuliza swali *~ they come*! wanakuja sasa. **H~ goes**! naanza sasa. 3 (*after prep*) *she lives near ~* anakaa karibu. 4 **~ and there** huku na huko. **~, there and everywhere** pote, kila mahali. **neither ~ nor there** haihusiani kabisa. **~ we go again** (*colloq*) yale yalee. 5 (*calling attention to sb/sth*) *my son ~ will show you* mwanangu atakuonyesha *~ is your book* kitabu chako ni hiki hapa. 6 (*when drinking to sb's health etc*) **H~'s to you** kwa afya yako! 7 (*compounds*) **~abouts** *adv* hapahapa. **~after** *adv* baadaye *n* wakati ujao, ahera. **~by** *adv* (*leg*) kwa njia ya, kwa kitendo cha. **~in** *adv* (*leg*) katika jambo hili. **~of** *adv* (*leg*) kwa kuhusu hayo, hicho. **~to** *adv* (*leg*) kwa shauri hili. **~tofore** *adv* (*leg*) mpaka sasa, awali. **~upon** *adv* (*formal*) kwa hayo. **~with** *adv* (*comm*) pamoja na hii.

heredity *n* urithi. **hereditament** *n* mali ya kurithika. **hereditary** *adj* -a kurithi.

heresy *n* uasi (hasa wa kidini). **heretic** *n* mwasi, mwenye kosa la uasi. **heretical** *adj*.

heritage *n* urithi. **heritable** *adj* -a kurithika. **heritor** *n* mrithi.

hermaphrodite *n* huntha. **hermaphroditic** *adj*.

hermetic *adj* -liozibwa kabisa (hata hewa haiwezi kuingia). **~ally** *adv*.

hermit *n* mtawa/walii anayekaa pweke. **~age** makao ya mtawa/walii pweke.

hernia *n* ngiri.

hero *n* 1 shujaa, nguli *~'s welcome* mapokezi ya kishujaa. **~ine** *n* mwanamke shujaa. **~ism** *n* ushujaa. **~-worship** kutukuza ushujaa. **~ic** *adj* -a kishujaa, -a kinguli. 2 kubwa mno *a statue of ~ size* sanamu kubwa mno. 3 (*of languages*) -a majisifu, -a maneno matupu. **~ics** *n* majisifu. **~ically** *adv*.

heroin *n* heroini: (dawa ya usingizi/ kulevya) itokanayo na afyuni.

heron *n* kulastara. **~ry** *n* kiota cha kulastara.

herpes *n* ugonjwa wa malengelenge ya neva ngozini.

Herr *n* (*German*) Bwana.

herring *n* heringi: aina ya samaki majichumvi. **~-bone** (*sewing*) mshono mwibasamaki.

hertz *n* (*phys*) hezi: kipimo cha mzunguko mmoja kwa nukta. **~ian** *adj* (*phys*) -a hezi. **~ian wave** sumakuumeme.

hesitate *vi* sita *don't ~ to* usisite, usiwe na wahaka.

hesitant *adj* -enye kusita; -enye wasiwasi, -a wahaka. **hesitantly** *adv*. **hesitance, hesitancy** *n*. **hesitation** *n* kusita, wasiwasi *without the slightest hesitation* bila ya kusita, bila ya wasiwasi wowote.

hessian *n* kitambaa-katani (nguo nzito ya katani au juti kama gunia).

hetero *pref* anuwai/mbalimbali; kinyume, tafauti. **~dox** *adj* -enye kufuata imani tafauti na wingi wa watu. **~doxy** *n*. **~geneous** *adj* tafauti/tafauti/aina aina/mbalimbali. **~geneity** *n*. **~sexual** *adj* -a kuvutiwa na mtu wa jinsi tafauti.

het-up *adj* -liosisimkwa, -liopagawa, -liochaga.

heuristic *adj* -a nadharia ya kujifunza kwa uvumbuzi, -a kubahatisha njia ya kufumbua matatizo kwa

kujaribujaribu.
hew *vt,vi* 1 ~ *down/away/off* tema, kata. ~ **down a tree** kata mti; (*colloq*) ~ *sb to pieces* katakata. 2 chonga ~*n timber* mbao zilizochongwa. 3 pata kwa shida/ juhudi kubwa ~ *out a career for oneself* jipatia kazi kwa shida na juhudi kubwa. ~**er** *n* (*colloq*) mkata miti (*colloq*) ~ *s of wood and drawers of water* watu wafanyao kazi ngumu, watwana, makabwela, wavuja jasho.
hex *n* uchawi. **put the ~ on** roga.
hexagon *n* pembe sita. ~**al** *adj*.
hey *int* ala! we!
hey-day *n* wakati wa ushababi/ furaha/neema.
hi *int halo*! mambo?
hiatus *n* ufa, pengo, pungufu.
hibernate *vi* 1 bumbwaa (ili kupitisha majira magumu). 2 kaa bila kazi. **hiberation** *n*.
hibiscus *n* haibiskasi (ua jamii ya bamia).
hiccup,hiccough *vi* -wa na kwikwi *n* kwikwi.
hick *n adj* (*sl. deroq*) mshamba.
hid *pt of* **hide**[1].
hidden *pp of* **hide**[1].
hide[1] *vt,vi* 1 ~ **(from)** jificha, ficha kitu *the stars were hidden by the clouds* nyota zilifichwa na mawingu. 2 jificha *don't* ~ usijifiche. ~ **and seek** *n* kibe *n* (*US = blind*) maficho ya wapiga picha/ wawindaji. ~**out/away** maficho. **hiding** *n* (*used of persons*) **be in/go into ~** enda mafichoni; jificha. **come out of ~** toka mafichoni ~ *place* maficho.
hide[2] *n* 1 ngozi ya mnyama (iliyotengenezwa tayari kwa kuuzwa). 2 (*colloq*) ngozi ya binadamu. **save one's** ~ jinusurisha (kutokana na adhabu au kipigo). **tan sb's** ~ piga mtu. ~-**bound** *adj* -enye akili finyu; -enye kufuata/ kushikilia sana sheria, mila, desturi n.k. **hiding** *n* kipigo *give sb a good* ~ piga mtu barabara.
hideous *adj* hunde, -enye sura mbaya sana; -a kutisha. ~**ly** *adv*.
hie *vi* (*archaic or joc*) enda chapuchapu.
hierarchy *n* 1 mfumo wa ngazi/ tabaka/msonge za madaraka, utawala msonge; kundi la watu wenye mamlaka; kundi la maaskofu (nchini); uongozi wa kikasisi. **hierarchic(al)** *adj*.
hieroglyph *n* 1 hieroglifu: picha inayowakilisha neno, sauti au silabi iliyotumiwa katika maandiko ya Wamisri wa kale n.k. 2 alama ya siri isiyoeleweka. ~**ics** *n* maandiko ya hieroglifu *adj* -a maandiko ya hieroglifu.
hi-fi *n, adj* (*colloq abbr.of*) **high fidelity** *see* **high higgle**
higgle *vi* bishana, shindania jambo. ~**dy-piggledy** *adj,adv* -a hobela-hobela, hobelahobela *n* fujo.
high[1] *adj* 1 -juu, -refu (kwa kwenda juu) *The clouds are ~ in the sky* mawingu yako juu angani *Kilimanjaro is the ~est mountain in Africa* Kilimanjaro ndio mlima mrefu kabisa barani Afrika. ~ **and dry**.(*of a ship*) -liokwama; nje ya maji; (*fig*) -liopitwa na wakati, -liotelekezwa, -liotengwa (*do sth*) *with a ~ hand* fanya jambo kwa kiburi. 2 -kuu, -a juu, muhimu. **a ~ official** afisa wa cheo cha juu ~ *society* tabaka la juu. **the Most ~** (*in the Bible*) Mungu. ~ **and low** watu wa matabaka yote katika jumuia, watu wote. 3 (*of sounds*) kali; -a kidato cha juu *speak in ~ tone* ongea kwa sauti kali ya kidato cha juu. 4 -a juu; kali; kubwa. ~ **prices** bei kubwa/ya juu. ~ **words** maneno makali. ~ **living** maisha ya juu, anasa. 5 ~ **time** wakati wa kufanya jambo *it is ~ time you left* wakati wa kuondoka umewadia, afadhali ufunge virago! 6 -enye heshima, ema, adili(fu) *a girl of ~ character* msichana mwenye tabia njema. ~ **ideals**

maadili mema. 7 **H~ Church** Kanisa la Anglikana la UMCA (ambalo huwapa maaskofu na mapadri mamlaka ya kutoa sakramenti). **H~-Churchman** muumini wa kanisa. 8 (*of food esp. meat and game*) -liovunda. 9 (*colloq*) -liolewa, -levi. 10 (*colloq*) -liolewa bangi/madawa. 11 *n* kiwango cha juu. **from (on) ~** kutoka mbinguni *the income reached a new ~ this year* mapato yalifikia kiwango cha juu mwaka huu. 12 (*compounds*) **~ ball** *n* (*US*) pombe kali na soda au maji (ndani ya glasi ndefu). **~est bidder** *n* mzabuni wa juu. **~ born** *adj* -a uzao bora, hababuu. **~boy** *n* (*US*) kabati refu lenye saraka. **~brow** *n adj* (*person*) -enye (mambo) makuu (agh. hutumiwa kwa kudharau). **~ chair** kiti kirefu cha mtoto. **~-class** daraja la kwanza/juu. **~ colour** (*of complexion*) rangi nyekundu iliyokolea. **H~ Commissioner** *n* Balozi wa nchi ya Jumuia ya Madola katika nchi nyingine ya Jumuiya ya Madola. **~ Court** Mahakama Kuu. **~ day** (*only in*) *~ says and holidays* sikukuu. **~ explosive** *n* baruti kali yenye mshindo mkubwa. **~ falutin** *adj* (*colloq*) -a mbwembwe. **~ fidelity** *n. adj* (*abbr. hi-fi*) (*of radios, records, tapes etc*) -enye kutoa sauti safi. **~-flier/flyer** *n* mtu mwenye tamaa kubwa ya kufanikiwa katika maisha. **~ flown** *adj* -enye makeke, -enye majisifu/mbwembwe. **~ flying** *adj* (*fig*) (*of persons*) -enye tamaa sana. **~ frequency** *n* (*abbr. hf*) -a masafa marefu. **H~ German** *n* Kijerumani sanifu. **~-grade** *adj* -a daraja ya juu. **~-handed** *adj* onevu, -dhalimu. **~-handedly** *adv*. **~hat** *adj, n* fidhuli, -enye makuu *vt* dharau, dhalilisha. **the ~ jump** *n* kuruka juu. **be for the ~ jump** (*sl*) stahili adhabu kali *you'll be for the ~ jump* utaipata, utakiona. **~ keyed** (*of sound*) kali; (*fig*) -enye mpapatiko. **~land** *n* milimani, uwanda wa juu. **~-level** *adj* (*attrib only*) (*of conferences etc*) -a ngazi ya juu. **~ life** *n* (a) maisha ya kisasa na ya anasa (*in W. Africa*) hailaifu: mtindo wa muziki na dansi. **~ light** *n* (*usu pl*) sehemu ya picha yenye kuakisi mwanga; (*fig*) sehemu yenye kuvutia au kuonekana waziwazi *vt* sisitizia; -pa umuhimu. **~ Mass** (*in R.C. Church*) Misa kuu. **~-minded** *adj* -enye msimamo, -enye maadili. **~-mindedly** *adv*. **~-mindedness** *n*. **~-necked** *adj* (*of a dress*) -a kukaba roho. **~-pitched** (*of sounds*) -kali, (*of roof*) -a paa, -liochongoka. **~-powered** *adj* -enye juhudi, -enye nguvu nyingi. **~-pressure** kanieneo ya juu; (*fig*) shupavu, -enye juhudi. **~-priced** *adj* ghali. **~ priest** *n* kuhani mkuu. **~-principled** *adj* -enye msimamo, nyofu. **~-ranking** *adj* (*of officers*) -enye cheo cha juu. **~ rise** *adj* maghohorofa marefu. **~ road** *n* barabara kuu, (*fig*) njia ya moja kwa moja. **H~ school** sekondari ya juu. **the ~ seas** bahari kuu. **~- sounding** *adj* (*of style*) -enye kuvutia; mbwembwe. **~-spirited** changamfu, -epesi, kunjufu; (*of a horse*) -enye kwenda mbio. **~ spot** *n* tukio muhimu. **~ street** *n* barabara kuu/muhimu (katika mji). **~ table** *n* meza kuu. **~ tea** mchanganyiko wa chai na chakula cha jioni. **~-tension** *adj* (*electric*) -enye volteji kubwa. **~ tide** *n* maji kujaa, maji makuu. **~ toned** -a juu (katika jamii au kisomo). **~ treason** *n* uhaini. **~ up** *n* (*colloq*) mtu mashuhuri; mtu wa cheo cha juu. **~ water** *see* **~tide.** **~-water mark** *n* alama yenye kuonyesha kikomo cha juu cha maji kujaa; (*fig*) upeo wa mafanikio. **~way** *n*. **~ road** barabara kuu. **H~ way Code** *n* kanuni/sheria za barabara. **~-way-man** *n* haramia, mnyang'anyi *adv* juu (*lit,fig*) lipa bei kubwa. **live** ~ ishi kitajiri (kwa vinono na vinywaji kochokocho). **fly** ~ (*fig*) -wa na tamaa kubwa. **hold one's head** ~ jiamini, jiona. **run** ~ (*of the sea*) kabiliwa na mkondo mkali na maji makuu; *(of the feelings)* chacharika. **search/look/hunt ~ and low (for sth)** tafuta kila mahali. **~ly** *adv* sana *he spoke ~ of her* alimsifu sana. **~ness** *n* 1 (*opposite of lowness*) hali/ sifa ya juu. 2 (*title*) Mstahiki, mtukufu.

hijack (*also* **high-jack**) *vt* teka nyara. **~er** *n* mteka nyara.

hike *vi* (*colloq*) tembea umbali mrefu (kwa burudani); matembezi marefu. **~r** *n* mtembeaji wa masafa marefu. **hitch-~** *vi* (*colloq abbr hitch*) omba lifti.

hilarious *adj* -a kikwakwa. **hilarity** *n* kikwakwa. **~ly** *adv*.

hill *n* 1 kilima. ~ **side** ubavuni mwa kilima *a steep ~* kilima kikali. ~ **top** juu ya kilima, kilele cha kilima. 2 mwinuko. 3 **ant~** kichuguu. **~y** *adj* -enye vilima. **~-billy** *n* (*colloq often used derog, in SE of the US*) mshamba, mkulima, mfanya kazi wa shambani/wa milimani; *(attrib)* -awakulima wa milimani.

hillock *n* kiduta.

hilt *n* mpini, (wa upanga, sime au jambia n.k.). **(up) to the** ~ kabisa.

him *pers pron* yeye (mwanamume); yule *give it to ~* mpe *that's ~* ndiye hasa (yeye). **~self** *pron* 1 (*reflex*) mwenyewe (mwanaume) *the injured man came to ~* mtu aliyeumia alipata fahamu tena *he found ~ in the ditch* alijikuta shimoni. **(all) by ~self** peke yake; bila msaada *he lives ~* anaishi peke yake. 2 (*emph*) mwenyewe *did you see the Director ~?* ulimwona Mkurugenzi mwenyewe? 3 hali ya kawaida (ya mtu) *he is not ~ today* hayupo katika hali yake ya kawaida leo.

hind[1] *n* paa jike.

hind[2] *adj* -a nyuma ~ *legs* miguu ya nyuma (ya mnyama). ~ **quarters** *n* (*of mutton or beef*) nyama ya miguu ya nyuma na kiuno. **~most** *adj* -a nyuma kabisa; -a mwisho. **~sight** *n* utambuzi (baada ya jambo kutokea).

hinder *vt* zuia ~ *sb from doing sth* zuia mtu asifanye kitu fulani; (*delay*) kawilisha, chelewesha. **~ance** *n* kizuizi, kipingamizi.

Hindi *n, adj* (*of a language*) Kihindi; -a Kihindi.

Hindu *n* Baniani, Mhindu. **~ism** *n* dini ya Kibaniani/Kihindu. **~stani** *adj* -a Kihindustani *n* Kihindustani (mojawapo ya lugha za Kihindi).

hinge *n* bawaba; (*fig*) kiini cha jambo; kanuni kuu (ya jambo fulani) *his mind is off its ~s* (*or un~d*) ana wazimu *vt,vi* 1 pigilia bawaba. 2 ~ **on/upon** tegemea.

hint *n* dokezo. **drop (sb) a** ~ dokeza kwa kufumbia. **take a** ~ tambua na fanya lililodokezwa *vt,vi* 1 ~ **(to sb)** dokeza. ~ **at**. 2 gusia, dokezea.

hinterland *n* bara.

hip[1] *n* nyonga. **smite ~ and thigh** shinda sana. **~-bath** *n* kipipa ambacho kinamfika mtu kwenye nyonga. **~-bone** n (*biol*) mfupa wa nyonga. **~-pocket** n mfuko wa pembeni (mwa suruali n.k.). **~-flask** *n* chupa ndogo (ya brandi) inayochukuliwa katika mifuko ya nyonga.

hip[2] *n* tunda la waridi mwitu.

hip[3] *adj* (*also hep*) (*sl*) kisasa, -nayofuata mambo/ mitindo ya kisasa.

hippie *see* **hippy**.

hippo *n* (*colloq abbr of*) **hippo potamus**.

Hippocratic *adj* ~ **oath** kiapo cha uaminifu cha madaktari.

hippodrome *n* (*in ancient Greece and Rome*) kiwanja cha mashindano ya magari ya kukokotwa.

hippopotamus *n* kiboko.

hippy,hippie (*late 1960s*) hipi, mwasi wa mila/utamaduni.

hire *vt* ~ **(out)** kodi, kodisha; panga, pangisha *~out boats* kodisha mashua; kodi *n* kodi, malipo ya kukodisha/kupangisha. **for** ~ kwa ajili ya kukodishwa. (**pay for/buy**) **on ~ purchase** bandika, (lipa/ nunua) kwa polepole; mkopo. **~ling** *n* (*derog*) mfanyakazi wa kukodiwa; mamluki.

hirsute *adj* -enye nywele kuruwili; -enye nywele na ndevu ndefu na za matimutimu.

his *adj, pron* -ake (mwanamume) *a friend of ~* rafiki yake.

hiss *vi,vt* 1 fanya sss kama nyoka. 2 ~ **(off)**; ~ **(at)** fanya zii! zomea *n* 1 sauti ya sss kama ya mlio wa nyoka. 2 sauti ya zii!

history *n* 1 historia. **make** ~ fanya kitendo/jambo la kihistoria. **ancient** ~ historia ya kale; hadithi ya zamani. **modern** ~ historia ya sasa (kuanzia 1453). 2 maelezo ya matukio ya zamani. 3 matukio yanayohusishwa na mtu au kitu *the inner ~of an affair* undani wa jambo. 4 **natural** ~ elimu viumbe; maelezo yenye mpango kuhusu hali za maisha. **historian** *n* mtaalamu wa historia, mwanahistoria. **historic** *adj* -a kihistoria, -enye kukumbukwa katika historia, -enye umuhimu kihistoria. ~ **times** nyakati ambazo historia yake ipo na imerekodiwa. **historical** *adj* 1 -a historia; si -a hadithi tu. ~ **events** matukio ya kihistoria halisi; -sio ya kufikiria tu. 2 -a kuhusiana na historia. **historically** *adv*. **historicity** *n* tabia ya historia, uhalisi wa matukio. **historiographer** *n* mwandishi wa historia. **historiography** *n* uandishi wa historia.

histrionic *adj* 1 tamthilia/thieta/ uigizaji. 2 -a unafiki, -a uwongo. **~s** *n* 1 maigizo (ya kwenye thieta). 2 tabia za kitamthilia au kithieta (hasa zilizotiwa chumvi).

hit *vt,vi* 1 piga, gonga ~ *sb on the head* piga mtu kichwani. ~ **a man when he is down**; ~ **a man below the belt** fanya kinyume cha sheria za masumbwi; (*fig*) shinda kwa hila. ~ **it**; ~ **the nail on the head** pata, patia kabisa. ~ **it off (with sb togather)** patana. **~-and-run** *attrib adj* (*of a road accident*) gonga mtu na kukimbia. 2 ~ **sb hard** hasiri. 3 pata, fikia. ~ **the right path** pata njia. ~ **the head lines** (*colloq of news*) pewa umuhimu wa kwanza katika gazeti; vuma sana gazetini. ~ **the road** (*colloq*) anza safari. 4 piga. ~ **out (against)** piga kwa nguvu; (*fig*) shambulia kwa nguvu. 5 ~ **on/upon sth** pata kwa bahati/ bila kutegemea. 6 ~ **sth/sb off** (*colloq*) elezea kwa kifupi na kwa usahihi; dokeza *n* 1 pigo. ~ **man** (*sl*) mtu anayelipwa ili aue. 2 ushindi. ~ **songs** nyimbo zinazovuma/zinazosifika sana. **make a ~ (with sb)** (*colloq*) pendeza sana mtu; penya moyoni. ~ **parade** *n* orodha ya rekodi mashuhuri zinazouzika sana. 3 utani mkali, kebehi, dhihaka.

hitch *vt,vi* 1 ~ **sth up** vuta. 2 funga, fungia; nasa ~ *a horse to a fence* fungia farasi bomani. 3 (*also*-**hike**) ~ **(a ride/lift)** (*colloq*) omba lifti/msaada wa gari *n* 1 mvuto; kumbo. 2 fundo. 3 kikwazo.

hither *adv* (*old use*) huku. **~-to** *adv* mpaka sasa.

hive *n* 1 (*also* **bee~**) mzinga wa nyuki; nyuki walio mzingani. 2 mahali penye watu wengi wanaoshughulika *vt,vi* 1 kusanya nyuki katika mzinga. 2 ingia mzingani; ishi pamoja kama nyuki. ~ **off (from)** (*fig*) jitenga (na kuwa chombo kinachojitegemea); gawa na fanya huru.

hives *n* ugonjwa wa mabaka ngozini.

hoar *adj* (*liter*) (*of hair*) -a mvi, (*of a person*) -enye mvi. **~frost** *n* jalidi. **~y** *adj* -enye mvi (kwa uzee); zee sana. ~**iness** *n*.

hoard *n* akiba, hodhi, hazina *vt,vi* ~ **(up)** weka akiba; hodhi. ~**er** *n*. (*US bill board*) *(often temporary)* ua wa mbao (unaotumika kwa matangazo).

hoarse *adj* 1 (*of voice*) -liopwelea, -a madende. 2 (*of a person*) -enye sauti iliyopwelea, -enye madende. ~**ly** *adv*. **ness** *n*.

hoax *n* mzaha, shere, dhihaka, hila *vt* dhihaki, cheza shere, fanyia mzaha, danganya kimzaha.

hob *n* bamba la chuma juu ya moto jikoni.

hobble *vt,vi* 1 chechemea; chopea, pecha. 2 funga miguu miwili ya mnyama (k.m. punda/farasi) ili asiende mbali *n* mwendo wa kuchopea. ~ **skirt** sketi inayobana sana (inayomzuia mvaaji kutembea vizuri).

hobby *n* 1 jambo alipendalo mtu; jambo la kupitishia muda (kwa kujiburudisha). 2 (*arch*) farasi mdogo. ~-**horse** *n* 1 farasi wa mbao (wa kuchezea/kwenye bembea), farasi wa fito au matete; (*fig*) (*of conversation etc*) mada anayoipenda mtu na anayoirudia rudia).

hobgoblin *n* pepo mbaya.

hobnail *n* njumu. ~**ed** *adj* (*of boots etc*) -enye njumu.

hob-nob *vi* ~ **(together) (with sb)** suhubiana (na); fanya urafiki (na).

hobo (*US sl*) mzururaji.

Hobson's choice *n see* **choice**.

hock[1] *n* goti la mguu wa nyuma wa mnyama.

hock[2] *vt* (*sl*) weka rehani *n* **in** ~ rehani.

hockey *n* hoki: mpira wa magongo. **ice** ~ hoki ya barafuni. ~ **stick** kigoe cha mpira wa magongo.

hocus-pocus *n* mrogonyo,udanganyifu *vt,vi* rogonya, vunga, chezea.

hod *n* chano, karai.

hodge-podge *n see* **hotch-potch**.

hoe *n* jembe *vt, vi* lima, palilia (kwa jembe). **Dutch** ~ jembe la kusukuma.

hog *n* nguruwe; (*fig*) mtu mchafu/ mlafi/mchoyo. **go the whole** ~ fanya kitu kwa ukamilifu. ~-**wash** *n* makombo, rojorojo; (*fig*) (*esp of sth said or written*) -sio na maana, upuuzi *vt,vi* chukua/-la zaidi ya unavyotakiwa; chukua/-la kwa ulafi na uchoyo. ~**ish** *adj* lafi na -enye choyo.

hogshead *n* 1 pipa kubwa, (hasa la kutilia pombe). 2 kipimo cha lita 240.

hoi polloi *n (derog)* **the** ~ (*pej*) makabwela, polo.

hoist *vt* inua, pandisha kwa roda. ~ **a sail** tweka tanga *n* chombo/kifaa cha kuinulia/kupandishia; roda; (*colloq*) kuvuta, kusukuma. **give sb a** ~ sukuma/vuta mtu ili kumsaidia kupanda.

hoity-toity *adj* (*colloq*) -enye kichwa kikubwa, -enye maringo/kujidai *don't be so* ~ usiwe na kiburi, usijidai.

hold[1] *vt,vi* 1 shika, kamata. ~ **oneself well** jiweka imara; simama vizuri. ~ **the line** shikilia simu. 2 zuia. ~ **one's breath** zuia pumzi (kwa woga n.k.). ~ **one's fire** acha kupiga risasi kwa muda. ~ **one's tongue/peace** nyamaza, kaa kimya. **there is no** ~**ing sb/sth** haizuiliki, haiwezekani kumzuia/kuzuia. 3 shikilia. ~ **oneself in readiness (for)** jitayarishe (kwa hatari), kaa tayari (kwa dharura). ~ **one's sides with laughter** shikilia mbavu, cheka sana/vunjika mbavu. 4 weka; -wa na uwezo wa kuweka; chukua *this tank* ~*s 30 litres* tangi hili linaweza kuweka lita 30. **(not)** ~ **water** (isiyo) kubalika. ~ **sth in one's head** kumbuka. 5 fanya watu wasikilize, sisimua *the speaker held his audience spellbound* msemaji aliwasisimua wasikilizaji wake. 6 ona; chukulia, amini. ~ **sb in high/ low esteem** heshimu/dharau mtu. ~ **sth dear/cheap** kuza/shusha thamani ya kitu, thamini sana/ kidogo. 7 linda, shikilia. ~ **the fort**

(*fig*) -wa na madaraka mwenyewe anapoondoka. ~ **one's ground** simama tisti. ~ **one's own** kacha, -torudi nyuma. 8 fanya, anzisha, endesha ~ *a meeting* fanya mkutano. ~ **court** (*fig*) karibisha, starehesha, kubali kuwa na maongezi na (washabiki/wapenzi). 9 -wa na haki ya, miliki. 10 -endelea vizuri. 11 shika nafasi. **office ~er** mwenye ofisi. 12 himili, beba *the new car ~s the road well* gari hili jipya linahimili barabara. 13 *(uses with adverbial particles and preps)*. ~ **sth against** acha kitu kiathiri wazo la mtu *don't ~ his political views against him* usimchukulie kuwa na makosa kwa sababu ya mawazo/ msimamo wake kisiasa. ~ **back** sita. ~ **sb/sth back** fanya mtu/kitu kisite; zuia, (*of secret*) ficha. ~ **sb/sth down** shikilia; kandamiza. ~ **a job down** (*colloq*) dumu kazini (kwa kuonyesha uwezo). ~ **forth** sema kwa kujikweza; jigamba, hubiri. ~ **sth forth** toa; pendekeza. ~ **sth in** zuia ~ *in one's temper* jizuia (hasira). ~ **off** jitenga, kaa/baki mbali; chelewesha. ~ **sb/sth off** zuia mtu/kitu mbali. ~ **on** simama imara (kwenye matatizo/hatari); (*usu imper*) acha ~ *on a minute* acha kwanza kidogo! ~ **on to** shikilia; -tokubali kutoa mali n.k.. ~ **sth on** shikilia; weka *bolts and nuts ~ the wheels on* parafujo na nati hizi inashikilia magurudumu mahali pake. ~ **out** shikilia, -tojisalimisha; dumu, endela kuwepo; *(of hand)* nyosha *the workers are still ~ing out for higher wages* wafanyakazi bado wanaendelea kudai mishahara ya juu. ~ **out on** kataa kupatana/ kushirikiana. ~ **sb/sth out** wa na mtu/kitu; toa. ~ **sth over** ahirisha. ~ **sth over sb** tumia kitu kutisha; tishia. ~ **to sth** fanya mtu atimize ahadi/mkataba, shikilia kuwa mwaminifu kwa; endelea kushikilia. ~ **sb to sth** fanya mtu aweke ahadi n.k.. ~ **sb (up) to ransom** shikilia mtu mateka (ili kudai vitu mbalimbali). ~ **together** shikamana. ~ **sb/sth together** fanya ishikamane. ~ **sb/sth up** shika, zuia; chelewesha; shikilia kwa nguvu/vitisho (ili kuibia n.k.). ~ **up** *n* ushikiliaji wa nguvu, wizi; fanya kuwa mfano. ~ **sb up to derision/scorn/ ridicule** dhihaki mtu. ~ **with sth** kubali.

hold[2] *n* 1 mshiko; kushika; uwezo wa kushika. 2 amri, madaraka *he has great ~ over him* ana madaraka makubwa juu yake. 3 mahali pa kushikia. 4 (*boxing and wrestling*) mashiko. **~all** *n* begi kubwa la kubebea nguo. **~er** *n* 1 kishikizi, kishikilia. 2 mwenye madaraka; mpangaji; mmiliki; mshikaji. **~ing** *n* kiwanja, shamba; umilikaji (agh wa ardhi). **small ~** *n* shamba dogo. ~ **company** kampuni mama.

hold[3] *n* sehemu ya meli ya kuwekea mizigo.

hole *n* 1 tundu, shimo. **make a ~ in** tumia kiasi kikubwa cha *the hospital charges made a large ~ in his savings* gharama za hospitali zilipunguza kiasi kikubwa cha akiba yake. **pick ~s in** tafuta kosa. **a square peg in a round ~** mtu asiyefaa katika cheo fulani. 2 (*colloq*) hali ngumu, mbaya; hali ovyo ovyo. 3 shimo la mnyama; (*fig*) maficho, pango. **~-and-corner** *adj* (*colloq attrib*) -a chinichini -a siri. 4. (*golf*) goli; pointi za magoli *vt,vi* 1 toboa. 2 ~ **(out)** tia mpira (wa gofu) shimoni. ~ **up** (*sl*) jificha.

holiday *n* 1 sikukuu; siku ya mapumziko. 2 (*often pl*) (US **vacation**) likizo. **~-maker** *n* mtu aliye likizoni; mtalii.

Holiness *n* utakatifu, uwalii. **His/ Your H** ~Baba Mtakatifu.

holler *vt,vi* (*sl*) piga makelele.

holloa *int halo.*

hollow 1 tupu, -a wazi. ~ **ware** kibia.

2 (*of sounds*) sauti kama itokeayo sehemu wazi/shimoni. 3 (*fig*) -enye hila; ongo, nafiki ~ *victory* ushindi wa kirahisi mno. 4 -a kuingia ndani; -a kubonyea. ~ **eyed** -enye macho ndani. 5 (*colloq; as adv*) **beat sb ~** shinda hasa, kabisa *n* shimo; kibonde *vt* ~ **(out)** fukua, komba.

holly *n* mholi: mti wenye majani yaliyo na ncha kali.

Hollywood *n* makao makuu ya utengenezaji filamu Marekani.

holm *n* kisiwa kidogo katika mto (hasa wakati wa mafuriko).

holm-oak *n* mwaloni.

holocaust *n* maangamizi makuu (hasa ya watu kwa kuchomwa moto, mabomu n.k.) *a nuclear ~* maangamizi ya watu kwa bomu la nyuklia.

holograph *n* holografu: maandishi yaliyoandikwa na mtu mwenyewe.

holster *n* mfuko wa bastola.

holy *adj* 1 -takatifu; -a kuhusiana na Mungu/dini. **the H~ Bible, H-Writ** Biblia Takatifu. **the ~ Land** nchi ya Palestina. **the ~ City** Yerusalemu. ~ **Week** Juma la Mateso. **~Communion** Komunyo; Ekaristi Takatifu. ~ **Father** Baba Mtakatifu. ~ **ground** sehemu takatifu. ~ **water** maji ya uzima. **a ~ war** jihad, vita vya kidini. 2 -a kumcha Mungu *a ~ man* mcha Mungu *live a ~ life* ishi kwa kumcha Mungu. 3 **a ~ terror** *(sl)* mtoto mtundu *n* **the ~ of Holies** chumba/mahali patakatifu, takatifu; (*fig*) mahali popote patakatifu.

holystone *n* jiwe la mchanga laini la kusugulia meli, sitaha ya meli *vt* sugua (kwa mchanga).

homage *n* 1 heshima kuu. **do/pay ~ (to sb)** toa heshima. 2 (*in feudal times*) heshima, utiifu kwa mtawala.

homburg *n* kofia laini.

home *n* 1 nyumbani, makazi, maskani. **at ~** nyumbani; (*football, etc*) uwanja wa nyumbani. **the ~ team** timu ya wenyeji/nyumbani; (*of invitation*) -wa nyumbani (kupokea wageni). **at ~** *n* tafrija ya nyumbani (ambayo wageni wanatarajiwa kufika wakati maalum). **not at ~ (to)** -tokaribisha/-topokea wageni. **make oneself/be/ feel/ at~** starehe, ondosha ugeni; jisikia nyumbani. **at ~ in** zoea. **be ~ and dry** (*colloq*) fanikiwa. **a ~ from ~** mahali mtu anapojisikia yu mwenyeji. **nothing to write ~ about** (*colloq*) hakuna cha ajabu/maana. 2 kituo cha wasiojiweza. 3 (*often attrib*) maisha ya kifamilia. ~ **economics** sayansi kimu. ~ **help** *n* (*GB*) mtu aliyeajiriwa kusaidia wasiojiweza. 4 (see **habitat**) maskani, makazi asilia. 5 (*in sport and in various games*) golini; kituoni. (*baseball*) **the ~ plate** kituo cha nyumbani. ~ **run** mzunguko wa mpigo mmoja. **the ~ straight/stretch** mwisho wa mbio fulani. 6 (*attrib*) **one's ~ town** makazi ya kudumu. **Ministry for H ~ Affairs** wizara ya mambo ya ndani. 7 (*compounds*) **~-baked** *adj* -liopikwa, -liotengenezwa nyumbani. ~ **brewed** pombe iliyotengenezwa nyumbani/ya kienyeji. **~coming** *n* kurudi nyumbani. **~cured** *adj* (*of food esp bacon*) -liokaushwa nyumbani. **the ~ front** raia (wakati wa vita). **~grown** *adj* (*of food*) -liopandwa/ -liozalishwa nchini. ~ **guard** *n* mwanamgambo wa Uingereza (1940-57). **~land** *n* nchi ya asili. ~ **made** *adj* (*of bread, cakes, etc.*) -liotengenezwa nyumbani. ~ **Rule** utawala wa wananchi wenyewe. **~sick** *adj* -a kutamania kukumbuka nyumbani. **~spun** nguo iliyofumwa kwa mkono; -a nyumbani. **~stead** *n* nyumba iliyozungukwa na shamba; (*US*) shamba lililotolewa na serikali kwa kuishi na kulima. ~ **thrust** *n* shambulio (kwa silaha au maneno) la nguvu. **~truth** *n* ukweli unaouma. **~work** *n* kazi ya nyumbani, zoezi (kwa mwanafunzi) la kufanyiwa nyumbani; *(colloq)* matayarisho (ya majadiliano, kuandika ripoti n.k.). ~ **less** *adj* -sio na makazi *like* ~ -a kama nyumbani. ~**ward** *adj* -a kuelekea nyumbani. ~**ward(s)** *adv* kwa kuelekea nyumbani *adv* 1 nyumbani, nchini. 2 hasa, barabara. **bring sth/come ~ to sb** fahamisha barabara. **drive a point/an argument** ~ eleza barabara. ~**ly** *adj* 1 -a kawaida *a ~ meal* mlo wa kawaida. 2 -a kama nyumbani, -a kukumbusha mtu nyumbani kwao. ~**liness** *n* (*US*) (*of people, their features*) -siovutia. ~**y** *adj* (*US colloq*) -a kama nyumbani. **homing** *adj* (*of pigeons*) -enye silika ya kurudi nyumbani; *(of torpedoes, missiles)* -enye uwezo wa kufikia shabaha iliyolengwa.

homicide *n* uuaji wa binadamu; muuaji wa binadamu. ~ **squad** (*US*) kikosi cha upelelezi wa mauaji hayo. **homicidal** *adj*.

homily *n* hotuba, mahubiri, waadhi. **homiletic** *adj*. **homiletics** *n* ustadi wa kuhutubia, kuhubiri.

hominy *n* uji.

homo[1] *n* (*lat*) mtu. ~ **sapiens** ukoo safu wa kisasa, binadamu.

homo[2] (*pref*) -a kufanana, -a jinsi moja. ~**genous** *adj* (*formed of parts*) -a jinsi moja. ~**geneity** *n* namna moja, hali moja. ~**genize** *vt* fanya kuwa -a jinsi moja; suka maziwa (ili kuchanganya mafuta na mtindi).

homocentric *adj* -enye kiinishirika.

homoeopathy *n* tiba inayotoa dalili za ugonjwa (kwa mtu asiye na ugonjwa huo) **homoeopath** *n* tabibu wa tiba hiyo.

homograph *n* homografu: neno lenye tahajia sawa na lingine lakini maana au matamshi tofauti.

homonym *n* homonimu: neno linalofanana na jingine lakini lenye maana tofauti.

homophone *n* homofoni: neno linalotamkwa kama jingine lakini tofauti katika tahajia, maana au chanzo.

homosexual *n* basha; msenge *adj* -a kibasha; kisenge, -enye kuvutiwa na jinsi yake. ~ **practices** vitendo vya kibasha (ubasha). ~**ity** *n* ubasha .

hone *n* kinoo, jiwe la kunolea *vt* noa.

honest *adj* -aminifu, -nyofu, -a kweli. **to be quite ~ about it** kusema ule ukweli. **make an ~ woman of sb** (*dated use*) oa mwanamke (baada ya kujamiiana). ~ **intention** nia njema. **earn an ~ penny** pata fedha kihalali. ~**ly** *adv* kwa uaminifu. ~**y** *n* uaminifu, ukweli.

honey *n* 1 asali ya nyuki (*fig*) ~-**dew** *n* asali ya mimea; utomvu; tumbaku tamu (tumbaku iliyotiwa asali). 2 (*colloq*) mpenzi. ~**ed** *adj* -a kama asali, tamu kama asali. ~-**comb** *n* 1 sega, (*piece of*) pambo lenye umbo la sega *vt* toboa matundu matundu.

honeymoon *n* fungate; (*fig*) kipindi cha maelewano mazuri mwanzoni mwa shughuli fulani *vt* kaa fungate.

honk *n* mlio wa bata bukini mwitu; honi *vi* piga/liza honi.

honour(*US* **honor**) *n* 1 heshima, utukufu, adhama *show ~ to one's parents* heshimu, onyesha heshima kwa wazazi. **do sb/do ~ to sb** toa heshima/heshimu mtu. **maid of ~** mpambe (hasa wa malkia) *guard of ~* gwaride la heshima. 2 sifa njema; uaminifu, uadilifu. **on one's ~** kwa sifa/uaminifu wake. **an affair of ~** (*hist*) pambano la kutetea hadhi. **be/feel in ~ bound to do sth** wajibika (sio kwa sheria). **one's word of ~** ahadi, kutimiza jambo. **pay/incur a debt of ~** lipa deni kwa heshima. **put sb on his ~** amini mtu. 3 (*in polite formulas*) kuheshimu, kustahi (mtu). **do sb the ~ of** fanyia mtu heshima. **have the ~ of/to** -wa na heshima ya *(formal style) I have the ~to write to you* nina heshima kukuandikia. 4 **Your/His ~** Mheshimiwa, Mtukufu. 5 **an ~** mtu/jambo lenye kuleta sifa *she is an ~to her group* yeye ni mfano mzuri kwa kikundi chake. 6

(*pl*) maadhimisho ya heshima, cheo, nishani. **full military** ~ heshima zote za kijeshi (agh. kwa mazishi ya shujaa au kukaribisha kiongozi wa heshima). **do the ~s** (*colloq*) (*of the table,house etc.*) karibisha. 7 *(pl)* (*in universities*) nafasi ya juu katika digrii. **~s degree** digrii ya daraja la juu. 8 (*in card games*) karata ya thamani kubwa *vt* 1 heshimu, tukuza, adhimu. 2 *(comm)* pokea na lipa kwa wakati maalum ~ *a debt* lipa deni ~ *one's signature* kiri/ kubali sahihi na kulipa fedha. **honorary** *adj* 1 (*shortened in writing to* **Hon**) (*of a position*) -sio na malipo *the ~ secretary* katibu asiyelipwa. 2 (*of a degree, rank*) -a heshima *an ~ member* mjumbe wa heshima. **honorarium** honoraria, tunzo (isiyodaiwa). **honorific** *adj* (*of expression*) -a heshima. ~ **able** *(US* **honorable)** *adj* 1 -a heshima, tukufu ~ *burial* mazishi ya heshima. 2 **~able** (*abbr.* **Hon**) Mheshimiwa. **Right** ~ (*abbr.* **Rt Hon**) jina la heshima kwa wenye vyeo maalum k.m. waziri n.k. **~ably** *adv*.

hooch *n* (*US sl*) pombe kali.

hood *n* kifuniko; (*of rain coats*) ukaya, (*of universities*) skafu, (*of cars*) kifuniko; *(US)* boneti *vt (chiefly in pp)* -funika na.

hoodlum (*also* **hood**) *n* jambazi (la kutisha).

hoodoo *n* (*chiefly US*) kisirani, ndege mbaya *vt* leta mkosi/bahati mbaya.

hoodwink *vt* ~ **sb (into)** hadaa.

hooey *n* (**sl**) upuuzi; puo.

hoof *n* kwato. **cattle on the** ~ ng'ombe wazima/hai *vt* piga kwa kwato; (*sl*) piga teke.

hook *n* 1 kiopoo. **a clothes ~/a crochet** ~ kulabu. **a fish** ~ ndoana/ chango. ~ **line and sinker** *(from fishing)* (*fig*) kabisa, zimazima, -ote. **a fruit** ~ kigoe, upembo. **be on the** ~ (*colloq*) -wa/kabiliwa na uamuzi mgumu wa kufanya. **be/get off the** ~ ondokana na tatizo. ~ **nosed** *adj* -enye pua iliyopinda. ~ **worm** tegu. 2 (*for cutting*) nyengo. **by ~ or by crook** kwa vyovyote vile. 3 (*cricket, golf*) pigo la kushoto; (*boxing*) pigo (la) kiko *vt,vi* 1 vua; ngoeka, koeka; ~ *a quiet husband* (*fig*) koeka mume mpole. 2 tengeneza ndoana/kiopoo. 3 ~ **it** *(sl)* toroka. 4 **~-up** *n* (*of radio*) idhaa mbili au zaidi zenye matangazo ya kufanana; idhaa muungano. **~ed** 1 -enye umbo la kulabu, -enye viopoo. 2 **~ed (on)** (*sl*) -lioathiriwa na; -liotawaliwa na. **~er** (*US sl*) malaya.

hookah *n* buruma.

hooky/hookey *n* **play** ~ *(US sl)* toroka (shuleni).

hooligan *n* mhuni. **~ism** *n* uhuni.

hoop[1] *n* pete (la chuma/plastiki/mti); (*of circus, game/croquet*) duara, gurudumu *put sb/go through the ~(s)* (*fig*) ingiza/pitia katika mateso, sumbua sana; (*of a cask*) zingirisha bamba mbavuni.

hoop[2] *see* **whoop**.

hooray *int see* **hurrah**.

hoot *n* 1 mlio wa bundi. 2 mlio wa honi. 3 sauti ya kuzomea. **not care a ~/two** ~ (*sl*) -tojali kabisa *vi,vt* 1 piga honi; lia kama bundi. 2 zomea *students ~ed and jeered at the teacher* wanafunzi walimzomea mwalimu. **~er** *n* king'ora, honi. *(sl, GB)* pua.

Hoover *n* kivuta vumbi *vt* safisha zulia n.k. kwa kivuta vumbi.

hooves *pl* of **hoof**.

hop[1] *n* 1 mhopi: mmea mrefu wa kutambaa. 2 *(pl)* mbegu za mhopi. **~garden/~field** *n* shamba/bustani ya mhopi. **~-pole** *n* nguzo/waya za kusimamisha mhopi. **~picker**, **~per** mchuma mhopi, mashine ya kuchuma mhopi *vi* chuma mhopi.

hop[2] *vi, vt* 1 (*of persons*) ruka kwa mguu mmoja, chupa (*of other living creatures* e.g. *frogs)* rukaruka. ~ **off/it** *(sl)* ondoka, ambaa. **~ping mad** (*colloq*) -liokasirika sana,

-liofura hasira. 2 vuka dimbwi kwa kuruka *n* 1 mruko wa mguu mmoja. **on the** ~ -a kuchachawa, -a mchachariko . **catch sb on the** ~ shughulisha mtu. 2 mruko mfupi, mchupo. ~ **skip/step and jump** zoezi la (mchanganyiko wa) kuchupa, kupiga hatua na kuruka; (*athletics*) miruko mitatu (*colloq*) densi isiyo rasmi. 4 (*flying*) kituo katika safari ndefu. ~ **scotch** *n* (*of children*) mchezo wa vipande/ vyumba. **~ped-up** *adj (US sl)* -liochajiwa kupita kiasi,-liozidishiwa nguvu. **~per** *n* chano, mdudu arukaye (k.m. tunutu, panzi n.k.); (*in Australia*) Kangaruu. **~-light/~-casement** *n* dirisha lifunguliwalo kwa juu lenye bawabu chini.

hope *n* 1 matumaini; tarajio *have ~ of sth* tarajia kupata kitu. **hold out some/no/little/not much ~ (of sth)** -wa na matarajio ya kitu fulani. **be past/beyond ~; not have a ~** -wa bila/ondoa matumaini *in the ~ of doing sth* kwa matarajio ya kufanya jambo fulani. **live in ~ (s) of sth** -wa na matarajio ya kitu fulani. **raise sb's ~s** -pa mtu moyo/ matumaini. 2 tegemeo, tumaini *the village farm was the ~ of the villagers* shamba la kijiji lilikuwa ndilo tegemeo la wanakijiji. ~ **chest** *n* (*US*) saraka la vifaa vya harusi (kwa msichana anayetaka kuolewa); *(GB see* **bottom drawer**) vt,vi tumaini; tarajia; tegemea *I ~ to do sth* natarajia kufanya jambo fulani. ~ **against** ~ endelea kutarajia ingawa matumaini hayapo *hoping to hear from you* natarajia utawasiliana nami. **~ful** *adj* 1 -enye matumaini. 2 -a kutia/leta matumaini. 3 (*as n*) **(young) ~ful** *n* mtoto anayeelekea kufaulu; tumaini. **~fully** *adv* 1 kwa mategemeo/matarajio. 2 natarajia; itarajiwe. ~ **fulness** *n*. **~less** *adj* 1 -sio na matumaini; -sioleta matumaini. 2 -sioponyeka. **~lessly** *adv*. **~lessness** *n*.

horizon *n* 1 upeo wa macho. 2 (*fig*) upeo wa fikira, elimu, ujuzi n.k.. **~tal** *adj* -a mlalo, (-a kwenda) sambamba na upeo wa macho ~ *bar n* mtaimbo wa mlalo. **~tally** *adv*.

hormone *n* homoni.

horn *n* 1 pembe (ya mnyama). 2 kitu/ chombo cha pembe *a ~ handle spoon* kijiko cha pembe. ~ **rimmed** *adj* (*of spectacles*) -enye fremu ya pembe. **a ~ of plenty** *see* **cornucopia**. 3 (*mus*) baragumu, siwa, mbiu, gunda. 4 honi *a motor ~* honi ya motakaa. 5 kitu kama pembe (k.m. kichwani mwa konokono). **draw in one's ~s** tulia, jivuta, jirudi. 6 pembe za mwezi mchanga. **on the ~s of a dilemma** kabiliwa na uchaguzi mgumu (kati ya vitu viwili visivyopendeza), -tokuwa na uchaguzi wa haja. 7 (*compounds*) ~ *bill n* hondohondo ~ *blower* mpiga baragumu/gunda/ siwa. **~pipe** *n* 1 dansi la baharia (la mtu mmoja) *vi* (*sl, only in*) ~ **in (on)** ingia bila kukaribishwa, dukiza, vamia. **~ed** *adj* -enye pembe. **a ~ed goat** mbuzi mwenye pembe. **~less** *adj* -sio na pembe. **~like** *adj* -a kama pembe. **~y** *adj* -a pembe; gumu kama pembe, sugu; *(sl)* -liojaa nyege, mshongo.

hornet *n* nyigu, mavu. **stir up a ~s' nest; bring a ~s' nest about one's ears** chokoza maadui; jiletea matata. **~pipe** dansi la baharia (la mtu mmoja).

horology *n* maarifa ya kutengeneza saa, wakati, usanifu saa.

horoscope *n* buruji (hasa kwa kutazama nyota zilivyo mtoto azaliwapo) *cast a ~* piga falaki. **horoscopy** *n* ufalaki, uaguzi.

horrendous *adj* -a kuogofya, -a kutisha. **~ly** *adv*.

horror *n* kitisho, tisho; chukizo. **chamber of ~s** makusanyo ya vitu, vielezo n.k. vya kutisha/kikatili. **strike with** ~ ogofya; shtusha. ~ **film** filamu ya kutisha. ~ **struck/**

stricken *adj* -a kutishwa, -a kustushwa. **horrible** *adj* 1 -a kuogofya; -a kutisha. 2 (*colloq*) -baya, -siopendeza. **horribly** *adv*.
horrid *adj* 1 -a kutisha. 2 (*colloq*) -a kuchukiza *be ~ to sb* fanyia vibaya, sumbua, chukiza mtu. **~ly** *adv*. **~ness** *n*. **horrific** *adj* (*colloq*) -a kutisha. **horrify** *vt* ogofya, shtusha, tisha.
hors de combat *pred adj* (*F*) -sioweza kuendelea kupigana (hasa kwa sababu ya kujeruhiwa).
hors-d'oeurve *n pl* kuchangamsha kinywa (mwanzo wa mlo).
horse *n* 1 farasi. **a dark ~** mtu ambaye bahati/nyota yake haijajulikana. **a ~ of another colour** jambo tofauti kabisa. **back the wrong ~** unga mkono mshinde katika shindano. **be/get on one's high ~** dai/kazania kupewa heshima inayostahili. **eat/work like a ~** -la sana/fanya kazi kwa. bidii. **hold one's ~** taradadi, sita. **look a gift ~ in the mouth** pokea kitu bila shukrani. **(straight) from the ~'s mouth** *(of tips, advice, information)* halisi, toka kwa mwenyewe/ mhusika. 2 (*collective sing*) askari wapanda farasi *~ and foot* askari wapanda farasi na wa miguu. **~ artillery** mizinga inayovutwa na farasi. 3 kiango, kitegemezi, farasi *a clothes ~* kiango cha kuanikia nguo *a towel ~* kiango cha kutundikia taulo. 4 (*compounds*) **~back** *n*. (*only in*) **on ~back** mgongoni mwa farasi. **~box** *n* gari la kubebea farasi. **~ breaker** *n* mfunga farasi. **~droppings/dung** samadi/mavi ya farasi. **~flesh** *n* nyama ya farasi; (*pl*) farasi. **~fly** *n* nzi mkubwa (asumbuaye farasi/ng'ombe). **~hair** *n* manyoya (ya shingo/mkia) ya farasi. **~laugh** *n* kikwakwa, kicheko cha kukwaruza na cha kelele. **~man** *n* mpanda farasi (hasa bingwa). **~manship** *n* ubingwa wa kupanda farasi. **~meat** *n* nyama ya farasi. **~ play** *n* mchezo wenye ghasia na kelele. **~pond** *n* bwawa la farasi la kuogea na kunywa maji. **~power (hp)** nguvu farasi. **~ race** *n* mashindano ya mbio za farasi. **~ sense** *n* busara ya kawaida. **~ shoe** njumu/kiatu cha farasi; (kitu) -enye umbo la kiatu cha farasi *a ~ shoe desk* dawati lenye umbo la kiatu cha farasi. **~ whip** *n* mjeledi/ kiboko cha farasi. **~ woman** *n* mwanamke mpanda farasi. **horsy** *adj* 1 -a kupenda farasi. 2 -a kuhusu farasi.
hortative *adj* (*formal*) -a kuonya; -a kutia moyo/ kuhimiza.
horticulture *n* kilimo cha bustani, ukulima wa bustani. **horticultural** *adj*. **horticulturalist** *n* mkulima wa bustani.
hosanna *n int* hosana (tamko) la kumsifu Mungu au kumwabudu).
hose[1] *n* mpira wa maji (wa kunyweshea bustani au kuzimia moto). **~pipe** bomba la mpira *vt* 1 **~ (down)** nywesha/mwagilia maji (bustani n.k.). 2 safisha (motokaa n.k.) kwa kutumia bomba la mpira.
hose[2] *n* (*collective, as pl*) soksi. **hosier** *n* mwuza soksi, nguo za ndani. **hosiery** *n* bidhaa za mwuza soksi, fulana n.k.
hospice *n* 1 nyumba ya kupumzikia wasafiri. 2 hospitali ya wagonjwa mahututi.
hospitable *adj* -karimu. **hospitably** *adv*. **hospitality** *n* ukarimu.
hospital *n* hospitali. **hositalize** *vt* laza mgonjwa hospitalini.
host[1] *n* 1 wingi. 2 (*arch*) jeshi.
host[2] *n* 1 mwenyeji, (mwenye kukaribisha wageni). 2 mwenye hoteli *reckon without one's ~* fanya mipango bila mawasiliano na wanaohusika. 3 *(bio)* kimelea. **~ess** *n* mwenyeji wa kike mhudumu wa kike. **air ~** mhudumu wa kike katika ndege.
Host *n* hostia: Mkate Mtakatifu.
hostage *n* 1 kole, mateka. 2 **give ~s to fortune** fanya uamuzi unaoweza

kudhuru baadaye.
hostel *n* hosteli, dahalia *youth ~* hosteli ya vijana. **~ry** *n* (*arch*) hoteli.
hostile *adj* -a adui, -a uhasama, -enye uadui. **~ly** *adv*. **hostility** *n* 1 uadui, uhasama. 2 *(pl)* vita.
hot *adj* 1 -enye joto, -a moto *it's ~ today* leo kuna joto *I like ~ tea* napenda chai ya moto. **be in/get into ~ water** -wa matatani, aibika. **be/get ~ under the collar** kasirika/pandwa mori. **make a place/make it too ~ for sb** *(fig)* fanyia mtu visa mpaka ahame. 2 -kali *this curry is ~* mchuzi huu ni mkali. 3 -a hasira, -a kisirani, -kali. **he has a ~ temper** ana hasira, mkali. **be ~ on the trail of sb/on sb's tracks** karibia windo (kinachofuatiwa). 4 *(in hunting)* kali, bichi. 5 *(of music, esp jazz)* motomoto. 6 *(sl)* (*of stolen goods*) -sioweza kuuzwa hadharani, bomu. 7 (*as adv*) sasa. **blow ~ and cold** *(fig)* yumbayumba (katika uamuzi), shindwa kuwa na uamuzi. **give it to sb ~** adhibu/karipia vikali. 8 -enye nyege. 9 (*special use with nouns and particles*) **~ air** maneno matupu/ahadi za uongo. **~bed** tuta lenye mbolea au samadi, la kuotesha mboga; *(fig)* mahali penye maovu (mabaya, fitina) mengi. **~blooded** -enye harara (ya moyo), -a hamaki. **~ cross bun** keki yenye alama ya msalaba (inayoliwa Ijumaa Kuu). **~ dog** soseji katika mkate. **~foot** *adv* kwa bidii, enda upesi. **~gospeller** *n* (*colloq*) mhubiri mwenye mhemko/bidii sana; **~head** *n* mkaidi, mkali. **~ headed** *adj* -enye harara, -kali, -kaidi. **~house** kibanda (agh. cha kioo) cha kuoteshea maua na matunda. **~ line** *n* simu ya moja kwa moja kati ya wakuu wa serikali mbalimbali. **~ money** *n* mfuko wa fedha unaopelekwa mahali penye kupata riba kubwa. **~ news** *n* habari motomoto. **~plate** kisahani cha jiko, jiko la kisahani kimoja. **~ potato** *n* (*fig*) (*colloq*) jambo gumu au lisilopendeza kushughulikia; suala nyeti. **~ rod** *n* (*US sl.*) gari lenye; mbio kuzidi magari yote. **the ~ seat** *n* kiti cha umeme (cha kunyongea); (*fig*) hali ya mtu ambaye analazimika kuamua mambo magumu (k.m. wakuu wa serikali). **~ spot** *n* (*colloq*) sehemu yenye matatizo/fujo za kisiasa. **~ spring** *n* chemchemi ya maji moto. **~stuff** *n* (*sl*) mtu/kitu bora. **~tempered** *adj* -enye hasira. **~water-bottle** *n* mpira wa majimoto *vt,vi* **~ sth up** (*colloq*) pasha moto; *(fig)* iva, shikwa na harara. **~ly** *adv* kwa harara, kwa hamaki.
hotchpotch *n* mchanganyiko *his article is a ~ of other people's ideas* makala yake ni mchanganyiko wa mawazo ya wengine.
hotel *n* hoteli. **residential ~** hoteli yenye makazi *the ~ trade* biashara ya hoteli. **~ier** *n* mtunza hoteli.
hottentot *n* 1 Mhotento/Mkhoisan (mtu mweusi wa kabila moja la Afrika Kusini). 2 Kikhoisan.
hound *n* 1 mbwa mkubwa wa kuwindia *follow the ~s* winda na mbwa *Master of H ~s* Mkuu wa Uwindaji. 2 *(dated, colloq)* mtu mbaya, (mjuvi), fidhuli, duni, mshenzi *vt* fukuza, winda na mbwa; fuatafuata, sumbua.
hour *n* 1 saa *a four ~s' journey* mwendo wa saa nne. **at the eleventh ~** (katika) dakika za mwisho. **the small ~s** usiku mkubwa/wa manane. **~glass** shisha. **~ hand** *n* akrabu, mkono wa saa. 2 kipindi, muda, wakati wa siku *come at an early ~* wahi, fika mapema *they bother me at all ~s of the day and night* wananisumbua wakati wote *in the ~ of danger* wakati wa hatari. 3 *(pl)* wakati agh wa kazi. **work long ~s** fanya kazi mchana kutwa. **after ~s** baada ya saa za kazi. **out of ~s** baada/nje ya saa za kawaida. **keep good/bad/early/**

late/ regular ~s amka/lala, anza/ maliza kazi ondoka/rudi nyumbani/ mapema/umechelewa. **~ly** *adj* -a kila saa, -a kutokea (kufanyika) kila saa moja *adv* baada ya kila saa, saa yoyote, wakati wowote.

houri *n* hurulaini.

house *n* 1 nyumba. **get on like ~ a on fire** (*of people*) elewana haraka sana, fanya urafiki baada ya muda mfupi wa kufahamiana. **under ~ arrest** kuzuiliwa nyumbani. 2 (*usu with a pref*) kibanda, jengo, nyumba *hen ~* kibanda cha kuku *store~* ghala. **ware~** bohari *custom~* jengo la ushuru. **the H~ of God** Nyumba ya Mungu, kanisa. **~ of cards** nyumba ya karata; (*fig*) mpango wa wasiwasi. **~ of ill fame** *(old use)* danguro. **on the ~** kwa gharama ya kilabu au kampuni. 3 bunge *enter the H~* chaguliwa kuwa mbunge. 4 **keep a good ~** fadhili/ kimu nyumba vyema. **keep open ~** -wa tayari kupokea wageni nyumbani wakati wowote, -wa mkarimu. **set/put one's ~ in order** nyoosha mambo yako. 5 ukoo, jamaa agh. ya watawala. 6 *(theatre)* hadhira. **bring down the ~/bring the ~ down** shangiliwa sana na wote waliopo. 7 (*compounds*) **~ agent** *n* wakala wa nyumba. **~boat** *n* mashua nyumba, mastakimu. **~bound** *adj* -liozuiliwa nyumbani **~ breaker** *(US* **~wrecker**) *n* jambazi (avunjaye nyumba ili aibe); mtu anayeajiriwa kubomoa majumba. **~coat** a koti la nyumbani. **~craft** *n* maarifa ya utunzaji wa nyumba. **~dog** *n* mbwa mlinzi/anayelinda nyumba. **~ father/ mother** *n* mlezi wa makazi ya watoto. **~ flag** bendera ya shirika la meli. **~fly** *n* nzi. **~ful** *n* nyumba iliyojaa (watu). **~hold** *n* kaya. **~hold guards** watumishi/wanajeshi wa mfalme. **~hold word** neno/jina litumikalo na wengi. **~holder** *n* mwenyeji, mwenye nyumba. **~keeper** *n* msimamizi/mtunzaji wa nyumba. **~lights** *n* taa za sinema (n.k.). **~maid** *n* mhudumu wa nyumbani. **~ maid's knee** *n* uvimbe wa goti. **~man** *n* (*GB*) daktari msaidizi wa mtaalam akaaye hospitali. **~master** *n* mwalimu mlezi wa bweni. **~ party** *n* wageni wa siku kadhaa shambani. **~ physician** *n* daktari akaaye hospitali. **~proud** *adj* -enye fahari kubwa ya kutunza nyumba. **~room** *n* nafasi. **~sparrow** *n* shorewanda. **~ surgeon** daktari mpasuaji akaaye hospitali. **~ top** *n* (*chiefly in*) **cry/publish/proclaim sth from the ~tops** tangaza hadharani. **~ trained** *adj* (*of domestic pets*) -liofunzwa, -liofundishwa kuwa safi katika nyumba. **~ warming** *n* sherehe ya kuhamia nyumba mpya. **~wife** *n* mke afanyaye kazi za nyumbani. **~ wifely** *adj* -a kuhusu mke afanyaye kazi za nyumbani. **~wifery** *n* kazi za mke wa nyumbani. **~work** *n* kazi za nyumbani *vt* 1 -pa nyumba, karibisha. 2 weka/hifadhi vitu (agh. vyombo na vitabu) *n* makazi. **housing association** shirika la kujenga na kugawa nyumba (bila kupata faida). **housing estate** eneo la nyumba za kupanga au kuuz(w)a.

hove *pt, pp of* **heave**.

hovel *n* kibanda kibovu.

hover *vi* 1 vinjari, zungukazunguka angani *the helicopter ~ed over the airport* helikopta ilizungukazunguka juu ya uwanja wa ndege. **~craft** *n* hovakrafti: chombo kiendacho majini na nchi kavu kwa kuelea juu ya hewa. 2 (*of persons*) ngojea. *(fig)* **~ between life and death** karibia kifo.

how *adv* 1 jinsi (gani); namna gani; je; kwa vipi *~ is the car driven?* gari linaendeshwa namna gani? *~ did they catch you*? walikukamata namna gani/walikukamataje? **~-d ye do** *n* (*colloq*) vurumai, hali ya mambo ni shaghalabaghala. 2 kiasi gani, -ngapi *~ much*? kiasi gani? ~

old are you una umri gani?/una miaka mingapi? **and ~!** naam! Sawa! Na kweli! 3 (*introducing an indirect statement*) jinsi, *he told me ~ he had been mistaken for a thief* alinieleza jinsi alivyodhaniwa kuwa ni mwizi. 4 (*in exclamations!*) ~ *intelligent he is*! ana akili kama nini! 5 (*in asking for opinion etc.*) ~ *is that* una maoni gani? unaonaje? una maana gani? **h~ come**? kwa nini; vipi ~ *come you are always late*? kwa nini unachelewa kila wakati. **h~ so** kweli? kwa vipi? unaweza kuthibitisha kuwa hivyo ndivyo? **h~ about going for a walk** unaonaje tukitembea kidogo ~ *do you find your new home*? unayaonaje makazi yako mapya? ~ **beit** *(conj. arch)* hata hivyo. **~ever** *adv* kwa hali yoyote, hata kama *I will never agree ~ ever hard you try to persuade me* sitakubali kwa hali yoyote/hata unishawishi namna gani *conj* hata hivyo. **~soever** *adv* kwa hali yoyote.

howdah *n* (*Ind*) kiti chenye mwavuli (kilichofungwa mgongoni mwa tembo).

howitzer *n* mzinga wa masafa mafupi.

howl *n* 1 mlio mkali (agh. wa mbwa mwitu). 2 kilio cha maumivu makali.3 (*of amusement*) kikwakwa. 4 (*of wind*) mvumo *vt,vi* lia kwa ukelele (k.m. mbwa); (*of wind*) vuma; (*with laughter*) cheka kwa sauti kubwa. ~ **down** zomea, zima ~ *down the lecturer* zima mhadhiri. **~er** *n* kosa la kijinga; kichekesho. **~ing** *adj (sl)* sana, mno, -a wazi, tupu *it was a ~ injustice* ulikuwa uonevu wa wazi kabisa. **a ~ing shame** aibu kubwa sana/tupu.

hoyden *n* jikedume, msichana mjeuri/shupavu. **~ish** *adj*.

hub *n* 1 hebu, kitovu cha gurudumu; *(fig)* kitovu cha shughuli (agh. biashara n.k.).

hubble-bubble *n* buruma.

hubbub *n* makelele, ghasia, zahama.

hubby *n (GB)* (*colloq*) mume

hubris *n (Gk)* kujiona, kiburi, kujivuna.

huckaback *n* kitambaa kigumu cha kutengenezea taulo.

huckster *n* mchuuzi.

huddle *vt,vi* 1 songa; songamana songana, banana. 2 ~ **up against** banana, jibana na. 3 rundika *n* rundo, chungu, mkusanyiko (wa vitu au watu). **be in/go in a ~** (*colloq*) (*of persons*) kutana pembeni/faragha.

hue[1] *n* rangi. **~d** (*in compounds*) -enye rangi.

hue[2] *n* (*only in*) ~ **and cry** makelele (agh ya kufukuza mwizi au kutoridhika) *raise a ~ cry* piga makelele.

huff[1] *n* hasira, chuki. **be in/get into a ~** nuna, -wa na shonde. **~ish**, **~y** *adj* -enye kuchukia upesi.

huff[2] *vi* pumua kwa nguvu, tweta.

hug *vt* 1 kumbatia. 2 *(fig)* ng'ang'ania, shikilia ~ *old beliefs* ng'ang'ania imani za zamani. 3 ~ **the shore** (*of a ship*) ambaa pwani. 4 ~ **oneself (with pleasure/delight) over sth** jawa na furaha, jipongeza *n* kumbatio.

huge *adj* -kubwa mno. **~ly** *adv*. **~ness** *n*.

hugger-mugger *n* vurugu; siri *adj* -enye vurugu; -a siri *adv* kwa vurugu; kwa siri.

hula *n* hula: dansi/ngoma kama nachi ya wenyeji wa Hawaii.

hulk *n* 1 (*old ship*) chombo cha zamani (kitumiwacho kama stoo, zamani kilitumiwa kama jela); meli ya ovyo. 2 jitu la ovyo, kubwa (na jinga).

hull *n* ganda, kumvi *vt* menya kumvi, ambua, goboa.

hullaballoo *n* ghasia, makelele.

hullo (*also* **hallo, hello**) *int* 1 aisee!, halo! 2 (*in answering a telephone*) halo!

hum *vi* 1 vuma (kama nyuki); imba (hali midomo imefungwa). **~ming bird** *n* ndege mvumaji. **~ming top**

n pia. 2 pamba moto, changamka. 3 *(sl)* nuka. 4 *(usu* ~ **and haw/ha** (*colloq*)) uma ulimi, sitasita katika kusema *n* mvumo.

human *adj* 1 -a binadamu, -a watu ~ *rights* haki za binadamu. 2 -enye ubinadamu, -enye utu. **~ly** *adv*. **~e** *adj* -ema, -enye huruma, pole. **~eness** *n*. **~ism** *n* 1 elimu ya ubinadamu (inayohusu binadamu kwanza na mahitaji yake kuliko misingi ya dini). 2 utu, moyo wa kupenda watu. 3 sanaa (karne 14-16) yenye misingi ya Ugiriki na Urumi. **~ist** *n* mwanafunzi/mfuasi wa elimu ya ubinadamu, mpenda utu; mwanafunzi wa sanaa ya Ugiriki/ Urumi *adj* -a ubinadamu. **~itarian** *adj* 1 -a hisani, -a fadhila, -a huruma *n* mfadhili, mwanahuruma. **~itarianism** *n*. **~ity** *n* 1 binadamu. 2 ubinadamu. 3 huruma, wema, utu. 4 *the ~ities* sayansi za jamii. **~ize** fanya/kuwa binadamu *vt* staarabisha; fanya -a utu. **~kind** *n* wanadamu, walimwengu.

humble *adj* 1 -nyenyekevu, -enye soni, -siyetaka makuu *eat ~ pie* omba radhi (kupita kiasi), piga magoti; jidhalilisha. 2 (*of persons*) -a chini, -nyonge, -siokuwa muhimu; (*of things*) -a kimaskini, duni *a ~ occupation* kazi duni *vt* dunisha, shusha hadhi, dhalilisha. **humbly** *adv*.

humbug *n* 1 unafiki; ghiliba, ulaghai. 2 mnafiki; laghai, ayari *(GB)* gubiti *int* upuuzi *vt* laghai, danganya ~ *sb into doing sth* ghilibu mtu atende jambo.

humdinger *n* (*US sl*) mtu/kitu kilicho bora au cha ajabu.

humdrum *adj* -a kuchusha; a kawaida.

humerus *n (pl)* muungabega.

humid *adj* (*esp of air, climate*) -enye unyevunyevu. **~ify** *vt* fanya nyevu. **~ity** *n* unyevu.

humiliate *vt* aibisha, fedhehesha; shushia/vunjia hadhi, dhalilisha.

humiliation *n* aibu, fedheha.

humility *n* unyenyekevu.

hummock *n* kilima kidogo, kiduta. **~y** *adj*.

humour/(US humor) *n* 1 kichekesho, uchekeshaji, ucheshi *sense of* ~ ucheshi *the book has a lot of* ~ kitabu kina vichekesho vingi. 2 hali ya mtu *he is in a good* ~ yu mchangamfu, yu mkunjufu *he is not in the ~ for playing with the children* hana moyo wa kucheza na watoto. **out of ~** kutojisikia kunjufu, kutofurahi, kusonona. 3 ridhisha, kubalia ~ *a patient* ridhisha mgonjwa (kwa kutimiza matakwa yake). **~ist** *n* mchekeshaji, chale. **~ous** *adj*. **~ously** *adv*.

hump *n* 1 kibyongo (*of a cow, camel etc.*) nundu. **~back** mtu mwenye kibyongo. **~backed** *adj* -enye kibyongo, -enye nundu. 2 kero, hasira; mfadhaiko. **have/give sb the ~** *(sl)* kera/kereka *vt* ~ **(up)** bong'oa, pinda.

humph *int* mmh! sauti ya kuonyesha wasiwasi/kutoridhika.

humus *n* mboji.

hunch *n* 1 kipande kinene; kibyongo; nundu .**~backed** -enye kibyongo. 2 **have a ~ that** *(colloq)* fikiri/hisi kwamba *vt* ~ **(up)** bong'oa, pinda.

hundred *n adj* mia *two* ~ mia mbili *~s* mamia ~ *of people* mamia ya watu *in ~s* kwa mamia *a ~ and one* mno *a ~ to one* kwa bahati sana. **~fold** *adj* -a mara mia *adv* kwa mia *adj* -a mia, -a sehemu mia kwa moja *n* sehemu mia kwa moja. **~weight** *n* ratili mia na kumi na mbili. **~th** *n*, *adj* sehemu moja ya mia; -a mia.

hung *pt,pp of* **hang**.

hunger *n* 1 njaa. **be/go on (a) ~ strike** goma kula (kwa sababu ya kupinga/kudai kufunguliwa. ~ **march** *n* maandamo ya wasio na kazi kutangaza mateso yao. **~marcher** *n*. 2 hamu, tamaa, shauku *a ~ for love* hamu ya mapenzi *vi* ~ **for** tamani/taka sana. **hungry** *adj* 1 -enye njaa; -enye kuleta njaa. 2 (*of soil, land*) -sio na rutuba. 3 *(fig)* -enye shauku ~ *for sth* -wa na shauku ya kitu fulani. **hungrily** *adv*.

hunk *n* kipande kinene (hasa cha mkate).

hunkers *n pl* (*colloq*) matako, mapaja. **on one's** ~ kwa kuchutama/ chuchumaa.

hunky-dory *adj (sl)* shwari, bora, -zuri.

hunt *n* 1 **a/the** ~ kuwinda; mawindo. 2 msako, kutafuta *the ~ for the criminals* msako wa wahalifu. 3 (*esp in GB*) kundi la wawindaji (wa mbweha na paa) wanaotumia mbwa na farasi; mawindoni. ~ **ball** *n* sherehe rasmi ya wawindaji. **~er** *n* mwindaji; farasi wa kuwindia. 4 saa ya mfukoni (yenye kifuniko cha chuma). **~ing** *n* kuwinda, uwindaji (*attrib*) ~ **horn** baragumu la kuwinda. ~ **ground** *(fig)* mawindoni: mahali penye mategemeo ya mtu kupata anachokitafuta. **happy ~ ground** *(joc)* mbinguni. **~ress** *n* (*liter*) mwanamke mwindaji *vi,vt* 1 winda. 2 tafuta, saka. ~ **for a lost pencil** tafuta kalamu iliyopotea. ~ **down** saka, tafuta na pata ~ *down a criminal* saka mhalifu. ~ **for/out/up** tafuta. ~ **out** tafuta. 3 fukuza ~ *the dog out* fukuza mbwa. **~sman** *n* 1 mwindaji. 2 kiongozi wa mbwa wa kuwindia.

hurdle[1] *n* 1 mwindaji. 2 kiongozi wa mbwa wa kuwindia.

hurdle[2] *n* 1 kiunzi (cha kufanyizia zizi la muda n.k.). 2 kiunzi, (kinachorukwa katika mashindano ya mbio na ya farasi) ~ *race* mbio za kuruka viunzi. 3 *(fig)* kikwazo, jambo lililo gumu kufanywa *vt,vi* 1 ~ **off** tenga kwa viunzi. 2 ruka viunzi. **~r** *n* mtengeneza viunzi; mruka viunzi.

hurdy-gurdy *n* kinanda, (agh hupigwa kwa kuzungusha mkono).

hurl *vt* tupa kwa nguvu, vurumisha *n* mtupo wa nguvu; kutupa kwa nguvu.

hurling *n* mchezo wa Ireland unaofanana na mpira wa magongo.

hurly-burly *n* makelele, fujo, ghasia, vurumai.

hurrah *int* mlio wa shangwe (wa kushangilia); riboribo! shangalia.

hurricane *n* tufani, kimbunga *~lamp/ lantern* kandili, fanusi, taa ya chemni.

hurry *n* 1 haraka. **in a** ~ haraka haraka. **don't** ~ usifanye haraka *be in a ~* -wa na haraka. 2 mapema, hivi karibuni *I won't go there again in a ~* sitaenda tena pale hivi karibuni *vt,vi* harakisha, fanya haraka. ~ **away** enda/ondoka haraka. ~ **up** fanya haraka, harakisha. **hurried** *adj* -liofanywa kwa haraka; -enye haraka. **hurriedly** *adv*.

hurt *vt,vi* 1 umiza; dhuru; uma, wanga. 2 (*of feelings*) tia uchungu, sononesha. 3 (*bad effect*) leta madhara *n* 1 maumivu; madhara. **~ful** *adj* -enye kuumiza; -a kudhuru; -enye kutia uchungu.

hurtle *vi* enda, ruka kwa mbio sana; vurumishwa.

husband *n* mume *vt* hifadhi, tumia kwa uangalifu ~ *one's strength* hifadhi nguvu. **~man** *n* (*old use*) mkulima. **~ry** *n* ukulima *animal ~* ufugaji.

hush *vt, vi* nyamaa, nyamaza, nyamazisha. **H~!** Nyamaza! kimya! ~ **sth up** ficha, fanya iwe siri *n* **a/the** ~ ukimya; utulivu. ~ **money** *n* (pesa) kifunga mdomo. **~-~** *adj* (*colloq*) -a siri sana.

husk *n* ganda, kapi, kumvi, kumbi *vt* koboa, ambua; fua. **~y** *adj* 1 kavu kama kapi. 2 (*of voice*) -a mikwaruzo, -liopwelea. 3 (*of a person*) (*colloq*) kipande *n* 1 mbwa wa Kieskimo. 2 kipande cha mtu. **~ily** *adv*. **~iness** *n*.

hussar *n* askari mpanda farasi, askari

wa farasi.
hussy *n* mwanamke asiye na maana/ thamani; msichana mjeuri/mjuvi.
hustings *n (pl)* **the** ~ kampeni ya uchaguzi (hotuba, mabango n.k.).
hustle *vt,vi* 1 songa, sukumiza, sukuma, harakisha (kwa mkukumkuku). 2 (*esp US*) (*colloq*) laghai, uza/pata kitu kwa nguvu (hasa kwa kudanganya). 3 (*US sl*) -wa malaya *n* (*sing only*) mkukumkuku *Manzese bus stop was a scene of ~ and bustle* kituo cha basi cha Manzese kilikuwa mahala pa mkukumkuku. **~r** *n* 1 pwaguzi, laghai. 2 (*US sl*) malaya.
hut *n* kibanda. **~ment** ago/kambi la vibanda. **~ted** *adj*.
hutch *n* tundu, kirimba, kizimba (hasa cha sungura).
hybrid *adj* mahuluti. ~ **maize** mahindi mahuluti *n* 1 chotara. 2 *(bio)* mvyauso. **~ize** *vt* vyausa, zalisha chotara. **~ization** *n* uvyausaji.
hydra (*myth*) *n* haidra: joka kubwa la baharini lenye vichwa vingi.
hydrant *n* bomba la maji (la mtaani linaloweza kutumika kuzima moto, kusafisha barabara n.k.).
hydrate *n (chem)* haidreti: chumvi maji *vt,vi* changanya kemikali na maji. **hydraulic** *adj* haidroli: -nayoendeshwa kwa maji/kioevu. **hydraulics** *n pl* haidroliki: sayansi ya matumizi ya maji kupata nishati.
hydro *prefix* haidro -a kuhusiana na maji, -a maji. **~electric** *adj* -a umeme wa nguvu za maji. **~foil**, ~ **plane** *n* boti mpao. **~logy** *n* haidrolojia: sayansi ya maji. **~meter** *n* haidromita: chombo cha kupimia uzito wa maji na viowevu. **~pathy** utabibu kwa kutumia maji. **~phobia** *n* 1 kalabi: ugonjwa wa kushindwa kunywa maji kwa sababu ya koo kujikaza; ugonjwa wa kichaa cha mbwa. 2 woga wa maji. **~phyte** kimeamaji (k.m. mpunga, magimbi). **~phitic** *adj* -a majini. **~tropism** *n* uelekeomaji. **~ponics** *n* haidroponi: sayansi ya kuotesha mimea kwenye maji. **~us** *adj* -a majimaji. **~gen** *n* haidrojeni. ~ **gen bomb** (*also* **H** ~) bomu la hidrojeni. **~carbon** *n* haidrokaboni. **~chloric** *adj* -a umeme wa nguvu za maji, -a haidrokloriki.
hyena, hyaena *n* fisi.
hygiene *n* elimusiha; usafi. **hygienic** *adj* -a afya, -a kuleta afya, -a bila vijidudu vya maradhi. **hygienically** *adv*.
hymen *n* kizinda.
hymn *n* wimbo wa kidini (wa kumsifu Mungu) *vt* tukuza Mungu kwa kuimba. **~al** *n* kitabu cha nyimbo za dini.
hyper *pref* -a zaidi, -a kupita kiasi. **~bole** *n* mbalagha: kutia chumvi sana katika kuelezea kitu. **~bolic** *adj*. **~critical** *adj* -enye kukosoa mno, -enye kuhakiki mno, enye kutafuta makosa. **~market** duka kuu (lenye eneo kubwa na aina zote za bidhaa agh nje ya mji).
hyphen *n* kistariungio (-) *vt* (*also* **~ate**) unganisha na kistari ungio.
hypnosis *n* kiinimacho; hiponozi: hali ya kuwa kama katika usingizi mzito ambapo mtu anaweza kukuamrisha na wewe ukatenda bila kujijua. **hypnotic** *adj*. **hypnotism** *n vt* laza/ pumbaza akili. **hypnotist** mtu apumbazaye akili.
hypochondrial *n* kunyong'onyea; unyong'onyevu, ulegevu wa moyo (hasa wa kuona mashaka juu ya afya). **hypochondriac** *adj*, *n*.
hypocrisy *n* unafiki, uzandiki. **hypocrite** *n* mzandiki, mnafiki. **hypocritical** *adj*. **hypocritically** *adv*.
hypodermic *adj* (*of drugs etc*) -a chini ya ngozi. ~ **syringe** sindano ya kuingiza chini ya ngozi *n* dawa ya kuingiza chini ya ngozi.
hypotenuse *n* kiegana: upande mrefu wa pembetatu, -enye pembe mraba.
hypothesis *n* nadharia tete. **hypothetical** *adj* -a nadharia tete;

-a kubuni, -sio na uhakika.
hysteria *n* 1 umanyeto, mpagao. 2 mpwitompwito (wa jumla), jazba. **hysterical** *adj*. **hysterically** *adv*.

I

I,i *n* herufi i; (herufi ya tisa katika alfabeti ya Kiingereza); namba moja (1) ya Kirumi *pron* mimi.

ibex *n* mbuzi mwitu (mwenye pembe kubwa zilizopinda) wa milima ya Alps na Pyrenees).

ibid, ibidem *adv* (*Lat*) katika kitabu (msitari, kifungu, ukurasa) kile kile kilichotajwa.

ibis *n* kwarara.

ice[1] *n* 1 barafu. **break the ~** *(fig)* anza kuchangamkiana na mgeni; anza kitu kigumu/nyeti, vunja ukimya *cut no ~ (with sb)* -toathiri, -toingia. **keep sth on ~** weka kwenye friji/jokofu; *(fig)* weka akiba *be skating on thin ~ (fig)* tembea mleoleoni, chezea hatari. 2 chakula kitamu kilichogandishwa. **cream ~s**, malai. 3 *(compounds)* **~ Age** *n* Enzi ya Barafu. **~ berg** *n* siwa barafu; *(fig)* mtu baridi. **~boat** *n* mashua barafu. **~ bound** *adj (of harbours, etc.)* -liokingwa na barafu. **~box** *n* sanduku la barafu (la kuwekea chakula). **~cap** *n* kilele barafu (k.m. kilele cha mlima wa Kilimanjaro). **~-cream** *n* aiskrimu. **~cube** *n* kipande cha barafu (agh. kilichogandishwa katika friji). **~ fall** *n* poromoko barafu. **~field** *n* uwanda barafu. **~floe** *n* barafu tandavu (inayoelea).**~-lolly** *n* shikirimu ya kijiti. **~ man** *n (US)* mtembeza/muuza barafu. **~pack** *n* mapande ya barafu yaliyotanda juu ya bahari; mfuko wa barafu (agh. hutumika kutuliza homa). **~-show** *n* maonyesho juu ya barafu. **~pick** *n* chombo cha kuvunjia barafu. **~rink** *n* uwanja wa ndani wa barafu. **~-skate** *n* kiatu cha kutelezea barafuni.

ice[2] *vt,vi* 1 fanya kuwa baridi sana. **~ d drinks** vinywaji baridi sana. 2 **~ over/ up** funika, funikwa na barafu;tanda kwa barafu *the pond was ~ over* bwawa lilifunikwa na barafu. **the wings of the aircraft had ~d up** mabawa ya eropleni yalifunikwa na barafu. 3 funika (agh. keki) kwa sukari unga.

icicle *n* mchirizi wa barafu.

icing *n* kiikizo. 2 mkusanyiko wa barafu kwenye mabawa ya eropleni.

icy *adj* -a kama barafu, baridi sana, -liofunikwa kwa barafu. **~ cold** baridi sana. **icily** *adv (lit, fig)* kwa kupooza.

ichneumon *n* 1 nguchiro mla mayai ya mamba. 2 (*also* ~ **fly**) nzi mtagia mayai kwenye mabuu ya wenzake.

icon *n* taswira *(in the Eastern Church)* ikoni: sanamu/picha ya mtakatifu, sanamu/picha takatifu. **~clast** *n* mpinzani wa mila ya kuabudu sanamu k.m. katika Ulaya Mashariki na Walokole wa Uingereza katika karne ya 17; *(fig)* mtenguamila.

id *n (psych)* **(the)** ~ silka.

idea *n* 1 dhana, wazo, nia *I have no ~* sijui, sina habari/wazo lolote. 2 *(plan)* mpango; azimio; nia, lengo. 3 *(opinion)* fikira, shauri. 4 *(feeling)* imani, hisia, jinsi ya kufikiri *the young ~* fikira ya kitoto. 5 *(conception)* kujua, kutambua, utambuzi. **put ~s into sb's head** mpe mtu tumaini. 6 *(in exclamations): what an ~!* haya mambo gani!

ideal *adj* 1 -lio bora, kamilifu. 2 *(unreal, fanciful)* -a njozi *n* maadili/ wazo/mfano bora/kamilifu. **~ly** *adv*. **~ize** *vt* fanya/ona kama kamilifu. **~ization** *n*. **~ism** *n* 1 kanuni za maisha fulani. 2 *(in art) (opposite of realism)* ulimbwende. 3 *(in philosophy)* udhanifu.**~ist** *n* mdhanifu. **~istic** *adj*.

identical *adj* 1 ~ **(to/with)** sawa sawa. 2 pacha, -a kufanana *be ~* fanana. 3 **~ twins** mapacha. **~ly** *adv*.

identify *vt* 1 tambua, tambulisha. 2 **~ sth with sth** fananisha. 3 **~ with sb/sth** jihusisha, tegemeza, shirikisha, funganisha. **identification** *n*. **identity** *n* 1 sura, kufanana, kuwa sawa kabisa *give one's ~* jitambulisha. **identikit** *n* sura ya mtu iliyochorwa (agh. ya mhalifu) *prove one's identity* thibitisha nafsi. **~ card/ disc/certificate** kitambulisho. 2 utambulisho.

ideogram *n*. **ideograph** idiogramu: maandishi yasiyohusishwa na sauti bali dhana au kitu. **ideographic** *adj*.

ideology *n* itikadi. **ideological** *adj*.

ideologically *adv*.
id est (i.e.) yaani.
idiolect *n* lugha ya binafsi.
idiom *n* 1 lugha; lahaja. 2 nahau; mbinu. **~atic** *adj* 1 -enye nahau, -a mbinu. 2 -a nahau. **~atically** *adv*.
idiosyncrasy *n* upekepeke, tabia (nia, desturi, mwenendo, mazoea n.k.) ya mtu peke yake.
idiot *n* 1 zuzu. 2 *(colloq)* mpumbavu. **idiocy** *n* uzuzu; *(folly)* upumbavu mtupu. **~ic** *adj*. **~ically** *adv*.
idle *adj* 1 -sio na kazi; -liotulia, -siotumika. 2 vivu, legevu. 3 -sio faa; -a bure *vi,vt* 1 ~ **(away)** -wa bila kazi; -wa vivu/ zembe. 2 *(of a car)* endelea kuwaka (wakati gari limesimama). **~r** *n*. **idly** *adv*. **~ness** *n*.
idol *n* 1 sanamu, kijimungu. 2 *(great favourite)* kipenzi *he is the ~ of his parents* anapendwa na wazazi wake. **~ater** *n* 1 mwabudu sanamu, mwabudu kijimungu. 2 mpenzi. **~atress** *n* mwanamke mwabudu sanamu. **~atrous** -a kuabudu sanamu. **~atrously** *adv*. **~atry** *n* 1 kuabudu sanamu; mapenzi makubwa. **~ize** *vt* abudu kama mungu; penda mno. **~ization** *n*.
idyll *n* 1 masimulizi mafupi (hasa mashairi) ya habari za maisha ya shambani/vijiji. 2 kipindi cha amani na furaha. **~ic** *adj* -zuri sana; -a kupendeza sana (kuhusu maisha ya shambani).
if *conj* 1 ikiwa, iwapo, kama *~ you ask me, I will help you* kama ukiniomba nitakusaidia *~ he should come please call me* iwapo atakuja niite *~ you will wait a moment I will help you* kama utasubiri kidogo nitakusaidia *~ I were rich I would buy a car* laiti ningekuwa tajiri ningenunua gari *~ we'd started in time we would have finished earlier* kama tungeanza mapema tungemaliza mapema. 2 *(if meaning when, whenever) ~ you mix yellow and blue you get green* ukichanganya manjano na buluu unapata kijani. 3 **(even)** ~ hata kama *we'll finish even ~ it takes us all week* tutamaliza hata kama itatuchukua wiki nzima *even ~* ingawa, ijapokuwa *I'll escort her even I'll be late for the movie* nitamsindikiza ingawa nitachelewa sinema. 4 **as** ~ kana kwamba *it isn't as ~ we don't know the work* si kana kwamba hatujui kazi. 5 *(colloq) (if replacing whether, to introduce an interrogative clause)* kama *let me know ~ you are coming* niambie kama utakuja. 6 *(a wish or unfulfilled condition)* ~ **only** laiti (kama) *n too many ~ s and buts* ngonjera, taraghani.
igloo *n* msonge (wa barafu).
igneous *adj (of rocks)* -lioundwa na volkano.
ignite *vt, vi* washa, tia moto. **ignition** *n* mwako. **ignition key** ufunguo wa gari.
ignoble *adj* -sioheshimika; -a aibu. **ignobly** *adj*. **ignominious** *adj* -a aibu, -a kufedhehesha, -a kutahayarisha, -a kuadhirika. **ignominy** *n* aibu, fedheha, utwezo.
ignorance, ~(of) *n* ujinga. **ignoramus** *n* mjinga. **ignorant** *adj* 1 ~ **(of)** -jinga, -siojua *(to) be ~ of a subject* kuwa mbumbumbu; -tojua jambo fulani. 2 -a kijinga *an ~ question* swali la kijinga.
ignore *vt* -toangalia, -tojali.
iguana *n* gongola: mjusi mkubwa kuliko gonda.
ikon *n see* **icon**.
il- *pref* kinyume cha, -sio.
ilk *n* **of that/his ~** *(colloq hum)* -a namna (jinsi, jina) ile.
ill *adj* 1 *(usu pred)* -gonjwa. **fall/be taken ~** -wa mgonjwa, ugua. 2 *(attrib)* baya, -ovu, -a madhara. **it's an ~ wind that blows nobody any good** *(prov)* hakuna baya lisilokuwa na uzuri wake. ~ **weeds grow apace** *(prov)* ubaya huvuma haraka kuliko wema. 3 *(compounds)* **~-advised** *adj* -sio na busara, pumbavu. ~ **affected (towards)** *adj* -siopendelea jambo

fulani.~-**bred** *adj* -liolelewa vibaya; jeuri. ~-**breeding** *n* tabia mbaya. ~-**favoured** *adj* -baya, -enye sura mbaya, -a kuchukiza. ~-**gotten** *adj* -liopatikana kwa njia mbaya (magendo, wizi n.k.). ~-**humoured** *adj* -enye usununu. ~-**judged** *adj* -lioamuliwa vibaya. ~-**looking** *adj* -enye sura mbaya. ~-**mannered** *adj* -sio na adabu nzuri, fidhuli. ~-**natured** *adj* -kali, -enye hasira. ~**omened** *adj* -enye bahati mbaya, kisirani, chimvi. ~-**tempered** *adj* -gomvi. ~-**timed** *adj* -liopangiwa muda mbaya, -liofanywa wakati mbaya/usiofaa *n* 1 madhara, uovu. **do** ~ fanya baya/uharibifu. 2 mkosi, kisirani; matatizo, shida *the ~s of life* matatizo ya maisha. 3 *(compounds)* ~-**disposed (towards)** *adj* -enye nia ya kudhuru; -a kutopenda jambo fulani. ~-**fated** *adj* -enye kisirani, -enye mkosi. ~-**luck** *n* bahati mbaya. ~-**starred** *adj* -enye bahati mbaya -enye nyota mbaya. ~ **treat**/~ **use** *vt* tesa, dhulumu. ~-**treatment**/~ **usage** *n* ukatili, uonevu, dhuluma. ~-**will** *n* uadui; ukatili, roho mbaya *adv* vibaya; ovyoovyo, -kwa kutoridhisha. **be/feel ~ at ease** -jiona vibaya/pweke, -ona haya. **speak ~ of sb** sema mtu vibaya, sengenya. ~**ness** *n* ugonjwa.

illegal *adj* haramu, -a kinyume cha sheria, -sio halali ~ *act* kitendo kinyume cha sheria. ~**ly** *adv*. ~**ity** *n*.

illegible *adj* -siosomeka. **illegibly** *adv*. **illegibility** *n*.

illegitimate *adj*. 1 -a kinyume cha sheria. 2 -a haramu ~ *child* mwana haramu. 3 *(of a conclusion in an argument, etc)* -sio na mantiki, -liohitimishwa vibaya. ~**ly** *adv*. **illegitimacy** *n*.

illiberal *adj* 1 -siostahili mtu huru; -siopenda uhuru (wa mawazo, maisha n.k.) -enye fikra finyu, -siokuwa na uvumilivu. 2 bahili. ~**ly** *adv*. ~**ity** *n*.

illicit *adj* haramu; -liyokatazwa ~ *trade* biashara ya haramu ~ *relationship* uhusiano usio halali/usioruhusiwa.~**ly** *adv*. ~**ness** *n*.

illimitable *adj* -kubwa sana, -sio na mipaka/kikomo.

illiterate *adj (person)* -tojua kusoma wala kuandika ~ *person* mtu asiyejua kusoma na kuandika; mjinga. **illiteracy** *n*.

illogical *adj* -sio na mantiki. ~**ly** *adv*. ~**ity** ~**ness** *n*.

illuminate *vt* 1 tia nuru, angaza, mulika. 2 pamba (barabara n.k.) kwa taa. 3 pamba herufi kwa rangi ya dhahabu. 4 *(explain)* eleza, fafanua. **illumination** *n* 1 mwanga, nuru, mwangaza. 2 *(pl) (coloured illustration)* herufi za mapambo za rangi ya dhahabu/fedha, rangi za kumetameta. 3 *(usu pl)* kupamba mji (barabara n.k.) kwa taa; taa za kupambia mji (barabara n.k.). **illumine** *vt (liter)* 1 tia nuru. 2 -pa mwanga wa kiroho.

illusion *n* 1 njozi, uongo *entertain (indulge) in* ~ jitia katika ndoto, fikra za uwongo. **be under an** ~ danganyika. **cherish an ~/the ~ that**... penda kuamini. **have no ~s about sb/sth** -todanganyika, fahamu fika 2. kudanganyika kimawazo. ~**ist** *n* mfanya mazingaombwe. **illusive, illusory** *adj* -a kinjozi, -a uongo.

illustrate *vt* 1 eleza kwa mifano, picha au kielezo. 2 chora picha/vielezo katika kitabu/jarida. **illustrator** mchoraji picha/vielezo katika vitabu. **illustration** *n* kielezo. 2 *(explanation)* kueleza kwa mifano. **illustrative** *adj* -enye kutoa ufafanuzi au mifano kwa jambo fulani. **illustrious.** *adj* maarufu, mashuhuri; adhimu. ~**ly** *adv*.

im- *(pref)* kinyume cha; siyo, pasipo, bila.

image *n* 1 sanamu, picha *an ~ of Jesus Christ* sanamu (picha) ya Yesu Kristo. 2 kifani, mfano, nakili *he is the ~ of his father* anafanana na baba yake *God created man in his own ~* Mungu amemuumba binadamu kwa mfano wake. **be the (very/spitting) ~ (of sth/sb)** fanana kabisa na mtu/kitu fulani. 3 taswira; fikra, dhana. 4 tamathali za usemi *speak in ~* zungumza/andika kwa kutumia tamathali za usemi. 5 sura (kama inavyoonekana katika kioo, maji, kamera n.k.). *vt* 1 chora/chonga sanamu, picha (ya kitu fulani). 2 akisi. **~ry** *n* matumizi ya tamathali za usemi katika mazungumzo/ maandishi; sanamu, picha, michoro.

imagine *vt* 1 *(for a mental picture of)* waza, fikiria, dhani *I can't ~ being a doctor* sifikirii kuwa daktari. 2 dhania, kisia, amini *I ~ him to be clever* namkisia kwamba yu hodari. **imaginable** *adj* -a kuweza kufikirika/ kubunika. **imaginary** *adj* -a mawazo tu, -a kufikirika, -a kubuni. **imagination** *n* 1 ubunifu. 2 wazo, fikra, dhana. **imaginative** *adj* bunifu, -enye uwezo wa kufikiri/kubuni; -enye mawazo/fikra nyingi.

imam *n* imamu.

imbalance *n* kutolingana uzito/nguvu, kutokuwa na urari (k.m. wa hesabu).

imbecile *adj* -punguani; -pumbavu *n* punguani; bozi, zembe, pumbavu. **imbecility** *n* 1 upuuzi; upunguani. 2 *(pl)* matendo/maoni ya kipumbavu/ kupuuzi.

imbed *vt see* **embed**.

imbibe *vt* 1 *(formal)* -nywa, sharabu. 2 *(learn)* jifunza, hifadhi akilini (mawazo, maarifa n.k.).

imbroglio *n* ghasia, machafuko, nazaa, (hasa ya kisiasa au hasira).

imbue *vt ~* **with** *(formal)* tia moyoni, jaza (shauku) *~d with sympathy/ hatred etc.* -liojaa huruma/chuki n.k.

imitate *vt* 1 iga, fuatisha, nakili *it is advisable to ~ good manners* ni bora kuiga tabia njema *parrots ~ human speech* kasuku huiga sauti ya binadamu. 2 fanana; fananisha na, wa kama *a paper was designed to ~ a Bank note* karatasi ilisanifiwa ili ifanane na noti ya benki. **imitator** *n* mwigaji. **imitation** *n* 1 uigaji. 2 mfano, bandia. 3 mwigo *imitations of animal cries* miigo ya sauti za wanyama. **imitative** *adj* -a kuiga; -a kufuatisha. **imitativeness** *n*.

immaculate *adj* safi kabisa, pasipo mawaa; pasipo kosa, pasipo dhambi. **the ~ conception** *(RC Church)* Bikra Maria, Mkingiwa Dhambi ya Asili. 2 **immaculacy** *n*. **~ly** *adv*.

immanent *adj ~* **(in)** *(of qualities)* -a ndani, -a asili; *(of God)* -a kuwepo kila mahali daima. **immanence** *n*.

immaterial *adj* 1 ~ **(to)** *(unimportant)* -sio na umuhimu/maana sana, si kitu *it is quite ~* haidhuru; haina maana *~ alterations* mabadiliko yasio na maana. 2 -sio na mwili, -a pepo, -a roho.

immature *adj* -changa, -siopevuka *~ seeds* mbegu changa *~ girl* kigori. **immaturity** *n* uchanga, hali ya kuwa bado kukomaa/kupevuka.

immeasurable *adj* -siopimika, -a kupita kiasi, -sio na mwisho/mpaka, kadiri. **immeasurability** *n*.

immediate *adj* 1 *(instant)* -a mara moja; -a sasa hivi *~ answers* majibu ya mara moja. 2 *(close)* -a karibu sana, -a jirani *the ~ relatives* ndugu wa karibu *the ~ heir to the throne* mrithi anayefuata wa ufalme. **immediacy** *n*. **~ly** *adv* 1 sasa hivi, papo hapo, moja kwa moja, mara moja. 2 karibu moja kwa moja *(conj)* mara tu *~ I have the news I will let you know* mara nipatapo habari nitakuambia. **~ness** *n*.

immemorial *adj* -a zamani za kale, -a kale sana. **from time ~** tangu zama (ni) za kale.

immense *adj* -kubwa sana. **~ly** *adv* mno, kwa kiasi kikubwa; *(colloq)* sana, kwa wingi, hasa, tele. **immensity** *n* ukubwa (wa kupita kadiri); (pl. **immensities**) vitu vikubwa mno.

immerse *vt ~* **(in)** 1 chovya, tosa, zamisha, tumbukiza. 2 *(occupy fully)* shughulisha, zama katika shughuli (mawazo, kitabu n.k.). **immersion** *n*

1 mchovyo, mzamo, tumbukio. 2 *(occupation)* kushughulika, uzamaji katika shughuli (mawazo, kitabu n.k.). ~ **heater** kichemshio (cha umeme).

immigrate *vi* ~ **(to/into)** ingia nchi kwa kusudi la kukaa, hamia nchi nyingine. **immigrant** mhamiaji. **immigration** *n* uhamiaji ~ *officer* ofisa uhamiaji.

imminent *adj (of events, esp dangers)* -a karibu sana, -a kuelekea kutokea upesi *rains are* ~ mvua ziko karibu *his death is* ~ kifo chake kiko karibu. ~ **ly** *adv*. **imminence** *n*.

immobile *adj* -sioenda, -siojijongeza, -sioweza kuendeshwa, tuli kabisa. **immobilize** *vt* -fanya isiweze kusogea/kujongea; simamisha kabisa, fanya jeshi/gari lishindwe kusonga mbele; zuia fedha zisitumike. **immobilization** *n*. **immobility** *n*.

immoderate *adj* -a kupita kiasi, -ingi mno, -a kukithiri, -sio na kadiri. **~ly** *adv*.

immodest *adj* 1 pasipo haya. 2 -chafu, -baya, -potovu ~ *acts* matendo machafu/ya upotovu. **~y** *n* upujufu, ukosefu wa haya/wa adabu. 2 uhayawani, upotovu. **~ly** *adv*.

immolate *vt* ~ **(to)** *(formal)* tolea kafara, dhabihu, tambika. **immolation** *n* kutolea kafara, kudhabihu, kutambika.

immoral *adj* 1 -baya, -ovu. 2 -enye tabia mbaya, -sio adilifu; *(licentious)* fisadi, fasiki asherati ~ *purposes* dhamira ya kifisadi, potovu. 3 *(of books)* chafu. **~ity** *n* 1 ubaya, uovu. 2 tabia mbaya, upotovu, ukosefu wa maadili; ufisadi *acts of* ~ vitendo vya kiovu/kifisadi.

immortal *adj* -a kuishi milele, -siokufa; -siosahauliwa *n* **the ~s** miungu ya Kiyunani na ya Kirumi; wasiokufa. **~ity** *n* maisha ya milele, uzima/uhai usio na mwisho, kuto kufa; sifa njema ya milele/inayodumu. **~ize** *vt* -pa maisha ya milele; -pa sifa za daima. **immovable** *adj* 1 -siohamishika (k.m. jengo, mimea) ~ *property* mali isiyohamishika. 2 thabiti, imara, madhubuti *n (pl)* **~s** mali zisizohamishika. **immovability** *n*. **immovably** *adv*.

immune *adj* ~ **(from/against /to)** 1 *(from disease)* -enye kingamaradhi; *(from harm by poison etc.)* -sioweza kudhurika kwa sumu n.k. **immunity** *n* 1 *(exemption)* kinga *diplomatic* ~ kinga ya kidiplomasia (kuhusu kodi ya forodha, upekuzi n.k.). 2 *(from disease)* kinga maradhi. **immunize** *vt* -pa kingamaradhi; kaga; fanya sugu. **immunization** *n*. **immunology** *n*. elimu ya kinga maradhi.

immure *vt (formal)* funga, tia ndani; weka kizuizini.

immutable *adj* (formal) -siobadilika, -siogeuka. **immutably** *adv*. **immutability** *n*.

imp *n* shetani mdogo, kishetani, pepo mbaya. **~ish** *adj* tundu. **~ishly** *adv*. **~ishness** *n*.

impact *n* ~ **(on)** 1 mgongano, dharuba. 2 athari, matokeo *vt* gonga; pambanisha; songanisha (kwa kugonga).

impair *vt* haribu, dhoofisha. ~ **ment** *n*.

impala *n* swalapala.

impale *vt* 1 fuma. **~ment** *n*.

impalpable *adj* -sioonekana, -sio shikika, -siohisika, -sioeleweka. **impalpability** *n*. **impalpably** *adv*.

impanel see **empanel**.

impart *vt* 1 ~**(to)** pa, pasha, gawa. 2 arifu, pasha ~ *news to sb* pasha mtu habari.

impartial *adj* adilifu, -adili; -siopendeka, -enye haki. **~ly** *adv* kwa uadilifu, kwa adili. **~ity** *n* uadilifu, idili.

impassable *adj* -siopitika *the rivers are* ~ mito haipitiki, haivukiki. **impassability** *n*.

impasse *n* 1 kichochoro kisichotoka, kilichofungwa mwishoni. 2 shida kubwa, kipingamizi, kizuizi.

impassioned *adj* -enye hamaki/hamasa.

impassive *adj* baridi, -tulivu, -sioonyesha hisia. **~ly** *adj*. **~ness** *n*.

impassivity *n.*
impatient *adj* 1 ~ **for sth/to do sth** -a haraka, -enye pupa, bila subira. 2 ~ **(at sth/with sb)** -sio vumilivu, -sio mili *grow* ~ kosa subira, -wa mwenye pupa. 3 **be ~ of** kasirishwa na kitu fulani. **~ly** *adj*. **impatience** *n*.
impeach *vt* 1 onyesha wasiwasi juu ya tabia ya mtu. 2 tuhumu. ~ **sb for/of/ with sth,** ~ **sb for doing sth** (*legal*) shtaki mtu (agh. kwa kosa la kutumia madaraka vibaya). **~ment** *n*.
impeccable *adj* maasumu, -siokosea, bila kosa. **impeccability** *n*. **impeccably** *adv*. **impeccant** *adj*.
impecunious *adj* (*formal*) fukara, mkata.
impede *vt* zuia, kwamisha. **impediment** *n* kizuizi, kikwazo (~ *of speech*) kigugumizi (~ *of marriage*) kipingamizi cha ndoa. **impedimenta** *n* (*pl*) mizigo ya msafiri, vikorokoro (agh. vya majeshi).
impel *vt* ~ **(to)** sukuma, lazimisha, himiza; chochea. **~lant** *adj, n* **~ler** *n*.
impend *vi* karibia, -wa karibu. **~ence, ~ancy** *n*. **~ing** *adj*.
impenetrable *adj*. ~ **(to)** 1 -siopenyeka, -siopitika ~ *to water* -siopenya maji. 2 (*unintelligible*) sioeleweka, -siotambulikana, -a fumbo. **impenetrability** *n*.
impenitent *adj* -siotubu, -a moyo mgumu. **~ly** *adv*. **impenitence** *n*.
imperative *adj* 1 -a haraka, muhimu -a kuangaliwa mara moja. 2 -a kuamuru; (*necessary*) -a lazima, -a sharti. 3 -a kusikiwa, -a kutiiwa; -liotolewa (-liofanywa) kwa thabiti *n* (*gram*) kitenzi cha kuamuru k.m. *Go!* Nenda! **~ly** *adv*.
imperceptible *adj* -sioeleweka, -siotambulika (kwa sababu ya udogo). **imperceptibly** *adv*.
imperfect *adj* 1 -enye dosari, -kosefu. (*in growth, development*) -viza, -liovia. 2 (*gram*) ~ **(tense)** isiotimilifu *n* (*gram*) hali inayoendelea/ isiyotimilifu. **~ion** *n*. **~ly** *adv*.
imperial *adj* 1 -a kifalme (hasa wa Kiingereza); -a kibeberu ~ *laws* sheria za ufalme, -a kifalme. 2 *(grand, magnificent)* bora, -kubwa. 3 *(of weights and measures)* -a Kiingereza ~ *measurements* vipimo vya Uingereza (k.v. painti, galoni *n* 1 kionja mchuzi. 2 kipimo cha ukurasa (63 x 95 cm). **~ly** *adv*. **~ism** *n* ubeberu (kiuchumi, kisiasa, kiutamaduni). **~ist** *n*. **~istic** *adj*.
imperious *adj* 1 -a kuamrisha *he is very* ~ anajiona; -a sharti. 2 -a haraka sana. **imperil** *vt* hatarisha. **imperiously** *adv*. **imperiousness** *n*.
imperium *n* dola, ufalme wenye mamlaka makubwa.
imperishable *adj* -sioharibika, -siooza; -a kudumu milele.
impermeable *adj*. ~ **(to)** *(formal)* -siopenyeka.
impermissible *adj* -sioruhusiwa.
impersonal *adj* 1 -sioathiriwa na hisia (za mtu binafsi); -siohusishwa na mtu maalum. 2 *(of verbs)* vitenzi visivyohusishwa na vitu hai *it is raining* mvua inanyesha. 3 -sio a kibinadamu ~ *forces* nguvu za asilia (k.v. upepo). ~ **ly** *adv*.
impersonate *vt* iga, jifanya (mtu mwingine), jisingizia. **impersonation** *n* 1 kuiga/kuigwa. 2 hali ya kuiga. **impersonator** *n*.
impertinent *adj* 1 -fidhuli, -safihi, -a ufyosi/fyosi *he was* ~ *at me* alinifidhulikia. 2 -siohusiana (na kitu kinachonenwa). **impertinence** *n*. **~ly** *adv*.
imperturbable *adj* (*formal*) 1 -tulivu, -siosisimka, -siohangaika/ hangaishwa. **imperturbability** *n*.
impervious *adj* ~ **(to)** 1 -siopitisha kitu, -siopenyeka ~ *to water* -siopenya maji, -siovuja. 2 *(fig)* -kaidi, -siosikia *he is* ~ *to criticism* hasikii ushauri.
impetigo *n* upele wa malengelenge.
impetuous *adj* 1 -a harara, -a haraka, -a bidii (bila kufikiri), -a kishindo. **~ly** *adv*. **impetuosity** *n*.
impetus *n* kichocheo, nguvu, msukumo.
impiety *n* 1 kufuru. 2 tendo/ neno la

kukufuru. **impious** *adj* -a kukufuru, bila heshima. **impiously** *adv*.

impinge *vi,vt* **~on/upon** athiri, husu. **~ment** *n*.

implacable *adj* -siosuluhishika, -sioridhika, -siotulizika. **implacability** *n*. **implacably** *adv*.

implant *vt* 1 ~ **in** tia/kaza/jenga fikira moyoni, tia/kaza ndani imara. 2 *(bio)* pandikiza, gandamanisha (mnofu au mmea) katika kiumbe kingine. **~ation** *n*.

implement *n* kifaa, chombo (cha kazi). **implement** *vt* tekeleza ~ *a contract* tekeleza mkataba. **~ation** *n*.

implicate *vt* ~ **(in)** husisha/ingiza mtu (lawamani/hatarini). **implication** *n* 1 kuhusisha/kuingiza lawamani/ hatarini. 2 maana, kidokezi.

implicit *adj* ~ **(in)** 1 inayojitokeza (bila kutajwa), -liodokezwa. 2 thabiti. ~ **belief** imani thabiti. **~ly** *adv*. **imply** *vt (indicate)* dokeza, -wa na maana, onyesha bila kutaja.

implore *vt* ~ **(for)** omba sana, sihi, rairai ~ *sth from sb* omba sana kitu kutoka kwa mtu fulani. **imploring** *adj*. **imploringly** *adv*.

implosion *n* mlipuko kwa ndani.

impolite *adj* -sio na adabu, pasipo heshima, -sio staha.**~ly** *adv*. **~ness** *n*.

impolitic *adj* -sio busara.

imponderable *adj (phy)* 1 -siokadirika, -sio nzito. 2 *(fig)* -siopimika, dogo sana *n (pl.* **~s)** visivyokadirika, visivyopimika, sifa/hisia zisizopimika.

import *vt* ~ **(from/into)** 1 ingiza bidhaa kutoka nchi za nje. 2 maanisha, -wa na maana; onyesha *n (usu pl)* 1 maduhuli: bidhaa ziingizwazo *~s & exports* maduhuli na mahuruji: bidhaa zinazoingia na zinazotoka. 2 uingizaji. 3 maana, umuhimu *matters of* ~ mambo ya maana. **~er** *n*. **~ation** *n*.

important *adj* 1 -a maana, muhimu. 2 *(of a person)* -enye madaraka makubwa, kubwa *look*~ jifanya kuwa mtu wa maana. **~ly** *adv*. **~ance** *n*.

importunate *adj* 1 -a kuombaomba, -a kuchosha kwa maombi, -enye udhia. 2 *(of affairs)* -a muhimu na haraka. **~ly** *adv*. **importunity** *n*. **importune** *vt* **importune (for)** 1 ombaomba sana. 2 *(of a prostitute)* dai, omba mno, tongoza.

impose *vt,vi* 1 ~ **on sb** amuru, lazimisha. 2 *(exact)* ~ **on** toza, lipiza ~ *a tax on sth* toza kodi ya kitu. 3 ~ **upon sth** tumia nafasi/nzuri/kasoro n.k. (kwa manufaa) ~ *an obligation upon sb* lazimisha mtu ~ *hands on sb* wekea mikono. **imposing** *adj* -a kuvutia (kwa sababu ya ukubwa, sura n.k). **imposingly** *adv*. **imposition** *n* kutoza, kuweka, kutumia (vibaya). ~ **of sth upon sb** kutoza mtu ushuru wa kitu ~ *of conditions* kuweka masharti.

impossible *adj* -siowezekana, -siofanyika *it is ~ for me to* haiwezekani *make it ~ for sb to* fanya iwe ngumu kwa mtu (kufanya) *you are* ~ wewe ni mtu mgumu, huwezekani. **the** ~ kisichowezekana *suppose the* ~ fikiria jambo lisilowezekana(kutokea).**impossibly** *adv*. **impossibility** *n* -siovumilika.

impost *n* kodi, ushuru, ada.

impostor *n* ayari, laghai (ambaye anajifanya mtu mwingine). **imposture** *n* ulaghai, utapeli.

impotent *adj* pasipo nguvu, dhaifu, -siofaa neno; *(of males)* hanithi, -siofaa. **~ly** *adv*. **impotence** *n*.

impound *vt* 1 kamata (mali) kisheria. 2 fungia (wanyama waliopotea) bomani.

impoverish *vt* 1 fukarisha, fanya kuwa maskini. 2 *(weaken)* punguzia nguvu, dhoofisha, chakaza. **~ed** *adj* maskini, -liochakaa, dhaifu. **~ment** *n* 1 umaskini, ufukara. 2 udhaifu.

impracticable *adj* 1 -siotekelezeka, muhali; *(of routes)* -siopitika, -sioweza kutumika. **impracticably** *adv*. **impracticability** *n*. **impractical** *adj* -siofaa/weza kutendwa, -sioweza kutenda.

imprecate *vt* ~ **on/upon sb** *(formal)*

laani mtu. **imprecation** *n* laana, apizo **imprecatory** *adj*.

imprecise *adj* -sio sahihi, -enye kosa. **imprecision** *n*. **~ly** *adv*.

impregnable *adj* -sioshindika; -a kuweza kuzuia/kuhimili, mashambulio yote, -sioingilika. **impregnably** *adv*. **impregnability** *n*.

impregnate *vt* ~ **(with)** 1 tia (-pa) mimba. 2 kifu. 3 jaza.

impresario *n* 1 meneja wa kikundi cha sanaa. 2 mdhamini wa burdani, hadhara.

impress *vt* ~ **(on/upon)/with** 1 gandamiza, *(imprint)* piga chapa, mhuri n.k. 2 *(influence)* shawishi; athiri, vutia ~ *sth on sb's memory* tia/athiri fikra za mtu *I was not much ~ed* sikuvutiwa sana *how did that ~ him?* jambo hilo lilimvutia namna gani? *be favourably ~ed* pendezwa mno *n* chapa; alama ya muhuri. **~ion** *n* 1 chapa, alama. 2 toleo, chapa (jumla ya nakala za vitabu zilizopigwa chapa pamoja). 3 *(notion)* fikra, wazo, maono; picha *it is my ~* nionavyo *be under the ~ that* fikiria kwamba, pata picha/wazo, ona. **~ionism** *n* mbinu ya uchoraji, uandishi, uandikaji (usiotiwa madoido). **~ionist** *n*. **~ionistic** *adj*. **~ionable** *adj* -epesi kuathiriwa, -epesi kushawishika. **~ionability** *n*. **~ive** *adj* -a kuvutia, -enye kuathiri, -enye kuchochea hisia (za ndani) ~ *ceremony* sherehe iliyovutia. **~ively** *adv*. **~iveness** *n*.

imprest *n* masurufu: fedha anayopewa mtumishi wa umma kutumia kwa kazi maalum.

imprimatur *n (RC Church)* kibali rasmi; ithibati ya kupiga chapa kitabu *the book has received the ~ of the Government* kitabu kimepata ithibati ya serikali; *(fig)* kibali, idhini.

imprint *vt* ~ **with/on** 1 chapa; piga muhuri. 2 tia moyoni *ideas ~ed on the mind* fikra zilizotiwa moyoni *n* alama, wazo moyoni.

imprison *vt* funga, tia kifungoni/gerezani/jela. **~ment** *n* kifungo *life ~ment* kifungo cha maisha.

improbable *adj* si yamkini, -sioelekea kuwa kweli, -sioelekea kufanyika *I think the story is ~* ninafikiri hadithi hii si yamkini. **improbably** *adv*. **improbability** *n* kutoelekea kuwa kweli.

impromptu *adj* -a papohapo, -siotayarishwa kabla ~ *speech* hotuba ya papo kwa papo (bila kutayarishwa kabla) *adv* papo hapo; bila maaandalizi *he spoke ~* aliongea pale pale.

improper *adj* 1 -siofaa *vulgar language is ~ before children* lugha ya matusi haifai mbele ya watoto; -sio vizuri, si adabu *it is ~ for children to shout while adults are talking* sio vizuri kwa watoto kupiga kelele watu wazima wanapoongea. 2 *(indecent)* -chafu. 3 -sio sawa, sio sahihi. **~ly** *adv*. **impropriety** *n* utovu wa adabu, *(indecency)* upujufu, uchafu; jambo lisilofaa.

improve *vt,vi* 1 endeleza; -wa -zuri zaidi; tengeneza vizuri zaidi. ~ **on/upon** tengeneza vizuri zaidi *things are improving* mambo yanaanza kutengemaa; *(of health)* pata nafuu. 2 tumia vizuri (wakati, faida hali). **~ment** *n* 1 kuendeleza. 2 maendeleo, kufanya vizuri zaidi. **improvable** *adj* -enye kutengenezeka, -enye kustawishika.

improvident *adj (formal)* -siofikiria wakati ujao, badhirifu. **~ly** *adv*. **improvidence** *n*. ubadhirifu.

improvise *vt,vi* 1 faragua. 2 tunga (tengeneza, vumbua) papo hapo *~d song* wimbo uliotungwa wakati ulipokuwa ukiimbwa; tengeneza kwa haraka bila vifaa vyake hasa. **improvisation** *n*. ufaraguzi.

imprudent *adj* -sio busara, -a kijinga. **~ly** *adv*. **imprudence** *n* tendo la kijinga.

impudent *adj* -fidhuli, -juvi, -safihi, jeuri. **~ly** *adv*. **impudence** *n* ufidhuli, usafihi.

impugn *vt (formal)* bisha, tia/tilia shaka. **~able** *adj* -enye kubisha, bishi.
impulse *n* 1 msukumo *give an ~ to* endesha, sukumiza; *(desire)* shauku, raghba, hamu, mihemko ya ghafula **on the ~ of the moment** mvuto wa ghafla *insane ~* msukumo wa kiwazimu *irresistible ~* msukumo usiozuilika. 2 mhemko wa ghafla *on (an) ~* mara moja, bila kutafakari. **impulsion** *n* 1 msukumo, kutaka kwa ghafla; kichocheo. **impulsive** *adj (of persons, their conduct)* -a msukumo, -a harara, -a kuamua ghafla. **impulsively** *adv*. **impulsiveness** *n*.
impunity *n* kupona/kuepuka adhabu. **with ~** bila hofu ya kuadhibiwa wala kuumia.
impure *adj* 1 -chafu, -enye najisi, -liochanganywa. 2 -a ashiki, -kware *n* unajisi. **impurity** *n* uchafu, takataka, najisi.
impute *vt ~* **(to)** (*formal*) shutumu, tuhumu, zulia; dhania. **imputation** *n* tuhumu, shutuma; kudhania, kuzulia *~ on a character* kusingizia, kusuta.
in[1] *adv part (contrasted with out)* 1 ndani ya *(used with many vv) come ~* ingia. **give ~** salimu amri. 2 **be ~** -wa nyumbani; fika, wasili *is the train ~ yet?* garimoshi limefika? *(of crops)* vunwa; patikana *mangoes are ~ now* embe zinapatikana sasa; ingia *the new fashion is ~* mtindo mpya umeingia *the new Director is ~ power* mkurungezi mpya ameshika madaraka/ameingia kwenye madaraka. 3 **be ~ for sth** patikana na jambo baya; -wa tayari kufanya jambo, pata. **have it ~ on sth** taka kulipiza kisasi. **be ~ on sth** *(colloq)* husika kwenye shirika, -wa na sehemu/fungu kwenye jambo/kitu. **day ~, day out, week ~, week out, year ~, year out** siku nenda rudi, kila siku, mara nyingi. **~ and out** kuingia na kutoka mara kwa mara. **be (well) ~ with sb** patana na, -wa katika hali ya urafiki na, elewana na mtu. 4 *(preceding as n)* **an ~-patient** mgonjwa aliyelazwa hospitalini.
in[2] *prep* (*for use of/ in/ with many nn and vv*) 1 *(of place)* ni, katika, kwenye *the village ~ which he was born* kwenye kijiji alichozaliwa *~ Tanzania* Tanzania; *children playing ~ the street* watoto wanaocheza barabarani *~ school/church/mosque* shuleni, kanisani, msikitini. 2 *(of direction)* kwa *~ this direction* kwa upande huu *~ all directions* (kwa) pande zote. 3 *(indicating direction of motion or activity)* ndani ya, katika *he put his hands ~ the pockets* aliweka mikono yake mifukoni *they fell~love* walipendana *cut the orange ~ two* kata chungwa katika vipande viwili. 4 *(of time when)* kwenye, mnamo, wakati wa *~ 1990* mnamo mwaka wa 1990, mnamo mwaka 1990 *~ his youth* katika ujana wake *~ the morning* wakati wa asubuhi. 5 *(of time)* katika, baada ya *~ the presence of* wakati akiwepo *I shall be back ~ a short-time* nitarudi katika muda mfupi/baada ya muda mfupi. 6 *(indicating inclusion)* kwenye *seven days ~ a month* siku saba kwenye mwezi *~ his thirties* kwenye miaka ya thelathini. 7 (*indication ratio*) kwa *one ~ five* moja kwa tano. 8 *(of dress etc)* -wa na/kwenye/katika, -liovaa *the woman ~ white* yule mwanamke mwenye nguo nyeupe *~ uniform* katika sare. 9 *(indicating physical sorroundings, circumstances etc) go out ~ the rain* nenda, toka kwenye mvua *sleep ~ the open* lala nje/sehemu ya wazi. 10 *(indicating state or condition) ~ good order* katika hali nzuri *~ a hurry* kwa haraka *~ secret* kwa siri *~ poverty* kwenye/katika umasikini. 11 *(indicating form, shape, arrangement) ~ three parts* katika sehemu tatu *~ groups* katika makundi. 12 *(indicating the method of expression, the medium, means, material etc) speaking ~ Kiswahili*

akisema kwa Kiswahili ~ *two colours* kwa rangi mbili ~ *few words* kwa maneno machache. 13 *(indicating degree or extent)* kwa ~ *large quantities* kwa kiasi kikubwa ~ *great numbers* kwa idadi kubwa. ~ **all** kwa jumla. 14 *(indicating identity) you will always have a good friend ~ me* nitakuwa rafiki yako siku zote. 15 *(indicating relation, reference, respect) ~ every way* kwa kila njia *young ~ year* mdogo kwa miaka *weak ~ the head* sio na akili, punguani. 16 *(indicating occupation, activity etc) he is ~ the army* ni askari. 17 ~ **camera** *(leg)* kwa siri, faragha, *(colloq)* kwa siri. ~ **that** kwa sababu, kwa kuwa. ~ **as/so far as** kwa kiasi kwamba, kwa vile. ~ **itself** hasa, katika uhalisi wake. ~ **as such much as** *adv* kwa sababu, kwa kuwa. 18 ~ **for it!** patwa, patikana *you are ~ for it!* umepatikana. **be ~ for sth** fungwa. **~lieu of** badala ya. ~ **itself** yenyewe.

in[3] *n (only in)* **the ~s and (the) outs** chama cha kisiasa kilichoshika hatamu na kile kilichoondoka; sehemu tofauti, undani wa jambo.

inability *n* kutoweza.

inaccessible *adj* -siofikika, -sioendeka *(of book)* -sioeleweka. **inaccessibility** *n.*

inactive *adj* 1 -a kimya, -liotulia, zima. 2 *(dull)* -vivu, -legevu, -zito. **inactivate** *vt* fanya kuwa tuli. **inactivity** *n.* **inaction** *n* kimya, kuzubaa.

inaccurate *adj* si sahihi. **inaccuracy** *n.*

inadequate *adj* ~ **for sth/to do sth** -siotosha, -siofaa, -pungufu. **~ly** *adv.* **inadequacy** *n.*

inadmissible *adj* -sioruhusiwa, si halali, -siokubalika, -a kutokubalika. **inadmissibility** *n.*

inadvertent *adj (formal)* si -angalifu, -a kupitiwa, -a kughafilika. **~ly** *adv.* **inadvertence** *n* kutokuwa mwangalifu, kupitiwa.

inalienable *adj (formal) (of rights etc)* -sioondolewa, -sioachanika, -sioachanishika.

inalterable *adj* -siogeuzika, -siobadilika. **inalterability** *n.*

inane *adj* -sio na maana, -puuzi, -pumbavu. **~ly** *adv.* **inanity** *n.*

inanimate *adj* 1 -fu, -siokuwa na uhai. 2 *(spiritless, dull)* baridi, -liopooza, chapwa ~ *conversation* mazungumzo (maneno) yaliyopooza.

inanition *n (formal)* 1 utupu. 2 udhaifu/ kuwa hoi kutokana na njaa.

inapplicable *adj* ~ **(to)** -siofaa, -siopasa.

inappreciable *adj* 1 -dogo sana. 2 -siothaminika, -siotambulika.

inapproachable *adj* -siosogelewa, -siofikika; *(of person)* -sioambilika.

inappropriate *adj* ~ **to** -siofaa. **~ness** *n.*

inapt *adj* 1 -siohusiana (na somo/jambo linalojadiliwa). 2 *(unskilled)* -si -stadi, mbumbumbu. **~itude** *n* kutohusiana, kukosa ustadi.

inarticulate *adj (of speech)* 1 -siotamkwa vizuri, -sioweza kusema dhahiri, -sioweza kujieleza kwa ufasaha. 2 -siounganika.

inattention *n* kutokuwa makini, uzembe, kutokuwa na usikivu. **inattentive** *adj.*

inaudible *adj* -siosikika (sauti ndogo sana). **inaudibility** *n.*

inaugural *adj* -a kuzindua, -a kuanzisha, -a kufungua ~ *ceremony* sherehe ya kuzindua. **inaugurate** *vt* 1 zindua, fungua, ingia rasmi. 2 *(begin)* anzisha, simika/tawaza. 3 tambulisha (afisa mpya, profesa n.k.) katika sherehe maalum/rasmi. **inauguration** *n.*

inauspicious *adj* -a ndege mbaya, -a kisirani, -a nuksi. **~ly** *adv.*

inboard *adj (naut)* -wa ndani ya kiunzi.

inborn *adj* -a kuzaliwa nao; -a asili, -a silika, -a maumbile.

inbound *adj (of ship)* -a kuelekea nyumbani.

inbred *adj* 1 -a kuzaliwa nao; -a asili. 2 -liozaliwa na wazazi wa nasaba moja. **inbreeding** *n* uzao baina ya wazazi wa nasaba moja.

incalculable *adj* 1 -siopimika (kwa kuwa -kubwa au -ingi). 2 -siotabirika. 3 *(of a person, character etc)* geugeu, -sioaminika.

incandescent *adj* -a kutoa nuru ikiwa na joto. **incandescence** *n*.

incantation *n* nuio, tabano.

incapable *adj* ~ **(of)** -sioweza. **drunk and** ~ -levi kabisa. **incapability** *n*.

incapacitate *vt* ~ **sb (for/from)** 1 ondolea nguvu/uwezo haki n.k.; -towezesha. 2 toa (kwa kutofikia kiwango), -topasisha. **incapacity** *n* ~ **(for sth/for doing sth/to do sth)** kutoweza; ukosefu wa uwezo.

incarcerate *vt (formal)* funga jela. **incarceration** *n*.

incarnadine *(poet) adj* -ekundu *vt* fanya kuwa nyekundu.

incarnate *adj* 1 -enye mwili (kiwiliwili), *(of sb's character)* -enye umbo (hasa la binadamu) *a devil* ~ shetani mwenye umbo la binadamu. 2 *(of an idea, ideal etc)* -a kujitokeza kama binadamu *vt* 1 -pa umbo la mtu; -pa mwili. 2 tekeleza wazo. 3 *(of a person)* -wa mfano wa binadamu (kisifa). **incarnation** *n* 1 kuwa na mwili; kuwa na umbo (hasa la binadamu). **the incarnation** kupata mwili (kwa Yesu Kristo). 2 kuwa mfano halisi (wa tabia n.k.).

incautious *adj* -sio hadhari, si -angalifu, -a harara. **~ly** *adv*.

incendiary *n* 1 *(person)* mchomaji mali (kwa moto) kwa nia mbaya. 2 mchochezi *adj* 1 -a kuchoma, -a kuteketeza, chochezi. 2 *(bomb)* -a kusababisha moto. **incendiarism** *n*.

incense[1] *n* ubani, udi; *(smoke)* buhuri *burn* ~ fukiza.

incense[2] *vt* kasirisha, ghadhibisha.

incentive *n* ~ **(to sth/to do sth/to doing sth)** kichocheo, kifuta jasho, marupurupu; motisha *give* ~ toa motisha.

inception *n (formal)* mwanzo, chanzo.

incertitude *n (formal)* wasiwasi, shaka.

incessant *adj* -a kufululiza; -naorudiwa, -siokwisha. **~ly** *adv*.

incest *n* kujamiiana kwa maharimu. **~uous** *adj* -a kujamiiana kwa maharimu, -enye kosa la kujamiiana baina ya maharimu.

inch *n* 1 inchi. 2 kiasi kidogo, chembe. ~ **by** ~ kidogo kidogo. **by ~es** kidogo tu *the bus missed me by ~es* basi lilinikosakosa kidogo tu; kidogokidogo. **every** ~ ni kabisa, hasa *she is every ~ a doctor* ni daktari hasa. **within an** ~ **of** karibu sana. **not yield an** ~ kutokubali hata chembe *vt,vi* sogea kidogokidogo.

inchoate *adj (formal)* -a kuanza; -lioanza tu; -siokamilika, -siokuzwa

inchoative *adj* -a kuonyesha mwanzo wa tendo/hali. *(gram)* ~ **verbs** vitenzi vianzishi (vya tendo/hali) k.m. *get* katika *get dark* na *fall* katika *fall ill*.

incidence *n* 1 jinsi jambo linavyoathiri mambo *the ~ of disease* jinsi ugonjwa ulivyoathiri (kwa kuenea, hatari zake n.k.). 2 *(phys)* tokeo *angle of* ~ pembe ya kuingilia.

incident[1] *adj* ~ **to** *(formal)* -a kawaida/ kutegemewa katika (jambo fulani) *the social obligations ~ to life in diplomatic services* shughuli za kijamii ambazo ni za kawaida katika kazi za kibalozi.

incident[2] *n* 1 kadhia, tukio. **border** ~ tukio (la mapigano madogo) mpakani. 2 *(in a play/poem)* tukio katika mchezo/shairi. 3 *(modern use)* tukio linalozibwazibwa na utawala (ili lisijulikane). 4 tukio linalovutia wengi. **~al** *adj*. ~ **(to)** 1 inayo-ambatana na (lakini si -a lazima). 2 -dogo -dogo; -a dharura; -a ziada. 3 -nayoweza kutokea; -a kawaida (katika mazingira fulani) *discomforts ~ to pregnancy* matatizo ya kawaida wakati wa ujauzito. **~ly** *adv*.

incinerate *vt* 1 choma (mpaka kuwa majivu), teketeza. **incinerator** *n* tanuri la kuchomea taka. **incineration** *n* uchomaji (mpaka kuwa majivu); uteketezaji.

incipient *adj* -a kwanza, -inayoanza.

incise *vt* kata, chanja, toka. **incision** *n* mkato, chanjo; *(small)* mtai; *(ornamental)* chale, tojo.

incisive *adj* 1 -kali, -enye kukata. 2 *(of a person's mind)* -enye akili, -erevu; -a kuenga. 3 *(of remarks)* -kali. **~ly** *adv*.

incisor *n (of human beings)* kato, chonge, meno ya mbele.

incite *vt* ~ **sb (to sth/to do sth)** chochea, shawishi, vuta. **~ment** *n*.

incivility *n (formal)* ufidhuli, utovu wa adabu, ujuvi.

inclement *adj (formal) (of weather or climate)* kali; baridi; -a dhoruba **inclemency** *n*.

inclination *n* mwinamo an ~ *of the head* kuinamisha kichwa *an ~ of the body* kuinama (kwa kuonyesha heshima) ~ *of a roof* mwinamo wa kipaa. 2 ~ *(to sth/to do sth)* mwelekeo; matakwa, kupenda. 3 *(math)* mbetuko. **incline** *vt,vi* 1 inama; inamisha; inika. 2 *(liter) (usu passive)* elekeza. 3 *(math)* betuka. 4 ~ **to/towards sth** elekea *n* mwinamo; mteremko.

inclose,inclosure *n see* **enclose, enclosure**.

include *vt* -wa pamoja na; tia/weka ndani, -wa na ndani *Price is sh. 500/= postage ~d* bei ni sh. 500/= pamoja na gharama za posta. **inclusion** *n*. **inclusive** *adj* ~ **(of)** 1 pamoja na. 2 -ote pamoja ~ *terms (at a hotel etc)* gharama ya huduma zote, bei yote (bila kuwa na gharama nyingine k.m. za chakula n.k.). **inclusively** *adv*.

incognito *adj* -liojificha; -siotambulika (kwa kutumia jina la bandia) *adv* bila kutambulika.

incognizant *adj* -a -sio na dhamira/ hisia, -a kutotambua *be ~ of sth* kutokuwa na habari. **incognizance** *n*.

incoherent *adj* -sioeleweka, *(of speech)* -sioshikamana, -siofungamana, -siona taratibu. **~ly** *adv*. **incoherence** *n*.

incombustible *adj (formal)* -siochomeka, -siowaka, -sioungua.

income *n* mapato, chumo, pato, kipato *live within one's ~* ishi kwa kutumia pato lake. **national** ~ pato la taifa. ~ **tax** kodi ya mapato.

incoming *adj* 1 -nayoingia, -liofika. ~ **tide** maji kujaa.

incommensurate *adj* ~ **(to/with)** 1 -siolinganishika, -siofananishika. 2 -siolingana (kwa ukubwa, hadhi n.k.) -siopimika, -siofanana.

incommode *vt (formal)* sumbua, udhi, bughudhi.

incommunicable *adj* 1 -sioelezeka. 2 *(of a person)* baridi. **incommunicado** *adj (of sb in confinement)* -liotengwa, -siowasiliana, -liokatiwa mawasiliano (na watu wengine). **incommunicative** -siowasiliana, -siosema.

incommutable *adj* -siobadilishika, -a hali moja. **incomparable** *adj* 1 ~ **(to/ with)** -siolinganishika, -sioweza kufananishwa, -siofanana (na kitu). 2 -a kupita -ote; bora sana. **incomparably** *adv*.

incompatible *adj* ~ **(with)** kinyume, -siopatana, -siochukuana (na) *excessive smoking is ~ with good health* kuvuta sigara kupita kiasi ni kinyume cha afya bora. **incompatibility** *n*.

incompetent *adj* -siojimudu, -sioweza. **~ly** *adv*. **incompetence/ incompetency** *n*.

incomplete *adj* -siokamili, pungufu. **~ly** *adv*.

incomprehensible *adj* -sioeleweka. **incomprehesion** *n* kutoelewa, kushindwa kuelewa.

incompressible *adj* -sioweza kushindiliwa; -siobanika; gumu sana.

inconceivable *adj* 1 -siowazika, -siofahamika, *(colloq)* -sioaminika; -a kushangaza.

inconclusive *adj (of evidence, arguments, discussions, actions)* -enye shaka: -siohitimishwa, -sioamuzi, -siosadikisha. **~ly** *adv*.

incondite *adj (of literary compostion etc)* -siosanifiwa, -sio -a kistadi.

incongruous *adj* ~ **(with)** -siopatana; -siofaa mahali. **~ly** *adv*. **incongruity** *n* hitilafu, tofauti.

inconsequent *adj* -siofuatana, -siofungamana (na yaliyosemwa au kutendwa hapo awali) *(of a person)* -nayesema/-nayefanya mambo bila mpango. **~ly** *adv*. **~ial** *adj*.

inconsiderable *adj* -dogo, -sio na thamani.

incosiderate *adj* -siojali hisia za wengine, -siofikiria wengine.

inconsistent *adj* **~(with)** 1 -siopatana, -siowiana, -siofuata utaratibu. 2 kinzani. **~ly** *adv*. **inconsistency** *n*.

inconsolable *adj* -siofarijika, -siotulizika.

inconsonant *adj* -siopatana.

inconspicuous *adj* -sioonekana kwa urahisi; -siojitokeza, -dogo sana. **~ly** *adv*.

inconstant *adj* -enye kubadilika, -sio (na) msimamo, geugeu. **inconstancy** *n*.

inconsumable *adj* 1 -sioungua 2 *(in Pol Econ)* -siofaa kutumiwa (bila kutengenezwa kwanza).

incontestable *adj* -siopingika, -siokanika, -siokanushika.

incontinent *adj* 1 -sioweza kujizuia; *(med)* -sioweza kujizuia kukojoa na kunya. **incontinence** *n*. **~ly** *adv (lit.)* mara moja, huria, holela.

incontrovertible *adj (formal)* -siokanika, -siopingika.

inconvenience *n* usumbufu, taabu, takilifu; maudhi *vt* sumbua, taabisha, udhi. **inconvenient** *adj* -sumbufu; -siofaa. **inconveniently** *adv*.

inconvertible *adj* -siobadilishika, -siosarifika. **inconvertibility** *n*.

incorporate *vt, vi* ~ **(in/into/with)** unga, unganisha, shirikisha, ungana na, -wa shirika. **incorporate** *adj* -liounganishwa; -lioshirikishwa. **incorporation** *n*.

incorporeal *adj (formal)* -sio na mwili (umbo la wazi).

incorrect *adj* -kosefu, -sio sahihi. **~ness** *n*. **~ly** *adv*.

incorrigible *adj (of a person, his faults, etc)* -siorudika, -siorekebishika.

incorruptible *adj* 1 -sioharibika, -siochakaa, -siooza. 2 *(honest)* -sioshawishika, -siohongeka. **incorruptibility** *n*.

increase *n* nyongeza, ongezo, ongezeko ~ *in* kuongezeka; kukua, kupanuka *be on the* ~ anza kukithiri, ongezeka *vt, vi* ongeza, zidisha kithiri. **increasingly** *adv*.

incredible *adj* -siosadikika; *(colloq)* -a kushangaza, -sioaminika, -a ajabu sana. **incredibility** *n* **incredibly** *adv*.

incredulous *adj* -siosadiki, -sioamini *be* ~ tosadiki ~ *smile* tabasamu la mshangao. **incredulity** *n*.

increment *n* 1 nyongeza. 2 faida, mapato. **~al** *adj*.

incriminate *vt* tia hatarini; ponza. **incrimination** *n*. **incriminatory** *adv*.

incrust *see* **encrust**.

incrustation *n* utando, mtomo, gamba; kufanya gamba.

incubate *vt, vi* 1 atamia (mayai); atamiza mayai (kwa kutumia taa kubwa). 2 *(of bacteria etc.)* pevuka, pevusha, kuza. **incubation** *n* kuatamiza, kukuza ~*period* muda wa kupevuka (agh. wa vijidudu vinavyoleta ugonjwa). **incubator** *n* kitamizi, kiangulio, kitotoa. **incubative** *adj*. **incubatory** *adj*.

incubus *n (nightmare)* jinamizi; ndoto mbaya; balaa.

inculcate *vt* ~ **sth (in sb)** *(formal)* funda, fundisha, kazia mawazo *inculcate in young people the 'ujamaa' ideology,* fundisha/kazia vijana itikadi ya ujamaa. **inculcation** *n*.

inculpate *vt (formal)* tia hatiani, shutumu; laumu **inculpative** *adj*. **inculpatory** *adj*.

incumbent *adj* **be ~ on/upon sb (to do sth)** hapana budi, -wa wajibu, -a kubidi *it is ~ upon me* imenipasa, imenibidi, ni wajibu wangu, ni juu yangu *n* 1 padri wa mji, kasisi. 2

mtu ashikiliaye cheo fulani ~ *Member of Parliament* mbunge aliyepo. **incumbency** *n*.
incur *vt* ingia/pata ~ *a debt* ingia, pata deni ~ *expenses* gharamia, lipia ~ *the expenses* lipia gharama.
incurable *adj* -sioponyeka, -siotibika *n* mtu asiyeponyeka. **incurably** *adv*.
incurious *adj* -siodadisi, -a kutodadisi. **incuriosity** *n*.
incursion *n* ~ **on/upon** vamio la ghafla (la askari wa adui); *(fig)* kuingilia, mwingilio.
incurved *adj* -liobonyea, -liobinukia ndani. **incurvation** n.
incus *n* fuawe (ya sikio).
indebted *adj* ~ **to sb** -enye kuwiwa, -enye deni; -a kupaswa kushukuru *be ~* wiwa, -wa na deni, paswa kushukuru, fadhiliwa *he is ~ to me* anawiwa nami. **~ness** *n*.
indecent *adj* 1 *(of behaviour, talk etc) (immodest, obscene)* -sio na heshima, -a aibu. ~ **assault** shambulio la kuaibisha mtu hadharani ~ *exposure* kuonyesha uchi hadharani. ~ **behaviour** tabia mbaya. 2 *(colloq)* -sio sahihi, -siofaa. **indecency** *n*. **~ly** *adv*.
indecipherable *adj* -siosomeka, -siotambulikana, -sioweza kueleweka, siosimbulika.
indecision *n* kusita moyoni, kutoamua, kutoweza kuchagua/kukata shauri. **indecisive** *adj* -a shaka, -sio dhahiri; -a kusita, -sio amuzi. **indecisiveness** *n*.
indecisively *adv*. **indeclinable** *adj (gram)* -sionyambulika.
indecorous *adj* (*formal*) -sio adilifu, -sio na heshima staha; -siofaa. **~ly** *adv*. **indecorum** *n* utovu wa adabu/heshima, staha; ufidhuli; jambo lisilofaa.
indeed *adv* 1 kweli, hasa, ndiyo, naam. 2 *(to intensify)* sana *I am very glad ~* nimefurahi sana *thank you very much ~* asante sana; hasha. 3 (*as a comment to show interest, suprise irony etc)* kweli, hasa *who is she ~!* kweli/hasa yeye ni nani!
indefatigable *adj* (*formal*) -siochoka, -siochoshwa.
indefeasible *adj (formal)* -siotanguka.
indefectible *adj* -sioshindwa, -siokosa, -sioharibika.
indefensible *adj* -siolindika ~ *behaviour* -a sioweza kutetewa.
indefinable *adj* -sioelezeka, siofasilika.
indefinite *adj* -si dhahiri, -sio na mwisho, -sio na mipaka *the ~ article, see* **a, an**. **~ly** *adv*.
indelible *adj (of marks, stains, ink or (fig) of disgrace)* -siofutika; -sioondoleka ~ *ideas* fikra zisizofutika ~ *pencil marks* alama za penseli zisizofutika.
indelicate *adj (of a person, his speech, behaviour etc)* si -a adabu, -siofaa, -chafu, pujufu. **indelicacy** *n*.
indemnify *vt* 1 ~ **sb (for sth)** lipa, fidia, (agh. gharama aliyoipata mtu mwingine). 2 ~ **sb (from/against sth)** linda, kinga. **indemnification** *n*. **indemnity** *n* fidia bima.
indemonstrable *adj* -sioonyesheka, -siodhihirika.
indent *vt,vi* 1 tia pengo, bonyeza. 2 *(in printing)* jongeza msitari ndani *you must ~ the first line of each paraghaph* lazima kujongeza ndani msitari wa kwanza wa kila aya. 3 ~ **(on sb) for sth** *(comm)* agiza bidhaa kwa njia ya agizo maalum *n (comm UK)* hati ya kuuza bidhaa nje; hati maalum ya kuagizia vitu. **~ation** *n* 1 kuagiza; kuagizwa. 2 pengo, kighuba; kujongeza.
indenture *n* 1 mkataba, (agh. wa watumishi au mwanagenzi) *take up one's ~s* pata/pokea/rudishwa nakala ya mkataba (baada ya kipindi kwisha), maliza mkataba (wa utumishi) *vt* fanya mkataba (wa utumishi).
independent *adj* 1 ~ **(of)** huru ~ *means* pato lisilotegemea kazi. 2 -enye kujitawala, -lio huru, -enye kujitegemea *n* ~ **MP** mbunge anayejitegemea. **~ly** *adv*.

independence *n* uhuru; upweke, upekee; kujitegemea. **independency** *n*.

indescribable *adj* -sioelezeka, -a kushangaza. **indescribably** *adv*.

indestructible *adj* -sioweza kuharibika. **indestructibility** *n*.

indeterminate *adj* -sio wazi, -sio -a dhahiri, si yakini. **indeterminable** *adj*. **indeterminably** *adv*. **indeterminacy** *n*. **indetermination** *n*.

index *n* 1 kielezo, alama, ishara. ~ **finger** kidole cha shahada. 2 faharasa *the ~ card* kadi ya faharasa. 3 **~number/figure** nambari faharasa. 4 *(alg)* nambapeo *vt* faharisisha, orodhesha. **~er** *n*.

India *n* Uhindi ~ *paper* karatasi nyembamba sana. **~man** (*formerly*) meli (iliyosafiri baina ya Uhindi na Ulaya). **~-rubber** *n* kifutio. **Indian** *n* 1 Mhindi. 2 *American ~/West ~* Mhindi mwekundu *adj* 1 -a Kihindi. ~ **Ocean** Bahari ya Hindi. ~ **club** rungu la mazoezi. ~ **corn** mahindi. **in ~ file** -moja baada ya ingine. ~ **ink** wino mweusi agh hutengenezwa Uchina na Ujapani. ~ **red** -ekundu, udongo mwekundu. ~ **summer** mwisho wa majira ya joto; *(US) (fig)* kurudiwa na mawazo ya ujana uzeeni.

indicate *vt (fig)* onyesha; elekeza; dokeza; ashiria. **indication** *n* 1 alama, dalili, ishara. **indicative** *adj* 1 -a kuarifu; ~ *mood* hali ya kuarifu. 2 ~ **of/that** -wa dalili, alama ya. **indicator** indiketa kiashirio, dalili, alama.

indices *pl of* **index**.

indict *vt (leg)* shitaki rasmi. **~able** *adj*. **~ment** *n* shtaka rasmi lililoandikwa.

indifferent *adj* ~ **(to)** 1 -siojali *he is ~ to everything* hajali chochote. 2 -a kawaida; *(of medium, quality)* -a vivi hivi, -a kadiri. **~ly** *adv*. **indifference** *n* kutojali, kutojiingiza, kutojihusisha *it is a matter of ~ to me* sijali.

indigenous *adj* ~ **(to)** -a asili, -enyeji. ~ **tribe** mbari/kabila la asili.

indigent *adj (formal)* fukara. **indigence** *n*.

indigestion *n* kuvimbiwa. **indigested** *adj* 1 -sio na umbo. 2 -siofikiriwa vyema, -siomeng'enywa -sio na mpango. **indigestible** *adj* -siomeng'enyeka.

indignant *adj* -a kuudhika, -enye uchungu (hasira, hamaki, hasa kwa sababu ya kudhulumiwa) *feel ~ at sth* udhika kwa jambo fulani *he was ~ to learn about the news* alikasirishwa na habari. **~ly** *adv*. **indignation** *n* uchungu,hasira (isababishwayo na dhuluma/tabia mbaya); msononeko.

indignity *n* ufidhuli, kitu kinachomvunjia mtu heshima.

indigo *n* nili. ~ **(blue)** bluu iliyoiva.

indirect *adj* 1 -sionyooka, -a kuzunguka, sio dhahiri ~ *rule* utawala wa kuwatumia viongozi wananchi usio wa moja kwa moja ~ *taxation* kodi isiyo dhahiri. 2 -siokusudiwa, -siolengwa *an ~ outcome* matokeo yasiyokusudiwa. 3 *(gramm)* ~ **speech** kauli taarifa iliyotajwa. ~ **object** yambiwa. **~ly** *adv*. **~ness** *n*.

indiscernible *adj* -siofahamika; -sio tambulika, -siobainika.

indiscipline *n* utovu wa adabu; ukosefu wa nidhamu.

indiscreet *adj* 1 si -a busara, akili. 2 -sio na hadhari; -sio na adabu. **indiscretion** *n* kuvunja miiko ya jamii; kusema/kutenda bila hadhari.

indiscrete *adj* -siogawanyika katika sehemu.

indiscriminate *adj* -sio chagua kwa busara/kwa mpango. **~ly** *adv*. **indiscrimination** *n*.

indispensable *adj* ~ **to** -a lazima/sharti/ kimsingi. **indispensability** *n*.

indisposed *n* 1 -gonjwa kidogo *he is ~* yu mgonjwa kidogo. 2 ~ **for/to do sth** -a kutopenda/kutotaka, kutoridhika *he is ~ to go* hapendi/ hataki kwenda. **indisposition** *n* 1 ugonjwa, kutojisikia vizuri. 2 ~ **for/to do sth** kutopenda, karaha.

indisputable *adj* -siokanika,

siopingika, dhahiri. **indisputability** *n.*
indissoluble *adj* 1 -siotanguka, -siovunjika, -a daima. 2 -sioyeyuka.
indistinct *adj* si wazi/dhahiri shahiri/ bainifu,-siotambulikana vizuri. **~ly** *adv.* **~ness** *n.*
indistinguishable *adj* -sio tafautishika, -siotambulikana, -siobainika, -sioonekana dhahiri.
indivertible *adj* -siogeuzika, -sioweza kupelekwa upande mwingine.
individual *adj* 1 -a binafsi, -a mmoja mmoja ~ *help* msaada wa mtu mmoja mmoja ~ *problems* matatizo ya binafsi *n* 1 mtu binafsi. 2 *(colloq)* mtu, binadamu. **~ly** *adv.* **~ism** *n* 1 ubinafsi. 2 nadharia ya ubinafsi. **~ist** mbinafsi; mfuasi wa nadharia ya ubinafsi. **~istic** *adj* -enye ubinafsi, -a kujipendelea; -a nadharia ya ubinafsi. **~ity** *n* 1 nafsi, (tabia, sifa za mtu binafsi). 2 hali ya pekee. 3 *(usu pl)* **~ities** (mapendeleo, matakwa) ya mtu binafsi. **~ize** *vt* 1 bainisha, pambanua. 2 shughulikia kipekee/kimoja kimoja. **~ization** *n.*
indivisible *adj* -siogawanyika, -sio changulika. **indivisibility** *n.*
Indo- *pref (in compounds)* -a Kihindi *I~ European language* familia ya lugha zizungumzwazo sehemu za Ulaya na Magharibi ya Asia.
indoctrinate *vt* ~ **sb with** funza, fundisha, funda (hasa dhana au fikra maalum), tia kasumba. **indoctrination** *n.*
indolent *adj* 1 -a ukunguni, -vivu, -tepetevu. 2 *(med)* -sioleta maumivu. **indolence** *n.*
indomitable *adj* -sioshindika, thabiti, -siokata tamaa.
indoor *adj (attrib only)* -a ndani (hasa ndani ya nyumba), -a kufanywa ndani ya nyumba. **~s** *adv* ndani ya nyumba, ndani *keep~s* kaa nyumbani.
indorse *see* **endorse**. **~ment** *n.*
indrawn *adj* 1 -liovutwa (ndani). 2 -sio changamfu, baridi, -liojivuta.
indubitable *adj* pasipo shaka, bayana, wazi, hakika.
induce *vt* 1 ~ *sb to do sth* vuta, shawishi, pembeja. 2 *(cause)* anzisha, sababisha ~ *labour (in child birth)* anzisha uchungu. 3 *(of electricity)* dukiza, toa umeme. **~ment** *n* mvuto, kishawishi, kivutio, motisha.
induct *vt* ~ **sb (to/into as)** ingiza; simika *(US)* ita jeshini. **~ion** *n* 1 kuingiza, kusimika. 2 kudukiza umeme, kupitisha umeme. 3 matumizi ya visa kufikia kanuni/wazo la jumla. 4 *(maths)* hoja tama. 5 *(US)* kuitwa jeshini. ~ **coil** *n* pindi la kuingiza umeme. ~ **-pipe** *n* bomba la kuingiza umeme. ~ **-valve** *n* vali ya kuingiza umeme. **~or** *n* kidukiza/kiingiza umeme. **~tive** *adj* 1 -a kufuata mantiki kupata wazo la jumla. 2 -a kudukiza, kuingiza umeme au sumaku.
indue *see* **endue**.
indulge *vt, vi* 1 endekeza/deka ~ *sb in his whims etc.* endekeza matakwa ya mtu. ~ **oneself** jipendeza, jiachia, jifurahisha. 2 ~ **in** jiingiza ~ *oneself in excessive drinking* jiingiza katika ulevi wa kukithiri ~ *oneself in prayer* jitoa kwa sala, shikilia sala ~ *in sin* jiingiza katika dhambi. **~nt** *adj* -pole, -ema mno, taratibu ~ *parents* wazazi -dekezi/wema mno. **~ntly** *adv.* **~nce** *n* 1 kudekeza, kuendekeza. 2 *(of desires)* ~ *in* kujiachia, kujitoa kwa kujiingiza katika uzoefu wa kujifurahisha. 3 *(rel)* rehema, kipenda roho, upendeleo. 4 kitu mtu anachopendelea, starehe *to have a cup of coffee every evening is my ~* kahawa ndio kitu ninachopendelea kila jioni.
induna *n* jumbe.
indurate *vt, vi* fanya sugu, -gumu, gandamiza, shupaza. **induration** *n.* **indurative** *adj.*
industry *n* 1 bidii ya kazi, uchapaji kazi. 2 viwanda, tasnia. **industrial** *adj* -a kiwanda. ~ **action** mgomo *take ~ action* goma. ~ **alcohol** alkoholi ya viwanda ~ *dispute* mgogoro wa kiwanda/kazi ~ *estate* eneo la viwanda ~ *workers*

wafanyakazi wa viwandani ~ *states* nchi za viwanda ~ *relations* uhusiano wa wafanyakazi kiwandani. ~ **revolution** mapinduzi ya viwanda. **industrialism** *n* utasinia, mfumo wa uchumi unaotegemea viwanda. **indutrialist** *n* 1 mwenye kiwanda, mtasinia. 2 shabiki wa viwanda. **industrialize** *vt* jenga kiwanda, anzisha/endeleza mfumo wa viwanda. **industrialization** *n* ujenzi wa viwanda. **industrious** *adj* -enye bidii ya kazi, -chapakazi.

indwelling *adj* (*formal*) -enye kukaa ndani, -enye kukaa moyoni.

inebriate *vt (formal or joc)* levya *n* mlevi *adj* -levi. **inebriation/ inebriety** *n* ulevi.

inedible *adj* -siolika .

ineffable *adj* (*formal*) -siyoelezeka **ineffable happiness** furaha isioelezeka, furaha isiyokifani.

ineffaceable *adj* -siofutika.

ineffective *adj* -sio na nguvu uwezo/ ufanisi, hafifu, dhaifu, -siofaa. **~ness** *n.*

ineffectual *adj* 1 -sioweza kufanikisha jambo, -siojiamini.

inefficient *adj* -zembe, -sio na ufanisi -siofanya kazi vizuri. **~ly** *adv.* **inefficiency** *n* uzembe.

inelastic *adj* yabisi/kavu, -sionyumbuka, -siovutika; -sioweza kubailika/kufaa hali fulani. **~ity** *n.*

inelegant *adj* si -zuri, -sio na madaha, -siopendeza. **~ly** *adv.* **inelegance** *n.*

ineligible *adj* ~ **(for)** -siostahiki, -siofaa, -siojuzu (kuchaguliwa/ kuteuliwa n.k.). **ineligibility** *n.*

ineluctable *adj* -siozuilika, -sioepukika, -siokwepeka *death is* ~ kifo hakiepukiki.

inept *adj* 1 -siostadi, -sioelekevu. 2 -pumbavu, -siofaa, -a upuuzi. **~ly** *adv.* **~itude** n upumbavu, upuzi.

inequality *n* 1 kutokuwa sawa; tofauti, (ya cheo, utajiri n.k.). 2 *(pl) (of surface)* kutokuwa tambarare.

inequity *n* upendeleo, dhuluma.

inequitable *adj (formal)* -sio haki.

ineradicable *adj* -sioondoleka, -siong'oleka, -siofutika.

inert *adj* -fu, kama kifu, kama kufa. 2 -tepetevu, baridi. **~ia** *n* 1 ukunguni, uzito. 2 *(phy)* inesha.

inescapable *adj* -sioweza kuepukwa, -sioepukika.

inessential *adj* -sio ya lazima, siyo muhimu, -sio ya kimsingi.

inestimable *adj* -siokadirika (kwa ukubwa, thamani, wingi, n.k.).

inevitable *adj* -sioepukika, -siozuilika ~ *accident* ajali isiyoepukika *accidents are* ~ ajali hazina kinga *(fig)* -a kuonekana/kusikika kila mara, -a kutarajia (kuwepo/kutokea). **inevitability** *n.*

inexact *adj* -sio sahihi, -enye kosa, -enye hitilafu, si halisi. **~itude** *n* *terminological ~itudes (joc euphem)* uongo.

inexcusable *adj* -siosameheka.

inexhaustible *adj* 1 -sioisha, -siomalizika (kwa kuwa ingi), -ingi mno. 2 *(unwearied)* -siochoka. **inexhaustibility** *n.*

inexorable *adj* -sio na huruma, -siosamehe, -kali, -siobadilika wala kuzuilika. **inexorably** *adv.*

inexpedient *adj* -siofaa, siyo faida. **in expedience** *n.* **inexpediency** *n.*

inexpensive *adj* -sio ghali, rahisi, -a bei nafuu. **~ness** *n.*

inexperience *n* ukosefu wa uzoefu/ ujuzi. **~d** *adj* -sio na uzoefu/ujuzi/ tajriba.

inexpert *adj* si -stadi, si -bingwa.

inexpiable *adj (of offence)* -siolipika; -siosameheka; *(of resentment etc)* -siotulizika, -siofutika.

inexplicable *adj* -sioelezeka; -siofumbulika.

inexplicit *adj* si wazi/bayana; dhahiri; -a mafumbo; -sio fafanuliwa.

inexpressible *adj* -sioelezeka ~ *sorrow* majonzi yasiyoelezeka. **inexpressive** *adj* -sioonyesha, -siojulisha, -sio elezeka kwa maneno ~ *of anger* (uso usioonyesha kukasirika).

inextinguishable *adj* -siozimika,

-siotulizika.
in extremis *adj* -a kukaribia kufa, mahututi *(fig)* -wa katika shida kubwa.
inextricable *adj* -siochangulika, -siodadavulika, -sioachanishika, -siochanganulika.
infallible *adj* 1 -enye hakika, -sioweza kukosa/kukosea. 2 -sioshindika, -sio kosea, -a uhakika. **infallibility** *n.*
infamous *adj* 1. -enye sifa mbaya, -ovu sana, -a aibu, fedheha. **infamy** *n* tabia/kitendo kibaya.
infant *n* 1 mtoto mchanga/mkembe ~ *school* shule ya awali/chekechea. ~ **mortality** vifo vya watoto wachanga. 2 *(leg)* mtoto (chini ya miaka 18). 3 *(attrib)* changa; -a kitoto. **~icide** *n* 1 kosa la uuaji wa mtoto mchanga. 2 uuaji wa watoto wachanga. **~ile** *adj* 1 -a kitoto ~ *paralysis* polio. 2 -a mwanzoni. **~ilism** (*med*) *n* kuvia. **infancy** *n* 1 ukembe. 2 mwanzo; uchanga *aviation is no longer in its ~* urukaji hewani umekomaa *a nation still in its ~* taifa linaloinukia. 3 *(leg)* utoto, umri chini ya miaka 18.
infantry *n* askari wa miguu. **~man** askari (katika kikosi cha miguu).
infatuate *vt* **be ~d with/by sb** pumbazwa, lewa (upendo, ashiki n.k.); tia ashiki (hamu, upendo); *(with worldly goods etc)* ghururika na dunia. **infatuation (for)** *n* hali ya kutia ashiki, kupenda mno/ovyo.
infect *vt* **(with)** ambukiza, eneza; chafua; *(fig)* athiri *become ~ed* ambukizwa; *(of wound)* ingiwa vidudu; *(air, water)* chafua. **~ion** *n* 1 maambukizo, ambukizo, kuambukiza, kuenea; kuingia vidudu. 2 ugonjwa wa kuambukiza. 3 *(fig)* athari **~ious** *adj* 1 -a kuambukiza, -a kuenea. 2 *(fig)* -enye kushawishi/kuvutia, -a kuambukiza.
infelicitous *adj* -siofaa, -siokubalika, -siostahili. **infelicity** *n* udhaifu.
infer *vt* **(from sth) (that)** ona, fahamu (kwa kujua sababu yake); hitimisha/amua (kutokana na). **~able** *adj.* **~ence** *n.* **~ential** *adj.*
inferior *adj* dhalili; -a chini, duni *n* mtu wa chini (kwa cheo, uwezo n.k.), udhalili. **~rity** *n* udhalili. **~rity complex** *n* udhalili, (hali ya) kutojiamini, kutojitosheleza.
inferno *n* jehanamu, motoni, tukio la kutisha (agh. mteketeo mkubwa). **infernal** *adj* -a jehanamu, -a shetani; ovu kabisa; *(colloq)* baya sana, -a kuchosha, -a kuchukiza. **~ly** *adv.*
infertile *adj* gumba, tasa; *(of land)* -sio na rutuba, kame. **infertility** *n.*
infest *vt (of rats, insects etc)* jaa tele, tapakaa/zagaa *a house ~ed with rats* nyumba iliyojaa/tapakaa panya. **~ation** *n*
infibulation *n* mfyato, ufyataji: hali ya kufunga kuma kwa bizimu/kushona kuzuia kujamiiana.
infidel *n* kafiri *adj* kafiri. **~ity** *n (conjugal)* uzinzi; udanganyifu, kukosa uaminifu.
infighting *n (boxing)* mapigano ya karibu; *(fig)* mashindano makali, mashindano ya kikatili.
infiltrate *vt,vi* ~ **sth (into sth);** ~ **(into/through)** (maji) penya; penyeza. ~ **soldiers** penyeza askari (katikati ya maadui); *(of ideas)* ingia akilini. **infiltration** *n.*
infinite *adj* 1 -sio na kikomo, -sio na mwisho, (*maths*) isiyokoma. 2 -siopimika, -kubwa sana; -ingi sana *n* **the ~ I** Mungu. **~ly** *adv.* **~simal** *adj* -dogo mno *(maths)* kiduchu. **infinitude** *n (formal)* wingi usio na mwisho, pasipo kiasi. **infinity** *n* pasipo mwisho/kikomo; *(maths)* namba isiyo na kikomo. **infinitive** *n (gram)* kitenzijina *adj* -a kitenzi -jina. **infinitival** *adj.*
infirm *adj* 1 dhaifu (hasa kwa sababu ya uzee au ugonjwa). 2 goigoi, -sio thabiti, pungufu wa akili/mawazo ~ *of purpose* -a kusitasita. **~ity** *n.* **~ary** *n* hospitali; *(schools etc)* zahanati. **~arian** *n.*
infix *vt* ambika kati *n (gram)* kiambishi

kati.

inflame *vt, vi* 1 washa, waka, tia moto, choma. 2 hamasisha, tia hamaki, chochea, kasirisha. 3 *(of sore etc.)* vimba, vimbisha. **inflammable** *adj* 1 -a kuwaka, -a kuwashika, -a kuchomeka, -a kushika moto. 2 -a hamaki. **inflammation** *n* 1 mwako, moto. 2 *(swollen place)* uvimbeuchungu. **inflammatory** *adj* 1 *(med)* -enye uvimbe. 2 -a kuhamakisha/kuhamasisha/chochea.

inflate *vt* ~ **sth (with)** 1 shinikiza, jaza (upepo). 2 *(expand)* vimbisha, panua *~d language* maneno mazuri yasiyo na maana. 3 *(fig)* tia moyo/kiburi/ tumaini. ~ **with pride** vimbisha kichwa. 4 *(enlarge)* ongeza, kuza; fumuka/futuka ~ *the currency* ongeza fedha katika nchi ili kupandisha bei ya vitu. **inflation** *n* 1 kuvimba. 2 kupanda kwa gharama za maisha (kutokana na ongezeko la fedha). 3 *(econ)* mfumko/mfutuko (wa bei). **inflationary** *adj*.

inflect *vt* 1 badili, geuza. 2 *(gram)* nyambulisha majina, vitenzi n.k. 3 pinda. 4 *(phy)* (*of light*) pindisha. 5 *(mus)* badili sauti. **~ive** *adj*. **~ion** *n* 1 mabadiliko. 2 *(gram)* unyambulisho wa maneno. 3 kupinda (nuru). 4 *(mus)* mahadhi.

inflexible *adj* 1 -siopindika, -sionyumbuka. 2 *(fig)* -gumu, -siobadili, -shupavu, thabiti, madhubuti. **inflexibility** *n*. **inflexibly** *adv*.

inflict *vt* ~ **sth (on/upon).** 1 piga, umiza, tesa ~ *a penalty* toa adhabu, tesa. 2 lazimisha, shurutisha ~ *one's friendship on sb* shurutisha urafiki. **~ion** *n*.

inflorescence *n* 1 shaziua: hali ya kuwa na maua. 2 *(lit or fig)* kuchanua; ustawi.

inflow *n* 1 kumiminikia ndani, kutiririkia ndani. 2 *(tech)* bomba la kutiririkia (maji). **~ing** *adj*.

influence *vt* athiri; vuta, shawishi *n* ~ **(on/upon)** 1 uwezo wa kuathiri/ kuvutia. 2 mvuto, ushawishi, athari. 3 uwezo (kutokana na nafasi) *he used his ~ to get his wife the job* alitumia uwezo wake kumpatia kazi mke wake. **influential** *adj* -enye kuvutia, -enye kushawishi, -enye uwezo *an ~ person* mtu mashuhuri. **influentially** *adv*.

influenza *n (colloq abbr flu)* mafua, homa ya mafua.

influx *n* kumiminikia ndani, kuingia kwa wingi.

inform *vt,vi* 1 ~ **sb (of sth)** julisha, arifu, pasha habari, fahamisha *a well-~ed person* mjuzi, mweledi wa mambo. **I am ~ed** nimeambiwa, nimesikia habari. 2 ~ **against/on sb** shtaki, toa habari juu ya, semea. **~ant** *n* kijumbe mtoa habari. **~er** *n* mtoa habari, mbega. **~ation** *n* 1 ~ **(on/ about)** kuarifu, kuarifiwa/ kupashwa habari. 2 habari, taarifa *a piece of ~* taarifa fupi. ~ **bureau** ofisi ya habari. **~ative** *adj* -enye taarifa nyingi, -a kuarifu; -a kujuvya, -enye kuelewesha.

informal *adj* 1 *(irregular)*-sio rasmi, si -a taratibu, -a kienyeji. 2 -lio nje ya taratibu. **~ly** *adv*. **~ity** *n*.

infra- *adv* chini, baadaye. ~ **dig** *pre adj* -siolingana na hadhi yake *pref.*~ **-red** *adj* -a miali isiyoonekana (chini ya upinde). **~-structure** *n* muundo msingi, kikorombwezo.

infraction *n* kosa, uvunjaji sheria.

infrequent *adj* -a mara chache, -a nadra. **~ly** *adv*. **infrequency** *n*.

infringe *vt* 1 vunja, asi, halifu. 2 ~ **(upon)** ingilia *don't ~ on other's rights* usiingilie haki za wengine. **~ment** *n*.

infuriate *vt* ghadhibisha, kasirisha sana.

infuse *vt* 1 ~ **into/with** jaza, tilia (moyo, ujasiri n.k.). 2 lowesha, lowana (ili kutoa ladha) nywesha, nywea. **infusion** *n* 1 kujaza, kutilia. 2 unyweshaji (dawa, mimea n.k.). 3 uchanganyaji ~ *of new blood* uchanganyaji wa damu mpya.

ingathering *n* mkusanyo, mavuno.

ingenious *adj* 1 *(of a person)* -erevu, stadi, bunifu, vumbuzi. 2 *(of things)* -liofanywa kwa maarifa/werevu. **~ly** *adv*. **ingenuity** *n*.
ingenuous *adj (formal)* -sio na hila, nyofu, -kunjufu, -adilifu, kweli. **~ly** *adv*. **~ness** *n*. **ingenue** *n* (msichana) mtulivu/mnyofu, mwanamwali (agh. katika tamthiliya).
ingest *vt (formal) (lit. or fig) (food etc)* akia, meza. **~ion** *n*.
inglorious *adj* 1 -a aibu, fedheha, pasipo heshima. 2 -siofahamika, duni. **~ly** *adv*.
ingoing *adj* -pya, -nayoingia, -nayohamia.
ingot *n* kipande, kidonge (cha metali chenye umbo la tofali); kibongemetali.
ingraft *see* **engraft**.
ingrained *adj* 1 -liotopea, -liokolea sana ~ *habits* tabia iliyotopea/iliyojengeka. 2 -ingi, -liojazana, -lioshika. ~ **dirt** uchafu ulioshika.
ingratiate *vt* ~ **oneself with sb** jipendekeza, jikomba, rairai. **ingratiatingly** *adv*.
ingratitude *n* utovu wa shukrani, kutokuwa na shukrani, kutoshukuru. **ingrate** *(arch) adj* -sio na shukrani, -siofadhili *n* mtu asiye na shukrani.
ingredient *n* kiambato.
ingress *n (formal)* kuingia, mwingilio; haki ya kuingia *free* ~ kusabilia, kuingia, kiingilio bure.
ingrowing *adj* -a kukua ndani, (k.m. ukucha). **ingrown** *adj*. **ingrowth** *n*.
inhabit *vt* sakini, ishi. **~able** *adj*. **~ant** *n* mkazi.
inhale *vt,vi* vuta hewa (hadi ndani ya mapafu), jaza mapafu *~cigaratte smoke* jaza moshi wa sigara ndani ya mapafu. **~r** *n* kivutia hewa.
inharmonious *adj* si -linganifu, -sio patana.
inherent *adj* -a asili ~ *defect* dosari ya asili. **~ly** *adv*.
inherit *vt,vi* rithi *she ~ed her mother's kindness* alirithi ukarimu wa mama yake. **~ance** *n* urithi; mirathi. **~or** *n*. **~able** *adj*.
inhibit *vt* zuia, kataza. ~ **sb (from doing sth)** zuia mtu kufanya jambo. **be ~ed** zuiwa; *(psych)* jizuia. **~ion** *n* kuzuia, kusita; *(psych)* kujizuia. **~ory** *adj*.
inhospitable *adj* -sio karimu; *(of places)* -siokalika. **inhospitality** *n* utovu wa ukarimu, kutokalika.
inhuman *adj* -a kinyama, -katili, sio -a kiutu. **~ity** *n* ukatili, unyama. **~e** *adj* -a kikatili, -sio na huruma.
inhume *vt* (*liter*) zika, fukia.
inimical *adj* ~ **(to)** *(formal)* a (kuleta) uhasama; -a kudhuru.
inimitable *adj (formal)* -sio na kifani, -sioigika.
iniquitous *adj (formal)* ovu sana, dhalimu. **~ly** *adv*. **iniquity** *n* udhalimu, uovu.
initial *adj* -a mwanzo, -a kwanza, -a awali ~ *capital* mtaji wa kuanzia ~ *letter* herufi ya kwanza; *(esp pl)* herufi za mwanzo za majina ya watu k.m. F.R. *(for Felix Rajabu) vt* tia herufi za kwanza za jina kama sahihi. **~ly** *adv*.
initiate *vt* 1 anza, anzisha. 2 ~ **sb into a group** ingiza mtu katika kikundi. 3 ~ **sb into sth** fundisha, funda. ~ **sb into traditional customs** tia mtu jandoni/ unyagoni/kumbini *n* mtu aliyeingizwa chamani/kundini; mtu aliyetiwa jandoni. **initiation** *n* mwanzo; kuingiza; kufundwa, kufunzwa n.k.; jando. **initiator** *n*. **initiative** *n* 1 ari, uwezo wa kuanzishia mambo/kuvumbua njia n.k.; moyo wa kujituma *he has no ~* hana ari mwenyewe *do sth on one's own ~* fanya jambo mwenyewe *have the ~* -wa na nafasi ya kuanzisha *take the ~ (in doing sth)* anza (kufanya jambo). 2 haki, uwezo wa raia wa kutoa hoja zao nje ya bunge (kama ilivyo Uswisi).
inject *vt* ~ **(sth into sb sth); ~sb/sth (with sth)** ingiza/jaza (uowevu) kwa nguvu; piga sindano ~ *sth into sb's arm* piga sindano mkononi mwa mtu.

~**ion** *n* 1 kuingiza. 2 (dawa ya) sindano *give an ~* piga sindano *fuel ~ions* utemaji fueli.

injudicious *adj (formal)* si -a busara, si -a akili, -sio -a hekima. ~**ly** *adv*.

injunction *n* (agh. amri ya kisheria iliyoandikwa) *prohibitory ~* amri ya kukataza.

injure *vt* 1 dhuru, umiza. 2 jeruhi. ~**d** *adj* -liojeruhiwa *~ sb's feelings* muumiza mtu. **the ~d** *n* majeruhi. **injurious** *adj ~* **(to)** -a kudhuru, -a kuumiza, -a kutia hasara. **injury** *n* 1 dhara; uharibifu *do sb an ~* umiza mtu. 2 jeraha *sustain no ~* nusurika, -topata jeraha.

injustice *n* udhalimu, jambo lisilo la haki *do sb an ~* elewa vibaya (bila sababu), -totendea (mtu) haki.

ink *n* wino. ~-**bottle/pot** *n* chupa ya wino, kidau. ~-**pad** *n* kikausho. ~**stand** *n* kishikizo cha chupa ya wino. ~-**well** *n* kidau *vt* paka/tia wino. ~ **in** andika kwa wino. ~ **out** futa kwa wino. ~**y** *adj* -liopakwa wino; -eusi kama wino, -a giza sana.

inkling *n* kidokezo, fununu *give sb/ have/get an ~ (of sth)* -pa/pata/sikia fununu (ya kitu).

inlaid *pt, pp of* **inlay**.

inland *adj* 1 -a bara *~ regions* mikoa ya bara. 2 -enye kupatikana ndani ya nchi.~ **Revenue** *(GB)* kodi ya bidhaa za ndani *(colloq)* Idara ya Kodi (ya bidhaa za ndani) *adv* kuelekea bara.

inlaws *pl (colloq) (of parents)* wakwe, *(sing.)* mkwe *father inlaw* baba mkwe; *(of sisters/brothers)*shemeji/ wifi.

inlay *vt* **(in/into/with)** tia njumu/ vipambo/vipande vya mbao/metali kwenye ubapa wa kitu k.m. sakafu, mlango n.k. *n* 1 njumu, vipambo, vipande vya mbao n.k.; kitu kilichotiwa njumu. 2 *(dentistry)* uzibaji/jino kwa dhahabu, plastiki n.k.

inlet *n* 1 njia; mlango. 2 *(creek)* hori, ghuba ndogo. 3 *(of cloth)* upapi.

in loco parentis *(Lat)* kwa niaba ya, badala ya wazazi.

inmate *n* mkazi (mwenzi) (agh. katika hospitali, jela n.k.).

in memoriam *(Lat)* ukumbusho.

inmost *adj* -a ndani kabisa, chokomeani; *(fig)* -a siri sana, -a faragha mno.

inn *n* hoteli, mkahawa. ~ **keeper** *n* mwenye hoteli. **I~ of Court** *(GB)* vyama vya mawakili; nyumba za vyama hivyo London.

innards *n pl (colloq)* 1 tumbo na matumbo. 2 sehemu ya ndani.

innate *adj* -a hulka, -a asili, -a maumbile. ~**ly** *adv*.

inner *adj* -a ndani, -a ndani zaidi. **the ~ man** nafsi, undani wa mtu; tumbo. ~**most** *adj* chokomeani.

inning *n (baseball/cricket)* 1 kipindi. 2 *(pl)* zamu ya timu kupiga mpira; *(fig)* muda wa kutawala (wa chama); kipindi cha harakati za maisha. **have a good ~s** *(colloq)* -wa na maisha marefu na ya furaha.

innocent *adj* 1 ~ **(of)** -sio na kosa/hatia; maasumu. 2 -sio na ubaya, -siodhuru. 3 -siojua/tambua uovu. 4 -jinga *n* 1 maasumu. 2 mjinga, punguani. ~**ly** *adv*. **innocence** *n*.

innocuous *adj* -siodhuru, -sio na madhara, -sioumiza.

innovate *vt* vumbua, anzisha jambo jipya. **innovator** *n* mvumbuzi. **innovation** *n* uvumbuzi, bidaa.

innuendo *n* kijembe, masengenyo, chongezi.

innumerable *adj* -siohesabika, -ingi mno.

inoculate *vt ~* **sb (with/against sth)** chanja (ili kukinga na maradhi); *(fig)* tia kasumba. **inoculation** *n* chanjo, kuchanjwa *have an ~ against small pox* chanjwa ndui.

inoffensive *adj* -siodhuru, -sio -kali, -sio shari.

inoperable *adj (of tumours etc)* -siotibika kwa operesheni; -sioweza kufanyiwa operesheni.

inoperative *adj (of laws, rules etc)* -siofanya kazi, -siotumika, -liotanguka.

inopportune *adj (esp. of time)* si -a wakati wake, -siofaa (kwa wakati ule) *it is* ~ si wakati wake. **~ly** *adv.*
inordinate *adj (formal)* -sio na mpaka, -siozuiliwa vizuri; -a kuzidi, -ingi mno. **~ly** *adv.*
inorganic *adj* 1 -sio na uhai; -sioelezeka kiitimolojia. 2 -sio -a kikaboni ~ *chemistry* kemia isiyo ya kikaboni. **~ally** *adv.*
in-patient *n* mgonjwa aliyelazwa hospitali.
inpouring *n (formal)* mmiminiko *adj* -enye kumiminika.
input *n* pembejeo.
inquest *n* ~ **(on)** uchunguzi rasmi wa kisheria (agh. wa kifo ambacho chanzo chake hakijulikani).
inquietude *n* wasiwasi, jakamoyo.
inquire *vt* 1 uliza ~ *the way* uliza njia ~ *how to do sth* uliza jinsi ya kufanya. 2 ~ **about/concerning/upon** ulizia, uliza kuhusu (jambo fulani) ~ *about the accident* uliza kuhusu ajali ~ *after* ulizia hali (ya afya ya mtu). ~ **for** taka, omba (kuona). ~ **into** chunguza, dadisi. **~r** *n* mdadisi. **inquiring** *adj* dadisi. **inquiringly** *adv.* **inquiry** *n* 1 maulizo, kuuliza *inquiries* maulizo. 2 kutafuta habari, uchunguzi *hold an* ~ *into* peleleza, chunguza *court of* ~ *(mil)* mahakama ya kuchunguza mashtaka (dhidi ya mtu) *preliminary* ~ uchunguzi wa awali. **inquisitive** *adj* dadisi, -a kulabizi, -enye udaku ~ *person* mdadisi, mdukizi. **inquisitively** *adv.* **inquisitiveness** *n.* **inquisition** *n* uchunguzi (agh. rasmi) *the* ~ *(also called the Holy Office)* Mahakama ya Kanisa Katoliki ya kukomesha uasi (hasa karne ya 15 na 16). **inquisitor** *n.* **inquisitorial** *adj.*
inroad *n* shambulio la ghafla (ili kuharibu). **make ~ on/upon** ingilia.
inrush *n* mmiminiko.
insane *adj* -enye wazimu, -enye kichaa ~ *asylum* hospitali ya vichaa. **~ly** *adv.* **insanity** *n* wazimu, kichaa.
insanitary *adj* -enye kudhuru afya, chafu, -sio safi (kiafya).
insatiable *adj* ~ **(of/for)** *(formal)* -siotosheka, -sioridhika kamwe/kabisa; -lafi. **insatiably** *adv.* **insatiate** *adj (formal)* -sioridhika, -siotosheka.
inscribe *vt* ~ **(on/in/with)** andika; weka alama, chora ~*d stock (comm)* bidhaa ambazo majina ya wanaozimiliki yameorodheshwa. **inscription** *n* mwandiko; maneno yaliyoandikwa kwenye mnara wa ukumbusho, sarafu, medali n.k.
inscrutable *adj* -siotambulikana, -siofahamika, -sioeleweka, -a fumbo.
insect *n* mdudu. ~ **powder** dawa (poda) ya kuulia wadudu. **~icide** kiuwa wadudu. **~ivorous** *adj* -enye kula wadudu.
insecure *adj* 1 -sio salama/imara/madhubuti; -a hatari. 2 -enye shaka, -enye wahaka. **insecurity** *n.*
inseminate *vt* 1 otesha, zalisha. 2 tia mbegu, himilisha. **insemination** *n* uhimilishaji *artificial* ~ uhimilishaji bandia, kuzalisha kwa chupa.
insensate *adj* 1 *(formal)* -sio hisi, -siotambua. 2 pumbavu, -siofikiri.
insensible *adj* 1 -liopoteza fahamu (kwa kuumia, ugonjwa n.k.); -siohisi, -siotambua. 2 ~ **(of)** -siofahamu. 3 ~ **(to)** -siohisi, -liokufa ganzi; -siojali; -sio na imani/huruma. 4 *(of changes)* dogo/-a polepole sana. **insensibly** *adv.* **insensibility** *n (formal)* kutoona, kutotambua, kutohisi.
insensitive *adj* ~ **to** -siohisi; -siojali (hisia za) wengine. **~ly** *adv.* **insensitivity** *n.*
insentient *adj* -sio na hisia, -sio na uhai.
inseparable *adj* ~ **(from)** -siotengeka, -siochangukana ~ *friends* marafiki wasiotengana, (marafiki wa) chanda na pete; marafiki wa damu.
insert *vt* ingiza, tia, weka *n* kitu kilichoingizwa. **~ion** *n* kuingiza, mwingizo; kitu kilichoingizwa/tiwa.
in-service *attrib adj* (-a) kazini ~ *training* mafunzo kazini.

inset *n* 1 kitu kilichotiwa (ndani ya kitu kingine). 2 kipachikwa: ramani/picha ndogo iliyopigwa chapa katika ramani/picha kubwa 2 *vt* ingiza, pachika.

inshore *adj, adv.* -a ufukoni, karibu na ufuko ~ *current* mkondo wa ufukoni.

inside *n* 1 ndani; upande wa ndani ~ *out* ndani nje (nje ndani) *(fig) know sth ~ out* fahamu fika/kwa undani, barabara *turn every thing ~ out* pindua kila kitu kabisa. 2 sehemu ya ndani ya barabara/njia. 3 *(colloq)* tumbo na matumbo *adj* -a ndani -a (kutoka) ndani. **the ~ track** *(in racing)* njia ya ndani; *(fig)* kushika mpini; hali ya kufaidika *an ~ job (sl)* wizi wa ndani (kwa msaada wa mmoja wa wahusika/wenye mali) *adv, prep* 1 ndani. ~ **of** *(colloq)* katika; chini ya *we cannot finish the construction ~ of two weeks* hatuwezi kumaliza kujenga kwa wiki mbili. 2 *(GB sl)* ndani, jela. **~r** *n* 1 alwatani, mwenyeji, mjuzi wa mambo (kutokana na nafasi yake katika chama, shirika n.k). 2 wanachama.

insidious *adj* -enye kudhuru kwa siri. **~ly** *adv.* **~ness** *n.*

insight *n.* ~ **(into/sth)** umaizi, utambuzi. **gain ~ into sth** pata ujuzi wa kitu.

insignia *n* alama za cheo (kama nishani, tepe, taji n.k.).

insignificant *adj* -sio na maana; -sio na thamani; -dogo. **~ly** *adv.* **insignificance** *n.*

insincere *adj* -nafiki, si -aminifu, -danganyifu. **~ly** *adv.* **insincerity** *n.*

insinuate *vt* 1 **~sth/oneself (into)** penyeza/jiingiza (polepole na kwa hila). 2 ~ **(to sb) that** dokeza, singizia; pigia kijembe. **insinuation** *n.*

insipid *adj* chapwa, -sio na ladha. **~ly** *adv.* **~ness** *n.* **~ity** *n.*

insist *vt,vi* ~ **on/that** sisitiza; shikilia. **~ent** *adj.* **~ence** *n.*

in situ *(Lat)* mahali pake pa asili.

insofar *see* **in.**

insole *n* soli ya ndani (katika kiatu), wayo wa ndani.

insolent *adj* 1 ~ **(to)** fidhuli, jeuri, -enye dharau. **~ly** *adv.* **insolence** *n.*

insoluble *adj* 1 *(of substances)* -sioyeyuka. 2 *(of problems etc)* -siotatulika, -siofumbulika.

insolvent *adj* 1 muflisi, -sioweza kulipa deni, -liofilisika *n* muflisi; suta, mtu asiyeweza kulipa deni. **insolvency** *n.*

insomnia *n* kurukwa na usingizi, kukosa usingizi. **~c** *n.*

insomuch *adv* hata, kwa kiasi. ~ **as/that** kwa kiasi kwamba.

insouciance *n* kutojali; kutohusika. **insouciant** *adj* -siojali.

inspan *vt* *(S. African)* fungia (farasi, ng'ombe n.k.) gari.

inspect *vt* kagua, angalia. **~ion** *n* kukagua; ukaguzi. **~or** *n* 1 mkaguzi ~ *of weights and measurements* Mkaguzi wa mizani na vipimo. 2 *(of police force)* mrakibu. **~orate** *n* ukaguzi.

inspire *vt* ~ **sth (in sb); ~ sb (with sth/to do sth)** 1 tia moyo, tia msukumo, vutia. 2 fungulia mlango wa heri. **~d** *adj* -enye wahyi. **inspiration** *n* 1 msukumo, kariha, zinduko. 2 ~ **(to/for)** mfano wa kuvutia, mtu/kitu kitiacho msukumo, mvuto. 3 wazo zuri/la heri lijalo ghafla. 4 ufunuo, wahyi, mwongozo wa kiungu.

instability *n* kutotengemaa; kuyumba-yumba, kutokuwa thabiti/imara, udhaifu, kutosimama tisti.

install, instal *vt* ~ **sb/sth (in sth)** 1 simika. 2 weka, funga chombo mahali (kwa matumizi). 3 sakini, jipanga. **~ation** *n* 1 msimiko; uwekaji wa chombo; usakini. 2 chombo kilichowekwa (kwa matumizi).

installment *n* sehemu, fungu (la deni, malipo, mali, maandiko, hadithi n.k.) hisa ~ *system* mfumo wa kubandika, mfumo wa malipo ya kidogo kidogo; *pay by ~s* lipa kidogo kidogo.

instance *n* 1 mfano, namna *for ~* kwa mfano, mathalani *in this ~* hapa, kwa upande huu/namna hii *in the first ~* kwanza. 2 *at the ~ of sb* kwa ombi la fulani *vt* toa kama mfano; taja.

instant *adj* 1 -a mara moja, -a papo hapo. 2 -a haraka. 3 *(abbr. inst) (comm; dated)* -a mwezi huu *the 2nd instant* siku ya pili ya mwezi huu. **~ly** *adv* mara moja *conj* mara *n* mara *do it this ~* fanya sasa hivi *wait an ~* ngoja kidogo, ngoja kwanza *I'll come in an ~* nitakuja sasa hivi. **~aneous** *adj* -a mara moja, papo hapo. **~aneously** *adv*.

instead *adv* badala ya *if Jimmy is not willing to go with you, take John ~* kama Jimi hataki kwenda nawe mchukue Joni badala yake. ~ **of** *(prep phrase)* badala ya.

instep *n* kiganja cha mguu (juu ya wayo); sehemu ya juu ya wayo.

instigate *vt* ~ **sth/sb to do sth** chochea. **instigator** *n* mchochezi. **instigation** *n* uchochezi *~ to revolt* chochea maasi.

instil *vt* ~ **sth into sb** 1 ingiza, tia taratibu/polepole, kidogo kidogo. 2 fundisha kidogo kidogo. **~lation** *n*.

instinct *n* silika *pred, adj* ~ **with** -liojaa *a poem ~ with sorrow* shairi lililojaa huzuni. **~ive** *adj* -a silika, bila kufikiri. **~ively** *adv*.

institute[1] *n* taasisi; chuo *~ of Kiswahili Research* Taasisi ya Uchunguzi wa Kiswahili *~ of Finance Management* Chuo cha Usimamizi wa Fedha.

institute[2] *vt* 1 anzisha, asisi *~ proceedings* anzisha mashauri. 2 ~ **sb (to)** teua. **institution** *n* 1 kuanzisha, asasi. 2 chama, shirika; taasisi. 3 sheria/desturi/ya kawaida. 4 jumba la ustawi wa jamii (k.v. nyumba ya watoto yatima/wazee). **institutional** *adj* -a jengo la ustawi wa jamii. **institutionalize** rasimisha, anzisha/geuza kuwa sheria/desturi; peleka/weka mtu (yatima, kichaa n.k.) katika nyumba ya ustawi wa jamii.

instruct *vt* 1 funza, fundisha. 2 *(give orders)* agiza, amuru. 3 pasha habari, arifu. **~or** *n* mwalimu. **~ion** *n* 1 mafunzo, mafundisho. 2 *(pl)* maagizo; mwongozo, maelekezo. **~ional** *adj* -a mafunzo; -a kielimu. **~ive** *adj* -a kufundisha, -a kuelimisha. **~ively** *adv*.

instrument *n* 1 chombo, zana, kifaa. 2 *(mus)* ala. 3 chombo, mtumishi. 4 *(leg)* hati rasmi. **~ation** *n* upangaji wa muziki wa ala; utengenezaji wa zana za kisayansi. **~al** *adj* 1 -a kutumika, -a kusaidia, -a kuhusika *he was ~ in her getting promotion* alihusika na kupanda kwake cheo. 2 -a ala *~ music* mziki wa ala. **~alist** *n* mpiga mziki wa ala. **~ality** *n* wakala, njia.

insubordinate *adj* asi; -kaidi, -a dharau. **insubordination** *n*.

insubstantial *adj* 1 -sio kitu/dutu, -sio halisi. 2 -sio na maana, -sio na msingi.

insufferable *adj* 1 -siovumilika -siostahimilika. 2 -enye majivuno mengi, -enye kujiona sana.

insufficient *adj* haba, pungufu, -siotosha. **~ly** adv. **insufficiency** *n*.

insular *adj* 1 -a kisiwa. 2 -enye tabia kama za watu wa visiwani; (agh) -enye mawazo, maarifa n.k. finyu ya mumo humo tu. **~ism**, **~ity** *n*.

insulate *vt* ~ **(from)** 1 funika kwa mpira, hami (ili nguvu ya umeme, joto isitoke n.k.). 2 tenga, kinga. **insulator** *n* kihami. **insulation** *n*.

insulin *n* insulini: dutu inayotumika kutibu ugonjwa wa kisukari.

insult *vt* tukana, fedhehesha *n* tusi. **~ing** *adj*. **ingly** *adv*.

insuperable *adj* -sioshindika, -siondoleka. **insuperability** *n*.

insupportable *adj* -siovumilika, -siostahimilika.

insure *vt* ~ **(against)** kata bima *~ one's life* kata bima ya maisha. **the ~d** mwenye bima. **the ~r** mweka kampuni ya bima. **the insurant** *(leg)* mlipaji wa bima. **insurance** *n* 1 bima. 2 malipo ya bima *~ policy* hati ya bima. 3 *(safeguard)* kinga.

insurgent *n* askari mwasi *adj* -asi,

pinzani.

insurmountable *adj* -sioshindika, -sioondoleka.

insurrection *n* upinzani (dhidi ya serikali); maasi. **~ary** *adv.* **~ist** *n* mpinzani, mwasi.

intact *adj* -zima, kamili; -sioharibiwa, salama.

intaglio *n* kutia nakshi kwa kuchonga; kito chenye nakshi.

intake *n* 1 kipenyo, kiingizio, mlango, mkondo. 2 idadi (iingiayo/iingizwayo katika kipindi fulani) *university ~* idadi iingayo chuo kikuu. 3 eneo lililokaushwa maji (yatokanayo na bahari n.k.).

intangible *adj* tatanishi, -sioweza kueleweka kwa urahisi, -sioshikika *~ ideas* mawazo yasiyoshikika *~ assets (of business)* mali isiyopimika (k.v. hadhi, uaminifu n.k.).

integer *n* namba kamili; kitu kizima; *(math)* namba kamili. **integral** *adj* 1 -a lazima, muhimu (katika kukamilisha kitu/jambo) *the arms and legs are ~ parts of a human being* mikono na miguu ni sehemu muhimu za mwili wa binadamu. 2 -zima, -kamilifu. 3 *(math)* -a rejeo; -lio na namba kamili. **integrally** *adv.* **integrate** *vt* 1 unganisha; tungamanisha; kamilisha; changanya. 2 fanya/-wa sawa. **integration** *n.* **integrity** *n* 1 uaminifu, uadilifu msimamo. 2 uzima, ukamilifu.

integument *n (formal)* kifuniko, ngozi, ganda.

intellect *n* 1 akili, uwezo wa kufikiri, bongo. 2 *(collective sing or in pl)* watu wenye akili. **~ual** *adj* 1 -a akili, -enye akili *~ development* ukuzi wa akili 2. -somi, -enye kupendelea taaluma *n* msomi. *n* 1 akili *~ test* jaribio la kupima akili. *~* **quotient** kiwango cha akili. 2 habari, taarifa *~ service/agency* shirika la ujasusi/ upelelezi. **intelligent** *adj* -enye akili. **intelligently** *adv.*

intelligentsia *n (usu collective sing the intelligentisia)* wamaizi, wasomi.

intemperate *adj (formal) (of a person or his behaviour)* -sio na kadiri, -sio na simile, -a kupita kiasi; -siojitawala *~ habits (esp)* ulevi wa kupita kiasi. **~ly** *adv.* **intemperance** *n.*

intend *vt* 1 *~* **(for)** kusudia, nuia, azimu, dhamiria *this was ~ed for us* hii ilikusudiwa sisi *what do you ~ to do?* unakusudia kufanya nini? 2 *~* **(by)** *(old use)* maanisha *what do you ~ by this word?* unamaanisha nini? **~ed** *n* mchumba (wa kike).

intense *adj* 1 *(of qualities)* -a nguvu, -kali sana *~ heat* joto kali sana. 2 *(of feelings etc) kali sana (of persons)* -enye jaziba/mhemko. **~ly** *adv* sana.

intensify *vt,vi* ongeza, zidisha (nguvu n.k.) ongezeka, zidi. **intensification** *n.* **intensifier** *n.* **intensity** *n* mkazo, nguvu, ukali. **intensive** *adj* 1 makini, shadidi *~ agriculture* kilimo shadidi. *~* **care** *n* uangalizi makini wa wagonjwa *~ care unit* kitengo cha wagonjwa mahututi. 2 *(gram)* -a nguvu na -a kutia mkazo.

intent *adj* 1 -enye dhamira/shauku, makini. 2 *~* **on/upon sth/doing sth (of persons)** -a kuazimia/ kudhamiria *n* 1 *(chiefly leg)* azimio, dhamira *criminal ~* dhamira ya jinai *with good ~* kwa dhamiri njema. *do sth with ~* fanya kitu kwa kudhamiria 2 *(pl) to all ~s and purposes* kwa kila hali. **~ion** *n* nia, kusudi, dhamira *for the ~ of* kwa kusudi la, kwa nia ya. **~ioned** *adj* -enye nia *well ~* -enye nia njema. **~ional** *adj* -a makusudi. **~ionally** *adv* kwa kudhamiria.

inter[1] *vt (formal)* zika.

inter[2] *(prep)* baina, kati ya; miongoni mwa.

interact *vi* athiriana, ingiliana, tendana. **~ion** *n.* **~ive** *adj.*

interalia *(Lat)* pamoja na mambo mengine.

interbreed *vt,vi* zalisha kwa kuchanganya damu (baina ya makabila, jamii n.k.), hulutiana.

intercalary *adj (of a day or month)* -a

siku iliyoongezwa (29 Feb); *(of a year)* mwaka mrefu.

intercede *vi* ~ **(with sb) (for sb)** ombea, tetea, sihi. **intercession** *n* kusihi; sala ya kuombea.

intercept *vt* 1 kamata, zuia njiani, ingilia kati. 2 (*math*) kutana. **~ion** *n*. **interceptor** *n* ndege ya kuzuia (adui).

interchange *vt* 1 *(of two persons etc.)* badilishana (mashauri n.k.) *we ~d books* tulibadilishana vitabu. 2 *(each of two things)* badili ~ *the position of two objects* badili nafasi za vitu viwili. **~able** *adj* -enye kubadilishana *n* 1 badiliko; badilisho. 2 *(also)* ~ *station* stesheni ya kubadilisha njia ya kusafiri. 3 mahali pa kuingilia baraste (bila kuvuka barabara nyingine).

intercollegiate *adj* baina ya vyuo ~ *games* michezo baina ya vyuo.

intercommunicate *vi* wasiliana, pashana habari. **intercommunication** *n*.

intercom *n (colloq)* mawasiliano ya ndani.

intercommunion *n* ibada ya pamoja (ya madhehebu mbalimbali) ya meza ya Bwana.

intercontinental *adj* kati ya mabara.

intercourse *n* 1 *(social)* maingiliano, ushirikiano, kubadilishana (mawazo, n.k.); *(comm)* biashara, kubadilishana vitu. 2 *(sexual)* ~ *see* **coitus**.

interdenominational *adj* baina ya madhehebu, -a kuhusu madhehebu mbalimbali.

interdepend *vi* tegemeana, husiana. **~ent** *adj* -a kutegemeana. **~ence** *n*.

interdict *vt (formal)* kataza, piga marufuku, zuia (kwa amri ya serikali *(rel)* tenga *n (esp RC)* ilani: amri ya Kanisa ya kutenga watu, ibada zake. **~ion** *n*.

interest[1] *n* 1 moyo wa kupenda kujua/ kujifunza jambo/kitu fulani, shauku *he has a considerable ~ in world news* anapenda sana habari za ulimwengu *he listened with great ~* alisikiliza kwa shauku kubwa. 2 mvuto, raghba *a novel of great ~* riwaya ya kuvutia sana. 3 upendeleo, kitu mtu anachopenda. 4 *his main ~is fashion* hasa anapenda mitindo; *(often pl.)* faida, manufaa, maslahi *public ~* manufaa ya umma *it is to your ~ to build a house* kujenga nyumba ni kwa faida/manufaa yako. 5 ushirika, hisa *have an ~ in a company* -wa na ushirika/hisa katika kampuni fulani *sell one's ~ in the company* uza hisa katika kampuni fulani. 6 riba *the society charges five per cent ~ on a loan* chama hutoza riba ya asilimia tano kwenye mkopo *lend at ~* kopesha kwa riba. **with ~** *(fig)* kwa nguvu/kiasi kikubwa zaidi *return sb's hospitality with ~* lipa ukarimu wa mtu kwa kiwango kikubwa zaidi. 7 *(often pl)* kikundi cha watu wenye kazi/biashara n.k. ya aina moja *the industrial ~s* wenye viwanda vya biashara kwa pamoja *the shipping ~s* maslahi ya kampuni za meli kwa pamoja *vt* **~ sb in (sth)** tia moyo wa kupenda, vutia, tamanisha. **~ed** *adj* ~ **(in)** 1 -a kupenda, -a kupendelea, -a kupendezewa. 2 -liovutika, -liovutiwa, -lioshawishika/shabikia. **~ing** *adj* -a kupendelea. **~ingly** *adv*.

interface *n* 1 eneo linalomilikiwa na sehemu mbili. 2 *(fig)* eneo/ kipengee kinachojitokeza katika nyanja mbalimbali.

interfere *vi* 1 ~ **(in sth/with)** *(of persons)* jiingiza, jitia kati, jidukiza, ingilia. 2 ~ **(with)** *(of persons)* chezea, haribu *do not ~ with this machine* usichezee mashine hii. 3 ~ **with**, *(of events, circumstances etc)* zuia, ingilia, pinza, katiza. **~nce** *n*.

interim *n* 1 muda, wakaa. **in the ~** kwa wakati huu; katika muda/kipindi fulani cha kati, -a muda ~ *order* amri ya muda ~ *constitution* katiba ya muda.

interior *adj* 1 -a ndani. 2 -a bara, si -a pwani. 3 -a nchini, si -a kigeni *n* **the ~** 1 upande wa ndani, ndani. 2 bara ya nchi. 3 *Ministry of the I~* Wizara

ya Mambo ya Ndani.
interject *vt* chachawiza, hanikiza. **~ion** *n* kihisishi: neno la kuonyesha mshangao (k.m. ee! loo! ati! kumbe! haya! hebu! weye!).
interlace *vt, vi* ~ **(with)** fumana, ingiana, sokotana. **~ment** *n*.
interlard *vt* ~ **with** *(formal)* changanya (hasa lugha na maneno ya kigeni), tia kati, ingiza kati.
interleave *vt* ~ **(with)** changanya kurasa tupu na zilizoandikwa kitabuni.
interleaf *n* gombo.
interlink *vt,vi* ungana, unganisha, fungana.
intelock *vt,vi* unganisha, fungamana, ungana.
interlocutor *n* 1 mshiriki katika mazungumzo/majadiliano. **interlocution** *n* mazungumzo. **~y** *adj* 1 -a mazungumzo. 2 *(law)* -a muda ~ *order (decree)* amri ya muda ~ *proceeding* katikati ya shauri.
interloper *n* mdukizi.
interlude *n* 1 pumziko kati ya matukio/ vipindi viwili. 2 pumziko kati ya maonyesho mawili ya mchezo; muziki unaopigwa wakati huu. 3 nafasi kati ya sehemu za nyimbo za dini/zaburi.
intermarry *vt* ~ **(with)** *(of tribes, races etc)* oana kimseto, changanya damu. **intermarriage** ndoa ya mseto.
intermeddle *vt* jitia kati, jishughulisha na (hasa mambo ya watu wengine), ingilia.
intermediary *n* 1 mwamuzi, mshenga, msuluhishi. 2 kitu cha kati *adj* ~ **(between)** -a kishenga, suluhishi kati. **intermediate** *adj* -a kati, -a baina ya *n* 1 mwamuzi, wasta. 2 kitu cha kati. **intermediately** *adv*.
interment *n* maziko; kuzika.
interminable *adj* pasipo mwisho, -a kufululiza; -a kuchosha, -a kuchusha (kutokana na urefu). **interminably** *adv* milele, dumu daima.
intermingle *vt,vi* ~ **(with)**, changanya, changamanisha, changanyikana; seta.
intermission *n* kituo; pumziko *without* ~ bila kituo/pumziko.
intermittent *adj* -a vipindi, -a kwenda na kurudi, si -a kufululiza. **~ly** *adv*.
intermix *vt,vi see* **mix** changanya. ~ **ture** mchanganyiko.
intern[1] *vt* funga, zuia. **~ment** *n*. **~ee** *n* mfungwa.
intern[2] *n (US also* **interne**) *(US)* daktari mkufunzi (anayemaliza mafunzo kwa kukaa hospitalini chini ya uangalizi wa daktari) *(GB houseman)*. **~ship** *n*
internal *adj* -a ndani ~ *injury* maumivu ya ndani. ~ **combustion** *n* 1 mwako wa ndani. 2 -a nchi yenyewe ~ *affairs* mambo ya ndani ya nchi. 3 -a asili, -a moyoni. **~ly** *adv*.
international *adj* -a mataifa, -a kati/ baina ya mataifa; -a kimataifa ~ *court of justice* mahakama ya mataifa ~ *conferences* mikutano ya kimataifa ~ *competitions* mashindano ya kimataifa. ~ **money order** hawala ya fedha ya kimataifa *n* **the 1st/2nd/3rd** ~ vyama vitatu vya Kisoshalisti vya kimataifa vilivyoundwa mwaka 1864, 1889 na 1919. **~ism** *n* umataifa, nadharia inayotetea maslahi ya kimataifa. **~ist** *n* mtu anayetetea/unga mkono umataifa. **~ize** *vt* fanya -a kimataifa, fanya mali ya mataifa. **~ization** *n*. **~ly** *adv*. **~e** *n*. **the ~e** wimbo wa kimapinduzi wa kijamaa. **interne** *n see* **intern**[2]
internecine *adj (usu of war)* -enye kuleta madhara pande zote.
internee *n see* **intern**[1]
interpellate *vt* 1 kata kauli (waziri); katiza kwa kuuliza swali (kutaka maelezo). **interpellation** *n* swali, ulizo. 2 kukatiza mtu kwa maswali.
interphone *n (US) see* **intercom**.
interplanetary *adj* -a baina ya sayari.
interplay *n* uhusiano, mwingiliano.
Interpol *n (International Police Commission)* Shirika la Polisi la Kimataifa.
interpolate *vt* 1 toma maneno, tia maneno (yasiyokuwamo katika kitabu, hati, maandiko) *the book has*

been ~d kitabu kimetomwa maneno yasiyokuwamo kilipoandikwa. 2 *(maths)* jaza nambari zihusuzo. **interpolation** *n.*

interpose *vt,vi* 1 weka kizuizi, pinga (k.m. kura ya turufu). 2 ingilia kati, jitia kati; chachawiza. 3 ~ **(oneself) between;** ~ **in** -wa kati ya, -wa kiungo kati ya ~ *between disputants* suluhisha ugomvi, amua. **interpositon** *n.*

interpret *vt* 1 *(translate)* fasiri. 2 *(explain)* eleza, fafanua. 3 *(consider)* dhani/fikiria (kuwa maana yake). 4 *(of dreams)* agua. **~ation** *n* 1 fasiri, maelezo; ufafanuzi ~ *of statutes* fasiri/ufafanuzi wa sheria, fasiri ya sheria ~ *of maps* ufafanuzi wa ramani. **~er** *n* mkalimani. 2 mwaguzi.

interracial *adj* -a kati ya; -a kuhusu watu wa mataifa/asili tofauti.

interregnum *n* kipindi ambacho mtawala mpya hajachaguliwa kushika nafasi ya mtawala wa zamani; pumziko, muda kati ya matukio mawili.

interrelate *vt,vi* husisha; husiana, shirikiana. **interrelation** *n* ~ *of/ between* uhusiano (wa pande zote baina ya). **interrelationship** *n.*

interrogate *vt* 1 hoji, saili, dodosa. **interogator** *n* mhojaji. **interrogation** *n* 1 masaili. ~ **point** alama ya kuuliza. 2 kuhoji, kuuliza, kusaili. 3 kutahini kwa mazungumzo. **interrogative** *adj* 1 -a kuuliza. 2 *(gram)* -a kuuliza *interrogative pronouns (eg. who, which)* viwakilishi vya kuuliza (k.m. nani, kipi). **interrogatively** *adv.* **interrogatory** *adj* -a kuuliza *order of interrogatories* amri ya maulizo.

interrupt *vt,vi* 1 dakiza, chachawiza. 2 ingilia, katiza, pinga. **~er** *n* mtu/kitu kinachopinga/katiza/chachawiza. **~ion** *n* madakizo, katizo, zuio, pingamizi *there were many ~s* vilikuweko vipingamizi vingi.

intersect *vt,vi* 1 gawa kwa kukata/ pitisha/laza kimkingamo. 2 *(of lines)* kingamana, katana. **~ion** *n* 1 kukatana, mkingamano. 2 *(maths)* ungano, nukta (mistari inapokingamana/kutana).

intersperse *vt* 1 ~ **among/between** changanya, tawanya 2. ~ **with** changanyika. **interspersion** *n* mchanganyo.

interstate *adj* -a kati ya nchi na nchi ~ *pact* mkataba kati ya majimbo.

interstellar *adj* baina ya nyota ~ *space* anga baina ya nyota.

interstice *n* ufa, mwanya, kipenyo, kitundu.

intertribal *adj* baina ya makabila ~ *war* vita baina ya makabila.

intertwine *vt,vi* pota, sokota, potana, sokotana.

interval *n* 1 muda/wakati baina ya matukio mawili (hasa maonyesho ya mchezo) *at ~s* kwa vipindi *at short ~s* mara kwa mara, kwa vipindi vifupi. 2 nafasi baina ya vitu/vituo viwili *coconut trees planted at ~s of ten meters* minazi iliyopandwa kwa nafasi ya mita kumi. 3 *(music)* tofauti ya sauti baina ya noti mbili.

intervene *vi* 1 *(of events, circumstances)* ingilia kati. 2 ~ **(in)** *(of persons)* jitia kati; ingilia. 3 *(of time)* -ja, (-wa) kati ya. **intervention** *n* 1 kuingilia, kujitia kati. 2 *(armed)* uvamizi.

interview *n* mahojiano, masaili *vt* hoji, saili, dodosa. **~er** *n* mhojaji. **~ee** *n* mhojiwa, msailiwa.

interweave *vt,vi* ~ **(with)** fuma, fumana sokota, sokotana.

interwind *vt,vi* sokota; sokotana, zongomeza.

intestate *adj* -sioacha wasia.

intestine *n* matumbo *small ~* chango, uchengelele *large ~* utumbo mpana. **intestinal** *adj* -a matumbo.

intimate[1] *adj* 1 -a ndani, -a moyo, -a moyoni.2 -a siri ~ *friend* msiri, mwandani. **be/get on ~ terms (with) sb** -wa rafiki/mwandani wa. 3 *(thorough, complete)* kamili, -a -ote; -a undani ~ *knowledge* kujua sana *n* msiri, rafiki mwema, mwandani.

intimacy *n* 1 urafiki wa karibu sana, mwandani; *(euphem)* ngono, kujamiiana. 2 *(pl)* vitendo vya kimapenzi (k.m. kukumbatiana, kupigana busu n.k.). **~ly** *adv*.
intimate[2] *vt* **~ sth (to sb); (to sb) that,** arifu, tangaza, eleza; onyesha wazi wazi. **intimation** *n*.
intimidate *vi* **~ (into)** tisha, ogofya. **intimidation** *n*.
into *prep* 1 *(indicating motion/direction to a point within)* katika, kwenye, ndani ya *come ~ the house* ingia ndani ya nyumba. 2 *(indicating change of condition/result)*-ni; kuwa; kwa *she 'll get ~ trouble* ataingia matatani *the rain changed ~ snow* mvua iligeuka kuwa theluji **be ~ sth** *(mod use, colloq)* jiingiza, zamia. 3 *(maths)* kwa *4 ~ 24 (= 24 divide by 4) goes 6* 24 kwa 4 huwa 6.
intolerable *adj* -siovumilika, -siostahimilika *it is an ~ situation* hali hii haivumiliki. **intolerably** *adv*. **intolerant** *adj*. **~ (of)** -siovumilivu, -siostahimili. **intolerantly** *adv*. **intolerance** *n*.
intonation *n* lafudhi; kiimbo.
intone *vt* ingiza kiimbo, tia kiimbo (sema kwa sauti ya kuimba).
in toto *(Lat)* kwa jumla.
intoxicate *vt* 1 levya, lewesha, lewa *he is ~d* amelewa. 2 rusha akili, tia jazba, shindwa kujitawala. **intoxicating** *adj*. **intoxication** *n*. **intoxicant** *n* 1 kileo, kilevi *adj* -a ulevi.
intra - *pref forming adj* -a ndani ya, katika *~cellular* -a ndani ya seli *~cranial* -a ndani ya fuvu la kichwa **~ molecular** *(physics)* -a ndani ya molekyula *~mural* -a ndani ya (kanisa, chuo n.k.) *~muscular* -a ndani ya musuli *~cuterine (med)* katika uzazi. **~uterine device** (IUD) kitanzi, kidude cha kuzuia mimba *~venous* katika mishipa.
intransigent *adj* -siotaka/kubali mapatano/maafikiano; -enye msimamo usiobadilika. **intransigence** *n*.
intransitive *adj* -sio kikomo. **~verb** *n* kitenzi kisoelekezi. **~ly** *adv*.
intrench *see* **entrench**.
intrepid *adj* -jasiri, shujaa, hodari, jabari. **~ly** *adv*. **~ity** *n*.
intricate *adj* tatanishi, -enye kutatiza, -enye kutatanisha. **~ly** *adv*. **intricacy** *n*.
intrigue *vi,vt* **~(with sb) (against sb)** -la njama, vutia sana *n* 1 kula njama, kigwena. 2 mapenzi ya kuibana. **intriguer** *n*.
intrinsic *adj (of value, quality)* -a asili, halisi *~ value of a coin* thamani ya madini ndani ya sarafu. **~ally** *adv*.
introduce *vt* 1 wasilisha. 2 **~ into/to** anzisha, anza, leta. 3 **~ sb (to sb)** tambulisha, *(make acquainted)* julisha. 4 **~ (into)**, ingiza, penyeza. **introduction** *n* 1 utambulisho, ufahamisho *letter of ~* barua ya utambulisho. 2 kutambulisha (watu). 3 utangulizi. 4 *(of a textbook)* kitabu cha msingi (wa somo fulani). **introductory** *adj* 1 -a mwanzo; -a kuanzisha. 2 -a utambulisho.
introspect *vt* jipima, jichungua, jifikiria (kupata hali halisi ya mawazo, hisia n.k.). **~ion** *n*. **~ive** *adj*.
introvert *vt (mind/thought)* geuza ndani, elekeza ndani, peleka ndani *n* mndani. **introversion** *n*.
intrude *vi,vt* **~ (oneself) on/upon sb; ~ (oneself sth) into sth** dukiza, ingiwa *~ on sb's privacy* ingilia faragha ya mwingine *~ into other people's affairs* ingilia/jidukiza katika mambo ya wengine; leta/ingiza pasipo adabu (kwa jeuri au ufidhuli), jipenyeza, jidukiza. **~r** *n*. **intrusion** *n* **~ (on/upon/into)** 1 kujipenyeza, kujidu kiza, kuingilia. 2 dukizo. **intrusive** *adj*.
intrust *see* **entrust**.
intuit *vt,vi* hisi, jua, ng'amua (kwa maono juu ya kitu). **intuition** *n* 1 *(power of)* kipaji/uwezo wa kuelewa/kuhisi kitu haraka (bila kufikiria sana). 2 welewa, ujuzi (usiohitaji

kufikiri/wala ushahidi) ~ *as to the character of a person* ujuzi (maono) juu ya tabia ya mtu (bila kuwa na sababu thabiti) *have an ~ of sth* hisi. **intuitive** *adj* -enye kuweza kuhisi. **intuitively** *adv*.

inundate *vt* ~ **(with)** gharikisha, funikiza maji, furika katika; *(fig) (fill up)* jaza, zidi, eneza, songa *be ~d with requests*-wa, lemewa na maombi mengi. **inundation** *n*.

inure,enure *vt,vi* ~ **oneself/sb to** zoeza, zoea, lemaza *~d to* -zoevu wa.

invade *vt* vamia, shambulia, ingilia ~ *a state* vamia nchi ~ *sb's privacy* ingilia faragha ya mwingine ~ *sb's rights* ingilia haki ya mtu. **~r** *n*. **invasion** *n* 1 uvamizi, shambulio. 2 *(encroachment)* kuingilia. 3 *(leg)* ~ *of sb's rights* kuingilia haki ya mtu. 4 *(med)* kuingia kwa maradhi. **invasive** *adj* -a kuingilia (kivita), -a uvamizi, -nayoelekea kusambaa.

invalid[1] *adj* batili, -liotanguka, -a bure *declare ~* futa (cheti, hati n.k.). **~ate** *vt* fanya batili, batilisha, tangua. **~ation** *n*. **~ity** *n*.

invalid[2] *adj* 1 -gonjwa, -sio na nguvu, -siojiweza. 2 -nayofaa kwa wagonjwa ~ *chair* kiti cha kiwete *vi,vt* tendea kama asiyejiweza ~ *sb home* achisha mtu (hasa askari) kazi kwa ugonjwa n.k.

invaluable *adj* ~ **(to)** -a thamani sana, -a tunu, -siokadirika kwa kuwa na thamani sana (kwa kuwa na manufaa n.k.).

invariable *adj* -siobadilika, -siogeuka, sawasawa. **invariably** *adv* sikuzote, kila wakati.

invective *n* shutuma; matusi. ~ **language** lugha chafu.

inveigh *vi* ~ **against sb/sth** sema kwa hasira, shutumu, kemea, shambulia kwa maneno.

inveigle *vt* ~ **sb into (doing) sth** vuta kwa werevu (hila n.k.), laghai; shawishi, ghilibu. **~ment** *n*.

invent *vt* 1 buni, vumbua. 2 tunga, unda. **~ive** *adj*. **~or** *n*. **~ion** *n* 1 uvumbuzi, ubunifu *(something invented)* bidaa. 2 *(untruth)* uwongo, hila. 3 *(inventiveness)* akili ya kuvumbua (kubuni n.k.), werevu.

inventory *n* 1 orodha, hesabu, (ya vitu/ bidhaa).

invert *vt* pindua, geuza. **~ed commas** alama za mtajo. **inversion** *n*. **inverse** *adj* 1. -a kinyume, mbalimbali, -a kupinduka, pindu. 2 *(math)* ~ *matrix* solokinyume/pindu *inverse property* tabia ya kinyume *n* kinyume; *(math)* ~ *of relation* kinyume cha uhusiano. **inversely** *adv*.

invertebrate *adj* 1 -sio na uti wa mgongo. 2 *(fig) (of person)* legelege *n* (*bio*) mnyama asiye na uti wa mgongo, msouti wa mgongo

invest *vt* 1 ~ **(in)** tega uchumi ~ *money* tega fedha (uchumi). 2 ~ **in** *(colloq)* nunua (kitu cha manufaa). 3 ~ **with** -pa, vika, pamba ~ *with authority* -pa madaraka. 4 *(besiege)* zunguka, zingira, fanya mazingira .**~ment** *n* kitega uchumi. **~or** *n*. **~iture** *n* usimikaji/uingizaji/kuweka (kabidhisha, ingiza) katika kazi (cheo, daraja n.k.).

investigate *vt* 1 chungua, chunguza, peleleza ~ *a murder* chungua mauaji. 2 tafuta habari ya, hoji, hakiki. **investigator** *n*. **investigation** *n*.

inveterate *adj (esp. of habits, feelings)* -a zamani; -a nguvu; -zoevu, -lojijenga *an ~ thief/drunkard etc* mwizi/mlevi kupindukia/mzoefu/ aliyekubuhu.

invidious *adj* chochezi, -nayo -leta chuki. **~ly** *adv*.

invigilate *vi* simamia (wanafunzi wanaofanya) mtihani. **invigilator** *n*. **invigilation** *n*.

invigorate *vt* tia nguvu (uzima), imarisha, tia moyo.

invincible *adj* -sioshindika, -sioshindikana (kwa sababu ya kuwa na nguvu nyingi). **invincibly** *adv*. **invincibility** *n*.

inviolate *adj* -a wakfu, -siodhurika, -siokiukwa. **inviolable** *adj* -siokiukwa, -siodhurika, wakfu; -a heshima.

invisible *adj* -sioonekana *become* ~ toweka, tokomea. ~ **exports/imports** fedha inayopatikana kutokana na huduma, riba ya mtaji, utalii n.k.. ~ **mending** mshono uliofichika. ~ **ink** wino ambao mwandiko hauonekani mpaka karatasi ipashwe moto. **invisibility** *n.* **invisibly** *adv.*

invite *vi* 1 *(guests)* karibisha, alika. 2 *(attract)* vuta, shawishi. 3 ita, taka, omba *n (colloq)* aliko. **inviting** *adj* **invitingly** *adv.* **invitation** *n.*

invoice *vt* tengeneza ankara/bili *n* ankara; bili.

invoke *vt* 1 omba kwa Mungu/sheria n.k. 2 ~ **sth on/upon** omba, sihi. 3 *(by magic)* ita. **invocation** *n.*

involuntary *adj* -siokusudiwa, pasipo kutaka, bila kujua. **involuntarily** *adv.*

involute *adj* -enye sehemu nyingi, -lio tata, -liosokotwa kuzunguka; (kwa jani) kunjwa kwa ndani pembeni. **involution** *n.*

involve *vt* 1 ~ **(in)** husisha; ingiza matatani *I 'm not ~d in this matter* sihusiki, simo katika shauri hili. 2 -wa sababu ya, sababisha, maanisha. 3 **~d** *adj* tata, -gumu. **be/become/get ~d in sth/with sb** husika kwenye kitu fulani na mtu fulani. **~ment** *n.*

invulnerable *adj* -siodhurika *be* ~ -todhurika. **invulnerability** *n.*

inward *adj* -a ndani; -a moyoni. **~s** *adv* ndani, rohoni. **~ly** *adv.* **~ness** *n.*

inwrought *adj* -liopambwa kwa urembo.

iodine *n* aidini: madini ya joto.

ion *n (phys)* ioni. **~ize** *vi,vt* badilika kuwa ioni. **~ization** *n* uionishaji. **~sphere** *n* tabakaiyoni.

iota *n* herufi ya Kigriki *(fig)* chembe, kiasi kidogo sana *not an ~ of truth in the statement* maneno haya si kweli hata kidogo.

IOU *n* = **I owe you** naahidi kulipa (deni), hati ya kukiri deni, hakiri deni.

ipse dixit *(Lat)* ni kauli halisi yake.

Iran *n* Uajemi. **~ian** Mwajemi, mwenyeji wa nchi ya Uajemi *adj* -a Iran, -a Kiajemi.

irascible *adj (formal)* -a hamaki, -epesi kukasirika. **irascibility** *n.*

irate *adj (formal)* -a hasira, furufuru, -a harara.

ire *n (poet or formal)* hasira, ghadhabu, ufurufuru. **~ful** *adj.*

iridescent *adj* -enye rangi kama upinde wa mvua, -a rangi upindemvua. **iridescence** *n.*

iridium *n* **(ir)** *(chem)* iridiamu.

iris *n* 1 mboni. 2 airisi: aina ya mmea -maua wa majani ya umbo la upanga.

Irish *adj* -a Ireland ~ **potatoes** mbatata, viazi mviringo ~ *stew* supu ya nyama ya kondoo *n* lugha ya Kiairishi. 2 **the I~** Waairishi, watu wa Ireland.

irk *vt* udhi, kera, sumbua *it ~s me to (do sth)* nakerwa (kufanya). **~some** *adj* -a kuudhi, -a kero, sumbufu.

iron[1] *n* 1 chuma *as hard as* ~ -gumu sana; -a kama chuma. **rule with a rod of ~/with an hand** tawala kwa ukali. **a man of** ~ mtu mgumu; mtu asiye na huruma, mkatili. **an ~ fist in a velvet glove** ukatili uliofichika. **strike while the ~ is hot** udongo upate uli maji; samaki mkunje angali mbichi. **I~ Age** *(prehistoric)* Enzi ya Chuma. ~ **curtain** *(fig)* pazia la chuma, mpaka baina ya nchi zisizobadilishana habari wala biashara. ~ **lung** mashine ya kuvutia hewa. ~ **rations** akiba ya chakula cha dharura. 2 *(esp in compounds)* vifaa vya chuma. **(flat)** ~ *n* pasi **fire ~s** koleo; kingoe chenye kichwa cha chuma; chombo cha kutilia chapa. **have too many ~s in the fire** -wa na mambo mengi ya kufanya kwa wakati mmoja. *(pl)* **~s** pingu, minyororo 3. *(compounds)* **~-clad** *adj* -liolindwa kwa chuma. **~-foundry** *n* kiwanda cha (kukalibu) chuma. **~-grey** *adj n* rangi ya chuma. **~-monger** *n* mfanyabiashara wa bidhaa za chuma. **~-mongery** *n* biashara ya vyombo vya chuma. ~-**mould** *n* doa la kutu/wino. ~-**side** *n* askari mpanda farasi wa karne 17; *(fig)* mtu mbishi; mkaidi. ~-**ware** vyombo vya chuma. ~-**work** *n* kifaa kilichotengenezwa kwa chuma k.v. reli. ~-**works** *n (usu with sing v)* kiwanda cha chuma *vt,vi* piga pasi ~ *out* ondoa kwa kupiga pasi k.v. mikunjo; *(fig)* ondoa, suluhisha k.v. ugomvi. ~**ing-board** *n* ubao wa kupigia pasi.

irony *n* 1 kejeli; kinaya. 2 jambo la kinyume. **ironic, ironical** *adj* -a kejeli, -a kinaya. **ironically** *adv*.

irradiate *vt (formal)* 1 angaza, mulika, *(fig)* toa mwanga (juu ya jambo), dokeza. 2 tia nuru; ng'arisha, -wa angavu (kwa furaha).

irrational *adj* 1 bila mantiki/akili. 2 bila sababu; *(math)* -siowiana, witiri ~ *numbers* namba witiri/zisizowiana. ~**ly** *adv*.

irreconcilable *adj (formal) (of persons)* -sioweza kupatanishwa; *(of ideas, actions)* -siopatana.

irrecoverable *adj (formal)* -siopatikana tena, -siorekebishika; -siolipika ~ *losses* hasara isolipika.

irredeemable *adj (of paper currency)* 1 -siobadilishika kwa sarafu *(of government annuities)* -siodaika. 2 -siorudishika, -siookoleka.

irredentist *n (In politics)* mtu anayedai kuunganishwa kwa nchi zenye asili moja/kitamaduni n.k.

irreducible *adj* ~ **(to)** *(formal)* 1 -isopunguka, -siopunguzika, -sioweza kupunguzwa. 2 -siorekebishika.

irrefutable *adj* -siokanikana, -siokanushika, kweli, dhahiri.

irregular *adj* 1 -si -a kawaida; -siofuata kanuni ~ *attendance* mahudhurio ya wasiwasi, kutohudhuria mara kwa mara. ~ **troops** askari wasio wanajeshi, askari wa mgambo. 2 -siolingana; -siokuwa na taratibu. 3 *(gram)* -siofuata kanuni za kunyambulika, -siotabirika *n (usu pl)* mwanamgambo. ~**ly** *adv*. ~**ity** *n*.

irrelevant *adj* ~ **(to)** -siopasa, -siohusu. **irrelevance; irrelevancy** *n*.

irreligious *adj* -sioshika dini, -a kupinga dini.

irremediable *adj* -siorekebishika, -sioponyeka.

irremissible *adj* -siosameheka.

irremovable *adj* -sioondosheka, imara, madhubuti.

irreparable *adj (of injury, loss etc)* -siorekebishika, -siotengenezeka.

irreplaceable *adj* -siofidika ~ *loss* hasara isiyofidika

irrepressible *adj* -siozuilika, -siotulizika, -siodhibitika.

irreproachable *adj* -siolaumika, -sio na hatia, -sio na kosa.

irresistible *adj* -siokatalika, -siozuilika, -siokanika.

irresolute *adj* -a kusitasita, -sio shupavu, -sio na uamuzi. **irresolution** *n*.

irrespective *adj* ~ **(of)** bila kujali; bila kuangalia/zingatia.

irresponsible *adj* 1 -siowajibika, -siopaswa. 2 *(unreliable)* -sioaminika, -siotumainiwa. **irresponsibility** *n* utovu wa nidhamu/uaminifu, kutowajibika.

irresponsive *adj* -nyamavu, baridi. **be** ~ -tojibu, kaa kimya.

irretentive *adj* -sahaulifu *have an* ~ *memory* kuwa msahaulifu.

irretrievable *adj* -siopatikana tena; -siotengenezeka.

irreverent *adj* -sioheshimu vitu vitakatifu, safihi (wa vitu vitakatifu). ~**ly** *adv*.

irreversible *adj* -siogeuka; -siotangulika, -siobadilika; *(math)* -siogeuzika.

irrevocable *adj* -a makataa; -siotenguka, -siobadilika.

irrigate *vt* 1 mwagilia, nywesha. 2 jenga mabwawa, mifereji kwa ajili ya umwagiliaji. 3 osha kidonda (jeraha n.k. kwa maji yanayotiririka). **irrigation** *n* umwagiliaji, *(attrib) an irrigation project* mradi wa umwagiliaji.

irritate *vt* 1 kasirisha, sumbua, kera, udhi. 2 washa; choma. **irritation** *n.* **irritable** *adj* -enye kuudhika upesi; -enye harara. **irritably** *adv.* **irritability** *n.* **irritant** *adj* -a kuwasha; -a kusumbua, -a kukera *n* kitu kinachowasha/sumbua.

irruption *n* kuingia kwa ghafla na nguvu; kudukiza.

isinglass *n* utandogundi (unaotengenezwa na vibofu hewa vya samaki).

Islam *n* Uislamu; Waislamu wote; nchi zote za Kiislamu. **Islamic** *adj* -a Kiislamu.

island *n* kisiwa, kitu kifananacho na kisiwa (kwa kuwa peke yake au kuzungukwa na kitu kingine) *traffic~* kizingwa barabara: mahali katikati ya barabara pa kutenga magari. **~er** mzaliwa/mkazi wa kisiwani.

isle *n (not much used in prose, except in proper names)* 1 kisiwa *the Zanzibar ~s* Visiwa vya Zanzibar. 2 kijisiwa kidogo.

ism *n* itikadi/nadharia maalumu.

isn't *see* **be**[1]

isobar *n* isobaa: mstarikani (sawa) unaochorwa kwenye ramani kuunganisha au kuonyesha sehemu zenye msukumo wa hewa wa kiasi kimoja.

isolate *vt* ~ **(from)** tenga. **isolation** *n.* ~ **(from)** 1 kukaa upweke, upekee; kutenga ~ *hospital/ward* hospitali/ wadi ya wagonjwa wa kuambukiza. **isolationism** *n (in international affairs)* siasa ya kujitenga (kutojihusisha na mambo ya nchi nyingine). **isolationist** mtu aungaye mkono siasa ya kujitenga.

isosceles *adj (of a triangle)* -a pembe/pande pacha. ~ **triangle** pande/pembetatu pacha.

isotherm *n* hali joto sawa: mstari wa ramani unaounganisha mahali penye kadiri ile ile ya joto.

isotope *n* isotopu: atomi yenye uzito tofauti na atomi nyingine.

Israel *n* Uyahudi.

issue *vt, vi* 1 ~ **(out/forth) (from)** -ja, toka. 2 ~ **(sth to sb)**, ~ **(sb with sth)** toa, gawa (kwa ajili ya matumizi). 3 ~ **(to)** chapisha, toa stempu/noti mpya *n* 1 kutoka; kitokacho. 2 kutoa. 3 toleo. 4 suala, hoja **join/take ~ with sb (on/about sth)** jadili/toa hoja (juu ya jambo); bishana. **the point/matter at ~** suala linalojadiliwa 5 matokeo. 6 *(leg)* mtoto, dhuria.

isthmus *n* shingo ya nchi (iunganishayo mabara mawili.

it *pron* 1 *(used of lifeless things, or animals; when sex is unknown or unimportant)* hiki, hicho; huyo; huyu; hii, huu ~ *is a book* hiki ni kitabu. 2 *(used to refer to group of words which follow infinitive phrases)* ~ *is easy to learn Kiswahili* ni rahisi kujifunza Kiswahili; *(construction with for)* ~ *was hard for her to live on beer brewing* ilikuwa vigumu kwake kuishi kwa kupika pombe; *(gerundial phrase)* ~ *is no use trying to win me back* haitasaidia kujaribu kurudisha roho yangu; *a clause: does ~ matter what you do next?* ina tofauti yoyote kuwa utafanya nini baadaye? 3 *(used to refer backwards or forwards to identify sb or sth except when the identity of the person is known)* ~ *is the milkman* ni muuza maziwa. 4 *(used as a formal or meaningless word to supply a subject) dealing with weather, atmospheric condition etc* kuna ~ *is hot* kuna joto; *(for time)* ni ~ *is 18th of January* ni tarehe 18 Januari ya; *(for distance)* ~ *is five kilometres to Kileleni* ni kilometa tano hadi Kileleni; *(vaguely for the general situation or for sth that is understood from context) you've had* ~ utakiona. 5 *(used to bring into prominence one part of a sentence)* ~ *was his second book which made him famous* ni kitabu chake cha pili kilichomfanya mashuhuri *(the object of a verb)* ~ *is* *the pocket dictionary that I want* ni kamusi ya mfukoni niitakayo *(the object of a prep) ~ was Jimmy I gave the book to ni Jimmy* niliyempa kitabu (*an adverbal adjunct) ~ was on Monday that I saw him* ilikuwa Jumatatu nilipomwona *~s (poss) adj* -ake *the dog wagged ~ s tail* mbwa alitikisa mkia wake. ~ **self** *reflexpron* -enyewe. **by ~self** -enyewe *the machine works by ~self* mashine inajiendesha yenyewe, peke yake.

italic *adj (of printed letters)* -a italiki, -a mlazo *n (pl)* herufi mlazo za italiki. ~**ize** *vt* piga chapa kwa herufi mlazo za italiki.

itch *n (with def or indef art but rarely pl)* 1 mwasho *I have an ~* kitu kinaniwasha; nawashwa. 2 *(usu with the indef art or a poss adj)* shauku; hamu, uchu *vi* 1 washa *my hand ~es* kiganja changu kinawasha. 2 ~ **for** *(colloq)* -wa na hamu. **have an ~ing palm** -wa na hamu ya kupata fedha/ utajiri. ~**y** *adj*.

item *n* 1 kitu kimoja (agh. katika orodha). 2 aya, maelezo, kipengee ~ *of news* kipengee cha habari *adv* pia, aidha *(used to introduce successive articles in a list) ~ three* kitu cha tatu. ~**ize** *vt* andika/toa kitu kimojakimoja; orodhesha; chambua.

iterate *vt* kariri, rudiarudia, sisitiza. **it eration** *n*.

itinerary *n* 1 mpango/utaratibu wa safari; njia ya safari. 2 shajara ya safari *adj* -a safari. **itinerant** *adj* -a kuzungukazunguka, -a kutembea-tembea, -a kuvinjari. **itinerate** *vi* vinjari, zungukazunguka, tembeatembea. **itineration** *n*.

it'll *it will*. **it's** *it is/it has*.

I've I have

ivory *n* meno/pembe ya ndovu; *(attrib)* rangi ya pembe ya ndovu. ~ **tower** mahali palipojitenga/fanana na hali halisi ya maisha.

ivy *n* mwefeu: aina ya mmea unaotambaa wenye majani yenye ncha tano. **ivied** *adj* -liofunikwa na mwefeu.

izzard *n (arch)* herufi z.

J

J,j *n* herufi ya kumi katika alfabeti ya Kiingereza.

jab *vt,vi* 1 ~ **at** dukua, piga mduke. 2 ~ **sth into sth/sb** piga kwa nguvu. 3 ~ **sth out** chokoa *n* mdukuo, kipigo cha nguvu, dharuba *(colloq)* sindano.

jabber *vt,vi* payuka, bwabwaja, bwata, kupayuka. **~er** *n* mpayukaji.

jacana *n* sile, maua.

jacaranda *n* mjakaranda.

jack *n* 1 *J~ (familiar form of)* **John.** ~ **Frost** jalidi. ~ **in Office** kiongozi mdogo mwenye makuu/kujikuza, mrasimu, kimangimeza. ~ **of all trades** mjuaji wa kila kitu, mwenye kujaribujaribu kila kazi. **before one can say J~ Robinson** kufumba na kufumbua. **J~ is as good as his master** mtumishi na mwajiri wake wote sawasawa. 2 *(colloq)* mtu. **every man** ~ kila mtu. 3 *(usu portable)* jeki. 4 *(in the game of bowls)* mpira. 5 bendera ya meli (kuonyesha utaifa). **the Union** ~ Bendera ya Uingereza. ~ **staff** mlingoti wa bendera kwenye meli. 6 *(in a pack of playing-cards)* mzungu wa tatu, ghulamu. 7 *(compounds)* **~-in-the-box** *n* mwanasesere katika kasha. **~-o-lantern** kitu kisichoshikika (mf. moshi, gesi) *(fig)* fikra za kinyozi; boga lililokatwa mfano wa uso wakati wa sherehe ya Halloween. **~rabbit** *n* sungura mkubwa. **~tar** *n (old name for)* baharia *vt* ~ **sth in** *(sl)* telekeza. ~ **sth up** inua kwa jeki.

jackal *n* mbweha.

jackanapes *n* 1 mtu mwenye majivuno; mtukutu. 2 mtoto mtundu/mtukutu.

jackass *n* punda dume; mpumbavu. **laughing** ~ *(in Australia)* mkumburu.

jack-boot *n* buti buti linalofika magotini (k.m. buti ya mpanda farasi).

jackdaw *n* ndege mweusi jamii ya kunguru.

jacket *n* 1 jaketi. **dust a person's** ~ piga mtu. 2 *(cover)* kifuniko, kidhibiti joto. 3 maganda ya viazi. 4 ganda (la kitabu) *vt* funika.

jack-fruit *n* fenesi.

jack-knife *n* kisu kikubwa cha kukunja *vi (esp of an articulated truck)* kunjika.

jack-plane *n* randa ya kati.

jackpot *n* jumla ya fedha za kushindaniwa katika mchezo wa karata. **hit the** ~ kuwa na bahati, pata ushindi mkubwa.

jacobin[1] *n* mwanamapinduzi wa wakati wa Mapinduzi ya Ufaransa (1789) *adj* -a kishindo. **~ism** *n.*

Jacobin[2] *n* njiwa mwenye kishungi.

jade[1] *n* jiwe la thamani lenye rangi ya kijani kibichi.

jade[2] *n* 1 farasi aliyechoka na kuzeeka. 2 *(either contemptuous or playful)* mwanamke. **~d** *adj* hoi.

jag *n* ncha chonge; jino (la msumeno). **~gy. ~ged** *adj vt* keketa, kata (pasua) na kufanya mapengo; chana ovyoovyo.

jaguar *n* chui (wa Amerika ya Kusini na Kati).

jail see **gaol**.

jakes *n* (sl) choo.

jalopy *n (colloq)* mkweche, gari au ndege mbovu.

jalousie *n* dirisha la luva.

jam[1] *n* mraba, jemu. **money for** ~ *(sl)* kitu kipatikanacho bure/kwa bahati. **~- jar/-pot** *n* kopo la jemu. ~ **session** *n* kupiga mziki papo kwa papo/ faraguzi la muziki.

jam[2] *vt,vi* 1 ~ **(in/under/between etc)** bana, banwa, shindilia. 2 ~ **(on)** kwama, kwamisha, funga kwa nguvu ~ *on the brakes* funga breki kwa nguvu. 3 songamana; rundika. 4 zuia, ingilia mawasiliano ya redio *n* 1 msongamano. 2 kukwama, mkwamo. 3 *(sl)* hali ngumu/matata/mashaka.

jamb *n* 1 mwimo, mhimili. 2 *(pl)* kuta za meko, mafiga.

jampack *vt (colloq)* furika; jaa pomoni.

jamboree *n* 1 jamborii: hafla ya furaha. 2 mkusanyiko mkubwa (wa watu) hasa wa maskauti.

jangle *vt,vi* lia ovyo, kwaruza (kama kengele zisizopigwa vizuri); *(quarrel)* gombana, zozana *n* ukelele; mikwaruzo.

janitor *n* 1 bawabu. 2 *(US)* mhudumu wa ofisi.

January *n* Januari, mwezi wa kwanza.
japan *n* vanishi ngumu nyeusi *vt* paka vanishi.
jape *n (old use)* mzaha, utani.
jar[1] *n* 1 *(usu harsh)* mkwaruzo/ mtetemeko (wa sauti). 2 mshtuko.
jar[2] *n* gudulia; chupa kubwa, dumu, mtungi. **~ful** *n vt,vi* 1 ~ **against/on** gonga na kutoa sauti inayokera. 2 ~ **on** chukiza, kera. 3 shtua; shtuka. 4 ~ **(with)** achana, gongana, farakana. **~ring** *adj* -a kusababisha mfarakano; kali. **~ringly** *adv*.
jardiniere *n* chungu/dumu lililopambwa (la kuwekea maua ndani ya nyumba au dirishani).
jargon[1] *n* (aina ya) madini ya zirikoni.
jargon[2] *n* 1 istilahi, lugha ya kitaalamu. 2 lugha isiyoeleweka.
jasmine *n* yasimini/asmini.
jaundice *n* homa ya nyongo ya manjano; *(fig)* wivu, husuda *vt (usu passive)* athiri kwa wivu/husuda.
jaunt *n* mandari, matembezi *vt* fanya mandari. **~ing car** *n* gari la farasi la mandari. **~y** *adj* -a madaha, -enye kujiamini/kutosheka. **jauntily** *adv*. **jauntiness** *n*.
javelin *n* mkuki (agh. katika michezo) ~ *throw* kutupa mkuki.
jaw *n* 1 **(lower/upper)** ~ taya, utaya. **~-bone** *n* mfupa wa taya. **~-breaker** *n (colloq)* neno gumu kutamka. 2 *(pl)* kinywa *(sing)* sehemu ya chini ya uso; taya la chini. 3 mwingilio wa bonde, pango (hasa wa mahali pa hatari) *(fig) into/out of the ~s of the death* ingia/toka kwenye hatari. 4 *(pl)* **(machine)** kibanio. 5 *(colloq)* kidomo, payo; soga kubwa. 6 *(colloq)* mahubiri/wasifu/hotuba ndefu na ya kuchosha. ~ **(at)** *(colloq)* piga domo; hubiri.
jay *n* ndege kama kunguru mdogo mwenye rangi nyingi na milio mingi; *(fig)* mlimi, mpayukaji. **~-walker** *n* mtu atembeaye bila kujali usalama barabarani. **~-walk** *vi* kata barabara bila kujali usalama barabarani.
jazz *n* jazi (muziki uliobuniwa na Wamarekani weusi tangu karne ya 20). ~ **dancer** mcheza jazi *vt* 1 cheza katika mtindo wa jazi. 2 ~ **sth up** *(fig, colloq)* changamsha. **~y** *adj (colloq)* -a kijazi; maridadi, -zuri -enye kelele.
jealous *adj* 1 -wivu. **be** ~ ona wivu. 2 ~ **(of sb/sth)** -enye ngoa kijicho. 3 ~ **(of sb/sth)**, -wa mwangalifu. 4 *(in the Bible of God)* -enye kutaka upendo wote. **~ly** *adv*. **~y** *n*.
jean *n* 1 aina ya kitambaa kigumu cha pamba. 2 **~s** jinzi.
jeep *n* jipu: aina ya gari la sulubu/kazi.
jeer *vi,vt* ~ **(at sb)** zomea. **~ingly** *adv*.
jehad *see* **jihad**.
Jehovah *n* Mungu (katika Agano la Kale).
jejune *adj (formal) (of writing)* -siovutia, -siosisimua, -sioridhisha, kavu, chapwa; -a kitoto, -a kipuuzi. **~ly** *adv*. **~ness** *n*.
jell *vi,vt (colloq)* (*cause to*) ganda, dhihirika (katika umbo), pangisha, tengemaa. **~(ish)** *adj* kama jeli.
jellaba *n* juba lenye kofia (linalovaliwa na waarabu wanaume).
jelly *n* jeli. **~-fish** *n* kiwavi (wa baharini) *vt,vi* gandisha kuwa jeli. **jelled** *adj* -a jeli.
jemmy/jimmy *n* 1 mtaimbo/mtalimbo, nondo (agh. hutumiwa na wezi kufungulia milango).
jeopardize *vt* hatarisha. **jeopardy** *n* **be/place put in** ~ -wa/weka/ingia hatarini.
jeremiad *n* malalamiko, manung'uniko (marefu).
jerk[1] *n* 1 *(of a thing/muscles)* mkutuo, mshtuko *the tractor started to move with a* ~ trekta lilianza kuondoka kwa mshtuko. 2 *physical* ~ *s (colloq)* michezo/mazoezi ya viungo. 3 *(sl)* boza, bwege, mpumbavu *vt,vi* shtua, shtusha, shtuka, kutua ~ *sb out of sth* shtua mtu atoke katika hali fulani. **~y** *adj*. **~ily** *adv*. **~iness** *n*.
jerk[2] *vt* ng'onda/hifadhi nyama kwa kuikata vipande virefu na kukausha

juani.

jerry *n* 1 ~ **builder/building** mjenzi/ujenzi wa nyumba duni. 2 **~can** jarikeni, kipipa. 3 *(army sl)* askari wa Kijerumani. 4 *(sl)* msala, chombo cha kujisaidia (chumbani).

jersey *n* 1 (~ **wool**) kitambaa cha sufu; fulana nzito, jezi, sweta. 2 ng'ombe wa kisasa (ambaye asili yake ni Jersey).

jest *n* 1 kichekesho, masihara, mzaha, utani. **in** ~ kwa mzaha, kimzaha *a standing* ~ kichekesho *vi* ~ **(with)** toa mzaha, chekesha, fanya masihara, tania *it's not a matter of* ~ si utani. **~ingly** *adv*. **~ing** *adj*. **~er** *n* mcheshi, damisi.

Jesuit *n* 1 Mjesuti: mwanachama wa chama kimojawapo cha Kikristo. 2 *(derog)* mtu mwenye hila/mwerevu sana. **~ical** *adj*.

Jesus Yesu: mwasisi wa dini ya Kikristo.

jet[1] *n* 1 mchirizi wa ghafla (wa maji, mvuke) kutoka kwenye upenyo. ~ **propulsion (engine)** injini ya jeti. ~ **(air craft/air liner/fighter)** *n* jeti. **the** ~ **set** matajiri (agh. husafiri sana kwa ndege). 2 upenyo, bomba (la kutokea maji, hewa, n.k.) *vt,vi* to(k)a kwa nguvu, bubujika, foka (kwa nguvu). 2 *(colloq)* safirisha kwa jeti.

jet[2] *n* 1 jeti: namna ya jiwe jeusi sana linalotumika kufanya vifungo na mapambo ya mavazi. ~ **black** *adj* -eusi tititi.

jetsam *n* shehena n.k. iliyotoswa baharini kupunguza uzito wa jahazi (meli, chombo n.k.); shehena iliyotupwa baharini na kukokotwa pwani. **flotsam and** ~ *(fig use)* watu wasio na mbele wala nyuma, watu wasio na kazi wala makazi.

jettison *vt* tupa shehena baharini (ili kupunguza uzito wa jahazi n.k.) tupa/acha kitu/jambo lisilohitajika ~ *redundant workers* fukuza/punguza wafanyakazi wasiohitajika.

jetty *n* gati, bunta.

Jew *n* Myahudi. **~ess** *n* Myahudi wa kike. **~ish** *adj*.

jewel *n* 1 kito (k.m. almasi). 2 almasi bandia. 3 *(fig) (beloved)* kipenzi; tunu, mtu/kitu cha thamani *vt* 1 pamba kwa vito *(usu in pp)* a *~led ring* pete yenye vito a *~led watch* saa yenye almasi bandia. **~ler** *n* muuza vito. **~ry. ~lery** *n* mapambo ya vito.

Jezebel *n (derog)* kahaba, malaya.

jib[1] *n* 1 tanga la mbele la pembe tatu. **the cut of man's** ~ sura ya mtu. 2 mkono wa winchi.

jib[2] *vi (of a horse, etc)* simama ghafla; kataa kwenda *(fig)* kataa kuendelea. ~ **at** *(fig)* sita.

jibe *vi (US)* 1 *see* **gibe**. 2 *see* **gybe**.

jiffy *n (colloq)* muda mfupi. **in a** ~ sasa hivi, punde, mara moja *I shall come in a* ~ nitakuja sasa hivi, punde.

jig *n* 1 muziki wa dansi la yosayosa. 2 *(appliance)* kiongozi *vt,vi* 1 cheza dansi la yasayosa. 2 rukaruka, rusharusha.

jigger *n* 1 tekenya, funza. 2 toti: kipimo cha pombe kali kwenye mabaa.

jiggered *adj (pred only, colloq)* 1 -lio shangazwa *(well) I 'm ~!* nimeshangazwa. 2 hoi, -liochoka *I'm ~* niko hoi.

jiggery-pokery *n (colloq)* udanganyifu, ulaghai, upuuzi, mapayo.

jiggle *vt,vi* tingisha, vuta/sogeza kwa kushtua taratibu.

jigsaw *n* msumeno mdogo wa kutengenezea mapambo. ~ **(puzzle)** mchezo-fumbo (wa kupanga vipande ili kupata picha kamili).

jihad *n* jihadi; vita takatifu; *(fig)* kampeni kali (inayopinga au kuunga mkono mafundisho ya jambo fulani).

jilt *vt* vunja uchumba/mapenzi *n* mvunja uchumba.

Jim Crow *(Us derog)* mtu mweusi.

jiminy *int (colloq)* lahaula.

jim-jams *n (pl (sl)* **the** ~ woga wa kupita kiasi; wasiwasi, kutetemeka (kwa woga).

jimmy *see* **jemmy**.

jingle *n* 1 mlio (wa njuga, sarafu, funguo, kengele n.k.). 2 maneno yenye vina (yenye lengo la kuvutia k.m. katika tangazo la biasahra) *vt* 1 liza (njuga, sarafu, funguo, kengele n.k). 2 *(of verse)* tia vina rahisi.

jingo *n (pl)* mzalendo bubu (anayedharau nchi nyingine); ushari (kwa sababu ya uzalendo huu). **By ~** *(dated sl)* lahaula, kweli (kabisa). **~ism** *n* ugomvi, ushari, tabia ya kutaka vita. **~ist** *n.* **~istic** *adj* zalendo mno; -a shari, -anayetaka vita.

jinks *n (only in)* **high ~** vigelegele, hoihoi, shangwe, vifijo.

jinn *n see* **genie**.

jinx *n (colloq)* mtu/kitu chenye mkosi, nuksi. **put a ~ on sb** tia mtu mkosi.

jitney *n (US colloq)* 1 *(old use)* senti tano. 2 basi dogo.

jitters *n (pl)* **the ~** *(sl)* wasiwasi; woga wa kupita kiasi; kutetemeka kwa woga.

jittery *adj* **~bug** 1 dansi la yosayosa (miaka ya 1940); mtu achezaye dansi hilo *vt* cheza dansi la yosayosa.

jive *n* jaivu: aina ya dansi.

job[1] *n* 1 kazi. **on the ~** *(colloq)* -wa kazini; -wa na shughuli. **be paid by the ~** lipwa kipande, malipo ya kipande. **make a good/fine ~ of sth** fanya kazi vizuri. **odd ~s** kazi ndogondogo (zisizohusiana). **odd ~ man** mtu anayeishi kwa kufanya kazi ndogondogo. 2 **a good ~** *(colloq)* afadhali, bahati njema. **give sb/sth up as a bad ~** *(colloq)* puuza kitu/mtu. **make the best of a bad ~** fanya kila hali kuokoa kinachowezekana, kubali/pokea hali ilivyo. 3 **be/have a (hard) ~ doing/to do sth** -wa na kazi ngumu/nzito. 4 *(colloq)* ajira, kazi ya kuajiriwa; wadhifa. **out of a ~** -wa bila kazi (ya kuajiriwa). **~s for the boys** *(colloq)* kupeana nafasi za kirafiki/kindugu. 5 **~ lot** bidhaa shelabela (zilizonunuliwa pamoja). 6 **just the ~** -enyewe hasa *(colloq)* barabara, kama ilivyotakiwa. 7 *(sl)* kazi ya hila, kwa manufaa ya binafsi. 8 *(sl)* uhalifu (hasa wizi) *vt,vi* 1 fanya kazi ndogondogo za namna nyingi. 2 *(on the stock exchange)* fanya kazi ya uwakili/udalali; nunua/uza hisa kwa niaba ya wengine. 3 *(colloq)* tumia wadhifa kwa kupendelea rafiki zako. **~ber** *n* 1 dalali. 2 kibarua wa kazi ndogondogo. **~bery** *n* matumizi ya hila kwa faida za kibinafsi.

Job[2] *n (from the Book of ~ in the old Testament)* Ayubu; mvumilivu, mstahamilivu. **try the patience of ~** -wa ngumu kuvumilia; kera sana, -wa sumbufu. **a ~'s comforter** mtu anayeongeza uchungu kwa mtu aliyetakiwa kumliwaza.

jockey *n* 1 mpanda farasi katika mashindano *vt,vi* hadaa, laghai, danganya, ghilibu. **~ for position** *(in racing)* kumbakumba washindani wengine ili kupata nafasi nzuri; *(fig)* jaribu kwa ufundi au ujanja kupata manufaa fulani.

jocose *adj (formal)* cheshi, -a mzaha. **~ly** *adv.* **~ness. jocosity** *n.* **jocular** *adj* cheshi, -a mzaha. **jocularly** *adv.* **jocularity** *n.* mzaha, masihara. **jocund** *adj (liter)* cheshi, changamfu, kunjufu. **jocundity** *n* ucheshi, uchangamfu, ukunjufu.

jodhpurs *n (pl)* jodipa: suruali za kupandia farasi.

jog *vt,vi* 1 shtua, shtusha; tingisha kidogo, kutua, piga kikumbo. *(sl)* **~ sb's memory** kumbusha fulani. 2 *(go slowly)* enda polepole kwa mwendo wa wasiwasi. 3 **~ along/on** jikongoja, endelea pole pole kwa uvumilivu. 4 *(mod colloq)* jogi: kimbia polepole kama zoezi la viungo. **~ger** *n* mkimbiaji wa zoezi la viungo. **~ging** *n* 1 kujogi, zoezi la viungo la kukimbia. 2 kikumbo, mkutuo. 3 *(also ~* **trot)** mwendo wa polepole.

joggle *vt,vi* tikisa, sogeza/vuta kwa kushtua taratibu *n* mtikiso mdogo wa pole pole.

john *n (sl)* choo.

John Bull *n* Mwingereza (yeyote); taifa la Waingereza; Mwingereza hasa, tabia ya Kiingereza.

joie de viure *n (F)* kufurahia maisha.

join *vt,vi* 1 ~ **sth to sth/~ things together/up** unga, unganisha ~ *battle* anza kupigana. ~ **hands** shikana mikono, *(fig)* ungana, shirikiana. ~ **forces (with...)** fanya kazi na shirikiana na. 2 jiunga na, ingia ~ *the university* jiunga na, ingia chuo kikuu ~ *the association* jiunga na, ingia chama. ~ **up** *(colloq)* jiunga na jeshi. 3 ~ **(sb) in sth** ungana na, changanyika na, fuatana na *the next group will ~ us tomorrow* kikundi kingine kitaungana nasi kesho *n* kiungo, fundo. **~er** *n* seremala (agh. katika ujenzi wa nyumba). **~ery** *n* useremala (agh. wa shughuli za ujenzi wa nyumba). **~t** *adj* -a pamoja ~ *account* akaunti ya pamoja ~ *communique* taarifa ya pamoja *during their ~ lives* walipokuwa wanaishi pamoja. **~ly** *adv* kwa pamoja *n* 1 maungio 2 kiungo, fundo. **out of ~** *(of bones)* teguka, shtuka. **put sb's nose out of ~** *(fig)* pindua; fadhaisha; komesha. 3 *(of an ox, a sheep etc)* pande la nyama (k.m. mguu, paja, mkono). 4 *(sl)* mahali pa kuchezea kamari, kunywea vileo au madawa ya kulevya. **clip ~** baa ya gharama kubwa. 5 *(sl)* sigara yenye bangi *vt* 1 unganisha kwa kiungo. 2 gawanya kiungoni.

jointure *n (leg)* urithi wa mke (mali inayowekwa kwa urithi wa mke baada ya mume kufariki.

joist *n* boriti *(for carrying deck of vessel)* darumeti.

joke *n* kichekesho, dhihaka, mzaha, masihara. **have a ~ with sb** fanyia masihara, taniana na. **make a ~ about** fanyia mzaha/kichekesho. **a practical ~** utani (wa vitendo). **play a practical ~ on sb** tania mtu (kwa vitendo). **it's no ~** siyo mchezo, sio utani. **the ~ of the village** kichekesho *vi* fanya mzaha/dhihaka/utani. **jokingly** *adv*. **~r** *n* 1 chale, mcheshi, mfanya mzaha (masihara). 2 *(sl)* jamaa. 3 *(playing cards)* jokari.

jolly *adj* -a furaha, -changamfu, -liochangamka *adv (colloq)* sana *he was ~ miserable* alikuwa na huzuni sana *he'll ~ well have to do it* lazima afanye *vt (colloq)* bembeleza. **jollification** *n* shamra shamra. **jollity** *n*.

jolly-boat *n* mashua (ya meli).

jolt *vt,vi* 1 shtua, tingisha, rusharusha; *(fig)* shtua *the news ~ed us* habari zilitushtua ~ *along the road* rushwarushwa (na gari n.k.) *n* 1 mshtuo, mtikisiko. 2 *(fig)* mshtuko. **~y** *adj*.

Jonah *n* kisirani; mtu atolewaye kafara ili asilete nuksi.

josh *(US) (sl) vt,vi* cheza shere,fanya utani, tania.

joss *n* (*China*) sanamu ya mungu (iliyochongwa kwenye jiwe). **~-house** *n* hekalu la Kichina. **~-stick** *n* udi.

jostle *vt,vi* songa, sukuma, kumba. **don't ~ against me** usinisukume.

jot[1] *vt* ~ **sth down** andika upesi/mara moja (ukumbusho). **~ter** *n* kidaftari. **~tings** *n pl* kumbukumbu.

jot[2] *n* kipande kidogo, nukta *there's not a ~ of truth in it* si kweli hata kidogo.

joule *n (electr.) (abbr.J)* jouli.

journal *n* 1 gazeti; *(periodical)* jarida. 2 shajara, kitabu cha mambo ya kila siku, habari za kila siku *(naut)* batli. 3 daftari la kuwekea hesabu kabla ya kuandika katika daftari kubwa. 4 *(sl)* **the ~s** (katika bunge) rekodi za shughuli za kila siku. **~ese** *n* lugha chapwa za magazeti. **~ism** *n* uandishi wa habari. **~ist** *n* mwandishi wa habari. **~stic** *adj* -a uandishi wa habari.

journey *n* safari, mwendo *prepare for a ~* funga safari *set out on a ~* anza safari. **pleasant ~** safari njema *vi* safiri.

joust *n (hist)* mapambano (vita) ya mikuki mirefu kwa kutumia farasi *vi* shindana (hasa kwa wapanda farasi).

Jove *n* Jupita: Mungu wa Kirumi. **by ~!** Loo!

jovial *adj* bashasha, -liojaa furaha. **~ly** *adj*. **~ity** *n*.

jowl *n* taya; mashavu. **~y** *adj*.

joy *n* furaha, shangwe, nderemo *full of ~* furaha tele *wish sb ~ (of sth)* kumtakia mtu furaha (ya). **~-bells** *n* kengele za shangwe. **~-ride** *n (sl)* matembezi kwa motokaa (agh. bila ruhusa ya mwenye gari). **~-stick** *n (sl) (aviation)* usukani *vt,vi* furahia, furahiwa na. **~ful** *adj*. **~fully** *adv*. **~less** *adj* -sio na furaha. **~lessly** *adv*. **~fulness** *n*. **~lessness** *n*. **~ous** *adj*. **~ously** *adv*. **~ousness** *n*.

jubilant *adj* -a shangwe; -a ushindi. **be ~** -wa na shangwe. **~ly** *adv*. **jubilation** *n*.

jubilee *n* jubilii; sikukuu ya ukumbusho. **silver ~** jubilii ya mwaka wa ishirini na tano. **golden ~** sikukuu ya ukumbusho wa mwaka wa hamsini. **diamond ~** sikukuu ya ukumbusho wa mwaka wa sitini.

Judaism *n* 1 Uyahudi. 2 dini ya Kiyahudi. **Judaic** *adj*.

Judas *n* 1 Yuda (aliyemsaliti Yesu), mhaini, msaliti. 2 **~-hole** (kwa mlango) kitundu cha kuchungulia.

judder *vi* tetemeka sana, tingishika sana.

judge[1] *n* 1 *(leg)* hakimu, kadhi *(High Court)* jaji. **~ made law** kanuni zinazotokana na maamuzi ya mahakama. 2 *(competition)* mwamuzi. 3 *(critics)* mhakiki, mtaalam *vt,vi* 1 hukumu, toa hukumu. 2 amua. 3 *(estimate)* kisia, dhani, ona *~ it good to do sth* ona vema kufanya jambo fulani *~ a man by his actions* mpime mtu kwa matendo yake. **~ment** *n* 1 hukumu *binding ~* makataa. **concurring ~** hukumu ya mwafaka *dissenting ~* hukumu isiyowafiki. **the Last ~/~ Day** siku ya kiyama/hukumu ya mwisho *sit in ~ on sb* hukumu mtu fulani *~ seat n* kiti cha hukumu. 2 *(opinion)* shauri, maoni *in my ~* kwa maoni yangu. 3 *(wisdom)* akili, busara, ujuzi. 4 *(taste)* akili ya kutambua au kuchagua mazuri *use your ~* tumia uamuzi wako.

judiciary *n* Idara ya Mahakama; jamii ya majaji *independence of the ~* uhuru wa mahakama. **judicature** *n* 1 usimamiaji haki. 2 jamii ya majaji. **judicial** *adj* 1 -a jaji, -a kimahakama *~ murder* hukumu ya kifo isiyo haki. 2 -a haki, -siopendelea. **judicious** *adj (formal)* -enye akili, -a busara. **~ly** *adv*. **~ness** *n*.

judo *n* judo: mchezo wa mieleka uchezwao sana na Wajapani.

jug[1] *n* 1 jagi, dumu. 2 *(sl)* gereza, jela. **~ful** *adj*.

jug[2] *vt* 1 *(usu in pp)* pika katika chungu kilichofunikwa. 2 *(colloq)* funga gerezani.

juggernaut *n* 1 imani ya kutoa kafara/mhanga. 2 *(colloq)* tela, gari kubwa la usafirishaji.

juggle *vi,vt* 1 ~ **(with)** fanya kiinimacho; fanya mizungu. 2 *(distort etc)* chezea (ili kudanganya); ghushi. **~r** *n*.

jugular *adj* -a shingo, -a koo *~ vein* halkumu.

juice *n* 1 maji ya matunda/nyama n.k.; juisi *(of grated coconut)* kasimile, tui. 2 *digestive/gastric ~* maji-tumbo. 3 *(colloq)* mafuta, umeme, gesi. **juicy** *adj* 1 -enye maji mengi. 2 *(colloq)* nayovutia (kwa sababu inaongelea tabia/kashfa za mwingine) *give me all the ~ details* , leta umbeya wote. **juiciness** *n*.

ju-jitsu *n* (*Japan*) mchezo wa mwereka wa kujilinda/kujihami.

juju *n* (*West Africa*) 1 uchawi, ushirikina, ulozi. 2 kinyago cha uchawi.

juke-box *n* sanduku la santuri.

July *n* Julai: mwezi wa saba.

jumble *vi,vt* ~ **(up)** changanya, vuruga, fuja *n* fujo, vurugu, mchanganyiko. **~-sale** *n* seli ya mtumba/vikorokoro.

jumbo *adj* kubwa sana.
jump[1] *n* mruko, ruko, chupo. **long/high** ~ (mchezo wa) kuruka chini/juu. 2 mshtuo. **give sb a** ~ shtua. **the ~s** *(colloq)* kutetemeka. 3 kupanda kwa ghafla *yesterday there was a ~ in the price of rice* jana bei ya mchele ilipanda ghafla *vi,vt* 1 ruka, chupa. ~ **down sb's throat** varanga. **~ing-off place** mahali pa kuanzia. **~ed-up** *adj (colloq)* -enye majivuno, -enye kujidai, mjivuni. 2 ruka juu yao. ~ **the rails/track** acha reli. 3 shtuka, chachawa. 4 panda ghafla, ruka *the price of oil has ~ed* bei ya mafuta imepanda ghafla. 5 ~ **at** ruka, pokea kwa furaha, vamia. ~ **to conclusions** fikia uamuzi bila kutafakari. ~ **on/upon** karipia. 6 ~ **(one's bail)** toroka dhamana. ~ **a claim** pokonya eneo la mwingine (kwenye machimbo). ~ **the gun** anza mapema, wahi. **(go and)** ~ **in the lake** *(colloq)* toka hapa. ~ **the queue** ruka foleni, *(fig)* -tofuata utaratibu.
jumper *n* 1 sweta. 2 *(US)* aproni. 3 mrukaji, kirukaji.
junction *n* 1 njia panda. 2 mwungano ~ *box* kasha la mwungano wa waya za umeme.
juncture *n* mwungano. 2 hali ya jambo. *(esp in the phrase)* **at this** ~ kwa hali ya mambo yalivyo/yalivyokuwa.
June *n* Juni: mwezi wa sita.
Jungle *n (usu* **the** ~ *sing, or pl)* msitu. **the law of the** ~ *(fig)* kanuni ya mwenye nguvu mpishe/mabavu. **jungly** *adj* -a kimsitu.
junior *n* mdogo (wa umri au cheo) *he is my* ~ yeye ni mdogo kwangu *(US schools and colleges)* mwanafunzi wa mwaka wa tatu (kati ya minne) ~ *common room* ukumbi wa wanafunzi *adj* -dogo (kwa umri) -a chini ~ *class* darasa la chini.
juniper *n* mreteni.
junk[1] *n* 1 *(rubbish)* takataka, vikorokoro. ~ **dealer/shop** mwuza/duka la vikorokoro/bidhaa kuukuu (zilizotupwa).
junk[2] *n* jahazi la Kichina.
junket *n* 1 mtindi mtamu. 2 mandari yenye chakula *vi* enda mandari ya chakula. **~ing** *n* kufanya karamu.
junkie,junky *n* mlevi wa madawa ya kulevya.
junta *n* halmashauri ya utawala, baraza la majeshi (waliopindua serikali).
Jupiter *n* 1 *(of ancient Rome)* Jupita: Mungu Mkuu wa Warumi. 2 Jupita (sayari iliyo kubwa).
jury *n* 1 baraza la wazee wa mahakama. **grand** ~ baraza la uchunguzi wa awali. ~ **box** *n* kizimba cha mzee wa mahakama. **coroner's** ~ wazee wa mahakama wanaotoa uamuzi wa sababu ya kifo. 2 *(in competition)* waamuzi *(fig) the ~ of public opinion* uamuzi wa umma. **~man** *n* mzee wa baraza; mwamuzi. **jurist** *n* mwanasheria. **juror** *n* mzee wa baraza. 3 mtu anayeapishwa, mtu anayekula kiapo. **juridical** *adj* -a sheria, -a taratibu za kisheria. **jurisdiction** mamlaka, mamlaka ya kisheria, utekelezaji wa sheria *the issue is within my jurisdiction* suala hili lipo katika mamlaka yangu. **jurisprudence** *n* 1 sayansi na falsafa ya sheria za binadamu. 2 maarifa ya sheria.
jury-mast *n (naut)* mlingoti wa muda (uliotiwa badala ya mwingine uliovunjika au kupotea).
just[1] *adj* 1 -a haki, nyofu, -adilifu *a ~ sentence* hukumu ya haki *a ~ person* (mtu) mwadilifu. 2 *(well-deserved)* -enye kustahiki, -liostahili. **~ification** *n* 1 kitu au sababu zinazothibitisha. 2 kuthibitisha jambo kuwa ni haki, kusadikisha. 3 haki, halali *without* ~ bila ya haki/uthibitisho. **in ~ (for/of sth/sb)** kwa kuthibitisha/kutetea jambo. **~ify** *vt* 1 tetea, thibitisha uhalali wa jambo/tendo ~ *the punishment you meted out* thibitisha uhalali wa adhabu uliyoitoa. 2 -wa na sababu ya kufanya jambo, halalisha *finishing your work early does not ~ your*

loitering kumaliza kazi kwako mapema sio sababu ya kukufanya uzurure. 3 *(of print)* rekebisha. **~ifiable** *adj*. ~ **ifiably** *adv*.

just[2] *adv* 1 used *(GB) in the perfect tenses and (US often) with the simple past tense placed with the v to indicate an immediate past (GB)* sasa hivi, ndio kwanza *I have ~ finished my work* ndio kwanza nimemaliza kazi yangu. ~ **now** sasa hivi. 2 *(followed by n phrases and clauses)* hasa *this is ~ the person wanted to see* huyu ndiye hasa mtu niliyetaka kumwona. 3 ~ **as (+adj+as)** sawasawa na *it is ~ as good as mine* ni kizuri sawasawa na changu *(introducing adverbials of time)* wakati *he brought it ~ as you were leaving* alikileta wakati ule ule ulipokuwa unaondoka *(introducing clauses of comparison)* jinsi ~ *as you find it difficult to depend on your pay* jinsi inavyokuwia vigumu kutegemea mshahara wako. 4 *(with adv)* ~ **here** hapa hapa. 5 *(used to indicate approximation)* takribani *it was ~ about 9.00 a.m.* Ilikuwa takribani saa 3.00. 6 asubuhi tu. (*only*) **He ~ managed to get the fare** amefanikiwa kupata nauli tu *I have ~ enough money for food* nina fedha za kununulia chakula tu *I am ~ an ordinary person* mimi ni mtu wa kawaida tu. 7 *(used in familiar colloqual style)* hebu ~ *look at this and see how good it is* hebu tazama hiki na uone jinsi kilivyo kizuri. 8 *(colloq)* sana, mno *the story was ~ too good* hadithi ilikuwa nzuri mno. 9 wakati huuhuu uleule. ~ **now** muda huu; muda kitambo, punde *Saida left ~ now* Saida ameondoka punde.

justice *n* 1 haki *treat all men with ~* tendea watu wote (kwa) haki. **do ~ to** tenda haki. **do oneself ~** jitendea haki, -fanya jambo kulingana na uwezo wako. 2 mamlaka ya kisheria. **bring sb to ~** peleka mhalifu mahakamani akahukumiwe. 3 jaji wa Mahakama Kuu. **Chief** ~ Jaji Mkuu. ~ **of the Peace** *(JP)* hakimu wa Amani. **Department of** ~ *(US)* Ofisi ya Mwanasheria Mkuu. **justiciary** *n* Mamlaka ya Jaji au Jaji Mkuu.

jut 1 *vi* ~ **out** tokeza. 2 *n* kutokeza.

jute *n* kitani.

juvenile *n* kijana, mtoto ~ *court* mahakama ya watoto ~ *books* vitabu vya watoto ~ *deliquency* uhalifu wa vijana.

juxtapose *v* weka sambamba, **juxtaposition** *n*.

K

K,k *n* herufi ya kumi na moja katika alfabeti ya Kiingereza).
kaaba *n* kaaba: jengo takatifu (linalozungukwa wakati wa hija, Makka).
Kaiser *n* Kaizari: mfalme wa Ujerumani kabla ya 1918.
kampong *n* (*in Malaysia*) boma, uzio, kijiji.
kale *n* kale: aina ya kabichi.
kaleidoscope *n* nelibini.
kangaroo *n* kangaruu. ~ **court** mahakama isiyo halali (iliyoundwa ili kuwaadhibu watu walioikosea jamii). **kaolin** *n* kauri.
kapok *n* sufi.
kaput *adj* (*pred only*) (*sl*) -lioharibika; -liokwisha.
karat *see* **carat**.
karate *n* kareti: mbinu za kujihami kwa mikono na miguu.
kayak *n* kayaki: mtumbwi wa Kieskimo uliofunikwa kwa ngozi ya sili.
kebab *n* mshikaki.
keel[1] *n* 1 meli ya wachimba mkaa, kuchukua mkaa. 2 shehena ya makaa.
keel[2] *n* mkuku. **(keep) on an even** ~ *(of a ship)* bila kuyumbayumba (*fig*) tulia *vi,vt* pindua, pinduka ~ **over** pinduka. ~ **haul** *vt* 1 buruza mtu majini nyuma ya meli (kama adhabu). 2 kemea/ adhibu vikali.
keen[1] *adj* 1 (*of feelings, points & edges etc*) kali, -enye makali; (*fig*) **a ~ wind** upepo mkali. 2 (*of persons, their character)* -enye bidii, hodari. 3 (*of the mind, interest*) sana, -enye kupenda sana. **be ~ on** (*colloq*) penda. **~ly** *adv*. **~ness** *n*.
keen[2] **(Irish)** *n* maombolezo *vi,vt* omboleza.
keep[1] *vt,vi* 1 weka, zuia; fanya kuwa ~ *the class quiet* nyamazisha darasa. ~ **sb indoors** zuia mtu asitoke nje. ~ **an eye on** (*colloq*) angalia kwa makini, linda. ~ **sth in mind** kumbuka. 2 endeleza, weka ~ *sb waiting* ngojesha, fanya mtu aendelee kungoja. ~ **sb going** wezesha mtu kuendelea *shs 10,000/= will ~ me going for four days* shiiling 10,000/= zitanitosheleza kwa siku nne. 3 ~ **sb/sth from doing sth** zuia, kinga *you must ~ the wall from falling* lazima uzuie ukuta usianguke *we couldn't ~ from crying* hatukuweza kujizuia kulia. 4 ~ **sth (back) (from)** ficha *I can't ~ anything (back) from you* siwezi kukuficha kitu; zuia, kata *the employer ~s back 3000/= a month for my pension* mwajiri wangu hukata 3000/= kila mwezi kwa ajili ya kiinua mgongo changu. ~ **sth to oneself** (*often imper*) hifadhi, dhibiti, kaa na (kitu) ~ *your views to yourself* usiseme/usitoe maoni yako; nyamaza. 5 (*with an implied complement*) timiza ~ *a promise* timiza ahadi ~ *the law* fuata sheria. 6 adhimisha ~ *one's birthday* adhimisha siku ya kuzaliwa. 7 linda. 8 hifadhi, tunza ~ *the money for me* nitunzie fedha zangu. ~ **a firm/tight hold on** shika imara. 9 ruzuku, kimu, fuga *his salary ~s him and his family* mshahara wake unamkimu yeye na familia yake *he ~s cattle on his farm* anafuga ng'ombe katika shamba lake. 10 weka ~ *a note of sth* weka kumbukumbu ya kitu ~ *a ledger* tunza daftari. ~ **accounts** tunza mahesabu. 11 -wa na, miliki ~ *a shop* -wa na duka. **shop~er** mwuza duka. 12 tunza, simamia. ~ **a house** tunza nyumba. ~ **open house** -wa tayari kukaribisha wageni/marafiki. 13 ~ **on/to** endelea. **K~ cool** (*fig*) tulia! poa! **~fit** kaa imara/bora wa afya ~ *to the left* enda upande wa kushoto ~ *straight on* enda moja kwa moja ~ *right* enda upande wa kulia. 14 ~ **(on) doing sth** endelea kufanya jambo, fanya jambo mara kwa mara ~ *smiling* endelea kutabasamu *my shoe ~s (on) coming off* kiatu changu kinatoka mara kwa mara. ~ **going** endelea bila kusimama/kukoma. 15 (*of food*) -toharibika, kaa *the food will ~ till tomorrow evening* chakula hakitaharibika/kitakaa hadi kesho jioni. 16 *(uses with adverbial particles and preps)* ~ **at sth** shikilia; kazania;

fanyia kazi, sikate tamaa. ~ **sb at sth** kazania mtu aendelee na jambo fulani, himiza, tia ari. ~ **away (from) (sth)** epuka, kaa mbali na ~ *away from the dog* mwepuke yule mbwa. ~ **sb/sth away (from)** epusha, zuia asikaribie. ~ **back (from sth)** kaa/baki nyuma. ~ **sb back** zuia mtu asiende mbele. ~ **sb down** gandamiza, dhulumu. ~ **sth down** zuia ~ *down your anger* zuia hasira yako; punguza ~ *down your expenses* punguza matumizi yako. ~ **in** (*eg of fire*) endelea kuwaka *the fire will ~ in till I come back* moto utaendelea kuwaka mpaka nitakaporudi. ~ **in with sb** endelea kuwa na uhusiano mzuri, elewana/patana. ~ **sb in** zuia kama adhabu. ~ **off** kaa mbali. ~ **off sth** -sikaribie kitu fulani, -tojihusisha na. ~ **sb/sth off** zuia ~ *your hands off me* usiniguse. ~ **on (doing sth)** endelea, shikilia. ~ **on working** endelea kufanya kazi. ~ **sth on** endelea kuvaa. ~ **sb on** endelea kumwajiri mtu. ~ **on at sb** sumbua kwa malalamiko, maswali n.k. ~ **out (of sth)** kaa mbali, -tojiingiza. ~ **sb/sth out (of sth)** zuia kuingia ~ *out of my business* usingilie shughuli zangu. ~ **to sth** timiza, fanya jambo lililokubaliwa ~ *to your promise* fanya kama ulivyoahidi, timiza ahadi yako. ~ **to oneself** jitenga, epuka kukutana na watu. ~ **sb/sth under** tawala, zuia ~ *the fire under* zuia moto usienee. ~ **up (with sb)** enda kwa kasi/mwendo sawa na mtu mwingine *Juma kept up with his classmates* Juma aliendelea sawa na wenzake. ~ **up with the Joneses** shindana na majirani (katika kuhodhi vitu) (gari, nguo n.k.). ~ **sb up** chelewesha mtu kulala mapema *Don't ~ the children up* usiwacheleweshe watoto kulala. ~ **sth up** zuia kitu kisizame au kuteremka chini ~ *up your courage* jijasirishe zaidi; fuata, heshimu ~ *up old customs* endeleza/fuata mila za kale; endelea *we will ~ up the discussion the whole day* tutaendelea kujadili mchana kutwa; tunza *it costs me a great deal to ~ up my farm* inanigharimu sana kulitunza shamba langu. ~ **it up** endelea *n* 1 riziki, chakula. 2 mnara wa ngome/boma. 3 **for** ~ (*colloq*) kwa kudumu, daima, abadani *this is mine for ~s* hii ni mali yangu kabisa/abadani. **~er** *n* 1 mlinzi, mwangalizi. 2 (*in compounds*) **gate** ~ bawabu. **park** ~ mwangalizi wa hifadhi. ~ *n* 1 hifadhi, ulinzi. **in safe ~ing** mahali pa usalama. 2 (*in verbal senses*) ufugaji. **in/out of ~ (with)** -a kupatana/-siopatana na. **~sake** *n* kumbukumbu, ukumbusho.

keg *n* kikasiki, kipipa.

kelp *n* 1 majani ya bahari, mwani. 2 majivu ya mwani.

ken *n* (*only in*) **beyond/outside my** ~ (*colloq*) nje ya ujuzi/utambuzi wangu *vt* (*Scot*) fahamu, tambua.

kennel *n* 1 kibanda cha mbwa. 2 chaa ya kufuga na kufundisha mbwa *vt,vi* weka/tunza mbwa.

kept *see* **keep**.

kerb (*also* **curb**) *n* ukingo wa barabara (wa kikuta). **~stone** jiwe la ukingo wa barabara.

kerchief *n* kitambaa; leso.

kerf *n* mkato wa msumeno.

kernel *n* kiini *wheat* ~ kiini cha mbegu ya ngano, (*fig*) ~ *of argument* kiini cha hoja.

kerosene *n* kerosini, mafuta ya taa.

ketch *n* mashua/chombo kidogo cha milingoti miwili.

ketchup *n* kechapu: nyanya na viungo tamutamu.

kettle *n* birika, kandirinya *put the ~ on* teleka birika.

kettle-drum *n* ngoma ya shaba nyeupe.

key[1] *n* 1 ufunguo (wa mlango, saa n.k.). ~ **hole** tundu la ufunguo. ~ **money** kilemba. **~ring** pete ya ufunguo. **master/skeleton** ~ ufunguo malaya. 2 ~ **(to)** (*fig*) ufumbuzi. 3 ufunguo wa saa. 4 (*of text book*) majawabu, (*translation*) tafsiri. 5 (*also attrib*) mlango *a ~ position* nafasi maalumu. 6 (*attrib*) muhimu ~ *industry* tasnia muhimu (kwa ajili ya uendelezaji wa viwanda vingine). **~stone** *n* (*archit*) jiwe la kiungo kwenye tao; (*fig*) msingi/jambo muhimu. 7 kibao cha tapureta/piano/ kinanda/filimbi ~ *board* msururu wa vibao hivyo. 8 *(music)* ufunguo (mfululizo wa noti wenye mfumo maalumu); (*fig*) namna/mtindo wa sauti/mawazo *in a minor* ~ kwa huzuni *all in the same* ~ bila kuonyesha hisia; kwa sauti ya namna moja. ~ **note** *n* noti ya msingi; (*fig*) wazo linalojitokeza.

key[2] *vt* linganisha sauti (kwa kukaza/ kulegeza nyuzi). ~ **sth in** patanisha kitu na vingine. ~ **sth into sth** patanisha/unganisha vitu. ~ **sb up** chochea/amsha mtu.

key[3] *n* kisiwa kidogo/tambarare (cha matumbawe).

khaki *n* kaki *adj* -enye rangi ya kaki, -a kaki.

khan[1] *n* khan: cheo cha watawala na maofisa wa Asia ya Kati, Afghanistan n.k. (*in olden times*) (jina la cheo la) mfalme wa Waturuki; Watarta wa Mongolia.

khan[2] *n* (*in the East*) hotel yenye ua (inayotumiwa na misafara).

kick[1] *n* 1 teke. **get more ~s than halfpence** shukrani ya punda ni mateke. ~ **back** *n* (*US sl*) bahashishi; kiasi cha fedha (apewacho mtu kwa kumpatia mwingine mapato). 2 (*colloq*) msisimko. **do sth for ~s** fanya kwa kusisimka. **be on a** ~ (*sl*) zama katika shughuli. 3 (*colloq*) nguvu. **he has no ~ left in him** amechoka, yu hoi. 4 kushtua kwa nguvu. ~ **start (er)** pedali ya kuwashia pikipiki *vt,vi* 1 piga teke. ~ **the bucket** *(sl)* fariki. ~ **a goal** (*Rugby football*) funga goli. ~ **one's heels** kaa bure/bila kazi. ~ **sb up stairs** (*fig*) toa mtu mahali fulani kwa kumpa cheo kikubwa zaidi. 2 *(of a gun)* shtuka baada ya kufyatuliwa. 3 (*special uses with adverbial particles and preps*) ~ **against/at** pinga, onyesha kuudhika/ kulalamika/kutoridhika; kaidi. ~ **off** *(football)* anza mchezo. ~ **sth off** vua kwa kupiga teke, kwa kutupa/kurusha miguu ~ *off one's slippers* vua ndara kwa kupiga teke. **~off** *n* kuanza. ~ **sb out** fukuza mtu. ~ **sth up** pandisha kitu kwa kukipiga. ~ **up a fuss/ shindy/row/stink** (*colloq*) sababisha fujo, leta vurumai kwa kubisha. ~ **up one's heels** (*of a horse*) rukaruka baada ya kutumikishwa; (*fig*) jifurahisha.

kibbutz *n* kibuzi; shamba/makazi (ya kijamaa Israeli). **~nik** mwanakibuzi.

kid[1] *n* 1 mwana mbuzi. 2 ngozi ya mwana mbuzi. ~ **gloves** glavu za ngozi ya mwanambuzi. **handle sb with ~ gloves** (*fig*) shughulikia kwa unyenyekevu (pasipo kuwa mkali). 3 (*sl*) mtoto (*US sl*) kijana *college ~s* vijana wa chuo. **~dy** *n* (*sl*) kitoto, mtoto mdogo *vt* (*of a goat*) zaa.

kid[2] *vt,vi* (*sl*) (kwa kuongopa) tania; danganya *don't ~ yourself*, usijidanganye.

kidnap *vt* iba mtoto; teka nyara *n* **~per** mtekaji nyara; mwizi wa watoto.

kidney *n* 1 figo. ~ **bean** haragwe jekundu. ~ **machine** mashine ya figo (mashine itumiwayo kufanya kazi ya figo kwa mgonjwa wa mafigo).

kill *vt,vi* 1 ua, fisha. ~ **sb/sth off** ua; ondosha ~ *time* jishughulisha wakati wa kungoja. 2 poteza, haribu, fifisha *the red carpet ~s your curtains* zulia jekundu linafifisha rangi ya) mapazia. 3 shinda; piga kura ya vito. ~ **joy** mtu anayeharibu furaha ya wengine. 4 vutia sana. ~ **sb with kindness** haribu mtu kwa kumfanyia huruma sana, dekeza sana. **dress to** ~ vaa ili kuvutia watu *n* 1 kuua. **be in at the** ~ shuhudia kuuawa mnyama. 2 (*in hunting*) windo. **~ing** *adj* (*colloq, dated*) -a kuchosha, -a kuchekesha sana *n* **make a ~ing** fanikiwa sana. **~ingly** *adv*. **~er** *n* muuaji.

kiln *n* tanuru, joko *vt* kausha jikoni.

kilo[1] *n pl* (*abbr of*) **~gram** kilo.
kilo[2] *pref 1000* **~gram**, kilo: (gramu 1000). **~metre** kilomita: mita 1000.
kilt *n* sketi ya mikunjo ifikayo magotini, kitambaa cha tarta. **~ed regiment** askari wa kiskoti wavaao sketi hizo.
kimono *n* kimomo: kanzu refu jembamba ya Kijapani.
kin *n* 1 aali; ukoo, mlango; jamaa, ndugu. **next of ~** ndugu wa karibu zaidi *n* **~dred** *n* 1 ukoo, udugu *claim ~ with sb* dai kuwa wa ukoo mmoja na fulani. 2 familia, ndugu, jamaa *adj* (*attrib only*) -a asili moja. 3 -a namna moja, -a kufanana. **~ly** *adj* 1 -ema, -pole. 2 (*of climate*) tulivu. 3 halali. **~liness** *n*.
kind[1] *adj* -ema, -enye huruma, -karimu. ~ **hearted** *adj* -ema, -enye huruma. **~ly** *adv* 1 kwa huruma/ ukarimu. 2 (*in polite formulas*) *will you ~ly close the door* tafadhali funga mlango. 3 kirahisi, kawaida *take ~ ly to* kubali kirahisi. **~ness** *n* wema, huruma. **out of ~** kwa huruma. **do/ show sb ~** onyesha huruma/wema. **~folk** *n* ndugu, jamaa. **~sman** *n* ndugu/jamaa wa kiume. **~swoman** *n* ndugu/jamaa wa kike.
kind[2] *n* 1 namna, kabila. 2 aina, ngeli, namna *a ~ of dog* namna ya mbwa *all ~s of things* kila aina ya vitu *coffee of a ~* kinywaji kama kahawa. **nothing of the ~** si kitu kama hicho, si hivyo; hata kidogo. **sth of the ~** kitu kama hicho *this ~ of* -a aina hii ya *what ~ of?* -a namna gani? **~ of/~ a** kwa kiasi fulani *I ~ of expected* nilitarajia kiasi. 3 asili, tabia *they differ in ~* wanatofautiana sana. 4 **in ~** (*of payment*) vitu/bidhaa (si fedha) *repay sb in ~* tendea fulani jinsi ulivyotendewa naye; lipiza kisasi.
kindergarten *n* shule ya chekechea, shule ya watoto wadogo, shule ya awali.
kindle *vt,vi* 1 washa moto. 2 *(excite)* amsha, chochea. **~ling** *n* vijiti vya kuwashia moto.
kine *n pl* (*old form*) ng'ombe.
kinetic *adj* -a mwendo. ~ **art** sanaa mwendo. ~ **energy** nishati mwendo. **~s** *n pl* (*with sing v*) elimumwendo.
king[1] *n* 1 mfalme. **turn ~ evidence** toa ushahidi dhidi ya mhalifu mwenzi. 2 mtu mashuhuri. 3 (*chess game*) kete kuu; (*playing cards*) mzungu wa nne. 4 kitu kikubwa katika kundi la vitu/ wanyama. **the ~ of beasts** simba. **the ~ of the forest** mwaloni. **the ~ of terrors** kifo. 5 (*compounds*) **~bird** shore. ~ **bolt** komeo kubwa. **~crab** kaa mkubwa. **~craft** ustadi wa kutawala. ~ **cup** ua kubwa la njano. **~fish** nguru. **~fisher** mdiria/ chepea. ~ **-maker** mtu mwenye kuathiri uteuzi wa mfalme/uchaguzi wa viongozi. **~pin** komeo; (*fig*) mtu muhimu. **~size(d)** *adj* kubwa sana *~ size cigarettes* sigara kubwa sana. **~like**, **~ly** *adj* -a kifalme; -a fahari, -kuu. **~ship** *n* ufalme, utawala. **~dom** *n* 1 ufalme, himaya. **the United ~ (the UK)** Uingereza. 2 (*of God*) ufalme wa Mungu *gone to ~dom come* (*colloq*) aga dunia. 3 migawano mikuu ya viumbe/ maumbile duniani *the animal ~* jamii ya wanyama na binadamu *the vegetable ~* jamii ya mimea *the mineral ~* ulimwengu wa madini/ miamba/mawe. 4 (*realm or province*) eneo, sehemu.
kink *n* 1 pindokombo; waya/nywele; kasoro, dosari. 2 (*fig*) wazo lisilo kawaida *vt,vi* fanya pindokombo. **~lay** *adj* -enye tabia ya ajabu, -a kichaa.
kiosk *n* 1 kibanda cha simu. 2 kibanda cha kuuzia bidhaa.
kip[1] *n* ngozi ya mnyama mdogo iliyotengenezwa.
kip[2] *n (GB. sl)* chumba, kitanda cha wageni (katika nyumba ya kupanga) *vi* lala, korota.
kipper *n* samaki aina ya heringi (aina ya samaki aliyekaushwa kwa moshi na kutiwa chumvi) *vt* kausha samaki

(aliyetengenezwa kwa chumvi).

kirk *n* (*Scot*) kanisa.

kismet *n* (Turk) kudura.

kiss *vt,vi* busu. ~ **the hand** busu mkono. ~ **the book** apa kwa neno la Mungu. ~ **the dust/ground** onyesha utii, uwawa. ~ **the rod** kubali adhabu ya viboko *~-in- the-ring n* mchezo wa watoto ambao mmoja humfukuza mwenziwe na akimkamata humbusu *n* 1 busu. 2 peremende. ~ **of life** kuingiza hewa ndani ya mtu kwa kutumia njia ya mdomo kwa mdomo. **~er** *n* (*sl*) domo, bakuli.

kit *n* (*collectivesing*) 1 vyombo, vifaa, zana (agh nguo) za askari au msafiri, *the whole ~ and Kaboodle* (*colloq*) (*US sl*) watu/vitu/vikorokoro vyote. **~-bag** fuko, shanta 2 vifaa vya kazi. 3 **do-it- yourself** ~ seti ya sehemu za kifaa zinazoungwa na mnunuzi *vt* ~ **sb out/up (with sth)** -pa vifaa vyote vinavyohitajika katika shughuli fulani.

kitchen *n* 1 jiko, meko; *(GB)* chumba cha kulia (chakula) pamoja na shughuli nyingine. **everything but the ~ sink** vitu vingi mno (zaidi ya inavyohitajika). **~-garden** *n* bustani ya mboga na matunda. **~-sink drama** (*GB in 1950's and 1960's*) tamthilia inayoakisi maishaya mfanyakazi (agh jinsi anavyotambua hali ya kisiasa, uchumi, kijamii n.k.). ~ **unit** vifaa vya jikoni vilivyounganishwa pamoja. **~ware** *n* vifaa vya jikoni. **~ette** *n* chumba kidogo cha kupikia chakula.

kite *n* 1 mwewe, kipanga. 2 tiara, kishada. **fly a** ~ (*fig*) pima mawazo ya watu kwa jambo fulani. **~-balloon** putotiara la kijeshi.

kith *n* (*only in*) ~ **and kin** jamaa, ndugu na marafiki.

kitsch *n adj* (*in the arts, design etc*) -enye ulimbwende/madoido yasiyo na maana.

kitten *n* 1 mtoto wa paka *have ~s* (*colloq*) -wa na wahaka/ wasiwasi, wayawaya. **~ish** *adj*. **kit** *n* mtoto wa paka.

kitty *n* 1 (*in some card games*) mfuko wa fedha za michezo; (*colloq*) mfuko wa fedha. 2 (*of a child's language*) nyau.

kiwi *n* kiwi; ndege (wa New Zealand) asiye na mbawa; (*sl*) mwenyeji wa New Zealand.

kleptomania *n* udokozi. **~c** *n* mdokozi.

knack *n* welekevu, weledi, ustadi *there's a ~ in it* lazima ujifunze kwa kutenda *get the ~* -wa na ustadi (ubingwa), elewa *have the ~ of doing sth* -wa na ustadi wa kufanya kitu.

knacker *n* 1 mchinja farasi. 2 mtu anayenunua nyumba, meli, mashine kuukuu ili avunje na kupata vifaa.~ **'s yard** mahali pa kuvunjia vyuma vikuukuu.

knackered *adj* (*GB*) -enye kuchoka sana, hoi.

knap *vt* vunja mawe kwa nyundo.

knapsack *n* shanta.

knave *n* 1 (*old use*) ayari, laghai. 2 (*playing cards*) mzungu wa tatu, ghulamu. **~ry** *n*. **knavish** *adj*. **knavishly** *adv*.

knead *vt* (*dough/clay/muscles*) kanda.

knee *n* 1 goti. **bring sb to his ~s** tiisha mtu. **fall drop on one's ~s** angukia (kwa kuomba msamaha). **be on/go down on one's ~s** piga magoti (kwa kuabudu). 2 sehemu ya nguo (agh suruali) inayofunika magoti. 3 (*compounds*) **~breeches** *n* suruali fupi iliyofungwa chini ya magoti. ~ **cap** *n* pia ya goti/kifuu cha goti/ kibandiko cha goti. **~-deep** *adj, adv* -nayofikia magoti. **~capping** kupiga risasi miguuni. **~high** *adj,adv* -a magotini.

kneel *vi* ~ **(down)** piga magoti.

knell *n* mlio wa kengele (ikigongwa moja moja kama kwa maziko); (*fig*) ishara ya mwisho/kifo cha kitu *vt* (*fig*) piga kengele (agh kama onyo).

knelt *pt, pp of* **kneel**.

knesset Bunge la Israeli.

knew *pt of* **know**

knickerbocker *n* ~**s** kaboka.

knickers *n pl* 1 (*US*) (*inform*) chupi ya

mwanamke. 2 (*old use*) kaptura mkunjo. **get one's ~ in twist** (*GB sl*) changanyikiwa.

knick-knack *n* kikorokoro.

knife *n* kisu; jisu, (*for tapping palm -trees)* kotama *pocket ~* kisu cha kukunja, kijembe. **get one's ~ into sb** dhamiria kudhuru. **war to the ~** uhasama mkali, kukinzana na, vita vya kufa na kupona *before you could say ~* kufumba na kufumbua. **~ edge of** makali ya kisu. **on a ~-edge** (*a person awaiting (an important outcome, result etc.*) -enye mashaka/wasiwasi mwingi *be/go under the ~* pasuliwa *vt* kata/choma kwa kisu.

knight *n* 1 (*in the Middle Ages*) shujaa wa ukoo bora anayepewa daraja la juu katika jeshi baada ya kuonyesha uhodari wote. **~ -errant** *n* shujaa wa ukoo bora aliyekwenda kutafuta ushujaa. 2 (*GB modern use*) cheo cha hadhi/heshima kinachotolewa kwa kulitumikia taifa (mwenye cheo hiki huitwa "Sir" kabla ya jina lake). 3 *(GB history)* ~ **(of the shire)** Mbunge wa jimbo. 4 (*game of chess*) kete yenye kichwa cha farasi *vt* pa cheo, tunza cheo cha 'Sir'. **~hood** *n* 1 cheo/heshima ya shujaa wa ukoo bora. 2 watu wenye cheo hiki. **~ly** *adj*.

knit *vt,vi* **~ sth (up (from/into)**, 1 fuma *~ a sweater* fuma sweta. 2 (*join closely*) unga; unganisha. 3 weka pamoja. **~ one's/the brows** kunja uso. **~ter** *n* mfumaji. **~ting** *n* 1 kufuma. 2 nyuzi za kufumia. **~-machine** *n* mashine ya kufumia. **~-needle** *n* sindano ya kufumia. **~wear** *n* (*trade use*) nguo zilizofumwa.

knives see **knife**.

knob *n* 1 kirungu. 2 kifundo, kinundu. **~ kerrie** *n* rungu, **~bly** *adj* -enye fundo. **~ble** kirungu kidogo.

knock[1] *n* 1 pigo, bisho *a ~ at the door* kupiga/kubisha hodi, bisho mlangoni *he got a slight ~ on the fore-head* alipata pigo hafifu pajini. **~ for ~** (*of an Insurance Company*) kulipia kile kile kilicholipiwa bima. 2 (*of a petrol engine*) kuvunjika, kuharibika, kunoki. 3 (*cricket*) zamu (ya kupiga). 4 (*sl*) lawama; hasara. **~er** *n* 1 mtu/kitu kinachobisha mlango. **~ up** mtu anayeamsha wafanyakazi asubuhi *vt,vi* 1 bisha, gonga *~ at the door* bisha mlango, bisha/piga hodi **~ against sth/sb** gonga/gongana na kitu/mtu. **~ one's head against a brick wall** (*fig*) jisumbua bure. 2 (*sl*) shangaza, shtusha 3 (*of a petrol engine*) noki, vunjika, haribika. 4 (*sl*) kosoa. 5 (*compounds*). **~-about** *adj* (*of clothes*) zinazofaa kwa kazi. **~-down** *adj* (*of prices eg at an auction*) -a bei nafuu; -a chini na mwisho: *(fig)* -a kushangaza, -a kuduwaza. **~-kneed** *adj* -enye magobwe. **~out** *adj n* (*abb KO*) pigo la ushindi/ushinde (kwenye mchezo wa masumbwi); (*sl*) -a usingizi (*of a tournament*) mashindano ya kutoana; (*colloq*) (*person, thing*) -a kuvutia, -a kupendeza, -a usingizi *~out pills* dawa za usingizi. 6 (*uses with adverbial particles and props*). **~ about** (*colloq*) kuzurura. **~ about (with sb)** -wa na uhusiano (wa kimapenzi) na, tembea na. **~ sb/sth about** piga mara kwa mara; fanyia ubaya. **~ sth back** (*sl*) -nywa *~ back a pint of beer* -nywa bia; shangaza. **~ sb down** angusha; gonga. **you could have ~ed me down with a feather** nilishangaa sana, niliduwaa/shikwa na bumbuazi. **~ sth down** bomoa, haribu; changua katika sehemu *~ down the furniture* fungua fanicha katika sehemu (kupata wepesi wa kusafirisha). **~ sth/sb down (to sth)** uzia mtu kitu kwenye mnada. **~ down prices** punguza bei. **~ sth in** pigilia, gongomea *~ in a nail* pigilia msumari. **~ off (work)**, pumzika. **~ sb off** (*sl*) tongoza na kutelekeza. **~ sth off** punguza tunga/maliza haraka;

(*cricket*) funga haraka haraka; *(sl)* vunja, iba ~ *off a bank* vunja benki. ~ **it off** (*sl*) acha! ~ **on** (*Rugby*) gonga mpira kwenda mbele wakati wa kujaribu kuudaka ~ *or effect n* (*colloq*) matokeo mabaya; mwambukizano. ~ **sb out** (*boxing*) angusha mpinzania kiasi cha kushindwa kuendelea; (*fig*) shangaza; duwaza, zimisha. ~ **sb out (of)** toa shinda (mpinzani). ~ **sth out** kung'uta ~ *out one's pipe* kung'uta kiko (ili kutoa tumbaku). ~ **(things) together** gonganisha/weka vitu haraka haraka, haraka/ovyo ovyo. ~ **your/their heads together** tumia nguvu kuzuia mtu/watu wasigombane, waache ujeuri, gonganisha vichwa vyenu. ~ **up (tennis)** zoezi fupi kabla ya mchezo. ~ **sb up**, (*GB colloq*) amsha mtu (*GB colloq*) chosha, taabisha, (*US sl*) shambulia, piga; (*US vulg sl*) (*of a man*) jamiina na; tia mimba. ~ **sth up** piga/rusha juu kwa ngumi; panga/weka/tengeneza pamoja haraka; (*of cricket*) funga. ~ **up copy** (*in newspaper etc*) tayarisha mswada kwa uchapishaji. ~ **into** fundisha kwa nguvu; kutana na (bila kutegemea). ~ **off** ua.

knoll *n* kilima kidogo; mwinuko, kiduta, kuchuguu.

knot *n* 1 fundo *tie/make a ~* piga fundo *make a ~* (*fig*) funga *the marriage ~* kufunga ndoa/pingu za maisha. 2 utepe wa mapambo (wenye mafundo). 3 shida, taabu, tatizo. **tie oneself in/up in/into ~s** jibabaisha; changanyikiwa. 4 (*of trees*) kifundo.~ **hole** shimo la kifundo. 5 (*of persons*) kikundi. 6 (*naut*) noti: mwendo wa futi 6080 (mita 1853) kwa saa *ship of 16 ~s* meli inayokwenda noti 16 kwa saa *vt,vi* fanya/funga fundo. **~ty** *adj ~ tree* mti wenye vifundo. 2 gumu kufahamu. ~ **problem** tatizo gumu kutatuliwa.

knout *n* mjeledi wa ngozi (uliotumika Urusi kutolea adhabu) *vt* piga kwa mjeledi.

know *vt,vi* 1 jua, fahamu, elewa, tambua ~ *one's business/what's what/the ropes/a thing or two* -wa na ujuzi wa jambo fulani, elewa utaratibu wa jambo fulani, -wa na uamuzi wa busara, jua unachofanya. ~ **better than to do sth** jua ni vizuri kutofanya jambo fulani. ~ **about/of** fahamu jambo fulani, -wa na habari kuhusu. 2 fahamu, tambua jua (mtu), fahamiana na; tofautisha/pambanua mtu/kitu. **make oneself ~n to sb** jitambulisha. **be ~n to** julikana na *he's ~n to the police* anajulikana na polisi. **be ~ as** julikana kama. ~ **sb from sb** tofautisha, pambanua. ~ **sth from sth** weza kutofautisha kitu. **not~ sb from Adam/from a bar of soap** (*colloq*) -tofahamu (mtu) kabisa. 3 jua vizuri. 4 weza kutambua. (*compounds*) **don't-~** *n* (*colloq*) msailiwa asiyejua maswali ya kura ya maoni. **~-all** *n (derog)* sogora, mjuaji. **~-how** *n* akili ya kutengeneza vitu n.k., ujuzi wa mbinu za utekelezaji; ufundi ustadi, ubingwa wa ufundi *n* (*only in*) **in the** ~ (*colloq*) -enye habari. **~able** *adj* **~ing** *adj*. -stadi, -juzi, -enye maarifa; -erevu, -janja. **~ingly** *adv* 1 kwa makusudi. 2 kwa ujuzi *in a ~ing manner* kwa ujuzi, kwa utambuzi. **knowledge** *n* 1 elimu, maarifa. **~able** *adj* -enye maarifa mengi/akili/fahamu. 2 ujuzi. 3 ufahamu, utambuzi.

knuckle *n* 1 konzi. 2 (*in animals*) goti, kongoro *vi* ~ **down to sth** (*colloq*) anza kazi fulani kwa bidii, zamia. ~ **under** jitoa, salimu amri.

koala *n* (*zool*) koala: dubu mdogo wa Australia migodini.

kohl *n* wanja wa manga.

kohlrabi *n* aina ya kabichi.

kola *n* mkola. ~ **nuts** kola.

kook *n* (*sl*) mjinga. **~y** *adj* -a ujinga.

kookaburra *n* (*Australia*) mkumburu.

kopec(k) *n* see **copeck**.

kopje, koppie *n* (*in South Africa*) kilima kidogo, mwisho, kiduta.

Koran *n* Kurani, Msahafu.
kosher *n adj* (*food, foodshop*) -enye kutimiza kanuni za Kiyahudi.
kourbash *n* (*in Turkey/Egypt*) mjeledi; kiboko.
kowtow, kotow *n* (*former Chinese custom*) kusujudu (kama ishara ya heshima/utii), kusujudia *vt* ~ (**to**), sujudia; rairai, nyenyekea.
kraal *n* (*in South Africa*) 1 kijiji (kilichozungushiwa boma). 2 zizi.
Kremlin *n* Kremlin: ngome ya mji wa Moscow. **the K** ~ Makao Makuu ya Chama na Serikali ya Urusi.
krona *n* korona: sarafu ya fedha ya Sweden.
krone *n* sarafu ya fedha ya Denmark au Norway.
kudos *n* (*colloq*) heshima (kwa sababu ya tendo); sifa.
kudu *n* tandala.
Ku-Klux-Klan *n* jumuia ya siri ya ubaguzi wa rangi Marekani.
kulak *n* (*Russian*) kulaki: mkulima tajiri.
kungfu *n* kungfu: riadha ya kujihami, karate ya Kichina.
kwashiorkor *n* unyafuzi, chirwa.
Kwela *n* (*South Africa*) Kwela: aina ya jazi.

L

Ll *n* 1 herufi ya kumi na mbili katika alfabeti ya Kiingereza. 2 namba 50 ya Kirumi.

la *n* (*music*) la: noti ya 6 katika muziki.

laager *n* 1 *(in S. Africa)* kambi iliyopangwa kati ya duara ya magari. 2 *(mil)* maegesho ya magari ya kivita *vt,vi* 1 egesha magari katika duara. 2 jihami nyuma ya magari.

lab *n* (*colloq*) (*abbr of*) **laboratory**.

label *n* 1 kitambulisho (chenye maelezo/anwani ya mzigo) *vt* weka kitambulisho chenye maelezo/anwani ya kitu/ mzigo. (*fig*) ~ **sb (as sth)** -pa/pachika mtu (cheo, sifa, jina) *he was ~led a thief* alipachikwa jina la wizi.

labial *adj* -a midomo; -a kufanyika kwa midomo; (*phon*) ~ *sounds* sauti za midomo k.m. m,p,b. **labio-** *pref* -a mdomo.

laboratory *n* maabara, lebo.

labour *(US)***labor** *n* 1 kazi *division of ~* mgawanyo wa kazi. **hard ~** kazi ngumu. **manual ~** kazi ya mikono/ sulubu. ~ **saving** *adj* -a kupunguza kazi. 2 kazi. **a ~ of love** kazi afanyayo mtu kwa upendo. 3 wafanyakazi. ~ **Exchange** ofisi ya leba. **the ~ Party** Chama cha Leba/ Wafanyakazi. ~ **leaders** viongozi wa Chama cha Leba; viongozi wa Chama cha Wafanyakazi. ~ **Day** (*US*) sikukuu ya wafanyakazi; Jumatatu ya kwanza ya mwezi Septemba. ~ **union** (*US*) Chama cha Wafanyakazi. 4 uchungu wa uzazi *a woman in ~* mwanamke mwenye uchungu *vt,vi* 1 fanya kazi, tumika; jitahidi. 2 enda/ pumua polepole na kwa shida. 3 ~ **under sb/sth** teseka, pata shida *~ under a disadvantage* teseka kwa shida *~ under a delusion* jidanganya. 4 fanya kazi kwa undani/urefu mno. **~ed** *adj* 1 -a shida/taabu. ~ **breathing** upumuaji wa shida, taabu. 2 -enye kutafakuri mno. **~er** *n* mfanyakazi, kibarua. **~ite** *n* mwanachama/shabiki wa chama cha Leba. **~ious** *adj* 1 (*of work etc*) -harubu, -a kuchosha. 2 -enye kuhitaji makini. 3 gumu. **~iously** *adv*.

labret *n* ndonya.

labyrinth *n* 1 njia za mzingo; (*fig*) matata mengi, mchanganyiko wa mambo. 2 (*bio*) sikio la ndani. **~ine** *adj*.

lace *n* 1 (*shoes*) kamba. 2 lesi, gangiri, kimia. **~-glass** *n* kioo chenye marembo. **~-pillow** *n* mto wa kufuma lesi *vt,vi* ~ **(up)** 1 funga viatu kwa kamba. 2 pamba nguo kwa lesi. 3 ~ **sth with sth etc** tia (pombe kali) kidogo n.k. 4 ~ **into sb** piga mtu. **lacing** *n*. **lacy** *adj* -a kimia, -a lesi.

lacerate *vt* 1 papura, kwaruza (agh. ngozi). 2 (*fig*) tia uchungu. **laceration** *n*.

lachrymal *adj* -a machozi *~ glands* tezi za machozi. **lachrymose** *adj* lizi, -enye machozi.

lack *n* utovu, ukosefu, upungufu, uhitaji *no ~ of* tele *for ~ of* kwa sababu ya ukosefu wa (*naut*) *~ of stability* mleoleo *vt,vi* 1 ~ **(in)** -tokuwa na; kosa, pungukiwa na, hitaji *we ~ books* hatuna vitabu *they ~ed for nothing* hawakuhitaji/hawakukosa kitu *he ~s good manners* hana adabu *the borrower ~s not, he who ~s is the owner of the vessel* mwenye kuazima hatoi, mtovu ni mwenye chombo; -tovu, -enye kukosa. **~-lustre** *adj* -a mazimbwezimbwe, bila uhai.

lackadaisical *adj* -enye kupuuza, -enye kuchoka, zembezembe, -sio na bidii. **~ly** *adv*.

lackey *n* mtumishi wa kiume; (*fig*) mnyonge; kikaragosi.

laconic *adj* -a maneno machache. **~ally** *adv*. **laconism** *n*.

lacquer *n* vanishi; behedani *vt* paka vanishi/behedani.

lactate *vt* tunga maziwa; nyonyesha maziwa *n* (*chem*) chumvi ya maziwa. **lactation** *n*. **lactic** *adj* -a maziwa *~ acid* asidi ya maziwa yaliyo-chachuka.

lactose *n* (*chem*) laktosi.

lacuna *n* uwazi, pengo. **~l, ~ r** *adj*.

lacustrine *adj* -a ziwa *~ dwelling* kijiji

cha ziwani ~ *plain* uwanda wa ziwa.

lad *n* kijana (mwanamume); mvulana. **~die** *n*.

ladder *n* 1 ngazi, (*naut*) kipande *mount/ climb the* ~ panda ngazi. 2 (*US=run*) kufumuka kwa soksi. ~ **proof** -siofumukika *vi (of stockings)* fumuka.

laddie *n see* **lad**.

lade *vt* pakia shehena, sheheni. **~n** (**with**) *adj* 1 -enye shehena, -enye mizigo, -liojaa. 2 (*over-burdened by grief*) -a kulemewa. **lading** *n* shehena, mizigo *bill of* ~ hati/idhini ya kuchukulia mizigo; orodha ya mizigo melini.

la-di-da *adj* -a mzofafa, -a mbwebwe; -a kujifaragua, kujidai.

ladle *n* (*of soup*) upawa, ukasi; (*of water*) kata *vt* ~ (**out**) gawa kwa upawa/kata; (*fig*) toa (heshima/sifa n.k.) kwa wingi. **~ful** *n*.

lady *n* 1 bibiye, mke wa lodi. 2 bibi. ~ **in-waiting** bibi mpambe. ~ **of the house** mama mwenye nyumba. 3 mwanamke yeyote (*pl*) mabibi. **Ladies and Gentlemen** mabibi na mabwana. 4 mke *your ~/wife* mke wako 5 **Ladies** (*used as sing n*) choo cha wanawake. 6 (*attrib*) -a kike *a ~ doctor* daktari wa kike. 7 *(compounds)* (*rel*) **Our L~** Bikira Maria **L~ Day** (*rel*) sikukuu ya kupashwa habari ya kuzaliwa bwana (tarehe 25 Machi). **~-killer** *n* (*slang*) mtekaji wanawake. **~-love** *n* mchumba/mpenzi (mwanamke). **~'s maid** *n* mtumishi wa bibi. **ladies' man** mwanaume anayependa wanawake. ~ **like** *adj* -a adabu, -a malezi mazuri.

lag[1] *n* (*sl*) mfungwa *an old* ~ mtu aliyefungwa mara nyingi *vt* 1 tia gerezani. 2 bamba.

lag[2] *vi* kawia, chelewa, enda polepole ~ *behind* kawia *n (time)* ~ muda wa kuchelewa. **~gard** *n* mvivu, goigoi mchelewaji.

lag[3] *n* kihami vt hami/fungia/ vingirishia kitu (kuzuia joto kupita).

lager *n* bia isiyo nzito wala kali sana;

lagoon *n* wangwa.

laic *adj* -siokuwa a dini, -a kawaida *n* mtu wa kawaida, mlei. **~al** *adj*. **~ize** *vt* toa katika utawala wa dini, fanya (agh. padri) awe mtu wa kawaida.

laity *n* mlei, watu wa kawaida (wasio weledi).

laid *pp of* **lay**.

lain *pp of* **lie**.

lair *n* 1 malalo ya mnyama wa mwitu; tundu/pango *(fig)* pango/maficho ya majambazi. 2 banda (la ng'ombe) *vt,vi* enda mlaloni; -wa/-weka mlaloni.

laird *n* (*Scot*) kabaila, mmilikaji ardhi, lodi.

laissez-faire *n* uholela: hali ya kuacha mambo yajiendee kiholela.

lake[1] *n* ziwa. ~ **dwellings** makazi fukweni mwa ziwa. **The Great ~s** (*N. America*) maziwa matano makubwa. **the L~ District** (*GB*) sehemu yenye maziwa mengi. ~ **poets** washairi waliokaa huko (Coleridge, Wordsworth n.k.)

lake[2] *n* (*colour*) ngeu.

lakh *n* (*India and Pakistan*) laki.

lam *vt,vi* (*sl*) bubuta, dunda, kung'uta. ~ **into sb** bubuta mtu, karipia.

lama *n* mchungaji/mtawa wa madhehebu ya Kibuda (Tibet na Mongolia). **~sery** *n* makao ya watawa wa kibunda.

lamb *n* 1 mwanakondoo, nyama ya mwanakondoo. 2 maasumu; mpenzi. **like a** ~ *(to the slaughter)* (kufa) kingoto, kimyakimya *vt* zaa (vikondoo), gwisha. ~ **kin** *n* mwanakondoo mchanga. **~skin** *n* ngozi ya mwanakondoo. **~'s wool** sufu ya mwanakondoo.

lambaste *vt* (*sl*) tandika, kong'ota, buta; karipia sana.

lambent *adj* (*liter*) 1 -a kumetameta. 2 (*of eyes/sky*) -a kung'aa. 3 (*of humour, wit*) bashasha. **lambency** *n*.

lame[1] *adj* 1 kiguru, kiwete *be* ~ chechea, -enda chopi he has *a ~ leg* amelemaa mguu. 2 (*of metre*) -a mikingamo. 3 (*unsatisfactory*) -siofaa, si -zuri, -a wasiwasi *vt* lemaza. **~ly** *adv*. **~ness** *n*.

lame[2] *n* kitambaa chenye nyuzi za dhahabu au fedha.

lament *vt, vi* **~ (for/over)** lia, omboleza; sikitika *n* 1 kilio, maombolezo; sikitiko. **~able** *adj*. **~ably** *adv*. **~ation** *n*.

laminate *vt, vi* fanya tabaka jembamba, chana (katika) tabaka; funika kwa tabaka. **~d** *adj ~ plastic sheets* fomeka.

lamp *n* 1 taa. street ~s taa za barabarani **table ~** taa ta jysinea (*lantern*) kandili, fanusi; kibatari. 2 **~light** mwanga/nuru ya taa. **~lighter** (*hist*) mwasha taa barabarani. **~-post** nguzo ya taa (barabarani). **~-shade** kifuniko cha taa.

lampoon *n* stihizai, kushtumu/ kukashifu mtu *vt* stihizai.

lance *n* (*hist*) mkuki, fumo, lansi *break a ~ with sb* bishana sana na mtu. ~ **corporal** *n* koplo lansi. **~r** *n* askari wa farasi. **~s** *pl* (*with sing v*) dansi ya watu wanane au zaidi. *vt* 1 choma kwa fumo; pasua, tumbua (jipu) n.k. **lancet** *n* kisu kidogo (kinachotumika kupasulia). **lancinating** *adj* (*of pain*) -a kuchoma, kali.

land *n* 1 ardhi, nchi kavu *travel over ~* safiri nchi kavu *go by ~* enda kwa gari, treni n.k. 2 shamba, konde; kiwanja *work on the ~* fanya kazi shambani. **~army** (*GB*) kikosi cha wafanyakazi wa kike wa shamba wakati wa vita vikuu vya pili *Our ~ is about ten hectares* shamba letu lina ukubwa wa hekta kumi. ~ **agent** (*chiefly GB*) (*US real estate agent*) mwangalizi/msimazi wa shamba, wakala wa mashamba/viwanja. 3 nchi, taifa (la asili ya mtu) *my native ~* nchi yangu ya asili *distant ~s* nchi za mbali. **the ~ of the living** maisha ya sasa *I'm still in the ~ of the living* bado nipo *the promised ~/the ~ of Promise* Nchi ya Ahadi (*Canaan*). 4 (*compounds*) ~ **fall** *n* kukaribia nchi kavu (kutoka majini). ~ **forces** *n* jeshi la nchi kavu. ~ **holder** *n* mmilikaji wa ardhi. ~ **lady** *n* mwanamke mwenye hoteli/nyumba ya kupangisha. ~ **locked** *adj* -liozungukwa na nchi kavu *~ locked countries* nchi zisizokuwa na bandari. ~ **lord** *n* kabaila; mwenye hoteli/ nyumba ya kupangisha. ~ **lubber** *n* (*used by sailor*) (mtu) asiye baharia. **~mark** *n* alama (k.m. mnara, n.k.); alama ya mpaka; (*fig*) jambo/tukio/ wazo muhimu (linalodhi hirisha) upeo au mabadiliko. ~ **mine** *n* mabomu ya ardhini. ~ **owner** *n* mmiliki ardhi. ~ **rover** *n* landrova: gari madhubuti la barabara mbaya. ~ **slide** *n* mporomoko wa ardhi; (*in election*) ushindi mkubwa *~slide victory* ushindi mkubwa sana. ~ **slip** *n* **slide.** **~s man** *n* mtu asiye baharia *vt,vi* 1 (*of aircraft*) tua (*of ship*) fika pwani, teremka pwani *the aeroplane ~ed at night* ndege ilitua usiku *the passangers ~ed when the ship anchored at the harbour* abiria waliteremka (pwani) meli ilipotia nanga bandarini. ~ **on one's feet** (*fig*) -wa na bahati; nusurika. 2 ~ **sb/ oneself in sth** ingia matatani. ~ **up** (*colloq*) wasili; jikuta, ishia *because of his bad behavior one day he ~ed up in jail* kutokana na tabia yake mbaya siku moja alijikuta jela *Juma ~ed up this morning unexpectedly* Juma aliwasili asubuhi hii bila kutegemewa. 3 (*colloq*) pata *~ a good job* pata kazi nzuri. 4 (*sl*) piga/ chapa (kibao/ngumi) *he ~ed him one*... alimpiga kibao kimoja ... **~ed** *adj* -a ardhi; -enye kumiliki ardhi/ shamba. **~less** -siokuwa na ardhi/ shamba. **~ing** *n* 1 kushuka/kutua/ kuteremka pwani (nchi kavu). ~ **craft** *n* meli ya kushushia pwani/ ufukoni (magari ya kivita, askari n.k.). ~ **field/strip** *n* kiwanja cha kutua ndege. ~ **gear** *n* marandio. ~ **net** *n* fuko la kutilia/kuzolea samaki.

2 (*also* ~ **place**) gati, bunta. ~ **party** kikosi cha askari (agh. wa kutuliza fujo). ~ **stage** kikwezo. 3 jukwaa la ngazi.

landscape *n* 1 mandhari, sura ya nchi. 2 uchoraji/usanii wa mandhari. ~ **gardening/ architecture** *n* usanifu wa bustani/majenzi kimandhari.

lane *n* 1 barabara nyembamba, uchochoro. **it is a long ~ that has no turning** hakuna marefu yasiyo na **language** ncha. 2 ujia; (*in sports*) mstari *inside* ~ mstari wa ndani. 3 njia ya meli/ndege n.k.

language *n* 1 lugha *the ~ of the Nyamwezi* Kinyamwezi. **dead** ~ lugha ya kale (ambayo haizungumzwi tena). ~ **laboratory** maabara ya lugha. **professional** ~ lugha ya kitaalam/ kieledi. 2 ishara zitumiwazo kwa mawasiliano. **computer** ~ lugha ya kompyuta. 3 maneno, misemo itumiwayo katika kikundi fulani. **technical** ~ lugha ya kifundi. 4 **bad/strong** ~ lugha chafu, kali, -liojaa matusi n.k.

languish *vi* nyong'onyea, dhoofika, fifia, punguka. ~ **for sb** taka mtu sana ~ *for love* teseka kwa mapenzi.

languid *adj* -legevu; -chovu, -nyong'onyevu *be* ~ nyong'onyea, choka. **~ly** adv. **languor** *n* unyong'onyevu, udhaifu, ulegevu; uchovu.

langur *n* ngedere (mwenye mkia mrefu).

lank *adj* 1 -embamba na refu, -a kimbaombao. 2 (*of hair*) -ilionyoka. **~y** *adj* (*of a person, his arms or legs*) -a njorinjori; -lonjo.

lanolin *n* lanolini: shahamu inayotokana na sufu.

lantern *n* fanusi, kandili. **~jawed** *adj* -enye mataya marefu mebamba.

lanyard *n* 1 ugwe wa filimbi. 2 kamba (ya kufungia vitu melini).

lap[1] *n* 1 paja, mapaja. 2 kipande cha vazi (kinachofunika mapaja). **be/live in the ~ of luxury** ishi maisha ya anasa. **in the ~ of the Gods** *(of future event)* kwa kutegemea kudra, mashakani. ~ **dog** kijibwa cha kupakata *vt,vi* 1 funika/funga kwa nguo n.k. 2 pitana, pandana *the iron sheets on the roof ~ over* mabati yamepandana *n* mapandano; mzunguko mmoja (katika mbio).

lap[2] *vi,vt* ~ **up** 1 -nywa (kwa kulamba kama paka). 2 (*colloq*)(*of human beings*) pokea, twaa upesi/kwa shauku, papia. 3 (*of water*) piga (piga), fanya sauti kama mnyama anayekunywa kwa ulimi (k.m. mawimbi madogo pwani). 4 -wa mbele kwa mzunguko mmoja (kwenye mashindano), zunguka wenzako *n* kunywa kwa ulimi, kulambalamba; sauti ya unywaji kwa ulimi.

lapel *n* mkunjo (wa koti) kifuani.

lapidary *adj* -enye kutia nakshi katika mawe/kito; -lionakshiwa; (*fig*) nadhifu, fasaha *a ~ speech* hotuba fasaha *n* mtianakshi mawe/kito.

lapis lazuli *n* kito cha nili na zari, rangi ya nili.

lapse n 1 kuteleza (kwa ulimi/matendo/ maandishi) ~ *of memory* kupitiwa ~ *of the tongue* kuteleza ulimi. 2 ~ **(from) (into)** kupotoka, kuanza kutoka kwenye mstari/kuwa na tabia isiyohisi. 3 (*of time*) kupita *the ~ of time* kupita kwa muda. 4 (*leg*) kupotea, kuisha kwa haki (kwa kutotumia au kutoiomba tena) *vi* 1 ~ **(from) (into)** potoka; shuka hadhi. 2 (*leg*) poteza haki (kwa kutodai au kutoihuisha).

lapwing *n* pigile: aina ya ndege.

larboard *n (arch see* **port side**).

larceny *n* (*leg*) wizi, wivi. **larcener** *n.*

larch *n* mti wa aina ya msonobari.

lard *n* mafuta ya nguruwe *vt* tia mafuta ya nguruwe (katika nyama), tia bekoni kuongeza utamu. ~ **with** (*fig*)(*often derog*) tia mbwembwe (hadi kuchusha).

larder *n* chumba au kabati ya kuhifadhia chakula na nyama.

large *adj* 1 (*in size, importance*)

-kubwa; (*in quantity*) -ingi. ~ **of limb** -enye miguu, mikono mikubwa. ~ **scale** kubwa ~ *scale farmer* mkulima mkubwa (mwenye shamba kubwa) ~ *scale map* ramani yenye vipimo/skeli kubwa. 2 (*liberal*) -ema, -karimu ~ *hearted* -ema, -a huruma, -karimu; ~ *minded* -enye kupokea mawazo ya wengine *n* (*only in*) **at** ~ huru *the bandits are still at* ~ yale majambazi bado hayajaka- matwa/yako huru; kwa undani *talk at* ~ zungumza kwa undani; kwa jumla; hobelahobela, bila lengo ~**ly** *adv* kwa majivuno *his failure was* ~ *due to laziness* kushindwa kwake kumetokana hasa na uvivu wake; kwa ukarimu, bure. ~**ness** *n*. **largish** *adj* kubwa kiasi.

largesse *US* **largess** *n* zawadi; ukarimu mkubwa.

largo (*music*) *adj* kwa polepole kabisa.

lariat *n* kamba ya kufungia mifugo (farasi, ng'ombe n.k.); kamba yenye kitanzi.

lark[1] *n* kipozamataza.

lark[2] *vi* cheza kwa furaha/kimzaha *n* mzaha, mchezo *what a* ~!, inafurahisha namna gani! furaha iliyoje!

larn *vt,vi* (*dial*) -jifunza/funza.

larrup (*colloq*) charaza viboko. **larva** lava; (*of mosquito*) kiluwiluwi; (*of a bee*) jana; (*of a fly*) buu; (*of a butterfly*) kiwavi. ~**l** *adj*.

larynx *n* zoloto: sehemu ya mwanzo ya koromeo inayohusika na utoaji sauti, **laryngitis** *n* uvimbe wa zoloto.

lascar *n* baharia wa Kihindi.

lascivious *adj* -kware, -a kiasherati. ~**ly** *adv*. ~**ness** *n*.

laser *n* leza: chombo cha kukuza na kushadidisha miale kuelekea upande mmoja. (*attrib*) ~ **beams** mwangaza leza.

lash *n* 1 mjeledi; mchapo, kiboko; kipigo cha mjeledi/kiboko. **the** ~ adhabu ya kupigwa viboko. 2 **eye** ~ kope *vt,vi* chapa, piga; sukuma (k.v. kiungo cha mwili) *the rain was ~ing* (*against*) *the window* mvua ilipiga dirishani. 2 ~ **sb into (a state)** amsha, chochea. ~ **out (against/at sb/sth)** shambulia (kwa kupiga au kwa maneno). 3 ~ **one thing to another**; ~ **things together** fungasha, funga pamoja kwa nguvu. ~ **sth down** kaza, funga. ~ **up** *n* chombo kilichofaraguliwa kilichoundwa kwa haraka/bila makini. ~**ing** *n* 1 kamba ya kufungia. 2 kipigo, mchapo. 3 (*pl, colloq*) tele, chungu nzima *mangoes with ~ings of cream* embe na malai chungu nzima *~ings of drink* vinywaji tele.

lass/lassie *n* msichana; mpenzi.

lassitude *n* uchovu, kuchoka.

lasso *n* kamba yenye kitanzi (ya kukamatia wanyama) *vt* kamata kwa kamba yenye kitanzi.

last[1] *adj* 1 -a mwisho. ~ **but not least** -a mwisho katika orodha lakini si kwa umuhimu *this is our* ~ *hope* hili ndilo tumaini letu la mwisho *he is the* ~ *person I would like to talk to* yeye ni mtu wa mwisho ambaye ningependa kuongea naye; nisingependa kuongea naye *the* ~ *thing in mass media* kitu cha mwisho/kitu kipya kabisa katika utawanyaji wa habari. 2 -liopita. ~ **year** mwaka uliopita/jana ~ *night* usiku wa kuamkia leo *n*. **the** ~ **of** mwisho. **breathe one's** ~ (*liter*) kata roho; fariki. **at (long)** ~ mwishowe, hatimaye. **to/till the** ~ hadi mwisho (*liter or rhet*) hadi kifo ~**ly**, adv (*in making a list*) mwisho, mwishoni. 2 mwisho *she was well when I saw her* ~ alikuwa na afya njema nilipomwona mara ya mwisho *vi* 1 ~ **(out)** endelea, dumu, kaa *will Salehe* ~ *in his new job*? Salehe atakaa kwenye kazi yake mpya? 2 tosha *we have enough food to* ~ (*us*) *four days* tuna chakula cha kututosha kwa siku nne. ~**ing** *adj* -a kudumu.

last[2] *n* foroma (kiatu); mguu: kibao cha kutengenezea viatu *stick to one's* ~ fanya yale tu uwezayo kuyamudu.

latch 1 kia; komeo, kiwi *the door is on the* ~ kitasa hakijafyatuliwa, mlango umefungwa kwa komeo. 2 kitasa, kikomeo. ~**-key** ufunguo wa kikomeo/ kitasa. ~**-key child** (*colloq*) mtoto anayeachwa peke yake (wazazi wake wanapokwenda kazini) *vt,vi* 1 funga kwa komeo. 2 ~ **on (to)** (*colloq*) ng'ang'ania; elewa.

late *adj* 1 -liochelewa, -liokawia *be* ~ chelewa. 2 (*of night*) -kuu, -kubwa ~ *night* usiku mkuu, usiku wa manane. 3 mwishoni ~ *summer* mwishoni mwa majira ya joto. 4 -pya, -a kisasa. 5 -liopita. 6 hayati, marehemu. 7 **of** ~ (hivi) karibuni. **at (the)** ~ **st** kabla au siyo zaidi ya *adv* 1 baadaye, kwa kuchelewa. **Better** ~ **than never** (*prov*) kawia ufike. ~ **in the day** baadaye sana. ~**r on** baadaye. **early** ~ wakati wote *and she is at school early and* ~ yuko shuleni muda wote. **sooner or** ~**r** sasa au wakati mwingine ujao. 2 karibuni. **latish** *adj* -enye kuchelewachelewa, -liotaahari. ~**ly** *adv* hivi karibuni, juzijuzi.

lateen *n* (*naut*) (*only in*) ~ **sail** tanga la pembe tatu.

latent *adj* fiche. ~ **ambiguity** utata fiche.

lateral *adj* 1 pembeni, -a mbavuni, -a kando. ~ **erosion** mmomonyoko wa kingoni. 2 (*phon*) kitambaa.

laterite *n* ngegu.

latex *n* ulimbo wa mpira.

lath *n* uwasa; upapi.

lathe *n* kerezo.

lather *n* 1 povu (la sabuni). 2 jasho jingi *vt,vi* 1 toa jasho. 2 toa povu. 3 (*colloq*) chapa, piga.

Latin *n* Kilatini; watu wenye asili ya Kilatini *adj* -a Kilatini. ~ **America** Amerika ya Kusini. **the** ~ **Church** Kanisa Katoliki; **the** ~ **Quarter** (*of Paris*) Sehemu ya ukingo wa kusini wa Mto Seine (wanakoishi wanafunzi na wasanii kwa karne nyingi). ~**ist** msomi wa Kilatini. ~**ize** *vt* fanya -a Kilatini. ~ **phases** nahau za Kilatini *I speak Latin* ninasema Kilatini.

latitude *n* 1 latitudo. 2 (*pl*) maeneo. **high** ~**s** maeneo yaliyo mbali na Ikweta. **low** ~**s** maeneo yaliyo karibu na Ikweta. 3 (*space, liberty, choice*) nafasi, uhuru hiari. 4 *(photo)* wakati wa salama wa kuangaza filamu. **latitudinal** *adj*. **latitudinarian** *adj,n* mvumilivu, mwenye upeo/ upana wa mawazo.

latrine n choo.

latter *adj* -a karibuni, -a baadaye. ~ **-day** -a sasa. 2 (*also as pron*) *the* ~ -a pili, (miongoni mwa yaliyotajwa), -liofuata. **the former and the** ~ -a kwanza na -a pili *adv* karibuni, sasa.

lattice kiunzi cha fito; waya zinazokingamana (*attrib*). ~ **window** dirisha la vipande vya vioo kwenye fremu ya risasi. ~**d** *adj*.

laud *vt* (*formal*) sifu; himidi *adj* -enye kusifika. ~**ably** *adv*. ~**atory** *adj* *(formal)* -a kusifu.

laudanum *n* laudanumu: dawa ya kupoza itengenezwayo kwa afyuni.

laugh *vi,vt* 1 cheka. ~ **at** chekeshwa (na); dhihaki; dharau; puuza. ~ **in sb's face** dharau bayana. ~ **one's head off** vunja mbavu (kwa kicheko). ~ **on the other side of one's face** badilika (kutoka kwenye furaha na kuwa na majonzi). ~ **over** cheka huku unaendelea kufanya jambo. ~ **up one's sleeve** cheka/ furahi kirohoroho/kwa siri. **He** ~**s best, who** ~**s last, He who** ~**s last** ~ **longest** (*prov*) kutangulia si kufika. 2 ~ **away** puuza kwa kucheka kwa dharau. ~ **down** nyamazisha kwa kicheko. ~ **off** ondoa aibu kwa kucheka. 3 -wa katika hali fulani kwa kucheka. ~ **oneself silly** vunja mbavu (kwa kucheka). **have the last** ~ shinda/fanikiwa hatimaye. ~**able** *adj* -a kuchekesha. ~**ably** *adv*. ~**ing** *adj* -a furaha/kuchekesha. ~ **gas** gesi ya usingizi. ~**ingly** *adv*. ~**ter** *n* kicheko.

launch[1] *vt,vi* 1 (*of a ship, esp one newly built*) shua, zindua. 2 ~ **sth (against/at)** (*fig*) anzisha/anza;

lenga; tuma. 3 anza ~ *a man into business* tia mtu katika biashara. ~ **out**; ~ **(out) into** anza *n* 1 kushua (merikebu, meli mpya). 2 kutuma chombo angani.

launch[2] *n* mashua (agh. itumiayo injini).

laundry *n* 1 udobi. 2 **the** ~ nguo chafu (zinazohitaji kufuliwa na kunyooshwa). ~ **man** dobi wa kiume. **launder** *vt,vi* fua na nyoosha nguo, -wa dobi. **launderette** mahala/ mashine ndogo ya kufulia (ya kukodi). **laundress** *n* dobi wa kike.

laureate *n poet* ~ malenga wa ushairi.

laurel *n* laurusi: mti aina ya mdalasini. **look to one's** ~ chunga heshima; fahamu jinsi ya kuwashinda washindani. **rest on one's** ~**s** ridhika na mafanikio mtu aliyoyapata. **win/ gain one's** ~**s** pata heshima/sifa. ~**led** *adj*.

lav (*colloq abbr of*) **lavatory**.

lava *n* lava.

lavatory *n* maliwato, msala.

lave *vt* (*poet*) nawa; ogesha; (*of a stream*) tiririka (polepole).

lavender *n* mrujuani; rangi ya urujuani. ~ **water** manukato ya mrujuani.

lavish *adj* 1 ~ **(of sth/in doing sth)** -karimu mno, paji mno. 2 (*of what is given*) -ingi mno, tele; -a kupita kiasi ~ *expenditure on luxuries* matumizi makubwa katika anasa *vt* ~ **on** toa kwa wingi; toa kwa ukarimu mno ~ *care on the first child* jali mno mtoto wa kwanza. ~**ly** *adv*.

law *n* 1 sheria ~-**giver** *n* mtoaji sheria (k.m. Musa kwa Wayahudi, Soloni kwa Wagiriki). ~-**officer** *n* (*esp*) mwanasheria wa serikali (*US*) polisi. **break the** ~ vunja sheria. **lay down the** ~ toa hoja ya nguvu; amuru, sema kwa nguvu. ~ **abiding** *adj* -enye kufuata/kutii sheria. ~ **breaker** mvunja sheria. **take the** ~ **in one's hands** jichukulia sheria mkononi. **go to** ~ **(against sb)**; **have the law on sb** (*colloq*) shitaki mahakamani. ~ **court** mahakama. ~ **suit** daawa, kesi; madai. 2 (*esp of games or art*) kanuni. **be a** ~ **unto oneself** puuza kanuni. 3 (*natural* ~) kanuni *the* ~ *of self-presevation* kanuni za kujihifadhi. ~**ful** *adj* -a kufuata sheria; halali. ~**fully** *adv*. ~**less** *adj* -a kuvunja sheria, halifu. ~ **acts** vitendo vya kihalifu. ~**lessly** *adv*. ~**lessness** *n*. ~**yer** *n* mwanasheria.

lawn[1] *n* (uwanja wenye) nyasi zinazotunzwa vizuri. **tennis**~ uwanja wa tenisi. ~-**mower** *n* mashine ya kukata nyasi. ~**tennis** tenisi.

lawn[2] *n* bafta.

lax *adj* 1 -zembe; -sio kali; -sio angalifu. 2 (*of the bowels*) -a kuhara *have* ~ *bowels* hara. ~**ity** *n*. ~**ly** *adv*. ~**ative** *n* haluli, dawa ya kuharisha *adj* -a kuharisha, -a kuendesha.

lay[1] *n* (*chiefly in*) **the** ~ **of the land** sura ya nchi.

lay[2] *adj* 1 (RC) -a mtu wa kawaida, -a mlei ~ *brother* bruda mfanyakazi. 2 -sio -eledi ~ *opinion* mawazo ya watu wa kawaida. ~**man** mtu mlei, asiye mtaalam.

lay[3] *n* (*lit*) wimbo, utenzi.

lay[4] *n* mwenzi katika kujamiiana/ kukazana.

lay[5] *vt,vi* 1 weka, laza; tandaza *he laid his hand on my shoulder* aliweka mkono wake begani mwangu. ~ **a snare/trap/an ambush (for sb/sth)** tega mtego/tegea mtu, tayarisha mtego/uvamizi. 2 (*of non-material things, and fig uses*) weka. ~ **(one's) hands on sth/sb)** nyang'anya; chukua *he keeps everything he can* ~ *his hands on* huchukua kila kitu anachokiona; umiza, jeruhi; pata; (*eccles*) bariki. ~**ing-on of hands** uwekaji wakfu; kufanya kasisi; uthibitisho. ~ **the blame for sth on sb** laumu, twisha/tupia lawama. ~ **a (heavy) burden on sb** pa kazi/ wajibu mzito; pa mateso. ~ **one's hopes on** wekea matumaini. ~ **a strict injunction on sb (to do sth to)** amuru. ~ **great/little store by/on sth**, thamini sana/kidogo. ~

stress/emphasis/weight on sth fanya kuwa muhimu, sisitiza. ~ **a tax on sth** toza kodi. 3 sababisha hali fulani. ~ **sb to rest** zika. ~ **sb under a/the necessity/obligation** lazimisha, shurutisha. ~ **sb under contribution** lazimisha mtu atoe mchango. ~ **sth to sb's charge** -pa wajibu. 4 (~ *+n, adj or adv phrases*) ~ **sth bare** onyesha kwa uwazi kabisa, fichua. ~ **sth flat** sambaza, tandaza. ~ **sth open** fichua, onyesha waziwazi, funua, eleza; kata. ~ **oneself open to sth** jiweka katika hali ya kulaumiwa, kushukiwa n.k. ~ **sth waste** angamiza, teketeza. 5 tuliza. ~ **sb's doubts** ondosha mashaka. ~ **a ghost/spirit** fukuza/ punga mizimu/mashetani. 6 *(of birds and insects)* taga mayai. 7 (*usu passive*) (*story*) tokea (katika mahali fulani). 8 tayarisha, andaa, panga ~ *the table* andaa meza ~ *the fire* tayarisha moto mekoni. 9 weka dau. 10 tandika, funika ~ *carpet on the floor* tandika zulia sakafuni. 11 (*sl*) jamiiana, kaza, tia. 12 (*use with adverbial particles and preps*) ~ **about one (with sth)** pigapiga, piga pande zote. ~ **sth aside** weka akiba; weka chini, acha (tabia fulani n.k.). ~ **sth back** laza geuza/geuka, pindua/ pinduka. ~ **sth by** weka akiba. ~ **sb/ oneself down** laza/jilaza. ~ **sth down** lipa; anza kujenga meli n.k.; geuza shamba kuwa sehemu ya malisho; hifadhi (divai) ghalani (agh. chini ya ardhi). ~ **sth down,** ~ **it down that** agiza, panga (kanuni, sheria, utaratibu n.k.). ~ **down one's arms** weka silaha chini (kama ishara ya kusalimu amri). ~ **down the** amuru. ~ **down one's life** jitolea mhanga. ~ **down office** jiuzulu. ~ **sth in** weka akiba ya. ~ **off** (*colloq*) acha kufanya kazi; pumzika; acha kufanya jambo la kuudhi. ~ **sb off** achisha kazi kwa muda. ~ **off** *n* muda ambao watu wanakuwa wameachishwa kazi. ~ **sth on** weka gesi, maji, umeme kwenye jengo; *colloq*) toa, panga. ~ **it on (thick/ with a trowel)** visha kilemba cha ukoka. ~ **sth out** tanda, tandaza; osha/tayarisha (maiti) kwa kuzika; (*colloq*) tumia fedha; panga. ~**out** *n* mpango; mpangilio wa (kurasa, tangazo, kitabu n.k.), utaratibu *vt* ~ *out one's money carefully* tumia fedha kwa uangalifu; weka mipango/ utaratibu wa kazi, panga. ~ **oneself out (to do sth)** jitahidi; jiandaa. ~ **over** (*US*) (GB **stop over**) (*journey*) simama kwa mapumziko. ~**over** *n* mapumziko ya safarini. ~ **sth up** weka akiba; jichimbia kaburi *you're ~ing up trouble for yourself in the future* unajichimbia kaburi; simamisha shughuli za meli kwa ajili ya matengenezo. ~ **sb up** (*usu passive*) sababisha (mtu abaki kitandani).

lay[6] *pt of* **lie**[2]

lay-about *n* (*GB sl*) lofa, mtu asiyetaka kufanya kazi.

lay/-by *n* (*GB*) sehemu ya kuegeshea magari kando ya barabara.

layer *n* 1 safu, tabaka, rusu. ~-**cake** keki ya rusu. 2 (*gardening*) chipukizi lililofungiwa ardhini. 3 kuku wa mayai *vt* panga juu kwa juu, fungia chipukizi/kichomozi cha mti ardhini; chomeka ardhini.

layette *n* mavazi na mahitaji mengine ya mtoto mchanga.

layfigure *n* sanamu ya binadamu (agh. hutumiwa kuvalishwa nguo kwa maonyesho).

lay-man *n see* **lay**.

lazar *n* (*arch*) mtu maskini mwenye ugonjwa (agh. mkoma). ~**etto** (*also* ~ **et,** ~**ette)** *n* 1 nyumba ya kuuguza maskini wenye ukoma na magonjwa ya kuambukiza. 2 jengo/meli iliyowekwa karantini.

Lazarus *n* ombaomba; fukara, fakiri.

lazy *adj* -vivu, -zembe, -tepetevu. ~-**bones** *n* mvivu, mkunguni, mtepetevu. **lazily** *adv*. **laziness** *n*.

laze (away) *vt,vi* jikalia, kaa kwa uvivu, -wa vivu.

lea *n* (*poet*) mbuga, uwanja wa nyasi.

leach *vt* chuja ~ *out/away* ondosha *n* mchujo ardhi, chujuko (la ardhi).

lead[1] *n* 1 risasi *an ounce of* ~ risasi ya bastola. **~-ore** *n* miamba iliyo na risasi. ~ **poisoning** ugonjwa unaosababishwa na sumu ya risasi. ~ **works** kalibu ya risasi. 2 *(also* **black** ~) risasi ya kalamu. 3 timazi; chubwi. **cast/heave the** ~ pima urefu wa maji. **swing the** ~ (*sl*) kwepa/kacha kazi kwa kulaghai. 4 (*pl*) bati la risasi, mapaa yaliyoezekwa na mabati ya risasi; fremu za risasi. **~ed** *adj*. **~en** *adj* 1 -a risasi. 2 -enye rangi ya kijivu. 3 zito. **~en heart** moyo mzito. **~ing** *n* nafasi kati ya mistari ya chapa.

lead[2] *n* 1 kuongoza; mwongozo, welekezo. **follow sb's** ~ fuata uongozi wa. **give sb a** ~ mpe mtu mfano/ dokezo. **take the** ~ tangulia, ongoza. 2 **the** ~ nafasi ya kwanza. (*attrib*) **the** ~ **story** (*journalism, news broadcasting*) habari iliyopewa uzito wa kwanza. **a** ~ kadiri ya kutangulia *have a* ~ *of five metres* tangulia kwa kiasi cha mita tano. **take over/lose the** ~ tangulia/rudi nyuma (katika shughuli). 3 kamba ya kuongoza mbwa, kigwe. 4 (*drama*) mhusika mkuu; mwigizaji mkuu. 5 mfereji (uelekeao kwenye kinu). 6 (*electr*) waya wa umeme. 7 (*in card games*) haki ya kucheza kwanza *vt,vi* 1 ongoza ~ *an army* ongoza jeshi ~ *the way* tangulia, ongoza njia. ~ **in** *n* utangulizi; waya wa simu za upepo na televisheni. 2 ongoza ~ *a blind man* ongoza kipofu. ~ **sb astray** (*fig*) potosha mtu, shawishi ~ *sb by the nose* tawala mtu kabisa. ~ **sb on** (*fig*) shawishi mtu afanye zaidi ya alivyotegemea ~ *a woman to the altar* (*joc*) oa. 3 tangulia. ~ **off** anza. 4 ongoza/athiri/ shawishi (mawazo au vitendo); fanya (kufikiri) *what led you to this idea* kitu gani kilikufanya ufikiri hivyo. 5 elekea (*fig)* sababisha, leta *your work seems to be ~ing no where* kazi yako inaonekana haielekei popote. ~ **up to** fanya matayarisho. **All roads ~ to Rome** (*fig*) kuna njia nyingi za kukufikisha mahali fulani. 6 (*cause sb to*) ishi, pitisha, endesha maisha. ~ **sb a dog's life** fanya mtu aishi maisha ya dhiki, taabisha (*in card games*) anza. 7 ~ **with** (*journalism)* pa uzito wa juu/kwanza. **~er** *n* 1 kiongozi, mkuu, msimamizi. 2 wakili mkuu (kwa kesi fulani). 3 (*GB*) (*newspaper*) habari yenye uzito wa kwanza. 4 chipukizi. 5 ukano. **~less** *adj*. **~ership** *n* uongozi. **~ing** *adj* kuu; -a kwanza; maarufu. **a** ~ **article** maoni ya mhariri. ~ **case** kesi ya msingi. ~ **light** (*colloq*) mtu maarufu. ~ **question** swali linaloelekeza kwenye jibu *n* uongozi, usimamizi. **~-rein** *n* hatamu (ya kuongoza farasi). ~ **strings** *n pl* kamba ya kumwongoza mtoto anayefundishwa kutembea. **in ~-strings** (*fig*) kuongozwa/ kuelekezwa kama mtoto mdogo.

leaf *n* 1 jani; (*of a coconut tree*) kuti; (*colloq*) petali. **in** ~ -enye majani. **come into** ~ ota majani. **~-bud** *n* sehemu jani linapoota. **~-mould** *n* mboji. 2 karatasi (katika kitabu). **take a ~ out of sb's book** fuata mfano wa mtu, -iga, chukua mtu kama mfano. **turn over a new** ~ ongoka, jirekebisha na anza upya. 3 bamba, kipande chembamba cha chuma (agh. cha dhahabu). 4 kipandemeza: ubao unaoweza kutolewa kufanya meza iwe ndogo zaidi *vi* ~ **through (a book, etc)** pitia (kwa kusoma) haraka haraka. **~less** *adj* -siokuwa na majani. **~y** *adj* -liofunikwa na majani, -enye majani .**~let** n 1 jani changa. 2 ukurasa (wenye matangazo).

league[1] mapatano baina ya watu/ vikundi/mataifa yenye malengo sawa; shirikisho, washiriki, wanachama katika mapatano. **The ~ of Nations** Shirikisho la Mataifa (1919-1946). **be in ~ with** shirikiana na; -wa na shauri moja na. 2 (*sports*) ligi *vt,vi* shiriki, shirikiana.

league[2] *n* (*old*) kipimo cha urefu (kama maili 3).

leak *vt,vi* 1 vuja. ~ **(out)** to (*of news, secrets etc*) (*cause to*) toka; fichuka, julikana *n* 1 upenyu, mvujo, ufa, tundu. 2 gesi/maji yanayovuja. **~age** *n* 1 kuvuja, mvujo. 2 kufichuka (siri). 3 kiasi kinachovuja/ kinachofichuka. **~y** *adj*.

leal *adj* (*Scot or lit*) -aminifu, -tiifu.

lean[1] *adj* 1 (*of persons and animals*) -embamba, -liokonda *become ~* konda, dhoofika; (*of meat*) -nofu, -siokuwa na mafuta. 2 -siozalisha; hafifu; *~ years* miaka ya mavuno machache/mwambo *n* mnofu, nyama isiokuwa na mafuta. **~ness** *n*.

lean[2] *vi,vt* 1 enda upande, egama. ~ **over backward(s) (to do sth)** (*colloq*) fanya juu chini kumridhisha mtu, kupata kitu. 2 ~ **(on/upon)** egemea. 3 egemeza. 4 ~ **towards** elekea. 5 **~on/upon** tegemea. **~ing** *n* (*of mind*) mwelekeo. **~-to** *n* kibanda kinachoegemea nyumba nyingine.

leap *vi,vt* 1 ruka, chupa. ~ **at** pokea/ kubali kwa furaha nyingi. **look before you ~** fikiri kabla ya kutenda. 2 ruka; rusha *~ a horse over a fence* rusha farasi juu ya ua *n* mruko; ruko. **by ~s and bounds** upesi sana. **a ~ in the dark** jaribio (ambalo matokeo yake hayabashiriki. **~-frog** mchezo wa kurukiana. **~-year** *n* mwaka mrefu (ambamo mwezi wa Februari unakuwa wa siku 29).

learn *vt,vi* 1 jifunza *~ one's lessons* jifunza masomo. ~ **by heart** kariri. 2 arifiwa, pata habari, ambiwa *I have yet to ~ if the train arrived* sijapata habari kama treni ilifika. 3 (*vulgar or dialect*) fundisha *I'll ~ you*! nitakufundisha! **~ed** *adj* -enye elimu, -juzi ~ **man** msomi *the ~ professions* utaalamu (mwalimu, hakimu, n.k.) *my ~ colleague* msomi mwenzangu. **~edly** *adv*. **~ed** *n* mwanafunzi. **~ing** *n* elimu, ujuzi, usomi *a man of great ~* mtu mwenye ujuzi, mtaalamu.

lease *n* mkataba wa kupangisha/ kukodisha nyumba, duka, shamba n.k.; hati ya kukodisha. **let on ~** pangisha, kodisha. **take on ~** panga, kodi. **give/get a new ~ of life** -pa/pata nguvu mpya *vt* panga/ pangisha, kodi/kodisha. **~hold** *n* 1 nyumba/duka/shamba lililopangishwa/iliyokodishwa *adj* -a kukodi, -a kupanga. **~holder** mpangaji.

leash *n* ukanda/ugwe wa kufungia/ kuongoza wanyama (hasa mbwa) *hold in ~* zuia kwa ukanda; (*fig*) dhibiti. **strain at the ~** (*fig*) wa na shauku kuwa huru; -wa na shauku kupata fursa ya kufanya jambo *vt* zuia/funga kwa ukanda/ugwe.

least *adj* 1 dogo kuliko -ote, -lio dogo. (*maths*) ~ **common multiple** kigawe kidogo cha shirika (KDS) ~ **common denominator** kigawe kidogo cha asili. **the ~ said the better** ni bora kukaa kimya *~ said soonest mended* (*prov*) heri kutosema zaidi. 2 (*phrases*) **at ~** angalau (*not*) *in the ~* kidogo tu; hata kidogo *to say the ~* (*of it*) bila kutia chumvi *adv* (*the*) ~ kidogo, kwa kiasi kidogo. ~ **of all** kabisa; jambo la mwisho *no one can object ~ of all Mariamu* hakuna anayeweza kupinga, hata Mariamu *I would ~ of all want to hurt you* jambo la mwisho ninalotaka kufanya ni kukuudhi wewe. **~wise, ~ways** *adv* walao, angalau.

leather *n* 1 ngozi (iliyotengenezwa iwe laini na isioze). 2 (*compounds*) ~ **jacket** *n* lava wa aina ya inzi. ~ **neck** *n* (*US,sl*) askari mwana maji *vt* chapa, piga (hasa na ukanda wa ngozi). **~y** *adj* -a ngozi, -gumu kama ngozi. **~ette** *n* ngozi mwigo/bandia.

leave[1] *vt,vi* 1 toka, ondoka; *we shall ~ here tomorrow* tutaondoka hapa kesho. ~ **for** ondoka kwenda/ kuelekea (mahali fulani) *~ for Nairobi* ondoka kwenda Nairobi. 2 (*of a thing, person, work, place*) acha *~ your books here* acha vitabu vyako hapa *~ a guest at home* acha mgeni nyumbani *she expects to ~ the job* anatarajia kuacha kazi *when did you*

~ *school*? ulimaliza shule lini? **be/get nicely left** (*colloq*) danganywa; telekezwa. ~ **sb/sth behind** sahau, acha *don't ~ me behind* usiniache. ~ **sb/sth alone** -tosumbua, -toingilia, -togusa. ~ **well alone** (*prov*) usitie ufundi kwenye kitu kizuri, acha mambo yalivyo. ~ **off** acha; koma, isha, hulu *where did we ~ off*? tulikomea/tuliachia wapi *when did you ~ off your spectacles*? lini umeacha kuvaa miwani yako? ~ **sth/sb out** ruka, acha (kumshughulikia). ~ **sth over** ahirisha, acha (kwa muda). ~ **it at that** achia hapo, acha kusema/kufanya zaidi. ~ **sb to himself/to his own devices** acha huru. ~ **sth unsaid** acha kusema jambo. ~ **much/a lot/sth/to be desired** -toridhisha. ~ **nothing to be desired** ridhisha. ~ **go/hold (of sth)** achilia. 3 baki, bakisha ~ *some money for clothes* bakisha kiasi cha fedha kwa ajili ya nguo *eight from ten ~s two* kumi ukitoa nane hubaki mbili. **to be left until called for** ikae/iachwe hadi mwenyewe anakuja kuchukua. 4 -pa, achia; kabidhi. ~ **word (with sb) (for sb)** -pa/achia maagizo n.k. ~ *the matter to sb* achia mtu shauri alishughulikie ~ *a teacher on duty in charge of the school* achia/kabidhi madaraka ya shule kwa mwalimu wa zamu. 5 ~ **sth (to sb)**; ~ **sb sth (at the time of one's death)** rithisha, acha/achia (mali, madeni, mjane, watoto n.k.). 6 (*of directions*) pita ~ *the post office on your right* pita posta upande wa kulia *n* 1 ruhusa, idhini. ~ **of absence** likizo/ruhusa (ya kutokuwepo) ~ *to appeal* ruhusa ya kukata rufaa. **by/ with your** ~ kwa ruhusa yako, kumradhi. 2 likizo, livu *emergency ~* likizo ya dharura *sick ~* likizo ya ugonjwa *take French ~* toroka, enda likizo bila ruhusa. **on** ~ likizoni. 3 kuondoka. **take (one's) ~ (of sb)** aga, agana na. ~ **taking** *n* kuaga/kuagana. **take ~ of one's senses** fanya kama mwenda wazimu; pata wazimu. **leavings** *n* (*pl*) mabaki, masalio, masazo, makombo.

leaven *n* 1 chachu, hamira. 2 (*fig*) athari, kichocheo *vt* 1 chachua, tia hamira. 2 athiri, geuza.

lecher *n* fisadi, fasiki, mzinzi, mkware (wa kiume). **~ous** *adj* -zinifu, kware, asherati. **~y** *n* ukware, uzinzi, uasherati.

lectern *n* marufaa: meza ya kusomea kitabu (agh. kanisani au darasani).

lecture *n* 1 mhadhara *deliver a ~* toa mhadhara; makaripio. 2 hotuba ya kuonya *vt,vi* 1 ~ **(on)** toa mhadhara. 2 ~ **sb (for)** kemea/onya (kwa hotuba ndefu); hubiri. **~r** *n* mhadhiri. **~ship** *n* uhadhiri.

led *pt, pp of* **lead**[2]

ledge *n* 1 kishubaka, shubaka, kibao (itokezacho ukutani). 2 (*of rock*) mwamba chini ya maji (hasa karibu ya ufukwe).

ledger *n* 1 leja: daftari kubwa ya hesabu. 2 **~/leger line** *n* (*music*) mstari mfupi chini au juu ya mistari mitano ya noti.

lee *n* mahali pasipoelekea upepo. ~ **(side)** demani *under the ~ of a house* upande wa nyumba usioelekea upepo. **~ward** *adj* -a demani. **~way** *n* 1 mwendo wa chombo kikichukuliwa upande wa demani. 2 (*fig*) uhuru wa kuwa na fikra/matendo tofauti *make up ~-way* fidia muda, rudia mahali.

leech *n* 1 ruba *stick like a ~* (*fig*) ganda. 2 mnyonyaji. 3 (*old use*) daktari.

leek *n* liki: mmea kama kitunguu (wenye tumba jeupe).

leer *n* jicho/tabasamu la husuda/ufisadi *vi* **~(at sb)** tazama kwa jicho la husuda/ufisadi.

lees *n* masira, masimbi. **drink/drain to the** ~ (*fig*) pata matatizo/mateso makubwa, teseka kupita kiasi.

left[1] *pt,pp of* **leave**. **~overs** *n* masazo, makombo; kiporo.

left[2] *adj,n,adv* kushoto; -a kushoto *~side* upande wa kushoto *turn ~*

geuka kushoto. **the ~ (wing)** wanasiasa wa mrengo wa kushoto (wapendao mabadiliko ya kijamaa). **~hand** *adj* -a kushoto. **~handed** *adj* (*of a person*) -enye kutumia mkono wa kushoto. **a ~ handed compliment** wasifu tata; wasifu wenye mashaka. **~ist** *n* mwanasiasa wa mrengo wa kushoto.

leg *n* 1 (*of animal, person, garment, chair, table, stool etc.*) mguu. **be all ~s** (*of a person*) -wa -lonjo, njorinjori. **be off one' s ~** pumzika. **be on one's ~s** (*or joc* **on one's hind ~s)** simama (ili kuzungumza/ kuhutubia); (*after an illness*) -wa mzima, pona. **be on one's last ~s** choka, -wa na mavune, -wa hoi; chungulia kaburi, karibia kufa. **feel/find one's ~s** (*of a baby*) anza kusimama/kutembea; (*fig*) tambua uwezo/kipaji, vipaji n.k,; jiamini. **give sb a ~ up** saidia mtu wakati wa shida. **pull sb's ~** tania. **~ pull, ~ pulling** *n* utani. **run sb off his ~s** chosha (mtu) kwa kazi *shake a ~* (*colloq*) cheza dansi; (*imper*) fanya haraka; anza *show a ~* (*colloq*) amka kitandani; (*imper*) ongeza bidii *not have a ~ to stand on* shindwa kujitetea *stretch one's ~s* nyoosha miguu (kwa matembezi), punga hewa *take to one's ~s* kimbia *walk one's ~s off*; *walk sb off his ~s* chosha mtu kwa kutembea. 2 (*support of a bed*) tendegu *be on its last ~s* karibia kwisha. 3 sehemu ya safari; sehemu moja ya mfululizo wa mashindano ya michezo. **~ged** *adj* (*in compounds*) *long ~* enye miguu ya milonjo, njorinjori *two ~* -enye miguu miwili *three ~ race* mbio za miguu mitatu (kufungana miguu). **three ~ stool** kigoda. **~ging** *n (usu pl)* soksi ndefu za ngozi/nguo. **~gy** *adj* -lonjo, njorinjori.

legacy *n* 1 urithi; hiba *leave a ~ to* rithisha, achia urithi; (*for religious purposes*) wakifia. 2 (*fig*) kitu kinachorithishwa na mababu au waliotangulia, urithi.

legal *adj* halali; -a haki; -a kisheria. **~advice** ushauri wa kisheria. **~ adviser** mshauri wa kisheria. **~ aid** msaada wa kisheria. **~ capacity** uwezo wa kisheria. **~ practitioner** mwanasheria ~ *profession* jamii ya wanasheria, uwakili ~ *tender* fedha halali kwa malipo. **~ly** *adv*. **~ism** *n* ushikiliaji mno wa sheria. **~ity** *n* uhalali; haki. **~ize** *vt* halalisha. **~ization** *n* uhalalisho.

legate balozi (wa Papa). **legation** ubalozi mdogo.

legatee *n* (*leg*) mrithi.

legend *n* 1 ngano, hekaya. 2 ngano na hekaya hizi kwa ujumla. 3 maandishi katika sarafu/medali/ramani n.k.. **~ary** *adj* -a hadithi za kale.

leger *see* **ledger**[2]

legerdemain *n* 1 kiinimacho, mizungu, miujiza. 2 (*fig*) hoja za uongo.

leghorn *n* 1 kuku wa Mediterania. 2 kofia ya majani makavu.

legible *adj* (*of handwriting, print*) -a kusomeka, dhahiri. **legibly** *adv*. **legibility** *n*.

legion *n* 1 kikosi cha askari 3,000-6,000 wa Kirumi. 2 **British L~** Chama cha askari wa Kiingereza waliotoka vitani 1921. **Foreign ~** (Ufaransa) askari wa kigeni wanaopigana vita katika nchi ya kigeni. **the L~ of Honour** nishani ya Wafaransa. 3 *(Lit or rhet*) wingi, jeshi. **~ary** *adj n* 1 askari wa Kirumi. 2 askari wa kigeni katika jeshi la Ufaransa *adj* -a askari wa Kirumi; -a askari wa kigeni wa jeshi la Ufaransa.

legislate *vt* tunga sheria. **legislation** *n* utungaji sheria; sheria zilizotungwa. **legislative** *adj* -a kutunga sheria. **~ assembly** baraza la kutunga sheria. **~ draftsman** msawidi sheria. **legislator** *n* mbunge. **legislature** *n* baraza la kutunga sheria, bunge.

legitimate *adj* 1 -halali, -a ndoa *~ son/ daughter* mtoto wa ndoa/halali. 2 -a maana *~ purpose* kusudi la maana. 3 halisi *the ~ theatre* tamthilia halisi. 4 halali. **~ly** *adv*. **legitimacy** *n*.

legitimatize *vt* halalisha.
legume *n* jamiikunde. **leguminous** *adj* -a jamii kunde.
leisure *n* 1 wasaa/nafasi/wakati (wa mapumziko). **at ~** bila kazi *at your ~* kwa nafasi yako. 2 (*attrib*) wakati wa mapumziko *~ time/hours* muda/saa za mapumziko. **~ly** *adv* taratibu, polepole *work ~* fanya kazi polepole. **~d** *adj* -enye wasaa/nafasi *the ~ classes* matabaka tajiri.
leitmotif/leitmotiv *n* dhamira kuu (yenye kujirudia); dhamira, ishara (inayoashiria wazo/mtu).
lemon *n* 1 limau. 2 mlimau. 3 rangi ya limau. 4 bwege. **~ drop** *n* bonge la sukari iliyochemshwa na kutiwa limau. **~ squash** *n* kinywaji cha limau. **~ squezer** *n* chombo cha kukamulia limau. **~ sole** *n* aina ya samaki mpana. 4 (*GB*) (*sl*) mtu mjinga na asiyevutia. **~ade** *n* maji ya limau (yaliyotiwa sukari na maji).
lemur *n* komba wa bukini.
lend *vt* 1 azima, (*of money*) kopesha. *~ a hand (with sth)* saidia, auni *~ an ear* sikiliza. **~ing-library** maktaba ya kuazimisha (vitabu). **~ sth to sb, ~ sb sth** azima/azimisha. 2 **~ sth to sth** changia, ongeza *his ideas lent expertise to the discussion* mawazo yake yalichangia utaalamu kwenye mjadala *his actions ~ credence to his good reputation* matendo yake yanaonyesha ukweli wa sifa yake. 3 **~ oneself to sth** kubali, -faa *it ~s itself to* inafaa kwa. **~er** *n.*
length *n* 1 urefu *be 5 miles in ~* -wa na urefu wa maili tano (*period of time*) muda wa *the ~ of our stay was two days* tulikaa kwa muda wa siku mbili. **at ~** mwishowe; hatimaye; kwa muda mrefu; kwa undani. **(at) full ~** lala kwa kujinyoosha *keep sb at arms ~* kataa urafiki na mtu, epa. 2 kadiri, kiasi *go to any ~ (s)* fanya kila linalowezekana (kupata utakacho). 3 kipande cha (nguo, bomba n.k. kinachotosha shughuli fulani) *I need a ~ of dress material* ninahitaji kipande cha kitambaa cha gauni. 4 kipimo cha kitu mwanzo hadi mwisho; urefu. **~en** *vt, vi* refusha. **~ways, ~wise** *adv,adj* kwa urefu. **~y** *adj* -refu mno.
lenient *adj* -pole, -enye huruma. **lenience/leniency n.** **~ly** *adv*. **lenity** *n* (*formal*) huruma, upole.
lens *n* lenzi, kioo (cha miwani, darubini n.k.) *concave ~* lenzi mbonyeo; *convex ~* lenzi mbinuko.
lent *pp of* **lend.**
Lent *n* kwaresima **~en** *adj* -a kwaresima *with a ~ face* -enye uso wa huzuni.
lentil *n* dengu, adesi.
lento *adj, adv* (*music*) polepole. **Leo** *n* Simba: alama ya Zodiaki. **~nine** *adj* -a kama simba.
leopard *n* chui. **~ess** *n* chui jike.
leper *n* mkoma, (*fig*) mtu anayeepukwa na wengi kwa ajili ya ufidhuli wake.
leprosy *n* ukoma. **leprous** *adj*.
leprechaun *n* (*Irish*) zimwi mwema. **lesbian** *n* msagaji *adj* -enye kusaga **~ism** *n.*
lese-majesty *n* 1 uhaini. 2 (*joc*) ujeuri.
lesion *n* donda, jeraha.
less *adj* 1 (*for what is measured by size, degree, duration, number etc*) -dogo zaidi, -dogo *there is ~ money these days* siku hizi fedha ni ndogo zaidi *no ~ a person than the President came* Rais ndiye aliyefika hasa *adv* kidogo (zaidi) *he drinks ~ these days* amepunguza kunywa. **any the ~** bado ... ingawa *I don't think any the ~ of her for failing her exam* bado ninamwamini ingawa ameshindwa mtihani wake. **even/still ~** sembuse/ seuze *I don't believe he stole the money still ~ the car* siamini kuwa aliiba pesa sembuse gari. **no ~ than** si chini ya *she bought no ~ than 6 pairs of khangas* alinunua siyo chini ya jozi sita za khanga. **none the ~** hata hivyo, walakini *I know he's cunning none the ~ he's very charming* najua ni mjanja hata hivyo ni mchangamfu *n* kidogo *the ~ the*

better kikiwa kidogo ni bora zaidi *in ~ than an hour* -siozidi saa moja; *prep* kasoro, kosa, toa *a month ~ two days* mwezi kasoro siku mbili; *500/= ~ 50/= tax* Shilingi 500/= kasoro Shilingi 50/= za kodi. **~en** *vt,vi* punguza, punguka; fanya -dogo. **~er** *adj* -dogo zaidi, -lio -dogo *to a ~er degree* kwa kiasi/kadiri ndogo zaidi.

lessee *n* (*leg*) mpangaji. **lessor** *n* mpangishaji.

lesson *n* 1 somo. 2 (*portion of Bible*) somo, sura. 3 onyo; fundisho *let that be a ~ to you* naliwe fundisho kwako *teach him a ~* mrudi, mwadhibu asifanye tena.

lest *conj* 1 ili...si; sijekuwa (kwa hofu) *take heed ~ he falls* tahadhari asije akaanguka *I hurried ~ I be late* niliharakisha ili nisichelewe. 2 (*after fear*) kuwa *we were afraid ~ he should get here too late* tulihofu kuwa atachelewa.

let[1] *vt,vi* 1 ruhusu, toa ruhusa, acha *her father ~ her go to the film with us* baba yake alimruhusu aende sinema nasi *~ me know* niarifu. 2 (*imperative use*) **~ 's go** twende *~ them all come* na waje wote *~ me see* hebu nione *~ the water boil* acha maji yachemke. 3 (*hire*) pangisha, kodisha *she ~s rooms in her house* anapangisha vyumba nyumbani mwake *he ~s his car* anakodisha gari lake. 4 (*with adj/n/v/prep*). **~ alone** licha ya, sembuse. **~ sb along** mwache, usimsumbue *~ him alone now* usimsumbue sasa. **~ be** acha *~ him be* mwache. **~ drive at** lenga, tupa (kupiga). **~ blood** toa damu. **blood-~ing** *n* kutoa damu. **~ down** angusha; (*clothes*) refusha *you'll have to ~ the hem down* itakubidi kurefusha gauni lako. **~ sb down** sikitisha *you ~ me down by not finishing the work* umenisikitisha kwa kutotekeleza kazi yako. **~-down** *n* sikitiko *~ drive/fly* piga kwa nguvu. **~ drop/fall** angusha (*fig*) toa siri (kwa makusudi au kwa bahati tu). **~ go** acha, achia huru, fungulia *~ pass* samehe, fumbia macho *the judge ~ the prisoner go* hakimu alimwachilia mfungwa *~ oneself go* acha kujizuia; jiachia. **~ in** ruhusu kuingia, fungua, fumbulia *he ~ Maria in on the secret* alimfumbulia Maria siri. **~ oneself (sb) in for** jiingiza/jitia bila kujua (katika taabu, shughuli n.k.). **~ into** ingiza, ruhusu kuingia *he ~ the children into the room* aliwaruhusu watoto waingie chumbani *the window ~s good air into the room* dirisha linaingiza upepo mzuri chumbani. **~ loose** acha huru, fungulia *he ~ the goat loose* alifungulia mbuzi; (*fig*) ondoa, acha, onyesha *he ~ loose his anger at us* alituonyesha hasira yake. **~ off** piga, fyatua (bunduki n.k.); samehe (fulani) *I'll ~ you off this time but don't do it again* sasa ninakusamehe lakini usirudie tena. **~ on** (*colloq*) toa (siri) *he didn't ~ on that he knew anything* hakuonyesha kuwa anajua mambo yoyote. **~ out** toa, ondoa *she ~ the water out of the sink* aliachia maji kutoka kwenye beseni; (*clothes*) ongeza upana *because she put on weight she had to ~ out her clothes* kwa sababu alinenepa ilimbidi aongeze upana wa mavazi yake. **~ sth pass** puuza; -totia maanani. **~ through** ruhusu kupita, pisha *please ~ me through* nipishe. **~ up** pungua ukali, punguza jitihada *the rain ~up after an hour* baada ya saa moja mvua imepungua *he never ~ up working hard* hapunguzi jitihada yake kazini. **~-up** *n* (*colloq*) pungufu, kikomo *it was raining all day without ~-up* mvua ilinyesha siku nzima bila kikomo.

let[2] *n* kupangisha, kukodisha *this room is a good ~* chumba hiki ni kizuri kupanga/kupangisha. **~ing** *n* chumba/nyumba ya kupangisha.

let[3] *vt* (*archaic*) zuia *n* kizuio, mgogoro, pingamizi.

lethal *adj* -a (kusababisha) mauti, -a kuua.

lethargy *n* uchovu, kukosa nguvu, uzito. **lethargic** *adj* -zito, -enye usingizi. **lethargically** *adv*.
lethe *n* (*Gr*) mto wa jehanamu unaosababisha kusahau yaliyopita.
letter *n* 1 (*of alphabet*) herufi. 2 barua, waraka. **~-bomb** *n* bomu la barua. **~-box** *n* (*US* **mailbox**) sanduku la posta. **~-case** *n* mkoba wa barua. **~head** *n* karatasi yenye anwani. **~-paper** *n* karatasi za barua. **~-perfect** *adj* -enye kujua kwa moyo. **~-press** *n* maandiko (katika kitabu cha picha). 3 *(phrases)* **keep (to) the ~ agreement** fuata sheria/ makubaliano neno kwa neno bila kuzingatia maana. **to the ~** kwa makini, kabisa. 4 (*pl*) elimu, fasihi, *a man of ~* mwandishi; msomi *the profession of ~s* uandishi. **~ed** *adj* -enye elimu *vt* chapa herufi; pamba na herufi za alfabeti. **~ing** *n* maneno; uandikaji wa herufi.
lettuce *n* saladi.
leucocyte *(US* **leuocyte)** *n* selidamu nyeupe.
leukaemia (*US*) **leukemia** *n* lukemia: ugonjwa wa damu.
levant *vi* toroka (hasa pasi kulipa gharama au madeni fulani).
levee *n* (*US*) boma la kuzuia maji, ukingo wa udongo/kitope.
level *n* 1 usawa *on a ~ with* sawa na (cheo, daraja, ardhi n.k.) *on different ~s* usawa usiolingana, mbalimbali *be on the ~* -wa sawa; (*fig*) sema ukweli; (*flat area*) mahali pa sawa *find one's ~* fikia kiwango chako sawa. 2 pimamaji. 3 kiwango *rise to higher ~s* fikia viwango vya juu zaidi; ngazi *top ~ officials* maafisa wa ngazi ya juu. 4 **on the ~** (*colloq*) kweli, wazi *adj* 1 sawa (bila kuinuka) *a ~ crossing* tambuka reli; njia panda ya reli na barabara, chekereni; makutano. 2 usawa *~ race* mbio za kukaribiana. 3 **have a ~ head** -wa tulivu, bila papara. **~ headed** *adj* tulivu. **do one's ~ best** fanya vizuri uwezavyo *vt,vi* 1 sawazisha. **~ sth down/up** linganisha/sawazisha vitu. 2 bomoa (nyumba, ukuta n.k.), angusha, shusha *~ to the ground* bomoa kabisa. 3 (*aim*) elekeza, lenga *~ a gun at* lenga shabaha. 4 **~ off** (*airplane*) fanya ndege iwe sambamba na ardhi; (*fig*) fikia kiwango (ambapo hutegemei kupanda zaidi). **~ler** *n* msawazishi: mtu ambaye anataka kuondoa tofauti zote za jamii.
lever *n* wenzo *vt* inulia (vitu vizito). **~age** *n* nguvu ya wenzo *(fig) n* nguvu, uwezo wa kushawishi.
leveret *n* mtoto wa sungura, kititi.
leviathan *n* 1 (*in the Bible*) lewiathani, mamba. 2 kitu chochote kikubwa mno; dubwana.
levitate *vt,vi* anga, angama, elea. **levitation** *n*.
levity *n* 1 purukushani. 2 utovu wa staha.
levy *vt,vi* 1 ~ **(on)** toza. 2 (*of soldiers*) andikisha kwa lazima. **~ war upon/ against** anzisha vita. 3 **~ on** twaa/ kamata kisheria *n* 1 ada, kodi. 2 *pl* makundi ya wanajeshi *development~* kodi ya maendeleo.
lewd *adj* -pujufu, fisadi, asherati, -zinifu. **~ness** *n*. **~ly** *adv*.
lexicon *n* 1 msamiati, maneno. 2 kamusi. **lexical** *adj* -a msamiati/maneno. **~ly** *adv*. **lexis** *n* msamiati. **lexicographer** *n* mwana leksikografia; **lexicography** *n* leksikografia; usawidi kamusi. **lexicology** *n* (*ling.*) elimu msamiati, leksikolojia: sayansi ya maana na matumizi ya maneno.
liable *adj* 1 **~ for** -a kuwajibika kisheria *John is ~ for his son's debts* John anawajibika kisheria kulipa madeni ya mwanae. 2 -a kupaswa, -a kustahili. **be ~ to sth** paswa, stahili *tax evaders are ~ to heavy penalty* wanaokwepa kodi wanastahili adhabu kali. 3 -a kuelekea, -enye kuwezekana. **be ~ to do sth** -wa na uwezekano wa kufanya jambo he is

~ *to get a loan* anaelekea atapata mkopo. **liability** *n* 1 dhima. **limited ~** dhima ya ukomo. **limited ~ company** kampuni ya dhima zenye ukomo. **public unlimited ~** dhima isiyo ukomo. 2 wajibu, kupaswa ~ *to military service* wajibika kujiunga na jeshi. 3 (*pl*) **liabilities** madeni; kuwiwa. 4 (*colloq*) kikwazo.

liaise *vi* ~ **(with/between)** (*colloq*) -wa kiungo kati ya kikundi kimoja na kingine, wakilisha, shirikiana, husiana. **liaison** *n* 1 ushirikiano, uhusiano, kiungo. ~ **officer** afisa ushirikiano. 2 kufanya mapenzi yasiyo halali.

liana *n* mtambaa.

liar *n* mwongo.

lib *n* **(colloq abbr for liberation)** ukombozi *women's* ~ ukombozi wa wanawake.

libation *n* tambiko/sadaka ya kinywaji (mvinyo, maziwa n.k.).

libel *n* 1 (kuchapisha) maandishi ya kukashifu; maandishi yenye kutweza hadhi ya mtu *criminal* ~ kashifa za kijinai. 2 ~ **on** (*colloq*) dhalala, kashfa *vt* kashifu (kwa maandishi), singizia vibaya/bure. **~ler** *n*. ~ **lous**,(*US*) ~ **ous** *adj*.

liberty *n* 1 uhuru; haki/uwezo wa kujiamulia la kufanya *people defended their* ~ watu walilinda uhuru wao. **at** ~ (*of a person*) huru *we are at ~ to stay with them* tuko huru kuishi nao. **set sb at ~** achia mtu, pa mtu uhuru, toa mtu utumwani. ~ **of conscience** uhuru wa kuamini agh. dini. ~ **of speech** uhuru wa kusema (fikra za mtu) hadharani. ~ **of the press** uhuru wa kuandika na kuchapisha (majarida, vitabu n.k.) bila kuingiliwa. 2 kutenda jambo bila ruhusa ya mwenyewe; kutenda yasiyo haki. **take the ~ of doing sth** jiamulia *he took the ~ of using my car while I was away* alijiamulia kutumia gari langu pasi na ruhusa yangu nilipokuwa sipo. **take liberties with sb** zoeana na mtu kupita kiasi. 3 (*pl*) fadhila au haki zilizotolewa na mamlaka fulani *the liberties given by Scopo* haki zilizotolewa na Scopo. **libertarian** *n* mpigania uhuru wa mawazo, dini, uhuru wa kufikiri na kutenda.

liberal *adj* 1 -karimu, -paji, -ema *she is ~ with her money* yu mkarimu na fedha zake. 2 -enye mawazo mapana na huru; -siokuwa na upendeleo. 3 (*of education*) -a elimu (ya kupanua mawazo). **the ~ arts** masomo ya sanaa na sayansi za jamii k.m. historia, lugha n.k. 4 *(politics in GB)* -a chama (cha *Liberal)* chenye kupendelea mabadiliko ya wastani *n* mpenda maendeleo na mabadiliko *n* mwanachama wa chama hicho. **~ism** **(views/ideas/principles)** *n* msimamo, fikra za kupenda mabadiliko. **~ize** *vt* panua, legeza masharti (ya biashara n.k.). **~ization** *n*. **~ity** *n* 1 ukarimu, upaji, ufadhili, kutobagua, kutopendelea *his ~ities have made him poor* ukarimu wake umemfilisi.

liberate *vt* ~ **from** komboa, fanya huru. **liberation** n ukombozi *liberation committee* kamati ya ukombozi.

libertine *n* 1 mwasherati, mkware *chartered* ~ mkware anayevumiliwa na jamii.

libido *n (psych)* ashiki, nyege. **libidinous** *adj* -a ashiki.

Libra *n* Mizani: alama ya Zodiaki.

library *n* 1 maktaba *a walking* ~ (*fig*) mjuzi. **mobile ~** maktaba inayosafiri *public* ~ maktaba ya umma *reference* ~ maktaba ya marejeo. 2 (*attrib*) -a maktaba ~ *edition* toleo la kitabu kikubwa na chenye jalada gumu. 3 chumba cha kuandikia na kusomea katika nyumba binafsi. 4 mfulululizo wa vitabu vya aina na jalada la namna moja vilivyotolewa na mchapishaji mmoja. **librarian** *n* mkutubi: mwangalizi wa maktaba **librarianship** *n*.

libretto *n* kitabu cha maneno ya opera.

lice *n pl of* **louse**.

licence (*US* **license**) *n* (*permission*) ruhusa, hati, leseni *driving* ~ leseni ya kuendesha gari *teaching* ~ hati ya kufundishia. **on** ~ *n* (*GB*) leseni ya kuuza vileo katika baa. **off** ~ *n* (*GB*) leseni ya kuuza vileo katika stoo (bila ruhusa ya kunywa hapo hapo), duka lenye vileo. 2 kupuuza sheria/kanuni/mila n.k.; ufisadi, kuutumia vibaya uhuru. **poetic** ~ uhuru wa kishairi (wa kukiuka kanuni za kawaida za lugha). **license** (*also* ~) *vt* pa leseni *shops ~d to sell alcohol* maduka yenye leseni ya kuuza vileo ~ *the hawker to sell clothes* -pa mchuuzi leseni ya kuuza nguo. **~e** *n* mtu mwenye leseni (hasa ya vileo). **~er** *n* mtoa leseni. **licentiate** *n* mtaalam mwenye leseni/cheti cha kazi yake. **licentious** *adj* -asherati, fisadi, -kware. **~ly** *adv*. **ness** *n*.

lichen *n* kuvu, ukungu (wa miti na miamba).

lich-gate/lychgate *n* lango la kupitishia maiti kanisani.

licit *adj* halali, -a sheria, -nayo kubalika kisheria.

lick *vt* 1 ramba. ~ **a person's boots** ramba miguu, jipendekeza sana. ~ **one's lips** jiramba kwa uchu. ~ **one's wounds** jipa nguvu baada ya kushindwa. ~ **sth off/~sth up** ramba. ~ **into shape** (*fig*) funza/tengeneza barabara. ~ **the dust** (*rhet*) anguka chini, shindwa kabisa; -fa. 2 (*esp waves/flames*) gusa gusa, pitia *the waves ~ed the banks of the river* mawimbi yalipita katika kingo za mto. 3 (*colloq*) shinda, piga sana, twanga. ~ **an opponent** shinda mpinzani wako. 4 (*sl*) piga mbio, enda mbio *as hard as one can* ~ upesi sana *n* 1 kuramba. **a ~ and a promise** (*colloq*) kunawanawa/kusafisha/kuogaoga. 2 (*also* **salt** ~) mahali mifugo inapopatia magadi/chumvi. 3 (*sl*) **at a great** ~; **at full** ~ mwendo mkubwa; kwa kasi sana. **~ing** *n* (*colloq*) kurambisha; kipigo; ushinde *Pan African FC got a ~ last night* timu ya Pan African ilipata kipigo/ilirambishwa mchanga.

licorice *see* **liquorice**

lid *n* 1 kifuniko, *tea pot* ~ kifuniko cha birika. 2 *eye* ~ ukope wa jicho. **~less** *adj*.

lie[1] *vi* danganya, sema uwongo *she is lying* anadanganya *n* uwongo *tell a* ~ sema uwongo. **give sb the** ~ shitaki mtu kwa kudanganya. ~ **detector** kijaluba cha kupimia mabadiliko kifiziolojia (k.m. mapigo ya moyo, kupumua hasa wakati mtu anapohojiwa); kibaini uongo.

lie[2] *vi* 1 lala, jinyosha juu ya kitanda, ardhi n.k. ~ *on ones back* lala chali ~ *back* jinyosha ~ *face downwards* lala kifudifudi *her body ~s at the cemetery* amezikwa makaburini. **take sth lying down** kubali kutukanwa pasi na ubishi. ~ **down under (an insult)** kubali bila kupinga. ~ **in** kawia kuamka (kutoka kitandani); -wa katika uchungu kitandani (ili kuzaa mtoto). **lying -in hospital** (*old use*) hospitali ya uzazi. ~ **up** lala kitandani au chumbani kwa ugonjwa. ~ **with** (*old use biblical, now usu* **sleep with**) jamiiana. **let sleeping dogs** ~ *(prov)* usimwamshe aliyelala, ukimwamsha utalala wewe. **~-a bed** *n 1* mvivu, asiyetaka kuamka kitandani. 2 (*of things*) -wa juu ya *the coat lay on the floor the whole night* koti lilikuwa juu ya sakafu usiku kucha. 3 (*of abstract things*) -wa, -wa katika hali fulani *I know where his interest ~s* nafahamu mambo anayoyapendelea *the car's trouble ~s in the gear box* tatizo la gari lipo katika gia boksi. ~ **at sb's door** husika, laumika *at whose door should the defeat ~?* nani alaumiwe kwa kushindwa kwetu? ~ **with sb** wajibika *it ~s with you to appoint your deputy* unawajibika kumteua naibu wako. **as far as in me ~s** kwa kadri ya uwezo wangu. 4 -wa mahali. ~ **to** (*of a ship*) karibia kusimama, kabili upepo. 5 kaa, baki *the youth are lying around idle in* *town* vijana wanakaa bure mjini *the soldier lay in the cell for one more night* askari alikaa rumande kwa usiku mmoja zaidi. ~ **heavy on sth** lemea, dhuru. ~ **over** ahirishwa kwa jambo. 6 enea, zagaa, tanda *the game lay before us* wanyama walizagaa kila mahali mbele yetu. **find out/ see how the land ~s** (*fig*) jifunze, chunguza, dadisi jinsi hali ya mambo ilivyo. 7 (*legal*) kubalika *his appeal will not ~ in the court of law* rufaa yake haitakubaliwa na mahakama *n* (*sing only*) mkao/mlalo wa kitu. **the ~ of the land** jinsi sura ya nchi ilivyo (*fig*) hali ya mambo.

lied *n* (*G*) wimbo/shairi la Kijerumani. **~er-singer** mwimbaji wa nyimbo hizo.

liege *adj* (*leg*) (*only in*) ~ **lord/ sovereign** (*feudal times*) mtawala, mwinyi. ~ **man** *n* (*pl)* watwana wa mwinyi.

lien *n* dai la kumiliki (mpaka deni limelipwa).

lieu *n* (*only in*) **in ~ (of)** badala ya.

lieutenant *n* 1 luteni. 2 (*in compounds*) *second ~* luteni usu *~colonel* luteni kanali *~general* luteni jenerali *~commander* luteni kamanda. 3 naibu, mbadala, wakili. **Lord ~ (of the Country)** Mwakilishi wa Malkia. **lieutenancy** *n* uluteni.

life *n* 1 uhai. ~ **force** nishati uhai. 2 viumbe/vitu hai (watu, wanyama na mimea). 3 maisha. **a matter of ~ and death struggle** mapambano ya kufa na kupona *~ insurance* bima ya maisha. **bring to ~** huisha. **come to ~** pata fahamu baada ya kuzimia; changamka. **run for ones ~/for dear ~** kimbia ili kujiokoa/kunusuru maisha. **this ~** maisha ya hapa duniani. **the other ~, future/ eternal/everlasting ~** maisha ya peponi; ahera. **with all the pleasure in ~** kwa raha mustarehe. 4 **take sb's ~** ua mtu. **take one's own ~** jiua, jinyonga. **a ~ for a ~** mtu kwa mtu, kulipiza kisasi. **can not for the ~ of one** haiwezekani hata kama mtu akijitahidi kiasi gani. **not on your ~!** (*colloq*) la hasha! thubutu. 5 kipindi katika maisha (k.m. kuzaliwa hadi kufa) *he lived here all his ~* aliishi hapa maisha yake yote *the ~ of the government* maisha ya serikali ilipokuwa inafanya kazi *he was given a ~ sentence* alipata kifungo cha maisha. ~ **annuity** fedha alipwazo mtu mpaka atakapokufa *for ~* kabisa, kwa maisha. ~ **cycle** hatua anuwai za maisha kamili ya kiumbe (k.m. mbu kuanzia yai, kiluwiluwi, pupa hadi mdudu kamili). ~ **interest** (*legal*) mapato (kutokana na mali fulani) apewayo mtu wakati wa uhai wake tu. ~ **peer** mjumbe wa baraza la malodi (Uingereza) ambaye cheo chake hakirithiki. **have the time of one's ~** (*colloq*) jistarehesha sana. **early/late in ~** mapema, mwanzoni/ mwishoni mwa maisha. 6 uhusiano, uchangamfu, starehe *there is little ~ in the villages* vijijini hakuna shughuli nyingi/hapakuchangamka; maisha yamedorora vijijini *the children are full of ~* watoto wamechangamka/wana raha. **true to ~** (*of a story, drama etc.*) -enye kutoa picha halisi ya maisha; (*of interest/way of living*) -a kupendeza, -a kuvutia *put more ~ in your work* fanya kazi yako ivutie, changamkia kazi zaidi. **the ~ (and soul) of the party** mtu aliye mchangamfu sana katika kikundi. 7 wasifu *a ~ story of Julius Nyerere* wasifu wa Julius Nyerere. 8 mfano/kielezo chenye uhai *a ~ drawing* picha iliyochorwa kwa kutumia mfano wa kiumbe hai, vitu hai. **to the ~** kwa usahihi. **as large as ~** -enye ukubwa wa kawaida (*colloq and in joke*) -enyewe, binafsi; kwa uhakika; pasipo shaka yoyote. 9 maisha baada ya kunusurika. 10 (*compounds*) **~belt** *n* mkanda wa kujiokolea. **~-blood** *n* kiini; damu muhimu kwa uhai; (*fig*) jambo lenye athari kubwa;

kitu kinachotia nguvu. ~-**boat** *n* mashuaokozi (ya kuokolea watu au inayochukuliwa melini). ~**buoy** *n* boyaokozi (chelezo cha kuopolea/ kuokolea watu katika hatari ya majini). ~ **estate** *n* milki ya maisha (ambayo mtu hutumia hadi anapokufa na hairithishwi). ~ **expectancy** miaka ambayo mtu anatarajiwa kuishi. ~-**giving** *adj* -a kuhuisha. ~-**guards** *n* walinzi, waokozi katika sehemu za kuogelea. **L~ Guards** *n* (*pl*) kikosi cha farasi katika jeshi la Kiingereza. ~ **history** *n* (*biol*) kumbukumbu ya maisha kamili ya kiumbe. ~ **insurance/assurance** bima ya maisha. ~-**jacket** *n* jaketi/koti okozi. ~**like** *adj* -enye kufanana na kiumbe chenye uhai; -enye kufanana na kiwakilishwa. ~**line** *n* 1 kambaokozi: kamba ya kuokolea maisha (ambayo hufungwa kwenye boya au meli); kamba ya wapiga mbizi; (*fig*) tegemeo kuu; kitu kinachotegemewa kwa uhai wa mtu. ~**long** *adj* -a maisha, -a maishani. ~-**office** ofisi ya bima ya maisha. ~-**preserver** *n* (*US*) ~ **jacket** (*GB*) rungu la kujilinda. ~-**saver** *n* (*colloq*) kitu/mtu amsaidiaye mwenzake katika matatizo (*esp in Australia*); mwogeleaji aokoaye watu waliozama. ~-**sentence** *n* adhabu ya kifungo cha maisha. ~-**size(d)** (picha) -enye ukubwa sawa na kitu chenyewe. ~-**span** *n* (*biol*) maisha ya kiumbe/ kitu. ~-**support system** *n* vifaa kwenye chombo cha anga/hospitali ambavyo humsaidia mtu kuishi. ~**time** *n* maisha. **the chance of a ~ time** bahati inayotokea mara moja katika maisha. **in sb's ~ time** katika maisha ya mtu. ~-**work** *n* kazi ya kudumu, kazi yenye kumshughulisha mtu maisha yake yote. ~**less** *adj* -fu, -liokufa; -siokuwa na uhai; -enye kuchusha, -siovutia. ~**lessly** *adv*. ~**r** *n* (*sl*) mtu aishiye kwa namna fulani (*sl*) mfungwa wa maisha.

lift *vt,vi* 1 inua, pandisha, nyanyua, kweza. ~ **up ones eyes (to)** angalia, tazama (juu). ~ **up one's voice** paaza sauti. 2 ~ **off** (*of a space craft*) tweka; ruka, ondoka. 3 (*of clouds, fog*) panda, potea *the fog began to ~* ukungu ulianza kutoweka. 4 chimbua; (*root crops*) ng'oa. 5 iba, sogeza. 6 ondoa (agh kizuizi, upigaji marufuku) *n* 1 kuinua; msaada. **give sb a** ~-pa mtu lifti/msaada, beba; (*of a person's spirits*) fariji, changamsha. 2 (*US elevator*) lifti ~-*and-force pump* pampu la kuvuta na kusukuma. ~-**attendant/boy/man** *n* opereta wa lifti.

ligament *n* kano.

ligature *n* 1 uzi, bendeji itumikayo kufunga mishipa n.k. 2 (*printing*) herufi zilizounganishwa f na l kuwa fl.

light[1] *adj* 1 (*of colour*) -liokoza, -sioiva angazi, a ~ *brown* kahawia isioiva, hafifu. 2 (*of a place*) -enye mwanga. ~ **coloured** *adj* -enye rangi isiyoiva *n* 1 nuru, mwanga *the ~ begins to fail* mwanga unaanza kufifia *day ~* mchana. **in a good/bad ~** (*of picture etc*) kuonekana vizuri/vibaya; (*fig*) eleweka vizuri/vibaya. **see the ~** (*liter or rhet*) zaliwa; baini; tangazwa; tambua; -okoka. **be/stand in one's ~** kinga nuru; (*fig*) zuia mtu mafanikio/maendeleo yake. **stand in one's own ~** zuia kazi yako isionekane, fanya kinyume na matakwa yako. ~ **year** (*astron*) kipimo cha umbali kati ya nyota. 2 taa. ~**s out** muda wa kuzima taa. **the northern/southern ~s** miali ya mwanga katika ncha za kaskazini na kusini. 3 mwako wa moto; kiberiti *strike a ~* washa moto, washa kiberiti. 4 uchangamfu (usoni mwa mtu). **the ~ of sb's countenance** (*biblical*) kupendezwa kwake. 5 ufafanuzi; uvumbuzi unaobainisha, kuelewa. **come/bring sth to ~** funua, funuka, (*ji*)tokeza, bainisha. **shed/throw ~/(a) new ~ on sth** fafanua zaidi, toa habari/taarifa mpya. **in the ~ of** kutokana na, kwa kuzingatia *by the ~ of nature* kwa akili za asili. 6 jinsi (ya utendaji), hali *I have never looked upon the matter in that ~* sijawahi kuchukulia jambo hili katika mtazamo huu. 7 uwezo, kipaji. **according to one's ~s** kufuatana/kulingana na kipaji chake. 8 mtu maarufu, mashuhuri, mtu anayechukuliwa/tolewa kama mfano. 9 dirisha, sehemu ya kupitishia mwanga. 10 (*paintings*) uangavu, sehemu ya mwanga (ya picha). 11 (*compounds*) **~house** *n* mnara wa taa wa kuongozea meli. **~ship** meli yenye taa za kuongozea meli nyingine *vt,vi* 1 washa. 2 toa mwanga, mulika. 3 ~ **up** washa, mulika *~ing-up time* muda wa kuwasha taa za barabarani pamoja na magari; (*colloq*) anza kuvuta/washa (sigara au kiko). 4 furahia mno. ~ **up (with)** (*of a person's face or expression*) -wa angavu. 5 ongoza; ongozwa kwa mwanga wa kitu. 6 ~ **sth up** fanya iwe na mwanga. **~er** *n* kiberiti cha chuma/plastiki. 2 mtu/kitu kihusikacho na kuwasha taa. **~en** *vt,vi* 1 ng'arisha, mulika. 2 -wa angavu. 3 toa mwale wa radi, metameta.

light[2] *adj* 1 (*in weight*) -epesi, rahisi, sahala. **~horse/~-armed** *adj* askari wenye silaha nyepesi. 2 polepole, -a makini, -tulivu, -angalifu *walk with ~ footsteps* nyemelea; nyata. **~-handed** *adj*. ~ **handedly** *adv* -a mkono mwepesi. **~-fingered** *adj* -epesi kutumia vidole; stadi katika kuiba. 3 pungufu, shoti. 4 (*of beer, wines*) -sio kali sana; (*of food*) laini; (*of meals*) -dogo; (*of sleep*) lepe, -sio zito; (*of books, plays, music*) -a kuburudisha; (*of soil*) laini, -epesi; (*of work*) rahisi -epesi; (*of taxes, punishment*) -dogo, -epesi; (*of a syllable*) -siokuwa na mkazo. **make ~ work of sth** fanya bila shida. 5 -sio nguvu, -sio muhimu, -dogo *a ~attack of illness* ugonjwa usiokuwa na nguvu/mdogo. **make ~ of** dharau. 6 pumbavu; -sio makini, -puuzi. **~minded** *adj*. **~mindedness** *n*. 7 changamfu. ~ **heart** moyo mchangamfu. ~ **hearted** *adj*. ~ **heartedly** *adv*. ~ **heartedness** *n*. 8 -enye tabia mbaya, fisadi, kware. 9 -a kizunguzungu. ~ **headed** *adj*. ~ **headedly** *adv*. ~ **headedness** *n*. 10 (*compounds*) **~-o-love** *n* mwanamke kigeugeu; malaya. **~weight** *n,adj* (*man or animal*) chini ya uzito wa wastani; (*boxing*) uzito mwepesi (kati ya kg 57 na 61); (*fig*) mtu asiye muhimu. **~-heavyweight** *n* mwanamasumbwi mwenye uzito kati ya kg 72.5 na 79.3 *adv* kwa wepesi, kwa urahisi *travel ~* safiri na mizigo michache. **~ly** *adv*. **~ness** *n*. **~en** *vt,vi* punguza, punguka uzito *~ a ship's cargo* punguza shehena melini. **~some** *adj* -epesi, -enye miondoko ya kupendeza, cheshi *vi* ~ **on/upon** bahatisha *~ upon a rare commodity in a village shop* bahatisha kupata bidhaa adimu katika duka la kijiji.

lighter *n* tishali *vt* safirisha kwa tishali. **~age** nauli ya tishali.

lightning *n* radi *a flash of ~* mwale/kimulimuli cha radi. **like ~** -epesi kama radi. **with ~ speed** haraka sana. **~bug** *n* (*US*) kimulimuli, kimetameta. **~rod-conductor** *n* ufito wa kuzuia radi. ~ **strike** *n* mgomo wa kushtukiza.

lights *n* mapafu, yavuyavu (ya wanyama kama kondoo, nguruwe nk.) kwa ajili ya chakula.

ligneous *adj* -enye mti, -a mbao.

lignite *n* makaamawe yasiokomaa.

like[1] *adj* 1 sawa, -a kufanana. **as ~ as** -enye kufanana kabisa, sawasawa kabisa. **in ~ manner** hivyo. **~ father ~ son** *(prov)* rupia kwa nyenzie, mtoto wa nyoka ni nyoka; kufanana kwa baba na mtoto. **be ~** fanana na, landa; -wa sawa, twaana. **~-minded** *adj* -lio na mawazo/malengo n.k. sawa *adv* 1 ~ **as** (*archaic*) kwa namna ile ile. 2 kwa uwezekano, labda. ~ **enough; most/very ~; as ~ as not** penginepo, kwa uwezekano mkubwa *conj* 1 kama *she can't cook ~ her father does*, hawezi kupika kama baba yake. 2 (*non-standard use*) kama vile, kana kwamba *it looks ~ rain* inaonekana kana kwamba mvua itanyesha *n* 1 mtu/kitu kama hicho *I never heard the ~ (of it)* sijasikia kitu kama hicho. 2 **the ~ of** (*colloq*) watu/ vitu vya namna hiyo *the ~ of us* watu kama sisi *prep* 1 kama, kama vile. **nothing ~** pasipo kifani. **sth ~** kitu kama. 2 elekea **feel ~** jisikia kama *do you feel ~ having a rest*? ungependa kupumzika? **looks ~** onekana kama *he looks ~ winning* inaonekana kama anashinda. 3 ndivyo ilivyo *that is just ~ him* ndivyo alivyo. 4 namna, kama *don't talk ~ that* usizungumze namna hiyo. 5 (*colloq, sl*). **~ anything** mno; kama inavyopaswa. **~ mad/ crazy** mno. **~ hell/blazes** kwa nguvu; (*as an int*) wala! **~n** *vt*. **~ sth to sth** fananisha, linganisha. **~ness** *n* 1 mshabaha, mlingano, ufanani *have a ~ness* -wa mfano mmoja, fanana, landa *they have a great ~* wamefanana sana. **in the ~ of** katika mfanano. 2 kifani, taswira, sanamu, picha inayofanana na mtu mwenyewe *take sb's ~* fanya mchoro wa sanamu ya mtu fulani.

like[2] *vt* 1 penda *she ~s him* anampenda. 2 (*In neg sentences*) kataa, sita, -topenda *I didn't ~ to disturb you* sikutaka kukusumbua. 3 (*with should, would*) *they would ~ to come* wangependa kuja. 4 pendelea, chagua, taka *I ~ this more than that* napendelea hii kuliko ile. **if you ~** kama unataka, ukipenda. 5 faa kiafya, penda *the food doesn't ~ me* chakula hiki hakinifai. **likable/~able** *adj* -enye kupendeka *she is likable/~able* anapendwa. **liking** *n* mapenzi, matakwa, upendeleo *have a ~ for* penda *to one's ~* kama mtu apendavyo.

likely *adj* kuelekea, -a kufaa, -a kutaka kuwa *it is ~ to* yaelekea ku *they are ~ to lose* wanaelekea kushindwa *he is not ~ to succeed* haelekei kufaulu *adv* huenda, labda. **very/most ~** huenda. **as ~ as not** haikosi. **~lihood** *n* uwezekano, uelekeo (wa jambo kutokea kuwa kweli n.k.) *there is small ~lihood that he is telling the truth* kuna uwezekano mdogo kuwa anasema ukweli.

likewise *adv* kadhalika, vivyo *do ~* fanya hivyo *conj* pia; zaidi ya hayo.

lilac *n* lilaki: maua ya rangi ya zambarau isiyoiva.

Lilliputian *n* kibeti, kiduranga *adj* -dogo sana, -a kibeti.

lilt *n* mwendo/mpigo wa wimbo/ngoma; mahadhi *vt* imba kwa mapigo yenye mkazo.

lily *n* yungiyungi. **~-livered** *adj* -oga. **~-white** *adj* -eupe pepepe

limb *n* 1 kiungo (mkono, mguu) *there is pain in all my ~s* maungo yote yaniuma. 2 tawi. **leave sb/be/go out on a ~** acha mtu; jitenga; (*colloq*) jiweka katika hali ya hatari. 3 (*colloq*) **~ of the devil/of satan** mtoto mkaidi. **~er** *adj* laini *vt,vi* **~ (oneself) up** -fanya mazoezi ya mwili (kwa ajili ya kuulainisha).

limbo *n* 1 **in ~** kusahaulika. 2 sehemu ya kuzika vitu. 3 limbo (*rel.*) sehemu ya ahera ziendako roho za watoto na watu wema wasiobatizwa.

lime[1] *n* ndimu. **~ tree** mdimu. **~ juice** juisi/maji ya ndimu.

lime[2] *n* 1 chokaa. 2 **~-kiln** *n* tanuu, chomeo la chokaa. **(bird) ~** ulimbo *vt* 1 paka kwa ulimbo. 2 nasa ndege kwa ulimbo. **~light** *n* taa yenye nuru kali (kwenye jukwaa) *he is fond of the ~ light* apenda kujitokeza, kujionyesha mbele ya watu. **be in the ~light** wa maarufu, julikana. **~stone** *n* gange, mawe ya chokaa.

limerick *n* shairi cheshi (lenye mistari mitano).

limey *n* (*US sl*) Mwingereza.

limit *n* 1 mpaka, upeo, kikomo *that's the ~* ! basi! *there's a ~ to my patience* uvumilivu wangu una kikomo *there's a ~ to every thing* hakuna lisilokuwa na kikomo *you're the* ~ umezidi, mtu hawezi kukuvumilia *set a* ~ weka mpaka. **within ~s** kwa kiasi fulani *city ~s* mipaka ya jiji. **without** ~ bila kikomo. **off ~s** ni marufuku. 2 *(of business)* mpango. 3 ua, mzingo *vt* 1 zuia, wekea mpaka/kikomo. ~ **ed** *adj* -dogo, finyu, chache; -enye mipaka. ~ **liability company (Ltd)** kampuni yenye dhima ya kikomo ~ *Monarchy* utawala wa kifalme ulio na mipaka. **~less** *adj* bila kikomo. **~ation** *n* 1 kikomo, mpaka. 2 ufinyu, upungufu; udhaifu *he knows his ~s* anafahamu udhaifu wake.

limn *vt* (*old use*) chora (picha), fanya taswira.

limousine *n* limuzini: gari la anasa (agh. kiti cha mbele na cha nyuma vimetengwa na kioo).

limp[1] *vi* chechemea, chopea *n* mwendo wa chopi.

limp[2] *adj* 1 teketeke, laini; legevu, -nyong'onyevu. 2 -sio na nguvu. **~ly** *adv*. **~ness** *n*.

limpet *n* 1 koanata. 2 (*fig*) mtu anayeshikilia (kwa kupachikwa/ ng'ang'ania cheo). **~ed mine** bomu linalotengwa kwenye meli.

limpid *adj* -eupe, -angavu. **~ly** *adv*. **~ity** *n* uangavu, weupe, usafi.

linchpin *n* kipini cha chuma (mwisho wa ekseli) kinachofanya gurudumu lisiachie; (*fig*) kiungo muhimu, mtu/kitu muhimu katika shughuli/ sehemu fulani.

line[1] *n* 1 (*cord*) kamba, ugwe, uzi, waya. **fishing** ~ ugwe wa kuvulia samaki *telephone* ~ simu, waya wa simu *hang the clothes on the* ~ anika nguo kwenye kamba. **party/shared** ~ simu inayomilikiwa na watu zaidi ya mmoja. 2 mstari (uliochorwa) (*games*) *cross the* ~ vuka mstari. **linage** *n* 1 idadi ya mistari. 2 malipo juu ya idadi ya mistari katika aya. 3 alama ya mstari mwilini, kunyanzi; mistari kwenye kiganja. 4 kontua; umbo la nje. 5 (*of people/things*) safu, foleni. **in (a)** ~ kwenye mstari *on the* ~ (*of exhibitions*) sawa na macho ya watazamaji. 6 mpaka *the ~ between Kenya and Uganda* mpaka kati ya Kenya na Uganda. 7 Ikweta *cross the* ~ vuka Ikweta. 8 reli, njia moja ya reli. **reach the end of the** ~ (*fig*) fikia mwisho, fikia kuachana. 9 shirika la usafiri *an air*~ shirika la usafiri wa ndege *shipping* ~ shirika la usafiri wa meli. 10 mwelekeo; mkondo; njia *you should keep to your own* ~ shikilia msimamo wako *communication ~s*, njia za mawasiliano. **choose/follow/take the ~ of least resistance** fuata njia iliyo rahisi. **take a strong/firm ~ (over sth)** chukua mweleko imara. **do sth along/on sound/correct etc ~s** tumia njia/mbinu sahihi. **(be) in/ out of ~ (with)** kubaliana/-tokubaliana na. **bring sth into** ~ patanisha, sababisha makubaliano. **come/fall into ~ (with)** kubali, shawishi maafikiano. **toe the** ~ (*fig*) -wa na nidhamu, tii. **the party** ~ itikadi ya chama. 11 mfuatano, ukoo. 12 (*writing/print*) mstari wa maneno. **drop sb a** ~ (*colloq*) andikia barua. **read between the ~s** (*fig*) ona maana iliyofichika. **Marriage ~s** (*GB colloq*) cheti cha ndoa. **~s** maneno ya mwigizaji; mistari inayoandikwa kama adhabu (agh. kwa wanafunzi wa shule za msingi). 13 mstari wa mbele. **front** ~ vikosi vilivyo mstari wa mbele karibu na adui. **all along the** ~ katika kila hali. **go up the** ~ enda mstari wa mbele. 14 *(mil)* safu ya mahema, vibanda kambini. 15 **the** ~ (*GB army*) jeshi la askari wa miguu; (*US army*) jeshi. 16 (*mil*) safu mbili sambamba za askari. 17 (*naval*) ~ **abreast** (meli) zilizokaa sambamba. 18 shughuli; kazi. **his ~ is banking** anafanya/kazi benki. 19 (*trade use*) aina ya bidhaa. 20 **Hard ~s** bahati mbaya! pole. 21 (*sl*) **shoot a** ~ jigamba. ~ **shooting** *n*. ~ **shooter** *n*. 22 (*colloq*) **give sb/get/have a ~ on**

sth toa/pata habari zaidi juu ya jambo fulani. **~ar** *adj* -a mstari,-a mistari ~ *measure* vipimo; (*maths*) ~ *combination* matangamano mstari ~ *equation* milinganyo mstari ~ *geometry* jometrii mstari ~ *translation* uhamisho mstari ~ *transformation* mbadiliko mstari. **~ation** *n* uchoraji mistari. **~man** *n* 1 (*electricity*) fundi (wa) waya (za simu/umeme). *vt,vi* 1 tia alama za mstari. **~d paper** karatasi zenye mistari ~ *in a contour* chora kontua kwenye ramani. 2 -wa na mistari, funika na mistari; kunjika katika mistari *pain had ~d her forehead* maumivu yalisababisha uso wake kujikunyata. 3 **~-up** *n* mpangilio, foleni, safu; ratiba ~ *up* panga mstari/foleni; simama mstarini. 4 fanya, panga mstari/jipanga *crowds of people ~d the street to cheer their leader* vikundi vya watu vilijipanga katika mtaa kumshangilia kiongozi wao.

line[2] *vt* ~ **sth (with sth)** 1 weka kitambaa ndani; ongeza vitu katika sanduku, mfuko. 2 (*fig*) jaza, -wa na fedha nyingi *he ~d his purse well* amepata pesa nyingi, alitengeneza pesa kweli.

lineage *n* nasaba, ukoo, jadi. **lineal** *adj* -a nasaba, ukoo, jadi. ~ *descendant* dhuria.

lineament *n* (*formal*) sura, umbo.

linen *n* kitani, nguo ya kitani (hasa shati na nguo za meza na kitanda). **~-draper** *n* mwuza nguo za kitani na pamba. **wash one's dirty ~ in public** toa siri za nyumbani hadharani *adj* -a kitani.

liner *n* 1 meli/ndege ya abiria 2 ~ **(train)/freight** ~ gari moshi la bidhaa.

linesman *n* (*sports*) mshika kibendera.

linger *vi* kawia, limatia, kaa karibu *n*. **~ing** *adj* -a muda mrefu, -a kudumu ~ *disease* ugonjwa wa muda mrefu. **~ingly** *adv*.

lingerie *n* nguondani za kike.

lingo (*joc or derog*) kilugha, lugha isiyofahamika; istilahi.

lingual *adj* -a ulimi, -a lugha. **audio-~methods** mbinu za kusikiliza na kusema. **bi~** -a lugha mbili. **multi~** -a lugha nyingi. **lingua franca** *n* lugha ya biashara/mawasiliano (k.m. Kiswahili katika eneo la lugha nyingi mbalimbali).

linguist *n* 1 mwana isimu. 2 mjuzi wa lugha kadha. **~ic** *adj* -a isimu, -a lugha. **~ics** *n* isimu: sayansi ya lugha (maumbo, miundo, matamshi, maana na matumizi). **applied** ~ isimu matumizi.

liniment *n* dawa ya kuchua, fututa.

lining *n* bitana. **every cloud has a silver** ~ (*prov*) baada ya dhiki faraja.

link[1] *n* 1 pete (ya mnyororo). 2 (*person or thing*) kiungo *missing* ~ kiungo muhimu kinachokosekana; mnyama (kiungo) kati ya sokwe na binadamu. **~man** mtu wa kati; (*in games*) mchezaji (wa) kiungo. 3 kifungo (cha mkono wa shati). 4 kipimo cha urefu (sawa na sentimita 20) *vt,vi* ~ **(up)** unga, ungana, jiunga na, unganisha; husiana, husisha *~arms* unganisha mikono. **~age** *n*. **~up** *n* unganisho.

link[2] *n* (*hist*) mwenge, tochi, taa. **~boy**, **~man** mbeba mwenge/tochi/taa. ~ **man** mtangaza programu.

links *n* (*pl*) 1 kiwanja cha kuchezea gofu. 2 mbuga za majani karibu na bahari.

linnet *n* biliwili (wa nchi za baridi).

lino, ~leum *n* zulia la mpira/plastiki.

Linotype *n* linotaipu: herufi za kupangwa.

linseed *n* mbegu za kitani. **~-oil** *n* mafuta ya kitani.

linsey-woolsey *n* kitambaa cha sufu na pamba hafifu.

lint *n* nyuzi za pamba, kitambaa (cha kufungia kidonda), bandeji.

lintel *n* linta.

lion *n* 1 simba. **a ~ in the way** pinga mizi. **the ~s share** fungu kubwa kabisa *put one's head in the ~'s mouth* jihatarisha. ~ **hearted** *adj* shujaa. 2 mtu mashuhuri. **~ess** *n* simba jike. ~ **hunter** *n* 1 mwindaji wa simba. 2 (*fig*) mtu anayekusanya watu mashuhuri. **~ize** *vt* tendea mtu kama mtu mashuhuri, tukuza.

lip *n* 1 mdomo. **bite one's ~** onyesha hasira/ghadhabu. **curl one's ~** onyesha dharau/beza. **pay/give ~ service to sth** unga mkono kwa maneno matupu au kinafiki. **hang on/upon sb's ~s** sikiliza kwa shauku *smack/lick the ~s* lambitia, onyesha (dalili za) furaha. **keep a stiff upper ~** jizuia, vumilia. 2 ukingo *pouring ~* mdomo wa chombo 3 (*sl.*) (maneno ya) ujuvi/ufidhuli *none of your ~* acha ufidhuli *vt* 1 gusa kwa midomo, busu. 2 tamka. 3 (*of waves*) lamba/piga (mwamba n.k.). **~ped** *adj* -enye mdomo/ukingo (*combined forms*) **~reading** (*to deaf people*) kusoma midomo. **~ring** *n* ndonya. **~salve** dawa ya midomo. **~-service** *n* maneno matupu. **~stick** *n* rangi ya midomo.

liquefy *vt,vi* yeyusha; yeyuka. **liquefice** yeyusha barafu. **liquefaction** *n*. **liquescent** *adj* epesi kuyeyuka, -nayoyeyuka.

liqueur *n* kinywaji kikali, kitamu.

liquid *n* 1 uwoevu kitu kama maji, kimiminiko. 2 (*phon*) konsonanti l au r *adj* 1 -oevu, -a majimaji, -a kimiminiko. ~ **gas** gesi oevu/ miminiko. 2 (*of sound*) laini, -ororo. 3 -eupe, angavu. 4 -enye kubadilika-badilika. 5 (*in finance*) epesi kusarifika ~ *assets* mali rahisi kubadilishika kwa pesa taslimu. **~ate** *vt,vi* 1 lipa deni. 2 filisi, filisika. 3 (*sl*) ua. **~ation** *n* ulipaji deni. **go into ~** kufilisi; kufilisika. **~ated** filisika/ filisiwa. **~ator** *n* mfunga hesabu (wa kampuni/duka), mfilisi. **~ity** *n* umajimaji, uoevu; uwezo wa kupata pesa, ukwasi. **~ize** *vt* ponda matunda n.k. yawe rojorojo. **~izer** *n* kigeuza maji, kioeshaji.

liquor *n* 1 (*GB*) pombe, kileo; (*US*) pombe kali. 2 (*cooking*) maji ya kupikia pombe. 3 maji yatokanayo na kupika/ kuloweka chakula *vt* chuja, keneka, tonesha. **~up** -lewesha na pombe kali. **~ish** *adj (of person)* -liopenda ulevi.

liquorice *n* urukususu, susi.

lira *n* (*sl.* **lire**) lira: fedha ya Kitaliano.

lisle *n* kitambaa kigumu cha pamba.

lisp *vt,vi* sema kitembe, piga kitembe *n* kitembe. **~ing** *adj*. **~ingly** *adv*.

lissom, ~e *adj* -epesi, -a madaha. **~ness** *n*.

list[1] *n* 1 orodha (*leg*) ~ **price** bei iliyotangazwa. **the active ~** orodha ya maofisa wa jeshi (wanaoweza kuitwa jeshini). **the free ~** bidhaa zisizolipiwa ushuru; watu wanaoingia senema/mchezoni nk. bila kulipa. 2 ukingo, mtanda (wa nguo). 3 (*arch*) *pl*. kiwanja cha mashindano *enter the ~ against* jiandikisha kushindana na *vt* orodhesha, andikisha.

list[2] *vi* (*of ship*) egemea, lala upande *n* kuegemea, kulala upande.

list[3] *vt,vi* (*old use*) sikiliza.

list[4] *vi* (*old use*) taka, chagua, penda *he does as he ~s* anafanya apendavyo.

listen *vi* sikiliza; sikia ~ *to sb singing* sikiliza mtu akiimba ~ *in (to) sb* pulikiza, sikiliza mtu katika redio; sikiliza (kwa siri). **~er** *n* msikilizaji. **~ing post** *n* (*military*) kituo cha kupulikiza maadui; (*fig*) mahali pa kupata maelezo mbalimbali.

listless *adj* -tepetevu, -legevu, -nyong'onyevu, -zito (kutokana na uchovu). **~ly** *adv*. **~ness** *n*.

lit *pt, pp. of light ~ up* (*sl.*) -liolewa.

litany *n* litania: sala za kuomba za padri na watu wakiitikia.

litchi *n see* **lychee**.

liter *n see* **litre**.

literal *adj* (*exact*) hasa, halisi, -a maneno yenyewe, -a maana iliyo wazi ~ *translation* tafsiri sisisi. 2 -a herufi ~ *error* kosa la kuruka herufi. 3 *(of person)* kavu, -a kawaida, -siobunifu. **~ly** *adv* neno kwa neno *he did ~ nothing* hakutenda chochote.

literacy *n* kujua kusoma na kuandika.

literary *adj* -a maandishi, -a fasihi; -a waandishi ~ *man* mwandishi au mpenda fasihi ~ *property* haki ya mwandishi/mtunzi ya mrabaha na faida zinazotokana na kazi yake; ~ *criticism* uhakiki wa fasihi. **literate** *adj* 1 -enye elimu, somi. 2 -enye kujua kuandika na kusoma *n* mtu ajuaye kuandika na kusoma, mwenye elimu ya kadiri/ya kutosha. **literati** *n* wasomi, maulama, wanazuoni. **literature** *n* 1 fasihi. 2 vitabu/maandiko mbalimbali (ya nchi au kipindi fulani). 3 maelezo; matangazo.

lithe *adj* -a kupinda/kunengua/kugeuka kwa urahisi, -epesi, -a madaha. **~ness** *n.*

lithography *n* lithografia: tendo la kuandika/kuchora na jiwe. **lithograph** *n* lithografu. **lithographic** *adj* -a lithografu.

litigate *vi,vt* enda mahakamani, fungua madai mahakamani. **litigation** *n.* **litigious** *adj* 1 gomvi, -a kupenda daawa. 2 -enye kuleta ubishi. **litigant** *n* mdai, mwenye daawa *adj* -a daawa.

litmus *n* (*chem*) litmasi: dutu/utomvu wa zambarau (ambao hugeuka kibuluu kwa asidi na mwekundu kwa alkali). **~-paper** karatasi iliyopakwa litmasi.

litotes *n* tamshi poza/kinyume lenye kurahisisha mambo agh. husemwa kinyumenyume k.m. si mbaya, nzuri n.k.

litre/liter *n* lita.

litter *n* 1 takataka. **~bin/~basket** pipa/kapu la takataka. ~ **bug** *n.* ~ **out** *n* (*colloq*) anayetupa takataka. 2 **a** ~ fujo, machafuko. 3 majani ya kulalia wanyama. 4 vitoto vyote vya uzazi mmoja (mkumbo mmoja); (*pigs*) vibwangala *vt,vi* 1 ~ **sth (up) with sth** chafua, fuja; tia takataka. 2 ~ **sth (down)** tandika majani chini. 3 *(of animals)* zaa.

little *adj* 1 -dogo, chache, haba *the ~ finger* kidole kidogo *a ~ money* pesa chache. 2 fupi *a ~ sleep* lepe la usingizi. 3 kijana *a ~ boy* mvulana mdogo *the ~ ones* watoto *the ~ Nyereres* Nyerere wadogo. **the ~ people/folk** (*esp. Ireland*) vichimbakazi. 4 (*to emphasize a feeling*) -zuri *she's a nice ~ thing* ni kisichana kidogo kirembo *her poor ~ efforts to please* jitihada zake ndogo za kupendeza *so, that's your ~ game* ndiyo mchezo wako ehe! *he knows his ~ ways* anajua hila zake. 5 **a** ~ kidogo *a ~ rice* wali kidogo. **not a** ~ (*euphem*) -ingi *not a ~ trouble* matatizo mengi. 6 (*of a person*) -dogo, -fupi *a ~ man* mtu mfupi. 7 (*insignificant*) -nyonge, hafifu, duni. 8 (*of intelligence*) pungufu *n* 1 kidogo. ~ **by** ~ kidogo kidogo *take up ~ by ~* chota kidogo kidogo *a ~ of everything* kidogo kila kitu *a ~ of this and a ~ of that* kidogo hapa na kidogo pale *a ~ makes us laugh* hata jambo dogo linatuchekesha. ~ **or nothing** si chochote, kidogo sana *he got a ~ of it* alipatapata *what ~ remained* kidogo kilichobaki. (*of time*) **after a** ~ baadaye kidogo. **for a** ~ kwa muda mfupi *adv* 1 kidogo, punde *a ~ complicated* -a matatizo kidogo *a ~ more* bado kidogo ~ *tired* -enye kuchoka kidogo ~ *more than a thief* ni mwizi kweli. 2 (*with verbs think, dream, suspect*) ~ *did I suspect* sikushuku hata kidogo *think ~ of sb* dharau. **~ness** *n* 1 udogo. 2 unyonge, udhaifu, uhafifu, uduni.

littoral *adj* -a pwani *n* pwani.

liturgy *n* liturujia: kawaida ya ibada na sala ya dini, kawaida ya Ushirika Mtakatifu. **liturgial** *adj.*

live[1] *adj* 1 -hai, -enye uhai ~ *weight* uzito wa mnyama hai. 2 -a moto, motomoto, -a kuwaka; (*of issues*) motomoto, -a kisasa, sasa hivi ~ *coals* makaa ya moto; (*of bullets, bombs*) -enye marisawa; (*elec*) -enye umeme. ~ **wire** waya moto/wenye umeme; (*fig*) (*persons*) mchangamfu. 3 *(radio/TV) a ~ broadcast* tangazo la moja kwa moja (lisilorekodiwa kabla). 4 ~ **-birth** mtoto aliyezaliwa hai. 5 -a nishati, mashughuli, -a

hima.
live[2] *vt,vt* 1 ishi, -wa na uzima, -wa hai. 2 endelea kuishi, dumu. ~ **on** jikongoja, endelea kuishi. **you/we ~ and learn** kuishi kwingi kuona mengi. ~ **and let** ~ -wa mvumilivu *long ~ sb*! adumu fulani maisha marefu! ~ *honestly* -ishi kwa uaminifu ~ *to be....* ishi hadi... ~ **through**, shinda majaribio mengi, vumilia ~ *as man and wife* kaa kinyumba. ~ **to oneself** jitenga, ishi pekee. 3 pata riziki. ~ **by** tegemea. **what does he ~ by** kazi yake nini? ~ **by one's wits** ishi kwa ujanja/mbinu. ~ **off the land** tegemea riziki kwa kilimo. ~ **on sth** ishi kwa kutegemea kitu. ~ *on your salary* ishi kwa kutegemea mshahara wako *what does he ~on* anaponea nini? ~ *on one's name/reputation* ishi kwa sifa/jina zuri. 4 ~**(in/at)** (*reside*) ishi, -kaa; (*of room etc*) *not fit to ~* haifai kuishi ndani yake, haikaliki. 5 ~ **on** (*in memory etc*) dumu, ishi katika kumbukumbu ya watu. ~ **together** ishi pamoja. ~ **in/out** (*of domestic servants*)ishi kazini/ nyumbani, nenda na kurudi kila siku. 6 nenda. ~ **up to sth** fuata; fikia matarajio fulani. ~ **sth down** sahaulisha yaliyopita. ~ **with sth** vumilia. 7 ~ **it up** ishi maisha ya mishughuliko na anasa, furahia maisha. 8 ishi uonavyo, chagua kuwa mwaminifu. ~ **a lie** ishi kinafiki.
livable, ~able *adj* 1 -a kukalika; -enye kufaa kuishi. 2 -a kuvumilika. **~lihood** *n* kazi, riziki. **earn a ~lihood** chuma riziki. **~long** *adj* (*only in*) **the ~long day** mchana kutwa. **the ~long night** usiku kucha *adj* 1 -epesi, changamfu, -cheshi, -kunjufu. 2 (*of non-living things*) -a kwenda mbio **have a ~ly time** sisimkwa, changamka. **look ~ly** changamka. **make things ~ly for sb** changamsha, sisimua mtu. 3 (*of colour*) kali, -enye kung'aa *n* 4 hai, kama kweli/halisi. **~liness**. **~n** *vt, vi* ~ **up** changamsha, sisimua; sisimka. **~r** *n* mtu apendaye kuishi kwa namna yake (nzuri au mbaya).
liver *n* ini. **~ish** *adj* -enye kuugua ini; -enye kukasirika ovyo.
livery *n* 1 mavazi maalum, sare ya mtumishi ~ *servant* mtumishi mwenye sare rasmi. **in/ out of** ~ -liovaa/-siova sare rasmi. 2 *(fig) (poet)* vazi. 3 ~ **(stable)** banda la farasi wa kukodishwa. **liveried** *adj* -liovaa vazi rasmi. ~ **man** mtunza farasi
lives *pl. of* **life**.
live-stock *n* (*esp. farm*) mifugo.
livid *n* rangi ya risasi, samawati, kijivu (*of person or his looks*) -liokasirika sana, -liofura kwa hasira. **~ly** *adv*.
living *adj* 1 hai, -zima *not a ~ soul* hakuna mtu yeyote. **within ~ memory** -enye kukumbukwa na watu walio hai. 2 (*of a likeness*) hasa, halisi *she is the ~ image of her mother* anafanana sana na mama yake. 3 -enye nguvu, hai, -enye kusisimua. **the** ~ *n* (watu) wanaoishi/ wazima *the ~ and the dead* wazima na wafu *n (conditions)* hali za kuishi ~ *standard* kiwango cha maisha. 2 maisha, riziki. **a ~ wage** mshahara wa kujikimu *earn one's/make a ~* pata riziki. **for** ~ ili kupata riziki ~ *costs* gharama za maisha. ~ **room** *n* sebule, baraza *good ~* maisha ya starehe, raha. 3 kazi na mshahara wa padri/mchungaji.
lixiviate *vt* tenga vitu vinavyoyeyuka na visivyoyeyuka kwa kuchuja.
lizard *n* mjusi; (*burrowing*) guruguru. **monitor** -~ kenge.
Llama *n* lama: mnyama kama kondoo wa Amerika ya Kusini.
lo *int* (*old use*) tazama. ~ **and behold** ajabu ilioje!
load *n* 1 mzigo, shehena; (*fig*) wajibu, madaraka makubwa (ya usimamizi au utunzaji wa jambo) *a heavy ~ on one's shoulders* madaraka makubwa aliyonayo mtu. **take a ~ off sb's mind** ondolea mtu mashaka. **~s of** (*colloq*) kiasi kikubwa, tele. ~ **line**

mstari wa ujazo/shehena ya meli. 2 kiwango cha kazi ifanywayo na dainamo, mota, injini n.k.; kiasi cha umeme kinachotolewa na jenereta. ~ **shedding** kukata umeme mahala fulani na kuupeleka unakohitajika zaidi *vt, vi* 1 ~ **sth into sth** pakiza, sheheni, pakia. ~ **sb with sth** twisha, bebesha; (*fig*) lemeza. 2 (*of a gun*) tia risasi *he ~ed him with favours* alimtendea/alimsheheneza fadhili nyingi. ~ **dice (against sb)** (*fig*) fanyia mtu jambo lisilokuwa na manufaa kwake *a ~ed question* swali lenye mtego. **~ed** *adj* (*sl*) -liojaa, -enye fedha nyingi. **~er** *n*. **~ing** *n* upakiaji.

loadstar/loadstone *n see* **lode**.

loaf[1] *n* 1 mkate, boflo *a ~ is better than none* afadhali kidogo kuliko kukosa kabisa. 2 ~ *sugar* sukari kibonge. 3 chakula chenye umbo la boflo. 4 (*sl.*) **use one's ~** fikiri kwa makini, tumia akili.

loaf[2] *vt, vi* (*colloq*) randa, zurura ~ *away one's time* zurura *n* kuzurura. **~er** *n* mzururaji, lofa.

loam *n* udongo tifutifu wenye rutuba. **~y** *adj*.

loan *n* 1 mkopo, karadha *take a ~* kopa. 2 kukopesha; kukopa; kuazima *have sth on ~ (from sb)* azima kitu, chukua kitu kwa mkopo ~ *collection* picha n.k. zilizoazimwa (kwa maonyesho). ~ **office** *n* ofisi ya mkopo, karadha. ~ **word** neno la mkopo *vt* (*of money*) kopesha; azima.

loath,loth *adj* (*pred only*) ~ *to do sth* -totaka kufanya jambo. **nothing ~** -enye kutaka; kwa hiari *be ~ for sb to do sth* -tokubali mtu kufanya kitu.

loathe *vt* chukia kabisa, zia *I ~ him* namchukia kabisa ~ *doing sth* chukia kufanya kitu; (*colloq*) -topenda. **loathing** *n* chuki; karaha. **loathsome** *adj* -a kuchukiza, makuruhu.

loaves *n pl.*of **loaf**.

lob *vi, vt* rusha mpira juu mfano wa tao *n* mpira uliorushwa juu.

lobby *n* 1 sebule, ukumbi. 2 *(division) ~ (in House of Commons) n* ukumbi wa mahojiano baina ya wabunge na watu wengine, ukumbi wa bunge, kikundi shawishi: kikundi kinachowashawishi wabunge juu ya mswada/ sheria fulani *vt* shawishi wabunge (ili kupigia au kutopigia kura mswada). **~ist** mshawishi wabunge.

lobe *n* 1 (*of an ear, lung, brain etc*) ndewe *adj* -enye umbo la ndewe. 2 kitu kinachofanana na umbo la ndewe.

lobster *n* kambamti; kambakoche. **~pot** *n* mtego wa kamba.

local *adj* 1 -a mahali maalum, -a mahali palepale. ~ **colour** mambo ya kienyeji (yanayoongezwa katika hadithi ili kuipa ladha). ~ **custom** mila ya mahali. ~ **government** serikali ya mitaa ~ *habitation* makao, makazi. ~ **option/veto** mfumo wa kukataza jambo kwa kupiga kura k.m. kukataza uuzaji wa pombe. ~ **purchase order** dhamana ya ununuzi ~ *relief not indicated by contours* sura ya mahali ambayo haikuonyeshwa kwa kontua. ~ **time** saa za mahali pale. 2 -a (kuathiri) sehemu ~ *anaesthetic* dawa ya ganzi *n* (*usu. pl.*). 1 mkazi wa mahali fulani, mwenyeji. 2 (*colloq*) kilabu, baa. 3 habari za mahali pale pale (katika gazeti). **~ly** *adv*. **~e** *n* mahali, mandhari. **~ism** *n* 1 kupendelea mambo ya mahali pake (mji, mkoa n.k.); fikra finyu (kutokana na kujua mambo ya mahali pake tu). 2 mbinu, nahau, matamshi (ya lahaja fulani). **~ity** *n* 1 mahali. 2 (*neighbourhood*) janibu, mtaa. 3 (*a sense*) utambuzi wa mahali. **~ize** *vt* fanya (kuwa) ya mahali fulani, weka/zuilia mahali maalum ~ *the disease* zuia maradhi katika eneo fulani tu. **~zation** *n*.

locate *vt* 1 tambua/onyesha mahali pa ~ *the industrial area on the map* onyesha eneo la viwanda katika ramani. 2 weka mahali. 3 **be ~d** -wa/wekwa mahali. **location** *n* 1

mahali maalumu. 2 kuonyesha/ kutambua mahali. 3 mahali pa kupigia (sehemu ya) picha za sinema. 4 *(South Africa)* kitongoji (walikolazimika kuishi Waafrika).

locative *n, adj* (*gram*) -a mahali.

loci *n pl of* **locus**.

lock[1] *n* 1 shungi la nywele. 2 *pl.* **~s** nywele.

lock[2] *n* 1 kufuli, kifungio *be under ~ and key* fungwa kwa ufunguo. **~ smith** mtengeneza makufuli. 2 (*of a gun*) mtambo. **~ stock and barrel** kitu kizima, zimazima; kabisa. 3 (*of canal*) mlango *~ chamber* mlango/chumba cha kuzuia maji. **~ keeper** *n* mlinda lango (la mfereji). 4 hali ya kukwama, kushikamana. **~jaw** pepopunda. **~nut** nati kifungo. 5 *(motoring)* mkato wa usukani *vt,vi* 1 funga kwa ufunguo. **~ the stable door after the horse has bolted/ has been stolen** fanya tahadhari baada ya mambo kuharibika. **~ sth away** hifadhi kitu mahali pa salama; *(fig)* tunzia/hifadhi (moyoni). **~ sb in** fungia mtu ndani. **~ sb out** fungia mtu nje; zuia mtu asiingie. **~ out** *n* kufungia nje (kuzuia wafanyakazi wasiingie sehemu zao za kazi mpaka masharti fulani yatimizwe). **~ sth/sb up** fungia kwa ufunguo; funga nyumba n.k. (kwa funguo); tia mtu ndani; weka/wa na rasilimali isiyouzika kwa urahisi. **~up** *n* korokoroni, mahabusi; (*colloq*) jela *adj* -enye kufungika kwa kufuli. 2 fungika. 3 funga; kwama. 4 fungamana. **~ on to** (*of a missile*) tafuta na fuata (shabaha) kwa rada. **~er** *n* 1 kabati ndogo (agh. ya kuwekea nguo za michezo, kazi, n.k.). 2 kasha/chumba kidogo melini (cha kuhifadhia nguo, risasi, mavazi, n.k.). **be in/go to Davy Jone's ~er** zama baharini.

locket *n* 1 kibweta kidogo (agh. huvaliwa shingoni kwenye mkufu).

loco *adj* (*sl*) mwendawazimu.

locomotion *n* mwendo, uwezo wa kwenda.

locomotive *adj* 1 -enye nguvu ya kwenda *n* kichwa cha garimoshi *~ works* kiwanda cha garimoshi.

locum (tenens) *n* padri/daktari anayekaimu/fanya kazi kwa muda badala ya mwingine.

locus *n* 1 sehemu/mahali maalum pa kitu; kituo. 2 (*maths*) mchirizo; lokaso. 3 **~ classicus** aya muhimu (katika somo fulani).

locust *n* nzige.

locution *n* msemo, mtindo wa kusema, mbinu ya kutumia maneno; nahau.

locutory *n* ukumbi, baraza (ya nyumba ya watawa).

lode *n* mstari, uzi wa madini ndani ya mawe; tabaka ya madini ardhini. **~star** *n* nyota iongozayo, nyota ya Kaskazini; (*fig*) mwongozo, kiongozi. **~stone** *n* sumaku.

lodge *n* nyumba/chumba cha bawabu, mpagazi, n.k. 2 nyumba ya shamba. 3 (*GB*) makao ya mkuu wa chuo. 4 nyumba ya kukutania wanachama *vt,vi* 1 pangisha mtu chumba cha kulala (kwa muda); weka (watu) kwa muda. 2 **~ at/with** panga. **lodging** *n* (*usu. pl.*) 1 nyumba/chumba/vyumba vya kupanga kwa muda *take ~s* panga (katika nyumba ya kupanga). *I'm ~ here* nimepanga hapa. 3 **~ in** ingia, kwama; tia; kwamisha. 4 *~ a complaint (against sb)* shtaki, toa lalamiko dhidi ya *~ an appeal* kata rufaa. 5 weka, tia. **~r** *n* mpangaji wa muda *take ~s* pangisha. **~ house** *n* nyumba ya kupanga.

lodgment *n* 1 kushtaki. 2 (*mil*) eneo lililotekwa kutoka kwa adui. 3 (*accumulation*) limbikizo.

loft[1] *n* 1 darini. 2 roshani (katika kanisa au ukumbi).

loft[2] *vt* (*of golf, cricket*) piga juu. **~y** *adj* 1 (*not used of persons*) -a juu sana, -refu. 2 (*of thoughts, aims, feelings etc.*) -a fahari sana. 3 -a kiburi, -a kujidai, shaufu. **~ily** *adv* **~ness** *n* urefu, kiburi, ubora.

log[1] *n* gogo la mti, kigogo *like a ~* ⊢

fahamu, bila kujitambua. **sleep like a ~** lala fofofo. ~ **cabin** nyumba ya magogo. ~ **jam** mkwamo wa magogo yanayoelea majini; (*US*) mkwamo. ~ **rolling** kuungana mkono. **~ging** *n* ukataji miti.

log[2] *n* 1 kipimamwendo wa meli baharini. 2 (*also* **~book**) batli: kitabu chenye habari zote za safari ya merikebu (meli). 3 kitabu cha safari za ndege, gari n.k.; (*colloq*) kitabu cha usajili wa motakaa *vt* andika katika batli.

logarithm *n* (*maths*) logi. **~ic** *adj.*

loggerheads *n* (*only in*) **at ~ (with sb)** gombana, -topatana, sigana.

logic *n* mantiki. **~al** *adj* -enye mantiki *a ~ argument* hoja yenye mantiki. **~ally** *adv*. **~ality** *n* kuwa na mantiki. **~ian** *n.*

logistics *n* (*mil.*) utaratibu wa ugavi na usafirishaji wa watu na vitu.

logo *n* nembo; msemo.

loin *n* 1 kiuno. **gird up one's ~** (*biblical*) jitayarisha kwa safari; jifunga kibwebwe. **sprung from the ~s of** zaliwa na. **~-cloth** *n* msuli.

loiter *vi* zurura, randa, tanga *n* mzururaji.

loll *vi,vt* ~ **(about/around)** 1 jikalia, pumzika/lala/kaa kivivu. 2 (*of a tongue*) ~ **out** ning'inia/ning'iniza ulimi nje *the dog ~ed its tongue out* mbwa amening'iniza ulimi nje.

lollipop *n* peremende kijiti. ~ **man/woman** *(colloq)* mtu avushaye watoto barabarani.

lolly *n* 1 *(colloq)* perememnde kijiti. **iced ~** aisikrimu ya kijiti.

lone *adj* 1 *(attr only)* -a pekee, -a kukaa peke yake. **play a ~ hand** *(fig)* fanya jambo pasipo msaada. **~ly** *adj* -pweke, bila rafiki, -a ukiwa *feel ~* jisikia upweke. 2 pweke, -siotembelewa mara kwa mara. **~liness** *n* upweke. ~ **some** *adj* pweke, -a ukiwa.

long *adj* 1 -refu. 2 (*in phrases*) kubwa; -enye uwezo. **have a ~ arm** onyesha madaraka. **the ~ arm of the law** uwezo mkubwa wa sheria. **make a ~ arm for** nyosha mkono (kuchukua). 3 -a muda mrefu, -a kukaa. ~ **time no** *see (colloq as greetings)* habari za siku nyingi/masiku. 4 *(in phrases concerned with extent in time)* ~ **bond** *(fin)* mkataba wa miaka ishirini au zaidi. **take a ~ cool/hard look at sth** fikiria kwa makini, fikiria kwa mapana na marefu. **take the ~ view** angalia mbali. **in the ~ term** kwa kuangalia mbali. ~ **term** *attrib adj* -a muda mrefu. 5 *(compounds)*. ~ **boat** *n* mashua kubwa kuliko zote melini. **~bow** *n* upinde mrefu. **draw the ~bow** tia chumvi, piga chuku. ~ **distance** *attrib adj* -a masafa marefu *a ~-distance runner (athletics)* mkimbiaji wa masafa marefu. ~ **drink** *n* kinywaji kinachoandaliwa kwenye bilauri kubwa k.m. bia. **a ~ dozen** kumi na tatu. **~hand** *n* mwandiko wa mkono (ukilinganisha na hati mkato). **~-haired** *adj* -enye nywele ndefu; *(fig)* -somi; -a sanaa; si -a kawaida. ~ **headed** *adj* -janja, erevu; -enye kuona mbali (kwa mawazo). **the ~ jump** *(athletics)* kuruka chini. ~ **metre** ubeti wenye mistari minne yenye silabi nane. ~ **odds** *n pl (in betting)* -siowiana kabisa, -a kupishana sana. ~ **play(ing) disc/record** *n (abbr LP)* sahani ya santuri ndefu. **~range** *attrib adj* -a muda mrefu/masafa marefu. ~ **shore-man** kuli. ~ **sighted** -a kuona mbali; -enye kufikiri mbele. ~ **time** *attrib adj* -a muda mrefu. ~ **ton** *n* ratili 2240. ~ **wave** mawimbi ya masafa marefu. **~-winded** *adj* -refu na -a kuchosha (katika mazungumzo/maandishi), -enye maneno mengi *n* 1 muda mrefu, kipindi kirefu *the experiments will take ~* majaribio yatachukua muda mrefu. **at the ~est** sanasana; muda mrefu kabisa *I can wait three days at the ~est* siwezi kungoja zaidi ya siku tatu. **the ~ and the short of it** hali ya jumla; yote yanayohitajiwa kusemwa. 2 *(esp in*

Latin) silabi ndefu *adv* 1 **(for)** ~ (kwa) muda mrefu. **as/so ~ as** (*conditional*) mradi *you may lend me some money as ~ as you do not attach strings to it* unaweza kunikopesha pesa mradi huweki masharti yoyote. 2 (*in numerous compounds*) **~-drawn out** *adj* -liorefushwa (bila sababu). **~lived** *adj* -lioishi sana, -enye maisha marefu. **~standing** *adj* -liodumu muda mrefu, -a muda mrefu (bila kutimizwa). **~-suffering** *adj* -stahamilivu. 3 muda mrefu, zamani. ~ **ago** zamani sana ~ *after her wedding* muda mrefu baada ya ndoa yake. 4 (*with n indicating duration*) -zima, -ote *all day ~* siku nzima; mchana kutwa *all my life ~* maisha yangu yote. 5 **no/ any/much ~er** zaidi (ya muda fulani), tena *I cannot wait any ~er* siwezi kungoja zaidi *she is no ~er working here* hafanyi kazi hapa tena hivi sasa. **~evity** *n* maisha marefu. **~itude** *n* longitudo. **~itudinal** *adj* 1 -a longitudo. 2 -a kukata kwa urefu. **~ways**; **~wise** *adv see* **lengthways**.

long[2] *vi* ~ **for sth/for sb to do sth** tamani sana. **~ing** *n* hamu, shauku *adj* -enye (kuonyesha) hamu/shauku *the children are ~ for a break* watoto wanatamani sana kupumzika. ~ **eyes** macho yaonyeshayo hamu/shauku (hasa ya mapenzi). **~ingly** *adv*.

loo *n* (*GB colloq*) msala.

loofah, loofa *n* dodoki.

look *vi,vt* 1 ~ **(at)** tazama, angalia. **to ~ at him/it etc.** (*in passing judgement*) ukimwangalia kwa nje. **L~ before you leap** (*prov*) hadhari kabla ya kufanya jambo. **~ing glass** *n* kioo (cha kujitazamia). ~ **sb/sth in the eye(s)/face** angalia mtu usoni; kabili. 2 onekana ~ *ill* onekana mgonjwa ~ *oneself* onekana kama kawaida ya mtu alivyo. **~one's age** lingania/oana na umri wake *you don't ~ your age* huonekani kuwa mzee kiasi hicho. ~ **one's best** pendeza *she ~s her best in skirts* anapendeza akivaa sketi. ~black **(at)** angalia kwa hasira. ~ **blue** ononeka; nuna. ~ **good** pendeza vutia; onekana kuwa na maendeleo mazuri. **~ing** *adj* -enye sura/umbo la kupendeza. ~ **small** onekana duni. **L~ alive!** Changamka! **L~ here!** Sikiliza! Angalia! **L~ sharp!** Changamka! Fanya haraka! ~ **well** *(of persons)* onekana mwenye afya njema; *(of things)* onekana -a kupendeza, vutia; *(of a person wearing sth)* pendeza. 3 ~ **like/as if** onekana kama, elekea *it ~s like we will win* inaelekea tutashinda. 4 angalia *l~ where you are going* angalia unakokwenda! 5 onyesha (kwa sura). 6 (*uses with adverbial particles and preps)* ~ **about (for sth)** tafuta; angalia kwa makini, chunguza. ~ **about one** fanya uchunguzi ~ **after sb/sth** tunza; sindikiza kwa macho. ~ **at sth** *(special uses)* **not ~ at sth** *(usu with will, would)* -toangalia, -tofikiria; -tochunguza; *(in polite requests)* angalia. **good/bad etc. to ~ at** -enye sura ya kupendeza/kuchukiza n.k,. onekana vizuri, vibaya n.k. ~ **away (from sth)** kwepesha macho. ~ **back (on/to sth)** *(fig)* tazama nyuma, kumbuka ya nyuma. **never ~ back** usirudi/tazame nyuma; endelea (bila kukatishwa). ~ **down on sb/sth** *(colloq)* angalia kwa dharau/chuki. ~ **for sb/sth** tafuta; tarajia *it is too early to ~ for results* ni mapema mno kutarajia matokeo. ~ **forward to sth** ngojea kwa hamu/shauku. ~ **in (on sb)** tembelea (mtu) kwa muda mfupi. **give sb/get a ~-in** *(colloq, sport, etc.)* toa/pata nafasi, fursa (ya kushinda n.k.) *you won't get a ~- in with such strong competition* hutapata fursa ya kushinda/huwezi kushinda katika ushindani mkali namna hiyo. ~ **into sth** chunguza; peleleza; soma kwa kupitia (kitabu n.k.); angalia ndani ya kitu. ~ **on** -wa mtazamaji, tazama, **~er on** mtazamaji. ~ **on/upon sb/sth as** ona kama *do you ~ on him as an authority on biology?* unamwona kama bingwa wa biolojia? ~ **on/ upon sb sth with** ona mtu/jambo kuwa ni *he seems to ~ on me with distrust* anaelekea kutoniamini. ~ **on to** elekea *the hotel room ~s on to the beach* chumba cha hoteli kinaelekea ufukoni. ~ **out (of sth) (at sth)** tazama. ~ **out on (to)/over** elekea. ~ **out (for sb/ sth)** jihadhari, -wa macho -wa tayari kwa. **L~ out!** Tahadhari! **~-out** *n* **keep a good ~-out (for); be on the ~-out (for)** -wa mwangalifu, -wa macho; *(mil)* mahali pa kulindia, ulingo; mlinzi *(sing only) (prospect)* jambo la kutarajiwa, matarajio *thats' your own ~ out!* shauri yako! ~ **sth out for sb** chagulia mtu kitu (baada ya kukichunguza). ~ **over sth** kagua, chunguza. ~ **sth over** kagua sehemu mojamoja. **~-over** *n* ukaguzi. ~ **round** *(fig)* angalia uwezekano (kabla ya kufanya jambo); geuza kichwa (kuangalia kila upande). ~ **round (sth)** tembelea/zungukia mahali, (ili kuangalia). ~ **through sth** durusu. ~ **sth through** kagua kitu kwa makini. ~ **to sth** chunga, angalia. ~ **to sb for sth/to do sth** tegemea mtu kwa jambo/kwa ajili ya kufanya jambo. ~ **to/towards** elekea. ~ **up** angalia juu; tengemaa, ongezeka bei au ufanisi. ~ **sth up** tafuta kitu kitabuni n.k. ~ **sb up** tembelea mtu. ~ **sb up and down** kagua mtu; tazama (mtu) kwa dharau *n* 1 mtazamo, kutazama *let me have a ~ at your leg* hebu nitazame mguu wako. 2 sura, kuonekana. **give sth/get a new** ~ -pa/pewa sura mpya. 3 *(pl)* sura (ya mtu). **~er** *n a good ~er* mtu mwenye sura nzuri.

loom[1] *n* kitanda cha mfumi.

loom[2] *vi (large)* 1 onekana kama -kubwa (kwa kutisha); *(fig)* tisha (kwa kufikiriwa kubwa).

loon *n (Scot and arch)* 1 mjinga, mkunguni. **~y** *n, adj (sl)* -enye kichaa, wazimu *he is a ~* ana wazimu. **~bin** *n (sl)* nyumba/hospitali ya wendawazimu.

loop *n* 1 kitanzi, kishwara; *(colloq) (contraceptive)*kitanzi. 2 *(also* **~line**) reli au waya wa simu wa mzingo. 3 mzingo (unaofuatwa na ndege au pikipiki) wenye umbo la kitanzi. 4 pindo katika herufi *vt,vi* 1 piga kitanzi. 2 pinda ili kufanya umbo la kitanzi. **~hole** *n* 1 kitundu (cha kupenyezea bunduki, kuangalia, kupitishia hewa n.k.). 2 *(way of escape)* mwanya, njia ya kuokoka.

loopy *adj (sl)* -enye wazimu, kichaa.

loose *adj* 1 *(unfastened)* -liofunguka, -lioachwa (huru), -lioachiwa. **break/ get** ~ funguka, jitoa kifungoni, toroka. **let sth** ~ achia huru. **~box** sehemu katika zizi/behewa ambayo humwezesha farasi kutembea tembea). **~leaf** *attrib adj (of a notebook)* -siounganishwa, -siofungwa. 2 *(not tight)* -siokazwa, -a kupwaya, -liolegea *a ~ tooth* jino linalolegea. **come** ~ legea. **have a screw** ~ (*colloq*) fyatuka akili, -wa na kasoro kichwani. **have a ~ tongue** ropokaropoka. **have ~ bowels** endesha, harisha. **ride with a ~ rein** achia farasi huru; *(fig)* achia mtu (afanye apendavyo); *(of a bolt etc)* legea. 3 -siofungika vizuri. **at a ~ end** (*fig of a person*) -wa bila shughuli, kutojua la kufanya. 4 *(of talk, behaviour etc)*. -potovu, -baya. **(be) on the** ~ -wa fisadi. **play fast and ~ (with sb)** chezea, ghilibu, danganya. 5 -sio sahihi; -siofuata taratibu. 6 *(of the human body)* -sioshikana vizuri, -siopangwa vizuri. 7 -legelege, zembe *vt* 1 legeza. 2 achia huru *vt,vi* **~n (up)** 1 fungua, fumua, legeza. 2 (*of soil*) chimbua, tifua.

loot *vt,vi* pora, teka nyara *n* 1 mali iliyoporwa; mateka; nyara; kuteka nyara. **~er** *n* mporaji, mteka nyara.

lop[1] *vt* ~ **(away/off)** kata, pogoa, punguza matawi.

lop[2] *vi (chiefly in compounds)* ning'inia. ~ **eared** *adj* -enye masikio yanayoning'inia. ~ **sided** *adj* -a kwenda upande.

lope *vi* tembea/ruka kwa hatua kubwa (k.v. sungura) *n* hatua za kuruka.

loquacious *adj* -enye domo, -enye maneno mengi, -semaji, -limi. **~ly** *adv*. **~ness, loquacity** *n*.

lord *n* 1 mtawala mkuu (wa kiume) *our sovereign~ and king* mfalme mtawala wetu. 2 **The L~** Mungu, Mwenyezi Mungu, Mola, Bwana. **~! Good L~! ~ knows!** Yarabi! **our L~**'s Bwana Wetu Yesu Kristu **the L~ Day** siku ya Bwana, Jumapili. **the L~'s Prayer** sala ya Bwana, Baba Yetu. **L~'s Supper** Ushirika Mtakatifu. 3 (*peer, nobleman*) lodi, mwungwana; gabi. **as drunk as** ~ -liolewa chakari. **House of L~s** Baraza la Malodi (Uingereza). 4 *(in feudal times)* bwana, mwinyi. 5 (*joc,also* ~ **and master**) mume; kiongozi wa tasnia *the ~ of creation* binadamu. 6 mtu mwenye cheo/ madaraka. 7 Mheshimiwa. **My ~** Mheshimiwa *vt* (*chiefly in*) ~ **it over sb** tawala/ongoza kimwinyi. **~ly** *adj* 1 -a heshima; -a fahari. 2 *(arrogant)* -a kama mwinyi; -enye kiburi. **~liness** *n*. **~ship** *n* 1 ~ **over** utawala, miliki, mamlaka. 2 *His/Your~* Mheshimiwa, Bwana.

lore *n* elimu, maarifa ya mapokeo.

lorgnette *n* miwani yenye mpini (ishikwayo mkononi).

lorn *adj (poet of hum)* pweke.

lorry *n* lori.

lose *vt,vi* 1 poteza *~a knife* poteza kisu *~ weight* konda. ~ **one's cool** (*colloq*) hamaki; haha. ~ **in** choka na, -tovutwa tena na. ~ **ones reason/ senses** pata wazimu, pandwa na jazba. ~ **one's temper** kasirika. ~ **A to B** nyang'anywa/pokonywa A na B. 2 *(passive)* potea, -fa, *they were lost in the forest* walipotea msituni. **be lost to** -toathiriwa na kosa, -tosikia *he is lost to shame* hasikii, hana aibu. **be lost in** shikwa/jawa na (mawazo, mshangao n.k.) *be lost in astonishment* shangaa, shikwa na mshangao *be lost in thought* zama katika mawazo. 3 poteza. ~ **one's place** (*in a book etc.*) poteza. ~ **oneself/one's way** potea. ~ **sight of** sahau, -tozingatia, -toweza kuona *he lost sight of the fact that* alisahau kwamba. 4 chelewa. 5 kosa kuona/ kusikia n.k. *lost the last part of the speech* sikusikia sehemu ya mwisho ya hotuba. 6 kosesha *your obstinacy will ~ you your job* ujeuri wako utakukosesha kazi yako. 7 shindwa *we lost the match* tulishindwa katika pambano *a lost cause* jaribio/tendo ambalo limeshindwa/litashindwa tu. **(play) a losing game** (cheza) mchezo wa kushindwa *~-out to* rithiwa na. 8 ~ *by/in/on sth* haribikiwa, pata hasara *the story does not ~ in the telling* hadithi haipotezi utamu katika kusimulia. 9 (*of a watch etc.*) chelewa, poteza majira. 10 poteza bure (muda, juhudi, nafasi n.k.) *I shall ~ no time in doing it* nitaifanya mara moja *be lost on* shindwa kushawishi/kuvutia *my arguments were not lost on him* hoja zangu zilimwingia. 11 ~ **oneself in sth** *(reflex)* zamia, jisahau *he lost himself in his work* alijisahau katika kazi yake. **~r** *n* mshinde kupotea, upotezaji, kupotewa *loss of blood* kupoteza damu *loss of expectation of life* kupoteza matazamio ya uhai *loss of memory* kupotewa na kumbukumbu *we retired without loss of life* tulirudi bila mtu kuuawa. 2 msiba, maangamizi. 3 hasara *insure against loss* katia bima za hasara *total loss* hasara tupu *loss leader (comm)* bidhaa inayouzwa kwa bei ndogo ili kuvutia wateja. 4 kukosa, kushindwa kupata *the loss of a contract* kukosa mkataba. 5 kipunguo, hasara *be a ~ deal (of a person)* -wa bure/hasara tupu. 6 *(in expressions) be at a loss* changanyikiwa, tatanika; -tojua (la kufanya/ kusema).

lot[1] *n (colloq)* 1 *the whole ~, all the ~*

idadi yote, -ote. 2 a ~ (of); ~s (and ~s) -ingi *a ~ of people* watu wengi, umati wa watu *a good ~* -ingi, -a kutosha *quite a ~* -ingi, -a kutosha. 3 (*used adverbially*) sana *he is a ~ better today* anajisikia afadhali sana leo.

lot[2] *n* 1 bahati nasibu *draw/cast ~s* piga kura (kwa kuokota karatasi kutoka kwenye kasha). 2 *the ~* uamuzi/ uchaguzi unaotokana na bahati nasibu *it fell to my ~* iliniangukia. 3 bahati (ya mtu) *cast/throw in one's ~ with sb* amua kushirikiana na. 4 namba ya kitu katika orodha ya vitu vinavyouzwa kwa mnada. 5 fungu la vitu vinavyofanana. 6 *a bad ~ (colloq)* mtu mbaya. 7 sinema, studio na uwanja unaoizunguka *(esp US)* kiwanja *a parking ~* mahali pa kuegeshea magari *a vacant ~* kiwanja cha kujengea. **~tery** *n* bahati nasibu. ~ **ticket** tikiti ya bahati nasibu *(fig) is marriage a ~?* Je, ndoa ni bahati nasibu? ~ **to** *n* mchezo wa bahati nasibu; bingo; tombola.

loth see **loath**.

lotion *n* losheni.

lotus *n* yungiyungi (la Misri na Asia). ~ **eater** *n* mpenda starehe, mtu anayejitumbukiza katika anasa.

loud *adj* 1 -enye sauti kubwa, -a makelele; -a kusikika kwa urahisi *a ~ speech* hotuba yenye kusikika kwa urahisi; kubwa. **~-hailer** *n* kipaza sauti. **~-speaker** *n* kipaza sauti, bomba. 2 (*of behaviour, colours*) -a kujitangaza, -a mvuto *adv* kwa sauti kubwa. **~ly** *adv*. **~ness** *n*.

lough *n (in Ireland)* mkono wa bahari, ghuba; ziwa.

lounge *vi* kaa, simama (kwa kujiegemeza) kivivu; jikalia, tandawaa. **~r** *n* mtu akaaye/ asimamaye namna hii *n* kukaa/ kusimama kivivu. 2 ukumbi, sebule (agh. katika hoteli) wa kupumzika. ~ **suit** suti (ya kiume). ~ **chair** *n* kiti cha kupumzikia. ~ **lizard** *(dated sl)* mwanamme ambaye analipwa kwa kucheza dansi na wanawake kwenye mahoteli. **~-bar** *n* baa nzuri katika nyumba ya vileo.

lour, lower *vi* 1 ~ **at/on/upon** nuna, onekana na hasira. 2 *(of the sky, clouds)* -wa zito sana. ~ **ingly** *adv*

louse *n* chawa. *(sl.)* **lousy** *adj* -enye chawa; *(colloq)* -baya, -ovyo *a lousy trick* hila mbaya; *(sl)* -ingi *be lousy with money* -wa na fedha nyingi, jaa kishenzi.

lout *n* baradhuli. ~ *adj*.

louvre, louver luva. **~d** *adj*.

love[1] *n* 1 upendo, mapenzi, huba *a mother's ~ for her children* mapenzi ya mama kwa watoto wake. **give/ send sb one's ~** tuma salamu (zenye upendo;). **play for ~** cheza kwa kujifurahisha tu. **not to be had for ~ or money** -sioweza kupatikana (kwa njia yoyote). **there is no ~ lost between them** hawapendani. **a labour of ~** kitu mtu anachofurahia kufanya; kumfanyia mtu kitu kwa sababu ya upendo. **for the ~ of** *(in appeals etc)* kwa jina la..... **~feast** *n (rel)* karamu ya pamoja (iliyoadhimishwa na Wakristo wa zamani kudumisha upendo); ibada ya pamoja. 2 mapenzi, mahaba. **be in ~ (with sb)** penda mwanamke/ mwanamme *John is in ~ with Mary*, John anampenda Mary. **fall in ~ (with sb)** penda mwanamke/ mwanamume. **make ~ (to sb)** lala; jamiiana, fanya mapenzi; onyesha kupendana na. 3 *(compounds)* ~ **affair** *n* uhusiano wa kimapenzi. ~ **bird** *n* kasuku mdogo *(pl)* watu waliopendana sana. **~-child** *n* mwanaharamu. **~-knot** *n* fundo mapenzi. **~-letter** barua ya mapenzi. **~-lorn** *adj* -a simanzi (agh. kwa kumkosa mpenzi); -a kunyong'onyea (agh. kutokana na mapenzi). **~-making** *n* kujamiiana (na mambo yote yanayohusiana na kitendo hicho). **~-match** *n* ndoa itokanayo na mapenzi tu. **~-philtre/-potion** *n* dawa ya mapenzi. **~-seat** *n* benchi mfano wa S yenye sehemu mbili za kukalia zilizopeana migongo. **~-sick** *adj* -a simanzi, nyong'onyevu (kwa sababu ya mapenzi). **~sickness** *n* ugonjwa wa mahaba. **~-song** *n* wimbo wa mapenzi. **~-story** *n* hadithi ya mapenzi/huba. **~-token** *n* hidaya. 4 *(colloq)* mpenzi, kipenzi (agh. mke, mme, au mtoto) *come here my ~* njoo hapa kipenzi changu. 5 mpenzi. 6 (*in games*) bila, bure. **~ all** bila bila; hakuna bao pande zote. **~less** *adj* -siopenda; -siopendwa; pasipo penzi *vt* penda *~ one's parents* penda wazazi. 2 abudu. 3 *(colloq)* penda sana; furahia. **lovable** *adj* -a kupendeka. **~ly** *adj* 1 -zuri sana, -a kupendeza, -a kufurahisha. 2 *(colloq)* safi, -a kuchangamsha, -a kuburudisha *what a ~ meal!* chakula safi sana. **~liness** *n*. **~r** *n* 1 mpenzi *they are ~rs* ni wapenzi. 2 *(of music, football etc.)* mpenzi, shabiki. **~like** *adj* -enye mapenzi. **loving** *adj* -enye upendo. **~-cup** *n* bilauri/kata ya pombe (ambayo huzungushwa kwa zamu kutoka mnywaji mmoja hadi mwingine). **~-kindness** *n* wema, huruma, *(of God)* rehema. **lovingly** *adv*.

low[1] *adj* 1 -a chini; fupi *a ~range of hills* vimilima vifupi *~ shoe* kiatu kisicho cha mchuchumio. **~-lying land** nyanda za chini. 2 -a chini ya (usawa wa) kawaida. **~ tide/water** maji kupwa. **~-water mark** alama ya chini kabisa, mwisho mwa kupwa. **be in ~ waters** *(fig)* wamba. 3 *(of sounds)* -a chini ya pole, -a kunong'ona *speak in a ~low voice* ongea kwa sauti ya chini; nong'ona. **~-keyed** *(fig)* -sio makeke. **~-pitched** *(music)* -a sauti ya chini. 4 *(of people)* -a tabaka duni/-a/chini; nyonge *men of ~ birth* watu wa tabaka duni. **be brought ~** dhalilishwa. 5 shenzi *~ manners* tabia za kishenzi *~ life* maisha ya kishenzi. 6 dhaifu, nyonge *he is in a ~ state of health* afya yake imedhoofu. **be in ~ spirits** sononeka; -wa nyonge; -tochangamka. **~spirited** *adj*. 7 *(of a supply of anything)* **be/run ~** punguka, karibia kwisha, -wa haba *food supplies are running ~ in this town*, kuna uhaba wa chakula mjini hapa, -a kiasi kidogo, -dogo, a chini. 8 *(of amounts) ~ prices* bei za chini. **~ latitudes** latitudo karibu na Ikweta. **have a ~ opinion of sb** -tomthamini. **L~ church** waumini (wasiopenda utawala msonge na ulibwende katika kanisa). **L~ churchman**. 10 *(phrases)* **bring/lay sb/sth ~** dhoofisha; *(bankrupt)* filisisha; fedhehesha; dunisha. **lie ~** *(fig)* kaa kimya; fichama. 11 *(compounds)* **~-born** *adj* -a koo duni. **~-bred** *adj* -enye tabia za kishenzi, -siostaarabika. **~brow** *n adj (person)* -siosomi, -siopendelea mambo ya kitaaluma, hasa sanaa. **~er case** *(in printing)* herufi ndogo. **L~er Chamber/House** Bunge (la kutunga sheria). **~ comedian** chale kwenye kichekesho. **~ comedy** vichekesho. **~er deck** *(in the navy)* baharia wa kawaida. **~-down** *adj (colloq)* -a kishenzi, -a fasiki. **give sb/get the ~ down (on sth/sb)** *(colloq)* toa/fahamu siri juu ya jambo/mtu. **~lander** *n* mkazi katika nyanda za chini. **~ lands** *n (pl)* (maeneo yaliyo katika) nyanda za chini. **~ Latin** Kilatini kisichosanifu (kikilinganishwa na Kilatini kikongwe). **~ Mass** Misa ndogo (agh. iendeshwayo bila ya nyimbo). **~ Sunday Week** Jumapili na Wiki mara baada ya Pasaka. **L~ermost** *adj* -a chini kabisa. **L~ness** *n adv* chini *buy ~ and sell high* nunua kwa bei ya chini uza kwa bei ya juu *n* kitu, jambo, hali ya chini. **~er** *vt,vi* 1 shusha, teremsha, inamisha *~ a flag* teremsha bendera. **L~ away** *(naut.)* teremsha/ shusha (mtumbwi, nanga, tanga n.k.). 2 punguza *~ the rent of a house* punguza kodi ya nyumba. 3 **~ oneself** -tojiheshimu, jishushia hadhi, jidhalilisha. 4 dhoofisha. **~ly** *adj* duni, -a hali ya chini. **~liness** *n*.

lower *vi see* **lour**.
loyal *adj* -aminifu, -tiifu. **~ist** *n* mwaminifu (kwa mkuu wa serikali). **~ly** *adv*. **~ty** *n* 1 uaminifu. 2 *(pl)* aina za mahusiano, uwajibikaji, utiifu.
lozenge *n* 1 pipi/peremende ya kifua. 2 msambamba; *(of playing cards)* uru, kisu.
LSD *n* dawa kali ya kulevya.
Ltd *see* **limited**.
lubber *n* mtu mzito.
lubricate *vt* 1 lainisha, legeza kwa mafuta. 2 *(fig)* rahisisha kufanyika kwa jambo. **lubricant** *n* mafuta ya kulainisha. **lubrication n** kutia mafuta, ulainishaji.
lucent *adj (liter)* 1 -angavu, -a kung'ara. 2 -eupe.
lucerne *n* luserini: majani ya kulisha ng'ombe *(US* alfalfa).
lucid *adj* 1 -a kufahamika kwa urahisi, wazi, dhahiri. 2 -enye akili timamu *~ interval* wakati wa mzinduko. 3 *(poet)* -angavu, -eupe. **~ly** *adv*. **~ity** *n* uangavu, weupe, udhahiri.
Lucifer *n* 1 shetani, ibilisi. 2 zuhura.
luck *n* 1 bahati, nasibu, sudi. **as ~ would have it** kwa bahati mbaya/ nzuri. **bad ~** bahati mbaya, shari, kisirani, nuksi. **bad~** pole! bahati Mbaya! *out of ~* -enye bahati mbaya *better ~ next time* bahati njema safari ijayo *good ~* kisimati *he is in ~* ana bahati nzuri; anapendelewa, ameneemeka *good ~ (to you)* nakutakia mafanikio/kila la kheri *it's just my ~* nina mkosi/nuksi. **be down on one's ~** *(colloq)* -wa na bahati mbaya, -wa na matatizo, -wa na nuksi *try one's ~* bahatisha *worse ~* kwa bahati mbaya. **~less** *adj* -enye kisirani. **~y** *adj* -enye bahati, -a bahati njema, -a heri. **be ~** wa na bahati nzuri, bahatika *he 's a ~ dog!* ana bahati njema! *how ~* bahati nzuri. **~ily** *adv*.
lucrative *adj* -a kuleta faida, -enye faida.
lucre *n (in a bad sense)* fedha, faida, mali; *(filthy) ~* fedha iliyopatikana kwa njia mbaya *for filthy ~* kwa hela tu.
ludicrous *adj* -a kuchekesha, -puuzi, -a mzaha; pumbavu.
ludo *n* ludo: aina mojawapo ya michezo ya kutumia dadu/kete.
luff *n (naut.)* mbele ya tanga *vt,vi (naut)* bisha.
lug *vt* kokota, burura, buruta; *n* mkokoto, mbururo.
luge *n (F)* luji: gari telezi katika theluji.
luggage *n* mizigo. **~ carrier** *n* uchaga wa mizigo. **~-rack** *n* kichaga cha mizigo kwenye basi au treni. **~-van** *n* behewa la mizigo.
lugger *n* chombo chenye tanga la pembe nne.
lugsail *n (naut.)* matanga pembe nne.
lugubrious *adj (formal)* -a majonzi, -zito. **~ly** *adv*. **~ness** *n*.
lukewarm *adj* 1 *(of liquids etc)* -a uvuguvugu, fufutende. 2 *(fig) be ~* vuvuwaa. **~ly** *adv*. **~ness** *n*.
lull *vt,* liwaza, bembeleza, tuliza *n* utulivu. **~aby** *n* wimbo wa kubembeleza mtoto; sauti nyororo zitokanazo na upepo au mawimbi.
lumbar *adj* -a kiuno. **~ago** *n* maumivu ya kiuno.
lumber[1] *n* 1 *(GB)* makorokoro. **~ room** *n* chumba cha kuhifadhia makorokoro. 2 *(timber)* mti; mbao; magogo. **~man, ~jack** *n* mkataji miti, mpasua mbao. **~ mill** *n* kiwanda cha mbao *vt* **~ sth (up) (with)** jaza makorokoro (takataka n.k.).
lumber[2] *vi* 1 enda kwa kishindo, -wa zito *the army tanks ~ed past* vifaru vya jeshi vilipita kwa kishindo.
luminous *n* 1 -a kung'aa *~paint* rangi ya mng'ao. 2 *(fig)* dhahiri, wazi; -a kufahamika kwa urahisi. **~ity** *n*. **luminary** *n* 1 jua, mwezi, nyota, kitu kingaacho angani. 2 *(fig)* mtu mashuhuri (kwa usomi au maadili yake).
lummy, lumme *(GB sl.)* lahaula!
lump[1] *vt (only in) ~* **it** *(colloq)* vumilia jambo, mezea *if you don't like it you can ~it* upende usipende inakupasa

kumezea.

lump[2] *n* 1 bonge, fumba; jumla. ~ **sum** malipo yote (kwa pamoja). **in the** ~ kwa bunda, kwa jumla, kwa pamoja. ~ **sugar** sukari ya kibonge. 2 uvimbe mwilini. **a** ~ **in the throat** msongo wa moyo, donge. 3 *(colloq)* mtu mnene na mzito *vt,vi* ~ **together** 1 tia pamoja, changanya; jumuisha. 2 budaa. **~ish** *adj (of a person)* fupi na nene, bongebonge; pumbavu; zito. **~y** *adj* -liobudaa, -enye mabongebonge *(of water)* -enye viwimbi.

lunacy *n* 1 wazimu, kichaa, umajinuni. 2 *(pl)* matendo ya kichaa. **lunatic** *n* kichaa, majinuni. ~ **asylum** hospitali ya kutibu vichaa *adj* -enye kichaa. ~ **fringe** kundi la watu wachache wenye siasa/mawazo makali, wenye vitendo vya ajabu.

lunar *adj* 1 -a mwezi a ~ *month* mwezi unaofuata kuandama kwa mwezi. 2 (kwa umbo) -a umbo la mwezi mwandamo ~ *module n* njia ya chombo kinachozunguka na kutua mwezini ~ *orbit n* kuzunguka mwezi.

lunch *n* chakula cha mchana *vt,vi* 1 -la chakula cha mchana. 2 karibisha kwa chakula cha mchana. **~eon** *n*.

lung *n* 1 pafu, buhumu; *(of animal)* yavuyavu *~ish n* kambaremamba. ~ **power** *n* nguvu ya sauti. 2 *(fig)* eneo wazi/uwanja karibu na jiji.

lunge *n* mwendo/mrukio wa ghafla mbele *vi* enda/rukia (k.m. kwa lengo ya kupiga) ~ *forward* enda/rukia mbele ~ *out at sb* lenga kupiga mtu ghafla.

lurch[1] *n* msepetuko *vi* sepetuka, enda mrama, pepesuka; *(naut)* lalia/elemea upande mmoja.

lurch[2] *n (only in)* **leave in the** ~ acha katika shida.

lure *vt* vuta, shawishi, tega *n* 1 *(bait)* chambo. 2 *(attraction)* mvuto, kishawishi.

lurid *adj* 1 -a rangi za kuwaka. 2 *(fig)* -a kutisha, -a kuogofya. **~ly** *adv*. **~ness** *n*.

lurk *vi* jificha, jibanza, vizia *~ing place n* mafichoni.

luscious *adj* 1 tamu sana; -enye harufu nzuri. 2 *(of the arts)* -enye madoido sana.

lush *adj* 1 *(of vegetation)* -a kusitawi sana. 2 -a anasa *n (us. sl.)* mlevi.

lust *n* ashiki, hawaa; tamaa *vi* ~ **after/for** tamani ~ *after a woman* tamani mwanamke. **~ful** *adj*. **~fully** *adv*.

lustre,luster *n* 1 mng'aro. 2 *(fig)* sifa, heshima, fahari. **lustrous** *adj*.

lusty *adj* 1 -a nguvu, -enye afya njema, siha. **lustily** *adv*.

Lutheran *adj* 1 -a Kilutheri, -a mfuasi wa Luther *n* Mlutheri.

luxuriant *adj 1* -a kuota sana, -a kusitawi sana, tele. 2 -liopambwa sana, -a ufasaha. **luxuriance** *n*.

luxury *n* 1 anasa. 2 *(attrib)* -a anasa. **luxury hotel** hoteli ya anasa. 3 *(rare pleasure)* tunu. **luxuriate** *vi (in)* furahia, jistarehesha. **luxurious** *adj* 1 -a anasa, -a tunu. 2 -enye kustarehesha/kuanisi. 3 tele. **luxuririously** *adv*. **luxuriousness** *n*.

lycee *n* shule ya sekondari Ufaransa.

lyceum *n (U.S)* ukumbi (wa mikutano, maonyesho n.k.).

lye *n* maji magadi.

lying[1] *see* **lie**[2] *adj* -nayolala *n* kulala. **~-in** *n* kuzaa.

lymph *n* 1 limfu ~ *glands* tezi za limfu. **~atic** *adj* 1 -a limfu. 2 *(of person)* tepetepe, zito. ~ **fluid** giligili ya limfu ~ *system* mfumo wa limfu.

lynch *vt* ua kiholela (agh kwa kunyonga na bila nafasi ya kujitetea) *the crowd ~ed him* kundi la watu lilimuua *n* ~ **law** kunyonga bila kufuata sheria.

lynx *n* linksi: pakamwitu mwenye macho makali sana. **~-eyed** *adj* -a macho makali sana.

lyre *n* kinubi.

lyric *n* shairi la hisia. 2 *(pl)* maneno ya wimbo. **~al** *adj* 1 -a shairi la hisia. 2 -enye kusisimka, -liojaa shauku. **~ist** mtunzi wa (maneno ya) nyimbo.

lysol *n* dawa ya mafuta inayotumika kama kidhurubakteria na kiuavijidudu.

M

Mm *n* herufi ya kumi na tatu katika alfabeti ya Kiingereza; alama ya Kirumi yenye maana ya elfu moja.
ma *(colloq abbr of)* mama
ma'am *n* bibie.
mac *see* **mackintosh**.
macabre *adj* -a kutisha; -a kuashiria kifo; uchuro. *n* **danse** ~ ngoma ya uchuro/kifo.
macadam *n* ~ **road** barabara (iliyotengenezwa kwa maki kadhaa za mawe na changarawe). **~ize** *vt* fanya barabara ya namna hiyo.
macaroni *n* makaroni: aina ya tambi.
macaroon *n* keki au biskuti ndogo iliyotengenezwa kwa sukari, yai na nazi/lozi.
macaw *n* aina ya kasuku wa Amerika Kusini (mwenye mkia mrefu).
mace[1] *n* 1 rungu. 2 *(of Parliament etc)* fimbo, mesi. ~ **bearer** *n (Parliament)* mbeba fimbo/rungu *a ceremonial* ~ fimbo rasmi.
mace[2] *n (spice)* basibasi.
macerate *vt* lainisha (kwa kulowesha majini), dhoofisha kuwa laini. **maceration** *n*.
Mach *n (aviat)* mechi. ~ **number** uwiano wa mwendo wa ndege na mwendo wa sauti.
machete *n* panga, mundu.
machiavellian *adj* -erevu, danganyifu.
machination *n* njama, hila.
machine *n* 1 mashine, mtambo; (*sewing*) cherahani. 2 kikundi kinachoongoza chama cha siasa. 3 *(of person)* mtu atendaye bila kufikiri. ~ -**gun** *n* bombomu. ~-**made** *adj* -liotengenezwa kwa mashine. ~ **tool** mashine ya samani *vt* endesha mashine, fanya kitu kwa kutumia mashine. **machinist** *n* mtengeneza mashine, mwangalizi wa mashine. **~ry** *n* 1 sehemu au vyombo vya mashine kwa jumla. 2 utaratibu (k.m. wa serikali, chama n.k.), urasimu.
machismo *n* ujana dume, udume.
mackerel *n* samaki wa jamii ya bangala. ~ **sky** mawingu yenye mistari.
mackintosh *n GB* koti la mvua, mpira.
macro- *(prefix)* -kubwa, -makro. ~ **biotic** -nayorefusha uhai. ~**biotic food** *n* chakula cha mboga asilia tu. ~**cosm** *n* ulimwengu, jumla.
macron *n* makroni: alama ya urefu (-) juu ya vokali.
mad *adj* 1 -enye wazimu, -enye kichaa. **go** ~ shikwa na wazimu, rukwa na akili. **drive sb** ~ sumbua sana mtu *a bit* ~ punguani. **as** ~ **as a hare/ hatter** kichaa kabisa. 2 -enye kutaharuki/jazba, -liojaa shauku, -enye mhemko. **be/go** ~ taharuki, hamaki, chukia sana. **like** ~ sana sana, mno. **be** ~ **about sb** penda sana mtu. 3 -enye kukasirika, -enye hasira. **be** ~ **about sth** kasirikia kitu/jambo. ~**cap** *n* mtu mwenye harara. ~ **house** *n* hospitali ya wendawazimu; *(fig)* ghasia nyingi, vurumai. ~ **man/woman** mwenda-wazimu. ~**ly** *adv* kwa hasira nyingi, kwa wazimu. *(colloq)* ~ **ness** *n* wazimu; ujinga. ~**den** *vt* tia wazimu, kasirisha sana; kera sana.
madam *n* 1 bibi, mama. 2 *(colloq)* kuwadi wa kike (anayeongoza danguro). 3 *(colloq)* mwanamke/ msichana mpenda kuamrisha (watu).
madame *n pl (sl)* Bibi (hutumika mbele ya majina ya wanawake walioolewa).
madder *n* 1 *(bot)* mmea utoao rangi nyekundu. 2 rangi nyekundu (ya mmea).
made *pt, pp of* **make**.
mademoiselle *n pl* **mesdemoiselle** Bi (kwa wasichana au wanawake wasioolewa).
Madonna *n (rel)* Bikira Maria (sanamu au picha yake). ~ **lily** lili (ua jeupe).
madrigal *n* 1 wimbo wa kupokezana. 2 shairi fupi la mapenzi.
maelstrom *n* 1 *(fig)* machafuko, fujo, msukosuko. 2 kizingia cha maji, chunusi.
maestro *n* bingwa wa muziki.
Mae West *n (sl)* koti la uokoaji (baharini).
maffick *vt* sherehekea sana ushindi.
Mafia *n* Mafia: chama cha siri katika Sisilia, Italia na Marekani kinachopinga serikali halali na kujishughulisha na ujangili na

ujambazi.
magazine *n* 1 ghala/bohari/stoo ya silaha na zana nyingine za vita. 2 chemba (ya risasi katika bunduki). 3 gazeti (agh la wiki/mwezi/mwaka).
magdalen *n* malaya aliyeongoka.
magenta *adj* -a rangi ya damu ya mzee *n* rangi ya damu ya mzee.
maggot *n* 1 funza, buu. 2 *(arch)* matamanio. **have a ~ in one's head** -wa na wazo la ajabu.
Magi *n* Majusi, Mamajusi.
magic *n* 1 uchawi. **as if by ~; like ~** -a kimaajabu, ajabu. **black/white ~** uchawi/uganga. 2 *(for finding offender)* mburuga. 3 *(conjuring)* mazingaombwe, kiinimacho, mzungu. 4 *(fig)* mvuto *adj* -a uchawi, -enye uchawi. **~ eye** *(colloq)* kiongozea mbali, kiongoza toka mbali n.k. **~ lantern** projekta. **~al** *adj* -a ajabu; -a mwujiza; -a kichawi. **~ally** *adv*. **~ian** *n* mchawi, mfanya mazingaombwe.
magistrate *n* hakimu, mwamuzi *District ~* Hakimu wa Wilaya *Resident ~* Hakimu mkazi. **magistracy** *n* uhakimu. **the ~** mahakimu kwa jumla. **magisterial** *adj* 1 -a hakimu, -a kihakimu. 2 -a nguvu, -enye mamlaka, -enye amri.
magnanimous *adj* karimu. **~ly** *adv*. **magnanity** *n*.
magnate *n* mkwasi: mtu tajiri sana.
magnesium *n (chem)* magnesi.
magnesia *n* 1 magnesi *~ oxide* oksidi ya magnesi.
magnet *n* 1 sumaku. 2 *(fig)* mtu/kitu kinachovutia. **~ic** *adj* 1 -a sumaku. **~ pole** ncha sumaku **~ field** ugasumaku **~ North** Kaskazini kisumaku. **~ tape** ukanda/utepe wa sumaku. 2 -enye nguvu ya kuvuta. **~ism** *n* 1 nguvu ya sumaku; usumaku. 2 *(fig)* nguvu ya kuvuta; mvuto. **~ize** *vt* tia sumaku; *(fig)* vuta (kwa ajili ya tabia, akili n.k.).
magneto *n (tech)* mashine ya umeme; magneto.
Magnificat *n (rel)* utenzi wa Maria.
magnificent *adj* -zuri kabisa, -tukufu, -adhimu. **~ly** *adv*. **magnificence** *n*.
magnify *vt* 1 kuza. 2 tia chumvi. 3 tukuza, adhimisha, sifu, kuza.
magnifier *n* kiookuzi. **magnification** *n* ukuzaji, uadhimishaji.
magnilloquent *adj* -a maneno; -a maneno ya fahari; shaufu, -piga domo. **~ly** *adv*. **magniloquence** *n*.
magnitude *n* 1 *(size)* ukubwa. 2 *(greatness)* ukubwa, ubora, ukuu, cheo.
magnolia *n* mti wenye majani meusi na maua yanayong'aa na kunukia.
magnum *n* chupa kubwa ya mvinyo (nusu galoni).
magpie *n* 1 *(bio)* ndege wa jamii ya kunguru. 2 *(fig)* mpiga domo. 3 *(fig)* kijizi, mdokozi.
magus *n see* **magi** mnajimu.
Mahatma *n (India)* jina apewalo mtu mwenye heshima kuu (kutokana na mapenzi na utu wake).
mahogany *n* 1 mkangazi, mbambakofi. 2 *(arch)* meza ya kulia. 3 rangi ya mbambakofi.
maid *n* 1 mwanamwali, mwali, bikira. **old ~** mwanamke asiyeolewa. **~ of honour** mtumishi wa malkia au binti yake; mpambe wa Malkia/Bibi arusi; matroni. 2 *(arch poet)* msichana. 3 *(house servant)* mtumishi mwanamke. **~en** *n* 1 *(arch or poet)* msichana, binti. 2 mwali, mwanamwali. 3 *(hist)* mashine ya kukata shingo *adj* 1 -a msichana/-a mwanamwali. 2 -a kwanza. **~ name** jina la ukoo (kabla ya kuolewa). **~ speech** hotuba ya kwanza Bungeni (kwa/Mbunge mpya). 3 -a bikira. 4 *(compounds)* **~ head** *n* ubikira. **~ like ~enly** *adj* -a kibinti; -enye adabu, pole, tulivu.
mail[1] *n* 1 barua za posta. **~ bag** mfuko wa barua za posta. **~ boat** *n* meli ya barua. **~ box** *n (US* **letter box***)* sanduku la posta. **~ man** *n* mtu anayepeleka barua. **~ order** *n* ununuzi kwa posta. **~ train** *n* gari moshi lenye behewa la posta. 2 posta

vt peleka kwa posta, postia. **~ing list** *n* orodha ya watu wanaopelekewa matangazo n.k.

mail[2] *n (arch)* daraya, nguo za pete za chuma. **the ~ed fist** (tishio la) wanajeshi.

maim *vt* lemaza, atilisha (mguu, mkono, jicho n.k.) *he was ~ed in the war* alilemazwa vitani.

main[1] *adj (attrib only)* 1 kuu *~ road* barabara kuu *~idea* wazo kuu, muhimu. 2 -ote, kubwa. **do sth by ~ force** fanya jambo kwa nguvu zote. 3 *(compounds)* ~ **deck** *n* sitaha kuu. **~land** *n* bara, *Tanzania ~* Tanzania bara. ~ **mast** *n* mlingoti mkuu. ~ **spring** *n* kamani ya saa; *(fig)* kiini, chanzo hasa cha jambo. ~ **stay** kamba itokeayo kwenye mlingoti mkuu hadi kwenye mlingoti wa mbele; *(fig)* tegemeo kuu, nguzo. ~ **stream** mwelekeo tawala, mawazo ya walio wengi. **~ly** *adv* kwa kiasi kikubwa, hasa.

main[2] *n* 1 *(often* **the ~s)** bomba kuu (la maji, gesi); njia kuu ya umeme; bomba/mfereji mkuu wa maji machafu. ~ **s set** redio ya umeme. 2 **in the ~** kwa kiasi kikubwa, kwa jumla, aghalabu. 3 *(poet)* bahari.

maintain *vt* 1 dumisha, endeleza *~ order* dumisha amani *~ friendship* dumisha urafiki. **~ an open mind on sth** wa tayari kusikiliza, kuzingatia maoni ya wengine. 2 *(support)* lisha, kimu, gharimia. 3 *(assert)* shikilia, sema, sisitiza, thibitisha. 4 tunza *~ roads* tunza/fanyia matengenezo barabara. 5 hifadhi, linda. **~able** *adj*. **maintenance** *n* 1 kukimu; matengenezo. ~ **order** *n (leg)* amri ya kukimu mke, mtoto au mume (itolewayo na mahakama). ~ **gang/ men** kikosi cha kufanya matengenezo ya barabara. **retail price** ~ udumishaji bei za rejareja.

maisonette *n* nyumba ndogo ya ghorofa moja.

maize *n* 1 *(plant)* muhindi. 2 (*grain*) mahindi. 3 *(cob)* gunzi, kigunzi, kibunzi. 4 *roasted ~* bisi. 5 *(flour)* unga wa mahindi; sembe; dona.

majesty *n* 1 ukuu wa enzi, utukufu, uadhama, ujalali/ujalalati. 2 **your/his/her M** ~ Mtukufu/jalali Mfalme, mtukufu, jalalati Malkia. **majestic** *adj* -adhimu, -tukufu, -a fahari. **~ally** *adv*

major[1] *adj* 1 -kubwa, kuu, -enye maana zaidi *~ road* barabara kuu *~ operation* operesheni kubwa. ~ **scale** *n (music)* skeli kuu *vi* ~ **in sth** taalimikia somo fulani katika chuo kikuu *~ in linguistics* taalimikia isimu.

major[2] *n* 1 meja. ~ **general** *n* meja jenerali.

major-domo *n* mtumishi mkuu wa nyumba kubwa (agh ya mwana mfalme/mtawala/mfalme mdogo).

majority *n* 1 wingi, zaidi ya nusu. 2 **a/ the ~ (of)** walio wengi *~ judgement* hukumu ya wengi. **be in the ~** -wa zaidi ya nusu. **a ~ verdict** uamuzi wa wengi. 3 *(full age)* umri wa utu uzima. **attain one's ~** fikia utu uzima kisheria; pata umeja (cheo cha meja).

make *vt,vi* 1 **~ sth from/(out) of sth; ~ sth into sth** 1 tengeneza *~ a brick* tengeneza tofali. ~ **a boat** unda boti ~ **a house** jenga nyumba; *(create)* umba, huluku *God made man* Mungu alimuumba, alimhuluku binadamu; *(of tea, coffee etc)* pika *~ tea* pika chai. **show sb/let sb see what one is made of** onyesha sifa/nguvu/uwezo wa mtu. **be as clever etc as they ~ them** -wa na akili sana. 2 chimba, toboa *~ a hole* toboa/chimba shimo *~ a hole in the ground* chimba shimo ardhini; punguza. ~ **a hole in ones finances** mega/punguza sana fedha. 3 tunga, weka *the laws were made to protect people* sheria zilitungwa kuwalinda watu. 4 fanya, sababisha (kufanyika kwa jambo) *~ a treaty* fanya mkataba *~ a disturbance* fanya fujo *the news made him sad* ile habari ilimsikitisha *his jokes made us* *laugh* masihara yake yalituchekesha. ~ **one's hackles rise** kasirisha. ~ **one's hair stand on end** tisha. ~ **sth go round** fanya kitu kitoshe/kidumu. ~ **oneself useful** saidia. ~ **it worth sb's while (to do sth)** lipa. ~ **do with sth** ridhika na. ~ **do and mend** mudu kwa kushikiza. 5 ~ **believe** jifanya, jisingizia. 6 kadiria, fikiria, chukulia *how large do you ~ the audience* unafikiria hadhira ni kubwa kiasi gani. 7 chukuana, enda pamoja; *(of persons)* -wa kufu ya *Asha and Ali are made for each other* Asha ni kufu ya Ali *bread and butter are made to be eaten together* mkate na siagi huliwa pamoja. 8 pata *he ~s nine hundred shillings every day* anapata shs 900 kila siku *he made a name for himself* alijipatia umaarufu. ~ **a pile/packet** *(colloq)* jipatia fedha nyingi sana. ~ **one's living** jipatia riziki. 9 *(of games)* funga; shinda. 10 *(of the tide)* anza *the tide is making fast* maji yanaanza kujaa kwa haraka. 11 fanikiwa. ~ **or break/mar** ama ushinde au uangamie. **a made man** mtu aliyefanikiwa. 12 lazimisha, shurutisha *she made me drink beer* alinishurutisha kunywa bia. 13 onekana kama, onyesha kama kwamba, fanya kuonekana kama. 14 lingana, -wa sawa na *twelve things ~ a dozen* vitu kumi na viwili ni sawa na dazeni moja. 15 **it ~ s sense!** ni sawa. 16 -wa *(in a series)* mara *this ~s the second time you are late* umechelewa (tena) kwa mara ya pili sasa. 17 *(colloq uses)* safiri/enda kitambo. ~ **it in time** wahi, fika kwa wakati uliotakiwa. 18 chagua, teua *he was made the Prime Minister* aliteuliwa kuwa Waziri Mkuu. 19 toa *he made two proposals* alitoa mapendekezo mawili. 20 ~ **sth of sb/sth; ~ sth/sb sth** fanya kuwa *the coach wants to ~ them an excellent team* kocha anataka wawe timu bora *don't ~ smoking a habit* usiwe na mazoea ya kuvuta sigara. 21 ~ **(an) application (to sb) (for sth)** omba. ~ **arrangements for** panga, fanya mipango. ~ **a decision** amua. ~ **a guess at** kisia. ~ **an impression on** vuta, vutia. ~ **a request for** omba. ~ **a success of sth** fanikiwa. 22 *(of arguments, evidence etc)* lenga. ~ **against** dhuru, haribu, athiri. 23 *(compounds)* ~ **shift** *adj* -a muda. ~ **up** *n* mpangilio wa chapa/herufi, tabia, hulka; vipodozi. ~ **weight** *n* punje, kiasi kidogo cha kujazia; *(fig)* kitu cha thamani ndogo kinachojazia pengo. 24 *(with adverbial particles and prepositions)* ~ **after sb** kimbilia; fukuza, fuatia. ~ **at sb** fuata kwa hasira. ~ **away with sth** -iba. ~ **away with oneself** jiua. ~ **for sb/sth** elekea; changia. ~ **off** toroka. ~ **off with** iba na kutoroka. ~ **sth out** elewa *I couldn't ~ out her handwriting* sikuelewa maandishi yake. ~ **out that/~ sb out to be** dai. **he ~s himself to be extremely wealthy** anajidai ni tajiri sana. ~ **out (with sb)** endelea, patana *how are you making out with your new boss?* unaendeleaje na mkuu wako mpya? ~ **out a case for/against/that** jenga hoja. ~ **over** badilisha, hamisha, hawilisha. ~ **sth up** kamilisha *we need one more player to ~ up the team* tunahitaji mchezaji mmoja zaidi kukamilisha timu yetu; buni *your reason for being late is made up* sababu ya kuchelewa kwako ni ya kubuni tu; *(colloq)* patana (baada ya kugombana); unda, -wa na *the committee is made up of ten people* kamati ina watu kumi; tayarisha, tengeneza; ongeza mafuta ~ *up a bed* tandika kitanda. ~ **sb/ oneself up** (ji)tayarisha (kwa mchezo n.k.) (ji)paka vipodozi. ~ **up one's/ sb's mind** fikia uamuzi juu ya jambo fulani. ~ **up for** fidia. ~ **up for lost time** harakisha (ili kufidia muda uliopotea). ~ **up to sb** jipendekeza. ~ **it up to sb** fidia mtu kwa kitu alichokosa au madhara/hasara aliyopata. ~ **it up (with sb)** maliza uhasama/ugomvi. *n* 1 utengenezaji, mtindo *these shoes are a good* ~ viatu hivi vimetengenezwa vizuri. **on the** ~ *(sl)* -enye kutaka faida; *(US sl)* -enye kutongoza. 2 *(elect)* kutana, kamilisha (mzunguko). **~r** *n* **the/our M~** Muumba, Mungu; *(esp in compounds)* mtengenezaji, muundaji. **making** *n* 1 kufanya, kusitawi, kuendelea. **be the** ~ **of** sababisha kustaiwi *be in the* ~ tayarishwa. 2 **have the makings of** -wa na sifa za/zinazostahili *he has in him the ~s of a leader* anazo sifa za kiongozi. 3 *(pl)* viambajengo, viambaupishi.

malacca *n* ~ **cane** bakora.

malachsite *n* malakati: jiwe lenye rangi ya chanikiwiti/kijani.

maladjusted *adj* -liorekebishwa visivyo; *(of a person)* -sioweza kujirekebisha kulingana na mazingira, -siochukuana na mazingira. **maladjustment** *n.*

maladroit *adj* -zito, -siostadi. **~ly** *adv.* ~ **ness** *n.*

malady *n* ugonjwa, uele, maradhi.

malaise *n* uchovu, unyonge.

malapropism *n* matumizi mabaya ya maneno (hasa kwa kuyafananisha).

malapropos *adj* -siofaa kimatumizi/ -ki wakati *adv* -sio kwa wakati, mahali pake.

malaria *n* malaria *adj* -a malaria.

malcontent *adj* -sioridhika *n* mtu asiyeridhika.

male *adj* 1 -a kiume. 2 *(of parts/ tools)* dume: enye kuingia ndani ya nyingine *n (man).* dume

malediction *n* laana, maapizo. **maledictory** *adj* -a laana.

malefactor *n* mwovu, mhalifu (k.m. mwizi, mwuaji n.k.).

maleficent *adj* -a kudhuru. **maleficient** *n* **malevolent** *adj* -enye nia mbovu/ mbaya, -a kukubuhu, habithi. ~ **ly** *adv.* **malevolence** *n.*

malfeasance *n* uhabithi; *(leg)* kutenda ubaya, tendo ovu/haramu (kinyume cha sheria).

malformation *n* hitilafu katika ujenzi/ uundaji/uumbaji. **malformed** *adj* -liolemaa, -enye kilema/hitilafu.

malfunction *vi* -wa na hitilafu/kasoro, -totenda ipasavyo *n* kasoro, kushindwa kutenda.

malice *n* ~ **(towards)** uovu, kijicho, nia ya kudhuru wengine. ~ **aforethought** uovu wa kudhamiria; kusudio la uovu. **bear** ~ **to sb** onea mtu kijicho. **malicious** *adj* -ovu, -enye kijicho, -enye nia mbaya.

malign *adj (of things)* -a kudhuru *vt* singizia, sengenya; kashifu. **~ancy** *n* 1 hali ya kuwa na uovu, ubaya, chuki. 2 *(of disease)* dhara, donda ndugu. **~ity n** chuki kuu, uovu mkuu. ~ **ant** *adj* 1 *(of persons)* -enye nia mbaya. 2 *(of diseases)* -enye kudhuru/kuua ~ *disease* ugonjwa unaoelekea kuleta kifo. **~antly** *adv.*

malinger *vi* jisingizia kuugua, tega (kwa visingizio). **~er** *n* mtegaji.

mallard *n* bata mwitu.

malleable *adj* 1 -a kufulika/kubadilika umbo. 2 *(fig) (of a person's character)* elekevu, -epesi kuongozwa; -enye kubambika. **malleability** *n* kufulika, kufulikana.

mallet *n* 1 nyundo ya mti. 2 rungu ya kuchezea polo.

malnutrition *n* utapiamlo.

malodorous *adj (formal)* -a kunuka vibaya, -enye harufu mbaya.

malpractice *n* mwenendo mbaya; upurukushani kazini, kuzembea kazi/wajibu.

malt *n* kimea cha pombe ~ *liquor* pombe ya kimea *vt,vi* (fanya) kuwa kimea. ~ **star** mtengeneza kimea.

malthusianism *n* nadharia ya **Malthus** (kuwa idadi ya watu inaongezeka haraka zaidi kuliko uzalishaji mali).

maltreat *vt* onea, dhulumu. **~ment** *n* uonevu, dhuluma.

malveration *n (formal)* matumizi mabaya (ya fedha za umma); ubadhirifu (wa fedha za umma).

mamba *n* **black** ~ songwe. **green** ~ hongo.

mamma/mama *n (colloq)* mama.
mammal *n* mamalia. **~ian** -a mamalia.
mammon *n* utajiri, ukwasi (unaofikiriwa kuwa na athari mbaya). **M** ~ Mungu wa uchoyo/ulafi.
mammoth *n* mamothi: tembo wa kale *adj* kubwa mno.
mammy *n* 1 *(child's word)* mama. 2 *(US derog)* yaya mweusi wa watoto wa wazungu.
man *n* 1 *(human being)* mwanaadamu, binadamu. **one's ~ of business** wakala, wakili wake (mtu). 2 *(individual person)* mtu *all men* watu wote. **a ~ about town** mpenda starehe/kula maisha. **~ of the world** mjuzi wa mambo ya ulimwengu. **a new ~** aliyebadilika (tabia, nia). **the ~ in the street** mtu wa kawaida. **a ~ of letters** msomi, mwandishi (wa vitabu, fasihi) **the inner ~** tumbo **old ~** mzee **young ~** mvulana, kijana **white ~** mzungu **I 'm your ~** nakubali shauri lako **best ~** kungwi, mfuasi mkuu wa bwana arusi. **every ~ for himself (and devil take the hindmost)** kila mtu na wake. **to a ~; to the last ~** wote. **be one's own ~** wa huru, fanya utakalo. 3 mwanamume *my young ~* mvulana wangu; mtu wa kiume! *how can a ~ stand it?* mtu awezaje kuvumilia? 4 *(husband)* mume *they are ~ and wife* wao ni mume na mke. 5 mtumishi wa kiume (jeshini, kazini, nyumbani). 6 *(of chess)* vipande. 7 *(as a vocative)* bwana *listen ~* sikiliza bwana! 8 *(in compounds)* **~ at-arms** *n (middle ages)* askari mpanda farasi **~ eater** *n* mlawatu. **~handle** *vt* vurumisha, sogeza kwa nguvu, sukuma. **~-hater** *n* siyependa wanadamu wanaume. **~-hole** *n* shimo kwenye maungio ya bomba. **~hour** *n* kazi inayofanywa na mtu mmoja kwa saa moja. **~-hunt** *n* uwindaji (wa watu). **~-made** *adj* -liyotengenezwa na watu. **~-of-war** *n* manowari. **~ -power** *n* ikama: idadi ya watu wanohitajika (kiwandani, vitani n.k.); utumishi. **~ servant** mtumishi wa kiume. **~-sized** *adj* kubwa; -a kufaa wanaume; -a kipimo cha mtu mzima. **~ slaughter** *n* uuaji wa mtu bila makusudi. **~-trap** *n* mtego wa kutegea watu *vt* 1 toa/peleka, tia watu (kwenye amali); pakia wanamaji; wekea wanajeshi. 2 **~ oneself** piga moyo konde. **~ful** *adj* shupavu. **~fully** *adv.* **~fulness** *n.* **~hood** *n* 1 utu uzima (wa mwanaume). 2 ujana-dume, urijali. 3 uanaume. **~ kind** *n* 1 wanadamu. 2 *(contrasted with womankind)* wanaume. **~like** *adj* -a kiume, -enye tabia (nzuri au mbaya) za kiume. **~nish** *adj* 1 -a kiume. 2 *(of a woman)* -a kama mwanaume.
manacle *n* pingu *vt* tia pingu.
manage *vt,vi* 1 ongoza; simamia: endesha. 2 *(control)* tawala, tiisha. 3 **~ (to do sth); ~ (with/without sth/ sb)** weza; fanikiwa *I could ~ another glass* naweza kunywa gilasi nyingine. 4 *(transact)* fanya shughuli; *(be in charge of)* tunza *I can ~ (do by myself)* naweza *we will ~ very well* tutafaulu vizuri. **~able** *adj* 1 -liowezekana. 2 *(tractable)* -a kutii, -tiifu, -sikivu. **~ment** *n* 1 uongozi; menejimenti. 2 *(skill)* werevu, shauri la akili, mbinu. **~r** *n* meneja. **~ress** *n* meneja wa kike. **~rial** *adj* -a meneja, -a uongozi, -a utawala.
manatee *n* nguva.
mandarin *n* 1 *(hist)* afisa wa juu katika serikali ya China. 2 Kichina sanifu. 3 mrasimu, kiongozi (agh mpinga maendeleo). 4 **~ duck** bata mdogo wa China. **~ orange** chenza, kangaja.
mandate *n* 1 amri, agizo, hukumu. 2 uwakili, mamlaka. 3 udhamini ~ *government* serikali ya udhamini *vt* weka chini ya udhamini (wa). **~d** *adj* 1 *see* **mandate**. 2 *(of country)* -a kudhaminiwa. **mandatory** *n* mtu, nchi iliyopewa uwakili, mamlaka, agizo au amri *adj* -a lazima ~ *injunction* amri ya kutenda; amri ya kulazimisha/lazima.

mandible *n* 1 utaya. 2 (kwa ndege) mdomo. **andolin** *n* gambusi.
mandragora *n* mandragora: mmea wenye sumu unaofanyiwa dawa ya kutapisha au ya usingizi.
mandrill *n (bio)* nyani mkubwa mkali wa Afrika ya Magharibi.
mane *n* manyoya ya shingoni (mwa mnyama k.v. farasi au simba); nywele za singa.
manes *n (lat)* mizimu (ya watu wa kale).
maneuver *n,v see* **manoeuvre**.
manganese *n* manganizi.
mange *n* ugonjwa wa upele wa wanyama. **mangy** *adj* 1 -enye upele huu. 2 hafifu, -liochakaa, duni. **mangily** *adv*.
manger *n* hori.
mangle[1] *n* guruto *vt* gurutia, kamua kwa guruto.
mangle[2] *vt* 1 rarua, tatua, pasua. 2 *(fig) (spoil)* haribu (kwa kufanya makosa mabaya).
mango *n (tree)* mwembe; *(fruit)* embe; *(large)* dodo.
mangrove *n* mkandaa, mkoko, msindi ~ *swamp* bwawa la mikoko.
mania *n* 1 wazimu. 2 ~ **(for)** moyo wa kupenda sana; shauku kubwa, ushabiki mkubwa *he has a ~ for dancing* anapenda sana kucheza dansi. **~c** *n*. **~cal** *adj*. **manic-depressive** *adj,n* (mtu) anayefurahi na kuhuzunika kupita kiasi.
manicure n 1 utunzaji wa mikono na kucha. 2 tiba ya mikono na kucha *vt* tunza kucha. **manicurist** *n* mtunzaji mkono na kucha.
manifest *adj* dhahiri, wazi, baini, bayana *vt* onyesha, toa wazi; dhihirisha ~ *oneself* jidhihirisha, jionyesha, jitokeza *n* orodha ya shehena melini. **~ation** *n* 1 onyesho, kufunua, kutoa wazi. 2 dalili, alama. ~ **ly** *adv*. **~o** *n* manifesto: hati/ilani ya kutangaza sera, kanuni n.k.
manifold *adj* -a namna nyingi, -a mara nyingi *vt (US duplicate)* rudufu *n* bomba.
manikin *n* 1 kibete, kijitu, mbilikimo. 2 *(figure)* sanamu ya binadamu.
manilla, *(US)* **manila** *n* 1 ~ **(hemp)** katani, mkonge. 2 ~ **paper/envolope** karatasi/bahasha ngumu. 3 biri la manila. 4 mji mkuu wa visiwa ya Philippine.
manioc *n* 1 muhogo. 2 wanga wa muhogo.
manipulate *vt* 1 fanya, endesha, tengeneza, tawala kwa ufundi. 2 *(of persons)* miliki/tawala kwa werevu au hila; chezea. **manipulation** *n*. **manipulator** *n*.
manna *n* 1 *(bible)* mana: chakula walichopewa Wayahudi walipokuwa jangwani. 2 *(fig)* kitu kinachotolewa/ patikana bila matarajio; kiburudisho cha roho kisichotarajiwa.
mannequin *n* 1 mwonyesha mitindo; mwanamke anayeonyesha mitindo ya nguo. 2 sanamu ya kujaribia/ kuonyesha nguo.
manner *n* 1 njia, jinsi, namna. **(as) to the ~ born** fanya jambo kama mtu amezaliwa nalo. 2 *(sing only)* mwenendo. 3 *(pl)* tabia, adabu. **comedy of ~s** mchezo wenye kichekesho kuhusu tabia za (sehemu fulani ya) jamii; dhihaka (ya tabia/ desturi). 4 *(literature/art)* mtindo. 5 aina, namna. **all ~ of** kila aina ya. **by no ~ of means** kwa vyovyote vile. **in a ~** kwa namna/kiasi fulani. **in a ~of speaking** kwa namna fulani. **~ed** *adj* 1 *(in compounds)* **ill ~** -enye tabia mbaya. **well ~** -enye tabia nzuri. 2 -enye kuonyesha upekee. **~ism** *n* 1 upekee (kitabia/mazungumzo). 2 mtindo (unaotumika mno) maalumu katika sanaa/fasihi. **~ly** *adj* -enye adabu njema, -enye heshima.
manoeuver, **maneuver** *n* 1 maneva, luteka. 2 werevu, hila, ujanja *vi,vt* 1 fanya maneva/luteka. 2 tumia hila/ werevu/ujanja, shawishi. **manoeuvrable** *adj* -a kushawishika. **manoeuvrability** *n*. **~er** *n*.
manor *n* 1 shamba kubwa la mwinyi/ kabaila. 2 *(modern use)* eneo la ardhi

linalozunguka jumba kuu. (~ **house**), ~**ial** *adj*.

mansard *n* ~ **(roof)** paa la migongo miwili (ambapo mmoja una mteremko mkali zaidi ya mwingine).

manse *n* nyumba ya mchugaji (hasa Scotland).

mansion *n* 1 kasri, jumba kubwa. 2 *(pl, in proper names)* jumba la ghorofa.

mantel maungio ya meko; *(in modern houses, usu ~ piece)* shubaka juu ya meko.

mantilla *n* mtandio, mdongea (unaovaliwa na wanawake wa Kihispania).

mantis *n* **(praying ~)** vunjajungu: aina ya panzi.

mantle *n* 1 joho; *(fig)* kifuniko. 2 utambi wa taa ya gesi *vt,vi* 1 funika, tanda. 2 *(old use or liter) (of blood)* ingia, jaza/jaa kwenye mishipa, enea; *(of the face)* iva.

manual *adj* -a mikono *(mil) ~ exercises* mazoezi ya mikono *~ labour* kazi za mikono *n* 1 kitabu cha mwongozo; kitabu cha kiada. 2 *see* **key board**.

manufacture *vt* 1 tengeneza, zalisha (katika kiwanda). 2 tunga, buni *n* 1 utengenezaji, uzalishaji. 2 *(pl)* vitu vilivyotengenezwa/kuzalishwa kiwandani. ~**r** mtengenezaji, mwenye kiwanda.

manumit *vt* achia huru, toa utumwani. **manumission** *n*.

manure *n* 1 samadi; mbolea *vt* tia mbolea katika ardhi.

manuscript *n* muswada. **in ~** bado kuchapishwa.

many *adj,n* 1 -ingi, maridhawa, tele, kadha wa kadha. **a great/good ~** kadha wa kadha, -ingi sana. **one too ~** zaidi, -ingi kuliko inavyotakiwa/ inayostahili. **have one too ~** *(colloq)* lewa kidogo. **be one too ~ for** shinda (kwa werevu), weza. **the ~** umma, kaumu. 2 ~ **a** *(used with sing n rather liter, usu replaced by many and pl n)* -ingi *~ a man* watu wengi. ~ **sided** -enye pande nyingi; *(fig)* -enye uwezo/vipengele vya aina nyingi.

Maoism *n* nadharia ya siasa na matendo ya Mao Tse-Tung. **Maoist** *n* mfuasi wa nadharia hiyo.

map *n* ramani *~ reading* usomaji ramani. ~ **reader** *n* msomaji ramani. ~ **scale** kipimia ramani, skeli. **off the ~** *(colloq)*, -siofikika/ingilika; mbali; *(fig)* -sio muhimu. **on the ~** *(colloq)* -a muhimu *vt* chora ramani; onyesha kwenye ramani. ~ **out** panga *~ out one's time* jipangia wakati.

maquis *n* **the ~** maki: wapigania uhuru/ jeshi la msituni la wazalendo wa Kifaransa wakati wa Vita Kuu II.

mar *vt* haribu, hasiri, umbua *be ~red* sawajika, umbuka, haribika. **make or ~** fanikiwa sana au haribu kabisa.

marabou *n (bird)* kongoti.

marabout *n* 1 murabiti: mtawa wa Kiislamu, hasa wa Afrika Magharibi. 2 hekalu juu ya kaburi la murabiti.

marasmus *n* nyongea.

marathon *n* marathoni: mbio za masafa marefu (kiasi cha maili 26); *(fig)* majaribio ya ustahamilivu.

maraud *vi* nyang'anya, teka nyara. ~**er** *n*.

marble *n* 1 marumaru. 2 *(pl)* sanaa za marumaru. 3 gololi. 4 *(attrib)* -a kama marumaru *a ~ breast* mtu asiye na huruma. ~**d** *adj* -enye kupakwa rangi ya marumaru.

marcel *n* utengenezaji wa mawimbi katika nywele.

March[1] *n* Machi: mwezi wa tatu.

march[2] *vi,vt* 1 tembea/enda kama askari *Quick ~!* mbele tembea! ~**ing orders** amri ya kwenda maneva, vitani n.k. *(fig)* kufukuzwa. ~ **out** toka (hasa kwa kususa/kukasirika). 2 peleka *n* 1 mwendo wa kijeshi. **a ~ past** gwaride. **steal a ~ on sb** wahi mtu. **on the ~** kwenda kama askari. **a line of ~** njia inayofuatwa na askari. **a forced ~** kutembea kwa haraka na dharura. 2 mwendo; safari. 3 *(time)* matukio. **the ~ of events** matukio, maendeleo ya mambo. 4 wimbo/muziki wa kijeshi. ~**er** *n*.

march[3] *n (usu pl) (hist)* mpaka wa nchi (hasa baina ya Uingereza na Uskoti au Walesi); eneo linalogombaniwa *vi* ~ **upon/with** *(arch)* pakana.

Mardi Gras *n (F)* siku ya mwisho kabla ya kuanza Kwaresma.

mare *n* farasi jike. **a ~'s nest** uvumbuzi wa uongo au usio na maana.

margarine *n* majarini.

margin *n* 1 ukingo, ubavu, pembeni. 2 *(of book, writing)* pambizo, nafasi (ya kandoni). 3 *(extra amount)* ziada. 4 sehemu/eneo karibu na mpaka/kikomo/mwisho. **escape sth by a narrow** ~ ponea chupu chupu. 5 tofauti baina ya bei halisi na bei ya kuuzia kitu; faida ya muuzaji *vt* eleza pembeni. **~al** *adj* -a pembeni. ~ **land** ardhi isiyo na rutuba. ~ **seat/constituency** kiti cha ubunge ambapo Mbunge alimzidi mpinzani wake kwa kura chache.

marijuana, marihuana *n (also called hashish, cannabis, pot)* bangi.

marimba *n (mus)* marimba.

marinade *n* marinadi: achari ya mvinyo, siki na viungo *vt* (*also* **marinate)** lainisha kwa kutia marinadi.

marine *adj* 1 -a bahari, -a baharini, -a mambo ya bahari ~ *painter* mchoraji picha za baharini. 2 -a meli, -a majini, -a biashara ya baharini ~ *insurance* bima ya meli na mizigo *n* 1 askari wa manowari. 2 *(shipping)* **merchant/mercantile** ~ jamii ya marikebu/meli zote za taifa fulani. 3 ~ **corps** jeshi la wanamaji. **the M~s** jeshi zima la wanamaji. **tell that to the ~s** acha uongo! waeleze watoto. **marina** *n* bandari, mapumziko/starehe (ya ngarawa za kujifurahishia). **maritime** *adj* -a bahari, -a ubaharia; -a pwani, iliyo pwani. **~r** *n* baharia, mwanamaji (hasa anayesaidia kuongoza meli). **master** ~ nahodha (wa meli ya biashara).

marionette *n* karagosi.

marital *adj* 1 -a ndoa. ~ **obligations** majukumu ya ndoa. 2 -a mume.

marjoram *n* majorama: aina ya kiungo cha chakula (pia hutumika kama dawa).

mark[1] *n* 1 alama; doa *a ~ on the face* alama usoni *a ~ on the shirt* doa kwenye shati. 2 dalili, ishara. 3 maksi. **give sb/get gain good/bad** ~ pa/maksi nzuri/mbaya. 4 shabaha. **be/fall wide of the** ~ kosa; kosea. **hit/miss the** ~ *(fig)* patia/kosea. **easy** ~ *(colloq)* mtu anayedanganyika kwa urahisi. **beside the** ~ haihusiki/haimo. 5 umashuhuri. **make one's** ~ -wa mashuhuri. 6 **the** ~ kiwango; kawaida *not be/feel (quite) up to the* ~ -tojisikia vizuri. **be up to/below the** ~ fikia/-tofikia kiwango. 7 mkato (ufanywao na mtu asiyejua kusoma na kuandika) badala ya saini. 8 *(athletics)* mstari (wa kuanzia mashindano) *on your ~ s* kwenye mstari. 9 *(with numbers)* alama ya kuonyesha aina ya chombo *vt* 1 ~ **sth on/with sth; ~ sth down/up** tia alama; piga chapa. **~-up** *n* ongezeko la bei. **~ing-in** *n* wino wa kutilia alama (usiofutika). 2 *(passive)* -wa na alama (ya asili/inayoonekana) *a zebra is ~ed by stripes* pundamilia ana mistari. 3 toa maksi; sahihisha. 4 tia alama ya pata/kosa. 5 zingatia, angalia. 6 ~ **my words** zingatia maneno yangu. **a ~ed man** mtu anayeangaliwa kwa jicho baya. 7 -wa kitambulisho cha; onyesha. 8 -wa dalili ya, ashiria. 9 ~ **time** chapa miguu; *(fig)* subiri (mpaka hali itakapo ruhusu kuendelea). 10 *(use with adverbial particles)*. ~ **sth off** weka alama juu ya kitu (kuonyesha mipaka, vipimo n.k.). ~ **sth out** tia mipaka ya kitu. ~ **sb out for sth** amua tangu mapema kumpa mtu kitu/cheo n.k. ~ **ed** *adj* dhahiri, wazi. **~edly** *adv*. **~ing** *n (esp)* madoadoa (ya manyoya, ngozi). **~r** *n* 1 mtu au chombo kitiacho alama. 2 mtu anayerekodi pointi/magoli/alama mchezoni. 3 alama ya bendera/jiwe n.k. lionyeshalo masafa.

4 msahihishaji.

mark[2] maki: fedha ya Kijerumani.

market *n* 1 soko. **the ~** sokoni. **(to) bring one's egg/hogs to the wrong ~** haribikiwa na mipango/shindwa kwa kuomba msaada pasipostahili. **~ day** chete, gulio. **~ place/square** sokoni. **~-town** *n* gulio. **go to ~** enda sokoni (kununua vitu). **go to a bad/good ~ (to)** fanikiwa. **~ garden** bustani ya ya mboga za kuuza. **~ price** bei ya sokoni. 2 utashi, kutakiwa kwa soko. 3 ununuzi na uuzaji. **be on/come on (to) the ~** uzwa. **be in the ~ for sth** -wa tayari kununua; *(fig)* -wa tayari kufikiria jambo fulani. **put sth on the ~** uza kitu. **up/down ~** -a tabaka la juu/chini. **~ research** utafiti wa soko *vi,vt* 1 uza/nunua sokoni. 2 peleka/ tayarisha kwa ajili -a kuuza. **~ able** *adj* -a kuuzika, -inayouzika. **~ing** *n* elimu ya soko.

marksman *n* mlengaji hodari. **~ ship** *n* uhodari wa kulenga.

marl *n* maga: udongo mzuri wenye chokaa *vt* tia maga.

marlinespike *n* kitenga mshipi, kipande cha chuma cha kutengea nyuzi za kamba.

marmalade *n* mamaledi: jemu iliyotengenezwa kwa machungwa.

marmoreal *adj (poet)* -eupe, baridi, -liong'arishwa kama marumaru; -a marumaru.

marmot *n* panyabuku.

marocain *n* marokoni: aina ya kitambaa chepesi cha hariri au sufu.

maroon[1] *vt* acha/weka/telekeza (mtu au watu) katika kisiwa au nchi isiyo na watu.

maroon[2] *adj* (rangi ya) damu ya mzee.

maroon[3] **marque** *n* fataki (agh. hutumika kama kitoa ishara/hadhari) *(hist) letters of ~* kibali cha uvamizi; mamlaka anayopewa mtu kutumia meli kwa mashambulizi, uvamizi, uharibifu n.k.

marquee *n* hema kubwa. **arquetry** *n* nakshi za fanicha.

marriage *n* 1 ndoa, nikahi. **ask in ~** posa. **give in ~** oza. **take in ~** oa/olewa. **~ lines** *(colloq)* cheti cha ndoa. 2 *(usu wedding)* harusi. **~able** *adj (of a young person)* -a kufaa kuoa/kuolewa *a person of ~able age* mtu aliyefikia umri wa kuoa/ kuolewa. **~ability** *n*. **married** *adj* 1 -enye kuoa/kuolewa *~ woman* mwolewa: mwanamke aliyeolewa. 2 -a ndoa. **marry** *vt,vi* 1 funga ndoa; *(of male)* oa; *(of female)* olewa. 2 *(of a priest, a civil official)* fungisha ndoa. 3 ~ **(off)** oza. 4 pata kwa ndoa. **~ wealth** pata mali kwa ndoa.

marrow *n* 1 uboho. **chilled to the ~** ona baridi kali. 2 *(fig)* kiini. **the pith and the ~** sehemu ya lazima. 3 *(vegetable)* mumunye, mung'unye.

Mars *n* 1 *(Roman myth)* mungu wa vita. 2 *(astron) Mars* (jina la Sayari mojawapo).

marsh *n* bwawa, ziwa lenye matope, kinamasi. **~-gas** mitheni. **~y** *adj*.

marshal *n* 1 jemadari. **field ~** jemadari mkuu. 2 msimamizi wa sherehe/matukio muhimu. 3 afisa wa mahakamani. 4 *(US)* mkuu wa idara ya polisi/zimamoto *vt* 1 panga. **~ling yard** mahali pa kupanga (mabogi ya) treni *vt* ongoza kwa heshima/ taadhima. **~ sb into a room** ongoza mtu chumbani.

mart *n* 1 soko, gulio. 2 duka la dalali/ mnadi.

martial *adj* 1 -a vita, -a kijeshi. **~ law** sheria za kijeshi. 2 shujaa; -enye kupenda vita. **~ly** *adv*.

martin *n* **(house)** ~ mbayuwayu.

martinet *n* kidikteta.

martingale *n* 1 hatamu. 2 *(of cards)* kamari marudufu.

martyr *n* shahidi (wa dini), mfiadini. **make a ~ of oneself** jitoa mhanga. **be a ~ to sth** teswa/umwa sana kutokana na *vt* ua/umiza kishahidi. **~dom** *n* mateso/kifo cha kishahidi.

marvel *n* 1 ajabu, kitu/ jambo la kushangaza, mwujiza, shani *its no ~* si ajabu. 2 **~ of sth** mfano wa ajabu/zuri/bora *vi* 1 **~ at sth** shangaa, staajabu, ona ajabu. 2 ~ **that/why etc** shangaa kwamba/kuwa/kwa nini. ~**lous** *adj* -a ajabu, -a kushangaza. ~**lously** *adv*.

Marxist *n* Mfuasi wa Maksi ~ *criticism* uhakiki wa Kimaksi ~ *party* chama cha Kimaksi. **Marxism** *n (esp)* Umaksi.

marzipan *n* lahamu au keki (ya unga wa mlozi na sukari).

mascara *n* wanja.

mascot *n* nyota (ya jaha); kileta bahati, mleta bahati.

masculine *adj* -ume, -a kiume, dume. *(gram)* ~ **gender** jinsia ya kiume. **masculinity** *n* uume.

maser *n* chombo cha kuongeza wimbimaikro.

mash *n (of food and feed)* 1 mseto (kwa ajili ya kuku, ng'ombe, nguruwe n.k.) 2 togwa. 3 viazi vya kupondwa *vt* 1 seta; ponda; ~ *ed potatoes* viazi vilivyopondwa. ~ **er** *n* kipondeo.

mask *n* barakoa; *(of head, face)* kinyago. **do sth under a/the ~ of friendship** jifanye rafiki, fanya kwa kujifanya; kificho; kisingizio. **throw off one's** ~ *(fig)* jifichua, jionyesha wazi (tabia na malengo ya mtu) **(gas)** ~ kichuja hewa *vt* 1 vaa kinyago/barakoa. 2 ficha.

masochism *n* kufurahia/kupata ashiki kutokana na kuumia/kudhalilishwa.

mason *n* mwashi. ~**ic** *adj*. ~**ry** *n*.

masque *n* tamthiliya ya muziki na ngoma.

masquerade *n* 1 dansi ya vinyago. 2 *(fig)* kujifanya kisingizio *vi* ~ **(as)** jifanya. ~**r** *n*.

mass[1] *n* 1 ~ **(of)** fungu; wingi, bonge. 2 **the ~es** umma *the great ~ of the people* idadi kubwa ya watu, watu wengi sana *in the ~* kwa jumla *the workers in the ~ did not want to strike* wafanyakazi kwa jumla hawakutaka kugoma. ~ **meeting** mkutano wa hadhara. ~ **communications; M~ Media** vyombo vya habari. ~ **observation** uchunguzi/ mafunzo ya desturi za watu wa kawaida. ~ **production** uzalishaji kwa wingi (wa biadhaa moja). 3 *(science)* masi/tungamo *vt, vi* kusanya; n kusanyika. ~**y** *adj* imara, kubwa sana, zito. ~**ive** *adj* 1 kubwa, -nene, -zito. 2 *(fig)* imara. ~**ively** *adv*. ~ **iveness** *n*.

mass[2] *n (rel)* misa *high* ~ misa kuu *low* ~ misa ndogo.

massacre *n* mauaji ya kinyama (ya watu wengi wasiokuwa na hatia) *vt* ua ovyo watu wengi.

massage *vt* kanda, chua *n* kuchua musuli, kusinga.

masseur *n* msingaji mwanaume. **masseuse** *n* msingaji mwanamke.

massif *n* mrundikano wa milima.

mast *n* mlingoti, nguzo. **sail before the** ~ fanya kazi kama baharia wa kawaida. ~ **head** *n* ncha ya mlingoti.

master *n* 1 tajiri, mwajiri. **be one's own** ~ -wa huru *(attrib)* stadi (anayejitegemea). 2 mkuu wa kaya mwanamme. **be ~ in one's own house** mudu mambo yako mwenyewe. 3 nahodha, kapteni. 4 mwenye mbwa, punda n.k. 5 mwalimu wa kiume *the Kiswahili ~* mwalimu wa Kiswahili. **head** ~ mwalimu mkuu (wa kiume). 6 ~ **of** waria, stadi *he is ~ of the language* ni stadi wa lugha hii; mwamuzi. 7 **the M~** Yesu Kristu. ~ **of Arts/ Science etc** shahada ya pili. 8 *(with a boy's name)* bwana mdogo, kibwana. 9 **old ~s** wachoraji maarufu wa karne kati ya 13 na 17; michoro ya wachoraji hawa. 10 ~**mind** *n* mwanzilishi mwamba. ~ **mind up** *vt* panga, endesha, anzisha mipango; *(attrib)* tawala, -a juu. ~ **thought** fikra tawala. 11 cheo. **M~ of Ceremonies** Msimamizi Mkuu wa Sherehe. 12 *(compounds)* ~ **at arms** *n* Afisa wa polisi katika manowari na melini. ~-**key** *n* ufunguo malaya. ~**piece** *n* kazi bora. ~**stroke** *n* ustadi mkubwa; tendo la akili sana. ~ **plan** *n* mpango mkuu *vt* 1 -wa mjuzi/ mweledi/mbuji/hodari n.k. 2 shinda, tawala. ~**less** *adj* -sio na ujuzi. ~**ful** *adj* 1 -enye makuu -enye kupenda kutawala wengine; stadi. ~**ly** *adj* stadi sana. ~**ship** *n* 1 utawala, madaraka. 2 ualimu. ~**y** *n* 1 ~ **(of)** ustadi, ujuzi, uwezo kamili, umahiri *(to) gain the ~ of* tawala (kabisa). 2 ~ **(over)** madaraka, utawala.

masticate *vt* tafuna. **mastication** *n*.

mastiff *n* mastini: jibwa lenye masikio lepelepe.

mastitis *n* uvimbe wa titi *(of animals)* kinyungi.

mastodon *n* mastodoni: mnyama mkubwa wa kale kama tembo.

mastoid *n* mfupa wa nyuma ya sikio. ~**itis** *n* uvimbe wa mfupa huu.

masturbate *vi,vt (of a man)* piga punyeto; *(of woman)* jisaga. **masturbation** *n*.

mat[1] *n* mkeka, kirago, jamvi, busati *vt* 1 tandika jamvi n.k. 2 tatizika, tatiza.

mat[2], **matt** *(US also* **matte**, *adj (of surfaces, eg paper)* -siong'aa.

matador *n* matadoo: mcheza ng'ombe.

match[1] *n* njiti ya kiberiti. ~ **box** *n* ganda la kiberiti. ~ **wood** *n* miti itumikayo kutengenezea viberiti; vipande vya mbao.

match[2] *n* 1 *(equal)* mwenzi; sawa; mshindani *be a ~ for* -wa sawa na, weza *be more than a ~ for* -wa na uwezo zaidi ya mwingine. 2 kulingana *we shall never see his ~* hututaona mtu anayefanana naye *they are a good/bad ~* wanalingana vizuri/vibaya. 3 mechi *return ~* mechi ya marudiano. 4 *(marraige)* ndoa; mwenzi wa ndoa. **make a ~ of it** oana. ~ **maker** *n* mtu apendaye sana kuwa mshenga *vt,vi* 1 lingana na, linganisha, landanisha. 2 shindanisha, pambanisha. 3 *(arch)* oza, oana.

matchet *n see* **machete**.

matchlock *n* goboli: bunduki ya kizamani.

mate[1] *n* 1 *(colloq)* mwenzi; rafiki *yes, no ~* ndio, siyo yakhe! aisee!. 2 *(colloq)* mume/mke. 3 *(naut)* sarahangi. 4 msaidizi *cook's ~* msaidizi wa mpishi *surgeon's ~* msaidizi wa mpasuaji. 5 *(of animals)* dume/jike *vt ~* **(with)** *(of animals)* pandana.

mate[2] *n,v (in chess) see* **checkmate**.

matelot *n* baharia.

material[1] *n* 1 nyenzo, vitu vya kutengenezea/kujengea vitu vingine: *raw ~* mali ghafi. 2 kitambaa. 3 vifaa **writing ~s** vifaa vya kuandikia. 4 taarifa inayotumiwa kuandikia maandiko.

material[2] *adj* 1 -a mwili. 2 yakinifu. 3 *(leg)* muhimu, -a kiini *~ evidence* ushahidi unaoathiri kesi. 4 muhimu, zito. ~**ism** *n* 1 uyakinifu. 2 tamaa ya vitu/anasa. ~**ist** *n* myakinifu. ~**istic** *adj*. ~**istically** *adv*. ~**ize** *vt,vi* 1 fanya kuwa kitu, tokea; pata umbo/mwili, timizwa/ kamilishwa. ~**ization** *n*.

maternal *adj* -a mama, -a upande wa mama. ~**ly** *adv*.

maternity *n* -a uzazi *~ nurse* mkunga *~ hospital* hospitali ya uzazi.

matey *adj* ~**(with)** *(colloq)* changamfu, -a rafiki; zoeana na *(to) get ~ with sb* fanya urafiki na mwingine.

mathematics *n (abbr* **maths**; *US* **math**) hisabati, hesabu. **mathematical** *adj*. **mathematically** *adv*. **mathematician** *n*.

matinee *n* maonyesho ya alasiri.

matins *n (rel)* sala ya alfajiri.

matriarch *n* mamamkuu (katika familia au kabila). ~**y** *n* utaratibu wa jamii ambapo mama ndio wakuu wa familia. ~**al** *adj*.

matric *n see* **matriculation**.

matricide *n* 1 kumwua mama yako. 2 aliyemuua mama yake.

matriculate *vt,vi* 1 ingiza; ingia katika Chuo Kikuu, ingizwa katika Chuo Kikuu; shinda mtihani wa kuingia Chuo Kikuu. 2 *(formally)* shinda mtihani wa mwisho. **matriculation** *n*.

matrilineal *adj* -a kufuata nasaba kukeni. **matrilocal** *adj* -enye mila ya maharusi kuhamia kukeni.

matrimony *n* ndoa, kuoana. **matrimonial** *adj* -a ndoa. ~ **cases** kesi za ndoa.

matrix *n* 1 chanzo. 2 *(mould)* kalibu. 3 mawe ya asili (yenye madini, vito n.k.). 4 *(math)* solo. 5 *(bio)* matriki.

matron *n* 1 matroni: mwanamke wa makamo anayetunza shule n.k. 2 mwanamke anayeangalia wauguzi wa hospitali. 3 mwanamke aliyeolewa au mjane. **~ly** *adj*.

matt *adj* = **mat**[2].

matted *adj see* **mat**[1].

matter *n* 1 mata, maada. 2 maudhui. 3 machapisho/maandishi. **postal** ~ waraka wa posta. **printed** ~ vitabu, magazeti. **reading** ~ -a kusomwa, vitabu n.k. 4 jambo, kisa, hoja, habari *defamatory* ~ kiumbuzi, kashifa. ~ **of fact** jambo la kweli (hakika). ~ **-of-fact** *adj (of a person, his manner)* -a kawaida, -lio baridi ~ *of law* jambo la sheria. **subject ~ of course** jambo la kawaida/kutarajiwa, desturi. **~-of course** *adj* -a kutarajiwa; -a kutegemewa. **no laughing ~** jambo zito, si mchezo, si masihara. **no ~** haidhuru, mamoja *what is the ~?* kuna nini? **hanging ~** kosa la kunyongwa *leave the ~ hanging* achia jambo hewani (bila ufafanuzi/jibu kamili) *as ~s stood* kama mambo yalivyokuwa. **for that ~** zaidi ya hayo *(to) make ~s worse* vuruga/chafua mambo. 5 umuhimu, maana. **(with/be) no ~** haidhuru, si kitu, isio na maana/umuhimu. **no ~ who/what/where etc** yeyote (awaye), chochote lolote (litokealo). 6 **be the ~ (with) -**wa na. 7 *(quantity, amount)* kadiri, kiasi cha *a ~ of 10 miles* kadiri ya maili kumi *vi* pasa, faa, -wa na maana/umuhimu *it ~s a lot* ni cha maana sana *what does it ~* kwani ina umuhimu/maana gani?

mattins *see* **matins**.

mattock *n* jembetezo.

mattress *n* godoro.

mature *vt,vi* 1 pevuka; pevusha; iva, komaa. 2 *(of bills)* -wa tayari (kwa madai) *adj* 1 -zima, -pevu, -bivu. 2 *(ready)* kwa makini, kamili, -liotengenezwa. 3 *(of bills)* tayari kulipa. **~ly** *adv*. **maturity** *n*. **maturate** *vi* pevuka. **maturation** *n* upevu, kukua.

matutinal *adj (formal)* -a kutokea asubuhi.

maudlin *adj* lizi, -epesi kuona huzuni kipumbavu.

maul *vt* umiza vibaya, ponda *the critics ~ed his new play* wahakiki waliponda tamthiliya yake mpya.

maulstick *n* fimbo nyepesi ishikwayo na mpiga rangi kusitiri mkono ulioshika brashi.

maunder *vi* enda, sema, tenda kivivu.

Maundy Thursday *n (rel)* Alhamisi Kuu.

mausoleum *n* kaburi kubwa (zuri).

mauve *n* (rangi ya) urujuani *adj* -enye rangi ya urujuani.

maverick *n (US)* 1 ndama wa mwaka mmoja asiyepigwa chapa. 2 mpinzani.

maw *n (of animals)* 1 tumbo, shingo/koo. 2 *(fig)* kitu cha hatari (kinachoweza kumeza/kuangamiza watu n.k.).

mawkish *adj* -a (kuonyesha) hisia ya kijinga. **~ly** *adv*. **~ness** *n*.

maxi-/ *pref* kubwa, refu.

maxilla *n (bio)* taya (agh. la juu).

maxim *n* neno la hekima, kanuni, methali.

maximum *n* upeo, mwisho *adj* -a mwisho, -a upeo. **maximize** *vt* ongeza hadi upeo. **maximization** *n*.

May[1] *n* Mei, mwezi wa tano. **M~ Queen** Malkia wa uzuri. **M~ Day** Mei Mosi; sikukuu ya wafanyakazi duniani. **~fly** *n* mdudu aonekanaye mwezi Mei tu.

may[2] *aux verb* 1 *(of possibility or probability)* weza; wezekana *I ~ go* naweza kwenda; labda nitakwenda; omba (ruhusa). 2 *(of permission) ~ I go?* Niende? ~ *you be happy* nakutakia heri. 3 (*to express purpose) we eat that we ~ live* tunakula ili tuishi. ~ **be** *adv* labda, huenda. **as soon as ~ be** mapema iwezekanavyo. **~day** *n (radio telephone)* (neno la) ishara/ilani ya kimataifa ya kuomba msaada wakati wa shida angani au baharini.

mayhem *n* 1 *(old use, and US)* kosa la kuharibu kiungo cha mwili. 2 msukosuko, fujo, vurumai.

mayonnaise kachumbari nzito ya mayai, malai, mafuta, siki n.k.

mayor *n* meya. **~ess** *n* 1 mke wa meya. 2 meya mwanamke. **~alty** *n* muda/cheo wa/cha umeya.

maze 1 mzingile, mwanambije. 2 tazaa, mazonge. **~d** *adj.*

me *object pron* mimi, -ni-; mi *it is ~* ni mimi *he called ~* aliniita *with ~* pamoja nami *from ~* toka kwangu.

mead *n* pombe ya asali.

mead,meadow *n* malisho, konde la majani.

meagre (*US*=**meager**) *adj* 1 *(of persons)* -embamba, -a kimbaombao. 2 *(of things)* haba, -chache, kidogo. **~ly** *adv.* **~ness** *n.*

meal[1] *n* 1 mlo. 2 chakula. ~ **time** wakati wa chakula/kula.

meal[2] *n* unga (wa nafaka). **~ly** *adj* 1 -a unga; *(of potatoes when boiled)* -enye unga. ~ **bug** *n* kidungata. **~y mouthed** *adj* -oga kusema ukweli, -enye kukwepa kusema wazi.

mealie *n (South Africa) (pl)* mahindi; kibunzi cha muhindi. ~ **meal** unga wa mahindi.

mean[1] *adj* 1 ovyo, baya, duni. 2 *(of behaviour)* -a aibu, -a hila *a ~ trick* hila *feel ~* ona haya/aibu. 3 bahili, -enye choyo. 4 *(US)* katili. 5 *(of rank)* chochole, kabwela, -sio nasaba. **~ness** *n.* **~ie, ~y** *n.*

mean[2] *adj* 1 -a kati, -a kadiri *~ price* bei wastani *n* 1 kati, wastani. **happy/golden ~** wastani wa kufaa. 2 *(maths)* wastani. 3 *(pl)* **~s** njia, uwezo jinsi, namna. **by all ~s!** hakika, Inshallah! **by any ~s!** kwa njia yoyote. **by fair ~s or foul** kwa njia yoyote ile. **by no ~s** hasha, hata kidogo *by some ~s or other* kwa namna, njia moja au nyingine. **by ~s of** kwa njia ya, kwa kutumia. **by no manner of ~s** haiwezekani kabisa *~s of communication* njia ya mawasiliano *~ of payment* njia ya malipo. **ways and ~s** njia/mbinu (hasa za serikali za kupatia pesa). 4 *(pl) (wealth)* fedha, mali, utajiri *a man of ~s* tajiri. **~s test** kipimo cha uwezo/kipato. 5 wasaa, maishilio, nafuu *it is within my ~s* nina uwezo. **(to) live beyond one's ~s** kuishi kupita kipato/kutumia zaidi ya uwezo wako.

mean[3] *vt* 1 *(of words, sentences etc)* maanisha *that's what I ~* hiyo ndiyo maana yangu *what did he ~ by saying that?* alikuwa na maana gani kwa kusema vile? *who do you ~?* nani? *it ~s* yaani; maana yake. 2 ~ **(by)** dhamiria, taka, kusudia vema. **(to) ~ business** *(colloq)* dhamiria sana (kufanya kitu); amua. **(to) ~ mischief** dhamiria madhara. **(to) ~ no offence** -todhamiria kosa. 3 ~ **sth to sb** -wa na maana. ~ **a lot to sb** pendwa na mtu *it ~s a great deal to me* ina maana kubwa kwangu. 4 ashiria, elekea. 5 ~ **well (by)** -wa na nia njema. ~ **ing** *n* maana, kusudi *adj* -lio na maana. **~ingful** *adj.* **~ingfully** *adv.* **~ingless** *adj* -sio maana. **~ingly** *adv.*

meantime *n see* **meanwhile. in the ~** kwa sasa.

meanwhile *adv* wakati ule ule; kitambo, sasa hivi, punde si punde.

measles *n* 1 surua. 2 *(of pigs)* tegu.

measly *adj* 1 -enye surua. 2 *(fig)* -enye tegu.

measure *n* 1 kipimo, kimo. **take sb's ~** *(fig)* pima/angalia tabia, akili, uwezo n.k. wa mtu. **give full/short ~** toa kiasi kamili/ pungufu *give extra ~* toa nyongeza. **made to ~** *(of clothes)* iliyopimwa *~ of spread* kipimo cha mweneo. 2 kiasi, kiwango. **in some ~** kwa kiasi fulani. **beyond ~** kupita kiasi. **without ~** bila kiasi. 3 (*music, poetry*) mapigo, mwendo. **tread a ~**

with sb cheza dansi na. 4 chenezo, kipimo, kigezo. **greatest common ~** *(abbr GCM)* namba kubwa kabisa inayogawa namba nyingi zote sawasawa/bila kuacha mabaki. 5 hatua, mashauri, matendo *take ~s to rectify the situation* chukua hatua za kurekebisha hali. **set ~s to** wekea mipaka. 6 sheria (iliyopendekezwa) *vt,vi* 1 pima (ukubwa/kiasi n.k.). 2 tathmini. ~ **sb** angalia tabia ya mtu. 3 ~ **up to the job** -wa na uwezo wa kufanya kazi. ~ **one's length** anguka kifudifudi. ~ **swords against/with sb** *(fig)* pimana nguvu na. ~ **one's strength (with sb)** jaribu nguvu/ uwezo. 4 fikia, -wa na (urefu wa n.k.) *it ~s six feet* urefu wake ni futi sita. 5 ~ **out/off** toa kidogo kidogo; pambanua. **~d** *adj* -a taratibu, -a sawasawa; *(of language)* -liofikiriwa, zito. **measurable** *adj* -a kupimika. **~less** *adj* bila kikomo, -sio na mipaka. **~ment** *n* 1 kipimo. **inside ~ment** vipimo vya ndani; *(transportation)* bidhaa zinazogharimiwa kwa kipimo badala ya uzito. 2 *(pl)* vipimo (vya marefu, mapana na kina).

meat *n* 1 nyama; *(without bones)* kinofu, chinyango; *(with rice etc)* kitoweo *lean ~* mnofu (bila shahamu); *(US of fruits, nuts, shellfish)* nyama. 2 *(arch)* chakula, mlo. **one man's ~ is another man's poison** halali yako ni haramu ya mwingine. ~ **and drink** kipenzi, -enye kupendwa sana *football is his ~ and drink* mpira wa miguu ni mchezo anaopenda sana, ndio ulevi wake. 3 *(fig)* uzito, mambo ya maana *this short article contains a lot of ~* makala hii ndogo ina mambo ya maana. 4 *(combined forms)* **~ball** kababu. ~ **chopper** kishoka. ~ **grinder** kisagio nyama *~loaf* bofulo ya nyama. **~-safe** kabati ya nyama, chakula. *(GB)* ~ **tea** chai kuu (jioni), chai pamoja na nyama. **~less** *adj* bila nyama. **~y** *adj (fig)* -enye maana, muhimu.

Mecca *n* 1 Maka. 2 *(fig)* tarajio, kivutio.

mechanic *n* 1 makanika, fundi mitambo. 2 mbinu *~s of writing short stories* mbinu za utunzi wa hadithi fupi. **~al** *adj* 1 -a umakanika, -a mitambo ~ *engineer* mhandisi mitambo ~ *advantage (of machine)* manufaa ya kimakanika ~ *efficiency (of engines)* ufanisi wa kimakanika (katika injini); -a kufanya, kufanyika kama kwamba kwa mitambo. 2 *(persons)* -enye kutenda bila kufikiria, -a kufanya kama mashine. **~ally** *adv* kimashine, bila kufikiri. **~s** *n* umakanika. **mechanism** *n* 1 mashine, mtambo. 2 utaratibu wa kufanya jambo. **mechanistic** *adj (phil)* ~ **theory** nadharia inayoamini kwamba asili ya ulimwengu na vitu vyote vilivyomo ni mata. **mechanize** *vt* tumia mashine. **mechanization** *n.*

medal *n* nishani. **~list** *n* mpewa nishani. **~lion** *n* nishani kubwa, pambo.

meddle *vi* 1 ~ **(in sth)** ingilia *don't ~ in other people's affairs* usiingilie mambo ya watu wengine. 2 ~ **(with sth)** gusa, chezea. **~r** *n* mdukizi, mdakuzi. **~some** *adj* -liopenda kudukiza.

media *n* **the** ~ vyombo vya habari, njia za mawasiliano (redio, magazeti n.k.).

mediaeval *see* **medieval**.

medial *adj* 1 -a kati. 2 -a wastani.

median *adj* -a kati *n (math)* kati.

mediate *vi,vt* 1 ~ **(between)** patanisha, suluhisha. 2 leta suluhu/mapatano *adj* -a kati ya. **mediation** *n* upatanisho.

medicine *n* 1 sayansi na fani ya kuzuia na kutibu maradhi; uganga, tiba, udaktari. 2 dawa *give ~ to* -pa dawa, nywesha dawa. **~-ball** *n* mpira wa babucheza. **~-chest** *n* sanduku la dawa. **~-glass** *n* bilauri ya dawa. 3 adhabu inayostahili. **take one's ~** *(fig)* stahimili machungu; adhabu. **get a dose of one's own ~** fanyiwa kama ulivyomfanyia mwenzako. 4 uganga (wa kienyeji) *practise ~* fanya uganga *vt (arch)* ponyesha; tibu. ~-

man *n* 1 mganga. 2 mchawi. **medic** *n* *(colloq abbr for) medical student* mwanafunzi wa tiba/uganga. **medical** *adj* -a tiba, -a uganga, -a dawa *to be under ~ orders/treatment* endelea na matibabu, tibiwa *~ man/practitioner* daktari, mganga, tabibu *~ examination* uchunguzi wa kitabibu *~ juris-prudence* sheria za tiba *n (colloq)* mwanafunzi wa tiba; matibabu. **medically** *adv*.

medicament *n* dawa. **Medicare** *(US) n* mpango wa serikali wa kutibu watu (agh. wazee).

medicate *vt* tibu, tumia dawa, wekea dawa. **medicated soap** sabuni yenye dawa. **medicinal** *adj* 1 -a dawa. 2 -a kuponya. **medico** *n (colloq)* daktari, mwanafunzi wa uganga.

medieval *adj* -a enzi za kati (mnamo miaka 1100-1500) . **~ist** *n* msomi wa mambo za zama za kati.

mediocre *adj* hafifu, duni, -a hivi hivi; -a kadiri. **mediocrity** *n*.

meditate *vt,vi* 1 taamali, tafakari, zingatia. 2 ~ **(up)** *(intend)* azimu. **meditation** *n* taamuli, tafakuri, mazingatio. **meditative** *adj* -a mazingatio. **meditatively** *adv*.

Mediterranean *n* 1 -a Mediterania *the ~ Sea* Bahari ya Mediterania.

medium *n* 1 wastani, tabia/sifa ya wastani. **the happy** ~ kukwepa misimamo, kutobana sana wala kulegeza mno, wastani wa kufaa. 2 *(means)* njia, chombo *~ of circulation* njia ya mawasiliano *by the ~ of* kwa njia ya *~ of exchange* kibadilishio. 3 mtu anayewasiliana na mizimu. 4 *(pl)* mazingira *adj* -a kati, -a kadiri, wastani. **~ wave** masafa/mawimbi ya kati (-a urefu kati ya mita 100 na 1000).

medley *n* 1 mchanganyiko. 2 *(mus)* wimbo mseto (unaochanganya nyimbo mbalimbali).

medulla *n (bio)* medula: kiunga ubongo cha wanyama.

meed *n* 1 *(poet) (reward)* tunzo, zawadi. 2 *(merit)* stahili.

meek *adj* pole, vumilivu, sikivu, nyenyekevu. **~ly** *adv*. **~ness** *n*.

meerschaum *n* shamu: udongo laini mweupe unaotumika kufanyizia viko vya tumbako. ~ **(pipe)** kiko cha mishamu.

meet[1] *adj (arch)* -zuri, -a kufaa, -a kustahili; -a haki *it is ~ and just* ni vyema na haki.

meet[2] *vt,vi* 1 kutana. ~ **(with)** pata/patwa, kumbana na *~ with impediments* kumbana na vikwazo. 2 fahamu, fahamiana, juana *they met the professor at the farm* walifahamiana na profesa shambani. 3 pokea, laki, ridhia *~ sb's wishes* ridhi(sha) matakwa ya mtu *~ sb's request* kidhi ombi la mtu *~ the requirements*. 4 faa. ~ **the case** tosheleza. ~ **sb half way** *(fig)* patana, fanya suluhu. ~ **all expenses** lipa gharama zote. 5 gusa, gusana, patana; kimu, tosheleza mahitaji. **make (both) ends** ~ ishi kulingana na mapato. 6 onekana, sikika. ~ **sb's eye/ear** onekana/ sikika. **there is more than ~s the eye** kuna mambo mengi zaidi ya yanayoonekana kwa macho, kuna mengi yaliyojificha. 7 -wa tayari, jiandaa kwa *~ with political changes* jiandaa kwa mabadiliko/mageuzi ya kisiasa. 8 pambana, pinga, kabili (kwa vita). **~ ing** *n* 1 mkutano, kusanyiko *annual general ~* mkutano wa mwaka *a secret ~* mkutano wa siri. **~-house** *n* jengo la mikutano (agh. ya Quakers) ya sala. **~-place** *n* mahali pa kukutania.

meet[3] *n* 1 *(GB)* mkutano (wa wawindaji, watu wanaosaka, wapanda baiskeli n.k.). 2 *(US)* mashindano *athletic ~* mashindano ya riadha.

megacycle *n* mibembeo milioni.

megadeath *n* kifo cha watu milioni kwa mpigo, hasa kwa (bomu la nyuklia).

megalith *n* megalithi: jabali, mnara wa (miamba mawe).

megalomania *n* (ugonjwa wa) kupenda makuu. **~c** *n* mpenda makuu.
megaphone *n* megafoni, bomba, paza sauti.
megaton *n* megatoni: nguvu ya baruti/ bomu sawasawa na tani milioni moja.
melancholy *n* ghamu, huzuni *adj* -enye uzito wa moyo. **melancholia** *n* ugonjwa wa ghamu. **melancholic** *adj* -enye huzuni, -enye uzito wa moyo.
melange *n* mchanganyiko.
melee *n* vurumai, ghasia nyingi.
meliorate *vt,vi* rekebisha, (kuwa zuri zaidi). **melioration** *n.*
meliorism *n* imani ya kuwa wanadamu wanaendelea kujirekebisha kuwa bora.
mellifluous *adj (of sounds)* -tamu, laini, -zuri, ororo.
mellow *adj (of fruit)* 1 -bivu, -lioiva vizuri, laini na tamu. 2 *(of earth)* -enye kukomaa vizuri. 3 *(of colour)* zito. 4 *(of sound)* ororo. 5 -enye busara, tulivu. 6 *(colloq)* changamfu, levi kidogo *vt,vi* iva, -wa tamu.
melodrama *n* 1 melodrama: mchezo wa kuigiza wa kusisimua hisia, kupiga chuku, kuchoma moyo, kusikitisha, kuhuzunisha (agh. wenye mwisho mwema). 2 tabia, lugha ya kutia chumvi. **~tic** *adj*. **~tically** *adv*.
melody *n* tuni, lahani. **melodic** *adj (mus)* -a sauti tamu. **melodious** *adj* -a tuni, -a maghani. **melodiously** *adv*.
melon *n* tikiti maji.
melt *vt,vi* 1 yeyusha; yeyuka. ~ **away** isha, malizika, yeyuka. ~ **sth down** yeyusha kitu (ili kukitumia kama mali ghafi). 2 *(of food)* lainisha, mung'unya; meng'enyeka. 3 *(of persons)* lainika, tia/sikia huruma ~ *into tears* toa machozi. 4 *(of colours)* fifia. **~ing** *adj (fig)* tamu sana, laini, ororo; -a kusikitisha. **~-pot** chungu cha kuyeyushia madini/metali; *(fig)* mahali pa mchanganyiko mkubwa wa wahamiaji. **~ing point** kiwango cha kuyeyukia.
member *n* 1 mwanajumuiya ~ *of a party, society etc* mwanachama *M~ of the household* mwanakaya. **M~ of Parliament (MP)** Mbunge (Mb). 2 sehemu, kiungo cha mwili *the unruly ~ (arch)* ulimi. ~ **ship** *n* uanachama.
membrane *n* utando. **membranous** *adj*.
memento *n* ukumbusho, kumbukumbu.
memo *see* **memorandum**.
memoir *n* 1 kitabu cha kumbukumbu. 2 *(pl)* habari za maisha.
memorandum *n* 1 taarifa ~ *of appeal* rufani ~ *of association* katiba ya kampuni. 2 maandiko ya kukumbusha habari.
memory *n* 1 kumbukumbu; kukumbuka; *(past event)* mambo yaliyokwisha pita. **commit sth to ~** kariri, hifadhi, tia moyoni. **repeat/ speak from ~** kariri *keep in ~* tia moyoni, kumbuka *not in the ~ of man* zamani sana (hata mtu hawezi kukumbuka). **to the best of my ~** kadiri ninavyokumbuka *childhood memories* kumbukumbu za utotoni. **in ~ of sb; to the ~ of sb** kwa kumbukumbu ya. 2 kipaji/uwezo wa kukumbuka; nafasi/kiasi cha kurekodi mambo (ndani ya kompyuta) *Asha has a bad ~* Asha ana kumbukumbu mbaya/hakumbuki. 3 kina (masafa) cha kuweza kukumbukia. **within living ~** wakati wetu *loss of ~* kupotewa na kumbukumbu *refresh one's ~* jikumbusha. 4 heshima baada ya kifo *of blessed ~* marehemu *of sad ~* -a kukumbusha majonzi. **memorable** *adj* -a kukumbukwa, -a sifa kubwa, mashuhuri. **memorably** *adv*. **memorial** *n* 1 kumbukumbu, ukumbusho/kumbukizi. 2 hati yenye maombi. 3 sanamu ya ukumbusho. 4 *(pl)* **memorials** *n* makumbusho *adj* -a kumbukumbu. **memorialize** *vt* 1 peleka hati ya maombi. 2 wekea ukumbusho. **memorize** *vt* kariri, soma kwa ghaibu. **memorization** *n.*
memsahib *n* mamsabu, bibi.
men *n pl of* **man**.
menace *vt* hamanisha, ogofya, kamia, tisha ~ *a country with war* tishia nchi kwa vita *n* hamaniko, tishio, kamio,

hatari. **menacing** *adj*. **menacingly** *adv*.

menage *n* kaya.

menagerie *n* nyumba za wanyama (kwa maonyesho), mkusanyiko wa wanyamapori (hasa wa sarakasi).

menarche *n* kuvunja ungo, kuingia hedhi mara ya kwanza.

mend *vt,vi* 1 rekebisha, fanyiza ~ *the clothes* tengeneza nguo ~ *matters* rekebisha mambo. 2 ongoka. **its never too late to** ~ bado kuna muda wa kujiongoa. 3 pona, pata ashekali *my leg is ~ing well* mguu wangu unapona vizuri. 4 ongeza ~ *the fire* chochea moto ~ *one's pace* ongeza mwendo. **on the** ~ -enye kupata nafuu/ahueni. **~er** *n* mtengenezaji. **~ing** *n* utengenezaji.

mendacious *adj* -ongo, danganyifu. **~ly** *adv*. **mendacity** *n (formal)* uwongo, udanganyifu.

Mendelian *adj* -a nadharia ya jenetiki ya Mendel.

mendicant *n* mwombaji *adj* -a kimaskini, -a ombaomba.

menfolk *n (pl) (colloq)* wanaume.

menial *adj* -a mtumishi wa nyumbani; -a chini, duni ~ *duties* utumishi, (kazi za) uboi *n* mtumishi wa nyumbani, boi.

meningitis *n (med)* uvimbe wa tando za uti wa mgongo na ubongo; homa ya uti wa mgongo.

menopause *n* (wakati wa) kukatika hedhi.

menses *n* hedhi.

menstruate *vi* -wa na hedhi, ingia mwezini. **menstrual** *adj*. **menstruation** *n*.

mensuration *n* 1 mpimo (wa marefu na maeneo). 2 elimu ya kupima marefu na maeneo. **mensurable** *adj*.

mental[1] *adj* 1 -a akili, -a kichwa. ~ **age** umri/ukomavu wa akili. ~ **arithmetic** hesabu za kichwa ~ *aberration* kosa la akili. ~ **cruelty** ukatili wa kiakili. 2 -enye ugonjwa wa akili; mwenye kichaa (wazimu). ~ **deficiency** upungufu wa akili ~ *health* utimamu wa akili. ~ **home/hospital** mahali pa wagonjwa wa akili. ~ **illness** ugonjwa wa akili. ~ **patient** mgonjwa wa akili. ~ **reservation** kusita kimoyomoyo. ~ **retardation** taahira ya akili. **~ly** *adv*. ~ **defective** -enye akili pungufu/taahira. **~ity** *n* akili; tabia, fikira.

mental[2] *adj* -a kidevu.

menthol *n* mentha. **~ated** *adj* -enye mentha.

mention *vt* taja nena. **not to ~; without ~ing** licha ya *it was expressly ~ed* ilitajwa wazi. **don't ~ it** si kitu, haidhuru *n* kutaja *she made no ~ of your coming* hakutaja lolote kuhusu kuja kwako. **honourable** ~ tuzo la sifa (ya mwanafunzi katika mtihani). **~ed** *adj*.

mentor *n* mshauri, mnasihi.

menu *n* menyu, orodha ya vyakula.

mercantile *adj* 1 -a biashara, -a kufanya biashara. ~ **marine** meli za biashara ~ *agent* wakala wa biashara ~ *law* sheria ya biashara. **mercantilism** *n* nadharia kongwe ya uchumi yenye kuthamini zaidi utajiri wa fedha.

Mercator's Projection mtupo Mercator: Uchoraji wa ramani ya dunia kwa mistari mustatili toka ikweta na meridiani.

mercenary *n* mamluki, askari wa kukodiwa *adj* -enye kufanya kwa tamaa ya fedha; -a kutaka faida tu *for ~ ends* kwa ajili ya faida.

mercer *n* mwuza nguo (za hariri, za pamba na za sufu). **~ize** *vt* imarisha nyuzi za pamba.

merchandise *n* bidhaa.

merchant *n* 1 mfanyi biashara; ~ *law* sheria ya biashara. ~ **navy** meli za biashara (za nchi moja); baharia/ mwanamaji wa meli hizo ~ *prince* mfanya biashara tajiri. 2 mwenye duka. 3 *(GB sl)* shabiki, mlevi, mtu mwenye tamaa (ya kitu) *a speed ~* shabiki wa spidi, mtu apendaye kuendesha gari kwa kasi sana. ~ **man** *n* meli merikebu ya kupakia bidhaa.

mercury *n* 1 *(chem)* zebaki. 2 **M ~ (Roman Myth)** Mjumbe wa miungo; *(astronomy)* Zebaki. **mercurial** *adj* 1 *(of persons)* geugeu. 2 -a zebaki. 3 *(fig)* changamfu, janja, erevu *n* dawa ya zebaki.

mercy *n* 1 rehema, huruma, upole, wema *they had no ~ on me* hawakunionea huruma. 2 *(pardon)* msamaha *beg for ~* omba msamaha. **be at the ~ of** -wa chini ya. **be left to the tender ~/mercies of** achiwa kwa/ uteseke. 3 bahati njema, faraja, liwazo. **~ killing** *(colloq) see* **euthanasia**, 4 **M~ on us!** Mungu! Tusamehe! **merciful** *adj* -enye rehema, -a huruma; -pole. **merciful (to)** -enye kuonyesha huruma **mercifully** *adv*. **merciless** *adj* dhalimu, katili, bila huruma, **merciless (to)** -sioonyesha huruma. **mercilessly** *adv*.

mere[1] *adj* tu, tupu *~ accident* ajali tu *~ words* maneno matupu. **~ly** *adv* tu *he said it ~ as a joke* alisema tu kwa utani.

mere[2] *n* dimbwi, ziwa dogo.

meretricious *adj* -enye uzuri wa sura tu; -enye kung'aang'aa tu, kudanganya macho. **~ly** *adv*.

merge *vt,vi* **~ (into/in/with)**, *(comm) (of business companies)* unganisha; ungana *our company ~d with the company which sells machines* kampuni yetu imeungana na kampuni inayouza mashine *the government will ~ the chemical industries* serikali itaunganisha viwanda vya kemikali. 2 **~ into** badilika polepole, geuka taratibu. **~r** *n* kuunganisha; kuungana; muungano.

meridian *n* 1 meridiani; nusu ya mzingo wa dunia (mstari toka Kaskazini hadi Kusini). 2 adhuhuri. 3 *(fig)* upeo, kipeo, usitawi.

meridional *adj* -a kusini, -a kusini ya Ulaya; -a meridiani.

meringue *n* keki (ya ute wa mayai uliopigwa na sukari).

merino *n* merino: namna ya kondoo mwenye manyoya marefu laini sana; nguo ya sufu merino; nguo ya sufu au pamba laini/nyororo.

merit *n* 1 ustahili, tabia nzuri, sifa njema. 2 matendo mema. **affidavit of ~s** kiapo cha ustahilifu *on its ~s* kwa ustahilifu wake. **make a ~ of sth** daistahili/utambuzi/kutambuliwa stahili. **he ~'s it** ni stahili yake, amestahili. **~ocracy** *n* mfumo wa serikali unaoongozwa na wataalamu na weledi. **~orious** *adj* -enye kustahili -a kupongeza/kutunuka. **~oriously** *adv*.

mermaid *n (in children's stories)* nguva (jike). **merman** *n* nguva (dume).

merry *adj* 1 -a furaha; -a kufurahisha, -changamfu, kunjufu *wish sb a ~ Christmas* takia mtu heri ya Krismasi *a ~ laugh* kicheko cha furaha. **make ~** -wa na furaha, -wa mchangamfu. **~ maker** *n* mcheshi, mtu mchangamfu. **~ making** kufurahi, kuwa na furaha. **~ go round** *n* bembea yenye farasi, magari ya kuwafurahisha watoto. 2 *(old use)* -a kufurahisha. 3 -liolewa kidogo.

mesalliance kuoana na mtu wa tabaka la chini.

mescal *n* meskali: aina ya mpungate.

Mesdames *n pl of* **madame**.

mesdemoiselles *n pl of* **mademoiselle**.

mesh *n* 1 tundu la wavu, kimia, jicho (la wavu). 2 *(pl)* **~es** wavu, kimia. *(mechanics)* **in ~** -lioingiana *vt,vi* tega, nasa. **~ (with)** ingiana, umana; *(fig)* patana. **~y** *adj*.

mesmerism *n (old use)* kiinimacho, kutia usingizi. **mesmeric** *adj*. **mesmerist** *n* mtia kiini macho. **mesmerize** *vt* 1 tia mtu usingizi, fadhaisha.

mess[1] *n* 1 fujo, machafuko, takataka *here's pretty ~* mambo gani haya! haya matata ya kutosha *make a ~ of things* haribu, fanya vibaya *vt,vi* **1 ~ sth (up)** vuruga. **~ up** 1 *n (colloq)* fujo, kutokuelewana. 2 **~ sth/sb**

about chezea; fanya mambo bila mpango, fanya purukushani *make a ~ of sth* vuruga watu. **~y** *adj* -a fujo, -chafu.

mess[2] kikundi cha watu wanaokula chakula pamoja (hasa wanajeshi); mlo; mesi, bwalo la kulia chakula. ~ **jacket** *n* jaketi la mesi. ~ **mate** *n* mwenzi mshiriki wa mesini *vt,vi* ~ **with sb;** ~ **together** -la chakula pamoja.

message *n* 1 habari, taarifa, agizo *special* ~ risala. 2 ujumbe.

messenger *n* mjumbe, mtume; tarishi.

Messiah *n* Masiha, Kristo. **Messianic** *adj* -a Masiha, Masiha, -a Kristo.

Messieurs *n pl of* **monsieur**

Messrs *n (abbr of* **Messieurs)** Mabwana.

messuage *n (leg)* nyumba pamoja na kiwanja.

met *pt pp of* **meet**.

Met *n (abbr of)* **Meteorological**.

metabolism *n* umetaboli: hali ya ujenzi na uvunjajivunjaji wa kemikali mwilini. **metabolic** *adj* -a umetaboli.

metacarpal *adj (anat)* -a mfupa wa mkono.

metacarpus *n* kiganja cha mkono.

metal *n* 1 metali. 2 ~ **work** kazi ya metali. ~ **worker** *n* 1 mfua metali/ chuma. 2 kitu cha metali. 3 kokoto (za kutengenezea barabara/reli. 4 *(pl)* reli ya gari moshi *the train left/ jumped the ~s* gari liliacha reli *vt* tengeneza barabara kwa kokoto. **~lic** *adj* -a metali. **~lurgy** *n* ufuaji metali; maarifa ya ufuaji wa metali. **~lurgist** *n* bingwa wa metali. **~lurgical** *adj*. **~-works** *n* kiwanda cha metali.

metamorphose *vt,vi* ~ **(sb/sth) (into)** geuza, badili kabisa (tabia, umbo). **metamorphosis** *n* metamofosisi: ugeuzaji kabisa umbo/tabia.

metaphor *n* sitiari. **~ical** *adj* -a sitiari. **~ically** *adv*.

metaphrase *n* tafsiri (inayokaribia) sisisi.

metaphysics *n* 1 metafizikia: falsafa ya kuchunguza chanzo cha uhai na maarifa. 2 mazungumzo ya hewani, udhanifu. **metaphysical** *adj*.

metatarsal *n (anat)* -a mfupa wa kiganja/unyayo wa mguu.

mete *vt* ~ **out** gawa. ~ **to** pimia.

meteor *n* kimondo. **~ic** *adj* -a kimondo; kimondo *(fig)* -a kuvuma kwa muda mfupi; -a haraka sana. **~ite** *n* mavi ya nyota; jiwe lililotoka katika nyota.

meteorology *n* metorolojia: elimu inayohusika na upimaji wa hali ya hewa. **meteorologist** *n* mwanametolojia. **meteoroligical** *adj*.

meter[1] *n* mita *electricity* ~ mita ya umeme.

meter[2] *see* **metre**.

methane *n* methani.

methinks *vi (old use)* nionavyo mimi.

method *n* 1 *(system, order)* utaratibu, desturi. **there is ~ in madness** jambo analolifanya si la kijinga. 2 *(way, plan)* mbinu; njia ~ *of teaching* mbinu za kufundishia. **~ical** *adj* -liofanywa kwa utaratibu; -enye utaratibu. **~ically** *adv*. **~ology** methodolojia.

Methodism *n* Umethodisti:madhehebu ya Kikristo yaliyoanzishwa na John Wesley. **Methodist** adj -a imani ya Methodist *n* muumini wa umethodisti.

methought *pt of* **methinks**.

meths *n pl (colloq abbr for)* **methylated spirits**.

Methuselah *n (in the Bible)* Methusela: mtu aliyeishi muda mrefu kuliko wote (miaka 969); *(fig)* mtu mwenye umri mkubwa sana.

methyl *n (chem)* ~ **alcohol** alkoholi methili. **~ated** *adj* -liyomethilishwa. ~ **spirit(s)** spiriti iliyomethilishwa.

meticulous *adj* -angalifu sana katika mambo madogo madogo; -angalifu na sahihi. **~ly** *adv*. **~ness** *n* uangalifu sana (katika mambo madogo).

métier *n* kazi/weledi/shughuli (inayomfaa hasa mtu); ubingwa wa mtu (katika kazi, biashara n.k.).

metre[1] *(US =* **meter)** *n* mizani,mapigo. **metrical** *adj* -enye mizani.

metre[2] *(US =* **meter)** *n* mita, meta. **metric** *adj* -a mita. ~ **system** mfumo wa mita. **metricize; metricate** *vt* geuza kuwa katika mfumo wa mita. **metrication** *n.* **metrical** *adj* -a mita.

Metro *n* **the** ~ metro: reli za chini ya ardhi.

metronome *n* metronomi: chombo cha kupiga/kuongoza mwendo wa mapigo (ambacho mwendo wake unaweza kubadilishwa); kupigia mapigo.

metropolis *n* mji mkuu wa nchi; makao makuu. **metropolitan** *adj* 1 -a mji mkuu. 2 -a uaskofu mkuu ~ *bishop* askofu mkuu (wa sehemu/jimbo lenye maaskofu wengi). ~ **France** Ufaransa *n* 1 mkazi wa makao makuu. 2 **M**~ askofu **metropole** nchi za kati *contradictions between the ~ and the periphery* mikinzano kati ya nchi za kati na nchi za pembezoni.

mettle *n* ushupavu, ujasiri. **be on ones ~; put sb on his** ~ amka/hamasisha mtu aonyeshe ushupavu wake. ~**some** *adj* hodari, kunjufu sana.

mew *n (also* **miaow**) nyau, mlio wa paka *vi* fanya mlio wa nyau *the cat is ~ing* paka analia nyau.

mews *n* 1 *(old use)* mtaa wa vibanda (mazizi) vya farasi nyuma ya mtaa wa makazi. 2 *(modern use)* mabanda yaliyogeuzwa kuwa nyumba/gereji.

mezzanine *n* mezanini: ghorofa kati ya ghorofa ya chini na ghorofa ya kwanza.

mezzo *adv (musical direction)* kwa sauti ya kati. ~ **soprano** *n* mwimbaji wa sauti ya kati (ya sauti ya kwanza na sauti ya pili).

mi,me *n (mus)* noti ya tatu (katika mfumo wa do-re-mi-fa).

miaou,miaow *n see* **mew**.

miasma *n* ukungu mbaya (wa kuleta ugonjwa); *(fig)* mazingira machafu; athari mbaya. ~**tic** *adj* -enye ukungu mbaya.

mica *n* ulanga. ~**ceous** *adj.*

mice *n pl of* **mouse**.

mickey *n* **take the ~ (out of sb)** *(sl)* kejeli, cheza shere.

mickle, *also* **muckele** *n (Scot)* wingi, chungu nzima *many a little makes a ~* haba na haba hujaza kibaba.

micro- *pref* mikro, dogo sana.

microbe *n* vijiumbe maradhi.

microbiology *n* mikrobiolojia.

microcosm *n* mfano mdogo wa ulimwengu; binadamu; mfano (mdogo); mwakilishi wa mfumo mzima *prisons are a ~ of society* magereza ni mfano mwakilishi wa jamii.

microdot *n* mikronukta: picha ambayo imepunguzwa hadi ukubwa wa nukta.

microelectronics *n* mikroelectroniki.

microfiche *n* kipande cha mikrofilamu.

microfilm *n* mikrofilamu: filamu ya picha zilizopunguzwa kabisa *vt* piga picha za mikrofilamu.

micrometer *n* mikromita:chombo cha kupimia vitu vidogo sana.

micron *n* mikroni: kipimo cha urefu cha moja ya milioni ya mita.

micro-organism *n* kijiumbe, kidubini.

microphone *n* mikrofoni.

microscope *n* hadubini. **microscopic; microscopical** *adj* dogo sana (kuweza kuonekana kwa macho).

microwave *n* wimbi mikro.

mid *adj* -a kati *in ~ air* angani *~ course* katikati ya njia *in ~ August* katikati ya mwezi wa Agosti *~ latitude* latitudo ya kati *pref (poet)* katikati ya, miongoni mwa. ~ **most** *adj,adv* (-lio) katikati kabisa. ~**day** *n* adhuhuri, jua la utosini, saa sita ya mchana *~day meal* chakula cha mchana. ~**land** *n* sehemu ya katikati ya nchi. **The M~s** Wilaya za kati ya Uingereza. ~**night** *n* 1 saa sita ya usiku. 2 *(atrrib)* usiku wa manane. **burn the ~night oil** kesha, kaa usiku kucha ukifanya kazi. **the ~night sun** jua la usiku la nchi za Aktiki na Antaktiki. ~**ship** *n* katikati ya meli/merikebu. ~**shipman** *n* mwanamaji manowarini (mwenye cheo chini ya Luteni); afisa mwanamaji mkurufunzi. ~**st** *n (lit or arch)* sehemu ya katikati. **in our ~**

miongoni mwetu *prep* katikati ya, miongoni mwa. **~stream** katikati ya mkondo, mto. **in ~ stream** *(fig)* katikati ya jambo/shughuli/ tukio n.k.. **~summer** *n* katikati ya majira ya joto ya ulaya. **M~ day** Juni 24. **~ madness** *n* kilele cha wendawazimu. **~way** *adj,adv* **~ way between** katikati (ya), nusu kwa nusu. **~- week** *n* siku za kati ya juma (Jumanne hadi Alhamisi, hasa Jumatano). **~ winter** *n* katikati ya majira ya baridi ya ulaya.

midden *n* fungu la taka au mavi.

middle *n* 1 **the ~** katikati *the ~ of the room* katikati ya chumba. **~ of the road (of policies)** kati kwa kati, -a kadiri. 2 *(colloq)* kiuno. 3 *(atrrib use)*. **~ age** utu uzima. **M~ Ages** Enzi ya kati. **~ aged** *adj* -a makamo. **~ spread** *(colloq)* kitambi (kinacho-tokana na kuanza kuzeeka). **~-class** *adj* tabaka la kati. **take/follow a ~ course** fuata njia ya kati. **~ distance** masafa ya kati. **~ finger** kidole cha kati. **the M~ Kingdom** *(old name for)* China. **~man** mtu wa kati; mlanguzi. **~most** *adj* -a kati kabisa, -a katikati. **~-watch** *n (on ships)* zamu (baina ya saa sita na saa kumi za usiku). **~ weight** *n* uzito wa kati (kati ya kilo 66.6 na 72.5). **~ blouse** blausi mpwayo. **middling** *adj* -a katikati; *(moderate)* -a wastani *adv* kiasi, kwa wastani *n (usu pl)* bidhaa za daraja la pili.

middy *(colloq)(abbr of)* **midshipman.**

midge *n* usubi.

midget *n* 1 kibete.2 *(attrib)*-dogo sana.

midriff *n* 1 kiwambotao. 2 fumbatio; tumbo.

midwife *n* mkunga. **~ry** *n* ukunga.

mien *n* sura ya mtu (inayoonyesha hali aliyonayo).

might *n* uwezo, nguvu, ukuu. **with all one's ~; with ~ and main** kwa nguvu zote *~ is right* mwenye nguvu umpishe. **~y** *adj* 1 *(lit, biblical)* -enye nguvu/uwezo/amri/ukuu. 2 kubwa sana. **high and ~** -enye majivuno sana *adv (colloq)* sana *think oneself ~ clever* jifikiria kuwa na akili sana. **~ily** *adv*.

migraine *n* kipandauso.

migrate *vi* **~ (from/to)** hama, hajiri; hamia. **migration** *n* kuhama, uhamiaji; wahamaji (kwa pamoja). **migratory** *adj* -enye tabia ya kuhama. **migrant** *n* mhamiaji *adj* -hamaji. **~ labour** wafanyakazi wahamaji.

mike *n (colloq abbr for)* **microphone**.

milady *n (dated form of address)* siti.

milage *n see* **mileage**.

milch *adj* -enye kutoa maziwa, -a maziwa *~ cow* ng'ombe wa maziwa.

mild *adj* 1 -pole; -dogo; laini *~ attack of fever* homa kidogo. 2*(of food, drink, tobacco)* sio kali. 3 **~ steel** chuma cha pua (kinachopindika bila kukatika). **~ly** *adv* kwa upole. **to put it ~** bila kutia chumvi.

mildew *n* kuvu,ukungu *vt,vi* ota ukungu/kuvu.

mile *n* maili *he is feeling ~s better today (colloq)* anajisikia afadhali sana leo. **~ometer** *n* mita inayoonyesha maili zilizosafiriwa na gari. **~stone** *n* jiwe la maili: *(fig)* jambo/tukio muhimu la kihistoria. **~age** *n* 1 umbali (kwa maili). 2 malipo/posho ya usafiri /usafirishaji (kwa maili).

millieu *n* mazingira.

militant *adj* -liotayari kupambana, -a kutaka mapambano *n* mtu anayepambana; mpigania haki (katika vyama vya wafanyakazi, siasa n.k.). **militancy** *n* mapambano, hali ya kuwa katika mapambano.

military *adj* -a kijeshi, -a kivita *n* **the ~**askari, wanajeshi; jeshi. **militarism** *n* kuamini/kupenda kutumia nguvu za kijeshi katika siasa. **militarist** *n* mtu apendaye/anayeamini katika nguvu za kijeshi. **militaristic** *adj*.

militate *vi* **~ against** zuia, pinga.

militia *n (usu* **the ~***)* jeshi la mgambo. **~man** *n* mwanamgambo.

milk *n* 1 maziwa **the ~ of human kindness** huruma ya kibinadamu.

It's no use crying over spilt ~ maji yaliyomwagika hayazoleki. ~ **and water** *(fig)* hafifu, baridi. 2 *(compounds)* ~ **bar** *n* mkahawa wa kuuzia vinywaji vya maziwa, shikirimu n.k. ~-**churn** *n* gudulia la maziwa. ~ **loaf** *n* mkate mtamu. ~**maid** *n* mkama maziwa (mwanamke). ~**man** *n* muuza maziwa (majumbani). ~-**powder** *n* maziwa ya unga. ~**round** *n* njia anayopitia mwuza maziwa. ~ **shake** sharubati, maziwa (baridi). ~**sop** *n* mwanamume mwoga/mnyonge;kijana mwoga. ~-**tooth** *n* jino la utoto. ~-**white** *adj* -eupe kama maziwa. 3 utomvu wa mimea/maji ya mimea (yaliyo kama maziwa) *coconut* ~ tui; maji ya nazi. ~ **weed** nyasi zenye utomvu kama maziwa. 4 dawa iliyo kama maziwa ~ *of magnesia* maziwa magnesi *v,vi* 1 kama ng'ombe/mbuzi/kondoo n.k.; gema utomvu n.k. (kutoka kwenye miti); *(fig)* kamua mtu (ili atoe fedha, habari). 2 toa maziwa. ~**ing machine** *n* mashine ya kukama ng'ombe. ~**y** *adj* -a maziwa; kama maziwa. the ~ way kilimia: nyota ndogo nyingi sana pamoja (kama wingu jeupe) mbinguni usiku.

mill *n* 1 kinu *flour* ~ *n* kinu cha kusaga unga *sugar* ~ *n* kinu cha kusindika miwa *steam* ~ *n* kinu cha mvuke *oil* ~ kinu cha kusindika mafuta. **put sb/go through the** ~ -pa/fanya mazoezi makali; pitisha/pitia katika hali ngumu. ~ **dam** bwawa la kinu. ~ **pond** *n* dimbwi (kinu) *(of the sea)* tulivu/shwari kabisa. ~ **race** mkondo wa maji kwa ajili ya kuzungusha gurudumu la kinu. ~ **stone** *n* jiwe la kusagia. ~ **stone round the neck** *(fig)* mzigo mzito. **be between the upper and nether** ~ **stone** banwa sana. ~**wheel** *n* gurudumu la kinu. ~**wright** mjenzi na mtengezaji wa vinu (hasa vya maji na upepo). 2 kiwanda; karakana. ~ **hand** mfanyakazi wa kiwanda. 3 kijimashine/kijikinu cha kusaga (k.m. kahawa, pilipili n.k.) *vt,vi* 1 saga kwenye kinu ~ *flour* saga unga. 2 unda kwenye kinu ~ *steel* unda chuma cha pua katika fito chuma. 3 fanya mikato kwenye ukingo (k.v. wa sarafu). ~ **about/around** *(cattle, crowds of people)* enda hobelahobela, zunguka/tembea katika makundi na bila mpango. ~**er** *n* msagishaji.

millennium *n* 1 kipindi cha miaka elfu. 2 *(rel)* milenia: miaka elfu ya utawala wa Kristo duniani kama ilivyotabiriwa katika Biblia *(fig)* kipindi cha baadaye cha furaha na neema ndani ya jamii. **millenarian** *n* mtu anayeamini kutokea kwa milenia. **millenary** *adj* -a miaka elfu, -a milenia.

millepede *n see* **millipede**.

millet *n* mtama; serena, lulu *bullrush* ~ wimbi, ulezi, uwele ~ *stalk* bua *stalks of sweet* ~ vikita ~ *flour* unga wa mtama.

milli- *pref* mili: sehemu moja ya elfu ya kipimo. ~**gram** miligramu. ~**litre** mililita. ~**metre** milimeta.

milliard *n (GB) (US see billion)* elfu moja milioni.

milliner *n* mshona kofia za kike; mwuza mapambo na kofia za kike; biashara ya kofia za kike na mapambo yake.

million *n* milioni, 1,000,000. **make a** ~ -wa milionea. ~**aire** *n* milionea; mtu mwenye dola/pauni milioni moja na zaidi; tajiri mkubwa. ~**th** *n* sehemu moja ya milioni *adj* -a milioni. ~**fold** mara milioni moja.

millipede jongoo.

milometer *n see* **mile**.

milord *n (Fr word formerly used for)* bwana (wa Kiingereza), Mwingereza tajiri.

milt *n* 1 *(spleen)* wengu. 2 *(of fish)* mbegu za samaki dume *vt (of fish)* toa mbegu za kiume. ~**er** *n* samaki dume atoaye mbegu.

mime *n* 1 uchezaji bubu. 2 mchezo bubu *vi* iga. ~**sic** *n* uigaji, ufananisho. ~**tic** *adj* -a kuiga,

-lioigwa. **mimic** *adj* -liyoigiwa *n* 1 mwigaji. 2 mwigo wa lafudhi *vt* 1 iga, (hasa kwa dhihaka). 2 *(of things)* fanana sana. **mimicy** *n* uigaji, wigo.

mimeograph *n* kirudufu *vt* rudufu.

minaret *n* mnara wa msikiti.

minatory *adj* -a kutisha, -a kuogofya.

mince *vt,vi* 1 kata vipande vidogo, saga (nyama n.k.). **not to ~ matters/ one's words** sema waziwazi, bila kuficha. 2 sema/tembea kwa kujifanya/kujifaragua/kujidaidai. *n* kima (nyama ya kusaga). **~meat** *n* minsi: mchanganyiko wa zabibu, matunda, mafuta, sukari, unga n.k. wa kufanyia keki. **make ~meat of** *(colloq)* shinda kabisa (mtu au majadiliano); maliza; *(US)* nyama. **~r** mashine ya kusaga (nyama). **mincing** *adj* -a madaha, -a maringo *take ~ steps* tembea kwa maringo. **mincingly** *adv*.

mind *n* 1 kukumbuka; kumbukumbu. **call/bring sth to ~** kumbuka. **have/ keep/bear sth in ~** kumbuka jambo fulani. **go/pass from/out of ones ~** sahaulika. **it passed from my ~** niliisahau. **put sb in ~ of sth** kumbusha. **out of sight out of ~** *(prov)* asiyekuwepo na lake halipo. **time out of ~** mara nyingi. 2 maoni; mawazo. **presence of ~** uwezo wa kuamua/kutenda haraka. **be out of one's/ not in one's right ~** -wa na wazimu. **be of the same ~** -wa na mawazo sawa; *(of one person)* shikilia wazo/uamuzi wa awali. **to my ~** kwa mawazo yangu, nionavyo. **bend one's ~** athiri, tia athari za kudumu katika mawazo ya mtu (kwa imani n.k.). **~ing** *adj* -a kuathiri mawazo ya mtu. **blow one's ~** *(colloq) (of drugs, extraordinary or sensational sight, sounds etc)* tia jazba (katika mawazo). **~-blowing** *adj* -a kutia jazba. **~ boggling** *adj* -a kustaajabisha. **have sth on one's ~** sumbuliwa na wazo fulani. **keep one ~ on** endelea kumakinikia/kufikiria. **read sb's ~** soma mawazo ya mtu. **~ reading** *n* kubuni, ung'amuzi. **~ reader** *n*. **take one's/sb's ~ off sth** (ji) sahau (lisha) (mawazo). 3 nia dhamira, dhati. **be of/in two ~s** sita; -wa na mashaka, vutwa huko na huko. **change one's ~** ghairi; badilisha mawazo/nia. **give one's ~ to sth** makinikia, shughulikia. **have a good ~ to (do sth)** taka, elekea (kuamua). **have half a ~ to do sth** elekea/vutiwa kufanya jambo. **know one's ~** jua unalotaka, -wa na uamuzi. **make up one's ~** amua, azimu, kusudia, kata shauri. **make up one's ~ to do sth** amua kufanya jambo; *(reconcile)* kubali *we are poor we must make up our ~ to that* lazima tukubali kwamba sisi ni maskini. **set one's ~ on doing sth** kusudia, dhamiria. **speak one's ~** sema ukweli wake bila kuficha. 4 moyo, fikra. **enter sb's ~** ingia katika fikra za mtu. **have/give one's ~ to sth** fikiria sana. **an open ~ on sth** -wa tayari kusikiliza, kupokea mawazo ya mwingine. 5 akili. **great ~s** watu mashuhuri; wataalam. **sound in ~**
-enye akili timamu. **person of unsound ~** mtu asiye na akili timamu *vt,vi* 1 *(observe watch)* angalia, tunza. **~ out (for sth)** jihadhari, angalia. **~ your own business** shika lako, usijitie (si yako). **~ ones 'S and Q's** wa na adabu nzuri. **~ you!** unajua!. sumbuliwa (na), jali *do you ~ my smoking?* naweza kuvuta sigara? *would you ~ shutting the door* tafadhali ufunge mlango. **never ~** haidhuru; usijali, si kitu. **~er** *n (in compounds)* mwangalizi *machine* mwangalizi wa mashine. **~ed** *adj* 1 **~ to do sth** -a kuelekea/kutaka kufanya. 2 -enye mawazo ya. **strong-~ed** jeuri, -enye msimamo, imara, -enye kujali. **~ful** *adj*. **~ of** zingatifu. **~fully** *adv*. **~fulness** *n*. **~less** *adj* 1 **~ of** -siojali; -sahaulifu. 2 -sio na akili, -siohitaji akili. **~lessly** *adv*. **~lessness** *n*.

mine[1] *n* 1 mgodi, shimo; chimbo (la

kuchimbulia mawe, madini, makaa n.k.); *(fig)* hazina; *(explosive)* bomu la kutega. ~ **detector** chombo cha kugundua mabomu. ~ **disposal** *n* kutegua mabomu. ~**-field** *n* sehemu iliyotapakazwa mabomu ya kutega; sehemu yenye migodi mingi. ~**-layer** *n* meli/ndege ya kutega mabomu baharini. ~**-sweeper** chombo cha kuondoa mabomu baharini *vt,vi* 1 chimba mgodi; chimba. 2 weka mabomu; haribu kwa mabomu. 3 *(fig)* dhoofisha. ~**r** *n* 1 mchimba madini. 2 askari wa kutega mabomu ardhini. ~**ral** *n* 1 madini *adj* -a madini. ~ **pitch** lami. ~ **water** maji yenye madini (hasa yanayoweza kutibu); *(GB)* maji ya soda. ~ **wool** sufu madini. ~**ralogy** *n* elimu madini. ~**ralogist** *n* mtaalamu wa madini. **mining** *n* uchimbuaji wa madini ~ *company* kampuni ya migodi.

mine[2] *poss pron* -angu *through no fault of* ~ si kosa langu *poss adj (in poet & biblical style only)* ~ *eyes* macho yangu.

mingle *vt,vi* ~ **(with)** changanyika, changanya.

mingy *adj (GB colloq)* -choyo,bahili.

mini *(pref)* dogo, fupi.

miniature *n* 1 kisanamu; mfano mdogo. **in** ~ -dogo. 2 *(atrrib)* -dogo ~ *model* mfano mdogo wa kitu. **miniaturist** *n* mtengenezaji wa sanamu/picha ndogo ndogo.

minim *n* minimu: nusu noti.

minimum *n* kiasi/kadiri iliyo ndogo iwezekanavyo *adj* -a mwisho (kwa dogo), -dogo sana; -a chini kabisa. ~ **wage** kima cha chini. **minimal** *adj* -dogo kabisa. **minimize** *vt* 1 punguza kabisa. 2 punguza sifa; dharau.

minion *n (derog)* mtumishi (anaye jipendekeza). **the ~s of the law** polisi; askari jela.

minister *n* 1 waziri *Prime M~* Waziri Mkuu ~ *without portfolio* waziri bila wizara maalumu. 2 mjumbe wa serikali (chini ya balozi). 3 ~ **of religion** mchungaji, mhubiri *vi* ~ **to** tumikia; saidia. ~**ial** *adj* 1 -a waziri. 2 -a wizara/baraza la mawaziri. **ministration** *n* utumishi; msaada. **ministry** *n* 1 wizara. 2 **the** ~ jamii ya makasisi na wachungaji; uchungaji. **enter the** ~ -wa mchungaji.

ministrant *n (attrib adj, (formal)* -a kutumikia *n* msaidizi, mtumikiaji.

minnow *n* samaki mdogo wa mtoni. **Triton among the ~s** mtu aonekanaye mkubwa mbele ya wanyonge.

minor *adj* 1 -dogo, -a chini, hafifu ~ *breach* uvunjaji mdogo. 2 *(mus)* **in a ~ key** *(fig)* kwa huzuni, kwa kusononeka *n (leg)* mtoto mwenye umri chini ya miaka kumi na nane. ~**ity** *n* 1 *(leg)* utoto. 2 wachache, walio wachache. **be in a** ~ -wa wachache; -wa na wafuasi wachache *I'm in a ~ of one* niko peke yangu. ~ **government** serikali ambayo ina chini ya nusu ya nafasi za wabunge. ~ **programme** (*TV, radio*) kipindi kwa ajili ya wachache. ~**judgement** hukumu ya wachache.

Minotaur *n (Gk myth)* Minoto: zimwi lionekanalo nusu mtu na nusu mnyama.

minster *n* kanisa kubwa.

minstrel *n* 1 *(in the Middle Ages)* manju. 2 kampuni ya burudani. ~**sy** *n* sanaa na nyimbo za watunzi na mwimbaji msafiri.

mint[1] *n (leaves)* nanaa;*(plant)*mnanaa.

mint[2] *n* 1 kiwanda cha kutengenezea/ kupiga chapa sarafu. 2 **make/earn a ~ (of money)** pata pesa nyingi. 3 *(atrrib of medals, stamps, prints, books etc)* -pya. **in ~ condition** -pya; safi kabisa *vt* 1 piga chapa sarafu. 2 buni (maneno n.k.).

minus *prep* kasoro, bila he came back *from the war ~ an arm* alirudi vitani bila mkono mmoja *adj* ~ **sign** alama ya kutoa *n* kutoa.

minuscule *adj* -dogo sana.

minute[1] *n* 1 dakika. ~ **gun** *n* mzinga unaopigwa kila dakika (k.m. wakati wa mazishi). ~ **hand** *n* mshale wa dakika. ~**man** *n* mwanamgambo (aliye tayari kupigana wakati wowote). 2 *(short time)* kitambo kidogo muda mdogo *just a* ~ ngoja kidogo, *any* ~ wakati wowote. **in a** ~ sasa hivi. **to the** ~ juu ya alama. **the** ~ **(that)** mara tu. **up-to-the** ~ *attrib adj* -a kisasa kabisa. 3 *(pl)* kumbukumbu (za mkutano n.k.) *vt* andika kumbukumbu.

minute[2] *adj* 1 -dogo sana, -dogodogo. 2 *(trifling)* hafifu. 3 *(exact)* halisi, barabara; angalifu sana. ~**ly** *adv*. ~**ness** *n*.

minutiae *n pl* mambo madogo madogo.

minx *n* msichana fidhuli, asiye na adabu.

miracle *n* 1 muujiza. ~ **play** *(in the Middle Ages)* maigizo ya maisha ya Kristo/Watakatifu wa Kikristo. 2 ~ **of** maajabu ya, mfano wa ajabu. **miraculous** *adj* -a muujiza; -a kustaajabisha. **miraculously** *adv*.

mirage *n* 1 mazigazi. 2 alinacha.

mire *n* kinamasi, matope. **be in the** ~ *(fig)* pata matatizo. **sink into the** ~ kwama. **drag sb/sb's name through the** ~ fedhehesha, chafua jina *vt,vi* 1 pakaza matope, kwamisha kwenye matope. 2 *(fig)* tatiza. **miry** *adj* -enye tope.

mirror *n* 1 kioo (cha kujitizamia). ~ **image** taswira geu. 2 *(fig)* kiakisi *vt* akisi.

mirth *n* furaha, kicheko. ~**ful** *adj*. ~**fully** *adv*. ~**less** *adj* bila furaha.

mis- *pref* -baya, vibaya; (ku)to...~**trust** kutoamini.

misadventure *n* shari. **death by** ~ kifo cha ajali.

misadvise *vt* potosha, shauri vibaya/ visivyo.

misalliance *n* uhusiano mbaya (hasa katika ndoa); ndoa ya wasokufu.

misanthrope *n* mchukia wanadamu wenziwe; mkaa pweke. **misanthropic** *adj* -a kuchukia watu, -a kudharau (kuepukana na) watu. **misanthropy** *n* kuchukia watu; chuki ya watu.

misapply *vt* tumia vibaya *the town council officials misapplied our development levy* maafisa wa halmashauri ya mji walitumia vibaya kodi yetu ya maendeleo. **misapplication** *n*.

misbecome *vt* -siowezekana.

misbecoming *adj* -siofaa.

misbegotten *adj* 1 mwanaharamu, haramu. 2 *(colloq)* duni, nyonge, -a kudharaulika, -a bure.

misbehave *vt,vi* kosa adabu, -wa na tabia mbaya. **misbehaviour** *(US=* **misbehavior)** *n*.

miscalculate *vt,vi* kokotoa vibaya, kosea. **miscalculation** *n*.

miscall *vt* ita kwa jina lisilo, kosea jina.

miscarry *vt* 1 *(of plans, etc)* -tofaulu, tokea vibaya, haribika, enda kombo *the plan miscarried* mpango haukufaulu/haukufanikiwa. 2 *(of letters etc)* kosa kufikishwa/kufika *the letter miscarried* barua haikufika. 3 *(of a woman)* haribu mimba. **miscarriage** *n* 1 kuharibika mimba. 2 ~ **of justice** upotoshaji wa haki. 3 kutowasilisha, kutofika mahala utakiwapo.

miscast *vt* 1 *(of a play)* pangia sehemu vibaya, chagua vibaya waigizaji. 2 *(of an actor)* pangiwa, pewa nafasi -siyoimudu.

miscegenation *n* uchotara, usuriama; kuzaa watoto chotara.

miscellaneous *adj* 1 anuwai. 2 *(of person)* mtu mwenye sifa/tabia anuwai/kadha/tafauti-tafauti. **miscellany** *n* mchanganyiko wa vitu vya namna mbalimbali. **miscellanea** *n* mchanganyiko wa maandishi.

mischance *n* bahati mbaya *by* ~ kwa bahati mbaya.

mischeif *n* 1 madhara, hasara, uharibifu. **to do sb a** ~ kumdhuru. 2 fitina. **make** ~ **(between)** tia fitina. ~ **making** kufitini. 3 utundu, utukutu *the child did it out of* ~ mtoto alifanya kwa utundu. 4 utani (usio na nia mbaya). 5 mtundu. **mischievous**

adj 1 -enye fitina. 2 -tundu. 3 -tani, -enye utani. **mischievously** *adv*. **mischievousness** *n*.
misconceive *vt,vi* 1 elewa vibaya. 2 ~ **of** elewa jambo visivyo. **misconception** *n*.
misconduct *n* 1 mwenendo mbaya, tabia mbaya *professional* ~ kinyume cha miiko ya weledi, tabia mbaya ya kazi. 2 uongozi mbaya *vt* 1 ~ **oneself (with sb)** -wa na tabia mbaya. 2 ongoza vibaya.
misconstrue *vt* elewa vibaya. **misconstruction** *n* welewa/ fasili mbaya.
miscount *vt,vi* 1 hesabu vibaya. 2 kosa makisio *n* 1 kuhesabu vibaya (hasa kura, vitu n.k.).
miscreant *n (dated)* baa, mtu mwovu.
misdate *vt* kosea tarehe.
misdeal *vt,vi (of playing cards)* gawa vibaya *n* mgawanyo mbaya (wa karata).
misdeed *n* tendo baya; kosa.
misdemeanour *(US)* **misdemeanor** *n (leg)* kosa dogo.
misdirect *vt* ongoza/elekeza/onyesha vibaya. ~**ion** *n*.
misdoing *n see* **misdeed**.
mise en scene *n (of a play)* mandhari; *(fig)* mazingira (ya tukio).
miser *n* bahili. ~**ly** *adj*. ~**iness**. **misery** *n* umaskini, taabu, mateso, maumivu *suffer ~ from the stomach ache* pata maumivu tumboni; teseka. **put the animal out of its** ~ ua mnyama (aliyeumia sana). 2 *(pl)* baa. 3 *(colloq)* hohehahe; mlalamishi. **miserable** *adj* 1 -enye taabu; maskini; duni, -nyonge *what a ~able life!* maisha gani haya ya taabu! 2 -enye kusababisha taabu/umaskini. 3 hafifu.
misfire *vi* 1 *(of a gun)* -tolipuka; -tofyatuka. 2 *(of motor-engine)* -towaka. 3 *(colloq of joke, etc)* -tofanikiwa *n* 1 kutofyatuka, kutowaka, kutolipuka, kutofanikiwa.
misfit *n* 1 vazi lisilo sawa na kimo, vazi lisilokaa. 2 *(fig)* mtu asiyefaa/ asiyechukuana na wenziwe.
misfortune *n* msiba, taabu, balaa; bahati mbaya.
misgive *vt* -wa na shaka, -wa na wasiwasi *my heart ~s me* moyo wangu umejaa wasiwasi. **misgiving** *n* -wasiwasi, mashaka.
misgovern *vt* tawala vibaya. ~**ment** *n*.
misguide *vt* 1 elekeza vibaya. 2 shauri vibaya. ~**d** *adj* -jinga, -liopotoka.
mishandle *vt* 1 shughulikia vibaya. 2 tendea mtu vibaya.
mishap *n* bahati mbaya; ajali.
mishear *vt* elewa vibaya, -tosikia vema.
mishmash *n* shaghalabaghala.
misinform *vt* potosha *I was ~ed* nilipotoshwa. ~**ation** *n*.
misinterpret *vt* tafsiri/elewa/eleza vibaya. ~**ation** *n*.
misjudge *vt,vi* pitisha uamuzi/kadiria vibaya; elewa/ fikiria vibaya.
mislay *vt* weka (kitu) pasipo pake, poteza (kwa kutokukumbuka ulipoweka) *I have mislaid my wallet* nimepoteza pochi yangu.
mislead *vt* potosha *be misled* potoshwa.
mismanage *vt* simamia/ongoza vibaya; haribu madaraka. (taratibu). ~**ment** *n*
misname *vt (usu possive)* taja kwa jina lisilo lake.
misnomer *n* matumizi mabaya ya neno/ jina; kosa, kioja.
misogamy *n* kuchukia ndoa. **misogamist** *n*.
misogyny *n* kuchukia wanawake. **misogynist** *n* mchukia wanawake.
misplace *vt* 1 weka mahali pasipo pake; weka mahali pasipofaa/pasipostahili. 2 *(usu passive)* penda mtu/kitu isivyo stahili.
misprint *vt* chapa vibaya *n* mategu.
misprision *n (leg)* kuficha kosa. ~ **of treason** kuficha uhaini.
mispronounce *vt* tamka vibaya. **mispronunciation** *n*.
misquote *vt* dondoa vibaya. **misquotation** *n*.
misread *vt* 1 soma visivyo. 2 elewa visivyo.
misrepresent *vt* wasilisha/hudhurisha visivyo, tafsiri vibaya.

misrule *n* kutawala vibaya *vt* tawala vibaya.

miss[1] *n* 1 **M~** binti, Bi. **M~ (Anna) Kyomo** Bi Anna Kyomo. 2 msichana; binti. 3 *(vocative)* dada, mama. **~y** *n (colloq familiar)* msichana; binti.

miss[2] *n* kukosa shabaha, kutopata, kutofanikiwa, kutofuma. **give sth a ~** *(colloq)* acha makusudi, kwepa. a **~ is as a good as mile** *(prov)* kukosa ni kukosa hata kama ni kidogo *vt, vi* kosa kupata/kuona/kusikia/kufuma. **~ the target** kosa shabaha,kosea lengo ~ *one's way* potea njia *he ~ed the train* alichelewa garimoshi *can't ~ it* huwezi kuikosa; usikose ~ *the obvious* toelewa iliyo wazi/dhahiri. 2 kumbuka (kwa hamu ya kuona tena) *we all ~ you* tunakukosa sote *we shall ~ you if you go* ukienda tutakukumbuka. 3 **~out (on sth)** *(colloq)* kosa nafasi, kosa kufanya jambo. **~ sth out** acha, sahau, -toingiza kitu. **~ing** *adj* -sioonekana, -liopotea.

missal *n (rel)* misale.

misshapen *adj* -lioumbuka, -lioumbika vibaya.

missile *n* kombora *(attrib)* ~ **site/base** kitu cha kurushia makombora. **guided** ~ kombora linaloongozwa kwa mitambo ya elektroniki.

mission *n* 1 ujumbe (kwa kazi maalumu) (agh. katika nchi ya kigeni). 2 *(rel)* misheni. 3 ~ **in life** wito. 4 *(esp. US)* kazi maalum. **~ary** *n* mmisionari *adj* -a misheni, -a misioni.

missive *n* (*hum)* barua (agh ndefu), waraka.

misspell *vt* kosea tahajia.

misspend *vt* tumia vibaya, poteza, fuja *Kiro misspent his youth* Kiro alitumia vibaya ujana wake.

misstate *vt* kosea kusema/kueleza. **~ment** *n*.

missus,missis *n (colloq/sl) (used with the, my, his, your)* mke *where is your ~* mke wako yuko wapi?

mist *n* 1 umande, ukungu. 2 utando machoni (agh. hutokana na machozi); *(fig)* ukungu; kitu chochote kinachosababisha mtu kushindwa kuelewa maana *vt, vi* ~ **(over)** funika na ukungu/utando. **~y** *adj*. **~ily** *adv*. **~iness** *n*.

mistake *n* kosa. **by ~** kwa makosa. **and no ~** bila shaka *he is a fool and no ~* yeye ni mpumbuvu bila shaka *vt, vi* 1 kosa, kosea, fahamu/fikiria visivyo. **there is no mistaking** ni dhahiri. 2 **~ sb/sth for** dhania visivyo kweli, changanya na *I always ~ Kurwa for Doto* mara kwa mara huwa nadhania Kurwa kuwa Doto. **be ~n (about sth)** kosea *if I'm not ~n* kama sikosei. **by ~** bila kukusudia.

mister *vt n always written* **Mr** Bwana (jina la kumtaja mwanamume pamoja na jina lake *Mr Mugabe* Bwana Mugabe.

mistime *vt* fanya kitu wakati usio wake.

mistletoe *n* mlimbo (mmea ambao matunda yake hutoa ulimbo).

mistook *pt of* **mistake**

mistranslate *vt* tafsiri visivyo. **mistranslation** *n*.

mistreat *vt* tesa, sumbua, fanyia/tendea vibaya. **~ment** *n*.

mistress *n* 1 mwanamke mkuu wa kaya; bimkubwa. 2 mwalimu wa kike *the Kiswahili ~* mwalimu (wa kike) wa Kiswahili. 3 bingwa/ mweledi wa kike *she is a ~ of handcraft* ni mjuzi wa kazi za mikono. 4 *(in stories of the 18th c)* bibi. 5 *(poet)* mpenzi. 6 kimada, hawara.

mistrial *n (leg)* kesi iliyobatilishwa / batili.

mistrust *vt* -toamini, onea shaka, dhania vibaya *n* ~ **(of)** shaka, tuhuma. **~ful** *adj* -enye kutia shaka. **~fully** *adv*.

misunderstand *vt* elewa visivyo,elewa vibaya. **~ing** *n* kutoelewana, kukosa maelewano, suitafahamu *there is some ~ between Mary and John* kuna suitafahamu kati ya Mary na John.

misuse *vt* tumia vibaya *n* matumizi

mabaya.

mite[1] *n* 1 kimchango, msaada kidogo *contribute one's* ~ toa uwezayo. 2 kitu kidogo *a* ~ *of a child* kitoto kidogo sana.

mite[2] *n* mdudu mdogo mharibifu (k.v. utitiri, nyenyere n.k.).

mitigate *vt,vi* punguza; punguka ukali (k.v. wa maumivu) ~ *pain* punguza maumivu. **mitigating circumstances** hali inayopunguza uzito/ukali wa makosa, madhambi n.k. **mitigation** *n.*

mitre*(US=* **miter)** *n* 1 kofia ya kiaskofu. 2 *(carpentry)* kingamo (namna ya kuunga vipande viwili vya mbao).

mitt *n* 1 glovu (yenye tundu moja la vidole vinne na moja la kidole gumba). 2 glovu ya besiboli. 3 *(sl)* ngumi; mkono.

mitten *n* 1 *see* **mitt** 2 glovu (inayo funika kiganja na nyuma ya kiganja tu).

mix *vt,vi* 1 changanya ~ *work with pleasure* changanya kazi na starehe. 2 ~ **(with)** *(of persons)* ishi pamoja (katika jamii/jumuiya) *he doesn't* ~ *well* haelewani na watu. 3 ~ **sth/sb up (with sth/sb)** vuruga, boronga; kosea (kwa kufananisha) *dont* ~ *me up with my brother* usinifananishe na kaka yangu. **be/get ~ed up in/ with sth** ingizwa/jihusisha na shughuli fulani *don't get ~ed up in this business* usijiingize katika shughuli hii. **~-up** *n* hali ya kutatanisha. **~ed -up** *adj* -enye kuchanganyikiwa *n* mchanganyo, mchanganyiko; mseto. **~ed** *adj* -enye mchanganyiko *a* ~ *school* shule ya mchanganyiko (wavulana na wasichana). **have ~ feelings (about sth)** wa na shaka/ wasiwasi juu ya mtu/kitu. ~ **blessing** kitu chenye faida na hasara/ uzuri na ubaya. ~ **farming** ukulima wa mchanganyiko/mseto. ~ **grill** nyama mchanganyiko iliyobanikwa. **~ed marriage** ndoa ya watu wasiokuwa na rangi/dini moja. ~ **metaphor** *n* sitiari mchanganyiko. **~er** *n* 1 mchanganyaji; kichanganyi. 2 *(colloq)* **a good (bad)** ~ mtu aishiye vizuri (vibaya) na watu. **~ture** *n* mchanganyo, mchanganyiko; *(medical)* dawa (ya kunywa) *a cough* ~ dawa ya kikohozi. **the ~ as before** *(colloq)* utaratibu ule ule (kama ilivyokuwa hapo nyuma).

miz(z)en *n (naut)* ~ **(mast)** galme. ~ **(sail)** tanga la galme.

mizzle *vi (dial or colloq)* nyunya.

mnemonic *adj* -a kusaidia kukumbuka. **~s** *n* mbinu elimu ya kumbukumbu.

mo *(sl abbr for)* **moment**.

moan *vi,vt* piga kite.

moat *n* handaki la maji (linalozunguka boma) *vt* zungushia (boma) handaki la maji.

mob *n* 1 kundi la watu wenye fujo, ghasia ya watu ~ *law/rule* sheria mkononi. 2 **the** ~ watu; umma; *(sl)* kundi la majambazi *vt,vi* songamana (kwa ghasia). **~ster** *n* mmojawapo wa majambazi.

mob-cap *n* kitambaa/ushungi/kofia ya mwanamke (ivaliwayo ndani ya nyumba inafunika nywele zote).

mobile *adj* 1 -a kwenda; -a kuweza kwenda. 2 *(of face, person)* -epesi kugeuka. ~ **clinic** kliniki itembeayo (agh. kwa gari). **mobility** *n.*

mobilize *vt,vi* andaa watu kufanya jambo, hamasisha. **mobilization** *n.*

mocassin *n* 1 ngozi ya swala; sapatu za ngozi ya swala. 2 *(bio)* ~ *snake* nyoka mkali kama pili (Amerika).

mocha *n* 1. moka: kahawa safi kabisa. 2 ladha ya mchanganyiko wa kahawa na chokleti.

mock *vt,vi* 1 ~ **sb;** ~ **at sb** dhihaki. **~ing bird** *n* 1 ndege mwigo (anayeiga milio ya ndege wengine). 2 katisha tamaa. **make a ~ of** fanyia mzaha/dhihaki. **~-up** *n* mfano wa kitu (kinachokusudiwa kutengenezwa); *(printing) n* pesta mwigo; mzaha; dhihaka *adj* -a kuiga; -a mzaha; bandia, -siohalali ~ *exam* mtihani wa majaribio. **~er** *n.* **~ingly** *adv.* **~ery** *n* dhihaka. **~-heroic** *n*

-enye kudhihaki ushujaa (katika fasihi).

mod *adj (colloq)* -a kisasa; -a madaha *n* **M~** *(1960 GB)* kijana aliyevaa nguo za kisasa na kupanda skuta.

mode *n* 1 namna; mtindo. 2 *(gram)* hali. 3 *(maths)* modi. 4 *(music)* hali ya ngazi. 5 *(commerce)* kati. **modal** *adj* 1 *(gram)* -a hali. 2 *(maths)* modi. ~ **class** daraja modi. **modality** *n* hali, namna. **~l** *n* 1 mfano, kielelezo, mtindo; kifani. 2 *artist's~* kifani cha msanii. 3 *(perfect example)* kitu/mtu mwendo, mfano mzuri. 4 mtu anayeonyesha mitindo mipya ya nguo *she is a fashion~* anaonyesha mitindo mipya ya nguo.

model *vt,vi* 1 **~ls (in)** finyanga, fanyiza (umba) kwa kufuata mfano; fanya mfano. 2 onyesha mtindo. 3 ~ **oneself on/upon sb** fuata mfano wa mtu mwingine, iga mtu mwingine. **~ler** *n* mfinyanzi. **~ling** *n* ufinyanzi; uonyeshaji mitindo.

moderate *adj* -a kiasi, -a kadiri, -a wastani *n* mtu mwenye siasa, tabia, mwendo wa kiasi. **~ly** *adv vt,vi* 1 punguza (joto, ukali, harara, nguvu); tuliza ~ *one's demands* punguza madai. 2 simamia mjadala/mtihani (wa chuo kikuu); rekebisha mtihani. **moderation** *n* 1 kiasi; kadiri; wastani; usimamizi wa mjadala/mtihani. 2 *pl* **moderations** (*also* **mods**). **moderator** *n* 1 msimamizi (wa mjadala, michezo n.k.) mtahini. 2 mpatanishi. 3 *(physics)* kipunguzo cha nutroni katika funguatomu. 4 msimamizi wa baraza/mahakama ya kanisa.

modern *adj* 1 -a kisasa. 2 -a siku hizi; -pya *n* mtu (mwandishi n.k.) wa kisasa. **~ism** *n* 1 usasa; zama hizi. 2 *(rel)* kufuata mambo ya kisasa badala ya desturi za kale. **~ist** *n* mtu wa kisasa. **~istic** *adj*. **~ity** *n* kuwa wa kisasa, usasa. **~ize** *vt* fanya kuwa -a kisasa, geuza upya. **~ization** *n*.

modest *adj* 1 -siojivuna. 2 -a wastani, -a kadiri. 3 -a staha. **~y** *n* staha; wastani *with due ~* pamoja na adabu zipasazo *in all ~* bila kujivuna.

modicum *n* kadiri, kiasi kidogo.

modify *vt* 1 geuza, badilisha, badili kidogo. 2 punguza (ukali, nguvu). 3 *(gram)* vumisha. **modifier** *n (gram)* kivumishi. **modification** *n* ubadili; badiliko; uvumishi. **modifiable** *adj* -a kubadilishika, -a kugeuzika.

modish *adj* -a kisasa, -a (kufuata) mitindo.

modiste *n (formal)* mshonaji (nguo).

modulate *vt,vi* rekebisha, geuza; *(mus)* badili ufunguo (sauti n.k.). **modulation** *n* kubadili sauti; urekebishaji. **modulator** *n*

module *n* 1 kipimo. 2 kitengo/kiunzi huru. 3 sehemu sawa/lingano. **command~** kiunzi/kitengo huru cha nahodha; chombo cha anga. **modular** *adj*.

modus operandi *(Lat)* utaratibu/mbinu ya utendaji, jinsi ya kufanya/kushughulikia jambo.

modus vivendi *(Lat)* namna ya kuishi; mapatano ya muda.

mogul *n (colloq)* mtu maarufu, tajiri, kigogo.

mohair *n* mahea: nguo/nyuzi/kitambaa kilichotengenezwa kwa manyoya ya mbuzi, (wa aina ya Angora).

Mohammedan *see* **Muhammad**.

moiety *n* sehemu/nusu ya kitu (kilichokatwa/gawanywa).

moil vi *(only in)* **toil and** ~ fanya/chapa kazi kwa bidii.

moist *adj* -a majimaji, -a unyevu; *(of tubers)* chelema *a ~ atmosphere* hewa yenye unyevunyevu. **~en** *vt* rowesha kidogo, tia maji kidogo. **~ure** *n* unyevu.

moke *n (GB sl)* punda.

molar *n* gego.

molasses *n* molasi.

mold *see* **mould**.

mole[1] *n (spot)* kiwaa cheusi, baka jeusi.

mole[2] *n* fuko: mnyama mdogo anayefukua chini. **blind as a ~ /bat** pofu, kutoona vizuri. **make mountains out of ~ hills** tia chumvi,

kuza jambo.
mole[3] *n (breakwater)* bomazuizi (baharini).
molecule *n (chem/physics)* molekuli.
molest *vt* sumbua, udhi, kera, (kwa makusudi). **~ation** *n.*
moll *n* mwanamke hawara/mwenzi wa mhalifu; malaya.
mollify *vt* tuliza, ridhisha mtu, bembeleza. **mollification** *n.*
molluce *(US* **mollusk)** moluska: vinyama kama konokono, koa; kombe, pweza, ngisi n.k.
mollycoddle *n* mlimbwende kupindukia *vt* engaenga; dekeza.
Moloch *n (Bible)* Mungu ambaye watoto walitolewa kwake kama dhabihu; *(fig)* tishio; janga.
Molotov *n (saying, mil)* ~ **cocktail** bomu la mkono.
molt *see* **moult**.
molten *pp of* **melt** *adj* -lioyeyuka, -a kuyeyusha ~ *metal* metali iliyoyeyuka.
molto *adv (mus)* sana.
mom *n US (colloq)* mama.
moment *n* 1 kitambo kidogo, muda mfupi sana, kufumba na kufumbua; wakati *at that ~* wakati ule ule *go this ~* nenda sasa hivi *for the ~* kwa sasa. **not for a ~** hata kidogo, kamwe! 2 **the ~** *(used as conj)* mara. 3 *(importance)* maana, thamani. **man of the ~** mtu mwenye sifa za siku hizi. **of great/small/little/no ~** -enye maana kubwa/ndogo/ n.k. sasa. **~ary** *adj* -a mara moja, -a kupita upesi sana; -a kuweza kutokea wakati wowote *be in ~ expectation of sth* tumaini kuwa jambo laweza kutokea wakati wowote (hivi karibuni). **~arily** *adv.* **~ous** *adj* -a maana sana. **~ously** *adv.* **~ousness** *n.*
momentum *n* 1 momenta: nguvu mwendo. 2 *(fig of events)* msukumo, nguvu.
monarch *n* 1 mfalme; *(fig)* mtawala mkuu. 2 *(biol)* kipepeo mkubwa (wa rangi nyeusi na ya machungwa). **~ic, ~al** *adj* **~ism** *n.* mfumo wa ufalme. **~ist** *n* mfuasi wa ufalme. **~y** *n* ufalme.
monastery *n* nyumba kubwa ya utawa.
monastic *adj* -a utawa; -a nyumba ya watawa. **~ism** *n* maisha ya utawa.
monaural *adj* -a sikio moja, -a kipazasauti kimoja, -a mono.
Monday *n* Jumatatu.
money *n* 1 fedha (sarafu, noti) inayotumika katika kuuza na kununua. **be coining/minting ~** tajirika harakaharaka. **be in the ~** *(sl)* tajirika. **make ~** chuma fedha. **(pay) ~ down** lipa fedha taslimu. **put ~ into sth** wekeza. **ready ~** fedha taslimu. **monetary** *adj* -a mambo ya fedha, -a fedha. ~ **policy** sera ya fedha. **monetize** *vt* 1 toa fedha zianze kutumika nchini. 2 panga thamani ya sarafu; utajiri. **marry ~** oana na tajiri. **get one's ~s worth** faidi; pata kitu cha thamani ya fedha alizotoa mtu. ~ **makes the marc go** fedha ni motisha ya mambo. *pl* **monies** raslimali, fedha, mali. 4 *(compounds)* ~ **bags** *sl* tajiri, kizito. **~-box** *n* sanduku la fedha. **~-changer** *n* mvunja fedha. **~-lender** *n* mkopesha fedha, mkopeshaji fedha. **~-order** *n* hawala ya fedha. **~-spinner** *n (colloq)* kitabu, mchezo, mradi wenye kumimina hela. **~ed** *adj* -enye mali *the ~ interest* mabepari. **~less** *adj* fukara.
monger *n* mfanyi biashara, mchuuzi, mwuzaji.
mongolism *n* upunguani wa kuzaliwa na kichwa bapa. **mongol** *n* punguani, taahira.
mongoose *n* nguchiro.
mongrel *n* 1 mbwa chotara; *(person) (derog)* chotara, suriama *adj* -a chotara, -a mchanganyiko.
monies *see* **money**.
monitor *n* 1 msimamizi; *(school)* kiranja. 2 *(radio)* msikilizaji na mtoaji habari za kituo cha nje. 3 *(warship)* manowari ndogo. 4 chombo cha kujaribia usafirishaji wa matangazo ya redio/TV; chombo cha

kufuatilia urukaji wa makombora, n.k. *vt, vi* fuatia, simamia; (*radio*) sikiliza kituo cha nje.

monk *n* mtawa wa kiume, sufii. **~ish** *adj*.

monkey *n* 1 *(small light)* tumbili, ngedere; *(small dark)* kima;*(colobus)* mbega. ~ **business** utundu. **have a ~ on one's back** *(sl)* -wa mlevi wa bangi n.k.; -wa na chuki kinyongo/ donge ~ *face* uso wa paka. **get one's ~ up** *(sl)* -wa na hasira, kasirika. **put sb's ~ up** *(sl)* kasirisha; mtu. *(compounds)* **~-bread** *n* buyu. **~-jacket** *n* koti fupi (livaliwalo na mabaharia). **~-nut** *n* karanga, njugu (nyasa). ~ **puzzle** *n* arokaria: mti usiopandika kwa sababu una miiba mingi. ~ **tricks** utundu. **~-spanner; ~ wrench** *n* 1 *(tech)* spana (ya matairi). 2 *(mischievous child)* mtundu. 3 *(sl)* pauni 500 au dola 500 *vi* ~ **about (with)** 1 chezea. 2 iga.

mono- *(pref)* -a moja tu, -a mara moja tu, -enye moja tu.

monocle *n* rodi: miwani ya jicho moja.

monochrome *n* picha/mchoro wa rangi moja *adj* -a rangi moja.

monoculture *n* kilimo cha zao moja.

monogamy *n* ndoa ya mke/mume mmoja. **monogamist** *n* mtu mwenye mke/mume mmoja. **monogamous** *adj* -a ndoa moja. ~ **marriage** ndoa ya mke/mume mmoja.

monogram *n* monogramu: chapa ya herufi mbili au zaidi zilizo changanyika pamoja, moja juu ya nyingine.

monograph *n* monografia: kitabu, makala yenye habari ya jambo/kitu/ elimu moja tu.

monolith *n* nguzo ya jiwe tu; nguzo imara. **~ic** *adj* -a mnara mkubwa; -a mfumo wa mawazo ya aina moja.

monologue *n* mazungumzo binafsi.

monomania *n* manomania: kushikia wazo moja. **~c** *n* -enye monomania; mgonjwa wa wazimu/ wazo moja.

monoplane *n* ndege ya bawa moja.

monopoly *n* 1 uhodhi; ukiriritimba. ~ **capitalism** ubepari kiritimbi. 2 haki ya pekee. **monopolist** *n* mhodhi. mkiritimba. **monopolize** *vt* kiritimba, hodhi. **monopolization** *n*.

monorail *n* reli moja; mfumo wa treni ya reli moja.

monosyllable *n* silabi moja k.m. la, tu *answer in ~s* jibu "ndiyo au la"; jibu kwa mkato. **monosyllabic** *adj*

monotheism *n* imani kwamba kuna Mungu mmoja tu. **monotheist** *n* mwamini Mungu mmoja. **monotheistic** *adj* -enye kuamini Mungu mmoja.

monotone *n* toni moja, kidatu kimoja *speak in ~s* sema kwa toni/kidatu kimoja.

monotonous *adj* -siobadilika, -a kukinaisha, kinaishi.

monotony *n* ukinaifu, kutobadilika mwenendo; uchovu (ubaridi, uchoshi) (kwa kutobadilika mambo). **~ly** *adv*.

monotype *n* monotaipu: mashine inayopanga/chapa herufi kwa herufi.

monsieur *n (Fr)* bwana.

monsoon *n* monsuni: pepo za msimu katika Bahari ya Hindi; masika (yatokanayo na pepo hizo).

monster *n* 1 jitu la kutisha, dubwana. 2 (unnatural) jinamizi. 3 *(brutal person)* mtu mkali, katili. 4 *(giant)* pandikizi.

monstrous *adj* 1 -kubwa mno, -a ajabu. 2 *(terrifying)* -a kuogofya, -a kuchukiza. 3 pumbavu, baya sana. monstrosity *n* dubwana; udubwana, kitisho; kioja. **~ly** *adv*.

montage *n* kupanga filamu.

montane *adj* -a milima.

month *n* mwezi *what ~ is it?* huu ni mwezi gani? *it is the fifth ~* ni mwezi wa tano. **a ~ of Sundays** muda mrefu sana. **~ly** *adj ~ pay* mshahara wa mwezi *n* 1 jarida linalotoka kila mwezi. 2 *(pl) (arch)*. **~lies** hedhi, damu, mwezi *adv* kila mwezi, a mwezi. **calendar ~** mwezi wowote katika mwaka. **lunar ~** kipindi mwezi unapokamilisha mzunguko wa dunia.

monument *n* 1 *(memorial)* jengo/ mnara/sanamu ya ukumbusho, kumbukumbu. 2 kazi ya mfano bora (istahiliyo kukumbukwa). **~al** *adj* -kubwa sana; -a sifa za daima; -a ukumbusho *~al ignorance* ujinga mkubwa mno *~al mason* mwashi wa mawekaburi.

moo *n* mlio wa ng'ombe *vt (of cows)* lia. **~-cow** *n (child's word for)* ng'ombe.

mooch *vt,vi* 1 ~ **(about)** *(colloq)* tangatanga, susurika, zurura; *(sl US)* doea.

mood[1] *n (gram)* hali.

mood[2] *n (temper)* hali ya moyo *be in the ~ for sth* tamani kitu; jisikia *have ~s* -wa na sununu. **~y** *adj* -enye tabia ya kubadilikabadilika, -enye kununa; -enye kukasirika. **~ily** *adv*. **~iness** *n* usununu.

moolah *n (sl)* fedha.

moon[1] *n* 1 **the** ~ mwezi *full ~* mwezi mpevu *new ~* mwezi mchanga. **once in a blue ~** *(colloq)* mara chache tu. **cry for the ~** taka sana kitu kisichowezekana. **promise sb the ~** toa ahadi nyingi. 2 *(compounds)* **~beam** *n* mbalamwezi, -mwali wa mwanga wa mwezi. **~-calf** *n* 1 dubwana. 2 mpumbavu. **~-face** *n* uso mviringo. **~light** *n* mbalamwezi *vi* fanya kazi nyingine na kulipwa (wakati umeajiriwa kwingine). **~light night** usiku wa mbalamwezi. **a/no ~** -a/sio mbalamwezi. **~lit** *adj* -liomulikwa na mwezi. **~ shine** mwanga wa mwezi; upuuzi; *(sl US)* gongo. 3 *(poet)* mwezi. **~less** *adj* bila mbalamwezi; usiku wa giza. **~stone** *n* kito rangi ya buluu yenye kijani kibichi. **~struck** *adj* -enye wazimu.

moon[2] *vi,vt* 1 **~(about/around)** zurura, susurika, zama ndotoni. 2 ~ **away** pitisha wakati ovyo. **~y** *adj* -enye kunyong'onyea.

Moor *n* chotara wa Kiberiberi na Kiarabu. **~ish** *adj*.

moor[1] *n* mbuga, nyika. **~-fowl/game** *n* kwale mwekundu. **~-cock** *n* kwale dume. **~ hen** *n* kwale jike. **~ land** *n* mbuga.

moor[2] *vt* funga chombo ufukoni; tia nanga. **~ing mast** *n* mlingoti wa kufungia chombo. **~ings** *n (pl)* 1 kebo, amari, minyororo. 2 maezi.

moose *n* aina ya kongoni (apatikanaye Amerika Kaskazini).

moot *adj (only in)* **a ~ point/ question** -nayohitaji kujadiliwa; -akinadharia, -sio na maana kiutendaji, -kuigiza *~ court* mahakama bandia *vt* leta kwa majadiliano.

mop[1] *n* 1 ufagio, tamvua. 2 *a ~ of hair* nywele za matimutimu *vt* 1 pangusa kwa ufagio, tamvua, piga deki. ~ **up** futa *~ up ones tears* futa machozi; *(colloq)* maliza, komesha. ~ **the floor with sb** shindwa kabisa.

mop[2] *n (arch only in)* ~ **and mow** kunja uso.

mope *vi* huzunika, jisikitikia, soneoneka **the ~s** huzuni. **~y** *adj* -enye huzuni/masikitiko.

moped *n* baiskeli moto.

moquette *n* kitambaa kizito cha mazulia.

moral *adj* 1 -adilifu, -nyofu. 2 -ema, adili. 3 *(having moral sense, free will)* -enye hiari/akili ya kuchagua mema au mabaya, -enye utashi. 4 -enye kuonyesha haki. **a ~ certainty** jambo linaloelekea kuwa kweli *~ law* kanunui ya mema na mabaya *a matter of ~ obligation* wajibu, lipasalo *he gained ~ victory* alishindwa, lakini akashinda uungwana/utu. **~courage/cowardice** moyo wa kuthubutu/kutothubutu. **give sb ~ support** saidia kwa kuunga mkono mawazo yake *n* 1 *(of story etc)* fundisho. 2 *(pl)* maadili *he has no ~s* mtu huyu si mwadilifu, hana murua *offensive to the ~s of the community* -a kukiuka maadili ya jamii. **~ly** *adv*. **~ist** *n* mwadilifu; mwalimu wa maadili. **~istic** *adj (often derog)* -enye kuhubiri. **~ity** *n* 1 uadilifu, murua; maadili. 2

(character) tabia. 3 ~ **(play)** mchezo/tamthiliya ya maadili. **~ize** *vt,vi* 1 fafanua/elezea wema au ubaya. 2 ~ **(about/on/upon)** adilisha. 3 *(often derog)* hubiri.

morale *n* moyo, imani, nguvu,hamasa.

morass *n* kinamasi; *(fig)* utata. **~y** *adj* -enye kinamasi.

moratorium *n* ruhusa ya kukawiza malipo ya deni/jambo lolote kwa muda.

morbid *adj* 1 -gonjwa, -enye kuugua. 2 *(of the mind)* chafu; -enye kuwaza mambo ya kutisha au mambo ya kuchukiza. **~ity** *n*. **~ness** *n*. **~ly** *adv*.

mordant *adj* -a kuuma; -a kukejeli.

more *adj* 1 zaidi. **neither ~nor less** si zaidi wala si pungufu. 2 **no** ~ hakuna tena zaidi *what ~?* nini tena. 3 *a little ~* kiasi kidogo zaidi *(of food) have some ~* ongeza (chakula) *have you any ~ apples* unayo matofaa mengine? *I have some ~* nina mengine kuzidi; *(of epidemics) ~ outbreaks* milipuko zaidi *~ than enough* zaidi kupita kiasi *~ than* kuliko, zaidi ya, fauka ya *see ~ of sb* ona mtu mara nyingi *adv* 1 zaidi *and what is ~* zaidi ya hayo *you need to rest ~* unapaswa kupumzika zaidi *~ beautifully* kwa vizuri zaidi *the ~* zaidi *you should work ~* fanya kazi zaidi. **be no ~** -fa, isha *grow /be/get ~* zidi kuwa. 2 tena, *once ~* rudia tena/mara nyingine *we saw him no ~* hatukumwona tena. 3 **~ or less** takriban, kwa kadiri. 4 **~ and ~** kwa hatua, zaidi na zaidi. **no ~ than** si zaidi ya *n* zaidi, nyongeza. **~over** *adv* aidha, zaidi ya.

mores *(pl)* desturi, mila, maadili.

Moresque *adj* -a Kiislamu.

morganatic *n* ~ **marriage** ndoa baina ya mume mwenye nasaba/hadhi ya juu na mke wa nasaba/hadhi ya chini.

morgue *n* 1 nyumba ya maiti. 2 *(in newspaper or office)* jalada la kumbukumbu ya maisha ya watu mashuhuri ambao hawajafa bado.

moribund *adj* mahututi, -a kukaribia kufa, kuisha.

morn *(poet)* asubuhi.

morning *n* 1 asubuhi *early ~* alfajiri, mapambazuko *good~!* subalkheri. **~s** *adv* asubuhi/kila asubuhi. **~-room** *n* sebule ndogo. **~-sickness** *n* kichefuchefu cha mjamzito asubuhi. **the ~-star** *n* zuhura, nyota ya asubuhi.

morocco *n* ngozi laini iliyotokana na ngozi ya mbuzi (hutumika kufanyia majadala ya vitabu.).

moron *n* punguani, taahira, mtu aliyevia akili, mtu mwenye akili afkani; *(colloq)* mpumbavu, zuzu. **~ic** *adj*.

morose *adj* uchusa, -enye huzuni, -enye kununa, -a chuki. **~ly** *adv*. **~ness** *n*.

morpheme *n (ling)* mofimu.

morphia, morphine *n* afyuni.

morphology *n* mofolojia; umbo. **morphological** *adj*.

morrow *n* 1 *(liter)* siku inayofuata/ iliyofuata, kesho yake *on the ~ of war* baada ya vita. 2 *(arch)* asubuhi.

morsel *n* chembe; funda.

mortal *adj* 1 -enye kufa *all human beings are ~* binadamu wote hufa. 2 -a kufisha; -liosababisha kifo. **~sin** dhambi ya mauti. 3 -a kudumu hadi kifo. ~ **enemies** uadui unaodumu hadi kufa/kifo. ~ **combat** mapambano baina ya watu wawili (hadi mmoja kufa) *(colloq)* sana, kubwa/ndefu sana *n* binadamu. **~ly** *adv* 1 kwa kufisha. 2 sana, mno. **~ity** *n* 1 hali ya kuweza kufa, mauti. 2 vifo. ~ **rate** kiwango cha vifo. 3 idadi ya vifo *there was a high ~* watu wengi walikuwa wanakufa. ~ **tables** (*insurance*) jedwali za makadirio ya uhai.

mortar *n* 1 *(for building)* mota. 2 *(for pounding)* kinu. 3 *(gun)* kombora *vt* changanya sementi na mchanga. **~-board** *n* 1 kibao cha udongo, ubao mota (mwashi anapojenga). 2 *(cap)* kofia inayovaliwa na wanachuo wa chuo kikuu.

mortgage *n* 1 rehani, poni.2 *(document)*

hati ya kuweka rehani *chattel*~ rehani ya chombo *vt,vi* ~ **(to) (for)** weka rehani. **be ~d up to the hilt** weka rehani kila kitu. ~**r** mwekewa rehani. **mortagagor** *n* mweka rehani.

mortician *n (US)* msimamizi wa mazishi.

mortify *vt,vi* 1 aibisha, dhalilisha. 2 ~ **the flesh** jinyima, jirudi, tawala matamanio. 3 oza. **mortification.**

mortise/mortice *n* tunduunganishi *vt* unga kwa kilimi; tia kilimi. ~ **lock** kia.

mortuary *n* nyumba ya maiti *adj* -a mazishi.

mosaic[1] *n* picha mpangilio; nakshi (za mawe n.k.) *adj* -a picha mpangilio.

Mosaic[2] *adj* -a Musa. **(the)** ~ **law** Taurati: vitabu vitano vya kwanza vya Agano la Kale.

mosey *vi (sl)* ~ **along** zurura, tembea tembea.

Moslem *n* Mwislamu *adj* -a Kiislamu.

mosque *n* msikiti.

mosquito *n* mbu. ~**net** *n* chandalua. ~ **proof** *adj* -siopitisha mbu. ~**craft** *n* manowari ndogo yenye (mwendo wa kasi).

moss *n* kuvumwani ~ *grown adj* -liofunikwa kwa kuvumwani. ~**y** *adj* -liofunikwa kwa kuvumwani. **a rolling stone gathers no** ~ *(prov)* mtu asiyetulia mahali pamoja hawezi kufanikiwa.

most *adj* -ingi, kupita -ote; -ingi sana. **at**~ si zaidi ya. **at the very** ~ sanasana, sio zaidi ya. **for the ~ part** kwa kawaida; kwa jumla *in ~ cases* mara nyingi ~ *people* karibu watu wote. **make the ~ of** tumia kila nafasi, tumia vizuri sana *adv* 1 kupita/kuliko yote ~ *faithful* mwaminifu kuliko wote. 2 hasa, zaidi *what pleased you* ~ ni kitu gani kilikufurahisha hasa zaidi? 3 kabisa, sana ~ *certainly* kabisa. 4 *(dial and US colloq)* karibu ~ *everyone enjoys football* karibu kila mtu anafurahia mpira. ~**ly** *adv* kwa kawaida; hasa; karibu yote.

mote *n* chembe (k.m. ya vumbi). **the ~ in sb's eye** kosa dogo alilofanya mtu (likilinganishwa na makosa ya wengine).

motel *n* moteli: hoteli ya wenye magari.

moth *n* nondo. ~ **ball** dawa ya mende. **in ~ balls** *(fig)* ghalani. ~ **eaten** *adj* 1 -lioliwa na nondo. 2 *(fig)* -liochakaa, -a zamani. ~**proof** -sioliwa na nondo. **clothes** ~ nondo mla nguo.

mother *n* 1 mama (mzazi, mlezi wa kike); *(term of respectful reference)* mama. 2 kiini, chanzo. **necessity is the ~ of invention** *(prov)* shida hufunza. 3 kiongozi wa jumuiya ya watawa (wa kike). **M~ Superior** Mama Mkuu. 4 **the ~ counrty** nchi ya kuzaliwa. ~**-of pearl** *n* lulumizi. ~ **in law** *n* mama mkwe. ~**liness** *n* umama. ~ **tongue** lugha mama, ya kwanza. ~ **wit** *n* 1 akili ya kuzaliwa. ~ **ship** meli inayopatia meli nyingine vifaa ~ *'s day* sikukuu ya mama. 2 asili, chanzo ~ *hood n* umama. ~ **less** *adj* -siokuwa na mama. ~ **like** *adj* kama mama. ~**ly** *adj vt* tunza/lea kama mama.

motif *n* motifu: wazo/kipengee kinachorudiwa (hasa katika muziki).

motion *n* 1 mwendo **put/set sth in** ~ sababisha kitu kiende. ~ **pictures** sinema. 2 msogeo. **go through the ~s** *(colloq)* fanya kitu kwa namna isiyo ya dhati. 3 *(proposal)* pendekezo, hoja *move a* ~ toa hoja/pendekezo. 4 (kwenda) choo *have a* ~ pata choo *vt* 1 ashiria, (kwa mkono); konyeza. 2 elekeza, ongoza. ~ **sb in** ashiria mtu aingie ndani. ~ **away** fukuza (kwa mkono). ~**less** *adj* -siojongea.

motive *n* 1 nia, maarubu, matilaba. 2 *(reason)* sababu (ya kutenda jambo) *adj* -enye kuendesha; -a kusogea/ tenda. **motivate** *vt* 1 tia hamasa/ motisha; sababisha. **motivation** *n* motisha; sababu ya kufanya jambo.

motley *adj* 1 -a rangi anuwai. 2 -enye tabia mbalimbali *n* vazi la mchekeshaji. **wear the** ~ cheza/fanya kama mpumbavu au mchekeshaji.

motor *n* 1 mota. **~-cycle; ~ bike** pikipiki *n* ~ *boat* motaboti. ~ **car** motokaa. ~ **cade** *n* msafara wa motokaa, pikipiki n.k.. ~ **coach** *n* basi la kitalii. **~way** *n* baraste kuu, barabara ya motokaa ziendazo kasi. ~ **man** *n* dereva wa garimoshi. 2 musuli wa mwendo. ~ **nerve** neva mwendo *adj* 1 -a mwendo. 2 -a musuli *vt,vi* enda kwa motokaa. **~ize** *vt,vi* tayarisha magari/motokaa/pikipiki kwa uchukuzi; patia magari. **~-vehicle** *n* motokaa.

mottle *vt* tia madoadoa. **~d** *adj* -enye madoadoa.

motto *n* wito.

mould/mold[1] *n* udongo wa mboji, udongo mweusi mzuri.

mould/mold[2] *n* 1 kalibu. 2 *(pattern)* kielezo. 3 tabia. **be cast in the same** ~ -wa na tabia zinazofanana *be cast in heroic* ~ -wa na tabia ya kishujaa *vt* ~ **sth (in/from/out of)** 1 *(in clay)* finyanga, umba. 2 *(in metal)* subu kwa kalibu. 3 *(character)* ongoza, nyoosha. **~ing** *n* 1 kusubu, kuumba. 2 *(of wood)* nakshi, mchoro.

mould[3] *n* 1 kuvu *development of* ~ kuota kuvu. 2 nyonyoka *vt* ota kuvu. **~ly** *adv*. **~er** *vi* oza, liwa na kutu, kuvu kama koga; vunjikavunjika; chakaa.

mound *n* 1 tuta.2 kilima. 3 lundo *vt* lundika (udongo, mawe), fanya chungu.

mount[1] *vi,vt* 1 panda, kwea ~ *the pulpit* panda mimbari ~ *a horse* panda farasi. ~ **the throne** tawazwa, kuwa mfalme. 2 *(of blood)* sisimka *his colour ~ed* alikuwa mwekundu (kwa hasira). 3 ~ **(up)** zidi; ongezeka. 4 onyesha mchezo jukwaani. 5 weka mahali pake; angika/tundika (picha); wekea fremu. 6 *(mil uses)* fanya. ~ **a guard (at over)** linda ~ *an offensive* fanya shambulio; *(of large animals)* panda (jike) *n* 1 *(of a picture)* kiunzi. 2 farasi. 3 baiskeli.

mountain *n* mlima, ~ **chain/range** safu ya/msururu wa milima. ~ **pass** ujia mwembamba mlimani. ~ **sickness** hali ya ukosefu wa oksijeni kwenye milima mirefu. ~ **dew** wiski ya kiskoti. **~eer** *n* 1 mkaa mlimani. 2 mpanda mlima. **~eering** kupanda milima. **~ous** *adj* -enye milima; kubwa sana. **mount** *n* mlima, kilima.

mountebank *n* ayari; mdanganyifu; tapeli.

Mountie *n (Canada colloq)* polisi mpanda farasi.

mourn *vt,vi* ~ **(for/over)** huzunika; omboleza; lilia huzunikia. **~er** *n* mwombolezaji. **~ful** *adj* -enye huzuni/majonzi. **~fully** *adj* kwa majonzi, kwa huzuni. **~ing** *n* 1 huzuni, majonzi, kilio, msiba. 2 **go into/be in** ~ anza kwenda eda/kuvaa nguo za kufiwa (nyeusi)/msiba. ~ **band** *n* utepe wa msiba. **~-ring** pete ya ukumbusho wa marehemu.

mouse *n* 1 panya; *(fig)* (mtu) mwoga. **~-trap** *n* mtego wa panya *vi (of a cat)* kamata. **~r** *n* paka akamataye panya. **mousy** *adj (esp of hair)* -a rangi kahawia kavu; *(of a person)* -oga, -enye haya.

mousseline *n* melimeli.

moustache *(US* **mustache)** *n* masharubu.

mouth *n* 1 mdomo. **by word of** ~ kwa mdomo. **down in the** ~ -enye majonzi, -nayosikitika. **out of the ~s of babes and sucklings** *(prov)* kauli ya busara/hekima inayotolewa na maasumu. **laugh on wrong side of one's** ~ lalamika; sononeka. **look a gift-horse in the** ~ pokea kitu bila shukurani. **put words into sb's** ~ ambia mtu la kusema, sema kuwa mtu amesema neno, singizia. **take the words out of sb's** ~ dakia maneno, wahi kusema. **~ful** *n* kinywa tele; funda. **~-organ** kinanda cha mdomo. **~piece** mdakale; chombo cha kupulizia kinanda au chombo cha muziki; msemaji (kwa niaba ya). 2 uwazi, tundu *vt,vi* 1 sema bila sauti. 2 sema kwa madaha. 3 kula; gusa kwa mdomo.

move *vt,vi* hama, sogeza; hamisha. ~ **heaven and earth** fanya kila liwezekanalo. 2 ~ **(house)** hamisha (vyombo, samani) kwenye nyumba nyingine. ~ **out** hama. ~ **in** hamia. 3 ~ **on** sogea, enda mbele (kwa shuruti). ~ **sb on** shurutisha mtu kwenda mbele/kusogea. ~ **along/ down/up** endelea mbele. 4 *(excite)* sisimua, gusa hisi. 5 *(advice)* toa pendekezo/hoja ~ *the court* omba mahakama (kufanya jambo fulani). 6 sukuma/tuma *Salome's appeal ~ed (us) to come* ombi la Salome lilitusukuma/vuta kuja. 7 ~ **for** omba rasmi. 8 endelea. 9 chukua hatua. 10 ishi, jinasibisha. 11 nya. 12 *(in compounds)* ~ **away** ondoka. ~ **forward** sogea mbele. **movable** *adj* 1 -a kusogezeka. 2 *(varying)* -a kubadilika *n (pl)* mali inayosogezeka/ hamishika (k.v. samani n.k.); mali binafsi *n* 1 mwendo. 2 *(turn)* zamu (katika mchezo). 3 *(action)* tendo, jambo (katika kazi). 4 **on the** ~ kusonga mbele; kuhamahama. **get a ~ on!** *(sl)* fanya haraka. **make a** ~ hamia mahali pengine; anza kufanya/ kutenda. 5 uhamisho. **~ment** *n* 1 mwendo, mwondoko; mabadiliko; tendo/kitendo. 2 mzunguko. 3 *(progress)* maendeleo; kubadili/ kuhama mahala. 4 *(of mus composition)* sehemu ya mtungo. 5 *(commerce)* kupanda na kushuka bei. 6 kunya. 7 *(of group)* tapo. **~r** *n* mtoaji hoja/pendekezo. **the prime** ~ mtu anayehusika hasa katika kuanzisha jambo; muasisi.

movie *n (colloq)* 1 filamu. 2 *the ~s* sinema.

mow *vt* 1 fyeka/kata majani, nyasi. ~ **down** fyeka. **~er** *n* mashine ya kukatia majani *n* rundo la majani ya ng'ombe; banda la majani.

Mozambique *n* Msumbiji.

Mr *(abbr)* Bwana, *see* **Mister**

Mrs *(abbr)* Bibi, mke wa.

Ms Bi, Bibi.

much *adj* -ingi, tele ~ *time* wakati mwingi ~*pain* maumivu mengi. **how ~ (is it)?** bei gani? kiasi gani; idadi gani? **be up to** ~ -wa na thamani/ maana ~ *trouble* matatizo mengi. **not ~ of a** si zuri, si -a haja. **make ~ of** elewa; tia maanani; kuza. **think ~ of** penda, heshimu. **this/that** ~ kiasi hiki (kidogo). **~as** ingawa. ~ **the same** vilevile. **(with)/without so ~ as** (na)/bila hata *adv* sana, mno *it is too ~ (costly)* ghali sana ~ *too dear* ghali sana/mno. ~ **more** zaidi sana. **be too ~ for** zidi nguvu, shinda, lemea. ~ **to sb's surprise** kwa mshangao.~ **more/less** seuze; sembuse ~ *as I hate it, I must...* ingawa nachukia, sina budi *I thought as ~* nilifikiri hivyo *it is as ~ (as) saying* ni kama kusema. **as** ~ bali kile kile; hivyo *so ~* mkubwa mno/ sana *so ~ so that* kwa kiasi kikubwa kwamba *not so ~ X as Y* y kuliko x. **~ness** *n (only in colloq phrase)* ~ **of a ~ness** karibu sawasawa, hakuna tofauti.

mucilage *n* ulimbo; gundi la mimea. **mucilaginous** *adj*.

muck *n* 1 samadi, uchafu. **~-raker** *(usu fig)* mdaku. ~ **raking** *n* udaku. 2 taka; *(colloq)* kitu kitiacho kinyaa *vt,vi* ~ **sth (up)** chafua, vuruga, haribu. 2 ~ **about** *(GB sl)* zurura. 3 ~ *out* safisha zizi. **heap** ~ lundo la taka. **make a ~ of sth** *(colloq)* chafua, haribu. ~ **y** *adj* chafu.

mucus *n* ute, utetelezi, kamasi, golegole. **mucous** *adj* -a kamasi, -a ute. ~ **membrane** utando telezi.

mud *n* tope ~ *hut* kibanda cha udongo ~ *wall* ukuta wa udongo. **fling/ sling/throw ~ at** paka mtu tope, haribia mtu jina. **~-bath** *n* kuoga tope za madini (dawa ya yabisi); kuoga matopeni. ~ **flat** *n* upwa tope. ~ **slinger** *n*. **~guard** madigadi *vt* tia tope, tibua; chafua, vuruga. ~ **dy** *adj*

1 -enye tope. 2 -a giza, -sio safi, -lio chafuka; *(fig)* -liokanganyikiwa.
muddle *vt,vi* 1 ~ **(up)** vuruga, tatanisha; chafua, tibua. ~ **sth/sb up with sth/sb** *(colloq)* changanya vitu/watu wawili. 2 ~ **along/on** boronga, bananga. ~ **through** maliza jambo kwa kubahatisha *n (usu a muddle)* mkanganyo. ~ **headed** *adj* pumbavu, -liokanganyika.
mudfish *n* kambare.
muesli *n* muzili: kiamshakinywa cha nafaka, njugu na matunda makavu.
muezzin *n* mwadhini.
muff[1] *n* nguo za kuzuia baridi (mikononi au miguuni).
muff[2] *n* 1 mchezaji mzito (hasa kwenye kriketi) *vt* shindwa kudaka mpira; shindwa kufanya vizuri, fanya kosa.
muffin *n* mafini: mkate mdogo wa mviringo.
muffle[1] *vt* 1 ~ **(up)** funika kwa nguo (hasa shingo na kichwa). 2 punguza kelele kwa kufunika (ngoma, kengele) kwa nguo. ~**r** *n* 1 kitambaa cha shingoni. 2 *(US) see* **silencer**.
muffle[2] *n* mdomo wa juu (wa mnyama k.v. panya).
mufti *n* 1 mufti. 2 *(usu* **in ~)** nguo za kiraia (avaazo mtu anayevaa sare).
mug[1] *n* 1 magi. 2 *(sl)* uso, mdomo.
mug[2] *n (sl)* mpumbavu *a ~'s game* kitu ambacho hakiwezi kuleta faida.
mug[3] *vt (colloq)* vamia mtu na kumwibia; iba kwa nguvu. ~**ger** *n* mvamizi, jambazi. ~**ging** *n* uvamizi.
mug [4] *vi (sl)* ~ **sth up** soma sana (kwa ajili ya mtihani). *n* mtu asomaye sana.
muggins *n (colloq)* mpumbavu.
muggy *adj (of the weather, a day etc)* -a joto na unyevu, -a jasho. **mugginess** *n.*
mugwump *n (US)* mshaufu.
Muhammad *n* Muhammad: Mtume na Mwasisi wa Uislamu.
mulatto *n* chotara, suriama.
mulberry *n* forosadi.
mulch *n* matandazo: majani yanayotiwa shinani mwa miche kuhifadhi unyevu *vt* weka matandazo.
mulct *vt* ~**(in/of)** 1 toza faini. 2 nyang'anya *n* faini.
mule *n* 1 nyumbu, baghala. 2 **as obstinate/stubborn as a** ~ kaidi sana. 2 *(colloq of a person)* mkaidi; shupavu. 3 aina ya mashine ya kusokotea. ~ **teer** *n* mwendesha nyumbu. **mulish** *adj* -kaidi, -shupavu. **mulishly** *adv.* **mulishness** *n.*
mull[1] *vt* unga, tengeneza (divai, bia) kuwa kinywaji moto (kwa sukari na viungo).
mull[2] *n* rasi.
mull[3] *vt* ~ **sth over/over sth** fikiria jambo.
mulla(h) *n* sufu, ulama.
mullet *n* aina za changu.
mulley *adj (US)* bila pembe. *n (US)* ng'ombe asiye na pembe.
mullion *n* nguzo ya mawe kati ya dirisha. ~**ed** *adj* -enye nguzo ya mawe kati ya dirisha.
multi- *(pref)* -enye -ingi. ~ **coloured** -enye rangi nyingi. ~**cellular** *adj* -enye seli nyingi. ~ **farious** *adj* -a namna nyingi, -ingi, tena mbalimbali. ~ **form** *adj* -enye maumbo mengi, -a namna nyingi. ~**lateral** *adj* -enye wahusika wengi ~ *trade* biashara kati ya nchi tatu au zaidi. ~ **millionaire** *n* tajiri sana (mtu mwenye kiasi cha milioni kadhaa za fedha). ~ **national** *adj* -a kimataifa; -a zaidi ya mataifa mawili. *n* kampuni ya kimataifa.
multiple *adj* -enye sehemu nyingi, -a mara nyingi. ~ **choice (question)** (swali) lenye majibu mengi *n* kigawe *40 is a multiple of 10,* 40 ni kigawe cha 10.
multiplex *adj* -enye sehemu/maumbo mengi.
multiply *vt,vi* zidisha, leta wingi. ~ **sth by sth** zidisha namba fulani kwa namba nyingine. **multiplican** *n* kizidishio; hesabu ya kuzidishwa. **multiplication** *n* kuzidisha. ~ **table** jedwali la kuzidisha. **multiplicity** *n* wingi. **multiplier** *n* kizidishi.
multitude *n* 1 wingi, kundi. 2 **the** ~

jeshi; umati, kaumu. **multitudinous** *adj* -ingi, tele.

mum[1] *adj (colloq)* **keep** ~ kaa kimya *int* kelele! kimya! **~'s the word** usiseme chochote, kimya, usimwambie mtu!

mum[2] *n (colloq)* mama. **~my** *n (chiefly child's word)* mama.

mumble *vt,vi* 1 munyamunya. 2 *(of eating)* mumunya.

mumbo-jumbo *n* marogonyo; mapayo.

mummer *n* mwigizaji wa mchezo bubu. **~y** *n* 1 mchezo bubu. 2 sherehe zisizo na maana (hasa za kidini).

mummify *vt* tia mumiani. **mummification** *n*. **mummy** *n* maiti iliyotiwa mumiani.

mumps *n* matumbwitumbwi.

munch *vt,vi* tafuna kwa nguvu.

mundane *adj* 1 -a ulimwengu huu, -a kidunia. 2 -a kawaida sana, -a kuchosha, -siosisimua. **~ly** *adv*.

municipal *adj* -a manispaa ~ *corporation* shirika la manispaa. **~ly** *adv*. **~ity** *n* manispaa, baraza la mji.

munificent *adj* -karimu, -paji. **munificence** *n (formal) (of sth given)* wingi wa ukarimu, ukarimu mkubwa. **~ly** *adv* kwa wingi.

muniments *n (leg)* nyaraka ambazo zimehifadhiwa kama ushahidi wa madai/haki.

munition *n (usu pl, in combination)* zana za vita, vifaa vya vita (hasa mizinga, makombora) *there was no shortage of ~s* hatukupungukiwa na silaha, tulikuwa na silaha tele *vt* -pa silaha. ~ **factory** *n* kiwanda cha zana za vita/silaha.

mural *adj* -a ukutani *n* sanamu/picha iliyochorwa ukutani.

murder *vt* 1 ua (kwa kusudi). 2 haribu, vunja *n* 1 kuua (kwa kudhamiria); mauaji yasiyo na sababu. 2 *(colloq)* mateso, jambo gumu kabisa. **cry blue** ~ *(colloq)* piga mayowe/ makelele sana. **M~ will out** *(prov)* mambo hayafichiki. **~er** mwuaji. **~ess** mwuaji wa kike. **~ous** *adj* 1 -a kiuaji. 2 katili. **~ously** *adv*.

murk *n* giza, utusitusi. **~y** *adj* -eusi, -enye giza. **~ily** *adv*.

murmur *vt,vi* 1 vuma. 2 ~ **(at/against)** nung'unika. 3 nong'ona *n* 1 mvumo. 2 manung'uniko. 3 mnong'ono.

murphy *n (sl)* kiazi, mbatata.

murrain *n* 1 ugonjwa wa kuambukiza wa ng'ombe k.m. kimeta. 2 *(old use) a ~ on you!* Mungu akulaani!

muscle *n* musuli, tafu, *(sinew)* ukano. **a ~ man** pande la mtu. *he did not move a ~* alitulia tuli *vi (colloq)* ~ **in (on sth)** jishirikisha kwa nguvu. ~ **-bound** *adj* -enye musuli, kakamavu, -lioshupaa. **muscular** *adj* 1 -a musuli. 2 -enye nguvu ya mwili, -enye maungo; -a kukakakawana.

muscovite *n* mkazi wa Moscow.

muse *vt* ~ **(over/on/upon)** fikiri, tafakari, waza, taamali *n* taamuli. **musingly** *adv*. **M~** *n (GK myth)* Mungu wa kike (kati ya watoto tisa wa Zeus waliolinda na kuendeleza ushairi, nyimbo, dansi n.k.). 2 kipaji/kipawa cha mshairi.

museum *n* (jumba la) makumbusho. **a ~ piece** kifaa/kitu kinachofaa kuhifadhiwa makumbusho; *(fig)* kitu/mtu aliyepitwa na wakati.

mush[1] *n* kitu kirojorojo; *(US)* uji (wa mahindi). **~y** *adj (colloq)* lizilizi; -enye kuonyesha hisia.

mush[2] *vi* tembea katika theluji (kwa gari linalokokotwa na mbwa) *n* matembezi katika theluji na mbwa.

mushroom *n* uyoga. *(attrib) ~growth* -liokua upesi ~ *cloud* wingu la bomu la nyuklia ~ *poisoning* sumu ya uyoga *vi* 1 **go ~ing** enda kung'oa uyoga mbugani. 2 enea, sambaa upesi.

music *n* muziki *(attrib) ~ lesson/ ~teacher* somo/mwalimu wa muziki. **face the ~** kabili matatizo/ wahakiki/shutuma kijasiri. **set/put sth to ~** tunga/tia sauti (ya muziki). ~ **box** *n* kisanduku cha muziki. **~-hall** *(GB)* ukumbi wa maonyesho. **~-stand** *n* dawati la kuimbishia. ~ **stool** *n* kigoda cha mpiga kinanda.

~al *adj* -a muziki, -enye kipaji cha muziki; -a kupenda muziki. **~-chairs** mchezo wa viti na muziki. ~ **comedy** *n* 1 komedi yenye muziki. 2 sinema yenye muziki. **~ally** *adv*. **~ian** *n* mwanamuziki. **~ianship** *n* ustadi wa muziki.

musk *n* 1 maski: tezi ya kulungu itumikayo katika utengenezaji wa manukato. **~deer** *n* kulungu asiye na pembe. ~ **rat** *n* panya wa majini. 2 mimea yenye harufu ya maski. ~ **melon** tikiti. ~ **rose** waridi lenye kunukia vizuri sana. **~y** *adj* -enye harufu ya maski.

musket *n* gobori. **~eer** *n* askari wa gobori. **~ry** *n* 1 maarifa ya kupiga bunduki. 2 *(old use)* kupiga gobori.

Muslim *n* mwislamu.

muslin *n* melimeli.

musquash *n* manyoya ya panya wa majini.

muss *n (US)* vurugu, fujo *vt* ~ **(up)** vuruga, chafua, paraganya.

mussel *n* kome.

must[1] *aux v* havina budi; sharti, lazima *you ~ go* sharti uende *he ~ be honest* yampasa kuwa mwaminifu *~ you shout!* kwani mpaka upige kelele! 2 hakika *it ~ be Mary* hakika ni Mary. *n (colloq)* jambo la lazima (la kuona au kusikia) *that film is a ~* ni lazima uone filamu hiyo.

must[2] *n* maji ya zabibu.

must[3] *n* ukungu, kuvu.

must[4] *n* hasira kali *adj (of male elephant or camel)* -kali sana. **go ~** pata wazimu; *(of animals)* kasirika.

mustanche *n (US) see* **moustache**

mustachio *n (arch)* masharubu (agh. marefu).

mustang *n* farasi mwitu.

mustard *n* 1 mharadali. 2 haradali. ~ **gas** *n* sumu ya mvuke (iliyotumika katika vita kuu ya kwanza). ~ **plaster** *n* plasta ya haradali. **as keen as ~** hodari, epesi sana. **grain of ~ seed** kitu kidogo kinachoweza kukua na kuwa kikubwa sana.

muster *n* gwaride. **pass ~** faa, tosha, kubalika *vt,vi* kutana, kutanisha; piga paredi. ~ **(up) courage** jipa moyo, thubutu; ita, kusanya nguvu.

musty *adj* 1 -enye koga/kuvu, -baya; *(fig)* -liopitwa na wakati, -liopooza. **mustiness** *n.*

mutate *vt,vi* badilika, badilisha. **mutable** *adj* -enye kuweza kubadilika. **mutability** *n.* **mutation** *n* mabadiliko.

mutatis mutandis *adv (Lat)* pamoja na mabadiliko yanayofaa.

mute[1] *adj* 1 kimya. 2 *(of a person)* bubu. 3 *(of a letter in a word)* hafifu. *n* 1 bubu. 2 *(of musical instrument)* kibana sauti. *vt* punguza sauti. **~ly** *adv.*

mute[2] *vi,vt (of birds)* -nya.

mutilate *vt* kata, ondoa, haribu sehemu ya, kata kiungo cha mwili; *(cripple)* lemaza; *(remove essential part)* ondoa (toa, haribu) sehemu yenye maana sana. **mutilation** *n* kuatilika.

mutiny *n* maasi, uasi, (agh. ya mabaharia na maaskari) *vi* ~ **(against)** asi, halifu. **mutineer** *n* mwasi. **mutinous** *adj* -a kuasi, halifu.

mutt *n (sl)* 1 mtu anayekosea bila kutambua, mjinga. 2 mbwa chotara.

mutter *vt,vi* 1 semea mashavuni/ chinichini. 2 nung'unika. 3 *(of thunder)* nguruma *n* manung'uniko. **~er n** mnung'unikaji.

mutton *n* nyama ya kondoo. **as dead as ~** -liokufa kabisa. ~ **dressed as lamb** (hutumika kwa) mzee anayevaa kama kijana; mzee kijana. **~-head** *n (colloq)* mpumbavu. **~-chop** *(fig)* sharafa.

mutual *adj* -a wote wawili, -a wenyewe; -a pande mbili *~ affection* upendano *~ agreement* maafikano, mapatano; *~ help* kusaidiana; *(in cultivating, building)* ujima *~ friend* rafiki wa wote wawili. ~ **insurance company** bima ya ubia *~ wills* wasia za kuhusiana. **~ly** *adv.*

muumuu *n* gauni pana na refu/kanzu.

muzzle *n* 1 pua na mdomo wa

wanyama (uliochongoka kama wa mbwa, mbweha, n.k.) 2 *(to prevent biting)* kifungo cha mdomo. 3 *(rifle)* mdomo, kitundu (cha kasiba, mtutu). ~ **velosity** mwendo wa risasi inapoacha mtutu *vt* fungia mdomo, tilia kifungo cha mdomo (wa mbwa n.k.); *(fig)* zuia (mtu, jamii, vyombo vya habari n.k.) kutoa habari, nyamazisha vyombo vya habari.

muzzy *adj* 1 -enye wasiwasi, -a kupumbazika. 2 -enye ukungukungu, -sio wazi.

my *poss adj* -angu.

mycology *n* maikolojia: sayansi/taaluma ya kuvu.

mya(h) *n* ~ **bird** mina: kwezi wa Asia anayeigiza sauti ya binadamu.

myelitis *n (path)* uvimbe wa neva kuu.

myopia *n* mayopia: kutoweza kuona mbali. **myope** *n* mwenye mayopia.

myriad *n* ~ **(of)** wingi sana, idadi kubwa mno.

myrimidon *n* mtu (mtumishi, mtumwa) atekelezaye amri bila kusaili, kibaraka.

myrrh *n* manemane.

myself *pron* mimi mwenyewe, nafsi yangu *I live by ~* naishi (mimi) mwenyewe. *I hurt ~* nilijiumiza (mwenyewe).

mystery *n* 1 fumbo, mwujiza. 2 siri; usirisiri. 3 matambiko. ~ **piay** tamthilia juu ya maisha ya Yesu. **mystic** *adj* -a siri, -sioelezeka, -a fumbo, -a maana/nguvu ya roho *n* mchaji (mtu ajaribuye kumshiriki Mungu kwa kujitoa na kutafakari sana habari za Mungu). **mystical** *adj* = **mystic**. **mysterious** *adj* -a fumbo, -sioelezwa, -a kiujiza, ajabu. **mysteriously** *adv*. **mysticism** *n* imani/mafundisho ya kumfikia Mungu kwa tafkira. **mystify** *vt* fumba, tatanisha, tatiza, changanya.

mystique *n* 1 fumbo ustadi wa siri/pekepeke.

myth *n* 1 kisasili: hadithi inayoeleza asili ya watu, matukio n.k. 2 *(fiction)* uwongo. 3 mtu/jambo lililobuniwa. **~ical** *adj* -a visasili, -a uwongo, -a kubuniwa. **~ology** *n* 1 mithiolojia: elimu ya visasili. 2 visasili. **~ologist** *n* mwanafunzi wa mithiolojia. **~ological** *adj* -a mithiolojia, -a visasili, -a kubuniwa.

N

N,n *n* herufi ya kumi na nne katika alfabeti ya Kiingereza.

nab *vt (colloq)* kamata, shika, bamba.

nabob *n (old use)* tajiri mpenda anasa.

nacelle *n* fumbatio/funiko la injini ya ndege.

nacre *n* lulumizi. **~ous** *adj*.

nadir *n* nyayoni; *(fig)* cheo (kadiri) cha chini, kilindi, lindi, sehemu ya chini kabisa.

nag[1] *n (colloq)* farasi (agh. mzee).

nag[2] *vt,vi* ~ **(at)** sumbua, kefya. **~er** *n*.

naiad *n (Gk myth)* zimwi wa maji.

nail *n* 1 ukucha. **fight tooth and ~** pigana kufa na kupona. **~-brush** *n* brashi ya kucha; **~-file** *n* tupa ya kusugua kucha. **~-scissors** *n* mkasi wa kucha. **~-polish/-varnish** *n* rangi ya kucha. 2 msumari. **as hard as ~s** -enye afya na nguvu kabisa; -sio na huruma, katili. **hit the ~ on the head** patia hasa, gonga. **right as ~s** kweli kabisa. **(right) on the ~** mara (moja) *vt* 1 kongomea, pigilia misumari. **~ a lie (to the counter)** thibitisha/ onyesha kuwa kauli fulani ni uongo. **~ sb down (to sth)** fanya/bana mtu aseme alichodhamiria. **~ sth down** gongomea, shikiza. **~ sth up** gongomea, fungia/shikizia (dirisha mlango) misumari. 2 vutia, teka (mtu), kamata.

nainsook *n* nguo laini ya pamba.

naive *adj* 1 -nyofu, -sio na hila; -jinga; shamba. **~ly** *adv*. **~te; ~ty** *n* usungo, ushamba.

naked *adj* 1 -tupu, uchi. 2 -siokuwa na ala *a ~ sword* jambia bila ala. **see sth with the ~ eye** ona kwa macho. **the ~ truth** ukweli mtupu. **~ly** *adv*. **~ness** *n*.

namby-pamby *adj (of persons, talk)* -enye hisia za kijingajinga *n* mtu mwenye hisia za kijingajinga, asiye na msimamo.

name[1] *n* 1 jina *change of ~* kubadili jina *full ~* jina kamili *list of ~s* orodha ya majina *assumed ~* lakabu *in one's own ~* kwa uwezo wa binafsi, kwa nguvu *do sth in sb's ~* fanya kitu kwa jina la fulani. **go under the ~ of** fahamika kwa jina la *know sb by ~* fahamu mtu kwa jina lake *mention no ~s* usitaje majina. **in the ~ of** kwa jina la; kwa ajili ya; kwa amri ya. **in the ~ of God** haki ya Mungu! kwa jina la Mungu, Bismillahi. **call sb ~s** tukana/kashifu mtu. **put enter down one's ~ for** jiandikisha, andikisha jina. **not have a penny to one's ~** -tokuwa na fedha kabisa. **lend one's ~ to** ruhusu jina litumike kwa faida ya wengine. **take sb's ~ in vain** tumia vibaya/kashifu jina la mtu. **~ day** siku ya sherehe ya somo. **~ dropping** tabia ya kujikombakomba kwa majina ya wakubwa. **~ drop** *vi* tumia majina ya wakubwa kujikomba. **~ part** *n* mshikilia jina la mchezo/mwajina. **~ plate** *n* kibao cha mlangoni. **~ sake** somo. 2 sifa *have a bad ~* -wa na sifa mbaya. **win a good ~ for oneself/make one's ~** fahamika, jipatia sifa njema.3 mtu mashuhuri *vt* 1 ~ **(after/**(*US*) **for)** -pa jina *the boy was ~d after his grandfather* kijana alipewa jina la babu yake. 2 taja *~ what you want* taja unachotaka. 3 ~ **(for)** teua. **~ for an office** -pa heo. 4 ainisha *~ all animals in Serengeti* ainisha/taja majina ya wanyama wote katika Serengeti. 5 toa bei *~ your price* sema uwezo wako, utatoa ngapi. **~less** *adj* 1 bila jina. 2 -siofaa kutajwa (kwa kuwa -baya mno). 3 -sioelezeka.

namely *adv* yaani.

nankeen *n* 1 marekani (nguo ya pamba ya manjano). 2 *(pl)* **~s** suruali ya marekani.

nanny *n* yaya.

nanny-goat *n* mbuzi jike.

nap[1] *n* usingizi kidogo *have a ~* lala kidogo *vi* lala kidogo. **catch ~ping** kuta usingizini; fuma, shtusha, shtukiza.

nap[2] *n* manyoya (nywele) mafupi ya nguo (zulia) *vt* (kwa nguo) tia/ tengeneza manyoya mafupi nguoni.

nap[3] *n see* **napoleon**[2].

napalm *n* napamu: aina ya grisi (ya kutegenezea mabomu). **~ bomb** bomu la (girisi la) napamu.

nape *n* kikosi, ukosi.

napery *n (old use)* vitambaa vya mezani; vitambaa/nguo za nyumbani.
naphtha *n* nafta: mafuta mepesi yanayowaka. **~lene** *n* naftalini: dawa yenye harufu kali inayotumika kufukuza wadudu (mende, nondo n.k.).
napkin *n* **(table)** ~ 1 kitambaa cha mikono/mezani. 2 winda, nepi.
napoleon *n* 1 sarafu ya dhahabu (ya Kifaransa ya faranga 20). 2 *(also nap)* mchezo wa karata.
nappy *n (GB colloq)* **napkin**.
narcissism *n (psych)* kujihusudu, kujipenda. **narcissistic** *adj* -enye kujihusudu, -enye kujipenda.
narcissus *n (bot)* nasisa.
narcotic *adj* -a dawa ya kutia usingizi *n* dawa ya kulevya. **narcosis** *n (med)* usingizi (wa dawa).
nark[1] *n (GB sl)* mpelelezi, kachero.
nark[2] *vt (GB sl)* kera, udhi.
narrate *vt* simulia, hadithia. **narrator** *n* msimuliaji. **narration** *n* usimuliaji, masimulizi. **narrative** *n* 1 hadithi, masimulizi. 2 *(attrib)* -a kusimulia ~ *literature* fasihi ya kusimulia.
narrow *adj* 1 -embamba. 2 dogo, chache; -a shida *living in ~ circumstances* ishi maisha ya shida. 3 chupuchupu, nusura. **a ~ escape** ponea chupuchupu. **a ~ squeak** *(colloq)* nusura. 4 halisi, hasa. 5 finyu. **~-minded** *adj* -lio na mawazo finyu. **~-mindedly** *adv.* ~ **mindedness** *n.* *vt,vi* -wa/fanya kuwa embamba ~ *sth down* fanya kuwa chache. **~ly** *adv* 1 kidogo tu, kwa shida *he ~ escaped failing* kidogo tu ashindwe 2. kwa uangalifu *watch his movement ~* angalia mwenendo wake kwa uangalifu. **~s** *n* mkono wa bahari/ mto. **~ness** *n.*
narwhal *n* nyangumi mwenye pembe.
nasal *adj* -a pua, -a puani, -a mwanzi wa pua, -a nazali ~ *sounds* sauti za nazali *n* nazali. **~ize** *vt* nazalisha, puza.
nascent *adj* -enye kuanza kuota/ kuondokea, chanzo.
nasty *adj* 1 baya, -siopendeza. 2 chafu, -sio murua, fisadi. 3 -enye chuki. 4 -enye hatari. 5 balaa, wasiwasi. **~crossing** tambukareli, balaa. **nastily** *adv.* **nastiness** *n.*
natal *adj* -a kuzaliwa, kwao. **~ity** *n* kima cha uzazi.
nation *n* taifa *law of ~s* sheria ya mataifa. **~-wide** *adj* -a taifa zima. **~al** *adj* -a taifa, -a watu wote (wa taifa fulani). **N~ Anthem** wimbo wa taifa. **N~ Assembly** Bunge. **the N~al Debt** Deni la Taifa. ~ **monument** kumbukumbu ya taifa. **~park** mbuga/ eneo la burudani (la taifa). ~ **service** kipindi cha kujenga taifa; jeshi la kujenga taifa *n* mtu wa taifa fulani; raia; mwananchi. *(pl)* **~als** wananchi. **~ality** *n.* **~alism** *n* 1 utaifa; uzalendo. 2 kupigania uhuru. **~alist** *n* 1 mfuasi wa utaifa; mzalendo. 2 mpigania uhuru. *adj* ~ **alistic** -a uzalendo/ kizalendo. **~ality** *n* uraia. **~alize** *vt,vi* 1 taifisha. 2 andikisha uraia. 3 geuza/ fanya taifa. **~alization** *n.*
native *n* 1 mzaliwa, mwenyeji. 2 *(of animals, plants)* asili ya *the black mamba is a ~ of Africa* songwe ni nyoka wa asili ya Afrika *adj* 1 ~ **land** nchi ya watu/kwao ~ *law and customs* sheria ya mila/kienyeji. 2 *(inborn, natural, original)* -a maumbile, hulka. **~intelligence** akili ya kuzaliwa. 3 ~ **to** *(of plants, animals)* **the lion is ~ to Africa** simba ni wa asili ya Afrika. 4 *(of metal)* halisi.
nativity *n* uzaliwa, siku ya kuzaliwa. **the N~** Kuzaliwa kwa Yesu Kristo. **a N~ Play** tamthilia ya kuzaliwa kwa Yesu.
natter *vt (GB colloq)* 1 piga soga. 2 nung'unika.
natty *adj (colloq)* 1 nadhifu, safi, malidadi. 2 -epesi, -stadi. **nattily** *adv.*
natural *adj* 1 -a asili, -a kawaida *she has a ~ ability in languages* ana kipaji cha lugha ~ *disaster* maafa ya asilia ~ *forces/phenomena* matukio

asilia. ~ **gas** gesi asilia. ~ **history** botania na zoolojia, elimuviumbe. ~ **justice** adili ya maumbile, idili. ~ **law** sheria/kanuni asilia. ~ **philosophy** *(old use)* sayansi agh. fizikia. ~ **religion** dini asilia (ya akili ya binadamu sio ya ufunuo). ~ **resources** maliasili. ~ **science** sayansi asilia (bayolojia, kemia na fizikia). ~ **selection** uchaguzi asilia (namna wanyama na mimea inavyoweza kulinganisha maisha yao na mazingira). 2 *(of abilities etc)* -a maumbile *he's ~ orator* ana kipaji cha usemaji. 3 -a kawaida *die a ~ death* -fa tu kwa kawaida *as is ~* kama ilivyo kawaida *running comes ~ to him* kukimbia ni kawaida kwake *(music)* noti/sauti ya kawaida 4. halisi *speak in a ~ voice* tumia sauti halisi. 5 *(inevitable)* pasipo budi, sharti ~ *result (consequence, effect)* tokeo la faradhi. 6 (*arch*) haramu. ~ **child** mwanaharamu *n* 1 **a** ~ **for sth** inayofaa/stahili *he's a ~ to win the race* bila shaka atashinda mbio. 2 *(old use)* punguani. 3 *(music)* alama ya kuashiria sauti ya kawaida. **~ism** *n* 1 tanakala/uasili. 2 *(philosophy)* falsafa asili (kueleza asili ya maumbile kwa historia ya viumbe). **~ist** *n* mwanaviumbe, mtaalam achunguzaye mimea, wanyama, wadudu. **~ize** *vt,vi* 1 andikisha uraia. **~ized citizen** raia wa kuandikishwa. 2 *(of words)* tohoa. 3 zoelea (tabia za nchi nyingine), zoelea (ugenini). **~ization** *n* kuandikisha uraia. ~ **papers** cheti cha uraia. **~ly** *adv* 1 kwa asili. 2 kwa urahisi, kwa desturi, kwa kawaida. 3 *(neccesarily)* bila shaka, wazi. 4 bila kujidai.

nature *n* *(world)* ulimwenguni, viumbe vyote *laws of ~* utaratibu wa jambo la asili, kawaida ya vitu vyote. *n* 1 *(world)* ulimwenguni, viumbe vyote *laws of ~* utaratibu wa jambo la asili, kawaida ya vitu vyote. ~ **study** elimu mimea/viumbe. ~ **worship** kuabudu nguvu za asili; (*natural appearance)* umbo, sura. **call of ~** haja *let ~ take its course* acha mambo yatokee kama kawaida yake. 2 asili, nguvu asili. **~cure** matibabu asilia. **pay the debt of/pay one's debt to ~** kufa. **in the course of ~** katika hali ya asili ya maisha *it's in the ~ of things* ni tabia zisizoepukika. **be in state of ~** hali ya asili; *(joc)* uchi. 3 *(habit)* desturi, mazoea, hulka *proud by ~* -enye desturi ya kujivuna *a woman with a kind ~* mwanamke mwenye desturi njema *a man's second ~* tabia nzuri/mbaya ya mtu *it's in my ~* ni tabia yangu. **by ~** kwa kawaida. **human ~** utu (dhidi ya unyama). **good ~** ukarimu. **good-/ill-~ed** -enye tabia njema/mbaya. 4 *(kind)* jinsi, namna, aina *anything of that ~* chochote cha namna hii. 5 kama, namna ya *a request in the ~ of a command* ombi la namna ya amri.

naturism *n* (ukaaji) uchi. **naturist** *n* mkaa uchi.

naught *n (old use and poet)* **all for ~** bure, kazi bure. **set at ~** dharau, beza. **bring to ~** haribu, shinda.

naughty *adj* 1 -tundu, -tukutu. 2 *(books, magazines)* -chafu. **naughtily** *adv*. **naughtiness** *n*.

nausea *n* 1 kichefuchefu, kigegezi. 2 kuchafuka moyo, kinyaa. **nauseous** *adj* -a (kuleta) kichefuchefu; -a kuchafuka moyo. **~te** *vt* tia kichefuchefu/kigegezi; chafua moyo.

nautch *n* nachi: maonyesho ya ngoma ya wasichana wa kihindi. ~ **girl** mcheza nachi/ngoma wa kike.

nautical *adj* -a baharia, -a ubaharia. ~ **mile** mita 1852.

nave *n* ukumbi wa kanisa.

navel *n* kitovu.

navigate *vt,vi* ongoza chombo majini/angani, safiri baharini; *(fig) ~ a Bill through Parliament* shawishi Wabunge kupitisha mswada. **navigable** *adj* 1 *(of rivers, seas etc.)* -a kupitika kwa chombo. 2 *(of ships etc.)* -a kuweza kusafiri majini/angani. **navigability** *n*. **navigation** *n*

1 uongozaji vyombo majini/angani *hazard to ~* hatari kwa usafiri (wa baharini/angani). 2 usafiri wa majini/angani. **navigator** *n* 1 nahodha. 2 baharia. 3 mwongoza njia.

navvy *n (GB)* kibarua.

navy *n* uanamaji, jeshi la wanamaji. **merchant ~** uanamaji wa biashara.

nay *adv* siyo, la, a-a *n* kura ya hapana *I will not take ~* sitakubali kukataa kwako.

naval *adj* 1 -a jeshi la majini. 2 -a manowari.

Nazi *n* Nazi: mwanachama wa chama kilichoanzishwa na Hitler *adj* -a Nazi.

neap *n* **~ (tide)** maji mafu.

near[1] *adv* 1 karibu *he lives ~ me* anaishi karibu nami. **as ~** karibu *as ~ as I can remember* kama ninavyoweza kukumbuka. **~ at hand** karibu, si siku nyingi *it is ~ on/upon* ni karibu *it lasted ~ a century* imedumu karibu karne moja. 2 bado *he was ~ dead with fright* alikaribia kufa kwa woga. 3 karibu na *be nowhere ~ sth* -wa mbali na kitu. **~by** karibu na, siyo mbali.

near[2] *adj* 1 -a karibu, (kwa jamaa) -wa jamaa ya *those ~ and dear* wale wapenzi na ndugu. 2 -a upande (wa gari ulio karibu na ukingo wa barabara) -wa kushoto/kulia. 3 -sio mbali. **a ~ thing/escape** kunusurika, kuponea chupuchupu. **~ miss** bomu linalolipuka karibu. 4 *(miserly)* -a choyo, bahili, -nyimivu *vt,vi* karibia, sogea, jongea *be ~ing completion* karibia kumalizika. **~ness** *n (prep)* karibu na *she lives ~ the bank* anaishi karibu na benki. **~ly** *adv* karibu, karibukaribu. **pretty ~** takriban. **not ~** mbali na *it is ~ one o' clock* inakaribia saa saba.

neat *adj* 1 nadhifu, malidadi, -liopangwa vizuri, -enye kuvutia (kwa sura na umbo). 2 -enye tabia ya unadhifu. 3 *(of liquor)* kavu, -siozimuliwa 4. *(colloq)* erevu. **~ly** *adv*. **~ness** *n*.

neath *see* **beneath**.

nebula *n* jamii ya nyota nyingi za mbali sana. **~r** *adj*. **nebulous** *adj* -a kama wingu, -a unyenyezi, si wazi, si dhahiri.

necessary *adj* -a lazima, -a faradhi, -a sharti, -a kujuzu *it is ~ for me to go* ni lazima niende *more than ~* a lazima hasa *as he deems ~* kama aonavyo ni lazima. *n pl* **necessaries** mahitaji muhimu ya lazima. **necessarily** *adv*.

necessitate *vt* lazimisha, sababisha juzu *misunderstandings often war ~* kutoelewana mara nyingi husababisha vita.

necessitous *adj (formal)* -a umaskini, -a ufukara.

necessity *n* 1 haja, shida *he was driven to steal by ~* shida ilimsababisha aibe **for use in case of ~** itumike wakati wa shida. **be under the ~ of** lazimishwa na. **bow to ~** kubali wajibu. **~ is the mother of invention** shida huzaa maarifa. **of ~** kwa vyovyote, haiepukiki, -a lazima. **make a virtue of ~** fanya jambo kwa moyo mkunjufu. 2 kitu cha lazima/muhimu *food and drink are necessities* chakula na kinywaji ni vitu vya lazima. **necessities of life** mahitaji muhimu ya lazima kwa kuishi. 3 hali ya ufukara *in ~* katika hali ya ufukara. 4 (jambo la) lazima *is it a ~ that you go to Tanga?* ni lazima uende Tanga?

neck *n* 1 shingo **break one's ~** *(fig)* fanya kazi kwa bidii. **breath down sb's ~** -wa karibu sana na mtu, fuata nyuma, fuatafuata, ingilia mno shughuli za mtu. **get it in the ~** *(sl)* umia sana, pata machungu; karipiwa sana. **have the ~** thubutu. **risk one's ~** jihatarisha. **save one's ~** *(infl)* okoka kunyongwa; epuka adhabu/fedheha. **stick one's ~ out** jiweka hatarini, thubutu. **win/lose by a ~** shinda/ shindwa karibu sana. **up to one's ~ in** *(fig)* -wa na shughuli nyingi. **~ and crop** kabisa. **neck and ~** bega kwa bega; sawa kwa sawa. ~

of the woods *(esp. US sl)* eneo/ sehemu ya *I don't know anyone in this ~ of the woods* sifahamu mtu yeyote hapa. ~ **or nothing** kufa na kupona. 2 rasi ~ *of land* rasi . 3 *(compounds)* ~ **band** ukosi. **~cloth** tai. **~erchief** leso. **~lace** mkufu. ~ **let** mkufu. ~ **line** *(women's clothes)* mstari wa juu (wa nguo). **~tie** tai. **~wear** *(comm)* tai n.k. *vi (sl)* busianabusiana.

necro *(pref)* -a kuhusu mauti. ~ **mancy** *n* ufundi wa kuwasiliana na mizimu (ili kufahamu mambo ya baadaye). **~mancer** *n*. **~polis** *n (esp. ancient)* makaburini, mava(ni). **~psy** *n* (pia **necroscopy**) uchunguzi wa maiti. **~sis** *n* kuoza kwa sehemu ya mwili.

nectar *n* 1 *(myth)* kinywaji cha miungu ya Kigiriki. 2 mbochi, nekta: majimaji matamu katika maua; kinywaji kitamu sana.

nectarine *n* nektarini: aina ya tini.

nee *adj* -a kuzaliwa *Mrs Brown ~ Robinson*, Bibi Brown aliyekuwa Robinson.

need *n* 1 ~ **(for)** haja (ya). **if ~ be** ikiwa lazima, ikibidi. **stand in ~ of** hitaji *there is no ~ for me to do this* hakuna haja ya mimi kufanya hivi *there is no ~ to hurry* hakuna haja ya kuharakisha. 2 mahitaji *my ~ s are few* mahitaji yangu ni machache. 3 *(poverty)* umaskini, ufukara; ukata. **a friend in ~ is a friend in deed** *(prov)* akufaaye kwa dhiki ndiye rafiki *vt,vi* 1 hitaji, taka *I ~ it* nakihitaji. 2 lazimika, -wa jambo la lazima *he ~ not come* si lazima aje *you ~ not have spoken* haikuwa lazima useme. **~ful** *adj*. **do the ~** fanya kinachohitajika; toa pesa (inayohitajika). **~fully** *adv*. **~less** *adj* -sio -a lazima, -a bure. **~less to say** ni wazi kwamba, inajulikana kwamba. **~lessly** *adv*. **~s** *adv* lazima, sharti. hakuna budi. **~s must when the devil drives** *(prov)* hali yatulazimisha. **~y** *adj* maskini.

needle *n* 1 sindano, *(packing)* shazia, *(magnetic)* dira *thread a ~* tunga sindano. **look for a ~ in a haystack** *(prov)* tafuta kitu kisichoweza kupatikana/ kuonekana. **as sharp as a ~** -enye akili kali, epesi. ~ **woman** mshonaji (mwanamke). **~craft/work** *n* ushonaji. 2 *(of wood etc)* kipande chembamba. 3 majani ya msonobari. 4 *(of mountain etc)* ncha. 5 *(of record player)* sindano. 6 **the ~** *(sl)* mhemko *give sb the ~* chokoza *vt* 1 shona. 2 *(fig)* chokoza.

ne'er *adv (poetic)* asilani, kamwe. **~-d/o-well** *n* mtu wa bure, mpotovu.

nefarious *adj* -ovu, -baya sana. **~ness** *n* ubaya, uovu. **~ly** *adv*.

negate *vt* 1 kana. kanusha. 2 tangua. **negation** *n* 1 kukana, kukanusha. 2 ukosekanaji (wa sifa au maana).

negative *n* 1 kukana *he replied in the ~* alikana/kataa.2 *(of photograph)* negativu. 3 *(gram)* kanusho.4 *(maths)* ukasi *adj* 1 -a kukana, -a kukanusha. 2 hasi ~ *number* namba hasi ~ *attitude* mwelekeo hasi ~ *criticism* uhakiki/maoni hasi. **the ~ pole** ncha hasi *vt* 1 kanusha. 2 *(render useless)* tangua. **~ly** *adv*. **negativism** *n* ukanaji.

neglect *vt* 1 -totunza, -toangalia, -tojali. 2 *(slight)* telekeza. **~ed child** mtoto aliyetelekezwa. 3 *(do carelessly)* zembea, puuza, purukusha *I ~ed to do that* nilipuuzia kufanya hivyo *n* 1 kupuuza, uzembe, upurukushani. 2 hali ya kutotunzwa. **~ful** *adj* -vivu, -zembe, sahaulifu. **~fuless** *n* uzembe, usahaulifu. **negligence** *n* uzembe, upurukushani. **gross ~** uzembe wa hali ya juu. **negligent** *adj* -zembe, -enye upurukushani *be ~ of sth* zembea jambo. **negligently** *adv*. **negligible** *adj* -sio muhimu; dogo sana.

neglige,negligee *n* vazi (la kike) la kulala; vazi pana lisilo rasmi.

negotiate *vt* 1 ~ **with sb** jadiliana na mtu, fanya shauri ili kuafikiana. 2 *(of money)* badili kwa fedha. 3 ~ *sth (with sb)* patana (juu ya). 4 pita.

negotiable *adj* 1 -a kuweza kujadiliwa *that dispute is* ~ ule ugomvi waweza kujadiliwa. 2 -a kubadilishika *the cheque is not* ~ cheki haibadilishiki. 3 *(of road etc)* -a kupitika *the bridge is* ~ daraja linapitika. **negotiator** *n* mpatanishi.

Negro *n* Mnegro (hasa anayeishi Marekani) *adj* -a Kinegro.

Negress *n* mwanamke mweusi. **Negroid** *adj* -a watu weusi; -a Kinegro, a kama watu weusi.

neigh *vi* lia (kama farasi) *n* mlio (wa farasi).

neighbour *n* jirani, mtu akaaye karibu *vt,vi* ~ **(on/upon)** -wa jirani, kuwa karibu. **~hood** *n* ujirani; (watu waishio katika) eneo (linaloongelewa) *that thief is feared by the whole* ~ mwizi yule anaogopwa na watu wote wa eneo lile *in the ~hood of* upande wa, karibu ya. **~ly** *adj* -a ujirani mwema, karimu; -ema. **~liness** *n*.

neither *adj pron (used with a sing n or pron)* si....o ote, si.... wala, wala *of the two* ~ *man lived here* kati ya hawa wawili hapana hata mmoja aliyeishi hapa. **~.... nor** si.... wala *I can* ~ *eat nor drink* siwezi kula wala kunywa ~ *Martin nor Selemani came* hakuja Martin wala Selemani. 2 *(after a negative clause etc)* wala, hata *I'm not going* ~ *is she* siendi mimi wala yeye.

Nelly *n (only in)* **not on your** ~ *(GB sl)* thubutu.

nemcon *adv* bila kupingwa; kwa kauli moja.

nemesis *n* 1 kudra; adhabu ya haki (iliyostahili kwa kosa lililofanywa); mshindani/adui asiyeshindika. 2 **N~** mungu wa kike wa kisasi.

neo- *(pref)* -pya, mamboleo. **~-colonialism** *n* ukoloni mamboleo.

neologism (*also* **neology**) *n* 1 neno jipya. 2 kuunda/kutumia maneno mapya.

neolithic *adj* -a neolithi, -a enzi ya mawe. ~ **man** *n* mtu wa neolithi/enzi ya mawe.

neon *n (chem)* neoni. ~ **sign** *n* tangazo la neoni. ~ **light** *n* taa ya neoni.

neophyte *n* muumini mpya (wa dini, imani).

neoplasm *n (path)* tezi, uvimbe.

nephew *n* mpwa (wa kiume); mtoto (wa kiume) wa kaka/dada.

nephritis *n* uvimbe wa/kuvimba kwa mafigo.

ne plus ultra *n (Lat)* kikomo, kiwango cha mwisho, kilele (cha kitu, jambo), upeo.

nepotism *n* upendeleo wa ndugu (agh katika kuajiri).

Neptune 1 *(Roman)* (mungu wa) bahari. 2 Neptuni: sayari mojawapo iliyo mbali sana na jua.

nerve *n* 1 neva. ~ **cell** *n* seli ya neva. ~ **centre** *n* fungu la seli neva; *(fig)* kuni. 2 *(pl)* wahaka, hali ya wasiwasi; msukosuko *in a state of ~s* katika hali ya wasiwasi. **get on one's** ~ sumbua, kera. **war of ~s** *n* vita vya kuumbuana/kuvunja moyo jitihada za kumshinda mshindani kwa kumvunja moyo. **~-racking** -enye kutisha/kuogofya sana; -enye kusumbua (hasa kihisi) *suffer from ~s* -wa na wahaka. 3 ujasiri, ushupavu *a man of* ~ mtu shupavu. **have the ~ to do sth** -wa na ujasiri; thubutu *he had the ~ to call me a liar* alithubutu kuniita mwongo *have a ~ (colloq)* thubutu **lose/regain one's** ~ ogopa/pata moyo. 4 *(old use)* ukano. **strain every ~ to do sth** jitahidi sana, fanya juu chini. 5 mbavu za kati za jani *vt* ~ **oneself for sth/to do sth** jipa moyo; kusanya nguvu. **~less** *adj* 1 legevu, dhaifu. 2 siotishika, tulivu. **~lessly** *adv*. **~lessness** *n*.

nervous *adj* -1 -a neva ~ *system* mfumo wa neva *a* ~ *breakdown* fadhaa; kuchanganyikiwa, kuharibikiwa akili. 2 -enye wahaka, -oga. 3 *(tense)* -enye wasiwasi, liokacha. **~ness** *n* wasiwasi, woga; kiherehere.

nervy *adj* 1 *(GB) (colloq)* -enye

wasiwasi/mfadhaiko. 2 *(sl)* -enye kudiriki, enye ukavu wa macho, fidhuli.

nescience *n (formal)* umbumbumbu. **nescient** *adj* -jinga *be ~ of sth* -tojua kitu fulani.

ness *n* rasi.

nest *n* kiota, tundu. **foul one's own ~** jiaibisha, nyea kambi. **~ egg** *n* akiba ya fedha (kwa matumizi ya baadaye). 2 mahali pa kupumzikia, starehe. 3 mkusanyiko wa vitu vya aina moja vinavyoingiliana (hasa, kasha meza n.k.). 4 *(fig)* maficho, kivuli *a ~ of crime* maficho ya majambazi *vi* 1 tengeneza/tumia kiota. **go ~ing** tafuta viota vya ndege (ili kuchukua mayai). **~le** *vt,vi* 1 ~ **(down)** tulia, starehe, jituliza (mahali pa starehe/ kupumzikia). 2 ~ **up (against/to)** jikumbatiza. 3 pakata, fumbata. **~ling** *n* kinda; *(chicken)* kifaranga.

net[1] *n* 1 wavu; kimia; jarife *mosquito ~* chandarua. 2 *(fig)* mtego. 3 ~ **ball** *n* mpira wa pete, netiboli. **the ~s** *(cricket)* sehemu ya mazoezi. **~work** *n* mistari ipitanayo, tandabui, mfumo mtandao. **spy ~work** mfumo wa upelelezi *vt* 1 vua kwa wavu. 2 funika kwa wavu. **~ting** *n* 1 wavu. 2 kutega wavu.

net[2], **nett** *adj ~ price* bei halisi (haipunguziki). ~ **gain/profit** faida halisi, faida tupu *vt* pata faida halisi.

nether *(arch)* -a chini *the ~ world* ahera, jahanamu; *(joking style)* ~ **garments** suruali. **~most** *adj* chini sana.

Netherlands *n* Uholanzi.**Netherlander n** Mholanzi.

nettle *n* upupu. ~ **rash** *n* mwasho wa upupu *vt* udhi *he was ~d by my words* maneno yangu yalimuudhi.

neural *-adj* -a neva, -a mshipa wa fahamu. **~gia** *n* ugonjwa wa neva (hasa kichwani).

neurasthenia *n* uchovu wa neva, udhaifu uletwao na uchovu wa neva. **neurasthenic** *adj n.*

neuritis *n* uvimbe wa neva.

neurology *n* nyurolojia; elimu ya neva. **neurological** *adj* -a nyurolojia. **neurologist** *n* mtaalam wa nyurolojia.

neurosis *n* fadhaa, kuchanganyikiwa, jakamoyo. **neurotic** *adj* -enye fadhaa/jakamoyo, -a kuathiri mfumo wa neva *n* mtu mwenye fadhaa/ jakamoyo.

neuter *(gram) adj* 1 -sio na jinsia; *(of verb)* -siochukua shamirisho. 2 *(of plants)* -siokuwa na pistili wala stameni *n* tasa; mnyama aliyehasiwa *vt* hasi.

neutral *adj* 1 -siosaidia upande wowote katika vita. 2 -siopendelea upande wowote. 3 -sio na sifa zinazobainika *I am ~* mimi simo *a ~ person* mtu asiyependelea upande wowote. 4 ~ **gear** gia huru, sioinjikwa. **~ity** *n* kutosaidia upande wowote katika vita *declaration of ~* tamko la kutokuwa upande wowote. **~ize** *vt* tangua, batilisha, zimua *~ a poison* zimua sumu.2 -tokuwa upande wowote. **~ization** *n.*

neutron *n* nutroni.

never *adv* 1 asilani, kamwe hata *she ~ goes to dances* haendi densini asilani *it has ~ been used* haijawahi kutumika *~ despair* usikate tamaa kamwe *~ ceasing ~-ending adj* -siokwisha *~-failing adj* -sioshindwa. **~-more** *adv* -si tena kabisa *~-to-be forgotten adv* -siosahaulika. 2 hata kidogo *~ slept a wink last night* sikulala hata kidogo. 3 *(phrases).* **well I ~ (did)!** lahaula. **n ~ mind!** usijali. **the n~ n ~ land** nchi iliyobuniwa. **on the ~- ~** kwa kubandika.

nevertheless *adv* hata hivyo.

new *adj* 1 -pya *nothing ~* hakuna (lolote) jipya. ~ **moon** mwezi mwandamo. ~ **Year** Mwaka Mpya. ~ **Testament** Agano Jipya *start/lead a ~ life* anza maisha mapya. ~ **World** Amerika *~ trial* kusikilizwa upya. 2 *(strange, novel)* -geni *she is ~ to me* yeye ni mgeni kwangu. **~from**

kutoka juzijuzi *a worker ~ from school* mfanyakazi aliyetoka shuleni juzijuzi. 3 *(modern)* -a siku hizi, -a kisasa. **a ~ fashion** mtindo wa kisasa *adv* karibuni *~-born adj* -liozaliwa karibuni *a ~born baby* mtoto aliyezaliwa karibuni *~-built adj* -liojengwa karibuni, -pya *~-coinedadj* -lioanzishwa karibuni; -liobuniwa karibuni *~-coined word* neno jipya. **~comer** *n* mgeni (asiye mwenyeji). **~ found** *adj* -liopatikana hivi karibuni. **~-laid** *(of an egg)* -liotagwa karibuni. **~ly** *adv* karibuni *a ~ married couple* waliooana karibuni. **~-weds** maharusi. **~ness** *n*.

newel n nguzo/mhimili a katikati ya ngazi.

news *n pl* 1 habari (za mambo yaliyotokea karibuni), taarifa. **the n ~s** *(on the radio)* taarifa ya habari *break the ~* toa habari (hasa ya msiba) *~ of death* tanzia *he is in the ~* habari zake zimechapishwa gazetini/ zimetangazwa redioni. **no ~ is good ~** *(prov)* ukisikia kimya jua ni shwari. **~agent** *n* mwuuza magazeti. **~agency** shirika la habari. **~cast** *n* taarifa ya habari. **~caster** *n* mtangazaji wa taarifa ya habari. **~-boy** *n* mvulana mwuuza magazeti (kwa kuyatembeza mitaani). **~ letter** *n* kijarida. **~monger** *n* mdakuzi, mmbea, mzushi. **~ paper** *n* gazeti *popular ~paper* gazeti pendwa. **~ paper man** *n* mwandishi wa magazeti/habari. **~-print** *n* karatasi za magazeti. **~reel** *n* filamu ya taarifa ya habari. **~-room** *n* 1 chumba cha habari (redioni n.k.). 2 chumba cha kusomea magazeti, maktaba. **~-sheet** *n* gazeti rahisi. **~-stand** kibanda cha kuuzia magazeti. **~less** *adj* -sio na habari. **~y** *adj* -enye michapo, -enye habari za mambo yaliyotokea.

newt *n* mnyama mdogo wa majini kama mjusi.

Newtonian *adj* linalohusiana na *Newton n* mfuasi wa Newton.

next *adj* 1 ~ **(to sth/sb)** -enye kufuata; kando *their house is ~ to ours* nyumba yao inafuata nyumba yetu *the ~ best (thing)* kitu kinachofuata kwa ubora *~ door* nyumba ya pili. **~ door to** *(fig)* inayokaribia. **~ but one** -nayofuata baada ya. 2 *(of time)* wakati -jao *~ week* wiki ijayo *in the ~ few days* siku chache zijazo *the ~ day* kesho yake *adv* baada ya hapo; halafu *what will you do ~?* utafanya nini baada ya hapo *come ~* fuata.

nexus *n* 1 kiungo. 2 mfululizo.

nib *n* nibu.

nibble *vt,vi* 1 ~ **(at)** nyofoa. 2 *(fig)* onyesha kuvutiwa (bila kutoa uamuzi) *n* unyofozi.

nice *adj* 1 -zuri, -a kupendeza; -ema, -enye hisani *a ~ fellow!* mtu mwema *it was ~ of you* nakushukuru kwa wema wako, ulifanya vema sana. 2 nyeti, -enye kuhitaji uangalifu. 3 *(ironic)* -gumu, -baya. 4 -a machagu. 5 -enye makini; -enye uangalifu. **~ly** *adv* 1 kwa vizuri; kwa wema. **to a ~** barabara, sawasawa kabisa. 2 *(colloq)* vizuri sana; sawa, barabara. **~ness** *n*. **~ty** *n* 1 usahihi. 2 *(pl)* **~ties** undani, mambo madogo madogo.

niche *n* 1 kishubaka, pembe. **have a ~ in the temple of fame** -wa na mafanikio yasiyosahaulika. 2 *(fig)* mahali pafaapo *make a ~ for oneself* pata sehemu inayofaa.

nick[1] *n* 1 (alama ya) mtai. 2 **in the ~ of time** wakati ufaao hasa. 3 *(sl)* **in the ~** korokoroni, jela *vt* 1 kata; tia mtai 2. *(GB) (sl)* iba *he ~ed my pen* aliniibia peni yangu.

nick[2] *n (sl) (only in)* **in good/poor ~** katika hali nzuri/mbaya.

nickel *n* 1 nikeli. 2 *(coin)* sarafu ya Marekani yenye thamani ya senti 5 *vt* chovya nikeli.

nicknack *see* **knick-knack**.

nickname *n* jina la utani, lakabu *vt* -pa jina la utani.

nicotine *n* nikotini; sumu iliyo katika tumbaku.

niece *n* mpwa (wa kike); mtoto (wa kike) wa kaka/dada.

niff *n (GB sl, dial)* mnuko. **~y** *adj (sl)* -enye mnuko.

nifty *adj (sl)* 1 maridadi, -zuri. 2 -enye mnuko. 3 -epesi, hodari.

niggard *n* mchoyo, bahili. **~ly** *adj* -a chonyo, -enye kutolewa roho upande. **~liness** *n* ubahili, uchoyo.

niggle *vi* shughulikia mambo madogo madogo; lalamikia mambo madogo madogo. **niggling** *adj* -dogodogo.

nigh *adv prep (arch and poet)* karibu *draw ~* karibia.

night *n* 1 usiku. **~ after night** kila usiku (uchao). **all ~ (long)** usiku kucha. **~ and day** usiku na mchana, kutwa kucha. **at ~** usiku. **by ~** wakati/majira ya usiku. **get a ~ off** pumzika kazi ya usiku. **last ~** usiku wa (kuamkia) leo. **to~** leo usiku, usiku huu. **have a bad ~** lala vibaya. **good ~!** alamsiki. **have a ~ out** enda kutembea jioni. **make a ~ of it** kesha kwenye starehe. **~ into day** fanya kazi ya mchana usiku. **work ~s** fanya kazi usiku. 2 *(compounds)* **~ bell** *n* kengele ya kumwamshia daktari usiku. **~-bird** *n* bundi; mtu atembeaye usiku, mzururaji. **~ cap** *n* kofia ivaliwayo usiku; *(usu alcoholic)* kinywaji cha kulalia. **~club** klabu ya usiku. **~-dress, ~ie, ~y** *n (colloq)* vazi (la kike) la usiku. **~ fall** *n* kuchwa, utusitusi. **~ jar** *n* upwaju. **~life** starehe za usiku. **~-light** *n* taa ndogo iwakayo kucha. **~-long** *adj* -a usiku kucha. **~mare** *n* jinamizi. **~ safe** *n* kisanduku cha benki (cha kuwekea amana usiku). **~-school** *n* masomo ya jioni. **~-shade** *n* mtunguja. **~shirt** shati refu (la kiume) la kuvaa usiku. **~-soil** *n* choo kizolewacho usiku. **~-time** *n* usiku. **~-watch** *n* mkeshaji; zamu ya kukesha. **in the ~-watches** wakati wa mkesha. **~-watchman** mlinzi wa usiku, korokoroni. **~ly** *adj,adv* -a usiku, -a kila usiku; kila usiku.

nightingale *n* ndege aina ya kinega.

nihilism *n* kano: ukataaji wa dini na sheria za ubinadamu zote. **nihilist** *n*. **nihilistic** *adj*.

nil *n* bila, sifuri *the result of the game was ~* matokeo ya mchezo yalikuwa bila.

Nilotic *adj* -a Niloti; -a mto Nile na kandokando zake.

nimble *adj* 1 -epesi, hodari (-a kazi), elekevu. 2 *(of the mind)* kali, epesi. **nimbly** *adv*. **~ness** *n*.

nimbus *n* 1 wingu la mvua. 2 halo: uzingo wa mtakatifu.

niminy-piminy *adj* -a kujidaidai; -a kujifanya/kujitendekeza.

nincompoop *n* mpumbavu, punguani, fala.

nine *adj, n* tisa *a girl of ~* msichana wa miaka tisa. **~ days' wonder** kitu kipya kivutiacho na kusahaulika mara. **dressed up to the ~s** -liovaa kilimbwende, -liovaa malidadi sana. **~ times out of ten** mara nyingi, karibu kila mara. **ninth** *adj,n* sehemu ya tisa; -a tisa. **the ninth hour** dakika ya mwisho. **~ to five,** saa (za kawaida) za kazi. **~teen** *adv,n* kumi na tisa. **a boy of ~teen** mvulana wa miaka 19. **(talk) ~teen to dozen** sema bila kunyamaza, bubujika. **~teenth** *adj,n* -a kumi na tisa; sehemu ya kumi na tisa. **~ty** *adj,n* tisini. **~ty times out of a hundred** karibu kila mara. **the ~ties** miaka ya tisini. **~ fold** *adj, adv* (-a) mara tisa.

ninny *n* mpumbavu, zuzu.

nip *n* 1 mminyo, mfinyo, mbinyo. 2 mkato. 3 pegi (ya kileo) *vt,vi* 1 minya, finya, binya, nyakua. 2 *(of dog)* uma. 3 *(destroy)* haribu. **~ sth in the bud** haribu mwanzoni, zuia maendeleo. 4 *(colloq)* **~ in (of car)** ingia; *(of dress)* punguza upana. **~ along** enda upesi. **~ping** *adj* kali, baridi sana. **~py** *adj (colloq)* 1 epesi. **look ~** fanya chapu chapu. 2 *(GB)* baridi sana.

nipper *n* 1 *(of crab)* gando, gendi. 2 *(pl) (colloq) (forceps)* kibano, koleo. 3 *(GB colloq)* kitoto.

nipple *n* 1 chuchu. 2 kitu chenye umbo la chuchu.

Nipponese *adj* -a Japani.

nirvana *n (in Buddhism)* nirvana: hali ya kujisahau binafsi kwa kuungana na Mungu.
nisi *n (Lat,leg)* isipokuwa. **decree** ~ amri halali isipokuwa pale inapokuwa na sababu za kubatilishwa katika muda uliowekwa.
nit *n* yai la chawa, utitiri, n.k.
nitrate *n* naitreti.
nitre/niter *n* shura. **nitrous** adj -a (kama) shura.
nitric *adj* -a naitrojeni, - enye naitrojeni. **nitrochalk** *n* mbolea ya kukuzia majani. **nitrogen** *n* naitrojeni. **nitrogenous** *adj* -enye naitrojeni, -a naitrojeni.
nitro glycerine n baruti kali.
nitty-gritty *n.* **the** ~ *(colloq)* kiini, masuala ya msingi.
nitwit/nit *n (colloq)* punguani. **~ted** *adj.*
nix *n (sl)* hapana, la *say ~ to* kataa.
no *adj* 1 hapana, hakuna, hamna *there is ~ food* hakuna chakula *I have ~ money* sina pesa ~ *doubt* hapana shaka ~ *mistake* hapana kosa, si kosa *it's ~ distance* si mbali *he had ~ luck* hakuwa na bahati *he is ~ fool* yeye si mpumbavu. 2 marufuku ~ *entrance* marufuku kuingia ~ *smoking* usivute sigara. ~ **nonsense!** hapana upuuzi! 3 *(in phrases)* **it's ~ go** *(colloq)* haiwezekani. **be ~ good/use** -wa bure. **be ~ wonder (that)** -tokuwa jambo la ajabu (kwamba). **in ~ time** haraka sana, mara moja. **~-go-area** *n* eneo ambapo polisi/jeshi hawawezi kuingia. **~-man's-land** *n* eneo katikati ya majeshi mawili ya maadui; eneo huru *rain or ~ rain* mvua inyeshe isinyeshe. 4 *(with -ing) there is ~ mistaking what was meant* haiwezekani kukosea ni jambo gani lilimaanishwa/lilikusudiwa *adv* 1 *(used with comp)* zaidi *he's ~ older* hajazeeka zaidi ~ *fewer than a hundred* haipungui mia moja *he will come ~ more* haji tena *whether or ~* kwa vyovyote *whether or ~ you will come* upende usipende utakuja *n* kukataa; hapana *I won't take ~ for an answer* hakuna kukataa *the ~es have it* wapingaji wameshinda *(particle)* hapana, la *are you tired? No* umechoka? hapana. **~body/~one** *(pron)* hakuna, si mtu *~body is there* hapana mtu *~body knows* hakuna ajuaye *a mere ~ body* mtu wa bure. ~ **how** *adv (colloq)* kwa njia yoyote ile.
nob[1] *n (sl)* mkubwa, tajiri, kizito, mtu wa hadhi (ya juu).
nob[2] *n (sl)* kichwa.
nobble *vt* 1 lewesha (farasi) ili asishinde mbio. 2 *(colloq)* pata kitu kwa ujanja.
noble *adj* 1 -a kilodi; *(Islam)* sharifu. 2 adili, -enye tabia nzuri *n (also)* **~man** *n* lodi; *(Islam)* sharifu; mtu mwenye cheo (daraja) kikubwa. **nobly** *adv* vema, vizuri, kwa uadilifu.
nobility *n* 1 ulodi; *(Islam)* usharifu. 2 *(character)* wema, uadilifu, uungwana. 3 *(class)* malodi, waungwana; *(Islam)* masharifu.
noctambulist *n* mtembea usingizini. **noctambulism** *n.*
nocturnal *adj* -a usiku.
nocturne *n* 1 *(music)* muziki wa polepole/wa kulaza. 2 mchoro unaohusu mambo ya usiku.
nod *vt,vi* 1 ~ **(to/at)** kubali/amkia kwa kichwa. 2 ~ **(off)** sinzia; angusha kichwa kwa kusinzia. **Homer sometimes ~s** *(prov)* hata mtu mashuhuri hufanya kosa. 3 ashiria kwa kichwa *n* 1 ishara ya kichwa. 2 **the Land of N~** usingizi. 3 **on the ~** *(US sl)* kwa mkopo.
noddle *n (colloq)* kichwa.
nodule *n* kinundu, kifundo, kivimbe. **nodular** *adj.*
Noel *n* Noeli, Krismasi.
nog *n* kileo (agh chenye mayai).
noggin *n* 1 kipimo kidogo (agh robo painti) cha pombe. 2 *(sl)* kichwa.
noise *n* 1 sauti, mlio, kishindo, uvumi. **make a ~ (about sth)** lalamika, piga

kelele. **make a ~ in the world** wa mashuhuri, pata umaarufu. 2*(uproar)* makelele, zahama. **a big ~** mtu maarufu *vt* ~ **sth abroad** tangaza, eneza habari. **noisy** *adj* -a makelele, -a kishindo kikubwa/ghasia. **noisily** *adv* kwa kelele, sauti. **~less** *adj* pasipo mlio/sauti; -a kimya. **~lessness** *n* ukimya.

noisome *adj* -a kuchukiza, -a kutia kinyaa, -a kukirihi.

nomad *n* mhamahamaji. **~ic** *adj* -nayohamahama. **~ism** *n* kuhamahama, uhamahamaji.

nom de plume *n* lakabu.

nomenclature *n* (mfumo wa) istilahi, utaratibu wa majina; kutia majina.

nominal *adj* 1 dogo ~ *consideration* malipo chembe ~ *rent* kodi ndogo ~ *value* thamani ndogo; thamani iliyotajwa, thamani bayana. 2 -a jina tu; iliyotajwa ~ *capital* rasilimali iliyotajwa, rasilimali bayana ~ *plaintiff* mdai wa jina tu. 3 si halisi. 4 *(gram)* -a nomino. **~ly** *adv* kwa jina, kwa maneno tu.

nominate *vt* ~ **sb (for)** pendekeza (jina la mtu kwa cheo/kazi, n.k.). 2 ~ **sb (to)** teua. **nominator** *n* mpendekezaji. **nomination** n1 pendekezo ~ *paper* hati ya mapendekezo. 2 uteuzi. **nominee** *n* 1 mtu aliyependekezwa. 2 mteule/mteuliwa.

nominative *n (gram)* -a kiima.

non- *(pref)* si, sio, -tokuwa. **~-alcoholic** *adj* sio kileo **~-alignment** *n* kutofungamana (na upande wowote). ~ **-appearance** *adj* kutoonekana (tena). ~ **aggression** *n* kutotaka ugomvi/vita, n.k. ~ **aggression pact** makubaliano ya kuzuia vita. **~-combatant** *n* mtu (agh mwanajeshi) asiyepigana vitani. **~-commissioned** *adj (esp. milit)* ofisa wa cheo cha chini. **~-committal** *adj* -siojihusisha (na upande wowote). ~ **-compliance** *n* kutoafiki, kutotekeleza. **~-conductor** *n* kisichopitisha umeme. **~conformist** *n* mtu asiyefuata desturi za jamii. ~ **conformity** *n* kutokukubaliana na kanuni za jamii. **~-consummation** *n* kutokamilisha ~- *of marriage* kutokamilisha ndoa (kwa kujamiiana). ~ **-contagious** *adj* sio ambukiza. ~ **-contentious** *adj* sio na ugomvi. **~-operation** *n* kutoshirikiana. **~essential** *adj* -sio ya lazima; -sio ya muhimu. **~-event** *n* *(colloq)* mpango uliovurugika. **~-existence** *n* kutokuwepo. **~-existent** *adj* -siokuwepo. -sio na uhai. **~-fiction** *n* maandishi yasiyo ya kubuni. **~-flammable** *adj* -sioshika moto. **~-intervention**, **~-interference** *n* kutoingilia. **~-moral** *adj* -siokuwa -a maadili. **~-observance** *n* kutofuata sheria/masharti. **~-payment** *n* kutolipa. **~-performance** *n* kutotimiza, kutotekeleza. **~-resident** *adj* -siomkazi *n* asiyeishi hotelini, n.k. **~-skid** *adj (of tyres)* -sioserereka. **~-smoker** *n* asiyevuta sigara; behewa la abiria wasiovuta sigara. **~-stick** *adj* -sionata. **~-stop** *adj,adv* bila kusimama, moja kwa moja. **~-union** *adj* 1 -siojiunga na chama/jumuia ya wafanyakazi. 2 -tofuata kanuni za chama/jumuiya. **~-violence** *n* kutotumia nguvu, kutumia njia za amani. **~acceptance** *n* kutokubali. **~-access** *n* kutofikia, kutoingilia. **~-affiliated** *adj* -siyoungana na ingine (k.m. kampuni, shirika).

nonage *n (leg)* utoto.

nonagenarian *n* mzee mwenye umri wa miaka kati ya 89 na 100 *adj* -enye miaka kati ya 89 na 100.

nonce *n (arch, or lit) (only in)* **for the ~** kwa wakati huu tu. **~-word** *n* neno linaloundwa kwa ajili ya muktadha maalumu.

nonchalant *adj* tepetevu; -sioonyesha kupenda; -sio na raghba, -sio na papara. **~ly** *adv.* **nonchalance** *n.*

non compos mentis *(Lat) (leg)* -sio na akili timamu; punguani; *(colloq)* -liochanganyikiwa.

nondescript *n,adj (person or thing)* -sioainishika, -sioelezeka vizuri, -a hivi hivi.

none *(pron)* 1 bila, kutokuwepo, hakuna ~ *of us* hakuna kati yetu. ~ **the less** hata hivyo. ~ **but** hakuna mwingine isipokuwa. ~ **other than** -enyewe *it was ~ other than the chairman* alikuwa ni mwenyekiti mwenyewe. 2 acha! ~ *of that* acha! ~ *of your stupidity* acha upumbavu wako *adv* sio, hapana *I am ~ the wiser for your information* sikunufaika na taarifa yako. **there are ~ so deaf as those who will not hear** *(prov)* wanaokataa kusikiliza ndio viziwi.

nonentity *n* 1 mtu asiye na hadhi, mtu duni. 2 hobelahobela 3. jambo la kuwazika tu, ndoto.

nonesuch, nonsuch *n* mtu/kitu kisicho kifani.

non-pareil *adj, n (formal)* teule, bila kifani, -sio kifani (kwa kuwa zuri, bora).

nonplus *vt* duwaza, pumbaza, shangaza.

nonsense *n* upuuzi. **nonsensical** *adj* -sio na maana; -a upuuzi.

non-sequitur *n (Lat) (logic)* hitimisho lisilofuata mantiki.

noodle[1] *n* baradhuli, mpumbavu.

noodle[2] *n* nudo: chakula aina ya tambi.

nook *n* pembe, kipembe; kificho, upenu.

noon *n* adhuhuri, saa sita mchana. **~day; ~tide** *n* adhuhuri.

no-one, no one *see* **nobody**.

noose *n* tanzi, kitanzi, shalaka, kishwara. **put one's head in the ~** *(fig)* (jisababisha) kukamatwa, jifunga mwenyewe *vt* tega ~ *a cord* fanya kitanzi katika kamba.

nope *int (sl)* la, hasha!

nor[1] *conj* wala *neither... nor* si... wala *neither Daudi ~ Abdallah* si Daudi wala Abdalla ~ *must we forget* wala tusisahau.

nor[2] *(pref)* **north**.

Nordic *n, adj* watu wa Kinodiki; -a nchi za Skandinavia (Denmark, Finland, Norway na Sweden).

norm *n* 1 kaida, kawaida, kanuni, cheo cha kawaida. 2 ngwe, kiwango. **~ative** *adj* -a kusanifisha, sanifu.

normal *adj* -a kawaida, desturi, -a siku zote. **a ~ school** chuo cha ualimu *n* kawaida. **~ly** *adv*. **~ity, ~cy** *n*. **~ize** *vt* fanya kawaida. **~ization** *n*.

Norse *n* lugha ya Norway *adj* -a Norway.

north *n* 1 kaskazini. **the ~** upande wa kaskazini, nchi za Kaskazini. 2 *(attrib)* -a kaskazini *n~ pole* ncha ya kaskazini ~ *winds* kaskazi. **~east** *n* kaskazini mashariki. **~west** *n* kaskazini magharibi. **the N~-West Passage** *n* njia ya baharini kutoka Atlantiki mpaka Pasifiki (kupitia Kaskazini ya Kanada na Alaska). **~-easter** *n* upepo kutoka kaskazini mashariki. **~-eastern** *adj* -a kaskazini mashariki. **~-eastward** *adj* (-a) kuelekea kaskazini mashariki. **~-western** *adj* -a kaskazini magharibi. **~erly** *adj (of winds)* -a kaskazini *adv (of wind)* kaskazini. **~wards** -a kuelekea kaskazini. **~ern** *adj* -a kaskazini. **the ~ern lights** miali ya kaskazini ya dunia. **~erner** *n* mwenyeji/mkazi wa sehemu ya kaskazini mwa nchi. **~ernmost** *adj* -a kaskazini kabisa.

Norwegian *adj* -a Norway; mtu wa Norway.

nose *n* 1 pua *speak through the ~* semea puani. **bite/snap sb's ~ off** jibu vikali. **count/ tell ~s** hesabu watu. **cut off one's ~ to spite one's face** kata pua uunge wajihi, jiumiza ili kulipa kisasi. **follow one's ~** enda mbele moja kwa moja. **keep a person's ~ to the grindstone** fanyisha kazi bila kupumzika. **look down one's ~ at sb** dharau; tendea ufidhuli. **pay through the ~** lipa gharama kubwa sana. **poke/stick one's ~ into** ingilia. **turn one's ~ up at** dharau. **as plain as the ~ on one's face,** dhahiri. **(right) under his very ~** palepale; mbele yake. 2 hisi za kunusa. 3 kitu chenye umbo kama pua, kitu kilicho mbele kabisa.

4 *(compounds)* ~-**bag** *n* mfuko wa chakula cha farasi. ~-**band** *n* sehemu ya hatamu (ipitayo juu ya pua). ~-**bleed** *n* mnoga, muhina; kutokwa na muhina. ~-**cone** *n* kichwa cha roketi. ~-**dive** *vi (of aircraft) n* mteremko wa kutanguliza kichwa. *vi* anguka kwa mteremko mkali huku kichwa kimetazama chini. ~-**flute** *n* zumari ya pua. ~ **gay** n fungu la maua. ~-**rag** *n (sl)* leso ya mfukoni. ~-**ring** *n* hazama. ~-**wheel** *n* gurudumu la mbele la ndege. ~**d** *adj* enye pua *long ~* -enye pua ndefu *short ~* -enye pua kipande *vt,vi* 1 sogea mbele polepole. 2 ~ **sth out** vumbua, gundua (kwa kunusa). 3 ~ **about (for sth)** nusa nusa; *(fig)* dadisi. ~ **into sth** dukiza, ingilia kati. ~**y,nosy** *adj* dadisi *n (sl)* mdadisi. ~ **parker** mdadisi.

nosh *n (GB sl)* chakula. ~-**up** *n* chakula kizuri *vi (colloq)* -la.

nostalgia *n* kiu/hamu ya nyumbani/ mambo yaliyozoewa. **nostalgic** *adj* -enye hamu/kiu ya nyumbani/ mambo yaliyozoewa. **nostalgically** *adv*.

nostril *n* tundu ya pua, mwanzi wa pua.

nostrum *n* dawa ya uwongo.

not *adv* si, siyo, hapana. ~ **so** sivyo. ~ **at all,** ~ **a bit** si kitu; hata kidogo, hasha. ~ **but what** hata hivyo; ingawa. ~ **to say**/~ **only** licha ya ~ *a man spoke* hakusema mtu hata mmoja *as likely as ~* huenda, labda.

nota bene *vt* angalia kwa makini.

notable *adj* -a kutambulika, -enye sifa, mashuhuri *n* mtu mashuhuri/maarufu. **notably** *adv*. **notability** *n*.

notary *n* ~ **public** mthibitishaji rasmi.

notation *n* mwandiko.

notch *n* 1 mkato wa umbo la *v*; *(US)* njia nyembamba katika milima; *(of arrow)* koleo. 3 *(in upright poles for building)* makwa *vt* fanya mkato wa umbo la v. ~ **up** *(colloq)* pata, fanikiwa.

note *n* 1 muhtasari. 2 *(memorandum)* ukumbusho; maneno ya kukumbusha. **marginal** ~**s** maelezo ya pembeni. ~ **book** *n* daftari. 3 barua; maneno machache *drop me a ~* niandikie barua. ~**paper** *n* karatasi ya barua. 4 *(music)* noti. **sound a ~ of warning (against sth)** onya, tahadharisha. **strike the right ~** *(fig)* gusa watu kwa maneno. **strike/sound a false ~** udhi watu. 5 **bank ~** noti. 6 *(fame)* sifa, jina *a person of ~* mtu mkubwa (mashuhuri) *worthy of ~* yafaa ifahamike, -a kufaa, bora. 7 fahamu *take ~!* fahamu. 8 maoni, tajriba *compare ~s* peana maoni *vt* 1 angalia, ona. 2 ~ **sth (down)** kumbuka, andika. ~**d** *adj* maarufu. ~**worthy** *adj* -a kufaa kuangaliwa.

nothing *n* hakuna kitu, si kitu *there is ~ to be done* hakuna lolote la kufanya *he has five foot ~* ana futi tano kamili.2 *(phrases)* **be ~ to** -tovutia, -topendwa. **come to ~** -tofanikiwa. **go for ~** -tokuwa na maana *all my work went for ~* kazi yangu ilikuwa bure. **have ~ to do with** -tohusu *it has ~to do with you* haikuhusu, -tohusika. **make ~ of** -toelewa, toka kapa. **mean ~ to** -tokuwa na maana kwa. **to say ~ of** sembuse. **think ~ of** chukulia (jambo) kuwa kawaida, -tojali. **think ~ of it** usijali. **for ~** bure, bila malipo; bila zawadi; bila lengo. ~ **but** tu. ~ **for it but** ila...tu *there's ~ for it but to* tunachoweza kufanya ni, hapana zaidi ya. **N doing!** la hasha! ~**ness** *n* hali ya kutokuwepo kitu.

notice *n* 1 notisi, taarifa, tangazo *put a ~ in the newspaper* tangaza gazetini *a ~ of marriage* tangazo/taarifa ya ndoa. ~-**board** ubao wa matangazo *our employer has given us a month's ~* mwajiri wetu ametupa notisi ya mwezi mmoja ya kusimama kazi *a tenant was given ~ to quit* mpangaji alipewa notisi ya kuhama nyumba. **do sth at short ~** fanya jambo bila kupata nafasi ya kujiandaa. 2 kuweka maanani/uangalifu, kufahamika. **be beneath one's ~** -wa kitu cha

kutotiwa/wekwa maanani. **bring sth to sb's ~** fahamisha mtu jambo fulani. **come to sb's ~** arifiwa/tambua/pata habari. **sit up and take ~** anza kupata ahueni. **make sb sit up and take ~** amsha. **take no ~ (of sth)** -tojali, -toangalia kwa makini. 3 uhakiki wa kitabu/mchezo mpya n.k. katika jarida *vt,vi* 1 angalia, fahamu, ona. 2 hakiki. **~able** *adj* -a kuonekana kwa urahisi. **~ably. adv.**
notify *vt* julisha, arifu, tangaza. **notification** *n* kutaarifu; taarifa **notifiable** *adj* -liolazimu kujulishwa (hasa magonjwa yanayopaswa kujulishwa kwa vyombo vinavyohusika).

notion *n* 1 wazo, fikira *I have no ~* sifahamu hata kidogo. 2 dhana. 3 *(pl) (US)* vikorokoro. **~al** *adj* 1 *(of knowledge)* -a kufikirika, -a kuwaza tu. 2 dogo, -a mfano.

notorious *adj* -enye sifa mbaya, -a kuvuma kwa ubaya. **~ly** *adv.* **notoriety** *n.*

notwithstanding *(prep)* licha *adv* hata hivyo *(conj)* ijapokuwa.

nougat *n* kashata.

nought *n* 1 si kitu, si neno. **come to ~** batilika, tanguka, shindikana. **bring sb/sth to ~** batilisha, tangua, angamiza, haribu. **set sb/sth at ~** -tojali, pinga, dhalilisha. 2 sifuri.

noun *n (gram)* jina, nomino.

nourish *vt* 1 lisha; stawisha; rutubisha. 2 tunza (jambo) moyoni. **~ment** *n* chakula.

nous *n* akili; busara.

nouveau riche *n (F)* mtu aliyetajirika hivi karibuni, tajiri wa juzijuzi.

novel[1] *adj* -pya, -geni *~ ideas* mawazo mapya. **~ty** *n* 1 upya, ugeni. 2 kitu kipya; shani. 3 *(fig) (pl)* vikorokoro.

novel[2] *n* riwaya. **~ette** *n* riwaya fupi. **~ist** *n* mwandishi wa riwaya. **~ize** *vt* badili iwe kama riwaya (k.m. tamthiliya). **~la** *n* riwaya sahili.

November *n* Novemba: mwezi wa kumi na moja.

novena *n (rel)* novena.

novercal *adj (arch)* -a mama wa kambo.

novice *n* 1 mwanafunzi, mwanagenzi; limbukeni. 2 mwanafunzi wa utawa, mnovisi. **noviciate, novitiate** *n.*

now *adv 1* sasa, sasa hivi, mara moja. **(every) ~ and then/again** mara kwa mara *~ then* ehe! sasa! *~then what's troubling you?* ehe nini kinakusumbua? **just ~** sasa hivi. **up to ~** mpaka sasa. **by ~** hadi/mpaka sasa. **~adays** *adv* siku hizi. **~aday** *adj* -a siku hizi. 2 *(conj)* kwa kuwa *~ (that) you mention it* kwa kuwa umetaja. **~... ~/then** mara ... mara *~ hot ~ cold* mara joto mara baridi.

noway *adv (sl)* si... haiwezekani, sahau *will you help me? noway, do it yourself* nisaidie! sahau ifanye mwenyewe.

nowhere *adv* si...mahali popote *I went ~* sikuenda popote *the man is ~ to be seen* yule mtu haonekani mahali popote. **be/come in ~** shindwa kabisa.

nowise *adv (old use)* kwa njia yoyote.

noxious *adj* -a kudhuru, -enye madhara, -a kuchukiza, -baya *~* **thing** kitu cha kudhuru. **~ly** *adv.* **~ness** *n.*

nozzle *n* ncha ya neli ya mpira/metali.

nuance *n* tofauti ndogo (katika maana ya neno, rangi, maoni n.k.).

nub *n* 1 *(fig)* kiini (agh cha jambo/ hadithi). 2 chenga (ya makaa).

nubile *adj* -a kuoleka, -liofikia umri wa kuolewa. **nubility** *n.*

nuclear *adj* 1 -a kiini. 2 -a nyuklia *~ weapons* silaha za nyuklia *~ energy* nishati ya nyuklia *~ energy plant* mtambo wa nishati ya nyuklia.

nucleus *n* 1 kiini. 2 chanzo, asili.

nude *adj* 1 tupu, -lio uchi, bila kuvaa nguo. 2 *(art)* bila mapambo *n* 1 uchi. **in the ~** uchi *paint from the ~* chora picha ya mtu aliye uchi. **nudist** *n* mtu anayependa kukaa uchi, anayeamini kuwa kukaa uchi juani na katika upepo/hewa huleta afya bora. **nudist camp/colony n** mahali pa wanaopenda kukaa uchi juani.

nudity *n* kukaa uchi.
nudge *vt* ashiria kwa kudukua/kugusa na kiwiko *n* muashirio wa kudukua/ kugusa na kiwiko.
nugatory *adj* hafifu, -sio na thamani, -a bure.
nugget *n* kipande, kibamba (cha dhahabu au madini).
nuisance *n* adha, usumbufu, kero *a perfect* ~ mchoshi. **be a** ~ -wa msumbufu.
nuke *n US (sl)* bomu la nyuklia.
null *adj* batili, -liotanguka. ~ **and void** tanguka, batilika, -fa. ~**ify** *vt* batilisha. ~**ity** *n*. ~**ification** *n*.
numb *adj* -enye ganzi, -zito *vt* tia/ fanya ganzi. 2 *be* ~ *to* -tosikia, -tojali. ~**ly** *adv*. ~**ness** *n*.
number *n* 1 hesabu, kiwango, idadi tarakimu *(written)* ~ *of people* watu kadhaa. **his/** ~ **your**~ **is up** *(colloq)* ame/umepatikana; utakufa. **in** ~ kwa idadi, kwa jumla. **to the** ~ **of** kufikia. **without** ~ -sio na idadi, -siohesabika. **times without** ~ mara nyingi mno; kila mara. ~ **plate** kipande cha namba ya gari. 2 namba. **the** ~ **three** namba tatu. ~ **one** wahedi. **look after/take care of** ~ **one** jiangalia, jitunza. **negative** ~ namba hasi. **nominal** ~ namba ya jina 3. *(of magazine, etc)* toleo. **back** ~ toleo la nyuma *(fig)* -liopitwa na wakati. 4 *(mus)* onyesho, wimbo (katika mfululizo). 5 *(gram)* idadi. 6 *(pl)* wingi *they defeatedus by ~s n* walitushinda kwa wingi wao. **in great** ~**s** tele, -ingi. 7 *(pl) (arithmetic)* hesabu *vt,vi* 1 tia hesabu/namba *my days are ~ed* sina siku nyingi za kuishi. 2 pata, fikia *the people ~ed fifty* watu walipata hamsini. 3 ~ **sb/sth among** hesabia. 4 *(mil)* ita, taja namba. ~**less** *adj* ingi, pasipo idadi, sio na namba, -siohesabika.
numbskull *(US) see* **numskull**.
numeral *adj* -a numerali, -a hesabu, -a tarakimu *n* numerali, tarakimu, herufi ya hesabu. **Arabic** ~ namba k.v. 1,2,3,4, n.k. **Roman** ~ namba k.v. I, II, III, IV, n.k. **numerable** *adj* -enye kuhesabika. **numerate** *adj* -enye ujuzi wa hesabu. **numeration** *n* hesabu, kuhesabu ~ *system* mfumo wa numerali. **numerator** *n* kiasi. **numerical** *adj* -a numerali ~ *methods* mbinu za numerali. **numerous** *adj* ingi.
numinous *adj* -a kuogofya; -a Mungu.
numismatics *n* elimu ya sarafu na nishani. **numismatist** *n* msomi wa elimu ya sarafu na nishani.
numskull *n* mpumbavu, baradhuli.
nun *n* mtawa wa kike(wa chama cha dini). ~**nery** *n* nyumba ya watawa wa kike.
nuncio *n* mjumbe au balozi wa Papa (Baba Mtakatifu). **nunciature** *n* ofisi ya mjumbe wa Papa.
nuptial *adj* -a arusi *n* arusi.
nurse *n* 1 muuguzi, nesi. 2 mlezi, yaya. ~ **maid** yaya; *(fig)* mtunzaji wa wengine. **wet**~ mama wa kunyonyesha. 3 kulea *put a child out to* ~ peleka mtoto kwa mlezi. ~-**child** *n* mtoto wa kupanga *vt* 1 *(of a baby)* nyonyesha *nursing mother* mama anaye nyonyesha. 2 tunza, uguza magonjwa, ponyesha. ~ **a cold** shughulikia mafua. **nursing home** hospitali ndogo ya binafsi. 3 angalia, tunza *she ~d her beer all evening* alitunza bia yake jioni (yaani isimalizike mapema). 4 *(in the mind)* weka, fikiri.
nursery *n* 1 ~ **(school)** shule ya watoto wadogo/vidudu/chekechea/awali. 2 chumba cha watoto. ~-**rhyme** wimbo wa watoto. 3 bustani ya miche. ~-**man** mtunza bustani ya miche. **nurs(e)ling** *n* 1 mtoto mchanga. 2 mmea mchanga.
nurture *n* 1 malezi. 2 mafunzo; elimu *vt* 1 lea. 2 elimisha.
nut *n 1* kokwa, njugu, lozi. **ground/ pea** ~ njugu nyasa, karanga; bambara. **hard** ~ njugumawe. **coco**~ nazi. **a hard** ~ **to crack** tatizo gumu, kitu/mtu ambaye vigumu kumshughulikia. ~-**brown** *adj* -enye rangi ya karanga iliyokaangwa.

~-**butter** *n* siagi ya karanga. ~**crackers** kitu cha kubanjia kokwa. ~**shell** *n* ganda, gamba la kokwa. *(fig)* **(put sth) in a ~shell** (sema) kwa muhtasari, kwa ufupi. 2 *(tech)* nati. ~**s and bolts** mambo ya msingi na rahisi. 3 *(sl)* kichwa. **off one's** ~ wazimu. ~-**house** hospitali ya vichaa. 4 *(pl)* vibonge vya makaa *vi* **go ~ting** chuma kokwa. ~**s** *adj (sl)* kichaa. **be ~s about/over sb/sth** penda sana, shabikia. ~**ty** *adj* 1 -enye ladha ya karanga/njugu. 2 -enye njugu nyingi. 3 *(sl)* -liopenda sana. 4 *(sl)* -enye wazimu. ~**tiness** *n*.

nutmeg *n* kungumanga; *(spice)*basibasi.

nutrition *n* lishe. **nutrient** *adj* -a virutubishi *n* kirutubishi. **nutriment** *n* chakula bora. **nutritious** *adj* rutubishi. **nutritive** *adj* rutubishi ~ *value* thamani ya chakula *n* mlisho.

nuzzle *vi,vt* 1 gusagusa/kumba kwa pua. 2 ~ **up (against/to)** sugua/sukuma kwa pua.

nylon *n* nailoni.

nymph *n* 1 mwanamwali mzuri. 2 *(fairy)* zimwi. 3 tunutu. ~**et** *n* mwanamwali anayetamaniwa. ~**o** *n* *(colloq)* *(abbr of* ~**omaniac)** *n* ugonjwa wa mwanamke kuwa na ashiki sana. ~**omaniac** *n,adj*.

O

O[1],**o** n 1 herufi ya kumi na tano ya alfabeti ya Kiingereza. 2 sifuri.

o[2],**oh** 1 *int sl o,oh* mlio wa mshangao/ hofu. 2 ee, enyi. 3 *(to stress)* oh no! la, hasha. **o'** *prep (abbr of) o'clock* saa tatu.

oaf *n* bwege. **~fish** *adj* **~shness** *n.*

oak *n* mwaloni *(attrib)* -a mwaloni *~ door* mlango wa mwaloni. **~en** *adj (esp. lit poetic)* -a mwaloni.

oakum *n* nyuzinyuzi za kamba iliyochakaa na kufumuliwa (hutumika kwa kukalafati).

oar *n* kasia; mpiga kasia. **pull a good ~** -wa mpiga makasia mzuri. **put/shove/ stick one's ~ in** jidukiza, jiingiza **rest/lay on one's oars** pumzika kwa muda (wakati wa kazi). **chained to the ~s** -liolazimishwa kufanya kazi kwa bidii na kwa muda mrefu. **~lock** *n* kishwara. **~sman/~swoman** *n* mpiga kasia. **~smanship** *n* upigaji wa kasia *vi* piga kasia.

oasis *n* oasisi (mahali penye miti na chemchemi katika jangwa); *(fig)* mahali/jambo lenye raha.

oast *n* **~-house** tanuru la kukaushia maua yatumiwayo kutengeneza pombe.

oat *n usu (pl)* shayiri. **sow one's wild ~s** piga maisha ujanani. **be off one's ~s** *(colloq)* -tojisikia vizuri. **feel one's ~s** *(colloq)* changamka. **~cake** keki ya shayiri. **~meal** unga wa shayiri.

oath kiapo, kasama, yamini; *(curse)* laana, apizo. **put on/under ~** apisha. **upon your ~!** apia! **exchange ~s** apiana *administer an ~* apisha *commissioner for ~* kamishina wa viapo *~ of allegiance* kiapo cha utii. *take an ~ on the Koran* apa yamini; kula yamini. **swear on /take an ~** kula kiapo.

obdurate *adj* shupavu, gumu, kaidi. **obduracy** *n.*

obeisance *n* kuinamisha kichwa (ishara ya kuheshimu, kustahi), kusujudu *pay ~* shika miguu.

obelisk *n* 1 mnara mrefu wenye pande mraba zilizochongoka juu. 2 *(printing)* alama (- au +) iliyotumika zamani katika maandishi.

obese *adj (of persons)* nene sana, -enye kitambi. **obesity** *n.*

obey *vt,vi* tii, sikia; tumikia. **obedient** *adj* -tiifu, -sikivu; (katika barua) *your ~ servant* wako mtiifu. **obedience** *n.* **obediently** *adv.*

obfuscate *vt* 1 fumba, tatiza, changanya. 2 tia giza. **obfuscation** *n.*

obi *n (Japan)* kibwebwe kivaliwacho na watoto/ wanawake.

obiterdictum *n* msemo wa kando.

obituary *n* tanzia *~ notices* taarifa ya waliofariki. **obituarist** *n* mtangaza tanzia.

object[1] *n* 1 kitu; jambo *~ lesson* somo linalofundishwa kwa vielezo; tukio/ hadithi yenye funzo/onyo. **no ~** bila kiuzi *money is no ~* fedha si kizuizi. 2 *(aim, purpose)* nia, kusudi, madhumuni *my ~ is* kusudi langu ni; nataka; ndiyo nitakayo. *fail in one's ~* shindwa kutimiza kusudi. 3 *(gram)* shamirisho *direct ~* yambwa *indirect* yambiwa *~ vt, vi* 1 kataa, bisha, pinga. **~ to sb** bishia mtu, katalia mtu. 2 **~ (against sb) that** pinga, toa sababu kupinga/dhidi ya. **~or** *n* mpinzani, mbishi. **~ify** 1 toa kielelezo ili kuthibitisha. 2 eleza waziwazi (kwa kuonyesha kitu hasa). **~ion** *n* 1 katazo, kinzano, kipingamizi, kizuizi *there is no ~* hakuna kipingamizi *raise ~ions* toa vipingamizi/vizuizi. 2 *(feeling of dislike)* uchungu, chuki, kutopenda; **take ~ to sth** pinga jambo. **~ionable** *adj* -a kuchukiza. **~ionably** *adv* .**~ive** *adj* 1 -a kuhusu jambo (kitu). 2 bila upendeleo *my advice is quite ~* shauri langu nimelitoa bila upendeleo. 3 *(gram)* -a shamirisho *n* 1 *(phil)* halisi. 2 *(mil)* lengo, shabaha. **~ivism** *n (phil)* nadharia inayotazama mambo kama yalivyo. **~ively** *adv*. bila upendeleo. **~ivity** *n* kutopendelea.

objurgate *vt (liter)* kemea, karipia. **objurgation** *n* kemeo, karipio.

oblate *adj (geom)* -a kubenuka.

oblation *n (rel.)* sadaka, dhabihu.

oblige *vt* 1 **~ sb to do sth** lazimisha/ taka mtu aahidi/afanye jambo. 2 **be**

~d to do sth shurutishwa, lazimishwa *we were ~d to shut the window* tulilazimishwa kufunga dirisha. 3 fadhili *~ me by closing the door* nifanyie hisani unifungie mlango/ tafadhali ufunge mlango. *Iam much ~d to you* nakushukuru sana. **obligate** *vt* **~ sb to do sth** wajibisha *he was ~ to help me* aliwajibika kunisaidia. **obligation** *n* 1 wajibu, faradhi, sharti *undertake an ~* wajibika *meet one's ~* timiza wajibu. 2 ahadi, lazima. 3 deni. **put/be under an ~** shurutisha; fadhili (ili naye aone anadaiwa). **obligatory** *adj* -a lazima, -a kujuzu, -a wajibu.

oblique *adj* 1 -a mshazari, -a kukingama *~ prism* mche shazari *~ line* mstari shazari. 2 -a kuzunguka; si wazi *~ reference to* mtajo usio wazi. **~ly** *adv* kwa kukingama. **obliquity** *n* 1 mshazari; mafyongo. 2 upotovu; ufidhuli.

obliterate *vt* futilia mbali, ondoa kabisa, haribu. **obliteration** *n*.

oblivion *n* hali ya kusahau/kusahauliwa, kutokumbukwa kabisa *buried in ~* sahauliwa kabisa.

oblivious *adj ~ of* -siotambua; -sio na kumbukumbu *be ~ of what was happening* -siotambua lililokuwa likitendeka.

oblong *adj* -a mstatili *n* mstatili.

obloquy *n* aibu, fedheha, masuto, kashfa.

obnoxious *adj* -a kuchukiza, makuruhu. **~ly** *adv*. **~ness** *n* makuruhu; karaha.

obscene *adj* -chafu, -a pujufu. **~ly** *adv*. **obscenity** *n*.

obscure *adj* 1 -agiza, -sioonekana/ eleweka vizuri *vt* fanya giza, zuia isionekane, vuruga. **~ly** *adv*.

obsecurity *n* 1 giza, uvunguvungu. 2 *(indistinctness)* fumbo. *live in ~* ishi katika mashaka. **obscurantism** *n* upingaji wa kupata maarifa/ufunuo. 2 kutoeleweka kwa makusudi, uvungaji wa (makusudi).

obsequies *n* mazishi.

obsequious *adj* **~ (to/towards)** -enye kutii kwa unyenyekevu sana, kujipendekeza sana, -a kurairai, -enye kujikomba. **~ly** *adv*. **~ness** *n* unyenyekevu; ukombi.

observe *vt,vi* 1 angalia kwa makini; chunguza; hoji. 2 fuata, shika kanuni; adhimisha (sherehe). 3 toa wazo. **~r** *n* 1 mwangalizi, mtazamaji, mchunguzi. 2 mfuata kanuni. **observing** *adj* -epesi kutambua. **observingly** *adv*. **observable** *adj* -a kuonekana; -a kutazamika. **observably** *adv*. **observance** *n* 1 kushika mila na desturi. 2 kanuni za dini, mila. **observant** *adj* 1 -epesi kutambua, -elekevu *be ~ of sth* angalia sana kitu fulani. 2 angalifu, chunguzi; sikivu, tiifu. **observantly** *adv*. **observation** *n* 1 kuangalia *by personal ~* kwa kutazama/ kuchunguza mwenyewe kwa macho. **be under ~** angaliwa. **keep sb under ~** angalia mtu kwa makini. **~ car** *(ina train)* gari la kuangalilia mandhari. **~ post** kituo cha uchunguzi/kuangalia maadui. 2 uelekevu wa kutambua *a man of no ~* mtu asiye na uelekevu. 3 *(remark)* wazo *make an ~* toa wazo. 4 *(usu pl)* (taarifa zilizokusanywa na kuhifadhiwa). **observatory** *n* mahali pa kuangalilia jua/mwezi/nyota.

obsess *vt (usu passive)* **~ed (by/with)** shika, shikilia, jaza *he is ~ed by fear* amejawa na hofu. **~ion** *n* 1 kushikwa na hofu/wazo n.k. 2 *(desire)* **~ (about/with sth/sb)** tamaa, shauku (inayojaa moyoni) isiyotulizika. **~ive** *adj* -enye kushika/shikilia (tamaa, shauku).

obsolete -siotumika siku hizi, -kongwe, -liopitwa, -siofaa (kwa neno) *it is ~* imefutwa, haifai. **obsolescent** *adj* -siofaa kwa sasa; -nayopitwa na wakati. **obsolescence** *n* hali ya kitu kutofaa kutumiwa sasa, hali ya kupitwa na wakati.

obstacle *n* kizuizi, kikwazo: *put ~s in the way* weka vizuizi njiani.

obstetric(al) *adj* -a ukunga; -a kuzalia;

-a uzazi *an ~ ward* wadi ya uzazi. ~**ian** *n* daktari wa uzazi. ~**s** *n* tiba ya uzazi.

obstinate *adj* 1 -kaidi, -ishi, -enye inadi. 2 *(of disease)* -siotibika kirahisi, -siokubali dawa kwa urahisi. ~**ly** *adv*. **obstinancy** *n* ukaidi, usugu.

obstreperous *adj* 1 tundu, tukutu. 2 -a makelele. ~**ness** *n*. ~**ly** *adv*.

obstruct *vt* 1 zuia, pinga, kinza. 2 ~ *a bill in parliament* zuia mswada bungeni. ~**ion** *n* 1 kuzuia. 2 *(obstacle)* kizuizi, kipingamizi. ~**ionism** uzuiaji, upingamizi. ~**ionist** *n* mzuiaji, mkinzani. ~**ive** *adj* -a kuzuia, -a kipingamizi. ~**ively** *adv*.

obtain *vt,vi* pata, jipatia; nunua. 2 *(of rules, customs)* kubalika; tumika. ~**able** *adj* -a kupatikana *it is ~* inapatikana; inakubalika.

obtrude *vt, vi* ~ **upon** jiingiza, jitia kati, jidukiza. **obtrusion** *n* kujidukiza, kujiingiza **obtrusive** *adj* -enye kudukiza. **obtrusively** *adv*.

obtuse *adj* 1 pumbavu. 2 butu ~ *angle* pembebutu. ~**ness** *n*.

obverse *n,adj* 1 sehemu ya juu ya sarafu. 2 uso wa kitu chochote kinachotarajiwa kuwakilishwa.

obviate *vt* ondoa; toa.

obvious *adj* wazi; dhahiri, -a kuonekana wazi; -a kueleweka *it was the ~ thing to do* lilikuwa jambo dhahiri kutenda. ~**ly** *adv*. ~**ness** *n*.

occasion *n* 1 nafasi, fursa, wasaa *take this ~ to do sth* chukua fursa hii kufanya jambo fulani. *(particular time)* wakati maalum (kwa jambo fulani); wakati ufaao *on the present ~* kwa wakati uliopo *we have met on several ~s* tumeonana mara nyingi. **on** ~ mara kwa mara; ikibidi. **rise to the** ~ onyesha uwezo unaohitajika. 2 haja; sababu *if the ~ arises* kama ikihitajika *this is no ~ for laughter* hakuna sababu ya kucheka. 3 tukio *vt* sababisha. ~**al** *adj* 1 -a mara moja *~ showers* rasharasha. 2 -a kufaa wakati fulani. ~**ally** *adv* mara chache.

Occident *n (liter) the ~* nchi za (Ulaya Magharibi na Marekani), Magharibi. ~**al** *adj* -a Magharibi. *n* mwenyeji wa nchi za magharibi.

occult *adj* 1 -a mizungu. 2 -liofichwa, -a siri, -a fumbo. **the** ~ kitu kilichofichwa (kinachofahamika kwa watu maalum).

occupy *vt* 1 twaa, shika, miliki, chukua. 2 ishi katika nyumba/miliki nyumba. 3 *(use, give work to)* chukua (muda), shughulisha, tumia. ~ **sb's mind** shughulisha akili ya mtu. 4 -wa na, shika ~ **an important post** -wa na cheo kikubwa. **occupant** *n* 1 mkaaji, mwenyeji. 2 mmiliki, mmilikaji. **occupancy** *n*. **occupation** *n* 1 shughuli, kazi, biashara. 2 *(taking possession)* kutwaa, kumiliki. 3 kipindi/muhula wa kumiliki. **occupational** *adj* -a shughuli, -a kazi. **occupier** *n* **occupant** *n*.

occur *vi* 1 tokea. 2 *(enter the mind)*. ~ **to** ingia mawazoni *an idea ~s to me* wazo hunijia. 3 -wapo *mistakes do ~* makosa hutokea. ~**rence** *n* tukio, kadhia *of frequent ~rence* -liotokea mara nyingi.

ocean *n* 1 bahari. ~ **going** *adj* -enye kusafiri baharini. 2 ~ *of (colloq)* -ingi *he has ~ of money* ana pesa nyingi. ~**ic** *adj* -a bahari kuu, -a kupita baharini; -a kuishi baharini. ~**ography** *n* elimu ya bahari.

ochre,ocher *n (red)* ngeu, ngegu, ukaria.

o'clock *n = (of the clock) what ~? it is eight ~* saa ngapi? saa mbili.

octagon *n* pembenane. ~**al** *adj* -enye pembe nane.

octane *n* oktani.

octave *n* 1 *(music)* sauti nane. 2 *(poetry)* ubeti wenye mistari minane.

october *n* oktoba: mwezi wa kumi.

octogenarian *n* mzee mwenye umri wa miaka themanini hadi themanini na tisa *adj* -enye umri wa miaka themanini.

octopus *n* pweza.

oculist *n* daktari wa macho. **ocular** *adj*

-a macho, kwa macho; kwa kuona. **ocularist** *n* mtengeneza macho ya bandia.

odalisque *n* suria, kimada.

odd *adj* 1 -moja (pasipo mwenzi wake); -moja au zaidi (katika seti/jozi). 2 *(number)* witiri ~ *degree* nyuzi witiri ~ *number* namba witiri ~ *power* vipeo witiri. 3 pamoja na -ingine *a hundred ~ shilings* shilingi mia moja na ushei. 4 -sio -a mara kwa mara, -a muda (mfupi), -sio a kawaida *at ~ times* katika nyakati fulani ~ *moments* nyakati fulani ~ *job* kazi za pembeni. 5 *(worthless)* -a ovyo, hafifu. 6 *(ridiculous)* -a mzaha; -a kuchekesha; -a ajabu ~ *man* mtu wa ajabu. **~ man out** mtu/kitu kilichobaki (baada ya vingine kuwa kwenye seti); *(colloq)* mtu aliyejitenga, aliyetofauti na wenzake wote *how ~!* ajabu! **~ly** *adj* kwa namna ya pekee. **~ity** *n* 1 ugeni, ajabu, shani, kioja. **~ments** *n* 1 *(pl)* vikorokoro. 2 mabaki, masalia.

odds *n (pl)* 1 nafasi/uwezekano (wa kufaulu au kushindwa kufanya jambo) *the ~ are in our favour* tuna nafasi nzuri ya ushindi. 2 kutokuwa sawa. **make ~ even** sawazisha mambo. 3 kutopatana. **be at ~ (with sb) (over/ on sth)** bishana, gombana, zozana. 4 tofauti **it makes no ~** hakuna tofauti; haidhuru; mamoja. **what's the ~**? haidhuru. 5 **~ and ends** takataka; vikorokoro. 6 **the ~s** *(gambling)* matumaini.

odium *n* chuki. **odious** *adj* -a kuchukiza, makuruhu, -a ikirahi. **odiously** *adv*.

odometer *n* odometa: chombo cha kupima masafa yaliyosafiriwa.

odour,(US)odor *n* 1 harufu, *(pleasant)* manukato; *(unpleasant)* uvundo; *(of body)* gugumu; *(of perspiration under armpits)* kikwapa, kutuzi. 2 sifa, upendeleo. **be in good (bad) ~ with** pendelewa (kutopendelewa) na. **~less** *adj* -sio harufu. **odoriferous** *adj* -a kunukia, -a manukato. **odorous** *adj (poet)* -a kunukia.

odyssey *n* safari ndefu (yenye matukio mengi).

oecumenical *adj see* **ecumenical**.

Oedipus complex *(psych)* (dhana ya) mapenzi ya binti kwa baba/mtoto wa kiume kwa mama yaliyofungamana na chuki ya binti kwa mama/mtoto wa kiume kwa baba.

o'er *adv see* **over**.

oesophagus *n see* **esophagus** **of** *(indicating separation in space or time)* kutoka, kutokea. 2 *(indicating origin, authorship)* -wa; ya/za. 3 *(indicating cause)* kutokana na, ya, wa. 4 *(indicatingrelief, riddance)* na. 5 *(indicating material or substance)* ya.

off[1] *adj* 1 *(of horses, vehicles)* -a upande wa kulia *the ~ front wheel* gurudumu la mbele upande wa kulia *the ~ horse (of a pair)* farasi aliye upande wa kulia. 2 -lio mbali zaidi. 3 -sio fanya kazi; -enye shughuli kidogo tu. ~ *hours* saa baada ya kazi maalum.

off[2] *adverbial particle* 1 *(distance)* mbali *the Universityis seven miles ~* Chuo Kikuu kiko umbali wa maili saba; *(time)* muda *the general elections are not far ~* uchaguzi mkuu hauko mbali; *(departure)* kuondoka *he's ~* ameondoka ~ *we go,* tunaondoka *take your hat ~!* ondoa kofia yako hiyo!. 2 vunjika, -tofanyika! *the meeting is ~/broken ~*, mkutano umevunjika/umevunjwa *the debate over language policy is ~* mjadala juu ya sera ya lugha hautafanyika. 3 katika *the water/ gas/electricityis ~* maji/gasi/umeme umekatika. 4 -a mapumziko *the workers were given a day ~*, wafanyakazi walipewa siku moja ya mapumziko. 5 *(of food)* -liochacha. 6 *(in a theatre)* -a nyuma au kando ya/ pembeni mwa jukwaa. 7 *(phrases)* **off of** *(US) ~ (prep)*. **on and ~; ~ and on**, mara chache *he comes here on and ~* huja hapa mara chache. **right/straight** ~ mara moja.

off[3] *prep* 1 toka, puuza *fall ~ a tree* anguka toka mtini *the car rolled ~ the slope,* gari lilibingirika kwenye mteremko *cut another piece ~ the material* toa kipande kingine kwenye kitambaa *cut ~ the price* punguza bei. *(of a road or street)* mchepuo, -liochepuka. 3 nje kidogo *a building ~ the swamp area* jengo karibu na kinamasi *an island ~ the coast* kisiwa nje kidogo ya pwani. 4 *(colloq)* acha (tabia fulani) *he is ~ drinking* ameacha tabia ya ulevi. **~ish** *adj (colloq)* -liojitenga (na shughuli za wengine). **~-licence** *n* liseni ya kuuza vileo vya kuchukua na kunywea kwingine; stoo/duka (linalouza vileo). **~-load** *vt* teremsha mizigo. **~-print** *n* lopoo: nakala (ya makala iliyochapishwa katika kitabu, jarida). **~-hand** *adv* bila maandalio, bila kufikiri, kwa haraka, mara moja *adj* -sioandaliwa *be ~-hand with sb* -tomjali mtu sana. **~-handed(ly)** *adj,adv (of behaviour)* -a kukatiza, bila kujali.

off[4] *pref (compounds)* **~-beat** *adj (colloq)* -si -a kawaida, tofauti. **~-day** *n (colloq)* siku mbaya.

offal *n* 1 matumbo/viungo vya ndani vya mnyama. 2 takataka

offence/offense *n* 1 **an ~ against** kosa, dhambi, hatia; kuvunja sheria *an ~ against the law* uvunjaji wa sheria *be convicted of an ~* onekana na kosa. **capital ~** kosa lenye adhabu ya kifo. 2 uchungu, chuki. **give/cause ~ (to sb)** chukiza (mtu). **take ~ (at sth)** chukizwa (na mtu). **no ~!** niwie radhi. 3 mashambulizi *weapons of ~* silaha za kushambulia. 4 kitu kinachoudhi/chukiza/kera. **~less** *adj*. **offend** *vi,vt* 1 **~ against** kosa; kosea. 2 chukiza, udhi; tia uchungu. 3 kasirisha, udhi. **offender** *n* mkosaji, mhalifu. **offensive** *adj* 1 -a kuchokoza; -a kuchukiza; -baya. **~ odour** harufu mbaya *offensive to the morals of the community* -a kuvunja murua wa jamii *~ words* matusi, maneno ya kuchukiza. 2 -a kukasirisha. 3 *(attacking)* -a kushambulia, -a shari, -a kutaka vita *~ weapon* silaha ya kudhuru. *n* shambulio, mashambulizi. **take the ~** anzisha/leta vita/mashambulizi. **peace ~** kampeni ya kuleta amani. **offensively** *adv*. **offensiveness** *n*.

offer *vt,vi* 1 **~ sth to sb; ~ sb sth; ~ sth for sth** toa; tolea, ahidi. **~ battle** -pa adui nafasi ya kupigana. **~ one's hand** toa mkono ili kusabahiana. **~ one's hand in marriage** posa. 2 **~ (to)** onyesha *~ no resistance* -toonyesha upinzani. 3 tukia, tokea. **as occasion ~s** nafasi inapotokea *n* 1 ahadi (ya kufanya jambo/kutoa kitu) *an ~ of marriage* posa. 2 bei inayotolewa. **goods on ~** bidhaa ziuzwazo. **be open to an ~** -wa tayari kupatana bei. **~ing** *n* 1 kutoa *the ~ of bribes* kutoa hongo. 2 sadaka. 3 kitu kitolewacho *peace ~* kitu kinachotolewa kurudisha maelewano baada ya ugomvi. **~tory** *n* sadaka (zinazotolewa kanisani).

office *n* 1 ofisi. **~-block** jengo (kubwa) la ofisi **~-boy** tarishi. 2 Wizara; Idara *planning ~* Idara ya mipango *the Foreign ~* Wizara ya Mambo ya Nje. 3 madaraka; cheo **~ bearer** mtu mwenye madaraka/cheo fulani. 4 wajibu. 5 fadhili, huduma, msaada *perform the last ~ for* zika, toa heshima za mwisho. **~r** *n* 1 ofisa *assessing ~* mthamini *public ~* ofisa wa serikali *superior ~* ofisa wa juu *police ~* afisa wa polisi *prison ~r* ofisa wa jela. 2 *(in the army/police)* afande. 3 mtu mwenye madaraka *~s of a society* viongozi wa chama *vt* **official** *adj* 1 -a serikali, -enye madaraka rasmi. **~ liquidator** mfunga hesabu rasmi. **~ receiver** mpokezi rasmi. **~ secrets** siri za serikali. 2 *(formal)* -a kawaida, -a taratibu *n* ofisa. **officially** *adv* kwa urasimu; kwa utaratibu. **officialdom** *n* utawala; urasimu. **officialese** *n* lugha ya kirasimu. **officiate** *vt* **(as)**

(at) 1 fanya kazi ya mtu wa cheo fulani. 2 *(rel)* salisha; ongoza.

officious *adj* -a kuingilia, -a kujitiatia. **~ly** *adv*. **~ness** *n*.

offing *n* sehemu ya bahari iliyo mbali (lakini inayoonekana) *gain an ~* zidi kuwa mbali toka pwani; *(fig)* karibu. **have sth in the ~** -wa na kitu kinachoelekea kutokea karibu.

off-scourings *n (usu fig)* takataka, uchafu; masimbi; machicha.

offset *vt* fidia; sawazisha *vi* chipua.

offshoot *n* chipukizi; *(liter or fig)* ziada.

off-shore *adj* 1 -a bara. **~ wind** pepo za bara. 2 mbali kidogo na pwani (kwa baharini). 3 **~ purchases** *(US)* bidhaa zinunuliwazo na Marekani kutoka nchi nyingine ili kutoa msaada kwa nchi nyingine.

off-side *adj; adv (football, hockey)* -a kuotea, -nayo otea.

offspring *n* mtoto; *(of bird)* kinda.

offstreet *n* mbali na barabara kuu.

oft *adv (in poetry)* mara nyingi. **~-times** *adv (archaic)* mara nyingi, mara kwa mara.

often *adv* 1 mara kwa mara, mara nyingi *more ~ (usually)* aghalabu, kwa kawaida, kwa desturi *many times and ~* mara nyingi. 2 *(in phrases)* **how ~?** mara ngapi? **as ~ as** kila mara. **as ~ as not/more ~ than not** mara nyingi sana, mara kwa mara; aghalabu. **every so ~** mara mojamoja. **once too ~** mara moja zaidi, mara ya mwisho.

ogle *vi, vt* **~(at)** tazama kwa matamanio.

ogre *n* 1 *(in fables)* zimwi. **~ish** *adj* -a kizimwi. **~ss** zimwi (la kike).

ohm *n (electricity)* omu: kizio cha nishati.

oho *int* aha!

oil *n* 1 mafuta *palm-~* mawese *cod-liver ~* mafuta ya samaki. 2 *(phrases)* **burn the midnight ~** soma usiku. **pour ~ on the flame(s)** kasirisha zaidi; zidisha ugomvi. **pour ~ on troubled waters** fanya/sema tuliza (kwa namna ambayo unamaliza ugomvi/hasira). **smell of the midnight ~** onekana kwamba umekesha ukisoma. **strike ~** pata mafuta (kwa kuchimba); fanikiwa *(fig)* tajirika sana *(compounds)* **~ bearing** *adj* tabaka ya jabali yenye (madini ya mafuta). **~ burner** *n* chombo kiendacho kwa mafuta. **~-cake** *n* mashudu. **~-can** *n* kopo la kutilia mafuta. **~-cloth** *n* kitambaa kisichopenyeza maji. **~-colours** *n* rangi za mafuta. **~ field** *n* eneo la visima vya mafuta. **~-fired** *n (of a furnace)* -enye kutumia mafuta kuwaka. **~- palm** mchikichi. **~-paper** *n* karatasi ya mafuta. **~-rig** mtambo/ mashine ya kuchimbia mafuta. **~-silk** hariri mafuta. **~-skin** kitambaa cha mafuta (kisichopenyeza maji). **~-tanker** *n* meli ya mafuta. **~-well** *n* kisima cha mafuta *vt* lainisha kwa mafuta *~ the machine* tia mafuta kwenye mashine (ili kuilainisha); *(fig)* fanya mambo yaende vizuri. *~ (more usu* **grease***) sb's palm* -pa mrungura/honga. **~ed** *adj (usu)* **(well-~ed)** *(sl)* -liolewa kidogo. **~er** *n* 1 kopo la mafuta. 2 fundi mafuta. 3 meli ya mafuta. **~y** *adj* 1 -enye mafuta. 2 laini. 3 janja. **~iness** *n also see* **oleaginous**.

ointment *n* lihamu; dawa ya kuchua.

okapi *n* okapi : aina ya paa wa Afrika ya Kati.

okay *(abbr* **OK***) adj, adv, (colloq)* sawa -safi *vt* kubali/kubalia *n* kukubali; kibali *I have got my ~ for* nimepata kibali cha.

okra *n (plant)* mbamia, mbinda; *(pods)* bamia, binda.

old *adj* 1 -enye umri wa *how ~ are you?* una miaka mingapi/umri gani? 2 zee; kongwe. **an ~ man** mzee, shaibu. **an ~ woman** ajuza; *(colloq)* mke. **~age** uzee; ukongwe. **~age pension** pensheni ya uzeeni. **~ and young** watu wote, kila mmoja; *(of things)* -a zamani, kuukuu, -liochakaa. 3 -a zamani; -a muda mrefu. **in the ~ days** zamani. **the good ~ days** nyakati njema za kale;

zama za. ~ **boy/girl** mwanafunzi wa zamani wa shule. **one of the ~ school** mtu wa kale, anayeshikilia mambo ya zamani. ~ **country** nchi ya zamani (mtu alikohama). **the ~ world** Ulaya, Asia na Afrika. ~ **soldier** askari wa zamani/muda mrefu. ~ **guard** mfuasi/shabiki wa zamani/muda mrefu. ~ **offender** mhalifu wa muda mrefu. **an ~ hand (at sth)** mtu mwenye ujuzi mwingi (kutokana na kufanya kazi fulani kwa muda mrefu). ~ **fashioned** -liopitwa na wakati, -a kale. ~ **hat** *(colloq)* -a kale ~ *time world* a wakati uliopita. ~ **timer** *n* mtu wa siku nyingi; mtu aliyejihusisha na mahali/kitu (fulani) kwa muda mrefu. **come the ~ soldier (over sb)** *(colloq)* dai kuwa na ujuzi mwingi kutokana na kufanya kazi muda mrefu; *(worn out)* -kuukuu, -liochakaa. 5 *(colloq) (used infront of names and addressing people)* mzee *listen ~ man* sikiliza mzee. ~ **Harry/ Nick/Scratch** Shetani. **the ~ man** baba; mume. **the ~ woman** mke. 6 *(used as intensifier) (sl)* sana. **a high ~ time** wakati mzuri sana (hasa katika starehe). **any ~ thing** kitu chochote kiwacho *n* zamani, kale. **in days of ~** siku za zamani. **the men of ~** watu wa kale. **~ish** *adj* -a zamanizamani; zeezee. **~en** *adj (archaic, liter)* -a zamani, -a kale. **in ~ days** siku za kale. **~ster** *n (colloq)* (mtu) mzee.

oleaginous *adj* -a mafuta; -a kuteleza, laini, -enye mafuta.

olfactory *adj* -a kunusa; -a kuhusu harufu ~ *nerves* neva za harufu.

oligarchy *n* utawala wa serikali ya wachache. **oligarch** mjumbe wa serikali hiyo.

olive *n* 1 ~ **(tree)** mzeituni. **wild ~ tree** mchekele ~ *grove* bustani ya mizeituni; *(fruit)* zeituni. 2 jani/tawi la mzeituni (alama ya amani). **hold the ~-branch** -wa tayari kuzungumzia amani *adj* -a zeituni. ~ **oil** mafuta ya zeituni.

Olympic *adj* -a Olimpiki: ~ *games* michezo ya Olimpiki. **Olympiad** *n* kipindi cha miaka minne baina ya Michezo ya Olimpiki.

Olympian *adj (of manners etc)* -zuri kabisa; -a kama Mungu *n* mmojawapo wa miungu ya Kigiriki.

ombudsman *n* **the O~** Mchunguzi Maalum (anayechunguza malalamiko ya wananchi).

omega *n* 1 omega: herufi ya mwisho ya alfabeti ya Kiyunani. 2 *(end)* mwisho. **alpha and ~** mwanzo na mwisho.

omelet(te) *n* kimanda, kiwanda *sweet ~* andazi la mayai lenye sukari na jam.

omen *n* ndege, fali; *(sign)* ishara, dalili *good ~* ndege njema, dalili ya bahati njema *bad ~* ndege mbaya, kisirani *of ill ~* ndege mbaya *vt* onyesha dalili, -wa ishara ya. **ominous** *adj* -a ndege mbaya, -a kisirani; -a kuogofya. **ominously** *adv*.

omit *vt* 1 ~ **to do/doing sth** acha, ruka, kosa, -shindwa *do not ~ to do that* usiache kufanya hayo. 2 ruka, acha. **omission** *n* 1 kitendo cha kuacha; kukosa kufanya, kutotenda; *(error)*. kosa2 jambo lililoachwa/lililorukwa.

omnibus *n (old use)* basi (gari kubwa la abiria) *(attrib)* makusudi mengi pamoja; jungu kuu *an ~ volume* vitabu vingi vilivyo katika jalada moja ~ *train* garimoshi la abiria.

omnipotence *n* kudura. **omnipotent** *adj* -enye kudura *the O~ God* Mwenyezi Mungu.

omniscience *n (formal)* maarifa/kujua yote. **omniscient** *adj* -enye maarifa yote.

omnivorous *adj* -a kula chochote; *(fig) an ~ reader* msomaji wa kila kitabu.

on[1] *adv part* 1 *(to show progress, activity) come ~* fanyafanya; fanya haraka. *work ~* endelea na kazi. **and so ~** na kuendelea, na kadhalika. **later ~** baadaye. ~ **and ~** bila kukoma/kusita. 2 *(to show places)* kuwa juu ya; kuvaa *your hat is not ~ straight* hukuvaa sawa kofia. ~ **to,** *prep* juu ya. 3 *(contrasted with off)* *the lights are* ~ taa zinawaka; endelea kuwepo *is water* ~? maji yangalipo?, maji yako? 4 *(combined with be and have in various meanings) what's* ~? kuna nini? *have you anything* ~ *tonight*? unafanya chochote leo usiku? **be ~ about sth** *(colloq)* endelea kuzungumzia/kulalamika juu ya jambo. **be ~ at sb** *(colloq)* sumbua, kera, fuatafuata. *be ~ to sb/sth* wasiliana na; jua juu ya *be ~ to a criminal* -wa na habari juu ya mhalifu. **be ~ to a good thing** shikilia jambo jema, fanikiwa. 5 kwa kuelekea. **head ~ collision** kugongana uso kwa uso.

on[2] *prep* 1 juu ya, -ni *put posters ~ the wall* bandika mabango/picha ukutani *suffer disaster ~ disaster* pata makosi juu ya mkosi. 2 *(indicating time) ~ Sunday* Jumapili *let's meet ~ 1st May* tukutane Mei Mosi ~ *Fridays* kila Ijumaa ~ *arrival* nitakapofika. ~ *time* kwa wakati unaotakiwa/ ulioahidiwa. 3 *(indicating direction)* **turn one's back ~ sb** -tojali mtu, -pa kisogo. 4 *(indicating charge) put tax ~ cigarettes* wekea sigara kodi. 5 *(indicating a proximity)* karibu na *a town ~ the coast* mji karibu ya pwani. 6 kuhusu, juu ya *a lecture ~ publications* mhadhara juu ya machapisho *be keen ~ the law* jihusisha mno na sheria. 7 *(indicating membership) she is ~ the commission* yeye ni mjumbe wa tume. 8 *(expressing the basis/reason for sth)* kwa *a book based ~ facts* kitabu kilichotokana na matukio halisi. 9 *(followed by n or adj) (indicating action, manner, state) ~ business* kikazi ~ *tour* kitalii *buy sth ~ the cheap (colloq)* nunua kwa bei rahisi *be ~ fire* ungua.

onanism *n* punyeto; kujamiiana kuliko-katishwa.

once *adv* 1 mara moja *Juma came here* ~ Juma alikuja hapa mara moja *we go to the cinema ~ a week* huwa tunakwenda sinema mara moja kwa wiki. ~ **more** tena, mara nyingine. ~ **or twice**; **~ and ~ again**; **in a while** mara chache tu. **(for) this ~; (just) for ~** mara hii tu. 2 hapo kale, hapo nyuma, wakati fulani *he ~ lived here*, hapo nyuma/wakati fulani aliwahi kuishi hapa. *(in story-tellingstyle)* ~ **upon a time** hapo zamani. 3 **never ~; not ~** hata mara moja *he never ~ agrees with us* hakubaliani nasi hata mara moja. 4 **at ~** mara moja, bila kuchelewa; papo hapo *come here at ~* njoo hapa mara moja *at ~ he collapsed* papo hapo alizirai; wakati huohuo; kwa wakati mmoja *don't do many things at ~* usifanye mambo mengi kwa wakati mmoja. **all at ~** ghafla *all at ~ I saw him* ghafla nilimwona. **get/give sb/sth the ~-over** *(colloq)* tupia kitu/mtu macho, pitia.

oncoming *adj* -nayofuata, -nayokuja. *n* kuja, kufika.

one *adj* 1 -moja ~ *hundred,* mia moja. 2 -a kwanza *standard ~* darasa la kwanza *book ~* kitabu cha kwanza *chapter ~* sura ya kwanza. 3 -moja (fulani) ~ *day* siku moja fulani, siku moja. 4 sawa *they all did it in ~ style* wote walifanya mtindo sawa/mmoja. **be at ~ (with sb)** -wa na mawazo sawa. **it's all ~ (to sb)** -ote sawa, ni mamoja. **become ~; be made ~** ungana; oana. 5 *(phrases)* **~ and all** kila mtu. **all in ~** (ote) kwa pamoja. ~ **or two** chache. **by ~s and twos** mmojammoja *people began to leave the meeting in ~s and twos* watu walianza kuondoka mkutanoni mmojammoja. ~ **up (on sb)** -wa na nafuu (zaidi ya mwingine), zidi. **number ~** *(colloq)* (mtu) mwenyewe. *he's always thinking of number ~* daima anajifikiria mwenyewe tu *indef pron* 1 kitu kimoja; mojawapo *the big book and the little~* kitabu kikubwa na kidogo *which ~ do you like* ni kipi unachokitaka? *pick me out some good ~s* nichagulie nzuri ~ *of my* *girls* mmojawapo wa wasichana wangu; *(colloq)* -le: *I want the red ~* nataka ile nyekundu. 3 *person pron* fulani. *the little ~s* watoto. **the Holy O~** Mungu. 4 ~ **another** -ana *they hate ~ another* wanachukiana. 5 *impers pron* mtu *she is not ~ to give up easily* yeye si mtu wa kukata tamaa kirahisi. 6 *(compounds)* **~-armed** *adj* -enye mkono mmoja. **~-armed bandit** *n (colloq)* mashini ya kamari inayoendeshwa kwa sarafu. **~eyed** *adj* chongo. **~-horse** *adj* -enye kuvutwa na farasi mmoja; *(fig)* -siokuwa na vitu vingi, duni. **~-idead** *adj* -lio na wazo moja tu. **~-man** *adj* -enye kufanywa na mtu mmoja tu. **~-sided** *adj* -a upande mmoja; -a upendeleo. **~time** *adj* -a zamani. **~track mind** -enye wazo moja tu. **~way street** *n* njia moja (hairudi). **~self** *reflex pron* mwenyewe *one must do it ~self* mtu lazima akifanye mwenyewe.

onerous *adj* -zito, -a kutaabisha; -a kuhitaji jitihada nyingi.**~ly** *adv*. **~ness** *n*. **on going** *adj* -enye kuendelea, -enye kufanyika muda wote.

onion *n* 1 kitunguu *spring, green ~* kitunguu kibichi. 2 *(sl)* kichwa. **be off one's ~** -wa na kichaa. *know one's ~s (sl)* fahamu kazi yako kutokana na uzoefu/tajriba. **~-skin** *n* ganda la kitunguu; karatasi nyepesi, nyembamba na ngumu sana.

onlooker *n* mtazamaji *the ~s sees most of the game (prov)* mtazamaji (ndiye) mfaidi yote.

only *adj* -a pekee, -a peke *~ child* mtoto pekee. *adv* 1 tu, basi *he ~* yeye tu *he can ~ say 'no'* anaweza tu kusema 'la' *if ~ he would come* laiti angekuja. 2 ~ **too** sana, kabisa. *I shall be ~ too glad* nitafurahi sana. *the news proved ~ too true* habari zilithibitika kuwa ni kweli kabisa *conj* ila, lakini, isipokuwa *I would do it with pleasure ~ I have no time* ningeifanya kwa furaha lakini sina nafasi. **~ that** isipokuwa, kwamba, ila tu.

onomatopoeia *n* onomatopia/tanakali sauti: ujenzi wa neno kwa kuiga sauti/mlio wa kitu.

onrush *n* mmiminiko mkali.

onset *n* 1 shambulio. 2 mwanzo (wenye nguvu) *at the first ~* mwanzoni mwa.

onshore *adj, adv* -a ufukoni; kuelekea ufukoni.

onslaught *n* shambulio, mvamio.

onto *prep see on.*

ontology *n* ontolojia: idara/nadharia (ya metafizikia) inayojishughulisha na asili ya uhai/maisha.

onus *n* **the ~** daraka, wajibu; mzigo, jukumu *~ of proof* dhima ya kuthibitisha *the ~ lies with you* wajibu wako (kuthibitisha)/kazi kwako (sasa).

onward *adj, adv* mbele.

oodles *n (sl)* ~ **of** wingi, chungu (nzima) *~ of money* pesa kibao/ chungu nzima.

oomph *n (sl)* mvuto, bidii.

ooze *n* matope, kinamasi *vt,vi* vuja, tona, chirizika *their courage ~ away* uhodari wao ulitoweka kama maji yalivyotiririka. **oozy** *adj* 1 -a matope, -a kinamasi. 2 majimaji.

opal *n* opali: kito chenye rangi ya maziwa na maji. **~escent** *adj* -a opali. **~ine** *adj* -a opali. *n* kito cheupe kinachobadili rangi.

opaque *adj* 1 -siopenyeka nuru. 2 -siometameta. 3 -pumbavu. 4 -gumu kuelewa; -enye utata wa maana. **opacity** *n* 1 hali ya kutopitisha nuru. 2 utata wa maana. **~ly** *adv*. **~ness** *n*.

opart *n* sanaa dhahania mauzauza inayotatanisha ya kisasa.

open *adj* 1 wazi, -eupe *the door is open* mlango u wazi. **~eyed** *adj* -enye macho wazi, -lio na makini; -a mshangao. **~-mouthed** *adj* -lafi; -liopigwa bumbuazi, -lioduwaa. ~ **vowel** irabu wazi. ~ **work** *n* nakshi/ urembo katika lesi n.k.. 2 -sio zingirwa, -sio ua, -sio na kizuizi. **the ~ sea** bahari kuu. **an ~ river** mto unaopitika bila kizuizi. 3

-siofunikwa, wazi, -siokipaa *an ~ boat* mtumbwi wazi *an ~ drain/sewer*, mtaro *in the ~ air* nje. **~-air** *attrib adj* -a kufanyika nje *an ~-air dance* dansi inayochezewa nje. **~ prison** kifungo/ jela ya nje; isiyobanabana. **~air theatre** *n* uwanja wa nje wa maonyesho; maonyesho ya nje, jengo la tamthilia lisilo na paa. 4 -liochanua; -liosambazwa *the flowers were all ~* maua yote yalikuwa yamechanua *the papers lay ~ on the floor* karatasi zilisambaa kwenye sakafu. **with ~ hands** kwa moyo mkunjufu, kwa wingi wa fadhila. **~handed** karimu. **~-hearted** (m) kweli. **with ~ arms** kwa upendo/ raghba. **~ order** *(of troops)* -lioachana sana kwa nafasi; -a watu wote, -a bure, -a wazi *an ~ competition* mashindano ya watu wote/wazi. **the ~ door** sera ya biashara bila ushuru, huru; kuruhusu wafanyabiashara wa kigeni nchini. **the ~ shop** kiwanda ambapo wafanyakazi wanachama na wasio wanachama wana maslahi na utetezi sawa **keep ~ house** -wa karimu kwa watu wote. 6 siotolewa uamuzi. **~ ended** *adj (of a debate etc)* wazi, -sio na hatima maalumu. **an ~ question** swali lisilokuwa na jibu moja/lisilohitaji kukatiwa shauri. **an ~ verdict** uamuzi usomshitaki mtu/ unaodhihirisha sababu ya kifo bila kusema kama ni cha ajali/makusudi/ faradhi n.k.. **have/keep an ~ mind (on sth)** -tofikia uamuzi; -wa tayari kupokea mawazo/mashauri mapya n.k. 7 dhahiri *an ~ scandal* -kashfa dhahiri. **an ~ letter** barua inayochapishwa jaridani. 8 -siolindwa, -siokingwa. **be/lay oneself ~ to sth** kaa bila kujikinga; karibisha. 9 -siohitimishwa, -siofungwa, -siokamilika. 10 *(phrases)* **~ and shut** wazi, dhahiri shahiri. **~ cast** *adj* -a juu ya ardhi. **an ~ cheque** hundi wazi. **~ court**, mahakama wazi/hadharani. **the ~ season** *(fishing and shooting)* msimu huru wa uwindaji/pasipo kuzuiwa. **an ~ secret** siri isiyokuwa siri; siri ya wazi. **the ~ University** chuo kikuu huria: chuo kikuu ambapo masomo yanaendeshwa kwa njia ya posta, redio, televisheni n.k.. **~ weather, an ~ winter** majira shwari ya baridi/yasiyo kuwa na barafu nyingi. *n* **the ~** nje. **come (out) into the ~** *(fig)* jitokeza, toa wazo/mpango n.k. hadharani *adv* waziwazi, bila siri; kwa ukweli; kwa watu wote. **~ness** *n* uwazi, unyofu ~ *vt,vi* 1 fungua; funguka; funua; funuka *~ the door* fungua mlango *~ the pot*, funua chungu. **~ one's eyes** shangaa; zinduka. **~ (sb's) eyes to sth** fumbua, elewesha. 2 toboa; kata *~ well* chimba kisima *~ a road through a forest* kata, toboa barabara katikati ya msitu. **~ sth up** fungua, fungulia, endeleza; tandaza, sambaza; kunjua *~ out a folding mat* kunjua/ tandaza mkeka. **~ one's mind/heart to sb** toa/tangaza maoni/hisia za mtu. 4 fungua/anzisha rasmi *~ a shop*, fungua(rasmi) duka *~ a meeting* fungua (rasmi) mkutano *~ a project* anzisha/zindua mradi. **~ the bidding** anza kunadi. **~ fire (at/on)** anza kupiga bunduki/risasi. 5 **~ with** anza na. 6 **~ out** onekana **~er** *n* mfungua, kifungua. **~ing** *n* 1 nafasi wazi *there's an ~ in the treasury* kuna nafasi ya kazi hazina. 2 kipenyo; mlango; tundu, ufa. 3 mwanzo; *the ~ of a speech* mwanzo wa hotuba. **the ~ing night** usiku wa kwanza wa kuonyesha. 4 nafasi/ uwanja wazi, upenu *adj* -a kwanza. **~ time** saa/wakati wa kufungua (shughuli).

opera *n* opera: mchezo wa kuigiza *comic ~* opera ya kuchekesha. **grand ~** opera kali (isiyo na mzaha). **~-cloak** *n* koti la usiku (la madaha). **~-glass** *n* darubini ya kutazamia opera. **~-house** *n* jumba la opera. **~tic** *adj*.

operate *vt,vi* 1 tenda kazi, endesha *~ a machine* endesha mashini. 2 *(med)* **~ (on sb) (for sth)** fanya operesheni, pasua. **operating-table/ theatre** *n* meza ya kupasulia. 3 *(of an army)* fanya maneva. 4 *(of a stock broker)* nunua na kuuza. **operable** *adj* -a kutibika kwa operesheni/kupasuliwa. **operation** *n* 1 kufanya kazi, kutenda; utendaji. **come into ~** tumika; anza kufanya kazi. **be in ~** tumika; shughulika. 2 kazi, shughuli. 3 *(med)* upasuaji. **~ set** vyombo vya kupasulia. 4 sehemu maalum ya kazi. 5 *(math)* tendo la kugawa, kuongeza, kuzidisha kutoa n.k., ukokotoaji. *binary ~* tendo jozi. 6 *(mil) (pl)* **operations** nyendo za vikosi vya jeshi, wakati wa vita/maneva. **~ room** chumba cha kudhibiti/kuongoza mambo. 7 *(polit)* operesheni, kampeni. **operational** *adj* 1 -a uendeshaji. **~ cost/expenditure** gharama ya uendeshaji. **~ research** uchunguzi wa njia bora za kutumikisha kifaa n.k. 2 -nayo fanya kazi *the ~ is already ~* kompyuta tayari inafanya kazi. **operative** *adj* 1 -a kutenda kazi; -a kutumika *become ~* tenda kazi, anza kutumika *this law became ~ on 1 April* sheria hii ilianza kutumika tarehe moja Aprili. 2 **~ words** maneno yenye athari za kisheria; maneno muhimu. 3 -a kupasua *n* mfanyakazi, fundi mitambo. **operator** *n* 1 mfanyakazi, mwendeshaji. 2 *(telephone)* mpokeaji/mumaji simu opereta. 3 *(sl)* mwerevu, hodari.

operetta *n (music)* opereta: opera fupi ya kuchekesha.

ophthalmia *n* ofthalmia: ugonjwa wa macho. **ophthalmic** *adj* -a ofthalmia. **ophthalmology** *n* ofthalmolojia **ophthalmoscope** *n* chombo cha kufanyia uchunguzi wa macho.

opiate *n* dawa (ya kutuliza) *adj* -a kutia usingizi *vt* tia afyuni.

opine *vt* **~ that** *(formal)* -wa na/toa maoni.

opinion *n* 1 oni, wazo, dhana. *expressed ~* kauli. **in my/your ~: in the ~ of sb** kwa maoni yangu/yako. **act up to one's ~s** tumia/ongozwa na maoni yako. **a matter of ~** jambo lisilohakika, si yakini, jambo linalojadilika. **be of the ~ that** dhani, ona. **have a good/bad/high/low ~ of sb/sth** heshimu/dharau n.k. mtu *I am of your ~* nakubaliana nawe. 2 maoni, imani, ya kundi *~ of the court* maoni ya mahakama. **public ~** maoni ya umma. 4 ushauri/shauri *get a lawyer's ~* pata shauri la mwanasheria. **~ated; ~ative** *adj* -lioshikilia maoni yake, -shupavu.

opium *n* afyuni. **~ den** maskani ya watumiaji/wavutaji afyuni *~ extract* afyuni *~ poppy* ua la afyuni; *(fig)* kasumba.

opponent *n* mshindani, mpinzani. *adj* -enye upinzani, pinzani, -shindani.

opportune *adj* 1 *(of time)* -a kufaa, -a wakati maalumu. 2 *(of event)* -liotokea wakati unaofaa. **opportunism** *n* msimamo wa liwezekanalo/kufuata upepo, kuongozwa na matukio katika kuamua jambo la kufanya. **opportunist** *n* mfuata upepo, mtu atumiaye matukio halisi katika maamuzi yake, mtu mwenye kuangalia masilahi yake zaidi kuliko haki au uhalali wa jambo. **~ly** *adv*.

opportunity *n* nafasi, fursa, wasaa *take the ~ of* tumia nafasi ya, tumia fursa.

oppose *vt* 1 pinga, shindana, kataa. 2 **~ (against/to)**-linganisha, shindanisha. **opposite** *adj* 1 **~ (to)** mkabala, -a kuelekeana, -a/-enye kukabili: *~ sides* pande zilizoelekeana. 2 kinyume. 3 wajina (wa), wa cheo/nafasi sawa (katika kundi jingine). **one's ~ number** mtu mwenye cheo sawa na chako katika asasi nyingine.

opposition *n* 1 upinzani. **be in the ~** -wa pinzani. 2 kuelekeana, kukabiliana; *(resistance)* upinzani, kupinga, uzuizi, pingamizi.

oppress *vt* 1 kandamiza, dhulumu, onea. 2 *(fig)* elemea, songa, taabisha. **~ion** *n* 1 ukandamizaji. 2 *(trouble)* mateso, kuteseka, kutaabika. **~ive** *adj* 1 -dhalimu, kandamizaji. 2 zito, -a kuelemea, -a kusonga, -a taabu. **~or**

n dhalimu, mkandamizaji. **~ively** *adv*.
opprobrious *adj (formal)* -a kuaibisha, -a aibu, -a kufedhehesha. **~ly** *adv*. **opprobrium** *n* dharau; aibu,fedheha, haya.

oppugn *vt* pinga, bishania.

opt *vi* 1 **~for sth** chagua, fanya uchaguzi, amua. 2 ~ **out of** amua kutoshiriki, jitoa.

optic *adj* -a macho *n* jicho **~s** *n* elimu ya nuru. **~al** *adj* -a macho. ~ **illusion** mazingaombwe, madanganyo ya macho, mauzauza ~ *instrument* ala ya macho (miwani, darubini n.k.). **~ian** *n* mtengenezaji/mwuzaji miwani.

optimism *n* msimamo wa kutegemea mazuri, kuwa na matumaini mema. **optimist** *n* mwenye msimamo wa kutegemea mazuri. **optimistic** *adj*. **optimistically** *adv*.

optimum *n* hali ya kufaa kabisa, bora kabisa, upeo *adj* -enye hali ya kufaa kabisa, -a juu kabisa.

option *n* 1 uchaguzi, hiari, haki ya kutenda *the ~ is yours* uchaguzi ni wako *there is no ~* hakuna budi, sharti, hakuna hiari, lazima *I have no ~ but to go* ni lazima niende *imprisonment without the ~ of a fine* kifungo bila hiari ya kulipa faini *none of the ~s is satisfactory* hakuna uchaguzi wa haja, uchaguzi wa aina yoyote hauridhishi. **local** ~ haki ya kuamua (jambo) kwa kura. 2 mambo ya kuchaguliwa. **leave one's ~s open** -tojifunga (na jambo) **~al** *adj*. **~ally** *adv*.

optometer *n* optomita: chombo kinachopimia macho nguvu ya kuona mbali. **optometrist** *n* mpimaji wa macho.

opulence *n* utajiri, mali; ukwasi. **opulent** *adj*. **opulently** *adv*.

opus *n* utungo (wa kitabu, wimbo n.k.). **magnum** ~ *n* utungo mkuu wa msanii.

or *conj* 1 au, ama. ~ **else** kama sivyo; la sivyo, ama sivyo. *whether you come ~ not it's all the same to* me uje usije ni mamoja kwangu. 2 ~ **so** kama hivyo, kitu kama hicho; hivi.

oracle *n* 1 *(ancient Greece) (place)* mizimuni; uaguzi; mwaguzi; jibu la mizimuni. 2 kahini/mwaguzi aliyetoa majibu hayo. 3 mshauri, mtu mwenye busara *work the ~ (fig)* fanikiwa kwa njia ya sirisiri. **oracular** *adj*.

oral *adj* -a mdomo, -a kinywa, -a kunena, -a maneno, -sioandikwa; simulizi ~ *exercises* mazoezi ya kusema ~ *literature* fasihi simulizi. **~ly** *adv*.

orange *n* chungwa; *(bitter)* danzi; *(mandarin)* chenza; kangaja; rangi ya machungwa. **~ade** *n* maji ya machungwa. **~-peel** ganda la chungwa. **~ry** *n* shamba la michungwa.

orang-outang *n* orangutangu: nyani mkubwa kama mtu wa Borneo na Sumatra.

orate *vi (joc)* hutubu. **oration** *n* hotuba rasmi. **orator** *n* msemi, msemaji, mhutubu, mwenye ufasaha wa kusema. **oratorical** *adj* -a ufasaha wa kusema; -a hotuba. **oratory** *n* ufasaha wa kusema/kuhutubu, usemaji.

oratory *n* kanisa dogo, kijumba cha kusalia.

orb *n* 1 tufe (hasa jua, mwezi au moja ya sayari). 2 kitu chenye umbo la tufe; mviringo; duara. 3 *(poetic)* jicho.

orbit *n* mzunguko; mzingo ~ *of the earth* mzingo wa dunia *the earth's ~ round the sun* mzingo wa dunia kuzunguka jua *eye-~* mzingo wa jicho *vt,vi* enda kwa mzingo, weka (kitu) katika mwendo wa kuzunguka. **~al** *adj*. ~ **velocity** mwendo wa kuliweka tufe kwenye mzingo.

orchard *n* shamba la/kiunga cha miti ya matunda *n ~man* mkulima wa shamba la (miti ya) matunda.

orchestra *n* 1 *(mus)* okestra: kundi la watu wapigao muziki pamoja. 2 ~ **pit** ukumbi wa wapigao muziki kwenye thieta. 3 ~ **stalls** viti vya mbele katika thieta. **~l** *adj* -a okestra. **~te** *vt (mus)* tunga; panga, tengeneza utaratibu (kwa ajili ya okestra). **~tion** *n*.

ordain *vt* 1 ~ **that** amua, amuru, agiza. 2 fanya kasisi/padri.

ordeal *n* 1 majaribu, mateso *go through an ~* pita katika majaribu *~ by fire* jaribu la moto *trial by ~* hukumu ya majaribu.

order *n* 1 mpango, taratibu *arrange in alphabetical ~* panga kialfabeti. **in ~ of** kwa kufuata, kwa mpango wa. 2 **in ~** sahihi, sawa. **in good ~** kwa utaratibu, hali ya utendaji safi *my watch is in good working ~* saa yangu inaenda sawasawa *the engine is not in good working ~* injini haiendi vizuri. **out of ~** bovu. 3 amani, utulivu *law and ~* sheria na amani. 4 nidhamu, taratibu (za midahalo). **call to ~** kumbusha nidhamu. **point of ~** swala la utaratibu. **be in ~ to do sth** ruhusiwa. **O~! O~!** tusikilizane! **~ of the day** taratibu ya siku/agizo la siku. 5 amri *he is under ~ to go* alipewa amri ya kwenda. **by ~of** kwa amri ya. **under the ~s of** amriwa na, chini ya amri ya. 6 agizo *we have received two ~s for ploughs* tumepata maagizo mawili ya plau. **on ~** imeagizwa. **made to ~** (kitu) kilichotengenezwa kwa maagizo *(colloq) a tall/large ~* jambo gumu la kutekeleza **~-book** kitabu cha maagizo; vitu vilivyoagizwa *your ~ has been sent* maagizo yako yamepelekwa. 7 maagizo (ya maandishi) ya kulipa fedha au kuidhinisha kutenda jambo. 8 aina, jinsi, cheo, daraja, tabaka *the lower ~* watu wa tabaka la chini *ability of a high ~* uwezo wa juu kabisa. 9 upadri, ukasisi. **be in/take (holy) ~** -wa padri/kasisi, pewa upadiri/ukasisi. 10 chama/shirika la watawa *The Franciscan ~* Shirika la Wafransiska. 11 kanuni *the ~ of prayers* kanuni ya sala. 12 *(bio)* oda. 13 hawala, hundi, hati *money ~* hawala ya fedha. 14 madhumuni, kusudi. **in ~ that/to** makusudi, ili. **in ~ to do that** ili kufanya hivyo. 15 kibali *I have an ~ to see the house nina* kibali cha kuangalia nyumba *vt* 1 panga. 2 amuru, agiza. 3 *(phrases)* ~ **about** amrishaamrisha, peleka huku na kule. ~ **away** fukuza. ~ **back** rudisha. **~ing** *n* mpango, mpangilio. **~ly** *adj* 1 kwa mpango, -zuri. 2 makini, -enye adabu, -a amani *n* askari mtumishi. **medical ~** msaidizi (katika hospitali ya jeshi). **~liness** *n*.

ordinal *adj* -a mpango. ~ **numbers** nambari za mpango.

ordinand *n* mtaka ukasisi. **ordination** *n* 1 utaratibu, mpango. 2 ibada/tendo la kufanya ukasisi/upadre. **Sacrament of O~** Sakramenti ya Upadre.

ordinance *n* 1 amri, agizo, sheria. 2 *(rel)* ibada.

ordinary *adj* 1 -a kawaida, -a desturi *~ days's work* kazi ya kawaida *an ~ person* mtu wa kawaida. ~ **way** ikiwa mambo ya kawaida. **in the ~ way** kama kawaida. *n* 1 kawaida. **in ~** -a kudumu; mara nyingi, kwa desturi. **out of the ~** si -a kawaida, -geni. 2 *(rel)* askofu. **ordinarily** *adv*. **ordinariness** *n*.

ordnance *n* 1 mizinga; zana za vita. 2 *(mil)* ~ **survey** upimaji halisi wa ramani *~ (survey) ~ map* ramani ya upimaji halisi wa nchi. ~ **corps** kundi linalohusika kutoa/kuagiza vifaa vya jeshi.

ordure *n* 1 mavi, kinyesi, taka, samadi.

ore *n* mbale: mawe yenye madini.

organ *n* 1 ogani: sehemu ya mwili au mmea ifanyayo kazi maalum k.v. mapafu, moyo, mizizi n.k. *~ of speech* ogani za matamshi. 2 chombo *~ of public opinion* magazeti, redio n.k.. 3 kinanda. ~ **blower** *n* mpuliza kinanda. **~ist** *n* mpiga kinanda. **~ic** *adj* 1 -a ogani; -a kiumbe hai. ~ **chemistry** kemia kaboni. 2 -a mfumo, -a sehemu zinazolingana. *an ~ whole* mfumo unaolingana. **~ically** *adv*. **organism** *n* kiumbehai, kiumbe cha kikaboni.

organdie *n* ogandi: kitambaa kama doria au shashi.

organization *n* 1 mpangilio, utaratibu, mfumo. 2 *(association)* chama, shirika. **organize** *vt* 1 simamia, andaa, ratibu, panga. 2 unda/anzisha chama cha wafanyakazi. **organized** *adj* -enye mpango/utaratibu *highly ~ forms of life* viumbe hai vyenye mfumo tata *~ labour* vyombo vya wafanyakazi. **organizer** *n* mtungaji; msimamizi; muandalizi.

orgasm *n (sexual)* mshindo, mshushio, upeo wa raha ya kujamiiana.

orgy *n* 1 karamu ya ulafi, ulevi na uasherati. **orgiastic** *adj* -a karamu ya ulafi n.k. 2 *(colloq)* kiasi kingi mno.

orient *adj* 1 *(of the sun)* -a mashariki, -a matlai, -a thamani *n* **the ~** nchi za Mashariki (k.v. Uchina, Japan n.k.). **~al** *adj* -a mashariki, -a pande za Asia *n* mtu wa nchi za mashariki. **~alist** *n* mtaalamu wa mambo ya nchi za mashariki. **~ate** *vt* 1 jenga kuelekea mashariki (kama ni kanisa ili upande wa madhabahu ukabili mashariki). 2 elekeza mahali *~ oneself* fanya uelewe mahali ulipo; elewa mazingira. **~ation** *n* maelekezo ya mazingira.

orifice *n* tundu, kitundu, kipenyo, mdomo.

origin *n* 1 asili, chanzo, mwanzo, chimbuko. 2 *(ancestry)* wazazi, ukoo, jadi, nasaba. 3 *(cause)* sababu. **~al** *adj* 1 -a asili, -a kwanza. 2 *(peculiar)* -pya, geni, ajabu. 3 *(inventive)* bunifu, -enye akili za kubuni. *n* 1 lugha ya kwanza/asili (ya utungo), mtindo wa kwanza. 2 asili. 3 *(of person)* mbunifu, mtu wa (mtindo wa) pekee. **~ality** *n* 1 kuwa na akili za kubuni (za kutunga, za kuvumbua). 2 *(singularity)* ajabu, upya. **~ally** *adv* 1 kwanza, kwa asili. 2 kwa ubunifu, kwa akili za kubuni. **originate** *vt,vi* **~ from/in sth; ~ from/with sb** tokana *her novel ~ from a short story* riwaya yake ilitokana na hadithi fupi. **~ator** *n* mwanzilishi, mtungaji, mwenye kubuni, mzushi, mvumbuaji.

oriole *n (bio)* kiambizi; **(golden) ~** umbia.

orison *n (archaic)* sala.

ormolu *n* 1 shaba iliyopakwa rangi kufanana na dhahabu. 2 vyombo vya shaba za dhahabu.

ornament *n* pambo, madoido *vt* pamba, remba, tia madoido. **~al** *adj* -a kupamba, -a urembo. **~ation** *n* 1 kurembwa, kutiwa madoido. 2 pambo, urembo.

ornate *adj* -a mapambo; -a/-enye madoido. **~ly** *adv*. **~ness** *n*.

ornery *adj (US colloq)* kaidi, -enye hasira.

ornithology *n* elimundege. **ornithologist** *n* **ornithological** *adj*.

orotund *adj (formal)* 1 -enye majivuno/kiburi. 2 -enye staha/hadhi.

orphan *n* yatima, (mwana) mkiwa *adj* -a yatima *vt* fanya yatima. **~age** *n* nyumba ya yatima.

orthodox *adj* 1 -enye imani kamili/halisi. 2 sahihi, halisi, barabara. **~y** *n* imani halisi/inayokubalika. matamshi sahihi yaliyokubaliwa.

orthography *n* tahajia; **orthographic** *adj*.

orthop(a)edics *n* tiba mifupa; orthopediki: utibabu wa kasoro na magonjwa ya mifupa. **orthopaedic** *adj* -a (kasoro na magonjwa ya) mifupa.

oryx *n* choroa.

Oscar *n (US)* zawadi (ya kila mwaka) ya mshindi wa sinema.

oscillate *vt,vi* 1 pembeza, bembe(z)a; *(fig)* wayawaya. 2 *(elect)* bembea. **oscillating current** mkondo bembeo. **oscillation** *n* mbembeo. **oscillator** *n* kibembeo; chombo cha kufanya mibembeo ya umeme. **oscillograph** *n (elect)* osilografu: kipima mibembeo. **oscilloscope** *n (elect)*. osiloskopu, kionyesha mibembeo.

osier *n* 1 aina ya matete. 2 ufito wa

kusukia viti, meza n.k..
osmosis *n (phy)* osmosisi: mfyonzo, mnyonyo wa uoevu.
osprey *n* furukombe.
ossify *vt,vi* fanya/fanyika ngumu kama mfupa; *(fig)* -tobadilika; fanya kutobadilika. **ossification** *n*. **osseous** *adj* -a mifupa, -a kama mfupa.
ossuary *n* mahali pa kupokea/hifadhi mifupa ya wafu; pango la mifupa.
ostensible *adj* 1 -a juu juu, -sio kweli/halisi. 2 -liobashiriwa, -liotangazwa. **ostensibly** *adv*.
ostentation *n* majivuno, kuonyesha ufahari, ushaufu. **ostentatious** *adj* shaufu, a kujidai/kujishaua. **ostentatiously** *adv*.
osteopathy *n* matibabu (ya magonjwa) kwa kuchezesha mifupa. **osteology** *n* elimu mifupa (ya watu na wanyama).
osteopath *n* mganga wa mifupa.
ostler *n (old use)* saisi.
ostracize *vt* 1 *(people)* tenganisha, tenga. 2 *(ancient Greece)* fukuza nchini (kwa miaka 5 hadi 10). **ostracism** *n*
ostrich *n* mbuni.
other *adj, pron* -ingine. **the ~** -a pili. **every ~** *(alternate)* kila -a pili; kila -ingine. **on the ~ hand** upande mwingine ~ *people* watu wengine. ~ **than** zaidi ya, -sipokuwa *some ~ day* siku nyingine. **the ~ day** juzijuzi. **one after the ~**; **one after an~** moja baada ya ingine; mfululizo. ~ **things being equal** kama mambo mengine yote yangekuwa sawa. **the ~s** -ingine. **or ~** fulani *someone or ~* mtu fulani. 2 tofauti *I do not want her ~ than she is* simtaki tofauti na alivyo. *prep* ~ **than** isipokuwa, ila *there's no teacher here ~ than me* hakuna mwalimu hapa isipokuwa mimi *adv* vinginevyo. ~-**worldly** *adj* -enye kuhusu/kufikiria dunia nyingine; -a kutopenda mambo/anasa za dunia. **~ness** *n* utofauti, wingine. **~wise** *adv* vinginevyo *he is stubborn but ~wise likeable* ni mkaidi vinginevyo hupendeka *all his speeches, political and ~wise* hotuba zake zote za siasa na vinginevyo. 2 kwa namna, upande mwingine *conj* la/ama sivyo *do it now ~wise you will regret it* ifanye sasa ama sivyo utajutia.
otiose *adj (formal)* -sio na maana, bila matumizi maalum, -siohitajika; -sio na kazi.
otoscope *n* otoskopu: chombo cha kupimia tundu la sikio.
ottoman[1] *n* kiti kirefu (kisicho na mgongo au mkono) chenye matakia.
Ottoman[2] *n* Uturuki; Mturuki. *adj* -a Kituruki.
oubliette *n* gereza la shimoni.
ouch *int* aaa! uui!
ought *(aux)* bidi; paswa, takiwa *I ~ to* napaswa, imenipasa, imenibidi.
ounce *n (abbr oz.)* 1 wakia. 2 *(pharm)* aunsi. **our** *adj* -etu. **O ~ Father** Mungu Baba. **O~ lady** Bikira Maria. **O ~ Lord** Bwana Wetu (Yesu Kristu). **~s** *pron, pred adj* -etu *a friend of ~s* rafiki yetu *~s was a lovely garden* bustani yetu ilikuwa nzuri *it became ~s by purchase* tulikipata kwa kununua. **~selves** *pron* sisi wenyewe! *we did it by ~selves* tulifanya sisi wenyewe. *We all by ~selves* sisi wenyewe (bila msaada); wenyewe (bila kufuatana na mwingine).
oust *vt* ~ **sb (from)** ondosha, toa, fukuza.
out *adv part* 1 (kwa) nje *he is ~* hayumo (nyumbani) *we don't go ~ these days* hatutoki/hatutembei siku hizi *be ~* -tokuwepo; *(of book in library)* tolewa, azimwa; *(of a dress)* -siotumika siku hizi; *(of workers)* goma; *(be mistaken)* kosa *I was ~ in my calculations* nilikosea katika hesabu zangu *you're not very far ~* hujakosea sana; *(of cricket)* tolewa. 2 toa, toka ~ *of the way*! simile! habedari! nipishe. ~ **with it** toa; sema! onyesha!. *(in expressions)* **be ~ and about** pata ahueni *the book is ~* kitabu kimetoka *the chickens are ~* vifaranga vimeanguliwa *the roses*

are ~ mawaridi yamechanua *the secret is* ~ siri imetoka, imejulikana, imefichuliwa *the sun is* ~ jua limechomoza. 3 huko (mbali) *my cousin is* ~ *in America* ndugu yangu yuko huko Amerika. 4 *(indicating exhaustion, extinction)* kwa kuzimika/kwisha *the light is* ~ taa imezimika *the lease is* ~ mkataba umekwisha. 5 *(indicating completion)* kwa kumaliza *before the week is* ~ kabla wiki haijamalizika. **cry one's eyes** ~ lia sana (hadi dukuduku linakwisha). ~ **and** ~ kabisa, kupindukia. ~ **and away** kwa mbali sana *she was* ~ *and away the most intelligent* aliwazidi wote akili kwa mbali sana. 6 kwa kutopatikana ~ *of print* -sichopatikana. 7 *(in phrases)* **be** ~ **for** tafuta. ~ **to** -enye nia, -enye kujaribu/kutarajia. **all** ~ kwa jitihada zote. 8 ~ **of** nje ya *fish cannot live* ~ *of water* samaki huishi majini tu; *(of motive or cause)* (ku)tokana na *he did it* ~ *of kindness* alifanya kutokana na huruma; *(from, among)* 5 ~ *of 10 failed* watano kati ya kumi walishindwa *(by the use of)* kutokana na *she made a shirt* ~ *of a kitenge* alishona shati kutokana na kitenge; *(without)* pasipo *I'm* ~ *of money* nimeishiwa (pesa) ~ *of work* pasipo na kazi *(origin or source)* kutoka/kutokea kwenye. **be** ~ **of it** -tokaribishwa, -tokubaliwa, pweke; -tohusika. 9 *(used as n)* **the ins and** (the) ~s wale walio ndani (ya shughuli fulani) na wasiokuwemo *(of details) adj* -a nje; -towezekana. *put the letter in an* ~ *tray* weka barua katika trei ya (vitu vinavyokwenda) nje *your request is* ~ *of question* ombi lako haliwezekani. vt *(sl or colloq)* timua, fukuza.

outback *adj, n (e.g. in Australia)* porini, mbugani, sehemu za mbali (na miji).

outbalance *vt* pita, shinda, zidi uzito.

outbid *vt* piku, shinda katika mnada.

outboard *attrib adj* -a nje ya chombo (cha majini).

out-bound *adj (of a ship)* -a kuelekea mbali.

outbrave *vt* kabili kishujaa.

outbreak *n* kuzuka (kwa maasi, vita); mlipuko (wa hasira, ugonjwa n.k.).

outbuilding *n* kibanda (zizi, jiko) nje ya nyumba kubwa.

outburst *n* kutoka kwa ghafla (k.m. hewa katika puto, mvuke n.k); mlipuko (wa hasira); kuangua kicheko.

outcast *n, adj* mtu aliyetengwa na jamii.

outcaste *n, adj (e.g. in India)* mtu asiye na tabaka.

outclass *vt* shinda, -wa bora kuliko.

outcome *n* matokeo *what will be the* ~ *of this?* matokeo yake yatakuwa nini?

outcrop *n* sehemu ya mwamba inayotokeza juu ya ardhi. ~ *rock* miamba nundu.

outcry *n* 1 makelele (ya hofu, ghadhabu, hasira), yowe. 2 makelele (ya kupinga).

outdated *adj* liopitwa na wakati.

outdistance *vt* acha nyuma.

outdo *vt* pita, shinda, zidi fanya vizuri zaidi *he was not to be outdone* alikuwa hakubali kushindwa.

outdoor *attrib adj* -a nje ~ *clothes* mavazi ya kutokea nje wakati maalum (k.m. wa baridi kali, mvua n.k.). ~**s** *adv, n* nje.

outer *adj* -a nje *the* ~ *man* umbo la nje la mtu (wajihi, vazi n.k.). ~ **most** *adj* -a mbali zaidi (kutoka kati); -a nje, juu kabisa.

outface *vt* tumbulia macho; thubutu; aibisha.

outfall *n* mdomo wa mto.

outfield *n (usu* **the** *~) (cricket and baseball)* sehemu ya uwanja mbali na mpiga mpira. ~**er** *n.*

outfight *vt* shinda katika pambano.

outfit *n* 1 mavazi (yote yanayohusu shughuli/kusudi maalumu); zana (zote zinazohusu shughuli fulani). 2 *(colloq)* kampuni *vt* visha; toa/uza

mavazi/zana. **~ter** *n* mwuza nguo.
outflank *vt* zunguka; *(outwit)* shinda kwa akili.
outflow *n* mbubujiko (wa maji, gesi n.k.).
outfox *vt* shinda kwa ujanja (mjanja mwenzake).
outgo *n* matumizi (ya hela).
outgoing *adj* 1 -nayotoka/hama, -nayoondoka ~ *tenant* mpangaji ahamaye. 2 changamfu. **~s** *n* matumizi.
outgrow *vt* kua sana (hata nguo hazifai kwa kuwa ndogo); pita (mwingine) kwa kukua upesi; acha katika kukua (desturi mbaya, fikira za utoto); -wa kubwa kuliko. ~ *one's strength* kua haraka mno.
outgrowth *n* 1 matokeo. 2 chipukizi.
out-herod *vt* ~ **Herod** shinda. (katika ukatili, ulafi n.k.).
outhouse *n* banda la uwani; *(US)* choo cha nje.
outing *n* matembezi, mandari: *go for an* ~ enda matembezi.
outlandish *adj* -a kigeni, -a ajabu. **~ness** *n*.
outlast *vt* ishi, dumu kuliko.
outlaw *n* haramia; mhalifu. *vt (ban)* harimisha; *(person)* fukuza (kwenye jamii). **~ry** *n*.
outlay *n* matumizi (kwa ajili ya shughuli).
outlet *n* 1 mlango, tundu la kutokea maji/mvuke n.k. 2 *(fig)* fursa ya kutoa (hisia n.k. kutumia nguvu n.k).
outline 1 mstari wa kuonyesha umbo au mpaka *a map in* ~ ramani ya mistari. 2 muhtasari. *vt* 1 chora mstari. 2 eleza kwa muhtasari.
outlive *vt* ishi dumu kuliko; dumu hata jambo lisahauliwe.
outlook *n* 1 mandhari. 2 matarajio. 3 mitizamo, msimamo (wa mambo).
outlying *adj* -a mbali, -a nje (na kiini).
outmanoeuvre *vt* shinda/pita kwa ujanja.
outmarch *vt* tangulia mbele ya, enda upesi kuliko.
outmatch *vt* shinda, pita.
outmoded *adj* -a mtindo wa zamani.
outmost *adj see* **outermost**
outnumber *vt* zidi, -wa -ingi kuliko.
out-of-date *adj* -liopitwa na wakati, -siotumika tena.
out-of-door(s) *see* **outdoor**
out-of-the-way *adj* 1 -siyo barabarani, mbali; -sio kawaida.
out-patient *n* mgonjwa asiyelazwa (hospitalini), mgonjwa wa nje.
outplay *vt (of games etc)* shinda, zidi (katika ustadi wa kucheza).
outpoint *vt (boxing etc)* shinda kwa pointi.
outpost *n* 1 *(mil)* mahali wanapolinda askari mbali na kundi kuu la jeshi. 2 makazi ya mbali, kituo cha mbali.
outpouring *n* 1 mbubujiko, miminiko. 2 *(usu*~**s***)* kutoa dukuduku/mihemko.
output *n* 1 mazao ya kiwanda, mgodi n.k.; nishati/nguvu inayotolewa; habari zitokazo kwenye kompyuta.
outrage *n* kitendo kiovu cha ukatili, jeuri, ufisadi *an ~ against morals* kitendo cha ufisadi kinachopinga kabisa maadili *vt* 1 tendea uovu, halifu. **~ous** *adj* 1 -a kufedhehesha; -a kifisadi, -a kikatili. 2 *(of price)* -a kuruka. **~ously** *adv*.
outrange *vt* -wa na masafa marefu zaidi.
outrank *vt* -wa cheo cha juu kuliko, zidi kwa cheo.
outre *adj* -enye kuvuka mipaka (ya maadili, desturi nk.).
outride *vt* kimbiza farasi kuliko. **~r** *n* msindikizaji msafara (kwenye farasi, pikipiki n.k.).
outrigger *n* mrengu, ndubi, parapi.
outrigged *adj* -enye mrengu.
outright *adv* 1 *(at once)* mara, papo hapo; moja kwa moja *he killed him* ~ alimwua papo hapo. 2 *(openly)* wazi, dhahiri *adj* -a wazi.
outrival vt shinda.
outrun *vt* shinda kwa mbio, tangulia mbele ya; *(fig)* zidi.
outsail *vt* safiri (baharini) haraka kuliko.
outsell *vt* uza kuliko nyingine.

outset *n* mwanzo. **at the ~** mwanzoni. **from the ~** toka mwanzo.

outshine *vt* shinda, pita (kwa uzuri n.k.).

outside *n* 1 upande wa nje *from the ~* kutoka nje *on the ~* nje. 2 sura *know only the ~ of sth* fahamu sura tu ya kitu. 3 *(limit)* upeo; mpaka. **at the (very) ~** sanasana. 4 jalada. 6 *(of football etc)* wingi *~ left* wingi wa kushoto *adj* 1 -a nje. 2 *(of place)* -a mwisho. 3 *(work)* -a nje ya kiwanda. 4 *(of price)* -a juu kabisa *adv* nje; barabarani; mbele ya nyumba *prep* nje ya *n* 1 mtu asiye wa jamii/kundi/ chama; mtu asiyekubaliwa na jamii. 2 *(colloq)* safihi. 3 *(racing)* farasi asiyetegemewa kushinda.

outsize *adj* kubwa sana. *n* kipimo kikubwa sana (cha nguo).

outskirts *n pl* kiunga (cha mjini), pembezo, kando.

outsmart *vt (colloq)* shinda kwa akili, hadaa.

outspan *vt,vi* fungulia farasi/ng'ombe punda katika gari.

outspoken *adj* -enye kusema yalivyo, bila kuficha *an ~ man* mtu asiyeogopa kusema ukweli. **~ly** *adv*. **~ness** *n*.

outspread *adj* -enye kuenea/ kutandazika; -lionyooka.

outstanding *adj* 1 -liobaki, -liosalia, -liopo *~ debts* madeni yaliyobaki. 2 *(prominent)* -liojipambanua/jitokeza.

outstation *n* kituo cha mbali/mbugani.

outstare *vt* kodolea sana macho (kushinda mwingine).

outstay *vt* kaa, baki zaidi kuliko muda unaofaa **~ one's welcome** kaa mahali muda mrefu mno (hata kuchukiza wenyeji wako).

outstretched *adj* -lionyoshwa sana (hasa mikono ya mtu).

outstrip *vt* shinda, pita, zidi.

outtalk *vt* hinikiza, shinda katika kuongea, mazungumzo.

outvalue *vt* -wa -a thamani kubwa kuliko; thaminisha zaidi.

outvie *vt* shinda (katika mashindano) *~ each other* shindana.

outvote *vt* shinda kwa kura nyingi zaidi.

outwalk *vt* shinda kwa mwendo.

outward *adj* 1 -a upande wa nje; -a kuonekana, -a usoni. 2 -a kuelekea nje **~ly** *(also* **~s***) adv* kwa nje, usoni. **~-bound** *adj (of ship)* -enye kuondoka kwenda mbali.

outwear *vt,vi* 1 dumu zaidi. 2 chakaa; chakaza mpaka isiwe na thamani tena.

outweigh *vt* 1 pita kwa uzito (kwa nguvu). 2 -wa na uzito/maana zaidi, shinda, (kwa uzito) maana zaidi.

outwit *vt* shinda kwa akili.

outwork *n* boma la mbele. *vt* shinda (kwa bidii, wepesi wa kazi).

ouzel *n* kizamiadagaa.

ova *pl of* **ovum. ovary** *n* ovari.

oval *adj* -enye umbo la yai.

ovation *n* makofi ya shangwe, vifijo.

oven *n* joko, oveni. **~ware** vyombo vinavyostahimilijoto/vinavyotumika jikoni.

over[1] *prep* 1 juu ya *spread a mat ~ the floor* tandika mkeka juu ya sakafu *the sky is ~ our heads* mbingu iko juu ya vichwaa vyetu *be ~ one's head (colloq)* shinda kuelewa. 2 -enye kutawala/kuongoza, -enye cheo cha juu zaidi *Juma is ~ me in the office* Juma ni kiongozi wangu ofisini. 3 -ote, sehemu zote *she has travelled all ~ Africa* ametembea Afrika kote. 4 kule, upande mwingine *who is ~ there?* nani yuko kule (upande mwingine) *look ~ the wall* angalia upande wa pili wa ukuta *~ the way* upande wa pili wa barabara. ~ mpaka mwisho wa muda wa, -ote, hadi *can you stay ~ Sunday* unaweza kukaa Jumapili yote. 6 zaidi ya *they worked for ~ three hours* walifanya kazi kwa zaidi ya saa tatu. **~ and above** zaidi ya (hayo). 7 wakati ule ule (wa shughuli) *he went to sleep ~ his work* alisinzia wakati akifanya kazi yake. 8 kuhusu *we talked ~ his problems* tulizungumza kuhusu matatizo yake *adv* 1 *(full,* *turn)* **fall** ~ angukia **turn** ~ geuka/geuza. **roll** ~ biringika. 2 *(upwards, outwards)* **boil** ~ furumia. 3 *(from start to finish)* **look** ~ pitia; angalia toka mwanzo hadi mwisho. **think** ~ fikiria. 4 tena *say it* ~ sema. **(all) ~ again** tena (toka mwanzo). ~ **and ~ again** tena na tena, mara nyingi. 5 kwa kuvuka/kwenda upande wa pili *come ~ to our house* karibu nyumbani. ~ **against** *(lit)* kinyume cha; kwa kukinzana na. 6 -nayobaki *is there any wine left ~?* kuna divai iliyobaki? 7 zaidi *children of thirteen and ~* watoto wenye miaka kumi na tatu na zaidi. 8 -liokwisha; -liofikia mwisho *the meeting is ~* mkutano umekwisha. 9 *(from one to another) go ~ to the enemy* jiunga na adui ~ *to you!* kwako! 10 sehemu zote, kote *she is famous all ~ Tanzania* ni maarufu kote Tanzania *pref* mno, -a kupita kiasi, -liozidi, sana. **~-cook** ivisha mno. **~-excited** -enye mpwitompwito, liohemka/sisimka mno. **~-payment** malipo yaliyozidi.

over[2] *n (cricket)* idadi ya mipira inayotupwa mfululizo.

overact *vt,vi* zidisha mbwembwe (hasa katika kuigiza).

overall *adj* -a jumla *adv* kwa jumla *n (pl)* ovaroli, bwelasuti.

overarch *vt* fanya tao juu ya. **overarm** *adj,adv (cricket etc)* -enye/kwa kurusha mkono juu ya bega.

overawe *vt* tisha, ogofya, fadhaisha; stahisha mno.

overbalance *vt,vi* 1 angusha, anguka. 2 pita, zidi (kwa uzito n.k.).

overbear *vt* shinda, tiisha. **~ing** *adj* -enye nguvu; -enye kutisha/ kulazimisha wengine; dhalimu.

overbid *vt,vi* 1 *(at an auction)* shinda bei. 2 toa bei zaidi ya thamani ya kitu. 3 *(bridge)* taja thamani isiyoweza kufikiwa; taja thamani zaidi ya mwenzio *n* kushinda bei; kutoa bei ya juu sana; *(bridge)* kutaja thamani zaidi.

overblown *adj* 1 *(of flowers)* liochanua, wazi kabisa lioanza kuharibika. 2 -enye madoido mengi mno, -a kupita kiasi.

overboard *adv* kutoka kwenye chombo, toka chomboni *fall/jump ~* anguka/ ruka kutoka kwenye chombo *throw sb ~ (fig)* tupa, telekeza. **go ~** *(colloq)* vutiwa mno na.

overbore,overborne *see* **overbear**.

overbuild *vt* jenga (nyumba) nyingi sana, jaza nyumba mno *over built area* eneo lililojaa nyumba.

overburden *vt* lemeza, twisha mawazo mazito mno (k.m. huzuni) *n* udongo wa juu ya ardhi (ambao ni sharti uondolewe ili kufikia mkaa wa mawe).

overcall *vt,vi see* **overbid**.

overcapitalize *vt* kadiria mtaji mkubwa kupita kiasi. **overcapitalization** *n.*

overcast *adj* 1 *(of the sky)* -liotanda mawingu *the sky is ~* mawingu yametanda angani. 2 *(fig)* -a huzuni, -a majonzi.

overcharge *vt* 1 toza fedha nyingi mno, uza ghali mno. *(overload)* tia -ingi mno *n* 1 malipo ya kupita kiasi. 2 *(electric)* chaji kubwa kupita kiasi. **overcloud** *vt* 1 tanda(za) (mawingu). 2 *(fig)* tia majonzi, huzuni, uzito.

overcoat *n* koti kubwa la kuvaa juu ya nguo nyingine.

overcome *vt* 1 shinda. 2 **be ~ with/by** dhoofishwa/lemaza/jawa na.

overcrop *vt* lima mno hadi ardhi inapoteza rutuba.

overcrowd *vt* songamana, songa.

overdo *vt* 1 fanya (kazi) kupita kiasi. 2 *(exaggerate)* tia chumvi, zidisha. 3 *(cooking)* ivisha mno.

overdose *n* kuzidisha kiasi cha dawa kinachohitajiwa *vt* -nywa/toa dawa kupita kiasi.

overdraft *n* ovadrafti: deni katika akaunti ya benki.

overdraw *vt* 1 toa, -wekua zaidi (kuliko fedha zilizopo) ~ *one's account* wekua fedha zaidi (kuliko zilizowekwa). 2 *(lit)* tia chumvi.

overdress *vt,vi* jionyesha kwa mavazi

(zaidi ya inavyopaswa).
overdrive *n* gia ya mbio (inayoongeza mwendo bila kutumia petroli nyingi).
overdue *adj* -a kuchelewa, -a kupitiliza muda *long ~* liopitiliza muda mrefu.
overeat *vt,vi* -la kupita kiasi, lafua.
over-estimate *vi* kadiria kupita kiasi thamini mno, kuza thamani *n* kisio la juu.
overfeed *vt,vi* -la/lisha mno.
overfill *vt,vi* jaa/jaza mno.
overflow *vt,vi* 1 furika *the toilet is ~ing* choo kimefurika. 2 ~ **with** -jaa, jawa na *the mother was ~ing with happiness* mama alikuwa amejawa na furaha *n* 1 mafuriko. 2 *(superfluity)* ziada. 3 *(outlet)* mahali pa kutokeza maji.
overgrown *adj* 1 -liokua upesi mno. 2 -liofunikwa kwa majani au miti.
overgrowth *n* 1 kukua upesi mno. 2 majani/mimea iliyoota sana na kufunika ardhi.
overhang *vt,vi* 1 tokeza juu ya. 2 elekea/tishia kutokea *n* sehemu inayotokeza.
overhaul *vt* 1 chunguza kwa makini (na kutengeneza ikibidi); *(of engine)* suka upya; *(colloq) go to the doctor to be ~ed* enda kwa daktari kwa uchunguzi (kuhusu afya).
overhead *adv* juu (ya kichwa). *adj* -a juu (ya kichwa). 2 *(of business)* -a uendeshaji; *(expenses/charges)* gharama za uendeshaji k.v. kodi, ushuru, mishahara n.k.
overhear *vt* sikia bila kukusudia; *(deliberately)* dukiza.
overheat *vt,vi* pata/pasha joto kupita kiasi chake.
overjoyed *adj* -a kufurahi mno, -liojaa furaha.
overkill *n* uwezo wa kuharibu/kuua n.k. uliyozidi kiasi.
overland *adv* kwa nchi kavu *adj* -a nchi kavu.
overlap *vt,vi* 1 pishanisha; pishana. 2 *(fig)* lingana kwa mambo mengine *n* kitu kilicho juu ya; sehemu inayolingana.
overlay *vt* tia/weka juu ya, funika, tandaza. ~ **sth with sth** funika kitu na kitu kingine *n* kifuniko.
overleaf *adv* upande wa nyuma/ pili wa (karatasi n.k.).
overleap *vt,vi* rukia upande wa pili; *(fig)* enda mbali, jaribu kupita kiasi, zidi.
overload *vt* jaza mno, pakia (gari n.k.) kuzidi kiasi; *(electr)* tia chaji nyingi zaidi.
overlook *vt* 1. tazama kutoka juu; -wa juu ya. 2 -togundua; -toangalia, -totilia maanani. 3 samehe. 4 simamia.
overlord *n (old)* kabaila.
overly *adv* mno, kwa kuzidi kiasi.
overmantel *n* rafu za mapambo (juu ya meko).
overmaster *vt* tawala kabisa; shinda.
overmuch *adj* -ingi mno *adv* kwa wingi mno.
overnight *adv* 1 usiku kucha *adj* -a usiku. 2 *(fig)* -a ghafla sana.
overpass *n* tambukabaraste.
overpay *vt* lipa mno. **~ment** *n.*
overplus *n* baki; ziada.
over-populated *adj* -lio na watu wengi mno. **overpopulation** *n.*
overpower *vt* shinda (kwa nguvu nyingi), tiisha. **~ing** *adj* -lioshinda kwa nguvu, -enye nguvu nyingi *an ~ stink* harufu mbaya tena kali sana. **oversimplify**
overprint *vt* 1 *(photog)* chapa kuwa nyeusi kuliko ilivyokusudiwa. 2 chapa nakala nyingi. 3 chapa maandishi juu ya maandishi mengine *n* maandishi yaliyogandamizwa.
over-produce *n* zalisha kupita kiasi. **overproduction** *n.*
overrate *vt* thamini zaidi kuliko inavyostahili.
overreach 1 shinda kwa hila, ghilibu, rubuni. 2 ~ **oneself** jiharibia kwa kutaka kufanya kupita kiasi.
override *vt* 1 puuza; fanya kinyume; *(of a horse, donkey etc)* chosha kwa kuendesha.

overrule *vt* batilisha, tangua.
overrun *vt* 1 *(mil)* tanda nchi/mahali, (agh. na kutia hasara). 2 enea *weeds have ~ the whole garden* magugu yameenea pote bustanini. 3 pitiliza (muda uliopangwa).
oversea(s) *adj* -a ng'ambo (ya bahari), -a ughaibuni *adv* ughaibuni, ng'ambo *from ~* toka ng'ambo.
oversee *vt* simamia. **~r** *n* msimamizi.
oversell *vt* uza kwa wingi mno (kuliko vitu vilivyoko); *(fig)* sifia mno; toa madai ya kupindukia.
overset *vt,vi* pindua, tibua; pinduka, tibuka.
oversexed *adj* -lio na ashiki kupita kiasi.
overshadow *vt* 1 tia kivuli juu. 2 *(fig)* toa maanani.
overshoe *n* buti inayovaliwa juu ya kiatu cha kawaida.
overshoot *vt* kosea shabaha (kwa kupiga juu au mbele zaidi). 2 *~ the mark* piga chuku, tia chumvi; zidi. 3 *(lit, fig)* enda mbali zaidi.
overshot *vt pt,pp of* **overshoot** *adj* *~* **wheel** *n* gurudumu lenye kuzungushwa na nguvu maji.
overside *adv* kwa upande, ubavuni (meli, jahazi, n.k.).
oversight *n* 1 *(error, neglect)* (kosa la) kupitiwa na jambo. 2 *(supervision)* usimamizi, uangalizi.
oversimplify *vt* rahisisha mno (hadi kupoteza maana). **oversimplification** *n*.
oversize *adj* kubwa kupita kiasi.
overskirt *n* sketi ya juu.
oversleep *vi* chelewa kuamka, pitiliza usingizi, lala mno.
overspill *n* kufurika (kwa watu/kitu), kuzidiana *~ town* mji unaojengwa kupokea watu waliofurika.
overstate *vt* tia chumvi; piga chuku. **~ment** *n* chuku, kutia chumvi.
overstay *vt* kaa zaidi ya muda unaotakiwa. *~* **one's welcome** chosha watu kwa kukaa.
overstep *vt* vuka/kiuka mipaka (ya jambo, madaraka n.k.).
overstock *vt* weka/nunua bidhaa nyingi kuliko inayoweza kuuzwa; weka mifugo zaidi ya unayoweza kulisha *n* mizigo (bidhaa n.k.) iliyozidi.
overstrung *adj* -epesi kusisimuka/ kuhemkwa.
overstuff *vt* jaza mno (kuliko inavyotakiwa). **~ed** *adj*
oversubscribed *adj (fig)* -liochangiwa/ ombwa kupindukia.
overt *adj* -a wazi, hadharani. *~* **and covert charges** mashtaka ya wazi na ya kisiri. *~* **market** soko mjinga.
overtake *vt* 1 kuta, pita. 2 pata kwa ghafla *he was ~n by a storm* alikumbwa na dhoruba.
overtax *vt* 1 toza ushuru kupita kiasi. 2 *(overstrain)* lemea; chosha *~ one's strength* kujichosha mno.
overthrow 1 pindua; angusha *~ a regime* angusha serikali. 2 *(ruin)* angamiza; shinda; vunja *n* maangamizi, mapinduzi.
overtime *n* ovataimu: saa za ziada *adv work ~* fanya (kazi ya) ovataimu.
overtone *n (pl) (music)* alama ya juu ya noti, kidokezo; *(often pl)(fig)* vidokezo vya maana halisi.
overtop 1 *(rise above)* inuka juu ya; nyanyuka. 2 *(excel)* shinda; pita (kiwango cha kawaida).
overtrump *vt* piku mapiku.
overture *n* 1 *(music)* lele, yaleli. 2 *(fig)* mwanzo. 3 *(often pl)* mazungumzo ya awali (kabla ya mjadala).
overturn *vt,vi* pindua; pinduka, angusha, anguka *n* mpinduko.
overweening *adj* -a kujivuna; -a kutakabari; -a kinaya.
overweigh *vt* zidisha uzito wa kawaida *vi* shinda kwa uzito.
overweight *n* uzito kupita kiasi cha kawaida/kilicho halali *adj* 1 *(of person)* nene sana. 2 -liozidi (kwa uzito). **~ed** *adj* liolemewa.
overwhelm *vt* 1 shinda kabisa, angamiza; *(of feelings)* zidi, jawa na *be ~ed with* jawa/shindwa na. 2 *(overrun)* ingia kwa shari/nguvu; funika, gharikisha. 3 *(cover)*

funikiza.

overwind *vt* jaza mno (saa).

overwork *vt,vi* fanya/fanyisha kazi ya kupita kiasi, chosha; *(fig)* tumia mno *n* kazi ya kupita kadiri.

overwrought *adj* 1 -liohamanikana. 2 -liotiwa madoido mengi.

ovulate *vi* fanya/taga mayai. **ovulation** *n*.

ovum *n (pl.)* ovari. **oviduct** *n* mirija ya ova. **oviform** *adj* umbo la yai. **oviparous** *adj (zool)* -enye kutaga mayai.

ovoid *n adj* -enye umbo la yai *n* kitu chenye umbo la yai.

owe *vt,vi* 1 ~ **sb sth**; ~ **sth to sb**; ~ **for sth** wiwa; -wa na deni *be ~d a debt* wia deni, dai *he ~s me money* namdai, awiwa nami; namwia. 2 *(owe to)* wajibika, paswa na pasa; -wa na (kitu) kwa sababu ya; -wa haki ya *I ~ respect to my father* inanipasa kumheshimu baba ~ *no thanks to sb* -tomwia mtu shukrani. 3 ~ **sth to sth** pata kwa, tokana na: *I ~ my wealth to my father* utajiri wangu unatokana na baba yangu *I ~ my succes to hard work* mafanikio yangu yanatokana na jitihada zangu. **owing** *adj* 1 -enye kudaiwa, -siolipwa bado *money is ~ by me* nawiwa fedha na mtu *prep* ~ **to** kwa sababu ya *it is all owing to you* yote ni juu yako kwa sababu yako. *owing to the floods the road is impassable* kwa sababu ya mafuriko barabara haipitiki.

owl *n* bundi. **~let** *n* bundi mchanga (kifaranga). **~ish** *adj* kama bundi; nzito; -enye busara; -a kujifanya/ kuonekana nzito. **~ishly** *adv*.

own *vt,vi* 1 miliki. 2 kiri, tambua. 3 ~ **up** kiri (kwa moyo) *adj* -enyewe *my ~* -angu mimi *be (all) on one's ~* peke yake *I live on my ~* nakaa peke yangu; -enyewe *she can work on her ~* anaweza kufanya kazi mwenyewe. **be one's ~ man/master** jitegemea, -wa huru *come into one's ~* stahili; onyesha. **hold one's ~** simama kidete, jihami, shikilia yako *he made the house his ~* alijifanya yuko kwake. ~ **brother/sister** ndugu wa mama na baba mmoja. **get one's ~ back** *(colloq)* lipa kisasi *n* **~er** mmilikaji mwenyewe. ~ **-driver** -a dereva mwenyewe. **~er occupied** -a kukaliwa na mwenyewe. **~less** *adj* bila mwenyewe. **~ship** *n* umilikaji.

ox *n* 1 ng'ombe. 2 maksai; ng'ombe wa kufugwa *strong as an ~* -enye nguvu nyingi sana. ~ **bow** *n* 1 nira ya ng'ombe. 2 ziwapinde (kwa mto). ~ **eye** *(bot)* mmea wenye maua kama jicho. **~-eyed** *adj* -a macho makubwa kama ya ng'ombe. ~ **hide** *n* ngozi ya ng'ombe. ~ **tail** *n* mkia wa ng'ombe. **oxbridge** *n* vyuo vikuu vya Oxford na/au Cambridge.

oxide *n* (*chem*) oksaidi *mercuric ~* oksaidi ya zebaki. **oxidize** *vt,vi* oksidisha. **oxidation** *n* uoksidishaji.

Oxonian *adj* -a Oxford *n* mwanafunzi wa Chuo Kikuu cha Oxford.

oxygen *n* oksijeni (hewa safi). ~ **mask** kifuniko cha oksijeni (cha uso). **~tent** kihema cha oksijeni. **~ate; ~ize** *vt* patia oksijeni.

oyes,oyez *int* (maneno ya kunyamazisha watu mahakamani) sikilizeni.

oyster *n* chaza. **-bed/bank** *n* mahali ambapo chaza huzaa. **~-knife** *n* kisu cha kufungulia chaza.

oz *abbrev of* **ounce**.

ozone *n (chem)* ozoni; *(fig)* kitu kinachochangamsha; *(colloq)* hewa safi ya kuburudisha pwani. ~ **layer** tabaka ozoni.

P

P, p herufi ya kumi na sita ya alfabeti ya Kiingereza. **mind one's ~'s and q's** -wa na adabu/ mwangalifu, ongea kwa adabu.

pa *n (colloq)* baba.

pabulum *n* chakula; *(fig) mental ~* kilisha akili, jambo la kutafakari.

pace *n* 1 hatua. 2 mwendo (wa kutembea, kukimbia). **keep ~ with sb/sth** enda sambamba/sawasawa na. **go at a good ~** enda/tembea kwa haraka. **go the ~** enda kwa kasi sana; *(fig)* fuja pesa. **set the ~ (for sb)** ratibu/ongoza mwendo; pimia mwendo *stand/staythe ~* himili, weza kufululiza na wengine. **~-maker/ setter** mwekaji/mwongozaji wa mwendo; kifaa cha kurekebisha mapigo ya moyo. **put sb through his ~s** pima uwezo wa mtu *vi,vt* 1 tembea polepole; enda dalji. 2 **~ sth off** tembea tembea, pima kwa hatua *~ off a room* pima chumba kwa hatua. 3 pima mwendo (wa mtu/mnyama katika mashindano/mazoezi).

pachyderm *n (zool)* pakidema: mnyama mwenye ngozi nene sana k.v. tembo, kiboko, kifaru.

pacifism *n* upinzanivita (nadharia ya kupinga vita vyovyote). **pacifist** *n* mpinzanivita. **pacify** *vt* suluhisha, patanisha, tuliza, fanya/leta amani. **pacifier** *n* 1 msuluhishi, mpatanishi. 2 mpira wa mtoto, titibandia. **pacific** *adj* -a kupenda amani, -tulivu, pole *n the P~/P~ Ocean* Bahari ya Pasifiki. **pacifically** *adv.* **pacification** *n* suluhu. **pacificatory** *adj.*

pack *n* 1 mtumba, furushi, bunda, robota, mzigo. 2 *(usu derog)* genge, kundi *-a ~ of thieves* kundi la wezi *a ~ of nonsense* upuuzi kabisa *~ of lies* uongo mtupu. 3 kundi la wanyama *wild dogs hunt in ~s* mbwa mwitu huwinda kwa vikundi. 4 jozi/seti ya karata. 5 kiasi (cha nyama, samaki iliyohifadhiwa makoponi kwa msimu mmoja). 6 *(compounds)* **~-animal/ horse** mnyama/farasi anayebeba mizigo. **~ man** *(arch)* mchuuzi. **~-saddle** saruji la mizigo. **~-thread** itani. 7 **~-ice** barafu tandavu baharini *vt,vi* 1 **~ (up) (in, into)** funga furushi/mzigo; fungasha. **~ one's bags** jiandaa/jitayarisha kuondoka. **~ it in** acha (jambo). **~ up** *(colloq)* acha kufanya kazi; *(sl)* anguka, shindwa. 2 songa, jaza; songamana. 3 funga kwa uangalifu kwa kuwekea vitu nyororo *~ the glasses in cotton* funga glasi kwa uangalifu kwa kutumia pamba. 4 *(sl)* pachika silaha. 5 **~ sb off** fukuza, ondosha harakaharaka. **send sb ~ing** fukuza mtu bila staha. **~er** *n* mtu/kitu kinachofungia mizigo/chakula. 6 funga/hifadhi makoponi. 7 chagua wanakamati (ambao unahisi wata kupendelea katika maamuzi). **~age** *n* kifurushi, kirobota. **~ deal/ offer** *(colloq)* pendekezo/mpango wa jumla. **~ tour** *(colloq)* safari ya utalii ambayo mambo yote yamelipiwa pamoja. **~ store** *(US)* stoo ya bia. **~aged** *adj* -enye kuwekwa pamoja *vt* funga katika furushi. **~ing** *n* 1 kufunga mizigo *do one's ~* funga mizigo. 2 *(stuffing)* kitambaa (majani makavu n.k.) cha kuzuia kitu kisivunjike au kuharibika wakati wa kusafirisha, kibibo, kisongo. **~-case** kasha la mbao. **~-needle** shazia.

packet *n* 1 kifurushi,pakiti,kichopa, kibumba. 2 *(GB sl)* taabu, tatizo *catch/stop/get a ~* umia/jeruhiwa sana. 3 *(sl)* kibunda, hela nyingi. 4 **~-boat** meli ya posta.

pact *n* maafikiano, mapatano; makubaliano.

pad *n* 1 kitu ororo cha kinga. 2 ngao/ kinga/pedi (ya mguu, mwili n.k.). 3 kitita/pedi ya karatasi za kuandikia. 4 pedi ya kupigia mhuri. 5 unyayo laini wa mbwa, mbwa mwitu, n.k. 6 jukwaa la kurushia makombora. 7 *(sl)* kitanda, chumba cha kulala *vt* 1 jaza vitu vyororo. 2 **~ sth out** *(books, speeches etc)* refusha bila sababu *~ded-cell* chumba chenye kuta zilizojaa vitu vyororo (katika hospitali ya wagonjwa wa akili). **~dig** *n* vitu vyororo vya kujazia *vt,vi* tembea, enda kwa miguu.

paddle *n* 1 kafi, kasia. 2 kupiga kasia/

kafi polepole. ~-**box** *n* ubao unaofunika sehemu ya juu ya gurudumu la kafi. ~ **steamer** meli inayoendeshwa na magurudumu ya kafi. ~-**wheel** gurudumu la kafi *vi,vt* 1 piga kafi; endesha mtumbwi kwa kafi ~ *one's own canoe* jitegemea. 2 tembeatembea majini (pasipo viatu). 3 *(colloq)* tembea, piga chapa. 4 piga ubao.

paddock *n* 1 uwanda wenye nyasi (hasa kwa ajili ya mazoezi ya farasi). 2 zizi la farasi wanapokusanyika kabla ya mashindano.

paddy[1] *n* mpunga. ~-**field** shamba la mpunga.

paddy[2] *n (colloq)* hasira.

Paddy *n* Mwairish (jina la kupanga). ~-**wagon** *(US sl)* karandinga la kupeleka washtakiwa gerezani.

padlock *n* kufuli *vt* funga kwa kufuli.

padre *n (GB colloq)* kasisi, padiri; *(mil)* padiri/mchungaji (jeshini).

paean *n* wimbo wa kusifu/shukrani.

paederasty ulawiti (hasa kwa kijana wa kiume).

pagan *n* mpagani *adj* -a kipagani. ~**ism** *n.*

page[1] *n* 1 *(hist)* askari mwanafunzi. 2 mtoto mtumishi, tarishi *vt* pitapita na kuita majina (hotelini, kilabuni n.k.).

page[2] *n* ukurasa, laha *vt* tia namba za kurasa. **paginate** *vt* tia namba za kurasa. **pagination** *n.*

pageant *n* 1 tamasha, mchezo wa kuigiza mambo (habari, matokeo) ya zamani. 2 *(vain show)* tamasha (sherehe) (hasa zenye maandamano) *beauty* ~ mashindano ya uzuri (ya wasichana). ~**ry** *n.*

pagoda *n (India, China, Japan etc)* hekalu.

paid *pt of* **pay**.

pail *n* ndoo. ~**ful** *n* ndoo tele.

paillasse, palliasse *n* godoro la majani.

pain *n* 1 maumivu, uchungu, kuumia. ~-**killer** *n* kituliza maumivu; dawa ya kutuliza maumivu. 2 *(stabbing pain)* kichomi. **labour** ~ s uchungu wa kuzaa. 3 *(mental ~)* huzuni, ghamu, sikitiko *it gives me ~ to tell you that* inanipa uchungu/ghamu, kukuambia kwamba. 4 *(arch)* adhabu. **on/under ~ of death** kwa kuchelea kifo. **a ~ in the neck** *(sl)* kero, adha *vi,vt* 1 umiza, tia uchungu. 2 huzunisha, kera. ~**ed** *adj* -a kuhuzunisha. ~**ful** *adj* -a kuumiza; -a kuhuzunisha. ~**less** *adj* bila maumivu, -sioumiza. ~**lessly** *adv.* ~**s** *n (pl)* jitihada, bidii. **be at ~s to do sth** jitahidi, jikalifu. **take (great) ~s (over sth/to do sth)** jitahidi sana. **spare no ~s** fanya kila liwezekanalo. ~**staking** *adj* -enye kujitahidi, -angalifu, -a bidii za kazi.

paint *n* 1 rangi. 2 dalia (ya uso). ~-**box** sanduku la rangi. 3 *(pl)* rangi (za kuchorea). ~-**brush** brashi ya kupakia rangi *vt,vi* 1 paka (tia) rangi ~ *the town red (colloq)* enda kustarehe sana; toka na kusherehekea sana jambo. 2 chora picha za rangi. ~ **sth in** ongezea picha kwa kuchora zaidi. ~ **sth out** ficha/futa kwa kuchora au kupaka rangi. 3 *(fig)* fafanua, eleza habari. **not so black as he is ~ed** siyo mbaya kama anavyoelezwa. 4 jirembesha ~ *one's face* paka dalia usoni. ~**er** *n* 1 mchoraji. 2 mpaka rangi. ~**ing** *n* 1 kupaka rangi. 2 kuchora picha (ya rangi). 3 picha/mchoro wa rangi; ustadi wa kuandika picha. ~**ress** *(arch)* mpaka rangi wa kike; mwandishi wa picha za rangi wa kike (mchoraji wakike).

painter *n* kamba za kufungia mashua. **cut the** ~ fungua kamba. 2 *(fig)* jitenga, achanisha.

pair *n* 1 jozi *a ~ of shoes* jozi ya viatu *a ~ of scissors* mkasi *a ~ of trousers* surali *a ~ of spectacles* miwani *adj* -a jozi, mbili mbili. 2 watu au wanyama wawili wanaoshirikiana sana; mume na mke *in ~s* wawili wawili *vt,vi* panga, weka, linganisha wawili; wa, lingana viwili/wawili/ mbili/n.k. ~ **off** weka/enda kwa jozi.

pajamas *(US) see* **pyjamas**.
pal *n (colloq)* mwenzi, rafiki *vi* ~ **up (with sb)** fanya urafiki. **~ly** *adj (colloq)* -a kirafiki, rafiki.
palace *n* 1 kasri, hekalu; jumba kubwa, jumba la mtawala/mkuu wa nchi/ mfalme/askofu n.k. 2 **the** ~ watu mashuhuri; vigogo. ~ **revolution** mapinduzi ya wenyewe kwa wenyewe, ya ndani. **palatial** *adj* -a jumba kubwa; -a anasa; -a kasri.
palaeo- see **paleo**.
palanquin *n* machela yenye paa.
palatable *adj* -tamu, -a kupendeza; *(fig)* -a kukubalika akilini *it was not ~ to them* haikuwapendeza.
palate *n* 1 kaakaa: paa la kinywa. 2 *(taste)* maonjo. **palatal** *adj* -a kaakaa. **palatalization** *n*.
palatinate *n (hist)* upalitanati (wilaya ya Ujerumani ya zamani).
palaver *n (hist)* baraza, majadiliano (kati ya wageni/ wenye biashara na wenyeji); *(colloq)* bughudha *vi* piga soga/gumzo.
pale[1] *n* 1 kiguzo. 2 mpaka. *(esp fig)* **beyond/outside the** ~ -liovuka mpaka, -siokubalika kijamii. **paling** *n* uzio/boma la viguzo. **palisade** *n* 1 boma, ua (wa viguzo vilivyo-chongoka). 2 *(pl) (US) n* genge (agh kando ya mto) *vt* tengeneza ua kwa viguzo.
pale[2] *adj* -liokwajuka ~ *blue* samawati, buluu hafifu *turn* ~ kwajuka, sawajika *vt,vi* sawajika, kwajuka. ~ **before/by the side of sth** *(fig)* shindikana; onekana dhaifu (mbele ya kitu kingine). **~ly** *adv*. **~ness** *n*. **palish** *adj* -enye rangi iliyofifia.
paleolithic (*also* **palaeolithic)** *adj* -a enzi ya zana za mawe.
paleontology *n* paleontolojia: elimu ya visukuku. **paleontologist** *n* mwanapaleontolojia.
palette *n* kibao cha kuchanganyia rangi. ~ **knife** *n* kisufugutu.
palfrey *n (arch, poet)* farasi (agh kwa ajili ya mwanamke).
palindrome *n* palindromu: neno linalo-someka kwa namna moja kwa mbele au kinyume k.m. ama, ana, ini n.k.
pall[1] *n* subaya, deuli. ~ **bearer** *n* 1 mbeba jeneza/msindikiza jeneza mazishini. 2 *(fig)* guo zito na jeusi *a ~ of smoke* moshi mzito.
pall[2] *vi* ~ **(on/upon)** chosha, kinaisha.
pallet *n* 1 godoro la majani makavu. 2 toroli, bao la kubebea mizigo.
palliasse *n also* **paillasse**.
palliate *vt (formal)* tuliza, punguza (maumivu, ugonjwa); punguza/ samehe ukubwa wa kosa (la jinai n.k.). **palliation** *n* urahisishaji kosa; setiri, upunguzaji wa maumivu. **palliative** *adj*. **palliation** *n*.
pallid *adj* -liokwajuka; -losawajika, -a kuonekana gonjwa (-a uso n.k.). **~ly** *adv*. **~ness** *n*. **pallor** *n* kukwajuka; msawajiko.
palm[1] *n* kiganja, kitanga cha mkono. **grease/oil sb's** ~ toa rushwa, honga. **have an itching** ~ penda kula rushwa/kuhongwa *in the ~ of one's hand* weka mkononi, tawala *vt* ficha katika kitanga cha mkono. ~ **sth off (on sb)** tapeli, toa/-pa kwa hila. **~ist** *n* mtabiri asomaye kitanga. **~istry** *n* usomaji kitanga.
palm[2] *n* 1 mti wa jamii ya mchikichi n.k. *coconut* ~ mnazi *date* ~ mtende ~ *tree* mchikichi ~ *kernel* kiini/ nazi/kokwa. **~oil** mawese. ~ **wine** *n* tembo. **P~ Sunday** Jumapili ya Matawi. 2 jani la mnazi (alama ya ushindi). **bear/carry off the** ~ shinda. **yield the ~ to sb** kubali kushindwa (na mwingine). **~y** *adj* -liositawi; -lioneemeka. **~er** *n (formally)* hujaji arejeaye kutoka Nchi Takatifu na jani la mnazi.
palpate *vt* chunguza kwa kugusa, papasa. **palpation** *n*. **palpable** *adj* 1 -a kugusika, -a kuhisika, -a dhahiri. **palpably** *adv*.
palpitate *vi* 1 *(of the heart)* pigapiga, puma. 2 *(of a person, his body)* tetemeka, pwita. ~ **with fear** papa kwa hofu. **palpitation** *n* mpapatiko wa moyo.

palsy *n* 1 kupooza. 2 ugonjwa wa kutetemeka mwili *vt* 1 pooza.2 tetemeka.
palter *vi* ~ **with** laghai, fanya mzaha.
paltry *adj* hafifu, dhaifu, -dogo, -a bure. **paltriness** *n.*
pampas *n (pl)* savana: mbuga za Amerika ya Kusini. ~ **grass** *n* nyasi.
pamper *vt* dekeza, engaenga.
pamphlet kijitabu, kabrasha.
pan[1] *n* 1 sufuria; kiokamikate. **frying** ~ *n* kikaango, tawa. **~cake** *n* gole, chapati ya maji. **P~cake Day** Jumanne ya kabla ya Kwaresima. ~ **cake landing** kutua kwa tumbo (dharura) kwa ndege; poda. 2 mtitio wa ardhi. 3 **brain** ~ *n* funiko la juu la ubongo. 4 sahani ya mizani.5 sinia la kusafishia metali anuwai. 6 mtambo baruti. 7 **hard** ~ *n* udongochi mgumu. 8 *(sl)* uso *vt* 1 ~ **sth off/out** safisha (mchanga wenye dhahabu) ndani ya sinia. ~ **out** toa dhahabu; *(fig)* faulu, fanikiwa; tokea. 2 *(colloq)* kosoa sana, kengemeka.
pan[2] *vi,vt (cinema and TV)* elekeza kamera kulia/kushoto (ili kuvinasa vitu vinavyojongea).
pan- *(pref)* -a -ote *~-African* -a Afrika yote.
panacea *n* suluhisho/utatuzi; dawa/tiba ya kila kitu.
panache *n* mbwembwe.
panchromatic *adj* -a pankromatiki: -enye kunasa/kupokea rangi zote.
pancreas *n* kongosho. **pancreatic** *adj* -a kongosho. *pancreatic juice* maji kongosho.
panda *n* panda: aina ya dubu wa rangi nyeusi na nyeupe apatikanaye Tibeti. **P~ car** *n (GB)* gari la doria la polisi. **P~ crossing** *n (GB)* kivuko milia cha kujiwashia taa.
pandemic *adj* 1 -a pote. 2 *(of disease)* -a kuenea kote *n* maradhi yaliyoenea nchi nzima.
pandemonium *n* makelele mengi, ghasia kubwa, vurumai, zogo.
pander *vi* 1 shawishi, tia moyo. 2 kuwadia *n* kuwadi.
pane *n* kioo cha dirisha.
panegyric *n* hotuba ya wasifu; maandishi ya wasifu. **~al** *adj* -a wasifu. **panegyricst** *n.*
panel *n* 1 paneli: kipande kimojawapo katika vipande mbalimbali vilivyoungwa kufanya mlango. 2 sehemu ya vifaa vya kuendeshea chombo. 3 jopo, orodha ya wanajopo. 4 paneli: kundi la wazungumzaji waliochaguliwa kuwa wasemaji wakuu katika majadiliano kadhaa. 5 *(leg)* majina ya wajumbe wa baraza la wazee *vt* pigilia/weka upapi ~ *a door* pigilia paneli mlangoni. **~ling** *n* paneli za ukutani.
pang *n* maumivu ya ghafla makali; kichomi, mchomo *~s of hunger* maumivu ya njaa *birth ~s* uchungu wa kuzaa.
panga *n* panga; mundu.
pangolin *n (bio)* kakakuona.
panhandle *(US) n* sehemu nyembamba ya nchi *vt (sl)* ombaomba. **~r** *n (sl)* mwombaji.
panic *n* 1 hofu kubwa inayomwingia mtu ghafla. 2 muda wa kushikwa na hofu. ~ **stricken** -lioshikwa na hofu kubwa ya ghafla hata kutofikiri sawasawa *vt,vi* -wa na wasiwasi, hangaika, shikwa na hofu. **~ky** *adj.* **~-monger** *n* mtiaji, mchochea hofu.
panjandrum *n* mkubwa, jina la mzaha (apewalo mkubwa mwenye majivuno); kizito.
pannier *n* shogi.
pannikin *n* kikombe cha bati, kopo, bilauri ya chuma; kitu kilichomo katika kikombe hicho.
panoply *n* 1 deraya. 2 *(fig)* mavazi maridadi. **panoplied** *adj.*
panoptic *adj* -enye kuonekana yote.
panorama *n* 1 mandhari yote. 2 picha za mandhari yote. 3 mfululizo wa mambo mbalimbali, maisha na matukio yake. **panoramic** *adj.*
pan-pipes *n* aina ya zumari.
pansy *n* 1 ua. 2 *(derog)* msenge.
pant *vi,vt* 1 tweta, hema, kukuta. 2 ~ **for** taka sana, tamani. 3 ~ **out** sema

pamoja na kutweta *n* mtweto wa harakaharaka.

pantaloon *n* 1 mhusika zuzu (katika mchezo). 2 *(US) (hist)* suruali.

pantechnicon *n (GB)* gari la kubebea kuchukulia samani.

pantheism *n* kuabudu miungu wengi; imani kuwa Mungu yumo ndani ya wengi; imani kuwa Mungu yumo ndani ya kila kitu na kuwa kila kitu ni Mungu. **pantheist** *n* mwabudu-miungu. **pantheistic** *adj* -a kuabudu miungu. **pantheon** *n* 1 hekalu la miungu yote. 2 miungu yote ya dini fulani.

panther *n* chui mweusi. **American ~** Chui wa Amerika.

panties *n (pl, (colloq)* suruali (kipande) za watoto; chupi.

pantile *n* kigae (cha kuezekea kilichobinuka/pinda).

panto *n (colloq abbr of)* **pantomime**.

pantograph *n* 1 pantografu: chombo cha kunakilia mchoro au ramani. 2 chombo cha kupokelea umeme ndani ya gari (toka waya za juu).

pantomime *n* 1 mchezo wa kuigiza kwa ajili ya watoto (uliojaa vichekesho, nyimbo n.k.). 2 mchezo bubu. **pantomimic** *adj* -a mchezo bubu.

pantry *n* 1 stoo ya vyombo vya kulia. **~ man** *n* mwangalizi wa stoo ya vyombo vya maakuli. 2 stoo ya chakula.

pants *n (pl)* **(pair of ~)***(GB)* chupi;*(US)* suruali. **bore/ scare/talk etc the ~ off one** chosha sana. **scare the ~ off** ogofya/tetemesha sana. **catch sb with his ~ down** fuma.

panty-hose *n see* **tights**.

panzer *adj* -a kikosi cha vifaru *n* kifaru.

pap *n* 1 uji, ubwabwa. 2 *(fig)* rahisi mno; vitabu/magazeti rahisi rahisi.

papa *n (child's word for)* baba.

papacy *n* cheo (kazi, utawala) cha papa. **papal** *adj* -a Baba Mtakatifu.

paper *n* 1 karatasi *a ~ bag* mfuko wa karatasi. **(be/look) good on ~** onekana zuri katika karatasi/kinadharia/ kimaandishi. **put pen to ~** *(dated for)* anza kuandika. **~ backed** *adj (of books)* -liojalidiwa kwa karatasi. **~ back** *n* kitabu chenye jalada la karatasi. **~hanger** *n* mgundisha karatasi ukutani. **~knife** *n* kisu cha kukatia/kufungulia barua. **~tiger** tishio la bure tu. **~mill** kiwanda cha karatasi. **~weight** *n* uzito wa kukinga karatasi (zisipeperushwe). 2 **news~** *n* gazeti. 3 **~money** *n* noti. 4 *(pl)* hati (ya kuonyesha cheo cha mtu). **~work** urasimu, kazi ya mafaili *send in one's ~s (mil)* jiuzulu. 5 maswali/ karatasi ya mtihani. 6 makala *vt* bandika karatasi (ukutani); funika kwa karatasi. **~ over the cracks** *(fig)* setiri/ficha makosa. **~ the house** toa tiketi za bure kwa mchezo (ili kurubuni watu). **~-stainer** *n* mtengenezaji wa viungo vya karatasi. **~y** *adj* -a makaratasi.

papier-mache *n* pepamashi: karatasi zilizosagwa au kukatwakatwa na kulowekwa maji zikafanywa kama plasta ya kutengeneza vitu k.m. trei n.k.

papist *n (derog)* mroma: mfuasi wa kanisa la kikatoliki.

papoose *n* mtoto; mbeleko.

paprika *n* pilipili hohoa.

papyrus 1 mafunjo. 2 karatasi za mafunjo zilizotengenezwa na Wamisri; maandiko yaliyo katika mafunjo.

par *n* wastani; kiwango/thamani, kiasi cha kawaida. **above/below /at ~** juu ya/ chini ya/katika wastani. **on a ~ (with)** sawa na. **up to ~** *(colloq)* vizuri kama kawaida. **~ of exchange** kiwango cha kawaida cha kubadilishana fedha.

parable *n* fumbo; hadithi ya mafumbo (yenye mafundisho) *speak in ~s* ongea kwa mafumbo. **parabolical** *adj* -a kimafumbo.

parabola *n* parabola, -a mchirizo/ mchoro wa pia. **parabolic** *adj* -a parabola.

parachute *n* mwavuli, parachuti. **parachutist** *n* mtu arukaye kwa parachuti.

parade *vi,vt* 1 *(of troops)* kusanya (kwa ajili ya gwaride; ukaguzi n.k.); fanya gwaride. 2 onyesha, tembeza *n* 1 gwaride. ~ **ground** uwanja wa gwaride. 2 maonyesho. **make a ~ of one's virtues** jaribu kuwavutia watu kwa kujionyesha. 3 njia ya matembezi aghalabu pwani.

paradigm *n* kielelezo (cha mfumo wa miundo agh kisarufi).

paradise *n* 1 peponi, barazahi. 2 furaha kuu. 3 Bustani ya Aden. 4 mahali pa raha. **paradisiac, paradisiacal** *adj* -a peponi, -a bustani ya Adeni.

paradox *n* kweli kinza(ni); kweli iliyo kama uwongo, neno linaloonekana kama kwamba ni la kinyume kumbe ni sahihi, fumbo la maneno. **~ical** *adj*. **~ically** *adv*.

paraffin *n* 1 ~ **(oil)** mafuta ya taa. 2 ~ **wax** nta ya mishumaa. **liquid** ~ mafuta ya nyonyo.

paragon *n* kifano; mfano bora.

paragraph *n* aya, ibara *vt* gawa katika aya.

parakeet *n* kasuku mdogo na mwenye milele mirefu.

parallel *adj (of lines)* -liosambamba. ~ **bars** nguzo zilizo sambamba (kwa ajili ya michezo ya viungo) *n* 1 msambamba. ~ **of latitude** msambamba wa latitudo. 2 mfano, kifani *without* ~ -sio na kifani. 3 kufananisha, mlinganisho *vt* 1 fananisha. 2 -wa sambamba. **~ism** *n (lit or fig)* usambamba. **~ogram** *n* msambamba.

paralyse, (US) paralyze *vt,vi* 1 pooza, poozesha. 2 fadhaisha, duwaza. **paralysis** *n* kiharusi; *(fig)* hali ya kutokuwa na nguvu, kupooza. **paralytic** *n, adj* 1 mtu aliyepooza; *(fig)* (mtu) asiyejiweza. 2 (mtu) aliyelewa sana.

parameter *n* parameta, kigezo.

paramilitary *adj* -enye hadhi ya kijeshi.

paramount *adj (formal)* kuu; kubwa ~ *chief* chifu mkuu *of ~ importance* muhimu sana, -enye umuhimu mkubwa. **~cy** *n*.

paramour *n (arch)* hawara, kimada (wa mtu aliyeoa).

paranoia *n* wazimu (agh) -siotibika wa kujiona unaonewa kila wakati. **~c**, **paranoid** *n,adj*.

parapet *n* 1 ukuta mfupi wa pembeni (mwa daraja n.k.). 2 *(mil)* kizuio (cha mawe, udongo n.k.).

paraphernalia *n* vikorokoro; vifaa, zana.

paraphrase *n* ufafanuzi, fasili, maelezo *vt* fafanua, fasili.

paraplegia *n (path)* paraplejia: kupooza kwa sehemu ya chini ya kiwiliwili. **paraplegic** *n, adj* mwenye/-enye paraplejia.

parasite *n* 1 kimelea. 2 *(of a person)* kupe, mnyonyaji. **parasitic, parasitical** *adj*.

parasol *n* mwavuli wa jua.

paratroops *n pl* jeshi la miavuli. **paratrooper** *n* askari wa miavuli.

parboil *vt* tokosa; *(fig)* tia joto sana.

parcel *n* 1 kifurushi. ~ **post** *n* upelekaji vifurushi kwa posta. 2 **part and ~ of** sehemu muhimu ya. **a ~ of land** sehemu ya ardhi *vt* ~ **out** gawa katika mafungu. ~ **up** funga vifurushi.

parch *vt (of heat, sun etc)* kausha, choma, tia joto.

parchment *n* 1 karatasi iliyotengenezwa kwa ngozi. 2 karatasi inayofanana nayo.

pardon *vt* samehe. **P~ me!** Niwie radhi! **beg sb's** ~ omba radhi. ~ **sb for sth** samehe *n* msamaha, samahani. **~able** *adj* -a kusameheka. **~ably** *adv*. **~er** *n (in the Middle Ages)* mtu mwenye leseni ya kuuza msamaha wa Baba Mtakatifu, muuza rehema.

pare *vt* menya; kata, punguza. **parings** *n (pl)* kilichomenywa; kilichokatwa. **nail-parings** kucha zilizokatwa.

paregoric *n* dawa ya kutuliza neva.

parent *n* mzazi. ~ **company** *(comm)* kampuni mama. **~age** *n* ukoo, nasaba, uzawa. **~al** *adj*. **~ally** *adv*. **~hood** *n* hali ya kuwa mzazi.

parenthesis *n* mabano. **in** ~ kwenye mabano; *(fig)* -liotengwa. **parenthetic, parenthetical** *adj*. **parenthetically** *adv*.

par excellence *adv (F)* kwa kiwango cha juu kabisa, hasa.

pariah *n (India)* mtu wa tabaka la chini; *(fig)* mtu aliyetengwa na jamii. **~-dog** *n (India)* mbwa koko.

pari passu *adv (L)* kwa wakati mmoja; sawasawa, sawia.

parish *n* parokia. ~ **pump** *(usu attrib)* -a kuhusu mtaa/sehemu ile. **~-register** kitabu cha parokia. **civil** ~ mtaa (katika serikali ya mitaa). **~ioner** *n* mkazi wa parokia. **go on the** ~ pata msaada (wa chakula n.k.).

parity *n* usawa; kulingana. ~ **of exchange** viwango rasmi vya kubadilisha fedha.

park *n* 1 bustani. **ball** ~ *(US)* kiwanja cha michezo.2 mbuga zinazozunguka nyumba ya shamba. 3 **car** ~ maegesho ya magari. 4 **national** ~ mbuga za taifa. 5 *(mil)* kiwanja cha kuwekea mizinga na zana *vt,vi* 1 egesha. 2 *(colloq)* weka kitu mahali. ~ **ing** *n* maegesho. ~ **lot** maegesho. ~ **meter** mita ya maegesho.

Parkinson's *adj* ~ **disease** *(path)* ugonjwa wa kutetemeka/kukakamaa. ~ **law** *(hum)* nadharia kwamba kasi ya kazi hufuatana na muda uliotengwa.

parky *adj (sl) (of air, weather)* -a baridi.

parlance *n* usemaji, msemo *common* ~ msemo wa kawaida.

parley *n* mkutano, mazungumzo (hasa baina ya maadui) *vi* ~ **(with sb)** fanya mashauri.

parliament *n* bunge. **~arian** *n* mbunge stadi/maarufu/mjuzi wa kanuni za bunge. **~ary** *adj* -a bunge.

parlour, *(US)* **parlor** *n* 1 ukumbi,sebule. ~ **maid** *(not US)* kijakazi angojaye meza; *(GB)* mhudumu wa mezani. ~ **games** michezo ya ndani (ya nyumba). 2 *(esp US)* chumba cha kupokelea wageni. 3 chumba cha wateja. **~-car** *n (US)* behewa la starehe.

parlous *adj (formal)* -a hatari.

parochial *adj* -a parokia; *(fig)* finyu *a ~ outlook* mtazamo finyu. **~ly** *adv*. **~ism** *n*.

parody *n* mwigo wa kubeza *vt* iga kwa kubeza.

parole *n* ahadi ya mfungwa kutotoroka; kifungo cha nje. **on** ~ achiwa huru baada ya kutoa ahadi hiyo. **break one's** ~ vunja ahadi kwa kujaribu kutoroka *vt* achia mfungwa baada ya kutoa ahadi hiyo.

paroquet *n see* **parakeet**.

paroxysm *n* mshtuko, mshindo (wa maumivu, hasira, kicheko n.k.) wa ghafla.

parquet *n* sakafu ya vipande vya mbao.

parricide *n* muuaji/mauaji ya baba au ndugu wa karibu.

parrot *n* 1 kasuku. 2 mtu anayeiga tu (kama kasuku). ~ **fever** homa ya kasuku *(see* **psittacosis)** *vt* iga kama kasuku.

parry *vt* zuia, pangua konde; *(fig)* epuka (swali) *n* kuzuia, kupangua.

parse *vt* changanua, ainisha, pambanua maneno kisarufi.

parsimony *n (formal)* ubahili. **parsimonious** *adj*.

parsley *n* kitimiri, kotimiri.

parson *n* mchungaji; *(colloq)* kasisi. **~'s nose** *(colloq)* kikundu cha kuku. ~ **age** nyumba ya mchungaji.

part *n* 1 sehemu, kipande, kiasi. **for the most** ~ kwa kiasi kikubwa. **in** ~ kwa kiasi fulani. ~ **owner** *n* mmiliki bia. **~-time** *adj* -a muda maalumu. **~-timer** *n* mfanyakazi wa muda maalumu. 2 *(pl)* janibu. 3 nafasi, wajibu. **play a big/small ~ (in sth)** -wa mshiriki mkuu, -wa na nafasi kubwa/ndogo (katika). **take ~ (in)** shiriki. 4 upande. **for my** ~ kwa upande wangu. **take someone's** ~

unga mkono. 5 **take sth in good ~** chukulia kitu vizuri/bila kinyongo. 6 **(spare) ~** kipuri, spea. 7 *(gram)* aina. **~s of speech** aina za maneno. 8 **person of many ~s** mtu mwenye vipaji vingi. 9 *(mus)* sauti. **~ly** *adv* *vt,vi* 1 gawa; tenga. 2 **~ with** acha, achia; achanisha, achana na. 3 **~ one's hair** piga wei. **~ing** *n* 1 wei, mpaka (wa nywele). 2 mfarakano; kuagana, kuachana, kuondoka. **at the ~ of the ways** njia panda; *(fig)* wakati wa kuchagua. **~ial** *adj* 1 -a sehemu, -sio kamili, -a kiasi. 2 **~ (towards)** -a kupendelea. 3 **~ to** a kupenda/ kupendelea. **~ially** *adv.* **~iality** *n* 1 pendeleo. 2 **~ for** kupenda. **~ition** *n* 1 kugawanywa; mgawanyo *The P~ of Africa* kugawanywa kwa Afrika. 2 kitenganishi. 3 sehemu, chumba. ~ *vt* gawa, tenga. **~itive** *n,adj* (-a) kugawa, (-a) kutenga.

partake *vt,vi (dated, formal)* **~ of sth** 1 shiriki, onja; chukua sehemu ya. 2 -wa (na hali/sifa fulani).

parterre *n* 1 *(in a garden)* sehemu tambarare yenye tuta la maua/nyasi. 2 *(in a theatre)* gorofa ya juu ya ukumbi, sehemu ya nyuma ya ukumbi.

parthenogenesis *n* kuzaa bila kujamiiana/kurutubisha yai.

Parthian *adj* -a Parthia. **~ shot/ shaft** neno la mwisho (katika ugomvi/ kuachana).

participate *vi* **~ (in)** shiriki, -wa katika. **participant** *n* mshiriki. **participation** *n* kushiriki.

participle *n (gram)* badiliko la kitenzi kuonyesha hali inayoendelea *present ~* wakati uliopo, hali ya kuendelea.

particle *n* 1 chembe. 2 *(gram)* kishirikishi.

parti-coloured, (US) **parti-colored** *adj* -a rangi mbalimbali kwa kila sehemu.

particular *adj* 1 -a pekee. 2 maalumu, mahsusi. **in ~** hasa. 3 -enyewe hasa, halisi, kamili kabisa. 4 **~ (about/over)** -enye kuchagua sana, -enye kujali sana; angalifu juu ya; gumu kuridhisha *n* habari (kwa urefu), ukamilifu. **go into ~s** toa habari kwa urefu/ukamilifu. **~ly** *adv* zaidi, hasa. **~ity** *n* ukamilifu. **~ize** *vt,vi* taja, orodhesha; pambanua.

partisan *n* 1 mfuasi mwenye ari (wa chama, kikundi). 2 mpiganaji mzalendo *adj* -enye kufuata bila kupima. **~ship** *n.*

partner *n* 1 mbia. 2 mwenzi; patna *vt* -wa mbia/mwenzi wa. **~ship** *n* ubia.

partridge *n* kware.

parturition *n* kujifungua, kuzaa.

party *n* 1 chama. **~ spirit** moyo na ushabiki wa chama (hasa cha kisiasa). **multi ~ system** mfumo wa vyama vingi. 2 mojawapo wa watu/ upande (katika ugomvi, mashauri, daawa). **~ wall** ukuta wa mpaka. 3 ushirika, kikosi (hasa cha shughuli, kazi). 4 dhifa, karamu. **lack the ~ spirit** -tofurahia karamu. **make up a ~** ungana kwa ajili ya karamu. 5 mshiriki. 6 *(hum)* mtu.

parvenu *n* mtu aliyetajirika/kupata ukuu kwa ghafla.

paschal *adj* 1 -a Pasaka ya Wayahudi. 2 -a Pasaka.

pasha *n (hist)* pasha. Mkuu wa mkoa katika serikali ya zamani ya Uturuki.

pass *n* 1 kufaulu mtihani. 2 kuwa katika hali fulani; hali. 3 **come to/ reach a pretty/sad/ strange ~** fikia hali ya ajabu. **come to ~** tokea. **bring to ~** tekeleza; timiliza. 4 pasi, kibali, pasipoti. 5 *(football)* pasi. 6 kupitisha mkono juu ya kitu (kama vile wafanyavyo wacheza mazingaombwe). 7 pigo la kwenda mbele (katika mchezo wa kupigana kwa panga). **make a ~ at (a woman)** *(sl)* tongoza. 8 *(card games)* kumruka mchezaji. **hold the ~** *(fig)* tetea hoja. **sell the ~** *(fig)* saliti. 9 njia nyembamba ipitiayo katika milima. 10 *(compounds)* **~-book** *n* kitabu cha benki; *(S Africa)* pasi. **~key** *n* ufunguo malaya, ufunguo mkuu. **~word** *n* neno la siri la kumtambulisha mtu kwa walinzi (agh. katika jeshi) *vi,vt* 1 pita, nenda. **~ er by** mpita njia. 2 acha mtu/kitu nyuma au katika upande fulani na kwenda mbele. 3 ruka, pitia. 4 *(of time)* tumika, malizika. 5 tumia (muda), pitisha. 6 **~ (from)** badilika toka hali moja hadi nyingine. 7 -pa, pitisha *please ~ me the book* tafadhali nipe kitabu hicho. 8 sema, tamka. **~ the time of day with sb** ongea/sogoa na *~ a comment* sema kitu. 9 tawanya *he was found guilty of ~ing subversive documents* alipatikana na hatia ya kutawanya maandishi ya kupotosha umma. 10 pitisha; pita; idhinisha, kubali *the bill ~ed and became law* mswada ulipitishwa na kuwa sheria *most of the candidates ~ed* watahiniwa wengi walishinda. 11 fikia mwisho; kufa; vuka mpaka. 12 fanyika, tendeka, tokea *what was ~ing between you two?* kulikuwa na nini kati yenu wawili? 13 **~ sth on sth/sb** hukumu, toa (uamuzi, ushauri n.k.) *~ sentence on an accused man* hukumu mshitakiwa. **~ one's word** toa ahadi. 14 *(card games)* ruka (zamu ya mchezaji). 15 *(in football, hockey etc)* pasia *Juma ~ed the ball to Daudi* Juma alimpasia Daudi mpira. 16 pita, kuwa nje ya mpaka, zidi. 17 kubaliwa bila lawama; pita bila kuonekana au kusailiwa. 18 enda, fanya kitu kiende au kijongee; pitisha. 19 pitisha majeshi mbele (kwa ajili ya kukaguliwa. 20 *(with adv and prep)* **~ sth/sb by** pita, puuza, -tojali. **~ for** kubalika kama/kuwa. **~ off** *(of events)* fanyika, tendeka; acha kujali/ kuangalia; *(of pain)* isha. **~ sth or sb off as** jifanye kuwa. **~ over** acha kuzingatia; tojali, acha, sahau. **~ out** *(colloq)* tumia. **~ out (of sth)** maliza. **~ sth on sb/sth** toa (uamuzi, ushauri n.k.). **~ in/into** chaguliwa. **~ sth off** kwepa. **~ up** puuza. **~ away** *(euphem)* -fa. **~ sth on** -pa mtu mwingine, pitisha. **~ing out ceremony/parade** sherehe/gwaride la kumaliza mafunzo. 21 **~ water** kojoa. **~able** *adj* 1 -a kupitika. 2 -a kadiri, -a wastani, -a kuridhisha. **~ably** *adv*. **~age** *n* 1 kitendo cha kupita, mpito. **a bird of ~** ndege wa kuhama, mpita njia. 2 njia, pito, upenyo. 3 safari. 4 **~ (way)** njia; (nyumbani) ukumbini. 5 yapitayo baina ya watu wawili katika mazungumzo *have angry ~ with sb* wa na mabishano makali. 6 **~ s of arms** *(fig)* mapigano; mabishano. 7 dondoo, maneno, fungu la maneno yaliyonukuliwa katika kitabu. 8 kupitishwa kwa mswada kuwa sheria. **~ing** *adj* -a kupita, -a mara moja *n* 1 kupita. 2 kifo; kufariki, kufa. **~-bell** *n* kengele ya kujulisha kifo/mazishi. **in ~** kwa kupitia tu, wakati wa kusema *adv (arch)* sana.

passe,passee *adj* -a zamani, -liopitwa (na wakati).

passenger *n* 1 abiria, msafiri, *(colloq)* mwanatimu, mwanachama, n.k. ambaye ni mzembe, mshiriki.

passepartout *n* utepe wenye gundi (wa kushikizia picha); ufunguo malaya.

passim *adv* kwa kutokea kila mara (katika kitabu); pote.

passion *n* 1 hisia kali; *(of anger)* hamaki; *(of love)* uchu, mapenzi makali; mlipuko wa hamaki *fly into a ~* kasirika sana. 2 **the P ~** mateso ya Yesu Kristo. **P~ Sunday** Jumapili ya Mateso. **P~ Week** Wiki ya Mateso (ya Yesu Kristo). **~-flower** *n* ua la mkarakara. **~-fruit** n karakara. **~less** *adj*. **~ate** *adj* -enye kutekwa na hisia kali, -enye kujawa na/-enye kuonyesha hisia kali, shauku, n.k. **~ately** *adv*.

passive *adj* -a kutoonyesha hisia, -a kukaa tu, baridi. **~ resistance** upinzani wa kimyakimya, baridi *(gram) ~ voice* kauli ya kutendwa; kauli iliyotajwa. **~ly** *adv*. **~ness** *n*. **passivity** *n*.

Passover *n* Pasaka (ya Wayahudi).

passport *n* 1 pasi, pasipoti. 2 *see* **pass**. 3 *(fig)* njia bora (ya kufaulu).

past *adj* 1 -liopita, -a zamani. ~ **master** mtu mwenye kumbukumbu au utaalamu mkubwa juu ya kitu/somo. 2 *(gram)* ~ **tense** -a wakati uliopita *n* 1 **then** ~ zamani, mambo ya zamani yaliyopita, wakati uliopita. 2 maisha ya nyuma (ya mtu). 3 *(gram)* wakati uliopita *prep & adv* 1 kupita *it is half ~ two* ni saa nane na nusu. 2 kufikia na kupita umbali wa ~ *the butcher's shop* kupita mbele ya duka la nyama. **be/get ~ it** *(colloq)* -toweza tena kufanya ya zamani. 3 kuvuka kiwango (cha kufanya kitu) *the old man is ~ work* mzee amevuka kiwango cha kufanya kazi/amekuwa mzee mno kuweza kufanya kazi *I'am ~ doing such things* siwezi tena kufanya vitu hivi.

pasta *n* pasta (k.v. tambi n.k.).

paste *n* 1 lahamu, gundi. 2 mchanganyiko laini wa unga na maji (wa kugandamishia karatasi n.k.). ~ **board** kitu laini mfano wa ubao kilichotengenezwa kwa kugandamanisha karatasi nyingi pamoja. 3 vyakula vilivyopondwa na kuwa laini. 4 *(poetic)* embwe. 5 *(of artificial gems)* vitobandia *vt* 1 gandamishia. ~ **sth down** funga kwa gundi. ~ **sth up** bandika/funga kwa gundi; *(of printing)* tengeneza kurasa za kitabu (kabla ya kuchapisha). 2 *(colloq)* twanga, kung'uta, ambatisha kwa mchanganyiko.

pastel *n* 1 picha iliyochorwa kwa rangi za krayoni. 2 ~ **shades** rangi zilizopakwa kwa juujuu na laini.

pastern *n* kiungo cha kwato ya farasi.

pasteurize *vt* ondoa vijidudu (hasa bakteria) katika maziwa kwa kupasha moto kutumia njia ya Louis Pasteur. **pasteurization** *n*.

pastiche *n* kazi ya sanaa iliyoigwa.

pastille *n* 1 kidonge (kidogo kitamu chenye dawa ya koo n.k.), pipi ya kikohozi.

pastime *n* burudani.

pastor *n (rel)* 1 mchungaji. ~**al** *adj,n* 1 -a ufugaji, -a kuchunga n.k.; *(rural)* -a maisha ya shamba. ~ **poem** shairi kuhusu maisha ya shamba. 2 -a mchungaji, -a askofu *(rel) ~ letter* barua ya askofu ~ *staff* fimbo ya askofu ~ *responsibilities* wajibu wa mchungaji. ~**alist** *n* mchungaji, mfugaji. ~**ate** *n* 1 *(rel)* upadre, ukasisi, uchungaji. 2 jumuia ya wachungaji.

pastry *n* vitobosha. ~**-cook** *n* mwoka vitobosha.

pasture *n* malisho ~ *right* haki ya kuchunga *vt,vi* 1 chunga. 2 lisha, -jilisha. **pasturage** *n*.

pasty *adj* 1 -a lahamu. 2 *(of face)* -eupe; -sio wa afya.

pat[1] *n* 1 kikofi (cha kuonyesha upendo, kupongeza, kushangilia, furaha n.k.). 2 kishindo kidogo (kama cha kupiga kwa kitu bapa). 3 kibonge, hasa cha siagi *vt, vi* pigapiga (kwa kikofi); papasa ~ *on the back* pongeza, shangilia. ~ **oneself on the back** jipongeza.

pat[2] *adv* kwa wakati ufaao, mara moja, bila kusita; sawia; papo hapo, papo kwa papo, mara. **stand** ~ kataa kubadili (msimamo/uamuzi), shikilia msimamo.

patch *n* 1 kiraka. ~ **pocket** mfuko wa kiraka. 2 plasta (ya kufungia kidonda). 3 kitambaa/pamba ya kufunga kwenye jicho lililoumia. 4 kidoa. 5 kiwanja, shamba dogo, kiunga, konde. 6 **not a ~ on** haifikii hata kidogo. 7 **go through/hit/strike a bad** ~ -wa/fikia wakati wa mkosi/mgumu wa majonzi. ~**work** nguo iliyoundwa kwa viraka mbalimbali vya nguo; *(fig)* kazi iliyofanywa kwa kuchanganya vitu vidogovidogo *vt* 1 tia kiraka. 2 ~ **up** tengeneza, chomelea, unganisha-unganisha ~ *up a quarrel* patana; patanisha kwa muda. ~**y** *adj*. ~**ily** *adv*. ~**iness** *n*.

pate *n (colloq)* kichwa.

patella *n* kilegesambwa.

patent *adj* 1 wazi, dhahiri, bayana ~ *ambiguity* utata dhahiri ~ *defect* dosari dhahiri. 2 **letters** ~ amri ya serikali ya kuruhusu utengenezaji wa kitu kilichogunduliwa na kukilinda kisiigwe na watu wengine. 3 -enye kulindwa na serikali isiigwe na watuwengine. 4 ~ **leather** ngozi iliyopakwa rangi ngumu inayong'aa sana. 5 -a asili, -a akili, -a mtu mmoja peke yake. **~ly** *adv* wazi *n* 1 hataza: kibali rasmi kilichotolewa kwa kutengeneza bidhaa. 2 chombo kipya au namna mpya ya kufanyiza bidhaa n.k.. ~ **office** ofisi ya hataza. ~ **agent** hataza *vt* andikisha hataza. **~ee** *n* mwenye hataza.

paterfamilias *n (hum)* baba, mkuu wa familia.

paternal *adj* 1 -a baba, -a kama baba. 2 -a kuumeni. **~ly** *adv*. **~ism** *n* kukimu watu bila kuwapa madaraka, kutawala watu kama watoto. **paternity** *n* ubaba, kuumeni ~ *suit* madai ya ubaba, kudai ubaba. **paternoster** *n (rel)* 1 Baba Yetu, sala ya Bwana.

path *n* 1 ~ **(way)**, **(foot)** ~ njia ya miguu. **~finder** mvumbuzi, mtangulizi; msaka njia; *(mil)* ndege tangulizi. 2 uwanja wa mbio. 3 njia ambamo kitu hupitia (k.m. mwezi).

pathetic *adj* 1 -a kusikitisha/kutia huruma. 2 *(colloq)* makuruhi, -a karaha, -a ovyo. 3 ~ **fallacy** upotokaji wa kuvihuisha visouhai. **~ally** *adv*.

pathology *n* patholojia: sayansi/elimu ya magonjwa. **pathologist** *n* mwanapatholojia. **pathological** *adj*. **pathologically** *adv*.

patience *n* 1 subira, uvumilivu; ustahimilivu. **be out of ~ with** -toweza kumvumilia tena/zaidi. **the ~ of Job** uvumilivu mkubwa. 2 mchezo wa karata wa mtu pekee tu. **patient** *adj* -stahimilivu, -enye subira *n* mgonjwa. **~ly** *adv*.

patina *n* mg'ao.

patio *n (Spanish)* 1 ua. 2 baraza, ukumbizo, ufinga.

patois *n* lahaja.

patrial *n* mtu mwenye sifa za kuwa raia wa Uingereza.

patriarch *n* 1 (mwanamume) mkuu wa familia au ukoo. 2 babu; mzee wa umri mkubwa anayeheshimika sana. 3 *(rel)* askofu mkuu. **~al** *adj*. ~ **ate** *n* chuo cha askofu mkuu; makao ya askofu mkuu.

patrician *(ancient Rome)* muungwana, mtoto wa watu, mtu wa ukoo bora.

patricide *n* 1 uuaji baba. 2 muuaji wa baba yake.

patrimony *n* urithi kutoka kwa baba. **patrimonial** *adj*.

patriot *n* mzalendo. **~ism** *n* uzalendo. **~ic** *adj*. **~ically** *adv*.

patrol *vt,vi* linda/fanya doria (katika mji, kambi n.k.) *n* 1 doria. 2 watu, meli au ndege za doria. 3 *(US)* ~ **wagon** *n* karandinga.

patron *n* 1 mlezi. 2 *(rel)* ~ **saint** mtakatifu mlezi. 3 mteja wa kila siku katika duka. **~ess** mlezi, (wa kike). **~age** *n* 1 ulezi; uungwaji mkono na mlezi. 2 haki/mamlaka ya kuteua watu. 3 udhalilishaji. 4 uteja (wa kudumu). **~ize** *vt* 1 lea, linda. 2 dhalilisha. 3 -wa mteja wa (mara kwa mara). **~izing** *adj*. **~izingly** *adv*. **~ymic** *n* jina la ukoo *adj* -a jina la ukoo.

patten *n* kiatu cha mti, mtalawanda.

patter[1] *vt,vi* tarakanya/taraganya, sema upesi upesi (bila kufikiri maana ya maneno) *n* 1 lugha ya kikundi cha watu fulani (k.m. wezi n.k.). 2 utaraganyo/mtarakanyo.

patter[2] *vi* fanya vishindo vidogovidogo (k.m. kwa kutembea) *n* vishindo vidogovidogo vya mfulizo *the ~ of footsteps on a floor* vishindo vya mtu anayetembea kwenye sakafu.

pattern *n* 1 kiolezo, ruwaza. 2 *(design)* bombwe. 3 sampuli. 4 pambo (la kwenye zulia, pazia au karata). 5 mkondo, mwelekeo, mpangilio *vt* 1 ~ **sth upon/after sth/sb** fuata mtindo/ fulani. 2 piga ruwaza. 3 pamba.

paucity *n (formal)* uchache, uhaba.

paunch *n* tumbo (hasa kubwa), kitambi. **~iness** *n*.

pauper *n* mkata, ombaomba, maskini. **~ism, ~ization** *n*. **~ize** *vt* fukarisha.

pause *n* kituo, mapumziko, pauzi. **give ~ to** fanya (mtu) asite na afikirie kwanza *he made a ~* alisita, alitua kwa muda *vt* tua kwa muda, pumzika kidogo.

pave *vt* tia kibamba. *(fig)* **~ the way for** andalia njia. **paving-stone** kibamba. **~r** *n* mtengenezaji vibamba. **~ment** *n* 1 njia ya miguu (iliyojengwa pande za njia kwa waenda kwa miguu), **~ment-artist** *n* msanii (wa vibamba, mawe njiani).

pavilion *n* 1 *(sport)* kibanda cha wachezaji na watazamaji. 2 banda la maonyesho.

paw *n* 1 wayo wa mnyama mwenye makucha *vt* 1 parura. 2 *(of person)* gusagusa.

pawky *adj* -janja, -a mzaha. **pawkiness** *n*. **pawkily** *adv*.

pawl 1 wenzogurudumu, wenzo-mtaimbo *vt,vi* kaza kwa wenzo-gurudumu.

pawn[1] *n* 1 kitunda. 2 *(fig)* kibaraka.

pawn[2] *n* rahani; uwekaji rahani *his watch is in ~* saa yake ameiweka rahani *vt* 1 weka/ tia rahani. 2 *(fig)* ahidi. **~ broker** *n* mweka rahani. **~shop** *n* duka la rahani. **~-ticket** tiketi ya rahani.

pawpaw *n* (*tree)* mpapai; *(fruit)* papai.

pax *n* 1 amani (neno la watoto wa shule wavulana lenye maana: tuache ugomvi bwana). 2 *(rel)* busu/alama/ ishara ya amani.

pay[1] *vt,vi* 1 lipa; lipia. 2 -pa zawadi; fidia. 3 lipa deni. **put paid to sth** komesha, maliza *~ a visit* enda kutazama, tembelea, zuru. **~ a compliment to** salimu, sifu. 4 **~ (to)** toa/-pa heshima; jali. 5 *n (phrases)* **~ one's way** lipa kila kitu, -toingia kwenye madeni. **~ as you earn (abbr PAYE)** kodi ya mapato (inayokatwa kwenye mshahara). **~able** *adj* 1 -a kulipwa *~ on demand* -a kulipwa idaiwapo *~ to bearer* -a kulipwa kwa aliye nayo. **~ee** *n* mtu wa kulipwa, mlipwaji. **~er** *n* mtu wa kulipa, mlipaji. 6 *(with adv particles and preps)* **~ sth back** rudisha (pesa n.k.). **~ sb back/out for sth** lipiza kisasi, adhibu. **~ for** lipa, lipia; adhibika kwa. **~ sth** weka fedha benki/katika akaunti. **~ sb off** lipa na kuachisha kazi; lipa malipo/madeni yote. **~ out** lipa/tumia fedha; *(naut)* legeza/achia kamba. **~ up** lipa yote. **~ dirt** *n* udongo wenye madini. **~ load** *n* shehena ya kulipiwa (k.v. mizigo, abiria n.k.); bomu katika kombora. **~master** *n* mlipaji. **~master general** *n* mkuu wa idara ya mishahara hazina. **~ off** *n* saa ya kumaliza deni/kulipiza kisasi. **~ office** *n* ofisi ya mishahara. **~packet** *n* (bahasha ya) mshahara. **~ phone/ station** *n (US)* kibanda cha simu. **~roll/sheet** *n* orodha ya wapokea mshahara. **~ slip** *n* karatasi ya maelezo ya mshahara na makato yake. **~ment** *n* malipo kulipa *deferred~* malipo yaliyoahirishwa. **~ voucher** hati ya malipo.

paynim *n (arch)* asiye mkristu.

pea *n* njegere, choroko, dengu, adesi; *(pigeon)* mbaazi; *(cow)* kunde. **as like as two ~s (in a pod)** -enye kufanana sana, pacha. **sweet ~** maua yanayofanana na njegere. **~-pod** *n* ganda la njegere. **~ soup** *n* mchuzi mzito wa njegere/kunde zilizokaushwa. **~ souper** *n* ukungu mzito. **~green** *adj* -enye rangi ya kijani, a njerege mbichi. **~-fowl, ~-hen** *n* tausi jike. **~-chick** *n* kinda la tausi.

peace *n* 1 amani. **make ~ (with)** leta amani, patana *disturb the ~* vuruga amani. **breach of the ~** fujo, ghasia, vurumai. **Justice of the P ~** Hakimu *keep the ~* kaa kwa amani, fuata sheria. 2 *(often* **P~***)* Mkataba/ Mapatano ya amani. 3 utulivu, kimya. **at/in ~** kwa amani. **at ~ with** hali ya mapatano. **hold one's ~** kaa kimya, acha ubishi. **make one's ~ (with sb)** maliza ugomvi. **~ maker** *n*

1 mpatanishi, msuluhishi. ~-**offering** *n* dhabihu, uradhi, kitulizo. ~-**officer** *n* ofisa amani mwenye dhamana ya usalama kama askari polisi. ~-**pipe** *n* kiko cha amani (cha Wahindi Wekundu) cha ishara ya amani kitumiwacho kama kielelezo cha amani. ~**able** *adj* -tulivu, -a kutaka amani, -siokuwa na ugomvi; -sokuwa na ghasia. ~**ableness** *n*. ~**ably** *adv*. ~**ful** *adj* 1 -tulivu, -enye kimya. 2 -a kupenda amani ~ *coexistence* kuishi pamoja kwa amani. ~**fulness** *n*.

peach[1] *vt vi* ~ **(against/on/ upon) sb** *(sl)* semea, saliti.

peach[2] *n* 1 *(tree)* mpichi, *(fruit)* pichi. 2 *(sl)* mtu au kitu kinachopendwa/ kinachothaminiwa sana. ~ **coloured** *adj* -enye rangi ya pichi. ~**y** *adj*. ~**ery** *n* shamba la pichi.

peacock *n* tausi dume. ~ **butterfly** kipepeo tausi. ~ **blue** buluu kali.

peak *n* 1 kilele, upeo, kikomo. 2 *(naut)* ~ *of sail* uberu *vi* 1 chongoka, fikia kilele/upeo. 2 ~ **and pine** dhoofika. ~**ed**, ~**y** *adj* -liochongoka; -liodhoofika.

peal *n* 1 mlio wa kengele. 2 seti ya kengele mbalimbali (zipigwazo pamoja). 3 *a* ~ *of thunder* ngurumo, radi *vt,vi* 1 lia, vuma, nguruma *the bell ~ed* kengele ililia. 2 vumisha, liza, piga.

peanut *n* njugu, karanga. ~ **oil** mafuta ya karanga. ~ **butter** siagi ya karanga. ~ **politician** *(US sl)* mwanasiasa uchwara.

pear *n (tree)* mpea; *(fruit)* pea.

pearl *n* lulu *vi* 1 tafuta lulu; chomeka/ pamba lulu. ~-**barley** *n* shayiri iliyo katika umbo la punje ndogondogo kama lulu. ~-**diver**, ~-**fisher** mzamia lulu. ~**oyster** chaza/kombe lulu. ~**ies** *n* vifungo vya rangi ya lulu. ~-**shell** *n* kombe ya lulu. ~-**white** *n* nyeupe pe. ~**y** *adj* -enye umbo kama lulu, -enye kutoa lulu. **cast ~s before swine** toa kitu cha thamani kabisa kwa mtu asiyekithamini.

peasant *n* mkulima (mdogo). ~ **farming** kilimo cha kujikimu. ~**ry** wakulima.

pease *n* ~-**pudding** *n* pudini ya njegere.

peat *n* mboji. ~-**bog** *n* shimo la mboji. ~**y** *adj*.

pebble *n* 1 changarawe, mbwe. ~-**dash** *n* chokaa yenye vijiwe au changarawe za mviringo. **pebbly** *adv*.

peccable *adj* -a kutenda dhambi.

peccadillo *n* vikosa/vidhambi vidogo.

peck[1] *n* 1 kipimo cha vitu vikavu (lita 9.091). 2 *(fig) a ~ of troubles* matatizo mengi.

peck[2] *vt,vi* ~**at** donoa, gogota; *(colloq)* onjaonja chakula. ~**ing order** *n* mpangilio wa nafasi katika jamii (kufuatana na nguvu, hadhi n.k.). 2 fanya/pata kwa kudonoa. 3 *(colloq)* busu mara moja *n* 1 mdonoo, udonoaji. 2 busu la haraka (lisilo na mapenzi). ~**er** *n (GB sl)* pua; *(US sl)* dhakari. **keep your ~er up** changamka; usikate tamaa. ~**ish** *adj* -enye njaa.

pectoral *adj* -a kifua, -a kidari. *n* 1 *(bio)* kifua cha chini cha panzi. 2 *(rel)* -liovaliwa kifuani. ~ **cross** msalaba wa Askofu (unaovaliwa kifuani).

peculate *vt,vi* iba mali ya umma. **peculation** *n* wizi wa mali ya umma. **peculator** *n* mwizi wa mali ya umma.

peculiar *adj* 1 -a pekee. 2 ~ **(to)** -a kupatikana/kutumika tu *an animal ~ to Africa* mnyama anayepatikana Afrika tu. 3 *(strange)* geni, ajabu. ~**ity** *n* 1 hali ya kitu kuwa cha pekee sana. 2 sifa au kitu bainishi; kitu cha ajabu, kioja. ~**ly** *adv*.

pecuniary *adj (formal)* -a fedha, -enye kuhusika na fedha.

pedagogy *n* ufundishaji. **pedagogic/ pedagogical** *adj*. **pedagogue** *n* mwalimu *(colloq)* mwalimu anayefuata mno mambo ya kanuni na elimu ya vitabuni.

pedal *n* pedali. ~-**board** *n* ubao wa pedali *vt* piga pedali *adj* -a miguu.

pedant *n* kalalahu: mtu ashikiliaye sana elimu ya vitabuni, elimu ya ufundi, na kushikilia mno sheria. **~ic** *adj* -enye kushikilia sana elimu ya vitabuni na sheria. **~ry** *n* tabia ya kutawaliwa na kanuni na elimu ya vitabuni.

peddle *vt,vi* 1 chuuza; uza rejareja. 2 eneza (umbea n.k.). **~r** mchuuzi. **peddling** *adj* -dogodogo, -siokuwa muhimu.

pederasty *n* ufiraji/ulawiti wa wavulana. **pederast** *n* mfiraji wa wavulana.

pedestal *n* 1 kiweko (cha nguzo au mnara). 2 kiegemezo. **knock sb off his ~** tweza mtu. **set sb on a ~** kweza mtu.

pedestrian *n* mwenda/mtembea kwa miguu *adj* 1 -a kuhusu kwenda kwa miguu. **~ crossing** kivuko cha wenda kwa miguu (barabarani). 2 *(of writing/speech)* -iso na mvuto; zito.

pediatrics *n* matibabu ya watoto (na magonjwa yao). **pediatrician** *n* mganga wa watoto.

pedicab *n* (Asia) garibaiskeli: gari la abiria wawili linaloendeshwa na baiskeli.

pedical,pedicle *n (bot)* kikonyo.

pedicure *n* utunzaji/tiba ya miguu (agh wa kucha, sugu n.k.).

pedigree *n* 1 ukoo, nasaba, jadi, hesabu ya vizazi. 2 *(of animals)* ukoosafu. **~d** *adj* -a ukoosafu. **~d cattle** ng'ombe wa ukoosafu.

pediment *n* kenchipambo: sehemu ya mbele ya nyumba; -enye umbo la pembe tatu.

pedlar,peddle *n see* **peddle.**

pedometer *n* pedomita.

pee *vi (colloq)* kojoa *n (colloq)* mkojo.

peek *vi* **~ (at)** chungulia *n* kuchungulia.

peek-a-boo *n (of children)* mchezo wa kuficha uso.

peel *vt,vi* **~ (off)** 1 menya, ambua/ ambuka, kemba. 2 *(skin)* chuna/ chunuka *n* ganda. **~er** *n* kimenyeo. **~ings** *n pl* maganda.

peep[1] *vi* lia (kama kinda la ndege au panya) *n* chi-chi: mlio wa kinda la ndege au panya.

peep[2] *vi* 1 **~ (at)** chungulia kwa kuibia. **~ing Tom** mtu achunguliaye watu kwa siri (bila wao kutambua). 2 chomoza, onekana (kwa sehemu tu) *the sun ~ed out from behind the clouds* jua lilichomoza kidogo tu katika mawingu *n* 1 kuchungulia kwa kuibia. 2 mapambazuko, mwanzo. **~-hole** *n* tundu la kuchungulia. **~-show** *n* nelikioo (ya filamu), (maonyesho yaliyomo ndani ya kisanduku chenye tundu). **~er** 1 mtu achunguliaye. 2 *(sl)* jicho.

peer[1] *n* 1 mwenzi, aliye sawa (kwa cheo n.k.) *you will not find his ~* hutaona mfano wake. **~ group** *n* rika. **~less** *adj* bila kifani. 2 *(GB)* lodi, mwinyi, mwanachama wa Baraza Kuu. **~ess** lodi mwanamke; mke wa lodi. **~age** *n* 1 *(GB)* mamwinyi, malodi. 2 umwinyi. **raise sb to the ~** teua kuwa lodi. 3 kitabu cha orodha ya mamwinyi.

peer[2] *vi* **~ (at/into)** kazia macho, angalia kwa makini.

peeve *vt (colloq)* kera, udhi. **~d** *adj (colloq)* -lioudhika/kereka. **peevish** *adj* -enye kuudhika. **peevishly** *adv.* **peevishness** *n.*

peg *n* 1 mambo, kigingi. **a square ~ in a round hole** mtu asiyefaa kwa kazi aliyonayo. **buy clothes off the ~** nunua nguo za kutungua. 2 mambo ya ubao/ya kuunganishia mbao. 3 **clothes ~** kibanio. **take sb down a ~ or two** aibisha, umbua. 4 *(plug)* kizibo. 5 *(music)* hesi (ya kulegeza kuvuta kamba za vayolini n.k.). 6 hoja, kisa, sababu. 7 pegi (agh. wiski, brandi n.k.). **~ board** bao lenye tundu na vijiti (kwa mchezo au maonyesho). **~-leg** mguu bandia *vt,vi* 1 **~ sth down** funga kwa mambo/kigingi. **~ sb down** *(fig)* bana. 2 **~ sth out** onyesha (mipaka/ ramani n.k.) kwa mambo. 3 *(of prices/wages)* weka kima cha bei/ mishahara. 4 **~ away at** endelea kwa kasi ileile kufanya kazi. ~ **out** *(colloq)* -fa, kata kamba. **level ~ing** *(fig)* endelea kwa kasi ileile.

peignoir *n* kanzu; vazi refu la nyumbani la mwanamke.

pejorative *adj* -a kukashifu. **~ly** *adv*.

pekoe *n* majani ya chai (ya daraja la juu).

pelf *n* (*usu derog or joc*) fedha, mali.

pelican *n* mwari: aina ya ndege kama mwendambize.

pelisse *n* *(arch)* joho refu la mwanamke.

pellet *n* 1 *(of gun)* marisawa. 2 *(med)* kidonge *vt* tengeneza/piga na marisaa.

pell-mell *adv* kwa vurumai, haraka haraka bila mpango *adj* -a fujo.

pellucid *adj (lit, fig)* angavu, -eupe, bayana. **~ly** *adv*.

pelmet *n* upapipazia.

pelt[1] *n* ngozi ya mnyama ikiwa na manyoya.

pelt[2] *vt,vi* 1 ~ **sth (at sb), ~ sb (with sth)** shambulia kwa kutupia vitu k.v. mawe n.k. tupia (mawe, matope n.k.), vurumishia, rujumu. 2 *(of rain)* nya sana, nyesha kwa nguvu *n* **at full ~** kwa kasi zote, haraka iwezekanavyo.

pelvis *n* fupanyonga. **pelvic** *adj*.

pen[1] *n* 1 kizizi, ua, kizimba, tundu. 2 kizimba cha nyambizi *vt* funga. ~ **sb up/in** funga (kama) katika kizizi/kizimba.

pen[2] *n* 1 kalamu (ya wino). 2 (mtindo wa) uandishi; kazi ya uandishi. 3 *(with compounds)* ~ **holder** mpini wa kalamu. ~ **and ink** vifaa vya kuandikia. **~-and-ink** *adj* -liochorwa kwa kalamu na wino. **~-friend/ ~-pal** rafiki wa kalamu. **~knife** *n* kisu kidogo cha kukunja. **~manship** *n* sanaa au mtindo wa kuandika. **~-name** lakabu. **~-pusher** *(colloq)* karani *vt* andika (barua n.k.).

penal *adj* -a adhabu. ~ **servitude** kifungo na kazi ngumu. ~ **code** kanuni ya adhabu. ~ **colony/ settlement** makazi ya kuadhibia. **~ly** *adv*. **~ize** *vt* 1 adhibu, tia hatiani. 2 **~ize sth (for sth)** taabisha, onea, pa adhabu. **~ization** *n*. **~ty** *n* 1 adhabu *inflict*~ tia adhabu. ~ **clause** *(comm)* ibara ya adhabu katika mkataba. **on/under ~ of death, etc** kwa adhabu ya kifo n.k.. 2 *(sports)* penalti. ~ **area** eneo la adhabu/ penalti.

penance *n* 1 kutubu; toba, malipizi. **do ~ (for sth)** tubu, ungama, fanya malipizi. 2 (RC) kitubio, maungamo.

pence *see* **penny**.

penchant *n* kupenda, upendeleo; mwelekeo. **a ~ for** upendeleo, mapenzi kwa.

pencil *n* 1 penseli, kalamu ya risasi. 2 *(with compounds)* **~-case** *n* mkebe wa penseli. ~ **sharpener** *n* kichonga penseli. **eyebrow ~** *n* wanja (wa penseli) *vt* andika/chora kwa penseli.

pendant *n* 1 lozi ya kidani; jebu. 2 *(naut) see* **pennant**.

pendent *adj* 1 -a kuning'inia. 2 *see* **pending**.

pending *adj* -a kungoja uamuzi *(prep)* 1 wakati wa. 2 kabla; mpaka.

pendulous *adj (formal)* -a kubembea, -a kuwayawaya, -a kuyumbayumba, -enye kuning'inia.

pendulum *n* 1 timazi. 2 mizani ya saa. 3 **the swing of the ~** *(fig)* kuyumbayumba kwa maoni ya watu (umma) kutoka upande hadi upande.

penetrate *vt* ~ **(into/to/ through)** 1 ingia, penya. 2 ingia moyoni. **be ~d with** ingiwa (moyoni)/jawa na; *(comprehend)* fahamu/ingia akilini, elewa maana. 3 enea. **penetrating** *adj* elekevu, -a akili nyingi. **penetratingly** *adv*. **penetration** *n* 1 kupenya/kuingilia; upenyaji; *(understanding)* busara, welekevu. 2 *(power of piercing)* nguvu ya kupenya, ukali. **penetrative** *adj* penyezi, ingizi, makini. **penetrable** *adj* 1 -a kupenyeka, -a kuingilika. 2 *(intelligible)* -a kueleweka.

penguin *n* 1 pengwini: ndege mnene wa majini mwenye rangi nyeusi na nyeupe na miguu mifupi asiyeweza kuruka juu.

penicillin *(med)* penisilini.
peninsula *n* *(geol)* rasi, musoma, mkono wa nchi. **~r** *adj* -a musoma, -a rasi, -a peninsula.
penis *n* uume, mboo, dhakari.
penitence *n* ~ **(for)** majuto (kwa kutenda mabaya/maovu/ dhambi). **penitent** -enye kutubu/kujuta *n (rel)* mtu anayetubu. **penitently** *adj*. **penitential** *adj* -a majuto, -a malipizi. **penitentially** *adv*. **penitentiary** *n* gereza, jela ya kuwarekebisha wahalifu sugu/ wakubwa *adj* -enye kurekebisha wahalifu.
pennant, **pennon** *n* bendera (ndefu nyembamba ya kuashiria au kutambulisha meli).
pennon *see* **pennant**.
penny *n* 1 *(until 1971 UK)* sarafu yenye thamani ya 1/12 ya shilingi. 2 thamani ya 1/100 ya pauni; 1/5 ya shilingi. 3 *(US colloq)* senti. 4 *(phr)* **(cost) a pretty** ~ pesa nyingi. **in for a ~, in for a pound** ukishaanza jambo huna budi kulimaliza. **(be) ~-wise and pound foolish** -wa mwangalifu katika mambo madogo lakini mfujaji wa makubwa. **a ~ for your thoughts** vipi? **take care of the pennies and the pounds will take care of themselves** kubwa hutokana na dogo. **turn/make an honest** ~ pata riziki kwa kihalali. 5 *(compounds)* **~-a-line** *adj* (maandishi) dhaifu, duni. ~ **dreadful** *(colloq)* riwaya ya thamani ndogo. **~-pincher** *n (colloq)* bahili. **~pinching** *adj* bahili. ~ **whistle** filimbi. **~-worth** *n* kiasi cha thamani ya peni. **a good/bad ~worth** bei nzuri/mbaya. 6 **spend a** ~ *(colloq)* kojoa. **the ~ dropped** maana ilieleweka. **penniless** *adj* fukara, siye na senti hata moja, hohehahe.
penology *n* elimu ya kifungo na adhabu za malipo; taaluma ya adhabu za sheria na uendeshaji wa jela.
pension[1] *n (F)* kiinua mgongo, pensheni, malipo ya uzeeni. **draw one's** ~ chukua/jiwekea pensheni. **on (a)** ~ pata pensheni *vt* lipa pensheni. ~ **sb off** lipa pensheni, staafisha mtu. **~able** *adj* -a kustahili pensheni. **~er** *n* mpokeaji pensheni.
pension[2] *n* nyumba ya kupangisha. **en** ~ kama mpangaji.
pensive *adj* -enye kufikiri kwa makini; -liozama katika mawazo. **~ly** *adv*. **~ness** *n*.
penstock *n* mlango wa maji (katika bwawa au mfereji).
pentagon *n* pembetano. **~al** *adj* -enye pembetano. **the P~** *n* Makao Makuu ya jeshi la Marekani.
pentameter *n (English verse)* shairi la mapigo matano.
Pentateuch *n* torati: vitabu vitano vya kwanza vya Biblia.
pentathlon *n (in modern Olympic Games)* mashindano ya riadha ambamo kila mchezaji hushiriki katika michezo mitano.
Pentecost *n* Pentekoste.
penthouse *n* 1 upenu. 2 *(US)* nyumba juu ya paa.
pentup *adj* -liobanwa; -liogandamizwa *~ up feelings* hisia zilizogandamizwa.
penultimate *n adj* (neno, silabi n.k.) -a pili kutoka mwisho.
penumbra *n* kivuli (chepesi); kisuka.
penurious *adj (formal)* masikini, bahili. **~ly** *adv*. **~ness** *n*. **penury** *n* umasikini.
peon *n* 1 *(in India and Pakistan)* tarishi, askari (wa zamu). 2 *(in Latin America)* mlowezi, kibarua. 3 *(hist)* mtumwa (Marekani). **~age** *n* uajiri wa vibarua/watumwa.
people *n (collective with pl v)* 1 watu kwa jumla. 2 watu wa eneo/jamii fulani *the ~'s army* jeshi la umma/wananchi/wanakijiji *the ~ of Gezaulole* wanakijiji wa Gezaulole. 3 watu, wananchi. 4 *(colloq)* jamaa, ndugu *come and meet my ~* njoo uonane na jamaa/ndugu zangu. 5 *(not collective)* taifa, mbari, kabila *vt fill with ~* jaza watu *a densely ~d village* kijiji kilichojaa watu.
pep *n (sl)* nguvu, msisimko. ~ **pill** kidoge cha kuchangamsha mwili *put*

some ~ into a fellow hamasisha mtu. ~ **talk** gumzo la kusisimua wasikilizaji *vt* ~ **up** tia nguvu, sisimua, hamasisha.

pepper *n* pilipili *(red)* ~ pilipili hoho ~ *corn n* pilipili manga. ~ **mill** mashine ya kusagia pilipili. ~ **box/pot** *n* kiwekea pilipili *vt,vi* 1 tia pilipili. 2 nyunyizia. 3 tupia, rushia, shambulia na ~ *sb with stones* tupia mtu mawe ~ *sb with questions* tupia mtu maswali. **~y** *adj* 1 -enye pilipili. 2 *(fig)* -epesi kukasirika, -enye harara. ~ **and salt** rangi ya nguo iliyofumwa kwa nyuzi zenye vidoa vyeusi na vyeupe.

pepsin *n* pepsini: enzaimu ya kusahilisha mmeng'enyo. **peptic** *adj* -enye pepsini, -a mmeng'enyo.

per *prep* kwa (kila) (moja) ~ *month* kwa (kila) mwezi (mmoja) ~ *cent* kwa kila mia.

peradventure *adv (arch)* 1 labda. 2 *(after if and lest)* kwa bahati *if ~ you meet him* iwapo utakutana naye kwa bahati.

perambulate *vi vt (liter)* tembea, randaranda. **perambulation** *n*. **perambulator** *n (common colloq abbr pram)* kigari cha mtoto.

perceive *vt (formal)* tambua, ona, fahamu. **perceivable** *adj* -a kuonekana, -a kutambulika. **perceptive** *adj* -a kuhusu utambuzi; tambuzi, ng'amuzi. **perceptible** *adj (formal)* -enye kuonekana, -a kutambulika. **perceptibility** *n*. **perception** *n (formal)* utambuzi. **perceptively** *adv*. **percipient** *adj (formal)* tambuzi.

percent *n* asilimia. **~age** *n* asilimia, sehemu *a small ~ of his income is taxed* sehemu ndogo ya mapato yake hutozwa kodi.

perch[1] *n* 1 kitulio cha ndege. 2 *(colloq)* wadhifa wa juu (alio nao mtu) *come off your ~* acha kujikweza. 3 *(also rod, pole)* kipimo cha urefu, agh. juu ya ardhi, yadi 5½ *vt,vi* tua; kaa juu ya; *(chiefly in pp) (of buildings)* -wa juu ya (kitu kilicho juu).

perch[2] *n* **nile** ~ (samaki) sangara.

perchance *adv (arch)* kwa bahati; labda.

percolate *vt,vi* ~ **(through)** *(of liquids)* penya, penyeza, chuja. **~r** *n* chungu, kunguto.

percussion *n* kugonganisha; mgongano, mshindo. **the ~ (section)** sehemu ya ngoma, tumba n.k. **~ist** *n* mpiga ngoma.

perdition *n (formal)* kuangamia kabisa; kuteseka milele.

peregrination *n (formal)* kusafiri; safari.

peremptory *adj (formal) (of commands)* -a kutuwa, -siopingwa, -siosailiwa; *(of a person, his manner)* -enye amri kali,-enye kuamuru. **~writ** *(leg)* amri ya kufika mahakamani. **peremptorily** *adv*.

perennial *adj* 1 -a mwaka. 2 *(of plants)* -a kuishi zaidi ya miaka miwili. 3 -a kudumu. **~ly** *adv*.

perfect *adj* 1 kamili, timilifu, -enye kila kitu. 2 bila kasoro. 3 sahihi, safi. 4 timamu *(attrib only)* zima, hasa. 5 -liofikia kiwango cha juu kabisa. 6 *(of grammar)* timilifu. **~ly** *adv* kabisa, vizuri kabisa, barabara *vt* kamilisha. **~ible** *adj* -enye kuweza kukamilishwa, -enye kuweza kusahihishwa. **~ibility** *n*. **~ion** *n* 1 ukamilifu. 2 upeo. 3 usitawi. 4 ubora. **~ionism** *n* nadharia ya ukamilifu. **~ionist** *n* 1 mtu aaminiye kwamba mwanadamu anaweza kushinda. 2 *(colloq)* mtu asiyeridhika na chochote mbali na anachofikiri kuwa ndicho.

perfervid *adj (formal)* -a bidii/juhudi nyingi.

perfidy *n* uhaini; hiana; usaliti, ulaghai. **perfidious** *adj (formal)* haini, saliti, laghai. **perfidiously** *adj*. **perfidiousness** *n*.

perforate *vt* toboa, pekecha, toboa safu za matundu. **perforation** *n* vitobo; kutoboa. **perforator** *n* kitoboleo.

perforce *adv* sharti, lazima, hapana

budi.

perform *vt,vi* 1 tenda, tekeleza ~ *one's duty* timiza wajibu. 2 cheza/imba/ piga muziki; onyesha (mbele ya hadhira). **~er** *n* mchezaji/mwimbaji/ mutribu. **~ance** *n* 1 utendaji, uigizaji, upigaji muziki, n.k. 2 *(achievement)* tendo bora, tendo kuu (la ujasiri, akili, ustadi n.k.). 3 *(action)* maonyesho, mchezo.

perfume *n* manukato, marashi, uturi *vt* tia marashi/manukato. **~r** *n* mtengeneza/mwuza marashi/uturi *a ~r's shop* duka la marashi. **~ry** kiwanda cha marashi.

perfunctory *adj* -a kutimiza wajibu; -a uzembe, bila uangalifu, -a purukushani; *(of persons)* zembe. **perfunctorily** *adv*.

perfuse *vt,vi* pulizia, nyunyiza, fukiza, eneza.

pergola *n* mtambalio wa mimea.

perhaps *adv* labda; huenda.

pericarp *n (bio)* perikapi, ganda.

pericranium *n* utandoubongo.

perigee *n* Perigi: sehemu ya njia ya sayari karibu kabisa na dunia.

perihelion *n* Perihelini: sehemu ya njia ya sayari karibu kabisa na jua.

peril *n* 1 hatari kubwa. 2 kitu au jambo lisababishalo hatari *vt* hatarisha. **~ous** *adj* -enye hatari. **~ously** *adv*.

perimeter *n* mzingo.

period *n* 1 kipindi. 2 wakati. 3 (kuingia) hedhi/mwezi. 4 nukta; kituo kikuu. 5 *(gram)* sentensi kamili. 6 kipindi cha ugonjwa. 7 *(astron)* muda wa mzunguko mmoja. 8 *(in school)* kipindi. **~ic** *adj* 1 -a muhula, -a kipindi, -a kurudiarudia, -enye kutokea kwa vipindi. 2 -enye aidini. **~ic table** jedwali ya dutu/elementi kwa uzito wa atomu na tabia za kawaida. **~ical** *n* jarida (litolewalo kila baada ya kipindi fulani). **~ically** *adv* kila baada ya kipindi fulani.

peripatetic *adj* 1 -a kutangatanga, -a kwenda huko na huko, -a kuzunguka, -a kurandaranda.

periphery *n* 1 ukingoni, pembezoni.

peripheral *adj* -a ukingoni; -a pembezoni.

periphrasis *n* 1 kuongea kwa mafumbo/kuzungukazunguka. 2 *(gram)* kutumia mafungu badala ya maneno ya mkato k.m. fanya aanguke badala ya 'angusha.' **periphrastic** *adj*.

periscope *n* periskopu: darubini ya kuonea juu ya upeo wa macho inayowezesha mtu aliye katika nyambizi n.k. kuona nje ya upeo wa macho yake. **periscopic** *adj* -a periskopu.

perish *vi vt* 1 -fa, hiliki, angamia. **~ the thought** Mungu apishe mbali. 2 *(of things)* chakaa, fifia; chakaza, fifisha. 3 toweka, isha, *(of cold)* sumbua, dhikisha. **~able** *adj (esp of food)* -a kuharibika upesi; si -enye kudumu. **~er** *n (sl)* mtundu; msumbufu.

peristyle *n (arch)* nguzo zizungukazo jengo, baraza yenye kinga za nguzo.

peritonitis *n* uvimbe wa ngozi ya fumbatio.

periwig *n see* **wig**.

periwinkle[1] *n* konokono mdogo wa pwani (anayeliwa).

periwinkle[2] *n* periwinka: aina ya mmea utambaao wenye maua ya samawati.

perjure *vt (reflex)* ~ **oneself** sema uwongo (baada ya kuapa kusema ukweli). **~r** *n* mtu asemaye uwongo (baada ya kuapa kusema ukweli). **perjury** *n* kosa la kusema uwongo (baada ya kuapa kusema ukweli).

perk[1] *vi,vt* 1 ~ **up** *(of a person)* changamka. 2 ~ **(sb/sth) up** changamsha; inua (kichwa), peleka kifua mbele. **~y** *adj* 1 -liochangamka. 2 -enye kujikweza. **~ily** *adv*. **~iness** *n*.

perk[2] *n (colloq, usu pl)* marupurupu.

perk[3] *vi,vt (colloq)* penya, jichuja.

permafrost *n* udongo jalidi.

permanent *adj* -a kudumu. ~ **wave** mtindo nywele wa kutia mawimbi ya kudumu. **~ly** *adv*. **perm** *n (colloq abbr for)* 1 *(permanent wave)* mawimbi ya kudumu. 2 *(football)* mabadiliko ya mpangilio wa bahati nasibu wa wachezaji *vt* tia nywele mawimbi ya kudumu. **permanence** *n* kudumu. **permanency** *n* 1 kudumu. 2 kitu cha kudumu.

permanganate *n* mrututu.

permeate *vt,vi* ~ **(through/among)** sambaa/penya na enea. **permeation** *n* upenyaji na ueneaji, usambaaji. **permeable** *adj*. **permeability** *n* uwezo wa kupenyeka; mpenyo.

permit *vt,vi* ~ ruhusu *n* ruhusa, idhini, kibali.

permissible *adj* -a kukubalika, -a kuruhusika. **permissibly** *adv*. **permission** *n* ruhusa, idhini. **permissive** *adj* 1 -enye kuruhusu. 2 -enye kutoa uhuru (wa kuona na kutenda). **permissiveness** *n*.

permute *vt* badili mpangilio. **permutation** *n* *(math)* hitari: mabadiliko ya mpangilio wa seti ya vitu.

pernicious *adj* ~ **to** -enye madhara; -a kudhuru. **~ly** *adv*. **~ness** *n*.

pernickety *adj (colloq)* -enye kujali mambo madogo madogo; -enye nongwa; -enye gubu/machagu.

peroration *n (formal)* muhtasari wa hotuba; maneno ya kuhitimisha hotuba.

peroxide *n (chem)* peroksaidi *hydrogen ~* peroksaidi ya haidrojeni *vt (of hair)* paka peroksaidi.

perpendicular *adj* ~ **(to)** -a wima, -a mstatili *n* mstari wima; hali ya kuwa wima. **~ly** *adv*.

perpetrate *vt* fanya kosa; -wa na hatia. **perpetrator** *n* mkosaji. **perpetration** ukosefu, kufanya kosa.

perpetuate *vt* dumisha, endeleza. **perpetuation** *n* udumishaji, uendelezaji. **perpetual** *adj* 1 -a kudumu; -a kuendelea kwa muda mrefu. 2 -a kurudiarudia, -siokoma/isha. **perpetually** *adv*. **perpetuity** *n* 1 kuendelea, kudumu. **in** ~ pasipo mwisho, milele. 2 *(leg)* ndondo mwaka/mali aushi.

perplex *vt* 1 ~ **(with)** tatiza, fadhaisha. 2 tatanisha, kanganya. **~ed** *adj*. **~edly** *adv*. **~ity** *n* 1 mfadhaiko; mkanganyo. 2 kitu kinachosababisha mfadhaiko/mkanganyiko.

perquisite *n* marupurupu.

per se *adv* peke yake.

persecute *vt* 1 tesa, adhibu (agh. kwa ajili) ya imani. 2 sumbua. **persecutor** *n* mtesaji. **persecution** *n* mateso, usumbufu.

persevere *vi* ~ **(at/in/with)** stahamili, vumilia. **persevering** *adj* -enye kuvumilia. **perseveringly** *adv* kwa uvumilivu. **perseverance** *n* uvumilivu.

Persia *n* Uajemi. **P~n** *n,adj* Mwajemi; lugha ya Kiajemi; -a Kiajemi.

persiflage *n* mzaha.

persist *vi* 1 ~ **in sth** shikilia, chagiza; kataa kubadili kauli/msimamo. ~ **in doing sth** ng'angania kufanya kitu. ~ **with** endelea kushughulikia. 2 endelea kuwepo/kuishi. **~ence** *n*. **~ent** *adj*. **~ently** *adv*.

person *n* 1 mtu; mwenyewe. **in** ~ kwa nafsi yake, mwenyewe *he was present in ~* alihudhuria yeye mwenyewe. **in the ~ of** ambaye ni. ~ **to ~ call** *(of telephone)* mwito binafsi. 2 mwili, kiwiliwili; maisha. 3 *(gram)* nafsi. **~a** *n (psych)* hulka bayana. ~ **a grata** *(Lat)* mtu anayekubaliwa nchini. **~a non grata** mtu asiyekubalika nchini. **~able** *adj* -enye sura nzuri; maridhia. **~age** *n* 1 mtu (mashuhuri). 2 mhusika katika michezo (ya kuigiza). **~al** *adj* 1 -a mtu binafsi. 2 -enyewe *make a ~ appearance* fika mwenyewe. ~ **assistant** msaidizi mahususi. 3 -a mwili *~ cleanliness* usafi wa mwili. 4 -a kushambulia mtu binafsi, -a kukashifu, -a kusuta, safihi. 5 ~ **property/estate** *(leg)* mali binafsi inayohamishika. 6 *(gram)* ~ **pronoun** kiwakilishi nafsi *n* makala fupi kuhusu mtu binafsi. **~ally** *adv* 1 kwa nafsi ya mtu, kwa mtu binafsi. **~ality** *n* 1 nafsi (ya mtu). ~ **cult** kuabudu mtu (agh. kiongozi wa siasa n.k.);

nafsi. 2 haiba; tabia, hulka. 3 masuto *(pl)* **~alities** maneno mabaya kuhusu mtu *indulge in* ~ toa maneno mabaya kuhusu mtu. 4 mtu mashuhuri. **~alize** *vt* 1 tia alama binafsi. 2 -pa kitu nafsi. 3 fanya chako. **~alty** *n (leg)* mali binafsi. **~ate** *vt* 1 igiza. 2 *see* **impersonate/impersonation** *n*. **~ify** *vt* 1 -pa nafsi. 2 *(sb)* -wa mfano wa. **~ification** *n* tashihisi. **the ~ of** mfano halisi wa sifa ya. **~nel** *n* watumishi; utumishi. **~ manager** meneja utumishi. **airline ~** watumishi wa shirika la ndege.

perspective *n* 1 taswira (kuandika picha kwa jinsi ya kulinganisha ukubwa, kimo urefu, upana n.k. kama vitu vionekanavyo kwa macho). **in ~** kwa mlingano, kionekanavyo. **out of ~** bila maono halisi. 2 uhusiano. **in the/its right/wrong ~** kwa/bila uhusiano sahihi/halisi. 3 *(lit, fig)* mtazamo; maono, wazo; matumaini.

perspex *n* plastiki ngumu (itumikayo kama kioo kwenye magari).

perspicacious *adj (formal)* -epesi kuelewa na kukata shauri. **perspicacity** *n*.

perspicuous *adj* dhahiri, bayana, wazi; *(of person)* -enye uwezo wa kueleza wazi. **perspicuity** *n*.**~ly** *adv*. **~ness** *n*.

perspire *vi* toa/toka jasho. **perspiration** *n* 1 (kutoa) jasho. 2 *bathed in ~* -liorowa jasho. **perspiratory** *adj* -enye kutoa jasho.

persuade *vt* 1 **~ sb that.., ~ sb of sth** shawishi. 2 fanya mtu ashawishike. 3 **~ sb into/out of (doing) sth** shawishi mtu kufanya/kutofanya kitu. **persuadable** *adj* -enye kushawishika. **persuasion** *n* 1 ushawishi, mvuto; kushawishi. 2 imani. 3 madhehebu, waumini; kundi la watu wenye imani fulani. **persuasively** *adv*. **persuasiveness** *n*. **persuasive** *adj*.

pert *adj* 1 -juvi, -fidhuli, safihi. 2 *(US)* changamfu. **~ly** *adv*. **~ness** *n*.

pertain *vi* **~ to** *(formal)* fungamana (na), faa.

pertinent *adj* **pertinent (to)** *(formal)* 1 -a kufaa, -a kupasa. 2 -a kufungamana na. **pertinence** *n*. **pertinently** *adv*.

pertinacious *adj (formal)* 1 *(resolute)* -siokata tamaa, thabiti, -shupavu, -enye kushikilia nia. 2 *(obstinate)* -kaidi. **~ly** *adv*. **pertinacity** *n*.

perturb *vt (formal)* sumbua; tia wasiwasi. **~ation** *n*.

peruke *n* nywele za bandia ndefu.

peruse *vt (formal)* durusu, soma kwa makini. **perusal** *n*.

pervade *vt* enea kote, sambaa/zagaa *ideas that ~ the society* mawazo yaliyoenea kote. **pervasion** *n*. **pervasive** *adj* -a kuenea kote, -a kusambaa pote. **pervasively** *adv*. **pervasiveness** *n*.

pervert *vt* 1 potosha *n* mpotovu.

perverse *adj* 1 *(of persons)* kaidi. 2 *(of circumstances)* -a kinyume (na matakwa ya mtu). 3 *(of behaviour)* -potovu. **~ly** *adv*. **~ness** *n*. **perversion** *n* upotovu. **perversity** *n* ukaidi.

pervious *adj* 1 -a kupenyeka; -a kuvuja. 2 -a kuingilika; *(fig)* -enye kusikiliza (ushauri, mawazo).

pesky *adj (colloq)* -enye matata, sumbufu, -enye kuchukiza/kuudhi.

pessary *n* dawa ya kutia ukeni; kingamimba.

pessimism *n* kukosa rajua: tabia ya kuona kuwa mambo yote ni mabaya (ya kutazamia misiba, taabu n.k.). **pessimist** *n* msorajua. **pessimistic** *adj* bila rajua.

pest *n* 1 mdudu/mnyama mharibifu. 2 *(colloq)* msumbufu. **~icide** *n* kiuadudu. **~ology** *n* pestolojia: elimu ya wadudu.

pester *vt* **~ sb/with sth/for sth/to do sth** sumbua, udhi, chokoza, chagiza.

pestiferous *adj* -ovu; -enye kuleta maradhi.

pestilence *n* ndwele yoyote yenye kufisha agh tauni. **pestilent, pestilential** *adj* 1 -a kudhuru, -enye madhara, -a kuharibu afya, -baya, -haribifu. 2 *(colloq)* sumbufu, -a maudhi.

pestle *n* mchi *vt* twanga, funda (kupata unga).

pet[1] *n* 1 kipenzi *his mother's ~* kipenzi cha mama yake. 2 mnyama kipenzi. **~ name** jina la kimapenzi. **~ aversion** kitu/mtu anayechukiwa sana *vt* busu, tomasatomasa, papasapapasa (kimapenzi).

pet[2] *n* chuki ya ghafula, mfundo wa moyo. **~tish** *adj* -a chukichuki. **~tishly** *adv*. **~tishness** *n*.

petal *n* petali.

petard *n* kombora dogo. **hoist with one's own ~** *(prov)* mchimba kisima huingia mwenyewe.

peter[1] *vi* **~ out** *(of supplies etc)* -toweka taratibu, isha taratibu.

Peter[2] *n* **rob P~ to pay Paul** kata pua uunge wajihi.

petit-bourgeois *n* *(F)* bwanyenye uchwara.

petite *adj (of person)* -dogo, -nadhifu.

petition *n* ombi *~ of right* ombi la haki; *(rel)* dua vt,vi 1 **~ for** omba. 2 **~ sb (for sth/ to do sth/that.)** lalama; lalamika. **~er** *n* mlalamikaji.

petrify *vt,vi* 1 geuza kuwa jiwe, fanya jiwe. 2 ogofya sana, tisha; *(fig)* ondolea uwezo wa kufikiri (kwa kutisha). **petrifaction** *n*.

petro 1 *pref*. 2 -a mwamba, -a petroli.

petrol *n* petroli, mafuta yaliyosafishwa na kutumika kuwashia injini. **~eum** *n* mafuta. **~eum jelly** grisi. **~ogy** *n* petrolojia: taaluma ya asilimwamba.

petticoat *n* gaguro shimizi.

petty *adj* 1 dogodogo, -dogo; -siokuwa muhimu. 2 **~ cash** fedha za kichele. **~ larceny** udokozi. 3 **~ officer** ofisa wa cheo cha chini wa manowari. 4 uchwara *~ trader* mfanyabiashara uchwara/mdogo. 5 *(of person/mind)* -enye kujishughulisha na mambo madogo madogo; finyu. **pettily** *adv*. **pettiness** *n*. **pettifogging** *adj* -enye kujishughulisha na mambo madogo madogo.

pettish *adj* -a chukichuki. **~ly** *adv*. **~ness** *n*.

petulant *adj* -sovumilivu; -enye kuudhika (bila sababu), -enye chukichuki. **~ly** *adv*. **petulance** *n*.

pew *n* benchi la kanisani; *(colloq)* kiti *take a ~* keti chini. **~-opener** *n* mtu anayeketisha/karibisha watu kwenye benchi hilo.

pewter *n* pyuta; mseto wa bati na risasi *(attrib) ~ mugs/dishes* vyombo vya pyuta.

peyote *n* peyote, dungusi, mpungate wa Mexico.

phagocyte *n (bio)* fagositi: seli nyeupe za damu.

phalange *see phalanx*.

phalanx *n* 1 falanksi: kikosi cha askari waliosongamana. 2 kundi la watu wenye nia moja. 3 kifupachanda.

phallus *n* picha/taswira ya dhakari (kama ishara ya nguvu ya uzazi). **phallic** *adj*.

phantasm *n* 1 zimwi. 2 njozi. **~agoria/ ~agory** sura/ taswira ya watu na vitu inayobadilika. **~al** *adj* -a njozi, -a kuwazika tu.

phantom *n* 1 zimwi (katika njozi). 2 *(vision)* njozi. **~ship** meli njozi.

phantasy *see* **fantasy**.

Pharaoh *n* Farao, Firauni.

pharisee *n* 1 mfarisayo. **pharisaical** *adj*. **pharisaism** *n*. 2 *(hypocrite)* mnafiki, mzandiki.

pharmacy *n* 1 famasia: utayarishaji na utoaji madawa. 2 duka la dawa. **pharmaceutic (al)** *adj* -a madawa. **pharmacist** *n* mfamasi. **pharmacology** *n* taaluma ya madawa. **pharmacologist** *n* mtaalamu wa madawa. **pharmacopoeia** *n* kitabu cha orodha ya madawa na matumizi yake.

pharos *n* mnara wa taa (baharini).

pharynx *n* koromeo. **pharyngeal** *adj*. **pharyngitis** *n* uvimbe wa koromeo.

phase *n* 1 awamu, mkupuo. 2 sura *~s of the moon* sura za mwezi *vt* panga (mipango) (agh. kwa awamu). **~ in/ out** ingiza/ondoa polepole; hatua kwa hatua.

pheasant *n* kwale. **~ry** banda/kiota cha

kwale.
phenobarbitone *n* finobabitoni: aina ya dawa ya usingizi; kitulizaji.
phenomenon *n* 1 *(fact)* kitu, jambo. 2 *(curiosity)* tukio, shani, ajabu, kioja. **phenomenal** *adj* 1 -a ajabu sana. 2 kubwa, -ingi mno. 3 -nayotambulika na hisia. **phenomenally** *adj*.
phew *int* uhu! lo! (mlio wa uchovu).
phial *n* chupa ndogo, kichupa (agh cha kuwekea dawa).
philander *vi* 1 zini, -wa zinifu. 2 bemba, laghai (katika mapenzi). **~er** *n* mzinifu, mwasherati, mbembaji.
philanthropy *n* huruma, ufadhili; mapenzi juu ya binadamu, uhisani. **philanthropic(al)** *adj*. **philanthropically** *adv*. **philanthropist** *n*.
philately *n* ukusanyaji wa stempu. **philatelist** *n*.
philistine *n* mshenzi, mshamba.
philology *n* filolojia: taaluma ya kukua kwa lugha. **philologist** *n*. **philological** *adj*.
philosophy *n* 1 falsafa. **moral** ~ falsafa ya maadili. **natural** ~ falsafa ya maumbile. **Doctor of P~** Daktari wa Falsafa. 2 *(calmness)* siasa. **philosophical** *adj* 1 -a falsafa. 2 -enye kufuata taratibu za mantiki. **philosophically** *adv*. **philosophize** *vi* toa falsafa. **philosopher** *n* mwanafalsafa: mtu achunguaye falsafa. **~'s stone** dutu maalum iliyoaminiwa kuwa ingebadili metali kuwa dhahabu. 2 mtu makini/mtulivu.
philtre *(US* **philter**) *n* dawa ya mapenzi.
phlebitis *n* uvimbe wa vena.
phlegm *n* 1 kohozi. 2 utulivu, upole/ usiri (wa utendaji). **~atic** *adj*. **~atically** *adv*.
phobia *n* hofu, woga wa kutopenda kitu fulani.
phoenix *n* finiksi: ndege wa hadithini Uarabuni ambaye baada ya kila miaka 500 au 600 alijichoma moto na kufufuka pale pale katika majivu.
phone[1] *n (ling)* foni. **phonics** *n* foniki: elimu ya kutumia sauti kufundishia kusoma. **~tic** *adj* -a jinsi ya kutamka, -a fonetiki ~ *transcription* unukuzi kifonetiki, unukuzi finyu. **~tician** *n* mwanafonetiki. **~tics** *n* fonetiki: elimu ya sauti za usemi. **phonic** *adj* 1 -a sauti; -a fonetiki. **phonograph** *n* gramafoni, santuri.
phone[2] *n (sl) see* **telephone**. simu *be on the ~* zungumza kwa simu *get sb on the ~* pigia mtu simu *hang up the ~* rudisha chombo cha simu; kata simu *vt,vi* piga simu.
phoneme *n (ling)* fonimu, sauti bainifu. **phonemic** *adj* 1 -a fonimu. 2 **phonemics** elifonimu, fonimiki.
phoney, phony *adj (sl)* -a bandia.
phonology *n* fonolojia: tawi la isimu linaloshughulikia mfumo wa sauti za lugha. **phonological** *adj*.
phosgene *n* fosjeni: gesi ya sumu isiyo na rangi ($COCL_2$).
phosphate *n* 1 fosfati: chumvi ya asidi fosforiki. 2 mbolea.
phosphorescence *n* mmemetuko: utoaji mwanga bila moto. **phosphorescent** *adj*.
phosphorous *n (chem)* fosforasi: elementi kama nta ya njano isiyo metali ambayo huwaka haraka; nyekundu ambayo hutengenezewa viberiti. **phosphoric/phosphorous** *adj* -a fosforasi.
photo *(pref)* 1 -a mwanga. **~-cell** *n adj* betri ya mwanga. **~-synthesis** *n* usanidinuru. 2 foto. **~genic** *adj* -enye kutoa mwanga; -enye kutoka vizuri katika mwanga. ~ **finish** mwisho wa karibu mno, mshindi wa kuamuliwa na picha. ~ **copy** *n* fotokopi, mashini ya kunakili kwa picha *vt* nakilisha kwa mwanga. ~ **electric** *n (phys)* -a umeme-mwanga, inayopata umeme kutokana na mwanga. **~print** *n (print)* chapa, foto, picha. **~telegraphy** *n* simu picha.
photograph *n* picha *vt* 1 fotoa, piga picha. 2 toka/onekana vizuri katika picha. **~er** *n* mpiga picha. **~ic** *adj* -a picha, -a kupiga picha. **~y** *n* 1

upigaji picha; sanaa ya kupiga picha. **photometer** *n (phy)* fotomita,kipima mwanga, kipimanuru. **photometric(al)** *adj (phys)* -a kupimia mwanga. **photometry** *n*.

photostat *n* fotostati: *see* **photocopy**.

phrase *n* 1 *(gram)* kirai: fungu la maneno ambalo ni sehemu ya sentensi. 2 msemo. **~-book** kitabu cha misemo. 3 *(mus)* kifungu cha muziki *as he ~d it* kama alivyosema. **~ology** *n* uteuzi wa maneno; jinsi ya kutumia maneno. **~ological** *adj*.

phrenetic *adj see* **frenetic**

phrenology *n* frenolojia: ujuzi wa tabia (moyo, akili n.k.) ya mtu kwa umbo la kichwa chake. **phrenological** *adj*. **phrenologist** *n*.

phthisis *n* kifua kikuu (cha mapafu). **~ical** *adj* -a kifua kikuu.

phut *vi* haribika, vunjika. *(lit or fig) (colloq)* **go ~** haribika.

phylum *n (bio)* jamii, ukoo, mgao wa juu kabisa katika ulimwengu wa wanyama.

physic *n (colloq)* dawa.

physical *adj* 1 *(natural)* -a maumbile; -a viumbe. 2 *(corporeal)* -a mwili *~ strength* nguvu za mwili *~ education* elimu ya mazoezi ya viungo *~ examination* kukaguliwa afya *~ science* sayansi ya vitu visivyo na uhai. 3 *(external)* -a nje, -a sura, -a asili. **~ly** *adv* kimwili *he is ~ly unfit* hajiwezi kimwili. **physician** *n* tabibu, daktari, mganga.

physics *n* fizikia. **physicist** *n* mwanafizikia, mtaalamu wa fizikia.

physiognomy *n* 1 (elimu ya kutambua tabia kwa kuangalia) uso. 2 sura/ umbo la nchi. **physiognomical** *adj*. **physiognomist** *n*.

physiology *n* fiziolojia. **physiological** *adj* -a fiziolojia. **physiologist** *n* mwanafiziolojia.

physiotherapy *n* tibamaungo. **physiotherapist** *n* mtaalamu wa tibamaungo.

physique *n* umbo, maungo, umbile.

pi *n* pai: herufi ya Kigiriki hasa itumiwapo katika hisabati kuashiria uwiano wa mzingo wa duara na kipenyo chake (3.14159).

piano *n* piano *adv (mus)* kwa sauti laini/ndogo. **pianist** *n* mpiga piano. **pianissimo** *adv (music)* sauti laini, kwa sauti ndogo sana.

pianoforte *see* **piano** *n*.

piazza *n* 1 *(Italy)* uwanja, soko, gulio. 2 (US) baraza.

pica *n* 1 pika: aina ya herufi katika uchapishaji. 2 ugonjwa wa kula kisichofaa (k.m. udongo).

picador *n* pikadore: mpanda farasi anayechokoza ng'ombe katika mchezo wa ng'ombe.

picaresque *(lit)* -nayohusu hadithi/visa vya wahuni.

picalilli *n* chatini.

pick[1] *n* 1 sululu, mchokoo. 2 chombo kidogo kama kijiti cha kiberiti *a tooth ~* kitu cha kuchokolea meno.

pick[2] *n* 1 uteuzi, uchaguzi. 2 kiasi kilichochumwa k.m. matunda. 3 kiteule, kitu kilicho bora. **the ~ of (the bunch)** kilicho bora kuliko vyote *vt* 1 chokoa. **~ holes in an argument** *(fig)* tafuta kasoro; *(of flowers)* chuma. **~ sb's brain** pata mawazo/habari kutoka kwa mtu; chota akili. **~ sb's pocket** chomoa/ iba fedha/mali mfukoni. **~ and steal** iba, dokoa. 2 chokonoa. **~ one's teeth** chokonoa meno. 3 chagua, teua. **~ a quarrel with** chokoza (kwa makusudi), anzisha ugomvi. 4 chambua. 5 onja, -la kidogo. **~ at** onja; *(of birds)* donoa. 6 *(of guitar)* piga (kwa kuvuta). *(special uses)* **~ at (sb)** karipia, kosoa. **~ sth off** chuma, ondoa. **~ sb off** piga risasi (mojamoja). **~ on** onea. **~ out** chagua *(recognise)* tambua. **~ sth out** elewa (kwa kusoma/angalia kwa makini). **~ over** chunguza/kagua na kuchagua. **~ up** inua, chagua. **~ oneself up** jiinua, inuka. **~ up (health)** pata nafuu. **~ up speed** ongeza/pata mwendo. **~ up with sb** fahamiana na. **~up** *n* sehemu ya santuri inayoshikilia sindano;

pikapu; *(sl)* mtu ambaye unafahamiana naye bila kujulishwa. ~-**me-up** *n* kinywaji cha kutia nguvu. ~**er** *n* mtu au kitu kinachookota kitu kingine; mchumaji. ~**ing** *n* kuchuma. ~ **and stealing** kuiba vitu vidogo vidogo/rahisi.

pick-a-back *adv* kiyongoa *carry*~ beba mgongoni au begani; yongoa *be carried*~ yongolewa.

picket *n* 1 kigingi. 2 askari wa doria. 3 watu waliowekwa mlangoni (wakati wa mgomo) ili kushawishi wengine wagome. ~**ing** *n vt,vi* 1 pigilia fungu kwa kigingi. 2 wekea walinzi, weka walinzi. 3 shawishi wengine kugoma; zuia. **flying** ~ wafanyakazi washawishi (kutoka mahali pengine).

pickle *n* 1 achali. 2 hali. **in a sad** ~ katika hali mbaya *vt* 1 hifadhi katika achali, tengeneza kwa achali. 2 ~**d** *(sl)* -liolewa.

picnic *n* 1 mandari. 2 *(colloq)* jambo rahisi *it's no* ~ si rahisi *vt* -la mandarini. ~**ker** *n*.

picture *n* 1 picha, sanamu, mchoro. 2 *(fig)* taswira; maono. 3 mfano, mithali. **be the** ~ **of health** onekana mzima sana *he is the* ~ *of his father* anafanana sana na baba yake. 4 masimulizi, maelezo. **be/put sb in the** ~ elewa/elewesha. 5 *(pl)* sinema, filamu. 6 *(compounds)*. ~-**book** kitabu cha picha/mapicha. ~-**card** mzungu. ~-**gallery** makumbusho ya sanaa/picha. ~-**goer** mshabiki wa sinema. ~ **hat** kofia ya kike yenye ukingo mpana. ~-**palace/theatre** jengo la sinema *vt* chora picha; sawiri. ~ **sth to oneself** waza, fikiria. ~**sque** *adj* 1 -enye sura nzuri, -a kupendeza macho. 2 *(of people, manner, dress etc)* -a ajabu ajabu, si -a kawaida. 3 *(of language)* -enye kusisimua. ~**squeness** *n*. ~**squely** *adv*. **pictorial** *adj* -a picha, -enye picha ~ *art* sanaa ya picha *n* gazeti lenye picha.

piddle *vt (colloq or children's lang)* kojoa *n* mkojo.

piddling *adj* dogodogo, -sio muhimu.

pidgin *n* pijini: maneno ya lugha mchanganyo yanayotumiwa kama lugha ya mawasiliano.

pie *n* pai. **have a finger in the** ~ jitia/ingilia kati; husika, jihusisha. **as easy as** ~ rahisi sana. ~ **in the sky** raha ya mbinguni; ndoto za mchana.

piebald *adj (of horse)* -a rangi mbili, -enye madoa ya rangi mbili.

piece *n* 1 kipande. **(be) in** ~**s** vipande vipande. **break (sth) to** ~**s** vunjika-vunjika (kutokana na ajali). **come/take (sth) to** ~**s** gawanya, vunjavunja). **go (all) to** ~**s** changanyikiwa, haribikiwa. **a** ~ **of cake** *(sl)* rahisi sana. ~ **by** ~ kimoja kimoja. **of a** ~ **with sth** *(fig)* -a tabia moja, -enye kulandana. 2 tukio/kipande *a* ~ *of luck* bahati *a* ~ *of advice* ushauri *a* ~ *of furniture* samani, fanicha. **give sb a** ~ **of one's mind** -pa mtu ukweli. **say one's** ~ toa maoni, nena; tongoa. 3 *(of cloth etc)* kipande, kipimo maalum/rasmi. ~ **goods** vitambaa. 4 *(in art generally)* kazi; *(mus)* tungo. 5 *(coin)* sarafu. 6 bunduki, mzinga. 7 sehemu/kitu kimoja kati ya seti. 8 *(of work)* kipande. ~ **work** kipande *vt* (~ **together**) unganisha. ~ **sth out** unganisha/kamilisha (hadithi; nadharia) kitu. ~**meal** *adv* kidogo kidogo, hatua kwa hatua *adj* -a kidogo kidogo ~ *meal solution* tanzuo la hatua kwa hatua.

piece *n (Fr)* ~ *de resistance* 1 chakula kikuu. 2 tukio kuu.

pied *adj* -a rangirangi, -a madoadoa; -a rangi nyeusi na nyeupe.

pied-a-terre *n* chumba/nyumba ya ziada/akiba.

pier *n* 1 gati (itokezayo baharini). 2 *(pillar)* msingi, nguzo. ~-**glass** *n* kioo kikubwa (cha kutundika ukutani).

pierce *vt,vi* 1 toboa, choma. 2 *(of ears etc)* toga, dunga. 3 *(of cold, pain etc)* penya, ingia moyoni, umiza *(of army)* penya. **piercing** -a kupenya, -kali, -a nguvu, -a kuchoma.
piercingly *adv*.

piety *n* uchaji Mungu. **filial** ~ adabu/ utiifu kwa mzazi.

piffle *n (colloq)* upuuzi *vi* ongea upuuzi. **piffling** *adj* -a kipuuzi, -sio na maana.

pig *n* 1 nguruwe. **buy a ~ in a poke** nunua kitu bila kukiona au kujua thamani yake. **bring one's ~s to the wrong market** shindwa katika kufanikisha jambo (k.m. kuuza kitu). **~s might fly** maajabu yanaweza kutokea, wapi! **~ headed** *adj* kichwa ngumu; jeuri. **~ headedly** *adv.* **~ headedness** *n.* **~ skin** ngozi ya nguruwe; *(sl)* shogi. **~sty** banda la nguruwe. **~tail** nywele zilizofungwa nyuma na kuning'inia mabegani. **~ wash/swill** chakula cha nguruwe. **~ boat** nyambizi. 2 *(colloq)* mchafu, mlafi, mwenye tabia mbaya. **make a ~ of oneself** -la sana, -wa mlafi. 3 **~ iron** mkuo wa chuma *vi* **~ it; ~ together** ishi pamoja kwenye mazingira machafu. **~gish** *adj (derog of a person)* kama nguruwe, -chafu; -lafi. **~gishly** *adv.* **~gishness** *n.* **~ gery** *n* shamba la nguruwe. **~gy** *n* 1 *(informal)* kiguruwe. 2 *(informal) (usu of a child)* mlafi, mchoyo. **~let** mtoto wa nguruwe.

pigeon *n* 1 njiwa. **green ~** ninga. **speckled ~** kinda. **clay ~** kisahani cha kupimia shabaha. 2 *(compounds)* **~-breast/chest** *n* kifua kilichotokeza nje. **~-hole** *n* tundu la njiwa; shubaka *vt* ahirisha kitu. **~ toed** *adj* -enye matege.

pigment *n* pigmenti: rangi ya asili *vt* paka pigmenti. **~ation** *n* kiwango cha rangi ya asili.

pigmy *see* **pygmy**.

pike[1] *n* 1 mkuki mrefu mwembamba. **~staff** *n* mpini wa mkuki. *(colloq)* **as plain as ~ staff** dhahiri/wazi kabisa.

pike[2] 1 barabara. 2 kodi ya barabara(ni).

pike[3] *n* samaki mkubwa wa maji baridi (anayefanana na ngege).

pilaf(f) *see* **pilau**.

pilaster *n* nguzo chomozi.

pilau *n* pilau; wali uliopikwa pamoja na nyama na viungo mbalimbali.

pilchard *n* dagaapapa.

pile[1] *n* 1 fungu, chungu, rundo. **funeral ~** chungu ya kuni za kuchomea maiti. 2 *(sl)* hela nyingi. **make one's ~** pata/chuma fedha. 3 jumba kubwa; maghorofa. 4 betri. **atomic ~** *n* kidhibiti atomu *vt,vi* 1 lundika, tuta, omekeza, jaza. **~ arms** simamisha silaha. **~ it on** piga chuku, tia chumvi. **~ on the agony** tia chumvi (katika kuelezea) machungu. 2 **~ up** lundikana, ongezeka, kusanyika; *(of a crash)* gongana mfululizo. 3 **~ into/out of** ingia/toka bila mpango.

pile[2] *n (post)* nguzo, mhimili wa chuma/saruji wa kushikilia daraja *vt* wekea nguzo. **~ driver** *n* kishindilia nguzo. **~ dwelling** nyumba iliyosimama juu ya nguzo.

pile[3] *n* manyoya laini (ya nguo, zulia n.k).

piles[4] *n* bawasiri, kikundu, futuri.

pilfer *vt* dokoa. **~age** *n* (hasara ya) udokozi. **~er** *n.*

pilgrim *n* haji, hujaji. **P~ Fathers** Waingereza waliolowea Marekani na kuanzisha koloni la Massachussets na Plymouth 1620 *vi* hiji. **~age** *n* hija *go on a ~* enda hija.

pill *n* kidonge, tembe *take a ~* meza kidonge. **sweeten/sugar the ~** punguza makali, lainisha mambo. **~ box** mkebe wa vidonge; *(mil)* ngome ndogo (chini ya ardhi). 2 **the ~** kidonge cha kuzuia mimba. **be/go on the ~** anza kutumia vidonge vya kuzuia mimba.

pillage *n* utekaji nyara, uporaji *vt* teka nyara, pora. **~** *n.*

pillar *n* 1 nguzo, mhimili, mwimo. **(driven) from ~ to post** endeshwa n.k. huko na huko. 2 *(fig)* **~ of the faith** muumini, mfuasi imara, shabiki. **~ box** *n* sanduku la barua barabarani.

pillion *n* 1 kiti cha nyuma (cha farasi, pikipiki, n.k.) *the ~ passenger n* abiria aliyekalia kiti cha nyuma.

pillory *n* mkatale (wa kumfungia mtu kichwa na mikono) *vt* 1 tia mkatale. 2 *(fig)* kashifu hadharani.

pillow *n* 1 mto, takia. **take counsel of one's ~** -toamua jambo mpaka siku ya pili. 2 mhimili *vt* pumzisha, beba; pumzika. **~-case/slip** *n* foronya. **~-fight** *n* (mchezo wa watoto wa) kupigana kwa kutumia mito.

pilot *n* 1 rubani. **drop the ~** achisha kazi mshauri anayeaminika sana. **P~ Officer** afisa wa chini katika jeshi la anga. 2 *(attrib)* -a majaribio *a ~ project* mradi wa majaribio. 3 *(with compounds) ~-balloon* puto chunguzi (ambalo hurushwa angani na kuangaliwa linavyokwenda ili kupima nguvu ya upepo na sehemu ambayo upepo unaelekea). **~-boat** *n* jahazi ongozi. **~-engine** *n* kiberenge. **~-fish** *n* samaki kiongozi. **~-light/burner** *n* mwenge mdogo *vt* ongoza, endesha ndege, meli, treni n.k.

pimento *n* 1 pilipili Jamaica. 2 mpilipili Jamaica.

pimp *n* kuwadi *vi* ~ **(for sb)** tongozea, kuwadia.

pimple *n* chunusi. **~d, pimply** *adj* -enye chunusi.

pin[1] *n* 1 pini. **~s and needles** mwasho baada ya mwili kufa ganzi. **don't care a ~** -tojali kabisa. **there isn't a ~ to choose between them** hawana tofauti. **neat as a new ~** safi sana. 2 **safety ~** pini, kikwasi. 3 *(compounds)* **~table** *n* meza ya kuchezea mchezo wa tufe. **~ball** *n* mpira wa tufe. **~ cushion** *n* kichomekea pini. **~ head** *n* *(colloq)* zuzu. **~ money** *n* pesa za matumizi madogomadogo (ambazo mke anapewa na mume). **~point** *n* ncha ya pini; ncha/eneo dogo *vt* baini; lenga. **~prick** *n* *(fig)* kikero, jambo dogo lenye kuchukiza. **~stripe** -enye mistari. 4 *(pl) (colloq)* miguu (ya mtu).

pin[2] *vt* 1 funga/bandika kwa pini. **~ sth on sb** sakazia, sukumia. **~ ones hopes on sb** tegemea. **~ up** *n* picha iliyobandikwa ukutani (ya mtu unayempenda). 2 bana. **~ sb down** bana (ili aeleze lengo lake/atimize ahadi). **~ sb down to sth** bana/fanya akubali (kutimiza ahadi, makubaliano n.k.).

pinafore *n* (namna ya) gwanda (linalovaliwa na mwanamke juu ya nguo nyingine ili kutozichafua).

pince-nez *n* miwani ya kupachika puani.

pincers *n (pl) (also a pair of ~)* koleo. **~ movement** *(mil)* shambulia mbele na nyuma kwa wakati mmoja.

pincette *n* kibano kidogo, kikoleo.

pinch *vt* 1 finya *he ~ ed his brother* alimfinya kaka yake. 2 bana sana *my finger was ~ed in the door* kidole changu kilibanwa mlangoni. **see where the shoe ~es** ona tatizo lilipo. 3 umia, pata athari ya *be ~ed with cold/hunger* banwa na baridi/njaa. **be ~ed for money** kosa fedha. 4 *(colloq)* iba, dokoa. 5 -wa bahili; bana matumizi. 6 *(sl) (of the police)* kamata, bamba *n* 1 mfinyo *give sb a ~* finya mtu. 2 shida, mashaka, dhiki *feel the ~* -wa katika mashaka/ dhiki. 3 mfinyo, kiasi kidogo. 4 **at a ~; if it comes to the ~** ikibidi; ikiwa hakuna budi.

pinchbeck *n* dhahabu bandia. *adj* -a bandia.

pine[1] *n* msonobari *adj* -a msonobari.

pine[2] *vi (~ away)* dhoofika, konda, sinyaa, nywea (kwa sababu ya ugonjwa, huzuni, n.k.). **~ for sth; ~ to do sth** tamani sana kitu.

pineapple *n (plant)* mnanasi; *(fruit)* nanasi.

ping *n (of bullet)* mlio wa "pa" *vi* lia kama risasi.

pingpong *n* mpira wa meza.

pinion[1] *n* kipapatio; *(poet)* bawa *vt* 1 kata kipapatio, bawa. 2 ~ **(to/ together)** funga mikono kwa pingu/ kamba.

pinion[2] *n* pinioni: ,mpinimeno.

pink[1] *n* (rangi ya) waridi. 2 *(flower)* waridi. **in the ~ of health** zima sana.

~ **eye** *n* ugonjwa wa macho *adj* 1 -a waridi. 2 *(colloq)* -enye kuelekea mrengo wa kushoto (katika siasa). **~ish** *adj*. **~ness** *n* wekundu mweupe. **~y** *adj* -a waridi.

pink² *vt* 1 choma, penyeza, (kwa upanga). 2 ~ **(out)** pamba/tia nakshi ngozi. **~ing shears** mkasimeno.

pink³ *vi (of internal combustion engine)* toa sauti ya mlipuko.

pinnace *n* mashua ya meli kubwa.

pinnacle *n* 1 mnara mrefu juu ya paa ya nyumba. 2 *(summit)* kileleta cha mlima. 3 *(culminating point)* upeo, kipeo *at the ~ of his prosperity* katika upeo wa usitawi wake *vt* weka mnarani, fanya mnara.

pint *n* painti *a gallon contains eight ~s of fluid* golani moja ina painti nane za kiowevu.

pioneer *n* 1 mtangulizi, mwasisi; mpelelezi. 2 *(mil)* payonia, askari wa kikosi tangulizi chenye kutengeneza njia na madaraja n.k. 3 **Young P ~s** Chipukizi *vi,vt* peleleza, ongoza; tangulia.

pious *adj* 1 -cha Mungu. 2 *(arch)* -a kutii wazazi. **~ly** *adv*.

pip¹ *n* **the ~** ugonjwa wa makamasi (wa kuku); *(fig)* maudhi, hasira. **give sb the ~** kasirisha, chukiza. **have the ~** -wa na hasira.

pip² *n* 1 alama katika dadu/karatasi. 2 *(GB colloq)* nyota (katika bega la vazi la askari). 3 mlio wa kuonyesha majira *the six ~s of the time-signal* milio sita ya kuashiria wakati.

pip³ *vi,vt* 1 piga risasi. 2 shinda. **be ~ped at the post** shindwa mwishoni kabisa.

pip⁴ *n* mbegu ya tunda/chungwa *vt* ondoa mbegu (kwenye tunda).

pipe *n* 1 bomba, paipu. 2 zumari, filimbi. 3 *(pl)* **the ~s,** *(bag ~s)* zumari ya Kiskoti. 4 (mlio wa) filimbi; wimbo wa ndege. 5 muluzi wa serahangi. 6 kiko, mtemba. **put that in your ~ and smoke it** itabidi ukubali upende usipende, kazi kwako. 7 koromeo. 8 *(compounds)* **~clay** mfinyanzi mweupe (wa kufinyanga viko); chaki. **~cleaner** kisafishia kiko. **~dream** ndoto ya mchana; njozi. ~ **laying** kuweka mabomba. **be in the ~line** -wa katika maandalizi. ~ **line** njia ya bomba. **~ful** *n* ujazo wa kiko, kichanja cha viko *vt* 1 piga filimbi/zumari. **~rack** ubao wa kuhifadhia mitemba. 2 pitisha uowevu/kimiminiko katika bomba. 3 piga king'ora. ~ **away** toa ishara kuondoka kwa meli. ~ **down** nyamaza. ~ **up** anza kuimba/kucheza/kusema. 4 pamba nguo kwa kichuruzio. **~r** *n* mpiga zumari. **he who plays the ~r calls the tune** anayegharamia (kitu) ndiye mwenye madaraka nacho/mwamuzi. **~tte** *n* kidodezi, kineli. **piping** *adj* 1 -enye sauti ya filimbi. **the ~ times of peace** wakati wa kusikiliza muziki wa burudani. 2 -enye sauti nyembamba (kama makinda ya ndege) *adv* ~ **hot** joto sana; *(of news)* motomoto *n* 1 kipande cha bomba. 2 sauti ya upigaji wa (zumari). 3 kichuruzio.

pipsqueak *n (sl)* kidude, kijitu.

piquant *adj* kali;(fig)-a kutia shauku, -a kuchangamsha.**~ly** *adv*. **piquancy** *n*.

pique *vt* 1 kera, udhi (kwa kutweza). 2 chokoza (udadisi, shauku). 3 ~ **oneself on sth** jivunia *n* kiburi, chuki, hasira.

pirate *n* 1 haramia; meli ya maharamia. 2 mwizi (wa haki za kunakili) *vt* iba (kazi ya mwingine). **piratical** *adj*. **piratically** *adv*. **piracy** uharamia; wizi.

pirouette *n* mzunguko kwa ncha za vidole vya miguu *vi* zunguka kwa kutumia ncha za vidole vya miguu.

pis aller *n* njia pekee/ya mwisho.

Pisces *n (Zodiac)* Samaki. **piscary** *n* 1 haki ya kuvua samaki (katika bwawa la mtu mwingine). 2 mahali pa kuvua samaki. **piscatorial, piscatory** *adj* -a wavuvi, -a kuvua samaki; shabiki sana wa kuvua samaki.

pisciculture *n* uzalishaji samaki (kwa kupandisha). **pisciculturist** *n*. **piscina** *n*. bwawa la samaki. **piscine** *adj* -a samaki.

piss *(vulg) vt,vi* 1 kojoa, kojolea. 2 **P~ off** Ondoka, Potea! **~ed** *adj* -liolewa kabisa. **~ed off** -liokasirika, -lioudhika *n* mkojo.

pistil *n* pistili: sehemu ya ua inayotoa mbegu.

pistol *n* bastola. **hold a ~ to sb's head** tisha mtu ili afanye kitu *vt* piga kwa bastola.

piston *n* pistoni. **~ engined** -a injini ya pistoni. **~ ring** ringi/pete ya pistoni. **~ rod** mkono wa pistoni.

pit[1] *n* 1 shimo. 2 *(mine)* mgodi, machimbo. **~head** *n* mlango wa mgodi (wa mkaa wa mawe). **~-man** *n* mfanyakazi mgodini. **~prop** *n* nguzo ya mgodini. 3 mtego wa shimo. **~fall** *n* mtego wa shimo uliofunikwa-funikwa; *(usu fig)* hatari isiyoonekana. 4 mvungu (katika mwili au mmea). **the ~ of the stomach** sehemu ya chini ya mbavu. 5 kovu ya ndui. 6 *(GB) (theatre)* viti vya kati sakafuni; watu wakaao hapo. 7 gulio la biashara maalumu *wheat-~* gulio la ngano. 8 **the ~** *(rhet, biblical)* jahanamu. 9 kituo cha huduma za magari (ya mashindano). 10 *see cock~ vt* 1 *be ~ted with* -wa na vishimo/makovu ya ndui. 2 **~ against** pambanisha.

pit[2] *n (US)* kokwa *vt* toa kokwa. **~-a-pat** *adv* kwa hatua/mapigo mepesi.

pitch[1] *n* lami, bereu. **as dark/black as ~** -eusi kabisa, giza kabisa *mineral ~* madini meusi *vt* paka lami (bereu).

pitch[2] *vt,vi* 1 weka piga (hema, kambi n.k.) *~ camp* piga kambi. 2 tupa, vurumisha. **~ fork** *n* uma ya nyasi *vt* tupa. 3 *(mus)* rekebisha sauti. 4 anguka, angusha. 5 *(sl)* simulia, hadithia. 6 enda mrama, tupwa huko na huko, sukasuka. 7 tua, tulia. 8 **~ in** anza kazi kwa bidii. **~ into** shughulika kwa bidii; piga. **~ on** kuta, angukia, patia, pata. **~ upon (sb)** chagua fulani kwa bahati. 9 tia mwinamo katika paa ya nyumba. **~ed battle** mapigano/vita vya majeshi yalioandaliwa rasmi *n* 1 mrama, msukosuko. 2 mtupo, mvurumisho. 3 uwanja wa kuchezea (kriketi n.k.). 4 mahali pa kuuzia vitu, hasa sokoni au barabarani. **queer sb's ~** vuruga/zima mipango ya mtu. 5 mwanguko (hasa wa paa); mshuko, mwinamo, anguko, mtelemko. 6 kiwango *come to a ~* iva, endelea sana *the highest ~* kipeo. 7 *(mus)* uzito wa sauti. 8 *(tech)* nafasi kati ya meno ya gurudumu.

pitcher *n* gudulia, jagi. **little ~s have long ears** watoto wadogo husikia upesi *n* mtupa mpira.

pitfall *see* **pit**[1].

pith *n* 1 moyo mwororo (laini) wa bua n.k.; kitu chororo; upande wa ndani wa ganda la chungwa; *(of coconut)* joya; *(of shoot of coco-nut tree)* kitale; kilele, shaha; *(bio)* ubongo; mtima. **~ hat/helmet** *n* kofia ya jua. 2 nguvu, juhudi, wepesi. 3 *(fig)* kiini, maana. **of ~ and moment** muhimu sana. **~y** *adj* -a nguvu; -a maana sana.

pit-pat *see* **pit-a-pat**

pittance *n* ujira mdogo (kuliko inavyostahili).

pitter-patter *n* ndondondo (mlio wa maji yanayodondoka).

pituitary *adj* **~ gland** tezi pituitari: teziubongo.

pity *n* 1 huruma. **for ~'s sake** kwa huruma; jamani! **out of ~** kutokana na huruma. **take/have a ~ on** onea huruma, hurumia. 2 jambo la kusikitisha *what a ~!* inasikitisha, bahati mbaya *vt* hurumia; sikitikia *I ~ you* nakusikitikia. **~ ing** *adj* -enye kuonyesha huruma/masikitiko. **~ingly** *adv*. **piteous** *adj* -a huzuni, -a kuhuzunisha, -a kutia huruma, **piteously** *adv*. **pitiable** *adj* 1 -a kusikitisha, -a kutia huruma, -a kuhuzunisha. 2 *(wretched)* baya; nyonge, hafifu. **pitiful** *adj* 1 -a

kusikitisha. 2 -a kudharaulika. **pitiless** gumu, -katili, -sio na huruma.
pivot *n* 1 egemeo; *(fig) (of discussion)* msingi/kiini. 2 *(mil)* mtu aendeshaye kikosi cha askari *vt,vi* ~ **on** egemeza; geuka (zunguka) katika egemeo. **~al** *adj* -a mnenguo/maana; *(fig)* -a maana sana, -a msingi.
pixie,pixy *n* kizimwi.
pizza *n* piza: chapati ya mseto wa nyanya/jibini n.k.
placard *n* bango *vt* bandika bango ukutani, tangaza habari kwa bango.
placate *vt* tuliza.
place *n* 1 mahali. 2 jiji, mji, kijiji n.k.. **go ~s** *(colloq)* fanikiwa zaidi na zaidi. ~ **name** *n* jina la mahali k.v. mlima, mji. 3 jengo/sehemu maalum. 4 ukurasa/sehemu katika maandishi. 5 cheo, daraja. **keep one's** ~ jua nafasi yako; heshimu wakubwa. 6 nafasi ya kitu au mtu (kati ya washindi). 7 hatua (katika majadiliano n.k.). **in the first/second, etc** ~ kwanza/pili. 8 nyumba, nyumbani. 9 *(in proper names)* mtaa. 10 *(football, Rugby)* ~ **kick** kiki ya kuweka mpira chini. 11 *(compounds)* **in** ~ katika nafasi yake; *(fig)* -a kufaa. **out of** ~ si katika nafasi yake; *(fig)* -siofaa. **in** ~ **of** badala ya. **give** ~ achia. **give** ~ **to** achia nafasi kwa, rithiwa na. **make** ~ **for** acha nafasi kwa ajili ya; achia; tanguliwa na. **take the** ~ **of** chukua nafasi ya, -wa badala ya. **take** ~ tukia. **pride of** ~ nafasi ya juu. ~ **man**, ~**-seeker** mtafuta cheo *vt* 1 weka (kitu) mahali fulani, panga (kitu) katika nafasi yake. 2 teua (mtu). 3 weka, wekeza. 4 agiza bidhaa. 5 uza/sukuma bidhaa. 6 ~ *confidence in* -wa na imani na. 7 kumbuka/tambua mtu. 8 *(racing)* shika nafasi. **be ~d** -wa kati ya washindani watatu wa mwanzo, -wa mshindi.
placebo *n* kipozauongo: dawa ya kutuliza/kupoza.
placenta *n* mji/kondo; kondo la nyuma.
placid *adj (of sea etc)* tulivu, mwanana, -pole. **~ly** *adv*. **~ity** *n*.
plafond *n* dari lililorembwa.
plage *n* ufuko.
plagiarize *vt* iba maandishi/mawazo/maandiko n.k. ya mtu mwingine (na kuyatumia bila kukiri kuwa ni yake). **plagiarism** *n* wizi wa maandishi/mawazo n.k. ya mtu. **plagiarist** *n* mwizi wa maandishi (mawazo).
plague *n* 1 **the** ~ tauni. ~ **spot** kovu la tauni; eneo lililoingiliwa na tauni; kiini/chanzo cha au dalili ya maadili potovu. 2 sababu ya msiba, baa, adha, n.k *vt* ~ **(with)** sumbua, kera (hasa kwa maombi mengi au kwa kuhoji), udhi, taabisha. **plaguy** *adj (colloq)* -enye kusumbua/kuudhi. **plaguily** *adv* kwa kusumbua, kuudhi; kwa uchokozi.
plaice *n* wayo.
plain[1] *adj* 1 *(clear)* dhahiri, wazi. ~ **sailing** *(fig)* rahisi na isiyo na matatizo *make one's meaning* ~ toa maana waziwazi. 2 rahisi, -a kawaida, sio na mapambo/marembo *in ~ clothes* -liovaa mavazi ya kawaida; raia ~ *clothes policeman* askari kanzu. 3 *(of persons, their thoughts, action etc)* nyofu, -a kweli. **to be ~ with you** kwa kusema kweli. **in ~ words** waziwazi ~ *dealing* unyofu; uaminifu. ~ **spoken** *adj* msema kweli. 4 *(of appearance)* si -zuri, dufu. ~ **song/chant** muziki wa sauti nyingi pamoja. **~ly** *adv*. ~ **ness** *n*.
plain[2] *n* uwanda, tambarare *coastal* ~ uwanda wa pwani. **~sman** *n* mkazi wa nyanda tambarare.
plaint *n* 1 *(leg)* dai, shtaka, mashtaka, hati ya mashtaka. 2 malalamiko, kilio. **~iff** mdai *nominal ~iff* mdai wa jina tu.
plaintive *adj* -a huzuni, -a majonzi. **~ly** *adv*. **~ness** *n*.
plait *n* 1 msuko; msokoto.2 *(braid)* kigwe, ugwe *vt* suka, sokota.
plan *n* 1 ramani ya jengo. 2 michoro ya mashine. 3 picha, ramani, kielelezo.

4 mpango. **(go) according to ~** (tokea/-wa) kama ilivyopangwa *vt* 1 nuia. **~ to do sth** panga, fanya mipango. 2 chora/tayarisha ramani. 3 **~ (out)** panga/fikiria mapema (jambo). **~ned economy** uchumi unaopangwa na kudhibitiwa na dola. **~ner** mpangaji, mwana mipango. **~less** -sio na mpango.

plane[1] *n* randa *vt* piga randa. **~ away/down** sawazisha kwa randa.

plane[2] *n* 1 uso (wa kitu) ulio sawa sawa, ubapa. **~ table** kipimapembe ubapa *on the same ~ as* katika usawa mmoja. 2 ubapa mkuu wa kuhimili ndege. 3 *(colloq)* ndege, eropleni. 4 *(fig)* hatua, kiwango *~ of development* kiasi (cha maendeleo). **~ sailing** (*see* **plain sailing)** *vi,vt* **~ down** paa, teremka, tua (bila kutumia injini) *adj* -enye uso ulio sawasawa (usioinuka wala kushuka). **~ geometry** jometri bapa.

planet *n* sayari. **~arium** *n* (jengo la) chombo cha kuigiza nyendo za sayari. **~ary** *adj* 1 -a sayari. 2 -a ardhi. 3 -a kuzunguka; -a kuhama. **~oid** *n* sayari ndogo.

plangent *adj (of sounds)* -a mwangwi, -a kutetemeka.

plank *n* 1 ubao mnene na mpana. **~ bed** kitanda cha chaga/mbao (bila godoro). 2 kanuni muhimu/ya msingi katika siasa *vt* 1 weka/funika kwa mbao. 2 **~ down** laza chini; *(colloq)* lipa mara moja.

plankton *n (bio)* planktoni.

plant *n* 1 mmea, mche. **~ louse** chawa (wa) mmea. 2 mtambo, vifaa, mashine (za viwandani). 3 kiwanda, karakana. 4 hila, mtego. 5 askari kanzu anayejiunga na majambazi ili awashike/ajue yao *vt* 1 panda, atika, pandikiza, otesha; *(fig)* ingiza wazo (akilini). 2 weka, kaza, simamisha, piga *~ a blow* piga ngumi *~ a bullet* piga risasi. 4 anzisha, asisi; lowea. 5 *(sl)* jifanya/jificha (ili kuhadaa); sakazia/tungia uongo. **~er** *n* mkulima mwenye shamba kubwa; mlowezi; mashine ya kupandia. **~ation** *n* shamba kubwa, mgunda.

plantain *n (fruit)* ndizi; *(plant)* mgomba.

plaque *n* 1 bamba la taarifa, mapambo n.k. ukutani. 2 *(med)* utando.

plash[1] *n* sauti ya mapigo ya maji k.m. wakati wa kupiga kasia *vt,vi* piga maji, maziwa n.k.

plash[2] *vt* pinda/suka matawi (kufanya uga).

plasm *n see* **plasma**.

plasma *n (biol)* plazma: maji ya damu.

plaster *n* 1 plasta, kikandiko, lipu: mchanganyiko wa chokaa, mchanga na maji. **~ board** *n* bao la karatasi na jasi. **~ cast** *n* ganda (la piopii); sanamu ndogo ya piopii. **~ of Paris** *(POP)* plasta ya jasi, piopi. 2 plasta (ya vidonda n.k.) *vt* 1 piga plasta, tia lipu; kandika *his hair is ~ed with oil* nywele zake zimetiwa mafuta mengi. 2 **~ sth with sth; ~ sth on sth** bandika, pakaza (dawa). **~ down** tia sakafu. **~er** *n* mpiga lipu. **~ed** *adj* -liolewa chakari.

plastic *adj* 1 *(of materials)* -a plastiki, kinamo, -a kunyumbuka. **~ explosive/bomb** bomu la plastiki. 2 -a kuumba/kutengeneza. **~ surgery** utengenezaji upya wa viungo. 3 *(fig)* -enye kuathirika kwa urahisi *n* plastiki. **~ity** *n* .

plasticine *n* plastisini: dutu kama udongo wa mfinyazi itumikayo kutengeneza modeli.

plate *n* 1 bamba, kipande cha chuma au glasi. **~ glass** *n* kioo cha dirisha. 2 sahani. **give sb sth on a ~** *(colloq)* -pa mtu kitu pasi yeye kukishughulikia. **on one's ~** -a kushughulisha. **have a lot/enough on one's ~** tingwa, -wa na mengi ya kukushughulisha. **~ rack** *n* kichanja cha vyombo. 3 vyombo vya fedha au dhahabu (kama vile vijiko, vikombe, sahani). **~ powder** *n* unga wa kusafishia na kung'arishia fedha. 4 *(in printing)* pleti, bamba; picha ya kitabuni. 5 kipande cha chuma chenye jina la mtu. **dental** ~ menobandia; 6 kombe la dhahabu (kwa ajili ya zawadi ya ushindi) *vt* 1 chovya vitu vya madini katika madini ya namna nyingine. 2 ~ **with** funika kwa bamba/chuma. ~**ful** *n* ujazo wa sahani moja; sahani tele. ~-**mark** *n* alama ya mtengenezaji. ~**r** *n* mchovyaji vyombo kwenye dhahabu, fedha n.k. **plating** *n* mpako/mchovyo. *gold* ~ mpako/mchovyo wa dhahabu *plating with gold* kuchovya dhahabu. **platter** *n* 1 *(US)* kombe. 2 *(GB arch)* chano. **platter** *n see* **plate.**

plateau *n* uwanda wa juu, nchi iliyoinuka ikawa tambarare.

platelayer *n* fundi wa reli.

platform *n* 1 jukwaa. 2 ulingo, mahali palipoinuka kando ya njia ya reli n.k. ~ *ticket* tikiti ya msindikizaji/kuingilia stesheni. 3 programu (ya chama cha siasa hasa itolewayo kabla ya uchaguzi). ~ **oratory** uzungumzaji wa kuvutia jukwaani.

platinum *n* platinamu: madini nzito tena nyeupe ya thamani. ~ **blonde** *(colloq)* mwanamke mwenye nywele nyeupe kama fedha.

platitude *n* maelezo ya kawaida/chapwa. **platitudinous** *adj* -lio kawaida.

Platonic *adj* -a Plato au mafundisho yake. ~ **love/friendship** mapenzi ya taamuli (si kwa ngoa, ashiki, wala tamaa).

platoon *(mil)* platuni: kundi la maaskari walio chini ya amri ya luteni.

platypus *n* kinyamadege: mnyama mdogo (wa Australia) ambaye hutaga na kunyonyesha.

plaudit *n* makelele, makofi vifijo, (vya kuunga mkono/kukubali).

plausible *adj* 1 -enye kuelekea; -enye kukubalika; *(of person)* -enye kutoa hoja za kukubalika. **plausibly** *adv*. **plausibility** *n*.

play *n* 1 mchezo. **a** ~ **on words** kucheza na maneno. **child's** ~ *n* kitu cha kawaida na rahisi. ~ **boy** *n* mpenda sana starehe. ~ **fellow/mate** *n* mwenzi (katika mchezo). ~-**ground** *n* kiwanja cha michezo. ~-**pen** *n* sanduku/tenga (ambamo mtoto huweza kuachwa akacheza). ~ **room** chumba cha michezo ya watoto. ~-**school group** *n* vichekechea: kundi la watoto wachezao pamoja chini ya uangalizi maalum. ~-**suit** *n* nguo za kuchezea. ~**thing** *n* *(fig)* mtu anayechezewa. ~ **time** *n* muda/kipindi cha kucheza, mapumziko. 2 kucheza, namna ya kucheza mchezo. **in/out of** ~ ndani/nje (ya uwanja). **fair** ~ *(fig)* usawa, haki kwa wote. **foul** ~ kinyume na sheria; *(fig)* njama. 3 zamu katika mchezo *it is John's* ~ ni zamu ya John. 4 kamari. 5 tamthilia. **as good as a** ~ -a kufurahisha, -a kupendeza, senema ya bure. ~ **acting** *n* kuigiza tamthilia; *(fig)* kujisingizia. ~-**bill** *n* tangazo la (tamthilia, mchezo n.k.). ~**goer** *n* mpenda kutazama tamthilia. ~**house** *n* jumba la kuonyeshea tamthilia. ~ **wright** mwandishi wa michezo ya kuigiza. 6 mwendo mwepesi. 7 nafasi ya kufanya jambo *allow full* ~ *to one's ability* toa nafasi ya kutumia uwezo wake. 8 kazi, kitendo, shughuli. **be in full** ~ tumika kikamilifu. **bring sth into** ~ anza kutumia/kutumika. **come into** ~ anza kufanya kazi, anza kushughulika *vt,vi* 1 cheza. ~ **with** jifurahisha. 2 ~ **(at doing sth)** jifanya kuwa unafanya kitu; fanya mzaha. 3 ~ **a joke/ prank/trick (on sb)** hadaa, tania. 4 shiriki katika mchezo; cheza *he* ~*s football for our club* huchezea mpira klabu yetu. 5 ~ **(as/at)** shika nafasi fulani katika mchezo *Juma* ~*s in goal/ as goalkeeper* Juma hushika nafasi ya mlinda mlango. ~ **sb as/at** ingiza katika timu. 6 *(cricket, football etc)* piga/gonga mpira kwa namna maalumu. ~ **ball (with)** *(fig, colloq)* -wa tayari kufanya kwa ushirika; shirikiana. 7 *(of chess)* sogeza (kete); *(of cards)* cheza (karata). ~ **one's**

cards well *(fig)* tumia nafasi yako vizuri. 8 ~ **fair** fuata kanuni/sheria; fanya kama inavyotakiwa. ~ **hard** cheza kwa bidii. ~ **the ball, not the man** cheza mpira usipige watu; *(fig)* -wa mwaminifu na kutenda haki. ~ **the game** fuata sheria za mchezo; *(fig)* -wa mkweli bila upendeleo; fuata haki. 9 piga chombo/ala ya muziki, fungua chombo cha muziki k.v. santuri ~ *the flute* piga zumari. ~ **(sth) back** piga kanda baada ya kuirekodi. ~ **back** *n* chombo kinachorudisha nyuma kanda iliyorekodiwa; kurudisha nyuma kanda. 10 igiza tamthilia, onyesha maigizo. ~ **the fool** fanya mambo kijinga. ~ **the man** fanya mambo kiume. 11 yumba-yumba, wayawaya, chezacheza. 12 endesha/enda kwa mfululizo. 13 ~ **(sth) on/upon sth** piga risasi. 14 ~ **a fish** chosha samaki kwenye mshipi. 15 *(special uses)* ~ **down to sb** zungumza kwa kujishusha (ili mtu asijihisi mnyonge na akuunge mkono). ~ **sth down** dhalilisha/ dumisha kitu kwa makusudi, punguza umuhimu wake. ~ **sb in,** ~ **sb into a place** pigia muziki wakati wa kuingia. ~**into sb's hands/the hands of sb** jiingiza/jiuza/pa faida. ~ **one person off against another** gonganisha/ chonganisha. ~ **(sth) off** *n* mchezo wa marudiano. ~ **on upon (sth)** chochea. ~ **sth out** fikia kikomo/kilele. **be ~ed out** kwisha; pitwa na wakati. ~**up** cheza kwa nguvu; *(colloq)* wa mtukutu. ~ **sth up** tukuza; taaradhi. ~ **up to sb** jipendekeza. ~ **(sb) up** *(colloq)* pa taabu, taabisha. ~ **with** chezea. ~**er** *n* 1 mchezaji. 2 *(arch)* mwigizaji. 3 mpigaji kinanda n.k.; rekodiplea, santuri. ~**ful** *adj* cheshi, -a kucheza, -a mzaha, -purupuru. ~**fully** *adv.* ~**ing** *n.* ~ **field** kiwanja cha michezo. ~**let** *n* tamthilia fupi.

plaza *n* uwanda (katika Hispania); *(US)* mahala penye soko/gulio.

plea *n* 1 *(leg)* maelezo ya mshitakiwa mahakamani. 2 ombi. 3 sababu, kisingizio *on the ~ of ill health* kwa sababu ya ugonjwa.

pleach *vt* suka.

plead *vt,vi* 1 ~ **for/against sb** wakilisha mtu mahakamani, kiri. ~ **guilty/not guilty** kiri/kana kosa. 2 tetea (mahakamani). 3 ~ **(with sb) (for sth to do sth)** sihi. 4 toa maelezo, jitetea. 5 tetea hoja. ~**ings** *n (pl) (leg)* maandishi rasmi ya utetezi. ~**ingly** *adv.*

please *vi,vt* 1 *(imper) (abbr of if you ~)* tafadhali. 2 pendeza; ridhisha *he is hard to ~* ni vigumu kumpendeza, hapendezeki *be anxious to ~ sb* -wa na hamu ya kumpendeza mtu. ~ **God** Mungu akipenda, Inshaallah; penda, taka *just as you ~* upendavyo, hiari yako as much as you ~ kadiri upendavyo. **if you** ~ *(ironic)* tafadhali, kama unaridhika. **pleasing** *adj* -a kupendeza, -zuri, -tamu, -a anasa. ~**d** *adj* -enye furaha. **pleasingly** *adv.* **as much as you ~**

pleasure *n* 1 furaha, anasa, starehe, ridhaa. **take ~ (in doing) sth** furahi kufanya kitu *I have much ~ in* ninayo furaha kuu *the pleasure is mine* ni furaha yangu *man of pleasure* mtu mpotevu, fisadi, asherati *sensual pleasure* furaha za mwili, ashiki. *(compounds)* ~- **boat** *n* meli, mashua ya starehe. ~- **-ground** *n* uwanja wa burudani ya starehe. ~ **-steamer** *n* meli ya starehe. ~ **-trip** *n* safari ya starehe *vt* **pleasure sb** *(arch)* furahisha mtu kwa kujamiiana naye. ~ **loving/** ~- **seeking** *adj* -a kutafuta starehe. 2 ridhaa, utashi. 3 kivutio, kipenda roho, vianisi. **pleasurable** *adj* -enye kuanisi. **pleasurably** *adv.*

pleasance *n* 1 *(arch)* furaha anasa, eneo la burdani. 2 bustani iliyounganishwa na nyumba. *adj* anisi, -a kufurahisha. **pleasantly** *adv.*

pleat *n* mkunjo, rinda *vt* kunja, fanya (tia) marinda, *(see* **plait)**.

plebeian *(also* **pleb)** *(colloq abbrev.)* *adj* mchochole *n* mtu wa hali ya

chini.
plebiscite *n* kura ya maoni.
plectrum *n* mnyakuo wa gita: chuma kivaliwacho kidoleni kupigia gita.
pled *pp of plead.*
pledge *n* 1 ahadi, dhamana, kiapo *under ~ of secrecy* katika siri, faragha. **take/sign the ~** ahidi kuacha pombe. 2 rehani, aburani *lying in ~* kuwa katika rehani *put in ~* weka rehani *take sth out of ~* komboa kitu cha rehani. 3 zawadi, ishara; *(fig)* **~ of love** mtoto. 4 kunywa kwa afya/ furaha ya. 5 mdhamini *vt* 1 weka rehani. 2 apa, apisha; ahidi *~ one's word of honour* jifunga kwa kiapo, weka sharti, diriki, ahidi. 3 -nywa kwa afya ya. 4 **~ oneself** jidhamini, jiwekea dhamana. **~ oneself for sb** mdhamini mtu.
plenary *adj* 1 -enye uwezo, -sio na mipaka kamili *~power* uwezo kamili. 2 *(of meeting)* -a wote. **plenarily** *adv.*
plenipotentiary *n* mjumbe mwenye mamlaka kamili *adj* -enye mamlaka kamili (kwa niaba ya serikali yake).
plenitude *n* ukamilifu, wingi.
plenty *n* **~ (of)** wingi (wa), maridhawa *~ of food* chakula tele. **the horn of ~** hali ya neema. **in ~** kwa wingi *live in ~* ishi katika anasa *adv (colloq)* sana. **plenteous** *adj* -a wingi, maridhawa. **plenteously** *adv.* **plentiful** *adj* -ingi, maridhawa. **plentifully** *adv.*
pleonasm *n* utumiaji wa maneno yasiyohitajika. **pleonastic** *adj.*
plethora *n* 1 wingi kupita kiasi. 2 ugonjwa wa kuwa na seli damu nyekundu nyingi kupita kiasi. **plethoric** *adj.*
pliable *adj* 1 -a kupindika kwa urahisi. 2 *(of mind)* -enye kushawishika kwa urahisi. **pliability** *n.* **pliancy** *n.* **pliant** *adj.* **pliantly** *adv.*
pliers *(pl) n* **(pair of) ~** koleo; chamburo.
plight[1] *n (arch)* 1 ahadi *give one's ~ to* toa ahadi kwa. 2 rehani *vt* ahidi *(only in)* **~ one's troth** ahidi kuoa.
plight[2] *n* hali mbaya, taabu.
Plimsoll 1 **~ line/mark** alama ya kudhibiti kiasi cha shehena. 2 *(pl)* **~s** raba.
plinth *n* msingi wa nguzo.
plod *vi,vt* jikokota (kufanya kazi/ kutembea n.k.) *~ through a textbook* soma kitabu kwa taabu *n* 1 kazi ngumu. 2 mshindo. **~der** mtu ajikokotaye/mzito lakini mwenye bidii. **~ding** *adj.* **~dingly** *adv.*
plonk[1] *n* chubwi: sauti ya kitu kiangukapo katika kioevu *vi* **~ (down)** dondosha.
plonk[2] *n (sl)* mvinyo rahisi.
plosive *adj (phon)* -a kipasuo *n* kipasuo.
plot n 1 *(of land)* kiwanja. 2 *(of story)* mtiririko/msuko (wa hadithi). 3 njama *vt,vi* 1 *(math)* chora, tia alama (kwa kuonyesha majira ya mshale n.k. katika ramani n.k.). **~ting paper** karatasi ya kuchorea ramani. 2 kula njama. 3 tunga mtiririko (wa hadithi). 4 **~ (out)** gawa, weka michoro/alama n.k. **~ter** *n.*
plough *(US)* **plow** *n* 1 plau *follow the ~* lima, -wa mkulima. **put one's hand to the ~** *(fig)* anzisha/anza kazi. **~ boy** kijana mwongoza plau. 2 zana kama plau. **snow ~** plau/kifaa cha kuondolea theluji njiani. 3 shamba lililolimwa kwa plau. 4 kundi la nyota zifanyazo umbo la plau *vt,vi* 1 **~ (back)** lima kwa plau; *(fig)* wekeza upya/tena. **~ a lonely furrow** *(fig)* fanya kazi bila msaada. **~ the sand** fanya kazi ya bure. 2 **~ through** kata, penya kwa nguvu *the ship ~ed through the heavy waves* meli ilikata mawimbi mazito. 3 *(sl)* kataa mtahiniwa *~ under* lima chini sana kwa plau. **~ up** fukua mizizi. *(compounds)* **~-beam** *n* mhimili wa plau. **~-disc** *n* kisahani cha plau. **~-handle** *n* plau. **~man** *n* mlimaji.
plover *n* kitwitwi.
plow *(US) see* **plough**
ploy *n* hila.
pluck *vt,vi* 1 nyonyoa (manyoya); futua. 2 **~ sth out/up** vuta, ng'oa

(magugu); chuma; konyoa. 3 *(sl)* ~ **at** ng'ang'ania, vuta ~ *sb by the sleeve* vuta usikivu wa mtu (kwa kumgusa). 4 *(GB sl)* ~ **up courage** piga moyo konde, jipa moyo. ~ **at sth** ng'oa kitu. 5 *(sl)* iba *n* 1 ujasiri, ushupavu. 2 kitu kilichotolewa ndani (k.m. moyo, ini n.k.). 3 manyakuo. **~y** *adj.* **~ily** *adv.*

plug *n* 1 kizibo; *(naut)* nguruzi. 2 plagi. 3 *(of tobacco)* bumba/msokoto/kibonge (cha tumbaku). 4 *(sl)* tangazo la biashara linalovutia. **pull the ~** tangaza kitabu *vt* 1 ziba, funga. 2 ~ **(sth) in** unganisha plagi. 3 *(sl)* piga risasi; piga konde. 4 ~ **(up)** unganisha na umeme. 5 *(colloq)* ~ **(sth) in, away at** shughulikia, fanyia kazi sana. 6 tangazisha, vumisha. **~ging** *n* 1 tendo la kuzuia kwa plagi. 2 pigo la ngumi.

plum *n* 1 plamu: tunda kama zambarau. 2 ~ **cake** keki ya plamu. 3 *(~-tree)* mplamu. 4 *(fig)* kitu bora, kazi yenye mshahara mzuri.

plumb *n* 1 timazi, chubwi. **out of** ~ si wima, tenge. 2 (kwa wima) uzi wa timazi *adj* 1 sawasawa, kiwima. 2 *(sl)* kabisa, sawasawa kabisa, halisi *adv* 1 sawa kabisa. 2 *(US colloq)* hasa *vt (fig)* fikia mizizi/kiini cha jambo. **~-rule** *n* rula ya bildi.

plumber *n* fundi bomba. **plumbing** 1 ufundi bomba. 2 mabomba, matanki n.k..

plume *n* nyoya. **borrowed ~s** *(fig)* -a kuazimwa tu *vt* 1 *(of birds)* jipuna. 2 ~ **oneself (on sth)** jipongeza; *(of birds)* jipuna. **plumage** *n* manyoya ya ndege.

plummet *n* timazi, chubwi, bildi *vi* poromoka.

plummy *adj* 1 -enye kazi bora; *(fig)* -zuri, -a kuvutia.

plump[1] *adj* -nenenene, -a mviringo; *(of animals)* -nono *vi* ~ **up/out** nenepa. **~ness** *n* unene, unono.

plump[2] *vi* 1 ~ **(one self/sb/ sth) down** anguka, dondoka; angusha/dondosha. 2 ~ **for** chagua, pigia kura *adv* 1 ghafla *come ~ into the water* tumbukia majini ghafla *run ~ into sth* gonga ghafla. 2 bila kuficha, waziwazi *adj* -a wazi, dhahiri.

plunder *vi,vt* ~ **(of)** 1 teka nyara. 2 pora *n* 1 nyara 2 mapato (kwa wizi, unyang'anyi n.k.). **~er** *n.*

plunge *vt,vi* 1 ~ **(into)** tumbukiza, tosa; tumbukia (majini n.k.). 2 *(of ship)* sukasuka, enda mrama. 3 *(of cards)* cheza karata/kamari sana; pata madeni. 4 piga mbizi *n* 1 mbizi. **take the** ~ *(fig)* chukua hatua kali, fanya uamuzi mkali. 2 mtupo, mwendo wa ghafula, mruko, mshindo. **~r** *n* kizibuo.

plunk *see* **plonk**.

plural *adj* 1 ingi. 2 *(gram)* wingi *n* wingi. **~ism** *n* 1 wingi. 2 *(usu derog)* kushika cheo zaidi ya kimoja. 3 *(phil)* mfumo unaotambua mawazo/misimamo/dini mbalimbali. **~ity** *n* 1 wingi; hesabu (namba) zaidi ya moja. 2 kushika vyeo zaidi ya kimoja *~ity offices* kuwa na ofisi nyingi. **~ize** *vi* fanya ingi.

plus *(conj)* pamoja na, zaidi ya, na *adj* -a kujumlisha; chanya *n* kujumlisha; alama ya +; *(fig)* sifa bora. **~-fours** *n (pl)* kaboka (suruali pana ya chini ya magoti).

plush *n* kitambaa kama mahameli *adj* -a anasa, -a kitajiri. **~y** *adj (sl)* safi, tanashati.

Pluto *n* 1 *(Roman myth)* Mungu wa kuzimuni. 2 *(astr)* Pluto. **~cracy** *n* utawala wa tabaka la matajiri wenye nguvu za kimadaraka/mamlaka. **~crat** *n* mtu ambaye ana mamlaka kutokana na utajiri wake. **~cratic** *adj* utawala wa kitajiri.

ply[1] *n (layer)* 1 tabaka (la mbao au kitambaa). **three ~-wood** tabaka kadhaa zilizogundishwa. 2 *(strand)* uzi ~ *wool for knitting* sufu ya nyuzi tatu (katika ufumaji).

ply[2] 1 fanya kazi. 2 enda na kurudi mara kwa mara. 3 ~ **a trade** fanya biashara. ~ **sb with** pa/lisha/nywesha kila wakati. 4 shambulia kwa maneno.

pneumatic *adj* -a hewa, -a kuendeshwa kwa nguvu/kani ya hewa ~ *tyres* tairi hewa. **~s** *n* elimu ya tabia ya hewa.
pneumonia *n* nimonia, kichomi.
poach[1] *vt* vukiza yai. **~ed eggs** yai la maji.
poach[2] *vt,vi* 1 ~ **(on/for)** chukua/winda iso halali. 2 *(fig)* ingilia kazi ya mwingine ~ *on sb's preserves* twaa kazi ya mwingine. **~er** *n* jangili. **~ing** *n* ujangili.
pock *n* kiduduiko, vishimo vya makovu ya ndui. **be ~ marked** duduika. **be ~ed with** -wa na/jaa vidimbwi.
pocket *n* 1 mfuko. **(be) in someone's ~** -wa kibaraka wa mtu fulani; nunuliwa na mtu. **pick sb's ~** -chomoa, chomolea. **put one's pride in one's ~** kubali aibu ili kutimiza lengo. **be/live in each other's ~s** -wa pamoja siku zote. **line one's ~s** jitajirisha (hasa kwa njia zisizo halali). **put one's hand in one's ~** kuwa tayari kutoa au kutumia pesa. 2 mali, fedha. **be in/out of ~** pata faida/hasara. **out-of ~ expenses** gharama/matumizi halisi. 3 kishimo, kifuko, kibonge, chungu *air ~* kifuko cha hewa *~s of resistance* upinzani wa hapa na pale *~ of gold in the rock* kibonge cha dhahabu katika jabali. 4 kitu kidogo *a ~ dictionary* kamusi ndogo *a ~ camera* kamera ndogo. 5 *(compounds)* **~-book** kitabu kidogo cha kuandikia; *(US)* pochi ~-*handkerchief* leso, hanchifu. ~ **knife** kisu kidogo cha kukunja; kijembe. **~-money** kichele, fedha kidogo za kununulia vitu vidogo vidogo. **~ful** *n* kiasi kinachojaa mfuko *vt* 1 tia mfukoni, futika. ~ **an insult** vumilia udhia. ~ **one's pride** ficha aibu. 2 shikilia (fedha n.k.) pasipo haki; iba.
pod *n* ganda *vt,vi* 1 menya kunde, harage *they are as like as two peas in the ~* wanafanana sana. 2 ~ **(up)** weka (ma)ganda.
podgy *adj (of person)* nene na fupi.
podium *n* 1 jukwaa. 2 mimbari.
poetry *n* mashairi; ushairi *write ~* tunga (buni mashairi *a line of* mstari/ubeti *a piece of ~* shairi. **poem** *n* shairi. **poesy** *n (arch)* ushairi, mashairi. **poet** *n* mshairi, mtunga mashairi. **poetess** *n* mshairi wa kike. **poetic(al)** *adj* -a mashairi; -a kishairi. **poetic justice** haki halisi. **poetically** *adv*. **poetics** *n* elimu ya ushairi.
pogrom *n* uuaji wa kikatili wa jumuiya ya watu.
poignant *adj* kali, -a kutia uchungu.
point *n* 1 ncha kali (ya kalamu, pini, kisu, n.k.). **not to put too fine a ~ on it** kusema ule ukweli. 2 ncha-chonge. 3 nukta (ifanywayo na kitu, kama vile kalamu). **decimal ~** desimali *four ~ six* nne nukta sita (4.6). 4 alama (halisi au ya kufikirika) ya eneo, mahali au wakati. **a ~ of view** mtazamo. *(US)* **at this ~** mahali hapa; sasa, wakati huu. **be at the ~ of death** -wa mahututi. **be on the ~ of doing sth** karibia kufanya jambo fulani. **if/when it comes to the ~** wakati ukifika. ~ **duty** zamu ya polisi wa usalama barabarani katika kituo maalum. 5 *(printing)* kizio cha kupimia ukubwa wa herufi. 6 alama (kwenye skeli); kizio cha kupimia, kiwango. **boiling ~** kiwango mchemko. **possession is nine ~ of the law** hamadi kibindoni. 7 pointi, alama, kizio cha kupatia pointi katika mchezo. **win/be beaten on ~s** shinda/shindwa kwa pointi. 8 *(of compass)* alama, nyuzi. 9 wazo (kuu/kiini), jambo. **carry/gain one's ~** shawishi mtu akubaliane na wazo lako. **come to/get to/reach the ~** sema kile (hasa) unachotaka kusema. **get/see/miss the ~** pata/ona/shindwa kuona ambacho mtu anajaribu kusema. **make one's ~** jenga hoja. **make a ~ of doing sth** chukua kitu kuwa muhimu au cha lazima kufanya. **stretch a ~** kwenda mbali zaidi ya kiwango kinachoruhusiwa. **take sb's ~** elewa/kubaliana na kile asemacho mtu. **(get/wander)**

away from/off the ~ sema kitu kisichohusiana na habari isemwayo. **a case in** ~ jambo/mfano halisi mmojawapo. **in** ~**of honour/ conscience** kitu muhimu kwa dhamiri/ hadhi ya mtu. 10 sababu **no/not much** ~ **in doing sth** hakuna sababu ya msingi (ya kufanya kitu fulani). **What's the** ~ Ya nini? usihangaike bure. 11 sifa. 12 soketi/njia ya kupitia umeme. 13 maungio (ya kubadilishia njia ya reli). ~**sman** mlinzi wa njia panda ya reli. 14 umuhimu *vt,vi* 1 ~ **(to)** elekeza; onyesha sehemu/uelekeo wa. ~ **sth at/towards** elekeza, lenga. 2 ~ **sth out** onyesha. 3 tia nukta; *(fig)* kazia, sisitiza. 4 kazia maungio ya matofali yaliyojengwa. 5 *(of a dog)* jiweka tayari. ~**ed** *adj* 1 -liochongoka, -enye ncha kali; *(fig)* -lioelekezwa dhidi ya mtu fulani. 2 *(fig)* -a wazi, -liolenga wazi. 3 kali. ~ **edly** *adv*. ~**er** *n* 1 mshale, akarabu. 2 fimbo (fito) ya kuelekezea/kuonyesha. 3 mbwa wa kuwinda, mwepesi kuonyesha alipo ndege au mnyama. 4 *(mil)* mlenga shabaha/mzinga. ~**less** *adj* 1 *(fig)* -sio na maana/sababu *a ~less speech* hotuba isiyo na maana. 2 *(sport)* -sio na pointi. ~**lessly** *adv*. ~-**blank** *adv* 1 *(of a shot)* papo kwa papo, kwa karibu mno. 2 kinagaubanga, waziwazi. ~**illism** *n* uchoraji wa kutumia nukta; utonaji.

poise *vt,vi* 1 weka sawasawa (kama mtungi n.k.) kichwani; tuliza sawasawa. ~ **oneself on one's toes** chuchumia, tengemea; *(fig)* -wa tayari. 2 pembeza, jinega; *(weigh)* pima; *(fig)* kujisawazisha. 3 *(hover)* elea angani. 4 ~**d in suspense** -wa na shaka, sitasita *n* 1 mwendo, mkao (k.m. kuinua kichwa, kusimama wima n.k.). 2 *(elements etc)* mtu mwenye kujiamini *a man of* ~ mtu makini.

poison *n* sumu *they hate each other like* ~ wanachukiana sana sana *die of* ~ -fa kwa sumu. ~ **gas** gesi ya sumu. ~ **pen** mtu aandikaye barua za kashifa zisizo na jina la mwandishi. ~ **pen letter** barua za kashifa. 2 maadili mabaya/maovu *vt* 1 tia/lisha sumu *I ave a ~ed hand* nina kidonda mkononi. ~**er** *n* msumishaji; muuaji atumiaye sumu. ~**ous** *adj* -enye sumu; ovu; fisadi.

poke *vi,vt* 1 sukuma, piga kikumbo; tia mdukuo. 2 chochea, choma, sukumiza ~ *the fire* chochea moto. ~ **fun at** dhihaki. 3 chakura; tomasa. 4 dukiza. ~ **one's nose into sb's business** jidukiza katika mambo ya watu. 5 ~ **(about)** papasapapasa kwa kutafuta. 6 fanya shimo kwa kudukua, kuchakura *n* msukumo, kikumbo, mdukuo.

poker[1] *n* mchokoo wa chuma.

poker[2] *n* poka: mchezo fulani wa karata. ~ **face** *(colloq)* uso ubao; uso usioonyesha mhemko/hisia.

poky *adj (of room)* dogo, -a maskini.

polar *adj* 1 -a ncha za dunia, -a nchi ya baridi sana. ~ **lights** nuru ya kaskazini au kusini. *(math)* ~ **coordinates** majiranguzo *n* ~ *front* mkabala/mkingamo wa ukanda wa baridi na joto. ~ **bear** dubu mweupe aishiye karibu na ncha ya kaskazini. 2 kingamo. ~**ity** *n*. ~**ize** *vt* kingamiza. ~**ization** *n*.

pole *n* 1 ncha *north P~* Ncha ya Kaskazini. ~**s** pembe za dunia. **be** ~**s apart** -wa mbalimbali kabisa, hitilafiana kabisa. 2 mwisho wa sumaku; pembe ya hatari ya umeme. ~**star** nyota ya kaskazini.

pole *n* 1 ufito; upondo/boriti; pao; mpiko; *(post)* mhimili, mwimo kiopoo. **up the** ~ *(sl)* kichaa kidogo. 2 kipimo cha urefu (yadi tano na nusu) *vt* 1 sukuma/endesha kwa upondo. 2 toa, andaa nguzo, mhimili n.k. ~ **vault** *n* (mchezo wa) kuruka kwa upondo; upondo wa kurukia.

pole-axe *n* 1 shoka la vita. 2 shoka la mchinjaji *vt* piga/chanja kwa shoka; *(fig)* chinja, haribu.

polecat *n* kicheche.

polemic *n* hoja; bishano, mikingamo; shindano, mjadala. ~**s** ubishi;

taaluma ya mjadala *adj (also* ~ **al**).
police *n* polisi *military* ~ polisi wa jeshi. ~ **constable** askari, konstebo. *vt* 1 simamia (mahali) kwa kutumia polisi ~ *the streets* zuia uhalifu barabarani. *(compounds)* ~ **dog** *n* mbwa wa polisi. ~ **force** *n* jeshi la polisi. ~**man** *n* polisi, askari polisi. ~ **office** *n* ofisi ya polisi. ~- **state** *n* (nchi yenye) utawala wa mabavu/ udikteta. ~-**station** *n* kituo cha polisi. ~-**woman** *n* polisi wa kike.
policy[1] *n* 1 sera *self-realice* ~ sera ya kujitegemea. 2 *(prudence)* busara.
policy[2] *n* hati *insurance* ~ hati ya bima. polio (*also* ~**myelitis**) *n* polio; kupooza (miguu/mikono n.k.).
polish *vt,vi* 1 ~ **up** ng'arisha, ng'arika; kwatua; sugua. 2 *(of character)* adibisha, ongoza, noa. 3 ~ **sth off** maliza haraka *n* 1 ulaini, mng'aro mwanga. 2 polishi: dawa ya kung'arisha/kukwatulia. 3 *(fig)* ustaarabu, malezi mazuri, adabu. ~**er** *n* mng'arishaji.
politburo *n* kamati kuu ya chama (hasa katika chama cha kikomunisti).
polite *adj* taratibu, pole, -a adabu, -a heshima. ~ **ly** *adv*. ~**ness** *n*.
politic *adj* 1 -a kufaa, -a busara. 2 **the body** ~ dola.
politics *n* siasa *racial* ~ siasa ya ubaguzi (wa rangi). **political** *adj* -a siasa, -a kisiasa ~ *party* chama cha siasa. ~ **asylum** hifadhi ya kisiasa. ~ **economy** uchumi/ikitisadi ya kisiasa. ~ **prisoners** wafungwa wa kisiasa ~ *offence* jinai ya kisiasa. **politician** *n* mwanasiasa. **politicize** *vt,vi* tia mwako wa kisiasa. **politick** *vi* jihusisha na siasa.
polity *n* 1 dola; serikali.
poll[1] *n* (~ **parrot**) kasuku.
poll[2] *n* 1 (upigaji) kura, kuhesabu kura. 2 kichwa. ~ **tax** *n* kodi ya kichwa. 3 kutafuta maoni ya watu kwa kuwahoji *vt,vi* 1 pata kura, piga kura. ~**ing booth/station** *n* kituo cha kupigia kura. ~**ing day** *n* siku ya kupiga kura. 2 tafuta maoni ya watu kwa kuwahoji. ~**ster** *n* mtafuta maoni. 3 kata ncha za matawi/pembe n.k..
pollard *vt* pogoa, kata kilele cha mti.
pollen *n* n chavua. **pollinate** *vt* chavusha. **pollination** *n*. mchavusho. **cross** ~ mchavusho tambuko. **self** ~ kujichavusha; mchavushopweke.
pollute *vt* chafua *waste from industries* ~ *the sea* uchafu kutoka viwandani huchafua bahari. **pollutant** *n* kichafuzi. **pollution** *n* uchafu.
polo *n* polo: mchezo wa wapanda farasi kupiga tufe kwa fimbo. **water** ~ *n* mchezo wa mpira wa waogeleaji ~ *stick* fimbo ya kuchezea polo.
poltergeist *n (in folklore etc)* pepo mbaya mwenye makeke/ghasia.
poltroon *n* mwoga *he is a* ~ yu mwoga. ~**ery** *n* woga.
poly *prep* 1 -ingi. 2 *(colloq abbr for)* **polytechnic**.
polyandry *n* mfumo ambao mwanamke anakuwa na waume wengi. **polyandrous** *adj*.
polychrome *adj* -a marangirangi, -liopakwa rangi aina aina. **polychromy** *n* utiaji rangi nyingi.
polygamy n mitala. **polygamist** *n* aoaye wake wengi. **polygamous** *adj* -a mitala, -a wake wengi ~ *marriage* ndoa ya wake wengi. *potentially* ~ *marriage* ndoa inayoweza kuwa ya wake wengi.
polyglot *adj* -a lugha nyingi. *n* mzungumzaji wa lugha nyingi.
polygon *n* pembenyingi, poligoni *a* ~ *is a many sided figure* poligoni ni umbo lenye pembe nyingi. ~**al** *adj* -a pembe nyingi.
polymorphous *adj* -a maumbile mengi; -enye kupitia hatua nyingi (za maendeleo, kukua n.k.). **polymorphic** *adj*. **polymorphism** *n*.
polyphony *n (music)* sauti nyingi. **polyphonous** *adj* -a sauti nyingi.
polypus *n see* **polyp**.
polysyllable *n* neno la silabi nyingi. **pollysyllabic** *adj* -enye silabi nyingi. ~ *word* neno lenye silabi zaidi ya tatu.

polytechnic *n* chuo cha ufundi anuwai *adj* -a ufundi anuwai.

polytheism *n* imani ya kuabudu miungu wengi. **polytheist** *n.*

polythene *adj* -a plastiki laini.

pomegranate *n* komamanga.

pommel *n* 1 mduara wa saruji/ matandiko ya farasi au punda. 2 kinundu cha mpini wa upanga.

pomp *n* fahari/ufahari; makuu, majivuno. **~ous** *adj* -enye makuu, -enye majivuno, -a kujidai. **~osity** *n* ushaufu, majivuno, makuu. **~ousness** *n.*

pompon *n* pambo-duara (liwekwalo kwenye kofia, nguo, viatu n.k.).

ponce *n* 1 kuwadi. 2 msenge *vi* ~ **about** -wa kama msenge.

poncho *n* poncho: joho kama kawa.

pond *n* dimbwi (hasa ambapo wanyama hunywa maji).

ponder *vt,vi* ~ **(over)** fikiri, tafakari, waza *he ~ed a variety of issues* alitafakari masuala kadhaa. **~able** *adj (phys)* -a kupimika, mambo yawezayo kufikiriwa, kukadiriwa n.k. **~osity** *n.* **~ous** *adj* 1 zito sana, kubwa. 2 *(dull)* zito, bwege. **~ly** *adv.*

pone *n (also* **corn** *~)* mkate wa mahindi.

poniard *(arch or poet)* jambia *vt* choma kwa jambia.

pontiff *n* 1 Papa, Baba Mtakatifu. 2 *(arch)* kuhani mkuu; askofu. **pontifical** *adj* 1 -a Papa, -a kuhani mkuu, -a askofu. **pontificals n** mavazirasmi ya maaskofu. 2 -enye makuu. **pontificate** *n* ofisi ya Papa; utawala wa Papa *vi* hubiri.

pontoon[1] *n* pantoni. ~ **bridge** *n* daraja la pantoni.

pantoon[2] *n* mchezo wa karata.

pony *n* 1 farasi mdogo. ~ **tail** *n* mtindo wa nywele. ~ **trekking** *n* kutembea kwa kumpakia kumpanda/farasi mdogo.

pooh-pooh *vt (colloq) (an idea etc)* dharau, beza, cheka.

pool[1] *n* 1 dimbwi. 2 **swimming** ~ bwawa la kuogelea. 3 kilindi cha mto.

pool[2] *n* 1 *(gambling)* fedha zilizowekwa poni na wacheza kamari. **football** ~ kamari ya kutabiri matokeo ya mpira. 2 mpango wa kubia biashara na kugawana faida (ili kuepuka ushindani). 3 *(US)* aina ya biliadi. 4 fedha/huduma za kuchangia;mchango wa ubia *vt* changa/changizana; fanya ubia.

poor *adj* 1 maskini, fukara. **the** ~ *n* mafukara, maskini. **~box** *n (in church)* kisanduku cha maskini. ~ **house** nyumba ya maskini (wanao hudumiwa na serikali). **~law** sheria ya kulinda/kuhudumia maskini. **~rate** *n* kodi ya kuwakimu maskini. **~relief** *n* msaada kwa maskini. 2 chache *a ~ supply of food* ugavi wa chakula kichache. 3 -a kustahili huruma/ msaada, nyonge *a ~ creature* maskini, kiumbe *~ me!* maskini miye! 4 duni, hafifu. ~ **consolation** kitulizo duni. **~ly** *adv* vibaya *adj* -gonjwa *feel* ~ -ugua, ona vibaya. ~ **off** maskini, -enye fedha kidogo. **~ness** *n* ukosefu, upungufu, uduni. ~ **-spirited** *adj* -oga; -liokata tamaa.

pop[1] *adj (colloq abbr for popular)* pendwa. ~ **art** sanaa pendwa/mpito. ~ **song** wimbo pendwa. ~ **festival** tamasha pendwa (la muziki n.k.) *n (colloq)* sanaa ya kupita, sherehe ya kawaida.

pop[2] *vt,vi* 1 *(of corks)* zibua. ~ **the question** *(sl)* posa. **~eyed** *adj* -enye macho pima, -enye macho ya popo. ~ **gun** bunduki ya kitoto (inayotumia vizibo). 2 *(with adv & prep)* ~ **in** pitia, tembelea. ~ **sth into sth** tia/ weka mara moja *~ sth into a drawer quickly etc* weka kitu katika saraka kwa haraka. ~ **off** ondoka ghafla; fariki. ~ **over/across to** tembelea. 3 *(sl)* weka rehani. **go** ~ enda kwa vishindo. 4 piga bunduki. 5 kaanga bisi. **~corn** bisi *n* 1 kishindo (kama kizibo kinapozibuka ghafla). 2 *(sl)* soda. 3 **in** ~ hali ya kuwa katika rahani.

pope *n* 1 Papa, Baba Mtakatifu. **~ry** *n*

(*in hostile use*) mambo ya Roma; ukatoliki. **popish** -a kikatoliki; -a upapa.
popinjay *n* 1 *(arch)* kasuku. 2 sanamu ya kasuku iliyowekwa mtini kwa kulengea. 3 maridadi, mfuauji (mwenye kujinaki).
poplar *n* mpopla: mti mrefu, mnyofu unaokua haraka sana.
poplin *n* poplini: aina ya kitambaa cha kutengenezea mashati, n.k.
poppet *n* kipenzi *(used to a child) come here my little ~* njoo hapa kipenzi changu.
poppy *n* mpopi: aina ya mmea/ua jekundu (hutumika kutengenezea kasumba).
poppycock *n (sl)* upuuzi.
populace *n* umma, wananchi.
popular *adj* 1 -a umma, -a watu ~ *government* serikali iliyochaguliwa na walio wengi. ~ **front** muungano wa kupinga ufashisti n.k. 2 pendwa. ~ **novel** riwaya pendwa. 3 inayopendwa *be ~* pendwa na wengi *make oneself ~* fanya mambo yatakayokufanya upendwe na watu ~ *science* sayansi ya kufaa watu kwa kadiri ya elimu yao. **~ity** *n.* **~ly** *adv.* **~ize** *vt* 1 *(spread)* eneza kwa watu. 2 *(simplify)* rahisisha, fanya ifae watu wa kawaida. **~ization** *n.*
populate *vt* jaza watu. **population** *n* 1 (idadi ya) watu (wa nchi, mji n.k.). 2 *(bio)* mimea au wanyama wa sehemu fulani. **populism** *n* mfumo wa serikali/siasa inayojali maoni na fikra za umma. **populist** *n* mtu anayefuata mfumo huo. **populous** *adj* -enye watu wengi, -a kujaa watu.
porcelain *n* kauri. ~ **clay** kaolini *adj* -a kauri.
porch *n* baraza.
porcine *adj* -a nguruwe, kama nguruwe.
porcupine *n* nungu, nungunungu.
pore[1] *n* kinyweleo, kitundu kidogo. **porous** *adj* -enye vinyweleo, -enye kunyonya/kunywa unyevunyevu -enye kuvuja. **porousness** *n.* **porosity** *n.*
pore[2] *vi* ~ **over sth** soma kwa makini.
pork *n* 1 nyama ya nguruwe. 2 *(US)* ~ **barrel** *(sl)* mradi wa serikali/ruzuku yenye kuzaa faida ya kujijenga kisiasa kwa watu. ~ **butcher** *n* muuza nyama ya nguruwe. **~er** *n* nguruwe wa nyama.
pornography *n* ponografia: picha au maandishi yenye kutia ashiki. **pornographic** *adj* -a kiponografia.
porphyry *n* mwamba wa kito chekundu.
porpoise *n* pomboo.
porridge *n* uji.
porringer *n* bakuli lenye kishikio.
port[1] *n* 1 *(harbour)* bandari. **free ~** bandari huru (ambayo iko wazi kutumiwa na nchi zote bila kutozwa ushuru). 2 mji/jiji lenye bandari (k.m. Dar es Salaam). 3 *(fig)* mahali pa usalama, kimbilio. **any ~ in a storm** mahali pa usalama (wakati wa shida). ~ **after stormy seas** mapumziko baada ya hali ngumu.
port[2] *n (naut)* mlango wa ubavuni mwa meli. **~hole** dirisha dogo ubavuni mwa meli/ndege; uwazi ubavuni mwa meli (kuruhusu mwanga/hewa).
port[3] *n* upande wa kushoto wa meli/ ndege (mtu anapokabili gubeti mbele).
port[4] *n* **(~-wine)** porto: divai nyekundu nzito tamu.
portal *n* mlango mkubwa, lango.
portcullis *n* mlango wa chuma wenye kuinuka na kushuka.
portend *vt (formal)* bashiri, tabiri. **portent** *n* 1 ishara. 2 kitu cha ajabu. **portentous** *adj* -a kutisha; -a ajabu. **portentously** *adv.*
porter[1] *n* bawabu, mngoja mlango. ~ **'s lodge** nyumba ya bawabu.
porter[2] *n* 1 hamali, mchukuzi; mpagazi; *(US)* mhudumu (katika behewa la kulala la treni). ~ **age** *n* upagazi; ushuru/gharama ya upagazi. **portable** *adj* -a kuchukulika, -a kubebeka. **portability** *n.* **porter-house** *n* ~ **(steak)** nyama ya kiuno.
portfolio *n* 1 mkoba, sanduku/jalada la

kutia hati, barua n.k.. 2 uwaziri. 3 *(of bank)* orodha ya fedha zilizowekwa kwa faida.

porthole *see* **port**[2].

portico *n (archit)* varanda yenye matao na nguzo.

portiere *n* pazia zito la mlangoni.

portion *n* 1 sehemu, fungu. 2 **marriage** ~ mahari. 3 *(inheritance)* urithi. 4 majaliwa *vt* 1 ~ **sth out (among, between)** gawa sehemu. 2 ~ **sth to sb** gawia, -pa.

Portland *n* **P~ cement** saruji.

portly *adj* nene, -enye kitambi.

portmanteau *n* kasha la ngozi la kuchukulia nguo. ~ **word** neno lililoungwa.

portray *vt* 1 chora picha/taswira. 2 eleza, simulia, fafanua. 3 igiza. **~al** *n*. **portrait** *n* picha, taswira. **portraitist** *n*. **portraiture** *n*.

Portugal Ureno. **Portuguese** *adj* -a Kireno *n* 1 Mreno. 2 (lugha ya) Kireno.

pose *n* 1 mkao; sura, hali. 2 *(pretence)* kujifanya, sura ya kinafiki *vt,vi* 1 panga/tayarisha mkao. 2 *(pretend to be)* jifanya, jidai. 3 leta/toa hoja/swali. 4 jiweka tayari kwa ajili ya kuchorwa/kupigwa picha. 5 ~ **as** jifanya. **~ur** *n (fem* **poseuse)** mpenda makuu, mnafiki.

posh *adj (sl)* maridadi, -zuri sana, -a anasa/tajiri *vt,vi (sl)* ~ **oneself up** jikwatua, jirembesha.

posit *vt* toa hoja, dai.

position *n* 1 *(place)* mahali. **in** ~ mahali pake, sawa. **out of** ~ -tokuwa mahali pake. 2 *(condition)* hali, namna. 3 msimamo *what's your ~ on this problem?* waonaje juu ya jambo hili? 4 uwezo *be in a ~ to* weza. 5 nafasi. 6 kazi, cheo *people of ~* watu maarufu! *vt* weka, panga. **~al** *adj* -a mahali.

positive *adj* 1 -a hakika, halisi. 2 *(definite)* waziwazi, bayana, dhahiri. 3 -a kujenga; -a kusaidia *a ~ suggestion* wazo la kujenga. 4 *(math)* chanya ~ *number* namba chanya. 5 *(electr)* chaji/umeme upatikanao kwa kusugua kioo na hariri, umeme utokanao na ukosefu wa elektroni. 6 *(of photo)* picha (sura kwenye karatasi). **~ness** *n*. **positivism** *n (phil)* falsafa umbile: falsafa inayozingatia tu mambo yanayoonekana na kujulikana vema na wanadamu. **positivist** *n*.

posse *n* 1 kikundi (cha sungusungu, polisi, wanamgambo).

possess *vt* 1 miliki, -wa na, hodhi. 2 tawala, shika *fear ~ed him* hofu ilimtawala. 3 ~ **oneself of** *(arch)* miliki. **be ~ed of** -wa na. 4 **be ~ed** pagawa, -wa na pepo *be ~ed by the devil* -wa na shetani. 5 kaza. **~ion** *n* 1 kumiliki; mali, miliki *take ~* shika, twaa, kamata. 2 kupagawa/kupandwa na pepo. 3 *(pl)* **~ions** mali. **~ive** *adj* 1 -a kumiliki, -enye tamaa (ya kumiliki), -enye tamaa ya kuweka kwenye kiganja. 2 *(gram)* milikishi, -enye kuonyesha kumiliki.

possible *adj* 1 yawezekana, yamkini *as soon as ~* upesi iwezekanavyo, kwa haraka sana. 2 -a kufaa *the one ~ man* mtu anayefaa. 3 -a yakini *n* mtu/kitu kiwezacho *do one's ~* fanya uwezavyo. **possibility** *n* 1 uwezekano. 2 kitu kinachowezekana. **possibly** *adv* labda, kwa kadiri iwezekanavyo *I cannot possibly do it* siwezi kabisa kuifanya (haiwezekani) *as soon as you possibly can* upesi uwezavyo/iwezekanavyo *how can we possibly do that?* tunawezaje kufanya hivyo?

possum *n (animal)* kifaurongo. **play** ~ jifanya (kulala n.k.).

post[1] *n* 1 mhimili, nguzo *lamp ~s* nguzo za taa *starting ~* mahali pa kuanzia mbio *winning ~* mahali pa kumalizia mbio. 2 *(door~)* mwimo, mhimili. 3 *(bed ~)* tendegu, mhimili wa kitanda *vt* 1 ~ **(up)** bandika; weka matangazo. 2 ~ **(over)** jaza matangazo. **~er** *n* 1 tangazo, picha kubwa (inayobandikwa ukutani), bango. 2 **bill (~ er)** mbandikaji matangazo/mabango.

post[2] *n* 1 posta *a heavy ~* mfuko mzito wa barua *has the ~ come yet?* barua zimefika? *by return of ~* kwa posta ijayo *send sth by ~* peleka kitu kwa posta. **~man** *n* mtu wa posta. **~mark** *n* mhuri wa posta. 2 *(post office)* posta. **the p~ office** Shirika la Posta. **~ office box** (P.O.) sanduku la posta (S.L.P.) *by registered ~* kwa rejesta. **~ free** *adj* -liokwisha lipiwa stempu; -enye kupelekwa bila malipo. 3 *(hist)* tarishi, mjumbe, tume *vt,vi* 1 peleka barua na vifurushi kwa posta, tia posta. 2 **(~ up)** andika katika daftari. 3 **keep sb ~ed** fahamisha fulani juu ya habari yote. 4 enda kwa farasi. **~card** *n* postikadi. **picture ~card** postikadi ya picha **~code** *n* simbo. **~ restante** *n (F)* mahali pa barua zinazongojea. **~master** *n* postamasta. **Postmaster General** Postamasta Mkuu. **postmistress** *n* postamasta (wa kike). **~-paid** *adj* -liokwisha lipiwa stempu. **~age** *n* ada ya posta. **~ stamp** stempu *extra ~* gharama zaidi ya posta *inland/foreign ~* gharama ya kusafirisha barani/nchi za nje kwa posta. **~al** *adj* -a posta. **~ order** hundi ya posta. **~ service** huduma za posta. **~ savings bank** benki ya akiba ya posta.

post[3] *n* 1 mahali pa kazi; *(mil)* kilindo. 2 *(of trade)* kituo cha biashara, mahali pa kufanya biashara (porini). 3 cheo, daraja, nafasi katika kazi. **the last ~** kamsa *vt* 1 panga/weka walinzi. 2 tuma/peleka mahali pa kazi.

post[4] *(pref* 1 baada ya *~ war* baada ya vita.. **~ natal** baada ya kuzaa *~ primary* baada ya msingi *vt* **~date** weka tarehe ya mbele.

posterior *adj* **~ (to)** -a nyuma; -a baadaye *n* matako *kick sb's ~* piga mtu matakoni.

posterity *n* 1 watoto. 2 vizazi vya baadaye.

postern *n* 1 mlango wa nyuma. 2 ujia au mlango wa pembeni.

postgraduate *adj* -a uzamili; -a masomo ya baada ya shahada ya mwanzo (ya Chuo Kikuu) *a ~ course* kozi ya uzamili *n (post-graduate student)* mzamili.

posthumous *adj* -a baada ya kufa *~ novel* riwaya iliyochapishwa baada ya mwandishi kufa. 2 *(of a child)* -liozaliwa baada ya kufa baba.

postiche *n* nywele za bandia.

postmeridiem *adv (p.m.)* muda tangu saa sita mchana hadi saa sita usiku.

post-mortem *n* 1 uchunguzi wa maiti. 2 *(colloq)* mapitio ya tukio n.k. la wakati uliopita *adj* -a uchunguzi wa maiti.

postpone *vt* ahirisha. **~ment** *n.*

postposition *n (gram)* mwao tamati.

postprandial *adj* -a baada ya chakula cha jioni.

postscript *n (abbr PS)* 1 nyongeza ya maneno kwenye barua. 2 taarifa za ziada au za mwisho.

postulant *vt* dai *n* dai, daawa, dhana. **postulation** *n.* **postulator** *n.*

posture *n* 1 mkao. 2 hali. 3 *(of mind)* msimamo *vt,vi* 1 weka/panga katika mkao. 2 jifanya, jidai. **posturing** *n.*

posy *n* 1 shada (fungu) la maua. 2 *(arch)* mithali.

pot[1] *n* 1 chungu, sufuria. **tea~** birika la chai *chamber ~* poti. 2 *(fig)* **a big ~** *(colloq)* kizito, mtu maarufu. 3 *(games) (colloq)* kikombe. 4 *(sl)* bangi. 5 *(colloq)* kiasi kikubwa. **~s of money** pesa kibao. 6 *(phrases and proverbs)* **go to ~** *(sl)* haribika. **keep the ~ boiling** -wa na fedha kusogeza siku; fanya jambo liendelee. **take ~ luck** chukua kilichopo, bahatisha. **the ~ calling the kettle black** nyani haoni kundule/mandole. 7 *(comp)* **~-bellied** *adj (of a person)* -enye kitambi; *(of a stove)* -enye kitako cha mviringo. **~-belly** *n* kitambi, kitumbotumbo. **~-boiler** *n* kitabu chapwa (cha kutafutia pesa tu). **~-bound** *adj (of a plant)* -enye mizizi tele. **~-boy**, **~-man** *n (hist)* mhudumu katika baa. **~-hat** *n (sl)* kofia mviringo. **~head** *n (sl)* mvuta bangi. ~ **herb** *n* kiungo. ~**-hole** *n* shimo barabarani; shimo refu katika mwamba. ~**-house** *n (arch)* kilabu (ya pombe). ~**-hunter** *n* msasi anayeua chochote anachokikuta msituni kwa kufikiria chakula au faida tu; mtu anayeingia katika mashindano kwa ajili ya kupata zawadi tu. ~**roast** *n* nyama iliyokaushiwa chunguni. ~ **shot** kupiga (risasi) ndege/mnyama aliye karibu. ~**-trained** *adj (of a small child)* -liofunzwa kutumia poti. ~**ter**[1] *n* mfinyanzi. ~**ter's wheel** gurudumu la mfinyanzi. ~**tery** *n* 1 vyombo vya udongo. 2 ufinyazi, mahali pa kufinyanga.

pot[2] *vt,vi* 1 hifadhi (nyama, samaki n.k.) katika chungu. 2 ~ **(up)** panda miche katika chungu. 3 piga risasi mnyama bila kulenga shabaha, ua kwa njia hiyo. 4 *(billiards)* ingiza mpira kwenye kishimo. 5 *(colloq)* weka (mtoto) kwenye poti.

potable *adj* -nayonyweka, -nayofaa kunywewa. **potation** *n (liter)* 1 kunywa. 2 kinywaji. 3 *(pl)* ulevi.

potash *n* (chumvichumvi za) potashi.

potassium n potasiamu. ~ **carbonate** magadi. ~ **nitrate** shure.

potato *n* kiazi, mbatata, kiazi ulaya *(fig/sl)* **small** ~ watu wadogo, akina yakhe. **sweet** ~**es** viazi vitamu ~ *bed* tuta. ~ **beetle** mdudu ashambuliaye majani ya viazi. ~**-masher** *n* kipondeo cha viazi.

poteen *n (Irish)* gongo.

potent *adj* -enye nguvu. ~**ate** *n* -a kuweza kuwa, -a kuwezekana *n* nguvu zisizodhihirika. ~**iality** *n* uwezekano. ~**ially** *adv*. ~**ial** *n* mtu mwenye nguvu, mkuu, mtawala.

pother *n* 1 vumbi/moshi wenye harufu kali. 2 ghasia *vt,vi* hangaisha, hangaika.

potion *n* (kiasi cha) dawa/sumu ya maji *a love* ~ dawa ya mapenzi.

pot-pourri *n* 1 mchanganyiko wa maua (makavu), miti shamba na viungo vingine. 2 *(music)* muziki mchanganyiko.

pot-sherd *n* kigae, gae, kigeranja, kigerang'enza.

pottage *n (arch)* supu nzito.

potted *adj (often derog)* -liofupishwa na kurahisishwa.

potter *(US* **putter)** *vi* 1 paraza, fanya kazi bila kutia makini; cheza cheza na kazi *vt* ~ *away one's time* poteza muda/wakati. 2 tembelea mahali, poteza wakati, wa mzembe.

potty[1] *adj (GB dated colloq)* 1 hafifu, dogo, -sio muhimu. 2 ~ **(about sb/ sth)** *(of a person)* pumbavu, -enye wazimu/kichaa.

potty[2] *n* poti: chombo cha mtoto cha kwendea haja.

pouch *n* 1 pochi, kifuko. 2 kifuko cha macho. 3 mbeleko ya kangaruu, kifuko cha mbegu katika mmea *vt* tia mfukoni, futika; futuka.

pouf, pouffe *n* 1 takia. 2 *(derog slang)* msenge.

poultice *n* dawa ya moto ya kubandika (kama ugali laini wa moto) *vt* ~ **sth** bandika dawa.

poultry *n* kuku, mabata n.k.. ~**-farm** *n* shamba la kuku. **poult** *n* kifaranga. **poulterer** *n* mwuza kuku, mabata n.k..

pounce *vi* ~ **on/at** rukia/shambulia ghafla, vamia.

pound[1] *n* 1 *(of money)* pauni. *(GB)* ~ **(sterling)** pauni: pensi mia moja. 2 *(of weight)* ratili: wakia/aunsi 16. ~**age** *n* 1 ushuru ulipwao kwa kila pauni/ratili. 2 asilimia ya jumla ya mapato ya biashara. ~**er** *n* kitu chenye uzani wa ratili fulani *a six* ~ mzinga wenye risasi za ratili sita.

pound[2] *n* zizi la kuwekea wanyama (ng'ombe, mbuzi, farasi n.k.) waliopotea; uga wa magari (agh. yaliyokamatwa).

pound[3] *vt,vi* ~ **(away) (at/on)** 1 twanga, ponda. 2 chakaza, funda. 3 enda, kimbia kwa nguvu. ~**er** *n* mchi au chombo chochote kinachotumika kwa kutwangia au kusagia.

pour *vt,vi* 1 mimina, mwaga. *(fig)* ~ **cold water on sth** katisha tamaa (mtu). ~ **missiles on a town** shambulia mji kwa makombora. ~ **oil on troubled water** tuliza fujo kwa maneno ya upole. 2 toka/ingia kwa wingi; miminika. 3 *(of rain)* mwagika, anguka kwa wingi *the rain is ~ing down* mvua inanyesha sana. **it never rains but it ~s** *(fig)* hakuna msiba usiokuwa na mwenziwe.

pout *vt, vi* bibidua midomo *n* kubibidua. **~ingly** *adv*. **~er** *n* 1 *(of person)* mwenye midomo mikubwa. 2 *(bio)* njiwa mwenye uwezo wa kuvimbisha gole.

poverty *n* 1 umaskini, ufukara, ukata. 2 *(deficiency)* upungufu. ~ **stricken** *adj* hohehahe, fukara.

P.O.W. *(abbr*. **prisoner of war)** *see* **prisoner**.

powder *n* 1 *(for face etc)* poda. ~ **puff** kisifongo poda. ~ **room** maliwato ya wanawake. 2 *(of soap etc)* unga. 3 baruti **not worth ~ and shot** -siostahili kupiganiwa. ~ **magazine** ghala ya baruti. ~ **flask/horn** kibweta cha baruti *vi* 1 paka poda. 2 tumia poda. **~ed** -enye ungaunga; -a mchangamchanga. **~ed milk** maziwa ya unga. **~y** *adj*.

power *n* 1 uwezo. **more ~ to your elbow** safi, endelea! ~ **boat** *n* (*see* **motor boat**). ~ **dive** *n* ndege ipigayo mbizi hewani. ~ **driven** -enye nguvu ya injini; -a mitambo/uwezo. ~ **house/station** *n* kituo cha umeme. ~ **point** *n* soketi. 2 nguvu. **mechanical** ~ uwezo makanika; randa. 3 mamlaka, kazi, amri *have sb in your* ~ -wa na mamlaka/amri juu ya, weza kudhibiti *the party in* ~ chama kinachotawala *have* ~ *over* miliki, tawala, wa na amri/mamlaka juu ya. 4 *(authority)* mwenye nguvu, mkubwa *the big ~s* mataifa makubwa. **the ~s that be** wenye madaraka/mamlaka. ~ **politics** siasa za mabavu. **Great P~s** mataifa makubwa. 5 *mental* ~ akili. 6 mungu, mzimu *the ~s of darkness* mashetani. 7 *(maths)* kipeo. 8 madaraka *the ~s of the President* madaraka ya Rais. 9 mtu/shirika lenye mamlaka (au uwezo wa kuathiri). 10 *(colloq)* kiasi kikubwa *the holiday did him a ~ of good* likizo ilimsaidia sana *vt* tia nguvu/nishati. **~ful** *adj* -enye nguvu, -enye uwezo. **~less** *adj* -sio na nguvu, -sioweza kufanya kitu fulani; dhaifu *become ~less* potewa nguvu.

pow wow *n* baraza la Wahindi wa asili; *(colloq)* baraza, mkutano *vi* fanya mkutano.

pox *n* 1 *(syphilis)* sekeneko, kaswende. 2 *(arch)* ndui.

practice *n* 1 mazoezi ~ *makes perfect* mazoezi huleta ufanisi *you must do a lot of* ~ lazima ufanye mazoezi sana *I am out of* ~ sijafanya mazoezi. 2 utekelezaji, utendaji *put a plan into* ~ tekeleza mpango *in* ~ kwa vitendo. 3 mazoea, desturi. **make a ~ of** -wa na mazoea/desturi ya *the ~ of closing shops on Sundays* desturi ya kufunga maduka Jumapili *a matter of common* ~ ni jambo la mazoea; jambo la kawaida. 4 *(of doctor, lawyer)* kazi, weledi ~ *of law* uwakili ~ *of medicine* udaktari. 5 hila. **sharp** ~ tendo la ujanja *(pl) currupt ~s* rushwa. **practicable** *adj* 1 -a kuweza kufanyika/kutumika. 2 *(of roads)* -a kuendeka, -a kupitika. **practicability** *n*.

practical *adj* 1 -a utendaji ~ *problems* matatizo ya kiutendaji. 2 *(of persons, their character)* -a busara. **practicality** *n*. **practically** *adv*. **practicably** *adv*.

practise (US **practice**) *vt, vi* 1 fanya mazoezi ~ *the piano* jizoea kupiga kinanda. 2 -wa na desturi, tenda. ~ **what you preach** tenda unavyosema. 3 fanya kazi/weledi ~ *medicine* tibu ~ *law* fanya kazi ya sheria. 4 ~ **on/upon;** ~ **to do sth** lalia; okota; lia njama. **~d** *adj* eledi, -liobobea.

practician *n see* **practitioner**.

practitioner *n (leg)* 1 mweledi (hasa daktari/mwanasheria). **general** ~ **(GP)** daktari wa kawaida. 2

fundinjaa.

praetor *n (also* **pretor**) *(ancient Rome)* hakimu.

pragmatism *n* 1 nadharia ya vitendo. 2 ubwana. **pragmatist** *n.* **pragmatic** *adj* -a vitendo. **pragmatically** *adv.*

prairie *n* uwanda mpana wa majani (usio na miti); mbuga pana katika Amerika ya Kaskazini.

praise *vt* 1 sifu, himidi. 2 *(glorify)* adhimisha, tukuza. *n* 1 kusifu; sifa, himidi. 2 **sing sb's/one's own ~s** sifia/jisifu sana. 3 sifa; utukufu. **~worthiness** *n.* **~worthy** *adj.* **~worthily** *adv.*

pram *n see* **perambulator**

prance *vi* 1 *(of horse)* rukaruka, chachawa. 2 *(of person)* tembea kwa madaha/mikogo; randa, chezacheza (kwa furaha).

prank[1] *n* mzaha *play a ~ on sb* fanyia stihizai, mzaha, n.k.. **~ish** *adj* -a mzaha; -enye kupenda mzaha.

prank[2] *vi* jipanga kiajabu (agh. kwa kivutia macho ya mtazamaji) *~ a meadow with flowers* pamba konde kwa maua. ~ **oneself (out)** jipamba; jiona.

prate *vt* ~ **about** bwata, bwabwaja *n* kubwata. **~r** *n.* **prating** *adj.*

prattle *vt,vi* bwabwaja, bubujika maneno; toa maneno mengi (kama mtoto); ongea kitoto *n* maneno ya kitoto; vijineno, mapayo. **~r** *n.*

prawn *n* kamba.

praxis *n* 1 desturi, mila. 2 matumizi ya sanaa, sayansi au ufundi.

pray *vt,vi* 1 ~ **(to God)(for sth)** sali. **past ~ing for** -wa mahututi. **~ for** ombea. 2 ~ **sb for sth/to do sth** *(liter rhet)* omba, sihi. 3 tafadhali, kumradhi *~ tell me* tafadhali niambie. **~er** *n* 1 dua, sala. ~ **leader** imamu, msalishaji *the Lord's P~* Sala ya Bwana *say a ~* sali. ~ **book** *n* kitabu cha sala. 2 ibada. **Evening P~** Ibada ya Jioni. ~ **meeting** mkutano wa maombi. **~-mat, ~ rug** *n* ms(w)ala. **~erful** *adj* -enye kuomba, -a kusali, zoevu kwa kuomba/kusali.

pre- *(pref)* kabla ya. **~selection** uchaguzi wa awali.

preach *vt,vi* 1 ~ **(to)** hutubu, hubiri, hubiria, shawishi, shauri. **~ify** *vi* hubiria mno.

preamble *n* dibaji.

prearrange *vt* panga kabla. **~ment** *n* mipango ya awali.

prebend *n* mshahara (wa kasisi utokanao na michango ya kanisa).

precarious *adj* -a hatari, -a mashaka, -a wasiwasi. **~ness** *n.* **~ly** *adj.*

precast *adj (of concrete)* -lioundwa/finyangwa mapema.

precaution *n* hadhari, uangalifu *take ~* jihadhari. **~ary** *adj.*

precede *vt,vi* tangulia, sabiki. **preceding** *adj* tangulizi, -liotangulia. **~nce** *n* nafasi ya kwanza, umuhimu wa kwanza. **have/take ~nce (over)** fikiriwa kwanza, pewa umuhimu wa kwanza. **~nt** *n* kigezo; kitangulizi (cha jambo). **set/create/establish a ~ (for sth)** weka kigezo; wa mfano (wa kurejelea). **~nted** *adj.*

precentor *n (rel)* mtoa kongwe; mkurugenzi wa muziki (kanisani).

precept *n* 1 maadili. 2 agizo, mwongozo.

preceptor *n (formal)* mwalimu.

precession *n (astron)* ~ **of the equinoxes** mabadiliko ya ikwinoksi.

precinct *n* 1 ua (hasa wa kanisa). 2 *(pl)* mazingira ya jirani. 3 mpaka. 4 *(US)* jimbo la uchaguzi; kituo cha polisi. 5 eneo (lenye masharti ya kulitumia). **pedestrian ~** eneo la wenda kwa miguu. **shopping ~** -a maduka tu.

precious *adj* 1 -a thamani, -a tunu, ghali *~ stone* kito. 2 -a thamani kubwa, -a kupendwa sana. 3 *(colloq)* kabisa, mno *a ~ fool* mpumbavu. 4 *(of language)* -a kujifanya fasaha (kupita kiasi). **~ly** *adv.* **~ness** *n.* **preciosity** *n* ufasaha uliokithiri.

precipice *n* genge, jabali, poromoko; *(naut)* ombwe. **precipitious** *adj* -a kama genge, -enye mwinuko mkali sana.

precipitate *vt,vi* 1 *(hasten)* himiza, harakisha. 2 angusha, poromosha, tupa chini. ~ **sth/sb into sth** tupa/ ingiza kwenye/katika. 3 *(chem)* tenganisha maungo na myeyusho. 4 poza mvuke *n* vumbi/taka liangukalo katika maji yakituama *adj* -a harara, -a haraka, -epesi. **~ly** *adv*. **precipitation** *n* 1 haraka nyingi; harara. 2 kutuama, kuanguka chini (k.m. vumbi katika maji). 3 kunyesha kwa mvua, theluji, n.k.

precis *n* muhtasari; ufupisho wa maneno, beti, barua, n.k. *vt* fupisha.

precise *adj* 1 *(accurate)* sahihi, sawasawa kabisa *at that ~ moment* wakati uleule. 2 wazi, dhahiri. 3 *(careful)* -a taratibu, -angalifu. 4 -a kushika desturi/kawaida barabara. **~ly** *adv* kwa usahihi/uangalifu; kabisa. **precision** *n* usahihi, utaratibu, kutokuwa na makosa mahususi.

preclude *vt* ~ **sb from doing sth** zuia. **preclusion** *n*. **preclusive** *adj*.

precocious *adj* 1 -enye kukomaa upesi akili. 2 -enye akili za mtu mzima. 3 *(of plant)* -enye kupevuka mapema. **~ly** *adv*. **~ness** *n*. **precocity** *n*.

precognition *n* 1 ubashiri. 2 kujua jambo kabla halijatokea.

preconceive *vt* waza kabla ya *~d notion* wazo kabla ya kuona/kujua. **preconception** *n*.

preconcerted *adj* -liokubalika mbele.

precondition *n* sharti la mwanzo.

precursor *n* mtangulizi, mjumbe. **~y** *adj* tangulizi, bashirifu.

predatory *adj* 1 -a kunyang'anya/ kuteka/kupora. 2 *(of animals)* -a kuwinda (na kula wanyama wengine). **predator** *n*.

predecease *vt (leg)* -fa mbele, tangulia kufa.

predecessor *n* 1 mtangulizi ~ *in title* mtangulizi katika milki. 2 kitu kilichotangulia.

predestinate *vt see* **predestine**. *adj* -liojaaliwa, -lioamuliwa/andikwa kabla. **predestination** *n* majaaliwa; nadharia ya kwamba yote yatokeayo ni maamuzi ya Mungu na binadamu hana utashi nayo; nadharia ya kwamba Mungu ameamua kuwa wengine watakwenda mbinguni na wengine motoni. **predestine** *vt* ~ **sb to sth/to do sth** *(of God, fate)* amua kabla, amulia kabla.

predetermine *vt* 1 amua kabla. 2 ~ **sb to do sth** shawishi (mtu) kufanya kitu (kabla hajaamua kukifanya). **predetermination** *n*

predicament *n* mashaka, hali ngumu, hatari *he was in the same ~* alikuwa katika mashaka yale yale.

predicate *vt* 1 *(formal)* semea, arifu. 2 sababisha, leta *n (gram)* kundi arifu; kiarifu: neno au kundi linalotoa maelezo/taarifa juu ya kiima, k.m. *is beautiful* yu mrembo, katika **Upendo is beautiful** Upendo yu mrembo. **predication** *n*. **predicative** *adj (gram)* arifu, -a maelezo.

predict *vt* tabiri, bashiri, agua. **~ion** *n*. **~able** *adj*. **~ability** *n*.

predigest *vt* andaa chakula ili kiweze kumeng'enywa kwa urahisi (kwa ajili ya mtoto).

predilection *n* **a ~ for** upendeleo.

predispose *vt (formal)* ~ **sb to sth/to do sth** elekeza, ongoza, vuta. **predisposition** *n* ~ **to sth/to do sth** kuelekeza; maelekezo.

predominate *vi* ~ **(over)** pita, zidi, shinda. **predominant** *adj*. **predominant (over)** -enye nguvu au athari juu ya wengine; kuu. **predominantly** *adv*. **predominance** *n*.

preeminent *adj* -a kushinda wengine wote, -enye sifa fahari, cheo, uzuri, n.k., zaidi **preeminence** *n*. **~ly** *adv*.

pre-empt *vt* 1 *(formal)* wahi kununua kabla ya wengine kupewa nafasi. 2 wahi kufanya jambo kabla ya wengine. **~ion** *n right of ~ ion* haki ya kununua kwanza (kabla ya wengine) au mbele. **~ive** *adj (leg)* -a haki ya shufaa.

preen *vt* 1 *(of birds)* puna manyoya kwa mdomo. 2 *(of person)*

jinadhifisha. ~ **oneself on** *(fig)* jivunia.
pre-exist *vi* wako/ishi kabla. **~ence** maisha ya roho kabla ya mtu kuzaliwa. **~ent** *adj*.
prefab *(colloq abbr of)* **prefabricated house** *see* **prefabricate**.
prefabricate *vt* tengeneza majengo kabla ya kuyaunganisha. **~d house** nyumba iliyojengwa kwa vifaa vilivyotengenezwa mbele/kabla.
preface *n* dibaji *vt* andika dibaji. ~ **sth with sth/by doing sth** anza. **prefatory** *adj* -a utangulizi (wa kitabu).
prefect *n* 1 *(ancient Rome)* gavana, hakimu mkuu. 2 *(school)* kiranja. 3 *(France, Japan)* mkuu wa wilaya; *(France)* mkurugenzi wa polisi wa Paris. **~ure** *n* 1 *(France, Japan)* wilaya. 2 *(France)* makao makuu ya polisi.
prefer *vt* 1 ~ **(to)** stahabu, hitari; penda zaidi *he ~s to die rather than (to) surrender* anaona heri kufa kuliko kujisalimisha 2. leta (mashtaka, maombi, n.k.). ~ **a charge/charges against sb** shitaki mtu. 3 ~ **sb (to sb)** pandisha cheo. **~able** *adj* afadhali, zaidi, heri, -ema zaidi, bora. **~ably** *adv*. **~ence** *n* 1 upendeleo, hiari *a mark of ~* alama ya upendeleo. 2 kiteule, kitu kilichohitariwa *his is my ~ence* napenda hiki. 3 hisa, uteuzi. ~ **share** hisa maalum ya upendeleo. **~ential** *adj* -a kupendelea/ upendeleo. **~ment** *n* kuzidisha cheo, kupandisha cheo; kupata kazi (daraja) bora.
prefigure *vt* 1 ona mbele. 2 onyesha/ bainisha/eleza kabla.
prefix *vt* ambisha awali; tia mwanzoni; tanguliza *n* 1 *(gram)* kiambishi awali. 2 neno au jina lililotiwa kabla ya jina la mtu, k.m. Bw., Bi, Dkt.
pregnant *adj* 1 -enye mimba ~ *woman* mjamzito. 2 *(of words, actions)* -a maana nyingi *this is a very ~ word* neno hili lachukua maana nyingi. ~ **with** -liojawa na. **pregnancy** *n* mimba, ujauzito. **pregnable** *adj (of fort etc)* -lioweza kukamatwa, kuingilika.
prehensile *adj (bio) (of tail etc)* -enye nguvu ya kushika.
prehistoric, **~al** *adj* -a kabla ya historia, -a zamani za kale. **prehistory** *n*.
prejudge *vt* kata maneno kabla ya kusikia kisa chake, hukumu bila kusikiliza. **~ment** *n*.
prejudice *n* 1 maoni/hisia za mapenzi/ chuki bila sababu. 2 *(leg)* athari, madhara, dhuluma *to the ~ of sb* kuelekea kumletea fulani madhara. **without ~ (to)** bila kuleta athari/ madhara kwa haki/madai yaliyopo *vt* 1 pendelea, bagua, chukiza. ~ **sb (against/in favour of sb/sth)** fanya upendeleo kwa/dhidi ya. 2 dhuru, athiri; haribu/punguza upendeleo wa mtu. **prejudicial** *adj*.
prelate *n* askofu. **prelacy** *n* uaskofu; jamii ya maaskofu.
prelim *(colloq abbr for* **preliminary)** 1 mtihani wa awali. 2 kurasa za mwanzo (kabla ya kurasa za matini).
preliminary *adj* -a mwanzo, tangulizi ~ *inquiry* uchunguzi wa mwanzo *n* 1 kitangulizi, utangulizi. 2 *(pl)* **preliminaries** mambo ya mwanzo/ awali.
prelude *n* ~ **to** mwanzo (wa matendo, habari, muziki n.k. unaotangulia matendo n.k. yenyewe hasa); dibaji *vt* anzisha, tangulia.
premarital *adj* -a kabla ya ndoa.
premature *adj* -a kabla ya wakati wake; -a haraka. ~ **baby** *n* kabichi/ (mtoto) njiti. **~ly** *adv* kabla ya wakati wake. **prematurity** *n*.
premeditate *vt* waza, azimu, panga mapema, dhamiria. **~d** *adj* -enye kudhamiriwa. ~ **murder** *n* mauaji yaliyodhamiriwa. **premeditation** *n* kudhamiria.
premier *adj* -a kwanza, -kuu *n* waziri mkuu. **~ship** *n* uwaziri mkuu.
premiere *n* onyesho la kwanza (k.m. la filamu, mchezo wa kuigiza n.k.).

premise/premiss *n* 1 kauli -gezi/ kigezo: kauli ambayo ndiyo msingi wa maelezo au hitimisho. 2 kigezo mantiki: mojawapo ya sehemu mbili za kwanza katika hitimisho la kimantiki. 3 *(pl)* kipande cha ardhi chenye majengo; nyumba au sehemu ya nyumba na eneo linaloandamana nayo. 4 *(leg)* maelezo ya mali na majina (ya wenye mali) katika sehemu ya kwanza ya mkataba wa kisheria *vt* ~ **(sth/that)** sema kwanza.

premium *n* 1 zawadi; bonasi. **put a ~ on sb** fanya mtu ashawishike kufanya jambo fulani. **put a ~ on sth** shawishi. 3 ada *insurance ~* malipo ya bima. 4 malipo ya uanagenzi. 5 thamani ya juu. **at a ~** *(fig)* -liothaminiwa sana.

premonition *n* wasiwasi, jakamoyo (ya kuwa jambo litatukia). **premonitory** *adj* -enye jakamoyo.

prenatal *adj* -a kabla ya kuzaliwa.

prentice *n (old use) (short for* **apprentice**) **try his ~ hand** jaribu kufanya bila ufundi.

preoccupy *vt* shughulisha; fikirisha. **preoccupation** *n* mshughuliko; jambo lenye kumshughulisha mtu.

prepackaged/prepacked *adj (of products)* -liofungwa kabla ya kuuzwa.

preordain *vt* amua, agiza kabla.

prepare *vt,vi* 1 tayarisha, andaa, zatiti *~ for examination* jiandaa kwa mtihani. 2 pika *~ a meal* pika chakula. 3 *(construct)* fanya. 4 **be ~d to** weza, kubali, -wa tayari. **~dness** *n.* **prep** *n (schoolboy slang for* **preparation)** kazi ya nyumbani.

preparation *n* 1 kutayarisha, matayarisho; kuandaa, maandalizi. 2 *(mixture)* mchanganyiko (wa chakula, dawa n.k.); *(medicine)* dawa. 3 *(colloq abbr prep)* kazi ya nyumbani. 4 *(usu pl)* maandalizi. **preparatory** *adj* -a matayarisho. **~ school** *(US)* shule ya matayarisho kwa sekondari/ chuo kikuu; *(GB)* shule ya msingi ya binafsi *adv* kwa njia ya matayarisho.

prepay *vt* lipa mbele/kabla; lipia ada mbele.

prepense *adj* -liokusudiwa mbele, -liopangwa kabla *malice ~* -a nia ya kudhuru. **~ly** *adv.*

preponderant *adj* -a kuzidi, -kubwa, -ingi (kwa uzito, nguvu, idadi n.k.). **preponderance** *n.* **~ly** *adv.* **preponderate** *vi* zidi, -wa na nguvu (nyingi); zidi kwa uzito, idadi, athari n.k.

preposition *n (gram)* kihusishi. **~al** *adj (gram)* -a kihusishi.

prepossess *vi (formal)* pendeza, vutia *his conduct ~ed me in his favour* tabia yake ilinivutia. **~ing** *adj* -a kuvutia, -a kupendeza. **~ion** *n* mvuto.

preposterous *adj* -sio na maana/ mantiki; -a upuuzi. **~ly** *adv.* **~ness** *n.*

prepuce *n* govi, zunga.

prerecord *vt* rekodi (ukanda) mapema.

prerequisite sharti *adj* -a sharti.

prerogative *n* haki/hiari/ ridhaa. **royal ~** haki ya pekee ya kifalme. **~ writ** haki ya pekee *be the ~ of* -wa haki ya.

presage *n* dalili, ishara (ya mambo yatakayo kuja); ndege (mbaya au njema).

presbyterian *n* **P~ Church** *n* kanisa la Kiprotestanti (linaloongozwa na wazee wenye cheo sawa); muumini wa kanisa hilo. **~ism** *n* Upresibiteri: mfumo wa uongozi wa kanisa la Presibiteri. **presbyter** *n* mzee wa kanisa. **presbytery** *n* 1 uongozi wa baraza la mkoa wa kanisa la Presibiteri. *(RC)* nyumba ya paroko.

prescient *adj (formal)* -enye kujua, -a kuweza kubashiri (mambo yatakayokuja). **~ly** *adv.* **prescience** *n.*

prescribe *vt* 1 agiza, amuru. 2 shauri. **~ sth (for sth)** shauri/agiza matumizi ya. **prescript** *n* amri, agizo. **prescription** *n* 1 maagizo. 2 agizo la daktari *make out a ~ for a medicine* andika maagizo ya matumizi ya dawa. **prescriptive** *adj* -enye kuagiza, -enye kuelekeza.

~ **grammar** *n* sarufi elekezi.

presence-chamber *n* baraza/ sebule kuu (wanamopokelewa watu wa heshima).

present[1] *adj* 1 -liopo *be* ~ -wapo *he is* ~ yupo. ~ **company excepted** *(colloq)* ukiacha waliopo. 2 -a sasa, -a siku hizi, -a wakati huu *the* ~ *government* serikali ya sasa. 3 *(arch)* -a mara moja, tayari; -a wakati wa kufaa. 4 ~ **to** -nayokumbukwa (na) *n* 1 wakati uliopo, wakati wa sasa, siku hizi. **at** ~ sasa, wakati huu. **for the** ~ kwa wakati huu. **up to the** ~ mpaka sasa. 2 *(gram)* wakati uliopo; 3 *(pl) (leg)* **by these** ~**s** kwa hati hii. ~**-day** *adj* -a siku hizi. ~**ly** *adv* 1 sasa hivi, hivi karibuni. 2 sasa. **presence** *n* 1 kuwapo mahali, sehemu n.k. *in the* ~ *of* mbele ya, machoni pa, panapo *your* ~ *is requested* kuwepo kwako kunahitajiwa. 2 sura, umbo; namna mtu anavyojichukua au anavyoonekana *vt* 1 ~ **sth to sb;** ~ **sb with sth** toa, tunukia, tuza ~ *a cheque at the bank (for payment)* toa hawala katika benki (kwa kulipwa fedha). 2 fichua, onyesha, dhihirisha. 3 ~ **sb to sb** tambulisha rasmi. 4 *(arms)* ~ **sth at sb** lenga. 5 *(mil)* ~ **arms** toa heshima (kwa silaha). 6 *(reflex)* hudhuria, fika. 7 *(theatre)* onyesha *n* zawadi, tuzo. **give away a** ~, **make sb a** ~ **of sth** tunukia, zawadia. ~**ee** *n* anayefikishiwa/anayepewa/tunukiwa zawadi. ~**er** *n* mtangazaji (wa kipindi cha redio/TV); mtoa zawadi. ~**ation** *n* 1 kupa, kutoa, kuwasilisha. **payable on** ~**ation** -liopasa kulipwa kwa kutoa kitu. 2 tuzo, zawadi (hasa iliyotolewa mbele ya watu). 3 maonyesho.

presentable *adj* -a kupendeza, -zuri, -a kufaa; -a kupendeza mbele ya watu. **presentably** *adv*.

presentiment *n* 1 wasiwasi, hofu *have a* ~ *of sth* -wa na wasiwasi kwamba kitu fulani kitatokea.

preserve *vt* 1 ~ **from** tunza, linda. 2 hifadhi (kwa kukoleza, kukausha, n.k.). 3 *(of game)* hifadhi *n* 1 jemu. 2 hifadhi (za wanyama). **poach on another's** ~ shiriki/ingilia kazi (ambayo kwa kawaida ni ya mtu mwingine). **preservable** *adj*. ~**r** *n* kihifadhi; mlinzi, mhifadhi, mwokozi. **preservation** *n* kulinda, hifadhi, kuhifadhi hali *be in a good state of* ~ -wa katika hali ya kutunzwa vizuri. **preservative** *adj* -a kulinda, -a kuponya, -a kuhifadhi *n* dawa ya kuzuia kitu kisioze.

preside *vi* 1 ~ **at** -wa mwenyekiti. 2 ongoza. ~ **over a company** ongoza kampuni ya biashara.

president *n* rais(i). ~**ial** *adj* -a rais(i) **P~ Commission** *n* Tume ya Rais(i). **presidency** *n* 1 uraisi(i). 2 ofisi ya rais(i).

presidium *(in communist countries)* Kamati ya Kudumu ya Utendaji.

press *n* 1 mgandamizo. 2 shinikizo, kisindiko; mtambo wa kusindika. 3 **the** ~ waandishi wa habari/magazeti. **the freedom of** ~ *n* uhuru wa magazeti. ~ **agent** *n* afisa uhusiano/mtangazaji (wa wasanii). ~**box** *n* kibanda cha waandishi wa habari. ~ **conference** *n* mkutano baina ya waandishi habari. ~ **cutting/ clipping** kipande kilichotolewa gazetini/jaridani (kwa kukata). ~**gallery** *n* ukumbi wa waandishi habari bungeni. ~ **lord** kizito wa magazeti. ~ **photographer** *n* mpiga picha wa gazeti. 4 upigaji chapa *(also printing ~)* kiwanda/mtambo wa kupiga chapa. **in the** ~ mtambo, vitabu, n.k.. ~ **mark** alama ya maktaba (kwenye kitabu). 5 umati (wa watu), msongamano; zahama. 6 kabati (la nguo, vitabu n.k.). 7 ~ **gang** kundi (la kukamata watu na kuwalazimisha wajiunge na jeshi) *vt,vi* 1 gandamiza. 2 minya; *(of button, etc)* bonyeza. 3 *(of fruit)* kama, sindika. 4 *(of clothes)* piga pasi, nyoosha. 5 *(mill)* bana. 6 *(argument)* ~ **sth on/upon sb** sisitiza. 7 ~ **for** sihi, dai sana, himiza. 8 **be** ~**ed for** pungukiwa na. 9 *(of people)* songamana. 10 ~ **sb for sth** dai;

sukuma. 11 **time ~es** hapana muda (wa kupoteza). 12 ~ **(down)/ (up) on sb/sth** lemea, gandamiza. 13 ~ **on/forward** endelea kwa bidii *adj* 1 -a haraka, -a hima. 2 muhimu. 3 -a kudai *n* chapa ya sahani ya santuri.

pressure *n* 1 shinikizo; kanieneo. ~- **cooker** sufuria ya mvuke. ~ **gauge** geji ya kanieneo. 2 mkazo, mbano, mlemeo *exert* ~ bana. **be/come under** ~ banwa. **bring ~ to bear on sb/put ~ on sb/put sb under ~ (to do sth)** shurutisha. ~ **group** kundi shawishi: kundi/shirika la watu linalojaribu kuvuta serikali/wabunge/wananchi wawe upande wao. **at high** ~ kwa nguvu/kasi sana. **pressurized** *adj (of an aircraft, a submarine etc)* -enye kudhibiti kanieneo.

prestidigitator *n* mfanya mazingaombwe. **prestidigitation** *n* mazingaombwe.

prestige *n* 1 sifa njema, hadhi kubwa (kwa ajili ya matendo, maarifa, tabia n.k. inayojulikana). 2 heshima, fahari kuu (inayotokana na mafanikio, mali, n.k.).

prestressed *adj* -liotiwa nondo.

presume *vt,vi* 1 dhania, kisia, waza. 2 *(dare)* thubutu, fanya pasipo ruhusa/pasipo haki. ~ **upon sth** tumia vibaya. 3 ~ **upon sb's good nature** tumia vibaya ukarimu wa mtu. **presuming** *adj*. **presumption** *n* 1 kiburi, ufidhuli, usafihi, ujuvi. 2 *(probability)* jambo linalowezekana. **presumptive** *adj* -a kutazamiwa, -a kusadikiwa, -a kutarajiwa *heir* ~ mrithi mdhaniwa ~ *evidence* ushahidi wa kukisiwa. **presumptively** *adv*. **presumptuous** *adj (formal)* -enye kiburi, fidhuli, -juvi; -enye kujiamini mno. **~ly** *adv*.

presuppose *vt* 1 dhani. 2 *(imply)* hitaji; maanisha. **presupposition** *n* dhanio.

pretend *vt,vi* 1 jifanya, jisingizia ~ *to be* jisingizia kuwa; jifanya kuwa. 2 danganya. 3 ~ **to** dai. **~edly** *adv*. **~er** *n*. **pretence** *n* (US **pretense**) 1 kujifanya, kujisingizia. **false ~s** *(leg)* hila, ulaghai. 2 kisingizio.

pretentious *adj* -a kujidai. **pretentiously** *adv*. **pretentiousness** *n*.

preternatural *adj* -sio -a kawaida, -si -a desturi, -a ajabu.

pretext *n* kisingizio.

pretty *adj* 1 -zuri; safi; -a kupendeza. 2 *(colloq)* -kubwa -ingi. **a ~ penny** pesa nyingi. 3 (kwa mwanariadha) hodari *n (used of a child)* kipenzi. **my** ~ kipenzi changu. **come to/reach a ~ pass** fikia hali ngumu *adv* kiasi. ~ **much/ nearly/almost** karibu *it is ~ hot* joto kiasi *I'm ~ well* sijambo kidogo/kiasi. **sitting** ~ *(colloq)* katika nafasi nzuri. **prettily** *adv*. **prettiness** *n*.

prevail *vi* 1 ~ **(over/against)** shinda. 2 enea, tapakaa. 3 ~ **on/upon sb to do sth** shawishi. **~ing** *adj* -a kawaida; -lioenea. ~ **winds** pepo za kawaida. ~ **fashions** mitindo iliyoenea. **prevalent** *adj (formal)* -lioenea, -a kuenea, tele. **prevalence** *n*.

prevaricate *vi (formal)* ongopa, epa kusema ukweli wote. **prevarication** *n*. **prevaricator** *n*.

prevent *vt* 1 ~ **sb (from doing sth; sth (from happening)** zuia, kinza, kataza. 2 *(arch)* ongoza. **~able** *adj*. **~ion** *n* kuzuia; zuio; kukinga, kinga. ~ **is better than cure** *(prov)* heri kuzuia kuliko kuponya; hadhari kabla ya hatari/athari. **~ive** *adj* -a kuzuia, -a kulinda, -a kukinga, -a hadhari. ~ **custody** kifungo cha hadhari. ~ **detention** kizuizini. ~ **medicine** utafiti wa dawa za kinga. ~ **officer** afisa forodha mzuiaji magendo. ~ *n* kinga.

preview *n* onyesho la awali (la filamu, mchezo n.k) kabla ya kuonyeshwa kwa wote *vt* onyesha mchezo, filamu, n.k. kabla ya kuonyeshwa kwa wote.

previous *adj* 1 -a kwanza, -liotangulia, -a zamani ~ *convictions* makosa ya zamani. 2 -a pupa/harara. 3 ~ *to* kabla. **~ly** *adv*.

prevision *n* utabiri.

prey *n* mawindo, mateka, nyara. **beast of** ~ mnyama mbua, mnyama mkali. **bird of** ~ ndege mbua k.m. tai. **be/fall** ~ **to** shikwa/kamatwa; *(fig)* sumbuliwa sana na. **be a** ~ **to fears** shikwa na hofu *vi* ~ **on/upon** 1 winda. 2 iba. 3 *(harass)* sumbua sana. ~ **on sb's mind** sumbua mtu kwa mawazo, chezea akili ya mtu.

price *n* 1 bei. **every person has his** ~ kila mtu anaweza kuhongwa. **put a** ~ **on sb's head** toa zawadi ya kumkamata mhalifu (akiwa hai au amekufa). **asking** ~ bei ya mwanzo/ya kuanzia kuuza kitu. ~ **control** *n* kudhibiti bei. ~**-list** orodha ya bei ya mauzo. **list** ~ *n* bei iliyopendekezwa na mtengenezaji. 2 thamani. **beyond/above/without** ~ -enye thamani isiyopimika. 3 dau **What** ~? kuna matumaini gani? *(used to sneer at the failure of sth)* ovyo! bure! *bride*~ mahari *vt* weka/panga bei. ~ **oneself/one's goods out of the market** weka bei kubwa mpaka bidhaa zisiuzike. ~**ly** *adj* ghali. ~**less** *adj* 1 -a thamani mno. 2 *(sl)* -a kuchekesha!

prick *n* 1 mchomo, maumivu (yatokeayo baada ya kuchomwa na sindano, mwiba, n.k.). **kick against the** ~**s** *(fig)* jiumiza, jisumbua bure. 2 alama/kitundu/kitobo (kitokeacho baada ya kuchomwa na sindano, mwiba, n.k.). 3 kitu kilichochomoza na chenye ncha kali k.m. pembe. 4 *(vulgar)* mboo *(term of abuse) you silly* ~ mpumbavu we! *vt,vi* 1 choma *(fig) his conscious ~ed him* dhamira yake ilimsuta/umiza. 2 toboa ~ *a hole in sth* toboa tundu. 3 hisi maumivu makali (kutokana na) kuchomwa au kutogwa. 4 ~ **sth out/off** atika, pandikiza katika kitu. 5 ~ **up one's ears** simamisha masikio, sikiliza kwa makini. ~**le** *n* mwiba *vt,vi* 1 chomachoma, washa. ~**ly** *adj* 1 -enye kuchomachoma; -enye miiba. ~**ly pear** mpungate. 2 ~**ly heat** vipele vya harara. 3 *(colloq)* -enye kuudhika haraka; -enye harara.

pride *n* 1 kiburi, majivuno, usodai. **false** ~ majivuno yasiyo na msingi. 2 *(display)* fahari, makuu; kujikweza mno. **take (a)** ~ **in sb/sth** ona fahari juu ya mtu/kitu. ~ **of place** nafasi yenye hadhi kubwa. 3 heshima *wound sb's* ~ haribu heshima ya mtu. 4 kitu cha kujivunia, kitu cha kusifiwa sana, tunu, kipenzi. 5 **the** ~ **of** kipeo. 6 kundi. ~ **of lions** kundi la simba *vt (reflex)* ~ **oneself on/upon sth** jidai, jivunia.

prie dieu *n* kibao cha kupigia magoti wakati wa kusali.

priest *n* 1 kasisi, padri. ~ **ridden** -liotawaliwa mno na mapadri. 2 kuhani. ~**craft** *n* ujanja wa makuhani au makasisi. ~**ess** *n* kasisi wa kike. ~**hood** *n* jumuiya makasisi. ~**ly**, ~**like** *adj* -a padri, -a kasisi, -a kuhani.

prig *n* 1 mjuvi, mtu anayejiona bora sana. ~**gish** *adj* juvi/-enye kujiona. ~**gishly** *adv*. ~**gishness** *n*.

prim *adj* 1 taratibu, -a makini *she is* ~ hataki upuuzi, yu baridi, ana makini. 2 nadhifu *vt* kunja uso/bibidua mdomo.

primacy *n* 1 ubora. 2 uaskofu mkuu.

primaeval *adj see* **primeval**.

prima facie *adv adj (L)* (kama) inavyoonekana mwanzoni. ~ **evidence** *(leg)* ushahidi wa kutosha (mpaka inapothibitika vinginevyo).

primary *adj* -a kwanza, -a awali, -a msingi. ~ **colours** rangi za msingi: nyekundu, buluu na manjano ~ *school* shule ya msingi ~ *assembly (meeting)* mkutano wa awali wa siasa. *(USA) primaries* uchaguzi wa mwanzo. 2 *(important)* -a muhimu, kuu, -a maana. **primarily** *adv* kwanza, hasa. **prima** *adj* 1 -a kwanza, -a asili. 2 *(important)* -kuu, -a msingi. **prima donna** mwimbaji mkuu wa kike katika opera; *(colloq)* -enye majivuno. **prima ballerina** mchezaji mkuu wa kike katika balei.

primate[1] *n* askofu mkuu. ~**ship** *n* uaskofu.

primate[2] *n* mamalia wa hali ya juu.

prime *adj* 1 -kuu, -a kwanza. **P~ Minister** Waziri Mkuu. **P~ Meridian** Meridiana kuu. 2 *(math)* tasa. **~ number** namba tasa. 3 bora *~ meat* nyama bora. 4 -a asili, -a msingi. **~ cost** bei ya uzalishaji tu. **~ mover** chanzo cha nguvu; *(fig)* mwanzilishi *in ~ condition* katika hali ya asili *n* 1 upeo, ukamilifu, usitawi, uzima *he is past his ~* amezeeka *the ~ of life* ujana. 2 sehemu iliyo bora. 3 mwanzo. 4 *(rel)* ibada ya alfajiri *vt* 1 andaa *~ a gun (hist)* tia baruti kwenye bunduki *~ a pump (fig)* weka rasilimali/fedha katika mradi (ili kuuendeleza). 2 somesha mafundisho ya kwanza, erevusha, julisha mambo. 3 -pa/jaza na chakula au kinywaji. 4 paka rangi ya mkono wa kwanza. 5 tia maji (mafuta, petroli) kidogo. 6 pewa/pa taarifa za kweli. *~ n 1 (of school)* kitabu cha kwanza 2 fataki (kwa kuwasha baruti) 3 mpako/mkono wa kwanza wa rangi. **priming** *n* 1 baruti. 2 mpako/mkono wa kwanza wa rangi.

primeval *(also* **primaeval)** *adj* 1 -a asili. 2 -a kale.

primitive *adj* 1 -a asili, -a kale. 2 -siostaarabika, shenzi *n* mchoraji au mchongaji wa zamani za kale. **~ly** *adv.* **~ness** *n.*

primogeniture *n* 1 uwanambee; kuwa mwanambee. 2 *(leg)* mfumo ambao kwao mali ya mzazi hurithiwa na mtoto wa kwanza wa kiume.

primordial *adj* 1 -a kwanza. 2 -a asili.

primp *vt see* **prink**.

primus *n* **(~ stove)** stovu.

prince *n* 1 mwana mfalme. **the P~ of Peace** Kristo. **P~ Consort** mme wa Malkia. **~dom** *n* dola ya mwana mfalme. 2 mtoto wa kiume katika ukoo wa kifalme. **~ly** *adj* -a kustahili ufalme; zuri, -a fahari. **~ss** *n* kibibi, binti mfalme. **principality** *n* himaya ya mwana mfalme.

principal *adj* -kuu *n* 1 mkuu. 2 *(fin)* rasilimali, mtaji. 3 wakala. 4 *(leg)* mhalifu mkuu. 5 *(of house)* kombamoyo kuu. **~ly** *adv* kwa kiasi kikubwa, kwa kawaida.

principle *n* 1 kanuni. 2 maadili; msimamo *of no ~s* -siokuwa na maadili. **in ~** kwa jumla, kimsingi. **on ~** kimsimamo. **~d** *adj* -enye msimamo/maadili.

prink *vt* **~ oneself (up)** vaa malidadi, *(of bird)* puna.

print *n* 1 chapa. 2 alama *foot ~s* nyayo *finger ~s* alama za vidole. 3 kitabu; chapisho. 4 kitambaa cha maua. 5 *(of a book)* **in ~** kilichochapishwa na kinachouzwa. **out of ~** kitabu kisichopatikana; kutopatikana *in large ~s* kwa maandishi makubwa. 6 picha, mchoro. 7 mwandiko wa wima. **~-seller** *n* mwuza michoro *vt,vi* 1 tia alama; *(fig) (impress)* ingiza moyoni, tia moyoni.2 piga chapa *his paper is now being ~ed* gazeti lake liko mtamboni. 3 **~ (off)** safisha picha; **~ out** *n* katarasi za kompyuta zilizochapwa. 4 *(of plate or film)* chapisha. 5 weka alama/mchoro (kwenye nguo/kitambaa). **~able** *adj* -a kuchapika. **~er** *n* mpiga chapa. **~ing - ink** *n* wino wa kupigia chapa **~ing -machine, ~ing press** *n* matbaa. **~ing office** *n* matbaa; kiwanda cha kupiga chapa.

prior[1] *adj* **~ (to)** -a awali, -a mbele, -liotangulia, kabla *~ claim* dai la awali *~ notice* taarifa ya awali/mbele *adv* **~ to sth** kabla ya jambo *~ to his appointment* kabla ya kuteuliwa kwake.

prior[2] *n (rel)* mkuu wa nyumba ya watawa. **~ess** *n* Mama mkuu wa nyumba ya watawa. **~y** *n* nyumba ya watawa.

priority *n* aula, kipaumbele, umuhimu wa kwanza, haki ya kutangulia. *first/top ~* aula ya kwanza.

prise *vt see* **prize**.

prism *n* mche. **~atic** *adj* 1 -a mche. 2 -enye rangi anuwai zilizoiva.

prison *n* gereza, jela *commit to ~* funga, peleka gerezani. **~ officer** ofisa wa magereza. **remand ~**

mahabusi. ~ **breaker** *n* mtoroka gerezani. ~-**breaking** *n* kutoroka jela. ~**er** *n* mfungwa. ~ **of conscience** *n* mfungwa wa kisiasa. ~ **of war** mfungwa wa vita.

pristine *adj (formal)* -a zamani za kale, -a asili; bichi, safi kabisa.

prithee *int (arch)* tafadhali.

private *adj* 1 -a binafsi ~ *property* mali ya binafsi. ~ **school** *n* shule ya kulipa/binafsi. ~ **enterprise** biashara binafsi. ~ **means** mapato binafsi (yatokanayo na mali/vitegauchumi vya mtu binafsi). 2 -a faragha, -a siri *keep sth* ~ weka vitu faraghani. ~ **parts** uchi, sehemu za siri. 3 -sio na kazi/cheo rasmi (katika serikali au shirika). **retire into** ~ **life** acha kazi ya serikali. ~ **member** *(GB)* mbunge huru asiye na chama. 4 ~ **soldier** askari (asiye na cheo) *n* 1 askari. 2 faragha, siri. **in** ~ faraghani, sirini. ~**ly** *adv*. **privacy** *n* 1 faragha *right to* ~ haki ya kutoingiliwa *do sth in strict*~ fanya kitu faraghani sana. 2 siri.

privateer *n (formerly)* merikebu mamluki: merikebu yenye ruhusa ya kufanya vita pekee. 2 nahodha wa merikebu. *(pl)* ~**s** mabaharia wa merikebu hii.

privation *n* 1 ufukara. 2 hali ya kukoseshwa/kunyimwa.

privilege *n* 1 marupurupu. 2 faida kubwa *listening to him was a* ~ ilikuwa ni faida kubwa kumsikiliza. 3 haki *diplomatic* ~ haki za kidiplomasia *parliamentary* ~ haki ya Bunge. 4 upendeleo, fadhila. 5 heshima *I was ~d to see the President* nilipewa heshima ya kumwona Rais *vt* pendelea. ~ *adj* -liobahatika. ~ **class** tabaka la matajiri. **under**-~ wachochole, maskini.

privy *adj* 1 *(leg)* -a siri. **be** ~ **to** jua siri, shiriki siri. 2 ~ **Council** Baraza (la ushauri la Mfalme). ~ **seal** lakiri ya Mfalme. **P**~ **Purse** ruzuku ya mfalme *n (arch)* choo. **privily** *adv* kwa siri. **privity** *n* 1 uhusiano ~ *of contract* uhusiano katika mkataba ~ *of estate* uhusiano katika miliki. 2 siri, maarifa ya siri.

prize[1], **prise** *vt* ~ **up (out, open)** fungua kwa nguvu (kwa mtaimbo, n.k.).

prize[2] *n* 1 tuzo, zawadi. 2 *(fig)* kitu cha thamani, azizi, dafina. 3 ~ **fight** *n* shindano la masumbwi la kulipwa. ~ **fighter** *n* bondia wa kulipwa. ~-**fighting** *n* mashindano ya masumbwi (ya kulipwa). ~**ring** *n* ulingo wa masumbwi. 4 ~**man** *n* mshindi wa tuzo ya uanazuoni. ~ **winner** *n* mshindi wa tuzo *vt* thamini sana, tunuka.

prize[3] *n* mateka, nyara (agh. meli au mizigo yake) wakati wa vita. ~-**money** *n* 1 fedha itokanayo na mauzo ya nyara. 2 dau.

pro[1] *n (usu only in)* **the ~s and cons (of sth)** ubaya na uzuri. ~ **and con** *adv* kwa ubaya na uzuri.

pro[2] *n (pl) (colloq) (abbr)* **professional (player)**.

pro- *(pref)* -enye kuunga mkono. ~-**government** -enye kuunga mkono serikali. ~**consul** kaimu balozi.

probable *adj* -lioelekea kutokea kuwa, yamkini *it is* ~ inaelekea *the ~ result will be* matokeo yake yanaelekea yatakuwa ~ *cause* sababu ya kumkinika *n* anayeelekea kuchaguliwa. **probability** *n* welekeo. **in all** ~ huelekea, yamkini *no ~ of* hakuna welekeo wa uwezekano. **balance of probabilities** kipimo cha welekeo **probably** *adv* huenda, labda, yumkini.

probate *n* uthibitisho wa wasia; kuthibitisha (wasia); hati ya uthibitisho (wa wasia) *vt* thibitisha.

probation *n* 1 majaribio *on* ~ katika majaribio. 2 **the** ~ **system** *(leg)* mfumo wa majaribio (ya wahalifu kuishi bila kufanya kosa). ~ **officer** ofisa wa majaribio. ~**ary** *adj* -a majaribio. ~**er** *n* 1 nesi mwanafunzi (katika majaribio). 2 *(leg)* mhalifu (aliye chini ya majaribio/uangalizi).

probe *n* 1 *(med)* kipima kidonda: kifaa

butu cha kupimia kina cha kidonda n.k. 2 *(journalism)* uchunguzi (wa jambo) *vt* 1 pima kina cha kidonda.2 chunguza jambo kwa undani/makini.

probity *n (formal)* uaminifu, unyofu, uadilifu.

problem *n* 1 tatizo; utata; mzozo; mgogoro. ~ **child** mtoto sugu/ mtukutu. ~ **play/novel** tamthiliya/ riwaya ya matatizo/maadili ya kijamii. 2 swali, hoja. 3 mashaka, fumbo, neno gumu. **~atic** *adj* tatanishi. **~atically** *adv*.

proboscis *n* 1 mkonga, mwiro. 2 *(of insect)* mrija. 3 *(joc)* pua ya mtu.

procedure *n* utaratibu. **procedural** *adj* -a utaratibu, -a mwenendo.

proceed *vi* 1 ~ **to sth/to do sth** endelea mbele, enda, shika njia *he ~ ed to say* aliendelea kusema. ~ **with sth** anza, endelea na. 2 ~ **from sth** toka. ~ **(from)** tokana (na) hali. 3 ~ **against sb** shtaki.

proceeding *n* 1 kutenda/utendaji (wa) jambo; namna ya kutenda jambo/ kitu. 2 tendo, jambo lililotendwa. 3 *(pl)* **take/start legal ~s (against sb)** shtaki, dai sheriani. 4 *(pl)* kumbukumbu, mashauri mafupi.

proceeds *n (pl)* mapato.

process *n* 1 njia, jinsi, namna. 2 mfuatano/mlolongo wa mambo; maendeleo. **in ~ of time** wakati wa. 3 mfanyiko tendani *the Bessemer ~* mfanyiko tendani wa Bessemer. 4 *(leg)* hati. ~ **server** muasilishi hati. **legal** ~ daawa, mashataka, hukumu. 5 **in** ~ wakati inapofanyika *vt* tengeneza, tenda; *(photography)* safisha. **~ing** *adj* -a utengenezaji *vi* andamana. **~ion** *n* mfuatano, msululu; *(demonstration)* maandamano *walk in a ~* andamana. **~ional** *adj* -a maandamano.

proclaim *vt* 1 tangaza, piga mbiu, eneza, toa ilani *~ sb a traitor* tangaza mtu kuwa haini. ~ **war** piga mbiu ya vita, tangaza vita. 2 onyesha, bainisha. **proclamation** *n*.

proclivity *n* ~ **(to/towards sth/ to do sth)** mwelekeo, tabia; *(aptitude)* welekevu *he has a ~ to steal* ana tabia ya kuiba.

procrastinate *vi* ahiri, kawia, chelewa, sitasita. **procrastination** *n*. **procrastination is the thief of time** *(prov)* kuchelewa ni kupoteza muda.

procreate *vt,vi* zaa. **procreation** *n*. **procreative** *adj*. **procreator** *n*.

proctor *n* 1 mlezi wa wanafunzi. 2 **the kings/Queen's P~** kadhi. **~ial** *adj*.

procure *vt,vi* 1 pata, patia. 2 *(arch)* sababisha, leta. 3 kuwadia, tuma. **procurable** *adj*. **~ment** *n*. **procuration** *n* 1 wakala; uwakala. 2 tendo lililoidhinishwa na mwanasheria, uteuzi wa wakala. 3 kukuwadia, ukuwadi. **procuratory** *n* uwakili. **~r** *n* kuwadi. **~ss** *n* kuwadi wa kike. **procurator** *n* 1 wakili. 2 **procurator fiscal** mwendesha mashtaka.

prod *vt* ~ **(at)** 1 dukua, chokoa. 2 *(fig)* chokoza, chochea *n* 1 mdukuo *give a ~* tia mdukuo. 2 uchochezi. 3 chombo chenye ncha. **prodigal** *adj* ~ **of** -fujaji, badhirifu *be ~ of sth* -wa mfujaji wa kitu. ~ **son** mwana mpotevu *n* mbadhirifu. **~ity** *n*.

prodigious *adj* 1 -a ajabu. 2 -ingi mno.

prodigy *n* mwujiza, ajabu, kioja. **infant ~** mtoto mwerevu sana, mtoto mwenye akili za ajabu.

produce *vt* 1 leta, onyesha.2 tengeneza, tunga, buni. 3 zaa, taga. 4 sababisha, leta, fanyiza. 5 *(maths)* ongeza urefu *(of play, book etc)* toa *~ a play* tunga mchezo *n* mazao, mavuno. **producible** *adj*. **~r** *n* 1 mfanyizaji, mtenda kazi, mzalishaji (mali). 2 *(of play)* mtoaji/mwonyeshaji mchezo.

product *n* 1 mazao bidhaa. 2 matokeo. 3 *(maths)* zao. **production** *n* 1 uzalishaji. ~ **line** *see* **assembly line**. 2 mazao; bidhaa. 3 *(of play)* utoaji/ uonyeshaji. **productive** *adj* 1 zalishi; *(of land)* -enye rutuba. 2 ~ **of** -enye kusababisha/kuzalisha, -enye kutoa, -ingi; hodari kwa kutoa (kufanyiza, kuzaa). 4 nayozaa matunda (ya kazi).

productiveness *n.* **productively** *adv.* **productivity** *n* tija. ~ **agreement** marupurupu (kutokana na uzalishaji zaidi).

profane *adj* 1 *(contrasted with sacred)* -a ulimwengu/dunia. 2 -enye kukufuru ~ *language* maneno machafu. **profanity** *n* mwenendo/tabia/lugha mbaya/chafu. 2 *(pl)* matusi. **~ness** *n.* **profanation** *n* utoaji maneno ya kufuru; utumiaji wa lugha chafu, upujufu.

profess *vt,vi* 1 tangaza, toa kauli/hoja, sema wazi. 2 *(rel)* shuhudia, ungama, kiri; weka nadhiri. 3 -wa mweledi, fanya kazi ya. 4 dai; jidai. **~ed** -nayojidai; *(rel)* -lioweka nadhiri *I don't ~ to be an expert* sijidai kuwa mtaalamu. **~ed** *adj.* **~edly** *adv.* **~ion** *n* 1 weledi, ubingwa. 2 ~ **of** kauli; ungamo, nadhiri. 3 *(leg)* **the** ~ jamii ya weledi/mabingwa/maulama. **~ional** *adj* 1 -a weledi. 2 -a kazi ya kulipwa (agh. katika michezo) *n* mchezaji wa kulipwa. **~ionalism** *n* 1 sifa za ubingwa/weledi. 2 *(of games)* uajiri wa wachezaji wa kulipwa. **turn ~ional** anza kuwa mchezaji wa kulipwa. **~or** *n* 1 profesa *assistant ~* profesa msaidizi *associate ~* profesa mshiriki *(US) full ~* profesa. 2 walimu. 3 mtangaza imani. **~orship** uprofesa. **~orial** *adj* -a kiprofesa.

proffer *vt* toa, -pa *n* zawadi. **~e** *n.*

proficient *adj* ~ **(in)** hodari, -enye maarifa, stadi, bingwa *be ~ in language* -wa stadi wa lugha. **proficiency in** *n* ustadi, n.k. **~ly** *adv.*

profile *n* 1 umbo kwa upande, sura ya (umbo la) mtu au kitu kwa upande (si kwa mbele yake) *in ~* kama -onekanavyo kwa upande. 2 ukingo wa kitu. 3 maelezo mafupi (juu ya mtu) *vt* toa sura ya umbo, toa maelezo mafupi; chora kwa upande *be ~d against sth* -wa mfano wa kitu.

profit *n* 1 mafaa, manufaa *to one's ~* kwa mafaa yake. 2 faida *at a ~* kwa faida *make ~ on sth* pata faida kwa kitu. ~ **and loss account** akaunti ya faida na hasara. ~ **margin** faida halisi. ~ **sharing** kugawana faida (waajiri na waajiriwa) *vt,vi* 1 ~ **from/by** faidi. 2 saidia; saidiwa (na), pata faida (kwa) *it ~ed him nothing* haikumfaidia chochote. 2 *(arch) (of things)* -wa na manufaa kwa. **~able** *adj.* **~less** *adj* **~lessly** *adv.* **~ably** *adv.* **~eer** *n* mlanguzi *vt* langua. **~eering** *n.*

profligate *adj* 1 *(of person)* fisadi, safihi, -asherati. 2 *(of money)* badhirifu *n* 1 mpotovu, fisadi, safihi, mwasherati. **profligacy** *n.*

pro-forma *n* kifani. ~ **invoice** ankara kifani.

profound *adj* 1 *(deep)* -a ndani sana, kina; kubwa, -a -ingi *~ sleep* usingizi mnono. 2 *(significant)* -a maana sana. 3 zito. 4 -a kuhitaji/kuonyesha maarifa mengi ~ *books* vitabu vyenye mambo mengi ~ *writers* waandishi wenye maarifa mengi ~ *thinkers* watu wenye fikra nyingi. **~ly** *adv.* ~ **ness n. profundity** *n.*

profuse *adj* 1 maridhawa, tele. 2 ~ **in** paji sana *be ~ in one's apologies* omba radhi mno. **~ly** *adv.* ~ **ness** *n.* **profusion** *n.*

progenitor *n* 1 mzazi; babu. 2 *(fig)* muasisi. **progeny** *n* uzao; watoto.

prognosis *n* 1 ubashiri, utabiri; ishara, dalili. 2 *(med)* ubashiri (wa maendeleo ya ugonjwa kutokana na dalili/ishara zake). **prognostic** *adj.* **prognosticate** *vt* bashiri, tabiri. **prognostication** *n.* **prognosticative** *adj.* **prognosticator** *n.*

program(me) *n* 1 utaratibu/mpango (wa mfuatano wa mambo ya kutekelezwa). ~ **music** muziki unaoashirika na hadithi/matukio yanayojulikana. ~ **note** maelezo mafupi juu ya maonyesho. 2 *(politics, etc)* programu, mpango. 3 *(of computer)* programu *vt* 1 tengeneza programu ya kompyuta. **~d course** kozi inayodhibitiwa hatua kwa hatua. **~d learning** kujifunza kwa kozi ya aina hiyo. **~r** *n* mtengeneza programu. 4 *(radio)* mfuatano wa vipindi.

progress *n* 1 mwendo wa mbele; kuendelea mbele; maendeleo *make ~* endelea. 2 safari ya kiserikali (inayofanywa na mkuu wa dola) *vi* endelea, songa mbele, piga hatua. **~ion** *n* 1 uendeleaji, kuendelea, kwenda *modes of ~* aina za miondoko k.m. kutambaa. 2 kuendelea mbele. **~ive** *adj* 1 -a kuendelea mbele. 2 -a kuongezeka hatua kwa hatua. 3 -a kupendelea maendeleo *~ movement* genge la kimaendeleo. 4 -a moja kwa moja, -a kidogo kidogo *n* mpenda maendeleo. **~ively** *adv*. **~iveness** *n*.

prohibit *vt* 1 **~ sb (from doing sth)** kataza, zuia; piga marufuku. **~ion** *n* 1 makatazo. 2 kizuizi. **~ionist** *n*. **~ive** *adj* 1 zuizi, -a kukataza. 2 ghali sana. **~ory** *adj* -a kukataza, -a kuzuia *~ injunction* amri ya kukataza.

project *n* mradi, mpango *vt,vi* 1 panga, sanifu. 2 **~ sth (on (to) sth)** tupa/ onyesha (mwanga, picha, mwali, n.k.). 3 **~ sth on to sb** singizia (bila kukusudia). 4 onyesha, toa picha/sifa. 5 vurumisha. 6 chomoza. 7 chora picha/ramani ya kitu. **~ile** *adj* -a kutupa, -a kutupwa mbele, -a kuvurumisha, -a kurusha *~ force* nguvu ya kutupa kitu *n* kombora. **~ion** *n* 1 mtupo, mvurumisho. 2 mchomozo. 3 usanifishaji mipango. 4 *(drawing)* sanamu, picha, ramani, utoaji/utupaji kivuli au picha mbele. **~ room** chumba cha projekta (chumba cha kuonyeshea picha za sinema katika kiambaza). **~ionist** *n* mwonyeshaji picha za sinema. **~or** *n* projekta: chombo kitupacho picha mbele k.m. katika sinema.

prolapse *vi (med)* chomoza, tokeza (mbele au chini), telezea (chini au mbele).

prolegomena *n (pl)* dibaji, maelezo ya kwanza (hasa katika kazi ya kitaaluma).

prole *n (colloq) see* **proletariat.**

proletariat *n* 1 (tabaka la) wafanyakazi. 2 *(arch)* tabaka la chini. **proletarian** *n* mfanyakazi (wa tabaka la chini) *adj* -a mfanyakazi *~ internationalism* mshikamano wa kimataifa wa wafanyakazi.

proliferate *vi,vt* kua/zaa/enea upesi; zaana/zaliana. **proliferation** *n*. **non proliferation treaty** mkataba wa kuzuia ueneaji wa silaha za nyuklia.

prolific *adj* 1 -a kuzaa sana. 2 *(active)* -a kufanya mengi.

prolix *adj (of speaker, speech, writer etc.)* -a kuchosha. **~ity** *n*.

prologue *n* dibaji, utangulizi, shairi la utangulizi.

prolong *vt* refusha. **~ed** refu sana, -liorefushwa. **~ation** *n* urefushaji.

prom *n (abbr of)* **promenade**.

promenade *n* 1 matembezi; mahali pa kutembelea *~ concert* maonyesho ambapo watazamaji/wasikilizaji wengi husimama. 2 *(US)* dansi rasmi ya vyuo au shule za sekondari *vi,vt* tembeatembea/tembezatembeza.

prominent *adj* 1 -a kutokeza; -a kuchomoza. 2 *(of persons)* -a kujulikana, mashuhuri, maarufu. **~ly** *adv*. **prominence** *n* 1 utokezo. 2 *(renown)* umaarufu, umashuhuri. **bring sth into ~** sifia. **come into ~** julikana, tokeza.

promiscuous *adj* 1 -liochangamana, -sio na taratibu, -a shaghalabaghala. 2 vivi hivi, -a fujofujo; -ovyoovyo. *(of sexual relation)* zinzi. **promiscuity** *n*. **~ly** *adv*.

promise *n* 1 ahadi. 2 kiaga, miadi. 3 agano. 4 matumaini, taraja *break a ~* vunja ahadi *keep a ~* timiza/tekeleza ahadi. **claim sb's ~** dai kilicho ahidiwa *vt,vi* 1 ahidi, toa ahadi. **the P~d land** Kanaan; Peponi. 2 *(give prospect of)* tia tumaini, elekeza. **~ well** onyesha matumaini, elekea kufanikiwa. **promising** *adj*. **promissory** *adj* -a/-enye ahadi. **~ note** waraka wa ahadi; hawala.

promontory *n* rasi.

promote *vt* 1 **~ to** -pa daraja, pandisha cheo. 2 saidia kuanzisha/kupanga/

kusimamia; kuza. 3 tangaza, jenga *milk ~s health* maziwa hujenga afya. ~ *n* mtangazaji; *(of sports)* mdhamini.
promotion *n* 1 kupanda cheo. 2 kuanzisha. 3 ukuzaji.
prompt[1] *adj* mara, -a papohapo. **~ly** *adv*. **~ness** *n*. **~itude** *n* upapo, wepesi.
prompt[2] *vt* 1 chochea, shawishi. 2 ~ *sb (of theatre)* kumbusha maneno (katika maonyesho ya tamthiliya); kukumbusha maneno. ~ **copy** *n* nakala ya mkumbushaji. **~-box** *n* mahali pa mkumbushaji. **~er** *n* mkumbushaji.
promulgate *vt* 1 tangaza rasmi, toa ilani. 2 eneza (imani, wazo, elimu). **promulgation** *n*. **promulgator** *n*.
prone *adj* 1 -a kifudifudi *fall ~* anguka kifudifudi. 2 ~ **to** -a kuelekea. **accident** ~ *adj* -a kupata ajali mara kwa mara. **~ness** *n*.
prong *n* kidole cha uma. **~ed** *adj,vt* choma, tumbua.
pronoun *n (gram)* kiwakilishi nomino. **pronominal** *adj (gram)* -a kiwakilishi nomino.
pronounce *vt,vi* 1 tamka *how do you ~ that?* unatamkaje hiyo? 2 nena wazi; tangaza. 3 ~ **for/against sb** *(leg)* pitisha/toa hukumu ~ *sentence* tamka adhabu. ~ **on/upon** toa wazo/maoni. **pronunciation** *n* matamshi **~able** *adj* -a kutamkika. **~d** *adj* wazi, thabiti. **~ment** *n* tangazo, maelezo (ya nia au ya shauri), hukumu.
pronto *adv (sl)* upesi, kwa haraka, mara moja, chapuchapu.
pronunciamento *n* manifesto, tamko.
proof *n* 1 ushahidi, thibitisho, ithibati *convincing~* ushahidi wa kutosheleza, ithibati. ~ *to the contrary* kinyume cha ushahidi. **the ~ of the pudding is in the eating** ukweli unajitokeza katika vitendo. 2 uelekezaji, hali ya kujaribu (kuona kama kitu ni cha kweli au la). 3 jaribio, uchunguzi (wa kuyakinisha). 4 prufu, nakala ya kitabu n.k. ya kujaribia. **~read** *vt,vi* soma/sahihisha prufu. ~ **reader** *n* msomaji wa prufu. 5 kiwango sanifu cha ukali wa vinywaji vikali *adj* 1 ~ **(against)** hodari, thabiti, imara ~ *against temptation* imara, -siovutwa na majaribio. 2 -siopenyeka -a *rain-~ coat* koti lisilopenyeka mvua. **fool-~** *adj* -sioshindika.
prop[1] *n* 1 mhimili, nguzo *(of person)* tegemeo *pit ~s* mihimili ya migodini ya kutegemeza upande wa juu wa mashimo ya makaa n.k. *he was the ~ of his parents during their old age* alikuwa tegemeo la wazazi wake wakati wa uzee wao *vt,vi* ~ **sth (up)** saidia, weka sawa; *(of a horse)* kataa kuruka kikwazo.
prop[2] *n (colloq abbr of)* **propellor/propeller.**
prop[3] *n (colloq abbr of)* **property**.
propaganda *n* propaganda; ueneaji habari; *(derog)* kauli/mawazo finyu. **propagandist** mweneza habari; mpiga propaganda. **propagandize** *vi* eneza habari.
propagate *vt,vi* 1 zaa, zalisha. 2 *(spread)* eneza, tangaza. **propagator** *n*. **propagation** *n*.
propane *n* propani (C 3 H 8): gesi (inayotumika kama fueli).
propel *vt* sogeza mbele, sukumia mbele, endesha. **~lant** *adj* -enye kusukumia mbele. *n* kitu kinachosukuma mbele. **~ler** *n* rafadha. 2 ~ **-blade** *n (tech)* jembe la rafadha. **~-shaft** *n (tech)* mtaimbo endeshi. **propulsion** *n* 1 nguvu ya kusogeza mbele, kusukuma, kupeleka mbele. 2 msukumo. **jet** ~ mwendo wa jeti.
propensity *n* ~ **to/towards sth/to do sth/for doing sth** mwelekeo, hulka.
proper *adj* 1 -a kufaa, -a kustahili, -stahiki, sawa. 2 -a adabu, -a heshima; sahihi, -zuri. 3 halisi *in ~ condition* katika hali halisi. ~ **fraction** sehemu halisi. 4 ~ **to** kuhusiana hasa na, maalumu kwa. 5 *(gram)* kamili. 6 *(colloq)* kabisa, hasa ~ *telling off* karipia *he was given a ~ telling off* alikaripiwa vikali. **~ly** *adv* 1 kwa kufaa, vizuri. 2

kikamilifu; hasa.

property *n* 1 miliki, rasilimali. 2 mali *immovable* ~ mali isiyohamishika. **a man of** ~ tajiri. **personal** ~ mali ya binafsi. **common** ~ mali ya wote. **real** ~ ardhi na majengo. 3 umilikaji. 4 tabia; asili, nguvu. 5 *(theatre, abbr. prop)* vitu, vyombo, vifaa. **stage** ~ vifaa vya jukwaani. ~ **man/master** *n* mtunzaji vifaa vya michezo ya kuigiza. **propertied** *adj* -enye mali.

prophet *n* 1 nabii, mtume. **The P~**, Mtume Muhammadi. 2 *(foreteller)* mwaguzi, mbashiri. 3 mwanzilishi, mwasisi. **prophecy** *n* uaguzi, ubashiri; utume, unabii. **prophesy** *vi vt* agua, bashiri, tabiri. **~ic** *adj* -a nabii, -a kubashiri *the ~ books* vitabu vya manabii. **~cal** *adj*. **~cally** *adv*.

prophylactic *adj* -a kukinga/kuzuia (ugonjwa/mikosi, n.k.) *n* dawa ya kukingia/kuzuia ugonjwa.

prophylaxis *n* tiba ya kuzuia maradhi.

propinquity *n* 1 *(of ideas)* ufananaji, mfanano. 2 udugu.

propitiate *vt* tuliza, ridhisha. **propitiation** *n*. **propitiatory** *adj*. **propitious** *adj* ~ **to sb/for sth** -a neema, -a heri, -a kupendelea *be ~ to sb* mpendelee mtu fulani. **propitiously** *adv*.

proponent *n* mpendekezaji, mtetezi.

proportion *n* 1 uwiano, urari. **in ~ to** kwa kuwiana na. **get sth/be out of (all/any) ~ (to)** fanya iwe/isiwe na uwiano na. 2 *(pl)* **~s** ukubwa, vipimo, kadiri. 3 sehemu, hisa. 4 *(math)* kadri ya uhusiano baina ya seti mbili za namba *vt* 1 ~ **(to)** linganisha. 2 gawanya, gawa. **~able** *adj*. **~al** *adj* **~al (to)** -a uwiano, -a kuwiana, -a urari. ~ *adj* -a uwiano, -a urari *vt* wianisha. ~ **ately** *adv*.

propose *vt,vi* 1 shauri. 2 pendekeza ~ *sb as a chairman* pendekeza mtu awe mwenyekiti. ~ **the toast** takia heri na afya. 3 ~ **marriage (to sb)** posa. **~r** *n*. **proposal** *n* 1 shauri. 2 pendekezo. 3 posa. 4 mradi.

proposition *n* 1 neno, shauri, kauli, tamko. 2 swali, fumbo, suala. 3 wazo, rai, pendekezo. 4 **a tough** ~ *(colloq)* mtu/jambo/suala gumu (kushughulikia).

propound *vt* 1 toa, leta, nena ~ *a riddle* toa kitendawili.

proprietor *n* mwenye mali; mmiliki mali. **proprietress** mwenye mali (wa kike). **proprietary** *n* kundi (la wenye kumiliki) *adj* 1 -nayomilikiwa, -a mwenyewe. 2 -a kama mmiliki. ~ **medicine** dawa ya pekee iliyohifadhiwa isiigwe.

propriety *n (formal)* 1 adabu, utaratibu, uzuri, makini. 2 urazini; usahihi *I doubt the ~ of doing that* nina shaka na usahihi wa kutenda hivyo.

pro rata *adv (Lat)* kwa uwiano, (kwa) kulingana na. **prorate** *vt* gawa sawa sawa.

prorogue *vt* ahirisha (kikao cha bunge). **prorogation** *n*.

prosaic *adj* -sio changamfu, -siovutia, baridi. **~ally** *adv*. **prosy** *adj (of speakers, authors)* baridi, -a kuchusha **prosily** *adv*. **prosiness** *n*.

proscenium *n (in theatre)* sehemu ya jukwaa mbele ya pazia.

proscribe *vt* 1 kataza (mtu) kisheria, piga marufuku. 2 *(arch)* tenga. 3 kana. **proscription** *n* kukataza; kukana; kupiga marufuku; kutenga. **proscriptive** *adj*.

prose *n* 1 nathari; lugha ya mjazo (isiyo ya kishairi).

prosector *n* mpasua viumbe vilivyokufa (kwa ajili ya mafunzo).

prosecute *vt* 1 ~ **sb (for sth)** shtaki; endesha mashtaka. 2 *(formal)* endelea na ~ *research on* endelea na uchunguzi wa. **prosecution** *n*. **prosecutor** *n*. **Public P~** *n* mwendesha mashtaka wa serikali.

proselyte *n* mbadili dini/imani/itikadi/chama. **proselytize** *vt* hamasisha/shawishi watu kubadili dini, itikadi, n.k.

prosody *n* arudhi. **prosodic** *adj* -a arudhi.

prosopopoeia *n* aina ya tashihisi.

prospect[1] *n* 1 mandhari; *(fig) (of the mind)* maono. 2 (pl) matazamio; matarajio *the ~s of heavy rains have diminished* matazamio ya mvua nyingi yamepungua. 3 matumaini. 4 mteja (wa kutumainiwa). **~ive** *adj* -a kutazamiwa. **~ively** *adv* kwa matazamio.

prospect[2] *vt* ~ **(for)** tafuta (madini). **~or** *n* mtafuta (madini). **gold ~** *n* mtafuta dhahabu. **~ing** *n.* kutafuta (madini); utafutaji (wa madini).

prospectus *n* muhtasari (wa chuo, kampuni, n.k.).

prosper *vi* sitawi, fanikiwa, -wa na heri; *(lit or rhet) (of God) ~ you* Allahu/Mungu bariki. **~ity** *n* usitawi neema, baraka, ghanima. **~ous** *adj* -enye usitawi; -a ghanima; -a neema. **~ously** *adv.*

prostate *n (anat)* ~ **gland** tezi kibofu (ya mamalia dume).

prosthesis *n* 1 elimu ya viungo bandia (meno, miguu, mikono). 2 viungo bandia. 3 *(gram)* kuongeza sauti mwanzoni mwa neno.

prostitute *n* malaya; kahaba *vt* 1 *(reflex)* fanya ukahaba. 2 tumia vibaya. **prostitution** *n* umalaya; ukahaba.

prostrate *adj* -a kifudifudi; *(fig)* -chovu; -lioshindwa *vt* 1 angusha chini. 2 sujudu, nyenyekea. 3 *(usu passive)* shinda, choka. **prostration** *n* uchovu, ulegevu (wa nguvu); unyong'onyevu, mavune.

protagonist *n (lit)* 1 nguli; mhusika mkuu. 2 mwongozaji.

protean *adj* geugeu, -a kugeukageuka.

protect *vt* hami, linda, hifadhi; *(of medicine)* zinga, kinga. **~ion** *n* 1 ulinzi; kinga *give ~* linda. **~ money** *n* fedha za ulinzi (pesa zinazodaiwa na wahalifu). 2 mfumo wa kulinda viwanda (dhidi ya ushindani wa viwanda vya nje). 3 ulinzi. **~onism** *n* ulindaji, ukingaji. **~ive** *adj* 1 -a kuhifadhi; -a kukinga. **~ shoes** *n* viatu vya kujikinga. ~ **colouring** *n* rangi ya kujikinga. 2 ~ **(towards)** -enye kutaka kulinda. ~ **foods** vyakula vya kinga mwili. **~or** *n* mlinzi, mhifadhi. **~orate** *n* nchi lindwa: nchi iliyo chini ya ulinzi wa nchi nyingine.

protege *n* mfuasi, mlindwa.

protein *n* protini.

pro tempore *(abbr* **protem***)* *adv* kwa sasa, kwa wakati huu.

protest *vt* lalamika; pinga. **~er** *n* mpinzani; mlalamikaji. **~ingly** *adv n* lalamiko, taarifa (ya kulalamika au kupinga), kupinga, upingaji. *under ~* kwa kupinga. **~ation** *n (formal)* kukataa; kushuhudia; shahada.

Protestant *n* 1 Mprotestanti. **P~ism** *n* uprotestanti, imani/mafunzo ya Uprotestanti *adj* -a kiprotestanti.

proto- *pref* 1 -a asili. 2 -a awali, -a kwanza.

protocol *n* 1 itifaki, protokali. 2 hati za awali.

protoplasm *n* protoplazimu: sehemu hai za seli. **~ic** *adj* -a protoplazimu.

prototype *n* sampuli kifani, sampuli ya awali; mfano wa awali.

protract *vt* 1 endeleza, refusha, zidisha. **~edly** *adv.* 2 chora kwa kipima pembe. **~or** *n* kipima pembe.

proton *n* protoni: dutu chanya (katika nyuklia ya atomu).

protrude *vt, vi* tokeza; benua; chomoza. **protrusion** *n.* **protrusive** *adj.*

protuberant *adj* -liotokeza; -liovimba; -liobinuka. **protuberance** *n.*

proud *adj* 1 *(in a good sense)* -a kujivunia. 2 *(in a bad sense)* -a kiburi, -a majivuno. 3 -a fahari *it was a ~ day for Tanzania* ilikuwa siku ya fahari kwa Tanzania. 4 ~ **flesh** *n* punye la kovu. 5 *(compounds)* **house ~** *adj* -enye kujali nyumba. **purse ~** -enye kujivuna kwa sababu ya utajiri. **~ly** *adv.*

prove *vt, vi* 1 ~ **(to)** thibitisha *until the contrary is ~d* mpaka ithibitike vinginevyo. **the exception ~s the rule** kawaida ni kama sheria. 2 *(run out)* tokea, onekana. **provable** *adj* -a kuthibitika, -a kuhakikika. **~n** *adj* *(leg)* -liothibitishwa, jarabati.

provenance *(US* **provenience)** *n* chimbuko; mahali (pa) asili.

provender *n* foda; chakula (cha ng'ombe au farasi); malisho, majani, nyasi; *(colloq)* chakula.

proverb *n* 1 methali. 2 **the Book of P~s** Mithali. 3 mfano halisi *he is a ~ for hypocrisy* ni mfano halisi wa unafiki. **~ial** *adj* -a kufahamika sana, -a kutumika sana.

provide *vt,vi* 1 ~ **for sb/sth** toa; andaa, auni. ~ **against sth** weka kinga, jikinga na. 2 taja; *(prepare)* weka wazi. 3 ~ **sth (for sb); ~ sb with/sth** kimu. *conj* **~d (that); providing (that)** kwa sharti kwamba; alimradi/ mradi. **provision** *n* utoaji wa vitu kwa siku za mbele. 2 kiasi kinachotolewa. 3 *(pl)* vyakula, chakula (bidhaa n.k.). ~ *n* 1 *(arch)* uwekevu; ubanifu (wa hali). 2 **P~** majaliwa, amri ya Mungu. **~nt** *adj* 1 -enye busara, -a kuona mbali. 2 -wekevu, -a kuweka akiba. **~ntly** *adv*. **~r** *n* mpaji, mkimu *a good ~r* mkimu mwema *a ~ of office supplies* mgavi wa vifaa vya ofisi. **~ntial** *adj* -a kudra, -a bahati njema; -a kufaa. **~ntialy** *adv*.

province *n* 1 jimbo, mkoa. 2 **the ~s** shamba, nje ya mji. 3 uwanja (wa kitaaluma). 4 jimbo la askofu.

provincial *adj* 1 -a jimbo, -a mikoani, -a bara. 2 mshamba. 3 -enye mawazo finyu. **provincially** *adv* kishamba, kigeni, kimawazo finyu. **provincialism** *n* 1 tabia, lugha/ mwenendo wa mtu wa kishamba/ kibara; ushamba, ubara.

provisional *adj* -a muda, -a kitambo. **~ly** *adv*.

proviso *n* kivuo, sharti. **~ry** *adj* -enye masharti.

provoke *vt* 1 chokoza, kasirisha. 2 chochea, sababisha. ~ **sb to do sth/ into doing sth** sababisha mtu kufanya kitu. **provoking** *adj*. **provocation** *n* 1 uchokozi, ushari. 2 kitu kinachokera/kinachoudhi. **provocative** *adj* 1 -a kukasirisha, -a kuchokoza.

provocatively *adv*.

provost *n* 1 mkuu (wa chuo kikuu), mudiri. 2 *(in Scotland)* meya. 3 ~ **marshal** *n* mkuu wa polisi jeshini.

prow *n* gubeti; omo.

prowess *n* ushujaa; uhodari; ujasiri; umahiri.

prowl *vt* zungukazunguka (katika kuwinda). **~er** *n*.

proximity *n (formal)* ujirani, kuwa karibu; kupakana na. **proximate** *adj (formal)* -a karibu; -a pili yake; -a jirani.

proxy *n* 1 wakili; wakala. 2 *(of voting)* **vote by ~** piga kura kwa kuwakilisha. ~ **vote** kura ya kuwakilisha.

prude *n* mtu mwenye adabu/staha mno; mtu anayejidai kuwa ana adabu. **~ry** *n*. **prudish** *adj*. **prudishly** *adv*.

prudent *adj* -enye busara, -a taratibu; -angalifu. **prudence** *n* busara, wekevu. **~ly** *adv*. **~ial** *adj* -enye kuhusu busara, -enye sifa ya busara.

prune[1] *vt* 1 ~ **sth from sth, ~ sth off sth, ~ sth away** punguza, kata; changa; pogoa (matawi). 2 *(fig)* ondoa kisichotakiwa. **pruning** *n*. ~ **knife** *n* kisu cha kupogolea. **~rs** *n* makasi ya kupogolea.

prune[2] *n* 1 plamu kavu. 2 mtu mjinga.

prurient *adj* -enye nyege mno, -enye ashiki kubwa. **prurience, pruriency** *n* ukware. **~ly** *adv*.

pry[1] *vi* ~ **(into)** chunguza, ulizia, dadisi, peleleza. ~ **(about)** dukiza. **~ingly** *adv*.

pry[2] *vt* 1 banua; inua. 2 *(fig) ~ a secret out of sb* toa siri toka kwa mtu.

psalm *n* zaburi ~ *book* kitabu cha zaburi. **~ody** *n* 1 sanaa ya kuimba zaburi. 2 kitabu cha zaburi na muziki wake. **~ist** *n* mtunga zaburi.

psalter *n* kitabu cha zaburi; zeze la kiyahudi.

psephology *n (US)* taaluma ya mwenendo wa uchaguzi **psephologist** *n*.

pseudo *(pref)* uongo, bandia *adj (colloq)* bandia, -a uongo, -a

kujifanya. ~**nym** *n* jina bandia; jina la kukopa, jina la kujipachika. ~**nymous** *adj* -enye kuandika kwa jina la bandia.
pshaw *int* mawe! bure! upuuzi!
psychedelic *adj (of drugs)* -a kuchochea njozi.
psyche *n* 1 roho, moyo (wa mtu). 2 akili.
psychiatry *n* taaluma na tiba ya magonjwa ya akili. **psychiatric** *adj*. **psychiatrist** *n*.
psychic[1] *n* bingwa wa maono.
psychic[2] *adj* -a akili.
psycho *pref* -a nafsi, -a akili, -a maono. ~**analysis** *n* tiba nafsia; uchunguzi nafsia. ~**linguistics** *n* isimu nafsia. ~**logical warfare** vita vya kimawazo/ kiimani.
psychology *n* saikolojia, elimu nafsia. **psychological** *adj*. **psychologist** *n* mwanasaikolojia.
psychopath *n* mgonjwa wa akili (hasa mwenye kutumia nguvu). ~**ology** *n* sayansi ya ugonjwa wa akili.
psychosis *n* kichaa; wendawazimu; kurukwa akili.
psychosomatic *adj (of disease)* -nayosababishwa na matatizo ya akili.
psychotherapy *n* matibabu ya kisaikolojia.
ptomaine *n* sumu iliyo katika vyakula vilivyooza.
pub *(abbr for* **public house***)* bwalo, baa.
puberty *n* ubalehe; kupevuka. **pubescence** *n* 1 kubalehe. 2 malaika laini ya miti (majani wadudu). **pubescent** *adj* -nayebalehe; -enye malaika laini.
pubes *n* see **pubic**.
pubic *adj* -a mbeleni, -a kinena ~ **hair** *(also pubes)* mavuzi.
public *adj* 1 -a watu wote; -a umma, -a wananchi, -a serikali. ~ **house** kilabu. ~ **transport** usafiri wa umma. ~ **enemy** adui wa jamii/ umma. 2 *(compounds) notary* ~ mthibitishi rasmi, wakili ~ *auction* mnada. ~ **address system** *n* mfumo wa kupaza sauti. ~ **affairs** mambo ya taifa. ~ **benefit** faida ya umma. ~ **document** hati ya serikali. ~ **highway** barabara kuu (ya wote). ~ **interest** manufaa/ maslahi ya umma. ~ **relations** *n* uhusiano. ~ **relations offficer** ofisa uhusiano. ~ **school** *(US and Scot)* shule ya serikali; *(GB)* shule ya kulipa. ~-**spirit** moyo wa kusaidia jamii. ~ **utilities** mashirika ya huduma za umma. ~-**spirited** *adj n* 1 **the** ~ watu, umma. 2 kundi la watu. **in** ~ hadharani, kadamnasi.
publican *n* 1 *(Roman time)* mtoza ushuru. 2 mwenye baa.
publication *n* 1 uenezi. 2 uchapishaji. 3 chapisho. **publicist** *n* mwandishi wa habari (agh. za kisasa zenye kuvutia umma), mwenezi habari. **publicity** *n* 1 kujulikana, kuwa hadharani. 2 utangazaji. ~ **agent** *n* afisa mwenezi. **publicize** *vt* tangaza, eneza habari. **publish** *vt* 1 chapisha. 2 tangaza. **publisher** *n* mchapishaji.
puce *n* hudhurungi.
puck[1] *n (in folklore)* kichimbakazi, mtundu. ~**ish** *adj* -tundu. ~**ishly** *adv*.
puck[2] *n* tufe la mpira wa magongo (hoki) barafuni.
pucker *vt,vi* ~ **(up)** kunja; finya, kunjamana, finyana, (ji)kunyata *n* kikunjo; finyo, kunyanzi.
pud *n (sl) see* **pudding**.
pudden *n (colloq) (only in)* ~ **-head** *n* zuzu, mpumbavu.
pudding *n* 1 pudini. ~ **face** uso mkubwa na mnene. 2 aina ya soseji. **black** ~ soseji ya utumbo wa nguruwe. 3 kitu kama pudini. 4 ~ **stone** mwamba wenye tabaka la vijiwe vidogo.
puddle *n* 1 kidimbwi. 2 tope (iliyochanganywa na mchanga) *vt* 1 kanda; kandika udongo. 2 koroga chuma (kilichoyeyushwa). ~**r** *n* mkandaji; mkandikaji, mkorogaji.
pudenda *n (pl) (formal)* sehemu ya nje ya uchi (agh. wa mwanamke).
pudgy *adj* kibonge, fupi na nene.

puerile *adj* -a kitoto; -a upuuzi. **puerility** *n* 1 utoto, upuuzi; uhafifu.
puerperal *adj* -a uzazi ~ *fever* homa ya uzazi.
puff[1] *n* 1 mpumuo, mpwito. 2 **(powder -)** ~ kipakazi (poda). 3 kitambaa laini kinachobandikwa kwenye nguo kama urembo. 4 ~**-pastry** kinyunga chepesi. 5 tahakiki inayosifia kupita kiasi. 6 ~**-adder** *n* bafe, kifutu. ~**-ball** *n* kuvu yenye umbo la mviringo (agh. hupasuka linapokomaa). ~**y** *adj*. ~**ness** *n*. uvimbevimbe.
puff[2] *vi,vt* 1 pwita, toa pumzi kwa nguvu, hema. 2 puliza. ~**ed up** -wa na kiburi, majivuno. 3 ~ **sth out** zima kwa kupulizia; furisha, vimbisha. 4 sifia kupita kiasi.
pug *vt* kanda (udongo wa kufanyia matofali), finyanga. *n* udongo uliokandwa.
pugilist *n* *(formal)* bondia; mwanamasumbwi, mwanadondi. **pugilism** *n* upiginaji ndondi. **pugilistic** *adj* -a ndondi.
pugnacious *adj (formal)* -gomvi, -piganaji. ~**ly** *adv*. **pugnacity** *n*.
puissant *adj (arch)* -enye uwezo mkubwa; mashuhuri. **puissance** *n*.
puke *vi,vt (sl)* tapika.
pukka(h) *adj (Anglo - Indian sl) (dated sl)* halisi; bora.
pulchritude *n (formal)* uzuri wa umbo. **pulchritudinous** *adj*.
pule *vi* lialia (kwa sauti ya chinichini).
pull *n* 1 uvutaji, unywaji mfululizo. 2 mvuto. 3 nguvu ya kwenda dhidi ya mvuto. 4 *(colloq)* uwezo wa kushawishi/kupata msaada. 5 kishikizio. 6 *(printing)* prufu; chapa (kwa ajili ya ukaguzi/masahihisho) *vt,vi* 1 vuta; kokota; buruta. ~ **to pieces** rarua vipandevipande; *(fig)* kosoa; maliza, burura. 2 *(of a boat)* pwezua, shua. ~ **in together** *(fig)* fanya pamoja, shirikiana. ~ **one's weight** wajibika. 3 ~ **at/on** vuta; -ng'oa, nyonya. 4 *(sl)* ~ **a fast one** *(colloq)* danganya. ~ **a muscle** umia msuli; shtuka musuli. ~ **proof** chapa prufu. 5 *(in games)* piga kushoto kwa makosa. 6 *(sl)* iba; vamia na kunyang'anya. 7 ~ **sb/sth about** vuta huku na huko; tendea mtu mabaya. ~ **sth apart** rarua (makala, maandishi, dhana n.k.). ~ **sth down** haribu. ~ **sb down** *(of illness, etc)* dhoofisha; *(fig)* dhalilisha. ~ **in (of a train)** ingia katika stesheni; *(of motor vehicle or boat)* elekea. ~ **sb in** vutia; *(colloq) (of the police)* kamata. ~ **oneself in** kaza misuli ya tumbo. ~ **sth in** *(colloq)* pata. ~ **sth off** egesha; simama pembeni.~ **out** toa, chomoka, chomoa; *(of person)* jitoa. ~ **out of sth** ondoka. ~ **(sb) out (of sth)** okoa. ~ **(sth) over** *(of a vehicle, boat, etc)* weka kando. ~ **(sb) round** saidia (kupata nafuu ya gonjwa/udhaifu, n.k.) mtu. ~ **through/~ round** fanikiwa (licha ya shida, n.k.). ~ **sb through** saidia (mtu) kupona; saidia mtu kuepukana na matatizo, saidia mtu ashinde mtihani. ~**-through** *n* tambara la kusafishia bunduki. ~ **oneself together** jizuia; jikaza. ~ **(sth) up** vuta juu, simama. ~ **sb up** kemea, karipia. ~ **up** simama, simamisha. ~ **up to with sb/sth** fanya uhusiano uwe wa karibu zaidi.
pullet *n* tembe.
pulley *n* roda, kapi. ~ **block** gongo lenye roda/kapi.
pullman *n (also* ~ **car)** behewa la kulala.
pullover *n* sweta.
pullulate *vi* zaa, chipua kwa wingi. **pullulation** *n*.
pulmonary *adj* -a mapafu.
pulp *n* 1 nyama ya tunda; moyo. 2 kitu chororo au laini. ~ **magazines/literature** magazeti/fasihi chapwa. 3 ubao uliosagwa kutengeneza karatasi; rojo ya ubao *vt* ororesha; lainisha. **beat sb to** ~ piga mtu sana. ~**y** *adj*.
pulpit *n* mimbari. **the** ~ mapadri, wachungaji.
pulsate *vt* 1 pigapiga; dundadunda; rindima, tetemeka. 2 tetemesha, rindimisha. **pulsation** *n* 1 pigo moja,

pigo la moyo. 2 kupigapiga, kudunda, kupuma. **pulse** *n* 1 papo, pigo la moyo; kipigo cha mshipa wa damu. 2 *(fig)* msisimko, mhemko. **feel sb's ~** pima papo *vt* puma. **pulsimeter** *n* kipimo cha papo.

pulse *n* jamii ya kunde.

pulverize *vt,vi* 1 ponda; saga; fanya unga; twanga; chua. 2 -wa unga/ vumbi; *(fig)* bomoa. **pulverization** *n.*

puma *n* puma: mnyama kama simba apatikanaye Marekani.

pumice *n* ~ **(stone)** fuwawe.

pummel *vt* piga mfululizo (kwa ngumi).

pump[1] *n* pampu: bomba ya kuvutia maji au mafuta; chombo cha kujazia upepo/hewa. ~ **room (at a spa)** chumba cha kugawanyia/sambazia maji ya dawa *vt* 1 vuta kwa bomba; jaza upepo. 2 sukuma *the heart ~s blood in the body* moyo husukuma damu mwilini. 3 *(fig)* dadisi, hoji; jaza maarifa.

pump[2] *n* viatu (bila gidamu vya kuchezea dansi).

pumpernickel *n* mkate (agh. mweusi).

pumpkin *n* boga.

pun *n* mchezo wa maneno *vi* ~ **(on/ upon)** chezea maneno. **~ster** *n* mchezea maneno.

punch[1] *vt* 1 piga ngumi/konde. 2 *(US)* chunga ng'ombe *n* 1 pigo la konde/ ngumi. ~ **ball, ~ing ball** gunia la kufanyia mazoezi ya ubondia. 3 *(fig)* ladha, nguvu. **pull one's ~es** shambulia kidogo tu, punguza nguvu ya mashambulizi. ~ **drunk** *adj (in boxing)* -liochanganyikiwa (baada ya kupigwa). ~ **line** kipeo cha hadithi. **~up** *n (colloq)* mapigano ya ngumi.

punch[2] *n* 1 panchi. 2 mhuri/chapa *vt* toboa kwa panchi.

punch[3] *n* panchi: kinywaji kilichotengenezwa kwa mvinyo au pombe kali (iliyochanganywa na maji ya moto yaliyotiwa sukari, limau, na viungo). ~ **bowl** *n* bakuli la mvinyo.

punch[4] *n* Panchi: nguli wa mchezo wa karagosi wa Uingereza. **as proud/ pleased as P~** -enye furaha; -enye majivuno.

punctilio *n* 1 umakinikiaji wa mila na desturi. 2 ushikiliaji sana itifaki. **~us** *adj (formal)* -enye kushikilia itifaki. **~usly** *adv.* **~usness** *n.*

punctual *adj* -a wakati upasao, -siochelewa. **be ~** wahi. **~ly** *adv.* **~ity** *n.*

punctuate *vt* 1 tenga maneno, weka vituo vya uandishi. 2 ingiza, ingilia mara kwa mara. **punctuation** *n.*

puncture *n* pancha *vt* toa/toka upepo, toboa; pata pancha.

pungent *adj (of smell, tastes; fig of remarks)* chungu, kali. **~ly** *adv.* **pungency** *n.*

punish *vt* 1 ~ **sb (with/by sth) (for sth)** adhibu, adhibisha. 2 chakaza; *(boxing)* twanga ngumi. 3 *(colloq)* kula/kunywa/tumia sana. ~ *an opponent* shinda vibaya; twanga. **~a dish** kula kwa hamu kubwa. **~able** *adj* -a kustahili adhabu, -a kupasiwa adhabu. **~ment** *n* 1 adhabu *administer* ~ tekeleza adhabu timiza adhabu **capital** ~ adhabu ya kifo *corporal* ~ adhabu ya viboko. **punitive/punitory** *adj* -a adhabu, -a kuadhibu.

punk *n* 1 mti uliooza (sehemu); uyoga wa mitini; uozo. 2 *(colloq)* uchafu, takataka. 3 mtu asiye na maana/wa ovyo.

punnet *n* kikapu/ungo mdogo (wa kuwekea matunda).

punt[1] *n* mashua (isiyo na mkuku) *vt* endesha mashua (kwa upondo); piga upondo. **~er** *n,* **~-pole** *n* upondo.

punt[2] *vt* betua *n* mbetuo.

punt[3] *vi (of card games)* pinga; weka dau *n* upingaji; uwekaji dau.

puny *adj* -dogo na dhaifu; dhalili, duni, -a hali ya chini.

pupa *n* pupa: hali ya mdudu kati ya kuwa kiluwiluwi na mdudu mzima; *(of bees)* jana.

pupil[1] *n* mwanafunzi. **~teacher** mkufunzi.

pupil[2] *n* mboni. **~lary** *adj.*

puppet *n* 1 karagosi. 2 *(fig)* kibaraka. ~ **play** *n* mchezo wa karagosi. **~ry** *n* ufundi wa kuchezesha karagosi. ~ **show** *n* mchezo wa karagosi. **~-state** *n* dola kibaraka.

puppy *n* 1 kitoto cha mbwa. 2 kijana mwenye majivuno/mjuvi, fidhuli. ~ **love** mapenzi ya kitoto; mapenzi ya kwanza/uzuzu. ~ **fat** *n* unene wa kitoto.

purblind *adj* 1 nusukipofu. 2 *(fig)* pumbavu. **~ness** *n* uzito (wa akili), upumbavu, uzito.

purchase *vt* 1 nunua. 2 pata kwa gharama *a dearly ~d victory* ushindi uliopatikana kwa hasara kubwa. ~ **tax** kodi ya mauzo. 2 kitu kilichonunuliwa. 3 *(sing only)* mshikilio. 4 thamani. **purchasable** *adj* -a kununulika. ~ **price** bei ya kununulia. **~r** *n* mnunuzi.

purdah *n* 1 buibui. 2 ukaya. 3 desturi ya kutawisha wanawake. **be in ~** tawa.

pure *adj* 1 safi. 2 menyu; tupu; halisi. 3 -sio na doa, safi kabisa. 4 *(of sounds)* dhahiri. 5 kwa ajili ya nadharia tu. 6 tu, tupu. ~ **and simple** tupu *stupidity ~ and simple* upumbavu mtupu. ~ **blood** *n* damu menyu, safi. ~ **ly** *adv* kabisa. **~ness/purity** *n* usafi, utakaso, utakatifu; udhu. **purifier** *n* kitakaso; kisafishi. **purify** *vt* 1 safisha; takasa, chuja. 2 fanya -ema. 3 *(correct)* sahihisha. **purification** *n* utakaso. **purist** *n* mtu anayesisitiza ufasaha. mkuntu. **purity** *n* 1 usafi, weupe, utakatifu. 2 tohara, udhu. 3 ufasihi, uhalisi, ubora. **purism** *n* 1 usafi; utakatifu; ufuauji. 2 hali ya kung'ang'ania mno usahihi wa taratibu.

puree *n* rojo ya matunda/mboga.

purge *vi* 1 takasa, safisha. 2 harisha (tumbo). ~ **sb (of/ from sth); ~ sth away (from sb)** 1 *(rel)* takasa. 2 safisha tumbo (kwa kuharisha). 3 *(leg)* lipiza, safisha. ~ **one's contempt** fanya itakiwavyo baada ya kudharau mahakama. 4 *(pol)* safisha (chama) kwa kuondoa wakorofi *n* 1 haluli. 2 kusafisha. **purgation** *n* 1 utakaso. 2 kusafisha tumbo (kwa kuharisha). **purgative** *n* haluli *adj* -enye haluli, -a kuharisha. **purgatorial** *adj* -a mahali pa kutakasia (dhambi ndogo). **purgatory** *n (rel)* 1 toharani. 2 mahali pa mateso ya muda.

purl[1] *vt* 1 pindapinda; fuma kwa kupindapinda. 2 pindua *n* 1 ugwe uliozungushiwa waya wa dhahabu na fedha. 2 mfumo uliopindwa.

purl[2] *vi* bwabwajika; (kwa mto) bubujika, tiririka *n* kubwabwajika.

purler *n* 1 anguko. **come a ~** anguka vibaya. 2 pigo.

purlieus *n* 1 kiungani. 2 ujirani. 3 pambizoni.

purlin *n* mwamba; mtambaa panya.

purloin *vt* iba, nyang'anya; kwepua. **~er** *n*.

purple *n* 1 zambarau. 2 vazi la kifalme; vazi la kadinali. **born in the ~** mwanafamilia ya kifalme. **raise sb to the ~** teua kuwa kadinali. ~ **heart** dawa ya kusisimua; nishani ya Marekani *adj* -a zambarau. **purplish** *adj*. -a zambarauzambarau.

purport *n* maana ya jumla, madhumuni *(purpose)* kusudi *vt* 1 elekea kumaanisha. 2 dai.

purpose *n* azma, nia; matilaba; kusudi. **on ~** kwa makusudi. ~ **built** -liotengenezwa maalumu. **of set ~** kwa makusudi. **to the ~** inayofaa. **to little ~** -enye athari ndogo. **serve/answer one's ~** faa *immoral ~* kusudi baya, mambo yasiyo ya maana. *vt (lit)* kusudia. **~ful** -enye nia, -enye maana. **~less** *adj* bure, -sio na lengo/maana. **~lessly** *adv*. **~ly** *adv* kwa makusudi; kwa madhumuni **purposive** *adj* -enye nia/kusudi. **~fulness** *n*.

purr *vt* *(of a cat)* koroma; toa sauti ya furaha.

purse *n* 1 pochi. **hold the ~ strings** dhibiti matumizi. **tighten/loosen the**

~ **strings** punguza/ongeza matumizi. 2 fedha. **the public ~** hazina. **~r** *n* mhasibu; afisa wa fedha katika meli. 3 fedha za kuzawadia. 4 mkoba.

pursue *vt,vi* 1 fuatilia, fukuzia. 2 andama, ganda, shikilia. 3 endelea na. 4 saka, shikilia, abudu. **~r** *n.*

pursuit *n* **(in) ~ of** ukimbizaji, ufukuziaji. 2 kazi *hot ~* ukimbizaji wa nguvu. *he is angaged in literary ~* anashughulika na uandishi.

purulent *adj* -enye usaha. **purulence** *n.*

purvey *vt* **~ (to)** patia (chakula/nyama) kama muuzaji, uzia (chakula/nyama). 2 **~ for** lisha (jeshi, shule, hospitali, n.k.). **~ance** *n* utoaji chakula; ulishaji. **~or** *n* mtoa chakula; mlishaji.

purview *n* 1 eneo. 2 upeo wa macho; uelewa/utambuzi. 3 vifungu vya sheria. 4 uwanja, medani.

pus *n* usaha, udusi.

push *vt,vi* 1 sukuma, sekua. **~ past** pita. ~ **questions** hojihoji. 2 himiza, shawishi **~ oneself** jitutumua. 3 uza madawa ya kulevya. 4 **~ sb for sth** sukuma, himiza. **be ~ed for sth** pata shida kupata/kuona kitu. 5 **~ sb/ oneself to sth/to do sth** himiza/ endesha mtu; jihimiza. 6 *(press)* bonyeza. 7 **be ~ing thirty/forty,** etc *(colloq)* karibia miaka thelathini/ arubaini, n.k. 8 *(compounds)* **~bike** baiskeli. *(special uses)* **~ along** *(colloq)* ondoka. **~ sb around** onea, sumbua. **~ forward on (to a place)** endelea kwa nguvu. **~ oneself forward** jitokeza; jitiatia. **~ off** *(colloq)* ondoka. **~ sb/sth over** angusha, pindua (mtu/kitu); ambaa; **~ (a boat, etc) off/out** sukuma mbali na ukingo. **~ sb through** wezesha kufanikiwa. **~ sth through** fikisha mwisho. **~ sth up** lazimisha kupanda. **~ up the daisies** *(sl)* zikwa kaburini *n* 1 msukumo. 2 jitihada. 3 **get the ~** *(sl)* fukuzwa (kazi). **give sb the ~** *(sl)* fukuza (mtu) kazi. 4 lengo la kujiendeleza. 5 **at a ~** ikibidi/ ikilazimu *until it comes to the ~* mpaka itakapolazimu.

pusillanimous *adj* -oga, -a kuogopa haraka. **pusillanimity** *n.*

puss, pussy *n* 1 paka; pusi (hasa hutumika katika kumwita). 2 *(vulgar)* kuma, tupu (ya mwanamke). 3 *(colloq)* msichana. **~foot** *vi* enda kimya kimya, enda kwa kunyapia.

pustule *n* chunusi, lengelenge. **pustular** *adj.*

put *vt* 1 weka, tia. 2 jiweka, weka. **~ oneself/sth in/ into sb's hands** kabidhi, weka mikononi. **~ sb in his proper place** shikisha/tia adabu. **~ oneself in sb's/sb else's position** jiweka katika nafasi ya. 3 pachika, wekea. **~ the blame on sb** tupia lawama. **~ pressure on** himiza sana; lazimisha. **~ a strain on sb/sth** elemea. 4 athiri maendeleo. **~ an end to** maliza, ondoa. **~ an end to ones life** jiua. **~ the brakes on sth** *(fig colloq)* punguza kasi/mwendo. 5 sababisha. **~ oneself to death** jiua. **~ sb to death** ua. **~ sb at his ease** tuliza. **~ sb to (great) expense** sababisha gharama (kubwa). **~ sb to (great) inconvenience** sumbua sana. **~ sb to the indignity of doing sth** dhalilisha/tweza. **~ sb in mind of sth** kumbusha. **~ sb/sth out of his/its misery** tuliza hofu, maumivu, n.k.; *(of animals)* ua. **~ sb on (his) oath** apisha. **~ sb/sth to the test** pima. **~ sb in the wrong** fanya (mtu) aonekane mkosaji. **~ sth right** rekebisha. **~ sb right/straight** sahihisha. 6 andika, weka alama. 7 **~ sth to sb, ~ it to sb (that)** pendekeza, ambia. 8 kadiria. **~ a price/value** kadiria bei/thamani. **~ sth at** kadiria. 9 tupa. **shot ~** kutupa tufe. 10 *(with adv particles and preps)* **~ (a ship) about** badilisha welekeo. **~ oneself about** hangaika; sononeka. **~ sth about** eneza. **~ sth across over** wasilisha. **~ across ideas** elewesha; *(of business)* fanikisha. **~ sth across sb** danganya, laghai. **~ sth aside** weka; *(of money)* limbikiza, dunduliza, weka akiba;

sahau. ~ **sth away** weka mahali pake; *(of money)* weka akiba; *(of food)* -la, -nywa mno!; *(give up)* sahau. ~ **sb away** weka kizuizini (agh. katika jela) au hospitali ya vichaa; *(of pets)* ua. ~ **back** rudi. ~ **sth back** rudisha; *(fig)* chelewesha. ~ **sth by** weka akiba. ~ **sth down** weka chini; *(of plan)* tua; *(store)* hifadhi; *(of accelerator)* kanyaga; *(of rebellion)* komesha; *(of note)* andika. ~ **sb down** tetemesha; dhalilisha; nyamazisha. ~ **down** *n* dhalilisho. ~ **sb down as** hesabu, fikiria. ~ **sb down for** andika jina (katika orodha ya mchango). ~ **sth/ sb down to** weka kwenye akaunti; dhania kuwa. ~ **sth forth** toa. ~ **sth forward in/for sth** pendekeza; tanguliza, peleka mbele. ~ **sb forward** pendekeza. ~ **in** ingilia. ~ **in/into** *(naut)* ingilia, tia nanga. ~ **in for sth** toa maombi rasmi. ~ **in for leave** omba likizo. ~ **sth in** ingiza; toa/leta rasmi, fanya. ~ **sth in/into sth** tumia. ~ **in a good word for sb** semea (ili kutetea). ~ **sb in** ajiri, wajibisha; *(politics)* chagua. ~ **off** *(naut)* ondoka. ~ **sth off** ahirisha; *(of clothes etc)* vua, ondoa. ~ **sb off (sth)** ahirisha mpango wa; *(excuses)* kwepa. ~ **sb off** zuia. ~ **sb off his stroke** sitisha. ~ **sth on** vaa; jifanya; ongeza; *(of show, etc)* panga, simamia; *(of clock)* peleka mbele. ~ **sb on** laghai. ~ **on** *n* ulaghai; *(of hotels)* zidisha bei. ~ **it on** jitiatia. ~ **money on** weka dau. ~ **out** *(naut)* ondoka. ~ **sth out** zima; *(of bone)* tengua; kopesha pesa kwa riba; *(produce)* zalisha; *(broadcast)* tangaza. ~ **one's hand out** toa mkono. ~ **one's tongue out** toa ulimi; tusi. ~ **sb out** sumbua, changanya, fadhaisha. ~ **sb out (of)** fukuza. ~ **sth through** fanikisha; kamilisha. ~ **sb/ sth through** unganisha. ~ **sb through sth** fanya apitie. ~ **sb through it** pima kwa uangalifu; *(of interrogation)* tesa. **be hard ~ to it to do sth** ona ugumu, wia ngumu. ~ **sth together** unda. ~ **one's heads together** shauriana. ~ **up at)** panga, kaa. ~ **up for sb** simama (katika uchaguzi). ~ **sth up** inua; *(of building)* jenga; *(of notice)* bandika; *(of rent, etc)* pandisha; *(store)* hifadhi; *(supply)* toa; *(of sword)* futika; *(of hunting)* shtua. ~ **sth up for auction** peleka mnadani. **a ~ up job** ulaghai, udanganyifu, kazi ya hila. ~ **sb up** karibisha. ~ **sb up for sth** pendekeza. ~ **sb up to sth** chochea. ~ **up with sb/sth** vumilia, stahimili.

putative *adj* -liodhaniwa ~ *father* baba wa kudhaniwa.

putrefy *vt,vi* oza, ozesha; vunda. **putrefaction** *n*. **putrescent** *adj* -a katika kuoza, -a katika kuvunda. **putrescence** *n*.

putrid *adj* 1 -liooza, inayovunda. 2 *(sl)* baya, chafu; -a kutia kinyaa. **putridity** *n*.

putsch *n* maasi, jaribio la mapinduzi.

putt *vt,vi (golf)* piga mpira kuelekezea shimoni. **~ing green** *n* eneo la shimo. **~ing - iron/er** *n* kigoe (cha gofu). **~ee** *n* patisi.

putter *vt,vi* see **potter**.

putty *n* puti. **~-knife** *n* kisu cha kujazia puti. *vt* jazia puti.

puzzle *n* 1 fumbo; kitendawili. 2 mkanganyiko. 3 chemsha bongo *vt,vi* kanganya. ~ **over sth** fikiria sana (jambo fulani). ~ **sth out** jaribu kupata ufumbuzi wa jambo. **~ment** *n* utata. **~r** *n* fumbo.

Pygmy *n* 1 mbilikimo. 2 kibete *adj* 1 -a mbilikimo. 2 -a kibete.

pylon[1] *n pl* pajama.

pylon[2] *n* 1 nguzo ya chuma (kiunzi cha chuma) ya kuegemeza nyaya za nguvu ya umeme. 2 mlango (wa hekalu la kimisri). 3 nguzo ya mipaka, nguzo ya pambo.

pyorrhoea *n* kimenomeno: ugonjwa wa ufizi kutoa usaha.

pyramid *n* haram, piramidi. **~al** *adj*.

pyre *n* kimbwi.

pyrethrum *n* pareto.

pyrotechnics *n pl* ujuzi wa fataki na baruti; maonyesho ya fataki; *(fig)* *(irony)* ufasaha. **pyrotechnical** *adj*.

Pyrrhic *adj* -a ushindi mgumu. ~ **victory** ushindi uliosababisha hasara kubwa.

python *n* chatu.

pyx *n (rel)* kikasha cha kuhifadhia Ekaristi.

Q

Q,q herufi ya kumi na saba ya alfabeti katika Kiingereza.

qua *conj* kama, -kiwa ni, -ilivyo.

quack[1] *vt* 1 lia (kama bata). 2 bwata, payuka *n* mlio (wa bata); ~- ~ bata (jina litumiwalo na watoto).

quack[2] *n* bingwatapeli: mtu ajifanyaye mjuzi/mtaalamu (hasa katika tiba), **~ery** *n* utapeli wa kitaalamu.

quadrangle, quad *n* 1 pembenne: umbo lenye pande nne na pembe nne k.m. mraba, mstatili. 2 *(court)* behewa kati ya nyumba; uwanja wenye nyumba (kari) pande zote. **quadrangular** *adj*.

quadrant *n* 1 roboduara. 2 chombo cha kupimia pembe za kimo.

quadratic *adj* 1 -a mraba. 2 *(maths)* ~ **equation** hesabu ya kipawa cha pili.

quadrennial *adj* -enye kudumu miaka minne, -a miaka minne.

quadrilateral *adj* -a pembenne.

quadrillion *n* 1 *(GB)* milioni kwa kipawa cha nne. 2 *(US)* milioni kwa kipawa cha tano.

quadroon *n* suriama wa chotara; mtoto wa chotara.

quadruped *n* mnyama wa miguu minne. **~al** *adj* -a miguu minne.

quadruple *adj* 1 -a sehemu nne. 2 -enye kukubaliwa na pande nne/watu wanne *n* mara nne *vt* zidisha kwa nne.

quadruplet *n* mmoja kati ya mapacha wanne (waliozaliwa).

quadruplicate *adj* -lionakiliwa mara nne. **in** ~ nakala nne.

quaff*(lit) vt, vi* gugumia, gugumiza. **~er** *n*.

quagmire *n* 1 bwawa, kinamasi. 2 *be in a* ~ kwama.

quail *vt* ~ **(at/before)** tetema kwa hofu, jikunyata, nywea.

quaint *adj* -enye kuvutia, -a kupendeza (kwa uzamani/ugeni wake). **~ly** *adv*. **~ness** *n*.

quake *vt,vi (of the earth, person, etc)* tetemeka ~ *with cold* tetemeka kwa baridi *n (colloq abbr for)* **earthquake** tetemeko la ardhi.

Quaker *n* 1 mwanachama wa Jamii ya Marafiki, kundi la Wakristo ambalo halipendelei mikutano rasmi na halipendelei ghasia au vita. 2 kitu kitetemekacho/mtu atetemekaye.

qualify *vi,vt* 1 ~ **sb to do sth** stahili; stahilisha, wezesha. ~ **for sth** stahili kuwa na, weza; ruhusu. 2 ~ **sb (for sth/to do sth/as sth)** wa na/pata sifa, -wa na uwezo. **~ing test** jaribio la ustahilifu. 3 wekea mipaka; pambanua. 4 *(gram)* vumisha. 5 ~ **sb as** elezea sifia. **qualified** *adj* 1 -enye sifa zinazostahili. 2 -enye mipaka. **qualifier** *n* 1 sharti. 2 *(gram)* kivumishi. **qualification** *n* 1 sifa (itokanayo na mafunzo, mtihani, n.k.), tabia, uwezo. 2 mipaka, kikwazo, sharti *he endorsed the plan without* ~ alikubali mpango bila kikwazo. **qualificatory** adj.

quality *n* 1 aina, ubora, tabia, jinsi. 2 sifa *a person of good* ~ mtu mwenye sifa, mtoto wa watu. *inferior* ~ duni, sifa duni. *marketable* ~ sifa ya kununulika. **qualitative** *adj* bora, stahilifu.

qualm *n* 1 shaka, wasiwasi. 2 kigagazi, kichefuchefu.

quandary *n* utata, shaka; mshangao.

quantify *vt* pima/eleza kiasi cha. **quantification** *n*. **quantitative** *adj* -a kiasi. **quantity** *n* 1 sifa ya kitu inayoweza kupimwa k.m. ukubwa, uzito, n.k. 2 kiasi, idadi, wingi. 3 *(often pl)* idadi kubwa. 4 **an unkown** ~ *(maths)* alama ionyeshayo idadi isiyofahamika; *(fig)* mtu/kitu kisichoweza kutabirika. ~ **surveyor** mkadiria ujenzi. **bill of** ~ bili ya makadirio ya ujenzi.

quantum *n* 1 kiasi, kinachotakiwa. 2 *(Physics)* namba za kwanta. ~ **theory** nadharia ya kwanta (kwamba katika unururishaji nishati ya elektroni hutolewa kwa kiasi maalumu, wala si mfululizo)

quarantine *n* karantini *vt* weka karantini.

quarrel *n* 1 ugomvi, mzozo **pick a ~ (with sb)** zusha ugomvi. 2 kisa cha ugomvi *vi* ~ **(with sb) (about sth)** 1 gombana. 2 ~ **with** -tokubaliana, -toafikiana; lalamikia. **~some** *adj* gomvi. **~someness** *n* ugomvi, ubishi.

quarry[1] *n* 1 windo, mnyama (ndege) awindwaye *become the ~ of* -wa mawindo ya.

quarry[2] *n* 1 machimbo. 2 karakana ya mawe *vt* chimba, chimbua; vunja mawe n.k. **~man** *n* mvunja/mchimba/ mpasua mawe.

quart *n* kwati, kisaga. **try to put a ~ into a pint pot** *(fig)* jaribu kufanya jambo lisilowezekana.

quarter *n* 1 robo: *a ~ of century* robo karne *a ~ of an hour* robo saa *a ~ of the price* robo ya bei. **a bad ~ of an hour** tukio la muda mfupi lisilopendeza. 2 robo saa *a ~ to eight* saa mbili kasorobo. 3 kwota: kipindi cha miezi mitatu ambapo kodi na malipo mengine hulipwa. 4 *(US)* senti ishirini na tano. 5 mguu na tako (la mnyama k.v. ng'ombe n.k.). 6 upande *from every ~* toka kila upande, kila mahali *nothing will come from this ~* hakuna kitakachotoka huku. 7 mtaa, makazi. **industrial ~** mtaa wa viwanda. **married ~s** makazi ya watu waliooa (hasa ya wanajeshi) *take up ~s* pangisha. 8 robo ya mwezi. 9 **at close ~s** karibu, karibu sana. 10 nafasi (hasa wakati wa kupigana) *ask for ~* omba msamaha/huruma. **give ~** samehe, hurumia. 11 *(compounds)* **~ binding** *n* jalada la ngozi nyembamba. **~day** *n (of payments)* siku ya robo mwaka. **~-deck** *n (naut)* shetri, sitaha ya nyuma. **~final** *n* robo fainali. **~ light** *n* kidirisha cha gari *vt* 1 gawa sehemu nne. 2 *(ml)* tafutia malazi. **~master** *n* 1 *(of a ship)* serehangi; baharia msimamizi. 2 *(army)* ugavi. **~ master general** Afisa Ugavi Mkuu. **~staff** *n* gongo. **~ly** *adj* -a mara nne kila mwaka, -a kila mwezi wa mitatu *adv* kwa kila mwezi wa tatu.

quartet *n* 1 (muziki wa) waimbaji/ wapigaji wanne.

quarto *n* 1 kwato. **~ size** ukubwa wa kwato. 2 kitabu chenye kurasa kadiri ya urefu wa inchi 12 na upana wa inchi 9.

quartz *n* kwatzi: namna ya jiwe gumu jeupe la kung'aa. **~ite** *n*

quasar *n (astron)* mawimbi, mwanga wa radio ya mbali sana.

quash *vt* 1 tangua, batilisha, tupilia mbali. 2 *(suppress)* komesha, nyamazisha.

quasi- *adj pref (with noun or adj)* kwa/ kama kiasi fulani.

quatercentenary *n* sherehe ya miaka mia nne.

quatrain *n (poetry)* tarbia, unne; ubeti wa mistari minne.

quaver *vi* 1 *(of voice/sound)* tetema, tetemeka. 2 imba/sema kwa sauti ya mtetemo *n* sauti ya mtetemo; mtetemeko. **~y** *adj* -a kutetemeka.

quay *n* gati, liko, diko, kikwezo. **~age** *n* ushuru wa gati.

queasy *adj (of food)* 1 -a kuchefua moyo, -a kichefuchefu. 2 *(of the stomach)* -a kuchefuka. 3 *(fig) (of person)* -enye wasiwasi, oga. 4 *(of person)* -enye kuchefuka kwa urahisi. **queasiness** *n.* **quesily** *adv.*

queen *n* 1 malkia. 2 mke wa mfalme. 3 **~ mother** mame malkia. **~ant/bee** malkia wa mchwa/nyuki. **~bee** *(fig)* mtu mwenye maringo. **beauty ~** mshindi wa shindano la urembo 4 *(sl)* rambuza *vt* **~ it over sb** tawala kama malkia. **~ly** *adv* kimalkia.

queer *adj* 1 -geni, -siokuwa -a kawaida. 2 -enye kusababisha wasiwasi. 3 **in ~ street** *(GB sl)* -enye shida, -enye madeni. 4 *(coll)* -gonjwa kidogo. 5 *(derog)* -senge, basha *n (derog) (sl)* rambuza, msenge *vt (sl)* haribu, potosha. **~ly** *adv.* **~ness** *n.*

queu *vt (poet and rhet)* zima.

quench *vt* 1 zima, zimisha (moto). 2 *(thirst)* kata (kiu). 3 *(hope)* ondoa, fisha, komesha. 4 poza (chuma) katika maji. **~less** *adj* -siozimika.

quern *n* kinu (cha mkono) cha kusaga.

querulous *adj* lalamishi, -gomvi. **~ ness** *n.* **~ly** *adv.*

query *n* 1 swali. 2 alama ya kuuliza *vt* 1 saili, taka maelezo zaidi juu ya jambo. 2 **~ whether/if** uliza, dadisi.

3 tia/weka alama ya kuuliza.
quest *n* 1 kutafuta, uchunguzi; *(old or lit use) vi* **in ~ of** tafuta, chunguza.
question *n* 1 swali *put a ~ to sb* uliza mtu swali. **~master** *n* mwenyekiti wa jopo la michezo ya maswali na majibu. **~ time** *n* kipindi cha maswali bungeni. **~ mark** alama ya kuuliza. 2 mada, suala. **in ~** -anayozungumziwa/ jadiliwa. **out of the ~** haiwezekani. **be some/no etc ~ of** -wa/-to kuwepo na mjadala. **come into ~** jadiliwa; -wa muhimu. **Q~!** swali! hoja! **put the ~** itisha/pigisha kura. 3 upingaji (kadamnasi); uonyeshaji wasiwasi. **beyond (all)/ without ~** bila shaka, dhahiri. **call sth in ~** saili suala, onyesha wasiwasi juu ya kitu *vt* 1 uliza, hoji saili. 2 **~ (whether/if)** *(doubt)* kuwa na shaka *I ~ whether* nina shaka kwamba *it cannot be ~ed* haiwezi kushukiwa. **~ able** *adj* -enye shaka, si hakika; tata. **~bly** *adv*. **~er** *n* msaili. **~ingly** *adv*.
questionnaire *n* hojaji, kidadisi.
queue *n* 1 foleni. 2 msururu wa magari. 3 msuko wa nywele (wa mkia) *vt* **~ (up) (for sth)** panga foleni; tia shungi.
quibble *n* kukwepa swala la msingi *vi* **~ (over)** jadili mambo yasiyo ya msingi (ili kukwepa swala muhimu). **~r** *n*. **quibbling** *adj*.
quick *adj* 1 -epesi, -a haraka *a ~ luncheon* mlo mwepesi *in ~ succession* kwa haraka, haraka; upesi *be ~* fanya haraka, harakisha; chapuka. **(in) ~ time** kwa mwendo wa kawaida (wa askari). **Q~ March** kwa mwendo wa haraka mbele tembea! **~change actor** mchezaji abadilishaye nguo haraka. **~ freeze** gandisha (chakula) haraka ili ladha isipotee. 2 hodari, -elekevu, -enye akili *~ at figures* -a kipaji cha hesabu. **a ~ wit** erevu. 3 (*arch*) hai, -zima, -enye uhai *~ with child* -enye mimba. **the ~ and the dead** wazima na wafu *n* 1 nyama chini ya ngozi (agh. kucha). **cut sb to the ~** choma sana moyoni. **~ly** *adv* upesi, haraka. **~ness** *n*. **~ change** *adj* -liobadilika kwa haraka. **~en** *vt, vi* 1 harakisha, ongeza mwendo. 2 chochea, sisimua, sisimka. 3 *(give life to)* huisha, fufua, fufuka. 4 *(of child in womb)* shtuka. **~set** *adj* -a ua wa miti. **~ie** *n* jambo lililofanywa kwa haraka. **~-lime** *n* chokaa isiyolowa maji. **~-lunch/bar** *n* mkahawa, hoteli ya kujihudumia. **~sand** *n* mchanga didimizi. **~ sighted** *adj* -enye macho makali. **~ silver** *n* 1 zebaki. 2 *(fig)* mabadiliko ya tabia, mwenendo. **~-tempered** *adj* -a hasira fupi. **~-witted** *adj* -erevu.
quid[1] *n* mshuku.
quid[2] *n (GB sl)* pauni ambayo haijavunjwa.
quid pro quo *n (Lat)* malipizo.
quiescent *adj* -siojongea, -liotulia; -tulivu, nyamavu. **~ly** *adv*. **quiescence** *n*.
quiet *adj* 1 -siojongea, tulivu. 2 -nyamavu/kimya. **be ~** nyamaza! *become ~* -wa kimya. 3 *(of colours)* -siong'aa. 4 -liofichika -a siri. **keep sth ~** fanya siri. **on the ~** kwa siri, *n* utulivu, kimya, amani *vt,vi (usually* **~en)** tulia, nyamaa, tuliza. **~ly** *adv*. **~ness** *n*. **~ism** *n* falsafa ya unyenyekevu; usufii. **~ist** *n* mnyenyekevu, msufii.
quietude *n (lit)* utulivu.
quietus *n (formal)* 1 malipo; stakabadhi. 2 *(death)* kifo, mauti *get one's ~* fariki dunia *give sb his ~* ua.
quiff *n* bwenzi, sunzu, junju.
quill *n* 1 **(~-feather)** unyoya mkubwa wa mkia. 2 unyoya wa kuandikia. 3 mwiba wa nungu.
quilt *n* mfarishi *vt* tengeneza mfarishi.
quin *n (colloq abbr of)* **quintuplet**.
quince *n* tunda aina ya pea.
quincentenary *n* adhimisho la miaka mia tano *adj* -a miaka mia tano.
quinine *n* kwinini.
quinquagesima *n (rel)* Jumapili kabla ya Kwaresima.
quinquennial *adj* -a kila mwaka wa tano, -enye miaka tano *n*

adhimisho la miaka mitano mitano. **quinquennium** *n (pl. quinquennia)* kipindi cha miaka mitano.

quinsy *n* halula.

quintessence *n* 1 mfano kamili, kiini halisi. 2 sehemu muhimu.

quintet *n* 1 *(mus)* sauti tano, waimbaji watano (watu watano wakiimba pamoja). 2 kikundi cha tano.

quintuplet *n* 1 moja kati ya tano. 2 **~s** watoto watano pacha.

quip *n* stihizai, kejeli, mzaha *vt* kejeli.

quire *n* kitita, fungu la karatasi (za kuandikia) ishirini na nne zilizokunjwa na kufanya kurasa nane.

quirk *n* mazoea/tabia fulani pekee ya mtu/kitu; mabadiliko ya ghafla.

quirt *n* fimbo yenye mkono mfupi ya kuchapa *vt* chapa kwa kutumia fimbo.

quisling *n* kibaraka, msaliti.

quit *vt* 1 *(leave)* acha, ondoka, ondosha *~ hold of sth* achilia kitu. **be ~ of** ondolewa *~ one's office* acha kazi *~ the army* acha jeshi. 2 *(acquit)* achilia. **~ter** *n* aachaye kazi kabla haijamalizika *adj* -lioachiliwa; lioondokana *we are well ~ of the thief* tumeondokana na mwizi huyo.

quite *adv* 1 kabisa; hasa, kamwe *~ blind* yu kipofu kabisa. **~ the thing** *(colloq)* kidhaniwacho/kifikiriwacho kuwa ni sahihi. 2 kwa kiasi fulani *~ a good singer* mwimbaji mzuri kiasi. 3 kweli *they were all ~ happy* kwa kweli wote walifurahi kweli. 4 *(indicatingagreement/understanding),* sawa, si kitu, sijali.

quits *adj* -a lipizo sawa (kwa kivita au kwa maudhi). **be ~ (with sb)** ridhiana, patana, peana sawa. **let's cry ~** tusameheane. **call it ~** acha (ugomvi) *I will be ~* nitalipa kisasi.

quittance *n* 1 agizo la msamaha, malipo. 2 msamaha (wa deni). 3 hati ya msamaha (wa deni); stakabadhi, risiti.

quiver[1] *vt,vi* tetemeka *n* mtetemo.

quiver[2] *n* podo, ziaka. **a ~ full of children** familia kubwa. **have an arrow left in one's ~** -wa na hoja (jambo).

qui vive *n (only in)* **on the ~** -wa macho (na jambo litakalotokea); -wa tayari, -wa na hadhari.

quixotic *adj* -enye ukarimu (kupita kiasi). **~ally** *adv.*

quiz *vt* jaribio la maswali, chemsha bongo, fumbo, mtihani mdogo *vt* 1 uliza maswali (hasa ya mtihani). 2 *(arch)* chokoza, dhihaki.~ *adj* 1 tani. 2 chokozi. **~ly** *adv.*

quoin *n* kona ya nje ya nyumba; pembe ya chumba. *vt* kaza, inua kona za nyumba.

quoit *n* pete (duara) ya chuma (ya mchezo).

quondam *adj* -a zamani, -a siku zilizopita (lakini si sasa).

quorum n akidi.

quota *n* sehemu ya haki (iliyopasa); idadi ya kikomo, kiasi (kilichopasa).

quotation *n* 1 kidondoa. 2 dondoo. **~-mark(s)** alama za kudondoa (' ') au (" ") *put words into ~ marks* weka maneno katika alama za dondoo.

quote *vt* 1 ~ **(from)** dondoa, tumia maneno ya mtu mwingine. 2 toa maneno kushuhudia. 3 taja *n (colloq)* dondoo. **quotable** *adj* -a kudondoleka. **quotability** *n.*

quoth *vt (arch)* asema; alisema; nasema.

quotidian *adj (of fevers)* -a kila siku, -a kawaida. *n ~ fever* homa inayorudia kila siku.

quotient *n (maths)* hisa.

Quran see **Koran**.

R

R,r *n* 1 herufi ya kumi na nane katika alfabeti ya Kiingereza. 2 **the three R's (reading, (w)riting and (a)rithmetic K3** kusoma, kuandika na kuhesabu (kama msingi wa elimu).

rabbi *n* 1 rabi: mwanasheria (wa sheria za Kiyahudi). 2 mwalimu/bwana: neno la heshima litumiwalo na Wayahudi. 3 kiongozi wa dini ya Kiyahudi. **~nate** 1 ofisi/muda/kipindi cha urabi. 2 jumuiya yote ya marabi. **~nic(al)** *adj* -a utaalamu wa dini/ sheria za Kiyahudi.

rabbit *n* 1 sungura. **~-hole/-burrow** *n* shimo la sungura pori. **~-hutch** *n* kijumba cha mbao cha sungura (afugwaye). ~ **punch** pigo la ngumi nyuma ya shingo. **~-warren** *n* eneo lililojaa mashimo ya sungura pori. 2 *(fig)* sehemu ya njia nyembamba na ya kupindapinda. 3 *(colloq)* mchezaji duni (agh. katika tenisi) *vt* winda sungura.

rabble[1] *n* 1 msongamano wa watu; umati wenye zogo. 2 **the** ~ *(contemptuous)* watu duni, wanyonge na wenye kudharauliwa; akina yahe.

rabble[2] *n* chuma chenye kupinda (upande mmoja) cha kukorogea; chuma kilichoyeyushwa.

rabies *n* 1 kichaa cha mbwa. **rabid** *adj* 1 *(of dogs)* -enye kichaa. 2 kali sana; -enye hasira iso na urazini *go* ~ ghadhibika, -wa mkali sana.

raccoon *see* **racoon**.

race[1] *n* 1 *(origin)* asili kabisa. 2 *(group)* jamii. 3 *(ancestry)* mbari. **racial** *adj* 1 -a jamii; -a mbari ~ *discrimination* utenganisho wa kimbari ~ *segragation* ubaguzi wa kimbari. 2 -a ukoo. **racialism** *n* 1 ukinzani wa kimbari/kijamii. 2 imani kuwa jamii au mbari ya watu fulani ni bora zaidi kuliko nyingine. **racism** *n* ubaguzi wa kimbari.

race[2] *n* 1 shindano la mbio *horse* ~ shindano la mbio za farasi *motor* ~ shindano la mbio za magari ~ *track* uwanja wa mbio. **~-card** *n* ratiba na orodha ya mbio za farasi. **~-course** uwanja wa mashindano ya mbio za farasi. **~horse** *n* farasi wa mashindano. **~-meeting** siku ya mashindano ya mbio. **~-track** *n* barabara ya mbio. 2 mkondo wa maji wa kasi. 3 *(lit)* njia ya jua au mwezi; *(fig)* maisha *vt,vi* 1 *(with/against sb)* shindana katika mbio. 2 miliki/ shindanisha farasi wa mbio. 3 kimbiza/endesha mtu/kitu kwa mwendo mkali. **racing** *n* mashindano ya mbio. **~r** *n* 1 mtu/farasi/baiskeli inayoshiriki katika mashindano ya mbio. 2 mtu, chombo, n.k. chenye mbio sana.

rack[1] *n* 1 uchaga/chanja. 2 shubaka la kuwekea mizigo ndani ya gari/basi. 3 chano cha wanyama. 4 chuma au reli yenye meno ambamo meno ya gurudumu huingia.

rack[2] *n* (*usu.* **the** ~) kitanda cha kutesea. **be on the** ~ *(fig)* teseka, -wa katika tabu, dhiki, shida kubwa *vt* 1 tesa, kwa kutumia kitanda cha kutesea; *(of disease or of mental agony)* tesa sana *he was ~ed with grief* aliteseka sana kwa huzuni. 2 ~ **one's brains** piga bongo, tafakari. 3 nyanyasa (wapangaji nyumba) kwa kuwatoza kodi kubwa. ~ **rent** kodi ya kinyonyaji.

rack[3] *n* 1 *(lit.)* mawingu madogo yanayopeperushwa. 2 *(only in)* ~ **and ruin** angamia.

racket[1] *n* 1 *(sing. only)* ghasia, makelele,zahama. 2 utapeli, ulaghai (wa kudanganya ili kupata fedha). 3 jaribio. **stand the** ~ kubali lawama, kubali adhabu yako; shinda jaribio. 4 msukosuko/pilikapilika *vi* ~ **(about)** piga kelele; ishi maisha ya pilikapilika. **~eer** *n* laghai, mlanguzi, tapeli. **~eering** *n*.

racket[2] *n* (*also* **racquet**) 1 raketi. 2 *(pl)* mchezo wa (kutumia) raketi. 3 kiatu cha kutembelea juu ya theluji.

raconteur *n* mtambaji, mweledi wa masimulizi.

racquet *n see* **racket**[2].

racy *adj* 1 *(of speech or writing)* changamfu, -enye kusisimua. 2 -enye tabia/sifa za namna yake; -enye kuvutia. ~ **of the soil** -enye kuchangamsha; -enye alama za uasili.

racily *adv*. **raciness** *n*.

radar *n* rada: chombo kitumiwacho na marubani kuonyesha vitu kwenye skrini vitu (k.m. ndege, nchi, n.k.) vinavyokaribia eneo lao.

radiate *vt* 1 nururisha. 2 ~ **from** ingia na kutoka katika umbo la miali; onyesha. 3 sambaa kama nusuvipenyo. **radiation** *n* mnururisho. **radiant** *adj* 1 -enye kupeleka miali ya mwanga; angavu, -a kung'aa, ng'avu. 2 *(of person)* ng'avu, -enye kuonyesha furaha/ upendo. 3 *(Phys)* -liosafirishwa kwa miali ~ *energy* nishati ng'avu. **radiance** *n*. **radial** *adj* -enye kuhusu miali au nusu kipenyo; -a miali; -liopangwa kama miali au nusu kipenyo. **radially** *adv*.

radiator *n* rejeta.

radical *adj* 1 -a kiini, -a msingi; -a mzizi. 2 *(politics)* -a siasa kali *n* 1 mtu mwenye siasa kali. 2 *(maths)* kipeo; *(chem)* radikali. **~ism** *n* siasa kali. **~ly** *adv* kimsingi; sana, kabisa.

radicle *n (bot.)* kitungamizizi.

radio[1] *n* 1 redio. 2 simu ya upepo. 3 matangazo ya redio. **~link** matangazo ya redio yanayounganisha sawia watu wa miji tafauti. **~gram**; **~gramophone** rediogramu. 4 ~ **telescope** darubini inayogundua nyota, sayari, n.k. kwa kutumia mawimbi na mwangi wa redio. **~set** chombo cha kupatia habari (katika meli, ndege n.k.).

radio[2] *(pref)* -a miali, -a radiamu. **~-active** *adj* nururishi, -enye uwezo wa kunururisha. **~-activity** *n* unururifu, chembe alfa au chembe beta za mnururisho. **~graph** *n* picha ya eksirei (miale-X). **~grapher** *n* mtaalamu wa picha za eksirei (miale-X). **~graphy** *n* fani ya upigaji picha za eksirei (miale-X). **~isotope** *n* isotopu (redio). **~location** *n* rada. **~logy** *n* rediolojia: taaluma inayohusu eksirei (miale-X) na radiamu nyingine. **~logist** *n* mtaalamu wa eksirei (miale-X). **~therapy** *n* tibaredio: matibabu kwa njia ya eksirei. **~therapist** *n* mtaalamu wa tibaredio. **~copy** *n see* **~logy**. **~telephone** *n* simu ya redio. **~telegraph** *n* simu ya upepo ya redio. **~ telegram** *n* telegramu ya redio.

radish *n* figili.

radium *n* radiamu.

radius *n* nusu kipenyo.

raffia *n* 1 chane (kama za ukindu). 2 *(palm)* mwale, mondo.

raffish *adj* safihi; -siopendelewa na watu, -enye tabia mbaya. **~ly** *adv*.

raffle *n* bahati nasibu *vt* **~sth (off)** uza (kitu) kwa kutumia bahati nasibu; (pigia) kura kwa fedha.

raft *n* 1 chelezo. 2 boya *vt,vi* safirisha kwa chelezo. **~er**; **~sman** *n* mtu anayesafirisha magogo/mbao kwa chelezo.

rafter[1] *n* kombamoyo, pao. **~ed** *adj* -enye kujengwa kwa kombamoyo/ pao.

rafter[2] *see* **raftsman**

rag[1] *n* 1 kitambaa (cha kusafisha). 2 tambara. **the ~ trade** *(sl)* biashara ya kutengeneza na kuuza nguo. 3 kitu kilichochakaa; mabaki ya kitu. **~-bag** *n* mfuko wa matambara; mchanganyiko wa vitu; *(sl)* mtu aliyevaa ovyo. 4 matambara ya kutengenezea karatasi. 5 *(used contemptuously)* gazeti. **~amuffin** *n* mtu/mtoto mchafu. **~ged** *adj* 1 (of clothes) -liopasuka, -liotatuka, lioraruka. 2 -sio sawa, -sio kamili. 3 -enye umbo/pande, usio sawa. **~gedness** *n*. **~gedly** *adv*.

rag[2] *vt, vi* tania; dhihaki, piga makelele *n (colloq)* makelele yenye fujo; sherehe/maandamano yenye makelele na shamrashamra nyingi. **~day** *n* siku ya sherehe ya wanafunzi (agh. mara moja kwa mwaka) yenye lengo la kutafuta pesa kwa ajili ya kuwasaidia wenye matatizo.

rage *n* 1 ghadhabu, kiruu, hasira kali. **be in/fly into a ~ with sth** kasirikia sana mtu. 2 tamaa, uchu. **all the ~** shauku kubwa ya kitu. ~ **for** kuwa shabiki wa. 3 **be (all) the ~** *(colloq)* tamaniwa sana, shabikiwa sana *vt,vi* 1 kasirika sana, ghadhibika, hamaki. 2 *(of storm)* chafuka, sukasuka. 3 *(of disease)* endelea vikali, chaga, -wa kali sana.

raglan *n* kikoti au sweta isiyo na vipindo kwenye mabega. ~ **sleeve** *n* mkono shingo.

ragout *n* mchuzi (wa nyama na mboga za majani).

ragtag *n the ~ and bobtail* watu hohehahe, makabwela.

ragtime *n (in the 1920s)* ngoma ya watu weusi Marekani.

raid *n* 1 shambulio la ghafla la vita. 2 uvamizi wa polisi. 3 shambulio la kupora fedha *vt,vi* 1 shambulia. 2 vamia. 3 pora. **~er** *n* mtu, meli, chombo n.k. kifanyacho mashambulio.

rail[1] *n* 1 mti/ubao/chuma ambacho ni sehemu ya ua/uzio. 2 ubao/mti/chuma cha kutundikia vitu; reli *go off the ~s (of train)* toka relini; *(fig)* haribika, enda kombo; *(colloq)* pata wazimu. **~ing** *n* kitalu. **~-car** *n* kiberenge. **~-fence** *n* kitalu. **~-head** *n* mwisho wa reli inayojengwa. **~-road** *(US)* njia ya reli *vt US* 1 safirisha mizigo kwa reli. 2 harakisha mtu kukubali kitu; pitisha hoja kwa haraka. 3 peleka mtu gerezani kwa hila. ~ **off/in** zungusha/zunguka kitalu. **~way** *n* reli. 2 mfumo wa reli. **~wayman** *n* mfanyakazi wa reli. **~way-yard** *n* karakana ya reli. **~way-station** *n* stesheni ya garimoshi.

rail[2] *vi* **~(at/against)** *(lit.)* kosoa, karipia, laumu, shutumu. **~ing** *n* ukosoaji.

raillery *n (liter)* utani.

raiment *n (liter)* nguo, mavazi.

rain[1] *n* 1 mvua. **long ~s** masika. **lesser ~s** vuli. **the ~s** mvua za mwaka *~ or shine* inyeshe isinyeshe. **~bow** *n* upinde wa mvua. **~cloud** *n* ghubari. **~coat** *n* koti la mvua. ~ **drop** *n* tone la mvua. **~fall** *n* mvua, kiasi cha mvua. ~ **forest** *n* msitu wa mvua. **~-gauge** kipimamvua. **~-maker** *n* mgimbi. **~-proof** adj -siopenya mvua. **~-shadow** *n* 1 ukame, demani. 2 *(fig)* **~check** tiketi/hundi rubuni; ahadi (ya kufanya tena).

rain *vi,vt* 1 nya, nyesha. ~ **cats and dogs** nyesha kwa wingi. 2 ~ **sth on/upon** toa kwa wingi. 3 tiririka *the tears ~ed down her cheek* machozi yalimtiririka. **~y** *adj* -enye mvua nyingi. **save/provide/putaway/keep sth for a ~ day** weka akiba kwa siku za shida.

raise *n* nyongeza (ya mshahara n.k.). vt 1 inua, pandisha, kweza *~ in pay* pandisha mshahara. ~ **glass to** kunywa (kwa afya ya), takia heri. ~ **one's hand** jongea kama utakaye kumpiga mtu. ~ **sb's hopes** pa mtu tumaini. ~ **a man to the peerage** teua kuwa lodi. ~ **the temperature** ongeza joto; *(fig)* ongeza mvutano, ongeza hali ya wasiwasi (kwa kuhamaki, kugomba, n.k.). ~ **one's voice** paaza/pandisha (sauti). 2 inua, nyanyua. ~ **sb from the dead** fufua. 3 sababisha, fanya kutokea. ~ **dust/commotion** *(sl)* sababisha fujo. ~ **a laugh** fanya kitu cha kuchekesha. ~ **cain/hell the devil/the roof** *(sl)* fanya/anzisha fujo. 4 leta mjadala/dakizo. ~ **a new point** leta mjadala mpya, dakiza. 5 *(crops)* otesha, lima; *(animals)* fuga; *(children)* lea. 6 *(money, loans etc)* pata, kopa, kusanya, changa. ~ **an army** andaa jeshi. ~ **funds for** changa pesa. 7 ongeza, kuza. ~ **an embargo** ondoa vikwazo. ~ **a siege/blockade** acha uvamizi. 8 *(naut.)* ~ **land** ona nchi kavu.

raisin *n* zabibu kavu.

raison d'etre *n (Fr)* sababu (ya kuwepo kwa kitu).

rake[1] *n* reki: zana yenye meno itumiwayo kuokotea taka; chombo kitumikacho kuzolea fedha kutoka meza ya kamari *vt* 1 sawazisha, palilia au vunjavunja ardhi (kwa reki). 2 pata/chukua *~ together dead leaves* chakura na kukusanya majani yaliyorundikana *~ out the fire* toa majivu mekoni. ~ **off** *n (sl)* bakshishi, mgawanyo wa faida (usio halali). ~ **sth in** *(fig)* chuma, pata pesa nyingi. ~ **sth up** fichua; fufua. 3 ~ *(over/ through) sth* tafuta sana katika makaratasi yako habari hiyo muhimu. ~ **one's memory** jaribu kukumbuka sana. 4 piga kwa bunduki na mizinga kutoka upande mmoja hadi mwingine.

rake[2] kijogoo, mfisadi, mwasherati. **rakish** *adj* 1 -a uasherati, zinifu. 2 kichale, -a madaha, -kimadaha.

rake[3] *n (slope) (naut)* hanamu, mwinamo *vt vi* enda hanamu. **rakish** *adj (of ship)* -a mjengeko mzuri/ malidadi na -a kuonekana; -enye kasi.

rally[1] *vt,vi* 1 ungana, unganika, kusanya, kusanyika; anza upya. 2 pata moyo/nguvu, tengenezesha, kusanya tena, rudisha ~ *one's wits* pata nguvu tena *n* 1 (kitendo cha) kujikusanya tena; kupata nguvu upya; kupata afua ya ugonjwa. 2 *(in tennis)* kurudishiana mapigo ya mpira kwa muda mrefu (kabla ya mmoja kufunga mwenzake). 3 mkusanyiko mkubwa wa watu (hasa uliokusudia kuamsha nguvu mpya). 4 *(car)* mashindano ya motokaa.

rally[2] *vt* tania.

ram *n* 1 kondoo dume (asiyehasiwa). 2 mtambo wa kusukumia/kubomolea. 3 *(of warship)* mdomo wa manowari (uliochongoka na utumiwao kutobolea ubavu wa meli ya adui) *vt* 1 shindilia, shindika. ~ **sth down one's throat** gongomeza; mwambie jambo mara nyingi mpaka akubali. 2 *(of a warship)* ponda mbavu, piga kwa nguvu. ~**rod** *n* mdeki.

Ramadan *n (rel)* Ramadhani: mwezi mtukufu (ambapo Waislamu hufunga).

ramble *vt* 1 enda kutembea/matembezi; *(fig)* semasema (bila mpango). 2 *(of plants)* tambaa *n* matembezi, mizunguko *go for a ~* enda matembezini, randa. ~**r** *n* mtu anayerandaranda; mmea mtambaa. ~ *rose* waridi tambaazi. **rambling** *adj* 1 *(of buildings)* siopangwa sawasawa, -liojengwa ovyo, si kwa taratibu. 2 *(of speech, essay)* -sio na mpangilio mzuri, -enye kuparaganywa paraganywa.

rambunctious *adj* tundu sana, -enye makelele, -enye fujo; -a maringo/ majivuno.

ramify *vi* 1 gawanyika katika matawi; zaa matawi. 2 fanya kimia; enea. **ramification** *n* kipengee (cha kitu kilicho tata).

ramp[1] *n* 1 mahali penye hanamu, mteremko wa kushukia au kupandia (k.m. hospitalini n.k.). 2 ngazi ya (kushukia au kuingilia katika) ndege. 3 tuta.

ramp[2] *n* 1 hila ya kupandisha bei. 2 *(swindle)* madanganyo, ulaghai.

ramp[3] *vt ~ about (usu joc.)* vamia, fanya vurumai; charuka.

rampage *n* ghasia, ukali. **be go/on the ~** fanya ghasia *vi* hamaki, ghadhibika. ~**ous** *adj*.

rampant *adj* 1 *(of disease, social evils, etc.)* -a kuenea pote, -liotapakaa. 2 *(of animals)* -enye kusimamia miguu ya nyuma tu. 3 *(of plants etc.)* -a kuenea kwa haraka na majani mengi. **rampancy** *n*.

rampart *n* 1 boma. 2 *(fig)* ngome; ulinzi.

ramshackle *adj* -liochakaa, bovubovu; -a karibu kuvunjika/kuanguka.

ran *pp of* **run**.

ranch ranchi: shamba la mifugo, (ng'ombe, kondoo, n.k.) *vt* fuga wanyama. ~**er** *n*.

rancid *adj* -a mafutaozo, -liooza, kali, -enye harufu au uonjo wa uozo, -liovunda.

rancour *n* uchungu/machukio/chuki ya muda mrefu sana. **rancorous** *adj*.

rand *n* fedha/sarafu ya Afrika ya Kusini.

random *n* **at ~** bila taratibu maalumu, bila mpango maalumu; kwa kubahatisha *adj* -sio kuwa na taratibu maalumu, bila kufikiria; -a kubahatisha, -a nasibu, iwezavyo vyovyote.

randy *adj* 1 -enye ashiki nyingi. 2

(Scot.) -a nguvu, jeuri, -enye makelele ya maudhi. **randiness** *n.*

rang *pt of* **ring**.

range[1] *n* 1 safu (hasa ya milima); mlolongo wa vitu ~ *of mountains* safu ya milima. 2 uwanja wa shabaha. 3 mfiko, mtupo (wa risasi ya mzinga, bunduki) *out of rifle* ~ nje ya mtupo wa risasi ya bunduki *at short* ~ kwa karibu *at long* ~ kwa mbali, baidi *take the* ~ piga shabaha. **~-finder** *n* kitafuta umbali/masafa. 4 umbali ambao mtu anaweza kuona au kusikia, au sauti inakoweza kufika. 5 eneo; kadiri *a wide* ~ *of prices* bei anuwai *a wide* ~ *of colours* rangi anuwai *the annual* ~ *of temperature* kadiri ya vipimo vya joto vya mwaka. 6 *(space)* nafasi. 7 jiko kubwa (lenye oveni, pleti, n.k.). 8 eneo la kuchungia au uwanda wa kuwindia.

range[2] *vt,vi* 1 *(arrange)* panga. 2 ~ **(through/over)** tembea, zunguka, tangatanga, zurura; zungumzia. 3 *(extend)* fikia, enea. 4 *(of guns)* fikia umbali/masafa fulani. **~r** *n* 1 mhifadhi, mwangalizi wa hifadhi ya msitu na mbuga za wanyama. 2 *(US)* askari polisi mpanda farasi. 3 *(US)* komando.

rank[1] *n* 1 safu (ya watu au vitu). 2 safu ya askari. **keep/break the** ~ -wa/toka katika msitari. 3 **the ~s; the rank and file; other ~s** askari wa kawaida *he has risen from the ~s* amepandishwa cheo na kuwa ofisa. **be reduced to the ~s** fanywa askari wa kawaida. *(US)* **the ~ing officer** ofisa mwenye cheo cha juu aliyepo. 4 cheo, kiwango, daraja, tabaka *high* ~ cheo kikubwa, daraja bora *he was promoted to the* ~ *of sergeant* alipandishwa cheo cha usajini. **pull ~s on sb** tumia cheo/madaraka (juu ya/ kumshinda mtu mwingine) *vt,vi* 1 weka (katika matabaka, safu, n.k). 2 -wa na cheo, wadhifa, n.k.

rank[2] *adj* 1 *(of plants)* -enye majani mengi mno; *(of land)* -lio na magugu mengi. 2 *(strong smelling)* -a kuvunda, -a kunuka. 3 baya kabisa, -a kupita kiasi *a* ~ *idler* mvivu kabisa ~ *a liar* mwongo sana. **~ly** *adv.* ~ **ness** *n.*

rankle *vi* endelea kuchoma moyo, tia uchungu; kereketa ~ *in sb's mind* tia mtu uchungu.

ransack *vt* 1 ~ **sth (for sth/to do sth)** pekua, chakura. 2 ~ **sth (of sth)** *(plunder)* nyang'anya, pora.

ransom *n* fidia/malipo ya kukomboa mateka. **hold one to** ~ teka mtu na kudai malipo (ili kumwachia huru). **worth a king's** ~ -enye bei/thamani kubwa sana *vt* komboa mtu kwa kulipa fedha.

rant *vt* jigamba kwa maneno (kana kwamba unaigiza mchezo jukwaani), jitapa *n* majitapo/majigambo yenye makelele. **~er** *n.*

rap[1] *n* 1 *(of sound)* kibao. **give sb a ~ on the knuckles** *(fig)* karipia. 2 *(colloq)* lawama, madhara. **take the ~ (for sth)** laumiwa, adhibiwa bila sababu. 3 *(US) (sl)* mazungumzo, majadiliano *vt,vi* 1 bisha, gonga, piga kibao, gota. 2 ~ **sth out** sema kwa ghafla au kwa ukali. 3 *(US) (sl)* zungumza, jadili.

rap[2] *n* **not care/give a** ~ kutojali kabisa sababu ya zamani isiyo na thamani *(phr) don't care a* ~ sijali kabisa.

rapacious *adj (formal)* -enye tamaa (hasa ya fedha). **~ly** *adv.* **rapacity** *n* tamaa ya mali.

rape[1] *n* 1 uporaji. 2 ubakaji *vt* pora. 2 baka. **rapist** *n* mbakaji.

rape[2] *n* rapa (aina ya mimea inayooteshwa kwa ajili ya chakula cha kondoo au nguruwe).

rapid *adj* 1 -epesi, -a kasi, -a haraka. 2 *(of a slope)* -a mteremko mkali *n* *(of river)* maporomoko, mkondo wa nguvu. **~ly** *adv.* **~ity** *n.*

rapier *n* upanga mwembamba. **~-thrust** *(fig)* jibu la mkato.

rapine *n (liter or rhet)* uporaji.

rapport *n* maelewano, mapatano. ~ **(with)** sikilizana na.

rapporteur *n* mwandishi, katibu (wa

mikutano).

rapprochement *n* kurejesheana uhusiano/urafiki.

rapscallion *n (old use)* mhuni.

rapt *adj* 1 -liozama (katika mawazo, mazungumzo, furaha n.k). 2 *(attention)* makini.

rapture *n* furaha nyingi kupita kiasi. *(pl)* **be in/go into/be sent into ~s (over/about)** -wa na furaha sana, -wa na shauku. **rapturous** *adj* -enye furaha (kupita kiasi).

rare[1] *adj* 1 *(scarce)* adimu. 2 zuri mno! -sio na kifani; -siyo ya kawaida. **~ly** *adv* 1 mara chache. 2 vizuri kabisa. **~ness** *n*. **rarity** *n* uadimifu; tunu *it is a great ~* ni adimu sana.

rare[2] *adj* bichibichi. **~meat** nyama mbichimbichi, -sioiva sana.

rarefy *vt,vi* 1 punguza, (hewa, gesi, n.k). 2 takasa, chuja.

raring *adj (colloq)* -liojaa hamu/uchu.

rascal *n* mhuni. **~ly** *adv*.

rase *see* **raze**.

rash[1] *n* vipele; ukurutu.

rash[2] *adj* pupa, -tokuwa na subira; -sio na simile. **~ly** *adv*. **~ness** *n*.

rasher *n* kipande cha nyama ya nguruwe cha kubanikwa au kukaangwa (au kilichokaushwa kwa chumvi).

rasp *vt,vi* 1 *~ sth (away/off)* kwaruza. 2 *(irritate)* kera, udhi. 3 toa sauti ya bezo *n* tupa (ya kukwaruzia); sauti ya mkwaruzo.

raspberry *n* 1 rasiberi: aina ya tunda. 2 *(sl)* sauti ya bezo *give sb the ~* beza.

rat *n* 1 panya. 2 **~ (on sb)** msaliti. **smell a ~** shuku hila. **(look) like a drowned ~** lowa na nyong'onyea. **the ~ race** vita vya cheo, hadhi, n.k.. **R~s** upuuzi! vt 1 winda (saka) panya. 2 vunja ahadi, saliti. **~ter** *n* mtu, mbwa au paka akamataye panya. **~ty** *adj (colloq)* -a kuudhi.

ratan *see* **rattan**.

rat-a-tat *see* **rat-tat**.

ratchet *n (also* **ratch)** gurudumu la menomeno *vt* fanya menomeno.

rate *n* 1 **birth/marriage/ death, etc ~** kiasi, kima. **accident ~** kiasi cha ajali. **~ of exchange** kiasi cha kubadilishana. **the discount ~** kiasi cha kipunguzi. **bank ~** kiasi/kiwango cha riba. 2 mwendo. 3 daraja. 4 **at this/that ~** mambo yakiendelea hivyo/kwa kiwango hiki. **at any ~** kwa vyovyote vile. 5 **(the) ~s** kodi, ushuru (wa serikali za mitaa). **~-payer** *n* mlipa kodi/ushuru *vt* 1 **~ (at)** kadiria, tathmini, thamini. 2 **~ sth (at)** tathmini kwa ajili ya kodi. 3 **~ sb as** -pa daraja/cheo. **~able/ ratable** *adj* 1 -liostahili kulipiwa kodi. 2 -enye kutathminika; **ratability/ ~ability** *n*. **rating** *n* 1 kukadiria thamani, kiwango cha kodi (ya ajira, ya cheo). 2 daraja. 3 *(navy)* baharia.

rather *adv* 1 *(moderately)* kidogo, kiasi *it is ~ hot* kuna joto kiasi! 2 *(preferably)* afadhali, heri *I would ~ die than be a slave* afadhali kufa kuliko kuwa mtumwa *she ought to have been chosen ~ than Juma.* alipaswa kuchaguliwa badala ya Juma *I would ~ not* nisingependa. 3 *(colloq GB)* hakika! kabisa! naam! 4 kwa usahihi zaidi.

ratify *vt* idhinisha, thibitisha, ridhia (kwa kutia sahihi au kutumia njia nyingine iliyo rasmi). **ratification** *n* idhini; uhakikisho, uthibitisho.

ratio *n* uwiano.

ratiocination mantiki. **ratiocinate** *vi* fikiria jambo kwa kutumia mantiki.

ration *n* 1 posho, mgawo. **~ card** kadi ya mgawo/posho. **be on short ~s** punguziwa posho/mgawo *vt* 1 wekea kiwango cha mgawo. 2 **~ (out)** gawa kwa kiwango kilichodhibitiwa.

rational *adj* 1 razini, -a kirazini. 2 -enye kuweza kufikiri kirazini. 3 -a kimantiki. 4 *(maths)* -a uwiano *~ expression*uonyesho wiano *~ number* namba wiano. **~ly** *adv*. **~ity** *n* taamuli, busara, mantiki. **~e** *n* urazini, sababu ya msingi. **~ism** *n* falsafa mantiki. **~ist** *n* mrazini. **~istic** *adj*. **~ize** *vt* 1 tazama jambo kimantiki, razini(sha). ~ **ones's fears/ behaviour** jipa moyo. 2 *(of industry etc)* panga upya (ili kuzuia ufujaji mali au kuepuka mambo). **~ization** *n.*

rat-line *(usu pl.)* *(also* **ratlin)** *n* kamba ndogo za ngazi ya kupandia juu na kuteremkia chini marekebuni.

rattan *n* *(also* **ratan)** 1 *(of E India)* mhinzirani. 2 mkongojo wa hinzirani. 3 ~ *stems (collectively)* chunga ya hinzirani.

rat-rat *(also* **rata-tat)** *n* tata: sauti ya kugonga.

rattle *vt,vi* 1 chacharisha, lia kama kayamba, gongagonga *the wind ~d the windows* upepo uligongesha-gongesha madirisha. 2 ~ **away; ~ sth off** sema, zungumza kwa haraka-haraka bila kufikiria au kwa kuonyesha furaha; bwabaja *n* 1 mgongano, mchachariko, mlio wa kugonganisha vitu (agh. chupa). 2 kayamba, manyanga. 3 mazungumzo ya upesi upesi, ubwataji. 4 ~ *snake (Am)* nyoka atoae sauti ya kuchacharika kwa mkia wake. 5 **(death)** ~ mkoromo wa mtu anayekufa. 6 **~-brain; ~ pate** *n* bozibozi, mjinga; domo kaya. **~-trap** *n* mkweche. **~r** *n* mtu/kitu kinacho-chacharika (hasa agh. nyoka). **rattling** *adj* 1 *(sl)* -a haraka, -a kasi; -a hali ya juu, safi kabisa *adv (sl)* sana *a ~ good speech* hotuba safi sana.

raucous *adj (of sounds)* -a kukwaruza; kali ~ *laughter* kicheko cha kukwaruza. **~ly** *adv.*

ravage *vt,vi* 1 teketeza, haribu *a house ~d by fire* jumba lililoteketezwa kwa moto. 2 *(of armies, etc.)* angamiza; nyang'anya mali kwa fujo na ghasia. *(pl)* **~s of** *n* 1 maangamizi, uharibifu. 2 *(pl)* athari (zinazoleta uharibifu/ madhara) *the ~s of heavy rains* athari/ madhara ya mvua kubwa. **~r** mwangamizi, mharibifu.

rave *vi* 1 ~ **(at/against/about sth)** sema kwa hasira, payapaya. 2 ~ **about sb/sth** sifia sana (bila kufikiri); sema kwa furaha iliyokifu (hata ukaonekana mjinga) (juu ya kitu). 3 ~ **it up** *(sl)* -la starehe. **~-up** *n* sherehe ya kusisimua *n* 1 *(colloq)* sifa nyingi. 2 *(sl)* sherehe, safari, dansi ya kusisimua. 3 shauku kuu *adv* kiwendawazimu, kichakaramu. **raving** *adj* -enye kupayuka, -enye kupayapaya. **ravings** *n* mazungumzo ya kiwenda wazimu.

ravel *vt,vi* 1 *(of knitted or woven things)* fumua, chambua. ~ **out** fumua, chambua, tatua. 2 tatanisha, funganisha, sokota; *(fig)* leta/ sababisha kuchanganyikiwa.

raven[1] *n* mdege mkubwa mweusi (hufanana na kunguru) *adj* -enye weusi ung'aao. ~ **locks** *n* nywele nyeusi.

raven[2] *vt* 1 paparika ovyo kwa kutafuta chakula. 2 lafua. 3 pora. **~ing** *adj* -kali, kinyama (kwenye chakula), lafi. **~ous** *adj* 1 -enye njaa kali. 2 -a kulafua, lafi, -enye pupa. **~ously** *adv.*

ravine *n* korongo.

ravish *vt* 1 jaza furaha, furahisha. 2 *(arch or poet)* pora. 3 *(arch)* najisi; baka. **~ing** *adj* -zuri mno. **~ment** *n* kupendezwa, kufurahishwa.

raw *adj* 1 bichi, -siopikwa. 2 ghafi ~ *materials* mali ghafi: vitu vya kufanyizia vitu vingine, k.m. pamba, katani, manyoya, mbata. **in the** ~ ghafi; -siyosafishwa/tengezwa; *(fig)* uchi. **~-hide** -liotengenezwa kwa ngozi ghafi. 3 *(of persons)* -sio na ujuzi/uzoefu *a ~ recruit* askari mpya asiyefundishwa bado; kuruta. 4 *(of weather)* -enye unyevuunyevu, baridi. 5 *(of wounds)* bichi, -enye damu; *(of a place on the flesh)* -liochunika ngozi. **~-boned** *adj* -enye mfupa mkubwa na nyama kidogo; mifupa mitupu. 6 *(artistically crude)* changa *his literary style is still rather ~* mtindo wa maandishi yake bado ni mchanga. 7 *(colloq)* kali, -onevu. **a ~ treatment; ~ deal** uonevu *n* ubichi katika ngozi (agh. ya farasi). **touch sb on the** ~ *(fig)* tonesha, umiza, tonesha hisia za mtu.

ray[1] *n* 1 mwali, mwonzi; *(fig)* matumaini. **not a ~ of hope** hakuna matumaini. 2 mstari wowote unaotoka kwenye kitovu cha kitu *vi, vt* toa miali.

ray[2] *n* taa: aina ya samaki.

rayon *n* rayoni: aina ya nguo ya hariri itengenezwayo kutokana na selulosi.

raze *(also* **rase)** *vt* bomoa, teketeza, haribu kabisa ~ *to the ground* teketeza.

razor *n* mashine ya kunyolea. ~ **blade** wembe. ~ **back** *n* (aina ya) nyangumi. **~edge** *n* 1 makali ya wembe. 2 hali ya hatari. ~ **backed** --enye mgongo mkali.

razzle *(also* **dazzle)** *n* **be/go on the** ~ *(sl)* chachawa; enda kustarehe.

re[1] *prep (in legal style)* mintarafu; ya juu; yahusu.

re[2] *n (mus)* noti ya pili.

re[3]- pref. 1 tena. 2 (fanya) kwa namna nyingine.

reach *vt,vi* 1 ~ **(out) (for)** nyosha mkono *he ~ed (out) (for) the knife* alinyoosha mkono kuchukua kisu *(fig) he ~ed out for help* aliomba msaada. 2 chukua, patia *please ~that book for me* tafadhali nipatie kitabu hicho. 3 fika, nenda hadi ~ *Tanga* fika Tanga. 4 enea, sambaa, fikia. **as far as the eye can** ~ kwa upeo wa macho. 5 ~ **me-downs** *n (pl) (sl)* mitumba *n* 1 *(sing) (only)* kitendo cha kunyoosha (mkono au kitu); mfiko. 2 uwezo (wa kufikia). **within** ~ karibu. **out of; beyond** ~ -siyofikika; nje ya uwezo. 3 mwendeleo (hasa wa mto).

react *vi* 1 ~ **to** jibu, onyesha hisia, pokea, furahia *~ed to the article* alijibu makala *the audience ~ed well to the play* hadhira iliufurahia mchezo. 2 ~ **on/upon** athiri *acid ~s on metal* asidi huathiri metali. 3 ~ **against** pinga, kataa, kacha; geukia. **~ion** *n* 1 jibu, mjibizo *what was his ~ to the news?* alizichukuliaje habari hizo. 2 athari. 3 upingaji mabadiliko/maendeleo; hali ya kurudi nyuma. **~ionary** *adj* -a kupinga maendeleo *n* mpinga maendeleo/ mabadiliko/mageuzi. **~ivate** *vt* fufua. **~or** *n.* **nuclear** ~ tanuri nyuklia; kinu kidhibiti nyuklia; mlundikano wa atomu.

read 1 *vt* 1 soma ~ *a news paper* soma gazeti. 2 tamka; soma kwa sauti. 3 soma; jifunza *he is ~ing physics* anasoma fizikia *you had better ~ the subject up* inakubidi ujifunze somo hili. 4 fasili/fafanua ~ *a dream* fasiri/agua ndoto. 5 onekana, toa picha (kama ni zuri) inaposomwa *the play ~s better than it acts* mchezo ni mzuri zaidi kuusoma kuliko kuona jukwaani. 6 chukulia kuwa ndivyo; fasili *silence mustn't be ~ as consent* kimya kisichukuliwe mara zote kama makubaliano. ~ **into** tia chumvi. ~ **between the lines** tafuta au gundua maana iliyojificha; fasiri. 7 *(of instruments)* onyesha *what does the clock~* saa inaonyesha ni saa ngapi? 8 bembeleza usingizi kwa kusoma. **~er** *n* 1 msomaji *he is not much of a ~* yeye si msomaji sana. *publisher's ~* msomaji/mpitiaji mswada. 2 *(GB)* profesa mshiriki; kitabu cha kusoma darasani; mfasiri. **~ership** *n* 1 *(GB)* uprofesa-mshiriki. 2 *(of periodical)* wasomaji. 3 kitabu cha kiada *supplementary~* kitabu cha ziada *he was having a quiet ~* alikuwa anasoma kwa utulivu. 9 *(pp with an adv) well ~* msomi mno *n* nafasi iliyotumiwa kwa kusoma **~ing** *n* 1 usomaji. ~ **glasses** *n* miwani ya kusomea. ~ **lamp** taa ya kusomea. ~ **room/library** chumba cha kusomea/ maktaba. 2 maarifa (hasa ya vitabu) *a man of wide ~* mtu aliyesoma maarifa mengi. 3 kiasi *temperature ~ was 40 degrees centigrade* hali ya joto ilikuwa nyuzi 40°C. 4 fasili/ufafanuzi *you are ~ing it wrongly* unaifasili vibaya. 5 usomaji wa kutumbuiza. **play-~** kukariri kwa kikundi mchezo ulioandaliwa. 6 *(GB parliament)* mapitio ya mswada kabla ya kupitishwa kwa mswada. 7 maandishi. (*compounds*) ~ **book** *n* kitabu cha kujifunzia kusoma; kitabu cha kusoma. **~able** *adj* nayo someka, -enye kusomeka. **~ability** *n*.

readdress *vt* badili anwani ya barua.

readily/readiness *see* **ready**.

readjust *vt* rekebisha tena/upya. **~ment** *n*.

ready *adj* 1 ~ **(for sth/to do sth)** tayari (kufanya kitu, kutumika) *be ~ to go* kuwa tayari kwenda. **make** ~ tayarisha, andaa. 2 -enye haraka *don't be so ~ to rush to conclusions* usiharakie kufanya mahitimisho; -epesi. 3 -enye kupatikana kwa urahisi *keep your weapon ~ for use* weka silaha yako tayari; karibu. ~ **money** fedha (sarafu au noti) iliyotayari kwa matumizi. ~ **reckoner** kitabu cha mikokotoo muhimu katika mambo kama biashara. 4 -liokwisha tayarishwa. **~made** *adj* 1 tayari kuvaliwa/kutumika; -a kutungua ~ *made clothes* nguo zilizo tayari kuvaliwa/nguo za kutungua, ntungulie ~ *made answers* majibu yaliyokwisha-tayarishwa; majibu ya papo kwa papo. 2 -siyo na upya. **readily** *adv* 1 bila kusita, bila wasiwasi. 2 bila shida. **readiness** *n* 1 hali ya kuwa tayari. 2 ukubalifu, ikibali. 3 wepesi, haraka.

reaffirm *vt* hakikish(i) -a tena, sisitiza tena, dhihirisha jambo.

reafforest *(also* **reforest)** *vt* panda miti upya, rudisha kuwa msitu. **~ation** *n*.

reagent *n (chem)* 1 kitendanishi: kitu cha kikemikali kisababishacho au kiletacho utendanaji wa kikemikali. 2 kitu kibainishacho kitu kingine.

real *adj* 1 halisi ~ *life* maisha halisi *the ~ thing* kitu halisi ~ *number* namba halisi. 2 *(leg)* ~ **property/estate** mali isiyohamishika. 3 *(US colloq as adv)* sana *I'm ~ sorry* nasikitika sana. **~ly** *adv* (kwa) kweli. **~ism** *n* uhalisia. **~ist** *n*. **~istic** *adj* -enye uhalisi; -enye kuwezekana; -a kweli. **~istically** *adv*. **~ity** *n* 1 uhalisi, hakika, hali ya kuwa kweli. **in ~ity** kwa kweli. 2 ukweli. **bring sb to ~ity** fanya (mtu) aone hali halisi; fanya (mtu) aache ndoto.

realize *vt* 1 elewa, tambua. 2 fanikisha ~ *one's hopes* fanikisha matumaini. 3 pata (faida, bei). 4 badilisha mali/hisa kwa fedha. **realizable** *adj* -a kupatikana, -a kufanyika, -a kuwezekana *it is ~* yaweza kufanyika. **realization** *n* 1 utambuzi. 2 matunda, matokeo. 3 kitendo chakubadilisha mali kwa fedha.

realm *n* 1 *(poet)* ufalme, dola *the laws of the ~* sheria za dola *the persons who are out of the ~* watu walio nje ya milki. 2 uwanja, eneo *the ~s of poetry* uwanja wa ushairi.

realtor *n (US)* wakala wa shamba.

ream *n* bunda la karatasi 480 (au 500 kwa Marekani) *~s and ~s* ingi sana, chungu nzima.

reanimate *vt* huisha; *(rally)* hamasisha.

reap *vt* vuna; chuma; *(obtain)* pata, pewa ~ *where one has not sown* pata faida/sifa kwa kazi ya mwingine. **sow the wind and ~ the whirlwind** vuna (kibaya) ulichopanda. **~er** *n* mvunaji. **~ing-hook** *n* mundu wa kufyekea. **~ing-machine** mashine ya kuvunia.

reappear *vi* tokea/tokeza tena. **~ance** *n*.

reappraisal *n* tathmini mpya: kitendo cha kukitazama kitu upya na kukifanyia uamuzi.

rear[1] *n* 1 nyuma. **bring up the ~** -wa mwisho *take the enemy in the ~* shambulia adui toka nyuma. 2 *(colloq)* matako. 3 ~ **admiral** ofisa wa jeshi la majini chini ya Makamu wa Mkuu wa jeshi la majini. ~ **guard** askari walindao nyuma ya jeshi. **a ~ guard action** mapigano baina ya jeshi linalorudi nyuma na adui. ~ **mirror** kioo cha kutazamia nyuma (katika gari). ~ **most** *adj* mwisho kabisa. **~wards** *adv* kwa nyuma, kuelekea nyuma.

rear[2] *vt* 1 lea, fuga. 2 simamisha,

inua. 3 *(of horse)* simama (kwa miguu ya nyuma). 4 *(of a monument)* jenga.

rearm *vt* -pa jeshi silaha tena/upya. **~ament** *n*

rearrange *vt* panga tena, panga upya. **~ment** *n.*

reason *n* 1 *(intellect)* akili, mantiki. **lose one's ~** pata kichaa/wazimu. 2 *(ground)* sababu, kisa, madhumuni. **by ~ of** kwa sababu/madhumuni ya. 3 *(sense)* maana; *(truth)* kweli; *(fairness)* haki; *(right)* adili; urazini. **bring sb to ~** shawishi mtu aache mambo ya kijinga/kipuuzi. **it stands to ~** imebainika, ni wazi. **do anything within ~** fanya chochote chenye maana (cha kiasi), zindua *there is no ~ in what you say* usemayo hayana msingi/mashiko. **listen to/hear ~** sikiliza ushauri. **~less** *adj vi* 1 tumia akili, fikiri, waza. 2 **~ with sb** toa sababu/hoja (ili kumshawishi mtu). **~ out** fikiri kwa kutumia mantiki. 3 **~ that** toa hoja kwamba. 4 jenga hoja. **lose all ~** kosa akili kabisa. **~able** *adj* 1 -a akili, -a maana; tayari kusikia hoja. 2 -a kiasi, -a kutosha *beyond ~ doubt* bila shaka yoyote *~ excuse* udhuru wa maana. **~ing** *n* hoja, utoaji hoja; *(intellectual process)* uwazaji wa kimantiki; kufikiri; fikira *adj* -enye weledi.

reassure *vt* thibitisha, ondolea shaka/hofu, -pa moyo, tuliza, poza. **reassurance** *n.* **reassuring** *adj.* **reassuringly** *adv.*

rebate *n* kipunguo cha bei (kwa sababu ya kulipa fedha tasilimu).

rebel *n* mwasi. **~lion** uasi, maasi *vt* asi, kataa. **~lious** *adj* asi, -kaidi. **~liousness** *n.* **~liously** *adv.*

rebind *vt* jalidi upya.

rebirth *n* 1 *(rel)* kuzaliwa upya; kuongoka. 2 kufufuka *~ of socialism* kufufuka kwa usoshalisti. **reborn** -liookoka.

rebound *vi* 1 **~ from** duta, rudi nyuma; rudishwa nyuma. 2 **~ on/upon** rudia *his words ~ed on him* maneno yake yalimrudia *n* tendo la kuduta/kurudi nyuma. **on the ~** wakati wa kuduta; *(fig)* mara baada ya kupata tatizo *she married Richard on the ~ (after being rejected by John)* aliolewa na Richard baada ya kukataliwa na John.

rebuff *vt* hakirisha, puuza; kataa kwa dharau *n* ukataaji wa kitu kikatili na kwa dharau; kupuuza, kupuuzwa. **~ to** hakirisha, dhalilisha. **meet with/suffer a ~** pata jibu kali na la dharau.

rebuild *vt* jenga tena/upya.

rebuke *vt* **~ sb (for sth)** karipia, kemea, shutumu, laumu *n* karipio, kemeo, onyo, lawama. **rebukingly** *adv.*

rebus *n* chemshabongo ya maneno na picha.

rebut *vt* jibu/pinga hoja; kanusha. **~tal** *n.*

recalcitrant *adj* kaidi, -siotii amri *n* mkaidi, sugu, kiloo. **recalcitrance** *n.*

recant *vt,vi* acha (wazo/imani uliyokuwa nayo); futa maoni yako (kwa kuona kuwa ni makosa). **~ation** *n.*

recall *vt* 1 **~ sb (from/to)** ita tena; rudisha. 2 kumbuka. 3 tangua, batilisha. 4 *(poetic) (revive)* fufua *n* 1 amri ya kurudi. **beyond/past ~** -sioweza kurudi, -siofanyika tena; -siyobatilika. 2 *(military)* alama (filimbi n.k.); mbiu ya kurudi. 3 uwezo wa kukumbuka.

recap[1] *vt,vi,n (colloq abbr)* **recapitulate**.

recap[2] *vt (US)* tengeneza tairi iwe mpya; tia tredi upya.

recapitulate *vt* rudia kwa muhtasari, eleza tena. **recapitulation** *n* muhtasari, ufupisho.

recapture *vt* 1 kamata tena, twaa tena, teka tena. 2 kumbuka (mambo/uzoefu wa awali).

recast *vt* 1 mimina katika kalibu tena, subu tena. 2 *(alter)* fanya vingine, fanya upya. 3 *(theatre)* badili wachezaji (waliochaguliwa kucheza mchezo fulani) *n* kufanyiza upya.

recede *vi* 1 **(~ from)** rudi nyuma. ~ **from view** tokomea. 2 -enda hanamu ~ *into the background* fifia. 3 rejesha nyuma (wazo). 4 pungua (k.m. katika thamani).

receive *vt* 1 pokea, pata ~ *sb into the Church* pokea mtu awe Mkristo ~ *a good education* pata elimu nzuri ~ *a letter* pata/pokea barua. **receiving-set** -redio. 2 pokea (wageni, wajumbe n.k.); kubali/ruhusu. **~d** *adj* -liokubaliwa ~ *pronounciation* matamshi yaliyokubaliwa. **receipt** *n* 1 stakabadhi, risiti. 2 kupokea, upokezi. 3 *(pl) (income)* mapato, uchumi, maduhuli *vt* andika stakabadhi. **~-book** *n* kitabu cha risiti, kitabu cha stakabadhi. **~-stamp** *n* muhuri wa stakabadhi. **receivable** *adj* -a kupokelewa. **~r** *n* 1 mkono wa simu. 2 mpokeaji **Official R~** Mfilisi. 3 mpokeaji *~r of stolen property* mpokeaji wa mali ya wizi. **reception** *n* 1 mapokezi; kitendo cha kupokea/kupokewa. ~ **desk** sehemu ya mapokezi ya wageni. ~ **clerk** karani mpokea wageni; *receptionist* mpokea wageni. ~ **room** chumba cha kupokelea wageni/habari. 2 tafrija, karamu. 3 makaribisho, kitendo cha kulaki; mlahaka. 4 upokeaji wa habari za redio; kusikika kwa (habari za) redio. **receptor** *n* kipokezi, mpokezi. **recipient** *n* mpokeaji, mwenye kupewa/kupata *adj* -a kupokea/kupewa/ kupata.

recent *adj* -pya, -a siku hizi, -a karibuni. **~ly** *adv*.

receptacle *n* 1 chombo cha kuwekea vitu mf. mfuko, kikapu, kasha, n.k. 2 *(bot)* kikonyo.

receptive *adj* sikivu; -epesi kupokea (mawazo, ushauri, n.k.). **receptivity** *n*.

recess *n* 1 kipindi cha mapumziko. 2 mafichoni, shubaka, kidaka *vt,vi* 1 pumzika. 2 weka nyuma. **~ion** *n* 1 *(comm)* kupungua/kushuka kwa uchumi/mdororo (wa uchumi). 2 kitendo cha kutoweko; kurudi nyuma. **~ional** *adj* -a mapumziko (ya bunge) *n* ~ **ional** *(hymn)* wimbo wa mwisho. **~ive** *adj* 1 -a kupungua; -a kurudi nyuma; *(bio)* -a selipumbazi.

rechauffe *n* kiporo kilichopashwa moto.

recherche *adj (of meals)* -lotayarishwa kwa uangalifu mno, -a mbwembwe mno.

recidivist *n* mhalifu sugu. **recidivism** *n*.

recipe *n* 1 mapishi; maelezo ya upishi. ~ **book** kitabu cha mapishi; maelekezo ya kufanya jambo. 2 hati ya dawa. 3 mbinu (ya kufanya jambo).

reciprocate *vt,vi* 1 rudisha, lipa, lipiza (k.m. fadhila, msaada, n.k.). 2 peana, tendana. 3 *(of parts of machine)* enda mbele na nyuma. **reciprocation** *n*.

reciprocal *adj* 1 -a kukubaliana, -a kupeana, -a wao kwa wao, -a kubadilishana ~ *affection* upendanaji ~ *action* kutendeana sawa sawa ~ *agreement* mapatano ya kukubalina. 2 -a kukubaliana kinyume. 3 *(gram)* -a kutendana/kutendeana. **reciprocally** *adv*. **reciprocal** *n (maths)* kinyume katika kuzidisha. **reciprocity** *n* kutendana/kutendeana.

recite *vt* 1 tongoa; ghani. 2 *(repeat by heart)* kariri (sema kimoyomoyo); soma kwa ghaibu; *(narrate)* simulia, nena, toa habari ya; *(publically)* soma mbele ya watu. 3 orodhesha. **~r** *n*. **recital** *n* 1 kitendo cha kutongoa; kughani; maonyesho (agh ya muziki). 2 kisa, masimulizi. **recitation** *n* 1 utongoaji; kughani; mashairi yanayotongolewa. 2 masimulizi. **recitative** *n (mus)* mtindo wa muziki ambao ni mchanganyiko wa kusema na kuimba.

reckless *adj* -siojali, -zembe ~ *fellow* mtu wa kujiendea, asiyejali mtu ~ *driving* kuendesha bila hadhari. ~ **ly** *adv*. ~ **ness** *n*.

reckon *vt,vi* 1 hesabu. ~ **up** jumlisha. ~ **sth in** ingiza katika jumla. 2 ~ **on (upon)** tegemea. 3 ~ **with sb**

shughulikia, lipiza; *(take into account)* zingatia, fikiria. 4 ~ **sb/sth as/to be; ~ that** dhania, fikiria. **~er** *n*. **~ing** *n* orodha ya madai (hasa ya hoteli). **day of ~** siku ya kulipa madeni (ya makosa); kiyama. 2 *(of ship)* kisa.

reclaim *vt* 1 rudisha katika hali nzuri (k.m. ardhi) *the desert was ~ed by hard work* jangwa lililimika baada ya kudhibitiwa kwa kazi kubwa. 2 dai kitu fulani kirudishwe. 3 *(reform)* ongoa, hidi. **~able** *adj*. **reclamation** *n*.

recline *vi,vt (lean on)* tandawaa, jinyoosha.

recluse mtu peke (ajitengaye na wenzake); sufii *adj* -enye kuishi peke yake.

recognizance *n* 1 mdhamana. **enter into ~** (mahakani) dhaminiwa. **on his/her own ~** kwa udhamini wake mwenyewe. 2 dhamana.

recognize *vt* 1 jua, tambua, fahamu, maizi *he ~d the danger of the journey* alitambua kuwa safari ilikuwa ya hatari *~ a new government* tambua serikali mpya. 2 *(acknowledge)* ungama, kiri, kubali. **recognizably** *adv*. **recognition** *n* 1 utambuzi. **alter/change beyond/out of (all) ~** badilika kabisa mpaka kutotambulika. **recognizable** *adj* -a kutambulika, -a kufahamika, -a kujulikana *he is no longer ~* hatambuliki tena.

recoil *vt* 1 ~ **(from)** rudi nyuma, jivuta nyuma. 2 *(of a gun)* rejea nyuma baada ya kutoka risasi. 3 *(shrink)* nywea; ogopa sana; kwepa, kimbia, sita. 4 ~ **on/ upon** *n* rudi, kurudi nyuma; kurejea.

recollect *vt* kumbuka *I couldn't ~ him* sikumkumbuka. **~ion** *n* 1 kumbukumbu *within my ~* kadri ya kumbukumbu zangu *it is outside my ~* sikumbuki. 2 jambo lililokumbukwa *have a dim ~ of sth* kumbuka kwa mbali.

recommence *vi* anza tena.

recommend *vt* 1 ~ **sth (to sb) (for sth); ~ sb; ~sb (for sth/as sth)** pendekeza, sifia. 2 *(advise)* shauri, nasihi *I have been ~ed to take cafenol* nimeshauriwa kutumia kafino. 3 pendeza *his behaviour does not ~ him* tabia yake haimpendezi. 4 ~ **sb to sb** kabidhi mtu kwa mtu. **~able** *adj*. **~ation** *n* 1 sifa. 2 kupendekeza; pendekezo *on the ~ of* kwa pendekezo la.

recompense *vt* jazi *n* jaza, fidia.

reconcile *vt* 1 **sb (with sb)** patanisha; suluhisha. 2 ~ **sth (with sth)** linganisha. 3 **be ~d to sth** kubali kuvumilia; ridhi **reconcilable** *adj*. **reconciliation** *n* upatanisho, suluhisho, suluhu. **reconciliatory** *adj* suluhishi, -a kupatanisha.

recondite *adj (of knowledge)* adimu; gumu.

recondition *n vt* rekebisha, tengeneza upya (kwa kutia vitu vipya), karabati.

reconnaissance *n* 1 *(mil)* upelelezi. ~ **party** kikosi cha upelelezi. ~ **planes** ndege za upepelezi. 2 uchunguzi/ ukaguzi wa awali.

reconnoitre *(US* **reconnoiter)** *vt, vi* peleleza, jasisi, piga reki.

reconstruct *vt* jenga tena, tengeneza upya. **~ion** *n*.

record *n* 1 kumbukumbu, taarifa iliyoandikwa; ushahidi *it is on ~ that* kuna ushahidi kwamba. **put me on ~ as saying that** andika kuwa nimesema. **off the ~** *(colloq)* isiandikwe/isichapwe. 2 sahani ya santuri. **~player** *n* santuri *gramophone ~* sahani ya santuri. 3 *(of games etc.)* rekodi. **beat/break the ~** vunja rekodi. ~ **holder** mshikilia rekodi. 4 sifa *a man with a good ~* mtu mwenye sifa nzuri *his ~ is against him* ana sifa mbaya; sifa yake inamwangusha. ~ *n* 1 *(GB)* jaji. 2 kinasa sauti. **tape ~** kinasauti. **video tape ~** video. 3 mwandishi wa kumbukumbu. 4 filimbi *vt* 1 andika. 2 *(of music etc)* rekodi. 3 *(of instrument)* onyesha. **~ing** *n* kipindi, muziki, harusi (iliyorekodiwa).

recount[1] *vt* hesabu tena *n* kuhesabu tena (hasa kura ili kuepuka makosa).

recount[2] hadithia, simulia.

recoup *vt* ~ **(for)** fidia ~ *one's losses* fidia hasara.

recourse *n* 1 njia (ya kupata msaada). **have ~ to** tafuta msaada. 2 msaada, kimbilio.

recover[1] *vt,vi* 1 pata tena (kitu kilichopotea) ~ *consciousness* pata fahamu tena baada ya kuzimia ~ *oneself* jikaza. 2 ~ **(from)** pona, pata nafuu/ashekali/ahueni. **~able** *adj* -enye kupatikana tena. **~y** *n* kupata tena; kupata nafuu tena.

recover[2] *vt* funika tena/upya.

recreant *adj* -oga; -saliti *n* mwoga; msaliti.

recreate *vt* buni, sanifu upya, kumbuka. **recreation** *n* burudani, mapumziko, burudiko. ~ **ground** kiwanja cha burudani. **recreational** *adj* -a burudani.

recrimination *n* shitaka/ lawama baada ya . shitaka (lililokwishatolewa). **recriminate** *vi* toa shitaka kufuatia shitaka dhidi yako. ~ **against sb** lipiza kisasi. **recriminatory** *adj indulge in recriminatories* baki kulaumiana.

recrudescence *n* kuanza tena, kuzuka tena (vita, matata, ugonjwa).

recruit *n (of army)* kuruta, askari mpya (anayejiunga); *(of a party)* mwanachama mpya *vt* 1 *(of military, association, etc)* andikisha. 2 pata kiasi/nafasi ya kutosha. 3 rudisha katika hali ya kawaida. **~ment** *n* 1 uandikishaji wa askari au wanachama.

rectangle *n* mstatili. **rectangular** *adj* -a mstatili.

rectify *vt* 1 sahihisha; rekebisha. 2 *(chem)* takasa; safisha. 3 *(electr)* badili mkondo. **rectifier** *n* 1 mtu/kitu kinachorekebisha, sahihisha. **rectification** *n (phys)* kirekebishi.

rectilineal/rectilinear *adj* -a mstari ulionyooka; -lio na mistari iliyonyooka.

rectitude *n* uadilifu, uaminifu, unyofu.

rector *n* 1 *(church of England)* paroko; mchungaji mkuu. 2 *(of a seminary)* mkuu wa chuo/shule; gambera. **~y** *n* nyumba ya paroko/mchungaji mkuu.

rectum *n (bio)* rektamu. **rectal** *adj* -a rektamu.

recumbent *adj (esp of a person)* -liolala, -a kulala. **recumbency** *n.*

recuperate *n, vt,vi* pata/rudisha nguvu tena (baada ya ugonjwa, kuchoka, n.k.). **recuperation** *n.* **recuperative** *adj.*

recur *vi* 1 rudia. 2 ~ **to** rejea ~ *to what I said yesterday* rejea maneno niliyosema jana. 3 *(of ideas, events, etc.)* -jia akilini tena. **~rence** *n* kutokea tena (mara kwa mara); kurudiarudia. **~rent** *adj (of events, fevers, etc)* -a kutokea mara kwa mara, -a kurudiarudia. **~expenditure** matumizi ya kawaida. *(maths)* ~ **series** mfululizo wa kurudiarudia.

recurve *vt,vi* pindia nyuma/chini. **recurvate** *adj* -liopindia nyuma/ chini.

recusant *adj* asi, kaidi (agh. Mkatoliki aliyekataa kujiunga na Waanglikana). **recusancy** *n* ukaidi.

red *adj* 1 -ekundu. **see ~** shindwa kujizuia kwa sababu ya hasira au kuonewa. **paint the town ~** *(colloq)* enda kustarehe kwa shangwe na vifijo. ~ **carpet** *n* zulia jekundu (kwa ajili ya wageni wa heshima) ~ *carpet welcome* mapokezi makubwa. 2 *(of Russia)* **R~ Army** *n* Jeshi la Urusi (wakati wa mapinduzi). 3 *(with compounds)* **R~ bricks** *n (UK)* vyuo vilivyoanzishwa karne ya 19 na baadaye. **~cap** *n (UK)* polisi wa jeshi; (US) mbeba mzigo katika kituo cha reli. **~coat** *n* askari wa Uingereza. **R~ Cresent** *n (in Muslim countries)* (mwezi mwekundu). **R~ cross** Msalaba Mwekundu: Chama cha Kimataifa cha kuwasaidia waliofikwa na maafa. **~deer** *n* aina ya swala wapatikanao Ulaya na Asia. **~ensign** (*or colloq* **~duster**) *n* bendera nyekundu yenye bendera a

Kiingereza pembeni mwake (itumiwayo na meli za wafanyibiashara wa Uingereza). **~flag** bendera ya hatari; alama ya mapinduzi. **~ handed** papohapo (penye kitendo) *catch~ handed* fuma, fumania. **~ hat** *n* kofia ya kadinali. **~head** *n* mtu mwenye nywele nyekundu. **~herring** *n* aina ya samaki wa maji ya chumvi aliyekaushwa kwa moshi; *(fig)* jambo la kupoteza lengo. **draw a ~ herring across the trail** poteza lengo (kwa kuleta mambo yasiyohusika). **neither fish, flesh, nor good ~ herring** -siyoeleweka. **~ hot** *adj (of a metal)* -enye moto sana (hata kuwa nyekundu); *(fig)* -liohemkwa, -liochachafika, -lioghadhabika sana. **~ Indian** *n (arch)* Mhindi Mwekundu, Mmarekani wa asili. **~lead** *n* kipande cha risasi nyekundu. **~-letter day** sikukuu; siku ya kumbukumbu. **~ light** *n* taa nyekundu, alama ya hatari. **see the ~ light** tambua hatari. **~-light district** mtaa wa makahaba, danguro. **~ meat** *n* nyama ya ng'ombe, mbuzi, kondoo n.k. **~ pepper** *n* pilipili hoho. **~ rag** *n*. **like a ~ rag to a bull** kichocheo, hasira. **~ tape** *n (fig)* urasimu *n* 1 rangi nyekundu. 2 nguo nyekundu. 3 *(colloq)* mkomunisti, mfuasi wa ukomunisti. 4 *(comm)* upande wa madeni katika mahesabu. **be in the ~** ishiwa; -wa na madeni. **~den** *vt,vi* tia wekundu, -wa -ekundu, iva usoni. **~dish** *adj* -ekundu kidogo.

redact *vt* hariri. **~ion** *n*.

redeem *vt* 1 ~ **(from)** komboa, okoa *~ one's right* komboa haki ya mtu. 2 timiza ahadi. 3 komboa (kwa kulipa). 4 fidia. **~able** *adj* -enye kuweza kukombolewa; -a kukomboleka. **the R~er** Yesu Kristo; Mwokozi. **redemption** *n* wokovu; ukombozi, fidia *the equity of~* haki ya ukombozi *past/beyond* -siokomboleka tena; -siyorekebishika. **redemptive** *adj* -a kuokoa; -a kufidia.

redeploy *vt* ondoa/hamisha na kupanga upya.

rediffusion *n* mfumo wa matangazo (ya redio, televisheni, n.k.) hadharani.

redo *vt* fanya/tengeneza upya.

redolent *adj* ~ **of** *(formal)* -enye harufu kali; -enye kunukia; *(fig)* -a kuleta kumbukumbu (za jambo fulani). **redolence** *n*.

redouble *vt,vi* 1 ongeza, zidisha *they ~d their efforts* walizidisha jitihada zao. 2 *(bridge)* fanya maradufu *n (bridge)* kufanya maradufu; kurudufu.

redoubt *n* kituo muhimu (katika ngome).

redoubtable *adj (liter)* mashuhuri, -a kuogofya *~ person* gogo.

redound *vi* **~to** *(formal)* endeleza, kuza, letea, changia *~ to his credit* inamletea heshima.

redress *vt* 1 rekebisha; fidia. 2 **~ the balance** sawazisha mambo tena *n* fidia, jazi, marekebisho *seek~* tafuta haki.

reduce *vt,vi* ~ **(to)** 1 *(lessen)* shusha, punguza, teremsha *~ one's expenditure* punguza matumizi. 2 *(subdue)* lazimisha *~ to silence* nyamazisha *~ to submission* tiisha *be ~d to begging* lazimishwa kuombaomba. **~ to the rank** nyang'anywa cheo. 3 *(change)* geuza umbile (kwa kuponda, kusaga, kushindika) *~ wood logs to pulp* shindika magogo. **reducible** *adj*. **reduction** *n* 1 kupunguza, kupunguka, upungufu *price ~* upunguzaji wa bei. 2 *(maps, photograph, etc)* kupunguza (ukubwa). 3 nakala ndogo. **reductio ad absurdum** *n* 1 (*Latin*) kukanusha hoja kwa kubeza; kugeuza/ kuonyesha kuwa hitimisho fulani ni upuuzi.

redundant *adj* 1 -siohitajika, -a kuzidi, -a ziada. **redundance, redundancy** *n* uziada; *(pl redundacies)* kufukuzwa kazi (kwa sababu ya kupunguza nafasi). **~ pay** malipo ya mfanyakazi anayepunguzwa kazi.

reduplicate *vt* radidi, rudia; rudufu. **reduplication** *n* uradidi, urudiaji; urudufu.
reed *n* 1 tete, mafunjo. **a broken** *~(fig)* kitu/mtu asiyeweza kutumainiwa. 2 *(pipe)* filimbi, kilimi. **~y** *adj* 1 -a matete. 2 *(of sounds, voices)* -enye usiyahi.
reef[1] *n* mwamba.
reef[2] *n* tanga *take in a ~* fupisha tanga; *(fig)* endelea kwa hadhari zaidi. **~-knot** *n* fundodufu, rifunoti *vt (of a sail)* punguza ukubwa.
reefer *n* 1 kizibao cha mabaharia. 2 *(sl)* sigara yenye mariwana/bangi.
reek *n* uvundo, rihi mbaya *the ~of tobacco* rihi mbaya ya tumbaku. 2 *(liter and Scot use)* moshi mzito, mvuke/ *vi* 1 nuka vibaya, toa mvuke/moshi. 2 ~ **with** jawa na, hanikiza.
reel[1] *n* kidonge, kigurudumu. **(straight) off the** ~ *(colloq)* bila kupumzika, moja kwa moja; *(cinema)* ukanda, rili *a seven ~film* filamu ya rili saba *vt* sokota uzi (katika kidonge). ~ **sth off** fanya/sema upesi upesi.
reel[2] *vi* 1 *(physically or mentally)* shtuka, shtushwa. 2 pepesuka, sepetuka, sesereka, yumbayumba *he ~ed like a drunken man* alipepesuka kama mlevi. 3 onekana kuchezacheza *the street ~ed before his eyes* aliona kama mtaa unachezacheza.
reel[3] *n* muziki wa ngoma ya kiskoti *vi* cheza ngoma ya kiskoti.
re-entry *n (of space craft)* kuingia tena (kwenye anga ya dunia).
reeve *n* 1 *(hist)* hakimu wa wilaya (au mji). 2 (*Canada*) mwenyekiti wa kijiji au halmashauri ya mji.
re-face *vt (of building)* sawiri upya, -pa sura mpya.
refection *n* viburudisho vya chakula na vinywaji. **refectory** *n* chumba cha kulia, mesini.
refer *vi* 1 ~ **sb/sth (back) ~ to sb/sth)** *(send)* peleka; *(send back)* rejesha, rudisha *~ a question to sb* peleka swali kwa mtu *~ a cheque to the drawer* rudisha hundi kwa mwenyewe. 2 ~ **to** nena, taja. **the person ~red to** mtajwa. 3 husu *this word ~s only to persons* neno hili lahusu watu tu. 4 tumia *~ to a dictionary* tumia kamusi. **~able** *adj*. **~ee** *n* 1 mwamuzi, refa *vt* chezesha. **~ence** *n* 1 kumbukumbu, marejeo *what is the ~* kumbukumbu ni nini? ~ **book** marejeo. ~ **library** maktaba ya marejeo *make a ~ to* fanya kumbukumbu, rejea. **terms of ~** hadidu za rejea. 2 udhamini. **give three ~s** taja wadhamini watatu. 3 **in/with ~ to** kuhusu. **without ~ to** bila kujali, bila kuhusisha na. **referential** *adj*.
referendum *n* kura ya maoni.
refill *vt* jaza tena, tia tena *n* ujazo; (kalamu) kijazi.
refine *vt* 1 takasa, safisha. 2 *(civilize)* adilisha, fanya ungwana, staarabisha. 3 ~ **upon** fanya kuwa nzuri zaidi; rekebisha. **~d** *adj*. ~ **sugar** *n* sukari safi. **~ment** *n* 1 utakaso, usafi, uhalisi *~ of language* ufasaha wa lugha. 2 adabu, ustaarabu, uungwana, makini, malezi mazuri. **~r** *n* msafishaji; kinu cha kusafisha sukari, metali n.k. **~ry** *n* kiwanda cha kusafisha sukari, metali, n.k.
refit *vt,vi (of a ship)* tengenezwa tena, karabati, unda upya *n* uimarishaji meli.
reflate *vt* rudisha uchumi/kiasi cha fedha katika hali yake ya awali.
reflect *vt* 1 akisi, rudisha (nuru, moto). **~ing telescope** darubiniakisi. 2 *(consider)* fikiri, waza, tafakari. 3 ~ **upon** (*disparage*) leta sifa nzuri/mbaya *his action ~ed great credit upon him* tendo lake lilimpatia sifa kubwa. 4 *(express)* akisi *literature ~s society* fasihi huakisi jamii. **~ion** *n* 1 kuakisi, kurudisha (nuru). 2 *(thoughts)* fikira, mawazo. 3 *(censure)* shutuma, masuto. 4 *(visual image, likeness)* mfano; picha (sanamu, mfano) katika kioo (maji). 5 *(maths)* pindu. 6 kitu kiletacho sifa

mbaya. **~ive** *adj* -a makini; -enye mawazo, -enye kuwaza. **~ively** *adv.* **~or** *n* kiakisi.
reflex *adj* 1 *(of action)* -a tendohiari, -a tendohisia (k.m. chafya); -a kujiendea. 2 ~ **camera** kamera akisi. 3 *(maths)* ~ *angle* pembekuu *n* tendohiari; tendohisia. **~ive** *adj (gram)* -a kujirejea.
reflexion *see* **reflection**.
refloat *vt* fanya kuelea tena, ibua.
reflux *n* kupwa, kurudi.
reforest *vt see* **reafforest**.
reform *vt,vi* rekebisha, ongoka, ongoa, hidi *n* 1 kurekebisha kuongoa; mageuzi ~ *school* shule ya kuadibisha. 2 . kurekebisha, sheria *law* ~ urekebishaji sheria. **~er** *n* mleta mabadiliko. **~ist** *n* mleta mabadiliko. **~tion** *n* 1 mageuzo, marekebisho. 2 **the R~** Mageuzo ya (mgawanyiko wa) Kanisa (la Kirumi karne ya 16). **~atory** *n* shule ya maadili; shule ya kuadibisha; -a kuadilisha. **~ed** *adj* -liotengenezwa, -lioongoka, -liogeuka kuwa -ema, -liotengemaa. **the R~ Church** kanisa la Protestanti hasa la mafundisho ya Kalvin; mafundisho ya Kalvin.
refract *vt (of water, air, glass, etc)* chepuka, pinda; pindisha. **~ion** *n* mchepuko, uchepukaji. **angle of ~** pembe mchepuko. **~ed ray** *adj* lenzi/ mwali mchepuko. **~or** *n.* **~ory** *adj* 1 -kaidi. 2 *(of substance)* -gumu. **~oriness** *n.*
refrain[1] *vi* ~ **(from)** jizuia, epuka, acha (kufanya) *please ~ from smoking* tafadhali acha kuvuta sigara; usivute sigara *please ~ from spitting* tafadhali usiteme mate.
refrain[2] *n* kiitikio, kipokeo.
refresh *vt* 1 burudisha/fariji, changamsha. 2 leta nguvu mpya; fanya mpya. 3 kumbusha. ~ **one's memory** jikumbusha. **~ingly** *adv.* 4 ~ **oneself** kula, kunywa. **~ing** *adj* -a kuburudisha, -zuri. **~er** *n* 1 *(leg)* ada ya ziada (alipwayo wakili wakati kesi bado inaendelea). 2 *(colloq)* kiburudisho, kinywaji. 3 kiamsha akili; kinoa ubongo *a ~ course* kozi ya kunoa ubongo, kozi ya kupiga msasa. **~ment** *n* 1 chakula, kinywaji, kiburudishacho *have some ~ment* pata kiburudisho. 2 hali ya kuburudika.
refrigerate *vt* fanya kuwa baridi; hifadhi chakula katika hali ya kutoharibika (kwa kukifanya kiwe katika baridi isiyobadilikabadilika); gandisha. **refrigerant** *n* kituliza joto, kipoza joto; **refrigeration** *n* utiaji kitu baridi. **refrigerator** *n* friji, jokofu, jorafu.
reft see **bereft**.
refuel *vt,vi* jaza tena mafuta (petroli, diseli, n.k.).
refuge *n* kimbilio, mahali pa salama pa kukimbilia *seek ~* omba/tafuta usalama *take ~ in silence* (jihami kwa) kunyamaza. **~e** *n* mkimbizi. **political** mkimbizi wa kisiasa ~ *camp* kambi ya wakimbizi.
refulgent *adj (formal)* -a kung'aa sana -nayong'aa sana. **refulgence** *n.*
refund *vt* rudisha/rejesha fedha; lipa *n* fedha zinazorudishwa.
refuse[1] *vt,vi* kataa, katalia, nyima; gahamu, iza *I was ~d entry* nilikataliwa kuingia *the child is refusing to eat today* leo mtoto anakataa kula. **refusal** *n* 1 kitendo cha kukataa. 2 **(the)** ~ *(with definite article)* haki/upendeleo wa kukubali au kukataa *if ever you decide to publish your manuscript please give me the first ~ of it* ukiamua kuchapisha muswada wako tafadhali nipe mimi fursa ya kwanza ya kufikiria kuuchapisha.
refuse[2] *n* takataka ~ *dump/heap* jalala, jaa (la takataka).
refute *vt* kanusha, thibitisha kuwa uwongo. **refutable** *adj.* **refutation** *n.*
regain *vt* 1 pata tena ~ *health* pona ~ *possession of sth* pata/miliki (kitu) tena. 2 rudia mahali.
regal *adj* -a mfalme, -a kustahili mfalme. **~ly** *adv.* **~ia** *n* 1 nembo/

mapambo ya mfalme. 2 nembo/ mapambano ya cheo fulani.

regale *vt,vi* ~ **oneself/sb (with sth)** anisi, furahisha sana; burudisha.

regard *vt* 1 *(arch)* angalia, tazama kwa makini; kodoa macho. 2 *(consider as one)* kuwa. 3 *(esteem)* stahi, jali, heshimu ~ *sb with esteem* heshimu mtu. 4 husu. **as ~s/~ing** mintarafu ya, kuhusu. **~ful** -ingi wa heshima *n* 1 *(arch lit.)* utazamaji wa kukodoa macho (kwa muda mrefu). 2 mazingatio. 3 heshima, staha, itibari *have little ~ for* -toheshimu. 4 salaamu (za upendo) *my ~s to* unisalimie. 5 suala. **in this ~** kuhusu suala hili. **in/with ~ to** kuhusu. **~ful (of)** *adj*. **~less** *adj*. **~lessly** *adv* bila kujali, pasipo kutia maanani.

regatta *n* mashindano ya mashua (ya kuendeshwa kwa makasia au matanga).

regenerate *vt,vi* 1 ongoa, ongoka. 2 fufua (jambo/chama, n.k.). 3 *(biol)* ota tena *adj* -lioongoka. **regeneration** *n* wongofu, ufufuo. **regenerative** *adj*.

regent *n* 1 kaimu, mtawala wa muda (badala ya mfalme); mtawala mshikiliaji. 2 *(US)* mjumbe wa Halmashauri (ya Chuo Kikuu cha jimbo, n.k.). **regency** *n* utawala wa pahala pa mfalme mwenyewe; kushikilia.

raggae *n* rege: muziki maarufu wa Visiwa vya West Indies.

regicide *n* 1 mwuaji wa mfalme. 2 uuaji wa mfalme.

regime *n* utaratibu/mfumo wa utawala.

regimen *n* kanuni za mlo, mazoezi, michezo n.k. kwa ajili ya kuleta afya.

regiment *n* 1 rejimenti: kikosi chini ya kanali. 2 *(fig)* ~ **of** jeshi ~ *of red ants* jeshi la siafu *vt* shurutisha, amuru. **~ation** *n* hali ya kuwa chini ya uongozi au udhibiti wa mtu mwingine; nidhamu kali ya kisiasa; udhibiti mkali. **~al** *adj* -a kuhusu rejimenti *n (pl)* mavazi ya askari wa rejimenti moja; mavazi ya kijeshi.

Regina *n* malkia anayetawala (hutumika wakati wa kutia sahihi tamko rasmi); (*leg*) dola ~ *vs Jones* dola dhidi ya Jones.

regnant *adj* -enye kutawala. **King ~** *n* mfalme anayetawala.

region *n* 1 eneo, uwanja, sehemu. **the lower ~s** jahanamu. 2 mkoa. **~al** *adj*. **~ally** *adv*.

register *n* 1 rejesta, daftari yenye rekodi. 2 kadiri ya sauti. 3 chombo (mashine) cha kuonyesha na kurekodi kasi, kani, namba. 4 kirekebishi (cha kupanua au kupunguza ukubwa wa tundu, uwazi, n.k.). 5 *(gram)* rejista: lugha itumikayo katika muktadha maalumu. 6 *see* **registry** *vt,vi* ~ **(sth/ oneself) (with sth/sb) (for sth)** 1 sajili, andikisha, rajisi ~ *voters* andikisha wapiga kura ~ *an association* sajili chama. 2 onyesha (hisia, kiasi cha joto, hali, n.k.) *his face ~ed anxiety* uso wake ulionyesha wasiwasi *the thermometer ~ed 40 degrees centigrade* pimajoto ilionyesha nyuzi 40 sentigredi. 3 tuma barua ya rejesta. **registrar** *n* 1 msajili, mrajisi *the ~'s office* ofisi ya msajili ~ *of companies* msajili wa makampuni ~ *of societies* mrajisi/msajili wa vyama. **~-general** *n* mrajisi mkuu. **registration** *n* 1 usajili, uandikishaji ~ *of deaths* usajili wa vifo ~ *plate* bamba la namba (ya kusajiliwa) ya gari. 2 ingizo; rekodi ya mambo. **registry** *n* 1 usajili *central* ~ usajili mkuu. 2 ofisi ya msajili *marriage* ~ ofisi ya msajili wa ndoa. 3 *(also* **register)** masijala.

regress *vi* rudi nyuma. **~ion** *n* kurudi nyuma. **~ive** *adj* -a kurudi nyuma.

regret *n* 1 majuto *have no ~s* usiwe na majuto *feel ~* jutia. 2 **(in** *pl.)* masikitiko *with many ~s* kwa masikitiko makubwa. **~ful** *adj*. **~fully** *adv,vt* 1 juta ~ *past actions* jutia vitendo vya nyuma. 2 *(feel sorry for)*: sikitikia *it is to be ~ted that* imesikitisha kwamba. **~table**

adj -a kusikitisha, -a kujutia. **~tably** *adv*.

regroup *vt,vi* kusanya/kusanyika tena, kusanya/kusanyika upya.

regular *adj* 1 -a kawaida, -a mazoea; -a kila siku ~ *customer* mteja wa kila siku ~ *hours* saa za kawaida ~ *habits* mazoea. 2 -enye sifa zinazotambulika/ zinazokubalika; -lopata mafunzo. 3 -enye kukubalika ~ *procedure* utaratibu unaokubalika. 4 -enye kufuata mpango, -enye utaratibu unaooana. 5 -enye kulingana na viwango vilivyokubaliwa. 6 *(rel)* -enye kufuata sheria za dini. 7 *(colloq)* kamili, kabisa. 8 *(gram)* -enye minyambuliko na mabadiliko ya kawaida. 9 -a kutokea/kufanyika/ kufanya mara kwa mara. 10 linganifu. 11 *(colloq)* safi, nzuri. **~ize** *vt* rekebisha, halalisha, panga/fanya kulingana na kanuni. **~ization** *n*.

regulate *vt* 1 rekebisha. 2 dhibiti; tiisha. **regulator** *n* mrekebishaji, kirekebishaji. **regulation** *n* 1 urekebishaji. 2 taratibu, kanuni; *(attrib)*-enye kufuata taratibu/ kanuni.

regurgitate *vt* cheua, tapika. **regurgitation** *n* mcheuo, matapishi.

rehabilitate *vt* 1 *(of building)* karabati, tengeneza upya. 2 rudisha cheo/ heshima/sifa njema; safisha. 3 *(of a disabled person, etc)* wezesha kuishi maisha ya kawaida. **rehabilitation** *n*.

rehash *vt* tumia tena kitu cha zamani *n* kitu (cha zamani) kilichotumiwa tena.

rehearse *vt* 1. fanya mazoezi. 2 kariri, simulia. **rehearsal** *n* 1 mazoezi (ya maigizo). 2 masimulizi.

reign *n* utawala, enzi *vi* ~ **(over)** tawala, miliki *he ~ed over the country for twenty years* alitawala nchi kwa miaka ishirini *silence ~ed* kimya kilitawala.

reimburse *vt* rejeshea gharama (alizotumia mtu). **~ sb (for) sth** rudishia, lipa. **~ment** *n*.

rein *n* hatamu. **give free ~s to** pa uhuru, achia. **assume/drop the ~s of government** chukua/acha madaraka. **draw ~** (*lit and fig*) punguza mwendo. **hold/take the ~s** (*lit and fig*) ongoza, shika hatamu. **keep a tight ~on** dhibiti vikali *vt* ongoza, zuia (kwa hatamu) *~up/back a horse* zuia/simamisha farasi.

reincarnate *vt* -pa roho mwili mpya *adj* -a kuzaliwa upya (roho) katika mwili wa kiumbe mwingine. **reincarnation** *n (Rel)* imani kuwa roho ya marehemu huingia katika mwili wa mtu mwingine.

reindeer *n* kulungu wa nchi za baridi.

reinforce *vt* imarisha, ongeza nguvu. **~d concrete** saruji iliyoimarishwa (kwa kutumia chuma). **~ment** *n* 1 uimarishaji; msaada, shime. 2 *(pl)* askari, manowari za kuongezea nguvu ya jeshi.

reinstate *vt* rejesha mahali pake, rudishia nafasi yake. **~ment** *n*.

reinsure *vt (of insurance comp)* weka bima katika kampuni kubwa zaidi **reinsurance** *n*.

reissue *vt* toa mara ya pili, toa tena *n* kitu kilichotolewa mara ya pili; chapa ya pili.

reiterate *vt* sema tena na tena, rudia kusema. **reiteration** *n*.

reject *vt* 1 kana, kataa. 2 tupa, *~ food* tapika. **~ion** *n* 1 mtu/kitu kilichokataliwa k.m. mali mbovu *export ~* bidhaa zilizokusudiwa kusafirishwa nje lakini zikakataliwa kutokana na kasoro/uhafifu au uduni wake. 2 kukatalia; kukataliwa.

rejig *vt (of factory, etc)* imarisha kwa kuongeza zana na vyombo vipya.

rejoice *vt,vi* 1 furahisha. 2 ~ **(over/at)** furahi, furahia, terema, shangilia. 3 ~ **in** -wa na *he ~s in the name of Kambare* jina lake ni Kambare. **rejoicing** *n* furaha, shangwe, shangilio, nderemo.

rejoin[1] *vt,vi* jiunga tena, rudia tena, rudiana tena, ungana tena.

rejoin[2] *vt,vi* jibu; *(leg)* jibu mashtaka. **~er** *n* jibu.

rejuvenate *vt,vi* rudishia ujana, rudishia nguvu za ujana.

rejuvenation *n.*
rekindle *vt,vi* washa tena; amsha tena. ~ **sb's zeal** amsha juhudi/raghba ya mtu.
relapse *vt,vi* ~ **(into)** rudia hali fulani tena (hasa uovu, mwendo mbaya, udhaifu, ugonjwa) *n* kuugua tena, kurudia hali mbaya, kurudiwa na ugonjwa. **relapsing fever** *n* homa ya vipindi.
relate *vt,vi* 1 ~ **(to)** simulia (hadithi, habari, n.k.). 2 ~ **to** toa maelezo ya kitu/jambo. 3 ~ **to/with** husisha, husika na. 4 **be ~d (to)** kuwa na mnasaba (na) *he is ~d to me* nina mnasaba naye.
relation *n* 1 masimulizi, maelezo. 2 *(also* **~ship)** uhusiano *the ~ship between husband and wife* uhusiano baina ya mume na mke *the oldman's death and Juma's disappearance have no ~(ship)* kifo cha mzee huyo na kutoweka kwa Juma havina uhusiano. **in/with relation to** kuhusu. 3 mahusiano *have business ~s* kuwa na mahusiano ya kibiashara *we have broken off all ~s with that company* tumevunja mahusiano yetu na kampuni ile. 4 udugu, mnasaba. **relative** *n* 1 ndugu, jamaa. 2 *(gram)* ~ **pronoun** kiwakilishi rejeshi *adj* 1 -a kuwiana na. 2 ~ **to** -enye uhusiano na, -nayohusu. ~ **motion** mwendo unaohusiana *with ~ ease* kwa urahisi bila shida. **relatively** *adv* kiasi.
relativism *n* imani kwamba maarifa na maadili ni mambo ya mpito yanayotawaliwa na uwezo wa ubongo na wakati.
relativity *n* 1 nadharia ya Einstein isemayo kwamba vipimo vya mwendo, nafasi na wakati vinawiana/kadiriana. 2 *(gram)* **linguistic ~** *(Sapir-Whorf hypothesis)* nadharia tete ya Sapir na Whorf isemayo kuwa lugha hutawala namna watu wanavyoufinyanga/wanavyouumba ulimwengu wao.
relax *vt,vi* 1 legeza, punguza. 2 *(relieve)* pumzika, pumzisha, burudisha; *(of bowels)* endesha, fungua ~ *the limbs* pumzisha/legeza viungo. **~ation** *n* ulegezaji, ulegevu; burudani.
relay[1] *n* 1 rilei : ubadilishanaji zamu wa wanyama, watu, n.k. kuchukua nafasi ya waliochoka. ~ **race** mbio za kupokezana *do by ~s* pokezana kazi. 2 *(telegraphy/broadcasting)* mtambo wa kupokea na kurushia habari *vt* rushia habari ~ *a message* peleka ujumbe.
relay[2] *vt* tandika (kebo, zulia) upya.
release *vt* ~ **(from)** 1 fungua, ruhusu kwenda, achia huru; ondoa *~sb of a debt* futa, samehe deni. 2 ruhusu kutolewa (kwa habari, filamu, n.k.). 3 *(leg)* achia mwingine haki/mali, n.k. *n* 1 ufunguliaji; ufunguliwaji, uachiaji huru. 2 kutolewa toleo (la filamu, n.k.) *the new ~s* filamu mpya. 3 wenzo unaoachilia au kufanya huru sehemu ya mashine.
relegate *vt* ~ **(sth/sb to sth)** 1 wakilisha. 2 teremsha, shusha ~ *a team to a third division* shusha timu kuwa daraja la tatu.
relent *vi* tulia, poa, punguza (hasira, ukali, n.k.). **~less** *adj* bila huruma *~less persecution* mateso yasiyo na huruma. **~lessly** *adv.*
relevant *adj* husika, -enye kuhusu (yajadiliwayo) *give him all the ~ books* mpatie vitabu vyote vinavyohusika. **~ly** *adv.* **relevance** *n* uhusiano.
relic *n* 1 *(of saints)* masalio. 2 ukumbusho, kumbukumbu. 3 *(pl)* maiti, mabaki ya binadamu.
relict *n (leg)* mjane, kizuka.
relief[1] *n* 1 *(of pain, distress, anxiety)* tulizo, shime, faraja, nafuu. 2 msaada (wa kuwapunguzia watu dhiki) *a ~ fund* mfuko wa msaada *be on ~* ishi kwa msaada wa serikali. 3 burudisho. 4 *(of a siege)* uimarishaji ngome; kukomboa. 5 *(taking turns)* mapokezano; mtu wa zamu ijayo; *(attrib)* -a ziada ~ *bus* basi la ziada.
relieve *vt* 1 fariji, punguza, tuliza *she*

was ~ to get the news alifarijika kupata habari zile. ~ **one's feelings** punguza mawazo/hisia. ~ **oneself** kojoa, tabawali. 2 -wa na zamu, pokea zamu. 3 ~ **sb of sth** mpokelea mtu kitu fulani, saidia; *(joc)* iba, ibia mtu; fukuza kazi, achisha kazi; vua madaraka. 4 dhihirisha, fanya ku(ji)tokeza.

relief[2] *n* 1 mbinu ya uchongaji/uumbaji inayofanya sanamu itokeze katika msingi wake. 2 sanamu iliyochongwa/ iliyoumbwa kwa kutokeza katika msingi wake. 3 *(in drawing etc)* uchoraji unaofanya kitu kitokeze katika msingi wake kwa kutumia vitu kama rangi. n.k. ~ **map** ramani ionyeshayo milima, mabonde, n.k. kwa kutumia rangi ili kuvifanya vitu hivyo vitokeze. 4 *(lit or fig)* uwazi, sura ya kutokeza *be/stand out in ~ against* tofautiana na; -wa kinyume na *his behaviour stood out in ~ against his principles* tabia yake ilitofautiana na taratibu zake.

religion *n* 1 dini: imani katika kuwepo kwa Mungu/kiumbe mwenye nguvu zaidi ya binadamu, aliyeumba na anayeudhibiti ulimwengu. 2 dini: mojawapo ya mifumo kadhaa ya imani na ibada zake (k.m. Ukristo, Uislamu, Ubudha). 3 utawa. 4 imani: kitu ambacho mtu huamini na kushikilia sana *she makes a ~ of keeping her house clean* anang'ang'ania sana usafi wa nyumba yake. **religious** *adj* 1 -a dini. 2 -a mcha Mungu. 3 -a utawa 4 -a imani. 5 -a kushikilia sana jimbo n mtawa, mchaMungu, mswalidina. **religiously** *adv*. **religiousness** *n*.

reline *vt (of garment)* tia bitana mpya.

relinquish *vt* acha, achilia ~ *a habit* acha tabia fulani. ~ **one's hold of/ over sb/sth** achilia mtu/jambo.

reliquary *n* sanduku/kibweta (cha kuwekea masalio).

relish *n* 1 ladha, utamu; mvuto, kivutio. 2 shauku, moyo *have no more ~ for sth* -tofurahia kitu, kinai kitu. 3 *(seasoning)* kiungo, kitoweo *vt* furahia, pendezwa na.

relive *vt* kumbukia, pitia tena, rudia.

relocate *vt, vi* hamisha; hamishwa; hamia makao mapya. **relocation** *n* kuhamia/kuhamishia makao mapya; *(of war)* kuhamishia wananchi katika makazi mapya.

reluctant *adj* ~ **(to do sth)** -totaka, sita, kaidi; -a kukalifu. **~ly** *adv*. **reluctance** *n*.

rely *n* ~ **on/upon** tumaini, tegemea; tawakali ~ *on oneself* jitegemea. **reliable** *adj* -a kutegemewa, -a kuaminika, -a kutumainiwa ~ *information* habari ya kuaminika. **reliably** *adv*. **reliability** *n* tegemeo, tumaini, uaminifu -a utawa. **reliance** *n* imani, tumaini, tegemeo *place ~ on* tumaini, aminia, tegemea. **self reliant** *adj* -enye kujitegemea *be self-reliant* jitegemee.

remain *vi* 1 baki, salia *nothing ~ed for us but* hatukuwa na la kufanya ila. 2 endelea kuwepo/ishi mahali fulani au katika hali fulani, bakia. **~der** *n* baki, salio. **~s** *n* 1 masalio, mabaki *(of food)* makombo; *(of building)* gofu. 2 *(also* **relics***)*. maiti.

remand *vt* weka mahabusi, weka rumande *n* rumande; mahabusi ~ *prison* mahabusi ~ *house/home* rumande ya watoto.

remark *vt,vi* 1 sema. 2 **~on/upon** toa maoni, zungumzia. 3 *(arch)* ona, tazama *n* 1 maoni, maneno *pass rude ~s about sb* toa maneno mabaya kuhusu mtu fulani. 2 kutazamwa. **~able** *adj* -a ajabu, -a kusifika, -sio kifani. **~ably** *adv*.

remarry *vt, vi* oa/olewa tena. **remarriage** *n*.

remedy *n* dawa; tiba *the ~ is worse than the disease* tiba yake ni mbaya kuliko ugonjwa wenyewe *vt* tengeneza, rekebisha. **remedial** *adj* -a kuponya, -a marekebisho, -a kutuliza ~ *classes* masomo ya kujirekebisha. **remediable** *adj* -a kuponyeka; -a kutulizika.

remember *vt,vi* 1 kumbuka, dhukuru. 2 **~ sb to sb** pa salamu, salimia *please ~ me to him* tafadhali mpe salamu zangu; unisalimie. 3 tunuka *~ someone in a will* tunuka katika wasia. **remembrance** *n* 1 ukumbusho, kumbukumbu *escape sb's ~* sahau. 2 salamu (zilizopelekwa kwa barua au kwa aliyetumwa).

remind *vt* **~ sb (to do sth/that..)**; **~ sb of sth/sb** kumbusha *that ~s me!* hiyo inanikumbusha. **~er** *n* kumbusho.

reminisce *vi* **~ (about)** kumbuka ya kale, (zingatia na zungumza juu ya mambo yaliyopita). **~nce** *n* 1 **~ (of)** ukumbukaji mambo ya kale. 2 *(pl)* makumbusho. **~nt (of)** *adj* -a kukumbusha; -a kukumbuka mambo yaliyopita. **~ntly** *adv*.

remiss *adj* **~ in/of** -zembe; vivu, ajizi. **~ly** *adv*. **~ness** *n*.

remit *vt,vi* 1. *(usu. of God)* ondolea dhambi, samehe. 2 *(of debts, penalty)* samehe, achilia, futa. 3 *(money, etc)* peleka kwa posta, lipa. **~tee** *n* mpelekewaji malipo. **~ter** *n* mpelekaji malipo. 4 *(of pain, effort, etc)* punguza, legeza. 5 **~ sth to sb** tumia mtu kitu *~ sth to higher authority* peleka kwa mamlaka ya juu (kwa uamuzi). **~tance** *n* 1 fedha; malipo. 2 upelekaji fedha; kiasi cha pesa kilichopelekwa mahali pengine. **remissible** *adj* -lioweza kusamehewa, -a kusameheka, -a kuhurumiwa. **remission** *n* 1 msamaha (wa dhambi unaofanywa na Mungu). 2 kusabilia deni au adhabu. 3 kupungua (kwa maumivu, bidii). **remissive** *adj*.

remnant *n* mabaki, masazo; makombo *~ sale* seli ya mabaki ya vitambaa.

remonstrate *vi* lalamika; pinga. **~ with sb about sth** pingana na mtu juu ya jambo fulani. **remonstrance** *n* ulalamikaji wa kupinga kitu/jambo.

remorse *n* 1 **~ (for)** majuto, toba. 2 huruma *without ~* bila huruma. **~ful** *adj*. **~fully** *adv*. **~less** *adj* pasipo kujuta, katili. **~lessly** *adv*.

remote *adj* 1 -a zamani *the ~past* zamani za kale. 2 -a mbali. *~ control* -enye kuendeshwa/kufanywa toka mbali, -liotengwa (kwa maono, kwa moyo wa kupenda). 3 *(feelings, interests, etc)* liopishana sana, liotengana, mbalimbali. 4 *(not friendly)* baridi. 5 *(insignificant)* dogo *I haven't the ~st idea* sijui hata kidogo, sina habari. **~ly** *adv*. **~ness** *n*.

remount *vt,vi* 1 panda tena. 2 *(of photographs, maps, etc)* weka katika fremu tena. 3 gawia mtu/wanajeshi farasi mpya *n* farasi mpya; ugawiaji watu farasi mpya.

remove *vt,vi* 1 **~ (from)** ondoa, ondosha. 2 **~ (from)** hama; hamisha, hawilisha, hajiri. **~ mountains** *(fig)* fanya miujiza. 3 *(of clothes)* vua; *(of bark)* ambua. 4 *(from office)* uzulu, fukuza. 5 *(erase)* futa. 6 *(of spell)* agua, eua, adua, tegua. 7 **~d** (*of cousins*) mtoto wa binamu *n* hatua *be one ~ from sth* pakana, karibiana na. **removable** *adj*. **removal** *n*.

remunerate *vt* **~ sb (for sth)** lipa, -pa ujira, tuza, -pa zawadi. **remuneration** *n* ujira, tunzo, zawadi. **remunerative** *adj* -a kuleta faida.

renaissance *n* (also **renascence) 1 the ~ (Europe)** kipindi mwamko-sanaa (katika karne ya 14, 15 na 16), kipindi cha kuchipuka upya. 2 mvuvumko.

renal *adj* -a mafigo.

rename *vt* pa jina jipya, batiza upya, ita upya.

renascence *n see* **renaissance**.

rend *vt,vi* 1 tatua, pasua, rarua; penya *~ one's hair (in grief)* timua nywele. 2 pokonya, pora.

render *vt* 1 **~ sth (to sb)** toa, lipa, rudisha, onyesha (heshima) *~ thanks* toa shukurani. 2 leta, peleka. **~ an account of oneself/one's behaviour** elezea, jieleza *~ed account* ankara iliyotolewa (kwa kulipwa). 3 fanya, geuza kuwa katika hali fulani *the drink ~ed him speechless* ulevi ulimfanya kuwa bubu. 4 **~ sth (down)** yeyusha; safisha siagi/samli kwa kuyeyusha. 5 *(of building)* piga lipu. 6 tafsiri, fanya, igiza. **~ing** *n* 1 *(translation)*tafsiri, fasili. **rendition** *n* 1 utambaji. 2 ufasiri, ufafanuzi.

rendezvous *n* 1 mahali pa kukutanika; mahali pa miadi. 2 makutano *vi* kutana (mahali palipochaguliwa).

renegade *n* 1 msaliti, haini; mwasi. 2 *(rel)* muritadi *vi* saliti, ritadi, asi.

renage, renegue *vi* 1 *(in card games)* kosa kucheza karata iliyochaguliwa hali unayo mkononi. 2 vunja ahadi au kauli.

renew *vt* 1 tengeneza/fanya upya, tia nguvu, -pa moyo. 2 pata/toa tena. 3 anza, rudia tena *~ one's youth* rudia ujana. **~able** *adj*. **~al** *n*.

renounce *vt* 1 *(refuse)* kataa, kanusha, kana. 2 burai (madai). 3 *(give up)* acha, jitoa katika jambo, achilia mamlaka ya mtu. **renunciation** *n* 1 kano, kanusho. 2 *(relinquishment)* kuacha, kujinyima, kujihini. **renunciatory** *adj*.

renovate *vt* rekebisha, fanyiza upya, karabati. **renovation** *n* 1 urekebishaji. 2 ukarabati; matengenezo. **renovator** *n* mtengenezaji.

renown *n* sifa, utukufu, umashuhuri, jina *a town of great ~* mji wa sifa kuu. **~ed** *adj* -enye sifa, adhimu, tukufu, mashuhuri.

rent[1] *pp of* **rend**.

rent[2] *n* kodi. ~ **rebate** kipunguo cha kodi *~ restriction* usimamiaji wa kodi *~ restriction board* halmashauri ya kusimamia kodi. ~ **collector** *n* mkusanya kodi. **~ier** mpangishaji, mtu ambaye mapato yake hutokana na kupangisha nyumba. **~-free** *adj* -siolipiwa, -siotolewa kodi, wakfu. **~-roll** *n* daftari ya upangishaji, orodha ya ukodishaji *vt,vi* ~ **to** pangisha, kodisha. **~from** panga, kodi. **~able** *adj* a kupangishika. **~al** *n* 1 kodi. 2 mapato ya kodi.

rent[3] *n* 1 mpasuko, mtatuko, ufa. 2 *(fig)* mfarakano, mtengano.

rep[1] *n* repu: kitambaa cha kufunikia viti.

rep[2] *(colloq) (abbr.)* **repertory, reputation, representative**.

repair[1] *vt* 1 karabati, fanya matengenezo; *(of clothes)* shona, tia kiraka *a road under ~* barabara inayofanyiwa matengenezo. 2 rekebisha, weka sawa *n* matengenezo, *(state)* hali (nzuri au mbaya) *in good ~* -nzima *in bad ~* bovu *keep in good ~* tunza vizuri *put in ~* fanya matengenezo. **~er** *n* mtengenezaji. **~ing** *n* utengenezaji, ushonaji wa kutia kiraka. **reparable** *adj* -enye kuweza kutengenezwa, -a kutengenezeka, -a kuweza kufidiwa, -a kulipika. **reparation** *n* 1 ulipaji fidia, kufidia (hasara, uharibifu). 2 fidia.

repair[2] *vi ~to* enda, zuru.

repartee *n* malumbano.

repast *n (formal)* mlo.

repatriate *vt* rudisha kwao, rejesha makwao *~a fugitive* rudisha mkimbizi kwao *n ~d person* mtu aliyerejeshwa kwao. **repatriation** *n*.

repay *vt,vi* 1 rejesha pesa, kitu, n.k. ulichochukua, lipa. 2 ~ **sth; ~sb (for sth)** lipiza; lipizia *adj* -a kulipika. **~ment** malipo, kulipa, kulipiza, malipizo.

repeal *vt* tangua, batilisha; futa, (sheria) *n* mtanguo, kufuta; ubatilifu.

repeat *vt* 1 rudia. 2 kariri, soma/sema kwa ghibu. 3 *(of numbers)* rudiarudia, tokea tena (mara nyingi). 4 *(of taste)* bakia mdomoni. 5 *(of commerce)* toa tena (bidhaa), rudia kutoa *n* 1 marudio k.m. mchezo, kipindi cha redio. 2 *(music)* alama ya kuonyesha mahali pa kurudia katika muziki. **~edly** *adv* -liofanywa tena na tena. **~er** *n* 1 bunduki inayotema risasi. 2 *(E.A)* mtu anayerudia (darasa n.k.). **~ing** *adj* -a kurudiarudia *~ decimal* desimali ya kurudiarudia. **repetition** *n* 1 kurudiarudia; urudiaji. 2 *(of poetry)* ukariri, usomaji wa ghibu. **repetitious, repetitive** *adj* -a kurudiarudia.

repel *vt* 1 fukuza. 2 kataa; zuia ~ *an enemy* fukuza adui. 3 chukiza. **~lent** *adj* -a kuchukiza; -a kukirihi *n* kiwinga.

repent *vt,vi ~(of)* tubu, juta. **~ance** *n* toba. **~ant** *adj* -a kutubu, -a kujutia *he is ~ant of his wrongs* anajutia makosa yake *n* mjutaji. **~antly** *adv*.

repercussion *n* 1 mruko/mtupo nyuma, mwangwi. 2 *(usu pl)* athari, matokeo hasi *be followed by ~s* fuatiwa na matokeo hasi (yasiyokusudiwa).

repertoire *n* mkusanyiko wa maonyesho (nyimbo, tamthilia, n.k.) ya msanii mmoja au kikundi kimoja cha sanaa.

repertory *n* 1 hazina (ya habari, maarifa, n.k. 2 *see* **repertoire** ~ *theatre company (abb. rep)* kikundi cha sanaa (kinachobadilisha wachezaji/tamthilia mara kwa mara).

repine *vi (formal)* **~(at)** onea uchungu. ~ **against** lalamikia *n*.

replace *vt* 1 rudishia mahali pake. 2 ~ **sb/sth by/with** chukua nafasi ya, ingia mahali pa, badilisha *~sb with a machine* badilisha mtu na/kwa mashine. **~able** *adj* -enye kuweza kubadilishwa, -a kubadilishika, -enye kuweza kuchukuliwa nafasi. **~ment** *n* ubadili; badala.

replay *n* marudio ya mchezo *vt* rudia mchezo *(colloq)* rudia kupiga kanda.

replenish *vt* ~ **(with)** jaza tena, sheheneza. **~ment** *n* ujazaji tena, ushehenezaji tena.

replete *adj* ~ **(with)** *(formal)* tele, -liojaa ~ *with food* -lioshiba. **repletion** *n (formal)* shibe *to eat to ~* kuvimbiwa *be full to ~* shiba mno/ kupita kiasi.

replica *n* nakala, nakili halisi; rupia/ shilingi kwa nyenziye. **~te** *vt* toa nakala, rudufu.

reply *vi* ~ **(to)** jibu, itika; peleka/tuma jibu. *n* jibu, itikio. ~ **paid** jibu lililokwishalipiwa.

report *vt,vi* 1 toa ripoti, toa taarifa, pasha habari; simulia mambo (uliyoona, uliyosikia, uliyofanya). ~ *progress* toa taarifa ya maendeleo. ~ **sth out** *(US)* rejesha pamoja na maoni. **~edly** kwa mujibu wa taarifa, inavyosemekana. **~ed speech** *n* kauli taarifa. 2 nakili, andika (kwa hatimkato). 3 **(oneself) (to sb/sth) (for sth)** ripoti ~ *to the manager* piga ripoti kwa meneja ~ *to the officer in charge* piga ripoti kwa afisa mfawidhi. 4 ~ **sb/sth (to sb) (for sth)** shtaki, lalamika ~ *a child to his parents* shtaki mtoto kwa wazazi wake. **~age** *n* (mtindo wa) utoaji habari (wa magazeti) *n* 1 ripoti, taarifa *annual* ~ taarifa ya mwaka *law* ~ ripoti ya kesi. 2 mshindo *it burst with a* ~ ilipasuka kwa kishindo. 3 uvumi, tetesi *the ~ goes* inasemekana kwamba, kuna uvumi kwamba. 4 sifa nzuri/njema *people of good* ~ watu wenye sifa nzuri. **~er** *n* mtoa habari; mwandishi wa habari.

repose[1] *vt,vi* 1 pumzisha, egemeza, weka, laza. 2 ~ **on** pumzika *n* kupumzika, utulivu, raha, kimya. **~ful** *adj* tulivu, -nyamavu, -lio kimya.

repose[2] *vt* **sth in sth/sb** amini ~ *on his promises* amini ahadi zake.

reposit *vt* weka (kitu) kwenye ghala (bohari). **~ory** *n* 1 hazina, mahali pa kuhifadhia vitu k.v. bohari, ghala, makumbusho n.k. 2 hazina, chemchemi ya habari *be ~r of* -wa na hazina ya.

repot *vt* hamishia (mmea) katika chungu kingine.

reprehend *vt* karipia, kemea, shutumu. **reprehensible** *adj* -a kulaumika. **reprehension** *n*.

represent *vt* 1 ~ **sth (to sb)**. 2 leta, toa, sawiri (picha, dalili) mfano wa *a picture that ~s the garden of Eden* picha iletayo mfano wa bustani ya Aden. 3 wakilisha, eleza. 4 fanya au sema kwa niaba ya. 5 igiza, iga. **~ation** *n* 1 picha, sanamu, fano, taswira. 2 kuonyesha, onyesho. 3 uwakili; uwakilishi. **proportional ~**

idadi fulani ya viti katika bunge kulingana na idadi ya kura ambazo chama kimepata. 4 *(statement)* maelezo (ya malalamiko) *false* ~ ghiliba. **~ative** *adj*. ~ **of** -wakilishi, -a uwakilishi, -a ujumbe ~ *government* serikali ya uwakilishi ~ *action* madai ya jumla *n* 1 mfano. 2 mwakilishi *legal* ~ mwakilishi wa kisheria *permanent* ~ mwakilishi wa kudumu.

repress *vt* zima, zuia, nyamazisha, komesha. **~ed** (*of emotions*) *adj* -liozimwa. **~ion** *n* 1 uzuiaji kwa nguvu; kunyamazisha, kuzimwa, uonevu. 2 *(psych)* mfadhaiko. **~ive** *adj* -a kuzuia, -a uonevu, -a kugandamiza, -a kukomesha ~ *government* serikali onevu.

reprieve *vt* ahirisha/cheleweshaadhabu (agh. ya kunyonga mtu aliyeua); *(fig)* -pa, toa nafuu, achilia kwa muda ~ *a debtor* achilia mdeni kwa muda *n* 1 *(leg)* uzuiaji kwa muda/ ucheleweshaji wa kunyongwa mtu aliyehukumiwa. 2 achilio la muda; kuachiliwa kwa kitambo.

reprimand *vt* karipia, kemea *n* karipio/ kemeo rasmi.

reprint *vt* piga chapa tena, toa kitabu mara ya pili *n* lopoo.

reprisal *n* 1 ulipizaji kisasi (kwa kufanya yale yale uliyotendewa) **take** ~ lipiza kisasi. 2 *(pl)* vitendo vya kulipiza kisasi (hasa nchi kwa nchi) katika vita.

reprise *n* kibwagizo, mkarara, kiitikio.

reproach *vt* ~ **sb (for/with sth)** laumu, suta, shutumu, kengemeka. ~ **oneself** jilaumu *n* 1 shutuma, lawama, kengemeko. 2 aibu, fedheha. **above/ beyond** ~ -sio fedheha/-laumika. **in** ~ ishi katika fedheha *heap ~s on sb* fedhehesha sana mtu. 3 ~ **(to)** kitu cha aibu/fedheha. **~ful** *adj* -a kushutumu, -a kulaumu. **~fully** *adv*.

reprobate *vt* -tokubali, kataa, chukia *n* baa, fisadi, fasiki, mpotovu *adj* -ovu, potovu. **reprobation** *n*.

reproduce *vt, vi* 1 nakili, fanya sura/ mfano/namna ya. 2 fuatisha, rudisha, toa tena, leta mara ya pili. 3 zaa. 4 ota upya. **~r** *n* mtu ambaye/kitu ambacho huzaa. **reproducible** *adj* -a kutengenezeka upya. **reproductive** *adj*; -a uzazi -a uwezo wa kuzaa (wanyama au mimea). **reproduction** *n* 1 kuzaa; uzazi. 2 nakala halisi. 3 *(fresh growth)* kuota upya; kitu kinachoota upya.

reproof *vt* fanya tena kitu (k.m. koti) kisipenyeke maji.

reprove *vt* ~ **sb (for sth)** shutumu, laumu. **reprovingly** *adv*. **reproof** *n* 1 lawama, mashutumu. 2 hali ya kuonyesha kulaumu/kushutumu *looks of reproof* uso wa kulaumu/ kushutumu.

reptile *n* mtambaazi: mnyama wa ngeli ya reptilia. **reptilian** *adj* -a reptilia, -enye kutambaa.

republic *n* 1 jamhuri. 2 jamii (ya waandishi n.k.). ~**an** *adj* -a jamhuri *n* 1 mtu apendaye serikali ya jamhuri. 2 *(US)* mwanachama wa *Republican Party*. **~anism** *n* falsafa/ sera ya serikali ya jamhuri.

repudiate *vt* 1 kana. 2 kataa kukubali/ kukiri. 3 kataa kutimiza wajibu; kataa kulipa ~ *a debt* kataa kulipa deni. **repudiation** *n*.

repugnant *adj* 1 -a kuchukiza, -a kukirihi, -a kutia kinyaa. 2 *(contrary)* kinzani, -a mgongano. **repugnance** *n* 1 kinyaa. 2 ukinzani, mgongano.

repulse *vt* 1 rudisha nyuma (maadui); shinda; fukuza. 2 kataa (msaada); fanya mtu asizoee, katisha tamaa kwa kufanyia inadi *n* 1 kufukuza/ kufukuzwa, kushindwa. 2 kanyo, makatazo *suffer a* ~ rudishwa nyuma (vitani). **repulsion** *n* 1 kinyaa. 2 kurudishwa nyuma, kufukuzwa. 3 *(phys)* hali ya vitu kukimbiana/ kutotangamana. **repulsive** *adj*. 1 -baya, chushi, -a kutia kinyaa, -a kukirihi. 2 -siovutia. **repulsiveness** *n*. **repulsively** *adv*.

reputation *n* sifa *of good* ~ -enye sifa njema *of bad* ~ -enye sifa mbaya *live up to one's* ~ ishi kufuatana na sifa

ya mtu. **reputable** *adj* -a sifa njema, zuri, -a kuheshimika. **reputably** *adv*.
repute *n* sifa *ill ~* sifa mbaya *a specialist of ~* mtaalamu mashuhuri *know sb by ~* fahamu mtu kwa sifa yake *vt* **be reputed as/to be** julikana/sifika kwa (*attrib.*) *adj* -a kusifika, -a kujulikana, -enye kusemekana *he is reputed to be the father* inasemekana kuwa ndiye baba. **~dly** *adv*.
request *n* ombi, matakwa *by ~* kwa maombi *I have a ~ to make* nina ombi *vt* **~ sth (from/of sb); ~ sb to do sth** taka, sihi, omba *may I ~ you* tafadhali *~ sb's presence* alika mtu, omba mtu ahudhurie.
requiem *n ~ mass* misa ya wafu.
require *vt* 1 *(need)* taka, hitaji *whatever is ~d* chochote kitakiwacho. 2 **~ sth (of sb; ~ sb to do sth; ~ that** *(often passive) (formal)* shurutisha, taka kwa nguvu, amrisha, lazimisha. **~ sb to do sth** shurutisha mtu kufanya jambo. **~ment** *n* mahitaji, matakwa, masharti.
requisite *n* **~ (for)** mahitaji *adj* -liotakiwa; lazima, -liohitajiwa.
requisition *n* hali ya kuhitaji/kutaka/kulazimisha(jambo lifanywe); mahitaji rasmi (ambayo agh huandikwa) *~ order* hati ya mahitaji. *vt* **~ (for)** andika/peleka mahitaji. *~ sb's services* taka/hitaji huduma za fulani.
requite *vt* 1 **~ sth/sb (with sth)** (*formal*) lipa. 2 lipiza kisasi. **requital** *n*.
reredos *n (church-altar)* pambo la ukutani nyuma ya altare.
re-run *n (cinema, TV)* marudio (ya kipindi, filamu, n.k.) *vt* rudia (filamu/sinema/kipindi), n.k.
rescind *vt (leg)* tangua, futa, vunja, batilisha. **rescission** *n*.
rescript *n* 1 agizo/tangazo rasmi (hasa litolewalo na mtawala). 2 agizo la Papa.
rescue *vt* **~ sb from sth/sb** okoa, saidia *a ~ team* kikosi cha waokoaji *n* wokovu, msaada, kuokolewa. **come/go to the ~/to sb's ~** saidia, okoa mtu. **~r** *n* mwokozi.
research *n* utafiti, uchunguzi *~ work* kazi za uchunguzi *vi* **~ (into)** chungua, tafiti. **~er** *n* mchunguzi, mtafiti.
reseat *vt* 1 toa, pa, kiti kipya *~ a chair* weka kitako kipya. 2 kaa tena.
resemble *vt* fanana, landa, shabihi *they ~ each other* wanafanana. **resemblance** *n*.
resent *vt* chukia, udhiwa, kasirikia, sonona *he ~s her coming* anachukia kuja kwake. **~ful** *adj* -enye chuki, -enye kero, -a kuudhi. **~fully** *adv*. **~ment** *n* uchungu, chuki, maudhi, hasira, mfundo.
reserve *vt* 1 weka akiba, limbika; ahirisha *the judgement was ~d* hukumu iliahirishwa. 2 setiri, bakiza, saza. 3 weka/shika/chukua nafasi. **all seats ~d** viti vyote vimechukuliwa. **all rights ~d** *adj (leg)* haki imehifadhiwa. **~d** *adj (person)* kimya, -siyoonyesha hisia kwa urahisi. **~dly** *adv*. **reservation** *n* 1 kusita, shaka; ajizi (ya kukubali jambo) *accept sth without ~* pokea kitu kwa moyo mkunjufu *accept a plan with ~* pokea mpango kwa shaka. 2 *(US)* ardhi iliyohifadhiwa kwa matumizi maalumu *the Indian ~* ardhi iliyotengwa kwa matumizi ya Wahindi wa Asili. 3 *(esp US)* kuishika/kuchukua/kuweka nafasi agh. ya usafiri *n* 1 akiba, limbiko *~ fund* mfuko wa akiba *a ~ player* mchezaji wa akiba. 2 *(mil)* **the R~** askari wa akiba (ambao wako nje ya jeshi lakini wanaweza kuhitajiwa wakati wowote); hali ya kitu kuwekwa kama akiba. 4 hifadhi *game ~* mbuga (za hifadhi ya wanyama) *a forest ~* hifadhi ya msitu. 5 kizuizi. 6 haya, kimya *~ of manner* mkimya. **reservist** *n* askari wa akiba/msaada.
reservoir *n* 1 hodhi, ziwa, bwawa, tangi la maji. 2 *(fig)* hazina.
reset *vt* 1 noa upya (msumeno, n.k.). 2

panga upya. 3 *(printing)* seti upya.
resettle *vt,vi* pa/pata makazi mapya.
reshuffle *vt* panga upya, badilisha, changanya ~ *the personnel* badilisha wafanyakazi ofisini ~ *the cabinet* badilisha baraza la mawaziri. *n* upangaji upya, ubadilishaji.
reside *vt* 1 ~ **(in/at)** ishi, kaa, -wa na nyumba/makao/makazi ~ *abroad* ishi ng'ambo. 2 ~ **in** (*of power, rights*) -wa mikononi mwa/chini ya. **~nce** *n* 1 kuishi, kukaa ~ *area* eneo la makazi. **in** ~ (*official*) nyumbani *(of students)* Chuoni. 2 nyumba. **~ncy** *n* nyumba ya balozi, makao ya wageni (wa nchi). **~nt** *n* 1 *(inhabitant)* mwenyeji, mkaaji, mkazi. 2 **R~** Balozi *adj* 1 -a mkazi, -a kukaa, a kuishi. ~ **magistrate** hakimu mkazi. ~ **physician** daktari mkazi (katika eneo la hospitali). **~ntial** *adj* -a kukaa watu, -a makazi *the ~ part of the town* eneo la makazi.
residue *n* mabaki, masalio, masazo, machicha. **residual** *adj* -a masazo, -a mabaki. **residuary** *adj* -liobaki, -a mabaki ~ *clause* ibara baki (masazo) ~ *legatee* muusiwa wa mabaki (masazo).
resign *vt,vi* 1 ~ **(from)** jiuzulu, jitanibu. 2 ~ **sb/oneself to sb/sth** toa, weka mtu chini ya madaraka ya fulani. 3 ~ **oneself to sth/be ~ed to sth** kubali bila kulalamika, -wa tayari kukubali, kubali matokeo ya maisha. **~ed** *adj*. **~edly** *adv*. **~ation** *n* 1 ~ kujiuzulu, kuacha kazi, kujitoa. 2 hati ya kujiuzulu (ya kuomba ruhusa kuacha kazi). 3 *(submission, acquiescence)* kukubali.
resile *vi* nyambuka, nepa, nesa. **resilience** *(also* **resiliency)** *n* unyumbukaji, mnepo, kuvutwa. **resilient** *adj* -a kunepa, -a kunyumbuka; *(of persons)* imara/ thabiti, epesi kujirekebisha/kurudia hali ya awali.
resin *n* utomvu *vt* tilia/pakaza utomvu. **~ated** -enye ladha ya utomvu; -liojaa utomvu. **~iferous** *adj* -enye kutoa utomvu. **~ous** *adj* -enye utomvu.
resist *vt* 1 pinga, kinza, bisha ~ *arrest* pinga kukamatwa. 2 stahamili, jizuia. 3 kataa kusalimu amri. **~er** *n* mpingaji, mkinzani. **~less** *adj* -sioweza kukinzika, -sioweza kukatalika. **~ance (to)** *n* 1 (uwezo wa) upinzani (k.m. dhidi ya adui) *they cannot overcome the enemy's ~* ~ hawawezi kushinda nguvu ya upinzani wa adui. ~ **movement** tapo, chama cha upinzani (dhidi ya maadui waliovamia nchi). 2 nguvu kinzi *the boat failed to overcome the ~ of the wind* boti ilishindwa kukabili nguvu kinzi ya upepo. **line of least** ~ uelekeo usio na nguvu kinzi kali; *(fig)* njia au mbinu rahisi zaidi. 3 uadui; uhasama. **~ant** *adj* kinzani, -enye upinzani, kinzi. **~or** *n (phys)* kikinzanishi: sehemu ya saketi inayopitisha umeme kwa shida.
resole *vt* tia soli mpya (kwenye kiatu).
resolute *adj* shupavu, imara, thabiti. **~ly** *adv*. **~ness** *n*. **resolution** *n* 1 hali ya kuwa shupavu/imara/ thabiti. 2 jambo lililoamuliwa, azimio. 3 utatuzi. 4 ahadi, nadhiri; nia, uamuzi (wa mtu, katika kufanya jambo). 5 mchanganuo, mgawo.
resolve *vt* 1 ~ **to do sth; ~ that...; ~ on/upon (doing) sth** azimu, nuia, kusudia, amua. 2 *(of a committe, public meeting etc)* amua kwa kupiga kura, pitisha. 3 tatua, maliza, komesha (kwa kutoa jawabu). ~ **sth (into sth)** vunja, gawa; geuza, geuka kuwa *the Parliament ~d itself into a committee* Bunge liligeuka kuwa Kamati *n* azma, azimio, nia, kusudi, uthabiti, ushupavu *adj* -lioamriwa, -liokatiwa shauri, -liazimiwa, -lionuia. **resolvable** *adj*. **resolvedly** *adv* kwa uthabiti.
resonance *n* mvumo, mwangwi; *(phon)* sauti yenye kuendelea (kwa mtetemo). **resonant** *adj* 1 *(of voice)* fululizwa (kwa mtetemo). 2 *(of room)* -a mwangwi, -a kuvuma. 3 (*of places*) mahali penye mvumo wa

sauti. **resonate** *vt,vi* vuma, toa mwangwi.

resort *vi* ~ **to** 1 kimbilia, ishia, tumia *finally they ~ed to blows* mwishowe waliishia kupigana makonde. 2 tembelea mara kwa mara *n* 1 msaada, kimbilio, tegemeo *the only* ~ msaada pekee uliopo. **in the last ~; as a last** ~ hapana budi; mambo yote mengine yakishindikana. 2 matembezi, mahali (maalum) pa kutembelea kutalii.

resound *vt,vi* ~ (**with**) 1 vuma na toa mwangwi, paza sauti. 2 *(of fame)* enea pote, julikana pote; vuma ~ *through the country* julikana pote nchini. **~ing** *adj* 1 -a mvuvumo, -a mwangwi. 2 kubwa sana *a ~ing victory* ushindi mkubwa sana. **~ingly** *adv*.

resource *n* 1 njia, nguvu, shauri, mali. 2 *(pl)* mali, rasilimali; uwezo *natural ~s* mali asili, rasilimali. 3 zana, msaada, nyenzo, kimbilio, tegemeo *open new ~s* tafuta njia mpya. 4 werevu, akili, burudani. **~ful** *adj* -a akili, elekevu, -erevu, -a hekima. **~fully** *adv*.

respect *n* 1 ~ (**for**) heshima, staha, taadhima. **have ~for sb** heshimu. 2 ~ (**for**) heshima, kuzingatia, upendeleo. **pay ~ to** zingatia, fikiria; heshimu; (*for persons*) upendeleo. (unaoambatana na ukwasi/hadhi/ nasaba). 3 kuhusu. **with ~ to** kuhusu/ juu ya. **in this ~** kwa hili/haya *in all ~s* kwa jumla/hali zote. **without ~ to** bila kujali. 4 *(pl)* ~**s** salamu *my ~s to Joha* nisalimie Joha *pay one's ~s to sb* zuru/tembelea (kama ishara ya heshima). 5 namna, jinsi ya. **in ~ of** kulingana na, kuhusu. **in some/any/ no ~s** kwa kiasi fulani; kwa namna yoyote, hata kidogo *vt* heshimu, stahi, jali, pendelea. ~ **oneself** jiheshimu. **~er** *n (only in)* **no ~er of persons** *n* mtu/kitu kisicho na ubaguzi wowote. **~ing** *prep* mintaarafu, kuhusu. **~able** *adj* 1 -a heshima, zuri, nyofu, stahiki. 2 (*moderate*) -a kiasi, -a kadiri. **~ably** *adv*. **~ability** *n* maadili, unyofu. heshima. 3 *(ironic use)* -a kushika/kufuata desturi/mila. **~ful** *adj* -stahifu, -a heshima, -a adabu. **~fully** *adv*.

respective *adj* 1 -a pekee, -a kulingana na, kuhusiana na. 2 *(relative)* kwa kadiri ya/kwa kila (mhusika) *they returned to their ~ homes* kila moja alirudi kwake. **~ly** *adv*.

respire *(formal) vt,vi* pumua, tanafusi. **respiratory** *adj* -a pumzi ~ *diseases* maradhi yanayohusiana na upumuaji. **respiration** *n* upumuaji, hali ya kutanafusi, mtweto. **respirator** *n* kipumulio.

respite *n* 1 ~ (**from**) nafasi ya kupumua, pumziko. 2 kukawiza, kuahirika katika adhabu *vt* ahirisha, -pa nafasi ~ *a condemned person* ahirisha kunyonga mhukumiwa kwa kitambo.

resplendent *adj* -zuri, -a kung'aa; -a sherehe, -a fahari. **~ly** *adv*. **resplendence, resplendency** *n*.

respond *vi* 1 ~ (**to**) (*of church services*) itika; itikia. 2 jibu. 3 ~ (**to**) (*react to*) shawishika, athirika, vutika; ongezeka, kubali, pokea *he always ~s to kindness* kila mara avutika na upole *the plane ~s to the controls* ndege inaendesheka vizuri kwa vyombo vyake. **~ent** *n (leg)* mshitakiwa, mjibu mashtaka; mtetezi (wa tasnifu), mjibu (hojaji n.k.) *adj* -a kulingana; -a kujibia. **response** *n* 1 jibu, itiko *bring no response* -toleta jibu lolote. 2 kiitikio, mkarara. **responsive** *adj* -a kujibu, -a kuitikia, -a kuvutika. **responsiveness** *n*.

responsibility *n* madaraka, jukumu, wajibu, dhima *undertake ~ of* chukua madaraka/dhima/wajibu *a position of ~* kazi yenye madaraka *be relieved of one's ~* pokewa/ uzuliwa madaraka, vuliwa madaraka. **rensponsible** *adj* 1 -enye madaraka/ wajibu/jukumu/dhima *a ~ office* kazi yenye madaraka mengi *make oneself ~ for* chukua dhamana. 2 *(trustworthy)* -aminifu, -ema. 3 **be**

~ **for sth** wajibika, husika *he is ~ for this mess* ghasia hii ameileta mwenyewe.

rest[1] *n* 1 pumziko, utulivu, raha; (*sleep*) usingizi *take one's ~* pumzika, lala. **at ~** tulivu; -lokufa. **be laid to ~** zikwa. **come to ~** simama, tua. **set someone's mind/ fears to ~** tuliza mtu. **~-cure** matibabu ya mapumziko. **~-day** siku ya mapumziko. **~-home** makazi ya wazee. **~-house** nyumba ya mapumziko (kwa wasafiri). 2 **~-room** (*US*) msala. 3 kiegemeo. 4 kituo. 5 **~ing-place** mahali pa kupumzikia; kaburi. **~ful** *adj* -a kutulia/kutuliza, -a kuliwaza. **~fully** *adv*. **~fulness** *n*. **~less** *adj* -siotulia, -enye wahaka. **~lessly** *adv*. **~lessness** *n* *vi, vt* 1 pumzika/pumzisha, starehe/starehesha. 2 tulia/tuliza *God ~ his soul in peace* Mwenyezi Mungu amweke mahali pema peponi. 3 **~ sth on/upon/ against** egemeza; egemea. **~ on one's oars** acha kupiga makasia kwa muda; *(fig)* pumzika kwa muda. 4 **~ (sth) on/upon** tandawaa; tegemea (mtu/kitu); *(of sight)* elekeza na kukazia macho sehemu moja.

rest[2] *n* **the ~** 1 baki, salio, mwisho. **and (all) the ~ (of it)** mengine yote. 2 *(pl)* wengine, vingine, nyingine. **for the ~** kuhusu wengine/nyingine/vingine *vi* 1 kaa, dumu *~ assured that I will do what I can* usiwe na mashaka/kaa ukijua kuwa nitafanya kadiri niwezavyo. 2 **~ with** -wa mikononi mwa *it ~s with him* ni juu yake, hiari yake, iko mikononi mwake. 3 **~ on/ upon** tegemea.

restate *vt* taja/tamka tena/upya. **~ment** n.

restaurant *n* mkahawa, hoteli *~-car* behewa mkahawa.

restrain *vt* ~ **(from)** zuia, rudisha. **~ed** *adj* -liozuiwa. ~ *n* 1 kizuizi; kuzuia. **be put under ~t** (*esp of a mentally ill person*) wekwa katika hospitali ya vichaa. **without ~** kwa uhuru; bila kuzuizi. 2 *(of persons) self~* kujihini. 3 *(in art, literature)* kutokuwa na mbwembwe.

restrict *vt* ~ **(to)** zuia, wekea mipaka, tilia amri/sharti, finya *~ed within narrow limits* -liozuiwa katika mipaka finyu *~ed code* sheria finyu; lugha finyu. *~ed area* eneo marufuku kuingiwa. **~ion** *n* kizuio, sharti; amri, mipaka. **~ive** *adj* -zuivu, -a kuzuia. **~ive practices** *(in industry)* vikwazo katika uzalishaji (k.m. matumizi mabaya ya wafanyakazi, mali ghafi, zana, n.k). **~ively** *adv*.

restructure *vt* unda/panga upya.

result *n* 1 matokeo, athari *the ~s of the war* matokeo ya vita *without ~* bila matokeo. 2 jibu, jawabu *vi* 1 ~ **(from)** tokana na, sababishwa na. 2 ~ **in** sababisha. 3 ishia. **~ant** *adj* -a kutokea (pande zote) *~ vector (math)* vekta tokeo.

resume *vt* 1 endelea, anza tena, rudia tena *~ one's work* anza kazi tena. 2 twaa/chukua tena *~ one's seat* twaa/ kalia kiti tena. **resemption** *n*.

resumé *n* ufupisho, muhtasari.

resurface *vt* 1 sakifu tena. 2 ibuka/ tokeza tena.

resurgent *adj* -liofufuka, -liofufuka tena, -lioamka tena, -lioinuka tena. **resurgence** *n*.

resurrect *vt,vi* 1 fufuka; fufua. 2 ondoa kaburini, fukua, *(colloq)* chimbua. 3 rudisha, anzisha tena (jambo), tumia tena. **~ion** *n* 1 **the R** ~ Ufufuo wa Yesu Kristo. 2 Ufufuko (wa wafu) *the day of ~* siku ya kiyama, siku ya kubaathiwa. 3 kufufua, kurudisha (desturi).

resuscitate *vt,vi* pata fahamu, rudishia fahamu; amsha, chochea. **resuscitation** *n*.

ret *vt* lowanisha (ili kulainisha).

retail *n* rejareja; uchuuzaji *adj* -a rejareja *vt,vi* 1 ~ **(at)** chuuza, uza rejareja. 2 *(circulate)* eneza (uvumi). **~er** *n* mwuuzaji rejareja.

retain *vt* 1 zuia; shika, weka. 2 *(hire)* ajiri (hasa wakili). 3 baki na, bakiza *~ sb's services* bakiza huduma ya mtu. **~er** *n* 1 *(arch)* mtumishi (wa mtu mwenye cheo kikubwa/wa nyumbani) wa siku nyingi. 2 *(lawyers' fee)* ada ya wakili, ada ya awali. **retention** *n* kuzuia; kufunga, kuweka; kubakiza. **retentive** *adj* ~ **(of)** -a kushika, -a kufahamu. **he has ~ memory** ana kumbukumbu nzuri. **retentively** *adv*. **retentiveness** *n*.

retake *vt* chukua/twaa/teka tena; piga (picha) upya/tena *n (esp. cinema, TV)* onyesho lililopigwa picha tena.

retaliate *vi* ~ **(against/ on/upon)** lipiza kisasi ~ *upon one's enemy* lipiza kisasi kwa maadui. **retaliation** *n*. **retaliative, retaliatory** *adj* -a kisasi, -a kulipiza kisasi.

retard *vt,vi* 1 kawilisha, chelewesha. 2 vunja (punguza) mwendo, rudisha nyuma. 3 dumaa/dumaza, via/viza *mentally ~ed person* mtu aliyevia akili, -a akili taahira. **~ation** *n* ucheleweshaji, mtindio, udumavu, taahira.

retch *vi* kokomoa, gooka *the sight makes one ~* kuona kitu (fulani) kunaleta kugooka/kinyaa *n* ukokomoaji, ugookaji.

rethink *vt,vi* fikiri(a) tena/upya.

reticent *adj* nyamavu, -kimya, -a maneno machache *be ~ on sth* -tosema mengi juu ya kitu. **reticence** *n* unyamavu, ukimya; hali ya kutosema maneno mengi.

reticulate *vt* gawa/gawanya katika miraba; fanya, panga/kama wavu/ kimia *adj* -a kimia, -a wavu. **reticulation** *n* mpangilio/mfumo unaofanana na wavu/kimia.

reticule *n (arch)* kifuko, kipochi, kibegi cha mwanamke.

retina *n* retina: sehemu inayopokea nuru ndani ya jicho.

retinue *n* jumla ya watu (wanaoandamana na mkubwa), msafara.

retire *vt,vi* 1 ~ **(from) (to)** jitoa, ondoka. 2 ~ **(to bed)** (*formal*) enda kulala *she ~s at 10 o'clock* analala saa nne usiku. 3 *(of an army)* rudi, rudisha; jiondoa ~ *an imprest* rudisha masurufu *(of an army)* rudi nyuma, jiondoa vitani. 4 staafu; ng'atuka, staafisha *the manager was ~d* meneja alistaafishwa. 5 ~ **from the world** ingia utawa/usafii, jitenga na mambo ya kilimwengu. ~ **into oneself** zama katika mawazo, ishi kipekee *n (army)* ishara ya kurudi nyuma. **~d** *adj* 1 (aliye) staafu *a ~ officer* ofisa mstaafu/aliyestaafu. 2 -enye kujitenga; pweke, kimya. **retiring** *adj* -a kujitenga. **~ment** *n* kustaafu; kujitenga *go into ~* staafu, ingia utawani.

retool *vt* weka vifaa vipya katika kiwanda.

retort[1] *vt,vi* 1 jibu vikali, rudisha maneno, itika kwa ukali ~ *an argument* jibu hoja. 2 *(rare)* lipiza kisasi, rudishia tendo *n* jibu kali.

retort[2] *n* 1 kigida (chenye shingo ndefu), chombo cha kutoneshea. 2 chombo cha kutakasisha zebaki na kutengenezea gesi.

retouch *vt (of photograph, painting etc.)* sahihisha, rekebisha kwa burashi.

retrace *vt* 1 fuatilia/fuata nyuma; rudi ulikotoka *he ~d his steps* alifuatilia nyayo zake. 2 rudia mambo yaliyopita.

retract *vt,vi* 1 futa (usemi, kauli, wazo n.k.). 2 rudisha, rudi *a snail can ~ its horns* konokono anaweza kurudisha ndani pembe zake. **~able** *adj* -a kuweza kurudi ndani. **~ile** *adj* 1 -a kurudishika ndani. 2 -a kufumbatika, -a kuweza kurudishwa nyuma. **~ion** *n* hali ya kurudi nyuma/ndani.

retread *vt* tia tredi upya *n* tairi lililotiwa tredi upya.

retreat *vi* ~ **(from) (to)** kimbia; rudi nyuma *n* 1 kurudi nyuma. 2 ishara ya kurudi nyuma *sound the ~* rudisha nyuma askari (kwa kutoa ishara). 3 utoaji wa ishara hiyo *beat a (hasty) ~ (fig)* jiondoa, kimbia, acha kufanya jambo. 4 *(refuge)* kimbilio; mahali pa raha/usalama faragha. 5

kujiondoa kwa muda; *(rel)* mfungo *go into* ~ funga.

retrench *vt,vi* punguza (gharama), bana matumizi. **~ment** *n* kubana matumizi.

retribution *n* rada, adhabu (anayostahili mtu), malipo. **retributive** *adj* -a kulipa, -a rada, -a kupatiliza, -a kuadhibu. **retributively** *adv*.

retrieve *vt,vi* 1 pata tena. 2 rekebisha, hidi. 3 ~ **(from)** okoa, rudisha; stawisha. 4 *(of trained dogs)* tafuta na kurudisha. **retrievable** *adj* -enye kuweza kupatikana tena. **retrieval** *n* upatikanaji tena. **~r** *n* mbwa wa msasi.

retro- *pref.* kuelekea nyuma, kinyumenyume, -nyuma.

retroactive *adj* *(of laws,etc)* *see* **retrospective**.

retroflex *adj* 1 -liopindika/-lioelekea nyuma, akisi. 2 -liobinuka, *(phon.)* -a kubinua ulimi.

retrograde *vi* rudi chini/nyuma; wa baya zaidi *adj* -a kurudi nyuma/chini; -lioelekezwa nyuma.

retrogress *vi* rudi nyuma; enda kinyumenyume. **retrogression** *n*. **retrogressive** *adj* -a kurudi nyuma; -enye kuelekea kurudi nyuma.

retro-rocket *n* roketi saidizi (ya kupunguza mwendo au kurekebisha njia ya chombo au bomu angani).

retrospect *n* kuwazia/kukumbuka mambo ya zamani. **in** ~ ona/fikiria ya zamani *n* hali ya kutazama yaliyopita. **~ive** *adj* 1 -a kutazama nyuma, -a kuhusu mambo ya nyuma, -liotangulia, -liopita. 2 *(of laws, etc.)* -a kuanzia nyuma. **~ively** *adv*.

retrousse *adj* -lioelekezwa juu (hasa pua), -lioinukia mwishoni.

retroversion *n* kugeuka nyuma; kuelekezwa nyuma.

return *vt,vi* 1 ~ **(to)** **(from)** rudi, rejea; rudisha. 2 ~ **to** rudia (hali ya kwanza) *~ to dust* rudi mavumbini, -wa mavumbi. 3 *(reply)* jibu, itika *~ sb's greeting* jibu salamu. 4 *(repay)* rudisha, lipa. ~ **thanks** toa shukurani (k.m. kusali kabla ya kula). **~ed empties** chupa, kreti, n.k. tupu zilizorudishwa. 5 *(give account of)* toa (hesabu, hukumu, faida, n.k.). 6 *(of constituency)* chagua mbunge/ mwakilishi. **~ing officer** msimamizi (wa kura). **~able** *adj* -a kurudishika *n* 1 kurudi au kurudishwa, kuja; kwenda; kutoa, kupeleka. **by** ~ kwa posta inayofuata. **on sale or** ~ kwa kurudishwa iwapo haitauzwa. **point of no** ~ -sioweza kurejea au kurejeshwa nyuma tena. **many happy** **~s** heri ya sikukuu (ya kuzaliwa). **in** ~ **(for)** kama malipo (ya). 2 hali ya kwenda au kurudi. ~ **ticket** tikiti ya safari kwenda na kurudi. ~ **match** mchezo wa marudiano. ~ **fare** nauli ya kwenda na kurudi. 3 *(often pl)* faida toka kitegauchumi au biashara. 4 taarifa rasmi (itolewayo kwa kufuata agizo maalumu) *annual ~s* ripoti ya mwaka.

reunite *vi,vt* kutana/kutanisha tena, ungana/unganisha tena; patana/ patanisha, suluhisha. **reunion** *n* kurudiana, kupatana, kuunganika tena *a family ~* kukutana kwa familia yote (katika siku maalumu).

rev 1 *(abbr)* **revolution**. 2 ~ *(colloq)* ongeza mwendo wa mzunguko (wa injini).

revalue *vt* thaminisha upya; ongeza thamani ya fedha. **revaluation** *n*.

revamp *vt* piga jeki, fufua, inua; *(colloq)* tengeneza/fanya upya.

reveal *vt* ~ **(to)** 1 funua, onyesha. 2 gundua (jambo jipya), fichua. **~ed religion** dini iliyoletwa na Mungu. **revelation** *n* ufunuo. *(Bible) the Book of R~* Ufunuo. 2 hali ya kudhihirisha kitu kilichokuwa siri/fumbo; kitu kilichodhihirishwa.

reveille *n* kizinduzi, tarumbeta (ya kuamsha watu, hasa jeshini).

revel *vi* 1 furahia, shangilia. 2 ~ **in** sherehekea *n* sherehe, tamasha, shangwe. **~ler** *n* mtu asherehekeaye *n* shamrashamra; makelele na vifijo vya sherehe.

revenge *vt* 1 lipiza kisasi. 2 **be ~d on sb, ~ oneself on sb** jilipiza kisasi *n* 1 ulipizaji kisasi. **get/take one's ~; take ~ on sb (for sth); have/get one's ~ (on sb) (for sth); do sth in/out of ~ (for sth)** lipiza kisasi. 2 hali ya kulipiza kisasi. 3 *(in sports)* nafasi ya kulipiza kisasi. **give sb his ~; get/take one's ~** -pa mtu nafasi ya kurudia. **~ful** *adj*. **~fully** *adv*.

revenue *n* 1 mapato, maduhuli; *(public)* mapato ya serikali (kwa kodi), ushuru *~ officer* afisa mapato/ ushuru. 2 vitu mbalimbali vya mapato vikiwa pamoja.

reverberate *vt,vi (of sound,)* 1 fanya mwangwi tena na tena, vumavuma, nguruma, rindima. 2 *(of light)* akisi. **reverberant** *adj*. **reverberation** *n (pl)* miangwi; *(fig)* athari. **reverberator** *n*. **reverberatory** *adj*.

revere *vt* heshimu sana, stahi sana, -cha, tukuza. **~d** *adj* 1 mahashumu, -enye kustahili heshima. 2 **the R~nd** mchungaji, padri, mheshimiwa. **~nce** *n* 1 heshima kuu, uchaji, unyenyekevu. 2 *(arch)* ishara ya kuonyesha unyenyekevu mkubwa/ kutoa heshima *vt* stahi. **~nt** *adj* -a kustahi sana. **~ntial** -enye kusababishwa (na) heshima; -ingi -a heshima/staha. **~ntly** *adv*.

reverie *n* 1 njozi, ruya. 2 muziki wa njozi/maliwazo.

revers *n* pinduo: sehemu ya mbele ya ukosi wa koti iliyo karibu na vifungo.

reverse *vt,vi* 1 pindua, geuza. **a ~d charge** gharama kwa mpigiwa (simu). **~ arms** *(mil)* mtutu chini. 2 rudi/ rudisha nyuma. 3 tangua, batilisha. **reversible** *adj* -a kupindulika, -a kutumika kuwili. **reversibility** *n*. **reversal** *n* 1 kupindua, upinduaji. 2 hali ya kupindua *adj* **~ (to/of)** -a kinyume, -a nyuma. **in ~ order** kuanzia mwisho, nyuma mbele. **~ly** *adv n* 1 **the ~ of** kinyume. 2 **the ~ (of)** nyuma. 3 kitu cha kurudishia nyuma (k.v. gia ya nyuma). 4 ushinde, mkosi.

revert *vi* 1 **~ (to)** rudi, rejea, rudia hali ya kwanza. 2 *(leg)* rudi (kwa mwenye mali wa kwanza). **~ible** *adj*. **reversion** *n* 1 hali ya kitu kurudi kwa mwenye mali. 2 haki ya kumiliki mali katika mazingira fulani maalumu; kitu kimilikiwacho katika mazingira hayo. 3 hali ya kitu kurejea katika hali yake ya awali (k.m. mimea). **reversionary** *adj*.

revetment *n* 1 safu (tabaka, utando) ya mawe (ya kuzuia, kuimarisha) ukingo. 2 ukuta. **revet** *vt* imarisha/zuia kwa mawe.

review *vt,vi* 1 angalia/fikiri/tafakari/ pitia upya *come under ~* chunguzwa/ kaguliwa. 2 kagua rasmi (majeshi, n.k.). 3 pitia maandishi, chambua, hakiki *n* 1 kutafakari/ kuangalia upya. 2 ukaguzi (wa majeshi). 3 jarida/gazeti la mambo ya leo. 4 uhakiki; mapitio; muhtasari *the book under ~* kitabu kinachohakikiwa, n.k. 5 kitendo cha kutafakari jambo (k.m. maisha ya mtu mwenyewe). **~er** *n* mhakiki.

revile *vt, vi* **~ at/against** tukana, shutumu, laani. **~r** *n*. **~ment** *n*.

revise *vt* 1 fikiria tena; pitia (ili kusahihisha na kufanya bora zaidi). **the R~d Version** nakala ya Biblia iliyofanywa 1870-84 ikiwa ni masahihisho ya tafsiri ya Biblia iliyofanywa 1611 *n* nakala iliyosahihishwa. 2 *(alter)* geuza, badili, tengeneza. **~r** *n* msahihishi. **revision** *n* kurudia masomo (k.m. kabla ya mtihani); masahihisho. **revisionist** *n* mbadilishaji wa itikadi ya siasa. **revisionism** *n*.

revive *vt,vi* 1 fufua; fufuka; huisha. 2 rudisha, anzisha, amsha; anza kutumika tena. **revival** *n* 1 ufufuaji. 2 uhuishaji, uamshaji, urudishaji (hali ya zamani). **revivalist** *n*. **revivify** *vt* rudishia nguvu/uzima, huisha; amsha. **revivification** *n*.

revoke *vt,vi* batilisha, tangua, futa, kanusha. **revocable** *adj* -a kufutika,

-a kutangulika, -a kubatilika.
revocation *n* utanguo, batilisho.
revolt *vi,vt* 1 ~ **(against)** asi. 2 ~ **(against/at/from)** chukizwa, nyarafiwa, kirihishwa. 3 kirihi, chusha *n* uasi, maasi. **~ing** *adj* -a kuchukiza, -a ķaraha. **~ingly** *adv* kwa namna ya kuchukiza.
revolution *n* 1 mapinduzi. **~ary** *adj* -a mapinduzi, -a kimapinduzi ~ *spirit* imani ya kimapinduzi ~ *movement* tapo la kimapinduzi. **~ist** *n* mwanamapinduzi. 2 mzunguko. **~ize** *vt* 1 fundisha kanuni za kimapinduzi, fanya mwanamapinduzi. 2 pindua, badili kabisa.
revolve *vt,vi* 1 ~ **(about/ around)** zunguka, zungusha. 2 *(consider)* tafakari.
revolver *n* bastola.
revue *n* maonyesho (ya ngoma, nyimbo, vichekesho, n.k.).
revulsion *n* 1 mageuzi ya fikira. 2 ~ **(against/from)** *(disgust)* machukio, makuruhu.
reward *n* 1 thawabu, jaza; zawadi, tuzo. 2 kiokosi, machorombozi, utotole, kiangaza macho *vt* ~ **sb (for sth)** -pa (mtu) zawadi (kwa..), zawadia, tuza; -pa thawabu *may God ~ you* Mungu akujaze heri.
rewire weka/suka/tandaza nyaya upya.
rewrite 1 andika upya. 2 ~ *as (ling)* andika/fasiri kama... *n (colloq)* maandishi yaliyoandikwa tena *(attr.) a ~ man* msanifu maandishi.
rhapsody *n* 1 maneno ya kuonyesha furaha/shauku, sifa/maneno ya nderemo. 2 *(music)* tungo isiyokuwa na ulinganifu/isiyofuata kanuni *vi* **rhapsodize ~ (about/over/on)** sema/ andika kwa shauku/furaha, sifia sana, husudu.
rheostat *n* reostati: kidhibitiumeme.
rhesus *n (North India)* ngedere mdogo mwenye mkia mfupi .
rhetoric *n* 1 balagha: elimu ya usemaji. 2 *(eloquence)* ufasaha wa kusema. 3 chuku. **~al** *adj* 1 -enye balagha, -a usemaji, -a ufasaha. 2 *(not serious)* -a kutia madoidoi tu. ~ **question** balagha, swali lisilodai jibu. **~ian** *n* mgambi, mbalagha.
rheum *n (arch)* majimaji yatokayo machoni au puani k.m. makamasi.
rheumatism *n* baridi yabisi, ongo, viungo. **rheumatic** *adj*.
rhinal *adj* -a pua.
rhinoceros (*abbr* **rhino**) *n* kifaru.
rhizom *n (bot)* rizomu: shina ukoka (k.m. tangawizi).
rhomb/rhombus *n* msambamba sawa. **rhomboid** *adj*.
rhubarb *n* 1 aina ya mmea ambao majani yake huliwa kama tunda. 2 *(colloq)* upuuzi. 3 mabishano.
rhyme, rime *n* 1 kina *without ~ or reason* bila maana, puuzi. 2 mashairi ya vina *nursery ~* mashairi/beti za watoto. 3 neno lifanyalo kina. 4 matumizi ya vina *vt, vi* 1 fanya mashairi ya vina. 2 -wa na sauti sawa mwishoni. 3 weka pamoja ili kujenga vina. **~ster** *n* mshairichapwa.
rhythm *n* 1 wizani; mfuatano wiani wa mkazo mkali na hafifu wa lafudhi, sauti; mahadhi n.k. (katika usemaji, muziki, dansi, n.k.). 2 mifuatano maalumu ya namna hiyo. **~ical** *adj* -enye mahadhi (mapigo, mdundo, mwendo) safi.
rib *n* 1 ubavu. **dig/poke sb in the ~** tekenya. 2 (*of ship*) taruma. 3 *(of coconut leaf)* ujukuti. 4 *(of leaf)* mshipa, chelewa *vt* 1 chana, nyambua. 2 *(US colloq)* kefyakefya, tania; tekenya.
ribald *adj* pujufu, safihi *n* mpujufu, mwenye mdomo mchafu. **~ry** *n* mizaha, maneno ya upujufu/usafihi.
riband *n (old use)* **ribbon**.
ribbon *n* 1 utepe, riboni *white ~* jandani. 2 ugwe matambara. 3 ~ **development** msururu wa majumba sambamba na barabaraba kuu.
rice *n (paddy/unhusk)* mpunga, sena, bungala; *(cooked)* wali; *(burnt layer at the bottom of the pot)* ukoko; *(burnt layer on top of cooked rice)* matandu; *(ground)* ubwabwa;

(husked) mchele, mashendea. ~ **paper** *n (Chinese)* karatasi la sanaa. ~**-water** *n* maji ya mchele.

rich *adj* 1 tajiri, -kwasi, -enye mali. 2 -a gharama, -a fahari. 3 ~ **in** -enye neema, -enye kutoa/kuzaa kwa wingi. 4 *(soil)* -enye rutuba nyingi. 5 *(of colours, sounds)* kali, -enye nguvu. 6 *(of food)* -enye mafuta mengi; -tamu sana, -enye ladha nzuri. 7 *(abundant)* -ingi, tele ~ *in minerals* -enye madini tele. 8 *(colloq)* -a kuanisi *that is ~!* yachekesha sana. ~**ly** *adv*. ~**ness** *n* utajiri. ~**es** *n (pl)* 1 mali, utajiri, ukwasi. 2 wingi, neema *amass great ~* kusanya mali nyingi.

rick[1] *n* lundo/kitita cha majani ya ng'ombe, farasi, mbuzi, n.k. (yaliyokatwa na kuhifadhiwa pamoja) *~ of corn* lundo la mahindi *~ of hay* kitita cha majani makavu *vt* tita, fanya chungu, lundika.

rick[2] *see* **wrick**.

rickets *n* matege, nyongea.

rickety *adj* dhaifu (hasa katika viungo) *~ old car* mkweche.

rickshaw *n* riksho.

rid *vt* ~ **of** safisha, ondoa. **be/get ~ of** ondoa, toa, epuka. ~**dance** *n (US)* **a good** ~ afadhali *their departure was a good ~* afadhali wameondoka.

riddle[1] *n* 1 kitendawili, fumbo. 2 mtu/kitu/jambo/hali ya kushangaza/kutatanisha.

riddle[2] *n (sieve)* chekecheke, chungio, kung'uto *vt* 1 chekecha, chunga, kung'uta. 2 ~ **(with)** toboa (k.m. kwa kupiga risasi); chomachoma *~ with bullets* toboa kwa risasi. **be ~d with** jawa na.

ride *n (of a car, bicycle, horseback)* 1 kupanda, usafiri (wa kupanda) *~ a child on one's shoulders* beba mtoto mabegani. **take sb for a ~** *(colloq)* danganya/laghai mtu. 2 njia ya farasi na watu (hasa ipitayo katika pori) *vi,vi* 1 panda/enda/chukuliwa kwa (farasi, baiskeli, n.k.), endesha. ~ **for a fall** endesha kwa fujo; *(fig)* omba maafa, fanya vitendo vinavyoweza kusababisha maafa au kushindwa. 2 shindana katika mbio za farasi/baiskeli. 3 ~ **on** panda, kaa kwa kutagaa/kutenganisha miguu kama mpanda farasi. 4 beba mtu mabegani (kwa kuning'iniza miguu yake shingoni). 5 *(of a jockey or other person)* -wa na uzito (fulani wakati wa kupanda farasi). 6 fanya matembezi/mazoezi kwa farasi. ~ **to hounds** enda kuwinda mbweha. 7 *(of ground, etc)* -wa katika hali fulani ya kuendesha farasi *the ground rode hard after the frost* uwanja ulikuwa mgumu baada ya jalidi. 8 elea baharini. ~ **out a storm** *(of a ship)* toka salama/okoka katika dhoruba. *(fig)* salimika, okoka kutoka kwenye matatizo, shambulio, n.k. **let it ~** *(colloq)* acha jambo liende bila kulijali/kulishughulikia;achamambo yalivyo. 9 ~ **sb down** fukuza mtu kwa farasi hadi kumfikia; angusha kwa farasi. 10 ~ **up** (*of an article of clothing*) ruka. ~**able** *adj*. **ridden** *(pp of* **ride***)* *(esp. in compounds)* 1 -liojawa na *~ by fears* jawa na hofu. 2 -liotawaliwa/sumbuliwa/nyanyaswa na *priest ~* wanaonyanyaswa na mapadri *police ~* wanaonyanyaswa na polisi. **riding-breeches** *n pl* suruali za mpanda farasi. **riding-habit** vazi la kike la kupandia farasi. **ridding-light/lamp** taa ya meli inapotia nanga. **riding master** mwalimu wa wapandafarasi.

ridge *n* 1 mgongo, kigongo, utiko. ~ **pole** mtambaapanya wa hema. ~ **tile** kigae cha mgongo wa paa la nyumba. 2 *(of hills)* mgongo wa safu vilima/milima/sehemu ndefu iliyoinuka. 3 mstari wa sehemu iliyoinuka inayotenganisha mito. 4 *(of farming)* tuta.

ridicule *vt* dhihaki, fanyia mzaha; kebehi, beza *n* bezo; mzaha; dhihaka. **hold up to ~** dhihaki. **lay oneself open to ~** jiaibisha, fanya vitendo vya kubezwa/kudharauliwa. **ridiculous** *adj*.

rife *adj (pred only)* 1 -liotapakaa/enea kote. **be ~** tapakaa. 2 **~ with** -liojawa na/enea.

riff *n* msemo unaotumika sana katika muziki.

riffle *n vt,vi* 1 changa karata. 2 pindua karatasi upesiupesi. **~ through sth** changa, geuza upesiupesi agh. kurasa.

riff-raff *n* **the ~** wahuni; makabwela; watu wasioheshimika (kutokana na tabia mbaya).

rifle[1] *vt* chakura, pekua (ili kuiba).

rifle[2] *n* bunduki; bunduki kubwa yenye mifuo; *(pl.)* kikosi cha askari wa bunduki. **~-range** *n* uwanja wa kujifunzia shabaha; mtupo wa risasi. **~-shot** mtupo wa risasi; mpiga bunduki mwenye shabaha. **~ man** askari wa kikosi cha bunduki.

rift *n* 1 ufa, mwatuko, mpasuko. **~-valley** bonde la ufa. 2 *(of friends)* ugomvi.

rig[1] *vt* fanya hila **~** *an election* pata ushindi katika uchaguzi kwa hila **~** *the market* fanya hila katika ununuzi/uuzaji wa hisa (ili kupata faida isiyo halali).

rig[2] *vt,vi* 1 **~ (with) (a ship)** weka/patia (meli) mlingoti/tanga; -wa na vifaa hivyo; -andaa kwenda baharini na vifaa hivyo. 2 **~ sb out/ in with sth** -pa mtu nguo/vifaa vinavyotakiwa; *(colloq)* nguo, mavazi (ya mtu). **~ sth up** unganisha, rekebisha kitu; tengeneza *n* 1 *(of a ship)* mpangilio wa mlingoti, tanga, n.k. 2 mtambo, vifaa vilivyowekwa pamoja kwa madhumuni maalumu. **test-~** mahali/mtambo wa kujaribia magari. 3 *(colloq)* mtindo wa mavazi; namna mtu aonekanavyo kutokana na mavazi yake. **~ging** *n* kamba za melini zinazoshikilia tanga na mlingoti. **~ger** *n* mfunga kamba melini; mwunda ndege.

right[1] *adj (contrasted with wrong)* 1 *(of conduct, etc)* nyofu, adilifu, -ema. 2 -a kweli, sawa, halisi, sahihi. **get sth ~** elewa sawasawa. **put/set sth ~** rekebisha, sahihisha. **R~ you are!/R~o! R~!** *int (colloq)* sawa!/kabisa! **All ~/ Al~** *int.* vema! vizuri sawa! **~ minded** *adj* -enye mawazo mazuri/misingi mizuri, -enye akili timamu. 3 -a kufaa, -enye afadhali, -a heri *he is the ~ man for the job* anafaa kwa kazi hii *she is on the ~ side of 40* hajafika miaka arobaini. **get on the ~ side of** fanya kupendwa/kupendelewa na. 4 **(all) ~** zima. **not (quite) ~ in the/ one's head** -enye wazimu (kidogo), haziko sawa. **not in one's ~ mind** haziko sawa. **~ as rain/as a trivet** *(colloq)* mzima, safi kabisa. 5 *(of an angle)* -a pembe mraba. **~ly** *adv* kwa kweli/haki, kwa usawa inavyotakiwa. **~ness** *n,adv* 1 hasa; moja kwa moja. **~ away/off** mara moja, moja kwa moja. **~ now** kwa sasa, sasa hivi. **~ on!** *int (colloq)* sawa! hasa! 2 kwa usahihi *if I remember ~* kama nakumbuka vizuri. **it serves him ~** ni haki yake; inamstahilia. 3 sana; kabisa. **~-down** *adj, adv (more usu down ~)* kabisa *n* 1 haki, ukweli. **be in the ~** -wa mkweli na mwenye haki. 2 haki *she has no ~* hana haki. **by ~ of** kwa sababu ya, kutokana na. **in one's own ~** kwa haki/uwezo wake mwenyewe. **~ of way** haki ya kutumia njia (ya jumuia/umma) *(in road traffic)* haki ya kupita barabarani. **by ~ (s)** kwa kufuata haki. **human ~s** haki za binadamu. **women's ~s** haki za wanawake. **stand on/assert one's ~s** tetea haki. 3 *(pl.)* hali halisi. **put/set things ~** rekebisha, nyoosha. **~s and wrongs** ukweli *vt* tengeneza/sahihisha/rekebisha kuwa sawa; simamisha (wima) *that fault will ~ itself* tatizo hili litajirekebisha lenyewe. **~ the helm (of ship)** weka katikati; elekeza mbele. **~eous** *adj* 1 adilifu, -a kutii amri. 2 -enye kukubalika kimaadili, -enye haki. **~ously** *adv.* **~ousness** *n.*

right[2] *adj (contrastedwith left)* -a kulia, -a kuume. **one's ~ hand/arm** *(fig)* msaidizi mkuu, mwenzi. **~ hand** -a bidii/nguvu zote *put one's ~ hand to the work* fanya kazi kwa bidii/nguvu zote. **~-handed** *adj (of a blow, etc)* -a kulia. ~ **hander** *n* anayetumia mkono wa kulia/kuume; *(of a blow, etc)* -a kulia; kofi la mkono wa kulia. ~ **turn** geuka kulia. ~ **about turn/face** geuka nyuma kwa kupitia mkono wa kulia *adv* kwa upande wa kulia. *(mil)* **Eyes ~!** macho kulia! *n* 1 (upande wa) kulia, kuume. 2 *(politics, usu ~* **the**) mrengo wa kulia: chama/vyama visivyopenda mabadiliko/ vinavyopinga mabadiliko. **~ist** *n* mwanachama wa chama cha mrengo wa kulia *adj* -a mrengo wa kulia.

rigid *adj* 1 -siopindika/kunjika, gumu, imara. 2 *(severe)* gumu; -siobadilika/ badilishwa, -isoshawishika. **~ness** *n* ugumu, ukavu, uimara; hali ya kutoshawishika vinginevyo. **~ly** *adv.*

rigmarole *n* 1 mapayo, upuuzi, porojo. 2 utaratibu wa kuchusha/kutatanisha.

rigour/rigor *n* 1 ukali/ugumu (wa) kufuata sheria; msimamo. 2 hali ngumu. **~mortis** *n* ukakamaaji wa misuli (baada ya kufa). **~ous** *adj* kali. **~ously** *adv.*

rile *vt (colloq)* kasirisha, ghadhibisha, kera, udhi *it ~d me* kilinikasirisha.

rill *n* kijito.

rim *n (of wheel)* rimu; ukingo, mzingo; *(of spectacles)* fremu. **red ~med** -enye macho mekundu *vt* tia/wekea ukingo/rimu; kuwa rimu ya kitu.

rime[1] jalidi *vt* gandisha. **rimy** *adj.*

rime[2] = **rhyme.**

rind *n* ganda, gome, *(of squeezed fruit)* kaka *vt* menya.

rinderpest *n* sotoka (maradhi ya ng'ombe).

ring[1] *n* 1 pete *nose-~* hazama *ear-~* hereni, kipuli *lip-~* ndonya. ~ **finger** kidole cha pete. 2 kizingo, kipete, kishikizo *key ~* kishikizo cha funguo *~ mail, ~ armour* ngao ya pete, deraya. 3 duara. **run/ make ~s round sb** zidi sana kwa kasi, ubora wa kufanya mambo. 4 jamii, kundi, genge la watu wafanyao kazi kwa pamoja kwa manufaa yao *a ~ of thieves* genge la wezi. 5 ulingo *boxing ~* ulingo wa masumbwi. ~ **master** *n* kiongozi wa kikundi cha wachezaji (hasa wa sarakasi). 6 uwanja (wa maonyesho ya mifugo). 7 *(compounds)* ~ **road** *n* barabara (inayozunguka nje ya mji). **~-side** *n* kando ya ulingo. **~worm** *n* choa, baka, bato. **~-leader** *n* kiongozi wa waasi/maasi/jambo baya *vt,vi* 1 zingira. 2 visha pete. 3 tupa shilingi. 4 *(of a hunted fox)* kimbia kwa kuzunguka. **~let** *n* 1 msokoto, songo la nywele. 2 pete ndogo. **~ed** *adj.*

ring[2] *vt,vi* 1 vuma, lia *the telephone rang* simu ililia. 2 ashiria, leta athari fulani baada ya kusikika, onyesha dalili. ~ **true** ashiria ukweli. 3 piga kengele ya tahadhari. ~ **(for)** ita kwa kengele. 4 piga/liza (kengele) *~ the alarm* piga kamsa. ~ **the bell** *(colloq)* faulu katika jambo. ~ **a bell** leta kumbukumbu kwa mbali. 5 vuvumka, jaa. 6 baki (katika masikio/ kumbukumbu). 7 ~ **(with)** *(of the ears)* wangwa *ears are ~ing* masikio yanawangwa. 8 ~ **sb (up)** pigia simu, wasiliana kwa simu. ~ **off** maliza mazungumzo ya simu, kata simu. 9 *(of a chime of bells)* tangaza (saa, kipindi, n.k). 10 toa ishara (kwa kupiga kengele, n.k. 11 ~ **the changes** *(of church bells)* piga kengele kwa namna mbalimbali; *(fig)* fanya/weka au panga vitu kwa namna mbalimbali. 12 tangaza au sherehekea kuanza au kwisha kwa jambo fulani (kwa kupiga kengele) *n* 1 sauti au mlio wa kengele (au chuma) ipigwapo. 2 *(sing only)* sauti kubwa na yenye kusikika. 3 kitendo cha kutoa sauti kama kengele. **~er** *n* mpiga simu/kengele; ala ya kupigia kengele.

rink *n* kiwanja maalum cha barafu cha kutelezea.

rinse *vt* 1 ~ **sth (out)**; ~ **sth out of sth** suuza, osha kwa maji safi; *(the mouth)* sukutua. 2 ~ **sth down**

telemsha (kwa kinywaji) *n* 1 kusuuza. 2 rangimaji (ya kubadilishia rangi ya nywele). **rinsing** *n.*

riot *n* 1 ghasia, fujo. **the R~ Act** sheria ya kuzuia fujo *read the R~ Act* soma sheria hii mbele ya wafanya fujo; *(joc)* kemea sana. **run ~** fanya fujo; *(of plants)* tanda haraka sana. 2 makelele, vurugu. 3 *(profusion)* **a ~ (of)** wingi; mvuvumko. 4 **a ~ (of)** kujiachia. 5 jambo linaloleta shauku kubwa, jazba, ghasia ~ *in* furaha. **~er** *n* mfanya fujo. **~ous** *adj.* **~ously** *adv.* **~ousness** *n.*

rip *vt* 1 pasua/pasuka/raruka/tatuka ~ *open* pasua. **~ sth/sb off** iba/ibia, ghilibu, tapeli. **~off** *n* utapeli, wizi. **~-cord** *n* ugwe wa mwavuli wa kurukia (ambao ukivutwa mwavuli hufyatuka na kujaa hewa). 2 kata kwa msumeno (mti, n.k.) kwa kufuata uelekeo wa nyama zake. **~ saw** msumeno wa kufanyia kazi hii. 3 *(of material)* chana/chanika. 4 endesha upesi; enda kwa kasi. **let things ~** acha kuvidhibiti; acha mambo yaende kwa namna yake *n* mpasuko mrefu; mahali palipopasuka. **~-roaring** *adj* -a makelele, -a ghasia, -a vurumai.

ripe *adj* 1 *(of fruit)* -lioiva, bivu; *(of grain)* -liokomaa; *(of drink)* -lioiva. 2 -liokomaa/pevuka. 3 ~ **for** tayari. **~ly** *adv.* **~n** *vt,vi* iva/ivisha; pevuka/pevusha; komaa/komaza. **~ness** *n* ubivu, upevu; *(perfection)* ukamilifu.

riposte *n* 1 jibu kali. 2 *(in fencing)* kukinga/kurudishia kwa haraka (baada ya kukwepa upanga) *vi* toa jibu kali/hima.

ripple *n* 1 kiwimbi, lembelembe. 2 mlio wa wimbi. 3 *(of sound)* sauti/kicheko cha kimawimbi *vt,vi* 1 lia kama wimbi. 2 -wa na viwimbi, fanya viwimbi *adj.*

rip-tide *n* mkondo mkali.

rise *vi* ~ **(up)** 1 *(of the sun, moon)* chomoza, tokeza 2 inuka. 3 amka, toka kitandani. 4 *(from the dead)* fufuka. 5 panda, inukia, enda juu. **the rising generation** kizazi kinachoinukia. **rising twelve** *(of a person's age)* karibia miaka kumi na miwili. **high ~** -enye maghorofa. 6 ongezeka (nguvu). 7 ibuka. 8 onekana juu ya uso wa nchi kwa mbali (k.m. vilima); tokeza. 9 panda cheo/hadhi n.k. 10 **~ to** weza kukabili. **~ to the occasion** weza kukabili hali. 11 *(of slope)* panda. 12 anzia. 13 **~ against** asi. **rising** *n* maasi *n* 1 mwinuko, kilima, kituta. 2 ongezeko (k.m. katika thamani, ukubwa, joto, n.k.). 3 *(lit)* kuchomoza, kutokeza (agh. kwa jua). 4 kuibuka kwa samaki, kuja juu ya maji. **get/take a ~ out of sb** ginginiza/chokoza/fanyia mzaha hadi kumuudhi. 5 mwanzo, asili. **give ~ to** sababisha, -wa chanzo. **~r** *n* 1 mwamkaji. **an early ~** mwamkaji mapema. 2 sehemu ya wima ya ngazi (inayounganisha vidatu viwili).

risible *adj* -a kucheka; -a kuchekesha. **risibility** *n*

risk *n* 1 hatari, mashaka. **run/take ~s/a ~** fanya mambo ya hatari; bahatisha; thubutu *to succeed you must take ~s* ili ufanikiwe sharti uthubutu. **run/take the ~ of doing sth** -wa na dhima, chukua jukumu. **at ~** -enye mashaka. **at the owner's ~** juu ya mtu mwenye mali. **one's own ~** juu yake mwenyewe. 2 *(insurance)* kiasi/thamani ya bima; kiasi ambacho mtu/kitu kimelipiwa bima; mtu au kitu kilicholipiwa bima *vt* hatarisha, bahatisha, jasiri *I will ~ it* hasara juu yangu. **~y** *adj* -enye hatari. **~iness** *n* hatari, jukumu. **~ily** *adv.*

risque *adj* -nayoweza kuudhi/kuaibisha.

rite *n* kanuni, kaida ya dini; ada, ibada *traditional ~* tambiko *initiation ~s* jando, unyago. **ritual** *n* 1 kaida za dini, (taratibu za) ibada; tambiko. **rituals** *n* matambiko. 2 taratibu *adj* -a kanuni kaida. **ritualism** *n.* **ritualist** *n.* **ritualistic** *adj.*

ritzy *adj (sl)* malidadi.

rival *n* mshindani, mpinzani *adj* shindani, pinzani *vt* shindana, taka kupita (kushinda); jaribu kuwa sawa na. **~ry** *n* ushindani.

rive *vt,vi* chana, pasua, tatua.

river *n* 1 mto. **sell sb down the ~** *(fig)* saliti mtu. 2 ~ *head* chanzo; chemchemi. **~-bed** *n* chini ya mto. ~ **basin** *n* bonde la mto. ~ **bank** ukingo wa mto. ~ **side** *n* kando ya mto. ~ **horse** *n* kiboko. 3 gharika, mafuriko makubwa (k.m. ya lava ya volkeno); kububujika kwa wingi (k.m. damu), umwagaji mwingi wa damu katika vita. **~-borne** *adj* (kwa miti) -a mto. **rivulet** *n* kijito.

rivet *n* ribiti *vt* 1 piga ribiti. 2 kaza. 3 vuta, vutiwa (na kitu). **~er** *n* mpiga ribiti.

roach/cock~ *n* 1 mende, kombamwiko. 2 *(sl)* kishina/kipande cha sigara ya bangi.

road *n* 1 barabara, njia. **on the ~** safarini, kusafiri. **take to the ~** -wa mzururaji. **rule of the ~** sheria/ kanuni za kupishana magari/meli, n.k. ~ **safety** usalama barabarani. 2 *(compounds)* ~ **bed** *n* jumla ya vifaa k.v. mawe, kokoto, kifusi n.k. vinavyotandazwa katika ujenzi wa barabara. **~-block** *n* kizuizi barabarani. ~ **book** *n* kielelezo cha barabara za mji/nchi. **~-hog** *(colloq)* dereva jahili/mbaya. **~house** *n* mgahawa wa barabarani, hoteli iliyopo kando ya baraba kuu. ~ **man/ mender** *n* mtengeneza barabara. ~ **metal** *n* kokoto za kutengenezea njia/ barabara. ~ **-sense** *n* akili ya udereva. ~ **show** maonyesho (yaonyeshwayo na kikundi cha sanaa kinachozunguka sehemu mbalimbali) ~ **side** *n* pembeni mwa barabara, njia kando ya barabara. **~stead** *n* bandari, maelezi pa kutia nanga. **~way** *n* (sehemu ya) barabara (yanapopita magari); sehemu ya kati ya barabara. 3 njia (apitapo mtu). 4 ~ **(to)** *(fig)* njia (ya kuelekea); namna *the ~ to success* njia ya kufanikiwa. **~ster** *n* gari ndogo iliyo wazi (agh ya watu wawili).

roam *vi, vt* tembeatembea; susurika, tangatanga, zururazurura *go ~ing about* zurura, kata mitaa *n*.

roan[1] *adj (of animals)* -enye rangi mchanganyiko hususan hudhurungi na nyeupe *n* farasi/ng'ombe wa rangi mchangayiko. **~antelope** *n* korongo.

roan[2] ngozi ya kondoo (itumikayo kujalidia vitabu).

roar *n* 1 ngurumo, rindimo *vt,vi* nguruma, rindima. 2 sema/imba kwa sauti kubwa. 3 ~ **oneself hoarse** pwelewa/kaukiwa na sauti (kwa kuimba au kutoa sauti kubwa/kali). ~ **sb down** zima. **~ing** *adj* 1 -a kunguruma, -a kurindima. 2 -a dhoruba. 3 -enye kustawi *adv* sana. **~ingly** *adv*.

roast *vt,vi* 1 choma, banika, oka. 2 pasha joto, moto. 3 weka katika hali ya joto ya namna fulani ~ *oneself in the sun* jianika juani. 4 kemea sana *n* 1 nyama iliyobanikwa/okwa; vipande vidogovidogo vilivyokatwa kutoka pande hili. 2 ubanikaji au uchomaji (nyama). **~er** *n* aina ya jiko la kubanikia nyama; chombo cha kuchomea kahawa/buni; aina ya chakula (k.m kuku) kinachoweza kubanikwa au kuchomwa. **~ed** *adj* -liyochomwa; -liobanikwa. **~ing** *n*. **give sb a good ~** *(fig)* karipia/kemea vikali.

rob *vt* ~ **sb/sth (of sth)** 1 ibia, nyanganya, pora. 2 nyima/zuia mtu (haki yake/kilicho chake). **~ber** *n* mwizi, mnyang'anyi, jambazi, mporaji. ~ *n* wizi, unyang'anyi. **daylight ~ bery** wizi wa kimachomacho, kupandisha bei mno.

robe *n* 1 joho. **bath ~** joho la kuogea/ bafuni; vazi rasmi (la kazi k.m. la mapadri, majaji, n.k.) *vt,vi* vaa/ visha.

robot *n* roboti: mashine ifanyayo kazi kama mtu/badala ya mtu; *(fig)* mtu afanyaye kazi kama mashine/bila kufikiri au kuuliza, n.k.

robust *adj* -enye afya/nguvu, imara. **~ly**

adv. **~ness** *n.*

roc *n* ndege mkubwa wa ajabu wa hadithini katika sehemu za Uarabuni.

rock[1] *n* 1 mwamba, jabali. **as firm/solid as a ~** isiotingishika, imara kabisa; *(of persons) (fig)* thabiti. **on the ~s** *(of a ship)* -liovunjika juu ya miamba; *(fig)* -liowamba; *(of a marriage)* -nayoelekea kuvunjika; *(US) (of whisky)* kwa barafu. **see ~s ahead** ona miamba/hatari mbele. **the R~ of Ages** Yesu. 2 jabali kubwa lijitokezalo juu ya ardhi au majini; *(of a person)* mtu aliyewamba. 3 genge la mwambajiwe, jiwe kubwa. 4 peremende ngumu. 5 *(used with compounds)* ~ **bottom** *n* kiwango cha chini kabisa. ~ **climbing** upandaji miamba (kwa msaada wa vifaa fulanifulani k.v. kamba). **~-crystal** *n* kwazi ya fuwele: namna ya jiwe gumu, jeupe la kung'aa. **~garden** tita kubwa la majabali na mawe na juu yake kukiwa kumeota mimea. ~ **plant** aina ya mmea unaoota katika sehemu za majabali au mawe. ~ **salmon** *see* **dogfish**. ~ **salt** chumvi ya mawe. **~ery** *n see* ~ **garden**. **~y** *adj* 1 -enye miamba. 2 -sio imara.

rock[2] *vt,vi* 1 *(swing)* pembeza; pembea, chuchia. 2 *(shake)* tikisa, tingisha ~ *the boat (fig)* yumbisha/vuruga, jambo. **~chair** *n* kiti cha bembea. **~ing-horse** *n* bembeafarasi: farasi bandia wa mbao wa kupandwa na watoto. **~er** *n* mguu tao (wa kiti cha bembea au farasi bandia). **off one's ~** -enye wazimu.

rock[3] *also* **~'n-roll** *n* roki: aina ya dansi la kurukaruka *vi* cheza roki.

rocket *n* 1 roketi. ~ **base** *n* kambi la makombora ya roketi. 2 fataki, fashifashi. 3 *(colloq)* karipio *give someone a severe ~* karipia vikali *vi* panda (kama roketi), paa *prices ~ed* bei zilipaa.

rococo *adj* -enye nakshi nyingi/kupita kiasi *n* mtindo wa rokoko.

rod *n* 1 ufito. 2 kiboko, fimbo ya kuadhibia. **make a ~ for one's own back** karibisha matatizo/adha. **spare the ~ and spoil the child** *(prov)* mchelea mwana kulia hulia yeye. **have a ~ in pickle for sb** wekea mtu adhabu yake. 3 kipimo cha urefu sawa na yadi 5½. 4 chuma chochote (chenye kipenyo kidogo) kirefu. 5 *(US sl)* bastola.

rodent *n* mnyama mgugunaji (k.m. panya, sungura, n.k.) *adj* -mnyama mgugunaji.

rodeo *n* 1 *(US)* kukusanya ng'ombe (kuwatia alama). 2 maonyesho/mashindano ya wachunga ng'ombe (kuhusu ufundi wao wa kufunza mifugo).

rodomontade *n* makeke, majivuno, maringo, kujidai *vi* jivuna.

roe[1] *n* ng'ofu: mayai ya samaki.

roe[2] *n* paa mdogo wa Ulaya na Asia. **~buck** *n* paa dume.

rogation *n (Rel.)* litania ya watakatifu. **R~ Days** siku za kuombea watakatifu, siku tatu kabla ya sikukuu ya kupaa.

roger *int (of radio communication)* nimeelewa! imefika!

rogue *n* 1 ayari, laghai, mjanja. 2 jambazi, jangili, mhuni. **~'s gallery** mkusanyiko wa picha za majambazi sugu/wahuni/wahalifu, n.k. 3 *(mischievous child)* mtundu. 4 mshari ~ *elephant* tembo mshari. **~ry** *n* 1 ujanja, hila, ulaghai. 2 *(fun)* mizaha, utundu, ucheshi. **roguish** *adj* 1 -a kilaghai, -a kihuni. 2 -a kitundu, -a kidhihaka.

roister *vi* piga makelele (ya furaha). **~er** *n* mfanya ghasia.

role *n* 1 wajibu, dhima. 2 nafasi (ya mwigizaji).

roll *vt,vi* 1 bingirisha; bingirika *heads will ~ (colloq)* watu watafukuzwa/umbuka. 2 ~ **(up)** sokota, kunja, zongomeza ~ *a cigarette* sokota sigara. 3 enda, pita *the clouds ~ed away* mawingu yalitoweka *tears ~ed down his cheeks* machozi yalimtiririka. 4 geukageuka. 5 *(make flat)* tandaza; sukuma (k.m. chapati);

futa; nyosha. **~ed gold** tabaka nyembamba la dhahabu (juu ya metali nyingine). 6 sukasuka, yumbayumba. 7 *(of surfaces)* tia mawimbi. 8 *(of waves)* panda na kushuka. 9 nguruma ~ **ones r's** sema kimadende. 10 ~ **at** *(of eyes)* geuzageuza, zungusha. 11 **~ing** *n (compounds)* ~ **mill** kiwanda cha kusukuma metali. ~ **pin** *n* kijiti/ mpini/kipande cha kusukuma unga. ~ **stock** *n* mabehewa, mabogi ya reli. 12 *(with adv particles and prep)* ~ **sth back** rudisha nyuma (k.m. adui). ~ **in** miminika, wasili/fika kwa wingi. **be ~ing in** jaa *they're ~ing in money* wamejaa. ~ **on** pita; fika haraka. **time ~ed on** wakati ulipita. ~ **on the weekend!** wikendi ifike haraka. ~ **sth on** vaa nguo kwa kuzungusha kwenye miguu. ~ **sth out** tandaza. ~ **out the red carpet** *(fig)* -pa mgeni. rasmi makaribisho makubwa; *(of pastry etc)* sukuma. ~ **up** *(of a vehicle)* fika na kusimama. **R~ up! R~up!** Njoo! Njoo. ~ **sth up** *(mil)* rudisha nyuma. ~ *n* 1 kitu chenye umbo la mcheduara (kutokana na kuviringwa; *(of cloth)* jora *(of paper)* gombo; *(of film)* filamu; *(of tobacco)* bumba; *(of bread)* skonzi. ~ **top desk** *n* deski lenye mfuniko unaokunjika. 2 ukingo uliogeuzwa (k.m. pindo la nguo lililogeuzwa). 3 mwendo wa kubingiria. 4 orodha rasmi (hasa ya majina). **~call** *n* kuita majina (ya wanafunzi, askari, n.k.) katika orodha. ~ **of honour** *n* orodha ya majina ya watu waliokufa kwa ajili ya nchi yao. **strike off the ~s** ondoa jina la mwanasheria katika orodha ya wale wanaoruhusiwa kufanya kazi ya uanasheira. 5 sauti ya mbingirio, ngurumo. **~er** *n* 1 chuma/mti/mpira - mcheduara (-a kukandamizia, n.k.). 2 rola: gurudumu aina ya mcheduara. **~skates** *n* rolasketi: magurudumu yanayofungwa chini ya kiatu/ubao kwa ajili ya kutelezea. 3 ~ **bandage** bandeji ya operesheni. 4 wimbi refu na kubwa.

rollick *vi* chachawa, cheza, dhihaki; rukaruka kwa furaha *n* kurukaruka kwa furaha, kucheza sana. **~ing** *adj* 1 -enye kelele/furaha/vifijo, -enye kuchachawa. 2 -a makelele.

roly-poly *n* 1 *(also ~* **pudding)** pudini yenye utando wa unga wa jamu iliyotengenezewa katika umbo la mcheduara na kuchemshwa. 2 *(colloq)* mtoto mfupi na mnene.

Romaic *adj* -a Kigiriki cha kisasa. *n* Kigiriki cha kisasa.

Roman *adj* 1 -a Kirumi. ~ **alphabet** alfabeti ya Kirumi. ~ **letters/type** hati za Kirumi. ~ **numbers** namba za Kirumi. 2 -a Kikatoliki. ~ **rite** ibada ya Kikatoliki. ~ **Catholic** Mkatoliki *n* 1 Mrumi. 2 Mkatoliki. **~ize** *vt,vi* fanya kuwa Urumi; tia tarakimu za Kirumi, fanya kuwa Katoliki; ongoa Kikatoliki.

Romance[1] adj ~ *languages* -a lugha za Kirumi (k.m Kifaransa, Kitaliana, Kireno, Kihispania) *n* lugha za Kirumi.

romance[2] *n* 1 *(love story)* hadithi ya mahaba (hasa dhanifu); fasihi ya mahaba. 2 mapenzi. 3 hali ya kuvutia/kuvutiwa na hadithi na vitendo/vituko vya mapenzi. 4 uzushi, maelezo yaliyotiwa chumvi *vi (usually romanticize)* piga chuku katika kuhadithia. **~tic** *adj* 1 *(of persons)* -enye mawazo/ hisia/njozi za mapenzi; -enye kupenda mambo yaliyotiwa chumvi/ya ajabu. 2 -enye hali ya ajabu/mahaba. 3 -enye kubuni ya usoni. 4 *(lit,etc.)* -enye kusisitiza hisia kuliko mantiki/akili *n* 1 mpenda mahaba. 2 mpendelea hisia na ubunifu. 3 mpiga chuku; mwota njozi. **~tically** *adv*. **~ticism** *n* tapo la sanaa linalosisitiza ubunifu na hisia. **~icist** *n* mfuasi,mshiriki wa mwelekeo huo. **~cer** *n* 1 mwandishi wa hadithi za mahaba. 2 kidhabi.

Romansque *n* mtindo wa uhandisi majenzi wa Kirumi.

Romany *n* 1 Mjipsi. 2 lugha ya Wajipsi *adj* -a kijipsi.

Rome *n* Roma. *(with different phrases.)* **R~ was not built in a day** usione vyaelea vimeundwa. **when in R~ do as the Romans do** fuatia maadili ya wenyeji.

Romish *adj* -a Kanisa la Katoliki.

romp *vi* 1 cheza, randa, rukaruka, chachawa. 2 shinda haraka/bila shida *n* 1 mchezo wa kurukaruka na kufanya makelele; kelele. 2 mtoto anayependa kuchezacheza na kurukaruka. **~er** *n (also* **a suit of ~ers)** ovaroli ya mtoto. **~ish** *adj* -a kuchezacheza.

Roneo *n* mashine ya kurudufu barua, nakala, n.k. *vt* rudufu kwa mashini.

rood *n* 1 ~ **(-tree)** *(arch)* msalaba ambapo Yesu alisulubiwa. 2 sanamu ya Yesu msalabani. 3 robo eka.

roof *n* 1 paa: sehemu inayufanika juu (ya nyumba, basi, gari, treni, n.k.). **raise the** ~ *(colloq)* piga makelele (ndani ya nyumba). ~ **garden** bustani juu ya jengo. ~ **tree** mti wa ulalo unaounganisha/unaoshikilia paa. 2 kilele, sehemu ya juu kabisa. 3 kakaa *vt* tia paa, tia dari, *(thatch)* ezeka, vimba. **~ing** *(also* **~ing material)** vifaa vitumiwavyo kuezekea; maezeko, mavimbo. **~less** *adj* sio na paa *(of person)* -siyekuwa na makazi/ nyumba.

rook[1] *n* ndege mkubwa mweusi kama kunguru. **~ery** *n* 1 makazi ya ndege huyo. 2 jamii ya penguini.

rook[2] *n* ayari, laghai *vt* danganya, ghilibu, laghai (katika kamari).

rook[3] *n* ngome katika sataranji.

rookie,rooky *n (sl)* askari mbichi/ kuruta.

room *n* 1 chumba. **~ed** *adj* -enye vyumba *a five ~ house* nyumba yenye vyumba vitano. 2 vyumba (vinavyokaliwa/tumiwa na mtu mmoja au familia moja). **~mate** mkazi-mwenza (katika chumba/ nyumba). 3 ~ **(for sb (sth)**; ~ **(to do sth)** nafasi *there is no ~ for doubt* hapana shaka yoyote. 4 mwanya, nafasi (ya kufanya jambo) *vi* panga chumba/ vyumba/nyumba. **~ing house** jengo lenye vyumba vingi vya kupanga (agh. wapangaji wakajihudumia wenyewe). **~er** *n (USA)* mpangaji. **~ful** *n* watu, samani, n.k. inayoweza kujaza chumba. **~y** *adj* -enye nafasi tele. **-ily** *adv*.

roost *n* kijiti cha kutulia; kituo cha ndege; banda la kuku. **come home to** ~ *(of words)* rudia *his words came home to ~* maneno yake yalimrudia. **rule the** ~ tawala (agh. nyumbani); *(of birds)* jikalia kiotani usiku.

rooster *n* jogoo, jimbi.

root[1] *n* 1 mzizi. **pull up one's ~s** *(fig)* hama (ili kuanza maisha mapya mahali pengine). **put down new ~s** *(fig)* anza maisha mapya baada ya kuhama maskani ya zamani. **take/ strike** ~ *(of plants)* anza kuota mizizi, anza kukua; *(fig)* anza kustawi. ~ **and branch** *(fig)* kabisa. 2 **~s,** ~ **crop** mazao yawekayo chakula katika mizizi (k.v. karoti). 3 *(of hair, tooth, nail)* kizizi. 4 *(fig)* asili, chanzo, kiini. **get at/to the ~ of sth** fikia/kabili kiini cha jambo. 5 *(gram)* mzizi: sehemu ya neno ambayo ndiyo kiini/kijenzi cha neno zima (k.m. pik- katika pik-a, pik-i-a, n.k). 6 kipeo (katika hesabu) *vt,vi* 1 *(of plants etc)* toa mizizi, anza, kukua. 2 weka/simama imara, kaza, pigwa bumbuwazi. 3 *(of ideas, principles)* kuwa na mawazo/misingi thabiti. 4 ~ **sth out,** ~ **sth up** ng'oa; ondoa kabisa (kitu kibaya); angamiza. **~less** *adj* bila mizizi, -sio na mashiko/asili.

root[2] *vt,vi* 1 ~ **about (for)** *(of pigs etc)* chimbua; *(of persons)* pekuapekua. ~ **sth out** gundua/fuma kwa kutafuta. 2 ~ **(for)** *(US sl)* unga mkono, shangilia, shabikia. **~er** *n*. **~le** *vi* ~ *about for (of pigs)* chimbua chimbua.

rope *n* 1 kamba, ukamba, ugwe. **the** ~ kitanzi (agh. kunyonga mtu). **the ~s** kamba za ulingo/jukwaa (la ndondi, n.k.). **show sb/know/learn the ~s** onyesha/jifunza namna ya kufanya jambo. **give sb (plenty of) ~** mpe uhuru wa kufanya jambo. **give sb enough ~ and he 'll hang himself** mwana akililia wembe mpe. 2 *(with compounds)* **~-dancer, ~walker** mchezaji juu ya kamba. **~-ladder** ngazi ya kamba. **~-walk/yard** sehemu ya ardhi inayotumika kusokota kamba. **~way** reli ya kamba. **~-yarn** uzi wa kamba. 3 vitu kadhaa vilivyosokotwa pamoja *vt* 1 funga kwa kamba. 2 **~ sth off** zungushia eneo kwa kamba. 3 **~ in** shawishi mtu ajiunge.

ropy *adj (sl)* hafifu, duni.

rosary *n* 1 rosari; tasbihi. 2 bustani ya waridi. 3 *(RC)* sala ya rozari.

rose[1] *n* 1 waridi. **a bed of ~s** maisha ya raha. **it is not all ~s** ina matatizo yake. **no ~ without a thorn** hakuna kizuri kisicho ila, hakuna furaha bila tabu. **gather life's ~s** tafuta raha za maisha. 2 rangi nyekundu-nyeupe. **see things through ~ coloured tinted spectacles** ona/bashiria mema tu (labda bila sababu). 3 vitu vyenye umbo la waridi. 4 *(with compounds)* **~-bed** tuta la waridi. **~ bud** tumba la waridi. **~ leaf** petali ya ua la waridi. **~red** waridi, nyekundu ya waridi. **~-water** marashi ya waridi. **~window** dirisha la duara na mapambo. **~wood** mwaridi (mti mwekundu na mgumu unaotumika kutengeneza fanicha) *adj* 1 -ekundu -eupe. 2 -a waridi. **~ate** *adj* -a waridi, -ekundu, -a rangi ya waridi. **rosy** *adj* 1 -a rangi nyekundu/nyeupe (hasa kwa shavu la uso) *turn rosy* geuka mwekundu. 2 *(fig)* -a kutia matumaini.

rose[2] *pt of* **rise**.

rosin *n* 1 ulimbo (wa baadhi ya miti kama sandarusi). 2 resini *vt* sugua kwa resini.

roster *n* rosta: orodha ya majina ya watu na kazi wapaswazo kufanya kwa zamu (pia rota). **by ~** kwa zamu.

rostrum *n* mimbari; jukwaa.

rot *vt,vi* 1 oza. 2 *(of society, prisoners, etc)* dhoofika, chakaa. 3 ozesha. **~-gut** *n* gongo chafu lenye kudhuru tumbo *n* 1 kioza, uoza/uozo. 2 *(US* **the ~)** ugonjwa wa ini wa kondoo. **(foot ~)** ugonjwa wa miguu wa kondoo. 3 *(sl) (nonsense)* upuuzi, mapiswa. 4 mfululizo wa kushindwa. **~ten** *adj* 1 bovu, viza; -liooza. **~ eggs** mayai viza. 2 -siyopendeza, baya sana *he is a ~ singer* ni mwimbaji mbaya sana.

rota *n (GB)* orodha ya zamu; zamu.

rotary *adj* 1 -a kuzunguka/-liozunguka sehemu maalumu ya kati. **R~ Club** Klabu ya *R~* (ya wanabiashara). **Rotarian** *n* mwanachama wa **R~y**. **rotate** *vt,vi* 1 zunguka kitu; zungusha; fuatana kwa zamu. 2 badilisha *~ the crops* badilisha mimea. **rotative** *adj*. **rotatory** *adj*. **rotation** *n* 1 mzunguko, mzingo. **~ of the earth** mzunguko, mhimili (wa dunia). 2 **in ~** kwa zamu.

rote *n* **by ~** kwa ghibu, kwa moyo *learn by ~* jifunza kwa ghibu.

rotor *n* rafadha.

rotter *(sl)* mkorofi, mwovu, mtu asiye na mwamana; mshenzi.

rotund *adj* 1 *(of person, his face; of voice)* nene; nzito; -a mviringo. 2 *(of speech, style)* -enye mbwembwe, -a majivuno. **~ly** *adv*. **~ity** *n*.

rotunda *n* jengo la duara (hasa lenye paa la duara).

rouble *n* rubo: sarafu ya Kirusi.

roue *n* fisadi, fasiki.

rouge *n* 1 poda nyekundu (ya kupaka kwenye mashavu). 2 poda ya kusafishia (fedha, kioo, n.k.) *vt* jipodoa (kwa kutumia rangi hiyo).

rough *adj* 1 *(of surfaces)* -a kukwaruza, -a kuparuza; *(of road)* -enye mashimoshimo; *(of sea)* -liochafuka. 2 kali, -enye fujo. **be ~ on sb** onea mtu, -wa mkali. **give sb the ~ side of one's tongue** karipia mtu. **give sb/have a ~ time** -pa/pata matatizo. **~ house** *(colloq)* ugomvi, zahama, ghasia. 3 ghafi, -siokamilika, -a kukadiria. **~ and ready** -enye kufaa kutumia (lakini si makini sana). **a ~ diamond** *(fig)* mtu wa thamani lakini asiyestaarabika. 4 *(of sounds)* nene na -enye kukwaruza. 5 *(with compounds)* **~-and-tumble** *adj* -a mkikimkiki; -enye vurumai, ovyo na gomvi. **~-neck** *n (US colloq)* mhuni, jambazi. **~-rider** *n* mfunza farasi (ili akubali kupandwa). **~shod** *adj (of horses)* -enye viatu vya njumu. **ride ~shod over sb** puuza kabisa. **~spoken** *adj* mwenye mdomo mchafu, mpujufu. **~ly** *adv* 1 kwa ukali, kwa kuparuza. 2 takribani, mnamo ~ *speaking* kwa kukisia. **~ness** *n* fujo, ghasia, ukatili; mparuzo, mkwaruzo *n* 1 jambazi, mhuni. 2 hali ya kutokamilika *in (the) ~ draft* drafti ya awali. 3 hali ya kukwaruza/kutokuwa sawa; kitu kibaya. **take the ~ with the smooth** *(fig)* kubali mabaya yanayoandamana na mema. 4 *(golf)* **the ~** sehemu ya majani marefu *vt,vi* 1 **~ sth (up)** vurugavuruga, timua timua. 2 **~ sb up** *(sl.)* tikisatikisa; pigapiga; fanyia fujo, sumbua. **~ sth in** sawidi. 3 **~ it** ishi maisha ya taabu/shida *adv* 1 kwa ugomvi/ukali/ukatili *play* ~ cheza kwa rafu. **cut up ~** *(colloq)* kasirika. **live ~** ishi kwa kubabia, ishi maisha ya ovyo. **sleep ~** lala majaani. **~en** *vt,vi* -wa/fanya rafu/fujo/vurugu.

roughage *n* chakula ghafi; vyakula vigumu.

roulette *n* mchezo wa kamari (uchezwao kwa gololi na kigurudumu).

round *adj* 1 -a duara, -a mviringo, -a kuviringa(na). **a ~ game** mchezo usio na timu au idadi maalumu ya wachezaji. 2 -enye kufanywa kwa kuzungukazunguka/kuzungushazungusha. **~ brackets** mabano upinde. **~ dance** ngoma ya kucheza katika duara. **~ robin** barua ya maombi/malalamiko yenye sahihi zinazofanya mviringo (ili kuficha ni nani aliyeanza kutia sahihi). **~ trip** safari ya kwenda na kurudi. 3 kamili, -ote; nzima. **in ~ numbers/figures** namba za makumi 10, 100, 1000. 4 wazi, dhahiri, kamili. 5 *(with compounds)* **~ arm** *adj* -a usawa wa bega. **~backed** *adj* -a kibiongo. **~eyed** *adj* kodozi; -enye macho makubwa. **~ hand** *n* mwandiko wa herufi za kuumba. **~-house** *n (hist)* gereza; *(naut)* chumba cha staha; karakana ya garimoshi. **~ shouldered** *adj* -enye matao *vt,vi* 1 fanya/-wa mviringo, viringisha. 2 zunguka. 3 **~ sth off** kamilisha jambo. **~ out** viringisha. **~ sb/sth up** leta pamoja, kusanya. **~ up (a figure/ price)** fanya (idadi) kamili. **a ~ up** msako. **~ on (upon)** geuka ghafla. **~ upon sb** geukia mtu na kumshambulia (kwa maneno au kwa vitendo) *n* 1 kitu kilicho na umbo la mviringo. 2 *(of sculpture)* umbo linalokiwezesha kitu kuonekana kutoka sehemu zote. **in the ~** *(arts)* -liotengenezwa/ fanywa ili kuonekana pande zote. **theatre in the ~** jukwaa linalozungukwa na watazamaji. 3 *(series)* mfululizo, mfuatano, mgawo, mzunguko. **make ones ~s** fanya raundi za kila siku/mara (k.m. kukagua). **go the ~ of; go the ~s** fikia (watu, mahali), sambaa, enea haraka *the news went the ~ of the school* habari zilisambaa haraka shuleni. 4 (*games contest, etc*) raundi *the third ~ of the super league* raundi ya tatu ya ligi kuu; duru. 5 mzunguko (wa kitu kinachogawiwa watu, k.m. kwenye unywaji wa pombe). 6 wimbo wa kupokezana. 7 mchezo wa dansi ambapo wachezaji hucheza katika mtindo wa duara *prep* 1 *(expressing movement)* kwa kuzunguka. **sleep/work ~ the clock** *(attr)* lala/fanya usiku na mchana, saa zote. 2 *(expressingmovement)* katika njia ambayo inabadili uelekeo kutoka upande mmoja wa kitu hadi upande mwingine. **~ the bend** *(sl)* kichaa. 3 *(expressing position)* kuwa katika pande zote za kitu *they were sitting ~ the table* walikuwa wamekaa kwa kuzunguka meza. 4 katika sehemu mbalimbali/zote. **show ~** tembeza. **go**

~ tembelea; zunguka. 5 sehemu mbalimbali kutoka kituo maalumu. 6 ~ **(about)** *(fig)* takribani *adv* 1 katika duara; kwa kuzunguka. 2 kwa kurudia mahali ulipoanzia. ~ **and** ~ kwa mizunguko kadhaa. **all ~, right** ~ kwa kuzunguka kabisa. **all the year** ~ kwa mwaka mzima. 3 kwa kuzunguka, katika mzingo. 4 ili kuwa katika duara. 5 kutoka sehemu/eneo/mtu mmoja hadi mwingine. **hand** ~ gawia/mpe kila mmoja. **go** ~ tosheleza. **taking it all** ~ kwa kulitazama (k.m.) katika ujumla wake/pande zake zote. **look** ~ tembelea. 6 kwa kutumia njia ndefu zaidi. 7 kwenye sehemu alipo mtu/atakapokuwa mtu. 8 ~ **(about)** jirani/katika mazingira jirani. **~ly** *adv* sana, wazi. **~about** *adj* -enye *adv* sana, wazi. **in a ~about way** kwa kuzunguka. **~about** kuzungukazunguka *n* 1 pembea. **you lose on the swings what you make on the ~abouts** *(prov.)* kata pua uunge wajihi. 2 kipulefti, kizingwa, kisiwa (cha trafiki).

roundel *n* 1 nishani. 2 nembo ya ndege.

roundelay *n* wimbo mfupi wenye kiitikio.

rounders *n* mchezo unaofanana na baseball.

roundsman *n* mchuuzi (wa nyumba hadi nyumba).

rouse *vt,vi* 1 amka/amsha, chochea. 2 ~ **sb (from sth to sth)** zindua/zinduka, sisimua; chachafya.

rout[1] *vt* shinda kabisa *n* 1 kushindwa *put the enemy to* ~ shinda adui kabisa. 2 *(arch)* umati/halaiki yenye ghasia. 3 *(arch)* tafrija, sherehe.

rout[2] *vt* ~ **sb out (of)** furusha; amsha (kitandani); winga, fukuza.

route *n* 1 njia. **en** ~ njiani. 2 *(mil)* **column of** ~ safu ya askari wanaotembea. **~-march** *n (mil)* safari ndefu ya miguu (ya mazoezi) *vt* peleka/tuma kwa njia fulani; panga njia ya safari.

routine *n* utaratibu, kawaida, desturi *business* ~ utaratibu wa biashara/shughuli *adj* -a kawaida.

rove *vi,vt* 1 tangatanga, zurura ~ *the streets* zurura barabarani. **a roving commission** wajibu/kazi zinazohitaji kutembea/kuzunguka sana. 2 *(of affections)* badilibadili. 3 *(of eyes)* tazama huko na huko; -totulia. **~r** *n* 1 mzururaji, mtembezi. 2 *(arch)* **sea** ~ haramia wa baharini. 3 skauti wa kiume mwandamizi.

row[1] *n* 1 makelele, ghasia, zahama. **kick up/make a** ~ anza ugomvi/mabishano. 2 ugomvi. 3 matata; karipio *vt,vi* 1 karipia, kemea. 2 ~ **with** gombana kwa makelele na mtu. **~dy** makelele, zahama, vurugu *n* mtu mwenye vurugu, mhuni. **rowdily** *adv* **rowdiness** *n*. **~dyism** *n*.

row[2] *n* safu; mstari; msafa *be in ~s* kuwa katika safu; *(colloq)* mfululizo *two weeks in a* ~ wiki mbili mfululizo. **a hard ~ to hoe** kazi ngumu sana; *(of things piled up)* rusu; *(of fish on a string)* mtungo, mtanda; *(of plants)* mpando wa ghasia.

row[3] *vt,vi* piga (vuta) makasia *n* kwenda katika mtumbwi. **~boat; ~ing boat** mtumbwi wa makasia; ngalawa. **~ing club** *n* klabu ya wapiga makasia. **~lock** *n* kileti, kishwara. ~ **er** *n* mpiga kasia.

rowel *n* kikuna farasi (kisumari cha kumchochea farasi mbavuni).

royal *adj* -a kifalme ~ *charter* idhini ya kifalme ~ *prerogative* haki za mfalme (kwa mujibu wa katiba); -zuri sana. ~ **road to success** njia rahisi/bora ya mafanikio *have a* ~ *time* starehe sana *n* mmojawapo wa familia ya kifalme. **~ist** *n* mfuasi wa ufalme. **~ty** *n* 1 hadhi, cheo, mamlaka ya mfalme/jamaa wa mfalme. 2 watu wa jamaa/aila ya mfalme. 3 mrabaha: malipo ya mwandishi.

rub *vt,vi* 1 chua; fikicha ~ *hands together* fikicha viganja ~ *the ears of wheat* fikicha ngano; ~ *shoulders with (fig)* changamana na watu wa aina mbalimbali. 2 sugua. 3 *(with adverbial particles and prep)* ~ **along** ishi. ~ **along (with sb/together)** ishi vizuri (pamoja), elewana. ~ **sb/oneself/a horse down** sugua vizuri na kwa nguvu (k.m. kwa taulo ili kukausha na kusafisha). ~ **sth down** sugua. ~ **sth in**; ~ **sth into sth** chua; sisitizia, tia mkazo. ~ **it in** kumbusha kila wakati. ~ **sth off/out** ondoa kwa kufuta. ~ **sb out** *(US sl)* ua. ~ **sth up** piga polishi, ng'arisha; fanya kiwe kipya. ~ **sb up the wrong way** udhi mtu *n* 1 usuguaji, (muda wa) kusugua. 2 *(esp in the phrase)* **(there's the ~)** tatizo, mahali ambapo ugumu unaanza kutokea. **~bing** *n* picha ya kusuguliwa.

rub-a-dub *n* mdundo.

rubber[1] *n* mpira. ~ **stamp** mhuri. ~-**stamp** *(colloq) vt* pitisha kitu/jambo bila kulizingatia. ~ **neck** *n (US) (colloq)* mtalii anayegeuka kila upande (ili ajaribu kuona kila kitu) *vi* 1 talii 2. kifutio, raba. 3 viatu vya mpira, raba. 4 mtu afutaye/kitu kitumiwacho kufuta (k.m. sehemu ya mashine) *vt* funga/funika kwa mpira. **~ize** *vt* funga/funika kwa mpira. **~y** *adj*.

rubber[2] *n (in cards)* 1 seti: michezo mitatu mfululizo ya karata. 2 mchezo wa tatu wa kutafuta mshindi.

rubbish *n* 1 taka, takataka; kitu cha kutupwa; kitu kisicho na faida/thamani. 2 upuuzi; mawazo/fikra zisizokuwa na faida *(as expression)* mawe! **~-bin/can** *n* pipa la taka *a heap of ~* jalala, jaa; *(of demolished house)* kifusi. **~y** *adj*.

rubble *n* 1 kifusi. 2 kokoto.

rube *n (US colloq)* mshamba.

Rubicon *n (esp in)* **pass/cross the ~** jiingiza katika mradi/jambo/uhusiano ambao haiwezekani kujitoa.

rubicund *adj (of person's face or complexion)* -ekundu.

ruble *n see* **rouble**.

rubric *n* 1 kichwa cha maandiko kilicho andikwa kwa rangi nyekundu. 2 utaratibu, maelezo. 3 utaratibu, mfumo.

ruby *n* 1 rubi: kito chekundu cha thamani. 2 rangi ya zambarau *adj* -ekundu.

ruck[1] *n* **the ~, the common ~** kabwela; vitu vya kawaida.

ruck[2] *n* kunyanzi katika nguo *vt,vi* ~ **(up)** kunjakunja, fanya kunyanzi.

rucksack *n* shanta.

ructions *n* maneno ya hasira au upinzani; ghasia, zahama; ugomvi wenye makelele.

rudder *n* usukani. **~less** *adj* bila usukani.

ruddy adj 1 -ekundu (na -enye afya). 2 *(of sky)* -ekundu (ekundu). **ruddiness** *n* wekundu (wa uso). **ruddily** *adv*.

rude *adj* 1 fidhuli, -juvi, -sio adabu. 2 -a kushtusha; -a fujo na ghasia; kali. **get a ~ awakening** tambua ghafla ukweli usiopendeza. 3 -a kishenzi. 4 ghafi. 5 -liofanywa kwa haraka-haraka; sahili. 6 -a nguvu. **~ness** *n*. **~ly** *adv* kishenzi.

rudiment *n* 1 *(beginning)* mwanzo, asili, msingi, hatua za kwanza. 2 chipuko, chanzo. **~al** *adj*. **~ary** *adj* 1 -a mwanzo. 2 -sioendelezwa; katika hali isiyokamilika.

rue *vt* jutia, sikitikia *to ~ the day when....* kujutia siku ya .... **~ful** *adj*. **~fully** *adv*. **~fulness** *n*.

ruff[1] *n* 1 kikunjo shingo, kitambaa chenye vikunjo cha kuvaa shingoni, matimutimu. 2 pete ya manyoya ya rangirangi shingoni mwa ndege au mnyama. **~ed** *adj* 1 -liokunjamana. 2 matimutimu.

ruff[2] *vt,vi* shinda kwa turufu.

ruffian *n* katili, mgomvi, jambazi, mhuni. **~ism** *n* uhuni; ujambazi, ukatili. **~ly** *adj* -gomvi, huni, -katili.

ruffle 1 *vt,vi* ~ **(up)** chafua, timua, vuruga *~ its feathers* timua manyoya (kwa hasira au kutoa baridi). 2 kasirika; chafuka, timka *easily ~d* -a kukasirika, -a kuudhika upesi *n* 1 vikunjo (vya nguo vya kuvaa shingoni; mwisho wa mikono ya vazi. 2 matatizo, shida. 3 kuchafuka, machafuko. **~d** *adj*.

rug *n* zulia dogo nene; blanketi nene la safari.

rugby *n* ragbi: mchezo wa mpira wa mikono.

rugged *adj* 1 -a mawemawe; -a kuparuza; -sionyooka. 2 -enye mikunjomikunjo; -a kunyanzi. 3 -sio laini/taratibu/pole. **~ness** *n* **~ly** *adv*.

rugger = **rugby**.

ruin *n* 1 maangamizi; uharibifu; utilifu *the ~ of my hopes* kuharibika kwa matumaini yangu. 2 *(in sing. only)* sababu ya kuharibika. 3 *(of buildings)* hali ya kuwa katika maanguko/magofu/mahame/mabaki *a ~ed house* gofu la nyumba, hame 4 *(business)* kufilisika *vt* vunja; angamiza; haribu; tilifisha. **~ation** *n* kuangamia, kuharibika; uangamiaji. **~ous** *adj* 1 -enye kuharibu. 2 -liovunjika (na kuanguka). **~ously** *adv*.

rule *n* 1 *(regulation)* amri, kanuni, sharti, desturi, mila. **by/according to ~** kwa mujibu wa kanuni/sheria. **work to ~** timiza mradi, -wa na mgomo baridi (kwa kufuata sana sheria kwa makusudi) kwa kiasi cha kurudisha nyuma uzalishaji (mali). 2 desturi. **as a ~** kwa kawaida/desturi. 3 utawala; mamlaka; dola; serikali. **~ of law** utawala wa sheria. 4 *(for measuring)* rula *vt,vi* 1 ~ **(over)** tawala, -wa na mamlaka. 2 *(usu passive) (control)* ongoza, athiri, tawala. 3 *(order)* amuru. 4 *(decide)* amua. **~ sth out** futilia mbali. 5 piga mstari. **~d paper** karatasi ya mistari mifuo. **~ sth off** kata, ondoa. **~r** *n* 1 mtawala, mfalme, mkuu. **absolute ~** dikteta, mtawala mmoja. 2 *(for measuring)* rula, chenezo, kigezo, futi. **ruling** *adj* -a kutawala, -a nguvu; -liopo *n* amri, hukumu, uamuzi.

rum[1] *n* aina ya pombe kali. **~ runner** mlanguzi (wa pombe zisizoruhusiwa); *(US)* pombe.

rum[2] *adj (colloq)* kioja; -a kigeni; -sio -a kawaida; ajabu. *see* **rummy**.

rumba *adj* rumba: dansi yenye asili ya Cuba.

rumble *vt,vi* 1 nguruma; vuma, tutuma; rindima. **~ along** enda kwa kunguruma. 2 **~ (out)** sema kwa sauti nzito *n* 1 ngurumo, uvumi, tutumo, tetemo, mdundo, rindimo. 2 *(colloq US)* mapambano ya vikundi vya wahuni mitaani.

rumbustious *adj (colloq)* -a ghasia, -enye kelele, -a makeke.

ruminant *adj* 1 -a kucheua. 2 *(of person)* -liozama katika fikra, -liokaa na kushika tuma *n* mnyama anayecheua. **~s** wacheuzi. **ruminate** *vt,vi* 1 cheua, tafuna. 2 waza, tafakari. **~ over (a plan)** fikiria jambo/azimio. **rumination** *n*.

rummage *vt,vi* 1 **~ (among, in, through)** geuzageuza vitu wakati unatafuta kitu, pekua, chakura. 2 **~ through** pekua/chakura sana, chunguza, kagua. **~ sale** *see* **jumbo sale** *n* 1 upekuzi mkali. 2 vitu vilivopatikana katika upekuzi. 3 vitu vikuukuu.

rummy[1] *adj see* **rum**.

rummy[2] *n (of cards)* mchezo wa karata uchezwao na jozi mbili.

rumour *n* uvumi, mnong'ono, tetesi, udaku *vt* vumisha; toa uvumi. **~ monger** mvumishaji, mzushi.

rump *n* 1 *(animal)* tako; *(bird)* mkiani. 2 *(derog)* mabaki, masazo (ya kundi kubwa la watu). **~ steak** *n* steki ya tako.

rumple *vt* kunjakunja, vuruga.

rumpus *n* zahama, ghasia, ugomvi wenye makelele/makeke. **kick up/make a ~** fanya ghasia.

run[1] *vt, vi* 1 kimbia, kimbiza **take a ~ning jump** kimbia na kuruka; *(sl)* ambaa, usiwe mpuuzi! 2 epuka, toroka, kimbia. **~ for it** kimbia (ili kukwepa jambo). **cut and ~** *(sl)* toroka. **a ~ning fight** mapambano ya manowari (kati ya wanaorudi nyuma na wanaowakimbiza). 3 shiriki katika mbio/mazoezi ya kukimbia. **also ran** *n* mshinde. 4 **~ for** gombea (uchaguzi, cheo, n.k.). 5 sababisha kukimbia/kushiriki (katika mashindano ya mbio); wasilisha/teua (kushika cheo). 6 sababisha kufikia hali fulani/mahali fulani (kutokana na kukimbia). ~ **sb clean off his feet/ legs** *(colloq)* shughulisha hadi kuchosha kabisa. ~ **oneself/sb into the ground** jichosha/chosha (mtu) kwa kazi/mazoezi magumu. 7 enda haraka. ~ **its course** kua, endelea kawaida; fuata mkondo wa kawaida. ~ **the streets** *(of children)* cheza barabarani (bila usimamizi). 8 jiweka wazi; jihatarisha. ~ **the danger/chance of sth** jiweka katika hali/hatari ya. 9 kimbiza, shindana na. ~ **sb/sth to earth** fuatilia hadi kupata/kushika. ~ **sb/sth close hard** karibia sana (katika mashindano). 10 *(of ships, etc)* enda safari; *(of fish)* ogelea. 11 *(of machines)* fanya kazi. 12 enda mbele kwa mwendo wa kuteleza au kuendelea; enda kama kwamba uko kwenye magurudumu. 13 *(of public transport)* pita; enda na kurudi (kila mara). 14 chukua (mtu katika gari, basi, n.k. na kumpeleka mahali). 15 peleka, safirisha. ~ **errands/messages** peleka ujumbe. ~ **arms/guns** ingiza silaha nchini kwa siri, fanya magendo ya silaha. ~ **liquor** fanya magendo ya vileo. 16 fanya kusogea au kupanuka kuelekea upande fulani. 17 *(of fire, news, emotions, etc)* enea haraka. 18 *(of liquids)* tiririka; churuzika, lowa. 19 fanya kumwagika/tiririka; fanya kuenea. 20 -wa/pitia katika hali fulani. ~ **riot** fanya fujo na ghasia; *(of plants)* enea ovyo. ~ **wild** kaa/kuwa bila mipango/nidhamu. ~ **a temperature** -wa na homa. 21 endesha, ongoza, simamia. ~ **a company** endesha kampuni. ~**ning costs** gharama za uendeshaji. ~ **the show** kuwa bosi katika kadhia fulani. 22 *(of thoughts, feelings memories, the eyes, etc)* pitia/pitisha mara moja/kwa haraka. 23 endelea/ endelezwa katika mpango maalumu *a scar that ~s across his cheek* kovu linaloanzia upande mmoja hadi upande mwingine wa shavu lake. **the ~ning commentary** tangazo mfululizo. 24 -wa na mwelekeo fulani (wa kitabia), -wa na bei ya wastani; -wa na kiwango cha wastani. 25 *(of colour)* -sambaa toka sehemu yenye rangi hadi isiyo na rangi 26 andikwa, simuliwa au semwa *the story ~s that* hadithi imeandikwa/yasemwa kuwa ---. 27 *(of woven or knitted material)* fumuka. 28 *(in special uses)* ~ **about** kwenda huku na huko. ~-**about** *n* matokaa ndogo (k.m. ya watu wawili); mtu atangatangaye kutafuta mambo mageni, raha, n.k. (hatulii katika sehemu moja). ~ **away** kimbia; jaribu kutoroka. ~**away** *n* mtu/farasi atorokaye. ~ **away with** tumia; toroka; iba; shinda vibaya sana washindani wengine; kubali wazo harakaharaka, fikia hitimisho lisilo na msingi; enda kwa kasi kubwa isiyodhibitika. ~ **back** rejea nyuma (katika mawazo). ~ **down** *(of a clock or other mechanism of the like)* simama (kwa kukosa kulishwa); *(of a person's health)* nyong'onyea, zidi kuwa mbaya (kwa sababu ya kazi nyingi, fikra nyingi, n.k.); *(of a battery)* isha; gonga/gongana; sema vibaya (mtu au kitu); fukuza na kupita/kamata; punguza nguvu. ~-**down** *n (colloq)* upunguzaji orodha/maelezo kamili. ~ **in** tembelea (mtu mahala) kwa muda mfupi; *(colloq of the police)* kamata, bamba; endesha kwa uangalifu kwa mara ya kwanza (gari/mashine mpya) kwa muda/umbali fulani ili kuiweka katika hali nzuri ya matumizi. ~ **into** gongana; sababisha kuingia katika (deni, ugomvi, n.k.). ~ **off** toroka (na); churuzika/tiririka (kutoka sehemu hadi sehemu); fanya kuchuruzika/kutiririka; andika au soma kwa ghibu (moja kwa moja bila kusita/kwa ufasaha); chapa; toa (makala/kitabu); amua baada ya watu kufungana baada ya majaribio; anzisha (k.m. mbio). ~-**off** *n* uamuzi mkata. ~ **sth on** unganisha/endeleza/ endelea; sema mfululizo; *(of time)* pita, isha, *time ~s on* wakati unapita; *(of disease)* endelea kutokea/ kusumbua. ~ **on/upon sth** *(of thought etc)* husika na. ~ **out** toweka; fikia mwisho, isha; *(of tide)* kupwa. ~ **out of** *(of tide)* kupwa. ~ **oneself out of breath** jichosha. ~ **out on sb** telekeza. ~ **over** *(of a vessel or its contents)* furika; pitia (ili kuzingatia au kushika akilini barabara); soma harakaharaka; gonga/kanyaga mtu (kwa gari); tembelea kwa muda mfupi. ~ **through** pitisha msitari (k.m. katika maneno yaliyoandikwa); choma kwa singe; tumia vibaya (bahati, fedha); chungua kwa haraka; shughulikia kwa haraka; *(of play)* fanya mazoezi. ~ **to** fikia; tosha/tosheleza. ~ **to fat** nenepa mno! ~ **to ruin** haribika. ~ **to waste** tumika vibaya. ~ **up** inua, simamisha (k.m. bendera kwenye mlingoti); jenga/ tengeneza harakaharaka; fanya kuongezeka kwa haraka; fikia kiasi cha/pata/ongeza mwendo kimbia (kabla ya kutupa mpira, mkuki, n.k.).

run[2] n kukimbia. ~**up** *n* 1 urefu (wa kukimbia) masafa; kipindi kabla ya tukio kubwa. **a ~ for one's money** malipo ya kazi au juhudi za mtu; -pa ushindani mkubwa. 2 ziara, matembezi *a ~ to Mikumi* ziara ya Mikumi. 3 *(of a ship)* umbali (wa mwendo kwa kipindi maalumu). 4 njia (ya mashua, meli, n.k.). 5 mshuko wa ghafula *price came down in a ~* bei zilishuka kwa ghafla. 6 mfululizo wa maonyesho (k.m. ya muziki, tamthiliya, n.k.). 7 kipindi; mfuatano *a ~ of bad luck* kipindi cha mkosi. *a ~ on sth*, kitu kinachohitajiwa ghafla na watu wengi. **in the long ~** hatimaye. 8 *(of domestic animals)* zizi, banda. 9 *(cricket and baseball)* pointi. 10 kawaida, mwelekeo, utaratibu *the common ~ of mankind* watu wa kawaida. ~-**of-the mill** kawaida, wastani. 11 kundi la samaki wakiwa katika mwendo. 12 *(colloq)* **give sb/get the ~ of sth** ruhusa ya mtu kutumia kitu bila kulipa. 13 mwelekeo. 14 *(music)* mfuatano wa nota zinazoimbwa/ zinazochezwa haraka na kufuata daraja mbalimbali. ~ **ner** *n* 1 mkimbiaji. ~ **-up** mshindi wa pili katika mashindano. 2 *(messenger)* mjumbe, tarishi. 3 *(surface root)* kitawi cha mmea utambaao chini. 4 *(plant)* mtambaazi. 5 *(cloth)* kitambaa kirefu, kipambo cha meza. 6 *(in compounds)* mfanya biashara ya magendo. **gun** ~ mfanya biashara ya magendo ya bunduki. ~**ning** *adj* 1 -a kukimbia. 2 *(successive)* moja kwa moja, -a mfululizo ~ *fire* mfululizo wa bunduki/wa mizinga. 3 *(after a pl n)* katika mfuatano *six days ~* siku sita mfululizo/moja kwa moja. 4 *(of water)* -a kuchuruzika. 5 *(discharging)* -a kutoka usaha *n* 1 mbio, kukimbia, kwenda mbio. **make the ~** ongoza mbio. **take up the ~** ongoza (baadaye) katika mbio. **in/out of the ~** *(of competitions)* -enye/ pasipo nafasi ya kushinda. 2 ~-**board** *n (old fashioned)* sehemu ya kukanyagia, kuingia garini. ~ **mate** farasi wa kuongoza mwendo; *(US)* mgombea umakamu wa rais.

rung[1] *n* 1 kidato (cha ngazi). 2 taruma la kiti.

rung[2] *pp of* **ring**[2].

runnel *n* 1 kijito, mlizamu, chururu. 2 mfereji wa wazi.

runt *n (colloq)* kibeti: mtu/mnyama aliyedumaa.

runway *n* 1 barabara ya ndege. 2 njia ya kusukumia miti iliyokatwa.

rupee *n* rupia.

rupture *vt,vi* 1 pasua/pasuka *be ~d* pasuliwa. 2 farakana *n* 1 kupasuka. 2 *(discord)* farakano. 3 *(of bowel)* henia.

rural *adj* -a vijijini, -a mashamba *~ planning* mipango ya vijiji.
Ruritanian *adj (of a State, its politics)* -liojaa hila na fitina.
ruse *n* hila, ujanja, werevu, mtego.
rush[1] *n* tete. **~light** *n* mshumaa uliotengenezwa kwa utete. **~y** *adj* -enye matete.
rush[2] *vi,vt* 1 ~ **(away/off/ out)** timua; kurupuka, kurupua *the workers ~ed out of the factory* wafanyakazi walikurupuka kutoka kiwandani. ~ **to conclusions** amua bila kufikiria. ~ **into print** chapisha bila kujali usahihi/ukweli. ~ **sth through** fanya jambo upesi sana. 2 shambulia, vamia *~ the bus* vamia basi. 3 harakisha. ~ **sb off his feet** harakisha; chosha. 4 ~ **(for sth)** *(sl)* langua *n* 1 mwendo wa kasi, kukurukakara, mkurupuko. 2 mahitaji makubwa ya ghafla *a ~ for rain-coats* mahitaji ya makoti ya mvua wakati wa mvua. **the ~-hour** wakati wa msongamano wa kutoka na kwenda kazini agh. katika miji mikubwa. 3 *(cinema, oftenpl)* toleo la kwanza kabla ya kukaguliwa na kuhaririwa.
rusk *n* tosti.
Russia *n* Urusi. ~ **leather** ngozi ya kujalidi. **~n** *adj* -a Urusi *n* 1 Mrusi. 2 Kirusi.
rust *n* 1 kutu. 2 *(on plants)* kizimwili *vt,vi* ingia/shika kutu ~ *preventive adj* -a kuzuia kutu; *(fig)* chakaa (kwa kutotumika); poteza thamani. **~less** *adj* -siopata kutu. **~y** *adj*. **~proof** *adj* 1 -enye kutu. 2 -enye kuhitaji mazoezi, -liozeeka, -a zamani. 3 *(of blackcloth)* -liochujuka. **~ness** *n*.
rustic *adj* 1 -a kishamba *~speech* msemo wa kishamba. 2 -a ovyoovyo *n* mshamba. **~ity** *n* ushamba.
rusticate *vt,vi* 1 ishi maisha ya kijijini. 2 *(GB)* fukuza (mwanafunzi kwa muda).
rustle *vt,vi* 1 chakacha. 2 *(US colloq)* iba (ng'ombe, farasi, n.k.). 3 ~ **sth up** fanya/tayarisha/tengeneza *n* mchakacho, mchakarisho. **~r** *n (US colloq)* mwizi wa ng'ombe/farasi.
rustling *n* sauti ya mchakarisho, *(pl)* mrudiorudio wa sauti hii.
rut[1] *n* 1 alama za magurudumu ya magari (katika mchanga, tope, n.k.). 2 *(fig)* utaratibu wa kufanya jambo. **be in/get into a** ~ fuata utaratibu ule ule siku zote bila kubadili wala kufikiria mwingine *vt* fanya mifuo njiani.
rut[2] *n* nyege ya vipindi ya mnyama *vi* -wa na nyege ya vipindi.
ruthless *adj* pasipo huruma; -katili, -korofi. **~ly** *adv*. **~ness** *n*.
rye *n* 1 shayiri *~-bread* mkate wa shayiri. 2 wiski ya shayiri.

S

S,s *n* 1 herufi ya kumi na tisa katika alfabeti ya Kiingereza. 2 *(pl) (suffix)* ishara ya wingi k.m. *boy-boys.* 3 *(tense suffix)* nafsi ya tatu katika umoja/ishara ya hali ya mazoea k.m. *she plays* anacheza. 4 *(possessive suffix)* ishara ya kumiliki k.m. *children's room* chumba cha watoto 5 *(colloq - short form of) is, he's here* yuko hapa *she's gone* ameondoka *let's go* twende.

sabbatarian *n* 1 Msabato anayefuata sana sheria ya Jumamosi. 2 msabato *n* usabato. **sabbath** n 1 Sabato; siku ya saba ya juma (kuanzia Ijumaa jioni hadi Jumamosi jioni). **break the ~** vunja sabato *keep the ~* adhimisha sabato. **sabbatical** *adj* 1 -a sabato. 2 *~ leave (of University teacher)* likizo ya kunoa ubongo.

saber *see* **sabre**.

sable *n* 1 mbelele: mnyama mdogo mwenye ngozi ya thamani; ngozi ya mnyama huyo. 2 ~ **antelope** palahala *adj (liter)* -eusi; -enye huzuni.

sabot *n* mtalawanda, magongo.

sabotage *n* hujuma *vt* hujumu. **saboteur** *n* mhujumu.

sabre (*US* **saber**) *n* 1 kitara *a ~ cut* kukata kwa kitara; kovu. **~-rattling** *n* vitisho vya kijeshi. **~-toothed** *adj* -enye meno (hasa mawili) yanayofanana na kitara *vt* shambulia/ jeruhi kwa kitara.

sac *n* 1 kifuko (cha maji au ute katika mwili wa mwanadamu/mnyama/ mmea). 2 uvimbe wa ngozi nyembamba (ya ndani ya mwili). **~cate** *adj* 1 -a kifuko, kama kifuko. 2 -a ndani ya kifuko.

saccharin *n* sakrani; unga mtamu.

sacchrine *adj* -a kama sukari; tamu sana; tamu mno.

sacerdotal *adj* -a kikasisi; -a kichungaji. **sacerdotism** mfumo wa serikali ambamo makasisi wana madaraka makubwa.

sachet *n* 1 kikoba chenye uturi. 2 pakiti ya uturi. 3 uturi, uvumba (wa nguo).

sack[1] *n* gunia, mfuko. **~ race** mashindano ya kukimbia katikamagunia. ~ **cloth** nguo ya gunia. ~ **cloth and ashes** kujutia kosa, majuto; matanga, kilio; gauni fupi na pana. **~ing** *n see* **cloth.**

sack[2] *n* **give sb/get the ~** *(colloq)* fukuza mtu kazi, fukuza; fukuzwa kazi. *vt* fukuza kazi.

sack[3] *vt (of a victorius army)* teka nyara, nyang'anya, pora *n* **the ~** kupora mali katika mji uliotekwa.

sack[4] *n (sl)* kitanda *hit the ~ (US)* enda kulala.

sacrament *n* sakaramenti (k.m. Ekaristi Takatifu; Ushirika Mtakatifu). **the Blessed/Holy S~** Komunyo Takatifu, Ekaristi. ~ **al** *adj* -a kisakramenti, -a Fumbo Takatifu.

sacred *adj* 1 -a Mungu; -takatifu. 2 -a dhati *a ~ promise* ahadi ya dhati 3 tukufu, -a heshima sana; -kuu. ~ **cow** *(colloq)* kitu cha kutukuzwa/ kuheshimika. **~ly** *adv.* ~ **ness** *n.*

sacrifice *n* 1 sadaka; dhabihu; kafara; kitu kitolewacho kwa tambiko. **offer an animal as** ~ toa mnyama awe kafara 2. *(victim)* mhanga, dhabihu *make ~* jitoa mhanga *vt,vi* ~ **(sth)(to)** dhabihu, toa sadaka/kafara. 2 toa/tolea kitu makusudi; jitolea mhanga. **sacrificial** *adj* -a sadaka/ tambiko/mhanga.

sacrilege *n* kufuru; jambo au tendo la kumchukiza Mungu; matumizi mabaya ya kitu kilicho wakfu. **sacriligious** *adj* -a kufuru.

sacristan *n (RC Church)* mtunzaji wa vifaa vya Kanisa. **sacristy** *n (RC Church)* sakristi: chumba cha kuvalia padre/kuhifadhia vyombo na nguo za kanisa.

sacrosanct *adj* 1 -takatifu sana, -tukufu; -lindwa kwa madhara yote (kwa sababu ya utakatifu). 2 *(fig)* -sioingilika.

sad *adj* 1 -a huzuni; -a kusikitisha; -enye majonzi; -sio na furaha *look ~* onekana -enye huzuni *make sb ~* huzunisha. 2 -a aibu, -a kashfa. **~ly** *adv.* ~ **ness** *n.* **~den** *vt,vi.* huzunisha, huzunika, sikitisha, sikitika, tia uchungu.

saddle *n* 1 tandiko (la farasi, punda, n.k.); shogi. **be in the ~** -wa juu ya farasi; *(fig)* -wa madarakani. **~-sore** jeraha la horji. ~ **of mutton/venison** pande la nyama ya mgongo iliyoshikana na mbavu. 2 kiti (cha baiskeli, trekta n.k.). 3 safu au milima iliyoinuka mwanzoni na mwishoni *vt* 1 weka tandiko (juu ya farasi). 2 ~ **sb with** -pa mtu jukumu kubwa) twisha mtu madaraka/mzigo n.k.. ~ **bag** *n* 1 shogi, horji. 2 mfuko wa vyombo vya kutengenezea baiskeli. **~er** *n* fundi/ mshonaji matandiko ya farasi/punda *n* 1 vitu vilivyotengenezwa na mshonaji matandiko ya farasi; ushonaji wa matandiko ya farasi.

sadhu *n* mtawa wa Kihindu.

sadism *n* 1 kupenda ukatili; unyama; utesaji. 2 kupata furaha/raha ya kimapenzi/kujamiiana kwa kufanya ukatili kwa mwenzio (wa jinsi nyingine). **sadist** *n* mtu katili; mpenda ukatili; mtesaji. **sadistic** *adj* -a ukatili; -penda ukatili; -tesaji.

sadomasochism *n* kupenda ukatili na mateso. **sadomasochist** *n* mtu afanyaye hivyo.

safari *n* msafara wa uwindaji/utalii (katika Afrika); safari.

safe[1] *adj* 1 ~ **(from)** -a salama, salama; -siodhuriwa au kuharibiwa. ~ **and sound** salama salimini *travel at a ~ speed* -enda kwa mwendo usio wa hatari. 2 -angalifu, -enye hadhari *a ~ statesman* mtawala mwadilifu. **be on the ~ side** chukua hadhari sana. 3 *(certain)* yakini, hakika, bila shaka, -sio na mashaka. ~ **conduct** *n* hati, cheti cha usalama; kibali (cha kusafiri/kupita). **~guard** *n* kinga; ulinzi *vt* **~guard (against)** linda; hifadhi; kinga *~guard oneself* jilinda, jikinga. **~-keeping** *n* ulinzi. **~ly** *adv* salama; kwa salama *I'll see you ~ ly home* nitakusindikiza (kwa usalama) nyumbani. **~ness** *n*.

safe[2] *n* 1 sefu. 2 kabati ya chakula. ~ **deposit** *n* nyumba ya sefu ya kuhifadhia vitu vya thamani. **~ty** *n* usalama ~ *first* usalama kwanza ~ *-belt n* mkanda wa usalama. ~ **curtain** *n* pazia la usalama. **~-glass** *n* kioo kisichopasuka vipande. **~-lamp** *n* kurunzi ya migodini, kurunzi. **~-match** *n* kiberiti. **~-pin** *n* pini. ~ **-razor** *n* wembe. **~-valve** *n* vali ya usalama. *(fig)* **sit on the ~ ty-valve** fuata siasa ya ukandamizaji. *n* ~ **bolt/catch/lock** kinga.

saffron *n* 1 zafarani. 2 rangi ya manjano *adj* -a zafarani; -enye rangi ya manjano *vt* paka zarafani.

sag *vi* 1 inama; zama; bonyea. 2 legea, nyong'onyea *n* kubonyea, kulegea.

saga *n (Norwegian)* 1 ngano. 2 hadithi ndefu, au msururu wa vituko. 3 *(colloq)* maelezo marefu ya tukio fulani.

sage *n* mtu mwenye hekima *adj* -a hekima, -a busara nyingi. **sagacious** *adj* -a busara; -a akili, hodari. **~ly** *adv* **sagacity** *n* busara, akili.

Sagittarius *n* Mshale: alama ya tisa ya zodiak.

sago *n* sago: moyo wa mti kama mtende; wanga wa moyo wa mtende utumikao kwenye chakula.

sahib *n (India)* bwana, mheshimiwa.

said 1 *pp of* **say**. 2 *attrib adj (leg)* -liotajwa.

sail *n* tanga. **under ~** ikitumia matanga yote. **set ~** anza safari. **take in ~** punguza tanga, vyombo (jahazi mashua n.k.) vya matanga; *(fig)* punguza midadi/nguvu. 2 safari ya chombo cha matanga. **~-arm** *n* mkono (wa kinu cha upepo). **~-boat** *n* mashua ya matanga. **~-cloth** *n* marudufu. 3 meli. 4 safari ya burdani melini. 5 *(of wind mill)* mabawa/ mapanga (ya kinu cha upepo) *vi,vt* 1 endesha kwa tanga; endesha (merikebu, meli, chombo). 2 safiri merikebuni, (chomboni); pita baharini. ~ **close to the wind** enda joshi; *(fig)* karibia kuvunja/kupinda sheria; *(start on a voyage)* tweka, funga safari chomboni. 3 mudu kuendesha chombo chenye tanga. 4 paa/elea polepole angani. **~ing-master** *n* nahodha. **~ing- ship** *n* merikebu ya matanga. **~ing vessel** *n* chombo cha matanga. **~ in** anza, fanya jambo kwa bidii. **~ into sb** karipia, shambulia. **~er** *n* chombo (mashua) cha matanga *a fast ~* mashua iendayo kasi sana. **~or** *n* 1 baharia; mwanamaji. 2 **a good/bad ~** mtu asiye/anaye chafukwa na tumbo kiasi/sana awapo chomboni. **~-suit** *n* vazi la mtoto linalofanana na la mwanamaji.

saint *n* 1 walii, sufii. 2 mtakatifu. **All ~s Day** Sikukuu ya Watakatifu Wote. 3 mtu mwema sana. **~ed** *adj* -liotangazwa kuwa takatifu, -lioheshimiwa kama takatifu. **~hood** *n* utakatifu, usufii. **~-like** *adj* kama mtakatifu. **~liness** *n* utakatifu. **~ly** *adj* -takatifu, kama takatifu. **~ Vitu's dance** kasoro katika neva.

saith *(old form)* **says**.

sake *n* **for the ~ of sb/sth; for sb's/sth's ~** kwa ajili ya *for my ~* kwa ajili yangu *talk for talking's ~* piga soga tu. **for goodness/God's ~** *(exclamation)* tafadhali sana/juu ya tafadhali.

salaam *n* salamu *vi* salimu.

salacious *adj (of speech books, pictures etc)* chafu, pujufu; -a kutia ashiki. **~ly** *adv*. **~ness** *n*. **salacity** *n*.

salad *n* 1 saladi; kachumbari. **~ days** *n* wakati wa ujana (wa kutojua mambo). **~ dressing** *n* kiungo (cha rojorojo) cha saladi. **~ oil** *n* mafuta ya kutia kwenye kachumbari. 2 **fruit ~** saladi ya matunda, fruti.

salamander *n* 1 salamanda: namna ya mjusi ambaye zamani alisadikiwa kwamba anaweza kuishi motoni.

salami *n* salami: soseji ya Kitaliano.

salary *n* mshahara. **salaried** *adj* -enye mshahara *~ posts* vyeo vinavyopewa mshahara.

sale *n* 1 kuuza; kuchuuza. **(up) for ~** inauzwa. **on ~** *(of goods in shops etc.)* inauzwa. **on ~ or return** zisiouzwa zirudishwe. **bill of ~** waraka wa kiwakilishi. **a ~s clerk** muuzaji, mhudumu dukani. **~s department** idara ya mauzo. **~s resistance** kusita kununua. **~s talk** *(colloq)*, **~s chat** maneno ya kuvutia mnunuzi. 2 mauzo, uuzaji. **on ~** -a kuuzwa *it is not for ~* haiuzwi. **cash ~** kuuza taslimu. **~ of goods** uuzaji wa bidhaa. **~ of credit** kuuza kwa muamana. **~s tax** kodi ya mauzo. 3 seli: mauzo yaliyopunguzwa bei. 4 *(auction)* mnada. **put up for ~** toa kwa mnada. *(compounds) ~s girl/ lady/woman/ man* mwuzaji *~s room* chumba cha kunadia. **~smanship** *n* ujuzi wa uuzaji. **~ able/salable** *adj* -a kuuzika.

salient *adj* 1 -a ku(ji)tokeza. 2 muhimu, -a maana, kubwa *n ~ angle* pembe ijitokezayo mbele (kuwapangua maadui). **saliency** *n*.

saline *adj* -a chumvi, -a munyu *a ~ solution* myeyusho wa chumvi na maji *n* ziwa/chemchemi/machimbo ya chumvi/munyu. **salinity** *n* uchumvi, umunyu.

saliva *n* mate, ute, udende, uderere. **~ry** *adj* -a mate. **~ glands** matezi ya mate. **~te** *vi* tokwa mate. **~tion** *n*.

sallow *adj (of skin)* -a rangi ya manjano *vt,vi* geuza au geuka manjano.

sally *n* 1 shambulio, tukio, tokeo la ghafla (kutoka boma lililozingiwa na adui). 2 mzaha, masihara (agh. ya kumdhihaki mtu) *vi* tokea; shambulia ghafla nje ya boma linalozingiwa. **~ out/forth** tembea; enda safarini.

salmon *n* samoni; samaki mkubwa mwenye nyama nyekundu.

salon *n* 1 sebule/chumba cha mapokezi chenye kuvutia *~ music* muziki laini (upigwao sebuleni). 2 **the ~** maonyesho ya mwaka ya wachoraji katika mji wa Ufaransa. 3 mkusanyiko wa watu sebuleni mwa mtu mashuhuri. 4 mahali panapotoa huduma zinazohusiana na mitindo.

saloon *n* 1 sebule kubwa, chumba kikubwa cha shughuli fulani *hair dressing ~* chumba cha kunyolea/

kutengenezea/kukatia nywele. 2 chumba cha kulia melini/garini. 3 (*US*) baa; kilabu ~ *keeper* mlinzi wa baa. 4 ~ *(car)* gari ndogo.

salt *n* 1 chumvi, munyu. **not/hardly worth one's ~** siostahili mshahara. **take sb/sth with a grain/pinch of ~** amini nusunusu; -wa na shaka kuhusu... **the ~ of the earth** watu wema/wenye haki. **rub ~ into the wound** tia chumvi/tonesha donda. 2 *(chem)* mchanganyiko wa metali na asidi. 3 **a ~/an old ~** baharia stadi. 4 haluli, *(sl)* kasi sana. 5 *(fig)* kikolezo. 6 *(compounds)* **~-cellar/shaker** kidau cha chumvi. **~-lick** mwamba wa chumvi (kwa wanyama kuulamba). **~-marsh** matope ya chumvi. **~-mine** mgodi wa chumvi. **~-pan** shimo la chumvi. **~ water** *n* maji ya chumvi. **~-water** *adj* -a bahari *~-water fish* samaki wa baharini. **~works** *n* kiwanda cha chumvi *vt* tia chumvi, koleza kwa chumvi. **~ sth down** hifadhi kwa chumvi. **~ away** *(colloq)* weka (agh fedha) akiba *adj* -enye chumvi, -a chumvi; -lioungwa chumvi **~-free, ~ less** *adj* isiyo na/bila chumvi. **~y** *adj*. **~ish** *adj*. **~iness** *n*.

saltpetre (*US* **saltpeter**) *n* shura.

salubrious *adj (of climate)* -a kuleta afya; -a kutia uzima, -enye rai. **salubrity** *n*.

salutary *adj* -a kufaa/kuburudisha mwili; -a kutia afya; -ema; -zuri.

salute *n* 1 saluti, mizinga (bunduki) ya salamu. 2 salamu. **take the ~** pokea saluti *vt,vi* 1 piga saluti. 2 amkia; salimu. **salutation** *n* salamu; maamkizi.

salvage *vt* okoa (agh. baharini) *n* 1 ada (ujira) ya uokoaji, malipo ya kuokoa. 2 uokoaji; (k.m. kuokoa meli hatarini). 3 kitu kilichookolewa (k.m. meli).

salvation *n* 1 wokovu, wokozi. 2 uokoaji. **~ Army** *n* Jeshi la Wokovu. **work out one's own ~** fanya jitihada za kujiokoa.

salve *n* 1 marhamu. 2 *(fig)* kitulizo cha hisia, dhamira n.k. *vt* 1 paka marhamu. 2 tuliza ~ *one's conscience* ficha/tuliza dhamira mbaya.

salver *n* sinia, trei la vyombo.

salvo *n* 1 kupiga bunduki nyingi kwa pamoja kama saluti. 2 vifijo/vigelegele vya pamoja.

salvolatile *n* shazasi.

Samaritan *n* Msamaria. **Good ~** Msamaria Mwema.

samba *n* samba: aina ya dansi yenye asili ya Brazil.

same *adj* **the ~** -a moja; sawa. **at the ~ time** wakati huohuo/huuhuu *they went to the ~ school* walisoma shule moja *in the ~ manner* kwa namna hiyo hiyo, hivyo hivyo, namna ile, kama. **all the ~** hata hivyo *at the ~ time* pamoja; hata hivyo, pamoja na hayo. **be all/just the ~ to sb** -wa mamoja. **come/amount to the ~ thing** ina maana ile ile. **the very ~** hilo hilo/huyo huyo. **one and the ~** sawa kabisa. **~ness** *n* 1 umoja; usawa; mfano mmoja; yale yale; vile vile. 2 *(monotony)* kuchosha, mambo yale yale.

sample *n* 1 kielelezo. **~ space** *(maths)* sampuli uwazi. 2 sampuli fulani/kifani *sale by ~* uza kwa kuonyesha sampuli. **up to ~** *(comm)* -nayofikia sampuli kwa ubora *vt* 1 onja. 2 jaribu. **~r** *n* kielelezo cha darizi.

samurai *n* (*Japan*) **the ~** 1 askari wa tabaka la kijeshi lililokuwa chini ya koo bora (wakati wa ukabaila). 2 mtu wa tabaka la watawala wa kijeshi katika kipindi hicho.

sanatorium/sanatarium *n* 1 hospitali/kituo cha afya ambacho kinawapa wagonjwa tiba, chakula maalum na mazoezi. 2 hospitali ya magonjwa ya muda mrefu. 3 *(lab)* chumba cha wagonjwa katika shule ya bweni.

sanctify *vt* takasa; fanya takatifu. **sanctification** *n*. **sanctimonious** *adj* -a kujifanya takatifu; nafiki. **sanctimoniously** *adv*.

sanctity *n* 1 utakatifu, usufii. 2 *(pl)* **sanctities** majukumu/maono thabiti.
sanctuary *n* 1 mahali patakatifu, (k.v. kanisa, msikiti, hekalu). 2 madhabahu. 3 *(refuge)* kimbilio *seek ~* tafuta kimbilio *be offered ~* pata kimbilio. 4 hifadhi (ya ndege, wanyama n.k.) *bird ~* hifadhi (mbuga) ya ndege. **Sanctum** *n* 1 mahali patakatifu. 2 *(colloq)* faragha.
sanction *n* 1 ruhusa, idhini; kibali. 2 kikwazo *economic ~s* vikwazo vya kiuchumi. 3 sababu ya kuheshimu kanuni. 4 adhabu *vt* 1 kubali. 2 ruhusu.
sand *n* 1 mchanga. 2 **the ~s are running out** muda unakwisha. 3 *(compounds)* **~bag** *n* mfuko wa mchanga (hutumika kama kinga/ngao wakati wa vita). **~bank** *n* ukingo wa mchanga mtoni/baharini. **~bar** *n* fungu la mchanga. **~-blast** *vt* kwangura/safisha kwa msukumo wa mchanga. **~boy** *n (only in)* **as happy as a ~boy** -enye furaha kubwa. **~ dune** *n* tuta la mchanga. **~-fly** *n* usubi. **~-glass** *n* shisha. **~paper** n msasa *vt* piga msasa. **~piper** *n* chamchanga. **~pit** *n* shimo lililojazwa mchanga (kwa ajili ya watoto kuchezea). **~-shoes** *n (pl)* raba za kutembelea mchangani. **~-stone** *n* jiwe mchanga. **~-storm** *n* dhoruba ya mchanga (agh. jangwani). **~y** *adj* 1 -a mchanga. 2 *(of hair etc.)* -a rangi ya lasi. *n (colloq)* jina la utani kwa mtu mwenye nywele za rangi ya lasi.
sandal *n* ndara; makubadhi, kandambili, malapa. **~led** *adj*.
sandalwood *n* msandali.
sandwich *n* sandwichi; vipande vya mkate vyenye nyama, jibini n.k. katikati. **~ man** mtangazaji anayebeba mabango ya kutangazia (moja kifuani na moja mgongoni). **~-board** moja ya mabango hayo. **~course** kozi ya nadharia (shuleni) na vitendo (kazini) *vt* **~ (between)** bana, tia mtu katikati.
sane *adj* 1 -a akili timamu, -sio kichaa. 2 -a busara, -enye akili sana. **~ views** mawazo ya busara. **~ly** *adv* kwa akili timamu, kwa busara. **~ness** *n*. **sanity** *n* 1 akili timamu. 2 busara.
sanforized *adj* -sioruka. **~ fabric** kitambaa kisichoruka wala kutoa rangi.
sang *(pt of)* **sing.**
sang froid *(F) n* utulivu, kutotishika, uimara (katika hatari au shida).
sanguinary *adj (formal old use)* 1 -a (kumwaga) damu nyingi; -uaji; -katili. 2 -a kupenda mauaji/ukatili. **~ ruler** mtawala katili.
sanguine *adj (formal)* 1 -a tumaini, -tumainifu, -a matarajio mema *a man of ~ disposition* mtu mwenye tabia ya kutazamia mema tu *~ of success* ya tumaini la ushindi. **~ness** *n* 2 -enye sura nyekundu. **~ous** *adj* -enye rangi ya damu.
sanitarium *n see* **sanatorium**.
sanitary *adj* 1 safi, -a kutia afya. 2 -a kulinda afya *~ inspector n* mkaguzi wa afya. **~-towel/napkin** sodo, mlembe. **sanitation** *n* usafi/udhibiti afya (kwa kuondoa, maji machafu na takataka).
sank *pt of* **sink.**
sans *pref (colloq)* bila *~ eyes* bila macho.
Sanskrit *n* Sanskriti: lugha ya Kihindi ya kale.
Santa Claus *n* Baba Krismasi; mtu ambaye huzawadia watoto wakati wa usiku wa Krismas.
sap[1] *vt* dhoofisha; toa nguvu/uhai wa mtu.
sap[2] *n* handaki. **~-head** kichwa cha handaki (sehemu ya mwisho wa handaki iliyo karibu kabisa na adui) *vt,vi* chimba handaki; tekua (ukuta) kwa kuchimba chini yake; *(fig)* vunja, dhoofisha matumaini/imani. **~ per** askari mjenzi wa barabara/ madaraja; mchimba mahandaki.
sap[3] *n (dated sl)* bwege, mpumbavu.
sap[4] *n* 1 maji (ya miti, majani); utomvu. **~ wood** safu laini za nje ya mti. 2 *(fig)* (chochote kitiacho) nguvu, hamasa. **~less** *adj* bila

maji/utomvu; kavu; -sio na nguvu. **~ ling** mti mchanga, chipukizi la mti; kimelea; *(fig)* kijana. **~py** *adj* -enye maji mengi; -changa, -enye nguvu.

sapient *adj (liter)* 1 -a busara. **~ ly** *adv*. **sapience** *n (often ironic)* busara.

sapphic *adj* 1 **S~ verse/stanza/ode (Prosody)** -enye mistari minne (mitatu iliyo sawa na mmoja mfupi). 2 mshairi (wa kike); msagaji wa Kigiriki *(Sappho)*.

sapphire *n* 1 johari (ya rangi ya samawati). 2 buluu ya kung'ara.

Saracen *n (name used by Europeans for)* Mwarabu na Mwislamu (wakati wa vita vitakatifu).

sarcasm *n* kejeli, kijembe. **sarcastic** *adj* -a kupiga kijembe, -a kejeli. **sarcastically** *adv*.

sarcophagus *n* jeneza la jiwe.

sardine *n* 1 sadini: samaki mdogo kama dagaa upapa (hupikwa na kutiwa makoponi). 2 dagaa. **packed like ~s** -liosongamana sana, -a kubanana sana.

sardonic *adj* -a dhihaka, -a mabezo *~ laughter* kicheko cha dhihaka. **~ally** *adv*.

sari *n* sari: vazi la wanawake wa Kihindi.

sarong *n* saruni.

sartorial *adj* -a (ushonaji) nguo (agh za wanaume).

sash[1] *n* mshipi.

sash[2] *n* **~-window** dirisha la kuinuka na kushuka.

sat *(pt of)* **sit**.

Satan *n* shetani, Ibilisi. **~ic** *adj* 1 -a shetani. 2 bilisi.

satchel *n* mkoba, mfuko, shanta.

sate see **satiate**.

satellite *n* 1 setilaiti nyota inayozunguka sayari, mwezi n.k. 2 *(fig, often attrib)* mtu/kitu tegemezi, kibaraka. **~ town** mji wa pambizoni.

satiate *vt (formal)* 1 shibisha, tosheleza. 2 kinaisha, chosha *be ~d with food* kinai chakula.

satiety *n (formal)* shibe; kinaa *to ~* (ushiba) mno hadi kukinai.

satiable *adj (formal)* -a kukinai, -a kuweza kukinaishwa, -enye kuweza kutoshelezwa/kuridhishwa.

satin *n* hariri, atlasi *adj* -a kung'aa kama atlasi. **~ y** *adj*.

satinwood *n* mbao nyororo na ngumu ya kutengenezea samani (fanicha).

satire *n* tashtiti. **satirical** *adj*. **satirically** *adv*. **satirist** *n* mwandishi wa tashtiti. **satirize** *vt* 1 andika tashtiti. 2 dhihaki.

satisfaction *n* 1 ridhaa, kuridhika; uradhi, raha mustarehe *it is a real ~ to see* inafurahisha kuona. 2 malipo, fidia, malipizi, kisasi. 3 *(atonement)* kipatanisho. **satisfactory** *adj* -a kuridhisha, -a kufaa, -a kutosha. **satisfactorily** *adv*. **satisfy** *vt,vi* 1 ridhisha, tuliza, tosheleza, kidhi *that does not ~ me* hiyo hainiridhishi *just to ~ one's conscience* kwa kuridhisha dhamira yake tu. 2 lipiza kisasi. 3 **~ sb (that .../of sth)** ridhisha. **satisfying** *adj*. **satisfyingly** *adv*.

satrap *n* liwali wa Kiajemi (wa kale); akida. **~y** *n*.

satsuma *n* chenza, kangaja.

saturate *vt* 1 **~ (with/in)** kifu, lowesha/koleza kabisa, shinikiza. 2 jaza kabisa. **~d** *adj* dabwadabwa. **saturation** *n* ukifish(w)aji; unywesh(w)aji; ulowesh(w)aji. **~ point** kiwango cha kuloa/kujaa kabisa; kiwango kifu; *(fig)* kipeo cha juu, hatua ambayo hakuna linaloweza kuingia/kukubalika/kupatiwa nafasi.

Saturday *n* Jumamosi.

Saturn *n* 1 Zohali. 2 *(myth)* Mungu wa kale wa kilimo wa Kirumi. **~alia** *n (pl)* 1 **Satanalia**: sikukuu ya Zohali, siku ya kufurahi/kucheza (na kufanya mengineyo yote). 2 wakati wa vurugu.

saturnine *adj (liter)* (kwa mtu) -zito, baridi, -enye kusononeka.

satyr *n* 1 *(Greek and Roman myth)* zimwi la mwitu (nusu mtu, nusu mnyama). 2 mwanaume mwenye nyege sana.

sauce *n* 1 sosi, mchuzi mzito, rojo. **what is ~ for the goose is ~ for the gander** *(prov)* sheria ni msumeno. **~-boat** *n* kibakuli. **~-pan** *n.* sufuria. 2 *(impudence)* mzaha *vt* fanya ujeuri. **saucy** *adj* 1 -tundu; -jeuri. 2 tanashati. **saucily** *adv* kwa utundu. **sauciness** *n* ujuvi; utundu. **~r** *n* 1 kisahani. **~eyed** -enye kutoa macho (kwa mshangao). 2 tufedishi lenye kupaa. 3 mbonyeo.

sauna *n* sauna: bafu ya mvuke.

saunter *vi* tembea polepole, tembeatembea *n* matembezi; kutembea polepole.

sausage *n* soseji. **~-meat** *n* nyama ya soseji. **~-roll** *n* mkate wa nyama.

saute *adj (of food)* -liokaangwa upesi (kwa mafuta kidogo) *vt* chovya mafuta moto, kaanga haraka haraka/ upesi.

savage *adj* 1 -shenzi; -siostaarabika. 2 -kali; katili, -uaji, nduli. 3 *(colloq)* -enye hasira sana, -a ghadhabu, -a kiruu *n* mshenzi *vt* shambulia kikatili, ng'ata, uma, kanyagakanyaga. **~ly** *adv.* **~ness** *n.* **~ry** *n.*

savanna(h) *n* savana: uwanda mpana (wenye miti hapa na pale).

savant *n* mwanazuoni, mtaalam, bingwa.

save[1] *vt,vi* **~ (from)** okoa, nusuru. **~ the situation** okoa jahazi/janga. 2 **~ (up) (for sth); ~ sth (up) (for sth)** weka akiba, dunduiza. 3 okoa; *(relieve)* punguzia adha *that will ~ you 5000 Shs a week* hiyo itakuokolea Shs 5000 kila juma. **~ one's breath** nyamaza (maneno hayatasaidia chochote). 4 **~ sb (from sth)** *(relig)* okoa katika dhambi. 5 weka hadhari/kinga *n (in football etc)* (tendo la) kuzuia kufunga goli. **~r** *n* 1 mwokoa roho; mwokoaji. 2 mtu adundulizaye pesa. **saving** *adj* -a kuokoa. **~grace** sifa nzuri (yenye kufidia tabia mbaya) *n* 1 uwekaji akiba, udundulizaji, kuokoa (muda n.k.). 2 *(pl)* akiba. **~s bank** benki ya akiba. **~s account** akaunti ya akiba.

save[2] *(also saving) prep* isipokuwa *all ~ him* wote isipokuwa yeye.

saviour *n* 1 mwokozi. 2 mkombozi *The S~ , Our S~* Yesu Kristo.

savoir-faire *n* kukoga/kujichukua mbele ya watu.

savour (*US* **savor**) *n* 1 **~ of** ladha. 2 *(arch)* harufu *vt,vi* 1 *(lit or fig)* furahia, pendelea. 2 **~ of** ashiria, onyesha dalili ya, -wa na dalili ya. **~y (-vory)** *adj* yenye ladha kali, chakula chenye viungo vikali *n* nyama, chumvi, n.k.

savoy *n* kabichi (yenye majani yaliyokunjamana sana.

savvy *vi (sl)* fahamu, elewa, jua *no ~* sijui, sielewi *n (sl)* werevu, ujuzi, akili.

saw[1] *(pt of)* **see**.

saw[2] *n* msumeno; jambeni *(compounds)* **~-dust** *n* vumbi/unga wa mbao. **~-horse** farasi ya mbao. **~-mill** kiwanda cha kupasulia mbao. **~ pit** shimo la kupasulia mbao. *vt,vi* 1 pasua kwa msumeno, tumia msumeno. **~ sth off** kata kitu (na kukiondoa) kwa msumeno. **~ sth up** katakata kitu, pasua vipande vipande (kwa msumeno). 2 enda/peleka mbele na nyuma. 3 pasulika *this wood ~s easily* gogo hili linapasulika kwa urahisi. **~yer** mpasua mbao.

saw[3] *n (maxim)* msemo; methali.

saxhorn *n* aina ya tarumbeta.

Saxon *n* 1 Msaksoni. 2 lugha ya Kisaksoni.

saxophone (*abbr* **sax**) saksafoni. **saxaphonist** *n* mpiga saksafoni.

say *vt,vi* 1 **~ sth (to sb)** sema, nena. **~ to** ambia. **go without ~ing** -wa dhahiri/wazi. **have nothing to ~ for oneself** kosa neno la kujitetea. **~ the word** kubali. **~ a good word for** sifu, pongeza. **~ one's ~** maliza kusema unayotaka/kusudia kusema, hitimisha (maneno). **~ one's prayers** sali. **so to ~** kama vile *that is to ~* yaani. **what do you ~** waonaje. **I ~** kumbe, ala/aisee! **they ~/it is said** yasemekana. **~ no** kataa, kana. 2

kadiria, sema, mathalan, huenda *I will run a mile in ~ three minutes* nitakimbia maili moja kwa dakika tatu hivi *let's ~ he agrees* mathalan/ tuseme anakubali *not to ~* sembuse *n (only in)* **have a ~ in** kuwa na neno/kauli/oni katika. **have no/not much ~ in the matter** -tokuwa na kauli, fursa nyingi katika jambo. **have one's ~** toa oni, sema. **~ ing** *n* neno, kauli; methali *as the ~ goes* kama methali isemavyo.

scab *n* 1 kigaga. 2 *(colloq)* mfanyakazi msaliti wa mgomo. 3 **~ies** *n* upele, ukurutu *vi* pata kigaga. **~ious** *adj* -enye gaga. **~by** *adj* -a kigaga; -enye vigaga.

scabbard *n* ala, uo.

scabrous *adj* 1 *(of animals, plants, etc)* si -ororo; kwarukwaru. 2 *(of subjects)* -enye utata. 3 *(of language)* chafu.

scaffold *n* 1 jukwaa, dungu. 2 jukwaa (wanaponyongewa wahalifu). **go to the ~** nyongwa. **~ing** *n* 1 (vifaa vya kujengea) jukwaa. 2 dungu, jukwaa.

scald *vt* 1 babua **~ing tears** machozi ya uchungu. 2 safisha (kwa maji moto au mvuke). 3 pasha moto *n* unguzo; lengelenge, kidonda cha kuungua moto.

scale[1] *n* 1 kitanga cha mizani. *(pl)* **(pair of) ~s** mizani. **hold the ~s even** amua sawasawa/kwa haki. **turn the ~(s)** kata neno na ondoa mashaka. **turn the ~(s) at** *(colloq)* -wa na uzito **I**wa. 2 mashine/mizani ya kupimia.

scale[2] *n (of fish)* gamba; *of metal, mineral)* mavi; makoko; *(scurf)* mba, kigaga; *(of teeth)* ukoko. **remove the ~ s from sb's eyes** *(fig)* fungua macho, gutusha; tambulisha mtu ukweli wa jambo *vt,vi* paa magamba, kwangua; anguka, toka *~ a fish* paa samaki. **~ off** bambuka. **scaly** *adj* -enye magamba.

scale[3] *n* 1 kipimo, alama (za vipimo); *(instruments)* vifaa vya kupimia (k.m. rula, mita, n.k.), kipimio, kigezo, mizani. 2 *(music)* jamii ya sauti (hasa sauti nane) *practise ~s* jizoeza (kinanda). 3 *(Maths)* mfumo wa vipimo *the decimal ~* kipimo cha desimali. 4 skeli: mlinganisho kati ya ukubwa wa kitu na ramani au mchoro. 5 ngazi. **salary ~ (s)** ngazi za mshahara. 6 kiwango. **on a large ~** kwa kiwango kikubwa/wingi. **on a small ~** kwa kiwango kidogo *vt* 1 panda, kwea *~ a mountain* panda mlima. **scaling-ladder** ngazi ya kupandia. **~ up/down** pandisha/ punguza *all prices were ~d up ten per cent* bei zote zilipandishwa kwa asilimia kumi. 2 nakili kwa kulinganisha ramani.

scallop *n (also* **scollop)** 1 kombe ya pwani. 2 *(p)* **~s** marinda, vikunjo *vt* kaanga katika kombe; pamba kitu kwa makombe.

scallywag *n (US* **scalawag)** mhuni.

scalp *n* ngozi ya kichwa na nywele zake *vt* chuna ngozi ya kichwa ikiwa na nywele. **out for ~** *(fig)* -enye kutafuta ushindi.

scalpel *n* kisu kidogo cha kupasulia.

scamp[1] *n* 1 mtundu, mtukutu. 2 mhuni.

scamp[2] *vt* lipua (kazi).

scamper *vi* enda mbiombio; kimbia; puruka. *n* mbio fupi za haraka.

scampi *n (pl)* kamba wakubwa.

scan *vt,vi* 1 chungua, kagua. 2 pitia haraka. 3 *(poetic)* soma kwa mapigo, mdundo; pima mapigo *~ well* fuata mapigo. 4 changanua picha, maandishi, michoro kwa mwale electroniki (kwa nia ya kunakili na kusafirisha). **~sion** *n.* **~ner** *n* skana: kisoma maandishi (kielektroniki) *n (poetic)* kufuata mapigo/mdundo wa kishairi.

scandal *n* 1 kashfa/hizaya. **~ mongering** uenezaji kashfa. 2 umbeya, masengenyo. **~ monger** mweneza/mchuuza uvumi, mmbeya. **~ize** *vt* kashifu; shtua. **~ous** *adj (of reports etc)* -enye (maneno ya) kashfa; *(of persons)* mwanahizaya; -mbeya. **~ously** *adv*.

Scandinavian *n/adj* mwenyeji wa Skandinavia (Denmark, Norway,

Sweden, Iceland).

scant *adj* ~ **(of)** -chache, haba, adimu *give ~ attention* -toangalia sana *with ~ courtesy* kwa adabu kidogo sana *vt* -bana, punguza. **~iness** *n*. **~ily** *adv*.

scantling *n* 1 boriti ndogo. 2 kipimo cha kukatiwa mbao, mti au jiwe.

scape *vi (arch) see* **escape**.

scapegoat *n* kisingizio; msingiziwa, bene.

scapegrace *n* baa.

scapula *n* 1 mtulinga, skapula. **~r** *adj*.

scar *n* kovu; baka *vt,vi* tia kovu, fanyika kovu; pona na fanyika kovu.

scaramouch *n* mtu mwenye majivuno.

scarce *adj* 1 haba. 2 -adimu, nadra. **be ~** adimika *food became ~* chakula kiliadimika. **make oneself ~** *(colloq)* potea, toweka, jifanya adimu *~ goods/commodities* bidhaa haba/adimu. **scarcity** *n*. **~ly** *adv* kwa shida, si sana, kidogo sana, kwa nadra; si yamkini *I ~ know what to say* hata sijui la kusema *he had ~ arrived when* alifika tu mara.

scare *vt,vi* 1 ogofya, gutua, tisha; ogopa, gutuka, tishika; *be ~d to death* tishika sana *~ away* fukuza. 2 winga, gutusha, shtusha. **~ sb to death/out of his wits/stiff** *(colloq)* gutusha/tisha sana *n* hofu; fadhaa; kitishotisho *give a ~* ogofya *~-crow n* sanamu (la kuwingia ndege). **~ headline** *n* kichwa cha habari za kutisha. **~ monger** *n* mzushi wa vitisho/mvumisha vitisho. **scary** *adj*.

scarf[1] *n* 1 skafu; shali *~-pin n* pini ya skafu *~-ring n* kishikizo cha skafu.

scarf[2] *vt* unganisha mbao, chuma (bila kupunguza au kuongeza unene) *n* kiungo.

scarify *vt* 1 *(in surgery)* chanja, piga mitai 2 *(fig)* chambua, chachafya/shambulia (kwa maneno makali). 3 papura, parura. **scarification** *n*.

scarlet *n* rangi nyekundu; wekundu *adj* -ekundu *turn ~* geuka ekundu. **~ fever** homa ya vipele vyekundu. **~ hat** kofia ya Kardinali. **~ runner** mmea wenye maua mekundu. **~ woman** *(old use)* malaya.

scarp *n* mtelemko mkali, genge; ngome *vt* fanya mtelemko mkali.

scarper *vi (sl)* toroka.

scat *int (sl)* ambaa.

scathe *n (arch)* 1 kuumiza (kwa dhihaka, kejeli, matusi); dhihaki. 2 jeraha *vt* 1 jeruhi. 2 umiza, (kwa dhihaka) shambulia, sema mtu (vikali). **~less** *adj*. **scathing** *adj (of criticism etc)* -kali, -enye kuumiza.

scatter *vt, vi* tawanya, tapanya. **~-brain** *n* mtu wa wasiwasi/asiyetulia pamoja/asiye makini. **~brained** *adj n* mtawanyo. **~ed** *adj* -liotengana sana; - a hapa na pale; -liotawanyika *~ villages* vijiji vilivyotengana sana. *~* **trees** miti iliyotawanyika *~ showers* mvua za hapa na pale.

scatty *adj (colloq)* 1 -punguani, a wazimu. 2 -puuzi, -a wasiwasi, sahaulifu.

scavenger *n* 1 *(GB)* msafisha mji. 2 ndege mla mizoga. 3 mwokotezaji. **scavenge for** *vt,vi* okoteza.

scenario *n* mpangilio wa maonyesho katika tamthilia; mpangilio wa matukio ya baadaye (yanayotabirika/buniwa). **scenarist** *n* mratibu wa maonyesho katika tamthilia.

scene *n* 1 mandhari; sehemu ya matukio. **quit the ~** ondoka; *(fig)* fariki. 2 *(in plays)* onyesho. **behind the ~** nyuma ya jukwaa; *(fig, of person)* -enye kuathiri mambo kisirisiri; *(of an event)* siri, -siofahamika na watu *be behind the ~* -toonekana, -wa nyuma ya jukwaa. **be/come on the ~** -wa katika eneo fulani; *(fig)* tokea. 3 (maelezo ya) tukio. 4 vituko, ghasia. **make a ~** fanya vituko/ghasia. 5 eneo, uwanja. **be on/make the ~** *(colloq)* -wa sehemu ya/kubalika. **~-painter** *n* mpamba jukwaa. **~-shifter** *n* mbadilisha mandhari katika jukwaa. **~ry** *n* 1 mandhari *a change of ~* mabadiliko ya mandhari (hasa safarini). 2 pambo la jukwaa (tamthilia). **scenic** *adj* -a mandhari nzuri, -a kupendeza macho. **scenically** *adv*.

scent *n* 1 harufu. 2 marashi, uturi, manukato. 3 udi, uvumba *~-bottle n* chupa ya uturi *~-spray n* kifukuzio cha uturi. 4 mtara (wa windo), harufu ya mnyama. **on the ~** -enye ishara/dalili/fununu. **off the ~** bila ishara/dalili/fununu. **be on the ~** fuatilia (jambo) kwa viashirio/vidokezo; *(track)* njia, wayo, dalili. **put sb off the ~** *(fig)* potosha; poteza kwa taarifa vidokezo vya uwongo *vt* 1 nusa, sikia harufu. 2 hisi *~ the air* sikia harufu hewani. 3 nukiza. **~less** *adj* -sioharufu.

sceptic (*US* **skeptic**) *n* mwenye kushuku. **~al** (US **skeptical**) *adj* -a kushuku *be ~ about* shuku. **~cally** *(US* **skeptically**) *adv*. **~ism** *(US* **skepticism**) *n* nadharia ya kushuku.

sceptre/*(US* **scepter**) 1 fimbo ya kifalme. 2 *(sovereignty)* enzi; ufalme *wield the ~* tawala. **~d** *adj* -a fimbo ya kifalme.

schedule *n* ratiba; jedwali *to ~ time* kupanga wakati. **on ~** kwa wakati uliopangwa. **behind ~** kwa kuchelewa. **according to ~** kama ilivyopangwa *vt* ~ **(for)** panga, ratibu.

schema *n (pl schemata)* kielelezo. **~ tic** *adj* 1 -a kielelezo. 2 -a mpango. **~tically** *adv*.

scheme *n* 1 mpango; taratibu. 2 hila, njama *vi,vt* 1 ~ **for sth/to do sth** fanya mpango/shauri. 2 *(fig)* fitini; pika majungu. 3 panga/fanya njama/hila. **~r** *n* mwenye hila, mjanja.

schism *n* farakano, utengano (hasa kidini). **~atic** *adj* -a kufarakana *n* mtu wa ufarakano.

schist *n* jiwe gumu linaloweza kupasuka vipandevipande **~ose, ~ous** *adj* -a kupasuka.

schizophrenia *n (med)* sizofrenia: kuchanganyikiwa (kiakili). **schizophrenic** *adj* mtu aliyechanganyikiwa.

scholar *n* 1 *(dated use)* mwanafunzi. 2 mwenye kupata msaada wa masomo. 3 mtaalamu, msomi, mwanazuoni. **~ly** *adj* -a kitaalamu/kisomi. **~ship** *n* 1 utaalamu. 2 msaada wa masomo.

scholastic *adj* 1 -a chuo, -a masomo, -a elimu *a ~ institution* chuo. 2 *(abstruse)* -a fumbo, -enye utata.

scholasticism *n* falsafa ya uwanazuoni (enzi za kati).

school[1] *n* 1 shule ~ *children* watoto wa shule *reform ~* shule ya kuadibisha, shule ya kutia nidhamu *boarding ~* shule ya bweni *day-* ~shule ya kutwa. **~-board** *n* halmashauri/bodi ya shule. **~-book** *n* kitabu cha shule. **~days** wakati wa shule. **~house** *n* nyumba ya shule. **~man** *n* mwanachuoni wa kale, mwalimu katika chuo kikuu. **~master/mistress** *n* mwalimu. **~mate** mwenzi shuleni. **~ time** saa za masomo. 2 kusoma. **~ age** *n* umri wa kwenda shule; darasa. 3 vipindi, masomo. 4 wanafunzi (watoto wa shule). 5 idara/kitengo (cha chuo kikuu cha kushughulikia somo fulani); *(followers)* wafuasi. 6 *(opinion)* tapo; madhehebu. 7 mtihani *be in for one's ~* -wa katika mafunzo *vt* 1 fundisha, adibu. 2 zoeza. **~ oneself to** jizoeza. **~ing** *n* elimu, kisomo.

school[2] *n (of fish)* kundi (kubwa la samaki).

schooner *n* 1 jahazi kubwa (lenye milingoti miwili au zaidi). 2 bilauri/gilasi ndefu.

shwa *n* (alama) katika sayansi ya fonetiki.

sciatic *adj* -a nyonga. **the ~ nerve** mshipa wa nyonga. **~a** *n* ugonjwa wa mshipa wa nyonga.

science *n* 1 sayansi. **the natural ~** sayansi asili (k.m. biolojia, zuolojia). **the physical ~** sayansi umbile (k.m. fizikia, kemia). **social ~s** sayansi jamii (mf. saikolojia, siasa). **applied ~** sayansi tumizi (k.m. uhandisi). **~ fiction** riwaya ya kisayansi. 2 maarifa, ujuzi, ubingwa. **scientist** *n* mwanasayansi. **scientific** *adj* 1 -a kisayansi; -a kanuni za sayansi ~

instruments vyombo vya kisayansi ~ *socialism* usoshalisti wa kisayansi 2. -a ujuzi/ maarifa. **scientifically** *adv*.

scimitar *n* jambia; hanjari.

scintilla *n* 1 cheche; chembe, atomi; mmeto *not a ~ of truth in his words* hakuna hata chembe ya ukweli katika maneno yake. **~te** *vi* 1 metameta, memeteka. 2 *(fig)* vutia. **~tion** *n* 1 mmeto, mng'ao. 2 mvuto.

scion *n* 1 kibwana/kijana (katika familia bora). 2 kitawishina, kipanda.

scissors *n (pl)* **(pair of ~)** mkasi, makasi. ~ **and paste** uandishi wa vitabu kwa kutumia sehemu za makala na vitabu vya watu mbalimbali.

sclerosis *n* ugonjwa wa kukacha kwa seli/tishu.

scoff[1] *vi* ~ **(at)** dhihaki, kejeli *n* neno la kejeli/dharau. **~er** *n* mfanya dhihaka. **~ingly** *adv*.

scoff[2] *vt (sl)* lafua, lapa *n* ulafi; *(sl)* chakula, maakuli.

scold *vt,vi* ~ **(sb) (for sth)** karipia, kemea *n* mkaripiaji **~ing** *n* ukaripiaji.

scollop *n, vt see* **scallop**

sconce *n* kiango, mwango.

scone *n* skonzi.

scoop *n* 1 upawa, ukasi, bambo, mkamshi. **~-net** *n* wavu wa kukombea chini ya mto. 2 *(fig)* mkupuo *he won pound 5000 at one ~* alipata pauni 5000 kwa mkupuo mmoja. 3 *(colloq)* habari inayotangazwa mara na gazeti moja kabla ya mengine; *(comm)* faida kubwa (inayotokana na kuwawahi wafanyabiashara wengine) *vt* 1 ~ **sth out/up** chota kitu kwa kijiko/ mkamshi. 2 ~ **(out)** chimba/kata (shimo/mtaro) kwa bambo. 3 *(colloq)* pata (faida, habari) kwa wingi (kutokana na kuwahi). **~ful** *n* upawa/ ukasi tele.

scoot *vi (colloq hum)* enda mbio, kimbia haraka, potea, toweka.

scooter *n* 1 *(motor ~)* skuta. 2 kiwambo.

scope *n* 1 nafasi, mawanda. 2 eneo, uwezo. **within the ~ of authority** katika eneo la madaraka.

scorbutic *adj* -a kiseyeye.

scorch *vt,vi* 1 unguza; choma, babua; *(of sun)* nyausha. **~ed earth policy** sera ya kuunguza mazao, majumba katika eneo la uvamizi. 2 pauka. 3 *(colloq of cyclists, motorists etc)* enda kasi sana, choma *n (of clothes)* baka hasa la kuungua. **~er** *n* 1 kitu/ mtu anayeunguza. 2 *(colloq)* siku yenye joto kali. **~ing** *adj* -enye joto kali, jahanam. **~ingly** *adv* kwa joto kali.

score *n* 1 ishirini, korija, fungu la ishirini. 2 hesabu katika mabao (katika mchezo). **pay/settle/wipe off old** ~ *(fig)* lipiza kisasi. 3 mfuo, mchoro, mtai, chale. 4 karatasi za muziki (zinazoonyesha manoti, matumizi ya sauti na vyombo). 5 *(sl)* tamko/hoja ya ushindi katika majadiliano. 6 *(sports)* goli, bao, pointi. **keep the** ~ rekodi magoli. ~ **board/book/card** ubao/kitabu/ kadi ya kurekodia magoli. 7 sababu, ajili. **on the ~ of** minajili ya. **on more ~ s than one** kwa sababu nyingi/zaidi ya moja. **on that** ~ kwa hoja/sababu hiyo *vt,vi* 1 tia bao, funga, hesabu. ~ **an advantage/a success** shinda, bahatika. 2 andika sehemu za muziki/ sauti za wimbo. 3 chora, tia pengo, kata. ~ **out** futa. ~ **under** piga msitari chini ya (neno). 4 ~ **off sb** *(colloq) ~ a point against/off/over sb* shinda; dhalilisha/aibisha mtu. 5 ~ **sth up (against sb)** weka kama kumbukumbu/rekodi dhidi ya mtu. 6 ~ **(up)** weka rekodi. **~r** *n* 1 mwandishi wa magoli/pointi (za mchezo). 2 mfungaji (magoli).

scorn *n* 1 dharau, bezo. **laugh sb/sth to** ~ cheka kwa mabezo. 2 kitu cha dharau vt dharau, beza *he ~s lying* anadharau uwongo. **~ful** *adj* -enye dharau. **~fully** *adv* kwa dharau.

scorpio *n* nge: alama ya nane ya unajimu. **~n** *n* nge.

scot *n (only in)* **pay ~ and lot** shirikiana katika kugharamia kitu.

get off/escape ~-free vuka salama/ bila madhara/bila adhabu; achiwa huru.

Scot *n* Mskoti mtu wa. **~land**.

Scotch[1] *adj* 1 -a kiskoti *n* lugha ya kiskoti. 2 **the** ~ Waskoti. 3 ~ *whisky* wiski ya kiskoti.

scotch[2] *vt* 1 *(arch)* jeruhi. 2 haribu ua; oza; vuruga; komesha. *n* chanjo, chale.

Scotland Yard *n* Makao Makuu ya idara ya upelelezi wa jinai Uingereza; Polisi wa London.

scoundrel *n* mwovu, baa. **~ly** *adv* kiovu, kwa ubaya.

scour[1] *vt* 1 sugua; ng'arisha/safisha kwa kusugua/kupitishia maji au dawa ~ *the bowels* harisha, endesha sana. 2 **~ sth (away/off)** ondoa kutu, doa n.k. ~ *the rust away/off from sth* toa kutu katika kitu. 3 safisha tundu/tanuri/ bomba (kwa kupitisha maji) *n* 1 kusafisha 2. dawa ya kusafishia/ kusugulia. **~r** *n* 1 kisugulio; sifongo. 2 msafishaji. **~ing** kusugua/ kung'arisha. ~ **powder** unga wa kusugulia.

scour[2] *vt,vi* 1 pitia haraka (katika kutafuta kitu); nenda haraka (hapa na pale). 2 **~ about after/for sb/sth** tafuta ~ *the country* pekua/saka nchini.

scourge *n* 1 mjeledi, kiboko. 2 *(punishment)* baa; njia ya kulipizia kisasi *vt* 1 piga na mjeledi. 2 *(fig)* tesa, umiza.

scout[1] *n* 1 **(Boy) s ~** skauti. **~master** *n* kiongozi wa maskauti. 2 msaidizi wa wenye magari barabarini. 3 mtu/ chombo kinachotangulizwa kupeleleza habari za maadui (katika vita). 4 mtafuta wasanii/wachezaji. ~ **about/ around (for sb/sth)** *vi* peleleza, kagua. ~ **about/around** tafutatafuta.

scout[2] *vt* kataa kabisa (kwa dharau).

scow *n* tishali.

scowl *vi* ~ **(at)** kunjia uso (kwa ghadhabu). ~ **at** tazama vikali *n* uso mkali, uso mkunjamano; tazamo kali. **~ingly** *adv*.

scrabble[1] *vi* ~ **about (for sth)** papasa papasa; kwaruza; charaza/andika ovyoovyo michoromichoro/ makwarukwaru.

scrabble[2] *n* mchezo wa kujenga maneno.

scrag *n* 1 kiumbe (mtu, kitu, mti, au mnyama) hafifu/ dhalili; gofu la mtu. 2 ~ **(-end)** sehemu ya mifupa ya shingo ya kondoo *vt* songa, kaba koo; nyonga. **~giness** *n* udhaifu, unyonge; ukondefu. **~gy** *adj* -embamba; -liokonda; -a kimbaombao; -gofu; ng'onda.

scram *vi (sl)* ambaa! potea! ondoka!

scramble *vt,vi* 1 sombera, kwea. 2 ~ **(for)** gombania, pigania, shindania, nyang'anyana. 3 ~ *(of eggs)* vuruga ~ *eggs* vuruga mayai *~d eggs* mayai ya kuvuruga 4 paraganya ujumbe (kwa simu) makusudi *n* 1 mchafuko, fujo, vurugu. 2 mashindano ya uparaganyo (mchanganyiko maalum). 3 kinyanganyiro. **~r** chombo cha kuparaganyia ujumbe, kiparaganyio.

scrap[1] *n* 1 masalio, mabaki. 2 takataka, kipande *not a* ~ hata chembe. ~ **heap** lundo la takataka, jaa. **~-iron** vipande vya chuma. **throw sth/sb on the ~ heap** tupilia mbali, fukuzilia mbali, telekeza. 3 vikorokoro; *(of food)* makombo. 4 picha, makala (toka gazetini). ~ **-book** kitabu cha picha, maandishi *vt* 1 *(discard)* tupa; samehe, acha makombo takataka. **~py** *adj* vivihivi, -a wasiwasi. **~ily** *adv*. ~ **iness** *n*.

scrap[2] *n (colloq)* mapigano, mzozo *vi* pigana, zozana.

scrape *vt,vi* 1 ~ **sth (from/off sth)**; ~ **sth (away/off)** paa, kwangua, komba, kwaruza. 2 ~ **sth (from/off sth)** chubua, umiza. ~ **one's boots** kwangua (taka) viatu. 3 ~ **sth (out)** chimba, toa. 4 pita, pitisha, pangusa. ~ **along** *(fig)* ishi kwa shida. ~ **through (sth)** shinda (kwa shida). **bow and** ~ *(fig)* toa heshima iliyozidiana, nyenyekea mno. ~ **past**

ambaa. 5 ~ **up an acquintance with** lazimisha urafiki, jipendekeza, jidukiza kwa fulani. 6 ~ **sth/sb together** kusanya kwa shida, pata kwa nguvu, pambanya, dunduliza ~ *the bow across the fiddle* piga fidla. ~ **a living** tarazaki, hemea (kwa shida), okoteza *n* 1 paruzo, mkwaruzo, mparuzo; kukwaruza. **a ~ of pen** mwandiko, mchubuko; *(fig)* shida, mashaka, mkasa, matata. **be in a ~** -wa matatani, pata mkasa *get out of a ~* ponea chupuchupu. 2 kisu, mbuzi, ukombo.

scratch *vt,vi* 1 parura, kwaruza. ~ **the surface** *(fig)* lipua, babia, fanya bila makini. 2 ~ **sth out** chora; kata, futa. ~ **out** futa. 3 piga makucha. 4 toa katika shindano. 5 kuna. ~ **one's head** kuna kichwa, onyesha kuchanganyikiwa. ~ **my back and I'll ~ yours** nipe nikupe ~ *a hole* fukua. 6 ~ **sth (out)** fukua ~ *out a hole* fukua shimo. 7 andika kwa haraka, paraza/charaza. ~ **pad** karatasi/bunda la kuandikia. 8 toa sauti ya mkwaruzo. 9 ~ **about (for sth);** ~ **sth up** tifua/chakura (katika kutafuta kitu) *n* 1 mtai, mchoro, mfuo; *escape without ~* okoka, vuka salama. **start from ~** anza upya; *(fig)* anza kwa shida; *(fig)* anza bila ya matayarisho. **be/come/bring sb up to ~** *(fig)* wa tayari/tayarisha (mtu) kufanya linalotarajiwa/takiwa *covered with ~es* -liojaa mitai. **a ~ of the pen** sahihi (mcharazo wa maneno machache). 2 mkuno. 3 mstari wa kuanzia (mbio). 4 bila dosari/kizuizi *adj* ovyo; -a watu wowote; -a bahati; -a kuokoteza ~ *paper n* karatasi ya mazoezi. ~ **wig** *n* wigi iliyofunika nusu ya kichwa. ~ **-work** *n* mchoro (kama pambo). **~y** *adj* 1 -enye sauti ya kukwaruza. 2 -a kuwasha. 3 -a kuchorwa, -liochorwa ovyo.

scrawl *vt,vi* kwaruza; chora ovyoovyo ~ *all over a sheet of paper* chorachora katika karatasi *n* makwarukwaru. **~ler** *n* mwandishi mbovu.

scrawny *adj* -liokonda, -a kimbaombao.

scream *vt,vi* 1 ~ **(out)** piga unyende; piga yowe, lalaika. ~ **one's head off** lia kwa nguvu. 2 nguruma *(of wind machines etc)* vuma *n* 1 yowe, unyende; ukemi. 2 kilio cha nguvu; mvumo, ngurumo. 3 *(colloq)* kigelegele *~s of laughter* vicheko, chereko; *(colloq)* mcheshi. **~ingly** *adv (colloq)* mno *n* 1 mpiga yowe.

scree *n* changarawe (usena).

screech *vi,vt* ~ **(out)** lia kwa/ukemi/maumivu/tisho(kwa sauti nyembamba); chuna *n* ukemi; kilio (cha sauti nyembamba, cha kukwaruza). **~-owl** *n* timvi, mkata-sanda. **~y** *adv*.

screed *n* 1 barua iliyopoa, maandiko marefu yasiyokolea (yasiyovutia). 2 hotuba ndefu. 3 ufito (sehemu ya kupakwa rangi).

screen *n* 1 kisitiri, kinga, kificho. 2 chekecheke. 3 kiwambo cha nguo. 4 *(cinema)* skrini, kioo. 5 kiambaza. 6 pazia *door/window-~* wavu wa mlango/dirisha *vt* 1 sitiri. 2 linda, chekecha, chuja. 3 onyesha filamu *she ~s well (of films)* anatokea vizuri. **~ing** *n (pl)* masalia (baada ya kuchekecha).

screw *n* 1 parafujo/skurubu. **~driver** bisibisi. **a ~ loose** hitilafu; *(fig)* kichaa, afkani. **~ball** *(US sl)* wazimu. ~ **topped** -enye kifuniko chenye hesi. 2 parafujo shinikizi: kitu kizungushwacho kama parafujo na kutumika kama shinikizi. **put the ~ on sb/give sb another turn of the ~** lazimisha, shurutisha; bana. 3 (kitendo cha) kuzungusha; mzungusho/mzunguko. 4 **~-propeller** majembe, mapanga, rafadha. 5 *(in games, billiards etc)* mpindisho/mbetuo (wa mpira). 6 *(twist)* msokoto. 7 *(colloq)* bahili. 8 *(GB sl) (wages)* mshahara, ujira. 9 *(GB sl)* askari jela. 10 mwenzi katika kutiana/kukazana *vt,vi* 1 tia skrubu, kaza kwa skrubu. **have one's head**

~ed on (the right way) -wa na busara/akili, -wa na uamuzi wa busara. 2 (*squeeze*) sokota, songa; kaza (kwa kuzungusha), fanya imara, thabiti. ~ **up one's courage** kaza moyo, piga moyo konde. ~ **up one's eyes** kaza macho. 3 (*extort*) kama, kamua. 4 *(sl)* **be ~ed** lewa. 5 kaza, jamiiana na, 6 ~ **sb up** vuruga *adj* (*sl*) *(GB, colloq)* kichaa; *(US colloq)* -a kijinga.

scrible *vt,vi* andika haraka, paruza, andika ovyo; chorachora. **scribbling block** karatasi za rafu *n* mwandiko wa mchorochoro. **~r** *n* mtu aandikaye ovyo; mwandishi chapwa.

scribe *n* 1 mwandishi -mweledi wa barua. 2 mnakili wa maandishi (kabla ya kugunduliwa kwa uchapaji).

scrimmage *n* ghasia, msukosuko, tandabelua *vi,vt* vurumishana, gombana.

scrimp *vi,vt* see **skimp**.

scrimshank *vi (mil. sl)* tega kazi; kwepa wajibu; toroka kazi. **~er** *n*.

scrip *n* hati ya muda (inayoonyesha haki ya kupewa cheti cha kumiliki baada ya kukamilisha urasimu).

script *n* 1 *(handwriting)* mwandiko wa hati ya mkono.2 *(short for)* mswada (wa mchezo/filamu n.k.). ~ **writer** *n* mwandishi wa mswada. **~ed** *adj* -liosomwa kutoka kwenye mswada. 3 karatasi ya majibu ya mtihani.

scripture *n* 1 **(Holy) S~; the (Holy) S~s** Biblia, maandiko matakatifu. **scriptural** *adj*.

scrofula *n* mafindofindo. **scrofulous** *adj*.

scroll *n* 1 hati ya kukunja (kwa kuvingirisha); hati ndefu (hasa kama zile za zamani). 2 nakshi, mapambo ya kuchora/kuchonga yanayoonekana kama hati.

scrooge *n* bahili.

scrotum *n (pl)* korodani, mfuko wa pumbu.

scrounge *vt (colloq)* doea, randia. ~ **a dinner** doea chakula. **~r** *n*.

scrub[1] *vt,vi* ~ **(out)** 1 sugua sana (hasa kwa brashi). 2 *(sl)* futa, tangua, batilisha *n* 1 *give a ~* safisha, sugua. **~bing-board** *n* ubao wa kusugulia. ~**bing-brush** *n* brashi ya kusugulia.

scrub[2] *n* 1 pori. 2 *(stunted)* kibeti. ~**by** *adj* 1 dogo, -lodumaa -sio laini.

scruff *n (only in)* **the ~ of the neck** ngozi ya kikosi *take by the ~ of the neck* shika mtu kikosini (na kumsukuma) *adj (colloq)* -a vigaga, chafu.

scrummage *see* **scrimmage.**

scrumptious *adj (colloq) (highly of food)* -tamu sana, -a kupendeza sana.

scrunch *see* **crunch**.

scruple *n* 1 haya, aibu *a man of no ~s* mtu asiye na haya *have you no ~* huoni haya. 2 kipimio kidogo (uzani wa gramu 20) *vt,vi* ona haya.

scrupulous *adj* 1-angalifu sana, -a hadhari sana. 2 adilifu. **scrupulosity** *n*. **scrupulousness** *n*. **scrupulously** *adv*.

scrutinize *vt* chunguza, angalia kwa makini. ~ **sb's face** angalia mtu usoni kwa makini. **scrutineer** *n* msimamizi/mkaguzi wa kura (karatasi za kura). **scrutiny** *n* 1 uchunguzi makini. 2 uchunguzi rasmi wa kura.

scud *vi* serereka, peperuka (kama jahazi, mawingu n.k.)*n* kupeperuka, kuserereka; ukungu, (unaopeperushwa na upepo).

scuff *vi,vt* 1 buruza/buruta miguu tembea kwa kuburuza miguu. 2 chakaza viatu kwa kuburura miguu, umiza miguu.

scuffle *vi* vurumishana *n* tandabelua; fujo, ugomvi.

scull *n* 1 kasia (mojawapo kati ya makasia mawili yatumiwayo na mpiga kasia). 2 kasia, upondo *vt,vi* endesha kwa kasia, piga/vuta kasia. **~er** *n* mpiga kasia.

scullery *n* chumba cha kuoshea vyombo vya nyumbani.

scullion *n (hist)* chokora wa jikoni.

sculpture *n* 1 sanaa ya uchongaji (wa sanamu). 2 sanaa ya kuchongwa, kinyago *vt,vi* chonga; tia nakshi. **sculptural** *adj* -a uchongaji nakshi. **sculptor** *n* mchongaji (wa sanamu katika mawe, mbao, shaba n.k.); mfinyanzi (sanamu). **sculptress** *n* mchongaji wa kike.

scum *n* 1 povu, fuo; taka za juu (ya maji). 2 **the ~ of** *(fig)* watu wasio na thamani/dini. **the ~ of the earth** watu duni kabisa; watu wabaya kabisa *vt,vi* engua povu/taka za juu n.k. **~my** *adj*.

scrupper *n* nguruzi, nguzi *vt* 1 zamisha meli. 2 *(colloq)* angamiza, lemaza.

scurf *n* mbaza (kichwani); ukoga, ukoko. **~y** *adj*.

scurrilous *adj* -a kutukana, -a matusi, -a kashfa. **scrurrility** *n*.

scurry *vi* ~ **(about) (for/through)** kimbia haraka, kurupuka, kimbia *n* 1 mwendo wa haraka. 2 ~ **(of)** manyunyu ya theluji; wingu la vumbi.

scurvy *n* kiseyeye, hijabu *adj* fidhuli. **scrurvily** *adv*.

scut *n* mkia mfupi wa mnyama (kama wa sungura, mbuzi).

scuttle[1] *n* tundu/upenyo/dirisha ubavuni mwa meli *vt* toboa meli ili kuizamisha. ~ **butt** *n* 1 pipa la maji matamu melini. 2 *(sl)* uvumi, umbeya.

scuttle[2] *vi* ~ **(off/away)** mbiombio. 2 kukwepa/kukimbia (shinda/matatizo/hatari); kupiga chenga.

scuttle[3] *n* chombo cha kuwekea makaa ya mawe.

scythe *n* fyekeo *vt* fyeka nyasi.

sea *n* 1 **the ~** bahari. **go to ~** safiri kwa meli; -wa safari ya chombo, anza kuondoka bandarini/pwani. **on the ~ (of a place)** pwani. **beyond/over the ~s** ng'ambo. **the high ~s** bahari ya mbali. **the freedom of the ~s** haki ya kufanya biashara katika eneo lolote la bahari. **the Red S~** Bahari ya Sham. **the Seven S ~s** *(poet)* bahari zote. 2 *(various phrases without articles)* **at ~** baharini; -sioelewa. **all/completely at ~** liochanganyikiwa. **by ~** kwa meli. 3 *(wave)* wimbi. **heavy ~** mawimbi makubwa. 4 **half ~s over** -levi, wingi wa. **~ of troubles** shida nyingi. 5 *(attrib and in compounds)* **~ air** *n* upepo wa bahari. **~ animal** *n* mnyama wa baharini. **~ bathing** *n* kuoga baharini/kuongelea baharini. **~ bed** *n* chini ya bahari. **~ bird** *n* ndege waishio karibu na bahari. **~ board** *n* eneo la pwani; ufukwe. **~ boat** *n* mashua. **~borne** *adj* -liobebwa na meli. **~ breeze** *n* upepo wa bahari. **~-coast** *n* pwani, ukingo wa bahari. **~ cow** *n* nguva. **~-dog** aina ya sili; baharia mkongwe. **~ eagle** *n* kwazi. **~ farer** *n* baharia. **~faring** *n* safari baharini *adj* -a bahari; -enye kufanya kazi/kusafiri baharini. **~faring men** wanamaji, mabaharia. **~fish** *n* samaki wa bahari/wa maji ya chumvi. **~food** *n* vyakula vya habarini. **~ front** *n* upande wa mji uliokabiliana na bahari. **~-girt** *adj (poet)* -liozungukwa na bahari. **~ going** *adj* 1 *(of ships)* -a kuvukia bahari. 2 *(of person)* -a ubaharia. **~-green** *n* kijani bahari *adj* -enye rangi ya bahari. **~ - lion** *n* sili mkubwa wa bahari. **~ man** *n* baharia. **~ manship** *n* ustadi wa ubaharia. **~ mile** *n* maili ya majini (futi 6080). **~plane** *n* ndege ituayo baharini/ziwani. **~port** *n* (mji wenye) bandari. **~power** *n* nguvu (ya jeshi la maji) ya kutawala bahari. **~-rover** *n* haramia; meli ya haramia. **~scape** *n* mandhari ya bahari. **~shore** *n* ufuko. **~sick** *adj* -a kichefuchefu cha baharini. **~ sickness** *n* kigegezi. **~side** *n* pwani, ufukoni. **~snake** nyoka wa baharini. **~-view** *n* mandhari ya bahari. **wall** ukuta/boma la kuzuia bahari. **~water** *n* maji ya bahari, maji ya chumvi. **~ way** *n* njia ya majini; mto unaopitika na meli za baharini. **~worthy** *adj (of a ship)* -a kufaa kusafiri baharini.

seal[1] *n* sili: mnyama wa baharini mwenye manyoya mazuri. **~ skin** *n* ngozi ya sili; vazi la manyonya ya sili. **~er** *n* mwindaji wa sili; meli itumikayo kuwinda sili.

seal[2] *n* 1 muhuri, chapa, alama. **given under my hand and** ~ *(leg)* -liotiwa saini na kupigwa muhuri na mimi. **under ~ of secrecy** *(fig)* kwa masharti ya siri. ~ **ring** pete yenye muhuri. 2 ~ **of** idhini *vt* 1 ~ **(up)** tia (piga) muhuri. ~ **(close)** ziba, funga kabisa. 2 ~ **sth in** fungia. 3 ~ **sth off** zingia, zuia. **my lips are ~ed** sitasema. **~ing-wax** *n* lakiri.

seam *n* 1 mshono; *(hemmed)* upindo; *(tacked)* bandia; *(strong)* jongo. 2 tabaka ya madini (ya makaa ya mawe n.k.) 3 *(wrinkle)* kikunjo, kifinyo, kunyanzi. 4 kiungo, ufa (kati ya mbao) melini *(of sail)* mlete *vt* shonesha/tia/onyesha (vikunjo, kovu n.k.). **~less** *adj* -a bila mshono, -liofumwa kipande kimoja. **~stress** *n* mshonaji wa kike.

seamy *adj (chiefly fig, esp in)* **the ~ side of life** upande mbaya (wa maisha) (k.m. umaskini, uhalifu n.k.).

seance *n* mkusanyiko wa kutafuta kuwasiliana na pepo n.k.

sear[1] *vt* 1 unguza (hasa kwa chuma cha moto); kausha, nyausha; fanya kavu. ~ **ing-iron** *n* chuma cha kuunguzia. 3 *(fig)* fanya (roho, moyo, dhamiri n.k.) kuwa sugu/gumu.

sear[2]**/sere** *adj (liter)* -liokauka; *(of flowers, leaves)* -lionyauka.

search *vt,vi* 1 ~ **(sb/sth) (for sb/sth);** ~ **sb/sth out** tafuta; chunguza; pekua, chakura. ~ **out** tafuta, saka. ~ **one's heart/conscience** chunguza dhamira, tafakari. **S~ me** *(colloq)* sijui kabisa. 2 *(lit)* penya; zama *n* kutafuta; upekuzi, mchakuro. **right of ~** haki ya manowari za nchi kusimamisha na kupekua meli nyingine wakati wa vita. **~light** kurunzi. **~-party** *n* kikundi cha watafutaji kinachotafuta mtu/kitu kilichopotea. **~-warrant** *n* hati ya upekuzi. **~er** *n*. **~ing** *adj* -a kuchunguza kwa undani; *(of a test)* -a mambo yote, kamilifu. **~ingly** *adv*.

season *n* 1 majira, msimu; muhula, kipindi. **wety/rain ~** masika, kusi. **dry ~** kiangazi, kaskazi. **cold ~** kipupwe. **the ~** pembe za mwaka. **closed ~** msimu usio ruhusu (agh. uwindaji). **it is in ~** ni muhula wake/kipindi chake. **~ in (~) and out of ~** nyakati zote. **the ~'s greetings** salamu za krismasi na mwaka mpya. **in/out of ~** *(of goods)* -a msimu/-sio msimu wake; -a msimu wa likizo, utalii/-sio na watalii. **a word in ~** ushauri wakati unaofaa. ~ **(-ticket)** *n* tiketi ya msimu; tiketi ya kuingia katika sehemu za burudani kwa kipindi maalum *vt,vi* 1 zoea; zoeshwa. 2 ~ **(with)** unga, koleza. 3 *(lit)* punguza makali. **~ing** *n* viungo. **~nable** *adj* 1 *(of the weather)* -a wakati wake, -a majira. 2 *(of help, gift, advice)* -a wakati unaofaa. **~al** *adj* -a majira, -a msimu, -a muhula. **~ally** *adv*.

seat *n* 1 kikalio (benchi, kigoda, kiti n.k.) *the back ~ of the car* kiti cha nyuma cha gari. **keep one's ~** endelea kukaa (kitini). **take a ~** keti, kaa kitako *take one's ~* kaa mahali pako. ~ **belt** mkanda wa usalama wa kiti (agh. katika ndege, gari). 2 makalio, kitako. 3 matako. 4 nafasi. **take one's ~** ingia Bungeni. **win/lose one's ~** shinda/shindwa katika uchaguzi wa Bunge. 5 makao, makazi; mkao. 6 *(country)* ~ jumba kubwa la mashambani. 7 mkao, ukaaji (hasa juu ya farasi) *vt* 1 ~ **oneself; be ~ed!** *(formal)* kaa/kaeni. 2 -wa na nafasi ya watu kukaa. ~ **ing-room** *n* sebule. 3 *(usu re~)* tengeneza kitako/makalio (agh. ya kiti, suruali).

sec *n (sl abbr of)* **second**.

secateurs *n pl* mkasi wa bustani.

secede *vi* ~ **(from)** jitenga, jiondoa; jitoa. **secessionist** *n* **secession** *n* kujitenga; kujitoa. *n* mtetezi wa/mwenye kujitoa.

seclude *vt* ~ **sb/oneself (from)** jitenga. **~d** *adj (esp. of place)* kimya; pekee, faragha. **seclusion** *n* kutengwa, kutenga; upweke.

second *adj* 1 *(abbr 2nd)* -pili ~ *child*

mtoto wa pili. ~-**best** *adj* -a pili kwa ubora *n, adv come off ~ best* shindwa, zidiwa. ~ **class** *adj* -a daraja la pili; hafifu, duni *n* daraja la pili *adv* kwa daraja la pili. ~-**floor** *n* ghorofa ya pili; *(GB)* ghorofa mbili; *(US)* ghorofa moja kutoka chini. ~-**hand** -liokwishatumika. ~ **hand bookshop** duka la vitabu vilivyokwisha tumika. **second-hand clothes** *n* mitumba; *(of news, knowledge)* -liopatikana kwa kupitia wengine, -sio mpya. ~ **lieutenant** *n* luteni usu. ~**rater** *n* mtu wa akili/uwezo mdogo. ~-**sight** *n* utabiri, uaguzi. ~ **teeth** *n* meno ya utu uzima. ~ **to none** bora kabisa. 2 -a ziada, zaidi. 3 ~ **advent/coming** Ujio wa Pili (wa Yesu Kristu). ~ **ballot** mtindo wa kuwapigia kura washindi wawili endapo wa kwanza anashindwa kufikia nusu ya kura zinazohitajika. ~ **nature** *n* desturi, silika. ~ **thoughts** kubadili mawazo (baada ya kufikiria upya). 4 -a kufuata, -a baadaye. ~ **childhood** *n* uzee unaoandamana na upungufu wa akili. **play ~ fiddle (to sb)** -wa chini ya (mtu fulani). ~**ly** *adv* baadaye; pili; zaidi; tena *n* 1 kitu cha pili *the ~ of June* tarehe mbili Juni. **get a** ~ pata daraja la pili. 2 mwingine, kingine. 3 *(pl)* bidhaa hafifu/duni. 4 *(pl)* nyongeza ya chakula. 5 msaidizi (katika ndondi n.k.) *vt* 1 saidia, unga mkono. ~**er** *n* mwuunga mkono azimio. ~**ment** *n* kuazima/kuazimwa. ~**ary** *adj* 1-a kufuata, -a baadaye, -a pili. ~ **education** elimu ya sekondari/upili. 2 -a naibu, wakilishi. ~**arily** *adv*.

secret *adj* 1 -a siri; -a faragha, -liofichwa ~ *ballot* kura ya siri. **the ~ service** idara ya ujasusi/usalama. ~ **agent** jasusi/afisa usalama. 2 *(of places)* tulivu, kimya, fichika. 3 *(of persons)* siri *n* 1 siri, jambo la siri *in ~* kwa siri, faraghani. **keep a** ~ weka/tunza siri *official~s* siri za serikali. **in the** ~ kati ya wasiri. **let sb into the** ~ ambia mtu siri. **(be) an open** ~ siri iliyofichukuka. 2 usiri. 3 mwujiza, ajabu. **the ~s of science** miujiza/maajabu ya sayansi. ~**ly** *adv*. **secrecy** *n* usiri, ufichaji, uwezo wa/tabia ya kuweka siri *swear/bind sb to ~* fanya mtu aahidi kuweka siri, apisha mtu (kuweka siri). ~**e** *vt* 1 ficha, setiri. 2 -nya, toa, nyunyuza. ~**ion** *n* utoaji, unyaji; utemaji; mnyunyizo; kuficha kuficha, kusetiri. ~ **ive** *adj* -siri, -fichaficha. **a ~ person** (mtu) msiri. ~**ively** *adv*. ~**iveness** *n*.

secretary *n* 1 katibu, mwandishi. **executive** ~ katibu mtendaji. **principal** ~ katibu mkuu. **private** ~ katibu myeka. **publicity** ~ katibu mwenezi. **S ~ General** Katibu Mkuu. 2 mhazili. 3 Waziri wa Nchi. ~ **of State** waziri. **secretarial** *adj*.

sect *n* 1 madhehebu. 2 kikundi. ~**arian** *adj* -a kikundi; -a madhehebu *n* mtu wa madhehebu (kikundi) (agh.mtu mwenye mtazamo/mawazo finyu); mlokoke wa madhehebu fulani. ~**arianism** *n* ufuasi wa madhehebu (au kikundi).

section *n* 1 sehemu, kipande *build in ~s* jenga kwa sehemu. 2 *(of book, paper)* fungu. ~ **of the law** fungu la sheria; *(of place)* eneo. **shopping** ~ eneo la maduka. 3 *(departiment)* idara *(of soldiers)* kikosi. ~**al** *adj* 1 -enye sehemu. 2 -a kupenda/kupigania sehemu (ya jamii). ~**alism** *n* ulokole; kujishughulisha na utengano.

sector *n* 1 kipindi. 2 sehemu ya medani; sekta; sehemu *public ~* sekta ya umma *private ~* sekta binafsi.

secular *adj* 1 -a kilimwengu; -a kidunia ~ *education* elimu isiyoendeshwa na dini (agh.shule za serikali). 2 -a nje ya nyumba ya utawa *the ~ clergy* mapadre (wasio watawa). ~**ism** *n* maoni kwamba dini isiwe msingi wa elimu na maadili. ~**ist** *n* 1 mpinga dini. 2 mfuasi wa malimwengu (mlimwengu). ~**ize** *vt* fanya -a kilimwengu; ondoa kwenye dini.

~ization *n* 1 kufanya -a ulimwengu. 2 kuondoa kwenye dini.

secure *adj* 1 salama, pasi hofu. 2 -a hakika, -a kudumu. 3 ~ **(against/ from)** salama. 4 thabiti; yakini *vt* 1 ~ **sth (against, from)** tunza, linda, hifadhi. 2 *(fasten)* funga, kaza. 3 pata, (ji)patia. 4 *leg)* dhamini. ~ **creditor** mwia mwenye dhamana. ~ **debt** deni lenye dhamana. **securable** *adj*.~**ly** *adv*.

security *n* 1 usalama. ~ **Council** Baraza la Usalama. ~ **forces/police** askari/ polisi wa usalama. ~ **risk** mtu wa hatari. 2 amana, rehani, dhamana. 3 *(bond)* hati, sharti.

securicor *n (Commercial)* kikosi cha usalama (agh. kwa vitu vya thamani).

sedan *n* 1 motokaa/gari ndogo. 2 ~- **chair** machela.

sedate *adj* -tulivu, -pole, -a makini *vt* tuliza (na dawa). ~**ly** *adv*. ~**ness** *n* **sedative** *adj (med)* -a kutuliza *n* kitulizo, kipozo.

sedentary *adj* 1 -a kukaa kitako, -a kukaakaa. 2 *(of persons)* -a kukaa sana/tu.

sedge *n (bot)* mafunjo, kangaga, njaanjaa. **sedgy** *adj*.

sediment *n* masimbi, mashapo (takataka za chini); shinda, chenga. ~**ary** *adj* -a mashapo. ~ **rock** mwamba masapo.

sedition *n* (uchochezi wa) maasi/uhaini. **seditious** *adj* chochezi, asi.

seduce *vt* ~ **sb (from/into sth)** 1 shawishi; potoa. 2 tongoza. ~**r** *n*. **seduction** *n* 1 kupotoa, upotofu, kupoteza, ushawishi. 2 utongozaji. 3 vivutio. **seductive** *adj*. **seductively** *adv*.

sedulous *adj* -tendaji kazi; *(fig)* -a bidii, -a jitihada, -a jududi. ~**ly** *adv*. ~**ness** *n*. **sedulity** *n*.

see[1] *vi,vt* 1 ona. ~**ing is believing** kuona ni kuamini. **be ~ing things** ota (ndoto). 2 ona. ~ **the back of sb** ondokana na, ona kwa mara ya mwisho. ~ **the last of sb/sth** achana na; malizana na. ~ **the sights** tembelea/zuru mandhari/sehemu maarufu. ~ **stars** ona maluwiluwi. ~ **visions** agua. ~ **one's way (clear) to doing sth** elewa namna ya kufanya jambo; jisikia. 3 *(imper)* tazama! angalia! 4 *(not in the progressive tenses)* elewa, tambua. **I don't** ~ sielewi/sioni kwa nini. ~ **for oneself** jionea mwenyewe. **not ~ the use/ good of doing sth** -toona umuhimu. **you** ~ unajua; kama ujuavyo. ~**ing that** kwa kuwa, madhali, maadam. 5 pata habari (kutoka gazetini n.k.). 6 pitia (katika maisha), ona *he'll never ~ forty again* ameshavuka miaka arobaini. **have ~n the day/time when** enzi zake. **it has ~n better days** wakati wake umepita. ~ **sb damned/in hell first** -tokubali kitu, kamua. 7 onana na. **Be ~ ing you/S ~you soon** *(colloq)* kwa heri ya kuonana. 8 acha (bila kusaidia). 9 angalia, hakikisha. ~ **that the door is locked** uhakikishe kwamba mlango umefungwa. 10 jiona, jifikiria. 11 *(with adv particles and preps)* ~ **about sth** shughulikia. ~ **sb about sth** ona, pata ushauri. ~ **sb across sth** elekeza/ongoza/ saidia kuvuka. ~ **(sb) around (sth)** tembeza, onyesha. ~ **you around** *(sl)* tutaonana. ~ **sb back/home** sindikiza. ~ **(sb) off** aga, -pa mkono wa buriani; sindikiza. ~ **sb off sth** toa. ~ **sb out** toa, sindikiza. ~ **sth out** endelea hadi mwisho. ~ **sb over/around sth** tembeza, onyesha. ~ **to** shughulikia. ~ **through sb/sth** ng'amua, baini, -todanganywa. ~ **through** *adj* -enye kuonyesha/kuona/ onyeshi. ~ **sb through (sth)** auni. ~ **sth through** piga moyo konde, shikilia; endelea hadi mwisho. ~**r** *n* mtabiri, mwaguzi.

see[2] *n* jimbo la askofu, dayosisi.

seed *n* 1 mbegu, punje. **run/to** ~ fika mwisho wa kuchanua na kuanza kutoa mbegu; *(fig)* acha kujitunza (mwili na mavazi). ~-**bed** *n* kitalu. ~ -**cake** *n* keki ya kisibiti. ~ **corn** shuke la mbegu za kupanda. ~**sman** mwuza mbegu. ~ **time** msimu wa upandaji mbegu. 2 asili; mwanzo, chanzo, chimbuko. **sow the ~s of discord** chonganisha. 3 *(off spring)* uzao, manii. 5 ~ **potato** kiazi cha mbegu (kinachooteshwa kabla ya kupanda). ~ **pearls** lulu ndogo. 6 *(sport)* mteule. **~ing-machine** n mashine ya kupandia (mbegu). **~less** *adj* -a bila mbegu . **~ling** *n* mche *vi,vt* 1 toa mbegu. 2 panda, otesha. 3 ondoa mbegu. **~ed grapes** mizababu isiyo na mbegu; teua, panga wachezaji bora ili wasikutane hadi sehemu za mwisho wa mashindano. **~y** *adj* 1 -enye mbegu nyingi. 2 -kuukuu, -liochakaa, -chakavu. 3 -gonjwa *be/feel* ~ -wa mgonjwa. **~iness** *n.* **~ily** *adv.*

seek *vivt* 1 tafuta. ~ **the truth** tafuta ukweli *the reason for his failure is not hard to* ~ sababu ya kushindwa kwake inaeleweka. 2 omba, taka *(much sought after)* -liotakiwa sana. 3 *(endeavour)* jaribu, jitahidi. 4 ~ **for** jaribu kupata. **~er** *n.*

seem *vi* onekana; elekea kuwa; -wa kama, fanana na *you ~ (to be) unwell* unaonekana mgonjwa *I don't ~ to fancy that* sielekei kupendelea hayo. **~ing** *adj* -a kujifanya; -a uwongo; -a juujuu. **~ingly** *adv* inavyoonekana kwa nje. **~ly** *adj* (*formal*) 1 sahihi, -a kufaa, *it is not ~ly* haifai. 2 -a heshima/adabu. **seemliness** *n.*

seen *pp of* **see**

seep *vi* vuja, penya. **~age** *n* upenyaji, uvujaji, mchuruziko.

seesaw *n* bembea *vi* bembea; *(fig)* sita kuamua (kati ya mambo mawili) *adv* pandashuka.

seethe *vi,vt* 1 ~ **(with)** chemka, sisimka, jaa (hasira, shauku n.k.) *Africa was seething with excitement* Afrika ilikuwa ikisisimka. 2 *(old use)* pika kwa kuchemsha.

segment *n* 1 mkato, sehemu. 2 kipande, pingili *a ~ of an orange* kipande cha chungwa. **a ~ of sugar cane** pingili ya muwa. 3 *(tech)* kitengwa *vt,vi* gawa katika sehemu. **~al; ~ary** *adj* -a pingili; -a sehemu, -a kipande.

~ation *n* ugawaji katika pingili.

segregate *vt,vi* tenga, tenganisha; bagua *adj (zool)* pekee. **segregation** *n* kutenga; *(racial)* ukabila, ubaguzi.

seigneur,seignior *n* mwinyi.

seine *n* juya *vt* vua kwa juya.

seismic *adj* -a tetemeko (la nchi). **seismograph** *n* kipimatetemeko. **seismology** *n* elimu ya tetemeko. **seismologist** *n* mtaalamu wa tetemeko.

seize *vi,vt* 1 kamata, twaa *be ~ with* patwa, shikwa na *be ~d by a fit of rage* patwa na hasira kali. 2 teka, nyang'anya, pokonya. 3 ~ **on/upon** elewa na kutumia ~ *upon an idea* fahamu vizuri wazo na kulitumia ipasavyo. 4 ~ **(up)** kwama, shikamana, goma. **seizure** *n* 1 kukamata; kukamatwa, ukamataji, utekaji. 2 shtuko la moyo; kifafa. kukwama, kugoma.

seldom *adv* mara chache, kwa shida/ nadra ~ *or never* mara chache au hata kidogo.

select *vt* chagua, teua *adj* -liochaguliwa, -teule. ~ **committee** Kamati ya Wabunge waliochaguliwa kufanya kazi rasmi. ~ **man** *n (US)* diwani. **~or** *n* mchaguzi, mteuzi. **~ion** *n* 1 uchaguzi, uteuzi. **natural~** (nadharia ya Darwin ya) uteuzi asilia. 2 vitu teule. **~ive** *adj* -chaguzi; -enye uwezo wa kuchagua, teule. **~ivity** *n* 1 uteuzi. 2 *(esp, of radio)* uwezo wa kupata idhaa za redio mbalimbali (bila tatizo). **~ively** *adv.*

selenium *n (chem)* saliniamu.

self *n* 1 nafsi, tabia *one's better ~* upande bora wa tabia/sifa za mtu. 2 mapendeleo (ya mtu binafsi) *she has no thought of ~* hajifikirii/ hajipendelei. 3 uenyewe.

self- *pref* -enyewe, -ji-, automatiki. **~-abasement** *n* kujishushia hadhi; kujidhalilisha. **~-abnegation** *n* kujinyima, kujitoa mhanga. **~-absorbed** *adj* -liozamia (katika mawazo, shughuli, n.k.). **~-abuse** *n* kujitukanisha, kujidunisha, kujidhihaki. ~-**accusation** *n* kujishtaki. ~-**acting** *adj* -a kujifanyia -enyewe; -a kujituma. ~ -**addressed** -lioandikwa anwani ya mwandikaji. ~-**activating** -a kujiendesha enyewe. ~-**adjustable** *adj* -a kujirekebisha, -a kujirudi. ~-**admiration** *n* kujiona; kujisifu, kujishauwa. ~-**advertisement** *n* ·kujionyesha, kujitangaza. ~-**apparent** *adj* wazi, bayana. ~-**appointed** -a kujiteua/kujichagua. ~-**assertion** *n* kujitanguliza/kujitokeza. ~-**assertive** *adj* - kujitanguliza, -a kujitokeza. ~-**assurance** *n* kujiamini. ~-**awareness** *n* kujitambua (utu, msimamo). ~-**binder** *n* mashine ya kuvunia ya automatiki. ~-**centred** *adj* -a kujifikiria mwenyewe tu, -a kimimimimi, -a kujipenda mno. ~-**closing** *adj* -a kujifunga -enyewe. ~-**collected** *adj* tulivu, -sio na harara. ~-**coloured** *adj* -a rangi moja. ~-**command** *n* kujitawala, kujiamuru. ~-**communion** *n* kujifikiria, kujihoji, kujitafakuri. ~-**complacent** *adj* -a kuridhika na jinsi ulivyo, -a kujiridhikia (tu). ~-**complacency** *n* kuridhika na jinsi ulivyo. ~-**conceited** *adj* -a kujipenda; -a kujiona, -a kujishauwa. ~-**confidence** *n* kujiamini. ~-**confident** *adj* -a hakika, -a kujiamini. ~-**conscious** *adj* -a kujitambua (hali, tabia, msimamo); -enye kujibaini; *(colloq)* -a kuona haya, -enye aibu. ~- **contained** *adj* 1 *(independent)* kinaifu. 2 -nyamavu, makini. 3 *(complete)* -a kujitosheleza, -a kujitosha, kamili; -enye yote ndani yake. ~-**contradictory** *adj* -a kujipinga. ~-**control** *n* kujidhibiti nafsi, kujiweza, kujitawala, kujizuia. ~-**cooling** *n* kujipoza. ~-**criticism** *n* kujihakiki, kujisahihisha, kujikosoa. ~-**deceit** *n* kujidanyanga, kujikanganya. ~-**deception** *see* **self-deceit**. ~-**defence** *n* kujitetea; kujilinda, kujihami, kujipigania. ~-**delusion** *n* kujidanganya, kujihadaa. ~-**denial** *n* kujihini, kujinyima, kujikana, kujizuia. ~-**dependence** *n* kujitegemea. ~-**desturction** *n* kujiangamiza, kujipoteza, kujifisha. ~-**determination** *n* kujitawala, uhuru; kujiamulia (mambo). ~-**display** *n* kujishaua, kujivuna, kujionyesha, kuranda. ~-**discipline** *n* kujiongoza, kujiwekea nidhamu. ~-**distrust** *n* kutojiamini, kujihisi. -~**educated** *adj* -a kujisomesha, -a kujielimisha *a ~ educated teacher* mwalimu aliyejifunza mwenyewe. ~-**effacing** *adj* -a kujificha, -enye soni. ~ -**employed** *adj* -a kujiajiri -a kujituma. ~-**esteem** *n* kujistahi, kujitukuza; kujiona, kiburi. ~-**evident** *adj* wazi, dhahiri, kinaganaga, bayana. ~-**examination** *n* kujichunguza, kujijaribu, kujihoji. ~-**explanatory** *adj* -enye kujieleza, -a waziwazi. ~-**generating** *adj* -a kujiongeza, -a kujizaa. ~-**governing** *adj* -a kujitawala. ~-**help** *n* kujisaidia mwenyewe, kujiweza. ~-**ignition** *n* kujiwasha. ~-**importance** *n* kujikweza, kujigamba; majivuno, makuu, kiburi. ~-**important** *adj* -a kujiona, -a kujikweza. ~-**imposed** *adj* -a kujitwisha; -a kujielemeza. ~-**improvement** *n* kujiendeleza. ~-**induction** *n (elect.)* kujichochea. ~-**indulgence** *n* -a kujiingiza/kujishughulisha mno na mambo. ~-**inflicted** *adj* -a kujiumiza, -a kujiadhibu, -a kujitaabisha. ~-**interest** *n* umimi, uchoyo. ~-**locking** *adj (tech)* -a kujifunga. ~-**made** *adj* -liojiendeleza/-liojitajirisha-enyewe. ~**mutilation** *n* kujihasiri, kujiharibu, kujilemaza, kujikata. ~-**opinionated** *adj* -kaidi, -bishi; shupavu. ~-**perception** *n* kujitambua. ~-**pity** *n* kujihurumia; kujionea uchungu. ~-**portrait** *n* kujichora, kujichonga (kuwa katika picha/sanamu). ~-**possessed** *adj* tulivu, a kujiamini. ~-**praise** *n* majisifu; kutamba; kujigamba. ~ -**preservation** *n* kujilinda, kujihami, kujitunza, kujikimu. ~-**propelled** *adj* -a kujiendesha (kwa rada, mapanga).

~-**raising** *adj (of flour)* -enye hamira. ~-**realization** *n* kujing'amua, kujibaini. ~-**recording** *adj* -a kurekodi -enyewe. ~-**reliance** *n* kujitegemea. ~-**reliant** *adj* -a kujitegemea. ~-**respect** *n* kujistahi/kujiheshimu (nafsi). ~-**restrained** *adj* -a kujikana, -a kujizuia; -a kujitawala. ~-**restraint** *n* kujitawala; kujizuia. ~-**righteous** *adj* -a kujidai, nyoofu. ~-**rule** *see* ~ **government**. ~-**sacrifice** *n* kujitoa mhanga; kujitolea. ~-**same** *adj* -le-le; pacha. ~-**satisfaction** *n* kujiona, majisifu; ukinaifu; kujiridhisha. ~-**satisfied** *adj* -a kujiona, kinaifu; -enye kiburi. ~-**sealing** *adj* -enye kujifunga -enyewe. ~-**seeker** *n* mtafuta/mtaka makuu; mwenye kujipendekeza. ~-**seeking** -a kujipendekeza, kutafuta/kutaka makuu *n* kujipendekeza. ~-**service** *n* kujitumikia, kujihudumia. ~-**sown** *adj* kimelea (-siopandwa), maotea. ~-**starter** *n* stata, kijianzishi. ~-**styled** *adj* -enye kujiita. ~-**sufficiency** *n* 1 utoshelevu. 2 kujitegemea. ~-**supporting** *adj* -a kujikimu, -a kujitegemea. ~-**taught** *adj* -liojielimisha; -liofunzwa na ulimwengu. ~-**will** *n* ukaidi, ushupavu. ~-**winding** *adj (of watch, clock etc)* -a kujilisha, -a kujitia ufunguo. ~-**hood** *n* ubinafsi, upeke. ~**ish** *adj* -a choyo, -enye ubinafsi. ~**ishness** *n* ubinafsi, uchoyo. ~**ishly** *adv*.

sell *vt,vi* ~ **sth (to sb);** ~ **sb sth** 1 uza; uzia. ~ **sth off** *(of stock of goods)* uza rahisi. ~ **sth out** uza sehemu au hisia zote; uza mali/vitu vyote. ~ **(sb) out** *(colloq)* saliti. ~ **out** *n* kuuza tikiti zote; *(colloq)* usaliti. 2 *(of goods)* uzika. ~**ing price** bei ya kuuzia/uzika *his new book is ~ing well* kitabu chake kipya kinauzika vizuri. 3 *(fig. uses)* ~ **the pass** *(prov.)* uza nchi; wa msaliti. 4 *(usu. pass)* danganya, tapeli. 5 **be sold on sth** *(colloq)* tekwa bakunja, kubali *n (colloq)* hila, ulaghai, ghiliba. **hard/soft** ~ mbinu kali/hafifu za kuuza. ~**er** *n* 1 mwuzaji. **a** ~**ers' market** *(comm)* wakati wa uhaba wa bidhaa. 2 bidhaa.

sellotape *n* selotepu: gundi ya karatasi.

selvage, selvedge *n* mtande.

semantic *adj* -a maana (katika lugha). **semantics** *n* semantiki, elimu-maana.

semaphore *n* 1 kuashiria (kwa kutumia bendera/taa/mikono n.k). 2 selo, ishara *vt,vi* ashiria.

semasiology *n* semasiolojia: elimu maana.

semblance *n* mfanano; sura, umbo; mfano.

semeiology, semeiotics *see* **semiology, semiotics.**

semen *n* shahawa, manii. **seminal** *adj* -a shahawa/manii, -a mbegu; *(fig)* -a msingi. **semination** *n* kupanda mbegu; utungaji mimba.

semester *n* muhula.

semi- *prep* 1 nusu. **a** ~-**circle** nusu duara. ~**circular** *adj* -a nusu duara. ~ **breve** *n (mus)* noti nzima. ~**quaver** *n (mus)* nusu kwiva. ~**tone** *n (mus)* nusutoni. 2 -a upande mmoja. ~-**detached** *adj (of a house)* -a upande mmoja. 3 kidogo ~ *civilized* -liostaarabika kidogo. 4 ~-**colon** *n* nukta mkato (;). ~-**conscious** *adj* -enye fahamu kidogo ~ **final** *n* nusu fainali . ~-**official** *adj* rasmirasmi, si rasmi sana. ~-**rigid** *adj* -a nusu yabisi. ~-**tropical** *adj* -a nusu tropiki. ~ **vowel** *n* nusu-irabu.

seminal *see* **semen**.

seminar *n* semina. ~**y** *n* seminari. ~**ist** *n* mseminari

semiology, semiotics *n* elimu ishara.

Semite *n* Msemiti. **Semitic** *adj* -a kisemiti.

semolina *n* semolina: punje/ngumu za ngano iliyosagwa.

sempstress see **seamstress.**

senate *n* 1 *(Fr, US)* seneti; (sehemu moja ya bunge). 2 baraza la uongozi wa Chuo Kikuu. **senator** *n* seneta. **senatorial** *adj* -a seneti.

send *vt,vi* ~ **sb/sth;** ~ **sth to sb** 1

peleka, tuma ~ *one's love to sb* salimia mtu, peleka salamu. 2 tupa, rusha, endesha, sukuma, jongeza ~ *sb sprawling* angusha mtu. ~ **sb packing/about his business,** *(colloq)* fukuza, timua. 3 sababisha kuwa, tia *the girl ~s me crazy* msichana (huyu) ananitia wazimu. 4 *(of God)* jalia. 5 *(phrases)* ~ **sb mad** tia fulani wazimu. ~ **sb away** ondoa/fukuza chuo; funga; shusha, teremsha. ~ **sth down** teremsha, shusha (bei, n.k) ~ **for sb (to do sth)** ita. ~ **sth forth,** *(formal)* toa. ~ **sth in** tuma, peleka. ~ **one's name in** pendekeza jina. ~ **sb off** sindikiza; *(of football)* toa uwanjani. ~ **sth off** tuma. ~ **sth on** tuma mapema; *(of letters)* tuma kwa anwani mpya. ~ **sth out** tawanya, gawa; chipua, toa. ~ **sb/sth up** dhihaki. ~ **up** pandisha (bei, n.k.). **~er** *n* mpelekaji, mtumaji.

senescent *adj* -a kuzeeka, -a kukonga. **senescence** *n.*

senile *adj* dhaifu (kutokana na uzee). **senility** *n* udhaifu, (utokanao na uzee).

senior *adj* 1 -kubwa (kwa umri, daraja, cheo). ~ **citizen** mzee; mstaafu. 2 andamizi ~ *magistrate* hakimu mwandamizi ~ *research fellow* mchunguzi mwandamizi. 3 *(after a person's name)* -a kwanza, -a kutangulia *n* 1 mkubwa *he is my ~* ni mkubwa wangu. 2 *(US)* mwanafunzi wa mwaka wa tatu/nne (katika sekondari au chuo). **~ity** *n* 1 ukubwa (wa umri, cheo); ukuu. 2 kutangulia.

senna *n* sanamaki.

senõr *n (spanish)* bwana ~ **Lopez** Bw Lopezi. **~a** *n* bibi. **~ita** Bi.

sensation *n* maono, hisi/kioja, shani; mhemko. **~al** *adj* -a kushtua, -a ajabu. **~al** *(of news papers)* -a vioja, -a mihemko. **~alism** *n* 1 nadharia (ya kifalsafa) isemayo kuwa dhana zote zatokana na michomo ya hisi. 2 utumiaji/uchokozaji wa mihemko. **~alist** *n* mpiga chuku.

sense *n* 1 *(perception)* hisi, fasili ya dhana akilini. **~-organ** *n* mlango wa hisi/fahamu *the ~ of smell, hearing, taste etc.* kunusa, kusikia, kuonja n.k. *pleasure of the ~s* anasa za mwili. 2 akili; busara *a man of good ~* mtu mwenye busara/akili nyingi *be out of ones ~s; lose one ~s* potewa na akili, rukwa na akili, fadhaika; *(faint)* zimia, zirai. **bring sb to her ~s** fanya mtu aache kufanya mabaya. **come to one's ~s** jirudi, acha kufanya upumbavu *recover one's ~s* jirudia, pata akili/fahamu tena. **have you taken leave of your ~s** una kichaa? 3 **(a/the)** ~ **(of)** kuthamini, kufahamu, kujua, kupambanua *he has moral ~* anapambanua mema na mabaya. 4 maana. **in a ~** kwa namna fulani. **in the ~ of** kwa maana ya kwamba *it has a bad ~* ina maana mbaya *in the legal ~* kisheria. **the figurative ~** -a tamathali. **make ~** fanya/leta maana, eleweka. **make ~ of sth** elewa maana. **talk ~** sema yenye maana. 5 maoni ya watu wengi *vt* hisi; tambua; fahamu, elewa. **~less** *adj* 1 pumbavu, -so akili; -sio na sababu. 2 -liozimia, -liozirai *he fell ~less* alizimia *become ~less* zimia, zirai *knock sb ~less* piga mtu mpaka azirai. **~lessly** *adv.* **~lessness** *n* upumbavu, upuuzi. **sensibility** *n* wepesi wa kuhisi. **sensible** *adj* 1 -a akili, tendaji, -a busara/hekima. 2 ~ **of** *(arch.)* -tambuzi. 3 *(arch.)* -a kuhisika. **sensibly** *adv.*

sensitive *adj* 1 -epesi kuhisi (kuona, kusikia, kunusa, kugusa, kuonja); *(issue)* nyeti. **the ~ plant** kifaurongo. 2 -epesi kuumia/kuathirika. 3 *(of instruments, institutions)* -a kuweza kuonyesha mabadiliko madogo-madogo. 4 *(of photographic film, paper)* -a kudhurika kwa mwanga. **sensitively** *adv.* **sensitivity** *n* kiwango cha hisi. **sensitometer** *n* kipima hisi. **sensitize** *vt* hisisha.

sensory *adj* -a fahamu ~ *nerves* neva fahamu.

sensual *adj* -a kupenda anasa/raha; tamanifu, -a ashiki. **sensualiasm** *n* upendaji anasa, utamanifu. **sensualist** *n* mpenda anasa, mkware. **sensuality** *n* kupenda anasa/matamanio, ashiki. **sensuous** *adj* -a hisi. **sensuously** *adv*. **sensuousness** *n*.

sent *pt, pp of* **send**.

sentence *n* 1 sentensi ~ *drill* jedwali (la mazoezi ya sentensi) ~ *patterns* sulubu/ruwaza za sentensi. 2 hukumu, fetwa. **pass/pronounce**~toa hukumu. 3 *(arch)* shauri, maoni *vt* hukumu, toa hukumu *he was ~d to death* alihukumiwa kifo/kunyongwa.

sententious *adj* 1 *(arch.)* -a -enye maneno ya akili. 2 *(mod. use)* - a kujifanya mwenye hekima, -a kujivuna; -a kuchosha **~ly** *adv*.

sentient *adj* -enye (uwezo wa) kuhisi.

sentiment *n* 1 mawazo, maono. 2 hisia za moyoni, pendo. 3 maoni, shauku *national* ~s maoni/hisia za taifa. **~al** *adj* 1 -epesi kuvutwa na upendo (huruma, ashiki), -a hisi za moyoni. 2 *(of things)* -a kuamsha/kuchochea hisi. **~ally** *adv*. **~alism** *n* 1 wepesi wa kuathiriwa na hisi za moyo. 2 kujitungia mawazo moyoni. **~ist** *n* mtu mwepesi kuathiriwa na hisi. **~ize** *vt, vi* athiri na hisi za moyoni. **~ity** *n* hali ya kuwa na/kuingiliwa na hisi vibaya.

sentinel *n see* **sentry** *stand ~ (over) (liter)* shika gadi.

sentry *n* askari wa zamu, gadi, mlinzi, mshika doria. **~-box** kibanda cha mlinzi. **on ~-go** *n* wajibu wa mlinzi kutembea mbele na nyuma akilinda.

sepal *n (bot)* sepali.

separable *adj* -a kutengeka, -a kugawanyika. **separably** *adv*. **separability** *n*.

separate *vt,vi* 1 ~ **from** tenga, tenganisha. ~ **sth (up) into** gawanya. 2 *(of a number of people)* achana, tengana, farakana. **separatist** *n* mpendelea ufarakano/utengano, mpenda kujitenga/utengano; mtenganishi mgawanyaji. **separator** *n* kigawaji; chombo cha kutenganisha (agh. krimu kutoka kwenye maziwa). ~ *adj* 1 -liotengwa; -liogawanyika. 2 -liotengana, mbali mbali, -moja -moja *n (trade use, pl)* mavazi yanayoweza kuvaliwa na mengine (agh. blauzi, shati n.k.). **~ly** *adv*.

separation *n* 1 utengano, kuachana, mfarakano, utenganisho. **judicial** ~ utenganishowakisheria/kimahakama ~ *agreement* mapatano ya kutengana. 2 kipindi cha utengano/ufarakano. 3 *(maths)* utengano ~ *by set* utengano wa seti. **separatism** *n* utengano; ubaguzi; hali ya mgawanyo.

sepia *n* 1 sipia: rangi ya kahawa. 2 maji meusi ya pweza.

sept,septi *(comb. forms)* saba. **~enary** saba, -a kuhusika na saba. **~angle** *n* pembe saba. **~angular** *adj* -a pembe saba. **~ennial** *adj* -a miaka saba, -a kila mwaka wa saba. **~et** *n* kundi la waimbaji wa sauti saba/ala saba za muziki.

September *n* Septemba, mwezi wa tisa.

septic *adj* -lioambukizwa; -a kuoza ~ *poisoning* kuoza kwa kidonda kutokana na bakteria. ~ **tank** tangi la maji machafu. **sepsis** *n* kuambukiza sumu ya kidonda kwenye damu. **~emia** *n* sumu katika damu.

septuagenarian *n (US)* mzee wa umri wa miaka kati ya sabini na sabini na tisa.

sepulchre *n* kaburi, (lililochongwa katika mwamba/lililotengenezwa kwa mawe). **The Holy ~** Kaburi la Yesu Kristo. **whited** ~ *n* mnafiki, mzandiki. **sepulchral** *adj* 1 -a kaburi (la mawe), -a mazishi. 2 -a huzuni kubwa, -a kuashiria mazishi.

sepulture *n* maziko.

sequel *n* 1 matokeo; mfuatano. **in the ~** baadaye, hatimaye. 2 mambo/ matukio ya baadaye (katika hadithi, yakihusiana na matukio ya awali).

sequence *n* mwandamano, mfuatano, utaratibu, mfululizo. ~ **of tenses** mfutano wa nyakati (katika vishazi) na kitenzi cha wakati. **sequent** adj (*formal*) -a kufuata, -a kuandama, -a kutokea; -a kutokana na. **sequential** *adj* -a kutokana na; -a kufuatana kwa wakati na mahala.

sequester *vt,vi* 1 *see* **sequestrate**. 2 tenga ~ *oneself* jitenga. **~ed** *adj (of places)* kimya, -liotengwa.

sequestrate *vt* 1 twaa mali ya mdaiwa kwa muda. 2 pora, nyang'anya. **sequestration** *n*. **sequestrator** *n*.

sequin *n* 1 puleki. 2 *(hist)* sarafu ya dhahabu iliyotumika Venice.

seraglio *n* 1 nyumba ya harimu. 2 harimu; *(hist)* Ikulu ya kiongozi wa Uturuki yenye maofisi ya serikali.

seraph *n (biblical)* serafi: (malaika wa daraja ya juu) *adj* kimalaika; -enye furaha na nzuri kama serafi. **~ic** *adj* -a kiserafi, -a malaika.

sere *adj see* **sear**.

serenade *n* muziki upigwao nje usiku (hasa kumwimbia mpenzi) *vt* chombeza, liwaza kwa wimbo. **~er** *n*.

serendipity *n* (kipaji cha) kubahatisha ugunduzi.

serene *adj* 1 -eupe, safi, -liotakata, bila mawingu. 2 tulivu, shwari *all* ~ mambo yote shwari. **~ly** *adv*. **serenity** *n*.

serf *n* mtwana/kijakazi. **~age** *n*. **~dom** *n* utwana; ujakazi.

serge *n* kitambaa cha sufu kigumu.

sergeant *n* sajini. **~-major** *n* sajini -meja.

sericulture *n* ufugaji wa nondo wa hariri; **sericultural** *adj*. **sericulturalist** *n* mfugaji wa nondo wa hariri.

series *n* mfuatano, mwandamano, mfululizo safu. **serial** *adj* -a sehemu ya;. -a mfululizo (wa maandishi) ~ *writer* mwandishi anayeandika mfululizo *n* 1 maandiko/matangazo ya kufululiza. **serially** *adv*. **serialize** *vt* chapisha kwa sehemu/mfululizo. **seriated** *adj* -liopangwa katika mfululizo (kwa sehemu zinazofuatana). **seriatim** *adv* mfululizo, kwenda sanjari, mojamoja, hatua kwa hatua, kaifa kwa kaifa.

seriocomic *n (of theatre arts)* mchezo wenye kuchekesha bila utani/mzaha.

serious *adj* 1 -zito, -siocheka. 2 -a maana -kubwa *a ~ offence* kosa kubwa. 3 -a kweli, -a kufikiria, -a dhati; makini *are you ~?* unasema kweli? 4 *(of illness)* -a hatari *a ~ illness* ugonjwa wa hatari. 5 *(of patient)* -enye hali mbaya, mahututi. **~ly** *adv*. **~ness** *n*. **in all ~ness** bila utani, kwa uzito kabisa.

serjeant *n* 1 wakili mkuu. **~-at-arms** msimamizi wa mahakama/bunge. 2 *(of arrest)* mshikaji.

sermon *n* 1 hotuba. 2 mahubiri. **~ize** *vt, vi* 1 hutubu, hubiri. 2 sema kama mhubiri.

serpent *n* nyoka *the Old S~* Ibilisi; *(fig)* ayari. **~-snake, ~-charmer** *n* mcheza nyoka, mjiriri (Kikwaya). **~ine** *adj* -enye mapindi, -a kupindikapindika (kama nyoka).

serrate(d) *adj* -a kukerezekakerezeka; -a menomeno; -liochongoka (kama msumeno).

serried *adj* -a kusongana, -a kusonganasongana, -a bega kwa bega.

serum *n (bio)* 1 majimaji ya damu. 2 chanjo ya dawa. **serous** *adj*.

serval *n* ngawa.

servant *n* mtumishi; hadimu. **domestic** ~ mtumishi wa nyumba. **civil** ~ mtumishi wa serikali. **public** ~ mtumishi wa umma. **your humble** ~ wako mtiifu.

serve *vt, vi* 1 tumikia, hudumia. 2 -wa mtumishi wa. ~ **on sth** -wa mjumbe wa. ~ **under sb** -wa jeshini chini ya. ~ **two masters** -wa na mabwana wawili. 3 ~ **sth (to sb)**; ~ **sb (with sth)**; ~ **sth (out)** gawa, hudumia *dinner is ~d* chakula tayari. 4 ~ **sb (for/as sth)** faa. ~ **for** faa mahali pa (badala ya) *this pen ~ me well* kalamu hii inanifaa. ~ **sb's needs/ purpose** kidhi haja/matakwa yake. **as occassion ~s** mara ipatikanapo fursa/ nafasi. 5 tendea. **it ~s her right** inamstahilia. 6 maliza muda/kipindi (cha kufanya kazi). 7 ~ **a sentence**; ~ **time** fungwa; maliza kifungo. 8 ~ **a summons/writ/ warrant on sb** *(leg)* pa samansi/hati za kisheria. 9 *(sports)* anzisha; pigia mpira. 10 *(of animals)* panda. 11 saidia, auni. 12 *(rel)* hudumia Misa. **~r** *n* 1 *(at a table)* mwandalizi. 2 *(tennis, volleyball etc)* mwanzisha mchezo. 3 mtumishi/ msaidizi kanisani. 4 trei ya vyombo. 5 vyombo vya chakula. **serving** *n* kiasi cha chakula apewacho mtu.

service *n* 1 (kazi ya) utumishi. **be in/go into/go out to** ~ ajiriwa kama mfanyakazi wa nyumbani. 2 uwasilishaji *personal* ~ kuwasilisha kwa mwenyewe *substitute* ~ kuwasilisha kwa badala. 3 *(use, employment)* manufaa *can I be of ~?* naweza kusaidia? 4 *(help)* fadhila, msaada. **do sb a** ~ saidia, auni. 5 huduma (za umma) *telephone* ~ huduma za simu. ~ **charge** gharama za huduma. ~ **road** ujia. 6 ibada, sala *divine* ~ ibada takatifu; fatiha, hitima. 7 *(sl) the ~s* uanajeshi. **on active** ~ jeshini. **the three ~s** jeshi la nchi kavu, jeshi la maji, jeshi la anga *quit the* ~ toka jeshini. **see ~ in sth** -wa jeshini *have seen (good)* ~ -liosaidia, -liotumikia. 8 *(of china etc)* seti ya vyombo vya chai. 9 uangalizi wa kitaalamu, ukaguzi. ~ **station** kituo cha petroli. **~-area** kituo cha petroli, vinywaji n.k. katika barabara kuu. 10 *(leg)* kutoa samansi. 11 *(sport)* kuanzisha mchezo *vt* 1 tengeneza na kutunza daima (baiskeli, meli, motokaa n.k.). 2 *(of animals)* panda. **~able** *adj* 1 -a kufaa, -enye manufaa. 2 -nayotumika, -gumu na -a kudumu. **~-line** *n* msitari wa kusevu (katika michezo kama mpira wa nyavu, tenesi n.k.). **~-pipe** *n* bomba la kupitishia (maji, hewa katika nyumba).

serviette *n* kipangusia mdomo.

servile *adj* 1 *(arch)* -a kitumwa, kinyonge. 2 nyonge, dhalili; barakala. **servility** *n*.

servitor *n (arch)* hadimu

servitude *n* utumwa.

servo *pref. (of machinery)* kidhibiti, sevo ~ *mechanism* mtambo-sevo ~- *motor* sevomota.

sesame *n* 1 ufuta ~ *oil* mafuta ya uto. 2 **open** ~ *(fig)* fungua!! *education is an open ~ to success* elimu ni ufunguo wa mafanikio.

sesquipedalian *adj* 1 -a silabi nyingi. 2 -a kuchosha; refu sana.

session *n* 1 kikao; baraza *be in* ~ -wa katika kikao. 2 *(US) (University)* muhula wa masomo.

sestet *n* mistari sita ya mwisho ya shairi.

sestina *n* shairi la beti sita la mistari sita sita.

set[1] *vt,vi* 1 tua, weka *the sun* ~ jua limetua *he ~ the load down* alitua mzigo ~ *the plate on the table* weka sahani mezani. 2 ~ **to/~ sth to sth** weka karibu, sogeza. ~ **the axe to** *(a tree)* kata (mti); *(fig)* haribu. ~ **fire/a match/(a) light-to** washa moto. ~ **pen to paper** anza kuandika *the farmers ~ to cultivating cotton* wakulima walianza kulima pamba. ~ **one's seal to sth**; ~ **the seal on sth** idhinisha, thibitisha ~ *forth/out on a journey* anza safari. 3 ~ **sb at his ease** fanya mtu ajisikie yuko nyumbani, ajisikie huru. **not/never ~ the world/Thames on fire** -sifanye maajabu. ~ **sb free/at liberty** achia uhuru. ~ **people at loggerheads/ variance** gombanisha. ~ **sth in order** panga vizuri. ~ **one's (own) house in order** *(fig)* jirekebisha kwanza kabla ya kukosoa. ~ **sb's mind at ease/ rest**; ~ **sb's doubts/fears/mind at rest** tuliza. ~ **sb's teeth on edge** sumbua, udhi, kera. ~ **sb right** *(fig)* kosoa mtu, onyesha njia, weka sawa; tia nguvu. ~ **sth/right/to rights** sahihisha, rekebisha (makosa). **be all ~ (for sth/to do sth)** -wa tayari. **be ~ on doing sth** dhamiria kufanya jambo. ~ **sb on his way** sindikiza. 4 anzisha, sababisha *the shadow ~ the dog barking* kivuli kilimsababisha mbwa kubweka his *joke ~ us laughing* masihara yake yalituchekesha. 5 weka, -pa ~ *the plate on the table* weka sahani mezani ~ *food before the guest* mpe mgeni chakula ~ *myself the task* jipa kazi ~ *eggs* weka mayai yaatamiwe. 6 ~ **(for)** tunga *they ~a difficult examination* walitunga mtihani mgumu. ~ **book** kitabu cha kiada/ kutahiniwa. ~ *(good) example* onyesha mfano mzuri. ~ **the fashion** anzisha mtindo. ~ **the pace/ stroke** rakibu mwendo. ~ **a thief to catch a thief** *(prov)* dawa ya moto ni moto. 7 *(with various grammatical objects)* ~ **against sth** pinga vikali. ~ **one's heart/hopes/mind on sth** pania kitu. ~ **eyes on sb** ona. ~ **one's face against** pinga. ~ **a price on sth** panga bei. ~ **a price on sb's head** toa zawadi ili kuuliwa mtu fulani. ~ **much/great/little/no store by sth** thamini/-tothamini kitu. 8 unganisha, rekebisha. ~**a watch** rekebisha saa. ~ **a broken bone** unganisha mfupa. ~ **a hen** weka ili aatamie. 9 ~ **hair** tengeneza nywele. ~ **a saw** noa msumeno. ~ **the scene** eleza mandhari. ~ **sail (from/to/for)** tweka tanga. ~ **the table** tandika meza. ~ **one's teeth** uma meno; *(fig)* dhamiria. ~ **a trap (for sth/sb)** tega/tegea. 10 ~ **sth in sth**; ~ **sth with sth** gongomea. 11 elekea, pata nguvu *the wind ~s eastward* upepo unaelekea matlai. 12 *(music)* ~ **sth (to sth)** tunga sauti ya wimbo/shairi. 13 *(plants, seed)* auka, zaa matunda. 14 *(of clothes)* kaa vizuri *this coat ~s well* koti hili linakaa vizuri. 15 ganda, *the cement is ~* saruji imeganda; *(of dog)* simama na kuashiria windo; *(of dancers)* simama kuelekea mwenzi wakati wa kucheza; *(rare) (of body etc)* komaa; kakamaa. 16 -a kulazimisha *a ~ smile* tabasamu ya kujilazimisha ~ *look* mtumbuo wa jicho ~ *purpose* nia thabiti; -liokwisha pangwa ~ *menu* menyu iliyokwisha pangwa; -siobadilika *he has ~ ideas* ana mawazo yasiyobadilika; -a kawaida ~ *prayers* sala za kawaida ~ *speech* hotuba iliyotayarishwa. 17 *(with adv particles and preps)* ~ **about sth** anza *we must ~ about solving the problems* lazima tuanze kutatua matatizo. ~ **about sth** *(colloq)* vamia, shambulia. ~ **sth about** eneza uvumi. ~ **one thing against another** oanisha. ~ **sb against sb** pambanisha. **sth apart/aside** weka akiba; puuza; *(leg)* futa. ~ **sth back** rudisha nyuma; -wa mbali na. ~ **sb/sth back** zuia; *(sl)* gharimu. ~**-back** *n* kipingamizi; *(sl)* gharama. ~ **sb down** shusha, teremsha abiria. ~ **sth down** shusha, weka chini; weka kwenye maandishi, andika. ~ **sb/ oneself down as** elezea/jieleza kama. ~ **down to sth** taja/eleza kuwa sababu ya. ~ **forth** anza safari. ~ **sth forth** tangaza. ~ **in** anza na elekea kuendelea; anza kuelekea. ~ **off** anza (safari, mbio n.k). ~ **sth off** lipua; tokea; fidia. ~ **sb off (doing sth)** chochea. ~ **on** songa mbele. ~ **on/upon sb** shambulia. ~ **out** anza (safari n.k). ~ **out to do sth** dhamiria, lenga, kusudia. ~ **sth out** eleza kinagaubaga; onyesha. ~ **sb over sb** mpa mtu madaraka. ~ **to** anza kufanya kitu/ugomvi. ~ **sth up** *vt* weka kitu mahala; asisi, jenga (chuo, shirika, hoja) ~ *up a statue* weka sanamu mahala. ~ **up an argument** jenga/andaa hoja. ~ **up** *n (colloq)* genge; njama, mpango *what is the ~ up here?* mambo yakoje, mnakaakaaje?; sababu *what has ~ up this confusion* vurugu hili limesababishwa na nini; piga yowe; andaa kuchapa ~ *up a book* andaa kitabu tayari kwa kuchapa. ~ **sb up** ponya, pa ahueni *exercises has ~ his physique up* mazoezi yamemrudishia mwili wake. ~ **(oneself) up as** jiingiza/jitangaza; taka kuwa; jidai ~ *onself up as a freedom fighter* jitangaza kuwa mpigania uhuru; jidai

~ *oneself up as* jidai kuwa. ~ **up house** anza kuishi nyumbani (badala ya kupanga). ~ **up house with sb/ together** anza kuishi pamoja. **be well ~ up** kaa vyema, jengeka, umbika *she has a well ~ up figure* ameumbika *be well ~ up with books* limbikiziwa/ jawa na vitabu.

set[2] *n* 1 seti *number ~* seti: (idadi ya) vitu vya aina moja. 2 kundi la (idadi ya) watu wanaoshirikiana/wenye mambo yanayofanana (k.m. vionjo, mapendeleo n.k.). 3 redio, televisheni n.k. 4 uelekeo; maelekeo/mwelekeo. 5 mkao: jinsi kitu/mtu anavyoonekana kiumbo; *(of clothes)* namna nguo zinavyomkaa/zinavyomchukua. 6 machweo. 7 kuashiria windo *make a dead ~ at* shambulia; jipendekeza. 8 mandhari ya filamu/mchezo. 9 chipukizi.

set-square *n* kiguni.

settee *n* kochi.

setter *n* 1 mbwa wa kuwindia. 2 *(in compounds)* mtu/kitu kinachounganisha kitu.

settle[1] *n* benchi ya kukalia, kiti kirefu.

settle[2] *vt,vi* 1 fanya makazi/koloni; lowea. 2 fanya makazi/ishi. 3 ~ **(on sth)** tua, tuama *the bird ~d on a branch* ndege alitua kwenye tawi. 4 *(decide)* hukumu, kata shauri (neno); amua, maliza *that ~s it!* tumeafikiana. 5 *(adjust)* patanisha, suluhisha ~ *out of court* patana nje ya mahakama. 6 sarifu ~ *property* sarifu mali. 7 *(of dust in the air)* tua, shuka; *(of a liquid)* tuama. 8 *(of the ground, foundation)* didimia. 9 *(with adverbial particles)*. ~ **down** pumzika/tulia. ~ **(sb) down** tuliza. ~ **(down) to sth** fanya kwa makini. ~ **down to married life; marry and ~ down** ishi maisha ya ndoa. ~ **for sth** kubali (kwa shingo upande). ~ **(sb) in** saidia mtu kuhamia kwenye nyumba, kazi mpya. ~**-in** zoea. ~ **sth on/upon sb** *(leg)* pa mtu (mali n.k.) kwa ajili ya matumizi. ~ **on/upon sth** chagua. ~ **up (with sb)** lipa deni. **have an account to ~ with sb** *(colloq)* -wa na kisa na fulani. **~d** *adj* 1 imara, thabiti, -tulivu, makini *a ~d country* nchi yenye amani; nchi iliyotengamana. 2 lio kwisha lipwa. **~ment** *n* 1 makazi, mji mpya; ulowezi 2 *(in heritance)* urithi, usia. 3 *(agreement)* mapatano, mwafaka, maafikiano, suluhu *amicable ~* mapatano ya hiari. 4 masarifu *family ~* masarifu ya familia *marriage ~* masarifu ya ndoa. **~r** *n* mlowezi,

seven *n* saba *a child of ~* mtoto wa umri wa miaka saba *adj* saba ~ *children* watoto saba. **~fold** *adj* mara saba *adv* kwa mara saba. **~teen** *n* kumi na saba *adj* -a kumi na saba. **~teenth** *adj* -a kumi na saba *n* kumi na saba. **~th** *adj* -a saba. **be in ~th heaven** jawa na furaha. **~th-Day** *adj* -a siku ya saba; -a Sabato/Jumamosi. **~thly** *adv* kwa saba. **~tieth** *adj* -a sabini *n* sehemu ya sabini. **~ty** *n* sabini *adj* -a sabini *she is ~* ana miaka sabini. **The ~ties** *n (pl)* miaka ya sabini.

sever *vt,vi* katika; *(fig)* kata; vunja; vunjika. **~ance** *n* kuvunjika; kutengana; kukatika.

several *adj* 1 kadhaa; baadhi ya ~ *of the people* baadhi ya watu ~ *boys* wavulana kadha wa kadha ~ *times* mara nyingi/kadha ~ *of us* baadhi yetu. 2 *(separable)* -moja -moja; kila -moja *each has his ~ points of view* kila mmoja ana maoni yake mbalimbali. **~ly** *adv* -mojamoja; kila mtu; *jointly and ~* kwa ubia na mbalimbali.

severe *adj* 1 -kali; -sio na huruma; -kalifu. 2 *(of style)* -futo, -a mfuto, bila urembo (pambo). 3 *(of weather, disease etc)* kali, baya. 4 -enye kuhitajia ustadi/uwezo/uvumilivu n.k. **~ly** *adv* kwa ukali. **be ~ ill** -wa mgonjwa mahututi. **severity** *n* 1 ukali. 2 uzito, nguvu, ukalifu.

sew *vi,vt* shona. ~ **in** kaza kwa uzi na sindano. ~ **up (sth)** funga kwa kushona; *(colloq)* panga, maliza *the deal is ~d up* mipango imemalizika. **~er** *n* mshoni. ~ *n* ushoni, mashono. ~ **machine** *n* cherahani. **~ing-press** *n* mashine ya kushonea vitabu.

sewage *n* maji machafu. ~ **system** utaratibu wa kuondoa maji machafu (kwa mfereji). **~-farm/works** karakana ya kusafisha/kushughulikia maji machafu.

sewer *n* mfereji wa uchafu; *(pl)* mifereji ya uchafu. **sewer gas** harufu chafu. **sewer rat** panya/buku wa miferejini. **sewerage** *n* utaratibu wa kuweka mifereji ya maji machafu.

sewn *pp of* **sew**.

sex *n* 1 jinsia; uke/ume *male* ~ jinsia ya kiume *female* ~ jinsia ya kike. 2 mapenzi. **~-maniac** *n* mkware. **~-appeal** *n* kuvutia kijinsia. 3 kujamiiana *have ~ with* jamiana na. **~less** *adj* 1 -so na jinsia. 2 *(frigid)* baridi. **~starved** *(colloq)* kutopata kujamiiana. **~y** *adj* *(colloq)* -a kuhusu mapenzi; a kuvutia kimapenzi. **~ism** *n* ubaguzi jinsia. **~ist** *adj*. ~ *adj* -a jinsia ~ *offences* makosa ya kinyumba ~ *pervert* asherati, kware **~ual intercourse** kuingiliana, ngono, kulalana, kujamiiana ~ *passion* nyege, ashiki, -goa ~ *organs (male)* sehemu za siri, mboo, uume, dhakari; *(female)* kuma, uke. **~uality** *n* 1 ujinsia. 2 ashiki.

sexagenarian *n adj* mtu wa umri wa miaka kati ya 59 na 70.

sextet(te) *n* mchanganyiko wa sauti/vyombo vya muziki/wachezaji sita.

sexton *n* mtunza kanisa pamoja na kiwanja.

shabby *adj* 1 chakavu, -liovaa malapulapu/midabwada. 2 baya *a ~ trick* hila mbaya. **shabbiness** *n* 1 ukuukuu; uchakavu. 2 ubaya. ~ **genteel** *adj* chakavu (lakini enye kujitahidi kuonyesha umalidadi). **shabbily** *adv*.

shack *n* banda *vi* ~ **up (with sb/ together)** *(sl)* ishi pamoja.

shackle *n* kiungo (cha pingu). *(pl)* **~s** pingu, silisili; *(fig)* kipingamizi *vt* 1 funga, pinga. 2. zuia, wekea mipaka.

shaddock *n (fruit)* furungu, balungi, pomelo *(tree)* mfurungu, mbalungi.

shade *n* 1 kivuli. **put sb/sth in/into the ~** zima; zika, dunisha. 2 giza, utusitusi. *(US)* ~ **tree** mti wa kuvuli. 3 mzimu, pepo *the ~s* makazi ya mizimu. 4 (kiasi cha) tofauti ndogo *a ~ of difference* tofauti ndogo *a ~ of colour* namna ya rangi. 6 *(of lamp)* chengeu *vt,vi* 1 tia kivuli, tia giza. 2 kinga jua mwanga. 3 *(of colour)* tia kivuli (kwa penseli n.k.), ingiana, oana. ~ **off (away)** badilika taratibu, fifia. **~d** *adj* 1 -liotiwa kivuli. 2 tiwa tabaka za rangi. **shading** *n* 1 kufanya kivuli. 2 utusitusi. 3 tofauti ndogo. **shady** *adj* 1 -a kivuli. 2 *(of action/ conduct)* -a hila; -si aminifu; -danganyifu; -erevu ~ *business* biashara/shughuli/jambo la hila; *(colloq) a ~ person* mtu laghai.

shadow *n* 1 kivuli. **coming events cast their ~s before them** dalili ya mvua ni mawingu. **be afraid of ones own ~** ogopa sana -wa mwoga sana. 2 giza. 3 *(illusion)* ndoto; wazo, njozi. 4 utusiutusi. **worn to a ~** amekonda sana. 5 mashaka, dalili *there is not a ~ of doubt* hakuna mashaka kabisa. 6 ingojeayo wakati wake ~ *factory* kiwanda kinachoweza kugeuzwa ili kutengeneza vifaa vya kivita inapobidi ~ *cabinet* baraza la mawaziri wa chama cha upinzani bungeni. 7 mwenzi *vt* 1 tia kivuli (giza). 2 fuata kwa siri, vizia. **~-boxing** *n* kufanya mazoezi kwa kumpiga ngumi mpinzani wa kufikirika/hewa. **~y** *adj* 1 -a kivuli, -a kinyenyezi; -sioonekana vizuri. 2 *(vague)* -siyo kiini, si hakika, si dhahiri.

shaft *n* 1 wano, mpini (wa mshale, mkuki); *(fig) ~s of envy/wit* kuonyesha husuda, kijicho. 2 gogo la kufungia punda, farasi n.k., nira. 4 shina. 5 shimo, dohani. **mine-~** shimo la mgodi. **ventilation ~**

dohani ya hewa. 6 *(tech)* mtaimbo *propeller* ~ mtaimbo endeshi. 7 mwale, mwanzi.

shag *n* tumbaku (iliyochambuliwa). **~gy** *adj* *(of hair)* -enye nywele za matimutimu. **~gily** *adv*. **~giness** *n*.

shake *vt,vi* 1 tikisa/tikisika, tetema/ tetemeka; tukuta, tingishika/tingisha. 2 tia shaka, dhoofisha, shtua ~ *sb's confidence* katisha tamaa/vunja moyo. 3 *(of voice)* tetema/tetemeka. 4 *(with preps and adverbials)* ~ **own** *(sl)* tapeli; *(colloq)* zoea (mazingira mapya); zoeana; pukusa/ pukutisha. **~down** *n* tandiko (la kwenye sakafu). ~ **sth from/out of sth** kung'uta kung'uta. ~ **sb off** kimbia/kwepa, poteza (mtu anayekufuata). ~ **sth off** ondoa, kung'uta; *(fig)* pona. ~ **out** *(mil)* sambaza, tawanya, tawanyika, sambaa *n* kupunguza wafanyakazi. ~ **sth out** tandaza kwa kukung'uta (k.m. kitambaa cha meza). ~ **sth up** changanya kwa kutikisa; rudisha katika hali ya awali (kwa kutikisa). ~ **sb up** shtusha mtu; changamsha. **shaking** *n* mtikiso, mshtuko. **~r** *n* mtikisaji/mshitushaji; chombo cha kutikisia chumvi, sukari n.k. *n* 1 mtikiso, msukosuko, tetemeko. 2 *(colloq)* muda. **in half a** ~ sasa/hivi. 3 *(pl)* **no great ~s** *(sl)* siyo nzuri sana *he's no great ~s as a driver* siyo dereva mzuri (yeye dereva mbaya). 4 **egg ~; milk** ~ *n* sharubati ya mayai/ maziwa. **shaky** *adj* 1 -a kutikisika, dhaifu, isoimara. 2 -sioaminika, -siosalama; -tojiweza. **shakily** *adv*. **shakiness** *n*.

shakespearian *adj* -a kuhusiana na **Shakespeare**.

shale *n* mwambatope *~-oil* mafuta ya mwambatope.

shall, should *aux v (to express future)* **I** ~ **go** -nitakwenda *you ~ go* utakwenda. 2 *(to express obligation)* lazima; lazimika *you ~/should go* huna budi kwenda. 3 *(in questions)* ~ **I go?** niende? 4 *(to express command) you ~/should not go there again* usiende kule tena; *(to express purpose/as a subjunctive equivalent)* weza. 5 *(to express expectation)* nadhani. 6 *(to express what is advisable)* -faa, -enye kufaa.

shallow *adj* 1 -a kina kifupi; *(fig)* -sio kweli, -a juu juu, -sio makini *n (pl)* maanga ~ *water* maji maanga *vi* punguka/punguza kina taratibu. **~ly** *adv*. **~ness** *n*.

shalt see **shall**.

sham *vt,vi* jifanya, jigeuza; iga; jisingizia *~ming dead* kufa uwongo ~ *sickness* jisingizia ugonjwa *adj* -a kuiga, -a uwongo, -bandia ~ *fight* vita ya kuigiza/mchezo wa vita *n* 1 mnafiki, mzandiki, laghai. 2 unaiki.

shamble *vi* enda kwa kukokoteza; jikokota *n* kukokoteza miguu.

shambles *n* 1 *(arch)* machinjioni; mahali pa kuuana; vurumai, mchafukoge *be in* ~ -wa katika hali ya vurumai, -wa shaghalabaghala.

shame *n* haya, soni, fedheha, tahayuri *it is a* ~ ni aibu *without* ~ bila haya. **for** ~ aibu! ~ **faced** *adj* -enye haya nyingi. ~ **facedly** *adv*. ~ **making** *adj* *(colloq)* 1 a kuaibisha wazee. 2 -a izara. **bring/heap** ~ **on someone** aibisha/fedhehesha/adhiri *n* 1 hizaya, fedheha, kujiaibisha. **cry** ~ **on sb** tangaza mtu kuwa mwanahizaya. 2 utwezo, jambo la aibu. **put sb to** ~ aibisha, fedhehesha. ~ **on you**! huna aibu, hebu ona aibu! mwana hizaya *vi,vt* aibisha, tahayari(sha), tia haya, fedhehesha. ~ **sb into doing sth** fanya mtu afanye kitu kwa kuogopa aibu. **~ful** *adj* -aaibu, -a kutahayarisha, -a kuaibisha. **~fully** *adv*. **~less** *adj* bila haya, -tovu wa haya, -kavu wa macho; pujufu *lead a ~less life* jipujua. **~lessly** *adv* kwa ukavu wa macho *act ~lessly* jipujua. **~lessness** *n* utovu wa haya; upujufu, uchafu.

shammy *n* ~ **(leather)** *see* **chamois**.

shampoo *vt* osha kwa shampuu (nywele, zulia n.k.) *n* shampuu; sabuni ya nywele *give sb a* ~

mwoshe mtu nywele.

shamrock *n* shamroki: mmea wenye vikonyo vya majani matatu; nembo ya *Ireland.*

shandy *n* shandi: mchanganyiko wa bia na soda.

shanghai *vt* 1 *(sl)* pora mtu kwa kumlevya ili kumfanya baharia. 2 laghai mtu (ili afanye kitu asicho penda).

shank *n* 1 muundi (wa mguu). **go on ~'s mare/ pony** enda kwa miguu. 2 mpini, kipini.

shan't *'shall not'.*

shanty[1] *n* kibanda (kwa kawaida cha mbao); kibanda cha muda tu. **~-town** *n* mtaa wa vibanda vibanda.

shanty[2] *n (U.S. Chantey) (naut)* hangamaji.

shape *n* 1 umbo, sura, tambo, muundo. **get/put sth into ~** panga kitu vizuri. **give ~ to** eleza kinaganaga. **take ~ in** jionyesha, jitokeza. **take ~** onekana, pata umbo. 2 **knock sth into/out of ~** weka kitu katika sura nzuri/mbaya. 3 hali *his business is in good ~* biashara yake iko katika hali nzuri. 4 kivuli, kitu/umbo (lisiloonekana vizuri). 5 kalibu; *(of hat)* faruma *vt,vi* 1 tengeneza, umba, unda; fanyiza. 2 pata umbo, kua, endelea. **~ up well** tumainiwa *things are shaping up well* mambo yanaendelea vizuri. **~less** *adj* -sio na umbo/sura nzuri; -sio nzuri. **~lessly** *adv*. **~lessness** *n*. **~ly** *adj* -zuri, -enye umbo la kupendeza.

shard, sherd *n* gae.

share[1] *n* 1 fungu, mgawo. **go ~s (with sb) (in sth)** gawana; kula bia, changa bia (na mtu fulani). 2 hisa. **deferred ~** hisa ya rajua. **distributive ~** hisa mgawanyo. **ordinary ~** hisa ya kawaida. **preference ~** hisa maalum. **~ certificate** *n* hati ya hisa. **~-cropper** *n* mkulima anayekodi shamba la mwinyi (na kutoa fungu la mazao yake kama kodi). **~holder** *n* mhisa. **~ list** *n* orodha ya hisa. **~ index** dira (ya bei za hisa). **~ pusher** *(colloq) n* mchuuza hisa *vt,vi* 1 gawa, gawana. **~ sth (out) (among/ between)** toa fungu kwa wengine; gawana. **~ sth with sb** gawana; gawia mtu. **~-out** *n* mgao. 2 **~ sth (with sb)** shirikiana, shiriki *~ a room with sb* kaa na mtu chumba kimoja *~ in sb's happiness* shiriki katika furaha ya mtu. **~ and ~ alike** gawana sawa.

share[2] *n* ulimi wa plau.

shark *n* papa. **~ oil** *n* mafuta ya papa. **~ skin** *n* 1 kitambaa laini. 2 ayari, laghai, mdanganyifu; mla riba.

sharp *adj* 1 -enye ncha kali, -liochongoka *a ~ needle* sindano yenye ncha kali. 2 wazi, dhahiri. 3 *(of slopes, corners, sounds, feelings)* kali *a ~ corner* kona kali *a ~ slope* mteremko mkali *a ~ sound* sauti kali *a ~ pain* maumivu makali *~ words* maneno makali. 4 *(quick)* -epesi kuona, -elekevu, hodari *a ~ student* mwanafunzi hodari *he is as ~ as a needle* ana akili sana. **~ shooter** *n* mpiga shabaha hodari (kwa bunduki). 5 *(bitter)* -chungu, -kali. 6 -danganyifu, -laghai *a ~ businessman* mfanyabiashara laghai *adv* 1 kamili *at eight o'clock ~* saa mbili kamili. 2 ghafla *turn ~ to the left* geuka kushoto ghafla. 3 *(music)* juu (kuliko inayotakiwa). 4 **look ~** harakisha; tahadhari. 5 **~ set** *adj* -enye njaa. **~en** *vt,vi* noa,tia makali, chonga; amsha.**~ener** *n* cherehe; kichongeo. **~ly** *adj*. **~ness** *n*. **~er** *n* ayari, mjanja, laghai, danganyifu. **card ~er** *n* laghai wa mchezo wa karata.

shat *pp of* **shit**.

shatter *vt,vi* vunjavunja, pondaponda, haribu haribu/ haribika kabisa.

shave *vi,vi* 1 ~ **(off)** nyoa *he does not ~ everyday* hanyoi kila siku *shaving brush* brashi ya kunyolea. **shaving cream** krimu ya kunyolea *shaving soap/stick* sabuni ya kunyolea. 2 **~ sth off** engua. 3 ambaa. **a close ~** kuwa karibu, kuponea chupuchupu. 4 **~n** *pp as adj* -lionyolewa *well ~n* -lionyolewa vizuri *n* kunyoa; unyoaji;

kuwa karibu *he had a narrow ~* aliponea chupuchupu. **~r** *n* 1 **(dry ~r)** mashine ya kunyolea. 2 *(colloq)* kijana mdogo. **~ling** *n (arch)* mtu aliyenyolewa; mtawa. **shavings** *n* takataka za mbao.

shawl *n* shali, kashida, mharuma.

she *pron* 1 yeye (mwanamke) *is the baby he or ~* ni mtoto wa kiume au wa kike *there ~ is*! huyo! *it is ~* ndiye. 2 *(as a pref)* -a kike, jike. **~ goat** mbuzijike, mbarika.

sheaf *n* 1 tita. 2 mganda (wa mikuki n.k.) *vt,vi* funga mganda. **~ binder** *n* kifungia mganda.

shear *vt* kata manyoya, nyoa (kondoo); *(fig)* nyima; vua *shorn of* poteza kabisa, nyolewa kabisa. **~s** *n* **(pair of) ~** mkasi mkubwa.

sheath *n* 1 ala, uo. **~ knife** kisu cha ala. 2 kifuko. **contraceptive ~** uo (wa kuzuia mimba), mpira, kondomu. 3 kibana mwili. **~e** *vt* 1 futika *~ the sword* futika upanga. 2 funika, zungushia. **~ing** *n* bomba la metali, mbao n.k. la kufunikia au kubandikiza (nje ya kitu).

sheaves *pl of* **sheaf** *n.*

shebang *n (sl)* nyumba, banda; jambo. **the whole ~** kila kitu, mambo yote.

shebeen *n* stoo bubu (hasa Ireland na Afrika ya Kusini); kilabu.

she'd *she had*; she *would.*

shed[1] *n* banda (la wanyama), zizi.

shed[2] *vt* 1 ambua, nyumbua *a snake ~ its skin* nyoka aliambua ngozi yake; pukusa *a tree ~ its* leaves mti ulipukusa majani yake. **~ (one's) blood** jeruhiwa, uawa; mwaga damu. **blood ~** umwagikaji wa damu. **~ tears** toa machozi. 2 toa, ondoa, vua. 3 eneza, tawanya *~ some light (fig)* toa mwanga.

sheen *n* mng'ao, kung'aa. **~y** *adj* -a kung'aa.

sheep *n* kondoo. **separate the ~ from the goats** tenga watu wema na wabaya *follow like a ~* fuata kama kondoo. **cast/make ~'s eyes at** kodoa/tumbua macho kimapenzi. **a wolf in ~'s clothing** chui aliyevaa ngozi ya kondoo. **as well be hanged for a ~ as a lamb** kama ni kula nguruwe basi chagua aliyenona. **~ dog** mbwa alindaye na kuchunga kondoo. **~-fold** zizi la kondoo. **~ hook** bakora ya mchunga kondoo. **~run** *(Australia)* malishoni. **~skin** *n* nguo iliyotengenezwa kwa ngozi ya kondoo; ngozi ya kujalidi; ngozi ya kuandikia mswada maalum; *(esp US)* diploma iliyoandikwa kwenye ngozi hiyo. **~-wash** *n* josho la kondoo. **~ish** *adj* 1 -enye haya. 2 -a kuona aibu, -a woga. **~ishly** *adv*. **~ishness** *n.*

sheer[1] *adj* 1 -tupu, tu *out of ~ malice* kwa nia ya kudhuru tu. 2 *(of textile)* -epesi, nyororo, laini. 3 -a kwenda juu, wima *adv* kabisa, moja kwa moja.

sheer[2] *vi* 1 **~ away/off** *(esp of ship)* kengeuka, enda upande; enda mrama. 2 **~ off** *(colloq)* ondoka, achana na.

sheet[1] *n* 1 shuka; shiti. 2 *(of paper)* karatasi *as white as a ~* eupe kama karatasi; *(of ice, iron, glass)* bamba. 3 eneo la maji/mvua theluji nyingi *the rain came down in ~s* mvua ilinyesha kwa wingi. 4 *(compounds)* **~-erosion** *n* mmomonyoko tandavu. **~-lightning** *n* umeme-tandavu. **~ing** *n* kitambaa cha kutengeneza mashuka.

sheet[2] *n* demani. **~-anchor** *n (usu fig)* kimbilio/tegemeo la mwisho.

sheik(h) *n* shehe, shekhe. **~dom** *n* ushehe.

shekel *n* 1 shekeli: sarafu ya kiyahudi ya zamani. 2 *(pl)* **~s** utajiri.

shelf *n* 1 rafu *on the ~* -lioachiwa, -liowekwa pembeni; *(colloq) (of a woman)* -liyepita umri wa kuolewa. 2 *(of a rock)* mwamba.

shell *n* 1 *(of fruit, nuts etc)* kaka, ganda. 2 *(of marine animals)* kombe, kauri, simbi, koa. **go/retire into one's ~** -wa msiri/mkinga; -wa na aibu, nyamaza. **come out of one's ~** changamka; ondoa aibu. **~-fish** *n* samakigamba, samaki wa magome. 3

gofu,kiunzi, bupuru. 4 mashua ya mashindano inayoendeshwa kwa makasia. 5 (*US* **cartridge**) risasi, kombora. **~-proof** *adj* -siopenya risasi. **~-shock** *n* kurukwa akili; wehu/kichaa kinachotokana na mshindo wa risasi *vt,vi* 1 bambua, ambua, menya. 2 tupa/rusha kombora. 3 ~ **out** *(colloq)* gharamia, lipia, lipa.

she'll *abbr she will, she shall.*

shellac *n* sandarusi *vt* paka sandarusi.

shelter *n* 1 kimbilio, hifadhi. 2 kinga mahali pa kujisetiri (agh. banda) *vt,vi* ~ **(from)** 1 funika, linda, hifadhi. 2 jificha, jilinda, jikinga *take ~ from rain* jificha mvua.

shelve[1] *vt* 1 panga/weka (agh. vitabu) katika rafu. 2 *(fig) (of problems, plans)* ahirisha, weka kando. 3 uzulu, toa/ achisha mtu kazi.

shelve[2] *vi (of land)* inamia, telemkia (kwa taratibu).

shepherd *n* mchunga kondoo *~'s crook* fimbo ya mchungaji. **~'s pie** pai ya viazinyama. **the Good ~** Yesu Kristo. **~'s plaid** kunguru wa rangi nyeusi na nyeupe *vt* 1 chunga. 2 ongoza (safari n.k.). **~ess** *n* mchunga kondoo wa kike; mwanamke mchungaji.

sherbert, sherbet *n* sharubati.

sheriff *n (US)* liwali. **~dom** *n* 1 usharifu. 2 uliwali.

sherry *n* sheri *~ glass* gilasi ya sheri.

she's *abbr. she is; she has*

shibboleth *n* 1 neno/ishara/desturi ya uanachama wa kikundi. 2 mila iliyoachwa *the ~s of the past are no longer valid* ya kale hayapo.

shield *n* 1 ngao. 2 *(of person) (fig)* kinga, mlinzi. 3 *(of machinery)* ngao, kinga *vt* linda, kinga *~ from* kingia, zuilia.

shift[1] *vt,vi* 1 ~ **sth (from/to)** hamisha, sogeza, hamia, sogea *~ to somewhere else* hamia mahali pengine. **~ one's ground** badilisha msimamo/ mtazamo. 2 badili, ghairi; *(motoring)* badilisha gia. 3 ~ **for oneself** jitegemea. **~y** *adj* -danganyifu, -a hila, -a kigeugeu *a ~ customer* mteja mwenye kigeugeu. **~ly** *adv*. **~iness** *n*.

shift[2] *n* 1 zamu, shifti *work in ~* fanya kazi kwa zamu. 2 kubadilisha nafasi; mabadiliko. 3 hila, ujanja maarifa (ya kuepa/kupata kitu). **make ~ (with sth/to do sth)** jitahidi, tumia maarifa, weza (kwa kila hali/njia). 4 shifti: gauni isiyo na marinda. 5 **(gear) ~** *n* kibadilisha gia, mkono wa gia. **~less** *adj* -zembe, -vivu, -siojimudu.

shilling *n* shilingi *take the queen's ~* -jiandikisha kuwa askari.

shilly-shally *vi* sitasita, yumbayumba *adj* - a kusitasita, -a kuyumbayumba *adv* kwa kusitasita *n* kusitasita, kuyumbayumba.

shimmer *vi* meremeta *n* mmeremeto. **~y** *adj*.

shin *n* muundi. **~guard** kinga ya muundi *vi* ~ **up** panda, paramia.

shinding *n* 1 *(sl)* sherehe ya vifijo/ shamrashamra. 2 ghasia, vurumai.

shindy *n (colloq)* ghasia, tandabelua *kick up a ~* fanya ghasia.

shine *vi* ng'aa, waka, angaza, mulika, waa; *(colloq)* ng'arisha (viatu n.k.) *n (sing only)* rangi ya viatu; mng'ao, uangavu *come rain or ~* inyeshe isinyeshe; *(fig)* lolote liwalo na liwe. **shiny** *adj* -liong'arishwa, -a kung'aa.

shiner *n* ngeu ya jicho.

shingle[1] *n* mbwe. **shingly** *adj* -a mbwe.

shingle[2] *n* 1 kiezekeo (cha kibao). 2 *(US colloq)* ubao (wa tangazo) *vt* 1 ezeka kwa kiezekeo/kibao.

shingles *n* ugonjwa wa vipele (agh. kiunoni).

shinto *n* Shinto; dini asili ya Wajapani.

ship *n* meli, merikebu, chombo *take ~* ingia chomboni *merchant ~* meli ya shehena. **war ~** *n* manowari. **passenger ~** meli ya abiria. **when my ~ comes home** nitakapotunukiwa bahati/nikitajirika. **the ~ of the desert** ngamia. **on ~-board** chomboni/melini; *(colloq)* chombo cha angani; *(US colloq)* eropleni. 3 *(compounds)* **~-breaker** *n* kontrakta anayenunua meli mbovu na kuzibomoa. ~**broker** *n* wakala wa meli. ~-**builder** *n* muunzi (wa meli). ~-**canal** mfereji (wa kuweza kupitisha) meli. ~**'s chandler** mfanyabiashara wa vifaa vya meli. ~-**load** shehena/abiria wa kujaza meli. ~**mate** *n* baharia-mwenzi. ~-**owner** *n* mwenye meli/tajiri wa meli. ~-**shape** *adj*, sawasawa, barabara, taratibu, safi. ~-**way** *n* eneo la kuingilia meli baharini. ~**wreck** *n* maangamizi ya meli baharini *vi* angamiza meli baharini. ~-**wright** *see ~-builder*. ~-**yard** *n* kiwanda cha meli *vt,vi* 1 sheheni, peleka shehena; *(comm)* peleka mzigo kwa reli/barabara. ~ **off** peleka ~ *off young men to war* peleka vijana vitani. 2 ~-**oars** toa makasia majini na kuyaweka chomboni. ~ **water;** ~ **a sea** jaa maji chomboni 3 ajiri baharia. ~**ment** *n* upakiaji wa shehena melini; shehena. ~**per** msafirishaji shehena. ~**ping** *n* meli zote za nchi. ~ **agent** *n* wakala wa meli. ~-**office** *n* ofisi ya wakala wa meli; ofisi ya mabaharia.

shire *n* mkoa. ~ **horse** farasi wa kuvuta mkokoteni.

shirk *vt* kwepa, tega. ~ **school** tega shule. ~**er** *n* mtegaji.

shirt *n* 1 shati. **in one's** ~-**sleeves** bila koti; -siovaa koti. **keep one's** ~ **on** *(sl)* jizuia, -tokasirika, tuliza hasira. **put one's** ~ **on** *(a horse etc.) (sl)* pinga kwa chochote ulichonacho. ~-**front** *n* upande wa mbele wa shati; ~-**waist** *n* blauzi. ~**ing** *n* kitambaa cha shati. ~**y** *adj (sl)* -lioghadhibika.

shish kabab *n* mshikaki.

shit *vt (vulg)* -nya. ~ **on sb** *(vulg sl)* tukana, chamba; ripoti (mtu) polisi *n (not in polite use)* 1 kinyesi, mavi. 2 *(sl)* bangi. 3 upuuzi. 4 upumbavu, ubwege *I dont give a* ~ sijali kabisa.

shiver[1] *vt* vunja vipande vipande, vunja kabisa *n* vipande vipande.

shiver[2] *vi* 1 tetemeka, gwaya *n* kitapo, mtetemo *have the ~s* tetemeka *it gave me the ~s* ilinitetemesha, iliniogofya. 2 *(pl)* **get/have/give sb the** ~**s** *(colloq)* tetemeka, ogopa; tetemesha, ogofya. ~**y** *adj*.

shoal[1] *n* 1 *(of sea)* sehemu ya kina kifupi. 2 *(pl fig)* hatari zilizosetirika/ zilizofichama *vi* pungua kina.

shoal[2] *n* kundi la samaki, usheha *vi* fanya kundi.

shock[1] *n* 1 tita kubwa (la ngano).

shock[2] *n* vunga. ~-**headed** *adj* -enye vunga/nywele matimtimu.

shock[3] *n* 1 shindo, tetemeko; shambulio kali. ~-**absorber** shokomzoba. ~-**tactics** mashambulizi ya askari/ nguvu nyingi (katika vita); *(fig)* matumizi ya nguvu/maneno makali ghafla (ili kufikia lengo). ~-**troops** kikosi cha mashambulio makali. ~-**brigade;** ~-**workers** *(USSR)* wafanyakazi wa mitulinga. ~**wave** wimbi la kishindo/kiatomiki. 2 *(of electricity)* mrusho, mshtuo. 3 mshtuko *I was ~ed to hear* nilishtuka kusikia. ~**treatment/therapy** tiba ya kushtua neva kwa umeme (au dawa) *vt* shtua. ~**er** *n* 1 mtu anayeshtua/ ogofya. 2 kitu kinachoshtu(sh)a/ ogofya. ~**ing** *adj* 1 -a kuchukiza; -baya sana. 2 -a kushtua/ kutisha. ~**ingly** *adv* 1 vibaya mno. 2 vibaya sana, mno, kabisa.

shod *see* **shoe** *v*.

shoddy *n* 1 kitambaa cha nyuzi kukuu/ duni. 2 kitu hafifu/duni *adj* hafifu, duni, -a bandia. **shoddily** *adv*. **shoddiness** *n*.

shoe *n (often pair of ~s)* 1 kiatu. **dead man's** ~ mali ya urithi. **be in/put oneself in sb's** ~**s** -wa kama/jifanya mtu fulani; chukua nafasi ya mtu mwingine; jifikiria/fikiria kuwa katika nafasi ya mtu fulani. **know where the** ~ **pinches** siri ya mtungi aijuaye kata. **that's where the** ~ **pinches**! hapo ndipo penye matatizo. 2 **(horse)**~ kiatu cha farasi. 3 *(compounds)* ~ **black** *n* mpiga viatu rangi. ~-**buckle** *n* bizimu ya kiatu. ~**horn** *n* kivalia viatu. ~ **lace** *n* gidamu. ~-**leather** *n* ngozi ya viatu.

~ **maker** *n* fundi/mshona viatu. ~ **string** *n* *(U.S)* gidamu. **do sth on a ~ string** fanya jambo (k.m. kuwekeza) kwa mtaji mdogo. ~ **tree** kibao cha kiatu. **live on a ~ string** *(fig)* sukuma wiki, ishi kwa fedha chache tu. 4 kipande cha breki *vt* 1 valisha viatu. ~ **with iron** tia njumu.

shone *pp of* **shine** *v.*

shoo *int* shi! shi! sauti ya kuwingia ndege *vt* winga (ndege). ~ **sth/sb away off** fukuza.

shook[1] *pt of* **shake** *v.*

shook[2] *n* 1 sehemu za kitu (ambazo hazijaunganishwa). 2 matita ya nafaka shambani.

shoot *vi,vt* 1 vurumisha, vurumuiza, tupa (kwa nguvu). ~ **a glance at sb** tupia mtu jicho. ~ **a bolt** funga komeo. ~ **one's bolt** fanya jaribio la mwisho. ~ **dice** rusha dadu. *(sl)* ~ **rubbish** tupa/mwaga takataka. ~**ing star** *n* kimwondo. 2 ~ **up** panda sana, ruka *prices shot up last month* bei zimepanda mwezi uliopita. 3 *(of plants)* chipua, mea. 4 *(of pain)* choma, shambulia ghafla *pain shot up my leg* maumivu yamenipata mguuni. 5 *(of boats)* pita kasi *he shot by me on the road* alinipita kwa kasi barabarani. 6 piga risasi/mzinga/upinde *he shot an elephant* alipiga tembo risasi *he was shot three times in the leg* alipigwa risasi tatu mguuni. ~ **away** anza na kuendelea kupiga risasi/kutupa mishale n.k.; *(fig)* takadamu, anza. ~**/get sth away** tapanya, sambaza, ondosha; maliza. ~ **sth down** tungua *the soldiers shot down the plane* wanajeshi waliitungua ndege. ~ **sth off** kwata (kwa risasi). ~ **a covert/an estate** winda (shambani). ~ **a line** *(US sl)* ongopa, danganya, tia chumvi. ~ **one's mouth off** *(US sl)* payuka, ropoka. ~ **a place up** *(US sl)* tisha; chachafya kwa risasi na mizinga. ~**ing** *n* haki ya kuwinda; eneo la kuwind(i)a. ~**-box** banda la wawindaji. ~**-gallery** *n* mahali pa mazoezi ya kupiga bunduki. ~**-party** *n* kundi la wawindaji. ~**-range** *n* upigaji shabaha. ~**-stick** *n* kiti cha mwindaji: fimbo ya mwindaji ambayo pia hutumika kama kiti. ~ **war** vita hasa. 7 toa maelekezo/utaratibu wa kupiga filamu (za senema). 8 piga filamu. 9 *(in sports)* piga shuti *n* 1 chipukizi. 2 maporomoko ya mto. 3 mahala pa kuwindia; kundi la wawindaji. ~**er** *n* *(in compounds)* bastola. **six-~** bastola yenye risasi sita.

shop *n (US store)* 1 duka, **chemist's ~** duka la madawa. **come/go to the wrong ~** *(colloq)* potea, -topata mtu wa kutoa msaada uliotarajiwa; fika/enda mahali pasipofaa/kwa mtu asiyefaa (ili kupata msaada). **keep ~** uza duka, fanya kazi dukani. **keep a ~** -wa na duka. **set up ~** anzisha/fungua duka, biashara ya rejareja. ~ **assistant** *n* mwuza duka. ~**-bell** *n* kengele ya duka. ~**-boy/girl** *n* msaidizi, kijana wa duka. ~ **front** mbele ya duka ~**-hours** *n* saa za mauzo. ~ **keeper** *n* mwenye duka. ~**-lift** *vi,vt* iba vitu dukani. ~**-lifter** *n* mwizi wa vitu dukani. ~ **lifting** wizi wa/kuiba vitu dukani. ~**-soiled/ worn** *adj* -liochakaa (kwa kukaa sana). ~ **walker** *n* mwelekezaji (katika duka kubwa). ~ **-window** *n* dirisha la kuonyesha bidhaa. **put all one's goods in the ~ window** *(fig)* toa/onyesha kila ulichonacho/ujuacho; jionyesha. 2 kazi, weledi, utaaluma. **talk ~** zungumzia mambo ya kazi. **shut up ~** *(colloq)* acha kufanya jambo. 3 kiwanda, karakana. ~**-steward** *n* mjumbe wa wafanyakazi kiwandani. **closed ~** mfumo wa uanachama wa lazima kazini. 4 **all over the ~** *(sl)* shelabela, bila mpango, ovyoovyo, kila mahali, mahali pote *vi,vt* 1 enda dukani, fanya ununuzi. ~ **around** *(sl)* enda huku na huko kutafuta bei nafuu. 2 ~ **on sb** *(sl)* shtaki mtu. ~**ping** *n* ununuzi dukani. ~**-centre** *n* madukani, mahali penye maduka mengi. **window** ~ *n* kutazama vitu dukani (bila kununua). **~per** *n* mnunuzi, mteja.

shore[1] *n* 1 pwani, ufuko *on (to, at, near) the* ~ pwani *go on* ~ shuka pwani. **off** ~ mbali na pwani ~ *leave* ruhusa ya kushuka pwani/kutoka melini. **~less** *adj* -sio na pwani/ ufuko. **~ward** *adj* -a kuelekea pwani *adv* kwa kuelekea pwani.

shore[2] *n* gadi, shikizo, makwa *vt* ~ **sth up** gadimu, shikiza.

shore[3], **shorn** *see* **shear**.

short[1] *adj* 1 *(opp of long, tall)* -fupi *a ~ while ago* muda mfupi uliopita ~ *steps* hatua fupi. **a ~ cut** njia ya mkato. ~ **circuit** *n* kosa/shoti/mkato wa umeme *vt,vi* fupisha, pata shoti; *(fig)* fupisha, rahisisha (utaratibu). **~list** *n* orodha (fupi) teule *vt ~ list* fupisha orodha (ya majina ya waombaji). **~lived** *adj* -liodumu/ishi muda mfupi. **a ~ range** *(of plans)* -a muda mfupi; *(of missiles)* -a masafa mafupi. **have a ~ temper** -wa na harara, -wa mwepesi kukasirika; kuwa na hasira za haraka. ~ **tempered person** mtu mwenye harara. **~term** -a muda mfupi *~term loan* mkopo wa (kulipwa kwa) muda mfupi. 2 chache, pungufu, adimu *sugar is in ~ supply these days* siku hizi sukari imeadimika. *the workers are on ~ time* wafanyakazi wanafanya kazi kwa saa chache kwa siku. **~change** rudisha chenji pungufu. **~-change sb** danganya mtu (kwa kumrudishia chenji pungufu). **be ~ of** pungukiwa na; -wa mbali na *the tyre burst when we were still ten km ~ of our home* gurudumu lilipasuka km kumi kutoka nyumbani. **little/nothing ~ of** kama *it was little ~of a miracle* ilikuwa kama mwujiza. **make ~ work of** shughulikia haraka, fanya chapuchapu. ~ **of breath** kuhema, kutapia hewa! ~ **coming** *n* kushindwa (kufikia lengo/ kiwango kilichowekwa); dosari, kasoro. ~ **drink** *n (or colloq)*; **a ~** pegi ya kinywaji kikali, wiski, jini n.k.. ~ **handed** *adj* -enye wasidizi wachache. **~sight** *n* kutoona mbali; *(fig)* ujinga, kutofikiria mambo ya wakati ujao. ~ **sighted** *adj* -sioona mbali; *(fig)* -tofikiria mambo ya wakati ujao. ~ **winded** *adj* -enye kuishiwa na pumzi haraka; -a kutweta. 3 *(in comm)* -enye kupevuka/kukomaa haraka. ~ **dated** *adj* -enye kupevuka baada ya muda mfupi. **~term capital** *n* mtaji wa muda mfupi. 4 *(of a person)* msema maneno machache; kusema kwa ufupi *the answer was ~* jibu lilikuwa fupi/la mkato. **for ~** kwa kifupi *Joseph is called 'Joe' for ~* Joseph huitwa Joe kwa kifupi. **in ~** kwa kifupi/muhtasari. **the long and the ~ of it** mambo yote yapaswayo kusemwa kwa jumla. 5 *(of cake, pastry)* -a kuvunjika kwa urahisi. ~ **pastry** *n* (kinyunya) chenye siagi nyingi. ~ **bread/cake** mkate/keki yenye siagi nyingi. 6 *(of vowels syllables)* fupi ~ *vowel* irabu fupi. 7 *(compounds)* ~ **fall** pungufu. ~ **hand** hati mkato. **by a ~ head** *(racing)* kwa kichwa/kitambo kisichozidi urefu wa kichwa cha farasi; *(fig)* kwa kiasi kidogo tu. ~ **horn** ng'ombe wa pembe mzingo/pinde. ~ **wave** *(radio, telegraphy)* masafa mafupi; (kati ya mita 10 na 100). **~ly** *adv* 1 mara moja; punde. 2 kwa ufupi, kwa mkato, kwa makali. **~ness** *n adv* 1 (kwa) ghafla, mara *stop ~* simama ghafla. **bring/pull/take sb up~** ingilia mtu ghafla. ~ **of** isipokuwa *they stole all the cattle ~ of the sick ones* waliwaiba ng'ombe wote isipokuwa wagonjwa tu. 2 kabla ya wakati wake (wa kawaida); kinyume cha matarajio. **come/fall ~ of** -wa pungufu ya (matarajio) *the production fell ~ of the manager's expectations* uzalishaji ulikuwa pungufu ya matarajio ya meneja **cut sth/sb ~** ingilia kati, katiza, fupisha; punguza. **go ~ (of)** kosa, -tokuwa na, pungukiwa,wa bila *you will go ~ of* *school fees* utakosa karo. **run ~ (of)** ishiwa, kaukiwa *the school's provisions ran ~* shule iliishiwa chakula. **be taken ~** *(colloq)* harisha gafla. 3 **sell ~** *(comm)* uza (bidhaa hewa/isiyokuwepo) mapema kwa matarajio ya kununua kwa bei nafuu baadaye. **sell sb ~** saliti, danganya; dhalilisha. **~age** *n* upungufu, uhaba; uchache *there is a ~ of rice* kuna upungufu wa mchele. **~en** *vt,vi* punguza, fupisha, -wa fupi, punguka. **~ening** *n* mafuta ya kukaanga kinyunya.

shorts *n (pl)* **a pair of ~** kaptura, suruali kipande, bombo.

shot *n* 1 mlio, mwaliko (wa bunduki, mzinga, bastola). **(do sth) like a ~** (fanya) mara bila kusita/kujali, haraka. **off like a ~** kwa mwendo mkali, haraka sana *he was off like a ~* alichomoka mbio. 2 jaribio la kupiga kitu/kufanya jambo, kujaribu kujibu swali; *(in football)* shuti. **a ~ in the dark** kubahatisha; bahati. **have a ~ (at sth)** jaribu kufanya jambo. **a long ~** jaribio la kufumbua jambo pasi kuwa na data/ushahidi wa kutosha. **not by a long ~** hata kama hali ingeruhusu; hata kidogo. 3 risasi, kombora. **~put** tufe. 4 **lead ~** marisau. **~gun** bunduki ya marisau. **~ proof** siopenya risasi 5 mpigaji (wa bunduki, picha n.k.). 6 picha *long ~* picha -liyopigwa kutoka mbali. 7 *(US)* sindano ya dawa. **give/get/have sb a ~ in the arm** piga mtu sindano; -pa mtu uwezo wa kufufua kitu mathalani uchumi. 8 **a big ~** *(slang)* mkubwa, kizito agh. anayejivuna. **~ n** sehemu ya gharama/wajibu (wa mtu).

should *see* **shall**.

shoulder *n* 1 bega, fuzi. **put one's ~ to the wheel** fanya kazi kwa bidii. **~ to ~** *(fig)* bega kwa bega. **stand head and ~ above (others)** zidi sana (kwa urefu, akili, uadilifu n.k.). **straight from the ~** *(fig, of rebukes, criticism)* bila kuficha, waziwazi. **~ blade** *n* jembe, mtulinga. 2 mabega, mgongo. **have broad ~s** weza kubeba mzigo mzito; *(fig)* weza kuchukua madaraka makubwa. **~-belt** *n* mkanda wa begani. **~-high** *adj* -a usawa wa bega. **the snow was ~-high** theluji ilifika mabegani. **~-strap** *n* ukanda wa bega, mikanda inayo shikilia vazi begani *vt* 1 chukua mabegani *~ a burden/the responsibility/*beba mzigo/madaraka. **~ arms** *(mil)* sogeza bunduki ikae wima mbele ya mkono wa kuume. 2 sukuma kwa bega, piga kikumbo.

shout *n* ukelele, yowe, unyende *vi,vt* 1 **~ out** piga kelele. 2 paaza sauti. **~ at sb** pigia mtu kelele. **~ with laughter** cheka kwa sauti kubwa. **~ sb down** zomea, pigia kelele ili asisikike, zima. **~er** *n* mpiga kelele. **~ing** *n* kupiga kelele. **it's all over but/bar the ~ing** mapambano yote yamekwisha (kilichobaki ni maneno vifijo/hoihoi tu).

shove *vt,vi (colloq)* sukuma, kumba, piga kikumbo, bimbirisha. **~ off** anza kuondoka ufukoni (ukiwa ndani ya mashua); *(fig)* ondoka mahali (kwa fujo) *push and ~ each other* sukumana, buburushana. **~ aside** sukuma kando kwa nguvu *n* kumbo, kikumbo.

shovel *n* sepetu, beleshi, koleo *vt* 1 chota, beba kwa beleshi. 2 ondoa/safisha kwa beleshi, pakua *~ food into one's mouth* bwakia. **~ -ful** *adj* koleo tele.

show *n* 1 kuonyesha. 2 maonyesho. **on ~** -a maonyesho; maonyeshoni. 3 *(colloq)* burudani, tamasha. **~ business** *(colloq)* **~ biz** biashara/shughuli ya burudani. 4 *(colloq)* jambo, kitendo *put up a good ~* fanya jambo vizuri, jitahidi, anisi *a poor ~* jambo lililoborongwa. **steal the ~** vutia watu wote *good ~!*; safi! *(colloq)* shughuli; biashara; *Juma is running the ~* Juma anaendesha biashara hii. **give the (whole) ~ away** fahamisha watu mambo yote yanayofanywa au yaliyopangwa kufanywa. 5 *(sing only; dated colloq use)* nafasi, fursa ya (kujitetea) *he was given a fair ~* alipewa fursa ya kujitetea. 7 sura, hali, dalili *he did not offer a ~ of resistance* hakuonyesha upinzani. 8 maringo, ushaufu, kujionyesha *he's fond of ~* anapenda kujionyesha. *(compounds)* **~boat** mashua/merikebu ya tamthilia. **~-case** *n* sanduku la maonyesho; *(fig)* nafasi ya kuonyesha/kutangaza (agh. kitu kipya). **~-down** *n* kuonyesha/kutangaza nguvu/dhamira ya mtu; kupeana ukweli. **~-girl** *n* mwanamke mchezaji. **~jumping** onyesho la ustadi wa kuruka viunzi kwa farasi. **~ man** *n* msimamizi wa/msimamia mipango (katika tamasha); mtafuta sifa (kwa kujitangaza). **~ manship** kujitangaza; uhodari wa kuvutia watu. **~place** sehemu ya utalii. **~-room** *n* chumba cha maonyesho (ya biashara ambamo sampuli za bidhaa huwemo). **~-window** n dirisha la kuonyesha bidhaa. **~y** *adj* shaufu, -a fahari, limbwende, -enye kuvutia. **~ily** *adv.* **~iness** *n* *vt,vi* 1 **~ sth (to sb); ~ sb sth** onyesha. 2 -onekana *his delight ~ed in his face* furaha yake ilionekana usoni pake. 3 **~ itself** jitokeza, onekana. **~ oneself** hudhuria (mkutano, sherehe n.k.). **~ one's face** tokea hadharani/mbele za watu. **~ fight** onyesha (dalili za) kuwa tayari kupigana. **~ one's hand/cards** *(fig)* tangaza/dhihirisha nia ya mtu. **~ a leg** *(colloq)* toka kitandani. **~ one's teeth** *(fig)* onyesha hasira, ghadhibika. **have nothing to ~ for it/sth** -tokuwa na ushahidi wa kitu alichopata au alichojaribu kupata. **~ mercy on sb** onea huruma mtu. 4 elekeza **~ sb in/into sth/out/out of sth** elekeza mtu njia ya kuingia/kutokea. **~ sb over/around/round, sth** tembeza, zungusha mahala. **~ sb the door** amuru mtu aondoke na msindikize hadi mlangoni. **~ sb the way** eleza mtu njia ya kufuata; *(fig)* onyesha mfano. 5 fanya wazi; hakikisha; elewesha. 6 **~ sb/sth off** onyesha kitu (ili uzuri wake utokeze vizuri). **~ off** onyesha/tangaza (utajiri, ubora); belenga; ringa; ringia *n* mtu anayeringa. **~ sb/sth up** eleza ukweli waziwazi. **~ up** onekana waziwazi; *(colloq)* onekana, hudhuria. **~ing** *n* hali; picha; uonyeshaji, kuonyesha. **on one's own ~ing** kwa kukiri mwenyewe.

shower *n* 1 manyunyu. **~ (bath)** bafu ya manyunyu. 2 wingi, vitu vingi vinavyokuja mfululizo *a ~ of stones* mawe mengi *a ~ of blessings* baraka nyingi. 3 *(US)* tafrija ya kumzawadia mwali kabla ya kuwa bi harusi *vt,vi* 1 **~ sth upon sb/~ sb with sth** -pelekea/tumia/miminia mtu kitu kwa wingi. **~ sb with questions** miminia mtu maswali/uliza mtu maswali mengi. 2 anguka kwa wingi; nyunyizia. **~y** *adj (of weather)* -a manyunyu ya mara kwa mara, -a manyunyumanyunyu.

shown *pp of* **show**.

shrank *pt of* **shrink**

shrapnel *n* marisau ya kombora au risasi.

shred *n* uchane, kipande. **tear to ~s** *(lit or fig)* chanachana; chana vipande vipande; haribu *there is not a ~ of evidence* hakuna hata chembe ya ushahidi *not a ~ of clothing on him* bila hata kipande cha nguo mwilini, uchi *vt* chana chana, pasua vipande vipande.

shrew *n* 1 mwanamke mwenye gubu, mwanamke mwenye ulimi mkali. 2 **~ (mouse)** panya mdogo. **~ish** *adj* -enye gubu/ulimi mkali. **~ishly** *adv.* **~ishness** *n.*

shrewd *adj* 1 -erevu. **~ly** *adv.* **~ness** *n.*

shriek *vt,vi* **~ (out)** 1 piga unyende (kwa hasira, maumivu n.k.). 2 tamka, taja kwa unyende *~ with laughter* angua kicheko unyende, kikwakwa.

shrift *n (old use)* maungamo. **give sb short ~** -pa mtu jibu la mkato; sikiliza shingo upande; -toshughulikia ipasavyo; *(old use)*

-pa mtu muda mfupi kati ya hukumu na kunyongwa.

shrike *n* kipwe.

shrill *adj (of sounds, voices)* kali, -a juu ~ *cries* ukelele, ukemi. **~y** *adv*. **~ness** *n*.

shrimp *n* uduvi, ushimba, duvi, kamba wadogo *vi* vua uduvi.

hrine *n* 1 madhabahu, mahali patakatifu. 2 sanduku lenye mabaki matakatifu. 3 sehemu ya heshima. **worship at the ~ of mammon** abudu mali/fedha *vt see* **enshrine**.

shrink *vi* 1 *(of clothes, leaves etc)* ruka, nywea, rudi. 2 ~ **(back) (from)** jitanibu, -wa na haya, sita. **~age** *n* urukaji wa nguo, kiwango cha urukaji nguo. ~ **proof** *adj* -sioruka/chupa.

shrive *vt (archaic of a priest)* ungamisha dhambi.

shrivel *vt,vi* ~ **(up)** kauka, nyauka, (kwa makunjokunjo) *he has a ~led face* ana uso wa makunyanzi.

shriven *see* **shrive**.

shroud *n* 1 sanda. 2 kifuniko, vazi. 3 ayari *vt* 1 kafini. 2 funika, gubika, ficha *~ed in darkness* -lioghubikwa gizani.

shrove *see* **shrive**.

Shrove Tuesday *n* Jumanne inayotangulia Kwaresima. **S~ tide** siku tatu kabla ya Jumatano ya majivu.

shrub *n* kichaka. **~bery** *n* eneo bustanini lililoota vichaka. **~bery** *n (pl)* vichaka. **~by** *adj*.

shrug *vt* pandisha/inua mabega (kwa ishara ya kusitasita). ~ **sth off** dharau *n* kupandisha mabega (kutoa ishara ya kutojali).

shrunken *see* **shrink**.

shuck *vt* menya, koboa ~ *corn/peas* menya mahindi/kunde *n* ganda *(fig)* kitu cha thamani ndogo. **S~**! *(int) (US)* oh! lo! afanaleki!

shudder *vi* tetema, tetemeka, gwaya *n* kitapo, tetemeko, mtetemo. **~ingly** *adv*.

shuffle *vt,vi* 1 ~ **one's feet** burura, kokoteza miguu. 2 *(of cards)* changa karata, geuzageuza, gugurusha. 3 boronga kazi; *(fig)* ~ *off responsibility upon others* sukumia wajibu wako kwa wengine. 4 taataa, tapatapa, furukuta *n* 1 kusowera; kuchanga karata. 2 kutaataa, mabadiliko *a Cabinet* ~ mabadiliko katika Baraza la mawaziri. 3 ulaghai, uongo. **~r** *n*.

shun *vt* 1 epukana na, jitanibu ~ *temptation* epukana na kishawishi. 2 *(a blow)* epa ~ *everybody* jitenga na kila mtu.

shunt *vt,vi* 1 *(of railway wagons)* chepua/geuza njia. **~ing-yard** uwanja wa kugeuzia gari moshi. 2 *(of a train)* peleka njia nyingine. 3 *(fig, colloq)* kwepa, ahirisha. 4 *(fig of a project)* weka, pembeni. **~er** *n* mgeuzaji reli.

shush *vt,vi* nyamaza ~ *him up* mnyamazishe; shsh!

shut *vt,vi* funga; fumba ~ *the door* funga mlango *(sl)* ~ *sb's mouth* nyamazisha mtu. **~-eye** *n (colloq)* usingizi; kulala, kujipumzisha. 2 fungika, unga *the window won't* ~ dirisha halifungiki/halifungi. 3 bana ~ *one's finger in the door* banwa kidole mlangoni. 4 *(special use with adverbial particles and preps)* ~ **(sth) down** funga ~ *down a factory* funga kiwanda ~ *down an engine* zima injini. **~-down** *n* kufungwa kwa kiwanda n.k. ~ **sb in** fungia/zuia/zingira mtu mahali fulani. ~ **sth off** funga, zuia kitu kisiingie/kisipite mahali fulani. ~ **sb/sth out** zuia mtu/kitu, fungia nje *don't ~ him out* usimfungie nje. ~ **sth up** funga, bana, hifadhi; fungia ~ *up one's treasures* fungia/hifadhi vitu vya maana vya mtu. ~ **(sb) up** *(colloq)* nyamazisha mtu ~ *him up* mnyamazishe. **~ter** *n* 1 kilango (cha mwanga katika kamera). 2 ubao wa dirisha. **put up the ~ters** funga kazi (kwa siku moja au kabisa) *vt* tia/funga vilango.

shuttle *n* kipisha-uzi; kipisho-mshindo. ~ **cock** mpira wa vinyoya. ~

diplomacy ushauriano wa kidiplomasia (ambao mabalozi hutembelea vikundi vinavyohusika). **space** ~ *n* sayari/roketi ya safari fupi za anga. ~ **service** safari fupi fupi za kwenda na kurudi *vt,vi* enda/-rudi/ peleka na kurudi.

shy[1] *adj* 1 *(of persons)* -enye haya/ soni. **fight ~ of** -epa. 2 *(of birds, animals, fish)* -epesi kutishwa, -siotaka kuonekana. 3 ~ **of** -enye wasiwasi/hofu/mashaka *she was ~ of telling him the problems* alikuwa na hofu kumweleza matatizo. **~ly** *adv*. **~ness** *n*.

shy[2] *vi* 1 ~ **(at sth)** *(of a horse)* geuka ghafla (kutokana na tishio). 2 ~ **(off, away)** epa *vt (colloq)* tupa, rusha ~ *a stone at sth* tupia (kitu) jiwe *n* 1 mtupo; mrusho *ten cents a ~* mtupo mmoja kwa senti kumi. 2 *(colloq)* jaribio *have a ~ at farming* jaribu kilimo.

shyster *n (US colloq)* mtu asiyeshika miiko ya kazi yake, (agh. mwanasheria) laghai.

Siamese *adj* -a Siam/Thai. **~twins** -liounganika; mapacha waliounganika; *(national)* Msiam/Mthai; *(lang)* Kithai/Kisiam.

sibilant *adj* -a sauti kama nyoka; -enye sauti ya mluzi *n* kifyonzo. **sibilance** *n*.

sibling *n* ndugu/umbu (wa baba mmoja mama mmoja).

sibyl *n* ajuza mtabiri, nabii wa kike wa zamani. **~-line** *adj* -a utabiri wa kimuujiza/ajabu.

sic *adv (lat)* vivyo hivyo (japo kwa makosa).

sick *adj* 1 *(pred only)* **be** ~ tapika. **feel** ~ sikia kichefuchefu/jelezi. **air/car/sea ~ness** *n* kigegezi. 2 -gonjwa, -uguzi *she's been ~ for two days* amekuwa mgonjwa kwa siku mbili. **be off ~ (with sth)** -tokuwepo kazini/shindwa kazi kutokana na ugonjwa. **fall ~** ugua. **go/report ~** *(mil)* enda kwa daktari (kwa matibabu). **the ~** *(pl)* wagonjwa. **~-bay** *n (navy)* zahanati ya melini, zahanati ya chuoni. ~ **bed** *n* kitanda cha mgonjwa. **~-berth** *n see* **~-bay. ~-headache** *n* kuumwa kichwa kutokana na nyongo nyingi. **~-leave** *n* likizo ya ugonjwa *he is on ~-leave* ana likizo ya ugonjwa. **~-list** *n* orodha ya wagonjwa. **~-parade** *(mil)* foleni ya wagonjwa. **~-pay** *n* malipo ya mfanyakazi mgonjwa. **~-room** *n* chumba cha wagonjwa. 3 ~ **(and tired/to death) of** *(colloq)* choshwa na kasirishwa na *I am ~ and tired of her complaints* nimechoshwa na malalamiko yake. 4 ~ **at heart** -enye majonzi makubwa. ~ **at/about sth** *(colloq)* -enye kusikitishwa na, enye kujutia jambo fulani. 5 ~ **for** -enye kutamani/ kulilia/kukumbuka sana. 6 *(sl)* -enye mawazo machafu *vt* ~ **sth up** *(colloq)* tapika. **~en** *vt,vi* 1 ~ **(for sth)** -wa katitka hatua za mwanzo (za kuugua). 2 chusha, kirihi, kasirisha. 3 ~ **at sth/to see sth** chukizwa/kinaishwa/udhiwa kutokana na/kwa kuona jambo fulani. 4 ~ **of sth** choka, choshwa na, kifu na. **~ening** *adj* -a kukifu, -a kuchosha. **~eningly** *adv*. **~ish** *adj* -a kuugua, kuuguza, gonjwagonjwa *feel ~* -a kutojisikia vizuri. **~ly** *adj* 1 -a kuugua mara kwa mara, -sio na afya nzuri. 2 dhaifu, legevu, -sio changamfu. 3 -enye kuchefua; -enye kukirihi. **~ness** *n* 1 ugonjwa magonjwa. **~ness benefit** *n* maslahi/ bima ya ugonjwa. 2 kichefuchefu; kutapika.

sickle *n* mundu ~ *shaped* -a umbo la mundu. **~-cell anaemia** *n* anemia selimundu.

side *n* 1 upande, janibu, pembeni. **other ~ of** upande wa pili wa; *(of river)* ng'ambo ya. ~ **by** ~ kwa pamoja, bega kwa bega. **by the ~ of**; **by one's ~** kandokando (ya); kwa kulinganishwa na. **on/from all ~s; on/from every ~** kutoka pande zote. **take sb on one ~** weka/ketisha pembeni. **on the right/wrong ~ of**

chini/juu ya. **do sth on the ~** kama kazi/mradi wa ziada; kisirisiri/ kimyakimya. **on the ~** pembeni. **on the cold ~** baridi kidogo. **lay on the ~** inika, laza kibavu. **put on/to one ~; (set ~)** weka, tenga; *(postpone)* ahirisha. 2 ubavu. **split/burst one's ~s (laughing)** vunja mbavu (kwa kucheka); angua kicheko. **~ splitting** *adj* -enye kuvunja mbavu (kwa kucheka). 3 kundi; timu, chama, n.k. *Tanzania has a strong ~* Tanzania ina timu nzuri. **be on sb's ~** unga mkono, wa upande/mfuasi wa. **let the ~ down** fanya vibaya. **off ~** kuotea. 4 *(descent)* nasaba, ukoo, upande *on the father's ~* upande wa baba. 5 kiburi, majisifu. **have no/be without ~** -tojidai, -tokuwa na maringo. **put on ~** jidai. 6 *(of animal)* ubavu. 7 *(compounds)* **~-arm** *n* silaha za kuvaa/kubeba ubavuni (k.m. upanga, jambia, bastola). **~-board** *n* kabati (la vyombo) **~-burns/boards** *n (pl)* sharafa. **~-car** *n* kigari cha pikipiki. **~-dish** *n* chakula cha ziada (k.m. saladi, matunda n.k.). **~-door** *n* mlango wa pembeni. **~-drum** *n* hanzua. **~ effect** athari. **~ face** kwa upande. **~-glance** *n* mtazamo wa chati. **~-issue** *n* jambo dogo/lisilo muhimu. **~ light** *n* taa ya pembeni; *(fig)* kiangaza: jambo lisilofungamana hasa na jambo lenyewe lakini linaliangazia. **~-line** *n* kazi ya ziada (isiyo ya kawaida); bidhaa za ziada; mstari wa pembeni. **on the ~ lines** *(fig)* pembeni, (kama) mtazamaji *vt* zuia kushiriki mchezoni (kwa kuumia) *a sore shoulder has ~ lined him* maumivu ya bega lake yamemzuia kushiriki mchezoni. **~ long** *adj* -a upande; -a kwenda upande *~long glance* tazamo la kitongotongo *adv* kwa kwenda upandeupande. **~ road** barabara ndogo. **~-saddle** *n* tandiko la farasi la mwanamke (ambalo humwezesha kuweka miguu yake upande mmoja) *adv* (panda) kike. **~-show** *n* onyesho dogo kwenye uwanja wa maonyesho, pambizo; shughuli/kazi ndogo. **~-slip** *vi* serereka *the car ~-slipped* gari liliserereka *n* kuteleza, kuserereka. **~sman** *(church) n* mtumishi/ msimamizi. **~-step** *n* (hatua ya) kukwepa *vi* 1 kwepea upande, epuka. **~-stroke** kuogelea kiubavuubavu. **~track** *n* ujia, njia ndogo ya kando; (reli n.k.). 2 weka/pita kando; *(fig)* ahirisha/epa. **~-view** *n* mandhari ya pembeni. **~ walk** *n (US)* ujia, njia (ya miguu). **~ whiskers** sharafa. **~ ways/ wards** *adv* kwa upande *vi* **~ with** chagua upande, unga mkono.

sidereal *adj* -a nyota.

siding *n* njia ya kando (ambapo treni hupanguliwa na kupangwa).

sidle *vi* **~ along/off** enda kwa woga/ wasiwasi/aibu. **~ in** ingia kwa siri. **~ up to (sb)** sogelea kwa wasiwasi.

siege *n* kuzingira (mji, boma n.k.). **lay ~ to** *(a town etc)* zingira (kwa lengo la kutwaa). **raise a ~** komboa; -tozingira *vt* zingia. **~ artillery/guns** *n* mizinga (ya kuzingira).

sienna *n* (aina ya) udongo utumiwao kama rangi.

sierra *n* mlolongo wa milima (agh. katika Hispania na Marekani ya Kusini).

siesta *n* usingizi wa mchana (kwa kujipumzisha).

sieve *n* chekecheke, chungio, chekeche. **have a head/memory like a ~** wa msahaulifu sana. *vt* chekecha; chunga.

sift *vt,vi* **~(out)/(from)** 1 chunga, chekecha; tia/tenganisha kwa kupitisha katika chekeche. 2 pekua; *(fig)* chunguza kwa makini. 3 dondoka; vuja, pita kama kwamba inachujwa. **~er** *n* kichungio, chekecho/chekecheke.

sigh *vi* 1 tanafusi, shusha/vuta pumzi; hema (kwa majonzi au kwa kuliwaza). 2 **~ for sth** tamani sana. **~ (out)** toa kwa kushusha pumzi *n* kushusha pumzi, kutanafusi *a ~ of relief* kutanafusi.

sight *n* 1 kuona, kutazama; *(range)* peo, eneo; (upeo/uwezo wa) kuona. **know sb by** ~ fahamu kwa sura. **catch ~ of; have/get a ~ of** anza kuona, fanikiwa/weza kuona. **keep ~ of; keep sb/sth in ~** -wa karibu ili kuweza kuona; kukumbuka, kuzingatia kuweka akilini. **lose ~ of** -toona; sahau. **at/on ~** papohapo. **at first ~** mwanzoni, kwa kuangalia mara ya kwanza. **at (the) ~ of** kwa kuona. **in/within ~ of** -enye kuweza kuonekana. **out of ~** -sioweza kuonekana. **come into ~** onekana, tokea. **go out of ~** toweka. **keep out of (sb's) ~** jificha, kaa mbali 2. maono, mtazamo *in the ~ of God* mbele ya Mungu. 3 mandhari, shani; *(pl)* sehemu maarufu (ya mahali). ~ **seeing** kutembelea, kutalii sehemu maarufu. ~ **seer** mtalii. **a ~ for sore eyes** faraja. 4 **a ~** *(colloq)* kioja, mtu wa ajabu. 5 *(often pl)* dira, shabaha. **take a ~** lenga shabaha. **gun ~** *n* jicho la bunduki. 6 **a ~** *(sl)* kiasi kikubwa sana, tele. **a ~ of money** pesa nyingi sana. **not by a long ~** kwa mbali, haikaribii *vt* 1 ona, tazama, angalia 2. lenga/piga shabaha. **~ing** *n* kuonekana; *(of the moon)* kuandama, kuonekana. **~ed** *adj*. **~less** *adj* kipofu. **~lessness** *n* upofu. **~ly** *adj* -a kupendeza; -a kuvutia, murua, malidadi. **~liness** *n*.

sign *n* 1 dalili, ishara *~s of suffering are to be seen on his face* dalili za mateso zajionyesha usoni mwake *there is no ~ of* hakuna dalili ya. ~ **and counter ~** maneno ya siri (ya kundi fulani); maneno ya ishara ya kutambulishana. 2 alama *multiplication ~* alama ya kuzidisha. **~post** kibao cha barabarani. 3 kionyo, dokezo, konyezo la (jicho/mkono); ishara *make no ~* -toonyesha ishara. ~ **language** *n* lugha ya bubu/kipofu ~ *of the cross* ishara ya msalaba. 4 ~ **(board)** ubao (wenye picha/jina/ habari) kibao. **~-painter** mchoraji/ mwandikaji vibao *vt,vi* 1 weka/tia sahihi/saini, tia mkono. ~ **sth away** toa haki/mali kwa kutia sahihi ~ *judgement* weka sahihi katika hukumu *~ed, sealed and delivered* imesainiwa, imepigwa muhuri na kuwasilishwa. **~er** mweka saini. ~ **(sb) in/out** andikisha jina kama kumbukumbu ya kufika/kuondoka. ~ **on** *(colloq)* jiandikisha ustawi wa jamii (kwa mtu asiye na kazi). ~ **sb on/up** andikisha, ajiri. ~ **sth over (to sb)** thibitisha mauzo kisheria. 2 ~ **for sb (to do sth)** ashiria. 3 ~ **on/off** *(radio)* anza/maliza. **~al** *n* 1 selo (ya meli, treni, garimoshi). 2 ishara, kichocheo, dalili, chanzo. 3 *(of radio, T.V. etc)* mawimbi *vi* toa ishara, ashiria. **~-box** *n* selo. **~-light** *n* taa za selo, ishara. ~ **man** *n* kandawala, mtoa ishara. **~aller** *n* mpelekaji/mpokeaji habari kwa ishara. **~atory** *n* mweka sahihi (katika mkataba, makubaliano, mapatano) *~ to a convention* mweka sahihi katika mapatano. **~ature** *n* 1 sahihi, saini. 2 **key ~** *(mus)* alama ya kuonyesha (kubadilishwa kwa) ufunguo. 3 ~ **tune** wimbo wa kipindi/idhaa.

signal *adj* kubwa, -a maana mashuhuri. **~ly** *adv* waziwazi. **~ize** *vt* tukuza, adhimisha, -pa heshima.

signet *n* 1 muhuri. 2 *(hist)* muhuri wa mfalme. **Writer to the S~** wakili wa *Scotland*. ~ **ring** *n* pete yenye muhuri.

signify *vt,vi* 1 onyesha *what does this~?* hii inaonyesha nini? 2 -wa na maana/ umuhimu. **significance** *n* maana, umuhimu *of no ~* bila maana. **significant** *adj* -enye maana; -enye umuhimu *the only ~ event* tukio pekee la maana. **significantly** *adv*. **signification** *n* 1 maana. 2 kumaanisha, kuashiria. **significative** *adj* -a kumaanisha.

signor *n* (*Italian*) bwana. **~a** bibi. **~ina** binti.

silage *n* sileji: chakula cha mifugo.

silence *n* kimya, unyamavu ~ *gives*

consent kimya ni dalili ya kukubali. **reduce sb to ~** nyamazisha mtu. **in ~** kimya (kimya) *vt* nyamazisha; *(int)* kelele! nyamaza! **~r** *n* kizuia kelele, kinyamazishi. **silent** *adj* -a kimya; -nyamavu, taratibu *be ~* -wa/kaa kimya; nyamaza. **~ partner** mtu asiyeshiriki waziwazi *(phon)* -sio tamkika, -siosikika. **silently** *adv*.

silhouette *n* taswira ya umbo, kivuli *vt* piga taswira.

silica *n* silika. **~te** *n* mchanganyiko wa madini yenye silika.

silicon *n* silikoni; mchanganyiko wa silikoni (inatumika katika rangi n.k.).

silicosis n *silicosisü* ugonjwa usababishwao na kuvuta hewa ya vumbi la kwazi.

silk *n* 1 hariri; *(tussore)* lasi. 2 vazi la hariri. **~-screen** *(printing)* uchapaji wa hariri. **~-worm** *n* nondo wa hariri. 3 *(GB)* mshauri (wa Malkia/Mfalme). **take ~** *(GB)* -wa mshauri wa Malkia/ Mfalme. **~en** *adj* 1 laini, -ororo. 2 *(old use or lit)* -a hariri, kama hariri. **~en voice** sauti nyororo, sauti laini. **~y** *adj* -ororo, laini. **~iness** *n*.

sill *n* kizingiti.

silly *adj* -pumbavu, -puzi. **a ~ thing** jambo la kipumbavu *the ~ season* msimu ambao magazeti hukosa habari za maana. **knock sb ~** bomoa mtu sana; *(colloq) n* mpumbavu. **silliness** *n*.

silo *n* 1 silo (la kuhifadhi chakula cha wanyama). 2 kituo (chini ya ardhi) cha kurushia makombora.

silt *n* mchangatope, mashapo ya mto *vt,vi* **~ (sth) up** jaa/jaza mashapo, ziba.

silvan *see* **sylvan**.

silver *n* 1 fedha. **~ plate** vyombo vilivyopakwa/chovywa fedha. **be born with a ~ spoon in one's mouth** zaliwa adinasi. 2 vitu vya fedha. 3 sarafu. 4 *(attrib)* -a fedha, kama fedha, -a rangi ya fedha; *(of sounds)* wazi, laini. **~ grey** *adj* -a rangi ya fedha inayong'aa. **the ~ screen** senema, kitambaa, ubao wa kuonyeshea senema. 5 -a pili (bora), -a fedha. **~ medal** nishani ya fedha (kwa mshindi wa pili). *(compounds)*~ **birch** *n* mti wa rangi ya fedha. **~ fish** *n* siridado. **~ jubilee** maadhimisho ya miaka 25. **~-paper** jaribosi; fedha. **~ side** *n* mnofu paja. **~ smith** mfua fedha; sonara (wa vitu vya fedha). **~-tongued** -enye ufasaha -enye kujua kuongea. **~-ware** vyombo vya fedha (agh vijiko, uma, visu). **~ wedding** maadhimisho ya miaka 25 ya ndoa *vt,vi* 1 paka rangi ya fedha, fanya kitu king'ae kama fedha. 2 geuka mvi. **~y** *adj*. **~n** *adj (arch)* fedha *speech is ~ but silence is golden* ni vyema kunyamaza kuliko kuongea.

simian *adj* -enye kufanana na nyani/ tumbili *n* nyani, tumbili.

similar *adj* **~ (to)** -a kufanana;-a hali moja *~ in shape* -enye kufanana kwa umbo. **~ity** *n* 1 kufanana; mfanano. 2 *(of features)* mlandano. **~ly** *adv* vile vile, vivyohivyo, hali kadhalika.

simile *n* tashbihi. **similitude** *n* mfanano, mlinganisho, tashbihi.

simmer *vi* 1 chemka polepole. 2 karibia kuwaka (kwa hasira n.k.). **~ down** *(fig)* poa (baada ya kukasirika sana) *~ with laughter* bana kicheko. **keep sth at a ~/on the ~** chemsha polepole *n* kuchemka polepole; kutokota.

simony *n (hist)* (kosa la) kutoa/ kupokea rushwa ili kupata cheo katika kanisa. **simonical** *adj*.

simoom, simon *n* upepo mkavu wa joto sana (unaovuma Uarabuni na jangwa la Sahara).

simper *vi* tabasamu/chekacheka ovyo/ kijinga/kipuuzi/kibembe *n* tabasamu ya kijinga/kipuuzi. **~ingly** *adv*.

simple *adj* 1 sahili. **~ interest** riba sahili *~ sentence* sentensi sahili. 2 rahisi, -epesi *~ English* Kingereza rahisi. 3 -a kawaida, -siorembwa, -siopambwa *~ food* chakula cha kawaida. 4 nyofu; wazi. **~ hearted** mkweli. **~minded** msema kweli;

punguani. 5 peke, tupu ~ *truth* ukweli mtupu (bila kutiwa chumvi). **pure and** ~ *(colloq)* kabisa. 6 mshamba, -a kudanganyika kwa urahisi *n (old use)* mtishamba, dawa asili. **~ton** *n* punguani, juha. **simplicity** *n* urahisi, wepesi. **be ~ itself** *(colloq)* -wa rahisi sana. **simplify** *vi* rahisisha, -fanya epesi. **simplification** *n* kurahisisha, kuondoa shida. **simply** *adv* 1 pasipo anasa, kawaida. 2 kabisa; hasa *we ~ have to do it* hatuna budi kuifanya. 3 tu *this medicine consists ~ of herbs* dawa hii ni mitishamba tu *it is ~ a mater of being careful* ni suala tu la kujihadhari.

simsim *n see* **sesame**.

simulacrum *n* sanamu/kielelezo cha mtu/kitu; mfanano, kielelezo cha picha.

simulate *vt* iga, igiza; jifanya, jidai, jisingizia. **simulation** *n* kujisingizia, uigaji. **simulator** *n* chombo kinachoonyesha hali bandia/kama ilivyo katika hali halisi.

simultaneous *adj* ~ **(with)** -a wakati ule ule; pale pale, papo hapo, sawia. ~ **equation** mlinganyo sawia. **~ness/ simultaneity** *n* wakati huo huo. **~ly** *adv* sawia.

sin *n* 1 dhambi. **live in ~ (dated)** ishi na kimada *confess ~* ungama dhambi. **original ~** dhambi ya asili. **mortal/ deadly ~** dhambi ya mauti. **the seven deadly sins** dhambi saba za mauti. **venial ~** dhambi nyepesi. 2 *(colloq)* kosa *vi ~ (against)* 1 tenda dhambi, potoka. 2 kosa. **~ful** *adj* -enye dhambi. **~fulness** *n*. **~less** *adj*. **~ lessness** *n*. **~ner** *n* mwenye dhambi, mkosefu.

since *adv* 1 tangu wakati ule; tena *I have not seen him ~* sijawahi kumwona tena. **ever ~** tangu wakati huo. 2 -liopita *I saw him many days ~* nilimwona siku nyingi zilizopita; *(prep)* tangu; *(conj)* 1 tangu *it is three days ~ he desappeared* ni siku tatu tangu atoweke. 2 kwa kuwa, maadam *~ we have no food we must work hard* kwa kuwa hatuna chakula lazima tufanye kazi kwa bidii.

sincere *adj* -aminifu, -nyofu, -a kweli, -enye moyo safi. **~ly** *adv* kwa kweli, kwa moyo safi; kwa unyofu. **yours ~ ly** wako mwaminifu. **sincerity** *n* unyofu, uaminifu.

sinecure *n* upataji wa cheo/kazi ya dezo/faida bila kuifanyia kazi.

sine die *adv* *(lat)* hadi hapo itakapotangazwa tena.

sine qua non *n* sharti/jambo la lazima.

sinew *n* 1 kano, mshipa. 2 *(pl)* misuli, nguvu, uwezo; *(fig)* namna/ njia ya kupata nguvu. **the ~s of war** pesa za kununulia mahitaji ya vita. **~y** *adj* -a nguvu, -shupavu; -enye misuli.

sing *vi,vt* 1 imba *you are always ~ing the same song* unaimba mambo hayohayo siku zote. ~ **another tune** badili mwenendo/usemi. ~ **small** *(colloq)* nyenyekea (baada ya kukemewa) *~ a baby to sleep* bembeleza mtoto kwa wimbo ili alale. 2 vuma, lia *my ears are ~ing* masikio yangu yanavuma 3 ~ **(of) sth** *(liter)* simulia kwa utenzi/ushairi, ghani. ~ **sb's praises** sifia sana, tukuza. 4 ~ **out (for)** ita kwa nguvu. ~ **sth out** tamka kwa sauti kubwa. ~ **up** imba kwa sauti/nguvu zaidi. **~er** *n* mwimbaji. **~ing** uimbaji. **~able** -nayoimbika. **~song** *n* 1 kuimba kwa pamoja (kwa kujifurahisha); *(attrib)* **in a ~ song voice/manner** kwa mahadhi ya kupanda na kushuka/kwa namna ya kuchosha.

singe *vt,vi* unguza, babua, choma. **become ~d** ungua *n* alama ya kuungua.

single *adj* 1 -moja (tu), peke yake, pasipo mwenzi. **walk in ~ file** tembea katika safu/msitari mmoja *the most important ~ event* jambo la maana kuliko yote. **~-barrelled** (bunduki) -a mwanzi/mtutu mmoja. **~-breasted** *(of a coat)* -enye mstari mmoja wa vifungo. ~ **handed** *adj,adv* peke yake; bila msaada, bila kusaidiwa. ~**minded** -enye lengo moja tu; thabiti. ~-**seater** *n* gari ndege ya kiti kimoja. ~**stick** *n* gongo/fimbo ya kupigania, mkwaju. ~-**track** *adj* 1 *(railway)* -enye njia moja. 2 mseja, mhuni -a mtu mmoja. ~ **room** chumba cha mtu mmoja *n* 1 *(tennis and golf)* mchezo wa wachezaji mmoja mmoja. 2 *(short for a)* ~ **ticket** tiketi ya kwenda tu 3. *(cricket)* pointi moja *vt* ~ **sb/sth out** chagua, teua; bagua. **singly** *adv*. ~**ess** *n*. ~**ness of purpose** umakini katika lengo.

singlet *(GB)* fulana.

singular *adj* 1 *(liter)* -a ajabu, -sio -a kawaida. 2 *(fomal)* -a kipekee ~ *matrix* solo shani. 3 *(gram) -a* umoja *n* umoja. ~**ity** *n*. ~**ly** *adv* kwa kipekee, hasa, ajabu. ~**ize** *vt*.

sinister *adj* 1 *(liter)* baya, -ovu; -a kisirani, -a shari ~ *beginning* mwanzo mbaya. 2 -a husuda, -baya. **a** ~ **face**, uso wa husuda. 3 *(on a shield)* -a kushoto. **bar** ~ alama katika ngao kuonyesha kizazi haramu.

sink[1] *n* 1 sinki, beseni la kuoshea vyombo vya jikoni. 2 shimo la maji machafu. 3 *(fig)* eneo la uovu.

sink[2] *vt,vi* 1 zamisha; zama. ~ **or swim** (jitosa) kufa na kupona. 2 shuka, didimia; topeza, lemewa *the foundation has sunk* msingi umedidimia *his heart sank* alisononeka. 3 chimba/zamisha ~ *a well* chimba kisima ~ *a post in the ground* chimbia zamisha nguzo. 4 ~ **in; ~ into/to sth** zama, topea, shuka ~ *into a deep sleep* topea katika usingizi mzito. 5 ~ **in; ~ into sth** *(of liquids, and fig)* zama. 6 pungua, angamia; punguza *he sank his voice* alipunguza sauti *let's ~ our differences* tusahau/ tuache tofauti zetu. 7 ~ **(in)** tega uchumi/fedha. ~**able** *adj*. ~**er** *n* chubwi, bildi. ~**ing** *n* 1 kuzama. 2 **a ~ feeling** hali ya kuona njaa/hofu. ~-**fund** *n* mfuko wa (serikali au shirika) wa kulipia madeni.

Sinology *n* Sinolojia: utaalam wa lugha na utamaduni wa Kichina. **sinologist** *n* mwana sinolojia.

sinuous *adj* -enye mapindi; -enye konakona; -a mzingo, -a kuzingamana. ~**ity** *n* mapindi, mizingo, kubetabeta.

sinus *n* uwazi katika mfupa (hasa ndani ya fuvu) unaowasiliana na mianzi ya pua. ~**itis** *n* uvimbe katika uwazi huo.

sip *vt,vi* konga, -nywa kidogo kidogo, -onja (kitu cha maji) n.k.

siphon *n* mrija, neli, kifyonzaji *vt* ~ **sth off/out** fyonza, nyonya *who has ~ed off all the petrol from my tank?* nani amenyonya petroli yote kutoka katika tangi langu?

sir *n* bwana, mzee, maulana, *(in letters) Dear* ~ Bwana, mheshimiwa, *(used before name of knight)* hababi.

sire *n* 1 *(old use)* baba, babu 2 *(old use)* mtukufu (cheo kilichotumiwa kumtaja mfalme). 3 mzazi dume wa mnyama *vt* *(esp of horses)* zaa *be the ~ of* kuwa mzazi wa.

siren *n* 1 *(hooter)* king'ora, honi. 2 mbembezi; mwanamke wa hatari; mwanamke mshawishi.

sirloin *n* sarara.

sirup *see* **syrup**.

sisal *n* mkonge, katani.

sissy *n (colloq; derog)* joga.

sister *n* 1 dada. **half** ~ dada wa kambo. ~ **in law** *(of ones wife)* shemeji; *(of ones husband)* wifi. 2 sista; mtawa wa kike. 3 mwuguzi (mwenye cheo). 4 *(attrib)* mwenzi, pacha. ~**hood** *n* 1 utawa; udada/ushoga. ~**ly** *adj* -a dada, kidada, kama dada. ~**liness** *n* udada.

sit *vt,vi* 1 kaa; keti, jilisi. ~ **to an artist/~ for ones portrait** kaa uchorwe (na msanii) ~ **(for) an examination** fanya mtihani. 2 ~ **tight** kaa imara; tulia tuli; *(fig)* shikilia jambo. ~ **for (a constituency)** wakilisha Bungeni jimbo (la uchaguzi). ~**ting member** *(at election)* mbunge wa zamani. 3 kalisha. 4 kutana, fanya mkutano/

kikao. 5 *(of birds)* tua. **~ting duck** kitu/mtu asiye na kinga. **~ting tenant** mpangaji aliyepo. 6 *(on eggs)* atamia; *(on heels)* chuchumaa; *(astride)* tagaa. 7 *(of clothes)* kaa *the dress ~s well on her* gauni linamkaa. 8 kalia. 9 *(with adverbial particles and prepositions)* **~ back** starehe; *(fig)* pumzika; kaa (na kutoshughulika). **~ down** keti. **~-down strike** mgomo katika eneo la kazi (ambapo wafanyakazi wanakataa kuondoka kiwandani hadi madai yao yanaposhughulikiwa. **~ down under** vumilia, kufa kiofisa, teseka bila malalamiko. **~ in** goma kwa kuvamia makazi na kubakia papo hapo. **~ in** *n* mgomo. **~ in on sth** hudhuria kama mtazamaji/msikilizaji. **~ on/ upon sth** -wa mjumbe; *(delay)* kwamisha; *(investigate)* chunguza, tafiti, peleleza. **~ on/upon sb** *(colloq)* kalia, gandamiza; -tojali. **~ out** kaa nje. **~ sth out** kaa/vumilia hadi mwisho; *(of dance)* -toshiriki. **~ up,** kesha; kaa/ kalisha vizuri. **~ (sb) up** kalisha/ kaa, keti(sha). **~ up straight**! kaa vizuri/sawasawa. **make sb ~ up (and take notice)** *(colloq)* shtua. **~ter** *n* 1 mtu anayechorwa picha na msanii. 2 kuku anayeatamia. 3 ndege rahisi kupigwa risasi; *(fig)* kitu rahisi kufanywa. **~ting** *n* 1 kikao, baraza, mkutano *a long ~* kikao kirefu. 2 mkao *at one ~* kwa mkao mmoja *her portrait was finished in one ~* picha yake ilichorwa kwa mkao mmoja. 3 mkupuo, awamu *be served at one ~* hudumiwa kwa awamu moja. 4 mayai ya kuatamiwa. 5 **~-room** *n* sebule, ukumbi.

site *n* mahali, eneo; *(for building)* kiwanja *vt* weka mahali.

situate *vt* weka mahali. **situated** *pred adj* 1 *(of town, building etc)* -liopo mahali *it is ~ in Egypt* iko Misri. 2 *(of a person)* -wa katika hali fulani *I am rather awkwardly ~* nina matatizo kidogo. **situation** *n* 1 mahali. 2 hali. 3 kazi *~ vacant* nafasi za kazi *be in a ~* ajiriwa, wa na kazi. *adj* sita. **~ of one and half a dozen of the other** ni mamoja; si tofauti sana. **at ~es and sevens** -liochanga- nyikiwa, -liovurugikiwa. **in ~es** sitasita. **~-footer** *n (colloq)* kitu/mtu mwenye urefu wa futi sita. **~- shooter** bastola ya risasi sita. **~fold** *adj, adv* mara sita. **~teen** *adj, n* kumi na sita. **~teenth** *n, adj* kumi na sita. **~th** *n adj* -a sita *~ form* kidato cha sita. **~ sense** *n* utambuzi wa moyoni. **~thly** *adv* ya sita. **~tieth** *n adj* -a sitini. **~ty** *n, adj* sitini *a man of ~* mtu wa umri wa miaka sitini. **~ties** *n (pl)* miaka ya sitini; miaka kati ya 60 - 69.

size[1] *n* 1 ukubwa *about the ~ of an orange* ukubwa wa chungwa. 2 kipimo, saizi *what ~ do you wear*? unavaa saizi/kipimo gani? **that is about the ~ of it** *(colloq)* ndivyo ilivyo, ndivyo ilivyokuwa, ndiyo hali yenyewe. 3 kiasi *vt* panga kwa saizi/ukubwa. **~ sb/sth up** *(colloq)* pima/tathmini mtu/kitu. **~d** *(suff) (in compounds)* -enye ukubwa fulani *medium ~* -enye ukubwa wa kati. **~able** *adj* kubwa kiasi.

size[2] *n* dondo, gundi ya kung'arisha karatasi/plasta *vt* tia dondo katika kitambaa, paka gundi katika karatasi/ plasta.

sizzle *vi n (colloq)* chachatika; chata *(fig) a sizzling hot day* siku ya hari.

skate[1] *n* **ice ~** reli za barafu, vyuma vifungwavyo kwenye viatu kutelezea kwenye barafu *vi* teleza kwenye barafu/sakafu. *(fig)* **~ on thin ice** ongelea swala nyeti. **~-board** *n* ubao mtelezo. **~-boarder** *n* mtumiaji wa ubao wa kuteleza. **skating** *n* mchezo wa kuteleza. **~-rin** kiwanja cha kutelezea. **~r** *n* mtelezaji.

skate[2] *n* samaki wa bahari mkubwa na mpana kama taa.

skedaddle *vi (colloq)* kimbia, toweka.

skein *n* 1 fundo/kibonge/donge (la uzi).

skeleton *n* 1 kiunzi cha mifupa *a mere ~* gofu la mtu; mifupa mitupu. **reduced to a ~** -liokonda sana (kutokana na njaa/ugonjwa), mifupa mitupu. **the ~ in the cupboard; the family ~** aibu iliyofichwa, jambo la kutia haya, siri ya ndani. 2 *(of plan, etc), (of building)* plani. 3 *(attrib)* **~ key** ufunguo malaya. **~ staff/crew/ service etc** wafanyakazi wachache kuliko kawaida; wafanyakazi wa kazi za lazima.

skep *n* 1 pakacha, *(wicker bee-hive)* mzinga wa nyuki uliotengenezwa kwa makuti.

skeptic *see* **sceptic**.

sketch *n* 1 mchoro wa haraka, picha ya haraka, kielelezo. **~ book/block** daftari ya kuchorea. **~-map** ramani yenye maelezo machache. 2 muhtasari, madokezo. 3 kichekesho (maandishi, mchezo wa kuigiza) *vt,vi* 1 chora upesi. **~ sth out** andika, sema, eleza kwa juu juu, andika muhtasari. **~er** *n*. **~y** *adj* a haraka haraka, hafifu. 2 -sio kamilifu. **~ily** *adv*. **~iness** *n*.

skew *adj* -a kukingama, -a mshazari, -a upande, -a upogo *~lines* mistari tengano. **~-eyed** *(colloq)* -enye makengeza. **on the ~** *(colloq)* -a upogoupogo.

skewbald *adj* *(of an animal)* -enye madoa meupe na ya hudhurungi.

skewer *n* kibaniko, mbano *vt* tunga (kama) katika kibaniko.

ski *n* skii, relitheluji: ubao mrefu ufungwao kwenye kiatu kutelezea kwenye theluji. **~-bob** *n* baiskeli ya skii *~-boots n* mabuti ya skii. **~jump** *n* mruko wa skii. **~-plane** *n* eropleni ya skii *water-~ n* skii ya majini *vi* teleza katika theluji kwa skii. **~er** *n* mtelezaji wa skii. **~ing**.

skid *vt* teleza, *the car ~ded* gari liliteleza *n* 1 kizuio mnyororo/ chuma cha kuzuia gurudumu lisiteleze. 2 nyenzogogo/bao (la kubingirishia magogo). **~-row** *n (US)* maskani ya wasikwao. 3 kuteleza. **~-pan** eneo la kuteleza. **put the~s under sb** *(sl)* harakisha (mtu) kuendelea. **~ proof** *adj* -sioshikwa na utelezi; -sioteleza.

skiff *n* skifu: mashua nyepesi ndogo tena nyembamba.

skiffle *n* mchanganyiko wa jazi na nyimbo za kienyeji.

skill *n* ustadi; ujuzi, umahiri, ufundi. **~ed** *adj* -stadi *~ workman* fundi stadi/hodari. **~ful** *adj* stadi, -bingwa, mahiri, -enye ujuzi. **~fully** *adv*.

skillet *n (US)* **(frying-pan)** kikaango (cha mkono mrefu).

skilly *n (GB)* supu, uji mwepesi.

skim *vt* **~ (off/from)** 1 engua, *~the cream off the milk* engua malai/ krimu. **~med milk** machunda. 2 ambaa, pitia juujuu upesi. 3 **~ (through) sth** soma kwa haraka; pitisha jicho, angalia juu juu. **~mer** *n* 1 mwiko, chujio. 2 kiparara.

skimp *vt,vi* 1 bania. 2 -wa bahili. **~y** *adj* 1 banifu 2 *(of a dress etc)* dogo mno. **~ily** *adv*. **~iness** *n* uchache, uhaba, udogo. **~ing** *n*.

skin *n* 1 ngozi. **~ and bone** gofu la mtu; embamba sana, ng'onda. **escape by the ~ of one's teeth** ponea chupuchupu. **get under one's ~** *(fig)* kera, udhi; vutia sana mtu. **have a thin/thick ~** *(fig)* -wa wa kuumia haraka/-wa sugu. **no ~ off my nose** *(colloq)* ni mamoja kwangu, haidhuru, fahuwa. **save one's ~** nusurika; jinusuru. **~-deep** *adj* -a juu juu tu; -enye unafiki. **~-flint** *n* bahili, mchoyo. **~-game** *n* kamari; utapeli. **~-graft** *n* kirakangozi. **~-tight** *adj* -a kubanabana. 2 *(of fruit, plant)* ganda, gome. 3 *(wine, water)* kiriba. 4 utando (wa maziwa) *vt,vi* 1 chuna. **keep one's eyes ~ned** -wa macho, kaa chonjo. 2 tapeli. **~ over** funikwa. **~ner** *n* mchuuzi wa ngozi. **~y** *adj* -kondefu, -gofu; -a kimbaombao *(colloq)* bahili.

skint *adj (GB sl)* maskini, fukara.

skip *vi* 1 chachawa, rukaruka. 2 *(of games)* ruka kamba. **~ping rope** *n* kamba ya kurukia. 3 ruka (sehemu ya kazi, kitabu n.k) *~it! (sl)* achilia!, acha!

skipper *n* 1 nahodha, rubani. 2 *(colloq)*

kapteni wa timu *~'s daughters* mawimbi makubwa yenye vishungi vyeupe *vt* ongoza.

skirl *n* sauti kali *vi* lia kwa sauti kali.

skirmish *n* mkwaruzano, mapigano madogo, vita vidogo, mabishano *vi* kwaruzana, pigana; bishana. **~er** *n* doria, mpiganaji; mpigani.

skirt *n* 1 sketi. 2 *(pl)* mpaka, ukingo, pambizo *vi,vt* 1 -wa mpakani, pakana na. 2 *(pass near)* pitia kando *~ along the coast* ambaa pwani. 3 **~ round sth** epuka (suala n.k.). **~ing-board** *n* *(of a house)* kiuno sakafu (mfano wa kiuno cha nyumba) unaozunguka chumba.

skit *n* kichekesho; igizo fupi la kuchekesha.

skittish *adj (of horses)* -enye makeke; -enye machachari *(of person)* -enye makeke, -bembe. **~ly** *adv*. **~ness** *n*.

skittle *n* pini: vibao mfano wa chupa. *(pl)* **~s** mchezo wa kudondosha pini kwa tufe. **(all beer) and ~s** furaha/ shangwe tupu/pekee. *vt* **~ out** *(cricket)* toa kwa urahisi, shinda kwa urahisi.

skive *vt* 1 *(of skin leather)* parura; chuna; chana, *(sl)* zembea. **~r** *n* 1 kisu cha kuchuna ngozi. 2 mchuna ngozi. 3 mzembe.

skivvy *n (GB sl) (derog)* kijakazi.

skua *n* (aina ya) shakwe mkubwa.

skulk *vi* jifichaficha kwa woga au kukwepa kazi. **~er** *n*.

skull *n* fuvu la kichwa, fuu, bupuru (la kichwa). **have a thick ~** -wa mzito wa kuelewa. **~ and cross-bones** alama ya hatari. **~-cap** *n* kibaraghashia.

skull-duggery *n (colloq)* ulaghai.

skunk *n* 1 *(bio)* kicheche. 2 mwovu, mshenzi.

sky *n* 1 mbingu, anga *clear ~* kweupe; hakuna mawingu *cloudy ~* anga lenye mawingu. **praise sb to the skies** sifia sana. **the ~ is the limit** hakuna kiwango/mpaka/kikomo. 2 *(often pl.)* hali ya hewa ~ the ball piga mnazi. **~ward (s)** *adj adv* (-a) kuelekea juu. 3 *(with compounds)* **~-blue** *adj* -samawi, samawati, **~-high** *adv* juu; *(sl)* kasisi, padri, mchungaji (katika meli ya vita). **~rocket** *vi (of prices)* panda haraka, paa *n* roketi. **~scraper** *n* maghorofa. **~-way** *n* njia ya angani. **~-writing** *n* maandishi ya moshi (yafanywayo na ndege ya matangazo).

slab *n* 1 ubamba (wa jiwe, ubao); bamba, kibamba. 2 kipande (cha mkate).

slack *adj* 1 goigoi -zembe, -vivu; -siomakini. **keep a ~ rein on sth** *(fig)* tawala kizembe/bila kujali. 2 -liolegea, -a kudorora, -a kudoda. 3 *(of water)* -a mwendo wa pole pole; -zito *vi* 1 **~ off** zembea, legea. **~ up** punguza mwendo. 3 **~ away** legeza (kamba, uzi n.k.). **~er** *n (colloq)* mvivu, mtegaji. **~ly** *adv*. **~ness** *n* 1 **the ~** sehemu ya kamba, mnyororo, n.k. inayoning'inia/iliyolegea. **take up the ~** kaza kamba; *(fig)* dhibiti viwanda ili vifanye kazi kwa ufanisi. 2 *(pl)* suruali. 3 vumbi la mkaa wa mawe. **~en** *vt,vi* 1 pungua/punguza, legeza/legea, zembea *the gale is ~ening a little* dhoruba inapungua kidogo. **~ away/off** legeza.

slag *n* mavi ya chuma/madini. **~-heap** *n* fungu la mavi ya chuma.

slain *pp of* **slay**.

slake *vt* 1 zima, tuliza, punguza, ridhisha. 2 *(of lime)* tia maji.

slalom *n* mbio mapindi (ya mashua au skii).

slam *vt, vi* bamiza, funga (mlango, dirisha) kwa kishindo *~ down* weka kwa kishindo, fungika kwa kishindo. **~ (to)** fungwa; jifunga kwa kishindo *n* mshindo, kishindo. **gland ~** kushinda yote.

slander *vt* kashifu *n* kashfa. **~er** *n*. **~ous** *adj* -liojaa uzushi/uongo/ kashifa.

slang *n* misimu, simo, lugha ya mitaani *vt* tukana. **a ~ing match** kutukanana *adj* -a msimu. **~ily** *adv*. **~iness** *n*. **~y** *adj* 1 -a msimu. 2 -liopenda kutumia msimu.

slant *vi, vt* 1 enda/elekea upande; inama, inamisha, elekeza upande. 2 ~ **the news** toa habari za upande mmoja tu *n* mwinamo. **on a/the** ~ katika mwinamo. 3 *(colloq)* wazo, mtanzamo *adj* hanamu; *(maths)* ~ *height* kimo hanamu. **~ingly/ ~wise** *adv*.

slap *n* kofi, kibao. **get a ~ in the face** *(fig)* kataliwa (kwa dharau); bezwa, dharauliwa. **give a ~ in the face** kataa (kwa dharau); puuza, beza, tweza *give a ~ on the back* pongeza mtu *vt* piga/ chapa/zaba kofi ~ *down* bamiza, weka kwa kishindo *adv* moja kwa moja. **hit ~ on** gonga, piga dango/shabaha. **run ~ into sb** gongana na (mtu) kwa ghafula. **~-bang** *adv* kwa nguvu, kwa kishindo, kwa vurumai. **~-dash** *adj* -zembe, -a harara, -purukushani *in a ~dash manner* kwa uzembe *in a ~dash adv* juujuu. **~-happy** *adj (colloq)* -siojali. **~-stick** *n (fig)* futuhi. **~-up** *adj (sl)* bora.

slash vt 1 kata, tema. 2 chapa (kwa kiboko). 3 laani/pinga vikali; shutumu. 4 *(colloq)* punguza sana. 5 chanja, toja *n* 1 mchanjo; mtemo; tojo. 2 *(vulg. sl)* kukojoa. **~er** *n* 1 kwanja, panga (la kufyekea nyasi), fyekeo. 2 kichanjio (kisu, wembe).

slat *n* 1 kibao, bamba. **~ed** *adj* -enye ubao, -liotengenezwa kwa vibao.

slate *n* 1 grife. 2 sleti, kibao. **a clean ~** *(fig)* rekodi safi, jina zuri *start with a clean ~* anza upya (baada ya kusamehewa/kusahau makosa ya nyuma). 3 rangi ya kijivu. 4 kigae. 5 jiwe jembamba *vt* 1 ezeka kwa vigae. 2 *(US, colloq)* pendekeza mtu kwenye cheo/madaraka. 3 *(colloq)* lima. **~-club** *n* chama cha kusaidiana. **~-pencil** *n* kalamu ya sleti/grife. **slaty** *adj* 1 -a sleti. 2 -a rangi ya kijivu. **~ing** *n (colloq)* karipio, kemeo, lawama.

slattern *n* mwanamke mchafu. **~ly** *adj (of dress)* -chafu, -sio nadhifu. **~liness** *n*.

slaughter *vt* chinja, ua kwa wingi *n* 1 kuchinja. ~ **house** machinjioni. 2 mauaji (ya watu). ~ **er** *n*.

slave *n* 1 mtumwa; mtwana; kitwana; *(female)* kijakazi; *(concubine)* suria; *(home- born)* mzalia; *(house hold)* kijoli; *(war)* mateka; *white ~* msichana/mwanamke anayeuzwa/ anayelazimishwa kuwa malaya. 2 mtumwa wa jambo fulani *a ~ to drink* mlevi kupindukia *vi* ~ **(away) at sth)** fanya kazi kama punda/za kuchosha. **~-dealer** *n* mchuuzi wa watumwa. **~-driver** *n* 1 mnyapara wa watumwa. 2 msimamizi katili. **~-hunter** *n* msaka watumwa. **~-owner** *n* mwenye watumwa. **~-ship** *n* meli ya kubeba watumwa. **~-states** *n (hist)* majimbo ya kusini mwa Marekani (ambako kulikuwa na watumwa). **~-trade** *n* biashara ya watumwa. **slavish** *adj* -a mtu asiye na uamuzi wa peke yake/huru -enye mawazo ya kitumwa; sio na uasili; dhalili. **slavishness** *n* **slavishly** *adv*. **~r** *n* meli ya watumwa, mfanyabiashara ya watumwa. **~ry** *n* 1 utumwa. 2 kazi za utumwa/ kushurutishwa. **~y** *n (sl)* kijana mtumishi.

slaver *vi* dolola, churuza (ute,udende, udelele, mate) *n* udende, mate.

Slavonic/slavic *adj* -a Kislavoni *n* lugha ya Kislavoni (agh. Kirusi, Kipoli n.k.). **slaw** *n (often* **cole** ~) saladi ya kabichi.

slay *vt (liter, or rhet)* chinja, ua (kwa kuchinja). **~er** *n* mwuaji ~ *with laughter (colloq)* vunja mbavu.

sleazy *adj (colloq)* -ovyo ovyo, chafu, -sio nadhifu *a ~ hotel* hoteli chafu.

sledge[1] *n* (*also* **sled**) sleji: kitoroli cha kuteleza juu ya theluji *vi* teleza kwa sleji.

sledge[2] *n* ~ **hammer** nyundo kubwa. *~-hammer argument* mabishano makali.

sleek *adj* 1 *(of hair etc)* laini, -ororo; -a kung'aa. 2 *(of a person)* mtanashati, malidadi. 3 **as ~ as a cat** *(fig)* -a kuraírai, -enye tabia ya kunyenyekea mno, laghai *vt* 1 lainisha, fanya ororo. 2 ng'arisha. **~ly** *adv.* **~ness** *n.*

sleep *n* 1 usingizi, kulala. **get to ~** pata usingizi, lala. **go to ~** lala. **have one's ~ out** lala mpaka usingizi uishe. **put sb to ~** laza, fanya mtu alale. **put (an animal) to ~** ua. 2 **a ~** kipindi cha usingizi *n* mtu atembeaye singizini, mzindukaji. **~less** *adj* bila usingizi. **~lessly** *adv.* **~lessness** *n vi,vt* 1 lala *be fit to ~ in* lalika *things to ~ on* malazi. **~like a top/log** lala fofofo. **~round the clock; ~ the clock round** lala kutwa kucha. 2 laza -wa na vitanda *this hotel ~s 300 guests* hoteli hii inavyo vitanda 300. **~ing-bag** *n (in compounds)* fuko la kulalia. **~ing draught/pill** dawa ya usingizi. **~ing car** *n* behewa la kulala. **~ing partner** *n (US) (silent partner)* mbiamsiri. **~ing sickness** *n* malale. **~er** *n* 1 mchapa usingizi *be a light ~* -wa mwepesi kuamka. 2 taruma (relini). 3 kitanda katika behewa la kulala. **~ around** *(colloq)* wa mkware. **~ in/out** lala kwenye/mbali na sehemu ya kazi. **~ sth off** pona kwa kulala usingizi. **~ on** endelea kulala. **~ on sth** fikiria (jambo) hadi kesho. **~ with sb**, jamiiana na. **~ through** endelea kulala (licha ya makelele, n.k.). **~y** *adj* 1 -zito wa macho, -enye usingizi, -a kusinzia, -enye lepe. **~ head** *n* msinziaji; mzito. 2 *(places, etc.)* tulivu; -liopooza *a ~ little town* mji mdogo uliopooza. 3 *(of some kinds of fruits)* -lioiva sana. **~ily** *adv.* **~iness** *n.*

sleet *n* mvua ya theluji *vi it ~s* inanyesha mvua ya theluji. **~y** *adj.*

sleeve *n* 1 mkono wa vazi (k.m. koti, shati). **laugh up one's ~** cheka kichinichini; cheka kwa siri. **roll up one's ~s** -wa tayari, jiandaa kupigana/kufanya kazi; jifunga kidete/ kibwebwe. **have sth up one's ~** -wa na mpango/wazo (la baadaye) la siri. **wear one's heart on one's ~** onyesha mapenzi waziwazi. **~less** *adj (dress garment)* -sio mkono. 2 gamba la rekodi. 3 *(mechanics)* mwanzi *~ coupling n (mech.)* kiunganishi mwanzi. **~d** *adj (of cloth)* -a mikono; -enye mikono.

sleigh *n* sleji inayokokotwa na farasi. **~-bell** *n* kengele ya sleji *vi,vt* safiri katika sleji inayokokotwa na farasi; safirisha mizigo kwa sleji.

sleight *n* werevu *(usu in)* **~ of hand** kiini macho, mazingaombwe.

slender *adj* 1 -embamba *a ~ waist* kiuno chembamba. 2 *(of persons)* -embamba; -sio nene. 3 -dogo, -chache, -pungufu, haba *a ~ income* pato dogo. **~ly** *adv.* **~ness** *n.* **~ize** *vt, vi* fanya/-wa -embamba.

slept *pt. pp of* **sleep**.

sleuth *n (colloq)* mpelelezi. **~-hound** *n* mbwa mpelelezi.

slew[1] *(US (slue)* *vt,vi* **~ (sth) round** geuka/geuza kwa nguvu.

slew[2] *pt of* **slay**.

slice *n* 1 ubale, kipande chembamba, cheche; *(of bread)* slesi. 2 *(share)* hisa, fungu, sehemu. 3 mwiko bapa. 4 *(in games)* mbetuo, pigo komba *vt* 1 checha; chanyata, lenga. 2 **~ off** pangua. 3 betua, piga kombo. **slicing** *n* kulenga.

slick *adj (colloq)* 1 laini, telezi. 2 -erevu, -a hila, janja, stadi *adv* moja kwa moja, barabara (sawasawa) *vt* lainisha *n* **oil ~** utando wa mafuta. **~er** *n* 1 *(colloq)* koti la mvua. 2 mwerevu, mjanja, alwatani.

slide *n* 1 kuteleza. 2 mtelezo. 3 *(photography, microscope etc)* slaidi *vi, vt* 1 teleza, nyiririka. **let things ~** acha mambo yalivyo, telekeza. **~ over sth** kwepa; gusia. 2 **~ into** ingia polepole, angukia, jikuta katika *~ into alcoholism* jikuta katika mazoea ya ulevi. 3 penyeza *(comp.)*. **~-rule** *n* kikokotoo telezi. **sliding-door** *n* mlango telezi. **sliding-scale** *n* mizani uwiano. **sliding seat** *n* kiti telezi (katika mashua ya mashindano).

slight[1] *adj* 1 -dogo, chembe, si muhimu. **not in the ~est** hata kidogo. 2 -embamba. **~ly** *adv* kidogo *I am ~ better today* sijambo kidogo leo. **~ness** *n.*

slight[2] *vt* dharau, tweza, puuza, beza *n* bezo, dharau, twezo *put a ~ on* dharau. **~ingly** *adv*.

slim *adj* 1 -embamba. 2 *(colloq)* -dogo; haba *~ hopes of success* matumaini kidogo ya mafanikio *vi* konda, punguza uzito *~ming exercises* mazoezi ya kujikondesha. **~ly** *adv*. **~ness** *n*.

slime *n* 1 kinamasi, tope la mfinyanzi. 2 ute. **slimy** *adj* 1 -a kuteleza (kama kamasi), -a kinamasi. 2 *(fig)* -danganyifu; -enye unafiki; -erevu.

sling *n* 1 kombeo, kumbwewe, teo. **~ shot** *n* manati. 2 tanzi *have one's arm in a ~* kuwa na mkono uliofungwa tanzi. 3 kutupa kwa kombeo *vt* 1 tupa kwa nguvu, vurumisha. **~ one's hook** *(sl)* ondoka. **~ sb out** tupa mtu nje. **~ mud at sb**. *(fig)* tukana. 2 ning'iniza, tundika. **~ one's coat over one's shoulder** ning'iniza koti begani. **~er** *n* mwenye kombeo/teo.

slink[1] *vi* 1 nyapa, nyata; nyiririka. **~ out** ondoka kisirisiri/kimyakimya.

slink[2] *n (of animals)* kuzaa kabla ya wakati; nyama ya mnyama huyo.

slip *n* 1 utelezi; kuponyoka; kosa dogo, kujikwaa. *(fig)* **~ of the tongue/pen** kosa dogo katika kusema/kuandika. **give the ~ to sb** ponyoka/toroka mtu. **there's many a ~ twixt (the) cup and (the) lip** *(prov)* binadamu hupanga Mungu akapangua. 2 *(of pillow)* foronya; *(underskirt)* gagulo. **gym-~** vazi la msichana la kuchezea sarakasi. 3 karatasi nyembamba. 4 chipukizi. 5 kijana mwembamba. 6 *(usu pl also* **~-way)** bunta, jahabu. 7 *(pl)* jukwaa dogo pembeni mwa jukwaa kuu. 8 *(for earthen ware)* tope la majimaji *vi* 1 teleza, serereka, sepetuka. 2 nyiririka, nyapa, nyata. 3 ponyoka, agaa, churupuka *the cup ~ped from his hand* kikombe kilimponyoka. **let sth ~** achilia jambo/kitu bila kukusudia; toa/fichua siri. **~ through one's fingers** *(lit or fig)* ponyoka. **~ one's mind** *(of a name, address, message)* potea (akilini). 4 vuta/sukuma/vua vuta upesi upesi; penyeza. 5 achia (makosa madogo, n.k.) kufanyika (hasa kutokana na uzembe). **~ up** *(colloq)* kosea. **~-up** *n* kosa dogo. 6 *(of ship, etc)* penya. 7 achia huru; funguka, toka ghafla; *(of a cow)* zaa kabla ya wakati wake. 8 *(compounds)* **~ carriage/ coach** *n* behewa la mwisho (linaloweza kuachanishwa bila kufanya treni isiende). **~-cover** *n* foronya; kitambaa cha kufunikia samani. **~-knot** *n* fundo la kitanzi; fundo linaloweza kufunguliwa kwa kuvuta ncha zake kwa urahisi. **~-road** *n (US)* **(access road)** barabara ndogo ya kuingia/kutoka baraste. **~-stream** *n* mkondo wa hewa kutoka katika rafadha au injini za ndege. **~per** *n* (*often* **pairs of ~s)** sapatu, ndara, makubadhi, koshi. **~ed** *adj* -liovaa sapatu/makubadhi. **~pery** 1 *(of surface)* telezi; *(fig) (of a subject)* nyeti, -enye kuhitaji uangalifu *be on a ~ slope (fig)* elekea hatarini. 2 *(fig of persons)* -janja, -erevu, -laghai. **~periness** *n* 1 utelezi. 2 ujanja. **~py** *adj (colloq)* 1 telezi, -a kuponyoka (kwa urahisi), -a kuchurupuka. 2 *(dated)* haraka *look ~* fanya haraka.

slipshod *adj* hobelahobela, ovyoovyo -a *~-style* mtindo wa ovyoovyo.

slit *vt* pasua, chanja, chana *n* mpasuko, ufa mdogo, mfuo, mwatuko.

slither *vi* telezateleza, nyinyirika. **~ly** *adj* -a kuteleza.

sliver 1 *n* kipande chembamba cha kitu; bamba la mbao *~ of cheese* kipande cha jibini *vi* enga, chanja.

slob *n (sl)* fasiki, baradhuli.

slobber *vi,vt* 1 dorora; toa udenda. **~ over sb** penda mno. 2 lowesha/ lowanisha kwa mate *n* 1 mate, udenda, ute. 2 mazungumzo ya mapenzi.

slog *vt,vi* **~ (at)** piga, charaza (hasa ndondi na kriketi); tembea kwa bidii; fanya kwa bidii. **~ger** *n* mchapa kazi.

slogan *n* wito.
sloop *n* jahazi. ~ **of war** manowari ndogo.
slop[1] *vt,vi* 1 *(of liquids)* mwagika pembeni. 2 ~ **over sb** penda sana. 3 mwaga ~ *beer over the table* mwaga bia mezani. 4 ~ **out** mwaga maji machafu/mkojo. 5 chafua ~ *tea all over the table* chafua meza yote kwa chai. 6 chezea uchafu/matope *n* ~**s** 1 maji machafu; mkojo; mavi (yaliyo kwenye chombo). ~**-basin** beseni la mabaki (mezani). ~**-pail** *n* ndoo ya mkojo (chumbani). 2 vyakula vya majimaji; uji, mchuzi, maziwa; chakula cha nguruwe.
slop[2] *n (pl) (esp. of sailors)* magwanda; matandiko. ~ **room** *(naut)* chumba cha nguo (melini). ~**-shop** *n* duka la mtunguo.
slope *n* mteremko, mwinamo, hanamu *vt,vi* 1 fanya mteremko; inama, inamisha; teremka. 2 ~ **off** *(colloq)* jiondokea (ili kuepa...). 3 ~ **arms** *(mil)* wa na bunduki begani. **sloping** *adj*. **slopingly** *adv*.
sloppy *adj* 1 -a majimaji, -liolowa mvua/tope. 2 *(of food)* -enye chakula cha majimaji *(colloq) (of work)* hobelahobela. 3 *(colloq) (of sentiments)* -a kibwege. **sloppily** *adv*. **sloppiness** *n*.
slosh *n* 1 piga, chapa. 2 ~ **about** garagara katika matope. 3 ~ **sth about** rusha (maji, matope, n.k.). ~**ed** *adj (sl)* -liolowa.
slot *n* 1 mpenyo, tundu jembamba. ~ **machine** mashine yenye kitobo (ya kuuzia vitu). 2 njia. 3 *(colloq)* nafasi (katika kipindi cha *TV*, redio, n.k.) *vt,vi* 1 fanya tundu. 2 kata njia. 3 pangilia/panga kati ya, penyeza.
sloth *n* uvivu, uzembe, ulegevu. ~**ful** *adj* -vivu, -zembe, -legevu.
slouch *vi* enda/simama/kaa kivivu, jikokota. ~ **about** tangatanga *n* 1 mwendo wa kujikokota. 2 *(colloq)* mtu. ~**ingly** *adv* mzito; mzembe. ~**ing** *adj*.
slough[1] *n* kinamasi.
slough[2] *n* ngozi kavu (ya kuambuka), gamba la nyoka *vt,vi* ~ **off** acha; ondoa; ambua ~ *a habit* acha tabia.
sloven *n* mkoo. ~**ly** *adj, adv*. ~**liness** *n*.
slow *adj* 1 -a polepole *a ~journey* safari ya polepole. 2 -zito. ~ **of wit** mzito. 3 *(of watches and clocks)* -a kuchelewa, -a nyuma *be ~ by 10 minutes* chelewa dakika kumi. 4 -a kuchosha, -siovutia. 5 *(compounds)* ~**-coach** *n* mtu mzito, mwenda pole. ~ **march** *n (mil.)* mwendo wa pole. ~**-match** *n* utambi wa kuwaka polepole. ~ **motion** *n (films)* mwendopole. ~**-witted** *adj* bozi. ~**ly** *adv*. ~**ness** *n adv* 1 polepole. **go** ~ enda polepole *(of workers)* fanya mgomo baridi. 2 kwa upole *vi,vt* ~ **(sth) up/down** punguka, punguza mwendo, enda polepole. ~**-down (strike)** *n* mgomo baridi.
sludge *n* 1 kinamasi. 2 uchafu (wa majimaji). 3 uchafu wa grisi/mafuta machafu. ~ **well** banduru. **sludgy** *adj*.
slue *see slew*[1].
slug[1] *n* konokono (asiye na gamba).
slug[2] *n* marisau.
slug[3] *vt,vi (US)* **slog**.
sluggard *n* mtu goigoi, mtu mvivu. **sluggish** *adj* -a polepole, -vivu, -zito, goigoi. **sluggishnness** *n*.
sluice *n* mlizamu *vi,vt* mwagia maji, lowanisha; tenga (madini na mchanga kwa kutumia maji). ~ **(out)** jaza na/osha kwa maji. ~ **out (of water)** toka kwa nguvu katika mlizamu. ~**-gate** *n* mlango mlizamu. ~**-valve** *n* vali mlizamu. ~**-way** *n* njia ya mlizamu.
slum *n* 1 **the** ~**s** maeneo ya ovyo, mtaa wa ovyo. 2 kibanda cha ovyo ovyo. ~ **clearance** ubomoaji na usafishaji wa mtaa wa ovyo *vi* 1 tembelea wakazi wa mtaa na kuwakimu. 2 toa msaada kwa maskini. 3 *(colloq)* ishi maisha ya chini. ~**my** *adj*.
slumber *vi, vt (liter. and rhet)* lala, sinzia, *n* usingizi. ~**er** *n* gonezi. ~**ous** *adj*.

slump *vi* shuka/anguka ghafula, jibwaga; *(of prices, trade, business etc)* shuka ghafula, poromoka *the stock ~ed* hisa zimeshuka bei *n* mbwago, mshuko wa ghafula wa bei, kupungua/kuanguka kwa biashara, mporomoko.

slung *pt pp of* **sling**.

slunk *pt pp of* **slink**.

slur *vt* 1 kokoteza maneno (au sauti). 2 ~ **over sth** pitia haraka (ili kuficha jambo) *n* 1 aibu, fedheha, hizaya, kashfa. **cast a ~ on sb** fedhehesha mtu, kashifu, umbua.

slurry *n* tope laini (la majimaji) la saruji, udongo n.k.

slush *n* 1 matope mepesi; theluji inayoyeyuka. 2 *(fig)* mhemko wa kipuuzi. ~ **fund** *(comm)* fungu la fedha za kuhonga maofisa wa umma. **~y** *adj*.

slut *n* 1 mwanamke mkoo; mwanamke mchafu. **~tish** *adj*.

sly *adj* 1 -janja, -enye hila, -danganyifu, -laghai *on the ~* kwa siri, kwa kificho *a ~ dog/boot* ayari, mtu mwenye siri. 2 *(playful)* tundu, tukutu, -enye usumbi. **~ly** *adv*. **~ness** *n*.

smack[1] *n* 1 kibao, kofi. **get a ~ in the eye** *(colloq)* pata hasara/kipingamizi. **have a ~ at sth** *(colloq)* jaribu kufanya jambo. 2 mwaliko, sauti *vt* 1 piga kofi, zaba kibao. 2 ~ **one's lips** rambitia *adv* ghafula; kwa kishindo *I hit him ~ in the nose* nilimpiga kibao puani. **~er** *n (colloq)* busu kali; *(pound)* pauni au dola (ya kimarekani). **~ing** *n* kupiga kofi; kualika.

smack[2] *n* mashua (ndogo) ya kuvulia samaki.

smack[3] *n* 1 *(taste)* mwonjo, ladha *have a ~ of* -wa na ladha/mwonjo wa *vi* -wa na ladha ya mwonjo wa; ashiria.

small *adj* 1 -dogo. ~ **fry** watu hohehahe; makabwela. 2 dogo, -sio muhimu. ~ **talk** porojo, soga. **be thankful for ~ mercies** shukuru kwa kidogo ulichopata. 3 *(attrib) ~ eater* mtu anayekula kidogo. 4 finyu; bahili, choyo. ~ **minded** *adj* -enye akili finyu. 5 -a hali ya chini, nyofu. **great and ~** watu wa matabaka yote. 6 *in a ~ way* kwa namna yake. 7 *(compounds)*. ~ **arms** *n* silaha nyepesi (bastola, bunduki). ~ **change** *n* sarafu ndogo; *(fig)* porojo. ~ **holder** *n* mkulima mdogo. ~ **holding** shamba. ~ **letters** *n* herufi ndogo. **~pox** *n* ndui. ~ **time** *adj (colloq)* duni, dogodogo. **on the ~ side** ndogo mno (kwa kiasi fulani). **look/feel ~** dhalilika. **~ness** *n*. **the ~ of** sehemu nyembamba. **the ~ of the back** kiuno. **~s** *(colloq)* vitu vidogo vidogo vya kuvaa (k.m. chupi; mkanda). **the still ~ voice** dhamira.

smarmy *adj (colloq)* -a kujipendekeza; -a kupaka mtu mafuta na mgongo wa chupa.

smart[1] *adj* 1 nadhifu, maridadi, -tanashati *a ~ young man/woman* mtanashati. 2 -erevu, stadi. 3 -a haraka, -a upesi *look ~!* chapuka, jikaze! 4 kali *(punishment)* adhabu kali. 5 -a kisasa, -a mitindo. **~ly** *adv* **~ness** *n* **~ten** *vt,vi* ~ **(oneself) (up)** (ji)nadhifisha.

smart[2] *vt,vi* 1 washa, cheneta, chonyota; uma *my eyes ~* macho yangu yanauma/yanawasha. 2 ona uchungu *~ under an injustice* ona uchungu kwa uonevu. 3 *~ for* adhibika *you shall ~ for it* utaona! utakiona! utaona cha mtema kuni! *n* kichomi, mwasho, maumivu makali.

smash *~ (up) vt* 1 vunja, ponda, seta. ~ **and grab raid** uporaji. 2 gonga. 3 vunja, shinda. 4 *(of a business firm)* filisika. 5 *(tennis)* piga kwa nguvu (mpira) *n* 1 mvunjiko. 2 kishindo. **go ~** angamia. 3 piga mpira uanguke chini. **a ~ hit** *(sl)* kitu (wimbo, mchezo) kilichotia fora. *adv* kwa nguvu. **go ~ into sth** gongana na; jibamiza, bamizana na *n (sl)* 1 pigo. 2 mtu/kitu kinachotia fora. **~ing** *adj (colloq)* -a kuvutia sana.

smattering *n (usu* **a ~ (of)**) fununu; ujuzi kidogo tu *I have a ~ of* *chemistry* ninafahamu kemia kidogo.

smear *n* doa; mpako; waa. ~ **word** neno la kashifa; neno la stihizai *vt,vi* 1 ~ **sth on/over/with** paka/ kidogo, paka/tia madoa (ya mafuta). 2 chafua (kwa grisi, mafuta); *(fig)* haribu jina la mtu, paka mtu matope. **a ~(ing) compaign** kumpaka mtu matope. 3 funika, fifisha. **~y** *adj*.

smell *n* 1 (mlango wa fahamu wa) kunusa. 2 harufu; kunuka, kunukia. 3 unusaji, kunusa. *(bad)* uvundo. 4 *(body)* gugumu. 5 *(armpits)* kikwapa, kutuzi. 6 *(fish)* vumba. *vi,vt* 1 nusa, sikia harufu. ~ **round/about** pita pita kupata habari. ~ **sth out** gundua, tafuta kwa kutumia hisi za mnuso au akili. 2 ~ **(of sth)** toa harufu; nukia; nuka. 3 shuku. ~ **of the lamp** *(of work)* -nayoelekea kuwa ilifanywa usiku sana kwa juhudi kubwa. **~ing salts** *n pl* shazasi. **~ing bottle** *n* chupa yenye shazasi. **~er** *n* 1 mnusaji; kinachohisi kwa kunusa (mbwa, paka). 2 *(sl)* pua. **~y** *adj (colloq)* -enye kunuka.

smelt[1] *vt* yeyusha madini.

smelt[2] *n* furu: samaki wadogo aina ya dagaa.

smelt[3] *pp. pt of* **smell**

smile *vi,vt* 1 ~ *(at/on/upon)* tabasamu. ~ **on** fadhili/bariki *John ~d his consent* *John* alitoa ridhaa yake. ~ **at** kejeli, furahia *keep smiling* vumilia. 2 kubali kwa tabasamu *n* tabasamu. **be all ~s** kwa tabasamu *n* tabasamu. **be all ~s** bubujika kwa furaha. **smilingly** *adv*.

smirch *vt* 1 chafua. 2 *(fig)* haribu jina, -toheshimu *n (fig)* aibu, doa.

smirk *vi* kenua *n* kukenua.

smite *vt,vi (arch)* 1 gonga; piga (kwa nguvu). 2 angamiza *God will ~ our enemies* Mungu ataangamiza maadui wetu. 3 choma, pasua.

smith *n (of iron)* mhunzi, mfua(ji); *(of gold, diamond etc.)* sonara. **~y** *n* kiwanda cha mhunzi/sonara, karakana ya mfua chuma.

smithereens *n* vigereng'enza, vipande vidogovidogo *break a glass into ~* vunja kioo katika vipande vidogovidogo.

smitten *pp of* **smite**.

smock *n* gwanda *vt* remba (kwa kutia makunjo madogo madogo). **~ing** *n* kufuma, kuremba (kwa kufuma).

smog *n* mchanganyiko wa ukungu na moshi.

smoke *n* 1 moshi. **end up in ~** isha pasi mafanikio. **go up in ~** teketea (kwa moto); *(fig)* kuwa bure/bilashi, ishia hivihivi/bila mafanikio. ~ **bomb** *n* bomu la moshi. **~-cured/dried** *adj* liokaushwa kwa moshi. **~-screen** *n* wingu la moshi (la kuficha manowari au ndege za vita); *(fig)* maelezo ya kuficha ukweli. **~-stack** *n* dohani; bomba la moshi. 2 kuvuta tumbaku; *(colloq)* sigara. **smoking** *n (in compounds)*. **~-car carriage/~ -compartment** behewa la wavutaji. **~-jacket** *n* vazi jepesi (la kuvaliwa nyumbani tu). **~-room** *n* chumba cha wavutaji hotelini n.k. **~less** *adj* pasipo moshi. **smoky** *adj* -enye moshi mwingi. **smokiness** *n* hali ya moshimoshi *vi,vt* 1 toa moshi, fuka. 2 vuta sigara (tumbaku). 3 kausha (nyama, tumbaku, samaki n.k. kwa moshi). 4 fukiza moshi. ~ **sth out** fukuza kwa moshi; *(fig)* fichua siri. **~r** *n* 1 mvutaji (sigara/tumbaku) *are you a ~?* wewe ni mvutaji? 2 behewa la wavutaji.

smooth *adj* 1 laini, -ororo, sawa, mfuto. ~ **bore** laini; *(of a gun)* -a mtutu laini, -a mtutu usio na mifereji. ~ **faced** *(fig)* nafiki. 2 rahisi; taratibu, tulivu *I am in ~ water now* nimetulia baada ya kupita vipingamizi vingi. **take the rough with the ~** chukulia mambo jinsi yalivyo/yanavyotokea. 3 *(of liquid mixture)* tamu; -liopondwa/kandwa vizuri; laini. 4 *(flattering)* -a kujipendekeza, -a kurairai. ~ **faced/spoken** *adj* nafiki, -enye kurairai. 6 *(compounds)* **~chinned** *adj* 1 -sio na ndevu. 2 -a kidevu mfuto *vt* 1 ~ *sth (down/out/*

away/over) sawazisha, lainisha, rahisisha, ondoa shida. ~ **sb's path** *(fig)* rahisisha mwendo/maendeleo. 2 piga randa; piga pasi, piga msasa, siliba. 3 tulia; tuliza, punguza. 4 *(compounds)* **~ing-iron** *n* pasi. **~ing-plane** *n* randa. **~ly** *adv* 1 bila kukwaruza. 2 kwa urahisi, kwa wepesi; bila taabu. ~ness *n* 1 ulaini, usawa. 2 upole, urahisi.

smorgasbord *n (Swedish)* mlo wenye vyakula anuwai.

smote *pt of* **smite**.

smother *vt* 1 songa roho, kaba roho. 2 ~ **sth/sb with sth** funika, gubika. 3 zima; punguza nguvu ya moto (kwa kufunika majivu). 4 zuia, ficha. ~ **one's anger** zuia hasira *n* (*usu.* **a smother**) wingu la moshi, mvuke, vumbi n.k.

smoulder *vi* ungua polepole (bila kutoa miali); *(fig) (of feelings)* endelea/ kuwepo kisirisiri. ~ **in sb's mind/ heart** kera akilini/moyoni *n* kuungua taratibu.

smudge *vt, vi* tia doa/alama/waa, chafua/chafuka *n* 1 alama, waa, doa (chafu). 2 *(chiefly US)* moto wa nje (wenye moshi mkubwa) wa kuzuia wadudu. **smudgy** *adj*.

smug *adj* -a kujisikia, -a kuridhisha nafsi. **~ly** *adv*. **~ness** *n*.

smuggle *vt, vi* fanya magendo. **~r** *n* mfanya magendo. **smuggling** *n* magendo.

smut *n* 1 doa la masizi, waa, uchafu. 2 fugwe. 3 *(colloq)* upujufu *vt* chafua. **~ty** *adj* 1 -liochafuka kwa masizi. 2 -enye lugha chafu. **~tily** *adv*. **~tiness** *n*.

snack *n* 1 kumbwe; asusa. ~ **bar counter** mkahawa wa kumbwe.

snaffle[1] *n* lijamu.

snaffle[2] *vt (GB sl)* iba, kwepua; nyakua, dokoa.

snag *n* 1 kisiki/mwamba uliojificha (unaoweza kusababisha hatari). 2 *(colloq)* kipingamizi (kilichofichika).

snail *n* konokono, koa. **at a ~'s pace** polepole sana.

snake *n* nyoka. *(fig)* **a ~ in the grass** laghai, mwovu, nyoka. **see ~s** weweseka. ~ **charmer** *n* mcheza nyoka, mzwiriri *vi* pindapinda, jizongazonga. **snaky** *adj*. 1 -enye/-a nyoka. 2 *(fig)* -enye hila, -enye mapindi.

snap *vt, vi* 1 ~ **(at) (sth)** ng'ata, ng'wafua, bana (kwa meno); *(fig)* chukua/kubali; nunua upesi. ~ **sth up** nunua kwa hamu, nunuliwa upesi upesi. 2 data; fungika/fungua kwa kelele, sema/zungumza kwa sauti kali; katika *the rope ~ped* kamba ilikatika. ~ **at sb** karipia mtu, sema mtu kwa hasira. ~ **one's fingers at sb/in sb's face** alika vidole mbele ya mtu mwingine kwa dharau. ~ **sb's nose/head off** karipia; dakiza (mtu katika mazungumzo), rukia maneno. 3 piga picha. 4 *(sl)* ~ **to it** anza kuondoka, ondoka upesi. ~ **out of it** acha (tabia/hali fulani), zinduka *n* 1 mwaliko. 2 **a cold ~** kipindi cha ghafula cha baridi. 3 *(colloq)* nguvu, ari, bidii. 4 keki ndogondogo. 5 *(usu in compounds)* **~-fasteners** (*also* **presstuds**) vifungo/vishikizo vya kubana. 6 *(attrib)* -a ghafla, -a haraka *a ~ election* uchaguzi wa ghafla. **~-lock** *n* kufuli lijifungalo kwa mwaliko. **make it ~py! Look ~py** *(sl)* changamka; harakisha, changamkia. 7 *(compounds)* ~ **shot** picha iliyopigwa haraka (agh. na asiye fundi wa kupiga picha). **~py** *adj*; **~pish** *adj* -a hamaki, -enye harara. **~pishly** *adj*. **~pishness** *n*.

snare *n* 1 mtego,kitanzi. 2 *(fig)* kishawishi, ghiliba. 3 ugwe ufungwao katika tako la ngoma ya pembeni. ~ **drum** ngoma nyugwe *vt* nasa, kamata, tega.

snarl[1] *vi vt* ~ **(at)** *(of dogs)* bwekea; *(of persons)* karipia, ng'aka, kemea *n* la kukemea, kemeo, karipio.

snarl[2] *n* 1 vurugu, msongamano (wa mambo). 2 msokotano wa nywele; *vt, vi* songamana. ~ **up** msongamano wa magari.

snatch *vt* 1 nyakua, pokonya, kwapua, chopoa. 2 twaa upesi, chukua upesi. ~ an **opportunity** tumia fursa chukua *n* 1 kukwapua, kunyakua *(attrib)* **a ~ decision** uamuzi wa ghafla. 2 kipindi kifupi *short ~es of music* vipindi vifupi vifupi vya muziki *work in ~es* fanya kazi kwa vipindi vifupi. **~er** *n* mkwapuaji, mnyakuaji.

sneak *vt,vi* 1 ~ **(on sb)** nyemelea, penyeza kimya kimya. 2 *(school sl)* chongea mwanafunzi mwenzio kisirisiri. 3 *(sl)* iba, kwapua *n* 1 mwoga, msaliti. 2 sakubimbi, mbukuzi. 3 *(school sl)* mbea, mchongezi. **~ing** *adj* -a kisirisiri. **~ers** *n (pl) (in US)* **a pair of ~ers** raba.

sneer *vi* ~ **(at)** kenua, cheka kwa dharau, dhihaki, beza *n* kukenua, dhihaka, dharau, bezo. **~ingly** *adv* kwa dhihaka, kwa dharau.

sneeze *n* chafya *vi* pigachafya, chemua. **not to be ~d at** *(colloq)* si mbaya; si haba *he is not to be ~d at* usimdharau. **sneezing** *n* kuchemua, kupiga chafya.

snick *vt* 1 chanja, kata kidogo. 2 *(of cricket)* betua kidogo; kata *n* pengo; mkato, mchanjo.

snicker *vi* 1 *(of a horse)* lialia. 2 cheka kichinichini; beza.

snide *adj* -a dhihaka, -a kejeli, -a kutweza.

sniff *vt,vi* 1 nusanusa, vuta kamasi. ~ **at** dharau, beua. 2 ~ **(at) sth; ~ sth up** vuta puani *n* kunusa; kuvuta hewa. **~y** *adj (colloq)* 1 duni, bayabaya. 2 -enye kunuka.

sniffle *vi see* **snuffle**.

sniffer *n (dated sl)* pegi; toli: kiasi kidogo cha pombe kali.

snigger *vi* cheka kidogo,cheka kichinichini; beua *n* kicheko cha chinichini au kebehi.

snip *vt,vi* ~ **(at) sth; ~ sth off** kata kwa mkasi. ~ **off** kata kipande *n* 1 mkato. 2 kipande *(fig)* kitu kidogo *(colloq)* jambo lipatikanalo kwa urahisi. **~ping** *n*. **snipe** *n* 1 kichonge: aina ya ndege.

snipe *vt* 1 ~ **(at)** tungua, dungua/adui mmoja mmoja kutoka mafichoni kwa risasi. 2 shambulia kwa hila *n* shambulio. **~r** *n* askari doria, mdunguzi.

snippet *n* 1 kijipande. 2 *(pl)* dondoo la habari.

snitch *vt,vi* 1 *(sl)* dokoa. 2 *(sl)* ~ **(on sb)** chongea, semea.

snivel *vi* 1 vutavuta kamasi, penga. 2 lialia kwa kujifanya *n* 1 kamasi. 2 kulia kwa manung'uniko. **~ler** *n* mpengaji (kamasi); mnung'unikaji.

snob *n* mpenda ukuu, mdharau wanyonge; mjivunia hadhi. **~bery** *n* kujiona, kupenda makuu. **~bish** *adj* -a kupenda makuu. **~bishly** *adv*. **~bishness** *n*.

snood *n* 1 wavu wa nywele. 2 kishipi (cha ndoana).

snook *n* **cock a ~ (at sb)** onyesha dharau kwa mtu (kwa kuweka dole gumba katika pua).

snooker *n* snuka: mchezo wa kugonga tufe mezani. **be ~ at** *(colloq)* tegewa, wekwa katika hali ngumu.

snoop *vt, vi (colloq)* ~ **(about/around)** peleleza, dadisi, dukiza ~ *into* jihusisha na mambo ya wengine. **~ er** *n*.

snooty *adj* -a kujidai, -enye dharau.

snooze *vi* sinzia, lala usingizi kidogo mchana *n* usingizi wa muda mfupi mchana.

snore *vi* koroma, forota *n* kukoroma, kuforota; koromo. **~r** *n*.

snorkel,schnorkel *n* neli ya hewa ya mzamia.

snort *vi (of animals)* koroma; toa pumzi puani *vt* ~ *defiance* tia shari, pandisha mori; *(colloq)* cheka kwa kikwakwa *n* kukoroma; kutoa pumzi puani. **~er** *n* 1 mkoromaji. 2 *(sl)* kioja. 3 dhoruba. **~y** *adv*.

snot *n* 1 kamasi. 2 mwenye kamasi. 3 *(sl)* kizabizabina. **~-rag** *n (sl)* kitambaa cha kamasi, leso. **~ty** *adj* 1 *(vulg)* -enye makamasi. 2 -epesi kwa hasira. 3 ~ **(nosed)** *(sl)* -a kujihisi, -a kujiona; mtu anayejidaidai; mwenye dharau.

snout *n* pua la nguruwe.

snow *n* theluji *vt,vi* -nya theluji, anguka (kama) theluji, tupia theluji; vuvumka. **be ~ed in/up** kwamishwa na 'theluji. **be ~ed under (with)** elemewa, zidiwa. **~ ball** *n* bonge la theluji; jambo/kitu kinachoongezeka kadiri kinavyokwenda; shindano la kutupiana tufe la theluji; kuongezeka haraka (kwa ukubwa, maana nk.). **~-blind** *adj* -liokiwishwa na mng'ao wa theluji. **~ blindness** *n* kukiwishwa na mng'ao wa theluji. **~-bound** *adj* -a kufungiwa/kuzuiwa na theluji. **~-cap** *n* kilele chenye theluji. **~-capped/ clad/covered** *adj* -liofunikwa na theluji. **~ drift** *n* chungu ya theluji (iliyokumbwa na upepo). **~ fall** *n* kuanguka kwa theluji; . **~-field** *n* mbuga ya theluji; upeo wa theluji. **~flake** *n* kipande kidogo sana cha theluji; chembe. **~-line** *n* mwanzo wa theluji isiyoyeyuka. **~-man** *n* sanamu ya mtu ya theluji. **~plough** *n* gari la kuondoshea theluji njiani. **~-shoes** *n* viatu vya theluji. **~-slide/~slip** *n* mmomonyoko wa/maporomoko ya theluji. **~-storm** *n* dhoruba ya theluji. **~-white** *adj* -weupe wa theluji, safi. **~y** *adj* -a theluji; -eupe sana. **~ily** *adv*.

snub[1] *vt* puuza, dharau, bera *n* dharau, bezo.

snub[2] *adj (only in)* **a ~-nosed** *adj* -a pua fupi.

snuff[1] *n* ugoro, tumbaku ya kunusa. **up to ~** *(colloq)* erevu; zima *vi* nusanusa; vuta hewa/tumbako puani. **~ box** kikopo/kijaluba cha ugoro. **~-coloured** *adj* -a rangi ya ugoro.

snuff[2] *vt,vi* 1 kata sehemu ya utambi (wa mshumaa) ilioungua. *(extinguish)* **~ sth out** *(lit or fig)* zima. 2 **~ out** *(sl)* -fa, fariki *n.* utambi wa mshumaa ulioungua. **~ers** *n (pl)* mkasi wenye kisanduku cha kudakia utambi wa mshumaa ukishaungua.

snuffle *vt* 1 sinasina. 2 semea puani *n* 1 king'ong'o. 2 kuvuta kamasi.

snug *adj* 1 buraha, -a raha mustarehe. 2 **as ~ as a bug in a rug** raha mustarehe. 3 nadhifu. 4 -a kubana *(of clothes);* -a kukaa. 5 -a kuridhisha. **~ly** *adv*. **~ness** *n*. **~gery** *n* mahali pa buraha.

snuggle *vt vi* 1 **~ (up) (to sb)** sogelea (ili kupata joto, faraja n.k). 2 **~ sb to sb** vuta karibu, kumbatia.

so *adv* 1 *(of degree)* kwa kiasi hicho *we didn't expect him to stay ~ long* hatukumtarajia kukaa kiasi hicho. 2 tafadhali *would you be ~ kind as to come tommorow* tafadhali njoo kesho. 3 kiasi kwamba *he was ~ tired that he could not walk the distance* alichoka kiasi kwamba alishindwa kutembea. 4 **~ as** (kiasi) kama *it is not ~ good a book as his earlierone* si kitabu kizuri kama kile alichoandika mwanzo. 5 sana *it's ~ easy* ni rahisi sana. 6 *(in phrases)* **~ far** hadi hapo. **~ far as** kwa kadiri. **~ far ~ good** mambo mazuri hadi hapo. **~ far from** badala ya, kinyume cha. **~ long as** ilimradi. **~ much/many** kiasi fulani. **not ~ much as** kama. **~ much** tupu. **~ much ~ that** kiasi kwamba *(of manner)* 1 hivyo, hivi, kwa namna hiyo, *~ it was* ndivyo ilivyokuwa. 2 *(in phrases) ~ called* -nayodaiwa kuwa *~ that* ili, mpaka, kusudi; kwa hiyo *~... that* kwa namna kwamba; kwa namna ambayo. **~ as to do sth** ili kufanya kitu/jambo. 3 hivyo *I told you ~* nilikwambia hivyo. 4 naam. 5 pia *~ did I* mimi pia. 6 *(various uses)* **or ~** kitu kama hicho. **and ~ on and ~forth** na kadhalika. **just ~** hivyo tu; safi. **~ to say/speak** kitu kama hicho. **~ and ~** *(colloq)* fulani; *(derog)* kisirani *conj.* 1 kwa hiyo; ndiyo maana. 2 *(exclamatory)* kumbe! alaa! **~ ever** *adv (usu as suffix to rel. prons, adv, adj)* -o ote -le, kwa vyovyote vile. **what end ~ ever** pamoja na mwisho wowote. **who ~ ever** *(rel. pron)* yeyote yule.

soak *vt,vi* 1 lowa, tota. 2 **~ sth (in sth)**

loweka/lowesha/lowanisha. ~ **oneself in sth** *(fig)* zama, zamia. 3 ~ **sth up** fyonza, nyonya. 4 *(of rain etc)* ~ **sb (through)** lowanisha, lowesha. **be ~ed to the skin** lowa chepe chepe. 5 ~ **through sth** penya/penyeza. 6 *(sl)* chukulia mtu pesa kwa kulipiza/lipisha zaidi. 7 *(colloq)* wa mlevi, kunywa pombe sana *n* 1 kulowana. **in** ~ kulowanisha. **put in** ~ lowanisha. 2 *(sl) (usu old soak)* mlevi. **~er** *n* 1 *(colloq)* mvua nyingi. 2 mlevi.

so-and-so *n* 1 fulani *Mr. so and so* Bw. fulani. 2 hohehahe.

soap *n* sabuni. **~-berry** *n* mharita. **~-box** *n* kikwezeo cha msemaji barabarani. **~bubble** *n* tufe la povu. ~ **opera** *(US)* mfululizo wa drama ya mivutano ya kijamii. **~suds** mapovu ya sabuni. **~-works** *n* kiwanda cha sabuni *vt* 1 paka sabuni, tia sabuni. 2 *(colloq)* sifusifu; jipendekeza, visha kilemba cha ukoka. **~y** *adj.*

soar *vi* 1 ruka juu kwa mabawa; puruka, paa angani. 2 *(of prices)* panda sana *prices are ~ing* bei zinapanda sana.

sob *vi* mamia. ~ **sth out** sema kwa kikweukweu *n* kikweukweu; kikwifukwifu. **~-story** *n* hadithi iliyotiwa chumvi ili kuhuzunisha. **~-stuff** *n* maneno/maandishi yenye chumvi. **~bingly** *adv.*

sober *adj* 1 tulivu, -enye busara, -a makini, -taratibu. ~ **colours** rangi zisizovutia/baridi. **~-minded** *adj* -enye tafakuri, -a taratibu. **~-sides** *n (dated colloq)* mtu makini. 2 -siolewa, si -levi. **~ly** *adv* **as ~ as a judge** siolewa hata kidogo *vt, vi* ~ **(sb) down** 1 tuliza. 2 ~ **(sb) up** toa ulevi.

sobriety *n* 1 utulivu. 2 kunywa kiasi.

sobriquet *n* msimbo, lakabu.

soccer *n* soka, kandanda, mpira wa miguu.

social *adj* 1 -a jamii, -a ushirikiano. ~ **position** hadhi. ~ **interests** matakwa ya jamii. ~ **integration** mwingiliano wa kijamii. ~ **roles** wajibu wa kijamii, wajibu katika jamii. ~ **services** huduma za jamii. ~ **system** mfumo wa jamii. ~ **status** hadhi ya kijamii katika jamii. ~ **stratification** tabaka za kijamii. ~ **order** utangamano wa jamii. ~ **security** ruzuku ya serikali (kwa wasiojiweza na wasio na kazi). ~ **Democrat** mjamaa (anayetaka kuleta ujamaa kwa njia ya mageuzi ya amani). ~ **club** chama. 2 bashasha, cheshi, changamfu. 3 *(of animals)* -a jumuiya/pamoja. ~ **work** *n* huduma za jamii. ~ **worker** *n* mfanyakazi wa huduma za jamii. **sociable** *adj* -changamfu, -kunjufu, bashasha. **sociably** *adv*. **sociability** *n*. ~ **welfare** *n* ustawi wa jamii.

socialism *n* ujamaa. **demagogic** ~ ujamaa wa domo. **traditional** ~ ujima. **socialist** *n* 1 mjamaa. 2 msoshalisti *adj* -a kijamaa *a socialistic transfromation* mageuzi ya kijamaa.

socialite *n (US) (colloq)* mtu mwenye hadhi ya juu (katika mfumo wa kibepari); tajiri; kizito. **socialize** *vt* ishi pamoja; endesha/fanya -a umma, juana. **socialization** *n*. **socially** *adv*. pamoja.

society *n* 1 maisha ya kuishi pamoja; mfumo wa jamii. 2 jamii. 3 shirika; umoja; chama. 4 tabaka la watu wa nasaba/koo bora.

socio *pref.* -a jamii *~-economic problems* matatizo ya kijamii na kiuchumi *~linguistics* isimu jamii. **~logy** *n* elimu-jamii, sosiolojia. **~logist** *n* mwana elimujamii, mwanasosiolojia. **~logical** *adj*. **~logically** *adv*.

sock[1] 1 *(often* **pairs of ~s***)* soksi. **pull one's ~s up** *(colloq)* fanya jitihada. **put a ~ in it**! *(sl)* kimya! kelele! nyamaza! 2 soli ya ndani ya kiatu.

sock[2] *n (sl)* kibao, pigo (la ngumi). **give sb a ~ on the chin** piga mtu ngumi ya kidevuni *vt* piga mtu ngumi *adv (sl)* barabara.

socket *n* 1 tundu, shimo (kama la jicho). 2 soketi.

sod[1] *n* tabaka la juu la udongo (pamoja

na majani au nyasi). **under the ~** kaburini.

sod[2] *n (vulgar) (sl)* 1 basha. 2 mshenzi. **s~ it!** shenzi. **~ off** toka hapa, potea.

soda *n* 1 magadi. **baking ~** magadi ya kuumulia. 2 soda. **~-fountain** *n* mgahawa. **~ water** *n* maji ya gesi ya kaboni. **~-pop** *n* soda.

sodden *adj* 1 chepechepe, majimaji. 2 -zito kama kinyunya kilicholowana. 3 levi sana, -liokunywa sana *vt,vi* lowesha, lowanisha; lowana.

sodium *n* sodiamu *~ carbonate* magadi. **~ chloride** chumvi.

sodomy *n* kufirana/ufiranaji; kulawiti/ulawitianaji. **sodomite** *n* mfiraji, mlawiti, basha.

sofa *n* sofa; kochi. **~ bed** kitanda cha sofa.

soft *adj* 1 *(of surfaces, of sounds etc)* -ororo, laini *a ~ pillow* mto laini *~ wind* upepo mworororo *~ fur* manyoya mororo *~ music* muziki mororo. **~ mud** kinamasi. **~ landing** utuaji salama. **~ land** tua salama. 2 *(of colours)* -sio kali, -liofifia. 3 *(of outlines)* -siokuwa wazi, -sio dhahiri. 4 *(of answers, words etc)* pole, -a kupendeza, tamu, laini. 5 *(of water)* -sio na chumvi. 6 *(orig US)* tamu, -si kileo. **~ drinks** vinywaji baridi. 7 -epesi, rahisi. **~ work** kazi nyepesi. **~ job** *(sl)* kazi nyepesi yenye malipo makubwa. 8 -nyonge, dhaifu. 9 -enye huruma *have a ~ spot for sb* penda; pendelea. 10 *(colloq)* -pumbavu; bwege. 11 *(compounds)* **~-boiled** *adj* -liochemshwa kidogo. **~ coal** mkaa hafifu (wenye kutoa moshi). **~ currency** *n* fedha zisizobadilishika kwa dhahabu au kwa fedha fulani fulani. **~ drug** *n* dawa baridi (k.m. bangi, kungumanga n.k.). **~ footed** *adj (of a person)* -a kunyata. **~ headed** *adj* bozi, zuzu. **~hearted** *adj* -enye huruma, -pole. **~ option** njia/uteuzi rahisi. **~ palate** *n* kaakaa laini *~ pedal (fig)* lainisha (agh. kwa maneno). **~ soap** *n* sabuni ya maji; *(fig)* kilemba cha ukoka. **~-spoken** *adj* -enye sauti nyororoo, -enye maneno mazuri. **~ solder** *n* lehemu/risasi laini *vt* lehemu/chomea na risasi laini. **~ware** *n* data, programu ya kompyuta. **~ witted** *adj* pumbavu. **~ wood** *n* mbao laini. **~ish** *adj*. **~ly** *adv*. **~ness** *n*. **~y** *n* 1 (mtu) bozi, zuzu. 2 (mtu) dhalili. **~en** *vt,vi* lainisha, punguza (ukali), rahisisha; lainika. **~ sb up** *(of enemy positions)* piga (kwa makombora n.k.) kabla ya kushambulia; *(of persons)* lainisha kwa kushawishi/kubembeleza. **~ener** *n* kilainishaji.

soggy *adj* chepechepe, chapachapa, dabwadabwa **sogginess** *n*.

soil[1] *n* 1 udongo *heavy ~* udongo mzito *light (sandy) ~* udongo wa kichanga. **~erosion** mmomonyoko wa udongo *~ conservation* kuhifadhi ardhi. **~ pipe** *n* bomba la choo cha maji *~ science* sayansi ya udongo *~ survey* uchunguzi wa ardhi. 2 nchi *one's native ~* nchi ya mtu fulani.

soil[2] *n* uchafu *vt, vi* chafua; chafuka. **~ one's hands** shiriki katika jambo baya.

soiree *n* tafrija ya jioni, tumbuizo la hisani (agh. kusaidia malengo ya jamii).

sojourn *vi* shinda; kaa kwa muda *n* kushinda. **~er** *n* mgeni; msafiri, mpita njia.

sol *n (hum) (often* **old s~***)* jua.

solace *n* faraja, tumbuizo, kitulizo; liwazo. **derive ~ from sth** pata faraja kutoka kitu fulani *vt* fariji, tuliza, tumbuiza, burudisha, liwaza. **~ oneself with sth** jifariji kwa kitu fulani.

solar *adj* -a jua, -a sola. **~ cell** beteri/seli ya nishati ya jua; kifaa kinachogeuza mwanga/nishati ya jua kuwa umeme. **~ energy** *n* nishati ya jua/sola. **~ calculator** *n* kikokotoo sola. **the ~ system** mfumo wa jua na sayari zake. **~ plexus** mishipa ya fahamu (nyuma ya tumbo) *the ~ year* kipindi cha dunia kuzunguka jua. **~ium** *n* chumba/jengo la tiba/

burudani linaloruhusu mionzi ya jua kuingia.

sold *pt,pp of* **sell**

solder *vt* lehemu; unganisha kwa lehemu, *n* lehemu, risasi ya kulehemia. **~er** *n* mlehemi, mlehani. **~ing iron** *n* nyundo ya kulehemia.

soldier *n* askari, mwanajeshi. **private ~** askari wa kawaida. **~ of fortune** mamluki, askari wa kukodiwa *vi* fanya kazi ya uaskari. **be tired of ~ing** choshwa na uaskari. **~ on** fanya kazi kwa ujasiri. **~ly; ~like** *adj* kama askari, kiaskari; kakamavu; jasiri. **~y** *n.*

sole[1] *n* 1 wayo. 2 soli *vt* weka soli.

sole[2] *adj* 1 pekee, -a peke yake. 2 -a mtu/kampuni, n.k. moja tu. **~ trader** *n* mfanyabiashara pekee. **~ly** *adv.*

sole[3] *n (of fish)* wayo: samaki bapa.

solecism *n* 1 kosa/kasoro (ndogo) katika matumizi ya lugha. 2 utovu wa adabu. 3 kosa la uvunjaji kanuni za kundi.

solemn *adj* 1 -a kuandamana na ibada/ sherehe (agh. za dini). 2 -enye taadhima. 3 makini, -a dhati, zito. **~ declaration** tamko la dhati/zito. **~ly** *adv.* **~ ness** *n* **~ity** *n* 1 makini, uzito, umuhimu. 2 taadhima. **~ize** *vt* 1 tekeleza ibada itakiwavyo. 2 -pa taadhima. **~ization** *n.*

solicit *vt,vi* 1 **~ sb (for sth)** omba, sihi. 2 *(of a prostitute)* tongoza. **~ation** *n.* **~or** *n* 1 mwanasheria; wakili. **~or and client costs** gharama za mwanasheria na mteja *S~ General* Mwanasheria wa Serikali. 2 mshawishi, mbembeleza (biashara n.k.). **~ous** *adj.* **~ (for/about/ sth/sb); ~ (to sth)** -enye kutaka kusaidia, -a kujihusisha (na mambo ya mtu mwingine); -enye kujali. **~ously** *adv.* **~ude** *n* kutaka kusaidia, kujihusisha (na mambo ya mtu mwingine); wasiwasi, mashaka.

solid *adj* 1 -a mango. **~ fuel** fueli mango. **~ state** *adj (of electronic devices)* -a transista tupu, -sio na vali. 2 yabisi; nene. 3 -a mfululizo, -zima *two ~ days* siku mbili mfululizo 4. -liozibwa kabisa *~ sphere* tufe. 5 thabiti, imara, gumu *~ furniture* samani imara. **be on ~ ground** -wa na hakika. 6 aminifu, -a kutegemewa *a man of ~ character* mtu mwaminifu/ mtegemewa. 7 tupu *~ gold* dhahabu tupu. 8 -enye umoja, -lioshikamana *we are ~ for our rights* tuna umoja juu ya haki zetu. **~arity** *n* umoja, mshikamano *workers ~* umoja/mshikamano wa wafanyakazi. 9 *(maths)* -enye kina, urefu na upana/ ujazo; -a mango *~ ball* tufemango *n* 1 mango, kitu kigumu. 2 *(geom)* mango. **~ly** *adv.* **~ity**. **~ness** *n* umango, uimara, uthabiti, madhubuti. **~ify** *vt, vi* 1 fanya gumu, damiza, ganda/ gandisha. 2 imarisha. **~ification** *n.*

soliloquy *n* mazungumzo ya nafsi, kusema na nafsi, kusema mwenyewe. **soliloquize** *vi* zungumza na nafsi.

solipsism *n* nadharia kwamba mtu anaweza kumudu ya nafsi tu.

solitaire *n* 1 *(of jewel)* kito kimoja. 2 *(of cards)* mchezo wa mtu mmoja.

solitary *adj* -a peke (yake), pweke, -moja tu, -a kujitenga, -kiwa. **~ confinement**, kutengwa, kifungo cha upweke. **in ~** (wa) katika kifungo cha upweke. **solitude** *n* 1 upekee, upweke; faragha, ukiwa 2 mahali pa upweke.

solo *n* 1 solo, wimbo wa mtu mmoja. 2 jambo linalofanywa na mtu mmoja *adj* -a mtu mmoja tu, peke yake *adv* kwa pekee, -peke yake. **~ist** *n* mwenye kuimba/ tenda peke yake.

solstice *n* solistasi: wakati jua linapokuwa kaskazini/ kusini kabisa mwa Ikweta.

solution *n* 1 **~ (to/for/of)** jibu, ufumbuzi (wa tatizo), utatuzi. 2 myeyusho, uoevu, mmumunyo. 3 mchanganyiko. **soluble** *adj* mumunyifu, -a kuyeyuka, -a kuyeyushwa. **solubility** *n* umumunyifu. **solute** *n (chem)* kioevu, kimumunyishwaji.

solve *vt (explain)* fumbua, tafuta jibu, fumbua ~ *a difficulty* tatua tatizo. **solvable** *adj* -a kutatulika. **~nt** *adj* 1 -a kuyeyusha; -a kumumunyisha. 2 *(comm)* -a kuweza kulipa (madeni) *n* kimumunyishaji, kiyeyushi. **~ncy** *n* uwezo wa kulipa madeni.

somatic *adj* -a mwili/maungo.

sombre *(US* **somber**) *adj* 1 -a giza, -eusi, -zito 2 -a huzuni, -a majonzi. **~ly** *adv*. **~ness** *n*.

sombrero *n* pama.

some *adj* 1 kiasi (tu) *I want ~ food* na taka chakula (kiasi). 2 -ingine, baadhi *~ children don't like school* watoto wengine hawapendi shule. 3 fulani *he works at ~ office in town* anafanya kazi katika ofisi fulani mjini. 4 kiasi kidogo/kikubwa *they spent ~ time looking for accomodation* walitumia muda mwingi wakitafuta malazi *adv* kama *~ fifty students demonstrated* wanafunzi kama/wapatao hamsini waliandamana *pron* baadhi/sehemu ya *~ of his friends do not agree with him* baadhi ya marafiki zake hawakubaliani naye. **~body/~one** *n* 1 mtu (fulani). 2 mtu maarufu *he is ~body* ni mtu maarufu/ wa maana. **~how** *adv* kwa namna fulani, kwa namna. **~-how or other** kwa namna moja au nyingine; vyovyote vile. **~ place** *adv (US informal)* mahali fulani. **~thing** *n* 1 kitu, jambo (fulani). 2 **or ~thing** *(colloq)* kitu kama hicho Juma *is a doctor ~* Juma ni daktari au kitu kama hicho. 3 **~ thing of** kama, hivi. **she is ~thing of a thief** yu mdokozi dokozi/ mwizimwizi. **~ thing like** kufanana kidogo, kadiri; kweli kweli; takriban *he is ~thing like his father* anafanana na baba yake; anamlanda babaye kwa namna *it must be ~thing like six o'oclock* haikosi inapata saa kumi na mbili. **~time** *adv* 1 siku moja, wakati/siku fulani. 2 *(also as adj)* aliyetangulia, aliyewahi kuwa. **~times** *adv* mara nyingine, wakati mwingine, pengine. **~way** *adv* kwa jinsi fulani. **~way or other** jinsi hii au nyingine. **~what** *adv* kidogo; kwa kiasi fulani *this is ~what hazy* hii si dhahiri *he is ~what of an artist* yeye kidogo ni msanii. **~where** *adv* mahali fulani *she was ~where about seventy* alikuwa karibu miaka sabini *~where around (time)* mnamo.

somersault *n* kichwa ngomba *vi* pinduka, kichwangomba.

somnambulism *n* kutembea usingizini. **somnambulist** *n*.

somnolent *adj* -a usingizi, -a kusinzia, -a kutia usingizi. **somnolence** *n*

son *n* mtoto wa kiume *the ~of God; the ~of Man Yesu Kristo the ~ of men* wanadamu. **~-in law** mkwe. 2 *(used as a form of address)* mwanangu *my ~* mwanangu! 3 *~ of* bin *a ~ of the soil* mkulima. **~ny** *n* kijana, bwana mdogo.

sonar *n* sona: chombo cha kugundua vitu vilivyomo ndani/chini ya maji kwa mawimbi ya sauti.

sonata *n (mus.)* sonata.

song *n* 1 wimbo. **~bird** *n* chiriku. 2 ushairi. **~-book** kitabu cha nyimbo. **buy sth for a ~/an old ~; go for a ~** uzwa kwa bei ya chini. **nothing to make a ~ and dance about** *(colloq)* isiyo na maana. **a ~ and dance** *(colloq)* usumbufu, makelele, maudhi. **~ster/stress** mutribu, mwimbaji.

sonic *adj* -a kuhusu sauti, mawimbi sauti au mwendo/kasi ya mawimbi sauti.

sonometer *n* sonometa:kipima mawimbi ya sauti.

sonorous *adj* 1 -a sauti kubwa (nene), -a kuvuma sana. 2 *(of language, words)* -a kuvutia. **sonorously** *adv*. **~ness** *n*. **sonority** *n*.

sonnet *n* soniti: utenzi wa mistari 14. **~eer** *n (usu derog)* mtunzi wa soniti.

sonsy *adj (scot)* tipwatipwa, (msichana) mcheshi.

soon *adv* 1 karibu, hivi punde *~ after* baadaye kidogo, mara baada ya;

hatimaye. 2 mapema, kabla ya *how ~?* mapema kiasi gani *she was there ten minutes too ~* alifika pale dakika kumi kabla ya wakati. 3 **as/so ~as** mara...po.. *as ~ as she came* mara alipofika, wakati uliotakiwa. **no ~er than** mara.. po.. mara moja; papo hapo. **no ~er said than done** fanyika mara moja. 4 *(in double comparative constructions)* **the ~er the better** mapema iwezekanavyo. **~er or later** hapana budi, siku moja; ipo siku. 5 *(suggesting comparison) (just)* **as ~ (as)** sawa *I would just as ~ walk as go by bus* ni sawa kutembea au kwenda kwa basi. **~er than** kulikoni *~er than cook he will skip his meal* atasamehe mlo kulikoni kupika *as ~ as not* mara moja; kwa moyo mkunjufu *I'd join the University as ~ as not* nitapenda sana kujiunga na chuo kikuu.

soot *n* masizi *he is as black as ~* ni mweusi tititi. **~y** *adj* -a masizi, -eusi sana *vt* paka masizi.

sooth *n (archaic)* kweli *in ~* kweli. **~ sayer** mtabiri.

soothe *vt* 1 tuliza, bembeleza. 2 punguza/poza (maumivu). **soothingly** *adv*.

sop *n* 1 kitonge (cha mkate, n.k.) kilichochovywa ndani ya mchuzi n.k. 2 **a ~ to sb** kitulizo, rushwa. **throw a ~ to Cerberus** honga/toa rushwa (kutuliza mtu) *vt* chovya/loweka katika mchuzi/maji n.k. **~ sth up** nyonya/fyonza uowevu. **~ping** *adj* -a kulowana, -a kutota.

sophism *n* hoja potofu **sophist** *n* mpotoshaji. **sophistry** *n* maneno ya hila, ghiliba, werevu, madanganyo.

sophisticated *adj* 1 staarabu. 2 -a kisasa 3 *(of mental activity)* changamano. **sophistication** *n*.

sophomore *n (US)* mwanafunzi wa mwaka wa pili chuoni.

soporific *adj* -a kutia usingizi. **soporiferous** *adj*.

soppy *adj* 1 chepechepe, chapachapa, dabwadabwa. 2 *(colloq)* -a hisia za kipuuzi.

soprano *n* soprano. **~ voice** sauti ya kwanza (ya kike au mtoto mdogo).

sorbet *n* see **sherbert**.

sorcerer *n* mchawi, mlozi (wa kiume).

sorceress *n* mchawi wa kike. **sorcery** *n* uchawi, ulozi, usihiri.

sordid *adj* 1 *(of conditions)* duni, hafifu, dhalili *living in ~poverty* ishi maisha ya hawinde. 2 bahili, -a kujihini. **~ly** *adv*. **~ness** *n*.

sore *adj* 1 -a kuumwa *I am ~ all over* ninaumwa mwili mzima. **like a bear with a ~ head** -enye ghadhabu/hasira, gomvi. **a sight for ~eyes** -a kuvutia macho, -a kuburudisha, -a kutuliza. 2 -a majonzi, -enye uchungu, sononi. 3 -a kutia uchungu, -a kero/maudhi. **a ~ point/subject** jambo nyeti. 4 *(old use; also adverbial)* mno, sana, kubwa. **in ~ distress** kwa uchungu mkubwa. 5 -enye kukereka/kuudhika *n* 1 kidonda, jeraha. 2 *(fig)* donda *don't bring up old ~* usitoneshe donda. **~ly** *adv* sana, mno *~ tempted* shawishika sana *military help is ~ needed* msaada wa kijeshi unahitajika mno. **~ness** *n*.

sorghum *n* mtama.

sorority *n* 1 udada, ushoga. 2 chama/ klabu ya mashoga.

sorrel *adj* -a rangi ya kahawia -nyekundu; -a rangi ya hudhurungi -nyekundu.

sorrow *n* huzuni, sikitiko, ghamu, simanzi, sononeko *more in ~ than in anger* kwa huzuni zaidi kuliko hasira. **the Man of S ~s** Yesu *vi ~* **(at, for, over)** sononeka. **~ful** *adj*. **~fully** *adv*. **~-stricken** *adj* -a kufikwa na majonzi, -a kuingiwa na huzuni.

sorry *adj* 1 -a huzuni, sikitiko, ghamu; -a majuto, toba. **be/feel ~ (about/ for sth)** sikitika; tubu. 2 **be ~ for sb** hurumia, sikitikia. 3 hafifu, nyonge, maskini. 4 *(used to express mild regret or apology)* samahani.

sort *n* 1 jinsi, namna, aina, mtindo;

what ~ of fellow is he? ni mtu wa namna gani? *of an African ~* -a Kiafrika *of a ~/of ~s -a* aina yake, -a namna fulani. 2 hali *I ~ of felt it* nilihisi hivyo. **a ~ of** -nyangalika. *(colloq)* **after a ~, in a ~**, kwa kiasi fulani 3 **a good ~** mtu mzuri, mwungwana. 4 **out of ~s;** *(colloq)* hoi, -gonjwa, ovyoovyo *(colloq) he is out of ~* hajiwezi, kidogo mgonjwa ~ *vi,vt* 1 ~ **sth (out)** ~ *(classify)* tenga, chambua, ainisha, changanua, piga mafungu ~ *out the good soldiers from the bad ones* ainisha askari wazuri na wabaya. ~ **sth out** *(colloq)* tatua, maliza *let developing nations ~ out their own problems* ziache nchi zinazoendelea zitatue matatizo yao. 2 **~-well/ill with** *(liter)* chukuana/achana na. **~er** *n* 1 mchaguaji, mtengaji (barua n.k.). 2 mashine ya kuchagulia/kuchambua. **~ing** *n* uchambuzi, kuchambua, uainishaji.

sortie *n* 1 shambulio la askari waliozingirwa (kwa waliowazingira). 2 shambulio moja la ndege ya vita.

SOS *n* 1 *(of ship, aerophane etc)* wito wa msaada. 2 yowe/kilio cha msaada.

so-so *adj* -a hivi hivi, -a kuvumilika *adv* hivi hivi tu *he played marimba only ~* alipiga marimba hivyo hivyo tu.

sot *n* mlevi *vt* -lewa sana. **~tish** *adj* -levi; -jinga (kwa sababu za ulevi). **~tishly** *adv*. **~ tishness** *n*.

sotto voce *adv* kwa sauti ndogo, kwa kunong'ona, kwa sauti ya chini, kwa pembeni.

sou *n* (*Fr*) senti; *(fig)* nduruiu *he hasn't a ~* hana hata nduruiu moja.

sough *vi* vuma (upepo) *n* uvumi, mvumo.

sought *pt,pp of* **seek**.

soul *n* 1 roho, nafsi. **heart and ~** nguvu zote. 2 akili; zinduko; moyo; hisia. 3 mtu *there was not a ~ to be seen* hapakuwa na mtu hata mmoja. **poor ~!** maskini! *he is the ~ of bravery* yeye ni shujaa hasa. **a dull ~** boza. 4 *the life and ~ of the party* tegemeo la kila mtu. 5 mfano bora, kielelezo. 6 *(US colloq)* sifa mwafaka; hisia za kidugu. ~ **music** muziki (wenye hisia za) kidugu. ~ **brother/sister** ndugu/mwenzi katika hisia zinduzi. **~ful** *adj* -a kuzindua moyo; zinduzi, -a kuamsha (kuleta, kuingiza) maono mema. **~fully** *adv*. **~less** *adj* -enye roho ngumu, katili. **~lessly** *adv*. 7 *(compounds)* ~ **destroying** *adj* dhalilishi; -a kuchusha. **~-stirring** *adj* -a kereketo; -a kuchangamsha -a kusisimua.

sound[1] *n* 1 sauti, mlio. 2 uvumi, mvumo. 3 maana (ya kichinichini). 4 *(compounds)* ~ **archive** *n* kumbukumbu za kanda. ~ **barrier** *n* mapatano ya spidi ya sauti na ya ndege. **~-box** santuri. ~ **effects** *n* mapambo ya sauti. **~-film** *n* filamu yenye sauti/maneno. ~ **proof** siopenya sauti. ~ **recording** *n* ukanda wa sauti bila picha. **~-track** *n* kifereji cha sauti (katika sahani ya santuri au utepe wa filamu). **~-wave** *n* wimbi la sauti. **~less** *adj* sio na sauti, bila sauti. **~lessly** *adv* *vt,vi* 1 toa sauti, lia, liza, piga (chombo cha) muziki ~ *a trumpet* piga tarumbeta. 2 tangaza; tamka. ~ **a note of alarm** tangaza hatari. ~ retreat amuru kurudi. 3 tamka (herufi n.k.). 4 pima/chunguza kwa kugonga. 5 onekana, elekea, toa picha, sikika. ~ **hollow** lia wazi. **~s queer** onekana kioja. 6 **~ing board** *n* kibao cha kupazia sauti; *(fig)* njia ya kuenezea maoni.

sound[2] *adj* 1 -zima, timamu, kamili. **a ~ mind in a ~ body** akili timamu ndani ya mwili wenye afya. ~ **in mind and limb** *(colloq)* mzima wa afya. **safe and ~** salama salimini. ~ **in health** -enye afya njema. 2 -a mantiki/busara; thabiti, imara. 3 angalifu, -a uwezo 4 kamili, barabara. **a ~ beating** pigo barabara/la haja. **~ly** *adv*. fofofo **~ness** *n adv fofofo be/fall ~ asleep* lala fofofo.

sound[3] *n* mlangobahari.
sound[4] *vt* 1 tia bildi, pima maji kwa bildi. **~er** *n* saunda: chombo cha kupokea na kupeleka habari kwa sauti. 2 jaribia moyo, hakikia shauri, hoji, dadisi. **~ sb (out) (about/on sth)** pata maoni ya; tikisa kibiriti usikie mlio wake. **~ings** vipimo; maoni, hisia; eneo la upimaji.
soup *n* supu. **in the ~** *(colloq)* matatani. **be in the hot ~** patikana na janga, -wa matatani. **~-kitchen** *n* pa kuwapea supu maskini bila malipo. **~ladle** *n* upawa wa supu. **~-plate** *n* sahani ya supu. **~-tureen** *n* bakuli la supu. *vt* **~ sth up** *(sl)* ingiza kifaa cha kuongezea injini nguvu/mwendo.
soupson *n (Fr)* (*usu* **a ~ of**) punje, ukufi, mnuko. **a ~ of clove** harufu kidogo ya karafuu.
sour *adj* 1 -kali. 2 chachu. **~ milk** mtindi. **turn ~** chachuka. 3 -a kisirani, -a chuki *vt,vi* chachua, chacha. **~ish** *adj* kalikali, si kali sana. **~ly** *adv*. **~ness** *n*. **~sweet** *adj* kali tamu, si kali wala si tamu. **~ dough** *n* kinyunya, chachu.
source *n* 1 chanzo, asili. **river ~** chanzo cha mto. **~ of law** asili ya sheria. 2 chemchemi, chimbuko, shina. 3 *(references)* kumbukumbu, rejeo. **~-book** *n* kitabu cha marejeo.
sour-sop *n* stafeli, topetope, tomoko.
souse *vt,vi* 1 chovya, mwagia maji mengi, suuza. 2 *(pickle)* loweka, weka katika maji ya chumvi, bambika *n* 1 kutengeneza achari. 2 *(sl)* ulevi; mlevi. **~d** *adj (sl)* -levi, -liolewa, chakari.
soutane *n* suteni: kanzu ya kasisi.
south *n* kusini. **the S~** upande wa kusini; nchi za kusini *adj* -a kusini, -a upande wa kusini. **the ~ star** ng'andu/zuhura. **~ winds** pepo za kusini.**~ Pole** Ncha ya Kusini. **~erly**; **~ern** *adj* -a kusini, -a upande wa kusini. **~ern cross** nyota nne za kusini mfano wa msalaba. **~bound** *adj* -a kuelekea kusini, -a kwenda kusini. **~east** *n* kusini mashariki *adj* -a kusini mashariki. **~-easter** *n* pepo zivumazo kutoka kusini mashariki, pepo za kusi. **~easterly** *adj* -a kutoka kusini mashariki; -a kuelekea kusini mashariki. **~-eastern** *adj* -a kusini mashariki. **~ west** *n* kusini magharibi. **~-wester; sou-wester** *n* pepo za kusini magharibi. **~-westerly**; **~-western** *adj* -a kutoka/kuelekea kusini magharibi. **~ward** *adj* kuelekea kusini. **~ward(s)** *adv* -a kuelekea kusini kwa kusini. *adj* -a kusini. **~ern** *n* mtu wa kusini. **~er** *n* **most** *adj* -a kusini kabisa; -a kusini nchani.
souvenir *n* ukumbusho, hedaya.
sovereign *adj* 1 -kuu; -enye enzi, -a kifalme **~** *state* dola huru. 2 bora; -a nguvu *n* 1 sarafu ya dhahabu (ya zamani, Uingereza). 2 mwenye enzi; mwenye nchi; mfalme/malkia. **~ty** *n* 1 mamlaka; enzi. 2 hukumu, utawala.
Soviet *n* 1 baraza la kirusi *the Union of S~ Socialist Republics* Jamhuri ya Mwungano wa Kisoshalisti ya Urusi. 2 raia wa Urusi, Mrusi *adj* -a kirusi, -a Urusi *the S~ Union* Urusi. **~ize** *vt* ingiza katika mfumo/siasa ya kisovieti.
sow[1] *n* nguruwe.
sow[2] *vt* 1 panda; sia. 2 *(fig)* tapanya; eneza **~** *terror* eneza hofu. **~er** *n* mpanzi; mpandaji. **he who ~s the wind must reap the whirlwind** anayepanda upepo huvuna tufani. **~ing** *n* kupanda. **~-machine** *n* kitemela, mashine ya kupandia.
soy/soya *n* **~bean** *(Far East)* soya (aina ya maharagwe meupe). **~sauce** *n* mchuzi wa soya.
sozzled *adj (GB.sl)* -liolewa chakari.
spa *n* 1 chemchemi ya maji ya madini. 2 mahali penye chemchemi.
space *n* 1 anga. **~-capsule** kibumba cha anga. **~craft/ship/vehicle** chombo cha anga. **~-rocket** roketi ya anga *~suit* suti/vazi la angani. **~station** kituo cha angani. **~travel** usafiri angani. 2 nafasi, kitambo, urefu kati ya *we were separated by a ~ of five*

feet kulikuwa na nafasi ya futi tano kati yetu. 3 uwanda, sehemu *open~* uwanda mtupu, nafasi iliyoachwa wazi. 4 uwazi ~ *vector* vekta uwazi ~ *between the lines* uwazi kati ya mistari ~-*bar* pao uwazi. 5 muda, kipindi *within the ~ of ten minutes* mnamo dakika *vt* ~ **sth (out)** panga kwa nafasi sawasawa. **spacing** *n* nafasi baina ya mistari, vitu n.k. *single/double* ~ (kuacha) nafasi moja/mbili kati ya mistari. **child** ~ *n* uzazi wa majira. **spacious** *adj* kubwa, -pana,-enye nafasi kubwa. **spaciously** *adv.* **spaciousness** *n.*

spade *n* 1 sepeto. **~work** *(fig)* kazi ngumu ya uanzishaji. **call a ~ a ~** sema waziwazi, 2 (karata) shupaza *vt* ~ **sth (up)** chimba/chimbua (kwa sepeto). **~ful** *n* kiasi cha sepeto.

spaghetti *n* spageti: aina ya tambi.

spake *(old or poet) pt of* **speak**.

spam *n* nyama ya nguruwe ya kopo.

span *n* 1 shubiri, futuri. 2 muda, kitambo. 3 *(bridge)* umbali, upana (kati ya mihimili); tao. 4 *(of horses/oxen etc)* jozi, -wili. 5 ~ **roof** mgongo wa tembo *vt* 1 pima kwa shubiri. 2 *(extend)* vuka a *bridge ~ned the river* daraja lilivuka mto. 3 dumu, ishi *his life ~ned almost 100 years* aliishi karibu miaka 100.

spangle *n* puleki *vi,vt* metameta, metuka, metesha, pamba kwa puleki.

spank *vt,vi* chapa/tandika matakoni. **~along** piga mbio. *n* kofi la matakoni.. **~ing** *n* kofi matakoni *adj* bora, safi sana.

spanner *n* spana. **throw a ~ into the works** *(fig)* vuruga/korofisha mambo, kwamisha.

spar[1] *n* 1 boriti, kombamoyo, mhimili, nguzo. 2 *(naut)* mlingoti, makiri. **~buoy** *n* mlingoti wa boya. **~-deck** *n* rosheni ya juu ya meli.

spar[2] *vi* 1 pigana ngumi (kwa mazoezi). 2 *(fig)* shindana, bishana *n* shindano, bishano. **~ring** *n.* ~ **partner** mpiga masumbwi wa mazoezi.

spare[1] *adj* 1 haba, -chache, kiasi ~ *of speech*-enye maneno machache. 2 -a akiba, ~ *tyre* tairi la akiba. 3 -embamba ~ *of build* -a kimbaombao ~ *rib* mbavu (tupu) za nguruwe *n* ~ *(part)* kipuri, spea. **~ly** *adv.* **~ness** *n.*

spare[2] *vi,vt* 1 acha kuumiza/kuharibu, hurumia. ~ **sb's feelings** epuka kuudhi mtu. ~ **the rod and spoil the child** mchelea mwana kulia hulia yeye. 2 ~ **sth (for sb/sth)**; ~ **sb sth** toa, -pa (muda, fedha n.k) *can you ~ me a minute*? naomba tuongee kidogo; *if our lives are ~d we'll see each other again* tukijaliwa tutaonana. 3 bania, tumia kidogo kidogo. **no expense(s)/pains ~d** tumia mali/juhudi zote *she is very sparing of her food* anabania chakula chake. **sparing** *adj* banifu, nyimifu, angalifu. **sparingly** *adv.*

spark[1] *n* 1 cheche; kimota. 2 *(fig)* chembe, dalili ya uhai *vi,vt* toa cheche, tatarika. **~-gap** *n* pengo katika ncha za waya za umeme. **~-plug/~ing-plug** *n* plagi. ~ **sth off** anzisha, chochea. **~le** *vi* 1 metameta, memetuka, ng'ara. 2 *(effervesce)* chemka *n* 1 mng'ao, mmeto 2 *(of wines)* kuchemka. **~er** *n* 1 kimulimuli, mng'ao. 2 *(pl) (sl)* almasi. **~ling** *adj (esp wine)* -liochemka, -enye kutoa viputo vidogo vidogo.

spark[2] *n (colloq)* mbeja, mmalidadi.

sparrow *n* shorewanda; jurawa.

sparse *adj* -chache, kidogo; -a kutawanyika; -a kusambaa. **~ly** *adv* kwa uchache. **~ness**; **sparsity** *n.*

Spartan *adj* 1 *(of person)* -vumilivu, stahamilivu. 2 *(of living conditions)* gumu, -siopenda starehe.

spasm *n* 1 mshtuko/mkazo wa ghafula (wa msuli) 2 tukio la ghafla. 3 mpasuko (wa nishati). 4 *(convulsion)* mtukutiko. **~odic** *adj* 1 -a (kutokea kwa) vipindi visivyo tabirika. 2 -a kushtushwa, ghafula; -a kubana, -a kusababishwa na mshtuko. ~**odically** *adv.*

spat[1] *pt pp of* **spit**.
spat[2] *vi* 1 gombana, korofishana. 2 piga kibao kidogo *n* 1 ugomvi mdogo na mfupi.
spat[3] *n (pl)* chaza wachanga.
spat[4] *n* **(a pair of)** ~ kitambaa kifunikacho kifundo cha miguu na sehemu ya juu ya viatu.
spatchcock *n* kuku aliyechinjwa na kupikwa mara moja *vt* ~ **(in/into)** *(colloq)* chopeka (maneno).
spate *n* 1 furiko *the river is* ~ mto umefurika. 2 *(fig)* kufurika (kwa biashara, vitu n.k.).
spatial *adj* -a kuhusiana na anga ~**ly** *adv*.
spatter *vt,vi* 1 ~ **sth (on/over sth)**; ~ **sth (with sth)** tapanya, tapanyika, nyunyiza ~ *mud over sb* tapanyia matope; *(fig)* chafulia jina; -nya matonematone *n* kunyunyiza; mtapanyiko; manyunyu.
spatula *n* mwiko mpana.
spavin *n* ugonjwa wa farasi (wa kuvimba miguu). ~**ned** *adj* -liolemazwa na ugonjwa wa uvimbe.
spawn *n* 1 mayai ya samaki au chura. 2 nyuzinyuzi za uyoga *vt,vi* zaa/taga mayai kwa wingi.
spay *vt (of female animals)* fanya tasa, toa viungo vya uzazi.
speak *vi* 1 sema, nena ~ *Kiswahili* sema Kiswahili ~ *the truth* sema kweli. 2 ~ **(to/with sb) (about sth)** sema, zungumza na, ongea na. ~ **for oneself** toa maoni yako, jisemea. ~ **for yourself**! jisemee mwenyewe ~ **to sb** karipia, kemea, sema. ~ **to sth** thibitisha. ~ **of the devil**! una maisha marefu! hufi upesi! husemwi! hutetwi! ~ **with sb** zungumza/ongea na mtu. **nothing to** ~ **of** kitu kidogo tu. ~ **out/up** sema kwa sauti (zaidi); toa mawazo/hoja bila woga/kusita. **not be on ~ing terms with sb** toongea na mtu kwa kutofahamiana; acha kuongea na mtu baada ya/kwa sababu ya ugomvi. **so to** ~ yaani, kwa maneno mengine. **strictly ~ing** kusema kweli. **~ing trumpet** chombo cha kusaidia kusikia. **~ing tube** *n* bomba la kupitisha sauti (k.m. katika meli). 3 toa ushahidi; onyesha dhahiri. ~ **volumes for** -wa ushahidi thabiti/wa kutosha. ~ **well for** tetea vizuri, toa ushahidi mzuri. 4 *(of language)* jua, (na mudu/weza kutumia). 5 hutubia. 6 sema, toa kauli. ~ **one's mind** toa maoni yako ya dhati, sema bila kuficha. 7 *(naut)* wasiliana kwa ishara (k.m. kupungiana bendera). 8 *(of a gun, musical instrument etc)* toa sauti. 9 ~ **easy** *n (US)* klabu/duka la pombe haramu. ~**er** *n* 1 mzungumzaji, msemaji. 2 *(abbr for loud ~)* spika, kipaza sauti. 3 **the** ~ *n* Spika, ~**ship** *n* uspika.
spear *n* 1 mkuki *vt* choma mkuki. ~**head** *n (usu fig)* 1 mtu au kikosi tangulizi kinachoongoza mashambulizi *vt* ongoza (mashambulizi). ~**man** *n* 1 askari mtumia mkuki.
spearmint *n* aina ya mnanaa ambao haulevyi bali hutumika kama kiungo na kutengenezea ulimbo wa kutafuna.
spec *(colloq abbr for) speculation*, **on** ~ kwa kuwazia tu.
special *adj* 1 -a namna, -a pekee; *(definite)* maalumu. ~ **constable** *n* konstebo maalumu, mwanamgambo/mgambo. ~ **delivery** upokeaji/ufikishaji barua vifurushi n.k. kwa njia maalum. ~ **licence** liseni maalum ya kibali cha ndoa. ~**ly** *adv* hasa. ~**ist** *n* mtaalamu. ~**ity** *n* 1 utaalam, kazi, shughuli maalum *this is his* ~ huu ndio utaalam wake/hii ndiyo kazi yake hasa/hii ndiyo shughuli aiwezayo hasa/hapa ndipo mahali pake. 2 hulka/sifa maalum. ~**ize** *vt, vi* 1 ~ **(in sth)** wa mtaalamu, bobea, topea. 2 wekwa maalum *a hospital with ~ized wards* hospitali yenye wodi maalum. ~**lization** *n*. ~**ty** *n see* ~**ity**.
specie *n* sarafu (za shaba, fedha, dhahabu). **in** ~ kwa sarafu.
species *n* 1 *(biol)* spishi (wanyama au

mimea) *the origin of the ~* chimbuko la spishi. 2 aina, namna.

specific *adj* 1 dhahiri, bayana. 2 maalum, mahususi. ~ **gravity** uzito linganifu mahususi. ~ **name** jina maalum la spishi. ~ **remedy** tiba maalum (kwa ugonjwa fulani). **~ally** *adv*. **~ation** *n* 1 ainisho; uonyeshaji uhalisi (wa kitu). 2 *(often pl)* vipimo kamili. **specify** *vt* taja, eleza bayana.

specimen *n* 1 kielelezo, sampuli. 2 *(med.)* sampuli ya choo, mkojo n.k. 3 mfano (wa kitabu n.k). 4 *(colloq)* kioja.

specious *adj* 1 -a hadaa, -enye uzuri wa juu juu tu, - enye kuonekana -zuri/ kweli (lakini siyo). 2 -a kughilibu, -a kujifanya. **~ness** *n* hadaa, ghiliba; kudanganya macho. **~ly** *adv*.

speck *n* alama/waa/doa dogo *vt* tia alama (doa, waa, kipakazo), chafua. **~ed** *adj*. **~less** *adj*.

speckle *n* doa. **~d** *adj* -a madoa madoa.

specs *n (pl) (colloq)* miwani.

spectacle *n* 1 tamasha, sherehe, maonyesho. 2 shani, kioja, kichekesho. 3 **~s**; **a pair of ~s** miwani. **put on ~s** vaa miwani. **~-case** *n* kifuko cha miwani, kijaluba cha miwani. **see everything through rose-coloured ~s** ona mema tu, **~d** *adj* -liovaa miwani. **spectacular** *adj* -a kustaajabisha; -a sherehe.

spectator *n* mtazamaji; mshangiliaji.

spectre *n* 1 kivuli, kioja; tishio. 2 spektra. **spectral** *adj* 1 -a kivuli; kama kivuli. 2 -a spektra. **spectroscope** *n*. spektraskopu: chombo cha kutoa, kuangalia na kupima spektra mbalimbali. **spectrum** n *(phys)* spektra mpangilio maalum wa taswira zinazotokana na miali ya mnunurisho.

speculate *vi* 1 *(consider)* otea, kisi, wazia 2 langua, uza/nunua kwa kubahatisha. **speculator** *n* mlanguzi. **speculation** *n* 1 kisio, kuotea. 2 bahatisho; ulanguzi *buy on ~* nunua kwa kubahatisha. **speculative** *adj* 1 -a kisio, -a kukisia. 2 -a kubahatisha. **speculatively** *adv*.

speech *n* 1 (uwezo/kipaji cha) kusema, kunena *have the power of ~* weza kunena. ~ **therapy** tiba ya matatizo ya kunena (k.m. kigugumizi). 2 *(mode)* msemo, usemi; kauli. **figure of ~** tamathali ya usemi. **direct ~** kauli halisi. **indirect/ reported/oblique ~** kauli iliyotajwa *parts of ~* aina za maneno *slow of ~* kusema pole pole. 3 hotuba, waadhi *make a ~* toa hotuba. ~ **day** *(school)* sikukuu ya wazazi. 4 lugha (ya taifa, kundi n.k.). **~less** *adj* -sioweza kunena (kwa sababu ya hasira, hofu n.k.) *be ~less* pumbaa, duwaa *be ~less with terror* pigwa na butaa. **~lessly** *adv*. **~ify** *vi* eleza.

speed *n* 1 mbio, kasi, haraka. **more haste less ~** *(prov)* haraka haraka haina baraka. 2 mwendo, spidi *at full ~* katika mwendo mkali. 3 *(sl)* dawa ya kusisimua. 4 *(compounds)* **~-boat** *n* mashua ya kasi. **~-cop** *n (sl)* askari wa usalama barabarani (agh. anayeangalia spidi za waendesha magari). **~-indicator/~ometer** *n* spidometa, kipima spidi. **~-limit** *n* kikomo rasmi cha spidi. **~merchant** *(sl)* mwendesha gari kwa mwendo wa kasi. **~way** *n* uwanja wa mbio (agh. kwa ajili ya pikipiki), *(US) baraste vt,vi* 1 enda/endesha kasi, zidisha mwendo. 2 peleka haraka; *(arch)* fanikisha *God ~ you* Mungu akupe heri. 4 ~ **(sth) up** ongeza kasi. **~-up** *n* kuongeza kasi. **~ing** *(of motorist)* kuzidisha kasi. **~ily** *adv* kwa haraka. **~y** *adj* haraka, -epesi, -a kasi.

spelaeology (*also* **spele**) taaluma ya mapango, elimu mapango. **spelaeologist** *n*.

spell[1] *n* 1 kipindi; muda *a ~ of bad luck* kipindi cha bahati mbaya *wait a ~* ngoja kidogo. 2 zamu *vt ~* **sb (at sth)** pokezana (zamu).

spell[2] *n* 1 laana/apizo *cast a ~ over sb (fig)* duwaza. ~ **bound** *adj* -enye kustaajabisha, -a kuteka usikivu.

~-**binder** *n* msemaji hodari. 2 *(fascination)* mvuto, (kwa uzuri n.k.).

spell[3] *vt* 1 taja/andika (tahajia za neno). **~ing pronunciation** matamshi ya tahajia. 2 ashiria *this weather ~s ruin to us* hali hii ya hewa inaashiria maangamizi kwetu *delay may ~ danger* kuchelewa kwaweza kuzaa hatari. 3 ~ **sth out** soma neno kwa neno kwa taabu; eleza kinagaubaga. **~er** *n* 1 kitabu cha tahajia. 2 mwendeleza maneno *be a good ~* -wa mwendelezaji hodari *be a bad ~* -wa mwendelezaji mbaya. **~ing** *n* tahajia.

spelt *pt of* **spell**.

spend *vt, vi* 1 tumia. ~ **money (on sth)** tumia pesa ~ *all his money on beer* tumia pesa zake zote kwenye bia. ~-**thrift** *n* mfujaji wa mali, mbadhirifu. 2 ~ **sth (on sth/ (in) doing sth)** tumia (yote/sana) ~ *a lot of energy on a project* tumia nguvu nyingi kwenye mradi. *how do you ~ your spare time* unatumiaje muda wako wa ziada. **~er** *n* mtumiaji. **spent** *adj* 1 hoi, -liokwisha. 2 -liotumiwa.

sperm *n* shahawa, manii. **~atozoa** *n* manii: seli za gameti za kiume zilizokomaa. ~-**whale** nyangumi atoaye spemaseti *low ~ count* shawawa dhaifu

spermaceti *n* spemaseti: nta/mafuta kichwani mwa aina ya nyangumi.

spew *vt,vi* tapika.

sphere *n* 1 tufe. 2 uwanja; fani. 3 eneo, mazingira ~ *of influence* eneo la mamlaka. **spherical** *adj* -a mviringo, -a tufe. **spheroid** *n* kitu kama tufe.

sphinx *n* 1 sanamu la jiwe huko Misri (lenye mwili wa simba na kichwa cha mwanamke). 2 msiri; mtu mgumu kueleweka mawazo na malengo yake.

spice *n* 1 kiungo, kikolezo; 2 *(fig)* mvuto, msisimko *vt* 1 tia kiungo, unga, koleza. 2 *(fig)* tia chumvi. **spicy** *adj* -liotiwa kiungo; *(fig)* -enye kusisimua. **spicily** *adv*. **spiciness** *n*.

spick *adj (only in)* ~ **and span** nadhifu, safi.

spider *n* buibui. ~'s web kimia/utando wa buibui. **~y** *adj (esp. of handwriting)* -refu na embamba.

spiel *n* 1 *(sl)* kupiga domo. 2 hadithi, maneno mengi *vi, vt* toa hotuba ndefu.

spigot *n* 1 mambo, kizibo. 2 bilula, mrija.

spike *n* 1 msumari, mwiba, uma, njumu. 2 kitu kilichochongoka. ~ **heel** *n* kiatu mchuchumio. 3 suke: (kanda) la mpunga (mtama, n.k.). 4 msuka. 5 **~s** *n* viatu vya njumu *vt* 1 choma/toboa (kwa msumari n.k.); haribu kwa kuchoma. 2 *(of cannon)* haribu kwa kutia msumari tunduni mwa fataki. ~ **sb's guns** haribu mipango ya mtu. **spiky** *adj* -a kuchongoka; -enye ncha kali; -a miiba.

spill[1] *vi,vt* 1 mwaga, tapanya. ~-**blood** mwaga damu, -wa na kosa la kuua au kujeruhi mtu *it's no good crying over spilt milk* maji yaliyomwagika hayazoleki. 2 *(of horse, cart etc)* mwaga, bwaga, angusha, dondosha *n* mwangusho, mbwago. ~-**over** *n (often attrib)* ziada (ya watu n.k.). ~-**way** *n* mfereji wa kupunguza maji ya mto/bwawa.

spill[2] *n* kibahaluli.

spilt *pt, pp of* **spill**.

spin *vt, vi* 1 ~ **(into, from)** pota, sokota. **~ning jenny** *n* mashine ya kusokota nyuzi (zaidi ya mmoja kwa wakati mmoja). **~ning-wheel** *n* gurudumu la kusokota nyuzi. 2 *(of a spider)* jenga kimia/utando. 3 *(fig)* tunga hadithi. ~ **a yarn** simulia hadithi. ~ **sth out** bania, tumia kitu kwa muda mrefu. 4 zungusha, rusha. ~ **a coin** rusha sarafu. ~-**drier** *n* mashine ya kukaushia. ~-**dry** *vt* kausha nguo kwa mashine. ~-**off** *n* faida ya ziada (isiyo tegemewa). 5 biringika, zunguka haraka; *(of bicycle etc)* enda kwa kasi. 6 **spun glass** glasi iliyosokotwa nyuzi (kwa moto). **spun silk** hariri duni (iliyochanganywa na pamba) *n* 1 mzunguko, kuzunguka. 2 matembezi (kwenye gari, baiskeli nk.). 3 *(of an aircraft)* mbiringiko/kugeuka ghafla. **be in a flat** ~ -wa na wasiwasi/harara.

spinach *n* spinachi; mchicha.

spinal *adj* -a uti wa mgongo ~ *cord/ column* uti wa mgongo.

spindle *n* 1 *(in spinning)* pia, mkono wa kisokotea nyuzi. 2 **~-legged/ shanked** *adj* -a miguu ya mironjo. **~-shanks** *n* njorinjori, mironjo. **spindly** *adj* -embamba na -ndefu.

spindrift *n* povu/manyunyu ya bahari.

spine *n* 1 uti. 2 *(of cactus, animals)* mwiba. 3 *(of a book)* mgongo. **~less** *adj* -sio na uti; *(fig)* oga. **spiny** *adj* -enye miiba.

spinney *n* kichaka.

spinster *n (usu official or leg)* (mwanamke) mseja. **~hood** *n* useja (wa kike).

spiral *n* mzunguko, pia *adj* -a mzunguko, -a pia *vi* zunguka, enda kwa mzunguko kama pia.

spire *n* mnara-pia (agh. wa kanisa).

spirit *n* 1 roho, nafsi. **the Holy ~** Roho Mtakatifu *the ~ is willing but the flesh is weak* roho inataka lakini mwili ni dhaifu. 2 kivuli, mzimu, pepo. **~-rapper** *n* mtambikaji. **~-rapping** *n* kutambika kwa mizimu. 3 *(fairy)* mzuka, kizimwi zimwi 4 uzima (pasipo mwili), pumzi *God is pure ~* Mungu ni pumzi ya uzima. 5 *(always with an adj)* mtu wa hekima, mwenye akili n.k. **moving ~** mwanzilishi, mtakadamu, mwasisi. 6 ari, uchangamfu, moyo (wa bidii, juhudi n.k.). 7 *(sing only)* hali (ya kimawazo/tabia) moyo wa kutenda, msimamo. 8 maana, kusudi, kiini *the ~ of his instructions* kiini cha maongozi yake. 9 *(pl) (state of mind)* hali/hisia za ubongo (k.m. madadi, hasira n.k.) ya mtu *in high ~s* -enye furaha,. 10 *(sing only)* mwelekeo; hali inayoleta maendeleo *the ~ of the 90's* mwelekeo wa miaka ya tisini. 11 **~ lamp/stove** taa/jiko la spiriti. **~-level** *n* pima maji. 12 *(usu pl)* kinywaji kikali (k.m. brandi, wiski, gongo n.k.). 13 *(pl)* mmumunyo katika alkoholi *vt* **~ sb/ sth away/off** torosha. **~ed** *adj*. 1 jasiri; -enye ari. 2 *(in compounds)* **high ~** -enye uchangamfu mwingi. **low-~** -enye majonzi. **~less** *adj* -sio na furaha, -liokata tamaa, -zito; -sio jasiri. **~uous** *adj (of liquids)* -a kulevya ~ *liquors* pombe kali. **~tual** *adj* 1 -a roho, - a kiroho. 2 -a pepo, -a mizimu. 3 -a kanisa; -a dini. **lords ~** *(GB)* maaskofu walioko katika bunge la malodi *n (Black American) ~ n* wimbo wa dini. **spiritually** *adv*. **spirituality** *n*. mambo ya roho, kuthamini mambo ya roho. **spiritualism** *n*. (imani katika) kuwasiliana na pepo (mizimu, mahoka n.k). **spiritalist** *n* mwenye kuamini kuwasiliana na mizimu/ pepo. **spiritualistic** *adj spiritualize vt* takasa, fanya -a kiroho. **spiritualization** *n*.

spirt *see* **spurt**.

spit[1] *n* 1 kijiti/chuma cha kubanika n yama *toast on a ~* banika. 2 musoma, sehemu nyembamba ya nchi kavu iliyoingia majini *vt* tunga (nyama) katika chuma/kijiti.

spit[2] *vt,vi* 1 ~ **(at/on/upon sb/sth)** tema, temea ~ *blood* tema damu; *(of a cat)* toa ukali. 2 ~ **sth (out)** tema; *(fig)* foka ~ *out threats* tishia. 3 *(of a fire, candle,)* alika; *(of a gun)* tema (risasi). **~-fire** *n* mwenye hasira nyingi. 4 *(of rain or snow)* nyunya, chonyota *n* 1 mate. 2 kutema ~ **and polish** kusafisha na kung'arisha. 3 **the dead ~ of; the ~ and image of; the ~ting image** sura moja na *the ~ting image of his father* sura moja na baba yake. 4 mate-povu (ya wadudu). **~tle** *n* mate. **~ton** *n* chombo cha kutemea mate.

spit[3] *n* kina cha koleo/sepetu.

spite *n* chuki, ukorofi, mfundo *he has a ~ against me* ananichukia. 2 inda *he sacked her out of ~* alimfukuza kutokana na inda. 3 **in ~ of** ingawa, ijapokuwa; bila kujali *he went in ~*

of the rain alikwenda bila kujali mvua *vt* chukiza, udhi. **cut off one's nose to ~ one's face** kata pua uunge wajihi. **~ful** *adj* -a chuki, -enye inda. **~fully** *adv* kwa chuki/inda. **~fulness**

spitle *n* 1 mate. **spittoon** *n* chombo cha kutemea mate.

spiv *n (dated GB sl)* tapeli.

splash *vt,vi* 1 **~ sth (about) (on/over sth)**; **~ sth/sb (with sth)** rushia, rashia (maji, matope n.k.) *the car ~ed mud over us* gari liliturushia matope. 2 *(of a liquid)* ruka, rukaruka. 3 tua, anguka (kwa kurushia maji). **~-board** *n (vehicle)* bamba la kuzuia maji. **~-down** *n* kutua kwa chambo cha anga majini. 4 **~ one's money about** *(sl)* tapanya pesa (kwa kujionyesha) *n* 1 sauti ya kurashia maji/matope. 2 madoamadoa ya rangi. 3 *(colloq)* kiasi kidogo cha soda *a whisky and ~* wiski na soda kidogo. 4 *(colloq fig)*. **make a ~** jionyesha kwa kutapanya fedha.

splay *adj (esp of feet)* -pana, bapa, liotanuka; -a kwenda upande *vt,vi* tanua. **~-foot** *n* (wayo) batabata.

spleen *n* 1 wengu, bandama. 2 *(fig)* chuki, hasira *vent one's ~ upon sb* onyesha chuki, kasirikia. **splenetic** *adj* -enye chuki/hasira.

splendid *adj* bora, -tukufu, -a fahari. **~ly** *adv* vizuri sana. **splendiferous** *adj (colloq often hum or ironic)* -zuri mno, -tukufu, -a fahari. **splendour** *n* 1 fahari, uzuri; wangavu; mng'ao. 2 ubora, utukufu.

splice *vt* 1 unganisha (kamba) kwa kusokota, fungamanisha *get ~d (sl)* oana. 2 *(tree)* ganga *n* mgango, mwungo kiungio.

splinter *n* 1 kibanzi, kichane, . 2 *(of glass)* kigeregenza *vt, vi* vunjavunja, chanachana; vunjikavunjika, chanikachanika. **~-group** *n (political)* genge la waasi. **~-proof** *adj* isiyo pata ufa *vt vi* **~ (off)** vunjika vipande vipande; toka kibanzi. **splint** *n* banzi, gango, kitata, kijiti *vt* ganga, funga kwa banzi.

split *vt,vi* 1 **~ (into)** pasua, pasuka, mamatua, (mamanua), chanja. 2 **~ (open)** pasuka, chanika. 3 **~ (up) into** gawa, gawanyika; *(of couple)* achana, tengana *lets ~ (mod colloq)* tuondoke. **~ the difference** afikiana (juu ya bei n.k.). **~ting headache** kuwanga kwa kichwa. **~ hairs** *(in an argument)* bishana juu ya tofauti ndogondogo. **hair ~ting** *adj*. **~ mind/personality** akili/tabia iliyogawanyika. **~ peas** njegere kavu zilizopasuliwa. **~ ring** kishika funguo. **a ~ second** punde. **~ one's sides (with laughter)** pasuka/vunjika mbavu. **side ~ting** *adj*. 4 **~ (on sb)** *(sl)* fichua; chongea; toboa siri *n* 1 mpasuko, ufa. 2 kugawanyika; mfarakano. 3 *(colloq)* nusu chupa ya soda.

splotch/splodge *n* waa, alama, doa *a ~ of rust* doa la kutu.

splurge *n (colloq)* mikogo *(colloq) vi* jivuna, koga, ringa, piga mbwembwe.

splutter *vt,vi* 1 tatarika, babaika (katika kusema). 2 **~ sth (out)** bwata. 3 *(water)* foka, bubujika. 4 tematema *n* sauti ya kimadende.

spoil *n* 1 mateka, ngawira; mali iliyoibiwa. 2 *(pl)* marupurupu. 3 taka, fusi *vt,vi* 1 haribu, dhuru, haribika, oza *~ the fun* haribu starehe. 2 *~t votes* kura zilizoharibika. **~ sport** mvurugaji starehe; *(a child)* dekeza. 3 *(look after)* endekeza. 4 **~ sb (of sth)** teka nyara, nyang'anya. 5 **be ~ing for sth** taka sana, -wa na shauku ya kitu, ashiki. **~age** *n* uharibifu; uozo. **~er** *n* mnyang'anyi, mtekaji; mharabu.

spoke[1] *n* 1 njiti; tindi, njukuti. **put a ~ in sb's wheel** zuia, tilia guu, vuruga mipango yake. 2 *(of a ladder)* kipago, kipandio.

spoke[2], **spoken** *pt and pp of* **speak**.

spokesman *n* msemaji mkuu; mwakilishi.

spoliation *n* unyang'anyi; utekaji nyara.

sponge *n* sifongo, sponji. **throw up/in the ~** kubali kushindwa. **pass the**

~ **over** futa, kubali kusahau *vt, vi* 1 ~ **sth (out)** safisha kwa sifongo. 2 ~ **sth up** fyonza kwa sifongo. ~ **out** futa, tangua. ~ **on/upon (sb)** *(colloq)* nyonya. ~ **sth (from sb)** doya, doea, chomoa. ~**r** *n* mdusi, mdoezi, mdumizi. **spongy** *adj* -a kama sifongo/sponji *n* yavuyavu; tipwatipwa. **sponginess** *n* uyavuyavu, wororo; utipwatipwa, usponji.

sponsor *n* mfadhili; mlezi *stand ~ to a child* fadhili mtoto *vt* fadhili. ~**ship** *n* ufadhili.

spontaneous *adj* -enyewe; hiari, -a kujianzia. ~ **combustion** mwako utokanao na mabadiliko ya kikemikali. **spontaneity** *n*. ~**ly** *adv*. ~**ness** *n*.

spoof *n* 1 *(sl)* hila, udanganyifu. 2 kichekesho, mzaha *vt* danganya; punja. ~**er** *n*.

spook *n (hum)* kivuli, pepo, mzuka. ~**y** *adj*. -a kuzindua, -a kutishia, -a mashetani/mizuka/pepo *the house is ~* nyumba inatisha.

spool *n* kidonge/kigurudumu cha uzi/ filamu *vt* viringisha (uzi n.k).

spoon[1] *n* kijiko. **serving** ~ mkamshi, upawa *vt* ~ **sth up/out** chota, teka kitu kwa kijiko/upawa. ~ **feed** *vt* lisha; *(fig)* endekeza, andalia kila kitu. ~**ful** *n* (kiasi cha) kijiko kimoja, kijiko tele.

spoon[2] *vi (dated colloq)* fanya mapenzi.

spoonerism *n* uspuna: kuchanganya herufi za mwanzo za maneno (bila kukusudia).

spoor *n* nyayo za mnyama *vt* fuata nyayo za mnyama.

sporadic *adj* -a hapa na pale, a-mtawanyiko, -a mara moja moja. ~ **ally** *adv*.

spore *n* kiiniyoga, kijimbegu.

sport *n* 1 mzaha, burdani *make ~ of* fanyia mzaha, dhihaki. 2 mchezo *football is a ~* mpira ni mchezo. 3 *country ~* uwindaji (kwa kujiburudisha). 4 *(colloq)* muungwana. 5 *(pl)* ~**s** mashindano ya riadha. 6 *(compounds etc) ~ car* gari lililotengezwa kwenda kwa kasi. ~ **coat/jacket** koti (lisilo rasmi). ~ **editor** mhariri wa michezo. ~**man** mpenda michezo; mchezaji; muungwana. ~ **manship** uungwana. ~ **manlike** *adj vt, vi* 1 chezacheza; jifurahisha. 2 *(colloq)* onyesha; koga, ringishia, ringia. ~**ing** *adj* -chezaji; uungwana; jasiri. ~**ingly** *adv*. ~**ive** *adj* -a kupenda mizaha, -a kuchezacheza, -a kuchangamka. ~ **ively** *adv*. ~**iveness** *n*.

spot *n* 1 waa, doa, paku, baka *can the leopard change his ~s?* chui aweza kubadili madoa yake? 2 *(pimple)* chunusi, kidundusi, kijiwe. 3 *(fig)* doa *a ~on sb's reputation* doa katika sifa ya mtu. 4 mahali *the very ~* palepale. **radio** ~ mahali pa matangazo ya biashara (katika kipindi). 5 (kiasi) kidogo *a ~ of leave* likizo fupi *a ~ of trouble* shida kidogo. 6 *(comm) ~ cash* nakidi, fedha taslimu *~ market* sokosawia *~ prices* bei za papo. 7 tone *a few ~s of rain* matone ya mvua. 8 *(phrases)*. **a ~ check** ukaguzi wa ghafula. **a tender ~** suala nyeti. **in a ~** *(colloq)* taabuni. **knock ~ of sb** shinda/zidi kirahisi *on the ~* pale pale, papo hapo; mara moja; *(sl)* katika matatizo *the person on the ~* mwenyeji; mhusika *put sb on the ~* ingiza (mtu) matatizoni; *(of gangsters)* amua kumwua mtu *put ones finger on/find sb's weak ~* tambua/ona kasoro ya mtu (kwa ajili ya kumshambulia) *vt, vi* 1 tia waa, pata madoa. 2 chafua, haribu/haribika. 3 ona, tambua. ~**ted** *adj* -a madoa madoa. ~**less** *adj* pasipo waa, -eupe, safi. ~**lessly** *adv*. ~**ty** *adj* -enye chunusi, -a wasiwasi (katika ubora). ~**ter** *n* mchunguzi, mpelelezi (kwa ndege, n.k.).

spotlight *n* 1 mwangaza (wa) *be in the ~* -wa katika mwangaza; *(fig)* -wa kivuta macho. 2 kiangaza *vt* angazia, mulika.

spouse *n (leg)* mume, mke.

spout *n* 1 mlizamu, mrizabu, neli.

2 bubujiko, mfoko wa maji. 3 mdomo wa birika *up the ~ (sl)* rahani; katika shida; mjamzito *vt, vi* 1 ~ **(out)** *(of liquids)* rusha/ruka, churuza; foka, bubujika, chirizika *the wound ~ed blood* kidonda kilitoa damu. 2 *(colloq)* piga domo, nena makuu; hubiri.

sprain *vt* tengua, tenguka *n* kutenguka.

sprang *pt of* **spring**.

sprat *n* sprati (namna ya samaki mdogo). **risk a ~ to catch a whale** toa kidogo upate kingi.

sprawl *vi* 1 jibwaga, tandawaa. 2 *(be spread out)* enea, tambaa, tapakaa, sambaa *n* kutandawaa, kuenea, kutapakaa; eneo pana lenye uchafu (hasa kwenye majengo).

spray[1] *n* 1 manyunyu; rasharasha. 2 vioevu (vyenye kunyunyizwa, k.m. marashi, viua wadudu, n.k.). 3 kinyunyizio. ~ **gun** kinyunyizio cha shinikizo *vt* ~ **sth/sb (with sth); ~sth (on sth/sb)** nyunyizia, pulizia. **~er** *n* 1 mnyunyizia/mpulizia (dawa, rangi, n.k.). 2 kinyunyizio.

spray[2] *n* kitawi; pambo (agh. la vito) lenye umbo la tawi.

spread *vt,vi* 1 **~ sth on/over sth; ~ sth with sth; ~ sth (out)** kunjua, tandika, tawanya/tawanyika. 2 **~ sth on sth; ~sth with sth** pakaza, paka. 3 eneza; enea. ~ **oneself** tandawaa; andika/ zungumza kwa upana juu ya kaifa fulani; toa bila kujizuia. 4 tandaa. 5 chukua muda, dumu. 6 ~ **eagle** *n* tai aliyejitandaza. ~ **eagle oneself** jitandaza. ~ **over** upangaji wa saa za kazi kulingana na mahitaji; upangaji wa shifti *n (rarely pl)* 1 mweneo; upana. 2 kuenea; upanuzi. 3 *(colloq)* meza iliyojaa vyakula vingi. 4 kitu kinachotandikwa k.m. shuka. 5 jina la jumla la vipakaza vya chakula *n* kitandaza, kipakaza, mpakazaji, mtandazaji.

spree *n* shamrashamra. **be on the ~; go out on a ~** -wa na/enda katika shamrashamra. **a spending/ buying ~** tukio la ufujaji wa fedha.

sprightly *adj* -epesi, -changamfu. **sprightliness** *n*.

spring[1] *vi,vt* 1 ruka ghafla, chupa. ~ **upon** rukia. ~ **to one's feet** simama ghafula. 2 ~ **(up)** chipuka, tokeza. 3 ~ **from** tokea/tokezea. 4 ~ **sth on sb** toa ghafla. 5 anzisha/ fyatua/tegua mtambo/mtego. 6 pasuka, atuka. ~ **a leak** -anza kuvuja *n* 1 kichipukizi, kitawi. 2 *(derog)* chipukizi, kijana *vt* pamba kwa chipukizi *n* 1 mtambo, springi. 2 *(of a watch)* kamani, utumbo. 3 *(water)* chemchemi, jicho la maji. 4 ruko, mruko. 5 mnyambuko, kuduta. 6 asili, mwanzo, chimbuko. 7 kisa, sababu. 8 *(compounds)* **~-balance** *n* mizani ya springi. **~-board** *n* ubao wa kuchupia. ~ **chicken** *n* kuku mchanga; *(fig)* kisichana. ~ **gun** *n* bunduki ya kutega. ~ **mattress** *n* godoro la springi. **~less** *adj*. **~y** *adj*.

spring[2] *n* majira ya kuchipua. **~tide** *n* bamvua. **~time** *n* majira ya kuchipua *vt* ~ **clean** safisha (nyumba, chumba) vizuri. **~like** *adj* -a kama majira ya kuchipua.

springbok *n* paa wa Afrika Kusini.

sprinkle *vt* ~ **sth (on/with sth)** nyunyiza; tia kidogo huko na huko, rashia. **be ~d about** tapakaa *n* 1 mnyunyizo/unyunyizaji. 2 utiaji kidogo (k.v. chumvi, sukari n.k.) ~ *of salt* mnyunyizo wa chumvi. **~r** *n* kinyunyizo; mrashi. **sprinkling** *n* 1 kidogo, uchache, uhaba *there was only a ~ of people present* watu wachache tu walihudhuria. 2 marasharasha.

sprint *vi* enda mbio sana (masafa mafupi), timka *n* mbio fupi. **~er** *n* mwanariadha wa mbio fupi.

sprit *n (naut)* boriti ndogo pembeni mwa tanga ~ *sail* tanga lililoshikwa kwa boriti ndogo.

sprite *n* jini, zimwi, pepo, kivuli.

sprocket *n* jino (la gurudumu). ~ **wheel** gurudumu lenye meno.

sprout *vi,vt* 1 ~ **up** chipuka, chipua, anza kumea, anza kuota. 2 anza kukua. 3 otesha, ota (ndevu, pembe, n.k.) *n* chipuko, chipukizi, kimea.

spruce[1] *n* ~ **(fir)** mti (jamii ya) msonobari. ~**-beer** *n* pombe iliyotengenezwa kwa majani ya msonobari.

spruce[2] *adj* nadhifu, -a malidadi *vt, vi* ~ **sb/oneself up** jifanya nadhifu, (ji)kwatua. ~**ly** *adv*. ~**ness** *n*.

sprung *pp of* **spring**.

spry *adj* -changamfu. **look** ~ onekana mchangamfu na mwepesi. ~**ly** *adv*. ~**ness** *n*.

spud *n* 1 *(colloq)* kiazi. 2 kijisepeto cha kupalilia. *vt* palilia chimbua (kwa kutumia kijisepeto).

spue *see* **spew**.

spume *n* povu *vi* toa povu. **spumy** *adj*. **spumous** *adj*.

spun *pp of* **spin**.

spunk *n* 1 *(colloq)* ujasiri, moyo wa ujasiri. 2 *(sl)* shahawa, manii *put* ~ *into sb* tia mtu moyo wa ujasiri. ~**y** *adj*.

spur *n* 1 *(of bird)* kipi, kikwaru. 2 kichokoo, mwiba, msumari. **win one's** ~**s** *(fig)* pata heshima na sifa. 3 tuta (ubavuni mwa kilima). 4 kichocheo. **on the** ~ **of the moment** mara moja, ghafula, hima *vt,vi* ~ **sb/sth (on)** 1 chochea, himiza, tia chonjo, chonjomoa ~ *a willing horse* tia chonjo farasi hodari. 2 piga mbio, pita kwa kasi.

spurious *adj* -a uwongo, -a kujifanya; si halisi, bandia. ~**ness** *n* uigaji; uwongo; hali ya kujifanya. ~**ly** *adv*.

spurn *vt,vi* 1 sukumia mbali, piga teke. 2 kataa kwa dharau, dharau, beua *n* ukataaji jambo kwa dharau.

spurt *vi* 1 ~ **(out) (from)** bubujika, foka *the water* ~*ed out* maji yalibubujika. 2 kurupuka, timka *n* 1 mfoko, mbubujiko. 2 mkurupuko, mtimko.

sputnik *n* sputniki: sateliti bandia ya kirusi isiyo na mwanaanga.

sputter *vi, vt* 1 bwabwajika. 2 tatarika.

sputum *n* mate; kohozi (hasa liashirialo ugonjwa).

spy *vt, vi* ~ **(into/on/up on sth)**; ~ **sth out** 1 peleleza, jasisi, duhusi, doya. 2 ona; tambua, gundua *n* 1 jasusi. 2 mpelelezi. ~ **glass** *n* darubini ndogo. ~ **hole** *n* kitundu cha kuchungulia (mlangoni).

squab *n* 1 kinda (hasa la njiwa). 2 kiti chenye takia laini. ~ **chick** ndege asiyeweza kuruka.

squabble *n* ugomvi, mzozo, mabishano *vi* gombana, bishana, zozana. ~**r** *n* mbishani, mgomvi.

squad *n* kikosi (agh cha jeshi) ~ *car (US)* gari la doria. ~**ron** *n* kikosi cha askari (hasa wapanda farasi au wahandisi); *(warship)* kundi dogo la manowari *(aircraft)* kundi la ndege. ~**ron-leader** *n* 1 mkuu wa kikosi. 2 mkuu wa jeshi la ndege.

squalid *adj* -chafu, -nyonge, -baya, dhalili. ~**ly**.

squall *n* 1 kilio kikali (cha maumivu). 2 dhoruba, upepo mkali (unaoambatana na mvua au theluji) *look out for* ~*s (often fig)* jihadhari na hatari/tatizo. ~**y** *adj* -a tufani, -a dhoruba.

squalor *n* uchafu; udhalili. ~**ly** *adv*.

squander *vt* fuja, tapanya. ~**er** *n* mfujaji mali, mtapanyaji, mbadhirufu.

square *adj* 1 -a mraba. ~ **dance/game** mchezo ambapo wachezaji katika mraba huangalia ndani ya mraba. 2 kama pembe mraba. ~ **brackets** mabano mraba. ~ **built** *(of a person)* -enye miraba minne, pande la mtu; pandikizi la mtu. ~**-rigged** *(of sails)* -enye matanga yaliyokuwa pembe mraba kutoka katika mlingoti. ~**shouldered** -enye mabega yaliyo pembe mraba kutoka shingoni. ~ **toed** -enye kupenda mambo rasmi. 3 sambamba, sawa na, liosawazishwa. **be (all)** ~ *(golf)* sare, enda suluhu; bila kudaiana. **get** ~ **with sb** lipa fedha; *(fig)* lipa deni. 4 -a mraba. ~ **km**. km za mraba. ~ **root** kipeo cha pili. 5 -a haki, a kweli. ~ **deal** maafikiano ya haki. **get/give**

sb a ~ deal mtendee mtu haki; mfanyie mambo mazuri. 6 kamili, -a kutosheleza kabisa. **a ~ meal** mlo kamili. **~ly** *adv* 1 kwa kuunda pembe mraba. 2 kwa haki/uaminifu. **fair and ~** kwa haki kabisa. 3 kwa mkabala. 4 moja kwa moja. **~ness** *n* 1 mraba. **back to ~ one** rudia mwanzo. 2 chochote kilicho mraba. 3 uwanja (wa pande nne) *barrack ~* uwanja wa kikosi cha askari. **~ bashing** *(sl)* gwaride la kijeshi (hasa la kutembea). 4 majengo na barabara zinazozunguka uwanja wa mraba. 5 majengo yaliyozungukwa na barabara nne. 6 *(maths)* kipeo. 7 filifili, rula ya T, kipima pembe. **out of ~** -sio pembe mraba. 8 **on the ~** nyofu, adili. 9 kikosi cha askari wa miguu katika umbo la mraba. 10 *(sl)* mshikilia ukale, mtu asiyekubali mawazo mapya *vt,vi* 1 fanya mraba. **~ the circle** jaribu jambo lisilowezekana. 2 fanya pembe mraba katika mstari. 3 sawazisha, patanisha. 4 zidisha namba kwa yenyewe. 5 **~ sth off** gawa katika miraba. 6 **~ (up) (with sb)** lipa deni la mtu; *(fig)* lipiza kisasi. 7 honga, -pa rushwa. 8 **~(sth) (with)** linganisha, oanisha. 9 **~up to sb** -wa tayari kupigana, kabili.

squash[1] *vt,vi* 1 ponda/pondeka; kamua. 2 bana, songa. 3 *(colloq)* nyamazisha mtu kwa kumkemea. 4 komesha (maasi) *n* 1 msongamano (wa watu), halaiki. 2 maji ya matunda. 3 mchezo wa skwoshi. **~ (rackets)** *n* mchezo uchezwao kwa kutumia ubao na mpira.

squash[2] *n* boga.

squat *vi* 1 chuchumaa, chutama. 2 *(colloq)* kaa kitako. 3 kalia ardhi bila ruhusa *adj* -fupi, -nene. **~ter** *n* 1 mwingiliaji ardhi (pasipo ruhusa), mvamiaji nyumba. 2 *(Australia)* mfugaji kondoo.

squawk *n* 1 *(chiefly of birds)* kilio cha maumivu (au hofu). 2 *(colloq)* kulalamika *vi* 1 toa kilio, lia, lalama. 2 *(sl)* saliti. **~er** *n*.

squeak *n* 1 mwaliko; kilio chembamba. 2 **a narrow ~** kuponea chupuchupu *vi* 1 alika. 2 **~ sth (out)** tamka/sema kwa sauti ya juu; *(colloq)* -wa mtoa habari, -wa shushushu. **~er** *n (colloq)* mtoa habari. **~y** *adj a ~ floor* sakafu inayoalika.

squeal *n* unyende: kilio chembamba kirefu (cha hofu au maumivu) *vi* 1 lia, toa sauti kali. 2 sema kwa sauti kali. 3 *(colloq)* - wa mtoa habari. **~er** *n* 1 mnyama mwenye sauti kali. 2 mtoa habari, shushushu.

squeamish *adj* 1 -jepesi kuugua, -gonjwa; epesi kutapika, -enye kichefuchefu. 2 -enye kuchukia haraka, enye kuchukizwa, -enye haya. 3 -a kichefuchefu *I feel ~* naona kichefuchefu. 4 -epesi kuona mashaka. **~ly** *adv*. **~ness** *n*.

squeeze *vt* 1 bana, minya, kaba *~ to death* kaba mpaka kufa; songa. 2 **~ sth (from/out of sth); ~ sth out** kamua. 3 penyeza, penya. 4 **~ sth out of sth/sb** toza, lipiza. 5 *vi* bonyea. **squeezable** *adj* -a kuminyika, -a kupenyeka, -a kupunguka *n* 1 kuminya; msongamano *a s~ of lemon* tone la limau. 2 **close/narrow/tight ~** kuponea tundu la sindano/ chupuchupu. 3 *(colloq)* sera ya kubana matumizi kwa kuweka viwango vya juu vya kodi, riba, n.k.; fedha za ziada zinazotozwa watu. **~r** *n* kibanio/kiminyio; kikamulio; mminyaji, mkamuaji.

squelch *vi* fanya sauti ya mfyonzo (k.m. mtu akitembea kwenye matope) *n* mfyonzo.

squib *n* 1 fataki (ya karatasi yenye baruti kwa kuchezea). **damp ~** jaribio lisilofanikiwa. 2 dhihaka (agh. iliyomo katika maandishi).

squid *n* ngisi.

squiffy *adj (sl)* -liolewa kidogo.

squiggle *vt* 1 *n* mcharazo, mstari mfupi/ mdogo uliopindika. **squiggly** *adj*.

squint *n* 1 makengeza. **~-eyed** *adj* -enye makengeza; *(fig)* -a kudhuru,

-a kuchukia, -a kutoridhia/kubali. 2 *(colloq)* mtupio wa jicho *vi* 1 -wa na makengeza. 2 ~ **at/through** tupia jicho; chungulia.

squire *n* 1 *(GB-ancient)* msaidizi wa lodi (aliyembebea ngao na silaha zake). 2 mwinyi katika kijiji. 3 msindikizaji wanawake; mpenda kukaa na wanawake. 4 *(US)* mwanasheria. 5 Bwana. **~archy** *n* mamwinyi, tabaka la mamwinyi *vt* *(of a man)* sindikiza/ shughulikia bibi.

squirm *vi* 1 furukuta, jinyonganyonga mwili. 2 *(be embarrassed)* fadhaika, tahayari *n* mfurukuto.

squirrel *n* kuchakuro.

squirt *vi,vt (of liquid)* foka *n* 1 kibomba cha kurushia maji. 2 maji yatokayo kwa nguvu katika tundu. 3 *(colloq)* mjuvi.

St *(abbr. of* **street***) and* **saint.**

stab *vt, vi* 1 ~ **(at)** choma (kwa kisu, upanga, mkuki). ~ **sb to the heart** choma moyoni. 2 uma, pwita *n* 1 mchomo. **a ~ in the back** *(fig)* masengenyo; usaliti. 2 *(colloq)* jaribio. **~ber** *n.*

stable[1] *n* zizi, chaa. **~-boy/man** *n* mtunza farasi. **~-companion/mate** *n* farasi; *(fig)* wenzi *vi* fuga farasi zizini. **stabling** *n* nafasi ya kulala farasi.

stable[2] *adj* thabiti, imara, tulivu, -liotulia. **stability** *n* uthabiti, utengemano; kutengemaa. **stabilization** *n.* **stabilize** *vt* dhibiti, tengemeza, tuliza, imarisha. **stabilizer** *n* mtu/kitu kinachoimarisha; kidhibiti umeme.

staccato *adv (music)* kidono: kila sauti na kishindo chake halisi.

stack *n* 1 kitita, rundo la nyasi, fito n.k. katika umbo la mviringo au mstatili. 2 bunduki zilizopangwa katika umbo la pembetatu. 3 *(brickwork or store work)* mabomba ya moshi; dohani. 4 rafu. 5 kundi la ndege zinazozunguka angani zikiwa zinasubiri zamu ya kutua. 6 rundo (la vitabu, kazi, n.k.); *(colloq)* idadi/kiasi kikubwa *vt* 1 ~ **(up)** rundika. 2 *(US)* *(of playing cards)* panga kwa hila, changia. **have the cards ~ed against one** *(fig)* -wa matatani, -wa katika hali ngumu. 3 panga ndege angani kufuatana na zamu ya kutua.

stadium *n* uwanja wa michezo (k.m. mpira, riadha n.k.).

staff *n* 1 fimbo, gongo; mkongojo ~ *of life (fig)* mkate. 2 fimbo rasmi. 3 nguzo. 4 wafanyakazi, watumishi. *(mil)* ~ **office** ofisi ya utumishi. 5 maafisa waandamizi wa jeshi. 6 *(mus)* mistari ya kuandika manota *vt* ajiri watumishi/wafanyakazi; wa mfanyakazi/mtumishi.

stag *n* 1 paa dume. **~-party** *n (colloq)* tafrija ya wanaume tu (agh. ya mkesha wa bwana harusi). 2 mhodhi, mlanguzi wa hisa.

stage *n* 1 jukwaa, dungu, ulingo. 2 *(in a theatre)* **the** ~ (kazi ya) uigizaji; weledi wa kuigiza. **be/go on the ~** wa mwigizaji. **~-craft** *n* ustadi wa sanaa za maonyesho. ~ **direction** *n* uongozi wa jukwaa. ~ **door** *n* mlango wa nyuma wa waigizaji. ~ **fright** *n* kiwewe cha jukwaani. ~ **manager** msimamizi/kiongozi wa michezo (ya kuigiza). ~ **struck** *adj* -enye kupenda kuwa mwigizaji. **~-whisper** *n* mnong'ono wa jukwaani. 3 *(fig)* tukio; mahala pa tukio. 4 hatua, wakati, kipindi *the baby has reached the talking* ~ mtoto amefikia wakati wa kusema. 5 mwendo kati ya vituo viwili. ~ **(-coach)** *n (hist)* gari la abiria linalokokotwa na farasi. **fare-~** *n* sehemu yenye nauli isiyobadilika *vt,vi* 1 fanya tamthilia; onyesha mchezo jukwaani. ~ **a come-back** rudi ulingoni/uwanjani (baada ya kuacha mchezo). 2 faa/-tofaa jukwaani. **staging** *n* 1 uonyeshaji wa tamthilia 2. jukwaa. **stagy** *adj* -a kuigiza, -a kuigizaigiza **~stagily** *adv.* **staginess** *n.*

stager *n (only in)* **an old ~** mtu mwenye ujuzi wa siku nyingi.

stagflation *n (fin)* kushuka kwa

thamani ya fedha bila ongezeko la uzalishaji viwandani.

stagger *vt,vi* 1 pepesuka, yumbayumba, pepa. 2 *(of blow or shock)* peperusha; *(of news)* duwaza, shangaza, tia bumbuazi, fadhaisha. 3 panga nyakati tofauti *n* 1 kupepesuka, kupepa. 2 *(pl) the ~s* kizunguzungu. **~er** *n*.

stagnate *vi* 1 tuama. 2 *(fig)* dorora, doda. **stagnation** *n*. **stagnant** *adj* 1 *(of water)* -liotuama. 2 *(fig)* -a kudoda/kudorora, -liokwama *the trade is ~* biashara imedoda/ imekwama.

staid *adj* -siopenda mabadiliko, tulivu na -liomakinika. **~ly** *adv*. **~ness** *n*.

stain *vt, vi* 1 tia waa (doa, alama, uchafu); *(fig)* chafua, haribu. 2 tia rangi. **~ed glass** kioo kilichotiwa rangi za kuona. 3 *(of material)* chuja, chafuka *n* 1 waa, alama, taka, doa. 2 tone, rangi *~ remover* kitoa madoa. **~er** *n* kipaka rangi, mpakaji rangi. **~less** *adj*. 1 pasipo waa, -eupe, safi. 2 -siopata kutu, -siopata alama. **~less steel** chuma cha pua.

stair *n* daraja, kipago. **up ~s** orofani, juu. **down ~s** chini. **flight of ~s** ngazi. **below the ~s** orofa ya chini ya nyumba. **at the foot/head of the ~** chini/juu ya ngazi *moving ~s* eskaleta: ngazi za umeme katika jengo. **~ carpet** *n* zulia la ngazi. **~ rod** chuma/ubao wa kushikilia zulia ngazini. **~case; ~ way** *n* ngazi.

stake *n* 1 mambo, kiguzo, kigingi. 2 nguzo ya kuchomea watu moto. **go to the ~** chomwa moto (kwa kufungwa kwenye nguzo); *(fig)* dhurika kwa kupata ushauri mbaya. 3 kitegauchumi. **at ~** hatarini, kufa na kupona, pata potea; *(fig) his life is at ~* maisha yake yamo hatarini. 4 dau *~ money* dau. **~holder** *n* mshika madau *vt* 1 shikilia kwa kiguzo/ mambo. 2 **~ sth (out/off)** weka mpaka wa eneo kwa mambo/viguzo. 3 **~ sth on sth** bahatisha, cheza kamari.

stalactite *n* stalaktiti: chokaa iliyogeuka kuwa jiwe na kuning'inia juu pangoni.

stalagmite *n* stalagmiti: chokaa iliyogeuka kuwa jiwe na kuenea chini pangoni.

stale *adj* 1 *(of food)* -liochina, -liochacha. 2 *(of athletes, pianists etc)* -a kulegea, -a kuchoka, -a kunyong'onyea. 3 baridi, ovyo *~ cheque* cheki iliyochina *~ debt* deni chakavu *vi* chakaa, china. **~ness** *n*.

stalemate *n* mvutano, mkwamo; *(fig)* kukwama, kufikia ukingoni *vt* shinda mpinzani katika mchezo wa sataranji.

stalk[1] *n* shina; bua, ubua; kikonyo.

stalk[2] *vt,vi* 1 tagaa, magamaga. 2 nyatia, nyemelea, nyapa, nyendea. **~ing-horse** *n* farasi wa kujikingia; *(fig)* kisingizio; njia ya kuficha ukweli *n* mnyemeleaji, mnyapiaji.

stall *n* 1 zizi. **~fed** *adj* -a kulishwa na kufungiwa ndani ya zizi. 2 genge. **~-keeper** *n* mchuuzi. 3 *(of a clergyman)* kiti maalum. 4 *(of an engine)* kusota. 5 *(usu. pl) (GB)* kiti cha mbele karibu na jukwaa *vt,vi* 1 fuga/weka zizini. 2 shindwa kuendelea kwa ukosefu wa kani. 3 *(of an aircraft)* shindwa kuwasiliana kwa ukosefu wa mwendo. 4 chelewesha jibu, kwepa jibu.

stallion *n* farasi dume (asiyehasiwa).

stalwart *adj* -a miraba minne, mwamba *n* mfuasi mkereketwa/mwaminifu, muumini hodari.

stamen *n* stameni.

stamina *n* 1 bidii/nguvu/uthabiti/ ushupavu wa kufanya jambo kwa muda mrefu. 2 kutochoka upesi, ustahimilivu; *(fig)* moyo mkuu.

stammer *vi,vt* 1 gugumia. 2 **~ sth (out)** gugumiza maneno *n* kigugumizi. **~er** *n* mwenye kigugumizi. **~ingly** *adv* kwa kigugumizi.

stamp *vt,vi* 1 **~ sth (on/with sth)** piga chapa, piga muhuri. **~ sth (out)** ponda ponda, seta, vyoga, komesha. **~ing ground** *n* eneo maalum la wanyama fulani k.m. tembo; eneo maalum wanapokusanyika watu wa aina moja. 2 **~ sth (on/with sth)**

chora, tia nakshi za mchoro, bandika mhuri wa jina n.k. 3 tia stempu, bandika stempu. 4 ~ **sth (out)** -pa umbo, finyanga. 5 *(fig)* jitokeza, thibitisha, dhihirisha; kosha *n* 1 muhuri, alama, chapa. 2 *(US sing)* namna, tabia *men of that* ~ watu wa aina ile ile. 3 kukanyaga, kuchapa mguu. 4 *(postage)* stempu *adhesive* ~ stempu ya kubandika. ~ **album** *n* kitabu cha kuwekea stempu, kitabu cha kukusanyia stempu. ~**-collecting** *n* ukusanyaji wa stempu (kwa kupenda au kwa sughuli maalum). ~**-collector** *n* mkusanyaji wa stempu. ~**-dealer** *n* mwuza stempu. ~**-duty** *n* ushuru wa hati. 4 *(usu. sing)* alama, ishara *her face bears the* ~ *of suffering* uso wake unaonyesha alama za mateso.

stampede *n (of animals)* kukimbia kwa haraka (kufanywako na mtu/mnyama), mkurupuko, mtimko *vt,vi* 1 kimbia ghafula, kurupuka. 2 ~ **sb into sth/doing sth** harakisha/tishia mtu katika kufanya jambo; kurupusha.

stance *n* mkao, namna ya kujiweka katika mchezo; msimamo.

stanch *vt* zuia, komesha, (hasa damu isitoke).

stanchion *n* nguzo; rubi, kiguzo *vt* funga kwenye nguzo; tia nguzo.

stand *n* 1 kusimama, kutuama *be brought to a ~still* simamishwa. 2 **make a** ~ zatiti. 3 nafasi, msimamo **take one's** ~ chukua/tangaza msimamo. 4 kinara, kiweko, kimeza. 5 jukwaa. 6 kibanda. **news** ~ kibanda cha magazeti. 7 kituo, stendi. 8 kigono, kambi, ago. **one night** ~ kujamiiana mara moja. 9 *(US)* kizimba *take the* ~ -wa kizimbani. 10 *(of crops) a good ~ of maize* mazao mazuri ya mahindi. 11 *(compounds)* ~**-pipe** bomba wima la maji. ~**point** *n* msimamo, maoni, mtazamo, fikira. ~**-still** *n* kusimama, kutua *vt,vi* 1 ~ **(up)** simama, -wa wima. 2 -wa na urefu wa *he ~s five feet* ana urefu wa futi tano. 3 tua, koma, tuama. 4 kaa, baki, dumu. ~ **firm/fast** baki pale pale; shikilia msimamo. ~ **clear (of sth)** kaa mbali/pembeni *the dishes ~ there* vyombo hivyo vinakaa pale. 5 weka, simamisha ~ *the ladder over there* simamisha ngazi pale. 6 vumilia, himili, kubali, chukua *he cant ~ him* hawezi kumvumilia/kumstahamilia. ~ **one's ground** -torudi nyuma; *(fig)* shikilia msimamo. ~ **(one's) trial** shitakiwa. 7 ~ **sb sth** hudumia; gharimia, kirimu *will he ~ us wine* atatukirimu kwa mvinyo? ~ **treat** gharimia viburudishi vya wengine. 8 *(phrases)* ~ **a good/poor chance to win/lose** -wa na nafasi nzuri/finyu ya kushinda/kushindwa. 9 *(adv. particles and preps)* ~ *aside* -tojishughulisha; -tojihusisha, kaa pembeni, sogea; jiuzulu, jitoa (katika orodha ya wagombeaji). ~ **at** fikia *the children's fund ~ s at* Shs. 10,000 mfuko wa watoto sasa umefikia shilingi elfu kumi. ~ **back** rudi nyuma; -wa mbali na *the house ~s back from the road* nyumba iko mbali na barabara. ~ **by** -wa mtazamaji; tazama tu; *(of troops etc)* kaa tayari. ~ **by sb** unga mtu mkono, tetea, kaa upande wa fulani. ~ *by sth* timiza ahadi. ~**by** *n* 1 kujizatiti, kujiandaa. 2 mtu/kitu cha kutegemewa/akiba *a ~ by player* mchezaji wa akiba. ~ **down** toka kizimbani *(of a candidate)* jitoa (katika uchaguzi, n.k.). ~ **for sth** maanisha; unga mkono; tetea, gombea; *(colloq)* vumilia. ~ **in (with sb)** shiriki katika kugharimia. ~ **in (for sb)** shikilia nafasi ya mwingine. ~ **in** *n* mshikilia nafasi ya mwingine. ~ **off** kaa mbali; sogea nyuma. ~ **off** achisha mtu kazi kwa muda. ~**-offish** *adj* kimya; baridi na -a kujitenga. ~**-offishly** *adv.* ~**-offishness** *n.* ~ **out** tokeza. ~ **out a mile** -wa dhahiri kabisa; endelea kupinga/kukaidi. ~ **over** ahirishwa. ~ **over sb** simamia mtu/kitu, angalia kwa makini. ~ **to** *(mil)* -wa macho/tayari. ~**-to** *n (mil)* alama ya kuwa tayari. **~-up** *adj (of collars)* -enye kusimama; *(of a meal)* -a kuliwa wima; *(of a fight)* -kali sana, -a kipigo kikubwa. **~ sb up** *(colloq)* vunja miadi. **~ up to sth** *(of materials)* dumu, stahimili, -wa na maisha marefu. **~ (well) with sb** elewana na.

standard *n* 1 bendera. **raise the ~ of revolt** *(fig)* anzisha mapambano na omba msaada. **~bearer** *n* mshika bendera; kiongozi mashuhuri wa jambo fulani. 2 *(often attrib)* kipeo sanifu, kipimo, kiwango; *(fig)* matarajio *conform to the ~s of society* zingatia matarajio ya jamii. **be up to/below ~** -wa juu/chini ya kiwango kilichowekwa *the work is below the ~* kazi haikufikia kiwango *~ Kiswahili* Kiswahili sanifu. 3 *(former)* darasa *~ four* darasa la nne. 4 **monetary ~** uwiano wa uzito wa metali na madini katika sarafu. **the gold ~** mfumo wa kukadiria thamani ya fedha na dhahabu. **abandon/go off the gold ~** achana na mfumo huo. 5 *(often attrib)* mhimili, nguzo, mwimo. **~ lamp** taa ya nguzo/mhimili. 6 chipukizi lililopandikizwa katika shina wima. **~ize** *vt* sanifisha, fanya kawaida, fanya wastani, fanya kuwa ya aina moja. **~ization** *n* kusanifisha, kufanya wastani, kufanya kawaida.

standing *adj* 1 -a kusimama *~ crop* mazao yaliyo shambani. 2 -a siku zote, -a kudumu. 3 **~ orders** taratibu kuu. 4 **~corn** mahindi ambayo hayajavunwa. **~jump** mvuko bila kukimbia. **~ army** wanajeshi wa kudumu *n* 1 nafasi, hadhi, cheo *a man of good ~* mtu mwenye cheo. 2 aushi, maisha, muda, wakati *of long ~* -a muda mrefu.

stank *pt of* **stink**.

stannary *n (GB)* mgodi wa madini ya bati.

stanniferous *adj* -enye madini ya bati.

stanza *n* ubeti/beti.

staple[1] *n* 1 tumbuu. 2 **stapling-machine; ~r** machine ya kubana (karatasi), kibanio.

staple[2] *n* 1 bidhaa kuu ya mahali, zao kuu la mahali. 2 dhana, wazo kuu *sports forms the ~ of his conversation* michezo hutawala sana mazungumzo yake. 3 aina ya uzi wa pamba/sufu *cotton of long ~* pamba ya uzi mrefu. 4 *(attr)* kuu.

star *n* nyota. **falling ~** kimondo *lucky ~* nyota ya jaha. **~fish** *n* kiti cha pweza. **~light** *n* mwanga wa nyota. **~lit** *adj* 1 -a kuangazwa kwa nyota. 2 umbo la nyota; kinyota. **see ~s** ona vimulimuli. **the S~-Spangled Banner** Bendera ya Taifa ya Amerika; wimbo wa taifa wa Amerika. **the S~ and Stripes** *n* bendera ya taifa ya Amerika. **S~ Wars** *n* vita vya anga. 3 *(of a person's fortune)* nyota *born under a lucky ~* mtu mwenye bahati. **~-gazer** *n (hum)* mnajimu. 4 mashuhuri, maarufu, nyota *a film-~* mchezaji maarufu wa sinema *vt, vi* 1 pamba, tia alama ya nyota. 2 **~ (sb) in** -wa nyota; tangaza mchezaji mchanga anayeelekea kwenye umaarufu. **~dom** kuwa nyota; umashuhuri. **~let** msichana mchezaji (anayeelekea kuwa nyota). **~less** bila nyota. **~y** *adj* -enye nyota, -a kung'aa, -a kumetameta *~-night* usiku wa nyota. **~-eyed** *adj (colloq)* dhanifu; -a kufikirika tu.

starboard *n* (*of a ship*) chini, upande wa kulia wa mtazamaji *vt* elekea/elekeza kulia.

starch *n* 1 wanga, nisha. 2 kanji, uwanga; *(fig)* urasimu; baridi; *(of manner)* ushupavu *vt* tia wanga. *(fig)* **a ~ed manner** tabia kakamizi. **~y food** vyakula vya wanga.

stare *vt, vi* **~ (at)** 1 kodoa/kodolea/kaza/kazia/tumbua/tumbulia macho. **make sb ~** shtua mtu. 2 **~ sb out (of countenance)** kodolea mtu macho kiasi cha kumtia kiwewe/wasiwasi. **~ sb out/down** kodolea mtu macho kupita anavyoweza kukukodolea wewe. **~ one in the face** kazia mtu macho; -wa mkabala na, -wa usoni mwa; -wa mbele ya *n* kukodoa kutumbua macho. **staring** *adj (of colours)* -kali, -a kuonekana *adv (only in)* **stark staring mad** kichaa kabisa.

stark *adj* 1 -gumu, -kavu, -siovunjika (hasa -liokufa). 2 -tupu, kabisa. **~ers** *pred adj (GB sl)* uchi wa mnyama, uchi kabisa. **~ness** *n*.

starling *n* kwezi.

start *vi,vt* 1 ~ **(out)** ondoka, anza (safari). 2 anza. 3 ~ **(on) sth** fanya mwanzo (wa) kitu. 4 ~ **(up)** shtuka, shtùsha, gutuka, gutusha *his eyes were ~ing out of his head* macho yalimtoka. 5 jongea/inuka/ruka ghafla. 6 *(of timbers)* dondosha; legeza, legea.7 anzisha, fanya kuwepo; sababisha kuanza. 8 *(with adv. part)* **~-back** anza kurudi. ~ **in (on sth/to do sth** *(colloq)* anza kufanya kitu. ~ **off** anza kuondoka, anza kwenda/ kujongea. ~ **out (to do sth)** *(colloq)* anza, takadamu; chukua hatua za mwanzo. ~ **up** inuka ghafla; ruka; tokea ghafla/bila mategemeo. ~ **sth up** *(an engine)* washa. 9 **to ~ with** kwanza kabisa, awali ya yote. 10 **~ing gate** *n* mstari/tepe/alama ambapo farasi huanzia mbio za mashindano. **~ing post; ~ing point** *n* mwanzo, mahali pa kuanzia. **~er** *n* 1 mshindanishi. (katika mbio) 2 mwanzishaji. **under ~'s orders** kusubiri amri ya mwanzishi. 3 *(tech)* stata. 4 *(colloq) (of meals)* kianzio *n* 1 *(fright)* shtuko, kushtuka, mshituko *you gave me a ~* umenishtua; *(shock)* kishindo. 2 mwanzo, awali, chimbuko; utangulizi *he gave his son a ~* alimtanguliza mwanawe *at the ~* mwanzoni *get a ~* tangulia, toka kwanza. **a head** ~ upendeleo, mwanzo mwema. 3 *(departure)* kushika njia, kuondoka *make an early ~* ondoka mapema. 4 *(pl)* **~s** vipindi.

startle *vt* shtua, shtusha, gutusha.

startling *adj* -a kushtusha. **startlingly** *adv*.

starve *vi,vt* shinda/shindisha na njaa; kosa/kosesha chakula; jinyima/nyima chakula, -fa kwa njaa. **be ~d of/ ~for** *(fig)* tamani; hitaji sana. **starvation** *n* 1 kukosa chakula, njaa, . 2 *(colloq)* kuona njaa. **~ling** *n* ashindaye na njaa, afaye kwa njaa/utapiamlo.

stash *vt* ~ **sth away** *(sl)* tumia; ficha.

state[1] *n* 1 hali ~ *of emergency* hali ya hatari. ~ **of play** *(fig)* hali ya mambo (katika mashindano). 2 cheo, daraja, hadhi. 3 fahari, heshima, enzi, sherehe *live in ~* ishi katika enzi. 4 dola; serikali, jimbo. **the United S~s** Marekani. **Head of S~** Mkuu wa nchi. **the S~ Department** *(US)* Wizara ya mambo ya nchi za nje. **S~ legislature** bunge la jimbo. **~'s evidence** shahidi wa serikali. **S~ House** *n* Ikulu. **lie in** ~ pewa heshima ya mwisho (baada ya kufa). 6 *(compounds)* **~-room** *n* chumba cha binafsi (melini). **~ly** *adj* -adhimu, bora; -a madaha. **~liness** *n* sherehe, fahari; madaha, madahiro. **~craft** *n* ujuzi wa uongozi. **~less** *adj* -sio na uraia/utaifa *~less person* asiye na uraia wowote. **~sman** mtawala, mwanasiasa mweledi; kiongozi wa siasa. **~sman like** *adj* -a akili, -a kama mtawala mweledi, -a busara *in a ~smanlike manner* kiungwana. **~smanship** *n* ustadi katika utawala; akili katika utawala; weledi wa utawala.

state[2] *vt* nena, sema, eleza, aridhia. **~d** *adj* -liotajwa. **~ment** *n* 1 kauli, habari, maelezo. 2 taarifa *contradictory* ~ maelezo yanayopingana.

static(al) *adj* tuli ~ *electricity* umeme tuli. **~s** *n* 1 elimu mituamo. 2 (*radio, TV*) mikwaruzo.

station *n* 1 kikosi, lindo. 2 stesheni/ kituo **~master** stesheni masta, **broadcasting** ~ *n* kituo cha matangazo. **police** ~ kituo cha polisi. 3 **(Australia)** zizi, ranchi. 4 kikao, manzili. 5 cheo, daraja, kiwango. 6 *(mil)* ngome, kituo cha jeshi. 7 **s~ of the cross** njia ya msalaba *vt* weka mahali pamoja, jikita, kalisha. **~ary** *adj* 1 -a kusimama pamoja, -liokazwa pamoja -siohamishika. 2 -sioondoleka, -siogeuka, liosimama.

stationer *n* mwuuza/vifaa. **~y** *n* vifaa vya kuandikia.

statistics *n* takwimu. **statistic(al)** *adj* -a takwimu. **statistician** *n* mtakwimu. **statistically** *adv*.

statue *n*. sanamu, umbo (la kitu katika mti, jiwe n.k.). **~sque** *adj* kama sanamu ya kuchonga. **~squeness** *n*. **~squely** *adv*. **~tte** *n* sanamu kijisanamu. **statuary** *n* (mchonga) sanamu *adj* -a kuchonga sanamu

stature *n* 1 kimo, urefu (wa mtu) *of short ~* -fupi; *(fig)* tabia/msimamo. 2 akili.

status *n* hadhi, hali, cheo, manzili *immigration ~* (hali ya) uraia *marital ~* hali ya ndoa *national ~* hali ya uraia. **~ symbol** ishara/alama ya ukubalifu/hadhi.

status quo *n* hali kama ilivyo. **~ ante** hali ilivyokuwa (kabla ya mabadiliko ya hivi karibuni).

statute *n* sheria; amri ya serikali, sharti la chama. **~ law** sheria za bunge. **~-book** *n* kitabu cha sheria za taifa. **statutory** *adj* -a sheria iliyoamriwa halali, -a sheria za bunge.

staunch[1]/stanch *vt* ziba, zuia umwagikaji (wa damu).

staunch[2] *adj* -aminifu, thabiti; imara, madhubuti. **~ly** *adv*. **~ness** *n*.

stave *n* 1 kipande cha pipa, kipandio kipago. 2 *(poem)* ubeti. 3 *(mus)* mistari mitano.

sterile adj 1 tasa, -a mgumba. 2 *(of land)* kame. 3 -sio na matokeo. 4 matunda yasio na bakteria, safi kabisa. **sterility** *n* 1 utasa, ugumba; ukame. 2 usafi kabisa. **sterilize** *vt* 1 hasi. 2 ondoa/fisha bakteria/vijidudu **sterilization** *n*. **sterilizer** *n* kifisha vijidudu.

sterling *n* 1 *adj (of gold and silver)* -enye thamani iliyokubaliwa. 2 *(fig)* halisi, bora *n* fedha za Uingereza. **the pound ~** pauni moja. **the ~ area** kundi la nchi linaloweka akiba yao kwa fedha za Kiingereza.

stern[1] *adj* -kali, -gumu, yabisi, bila huruma. **~ly** *adv* kwa ukali, bila huruma. **~nes** *n* ukali, ugumu.

stern[2] *n* 1 shetri, tezi. **~wheeler** stima yenye kasia la gurudumu. 2 nyuma, matako, mkia. **~-sheets** *n* eneo la viti vya abiria.

sternum *n* mfupa wa kidari.

stertorous *adj* -a kukoroma, -a kukorota. **~ly** *adv*.

stet *vi (of print)* acha ilivyo, usifute, ibaki.

stethoscope *n* stetoskopu; chombo cha kusikilizia mapafu/mapigo ya moyo.

stetson *n* pama.

stevedore *n* kuli.

stew *vt,vi* chemsha pole pole. **~ fruit** tokosa matunda. **let him ~ his own juice** shauri yake. **~ in one's own juice** jipalia makaa. **~-pan** *n* sufuria yenye kina (ya kutokosea) *n* 1 mchuzi, nyama/samaki/mboga zilizotokoswa. 2 **be in/get into a ~ (about sth)** *(colloq)* hamaki, -wa na kiherehere; ingiwa na wasiwasi *in a great ~* -enye kiherehere sana. **~ed** *adj (sl)* -liolewa.

steward *n* 1 *(of aircraft, ship, train)* mtumishi, mhudumu (wa abiria). 2 mwandalizi (wa dansi, mikutano n.k). 3 mkadamu. 4 afisa ugavi (wa kilabu, chuo n.k). **~ess** *n* (*of aircraft, ship, train*) mtumishi wa kike. **~ship** *n* utumishi; usimamizi; ukadamu; kipindi cha kutumikia kazi hizo.

stick[1] *n* 1 fimbo, ufito. 2 kiboko, kibarango *(walking)* bakora, mkongojo. **give sb the ~** chapa mtu fimbo/kiboko; *(fig)* adhibu mtu. **get hold of the wrong end of the ~** changanyikiwa, -toelewa kabisa, **the big ~** *(fig)* tishio la kutumia nguvu *a policy of the big ~* siasa ya mabavu. 3 *(colloq)* fala, mtu aliyezubaa na mnyamavu. 4 **the ~s** *(colloq)* mashenzini. **out in the ~s** porini;

mbali na kiini cha jambo. 5 *(of soap etc)* mchi, kinoo, mkuo *vt* shikilia kwa fito.

stick[2] *vt, vi* 1 ~ *sth (in)* choma; chomekwa; chomeka. ~ **a pig** *(in sport)* ua nguruwe kwa mkuki. 2 *(of sth pointed)* ng'ang'ania, shikilia, nasa. 3 ganda, gandamana, gundika. **be/get stuck with sb/sth** *(colloq)* sukumiziwa, bebeshwa, fungwa na shindwa kuachana na mtu/kitu. **~ing plaster** *n* plasta. 4 *(colloq)* futika, weka haraka au ovyo ovyo *he stuck the money in his pockets* alifutika fedha mfukoni mwake. 5 ~ **(in)** ng'ang'ana, nasa, kwama *the key stuck in the lock* ufunguo ulinasa katika kufuli. ~ **in one's throat** *(of proposals)* -tokubalika, -wa ngumu kuelezeka. ~ **-in-the-mud** *attr. adj* -a kung'ang'ania ya kale. 6 *(colloq)* vumilia. ~ **to it** shikilia. 7 *(special uses)*. ~ **around** *(sl) (of a person)* -toenda mbali, kaa karibu. ~ **around!** usiende mbali. ~ **at sth** sitasita; endelea na jambo (k.v. kazi) kwa kipindi kirefu. ~ **sth down** *(colloq)* weka chini; *(colloq)* andika; gundika; bandika. ~ **on sth** bakia, shikilia. ~ **sth on** bandika. ~ **it on** *(sl)* langua sana. ~ **sth out** toa (kitu) nje *he stuck his head out of the window* alitoa kichwa chake nje ya dirisha. ~ **out for sth** ng'ang'ania. ~ **to sb/sth** -wa mwaminifu; endelea hadi mwisho wa jambo. ~ **together** *(colloq) (of persons)* chukuzana, bakia marafiki, shikamana. ~ **up** jitokeza. ~ **sb/sth up** *(sl)* tishia kumpiga mtu risasi ili kumwibia. ~ **your hands up** mikono juu. ~ **up for sb/oneself/sth** unga mkono, tetea; jilinda. ~ **with** *(sl)* shikamana na, shikilia *n* 1 kitu kinachong'ang'ania; mshikiliaji (wa jambo). 2 kibandiko, karatasi ya gundi. **~ler** *n (for sth)* mrasimu, mtu anayesisitizia umuhimu wa kitu (k.m. ukamili, sheria, adabu, urasimi n.k.). **~y** *adj* 1 -a kunata; *(of earth)* -a mfinyanzi. **be on a ~ wicket** *(fig)* -wa katika hali ngumu. 2 *(sl)* baya, gumu **come to a ~y end** kufa vibaya kwa mateso makali. 3 *(colloq)* gumu (kutoa n.k.). **~ily** *adv*. **~ness** *n* **~pin** *n (US)* 1 pini ya tai, pete ya tai. 2 pini.

stiff *adj* 1 *(unyielding)* -gumu, -zito; *(of body)* -enye mavune; -enye kushupaa; *(rigid)* -kavu. **keep a ~ upper lip** kaa imara, stahamili. **~-necked** *adj* -enye kiburi, kaidi. 2 *(of manners, behaviour)* -si kunjufu, baridi, rasimu *a ~ reception* mapokezi baridi. 3 -ingi *a ~ drink* kinywaji kingi/kikavu; kali ~ *wind* upepo mkali *adv* sana, mno, kabisa *it bore me ~* ilinichusha sana *n (sl)* 1 maiti. 2 *(sl)* mpumbavu. **~ly** *adv*. **~ness** n ugumu, mavune, uzito; *(of manners etc)* ukali. **~en** *vi,vt* 1 fanya -gumu, kausha, kaza; kauka. **~ening** *n* kiimarishaji. **~ener** *n* kitu cha kuimarishia.

stifle *vt,vi* 1 songa, songwa, kaba, kabwa. 2 katiza, zimisha, komesha; zuia ~ *a flame* zima moto.

stigma *n (pl)* 1 makovu (yanayofanana na ya Yesu baada ya kusulubiwa). 2 *(fig)* doa/alama (ya aibu/fedheha). 3 stigma. **~tize** *vt* 1 shutumu. 2 *(fig)* tia waa.

stiletto *n* 1 kisu chembamba kirefu. 2 **~heel** stileto: kisigino cha kiatu kirefu.

still[1] *n* kikeneko: mtambo wa kukenekea vinywaji vikali (k.m. wiski, gongo, brandi n.k.). ~ **room** stoo ya mwangalizi wa nyumba (katika jumba kubwa).

still[2] *adj,adv* 1 -tulivu; kimya *be ~* tulia, nyamaza ~ *water* maji mafu, maji matulivu. **the ~ small voice** sauti ya dhamira. **~-life** *n* michoro ya vitu visivyo hai (k.m. matunda). ~ **birth** *n* mtoto asiye riziki. **~-born** *adj (of a child)* aliyezaliwa mfu. 2 *(of wines)* -sio na gesi *n* 1 *(poet)* kimya kabisa. 2 picha ya kawaida (iliyotofautishwa na sinema) vt nyamazisha; tuliza. **~y** *adj (poet)* tulivu, kimya. ~**ness** *n*.

still[3] *adv* bado, hata sasa, hata hivyo *she ~ hopes to go* bado anatarajia kwenda *he is sick but ~ he will do it* ni mgonjwa lakini hata hivyo atafanya.

stilt *n (often)* **(pair of ~s)** 1 mronjo. 2 nguzo. ~**ed** *adj* rasmi mno, -zito, -siochangamka. ~**edly** *adv*. ~**ness** *n*.

stimulate *vt* changamsha, amsha, chachawisha, chechemua. **stimulating** *adj*. **stimulation** *n* mchangamsho; kiamsho; kichechemo; uchangamshaji. **stimulant** *n* kichangamsho, kichocheo; kiburudisho *adj* -a kuamsha, -a kuchangamsha; -a kuchochea. **stimulus** *n* kichangamsho; kichocheo; kiamshi, kichokoo.

sting *n* 1 mwiba (wa nyuki, ng'e jani, miti n.k.). 2 ukali, uchungu (unaotokana na kuumwa na mdudu). 3 kichomi *~s of remorse* majuto, kuona vibaya *vt,vi* 1 uma, choma. 2 chonyota, chenyeta. 3 ~ **sb (to/into sth/doing sth)** tia uchungu, sononesha, kasirisha. 4 *(colloq)* ~ **sb (for sth)** ibia, langua, gonga *n* kinachouma; inayochonyota; mwiba. ~**less** *adj* bila mwiba, -siochoma.

stingy *adj* -a choyo, -nyimi, -a kunyima, bahili. **stingly** *adv*. **stinginess** *n*.

stink *vi,vt* 1 ~ *(of sth)* nuka. 2 **cry ~ing fish** chukia bidhaa zako mwenyewe; *(sl)* jaa tele. **he ~s of money** ana fedha tele. 3 ~ **sb/sth out** ondoa/ fukuza kwa kutumia harufu mbaya (k.m. kutoa ushuzi); jaza harufu mbaya; fukiza/puliza *n* 1 uvundo, harufu mbaya, kunuka. 2 *(sl)* fujo, vurugu. **raise/kick up a ~ (about sth)** *(colloq)* fanya fujo/vurugu. ~**er** *n (sl)* 1 barua kali/chafu. 2 mwenye roho mbaya. 3 *(colloq)* kitu/jambo gumu *the exam was a ~* mtihani ulikuwa mgumu.

stint *vt,vi* ~**sb (of sth)** nyima; toa kidogo; bana sana *she ~ed herself of food* alijinyima chakula. *n* 1 *(usu)* **without** ~ bila mipaka, bila kujizuia. 2 ngwe. ~**ingly** *adv* kinyiminyimi, kidogokidogo, kwa unyimivu.

stipend n mshahara, ujira (agh. wa kasisi). ~**iary** *adj* -a kupokea mshahara, -a kulipwa *n* hakimu wa kulipwa.

stipple *vt* tona, chora kwa kutona.

stipulate *vt, vi* 1 tamka/weka masharti. 2 ~ **for sth** sisitiza (kitu kuwa sehemu ya mapatano/mkataba). **stipulation** *n* masharti; mapatano.

stipule *n* kikonyo, kijijani kiotacho kati ya shina na jani.

stir[1] *vt,vi* 1 tingisha, tikisa. **not ~ an eyelid** -tojishughulisha na jambo lolote, toonyesha wasiwasi juu ya kitu. **not ~ a finger** -toonyesha jitihada yoyote ya kufanya kitu, -tosaidia. ~ **one's stumps** *(colloq)* fanya/tembea haraka. 2 ~ **sth** *(up)* koroga; *(fig)* vuruga; chokonoa. ~ **the fire** chochea moto. 3 ~ **sb to sth,** ~ **sth (up)** shtua, shtusha, amsha/ amka. ~ **sb's blood** sisimua. ~ **heaven and earth** jaribu kila liwezekanalo *n* 1 kukoroga. 2 kuvuruga, vurumai. 3 msisimko. ~**rig** *adj* -a kusisimua. ~**ringly** *adv*.

stir[2] *n (sl)* gereza.

stirrup *n* 1 kikuku (cha kupandia farasi). 2 mfupa katika sikio. ~-**cup** *n* kinywaji cha kuagana.

stitch *vt* shona *n* 1 mshono, kushona. **without a ~ on** uchi. ~ **in time saves nine** *(prov)* usipoziba ufa utajenga ukuta *he hasn't a dry ~ on him* amelowa chepechepe. 2 kichomi.

stock *n* 1 **take ~ of sth/sb** *(fig)* tathmini, pima, kadiria (hali, uwezo wa mtu n.k). 2 ~-**in trade** n mahitaji ya biashara/kazi *(attrib)* -enye kupatikana; *(fig)* -nayotumika mno, -a kawaida mno. ~ **answers** majibu yale yale. ~ **company** kikundi cha sanaa chenye michezo fulani fulani tu. 3 akiba. ~ **piling** kuweka akiba; kuhodhi bidhaa, mali. **make ~ of** faidi. **(be) in/out of ~** kuwepo/ kutokuwepo kwa bidhaa (fulani). ~-**list** *n* orodha ya bidhaa/mali (iliyopo). ~-**room** *n* bohari, ghala/stoo ya bidhaa. **take** ~ hesabu mali. ~-**taking** *n* kuhesabu mali. 4 **(live)** ~ mifugo. ~-**breeder/farmer** *n* mfugaji wa wanyama. ~-**car** *n* behewa la ng'ombe. ~**yard** *n* zizi (la muda). ~**car racing** mashindano ya mbio za magari (ya kawaida). 5 rasilimali; hisa. ~**broker** *n* dalali, mnadi (wa hisa). ~ -**exchange** *n* soko la hisa, mnada. ~**holder** *n* mwenye hisa. ~-**jobber** *n* mfanyabiashara wa hisa; mlimb ikizaji katika mnada wa bidhaa. ~**list** orodha ya bei za hisa shina. 6 nasaba, jadi, kizazi, ukoo. 7 ~ **s and** ~**stones** vitu visivyokuwa na uhai. ~-**still** *adv* kimya kabisa, tuli. **laughing** -~ kichekesho. 8 malighafi. 9 mchuzi, maji ya nyama/mifupa, supu. ~**pot** sufuria ya kuchemshia mchuzi. 10 *(of gun, etc)* tako, uti, mti. **look** ~**and barrel** kabisa. 11 shina. 12 daraja la kutengenezea meli. **on the** ~**s** -nayotengenezwa/jengwa. 13 skafu *vt* jaza, -wa na bidhaa (dukani). ~**ist** *n* mwekaji bidhaa (dukani n.k.).

stockade *n* boma, ua *vt* weka ulinzi kwa boma.

stocking *n* stokingi, soksi ndefu. **in one's** ~ **feet** -enye soksi (bila viatu).

stocky *adj* -fupi, -nene; **stockily** *adv*.

stodge *n (sl)* chakula kizito mno.

stodgy *adj* 1 *(of food)* -zito, sana. 2 *(of books etc)* -siovutia; -liojaa takwimu mno; *(of persons)* baridi, -siochangamka.

stoep *n (S. Africa)* baraza.

stoic *n* mvumilivu; mkakamavu. ~**al** *adj*. ~**cally** *adv*. ~**ism** *n* uvumilivu; ustahimilivu.

stoke *vt* chochea, chocheleza; tia makaa tanurini. ~ **hold/hole** *n (in a ship's furnaces)* mahali makaa yachochewapo; mdomo wa tanuri. ~**r** *n* mchocheaji makaa; kifaa cha kuchochea makaa.

stole[1] *n* mharuma.

stole[2], **stolen** *pt, pp of* **steal**

stolid *adj* -zito; -siyoonyesha hisia kwa urahisi. ~**ly** *adv*. ~**ness** *n*. ~**ity** *n*.

stomach *n* 1 tumbo, fuko. 2 hamu, shauku. **have no** ~ **for sth** -topenda/-topendelea kitu *vt* vumilia; stahamili ~ *an affront* vumilia mkingamo. 3 *(compounds)* ~-**ache** *n* msokoto wa tumbo, kuumwa tumbo. ~ **pump** bomba/pampu ya tumbo. ~**ful** *n* 1 shibe, kiasi cha kujaza tumbo.

stomp *vi* ~ **about** kanyaga (kanyaga).

stone *n* 1 jiwe. **S~ Age** *n* zama za zana za mawe. ~-**axe** *n* shoka la mawe. ~ **blind/cold/dead/-sober** *adj* -pofu/baridi/fu/macho kabisa. ~ **breaker** *n* mvunja/kivunja mawe. ~-**cutter** *n* mkata mawe. ~-**hammer** *n* nyundo ya (kupondea) mawe; nyundo ya mwashi. ~-**mason** *n* mwashi. ~-**pit** *n* shimo la mawe. ~-**quarry** *n* machimbo ya mawe; kiwanda cha mawe. ~**wall** *vt (cricket)* cheza kwa hadhari sana; *(fig)* zorotesha mjadala bungeni (kwa hotuba ndefu). ~**walling** *n*. ~ **waller** *n* uzoroteshaji/mzoroteshaji mjadala. ~**ware** *n* vyombo vya udongo na mawe. ~-**work** *n* uashi, mjengo wa mawe. 2 mawe; changarawe; kokoto. **leave no** ~ **unturned (to do sth)** fanya kila linalowezekana; fanya kila jitihada/tumia kila njia (kufanya jambo). **throw** ~ **at** *(fig)* kashifu. **within a** ~ **'s throw (of)** pua na mdomo, karibu sana, hapa hapa. 3 **(precious)** ~ kito, johari. 4 kilo 6.34 ratili 14. 5 kokwa. ~ **fruit** matunda yenye kokwa. **hail** ~ jiwe (la mvua ya mawe) *vt* 1 tupia mawe, rujumu. 2 toa kokwa, bujua. ~**less** *adj* pasipo mawe, bila kokwa. ~**d** *adj (colloq)* levi. **be** ~**d** lewa bangi/madawa.

stony *adj* 1 -a mawe, -enye mawe. 2 -gumu bila huruma. **a** ~ **stare** kukazia macho *(sl)* ~/-**broke** *adj* bila fedha kabisa; waya. ~-**hearted** *adj* katili, pasi huruma; -kaidi. 3 **stonily** *adv* bila huruma.

stood *pt, pp of stand.*

stooge *n* 1 *(colloq)* barakala, kibaraka. 2 mchekeshaji *vi* ~ **for sb** -wa kibaraka wa mtu.

stool *n* 1 stuli, kigoda, kiti kidogo. **fall between two ~s** poteza nafasi kwa kusita/kuyumba kwenye uamuzi. 2 choo, mavi, kinyesi. 3 **(foot) ~** kibago. **~-pigeon** *n* njiwa chambo: njiwa wa kuvutia wenziwe tunduni; *(fig) (of person)* shushushu chambo: mtu atumiwaye kukamatisha wahalifu.

stoop[1] *vi,vt* 1 inama. 2 **~ to sth** *(fig)* jishusha, jitweza *n* 1 kibiongo.

stoop[2] *n (in America)* kibaraza, baraza.

stop *vt,vi* 1 simamisha, komesha; zuia. 2 **~ sb (from) (doing sth)** zuia; sitisha 3 acha (kufanya jambo. **~ it!** *(imper)* Acha! 4 **~ (at)** nyamaza, tulia; isha, katika *the rain ~ed early* mvua iliisha/katika mapema. 5 **~ (at)** simama. **~ dead** simama ghafla. **~ short at sth** ishia, komea. 6 **~ sth (up)** jaza, ziba funga. **~ tooth** ziba jino. **~ one's ears** *(fig)* -tosikiliza/kataa kusikiliza. 7 simamisha, zuia. **~ sth out of sth** punguza kitu toka kitu (k.m. mshahara n.k.). 8 *(colloq)* kaa, fikia. **~ off (at/in)** katiza safari, ahirisha; shinda mahala. **~ off/over (at/in)** lala mahala. **~-over** *n* katizo la safari; mapumziko, kituo. **~ up (late)** kesha. **~ing** kiziba jino (k.m. risasi, dhahabu n.k.) *n* kituo; kikomo, mwisho, kusimamish(w)a; kukomesha. **put a ~ to sth, bring sth to a ~** simamisha/ komesha jambo. 1 *(music)* kizuio, kizuizi, kizibo. **pull out all the ~s** *(fig)* fanya kila juhudi/jitihada; bembeleza kwa kila hali. 2 *(in writing)* nukta, kituo. 3 *(phonetic)* konsonanti mpasuko (p,b,k,g,t,d.). 4 *(in a camera)* kidhibiti/kirekebisha mwanga. 5 *(compounds)* **~cock** *n* bilula. **~gap** *n* 1 badala; kuweka kwa muda. **~- light** *n* taa (ya kusimamisha). **~page** *n* kusimama kwa kazi (kutokana na mgomo); kipingamizi, kikwazo, kizuizi. **~per** *n* kizibo, kifuniko. **put a ~per/the ~pers on (sth)** *(fig)* komesha kitu au jambo, zima. **~-press** *n* habari mpya/ moto. **~-valve** *n* vali (izuiayo au kuruhusu maji n.k.). **~-watch** *n* saa ya michezo (ya kupima muda fulani).

store *n* 1 akiba. 2 **in ~** tayari *there is sth in ~ for you* kuna akiba yako. 3 vifaa, zana. 4 *(US)* duka. 5 *(pl)* duka kubwa (la bidhaa anuai). 6 **set great/little/no/not much ~ by** thamini sana/kidogo. **~ (house)** *n* bohari, ghala; *(fig)* hazina; bahari ya maarifa; **~keeper** *n* 1 mtunza ghala. 2 *(US)* mwenye duka; mwuuza duka. **~-room** *n* ghala, stoo *vt* 1 **~ sth (up)** weka, kusanya, dunduliza. 2 *(furnish)* patia, -pa, jaliza; pamba. 3 *(furniture etc)* tunza, hifadhi.

storey, *n US* **story** orofa, ghorofa. **third ~** orofa ya tatu; *(fig) the upper ~* akili. **have sth wrong in the upper ~** -wa punguwani. **~ed** (*US* **storied**) *adj* -enye ghorofa.

stork *n (bird)* korongo *African Woolly ~* korongo shingo -hariri *marabou ~* korongo mfuko-shingo *whale-headed ~* korongo nyangumi *white-bellied ~* korongo-samawati *yellow bellied ~* korongo uso-mwekundu; kongoro domo -njano.

storm *n* 1 dhoruba, tufani, mvua kubwa. **a ~ in a teacup** makelele/ wasiwasi wa bure; wasiwasi mkubwa kwa kitu/jambo dogo. **~-beaten** *adj* -lioharibiwa kwa dhoruba. **~-bound** *adj* -lioshindwa kuendelea na safari kutokana na dhoruba. **~- centre** *n* kitovu cha dhoruba; *(fig)* kiini cha matatizo. **~-cloud** *n* wingu zito (la mvua linaloashiria dhoruba). **~-cone/ signal** *n* alama ya kuashiria dhoruba. **~-lantern** *n* kandili, fanusi. **~-proof** *adj* -siodhurika kwa dhoruba. **~-tossed** *adj* -lioharibiwa/ -liopeperushwa kwa dhoruba. 2 mlipuko, hisia za ghafla. **a ~ of cheering** vifijo. **bring a ~ about one's ears** anzisha zahama, chokoza nyuki. 3 **take by ~** vamia, teka/twaa kwa nguvu. **~-trooper** *n* kikosi cha mashambulizi makali *vt,vi* 1 **~ (at)** foka (kwa hamaki). 2 teka kwa kuvamia, ingia kẃa nguvu. **~y** *adj* 1

-a tufani/dhoruba, -a mvua kubwa *a ~ wind* tufani. 2 -a hasira/ghadhabu. **~ly** *adv*.

story[1] *n* 1 hadithi, kisa, hekaya, masimulizi. **~-book** *n* kitabu cha hadithi. **~ teller** mtambaji, mhadithiaji. 2 uzushi, uwongo. 3 *(journalism)* makala; tukio *according to his own ~* kufuatana na maelezo yake. **storied** *adj* 1 -liohadithiwa sana. 2 *(of legends)* mashuhuri.

story[2] *see* **storey.**

stoup *n* 1 kombe, jagi. 2 chombo cha maji matakatifu.

stout *adj* 1 -nene, -a imara, thabiti, madhubuti. 2 jagina. **a ~ heart** moyo hodari. **~ hearted** *adj* jasiri. 3 *(of a person)* -nenenene, -enye uelekeo wa kunenepa *n* stauti: (bia) nzito/kali sana. **~ly** *adv*. **~ness** *n*.

stove[1] *see* **stave**[2]

stove[2] *n* stovu, (jiko la mafuta/gesi; n.k.). **~-pipe** *n* bomba la moshi wa stovu.

stow *vt* **~ sth (away); ~ sth into/with sth** weka, pakia, fungasha, hifadhi. **~ away** *n* mzamia/mdandia meli/ndege.

straddle *vt,vi* 1 tagaa, magamaga, panua miguu. **~ a chair** kaa kwa kutagaa. 2 simama kwa kutagaa.

strafe *vt (colloq)* 1 shambulia (kwa mizinga), lipua. 2 adhibu; laumu, karipia.

straggle *vi* 1 tawanyika, tapakaa, enea. 2 baki nyuma; potea *n* mchelewaji, aliye nyuma; mpoteaji. **straggly** *adj* -liotawanyika, -liotapakaa.

straight *adj* 1 sawa, -nyoofu, -siopinda. 2 sambamba na, -sawa. 3 safi, sawa, nadhifu. **put sth ~** nyoosha, weka sawa. **put the records ~** toa maelezo sahihi. 4 *(of a person)* aminifu, -kweli, -nyoofu. 5 *(colloq) (of a person)* -a kawaida, -a kupenda jinsi nyingine; -a kufuata taratibu. 6 *(phrases)* **a ~ fight** *(in politics)* michuano ya wagombeaji kura wawili tu. **a ~ play** drama ya kawaida. **a ~ tip** dokezo kutoka kwa mtu anayeaminika. **keep a ~ face** -toonyesha hisia, jizuia kucheka. 7 *(of alcoholic drinks)* kavu (isiyochanganywa na maji n.k.) *two ~ whiskies please* naomba wiski mbili kavu *n (colloq)* mtu wa kawaida, mwaminifu, mkweli, mnyoofu. **~en** *vt,vi* **~ (out/up)** nyosha, fanya sawa, tengeneza *~ your dress* tengeneza gauni lako. **~ness** *n, adv* 1 moja kwa moja. **keep ~ on** nenda moja kwa moja. 2 bila kuchelewa; bila kupinda; bila kubadili njia. **come ~ to the point** sema waziwazi, acha utondoti. 3 **~ away/off** mara moja. **~ out** bila kusita. 4 **go ~** *(fig)* -wa mwaminifu (baada ya kuishi kilaghai), acha uhalifu *n (usu* **the ~**) usawa, moja kwa moja; sehemu iliyonyooka/ ya mwisho. **~ forward** *adj* 1 -nyofu, halisi, waziwazi. 2 rahisi, -epesi. **~ forwardly** *adv*. **~way** *adv (arch)* mara moja, papo hapo, pale pale, bila kukawia.

strain *n* 1 mkazo, kulazimishwa, kulazimika. 2 majaribu, mvuto. **the ~ of modern life** majaribu/mvuto wa maisha ya kisasa. 3 uchovu, machofu, mavune. 4 kuteguka. 5 mtindo (wa kusema/kuandika). 6 mwelekeo, dalili *a ~ of insanity* dalili ya kiburi. 7 *(of animals, insects)* uzao, ukoo, safu mbegu *a goat of a good ~* mbuzi wa uzao bora. 8 *(poet usu pl)* wimbo *vt,vi* 1 vuta kwa nguvu, kaza. 2 tumia -ote vizuri (agh. uwezo, rasilimali), jitahidi, kakamka. 3 *(of muscles)* tegua, teguka, shtua; *(of eyes etc)* umiza. 4 **~ (at/on)** fanya kwa bidii sana. 5 *(fig)* geuza maana, lazimisha maana. 6 *(liter)* kumbatia, binya *she ~ed the child to her bosom* alimkumbatia mtoto kifuani. 7 **~ (off/out)** chuja. 8 **~ at sth** chunguza sana, chagua, sita. 9 *(esp. of feelings and behaviour)*-a kulazimishwa, -a shida, -a mashaka *a ~ed laughter* kicheko cha kulazimisha. **~ed relations** uhusiano wa kulazimisha. **~er** *n* kung'uto, kifumba, chujio, kichujio *coconut* ~ kung'uto *a tea* ~ kichujio cha chai.

strait *n* 1 mlango bahari. 2 matatizo, shida, dhiki, mashaka, *be in dire ~s* pata mashaka, dhikika, kuwa shidani, taabika. 3 *adj (old use)* -embamba, -a mkazo. ~ **jacket** jaketi (la mkono mirefu) la kufungia mikono ya wendawazimu; *(fig)* kizuizi cha maendeleo. ~**-laced** adilifu mno; -enye maadili finyu. **~en** *vt* songa, kaza, dhikisha, taabisha. **~ened circumstances** katika dhiki/mwambo.

strand[1] *n* 1 ncha, jino la kamba *a rope of three ~s* kamba ya meno matatu. 2 *(fig) (in a story)* tazamo, mwelekeo.

strand[2] *n (poet or rhet)* pwani ya mchanga *vt,vi* 1 *(of a ship)* kwamisha, kwama. 2 **be (left) ~ed** *(of a person)* kwama, -achwa katika shida *be ~ed in a railway station* kwama katika kituo cha reli.

strange *adj* 1 -geni; -a ajabu; -a kigeni. ~ **to say**... ni ajabu kwamba... 2 *(pred)* ~ **to sth** -pya, jinga, -siozoea, -geni. **be ~ to sth** -tozoea jambo fulani. **~ly** *adv* 1 ajabu, kiajabuajabu, kwa jinsi isiyo ya kawaida; vingine kabisa. **~ness** *n* 1 ugeni. 2 upya, ajabu. **~r** *n* mgeni *he is a ~ to me* simjui; mgeni kwangu *you are a ~ these days* umeadimika sana siku hizi *~ to proceedings* mgeni kwa mashauri *he is no ~ to poverty* -sio mgeni wa umaskini.

strangle *vt* 1 nyonga, songa kwa kamba, kaba roho. 2 komesha, zuia. ~ **hold** *n (usu fig)* msongo, kukaba *have a ~ hold on sth* kaba, bana kwa nguvu. **strangulate** *vt* 1 kaba roho. 2 gandamiza mshipa, (utumbo). **strangulation** *n* 1 msongo wa mshipa. 2 kunyonga, unyongaji.

strap *n* ukanda; ugwe; kigwe. ~ **hanger** *n* wasafiri wasimamao na kushikilia ukanda *vt* 1 ~ **sth (on/upon)** funga (ganga, kaza) kwa ugwe. 2 piga kwa kanda. **~ping** *adj* -refu, -enye siha nzuri, bonge, kubwa. **~pado** *n* adhabu ya kumning'iniza mkosaji kwa kamba.

strata *pl. of* **stratum**.

strategy *n* mkakati, maarifa. **stratagem** *n* (utumiaji wa) hila, werevu. **strategic(al)** *adj* 1 kimkakati. 2 -a hila ~ *material* vifaa muhimu vya vita. **strategically** *adv*. **strategist** mtu mwenye mikakati.

stratosphere *n* eneo la anga juu ya hewa ya kawaida (kati ya kilomita 10 na 60 juu ya ardhi).

stratum tabaka. **stratification** *n* utabakishaji, kufanyika kwa matabaka. **stratify** *vt* fanya tabaka, tabakisha, gawanya.

stratus *n* mawingu ng'amba.

straw *n* 1 majani makavu; *(of wheat, barley, rice)*, mabua. **make bricks without ~** fanya kitu bila maandalizi kamili/nyenzo. **a man of ~** mpinzani wa kubuni/wa kubuniwa/anayeshindwa kirahisi. ~ **board** *n* karatasi nene kama ubao mwembamba uliotengenezwa kwa mabua. ~ **coloured** *adj* njanonjano. 2 mrija. **catch at a ~/clutch at ~s** tapatapa. **not care a ~** -tojali hata kidogo. **not worth a ~** bure ghali. **a ~ in the wind** fununu. **a ~ vote** kura ya maoni, (isiyorasmi). **the last ~** pigo la mwisho *vt* tandaza majani/nyasi; funika na nyasi.

strawberry *n* stroberi ~ *colour* rangi ya stroberi. **~-mark** *n* alama/baka (kwenye ngozi).

stray *vi* potea, tangatanga; yugayuga, potewa na njia *(attrib)* 1 -liopotea. 2 -a bahati nasibu, chache *n* 1 mpotevu. 2 asiye na asili wala fasili. **waifs and ~s** watoto wasio (na) makwao.

streak *n* 1 mstari, mchirizi, mfuo, mlia. 2 dalili *he has a ~ of cruelty* ana dalili ya ukatili. 3 kipindi kifupi. **a ~ of good luck** kipindi cha bahati nzuri. **hit a winning ~** shinda mfululizo *vt* 1 piga milia, chiriza. 2 *(colloq)* kurupuka, kimbia kwa kasi sana. **~y** *adj* -enye milia, -a mistarimistari.

stream *n* 1 mto, kijito *navigable* ~ mto unaosafirika. **go up** ~ kata maji, enda dhidi ya mkondo (wa mto). **go down** ~ fuata maji. 2 *(current)* mkondo *(flow)* mfululizo; mmiminiko; msururu, mwelekeo, mvuto. *(fig)* **go with the** ~ fuata mkondo. ~ **of consciousness** mtiririko wa mawazo; *(lit)* mtindo unaofuata mtiririko wa mawazo ~ *of people* msururu wa watu. 3 *(educ)* mkondo *vi,vt* 1 miminika, tiririka. 2 pepea. **~er** *n* 1 bendera nyembamba ndefu; utepe. ~ **headline** kichwa cha habari (chenye maandishi makubwa). 2 mwali. **~let** *n* kijito kidogo.

streamline *vt* nyoosha, leta ufanisi (kwa kurahisisha). **~d** -lionyooka, -sio na mizengwe/vikwazo.

street *n* mtaa. **~-car** *n (US)* tramu. ~ **door** *n* mlango wa mbele/nje (katika nyumba). **~-lighting** *n* taa za barabarani *the man in the* ~ mtu (wa kawaida); mwananchi. **not in the same** ~ **(as)** si -zuri kama, -tolingana kabisa, tofauti kabisa. **~s ahead of** *(colloq)* mbali na; mbali sana; mbele kabisa (ya). **(right) up one's** ~ *(colloq)* -a kufahamika katika uwanja/utaalamu/eneo/mapendeleo ya. **go on the** ~ piga umalaya. ~ **girl/ mwalker** malaya. **~-sweeper** *n* mfagiaji barabarani.

strength *n* 1 uwezo *by sheer* ~ kwa kudura. **on the** ~ **of** kwa kutegemea. 2 wingi *they came in great* ~ walimiminika kwa wingi. **bring sth/be up to** ~ timia/timiza. 3 nguvu, tegemeo. **~en** *vt,vi* tia nguvu, imarika/imarisha, wezesha, fanya thabiti.

strenuous *adj* -enye kutumia/kuhitaji nguvu nyingi; -a kazi -enye bidii sana. **~ly** *adv*. **~ness** *n*.

stress *n* 1 mfadhaiko utokanao na shida/ taabu, dhiki, matatizo, msongo (wa mambo); shinikizo *work* ~ dhiki ya kazi. 2 shada, mkazo. ~ **mark** dhiki ya alama ya mkazo. 3 *(mech)* msongo, kani. 4 mkazo, uzito, msisitizo, himizo. **lay** ~ **on** sisitiza, tia mkazo *vt* sisitiza, kazia.

stretch *vt,vi* 1 nyosha/nyoka. ~ **one's legs** nyosha miguu. 2 eneza/enea. 3 ~ **(oneself) out (on)** jinyoosha, jitandaza. 4 pinda, panua, zidisha. **be fully ~ed** tumika zaidi ya kiasi. ~ **the law** pinda/panua sheria *n* 1 kujinyoosha; kupinda. **by any/no** ~ **of imagination** vyovyote vile ifikiriwavyo; hata ufikirie nini. **at full** ~ kwa nguvu zote. 2 kipindi, eneo mfululizo linaloendelea. **at a** ~ bila kusita, mfululizo. 3 *(of race course)* upande ulionyooka. **~er** *n* 1 kitanda cha mgonjwa/machela. 2 taruma. 3 kiti cha mataruma. 4 kitu cha kunyosha. **~er-bearer** *n* mbeba machela. **~er party** kikosi cha kubeba machela.

strew *vt* **(on/over sth); ~ sth with sth** tawanya, tapanya, tupatupa, nyunyiza, zagaza. ~ **the floor with sand** zagaza sakafu mchanga.

striated *adj* -a vifereji, -enye chanjo; -a milia, -enye mifuo.

stricken (*pp of* **strike**) adj -liojeruhiwa, -lioathiriwa, -liojaa huzuni, -liofikiwa na maafa ~ *with grief* -liojaa majonzi. ~ **in years** *(arch)* zee na dhaifu.

strict *adj* 1 -kali -a shuruti, -enye kutiisha. ~ **discipline** nidhamu kali. 2 halisi, hasahasa, kamili, tupu; -liotongolewa sawa sawa ~ *truth* kweli tupu. **~ly** *adv* hasa hasa, kabisa, kwa kweli, kwa akali. **~ness** *n*.

stricture *n* 1 shutuma, suto, karipio. 2 msongo wa mshipa.

stride *vi,vt* 1 tembea kwa hatua ndefu, piga hatua ndefu. ~ **over/across sth** chupa, ruka (kwa hatua moja). 2 panua/tanua miguu; tagaa *n* hatua ndefu. **take sth in one's** ~ fanya bila taabu. **make great ~s** endelea sana; fanya maendeleo ya haraka.

strident *adj* -a makelele, kali, -a kukwaruza. **stridence/stridency** *n* makelele, mkwaruzo. **~ly** *adv*.

stridulate *vt* fanya mlio kama kereng'ende. **stridulation** *n*.

strife *n* ugomvi, mabishano; migongano, vita.

strike *vt vt* 1 piga, gonga, bisha, chapa. ~ **at the root of sth** kata mzizi wa (fitina n.k.), ondoa kiini cha (tatizo n.k.). ~ **while the iron is hot** *(prov)* samaki mkunje angali mbichi; tenda bila kuchelewa. **a ~/striking force** kikosi cha mashambulizi. **within striking distance** karibu vya kutosha kushambulia (kwa urahisi). ~ **a blow** piga dafurao. 2 washa/choma. ~ **a light** washa taa/kiberiti. 3 fikia, pata. ~ **a balance** afikiana, patana. ~ **a bargain (with sb)** kubaliana na, barikiana. 4 *(coin)* piga chapa. 5 *(sail)* tua, shusha. ~ **one's flag** shusha bendera, salimu amri. ~ **tents/camp** vunja kambi. 6 *(on rock)* ingia/panda mwambani, kwama. 7 *(discover)* gundua. ~ **oil** gundua/pata mafuta; *(fig)* pata nyota ya jaha, tajirika. ~ **it rich** tajirika ghafla. 8 ~ **(for/against)** goma. 9 *(effect)* ingia moyoni, shtusha, choma, pata/toa, picha; gonga *he was struck by fever* alipata homa. 10 *(clock)* gonga, toa gusia. ~ **a note of** onyesha dalili ya, toa ishara ya; gusia ~ *a note of warning* toa tahadhari. 11 ~ **(off/out)** ondoka, enda, elekea. 12 fanya kuwa **be struck dumb/blind** kuwa bubu/ pofu, pigwa bumbuazi. 13 panda. ~ **a cutting** panda/pandikiza kipande/ kitawi. ~ **root** ota, toa mizizi. 14 kaa, nega. ~ **as pious** kaa kisalihina. 15 ~ **fear/terror/alarm into sb** jaza/tia hofu/homa/wahka. 16 *(with adv. particles and prep)* ~ **sb down** angusha, bwaga, andama; *(of disease)* shambulia. ~ **sth off** fyeka, chanja, kata; chapa. ~ **sth off (sth)** ondoa, futa. ~ **on/upon sth** gundua, vumbua, (kwa bahati). ~ **out** ~ ogelea kwa nguvu (kwa mikono na miguu); tupa ngumi/mikono; anza/fuata utaratibu mpya/wa pekee. ~ **sth out/through** futa, kata. ~ **(sth) up** anza, anzisha. ~ **up sth (with sb)** anza urafiki/uhusiano na *n* 1 ugomaji; mgomo. **be/go/on ~; be/come/go out on** ~ goma, anza mgomo. **a general** ~ mgomo wa wafanyakazi wote. ~ **bound** *adj* -lio athiriwa na mgomo; -liofungwa/simama kwa sababu ya mgomo. ~ **breaker** *n* mvunja mgomo, mbadala wa mgomaji. ~ **fund** *n* mfuko wa mgomo. ~ **leader** kiongozi wa mgomo. ~ **pay** malipo ya mgomo. 2 *(of oil etc)* ugunduzi. **lucky** ~ ugunduzi wa bahati; kupata bahati. 3 mashambulizi ya ghafla ya ndege. 4 pigo. **~r** *n* 1 mgomaji. 2 *(football)* mshambuliaji. **striking** *adj* 1 -a kuvutia. **the effect was not** ~ matokeo hayakuvutia. 2 -enye kugonga (k.m. kwa saa n.k.). **strikingly** *adv*.

string *n* 1 uzi, kamba, ugwe. 2 **have two ~s to one's bow** -wa na njia nyingine ya kutimiza lengo. **the first/second** ~ tegemeo la kwanza/ pili (katika kufikia lengo). 3 uzi **keep harping on one ~/on the same** ~ endelea kuzungumzia au kuandika juu ya mada moja/ileile, rudia yale yale. **the ~s** vyombo vya muziki vyenye nyuzi/waya n.k. ~ **orchestra/band** bendi ya vinanda. **~ed** -a vinanda. 4 nyuzi zinazoendesha mwanasesere. **have sb on a** ~ tawala (mtu). **pull the ~s** dhibiti vitendo vya watu wengine (kana kwamba wao ni mwanasesere). **pull** ~ tumia mbinu. **no ~s (attached); without** ~ *(colloq)* bila masharti yoyote. 5 mtungo **a ~ of beads** mtungo wa shanga. 6 ufumwele. ~ **bean** harage bichi. **~y** *adj* -a nyuzinyuzi *vt,vi* 1 funga uzi/ ugwe katika upinde, kinubi n.k. **~ed instrument** ala ya muziki yenye nyuzi. 2 **strung up** *(of a person, his senses)* chachawika. **highly strung** -liochachawika sana. 3 tunga (shanga) katika uzi. 4 ~ **(up)** funga/ tunga/tundika katika uzi. 5 ~ **sb along** potosha mtu kwa makusudi, laghai. ~ **along with sb** endeleza urafiki kukidhi haja pasipo na ahadi zozote. ~ **out** tanda/sambaa; tupatupa, tandiza, sambaza. ~ **sb up** *(sl)* nyonga mtu kwa kitanzi.

stringent *adj* 1 -kali, -liopasa kutiiwa, -a nguvu. 2 *(of the money-market)*, -a mwambo. **stringency** *n* ukali, mwambo. **~ly** *adv*.

strip *vi,vt* 1 ~ **(off)** ~ **sth/sb (off); ~ sth (from/off sth); ~ sth/sb (of sth)** *(of clothes)* vua/vulia *he ~ped his shirt off* alivua shati lake. ~ **sth down**, *(of an engine)* pambua, kongoa. **~tease/~ show** *n* mchezo wa kujiambua ambapo mtu huvua vazi moja baada ya jingine. **~per** *n* mtu anayejiambua. **~poker** *n* poka ya kujiambua. 2 ~ **sb of sth** nyima, nyanganya. 3 chukua, chomoa, safisha *the thieves ~ped the sitting room of all its furniture* wezi walisafisha fanicha zote sebuleni. 4 minya, kamua *n* 1 *(of land)* kishoroba *a ~ of garden* kishoroba cha shamba, chane, ubale, papi *~s of grass* miyaa. ~ **lighting** utumiaji taa ndefu za umeme. ~ **cartoon** *n* mfululizo wa michoro ya katuni ~ *of bark (fibre)* utangule; *(plaited)* ukili; shupatu; nyiza. 2 *(colloq)* nguo za wachezaji.

stripe *n* 1 milia. 2 *(mil)* utepe (cheo cha askari/mwalamu), mstari. **the Stars and ~s** Bendera ya taifa ya Marekani. 3 pigo, mchapo (wa kiboko). **~d** *adj* -liotiwa mistari, milia. **~y** -enye milia.

stripling *n* mvulana mvuli.

strive *vi* 1 ~ **(with/against sth/sb)** pambana. 2 ~ **for sth/to do sth** jitahidi, hangaikia, pania ~ *with one another* pambana. **~r** *n* mtu anayejitahidi.

strode *pt of* **stride**.

stroke *n* 1 pigo. 2 mkambi; kasia, kafi; mpiga makasia. 3 kiongozi; jaribio moja, tokeo la jaribio hilo. **at a/one ~** kwa mkupuo (mmoja). 4 mlio wa saa/ kengele *what a ~ of luck* bahati iliyoje. 5 alama ya kalamu, mstari. 6 kihàrusi, upoozaji, ugonjwa wa ubongo (unaosababisha kupooza) *vt* singa, sugua, papasa. ~ **up the wrong way** shusha, chukiza, kasirisha. ~ **down** tuliza, poza *n* kupapasa, kusinga.

stroll *n* kutembea pole pole; matembezi *vi* tembea polepole, vinjari. **~er** *n* 1 mvinjari. 2 mtembezi.

strong 1 *adj* -a nguvu, hodari, thabiti, imara. **as ~ as a horse** -enye nguvu sana. **one's ~ point** ustadi, jambo ambalo mtu analifanya vyema. **~-arm** *adj* -enye nguvu, mabavu. **~-box** *n* sefu, sanduku la chuma. **~-headed** *adj* -enye kiburi, -enye majivuno, kichwa ngumu. **~-headedness** *n* majivuno, kiburi; ushupavu. **~hold** *n* ngome, boma; *(fig)* chimbuko, kiini. **~minded** *adj* 1 -a ubongo wenye uwezo na mkali, -enye msimamo. **~willed** *adj* -enye msimamo wa nguvu. **~-room** *n* chumba cha hazina. 2 *(of smell, drink, flavour etc)* zito, kali. **a ~ tea** chai nzito. 3 -a athari kubwa, -a kero, tusi. ~ **language** *n* lugha kali/ ya matusi. 4 ~ **drink** pombe kali, -enye alkoholi. 5 *(adverbial use)* **going ~** *(colloq)* buheri wa afya, -enye afya/siha njema. **come/go it (rather/a bit) ~** *(colloq)* kuza, tia chumvi. **~ly** *adv*. 6 *(comm) (of prices)* -enye kupanda kwa utaratibu, isiyoyumba.

strop *n* kinoo cha wembe *vt* noa wembe.

strophe *n* sehemu ya wimbo, ubeti.

strove *pt of* **strive**.

struck *pt, pp of* **strike.**

structure *n* 1 muundo, umbile *the ~ of the human body* muundo wa mwili wa binadamu *the ~ of a sentence* muundo wa sentensi. 2 jengo; kiunzi. **structural** *adj*. **structurally** *adv*.

struggle *vi* ~ **(against/with)** shindana, pambana; kakamka, jitahidi sana. **they ~d up the hill** walijitahidi kukwea mlima *n* 1 mapambano, harakati. 2 shindano *the class ~* harakati za kitabaka.

strum *vi* pigapiga (kinanda) ovyo

ovyo.

strumpet *n (arch)* malaya, kahaba.

strung *pt,pp of* **string.**

strut[1] *vi* enda dalji/kwa mkogo *n* mwendo wa mikogo; kwenda dalji.

strut[2] *n* taruma, gadi, kiegemeo.

strychnine *n* sumu kali (ya kusisimua neva).

stub *n (of a tree)* kisiki, kigutu; *(of a cigerette)* kishungi; *(of a counterfoil)* kibutu/kipande *vt* 1 ~ **sth out** zima; vuta na kutoa, ng'oa, gonga. ~ **by** *adj* -fupi na -nene.

stubble *n* 1 mashina ya mabua/nyasi yaliyokatika. 2 ndevu fupi ngumu.

stubbly *adj* -a vishina vingi; -enye vishina.

stubborn *adj* -kaidi, -shupavu, sugu. **as ~ as a mule** kaidi sana. **~ly** *adj* kwa ukaidi. **~ness** *n* ushupavu; ukaidi.

stucco *n* lipu, chokaa ya kukandikia *vt* piga lipu, kandika.

stuck *pt,pp of* **stick.**

stuck-up *adj (colloq)* -a kiburi, -enye majivuno, -a kutakabari.

stud[1] *n* farasi waliofugwa kwa madhumuni maalum.

stud[2] *n* 1 kishikizo; kifungo. 2 njumu, msumari *vt* pigilia njumu/misumari. **~ded** *adj* -liopigiliwa njumu; -liotapakaa.

studio *n* 1 studio: chumba cha kurekodia na kutangazia vipindi vya redio, T.V. n.k. ~ **audience** washangiliaji katika studio. 2 studio: chumba cha msanii, mpiga picha n.k. (chenye mwanga mzuri). ~ **couch** kochi kitanda. 3 chumba/bwalo la kuigizia/kupigia filamu.

study *n* 1 kujifunza, mtalaa/mtaala; masomo. 2 uchunguzi, utafiti. 3 chumba cha kusomea. 4 **be in a brown** ~ potea/zama kimawazo *make a ~ of* chunguza. ~ **group** kikundi cha wasomi. 5 zoezi, mchoro wa mazoezi/majaribio. 6 *(old use)* bidii *vt,vi* 1 soma, talii. ~ **to be a doctor** somea udaktari. 2 tafiti, chunguza ~ *the programme* chunguza mpango. 3 shughulikia, zingatia. **studied** *adj* -a kusudi, -liodhamiriwa, -enye makusudi. **student** *n* mwanafunzi. 2 mwanachuo. **studious** *adj* 1 -enye bidii ya mafunzo. 2 -angalifu. **studiously** *adv*. **studiousness** *n* bidii ya kusoma.

stuff *n* 1 vitu, vyombo, zana, vikorokoro *I can't carry all that ~* siwezi kubeba vikorokoro vyote vile *what ~ is he made of* ni mtu wa namna gani? ~ **and nonsense!** upuuzi mtupu! 2 *(sl uses)* **do your ~** onyesha uwezo wako. **know one's ~** wa mtaalam, jua kazi yake. 3 *(old use)* kitambaa cha sufi *vt,vi* 1 ~ **sth with/into sth; ~ sth up** shindilia. **a ~ed shirt** *(colloq)* msaufu, mtu mwenye maringo. 2 ~ **(with)** *(colloq)* jazia (uongo n.k.), dangaya. 3 jaza ndani ya ngozi (ya mnyama/ndege aliyekufa ili kutoa umbo lake halisi). 4 jaza viungo ndani ya mbuzi/kuku (kabla ya kumpika). 5 lafua. 6 ~ **it/sth** *(sl)* fanyia upendavyo. 7 *(vulg sl)* kaza, tia, jamiiana na. **~ing** *n* 1 vijazio. **knock the ~ing out of a person** toa jeuri/komesha; maliza nguvu, dhoofisha. 2 viungo vinavyowekwa ndani ya nyama kabla ya kupika.

stuffy *adj* 1 *(of a room)* pasipokuwa safi. 2 *(colloq)* nunaji, gomvi, -enye hasirahasira. 3 *(colloq of a person)* -enye kuudhika haraka, -siostahimili mambo. 4 rasimu; baridi. **stuffiness** *n*.

stultify *vt* 1 pumbaza. 2 onyesha upuuzi wa; vuruga. **stultification** *n* kupumbaza.

stum *n* maji ya zabibu, divai isiyo chungu (isiyotiwa chachu) *vt* zuia kuchacha/kuchachuka.

stumble *vi* 1 jikwaa. ~ **across/upon** kuta/pata kwa bahati. **stumbling-block** kikwazo, pingamizi, kizuizi, kigingi. 2 ~ **about/along/around** yumbayumba. 3 *(in speech)* babaika *n* 1 kujikwaa. 2 kosa. **stumblingly** *adv*.

stump *n* 1 *(tree)* kisiki, gutu. ~

oratory/speeches hotuba za kuhamasisha. **on the** ~ *(colloq)* -enye kushiriki katika siasa. 2 *(limb)* kigutu; *(arm)* kikono. **stir ones ~s** *(colloq)* kaza mwendo. 3 *(cricket)* kijiti. **draw ~s** *(in cricket)* maliza (mchezo) *vt,vi* 1 *(colloq)* fumba, tatiza, shinda. **be completely ~ed** duwaa, shindwa kabisa. 2 zunguka na kuhutubia ~ *a district* zunguka wilaya na kuhutubia. 3 **(along, about)** tembea/enda kwa vishindo. 4 ~ **money up** *(sl)* lipa/toa pesa. 5 *(cricket)* toa (kwa kugonga kijiti). **~er** *n (colloq)* swali/tatizo gumu. ~ *adj* -fupi na nene, kibonge.

stun *vt* 1 fanya kupoteza fahamu, ziraisha. 2 fadhaisha, tia bumbuazi; shtua. **~ning** *adj (colloq)* -zuri mno. **~ningly** *adv*. **~ner** *n (colloq)* mcheshi, mchangamfu; zuri mno.

stung *pt,pp of* **sting**.

stunk *pp of* **stink**.

stunt[1] *n* mkogo, tendo la madahiro/ kuvutia. **~man** *n* mbadala wa mwingizaji, mtu achukuaye pahala pa mwigizaji katika senema wakati wa kuigiza/kufanya vitendo vya hatari.

stunt[2] *vt* viza. **be ~ed** via, dumaa.

stupendous *adj* -kubwa sana, ajabu. **~ly** *adv*.

stupid *adj* 1 -pumbavu, -zuzu. 2 -liochanganyikiwa, -liopumbaa, -liofadhaika *n (colloq)* mpumbavu, baradhuli, zuzu. **~ity** *n* upumbavu, uzuzu *it's sheer* ~! upumbavu mtupu! **~ly** *adv*.

stupor *n* mzubao *in a drunken* ~ -liolewa chakari. **stupefy** *vt* tia bumbuazi, duwaza, pumbaza, poteza akili ~ *with drugs* pumbaza kwa madawa. **stupefaction** *n* fadhaa, bumbuazi, mpumbao.

sturdy *adj* shupavu, -enye nguvu, imara. **sturdily** *adv*. **sturdiness** *n*.

stutter *vt* gugumiza, gogota maneno *n* kugugumiza, kigugumizi, kitata. **~er** *n*. **~ingly** *adv*.

sty(e)[1] *n* chekea.

sty[2] *n see* **pigsty**.

stygian *adj (fig)* agiza.

style *n* 1 mtindo (katika maandishi/ usemaji). 2 ufahari. **in** ~ kifahari. 3 *(fashion)* mtindo (katika mavazi, vitu vya anasa n.k.) 4 cheo, jina. 5 kalamu (ya kuandikia) *vt* 1 ita, taja. 2 buni, sanifu. **stylish** *adj* -a mitindo; -a fahari kupita. **stylishly** *adv*. **stylishness** *n*. **stylist** *n* 1 mwenye mtindo bora (agh. katika uandishi). 2 *(comm)* msanifu mitindo *hair stylist* msusi. **stylistic** *adj* -a mtindo **stylistics** *n* elimu mitindo. **stylize** *vt* shikilia mtindo, igiza mtindo, weka katika mtindo. fulani.

stylus *n* sindano ya santuri.

stymie *n* kizuizi, kipingamizi *vt* zuia.

styptic *adj* -a kuzuia damu *n* dutu ya kuzuia damu kutoka.

styx *n (Gk myth)* mto unaozunguka ahera *cross the* ~ -fa, fariki dunia.

suasion *n* uasaji, ushawishi. **moral** ~ uasaji (usiotumia nguvu).

suave *adj* -a adabu/pole (lakini pengine kwa unafiki). **suavity** *n*. **~ly** *adv*.

sub[1] *(pref)*. 1 -dogo, -a chini ~ **committee** kamati ndogo. 2 -a kukaribia. **~tropical** -a karibu na tropiki *n* 1 *(colloq) (abbr of.* **~marine**) nyambizi. 2 *(of ~scription)* mchango. 3 *(of ~ lieutenant)* luteni -usu. 4 *(of ~ editor)* mhariri msaidizi. ~ **(for sb)** - wa mbadala wa (mtu). 5 *(colloq, abbr of* **~edit)** hariri, -wa mhariri msaidizi.

subaltern *n* afisa jeshi mdogo (kuliko kapteni).

subaqueous *adj* -a chini ya maji, -a kutumika majini.

subconscious *adj* -a kufichika akilini *the ~ (self)* nafsi iliyofichika *n* **the** ~ akili iliyofichika **~ly**. *adv*. **~ness** *n*.

subcontinent bara kubwa ndani ya kontinenti k.m. India.

subcontract *n* mkataba mdogo (uliotokana na mkataba mkubwa) *vt* toa/chukua mkataba mdogo. **~or** *n* mpokea mkataba mdogo, kandarasi msaidizi.

subcutaneous *adj* -a chini ya ngozi.
subdivide *vt,vi* gawa tena/zaidi, gawanyika **subdivision** *n* kijisehemu; mgawo *plan of ~* ramani ya ugawanyaji.
subdue *vt.* 1 tiisha, shinda; dhibiti. 2 *(quiet)* tuliza, lainisha; punguza nguvu. **~d** *adj* polepole, taratibu.
sub-edit *vt.* hariri, -wa mhariri msaidizi. **~or** *n* mhariri msaidizi.
subfusc *adj (colour)* -siong'ara, -a kiwikiwi; *(fig)* -siovutia.
subheading *n* kichwa kidogo (cha habari).
subhuman *adj* 1 si -a utusi -a binadamu, -katili, -a kinyama. 2 *(arch)* nusu mtu, -enye sifa (umbo la) mtu.
subjacent *adj* -a chini.
subject *adj.* 1 -sio huru, -liotawaliwa na serikali ya kigeni. 2 **be ~ to** paswa kutii. 3 **~ to** -enye uelekeo wa, -enye kupatwa mara kwa mara na *are you ~ to malaria* unapatwa na malaria mara kwa mara? 4 **~ to** *(adj, adv)* kwa kutegemea, kwa sharti ya *this plan is ~o approval* mpango huu unategemea kukubaliwa kwake. **~ to contract** *(leg)* kutegemea mkataba. **~ to prior sale** kutegemea kutotokea kwa mshitiri mwingine kabla ya siku ya mauzo/mnada *n* 1 raia, mwananchi. **Tanzanian ~** raia wa Tanzania. 2 mada, suala, habari, mazungumzo. **change the ~** badilisha mazungumzo. **on the ~ of** kuhusu. **~ matter** *n* maudhui. 3 *(at school)* somo. 4 mhusika. 5 **~ for sth** sababu/chanzo. 6 mtu (mwenye mwelekeo fulani agh. mbaya) *an irritable ~* mtu mwenye hamaki. 7 *(gram)* kiima. 8 *(mus)* kiini *vt* 1 **~ to** tawala. 2 athiri; toa; jitoa *~ sb to torture* toa mhanga; tesa. **~ion** *n* 1 kugandamizwa, kutawaliwa. 2 kukomesha; kutawaliwa. **~ive** *adj* 1 *(of ideas, feelings, etc.)* -a nafsi, -a dhahania. 2 -a kiima. **~ivism** *n* udhanifu, udhahania, unafsi. **~ctively** *adv.* **~ivist** *n* mdhanifu, mdhahania. **~ivity** *n.*
subjoin *vt. (formal)* ambatisha, ongeza mwishoni.
subjudice *adj (lat)* -nayoshughulikiwa na mahakama.
subjugate *vt* tiisha, shinda; komesha.
subjugation *n* kutiisha, kutumikisha. **subjugator** *n.*
subjunctive *(gram)* **~ mood** dhamira tegemezi; dhamira ionyeshayo matarajio (ambayo agh hayapatikani).
sublease *vt* kodisha nyumba/shamba ulilokodishwa.
sublet *vt,vi* 1 pangisha nyumba/sehemu ya jengo uliyopanga. 2 toa sehemu ya mkataba kwa kontrakta mwingine.
sublime *adj* 1 -a hali ya juu sana, adhimu, -kuu, -tukufu. 2 -a shani, -a kioja *n* **the ~** adhama, fahari, utukufu. **(go) from the ~ to the ridiculous** toka kwenye utukufu/hadhi/mambo ya maana na kuingia kwenye uchwara/upuuzi. **~ly** *adv* kwa ubora, kwa utukufu. **sublimity** *n* fahari, adhama. **sublimate** *vt* 1 *(chem)* safisha kwa kufanya mvuke/kuchemsha/kuweka juani n.k. na kurudisha katika hali yake ya awali. 2 *(psych)* takasa (hisia n.k.). **sublimation** *n.*
subliminal *adj* -isiyohisika, -a mbali na fahamu.
submarine *adj* -a chini ya bahari *n* sabmarini, nyambizi. **~r** *n* mwana nyambizi.
submerge *vt,vi* 1 zamisha, didimiza. 2 piga mbizi, zama *adj* -a chini ya. **~nce/submersion** *n* kuzamisha, kuzama.
submit *vt,vi* **~ oneself to sb/sth** 1 tii, jiweka chini. 2 **~ sb to sth** lazimisha mtu afanye jambo. 3 **~ sth (to sb/sth)** toa, wasilisha. 4 *(leg)* toa hoja. 5 **~ to sb/sth** jisalimisha, ridhia, vumilia *she ~ted to illtreatment* alivumilia maovu yote. **submission** *n* 1 kutii; kujisalimisha; kukubali. 2 utufu, unyenyekevu *with all due ~* kwa heshima na taadhima. 3 *(leg)* oni/wazo (lililowasilishwa kwa hakimu). 4 uwasilishaji.

submissive *adj* tiifu, nyenyekevu; nyonge. **submissively** *adv*. **submissiveness** *n*.
subnormal *adj* -pungufu *n* punguani.
subordinate *adj* 1 ~ **(to)** -a chini, -dogo, saidizi, 2 *(gram)* tegemezi. ~ **clause** kishazi tegemezi *vt* ~ **sth (to)** weka chini *n* mdogo, msaidizi, mkadamu. **subordination** *n*. **subordinative** *adj*.
suborn *vt* shawishi (agh kwa hongo). **~ation** *n*.
subpoena *n (leg)* hati ya kuitwa mahakamani, kuitwa shaurini *vt* ita mahakamani.
subrogate *vt* hawilisha hati ya madai. **subrogation** *n*.
sub rosa *adv (lat) (of communication etc)* kwa siri kuu.
subscribe *vt* 1 ~ **(sth) (to/for)** changa, toa fedha, toa mchango. 2 ~ **to sth** *(of magazine etc.)* lipia; *(of ideas)* unga mkono ~ *for a book* kubali kununua kitabu kabla ya kuchapishwa kwake. 3 tia sahihi, tia mkono. **~r** *n* mchanga fedha; mteja. **subscription** *n* 1 mchango, ada. 2 utiaji sahihi. ~ **concert** maonyesho ambapo tikiti zote zinauzwa kabla ya siku.
subsequent *adj* ~ **(to)** -a baadaye, -a kufuatia, -a kutokea *adv* baadaye, kisha.
subserve *vt* faa, saidia, auni.
subservient *adj* 1 ~ **to** nyenyekevu, tiifu mno 2. -a kufaa, -a kutumikia. **~ly** *adv*. **subservience** *n*.
subside *vi* 1 *(of flood etc)* shuka, pungua. 2 *(land)* didimia, titia. 3 *(of buildings)* didimia. 4 *(of winds, emotion)* tulia; poa 5 *(hum) (of a person)* zama. **~nce** *n* kutitia; kudidimia; kushuka.
subsidiary *adj*. 1 **~(to)** saidizi, dogo, -a kusaidia. ~ **law** sheria ndogo. 2 tanzu. ~ **company** kampuni tanzu *n* 1 msaidizi; kisaidizi. 2 (kitu) tanzu, (k.v. kampuni).
subsidy *n* ruzuku. **food** ~ ruzuku ya chakula. **subsidize** *vt* toa ruzuku, saidia, toa fedha ya msaada.
subsidization *n*.
subsist *vi* ~ **(on)** ponea/ishi kwa (kutumia), jikimu. **~ence** *n* riziki. ~ **crops** mazao ya chakula. ~ **allowance** posho ya kujikimu. ~ **economy** uchumi wa kijungujiko.
subsoil *n*. 1 udongo wa chini. 2 tabaka chini la udongo.
subspecies *n* spishi ndogo.
subsonic *adj (of speed)* -ndogo kuliko ya sauti.
substance *n* 1 dutu. 2 kiini. 3 *(strength)* nguvu, uthabiti. 4 mali, utajiri *a man of* ~ tajiri *waste one's* ~ ponda mali, fuja mali. **substantial** *adj* 1 imara, thabiti. 2 kubwa, maridhawa. 3 tajiri, kwasi. 4 hususa, -a msingi. 5 kweli, halisi. **substantially** *adv*.
substandard *adj* chini ya wastani, chini ya kiwango kinachotakiwa; hafifu, -a kiwango cha chini.
substantiate *vt* thibitisha, hakikisha, yakinisha. **substantiation** *n*.
substantival *adj (gram)* -a jina, -a nomino.
substantive *n (gram)* jina, nomino *adj* huru; halisi, -a kweli ~ **rank** *(GB)* cheo (cha kudumu).
substation *n* stesheni ndogo, kistesheni.
substitute ~ **(sth/sb) (for)** vt badili, weka badala ya, chukua nafasi ya *n* badala. **substitution** *n* kibadala.
substratum *n* 1 tabaka chini, safu ya chini. 2 msingi, punje ~ *of truth* punje ya ukweli.
substructure *n* msingi.
subsume *vt* ~ **(under)** ingiza, jumlisha.
subtend *vt* kingama, kabili, elekeana na, ngoeka.
subterfuge *n* hila, werevu, kisingizio; ghiliba.
subterranean *adj* -a chini ya ardhi.
sub-title *n*. 1 kichwa kidogo (cha habari). 2 *(pl) (of films)* tafsiri za mazungumzo.
subtle *adj* 1 -gumu kueleza/kutambua, -a kutatiza. 2 erevu, -a akili. 3 stadi, pambanuzi. **subtly** *adv*. **~ty** *n*.
subtract ~ **(from)** *vt* 1 toa; ondoa. 2 punguza. **~ion** *n*.

suburb *n* kando ya kiunga cha mji, pambizoni mwa mji. **the ~s** viunga, vitongoji. **~an** *adj* 1 -a kiungani, -a pambizoni, -a pembeni, -a kando ya mji. 2 *(derog)* -a kienyeji, -siostaarabu, -enye mawazo finyu. **~ia** *n* 1 vitongoji, kando ya mji, viunga. 2 *(derog)* (maisha/ mtazamo wa) wakazi wa viunga.

subvention *n* fedha ya msaada, ruzuku.

subvert *vt* pindua, angamiza, chochea.

subversion *n* kupindua, maangamizi, mapinduzi; uchochezi. **subversive** *adj* -a kupindua, angamizi; chochezi.

subway *n* 1 njia ya chini kwa chini. 2 *(the subway) (US)* treni ya chini kwa chini.

succeed *vi,vt* 1 fuata, andama. 2 ~ **(to)** rithi ~ *to property* rithi mali. 3 ~ **(in)** fanikiwa, pata, faulu, fuzu. **success** *n* mafanikio, ufanisi. **nothing ~s like success** *(prov)* ufanisi huzaa ufanisi *meet with* ~ faulu *without* ~ bila mafanikio. **successful** *adj*. **successfully** *adv*. **succession** *n* 1 kufuatana, mfuatano, maandamano. **in ~** mfululizo, mfuatano, moja baada ya nyingine. 2 mfululizo, msururu. 3 urithi ~ *duty* ushuru wa mirathi. **the Apostolic S~** urithi wa upapa (kuanzia Mtakatifu Petro). **successive** *adj* -a kufuatana, chanjari, -a mojamoja, mfululizo. **successively** *adv*. **successor** *n* mrithi.

succinct *adj* -a maneno machache ya wazi, mafupi na dhahiri. **~ly** *adv*. **~ness** *n*.

succour *n* msaada, muawana *vt* saidia/ auni, (wakati wa dhiki/shida).

succubus *n* shetani, jini la kike (linaloingiliana na wanaume waliolala usingizini).

succulent *adj* 1 tamu. 2 *(of stems, leaves)* -nene; *(of plants)* nene, -enye utomvu mwingi. **succulence** *n*.

succumb *vi* 1 ~ **to** shindwa. 2 -fa. ~ **to one's injuries** - fa kwa sababu ya majeraha.

such *adj* 1 **~... as** ... kama ~ *politicians as Nyerere* wanasiasa kama Nyerere. 2 jinsi. ~ **as it is** jinsi ilivyo. ~ **as to**, kiasi cha ~ *as to scare me* kiasi cha kunitisha. 3 ~ **that; ~... that** kiasi kwamba *the work was ~ that he had no time for lunch* kazi ilikuwa kubwa kiasi kwamba hakuwa na muda wa kula mchana. 4 hivyo, hivi *don't be such a fool* usiwe mpumbavu hivyo. 5 *(intensive)* mno, hasa *she was ~ a good player* alikuwa mchezaji mzuri mno. 6 *(pred use)* hii, hiyo ~ *is life* hayo ndiyo maisha. ~ **and** ~ *adj* fulani. **~-like** *adj (colloq)* -a kama hiyo, -a jinsi hiyo, -liofanana na hiyo; *(pron)* hiyo, hayo, huyu n.k. **as ~** kikwelikweli, hasa (hasa).

suck *vi,vt* 1 ~ **sth (in/out/up/through etc) from/out of etc)** fyonza ~ *the juice from an orange* fyonza chungwa. 2 nyonya ~ *the breast* nyonya ziwa. 3 mung'unya ~ *sweet* mung'unya peremende. 4 ~ **sth up** nywa, sharabu *the fabric that ~s up water* kitambaa kinachokunywa maji. 5 vuta *the current ~ed the child (down)* mkondo ulimvuta mtoto. 6 ~ **up (to)** *(sl)* rairai, sifusifu, jipendekeza (kwa) *n* kufyonza; kumungunya. **give ~ to** nyonyesha, -pa ziwa. **~er** *n* 1 mnyonyaji, mfyonzaji. 2 *(colloq)* baradhuli, mpumbavu, zuzu. 3 *(of plants)* chipukizi. 4 mpira wa kunata kwenye dutu. **~le** *vt,vi* nyonyesha, nyonya. **~ling** *n* mtoto mchanga. **babes and ~lings** malaika. **suction** *n* 1 ufyonzaji; uvutaji na uondoaji (wa hewa, kioevu n.k.). 2 mvuto, mfyonzo. **~-pipe** *n* bomba la kunyonyea. **~-pump** *n* pampu fyonzaji/fyondaji. **~-valve** *n* vali fyonzaji/fyondaji.

sudden *adj* -a ghafula, -a mara, -siotazamiwa *n (only in)* **all of a ~** ghafula, mara. **~ly** *adv*. ghafula, mara, papo hapo. **~ness** *n* ghafula, ughafula.

suds *n (pl)* mapovu.

sue *vt,vi* ~ **(for)** 1 shtaki, fungulia mashtaka. 2 sihi, omba.

suet *n* shahamu (izungukayo figo). **~y** *adj*.

suffer *vt,vi* 1 **~ from** umwa, teseka, sumbuliwa na. 2 patwa na, pitia *~ hardship* pitia mateso, teswa, shindwa. 3 kubali, ruhusu *I won't ~ such conduct* sitakubali tabia kama hii. 4 *~ (endure)* vumilia. **~ fools gladly** vumilia wapumbavu. **~er** *n*. **~able** *adj*. **ing** *n* 1 mateso, taabu. 2 *(pl)* maumivu. **~ance.** *n* **on** ~ kwa ruhusa/kibali *he is here on ~* ameruhusiwa (lakini hatakiwi).

suffice *vt* 1 **~ (for)** tosha, kifu, kidhi. **~it to say that** inatosha kusema kwamba. 2 tosheleza. **sufficient** *adj* -a kutosha, -a kuridhisha, -a kukifu *it is ~* yatosha; basi *n (usu* **a sufficiency of sth)** kiasi cha kutosha. **sufficiently** *adv*. **sufficiency** *n* utoshelevu.

suffix *n* kiambishi tamati *vt* ambisha mwishoni.

suffocate *vt,vi* 1 songa, kaba roho, nyonga. 2 kosa hewa. **suffocation** *n* kusonga roho, msongo wa pumzi, kukosa hewa.

suffragan *n* **~ bishop, bishop~** askofu msaidizi.

suffrage *n* kura, haki ya kupiga kura *universal ~* haki ya kupiga kura kwa wote. **~tte** *n* mwanamke aliyedai haki ya kupiga kura (mwanzoni mwa karne ya 20 (huko Uingereza). **suffragist** *n* mdai haki ya wanawake kupiga kura.

suffuse *vt* jaa, enea *her eyes ~ with tears* macho yake yalijaa machozi. **suffusion** *n* kujaza.

sugar *n* sukari. **unrefined** ~ sukari guru *vt* tia sukari. **~-beet** *n* kiazi sukari *~-bowl n* bakuli la sukari. **~-cane** *n* muwa. **~ coated** *adj* -liopakwa sukari; *(fig)* -a kuvutia, -a kudanganya. **~ daddy** *n* mzee kijana (atumiaye mali kutongozea wanawali). **~ loaf** *n* bonge la sukari. **~ lump** kibonge cha sukari. **~-refinery** *n* kiwanda cha sukari. **~-tongs** *n* kishikio cha sukari. **~y** *adj* -a sukari; kama sukari; -tamu; *(fig)* -a kupaka mafuta.

suggest *vt* 1 **~ sth (to sb); ~ (to sb) that...; ~ doing sth** toa rai, toa shauri, pendekeza. 2 ashiria, dokeza; maanisha. 3 *(reflex)* jia *an idea ~ itself to me* wazo linanijia. **~tion** *n* 1 rai, maoni, ushauri, pendekezo. **~ box** sanduku la maoni. 2 dokezo, dalili. 3 kutia wazo akilini. **hypnotic ~** *n* kuingiza mawazo akilini mwa mtu aliye usingizini. **~ive** *adj* 1 -a kushawishi, dokezi. 2 pujufu. **~ively** *adv*. **~ible** *adj* -a kushawishika, -a kushaurika, -a kupendekezeka.

suicide *n* 1 kujiua; mtu anayejiua *commit ~* jiua. 2 kujiangamiza. **suicidal** *adj* -a kujiua, -a kujiangamiza.

suit[1] 1 *n* suti *a two/three piece ~* suti ya vipande viwili/vitatu *in one's birthday ~* uchi. **~case** *n* sanduku (la nguo). 2 **law ~** madai, daawa, mashtaka. **file ~** fungua madai/ mashtaka. 3 haja, maombi. 4 *(lit or old use)* kuposa, poso. 5 jamii ya namna moja ya karata. **follow ~** fuata jamii ya karata; *(fig)* fuata mkumbo, iga, fuata. **~ing** *n* kitambaa cha suti. **~or** *n* 1 mchumba mtu anayechumbia. 2 mdai.

suit[2] *vt* 1 faa, juzu, stahili, stahilia *that car ~s me* ile motakaa inanifaa. **~ oneself** fanya anavyopenda. **~yourself** hiari/shauri yako, upendavyo. **~ sb down to the ground** faa sana/hasa. 2 *(espec of clothes etc)* kaa vyema, pendeza. 3 **~ sth to** linganisha, patanisha, oanisha. **~ the action to the word** tekeleza kama ulivyonena. 4 **be ~ed (to/for)** faa. **~able** *adj* -a kufaa, -a kustahili, -stahiki *that would not be ~table* haifai. **~ably** *adv*. **~ability** *n* kufaa. **~ tableness** *n*.

suite *n* 1 msafara wa mkuu. 2 *(series, set)* jamii (ya meza, viti, n.k.), seti ya vitu *a ~ of rooms* seti ya vyumba (vikiwemo chumba cha kulala, sebule na maliwato).

sulk *vi* nuna. **the ~** kununa. **~iness** *n* kununa. **~y** *adj* nunaji, -siopenda watu.

sullen *adj* 1 -chukivu, -enye kinyongo -a chuki, -enye kununa. 2 *(gloomy)* -zito, -a utusitusi. **~ly** *adv*. **~ness** *n* chuki, kinyongo.
sully *vt usu (fig)* chafua, vunjia hadhi, paka matope.
sulpha *US* **sulfa** *n see* **sulphonamides**.
sulphate *(US)* = **sulfate**. *n* sulfeti. ~ **of magnesium** magnesi sulfate, haluli ya chumvi.
sulphide *(US)* = **sulfide**) *n* salfaidi.
sulphonamides *(US)* = **sulfonamides** *n* salfonamaidi.
sulphur *(US)* **sulfur** *n* salfa **~etted** *adj* -enye salfa. **~ous** *(US) ~eous* -enye salfa, -enye kufanana na salfa. **~ic** *adj*. **~ic acid** *n* asidi sulfuriki. **~-spring** *n* chemchemi ya maji yenye salfa.
sultan *n* sultani. **~ate** *n*. usultani; himaya ya sultani. **~a** *n* mke, dada au binti ya sultani.
Sultana *n* zabibu kavu nyeupe.
sultry *adj* 1 *(of weather)* -a hari, -a joto kali na hewa nzito. 2 -enye ashiki nyingi, bembezi. **sultriness** *n*.
sum *n* 1 *(also ~* **total)** jumla, majumlisho. 2 hesabu, fumbo la hesabu *do a ~ in ones head* fanya hesabu kichwani. 3 kiasi cha fedha *pay a large ~ of money* lipa kiasi kikubwa cha fedha, lipa fedha nyingi. 4 **in** ~ kwa kifupi, kwa maneno machache *vt,vi* ~ **(sb sth) up** toa jumla ya; toa muhtasari; soma *she ~med up his character at once* alimsoma tabia yake mara moja. **~ming up** *n* muhtasari/mapitio ya jaji kuhusu ushahidi katika kesi. **~mary** *n* muhtasari *adj* -a mara moja, -a papo hapo, bila kukawia; *(of law)* bila kufuata utaratibu, kienyeji. **~marily** *adv*. ~ **marize** *vt* fanya muhtasari, fupisha. **~mation** *n* 1 kujumlisha; jumla. 2 muhtasari.
summat *n (sl and dial)* kitu.
summer *n (in countries outside the tropics)* majira ya joto *vi* kaa/fanya makazi mahali wakati wa joto. **~-house** *n* banda la kukaa (bustanini n.k.). ~ **school** *n* kozi agh. za chuo kikuu wakati wa majira ya joto. ~ **time** majira ya joto/hari, kipindi ambacho saa hurudishwa nyuma kwa saa moja katika nchi kadhaa. **~y** *adj*.
summersault *vt* jipindua (kwa kuanza na kichwa na kuangukia mgongo).
summit *n* kilele; *(fig)* upeo. ~ **meeting/talk** mkutano wa wakuu wa nchi.
summon *vt* 1 ~ **sb (to sth/to do sth)** ita; ita kortini. 2 ~ **sth up** kusanya ~ *up one's energy* kusanya nguvu. **~s** *n* 1 kuitwa shaurini. 2 amri ya kufika mahali/kufanya jambo fulani *vt* ita shaurini.
sump *n* sampu; shimo la viowevu.
sumpter *n (old use)* mnyama mpagazi/hamali (k.m. punda, ngamia) *~-horse n* farasi wa mizigo.
sumptuary *adj* -a kudhibiti matumizi/anasa binafsi.
sumptuous *adj* 1 -a anasa, -a gharama nyingi, -a thamani. ~ **clothes** nguo za anasa. **~ly** *adv*. **~ness** *n* anasa.
sun *n* 1 **the** ~ jua. **rise with the** ~ rauka, damka, jihimu. **the midnight** ~ jua kama linavyoonekana katika maeneo ya aktiki na antaktiki. 2 **(the)** ~ (mwanga/joto la) jua. **bask in the** ~ ota jua, kaa juani. **under the** ~ popote duniani. **give sb/have a place in the** ~ *(fig)* -pa/-wa na nafasi/hali inayoruhusu maendeleo. 3 nyota. 4 *(compounds)* **~baked** *adj* -a kuanikwa/kukaushwa juani. ~ **bathe** *vi* ota jua, jianika juani. ~ **beam** *n* mwale wa jua; *(colloq)* mtu mchangamfu, mcheshi. **~-blind** *n* kizuia jua (dirishani); pazia. **~-bonnet/hat** *n* kofia ya jua. **~burn** *vi* babuka kwa jua, badilika rangi kwa sababu ya kuungua na jua *n* mbabuko (unaotokana na jua). **~burnt/~burned** *adj* -liobabuka kwa jua. **~burst** *n* kutokeza ghafla kwa jua. ~ **dial** *n* saa ya kivuli. **~down** *n* machweo, magharibi kuchwa (jua). ~ **downer** *n (colloq)* kinywaji cha jioni; *(Australia)* mzururaji anayefika kwa watu jioni. **~-drenched** *adj*

-enye kupata jua sana. ~**dried** -liokaushwa kwa jua. ~ **flower** *n* alizeti. ~**glasses** *n* miwani ya jua. ~-**god** *n* mungu jua. ~-**helmet/hat** *n* pama. ~-**lamp** *n* taa ya mionzi mikali kama ya jua. ~**light** *n* mwanga wa jua, nuru ya jua. ~**lit** *adj* -a kuangazwa na jua. ~ **lounge/porch/ parlour** *n* sebule (au chumba) chenye kuta za vioo kuruhusu mwanga wa jua. ~**proof** *adj*; -siopenya/penywa na jua. ~-**ray** *n* mwonzi/mwali wa jua. ~**rise** *n* macheo, mapambazuko. ~ **roof** *(or less usu* ~**shine roof)** paa la gari lenye sehemu ya kuruhusu mwanga jua/hewa. ~**set** *n* magharibi, machweo, kuchwa. **from ~set to ~rise** usiku kucha. **from ~rise to ~set** mchana kutwa. ~**shade** *n* mwavuli wa kukinga jua; kivuli. ~**shine** *n* jua, mwanga wa jua; *(fig)* mchangamfu. ~-**spot** *n (astron)* alama (doa) jeusi katika jua. ~**stroke** *(colloq)* mahali palipo na jua jingi *n* ugonjwa kutokana na jua kali. ~-**tan** mbabuko wa jua, kugeuka rangi ya ngozi kutokana na kubabuka. ~ **trap** *n* mahali penye joto na jua (bila upepo). ~-**up** *n (colloq)* macheo, mapambazuko. ~-**worship** *n* kuabudu jua; *(collq)* kupenda kuota jua/ kujianika juani. ~**less** *adj* pasipo jua, -a giza. ~**ny** *adj* 1 -a jua. ~ **side up** *(US) (of an egg)* -liokaangwa upande mmoja. 2 *(joyous)* -a furaha, changamfu. ~**nily** *adv*.

sundae *n* krimu ya matunda na barafu.

Sunday *n* Jumapili. **one's ~ clothes/best** *(colloq, joc)* nguo za kutokea, nguo nzuri. ~ **school** *n* shule ya Jumapili (hufundisha dini kwa watoto). **a month of ~** kipindi kirefu.

sunder *vt (old use or liter)* tenganisha, pasua *n (only in)* **in ~** kutengana.

sundries *n (pl)* vikorokoro, vitu vidogovidogo kwa pamoja.

sundry *adj*, baadhi, kadha wa kadha; -ingine, anuwai. **all and ~** *(colloq)* kila mtu/kila kitu.

sung *pp of* **sing**

sunk *pt pp of* **sink**

sunken *pp of* **sink**

sup *vt,vi* 1 ~ **(up)** *(esp Scot. and N. Eng)* nywa kidogo kidogo *n* kiasi kidogo (cha kioevu). 2 ~ **on/off** *(rare)* -la kidogo. **he that ~s with the devil must have a long spoon** *(prov)* jihadhari na mtu usiyejua tabia yake barabara.

super[1] *adj (colloq)* bora, -a kupendeza, safi sana; -a kukithiri *n (colloq)* mrakibu wa polisi; ziada.

super[2] *(prefix)* zaidi yai a kupita kiasi, a juu.

superable *adj* -a kuweza kuzuiwa/ kuzimwa, -enye kushindika.

superabundant *adj* -ingi mno, maridhawa, tele. **superabundance** *n*. **superabound** *vi* zidi kiasi, kuwa maridhawa, kuwa tele.

superadd *vt* ongeza sana, zidisha, fanya ziada.

superannuate *vt* staafisha; -pa mfanyakazi kiinua mgongo chake. 2 ~**d** *adj* -zee mno kwa kazi/matumizi; -a zamani; *(colloq)* -liopitwa na wakati. **superannuation** *n*.

superb *adj* -zuri sana, bora; -a daraja la kwanza. ~**ly** *adv*.

supercargo *n* karani wa shehena.

supercharge *vt* chochea zaidi. ~**r** kiongeza oksijeni (ndani ya injini). ~**d** *adj* -liotiliwa kiongeza oksijeni.

supercilious *adj* -juvi, sodai, -a kujivuna *a ~ look* macho ya kiburi. ~**ness** *n* ujuvi, kiburi, dharau, majivuno, usodai. ~**ly** *adv*.

supercool *vt* poza mno.

superego *n* **(the)** ~ *(psych)* dhamiri.

supererogation *n* kufanya zaidi ya kiwango/mategemeo.

supererogatory *adj* zaidi ya kiwango/ mategemeo.

superfatted *adj (of soap)* -enye mafuta mengi/yaliyozidiana.

superficial *adj* 1 a juujuu *a ~ wound* jeraha la juu juu/dogo. 2 -sio makini, -a wasiwasi, -a kubabiababia. ~**ly** *adv*. ~**ity** *n* upurukushani; ujuujuu.

superficies *n (pl)* sura ya juu/nje; eneo

la juu juu/nje.

superfine *adj* -zuri sana, bora kabisa, iliyochujwa sana.

superfluous *adj* -liozidi, -a kupita kiasi. **~ly** *adv*. **superfluity** *n*.

superheat *n* kiasi cha joto kupita maji yanayochemka, joto kali.

superhighway *n* barabara kuu.

superhuman *adj* -a mungu,-a kupita uwezo wa binadamu; -kubwa mno.

superimpose *vt* weka juu ya.

superintend *vt* simamia, amuru kazi, ongoza, rakibu. **~ence** *n* usimamizi, uongozi, urakibu. **~ent** *n* mrakibu; msimamizi, mwangalizi, mwongozi, mkurugenzi.

superior *adj* 1 bora, aula, -ema zaidi. 2 kubwa/ingi zaidi. 3 ~ **to** -a kupita -ingine, -sioshindwa, -enye kuzidi; -a cheo cha juu. ~ **to** -sioshindwa na; -sioshawishika na *he is ~ to bribes* hahongeki. 4 - enye usodai/kiburi *n* 1 mkuu. 2 mkuu wa jumuiya ya dini. **~ity** *n* ukubwa, ukuu; ubora (kuliko -ingine); kiburi. **~ity complex** hisia za kujifanya bora (kwa sababu ya kujihisi kuwa unadunishwa), majikwezo, ubwana mkubwa.

superlative *adj* bora kabisa; *(gram)* sifa ya juu kabisa. **speak in ~s** tumia lugha yenye sifa zilizozidiana, tia chumvi.

superman *n* mtu mwenye uwezo kupita kiasi.

supermarket *n* duka kuu la kujihudumia la vyakula na vifaa.

supermundane *adj* takatifu, -a kiungu.

supernal *adj* -a kutoka juu, -a kutoka mbinguni, -a kiungu.

supernatural *adj* 1 si -a ulimwengu, -a kupita akili, si -a dunia hii. 2 -a rohoni. 3 -a mwujiza *n the ~* yasiyoonekana k.m. mashetani/ malaika/majini. **~ly** *adv*.

supernormal *adj* -isiyo ya kawaida, kioja.

supernumerary *adj* -a zaidi kuliko ilivyopasa *n* ziada, zaidi ya matarajio; mtu afanyaye kazi ndogo ndogo; mtu aigizaye sehemu ndogondogo.

superpose *vt* weka juu ya kitu kingine, pagaza. **superposition** *n* kuweka juu ya.

superpower *(US)* *n* taifa kubwa.

superscription *n* andiko la juu.

superscribe *vt* andika juu ya (kitu). **superscript** *n (math)* namba juu ya nyingine.

supersede *vt* chukua nafasi ya. **supersession** *n*.

supersonic *adj (of speeds)* -a zaidi ya mwendo wa sauti.

superstition *n* ushirikina; usihiri; imani ya uchawi, majini, mazimwi na itikadi za kidhana. **superstitious** *adj* -a ushirikina. **superstitiously** *adv*.

superstructure *n* jengo juu ye jengo jingine, vikorombwezo.

supertax *n* kodi kabambe/kamambe (kwa matajiri sana).

supervene *vi* tukia baada, zuka, tokea; **supervention** *n* kuzuka/kutokea baadaye.

supervise *vt,vi* simamia, angalia, ongoza. **supervision** *n* usimamizi, uangalizi. **supervisor** *n* msimamizi, mwangalizi. **supervisory** *adj* -a uangalizi, -a usimamizi.

supine *adj* 1 -chali, kimgongo. 2 *(slack)* -legevu, -zito, -zembe; vivu. **~ness** *n* ulegevu, uzito, uzembe. **~ly** *adv*.

supper *n* chajio; chakula cha jioni/ usiku. **~less** *adj* pasipo chajio.

supplant *vt* twaa mahali pa, chukua nafasi ya, badiliwa na. **~er** *n*.

supple *adj*. nyumbufu. **~ness** *n* unyumbufu.

supplement *n* 1 nyongeza, ziada. 2 jalizo, kijalizo *vt* 1 ongeza. 2 jaliza. **~al** *adj* -a nyongeza, -a kama nyongeza, -a kuongezea. **~ary** *adj* 1 -a kuongeza, -a ziada, -a kutimiliza. 2 -a kujaliza *~ examination* mtihani wa kurudia/nyongeza.

suppliant *adj* -a kuomba, -ombaji *n* mwombaji.

supplicate *vt,vi* omba, sihi. **supplication** *n* maombi (ya unyenyekevu). **supplicant** *n* mwombaji.

supply *vt* ~ **sth to sb; ~ sb with sth** 1 toa, leta, weka, -pa. 2 kimu, ruzuku *n* 1 kutoa, kuleta, kuweka. 2 akiba, ugavi. ~ **and demand** ugavi na mahitaji. ~ **curve** mchirizo wa ugavi. **be in short** ~ pungua, adimika. 3 *(pl)* **supplies** vifaa. 4 **supplies** *(GB)* ruzuku ya bunge kwa serikali. 5 **be/go on supplies** shikiza (kazi); -wa mshikizio. **supplier** *n* mgawaji, mtoaji.

support *vt* 1 *(bear weight)* chukua, tegemeza, egemeza, himili. 2 *(endure)* vumilia, stahimili. *I can't ~ him* siwezi kumvumilia. 3 *(help)* unga mkono, saidia, auni, fadhili. 4 *(maintain)* lisha, ruzuku, kimu *n* 1 kuchukua, kutegemeza *in ~ (of troops)* -a akiba. **(be) in ~ of sb/sth** pa msaada. 2 tegemeo, nguzo, mhimili. 3 kukimu. **means of ~** riziki, chakula. 4 msaada, muawana, shime. 5 kuunga mkono. 6 mtetezi. **price ~s** *(US)* ruzuku. **~able** *adj*. **~er** *n* 1 msaidizi, mfuasi, mwunga mkono, shabiki. 2 kitegemeo. **~ive** *adj*.

suppose *vt* 1 dhani, fikiri. kisia. 2 chukulia kwamba; tuseme ~ *they differ* tuseme wanaachana/ wanafarakana. 3 *(used as imper. or to make a suggestion) ~ we go* tuondoke, waonaje tukiondoka. 4 **be ~d to** tarajiwa, takiwa *(colloq) (in neg)* -totakiwa, -topasa. **supposing** *conj* kama, iwapo. **~d** *adj* -a kudhaniwa. **~dly** *adv* kwa kudhani, kwa kuwazia. **supposition** *n* kukisia. **on this ~; on the ~ that** kwa kufikiria kwamba.

suppository *n* kidonge (cha kutiwa tupuni).

suppress *vt* 1 kandamiza, shinda, komesha ~ *a rebellion* komesha uasi. 2 ficha; zuia; zima. **~ion** *n* 1 ukandamizaji. 2 uzuiaji. **~ive** *adj* -a kukandamiza, -a kunyamazisha. **~or** *n* mkandamizi, mkomeshaji; kizuiaji.

suppurate *vi (formal)* tunga usaha. **suppuration** *n* kutunga usaha. **suppurative** *adj* -enye usaha.

supra *adv (latin formal)* juu, mapema (kitabuni, n.k.).

supranational *adj* -a juu ya mataifa.

supreme *adj* 1 -kubwa kabisa, -a juu kabisa. 2 -enye mamlaka/uwezo mkubwa kabisa. **the ~ Being** Mungu. **supremacy** mamlaka ya juu kabisa, uwezo wa juu kabisa. **supremacy over** kuwa na mamlaka ya juu dhidi ya. **~ly** *adv* sana, mno.

surcharge *n* 1 malipo ya ziada (k.m. adhabu). 2 mzigo wa ziada. 3 mhuri wa posta unaobadilisha thamani ya stampu *vt* 1 toza kodi ya ziada, chaji zaidi. 2 ongeza mzigo, zidisha uzito.

sure *adj* 1 -a hakika, -a yakini **be/feel ~ (about sth)** -wa na hakika (juu ya jambo fulani). **be/feel ~ of sth/ that** -wa na hakika/imani kwamba. **be/feel ~ of oneself** jiamini. **be ~ to do sth**; *(colloq)* **be ~ and do sth** usiache/ usishindwe kufanya, hakikisha unafanya, usikose kufanya. **to be ~** ni/kwa kweli. **make ~ that/of sth** -wa na hakika, hakikisha *I made ~ that he finished the work* nilihakikisha kuwa anamaliza kazi yote. 2 -a kuaminika *a ~ messenger* tarishi anayeaminika. **~ footed** *adj* -siyoteleza, -siyotetereka *adv* 1 ~ **enough** kwa hakika, kwa kweli. **for ~** kwa hakika, hapana shaka. 2 **as ~ as** kwa hakika, kwa yakini; kweli tupu. 3 *(colloq) (US)* kwa hakika. **~ly** *adv* 1 kwa hakika, bila shaka, haikosi. 2 *(safely)* kwa salama. **~ness** *n*. uthabiti, uhakika, kweli.

surety *n* dhamana, mdhamini, *stand ~ for sb* dhamini, mtu.

surf *n* povu la mawimbi ya maji; mawimbi ya kuumuka. **~ing/~riding** mchezo wa kuteleza katika mawimbi meupe kwa ubao. ~ **boat** mashua ya kusafiria katika mawimbi meupe.

surface *n* 1 uso *the ~ of the earth* uso wa dunia. 2 juu, sehemu ya juu ya kitu/maji. 3 ~ **mail** barua zinazotumwa kwa njia ya kawaida. ~ **to/air missiles** makombora ya kutungulia ndege yanayopigwa kutoka ardhini au manowarini. 4 sura/umbo la nje *on the* ~ kijuujuu. 5 *(attrib.)* -a nje, -a juu. ~ *politeness* heshima ya kijuujuu *vt,vi* 1 -wa na/weka tabaka la juu ~ *the road with tarmac* weka tabaka la lami katika barabara. 2 *(of submarine, skin diver)* ibuka.

surfeit *n* **a ~ of** wingi wa vitu hasa vyakula, vinywaji, n.k.; shibe; kinaya *vt* shibisha; kinaisha; jikinaisha. ~ **sb/oneself (with)** (ji) jazia, jawa na.

surge *vt* 1 enda mbele, bingirika, tapakaa, (kama mawimbi) *the floods ~d over the valley* mafuriko yalitapakaa bonde lote. 2 vimba, fura *n* mfuro wa mawimbi.

surgery *n* 1 ugangaji; upasuaji. 2 *(GB)* chumba/ofisi ya daktari (ambamo hutibia watu). ~ **hours** saa za kuganga/kupasua. **surgical** *adj* -a kuganga, -a kupasulia, -a upasuaji. ~ **instrument** zana za kupasulia. **surgically** *adv.* **surgeon** *n* 1 daktari mpasuaji. **dental** ~ daktari mpasuaji meno. ~ **house** daktari mpasuaji mkazi (wa hospitali fulani). 2 daktari wa jeshi la majini.

surly *adj* -kali, -gomvi. **surliness** *n.* **surlily** *adv.*

surmise *vi* dhani, kisia, bahatisha, buni *n* dhana; kisio.

surmount *vt* 1 shinda (matatizo); pita (vikwazo). 2 *(passive)* **be ~ed by/with sth** -wa na kitu juu yako. **~able** *adj* -a kushindika.

surname *n* jina la ukoo *vt* -pa jina la ukoo.

surpass *vt* pita, shinda, zidi kiwango; kulula *he ~es John in power* ana nguvu kumshinda John. **~ing** *adj* -a kupita -ote, -a kushinda -ote, - sio na kifani. **~ingly** *adv.*

surplice *n* kanzu (ya kupwaya) ya kasisi. **~d** *adj* -liovaa kanzu, -enye joho.

surplus *n* ziada ~ *production* uzalishaji wa ziada ~ *labour* wafanyakazi *wa ziada* ~ *value* thamani ya ziada.

surprise *n* 1 mshangao, mastaajabu, mzimbao *cause* ~ shangaza. **take sb by** ~ fumania, shutukiza tokea mtu kwa ghafla (pasi na yeye kutarajia). **take a town by** ~ teka/shambulia mji (kwa ghafla), vamia kwa shambulio. 2 *(attrib.)* kitu/jambo la kushtukiza/ lisilotarajiwa *vt* 1 staajabisha, ajabisha, shangaza, shitusha, duwaza. 2 **be ~d** shangaa, ona ajabu. 3 shtukiza, fumania. 4 ~ **sb into doing sth** shtua, harakisha mtu afanye jambo fulani. **surprising** *adj* -a kushangaza. **~d** *adj.* **surprisingly** *adv.* **~dly** *adv.*

surrender *vt,vi* 1 salimu amri, jisalimisha, kubali kushindwa *the rebels have ~ed* waasi wamesalimu amri. 2 acha. ~ **one's rights** acha kupigania haki. ~ **to justice** jitoa mbele ya sheria ili uhukumiwe. 3 ~ **(oneself) to** jiachia *n* kusalimu amri, kujisalimisha, kujitoa, kuacha. ~ **value** thamani ya kufunga bima.

surreptitious *adj* -a hila, -a kichinichini, -a siri. **~ly** *adv* kwa hila, kwa siri.

surrogate *n* naibu, makamu, badala (hasa wa askofu anayeweza kutoa leseni ya ndoa bila matangazo mara tatu). ~ **mother** mama mwenye kuchukua mimba kwa ajili ya familia nyingine.

surround *vt* zunguka, zingira, zingia, zinga. **~ing** *adj* -a mazingira, -a jirani. **~ings** *pl n* mazingira, mastakimu.

surtax *n* kodi ya ziada ya mapato *vt* toza kodi ya ziada ya mapato.

surveillance *n* upelelezi, uchunguzi *be under* ~ pelelezwa/chunguzwa.

survey *vt* 1 aua, tazama, kagua. 2 pitia (kwa jumla). 3 pima ramani, pima kwa kuhesabu. 4 kagua jengo, shamba, n.k. *n* kutazama mandhari, uchunguzi, kupima; mapitio. **~ing** upimaji wa ardhi. **quantity ~ing** ukadiriaji majenzi. ~ **or** *n* mkaguzi wa mizani na vipimo, barabara, n.k. mkadiriaji (majenzi, ardhi, n.k.).

survive *vt,vi* endelea kuishi (baada ya

maafa), okoka, ponea chupuchupu. ~ **one's usefulness** endelea kuishi/kushika nafasi bila manufaa; baki, salia. **survivor** *n* mwenye kuokoka, msaliaji. **survival** *n* 1 kusalia, kupona, (hali ya) kuendelea kuishi/kudumu. 2 *(remainder)* baki, masalio, masazo ~ *of rights* kudumu kwa haki.

susceptible *adj* 1 -enye kuathirika kwa urahisi (na hisia). 2 -epesi kuhisi. 3 ~ **of** -enye kuweza. ~ **of truth** -enye kuweza kuaminika. **susceptibility** *n* 1 uathirikaji. 2 wepesi wa kuhisi.

suspect *vt* 1 shuku, tuhumu, tilia shaka. 2 dhani, kisi, waza. 3 ~ **sb (of sth)** tilia shaka, tuhumu *adj* -a shaka, -a tuhuma *n* mtuhumiwa *pred adj* -enye/-a kutilia shaka.

suspend *vt* 1 ~ **sth (from)** tundika, angika, ning'iniza. 2 elea. 3 ahirisha, weka kando; subirisha. 4 simamisha, (kwa muda), zuia ~ *a sitting* simamisha baraza. ~ **judgement** ahirisha hukumu. **suspension** *n* 1 kutungika, kuangika; kuondoshwa kwa muda, kusimamishwa; kuacha chuki ~ *of payment* kusimamisha malipo. 2 *(of motor vehicle)* viangiko (k.m. springi, shokamzoba n.k.). ~ **bridge** daraja linaloning'inia. **~er** *n* *(pl) (a pair of)* **~ers** ukanda/vazi la kuzuia suruali/soksi isidondoke.

suspense *n* shaka, wasiwasi, hangaiko, taharuki. **keep sb in** ~ weka/tia/acha mtu katika hali ya wasiwasi.

suspicion *n* 1 shaka, wasiwasi, tuhuma. **above** ~ -sioweza kutiliwa shaka, -a kuaminika. 2 **a** ~ **(of)** dalili ya mbali. **suspicious** *adj* -enye shaka, -a kuleta shaka, -a kutuhumu, a wasiwasi, **be/become/feel** ~ **about/of sb)** tilia shaka. **suspiciously** *adv.*

suss *vt* 1 ~ **sth out** *(colloq)* gundua. 2 fanya doria.

sustain *vt* 1 chukua, himili. 2 patwa na/pata (tatizo). 3 *(leg)* kubaliana na, toa idhini, idhinisha. 4 fululiza, endeleza. **sustenance** *n* 1 riziki. 2 mlo

suture *n* mshono wa kidonda; uzi wa kushonea vidonda.

suzerain *n* mfalme, sultani, mtawala. **~ty** *n.*

svelte *adj* (F) *(of a person)* -embamba, -enye madaha.

swab *vt* pangusa, safisha (kwa pamba, kitambaa), piga deki *n* 1 pamba/tambara la kupigia deki/kupangusia uchafu. 2 sifongo/, sponji.

swaddle *vt* fungafunga (mtoto) katika vitambaa/kamba za vitambaa. **swaddling - clothes** *n* vitambaa vya kumfungia mtoto, nguo za mtoto mchanga *still in his swaddling clothes (fig)* -enye kubanwabanwa bado.

swag *n* 1 *(sl)* mali iliyoibiwa/iliyoporwa, vitu vilivyopatikana kwa magendo/njia isiyo halali. 2 *(Australia)* virago.

swagger *vt* tamba, randa, enda kwa mikogo *n* majivuno, makuu, mikogo, jeuri *adj* *(sl)* -a mikogo. **~er** *n.*

Swahili *n* 1 *(person)* Mswahili. 2 *(language)* Kiswahili *adj* -a kiswahili.

swain *n (arch)* mtu wa shamba; *(joc)* mpenzi/kipenzi (wa kiume).

swallow[1] *n* kijumbamshale, mbayuwayu. **one ~ doesn't make a summer** *(prov)* si busara kuamua jambo kutokana na tukio moja.

swallow[2] *vt,vi* 1 ~ **(up)** meza, akia. 2 *(fig use)* mezea. 3 *(funds)* kausha, potea, toweka; jirudi *n* 1 kumeza. 2 funda.

swam *pt of* **swim**.

swamp *n* kinamasi *vt* 1 jaza maji, tapakaza maji, tosa majini. 2 ~ **(with)** *(fig)* lemewa na, lemea, zidi, zidiwa na *I am ~ed with work* nimelemewa na kazi. **~y** *adj* -a majimaji, -a kinamasi, -a topetope.

swan *n* bata maji (wa shingo ndefu). ~ **dive** mbizi ya mbayuwayu. ~ **song** tendo/wimbo wa mwisho (kabla ya kustaafu/kufa). ~ **'s down** manyoya mororo aina ya bata; kitambaa chenye manyamunyamu *vi (colloq)* ~ **off/around** enda matembezi, zurura, randaranda.

swank *vi (colloq)* tamba, jigamba *n* majigambo, makuu. **~y** *adj* maridadi sana, -a kutamb(i)a.

swap *vt,vi see* **swop**.

sward *n (lit)* uwanda, mahali penye nyasi nzuri fupi.

swarm[1] *n* 1 kundi kubwa la wadudu/ ndege n.k. *a ~of bees* bumba la nyuki *vi (of bees)* enda pamoja katika kundi. 2 **be ~ing with; ~ with** songamana, jawa na *the region ~s with locusts* eneo limejaa nzige. 3 -wa kwa wingi, songamana, tembea katika kundi.

swarm[2] *vt* ~ **(up)** paraga, sombea, paramia.

swarthy *adj* -eusieusi. **swarthiness** *n* weusi.

swashbuckler *n* mwonevu, mchokozi; mtu mwenye majigambo, mjeuri. **swashbuckling** *n* ugomvi, uchokozi; kugombana, kuchokoza.

swastika *n* swastika: nembo ya msalaba wa jua yenye kuashiria futahi au Unazi.

swat *vt* piga, chapa, ua (mdudu) *n* 1 mchapo. 2 kichapo.

swath *n* 1 fungu la nafaka, nyasi, lundo la nafaka iliyokatwa; kiduta cha nafaka iliyokatwa. 2 mkuza (nafasi iliyoachwa wazi baada ya kufyeka).

swathe *vt* zingia kitambaa, fungiafungia vitambaa, zungushia (zongomeza) kitambaa *n (bandage)* bendeji.

sway *vt,vi* 1 yumbisha, yumba, sukasuka, chuchia. 2 *(influence)* geuza, shawishi, vuta; tawala, *n* 1 kuyumba. 2 himaya, enzi, utawala, nguvu, mvuto *be under the ~ of* tawaliwa na.

swear *vt,vi* 1 apa, kula yamini. 2 apisha. ~ **sb in** apisha mtu, lisha kiapo. ~ **sb to secrecy** apisha kuweka siri. ~ **a witness** apisha shahidi. **sworn enemies** maadui wa jadi. **sworn friends** masahibu. 3 ~ **by sth** apia kama shahidi; *(colloq)* tegemea; jetea. ~ **off** *(colloq)* apa kuacha. ~ **to sth** apa kabisa, sema kwa dhati. *vt* ~ **(at sb)** laani, apiza; tukana *n* kutukana. **~er** *n* mwapizaji; mtukanaji. **~-word** *n* (neno la) tusi.

sweat *n* 1 jasho. **~-band** utepe (wa kofia wa kunyonya jasho). ~ **shirt** fulana ya jasho. 2 **a** ~ hali ya kutokwa jasho. **be in a cold** ~ kuwa katika hali ya woga na wasiwasi. **all of a** ~ *(colloq)* -wa/loa chepe kwa jasho; *(fig)* -wa na woga na wasiwasi. 3 *(colloq)* kazi ngumu, sulubu. 4 **an old** ~ *(sl)* askari mkongwe wa kazi. 5 majimaji, unyevu *vt,vi* 1 toa/toka jasho. 2 toa kitu. ~ **blood** *(fig)* fanya kazi kama punda. ~ **out a cold** ondoa mafua. 3 toza jasho. 4 fanyisha kazi ngumu, himiza, nyonya. **~ed goods** matunda ya jasho/kazi ngumu. **~ed labour** kazi ya malipo ya unyonyaji/dhulma. **~y** *adj* -iliyojaa jasho; -enye kutoa jasho.

sweater *n* sweta: fulana ya joto (ya mikono mirefu).

sweep *n* 1 ~ **(up/out)** kufagia. **make a clean** ~ **(of sth)** kumba, ondoa, zoa, fagilia mbali. 2 pigo la ghafula. 3 mkupuo. 4 mwendo wa nguvu, mkondo wa nguvu, mkondo. 5 *(range)* eneo, upeo. 6 **(chimney)** ~ msafisha dohani. 7 kafi, kasia. 8 upondo. 9 ~ **(stake)** bahati nasibu *vt,vi* 1 ~ **sth (from sth); ~ sth (free) of sth; ~ sth up/away** etc. fagia, futa, pangusa; kokoa. 2 peperusha, zoa, safisha *the wind swept the pieces of paper away* upepo ulipeperusha karatasi *the currents swept the branches along* mawimbi yalizoa matawi. ~ **all before one** -wa na mafanikio mfululizo. ~ **the board** pata fedha yote iliyokuwa ikichezwa kamari; shinda zawadi zote. **be swept off one's feet** *(fig)* emewa, jawa na jazba. **swept back** *adj (of aircraft wings)* -liofungwa usawa wa pembekali kutoka katika muhimili wa ndege; *(of hair)* -liolazwa kuelekea nyuma. 3 kumba *the storm swept the coast* tufani ilikumba pwani. 4 enda kwa fahari. 5 enea, tanda. 6 angaza *his eyes swept the room* macho yake yaliangaza chumbani. 7 pita upesi *the fingers swept the keys of the* piano vidole vilipita haraka kwenye vipande vya kinanda. 8 inama, piga goti kwa madaha. **~er** *n* 1 mfagiaji, mfagizi; ufagio. 2 *(football)* mlinzi. **~ing** *adj* kubwa; -a jumla ~ *changes* mabadiliko makubwa ~ *statement* kauli ya jumla. **~ingly** *adv*. **~ings** *n pl* vumbi, takataka, uchafu. **~stake** *n* bahati nasibu ya fedha (katika shindano).

sweet *adj* 1 -tamu. **have a ~ tooth** penda vitu vitamu. **~wine** mvinyo mtamu (wenye ladha ya matunda). 2 -a kupendeza, zuri, -a kuvutia. **a ~ voice** sauti ya kuvutia. 3 safi *keep a room ~* weka chumba katika hali ya usafi. 4 -a kunukia, -a kufiridi *(to) smell ~* (ku)nukia vizuri. **~ scented** *adj* -enye kunukia. 5 *(phrases)* **at one's own ~ will** apendavyo mwenyewe. **be ~ on (sb)** *(colloq)* penda sana. 6 *(compounds)* **~ bread** kongosho la ndama au kondoo. **~briar/brier** waridi mwitu. **~ corn** mahindi matamu. **~heart** mpenzi. **~ meat** halua. **~ potato** kiazi kitamu. **~tempered** *adj* -tulivu, -pole *n (US)* peremende, lawalawa, tamutamu (chokoleti). 2 *(US ~ dessert)* chakula kitamu, agh pudini. 3 *(pl)* furaha, anasa, maraha. 4 mpenzi, kipenzi. **~ly** *adv*. **~ness** *n*. **~ish** *adj* **~en** *vt,vi* tia utamu, tia sukari, koleza; -wa tamu; geuka kuwa -tamu. **~ening** *n* kikoleza utamu. **~ie** *n* 1 tamutamu, lawalawa. 2 mpenzi, kipenzi. **~y** *n* 1 peremende. 2 mpenzi.

sweet-and-sour *adj* tamchachu (siki yenye sukari).

swell *vi,vt* 1 **~ (up) (with)** vimba, tuna, vimbisha, tunisha. 2 **have/suffer from a swollen head** jivuna; -wa na kiburi, vimba kichwa *swollen headed* -enye kiburi. 3 **~ (out)** tanuka, vimbisha *n* 1 mvuvumko. 2 *(sing only)* mawimbi makubwa (baada ya tufani). 3 *(dated colloq)* mlimbwende, mtanashati. **come the heavy ~ over sb** *(sl)* jifanya maarufu ili kuweza kushawishi (mtu), jidai *adj (US colloq)* 1 -malidadi, -tanashati. 2 bora/sana, -a kiwango cha juu. **~ing** *n* 1 uvimbe. 2 nyongeza, ziada.

swelter *vi* ona hari, jisikia vibaya (kwa sababu ya joto).

swept *pt,pp of* **sweep**.

swerve *vt,vi* 1 chepuka, pinda ghafla, enda upande. 2 epa *n* mchepuko, kwenda upande; kupinda ghafla.

swift[1] *adj* -epesi, -a mbio, -a haraka, -a ghafula. **~ly** *adv* upesi, hima, kwa haraka. **~ness** *n* wepesi, mbio, kasi *~-flowing adj* -a kutiririka/ kumiminika kwa kasi *~-footed*-enye mbio, -a mbio, -a kasi. **~-handed** *adj* -enye mikono myepesi; -a haraka (katika kazi za mikono).

swift[2] *n* mbayuwayu, barawai.

swig *vt,vi* **~ (down/off)** *(colloq)* -nywa, piga funda *n* funda *take a ~ at a bottle of beer* kunywa bia moja kwa moja kutoka kwenye chupa; piga tarumbeta.

swill *vt,vi* **~ sth (out)** 1 osha, suuza. 2 *(colloq)* -nywa kwa pupa *n* 1 kusuuza, msuuzo. 2 makombo, masazo hasa ya kiowevu. **~er** *n*.

swim *vt,vi* 1 ogelea. **~ with the tide/ the stream** fuata mkondo/ mkumbo. **~ming bath/pool** *n* bwawa la kuogelea. **~ming costume/suit** vazi la kuogelea. **~ming trunks** vazi la kiume la kuogelea. 2 vuka kwa kuogelea; shindana (na mtu) kuogelea. 3 **~ with; ~ in/on** jawa na. 4 ona kizunguzungu, sulika, shikwa na gumbizi; zunguka (zunguka) *n* 1 kuogelea. 2 **the ~** matukio ya wakati uliopo, mambo yanayotokea sasa. **be in/out of the ~** wamo ndani ya, shiriki/-toshiriki, fahamu/-tofahamu mambo yanayotokea sasa. **~mer** *n* mwogeleaji. **~imingly** *adv* bila matatizo; vizuri kabisa.

swindle *vt* **~ sth out of sb; ~ sb of sth** tapeli, ghilibu, danganya, laghai ~

money out of sb tapeli; chukulia mtu fedha zake kwa ulaghai *n* ujanja, hila, ulaghai; kitu kilichouzwa ambacho hakina thamani iliyotajwa. ~r *n*. ayari, dhalimu, laghai.

swine *n* 1 nguruwe. **~-herd** *n* mchungaji wa nguruwe. 2 *(derog)* mshenzi; mnyama, mpujufu. **~ry** *n* banda la nguruwe. **swinish** *adj* -a kinyama/kishenzi.

swing *vt,vi* 1 bembea, bembeza; pembea. ~ **for sb/sth** *(colloq)* nyongwa (kwa kuua). **no room to ~ a cat in** *(of an enclousure)* nafasi ndogo sana. 2 tembea/kimbia kwa/ bila ukakamavu. 3 cheza/chezesha dansi au ngoma *(sl)* changamka, fuata mambo ya kisasa. 4 geuka, geuza, enda upande. 5 pembea *n* 1 kubembea. 2 mdundo. **go with a ~** *(of music, poetry)* -wa na mdundo mzuri; *(fig) (of an event, entertainment, etc.)* endelea vyema/ bila matatizo. **be in full ~** pamba moto. 3 bembea, pembea. **~ing** *adj (sl) (of persons)* -a kisasa, changamfu; *(of events, entertainment etc)* -a kuburudisha. **~-door** *n* mlango wa kufungulia upande wowote.

swinge *vt (arch)* tandika, piga chapa. **swing** *adj* -kubwa sana, -a nguvu.

swipe *vt (colloq)* 1 piga kwa nguvu, twanga, kung'uta. 2 *(colloq)* iba *n* pigo la nguvu.

swirl *vi* zunguka upesi upesi, zungusha upesi upesi *n* kuzungushazungusha, kuzingia. **a ~ of dust** chamchela, kimbunga.

swish *vt,vi* 1 ~ **sth (off)** vurumisha. 2 chakarisha, piga (kwa mjeledi) *n* kuvurumisha; kuchakarisha; *(colloq) adj*.malididi, -a mtindo.

switch *n* 1 ufito, mchapo. 2 swichi. 3 mtambo wa kubadilisha njia za reli. **~-engine** *n* injini ya kuunga mabehewa. **~-man** *n* mbadilisha njia ya reli. 4 *(of hair)* kishungi bandia, mwengo, mgwisho. 5 **~-back** *n (of railway)* reli za mteremko mkali katika viwanja vya michezo; (*of roads*) barabara yenye vilima vingi. 6 badiliko, uhamisho *vt* 1 ~ **on** washa, fungua. ~ **off** zima. 2 ~ **sb on** *(sl)* sisimua. 3 *(of railway)* geuza njia, hamisha njia. 4 ~ **(to)**; ~ **over to** badili, hamia. 5 chapa kwa fito. 6 geuka ghafla; pokonya.

swivel *n* 1 pete yenye kuzunguka. 2 ekseli *vt,vi* zunguka; zungusha.

swiz *n (sl)* uchungu mkubwa; ulaghai.

swob *see* **swab**.

swollen *pp of* **swell** *esp. as adj*. ~ **glands** hijabu. **(painful) ~ glands** mtoki.

swoon *(arch) vi* zimia, zirai *n* kuzimia, kuzirai, kupoteza fahamu *she went off in a ~* alizirai.

swoop *vt,vi* 1 ~ **(down) (on)** shuka kwa kasi kutoka angani (kama tai, kipanga), chupa, ruka chini. 2 ~ **sth up** pokonya, pora *n* kuchupa, kushuka kwa kasi (kama ndege, tai, kipanga atokapo angani); ruko la ghafula. **at one (fell) ~** kwa dharuba moja.

swop *vt (also* **swap**) (*colloq*) badili mali kwa mali. ~ **market** *n* soko la mali kwa mali; mali kwa mali. ~ **yarns** simuliana hadithi za matukio. ~ **places with sb** badilishana nafasi. **don't ~ horses in mid-stream** *(prov)* usifanye mabadiliko wakati wa msukosuko *n* ubadilishanaji (wa mali kwa mali).

sword *n* upanga kitara. **the ~ of justice** upanga wa haki. **cross ~ with sb** *(fig)* gombana na. **draw/sheath the ~** *(rhet)* anza/maliza vita. **put to the ~** *(rhet)* ua. **at the point of the ~** kwa kutishwa. **~-arm** *(usu) n* mkono wa kulia. **~-bearer** *n (hist)* mbeba upanga wa mfalme. **~-belt** *n* mkanda wa upanga. **~-cane/~ stick** *n* upanga wa ala/fimbo ya upanga. **~-cut** *n* jeraha la upanga; pigo la upanga. **~-dance** *n* hanzua, tari, mchezo wa sime. **~-fish** *n* chuchunge. **~-play** *n* mchezo wa kupigana kwa upanga; *(fig)* malumbano. **~sman** *n* askari/mtu hodari wa kutumia upanga. **~smanship** *n* ustadi wa kupigana kwa upanga.

swore, sworn *see* **swear**.

swot *vi, vt* ~ **(for sth)** bukua, soma/ somea sana; jiandaa kwa kusoma sana. ~ **sth up** somea sana *n* 1 mbukuaji. 2 kazi nzito.

swum *pp of* **swim**.

swung *pp of* **swing**.

sybarite *n* mtu wa anasa nyingi, mpenda anasa. **sybaritic** *adj*. -a anasa, -a kupenda raha.

sycamore *n* mkuyu.

sycophant *n* mtu anayejikomba/ anayejipendekeza. **~ic** *adj*.

syllable *n* silabi. **syllabary** *n* orodha ya viwakilishi vya silabi (k.m. katika Kijapani). **syllabic** *adj* -a silabi. **syllabicate**; **syllabize, syllabify** *vt* taja neno kwa silabi moja moja, gawa katika silabi. **syllabification** *n* kugawa katika silabi.

syllabus *n* muhtasari (wa masomo au mafundisho).

syllogism *n* hitimisho linalotokana na hoja mbili (k.m. mtu ana miguu miwili, nyoka hana miguu; kwa hiyo mtu si nyoka). **syllogistic** *adj* **syllogize** *vt* hitimisha kwa mantiki.

sylph *n* hurulaini; *(fig)* mwanamwali mwembamba mzuri. **~-like** *adj* -embamba na -enye madaha.

silvan *adj (liter)* -a mwitu/porini.

symbiosis *n* ufaano, hali ya utegemeano baina ya viumbe wawili. **symbiotic** *adj* -a kutegemeana (japo si wa jamii moja).

symbol *n* alama, dalili, ishara. **~ic; ~ical** *adj* 1 -a ishara. 2 -enye maana. **~ics** *n* 1 taala za mifano (ishara) ya kale na sherehe. 2 theolojia ya kihistoria ya Kikristo. **~ize** *vt* 1 onyesha kwa ishara, ashiria, -wa ishara ya. 2 wakilisha dhana kwa ishara. **~ization** *n*. **~ism** *n* 1 kuashiria, uashiriaji. 2 mfumo wa alama fulani zitumiwazo kuwakilisha kundi fulani la mawazo.

symmetry *n* ulinganifu (mzuri); mlingano, usawa; *(maths)* pacha. **symmetrical** *adj* -linganifu, -a pacha, -a sawa. **symmetrically** *adv* kwa ulinganifu (mzuri).

sympathy *n* huruma; upole; utu wema. **in ~ with** katika/kwa kukubaliana na *letter of ~* barua ya kuliwaza. **sympathetic** *adj* -a huruma, -pole, -a moyo mzuri. ~ **strike** *n* mgomo wa kuwaunga mkono wafanyakazi wenzi ~ *pregnancy (in man)* umito. **sympathetically** *adv* kwa huruma, kwa upole. **sympathize** *vi* 1 -pa makiwa, pa pole, -sikitikia. 2 onea huruma, hurumia, liwaza. **sympathizer** *n* anayeonea huruma (m)wenziye, mwenye kuwaunga mkono wenzake.

symphony *n* simfoni: aina ya muziki upigwao kwa kutumia ala nyingi kwa pamoja. **symphonic** *adj* -a simfoni.

symposium *n* 1 kongamano: mkutano wa majadiliano juu ya suala fulani. 2 mkusanyiko wa makala za aina moja, majadiliano ya pamoja.

symptom *n* ishara, dalili. **~atic** *adj* -a ishara, -a dalili. **~atically** *adv*. **~atology** *n* simptomatolojia: tanzu ya talaa za ishara katika udaktari.

synagogue *n* sinagogi: hekalu la kiyahudi.

synchronize *vt* patanisha, oanisha; **synchronization** *n* kupatanisha, kurekebisha, kuoanisha. **synchromesh** *n* utaratibu wa kubadili gia katika gari.

syncopate *vt* 1 *(of music)* badili mdundo. 2 geuza mdundo wa kawaida. **syncopation** *n*.

syncope *n* 1 *(med. term)* kuzimia, kuzirai, kupoteza fahamu. 2 udondoshajikati ; kudondoshwa kwa sauti katikati ya neno.

syndic *n* mjumbe (agh. wa chama/ taasisi fulani). **~alism** *n* nadharia inayodai kwamba madaraka ya kisiasa yanapaswa kuwa mikononi mwa vyama vya wafanyakazi. **~alist** *n* mfuasi wa nadharia hiyo. **~ate** *n* 1 ushirika wa mashirika yenye lengo moja. 2 ushirika wa wachapishaji makala/katuni katika magazeti *vt* chapisha (makala, katuni) katika magazeti mengi kupitia shirika fulani.

syndrome *n (med.)* dalili za ugonjwa; *(fig)* mkusanyiko wa vitendo/mawazo ya mtu yanayoweza kutokea/ kujitokeza kwa pamoja.

synod *n* 1 sinodi: eneo la majimbo ya kanisa. 2 mkutano wa majimbo ya kanisa kujadili na kutoa maamuzi juu ya sera, serikali, mahubiri n.k. **~al** *adj* -a sinodi.

synonym *n* kisawe: moja kati ya maneno mawili au zaidi yanayokaribiana sana katika maana. **~ous** *adj* -enye maana (karibu) sawa, -a kuhusiana katika maana. **~y** *n* usawe, hali ya maneno kuwa na maana (karibu) sawa.

synopsis *n* ufupisho, muhtasari, kidokezo. **synoptic** *adj* -a vidokezo, -a muhtasari, -a ufupisho. **synoptist** *n* mwandishi wa vitabu vya Injili (Matayo, Marko na Luka).

syntax *n* sintaksi: tawi la isimu linaloshughulikia kupanga na kuhusisha vipashio na maneno kisarufi. **syntactical** *adj* -a sintaksi; -enye kuhusu sintaksi. **syntactically** *adv*.

synthesis *n* usanisi. **synthesize** *vt* sanisi; unganisha (maneno). **synthetical** *adj* 1 -a usanisi. **synthetic chemistry** kemia sanisi. 2 *(of language)* -a maneno ambatani. **synthetically** *adv*.

syphilis *n* kaswende, sekeneko. **syphilitic** *adj* -a kaswende, -a sekeneko.

syphon *see* **siphon**.

syringe *n* sirinji *vt* tia kwa sirinji.

syrup *n* shira. **~y** -a (kama) shira, tamu mno.

system *n* 1 mfumo. **railway ~** mfumo wa reli. 2 utaratibu. **~atic** *adj* -a hatua kwa hatua; -a utaratibu, -a mfumo. **~atically** *adv*. **~atize** *vt* weka katika mfumo, -patia mfumo, utaratibu maalum, panga. **~atization** *n*.

T

T,t herufi ya ishirini katika alfabeti ya Kiingereza; hutumika mbele ya jina la kitu chenye umbo la T (k.m. *T-shirt* vesti ya mikono mifupi, *T-joint* kiungio).

ta *int (colloq)* ahsante.

tab *n* 1 nembo (agh. kwenye nguo), kitanzi (kinachoshonewa kwenye nguo). 2 *(colloq)* mahesabu, usimamizi. **keep a ~ on sth/sb** simamia; weka kumbukumbu; chunguza.

tabard *n (hist)* jambakoti, kizibao.

tabby *adj* ~ **(cat)** -a milia ya kahawia au kijivu.

tabernacle *n 1 (rel)* tabenakulo: hema takatifu linalotumiwa na Wayahudi katika ibada zao. 2 kisanduku kinachotumiwa kuwekea hostia.

table *n* 1 meza *she is at ~* anakula. **~-cloth** kitambaa cha meza. **~-knife** kisu cha mezani. **~-linen** *n* vitambaa vya mezani. **~-spoon** kijiko kikubwa cha kulia chakula. **~-talk** *n* mazungumzo ya wakati wa mlo. **~-tennis** *n* mpira wa meza. **~-ware** vyombo vya kulia chakula. 2 *(sing. only)* watu waliokaa mezani. 3 *(sing. only)* mlo ulioandaliwa mezani *he keeps a good ~* anaandaa mlo mzuri. 4 ~ **(-land)** uwanda wa juu. 5 orodha, jedwali, ratiba *a bus time ~* ratiba ya safari za basi. 6 *(phrases)* **lay sth on the ~** weka mezani; *(in parliament)* ahirisha jambo (kwa kipindi kisichojulikana). **turn the ~on sb** pindua mambo; unukia; shinda. 7 *(in the Bible)* jiwe; maandishi kwenye jiwe hilo. **the ~ of the law** amri kumi za Musa alizopewa na Mungu *vt* 1 pendekeza. 2 orodhesha, andika/ panga katika jedwali.

tableau *n (often ~* **vivant***)* uwakilishaji (bila maneno au vitendo) wa picha/mandhari fulani.

table-d'hote *adj adv. (Fr) (of a restaurant meal)* -a bei moja.

tablet *n* 1 kibao cha kuandikia. 2 ubamba wa madini wenye maandiko. 3 padi, bunda la karatasi (zilizofungwa pembe moja). 4 kibonge cha sabuni; kidonge kidogo cha dawa (k.m. aspirini).

tabloid *n* gazeti dogo (lenye picha na vichekesho).

taboo *n* mwiko; haramu *vt* haramisha *adj* haramu; -a mwiko *~ words* maneno haramu/-a mwiko.

tabor *n* tari: ngoma ndogo.

tabulate *vt* orodhesha, pangilia, panga katika jedwali. **tabulator** *n* mashine ya kuorodhesha/kupangilia. **tabulation** *n*. **tabular** *adj* -lioorodheshwa, -a jedwali.

tachograph *n (of motor vehicle)* kirekodi mwendo na muda wa safari.

tacit *adj* -a kimya; -lioeleweka pasipo kunena *~ agreement* makubaliano ya kimya kimya *he gives a ~ consent* anaridhia kimya kimya. **~ly** *adv* kwa kimya, bila kusema. **~urn** *adj* nyamavu, -a kimya, stirifu. **~urnity** *n* unyamavu, kimya.

tack *vt,vi* 1 *(of ship)* bisha, enda zigizaga. 2 *(in sewing)* shikiza, piga bandi. 3 *(nail)* bana kwa misumari midogo (yenye kichwa kipana) *n* 1 msumari mdogo mfupi. 2 *(of ship)* **~ing** mbisho. **be on the right ~** *(fig)* fuata mwelekeo mzuri. 3 *hard ~* biskuti ngumu (za melini). 4 mshikizo.

tackle *n* 1 *(of ship's sails)* kamba, ayari. 2 zana, vifaa, vyombo *fishing ~* vyombo vya kuvulia samaki. 3 *(rugby or American football)* kumkamata na kumwangusha mpinzani; kumvaa. 4 *(soccer)* kunyang'anya mpira *vt,vi* 1 shughulikia (jambo, kazi). **~ sb about/over sth** zungumza waziwazi bila kuficha jambo. 2 kamata kwa nguvu (mwizi au mchezaji wa ragbi). 3 shambulia *he ~s fearlessly* anashambulia vikali.

tacky *adj* 1 -a kunata, -siokauka. 2 *(US)* chafu.

tact *n* busara, hekima. **~ful** *adj* -a busara/hekima. **~fully** *adv* kwa busara. **~less** bila busara. **~lessly** *adv.* **~lessness** *n.*

tactic *n* 1 mbinu. 2 *(pl)* harakati za kivita; *(fig)* mpango/njia/mbinu za utekelezaji wa sera. **~al** *adj* 1 -a mpango au njia, -a namna maalum. 2 -a harakati. ~**ally** *adv*. ~**ian** *n* stadi wa mbinu.

tactile/tactual *adj* -a kugusika; -a uwezo wa kugusa; -a fahamu ya kugusa.

tadpole *n* kiluwiluwi.

taffeta *n* tafeta: kitambaa chembamba, kigumu (chenye kumeta cha hariri).

taffrail *n (of ship)* kizuia chuma/reli katika shetri.

taffy *n (US)* 1 tofi (peremende). 2 sifa za ghiliba; kilemba cha ukoka.

tag *n* 1 kishikizo: kipande kidogo kilichofungiwa kitu kingine. 2 msemo unaonukuliwa mara nyingi na watu. 3 kibandiko cha bei. 4 (*gram*) **question ~s** kirai shawishi. 5 mchezo (wa watoto) wa kukimbizana na kugusana *vt* 1 bandika (bei, anwani, n.k. 2 ~ **sth on (to)** ambatisha, fungia. 3 ~ **along/behind/after** fuata karibu sana. 4 unga, unganisha.

tail *n* 1 mkia; *(dry)* mgwisho, mwengo *put the ~ between the legs* fyata mkia. **turn** ~ kimbia *wag the ~* tikisa/chezesha mkia. ~**s up** *(of persons)* changamfu, -enye furaha. 2 kitu mfano wa mkia. **the ~-board/gate** *n* mlango wa nyuma wa lori, pikapu n.k. **the ~ end (of)** mwisho. ~ **feather** *n* mleli, mlele. ~ **light** *n* taa za nyuma za gari/treni. ~ **piece** *n (in a book)* pambo linalochorwa/pangwa mwisho wa sura; nyongeza ya kitu mwisho. ~ **spin** *(of aircraft)* kupiga mbizi ~ *of the eye* pembe ya jicho. 3 upande wa sarafu usio na kichwa cha mtu. 4 **tails** *(colloq)* koti lenye mkia. 5 *(colloq)* mchunguzi anayemfuata mtuhumiwa *vt,vi* 1 ~ **after sb** fuata mtu karibu sana. 2 ~ **a person** fuatia mtuhumiwa. ~ **off/away** pungua idadi/ukubwa; *(of remarks etc)* malizia kwa wasiwasi; baki nyuma. ~**ed** *adj (in compounds)* **long/short ~ed** -enye mkia/mfupi. ~**less** *adj* -sio na mkia.

tailor *n* mshoni wa nguo, mshonaji, fundi cherahani *vt* 1 kata na kushona. 2 rekebisha kulingana na malengo/hadhira. ~-**made** *adj* -lioshonwa na fundi cherehani; -a kupimisha; *(fig)* inayostahiki/faa.

taint *n (blemish)* waa, doa *(smell)* uvundo *vt, vi* tia doa; ozesha; oza. ~**less** *adj* -sio waa, safi.

take *vt,vi* 1 twaa, shika. ~ **hold of sth** shika, kamata. 2 teka; shinda; vamia ~ *a fortress* teka boma *the rat was ~n in a trap* panya alinaswa katika mtego. ~ **cold** shikwa na mafua. **be ~n ill** ugua, shikwa na ugonjwa. ~ **sb's fancy** furahisha, burudisha. ~ **sb at a disadvantage** lalia, onea, endea/shambulia mtu akiwa katika hali mbaya/ya kutojiandaa. ~ **sb unawares/by surprise** vamia, shtusha, shtukiza. 3 *(gain, obtain)* pata, jipatia; -la, nywa. ~ **a bath** oga. ~ **a holiday** pumzika; enda likizo ~*a meal* -la ~ *a deep breath* pumua sana ~ *pride/an interest in one's work* fanya kazi kwa nia (moyo) ~ *a taxi* kodi teksi ~ *a small house* panga nyumba ndogo. 4 kubali, pata pokea *I will ~ 100000 shs for it* nakubali kuiuza kwa shilingi laki moja *which newspaper do you ~ each day?* unapata gazeti gani kila siku? ~ *no nonsense* -toruhusu upuuzi wowote. ~ **one's chance** jaribu bahati yako. ~ **a chance (on sth)** kubali uwezekano wa kukosa. ~ **it from me**; ~ **my word for it** niamini. **be able to ~ it; can ~ it** vumilia, himili. 5 ~ **(down)** weka kumbukumbu/andika, piga (picha) ~ *(down) notes of the lesson* andika kumbukumbu za mafundisho ~ *a photograph* piga picha. 6 *(of time, need)* chukua; hitaji; tumia. ~ **one's time (over sth)** jipa muda, fanya bila haraka; *(ironic)* tumia muda zaidi ya ule utakiwao/kawaida. **it ~s two to make a quarrel** *(prov)* hakuna shari ya mtu mmoja. ~ **a lot of doing** hitaji jitihada/ufundi mwingi. 7 *(convey, conduct)* chukua; peleka ~ *children to the movie* peleka watoto sinema; ~ **home pay/wages** *(colloq)* mshahara (baada ya makato). 8 pima ~ *temperature/measurements* pima joto/saizi. 9 *(use)* tumia; chukua bila idhini, iba. 10 *(remove)* toa, ondoa. 11 fanikiwa *the novel did not ~* riwaya haikufanikiwa. 12 *(accept)* kubali. 13 ~ **sb/sth for** ...; ~ **sb/sth to be** ... dhani, fikiria *he was ~n for an Englishman* alidhaniwa kuwa Mwingereza. ~ **it (from sb) that** jichukulia kuwa/kwamba. 14 ~ **sth as** + *pp* chukulia (kuwa). ~ **sth as read** chukulia kuwa hakuna sababu ya kusoma. ~ **(it) as read that**.... chukulia kwamba. 15 *(with nouns)* ~ **(a) delight/an interest/(a) pleasure/ -a pride in sth** furahikia/ jivunia. ~ **an examination** fanya mtihani. ~ **fright (at sth)** ogopa, tishika. ~ **a gamble (on sth)** bahatisha. ~ **sb in hand** wajibika kwake, shughulikia. ~ **heed** zingatia, angalia. ~ **a liking to** penda. ~ **the opportunity of doing/to do sth** chukua nafasi/fursa ya kufanya kitu. ~ **(holy) orders** -wa kasisi, pata upadri. 16 ~ **after sb** fanana na, shabihi, landa. ~ **sth apart** bomoa, fungua, funua, pungua. ~ **(away) from** punguza, dhoofisha, fifiza. ~ **sth/sb away (from sb/sth)** ondoa/ondosha. ~**away** *n* (kitu cha) kuondoka nacho/kulia mbele ya safari. ~ **sth back** futa (kauli); kubali kupokea/kurudishiwa (kilichokwisha uzwa/tolewa). ~ **sb back (to)** kumbusha/rejesha (mtu) katika mambo/kipindi cha zamani. ~ **sth down** shusha, teremsha; bomoa; andika. ~ **sb down a peg (or two)** dhalilisha, shushia hadhi; tiisha. ~ **sth in** pokea (kazi) ya kulipwa (ya kufanyia nyumbani; elewa, fahamu; ingiza, weka, -wa na..... ndani; punguza (nguo); miliki/twaa (ardhi, n.k.); chungulia, ng'amua, ona mara; sikiliza/angalia kwa msisimko; lipia na kupokea kila wakati (k.m. jarida). ~ **sb in** -pa chumba/nyumba, pokea, laza, pangisha; ghilibu, danganya. ~ **off** anza kuruka; ruka. ~**off** *n* mahala pa kuanzia kuruka; *(of aircraft)* kuruka/kupaa. ~ **sth off** ondoa, vua; *(kettle)* ipua. ~ **sth off (sth)** hamisha, ondosha; punguza. ~ **sb off** peleka, ongoza (njia). ~ **sb off sth** okoa, ondoa; dhihaki (kwa kuiga) iga. ~ **off** *n* kichekesho; dhihaka. **not/never ~ one's eyes off sth/sb** kodolea macho, angalia kwa makini. ~ **on** *(colloq)* sisimkwa, hemkwa; *(colloq)* vuma, fahamika, -wa mashuhuri. ~ **sth on** jitwisha; geuka kuwa, chukua. ~ **sb on** shindikana, -wa mshindani; ajiri; *(of a bus, etc.)* pakia, ingiza; pitisha kituo. ~ **out sth** ng'oa, kamua; pata, kata; toa, ondoa. ~ **out insurance** kata bima. *(escort)* ~ **sb out** sindikiza, toa, fuatana na, peleka; chukua dau kubwa zaidi. ~ **out a tooth** ng'oa jino. ~ **it out in sth** kubali kuchukua (kitu) kama fidia. ~ **it out of** chosha; dhoofisha. ~ **it out on sb** tolea mtu hasira zako zote. ~ **sb over (to)** vusha. ~ **sth over (from sb)** chukua/twaa madaraka ya kitu; rithi cheo/uongozi/miliki (ya shughuli); *(of Government)* taifisha. ~**over** *n* badilisha uongozi/miliki ya shughuli/kampuni. ~ **over (from sb)** twaa/kubali wajibu/kazi/madaraka. ~ **to sth** fanya mazoea, zoea (tabia/ mwenendo, n.k.); tumia kama njia ya kuepuka/kutoroka; toroka, kimbia. ~ **to sth/sb** penda, pata tabia ya kupendelea kitu. ~ **sth up (in the hand)** inua; *(of train, etc.)* simama kuchukua abiria; *(a liquid)* fyonza, sharabu; yeyusha; *(occupy)* -wa kazi ya, taka, jishughulisha; fuatilia; anza upya; *(time, space)* chukua, maliza, bana; shika imara. ~-**up spool** kiroda cha kupokea filamu, ukanda. n.k. ~ **sth up (with sb)** zungumza, andikia kuhusu.... ~ **sb up** fanya urafiki na; saidia. ~ **sb up on sth** kubali mwaliko/changamoto, mwito. **be ~n up with sb/sth** penda, tekwa. ~ **sb up sharp/short** ingilia, katiza na kusahihisha. ~ **up one's residence at** *(formal)* hamia. ~ **sth upon/on oneself** jitolea, kubali jukumu, chukua dhima. ~**n** *adj* -liopatwa. **be**

~ **by sb's behaviour** tekwa na vutiwa/zuzuliwa na tabia ya mtu fulani. **~r** *n* mwenye kupinga, mpigadau.

taking *adj* -a kuvutia *n (pl.)* mapato/ mauzo.

talcum *n* ulanga. ~ **powder** poda ya ulanga.

tale *n* 1 hadithi, kisa, ngano, hekaya. 2 taarifa, maelezo. **tell ~s of** sengenya, toa siri ya mtu, vua mtu mbeleko; *(relate)* hadithia, simulia, elezea. **~bearer/teller** *n* mchongezi, mmbeya, dukizi, sakubimbi; msimulizi.

talent *n* 1 *(faculty, etc)* kipaji, kipawa. 2 watu wenye vipaji *the local ~* wasanii wa ridhaa wa mahali wenye vipaji. **~ed** *adj* -elekevu, -enye kipaji. **~less** *adj* bila kipaji.

talisman *n* talasimu, hirizi, zindiko.

talk *vi,vt* ~ **(to/with sb) (about/of sth)** sema, ongea, zungumza. ~ **about** semea, nena, zungumzia. **be ~ed about** sengenywa, semwa. ~ **against** sema, pinga. ~ **at sb** hubiri. ~ **away** piga porojo/gumzo. ~ **back (to sb)** jibu, jibiza. ~ **big** jiona, ringa, piga makuu, taaradhi. ~ **sb down** nyamazisha, zima, hinikiza. ~ **down an aircraft** elekeza rubani wakati wa kutua. ~ **down to sb** sema kwa namna ya dharau. **~ing of** mintarafu, kuhusu; ama kuhusu (jambo/kitu n.k. hicho). ~ **in one's sleep** weweseka. ~ **nonsense** payuka, bwata, bwabwaja. ~ **round sth** zungumzia jambo kwa kuzunguka au bila kufikia mwisho. ~ **sth over** zungumzia, jadili. ~ **to sb** *(colloq)* kemea karipia. **~ing to** *n* 1 karipio. 2 weza kusema, sema. 3 mudu lugha, sema, tumia. 4 jadili. **~ ing point** cha kuzungumzia, mada inayoelekea kuzua ubishi; wazo linaloelekea kushawishi mtu. 5 amba, nena, toboa. 6 shawishi. ~ **sb into/out of doing sth** shawishi/asa kufanya/ kutofanya jambo. ~ **sb round/over** shawishi (mtu) akubali. ~ **through the nose** semea puani, sema king'ong'o. ~ **to** sema na, ongea na. 7 piga porojo; toa taarifa; iga. **~ative** *adj* msemaji, domo kaya *n* msemi/ mzungumzaji; mpiga domo *n* 1 mjadala; mazungumzo. 2 hotuba, mhadhara (usio rasmi). 3 *(phrase)* **small ~** porojo, domo. ~ **of the town** jambo linalovuma *be all ~* mazungumzo mengi yasiyo na matokeo.

talkie *n (dated colloq)* filamu yenye sauti.

tall *adj* 1 *(of persons, objects, etc)* -refu. ~ **boy** *(GB)* kabati la nguo. 2 -a urefu maalum *he is six foot ~* ana urefu wa futi sita. 3 muhali, -a kuzidi. **a ~ order** kazi ngumu sana kufanya; maombi yaliyo muhali kutekelezwa. **a ~ story** hadithi yenye shaka; hadithi ngumu kuaminika/isiyoaminika *adv* **talk ~** jivuna. **walk ~** jivunia. *adj* **~ish**. **~ness** *n* urefu, kimo; tambo.

tallow *n* shahamu (agh. ya kutengenezea mishumaa). **~-chandler** *n* mwuza/mtengeneza mishumaa.

tally *vi* ~ **(with)** *(of stories, amount, etc)* patana, lingana *n* 1 hesabu, kuweka hesabu. 2 tiketi, kitambulisho, cheti chenye maelezo. ~ **clerk** *n* karani wa forodha (wa kukagua mizigo). **~man** *n* guoguo, mwuza mali anayelipwa kwa wiki.

tally-ho *(int)* ukelele wa kuitana wawindaji, yulee!

Talmud *n* buku la sheria na maadili ya Kiyahudi.

talon *n* kucha (la ndege), ukucha.

tamarind *n (tree)* mkwaju; *(fruit)* ukwaju.

tambourine *n* kigoma, tari.

tame *adj (of animals)* 1 -a kufuga, -liofugwa; sio kali 2 *(of person)* nyonge, nyenyekevu/tiifu mno; *(mild, dull, feeble)* -liopooza, -siochangamka, dhaifu, baridi *vt* 1 fuga; tiisha, tawala; *(reclaim)* ongoza, ondolea ushenzi. **~r** *n (usu in compounds)* mfugaji. **tamable** *adj* -a kuweza kufugwa, -a kuweza kugeuzwa hali. **~ly** *adv* bila ukaidi.

~**ness** *n* unyonge, utulivu, upole.

Tammany *n* ~ **(Hall)** Makao Makuu ya Chama cha Kidemokrasi, (New York).

tamp *vt* ~ **sth down** shindilia, pigapiga, gongagonga.

tamper *vi* ~ **(with)** geuza; vuruga, chezea (kwa hila, fedha, uwongo, n.k.) ~ **with a lock** haribu/chezea kufuli.

tampion *n* kizibo cha mti, metali, plastiki n.k.

tampon *n* kisodo kinachotiwa ndani ya tupu ya mwanamke kufyonza majimaji, damu, n.k.

tan *n* 1 hudhurungi *vt,vi* ~ *leather shoes* viatu vya ngozi ya hudhurungi; *(of an animal's skin)* tengeneza/tia rangi ya hudhurungi (kwa asidi). ~ **sb's hide** *(sl)* chapa (mtu) sawasawa. 2 geuka hudhurungi kwa jua. ~**ner** mtengeneza ngozi. ~**nery** tasnia ya ngozi.

tandem *n* tandemu: baiskeli ya watu wawili; baiskeli mbili katika moja *adv* **(in)** ~ *(of horses in harness or two persons on a ~bicycle)* mmoja nyuma ya mwingine.

tang *n* ladha kali; harufu kali *there is a ~ of fish out here* hapa kuna harufu kali/shombo. ~**y** *adj*.

tangent *n* ~ **line** mstari unaogusa duara bila kulikata, mstari mguso, kwenda upande. **go (fly) off at a** ~ *(fig)* ghairi kwa ghafula; geuza mawazo ghafla.

tangerine *n* chenza; kangaja.

tangible *adj* 1 -a kugusika. 2 wazi, dhahiri, halisi, hakika ~ *proof* thibitisho dhahiri. **tangibly** *adv*. **tangibility** *n* uwezo wa kuonekana.

tangle[1] *n* 1 mfungamano, msokotano (wa nyuzi, nywele, n.k.). 2 msongamano, mvurugano, mvurugiko, vurugu *get into a* ~ ingia utata *vt, vi* 1 vuruga; vurugika; sokotana; songamana ~ *hair* nywele timtimu. 2 ~ **with sb** *(colloq)* gombana na, zozana na; pigana na.

tangle[2] *n* aina ya mwani.

tango *n* tango: densi ya Amerika ya Kusini.

tank *n* 1 birika, hodhi, tangi (kubwa la kuhifadhi vimiminiko, gesi n.k.) *the petrol* ~ tangi la petroli. ~-**car** behewa/gari la kubebea petroli, n.k. 2 *(in India and Pakistan)* bwawa; *(armoured car)* kifaru. ~ **trap** kizuizi/ mtego wa vifaru *vi* ~ **sth up** jaza petroli kwenye gari. **be/get ~ed up** *(sl)* elewa. ~**er** *n* meli/ndege ya shehena ya mafuta; lori/gari ya kubebea mafuta/maziwa/kibuku, n.k. ~**ard** *n* bilauri, kombe kubwa la kunywea (agh. bia).

tannin *n* tanini: asidi ya magamba ya miti (fulani).

tannoy *n* (aina ya) kipaza sauti.

tantalize *vt* tia shauku, tamanisha bure.

tantamount *adj* ~ **to** sawa na *it is ~ to saying 'no'* ni sawa na kusema hapana.

tantrum *n* hamaki, ghadhabu.

TANU *n (abbr) Tanganyika African National Union.*

Tanzania *n* Jamhuri ya Muungano wa Tanganyika na Zanzibar.

tanzanite *n* tanzanaiti: madini ya kibuluu yapatikanayo Tanzania tu.

tap[1] *n* 1 kugonga; kipigo chepesi. ~ **dance** densi ya kugongagonga miguu chini. 2 *(pl.)* ~**s** *(US armed forces)* ishara ya kuzima taa usiku *vt, vi* gonga, bisha, babata, ng'ota.

tap[2] *n* 1 bilula, bomba. **on** ~ *(of beer etc)* kwenye pipa lenye bilula; *(fig)* tayari kwa mhitaji. ~ **room** *n (in an inn)* chumba cha kuhifadhi mapipa ya bia. ~**ster** *n* mwuza pombe, bia. ~ **root** *n* mzizi mkuu ~ *water* maji ya bomba/mfereji. 2 kizibo *vt* ~ **(off) sth (from sth)** 1 fungulia, fyonza; kinga; gema ~ *coconut trees* gema ~ *information from a child* pata habari kutoka kwa mtoto. 2 ingilia kati *the phone is being ~ped* simu inanaswa/ inaingiliwa/inasikilizwa na mtu baki. 3 wekea bilula/bomba/mfereji.

tape *n* 1 utepe, ugwe; kamba. ~ **measure** chenezo: kamba/utepe wa kupimia. ~ **worm** *n* tegu. 2 ~ **(ticker)** karatasi nyembamba za mashine ya telegrafu. **insulating** ~ tepu/gundi (ya kuunganisha nyaya za umeme). **magnetic** ~ tepu ya kurekodi sauti. ~ **deck/~recorder** kinasasauti/ tepurekoda. 3 utepe (wa kumalizia mashindano ya mbio) *vt* 1 funga kwa ugwe/utepe. 2 rekodi (sauti) kwenye kinasasauti. 3 *(colloq)* **have sth/sb ~d** elewa kitu/mtu barabara.

taper[1] *n* mshumaa mwembamba sana; ugwe/utambi wa mshumaa.

taper[2] *vt vi* chonga; chongoka nchani. **~ing** *adj* -a kuchongoka, -a kupunguka unene taratibu (mpaka kufanya ncha).

tapestry *n* kitambaa kilichofumwa/ pambo la sufi, la ukutani; zulia la ukutani. **tapestried** *adj*.

tapioca *n* udaga, makopa ya mhogo.

tar *n* lami, bereu *vt* paka/weka lami. ~ **and feather sb** adhibu mtu kwa kumpaka lami na kumpamba manyoya. **~red with the same brush** -enye makosa yaleyale. **~mac** *n* mchanganyiko wa lami na kokoto (kwa kusakafu barabara). **~ry** *adj* -a lami, -enye lami, kama lami.

taradiddle *n (US) (colloq)* uwongo.

tarantula *n* buibui mkubwa mwenye sumu.

tarboosh *n* tarbushi.

tardy *adj* -a kuchelewa, siri, -a kulimatia, ajizi. **tardily** *adv*. **tardiness** *n*

tare[1] *n* kigugu mwitu.

tare[2] *n* turuhani.

target *n* 1 dango, shabaha. 2 lengo, kusudio ~ *area* eneo la kupiga bomu

tariff *n* 1 *(customs duties)* ushuru wa forodha. 2 orodha ya bei (za vyakula, vyumba, n.k).

tarn *n* ziwa dogo la milimani. **tarnish** *vt,vi* **tarn** 1 fifisha mng'ao/nuru. 2 *(disgrace)* aibisha, haribu sifa *n* 1 kufifia, kupoteza mng'ao. 2 *(disgrace)* aibu. 3 doa, waa.

taro *n* myugwa; *(root)* jimbi.

tarpaulin turuba(l)i.

tarry *vi* 1 *(arch. liter)* kawia, chelewa, limatia. 2 *(wait)* ngoja, baki; ngojea, kaa kungojea.

tart[1] *adj* chungu, kali; -a asidi. **~ly** *adv*. **~ness** *n*.

tart[2] *n (derog sl)* malaya *vt* ~ **sth/sb up** *(colloq)* remba, pambapamba.

tart[3] pai (ya) matunda.

tartar[1] *n* mkorofi, mkaidi. **catch a** ~ pambana na mkorofi.

tartar[2] *n (of teeth)* ukoga, ugwagwa.

task *n* kazi (ya kufanya). **take sb to** ~ **(about/for sth)** kemea, karipia, laumu, shutumu. ~ **force** kikosi maalum cha kijeshi; *(fig)* kikosi cha kazi. **(hard) ~-master/mistress** *n* msimamizi (mkali) *vt* taabisha, chosha, kalifu.

tassel *n* manyamunyamu; shada. **~led** *adj* -enye shada.

taste[1] *vt, vi* 1 dhuku, chapukia, -wa na ladha ya. 2 ~ *(of)* hisi, pata ladha. 3 onja, twaa kidogo *he had not ~d food for several days* hajaonja chakula kwa muda mrefu. 4 *(fig)* pitia, ona. ~ **of** pitia; jua ~ *the joys of freedom* furahia uhuru. **~r** mwonjaji.

taste[2] *n* 1 **the** ~ utamu, ladha. ~ **bud** kundi la seli onji. 2 kionjo, ladha. **leave a bad/nasty ~ in the mouth** *(fig)* chefua, -wa na kichefu *give a nice ~ to (food)* koleza, unga. 3 **a** ~ **(of)** (kionjo) kidogo. 4 ~ **(for)** tamaa; upendo *have a ~ for* penda, pendelea. 5 kipaji cha kufurahia uzuri, akili za kupambanua mazuri, ustaarabu; kipawa. **(be) in good/ bad/poor/excellent** ~ vutia, pendeza/ topendeza, -tovutia *a man of ~* mtu wa akili, mchaguzi, mteuzi, mstaarabu; **~ful** *adj* -a akili; staarabu nzuri; fasihi. **~less** *adj* 1 bila ladha; -sio staarabu. 2 *(dull, flat)* chapwa, baridi. ~ **tasty** *adj* tamu, -a kukolea.

tat *vt,vi* fanya mafundo. **~ting** *n* utengenezaji mafundo mazuri.

ta-ta *(baby language)* kwa heri.

tatter *n* matambaa/marapurapu. **~-demalion** *n* mtu aliyevaa matambara machachafumachafu. **~ed** *adj (clothes)* bovu bovu; -liotatukatatuka.

tattle *n* mapayo, porojo, upuuzi, umbeya *vi, vt* payapaya, tatarika, bwabwaja; piga domo/umbeya. **~r** *n.*

tattoo *n* chanjo, chale, mchoro *vt* piga chale, chora *n* 1 milio ya ngoma (kuita askari), mbiu. 2 *(US)* mdundo (n.k.) wa kuita askari; mipigo, midundo. 3 tamasha/tafrija (ya maaskari).

taught *pt, pp of* **teach**.

taunt *vt* ~ **sb (with sth)** suta, tusha; dhihaki, tiriri *n* suto, tayo; dhihaka. **~ingly** *adv.*

Taurus *n (astrol)* ng'ombe.

taut *adj (of ropes, wires, etc.)* -a kukaza, -liokazwa, -a kudinda; *(fig) (of nerves)* -epesi kushtuka, -liokacha, kavu *a ~ smile* kicheko kikavu. **~ness** *n.* **~ly** *adv.*

tautology *n* marudiorudio, kutumia maneno yayo kwa yayo, kusema yale yale tu. **tautological** *adj.*

tavern *n* kilabu ya pombe.

tawdry *adj* -shaufu, -a pambo duni; shooshoo. **tawdrily** *adv.* **tawdriness** *n.*

tax *n* 1 kodi, ushuru. **poll ~** kodi ya kichwa. **entertainment ~** kodi ya starehe. **sales ~** kodi ya mauzo. **~ payer** mlipa kodi. **~ collector** mtoza/ mkusanyaji kodi/ushuru. **~ free** *adj* -siolipiwa kodi; *(of dividends or interest)* -liokwisha katwa kodi. 2 **a ~ on** mzigo *a ~ on my strength* mzigo kwangu *vt* 1 toza kodi, lipisha ushuru. 2 *(put strain on)* elemea, kalifu; sumbua. ~ **sb with sth** shtaki, laumu. 3 *(leg)* chunguza na kutoa uamuzi (kuhusu gharama za daawa). **~able** *adj* -a kutoza/kutozwa kodi/ushuru. **heavy ~ation** *n* kutoza kodi/ushuru mwingi *indirect ~ation* kodi isiyo dhahiri.

taxi *n* teksi *~-driver* dereva wa teksi. **~ meter** mita ya nauli (katika teksi). **~ rank** kituo cha teksi *vt, vi (of aeroplane)* ambaa chini.

taxidermy *n* sanaa ya kurudisha sura ya mnyama kwa kujaza vitu ndani ya ngozi yake.

taxonomy *n* (nadharia ya) uainishaji.

tea *n* 1 chai. **not my cup of ~** *(fig)* sio jambo ninalolipendelea. **~ bag** kifuko cha majani ya chai. **~ break** *n* mapumziko ya chai. **~-caddy** *n* kopo la majani ya chai. **~ chest** *n* sanduku (la mbao) la kusafirishia (majani ya) chai. **~ cloth** *n* kitambaa cha meza/ trei ya chai; kitambaa cha kukaushia vyombo. **~cup** kikombe cha chai. **a storm in a ~ cup** kelele za bure. **~ garden** mkahawa wa (chai) wa bustanini; shamba la majani ya chai. **~ house** mkahawa wa chai. **~-kettle** *n* birika la chai, buli. **~-leaves** *n* majani ya chai. **~-party** sherehe/ tafrija ya chai. **~room** *n* mkahawa. **~ service/-set** vyombo vya chai. **~ spoon** *n* kijiko cha chai. **~ spoonful** *n* (ujazo wa) kijiko kimoja cha chai. **~-strainer** *n* chujio la chai. **~-table** *n* meza ya chai. **~ things** *(colloq)* vyombo, seti ya vifaa vya chai. **~-time** *n* wakati wa chai, saa ya chai. **~towel** taulo/kitambaa cha kufuatia/ kukaushia vyombo. **~-tray** *n* treya ya kuandikia chai. **~ urn** *n* chombo cha kuchemsha maji ya chai. **~trolley/ wagon** *n* toroli la kuandikia chai. 2 kipindi cha chai ya chajio. **high ~** chajio.

teach *vt vi* 1 *(knowledge)* funda, funza, fundisha. 2 *(manners)* tia adabu, adibisha. 3 *(generally)* ongoza, lea, onya, zoeza. ~ **sb not to do sth** onya mtu asifanye jambo fulani. **~ in** *(colloq)* malumbano juu ya mada fulani. **~able** *adj* -elekevu, -sikivu, -a kufundishika. **~er** *n* mwalimu, mfundishaji. **~er's college** *n* chuo cha ualimu. **~ing** *n* 1 kufundisha, ufundishaji. 2 mafundisho.

teak *n* msaji; *(East Africa)* mvule.

team *n* 1 farasi/ng'ombe wanaokokota gari n.k. 2 timu. **~ work** *n* kazi ya kikoa/pamoja. **~ spirit** moyo wa ushirikiano *vi* **~ up (with sb)** *(colloq)* shirikiana na, ungana na.

~ster *n* saisi *(US)* dereva wa lori.
tear[1] *vt vi* 1 chana, pasua, rarua, tatua ~ *a piece off* kwangua, nyakua; *(of meat with the teeth)* ng'wafua. ~ **off (skin)** ambua; *(clothes)* vua upesi; *(boughs)* kwanyua, konyoa, kongonyoa. 2 *(divide)* tenga, vuruga gawanya. ~ **oneself away (from)** acha, ondoka; jiondokea, achana na. **torn between** pata shida ya kuchagua kati ya mambo the country was torn *by civil war* nchi ilivurugwa kwa vita vya wenyewe kwa wenyewe. 4 *(move/ go quickly)* puruka, kurupuka. ~ **away** *adj,n (colloq)* mtu mwenye harara. 5 acha, zima, futa ~ *in stripes* chana ~ *in pieces*, chanachana, chambua; *(of person* chamba, onyesha udhaifu *n* 1 mpasuo; mpasuko, mtatuko. 2 *(split)* ufa.
tear[2] *n* chozi *shed ~s, burst (break) into ~s* bubujika/toa/toka machozi. **in ~s** kilia. **~- drop** *n* chozi. **~-gas** *n* gesi/ moshi wa machozi. **~ful** *adj* -enye machozi, -a kulia. **~ fully** *adv*. **~less** *adj* pasipo machozi, kavu ~ *eyes* macho makavu.
tease *vt* 1 chokoza, sumbua, tashtiti, sunza, tania. 2 chamvua, chambua *n* mtani. **~r** *n* 1 fumbo; tatizo. 2 mchokozi, mwudhi. 3 mcheshi. **teasingly** *adv* kwa utani/uchokozi.
teat *n* chuchu; titi.
tec *n (sl abbr for)* **detective**.
tech *n (colloq abbr for)* **technical college**.
technical *adj* -a ufundi; -a kifundi, stadi ~ **college** *n* chuo cha ufundi. ~ **terms** istilahi: maneno ya kiufundi *the ~ skill of a pianist* ustadi wa mpiga kinanda. **~ly** *adv*. **technics** *n* njia za ufundi, mbinu, tekniki. **~ity** *n* neno/ kifungu/jambo la kifundi. **technician** *n* fundisanifu.
technicolor *n (photography)* ufundi rangi; njia ya kutengeneza filamu za rangi katika senema.
technique *n* mbinu: jinsi ya kufanya kazi.
technocracy *n* teknokrasia: mfumo wa serikali ya mabingwa. **technocrat** *n* mfuasi wa teknokrasia.
technology *n* teknolojia: elimu ya ufundi. **technologic(al)** *adj* -a teknolojia; -a maarifa ya ufundi. **technologist** *n* bingwa wa teknolojia, mwanateknolojia.
techy *see* **tetchy**.
teddy bear *n* mwanasesere wa dubu.
tedious *adj* -a kuchosha, chushi, -a taabu, -a kutaabisha. **~ness; tedium** *n* uchushi **~ly** *adv*.
tee *n* 1 *(golf)* kichungu kidogo, kichungu; kitii (cha mpira wa gofu). 2 herufi T; kitu chenye umbo la T. **T ~-shirt** fulana ya mikono. **to a tee/T** barabara, sawasawa, kamili *vt,vi* ~ **(the ball) up** wekea mpira (wa gofu) kitii. ~ **off** anza.
teem *vt* 1 wapo kwa wingi; jaa tele *the fish ~ in the river* samaki wamejaa tele mtoni. 2 ~ **with** jawa, jazana. ~ **(down) (with)** miminika, mwagika, nyesha sana.
teens *n* 1 ujana (kati ya miaka 13 na 19) *teen years* miaka ya ujana. 2 umri kati ya miaka kumi na tatu na ishirini. **teenage** *adj* -a ujana. **teenager** *n* kijana.
teeny *adj see* **tiny**.
teeter *vi* yumba, yumbayumba, pepesuka.
teeth *n pl of* **tooth** ~ *vi* ota meno. ~ **ing troubles** maumivu ya kuota meno, *(fig)* matatizo ya kuanza/ya awali.
teetotal *(US) adj* -siyekunywa vileo vya namna yoyote. **~ler** *n* mtu asiyekunywa namna yoyote ya kileo, mpiga vita ulevi. **~ism** *n* kutokunywa namna yoyote ya kileo; kupiga vita ulevi/aina yoyote ya kileo.
teetotum *n* pia ya mraba yenye namba kila upande.
tegument *n (more usu.* **integument)** gamba (la mnyama).
tele *-(pref)* -a mbali sana.
telecast *n* kutangaza kwa televisheni.
telecommunication *n* mawasiliano (ya kutumia) simu, redio au televisheni.
telegram telegramu.

telegraph *n* telegrafu: njia ya kupeleka ujumbe kwa mawimbi ya umeme kwa waya au kwa upepo; simu ya upepo ~ **post/pole** mti wa simu. ~ **wire/line** waya wa simu. **bush** ~ kupeleka ujumbe kwa moshi/sauti/ngoma *vt,vi* peleka habari/ujumbe kwa telegrafu. ~**er** *n* mtaalamu wa kupeleka na kupokea telegrafu. ~**ically** *adv*. ~**ese** *n* mtindo (wa lugha) wa ishara ya telegrafu. ~**y** *n* telegrafia: sayansi ya upelekaji na upokeaji simu (za upepo).

telemeter/telemetry *n* telemeta: ujipitishaji na ujipimaji wa data kutoka mbali (agh. kwa redio).

teleology *n* teleolojia: nadharia/mafundisho/imani/fikra kwamba viumbe vyote viliumbwa na Mungu kwa kusudi maalum. **teleological** *adj*. **teleologist** *n*.

telepathy *n* telepathia: uwezo wa kupashana mawazo/fikra bila kutumia njia za hisia za kawaida (kusema, kusikia, kuona, kugusa, kunusa); *(colloq)* kuweza kubaini mara moja nia za wengine, uwezo wa kuwasoma wengine. **telepathic** *adj*. **telepathis** *n* mtaalamu/mwanatelepathia.

telephone *n* simu (ya mdomo). ~ **booth** kibanda cha simu. ~ **directory** anuani/orodha za simu, kitabu cha simu. ~ **exchange** maungio ya simu *vt, vi*. piga simu. **telephony** *n* telefonia: njia/taratibu za kupeleka na kupokea simu. **telephonic** *adj* -a simu. **telephonist** *n* opereta, mpiga/mhudumu wa simu.

telephoto *n* ~ **lens** lenzi ya kuona mbali. ~**graph** picha iliyopigwa na lenzi ya aina hii; picha iliyotumwa au kupokelewa na lenzi ya mbali. ~**graphy** *n* 1 telefotografia: kupiga picha mbali. 2 upelekaji na upokeaji wa picha za mbali.

teleprinter *n* teleprinta: printa ya taarifa za mbali.

telescope *n* darubini *vt,vi* ingiana (kama sehemu za mtutu wa darubini); fupisha. **telescopic** *adj* -a darubini, -a kutazama mbali; -a kuonekana kwa darubini; -enye sehemu za mtutu (kama darubini).

teletype-writer *n see* **teleprinter**.

television *n (abbr* **TV** *or colloq* **telly**) ~ **set** televisheni. **televise** *vt* tangaza/peleka kwa televisheni.

telfer *see* **telpher**.

telex *n* teleksi: mfumo wa mawasiliano kwa teleprinta.

tell 1 *vt,vi* ~ **sth (to sb)**, ~ **sb sth** ambia. **I told you so** nilikwambia. **you are ~ing me**! sawa/kweli kabisa, wacha Bwana; naafikiana nawe kabisa. ~ **me another** sikuamini, wacha Bwana. ~**'the world** *(colloq)* tangazia kila mtu. 2 *(relate)* sema, simulia. ~ **the truth** sema kweli. ~ **a story** simulia hadithi. ~ **the tale** *(colloq)* toa hadithi ya kusikitisha (ili kuhurumiwa). ~ **tales about/on sb** chongea, fitini. ~**tale** mfitini; kidomodomo, mmbeya. 3 *(count)* hesabu. **all told** kwa jumla. ~ **one's beads** vuta uradi/tasbihi. ~ **sb off (for sth/to do sth)** pangia kazi; *(colloq)* simanga, karipia. 4 *(discover)* fahamu, jua, ng'amua, ona. ~ **the time** jua majira. **you can never ~; you never can ~** huwezi kujua; ajuaye Mungu. **there is no ~ing** haijulikani, haiwezekani kutabiri. 5 *(order)* amuru, agiza *do as you are told* fanya kama ulivyoamriwa. 6 ~ **(on/upon sb)** athiri. ~**ing** *adj* -a nguvu. ~ **sb/sth (from sb/sth)** baini tofautisha. 7 ~ **(on sb)** *(colloq)* fichua, umbua, chongea.

teller *n* 1 *(counter)* mwenye kuhesabu. 2 mhesabu kura bungeni.

telly *n see* **television**.

telpher *n* usafirishaji wa mizigo (k.m. mawe) kwa kebu za juu.

Telstar *n* satelaiti ya mawasiliano ya simu na televisheni.

temerity *n* (ujasiri wa) harara; ujasiri wa kijuvi.

temper *n* 1 *(disposition)* tabia, moyo, hali, mwenendo *good* ~ upole, ukunjufu *bad* ~ hasira, harara, hamaki. **get/fly into a ~** kasirika, hamaki, panda mori. **keep one's ~** tulia, poa, jiweza; jizuia. **lose one's ~** kasirika, hamaki. **out of ~ (with)** -liokasirikia. **~ed** *adj*. **~edly** *adv vt,vi* 1 *(mitigate)* tuliza, punguza ukali/nguvu n.k. ~ *justice with mercy* wa na huruma wakati wa kutoa adhabu. 2 *(metal)* tia matiko, chovya; *(clay)* kanda; finyanga.

tempera *n see* **distemper**.

temperament *n* tabia, moyo, hali, mwenendo, silika (inayodhibiti ukali/upole/mhemko wa mtu). **~al** *adj* 1 -lioletwa na tabia, hali. 2 -epesi wa kubadili tabia/hali; -epesi kukasirika/kuhamaki. **~ally** *adv*.

temperance *n* 1 kiasi; kadiri; kujiweza, kujirudi. 2 kutokunywa kileo cha namna yoyote ~ *society* jumuiya isiyokunywa vileo/ulevi; jumuiya inayopigania kupigwa marufuku kwa vileo.

temperate *adj* 1 -a kiasi, -a kadiri. 2 *(of climate)* -a wastani. **~ zone** ukanda (wa dunia) wenye halijoto wastani. **~ly** *adv*. **~ness** *n*.

temperature *n* 1 halijoto, hali ya kuwa na joto au baridi. **high ~** halijoto kali. **low ~** halijoto chini/kidogo. 2 homa. **have/run a ~** -wa na homa.

tempest *n* tufani, dhoruba; *(fig)* ghadhabu. **~-swept/tossed** *adj (liter)* liokumbwa na tufani. **~ous** *adj* -a tufani, -a dhoruba; *(sea)* -enye kuchafuka sana; *(debate)* -a ugomvi mwingi, -a kubishana.

template, templet *n* kiolezo; kigezo.

temple[1] *n* hekalu.

temple[2] *n (forehead)* panda.

tempo *n* mwendo.

temporal *adj* 1 -a maisha, -a dunia hii. 2 a wakati. **~ity** *n (usu pl) (arch)* mali; rasilimali *~llities of the church* mali za kanisa. **~ ity** *n* ulei; walei.

temporary *adj* 1 -a muda, -a wakati, -a kitambo (si -a siku zote) ~ *loss of memory n* chechele ~ *employment* ajira ya muda. **temporarily** *adv* kwa muda. **temporariness** *n* muda mfupi, kitambo kidogo.

temporize *vi* chelewesha, kawiza (jambo); pitisha muda (kwa makusudi). **temporization** *n* kusitasita, kukawia.

tempt vt 1 **~ (to sth/into doing sth)** *(mislead)* shawishi/vuta (kwa mabaya). 2 *(excite desire)* tamanisha. 3 *(old use) (test)* jaribu. **~ providence** jaribu Mungu, bahatisha. **~ingly** *adv*. **~er** *n* mshawishi. **the ~** Shetani. **~ress** *n* mwanamke mshawishi. **~ation** *n* kishawishi, ushawishi, majaribu; matamanio.

ten *n* kumi. **~ to one** kumi kwa moja; bila shaka; yumkini *adj* (sehemu) -a kumi. **~ old** *adv* mara kumi zaidi. **~thly** *adv*. **~ pence** *n (GB)* sarafu ya thamani ya mapeni kumi. **~ner** *n (colloq) (GB)* pauni kumi; noti ya pauni kumi.

tenable *adj* 1 -a kushikika, -a kulindika; -a kuweza kutetewa *the fortress is not ~* boma halilindiki *his argument was hardly ~* hoja yake haikuwa na utetezi. 2 *(of an office or position)* -a kudumu kwa muda fulani. **tenability** *n*.

tenacious *adj* 1 -enye kushika sana, -a kunata, -a kushikamana. 2 *(obstinate)* ng'ang'anifu; shupavu, gumu, -a kushikilia kauli yake *be ~ of one's rights* ng'ang'ania haki za binafsi. **tenacity** *n* 1 nguvu ya kung'ang'ania/kushikama/kunata. 2 ushupavu, ugumu, uthabiti.

tenant *n* mpangaji ~ *farmer* mkulima wa mfumo wa nyarubanja; mpangaji ardhi ya kulima *vt (usu passive)* panga. **tenancy** *n* 1 upangaji. 2 kipindi cha upangaji. **life tenancy** upangaji wa maisha. **~ry** *n (collective sing)* wapangaji wenzi (wa shamba/nyumba).

tend[1] *vt (take care of)* tunza; chunga.

tend[2] *vi* elekea *prices are ~ing upward* bei zinaelekea kupanda. **~ency** *n* mwelekeo, uelekeo.

tendentious *adj (of speech, writing,*

etc) -enye dhamira/ujumbe maalum, -nayoelemea upande mmoja, -a propaganda. **~ly** *adv*. **~ness** *n*.

tender[1] *vt, vi* toa *he ~ed his resignation* alitoa hati/barua ya kuacha kazi, alijiuzulu. 2 **~ for** zabuni, toa zabuni *n* 1 zabuni. 2 **legal** ~ pesa halali ya kulipia deni.

tender[2] *adj (soft, delicate)* -ororo, laini, -epesi kudhurika/kuharibika/ kuumia ~ *subject (fig)* suala nyeti *of ~ age/years* changa, -siopevuka. -toto, ~ **foot** *n* mgeni katika mazingira magumu. ~-**hearted** *adj* -a huruma, -a upendo, -pole. 2 *(of meat)* laini. ~ **loin** *n* sarara. 3 -ema, -a upendo ~ *parents* wazazi wema. **~ly** *adv*. **~ness** *n*.

tender[3] *n* 1 mtunzaji; mwangalizi, mlinzi. 2 melisaidizi. 3 behewa la mafuta na maji (nyuma ya gari moja).

tendon *n* kano.

tendril *n* ukono, kikonyo (cha mmea).

tenement *n* 1 ~ **(house)** nyumba ya vyumba vingi vya kupangisha kwa kodi nafuu. 2 *(leg)* nyumba, makao; mali yoyote ya kudumu.

tenet *n* imani, mafundisho, itikadi, kanuni.

tennis *n* tenisi. ~-**court** *n* kiwanja cha tenisi.

tenon *n (of wood)* ulimi.

tenor[1] *n* mwendo, mwelekeo, utaratibu (wa maisha).

tenor[2] *n* 1 sauti ya tatu (nyembamba ya mwanamume). 2 *(of instruments)* ala zenye sauti kama hiyo.

tense[1] *n (gram) n* njeo: kategoria ya kisarufi ambayo huwakilisha muda au wakati ambapo tendo hufanyika.

tense[2] *adj* 1 *(lit or fig)* -a kukakamaa, -liovutwa sana, liokazwa, -a kudinda. 2 -enye fadhaa/wasiwasi. 3 *(gram)* kaze: -enye kutumia nguvu nyingi za musuli katika kutamkwa, -a kuonyesha fadhaa *their faces were ~ with anxiety* nyuso zao zilionyesha fadhaa *vt* kaza, shupaza, kakamaa. **be/get ~d up** jawa na wasiwasi. **~ly** *adv*. **~ness** *n* fadhaa. **tensile** *adj* -a kutanuka; -a kunyosheka; -a mkazo.

tension *n* 1 kunyosha; kutanuka; mkazo; *(tech)* mvuto. 2 *(excitement)* fadhaa, hangaiko, wasiwasi. 3 mgogoro ~ *relations* mvutano/ mgogoro kati ya watu. 4 *(elec)* nguvu ya umeme. 5 fosi/nguvu za mtanuko wa gesi au mvuke. **tensity** *see* **tenseness**.

tent hema. **oxygen** ~ mfuniko wa kichwa kwa anayeongezewa oksijeni. **~cloth** *n* turubali. ~-**peg** *n* kigingi. **~stitch** mshono wa mshazari.

tentacle *n* mkono, mnyiri, mwinyo, mkia.

tentative *adj* -a kujaribia ~ *suggestion* pendekezo la kujaribia. **~ly** *adv* kwa majaribio.

tenterhooks *n (pl only in)* **on** ~ -enye fazaa/wasiwasi.

tenuous *adj* 1 -embamba. 2 dhaifu.

tenuity *n* 1 wembamba. 2 udhaifu.

tenure *n* 1 kumiliki; wakati/muda wa kumiliki; *(conditions)* masharti ya kumiliku. 2 kushika cheo, wakati/ muda wa kushika cheo.

tepid *adj* 1 -a (u)vuguvugu, fufutende. 2 *(of feelings)* baridi, fufumavu. **be** ~ vuvuwaa. **~ly** *adv*. **~ness** *n*. **~ity** *n* uvuguvugu.

tercentenary *n* kumbukumbu ya miaka mia tatu; sherehe za kumbukumbu hiyo. **tercentennial** *adj* -a miaka mia tatu.

tergiversate *vi (formal)* badili nia/ msimamo; jipinga. **tergiversation** *n*.

term *n 1 (period)* muda, kipindi. 2 *(word)* neno; istilahi, mtajo. 3 *(of school, etc)* muhula. 4 *(pl) (conditions)* sharti. ~ **implied** masharti fahamivu. **make ~s, come to ~s (with sb)** patana; kubaliana. **come to ~s with sth** kubali. **do sth on one's own ~s/sb else's ~s** fanya jambo kwa kufuata matakwa yako/ masharti ya mwingine. 5 *(pl)* uhusiano **be on good/friendly/bad ~s (with sb)** -wa na uhusiano mwema/mbaya; patana/-topatana na. **on equal ~s** kwa usawa, bila kubaguana, kwa kulingana. 6 *(leg)* wakati wa kazi wa mahakama. 7 *(pl)* jinsi/namna ya kueleza. **in flatttering/ abusive ~s** kwa kupaka mafuta/ kutusi/matusi. **a contradiction in ~s** kauli inayojipinga. 8 *(maths)* sehemu, mafungu *vt* taja, ita. **~inology** *n* istilahi. **~inological** *adj a ~ inexactitude (hum)* uongo.

termagant *n* mwanamke mgomvi, mwenye gubu.

terminal *n* 1 kituo cha mwisho; (cha reli, basi, n.k.) kituo maalum cha basi (kwa ajili ya abiria wa ndege, n.k.). 2 *(of battery)* kichwa/ncha za umeme/ betri, temino *adj* 1 -a kipindi, -a muhula. 2 -siyotibika/sikia dawa, -a kufa. **~ly** *adv*. **terminus** *n* kituo/ stesheni ya mwisho (ya reli n.k.).

terminate *vt (formal)* koma, isha, vunjika; komesha, vunja, toa, haribu *~ a pregnancy* toa mimba. **termination** *n* 1 kikomo, mwisho, uvunjaji. 2 *(gram)* silabi au herufi ya mwisho wa neno. **terminable** *adj* -nayoweza kusimamishwa/komeshwa/ achishwa *the contract is ~ by both parties* mkataba unaweza kusimamishwa/kufutwa na wote wanaohusika.

termite *n* mchwa; *(winged)* kumbikumbi.

tern *n* membe.

terrace *n* 1 mahali palipoinuka pa kutembelea au penye nyumba. 2 *(on hill)* mfululizo wa ngazi pana. 3 matuta ya mkingamo. 4 mlolongo wa majumba katika kitalu *vt* 1 fanya matuta ya mkingamo. 2 chimba na kusawazisha. **~d** *adj*.

terracotta *n* terakota: udongo mwekundu mgumu wa ufinyazi.

terra-firma *n (lat)* nchi kavu.

terra incognita *n (lat)* eneo lisilojulikana/lisilovumbuliwa.

terrain *n* mandhari, upeo (wa sehemu ya nchi).

terrapin *n* kasa.

terrestrial *adj* 1 -a dunia, -a mfano wa dunia. 2 -a nchi kavu.

territory *n* 1 eneo/nchi (chini ya himaya moja). 2 eneo (la wilaya). 3 *(US)* wilaya (kabla ya kuwa jimbo). **territorial** *adj* -a nchi/taifa (fulani) *~ water* maji ya taifa *the T~ Army (GB)* jeshi la mgambo *T~ (US)* -a wilaya ya Marekani *n* (mwana) mgambo.

terror *n* 1 woga/hofu kuu. **strike ~ into sb** tia hofu, tisha. **~ struck/stricken** -liojawa na hofu. 2 (mtu) matata/ shetani msumbufu. **~ism** *n* ugaidi, matumizi ya vitisho na ukatili (hasa kwa sababu za kisiasa). **~ist** *n* gaidi. **terrify** *vt* ogofya, tisha. **~ize** *vt* tisha sana. **terrible** *adj* 1 -a kuogofya, -a kutisha. 2 *(excessive);* a bughudha, sumbufu; baya. 3 *(colloq)* ovyo, baya sana. **terribly** *adv* sana, mno. **terrific** *adj* 1 -a kuogofya, -a kutisha. 2 *(colloq)* -kubwa mno, ingi mno. **terrifically** *adv*.

terse *adj* -a maneno machache/ya mkato. **~ly** *adv*. **~ness** *n*.

tertian *adj (of fever)* -a kila siku ya pili *~ fever* homa ya kila siku ya pili.

tertiary *adj* -a tatu *~ education* elimu ya juu.

terylene *n (GB)* terelini.

tesselated *adj* -a vijiwe vya rangirangi.

test *vt* jaribu, tahini; pima. **the ~** *n* jaribio, mtihani, kipimo, upimaji. **a ~-case** *(leg)* kesi ya kupimia kanuni, kipimo. **~ drive** uendeshaji wa majaribio (wa gari la kununuliwa). **~ pilot** rubani wa majaribio (ya ndege mpya). **driving ~** jaribio/mtihani wa udereva. **put sth to the ~** pima umadhubuti/thamani ya kitu. **~ match** mchezo wa kimataifa (wa kriketi au ragbi). **~ tube** neli ya majaribio. **~ tube baby** mtoto wa maabara: mtoto ambaye mimba yake ilitungiwa kwenye maabara.

testament *n* 1 *(often* **last will and ~)** hati ya wasia, wosia. 2 **Old ~** Agano la Kale. **New ~** Agano jipya. **~ary** *adj* -wa wasia.

testate *adj* -enye kuachia wasia ~ *succession* mrithi kwa wasia.
testor *n* mwenye kuandika wasia, mwusia, muusia.
testatrix *n* mwusia wa kike.
testicle *n (also* **testis***)* pumbu, korodani, kende.
testify *vt,vi* ~ **that;** ~ **to sth;** ~ **against/in favour of sth** shuhudia; toa ushahidi, thibitisha, wa ishara ya *your work testifies your ability* kazi yako inathibitisha uwezo wako. **testifier** *n* shahidi. **testimonial** *n* hati/barua ya sifa (ya kushuhudia kazi njema) zawadi ya kusifu/shukrani. **testimony** *n* 1 ushahidi; ushuhuda *conflicting* ~ ushahidi wa uwongo *sworn* ~ ushahidi wa kiapo *bear* ~ *to sth* shuhudia. 2 kauli, tamko, maoni (rasmi).
testis *n see* **testicle**.
testy *adj* -a harara/hamaki/hasira; -epesi kukasirika, kali. **testily** *adv* kwa hasira, vikali. **testiness** *n* hamaki, hasira; wepesi wa hasira (n.k).
tetanus *n* pepopunda.
tetchy *adj* -a hasirahasira. **tetchiness** *n.*
tete-a-tete *n* maongezi ya faragha ya watu wawili tu.
tether *vt* funga (mnyama) kwa kamba katika kigingi *n* kamba ya kufungia mnyama katika kigingi. **I am at the end of my** ~ *(fig)* nimeishiwa nguvu (mali, uwezo, n.k.), nimefikia kikomo.
text *n* 1 maandiko, matini. 2 *(verse)* mlango/kifungu/aya (ya kuhubiria au kujadilia). 3 *(subject)* maneno halisi (ya mwandishi). 4 ~ **(book)** *n* kitabu cha kiada. **~ual** *adj* -a maandiko/ maandishi ~ *errors* makosa ya maandishi.
textile *adj* -a kutengeneza nguo/ vitambaa ~ *industries* viwanda vya nguo *n* nguo; kitambaa; *(pl.)* nguo, vitambaa.
texture *n* 1 msokotano (wa kitamba). 2 umbile asili, (k.m. laini, kukwaruza, -nene, -embamba, n.k.). 3 tishu *a skin of fine* ~ ngozi nyororo.
than *conj* 1 kuliko, zaidi ya, kupita, kushinda *this is better* ~ *that* hii ni bora kuliko ile. 2 *(in phrases)* **no other** ~ sio mwingine bali, -enyewe. **nothing else** ~ sio chochote kingine ila, tu *other* ~ ukiacha *sb else other* ~ *Juma* mtu mwingine ukiacha Juma.
thank *vt* 1 ~ **sb (for sth)**. ~ **you** asante, shukrani. **no** ~ **you** (hapana) asante. 2 *(in peremptory requests, future tense)* tafadhali, ningekushukuru *I'll* ~ *you for that money* tafadhali nipe ile pesa *n (pl.)* shukrani; kushukuru. **~s/no ~s** asante/(hapana) asante. **~s to** kwa msaada wako. **small ~s to** *(ironically)* bila msaada wako. **~-offering** *n* sadaka ya shukrani. **~s-giving** *n* (sala ya) shukrani; *(US)* **T~s giving Day** sikukuu ya kutoa shukrani: Alhamisi ya nne ya mwezi Novemba. **~fulness** *n* shukrani, kushukuru. **~less** *adj* -sio na shukrani; -sio na faida.
that *adj, pron* 1 *(demonstrative)* -le (yule, ile, n.k.). 2 *(relative)* huo, n.k. *I like* ~ *song* napenda wimbo huo/ule *adv (colloq)* kiasi hicho/kile, hivi/ hivyo *its about* ~ *high* ni refu hivi *it isn't all* ~ *cold* sio baridi kiasi hicho *conj* 1 (ya) kwamba, ya kuwa *the problem is* ~ *he failed the exam* tatizo ni kwamba alishindwa mtihani. 2 **so** ~; **in order** ~ ili. 3 *(introducing clauses of result)* (kiasi) kwamba *he was so tired* ~ *he fell asleep in the bus* alichoka kiasi kwamba alilala kwenye basi. 4 *introducing clauses of condition)* kama *supposing* ~ *he comes* je akija/kama akija *on condition* ~ ili mradi. 5 *(rhet) (in exclamations)* laiti *oh* ~ *I could see her again* laiti ningemwona; *(rel pron)* -e, -o, amba(ye, o, vyo, n.k.) *the letter* ~ *came* barua iliyokuja *the boy* ~ *ran away* mvulana aliyekimbia /mvulana ambaye alikimbia.
thatch *vt* ezeka/vimba nyumba kwa makuti/nyasi *n* 1 maezeko; *(coconut leaves)* makuti *strip off* ~ ezua,

vimbua *put on ~* ezeka, vimba. **~ed** *adj* -lioezekwa makuti/majani, n.k. *~ed roof* paa la kuezeka. **~er** *n* mwezekaji.

thaw *vt,vi* 1 ~ **(out)** *(snow and ice)* yeyusha; yeyuka. 2 *(of persons/ behaviour)* changamka, changamsha *n* myeyuko, kuyeyuka kwa theluji.

the *(def art)* 1 *(usu not translated, expect when used as a less specific form of that)* -le, yule, wale, ile, n.k. *A boy and a girl live nearby* mvulana na msichana wanaishi karibu *t~ boy is very naughty* mvulana yule ni mtundu sana. 2 *(reference to sth obvious) she went to the kitchen* alienda jikoni. 3 *(reference to sth unique) T~ OAU* Umoja wa Nchi Huru za Afrika *adv* kwa kiasi/kiwango fulani *~ sooner ~ better* mapema iwezekanavyo.

theatre/theater *n* 1 jumba/uwanja wa maonyesho tamthilia. **~goer** *n* shabiki wa kuangalia tamthilia, mpenzi wa tamthilia. 2 *(scene of important events)* eneo (la tukio maalum). 3 thieta/ukumbi wa mhadhara, n.k. **operating ~** chumba cha kupasulia. 4 (sanaa ya) maonyesho, tamthilia *be good ~* -wa onyesho zuri. **theatrical** *adj* 1 -a maonyesho/tamthilia. 2 -a kujifanya; *(usu amateur)* maonyesho. **theatrically** *adv*.

thee *pron see* **thou**.

theft *n* wizi, wivi, kuiba.

their *poss pron, adj* -ao *they love ~ parents* wanapenda wazazi wao. **~s** *pron* -ao, -a kwao, n.k. *our house is smaller than ~s* nyumba yetu ni ndogo kuliko yao.

theism *n* imani kwamba Mungu yupo na ni muumba na mtawala wa dunia.

theist *n* muumini wa imani hiyo. **theistic/theistical** *adj*.

them *pron see* **they**.

theme *n* 1 *(of writing, etc.)* dhamira, wazo. 2 *(US)* (mada ya) insha (ya wanafunzi); sauti mrejeo: sauti inayorudiwarudiwa. **~ song** *n* wimbo unaorudia mara kwa mara katika mchezo/senema. **thematic** *adj* -a kiini; -enye kisa.

themselves *pron (reflex)* 1 wenyewe *they ate by ~* walikula wenyewe *they hurt ~* walijiumiza *they went ~* walikwenda wenyewe. 2 *(emphat) they ~ saw him* wao wenyewe walimwona.

then *adv* 1 *(time)* wakati ule/huo; zamani zile *the ~ Regional Commissioner* Mkuu wa Mkoa wa wakati huo/ule, toka wakati ule. 2 *(next, after)* baadaye, halafu, kisha. **till ~** hadi hapo. 3 *(US at the end of a sentence)* basi, kwa hiyo. 5 *(furthermore)* aidha, tena, tena basi. 6 **now ~** sasa basi. **~ce** *adv (formal)* toka huko; kwa sababu hiyo. **~ceforth, ~ceforward** *adv* tokea hapo/pale/wakati huo/wakati ule.

theocracy *n* (nchi yenye) mfumo wa utawala/serikali ya makasisi. **theocratic** *adj*.

theodolite *n (surveyors)* kipimiapembe: chombo cha kupima pembewima na pembemlazo.

theology *n* teolojia: elimu ya dini; nadharia ya madhehebu. **theologian** mwanateolojia. **theological** *adj* -a teolojia. **theologically** *adv*.

theorem *n* 1 uhakiki wa kimantiki. 2 *(maths)* uhakiki.

theory *n* nadharia. **in ~** kinadharia *(guesswork)* makisio, wazo *my ~ is that* nakisia kwamba. **theorist** *n* mnadharia. **theoretic(al)** -a nadharia, si -a matendo. **theoretician** *n* mnadharia. **theoretics** *n* elimunadharia. **theorize** *vi* **~ (about sth)** toa nadharia, ongea kinadharia; kisia.

theosophy *n* teosofia: imani ya kuwa wanadamu wanaweza kumfahamu Mungu na kuwasiliana naye kwa kutulia kabisa na kutafakari elimu. **theosophist** *n* mwenye imani hii. **theosophic(al)** *adj* -a imani ya utakatifu.

therapy *n* matibabu, tiba. **radio~** matibabu kwa eksirei/mionzi. **therapeuti(al)** *adj* -a kutibu/kuponya magonjwa, maradhi. **therapeutics** *n* maarifa ya kutibu/kuponya magonjwa, utabibu. **therapist** *n* mtaalam wa maṭibabu.

there *adv* 1 *(place, direction)* pale/kule, hapo/huko *she works ~* anafanya kazi pale. 2 *(for emphasis)* -le *t~ goes!* Ileee! *T~ they come!* Walee. 3 *(in argument etc)* hapo, pale *~ you are wrong* hapo umekosea. 4 *(in phrases)* **over ~** kule. **then and ~; ~and then** palepale, hapohapo. 5 *(colloq) you ~!* wewe!. 6 *(after prep and adv) in ~* mle *under ~* hapo chini, chini pale. 7 *(to introduce sentence)* kuna, pana *t ~'s a new teacher* kuna mwalimu mpya. **~about(s)** *adv* karibu, kama hivi, kitu kama hicho. **~after** *adv (formal)* baadaye, halafu, kuanzia/kutokea hapo. **~fore** *adv* kwa hiyo, kwa sababu hiyo. **~in** *adv* humo, mle. **~inafter** *adv* -a (mahali) pale, -a hiyo. **~on** *adv* juu yake. **~to** *adv* pamoja na hayo, kuhusiana na hiyo/ile. **~under** *adv* chini ya. **~upon** *adv* kwa sababu hii, kwa hiyo; pale, papo; kuhusu hiyo. **~withal** *adv (archaic)* aidha, zaidi ya hayo.

therm *n* kipimo cha matumizi ya gesi. **~al** *adj* -a moto; -a joto *~ belt* ukanda wa joto *~ spring* chemchemi ya moto. **~ capacity** *(phys)* ujazifu -joto: kiasi cha joto cha kupandisha halijoto digrii moja. **~ionic** *adj* -enye kushughulikia utoaji wa elektroni katika hali ya joto ya juu. **~ic valve** vali ya electroni. **~o** *(in compounds)* -a joto. **~odynamic** *adj* -a mwendojoto. **~odynamics** *n* mwendojoto: sayansi ya uhusiano wa joto na kazi za mitambo. **~o electric** *adj* -a umemejoto. **~o nuclear** -a nukliajoto. **~o-plastic** *adj, n* (-a) kugeuka sandarusi/plastiki kwa joto. **~o-setting** -enye (kupata) ugumu wa kudumu baada ya kuandaliwa kwa joto. **~ostat** *n* thermostati, kirekebisha joto. **~ostastic** *adj*. **~otheraphy** *n* tibajoto. **~meter** *n* kipimajoto.

thermos *n* (*also* **~oflask**) chupa ya chai, themosi.

thesaurus *n* 1 hazina, kusanyiko. 2 *(dictionary)* thesauri: kamusi ya maneno na mafungu yaliyokusanywa pamoja kwa vikoa vya maana.

these *pl of* **this**.

thesis *n* 1 tasnifu. 2 hoja, wazo (linalotolewa kimantiki).

Thespian *adj* -a tamthilia *n* mwigizaji/tamthilia.

thews *n (pl)* maungo, misuli. **~ and sinews** nguvu ya mwili.

they *pers pron* wao, -wa *~ came* (wao) walikuja *~ say* watu wanasema/inasemekana. **them** *pers pron* -wa *I saw them* niliwaona. **~'d/~ had** wali *~ would* wange, wata-. **~'ll/~ will** wata. **~'re/~ are** wana.

thick *adj* 1 -nene, -enye maki kubwa. **~ lipped** *adj* -enye midomo minene. **~ skinned** *adj (fig)* -siyejali wengine, sugu. 2 *(crowded)* -ingi, -a kusongamana. **~-set** -fupi; -nene; a miraba minne; *(of hedge)* -liofungamana. 3 **~ with** -enye -ingi, -enye kujaa. 4 *(of voice)* -enye mikwaruzo. 5 *(of liquids)* -zito. 6 *(colloq)* pumbavu, bozi. **~ headed; ~ skulled, ~ witted** *adj* mpumbavu. 7 *(colloq)* sahibu, rafiki. **as ~ as thieves** marafiki sana. 8 *(various colloq uses)* **a bit ~; rather ~** -enye kuzidi; -enye kuvuka mpaka. **give sb a ~-ear** zaba kibao (mpaka sikio livimbe). **lay it on ~** *(sl)* tapakaza sifa/heshima, sifia/shukuru mno, visha kilemba cha ukoka *n* 1 sehemu iliyojaa/songamana. **through ~ and thin** kwa heri na kwa shari, kwa vyovyote vile, katika hali yoyote. **in the ~ of it** katikati. 2 sehemu nene zito *adv* kwa wingi. **~ly** *adv* kwa wingi; katika vipande vikubwa *vt* -wa zito/nene zaidi, gandamana *the plot ~ens* mambo yanaiva. **~ening** *n* dutu la kufanya kioevu kuwa kizito. **~ness** *n* 1 uzito, unene. 2 tabaka. **~ish** *adj* -nene kidogo.

thicket *n* kichaka, chaka; *(of mangroves)* koko.

thief *n* mwivi, mwizi, mkwepuzi.

thieve *vi,vt* iba; ibia. **theivery** *n* wizi, uibaji. **thievish** *adj* kijivi, kiibaji, kidokozi. **thievishness** *n* tabia ya kuiba. **thievishly** *adv*.

thigh *n* paja, kiga, kiweo. ~**ful-bone** *n* fundabeka.

thimble *n* kastabini, subana, tondoo. ~**ful** *n* tone (la maji, pombe, n.k.).

thin *adj* 1 -embamba. ~-**skinned** *adj* *(fig)* -epesi kuudhika/kuumia/ kukasirika; -siopenda kukosolewa. 2 -epesi, -a kutokuonekana. ~ **air** katika hali ya kutokuonekana *vanish into ~ air* toweka kabisa. 3 *(opp of fat)* nyaufu, -kondefu, -embamba. 4 pungufu, haba, siojaa *a ~ audience* hadhira ndogo sana. 5 *(liquid)* -a majimaji; dhaifu, hafifu. 6 chapwa, -sio kamili *~ humour* kichekesho chapwa. 7 *(colloq)* -a kubughudhi; ovyo. **have a ~ time** bughudhika, endewa mambo ovyo, pata tabu *adv* sana *so as to be ~* ili kuwa nyembamba sana *vt,vi* punguza; punguza miche; -wa -embamba, punguka; konda, vyorora, dhoofu. ~ **(out)** pungua/punguka *~ down* zimua, tia maji. ~**ly** *adv*. ~**ness** *n*.

thine *pron see* **thy**

thing *n* 1 kitu. 2 *(pl)* vitu (vya mtu); vitu vijulikanavyo kutokana na muktadha. 3 njozi **be seeing ~s** pagawa, ona mambo, pata njozi. 4 suala. 5 hali, tukio *~s are getting worse* hali inakuwa mbaya. **for one ~** kwanza. **taking one ~ with another** kwa jumla/kuzingatia kila hali. 6 *(used of person or animal expressing an emotion) poor ~* masikini! *a silly ~* maskini ya mungu. 7 **the ~** kinachofaa (kwa mazingira maalumu) *say the right ~s* sema kinachofaa *quite the ~* naam, -a kisasa. 8 *(phrase)* **the ~** suala ni, tatizo ni, la muhimu/ msingi ni. **first ~** awali ya yote, kwanza. **the general/common/usual ~** kawaida, uzoefu. **a near ~** bahati, kuponea chupuchupu. **an understood ~** kilicho muwafaka; **do one's (own) ~** *(colloq)* fanya/upendavyo/ujuavyo/ uonavyo. **have ~ about** *(colloq)* penda/chukia sana. 9 *(pl)* mambo *~s Tanzanian* mambo Kitanzania. 10 *(leg)* ~**s personal/real** mali ya mtu/ halisi. ~**ummy/~(u) mabob/~(u) majig** *n (colloq)* nanihino.

think *vt,vi* 1 *(reflect)* fikiri, tafakari, waza. ~ **aloud** toa mawazo yako (kama yanavyokujia akilini) bila kupanga. ~ **tank** jumuiya ya washauri mabingwa. 2 *(suppose)* dhani, fikiri. 3 *(neg with can/could)* fikiria/elewa/jua (katika fikira). 4 dhani, fikiri *I ~ I can drive well* nadhani naweza kuendesha vizuri. 5 tafakari, waza, piga bongo. 6 tegemea, tarajia, kusudia, nuia. **I thought as much** nilitegemea hivyo. 7 *(with adverbial particles and preps)* ~ **about sth** tafakari/chunguza (hasa kitu/jambo kuona uwezekano wake). ~ **of sth** fikiria, zingatia; wazia (bila kufikia hitimisho); toa wazo, pendekeza; kumbuka; wa na/ kubali wazo. ~ **highly/well/not much/little, etc of sb/sth** heshimu/ penda/dharau/-tojali mtu/kitu. ~ **nothing of sth/doing sth** chukulia kuwa (kitu/kufanya kitu) si kitu. ~ **nothing of it** usijali! ~ **better of sb** heshimu sana mtu. ~ **better of sth** achana na/tupilia mbali. ~ **sth out** fikiria kwa makini na kufanyia mpango. ~ **sth over** fikiria tena jambo. ~ **sth up** buni, vumbua *n (colloq)* muda wa kutafakari. ~**able** *adj* -a kuweza kufikirika; -a kuwazika *it is hardly ~* haifikiriki. ~**er** *n* mtu (wa fikara nyingi, wa akili) *be a slow ~* -wa mzito wa kufikiri. ~**ing** *n* kufikiri, kutafakari, fikira, mawazo *do some hard ~* piga bongo *adj* -a kufikiri; -enye akili. **put on one's ~ cap on** *(colloq)* wazia, fikiria (tatizo/jambo).

third *n* theluthi, fungu la sehemu ya tatu *adj* -a tatu/upande wa tatu *~ class adj* -a daraja la tatu; hafifu. ~ **party** mtu wa tatu. ~ **degree** usaili wenye mateso, kusaili sana. ~ **rate**

adj -ovyo, duni. ~ **rater** *n* mtu duni. **the T~ World** nchi zinazoendelea, ulimwengu wa tatu. **~ly** *adv* tatu.

thirst *n* 1 kiu. 2 *(fig) (desire, yearning)* shauku, tamaa *vt* ~ **(for)** ona kiu, -wa na kiu. ~ **for** onea shauku, tamani, taka sana. **~y** *adj* 1 -enye kiu *I am ~* nina kiu. 2 *(dry)* kavu. **~ly** *adv*.

thirteen *n* kumi na tatu *adj* -a kumi na tatu. **~th** *adj* -a kumi na tatu *n* fungu la sehemu ya kumi na tatu.

thirty *adj* -a thelathini *n* thelathini *the thirties* miaka ya thelathini (30-39). **thirtieth** *adj n* -a thelathini.

this *adj,pro* 1 huyu, hiki, hii, hili, n.k. 2 fulani *adv (colloq) to ~ degree* kwa kiasi/kiwango hicho; kwa hiyo.

thistle *n* mbaruti. **~-down** *n* mbegu ya mbaruti *as light as ~ down* -epesi kama mbegu za mbaruti.

thither *adv (arch)* huko; kule. **hither and** ~ huku na kule, kote.

tho' *adv conj* **though**.

thole *n (also ~* **pin***)* pingu za makasia, kikuku.

thong *n* kigwe, ugwe, kikanda, mjeledi.

thorax *n* kifua; kidari.

thorn *n* mwiba *be on ~s* ona wasiwasi, hangaika, fadhaika sana, sumbuka mno. **a ~ in one's flesh/side** *(fig)* kero, usumbufu maudhi. ~ **bush** *n* mchongoma, mkwamba. **~y** *adj* 1 -enye miiba. 2 *(fig)* sumbufu sana, gumu, -enye kusababisha mzozo/ubishi.

thorough *adj* kamili, kamilifu, -zima, -a kweli *a ~ rascal* ayari wa kupindukia. **~-going** *adj* kamilifu, - a kwelikweli; hasa. **~ly** *adv* kabisa, kwa bidii sana, kamili, kwelikweli; kikamilifu. **~ness** *n* 1 ukamilifu. 2 bidii nyingi.

thorough-bred *n adj* mbegu njema, -liofunzwa vema, -a asili bora *n (esp. a horse)* mnyama wa mbegu/asili bora.

thoroughfare *n* mtaa, barabara, njia (iliyo wazi).

those *pl. of* **that**.

thou *pron (arch)* wewe *(sing)* **thee** wewe.

though *conj* 1 *(also* **al~***)* ingawa, japo, ijapokuwa. 2 *(also* **al~** *and* **even ~***)* hata kama. 3 **what ~** *(liter)* hata kama. 4 *(also* **al~** *)* ingawa; hata hivyo *adv* lakini, hata hivyo *we won ~* tulishinda hata hivyo.

thought[1] *pt, pp of* **think**.

thought[2] *n* 1 wazo, fikira **on second ~** baada ya kufikiri tena. **~-reader** *n* mtu anayejifanya kujua mawazo ya wengine. **~ transference** uhawilishaji fikira. 2 ~ *(for) (caution)* hadhari, uangalifu. **take ~ for** angalia, zingatia. 3 kufikiri, kuwaza; mawazo *as quick as ~* upesi sana. 4 **a ~** kidogo. **~ful** *adj* 1 -a kufikiri, -a mawazo. 2 *(careful)* -a hadhari, angalifu *that was ~ of you* nashukuru kwa msaada wako/kwa kunifikiria. **~-fulness** *n* uangalifu. **~less** 1 -zembe, -siyojali. 2 choyo, -siyofikiria wengine, -a haraka, -pumbavu *it was very ~less of you* hukutumia busara hata kidogo. **~lessly** *adv*. **~lessness** *n* uzembe, upurukushani, kutoangalia *~ of others* kutokujali/kutofikiria wengine.

thousand *n* elfu *two ~* elfu mbili *adj* 1 -a elfu. 2 tele, elfuelfu *~ thanks* shukrani nyingi mno. **a ~ to one (chance)** (uwezekano) mdogo sana. **one in a ~** nadra sana. **~fold** *adj, adv* elfu mara. **~th** *adj* -a elfu *n* fungu la sehemu ya elfu.

thrall *n* mtumwa; utumwa *he is (in) ~ to his passions* ni mtumwa wa ashiki zake. **thraldom** *n* utumwa.

thrash *vt,vi* 1 piga (kwa mjeledi/fimbo), charaza *he ~ed her with a whip* alimcharaza kwa mjeledi. 2 *(colloq) (in competition) (beat)* shinda. 3 **~ sth out** *(colloq)* tatua tatizo kwa majadiliano; fikia maamuzi/ukweli kwa majadiliano. 4 shikashika, tikisa, tosa, tupatupa. 5 *see* **thresh**. **~ing** *n* 1 kupura; kupiga. 2 *(defeat)* ushinde *give sb a ~ing* shinda mtu.

thread *n* 1 uzi. **hang by a ~** *(fig)* -wa

katika hatari kubwa, -wa mahututi. 2 kitu chembamba kama uzi. 3 mlolongo (unaounganisha sehemu za hadithi). 4 hesi *vt* 1 tunga uzi (katika tundu la shindano), tungia. 2 *(pass through)* penya. ~ **one's way** penya (kati ya kundi la watu). 3 *(of hair)* -wa na milia. ~**bare** *adj* 1 kuukuu, bovu. 2 *(fig) (uninteresting)* baridi, chapwa, -a kuchusha, -sio na thamani. ~ **bareness** *n* 1 uchakavu. 2 ubaridi. ~ **like** *adj* -a kama uzi, -a nyuzi nyuzi; embamba na refu. ~**worm** *n* mchangouzi.

threat *n* 1 tishio, kitisho *there is a ~ of rain* kuna tishio la mvua. 2 **a/the ~ (to sb/sth) (of sth)** dalili/ ishara (ya hatari). ~**en** *vt,vi* 1 ~**en sth; ~en to do sth** tisha, wa kitisho, ogofya. ~**en sb (with sth)** ogofya, tisha mtu. 2 *(indicate)* toa onyo/ishara ya; onya. 3 elekea kuja/kutokea. ~**ened with** tishwa na, elekea kupata. ~**ening** *adj* 1 -a kutisha, -a kuogofya. 2 -enye dalili ya shida. ~**eningly** *adv.*

three *n* tatu *adj* -a tatu ~ *times* ~ tatu mara tatu. ~**cornered** *adj* -a pembe tatu ~ *course meal* mlo wa hatua tatu. ~**-decker** *n* sandwichi ya vipande vitatu vya mkate; chombo chenye sitaha tatu. ~ **dimensional** *adj (abbr* **3-D***)* -a pande tatu.~**-figure** *adj* -enye tarakimu tatu (yaani namba kati ya 100 na 999). ~ **fold** *adj* -a mara tatu *adv* kwa mara tatu. ~ **lane** *adj* (*of a roadway)* -enye njia tatu. ~**-legged** *adj* -a miguu mitatu; mbio za miguu mitatu ~*-legged stool* kigoda. ~ **pence** *n* peni tatu. ~ **penny** *adj* -a peni tatu. ~**-per cent** *n* asilimia tatu. ~**-piece** *adj* -a vipande vitatu *a ~ piece suit* suti na kizibau; *(of a woman)* sketi/ suruali, blauzi na koti. ~**-ply** *adj* -enye tabaka/nyuzi, n.k. tatu. ~ **quarters** *adj* robo tatu; ~**score** *n, adj* sitini, korija tatu. ~**-seater** *adj* -enye (kukaliwa na) watu watatu. ~**some** *n* kundi la/mchezo wa watu watatu. ~**-storied** *adj* -a ghorofa tatu. ~ **wheel** *adj* -a magurudumu matatu.

threnody *n* wimbo wa maombolezo; wimbo wa mazishi.

thresh *vt,vi* pura, kafua, puta, pukuta; pukuchua. ~**ing-floor** *n* uga (wa kupuria nafaka). ~**er** *n* 1 mpuraji, kipuraji. 2 papa mkubwa mwenye mkia mrefu. ~**ing-machine** *n* mashine ya kukafulia.

threshold *n* 1 kizingiti (cha mlango) *cross the ~* ingia nyumbani. 2 *(fig)* lango, mwanzo; kitovu *a pain ~* kitovu cha maumivu. 3 *(physio; psych)* kilele, kiwango cha juu.

threw *pt of* **throw**.

thrice *adv* mara tatu ~*-blessed adj* -enye kubarikiwa mara tatu.

thrift *n* uwekevu; iktisadi, uangalifu katika kutumia fedha/mali. ~**iness** *n* iktisadi, uwekevu. ~**less** *adj* -tapanyaji mali, fujaji (wa mali), badhirifu. ~**y** *adj* 1 wekevu, -a iktisadi, -angalifu (kwa mambo ya mali). 2 -a fanaka, -enye mafanikio.

thrill *vt,vi* sisimua; sisimka *n* msisimko. ~**er** *n* tamthilia/filamu/ riwaya ya kusisimua. ~**ing** *adj* -a kusisimua.

thrive *vi* (*arch)* ~ **(on sth)** neemeka, fanikiwa, sitawi, tononoka. **thriving** *adj* -enye ufanisi, -liostawi.

thro' *(informal spelling of)* **through**.

throat *n* 1 koo. **cut** ~ *(attrib) adj (of razor)* -enye wembe mrefu uliotiwa katika mpini; *(of competition)* kali na -a kikatili. **cut one's own** ~ jiua (kwa kukata koo); *(fig)* jiharibia (nafasi/maisha/bahati). 2 umio. **force/thrust sth down sb's** ~ *(fig)* jaribu kumfanya mtu akubali jambo/maoni yako. **stick in one's** ~ *(fig)* -tokubalika kwa urahisi. ~**y** *adj (of voice)* -a kukwaruza, - a kooni.

throb *vi (of the heart, pulse)* puma, pwita, tuta, gonga *his head ~bed* kichwa kilimgonga *n* mapigo, kututa *a ~ of pleasure* mpwitompwito. ~**bing** *adj* -a kupwita, -a kugonga.

throe *n* ~s maumivu makuu, uchungu. **in the ~s of sth/of doing sth** *(colloq)* katika jitihada za kufanya jambo; katika mapambano na.

thrombosis *n* mvilio moyoni/kwenye mshipa wa damu.

throne *n* 1 kiti cha enzi; uwalio. 2 **the** ~ ufalme; enzi.

throng *n* msongamano, halaiki, umati, msukosuko *vi, vt* songamana, songana, banana; songa, bana.

throttle *vt* 1 songa roho, kaba, kwida. 2 *(machine)* ~ **(back/down)** dhibiti mmiminiko wa mvuke/mvuke hewa wa petroli, n.k. katika injini *n* ~ *(valve)* kilango/vali (inayodhibiti mmiminiko wa mvuke wa petroli, n.k. katika injini).

through[1] *(US informal* **thru'***).* 1 *(of places)* toka upande hadi upande, kupitia *the road goes ~ Serengeti* barabara inapitia Serengeti. 2 *(fig uses) go ~ an experience* pata hisia/mwonjo wa jambo, pitia tukio *go ~ an examination* pasi/faulu mtihani. 3 *(because of/by means of)* kwa sababu ya, kwa njia ya, kwa kutumia. 4 -a moja kwa moja. 5 *(of time)* tangu mwanzo hadi mwisho moja kwa moja *live ~ the night* ishi mpaka asubuhi. 6 *(US)* hadi.

through[2] *adv* 1 kuanzia mwisho hadi mwisho/kuanzia mwanzo hadi mwisho, kuanzia upande mmoja hadi upande wa pili. **all** ~ muda/wakati wote. 2 hadi mwisho. **be ~ (with)** maliza, malizana (na); *(colloq)* choshwa na. **go ~ with sth** endelea hadi kumaliza. **see sth** ~ wapo/saidia katika jambo hadi lifikie mwisho. ~ **and** ~ kabisa. 3 moja kwa moja (hadi), mfululizo. 4 *(telephoning) (GB)* unganishwa, pewa, tayari *you are ~* umeunganishwa/umepata/tayàri; *(US)* isha (kuzungumza). 5 *(as modifier)* -a kupita/kupita *a ~train/ticket/passeger* treni/tikiti/abiria -a kupita. **~put** *n* matokeo, mazao. **~way** *n (express way)* baraste.

throughout *prep,* popote, kotekote *adv* kote, kabisa.

throve *see* **thrive**.

throw *vt,vi* 1 tupa, gea, rusha. 2 **(on, over, off)** tupia, valia, vua; haraka (haraka) *~off clothes* vua nguo haraka (haraka). 3 *(of a rider)* angusha, rusha; *(of animals)* zaa; *(of snake)* bambuka (ngozi). 4 **(out, up, down, about)** tapanya. ~ **away** tupa, poteza/tumia bure, fuja. ~ **back** rejeza, rudisha. ~ **out** toa. 5 *(pottery)* finyanga, umba 6. *(silk)* sokota. 7 *(colloq)* vuruga akili; sumbua, kera. 8 *(sl)* ~ **a party** fanya sherehe/karamu/tafrija. ~ **a fit** shtuka/kasirika sana. 9 ~ **sth open (to)** shirikisha kila mtu; ruhusu kila mtu kushiriki. 10 *(with adv, particles and prep)* ~ **sth about** tapanya; *(fig)* tumia ovyo. ~ **oneself at** vamia, angukia; jipendekeza. ~ **sth away** poteza (kitu) (kwa uzembe/ujinga); tamka/sema kikawaida. **~away** kitu kisicho na faida tena baada ya matumizi. ~ **back** rejea uasili, kale. ~ **sb back on/upon sth** lazimisha (mtu) kurudia kitu (kwa kukosa kingine). ~ **down** angusha, angua; *(a load)* bwaga. ~ **oneself down** jibwaga, jinyoosha chini. **~sth in** changia, ongeza, tia nyongeza, tia bure; *(remark)* ng'aka, sema; *(football)* rusha/tupa. **a ~ in** *n* mpira wa kurusha/kutupa. ~ **in one's hand** kata tamaa; kiri kwamba huwezi kufanya (kitu). ~ **in one's lot with sb** kula bia, fanya pamoja, jiunga. ~ **in the towel/sponge** *(colloq)* shindwa, kubali kushindwa. ~ **oneself into sth** anza kufanya kazi kwa bidii. ~ **sb/sth off** jikomboa, pata uhuru, ondokana na. ~ **sth off** tunga/sanifu kwa urahisi. ~ **oneself on/upon sb/sth** egemea, tegemea. ~ **sth out** tamka; *(reject)* kataa; *(construct)* ongeza/panua, (jengo). ~ **sb out** fukuza; changanya/vuruga akili. ~ **sb over** telekeza, tupa, acha, tenga. ~ **sth up**; *(resign)* acha, toka, jitoa; *(vomit)* tapika. ~ **sth up** tangaza, toa ilani. ~ **sth together** kutanisha; unganisha haraka; kusanya/tengeneza haraka. ~ **people together** kutanisha watu. ~ **up one's hands in horror** nyanyua mikono kwa woga mtupo, mrusho. **within a**

stone's ~ (of) karibu, machoni. **~er** *n* 1 mtupaji. 2 mtoaji.
thrown *pp* **throw**.
thru *see* **through**.
thrum *vi,vt* ~ **(on) sth** donoa nyuzi za zeze ~ *on a guitar* suka nyuzi za gita; pigapiga (ngoma).
thrush *n* ugonjwa wa kuvimba ndani kwa ndani mwilini.
thrust *vt,vi* kumba, sukuma, songa; *(with a word)* choma (kwa nguvu). ~ **aside** deua, geuza *n* 1 pigo, kumbo, chomo, maneno makali; shambulio. 2 nguvu, msukumo. **~er** *n* mtu anayejitia kimbelembele.
thud *n* mshindo *vi* piga/anguka kwa mshindo.
thug *n* jambazi; mwuaji. **~gery** *n*.
thumb *n* kidole (cha) gumba. **(one's fingers) be all ~s; have ten ~s** -tokuwa stadi/hodari; -wa mzito sana. **rule of** ~ kanuni (zitokanazo na) mazoea, desturi. **under sb's** ~ chini ya, katika twaa ya. ~ **up/down** hongera; pole/hiloo, zii. **~-latch** *n* kitasa cha kuminya kwa kidole. **~-mark** alama ya dole gumba. **~nail** *n* ukucha wa dole gumba. **~nail sketch** muhtasari, picha/mchoro mdogo. ~ **screw** *n* skurubu inayoweza kufunguliwa kwa urahisi/kwa gumba; chombo cha zamani kilichotumika kutesea watu kilichominya magumba. **~-stall** *n* bandeji, kinga ya gumba jeruhi. **~-tack** *n* mshikizo mkubwa; *(US)* pini vt chafua kwa kugeuza-geuza; geuza (kurasa). ~ **a lift** omba lifti barabarani. ~ **one's nose at** beza.
thump *n* ngumi, pigo la ngumi; mshindo mzito *vt,vi* gonga, twanga, piga, dunda. **~ing** *adj (colloq)* sana, mno.
thunder *n* radi. ~ **bolt** *n* radi; *(fig)* jambo la kushtusha sana. **~-clap** *n* radi, ngurumo; *(fig)* tukio/habari mbaya ya ghafla, habari mbaya. ~ **cloud** *n* wingu la radi na ngurumo. ~ **storm** *n* mvua ya radi. ~ **struck** *adj (pred fig)* -enye kushangaa/kuduwaa/ kushikwa na bumbuwazi. **steal sb's** ~ kata bogi, wahi mtu (hivyo kumvurugia mpango) *vi* 1 piga radi, nguruma. 2 tia kishindo *it ~ed yesterday* jana kulipiga radi. ~ **(out) against** foka, fokea, nguruma. **~ous** *adj* -a radi, -a mshindo, -a makeke. **~y** *adj* - enye radi, -a ngurumo.
thurible *n* chetezo.
Thursday *n* Alhamisi.
thus *adv* hivi, hivyo, vivi hivi, ndivyo. ~ **far** mpaka hapa.
thwack *vt* piga kwa nguvu, dunda, twanga, gonga *n* pigo la nguvu, kikumbo.
thwart *vt* zuia, wekea vipingamizi *be ~ed* zuiwa *n* kiti cha mvuta kasia.
thy/thine *adj (arch)* -ako. **~self** *adj* (wewe) mwenyewe, nafsi yako.
thyroid *n* kikoromeo, dundumio. ~ **gland** tezi dundumio.
ti *n (also* **si***)* noti ya saba katika skeli ya muziki.
tiara *n* taji, tiara.
tibia *n* muundi goko.
tic *n* mtetemo wa kineva.
tick[1] *n* mfuko wa godoro/mto; kitambaa cha mfuko huo.
tick[2] *n* 1 ta: pigo jepesi (kama la saa). 2 alama ya vema (v) ya kuonyesha kuwa kitu ni sahihi; *(colloq)* muda, wakati. 3 nukta, punde. 4 **~tack** mfumo wa ishara za mawasiliano kati ya wapokea dau kwenye mashindano ya farasi *vt, vt* 1 piga/enda ta-ta. **in two ~s** kwa mapigo mawili. **what makes sb/sth** ~ *(colloq)* kitu gani kinammotisha. 2 tia alama. ~ **away** *(of a clock)* pita, pitisha. 3 ~ **over** *(of an engine)* waka/washa. ~ **sth off** weka tiki. *(colloq)* ~ **sb off** karipia, kemea.
tick[3] *n* 1 *(cattle)* kupe. 2 papasi.
tick[4] *n (colloq)* mkopo. **on** ~ kwa kukopa.
ticker *n* 1 *(colloq)* saa. 2 *(sl)* moyo. 3 mashine ichapishayo habari yenyewe. ~ **tape reception** mapokezi ya shangwe sana.
ticket 1 tiketi. **~-collector** *n* mkusanyaji tiketi. ~ **inspector** *n* mkaguzi wa

tiketi. 2 kipande (cha karatasi) kilichotiwa kwenye kitu kuonyesha bei, n.k. 3 *(US)* orodha ya wagombea wa chama kimoja. 4 taarifa ya kosa la barabarani. 5 **the** ~ *(sl)* jambo hasa/halisi la kufanya. 6 ~ **of-leave** *n (arch)* kifungo cha nje. 7 cheti chenye sifa za rubani *vt* weka alama/kipande.

tickle *vi, vi* 1 tekenya, nyegeresha. 2 *(amuse)* chekesha, furahisha; *(colloq) be ~d to death at sth* furahishwa sana. 3 washa. **~r** *n (colloq)* fumbo; kitendawili. **ticklish** *adj* 1 -a kutekenya. 2 gumu, tata.

tiddler *n (colloq)* 1 samaki mdogo sana. 2 mtoto mchanga.

tiddley *adj (colloq)* 1 dogo. 2 -liolewa kidogo.

tide *n* 1 maji kujaa na kupwa. **high/flood** ~ *(maximum)* bamvua. **low/neap** ~ maji kupwa, maji mfu. **spring** ~ bamvua kubwa. ~ **mark** *n* alama ya maji kupwa na kujaa. **~-way** mkondo wa bahari. 2 mwelekeo, mkondo. 3 *(old use)* wakati/msimu *(in compound)* **Easter-~** wakati wa Pasaka *vt* ~ **sb over (sth)** vusha/kwamua mtu kutokana na matatizo fulani. **tidal** *adj* -a maji kupwa na kujaa; -enye maji kupwa na kujaa ~ *flats* jangwa ~ *movements* maji mkimbizi. ~ **wave** *n* kabobo.

tidings *n pl (arch)* habari, taarifa.

tidy *adj* 1 nadhifu, safi, -liopangwa vizuri. 2 *(colloq)* kubwa/ingi kiasi ~ *sum of money* kiasi kikubwa cha fedha *cost a ~ penny* gharimu fedha nyingi *n* chombo/kibweta/kijaluba cha kuwekea mabaki ya jikoni/cha vikorokoro vya chumbani *vt,vi* ~ **(up)** panga vizuri *I must ~ myself* sina budi kujinadhifisha. **tidily** *adv.* **tidiness** *n* unadhifu, utanashati, usafi, ufuauji.

tie *vt, vi* funga, boba ~ *up a parcel* funga kifurushi. ~ **sb down** nyima mtu uhuru, bana, zuia. ~ **sb down to sth** bana mtu kwa masharti. ~ **oneself down to sth** kubali mipaka ya uhuru wako, jibana. ~ **(sth) in with sth** unganisha, husisha. ~ **sth up** *(of capital)* tenga, changia; wekea, masharti; *be/get ~ up with sth/sb* banwa na kitu/mtu; husishwa, husiana. ~ **up** *n* 1 mwungano, bia. 2 ~ *sth (on)* fungia kwa. **~-on attrib** *adj* kipande (cha anwani). 3 piga fundo. 4 fungiwa *does this sash ~ infront or at the back?* mshipi huu unafungiwa mbele au nyuma? 5 ~ **(with) (for)** *(of players, teams, candidates in competitive exams)* fungana, enda sare/suluhu *n* 1 kifungo, kiungo, fundo; *(US)* taruma *the ~ of friendship* mshikamno wa kirafiki. 2 *(necktie)* tai. 3 *(in games, etc)* sare; suluhu. 4 *(music)* tao (linalounganisha noti za sauti moja). 5 kizuzi, kipingamizi.

tier *n* safu; daraja, rusu.

tiff *n* ugomvi mdogo.

tiffany *n* bushashi.

tiffin *n* mlo mwepesi wa mchana.

tiger *n* 1 chui mkubwa mwenye milia. **~ish** *adj* katili, buka. **tigress** *n* chui jike.

tight *adj* -liokazwa, -liobana, -liofungwa vizuri. **~-lipped** *adj* -a kubana midomo; kimya, -a maneno machache; *(fig)* -enye uso mkali. 2 -liounganishwa vizuri. **water** ~ siovuja maji. **air** ~ -siopitisha hewa. 3 lionyooshwa sana, -liokaza sana, liowamba. 4 *(of money)* adimu, gumu kupata. 5 **~-fisted** -enye choyo, bahili, -nyimivu. **~wad** *n (sl)* bahili. 6 *(of clothing, etc)* -enye kubana, -a kufinya *a ~ corner* jambo lenye hatari (shida, dhiki) ~ *schedule* ratiba iliyojaa mishughuliko mingi ~ *squeeze* msongamano mkubwa. 7 *(colloq)* -liolewa, levi. **~ly** *adv* kikiki, kwa kukaza. **~ness** *n* kukaza, kubana. **~en** *vt,v* kaza, bana ~ *the rope* kaza kamba. ~ **one's belt** bana matumizi, bania. **~s** *n* 1 soksi ndefu (za wanawake) za kubana. 2 taiti; nguo zinazobana mwili mzima (zinazovaliwa na wanasarakasi).

tike *n see* **tyke**.

tilde *n* tilde, kiwimbi *(~)*.

tile *n* kigae (cha kuezekea, cha kubandikia ukutani au sakafuni). **be (out) on the ~s** *(sl)* shereheka. **have a ~ loose** *(sl)* ehuka *vt* ezeka kwa vigae. **~r** *n* mwezekaji vigae. **~ry** *n* kiwanda cha vigae.

till[1] *n* kikasha/mtoto wa meza *he was caught with his hand in the ~* alishikwa wizi.

till[2] *conj, prep* hata; mpaka, hadi *she waited ~ I came* alisubiri mpaka nilipofika.

till[3] *vt* lima. **~age** *n* ukulima, ulimaji, ukatuzi; ardhi iliyolimwa, ucheu. **~er** *n* mkulima, mlimaji. **~able** *adj* -a kulimika.

tiller *n* kana, mkombo. **~ rope** mjarari, ujari.

tilt *vt,vi* 1 inamisha, laza upande, inama, lala upande *don't ~ the barrel* usiinamishe pipa/kasiki. 2 **~ (at)** *(hist) (of men on horseback)* pigana kwa farasi na mikuki mirefu; *(fig)* shambulia kwa maandishi/maneno. **~ at windmills** pigana na maadui wa kubuni/wa kufikirika *n* 1 mwinamo. 2 kupigana kwa farasi na mikuki mirefu. **have a ~ at sb** *(fig)* shambulia/lima (mtu) (kirafiki) katika majadiliano. **(at) full ~** kwa kasi; kwa nguvu nyingi. **~-yard** *n* kiwanja cha mazoezi ya kupigana kwa farasi.

tilth *n* ucheu, weu.

timber *n* 1 mbao *~ merchants* wafanya biashara wa mbao *dressed ~* mbao zilizo tayari kwa matumizi. 2 *(also* **standing ~***)* miti *put fifty acres of land under ~* panda miti (ya mbao) ekari hamsini. 3 boriti. 4 *(in fox hunting)* uzio na lango (la miti). **~ed** *adj* -liojengwa/tengenezwa kwa mbao.

timbre *n* tabia/sifa ya sauti.

timbrel *n* kigoma, tari.

time *n* 1 wakati *past, present and future ~* wakati uliopita, uliopo na ujao. 2 majira, muda. **~ waits for no man** *(prov)* muda haumngoji mtu. 3 *(also)* **a** + *adj* + **~** kipimo cha muda *six hours is a period of ~* saa sita ni kipindi cha muda *we have no ~ to lose* hatuna muda wa kupoteza. **behind ~** -liochelewa *the bus is two hours behind ~* basi -limechelewa saa mbili. **on ~** -liowahi, katika/kwa wakati wake *she came on ~* aliwahi. **in no ~** mara moja, haraka sana. **(from/since) ~ immemorial; (from/since) ~ out of mind** zama za kale. **gain ~** vuta muda (kwa mbinu). **all the ~** kwa kipindi chote kile (kinachozungumziwa); wakati wote, muda wote. **half the ~** nusu ya wakati uliotolewa, kwa muda mrefu, mara nyingi, karibuni wakati wote. 4 saa *what is the ~?* ni saa ngapi? 5 kipindi (miaka, miezi, saa, dakika, n.k.), muda. **keep good/bad ~** *(of a clock or watch)* enda sawa/poteza majira. **the ~ of the day** muda unayoonyeshwa kwenye saa. **pass the ~ of day (with...)** amkiana/salimiana na mtu. 6 wakati *it is breakfast ~* ni wakati wa staftahi/kifungua kinywa *it is ~ to go* ni wakati wa kuondoka *~ is up* wakati umekwisha. **(work, etc) against ~** harakisha (kutokana na upungufu wa muda). **at the same ~** kwa pamoja, kwa wakati mmoja, sawia; hata hivyo; pamoja na hayo, lakini *he is poor at the same ~ he is generous* ni fukara hata hivyo ni mkarimu. **at ~s; from ~ to ~** mara nyingi, mara kwa mara. **at all ~s** wakati wote, mara zote. **at your ~ of life** katika umri wako. **in ~** mapema *she was in ~ for the lesson* alifika mapema kwa somo; baada ya muda fulani, hatimaye *you will succeed in ~* hatimaye utafanikiwa. **near her ~** *(of a woman)* karibia kujifungua. **do ~** *(coloq)* tumikia kifungo. **serve one's ~** -wa mwanagenzi kwa muda fulani; tumikia kifungo. **his ~ is drawing near** wakati wake unakaribia. 7 mara *for the last ~* kwa mara ya mwisho *he failed five ~s* alishindwa mara tano. **at one ~** wakati fulani *at one ~ she sent a nasty letter* wakati fulani alituma barua kali. **at other ~** wakati mwingine. **~ and ~ again, without number** mara kwa mara; kila mara. **many a ~; many ~s** mara nyingi, mara kwa mara. **one at a ~** moja moja *take two tablets at a ~* meza vidonge viwili kwa kila wakati mmoja. 8 *(pl) (maths)* mara *six ~s three* sita mara tatu. **her house is two ~s bigger than mine** nyumba yake ni kubwa mara mbili zaidi ya nyumba yangu. 9 *(often pl)* (hali ya) maisha; enzi *in the ~s of the chiefs* katika enzi ya watemi. **ahead of one's ~; born before one's ~** -wa mbele kimawazo; zaliwa kabla ya wakati wako. **(even) at the best of ~s** hata wakati wa neema. **behind the ~s** -wa na mawazo ya kizamani; liopitwa na wakati. **have a good ~** burudika, starehe. **have the ~ of one's life** *(colloq)* furahia kupita kiasi. 10 *(of music)* mdundo. **in /out of ~** inayofuata/isiyotuata mdundo. **double-quick ~** kwa kasi sana. **beat ~** onyesha mapigo ya mdundo kwa mkono au fimbo. **keep ~** cheza au imba kwa kufuata mdundo. 11 *(compounds)* **~-ball** *n* mpira wa kuashiria muda maalum. **~-bomb** *n* bomu lililotegeshwa kulipuka kwa muda maalum. **~ card/sheet** *n* kadi ya mahudhurio ya wafanyakazi. **~-expired** *adj (of soldiers and sailors)* waliostaafu. **~ exposure** *n* uachiaji wa mwanga kuingia kwenye filamu kwa zaidi ya nusu sekunde. **~-fuse** *n* fyuzi inayowaka kwa muda maalumu. **~-honoured** *adj* -a kuheshimiwa kutokana na ukale wake. **~-keeper** *n* mdhibiti/kidhibiti majira/muda; *(of a watch, etc)* saa inayokwenda vizuri/ isiyopoteza majira. **~-lag** *n* kawio, muda kati ya matukio mawili. **~-limit** *n* muda maalumu; kiwango maalum cha muda. **~-piece** *n* saa. **~-server** *n* mnafiki, ajipendekezaye; barakala. **~-serving** *adj* geugeu. **~signal** *n* kiashiria muda. **~-switch** *n* swichi ya wakati/majira. **~-table** *n* ratiba. **~-work** *n* kazi ya kibarua/ya kipande/ kulipua **~-worker** *n* kibarua. **~ worn** *adj* kuukuu, -a zamani. **~ zone** *n* ukanda wa kijiografia unaotumia majira yanayofanana *vt* 1 chagua/ panga saa (ya kutenda jambo). 2 pima muda. 3 rekebisha *~ one's steps to the music* rekebisha hatua zilingane na mdundo wa muziki. **timing** *n* mpangilio/urekebishaji wa muda. **~less** *adj (liter)* -a milele, -a aushi, -siopimika. **~ly** *adj* -a wakati wa kufaa, -a kuja wakati mzuri. **~liness** *n* wakati mzuri/wa kufaa.

timid *adj* -oga, epesi kutishwa. **~ity** *n* woga; haya. **~ness** *n*. **~ly** *adv*.

timorous *adj* -oga, -a kutishika. **~ly** *adv*. **~ness** *n*.

tin *n* 1 bati. **~ plate** *n* chuma kilicho-bambikwa/ambikwa madini ya bati. **~-foil** *n* jaribosi (bati). **a (little) ~ god** kijiungu (njaa). **~ hat** *n (sl)* kofia la chuma. **~-pot** *adj* hafifu; ovyoovyo. **~man/~smith** *n* mfua bati. 2 mkebe, kopo, debe. **~-opener** *n* kiboko/kifungulia kopo. 3 hela *adj* -a bati *vt* tia bati; ambika/bambika madini ya bati *pack in ~s* tia katika makopo (mikebe). **~ny** *adj* -a kama bati; -a mlio wa bati. **~ker** *n* 1 mfua bati, mtengenezaji vyombo vya bati, mhanja. **I don't care/give a ~ker's damn/cuss** sijali kitu. 2 kukorokochoa *vi* **~ (at/with)** bambanya, babia, babaisha.

tincture *n* 1 dawa (iliyo ndani ya alkoholi). 2 **a ~ (of)** dalili (ishara), alama (ya), kiashirio (cha) *vt* tia rangi/ladha kidogo.

tinder *n* vitu (visivyo vioevu) vinavyoshika moto haraka. **~ box** *n* sanduku la vifaa vya moto. **~y** *adj* -a kulipuka upesi.

tine *n* meno (ya msumeno au rato/uma n.k.) **~d** *adj* -enye meno.

ting *n* ngoo!!: mlio wa kengele; kupiga kengele *vi,vt* liza, piga kengele; lia.

tinge *vi* **~ sth (with)** tia rangi kidogo, athiri kidogo *n* dalili/ishara/ athari/alama ndogo.

tingle *vi* ona mnyeo; hisi mchonyoto;

washa, chachatika damu; *(fig)* sisimkwa *n* mnyeo, msisimko.

tinkle *vi* lia kama njuga *n* mlio wa njuga.

tin pan alley *n* jamii ya watunzi/ waimbaji wa muzikipendwa.

tinsel *n* 1 zari, mapambo ya kumetameta. 2 jambo la bandia/ mikogo *adj* 1 -a zari; -a urembo. 2 *(unreal)* -a bandia *vt* tarizi kwa zari.

tint *n* rangi ya kivulivuli *vt* tia rangi (kidogo) *~ed glasses* miwani iliyotiwa rangi.

tintinnabulation *n* mlio wa kengele.

tiny *adj* -dogo sana.

tip[1] *n* 1 kionyo, kidokezi, shauri *take sb's ~* fuata shauri. 2 bahshishi. 3 kikofi *vi* 1 gusa; gonga kidogo. ~ **and run** *adj* -a kupora na kukimbia. 2 -pa zawadi/bahshishi. ~ **sb off** *(colloq)* asa, dokezea, tahadharisha. ~ **off** *n* onyo, hadhari. **~sb the wink** *(colloq)* -pa habari ya siri. ~ **the winner** bahatisha/chagua mshindi kabla. **~ster** *n* mtabiri (wa mashindano ya farasi).

tip[2] *n* 1 *(end)* ncha, mwisho. 2 *(of a mountain, hill)* kilele, kileleta. 3 *(pointed part)* ncha, sehemu iliyochongoka, mchonge. 4 **(have sth) on the ~ of one's tongue** karibia/ taka kukumbuka/kusema kitu. 5 kichungi *vt* tia ncha/kichungi. **~top** *adj (colloq)* bora kabisa, safi.

tip[3] *vt,vi* 1 ~ **(sth) (up)** inama; inamisha upande mmoja, weka upande. ~ **sth (over)** pindua. ~ **the scale (at)** zidisha; *(fig)* amua; pima. **~up seat** kiti cha kukunja. 2 ~ **sth (out)**; ~ **sth (out of sth)/(into sth)** mwaga, tupa *n* jalala, jalalani, dampo; *(colloq)* mchafukoge. **~-lorry**; **~per** *n* tipa.

tipple *vi,vt* nywa sana; nywa kileo; lewa *n* kileo; *(hum)* kinywaji chochote. **~r** *n* mlevi.

tipsy *adj (colloq)* -liolewa kidogo; -levi kidogo. **tipsiness** *n* hali ya kulewalewa/kilevilevi/ulevilevi.

tip-toe *adv* **on** ~ kwa ncha za vidole, njongwanjongwa, mzofafa *stand on ~* chuchumia *be on ~ (of expectation)* tazamia kwa uchu sana *vi* enda njongwanjongwa, nyatia, enda kwa kuchuchumia, enda mzofafa.

tirade *n* makaripio, msuto.

tire *see* **tyre**.

tire *vi,vt* ~ **(sb) (out)**; ~ **of** chosha; nyong'onyea. ~ **(sb) (out)**; ~ **of** chosha mtu. **be ~d of** choshwa na *be ~d of each other* chokana. **~d** *adj* hoi, -liochoka, -liolegea kwa uchovu. **be ~d out** hoi kabisa. **~dness** *n* uchovu, kuchoka, mavundevunde, unyong'onyevu. **~less** *adj* -siochoka (kwa urahisi); siokwisha. **~some** *adj* -a kuchosha, -a kutaabisha, sumbufu, -tukutu. **~lessly** *adv* bila kuchoka, pasi kuchoka. **tiring** *adj* -a kuchosha, -a kutaabisha.

tiro, tyro *n* mwanagenzi.

tissue *n* 1 kitambaa kilichofumwa. 2 *(collection, series)* jamii, mfuatano; *a ~ of lies* uwongo mtupu. 3 *(substance)* kitu, mkusanyiko wa seli mwilini, tishu. 4 ~ **paper** *n* karatasi ya shashi *toilet~* karatasi ya chooni/ kuchambia.

tit[1] *n* mtama wa bibi (domo fupi).

tit[2] *n (only in)* ~ **for tat** nipe nikupe; jicho kwa jicho.

tit[3] **teat (vulg sl)** chuchu, ziwa.

titan *n* 1 *(GK)* moja ya majitu yaliyotawala dunia. 2 jitu, jitu maarufu. **~ic** *adj* kubwa mno.

titbit *n* vipande vidogo vizuri (vya chakula/habari, n.k.).

tithe *n* 1 *(rel)* zaka, sehemu ya kumi ya mavuno iliyotolewa kwa kanisa. 2 sehemu ya kumi ya chochote *not a ~* hata kidogo.

titillate *vt* tekenya, nyegeresha, amsha, sisimua. **titillation** *n* mnyeo, msisimko.

titivate *vi,vt (colloq)* kwatua, rembua. ~ **oneself** jiremba, jipamba.

title *n* 1 *(address)* anwani. 2 jina (la heshima), cheo. 3 kichwa (cha makala, n.k.). ~ **page** ukurasa (wa kwanza) wenye jina la kitabu na mwandishi. ~ **role** jina la mhusika ambalo pia ni jina la tamthilia (k.m. Kinjekitile, Hamlet). 4 *(claim, right)* haki, miliki. ~ **to sth/to do sth** *(leg)* haki (ya kudai/kumiliki kitu). ~ **deed** hati ya kumiliki. 5 **credit** *~(credits)* majina ya wasanii wa sinema/TV, n.k. **~d** -enye cheo/jina/anwani. **~d** *adj* -enye jina la heshima (k.m. *Sir, Lord* n.k).

titter *vi* jichekea, fanya kicheko, chekelea *n* kicheko.

tittle *n* **not one jot or ~** hata kidogo/ punje/chembe.

tittle-tattle *n* udaku, umbeya, porojo, soga *vi* piga porojo/soga.

titular 1 *adj* -a jina tu *the ~ ruler* mtawala wa jina tu. 2 -a cheo.

tizzy *n* **be in a ~** *(colloq)* -wa na wasiwasi.

T-junction *n* kiungo cha T (barabara mbili, bomba mbili, n.k.).

TNT *n* baruti kali.

to[1] *prep* 1 -ni *go ~ work* nenda kazini. 2 *(fig uses)* hadi, mpaka *drive sb ~ surrender* chemsha mtu mpaka asalimu amri. 3 *(introducing an indirect object)* -i/-ea kwa *she threw it ~ me* alinitupia kitu. 4 *(of time) quarter ~ six* saa kumi na mbili kasorobo. 5 *(indicating comparison, ration, reference)* kuliko, kwa *I prefer walking ~ running* napenda kutembea kuliko kukimbia *we defeated them three goals ~ one* tuliwafunga mabao matatu kwa moja. 6 -a, ya, wa *key ~ the door* ufunguo wa mlango. 7 kwa heshima/ajili ya *we are drinking ~ your health* tunakunywa kwa ajili yako. 8 hadi *from Monday ~ Friday* Jumatatu hadi Ijumaa. 9 kwa (kila) 100 *cents ~ a shilling* senti 100 kwa (kila) shilingi.

to[2] *adv* 1 *(used after many vv)* ku- *I want ~ play* nataka kucheza. 2 *(with adverbial functions of purpose, result, outcome)* ili- *they came ~ help* wamekuja ili wasaidie. 3 *(used with an inf as a n)* ku- *it is wrong ~ steal* ni vibaya kuiba. 4 *(as a substitute for the inf)* -fanya hivyo *we didn't want ~ go but we had ~* hatukutaka kwenda lakini ilitubidi kufanya hivyo.

to[3] *adv* barabara, imara, kabisa kabisa.

toad *n* chura. ~ **stool** *n* uyoga, kiyoga (agh. wenye sumu)

toady *n* mnafiki, mtu anayejipendekeza, barakala *vt,vi* ~ **(to sb)** wa mnafiki ili kufanikiwa, -jipendekeza kwa rairai, sifusifu mno; lamba miguu.

toast[1] *vt* 1 choma (moto), banika; choma tosti/tosi ~ *one's hands* pasha moto mikono *n* tosti/tosi mkate uliochomwa. ~ **rack** *n* kichaga (cha chuma) cha kuwekea tosti/tosi. **~er** *n* chombo (cha umeme) cha kuchomea tosti/tosi.

toast[2] *vt* pongeza, takia kheri/afya (kwa glasi ya kinywaji) ~ *the bride and bridegroom* nywa kwa afya ya bibi na bwana harusi *n* kupongeza, kutakia kheri *drink a ~* nywa kwa kumpongeza (fulani). **~-master** *n* mtangazaji wa pongezi katika karamu.

tobacco *n* tumbaku. *(pl)* **~nist** *n* mwuza tumbaku/sigara. **~-pouch** *n* mkoba (mfuko) wa kutilia tumbako.

tobaggan *n* sileji (nyembamba ya kupinda mbele) *vi* teleza kwa sileji.

toby-jug *n* bilauri (yenye umbo la mwanadamu.

tocsin *n* kamsa.

tod[1] *n (Scot & N Eng)* mbweha

tod[2] *n* *(sl) on one's ~* pekee, peke yake.

today *n, adv* 1 leo, leo hivi, siku hii *a week ~* baada ya wiki moja kuanzia leo. 2 *(the present time)* siku hizi *the young men of ~* vijana wa siku hizi.

toddle *vi* nyatua, demadema; enda dede; *(colloq)* tembea ~ *off to see a neighbour* enda kumwona jirani. **~r** *n* mtoto anayeanza kutembea/kwenda dede.

toddy *n* 1 kileo (agh wiski) na maji ya moto. 2 tembo.

to-do *n* matata; ghasia, tandabelua, fujo *don't make a ~ about such a small* *matter* usifanye matata juu ya jambo dogo hivi.

toe *n* 1 kidole cha mguu. **from top to ~** toka utosini hadi kidoleni; kamilifu. **step/tread on sb's ~** *(fig)* umbua mtu. **on one's ~** *(fig)* -wa macho. **~-cap** *n* sehemu ya juu ya kiatu inayofunika vidole (agh. buti). **~-hold** *n* kidato wasiwasi. **~ nail** *n* ukucha wa kidole cha mguu. 2 sehemu ya mbele ya soksi/kiatu (inayofunika vidole) *vi* gusa kwa vidole **~ the line** *(of a race)* gusa mstari wa kuanzia mbio kwa vidole; *(fig)* fuata, tii masharti ya chama.

toff *n (slang)* mtu maridadi, mmbuji, mlimbwende.

toffee, toffy *n* tofi; peremende iliyotengenezwa kwa sukari ya kuchemshwa na siagi.

tog *n* **~s** *(colloq)* nguo *vt (slang)* valia. **~ neself up/out (in)** jipamba; valia kilimbwende/kitanashati.

toga *n (Rome)* mgolole.

together *adv* 1 pamoja, -ote, *they went ~* walikwenda pamoja *fight ~* pigana *meet ~* kutana *talk ~* semezana. **~ with** pamoja na. **be ~** -wa pamoja. **get sth/it ~** *(sl)* panga, (ji) kusanya, dhibiti. **put your/our etc, heads ~** shauriana, jadiliana. 2 kwa wakati mmoja *the troubles came ~* matatizo yalianza kwa wakati mmoja/mfululizo *he was absent for a week ~* hakuwepo kwa wiki mfululizo. **~ness** *n* umoja, udugu, mshikamano.

toggle *n* kibanio.

toil *n* kazi, kazi ya taabu, kazi ya sulubu *vi* **~ at** fanya kazi kwa bidii/kwa taabu sana/muda mrefu; jikokota; *(go painfully)* enda kwa taabu, jikokota; *~ up a hill* jikongoja katika kilima. **~er** *n* mvuja jasho. **~some** *adj* -a sulubu.

toilet *n* 1 choo, msala. **~-paper, ~-rol** *n* karatasi (laini) ya chooni. 2 *(attrib) a ~ set* jumla ya vifaa vyote vya kujipambia. **~-powder** poda. **~-table** *n* meza ya vipodozi yenye kioo. 3 kunawa na kuvaa (nguo, n.k.); kujikwatua *make one's ~* vaa, valia.

token *n* 1 *(sign)* dalili, ishara, alama *a white flag is a ~ of surrender* bendera nyeupe ni alama ya ushinde. **in ~ of** kama ushahidi/ishara. **gift ~** zawadi. 2 *(attrib)* kianzio, chanzo, chambele. **~ payment** malipo ya mwanzo/kianzio. **~ strike** mgomo wa kutishia/wa muda mfupi. **~ vote** kura ya bunge ya kukubali matumizi ya fedha za kianzio.

told *pt, pp of* **tell**

tolerate *vt* vumilia, stahimili. **tolerable** *adj* -a kuvumilika, -a kustahimilika, -a kuchukulika; zuri kiasi. **tolerably** *adv* kadiri, kiasi, wastani. **tolerance** *n* stahamala (ya mawazo, maoni, fikra, n.k. za wengine). **tolerant** *adj* -a kuvumilia, -a kuchukuana, stahimilivu *she is very ~* ni mvumilivu sana. **tolerantly** *adv*.

toll[1] *vt, vi* piga/lia polepole (kwa mapigo/sauti ya kurudiarudia) *~ sb's death* piga kengele kuashiria kifo cha fulani *n* mlio wa kengele (inayopigwa pigo moja moja polepole).

toll[2] *n* 1 ushuru, kodi, ada (agh ya kivuko, barabara, bandari). **~-bar** *n* mlangoni pa kulipia kodi ada, n.k. **~-house** *n* nyumba ya watoza kodi. 2 *(fig)* maafa, gharama/hasara ya vifo vingi. 3 **~ call** *n* simu ya gharama kubwa kuliko simu za kawaida; simu ya mbali.

tomahawk *n* shoka: aina ya silaha ya Wamarekani wa asili *vt* piga kwa shoka.

tomato *n (plant)* mnyanya, *(fruit)* nyanya, tungule *~soup* supu ya nyanya.

tomb *n* kaburi. *(fig)* **~stone** *n* jiwe la kaburi.

tombola *n* tombola: aina ya mchezo; bahati nasibu.

tom-boy *n* mtoto wa kike mwenye mwendo/tabia ya watoto wa kiume.

tom-cat *n* paka dume.

tome *n* kitabu kikubwa/kizito, juzuu; buku.

tomfool *n* mpuuzi, mpumbavu; *(attrib)* -pumbavu ~ *speech* hotuba ya kipumbavu. **~ery** *n* upumbavu, upuuzi.

tommy-gun *n* bunduki (nyepesi) ya kutema risasi.

tommy-rot *n (colloq)* upuuzi kabisa *that's all* ~ huo ni upuuzi mtupu.

tomorrow *n,adv* kesho *day after* ~ kesho kutwa; *(third day after)* mtondo; *(fourth day after)* mtondogoo ~ *night* kesho usiku. ~ **week** siku nane baadaye.

tomtom *n* ngoma (agh msondo, mrungura).

ton *n* 1 tani: kilo elfu moja *(of a ship)* shehena ya ujazo futi arobaini za mraba. 2 **the** ~ *(sl)* kasi ya maili mia moja kwa saa *vi* ~ **up** endesha kwa kasi kubwa katika mashindano ya pikipiki. 3 *(colloq)* tele, chungu mzima *he is worth ~s of money* yeye ni tajiri kabisa *~s of* wingi wa ~ *of people* watu chungu nzima. **~nage** *n* 1 ukubwa wa ngama. 2 uwezo wa kusheheni. 3 jumla ya ukubwa wa ngama kwa meli za nchi moja. 4 gharama za usafirishaji kwa tani moja ya shehena.

tonne *n* tani moja ya metriki (kilo elfu moja).

tone *n* 1 *(sound)* sauti; toni: namna ya tabia ya sauti *in angry ~s* kwa sauti ya hasira. **~-deaf** *adj* sioweza kutofautisha toni. **~-poem** *n* muziki wa kuashiria wazo la kishairi au kisa fulani. 2 *(manner, style)* tabia, hali, mwelekeo *the ~ of the school is good* tabia ya shule ni nzuri. 3 kupanda na kushuka kwa sauti. 4 *(of colour)* kiwango cha rangi. 5 siha nzuri ya viungo vya mwili *good, muscular ~* maungo mazuri. **~d** *adj* -enye toni/ sauti fulani. **~less** *adj* -sio na rangi/moyo hai; baridi. **~lessly** *adv*. **tonal** *adj* -a toni; -a sauti. **tonality** *n (mus)* mpangilio wa sauti/muziki kufuatana na ufunguo, n.k. *vt,vi* 1 ~ **(sth down)** pungua; tuliza, zimua *the crowd soon ~d down* umati wa watu ulitulia upesi. ~ **(sth) up** zidisha rangi, ongeza nguvu, sisimua. 2 ~ **in (with)** *(colours)* chukuana *the colour ~s well with the others* rangi hii inachukuana vizuri na nyingine. 3 toa/geuza toni/sauti; geuza rangi.

tongs *n* **(pair of)** ~ koleo; kishikio *coal* ~ kishikio cha mkaa.

tongue *n* 1 ulimi. **find one's ~** weza kusema (baada ya kuondokana na aibu). **have/say sth with/speak with one's ~ in one's cheek** geresha, fanya utani. **lose one's ~** kaukiwa, vuta ulimi, ona aibu kuzungumza. **have a ready ~** -wa fasaha, -mwepesi kujibu. **hold one's ~** nyamaza. **keep a civil ~ in one's head** -wa na adabu, tokuwa jasiri. **~-tied** *adj* nyamavu, bubu. **~-twister** neno gumu (kutamka). 2 lugha. **one's mother ~** lugha asili (ya mtu), lugha ya kwanza. 3 nyama ya ulimi *ham and ~ sandwiches* sandiwichi ya hemu na nyama ya ulimi. 4 *(of land)* rasi. **~d** *adj (in compounds)* -enye ulimi *a sharp ~d women* mwanamke mwenye ulimi wa upanga.

tonic *adj* 1 -a kutia afya na nguvu. 2 -a sauti, -a mkazo *n* dawa ya kuchangamsha mwili. ~ **water** toniki.

tonight *n,adv* usiku huu, usiku wa leo ~ *s concert* mchezo wa leo usiku.

tonsil *n* tukwa, findo. **~litis** *n* mafindofindo.

tonsorial *adj* -a kinyozi.

tonsure *n* kipara cha utosini, kunyoa kipara cha utosini *vt* nyoa kipara cha utosini.

tontine *n* mgawanyo wa mapato (agh. ya bima) ambayo huongezeka kila mbia anapofariki.

too *adv* 1 mno, kupita kiasi *that is ~ small* (hiyo) ni ndogo mno. 2 *(in addition)* pia, vilevile. 3 *(phrases)* **all ~ soon/quickly** upesi/haraka mno. **none ~ soon** kwa kuwahi kidogo **have one ~ many** kunywa zaidi ya kipimo.

took *pt of* **take**.

tool *n* 1 chombo; kifaa, ala, zana

a bad workman always blames his ~s mchagua jembe si mkulima. **~-bag** *n* mkoba wa vifaa (vya ufundi). **~-box** *n* kisanduku cha vifaa. **~-holder** *n* kipingo cha ala. 2 karagosi, kibaraka *vt* 1 nakshi (ncha za jalada la kitabu) kwa kifaa cha moto. 2 ~ **up** weka vifaa vya kazi katika kiwanda.

toot *vt* piga honi; *(fig) ~ one's own horn* jivuna ~ *the whistle* piga mbinja *n* mlio wa honi/filimbi/tarumbeta.

tooth *n* 1 jino; *(incisor)* jino la mbele; *(molar)* gego, chego. **(eye ~)** chonge. **false** ~ jino bandia *go to have a ~ out* enda kung'oa jino. **armed to the teeth** -enye silaha nyingi; -enye ulinzi mkali. **cast sth in a person's teeth** karipia, gombeza mtu. **escape by the skin of one's teeth** ponea chupuchupu. **fight ~ and nail** pigana kufa na kupona. **get one's teeth into sth** fanya kazi kwa bidii. **lie in one's teeth/throat** danganya bila aibu. **long in the ~** zee. **show one's teeth** tishia, ogofya. **have a sweet ~** penda vyakula vitamu. **in the teeth of** dhidi ya/kwa kukabiliana na. **~ache** maumivu ya jino. **~-brush** *n* mswaki. ~ **paste/powder** *n* dawa ya meno. ~ **pick** kimbaka, kichokoa meno. 2 kitu mfano wa jino. **fine-~ comb** chanuo/ kitana chenye meno ya karibukaribu. **go over/through sth with a fine-~ comb** chambua kitu kwa makini. 3 *(pl coloq)* nguvu. **~ed** *(attrib)* -enye meno. **~less** *adj* kibogoyo, -sio na meno. **~some** *adj (liter) (of food)* tamu; -a kuchapukia.

tootle *vi* puliza (filimbi) taratibu au kwa mfululizo.

top[1] *n* pia. **sleep like a ~** lala kama pono, lala fofofo.

top[2] *n* 1 *(usu* **the ~ (of**) kilele; upeo; sehemu ya juu. **on ~** juu. **on (the) ~ of** juu ya; zaidi ya hayo. **~ to bottom** kabisa, juu mpaka chini. **blow one's ~** *(colloq)* hamaki. 2 sehemu ya juu ya kitu/upande wa juu. **bottle ~** kizibo, kifuniko. **go over the ~** *(mil)* toka handakini na kumshambulia adui; *(fig)* tenda mara moja baada ya kusitasita. **on ~ of the world** *(colloq)* -enye furaha kupita kiasi. 3 (nafasi ya) juu/mbele. **come to the ~** *(fig)* pata/heshima/mafanikio. **reach/be at the ~ of the ladder** fikia/-wa katika ngazi ya juu. 4 kipeo, kikomo. 5 *(motoring)* **in ~ gear** katika gia ya juu. 6 majani (ya mmea ambao huliwa mizizi yake); kisamvu. 7 **the big ~** hema kubwa la sarakasi. 8 *(compounds and attrib)* **~-boot** *n* buti refu (la magotini). ~ **coat** *n* koti. **be ~ dog** *(sl)* mshindi. ~ **drawer** *n* tabaka la juu (katika jamii). **~-dress** *vt* sambaza/tandaza mbolea ardhini. **~-dressing** kutandaza chokaa katika shamba. **~-flight/~-notch** *attr (colloq)* bora, -a daraja la juu. **~-gallant** *adj, n* tanga la tatu. **~hat** (*also* **~ per**) *n* kofia refu ya hariri. **~-heavy** *adj* -liozidi uzito kwa juu. **~-hole** *adj (dated sl)* zuri/safi sana. **~knot** *n* shungi. **~mast** *n* cheleko, mstamu. **~most** *adj* -a juu kupita zote. **~ people** watu wenye madaraka ya juu. **~-ranking** *adj* -a daraja la juu. **~sail** *n* tanga la miaa. ~ **secret** siri kuu/kubwa. **~less** *adj (of a woman's dress)* -a kifua wazi; -a matiti nje *vt* 1 funika, weka sehemu ya juu. 2 fikia kilele; -wa kileleni, -wa juu. 3 ~ **(sth) up** jazia, ongeza nguvu. ~ **(sth) out** zindua jengo refu kwa sherehe. 4 vuka, zidi, tendesa, tia fora. **to ~ it all** juu ya yote; kana kwamba hayo yote hayatoshi. 5 kata ncha; chuma majani (ya mimea ya mizizi). **~ping** *adj (colloq)* -zuri sana, -a kupendeza sana. **~pingly** *adv.* **~s** *n (pl) (usu* **the ~s**) *(colloq)* nzuri kupita -ote, bora kabisa.

topaz *n* topazi: madini ya njano ya kung'aa; kito cha madini haya.

tope *vi, vt (dated)* lewa; kunywa kila wakati; kuwa mlevi. **~r** *n* mlevi (wa kila siku).

topiary *n* ustadi wa kukata (majani, uzio, miti midogo, n.k.).

topi,topee *n* helmeti la jua.

topic *n* mada *~s of the day* mada za siku. **~al** *adj* -a (manufaa/ mapendeleo) ya wakati uliopo, -a siku hizi *a ~ news/film* filamu ya matukio ya wakati huu.**~ally** *adv*.

topography *n* topografia: maelezo juu ya mandhari ya nchi. **topographical** *adj* -a mandhari/sura ya nchi; -a topografia. **topographically** *adv*.

topple *vt,vi* tikisa, pindua, anguka, angusha *the dictator was ~d from power* dikteta alipinduliwa.

topsy-turvy *adv (colloq)* kichwa chini, kwa kupinduka, shaghalabaghala *adj* -a fujo, -liochafuka, -liovurugika. **~dom** *n* mchafuko, ghasia; fujo.

tor *n* kilima/kilele chenye majabali.

torch *n* 1 tochi, mwenge; *(fig)* nuru *hand on the ~* endeleza elimu. **carry a ~ for sb** penda mtu asiye kupenda. **~ light** *n* mwanga wa kurunzi/tochi. **~-race** *n (in ancient Greece)* mbio za mwenge. **~-singer** *n* mwanamke anayeimba nyimbo za mapenzi.

tore *pt of* **tear**.

torment *n (pain)* maumivu makali, mateso, uchungu; maudhi *vt* 1 tesa, tia maumivu makali; tia uchungu, umiza vibaya, udhi *~ed with hunger* teseka kwa njaa. 2 *(worry)* sumbua, udhi, hangaisha, tia wasiwasi *don't ~ him with stupid questions* usimsumbue na maswali ya kipumbavu. **~or** *n* msumbufu.

torn *pp of* **tear**.

tornado *n* kimbunga, chamchela.

torpedo *n* topido, kombora. **~-boat** manowari ya kurushia topido *vt* piga kwa topido; *(fig)* shambulia (sera, taasisi, n.k.) na kuizika. **~-plane** *n* ndege ya kurushia topido. **~-tube** *n* neli ya kurushia topido.

torpid *adj* 1 legevu, goigoi. 2 (*of animals that hibernate*) bila kusogea, tuli kabisa, bila hisi. **~ly** *adv*. **~ness; ~ity** *n* uzito, ugoigoi.

torpor *n* usingizi, uzito, ulegevu, unyogovu.

torque *n* 1 mkufu wa chuma. 2 nguvu ya kuzungusha kitu kama vile propela, msongonyo.

torrent *n* 1 mvo, mfoko/mbubujiko wa nguvu (hasa wa maji). **a ~ of abuse** mbubujiko (wa matusi/meneno). **~ial** *adj* -ingi sana na -enye nguvu nyingi *~ rain* mvua nyingi.

torrid *adj (of the weather, a country)* -a hari sana, -a joto jingi, -a tropiki *~ zone* sehemu ya dunia iliyo katikati ya tropiki. **~ ity** *n* hari, joto kali.

torsion *n* msokoto; kusokota, usokotaji. **~al** *adj*.

torso *n* 1 pingiti. 2 sanamu (bila kichwa, miguu, wala mikono).

tort *n* kosa la daawa; utesi. **~feasor** *n* mtenda kosa la kidaawa.

tortilla *n* kiwanda cha Mexico.

tortoise *n* kobe. **~-shell** *n* gamba la kobe.

tortuous *adj* -a vizingo vingi, -a kupindapinda, -a mapindi, -a minyongo; *(fig)* -enye hila, danganyifu, laghai. **~ly** *adv*.

tourture *n* mateso, maumivu makali *an instrument of ~* chombo cha kutesea (mtu) *put to the ~* tesa *~ of the damned* mateso ya kuzimu/motoni *vt* tesa umiza/vibaya. **~r** *n* mtesaji.

tory n *see* **conservative**

tosh *n (sl)* upuzi, upumbavu.

toss *vt,vi* 1 rusha (juu), tupa. **~ sth aside** tupa (kitu) pembeni. **~ (up) a coin, toss (sb) for sth; ~ up** rusha sarafu hewani (kwa kupiga kura). **~ -up** *n* urushaji wa sarafu (ili kupiga kura), bahati nasibu. 2 sukasuka, tikisika, gaagaa, furukuta *the sick child ~ed about in its sleep* mtoto mgonjwa aligaagaa usingizini. 3 **~ sth off** nywa -ote; toa/zalisha kitu harakaharaka bila taabu/juhudi *n* 1 urushaji *a contemptuous ~ of the head* mdekuo *take a ~* tupwa na farasi. 2 **win/lose the ~** bahatisha/ kosa mtupo. **~er** *n* mrushaji.

tot[1] *n 1 (often* **tiny ~**) kitoto kidogo. 2 *(colloq) (of liquor)* toti: kiasi kidogo cha kileo kikali.

tot[2] *vt,vi* **~ (sth) up** *(colloq)* jumlisha; fikia *expenses ~ting up to $100* gharama zinazofikia $100.

total *n* jumla *adj* -ote, kamili, zima, tupu. ~ **war** vita kamili *vt,vi* jumlisha; tia fikia. **~ly** *adv* kabisa ~ *blind* kipofu kabisa. **~ity** *n* jumla; ukamilifu, utimilifu.

totalitarian *adj (of govt)* -a imla, -a chama kimoja; isiyopingwa/isiyo na upinzani. **~ism** *n*.

tote *vt (sl)* beba (bunduki).

totem *n* 1 mnyama; kizimu: kitu kiwakilishi cha uungu/mizimu. 2 sanamu/ishara za mungu/mzimu. **~ism** *n* imani ya tambiko, utambikaji; usira. ~ **pole** *n* mti wa mzimu.

totter *vi* 1 pepa, pepesuka, yumbayumba, jikongoja, jikokota. 2 tikisika, tetema, tetereka. **~y** *adj*.

touch[1] *n* 1 kugusa; mguso. **at a ~** kwa kuguswa tu. 2 hisi ya kugusa *soft to the ~* laini, nyororo. **~stone** *n* kipimo, kigezo, kiwango. 3 rekebisho (la mwisho) *final ~es of sth* marekebisho ya mwisho mwisho ya jambo fulani. 4 **a ~ (of)** kiasi kidogo, dalili *there is a ~ of hatred in his speech* ipo dalili ya chuki katika hotuba yake. 5 mtindo, ufundi, namna ya kupiga/kutengeneza kitu n.k. **~-type** *vi* piga mashine bila ya kutazama. 6 mawasiliano, mahusiano. **in/out of ~ (with)** -enye kuwasiliana/kutowasiliana na, -wa/-tokuwa na habari kuhusu. **lose ~ (with)** potezana, -towasiliana. 7 *(football and Rugby)* nje ya uwanja. **~lines** pembe za chaki. 8 **a near ~** *n* sura, ponea chupuchupu. **~-and-go** *adj (colloq)* -a bahati nasibu, -a kubahatisha. 9 **a soft/easy ~** *(sl)* mtu aliye rahisi kuombwa au kukopwa *vt,vi* 1 gusa; gusana; gusanisha; *(lightly)* papasa; *(reach)* fikia kikomo cha huzuni, n.k. ~ **wood** pisha mbali. 2 *(concern)* pasa, husu. 3 *(affect)* athiri, sikitisha, huzunisha ~ *sb on a tender place (lit or fig)* gusa/umiza mtu. 4 *(usu neg)* -la, onja (chakula) *she hasn't ~ed food for three days* hajaonja chakula kwa siku tatu. 5 *(equal, rival in merit)* faa, shinda; lingana na; fikia *no one can ~ him as a novelist* hakuna anayelingana naye kwa uandishi wa riwaya. 6 (*pp* **~ed**) *(colloq)* punguani, -enye wazimu *he seems to be ~ed* kama punguani/ana kichaa. 7 weza, jaribu; shughulikia *she couldn't ~ the first two questions* hakuweza kufanya hata maswali mawili ya mwanzo. 8 bonyeza, sukuma taratibu *he ~ed the bell* alipiga kengele (kwa kubonyeza swichi). 9 umiza/haribu kidogo, gusa. 10 *(special uses)* ~ **at** *(of a ship)* tia nanga. ~ **down** *(rugby) funga goli; (of aircraft)* tua. ~ **sb for sth** *(sl)* pata fedha (agh kwa kuomba). ~ **sth off** ipua (mzinga; n.k.); *(fig)* anzisha, sababisha. ~ **on/upon sth** gusa, gusia, shughulikia jambo kwa muda mfupi. **~sth up** rekebisha, remba. **~able** *adj* -a kuweza kugusika. **~ing** *adj* huzunishi, -a kutia huruma *prep* kuhusu, kuhusiana na. **~ingly** *adv*. **touchy** *adj* -enye hamaki, -a/-enye harara. **~ily** *adv*. **~iness** *n*.

tough *adj* 1 *(of meat, material also)* gumu. 2 *(of material/thing)* -siotatuka/katika/zeeka kwa urahisi. 3 thabiti, stahamilivu. 4 (*of persons*) mbabe; mjeuri; katili. ~ **customer** *(colloq)* fidhuli, mkorofi. 5 korofi, -enye kiburi, sugu. **be/get ~ (with sb)** shupalia (jambo). 6 gumu kutekelezwa ~ *job* kazi ngumu. 7 ~ **luck** *(colloq)* mkosi, bahati mbaya *n (also* **~ie**) *(colloq)* mjeuri; mbabe. **~ly** *adj* **~ness** *n*. **~en** *vt,vi* imarisha, shupaza; shupaa.

toupee *n* kibandiko cha nywele za bandia; kichungi.

tour 1 utalii, safari ya kutalii/kutazama/kuona nchi. 2 matembezi. **on ~** safarini. 3 *(inspection)* ziara. 4 kipindi cha kazi ng'ambo *vt,vi* talii; tembelea ~ *about a country* zunguka nchi, safiri ~ *a country* tembelea nchi. **~ing** *n,adj*, ~ *car* gari la utalii ~ *party* kikundi cha utalii. **~st** *n* mtalii *(attrib)* -a utalii *a ~ agency*

wakala wa utalii ~ *ist class (of liners, airliners)* daraja la pili. **~ism** *n* utalii.
tour de force *n* mashindano ya kupimana nguvu, ubabe/ubingwa.
tournament *n* 1 mashindano. 2 *(middle ages)* mashindano kati ya wapanda farasi wawili.
tourney *n see* **tournament**
torniquet *n* fundo (la kuzuia damu).
tousle *vt* chafua, vuruga, timua *~d hair* nywele timtimu.
tout *vi,vt* ~ **(for)** tangaza/tangazisha (mali au huduma) ili inunuliwe na kutumiwa *n* mwuza bahari (hasa kuhusu mashindano ya farasi) *ticket~* mlanguzi wa tiketi.
tout ensemble *n* yote kwa pamoja, jumla yote.
tow *vt* vuta (kwa kamba), fungasha *n* 1 kamba/mnyororo wa kuvutia. 2 uvuto/uvutwaji kwa kamba, n.k. **have/take sth in ~** vuta kitu **have a family in ~** *(colloq)* andamana na familia. **~/~ing path** njia pembezoni mwa mfereji au mto inayotumika kwa kuvutia chombo.
toward(s) *prep* 1 kuelekea *walking ~ the sea* tembea kuelekea baharini. 2 juu ya, mintarafu ya, kuhusu/kuhusiana na *what is your stand ~ this plan* una msimamo gani mintarafu ya mpango huu. 3 kwa ajili ya (kusaidia) *save money ~ the children's education* weka fedha kwa ajili ya elimu ya watoto. 4 *(of time)* karibu *~ the end of the year* karibu ya mwisho wa mwaka.
towel *n* taulo. **~rack/horse** kining'inizia/kiangika taulo. ~ **rail** chuma cha kuangikia taulo *vt* futa kwa taulo. **~ling** *(US* **~ing**) kitambaa cha kutengenezea taulo.
tower *n* 1 mnara. 2 *(fig)* **a ~of strength** mtu wa kutegemewa wakati wa matatizo. 3 **water ~** mnara wa tangi la maji. ~ **block** jengo lenye ghorofa nyingi *vi* enda juu sana. ~ **above sb** *(fig, of eminent persons)* pita sana kwa uwezo, akili au maadili. **~ing** *adj (esp) in a ~ range* -enye hasira kali.
town *n* 1 mji. **be /go out on the ~** enda kustarehe (mjini). 2 *(attrib)* -a mji. ~ **clerk** karani wa Halmashauri ya mji. ~ **councillor** diwani (wa mji). ~ **hall** (jengo la) Halmashauri ya mji. ~ **house** nyumba ya mjini. ~ **planning** mipango miji; eneo/mahala pa biashara/maduka/majumba, n.k. *goto ~ (sl)* tembea/vinjari mjini (na kumwaga fedha). 4 **man about ~** (mtu) mpenda starehe za mji, alwatani. 5 **the ~** wakazi wa mji. 6 **the ~** mji kwa ujumla, mjini. 7 ~ **folk** *n (pl)* watu wa mji fulani; watu waishio mijini *~ people* wana mji. **~sman** mwana mji, alwatani, mzaliwa wa mjini. **~ee** *n (derog)* mwanamji asiyejua mambo ya vijijini. **~ship** *n.* 1 *(US, Canada)* mji na pambizo; eneo (lote) la mji. 2 (*Australia*) eneo lililotengwa kwa ajili ya mji. 3 (*S. Africa*) kitongoji: eneo wanamoishi watu wasio wazungu.
toxic *adj* -a sumu. **~ity** *n* kiwango cha kusumisha. **~ology** elimu juu ya asili na athari za sumu. **toxicological** *adj* -a kuhusu sumu au taaluma ya sumu **toxin** *n* sumu; toksini. **toxaemia** (*also* **tox-emia**) *n* kusumu damu.
toy *n* mwanasesere; kidude/kitu cha kuchezea watoto *~ trade n* biashara ya vitu vya kuchezea watoto *vi* chezea; chezacheza na. ~ **with sth** chezacheza na kitu fulani.
trace *n* 1 dalili; alama; (*track*) nyayo *(of thing crawling) utambazi;* (*of thing dragged*) mkokoto, maburuzo, mburuzo. 2 kiasi kidogo sana, chembe *without a ~ of pity* bila huruma, hata kidogo *vt,vi* 1 ~ **sth (out)** chora, fuata nyayo/alama. 2 *(copy)* fuatisha, nakili (kwa kutumia karatasi angavu). ~ **a line** fuatisha mstari. 3 andika polepole/kwa shida. 4 fuata/gundua (mtu/kitu) kwa kutumia alama, nyayo na vidokezo vingine. ~ **(sth/sb) back to sth)** tafuta/pata asili ya kitu kwa kuangalia miaka ya nyuma; tafuta

asili ya kitu kwa kutumia ushahidi kutokana na. 5 gundua mahali au ukubwa wa kitu kutokana na mabaki yake. **~able** *adj* -a kuonekana/ kutafutika/kufuatilika. **~ r** *n* 1 mfuatiliaji, mtafutaji. 2 mfuatishaji, mnakilishi. 3 chombo cha kunakilia. 4 *(often ~r bullet/shell)* risasi/kombora linayosafiri kwa kuacha moto/moshi nyuma. **~r element** element katiti. **tracing** *n* kunakili. **~ paper** *n* karatasi ya kunakilia.

trace *n* hatamu **kick over the ~s** *(fig)* goma; asi; kosa nidhamu.

tracery *n* pambo la mistarimistari (ya miliamilia); pambo la mawe dirishani.

trachea *n* koo, umio wa pumzi.

trachoma *n* trakoma: mtoto wa jicho.

track *n* 1 alama (za nyayo, gari, n.k.); mkokoto, mburuzo uachwao na magari, watu, wanyama, n.k. **be on sb's ~/on the ~ of sb** fuata/saka mtu fulani. **cover up one's ~ s** ficha nyendo/shughuli zako. **have a one ~ mind** fuata/shikilia mtazamo mmoja. **keep/lose ~ of sb/sth** fuatia/shindwa kufuatia (mtu/kitu). **make ~** *(colloq)* ondoka; kimbia. **make ~s for** *(colloq)* elekea, ongoza *in one's ~ (sl)* papo, mahali mtu asimamapo. **off the ~** *(fig)* mbali na makusudio, nje ya mada; (fuata) njia potovu. 2 reli za garimoshi *the train left the ~s* garimoshi limeacha njia. **on/from the wrong side of the ~** (*US*) (toka) upande wa watu wa chini katika jamii. 3 uwanja wa mbio za miguu/ magari/baiskeli, n.k. **~ suit** suti ya ridhaa. 4 minyororo (ya matrekta au vifaru vya jeshi inayotumika badala ya magurudumu) *vt* 1 fuatia (njia, mkondo, nyayo, mkokoto). **~ing station** kituo kinachoongoza vyombo vya angani. **~sb/sth down** kamata, fuma. **~ out** fuatilia. 2 (sinema, TV) zungusha kamera huko na huko ili kupiga picha. **~ and field** *adj* -enye njia za kupitia. **~er** *n* mwindaji. **~erdog** *n* mbwa mfuatiaji/ anayefuatilia wahalifu. **~layer** *n* mtandika reli. **~laying** *n* kazi ya kutandika reli. **~ man** *n* mwanariadha. **~ way** *n (of train)* reli.

tract[1] *n* eneo; nchi; jimbo. 2 mfumo wa viungo (vya mwili).

tract[2] *n* kijitabu kinachohusu mambo ya dini.

tractable *adj* -elekevu, -a kutii, tiifu, -sikivu. tractability *n* utii, usikivu, usikizi, welekevu.

traction *n* nguvu ya kuvutia. **~ engine** injini ya kuvutia mizigo mizito.

tractor *n* trekta, tingatinga.

trad *n (colloq) abbr of* **traditional**.

trade 1 biashara. **the ~** *(colloq)* watengenezaji na wauzaji wa bidhaa fulani; *(fig)* sifa bainifu. **~ name** *n* jina la bidhaa. **~ price** *n* bei ya jumla. **~ (s) union** chama cha wafanyakazi. **~ unionism** mfumo wa vyama vya wafanyakazi. **~unionist** mwanachama wa chama cha wafanyakazi. **~ wind** *n* pepo kali zinazovuma daima dumu kuelekea ikweta zikitokea kusini mashariki na kaskazini mashariki. **the T~s** pepo hizo. 2 kazi (agh. za ufundi), shughuli za uchumi. **~folk; ~ s people** *n* wafanyabiashara, wauza duka wachuuzi. **~s man** mwuza duka *vi,vt* 1 **~ (in) (with)** fanya biashara. **trading estate** eneo la viwanda. **trading stamp** kuponi za kupatia bidhaa au pesa. 2 **~ sth for sth** badilishana; uza mali kwa mali. 3 **~ sth in** toa mali ya zamani kama sehemu ya manunuzi ya mali mpya. 4 **~ on/upon** tumia (kitu) vibaya kunufaika. 5 nunua; jinufaisha. **~r** *n* mfanyabiashara, mchuuzi. **trading** *n* biashara *adj* -a biashara.

tradition *n* desturi; mila; mapokeo, mafundisho yaliyotokea zamani. **~al** *adj* -a mapokeo, -a desturi. **~ ally** *adv* kimapokeo. **~ alism** *n* imani juu ya mapokeo. **~ alist** *n* mfuata mapokeo/desturi.

traduce *vt (formal)* chongea, singizia, kashifu/zulia *n* mchongezi, msingiziaji, mzushi.

traffic *n* 1 nyendo/wendaji wa watu/ magari barabarani/ndege angani; watu, magari yanayopitapita barabarani/ ndege angani. **~ circle** kiplefti, panda, kizingwa. **~ indicator/~ator** *n* indiketa ya gari, ishara, kiashiria. **~ic jam** msongamano wa magari barabarani. **~ light(s)** taa zinazoongoza magari. 2 (biashara ya) usafirishaji watu/mizigo kwa barabara, meli, ndege na reli; mizigo, watu wanaosafirishwa kwa magari, meli, reli, ndege. 3 magendo, biashara haramu ya madawa ya kulevya. 4 wanunuzi wanaotembelea eneo la biashara. 5 mawasiliano/shughuli baina ya watu *vi* **~ in sth (with sb)** fanya biashara ya (na), chuuza, badilishana mali. **~er** *n* mfanyabiashara (hasa) ya magendo. **a drugs ~** muuza madawa ya kulevya.

tragedy *n* 1 (mchezo wa) tanzia. 2 (*disaster*) msiba, sikitiko, tanzia, jambo liletalo huzuni. **tragedian** 1 mwandishi wa (michezo ya) tanzia. 2 mchezo tanzia. **tragedienne** *n* mwanamke mcheza tanzia. **tragic** *adj* -a tanzia, -a msiba, -a huzuni, -a majonzi. **tragicomedy** *n* tanzia-ramsa. **tragicomic (al)** *adj* -a tanzia-ramsa. **tragically** *adv*.

trail *n* 1 alama, mabaki, nyayo, mchirizo **~** *of destruction* alama za ufisadi, mabaki ya maangamizi. 2 mkondo, utambao, harufu. **hot on the ~ (of)** *(lit or fig)* -lio karibukaribu/ -nayofuata karibu. 3 *(path)* njia; ujia *vi,vt* 1 vuta, burura, buruza. 2 andama, fuata alama/mchirizi, n.k. 3 *(of plant) tambaa; (of person)* jikongoja, jikokota. **~er** *n* 1 *(of lorry)* tela; *(of cinema)* trela. 2 mtambaazi.

train[1] *vt,vi* 1 **~** *(for)* fundisha, funza, jifundisha, jifunza. 2 elekeza. **~ sth on/upon sth** lenga, elekeza. **~ee** *n* mkurufunzi. **~er** *n* 1 mkufunzi; mazoezi. **in/out of ~ing** -wa/-tokuwa na afya (k.m. kwa mashindano). **go into ~ing** fanya mazoezi. **~ing college** *n* chuo cha mafunzo. **~ing-ship** meli ya kufunzia ubaharia.

train[2] *n* 1 *(locomotive)* garimoshi, treni. **~ferry** *n* kivuko cha treni. **~-man** *n* mfanyakazi wa garimoshi. 2 msafara, msururu. 3 mfuatano, mfululizo. 4 *(of dress)* mkia (sehemu ya vazi inayokokotezwa). **~bearer** *n* mshika mkia. 5 mstari wa baruti. **in ~** -nayoandaliwa.

traipse *vi (colloq)* jikongoja, jivuta.

trait *n* tabia, sifa pambazi/bainishi.

traitor *n* **~to one's party** saliti chama. **turn ~** -wa msaliti. **~ous** *adj* haini. **traitress** *n* msaliti wa kike. **~ously** *adv*.

trajectory *n* tao la mtupo angani.

tram[1] *n* uzi wa hariri.

tram[2] *n (also* **~ car**) tramu: treni ya umeme ya abiria (mijini). **~ line** reli ya tramu.

trammel *n (pl)* **~s** vipingamizi, vikwazo *vt* kwaza.

tramp ti,vt 1 enda kwa miguu. 2 tembea kwa kishindo *n* 1 **the ~ of** mshindo wa miguu. 2 mwendo mrefu. 3 mzururaji (agh. msokwao). 4 mashua sanyi.

trample *vt,vi* 1 **~ sth (down)** kanyaga, vyoga, liwata. 2 **~ on** kandamiza. 3 **~ about** tembea kwa kishindo *n* mshindo wa miguu.

trampline *n* turubali (la wanasarakasi).

trance *n* 1 kupagawa/mpagao. 2 kuzubaa/mzubao.

tranquil *adj* tulivu, -a raha, anana; (*sea*) shwari. **~ ly** *adv*. **~ity** *n* utulivu *political~* amani. **~ lize** *vt,vi* poza, tuliza maumivu (mara nyingi kwa dawa); tulia, poa. **~lizer** *n* kitulizaji/kitulizo, dawa ya kutuliza.

trans pref 1 -a kuvuka; -a ng'ambo/ ughaibu. 2 -a kupitia. 3 -a kubadili.

transact *vt* **~ sth (with sb)** shughulika na, endesha (biashara/shughuli na fulani). **~ion** *n* **the ~ a of** mapatano (ya kibiashara). 2 shughuli, amali. 3 *(pl)* **~s** *(record)* kumbukumbu.

transalpine *n* -a ng'ambo ya/kuvuka.

transatlantic *adj* -a ng'ambo ya bahari

ya atlantiki, -a kuvuka atlantiki.

transcend *vt* vuka mipaka; pita/zidi sana (uwezo wa binadamu); fanya miujiza. **~ental** *adj* 1 -a kupita uwezo wa binadamu, -a ruiya/njozi. 2 *(colloq)* vungivu. **~entally** *adv*. **~entalism** *n* unjozi: imani kwamba maarifa hutokana na kuchunguza shughuli ndani ya ubongo, licha ya tajriba, mazoea n.k. **~entalist** *n* mruiya.

transcontinental *adj* -a kuvuka kontinenti.

transcribe *vt* nakili; nukuu **transcript** *n* nakala, kitu kilichonakiliwa. **transcription** *n* kunakili; unukuzi.

transept *n* upande wa (kulia na kushoto wa) kanisa.

transfer[1] *n* uhamisho, hawilisho. **~ fee** ada ya uhawilisho *vt,vi* ~ **(sb/sth) (from) (to)** 1 hawilisha, hama, hamisha. 2 kabidhi. 3 nakili, hamisha. 4 badili (treni, basi, n.k.). **~ able** *adj* -a kuhamishika/kubadilishika. **~ ability** *n* uhamisho, uhawilishi.

transfigure *vt* geuza, badilisha (hasa kuwa -zuri zaidi), remba. **transfiguration** *n* mabadiliko; kugeuza; kuremba.

transfix *vt* 1 choma (kwa mkuki, mshale, n.k.). 2 *(with terror)* duwaza, stusha, piga bumbuazi.

transform *vt* ~ **sth (into sth)** geuza/badili (umbo la kitu). **~ sb beyond recognition** sawiji. **~able** *adj* -enye kuweza kugeuzika. **~ation** *n* 1 mgeuzo; kubadili; mbadiliko. **~er** *n* transfoma, kigeuzi.

transfuse *vt* -pa damu **transfusion** *n* kupa damu; upaji wa damu.

transgress *vt* 1 vuka mpaka. 2 vunja (sheria, mapatano). 3 kosa, vunja mwiko, tenda dhambi. **~ion** *n* 1 kosa. 2 dhambi. 3 uhalifu. **~or** *n* 1 mkosaji; mhalifu, mvunja sheria; mtenda dhambi.

transient *adj* -a kupita, siodumu; -a mara moja tu; -a muda mfupi tu. **transience/transiency** *n*.

transistor *n* 1 transista: kidude cha elektroniki (kitumikacho) badala ya vali. **~ized** -enye transista. 2 redio (ya transista).

transit *n* 1 kupita, kupeleka, kuchukua. **in ~** njiani, safarini. **goods in ~** bidhaa zinazosafirishwa. **~ camp** kambi ya wasafiri/wapita njia. **~ visa** visa ya kupita. 2 njia ya sayari ipitayo katika eneo la sayari nyingine. **~ion** *n* mabadiliko, mageuzi, mpito. **~ ion period** muda wa mabadiliko/mageuzi. **~ional** *adj* -a mpito/kupita /kubadilika/kuvuta, -a muda. **~ionally** *adv*. **~ory** *adj* -a kupita, -a kitambo, -a muda mfupi tu, -siodumu.

transitive *adj (gram)* elekezi. **~ly** *adv*

translate *vi,vt* ~ **sth (from) (into)** 1 tafsiri, fasiri; *(transfer)* weka pengine, hamisha sambamba. 2 hamisha (askofu); *(in the Bible)* paza (mbinguni). **translation** *n* 1 kufasiri, tafsiri, fasiri. 2 *(maths)* mhamisho sambamba. **translator** *n* mfasiri.

transliterate *vt* ~ **sth (into)** nukuu kwa mfumo tafauti. **transliteration** *n* kunukuu; unukuzi.

translucent *adj* -a kupenya nuru, -enye kupenyeka nuru. **translucence** *n* upenywaji nuru.

transmigrate *vt* 1 hama. **transmigration** *n* kuhama, mhamo. **~ of the soul** roho ya mtu kuingia katika mwili mwingine mtu afapo.

transmit *vt* 1 ~ **sth (to)** peleka; *(of disease)* ambukiza. **~ter** *n* transimita/kitu au chombo cha kupeleka ishara, sauti, n.k. 2 ruhusu, pitisha. **transmission** *n* 1 upelekaji, upitishaji; *(of disease)* uambukizaji; *(ofprogrammes)* utangazaji. 2 klachi, gea na wenzo pamoja.

transmogrify *vt* geuza sura au tabia kiajabuajabu au kwa kiinimacho. **transmogrification** *n* ubadilishaji sura/tabia kabisa (hasa kwa kiinimacho au miujiza).

transmute *vt* ~ **sth (into)** geuza, badili. **transmutable** *adj* -a kugeuka; -a kubadilika. **transmutation** *n* ugeuzi,

badiliko, mgeuko.
transoceanic *adj* -a kuvuka bahari ~ *flight of birds* msafara wa ndege kuvuka bahari.
transom *n* kizingiti cha juu.
transparent *adj* 1 -angavu; -a kuonya/kuona. 2 *(clear, obvious)* wazi, bayana, dhahiri. 3 *(of person)* -nyofu. **~ly** *adj*. **transparence** *n* uangavu.
transpire *vi* 1 julikana, tangaa, bainika. 2 toa jasho/mvuke. 3 *(colloq)* tukia. **transpiration** *n* kutoa jasho/mvuke.
transplant *vi,vt* 1 atika, pandikiza. 2 hamisha kiungo cha mwili. 3 *(fig)* hama, hamisha (toka mahala hadi pengine). **~ation** *n* 1 kuatika, mwatiko. 2 kuhamisha (kiungo cha mwili, ogani, tishu, n.k.).
transpolar *adj* -a kupitia ncha ya dunia.
transport *vt* 1 safirisha, peleka. 2 *(hist) (of criminals)* hamishia nchi nyingine. 3 **be ~ed with** *(liter)* pata, ingiwa jazba, hemkwa, chomwa moyo *be ~ed with joy* jawa/tekwa na furaha *be ~ed with anger* chomwa/umwa moyo kwa ghadhabu. **~able** *adj* -a kuchukulika *n* 1 uchukuzi, usafiri, upagazi. **~ cafe** mkahawa wa barabarani. 2 *(often pl)* furaha kubwa. **in a ~/in ~s of** *(liter)* -liojaa, -liohemkwa/sisimkwa. **in ~s of delight** kwa furaha isiyosemeka. 3 **(troop)** ~ meli/ndege za kijeshi (za uchukuzi). **~ation** *n* 1 usafirishaji, kuchukua, uchukuzi, uhamali, upagazi. 2 uhamisho. **~er** *n* msafirishaji, mchukuzi; chombo cha uchukuzi.
transpose *vt* 1 badilishana nafasi (herufi, n.k.). 2 *(music)* badili ufunguo. **transposition** *n* 1 kubadilisha; kubadilika. 2 *(maths)* hitari, uchaguzi.
transsexual *n (psych)* na hisia za jinsi nyingine, mtu aliyegeuzwa jinsi nyingine, mtu aliyegeuzwa jinsi kwa uganga/operesheni.
trans-ship *vt* badili meli; hamisha shehena; hawili, hawilisha. **~ment** *n*
transubstantiation *n (RC Church)* itikadi kwamba mkate na mvinyo hubadilika kuwa mwili na damu ya Yesu.
transverse *adj* kingamo, -a kukingama.
transversal *adj* -a kukingama *n* mstari wa kukingama, mkingamo. **~ly** *adv*.
transvestism *n (psych)* tabia ya kuvaa nguo za jinsi tafauti. **transvestite** *n* mtu wa tabia hiyo.
trap *n* mtego, *(spring)* mtambo; *(fig)* hila, njama. 2 *(bend in pipe)* pinda, kuruba (la bomba la kuwekea maji kidogo ili kuzuia harufu isirudi). 3 *(carriage)* toroli, gari lenye magurudumu mawili (la kukokotwa na farasi). 4 **~-door** *n* mlango wa sakafuni/darini (wa kuinuliwa juu au unaoning'inia). 5 *(sl)* kinywa/domo *vt* tega; nasa. **~per** *n* mtega wanyama.
trapeze *n* pembea.
trapezium *n* tenga; msambamba tenge.
trappings *n* 1 matandiko (ya farasi, n.k.); mapambo ya farasi. 2 *(fig)* mavazi rasmi, nishani, n.k.
trash *n* 1 *(US)* takataka. 2 upuuzi, maandishi chapwa *adj* -a ovyo, -sio na thamani, -siofaa kitu; chapwa.
trauma *n* kiwewe. **~tic** *adj*.
travail *n* 1 *(arch)* uchungu wa kuzaa. 2 kazi ngumu *vi* 1 shikwa na/ona uchungu wa kuzaa. 2 *(toil painfully)* taabika, lika.
travel *vi,vt* 1 safiri, abiri. **~ agent** wakala wa safari. **~ agency/bureau** *n* ofisi ya usafiri. **~ling fellowship** ruzuku ya safari za taaluma. 2 **~ (in sth) (for sb)** tembeza (mali). 3 *(of sound, moving objects)* enda, pita. 4 pitia, talii *n* 1 kusafiri; usafiri. **~ling bag** begi la safari. **~ling sickness** kichefuchefu (wakati wa safari). **~ling expenses** masurufu. 2 ziara, misafara. 3 mwendo. **~led** *adj* aliyesafiri sana. **~ler** *n* 1 msafiri, abiria. **~ler's cheque** *(US* **~ler's check***)* hundi ya msafiri. 2 *(often* **commercial ~ler**) mtembeza bidhaa. **~ogue** n mhadhara/filamu juu ya safari.

traverse *vt (travel over)* pita, pitia *n* 1 kingamo. 2 kinzo.

travesty *n* mwigo, wigo bezi *vt* dhihaki kwa kuiga.

trawl *vt,vi* vua samaki kwa kukokota wavu chini chini; kokoora. **~ler** *n* kikokoozi, chombo cha kuvulia samaki kwa wavu chini chini; kokoozi *n* 1 ~ **(net)** kokooro chini chini. 2 **~-line** *n* mvulio.

tray *n* chano, trei. **in/out** ~ trei ya majalada ya kuingia/kutoka.

treacherous *adj* 1 -ongo, siaminifu, saliti. 2 -danganyifu, si -a kutegemea. **~ly** *adv*. **treachery** *n* udanganyifu; usaliti, *(pl)* vitendo vya udanganyifu.

treacle asali ya miwa. **treacly** *adj* kama asali ya miwa; *(fig)* tamu mno; anisi.

tread *vt,vi* 1 ~ **(on sth)** kanyaga, vyoga, liwata. ~ **on air** jawa na furaha. ~ **on sb's corns/toes** *(fig)* udhi mtu. ~ **on sb's heels** *(lit or fig)* fuata karibu. 2 ~ **(out/down)** kanyaga, ponda, kandamiza (kwa miguu). 3 tengeneza (njia) kwa kutembea/kupitia. 4 kanyaga, pita; *(fig)* fuata. ~ **a dangerous path** fuata njia ya hatari. ~ **water** elea majini (kwa kupiga miguu) *n* 1 kishindo. 2 kidaraja cha ngazi; *(of tyre)* tredi (sehemu inayogusa chini). **~mill** *n* 1 kinu cha kuendesha kwa miguu. 2 kazi ya kuchusha.

treadle *n* mdoshi, kanyagio *vi* endesha mdoshi.

treason *n* uhaini. **high** ~ uhaini mkubwa. **~able** *adj* -a uhaini *~able offence* kosa la uhaini. **~ous** *adj*. **~ably** *adv*.

treasure *n* 1 hazina. ~ **house** hazina. **~-trove** *n* dafina. 2 tunu; kitu/mtu anayethaminiwa sana. 3 *(beloved)* mpenzi, kipenzi; mtu mwema sana *vt* 1 ~ **sth (up)** hifadhi, tunza. 2 thamini sana. **~r** *n* mhazini, mtunza/mweka hazina; bwana fedha. **treasury** *n* 1 hazina; *(public funds)* mali ya serikali. **the Treasury** Hazina. **First Lord of the T~** *(GB)* Waziri Mkuu. ~ **bill** hawala za serikali. ~ **note** noti. 2 hazina (ya habari, n.k).

treat *vi, vt* 1 ~ **(as)** tendea, ~ **sb well** tendea fulani vyema. 2 **~as** chukulia kama ~ *it as a joke* chukulia kama utani. 3 shughulikia; jadili, eleza. 4 ~ **(of)** *(formal)* husu, zingatia, shughulikia. 5 *(med)* tibu. 6 ~ **with (sb)** fanya shauri (na). 7 ~ **sb/oneself (to sth)** karibisha; lipia gharama; (ji) patia. 8 ~ **with sb** jadiliana (na), panga (na), fanya shauri (na). 9 tia, paka, chovya *n* 1 *(feast)* karamu, sherehe. 2 fadhila. **stand** ~ *(colloq)* gharimia (takrima/sherehe). 3 *(pleasure)* jambo la furaha, mapendezi. **~ment** *n* utendeaji/ jinsi ya kutenda; utendewaji/jinsi ya kutendewa; *(med)* matibabu, utabibu *be under ~ment* alikwa, tibiwa.

treatise *n* ~ **(on/upon)** tasnifu, maandiko, makala (yenye kuhusu mada moja).

treaty *n* 1 mkataba. ~ **port** bandari inayoruhusu bidhaa za nje kwa mkataba ~ *of friendship* mkataba wa urafiki. 2 mapatano, maafikiano. **be in ~ with sb for sth** afikiana na mtu kwa kitu.

treble[1] *vt,vi* zidisha mara tatu; zidi mara tatu *adj* mara tatu ya. ~ **chance** (aina ya) bahati nasibu (ya matokeo ya mpira). **trebly** *adv*.

treble[2] *n (mus)* sauti ya kwanza (ya mtoto wa kiume); chombo chenye sauti nyembamba.

tree *n* 1 mti. **family** ~ nasaba, ukoo. **up a (gum)** ~ *(colloq)* -liokwama/ -liobanwa. **at the top of the** ~ upeo wa ubingwa/weledi. 2 kipande *exle* ~ ekseli. **~less** *adj* pasipo miti. **~like** *adj* -enye kufanana na mti, kama mti. **~-top** *n* kilele cha mti. **~-trunk** *n* shina la mti *vt* kimbiza mtini *the lion ~d the hunter* simba alimkimbizia mwindaji mtini.

trefoil *n* mimea ya majani matatu; pambo linalofanana na mmea wa majani matatu.

trek *vi* 1 enda safari ndefu *n* safari ngumu na ndefu.

trellis *n* vijiti/fito za wima (agh. za kushikia mimea inayotambaa) *vt* weka/simika vijiti/fito. **~-work** *n* *(screen)* 1 kiambaza cha fito. 2 ua wa fito.

tremble *vi* 1 tetema, tetemeka, gwaya *my fate ~d in the balance* maisha yangu yalikuwa mashakani. 2 *(be anxious or perturbed)* -wa na hofu/ wasiwasi sana. **all of a ~** *(colloq)* -enye kuhamanika. **in fear and trembling** katika hofu na mashaka mengi. 3 *(of bridge etc)* yumba, tingishika, tikisika *n* mtetemo, tetemeko, mtikisiko.

tremendous *adj* -kubwa mno, -ingi, -a nguvu sana *(colloq)* -a ajabu; zuri mno. **~ly** *adv* vizuri mno.

tremolo *n (music)* mdendego.

tremor *n* mtetemo, tetemeko, utukuto, tukutiko.

tremulous *adj* 1 tetemi, -a kuvinyavinya. 2 *(timid)* -oga, -enye hofu, -a kusitasita. **~ly** *adv*.

trench *n* 1 ufuo, mfereji; *(mil)* handaki *irrigation~* mfereji wa umwagiliaji. 2 *(for foundation)* msingi *vt* chimba handaki/mfereji/ufuo; zungusha mahandaki.

trenchant *adj (of language)* kali; -a mkato. **~ly** *adv*. **trenchancy** *n* 1 ukali; mkato.

trencher *n (hist)* chano; **~man** *n* mlaji *a good ~man* mlaji sana. *a poor ~man* mlaji kidogo.

trend *n* mwelekeo *the ~ of opinion* mwelekeo wa maoni. **set the ~** anzisha mtindo. **~ setter** mwanzisha mtindo. **~ setting** *n,adj (sl often derog)* -a kupenda mno mtindo/ mamboleo/usasa, *vi* 1 elekea. 2 *(with prices) ~ upwards* panda.

trepan *n* 1 *see* **trephine**. 2 kitoboleo (cha mgodi) *vi see* **trephine**. **~ation** *n*.

trephine *n* msumeno (mzingo) wa kutobolea fuvu *vt* toboa fuvu (na kuondoa sehemu).

trepidation *n* hofu, kiherehere, wasiwasi.

trespass *vi* 1 **~ (on/upon)** ingia bila ruhusa *no ~ing* usiingie bila ruhusa. 2 **~ on/upon** ingilia; tumia mno. 3 **~ (against)** *(arch) (sin, commit an offence)* kosa, kosea; tenda dhambi *n* 1 kupita bila ruksa; mwingilio usio ruhusa. 2 *(old use biblical)* dhambi, kosa *n* mwingiaji (bila halali).

tress *n* 1 *(pl) (poet or lit)* nywele, (agh. za mwanamke). 2 msuko, msokoto (wa nywele).

trestle *n* 1 egemeo (la meza, benchi, n.k. lenye matendegu matatu au manne). 2 panda/farasi ya kuwekea mbao. **~ bridge** *n* daraja la panda. **~ table** meza panda.

tri *pref* tatu.

triad *n* seti ya watu/vitu vitatu vinavyohusiana sana.

trial *n* 1 kujaribu; majaribu; maonjo; jaribio *give sb a ~* jaribu mtu *on ~* kwa majaribio; baada ya majaribio. **~ and error** -a kubahatisha. 2 *(attrib)* a majaribio. 3 *(leg)* kesi, daawa. **be/ go on ~ (for sth)** shtakiwa. **bring sb to ~; bring sb up for ~; put sb on ~** shtaki upya. **stand (one's) ~** shtakiwa. 4 *(trouble)* taabu, shida, usumbufu, udhia. **be a ~** kuwa matata/msumbufu. **~s and tribulations** adha/maudhi na kero.

triangle *n* 1 pembetatu. 2 ala ya pembe tatu. 3 kundi la watatu. **the eternal ~** mapenzi ya wawili kwa mmoja. **triangular** *adj* 1 -enye pembetatu, mche pembetatu. 2 -a watu/ wagombea watatu. **triangulate** *vt* gawa katika pembetatu; pima kwa pembetatu; fanya pembetatu. **triangulation** *n* kupima (kwa kutumia) pembetatu.

tribe *n* 1 kabila; mbari. 2 *(bot, zool)* kundi (la mimea na wanyama) (kati ya jenasi na ukoosafu). 3 genge.

tribal *adj* -a kikabila/kimbari. **~sman** *n* jamaa katika kabila. **tribalism** *n* ukabila.

tribulation *n* (sababu ya) taabu, matata, majonzi.

tribunal *n* mahakama, baraza (la

hukumu) *military* ~ baraza la kijeshi.

tribune[1] *n* ulingo, dungu; jukwaa.

tribune[2] *n* 1 afisa mteule wa watu katika Roma ya kale. 2 kiongozi mpendwa; *(fig) (demagogue)* msukumizi.

tributary *adj* 1 *(of a state, ruler, etc)* -a kulipa kodi (kwa nchi nyingine). 2 *(of river)* -a kuingia mto mwingine *n* 1 (mtawala wa) nchi inayolipa kodi kwa nchi nyingine. 2 *(stream)* kijito.

tribute *n* 1 ushuru, kodi (kwa nchi nyingine). **pay ~; lay a nation under ~** lipisha/toza kodi kwa nchi. 2 jambo/neno/kitendo cha kuonyesha shukrani/kusifia *pay ~ to a person;* shukuru; tukuza.

trice[1] *n* 1 **in a ~** mara, kufumba na kufumbua.

trice[2] *vt* ~ **sth up** *(naut)* vuta (tanga, n.k.) kwa kamba.

trick *n* 1 hila, kitimbi, madanganyo, mbinu. **~s of the trade** mbinu za biashara. 2 shere, mzaha **she likes playing ~s on people** anapenda kuwachezea watu shere. **dirty ~** mchezo mbaya, kitendo cha ufasiki/ushenzi. 3 *(conjuring)* kiinimacho, mazingaombwe, mizungu, mauzauza. **do the ~** faa. **a ~ worth two of that** *(colloq)* njia bora ya kufanya jambo. **get/learn the ~ of it** elewa/jifunza mbinu zake. 4 *(habit)* mazoea, desturi *it's a ~ of his* ni desturi yake. 5 *vt,vi* 1 *(naut)* zamu ya kushika usukani. ~ **sb (into/ out of sth)** dangaya, laghai, ghilibu, hadaa. 2 ~ **sb/sth out/up** pamba; remba. **~ery** *n* udanganyifu, ulaghai, uayari. **~ster** *n* mwerevu, laghai, mghilibu, ayari. **~y** *adj* 1 danganyifu. 2 *(of work, etc)* gumu, tata.

trickle *vi,vt* churura, churuzika, churirika; churuza, chururisha. *n* chururu, mchuruziko, mchuruzo. ~ **charger** *n* chombo cha kuchajia.

tricolour *n* bendera ya rangi tatu. **The T~** bendera ya Ufaransa *adj* -a rangi tatu.

tricycle *n* baiskeli ya magurudumu matatu.

trident *n* 1 chusa chenye ncha tatu, mkuki wa vyembe vitatu. 2 alama yanguvu ya bahari.

tried *pt,pp of* **try**.

triennial *adj* (-a kila) miaka mitatu.

trier *n see* **try**.

trifle *n* 1 jambo dogo/hafifu, kitu kisicho cha thamani, takataka. **not stick at ~s** kutoruhusu mambo madogo kuingilia mpango wa mtu. 2 kiasi kidogo, cha fedha *she paid only a ~* alilipa fedha kidogo sana. 3 **a ~** *adv* kidogo kiasi *a ~ tough* gumu kidogo. 4 tamutamu *vt,vi* 1 ~ **with** chezea. 2 ~ **sth away** tupa/poteza (muda, nguvu, n.k.); fuja (fedha). **~r** *n* mpuuzi, kijoyojoyo. **trifling** *adj* dogo; hafifu, pumbavu *its no ~ matter* sio mchezo.

trigger *n* chombo cha kufyatulia risasi. **be quick on the ~** -wa mwepesi kufyatua bunduki. **have one's finger on the ~** *(fig)* tawala, mudu (hali). **~-happy** *adj (sl)* tayari kufyatua bunduki (bila hata sababu); -enye kupenda kutumia mabavu *vt* ~ **sth off** chokoza/chokonoa mambo.

trigonometry *n* trigonometria: elimu (ya hesabu) ya uhusiano kati ya pembe na pande tatu za pembetatu. **trigonometric** *adj* -a trigonometria.

trike *(colloq)* **tricycle**.

trilateral *adj* -enye pande tatu.

trilby *n* ~ *(hat)* kofia (ya mwanamume).

trill *vt,vi* tetemesha sauti katika kuimba, tia madoido (madende katika kuimba) *n* 1 mtetemo wa sauti. 2 *(mus)* madoido (katika kuimba). 3 *(of speech/sound)* kimadende.

trillion *n* trilioni; (*GB*) milioni milioni milioni; (*US*) milioni milioni.

trilogy *n* tamthilia/riwaya /opera yenye sehemu tatu mfululizo zenye maudhui moja (ambamo kila sehemu hujitegemea).

trim *vt* 1 *(adjust balance)* chenga/punguza; puna. 2 punguza gharama;

sawazisha, nadhifisha. 3 ~ **sth (with sth)** *(decorate)* pamba, remba. 4 sawazisha, panga (shehena); kisi/badili matanga (kufuatana na upepo) *adj* nadhifu, safi, -enye utaratibu mzuri/kuwa tayari *get into ~ for the competition* jiweka/katika hali nzuri tayari kwa mashindano *in perfect ~* katika hali nzuri kabisa. **~mer** *n* msawazishaji, mpambaji; mpunaji. **~ming** *n* pambo. **~ly** *adv.* 4 *(politics)* fuata upepo; chukua msimamo wa kati/badili msimamo (ili kupendwa na watu).

trinitrotoluene *n (usu TNT)* baruti kali.

trinity *n* utatu. **The (Holy) T~** Utatu Mtakatifu. **T~ Sunday** Jumapili ya Utatu Mtakatifu.

trinket *n* kipambo kidogo kizuri cha thamani ndogo (agh kishaufu, pete, kipini).

trio *n* 1 watatu pamoja. 2 *(mus)* muziki wa kuimbwa/kupigwa na watu watatu.

trip *vi,vt* 1 tembea/kimbia/cheza dansi kwa hatua nyepesi. 2 ~ **(over) (sth)** jikwaa. ~ **(sb) (up)** piga mweleka/ngwala/ngoe; *(fig)* babaisha mtu, kosesha. 3 ~ **(out)** *(sl)* ota ndoto/njozi (zinazotokana na madawa ya kulevya). 4 ~ **a measure** *(arch)* cheza dansi kwa hatua nyepesi za haraka n 1 safari, matembezi. 2 kujikwaa; *(fig)* kosa. ~ **wire** mtego wa waya ardhini. 3 *(sl)* njozi/maluweluwe (yanayotokana na madawa ya kulevya). **~per** *n* mtalii. **~ping** *adj* -a kurukaruka. **~pingly** *adv.*

tripartite *adj* 1 -enye sehemu/pande tatu. 2 -enye kuhusu watu/pande/vikundi vitatu.

tripe *n* 1 *(of cow, ox, etc)* utumbo (unaoliwa). 2 *(sl)* upuuzi, maandishi, mazungumzo mawazo ya kipuuzi. **~t** *n* 1 *(pl)* pacha (tatu). 2 seti ya vitu vitatu. **~x** *adj* -a tabaka tatu; -a mara tatu. **~x (glass)** kioo cha tabaka tatu.

triplicate *vt* fanya nakala tatu *n* **in triplicate** nakala tatu.

tripod *n* kiweko chenye miguu mitatu.

triptych *n* picha kwenye vibao vitatu vya pamoja (agh kanisani).

trisect *vt* kata katika vipande vitatu (agh sawa). **~ion** *n* kukata vipande vitatu.

trisyllable *n* neno lenye silabi tatu.

trisyllabic *adj* -a silabi tatu.

trite *adj (of remarks, ideas, opinions)* -a kawaida mno, -sio na upya wowote. **~ly** *adv.* **~ness** *n.*

triumph *n* 1 (furaha/shangwe ya) ushindi, shangwe. 2 *(in ancient Rome)* maandamano ya kusherehekea ushindi *vi* ~ **(over)** shinda, pata ushindi; shangilia ushindi; *adj* -a ushindi. **~ant** *adj.* **~antly** *adv.*

triumvir *n (in ancent Rome)* mtawala mmoja (anayeshika madaraka sawa na watawala wawili au zaidi). **~ate** *n* utawala wa watu watatu.

triune *adj* nafsi tatu kwa mmoja.

trivet *n* kipande chenye miguu mitatu. **as right as a** ~ safi kabisa, murua, -a afya.

trivial *adj* 1 -a upuuzi, -sio na maana/thamani, dogo. 2 -a kawaida, -a siku zote. 3 *(of a person)* mpurukushani. **~ly** *adv.* **~ity** *n* upuuzi, jambo dogo lisilo na maana. **~ize** *vt* puuza, dhalilisha, toa umuhimu. **trivia** *n* mambo madogomadogo, mambo ya kipuuzi.

trod, ~den *pt, pp of* **tread**.

troglodyte *n (ancient)* mkaa pangoni.

troika *(Russian) n* 1 troika: gari la kirusi (likokotwalo na farasi watatu). 2 kikundi cha watu watatu (agh viongozi wa kisiasa).

Trojan *n* mwenyeji wa Troy. **work like a** ~ fanya kazi kama punda. ~ **horse** *(fig)* mwarabu na ngamia; kitu/mtu kutoka nje aingiaye katika maadui na kusababisha kuanguka/kushindwa kwao.

troll[1] *vi* vua samaki kwa mshipi (kwa kuvuta chambo nyuma ya mashua).

troll[2] *n (Scandinavian myth)* zimwi.

trolley, trolly *n* 1 toroli. 2 kiberenge. 3 ~ **bus**, *(US)* ~ **car** tramu. 4 meza ndogo ya magurudumu (ya kuandikia chakula). 5 kigurudumu (kiñachogusisha tramu na waya wa umeme wa juu).

trollop *n* 1 *(colloq)* mkoo. 2 malaya, kahaba.

trombone *n* tromboni: **trombonist** mpiga tromboni.

troop *n* 1 kundi, jeshi. 2 *(pl)* wanajeshi, askari, kikosi cha wanajeshi. ~ **carrier** *n* meli/ndege/gari la kubebea wanajeshi. ~ **ship** *n* meli ya kubebea wanajeshi. 3 kikosi cha askari wa mizinga, vifaru au farasi. 4 kombania ya maskauti wa kiume *vt,vi* 1 enda katika kundi. 2 ~ **the colours** *(GB mil)* onyesha/tembeza bendera katika kikosi. **~ing the colour** sherehe ya kuonyesha bendera za kikosi. **~er** *n* 1 askari wa farasi au vifaru. 2 *(US)* askari polisi wa jimbo. **swear like a ~per** tukana sana, toa matusi sana.

trope *n* tamathali.

trophy *n* 1 kikombe. 2 kumbukumbu ya ushindi. 3 nyara.

tropic *n* 1 tropiki. 2 **the ~s** nchi za joto/tropiki. **~al** *adj* 1 -a tropiki, -a joto jingi, -a hari nyingi. **~ally** *adv*.

trot *vt,vi* 1 enda matiti. 2 enda shoti, kimbia kwa hatua fupifupi; *(colloq)* tembea. 3 ~ **sth out** *(colloq)* toa, onyesha. 4 tembeza mtu *n* 1 *(sing only)* mwendo wa matiti. **on the ~** *(sl)* mfululizo, moja baada ya nyingine. **be on the ~; keep somebody on the ~** *(colloq)* shughulika, shughulisha, enda/peleka mbio; *(sl)* kimbia, toroka (jela) *be on the ~ (US) have the ~s (colloq)* harisha, endesha. 2 kipindi/ wakati wa kutembea. **~ter** *n* 1 farasi aliyefunzwa kwenda matiti. 2 *(usu pl)* makongoro/ kwato ya kondoo au nguruwe.

troth *n (arch)* **plight one's ~** ahidi (agh. kufunga ndoa).

troubadous *n (hist)* mshairi/mwimbaji mtembezi.

trouble *vt,vi* 1 taabisha, chokoza, sumbua. 2 ~ **sb to do sth; ~ sb for sth** sumbua mtu *may I ~ you for a cigarette* naomba sigara. 3 jisumbua. 4 tia wasiwasi, hangaisha. **fish in ~d water** jaribu kunufaika kutokana na vurugu *n* 1 hofu, fadhaa; taabu, shida. **in ~** matatani; mashakani; -enye mateso. **ask/look for ~** *(colloq)* jitakia taabu/adha. **get into ~** jitia katika matatizo. **get sb into ~** kalifisha; *(sl)* tia mimba (msichana asiyeolewa). 2 *(sing only)* msumbufu; usumbufu, taklifu, shida. 3 fujo/machafuko/vurugu (la kijamii au kisiasa). 4 ugonjwa; tatizo (la afya). 5 *(compounds)* ~ **maker** *n* mchochezi; mkorofi. ~ **shooter** msuluhishi. **~some** *adj* -a udhia, sumbufu, -a taabu, -chokozi. **~spot** mahali pa fujo/machafuko (ya kisiasa au kijamii). **troublous** *adj (lit)* -a shida, -liochafuliwa.

trough *n* 1 kihori. 2 chombo cha kukandia mikate. 3 bonde kati ya mawimbi baharini. 4 ukanda wa hewa nyepesi kati ya kanda mbili za hewa nzito.

trouce *vt* shinda sana, chapa sana; karipia. **trouncing** *n*.

troupe *n* kundi (la wachezaji, waimbaji, n.k.). **~r** mwanachama wa kundi la waigizaji *he is a good ~ n* mchapa kazi bora.

trouser *n* **(pair of) ~s** suruali; *(attrib)* -a suruali.

trousseau *n* marembo na mavazi (agh ya bibi arusi).

trove *n see* **treasure**.

trowel *n* 1 mwiko wa mwashi. 2 kikoleo cha kupandia mimea.

troy *n* tola.

truant *n* mtoro (shuleni). **play ~** toroka (kazi, chuoni); *(attrib) (of persons their conduct, thoughts, etc)* -tegaji, -zururaji, -toro. **truancy** *n* utoro, utegaji, uzururaji.

truce *n* (makubaliano ya) kusimamisha vita kwa muda/kusitisha vita (k.m. kwa ajili ya kuondoa majeruhi).

truck[1] *n* 1 kubadilishana (bidhaa), mali kwa mali. **have no ~ with** -tokuwa na uhusiano na. 2 **garden ~** *(US)* mazao ya bustani (matunda/mboga) ya kuuza sokoni. 3 ~ **(system)** *(hist)* malipo ya ujira kwa bidhaa/vitu.

truck[2] *n* 1 *(GB)* behewa la mizigo. 2 *(US)* lori. 3 toroli, mkokoteni.

truckle[1] *vi* ~ **to** kubali/salimu amri kwa woga.

truckle[2] *n* ~ **bed** *n* kijitanda (hasa chenye vigurudumu katika matendegu yake kinachoweza kusogezwa ndani ya kingine).

truculent *adj* gomvi; -a kutaka shari/ugomvi. **truculence** *n* **truculency** *n* ugomvi, shari.

trudge *vi* burura miguu, jikokota, enda kwa taabu/uchovu *n* mwendo mrefu wa kuchosha.

true *adj* 1 kweli. **come** ~ tokea (kuwa) kweli. 2 ~ **(to)** amini, aminifu. ~ **blue** *n,adj* mwenye msimamo. ~ **hearted** *adj* aminifu. ~**love** *(n)* mpenzi (wa dhati). 3 halali, halisi. 4 ~ **to type** -enyewe hasa, -enye kufuatana na aina/jinsi yake. 5 imara, -liofungwa kwa usahihi. 6 sawa, sahihi, halisi *a ~ copy of document* nakala halisi *n (only in)* **out of** ~ -siyo halisi/isiohalisi; -siyo sahihi *adv (with certain vv)* kweli, kwelikweli, hakika *vt* ~ **sth up** fanya halisi, rekebisha, sawazisha. **truism** *n* kauli ya kweli/ya wazi mno (kiasi kwamba hakuna hata haja ya kuitoa). **truly** *adv* 1 kweli. 2 kwa hakika; kwa dhati. **truth** *n* 1 ukweli. **moment of** ~ kilele cha tatizo/majaribu; ufunuo. 2 (maneno ya) kweli. **tell the** ~ sema kweli. **to tell the** ~ *(when making a confession)* kusema kweli, kwa kweli. 3 imani. ~**ful** *adj* 1 *(of persons)* kweli. 2 kweli. **truthfully** *adv.* **truthfulness** *n* ukweli.

truffel *n* aina ya uyoga (unaokua chini ya ardhi).

trump[1] *n* 1 turufu. **play one's ~ card** *(fig)* jaribu kupiku, tumia silaha ya mwisho, tumia kitu bora ulicho nacho ili kushinda. **turn up ~s** *(colloq)* fanikiwa/pata matokeo mazuri kuliko ilivyotazamiwa; bahatika, -wa na sudi. 2 *(colloq)* muungwana, rahimu, karimu *vt, vi* 1 piku, cheza turufu. 2 *(usu passive)* ~ **sth up** tunga, zua.

trump[2] *n (lit)* (mkowa) tarumbeta/parapanda. **the last ~; the ~ of doom** parapanda ya kiama.

trumpery *n* mambo ya kishaufu/ovyo; upuuzi *adj* shaufu, hafifu, -a ovyo.

trumpet *n* 1 tarumbeta; baragumu, parapanda. **blow one's own** ~ *(fig)* jivuna, jisifu. 2 sauti ya tarumbeta *vt,vi* 1 eneza, vumisha, tangaza (kwa kusifu). 2 *(esp of elephant)* piga makelele.

truncate *vi* kata, fupisha.

truncheon *n* kirungu, rungu, kibarango.

trundle *vt,vi* sukuma; vingirisha, bingirika. ~ **bed** *(US) see* **truckle bed**.

trunk *n* 1 shina. 2 pingiti, kiwiliwili (bila kichwa, miguu wala mikono). 3 *(of elephant)* mkono, mkonga, mwiro. 4 sanduku, kasha. 5 *(pl)* kaptura. 6 *(US)* buti la gari. 7 *(attrib)* ~ **call** *n* simu ya mbali. ~ **line** *n* reli kuu; njia ya simu ya mbali. ~-**road** barabara kuu.

truss *n* 1 *(GB)* mzigo wa majani/nyasi/chakula (cha ngombe, farasi, n.k.), robota, mtumba. 2 mhimili, farasi. 3 mkanda avaao mgonjwa wa henia *vt* ~ **sth (up)** funga, fungasha. tegemeza, egemeza, himili.

trust *n* 1 ~ **(in)** imani. **on** ~ bila ushahidi/uchunguzi/ithibati; kwa itibari. 2 wajibu. 3 *(leg)* amana. ~ **money, ~ fund** mfuko wa dhamana, fedha ya amana. 4 ushirika wa wafanya biashara *vt,vi* 1 amini, -wa na imani na. ~ **in sb** amini. 2 ~ **to sth** tegema kitu. 3 ~ **sth to sb** aminisha, kabidhi. 4 amini, ruhusu. 5 kopesha. 6 tegemea, tumaini. ~**fully**. ~**ful; ~ing** *adj* -enye kuamini, -enye imani. ~**ingly** *adv.* ~**worthy** *adj* aminifu, -a kutegemewa. ~**worthness**. *n* ~**ee** *n* mdhamana. ~**eeship** *n* 1 uamana. 2 udhamini *T~eeship Territory* Nchi ya Udhamini (wa Uingereza) *Public T~ee* kabidhi wasii *adj (arch or hum)* -aminifu, tumainifu, -a kutegemewa; *n* mfungwa aliyepewa marupurupu jela kwa ajili ya maadili mema/uaminifu wake kwa utawala wa jela.

try *vt, vi* 1 jaribu, jitahidi, fanya bidii. 2 *(judge by law)* shtaki; sikiliza (kesi). 3 *(test, examine)* jaribu. ~ **sth on** jaribu (nguo, n.k.); *(colloq)* jaribu, thubutu. ~ **sth out** tumia kwa majaribio. ~**-out** *n* jaribio la awali. 4 ~ **for sth** jaribu kupata/omba kitu, (k.m. kazi). 5 sumbua, chosha. **tried** *adj* -liojaribiwa, mjarabati; -a kutegemewa. **trier** *n* asiyechoka kujaribu/kujitahidi. ~**ing** sumbufu, -a kusumbua; -a kuchosha *n* 1 jaribio. 2 *(rugby)* bao, goli.

tryst *n (arch)* (miadi ya) kuonana (agh ya wapenzi).

Tsar *n* Tsarina *see* **czar, czarine**.

tsetse, ~fly *n* mbung'o, chafuo, ndorobo.

T-shaped *adj* -enye umbo la herufi T.

T-shirt fulana ya mikono.

T-square *n* kipande chenye umbo la herufi T kinachotumika katika kuchora picha, michoro, n.k.

tub *n* beseni, hodhi, pipa. ~ **thumper** *n* 1 mhamasishaji (sana). 2 *(colloq)* bafu. 3 *(also* ~**ful***)* *n* beseni/bafu tele. 4 *(colloq)* boti lililozeeka/kuukuu.

tubby *adj* nenenene.

tube *n* 1 neli, bomba. ~ **well** kisima cha neli. 2 kioo/taa ya TV. 3 *(London)* reli ya chini ya ardhi. 4 *(of toothpaste, etc)* tyubu. 5 *(med)* (ki)fuko, neli. **tubing** *n* kifaa cha neli/bomba. **tubular** *adj* -enye umbo la neli. ~**less** -sio na tyubu.

tuber *n* kiazi, tunguu, mzizi unaohifadhi chakula cha mmea (agh huwa mnene).

tuberculosis (*abbr* **TB**) *n* kifua kikuu. **tuberculous** *adj* -a kifua kikuu. **tubercular** -loathiriwa na kifua kikuu.

tuck *n* 1 kunjo, pindo, kunyanzi. 2 *(GB)* chakula, (hasa keki, n.k.). ~**-shop** *n* duka la vyakula vitamu (agh. shuleni/chuoni) *vt,vi* 1 weka, chomekea, ingiza ~ *in a shirt* chomekea shati ~ *in a child* futika mtoto. 2 ~ **in** -la kwa furaha/uchu. ~ **into sth** -la kwa furaha. ~ **in** *n* mlo kamili.

tucker *n* mtandio. **one's best bib and** ~ *(colloq)* nguo za kutokea.

Tuesday *n* Jumanne.

tuft *n* kishungi, kishada; bwenzi *a ~ of grass* kishungi cha majani *adj* -enye kishungi.

tug *vt,vi* ~ **(at)** vuta kwa nguvu, vuta ghafla *n* 1 mvuto wa nguvu/ghafla; mchezo wa kuvuta jugwe, jugwe; mvutano, vuta nikuvute. 2 ~ **(boat)** stima ya kuvuta meli kubwa.

tuition *n* 1 mafundisho binafsi. 2 *(tuition fee)* ada ya mafundisho.

tulle *n* hariri nyororo.

tumble *vi,vt* 1 anguka ghafla na kwa vurumai, poromoka. 2 gaagaa, enda juu na chini, huku na huko bila kutulia. 3 dhoofu, konga, chakaa. ~ **down** *(attrib) adj* -liochakaa, bovu. 4 ~ **to sth** *(colloq)* gundua, tambua, ng'amua (kitu). 5 chafua, fuja, vuruga. 6 angusha, mwaga, pindua *n* 1 mwanguko, anguko. **a nasty** ~ anguko baya. 2 vurugu. ~ **weed** *(US)* jani liotalo jangwani.

tumbler *n* 1 *(glass)* bilauri. 2 *(small movingpart)* ulimi/kipande (ndani ya kufuli au kitasa). 3 *(acrobat)* mwana sarakasi. 4 njiwa ajipinduaye wakati wa kuruka. ~**ful** *n* bilauri tele.

tumbrel/tumbril *n (hist)* mkokoteni (hasa uliotumiwa kubebea wafungwa kwenda kukatwa vichwa wakati wa mapinduzi ya Ufaransa).

tumescent *adj* -liovimba; -enye kuvimba; **tumescence** *n*.

tumid *adj* 1 *(of parts of the body)* -liovimba. 2 *(style)* -liotiwa chumvi. ~**ity** *n* 1 uvimbe. 2 *(fig of style of writing)* -enye mbwebwe/mikogo, -a maneno magumu.

tummy *n (colloq)* tumbo.

tumour/tumor *n* kivimbe, uvimbe. ~**ous** *adj* -enye uvimbe.

tumult *n* 1 ghasia; makelele, zahama, msukosuko. 2 mfadhaiko, kuchanga-

nyikiwa. **~uary** *adj* - a makelele, -liochafuka, -enye fujo/ghasia, -a zahama. **~uously** *adv*.
tumulus *n* kichuguu (agh. juu ya kaburi la zamani).
tun *n* kasiki kubwa la bia/mvinyo (galoni 252) *vt* weka katika kasiki.
tuna *n* tuna jodari.
tundra *n* tundra: tambarare pana isiyokuwa na miti (katika Urusi na Siberia).
tune *n* 1 tuni, lahani. 2 mafuatano ya sauti, mlingano, ulinganifu wa sauti, utaratibu. 3 **in/out of ~** fuata/-tofuata mahadhi. 4 *(fig)* wiano, uelewano. 5 *(fig uses)* **change one's ~; sing another ~** badili mwenendo/tabia/msimamo. **to the ~ of** *(colloq)* kiasi cha *vt,vi* 1 rekebisha sauti/lahani. **~ up** anza kurekebisha sauti, lahani. **tuning fork** uma ya tuni. 2 **~ in (to)** rekebisha ili kupokea sauti za angani; sikiliza; *(fig)* elewa/fahamu mambo yasemwayo na watu wengine. 3 rekebisha/tuni injini (ya gari, pikipiki, n.k.). **~r** *n* mrekebishaji sauti/injini; kipokea ishara, mawimbi (katika redio). **~ful** *adj* **~fulness** *n*.
tung-oil *n* mafuta/utomvu wa vanishi.
tungsten *n* madini ya kutengeneza chuma cha pua na filamenti za taa za umeme.
tunic *n* 1 gwanda. 2 blauzi. 3 koti refu; kanzu fupi.
tunne *n* njia ya barabara/reli n.k. ya chini kwa chini mwa mlima, mto, n.k.; shimo la kupenya ndani *vi,vt* **~ (into/through)** chimba upenyo chini ya.
tup *n* kondoo dume.
tuppence *n* *(colloq)* peni mbili.
tuppeny, tupenny *adj* - a kugharimu peni mbili; *(fig)* isiyo na thamani kubwa; bure ghali.
tu quo-que *n* *(lat)* *(used in retort)* hata wewe!
turban *n* kilemba. **~ed** *adj* -liovishwa kilemba, -enye kilemba.
turbid *adj* 1 *(of liquid)* -liotibuliwa, -enye matope, -liochafuka. 2 *(fig)* -liochanganyikiwa, -liovurugika. **~ness, ~ity** *n*.
turbine *n* tabo: injini za maji/mvuke/hewa/gesi. **turbogenerator** *n* tabo; jenereta; genereta la mvuke/gesi.
turbo-jet *n* tabo: jeti; ndege yenye injini ya mvuke/gesi.
turbo-prop *see* **turbo-jet**.
turbulent *adj* -a ghasia, -siyodhibitika, -siotawalika. **turbulence** *n* fujo, ghasia, zahama, maasi. **~ly** *adv*.
turd *n* *(sl)* kimba, jivi.
tureen *n* bakuli la mchuzi/mboga.
turf *n* 1 majani mororo na udongo wake. **the ~** uwanja wa mashindano/mbio za farasi; weledi/shughuli za mashindano ya farasi. **be on the ~** jishughulisha na mambo ya mashindano ya farasi. **~ accountant; ~ commission agent** *see* **book maker**. 2 pande la majani na udongo wake lililokatwa *vt* 1 funika ardhi na pande la majani lenye udongo wake. 2 **~ out** *(GB sl)* tupa nje, fukuza.
turgid *adj* 1 -liovimba, -liotutuka, -liotutumka. 2 *(of language)* -a kujivuna, -a kiburi, -a kutakabari; -a maneno makuu; -a kujishaua. **~ly** *adv*. **~ity** *n* 1 uvimbe; kuvimba. 2 kiburi, majivuno.
Turk *n* Mturuki. **~ish** *n* ~ *adj* -a Mturuki/Kituruki. **~ish bath** josho la mvuke halafu kwa maji na mchuo; hamamu. **~ish delight** halua. **~ish towel** taulo (yenye nyuzinyuzi zenye kunywa maji).
turkey *n* 1 batamzinga. 2 *(US sl)* ushinde. **cold ~** uachaji ghafla wa kula dawa za kulevya; zimbaa; kauli thabiti. **talk ~** *(US sl)* sema wazi bila kuficha.
turmeric *n* bizari, manjano.
turmoil *n* ghasia, zahama, machafuko, msukosuko.
turn *n* 1 mzunguko *three ~s of the wheel* mizunguko mitatu ya gurudumu. **~ of the century** mwanzo wa karne mpya. **on the ~** karibu ya kugeuka. **done to a ~** *(of food)* iva/pikwa vizuri kabisa. 2 badiliko la

uelekeo, kona, kuruba *sudden ~s in the road* kona za ghafla barabarani. **at every ~** *(fig)* mara kwa mara. 3 badiliko la hali *the sick man took a ~ for the better* mgonjwa alipata ahueni. 4 zamu (ya kufanya kitu). **(do sth) ~ and ~ about** *(of two or more persons)* (fanya) mmoja baada ya mwingine, fanya jambo kwa zamu. **by ~s** *(of persons)* kwa mzunguko/duru; kwa zamu. **in ~** *(of two persons)* kwa zamu. **out of ~** kabla/baada ya zamu (yako). **take ~ (at sth)**; **take ~s about** fanya kwa zamu, fanya kwa kupokezana. 5 tendo, kitendo (kinachoathiri mtu). **one good ~ deserves another** *(prov)* matendo mema sharti yalipwe. **do sb a good/bad ~** tendea mtu wema/ubaya; saidia/-tosaidia. 6 uelekeo asilia; kipaji *a boy with a mechanical ~* mtoto mwenye uelekeo wa kiufundi/kipaji cha ufundi. 7 nia, matakwa, haja. **serve one's ~** kidhi matakwa/haja ya mtu, faa. 8 kipindi, kifupi cha mishughuliko *I'll take a few ~s before I go for lunch* nitazunguka/tembea kidogo kabla ya kwenda kula chakula cha mchana. 9 *(colloq)* mshituko, fadhaa, hofu *it gave me quite a ~* ilinishtusha/tia hofu. 10 igizo fupi. **star ~** igizo linalopendwa sana, igizo maarufu (kwenye TV) *vt,vi* 1 zungusha, zunguka; pindua, pinduka; geuza, geuka *the earth ~s round the sun* dunia hulizunguka jua. **~ one's mind/thoughts/attention to sth** elekeza mawazo yako, n.k. upande fulani. **~ one's hand to sth** (weza ku)fanya jambo/kazi fulani. **~ a deaf ear to sth** -tosikiliza, -tojali. **~ sb's flank; ~ the flank of sb** zingira ili kushambulia; *(fig)* shinda kwa akili; shinda katika malumbano. 2 **~ (sth) (into sth)**, geuza, geuka, badilika, badilisha. **~ sb's brain** vunga/rusha akili, tia wazimu. **~ sb's head** vimbisha kichwa. 3 fikia (kiwango fulani) na kupita *he has ~ed four* amefikia miaka minne, ana miaka minne sasa. 4 kereza; *(fig)* -pa umbo la kupendeza *wood/metal that ~s* mbao/chuma kinachoweza kukerezwa. 5 *(of garment)* shona (kwa kupindua ndani nje) **~ coat** *n* mtu anayehama chama kimoja na kujiunga na kingine; msaliti. *(compounds)* **~cock** *n* mtumishi anayefunga/fungulia maji. **~key** bawabu; askari jela. **~pike** *n (hist)* lango/kizuizi katika barabara inayolipiwa ushuru wa barabara; *(US)* barabara inayolipiwa ushuru. **~spit** *n (hist)* mbwa/mtumishi anayegeuza kibanio cha nyama inayookwa. **~table** *n* kikalio cha sahani za santuri. 7 *(special uses with adverbial particles and preps)* *~ (sb) about* geuza. **about ~** *(as a military command, in drills, etc)* nyuma geuka. **~ sb adrift** telekeza, tupa. **~ (sb) against sb** chukiza, chochea uadui na. **~ (sb) aside (from)** *(more usu* **~ away**) geuza mtu (aelekee upande mwingine). **~ sb away** geuka (upande) mtu asikuangalie; kataa (kuangalia/kukaribisha, n.k.). **~ (sb/sth) back** rudisha; rudi. **~ (sth) down** kunja (k.m, ukosi n.k.); teremsha (k.m. utambi wa taa); punguza; pindua karata. **~ sb/sth own** katalia. **~ in** *(colloq)* enda kulala. **~ in on oneself/itself** jitenga. **~ sb in** *(colloq)* peleka mtu polisi. **~ (sth) in** kunja/ingiza ndani. **~ sth in** *(colloq)* kabidhi/rudisha kwa mhusika; elekea/elekeza ndani. **~ sth off** unga (bomba) zima (mitambo, redio, taa). **~ sb off** *(sl)* ondolea hamu/haja/nia; chusha. **~off** *n* kitu/mtu anayekatisha (watu) tamaa. **~ sth on** fungua/washa. **~ the lights on** washa taa. **~ the tap on** fungua bomba. **~ (sb) on** *(sl)* sisimua, sisimka, burudisha, furahisha. **~ on** *n* kitu/mtu anayeburudisha/furahisha. **~ on sth**, tegemea. **~ on sb** shambulia, chukia mtu fulani. **~ out well** -wa bora mwishowe. **~ (sth) out** chomoza nje. **~ sth out;** zima/funga kung'uta (mifuko); safisha (chumba). ~ **sb/sth out** toa/zalisha *the school has ~ed out some first-rate scholars* shule imetoa wanazuoni bora. ~ **(sb) out** fika (kazini, kwenye shughuli, n.k.); *(colloq)* amsha, toka kitandani. ~ **sb out (of/from sth)** fukuza kwa nguvu/ vitisho, n.k. **~ed out** *(of a person, equipment, etc)* liovalia; liovishwa. ~ **out** *n* mahudhurio; (kipindi cha) usafi; hali ya unadhifu; mali iliyozalishwa/ tengenezwa. ~ **(sb/sth) over** pindua, pinduka. ~ **sth over** pata, patia; hariji *his business ~s over sh 90000/= a week* biashara yake humpatia shs 90000/= kwa wiki. ~ **sth over in one's mind** fikiria/fikiri (kabla ya uamuzi). ~ **sth/sb over (to sb)** kabidhi kitu/mtu fulani kwa mtu mwingine. **~over** *n* mapato na matumizi; kiasi (cha watu, wanafunzi, wafanyakazi, n.k.) waliofika kujaza nafasi; pai yenye jamu, nyama, n.k. ndani. ~ **(sth/sb) round** geuza, geuka. ~ **round** *n* (*esp of a ship or aircraft*); kipindi cha kujiandaa na kuanza safari nyingine (baada ya kufika. ~ **to** fanya kazi. ~ **to sb** endea au omba msaada kwa. ~ **up**, fika, hudhuria; onekana hasa kwa bahati; *(of an opportunity, etc)* fika, wadia, patikana. ~ **(sth) up** kunja (kuelekea juu). ~ **up your sleeves** kunja mikono yako; onyesha, weka wazi. ~ **sb up** *(colloq)* tapisha; chafua roho. ~ **up one's nose at sth** *(fig)* dharau, beza. ~ **up** *n (for a book)* tukio la kushangaza lisilotarajiwa; *(of trousers)* mkunjo (mguuni). ~ **upon** shambulia. **~ning** 1 kona, njia panda. **~point** *n* 1 *(fig)* kipindi muhimu. 2 mahala pa kugeuka. 3 jambo kuu/ muhimu.

turnery *n* 1 kiwanda cha kukereza. 2 vitu vilivyofanyizwa kerezo. **turner** *n* mkereza.

turnip *n* ua la tanipu.

turpentine *n* terafini: mafuta yapatikanayo kwenye miti fulani (agh. hutumika katika kuyeyushia na kuchanganyia rangi, vanishi, n.k.).

turpitude *n* uovu, ufisadi, upotovu.

turps *n (colloq abbr for)* **turpentine**.

turquoise *n* (rangi ya) feruzi.

turret *n* 1 mnara mdogo (hasa ulio kwenye kona ya jengo/ngome). 2 *(in man-of-war)* ngome, banda la chuma lenye mizinga.

turtle[1] *(usu)* **~-dove** hua.

turtle[2] *n, vi* kasa. **turn** ~ *(of a ship)* pinduka. **~-neck(ed)** *adj (of a garment)* kaba-shingo. **~-shell** *n* gamba la kobe.

tusk *n* jino; *(elephant's)* pembe; *(middle-sized)* buri; *(small)* kalasha; *(of boar)* upamba; *(of rhinoceros)* kipusa. **~er** *n* ndovu/nguruwe mwitu aliyekomaa.

tussle *vi* (**with**) (*colloq*) pambana vikali *n* pambano.

tussock *n* kilima cha majani.

tut, tut-tut *n* ebo! tamko la kuonyesha dharau; karipio; kutokubali *vi* onyesha kutokubali/dharau.

tutelage *n (formal)* ulezi, malezi.

tutelary *adj (formal)* -a ulezi, -a mlezi.

tutor *n* 1 *(at colleges, etc)* mkufunzi. 2 mdarisi, mwalimu binafsi. 3 *(GB)* mwalimu wa chuo kikuu, mhadhiri *vt* 1 fundisha, funda; darisi. 2 jizoeza, dhibiti, chunga. **~ial** *adj* -a ukufunzi *n* semina ya ukufunzi.

tutti-frutti *n* aiskrimu ya matunda; furuti.

tutu *n* sketi fupi ya wacheza baleyi.

tuxedo *n* koti (rasmi) la mlo wa jioni.

twaddle *n* upuuzi, mapiswa *vi* payapaya, payuka, bwata.

twain *n (arch)* jozi; viwili *cut in ~* kata sehemu mbili *adj* wili.

twang *n* 1 mlio wa uzi wa zeze au upinde, n.k. ukipigwa. 2 *(nasal)* king'ong'o *vt,vi* liza zeze/upinde, n.k. kwa kukwanyua, kuvuta nyuzi zake.

twas (*arch or poet*) **it was.** ilikuwa.

tweak *vi* binya, finya *n* kufinya.

twee *adj* -a kujidaidai (kwa uzuri).

tweed *n* 1 nguo ya sufu. 2 *(pl)* **~s** nguo

za sufu.

tween *adv, prep (arch or poet)* katikati. ~ **decks** katikati ya sitaha.

tweet *n* mtwito: mlio mkali (agh. wa ndege) *vi* toa mlio mkali. **~er** *n* kipaaza sauti (chenye noti za juu).

tweezers *n (pl) (pair of)* kikoleo; kibanio.

twelve *n, adj* kumi na mbili, thenashara. **The T~** mitume thenashara wa Yesu Kristo. ~ **month** *n (archaic)* mwaka. **twelfth** *adj* -a kumi na mbili *n* kumi na mbili, sehemu ya kumi na mbili. **twelfth man** *(in cricket)* mchezaji wa akiba. **Twelfth night** mkesha wa Epifania.

twenty *n, adj* 1 ishirini *a young girl of ~* msichana wa miaka ishirini. 2 (pl) **twenties** miaka ya ishini. **twentieth** *adj* -a ishirini *n* sehemu ya ishirini ishirini *adj, adv* mara ishirini.

twere *(arch or poet)* **it were** ilikuwa.

twerp *n (sl)* kidumbwana, kinyangarika, bwege, fala.

twice *adv* mara mbili. **think ~ about doing sth** fikiria mara mbili kabla ya kutenda. **a ~-told tale** hadithi inayofahamika vizuri.

twiddle *vt, vi* 1 sokotasokota (bila mpango). 2 ~ **with sth** chezeachezea kitu, chezacheza, chezesha chezesha *n* kusokotasokota, kugeuzageuza. **twiddly** *adj*.

twig[1] *n* kitawi, kijiti. **~gy** *adj*.

twig[2] *vt,vi (GB colloq)* elewa, fahamu; tambua, gundua, ng'amua.

twilight *n* 1 utusiutusi wa asubuhi au jioni. 2 *(fig)* zama za kale (zisizofahamika). **twilit** *adj* -enye mwanga hafifu.

twill[1] *n* aina ya kitambaa kigumu cha sufi.

twill[2] *(arch or poet)* **it will** ita.

twin *n* 1 pacha. 2 sawa, mwenzi, mfano mmoja *~ houses* nyumba pacha *adj* -a mfano mmoja; -a pacha *vt* ~ **(with)** ungana na; fanya jozi. **~ned** *adj (attrib)* ~ **(with)** -a jozi, -lioshikamana/(na) ungana.

twine *n* 1 kitani, uzi. 2 songa, sokota; *(twist)* sokotasokota.

twinge *n* mchomo (wa maumivu); kichomi. ~ **of conscience** mchomo wa dhamira.

twinkle *(bi)* 1 metameta, meremeta. 2 *(of eyes)* ng'aa *n* kumetameta. 2 *(of eyes)* ung'avu. **twinkling** *(sing only)* **in the twinkling of an eye**, kufumba na kufumbua, mara moja.

twirl *vt* zungusha; zunguka; zongomeza, songoa *n* msokoto; kusongoa.

twist *vt,vt* 1 *(string, rope, etc)* zungusha nyuzi juu ya nyuzi nyingine. 2 suka, sokota. 3 geuza, pinda, songoa, popotoa. ~ **sth off** songonyoa. ~ **sb's arm** popotoa mkono wa mtu; *(fig) (colloq)* lazimisha (kwa upole/ nguvu). ~ **sb round one's little finger** *(colloq)* fanya (mtu) afanye unalotaka. 4 geuza maana ya maelezo ya mwingine. 5 betabeta, pindapinda. 6 nengua *n* 1 kusokota; usokotaji. 2 misokoto, mpopotoo. 3 *(of dance)*. **the ~** twisti, mnenguo. **~er** *n* 1 *(colloq)* laghai, mrubuni. 2 tatizo, jambo gumu. **tongue-~er** neno/sentensi inayotatiza katika matamshi. **~y** *adj* 1 -enye kubetabeta. 2 -sio nyofu laghai.

twit[1] *vt* tania, sutasuta.

twit[2] *n (sl)* mpumbavu; punguani.

twitch *n* 1 mshtuko (agh. wa musuli); mtetemo wa uso. 2 kuvutwa (kwa ghafula); mpokonyo (wa ghafula) *vt,vi* 1 shtuka, shtusha *the dog ~ed its nose* mbwa alishtusha/tikisa pua yake. 2 vuta/nyakua/pokonya ghafla.

twitter *vi (of birds)* lia (kwa sauti nyororo), imba; *(of a person)* bubujika maneno, sema harakaharaka kwa sababu ya woga/ msisimko fulani *n* 1 mlio (wa sauti nyororo). 2 *(of persons) (colloq) (esp in)* **all of ~** katika msisimko fulani, -enye kiherehere.

twixt *prep (arch or poet)* **betwixt**.

two *n,adj* mbili, -wili, pili. **break/cut sth in ~** vunja/kata kitu katika sehemu mbili. **put ~ and ~ together**

fahamu kitu kutokana na mtu anavyoona, sikia, jifunza, n.k. **by ~s and threes** wawili wawili au watatu watatu kwa mpigo. **T~ can play (at) that game** tutaonana, wee ngoja tu! utaona! *(compound)* **~-edged** *adj (of a sword, etc)* -enye makali kuwili; *(fig) (of an argument, etc)* -enye maana mbili kinzani. **~-faced** *adj (fig)* nafiki, danganyifu. **~-fold** *adj, adv* -a mara mbili, mara dufu, mara mbili. **~-handed** *adj (of a sword)* -a mikono miwili; *(of a saw)* -a (kushikwa na) watu wawili. **~ penny piece** sarafu ya peni mbili. **~ penny half penny** -a peni mbili na nusu; *(colloq)* bure ghali, -sio na thamani. **~-a- penny** *adj* iliyo rahisi kupatikana, rahisi, -sio na thamani. **~ piece** *n* seti ya vazi la aina moja k.m. suruali na koti lake, sketi na kikoti chake, n.k. **~-ply** *adj* ncha mbili/unene wa aina mbili tofauti, - a tabaka mbili za unene. **~-seater** gari/ ndege, n.k. yenye viti viwili tu. **~-sided** -a njia mbili, -a pande mbili. **~some** *n* mchezo wa watu wawili tu. **~ stroke** *adj (of an engine)* -enye mapigo mawili, -a pistoni mbili. **~-timing** *adj* laghai, danganyifu. **~ -tongued** kigeugeu. **~-way** *attrib adj (of a switch)* -enye pande mbili za kuwasha na kuzima; *(of a road)* njia yenye panda mbili, -a njia mbili; *(of a radio)* inayopokea na kupeleka habari.

twould *(arch or poet)* **it would** inge.

tycoon *n (colloq)* tajiri (mwenye biashara au viwanda) maarufu, muki, bepari.

tying *pres p of* **tie**.

tyke, tike *n* 1 mbwa koko. 2 *(as a term of abuse)* mtu duni, bwege, mshenzi.

tympanum *n* 1 *(anat)* 1 kiwambo cha sikio. 2 sikio la kati.

type *n* 1 *(printing)* herufi (za kupigia chapa. 2 *(of a person, thing, event, etc)* kielezo, mfano, kifani. 3 *(genus/specie)* aina, jinsi, jamii *men of his* ~ watu wa aina yake. **true to ~** mwakilishi wa jamii yake.

typology *n* taipolojia; uainishi. 4 *(compounds)* **~ face** aina ya chapa. **~ script** *n* kazi iliyopigwa chapa tayari kwa kuchapishwa. **~ setter** mtayarishaji wa chapa. **~ writer** mashine ya chapa. **~ written** *adj* iliyopigwa chapa *vt,vi* 1 piga taipu. 2 panga katika aina, jinsi, jamii. **typist** *n* mpiga taipu. **typify** *vt* -wa mfano wa, wakilisha kundi/jamii fulani. **typography** *n* taipografia: sanaa/ taaluma ya kupiga chapa. **faults of ~** makosa ya kuchapa. **typographer** *n.* mchapaji. **typographic** *adj.* **typographically** *adv.*

type-cast *vt (theatre)* panga mtu kuchukua sehemu anayoiweza zaidi/ inayofanana na tabia zake.

typhoid *n (fever)* homa ya matumbo (kuhara damu).

typhoon *n* tufani, kimbunga.

typhus *n* homa kali iletwayo na chawa.

typical *adj* **~ (of)** -a mfano mmoja, -a mfano hasa, -a kufanana sana na asili; -a namna ile ile; -a kuwakilisha (aina/tabia,n.k.). **~ly** *adv* kwa kufanana hasa.

tyranny *n* 1 uonevu, udhalimu. 2 *(despotism)* udikteta, utawala kwa mtu mmoja peke yake, utawala wa mabavu. **tyrannical** *adj* dhalimu, -a kikatili, -a kidikteta. **tyrannize** *vi* **~ (over)** onea, dhulumu, tawala kwa mabavu, kandamiza. **tyrannous** *adj* onevu.

tyre *n (US* **tire***)* tairi, mpira.

tyro *n see* **tiro**.

tzar, tzarina *n see* **tsar**.

U

U,u *n* herufi ya ishirini na moja ya alfabeti ya Kiingereza. **~-boat** *n* nyambizi ya (ya) Kijerumani. **~bolt** *n* bolti ya **U.** **~ turn** mgeuko.
ubiquitous *adj (formal)* -a kuwapo kotekote (kwa wakati mmoja); -a kuenea kila mahali. **they are ~** wapo kila mahali. **ubiquity** *n* kuwapo mahali pote (mahali pengi sana); kuenea pote.
udder *n* kiwele.
udometer *n* udometa: chombo cha kupimia kiasi cha mvua; kipimamvua.
ugh wai!: sauti ya kuonyesha kero/tisho.
ugly *adj* 1 baya, hunde. 2 -a kutisha, -siovutia. **~ customer** *(colloq)* mtu wa hatari; mtu mgumu kushirikiana naye. **uglify** *vt* fanya -baya.
ukase *n (hist)* agizo la mfalme wa Urusi; amri isiyo kanuni.
ukulele *n* (*Hawaii*) kigita kidogo cha Hawaii (chenye nyuzi nne).
ulcer *n* donda; kidonda; *(fig)* athari/hali ya kupotosha. **~ous** *adj* -a kidonda. **~ate** *vt,vi* fanya/geuka. **~ation** *n* kidonda; kufanya kidonda.
ulna *n* (*anat*) mfupa wa mkono. **~r** *adj*. -a ulna.
ulster *n* joho lenye mkanda.
ulterior *adj* 1 -a baadaye, -a zaidi. 2 *(undisclosed)* -a siri, -a moyoni; -liofichika. **~motive** nia iliyofichika.
ultimate *adj* -a mwisho, -a mbali sana, -a msingi *~ cause* sababu ya msingi. **~ly** *adv* hatimaye, mwishowe.
ultimatum *n* sharti la mwisho, kauli ya mwisho; makataa *deliver an ~ to a government* kutoa makataa kwa serikali.
ultimo *adj* (*abbr* **ult**) -a mwezi uliopita; *the 30th ~* tarehe 30 mwezi uliopita.
ultra- *pref* -a kupita kiasi; -a kuzidi mno *(of person)* -enye mtazamo mkali. **~-fashinable** *adj* (kwa nguo) -a mtindo wa kisasa; -a kisiku hizi mno. **~ist** *n* mpinzani, mwenye mawazo makali. **~ism** *n* unazi.
ultramarine *n* rangi ya samawi *adj* -a (rangi ya) samawi.
ultramontane *adj (RC church)* -a uamini uwezo kamili wa Papa.
ultrasonic *adj* -a sauti isiyosikika kwa sikio la binadamu.
ultra-violet *adj* -a urujuani, -usioonekana kwa jicho la binadamu. **~ rays** miali isiyoonekana kwa jicho.
ultra vires *adj,adv (Lat)* -a kupita uwezo wa kisheria.
ululate *vi* piga vigelegele, piga vifijo. **ululation** *n* upigaji vigelegele, vifijo.
umber *n* kijani kibichi/chanikiwiti. **burnt ~** kahawia.
umbilical *adj* -a kitovu. **~ -cord** kiunga mwana.
umbrage *n* **take/give ~ (at sth)** jihisi kudharauliwa.
umbrella *n* 1 mwavuli. 2 *(fig)* kinga ya ndege za vita. 3 hifadhi, ufadhili, ulezi *under the ~ of the UNO* chini ya hifadhi ya Umoja wa Mataifa.
umlaut *n (in Germanic language)* umlati: utamkiaji mbele wa irabu za nyuma k.m. U ü.
umpire *n* mpatanishi; *(of games)* mwamuzi; *(of dispute)* msuluhishi. **be ~** amua *vi,vt* patanisha; amua; suluhisha.
umpteen *adj (slang)* chungu nzima; -ingi sana. **~th** *adj for the ~ time* sifahamu ni mara ngapi.
un *(pron) (colloq)* mtu; kitu *he is a good ~* ni mtu mwema *that's a good ~* ni mfano mzuri.
un- *(pref) (before adj. adv.)* 1 sio, hapana; *~certain* si yakini. 2 *(before (v)* tenda kinyume. **~tie** fungua. 3 *(before n)* huonyesha kutokuwa na uhakika; kutokuwa yakini; kutotaka.
unabashed *adj* -sioona haya, -sioogopa.
unabated *adj (of a storm, etc)* -a nguvu ileile, -siopungua.
unable *adj (pred only)* **~ to do sth** toweza, tokuwa na nguvu *I am ~ to go* siwezi kwenda.
unaccompanied *adj* 1 peke, -siosindikizwa *he was ~* hakusindikizwa. 2 *(of mus)* -nayopigwa pekee.
unaccountable *adj* -sioelezeka. **unaccountably** *adv* kwa namna isivyoelezeka.
unaccustomed *adj* 1 **~ to** -siozoea; -sio na mazoea ya. 2 -sio -a kawaida, -a

ajabu *his ~ silence* kimya chake kisicho cha kawaida.
unadvised *adj* bila ushauri/kushaurika, -enye kufanywa bila busara; -a harara, -a haraka. **~ly** *adv*. unaffected *adj* 1 -a kweli, nyofu. 2 *(unchanged)* **~ by** -siogeuzwa, -sio athiriwa/athirika *remain ~* -tobadilika *~ by acid* -siodhuriwa na asidi.
unalienable *adj* -siofarakanishwa, -siotenganishwa na.
unalloyed *adj* safi, halisi, -sioghushiwa, sio na mchanganyiko.
unalterably *adv* kwa kutobadilika, kwa uthabiti; kwa namna isiyobadilika.
unanimous *adj* -a kauli moja, -a pamoja, -siopingwa *the committee expressed the ~ opinion that* kamati ilikubaliana kwa kauli moja kwamba. **unanimity** *n* umoja *with ~* kwa umoja. **~ly** *adv* kwa kauli moja.
unannounced *adj* bila/pasipo kutangazwa *he walked into the room ~* aliingia pasipo watu kutangaziwa.
unanswerable *adj* -siokanika, -sioweza kukanushwa *the claim is ~* lile dai halikaniki. **unanswered** *adj* -siojibiwa *leave a letter ~* -tojibu barua.
unapproachable *adj* -sioingilika, -a baridi/kali.
unarmed *adj* bila silaha.
unasked *adj* ~ **(for)** bila kuombwa/ kuulizwa/kualikwa/kukaribishwa.
unassuming *adj* -siojitanguliza, -siojitia; -enye haya. **~ly**. *adv*.
unattached *adj* 1 -siofungamana na, huru, -siohusiana na. 2 -sioolewa, -sioposwa, -siochumbiwa *~ young lady* msichana asiyeolewa.
unattended *adj* 1 bila ya watumishi, -siosindikizwa. 2 -siohudumiwa.
unavailing *adj* bila jitihada, bila mafanikio, -a bure.
unavoidable *adj* -sioepukika *~ accident* ajali isiyoepukika. **unavoidably** *adv*.
unaware *adj (pref)* **~ of sth/that** -tofahamu, -tojua, -totambua *he was ~ of my presence* hakufahamu kuwa nipo. **~ness** *n* hali ya kutofahamu. **~s** *adv* 1 ghafula, bila kutazamiwa. **take sb ~s** stusha mtu. 2 bila kutambua. **he dropped the money ~s** aliangusha fedha bila kutambua.
unbacked *adj* 1 *(of a proposal)* bila kuungwa mkono. 2 *(of horse in a race)* bila kuwekewa dau/ kudhaminiwa.
unbalanced *adj (esp of a person, the mind)* kichaa, -enye wazimu, -liochanganyikiwa.
unbar 1 ondoa vyuma vya mlango;*(fig)* fungua/ondoa vikwazo. 2 achia wazi.
unbearable *adj* -siovumilika *his conduct is ~* tabia yake haivumiliki. **unbearably** *adv* kwa namna isiyovumilika.
unbecoming *adj* 1 -siofaa *it is ~ of sb to wear a short dress* haifai kuvaa gauni fupi. 2 ~ **to/for** si -zuri, baya.
unbeknown(st) *adj (colloq)* -siojulikana, bila kujua; *~ to anyone* bila kujulikana kwa mtu yeyote.
unbelief *n* 1 kutoamini. 2 kutokuwa na imani, ukafiri. **unbeliever** *n* asiyesadiki, mtu asiyemwamini Mungu. **unbelieving** *adj* -siyekuwa na imani; -sioamini.
unbend *vt,vi* 1 kunjua; pindua; nyosha, legea. 2 tulia, changamka, burudika, legeza maungo. **~ing** *adj* 1 -siokunjuka, -siopindika. 2 *(resolute)* -gumu; -shupavu; -siolegeza msimamo, -sioteteréka.
unbeseeming *adj (arch & impersonal)* -siofaa, -siostahili *it is ~ for you to do that* hustahili kufanya hivyo.
unbiased/unbiassed *adj* -a haki, -adilifu, -siopendelea.
unbidden *adj (formal)* -sioalikwa, -siokaribishwa, -sioitwa, pasipo kuamriwa *do sth ~* kufanya jambo pasipo kuamriwa.
unbind *vt* fungua; ondoa vifungo.
unblushing *adj* -sioona haya, -a/-enye kushupaa, -fidhuli, -pujufu *~ deeds* vitendo vya aibu.
unborn *adj* -siozaliwa bado, -a baadaye.
unbosom *vt* **~ oneself (to sb)** ungama,

fichua (siri) kwa mtu mwingine, toa siri zake.
unbounded *adj* pasipo kiasi, pasipo mpaka, bila kikomo.
unbowed *adj* -siokubali kushindwa, imara, thabiti.
unbrace *vt* fungua, legeza; tulia.
unbreakable *adj* -siovunjika.
unbridled *adj (esp fig)* -sio na nidhamu, -jeuri, -siodhibitiwa.
unbroken *adj* 1 -zima, kamili. 2 -siovunjika, -siobatilika/tangulika *the ~ law* sheria isiyobatilika/tangulika. 3 *(of horses)* -siofunzwa, -siofugwa. 4 *(of soil)* -siolimwa. 5 *(of records)* -siovunjwa. 6 mfululizo.
unbrotherly *adj* -sio kama ndugu, -siokuwa na upendo.
unbuckle *vt* fungua/legeza bakoli.
unburden *vt* **~ oneself/sth (of sth)** toa siri. funua siri/moyo; tua mzigo *~ oneself sth (of sth)* jiondolea hofi, ondosha mashaka *~ one's heart* jiondolea mashaka.
unbutton *vt* fungua kifungo *~ oneself* -jifungua vifungo. **~ed** *adj* 1 -liofunguliwa vifungo. 2 *(fig)* -sio na kiherehere, -sio na urasmi, huru.
uncalled *adj* -siotakiwa, -sio -a lazima, sio -a haki, -siohitajiwa.
uncanny *adj* -a ajabu, si -a kawaida, -sio -a desturi, -sio -a mazoea. **uncannily** *adv*.
uncap *vt,vi* 1 vua kofia. 2 ondoa kifuniko.
uncared-for *adj* -siotunzwa vema, -siolelewa vizuri, -liotupwa.
unceasing *adj* -a daima, -siokwisha, -a kuendelea bila kukoma. **~ly** *adv* daima, sikuzote, bila kukoma, mfululizo.
unceremonious *adj* -sio rasmi; -siofanywa kwa heshima, -liopuuzwa, -liodharauliwa. **~ly** *adv* bila heshima. **~ ness** *n*.
uncertain *adj* 1 -sio (na) hakika. 2 sioaminika; -a mashaka, geugeu; -a kubadilikabadilika *in no ~ terms* waziwazi, kwa kauli thabiti. **~ly** *adv*. **~ty** *n* 1 mashaka. 2 utovu wa hakika.
uncertified *adj*. -siohakikishwa, -siothibitishwa.
unchain *vt* fungua, fungulia minyororo.
unchallenged *adj* -siokanushwa, -siokaidiwa, -siopingwa.
unchangeable *adj* -siobadilika, thabiti, imara, madhubuti.
uncharitable *adj* -gumu, -siohuruma, -kali. **~ness** *n* ugumu wa moyo; utovu wa huruma.
uncharted *adj* 1 -siochorwa/onyeshwa kwenye ramani au chati. 2 *(lit or fig)* -siopimwa, -siopelelezwa.
unchecked *adj* 1 -siozuiwa; -siodhibitiwa*(untested)*-siotazamwa. 2 -siojaribiwa; -siopimwa *advance ~* kimyakimya.
unchristened *adj* -siobatizwa.
unchristian *adj* 1 -siyekuwa Mkristo, si -a kikristo, kinyume na maadili ya kikristo. 2 *(colloq)* -siofaa, -siostahili, -sio murua.
unchurch *adj* tenga/vua ukristo.
uncircumcised *adj* -siotahiriwa.
uncivil *adj* -siokuwa na adabu, siokuwa na uungwana/wema. **~ized** *adj* -siostaarabika, -shenzi.
unclaimed *adj* -siodaiwa na mwenyewe.
unclassified *adj* 1 -sioainishwa, -siopangwa taratibu. 2 -sio -siri.
uncle *n (mother's brother)* mjomba; *(father's brother)* amu; *(older than father)* baba mkubwa; *(younger than father)* baba mdogo. **U~ Sam** Marekani.
unclean *adj (of animals)* -chafu, -najisi, haramu.
unclouded *vt (the sky)* safi; *(fig)* -angavu, -sio na matatizo.
unco *(Scot) adj* -geni, -sio -a kawaida, -a ajabu *adv* ajabu.
uncoil *vi* nyoosha, kunjua, kunjuka.
uncoloured *adj (fig)* -siotiwa chumvi.
uncome-at table *adj (colloq)* -sioingilika, -siofikika.
uncomfortable *adj* -siotulia, -sio na raha; -siostarehesha; -a wasiwasi sana. **uncommitted** *adj* **~ (to)** -

-siofungamana, -siojifunga; huru.

uncommon *adj* -geni, ajabu, sio -a kawaida, si -a siku zote. **~ly** *adv*.

uncomplimentary *adj* -sio -a adabu, -fidhuli, -safihi, -a kuchukiza.

uncompromising *adj* -gumu, -a kushikiliashauri,-siobadilimsimamo.

unconcealed *adj* wazi.

unconcern *n* kutojali; -sio haya/hamu. **~ed** *adj* 1 -siojali. **~ed in sth** -siohusika na. **~ed with sth/sb** -siojali, -sio na uhusiano na -siojali, -sio na mawazo. 2 ~ **edly** *adv* kuwa pekee, kutohusika.

unconditional -enye kutokuwa na/-sio na masharti ~ *apology* radhi bila sharti. **~ly** *adv*. **unconditioned** *adj* 1 -sio (wekewa) masharti. 2 huru, -siotawaliwa ~ *reflex* mshtuko huru.

unconnected *adj* -a mbalimbali, -siohusiana, -siofungamana, -siounganika.

unconscionable *adj* -a kupita kiasi, mno, kabisa; -siokuwa na busara.

unconscious *adj* bila kufahamu, bila kujijua; sio na fahamu, -liozimia/ -liopoteza fahamu. **the** ~ *(psych)* sehemu ya ubongo isiyofikika (kiakili). **~ness** *n*. **~ly** *adv* bila kufahamu, bila kujua.

unconsidered *adj* 1 *(of words)* -siopimwa. 2 -siotiwa maanani, -enye kupuuzwa, -a kupuuzia.

unconstitutional *adj* -sio -a kikatiba, kinyume cha katiba.

unconstrained *adj* -siozuiwa, -sioshurutishwa, hiari, -siobanwa.

unconstricted *adj* -siobanwa.

uncontaminated *adj* -siochafuka, -sio najisi, safi, -sioambukizwa.

uncontemplated *adj* 1 -siokusudiwa, -sionuiwa. 2 -siotazamiwa, -siotarajiwa.

uncontested *adj* -siobishaniwa, -sioshindaniwa, -siogombewa.

uncontrolled *adj* -siozuiwa, -siotawali wa, -siodhibitiwa, -sioongozwa.

uncontrollable *adj* -siozuilika, -siotawalika, -sioongozeka, siodhibitika.

unconventional *adj* -sio -a kawaida, -siofuata kaida. **~ity** *n* hali ya kutofuata desturi/kaida.

unconverted *adj* -siobadilishwa, -sioongoka, -siogeuzwa. **unconvertible** *adj* -sioweza kubadilika, -sioweza kuongoka, -siogeuzika.

unconvicted *adj* -siotiwa hatiani.

unconvinced *adj* -sioshawishika, -siosadiki. **unconvincing** *adj* -siohakikisha, -sioaminisha.

uncooked *adj* -siopikwa, bichi.

unco-ordinated *adj* -sioratibiwa, -siokuwa na mpango.

uncork *vt* zibua.

uncorrected *adj* -siosahihishwa, -siotolewa makosa.

uncorroborated *adj* -sioshuhudiwa, -siothibitika.

uncorroded *adj* -sioliwa na kutu.

uncorrupted *adj* -siopotoka, -siopevuka, siokula rushwa, -siohongeka.

uncountable *adj* -siohesabika, -siokuwa na idadi ~ *noun* nomino isiyokuwa na wingi.

uncounted *adj* -siohesabiwa, -siofanyiwa hesabu.

uncouple *vt* fungulia, achanisha.

uncourteous *adj* -sio na adabu/ heshima. **~ness** *n* utovu wa adabu/ heshima.

uncourtly *adj* -sio adabu.

uncouth *adj* *(of persons, their behaviour)* -mbovu, shenzi, -baya; utovu wa adabu. **~ness** *n* utovu wa adabu, ushenzi. **~ly** *adv*.

uncover *vt* 1 funua, weka wazi; *(fig)* fichua, gubua. 2 gundua. 3 *(arch)* makofia. 4 funua (ili kushambulia).

uncoveted *adj* -siotamanika; *(unrespected)* -sioheshimika.

uncredited *adj* -siotamanika, -sio tumainika.

uncritical *adj* -siohakiki, -sioweza kupambanua, -nayokubali bila kupima.

uncropped *adj* 1 *(hair)* -siopunguzwa, -siokatwa na kuwa fupi. 2 *(of land)*

-siolimwa.

uncross *vt (legs, arms, knife)* -siokunjwa, -siofungwa. **~ed** *adj (of a cheque)* -siofungwa.

uncrowded *adj* -enye watu wachache; -siosongamana.

uncrown *vt* ondoa/ondoa kwenye ufalme. **~ed** *adj* 1 -siotiwa taji bado, -siotawadhwa. 2 -enye uwezo pasipo cheo cha ufalme. 3 **the ~ed king/ queen** mtu maarufu zaidi katika uwanja wake.

uncrushable *adj* -siopondeka, -sioangamizika; (*lit*) -siovunjika.

uncrystallized *adj* -sio dhahiri; -siofanywa fuwele.

unction *n* 1 kupaka mafuta **Extreme U~** mpako mtakatifu. 2 udanganyifu.

unctuous *adj* 1 -a mafuta, laini, -ororo. 2 nafiki. **~ly** *adv*.

uncultivated *adj* 1 -siolimwa, -siotengenezwa. 2 *(mind)* -sio na elimu, -jinga, -sio na malezi mema.

uncultured *adj* -siolelewa vizuri, -siokuwa na adabu, -siostaarabika.

uncurbed *adj* -siozuiwa, -siokinzwa.

uncured *adj* 1 -siopona. 2 *(meat)* -siokaushwa; *(of tobacco)* -siokanzwa.

uncurl *vt,vi* legeza; legea; *(straighten)* nyoosha, toa mapindi, nyooka *vi* legea, nyooka, toka mapindi.

uncurtailed *adj* -siofupishwa.

uncushioned *adj* -siokuwa na mto.

uncustomary *adj* -siokuwa na desturi, -siokuwa -a kawaida, -siokuwa -a mazoea.

uncut *adj (of a book or film)* -siopunguzwa, -siofupishwa; siokatwa; siokaguliwa.

undamaged *adj* -sioharibiwa.

undated *adj* -siotiwa/-sioandikiwa tarehe.

undaunted *adj* pasipo hofu, -siotishika, -jasiri.

undebatable *adj* -siobishanika, -siojadilika, -sio na mjadala.

undeceive *vt* fumbua (mtu) macho, eleza, bainisha.

undecided *adj* -siokata shauri bado, -a kusitasita.

undeclared *adj* 1 -sioonyeshwa (kwa afisa forodha). 2 -siotangazwa, kimyakimya.

undefeated *adj* -sioshindwa.

undefended *adj* -siolindwa, -siohifadhiwa, -siokingwa; *(of lawsuit)* -siotetewa.

undefiled *adj* -safi, -siochanganyika (na kitu duni), -sioghushiwa, -sionajisiwa.

undefined *adj* -siowekwa dhahiri/ wazi; -sioelezwa, sio fasiliwa. **undefinable** *adj* -siodhihirika, -sioelezeka waziwazi, -sioainishika.

undelayed *adj* -siokawizwa, -siocheleweshwa; -sioahirishwa.

undelivered *adj* -siokabidhiwa, -siotolewa, -siofikishwa.

undemonstrative *adj* -sioonyesha hisia. **undemonstratable** *adj* -sioonyesheka, -siofafanulika, -siothibitika. **undemonstrated** *adj* -sioonyeshwa, -siothibitishwa.

undeniable *adj* -siokanikana, -siokanushika, pasipo mashaka, -a wazi. **undeniably** *adv*.

undenominational *adj* -siohusu madhehebu yoyote, -siofungana na madhehebu.

undependable *adj* -siotegemewa, -siotumainika *he is ~* hatumainiki.

under[1] *adv* 1 chini *the ship went ~* meli imezama. 2 *(used to modify n)* -dogo; -enye cheo cha chini *~ secretary* naibu katibu mkuu.

under[2] *prep* 1 chini ya *the dog is ~ the tree* mbwa yuko chini ya mti. 2 -wa ndani ya, kufunikwa na, chini *the pillow is ~ the bedsheet* mto uko chini ya/umefunikwa na shuka. 3 -pungufu/dogo kuliko, chini ya *~ two acres* pungufu/chini ya eka mbili *children ~ twelve* watoto chini ya miaka kumi na mbili. 4 *(indicating various conditions) ~ fire* katika mashambulizi; *~ repair* katika matengenezo; *~ sentence* katika adhabu ya kifungo. 5 -liolemewa *marching ~ a heavy load* lemewa na mzigo mkubwa k.m. kodi, ada n.k.

underact *vt* igiza bila msisimko/mori/shauku. **~ion** *n* kitendo kidogo, kitendo kisicho kawaida au kisichotosheleza.
underarm *adj adv (cricket, tennis)* chini ya usawa wa bega/kiwiko.
underbid *vt* toa bei ndogo kuliko wengine.
underbred *adj* -enye mabaya, -siojua desturi, -tovu wa adabu.
underbrush *n see* **undergrowth**.
undercarriage *n see* **landing gear.**
undercharge *vt* toza pungufu ya thamani halisi (ya kitu kuliko ilivyo kawaida) *n* bei ya chini.
underclothing, underclothes *n (pl)* nguo za ndani.
undercover *adj* siri, chinichini ~ *agent* jasusi, shushushu.
undercurrent *n* 1 mkondo wa chini. 2 hisia/fikra za kichinichini.
undercut *vt* uza au fanya kazi kwa bei ndogo dhidi ya mshindani *n* nyama ya ng'ombe ya kiunoni, salala.
under-develop *vt* kwamisha/zuia maendeleo; *(of muscles etc)* dumaza. **~ed** *adj* -sioendelea.
underdo *vt* tenda kwa upungufu kuliko ipasavyo.
underdog *n* 1 *(often* **the** *~)* anayeonewa; mkandamizwaji, hohe hahe. 2 mtu anayedhalilishwa.
underdone *adj (esp of meat)* -bichi, -siopikwa/-sioiva vizuri.
underdose *n* kiasi cha dawa kidogo kuliko ilivyo pasa kuwa, pungufu.
underestimate *vt* kadiria pungufu, shindwa kupima nguvu n.k.
underfed *adj* -siolishwa ya kutosha.
underfloor *adj (of systems for heating)* chini ya sakafu.
underfoot *adv* chini ya miguu.
undergarment *n* nguo ya ndani k.m. gaguro n.k.
undergo *vt* pitia, fanya.
undergraduate *n* mwanafunzi wa Chuo Kikuu wa shahada ya kwanza.
underground *adj* chini *n* 1 chini ya ardhi. 2 *(fig)* siri *the ~ movement* chama cha siri *the ~ army* jeshi la siri *n* 1 **(the)** ~ reli ya chini ya ardhi. 2 tapo la chini chini.
undergrowth *n* magugu, vichaka; *(in mangrove swamp)* makoko.
underhand *adj* -a hila, -danganyifu, -janja ~ *dealings* njama *adv* kwa siri; kwa udanganyifu. **~ed** *adj*.
underhung *adj (attrib) (of the lower jaw)* -linalojitokeza kuzidi taya la juu.
underlay n mpira unaotandazwa chini ya zulia/godoro. **~er** *n* tabaka la chini.
underlet *vt* kadiria thamani kidogo kuliko ilivyopaswa, pangisha nusu; pangisha kwa kodi ya chini.
underlie *vt* -wa chini ya; -wa msingi wa (nadharia, tabia, imani n.k.).
underline *vt* chora/pigia mistari chini; *(fig)* sisitiza, kaza *n* mstari ulio chini ya maneno.
underling *n (usu contemptuous)* mdogo kwa cheo, kazi.
undermanned *adj (of a ship, factory etc)* -siokuwa na wafanyakazi/watumishi wa kutosha.
undermentioned *adj* -liyotajwa hapa chini; ifuatayo (baadaye).
undermine *vt* 1 fukua chini (kwa makusudi ya kubomoa); ekua; dhoofisha kwa chini/ndani. 2 dhoofisha kidogo kidogo.
undermost *adj* -a chini kabisa.
underneath *prep* chini *adv* chini ya *n* chini, sehemu ya chini ya kitu.
undernourished *adj* -siolishwa chakula cha kutosha. **undernourishment** *n*.
underpants *n* chupi.
underpaid *pt of* **underpay**
underpass *n* sehemu ya barabara inayopita chini ya barabara nyingine au reli.
underpay *vt* punja, lipa mshahara/ujira pungufu, lipa isivyo halali. **~ments** *n.*
underpin *vt* tegemeza, imarisha kwa miti (nguzo n.k.), gadimu; *(fig)* unga mkono, jenga hoja.
underpopulated *adj (of a country or*

area) -enye idadi ndogo ya wakazi (kulingana na raslimali ya nchi).

underprivileged *adj* -lionyimwa haki za kimsingi za kijamii, -lionyimwa nafasi ya kujiendeleza/kuishi vema.

underproduction *n* kuzalisha mazao pungufu (ya kiasi kilichotegemewa), uzalishaji pungufu (wa bidhaa, n.k.).

underquote *vt* weka/toa ndogo (kuliko ilivyo kawaida).

underrate *vt* toa thamani/makadirio madogo, dunisha, dharau, shindwa kubaini (nguvu, thamani n.k.).

underscore *vt see* **underline**.

under-secretary *n* katibu mkuu. **~ship** *n* ofisi ya (cheo cha) katibu mkuu.

undersell *vt* uza rahisi kuliko (mwuzaji mwingine).

undersexed *adj* -enye nyege/hamu/ matamanio kidogo (kuliko kawaida).

under-shirt *n* fulana.

undershoot *vt (of an aircraft)* tua kabla (ya kufikia kiwanja).

underside *n* chini, upande wa chini.

undersign *vt* tia sahihi; andika jina chini *the ~ed* wale wenye sahihi zao hapa chini/waliotia sahihi.

undersized *adj* -dogo, -liovia, -liodumaa.

underskirt *n* gaguro, kitema, rinda.

understaffed *adj* -enye watumishi pungufu, -enye ikama haba.

understand *vt,vi* 1 fahamu, elewa, sikia, maizi. **make oneself understood** jieleza wazi wazi. **(now) ~ me** tuelewane, nielewe. **~ one another** *(of two person, parties)* elewana; elewa hisia, mawazo, makusudi ya mwingine. 2 fahamu (tokana na taarifa iliyopatikana); jua; (ji)chukulia. **give sb to ~ (that....)** fanya mtu afahamu (kwamba), -pa picha. 3 fahamu akilini. **~able** *adj* inayoeleweka.**~ably** *adv*. **~ing** *adj* -enye kuelewa hisia za wengine *n* 1 uwezo safi wa akili, uwezo wa kuwaza vizuri, ufahamu. 2 huruma, kiwango cha kufahamu hisia za wengine. 3 *(often an understanding, but rarely pl)* mapatano, maafikiano, makubaliano. **on this ~ing** katika hali hii. **on the ~ing that....** kwa masharti kuwa... **~ingly** *adv* kwa kujua, kwa kuelewa, kwa kufahamu.

understate *vt* -shindwa kueleza kikamilifu, toa maelezo pungufu; rahisi; jizuia katika kusema. **~ment** *n* kutoeleza kikamilifu; urahisishaji; maelezo pungufu; kutosema ukweli wote.

understock *vt* pungukiwa (bidhaa); weka wanyama pungufu (shambani).

understood *pt of* **understand**.

understudy *n* kujifunza kazi ya mtu mwingine; mtu mwenye kujifunza/ kuweza kufanya kazi ya mtu mwingine *vt* jifunza kazi ya mtu mwingine (hasa mwigizaji).

undertake *vt* 1 ~ **(to do) sth,** kubali/ jitolea/jiandaa kufanya jambo. 2 anza kazi. 3 thibitisha, ahidi.

undertaking *n* 1 kazi/shughuli (aliyokubali/jitolea/jiandaa kuifanya). 2 ahadi; dhamana.

undertaker *n* mwenye kutayarisha maziko, mzishi, mpambaji.

undertaking *n* kazi ya kuzika.

undertenant *n* mpangaji mdogo.

undertone *n* 1 sauti hafifu ya mnong'ono. 2 hali/dalili (isiyo dhahiri) *an ~ of discontent* manung'uniko. 3 rangi nyepesi.

undertook *pt of* **undertake**

undertow *n* mkondo wa chini (kinzi).

undervalue *vt* -pa thamani pungufu/ ndogo, dunisha. **undervaluation** *n*.

underwater *n* chini ya usawa wa maji, chini ya maji.

underwear *n* nguo za ndani, chupi.

underwent *pt of* **undergo**.

underwood *n* magugu, vichaka.

underworld *n* 1 *(in GK myths)* jahanamu. 2 jamii ya wahalifu/watu waovu (wevi n.k.) wa mji.

underwrite *vt* kubali jukumu, chukulia bima; dhamini; chukua jukumu la kununua hisa zote za kampuni zilizobaki, (hasa kwa meli ya shehena). **~r** *n* mdhamini; mwenye kukubali jukumu (hasa la meli ya

shehena).
undeserving *adj* -siostahili, -siostahiki.
undesigned *adj* -siokusudiwa; -siotabiriwa/bashiriwa.
undesirable *adj* -siotakiwa, -siofaa, -baya *n ~ person* mtu asiyetakiwa.
undetachable *adj* si -a kutenga, si -a kutoa, si -a kubandua, -sioweza kutenganishwa na.
undetected *adj* -siogunduliwa, -siofahamika *adv* bila kugunduliwa.
undetermined *adj* -sioyakiniwa, -sioazimiwa, -siokusudiwa, -sionuiwa.
undeterred *adj* -sioogopeshwa, -siozuiwa, -siotishwa.
undeveloped *adj* -siostawishwa, -siostawi, viza.
undid *pt of* **undo**
undies *n pl (colloq)* nguo za ndani za mwanamke.
undifferentiated *adj* -siotofautishwa, -sopambanuliwa.
undigested *adj (of food)* 1 -siomeng'enywa. 2 *(of news)* -sioeleweka/fahamika. **undigestible** *adj* -siomeng'enyeka.
undignified *adj* -sio adabu, -siofaa, -sio heshima.
undiluted *adj* -siozimuliwa, -siofifishwa.
undimmed *adj* -a wazi, -a kuonekana, -a kueleweka, dhahiri.
undiplomatic *adj* si suluhishi, si -a busara, -sio -a kidiplomasia; -enye kusema wazi/bila kuficha.
undirected *adj* -siyoelekezwa, -siopangwa, -sioongozwa.
undiscerning *adj* -jinga, -sio juzi, -siotambuzi, -sioona.
undischarged *adj (of cargo)* -siosushwa/pakuliwa,-sioachiliwa;*(of debt)* -siolipwa; *(of person) ~ bankrupt* mufilisi asiyeachiliwa.
undisciplined *adj* -siozoezwa kutii amri, -a ovyo; -sioadibishwa, -sio na nidhamu.
undisclosed *adj* -siodhihirishwa, -siotangazwa.
undiscouraged *adj* -siovunjika moyo, -siopingwa, -siozuiwa, -siokatishwa tamaa.
undiscovered *adj* -siogunduliwa.
undiscriminating *adj* -siopambanua, -siochagua, -sitofautisha. **~ly** *adv* bila tofauti.
undiscussed *adj* -siozungumziwa, -sioongelewa, -siojadiliwa.
undisguised *adj* 1 -siofichwa, -siogeuzwa. 2 wazi, dhahiri, bayana. **~ly** *adv*.
undismayed *adj* -siotishwa, -siofadhaishwa; -siohofu, -siofadhaa.
undisputed *adj* wazi, -sioubishi/ bishaniwa.
undissolved *adj* 1 *(parliament)* -siovunjwa, -siokomeshwa. 2 -sioyeyuka; -siotanguka, -sioamuliwa.
undistinguishable *adj* -sioweza kupambanuliwa, -sioainishika.
undistracted *adj* -sioingiliwa, -siovurugwa.
undistributed *adj* -siogawanywa, -siosambazwa.
undisturbed *adj* -tulivu; bila usumbufu. **~ly** *adv* -siosumbuliwa.
undivided *adj* -siogawanyika, -zima, -ote, kamili.
undo *vt* 1 tangua, fundua, futua. 2 *(stitches)* fumua, shonoa. 3 *(arch)* angamiza, haribu. **what is done cannot be ~ne (prov)** yaliyokwisha kumwagika hayazoleki. **~ing n** (sababu ya) kuangamia.
undone *pred adj* siofanywa, -siokamilika.
undock *vt (of space craft)* achanisha/ tenganisha sayari/vyombo vya anga.
undomesticated *adj* koko; -siyovutiwa na mambo ya nyumbani, -siyofugwa. -siokalishwa nyumbani.
undoubted *adj* -a hakika, halisi, bila shaka, -sio (na) walakini, -a kweli. **~ly** *adv* pasipo/bila shaka.
undreamed, undreamt *adj (usu) ~* **of** -siowazika; -siootwa, -siofikirika.
undress *vt, vi* vua nguo *(of state)* 1 utupu, uchi; nusu uchi. 2 *(of clothing)* ya kawaida, sio rasmi.
undue *adj* -siyostahili, -liokiuka

mpaka.
unduly *adv* mno.
undulate *vi* piga mapinde; inuka na kushuka. **undulant** *adj*. **undulation** *n* 1 mapinde, mwendo wa wimbi, kuinuka na kushuka kama mawimbi, vilima na mabonde. 2 *(rising ground)* kiduta, mwinuko. **undulatory** *adj* 1 -a kuinuka na kushuka; -a mapinde/ mawimbi, -enye vilima na mabonde. 2 -a mwendo wa wimbi.
undying *adj* -siokufa, -sioisha, -a aushi, -a milele.
unearned *adj* 1 -siochumwa, bwerere ~ *income* mapato yasioyochumwa ~ *increment* nyongeza bwerere. 2 -siostahili, -siohaki.
unearth *vt* gundua; fukua, zikua ~ *a buried treasure* zikua/fukua hazina iliyozikwa ~ *new facts about the life of someone* gundua mambo mapya juu ya ·maisha ya mtu fulani.
unearthly *adj* 1 -sio -a dunia hii, -a peponi, -a shetani. 2 -a ajabu, -a miujiza, -a kuogofya. 3 *(colloq)* bovu *at an ~ hour* saa mbovu.
uneasy *adj* -sio na raha/utulivu; -a mashaka, -a wasiwasi. **uneasiness/ unease** *n* kutaradadi; mashaka, wasiwasi, hangaiko. **uneasily** *adv*.
uneatable *adj* -siolika, -siofaa kwa chakula.
uneaten *adj* -sioliwa.
uneconomic *adj* -a hasara, -siolipa, -sio na faida ya kutosha.
uneconomical *adj* fujaji, tapanyi.
unedited *adj* -siohaririwa.
uneducated *adj* -siofundwa, -siosoma, -sioelimishwa, -sioelimika
unemployed *adj* -sio na kazi, -sioajiriwa *n the* ~ watu wasio na kazi. **unemployable** *adj* -sioajirika *n (person)* -siofaa (kwa kazi).
unemployment *n* 1 kutokuwa na kazi. 2 nguvu ya kazi inayopotea bure. 3 *(attrib)* ~ *insurance/benefit/pay* ruzuku kwa wasio na kazi.
unenclosed *adj* -siozungushiwa kabisa, -siozingirwa kabisa, -siotiwa/fungwa ndani (ya furushi/bahasha ua kasha).
unencumbered *adj* -sio na vipingamizi/ vizuizi, huru kabisa.
unending *adj* -sioisha, -sio na mwisho, -sio na mpaka *(colloq)* -a mara kwa mara. **~ly** *adv*.
unendowed *adj* -siojaliwa, -siokipaji, -siokabidhishwa mali.
unendurable *adj* -siovumilika; -siochukulika.
unengaged *adj* -sioposwa; -sioajiriwa; -siotumwa/-sio na shughuli; -siochumbiwa.
unengaging *adj* -a kuchukiza, -siopendeza, -siovutia.
un-English *adj* (*characteristic of*) si -a Kiingereza.
unenlightened *adj* -sioelimishwa, -sio (na) habari, -jinga, -a gizani, -shirikina. **unenlightening** *adj* -sioeleza chochote, -sioelimisha, -siotoa mwanga/fununu.
unenterprising *adj* -siojasiri, -oga.
unentertaining *adj* -siopendeza, -siofurahisha, -sioburudisha.
unentitled *adj* -sio na haki, -siostahili.
unenviable *adj* -siotamanika, -sioonewa wivu, si -a kutaka.
unequal *adj* ~ **(to sth)** 1 -sio sawa. 2 -siolingana, -a kuhitilafiana. 3 dhaifu, -sioweza *be ~ to doing sth* -toweza kufanya kitu. **~ly** *adv*. **~led** *adj* -sio kifani, -zuri kabisa.
unequipped *adj* -sioandaliwa, -siotengenezwa, -sio jiandaa.
unequivocal *adj* -a kauli/maana moja, dhahiri, -sio -a ndumila kuwili, -sio kauleni ~ *plea* ikirari isiyo kauleni.
unerring *adj* -siokosea, -a hakika. **~ly** *adv*.
UNESCO *(abbr)* Shirika la Elimu, Sayansi na Utamaduni la Umoja wa Mataifa.
unessential *adj* -sio -a lazima, si -a maana sana, -si -a muhimu *n the ~ s* mambo yasiyo maana.
uneven *adj* -sio sawa *(of numbers)* witiri, -sio shufwa. **~ness** *n*.
uneventful *adj* -sio na matukio ya ajabu; -a vivi hivi, -a matukio ya

kawaida.

unexampled *adj* -sio na kifani, -a pekee, -siofikiwa.

unexçelled *adj* -sioshindika, -siopitika, -siozidiwa.

unexceptionable *adj* -zuri, safi, -sio na doa/lawama, kamili.

unexcited *adj* -sioamshwa, -siochochewa, -siosisimka.

unexecuted *adj* -siofanyizwa, -siotekelezwa.

unexpected *adj* -siotazamiwa, -a ghafula. **~ly** *adv* bila kutazamiwa, ghafula.

unexplained *adj* -sioelezwa, -siofasiriwa, -siofafanuliwa, -siofumbuliwa.

unexploded *adj* -siolipuka, -siolipuliwa *an ~ shell* bomu lisilolipuka (bado).

unfailing *adj* -a daima, -siokwisha, -siokwama. **~ly** *adv*.

unfair *adj* -sio sawa, -sio haki. **~ly** *adv*. **~ ness** *n*.

unfaithful *adj* 1 -sio -aminifu. 2 *(adulterous)* -zinifu, -zinzi. **~ly** *adv*. **~ness** *n*.

unfaltering *adj* imara, thabiti, -siosita, -siobabaika. **~ly** *adv*.

unfamiliar *adj* 1 ~ **(to)** -siojulikana sana. 2 ~ **with** si zoevu, -geni *be ~ with sth* -tozoea kitu.

unfashionable *adj* -sio -a siku hizi, -a zamani, -liopitwa na wakati.

unfasten *vt* fungua, komoa, fundua.

unfathomable *adj* 1 -siofikika chini; -a kina kirefu sana. 2 *(fig)* -gumu sana, -sioweza kueleweka; -geni mno.

unfathomed *adj (of depth)* -siopimika; *(of person)* -sioeleweka; *(of crime)* -siofumbuliwa.

unfavourable *adj* -siofaa.

unfeasible *adj* -siowezekana, -siotendeka.

unfed *adj* -siolishwa, -siochungwa; *(fire)* -siochochewa.

unfeeling *adj* -sio na huruma, -a moyo mgumu; -siowezakuonea huruma. **~ly** *adv*.

unfeigned *adj* -a kweli, halisi. **~ly** *adv*.

unfermented *adj* -siochachuka, -siochacha.

unfertile *adj* -sio na rutuba, tasa, gumba.

unfertilized *adj* -siotiwa mbolea/samadi; -siotiwa mbegu/mimba.

unfetter *vt* fungua (pingu).**~ed** *adj* huru, -sio na vikwazo; *(of a prisoner)* -liofunguliwa mnyororo, -lioachwa huru.

unfilled *adj* -siojazwa, -siojalizwa, -siofukiwa, -sioshibishwa.

unfinished *adj* -siokwisha, -siokamili, -siomalizwa.

unfit *adj* ~ **(for sth/to do sth)** -siofaa, -siostahili; dhaifu *vt* ~ **sb for sth** dhoofisha, ondoleanguvu/uwezo n.k. **~ness** *n*.

unflagging *adj* -siochoka; -siokatizwa.

unflappable *adj (colloq)* -sioyumba/yumbishwa.

unflavoured *adj* -siokolezwa, -siotiwa viungo, -sioungwa.

unfledged *adj* 1 *(of a bird)* -sioweza kuruka bado. 2 *(fig) (of a person)* -siokomaa; -sio na uzoefu.

unflinching *adj* -sioogopa; -siosita, -siolegea, thabiti.

unfold *vt,vi* 1 kunjua. 2 onyesha, tangaza; (ji)tokeza.

unforeseen *adj* -siotazamiwa, -a ghafula, -siofikiriwa. **unforeseeable** *adj* -siofikirika; -siotabirika, -siobashirika.

unforgettable *adj* -siosahaulika. **unforgotten** *adj* -siosahauliwa. **unforgiving** *adj*-siosamehe.

unformed *adj* -changa, -siokomaa, -siokuzwa.

unfortified *adj* -siojengewa ngome, -sioimarishwa.

unfortunate *adj* -a bahati mbaya; -a kusikitisha. **~ly** *adv* kwa bahati mbaya.

unfounded *adj* -siothibitishwa, -sio na msingi ~ *rumours* uvumi usio na msingi.

unfrequented *adj*-siopitiwa/tembelewa mara nyingi.

unfriendly *adj* -a kiadui, si -a rafiki,

-kali. **unfriendliness** *n* uadui, ukatili.
unfrock *vt (of a priest guilty of bad conduct)* fukuza upadre.
unfruitful *adj* 1 -siozaa, tasa. 2 -a bure, bila mafanikio.
unfulfilled *adj* -siotimizwa, -siotimilizwa.
unfurl *vt, vi* fungua, kunjua, funguka, kunjuka; *(of sail, flag* n.k.) tweka.
unfurnished *adj (house, apartments)* -sio na samani.
ungainly *adj* si -zuri, -zito, -ovyoovyo.
ungenerous *adj* -sio -karimu, -nyimivu, bahili.
un-get-at-able *adj* -siofikika, -sioambilika.
ungifted *adj* -siojaliwa, si hodari, -sio (na) kipawa.
ungird *vt* vua mshipi/mkanda/msombo n.k.
ungodly *adj* 1 si -cha Mungu, -ovu. 2 *(colloq)* -a maudhi/kero. 3 *(colloq)* -bovu, -siofaa.
ungovernable *adj* -siodhibitika, -siozuilika, -siotawalika *an ~ temper* hasira isiyozuilika.
ungraceful *adj* -sio -zuri, -sio -a madaha; -zito. **~ly** *adv*. **~ness** *n*.
ungracious *adj* 1 *(arch)* -ovu. 2 -sio -a adabu. 3 -siopendeza. **~ly** *adv*. **~ ness** *n*.
ungrammatical *adj* -sio -a kisarufi, -sio sahihi (kisarufi). **~ly** *adv*. **~ity** *n*.
ungrateful *adj* 1 -sio na shukrani. 2 *(of a task)* -siovutia. **~ness** *n*.
ungrounded *adj* bila kisa/sababu/hoja; -siothibitishwa.
unguarded *adj* 1 *(esp of a person and what he says)* -sio na hadhari, bila kufikiri; -sio -a busara. 2 -siolindwa. **~ly** *adv*.
unguent *n* mafuta (ya dawa).
unhallowed *adj* 1 -siofanywa takatifu; -siowekwa wakfu. 2 -ovu, -baya, -a shetani, najisi.
unhampered *adj* -siozuiwa, -siotatanishwa.
unhand *vi (arch)* achilia; ondoa mikono.
unhandsome *adj* hunde.
unhandy *adj* -sioelekevu wa kazi, -siofaa; -zito, -gumu.
unhanged *adj* -sionyongwa.
unhappy *adj* 1 -a huzuni, -a majonzi, -sio na furaha, -a moyo mzito. 2 siofaa/stahili. **unhappily** *adv*. **unhappiness** *n*.
unhealthy *adj* -sio na afya, dhaifu, -a kuleta magonjwa; *(colloq)* -a hatari. **unhealthily** *adv*.**unhealthiness** *n*.
unheard -siosikiwa, -siosikilizwa. **go ~** -tosikilizwa; -tokuwa na mtu wa kusikiliza. **~-of** *adj* -a ajabu, -geni, -sio na kifani, -pya kabisa.
unheeding *adj* -sioangalia, -sioangalifu, si makini.
unheeded *adj* -siosikilizwa, -sioangaliwa, -siofuatwa, -a kudharauliwa.
unheedful *adj* -zembe, -siyeangalia, -siyejali.
unhelpful *adj* kimyakimya, -siosaidia.
unhesitating *adj* bila hofu/kusita. **~ly** *adv* bila kusitasita.
unhindered *adj* -siozuiwa, -siopingwa, -siocheleweshwa.
unhinge *vt* 1 ondoa (mlango n.k.) kwenye bawabu zake. 2 rusha akili, tia wazimu.
unholy *adj* 1 -ovu, -a shetani, -chafu, najisi. 2 bovu.
unhonoured *adj* -sioheshimiwa, -siojaliwa, -siotukuzwa.
unhook *vt* fungua, toa katika ndoana.
unhoped-for *adj* -siotegemewa kutokea, -siotarajiwa.
unhorse *vt* tupa, rusha, ondosha kutoka juu ya farasi.
unhurt *adj* bila kuumia, bila kuumizwa, bila kupata madhara, -siodhurika.
unhygienic *adj* si -a afya, -a kuleta madhara kiafya; -sio safi, -siofuata kanuni za usafi.
uni- *pref* moja.
uniaxial *adj* -enye ekseli moja.
unicameral *adj (of -a parliament)* -enye chumba kimoja tu; -enye bunge moja.

unicellular *adj* -a seli moja, -enye mwili wenye seli moja tu.
unicolour *adj* -a rangi moja.
unicorn *n (in old stories)* mnyama kama farasi mwenye pembe moja.
unidentified *adj* -siotambuliwa. ~ **flying object** *(abbr UFO) see* **flying saucer.**
uniform *adj* -a mfano mmoja, sawasawa, -a kulingana; sare *make* ~ fanya sare/sawa, sawazisha/ yunifomu/sare. **in** ~ -liovaa yunifomu sare. **~ed** *adj* -liovaa sare. **~ly** *adv.* **~ity** *n* kuwa sawa, umoja, ulinganifu.
unify *vt* 1 fanya kuwa -moja, unganisha. 2 fanya sare.
unification *n* kuunganisha.
unilateral *adj* -a kuhusu upande (mtu, taifa) moja tu; -a upande mmoja.
unimaginable *adj* -siofikirika, -sioeleweka, -siowazika.
unimpaired *adj* -sioharibika, -siodhurika, -siodhoofika.
unimpeachable *adj* safi kabisa, -sio na shaka, -a kuaminika kabisa.
unimpeded *adj* -siozuiwa, -siopingwa.
unimportant *adj* -sio muhimu.
unimpressed *adj* -siovutiwa; -sioingiwa.
uninfected *adj* -sioambukizwa.
uninflammable *adj* 1 -sioshika moto, -gumu kushika moto. 2 si harara, gumu kukasirika.
uninfluenced *adj* -siovutwa, -sioshawishiwa, -siogeuzwa, -sioathiriwa.
uninfluential *adj* -sio na nguvu ya kushawishi.
uninformed *adj* -siokuwa na taarifa, -siojua.
uninhabitable *adj* 1 -sipokalika.
uninhabited *adj* -sipokaa watu. 2 -kiwa, mahame.
uninhibited *adj* huria,-siobanwabanwa.
uninitiated *adj* -siofundishwa, -siofundwa, -sioingizwa (katika chama, madhehebu n.k.); -siopitia jando/unyago.
uninspired *adj* -siovutia, chapwa, -a kuchusha, chushi.
uninstructed -siofundishwa, -sioelekezwa.
uninsured *adj* -siowekewa bima, -siodhaminiwa.
unintelligent *adj* -sio na akili, -siotambuzi, zezeta.
unintelligible *adj* -sioeleweka, -siotambulikana.
unintended *adj* -siokusudiwa, -sionuiwa, -sioazimiwa, -siodhamiriwa. **unintentional** *adj* -siokusidiwa, si -a makusudi.
uninterested *adj* ~ **(in)** -siovutwa, -siopendezwa, -sio na hamu.
uninterrupted *adj* -siokatizwa, mfululizo; bila kuzuiwa/kuingiliwa.
unintimidated *adj* -siotishiwa, -siokamiwa.
unintoxicating *adj* -siolevya, -siorusha akili.
uninventive *adj* -sio vumbuzi, -sio bunifu, -sio elekevu.
uninvited *adj* -siokaribishwa, -sioalikwa *come* ~ kuja bila kukaribishwa/kualikwa. **uninviting** *adj* si -a kutamanisha, si -a kuvutia.
union *n* 1 muungano, umoja. 2 *(colloq)* mapatano, maafikiano *a happy* ~ ndoa yenye furaha. 3 *(society)* jamii, chama. **U~ Jack**, bendera ya Waingereza ~ *of sets* mwungano wa seti. 4 *(tech)* kiungo. **~ism** *n* falsafa ya umoja. 5 **~ist** mwanachama wa chama cha wafanyakazi; mtetezi wa vyama vya wafanyakazi. **U~ist** *(GB Politics)* mpinzania wa kujitenga kwa Ireland; *(US)* mtetezi wa serikali ya muungano.
unique *adj* -a pekee, -sio na kifani ~ *solution* ufumbuzi wa pekee. **~ly** *adv.* **~ness** *n.*
unisex *adj (of clothes)* mtindo utumiwao na jinsi zote; -a jinsi zote.
unison *n* **(in)** ~ kwa mapatano/ maafikiano *act in* ~ tenda/fanya kwa pamoja.
unissued *adj* -siotolewa.
unit *n* 1 kitu kimoja, jamii ya vitu/ watu; kitengo. 2 kizio ~ *square* kizio mraba. 3 namba nzima ndogo

kuliko zote; namba moja. 4 *(compounds)* **kitchen** ~ vifaa vya jikoni. ~ **furniture** seti ya samani. ~ **trust** amana ya kikundi. **~ary** *n, adj* -a moja.

Unitarian *n* Mkristu asiyeamini utatu Mtakatifu. **~ism** *n.*

unite *vt, vi* 1 unga, unganisha. 2 ungana, unganika, -wa shauri moja, patana. 3 ~ **(in sth/to do sth)** fanya pamoja. **~d** *adj* 1 -lioungana (kiroho/ kisiasa); -liounganishwa. 2 -a pamoja. **~dly** *adv.* **unity** *n* 1 umoja, mapatano, ulinganifu ~ *is strength* umoja ni nguvu. **the dramatic unities; the unities of place, time and action** uwiano wa mahali, muda na vitendo katika mchezo wa kuigiza. 2 mwoano, makubaliano (ya hisia, malengo n.k.).

universal *adj* -a -ote; -a watu wote; -a kuenea pote, -a wakati wote, -a mahali pote, -a kazi zote. **a ~ joint** kiungo kinachoruhusu matumizi ya pande zote. **a ~ rule** kanuni, faradhi. ~ **suffrage** kura kwa wote. **~ism** *n* falsafa ya kilimwengu, malimwengu. **~ity** *n.* **~ly** *adv* kilimwengu. **~ize** *vt* fanya kilimwengu.

universe *n* 1 **the U~** Ulimwengu, vitu vyote. 2 mifumo ya sayari.

university *n* chuo kikuu.

unjust *adj* -sio haki, -dhalimu, onevu; -siostahili. **~ifiable** *adj* -sioweza kutetewa; -siothibitika. **~ified** *adj* sio -a haki, -siothibitishwa. **~ly** *adv* bila haki, kwa udhalimu.

unkempt *adj* chafu; *(esp of hair)* timtimu, -siochanwa.

unkind *adj* -sio na huruma; -sio -ema. **~ly** *adv.* **~ness** *n* ukosefu wa huruma.

unknowing *adj* -siofahamu; -sio na habari, -siojua. **~ly** *adv* bila kujua/ kuwa na habari.

unknown *adj* -siojulikana, -siobainika ~ *to me* nisilolijua.

unlabelled *adj* -siobandikwa/tiwa/ fungiwa kipande; -siowekwa alama.

unlace *vt* fungua (kamba).

unlawful *adj* kinyume cha sheria, haramu, isiyo halali ~ *assembly* mkutano haramu, mkutano bila idhini, mkutano usioidhinishwa.

unlearn *vt (ideas, habits etc)* ondoa/ acha (mawazo, tabia n.k.), jisahaulisha.

unleash *vt* fungulia mnyororo, *(fig)* achia huru.

unleavened *adj (of bread)* -siotiwa chachu/hamira.

unless *conj* ila; isipokuwa *he cannot work ~ he drinks coffee in the morning* hawezi kufanya kazi asipokunywa kahawa asubuhi.

unlettered *adj* -sio na elimu, -siosoma; -siojua kusoma.

unlicensed *adj* bila leseni, -sio na leseni.

unlike *adj* si sawa, tofauti na, -isofanana, -enye kuachana. **~ly** *adj* -sioelekea (kutokea/kuaminika); -sioyamkinika.

unlimited *adj* -sio na mpaka/ukomo ~ *liability* dhima isiyo ukomo.

unlined *adj* 1 *(of paper)* pasipo mistari. 2 *(of clothes)* bila bitana.

unload *vt, vi* 1 shusha, tua, pakua shehena. 2 ~ **(on to)** *(colloq)* ondolea, ondosha (mzigo/kitu kisichotakiwa), tua tatizo.

unlock *vt* fungua ~ *the door* fungua mlango.

unlooked-for *adj* -siotazamiwa, -siotarajiwa.

unloose *vt* fungua; fungulia, achilia huru.

unlucky *adj* -sio na bahati; -a kisirani, -a ndege mbaya *be ~* -wa na bahati mbaya/mkosi **unluckily**. adv kwa bahati mbaya.

unman *vt* legeza moyo, katisha tamaa, dhoofisha. **~ly** *adj* 1 dhaifu, oga. 2 *(of a man)* -a kike.

unmanageable *adj* -sioweza kuongozwa; -sioongozeka, -sioweza kuzuiwa, -siodhibitika.

unmanned *adj* -sio na rubani.

unmannered/unmannerly *adj* -sio na adabu, -fidhuli, -safihi.

unmarked *adj* -sio na alama, -siotambuliwa, -siogundulika.

unmarketable *adj* -siouzika, -sionunulika.
unmarried *adj* kapera, -seja, sio oa/olewa.
unmask *vt,vi* 1 vua sanamu. 2 funua, fichua.
unmatchable *adj* -siofananishika, -siolinganishika; -sio na kifano.
unmatched *adj* -sio na kifani.
unmentionable *adj* -siotajika, -siosemeka, -baya sana. **~s** *n (arch or hum)* chupi, nguo za ndani.
unmerciful *adj* -sio na huruma, -kali, katili.
unmindful *adj* ~ **(of)** -siokumbuka, -sahaulifu, -siozingatia, -siojali.
unmistakable *adj* dhahiri, wazi, bayana. **unmistakably** *adv.*
unmitigated *adj* kamili, kabisa.
unmixed *adj* safi, -sioghushiwa, -sio changanywa.
unmodified *adj* -siorekebishwa, -siobadilishwa/geuzwa.
unmoved *adj (of person)* -sioathirika/ingiwa na hisi; -sioshtuka.
unnamed *adj* -siotajwa jina, bila jina, -sio jina.
unnatural *adj* si -a asili, sio -a kawaida; -a kikatili ~ *offence* kosa kinyume cha maumbile/la kikatili. **~ly** *adv* -si kwa asili, si kwa urahisi, si kwa desturi, si kwa kawaida.
unnavigable *adj* -si -a kuendeka kwa meli, -sioabirika.
unnecessary *adj* -siohitajika, si -a lazima *it is ~ to say that* si lazima kusema hivyo. **unnecessarily** *adv.*
unneighbourily *adj* siema, -sio fadhili.
unnerve *vt* ogofya, fadhaisha, legeza moyo, tia kiherehere.
unnoted *adj* -siofahamika, -siokumbukumbu, -sioandikwa.
unnoticed *adj* bila kuonwa, -sioonwa, -siotambuliwa, -sioshughulikiwa, hivihivi.
unnumbered *adj* 1 bila namba/siohesabika. 2 -ingi mno.
unobtainable *adj* -siopatikana, -lioadimika, adimu.
unobtrusive *adj* 1 -liofichama, -siojitokeza. 2 -siojitanguliza. -siojitia.
unoccupied *adj* -siyo na mkaaji/mkazi; -siotumika, tupu.
unofficial *adj* si rasmi.
unopposed *adj* bila kupingwa *be returned ~* pita bila kupingwa.
unorganized *adj* 1 -siopangwa. 2 -sio na tabia za kiumbe hai. 3 -sio mwanachama wa chama cha wafanyakazi.
unoriginal *adj* -sio -a asili/-sio na uasili, -a kufuata wengine.
unorthodox *adj* -si -a desturi, tofauti na kawaida.
unpack *vt* fungua (mizigo); toa (kutoka mahali).
unpalatable *adj* -a kuchukiza, chapwa, -sio na ladha.
unparalleled *adj* -sio na kifani, -a pekee.
unpardoned *adj* -siosamehewa, -sioachiliwa. **unpardoning** *adj* -siosamehe; -a kisasi. **unpardonable** *adj* -siosameheka.
unparliamentary *adj (of language, conduct)* -siofaa kutumiwa bungeni.
unpatriotic *adj* -sio -a uzalendo; -siopenda nchi yake.
unperforated *adj* -siotobolewa.
unpersuaded *adj* -siosadikishwa; -siokubali ushauri, -sioshawishika.
unpersuasive *adj* -siosadikisha, -sioshawishi.
unperturbed *adj* -tulivu, -sioshtuka.
unplaced *adj (in competition)* -sio mmoja ya watatu wa kwanza.
unplastered *adj* -siopigwa lipu; -siochapiwa/kandikwa.
unplayable *adj (of a ball in game)* -siochezeka; *(of ground)* -siofaa kuchezea.
unpleasant *adj* -baya, -siopendeza, -a kuchukiza. **~ness** *n* ugomvi, chuki, maudhi, ubaya.
unpleasing *adj* -siopendeza, -siofurahisha.
unpledged *adj* -siofungwa kwa ahadi, -sioahidiwa.

unploughed *adj* -siolimwa kwa plau, -siotifuliwa.
unplug *vt* zibua, toa kizibo, toa plagi.
unpoetic(al) *adj* si -a kishairi.
unpolished *n adj* 1 -siong'arishwa, -siosuguliwa. 2 -sio na adabu/staha.
unpolitical *adj* siopendelea siasa, -siojishughulisha na siasa.
unpolluted *adj* safi; -siochafuliwa, -sionajisi.
unpopular *adj* -siopendwa (na wengi). **~ity** *n* kutopendwa na watu.
unpractical *adj* si -a amali, si -tendaji.
unpractised *adj* -sio -zoevu, -sio stadi.
unprecedented *adj* -siowahi kutokea, -sio na kifani; -a pekee.
unpredictable *adj* -siobashirika, -siotabirika, sio na uhakika.
unprejudiced *adj* -siopendelea, -enye haki, -adilifu.
unpremeditated *adj* -siofikiriwa kabla.
unprepared *adj* si tayari, bila kujitayarisha *be caught ~* tekwa bakunja.
unpretending, **unpretentious** *adj* -siojifanya, -siojikuza, -siojidai.
unpreventable *adj* -siozuilika *it was ~* haikuweza kuzuilika.
unprincipled *adj* -potovu; -a tabia mbaya; sio aminifu, sio na msimamo/maadili.
unprinted *adj* -siochapwa; -siopigwa chapa. **unprintable** *adj (of words)* -siofaa kuchapa (kwa sababu ni chafu).
unprivileged *adj* -sio na haki, -sio na bahati, -lioonewa.
unprocurable *adj* -siopatikana, -sioweza kupatikana.
unproductive *adj* -siozaa, -sioleta faida, -a bure.
unprofessional *adj (esp of conduct)* -siofuata maadili ya weledi.
unprofitable *n adj* -sioleta faida; -sio manufaa.
unprompted *adj* -sioongozwa, -siosukumwa, -siochochewa.
unpropitious *adj* -a ndege mbaya, kisirani, -a bahati mbaya.
unprosperous *adj* -siositawi, -sioleta faida.
unprotected *adj* -siolindwa. **unproved** *adj* -siothibitishwa, -sioshuhudiwa, -siohakikishwa.
unprovided *adj* 1 ~ **for** bila msaada. 2 ~ **with** bila kupewa.
unprovoked *adj* -siochochewa, -siochokozwa.
unpublished *adj* -siotangazwa, -siochapishwa.
unpunished *adj* -sioadhibiwa, -sio adibishwa.
unpurified *adj* -siotakaswa, safishwa, -siochujwa.
unputdownable *adj (colloq) (of a book etc)* cha kuvutia kiasi cha msomaji kutoweza kukiweka chini, -sioachika.
unqualified *adj* 1 -sio na kiwango/upeo kamili. 2 ~ **as sth/to do sth** sio na uwezo/sifa za kufanya jambo.
unquenchable *adj* -siozimika, -siotulizika.
unquestionable *adj* pasipo shaka, -a hakika, -siokanikana, -siokanushwa. **unquestionably** *adv* bila shaka. **unquestioned** *adj* -sioulizwa, -sioonewa mashaka; -siopingika. **unquestioning** *adj (obedience)* bila kuuliza/kupinga.
unquiet *adj (formal)* -sio tulivu; -enye vurugu/msukosuko.
unquote *(vi (imper only) (in a telegram, telephone message)* funga alama za msemaji; maliza unukuzi *n* mwisho wa kunukuu. **unquotable** *adj* -siodondoleka; -sionukulika.
unratified *adj* -siotiwa idhini.
unravel *vt,vi* 1 fungua, fumua. 2 *(explain)* fumbua, tatua.
unreadable *adj (of a book, articles)* -siosomeka.
unreal *adj* -a ndoto, -a njozi, sio -a kweli, -sio halisi.
unrealized *adj* -sioonwa kuwa kweli, -siong'amuliwa; -siotekelezwa.
unreasonable *adj* -sio na busara/mantiki; -enye kuzidi, muhali. **unreasoning** *adj* -siotumia busara/akili.

unrecognized *adj* -siotambuliwa, -siofahamika, -siong'amulika, -siohisiwa.
unrecorded *adj* -sioandikwa, -siorekodiwa.
unrecoverable *adj* si -a kupatikana tena.
unrectified *adj* -siosahihishwa, -siorekebishwa.
unredeemable *adj* -siokombolewa; -siofidiwa, -siokomboleka.
unreel *vt (of thread)* kunjua.
unrefined *adj* 1 -siotakaswa, -siosafishwa. 2 -sioadilishwa, shenzi -siostaarabika.
unregistered *adj* -sioandikishwa, -siosajiliwa, -siorajisiwa.
unrelated *adj* -sio na uhusiano.
unrelenting *adj* -sioachilia, -siopunguza (ukali/ugumu), -siolegea.
unreliable *adj* si -aminifu, -siotumainiwa, -siotegemewa. **unreliability** *n*.
unremembered *adj* -siokumbukwa, -siodhukuriwa.
unremitting *adj* -siolegea/pumzika/ choka/simama; -a kufuliliza, -a kudumu, -a kuendelea.
unremunerative *adj* -sioleta faida, -a bure, siolipa.
unrepentant, **unrepenting** *adj* -siotubu, -siojuta.
unreported *adj* -siosimuliwa, -siotolewa taarifa; -sioshitakiwa.
unrequested *n,adj* siosihiwa, sioombwa, -siotakiwa.
unrequited *adj* -siolipizwa; -siotuzwa.
unresented *adj* -siochukizwa na.
unresentful *adj* -siochukia, -sio na chuki. **unreserved** *adj* 1 *(of a person, his character)* wazi, kunjufu. 2 kamili, -sio na kikomo. **~ly** *adv*.
unresolved *adj* -siofumbuliwa.
unresponsive *adj* -sioitika, -sioshawishika, -siovutika.
unrest *n* vurugu, msukosuko.
unrestored *adj* 1 -siorudishwa; -siolipwa. 2 -siotengenezwa. 3 -sioponya.
unrestrained *adj* -siozuiwa; bila simile.
unrestricted *adj* -siozuiwa, sio na mpaka, -sio na sharti, -siofungwa.
unrevealed *adj* -siofunuliwa, -siofichuliwa, -sioonyeshwa.
unrevenged *adj* -siolipizwa kisasi.
unrewarded *adj* -siopewa zawadi, -siotunzwa.
unrighteous *adj* -ovu, dhalimu, -a dhambi, si -a haki. **~ly** *adv*. **~ness** *n*.
unripe *adj* -bichi, -changa.
unrivalled *adj* -sio na kifani, -a kupita -ote, -a kushinda -ote, -sio na mshindani.
unroll *vt* kunjua.
unruffled *adj* -tulivu.
unruled *adj (of paper)* -sio na mistari.
unruly *adj* -kaidi, -tundu, -tukutu, fidhuli.
unsaddle *vt* 1 tandua, ondoa matandiko (ya farasi n.k.). 2 *(of a person)* ondoa madarakani.
unsafe *adj* -a hatari.
unsaid *adj* -sionenwa, siosemwa.
unsaleable *adj* -siouzika *it is ~* haiuziki.
unsalted *adj* -siotiwa chumvi.
unsanctioned *adj* 1 -siopewa idhini, sioidhinishwa, -sioruhusiwa, -sioridhiwa. 2 -siowekewa.
unsatiated *adj* -sioshibishwa, -siokinaishwa, -siotoshelezwa.
unsatisfactory *adj* -sioridhisha, -siofaa. **unsatisfactorily** *adv*. **unsatisfied** *adj* -siotosheka,-sioridhika. **unsatisfying** *adj* siotosha.
unsavoury/(US unsavory) *adj* -siopendeza; -a fidhuli.
unsay *vt (lit)* futa/tangua usemi.
unscathed *adj* pasi kuumizwa, bila kuumia, -siodhurika, salamasalimini.
unscholarly *adj* -sio -a kitaaluma.
unscientific *adj* si -a kisayansi.
unscramble *vt (of scrambled message)* weka upya ili ieleweke, paraganyua.
unscratched *adj* -siokunwa, -siokwaruzwa, -siochanjwa.
unscreened *adj* -siosetiriwa, -siofunikwa, -siochunguzwa/ kaguliwa -siofichwa;

unscrew *vt* 1 toa parafujo (msumari wa hesi, skrubu), kongoa. 2 fungua (chupa n.k.).
unscripted *adj* -sioandikwa (kabla); -siosawidiwa.
unscrupulous *adj* si-nyofu, -a tabia mbaya, -sio na maadili, fidhuli. **~ly** *adv.* **~ness** *n.*
unseal *vt* vunja lakiri.
unseasoned *adj (of wood)* -changa *(of food)* -sio tiwa viungo.
unseat *vt* 1 ondosha madarakani. 2 rusha kutoka juu ya farasi.
unseconded *adj* -siosaidiwa, siotiwa moyo; -siopewa kazi maalumu; sioungwa mkono.
unseemly *adj (of behaviour, etc)* -siofaa, si -a adabu; si -zuri, -chafu.
unseen *adj* -sioonekana *n* 1 **the ~** peponi. 2 matini ya kutafsiri (bila ya kujiandaa kwanza).
unselfish *adj* -sio -choyo, -a hisani, -siojipendelea, karimu. **~ly** *adv.* **~ness** *n.*
unserviceable *adj* -siofaa, -siotengenezeka, liochakaa kabisa.
unsettle *vt* vuruga, tia wasiwasi, fadhaisha, hangaisha. **~d** *adj* geugeu, -a kubadilikabadilika, -a wasiwasi, -a kuhangaika.
unsex *vt* ondosha jinsi. **~ed** *adj* siotengwa/ainishwa kijinsi.
unshackle *vt* 1 fungua pingu. 2 ondoa kizuizi.
unshaken *adj* thabiti, imara, -siotikiswa. **unshakable** *adj* -siotikisika; -siodhoofika; -siotetemesheka.
unshapely *adj* -baya, -enye umbo baya, sio na umbo.
unshaved *adj* -sionyolewa; -siochegwa.
unsheltered *adj* -siofichwa; -siohifadhiwa, -siokingwa.
unship *vt* shusha kutoka melini.
unshod *adj* bila viatu.
unsightly *adj* -siopendeza macho, -a kuchukiza. **unsightness** *n.*
unsigned *adj* -siotiwa sahihi, -sioandikwa jina.
unskilled *adj (of work)* si stadi, -sio ujuzi/utaalamu. **~ labour** *n* kazi isiyo na ujuzi/utaalamu, kazi ya kibarua.
unskilful *adj* si -bingwa, si -stadi, -siojua kazi. **~ness** *n.*
unskimmed *adj (of milk)* -sioenguliwa, -sioondolewa mafuta.
unsmiling *adj* -siotabasamu, -a kukunja uso.
unsociable *adj* -siopenda kukaa na watu.
unsold *adj* -siouzwa.
unsolicited *adj* -sioombwa *he did it ~* alifanya bila kuombwa.
unsolved *adj* -siotatuliwa, -siofumbuliwa.
unsophisticated *adj* -sio na uzoefu; -a kishamba.
unsought *adj* -siotafutwa, -sioombwa.
unsound *adj* si -zima, -pungufu, -sioridhisha *person of ~ mind* mtu asiye na akili timamu.
unsparing *adj* sio nyimi, -siojizuia; -paji.
unspeakable *adj* -siosemeka, -sioelezeka; *(colloq)* -baya sana, -a kuchukiza kabisa. **unspeakably** *adv.*
unspecified *adj* -siotajwa, -sioainishwa.
unspectacular *adj* -a kawaida, si -a tamasha, si -a sherehe.
unspent *adj* -siotumiwa.
unspoiled *adj* -sioharibiwa, -siodekezwa, -sioengwaengwa.
unspoken *adj* -siosemwa, -sionenwa; -siotangazwa.
unspotted *adj* pasipo mawaa/doa; *(fig)* -eupe, safi.
unstable *adj* -si thabiti, si imara, geugeu.
unstained *adj* pasipo mawaa, -eupe, safi.
unstamped *adj (of letter)* -siobandikwa stempu; -siopigwa mhuri.
unsteady *adj* si thabiti, -si imara, -a kutetereka, geugeu.
unstinted *adj* -ingi *give (sb) ~ praise* -pa mtu sifa nyingi.
unstinting *adj* karimu, -paji:

unstintingly *adv*.
unstratified *adj* -siofanya safu, -siofanywa tabaka, -siotabakishwa.
unstressed *adj* -siokazwa, -siotiwa mkazo.
unstrung *adj* 1 *(mental)* -liochanganyikiwa. 2 -liofumuka.
unstruck *adj* siobandikwa. **come ~ (badly)** *(colloq)* vurugika, shindikana.
unstudied *adj (of behaviour)* -sio makusudi, -siokusudiwa, -siolazimishiwa, -a asili.
unsubstantial *adj* 1 -epesi, -embamba, hafifu. 2 -a kama ndoto.
unsubstantiated *adj* -siothibitika.
unsuccessful *adj* -siofanikiwa, -siositawi, -siofaulu *my attempt was ~* jaribio langu halikufanikiwa.
unsuitable *adj* -siofaa, -siostahili. **unsuitability** *n* kutofaa; kutostahili.
unsung *adj* -sioimbiwa, -sioghaniwa, -siosifiwa/tambuliwa (kwa nyimbo, mashairi n.k.), -liosahaulika.
unsupervised *adj* -siosimamiwa, -sioangaliwa, -sioongozwa.
unsupported *adj* -siochukuliwa, -siotegemezwa; -siosaidiwa, -siovumiliwa; -sioungwa mkono. **unsupportable** *adj* -siochukulika, si -a kuvumilika, si -a kustahimilika.
unsure *adj* si -a hakika, -a kutojua sana.
unsuspected *adj* -sioshukiwa, -siotuhumiwa, -sioonewa mashaka. **unsuspecting** *adj* -siotuhumu/shuku. **unsuspicious** *adj* -siodhania uovu, -sio na mashaka, -sio shuku, si -a kutuhumu.
unswayed *adj* -siogeuzwa, -sioshawishiwa, -sioyumbishwa.
unswerving *adj* thabiti, imara.
unsworn *adj* -sioapishwa; -sioapiwa *~ statement* maelezo yasiyoapiwa *~ testimony* ushahidi bila kiapo, ushahidi usioapiwa.
unsyllabic *adj* -sio silabi, -sio -a silabi.
unsympathetic *adj* -sio na huruma.
unsystematic *adj* -sio na mpango maalumu; -a bila taratibu.
untainted *adj* -siowaa, -sio aibu; -siooza, -siovunda.
untalented *adj* -siojaliwa, -sioelekevu, -siokuwa na kipaji.
untamable *adj (of animals)* -siofugika, -sio zuilika. **untamably** *adv*. **untameness** *n*. **untamed** *adj (of animals)* -siofugwa, -siozuiwa.
untangle *vt* tegua, rahisisha, achilia; weka wazi, fanya ieleweke.
untanned *adj (of skin)* -siotiwa dawa, -sio na rangi nyekundu.
untapped *adj* -siogemwa, -siotumia (bado).
untasted *adj* -sioonjwa/dhukiwa *the dish remained ~* chakula hakikuonjwa.
untaught *adj* -siofunzwa, -sioadibishwa, -sioongozwa.
untenable *adj* -siothibitika, -sioshikika; -siolindika; -sioweza kutetewa.
untested *adj* -siojaribiwa; -siothibitishwa.
unthankful *adj* sio shukurani, -sio na shukrani.
unthatched *adj* -sioezekwa.
unthinkable *adj* -siowazika.
unthinking *adj* -a pupa, bila kufikiri *done in an ~ moment* fanywa bila kufikiri. **~ly** *adv*.
unthought of *adj* -siofikiriwa, -siotarajiwa.
unthread *vt* 1 *(a needle)* fumua. 2 *(fig)* fumbua, funua.
untidy *adj (of a room, desk etc)* -siotengenezwa, chafu, -liofujika; *(of person)* chafu, -sio nadhifu/tanashati. **untidily** *adv*.
until *prep conj see* **till**.
untimely *adj* -a wakati usiofaa, -sio wakati wake, -a mapema mno.
untiring *adj* -siochoka, -enye bidii; -siochosha.
unto *prep arch see* **to** *(prep)*.
untold *adj* 1 *(beyond counting)* kemkem, -siohesabika. 2 -siosimuliwa, -siohadithiwa.
untouchable *adj* 1 -siguswa. 2 *n (pl)* **the ~s** jamii ya Wahindi wa tabaka la chini kabisa.

untouched *adj* -sioguswa/ shughulikiwa; -siojadiliwa/elezwa; bila kuonjwa/kubadilishwa; bila kuguswa/kuathiriwa.
untoward *adj (formal)* -siopendelewa, -a bahati mbaya, -siofaa, -sumbufu.
untraceable *adj* -siopatikana, -sioonekana.
untrained *adj* -siofundishwa, -jinga; -siofundwa, -siofugwa; -siofunzwa.
untrammelled *adj* -siozuiwa, -siopingwa, huru, -siodhibitiwa.
untransferable *adj* -siobadilishika, -siohamishika.
untranslatable *adj* -siofasirika, -siotafsirika.
untranslated *adj* -siofasiriwa, -siotafsiriwa.
untravelled *adj* -siosafiriwa, -sioabiriwa, -siosafiri.
untried *adj* 1 -siojaribiwa, sio mijarabu. 2 -siohukumiwa.
untrodden *adj* 1 -siokanyagwa, -siovyogwa. 2 -siotumiwa (bado).
untroubled *adj* -siotaabishwa, -siosumbuliwa.
untrue *adj* si kweli, si hakika, -a uwongo. **untruth** *n* uwongo. **untruthful** *adj* -a kusema uwongo; -ongo. **untruthfully** *adv*.
untrustworthy *adj* -sioaminika.
untutored *adj* -siofunzwa, jinga; -a asili.
untwine *vt* sokotoa.
untwist *vt* fumua, tatanua, sokotoa.
unused *adj* 1 -siozoewa, -siozoelewa, -siotumika. 2 ~ **to** siozoea.
unusual *adj* -sio -a kawaida, -sio -a desturi, -geni. ~**ly** *adv*.
unutterable *adj* -sioneneka, -siosemeka, -sioelezeka.
unvalued *adj* -sio (na) thamani; -siotiwa thamani.
unvanquished *adj* -sioshindwa, siopigwa, -siotiishwa.
unvariable *adj* -siogeuka, -siobadilika.
unvaried *adj* -a namna moja, ile ile, -siobadilishwa.
unvarnished *adj* 1 -siopakwa vanishi. 2 *(plain, simple)* -a kweli tupu, -siotiwa chumvi ~ *truth* kweli tupu.
unveil *vt* 1 funua; tandua, ondoa shela. 2 onyesha (kwa mara ya kwanza).
unventilated *adj* -siopitisha/ruhusu hewa safi.
unverified *adj* -siohakikishwa, -siothibitishwa.
unversed *adj* -sio juzi, -sio (na) maarifa ya; si zoevu.
unvisited *adj* -siotembelewa, -sioangaliwa, -siozuriwa.
unvoiced *adj* -siosemwa, -sionenwa, -siotajwa.
unwanted *adj* -siotakiwa, -siohitajika.
unwarrantable *adj* -sioidhinishika, -sio tetewa; -sio kisingizio.
unwarranted *adj* bila sababu, sio kisingizio; -siothibitishwa, -sioidhinishwa.
unwary *adj* si -enye hadhari, -zembe.
unwashed *adj* -siooshwa, -sioogeshwa.
unwatched *adj* -siolindwa.
unwavering *adj* bila kusita, thabiti, imara, sioyumba.
unweaned *adj* -sioachishwa ziwa, -sioachishwa, -siolikizwa.
unwearied *adj* si -legevu, -siochoka, -a kudumu, -enye bidii.
unweave *vt* fumua.
unwed(ed) *adj* -siofunga ndoa; *(of women)* -sioolewa.
unwelcome *adj* -siopende za, -siotakiwa, -baya.
unwell *adj* -gonjwa, -sioweza, -siojiweza.
unwept *adj* -sioliliwa, -siotolewa machozi, -siohuzunikiwa.
unwholesome *adj* -a kudhuru afya, -a kuleta ugonjwa, -sio na afya, -baya.
unwieldy *adj* -kubwa, -zito. **unwieldiness** *n* uzito. **unwieldly** *adv*.
unwilling *adj* -siotaka/penda, -a kujikalifu/kujishurutisha. ~**ly** *adv*. ~**ness** *n* kutotaka, kutokubali.
unwind *vt* 1 fumua, fungua, sokotoa, zongoa. 2 *(colloq)* pumua, pumzika.
unwinking *adj* -sio pepesa; -angalifu, mahiri, hadhiri.
unwise *adj* -sio akili, -sio busara.

unwitnessed *adj* -sioonwa, -sioshuhudiwa, -siotazamwa, -siothibitishwa.

unwitting *adj* pasipo kujua, -siokusudiwa, si -a kusudi. **~ly** *adv* bila kujua, bila kukusudia, kwa ujinga.

unwomanly *adj* si -a mwanamke, si kama mwanamke, kidumedume.

unworkable *adj* -sioweza kufanyika, siofanyika.

unworkmanlike *adj* -baya, -a kazi mbaya, -sio stadi, si -a ufundi.

unworldly *adj* 1 si -a ulimwengu. 2 -nyofu. **~ iness** *n.*

unworthy *adj* -siostahili, -siofaa; -siothamani.

unwrinkled -siokunjamana, pasipo vifinyo, -siosinyaa, -siojikunyata.

unwritten *adj* -sioandikwa, -a kufahamika kwa akili tu, -a mapokezi, simulizi, -a desturi. **an ~ law** sheria ya mila na desturi (isiyoandikwa).

unyielding *adj* -gumu, -sionyororo, -siokubali kushindwa.

unyoke *vt* fungulia.

unzip *vt* fungua zipu.

up[1] *adv* 1 juu. **what's ~** *(colloq)* kuna nini, habari gani. **~ to you** juu yako. **~ and about** hapa na pale. 2 zaidi *two degrees ~* nyuzi mbili zaidi. 3 hadi *travel ~ to Dodoma* safiri hadi Dodoma. 4 kabisa *we are hard ~* tumeishiwa kabisa. 5 sana, kwa sauti/nguvu zaidi *speak ~* sema sana. 6 **~ against sth** -enye kupambana/kukabiliwa na. **be ~ before sb** shtakiwa. **~ and down** mbele na nyuma, huku na huko; juu chini. **~s and downs** *(fig)* majaliwa, pata potea, mema na mabaya. **on the ~ (and up)** *(colloq)* inayoendelea/stawi. **~ for sth** -enye kushtakiwa kwa jambo; pendekezwa/fikiriwa kwa jambo. **be well ~ in/on sth** -wa bingwa/mahiri wa jambo. **~ to sth** -enye mashughuli na; sawa sawa na. **~ to sb** ni juu ya mtu, wajibu. **~ and coming** *(of person)* shababu, makini. -enye kupanda. *vi,vt (hum or colloq)* amka, ruka; *(colloq)* pandisha, ongeza.

up[2] *pref* (kuelekea) juu.

up-beat *n (mus)* pigo lisilo na mkazo; *(colloq)* uchangamfu.

upbraid *vt* **~ sb (for doing sth/with sth)** karipia, kemea, laumu, shutumu. **~ing** *adj* -a kukaripia, -a lawama. **~ingly** *adv.*

upbringing *n* malezi.

up-country *adv* bara (mbali na pwani) *go ~* enda bara *adj* -a bara.

update *vt* fanya (kuwa) -a kisasa, tengeneza upya.

up-end *vt* 1 angusha chini. 2 shinda. 3 fanya kusimama pembe. 4 shtua.

up-grade *n (esp)* **on the ~** kusitawi, kupiga hatua. *vt* pandisha daraja/cheo.

upgrowth usitawi; kumea, kukua (kwa kuelekea juu).

upheaval *n* mageuzi, mabadiliko (makubwa ya ghafla) *the country was in a state of ~* nchi ilikuwa katika hali ya mageuzi makubwa.

upheld *pt pp of* **uphold**.

uphill *adj (sloping)* -a mwinuko, -a kupanda; *(fig)* -a shida, -gumu, -zito, -a taabu. **on ~ task** shughuli ngumu sana *adv* kwa kupanda (kilima).

uphold *vt* 1 tetea, unga mkono. 2 *(confirm)* thibitisha.

upholster *vt (of a room)* weka zulia/pazia na kochi; *(a chair)* tia matakia, funika kwa nguo/ngozi. **~er** *n* mwuza mapambo ya samani/chumba. **~y** *n* vifaa vya kutengeneza makochi/matakia; biashara ya kutengeneza makochi/matakia.

upkeep *n* harija, gharama (za matunzo).

upland *n (often pl)* sehemu za mwinuko, nyanda za juu.

uplift *vt (fig)* inua (moyo); tia moyo.

upmost *adj see uppermost*

upon *prep (formal) see* **on**.

upper *adj* -a juu, bora. **the ~ crust** *(colloq)* waungwana. **the ~ storey** *(fig colloq)* bongo, akili. **gain/have/get the ~ hand (of)** shinda, dhibiti.

the U~ House *(in parliament) (GB)* Bunge la Malodi. ~ **cut** *n (boxing)* (m)chokonoo, (m)tunguo, ngumi ya kuchomeka *n* sehemu ya juu ya kiatu. **be down on one's ~s** ishiwa, dhikika, -wa maskini, fukarika. **~most** *adj* -a juu kabisa; -kuu, -enye kutawala *adv* juu *he said whatever came ~ most* alisema kile kilichomjia kwanza akilini.

uppish *adj (colloq)* -juvi, -a kujigamba, -enye kiburi. **~ness** *n*. **~ly** *adv*. **uppity** *adj (colloq)* -juvi.

upright *adj* 1 -a wima, -a kiwimawima. ~ **piano** piano yenye nyuzi za wima. 2 *(honest)* aminifu, -adilifu; -a kuheshimika, -enye heshima *n* mhimili, mwimo, nguzo. **~ly** *adv*. **~ness** *n* 1 unyofu, uaminifu. 2 wima.

uprising *n* maasi, machafuko.

uproar *n (sing only)* vurumai, makelele, fujo, ghasia *the meeting ended in an ~* mkutano uliisha kwa ghasia; katika hali ya vurumai. **~ious** *adj* -a makelele (agh. ya vikwakwa). **~iously** *adv*.

uproot *vt* ng'oa.

upset *vt,vi* 1 pindua, pinduka. 2 vuruga, tibua, fadhaisha ~ *ones stomach* tibua tumbo *n* 1 vurugu, mshtuo. 2 *(sport)* matokeo yasiyotarajiwa.

upshot *n* **the ~ (of sth)** matokeo *what is the ~ of it going to be* matokeo yake yatakuwaje?

upside-down *adj* juu chini, pindu; *(fig)* shaghalabaghala, shelabela.

upstage *adj (colloq)* -a kujigamba/kujisifu, juvi *adv* (kuelekea) nyuma ya jukwaa *vt* piku, vutia kwako/upande wako.

upstairs *adv* 1 ghorofani; juu. 2 *(attrib)* -a juu, -a ghorofani.

upstanding *adj* kititi, wima; -enye siha, -enye nguvu, adilifu, imara.

pstart *n (person)* mtu aliyepanda cheo/hadhi ghafla na ambaye anajidaidai sana; fidhuli.

upstream *adv* kwa kukata maji; -a kilimani, dhidi ya mkondo wa maji.

upsurge *n* mfoko wa wasiwasi/ghadhabu.

upswing *n* ongezeko.

uptake *n* **quick/slow on the ~** *(colloq)* wepesi/zito kuelewa jambo (lililodokez(e)wa).

uptight *adj*. ~ **(about)** *(sl)* 1 -enye fazaa/wahaka/kiherehere; -a upendeleo; -enye chuki; -a kuogofya.

up-to-date *adj* -a kisasa, -a siku hizi, mpya kabisa.

up-town *adj (US)* sehemu ya mji yenye makazi ya watu, kiungani.

upturn *n* unafuu.

upward *adj* 1 -a kwenda juu, -a kuelekea juu *adv* **(often ~s)** -a kuelekea sehemu ya juu; zaidi ya.

uranium *n* urani.

Uranus *n (astron)* Uranus: sayari ya saba kutoka jua.

urban *adj* -a mji, -a mjini, -a jiji, -a biladi ~ *planning* mipango miji. **~ization** *n*. **~ize** *vt* kuza/anzisha mji, fanya kuwa -a miji.

urbane *adj* ungwana; -a adabu sana, -enye malezi mazuri. **urbanity** *n* uungwana, adabu; utu wema; *(pl)* **urbanities** adabu njema. **~ly** *adv*.

urchin *n* mtukutu, msumbi; *(often* **street ~)** mtoto wa kikopo/mapipani/barabarani.

urge *vt* 1 ~ **sb (to sth)** sihi sana, bembeleza, nyenga. 2 ~ **sb/sth (on) onward/forward** sukuma, sukumiza. 3 ~ **sth (on/upon sb)** sisitiz(i)a kitu *n* hamu kubwa, tamaa, uchu.

urgent *adj* 1 -a haraka, muhimu. 2 *(of person, his voice)* -a kusisitiza. **urgency** *n* haraka, umuhimu. **urgency** *adv* kwa haraka. **~ly** *adv*.

urine *n* mkojo. **urinal** *n* 1 *(bed urinal)* chombo cha kukojolea kitandani. 2 *(public urinal)* msala, sehemu ya kutabawali. **urinary** *adj* -a mkojo *the ~ system* mfumo wa mkojo.

urinate *vi* kojoa, tabawali. **uric** *adj* -a mkojo.

urn *n* 1 chombo kirefu cha udongo au madini (hasa cha kutilia majivu ya maiti aliyechomwa). 2 buli.

ursine *adj* -a dubu.

us *pron* sisi; -tu *she saw* ~ alituona.
use *n* 1 matumizi, kutumia. **in** ~ -nayotumika. **out of** ~ -siotumika (tena). **come in** ~ anza kutumika. **go/fall out of** ~ -totumika tena. **make (good/the best)** ~ **of** tumia (vizuri). 2 kazi. 3 faida. 4 uwezo (wa kutumia). 5 ruhusa (ya kutumia). 6 mazoea *vt* 1 ~ **(for)** tumia *you* ~ *a knife to cut meat* unatumia kisu kukata nyama. 2 ~ **sth (up)** tumia yote *he has ~d up all his strength* ametumia nguvu zake zote. 3 tumia (watu), tendea, fanyia *adj*. **~d** -liotumika, -sio mpya ~ *car* gari lililotumika. **usable** *adj* -a (kuweza) kutumika. **~r** *n* mtumiaji. **~ful** *adj* 1 -a manufaa, -a matokeo mazuri. 2 *(colloq)* -enye uwezo, -a ufanisi. **~fully** *adv*. **~fulness** *n*. **~less** *adj* 1 bure, -siofaa. 2 -sio na maana, -siosaidia/-sio na manufaa. **~lessly** *adv*. **~lessness** *n*. **usage** *n* 1 matumizi. 2 desturi, mazoea.
used[1] *anom fin* ~ *to* + *inf* -wa na desturi/mazoea huko nyuma I ~ *to walk to work every day* huko nyuma nilikuwa na desturi ya kutembea hadi kazini kila siku *there* ~ *to be* zamani kulikuwepo na *there* ~ *d to be lions in Kawe* zamani kulikuwa na simba huko Kawe.
used[2] *adj* ~ **to** -a kuzoea *I am* ~ *to hard work* nimezoea kazi ngumu.
usher *n* bawabu *vt* 1 peleka, ongoza, hadi ~ *sb into the sitting-room* peleka mtu sebuleni. 2 ~ **sth in** ashiria, anzisha.
usual *adj* -a kawaida, -a desturi. **as** ~ kama kawaida. **~ly** *adv* kwa kawaida, aghalabu.
usurp *vt,vi* jitwalia bila haki, nyang'anya ~ *on sb's rights* nyang'anya haki. **~ation** *n* kunyang'anya. **~er** *n* mnyang'anyi (ufalme, usultani, mamlaka n.k.).
usury *n* kula riba, kukopesha fedha kwa riba. **usurer** *n* mla riba. **usurious** *adj* -a riba, -a kula riba.
utensil chombo; ala; *(pl)* ~*s* vyombo vya nyumbani.
uterus *n* *(anat)* mji wa mimba, uterasi. **uterine** *adj* 1 -a mama mmoja, -a tumbo moja (baba mbalimbali). 2 -a uterasi.
utility 1 manufaa, matumizi. 2 *(public)* huduma za umma (k.v. umeme, usafiri n.k.).
utilize *vt* tumia. **utilization** *n* kutumia; matumizi. **utilizeable** *adj* -a kuweza kutumia. **utilitarian** *adj* 1 -a kutafuta faida, -a kufaa, -a kuzingatia matumizi/manufaa tu (badala ya uzuri, haki, uadilifu n.k.). **utilitarianism** *n* falsafa kwamba njia bora katika maisha ni kutafuta kuridhisha watu wengi iwezekanavyo na kupima vitendo vya watu kwa kigezo hicho; -enye mawazo ya kuleta faida.
utmost *adj* -a juu/kubwa sana *of the* ~ *importance* muhimu sana *n* **one's/the** ~ kipeo *do one's* ~ fanya kila linalowezekana.
Utopia *n* jamii kamili/timilifu ya kufikirika. **~n** *adj* -a njozi, -a kufikirika.
utter[1] *adj* kabisa, kamili, -tupu ~ *darkness* giza/kiza totoro. **~ly** *adv* kabisa (kabisa). **~ness** *n*.
utter[2] *vt* 1 toa sauti/tamka. 2 nena, sema ~ *a curse* laani, apiza. 3 eneza (agh. pesa bandia). **~ance** *n* 1 usemi. 2 matamshi, maneno.
uttermost *n adj see* **utmost**.
uvula *n* kidakatonge, kimeo. **uvular** *adj* -a kidakatonge, -a kimeo.
uxorious *adj* -a kupenda mno mke, -enye mapenzi sana na mkewe. **~ly** *adv*. **~ness** *n*.

V

V, v *n* 1 herufi ya ishirini na mbili ya alfabeti ya Kiingereza. 2 alama ya kirumi ya kuwakilisha namba tano. 3 alama ya ushindi.

vac *n (colloq) (abbr of vacation)*, likizo.

vacant *adj* 1 -tupu ~ *space* nafasi tupu, pasipo kitu/mtu. 2 wazi. **a ~ possession** tangazo la kuwa nyumba wazi (isiyo na mpangaji). 3 *(of time)* -a kupumzika. 4 *(of mind)* -sio na wazo; *(of the eyes)* -sio na (dalili za) shauku/wazo.**~ly** *adv*. **vacancy** *n* 1 kuwa -tupu, uwazi, pasipo kazi. 2 kutotumika. 3 ujinga, ukosefu wa mawazo. 4 *(post unfilled)* nafasi wazi.

vacate *vt* 1 hama, ondoka. 2 acha wazi, achilia mbali. 3 *(formal)* samehe.

vacation n 1 *(formal)* kuacha, kuhama, kuondoka. 2 likizo, livu, muda wa kupumzika *court ~* likizo ya mahakama. **on ~** likizoni *vi* ~ **at/in** *(US)* enda likizo. **~ist** *n (US)* mtu aliye likizoni.

vaccinate *vt* ~ **sb (against sth)** chanja. **vaccination** *n* chanjo; kuchanja. **vaccine** *n* dawa ya chanjo.

vacillate *vi* ~ **(between)** yumba, babaika, kosa msimamo. **vacillation** *n* kutangatanga, kukosa msimamo, kubabaika; kuyumba.

vacuous *adj* -tupu, -sio na akili. **~ly** *adv*. **vacuity** *n*.

vacuum *n* ombwe, tupu. ~ **cleaner** kivuta vumbi. ~ **flask/bottle** themosi, chupa ya chai. ~ **pump** kivuta hewa; kivuta maji. ~ **tube/valve** neli/vali ombwe (ya kuchunguza mkondo wa umeme).

vade-mecum *n* kitabu (ambacho mtu anaweza kutembea nacho) cha kurejelea.

vagabond *n* msikwao; mzururaji, mhuni *adj* -sio na kwao; zururaji. **~age** *n* uhuni; usokwao, uzururaji. **~ism** *n* uhuni, hali ya mtu kutokuwa na kwao.

vagary *n* tukio au wazo lisilo la kawaida na lisilo na sababu.

vagina *n* kuma, uke. **~l** *adj* -a uke.

vagrant *n* mzururaji *adj* -zururaji, -a kutangatanga. **vagrancy** *n* uzururaji, kutangatanga.

vague *adj* 1 -sio dhahiri, -a mashaka, -sio wazi, si yakini *he was ~ on that subject* hakuwa wazi katika mada hiyo. 2 *(of persons, behaviour)* -a wasiwasi; -sio na uhakika. **~ness** *n*. **~ly** *adv*.

vain *adj* 1 *(useless)* ovyo, -siofaa, bure. 2 **in ~** bure *their efforts were in ~* jitihada zao zilikuwa bure; -sio na heshima, -a kufuru *take the name of God in ~* kufuru. 3 -a kujishaua, -a majisifu. ~ **glory** *n* kiburi; kujiona; majivuno; majisifu, makuu. **~glorious** *adj* 1 -a kujiona, -a kujisifu, -a kuona makuu. **~ly** *adv 1* bure. 2 *(conceitedly)* kwa kiburi.

valance, valence *n* pazia fupi (la maridadi).

vale *n (lit except in place names)* bonde.

valediction *n* (maneno ya) kuaga, kuagana. **valedictory** *adj* -a kuaga, -a kuagana a ~ *speech* hotuba ya kuagana.

valence[1] *n (chem)* valensi.

valence[2] *n see* **valance**.

valency *n (chem)* kizio cha valensi.

valentine *n (of letter, card etc)* barua inayotumwa kwa kipenzi/sahibu (bila jina la mwandishi) tarehe 14 Februari.

valet *n* mtumishi (wa kiume) afanyaye kazi za udobi *vt* fanya kazi za udobi.

valetudinarian *n* mwele, mgonjwa *adj* -dhaifu; -gonjwa, nyong'onyevu.

valiant *adj* shujaa, jasiri, hodari. **~ly** *adv*.

valid *adj* 1 *(leg)* halali; -enye sababu thabiti, -a nguvu, -a akili. 2 -a sheria halali. **~ly** *adv*. **~ity** uhalali, uthabiti. **~ate** *vt* halalisha, thibitisha.

valise *n* mfuko, begi dogo la nguo (agh. la safari); mkoba.

valley *n* bonde.

valour (*US* **valor**) *n* ujasiri (agh. wa vitani), ushujaa. **valorous** *adj* jasiri, shujaa.

value *n* 1 thamani. ~ **added tax** *(abbr VAT)* kodi ya nyongeza; thamani ya *set a ~ on* thamini. 2 faida, manufaa *this is of great ~* hii ina manufaa makubwa. 3 *(in painting)* uhusiano wa mwanga na kivuli; *(in language)* maana; athari; *(pl)* maadili. **artistic ~s** viwango vya sanaa *vt* thamini/tia thamani, kadiria. **~d** *adj* -liothaminiwa; -a thamani *a ~ friend* rafiki halisi. **~less** *adj* hafifu, -siofaa, bure, -sio na thamani. **~r** *n* mthamini. **valuable** *adj* -a thamani; -a tunu. *n (pl)* **valuables** vitu vya thamani (k.m. vito n.k.). **valuation** *n* kukadiria; ukadiriaji *draw up a ~ of sth* kadiria thamani ya kitu. **valuator** *n* mkadiria thamani.

valve *n* kilango, vali. **valvular** *adj* -a vali za moyo/mishipa ya damu.

vamoose *vi (US sl)* ondoka haraka, potea, ambaa.

vamp[1] *n* kipande cha mbele cha kiatu/buti *vt,vi* 1 tia kiatu kiraka. **~ sth up** *(fig)* ungaunga. 2 tunga tuni ya wimbo; fuatisha wimbo kwa ala ya muziki.

vamp[2] *n* kiberenge.

vampire *n* mnyonya damu. **~ (bat)** popo mnyonya damu. **vampiric** *adj*

van[1] *n* 1 gari la mizigo/bidhaa 2 *(GB)* behewa la mizigo, bogi.

van[2] *n (of army)* kikosi cha mbele.

vandal *n* mharabu, mshenzi. **~ism** *n* uharabu (wa kishenzi).

vane *n* 1 kishale (kinachoonyesha uelekeo wa upepo). 2 propela/tanga liendeshwalo kwa upepo/maji.

vanguard *n* kikosi cha mbele *(fig)* watangulizi, viongozi wa maandamano au wa chama; tapo.

vanilla *n* lavani, vanila.

vanish *vi* toweka, tokomea, yoyoma. **~ into thin air** tokomea, yeyuka. **~ing cream** krimu ya ngozi (inayofyonzwa haraka na mwili). **~ing** kutokomea, kufifia. **~ing point** mahala mistari sambamba inapoelekea kukutana.

vanity *n* 1 majivuno, majisifu, kiburi. 2 upuuzi, kutoridhisha. **~ bag/case** kikoba cha vipodozi.

vanquish *vt* shinda, tiisha.

vantage *n* manufaa. **~ point** *(lit. or fig)* mahali pafaapo kutazamia jambo fulani.

vapid *adj* -chapwa, -dufu, baridi. **~ly** *adv.* **~ness** *n.* **~ity** *n* uchapwa, udufu, ubaridi.

vapour *n* 1 mvuke. **~ bath** mafusho, buhuri. 2 kitu cha udhanifu; kitu kisicho na maana, upuuzi. 3 **the ~s** *(arch)* majonzi. **vaporize** *vt,vi* fusha, fanya mvuke. **vaporization** *n* kuvukisha, mvukisho. **vaporizer** *n* kivukisho. **vaporous** *adj* 1 -a mvuke. 2 *(fig)* -a njozi.

variable *adj* -a kugeuka, -a kubadilika, -geugeu. *n* kigeugeu. **variably** *adv.* **~ness** *n.* **variability** *n* ugeukaji-geukaji, ubadilikajibadilikaji.

variant *n* 1 tofauti. 2 kibadala *adj* -a tofauti, -ingineyo. **variance** *n.* **at ~ (with)** kuhitilafiana, kutofautiana; *(maths)* achano.

variation *n* 1 (kiwango cha) kubadilika; badiliko, mageuzo, tofauti. 2 *(of music)* lahani iliyorudiwa kwa utata zaidi. 3 mabadiliko ya mwili (yatokanayo na hali mpya). 4 *(maths)* muachano.

varicoloured *adj* -a rangirangi.

varicose *adj (esp.* **~ vein)** (veni) -liovimba daima.

variegated *adj* -a rangi rangi, -a rangi mbalimbali, -a namna nyingi mbalimbali. **variegation** *n.*

variform *adj* -enye maumbo mbalimbali.

various *adj (usu attrib)* mbalimbali, anuwai, -a tofautitofauti, ainaaina.

varlet *n (arch)* mshenzi, mwovu.

varnish *n* 1 vanishi. 2 mng'ao; *(fig)* sura/taswira danganyifu *vt* 1 paka vanishi. 2 pamba, puna; *(fig)* ficha kosa au dosari fulani. **~er** *n* mpaka vanishi.

varsity *n (colloq)* chuo kikuu.

vary *vt,vi* geuza, badili, badilisha; geuka, -wa mbalimbali. **varied** *adj* 1 mbalimbali, tofauti, -a namna nyingi. 2 -enye mabadiliko mengi; -enye tofauti nyingi.

variety *n* 1 tofauti. 2 *(collection)* jamii

(ya vitu mbalimbali) *a ~ of reasons* sababu mbalimbali. 3 (*species*) namna; *(many kinds)* namna nyingi. 4 maonyesho (ya aina mbalimbali k.v. sarakasi, nyimbo, igizo n.k.).

vascular *adj* -enye mishipa ya damu/utomvu.

vase *n* chombo (cha kuwekea maua), jagi.

vasectomy *n* kuhasi: operesheni ndogo ya kumhasi mwanaume.

vaseline *n* vaselini.

vassal *n (hist)* 1 mtwana, kijakazi; *(fig)* kibaraka. 2 mtumwa; mtumishi. **~age** *n* 1 utwana; *(fig)* ubarakala. 2 utumwa.

vast *adj* -kubwa mno, -ingi mno. **~ness** *n*. **~ly** *adv* sana, mno.

vat *n* pipa kubwa.

Vatican *n* Makao ya Papa/Baba Mtakatifu, Vatikani; *(fig)* serikali ya Papa.

vaudeville *n* vichekesho, maonyesho (ya aina mbalimbali).

vault[1] *vt,vi* ruka; ruka juu (kwa kujitegemeza au kwa msaada wa upondo). **~ing-horse** zana ya mazoezi ya kuruka *n* mruko. **~er** *n* mrukaji (wa upondo).

vault[2] *n* 1 kuba. 2 chumba cha chini kwa chini, ghala ya chini. 3 mfuniko wa kikuba *the ~ of heaven (poet)* anga. **~ed** *adj* -enye kuba.

vaunt *vt,vi (liter)* jivuna, (ji)sifu, jigamba. **~er** *n*. **~ingly** *adv*.

veal *n* nyama ya ndama.

veer *vi (esp of the wind), (fig of opinion, talk)* badili welekeo.

vegetable *n* mboga *~ soup* supu ya mboga (za majani) *adj* -a mboga, -a kuhusu mboga (za majani). **vegetarian** *n* mla mboga (za majani) *adj* -a kula mboga (za majani); **vegetarianism** *n* ulaji mboga.

vegetation *n* 1 uoto, uotaji. 2 mimea.

vegetate *vi (be idle)* jikalia, -la na kulala tu, ishi kama mmea bila kutumia akili.

vehement *adj* 1 *(of feeling)* -kali, shupavu. 2 -a nguvu, -a juhudi, -a bidii. **vehemence** *n* 1 ukali, harara. 2 juhudi, bidii, nguvu. **~ly** *adv*.

vehicle *n* 1 gari. 2 *(instrument, means)* chombo. **vehicular** *adj* -a magari.

veil *n* utaji, shela, barakoa; *(fig)* utando. **draw a ~ over sth** ficha. **take the ~** kuwa mtawa *vt* funika kwa shela; *(fig)* ficha, fanya siri. **~ed** *adj* 1 -enye kuvaa utaji/shela/barakoa. 2 *(concealed)* -liofichwa, -sio wazi. **~ing** *n* kitambaa cha shela, mtandio.

vein *n* 1 vena. 2 *(in leaf)* vishipajani. 3 *(in rock)* bamba la jiwe, ufa mwambani. 4 mwelekeo wa mwanzo; hali. **~ed** *adj* -enye nyuzinyuzi. **~ous** *adj* -a vena, -a mshipa wa damu.

velar *adj* -a kaakaa laini.

veld *n (S. Africa)* mbuga, tambarare, uwanda.

vellum *n* karatasi ya ngozi.

velocipede *n (hist)* baiskeli ya awali. *(US)* baiskeli ya watoto.

velocity *n* kasimwelekeo.

velouri *n* kitambaa kama mahameli.

velvet *n* mahameli, kiludhu. **an iron hand in a ~ glove** ukatili uliojificha *adj* laini (kama mahameli), -a mahameli/bahameli. **~een** *n* nguo kama mahameli. **~y** *adj* laini (kama mahameli).

venal *adj* 1 *(of persons)* -a kula rushwa, -a mrungura/hongo *~judges/politicians* mahakimu/wanasiasa wala rushwa. 2 *(of conduct)* -a kuhongwa. **~ity** *n* ulaji wa rushwa.

venation *n* vishipajani, mveneko.

vend *vt (chiefly legal)* uza, chuuza. **~ing machine** mashine sarafu (ya kuuzia bidhaa ndogondogo). **~ee** *n* mnunuzi. **~er**. **~or** mchuuzi.

vendetta *n* kisasi cha kurithi cha mauaji baina ya jamaa na jamaa.

veneer *n* 1 ubao-vene: ubao safi mwembamba unaobandikwa juu ya ubao usio bora. 2 *(fig)* uzuri, upole wa kujifanya/bandia *vt* bandika urembo.

venerable *adj* 1 -a kuheshimiwa (kwa sababu ya uzee, n.k.); -a heshima, -a kustahiwa. 2 *(church of England)* Dikoni mkuu. **venerate** *vt* heshimu, stahi, tukuza, jali. **veneration** *n.*

venereal *adj* -a zinaa ~ *disease* (*abbr* **VD**) ugonjwa wa zinaa.

vengeance *n* 1 kisasi *take* ~ lipiza kisasi. 2 **with a** ~ *(colloq)* kwa nguvu, sana, kabisa. **vengeful** *adj* -a kisasi, -a kutaka kulipa kisasi. **~ness** *n* kutaka kulipa kisasi.

venial *adj (of a sin/error/fault)* -a kusameheka, -dogo, -epesi. **~ity** *n (of sin)* udogo.

venison *n* nyama ya paa.

venom *n* sumu (ya nyoka, au mdudu); *(fig)* chuki, inda. **~ed** *adj* -a sumu; *(fig)* -a inda, chuki. **~nous** *adj* 1 -a sumu. 2 -a chuki, -a inda. **~ously** *adv.*

venous *adj* 1 -a vena ~ *blood* damu ya vena. 2 *(bot)* -enye vena ~ *leaf* jani lenye vishipajani.

vent *n* 1 tundu, kitundu cha kutokea gesi/hewa/maji. ~ **hole** *n* tundu la kutolea moshi, harufu, mvuke. 2 *(trade use)* mchano. 3 njia ya kutorokea/kupitia. 4 *(sing only)* liwazo. **give ~ to** *(fig)* toa mawazo bila woga *vt* ~ **sth on sb/sth** toa nje.

ventilate *vt* 1 pitisha hewa safi, burudisha kwa hewa. 2 *(fig)* eneza, tangaza, jadili. **ventilation** *n.* **ventilator** *n* tundu la (chombo cha) kupitisha hewa.

ventricle *n* ventrikali: uwazi (ndani ya mwili/ogani n.k.).

ventriloquism *n* kutoa sauti kama kwamba inatoka kwa mtu mwingine mbali kidogo. **ventriloquist** *n.*

venture *n* jambo la hatari ~ **scout** skauti mwandamizi; *vt, vi* thubutu, jasirisha **nothing ~, nothing gain/win/have** *(prov)* kujaribu si kushindwa. 1 -a kujaribu *(of persons)* 2 jasiri, hodari. 3 *(of acts, behaviour)* -a hatari; -a kubahatisha. **venturous** *adj.* **~some** *adj* -a ujasiri.

venue *n* mahali pa kukutanikia, makutano.

Venus *n* 1 *(astron)* ng'andu, zuhura. 2 *(Roman myth)* mungu wa kike wa mapenzi/uzuri.

veracious *adj (formal)* -a kusema kweli, -a kweli, -nyofu. **~ly** *adv.* **veracity** *n* 1 kweli, ukweli. 2 unyofu.

veranda(h) *n* veranda, baraza; roshani.

verb *n* kitenzi, *auxiliary* ~ kitenzi saidizi. **~al** *adj* 1 -a tendo; -a mdomo. 2 -a maneno tu. 3 *(literal)* sisisi. 4 -a kitenzi. **~ally** *adj* kwa maneno (si kwa maandishi), kwa kusema. **~alism** *n* 1 msemo. 2 msamiati. 3 maneno tu. **~alist** *n* msemaji ovyo, mropokaji. **~alize** *vt* sema, toa kauli. **~atim** *adv, adj* sisisi; kwa maneno yenyewe hasa, kwa kunukuu, kama ilivyosemwa. **~iage** *n (use of)* domo, maneno mengi ya bure, maelezo ya mzunguko. **~ose** *adj* -a maneno mengi. **~osely** *adv.* **~oseness**. *n* **~osity** *n.*

verdict *n* 1 hukumu, uaamuzi. 2 *(decision)* maoni, mkataa.

verdigris *n* kutu ya shaba.

verdure *n (lit)* majani, miti, mimea, majani ya chanikiwiti.

verdant *adj* 1 *(lit) (esp of grass, vegetation field)* -a majani mabichi, -a chanikiwiti; -a kustawi. 2 *(fig)* jinga, -siojua mambo, shamba. **verdancy** *n.*

verge *n* ukingo, kando; *(limit)* mpaka, mwisho. **be on the ~ of. bring (sb) to the ~ of** karibia; leta karibu karibu ya/katika ukingo *vi* ~ **on/upon** pakana (na), karibia.

verger *n* 1 *(church of England)* msimamizi (awaonyeshaye watu mahali pa kukaa). 2 mbeba rungu (la askofu au makamu wa mkuu wa chuo).

verify *vt* 1 thibitisha, hakikisha. 2 dhihirisha. **verifiable** *adj* -a kuthibitika. **verification** *n* hakika, thibitisho.

verily *adv (arch)* kweli.

verisimilitude *n* kuonekana kama kwamba ni kweli. **verisimilar** *adj* kinachoelekea ukweli, -a kuaminika.

verity *n* 1 *(old use)* kweli. **the eternal verities** sheria za Mungu. **veritable** *adj* -a kweli, -a hakika. 2 kanuni.

vermicelli *n* tambi.

vermicular *adj* -a funza, -a mchango, -a mnyoo. **vermiform** *adj* -enye umbo la mnyoo.

vermilion *n* rangi nyekundu kama damu *adj* -ekundu, -a rangi ya damu.

vermin *n* mnyama/mdudu mharibifu; *(of human) (fig)* doezi; rondezi **~ous** *adj* 1 haribifu, angamizi. 2 -enye kupe/chawa/utitirin.k;-liosababishwa na wadudu/wanyama waharibifu. **vermiverous** *adj* -enye kula wadudu.

vernacular *n* 1 lugha ya wenyeji; lugha ya kwanza/asili. 2 lahaja *in the ~* kwa lahaja ya kienyeji *adj* -a lahaja

vernal *adj* -a majira ya kuchipua/ kumea. **the ~ equinox** tarehe 21 Machi

verruca *n* dutu, sugu ya mguu.

versatile *adj* 1 hodari na -enye kupendelea mambo mbalimbali. 2 -enye akili nyepesi, elekevu sana. 3 *(changeful)* -geugeu, -badilifu, si thabiti; -enye matumizi mbalimbali. **versatility** *n.*

verse *n* 1 ushairi. 2 *(of Bible/ Koran)* aya. 3 ubeti. **give chapter and ~ for** toa kumbukumbu halisi; tongoa mstari wa shairi. **~-reading** *n* usomaji wa mashairi (beti na vipande). **versification** *n* 1 sanaa ya ushairi. 2 muundo wa shairi. **versifier** *n* mtunga mashairi (hasa ya ovyo). **versify** *vt,vi* tunga mashairi; geuza kuwa mashairi.

versed *adj* **~ (in)** -juzi, -enye maarifa ya *be ~ in sth* topea katika jambo.

versicolour *adj* -enye rangi nyingi, -a rangirangi.

version *n* 1 tafsiri. 2 *(account)* masimulizi, habari kama ilivyotolewa na mtu.

verso *n* ukurasa wa kushoto; upande wa pili wa sarafu.

verst *n* kipimo cha kirusi sawa na futi 3500.

versus *prep (often shortened to V or vs)* dhidi ya.

vertebra *n (pl)* 1 pingili la uti wa mgongo. 2 *(pl)* wanyama wenye uti wa mgongo. **~l** *adj* -a uti wa mgongo. **~ column** uti wa mgongo. **~te** *adj* -enye uti wa mgongo *n* mnyama mwenye uti wa mgongo.

vertex *n* kilele, kipeo.

vertices *n see* **vertex.**

vertical *adj* -a wima; *(overhead)* utosini. **~ly** *adv.*

vertigo *n* kisulisuli, kizunguzungu, kisunzi. **vertigious** *adj* -enye kuleta kizunguzungu.

verve *n* raghba, moyo, hamasa.

very *adj* 1 -enyewe; kweli, hasa. **in ~ deed** hasa, bila shaka *in ~ truth* kwelikweli, kwa kweli. 2 -ileile *the ~ same* yule yule *in this ~ place* papa hapa *come here this ~ minute* njoo sasa hivi *adv* 1 sana, kabisa; *(with superlative adj) the ~ lowest* ile ya chini kabisa. 2 *(to emphasize/ sameness or difference) the ~ same colour* rangi ileile. 3 *(to intensify adj and adv) ~ good* nzuri sana. **~ well** vizuri sana; *(often indicating agreement)* haya! vema! 4 *(to emphasize possession) my ~ own* -angu mwenyewe.

Very, Verey *adj* **~ light** fataki ya rangi (kama ishara ya matatizo baharini).

vesicle *n* kilengelenge. **vesicular** *adj* -a lengelenge.

vesper *n* 1 nyota ya jioni, zuhura. 2 *(pl)* **~s** sala za jioni.

vessel *n* 1 chombo (kama kikombe, bakuli). 2 *(ship)* chombo, jahazi, meli, merikebu. 3 *(vein)* mshipa.

vest[1] *n* 1 fulana 2 (*waistcoat*) kizibao.

vest[2] *vt,vi* 1 **~ sth in sb, ~ sb with sth** weka, wekea, kabidhi -pa. **have a ~ed interest in sth** -wa na maslahi. 2 **~ in** *(of property etc)* -wa na. kabidhiwa, pewa. 3 vaa, vika. **~ed** *adj.*

vestibule *n* 1 ukumbi. 2 ukumbi wa nje (wenye lango la kanisa). 3 chumba maalum mwishoni mwa behewa.

vestige *n* 1 alama, dalili baki, sazo. **vestigial** *adj* -a alama, -a mabaki; -a kumbukizi. 2 *(anat)* (kiungo/sehemu) salio la kitu kilichokuwepo zamani *adj* -liobaki kama salio.

vestment *n* vazi rasmi (hasa la kasisi).

vestry *n* 1 chumba cha kuvalia nguo kanisani. 2 *(parish council)* baraza la waumini. 3 chumba cha sala/ mafundisho ya dini/mikutano. **~clerk** *n* karani (wa baraza la waumini). **~man** *n* mjumbe wa baraza la parokia.

vesture *n* mavazi *vt* visha.

vet *n (colloq abbr for* **veterinary surgeon**) mganga wa mifugo *vt* 1 *(colloq) (hum)* pima mtu (afya yake). 2 *(manuscript)* hakiki, chunguza kwa makini.

veteran *n* mkongwe; *(of cars)* -liotengenezwa kabla ya 1916; *(in US)* askari mstaafu *adj* -kongwe, aliyebobea. **V~s Day** Siku ya kukumbuka mwisho wa vita ya Kwanza ya Dunia (Novemba 11).

veterinary *adj* -a kuhusu elimu ya maradhi ya wanyama. ~ **surgeon** mganga wa wanyama ~ *service* huduma ya utabibu wa mifugo.

veto *n* kura ya turufu (ya kisheria) ya kukataza jambo lisifanyike *vt* kataza, chelewesha, piga marufuku; tilia guu.

vex *vt* 1 chokoza, udhi, chukiza. **~ed question** suala tata lenye kuzua mabishano mengi (lakini lisilokatika). 2 *(poet, rhet)* chafua (bahari) **~ation** *n* 1 uchokozi, maudhi; chukizo/ chusho. 2 jambo la uchokozi, maudhi na chuki. **~atious** *adj* -chokozi, -a kuudhi, chushi.

via *prep* kupitia, kupita kwa njia ya.

viable *adj* -a kuweza kuwapo, -enye uwezo wa kujitegemea. **viability** *n* kuwezekana, kujitosheleza.

viaduct *n* daraja refu linalovuka bonde au korongo.

vial *n* kichupa kidogo (hasa cha dawa ya maji).

via media *(lat)* njia/mrengu wa kati.

vibes *n (sl)* hali/upepo.

vibrate *vt,vi* 1 tikisa, tingisha; tikisika, tingishika. 2 yumbayumba, wayawaya, taharuki. **vibrant** *adj* -a kutetemeka, -a kutikisika; -a kutaharukia/kusisimua. **vibrancy** *n.* **vibration** *n* mtetemo; mtikisiko; **vibrator** *n* kitingishi.

vicar *n* (*Anglican*) kasisi/padre wa usharika; (*RC*) mwakilishi, naibu wa ~ *of Christ* wakili wa Kristu. **~age** *n* nyumba/maskani ya padri/kasisi. **~ious** *adj* 1 -a kuwakilishwa. 2 -liofanywa kwa ajili ya wengine; -liotendwa kwa niaba ya. **~iously** *adv*.

vice[1] *n* 1 uovu. 2 *(in a horse)* tabia/ mazoea mabaya. **vicious** *adj* 1 -ovu, -enye makosa *a ~ argument* hoja potofu. 2 -a inda, -fisadi, fasiki. ~ **circle** mzunguko/hali inayoashiria mkwamo. ~ **spiral** upandaji wa bei unaotokana na upandaji bei ya kitu kingine *(animal)* -kali, -baya. **viciously** *adv* kwa ukali, kwa uovu; kwa makosa. **viciousness** *n* ubaya, ukali.

vice[2] *n* jiliwa ya seremala *as firm as a ~* imara sana *a ~ like grip* mbano imara sana.

vice[3] *(pref)* -dogo , naibu; makamu. **~-admiral** *n* makamu wa admirali. **~-chairperson** *n* makamu mwenyekiti. **~-chancellor** *n* makamu mkuu wa chuo kikuu. **~-premier** *n* naibu waziri mkuu. **~president** *n* makamu wa rais. **~-presidency** *n* umakamu wa rais.

viceroy *n* kaimu mfalme, mwakilishi wa mfalme/gavana mkuu. **viceregal** *adj* -a makamu mfalme. **vicereine** *n* mke wa makamu mfalme.

vice versa *adv* kinyume chake.

vicinity *n* 1 ujirani, kuwa karibu. 2 jirani.

vicissitude *n* mabadiliko, mageuko (hasa katika bahati ya mtu maishani).

victim *n* 1 kafara, mhanga. 2 mwathiriwa na janga (ambalo hakulisababisha yeye, mtu (au mnyama) anayesumbuka au kuuawa

au kupatwa na mabaya asiyostahili, kwa ajili ya mwingine. **~ize** *vt* onea, sumbua. **~ization** *n* maonevu, uonevu.
Victorian *n,adj (person)* (-a enzi ya) Malkia Victoria.
victory *n* ushindi. **victor** *n* mshindi, mshindaji. **~ious** *adj* -lioshinda, -liofaulu, -a shangwe, -a ushindi, (-shindi). **~iously** *adv*.
victual *vt,vi* 1 wekea akiba ya vyakula; -pa vyakula. 2 pakia vyakula (melini n.k.) *n (pl)* vyakula na vinywaji. **~ler** *n* 1 mfanya biashara ya vyakula. 2 **licensed ~ler** *(GB)* mwenye leseni ya baa na hoteli.
vide *vt (lat)* tazama. ~ **infra** tazama chini. ~ **supra** tazama juu.
videlicet *adv (common abbr viz)* yaani.
video *adj* 1 -a video; -a (matangazo ya) televisheni. 2 -a kunasa sauti na picha *n* 1 *(colloq)* video. 2 *(US)* televisheni. ~ **tape** ukanda wa televisheni/video *vt* piga picha za video.
vie *vi* ~ **(with sb) (for sth)** shindana na/chuana.
view *vt* 1 tazama, angalia; kagua. **an order to ~** hati/madaraka ya kukagua nyumba n.k. 2 fikiria. **~er** 1 mtazamaji televisheni. 2 kifaa cha kukuzia picha. **~less** *adj* 1 -sioonekana. 2 *(US)* bila maoni *n* 1 kutazama, kuangalia; upeo wa macho. **in ~ of** kwa kuzingatia. **in full ~ of** -enye kuonekana waziwazi. **on ~** -nayoonyeshwa. **come into ~** onekana, tokeza. **come in ~ of** weza kuona. 2 sura, mandhari; picha ya mandhari. 3 nafasi ya kuona; ukaguzi. 4 *(opinion)* maoni, rai, shauri. **fall in with/meet sb's ~s** kubaliana na. 5 nia, kusudio. **with a/the ~ to/of** kwa nia/matumaini ya. 6 *(compounds)* ~ *finder* kioo katika kamera cha kutafutia taswira.
vigil *n* 1 kukesha; ukeshaji (kwa ibada/ ulinzi) *keep ~* kesha. 2 mkesha (wa shughuli za dini).
vigilance *n* hadhari, uangalifu, kuwa macho. ~ **committee** kamati ya sungusungu/wazalendo ya kudumisha amani katika jamii au mahali ambapo hapana uongozi. **vigilant** *adj* macho, -angalifu, -enye hadhari. **vigilantly** *adv*. **vigilante** *n* mjumbe wa kamati ya wazalendo.
vignette *n* 1 nakshi/sanamu/picha ndogo nzuri (hasa kwenye jalada la kitabu au mwanzo/mwisho wa sura). 2 picha ya kichwa na mabega (ya mtu). 3 muhtasari wa tabia ya mtu.
vigour (*US* **vigor**) *n* 1 nguvu. 2 wepesi, bidii, juhudi. 3 makali (ya lugha). **vigorous** *adj* 1 -a nguvu. 2 -a juhudi, -epesi, hodari. **vigorously** *adv*.
Viking *n* mmoja wa maharamia wa Scandinavia walioshambulia na kuteka nyara pwani ya Ulaya kati ya karne ya 8 na ya 10.
vile *adj* 1 -enye kutia aibu; -a kuchukiza; ovu. 2*(colloq)* -baya. 3 *(old use)* -a bure, -sio na thamani. **~ly** *adv*. **~ness** *n* uovu, upotovu, ubaya.
vilify *vt* tukana, singizia, kashifu; sengenya. **vilification** *n* masingizio, maovu, masengenyo
villa *n* nyumba ya shamba yenye bustani kubwa.
village *n* kijiji, kitongoji. **~r** *n* mwanakijiji.
villain *n* mhalifu, mwovu. **~ous** *adj* -baya sana, ovu, halifu. **~y** *n*.
villein *n* mtwana/kijakazi (wakati wa enzi za ukabaila). **~age** *n*.
vim *n (colloq)* nguvu, juhudi, *full of ~* -enye nguvu.
vinaigrette *n* achari (ya siki, mafuta na viungo).
vindicate *vt* thibitisha. vindication *n* uthibitisho.
vindictive *adj* -siosamehe; -a kutaka kulipa kisasi. **~ly** *adv* kwa kulipiza kisasi. **~ness** *n* ulipizaji kisasi.
vine *n* mzabibu. **~-dresser** *n* mlimaji (mtunza) wa mizabibu. **~ry** *n* nyumba inamomea mizabibu. **~yard** *n* shamba la mizabibu.
vino *n (colloq)* divai, mvinyo. **~us** *adj* -a divai, kama divai.

vint *vt* tengeneza divai. **~age** *n* 1 msimu wa zabibu. 2 divai ya msimu fulani. 3 -a kipindi kilichopita/kilichosifika kwa ubora ~ *car* motokaa iliyoundwa kati ya mwaka 1916 - 1930. **~ager** *n* mvunaji mizabibu. **~ner** *n* muuza divai **~nery** *n* ghala ya divai.

vinegar *n* siki. **~y** *adj* kama siki; *(fig)* -enye kughadhibika, -a hamakihamaki.

vinyl *n* ngozi ya plastiki (ya kutengenezea mikoba, masanduku, viatu, busati n.k.).

viola *n* fidla kubwa (la sauti nyembamba).

violate *vt* 1 kiuka (kiapo, mkataba n.k.). 2 ingilia (faragha ya mtu, sehemu iliyo wakfu) bila heshima. 3 baka, ingilia mtu kwa nguvu. **violation** *n.* **violator** *n* mvunja sheria.

violent *adj* 1 -a nguvu nyingi 2. -kali sana. **~ly** *adv.* **violence** *n* vurugu, nguvu *robbery with ~* wizi wa nguvu. **do ~ to sth** *(fig)* kuwa kinyume cha; kasirisha.

violet n urujuani.

violin *n* fidla. **~ist** *n* mpiga fidla.

viper *n* kipiribao: nyoka mwenye sumu kali; *(fig)* mtu wa hila, inda na udanganyifu.

virago *n* mwanamke mgomvi, mwenye makelele.

virescence *n* hali ya kuwa kijani kibichi. **virescent** *adj* -a kijani kibichi.

virgin *n* bikira, mwanamwali. **(the Blessed) V~ (Mary)** Bikira Maria *adj* 1 -safi kabisa, -sioguswa ~ *snow* theluji safi isiyoguswa. 2 -liotakaswa **the ~ birth** uzao mtakatifu. 3 -a asili,-siotumika ~ *forest* msitu usioguswa bado ~ *soil* ardhi isiyolimwa bado. **~al** *adj* 1 -a mwanamali, -a bikira 2. -safi. **~ity** *n* ubikira.

virgo *n* mashuke.

virgule *n* mkwaju/mstari wa mshadhari wa kutenga maneno (kama katika na/au).

viridescent *adj* -a kijani kibichi. **viridescence** *n.* **viridity** *n* 1 kijani kibichi. 2 ulimbukeni, ushamba.

virile *adj* 1 -a kidume, -enye nguvu na tabia za kidume, -a nguvu. 2 *(of man)* rijali, -enye nguvu za kiume. **virility** *n* urijali; nguvu za mwanamume za uzazi.

virtu *n (only in)* **articles/objects of ~** vitu vya kupendeza kutokana na usanifu wa sanaa yake/utunu wake n.k.

virtual *adj* -a kweli (lakini si bayana). **~ly** *adv.*

virtue *n* 1 wema, maadili. **make a ~ of necessity** fanya jambo la lazima na kujitia ni kutokana na wema. **v~ is its own reward** *(prov)* tenda wema wende zako. **the cardinal ~s** nyemi/nemsi za asili. **the theological ~s** nyemi/nemsi za kidini. 2 utakatifu, usafi. 3 nguvu, uwezo. 4 ubora; manufaa. 5 **by/in ~ of** kwa sababu, kwa ajili ya. **virtuous** *adj* -ema/adilifu; -enye huruma; -lio bora; -lio safi, takatifu. **virtuously** *adv.*

virtuoso *n* stadi wa elimu hasa ya muziki; mweledi, mtu mwenye maarifa/vionjo vya kazi za sanaa. **virtuosity** *n* ujuzi wa mwana sanaa. weledi.

virulent *adj (of poison)* -kali, -a kuua; *(of words)* kali sana; *(of diseases)* -enye sumu kali. **~ly** *adv.* **virulence** *n.*

virus *n* virusi: viumbe hai ambao kiumbile hawajafikia ngazi ya seli. **virology** *n* virolojia, elimuvirusi.

visa *n* viza *vt* -pa viza.

visage *n (liter)* uso, sura (ya mtu). **~d** *adj (suff)* -enye uso.

vis-a-vis *adv* 1 uso kwa uso, -a kuelekeana. 2 *(fig)* kwa kulinganisha na, kwa kuhusiana na *n* kitu kinachoelekeana na kingine; mwenzi.

viscera *n* viungo vya ndani (hasa matumbo). **~l** *adj* -a viungo vya ndani; -a hisia za ndani.

viscid/viscus *adj* -a kunata (kama

ulimbo). **~ity** *n* 1 kunata; unato, mnato. 2 uzito. **viscosity** *n*.

vise *n (US)* jiliwa.

visible *adj* -a kuonekana wazi. **visibility** *n* hali ya kuonekana wazi ~ *is bad* mwangaza hautoshi. **visibly** *adv* wazi.

vision *n* 1 kuona. 2 maono; kivuli, ndoto. 3 *(insight)* uwezo wa kuona mbali/mbele, busara. 4 mwanga, nuru. **~ary** *adj* 1 -a kubuni tu, si hakika; -a njozi, -a ndoto. 2 *(of persons)* -enye fikra za kinjozi; -enye uwezo wa kuona mbali *n* ~ *person* mtu mwenye uwezo wa kuona mbali.

visit *vt,vi* 1 zuru, enda kuamkia, tembelea. 2 *(chiefly US)* kagua. 3 *(chiefly US)* ~ **with** tembelea, ongea na. 4 ~ **sth on sb** *(biblical use)* patiliza, adhibu. ~ **the sins of the fathers upon the children** adhibu watoto kutokana na makosa ya wazazi. **~ant** *adj,n* 1 *(liter)* mgeni mashuhuri, mzuka. 2 ndege mhamaji *n* kuzuru, kutembelea; ziara. **~ing** *n* kutembelea, kuzuru. **~ation** *n* 1 tume rasmi. 2 mapatilizo/adhabu ya kidini (agh. baa). 3 *(of animals)* mkurupuko. **~or** *n* 1 mgeni *state* ~ mgeni wa serikali ~*'s book* kitabu cha wageni. 2 mkaguzi.

visor *n* **(sun)** ~ kioo cha gari kinachopunguza mwanga.

vista *n* 1 taswira, upeo unaoonekana katika nafasi nyembamba; mandhari. 2 *(fig)* mfululizo wa taswira/mandhari/matukio n.k.

visual *adj* -a kuona, -a macho. ~ **aids (in teaching)** vielelezo (vya kufundishia). **~ly** *adv*. **~ize** *vt* pata sura, piga taswira kichwani. **~ization** *n*.

vital *adj* 1 -a uzima, -a uhai, -a lazima kwa uzima/kwa uhai. **the ~ force/principle** roho/uhai. ~ **statistics** takwimu muhimu (inayohusu urefu wa maisha na uzazi, ndoa na vifo); *(colloq)* vipimo vya mwanamke, vya kifua, kiuno na mapaja. 2 -kuu, -a kiini hasa. **~s** *n (pl)* viungo muhimu vya mwili hasa mapafu, moyo, ubongo. **~ly** *adv*. **~ism** *n* imani ya kuwa kuna nguvu katika viumbe inayotawala uhai/roho mbali na ile ya kikemia. **~ist** *n*. **~ity** *n* uzima, uhai, nguvu tendaji; uchangamfu. **~ize** *vt* jazwa na nguvu, ingiza nguvu, jipa tumaini, jadhubisha.

vitamin *n* vitamini.

vitiate *vt* haribu, punguza nguvu, rahisisha, dhoofisha. **vitiation** *n* 1 kuharibu; kuharibika. 2 upunguo/upungufu, urahisisho.

vitrify *vt,vi* geuza kuwa kioo; geuka kioo. **vitrification** *n* mageuzo (hasa kuwa kioo). **vitreous** *adj* -a kioo, kama kioo.

vitriol *n* mrututu, asidi ya salfa; *(fig)* kejeli. **~ic** *adj (fig of words feeling)* chungu, kali; -a kejeli. **~ize** *vt*.

vituperate *vt* tukana; laani. **vituperative** *adj* -a kutukana. **vituperation** *n* matusi; laana, maneno ya kulaani.

viva *n (colloq) see* **viva voce**; *interj*. idumu!

vivace *adv (music)* kwa kuchangamka/uchangamfu.

vivacious *adj* 1 -changamfu, kunjufu, -a furaha, cheshi, -enye bashasha. **~ly** *adv*. **vivacity** *n* uchangamfu, ukunjufu, bashasha, ucheshi.

viva-voce *adj* -a mdomo ~ *examination or test* mtihani wa mahojiano; jaribio la kuzungumza.

vivid *adj* 1 *(of colours etc)* -lioiva, nga'vu. 2 -liochangamka. 3 wazi, dhahiri. **~ly** *adv* 1 kwa dhahiri, waziwazi. 2 kama kwamba ni kweli. **~ness** *n* udhahiri, ung'avu; kung'aa.

vivify *vt* 1 *(esp fig)* tia uhai, amsha, huisha. 2 chochea. **vivification** *n*.

viviparous *adj (zool)* -a kuzaa watoto.

vivisect *vt* pasua/fanya jaribio la kisayansi (kwa viumbe hai). **~ion** *n*. **~ionist** *n*.

vixen *n* 1 mbweha jike. 2 mwanamke mgomvi/mwenye gubu/hasira. **~ish** *adj* -gomvi.

viz *adv (lat videlicet, usu spoken)* yaani,

ndiyo kusema.

vizier *n (in some Muslim countries)* waziri *grand ~* waziri mkuu.

vocable *n* neno (hasa muundo wake).

vocabulary *n* 1 msamiati. 2 maneno.

vocal *adj* 1 -a sauti *the ~ organs* ala za sauti (ulimi, midomo n.k.) *~ music* muziki wa kuimbwa. **~ly** *adv* kwa sauti. **~ist** *n* mwimbaji. **~ic** *adj* -a vokali, -a irabu. **~ism** *n* 1 utumiaji sauti (katika kusema (kuimba). 2 mfumo wa irabu. **~ize** *vt* sema/imba kwa sauti, toa sauti ya kusikika; tia/andika irabu *vi* toa sauti, piga kelele. **~ization** *n.* **vocative** *adj, n* kauli ya mneni.

vocation *n* 1 *(sing only) (of social or religious)* wito. 2 *(special attitude)* welekevu, moyo, uwezo. 3 kazi, shughuli, utaalamu; weledi. **~ al** *adj* -a kazi, -a utaalamu.

vociferate *vi,vt* piga makelele. **vociferation** *n* sauti kubwa, makelele. **vociferous** *adj* -a makelele. **vociferously** *adv* kwa makelele.

vodka *n* vodka: pombe kali ya Kirusi.

vogue *n* 1 mtindo wa sasa, fashini. 2 kupendelewa/kupendwa kwa jambo; -kupokelewa; kukubalika. **be in/come into ~, be/go out of ~** -wa/-tokuwa katika fashini, pendelewa/ -topendelewa. **all the ~** mtindo unaopendwa kote.

voice *n* 1 sauti, mlio. 2 (uwezo wa) kutoa sauti. 3 sauti ya mtu *in a loud ~* kwa sauti kubwa. **lift up one's ~** *(old use)* toa sauti (imba, sema). **shout at the top of one's ~** toa usiyahi. **with one ~** *(liter)* kwa kauli moja. 4 **a/some/no etc ~ in sth** haki/ kutokuwa na haki ya kutoa maoni. 5 wito; hiari; maono; hisia *the ~ of God Nature; the ~s of the night* dhamira. 6 *(in phonetic)* sauti irabu/-konsonanti. 7 *(gram)* kauli (ya kutenda/kutendwa *vt* 1 sema, eleza. 2 tamka irabu/ konsonanti. **~d** *adj (in compounds)* -a ghuna. **~less** *adj* -sighuna (mfano p,f).

void *adj* 1 tupu, pasipo mtu, wazi. 2 *~ of* -siokuwa na, bila, bure. 3 **null and ~** *(leg)* batili, -siofaa *n* uwazi, upweke *vt (leg)* tangua, batilisha; futa. **~able** *adj* -a kufutika, -a kubatilika. **~ance** *n.*

voile *n* kitambaa chepesi cha gauni.

volatile *adj* 1 *(of a liquid)* fukivu/ fushi, -a kugeuka hewa (mvuke). **volatilize** *vt,vi* fukiza, geuza kuwa hewa/mvuke, fusha. **volatilization** *n.* 2 *(of a person)* cheshi, changamfu, -enye kuingilika, -a watu; epesi kubadilika. **volatility** *n* kugeuka hewa.

volcano *n* volkano. **volcanic** *adj* -a volkano.

vole *n* buku.

volition *n* hiari, ridhaa; chaguo, moyo, akili *of one's own ~* kwa hiari. **~al** *adj.*

volley *n* 1 mshindo (wa makombora, bunduki nyingi n.k. zikipigwa pamoja). 2 mfululizo (wa maapizo, matusi, maswali n.k). **~-ball** *n* mpira wa wavu *vt,vi* 1 *(of guns)* lia sawia; *(of tennis)* jibu pigo (kabla mpira kugonga chini).

volt *n* volti, kizio cha nguvu ya umeme. **~age** *n* volteji. **~aic** *adj.*

volte-face *n* mgeuko, badiliko kamili; ugeukaji kabisa.

voluble *adj* msemi, -semaji, -epesi/ hodari wa kusema. **volubility** *n* usemaji. **volubly** *adv.*

volume *n* 1 juzuu. **speak ~s for** shuhudia sana, onyesha wazi. 2 nafasi, ujazo. 3 *(great quantity)* ukubwa, wingi, chungu *~ of production* wingi wa uzalishaji (bidhaa). 4 nguvu ya sauti, sauti kubwa. **voluminous** *adj* -kubwa; -enye kuchukua nafasi kubwa; *(of an author)* -enye kuandika vitabu vingi.

voluntary *adj* 1 -a hiari, bila kulazimishwa; -a kupenda mwenyewe. 2 -a bure, pasipo mshahara, -a kujitolea. 3 *(of muscle)* -nayodhibitiwa na utashi wa mtu *n* wimbo wa kinanda unaopigwa nje ya ibada. **voluntariness** *n* hiari.

voluntarily *adv*.
volunteer *n* 1 mtu ajitoaye. 2 askari wa kujitolea *vi,vt 1* ~ **sth/to do sth/for sth** jitolea kitu/kufanya kitu/kwa kitu (kwa kazi fulani) jiandika (kwa hiari). 2 *(offer freely)* toa kwa hiari.
voluptuous *adj* -a anasa nyingi, -a ashiki, -a kutia ashiki, nyegereshi.
voluptuary *n* mpenda anasa/maraha, mwenye ashiki. **~ness** *n* ashiki. **~ly** *adv*.
vomit *vt,vi* 1 tapika. 2 *(emit)* toa, foka, bubujisha *n* matapiko, matapishi.
voodoo *n* uchawi, ulozi, vuudu ~ *doctor* mchawi.
voracious *adj* -lafi; -enye uroho. **~ly** *adv* kwa uroho. **~ness. voracity** *n* ulafi, kula sana, uroho.
vortex *n* 1 kizingia (cha maji/hewa). 2 *(fig)* hekaheka, mvuto (katika shughuli fulani); mishughuliko. **vortical** *adj* -a kuzingia. **vortiginous** *adj (arch)* -liozingia.
votary *n* mfuasi (wa jambo fulani).
vote *n* 1 (haki ya kupiga) kura. **put sth to the** ~ pigia kura. 2 idadi ya kura. 3 kasma *vi,vt* 1 ~ **for/against sb/sth** pigia mtu kura ya ndiyo/hapana. ~ **on sth** pigia kura. 2 ~ **sb/sth (for sth)** -pa/toa fedha kwa madhumuni fulani. 3 ~ **sth down** shinda kwa kura. ~ **sth through** pitisha, kubali, idhinisha (kwa kura). 4 *(colloq)* tangaza kwa kutumia maoni ya watu. 5 pendekeza, shauri. **~r** *n* mpiga kura. **~less** *adj* -sio na haki ya kupiga kura.
votive *adj* -liotolewa/wekwa wakfu ili kuondoa nadhiri.
vouch *vi,vt* ~ **for sb/sth** dhamini, chukua dhima, amini/kiapo.
voucher *n* vocha, hati ya malipo. **gift** ~ vocha ya kupewa zawadi. **luncheon** ~ vocha ya kupewa chakula cha mchana hotelini.
vouchsafe *vt (formal)* kubali, toa/fanya kwa moyo.
vow *n* kiapo; nadhiri *vt* weka nadhiri.
vowel *n* irabu, vokali *back* ~ irabu nyuma *front* ~ irabu mbele.
vox *n (Lat)* sauti. ~ **populi** sauti ya umma; maoni ya watu.
voyage *n* safari (baharini n.k.) *vt* safiri (kwa chombo, katika jahazi, meli), abiri. **~r** *n* abiria, msafiri (melini, chomboni).
voyeur *n* mtu apataye burudani/ashiki kwa kuchungulia uchi wa mtu au watu wakijamiiana.
vulcanite *n* plastiki ngumu, vulkaniti. **vulcanize** *vt* vulkanisha; changanya mpira na salfa kutengeneza plastiki ngumu. **vulcanization** *n*.
vulgar *adj* 1 -sio na adabu, -a kishenzi, -tovu wa adabu, pujufu. 2 -a kawaida, -a watu wote; -a wingi wa watu. ~ **fraction** fraksheni ya kawaida. (mf ½). **the** ~ **herd** makabwela. **the** ~ **tongue** lugha ya kienyeji. **~ly** *adv*. **~ian** *n* mtu tajiri mwenye tabia ya kishenzi. **~ism** *n* usemi (neno) wa kishamba. **~ity** *n* ushenzi, ufidhuli, ujuvi, usafihi, ukosefu wa adabu, utovu wa adabu; upujufu. **~ize** *vt* tweza; rahisisha; eneza kwa watu wote, fanya -a watu wote. **~ization** *n*.
vulnerable *adj* -enye kuweza kudhuriwa, -sio salama; -siolindwa. **vulnerability** *n*.
vulpine *adj* 1 kama mbweha. 2 *(cunning)* -erevu, -janja.
vulture *n* 1 tai. 2 mtu mchoyo anufaikae kutokana na mikosi ya wengine. **vulturous, vulturine, vulturish** *adj* -a tai, kama tai.
vulva *n* kuma.
vying *vt see* **vie**.

W

W,w *n* herufi ya ishirini na tatu ya alfabeti ya Kiingereza.
wacky *adj (of people, ideas, behaviour) (sl)* -a kipuuzi, pumbavu.
wad *n* 1 fusho, matambara/takataka laini za kufungashia/tenganishia vitu. 2 *(of notes)* bulungutu: kibunda cha noti (fedha) *vt* 1 ziba/jaza kwa pamba/matambara/takataka laini n.k. **~ding** kitu chororo (agh. pamba) cha kushindilia na kuzuia vitu visicheze.
waddle *vi* tagaa *n (sing only)* mtagao.
wade *vi,vt* enda/pita/jivuta kwa shida (matopeni, n.k.). **wading bird** ndege atembeaye majini kama kitwitwi. **~ in** shambulia kwa nguvu. **~ into sth** shambulia vikali. **~r** *n* 1 kitwitwi, kiulimazi. 2 *(pl)* **~rs** gambuti: viatu virefu vya juu ya magoti.
wadi` *n (in the middle East, Arabia, Northern Africa)* korongo kavu la mto.
wafer *n* 1 biskuti nyembamba. 2 mkate wa ushirika mtakatifu.
waffle[1] *n* keki ndogo ya rojo ya unga, maziwa na mayai iliyookwa kwenye kikaango.
waffle[2] *vi (GB colloq)* bwabwaja, bwata, payuka *n* mapayo.
waft *vt,vi* peperusha, peperuka, chukuliwa (na upepo, maji) *n* 1 pumzi; harufu nzuri (ya kunukia) n.k. 2 mwendo wa mawimbi.
wag[1] *vt,vi* tikisa *~ ones finger at sb* onyesha kidole mtikiso, mtikisiko. **~ tail** *n* kitwitwi.
wag[2] *n* mcheshi, bashasha. **~gery** *n* bashasha, ucheshi. **~gish** *adj* cheshi. bashasha. **~gishly** *adv.*
wage[1] *vt* endeleza, pigana, fanya (vita, kampeni).
wage[2] *n (usu pl)* 1 ujira, ijara; mshahara *a living ~* mshahara wa kujikimu *minimum ~* kima cha chini cha mshahara. **~ claim** dai la mshahara. **~ earner** mfanyakazi. 2 *(old use; pl in form with sing v)* malipo.
wager *n* dau. **lay a ~** pinga *vt,vi* weka dau, pinga.
waggle *vt,vi* tikisatikisa.
waggon *(US usu* **wagon)** *n* 1 mkokoteni; gari la kukokotwa na farasi maksai. **on the (water) ~** *(colloq)* siye kunywa pombe. 2 *(US freight car)* chakara: behewa la wazi la mizigo. **station ~** *n (US)* gari dogo la abiria na mizigo. **~er** *n* mwangalizi wa gari la kukokotwa na farasi wake. **~-lit** *n* behewa la kulala.
wagtail *n see* **wag**.
waif *n* msokwao (hasa mtoto). **~s and strays** watoto wasokwao na waliotelekezwa.
wail *vi,vt* omboleza, lia kwa huzuni; *(of the wind)* fanya sauti kama mtu anayelia *n* maombolezo; uliaji.
wain *n (old use or poet)* mkokoteni mkubwa wa shambani (wa kukokotwa na farasi).
wainscot *n* mbao za ukutani (ndani ya nyumba) agh. kuanzia chini hadi kufikia nusu ya ukuta *vt* **~ed** *adj* -liowekwa mbao za ukutani.
waist *n* 1 kiuno. **~band** *n* mkanda wa nguo. **~-cloth** *n* shuka, kikoi. **~ deep** *adj, adv* -a kufika kiunoni. **~ high** -a kufika kiunoni. **~line** kiuno. 2 *(naut)* sehemu ya kati ya meli. **~coat** kizibao.
wait *n* 1 (kitendo cha) kungoja, kusubiri. 2 **lie in ~ for** *(less usu)* **lay ~ for** vizia, jificha ili kushambulia. 3 *(pl)* **the ~s** waimbaji wa nyimbo za Noeli waendao nyumba hadi nyumba *vi,vt* 1 **~ (for)** ngoja, ngojea, subiri. **keep sb ~ing** ngojesha mtu. **~ up (for sb)** kesha. **No ~ing** usingoje *~ and see* ngoja uone *this can ~* hii inaweza kusubiri. 2 **~ (for)** ahirisha. 3 **~ on/upon sb** tumikia, -wa kama mtumishi wa kutumwa. **~ on sb hand and foot** kidhia haja zote, tumikia kwa kila hali; *(colloq) (old use)* tembelea, zuru. 4 **~ at/on** hudumia mezani. 5 **~ing list** orodha ya wanaosubiri. **~ing-room** *n* chumba cha wanaosubiri. **~er. ~ress**

n mhudumu, mwandikaji.

waive *vt* 1 samehe, acha kudai (haki au dai). **~r** *n (leg) (written statement)* hati ya kusamehe madai.

wake[1] *vi,vt* 1 ~ **(up)** amka. 2 ~ **sb up** amsha, zindua. 3 ~ **sb (up)** chochea, changamsha. 4 sumbua kwa makelele. **waking** *adj,n* -wa macho *vt,vi* amsha, amka. **~ful** *adj* -a kukesha, -a kukosa usingizi.

wake[2] *n* mkondo (wa chombo). **in the ~ of** baada ya *follow in sb's ~* fuata nyayo za mtu.

wale *n see* **weal, welt**.

walk[1] *n* 1 matembezi, kutembea kwa mguu. 2 namna ya kutembea. 3 njia. 4 ~ **of life** weledi, wito, kazi (katika maisha) *vi,vt* 1 *(of persons)* tembea, enda kwa miguu; *(of animals)* -enda. **~-about** *n (Australian sl of Aborigines in the desert)* safari; *(colloq)* kuzunguka kwa mgeni rasmi na kusalimu watu njiani. ~ **away from** shinda kwa urahisi/bila taabu. ~ **away** *n* ushindi wa bure/rahisi. ~ **away with sth** shinda kwa urahisi.~ **off with sth** *(colloq)* chukua. ~ **into** *(sl)* kula kwa raha/buraha; shutumu, tukana; jipeleka. ~ **on** *(drama)* tokea jukwaani. **~-out** *(colloq)* goma. ~ **out** *n* mgomo. ~ **out on sb** *(sl)* acha, telekeza. ~ **out with sb** *(dated colloq)* chumbia; posa. ~ **over sb** shinda mtu kirahisi. ~ **over** *n* ushindi rahisi. ~ **up** pitia; panda juu; *(inviting people to)* karibuni! ~ **up (to sb/sth)** karibia, endea, jia. 2 tembeza, fanya kutembea. ~ **sb off his feet/legs** chosha mtu kwa kumtembeza. 3 tembea/pita kwa miguu. 4 *(with various n)* ~ *the wards* -wa mganga mwanagenzi ~ *the streets*-wa malaya. **~er** mtembeaji. **~ing** *n (in compounds)* ~ **shoes** viatu vya matembezi. **~-stick** *n* bakora, fimbo ya matembezi. **walkie-talkie** *n (colloq)* redio (ya mkononi) ya kupokea na kupeleka habari.

wall *n* 1 ukuta, kiambaza. **with one's back to the ~** kwa kubanwa sana; kwa kuzingirwa. **be/go up the ~** *(sl)* hamaki, chukia; udhika sana. **bang/run one's head against a (brick) ~** jaribu kufanya jambo ambalo wazi haliwezekani; piga ngumi ukutani. **see through a brick ~** ona mambo yajayo, ona mbali. 2 *(fig)* kizuizi, (kitu kinachofanana na) ukuta. 3 upenuni, kando *(chiefly fig)* **go to the ~** tupwa nje (katika mashindano), shindwa kabisa. **push/ drive sb to the ~** shinda. 4 *(compounds)* ~ **flower** aina ya maua ya bustani; mtu aliyekosa mwenzi katika dansi. ~ **painting** picha ya ukutani. ~ **paper** karatasi za rangi za kupamba ukutani *vt* 1 *(usu pp)* zungushia ukuta. 2 ~ **sth up/off** ziba (kwa matofali n.k.).

wallaby *n* kangaruu mdogo.

wallah *n (sl in India)* mtumishi (aliyeajiriwa kwa kazi maalumu).

wallet *n (US* **pocket book**) pochi, mkoba wa kuwekea karatasi/noti za benki.

wall-eyed *adj* -enye makengeza; -a kama makengeza.

wallop *vt (sl or hum)* piga sana, twanga, kung'uta; shinda sana/vibaya *n* konde zito; ushinde. **~ing** *adj* -kubwa sana.

wallow *vi* gaagaa, vingirika matopeni/ majini; *(fig)* zamia, jiachia. **be ~ing in money** *(colloq)* -wa mkwasi, tajirika sana *n* magaagao ya wanyama, mahali ambapo wanyama huenda kugaagaa.

Wall-Street *n (used for)* soko la fedha la Marekani.

walrus *n* sili wa bahari, mwenye pembe.

waltz *n (music)* msowero: aina ya dansi ya watu wawili wawili kuzunguka pamoja *vi* sowera. ~ **in/out/into/out of** ingia/toka kwa mwendo wa furaha.

wampum *n* kauri; simbi (pambo au fedha).

wan *adj* 1 *(of person, his look etc)* -liosawajika; -a/-enye huzuni, wasiwasi. 2 (*of light, the sky*) -lofifia, -eupe, -enye rangi kidogo isiyong'ara. **~ly** *adv*. **~ness** *n*.

wand *n* 1 kijifimbo cha mcheza mazingaombwe/kiongozi wa muziki, n.k. 2 fimbo rasmi ionyeshayo madaraka.

wander *vi* 1 zurura. 2 (*stray*) potea ~ *from the subject* -tofuata suala linalozungumzwa. 3 changanyikiwa, weweseka. **~er** *n* 1 mhamaji, mzururaji. 2 mwenye kupotea njia. **~ings** *n* 1 mizunguko, safari ndefu. 2 *(mental)* upayukaji maneno (kutokana na ugonjwa hasa wakati wa homa kali). **~lust** *n* shauku ya kusafiri.

wane *n* 1 ufifiaji, kufifia. 2 *vi* pungua, fifia, dhoofu. **on the ~** katika kufifia; *(of moon)* kuingia ndani.

wangle *vt (sl)* pata, panga kwa hila/ mbinu *n* hila, mbinu.

wank *vi (GB vulg sl)* piga punyeto *n* punyeto. n.k.

want[1] *vt,vi* 1 taka, hitaji; *(be without)* kosa, -takiwa; -tafutwa. **~ed** *adj,n (colloq)* tangazo (gazetini) la kazi. 2 (*desire*) tamani, -wa na hamu, taka. 3 hitaji, paswa, dai. 4 *(progressive tense only)* **be ~ing** kosekana, -wa pungufu. **be ~ing (in sth)** kosa/ kosekana; pungua/pungukiwa na. **be found ~ing** *(with human subject)* -totosheleza, -toridhisha. 5 *(impers)* pungua, baki *it ~s one hour to the class* imebaki saa moja kabla ya darasa. 6 -wa katika dhiki. **~ for nothing** jitosheleza kwa kila kitu. **~ing** *(prep)* bila; ikikosekana.

want[2] *n* 1 (*lack*) upungufu, ukosefu, uhaba. 2 *(felt need)* hitaji, haja; dhiki. 3 matamanio, uchu, matakwa.

wanton *adj* 1 *(lit)* -tundu, tukutu, -a kuchezacheza. 2 -siozuilika; tele, -a kuzaa sana, -enye kustawi sana; korofi. 3 -sio sababu, harabu. 4 *(arch)* asherati, kware, -a kikware, fasiki *n* kiberenge, mwasherati *vi (lit)* chezacheza. **~ly** *adv*. **~ness** *n*.

war *n* 1 vita, kondo, kitali. **at ~** katika hali ya vita. **carry the ~ into the** *enemy camp* shambulia (baada ya kuridhika na kujihami/kujilinda). **declare ~ (on)** tangaza vita. **go to ~ against** anza vita (dhidi ya). **have been in the ~s** *(colloq or hum)* umia (k.m. kutokana na ajali). **make/ wage~ on** pigana na. 2 **~ baby** *n* mwanaharamu (wa vita) (ambaye baba yake ni askari). **~ bride** mke wa askari (aliye vitani). **~ cloud(s)** *n* dalili za vita. **~-cry** *n* ukelele wa kutiana shime (vitani). **~ dance** *n* ngoma ya vita. **~ god** *n* mungu wa vita. **~-correspondent** *n* mwandishi wa habari za vita. **~-head** *n* kichwa cha kombora; bomu halisi (lenye baruti). **~ horse** *n* farasi wa vita. **~ lord** *n (rhet)* jemadari wa vita. **~ monger** n mchochezi wa vita. **~ office** Idara ya vita. **~ paint** *n* rangi inayopakwa mwili mzima (kabla ya kwenda vitani); *(fig)* mavazi rasmi ya askari; *(sl)* vipodozi. **~ path** *n (only in)* **on the ~ path** tayari kupigana. **~ ship** *n* manowari, meli ya vita. **~ torn** *adj* -lioharibika na vita, -lioangamizwa na vita. **~ widow** *n* mjane wa mwanajeshi aliyefia vitani. 3 sayansi au sanaa ya vita/mapigano/ matumizi ya silaha. 4 *(fig)* mapambano ~ *against bribery* mapambano dhidi ya hongo ~ *of words* mizozo. **~fare** *n* vita, mapigano; mambo ya vita. **~ like** tayari kwa vita; -nayoashiria vita; -enye kupenda vita. **~ time** wakati wa vita. **~rior** *n (lit or rhet)* mpiganaji; askari wa vita.

warble *vi,vt (esp of birds)* imba (hasa kwa madende/madoido) *n* wimbo, kuimba (kwa sauti nyororo kama ya ndege). **~r** *n* (aina ya) ndege mwimbaji.

ward *n* 1 **keep watch and ~** linda. 2 *(guardian)* ulinzi, ulezi; mtu (hasa mtoto) aliye chini ya mamlaka ya mahakama. 3 *(of a government area)* kata. 4 *(of hospital)* wadi *isolation ~* wadi iliyotengwa. 5 *(of lock, key)* mtoto, jino *vt* **~ sth off** kinga, epuka.

kwepa kitu.

warden *n* 1 msimamizi, mwangalizi. **traffic** ~ msimamizi wa maegesho ya magari *the ~ of the hall of residence* mwangalizi wa bweni *game-~* bwana nyama. 2 *(old use except in a few cases)* mkuu (wa chuo n.k.). 3 *(US)* askari jela. **warder** *n (GB)* askari magereza/jela. **wardress** *n* askari magereza wa kike.

wardrobe *n* 1 kabati la nguo. 2 nguo, mavazi. 3 maleba: mavazi ya kundi la sanaa za maonyesho.

ward-room *n* vyumba vya maofisa wa manowari (isipokuwa nahodha).

ware[1] *(imper)* angalia! jihadhari! habedari!

ware[2] *n* 1 *(in compounds)* bidhaa; chombo *silver ~* bidhaa za fedha 2 *(pl)* bidhaa, vitu vya biashara. **~house** *n* ghala, bohari *vt* weka/hifadhi ghalani.

warm *adj* **1** -a vuguvugu, -fufutende. ~ **work** kazi ya kusisimua mwili; kazi ya sulubu/hatari. **make things ~ for sb** letea matata, adhibu mtu. ~ **blood** damu ya mamalia na ndege. ~ **blooded** *adj* -a damu moto; motomoto; -enye mihemko ya haraka. 2 *(hearty)* -a shauku. 3 *(angry)* -a hasira. 4 *(cordial)* kunjufu, -ema. **~-hearted** *adj* -ema, -kunjufu, -a huruma, -a upendo. **~-heartedness** *n* *(of scent)* bichi; *(of children games)* -a kukimbia. **~ly** *adv* -kwa ukunjufu/upendo; kwa kuzuia baridi. **~th** *n* 1 hasira. 2 uvuguvugu, ukunjufu; wema mwingi *vt,vi* ~ **(sth) (up)** pasha/pata moto. ~ **to one's work/task/sb** changamkia kazi/mtu. **~ing-pan** *n (hist)* kipashi joto (cha kitanda). **~er** *n* kipasha joto.

warn *vt* onya, asa, hadharisha. ~ **sb off** katàza mtu (asiingie/asikaribie). **~ing** *n* onyo, ilani *without a moment's ~* kwa ghafula *give a month's ~* toa notisi ya mwezi mmoja *adj* -a onyo, -a ilani.

warp[1] *vt,vi* 1 *(bend)* pinda, pindika. 2 potoka; potosha *n* kupinda.

warp[2] *n* **the** ~ mtande.

warrant *n* 1 haki, sababu 2 hati (ya idhini ya kufanya kitu); kibali, waranti *search ~* hati ya upekuzi. 3 *(marine)* hati ya kuteua askari asiye afisa *vt* 1 tetea; halalisha; -wa na sababu. 2 thibitisha; *(colloq)* thibitishia, hakikishia. **~ee** *n* mtu anayepewa hati (ya kutengeneza/kubadilisha bidhaa); mdhaminiwa. **~or. ~er** *n* mdhamini. **~-officer** *n* askari asiye afisa. **~y** *n* 1 hati (ya kutengeneza/kubadilisha bidhaa). 2 mamlaka.

warren *n* eneo lenye mashimo na sungura wengi; *(fig)* maskani yenye watu/mitaa mingi.

wart *n* chunjua, sugu, dutu. **~-hog** *n* ngiri. **~y** *adj*.

wary *adj* -a hadhari, -angalifu, -enye kuwa macho. **warily** *adv* kwa hadhari, kwa uangalifu. **wariness** *n*.

was *see* **be**.

wash *vt,vi* 1 osha; (*bathe*) oga,ogesha; (*hands*) nawa. ~ **one's hands of sth/sb** jitoa kabisa katika jambo, nawa mikono. ~ **clothes** fua nguo. ~ **sth down** safisha (hasa kwa mtiririko wa maji. ~ **sth away/off/out** ondoa kwa kuosha, safisha kwa maji. **be/look/feel ~ed out** *(fig colloq)* jisikia hoi, choka sana. ~ **up** (*GB*) osha vyombo (baada ya mlo); *(US)* nawa uso na mikono. **~ing up** *n* uoshaji vyombo. **(all) ~ed up** *(colloq)* -liokwisha. 2 *(of material)* fulika; *(fig)* kubalika. 3 *(of sea, river)* -la; pita. 4 *(of moving liquid)* beba, tupa, chukua. ~ **sth down with** telemshia. **~ed out** *(of games)* lioahirishwa, -lioshindikana (kwa sababu ya mvua au mafuriko); *(of roads etc)* -siopitika. 5 chimba (mchanga) kwa maji. 6 *(ceremonially)* -toharisha, eua ~ *sb of his sins* toharisha/takasa mtu dhambi zake. 7 mwagika. 8 *(in compounds often used as a substitute for ~ing)* ~ **basin/bowl/hand-basin** beseni/bakuli la kunawia; karai. ~ **board** *n* ubao wa kufulia. **~cloth**

kitambaa cha kunawia uso. ~-**day** *n* siku ya kufua. ~**drawing** picha ya rangi za maji. ~**house** *n* chumba/ banda la kufulia nguo. ~-**leather** *n* ngozi laini ya kusafishia. ~**out** *n* sehemu iliyobomolewa na mafuriko; *(fig)* mtu wa bure; kushindwa kabisa. ~ **room** *(US)* msala. ~-**hand stand** *n* meza ya kunawia. ~**tub** *n* pipa la kufulia nguo. ~ **able** *adj* -a kufulika *n* 1 kuosha, josho *have a ~ and brush up* koga na kujinadhifisha, jitakasa. 2 *(sing only)* nguo, za kufua; mahali pa kufulia/kufanyia udobi. 3 *the ~ (ed)* mkondo; sauti inayotokana na mtiririko wa maji; kitu cha maji (kilichotayarishwa kwa shughuli maalum *white ~* chokaa wangwa; *(sediment)* kitope. 4 majimaji. 5 mashata. ~**er** *n* 1 washeli: pete bapa ya chuma/plastiki/mpira au ngozi iliyotobolewa, mashine ya kufulia/kuoshea vyombo. 2 ~**erman/ woman** *n* dobi. ~**ing** *n* 1 kuosha/ kuoshwa. 2 kufua; nguo zinazofuliwa au za kufua *~ day see* ~**day** *~ machine* mashine ya kufulia. ~ **soda** magadi. ~**y** *adj (of liquids)* -a majimaji; *(of feeling style)* dhaifu *(of colours)* hafifu; *(of ideas, thoughts etc)* chapwa.

wasp *n* nyigu. ~**waisted** *adj* -enye kiuno chembamba. ~**ish** *adj* -a chukichuki; kali.

wassail *n* 1 *(arch)* tafrija/sherehe ya vileo. 2 kileo kinachonywewa katika sherehe hiyo.

waste *adj* 1 -ovyo, -siofaa, -a takataka, -a bure. 2 *(of land)* -siotumika; -sio na rutuba. ~ **land** *n* kame, ardhi isiyotumika, mbaya; ardhi iliyoharibiwa na vita n.k. *(fig)* maisha/jamii iliyoharibika. **lay** ~ angamiza, haribu *vt,vi* 1 ~ **sth (on sth)** tumia vibaya, poteza, fuja, tapanya. ~ **one's breath** poteza nguvu bure. ~ **not, want not** *(prov)* atumiaye vyema hakosi kitu. 2 angamiza/haribu (ardhi). 3 dhoofika, lika, chakaa. 4 potea bure *n* 1 upotevu, uharibifu, ufujaji **go/run to** ~ potea bure *it is a ~ of time* ni kupoteza wakati. 2 *(of land)* jangwa; mbuga. 3 takataka. ~-**basket/bin** *n*. ~ **paper basket** jaa/kapu/pipa la taka. ~ **pipe** *n* bomba la kuondolea maji machafu. ~**r** *n* mharibifu, mfujaji. ~ **ful** *adj* haribifu, fujaji, potevu. ~**fully** *adv*.

wastage *n* 1 hasara; uharibifu. 2 takataka. **wastrel** *n* mfujaji; mzembe; mhuni.

watch[1] *n (time piece)* saa (ya mfukoni au mkononi). ~ **glass** *n* kioo cha saa. ~-**guard/chain** mnyororo wa kufungia saa nguoni. ~-**key** *n* ufunguo wa saa. ~-**maker** *n* fundi saa.

watch[2] n 1 ulinzi, lindo. **be on the ~ (for)** tazamia, weka hadhari, vizia. **keep ~ (on/over)** linda, chunga, tunza. ~-**dog** mbwa wa kulinda nyumba; *(fig)* mtu/kitu kinacholinda. ~-**tower** mnara wa doria kuchunga moto n.k. 2 **the** ~ *(hist)* walinzi (hasa wa usiku). 3 *(in ships)* zamu (kipindi cha saa mbili, au nne. **the first** ~ zamu ya saa mbili usiku hadi saa sita usiku. **the middle** ~ zamu ya saa sita usiku hadi saa kumi usiku. **the dog ~es** nusu ya zamu. **keep** ~ wa zamu. 4 *(old use)* mkesha. ~ **night service** ibada ya usiku/mkesha (wa kidini). ~**er** *n* mlinzi, mwangalizi. ~**man** *n* mlinzi wa usiku. ~**ful** *adj* -a hadhari, -angalifu, -chunguzi. ~**fully** *adv*. ~**fulness** *n*. ~**word** *n* neno la siri la kulindia; wito/neno la shime/kutia hamasa *vt,vi* tazama, angalia, chunga. ~ **one's step** -wa mwangalifu; fanya jambo kwa makini na tahadhari -wa na hadhari. ~ **one's time** vuta subira, subiri wakati unaofaa. ~ **the time** jali wakati, angalia saa ili (usichelewe). ~ **(out) (for sth)** -wa macho, angalia. ~ **out** jihadhari. ~ **(over) sth** linda, hami; *(old use)* kaa macho, kesha.

water *n* 1 maji *salt ~* maji chumvi *cold ~* maji baridi *by ~* kwa dau/meli/boti n.k: **in deep ~(s)** matatani. **in smooth ~** -enye kuendelea vizuri. **on the ~** katika dau, meli n.k. *under ~* -liojaa maji, -liofurika. **be in/get into hot ~** pata matatizo (kutokana na mwenendo mbaya). **cast/throw one's bread upon the ~(s)** tenda wema nenda zako (ingawa unaweza kulipiziwa baadaye). **drink the ~s** -nywa maji ya chemchemi kama dawa. **go through fire and ~ (for sb/sth)** pitia matatizo na majaribu makubwa (kwa ajili ya mtu/kitu). **hold ~** *(of theory etc)* thibitika inapojaribiwa. **keep one's head above ~** epuka matatizo ya kifedha. **make ~** kojoa; *(of a ship)* vuja. **spend money etc like ~** fuja mali, tumia, fedha kwa wingi. **throw cold ~ on (a plan etc)** tilia mashaka, pinga. **like a fish out of ~** -enye kujisikia/vibaya kutokana na mazingira asiyozoea; -enye kujihisi ugenini/upweke. **still ~s run deep** *(prov)* kimya kingi kina mshindo mkuu; simba mwenda kimya ndiye mla nyama. **written in ~** *(of a name, reputatio n etc)* -epesi kusahaulika. **the ~s of forgetfulness** usahaulifu. **table/mineral ~s**, maji ya kunywa (yenye madini). 2 hali ya maji kupwa/kujaa. **in low ~s** *(fig)* -pungufu ya fedha, -enye fedha kidogo. 3 *(pl)* bahari. **Tanzania ~s** bahari karibu ya Tanzania. 4 *(usu pl)* ziwa, mto *~s of the Nile* ziwa ambalo ndio chanzo cha mto Nile. 5 kimiminiko, maji. **rose ~** -a maji ya waridi. 6 **of the first ~** bora sana *a diamond of the first ~* almasi bora sana. 7 *(in compounds)*. **~-bed** *n* godoro la mpira lililojazwa maji. **~-borne** *adj* 1 *(of goods)* -a kuchukuliwa kwa meli, dau n.k.; *(of diseases)* -a kuenezwa na maji machafu. **~-bottle** *n* kiriba, chupa ya maji. **~ buffalo** *n* nyati wa kufugwa. **~ cannon** *n* bomba la maji (lenye kanieneo kubwa). **~-cart** *n* gari lenye tangi la maji ya (kunyunyizia barabarani au kuuza). **~-chute** *n* poromoko la maji; mfereji wa maji unaotelemka. **~-closet** *n (common abbr* **w.c.**) choo cha kuvuta, choo cha maji. **~-colour** *n* rangi za maji; picha ya rangi za maji; uchoraji wa rangi za maji. **~-colourist** *n.* **~-cooled** *adj* -enye kupozwa kwa maji. **~-cooler** *n* gudulia la maji baridi. **~-course** *n* kijito, mfereji wa maji, korongo. **~fall** *n* maporomoko ya maji. **~fowl** *n* ndege wa majini. **~front** *n* mwambao. **~ glass** ute mzito wa kukandia yai ili lisiharibike. **~-hole** *n* dimbwi, shimo la maji. **~-ice** *n* peremende barafu. **~ jacket** *n* fuko la maji la kupozea. **~ jump** kikwazo chenye mfereji wa maji (katika mashindano ya farasi). **~less** *adj* -kavu kame, pasipo maji. **~-level** *n* kina cha maji. **~-lily** *n* yungiyungi. **~-line** *n* msitari maji: mstari ubavuni mwa meli panapofikiwa na maji. **~ -logged** *adj (of boat, ship, wood, etc)* -liojaa maji. **~-main** *n* bomba kubwa la kuleta maji. **~man** *n* mwanamaji; mvushaji. **~-mark** *n* 1 kipimo cha kina. 2 *(on paper)* alama maalum ionekanayo kwa kuelekeza karatasi kwenye mwanga). **~ melon** *n* tikiti maji. **~-meter** *n* kipimamaji. **~-mill** *n* kinu cha gurudumu maji; kinu kiendeshwacho kwa gurudumu linalozungushwa na maji. **~-pipe** *n* bomba la kupitishia maji. **~ polo** mchezo wa mpira wa mikono majini. **~-power** nishati ya maji (ya kuendeshea mashine). **~-proof** *adj* -siopenya maji *~proof coat n* koti (isiyopenya maji) *vt* fanya maji yasipenye. **~-rate** *n (GB)* malipo ya kutumia maji. **~-shed** *n* eneo la mwinuko linalogawa mito; *(fig)* eneo la mwachano wa mambo, matukio; njia panda. **~side** *n* ukingo. **~-skin** *n* kiriba cha maji. **~-softener** *n* dawa ya kulainisha maji. **~-spout** *n* chamchela ya maji (hasa ya baharini); *(of a roof)* mlizamu. **~-supply** *n* ugavi wa maji. **~-table** *n* tabaka maji (chini ya ardhi). **~-tank** *n* tangi la maji. ~-**tap** *n* bomba la maji. ~**tight** *adj* -siovuja maji; -siopitisha maji; *(of an agreement)* thabiti, -siopindika. ~-**tower** *n* mnara wa maji. ~-**wagon** *n* gari la kubebea maji. ~**way** *n* njia ya majini. ~-**wheel** *n* gurudumumaji; gurudumu lizungushwalo na maji. ~-**wings** *n (pl)* vyelezo vilivyojazwa hewa na kufungwa mabegani (ili kumsaidia ajifunzaye kuogelea). ~- **works** *n (pl)* mfumo wa ugavi wa maji; chemchem za maji zilizopambwa; *(colloq)* (kazi za) kibofu; *(colloq)* machozi. ~**y** *adj* -a majimaji; chepechepe *vt,vi* 1 mwagia/nyeshea/nyunyiziamaji.~**ing can** *n* ndoo ya kunyweshea. ~**ing cart** *n* gari la kumwagia maji barabarani (agh. kuondoa vumbi). 2 patia maji. 3 *(of the eyes)* jaa machozi; *(of the mouth)* jaa mate/maji. **mouth** ~**ing** *adj* -a kutia hamu sana. 4 ~ **sth down** tia/ongeza maji; *(fig)* fanya hafifu. 5 *(fin)* ongeza deni au mtaji wa kampuni kwa kutoa hisa mpya bila kuongeza mali. 6 ~**ed** *(pp as adv)* -liopatiwa maji, -lio na maji. ~ **silk** hariri iliyotengenezwa na kuwa na mawimbi. 7 ~**ing place** dimbwi wanaponywea wanyama; *see* **spa;** mahali pa kupumzikia pwani.

Waterloo *n* **meet one's** ~ komeshwa, koma (baada ya mafanikio mengi).

watt *n* wati: kipimo cha umeme. ~**age** *n* kipimo cha umeme kwa wati.

wattle[1] *n* 1 ufito. ~ **and daub hut** nyumba ya mbavu za mbwa; kibanda cha fito kilichokandikwa. 2 miwati ~-*bark n* magome ya miwati.

wattle[2] *n (of a bird etc)* upanga/ndevu.

wave *vt,vi* 1 ~ **(at/to/in)** peperusha, peperuka; punga; tikisika. ~ **sth aside** *(fig)* tupilia mbali. 2 *(of a line or surface, of hair)* fanya mawimbi, mapindi *n* 1 wimbi. **the** ~**s** *(poet)* bahari. **in** ~**s** kwa mawimbi. 2 mpepeo, mpungo, mtikisiko. 3 *(of hair)* msuko. 4 ongezeko *a crime* ~ ongezeko la uhalifu. 5 wimbi la joto, sauti, mwanga, sumaku. **long/ medium/short** ~ **(radio)** mawimbi ya sauti ya masafa marefu/ kati/mafupi. ~ **length** *n* masafa; urefu wa wimbi. **wavy** *adj* -enye mawimbi, -a kuinuka na kushuka, -enye mapindi *a wavy line* mstari mawimbi.

waver *vi* 1 yumbayumba, pepesuka, tetereka. 2 -wa na shaka, sitasita. ~**er** *n*.

wax[1] *n* nta. ~-**chandler** *n* mtengenezaji mishumaa; mchuuzi wa mishumaa. ~-**paper** *n* karatasi nta: karatasi isiyosharabu maji kwa sababu ya tabaka la nta. ~ **work** *n* sanamu ya nta *(pl)* ~ **works** maonyesho ya sanamu za nta vt tia nta. ~. ~**en** *adj* -anta; -a kama -a nta. ~**y** *adj* -a kama nta; -ororo na -eupe.

wax[2] *vi* 1 *(esp of moon)* pevuka. ~ **and wane** pevuka na kupungua. 2 kua. ~**merry** furahi, -wa na furaha.

wax[3] *n (sl)* hasira. ~**y** *adj* -enye hasira.

way *n* 1 njia, barabara. **pave the** ~ **for** andalia, andaa. **The W**~ **of the Cross** Njia ya Msalaba. 2 mapito; njia (ya kupitia/kutumia). **go one's** ~**(s)** ondoka. **go out of one's** ~ **to do sth** fanya bidii kubwa, fanya jitihada maalum. **lead the** ~ ongoza njia, toa mfano. **make one's** ~ **in life** fanikiwa. **make the best of one's** ~ fanya hima, enda haraka iwezekanavyo. **make one's** ~ **(to/ fowards)** enda, jiendea. **pay one's** ~ epuka madeni; jilipia gharama. **the parting of the** ~**s** *(fig)* njia panda. **by** ~ **of** kupitia. **out of the** ~ geni, tunu, -sio -a kawaida, -a ajabu, miujiza. **out-of-the-** ~ *(attrib)* -a mbali, siofikika kwa urahisi. 3 **by the** ~ njiani; safarini; *(fig)* pamoja na hayo. **on the/one's** ~ njiani. **on the** ~ **out** *(colloq)* -nayokaribia kupitwa na wakati, -nayoelekea kupoteza umaarufu. 4 njia; mkakati, mbinu. **where there's a will there's a** ~ *(prov)* penye nia pana njia. ~**s and means** mbinu, njia. **have/get one's**

own ~ pata/tenda/fanya mtu atakavyo; fuata njia yako. **go/take one's own** ~ fuata matakwa yake mtu, fanya mtu aonavyo. 5 *(sing only)* masafa, hatua, umbali. 6 upande; welekeo *look this* ~ tazama upande huu. **put sb in the** ~ **of (doing) sth** saidia mtu kuanza jambo. 7 *(colloq)* karibu na, upande wa. 8 maendeleo, kufuata uelekeo fulani. **be under** ~ **have** ~ **on** *(of ship)* kata maji, enda. **gather/lose** ~ kaza/legeza mwendo; ongeza/poteza kasi. **get under** ~ anza kwenda, -wa mbioni. **make** ~ *(lit or fig)* piga hatua. 9 nafasi/mwanya wa kusonga mbele, uhuru wa kuendelea. **be/put sth out of harm's** ~ -wa/weka katika hali ya usalama, salimisha. **get sth out of the** ~ ondosha. **make** ~ **(for)** pisha. **put sb out of the** ~ ondoa (kwa kufunga/kuua kisirisiri) fanya atoweke. **put sb in the** ~ **of (doing) sth** saidia kuanza/kupata. **see one's** ~ **(clear) to doing sth** ona jinsi/namna ya kufanya mambo, -wa na hakika ya kufanya jambo. 10 mwenendo, desturi *good old* ~*s* desturi njema za zamani. **to my** ~ **of thinking** kwa maoni yangu. **the** ~ *(colloq adv)* kama, jinsi. **mend one's** ~s jirekebisha, jirudi. 11 namna. **no** ~ *(sl)* katu, hasha *they are in no* ~*s similar* hawafanani hata kidogo kwa namna yoyote ile. 12 hali *in a bad* ~ katika hali mbaya. **any** ~ vyovyote vile iwavyo. **each** ~**/both** ~**s** kote kote, kila upande. **have it both** ~ **s** taka kote kote. **be in the family** ~ -wa mjamzito. **in a big/small** ~ kikubwa/kidogodogo. 13 mwendo, utaratibu *the law had its* ~ sheria ilifuatwa. 14 **by** ~ **of** kwa kusudi ya; kwa namna ya. 15 *(pl)* ~s *see* **sleepway**. 16 *(compounds)* ~ **bill** *n* orodha ya mali ya abiria (shehena). ~**farer** *n* msafiri (agh. kwa miguu). ~**faring** *adj* -a kusafiri; -a kupenda kusafiri *n* safari. ~ **leave** *n* haki ya kupita njia. ~**side** *n* kando ya njia *adj* kando ya njia *adv* mbali. ~ **behind** nyuma; kwa mbali sana ~ *back in my boyhood* zamani katika siku zangu za utotoni. ~ **out** *adj (colloq)* -a ajabu. ~**lay** *vt* vizia *we were* ~*laid* tuliviziwa. ~**ward** *adj* kaidi, tundu, tukutu. ~**wardness** *n* ukaidi, utukutu.

we *(pron)* 1 sisi. 2 *(by king, Pope etc)* mimi; ni-.

weak *adj* 1 dhaifu, hafifu ~ *in will* -enye moyo dhaifu. ~-**kneed** *adj (fig)* -nyonge, -sio na dhamira, -enye moyo dhaifu. 2 *(of senses etc)* -pungufu; chini ya kiwango cha kawaida ~*-headed adj* -enye akili pungufu ~ *minded adj* -enye akili chache, -enye akili afkani. 3 *(of solutions, liquids)* majimaji; si -kali ~ *wine* divai isiyo kali. 4 baya, bovu ~ *in history* ni dhaifu katika historia. 5 *(gram)* hafifu. ~ **verb** kitenzi hafifu. ~ **form** maumbo yasiyotiwa mkazo. ~**ling** *n* mnyonge/mdhaifu. ~**ly** *adv* kwa udhaifu, kwa uhafifu, bila nguvu. ~**ness** *n* 1 udhaifu. 2 ubovu. 3 kutojiweza. **have a** ~**ness for** penda mno (hadi kuonekana mjinga) *vi,vt* dhoofu, dhoofika, legea, dhoofisha, punguza nguvu.

weal[1] *n* kovu: alama ya pigo katika ngozi.

weal[2] *n* usitawi, neema *for the public general* ~ kwa ajili ya neema ya watu wote. **in** ~ **or woe** katika dhiki au faraja.

weald *n (GB)* mbuga.

wealth *n* 1 utajiri, ukwasi; mali nyingi *a man of* ~ tajiri, mwenye mali. 2 wingi wa mali, wingi wa neema. ~ **of a/the** -ingi sana. ~**y** *adj* -tajiri, -kwasi, -enye wingi wa neema. ~**ily** *adv* kwa ukwasi.

wean *vt* 1 likiza: achisha mtoto ziwa. 2 ~ **sb from sth** fanya kuacha (tabia, marafiki wabaya n.k.) ~ *sb of a habit* tengua tabia ya mtu ~ *sb from bad company* ondoa mtu kutoka kwenye kundi baya/marafiki wabaya.

weapon *n* silaha. ~**less** *adj* bila silaha.

wear[1] *vt,vi* 1 vaa; valia; paka ~ *a hat* vaa kofia ~ *red lipstick* paka rangi nyekundu. ~ **the crown** tawazwa ufalme, -wa mfalme; wa shahidi. 2 chakaa; chakaza; -la, lika. ~ **away** chakaa, potea. ~ **sth away** chakaza. ~ **down** konga, dhoofu, lika. ~ **sth down** chakaza. ~ **sth/sb down** dhoofisha kitu kwa kushambulia/ kusuta mara kwa mara. ~ **off** pita, pungua, isha. ~ **sth off** maliza (kidogo kidogo). ~ **sth/sb out** chosha. ~ **(sth) out** chakaza, chakaa. **worn out** chakavu. 3 toboa, tia alama, tengeneza. 4 stahimili, dumu. 5 ~ **on/ away** *(of time)* potea, pita pole pole. **~er** *n* mvaaji. **~able** *adj* -a kuvalika, -a kufaa kuvaliwa. **~ing** *adj (exhausting)* -a kuchosha.

wear[2] *n* 1 vazi, kuvaa. 2 uchakavu. ~ **and tear** uchakavu (kwa matumizi). 3 ustahamilivu. 4 *(as in compounds)* **under** ~ chupi. **foot~** viatu. **~ily** *adv* kwa taabu, kwa hali ya kuchoka. **~iness** *n* kuchoka, kuchosha. **~isome** *adj* -a kuchosha, -a taabu, -sumbufu. **~y** *adj* 1 chofu. 2 choshi. 3 -a dalili ya kuchoka/uchovu *vt,vi* **~y sb (with sth)**. **~y of sth** chosha/choka.

weasel *n* mnyama mdogo kama cheche. **~-faced** *adj* -enye sura ya panya.

weather[1] *n* 1 hali ya hewa. **be/feel under the** ~ *(colloq)* umwa, jisikia vibaya. **keep a/ one's ~ eye open** -wa na hadhari, -wa macho, kaa chonjo, jiandaa. **make good/bad** ~ pambana na hali ya hewa nzuri/mbaya. **make heavy ~ of sth** sumbuliwa, taabishwa. **under stress of** ~ kwa sababu ya dhoruba n.k. 2. *(compounds)* **~ beaten** *adj* -iloathiriwa na hali ya hewa. ~ **boarding/boards** *n* mbao za kukinga mvua. ~ **bound** *adj* -liozuiwa safari kutokana na hali ya hewa mbaya. ~ **bureau** *n* ofisi ya hali ya hewa. ~ **cock** kieleleza upepo (kifananacho na jogoo). ~ **man** *n* mtabiri wa hali ya hewa. **~-glass** *n* barometa. **~proof** *adj* -sioathiriwa na upepo/mvua/ baridi. **~-ship** *n* meli ya hali ya hewa. **~-report** *n* ripoti ya hali ya hewa. **~-side** *n* upande wa joshi.

weather[2] *vt,vi* 1 pona, pita, epuka. 2 enda joshi. 3 acha nje. 4 kwajuka, nyauka.

weave *vt, vi* 1 ~ **sth (up) into sth.** ~ **sth (from sth)** fuma kitu. 2 *(fig)* tunga, sanifu, buni. **get weaving (on sth)** tia/fanya shime, anza kwa nguvu. 3 nyonganyonga, pindapinda *n* mtindo wa ususi/ufumaji *plain* ~ mfumo wa kawaida. **~r** *n* mfumaji. **~r bird** *n* mnana.

web *n* 1 kilichofumwa; mfumo. 2 *(of spider)* utando; tandabui, kimia; *(of waterbird's feet)* utando wa ngozi kati ya vidole. **~bed** *adj* -enye utando (wa hila, njama, wongo n.k.). **~-footed/toed** *adj* -enye ngozi kati ya vidole vya miguu.

we'd *we had, we would, we should.*

wed *vt,vi* oa; olewa, funga ndoa; *(lit)* ungana. **~ded to** *adj* -enye kushika sana; -enye kung'angania. **~d** *n* arusi, ndoa. **golden ~d** sikukuu ya 50 ya ukumbusho wa ndoa *adj* -a arusi. **~d-breakfast** chakula cha maarusi, ndugu na jamaa baada ya harusi. **~d garment** nguo za harusi. ~ **cake** *n* keki ya ndoa. **~d-card** *n* kadi ya taarifa; tangazo la ndoa (kwa marafiki); kadi (ya mwaliko) ya arusi. **~d-ring** *n* pete ya ndoa. **~lock** *n (legal)* ndoa *in ~lock* katika ndoa, -a ndoa.

wedge *n* 1 chembeo, kabari. **the thin end of the** ~ *(fig)* jambo dogo au badiliko dogo linaloelekea kuzaa jambo kubwa au badiliko kubwa. 2 kitu chenye umbo kama kabari *vt* tia chembeo, zuia kwa chembeo; bania. **~-shaped** *adj* -enye umbo la kabari, kama kabari.

Wednesday *n* Jumatano.

wee[1] *adj* dogo sana. **a ~ bit** *(adverbial)* kidogo. **the ~ folk** pepo, mazimwi n.k. **the ~ hours** *(US)* usiku wa manane, baada ya saa sita za usiku. **bide a** ~ kaa kidogo.

wee[2]**,wee-wee** *n (used by and to children)* mkojo *vi* kojoa.

weed *n* 1 gugu; majani. ~ **killer** kiua

magugu. 2 mtu mwembamba dhaifu, mtu hafifu. 3 *(dated sl)* sigara, biri, tumbaku; *(modern sl)* bangi *vt* palia magugu. ~ **sth/sb out** ondoa vitu hafifu (visivyofaa kitu), pembua, chagua. *adj* 1 -enye magugu. 2 *(sl)* -refu -embamba na dhaifu.

weeds *n (pl)* **widow's ~s** nguo (za nyasi) za mjane.

week *n* 1 juma, wiki. ~ **in** ~ **out** endelea bila kukoma. **~-end** *n* wikiendi, Jumamosi na Jumapili *~-end ticket* ruhusa ya Jumapili *vi* enda wikiendi. **long ~-end** wikiendi ndefu. 2 siku za juma za kazi. **~-day** *n* siku yo yote ya juma (isipokuwa Jumapili). **~ly** *adv* kwa juma *three times* ~ mara tatu kwa juma *n* gazeti litolewalo kila juma.

weeny *adj (colloq)* (often **teeny ~**) -dogo sana.

weep *vt,vi (liter)* 1 lia, toa machozi ~ *for joy* tokwa na machozi kwa furaha. 2 *(drip)* tona. 3 omboleza. **~ing** *adj* 1 -nayolialia. 2 *(arch)* -a mvua, majimaji; *(of trees)* -enye matawi membamba ya kuinama. **~y** *adj* -epesi kutoa machozi.

weevil *n* mdudu alaye nafaka.

weigh *vt,vi* 1 pima uzito. ~ **sth out** pima. ~ **(oneself) (in)** (*for a boxer etc*) pimwa uzito kabla ya mchezo. ~ **in (with)** *(of arguments, facts etc)* toa hoja zenye nguvu/za maana. ~ **bridge** *n* ya kupimia uzito wa magari. **~ing machine** *n* mizani. 2 -wa na uzani wa. 3 *(of a machine)* -wa na uwezo wa kupima. 4 ~ **sth (with/against sth)** pima (ubora, umuhimu wa kitu) dhidi ya kingine. ~ **sth (up)** fikiria kwa makini; hakiki. 5 ~ **sth down** lemea, inamisha. ~ **sb down** lemeza, chosha, sumbua. ~ **on sb/sth** sumbua, shughulisha. ~ **with sb** shawishi, athiri. 6 ~ *anchor* ng'oa nanga.

weight *n* uzito, uzani. **under/over ~** -enye uzito mdogo/mkubwa. **put on ~** nenepa: ongezeka uzito. **throw one's ~ about** *(colloq)* tamba, onyesha ukubwa/ubwana, onea. 2 **a/the ~ (of)** uzito (wa kubebwa), mzigo. 3 umaarufu, maana. **carry ~** -wa na maana, -wa muhimu. 4 jiwe la mizani. **~-lifting** *n* mchezo wa kuinua vitu vizito. 5 mfumo wa vipimo *vt* 1 tia, ongeza uzito; -pa nguvu, lemeza. 2 ~ **sb down** lemeza. 3 tumia madawa kufanya kitambaa kuwa kigumu. **~less** *adj* -sio na uzito. **~y** *adj* zito, -a maana. **~ily** *adv*. **~iness** *n* 1 uzito. 2 umuhimu, maana. **~lessness** *n*.

weir *n* 1 boma la kuzuia maji, kikinga mto. 2 mtego wa samaki.

weird *adj* 1 -a miujiza, sio -a kawaida, -a kuogofya. 2 *(colloq)* -a ajabu. **~ly** *adv*. **~ness** *n*. **~ie** *n (sl)* mtu mwenye tabia ya pekee.

welcome *adj* 1 -a kupokewa/kukaribisha kwa furaha, -a kufurahia, -a furaha, -a kufurahisha. 2 -enye kuruhusiwa/kuachiwa. ~ **to do sth.** ~ **to sth** pewa ruhusa ya kutumia bure; pewa bure. **you are ~** karibu; usijali. 3 *(as an interj)* karibu *n* mapokezi, makaribisho *vt* karibisha vizuri; pokea kwa furaha *go out to ~* laki.

weld *vt* lehemu, unga, tia weko, unganisha (chuma, madini) kwa kufua *n* kiungo kilichofanywa kwa weko. **~er** *n* mtia weko.

welfare *n* ustawi, hali njema, neema, afya *child ~* ustawi wa watoto. **the W ~ State** nchi yenye (mpango wa) kutoa huduma za jamii bure; *(US)* Ustawi wa Jamii. ~ **worker** afisa ustawi.

welkin *n (poet)* mbingu; anga.

we'll *we will, we shall.*

well[1] *n* 1 kisima. ~ **water** maji ya kisima *n* **oil ~** kisima cha mafuta. 2 chemchemi; *(fig)* chanzo, chimbuko. **~-head** *n* chanzo cha mto/chemchemi. 3 chumba cha lifti au ngazi katika jengo. 4 *(GB)* ulingo wa mawakili katika mahakama. 5 **~-deck** *n* nafasi katika staha kuu ya meli iliofungiwa. ~ **out (from/of)** bubujika. ~ **over** furika. ~ **up (in)** foka, chemka.

well[2] *adv* 1 -zima, vema, vizuri, barabara. **do ~** fanya, endelea vizuri, sitawi. **be doing ~** *(progressive tense only)* pata nafuu/ahueni. **do oneself ~** jipatia mambo ya starehe au anasa. **do ~ by sb** fanyia mtu ukarimu. **wish sb ~** takia mtu heri. 2 *(with praise or approval)* vizuri, sifia au unga mkono. **stand ~ with sb** pendwa na. 3 kwa bahati njema. **be ~ out of sth** jitoa katika jambo bila matatizo/ hasara. **~ off** -enye mali, -enye neema, tajiri; -enye bahati. **~ off for** hajambo kwa; -liojawa na *~off for food* hajambo kwa chakula; ana chakula kingi. **come off ~** *(of a person)* fanikiwa; *(of an event)* -liokuwa nzuri, -wa na matokeo ya kuridhisha. **do ~ to** + *(inf)* fanya vizuri. 4 kwa haki. *you may ~ be surprised* una haki ya kushangaa. 5 **may (just) as ~** hivyohivyo, vilevile, pia. **be just as ~** (-wa) afadhali. 6 *(end position)* sana, kabisa *shake the bottle ~* tikisa chupa sana. 7 kwa kiasi kikubwa. **~ away** -enye kuendelea vema; *(colloq)* -enye kukaribia (kulewa); -enye kuwaka. **leave/let ~ alone** usiingilie. 8 **as ~ (as)** pamoja na; vilevile. 9 *(with another adv)* **pretty ~** karibu. *pred adj* 1 -zima, -enye afya. **get ~** pona, pata nafuu *I am pretty ~* karibu sawa! si mbaya! sijambo. 2 sawa; -ema, -a hali njema, heri. **its all very ~** *(used ironically)* ni sawa. 3 -a bahati *it was ~ for you* ilikuwa bahati yako. 4 afadhali, bora *int* 1 *(expressing astonishment)* lo! **~ then** je, nini basi? 2 *(expressing relief)* haya! *~, here we are at last* haya, mwishowe tumefika hapa. 3 *(expressing resignation) ~, it cant be helped,* haya, hatuna la kufanya. **~-being** *n* ustawi; hali njema; afya, raha. **~-doing** *n (arch)* ufadhili, kutenda mema. **~-nigh** *adv (arch)* karibu *he was ~- drowned* alikuwa karibu azame majini. **~-off** *adj* -tajiri, -enye neema. **~-to-do** *adj* tajiri, -enye neema *n the ~ to do* matajiri **~-wisher** *n* mtakia heri. **~ doer** *n* mfadhili, mhisani. **~ advised** -a busara. **~balanced** -enye busara. **~appointed** *adj* -enye zana/vyombo vyote. **~born** -a ukoo bora. **~-bred** *adj* -enye adabu, -enye malezi mazuri, -ungwana, -a kiungwana; *(of animals)* -liofugwa vizuri. **~-chosen** *adj* -liochaguliwa vizuri. **~-conditioned** *adj* -enye hali njema; -a adabu, -enye malezi mazuri. **~-conducted** *adj* -lioendeshwa/ pangwa/ongozwa vizuri. **~connected** *adj* -enye uhusiano na watu (wa nasaba) bora (kwa damu/ndoa). **~-disposed** *adj (towards)* -fadhili, -a hisani, -ema; -a kupendelea. **~-favoured** *adj (old use)* -zuri, -a kupendeza, -enye sura nzuri **~-fed** *adj* -liolishwa vizuri **~-found** *adj* -enye zana/vyombo vyote. **~-founded** *adj* -enye ukweli. **~-groomed** *adj* maridadi, safi. **~ -grounded** *n* -enye ukweli; -enye mafunzo bora; -enye misingi imara. **~-heeled** *n (sl)* kwasi, kizito. **~-informed** *adj* -enye kujua, kutambua *be ~-informed on a subject* jua vema somo fulani. **~-intentioned** *adj* -enye nia safi. **~-knit** *adj* kakamavu; -shupavu, kakawana. **~-known** *adj* maarufu, mashuhuri, -nayojulikana sana. **~-lined** *adj (of a purse, colloq)* -liojaa fedha. **~-mannered** *adj* -enye tabia njema. **~-marked** *adj* -liodhahiri, bainifu. **~-meaning** *adj* -enye nia safi. **~-meant** *adj* -liosemwa/fanywa kwa nia safi. **~-paid** *adj* -enye malipo (ujira, mshahara) mazuri. **~-read** *adj* -a maarifa (elimu) nyingi, -liosoma sana. **~-rounded** *adj* -liokamilifu na linganifu; -enye maarifa mengi. **~-set** *adj* shupavu, kakamavu. **~-spoken** *adj* -enye lugha fasaha, -enye kusema kwa adabu/heshima. **~-timed** *adj* -a wakati wa kufaa. **~-tried** *adj (of methods)* -liojaribiwa mara nyingi (na kuonyesha kufaa kwake), mujarabu. **~-turned** *adj (of a compliment, phrase, verse)* fasaha, sanifu, -liotungwa vizuri. ~-**worn** *adj* -liotumika mno, -liopoteza maana/ ladha (kwa sababu ya kutumika).

welsh *vt,vi* 1 ~ **on sth/sb** kwepa kulipa; toroka bila kulipa. 2 vunja kauli/ ahadi. ~**er** *n.*

welt *n* 1 mshono (unaounganisha ngozi ya kiatu na unyayo wake). 2 alama ya pigo.

welter[1] *vt* gaagaa, vingirika; jinyonga-nyonga; tota katika damu n.k. *n (sing only)* vurugu, ghasia, machafuko *the ~ of the waves* msukosuko wa mawimbi.

welter[2] *n* ~ **weight** *(esp in boxing)* uzito wa wastani (agh. kati ya kilo 61-66.6). ~ **race** mbio za wapanda farasi (wenye uzito mkubwa).

wen *n* tezi, uvimbe wa kudumu (agh. kwenye upara, n.k.); *(fig)* mji mkubwa uliopanuka mno.

wench *n* 1 *(arch)* msichana, mwanamwali. 2 malaya *vi* zini.

wend *vt (old use, only in)* ~ **one's way (home)** -enda, elekea (nyumbani).

went *pt of* **go.**

wept *pt of* **weep.**

were *see* **be.**

we're *we are.*

werewolf *n (myth)* mtu bweha.

west *n* 1 magharibi, machweo ya jua. **The W** ~ Ulaya na America; *(world of politics)* Ulaya Magharibi na Bara; *(US)* eneo la kati ya mto Mississippi na bahari ya Pasifiki; sehemu ya magharibi ya nchi yoyote. 2 *(attrib)* toka magharibi. ~ **end** *adj* -a magharibi. **go** ~ *(sl)* potea, dhurika. ~ **of** magharibi zaidi ya. ~**ward(s)** *adv* enda upande wa magharibi. ~**erly** *adv, adj* -a magharibi, -a upande wa magharibi. ~**ern** *adj* -a (toka) magharibi the ~**ern Hemisphere** Amerika ya kaskazini na kusini *n* 1 filamu ya makauboi. 2 riwaya ya makauboi. ~**erner** *n* mwenyeji wa magharibi. ~**ernize** *vt,vi* fanya -a kimagharibi; leta utamaduni wa kimagharibi. ~**ernization** *n.* ~**ernmost** *adj* -a magharibi ya mbali.

wet *adj* 1 -a majimaji, chepechepe, -liolowa maji. ~ **dock** *n* gati lenye maji. ~ **nurse** *n* mwanamke aliyeajiriwa kunyonyesha mtoto wa mwingine. 2 -a chepechepe, -a mvua. ~ **paint** rangi ambayo haijakauka; rangi mbichi. 3 -enye kuhusu pombe. 4 *(sl) (of a person)* -oga, -a wasiwasi *n* 1 **the** ~ mvua. 2 unyevu, tia maji, lowesha, nyunyiza maji. ~**ting** *n* kulowanishwa, kulowana.

wether *n* ndafu: kondoo maksai,

we've *we have.*

whack *vt* piga kwa kishindo (mtu/kitu) *n* 1 *(sound of)* pigo. 2 *(sl)* mgawo, mgawanyo. ~**ed** *adj (colloq) (of a person)* -liochakaa, -liochoka, hoi. ~**ing** *n* kipigo, kuchapa (barabara). *adj (colloq)* kubwa ya aina yake/ sana. *adv (colloq)* sana. ~**er** *n* kitu kikubwa cha aina yake.

whale *n* 1 nyangumi. ~ **bone** mfupa wa kinywani mwa baadhi ya aina za nyangumi. 2 *(colloq)* starehe. **a** ~ **of a time** starehe/furaha sana *vi* winda nyangumi. ~**r** *n* 1 mwinda nyangumi. 2 chombo cha kuwindia nyangumi. **whaling-gun** *n* bunduki ya kuulia nyangumi.

whang *vt (colloq)* piga kwa nguvu/ kishindo *n* pigo, mshindo *adv (colloq)* sahihi, hasa, hapo hapo.

wharf *n* gati. ~**age** *n* 1 ada, ushuru (hasa unaotozwa kwa kutumia gati). 2 gati. 3 kupakia (pakua) gatini. ~**man** *n* kuli. ~-**master** *n* mwenye gati; msimamizi wa gati.

what *adj* 1 *(interr)* ipi, gani. 2 (*exclamatory*) unasemaje! kweli! 3 chochote (ambacho); *(pron) (inter)* nini. ~ **for** kwa kazi gani, kwa nini. ~ **for** *n (colloq)* adhabu. ~ **like** yukoje. ~ **if** itakuwaje, itakuwa vipi ~ **though** *(liter)* ijapokuwa, ingawa, hata kama. ~ **about/of** kuhusu nini; kuna habari gani kuhusu. ~ **of it?** *(or, mod colloq)* **So** ~ kwa hiyo? sasa? **and** ~ **not** na kadhalika. **and or** ~ **have you** pamoja na hayo, kadha wa kadha, na kadhalika. ~ **not** na vinginevyo; kibweta. **I know** ~ nina wazo/pendekezo, najua. **I/I'll tell you** ~ (hebu) sikiliza. **know ~s** tumia akili, elewa mambo. ~ **do you call him/her/it/them.** **~'s his/her its/their name** ni nani hii, nani hino,*(rel) (pron)* kitu chacho. ~ **with ... and (~ with)** kutokana na (sababu kadhaa). **~ever** *adj* 1 *(emphatic for what)* -o -ote ile, iwayo yote. 2 *(placed after n in a negative contex, giving emphasis to the negative)* kabisa *do ~ ever you like* fanya upendalo *(pron)* 1 hata iweje. 2 chochote. 3 **~ever** *(colloq)* lolote lingine, -o -ote ingine. **~-so-e'er** *(poet for)* **~-so-ever** *(emphatic for)* **~ever, whate'er** *(US) adj* **whatever**.

wheat *n* ngano ~ *crop* mavuno ya ngano. **~en** *adj* -a ngano, -a unga wa ngano.

wheedle *vt* ~ **(into/out of)** bemba, bembejea, bembeleza, shawishi, rairai. **~r** *n* mbembelezaji.

wheel *n* 1 gurudumu. **~s within ~s** *(fig)* matata mengi; mchanganyiko wa mambo. **put one's shoulder to the** ~ jitahidi; saidia **the man at the** ~ dereva, mwendeshaji. **~barrow** *n* toroli. ~ **base** *n* kitako cha gari. **~chair** *n* kiti cha magurudumu. **~house** *n* chumba cha nahodha katika meli. **~-man** *n* mpanda baiskeli. **~wright** *n* fundi wa magurudumu. 2 **potter's** ~ *n* gurudumu la kufinyangia vyungu, kurugo. **paddle** ~ *n* makasia. 3 mwendo wa gurudumu *vt,vi* 1 sukuma, vuta; beba, peleka. 2 enda; pinda, kata. ~ **and deal** *vi* fanya hila katika siasa/biashara.

wheeze *vt,vi* korota, forota, pumua kwa shida. ~ **sth out** sema kwa kukorota. *n* 1 mkoroto, mkoromo 2. hila, vitimbi. **wheezily** *adv*. **wheeziness** *n*.

whelk *n* aina ya konokono wa pwani.

whelp *n* 1 mtoto wa mbwa, simba, chui, mbweha, dubu n.k. 2 kijana fidhuli *vi* zaa.

when *(an inter adv)* lini? wakati gani? hadi lini *since* ~ tangu lini *adv (with day, time, etc as antecedent)* siku/saa zipi? *(rel) adv* amba *conj* 1 -po, ambapo. 2 ingawaje, ingawa. 3 kama, endapo. 4 wakati ambapo. **~ce** *adv (form)* 1 *(in questions)* kuanzia kutoka wapi? ~ *does he come?* atoka wapi? 2 *(in statements)* ambapo/ko/mo toka wapi. 3 kwenye sehemu atokako/aliko kuwa. **~ever** *adv (conj)* 1 wakati wowote. 2 kila. 3 ~ *(colloq)* wakati wowote.

where *inter adv* 1 wapi, mahali gani. 2 *(with a prep following the v)* mahali gani, wapi; *(rel) adv* ambapo/-ko/ -mo -po, alipo/ko/mo. **~abouts** *adv* wapi, sehemu gani *n* makazi *I don't know his ~abouts at present* sijui alipo sasa. **~as** *conj (esp leg)* kwa maana; kwa kuwa, lakini, wakati ambapo. **~at** *adv (old use)* na hapo, kwa hiyo, hivyo. **~fore** *adv (old use)* kwa nini? kwa sababu hii, sababu, kisa. **the whys and the ~fores** kwa nini na kwa sababu gani? kisa na mkasa. ~ **by**, **~in** *adv* katika hii; -ko -mo, -po; katika nini. **~of** *adv (formal)* ya kitu gani? **~through** *adv* ambacho kwacho. **~upon** *adv* hapo; baadaye; ndipo, kwa hiyo, katika. **~ver** *adv* kokote, po pote ~ *he likes* kokote/popote apendapo ~ *that may be* popote kiwapo. **~with** *adv* kwa hii, na hii, -enye hii, kwa (na). **~withal** *adv (old use)* **~with** *n* **the ~withal** *(colloq)* mali, uwezo, nafasi.

wherry *n* mashua ndogo nyepesi (kwa abiria). ~ **man** *n* mfanyakazi katika mashua ndogo nyepesi.

whet *vt* noa, tia makali; *(fig)* chochea, amsha, zidisha (tamaa ya chakula, kinywaji). ~ **stone** *n* kinoo.

whether *conj* 1 *(introducing an indirect question)* kama. ~ **or no** kwa vyovyote, ukipenda usipende. 2 *(introducing an infinitive phrase)* kama. ~ **or not** kwa vyovyote vile.

whew *(often in joke)* loo!!

whey *n* maji baada ya maziwa kuganda.

which *adj* 1 -ipi *(int adj/pron)* gani. 2

(rel adj) amba (-ye, -yo-, -zo-); kitu ambacho, -o ~ *story he believed* hadithi ambayo aliiamini; *(rel prons (of things) only not of persons)* -o: amba-o *the book* ~ kitabu ambacho/ kilicho. **~ever** *adj pron* 1 -o- -ote (yo yote, chochote) *~ever you wish* chochote utakacho. 2 ye yote, cho chote, yoyote. **~soever, ~ever**.

whiff *n* 1 mpumuo wa ghafla, mpulizo wa ghafla. 2 kishindo cha ghafla cha upepo ~ *of fresh air* mpulizo wa hewa safi. 3 harufu *vt,vi* vuma, puliza hewa kidogo kidogo.

while *n* muda, wakati. **once in a ~** mara moja moja *vt (only in)* **~ sth away** pitisha muda/wakati ~ *waiting* nilipokuwa nikingoja, wakati huo, papo hapo.

whilst *also* **while**.

whim *n* haja; wazo la ghafla.

whimper *vt,vi* 1 lialia (kwa sauti ndogo), kama mtoto mgonjwa. 2 nung'unika, lalama *n* sauti ya kulalama.

whimsy, whimsey *n* 1 kinjozi, ruya. 2 kichekesho cha ajabu ajabu **whimsically** *adv*. **whimsicality** *n*. **whimsical** *adj*.

whine *vi,vt* lia (kama mbwa anayeogopa); *(of person)* nung'unika. **~r** mlalamishi; mtu/mnyama anayetoa mlio huu *n* mlio (wa mbwa anayeogopa); mlio mkali wa kunung'unika (unaoendelea kwa muda mrefu). **whinny** *vi (of horse)* lialia *n* mlio wa farasi.

whip[1] *n* 1 kiboko, mjeledi. **have the ~ hand (over sb)** tawala, dhibiti, -wa na madaraka juu ya mtu. **~cord** kigwe cha nguvu; nguo ngumu kuchanika. 2 *(also* **~per in)** msimamizi wa mbwa (katika kuwinda). 3 mratibu wa chama cha siasa au shughuli za bunge (anayehakikisha wanachama wanahudhuria na kupiga kura bungeni); amri ya kuhudhuria na kupiga kura. **a three line ~** amri kali ya (kuhudhuria na kupiga kura) kikao cha bunge. 4 kupigapiga mayai, malai n.k.; mpigaji mijeledi.

whip[2] *vt,vi* 1 chapa, piga (mjeledi). 2 **~ sth (into sth)** piga, pigapiga, koroga. 3 *(colloq)* shinda sana, chapa. 4 chukua, chukulia; -ondoka, -ondoshwa, toa, toka (kwa haraka). 5 *(GB colloq)* iba. **~ round for money etc** changisha fedha kwa marafiki au wanachama (ili kununua zawadi). **~ round** *n* mchango huo. 6 shona pindo. **~ping** *n* kuchapa kiboko/ fimbo. **~-boy** *n (hist)* mtwana: kijana anayesoma na mtoto wa mfalme na kuadhibiwa badala yake; *(scapegoat)* msingiziwa bene. **~-post** *n (hist)* nguzo walipofungwa watu na kuchapwa viboko. **~-top** *n see* **top.**

whipper-snapper *n* mtu/kijana anayejidai/jikweza sana (pasipo kustahili).

whippet *n* mbwa wa mashindano ya mbio.

whippy *adj* -a kunyumbuka, -a kunepa, -a kunesa.

whir *see* **whirr.**

whirl *vt,vi* 1 zunguka/zungusha kwa kasi. 2 pita/pitisha kwa kasi, vurumisha. 3 *(of brain, the senses)* zunguka/vurugika; *(of thoughts)* changanyikiwa *n* 1 *(sing only)* mzunguko wa kasi; *(fig)* kuchanganyikiwa. 2 harakati, michakato, vuguvugu la maisha. 3 *(compounds)* **~ pool** *n* kizingia cha maji, mzunguko wa maji. **~ wind** kimbunga, kinyamkela, chamchela. **sow the wind and reap the ~ wind** *(prov)* panda upepo uvune tufani. **~igig** *n* 1 pia. 2 mzunguko. **the ~ of life** mzunguko wa maisha.

whir(r) *vi* vumisha *n (sing only)* uvumi (wa kitu kinachozunguka); mvumo.

whisk *n* 1 *(brush)* brashi (ya kupangusia nguo) *fly* ~ usinga, brashi ya nzi (iliyotengenezwa kutokana na manyoya). 2 mchapo (mayai). 3 pigo jepesi la upesi, panguso. *vt, vi* **~ sth/sb off/away** 1 pangusa upesi. 2 tingisha, punga mkia hewani. 3 chukua/twaa/peleka kwa ghafla. 4

(egg etc) koroga, pigapiga, chapa.

whisker *n* **~(s)** 1 *(person)* sharafa, ndevu za mashavuni. 2 *(animals)* sharubu. **cat's ~s** *(sl)* kitu kizuri/mtu mzuri. **~ed** *adj* -enye sharafa.

whisky *n* wiski: pombe kali.

whisper *vt,vi* 1 ~ **to** nong'ona, nong'oneza. **~ing gallery** ukumbi wa kunong'ona. 2 vuma, vumisha, fanya nywinywila; eleza kwa siri/faragha. **~ing campaign** kampeni za sirisiri za uvumi (dhidi ya mtu). 3 *(of leaves)* chachatika *n* 1 mnong'ono, manong'onezo. 2 uvumi. **~er** *n* mnong'onezaji; mnong'onaji; mvumishaji.

whistle *n* 1 mluzi, mbinja, mlio. **~ stop** *n (US)* kusimama kwa muda mfupi (ili kuzungumza na watu). 2 filimbi, kipenga. 3 **wet one's ~** *(sl)* nywa, pata kinywaji *vt,vi* 1 piga mluzi/ mbinja/filimbi, lia. **~ for sth** ahidiwa/tegemea/-wa na ahadi ya uongo. **~ down the wind** telekeza kitu. **~ in the dark** fanya jambo la kujitoa woga. 2 **~ (up)** piga mbinja, toa ishara, ita kwa mbinja. 3 pita haraka, (na kutoa mlio wa mluzi).

whit *n* **not a ~. no ~** hapana hata kidogo/chembe.

white[1] *adj* 1 -eupe. **bleed (sb/sth) ~** *(fig)* kamua/nyonya mtu. 2 *(compounds)* **~ alloy** fedha ghushi. **~ ant** mchwa. **~ bait** dagaa. **~ bear** dubu mweupe. **~caps** *n* mawimbi meupe. **~ collar** kazi isiyo ya sulubu. **~ coffee** kahawa yenye maziwa. **~ flag** ishara ya kusalimu amri. **~ heat** joto kali linalofanya chuma kuwa cheupe; *(fig)* hamaki, harara kali. **~ hot** *adj* -a harara, -enye hamaki. **the W~ House** Ikulu (ya Rais wa Marekani); sera ya serikali ya Marekani. **W~hall** *n* mtaa wa London (ambapo kuna ofisi za serikali); sera ya serikali ya Uingereza. **~ lead** *n* risasi nyeupe (yenye sumu inayotumiwa katika utengenezaji rangi). **~lie** uongo mtakatifu, uongo usiodhuru, maneno ya kupoza/kuondosha njiani. **~ lipped** *adj* -enye midomo myeupe (kwa woga). **~ livered** *adj* oga, mwoga. **~ man/woman** mzungu. **~ meat** nyama ya kuku, ndama au nguruwe. **~ metal** *see* **~ alloy**. **W~ paper** *(GB)* waraka/ripoti rasmi ya serikali ya habari maalum. **~d sepulchre** mnafiki. **~ slave** msichana anayelazimishwa kuwa malaya/ kahaba (hasa kwa kudanganywa kwenda ng'ambo kwa ahadi ya kuajiriwa). **~smith** *n* mfua bati; chokaa. **~thorn** miti ya miiba inayotumiwa kujengea wigo. **~ tie** vazi rasmi la jioni; tai ndogo nyeupe. **~ wash** chokaa; *(fig)* mbinu ya kuficha makosa ya mtu *vt (fig)* ficha makosa ya mtu.

white[2] *n* 1 rangi nyeupe. 2 mzungu, mtu mweupe. 3 ute wa yai. 4 mtoto wa jicho. **~ness** *n* weupe. **~n** *vt,vi* fanya -eupe, paka/tia rangi nyeupe; geuka kuwa -eupe. **~ning** *n* chaki, chokaa.

whither *adv (old use)* -ko, wapi? kwenda wapi? *Let him go ~ he will* aende apendako. **~soever** *adv (old use)* popote; kokote.

whiting[1] *n* chokaa, chaki.

whiting[2] *n* dagaa.

whitlow *n* mdudu (katika kidole).

whittle *vt,vi* 1 **~ (sth) away** chonga, kata vipande vyembamba; *(fig)* punguza. **~ (away) at sth** chongachonga. **~ sth down** chongachonga. 2 punguza vipande vidogo vidogo; *(fig)* punguza idadi/ kiasi. 3 chonga.

whiz *n* mvumo: mlio wa kitu kilichovurumishwa *vi* vuma.

whizz-kid *n (sl)* kijana mwerevu (anayefanikiwa haraka).

WHO Shirika la Afya Duniani.

who *interpron (used as the subject and only of persons; object form whom)* 1 nani. **(know) ~'s who** fahamu watu vizuri (maisha yao, kazi yao n.k.). 2 yupi, nani; *(rel)pron* ambaye/o, -ye-, -o-. **~ the gods love die young**

wazuri hufa mapema; chema hakidumu. **~ever** *pron* yeyote; -o-ote *~ever he is* yeyote awaye.

whodun(n)it *n (who done it (sl) for who did it)* riwaya ya upelelezi/ kusisimua/ujasusi.

whole *adj* 1 -zima, kamili, -timilifu, -ote. 2 -ote, zima. ~ **note** *(US)* noti zima. ~ **number** namba nzima. ~ **wheat meal** unga wa ngano isiyokobolewa, unga ambao haukukobolewa. ~ **milk** maziwa halisi. 3 **the/one's ~** -ote, kamili. **do sth with one's ~ heart** fanya kwa moyo mkunjufu/mmoja. 4 **~hearted(ly)** *adj,adv (attrib with pl n)* kamili, zima. 5 *(old use, biblical)* -enye afya njema, zima *n* uzima, kitu kizima. **on the** ~ kwa jumla; kwa kuzingatia yote. **(taken) as a ~** kwa kujumuisha, kwa pamoja. **wholly** *adv* kabisa. **~some** *adj* -enye (kuleta) afya, siha.

wholesale *n* jumla; biashara ya jumla *adj* -a jumla. **~r** *n* mwuza jumla.

who'll *who will* nani ata-.

whoop *n* 1 ukelele (wa shangwe, furaha). 2 sauti ya kikohozi. **~ing cough** kifaduro *vt,vi* piga ukelele wa shangwe/furaha. ~ **it up** *(sl)* -la starehe sana. **~ee** *n*. **make ~ee** *(sl)* sherehekea, fanya shamrashamra.

whop *vt (sl)* piga, shinda. **~per** *n* kitu/ jambo kubwa (agh uongo mkubwa); kitu kikubwa cha aina yake; kubwa sana. **~ping** *adj*.

who're *who are*.

whore *n (derog)* kahaba, malaya. **~dom** *n* umalaya; uasherati. **~-master** *n* asherati.

whorl *n* mzingo (duara au kama duara). **~ed** *adj* -enye mzingo, -a mzingo, (kama alama zilizo katika ngozi ya ncha za vidole).

whose *poss pron (who, of whom; of which)* 1 -a nani? **whose is that?** h-o ni -a nani? 2 *(in rel, defining clauses)* amba -ye/o/cho .... ke/ao *she is the woman ~ son went to University* yeye ni yule mwanamke ambaye mtoto wake alienda Chuo Kikuu.

whoso, whosoever *(old use) see* **whoever**.

why *adv* 1 *(interr)* kwa nini? mbona? kwa sababu gani. 2 *(rel adv)* sababu, (kwa nini) maana! *I will tell you ~* nitakuambia sababu *this is ~* ndiyo sababu/maana; *(int)* lo!; *(expressing surprise)* kumbe! *~ look at that!* kumbe! ona sasa!; *(expressing protest) n* sababu, kisa, hoja. **the ~s and the wherefores** kisa na mkasa.

wick *n* utambi, mjali, kope.

wicked *adj* 1 *(of person, his acts)* -ovu, habithi. 2 -enye inda, -a kuumiza. 3 tukutu, tundutundu. **~ly** *adv* kwa uovu. **~ness** *n* uovu; ufisadi.

wicker *n* fito (henzerani, matete) zilizosukwa. ~ **work** *n* vitu vilivyotengezwa kwa fito.

wicket *n* 1 ~ *(door or gate)* kilango. 2 kidirisha cha kuuzia tikiti. 3 *(cricket)* kilango cha vijiti vitatu kinacholindwa na mwenye kushika beti *take a ~* shinda mshika beti. **~-keeper** *n (cricket)* mdaka mpira aliye nyuma ya kilango.

wide *adj* 1 -pana, -liotanuka. 2 ingi, kubwa, pana. 3 wazi kabisa. 4. nje ya, -a mbali. 5 *(sl)* janja, danganyifu; -enye uhodari wa biashara. ~ **boy(s)** mtu mjanja/mdanganyifu; mfanyabiashara hodari *adv* 1 mbali. 2 wazi kabisa. ~ **awake** *adj (fig)* makini, -a macho. **be ~ awake** -wa macho/tayari. 3 kwa mapana. ~ **spread** *adj* -liotapakaa, -lioenea pote, -a kusambaa. **~ly** *adv* 1 sana, kwa kiasi kikubwa *be ~ly read* somwa sana. 2 hapa na pale, kwa vipindi vipana. 3 kwa kuenea/kutapakaa. **~n** *vt,vi* tanua, panua, eneza.

widgeon *n* aina ya bata mwitu.

widow *n* mjane mwanamke. **~er** *n* mjane mwanamume. **~ed** *adj*. **~hood** *n*.

width *n* 1 upana; *(fig)* upana wa mawazo, akili. 2 (kipimo cha) upana. 3 kitambaa cha upana fulani.

wield *vt* twaa/shika na kutumia ~

power shika madaraka, tawala ~ *an axe* tumia shoka.

wife *n* mke *take a* ~ oa *she will make a good* ~ atakuwa mke mwema. **old wives' tale** hadithi za kijinga/ kishirikina. **~like. ~ly** *adj* kama mke/ ahali; -a mke, -a kuhusu mke. **~ly duties** majukumu ya mke.

wig[1] *n* nywele bandia. **~ged** *adj* -liovaa nywele bandia.

wig[2] *vt* karipia, kemea. **~ging** *n (colloq)* karipio, kemeo *get/give sb a good* ~ kemewa, kemea mtu vikali.

wiggle *vt,vi* gaagaa; furukuta, jisombogoa; chezeshachezesha.

wight *n (arch)* binadamu, mtu. *a luckless* ~ mtu mwenye kisirani.

wigwam *n* hema (la ngozi au mkeka) (la Wamarekani wa asili).

wild *adj* 1 *(animals)* -a mwitu, -siofugwa ~ *animal* mnyama mwitu; *(plants)* -a gugu, -a kujiotea -enyewe, -a porini. ~ **cat** paka shume; *(attrib adj)* -a uenda wazimu, -siowezekana; -siopangwa. ~ **fowl** *n (esp)* ndege wa kuwindwa. ~ **goose** *n* bata mwitu. ~ **goose chase** shughuli isiyo na manufaa. 2 *(of horses, game birds)* -a kukurupuka. 3 *(of persons, tribes etc)* -shenzi, -siostaarabika, kali. 4 *(of scenery, areas of land etc)* -a mahame, -a pori, -siokaliwa. 5 *(violent)* -a nguvu nyingi, -a dhoruba. 6 *(ungoverned)* -liohemkwa/ vurugikiwa, -sio makini; -a kuchanganyikiwa ~ *with anger* -liohamaki sana. 7 *(colloq)* -a kupenda sana, -a shauku/raghaba/ hamu. **be ~ about sb/sth** fia mtu/ kitu, -wa na hamu juu ya kitu. 8 ovyo, mchafukoge. ~ **shooting** kufyatua risasi ovyo. **run** ~ tenda upendavyo (bila kudhibitiwa). **spread like ~ fire** *(of reports, rumours)* enea haraka sana. 9 *(of a playing card)* -enye thamani yoyote *n* **the ~s** mwitu, pori, nyika *adv* ovyo ovyo. **~ly** *adv* ovyo ovyo, bure, bila mpango. **~rness** *n.*

wildebeest *n* kongoni.

wile *n* hila, ujanja, werevu. **wily** *adj* -erevu, janja.

wilful *adj* 1 -kaidi, -gumu. 2 -a kusudi, -liokusudiwa ~ *damage* hasara ya kusudi. **~ly** *adv* makusudi; kwa kusudi, kwa kutaka. **~ness** *n* ukaidi, ugumu, ushupavu.

will[1] *n* 1 *the* ~ hiari, ridhaa *an iron* ~ nia thabiti *against sb's* ~ dhidi ya ridhaa ya mtu. 2 *(also* ~ **power)** utashi, rada. 3 dhamira. **take the ~ for the deed** shukuru kwa nia njema ya mtu (japo hakutenda). **of one's own free** ~ kwa hiari. **at** ~ upendavyo. **tenant at** ~ *(legal)* mpangaji anayeweza kuondolewa wakati wowote. 4 raghaba, hamasa, bidii, juhudi. 5 mapenzi, kudura. 6 **good/ill** ~ makusudi mema/mabaya, matlaba. 7 *(also* **last ~ and testament)** wosia.

will[2] *vt (pt would)* 1 taka, penda *what would you?* ungetaka nini. 2 *(the subject is often omitted)* -nge *would it were otherwise* laiti ingekuwa vinginevyo. 3 chagua, tamani, pendelea. **would be** *attrib adj* -naotarajiwa, -jao *the would ~-be authors* waandishi wanaotarajiwa, wanaoinukia *vt,vi* 1 fanya iwe; dhamiria, taka. 2 andika, jaalia. 3 athiri; taaradhi; tawala. 4 ~ **sth to sb.** ~ **sb sth** rithisha.

will[3] 1 *(used as an auxiliary verb of the future tense) (to express willingness, consent, offer, promise etc)* -ta *tomorrow* ~ *come* kesho itafika *she* ~ *come* atakuja *all right I'll come* sawa, nitakuja. 2 *(used with the 2nd person in questions, making polite request)* tafadhali *give me the book,* ~ *you* tafadhali nipatie kitabu. 3 kazania, shikilia; wa lazima *he* ~ *go to the dance* anashikilia kwenda kwenye dansi. 4 -wa na mazoea, tabia, desturi. 5 *(to indicate probability or likelihood)* majaliwa, labda, huenda. 6 *(conditional)* -nge-, -ngali, kama *they would have seen the thief if they had arrived earlier* wangalimwona yule mwizi endapo wangefika mapema.

willies *n (pl) (sl)* wasiwasi, woga.

willing *adj* 1 tayari, radhi. 2 -sio swali, bila kusita, bila makeke. **~ly** *adv*. **~ness** *n*.

will-o'the-wisp *n* mwanga uonekanao katika kinamasi; *(fig)* kitu/mtu mgumu kufikiwa/kupatikana.

willow *n* mti umeao karibu na maji. **~y** *adj* -refu -embamba.

willy-nilly *adv* taka usitake, bila hiari au kwa hiari, vyovyote vile.

wilt[1] *vi (of plants, flowers)* nyauka, dhoofu; pungukiwa na nguvu/uzuri *(of persons)* nywea, ishiwa nguvu.

wilt[2] *vt (arch form of)* **will**.

wily *adj see* **wile**.

wimple *n* ukaya/utaji/shela ya hariri yenye marinda *vt* weka marinda katika shela/utaji.

win *vi,vt* 1 shinda, pata, jipatia (kwa jitihada); tia fora. **~ the day/the field** shinda, pata ushindi. **~ free/clear/out through** shinda/pita/jinasua/ondokana na matatizo kwa jitihada. **~ hands down** *(colloq)* shinda kwa urahisi. 2 **~ sb over (to sth).** *(less usu)* **~ sb to do sth** vuta, shawishi mtu (kufanya jambo). 3 fikia (mahali) (kwa jitihada) *n* kushinda, ushindi *we had four ~s* tulishinda mara nne. **~ner** *n* mshindi. **~ning** *adj* -enye kushinda. 2 -a kushawishi, -shawishi, -a kuvutia. **~nings** *(pl) (esp)* fedha za ushindi. **~ning post** *n* kifundo: kiguzo cha kumalizia mbio, mwisho.

wince *vi* nywea, shtuka (kutokana na kuumia kama mtu aliyeumizwa sana kwa kitu au maneno) *he heard the news without wincing* alisikia habari bila kushtuka *n* mshtuko.

winceyette *n* kitambaa cha pamba au sufu.

winch *n* winchi, manjanika *vt* sogeza kwa winchi.

wind[1] *n* 1 *(often)* **the ~** upepo. **fling/ throw caution/prudence, etc to the ~s** acha kabisa, tahadhari. **get/have the ~ up** *(sl)* ogopa, tishika. **raise the ~** *(sl)* pata fedha zinazotakiwa. **put the ~ up sb** *(sl)* tisha/ogopesha mtu. **see/find out how the ~ blows** tafuta/sikiliza watu wasemavyo. **take the ~ out of sb's sails** wahi mtu; tafuta mwelekeo wa mambo, zuia mtu kusema/kutenda jambo; katiza faida yake ghafla. **there is sth in the ~** kuna njama/mpango wa siri (unaoandaliwa). 2 *(pl)* pande kuu nne za pepo *the papers were blown to the four ~s* karatasi zilipeperushwa pande zote. 3 pumzi. **get one's second ~** pata pumzi tena; *(fig)* pata nguvu mpya kutekeleza jambo. **sound in ~ and limb** buheri wa afya, katika siha nzuri, mabusuti. 4 harufu, fununu. **get ~ of** *(fig)* nusa harufu ya, pata fununu ya. 5 maneno matupu, upuuzi. 6 upepo/gesi (ya tumboni). **break ~** jamba, shuta. 7 **the ~** ala za kupuliza (za muziki). 8 *(compounds)* **~bag** *n (colloq)* mpiga porojo, mwenye kupayapaya. **~break** *n* kikinga upepo. **~cheater** (*US* **~ breaker**) *n* koti ya kukinga upepo. **~fall** *n* tunda lililoanguliwa na upepo; *(fig)* nyota ya jaha. **~-gauge** *n* kipimaupepo. **~ instrument** *n* ala ya muziki ya kupuliza. **~-jammer** *n* *(colloq)* chombo (jahazi n.k.) cha mfanyabiashara. **~mill** *n* kinu cha upepo. **fight/tilt at ~mills** pigana na adui, maovu ya njozi/kubuni. **~pipe** *n* koromeo. **~ screen** (*US* **shield**) *n* kioo cha mbele cha gari. **~-sock** *n* fuko la upepo. **~storm** *n* dhoruba (ya upepo mwingi na mvua kidogo). **~swept** *adj* wazi kutokana na upepo, -liofagiliwa na upepo; -a kukabiliana na upepo. **~less** *adj* -sio na upepo. **~ward** *adj* -a upande wa upepo wa joshini *n* upande wa upepo. **get to the ~ward of sb** epa harufu ya mtu. **~y** *adj* 1 -a upepo mwingi. 2 -a maneno mengi. 3 *(sl)* -enye hofu. **~ly** *adv*. **~iness** *n*.

wind[2] *vt* 1 gundua kitu kwa harufu. 2 kosa pumzi; kosesha pumzi. 3 -pa nafasi ya kupumua.

wind[3] *vi,vt* 1 zunguka, pinda, nyonganyonga; zungusha, pindisha. 2 sokota (kitu) kwa mfano wa mpira. ~ **sth off** sokotoa; fumua. ~ **sb round one's (little) finger** fanya mtu atende kila utakalo. 3 ~ **sth round sb/sth.** ~ **sb/sth .** ~ **sth** funika vizuri, kumbatia. **~ing sheet** *n* sanda. 4 ~ **sth (up)** zungusha, nyonga; pandisha kwa kunyonga mpini. 5 jaza ufunguo, lisha saa. 6 **wound up (to)** sisimka, changamka; panda. 7 ~ **(sth) up** maliza, katisha, komesha. ~ **up a business/company** kamilisha kila kitu kabla ya kufunga kampuni. ~ **up one's affairs** kamilisha na kufunga shughuli *n* mzunguko mmoja.

windlass *n* winchi.

window *n* dirisha. ~ **box** *n* sanduku la kuoteshea maua dirishani. **~-display** *n* maonyesho ya bidhaa dirishani. **~-dressing** *n* 1 mpangilio wa bidhaa (dirishani). 2 *(fig)* (ustadi wa) kujionyesha vizuri/kujipendezesha, upendezeshaji. **~-ledge** *n* ukingo wa dirisha. ~ **envelop** *n* bahasha -enye kioo/kidirisha). **~-pane** *n* kioo cha dirisha. **~-seat** *n* kiti cha dirishani. ~ **shopping** *n* kutia macho nuru, kuangalia bidhaa dirishani. **a ~ on the world** *(fig)* kifunua macho; njia yoyote ya kujua ulimwengu vizuri zaidi.

wine *n* divai, mvinyo. **new ~ in old bottles** mambo mapya yasiyoweza kuzuilika. ~ **glass** *n* bilauri ya divai. **~-grower** *n* mlimaji zabibu. **~-press** *n* kisindika zabibu. **~-skin** *n* 1 mfuko (wa ngozi yote ya mbuzi) wa divai. **~-taster** *n* mwonja divai. 2 pombe (inayofanana na divai). **palm ~** tembo *vi,vt* kunywa mvinyo. ~ **and dine sb** karibisha mtu chakula (na mvinyo). **~ry** *n* kiwanda cha mvinyo.

wing *n* 1 bawa, ubawa. **clip the ~s of** zuia. **lend/add ~s to** fanya kuchapuka. **take (to itself) ~s** potea, toweka. **take sb under one's ~** linda, hami, engaenga. ~ **nut/screw** nati. **~span, ~-spread** *n* kipimo cha ubawa toka ncha mpaka ncha. 2 *(of building. army)* upande, pembe; sehemu. 3 *(mil)* vikosi vya pembeni. 4 wakereketwa, wanazi; wenye msimamo mkali. 5 pembe za chaki. 6 **on the ~** -nayoruka/puruka. **take ~** anza kuruka. 7 kitu kama ubawa. 8 *(football, hockey)* wingi. 9 *(GB)* vikosi viwili au zaidi vya jeshi la anga; *(pl)* beji ya rubani. ~ **-commander** *n* ofisa wa jeshi la anga. **~ed** *adj* 1 -enye mabawa. **~less** *adj* bila ubawa. **~er** wingi.

wink 1 *vi,vt* ~ **(at)** pesa, pepesa, kupia, konyeza. **as easy.... as ~ing** rahisi sana. ~ **at sth** achilia, samehe, fumbia macho, jidai huoni. 2 *(of star)* meta *n* 1 ukope, konyezo *give a ~ to* kupia, konyeza. **a ~ is as good as a nod** ishara ni sawa na kuitikia/kukubali. 2 muda mfupi sana. **forty ~s** usingizi kidogo. **tip sb the ~** pasha mtu habari (kwa siri), nong'oneza mtu.

winkle *n* konokono wa pwani. *vt* **~sb/ sth out** chokoa/chokonoa kitu (mpaka kukitoa).

winnow *vt* pepeta, pembua, puliza.

winsome *adj* -a kuvutia, -a kupendeza. **~ly** *adv*. **~ness** *n*.

winter *n* majira ya baridi (kali) *a man of 50 ~s* mwenye umri ya miaka 50. ~ **garden** mimea ndani ya chumba cha glasi *vi,vt* kaa majira ya baridi ~ *in France* kaa Ufaransa majira ya baridi. **~tide** *n* kipindi cha baridi. ~ **wintry** *adj* -a majira ya baridi, -a baridi kali; *(fig)* baridi, a uongo *-a ~y smile* tabasamu baridi.

wipe *vt* pangusa, safisha kwa kufuta, futa. ~ **the slate clean** anza upya. ~ **sth away** futa, pangusa. ~ **sth off** pangusa; ondosha, maliza, futa. ~ **sth out** pangusa (ndani ya), ondosha, futa, sahau; angamiza, teketeza kabisa. ~ **sth up** kausha *n* kufuta. **~r** *n* 1 kifuto. 2 waipa.

wire *n* 1 waya. **pull (the) ~s** *(fig)* tumia njia za siri kupata jambo; endesha kikaragosi. **live ~** waya wenye umeme; *(fig)* mashughuli, mtu afanyae kazi kwa bidii. **~-cloth** *n* wavu wa nyuzi za chuma. **~-cutter** *n* chombo cha kukatia waya. **~-netting** *n* wavu wa nyuzi za chuma (shaba). **~-puller** *n* mtu avutaye mambo kwa siri. **~-pulling** *n* 1 ushawishi. 2 shauri la siri. **~ rope** *n* kebo, kamba ya waya. **~haired** *adj* -a kipilipili. **~ wool** *n* kumbi la waya/chuma. 2 *(colloq esp US)* simu ya upepo *vt,vi* 1 funga, kaza kwa waya. 2 weka, tia (nyuzi za) umeme. 3 *(telegraph)* piga simu, arifu kwa simu. 4 tega/nasa kwa waya. **wiring** *n* (mfumo wa) waya za umeme. **wiry** *adj* -embamba na shupavu. **~less** *n* simu ya upepo; redio *vt* peleka habari kwa redio *adj* -a redio, -a simu *~less station* stesheni ya simu ya upepo.

wise[1] *n (sing only old use)* namna, jinsi. **in no ~** sivyo kabisa, sivyo kwa jinsi yoyote.

wise[2] *adj* -a busara/hekima. **be none the ~r** -tojua zaidi kuliko mwanzo. **be/get ~ to sb/sth** *(sl)* zinduka. **put sb ~ to sb/sth** pasha, letea fulani habari, eleza. **~acre** *n* mtu ajifanyaye mjuzi; mchushi. **~crack** *n (sl)* mzaha, msemo *vi* toa mizaha/misemo. **~ly** *adv* kwa hekima *vt,vi* **~ up** *(US infml)* pata habari. **wisdom** *n* 1 busara, hekima, idili. **~ tooth** gego la mwisho. 2 mawazo ya busara, methali, misemo.

wish *n* 1 matakwa, mapenzi, matamanio. **if ~s were horses, beggars might ride** *(prov)* atakalo mtu hapati hupata ajaliwalo. **the ~ is father to the thought** *(prov)* tunaamini tunalotaka kuamini. 2 kitakiwacho, matilaba. **~ful** *adj* tamanifu, -enye kutaka. **~ thinking** ndoto za mchana. **~fully** *adv vt,vi* 1 **~ (that)** taka; penda; tamani. 2 **~ sb well/ill** takia mema/mabaya. 3 taka *she ~s to be alone* anataka faragha *I ~ you would be more careful* tafadhali kuwa mwangalifu zaidi. 4 **~ for** -wa na hamu, tamani, ombea jambo. **~ bone** *n* mfupa wa kuku ulioko kati ya shingo na kifua. **~ing cap** *n (in fairy tales)* kofia ya kuombea. 5 **~ sb/sth on sb** *(colloq)* takia baa/balaa. **~er** *n* mtakia bahati.

wishy-washy *adj (of soup, tea etc)* -dufu, -rojorojo; *(of talk, person)* chapwa, -sio na nguvu/msimamo, -a wasiwasi.

wisp *n* kichopa, kitita *adj* -a kitita, kama kitita/kichopa.

wistful *adj* -enye kusononeka; -enye kutamanitamani; -enye tamaa isiyoridhishwa. **~ly** *adv*.

wit[1] *adv* **to ~** *(leg)* maana yake, yaani, ndiyo *God ~* Mungu anajua.

wit[2] *n* 1 akili. **be at one's ~'s end** taka kuchanganyikiwa, -tojua la kufanya. **out of one's ~s** -liochanganyikiwa, -enye wazimu, -enye fadhaa. **have a ready ~** -wa na majibu/vichekesho vya haraka. **have/ keep one's ~s about one** -wa mahiri, tayari kung'amua na kutenda. **live by one's ~s** ishi kwa ujanja. 2 mwerevu, mtu hodari na mcheshi. 3 werevu, ucheshi, mzaha, utani. **~ty** *adj* cheshi, chekeshi. **~ticism** *n* misemo au maneno ya akili/kuchekesha. **~less** *adj* -pumbavu.

witch *n* 1 mchawi, mlozi mwanamke; *(fig)* mwanamke mwenye ucheshi, mvuto ajabu. **~craft** *n* ulozi, uchawi, usihiri *remove ~craft* adua, sua, zingua, tegua. **~doctor** *n* mlozi wa kiume, mganga, mchawi. **~hunt** *n* msako wa wachawi. 2 *(fig)* msako na uonevu wa watu (k.m. wale wanaodhaniwa kuwa wasaliti). **~ery** *n* 1 uchawi. 2 *(fascination, charm)* ucheshi, ushawishi wa kushinda moyo, uzuri wa kupoteza akili, mvuto, maliwazo *vt,vi* fanya uchawi, loga. **~ing** *adj*.

with *prep* 1 *(equivalent to constructions with have)* -enye, na, -a, kwa. **~ child** *(of woman)* mjamzito. **~ young** *(of an animal)* mwenye mimba. 2 *(to indicate what is used for filling, covering)* na, kwa *fill ~ sand* jaza na/kwa mchanga. 3 *(means or instrument)* kwa, na *write ~ a pen* andika kwa kalamu. 4 *(accompaniment or relationship)* na, pamoja na *discuss a problem ~* jadiliana tatizo na. **in ~** -enye kushirikiana na. 5 *(antagonistic, opposing)* -ana na *quarrel ~* gombana na *compete ~* shindana na. **fall out ~** gombana na. 6 *(causal)* kwa sababu ya, kwa *tremble ~ fear* tetemeka kwa (sababu ya) woga. 7 *(manner)* kwa *handle ~ care* shughulikia kwa uangalifu. 8 sawa na, pamoja; wakati mmoja na *move ~ time* enda na wakati. 9 *(indicate care, charge or possession)* -wa na *had no money ~ him* hakuwa na fedha. 10 *(separation)* -ana na *break ~* achana na. 11 *(in agreement or sympathy)* -ana na *I am ~ you* naafikiana na wewe. **be/ get ~ it** *(sl)* enda na wakati. 12 licha ya ~ *all our effort* licha ya juhudi yetu yote.

withal *adv (arch)* zaidi, tena, juu ya hayo, aidha.

withdraw *vt,vi* 1 chukua. **~ sth/sb (from)** toa, jitoa; ondoa/ondoka; chukua. 2 futa, tangua ~ *a charge* futa mashtaka, ondoa mashataka. 3 rudi nyuma, rudisha nyuma; (ji) tenga. **~al** *n* kuondoa, kuondoka; kufuta, kuchukua. **~ symptoms** kujitenga; hali (ya kimaumbile/kiakili) itokeayo kutokana na kuachishwa kitu ulichozoea (agh. madawa ya kulevya) *adj* pweke, kimya, -liojitenga; -enye mawazo ya mbali.

withe, withy *n* ufito, ubugu.

wither *vi,vt* 1 ~ **(sth) up.** ~ **(away)** chakaa, nyauka, -fa, fifisha, nyausha. 2 aibisha, fadhaisha *she gave him a ~ing glance* alimtupia jicho la kufadhaisha. **~ingly** *adv*.

withers *n (pl)* nundu (ya farasi n.k.).

withheld *pt,pp* **withhold.**

withhold *vt* ~ **sth (from)** nyima, katalia, zuia ~ *consent* kataa ~ *the truth from sb* ficha mtu ukweli.

within *(prep)* ndani ya; karibu; chini ya ~ *an hour* haipati saa ~ *my power/ strength* chini ya uwezo wangu ~ *call* karibu *adv (lit)* ndani.

without *(prep)* 1 bila, pasipo. ~ **fail** bila kukosa ~ *doubt* kwa hakika, bila shaka. 2 *(before gerunds)* bila, pasi *people can't live ~ eating* watu hawawezi kuishi bila ya kula. **go ~ saying** wa wazi mno, fahamika pasi kuelezwa. 3 *(old use)* nje *adv (lit or old use)* nje.

withstand *vt* himili.

withstood *pt pp* **withstand.**

withy *n see* **withe.**

witness *n* 1 *(often* **eye** ~) shahidi. ~ **box** *(US also* **~stand)** kizimba cha shahidi kortini. 2 ushuhuda, ushahidi. **bear ~ to sb/sth** unga mkono; thibitisha sahihi. 3 shahidi, mtu anayethibitisha sahihi ya mtu mwingine. 4 kielezo cha ushahidi, kithibitisho *vt,vi* 1 shuhudia, ona -enyewe. 2 ~ **to sth/ doing sth** toa ushahidi. 3 thibitisha sahihi ya mtu mwingine. 4 onyesho, thibitisha.

witticism *n see* **wit.**[2]

wittingly *adv* kwa makusudi; kwa kujua.

witty *adj see* **wit.**[2]

wive *vt,vi (arch)* oa.

wizard *n* 1 mchawi, mlozi. 2 mtu mwenye uwezo wa ajabu *adj (sl)* safi sana; bora, -zuri sana. **~ry** *n* uchawi ulozi.

wizen *adj* -liosinyaa, -liokauka, -kavu.

wobble *vi,vt* 1 yumbayumba, wayawaya, sesereka. 2 *(fig)* sitasita, yumba; -tokuwa na uhakika *n* mtu/ kitu kinachoyumba. **wobbly** *adj* -a kutikisika, legelege, -sio imara.

woe *n* 1 *(chiefly poet; sometimes hum)* huzuni majonzi, masikitiko. 2 *(pl)* sababu za huzuni; matatizo; shida. ~ **begone** *adj* -a huzuni. **~fully** *adv* -a huzuni nyingi, -a kuhuzunisha. **~ful** *adj*.

woke *pt* **wake**.

wold *n* pori, mbuga, nyika.

wolf *n* mbwa mwitu. ~ **cry** kilio cha uongo. **a ~ in sheep's clothing** chui aliyevaa ngozi ya kondoo. **keep the ~ from the door** weza kujikimu. **~-cub** *n* mtoto wa mbwa mwitu. **~-hound** *n* mbwa wa kuwindia mbwa mwitu. **~ whistle** *n* mluzi wa ashiki *vt* lafua, la kwa pupa. **~ish adj** -a kama mbwa mwitu.

wolfram *n see* **tungsten.**

woman *n* 1 mwanamke; *(young, unmarried)* msichana, mwanamwali; *(old)* (bi)kizee, ajuza; *(slave)* mjakazi, kijakazi. 2 *(without article)* jinsi ya kike. 3 tabia ya kike. **~hood** *n* 1 *(collective)* uanamama; wanawake. 2 hali ya kuwa mwanamama. **~ish** *adj* -a kike; -a kikekike; -enye tabia ya kike. **~ize** *vt,vi* fuata wanawake sana. **~izer** *n* mfuata wanawake. **~kind** *n* akina mama, wanawake wote. **~like. ~ly** *adj* -a kike, kama mwanamke. **~folk** *n* akina mama; wanawake wa familia ya mtu.

womb *n (anat)* 1 uterasi: tumbo la uzazi, mji wa mimba. 2 *(fig)* **it still lies in the ~ of time** muda ndio utafichua yote.

won *pt, pp* **win**.

wonder *n* 1 mshangao. **no/little/small ~** si shani/ajabu. **~land** nchi ya neema; nchi ya kubuni/kufikirika lioduwaa/kinduwaa. **~struck** *adj* -liopigwa na bumbuwazi, -a kustaajabu, -lioshangaa mno. 2 ajabu, kioja, mzungu, shani. **signs and ~s** miujiza. **work~s** fanya miujiza, fanya vizuri sana. **a nine days' ~** shani ya muda mfupi; kitu kinachovuma kwa muda mfupi. **for a ~** ni ajabu. **it is a ~ (that)** ni ajabu kwamba. **what a ~** ajabu ilioje! *vi,vt* 1 ~ **(at sth)** staajabu, shangaa, ona ajabu. 2 ~ **(about sth)** fikiria, wazia. 3 jiuliza. **~ingly** *adv* kwa ajabu, kwa mshangao. **~ful** *adj* -a ajabu, -a shani, -a kustaajabisha, -zuri sana. **~fully** *adv*. **~ment** *n* ajabu, mshangao. **wondrous** *adj (arch, or liter)* -a ajabu/shani, -a kustaajabisha, -a kushangaza *adv (only with adj) he was ~ kind* alikuwa mwema ajabu.

wonky *adj* 1 *(GB)* -a wasiwasi, goigoi, bovu. 2 -dhaifu. **feel ~** -tojiweza, jisikia vibaya.

wont *n (arch or lit) (sing only)* mazoea, desturi. **use and ~** desturi/ada /tabia madhubuti. *pred adj* **be ~ to** zoea *he is ~ to travel* amezoea kusafiri, mara kwa mara husafiri. **~ed** *attrib adj* -a desturi; -a kawaida.

won't *short form of* **will not**.

woo *vt* 1 *(old use)* chumbia, bembeleza (kwa nia ya kuoa). 2 tafuta, jaribu kupata (mafanikio, sifa, usingizi n.k.). 3 tafuta kuungwa mkono (na wapiga kura, wateja, wafanya biashara n.k.). **~er** *n*.

wood *n* 1 mbao, ubao. 2 *(often pl)* msitu mdogo, kituka, kichaka. **out of the ~s** *(fig)* -liookoka, -liopona toka hatarini/mashakani. **be unable to see the ~ for the trees** *(fig)* shindwa kuona vema kutokana na msongamano. 3 **in/from the ~** ndani/kutoka kwenye kasiki. 4 *(compounds)* **~ alcohol** *n* spiriti ya mti. **~-block** *n* gogo la kuchongea vinyago. **~-carving** *n* kuchonga vinyago; uchongaji vinyago. **~-craft** *n* ujuzi wa misitu, uzoefu wa mambo ya misitu; ufundi wa kuchonga miti. **~cut** *n* muhuri wa mbao wa herufi au picha. **~cutter** *n* mtema kuni. **~land** *n* eneo lenye miti, mwitu, msitu. **~man** *n* 1 bwana miti; mkata miti. **~sman** *n (esp US)* bwana miti; mkata miti. **~-pecker** *n* gogonola, kigogota, gogota. **~ pile** lundo la kuni. **~ pigeon** *n* bua. **~-pulp** *n* ubao uliosagwa (kwa ajili ya kutengeneza karatasi). **~ shed** banda la kuwekea kuni. **~-wind** *n* filimbi ya mti. **~-work** *n* vitu vya mbao, sehemu ya jengo la miti/mbao; useremala. **~worker** *n* seremala. **~ed** *adj* -a mwitu, -a msitu, -enye miti. **~en** *adj (attrib)* -a mti, -a mbao, -a miti. **~ headed** *adj* zito, -a akili ngumu, rasimu. **~y** *adj* 1 -enye miti. 2 -a mwitu, -a msitu.

woof *see* **weft**.
woofer *n* kipaza sauti kinachotoa sauti ya chini chini.
wool *n* manyoya, sufu. **dyed in the ~** -liotiwa rangi kabla ya kufumwa; *(fig)* barabara, kamilifu. **much cry and little ~** maneno mengi yenye matokeo haba; pigia kelele kitu kisicho na maana. **pull the ~ over sb's eyes** danganya mtu. **~ gathering** *n* 1 usahaulifu, chechele *adj* -enye kusahausahau. 2 kitu kama sufu. 3 *(of a person)* nywele nene zilizosokotwa, nywele za kipilipili. **lose one's ~** *(colloq)* kasirika. 4 *(compounds)* **~-ball** *n* bonge la sufu. **~-carder** *n* mchambuaji sufu. **~-carding** *n* utengenezaji wa sufu fupi na ndefu tayari kwa kufumwa. **~len** *(US woolen) (attrib adj)* -a sufu. **~lens** *n (pl)* nguo za sufu. **~ly** *adj* 1 -enye manyoya mengi, -a sufu; *(fig) (of the mind, ideas, arguments)* -liochanganyikiwa, -siodhahiri *n (colloq)* nguo za sufu (agh. sweta). **~-shears** *n* makasi ya sufu.
word *n* 1 neno. **a play on/upon ~s** ulimbuwaji maneno. **be not the ~ for it** -tokuwa maelezo yake; -wa maelezo yasiyoridhisha. **(repeat sth) ~ for ~** (rudia) neno kwa neno **(translate sth) ~ for ~** tafsiri sisisi/kwa neno. **in a/one ~** kwa kifupi. **by ~ of mouth** kwa mdomo. 2 taarifa, kauli, neno. **eat one's ~s** kiri kosa; futa kauli na kuomba radhi. **have a ~ with sb** zungumza na mtu. **have ~ (with sb)** gombana na. **have the last ~** funga mjadala. **put in/say a good ~ (for sb)** tetea mtu. **suit the action to the ~** timiza mara moja jambo ulilosema. **take sb at his ~** amini kauli yake. **big ~s** majigambo, majisifu,. **on/with the ~** mara tu baada ya kusema. **a ~ in/out of season** ushauri unaotolewa wakati unapohitajika/usipohitajika. **the last~ on (a subject)** neno la mwisho. **the last ~ (in sth)** taarifa/habari motomoto, -a kisasa, bora kabisa. 3 *(sing, without def art)* habari, taarifa. 4 *(sing only with a possessive)* ahadi, uthibitisho. **be as good as one's ~** timiza ahadi. **give sb one's ~ (that)** ahidi. **keep/break one's ~** timiza/vunja ahadi. **take sb's ~ for it** amini mtu asemacho. **upon my ~** kweli kabisa; lo, lahaula. 5 *(sing only)* amri; ishara. 6 *(in the Christian religion)* **the W~** *(of God)*. **God's W~** Neno (la Mungu) (agh. Injili), (jina la) Yesu Kristo. 7 *(compounds)* **~ book** *n* kamusi ndogo; faharasa. **~ division** *n* kutenga neno katika sehemu. **~-formation** *n* uundaji wa maneno. **~ painter** *n* mtu hodari wa kujieleza kwa maneno. **~-painting** *n* kueleza kwa maneno. **~-perfect** *adj* -enye kujua somo kwa moyo, hodari wa kusoma kwa ghibu; -lokariri. **~-picture** *n* taswira ya maneno, maelezo (mafafanuzi) stadi (kwa maneno). **~-play** *n* mchezo wa maneno. **~-processor** *n* kichambua maneno, kompyuta. **~ splitting** *n* 1 udanganyifu; utengaji maana za maneno *vt* eleza kwa maneno *(sing only)* jinsi jambo linavyoelezwa; uteuzi wa maneno katika kuelezea maana. **~less** *adj* kimya; bila maneno. **~y** *adj* -a maneno mengi (pasi lazima). **~ily** *adv* kwa maneno mengi. **~iness** *n*.
wore *pt* **wear**.
work *n* 1 kazi. **make hard ~ of sth** fanya kitu kionekane kigumu kuliko kilivyo, taabika na. **make short ~ of sth** maliza (kazi) haraka. **set/get to ~ (on sth/to do sth)** shika/anza kazi. **set/go about one's ~** anza kufanya kazi, shughulikia. **at ~ on (sth)** -wa kazini. **all in the day's ~** kawaida. 2 ajira, kazi ya kipato, kibarua. **at ~** kazini. **in/out of ~** -enye/sio na kazi. 3 shughuli (yoyote). 4 vifaa vya kazi. **~ bag/basket/box** *n* begi n.k. la kuwekea vifaa vya kazi (hasa vya ushonaji). 5 kazi, zao, kipande, kila kilichozalishwa kwa kazi. 6 kazi za akili (k.m. kitabu, muziki n.k.). 7

(pl) mashine (sehemu inayofanya kazi). **the ~s of a watch** mashine ya saa. 8 *(pl with sing or pl v)* (jengo la) kiwanda. **brick ~s** jengo la kiwanda; kiwanda cha matofali. **~s council/ committee** baraza/ kamati ya pamoja ya waajiri na waajiriwa. 9 **public ~s** ujenzi (wa barabara, madaraja n.k. na idara ya serikali). 10 *(pl v)* ngome. 11 *(compounds)* **~ bench** *n* benchi la makanika. **~-day** *n* siku ya kazi. **~force** wafanyakazi wote (wa mahali/ taasisi fulani). **~house** *n (GB hist)* nyumba ya serikali kwa wasio na makazi; *(US)* jela ya wahalifu wenye makosa madogo ambapo wanafanyakazi. **~man** *n* kibarua, mtendaji, mfanyakazi, fundi (wa kazi fulani), msanii. **~-manlike** *adj* -stadi, -a ufundi. **~manship** *n* ustadi, usanii. **~-room** *n* chumba maalum kufanyia kazi. **~shop** *n* karakana; warsha. **~-shy** *n,adj* vivu, -zembe, goigoi. **~study** *n* utafiti wa utendajikazi. **~table** *n (esp)* meza yenye saraka za kuwekea vifaa vya ushonaji *vi,vt* 1 fanya kazi. **~ in** *n* mgomo wa kuendelea kufanya kazi (kupinga amri ya kufukuzwa n.k.). 2 *(of a machine, apparatus, bodily organ, plan, method etc)* fanya, tenda kazi iliyokusudiwa; fanikiwa. 3 fanyisha kazi, tendesha kazi. 4 faulu, fanikiwa. **~ one's passage** pata nauli kutokana na kazi (kwenye chombo). **~ ones way (through college etc)** fanya kazi ili ulipe gharama za kusoma chuo. **~ one's will (on sb)** fanya mtu afanye utakavyo. **~ it** *(sl)* fanya mpango. 5 shughulikia, hudumia; dhibiti. 6 sogea, penya, fikia; sogeza, penyeza, fikisha. 7 umba, unda/finyanga. **~ clay** finyanga udongo. **~ dough** sukuma unga. 8 umuka; vimba; chemka; shtukashtuka *the yeast began to ~* unga ulianza kuumuka. 9 tarizi. 10 *(special uses with adverbial particles and preps)*. **~ away (at sth)** endelea kufanya/kuchapa kazi. **~ in, ~ into sth** penya, ingia. **~ sth in/into** ingiza, tia *~ a few jokes into your story* ingiza/tia utani kidogo katika hadithi yako. **~ sth off** ondoa, achana na; shughulikia. **~ on/upon sb/sth** athiri, gusa; shughulikia. **~ out** toa ufumbuzi/jawabu; tokea; fanya mazoea. **~ out** *n* (muda wa) mazoezi. **~ sth out** kisia, toa hesabu; pata jawabu, unda, buni, panga fumbua; *(usu passive)* maliza -ote, tumia -ote. **~ up to sth** panda taratibu (hadi upeo), fanya kwa hatua, endeleza; sisimua, amsha, hamasisha. **~ sb/ oneself (into)** pandisha (furaha, huzuni n.k), endelea, jazibisha. **~ upon sb/sth** *see* **~ on.** **~able** *adj* -nayowezekana. **~er** *n* mfanyakazi. **~ing** *n* 1 machimbo (ya madini, mawe) n.k. 2 utendaji kazi. **in ~ order** -enye kufanya kazi vizuri. *(attrib) (in various senses of the v)* **~ breakfast/ clothes** nguo za kazi. **~breakfast/ lunch/dinner** kifunguakinywa/ chakula cha mchana/jioni kinachoambatana na mazungumzo ya kikazi. **~ capital** mtaji. **~ day** siku ya kazi; muda wa kazi (kwa siku moja). **~ hypothesis** dhanio. **~ knowledge** maarifa yanayotosheleza kusudio. **~ out** upangaji, makisio (ya matokeo ya kazi); utekelezaji. **~ party** kamati teule (ya kazi/shughuli fulani). **~ part** *adj* -enye kuchapa kazi *a hard ~ woman* mwanamke mchapa kazi. **the ~ class** tabaka la wafanyakazi (za mikono/sulubu).

world *n* 1 **the ~** dunia, nchi zake na watu wake. **the Old ~** Ulaya, Asia na Afrika. **the New W~** Marekani. **make a noise in the W~** vuma, -wa maarufu. **a citizen of the ~** raia wa dunia. **It's a small ~!** vilima havikutani. 2 *(as 1 above; used attrib)* -a dunia, -a ulimwengu *a ~ language* lugha ya ulimwengu. **the W ~ Bank** Benki ya Dunia. **~ wide** *adj* -a duniani kote. 3 wakati, maisha *this ~ and the next* maisha ya sasa na baada ya kifo. **~ weary** *adj* -liochoka kuishi. 4 ulimwengu. **in the ~**

ulimwenguni. **all the ~ like sb/sth** -nayofanana kabisa na. **be all the ~ to sb** -wa pekee kwa mtu fulani. **not for the ~** kamwe, kabisa, asilani. **be/feel on top of the ~** jawa na furaha/hamasa. **be out of the ~ (of sth)** *(sl)* -wa bora sana, -wa -a ajabu. **carry the ~ before one** fanikiwa. **a ~ of sth** (-ingi/kubwa) sana. **think the ~ of sb/sth** penda/husudu/stahi sana mtu/kitu. 5 vitu/shughuli za watu, mambo ya dunia. **the ~, the flesh, and the devil** majaribu. **the best of both ~s** mema kutoka pande zote (hata yakikinzana). **for-sake/renounce the ~** fuata mambo ya kiroho, hama dunia. 6 mambo ya kibinadamu; maisha, malimwengu. **know the ~** pata uzoefu wa maisha. 7 ulimwengu, jamii *the ~ of sports* ulimwengu wa michezo. 8 **the ~** watu, jumuia (pamoja na taasisi na kawaida zake) *what will the ~ say?* watu watasemaje? **~ly** *adj* -a dunia; -a malimwengu, -a kupenda anasa za dunia. **~ wisdom** akili/hekima ya kuendeleza maisha. **~ liness** *n.*

worm *n* 1 **(in earth ~)** mnyoo; funza; *(in bowels)* mnyoo, mchango. **~ cast** kichuguu cha mnyoo. **the ~ of conscience** majuto, toba. 2 *(in compounds)* **~-eaten** *adj* -liotobolewa na funza; *(fig)* -liochakaa, -a zamani. **~ hole** *n* tobo la funza katika tunda/mti. 3 *(fig)* bwege, boza. **even a ~ will turn** *(prov)* uvumilivu una kikomo, hata bubu atasema, msalie mtume. 4 miduara/nyuzi za hesi *vt* 1 **~ oneself/one's way in/into/through** penya/pita (polepole au kwa shida). **~ out (of sb)** pata habari (kwa kusaili sana). 2 toa minyoo. **~y** *adj*-enye minyoo, -kama minyoo; -lioharibiwa na minyoo.

worn *pp* **of wear.**[2]

worry *vt, vi* 1 udhi, sumbua, hangaisha. 2 **~ (about/over sth)** kerwa na jambo fulani, ona wasiwasi juu ya jambo fulani. **~ along** *(colloq)* jikongojakongoja. 3 *(esp of dogs)* kamata kwa meno na kutikisa, ng'ata. 4 **~ a problem, etc out** shughulikia tatizo tena na tena hadi liishe, *n* 1 (hali ya kuwa na) wasiwasi/wahaka/kiherehere. 2 *(usu pl)* masumbuko. **worried** *adj* -enye wasiwasi, wahaka. **~ing** *adj.* **~ingly** *adv.* **worrisome** *adj* sumbufu; -enye kutia wasiwasi.

worse *adj* 1 -baya zaidi *make things ~* tibua, fanya mambo yawe mabaya zaidi. **the ~ for wear** -liochakaa sana; *(fig)* hoi, -liochoka sana. 2 *(pred only)* dhaifu; duni; gonjwa. **be none the ~ (for sth)** -todhurika, -toumizwa (nacho) *adv* 1 vibaya zaidi *he has been taken ~* hali yake imekuwa mbaya zaidi. **none the ~** vilevile. 2 *(used to intensify)* zaidi *n* ubaya zaidi, mambo mabaya zaidi *a change for the ~* badiliko linaloleta matatizo zaidi. **~n** *vi,vt* ongeza/ongezeka (ubaya). **worst** *adj* -baya kuliko -ote, baya kabisa *n* sehemu/hali/tukio baya kuliko yote. **if the ~ comes to the ~** mambo yakiwa mabaya kabisa. **get the ~ of it** komolewa, shindwa kabisa. **the ~ of it is that** baya zaidi ni kwamba. **at (the) ~** mambo yakiwa mabaya. **do your ~/let him do his ~** fanya upendalo/afanye apendalo *vt* shinda.

worship *n* 1 ibada. 2 heshima kubwa, pendo kuu. 3 **your/his W~,** *(GB)* Mheshimiwa, Mstahiki *vt,vi* abudu; sali. **~per** *n (US* **~er)** mwabudu. **the ~ers** watu waabuduo. **~ful** *adj (in GB titles of respect)* -a kustahili heshima, mstahiki.

worsted n uzi wa sufu; nguo za sufu (iliyosokotwa) *adj* -a sufu.

worth *pred adj* 1 -enye thamani fulani. **for what it is ~** bila ahadi juu yake. **~while** *adj* -a kufaa, -a maana. 2 -enye mali ya thamani fulani. **for all one is ~** *(colloq)* kwa bidii zote. 3 -ema, zuri, stahili *the book is ~ reading* kitabu ni kizuri kukisoma *n* 1 thamani. 2 kiasi chenye thamani fulani. **~less** *adj* bure ghali, -siofaa kitu, -sio na thamani. **~lessness** *n*. **~y** *adj* 1 ~ **(of sth/to be sth)** -a kustahili. 2 *(often ironic or used with a patronizing effect)* -a kustahili heshima *n* 1 mtu mashuhuri (wa kipindi fulani). 2 *(hum or ironic)* mheshimiwa. **~ily** *adv*. **~iness** *n*. **wot God ~** *(arch or hum)* Mungu anajua, ajuaye Mungu, allahu yaalamu.

wotcher *int (GB sl) (as a greeting)* halo!, mambo! vipi!

would *see* **will**.

wound[1] *n* 1 jeraha. 2 kidonda, mchubuko (katika mti n.k.). 3 *(of feelings)* uchungu, maumivu *vt* 1 jeruhi, umiza, tia jeraha. 2 udhi, choma moyo, tia uchungu.

wound[2] *pt, pp of* **wind**.

wove, woven *pt, pp* **weave**.

wow[1] *n (sl)* mafanikio makubwa; ushindi wa kustusha. *int* la-la-la-la, -lo.

wow[2] sauti ya kupanda na kushuka inayotokana na kasoro katika kinasa sauti.

wrack *n* mwani (majani) wa baharini uliotupwa ufukoni.

wraith *n* mzuka, pepo.

wrangle *vi* 1 ~ **(with sb) (about/over sth)** zozana, gombana *n* mzozo ugomvi. **~r** *n* mgomvi.

wrap *vt,vi* ~ **(up) (in sth)** 1 fungia, setiri, funika. ~ **sth up** *(sl)* kamilisha. 2 ~ **sth round sth** viringishia, zungushia. 3 **be ~ed up in** fungwa, fungashwa; *(fig)* fichwa; zamia, penda sana *n* vazi la nje kama skafu, vazi la kufunika au la kujitanda. **keep sth under ~s** ficha. **take off the ~s** onyesha (kwa mara ya kwanza). **~per** *n* 1 shali, nguo ya kujifunika. 2 karatasi ya kufungia kitu, k.m kifurushi. 3 kitambaa (kama khanga) cha Afrika Magharibi, vitu vya kufunikia/kufungia. **~ping** *n*.

wrath *n (lit)* ghadhabu, hasira. **~ful** *adj* -enye ghadhabu, -enye hasira. **~fully** *adv*.

wreak *vt* ~ **sth (on sb)** *(lit)* tolea, lipiza.

wreath *n* 1 shada la maua. 2 zingo (la moshi n.k.). ~ *vt,vi (esp in pp)* funika; zingira. ~ **itself round** jizingia, zongomea/viringisha. 3 ~ **sth into** fanya taji. 4 *(of smoke, mist etc)* fanya kuwa katika mzingo kama wa shada.

wreck *n* 1 kuvunjika (hasa chombo, merikebu, jahazi, meli), kupanda mwamba, *(fig)* kuvunjika kwa mipango, matarajio ya mtu. 2 meli iliyopata baa la kuvunjika. 3 gofu, chombo au jengo lililoharibiwa sana; mtu aliyetambarika *vt* haribu, bomoa; angamiza. **~age** *n* 1 mabaki ya chombo (kilichovunjika). **~er** *n* 2 mtu anayelipwa kurudisha meli iliyoharibiwa; mbomoaji majengo ya zamani. 3 *(hist)* msababisha kuvunjika kwa meli (ili apore).

wrench *vt* 1 sokota, vuta kwa ghafula. 2 umiza kwa kusokotoa/kutegua. 3 *(fig)* potosha, haribu maana *n* 1 kusokota/kuvuta kwa ghafla. 2 uchungu mkali kutokana na kuachana/kutengana na. 3 spana malaya, spana (inayorekebishwa).

wrest *vt* 1 ~ **sth from/out of** pokonya, nyang'anya. 2 ~ **sth from** pata kwa juhudi. 3 geuza, potosha maana.

wrestle *vi* ~ **(with sb)** piga mwereka; *(fig)* shindana (na vishawishi, majaribu n.k.) *n* shindano la mwereka, pambano. **~r** *n* mpigaji mweleka.

wretch *n* 1 maskini, fukara, mtu mnyonge. 2 fidhuli. 3 bazazi; mhuni. **~ed** *adj* 1 nyonge, -a huzuni, duni, dhalili. 2 -a kudhalilisha. 3 duni, -baya, -a ovyo. ~ **edly** *adv*. **~edness** *n* 1 ufukara, unyonge, umaskini. 2 aibu. 3 wasiwasi.

wrick, rick *vt* shtusha, tegua kidogo *n* shtuo, teguko.

wriggle *vi,vt* 1 jinyonganyonga, (ji)pindapinda. ~ **out** okoka kwa hila/werevu. ~ **one's way into sth** jiingiza katika jambo. 2 chezesha *n* kujinyonganyonga, kugaagaa, mapindi. **~r** *n* buu la mbu.

wright *n (rare except in compounds)* fundi stadi.

wring *vt* 1 popotoa, songonyoa. **~ one's hands** minya mikono. 2 **~ sth out. ~ sth out of/from sth** kamua; *(fig)* lazimisha kutoa (habari). **~ing wet** *(of clothes)* -liolowa chepechepe, -liotota *n* kamuo, mpopotoo. **~er** guruto.

wrinkle[1] *n* kunyanzi; mkunjo *vt,vi* **~ (up)** fanya makunyanzi, kunyata, kunjakunja, kunjikakunjika. **wrinkly** *adj*.

wrinkle[2] *n (colloq)* kidokezi cha kufaa, shauri la manufaa.

wrist *n* kifundo (cha mkono). **~ band** sehemu ya shati ifikayo kwenye kifundo cha mkono. **~watch** saa ya mkono. **~let** utepe, pambo la mkononi.

writ *n* 1 hati *serve a ~ on* mpa mtu hati ya kumwita mbele ya mahakama. 2 **the Holy W~** Maandiko Matakatifu ya Biblia.

write *vt,vi* 1 andika. 2 **~ sth down** andika; punguza bei/thamani. **~ sb down as** kumwelezea mtu. **~ in for sth** omba kwa barua. **~ off (for sth)** agiza kwa barua. **~ sth off** tunga haraka haraka; futa, maliza. **~ off** *n* kitukisicho na thamani tena, kilichokwisha. **~ sth out** andika kwa kirefu. **~ sth up** andika vizuri, kamilisha; tia thamani kubwa kuliko; elezea, sifia. **~ up** *n* maandishi ya tukio. 3 *(of book etc)* andika, tunga. 4 **~ (to)** -andikia. 5 *(US pass)* onyesha wazi; dhihirisha. **written** (*also* **writ**) **large** dhahiri, wazi. **~r** *n* 1 mwandishi. **~r's cramp** kibibi (cha mkono). 2 *(GB)* karani. 3 *(author)* mwandishi wa vitabu, mtunzi. **writing** *n* 1 mwandiko. 2 *(pl)* maandishi *give sth in ~ writing* eleza jambo kwa maandishi. **~-desk** *n* dawati. **~-ink** *n* wino (wa kuandikia). **~-pad** *n* kitita cha karatasi za kuandika. **~-paper** *n* karatasi ya kuandikia (agh. barua).

writhe *vi* jinyonga, tapatapa, furukuta, gaagaa; *(fig)* sononeka, umia/teseka akilini. **~ with shame** jikunyata kwa aibu.

written *pp of* **write**.

wrong *adj* 1 -baya, -ovu, -a dhambi. 2 *(mistaken)* -enye (ma)kosa, si sawa, si sahihi. **~ side out** nje/ndani. **be caught on the ~ foot** fumaniwa, shtukizwa, fumwa, kutwa bila kujitayarisha. **get out of bed on the ~ side** amka vibaya; amka na hasira. **get hold of the ~ end of the stick** kosa kabisa kuelewa jambo fulani, kuwa na dhana tofauti ya jambo, elewa vingine. **in the ~ box** mahali pasipostahili/pasipofaa. **on the ~ side of fifty etc** zidi/vuka miaka hamsini n.k. **~headed** *adj* -kaidi; -potovu. **~ headedly** *adv*. 3 -enye shida, hali mbaya *adv* vibaya; visivyo, kwa makosa. **get sth ~** elewa/hesabu vibaya kitu. **go ~** potea njia/barabara; -shindwa, tofaulu; vurugika; *(colloq) (of a machine etc)* haribika *n* 1 ubaya, dhambi, uovu. **~-doer** mwovu, mtenda mabaya/dhambi; mhalifu. **~ doing** *n* utendaji maovu, dhambi; uhalifu. 2 dhuluma, uonevu. 3 **in the ~** -enye makosa *vt* tendea ubaya, onea, dhulumu, hasiri. **~ful** *adj* si a haki, si sawa, kinyume cha sheria. **~fully. ~ly** *adv*.

wrote *pt of* **write.**

wroth *adj (pred only, poet, biblical or in mod use, hum)* -lokasirika/ghadhibika, -enye hasira.

wrought 1 -liyofuliwa (agh. metali). **~ iron** *n* chuma mfuo. 2 *(arch or lit)* **~ on/upon sb/sth** hemsha; gusa. **~-up** *adj* -liohemkwa, -liohamanika.

wrung *pt of* **wring.**

wry *adj* -a upande, -liojikunyata/kunjika. **make a ~ face (mouth)** kunja/finya uso *a ~ smile* tabasamu ya kulazimisha. **~ly** *adv*.

X

X,x *n* 1 herufi ya ishirini na nne ya alfabeti ya Kiingereza. 2 (ishara ya Kirumi) kumi. 3 (*algebra*) idadi isiyojulikana; *(fig)* jambo lisilo na uhakika. 4 *(of film)* (hati ya kuonyesha) watu wazima tu.

Xeno- *(pref)* -geni, -a nje. **~phobia** *n* chuki/hofu ya wageni (wa nchi).

Xerox *vt see* **photocopy**.

Xho'sa *n (person)* Mhosa; Mbantu wa Afrika ya Kusini mwenye nasaba wa Wazulu; *(language)* Kihosa.

X-ray *n* eksirei ~ *examination* uchunguzi kwa eksirei. ~ **picture** picha ya eksirei *vt* piga picha ya eksirei.

xylem *n* tishu ngumu za mti.

xylography *n* usanii wa kuchonga vinyago. **xylographer** *n* msanii wa kuchonga vinyago.

xylophone *n* marimba.

X-mas *see* **Christmas**.

Y

Y,y *n* herufi ya ishirini na tano ya alfabeti ya Kiingereza.

yacht *n* 1 yoti: boti dogo/jepesi la mashindano *vi* tembea/shindana katika yoti. **~-club** *n* klabu ya wenye yoti. **~ing** *n* mashindano ya yoti; kutembea na yoti. **~sman** *n* mwanariadha wa yoti. **~smanship** *n* ustadi wa kuimudu yoti.

yak *n (Central Asia)* nzao wa manyoya marefu.

yam *n* 1 kiazi kikuu. 2 *(US)* kiazi kitamu.

yammer *vi (colloq)* 1 lalamalalama, nung'unika. 2 bwabwaja, bwata.

yank *(colloq) vt* vuta kwa nguvu/ghafula *n* mvuto mkali.

Yankee *n* 1 *(colloq) (outside U.S.A) (sl)* mtu wa Amerika, Mmarekani. 2 *(US)* mwenyeji wa New England. 3 *(American Civil War)* mwenyeji wa Majimbo ya Kaskazini.

yap *vi* 1 *(of dogs)* bwekabweka kwa sauti kali. 2 *(sl)* bwata, payuka *n* mbweko.

yard[1] *n* 1 yadi, mita (0.914). **~ measure** *n* yadi, fimbo n.k. ya kupimia (ya yadi moja). **~-stick** *n (fig)* kigezo, kipimo. 2 *(naut)* foromali. **man the ~s** panga watu mstarini ili kutoa heshima. **~age** *n* jumla/idadi ya yadi.

yard[2] *n* 1 *(enclosure)* ua, uga, *(US)* kitalu; uwanja *school ~* uwanja wa shule *railway ~* yadi. **~-master** *n* bwana yadi. 3 *(usually in compounds)* **(work ~)** kiwanda, karakana. **brick -~** kiwanda cha matofali. 4 **the Y~** *(colloq abbr for)* **New Scotland Y~** Makao Makuu ya Upelelezi ya Uingereza.

yarn *n* 1 kitani, nyuzi zilizosokotwa. 2 *(colloq)* hadithi, kisa, masimulizi. **spin a ~** simulia hadithi *vi* simulia hadithi.

yashmak *n* barakoa, ukaya.

yaw *vi (of ship or aircraft)* enda mrama *n* kwenda mrama.

yawn *vi* 1 piga miayo. 2 *(lie open)* fumbuka, -wa wazi (kama pango) *n* mwayo.

yaws *n (pl)* buba.

ye[1] *pron (old formal you)* ninyi.

ye[2] *(old written form of)* **the**

yea *adv in (arch)* ndiyo, naam *n the ~s* wasemao ndiyo, waunga mkono. **~h** *adv (sl)* ndiyo.

year *n* 1 mwaka; kipindi tangu Januari 1 hadi Desemba 31 (mwaka wa kalenda). **~ in ~ out** mwaka hadi mwaka, awamu baada ya awamu, mwaka baada ya mwaka. **all (the) ~ round** mwaka mzima. **~ of grace; ~ of Our Lord** mwaka (wowote uliobainishwa baada kuzaliwa Yesu), mwaka. **the ~ dot** *(colloq)* zama za kale. 2 mwaka, kipindi chochote cha siku 365 mfululizo. **~-book** *n* kitabu cha taarifa (ripoti, takwimu n.k.) za mwaka. **~ long** *adj* -a mwaka mzima mfululizo. **the academic ~** mwaka wa masomo. **the financial/fiscal ~** mwaka wa fedha. 3 *(pl)* umri. **~ly** *adj* -a kila mwaka *adv* (kwa) kila mwaka. **~ling** *n* mnyama wa umri kati ya mwaka mmoja na miwili.

yearn *vi* ~ **(for sth/to do sth)** tamani sana, taka sana, onea shauku. **~ing** *n* tamaa, uchu, shauku, kiu *adj* -enye uchu/shauku. **~ingly** *adv* kwa shauku/uchu.

yeast *n* hamira, chachu. **~-powder** *n* unga wa hamira (chachu). **~y** *adj* -enye povu, -lioumuka, kama chachu.

yell *vi,vt* 1 piga yowe, piga kite. 2 **~ sth (out)** sema kwa sauti kubwa *n* ukelele (wa hofu, mashindano, maumivu n.k.).

yellow *adj* 1 -njano, -a rangi ya manjano. **~ flag** bendera ya manjano (inayopeperusha na meli iliyopigwa karantini). **~ press** magazeti yenye lengo la kusisimua tu. **~ fever** homa ya manjano 2. -oga. **~ bellied** oga, -enye hofu *n* 1 rangi ya manjano *vt,vi* geuka kuwa manjano, geuza manjano. **~ish** *adj* -a njanonjano. **~ness** *n* unjano.

yelp *vi* piga unyende, lia (kama mbwa akipigwa) *n* unyende, mlio mkali na mfupi.

yen[1] sarafu ya Kijapani.

yen[2] *n* ~ **for** *(colloq)* tamaa, uchu,

shauku *vi* tamani sana, ona shauku (ya kufanya kitu).
yeoman *n* 1 *(hist)* mkulima. ~ **service** utumishi bora wa muda mrefu; msaada (wakati wa matatizo /dhiki). 2 ~ **of signals** *(GB)* mwanamaji ahusikaye na ishara (kwa kutumia bendera, taa n.k.) *(US)* afisa mdogo mwenye kazi za ukarani. 3 askari mkulima. **~ry** *n* kundi la wakulima askari (wa kujitolea).
yes *particle* ndiyo, naam, vema, vyema *n* ndiyo, kibali. **~-man** *n* barakala, bwana ndiyo.
yester- *pref* a kabla ya hivi. **~day** *n* jana *~day week* siku nane zilizopita *~ morn(ing) adv* jana asubuhi. **~night** *adv* jana usiku, usiku wa jana. **~year** mwaka jana.
yet *adv* 1 *(in neg and conditional contexts)* bado; **-ja-** *he has not ~ come* hajaja (bado) *they haven't ~ done anything* hawajafanya kitu bado. 2 *(in interr and neg contexts)* bado sasa *there is ~ time* bado kuna wakati *need you go ~* lazima uende sasa. 3 *(in affirm sentences)* bado -ngali *be thankful you are ~ alive* shukuru bado ungali hai. 4 tena, baadaye, bado *the enemy may strike again ~* adui huenda akashambulia tena baadaye. 5 **as ~** hadi sasa *we have not discussed the matter as ~* hatujayajadili mambo hadi sasa. **nor ~** *(lit)* wala *nor ~ beautiful* wala sio mzuri *conj* hata hivyo, lakini *he worked well ~ he failed* alifanya kazi vizuri lakini akashindwa.
yeti *n* mnyama afananaye na binadamu ambaye yasemekana anaishi katika milima ya Himalaya.
Yiddish *n* Kiyahudi (kinachotumika hasa Ulaya ya Kati).
yield *vt,vi* 1 acha, jitoa, shindwa 2. toa matunda, zaa *the cow ~s three litres of milk* ng'ombe anatoa lita tatu za maziwa. 3 *(of material, objects)* topea, bonyea, nepa. 4 ~ **(to sb/ sth)** kubali (kushindwa). ~ **(up) sth (to sb)** salimu amri, ruhusu, acha upinzani, acha, achia. ~ **up the ghost** *(lit or rhet)* -fa *n* mazao, mavuno, chumo, mapato. **~ing** *adj* laini, teketeke, -a kubonyea; *(fig)* -tiifu, -epesi kushawishika. **~ingly** *adv*.
yippee *int* huree!
ylang-ylang *n* mlangilangi; langilangi.
yob yobbo yobo *n (GB sl)* mhuni.
yodel *vi* imba kwa madoido *n* wimbo (wa madoido).
yoga *n* 1 yoga, mfumo wa kihindu wa kutafakari na kujidhibiti. 2 mfumo wa mazoezi ya maungo na kudhibiti pumzi. **yogi** *n* mwalimu bingwa wa yoga.
yogurt, yoghurt, yoghourt *n* mtindi.
yo-heave-ho *int* halambe! harambee! hrrrrr - tii!.
yoke *n* 1 *(for cattle)* nira. 2 *(slave's)* kongwa, mkatale. 3 *(pair)* (la maksai) jozi. 4 (*bondage*) utumwa; *(authority, power)* mamlaka, himaya *the marriage ~* pingu za maisha *vt,vi* 1 fungia nira, fungasha, vaa nira. 2 unganisha; oza *n* mshamba.
yolk *n* kiiniyai.
yon *(arch or dial) adj* -le/ko *adv* kule, huko. **~der** *adj,adv (liter)* kule, huko.
yore *n* **of** ~ kale, hapo kale, zamani.
you *pron* 1 wewe; u-; -ku-; *(pl)* ninyi, m-, -wa- *between ~ and me* kati yako wewe na mimi. 2 *(colloq)* yeyote *~ can never tell* haijulikani, huwezi kujua. 3 *(preceding a n, esp. in vocatives)* wee, *(pl)* nyie/nyinyi. ~ **girls** nyie wasichana. **~r** *adj* -ako, *(pl)* -enu *give me ~ book* nipe kitabu chako *this is ~ room* hiki ni chumba chenu. **~rs** *pred adj, pron* 1 -ako; -enu *is this cup ~?* je, kikombe hiki chako? 2. *(at the end of a letter)* wako. **~rself** (*reflex pron)* mwenyewe, -ji- *did you make it ~?* umeitengeneza mwenyewe? *did you make it for ~?* umejitengenezea? *come by ~rselves* njooni peke yenu. **(all) by ~rself** peke yako; bila msaada. **~'re ~are ~'d ~ had; ~ would**. **~'ll ~will. ~'ve ~ have**
young *adj* 1 changa. 2 -bichi *the night*

is still ~ usiku bado mbichi. 3 **the ~er** mdogo. **be sb's ~er** wa mdogo kuliko mwingine. 4 *(used to distinguish a son from his father)* kijana, mdogo ~ *Ali* kijana Ali, Ali mdogo. 5 *(as a familiar or condescending form of address)* ~ *man/woman* bwana mdogo/bi mdogo. 6 -sio na uzoefu, chipukizi *he is ~ in crime* ni mhalifu chipukizi. 7 ~ **and old** kila mtu, wazee na vijana. **the** ~ watoto; vijana *n* mtoto; *(of birds)* kinda; *(of animals)* ndama. **with** ~ *(of an animal)* -enye mimba, mjamzito. **~ish** *adj* -a ujana kiasi; kijana kijana. **~ster** *n* mtoto; kijana.

youth *n* 1 ujana, ushababi. 2 vijana; shababi. 3 mvulana,ghulamu, kijana. ~ **festival** tamasha la vijana. **~ful** *adj* ujana, shababi. **~fully** *adv*. **~fulness** *n.*

yowl *vi* piga unyende/ukelele, piga yowe.

Y-shaped *adj* -enye umbo la Y, -a panda.

yule *n* (*also* **yule-tide**) *(arch)* sikukuu ya Krismasi; sikukuu ya kuzaliwa Yesu. **~log** *n* kigogo kinachochomwa mkesha wa Krismasi.

Z

Z,z *n* herufi ya z: herufi ya mwisho katika alfabeti ya Kiingereza.

zany *n* mcheshi kidogo; mpumbavu, mpuuzi *adj* pumbavu, puuzi.

Zap *(sl)* piga; shambulia; shinda.

Zanzibar *n (town)* Unguja; *(Island)* Kisiwa cha Unguja; *(Country)* Visiwa vya Unguja na Pemba. **a Z~ Islander** Muunguja, Mzanzibari. **Z~ dialect** Kiunguja.

zeal *n* ari, raghba, moyo, ghera. **~ous** *adj* -enye raghba. **~ously** *adv*.

zealot *n* mlokole, mnazi, shabiki; mkereketwa. **~ism** *n* ulokole, unazi, ushabiki. **~ry** *n*.

zebra *n* punda milia. ~ **crossing** alama (ya milia) ya kuvuka barabara kwa miguu.

zebu *n (in Asia and E. Africa)* zebu: ng'ombe mwenye nundu.

zee *n (US)* jina la herufi Z.

zenith *n* anga; *(fig)* upeo (wa ustawi, umashuhuri) wa watu/mtu, ufanisi. **~al** *adj* -a juu sana, -a kiwango cha juu.

zephyr *n* pepo za magharibi; *(poet)* upepo mwanana.

Zeppelin *n* zepelini: puto kubwa lililotumiwa na Wajerumani katika vita kuu ya kwanza.

zero *n* 1 sifuri, ziro, alama 0. 2 nukta kati ya hasi na chanya. ~ **hour** *(mil)* saa ya kuanza mashambulizi. ~ **in (on)** *(sl)* jizatiti, kaa tayari, -wa makini, elekeza mawazo kwenye.

zest *n* 1 bidii, shauku kubwa. 2 *(often with indef art)* ladha, kiungo cha kukoza.

zeta *n* herufi ya sita ya Kigiriki.

zigzag *adj* -a mshazari, zigizaga, -a kupindapinda *n* zigizaga *adv* kwa zigizaga, pindapinda, mshazari.

zinc *n* zinki. ~ **plate** bamba la zinki, zinki ferasi *adj* -enye zinki.

zing *n (sl)* bidii, nguvu.

zion *n* Uyahudi: Israel *n*. **~ist** *n*.

zip *n* 1 sauti ya risasi hewani. 2 *(fig)* bidii *put a ~ into it* tia bidii katika jambo *vt* fungua. ~ **sth open** fungua kitu kwa zipu. ~ **sth up** funga kitu kwa zipu. ~ **fastener; ~per** *n* zipu.

zipcode *n (US) see* **postcode**.

zither *n* nanga; zitha: ala ya muziki. **~ist** *n* mpiga zitha.

zodiac *n* 1 zodiaki: ukanda wa anga wenye njia za sayari zote kuu. **signs of the ~** nyota (za unajimu). 2 mchoro wa zodiaki.

zombi(e) *n* 1 dubwana; kizuu. 2 *(colloq)* zuzu, punguani, afkani.

zone *n* 1 ukanda, zoni *northern ~* ukanda wa kaskazini *equatorial ~* ukanda wa ikweta. 2 eneo maalum. **zonal** *adj* -a kanda, -a zoni *vt* gawa katika kanda. **zoning** *n* ugawanyaji wa maeneo mbalimbali.

zoo *n (zoo)* mahali wafugwapo wanyama pori; bustani ya wanyama. **~logy** *n* zuolojia: sayansi ya miundo, umbo na ugawanyikaji wa wanyama. **~logical** *adj* -a zuolojia. **~logical gardens** bustani kubwa za wanyama. **~logist** *n* mwana zuolojia.

zoom *vi* 1 panda/ruka juu kwa kasi sana. 2 *(of a camera)* vuta picha. ~ **in/out** vuta karibu/mbali *n* 1 mlio wa eropleni inayopuruka kwa kasi. 2 ~ **lens** *(of a camera)* lenzi ya kuvuta.

zoophyte *n* matumbawe zufiti: mnyama au mdudu kama mmea, yaani nusu mnyama nusu mmea.

zucchini *see* **courgette**.

Zulu *n* 1 Mzulu: mwenyeji wa Afrika ya Kusini. 2 lugha ya Kizulu *adj* -a kizulu.

zygote *n* zaigoti: seli ya gameti mbili; kiumbe kichanga.